*The Dictionary of Art · volume nineteen*

# The Dictionary of Art

EDITORIAL ADVISORY BOARD

Terukazu Akiyama; Carlo Bertelli; Whitney Chadwick; André Chastel; Oleg Grabar;

Francis Haskell; Alfonso E. Pérez Sánchez; Jessica Rawson; Robert Rosenblum;

Willibald Sauerländer; Peter Thornton; Irene Winter

CONSULTING EDITOR Hugh Brigstocke

EDITOR Jane Turner

## 19

Leather

TO

Macho

GROVE

© Macmillan Publishers Limited 1996

*The Dictionary of Art*

edited by JANE TURNER, in thirty-four volumes, 1996

Reprinted with minor corrections, 1998, 2002

This edition is distributed within the United Kingdom and Europe
by Macmillan Publishers Limited, London, and within the United States and Canada by
Grove's Dictionaries Inc., New York.

Text keyboarded by Wearset Limited, Sunderland, England
Database management by Pindar plc, York, England
Imagesetting by William Clowes Limited, Suffolk, England
Printed and bound by China Translation and Printing Services Ltd, Hong Kong

*British Library Cataloguing in Publication Data*

The dictionary of art
  1. Art - Dictionaries 2. Art - History -
    Dictionaries
I. Turner, Jane
703

ISBN 1-884446-00-0

*Library of Congress Cataloging in Publication Data*

The dictionary of art / editor, Jane Turner.
  p.  cm.
  Includes bibliographical references and index.
  Contents: 1. A to Anckerman
  ISBN 1-884446-00-0 (alk. paper)
  1. Art—Encyclopedias.
  I. Turner, Jane, 1956–
N31.D5  1996              96–13628
703—dc20                    CIP

# Contents

# *General Abbreviations*

The abbreviations employed throughout this dictionary, most of which are listed below, do not vary, except for capitalization, regardless of the context in which they are used, including bibliographical citations and for locations of works of art. The principle used to arrive at these abbreviations is that their full form should be easily deducible, and for this reason acronyms have generally been avoided (e.g. Los Angeles Co. Mus. A. instead of LACMA). The same abbreviation is adopted for cognate forms in foreign languages and in most cases for plural and adjectival forms (e.g. A.= Art, Arts, Arte, Arti etc). Not all related forms are listed below. Occasionally, if a name, for instance of an artists' group or exhibiting society, is repeated within the text of one article, it is cited in an abbreviated form after its first mention in full (e.g. The Pre-Raphaelite Brotherhood (PRB) was founded... ); the same is true of archaeological periods and eras, which are abbreviated to initial letters in small capitals (e.g. In the Early Minoan (EM) period... ). Such abbreviations do not appear in this list. For the reader's convenience, separate full lists of abbreviations for locations, periodical titles and standard reference books and series are included as Appendices A–C in vol. 33.

| | | | | | |
|---|---|---|---|---|---|
| A. | Art, Arts | Anthropol. | Anthropology | Azerbaij. | Azerbaijani |
| A.C. | Arts Council | Antiqua. | Antiquarian, Antiquaries | B. | Bartsch [catalogue of Old Master prints] |
| Acad. | Academy | app. | appendix | | |
| AD | Anno Domini | approx. | approximately | *b* | born |
| Add. | Additional, Addendum | AR | Arkansas (USA) | BA | Bachelor of Arts |
| addn | addition | ARA | Associate of the Royal Academy | Balt. | Baltic |
| Admin. | Administration | | | *bapt* | baptized |
| Adv. | Advances, Advanced | Arab. | Arabic | BArch | Bachelor of Architecture |
| Aesth. | Aesthetic(s) | Archaeol. | Archaeology | Bart | Baronet |
| Afr. | African | Archit. | Architecture, Architectural | Bask. | Basketry |
| Afrik. | Afrikaans, Afrikaner | Archv, Archvs. | Archive(s) | BBC | British Broadcasting Corporation |
| A.G. | Art Gallery | Arg. | Argentine | | |
| Agrar. | Agrarian | | | BC | Before Christ |
| Agric. | Agriculture | ARHA | Associate of the Royal Hibernian Academy | BC | British Columbia (Canada) |
| Agron. | Agronomy | | | BE | Buddhist era |
| Agy | Agency | ARIBA | Associate of the Royal Institute of British Architects | Beds | Bedfordshire (GB) |
| AH | Anno Hegirae | | | Behav. | Behavioural |
| A. Inst. | Art Institute | Armen. | Armenian | Belarus. | Belarusian |
| AK | Alaska (USA) | ARSA | Associate of the Royal Scottish Academy | Belg. | Belgian |
| AL | Alabama (USA) | | | Berks | Berkshire (GB) |
| Alb. | Albanian | Asiat. | Asiatic | Berwicks | Berwickshire (GB; old) |
| Alg. | Algerian | Assist. | Assistance | BFA | Bachelor of Fine Arts |
| Alta | Alberta (Canada) | Assoc. | Association | Bibl. | Bible, Biblical |
| Altern. | Alternative | Astron. | Astronomy | Bibliog. | Bibliography, Bibliographical |
| a.m. | ante meridiem [before noon] | AT&T | American Telephone & Telegraph Company | Biblioph. | Bibliophile |
| Amat. | Amateur | attrib. | attribution, attributed to | Biog. | Biography, Biographical |
| Amer. | American | Aug | August | Biol. | Biology, Biological |
| An. | Annals | Aust. | Austrian | bk, bks | book(s) |
| Anatol. | Anatolian | Austral. | Australian | Bkbinder | Bookbinder |
| Anc. | Ancient | Auth. | Author(s) | Bklore | Booklore |
| Annu. | Annual | Auton. | Autonomous | Bkshop | Bookshop |
| Anon. | Anonymous(ly) | Aux. | Auxiliary | BL | British Library |
| Ant. | Antique | Ave. | Avenue | Bld | Build |
| Anthol. | Anthology | AZ | Arizona (USA) | Bldg | Building |

| | | | | | |
|---|---|---|---|---|---|
| Bldr | Builder | Chin. | Chinese | Cur. | Curator, Curatorial, Curatorship |
| BLitt | Bachelor of Letters/Literature | Christ. | Christian, Christianity | | |
| BM | British Museum | Chron. | Chronicle | Curr. | Current(s) |
| Boh. | Bohemian | Cie | Compagnie [French] | CVO | Commander of the [Royal] Victorian Order |
| Boliv. | Bolivian | Cinema. | Cinematography | | |
| Botan. | Botany, Botanical | Circ. | Circle | Cyclad. | Cycladic |
| BP | Before present (1950) | Civ. | Civil, Civic | Cyp. | Cypriot |
| Braz. | Brazilian | Civiliz. | Civilization(s) | Czech. | Czechoslovak |
| BRD | Bundesrepublik Deutschland [Federal Republic of Germany (West Germany)] | Class. | Classic, Classical | $ | dollars |
| | | Clin. | Clinical | *d* | died |
| | | CO | Colorado (USA) | d. | denarius, denarii [penny, pence] |
| Brecons | Breconshire (GB; old) | Co. | Company; County | | |
| Brez. | Brezonek [lang. of Brittany] | Cod. | Codex, Codices | Dalmat. | Dalmatian |
| Brit. | British | Col., Cols | Collection(s); Column(s) | Dan. | Danish |
| Bros | Brothers | Coll. | College | DBE | Dame Commander of the Order of the British Empire |
| BSc | Bachelor of Science | collab. | in collaboration with, collaborated, collaborative | | |
| Bucks | Buckinghamshire (GB) | | | DC | District of Columbia (USA) |
| Bulg. | Bulgarian | Collct. | Collecting | DDR | Deutsche Demokratische Republik [German Democratic Republic (East Germany)] |
| Bull. | Bulletin | Colloq. | Colloquies | | |
| *bur* | buried | Colomb. | Colombian | | |
| Burm. | Burmese | Colon. | Colonies, Colonial | DE | Delaware (USA) |
| Byz. | Byzantine | Colr | Collector | Dec | December |
| C | Celsius | Comm. | Commission; Community | Dec. | Decorative |
| C. | Century | Commerc. | Commercial | ded. | dedication, dedicated to |
| *c.* | *circa* [about] | Communic. | Communications | Democ. | Democracy, Democratic |
| CA | California | Comp. | Comparative; compiled by, compiler | Demog. | Demography, Demographic |
| Cab. | Cabinet | | | Denbs | Denbighshire (GB; old) |
| Caerns | Caernarvonshire (GB; old) | Concent. | Concentration | dep. | deposited at |
| C.A.G. | City Art Gallery | Concr. | Concrete | Dept | Department |
| Cal. | Calendar | Confed. | Confederation | Dept. | Departmental, Departments |
| Callig. | Calligraphy | Confer. | Conference | Derbys | Derbyshire (GB) |
| Cam. | Camera | Congol. | Congolese | Des. | Design |
| Cambs | Cambridgeshire (GB) | Congr. | Congress | destr. | destroyed |
| *can* | canonized | Conserv. | Conservation; Conservatory | Dev. | Development |
| Can. | Canadian | Constr. | Construction(al) | Devon | Devonshire (GB) |
| Cant. | Canton(s), Cantonal | cont. | continued | Dial. | Dialogue |
| Capt. | Captain | Contemp. | Contemporary | diam. | diameter |
| Cards | Cardiganshire (GB; old) | Contrib. | Contributions, Contributor(s) | Diff. | Diffusion |
| Carib. | Caribbean | Convalesc. | Convalescence | Dig. | Digest |
| Carms | Carmarthenshire (GB; old) | Convent. | Convention | Dip. Eng. | Diploma in Engineering |
| Cartog. | Cartography | Coop. | Cooperation | Dir. | Direction, Directed |
| Cat. | Catalan | Coord. | Coordination | Directrt | Directorate |
| cat. | catalogue | Copt. | Coptic | Disc. | Discussion |
| Cath. | Catholic | Corp. | Corporation, Corpus | diss. | dissertation |
| CBE | Commander of the Order of the British Empire | Corr. | Correspondence | Distr. | District |
| | | Cors. | Corsican | Div. | Division |
| Celeb. | Celebration | Cost. | Costume | DLitt | Doctor of Letters/Literature |
| Celt. | Celtic | Cret. | Cretan | DM | Deutsche Mark |
| Cent. | Centre, Central | Crim. | Criminal | Doc. | Document(s) |
| Centen. | Centennial | Crit. | Critical, Criticism | Doss. | Dossier |
| Cer. | Ceramic | Croat. | Croatian | DPhil | Doctor of Philosophy |
| cf. | confer [compare] | CT | Connecticut (USA) | Dr | Doctor |
| Chap., Chaps | Chapter(s) | Cttee | Committee | Drg, Drgs | Drawing(s) |
| | | Cub. | Cuban | DSc | Doctor of Science/Historical Sciences |
| Chem. | Chemistry | Cult. | Cultural, Culture | | |
| Ches | Cheshire (GB) | Cumb. | Cumberland (GB; old) | Dut. | Dutch |
| Chil. | Chilean | | | Dwell. | Dwelling |
| | | | | E. | East(ern) |

| | | | | | | |
|---|---|---|---|---|---|
| EC | European (Economic) Community | figs | figures | Heb. | Hebrew |
| Eccles. | Ecclesiastical | Filip. | Filipina(s), Filipino(s) | Hell. | Hellenic |
| Econ. | Economic, Economies | Fin. | Finnish | Her. | Heritage |
| Ecuad. | Ecuadorean | FL | Florida (USA) | Herald. | Heraldry, Heraldic |
| ed. | editor, edited (by) | *fl* | *floruit* [he/she flourished] | Hereford & Worcs | Hereford & Worcester (GB) |
| edn | edition | Flem. | Flemish | | |
| eds | editors | Flints | Flintshire (GB; old) | Herts | Hertfordshire (GB) |
| Educ. | Education | Flk | Folk | HI | Hawaii (USA) |
| e.g. | *exempli gratia* [for example] | Flklore | Folklore | Hib. | Hibernia |
| Egyp. | Egyptian | fol., fols | folio(s) | Hisp. | Hispanic |
| Elem. | Element(s), Elementary | Found. | Foundation | Hist. | History, Historical |
| Emp. | Empirical | Fr. | French | HMS | His/Her Majesty's Ship |
| Emul. | Emulation | frag. | fragment | Hon. | Honorary, Honourable |
| Enc. | Encyclopedia | Fri. | Friday | Horiz. | Horizon |
| Encour. | Encouragement | FRIBA | Fellow of the Royal Institute of British Architects | Hort. | Horticulture |
| Eng. | English | | | Hosp. | Hospital(s) |
| Engin. | Engineer, Engineering | FRS | Fellow of the Royal Society, London | HRH | His/Her Royal Highness |
| Engr., Engrs | Engraving(s) | | | Human. | Humanities, Humanism |
| | | ft | foot, feet | Hung. | Hungarian |
| Envmt | Environment | Furn. | Furniture | Hunts | Huntingdonshire (GB; old) |
| Epig. | Epigraphy | Futur. | Futurist, Futurism | IA | Iowa |
| Episc. | Episcopal | g | gram(s) | ibid. | *ibidem* [in the same place] |
| Esp. | Especially | GA | Georgia (USA) | ICA | Institute of Contemporary Arts |
| Ess. | Essays | Gael. | Gaelic | | |
| est. | established | Gal., Gals | Gallery, Galleries | Ice. | Icelandic |
| etc | *etcetera* [and so on] | Gaz. | Gazette | Iconog. | Iconography |
| Ethnog. | Ethnography | GB | Great Britain | Iconol. | Iconology |
| Ethnol. | Ethnology | Gdn, Gdns | Garden(s) | ID | Idaho (USA) |
| Etrus. | Etruscan | Gdnr(s) | Gardener(s) | i.e. | *id est* [that is] |
| Eur. | European | Gen. | General | IL | Illinois (USA) |
| Evangel. | Evangelical | Geneal. | Genealogy, Genealogist | Illum. | Illumination |
| Exam. | Examination | Gent. | Gentleman, Gentlemen | illus. | illustrated, illustration |
| Excav. | Excavation, Excavated | Geog. | Geography | Imp. | Imperial |
| Exch. | Exchange | Geol. | Geology | IN | Indiana (USA) |
| Excurs. | Excursion | Geom. | Geometry | in., ins | inch(es) |
| exh. | exhibition | Georg. | Georgian | Inc. | Incorporated |
| Exp. | Exposition | Geosci. | Geoscience | inc. | incomplete |
| Expermntl | Experimental | Ger. | German, Germanic | incl. | includes, including, inclusive |
| Explor. | Exploration | G.I. | Government/General Issue (USA) | Incorp. | Incorporation |
| Expn | Expansion | | | Ind. | Indian |
| Ext. | External | Glams | Glamorganshire (GB; old) | Indep. | Independent |
| Extn | Extension | Glos | Gloucestershire (GB) | Indig. | Indigenous |
| f, ff | following page, following pages | Govt | Government | Indol. | Indology |
| | | Gr. | Greek | Indon. | Indonesian |
| F.A. | Fine Art(s) | Grad. | Graduate | Indust. | Industrial |
| Fac. | Faculty | Graph. | Graphic | Inf. | Information |
| facs. | facsimile | Green. | Greenlandic | Inq. | Inquiry |
| Fam. | Family | Gr.-Roman | Greco-Roman | Inscr. | Inscribed, Inscription |
| fasc. | fascicle | Gt | Great | Inst. | Institute(s) |
| *fd* | feastday (of a saint) | Gtr | Greater | Inst. A. | Institute of Art |
| Feb | February | Guat. | Guatemalan | Instr. | Instrument, Instrumental |
| Fed. | Federation, Federal | Gym. | Gymnasium | Int. | International |
| Fem. | Feminist | h. | height | Intell. | Intelligence |
| Fest. | Festival | ha | hectare | Inter. | Interior(s), Internal |
| fig. | figure (illustration) | Hait. | Haitian | Interdiscip. | Interdisciplinary |
| Fig. | Figurative | Hants | Hampshire (GB) | intro. | introduced by, introduction |
| | | Hb. | Handbook | inv. | inventory |

| | | | | | |
|---|---|---|---|---|---|
| Inven. | Invention | m | metre(s) | Moldov. | Moldovan |
| Invest. | Investigation(s) | m. | married | MOMA | Museum of Modern Art |
| Iran. | Iranian | M. | Monsieur | Mon. | Monday |
| irreg. | irregular(ly) | MA | Master of Arts; Massachusetts (USA) | Mongol. | Mongolian |
| Islam. | Islamic | | | Mons | Monmouthshire (GB; old) |
| Isr. | Israeli | Mag. | Magazine | Montgoms | Montgomeryshire (GB; old) |
| It. | Italian | Maint. | Maintenance | Mor. | Moral |
| J. | Journal | Malay. | Malaysian | Morav. | Moravian |
| Jam. | Jamaican | Man. | Manitoba (Canada); Manual | Moroc. | Moroccan |
| Jan | January | Manuf. | Manufactures | Movt | Movement |
| Jap. | Japanese | Mar. | Marine, Maritime | MP | Member of Parliament |
| Jav. | Javanese | Mason. | Masonic | MPhil | Master of Philosophy |
| Jew. | Jewish | Mat. | Material(s) | MS | Mississippi (USA) |
| Jewel. | Jewellery | Math. | Mathematic | MS., MSS | manuscript(s) |
| Jord. | Jordanian | MBE | Member of the Order of the British Empire | MSc | Master of Science |
| jr | junior | | | MT | Montana (USA) |
| Juris. | Jurisdiction | MD | Doctor of Medicine; Maryland (USA) | Mt | Mount |
| KBE | Knight Commander of the Order of the British Empire | | | Mthly | Monthly |
| | | ME | Maine (USA) | Mun. | Municipal |
| KCVO | Knight Commander of the Royal Victorian Order | Mech. | Mechanical | Mus. | Museum(s) |
| | | Med. | Medieval; Medium, Media | Mus. A. | Museum of Art |
| kg | kilogram(s) | Medic. | Medical, Medicine | Mus. F.A. | Museum of Fine Art(s) |
| kHz | kilohertz | Medit. | Mediterranean | Music. | Musicology |
| km | kilometre(s) | Mcm. | Memorial(s); Memoir(s) | N. | North(ern); National |
| Knowl. | Knowledge | Merions | Merionethshire (GB; old) | n | refractive index of a medium |
| Kor. | Korean | Meso-Amer. | Meso-American | n. | note |
| KS | Kansas (USA) | | | N.A.G. | National Art Gallery |
| KY | Kentucky (USA) | Mesop. | Mesopotamian | Nat. | Natural, Nature |
| Kyrgyz. | Kyrgyzstani | Met. | Metropolitan | Naut. | Nautical |
| £ | libra, librae [pound, pounds sterling] | Metal. | Metallurgy | NB | New Brunswick (Canada) |
| | | Mex. | Mexican | NC | North Carolina (USA) |
| l. | length | MFA | Master of Fine Arts | ND | North Dakota (USA) |
| LA | Louisiana (USA) | mg | milligram(s) | n.d. | no date |
| Lab. | Laboratory | Mgmt | Management | NE | Nebraska; Northeast(ern) |
| Lancs | Lancashire (GB) | Mgr | Monsignor | Neth. | Netherlandish |
| Lang. | Language(s) | MI | Michigan | Newslett. | Newsletter |
| Lat. | Latin | Micrones. | Micronesian | Nfld | Newfoundland (Canada) |
| Latv. | Latvian | Mid. Amer. | Middle American | N.G. | National Gallery |
| lb, lbs | pound(s) weight | Middx | Middlesex (GB; old) | N.G.A. | National Gallery of Art |
| Leb. | Lebanese | Mid. E. | Middle Eastern | NH | New Hampshire (USA) |
| Lect. | Lecture | Mid. Eng. | Middle English | Niger. | Nigerian |
| Legis. | Legislative | Mid Glam. | Mid Glamorgan (GB) | NJ | New Jersey (USA) |
| Leics | Leicestershire (GB) | Mil. | Military | NM | New Mexico (USA) |
| Lex. | Lexicon | Mill. | Millennium | nm | nanometre ($10^{-9}$ metre) |
| Lg. | Large | Min. | Ministry; Minutes | nn. | notes |
| Lib., Libs | Library, Libraries | Misc. | Miscellaneous | no., nos | number(s) |
| Liber. | Liberian | Miss. | Mission(s) | Nord. | Nordic |
| Libsp | Librarianship | Mlle | Mademoiselle | Norm. | Normal |
| Lincs | Lincolnshire (GB) | mm | millimetre(s) | Northants | Northamptonshire (GB) |
| Lit. | Literature | Mme | Madame | Northumb. | Northumberland (GB) |
| Lith. | Lithuanian | MN | Minnesota | Norw. | Norwegian |
| Liturg. | Liturgical | Mnmt, Mnmts | Monument(s) | Notts | Nottinghamshire (GB) |
| LLB | Bachelor of Laws | | | Nov | November |
| LLD | Doctor of Laws | Mnmtl | Monumental | n.p. | no place (of publication) |
| Lt | Lieutenant | MO | Missouri (USA) | N.P.G. | National Portrait Gallery |
| Lt-Col. | Lieutenant-Colonel | Mod. | Modern, Modernist | nr | near |
| Ltd | Limited | Moldav. | Moldavian | | |

| | | | | | |
|---|---|---|---|---|---|
| Nr E. | Near Eastern | Per. | Period | Ptg(s) | Painting(s) |
| NS | New Style; Nova Scotia (Canada) | Percep. | Perceptions | Pub. | Public |
| | | Perf. | Performance, Performing, Performed | pubd | published |
| n. s. | new series | | | Publ. | Publicity |
| NSW | New South Wales (Australia) | Period. | Periodical(s) | pubn(s) | publication(s) |
| NT | National Trust | Pers. | Persian | PVA | polyvinyl acetate |
| Ntbk | Notebook | Persp. | Perspectives | PVC | polyvinyl chloride |
| Numi. | Numismatic(s) | Peru. | Peruvian | Q. | quarterly |
| NV | Nevada (USA) | PhD | Doctor of Philosophy | 4to | quarto |
| NW | Northwest(ern) | Philol. | Philology | Qué. | Québec (Canada) |
| NWT | Northwest Territories (Canada) | Philos. | Philosophy | *R* | reprint |
| | | Phoen. | Phoenician | *r* | *recto* |
| NY | New York (USA) | Phot. | Photograph, Photography, Photographic | RA | Royal Academician |
| NZ | New Zealand | | | Radnors | Radnorshire (GB; old) |
| OBE | Officer of the Order of the British Empire | Phys. | Physician(s), Physics, Physique, Physical | RAF | Royal Air Force |
| | | | | Rec. | Record(s) |
| Obj. | Object(s), Objective | Physiog. | Physiognomy | red. | reduction, reduced for |
| Occas. | Occasional | Physiol. | Physiology | Ref. | Reference |
| Occident. | Occidental | Pict. | Picture(s), Pictorial | Refurb. | Refurbishment |
| Ocean. | Oceania | pl. | plate; plural | *reg* | *regit* [ruled] |
| Oct | October | Plan. | Planning | Reg. | Regional |
| 8vo | octavo | Planet. | Planetarium | Relig. | Religion, Religious |
| OFM | Order of Friars Minor | Plast. | Plastic | remod. | remodelled |
| OH | Ohio (USA) | pls | plates | Ren. | Renaissance |
| OK | Oklahoma (USA) | p.m. | post meridiem [after noon] | Rep. | Report(s) |
| Olymp. | Olympic | Polit. | Political | repr. | reprint(ed); reproduced, reproduction |
| OM | Order of Merit | Poly. | Polytechnic | | |
| Ont. | Ontario (Canada) | Polynes. | Polynesian | Represent. | Representation, Representative |
| op. | opus | Pop. | Popular | Res. | Research |
| opp. | opposite; opera [pl. of opus] | Port. | Portuguese | rest. | restored, restoration |
| OR | Oregon (USA) | Port. | Portfolio | Retro. | Retrospective |
| Org. | Organization | Posth. | Posthumous(ly) | rev. | revision, revised (by/for) |
| Orient. | Oriental | Pott. | Pottery | Rev. | Reverend; Review |
| Orthdx | Orthodox | POW | prisoner of war | RHA | Royal Hibernian Academician |
| OSB | Order of St Benedict | PRA | President of the Royal Academy | RI | Rhode Island (USA) |
| Ott. | Ottoman | | | RIBA | Royal Institute of British Architects |
| Oxon | Oxfordshire (GB) | Pract. | Practical | | |
| oz. | ounce(s) | Prefect. | Prefecture, Prefectural | RJ | Rio de Janeiro State |
| p | pence | Preserv. | Preservation | Rlwy | Railway |
| p., pp. | page(s) | prev. | previous(ly) | RSA | Royal Scottish Academy |
| PA | Pennsylvania (USA) | priv. | private | RSFSR | Russian Soviet Federated Socialist Republic |
| p.a. | per annum | PRO | Public Record Office | | |
| Pak. | Pakistani | Prob. | Problem(s) | Rt Hon. | Right Honourable |
| Palaeontol. | Palaeontology, Palaeontological | Proc. | Proceedings | Rur. | Rural |
| | | Prod. | Production | Rus. | Russian |
| Palest. | Palestinian | Prog. | Progress | S | San, Santa, Santo, Sant', São [Saint] |
| Pap. | Paper(s) | Proj. | Project(s) | | |
| para. | paragraph | Promot. | Promotion | S. | South(ern) |
| Parag. | Paraguayan | Prop. | Property, Properties | s. | solidus, solidi [shilling(s)] |
| Parl. | Parliament | Prov. | Province(s), Provincial | Sask. | Saskatchewan (Canada) |
| Paroch. | Parochial | Proven. | Provenance | Sat. | Saturday |
| Patriarch. | Patriarchate | Prt, Prts | Print(s) | SC | South Carolina (USA) |
| Patriot. | Patriotic | Prtg | Printing | Scand. | Scandinavian |
| Patrm. | Patrimony | pseud. | pseudonym | Sch. | School |
| Pav. | Pavilion | Psych. | Psychiatry, Psychiatric | Sci. | Science(s), Scientific |
| PEI | Prince Edward Island (Canada) | Psychol. | Psychology, Psychological | Scot. | Scottish |
| Pembs | Pembrokeshire (GB; old) | pt | part | Sculp. | Sculpture |

| | | | | | |
|---|---|---|---|---|---|
| SD | South Dakota (USA) | suppl., suppls | supplement(s), supplementary | Urb. | Urban |
| SE | Southeast(ern) | Surv. | Survey | Urug. | Uruguayan |
| Sect. | Section | SW | Southwest(ern) | US | United States |
| Sel. | Selected | Swed. | Swedish | USA | United States of America |
| Semin. | Seminar(s), Seminary | Swi. | Swiss | USSR | Union of Soviet Socialist Republics |
| Semiot. | Semiotic | Symp. | Symposium | UT | Utah |
| Semit. | Semitic | Syr. | Syrian | *v* | *verso* |
| Sept | September | Tap. | Tapestry | VA | Virginia (USA) |
| Ser. | Series | Tas. | Tasmanian | V&A | Victoria and Albert Museum |
| Serb. | Serbian | Tech. | Technical, Technique | Var. | Various |
| Serv. | Service(s) | Technol. | Technology | Venez. | Venezuelan |
| Sess. | Session, Sessional | Territ. | Territory | Vern. | Vernacular |
| Settmt(s) | Settlement(s) | Theat. | Theatre | Vict. | Victorian |
| S. Glam. | South Glamorgan (GB) | Theol. | Theology, Theological | Vid. | Video |
| Siber. | Siberian | Theor. | Theory, Theoretical | Viet. | Vietnamese |
| Sig. | Signature | Thurs. | Thursday | viz. | *videlicet* [namely] |
| Sil. | Silesian | Tib. | Tibetan | vol., vols | volume(s) |
| Sin. | Singhala | TN | Tennessee (USA) | vs. | versus |
| sing. | singular | Top. | Topography | VT | Vermont (USA) |
| SJ | Societas Jesu [Society of Jesus] | Trad. | Tradition(s), Traditional | Vulg. | Vulgarisation |
| Skt | Sanskrit | trans. | translation, translated by; transactions | W. | West(ern) |
| Slav. | Slavic, Slavonic | Transafr. | Transafrican | w. | width |
| Slov. | Slovene, Slovenian | Transatlant. | Transatlantic | WA | Washington (USA) |
| Soc. | Society | Transcarpath. | Transcarpathian | Warwicks | Warwickshire (GB) |
| Social. | Socialism, Socialist | transcr. | transcribed by/for | Wed. | Wednesday |
| Sociol. | Sociology | Triq. | Triquarterly | W. Glam. | West Glamorgan (GB) |
| Sov. | Soviet | Tropic. | Tropical | WI | Wisconsin (USA) |
| SP | São Paulo State | Tues. | Tuesday | Wilts | Wiltshire (GB) |
| Sp. | Spanish | Turk. | Turkish | Wkly | Weekly |
| sq. | square | Turkmen. | Turkmenistani | W. Midlands | West Midlands (GB) |
| sr | senior | TV | Television | | |
| Sri L. | Sri Lankan | TX | Texas (USA) | Worcs | Worcestershire (GB; old) |
| SS | Saints, Santi, Santissima, Santissimo, Santissimi; Steam ship | U. | University | Wtrcol. | Watercolour |
| | | UK | United Kingdom of Great Britain and Northern Ireland | WV | West Virginia (USA) |
| SSR | Soviet Socialist Republic | Ukrain. | Ukrainian | WY | Wyoming (USA) |
| St | Saint, Sankt, Sint, Szent | Un. | Union | Yb., Y.-b. | Yearbook, Year-book |
| Staffs | Staffordshire (GB) | Underwtr | Underwater | Yem. | Yemeni |
| Ste | Sainte | UNESCO | United Nations Educational, Scientific and Cultural Organization | Yorks | Yorkshire (GB; old) |
| Stud. | Study, Studies | | | Yug. | Yugoslavian |
| Subalp. | Subalpine | | | | |
| Sum. | Sumerian | Univl | Universal | Zamb. | Zambian |
| Sun. | Sunday | unpubd | unpublished | Zimb. | Zimbabwean |
| Sup. | Superior | | | | |

# *A Note on the Use of the Dictionary*

This note is intended as a short guide to the basic editorial conventions adopted in this dictionary. For a fuller explanation, please refer to the Introduction, vol. 1, pp. xiii–xx.

**Abbreviations** in general use in the dictionary are listed on pp. vi–xi; those used in bibliographies and for locations of works of art or exhibition venues are listed in the Appendices in vol. 33.

**Alphabetization** of headings, which are distinguished in bold typeface, is letter by letter up to the first comma (ignoring spaces, hyphens, accents and any parenthesized or bracketed matter); the same principle applies thereafter. Abbreviations of 'Saint' and its foreign equivalents are alphabetized as if spelt out, and headings with the prefix 'Mc' appear under 'Mac'.

**Authors' signatures** appear at the end of the article or sequence of articles that the authors have contributed; in multipartite articles, any section that is unsigned is by the author of the next signed section. Where the article was compiled by the editors or in the few cases where an author has wished to remain anonymous, this is indicated by a square box (☐) instead of a signature.

**Bibliographies** are arranged chronologically (within section, where divided) by order of year of first publication and, within years, alphabetically by authors' names. Abbreviations have been used for some standard reference books; these are cited in full in Appendix C in vol. 33, as are abbreviations of periodical titles (Appendix B). Abbreviated references to alphabetically arranged dictionaries and encyclopedias appear at the beginning of the bibliography (or section).

**Biographical dates** when cited in parentheses in running text at the first mention of a personal name indicate that the individual does not have an entry in the dictionary. The presence of parenthesized regnal dates for rulers and popes, however, does not necessarily indicate the lack of a biography of that person. Where no dates are provided for an artist or patron, the reader may assume that there is a biography of that individual in the dictionary (or, more rarely, that the person is so obscure that dates are not readily available).

**Cross-references** are distinguished by the use of small capital letters, with a large capital to indicate the initial letter of the entry to which the reader is directed; for example, 'He commissioned LEONARDO DA VINCI . . .' means that the entry is alphabetized under 'L'.

# L

## [continued]

**Leather.** The preserved hide of animals. It can be divided into two main categories: hides, which are taken from the skins of large animals such as horses and buffaloes; and skins, which are taken from small animals such as pigs, goats, sheep, reptiles and birds. Both hides and skins are composed of three layers: the top layer, or epidermis, which has fur or hair growing out of it; the middle layer, or corium; and the bottom layer of fat or flesh (adipose tissue). The top and bottom layers are destroyed before the tanning process, and only the corium is used to make leather. The surface of the corium is marked by a grain, formed by the holes of the hair follicles, from which the origin of the leather can be determined.

Leather is strong yet flexible, and it can be treated to be as firm as board or as soft as woven cloth. Its fibrous structure enables it to be moulded and set, and it will also take many forms of decoration. It is used for clothing and footwear, armour, harness and saddlery, bookbinding, upholstery and various decorative and utilitarian items.

1. Types. 2. Techniques. 3. History and uses. 4. Conservation.

1. TYPES. The main types of hides are: 'sole bends', which are taken from half of the back of a hide and become one of the finest quality leathers; 'harness' or 'strap backs', made from the hide once the belly and shoulder have been removed; 'bag' or 'case' leathers, made from hides that have been split to a thickness of *c*. 1.5 or 2 mm; and 'upholstery hide', a soft leather, of which the surface has been brought up by 'boarding' (i.e. folding the leather grain to grain and rolling it in two directions). The main types of skins are: 'calf', which is soft and fine-grained; 'modelling calf', which has no surface finish or colouring; and 'morocco leather', which is made of goat skin tanned with sumach, its grain worked by boarding to produce a characteristic pattern.

2. TECHNIQUES.

*(i) Preparation.* Leather is treated (see fig. 1 (top)) to protect it from decay and to develop such properties as strength, pliability and water resistance. The hides or skins are soaked in lime and water and the epidermis and adipose tissue removed. The leather then undergoes one or more of the three basic tanning processes: 'oil tannage' or 'chamoising', where the skin is treated with oil or fat; 'mineral tannage' or 'tawing', in which it is immersed in a

1. Processes of treating and decorating leather in a workshop: (top) soaking, beating, stretching, cutting and drying the leather; (bottom) applying varnish to gilt leather; from D. Diderot and J. d'Alembert: *Suite de recueil de planches* (Paris, 1777), no. 120 (supplement to the *Encyclopédie*)

mixture of mineral salts, often alum; and 'vegetable tannage', in which it is soaked in astringent liquids, originally obtained from a variety of vegetable sources including oak bark and sumach. The different types of animals produce skins that require different tanning treatments. The leather is dried and then softened by 'staking', which involves stretching the damp skins over a blunt-edged blade of metal or wood. Sometimes there is a final treatment known as 'stuffing', in which the leather is rubbed with such lubricants as egg yolk.

The cutting of leather requires considerable skill. The natural tendency of the skin to stretch in certain directions

1

must be taken into account, as must the type of leather required and the use to which it will be put. The softer leathers are often delicate. Defects and areas of excessive thickness must be avoided, but wastage should be kept to a minimum.

The half-moon cutting knife has been used since at least 1500 BC, but the knife most commonly used has the cutting edge on a curve ground out at one side near the top of the blade. The cut edges of the leather are often bevelled or chamfered; on good-quality leathers they may be treated with mixtures of glue, dye and wax and then rubbed up well. Separate pieces of leather are joined by sticking (usually with animal glue), sewing with waxed thread (the holes being made with an awl) and riveting.

*(ii) Decoration.* Leather can be decorated in many ways. Cutting, piercing and scoring were used from the earliest times, as was dyeing (fragments of red leather have been found in Predynastic graves in Egypt). Leather is dyed by immersion in a dye bath. The dyes came from vegetable or mineral sources until the mid-19th century, when chemical dyes were gradually introduced, which made more brilliant colours possible.

Another early method of decoration was gilding. The design is traced on to the surface of the leather and then lightly impressed with heated tools. Glair (beaten egg white) or gold size is applied to the design, and the gold leaf laid over it. The gold is gone over with heated tools and the superfluous leaf brushed away. In 'gilt' leather the effect is achieved by facing the skins with silver or tin foil, which is then punched with small patterns that reflect the light. The main pattern is painted on top and the metalled areas that remain unpainted are glazed with a yellow varnish to simulate the appearance of gold (see fig. 1 (bottom)). One of the earliest references to gilt hangings is in an inventory of 1380 made for Charles V of France, but no examples of such leatherwork survive from before the mid-15th century.

Leather can also be embossed. The earliest method for this was probably a Spanish invention developed from the early practice of hand-stamping leather bookbindings. The design is engraved on metal plates that give fine detail but only a low degree of relief. The plates are then heated, the leather placed between them and the embossing carried out through pressure applied by a screw press. This method is not suitable for large areas and was superseded by smaller metal plates from which impressions were punched over the surface. The most important method of embossing uses moulds in a roller press. The first mould is produced by cutting a design into a wooden block (see fig. 2) composed of dovetailed sections about 10 mm thick, strengthened with battens on the back. A counter-mould is then prepared by pouring on to a sheet of board a special paste made of pieces of soaked leather. A sheet of paper is glued over the paste and the combination placed face downwards. It is run through the roller press several times and allowed to dry, producing a hard counter-mould of the original mould. Then the damp leather, already silvered and varnished, is put between the mould and counter-mould and passed between rollers to produce an embossed panel.

2. Mould for embossing leather (detail), wood, 927×749 mm, Spanish, 17th century (London, Victoria and Albert Museum)

Leather may also be decorated by tooling, punching, modelling (with a small tool called a 'spade' that depresses the background to leave other areas in relief), other forms of embossing (working the reverse of damp leather with a ball tool) and carving. 'Scorched' leather is a reddish-brown leather on which a pattern has been made by pressing a heated metal plate on the front surface against a mould at the back. The effect is similar to damask, and it is likely that the 'leather damask' referred to in inventories is in fact scorched leather.

*(iii) Moulding.* Leather has a unique fibrous structure that allows it to be moulded. In the process known as cuir-bouilli, vegetable-tanned leather is soaked in cold water until it becomes saturated and highly pliable. It can then be moulded by hand over wooden forms or in a press. The surface may be decorated by punching or incising while it is still soft, after which it is dried in a moderate heat. The term has been used since the medieval period, and it has been suggested that the leather was boiled in order to harden it, but it seems more likely that 'bouilli' merely refers to the application of heat. Cuir-bouilli was used for armour and shields as a cheap alternative to metal.

3. HISTORY AND USES. In the Palaeolithic period untreated skins were used for clothing; the process of making leather was not developed until the Neolithic period. In Predynastic Egypt leather was used for bags, bottles, clothing and sandals. The use of alum for tawing probably originated in East Asia: later it was known throughout the antique world. The Romans called alumed leather *aluta* and its makers *alutarii.*

*(i) Decorative objects.* It is often difficult to attribute the date and provenance of European leather, but parallels can be drawn with other forms of decorative art, particularly textiles. Early Spanish leather, for example, was decorated with geometric patterns similar to those on Moorish tiles, but by the 17th century the designs were based on contemporary textiles. These later hangings were made to imitate costly brocades and damasks: heavy Baroque designs were combined with dense floral ornamentation, and flowers, fruit, foliage, putti and pomegranate patterns became increasingly popular. Vernacular motifs were copied by rival leatherworkers throughout Europe, and, since moulds and plates were expensive to produce, many of the same designs recur over a considerable period of time.

*(a) Spain.* One of the main centres of leather production was Córdoba, which was famous by the 10th century for its *guadameci*, a particular type of soft leather. The term was derived from the Libyan town of Ghadames, which produced a similar type of soft goatskin dressed with alum. Córdoba (hence the English term 'cordwainer') produced *guadameci* in its natural white form or dyed red with kermes. The leather was sometimes covered with gold or silver foil, and during the 14th century this metallized surface was punched. During the early 17th century, designs were embossed on silvered leather using moulds in a modified printing press. Other centres of production in Spain were Granada, Seville and Valencia.

The leather was used for upholstery, cushions, floor coverings, wall and bed hangings and ecclesiastical purposes (antependiums, kneelers and vestments). In the Sala de los Reyes (or de la Justicia) at the Alhambra, Granada, there are two leather-covered cupolas dating from the end of the 14th century. In 1570 Catherine de' Medici ordered from Córdoba four sets of *guadameci*, with designs of flowers, fruits and grotesques on a polychrome ground, to decorate rooms in the Palais du Louvre, Paris. A small number of expensive leather hangings, including one bearing papal arms, were exported from Spain to the Vatican in 1556 and 1559. In 1604 the majority of Cordovan leatherworkers were engaged on a contract for the palace of Philip II in Valladolid. Their contracts clearly state both the colours and designs to be used. Where particularly sophisticated work was required, it is likely that professional painters were employed.

*(b) France, Italy, the Low Countries and Portugal.* Though developed in Spain, decorated leather was soon copied and adapted throughout Europe. In France a charter was granted in 1594 to the 'doreurs sur cuir, garnisseurs et enjoliveurs', allowing them to make gilt-leather hangings and such leather furnishings as cabinets, coffers and frames; the craftsmen also acquired a special stamp with which they were required to mark their work. After some conflict, the leatherworkers amalgamated with two other guilds, the sheathmakers and the silverers. During this period, however, much of the leather used in France was probably imported, and import duties were imposed on gilt leather in 1664. Leather hangings were often put up in the summer to replace the woollen hangings used in the winter.

3. Leather sword scabbard (detail), l. 844 mm, w. 89 mm, Italian, *c.* 1500 (London, Victoria and Albert Museum)

Italian craftsmen developed their own techniques for decorating leather with the bold designs and coloured glazes that are characteristic of their work. Surviving examples of Italian leatherware include shields and coffers, often with punched decoration. Few gilt-leather hangings survive in Italy, but they were certainly known during the Renaissance; for example, they are depicted in Titian's *Venus of Urbino* (*c.* 1538; Florence, Uffizi). A particularly sophisticated group of cuir-bouilli objects from Renaissance Italy includes a 14th-century crozier case (London, V&A), carefully modelled into five compartments and covered in punched ornamentation, including the arms of a bishop of the Aldobrandini family. The same museum also houses an unfinished sword scabbard of black leather (see fig. 3), bearing the monogram of Cesare Borgia, that was described by Henry Cole as the 'finest piece of art in leather known'. It was worked in very high relief to simulate bronze. Italian leatherworkers used cuir-bouilli for book covers, knife and scissor cases, and even church plate (for example chalices, patens, pyxes).

By the end of the 16th century the Low Countries had become the most important centre of production, and the majority of surviving leather panels are either Flemish or Dutch. Mechelen in Flanders (now Belgium) was the most important centre, but leather was also produced in Antwerp, Liège and Brussels. The main centre in the northern Netherlands was Amsterdam. A complex and sophisticated style of decoration developed, based on contemporary textiles and using bold pomegranate forms. At a time when tapestries and silk wall hangings were prestigious and expensive, gilt-leather panels became an affordable alternative. Indeed, the Dutch continued to cover the walls of their houses with lavish gilt leather well into the 18th century, by which time it was no longer fashionable in other European countries. At this later period designs of small flowers and flowing ribbons predominated. A leather industry also existed in Portugal as early as 1644, when leather was exported from Lisbon to the port of Antwerp; but it was clearly unable to compete with the Flemish market.

*(c) England and Scandinavia.* In England the production of cuir-bouilli was widespread from the 15th century. The most popular product was a type of tankard known as a blackjack. A larger tankard was also made, known as a bombard since it resembled a cannon of the same name. The body, complete with handle, was cut in one, but the round bottom was a separate piece. Once the moulded

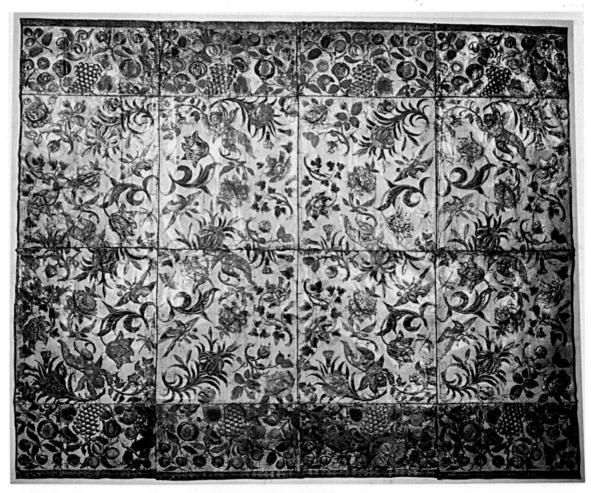

4. Leather hanging in the Marble Dining-room at Ham House, Surrey, 1670–80

5. Leather hanging of *The Battle*, detail from the story of Antony and Cleopatra, in the gallery at Dunster Castle, Somerset, mid-17th century

leather had set, molten pitch or resin was poured into the container to prevent liquids soaking into it.

Some form of gilt-leather industry existed in England by 1601 when the inventory for Hardwick Hall, Derbys, listed 50 pieces of 'wrought' gilt leather and 34 pieces of leather 'silvered but not finished'. Further evidence that England was producing leather by the mid-17th century can be found in the diary of Samuel Pepys. On 19 October 1660 he wrote, 'This morning my dining room was finished with green serge and gilt leather which is very handsome.' On 5 November 1668 he selected his first vehicle, 'a little chariot whose body was framed...to be covered with leather.' He watched impatiently while successive coats of yellow varnish were applied and explained that most coaches were then 'done so, and it is very pretty when laid on well, and not too pale, as some are, even to show the silver'. Surviving trade cards indicate that a small but important group of leather gilders were working in London around St Paul's Cathedral between 1714 and 1785.

Gilt leather, whether English or imported, became an increasingly popular form of interior decoration; examples can be found at Longleat House, Wilts, Chatsworth, Derbys, Prestonfield House, Edinburgh, and Ham House, Surrey (see fig. 4). Perhaps the most important surviving leather hangings are those at Dunster Castle, Somerset (see fig. 5). These depict the story of Antony and Cleopatra and are mentioned in inventories of 1741 and 1744, when

they were valued at £21. Unfortunately their provenance is unknown, but their similarity to mid-17th-century engravings and tapestries suggests that they came from France or Flanders. The battle scene, in particular, is closely related to a Brussels tapestry of 1661 by Justus van Egmont. Comparable sets of narrative leather hangings are extremely rare; there are some from Rouen, now at Ecouen, one in the château at Lunéville and two of 1688 in the royal palace at Drottningholm, Sweden. It is likely that they all originated from the same workshop. Other interesting examples of leather hangings are those in the closet at Honington Hall, Warwicks, where panels of chinoiserie leather are set in the wainscot.

The widespread taste for objects 'à la chinoise' that developed in Europe in the early 18th century influenced contemporary leather production. Chinoiserie screens became particularly fashionable for rooms and closets in this style, and leather was often used in preference to such delicate fabrics as chintz, silk or printed calico. Leather was eminently suitable as it was solid, practical and reasonably priced. It could be japanned or varnished in imitation of lacquer (*see* LACQUER, §II, 2), which made it a popular background for objects from East Asia and an appropriate substitute for true lacquer screens, which were then very expensive. The designs for these chinoiserie screens usually consist of an ideal landscape densely decorated with houses, flowers, birds and characters in oriental costume. The borders are generally decorated with single vases and other objects similar to the auspicious symbols frequently found in Chinese ceramics and decorative arts.

By the end of the 18th century leather gilders' trade cards indicate that paper hangings were among the wares they sold. Gradually, as a result of changing fashion, they channelled their skills into the production of embossed wallpapers. The catalogue of the Great Exhibition of 1851 in London lists only one exhibit of gilt, embossed and painted leather, but leather panels were occasionally produced in the 1890s for rooms decorated in the Art Nouveau style.

Leather was used in Scandinavia in the 17th and 18th centuries. Several sets of room hangings survive in Swedish and Danish country houses, and in the Swedish Royal Collection there are two sets, one depicting the Turkish siege of Vienna of 1683 and the other based on a series of mythological paintings by the Swedish court painter David Klöcker Ehrenstrahl. In the Nationalmuseum, Copenhagen, there is a set of hangings from the Jutland country house of Gamle Estrup.

*(ii) Furniture.* In England leather covers for beds and tables are mentioned as early as 1423, in an inventory of the wardrobe of Henry VI. By the 17th century gilt leather was sometimes used to cover chairs, but plain leather was more common. Scorched leather was used for protective covers (e.g. the celestial and terrestrial globes at Ham House, Surrey, dated *c.* 1730) and for upholstery on chairs. In 17th-century Italy and Spain there was a fashion for chairs upholstered in heavily tooled gilt leather comparable to bookbindings, and in the early 18th century many chairs in Scandinavia and central Europe were covered with gilt

leather, but such covers are rarely found in France and England.

Some pieces of leatherwork in revivalist styles were made in the 1920s, for example the leather boxes with polychrome Moresque decoration made by Alex Behrens and painted by Louis Churchill for Studland Art Industries in Dorset. Leather also became a major component in such designer classics as Charles Eames's lounge chair and ottoman (1956; see UNITED STATES OF AMERICA, fig. 37), as well as playing a predominant role in the furniture industry, particularly in Italy, where such designers as Vico Magistretti consistently used leather in their work.

See also AFRICA, §V, 9; EGYPT, ANCIENT, §XVII, 10; MONGOLIA, §IV, 6; NATIVE NORTH AMERICAN ART, §XIII; and ROME, ANCIENT, §X, 7.

BIBLIOGRAPHY

D. Diderot and J. D'Alembert: *Encyclopédie*, v/54 (Paris, 1755); *Supplément*, ii/735 (Paris, 1762); plates: *Planches*, iii, *Doreur* (Paris, 1763); *Suite de recueil de planches*, 120 (Paris, 1777);
A. D. Fougeroux de Bondaroy: 'Art de travailler les cuirs dorés ou argentés', *Description des arts et métiers* (Paris, 1762)
F. Lenygon: 'Gilt Leather Rooms', *A. J.* [London] (1911), p. 281
H. Clouzot: *Cuirs décorés*, 2 vols (Paris, 1925)
A. Lucas: *Ancient Egyptian Materials and Industries* (London, 1934)
H. Huth: 'English Chinoiserie Gilt Leather', *Burl. Mag.*, lxxi (1937), pp. 25–35
G. R. Faber: 'Dyeing and Tanning in Classical Antiquity', *Ciba Z.*, ix (May 1938)
J. W. Waterer: *Leather in Life, Art and Industry* (London, 1946)
C. Singer, E. J. Holmyard and A. R. Hall: *A History of Technology* (Oxford, 1956), i, *passim*; ii, pp. 147–86, 187–90
J. W. Waterer: *Leather Craftsmanship* (London, 1968)
G. A. Bravo and J. Trupke: *10,000 Jahre Leder* (Basle and Stuttgart, 1970)
J. W. Waterer: *Spanish Leather* (London, 1971)
D. Dodd: *Dunster Castle* (London, 1986)

BATHSHEBA ABSE

4. CONSERVATION. Leather is a complex organic material made up of skin protein, tanning compounds and lubricants (see §2(i) above). The character and, to a large extent, the type of deterioration is determined by the nature of the tanning compounds.

The most widely encountered leather is vegetable tanned. This is to be found on saddlery and harness, military accoutrements, upholstery and items that require tooling and embossing, for example screens and panels for wall hangings. Other types of tannage are alum tawing, which produces a white leather used principally for such costume as gloves and furs, and oil tanning, which produces buff leather from which gloves and jerkins were made.

One of the commonest and most damaging forms of deterioration is the chemical breakdown known as 'red rot'. This only occurs with vegetable-tanned leather. The deterioration is characterized by the reddish coloration of the leather, delamination, embrittlement and, in extreme cases, a total loss of strength of the leather fibres, which turn to powder when rubbed. It is caused by the action of acidic gases from the atmosphere (principally sulphur dioxide), which are absorbed and converted into acids within the leather. Once the deterioration has begun, specialist help must be sought to stabilize the leather. Acid-deteriorated leathers may be in a very fragile condition and, if this is the case, consolidation and support treatments will need to be carried out after stabilization. A similar form of deterioration is caused by contact with

iron; it is known as 'black rot', as badly affected leather fibres turn black. It leads to embrittlement, delamination and loss of strength.

Leather objects can be very hard and inflexible. Sometimes this is an intentional property, as in cuir-bouilli, but for objects that have lost flexibility the application of a lubricant may be required. Lubricants should be applied as solutions or emulsions; undiluted salves should be avoided as they tend to lead to over-application of oil. Lubricants should never be applied to the front surface of leathers that have been painted or varnished, but always on the reverse or flesh side. Lubricants may darken light-coloured leathers, and advice should be sought about their suitability.

Breakdown of oils within the leather can lead to a white bloom forming on the leather surface; this is termed 'fatty acid spue'. It is easily removed with organic solvents, but the potential for further spue formation will always be present.

In common with other organic materials, leather is affected by extremes in temperature and relative humidity. Long-term exposure to heat and high/low humidity cycles can lead to a cumulative hardening and loss of flexibility. Surface checks may also occur, and these may eventually develop into cracks and splits especially if the leather also suffers from chemical deterioration.

If leather is stored at too high a relative humidity (above 65% RH), mould growth may occur. When this happens the leather items should be immediately removed from contact with other objects to prevent contamination and placed in a dry environment. The mould can be removed by brush or with a vacuum and the surface swabbed with alcohol or a fungicide solution to destroy the growth.

The best conditions for the storage or display of leather are moderate temperatures and a relative humidity of 55–65% RH. Direct sunlight and high light levels should be avoided as these can lead to fading, cracking and embrittlement. For painted leather surfaces (e.g. screens and wall hangings), recommended light levels should be similar to those for oil paintings. Leather should be kept free from dust by being enclosed, if displayed, or by being wrapped in acid-free tissue, if stored. However, enamelled or patent leather objects should not be wrapped as the tissue may with time become attached to the leather surface. Leather is very prone to deformation: if it is not correctly supported it may stretch and distort, and if folded it may develop crease lines. This applies particularly to leather used in clothing, so costume accessories should be padded with acid-free tissue and garments hung on padded hangers or laid flat without folding.

See also BOOKCOVER AND BOOKBINDING, §3.

BIBLIOGRAPHY

P. E. Guldbeck: *The Care of Historical Collections* (Nashville, 1972)
J. W. Waterer: *A Guide to the Conservation and Restoration of Objects Made Wholly or in Part of Leather* (London, 1972)
H. Kühn: *Erhaltung und Pflege von Kunstwerken und Antiquitäten*, i (Munich, 1974, rev. 2/1981; Eng. trans., London, 1986)
S. Fogel, ed.: *Recent Advances in Leather Conservation* (Washington, DC, 1985)
*ICOM International Leather and Parchment Symposium: Leathercraft and Related Objects: Offenbach am Main, 1989*
C. N. Calnan, ed.: *Conservation of Leather in Transport Collections* (London, 1991)

C. N. Calnan and B. M. Haines, eds: *Leather: Its Composition and Changes with Time* (Northampton, 1991)

CHRISTOPHER CALNAN

**Leb, Wolfgang** (*b* ?Salzburg, ?1460; *d* Wasserburg, Upper Bavaria, ?1520). German sculptor. His father was a painter, and he may have been one also. He was recorded in Wasserburg in 1496 and mentioned there for the last time in 1519. His sculptural work embodies traditional forms in a new statuesque manner, and his red marble tomb sculpture is rooted in the work of the Bavarian sculptor Erasmus Grasser and the Master of the Chapel of Schloss Blutenburg, near Munich.

Leb made a great number of tomb slabs, of which two are signed and dated. The tomb of the founder of the former monastery of Ebersberg, Upper Bavaria, is dated 1500. The slab, made of red marble from Adnet and measuring 3.86×1.61 m, is the richest in the region. It shows the kneeling Count Ulrich and his wife, presenting a model of the monastery church to the Virgin and Child. Below is a smaller figure of Abbot Sebastian Häfele (*d* 1500). The strong symmetry of the design is underlined by the figures of SS Sebastian and Benedict near the border. With its flat background the whole composition recalls a shrine. The corners of the tomb box are accentuated by six figures of monks, seated and reading books, who may be a final reflection of the weepers of Burgundian tombs. The inscribed and turned ribbons framing the slab are characteristic of Leb's work.

The second dated tomb is that of the founder of the former monastery of Attel, near Wasserburg. Here, the model of the church is presented by the standing Graf Engelbrecht of Limburg and his wife. It is similar to the Ebersberg tomb, but much simplified. In the upper corners of the slab are busts of the Virgin and Child with an angel, with three escutcheons below. The inscription is on the border: *hanc sculpturam fecit fieri pater leonhardus abbas per manus magistri wolfgangi leb anno 1509*. Other tomb slabs attributed to Leb are those of the burgomaster Hans Baumgartner (*d* 1493; Kufstein, Tyrol, parish church) and of the knight Hans Baumgartner (*d* 1500; Wasserburg, parish church).

BIBLIOGRAPHY

*NDB*; Thieme–Becker

P. M. Halm: *Studien zur süddeutschen Plastik*, 2 vols (Augsburg, 1926), i, pp. 139–75

W. Pinder: *Die deutsche Plastik vom ausgehenden Mittelalter bis zum Ende der Renaissance* (Potsdam, 1929), pp. 447–8

T. Müller: *Alte bairische Bildhauer* (Munich, 1950), pl. 90

——: *Sculpture in the Netherlands, Germany, France and Spain, 1400–1500*, Pelican Hist. A. (Harmondsworth, 1966), p. 176

——: *Gotische Skulptur in Tirol* (Bolzano, 1976) p. 40, pl. 199

VINCENT MAYR

**Lebanon**, Republic of [Arab. Al-Jumhūriyya al-Lubnā-niyya]. Country in the Middle East *c.* 10,400 sq. km in area, with a coastline along the eastern Mediterranean Sea, bordered in the north and east by Syria and in the south by Israel. The limestone Mt Lebanon range runs from north to south, dividing the coastal plain from the fertile Beqaʻa Valley. The modern state, with its capital at Beirut, was created out of the Ottoman province of Lebanon with additional Syrian territory. Formerly with a Christian majority, the population was estimated in 1983 as 34%

Christian (the largest sects are Maronite Catholic, Greek Orthodox and Greek Catholic), 33% Shiʻa Muslim, 25% Sunni Muslim and 8% Druze; the total population (1990 estimate) is *c.* 3,340,000. The division of political power on a sectarian basis, dominated by the Christians, and factional rivalries exacerbated by the Palestinian issue were at the root of the conflicts that erupted into civil war in 1975. Intermittent peace was achieved in the early 1990s after agreement on a new division of power. This article covers the art produced in the country in the late 19th century and the 20th. For its earlier history *see* EARLY CHRISTIAN AND BYZANTINE ART; GREECE, ANCIENT; ISLAMIC ART; ROME, ANCIENT; and SYRIA–PALESTINE.

In the late 19th century Beirut was a small town with red-tiled villas of sandstone, two or three storeys high, with elaborate façades and decorative stairways and balconies. In the early 20th century Beirut expanded rapidly; new materials and construction techniques were used, particularly concrete. Two architects who trained in Paris, Farid Trad and Antoine Tabet, used the new materials sensitively. Tabet's St George's Hotel (1929; destr.), for example, made with precast concrete components, had an elegant design. In the construction boom after World War II many multi-storey blocks in reinforced concrete with glass façades and aluminium frames were built, but little work was entrusted to qualified architects. Beirut was devastated between the 1970s and the early 1990s; Tripoli and Sidon were also badly damaged, while Tyre declined because of its proximity to the closed Israeli border.

The vernacular architecture of Lebanon used stone. Five types of houses are known: the closed rectangular house with a flat roof; the gallery house, usually of two storeys open to the outside by an arcade or colonnade; the iwan and courtyard house; the central hall house (the most prevalent), usually of two storeys, in which the central hall, expressed externally by a triple-arch motif, is the nucleus to which rooms are added; and the combination type.

Close relations with the West, missionary education and the flourishing printing press stimulated the practice of art in Western styles. In the late 18th century and early 19th such Lebanese Christian artists as Moussa Dib (*d* 1826) and Kenaan Dib (*d* 1873) painted religious subjects and portraits of clergy. In the 19th century a number of young Lebanese studied in the Ottoman military and naval academies in Istanbul, and some were inspired by the style of painting prevalent among Turkish soldier–painters. The influence of the latter was felt in the Lebanese 'marine' school of painting. Among the painters of this school were ʻAli Jamal, Hassan Tannir, Ibrahim al-Najjar, Ibrahim Sarabiyye, Muhammad Said Miri, Najib Bekhazi, Najib Fayyad and Salim Haddad. Many works by 19th-century Lebanese artists are now lost.

Among the first Lebanese painters to study in Europe were DAOUD CORM and Habib Srour (1860–1938), both of whom studied in Rome; they gained recognition for their portraits and religious paintings in churches and convents. Khalil Saleeby (1870–1928) studied in Edinburgh and then in Paris under Puvis de Chavannes; he was inspired by Impressionism, particularly the work of Renoir. Gibran Khalil Gibran (1883–1931), the painter and writer, trained in Paris before settling in New York;

Beirut, Nicolas Ibrahim Sursock Museum, 19th century

his work included some notable portraits and drawings of nudes.

There was a greater sense of freedom among artists after World War I. Familiar with the new European movements while retaining links with their national culture, they depicted Lebanon and its people. Such artists as César Gemayel (1898–1958), Omar Onsi (1901–69), Mustafa Farroukh (1901–57), Rashid Wehbé (*b* 1917) and SALIBA DOUAIHY (*b* 1915) are seen as the founders of modern art in Lebanon. Their paintings of villages and mountain landscapes, with details of local customs and architecture, constituted a distinctive movement in Lebanese art. Among these painters, Douaihy later developed the abstract element in his work.

After World War II such artists as Etel Adnan (*b* 1925), Said Akl (*b* 1926), Rafic Charaf (*b* 1932) and Hussein Madi (*b* 1938) derived inspiration from Lebanese history, folk culture and Arabic calligraphy. Other artists followed international trends such as Expressionism, Surrealism and abstract art; among this group were Chafic Abboud (*b* 1926), Paul Guiragossian (*b* 1926), Yvette Achkar (*b* 1928), Amine Elbacha (*b* 1932) and Juliana Séraphim (*b* 1934). An important figure in the birth of modern Lebanese sculpture was YOUSSEF HOYECK, who studied in Rome and Paris before settling in Beirut in 1939; his work was influenced by the art of Rodin. Youssef Ghassoub (1898–1967) studied under the Egyptian sculptor Mahmud Mukhtar and executed works in an academic

style. The brothers Michael Basbous (1921–81), Alfred Basbous (*b* 1924) and Joseph Basbous (*b* 1929) also produced important work. Intellectual freedom, prosperity, a proliferation of exhibitions, commercial galleries and periodicals made Beirut in the 1960s a dynamic artistic centre. With the outbreak of civil war in 1975 art patronage largely ceased, and numerous artists left the country to live abroad.

Exhibitions of art were encouraged by the French authorities and continued after independence. In 1937 the Lebanese Academy of Fine Arts was founded in Beirut and attracted Arab and European teachers. In 1954 the Department of Fine Arts opened at the American University of Beirut, and in 1957 the Association of Lebanese Artists, Painters and Sculptors was founded in the capital. In 1961 the first art salons were held at the Nicolas Ibrahim Sursock Museum (see fig.), a 19th-century mansion bequeathed to the Beirut Municipality by Nicolas Ibrahim Sursock; this museum also organized exhibitions in Beirut and abroad. The Fine Arts Institute at the Lebanese University was established in 1965.

Lebanon was the home of the Phoenicians (*see* PHOENICIAN) in the 1st millennium BC, when TRIPOLI was founded. There is a rich mixture of sites dating from the Neolithic and Bronze Age periods, Greco-Roman and Christian–Islamic eras. Archaeological exploration started in the 19th century at BAALBEK, SIDON and TYRE; French teams began excavations at BYBLOS in the 1920s; the early Islamic site of ANJAR was investigated from the 1950s onwards. There are notable crusader castles (e.g. at Byblos, and Beaufort Castle nr Tyre) and palaces of the amirs of Mt Lebanon, such as the early 19th-century palace at BAYT AL-DIN. Numerous artefacts were taken in the 19th century for Western museums (e.g. Paris, Louvre) and to Istanbul. In the civil war some archaeological sites were destroyed (e.g. the Late Bronze Age site of KAMID EL-LOZ) or dug up by amateurs (e.g. the Roman cemeteries nr Tyre); Phoenician and Greco-Roman artefacts were illegally exported, mainly to the West; others were badly damaged (e.g. Phoenician sarcophagi).

During the Mandate the French set up a Department of Antiquities, which continued after independence. The National Archaeological Museum, founded in Beirut in 1919, was badly damaged during the civil war; it contains important Phoenician, Egyptian and Roman artefacts, as does the Archaeological Museum of the American University of Beirut, which was robbed in the early 1990s. In Bshirri (Bcharré), where Gibran Kahlil Gibran is buried, a museum contains some of his paintings and drawings.

BIBLIOGRAPHY

R. S. Ghosn: 'Beirut Architecture', in R. Saidah and others: *Beirut: Crossroads of Cultures* (Beirut, 1970), pp. 185–202
J. Gibran and K. Gibran: *Khalil Gibran: His Life and World* (Boston, MA, 1974)
E. Lahoud: *Contemporary Art in Lebanon* (Beirut and New York, 1974)
F. Ragette: *Architecture in Lebanon: The Lebanese House during the 18th and 19th Centuries* (Beirut, 1974)
A. Raphael: *Twenty Drawings by Khalil Gibran* (New York, 1974)
F. El-Khoury: *Domestic Architecture in the Lebanon* (London, 1975)
R. Chahine: *One Hundred Years of Plastic Arts in Lebanon, 1880–1980*, 2 vols (Beirut, 1982)
B. Fakhoury: *Art Education in Lebanon* (diss., U. London, Inst. Educ., 1983)
C. Aboussouan, ed.: *L'Architecture libanaise du XVe au XIXe siècle* (Beirut, 1985)
A. Bahnassi: *Ruwwād al-fann al-ḥadīth fi'l-bilād al-'arabiyya* [Pioneers of modern art in the Arab countries] (Beirut, 1985)
F. Debbas: *Beirut our Memory: An Illustrated Tour in the Old City from 1880 to 1930* (Beirut, 1986)
S. Saleeby: *Khalil Saleeby: A Painter from Lebanon* (Beirut, 1986)
*Romantic Lebanon: The European View, 1700–1900* (exh. cat., British Lebanese Association; London, Leighton House A.G. & Mus., 1986)
H. Khal: *The Woman Artist in Lebanon* (Beirut, 1988)
*Contemporary Lebanese Artists* (exh. cat., London, Kufa Gal., 1988)
W. Ali, ed.: *Contemporary Art from the Islamic World* (London, 1989), pp. 196–204
*Lebanon—The Artist's View: 200 Years of Lebanese Painting* (exh. cat., British Lebanese Association; London, Barbican Cent., 1989)

**Lebarbier** [Le Barbier], **Jean-Jacques-François** (*b* Rouen, 11 Nov 1738; *d* Paris, 7 May 1826). French painter, illustrator and writer. He began his studies in Rouen and, at 17, won first prize for drawing at the city's Académie. Shortly afterwards he travelled to Paris, entering the Académie Royale de Peinture et de Sculpture as a student of Jean-Baptiste-Marie Pierre. In 1767–8 he was in Rome, a fact confirmed by a number of dated and inscribed drawings and paintings, including the pen, ink and wash drawing *Landscape Inspired by the Gardens of the Villa d'Este at Tivoli* (Paris, Ecole N. Sup. B.-A.). He was in Switzerland in 1776, where he spent several years drawing illustrations for Beát Zurlauben's *Tableau de la Suisse ou voyage pittoresque fait dans les treize cantons du Corps Helvétique* (Paris, 1780–86). In 1780, having returned to France, he was approved (*agréé*) by the Académie Royale

and received (*reçu*) in 1785 with *Jupiter Asleep on Mount Ida* (Paris, Ecole N. Sup. B.-A.). Thereafter he regularly exhibited moralistic pictures at the Salon until 1814, including the *Canadians at the Tomb of their Child* (Rouen, Mus. B.-A.) and *Jeanne Hachette at the Siege of Beauvais* (Beauvais, Hôtel de Ville, destr. 1940) in 1781, *Aristoumenos and the Spartan Girls* (Paris, Louvre) in 1787 and pictures of *St Louis* and *St Denis* in 1812, both of which indicate his interest in depicting religious themes and incidents from earlier French history.

Lebarbier was swift to take up the increasingly fashionable Neo-classical style of Joseph-Marie Vien and Jacques-Louis David, and his works in this vein include the *Tomb of Sextus* (Angers, Mus. B.-A.). He also wrote a minor contribution to the literature of Neo-classicism, the treatise *Des Causes physiques et morales qui ont influé sur les progrès de la peinture et de la sculpture chez les Grecs* (1801). However, his drawing (1784; Paris, Carnavalet) of the Neo-classical hôtel (destr.) designed and built in the Chaussée d'Antin quarter of Paris for Mme Marie-Jeanne Thélusson by the architect Claude-Nicolas Ledoux shows that Lebarbier's artistic interests were not confined purely to painting and sculpture.

In 1786 Lebarbier painted cartoons for a set of four Beauvais tapestries on the theme of the *Four Parts of the World* (London, Osterley Park House, NT). His designs for two of the tapestries, *America* and *Europe*, emphasize the assistance given by France to American colonists during their struggle to throw off British rule. These designs reveal the warmth of Lebarbier's own republican sympathies, to which he gave free rein in his art during the French Revolution (1789–95). In 1786 he also began working on a series of illustrations for the *Works* of the Swiss poet and painter Salomon Gessner. While many of these attest to his Neo-classical bias, there are some, for example *Eraste*, that owe more to Jean-Baptiste Greuze's influence. Lebarbier worked on Gessner's illustrations until 1793, but he also provided designs for works by Ovid, Racine, Jean-Jacques Rousseau and Jacques Delille.

In 1790 the Assemblée Nationale approached Lebarbier to commemorate an early act of Revolutionary zeal; this resulted in *The Heroic Courage of the Young Desilles at the Nancy Affair, 30 August 1790* (Nancy, Mus. Hist. Lorrain). He also made a drawing of this same army officer, *Desilles Presented to Henry IV by Minerva in the Elysian Fields* (untraced; engr. by François Girard). By 1795, however, when the painting was shown at the Salon, the political climate had changed, and Antoine-Joseph-Marc Desilles was no longer seen as a hero but as a counter-revolutionary traitor. Lebarbier's portrait of the South American general *Francisco de Miranda* (1795; Caracas, Pedro Vallenilla Echeverria priv. col.) depicts another individual who was in turn fêted and hounded during the Revolution. Miranda (1756–1816) collected works of art, with Lebarbier acting as adviser and agent. Lebarbier's two daughters, Elise Bruyère (1776–1842) and Henriette, were both painters; Elise became a moderately successful portrait- and flower-painter.

WRITINGS
*Des Causes physiques et morales qui ont influé sur les progrès de la peinture et de la sculpture chez les Grecs* (Paris, 1801)

BIBLIOGRAPHY

J. Renouvier: *Histoire de l'art pendant la Révolution* (Paris, 1863)
G. W. Digby: 'A Set of Beauvais Tapestries Alluding to the War of American Independence', *Burl. Mag.*, xcii (1950), pp. 251–5
M. N. Benisovich: 'Le Général Francisco de Miranda et ses amis parisiens', *Gaz. B.-A.*, n.s. 5, lix (1962), pp. 345–51
J. Vergnet-Ruiz: 'Une Inspiration de Delacroix: La *Jeanne Hachette* de Lebarbier', *Rev. Louvre*, xxi/2 (1971), pp. 81–5
*French Landscape Drawings and Sketches of the Eighteenth Century* (exh. cat., intro R. Bacou; London, BM, 1977), p. 87
*French Painting: The Revolutionary Decades, 1760–1830* (exh. cat., ed. A. Serullaz, H. Toussaint and J. Vilain; Sydney, A.G. NSW; Melbourne, N.G. Victoria, 1980), pp. 170–73

JOSHUA DRAPKIN

**Le Barc de Boutteville, Louis** (*d* Paris, Oct 1896). French dealer. He was the first commercial dealer to show the works of the Nabi group and of other independent artists working in Paris in the 1890s, thereby helping to establish their reputations at the outset of their careers. Having worked as a dealer in Old Master painting, Le Barc de Boutteville was apparently on the point of retiring, when he decided, on the advice of the young painter Paul Vogler (1852–1904), to invest in and support the efforts of these young and as yet unknown painters. He mounted a first exhibition by the 'Peintres Impressionnistes et Symbolistes' in December 1891, and thereafter his gallery, at 47 Rue Le Peletier, Paris, mounted 15 exhibitions in all, two after his death. Regularly shown at Le Barc's gallery were works by such artists as Louis Anquetin, Emile Bernard, Pierre Bonnard, Maurice Denis, Ker-Xavier Roussel and Edouard Vuillard, as well as by members of the Neo-Impressionist movement such as Charles Angrand, Henri Edmond Cross, Maximilien Luce and Lucien Pissarro. Among the notable independents whose work Le Barc supported was Henri de Toulouse-Lautrec. Le Barc invited sympathetic critics (e.g. Georges-Albert Aurier and Camille Mauclair) or one of the participating artists to write prefaces for his exhibition catalogues. In addition to these group shows where each artist contributed a limited number of works and none was given a pre-eminence, the Le Barc de Boutteville gallery also mounted some thematic and one-man shows. A small retrospective exhibition of 16 works by van Gogh was arranged by Emile Bernard in 1892. An exhibition entitled *Portraits du prochain siècle*, including portraits by Georges Seurat, Paul Gauguin, Paul Cézanne and Vuillard, was held in 1893, and one-man shows were held for Maxime Maufra, Georges d'Espagnat and Armand Séguin, the latter, in 1895, with a preface written by Gauguin during his final stay in Paris.

BIBLIOGRAPHY

F. Jourdain: *Né en 76* (Paris, 1951)
C. Guy: 'Le Barc de Boutteville', *L'Oeil* (April 1965), pp. 31–6, 58–9

BELINDA THOMSON

**Lebas, Jacques-Philippe** (*b* Paris, 8 July 1707; *d* Paris, 14 April 1783). French engraver. He was brought up in poverty by his widowed mother. At the age of 14 he joined the studio of Antoine Herisset (1685–1769), a mediocre architectural engraver, and he also had lessons from Nicolas-Henry Tardieu. His training, however, was chiefly based on close study of 17th-century engravings, particularly those of Gérard Audran. As a result, he retained throughout his life a marked predilection for free engraving, using an etched base with rich tonal contrasts. In 1729 Pierre Crozat commissioned from him an engraving of *St John the Baptist Preaching to the Multitude* (Paris, Louvre) after Pier Francesco Mola (ii). Lebas rapidly became successful; around 1733 he opened a studio, which soon became the busiest in Paris. He began to assemble an important collection of plates as a long-term resource; he set all his pupils to work on these, restricting himself to giving unity and harmony to plates that had been worked by others. His remarkable technical skill enabled him to put right his pupils' work with a few strokes, sometimes even in drypoint (he was also the first engraver to use drypoint for skies). The practice of collaborative working caused him difficulties with membership of the Académie Royale de Peinture et de Sculpture, Paris. He was accepted (*agréé*) in 1735, but the portraits of *Pierre-Jacques Cazes* (SG 70) and *Robert Le Lorrain* (both Versailles, Château; both after Jacques Aved), which he had been required to submit as *morceaux de réception*, were refused in 1741 because of a rumour that Lebas had said to his pupils 'Rejoice, Messieurs; you are about to be received by the Académie'. He was once again *agréé* in 1742 and was received (*reçu*) in 1743 with a *Conversation galante* (London, Wallace) after Nicolas Lancret. In 1771 he was elected a Conseiller de l'Académie.

The prints made by Lebas or by his studio (a difficult distinction, as Lebas signed plates on which he had scarcely worked) perfectly reflect the tastes of 18th-century collectors. He appears to have been primarily motivated by self-interest; he sometimes complained about changes in taste but would not have considered working on prints that would not sell well. He thus engraved hardly any paintings of the Italian school or the French school of the previous century. His collection of plates was based on Dutch and Flemish painters, particularly David Teniers (ii), after whom he made more than 90 engravings, Philips Wouwerman (15 engravings) and Salomon van Ruysdael, after whom he made 11 engravings. Fashion dictated Lebas's choice of contemporary French artists: thus in the 1730s he engraved *L'Assemblée galante* (1731; untraced, SG 497) after Antoine Watteau; *Roman Charity* (1735; untraced, SG 141) after Noël-Nicolas Coypel; and the *Italian Meal* (1738; London, Wallace) after Nicolas Lancret. In the 1740s Lebas concentrated on Jean-Baptiste Oudry, François Boucher and Jean-Siméon Chardin. After 1755 he worked for the most part after Joseph Vernet (43 prints); in collaboration with Charles-Nicolas Cochin II he made after Vernet the 15 best-selling prints of the century, the *Ports of France* (Paris, Mus. Mar.). During the first phase (1758–67) of this enterprise, Lebas and Cochin engraved 14 paintings of ports with such success that they decided to continue the series. They engraved Vernet's *Port of Dieppe*, and Cochin was to draw a view of the *Port of Le Havre* and two of the *Port of Rouen*, but the latter two plates had not been finished at the time of Lebas's death.

Between 1768 and 1773 Cochin also commissioned Lebas to engrave four of the plates in the series of *Les Conquêtes de l'Empereur de la Chine* (SG 62) for the Compagnie des Indes; it was Lebas's efficiency and ability to direct his pupils' work that had gained him the greater part of this prestigious commission. A good many of the best engravers of the century came, in fact, from his studio; the list of 25 engravers known to have worked for him includes such artists of varied talents as Jacques Aliamet, Louis-Jacques Cathelin, Charles-Etienne Gaucher, Noël Le Mire, Joseph de Longueil, Jean-Michel Moreau (1) and even the Comte de Caylus. The end of Lebas's life was troubled by financial difficulties; many of his plates were no longer fashionable, and his last enterprise, the *Figures de l'histoire de France*, was paralysed by the procrastination of Moreau, who was the draughtsman and who was perhaps calculating that on Lebas's death he would complete a profitable collection alone.

BIBLIOGRAPHY

Y. Sjöberg and F. Gardey: *Inventaire du fonds français: Graveurs du dix-huitième siècle*, Paris, Bib. N., Cab. Est. cat. (Paris, 1930–74), xiii, pp. 78–320 [incl. bibliog.] [SG]

CHRISTIAN MICHEL

**Le Bas, James** (*b* London, 1772; *d* London, 1845). English silversmith, active in Ireland. He was apprenticed in London to his father, William Le Bas (1757–1827), on 1 November 1786. From December 1786 he worked for Samuel Merton, a silversmith and turner in Foster Lane, London, and from February 1793 for William Pitt, a goldsmith in Lithfield Street, Westminster. He moved to Dublin *c.* 1800 and was made a freeman in 1820. He set up a manufacturing workshop at 45 Great Strand Street and 15 months later moved to no. 41. He was described as a plateworker in 1813, William Middleton being his chief silversmith. Le Bas also manufactured tea sets (priv. cols, see Bennett) decorated with birds, foliage and flowers, developing a technique for applying cast decoration to existing chasing. He had two sons, William Robert Le Bas (1802–63) and Benjamin Le Bas, both of whom were silversmiths and worked in the family firm.

BIBLIOGRAPHY

D. Bennett: 'A Dublin Silversmith: James Le Bas, 1772–1845', *Ant. Colr*, xlv/6 (1974), pp. 36–41

For further bibliography *see* IRELAND, §IX.

DOUGLAS BENNETT

**Lebas** [Le Bas], **Louis-Hippolyte** (*b* Paris, 31 March 1782; *d* Paris, 12 June 1867). French architect and teacher. His father was an avid amateur of landscape painting and brother-in-law of Antoine-Laurent-Thomas Vaudoyer. Lebas began his formal studies with Vaudoyer in 1796 but soon transferred to the atelier of Charles Percier; the architecture of Percier and Pierre-François Léonard Fontaine, and the scope of their practice, including furniture and the decorative arts, marked Lebas for the rest of his life. Although he never won the Prix de Rome, he travelled extensively in Italy in 1804, 1806–8 and again in 1811. In 1806–8, when he was also doing military service in Italy, he spent much time sketching views and travelling with François Debret, also from Percier's studio, with whom he began to compile a lavish volume of measured drawings and views of all the executed work of Jacopo Vignola. During this second Italian journey Lebas also produced designs for furniture and decorative arts, notably for Jacob frères, the Sèvres manufactory, and for the new industrial textile and wallpaper works organized by Christophe-Philippe Oberkampf at Jouy; Lebas later designed buildings for Oberkampf and his works.

Lebas's official architectural career began with inspectorships on two of Paris's most prominent public monuments of the period: the Bourse (built 1808–26 by Alexandre-Théodore Brongniart), where he served on site for a decade, and the Chapelle Expiatoire in the Place Louis XVI by Fontaine, where he was responsible for much of the ornamental work from 1816, enlarging the repertory of classical ornamentation to encompass the austere styles of Etruscan and Pompeiian funerary architecture. Lebas's official favour under the Bourbon Restoration was confirmed with his commission (1822) to design a monument to Chrétien Guillaume de Lamoignon de Malesherbes, the lawyer who had defended Louis XVI; this took the form of a wall aedicula in the vestibule of the Palais de Justice, Paris, with sculpture by François-Joseph Bosio and Jean-Pierre Cortot. Lebas also developed an extensive private practice, which by 1824, according to his own letter of candidacy to the Académie, included several tombs at Père-Lachaise Cemetery, Paris (e.g. that of Brongniart, 1813), houses for the Comte de St Mory at Hondainville (Oise) and the Comte De Choiseul-Gouffier on the Champs-Elysées, Paris, and a jewellery shop in the Rue Vivienne, Paris, in the Pompeian style.

After 1819 Lebas became one of the most influential teachers of the day as effective head of Vaudoyer's atelier. He also achieved renown for his victory in two unusual closed competitions (1823 and 1825) organized by the Prefect Chabrol: for Notre-Dame-de-Lorette, a new parish church in the expanding northern suburbs (*see* FRANCE, fig. 11), and for a model prison, La Petite Roquette (1823–36; destr. 1973), Paris. Both buildings were intended to establish standards, both of building type and aesthetic refinement, and in both of them Lebas demonstrated his belief in the potential for modern reinterpretation of historical plans. Notre-Dame-de-Lorette (1823–35) renewed the basilican type for church design but incorporated archaeological details from the portico of the Doric temple at Cori, south-east of Rome, and the Corinthian capitals of the Temple of Antoninus and Faustina in the Forum Romanum. The church was most noted for its rich interior painted decoration, both frescoes and panel paintings in the nave clerestory, as well as for its subtle adaptation to the new axes of the city suburbs. For the prison Lebas turned to the radial plan type long postulated as the ideal configuration for a penitentiary but until then not fully realized in France, producing a very important statement of the form.

These two successes led to Lebas's election to the Académie des Beaux-Arts in 1825 and made him one of the most respected voices in French architecture. In 1832 he succeeded Vaudoyer as official architect of the Institut de France, building the courtyards of residential and office accommodation on the Rue Mazarine. In 1840 he succeeded Jean-Nicolas Huyot as Professor of Architectural History at the Ecole des Beaux-Arts, using his platform to reassert his belief in eternal classical values in architecture. He was much embittered by losing his post to Viollet-le-Duc after the short-lived reforms of the Ecole in 1863 (*see* FRANCE, §XV).

UNPUBLISHED SOURCES

Paris, Inst. France [letter of candidacy for Académie des Beaux-Arts, 18 May 1824; MS. of his course on architectural history at the Ecole des Beaux-Arts]

Santa Monica, CA, Getty Cent. [Lebas's letters from Italy]

WRITINGS

with F. Debret: *Oeuvre complète de Jacques Barozzi de Vignole* (Paris, 1812)

BIBLIOGRAPHY

*Catalogue des oeuvres de feu Hippolyte Lebas* (sale cat., Paris, Drouot, 3–4 Dec 1867)

L. Vaudoyer: 'Notice historique sur la vie et les ouvrages de M. Le Bas, architecte', *Rev. Gén. Archit.*, xxvii (1869), pp. 244–51

V. Petridou: *La Doctrine de l'imitation dans l'architecture française dans la première moitié du XIXe siècle. Du Néoclassicisme au Romantisme à travers l'oeuvre de Louis-Hippolyte Lebas (1782–1867)*, 2 vols (diss., U. Paris IV, 1992)

BARRY BERGDOLL

**Lebeau, (Joris Johannes) Chris** [Christiaan] (*b* Amsterdam, 26 May 1878; *d* Dachau, 2 April 1945). Dutch painter, designer and applied artist. He trained in design and decorative painting at the Quellinus school and the Rijksschool voor Kunstnijverheid (National School of the Applied Arts) in Amsterdam from 1892 to 1899. He was assigned to assist with the decoration of the Dutch pavilion at the Exposition Universelle in Paris in 1900. A number of his designs for the pavilion were executed in batik, a Javanese technique that had been recently introduced in the Netherlands. In subsequent years Lebeau developed a very personal approach to batiking and within a short time became the leading Dutch artist in this field. His batiked screens in particular were widely acclaimed (examples in Assen, Prov. Mus. Drenthe) and are considered masterpieces of Dutch *Jugendstil*.

Lebeau is one of the most important representatives of the severe, geometrical trend in Dutch applied arts of the early 20th century. From 1903 he designed damask tablecloths and household linen for the Van Dissel Co. in Eindhoven. Until the outbreak of World War II he regularly created new decorative patterns for the company, and his designs remained on the market until long after the war. During the 1920s he practised the art of glassmaking. In 1924–5 he designed mass-produced glassware for the Leerdam Glass Factory, near Utrecht, and also supervised the blowing of unique creations. After a disagreement there he worked in Bohemia in 1926, 1927 and 1929 in the glass factory of Ludwig Moser (1833–1916) at Adolf, near Winterberg (now Vimperk, Czech Republic). The glass items produced there under his direction and personal supervision, with their crackle decorations reminiscent of snowflakes, are considered a culmination point of European Art Deco.

Interested in nearly all areas of art, Lebeau also made stage scenery (1914–17), designed a number of stained-glass windows (e.g. *The Creative Idea*, 1926; Amsterdam, Rijksmus.) and the complete interior of a movie theatre, the Asta, in The Hague (1921). He painted the first-class marriage hall in the Stadhuis in Amsterdam (1926–7) and the interior of the Oud-Katholieke Kerk in Leiden (1926–9), illustrated books and designed posters and postage stamps (see 1987 exh. cat., pl. XII). He made drawings and prints and, particularly after 1930, paintings, including several self-portraits (e.g. 1933; Assen, Prov. Mus. Drenthe) and a portrait of the painter *Hannah Höch* (1933; Assen, Prov. Mus. Drenthe). As a teacher at the Haarlem Kunstnijverheidsschool from 1904 to 1914, he was influential in giving the principles of systematic design to many younger artists.

BIBLIOGRAPHY

H. E. van Gelder: 'Chris Lebeau', *Ned. Ksthist. Jb.*, xvi (1965), pp. 159–98

*Chris Lebeau* (exh. cat. by R. Dippel and M. S. Lebeau-Herman, The Hague, Gemeentemus., 1966)

F. Leidelmeijer and D. van der Cingel: *Art Nouveau en Art Deco in Nederland* (Amsterdam, 1983), pp. 55–7, 175–7

*Chris Lebeau, 1878–1945* (exh. cat. by M. de Bois, Assen, Prov. Mus. Drenthe; Haarlem, Frans Halsmus.; 1987) [extensive bibliog.]

JAN JAAP HEIJ

**Lebedev, Mikhail (Ivanovich)** (*b* Dorpat [now Tartu], Estonia, 16 Nov 1811; *d* Naples, 4 Aug 1837). Russian painter of Estonian birth. He studied from 1829 to 1833 at the Academy of Arts, St Petersburg, under the landscape painter Maksim Vorob'yov (1787–1855). For official commissions he painted in a classical vein, as in *View of Petrovsky Island in St Petersburg* (1832; St Petersburg, Rus. Mus.), while privately indulging in a freer treatment of Romantic themes, as in *Windy Weather* (*c.* 1833; Moscow, Tret'yakov Gal.). He was noted for a lyrical approach, as in his landscape *Vasil'kovo* (1833; Moscow, Tret'yakov Gal.).

Lebedev's Romantic style matured in Italy, where he was sent in 1834 on an Academy scholarship. The sombre colouring of his Russian landscapes was replaced by the bright light of the Mediterranean. He boldly juxtaposed shady foreground and bright background, as in *Ariccia near Rome* (1835; Moscow, Tret'yakov Gal.). Soon he began to treat space and light in a much more vigorous manner, especially in *Path at Albano near Rome* (1836; Moscow, Tret'yakov Gal.). Like the landscape painter Sil'vestr Shchedrin, Lebedev continued to maintain a decorative element within his work, but he also came close to *plein-air* painting, as with *In the Ghigi Park* (1837; Moscow, Tret'yakov Gal.). Lebedev's work was an important model for the landscapes of Fyodor Vasil'yev.

BIBLIOGRAPHY

T. V. Yurova: *Mikhail Ivanovich Lebedev* (Moscow, 1971)

V. M. VOLODARSKY

**Lebedev, Viktor (Vladimirovich)** (*b* Moscow, 2 Sept 1909). Russian architect. He studied from 1930 to 1936 in the architectural faculty of the Academy of Arts, Leningrad (now St Petersburg), under Lev Rudnev (1885–1956), under whose direction he began work in Moscow. His first buildings were in the style of St Petersburg classicism and were built in collaboration with Pavel Shteller (1910–77), for example the administrative building (1947) on the Petrovka, Moscow, and the Pavilion of the Central Black Earth Regions (1953) at the All Union Agricultural Exhibition, Moscow; they are notable for their integration with the surroundings and their virtuoso use of detailing. At the end of the 1950s he turned to the principles of Rationalism, forming sculptural, expressive compositions, such as the Prospekt Mira Radial Line metro station (1957; with Shteller) and the residential complex (1958–64; with others), at the junction of the Volokolamskoye and Leningradskoye roads, both in Moscow. The compact, enclosed composition of the Choreographical College

(1967; with Sergey I. Kuchanov and Alexandr D. Larin) of the Bol'shoy Theatre, Moscow, is marked by a calm balance. He led the design and construction of large residential districts in western Moscow, such as Veshnyaki-Vladychino (from 1968) and Ivanovskoye (1970), which were executed using industrially prefabricated units and followed the concept of vast, hierarchically arranged spatial groupings, centred on self-contained, enclosed residential structures. The building of the Perovsk Regional and Executive Committees of the Communist Party (1974; with Alexandr S. Tsiv'yan and E. V. Yavorsky), Perovo, Moscow, with the strong rhythm of its vertical pylons, shows a revival of interest in monumental architecture. In the Pioneer Palace (1987; with Yurii N. Konovalov and Igor K. Chalov), Perovo, suggestions of a traditional character are combined with an elegant geometry of generalized forms in a poetic 'game-building', whose character approaches that of Post-modernist designs.

WRITINGS
'Bez idei net arkhitektury' [Without ideas there is no architecture], *Arkhit. SSSR*, 5 (1984), pp. 44–9

BIBLIOGRAPHY
A. Zhuravlyov: 'Viktor Lebedev', *Zodchestvo*, 1 (1975), pp. 132–42

A. V. IKONNIKOV

**Lebedev, Vladimir (Vasil'yevich)** (*b* St Petersburg, 26 May 1891; *d* Leningrad [now St Petersburg], 21 Nov 1967). Russian poster artist, painter and illustrator. He began to publish caricatures in journals even before he enrolled at the Academy of Arts (1910–14) and at the School of Drawing, Painting and Sculpture (1912–16), St Petersburg, run by M. D. Bernshteyn (1875–1960) and Leonid Shervud. However, his most original period belongs to the 15 years after the October Revolution of 1917. Appointed professor at the Petrograd (St Petersburg) State Free Art Studios (Svomas; 1918–21) and assistant head of the poster department of the Russian Telegraphic Agency's Northern Region office (the Petrograd ROSTA; 1920–22), he was at the forefront of the development of the 'ROSTA Windows': revolutionary posters that used the forms of *lubok* folk prints for propaganda effect (e.g. *Uncle Prov*, *c*. 1920; St Petersburg, Rus. Mus.). In his posters made from coloured linocuts, such as *Provisions Tax* (1921; St Petersburg, Rus. Mus.), he developed the earlier Neo-primitivism of Vladimir Tatlin and Kazimir Malevich into a distinctive laconic formal composition marked by decorative and rhythmical contrasts of simple blocks of colour, form and text. In his painting Lebedev experimented with the abstract forms created by faceted planes in Cubism and Futurism, as in *Woman Ironing* (1920) and *Cubism* (1922; both St Petersburg, Rus. Mus.). He favoured the subject of the female figure throughout his life, and he also conducted stylistic experiments on single themes, such as the woman ironing, as in *Laundress* (1920; St Petersburg, Rus. Mus.) where he effectively combined the tenets of signboard painting with those of Cubist collage. Lebedev was the art editor of Detgiz Publishing House in Leningrad (1924–33) and was responsible for establishing the innovative Leningrad school of illustrated children's books, which was marked by the novel integration of stylized decorative elements and content, employing artists such as Nikolay Tyrsa and Vera Yermolayeva. Prime examples of his own illustrations are in Samuil Marshak's books *Morozhenoye* ('Ice-cream'; 1925) and *Mister Tvister* ('Mr Twister'; 1933).

PRINTS
*V. V. Lebedev: Risunki—Al'bom* [V. V. Lebedev: Drawings—an album], intro. by V. Pushkareva (Leningrad, 1974)

BIBLIOGRAPHY
N. Punin: *V. V. Lebedev* (Leningrad, 1922), also in *Russkoye i sovetskoye iskusstvo* [Russian and Soviet art] (Moscow, 1976), pp. 220–36
V. Petrov: *Vladimir Vasil'yevich Lebedev, 1891–1967* (Leningrad, 1972)
G. Pospelov: 'Vladimir Lebedev', *Iskusstvo sovetskogo soyuza* [The art of the Soviet Union], ed. G. Nedoshivin and others (Leningrad, 1985), pp. 316–29
N. Misler: 'A Public Art: Caricatures and Posters of Vladimir Lebedev', *J. Dec. & Propaganda A.*, 5 (1987), pp. 60–75
Yu. Gerchuk: 'Detskiye knigi V. V. Lebedeva' [The children's books of V. V. Lebedev], *Khudozhestvennyye miry knigi* [The artistic worlds of books] (Moscow, 1989), pp. 160–87
——: *Vladimir Lebedev* (Moscow, 1990)

JEREMY HOWARD

**Lebedeva, Sarra (Dmitriyevna)** (*b* St Petersburg, 23 Dec 1892; *d* Moscow, 7 March 1967). Russian sculptor. She trained in St Petersburg in the studio of Leonid Shervud as well as in other studios. From 1925 she lived and worked in Moscow. In her mature works impressionistic modelling, extraordinarily sensitive to surface nuances of texture and light and shade, blends with a structural logic that bears witness to a heartfelt absorption of the lessons of Cubism. The profoundly psychological quality of Lebedeva's work springs from her expressive modelling of her material and endows her subjects with a symbolic significance, while in no way overshadowing their individuality. For example, her bronze portrait of the chief of the secret police, *Feliks Dzerzhinsky* (1925; Moscow, Tret'yakov Gal.), is a striking embodiment of a menacing and merciless power. Lebedeva created a remarkable portrait gallery of personalities prominent in Russian culture (e.g. *S. Mikhoels*, 1939; *A. Tvardovsky*, 1943; both bronze, Moscow, Tret'yakov Gal.; and *V. Tatlin*, limestone, 1943–4; St Petersburg, Rus. Mus.). Her headstone for the grave of Boris Pasternak (sandstone, 1965) at Peredelkino, near Moscow, a stele, severe in its form, with a romantic, emotionally charged portrait of the poet in deep relief, is among the best examples of Russian memorial sculpture. She also created sculptures of a neo-classical equilibrium, such as *Girl with Butterfly* (plaster, 1935–6; hammered copper, 1956; St Petersburg, Rus. Mus.), and models for decorative items and sculptures in glazed earthenware (1934–6).

BIBLIOGRAPHY
B. Ternovets: *Sarra Lebedeva* (Moscow, 1940)
*Posmertnaya vystavka proizvedeniy S. D. Lebedevoy* [Posthumous exhibition of works by S. D. Lebedeva] (exh. cat., ed. N. N. Dubovitskaya and Ye. V. Savelova; Moscow, Tret'yakov Gal., 1969)

M. N. SOKOLOV

**Lebensztejn** [Lebenstein], **Jan** (*b* Brześć nad Bugiem [now Brest, Belarus'], 5 Jan 1930). Polish painter, draughtsman, printmaker and illustrator, active in France. From 1949 to 1954 he studied at the Academy of Fine Arts in Warsaw. After winning the Grand Prix de la Ville de Paris at the Biennale des Jeunes in 1959 he settled permanently in Paris. His early works (1954–6) are a direct response to the Socialist Realist devaluation of iconography and the studio. His masterly, picturesque *Landscapes from Rembertów* depict a world of mean suburbs banished to the periphery of official mythology through the image of an industrialized town and industrious countryside. People vanishing from run-down outlying districts appear elsewhere as *Figures in Interiors*—dumb, hieratic beings imprisoned in cramped, anonymous spaces. In the extensive series *Axial Figures* (1956–60) the shapes change into semi-insects bordering on abstraction; reduced to an impastoed skeleton by thick layers of paint with a texture resembling sand and stone, they are transformed into creatures of inanimate matter. The *Abominable Creatures* (a series of 1960–65) are half-human, half-bestial monsters; represented in dark colours, the figures come to life, quietly threaten each other and perform gloomy and secret rituals. Beginning with the *Bestiaria* series (1966–74), oneiric, mythological scenes steeped in *fin-de-siècle* eroticism are transferred to the modern metropolis: to metro stations, cheap cinemas, sleazy bars, hotels, and salons of the demi-monde (e.g. *Café Vanitas*, 1976). In the works of the 1970s, drawing, chromolithography and gouache gradually begin to prevail. The mythology of minotaurs, sphinxes and satyrs blends with images from 'high' and 'mass' urban culture and resembles the art of the comic strip, while at the same time echoing the conversation-piece tradition and the prints of Hogarth. There are quotations from Max Ernst and improvisations on subjects taken from Arnold Böcklin and August Strindberg. Lebensztejn's range of subjects was broadened by his illustrations to the Polish edition of George Orwell's *Animal Farm* (*Farma zwierzt*, Paris, 1974), to the *Book of Job* (*Ksiega Joba*) and the *Apocalypse* (*Apokalipsa*). In his later works the earlier stylizations are intermingled with allusions to medieval miniatures.

BIBLIOGRAPHY

G. Gassiot-Talabot: 'Lebenstein et l'Ankylose', *Opus Int.* (April 1968), no. 6, pp. 36–9
M. Hermansdorfer: 'Kosmogonie', *Projekt* (1977), no. 5
*Jan Lebenstein* (exh. cat., ed. M. Hermansdorfer; Wrocław, N. Mus., 1977)

EWA MIKINA

**Leber, Wolfgang** (*b* Berlin, 15 Feb 1936). German painter, printmaker and draughtsman. He studied at the Werkkunstschule in Charlottenburg, Berlin, from 1957 to 1961 and at the Hochschule für Bildende Künste in Charlottenburg in 1961. He began his career as a draughtsman and printmaker, before concentrating on painting in the late 1960s. Leber was able to transfer his feeling for figure and space from his graphic work to his paintings through the use of monochrome surfaces to help convey depth. He was not an experimental artist but belonged to the generation of artists in Berlin that developed their pictorial ideas within a modernist tradition that ran from Cézanne to Oskar Schlemmer, rejecting realism on the one hand and pure abstraction on the other. Leber was mainly concerned with the human figure, and in dealing with it he simplified the human form and the space enclosing it to form a framework. The figural bearing of his figures is reminiscent of Schlemmer's large studies, although Leber did not set out to achieve Schlemmer's monumental effect. In his interiors he aimed more at the internalization of the structure of movement, making it possible to experience the intimate nature of the subject despite the simplification of external features.

BIBLIOGRAPHY

*Wolfgang Leber* (exh. cat. by G. Brandler, E. Berlin, Gal. Arkade, 1981)
*Wolfgang Leber* (exh. cat. by M. Flügge, E. Berlin, Gal. Unter den Linden, 1984)
*Wolfgang Leber* (exh. cat. by I. Kerkin, E. Berlin, Gal. Rotunde Alten Mus., 1984)
*Wolfgang Leber* (exh. cat. by L. Böhme, E. Berlin, Gal. Mitte, 1986)

EUGEN BLUME

**Lebes.** Ancient vessel form, used as a mixing bowl and as a cauldron for boiling meat (*see* GREECE, ANCIENT, fig. 71).

**Lebes gamikos.** Ancient vessel form, often presented as a wedding gift (*see* GREECE, ANCIENT, fig. 71).

□

**Le Blanc, Horace** (*b* Lyon, ?*c.* 1580; *d* Lyon, 1637). French painter. He was in Rome in 1600, where he was cited in a lawsuit against Caravaggio; he was a member of the city's Accademia di S Luca. Although no Roman works by him have been identified, early sources place him in the circle of Giovanni Lanfranco and also describe him as a pupil of Palma Giovane, which suggests that he may have spent some time in Venice. He returned to Lyon in 1610, and in that year was appointed master of the painters' guild, an office he filled several times until 1629. He was soon much in demand, producing religious works for monastic establishments in and around Lyon. In 1621 he painted an *Ecstasy of St Teresa* (Lyon, Mus. B.-A.), probably for a Carmelite house, and an *Entombment* (Grenoble, St André) that includes portraits of *François, Duc de Lesdiguières*, and his wife.

In 1622 Le Blanc was responsible for the temporary decorations for the entry of Louis XIII and Anne of Austria into Lyon, a scheme perhaps recorded in a drawing of the *Apotheosis of Louis XIII* (Dijon, Mus. B.-A.). The following year he was commissioned to decorate the gallery of the château of Grosbois, Val-de-Marne, providing military scenes that are known from a description by Pierre-Jean Mariette and a drawing (Darmstadt, Hess. Landesmus.). In 1624 Le Blanc painted a *St Sebastian* (Rouen, Mus. B.-A.) for the Capuchins of Rouen. He returned to Lyon with the title of Peintre Ordinaire du Roi, and then of Peintre de la Ville.

Two further works by Le Blanc are known: the *Virgin and Child with Four Saints* (Tournon, St Julien) and the *Apparition of the Trinity to St Ignatius and his Companions*, painted in 1627 for the church of the La Trinité in Lyon (*in situ*). Jacques Blanchard and François Perrier trained in Le Blanc's studio.

BIBLIOGRAPHY

Mariette
G. Chomer: 'Charles Le Brun, 1646', *La Peinture d'inspiration religieuse à Rouen au temps de Pierre Corneille, 1606–1684* (exh. cat., Rouen, St Oucn, 1984), pp. 112–16
——: 'Horace Le Blanc: Essai de catalogue raisonné', *Bull. Mus. & Mnmts Lyon.*, 3 (1987), pp. 20–21
J. Foucart: 'La *Transverbération de sainte Thérèse*: Un Nouvel Horace Leblanc (1621) pour le musée de Lyon', *Bull. Mus. & Mnmts Lyon.*, 3 (1987), p. 25

THIERRY BAJOU

**Le Blanc,** Abbé **Jean-Bernard** (*b* Dijon, 3 Dec 1707; *d* Paris, 1781). French writer and critic. Having taken holy orders, he chose to pursue a literary career in Paris. He wrote poems and plays, with mediocre success until the publication of his *Lettres d'un Français* (1745), a critique of French standards of taste that found favour with Mme de Pompadour. His acceptance into her circle in 1746 led to his role as a leading art critic championing officially accepted standards of taste. She obtained for him the sinecure post of Historiographe des Bâtiments du Roi, and in this capacity he accompanied her brother, Abel-François Poisson de Vandières, soon to become the Marquis de Marigny, on his tour of Italy (1749–51). In the face of growing criticism, Le Blanc launched a defence of state patronage of the arts, beginning with his 'Lettre de Milton' (1746), in which he argued that the sole purpose of art education is to produce informed patrons. In his next work, *Lettre sur les tableaux exposés au Louvre* (1747), he openly attacked critics of official art; and in his *Observations sur les ouvrages de l'Académie de peinture et de sculpture* (1753) he accused those claiming to believe that state patronage results in conventional subjects, uninspired interpretation and mediocre execution (particularly Etienne La Font de Saint-Yenne) to be motivated only by self-interest, their reviews intended to attract attention to themselves through mere sensationalism. Le Blanc failed 30 times to be elected a member of the Académie Française; this, together with his extreme royalist views and the death of Mme de Pompadour, led to his eclipse. He died in poverty.

*Lettres d'un Français concernant le gouvernement, la politique et les moeurs des Anglois et des François*, 3 vols (The Hague, 1745)
'Lettre de Milton, où il propose une nouvelle manière d'élever la jeunesse d'Angleterre (traduit de l'anglais)', intro. to C. de Nonncy de Fontenay: *Lettres sur l'éducation des princes* (Edinburgh, 1746)
*Lettre sur les tableaux exposés au Louvre, l'exposition des ouvrages de peinture, sculpture, etc., de l'année 1747 et en général sur l'utilité de ces sortes d'expositions* (n.p., 1747)
*Réflexions nouvelles d'un amateur des beaux-arts pour servir de supplément à la 'Lettre sur l'exposition'* (Paris, 1747)
*Observations sur les ouvrages de l'Académie de peinture et de sculpture, exposés au Salon du Louvre, en l'année 1753, et sur quelques écrits qui ont rapport à la peinture* (Paris, 1753)

BIBLIOGRAPHY

E. de Broglie: 'Un Candidat malheureux à l'Académie française: Le Blanc et ses lettres', *Les Portefeuilles du Président Bouhier* (Paris, 1896), pp. 99–147
L. Muhlhofer: *Abbé J. B. Le Blanc: Sein Leben und Werk* (Würzburg, 1936)
H. Monod-Cassidy: 'Un Voyageur philosophe au XVIIIe siècle', *Harvard Stud. Comp. Lit.*, xviii (1941)

JUANITA M. ELLIAS

**Le Blon, Jacob** [Jakob] **Christoph** [Christof] (*bapt* Frankfurt am Main, 23 May 1667; *d* Paris, 15 May 1741). German printmaker, painter and tapestry manufacturer, active in the Netherlands, England and France. He was the son of the engraver and bookseller Christoph Le Blon II (1639–after 1706), whose mother was a daughter of Matthäus Merian (i), granddaughter of Johann Theodor de Bry and half-sister of Maria Sibylle Merian. Between 1696 and 1702 Le Blon was in Rome and was perhaps a pupil of Carlo Maratti. He then moved to Amsterdam in 1702, where he worked as a miniature painter until 1717. He visited London in 1710 and lived there from 1718 to 1734. He began experimenting with colour-printing in 1710, and in 1719 was granted a privilege by George I to reproduce pictures and drawings in full colour (*see* PRINTS, §III, 6). However, the company he set up failed in 1725. In that year he published *Coloritto: Or the Harmony of Colouring in Painting*, in which he presented his theory that any colour as well as black could be achieved by mixing in varying proportions just three colours (red, yellow and blue—not, as has been suggested, based on Newton's colour theory). In 1727 he was granted a privilege to weave tapestries on the basis of his colour theory and set up a factory. Once again this failed, and, in 1734, he fled to Paris where Louis XV granted him a privilege in 1737 for colour-printing. His mezzotints, which were specifically designed to reproduce painting, were much admired by the French. As well as reproducing his own work (e.g. *George I*; see Singer, no. 37), Le Blon engraved after Barocci (e.g. *Virgin and Child*; see 1987 exh. cat.), Correggio and Hyacinthe Rigaud, as well as van Dyck. His full-colour reproductions were reproduced from three mezzotint plates, using red, yellow and blue ink (e.g. the colour separation plates for the portrait of *Cardinal de Fleury* after Rigaud are preserved in London, BM, 1929–24–3/4/5/6; see Lilien, figs 52–6)—one colour per plate; later he often added a black plate. His techniques had been forgotten by the mid-19th century, but his theory survived in chromolithography and is the basis of modern colour-printing (*see* LITHOGRAPHY, §§I and II).

WRITINGS

*Coloritto: Or the Harmony of Colouring in Painting* (London, 1725) [*R* in Lilien, 1985, pp. 178–225]

BIBLIOGRAPHY

H. W. Singer: 'Jacob Christoph Le Blon', *Mitt. Ges. Vervielfält. Kst* (1901)
A. M. Hind: *A History of Engraving and Etching from the Fifteenth Century to the Year 1914* (London, 3/1925/*R* New York, 1963)
O. M. Lilien: *Jacob Christoph Le Blon, 1667–1741: Inventor of Three- and Four-colour Printing* (Stuttgart, 1985) [with extensive bibliog. incl. early sources]
*The Image Multiplied* (exh. cat. by S. Lambert, London, V&A, 1987)

AD STIJNMAN

**Le Blon** [Blondus; Leblon; Le Blond; Leblond], **Michel** (*bapt* Frankfurt am Main, 9 July 1587; *d* Amsterdam, 1656). German goldsmith and engraver, active in the Netherlands and England. He was of Huguenot descent and trained as a goldsmith but was already active as an engraver in 1605, the date of his earliest-known engravings (London, BM) of grotesque ornament suitable for jewellery. He may have studied under Theodor de Bry and Johann Theodor de Bry. Le Blon probably settled in Amsterdam in about 1610. His *Eenvoldige vruchten en spitsen voor d'ancomen kunst liefhebbende ieucht* was published in 1611, comprising 14 plates of ornament for goldsmiths' work: borders and friezes, with exotic birds, animals, insects, fish, flowers, vegetables, fruits and leaves. He also published engravings for the decoration of knife-handles and sword-handles, as well as heraldic shields and mantling for engraving on silver and some almost Auricular-style strapwork designs. In 1627 he issued a collection of engraved shields, emblems and small pictorial scenes, some religious, for the decoration of box-lids and watches. In the same year he travelled to Italy, possibly with Joachim van Sandrart. Le Blon also spent many years in England as an agent of the Swedish court and frequently visited Stockholm in this capacity. An English tankard (*c.* 1620–30; London, V&A) bears one of his designs. He signed his work *Blondus, Michaël Blondus* or with a monogram of the letters M and B.

BIBLIOGRAPHY

Bénézit; Thieme–Becker

A. E. Copp: 'On Portrait Medals or Plaques of Silver by Simon de Passe and Michel le Blond', *Connoisseur*, iii (1902), pp. 81–2

C. Dodgson: 'The Earliest Signed Works of Michel le Blon', *Burl. Mag.*, viii (1905–6), pp. 129–34

**Le Blond** [Leblond]. French family of artists. (1) Jean Le Blond (i) and (2) Jean Le Blond (ii) worked as painters, engravers and print publishers. Much the most important member of the family was the architect and garden designer (3) Alexandre-Jean-Baptiste Le Blond, who designed several hôtels in Paris as well as contributing to various influential books on architecture and garden design. In 1716 he moved to Russia, where he worked for Tsar Peter the Great.

**(1) Jean Le Blond (i)** (*b* Paris, *c.* 1594; *d* Paris, ?24 May 1666). Painter, engraver and print publisher. He was the eldest son of the print publisher Nicolas Le Blond I (*d* 1610), and was primarily a painter, described as 'peintre ordinaire du Roy' from 1629. None of his paintings is now known. He followed his father in publishing prints and inherited his stock on his death. His earlier publications were popular prints made by rather heavy-handed engravers such as Jeremias Falck and Willem de Gheyn (*d* after 1650): the slightly lascivious series *Le Miroir des plus belles courtisanes de ce temps* (1630) was clearly not aimed at the connoisseur of technique. He later employed more talented engravers and published works by Abraham Bosse, Pierre Brébiette, Israël Silvestre and others.

**(2) Jean Le Blond (ii)** (*b* Paris, *c.* 1635; *d* Paris, 13 Aug 1709). Painter, engraver and print publisher, nephew of (1) Jean Le Blond (i). He achieved greater official success as a painter than his uncle, being approved (*agréé*) by the Académie Royale de Peinture et de Sculpture in 1665 and received (*reçu*) as a full member in 1681. His *morceau de réception*, the *Fall of the Titans* (Paris, Ecole N. Sup. B.-A.), is his only known painting. He was also active as a print publisher, particularly of architectural subjects—between 1680 and 1685 he worked for Louis XIV producing plans and elevations of the château of Versailles. He wrote *Parallèle des cinq ordres d'architecture tiré des exemples antiques les plus excelens et des quatre principaux auteurs modernes que en ont écrit savoir Paladio, Scamozzi, Serlio et Vignole* (Paris, 1683).

BIBLIOGRAPHY

R.-A. Weigert and M. Préaud: *Inventaire du fonds français: Graveurs du XVIIe siècle*, Paris, Bib. N., Cab. Est. cat., vii (Paris, 1976), pp. 296–380

M. Préaud and others: *Dictionnaire des éditeurs d'estampes à Paris sous l'Ancien Régime* (Paris, 1987), pp. 203–5

**(3) Alexandre-Jean-Baptiste** [Jean-Baptiste-Alexandre] **Le Blond** (*b* Paris, 1679; *d* St Petersburg, Aug 1719). Architect and garden designer, son of (2) Jean Le Blond (ii). He began his training under the designer and engraver Jean Le Pautre, best known for his ornamental interiors. He also received encouragement from his uncle

Jean Girard, who served as architect to Philippe II, Duc d'Orléans. His most important teachers, however, were another uncle, André Le Nôtre, the major garden designer of the period, and the Architecte du Roi, Jules Hardouin Mansart.

The elegant simplicity of Mansart's style characterized Le Blond's designs for the Hôtel de Vendôme (also called Hôtel de Chaulnes; 1706–7, enlarged 1714–16) and the Hôtel de Saissac (also called Hôtel de Clermont; 1708–14; destr.), both in Paris. Both were planned as elongated rectangles surrounded by a complex series of courts and lower courts separated by grillwork and terraced gardens. The ground-floor plan of the Hôtel de Saissac was dominated by a long gallery flanked by a bedroom and salon on the garden side, in contrast to the Hôtel de Vendôme, which included a series of relatively small rooms looking on to the garden. An unusual feature of the latter hôtel is a large library located on the court side of the building. The sloping mansard roof and tightly spaced windows of the Hôtel de Vendôme make it look old-fashioned and crowded by comparison with the more widely spaced windows and flat balustraded roof *à l'italienne* of the Hôtel de Saissac. The Hôtel de Saissac is often seen as the inspiration for many houses of the later regency period, and Le Blond was given credit by his contemporaries for initiating the *style moderne* (later called Rococo) in architectural design.

Le Nôtre's influence is also apparent in Le Blond's designs, which often incorporated an elaborate, carefully planned garden. This was evident at the country house (destr.) Le Blond built for M. Regnault at Chatillon-sous-Bagneux, near Paris, at an unknown date. The relatively small, two-storey house overlooked a dramatic park, which descended from the garden façade in a series of elaborate terraces. The floor-plan of the house reflects his kinship to Germain Boffrand in its incorporation of a centrally located oval salon projecting on to the terraced garden and including a series of radiating rooms. More typical of Le Blond were the restrained elevations of the façades, which were similar in style to those of Mansart. The court façade included a slightly projecting *avant-corps* supported by Ionic and Corinthian columns and crowned by a pediment. This was flanked by three bowed windows, decorated with small trophies, on either side of the ground-floor and three rectangular windows either side on the upper storey. This façade was terminated by rusticated pilasters, while the garden façade was dominated by three simple central arches topped by three rectangular windows separated by Corinthian pilasters. The whole was crowned by a high, sloping roof with decorative urns at the base.

Le Blond is also credited with the design for a country house at an unknown location published by Mariette. This small, rectangular building was his simplest and most clearly organized work. He is thought to have been responsible for the gardens only at Château de Houger, Chatillon-sous-Bagneux. Other works include the gardens of Le Cannet, near Narbonne, and the unfinished archbishop's palace at Auch, Gascony.

Le Blond was involved with the illustration and publication of a number of books on both architecture and garden design. He contributed five of the twelve plates in J. F. Félibien's *Histoire de l'abbaye royale de Saint Denis en*

*France* (1706). He added a 32-page supplement and 29 plates to the edition of 1710 of Augustin-Charles d'Aviler's *Cours complet d'architecture* (1691), and he is believed to have produced almost all the illustrations (and possibly some of the text) in the third edition (1722) of Antoine-Joseph Dezallier d'Argenville's *Théorie et physique du jardinage* (1709). This latter publication popularized the French formal garden throughout Europe. In it Le Blond stressed four main principles: that design should be subject to nature; that the garden must not be too shady; that the garden must not be too exposed; and that the design should enhance the feeling of the size of the garden. He stressed the importance of the garden designer, describing him as a 'geometrician, architect, draughtsman, [one who] knows the character of plants and ornament'. Although the book encouraged variety in the selection of plants, it warned against too much dividing and subdividing of space and ornamental shell work and basins.

The best known of Le Blond's patrons was Tsar Peter the Great of Russia, for whom he served as general architect in St Petersburg. He arrived in the city in August 1716 accompanied by his family and an entourage of artists and craftsmen that included the interior designer Nicolas Pineau. Asked to elaborate a pre-existent general plan for St Petersburg, Le Blond produced a design for an oval city that incorporated three islands on the River Neva, all linked by an elaborate system of canals, reminiscent of Venice and Amsterdam. This original plan, called the 'ville idéale', was not executed due to its tremendous cost and because of the quarrels Le Blond had with the powerful Prince Menshikov. (Le Blond's argumentative personality is sometimes given as the reason for his departure from France.) He did, however, lay out a summer garden for the city in the style of Le Nôtre.

Le Blond also executed designs for two country residences: Strel'na (completed by Niccolò Michetti) and PETERHOF. Located on the Baltic, Peterhof was conceived as an elaborate summer palace for the Tsar and was modelled on the château of Versailles. Le Blond's palace (later altered and enlarged by Bartolomeo Francesco Rastrelli) had a mansard roof and interiors by Pineau and opened on to a magnificent French formal garden highlighted by a grand cascade. The garden, which was divided into upper and lower sections, included many beech, lime, fruit and other trees brought from elsewhere in Europe. There were numerous fountains and sculptural works, as well as two small pleasure pavilions (Monplaisir and Marly) also designed by Le Blond.

Le Blond's untimely death from smallpox in 1719 left many of his designs incomplete, although some of the documentation is preserved in the archives of the Ministry of Foreign Affairs, Moscow, and in the Hermitage Museum, St Petersburg. Other designs by Le Blond also survive (Brussels, Bib. Royale Albert 1er; Stockholm, Nmus.).

BIBLIOGRAPHY

J. Mariette: *L'Architecture français* (1727); ed. L. Hautecoeur (Paris and Brussels, 1927–9), ii–iii

J. F. Blondel: *Cours d'architecture*, 6 vols (Paris, 1771–7)

A.-N. Dézallier d'Argenville: *Vies des fameux architectes et sculpteurs* (1788)

H. Hymans: *Catalogue des estampes d'ornement faisant partie des collections de la Bibliothèque Royale de Belgique* (Brussels, 1907)

N. Roudnitski: *Istoricheskaya vystavka architecturii* [Historical exhibition of architecture] (St Petersburg, 1911)

L. Reau: *Saint-Petersburg* (Paris, 1913)

M. Gothein: *A History of Garden Art*, ii (New York, 1928)

B. Lossky: 'L'Hôtel de Vendôme et son architecte Alexandre Le Blond', *Gaz. B.-A.*, n. s. 5, xii (1934), pp. 30–41

——; 'J. B. A. Le Blond, architecte de Pierre le grand: Son Oeuvre en France', *Bull. Assoc. Rus. Ric. Sci. Prague*, iii (1936), pp. 179–216

C. Marsden: *Palmyra of the North: The First Days of St. Petersburg* (London, 1942)

L. Hautecoeur: *Première moitié du XVIIIe: Le Style Louis VI*, iii of *Histoire de l'architecture classique en France* (Paris, 1950)

R. Strandberg: 'André Le Notre et son école: Dessins inédits ou peu connus dans la collection Tessin—Harleman au Musée National de Stockholm', *Bull. Soc. Hist. A. Fr.* (1960), pp. 124–6

M. Gibellino-Krasceninnicowa: *L'architettura russa nel passato e nel presente* (Rome, 1963)

I. Dennerlein: *Die Gartenkunst der Regence und des Rokoko in Frankreich* (Bamberg, 1972)

M. Gallet: *Paris Domestic Architecture of the Eighteenth Century* (London, 1972)

A. Kennett: *The Palaces of Leningrad* (London, 1973)

J. Cracraft: *The Petrine Revolution in Architecture* (Chicago and London, 1988)

G. A. Langlois: 'Renaissance de la Folie-Desmares à Chatillon', *Sites & Mnmts*, 121 (1988), pp. 31–5

KATHLEEN RUSSO

**Leboeuf, Charles-François.** *See* NANTEUIL, CHARLES-FRANÇOIS.

**Lebourg, Albert-Charles** (*b* Montfort-sur-Risle, Eure, 1 Feb 1849; *d* Rouen, 7 Jan 1928). French painter. He had an early interest in architecture and studied under the architect Drouin at the Ecole Municipale de Dessin in Rouen. He became increasingly interested in art and through Drouin met the landscape painter Victor Delamarre (1811–68) who advised and taught him. Giving up architecture altogether, he then attended the Ecole Municipale de Peinture et de Dessin in Rouen under Gustave Morin (1809–86). In 1871 he met the collector Laperlier through whom he obtained the post of professor of drawing at the Société des Beaux-Arts in Algiers. He remained there from 1872 to 1877, producing works such as *Street in Algiers* (1875; Rouen, Mus. B.-A.). He also experimented with depicting a single site in a variety of different lights, in a manner similar to the late works of Monet. After giving up his teaching post in Algeria in 1877 he returned to Paris where he attended Jean-Paul Laurens's studio from 1878 to 1880. It was at this point that he became aware of Impressionism; later he became friendly with Degas, Monet and Sisley. He first exhibited at the Salon de la Société des Artistes Français in 1883 and again in 1886, and after the foundation of the Société Nationale des Beaux-Arts (1889) he exhibited there regularly from 1891 to 1914. Between 1884 and 1886 he spent much time in the Auvergne region, producing such Impressionist works as *Snow in Auvergne* (1886; Rouen, Mus. B.-A.), in which a river re-establishes the habitual presence of water in his work. After living and working in numerous places in northern France, Lebourg travelled in the Netherlands (1895–7), and in 1900 he spent a short period in Britain, which confirmed his love of Turner, Constable and Gainsborough. He continued working in a luminous Impressionist style with landscapes such as *Small Farm by the Water (Ile de Vaux)* (1903; Rouen, Mus. B.-A.) up until 1921 when he was paralysed by a stroke.

BIBLIOGRAPHY
L. Bénédite: *Albert Lebourg* (Paris, 1923)

**Le Bourguignon, Jean.** *See* CHANGENET, JEAN.

**Le Breton, Gilles** (*b* Paris, *c.* 1500; *d* Paris, *c.* 1552). French master mason. He played a crucial role in the works initiated by Francis I at Fontainebleau from 1527, although the exact nature of his duties is difficult to determine. It is possible that he was the architect responsible for the design as well as the execution of the first phase of works, even though the building accounts imply only that he was active as a master mason; some scholars have suggested instead that the designs for certain parts with which Le Breton's name is associated may have been provided by the Italian Rosso Fiorentino.

Le Breton was the most prominent member of a long line of master masons and probably learnt his trade as apprentice to his father at the château of Chambord (Loir-et-Cher). He was also involved with repairs to the Trinitarian abbey near the château in Fontainebleau. In 1527 he was named master mason of the Bâtiments du Roi at Fontainebleau, and he worked there until his death *c.* 1552. In early 1553 Henry II named Philibert de L'Orme to replace him as general master of the Bâtiments du Roi, a title conferred on Le Breton in 1548.

Le Breton's name appears in three contracts (1528, 1531, 1540) and in building accounts and patent letters at Fontainebleau. He was in charge of the King's scheme to renovate and enlarge the old château, to build the new lower court (later known as the Cour du Cheval Blanc) and the Galerie François I to connect the former with the old wing, the Cour Ovale. In this capacity he was responsible for the three-storey tower known as the Porte Dorée (1528), which was to serve as the new entrance pavilion to the Cour Ovale, a work typical of the early phase of Renaissance architecture in France in its combination of a medieval structural type with Italianate details. The Porte Dorée, no longer a fortified entry, retains elements of the medieval château in the vertical continuity of the windows, the asymmetry of the towers and the attic roofs, but it has open barrel-vaulted loggias, Italian in inspiration though lacking the refinement and symmetry of Renaissance precursors. It is faced simply with plaster walls and grey sandstone (*grès*) dressings, a combination of materials characteristic of those parts of the château attributed to Le Breton. Documents in 1534 record payments to Le Breton for the great garden, the walls and cloisters, the embankments of the ponds, the canals and foundations. Contracts of 1531 and 1540 allude to building within the Cour Ovale, namely the portico, the grand staircase (which may have been inspired by a design by Rosso Fiorentino), the peristyle and the reconstruction of the Chapelle St-Saturnin. The latter is comprised of two superimposed chapels, the lower chapel of the Cour Ovale and the one above known as the King's Chapel. The staircase (destr. 1540) provided an impressive access to the royal suites, two flights converging in a central one, culminating in a triumphal arch portico, seemingly appropriate for regal celebrations.

While Le Breton's early work in the Cour Ovale shows his assimilation of style characteristic of the châteaux of Madrid (Neuilly, nr Paris) and Chambord, the portico of the great stairway and the Chapelle St-Saturnin reflect a knowledge of antique sources. His work *c.* 1540 in the south wing of the Cour du Cheval Blanc bears the influence of Serlio and the contemporary architecture of the Italian Renaissance. In his late years Le Breton worked on town houses in Fontainebleau for the retinue of Henry II, including the Hôtel d'Albon (1547–50) for Jacques d'Albon, the Maréchal de Saint-André, as well as the Hôtel La Guette (1548). For Côme Claussé, he built the Hôtel de Marchamont (1548) and probably worked on the oldest forecourt wings of his châteaux at Courances (Essone) and at Fleury-en-Bière (Essone; 1550–52). Le Breton also built a hôtel for himself on the Rue de la Bauldroirie in Paris (1551). A posthumous inventory dated 1553 shows a well-appointed house replete with works of art, objects of devotion and nine books on architecture, including Serlio's *Regole generali*, published in Antwerp in 1541.

Bauchal

BIBLIOGRAPHY
L. de Laborde: *Les Comptes des bâtiments du roi (1528–71)*, i (Paris, 1877), pp. 50–65
F. Herbert: 'Les Travaux de Philibert Delorme à Fontainebleau', *An. Soc. Hist. & Archéol. Gatinais*, xii (1894), pp. 153–63
H. Stein: 'La Famille de l'architecte Gilles Le Breton', *An. Soc. Hist. & Archéol. Gatinais*, xxvii (1909), pp. 169–83
M. Roy: 'Quelques hôtels de Fontainebleau au XVIe siècle', *An. Soc. Hist. & Archéol. Gatinais*, xxxii (1914), pp. 230–32, 244–5
F. Gebelin: *Les Châteaux de la Renaissance* (Paris, 1927)
A. Bray: 'Le Premier Grand Escalier du château de Fontainebleau et les anciens escaliers de la cour ovale', *Bull. Mnmtl.*, xcix (1940), pp. 192–203
A. Blunt: *Art and Architecture in France, 1500–1700*, Pelican Hist. A. (Harmondsworth, 1953/R 1977), pp. 56–8
P. Vanaise: 'Gilles Le Breton, maître-maçon, entrepreneur ou architecte parisien du XVIe siècle', *Gaz. B.-A.*, lxviii (1966), pp. 241–64
A. Chastel: 'L'Escalier de la cour ovale à Fontainebleau', *Essays in the History of Architecture Presented to Rudolf Wittkower*, ed. D. Fraser, H. Hibbard and M. J. Levine (London, 1967), ii, pp. 74–80

NAOMI MILLER

**Le Brocquy, Louis** (*b* Dublin, 10 Nov 1916). Irish painter and decorative artist. His mother, Sybil le Brocquy, was a writer and his sister, Melanie le Brocquy (*b* 1919), a distinguished sculptor. In 1934 he joined the family business, at the same time studying chemistry at Trinity College, Dublin, and teaching himself to paint. He first exhibited a painting and a sculpture at the Royal Hibernian Academy in 1937 and from 1938 spent two years studying Old Master paintings at the National Gallery, London, the Louvre, the Prado, and in Venice and Geneva. Inspired by Velázquez and Goya, he adopted a palette of luminous greys and whites, as in *Girl in White* (1941; Belfast, Ulster Mus.), a full-length profile portrait influenced by Whistler.

While staying near Tullamore in 1945, le Brocquy commenced a series of paintings of tinkers, which were to occupy him for the next four years; these culminated in the large tapestry *Travellers* (edition of 10, 1948; see *Seven Tapestries, 1948–1955*, exh. cat., Belfast, Ulster Mus., 1966, opposite p. 2), commissioned by the Edinburgh Tapestry Weavers, and inaugurated a series of important tapestries in which human images acquired an allegorical significance. After moving to London in 1946 to teach at the Central School of Arts and Crafts, he began to participate in international exhibitions including the Venice Biennale in 1956, at which he was awarded the Premio Prealpina. His paintings and other works of this period include *Self-portrait* (1947; Dublin, N.G.; see fig.), a subject to which he often returned in later years. From 1950 to 1955 he examined the isolation of the individual in grey paintings such as *A Family* (1951; Milan, La Prealpina, see 1966 exh. cat., p. 35), a picture that caused great controversy when exhibited in Dublin in 1951; it shows a couple, their child and cat in a room divided into distinct geometric spaces as a metaphor of their separateness.

From 1956, shortly before his move in 1960 to the Alpes-Maritimes, le Brocquy turned again to white paintings that examined the theme of existence, for example in *Isolated Being* (1962; Dublin, Hugh Lane Mun. Gal.), in which a three-quarter-length figure painted in white impasto emerges from a pale uniform ground. From 1964 his chief subject was the human face, sometimes in the form of portraits of writers such as Beckett, Yeats, Lorca and Joyce; the Celtic heads on medieval Irish buildings such as Clonfert Abbey served as his point of reference. As the series progressed, the pairing of a head and a hand, in paintings such as *Head 293* (1971; Dublin, A.C. Ireland), became expressive of human emotion and horrific experience. Later paintings in his characteristic white tones, such as *Fantail Pigeons* (1986; Cork, Crawford Mun. A.G.), are gentler works. He illustrated the Irish epic narrative *The Táin* (Dublin, 1969, 3/1985), translated by Thomas Kinsella, and *Dubliners* (Dublin, 1986) by James Joyce, among other works. During the 1990s he painted watercolour landscapes and a series of *Images of Seamus Heaney* (1994; Cork, Crawford Mun. A.G.).

BIBLIOGRAPHY

*Louis le Brocquy: A Retrospective Selection* (exh. cat., intro. A. Crookshank and J. Dupin; Dublin, Hugh Lane Mun. Gal.; Belfast, Ulster Mus.; 1966)

*Irish Art, 1943–1973* (exh. cat. by C. Barrett, Cork, Crawford Mun. A.G., 1980)

D. Walker: *Louis le Brocquy* (Dublin, 1981)

*Louis le Brocquy: Images, 1975–1987* (exh. cat. by J. Montague and others, Dublin, A.C. Ireland, 1987)                    □

**Le Brun, Charles** (*b* Paris, *bapt* 24 Feb 1619; *d* Paris, 12 Feb 1690). French painter and designer. He dominated 17th-century French painting as no other artist; it was not until over a century later, during the predominance of Jacques-Louis David, that artistic authority was again so concentrated in one man. Under the protection of a succession of important political figures, including Chancellor Pierre Séguier, Cardinal Richelieu and Nicolas Fouquet, Le Brun created a series of masterpieces of history and religious painting. For Louis XIV and his chief minister Jean-Baptiste Colbert he executed his greatest work, the royal palace of Versailles: an almost perfect ensemble of architecture, decoration and landscape. After Colbert's death in 1683, he was no longer able to count on prestigious commissions and, apart from finishing the decoration of Versailles, he concentrated on smaller-scale religious painting.

1. Life and work. 2. Posthumous reputation.

## 1. LIFE AND WORK.

(i) Training and early work. (ii) Rise to prominence. (iii) Triumphs in the royal service. (iv) Last years.

*(i) Training and early work.* Le Brun was the son of Nicolas Le Brun (*d* 1648), a master sculptor, and Julienne Le Bé, several members of whose family were writing-masters to Louis XIII, to the children of Chancellor Séguier and subsequently to Louis XIV. While still a child, Le Brun apparently produced a number of small sculptures, and, in his adolescence, he spent a short time in the studio of the painter François Perrier. Séguier was instrumental in furthering Le Brun's career from about 1633–4, for he recommended the young artist to Simon Vouet, who, during the mid-1630s, was working on the decoration of Séguier's Hôtel de Bellegarde. Le Brun, apparently dissatisfied with the secondary work entrusted to him, left this project, in order to study the royal collections of paintings and antique sculpture, as well as the Mannerist decorations in the château of Fontainebleau. His earliest surviving painting, dated 1637, is a small *Crucifixion* (St Petersburg, Hermitage), which, despite traces of the influence of Perrier and Vouet, is already strikingly individual. He also designed a number of engraved frontispieces and book illustrations, including several for works by Précieux authors, in whose circle he probably moved. In 1638 he designed the thesis of *La Providence présentant le Dauphin à Louis XIII*, to celebrate the birth of the future Louis XIV.

Le Brun's first important paintings were commissioned *c.* 1639–41 by Richelieu for his Palais Cardinal in Paris (now the Palais-Royal). The only one to survive, *Hercules*

Louis le Brocquy: *Self-portrait*, raw umber on paper, 150×113 mm, 1947 (Dublin, National Gallery of Ireland)

1. Charles Le Brun: *Horatius Cocles Defending the Bridge*, oil on canvas, 1.22×1.72 m, *c*. 1642–6 (London, Dulwich Picture Gallery)

*and the Horses of Diomedes* (*c*. 1640; Nottingham, Castle Mus.), displays power, vigour, lyricism and a taste for colour, qualities that were rare and highly valued in Paris at the time. Poussin declared, on seeing Le Brun's paintings, that if they were the work of a young man, he would one day be one of the greatest painters of all time; and if they were by an older painter, he could justly call himself a most capable artist. These youthful works show a feeling for archaeology, combined with an intensity that Le Brun was never to lose. Moreover, he made masterly use of several sources of light and of dynamic composition in, for example, the *Martyrdom of St John the Evangelist* (Paris, St-Nicolas-du-Chardonnet), presented in 1642 to the Corporation des Peintres et Sculpteurs.

Le Brun was thus an accomplished artist when he accompanied Poussin to Rome in 1642. His visit was at the expense of his protector, Séguier, who also recommended him to Antonio Barberini, a nephew of Urban VIII. Even though in 1643 Le Brun unsuccessfully sought Séguier's permission to return to Paris, he was fully occupied in Rome for three years; he made copies after Raphael and the Antique, and learnt nature painting through contact with Poussin. He displayed a powerful realism in details and made rich use of values borrowed from the painters of Rome and Bologna, as in his *Death of Cato* (1646; Arras, Mus. B.-A.). He also produced for Séguier a number of religious works (all untraced) and works with subjects from ancient history, including *Horatius Cocles Defending the Bridge* (London, Dulwich Pict. Gal.; see fig. 1) and *Mucius Scaevola before Porsena* (Mâcon, Mus. Mun. Ursulines).

*(ii) Rise to prominence.*

*(a) Work in Paris, 1645–58.* In 1645, following the election of Pope Innocent X, who favoured Spain rather than France, Le Brun decided to return to Paris, where, after a short stay in Lyon, he arrived in March 1646. He immediately achieved prominence, being appointed Peintre Ordinaire du Roi on his arrival. He found, however, that taste had changed there; Eustache Le Sueur, Laurent La Hyre and Philippe de Champaigne were following Vouet's lead in practising a light-toned, classicizing manner of painting, and Le Brun, if he wished to succeed, would have to take account of this 'Parisian Atticism'. Séguier introduced him to the devout circle of Cardinal Pierre de Bérulle, and he seems to have been equally welcomed by the Précieux social world of Madeleine Scudéry and Georges Scudéry. On 26 February 1647 he married Suzanne Butay, daughter of Robert Butay (*d* 1662), Peintre du Roi.

Le Brun produced some more designs for frontispieces at this time and on two occasions executed the May of Notre-Dame (a painting on a theme from the Acts of the Apostles, which was annually presented to the cathedral of Notre-Dame-de-Paris by the goldsmiths' guild): the two works (both *in situ*) were the *Stoning of St Stephen* (1647) and the *Crucifixion of St Andrew* (1651). Whereas in the first May he demonstrated his ease of adaptation to the new Parisian taste by playing down realistic effects and Caravaggesque contrasts of light and dark, in the second one he demonstrated extreme fidelity to archaeological truth; he later told his colleagues at the Académie Royale de Peinture et de Sculpture, Paris, that on his return from Italy he had seen in Chartres Cathedral an antique low relief of a deacon attired in a manner that had served him as an example for his painting. In 1648 Le Brun was one of the 12 founder-members of the Académie Royale. Thanks to Séguier's protection, he was able, in 1654, to carry out some reforms; no easy task, since the young artists had to struggle against several traditions, notably that of the supreme authority of the Corporation des Peintres et Sculpteurs.

Like Vouet and Le Sueur, Le Brun went on to establish himself as a major decorative painter. In 1652 he supplied mythological paintings to decorate the *hôtel particulier* in Paris of the Chancellor Louis de La Rivière; two ceiling panels (*Dawn* and *Mercury Abducting Psyche*) are in the Musée Carnavalet, Paris. In 1653, to commemorate the defeat of the Fronde rebellion, he designed a thesis dedicated to the King, 'pio, forti, pacifico, triomphanti', representing him in the company of Mars and Hercules and alluding to France's monarchs of former times, for example Clovis, Dagobert, Charlemagne and St Louis. Le Brun demonstrated an aptitude for relating national issues to the heroic past, emphasizing the foundation of the monarchy in the Middle Ages and its dynastic legitimacy.

In 1654 Le Brun signed a contract with Jean-Jacques Olier, Superior of the seminary of Saint-Sulpice, to decorate the chapel there; in this task he was assisted by Charles de La Fosse, Gilbert de Sève and Pierre de Sève (1623–95). In 1656 Le Brun obtained from the King the extremely rare privilege forbidding the unauthorized reproduction of his works, particularly by means of engravings. In 1658 Jean Valdor (1616–70), Graveur du Roi, commissioned from Le Brun six or seven paintings of scenes from the story of Meleager, two of which, the *Hunt of Meleager and Atalanta* and the *Death of Meleager*, are in the Musée du Louvre, Paris. During the same period he carried out the decoration of the Galerie d'Hercule in the Hôtel Lambert, in collaboration with Le Sueur and Louis Le Vau. Besides painting the *Apotheosis of Hercules*, Le Brun arranged imitation sculptures and designed low reliefs for the sculptor Gerard van Opstal.

(b) *Vaux-le-Vicomte and entry into royal service, 1658–64.* The death of Le Sueur in 1655 confirmed Le Brun's position as the most prominent and successful decorative painter in France, and it was natural that the ambitious Surintendant des Finances, Nicolas Fouquet, should commission him to work at his extravagant new palace at VAUX-LE-VICOMTE, the most magnificent building enterprise of the period. Between 1658 and 1661 Le Brun was employed solely as a painter, but he then succeeded in becoming decorator and arranger of entertainments and took charge of the smallest details of sculptures and the gardens. He decorated the walls and ceilings of the royal apartment, the Salon d'Hercule and the Salon des Muses. He was not, however, able to complete his plan for a painting of the Palace of the Sun in the vault of the Salon Ovale; it is known only from a design (Paris, Louvre), which shows that he had long and brilliantly pondered the most 'Baroque' Roman ceilings.

The tapestries that Le Brun designed were woven at the Maincy factory. On 17 August 1661 Fouquet entertained the King and court there at a sumptuous festivity, the splendour of which hastened his impending financial disgrace. Vaux-le-Vicomte, however, had met with so much admiration and success that Le Brun's work there gave a new turn to his career. In 1659 he was presented to Cardinal Mazarin, who commissioned him to design the triumphal arch for the entry into Paris in 1660 of Louis XIV and his bride Maria-Theresa. Soon afterwards the young King made Le Brun responsible for his most important building projects.

While still working at Vaux, Le Brun found time to execute at Fontainebleau, under the King's personal supervision, a painting of the *Queens of Persia at the Feet of Alexander* (1660; Versailles, Château). Every detail of this work is derived from an ancient narrative, and the figures are subtly distinguished from each other by the individual expressiveness of their attitudes. In describing the picture, André Félibien was able to perceive, in the figure of Alexander alone, 'compassion, clémence, amitié et civilité', while the inclination of the head was said to show fidelity to a tradition to which Alexander could not bow because of a wounded thigh. This work was admired, discussed and studied at the Académie Royale; until the French Revolution (1789–95), it was regarded as a paradigm of the true theory of painting.

In 1662 Louis XIV granted the painter a patent of nobility and in 1664 confirmed his appointment as Premier Peintre du Roi, finally entrusting to him administrative and artistic responsibilities that were to set French art on a new course and to place the royal building projects in the first rank of importance. Le Brun's magnificent career was the product both of an immense talent and of a real aptitude for securing the favour of the great and powerful. Appointed Chancellor of the Académie Royale in 1663, he encountered hostility from Pierre Mignard and Charles-Alphonse Du Fresnoy, who refused to become members. This led Le Brun to secure an edict from the King's Council, forbidding any non-member of the Académie Royale to use the title of Peintre du Roi. The King further showed his esteem for Le Brun by putting him in charge in 1664 of the royal collection of paintings and drawings, officially confirming the confidence placed in his connoisseurship; this suggests that Le Brun advised Louis XIV on his acquisitions.

(iii) *Triumphs in the royal service.*

(a) *Gobelins.* In 1663 Jean-Baptiste Colbert, who had become Vice-Protector on Mazarin's death in 1661, decided to unite on one site the royal workshops at Paris and Maincy and requested Le Brun to organize at Gobelins the new Manufacture Royale des Meubles de la Couronne, where he became the head of a huge team of artists and craftsmen (*see* GOBELINS, §§1–3). The enormous annual salary that he received—4000 livres for the management of Gobelins, 3200 livres as Premier Peintre and 4800 livres as supervisor of royal paintings, with additional payments on the completion of important projects—testifies to the magnitude of his responsibilities. He created at Gobelins a school where the best artists, for example Louis Licherie (1629–87), could train apprentices. Such cabinetmakers and silversmiths from the Louvre workshops as André-Charles Boulle and Claude Ballin (i) also worked under his supervision on furnishings for royal residences. Painters and sculptors from the Académie Royale provided active support by teaching drawing, both from the Antique and from nature.

Between 1663 and 1690 the highly qualified craftsmen of Gobelins, some 250 of them, produced richly decorated and inventive furnishings that set a standard for the whole of Europe: they included 19 sets of high-warp hangings and 34 of low-warp hangings, each set comprising from 2 to 14 pieces and representing such subjects as *The Months* (Paris, Mobilier N.), the *History of the King* (Versailles, Château) and the *Battles of Alexander the Great* (two pieces in Fontainebleau, Château). For these Le Brun, assisted by Adam Frans van der Meulen, Noël Coypel, Louis Boullogne *le père* and René-Antoine Houasse, supplied cartoons that are actual paintings (Paris, Louvre; Versailles, Château). Le Brun also designed the silver furniture (designs in Stockholm, Nmus.), which was melted down in 1689 to help pay for the war against the League of Augsburg, as well as the carriage presented to the Great Mughal, the models of the royal arms for Brisach and Philipsbourg and the gold mounts for objects of vertu, some of which are displayed in the Galerie d'Apollon in the Musée du Louvre; for him, the smallest object in common use had to be of the finest quality. The factory functioned so smoothly that Le Brun, although greatly in demand, could devote himself to painting, his chief passion. Among his works, the *Battles of Alexander the Great* (1665–73; the cartoons for the tapestries woven at Gobelins), huge, vigorous and brilliant, is painted with immense authority, which won praise, almost a century later, from Pierre-Jean Mariette.

*(b) Lectures at the Académie Royale and role in art education.* In 1667 Le Brun inaugurated a series of Conférences of the Académie Royale, based on paintings in the royal collection; he himself gave an extremely important lecture on the subject of Poussin's *Israelites Gathering the Manna* (Paris, Louvre). His demonstration that painting is a matter of intelligence and theory stemmed from the discussions on this subject that he had been conducting from 1660 with Abraham Bosse and Sébastien Bourdon. In 1668 Le Brun gave a lecture on physiognomy: as well as comparing the facial expressions of humans and animals, he used Descartes's theory of the brain as the seat of the soul to show how human psychological characteristics were reflected in the expression, illustrating his discourse with numerous drawings (Paris, Louvre; *see also* EXPRESSION, fig. 1).

In 1671 the Quarrel of the Colours erupted, concerning the relative importance in painting of colour and drawing. In debating the respective merits of Titian and Raphael, such academicians as Jean-Baptiste de Champaigne, Nicolas-Pierre Loir and even van der Meulen, Le Brun's relation and protégé, set out to attack him in respect of his art, his theories and his authority. In his *Abrégé de la vie des peintres*, Roger de Piles, spokesman of the colour party, went further, claiming that in Le Brun's paintings the attitudes of the figures were always the same, that his colours, both of garments and of flesh, were too generalized and that his background colour gave no impression of fidelity to nature. Le Brun maintained his role of impartial arbitrator, defending the importance both of composition and of colour; the fact that in 1669 Bourdon had described Le Brun's *Battle of Arbella* (Paris, Louvre; see fig. 2) as a 'marvellous picture' shows that the lines of battle were not too firmly drawn, and that the quarrels were not final, only Pierre Mignard remaining intransigent.

Le Brun's attitude demonstrates one of the less obvious aspects of his character—his concern for art education, including both theory and technique; it had already led to the establishment, in 1663, of a competition for entry to the academy's school, while in 1666 he had founded the Académie de France in Rome (and silenced Charles Errard

2. Charles Le Brun: *Battle of Arbella*, oil on canvas, 4.70×12.65 m, 1669 (Paris, Musée du Louvre)

*le fils*, one of his principal critics, by appointing him Director). Around 1675 he conceived the notion of 'twinning' the Académie Royale in Paris with the Accademia di S Luca in Rome, so that each country's academicians would enjoy the same advantages and status in the other country. Although Domenico Guidi visited Paris, and Le Brun was twice appointed *principe* of the Accademia (1676 and 1677), the project came to nothing.

*(c) Versailles.* Louis XIV had decided in 1669 to transform the small palace at Versailles into his grandest residence (*see* VERSAILLES, §§1 and 2). Le Brun was involved from an early stage, and he oversaw even the smallest details of decoration, for example the sculptures for the park, of which he designed a large group in 1674, and firework displays for festivities. The ceilings of the Grands Appartements give a limited idea of his role; at the same time as working on the two great suites of rooms for the King and Queen, he also designed and executed the decoration of the Escalier des Ambassadeurs (1674–8; destr.) and of the Galerie des Glaces (1678–84). His history paintings were on subjects taken from neither mythology nor ancient history but from recent episodes in the King's reign. In the Escalier des Ambassadeurs he juxtaposed the Classical parabola shape with depictions in the antique manner of victories or important political events, for example the *Passage of the Rhine* and the *Submission of the Franche-Comté* (see fig. 3). In the Galerie des Glaces similar events were recounted in a more naturalistic manner, the artist's style being modified accordingly. Around the windows of the Escalier, which almost sprang out from the false perspective of the vaulting, were images representing the months, Classical deities and allegorical figures, arranged according to no particular concept. On either side of the King's Grand Appartement were exuberant representations of military or amorous subjects from Classical antiquity, despotic oriental princes, for example Alexander or Ptolemy, being preferred to figures from democratic Greece or republican Rome. In these two huge rooms Le Brun seems to have stressed perspective, brilliant colouring and dynamism, such as would appeal to the young King at the head of a brilliant court.

Le Brun had assistance in the execution of his project, but the concept was all his own: displaying the Escalier des Ambassadeurs to the Spanish ambassador in 1679, Louis XIV referred to it as 'M. Le Brun's staircase', and in order to plan the Galerie, the artist shut himself away for two days. Compared with André Le Nôtre's great perspectives, his projects in the gardens of Versailles—the fountains and groups of statuary for the Parterre d'Eau—appear to be those of a man of limited vision. His work in the interior, however, on the staircase and the gallery, and his plan of 1672 for a chapel, display an inventive and perfectly confident personality; his imagination and the breadth of his repertory informed all his decorative work. His touch is less sure in the large collaborative projects in

3. Charles Le Brun: *Submission of the Franche-Comté*, oil on canvas, 0.93×1.40 m, *c.* 1678 (Versailles, Château)

the Grands Appartements, especially in the evocation of antiquity.

*(iv) Last years.* In 1683 Colbert died; he was succeeded in his post by the Marquis de Louvois. Le Brun, who in 1668 had become Rector of the Académie Royale, tendered his resignation, which was refused. In 1683 he drew up, with truly scientific exactitude, an inventory of the King's pictures. In it, paintings are grouped according to their previous owners, such great collectors as Mazarin, Everard Jabach, Armand-Jean du Plessis, Duc de Richelieu, Fouquet and Prince Camillo Pamphili. Moreover, the attributions proposed by modern scholars show Le Brun as a true connoisseur of, for example, Bolognese painting. His work at Gobelins, which for a number of years he had been finding increasingly burdensome, presented new problems, as Louvois, who was Mignard's patron, immediately revealed his partisanship to the Académie Royale and gave a new direction to major new commissions. Le Brun's adversaries hoped to see him removed from his post, going so far as to accuse him of embezzlement and forcing him to defend himself before the King, who continued his salary until his death. In the absence of important commissions, Le Brun turned to painting such smaller-scale religious pictures as two versions of the *Adoration of the Shepherds* (both 1689; Paris, Louvre; see fig. 4) and *Christ's Entry into Jerusalem* (Paris, Louvre).

Le Brun must be regarded as an artist for whom painting demanded not merely intelligence and reason but also passion and imagination. His designs for the chapel at Versailles show the influence of Rubens, whose work the Parisian public was then rediscovering in the new collection of the Duc de Richelieu. Le Brun's battle scenes were influenced by Raphael's Vatican frescoes, but the two *Adorations* combine Correggio-like lightness and concentrated richness; a repose to succeed his earlier dynamism. It is as if Le Brun wished to show his detractors that he remained fully able to respond to the demands of his art. In his large cartoons for decorative work, for example *Calliope* (Paris, Louvre), the emotion revealed does not enfeeble the vigour of his line. He was a strict theoretician, who, in such works as the *Passage of the Rhine* and the plans for the chapel at Versailles, never renounced the splendour of colour and fire.

2. POSTHUMOUS REPUTATION. The name of Charles Le Brun has become closely identified with the Académie Royale, which commissioned a portrait of him by Nicolas de Largillierre (1683–6; Paris, Louvre; *see* PARIS, fig. 16), and his reputation has fluctuated with that of the academic style that it promoted. While even the most ardent republicans would not deny the perfection of Versailles and, to a lesser extent, of Vaux-le-Vicomte, Le Brun's artistic domination became equated with the political despotism of his master Louis XIV. During the 18th century, however, Le Brun's works, notably the battle scenes, were regarded as models of history painting, and the fame of such works as the *Penitent Magdalene* (1656–

4. Charles Le Brun: *Adoration of the Shepherds*, oil on canvas, 1.51×2.13 m, 1689 (Paris, Musée du Louvre)

7; Paris, Louvre) was almost unmatched by any other French work of art. Moreover, his lectures on the theory of art were translated into numerous European languages, and they became a standard textbook for art students. During the 19th century, as academic practice was gradually called into question, Le Brun came to be reviled and was even held to be a villain who had been responsible for the death of his rival, Eustache Le Sueur. It was not until the great *Le Brun* exhibition organized by Jennifer Montagu and Jacques Thuillier at Versailles in 1963 that art historians were able to judge the quality and range of his achievement, and he was recognized as one of the most innovative and versatile artists of the French school.

For further illustration *see* FRANCE, fig. 22.

UNPUBLISHED SOURCES
Paris, Bib. N. [MS. Fr. 12987 of C. Nivelon: *Vie de Charles Le Brun et description détaillée de ses ouvrages, par Claude Nivelon (c.* 1700)]

WRITINGS
*Méthode pour apprendre à dessiner les passions proposée dans une conférence sur l'expression générale et particulière* (Amsterdam and Paris, 1698)

BIBLIOGRAPHY
H. Jouin: *Charles Le Brun et les arts sous Louis XIV* (Paris, 1889)
J. Guiffrey and P. Marcel: *Inventaire général des dessins du musée du Louvre et du musée de Versailles: Ecole française,* vii (Paris, 1912), pp. 110–29; viii (Paris, 1913), pp. 2–129
A. Blunt: 'The Early Work of Charles Le Brun', *Burl. Mag.,* lxxxv (1944), pp. 165–73, 186–94
J. Montagu: 'The Early Ceiling Decorations of Charles Le Brun', *Burl. Mag.,* cv (1963), pp. 395–408
*Charles Le Brun, 1619–1690: Peintre et dessinateur* (exh. cat. by J. Montagu and J. Thuillier, Versailles, Château, 1963) [almost complete cat. of ptgs and exhaustive bibliog.]
D. Wildenstein: 'Les Oeuvres de Charles Le Brun d'après les gravures de son temps', *Gaz. B.-A.,* n. s. 5, lxvi (1965), pp. 1–58
J. Thuillier: 'Charles Le Brun (1619–1690)', *Au Temps du Roi Soleil: Les Peintres de Louis XIV (1660–1715)* (exh. cat., Lille, Mus. B.-A., 1968), pp. 23–8
R. Bacou: 'Cartons et dessins de Le Brun pour l'Escalier des Ambassadeurs au musée du Louvre', *Liber amicorum Karel G. Boon* (Amsterdam, 1974)
R. A. Weigert and M. Préaud: *Inventaire du fonds français: Graveurs du dix-septième siècle,* Paris, Bib. N., Dept Est. cat., vii (Paris, 1976), pp. 395–6
D. Meyer: *L'Histoire du roy* (Paris, 1980)
*Le Classicisme français: Masterpieces of Seventeenth-century Painting* (exh. cat. by S. Laveissière, Dublin, N.G., 1985), pp. 32–7
*Versailles à Stockholm: Dessins du Nationalmuseum, peintures, meubles et arts décoratifs des collections suédoises et danoises* (exh. cat. by G. Walton, Paris, Cent. Cult. Suéd., 1985)
*Le Brun à Versailles* (exh. cat. by L. Beauvais and J. -F. Méjanès, Paris, Louvre, 1985–6)
A. Brejon de Lavergnée: *L'Inventaire Le Brun de 1683: La Collection des tableaux de Louis XIV* (Paris, 1987)
L. Beauvais: 'Les Dessins de Le Brun pour "L'Histoire d'Alexandre"', *Rev. Louvre,* 4 (1990), pp. 285–95
*Charles Le Brun: Le Décor de l'Escalier des Ambassadeurs à Versailles* (exh. cat. by L. Beauvais and others, Versailles, Château, 1990)
*Courage and Cruelty: Le Brun's 'Horatius Cocles' and 'The Massacre of the Innocents'* (exh. cat., ed. J. Montagu and N. Kalinsky; London, Dulwich Pict. Gal., 1990–91)
M. Gareau with L. Beauvais: *Charles Le Brun, Premier Peintre du Roi Louis XIV* (Paris, 1992; Eng. trans., New York, 1992)

CLAIRE CONSTANS

**Le Brun [Lebrun], Jean-Baptiste-Pierre** (*b* Paris, 16 Feb 1748; *d* Paris, 6 Aug 1813). French dealer, collector, writer and painter. He was the son of a painter, Pierre Le Brun (*c.* 1703–1771), and great-nephew of Charles Le Brun. He studied painting with Jean-Baptiste Deshays, François Boucher and Jean-Honoré Fragonard, before becoming a leading connoisseur and art dealer. In 1776 he married the

painter Elisabeth Vigée (*see* VIGÉE LE BRUN, ELISABETH-LOUISE). In some of his articles (1771–81) published in the *Journal de Paris* he put forward the concept of a centralized museum. He served as Louis XVI's agent at art sales and was curator of paintings to the King's brother, Charles-Philippe de Bourbon, Comte d'Artois (later Charles X), and to Louis-Philippe-Joseph, Duc d'Orléans (1747–93); he subsequently acted as intermediary for foreign collectors, including Catherine the Great of Russia.

Between 1771 and 1813 Le Brun conducted 165 sales, including the collections of Joseph-Hyacinthe, Comte de Vaudreuil, Bailli de Breteuil and Joseph Vernet, which he displayed in the magnificent exhibition room he had added to his house in the Rue de Cléry, Paris. He set a new standard with his sale catalogues, in which he described each work, giving the dimensions and sometimes a judgement of its quality and account of its provenance. For important sales he included a preface with a biography of the collector.

Le Brun was tireless in travelling abroad to buy works of art for himself, which he dispersed in large sales. One of the two most important of these, held in 1791 (Paris, 11–30 March), included not only paintings, but also drawings, antiquities, armour, porcelain and furnishings. Le Brun, who often claimed to have rediscovered artists, was instrumental in defining schools of art. He emphasized the northern European school; among his 'rediscovered' artists was Hans Holbein the younger, whose *Ambassadors* (London, N.G.) he exported to England in 1792. In his *Galerie des peintres flamands, hollandais et allemands* (1792–6) he introduced the painting of northern Europe to a wider audience. Many of the illustrations in this three-volume publication represent works from his own collection.

Mme Vigée Le Brun, whose work brought her into close association with the court, had left France in the early days of the Revolution (October 1789). Le Brun campaigned vigorously but unsuccessfully to keep her from being listed as an émigré; in order to avoid the consequent forfeiture of their property, he was obliged to divorce her in 1794. They were reunited when, following the end of the Revolution, she returned to France after a 12-year absence. Le Brun himself had opposed the principles of the Revolution and did not participate in the activities of the Commission des Monuments. He campaigned against the Commission des Musées and argued that connoisseurs, not painters, should select works for museums, and he strongly criticized the destruction of works of art by poor restoration.

In 1810 (Paris, 20–24 March) Le Brun held a second major sale of his collection, which included paintings attributed to such artists as Raphael, Titian, Rembrandt, van Dyck, Murillo and David Teniers the younger; the two-volume catalogue contains 179 plates classified by school, as well as brief biographies of the painters and the provenances of their works. In 1814 the remainder of Le Brun's collections was dispersed in two posthumous sales in Paris (Paillet & fils Constantin, 23–9 May; Roux, 27 Dec).

WRITINGS
*Galerie des peintres flamands, hollandais et allemands,* 3 vols (Paris, 1792–6)
*Précis historique de la vie de la citoyenne Le Brun, peintre* (Paris, 1793)

*Essai sur les moyens d'encourager la peinture, la sculpture et la gravure* (Paris, 1794–5)

BIBLIOGRAPHY

G. Emile-Mâle: 'Jean-Baptiste-Pierre Le Brun (1743–1813): Son rôle dans l'histoire de la restauration des tableaux du Louvre', *Paris & Ile de France: Mem.*, viii (1956), pp. 371–417

A. P. de Mirimonde: 'Les Opinions de M. Lebrun sur la peinture hollandaise', *Rev. des A.*, vi (1956), pp. 207–14

M. Gallet: 'La Maison de Madame Vigée-Lebrun, rue du Gros-Chenet', *Gaz. B.-A.*, n.s. 5, lvi (1960), pp. 275–84

F. Haskell: *Rediscoveries in Art: Some Aspects of Taste, Fashion and Collecting in England and France* (London, 1976), pp. 18–23

C. B. Bailey: 'Lebrun et le commerce d'art pendant le blocus continental: Patriotisme et marge bénéficiaire . . .', *Rev. A.*, lxiii (1984), pp. 35–46

**Leca, Miguel Mañara Vicentelo de.** *See* MAÑARA VICENTELO DE LECA, MIGUEL.

**Le Camus, Louis-Denis** ( *fl* 1742–75). French architect. He is almost invariably confused with his namesake and contemporary, Nicolas Le Camus de Mézières. In 1742 he came second in the Prix de Rome competition with a design for a façade of a town house. From 1762 he was engaged, for Etienne-François, Duc de Choiseul, in restoring and enlarging the Château of Chanteloup (destr.), where in 1775 he built an extraordinary tower (extant). This hybrid monument to the alternative court that the exiled Choiseul maintained at Chanteloup takes the form of a pagoda but is articulated with a Doric order, the whole being an elaborate example of stone-cutting. Choiseul also employed Le Camus to design the Quartier Choiseul in Paris and the Colisée des Champs-Elysées, an extended series of pleasure pavilions, opened in 1771 and demolished in 1785. The creative use of light and the exciting spatial effects achieved in this short-lived pleasure garden can be judged from the sketches of Gabriel-Jacques de Saint-Aubin, who had a commercial interest in the enterprise. A domed and colonnaded circular central hall was surrounded by a number of variously shaped gaming-rooms, which led into differently sized oval, octagonal and kidney-shaped courtyards.

BIBLIOGRAPHY

G. L. Le Rouge: *Description du colisée élevé aux Champs-Elysées* (Paris, 1771)

R. Edouard-André: 'Documents inédits sur l'histoire du château et des jardins de Chanteloup', *Bull. Soc. Hist. A. Fr.* (1935), pp. 21–39

A. C. Gruber: 'Les "Vauxhalls" parisiens au XVIIIe siècle', *Bull. Soc. Hist. A. Fr.* (1971), pp. 125–43

RICHARD JOHN

**Le Camus, Pierre Duval.** *See* DUVAL LE CAMUS, PIERRE.

**Le Camus de Mézières, Nicolas** (*b* Paris, 26 May 1721; *d* Paris, 27 July 1793). French architect and writer. He studied at the Académie d'Architecture, Paris, where he won the second prize for architecture in 1742. From 1751 to 1792 he practised as 'architecte expert-bourgeois', an expert in the building of town houses (hôtels). When some timber joists were being replaced at the Ecole Militaire in 1762, he took the opportunity to study the use of timber in building, becoming an expert in the subject and subsequently publishing a manual on carpentry and a treatise on the strength of timber. In 1762 he received a commission to design what became his best-known scheme, the corn exchange or Halle au Blé (1763–9; rebuilt 1889 as the Bourse de Commerce; one staircase survives from the original scheme), built on the site of the old Hôtel de Soissons. It consisted of a vast circular courtyard 40 m across, surrounded by a double gallery with groined vaults resting on columns. The first floor of the gallery, which served as the granary, was covered by a barrel vault built of brick and stone. The exterior consisted of an arcade divided by broad piers, with small mezzanine windows to illuminate the granaries. The Halle au Blé was widely celebrated by contemporaries of Le Camus for the novelty of its design, notably its entirely isolated circular form, its elegant exterior and the ingenuity of its planning, its vaulting and its intertwined, double flights of oval stairs. The courtyard was later covered by a glass and timber dome (1781; *see* MOLINOS, JACQUES) and subsequently by a pioneering cast-iron dome (1808–13) by FRANÇOIS-JOSEPH BÉLANGER.

While the Halle au Blé was under construction, Le Camus was in charge of several other building projects in Paris. In 1764 he constructed the monumental gateway to the Collège Louis-le-Grand, built in a severe classical style. He also designed a barracks (begun 1765) for the Gardes Françaises on the Rue Mouffetard. Exploiting his special knowledge of carpentry, he constructed an exceptionally light floor for this building, but the economies made were contrary to established practice and aroused the opposition of the carpenters' guild. Another building, the hôtel for the Prince de Beauvau on the Rue du Faubourg Saint-Honoré, Paris (completed 1769; now occupied by the Ministère de l'Intérieur), reveals his skill at exploiting sites with awkward shapes. Here a semicircular plan allowed him to achieve a successful scenic effect: two wings with concave façades flank an imposing entrance composed of an entablature supported by four pairs of columns through which the façade of the hôtel may be glimpsed across the courtyard. He also built a house (destr. 1929) for himself at 5, Rue St–Blaise in the Charonne suburb of Paris and prepared a set of drawings for a Carmelite church (unexecuted), planned for the Rue de Grenelle, Paris.

After a business setback in the late 1760s, and in the absence of further architectural commissions, Le Camus devoted himself to the publication of his writings, including an illustrated account of the Halle au Blé, which he sought to present as a model of civic architecture. He owed much of his fame to his *Le Génie de l'architecture, ou l'analogie de cet art avec nos sensations* (1780), a book in which greater stress is laid on the character and atmosphere of a building than on adherence to traditional rules of composition. Le Camus later published various technical manuals, the products of his experience as a practising architect. Le Camus kept abreast of the principal developments in philosophy and science and was an educated and enlightened architect. His writings reveal a concern with public welfare, a confidence in the progress of the Enlightenment and an admiration of Georges Louis Leclerc de Buffon (1707–88) and Duhamel du Monceau. Several buildings by his namesake Louis-Denis Le Camus, architect to the Duc de Choiseul, are often incorrectly attributed to Le Camus de Mézières; these include the Colisée (destr. 1785), a vast amusement palace on the Champs-Elysées, the pagoda at Chanteloup and the development of the Comédie Italienne, Paris.

WRITINGS

with F. A. Babuty Desgodetz: *Dissertation de la compagnie des architectes experts des bâtiments à Paris . . . sur la théorie et les pratiques des gros bois de charpente* (Paris, 1763)

*Recueil de différents plans et dessins concernant la nouvelle halle aux grains* (Paris, 1769)

*Le Génie de l'architecture, ou l'analogie de cet art avec nos sensations* (Paris, 1780)

*Guide de ceux qui veulent bâtir* (Paris, 1781)

*Traité de la force des bois* (Paris, 1782)

BIBLIOGRAPHY

F. Boudon: 'Urbanisme et spéculation à Paris au XVIIIème siècle: Le Terrain de l'hôtel de Soissons', *J. Soc. Archit. Hist.*, xxxii/4 (1973), pp. 267–307

R. G. Saisselin: 'Architecture and Language: The Sensationalism of Le Camus de Mézières', *Brit. J. Aesth.*, xv (1975), pp. 239–53

M. Deming: *La Halle au Blé de Paris* (Brussels, 1984)

GÉRARD ROUSSET-CHARNY

**Le Carpentier, Antoine-Mathieu** (*b* Rouen, 15 July 1709; *d* Paris, 13 July 1773). French architect. He was the son of a cabinetmaker and wood–carver, Mathieu Le Carpentier (*fl* 1723–35), and worked in his father's shop and that of a local sculptor, François. He studied architecture on his own and came to the attention of officials in Rouen, who provided introductions for him in Paris. He worked in Orléans in 1733 under an engineer, Defroche, and in Paris under Jacques Gabriel V on the Chambre des Comptes (1738–40; destr. 1871). By the early 1750s Le Carpentier had established a busy residential practice serving prominent nobles and financiers. Most of his work was in Paris, and it included interior and exterior remodellings as well as new construction. His architectural taste was conservative; in plan and massing, his hôtels and châteaux reflected the practices of the first half of the 18th century, but he employed Neo-classical motifs in his detailing. He was elected to the Académie Royale d'Architecture in 1756.

Notable among Le Carpentier's commissions was the Pavillon de la Boissière on the Rue du Clichy in Paris (1751; enlarged *c.* 1770 by his pupil, Guillaume-Martin Couture; destr.). This elegant weekend house was conceived as an Italianate villa consisting of a single storey set on a base. Round-arched windows separated by columns dominated the elevations that enclosed a series of intimate oval and polygonal rooms. In 1765 he was employed at the Palais-Bourbon, rebuilding considerable portions of the *corps de logis* and adding two long wings on either side of the principal courtyard. Among his other buildings were the church of the Collège de Grandmont, Paris (1759; destr.), the Château de Courteilles, Eure (1754–62; destr.), and the Pavillon de Croix-Fontaine, Seine-et-Marne (*c.* 1755; destr.), commissioned by Michel Bouret as a hunting retreat for Louis XV.

In 1755 Le Carpentier was commissioned by the town council of Rouen to prepare a master-plan for his native city that was to include recommendations for street improvements, new quays along the Seine and designs for a town hall, a paymaster's office and a public garden. Although none of the major components of the plan was realized, it represented a valuable contribution to urban-planning theory in the mid-18th century.

Le Carpentier sought simultaneously to beautify the city and to improve its ability to function as a commercial centre. The key to his proposal was the control of traffic through Rouen to facilitate the flow of goods and to guide visitors to the city's architectural monuments. He conceived the Rue du Gros Horloge as a monumental axis linking the cathedral and its parvis to the proposed town hall, which was to occupy one side of a *place royale* honouring Louis XV.

The rectangular Place Louis XV, like the contemporary *places royales* built in Reims and Nancy, was to have been lined with buildings with façades composed of a rusticated base supporting a giant order framing two upper storeys. This scheme was a convention for *places royales*, which had been established in the late 17th century by the Place des Victoires and the Place Vendôme in Paris. At the centre of the square was to have been a statue of Louis XV designed by Le Carpentier and the sculptor Jean-Baptiste Lemoyne (ii). Their design departed from the conventional device of portraying the monarch in Roman military costume and instead depicted him in contemporary dress standing on a shield supported by three Gallic soldiers. This unique composition was to have reminded the citizens of Rouen that the authority of the king ultimately issued from the people.

WRITINGS

*Recueil des plans, coupes et élévations du nouvel hôtel de ville de Rouen* (Paris, 1758)

BIBLIOGRAPHY

P. Chirol: 'L'Architecte Le Carpentier et le projet du nouvel hôtel de ville de Rouen', *Congrès du Millénaire de la Normandie (911–1911)*, ii (Rouen, 1912), pp. 373–405

L. Hautecoeur: *Architecture classique* (1943–57), iii, iv

M. Gallet: *Stately Mansions: 18th-century Paris Domestic Architecture* (New York, 1972)

R. Cleary: *The Places Royales of Louis XIV and Louis XV* (diss., New York, Columbia U., 1986)

RICHARD CLEARY

**Lecce** [anc. Lupiae]. Italian city in Apulia, *c.* 40 km southeast of Brindisi and 12 km inland from the Adriatic Sea. The city is characterized by a maze of narrow medieval streets around three piazzas, S Oronzo, Duomo and Castello; its architectural significance derives from its wealth of churches and palaces built between the 16th and 18th centuries in an exuberant style generally referred to as 'Leccese Baroque' (see below).

Lecce was founded by the Mesappii, who spoke an Illyrian dialect, and in Roman times it was a prosperous town linked to an important port near San Cataldo, built *c.* AD 130 by Emperor Hadrian. Part of a large Roman amphitheatre was uncovered in the town centre (Piazza S Oronzo) in 1901. After the fall of the Western Empire, Lecce was ruled by the Byzantine governor in Otranto, and from 1043 it was held by Norman counts. Their chief surviving monument is the church of SS Niccolò e Cataldo (founded 1180) to the north-west of the centre beyond the Porta Napoli (1548); the central part of the church's Romanesque façade, including the decorated door and small rose window, was retained in a Baroque remodelling (*c.* 1716) by Giuseppe Cino (1644–1722). The Normans maintained an almost independent fiefdom until 1463, when Ferdinand I, King of Naples, added the principality of Taranto and the county of Lecce to the Aragonese domains in Italy. From then on Lecce shared the history of the Spanish rule in Naples and Sicily.

The buildings of Lecce's splendid Renaissance and Baroque phases are characterized by carved decoration facilitated by the nature of the local limestone (*pietra leccese*), which is very easy to carve but hardens after a few years' exposure. Such decoration gave rise to the stylistic term 'Leccese Baroque', although its use has been challenged on the grounds that the decoration is generally applied to such flat surfaces as the façades of churches, most of which have rectangular or Latin-cross plans with none of the curvilinear character associated with the Baroque elsewhere. Palaces feature complex window architraves, while in town houses florid decoration is generally limited to the brackets of balconies, carved in the shape of animals, monsters or human figures. The first important Baroque building of Lecce, and the most notable, is the basilica of Santa Croce (founded 1353; rebuilt after *c*. 1550), of simple, rectangular plan with a smaller, rectangular presbytery. The flat façade (see fig.), richly encrusted with decoration, is articulated by columns that in the lower storey have zoomorphic capitals and in the upper storey, bands of lotus leaves. Medieval reminiscences appear in the form of a large rose window and in brackets carved as grotesque figures supporting the balcony that runs across the façade. The lower half of this frontispiece is the work of Gabriele Riccardi (*d* 1582–6), the upper (1644) by Cesare Penna (1607–*c*. 1697). The adjacent Celestine monastery (now the Prefettura) is the work of Giuseppe Zimbalo ('lo Zingarello'; 1620–1710), who, with his pupil Giuseppe Cino (*fl* mid-17th century), was the leading architect of Lecce's Baroque phase; the rusticated pilasters of the monastery's two storeys frame a series of windows with florid architraves.

Lecce, façade of Santa Croce, late 16th century–mid-17th

The Piazza del Duomo, devoid of shops and accessible only through its north side, is a remarkable piece of unified townscape, the main components of which derive from the patronage of Bishop Luigi Pappacoda. They include the 12th-century cathedral of S Oronzo, rebuilt in Baroque style (1659–70) by Zimbalo, who also built its campanile; the cathedral's north entrance towards the piazza, more sumptuous than the west front, is surmounted by a triumphal arch crowned by a figure of S Oronzo, the city's patron. The adjacent bishop's palace (Palazzo Vescovile; 1420–38; rebuilt 1632; rest. 1761), with a loggia on the *piano nobile* above a rusticated base, is in turn linked to the Palazzo del Seminario (1694–1709), built by Cino, which has a giant order of rusticated pilasters.

Other notable churches of this period in Lecce include S Maria del Rosario (1691–1728), Zimbalo's last major commission, which has a west-front upper zone adorned with floreate pinnacles and stone fruit-bushes capped by birds. The only church in the city that displays the inflections of normative Baroque is S Matteo (1667–90) by Achille Carducci (1644–before 1712): its façade (1700) sets a convex lower storey against a concave upper one in a manner recalling that of Francesco Borromini's S Carlo alle Quattro Fontane, Rome. The entrance bay of S Matteo is covered in stone scales, a feature seen elsewhere in Lecce on the columns of doorways. The Baroque architecture of Lecce is the most striking example of an idiosyncratic style that can also be seen in other small towns in the Salentino region. The influence of Spain, once thought to have been prevalent, is now discounted, and the area was likewise culturally independent of Naples. No convincing explanation has been suggested for the distinctive character of the architecture, which was maintained with remarkable consistency for over a century. Lecce was also noted in the 17th and 18th centuries for its papier-mâché statuary, where remarkable effects were achieved in facial expression and folds of drapery; a revival of this art took place in the late 20th century. Lecce's principal museum, the Museo Provinciale 'Sigismondo Castromediano', has important archaeological and ceramics collections as well as an art gallery.

BIBLIOGRAPHY
L. De Sanctis: *La basilica di Santa Croce* (Lecce, 1912)
M. Calvesi: 'La chiesa e il convento dei Celestini, monumento principe dell'architettura leccese', *Commentari*, v (1954), pp. 316–29
M. Calvesi and M. Maniera Elia: *Architettura barocca a Lecce e in terra di Puglia* (Rome, 1971)
T. Pellegrino: *Piazza del Duomo a Lecce* (Bari, 1972)
C. D. Fonseca and others: '*Barocco' leccese* (Milan, 1979)
M. Paone: *Lecce: Elegia del barocco* (Galatina, 1979)
M. D. Elia, ed.: *La Puglia tra barocco e rococo* (Milan, 1982)

**Lecce, Matteo da.** *See* PÉREZ DE ALESIO, MATEO.

**Lechler** [Lacher], **Lorenz** (*b c.* 1460; *d* after 1516). German architect, sculptor and military engineer.

1. LIFE AND ARCHITECTURAL AND SCULPTURAL WORK. On 23 June 1489 the Milan City Council rejected a recommendation from Simon Brunus, German, that 'Master Laurentius, engineer' should come to Milan for the task of completing the tiburium (?ciborium, baldacchino) for the cathedral. It has generally been thought that

this letter referred to Lorenz Lechler, for on 25 August 1489 the City Council of Esslingen (near Stuttgart) also recommended Lechler to the Milanese for the completion of their cathedral. Lechler had constructed the sacrament house and choir-screen for St Dionysius, Esslingen, and he was commended to the Milanese for his 'ingenuity, industry and art'.

Circumstantial evidence suggests that Lechler may have been involved with the construction of the sacrament house and choir-screen at Speyer Cathedral in the late 1490s. In 1509 he was called back to Speyer to supervise the completion of the *Mount of Olives* located just outside and south of the cathedral nave, which had been begun by HANS SYFER. Although Seeliger-Zeiss (1967) has attributed to Lechler most of the responsibility for the design of this monument, his exact share is disputed.

Lechler enjoyed a multifaceted career, as demonstrated by the agreement that he reached in 1503 with Philip, Count Palatine (*reg* 1476–1508), to become the Artillery Master and Master Builder of the Palatinate, with lifelong tenure. In 1508 Philip's successor Ludwig VI (*reg* 1508–44) renewed this agreement, and under Ludwig's patronage Lechler was apparently involved with several major building projects in the Count's living quarters at Heidelberg Castle: the Ladies' Wing, the Ludwig Wing and the Library Wing. Archival documentation for these attributions, however, and indeed for Lechler's career after 1509, is very thin.

The last clearly documented date in Lechler's life is from his own design booklet, written in 1516 for the 'instruction of my son, Moritz' (*see* §2 below). In 1538 Moritz (*fl* 1538–55) was appointed to the same position as Artillery Master and Master Builder of the Palatinate that his father had held. Since no other holder of this office is documented between 1508 and 1538, Lorenz may have served until he was directly succeeded by his son, although by 1538 he would have been in his 70s.

Lechler's career is still a puzzle. On the one hand are the ornamental church fittings at Esslingen and Speyer that he designed, and for which he probably did some of the sculpture. On the other hand he served for many years for the Palatinate. In his 'Instructions' he alluded to his long experience in military fortification, yet none of these projects has been identified, even at Heidelberg Castle. His 'Instructions' are primarily concerned with techniques for designing the choirs of city and parish churches, but no such churches built in the Neckar region during his lifetime have been attributed to him. Although he clearly enjoyed a strong reputation in this region, most of his architectural projects have either not been identified or have subsequently been destroyed.

2. DESIGN THEORY AND BOOKLET OF 1516. Lechler's Gothic design booklet, written in 1516, was not printed at the time. Three manuscript copies were made near the end of the 16th century. The copy now preserved in Cologne (Hist. Archv, MS. W. f° 276*; for illustration *see* TEMPLATE) was made by Jacob Facht, a master carpenter from Andernach who dated his copybook 1593–6. It was printed in 1856. Another copy appeared in the manuscript market in 1975 and was purchased by the Heidelberg University Library (Heidelberg, Ubib., MS.

3858). It was made by Hans Düring, a Swiss master mason who returned from Strasbourg to Berne in 1596 to direct work on the minster. Watermarks date the paper used by Düring to the period 1598–1603.

Handwriting analysis suggests that the anonymous third copy (Karlsruhe, Bad. Landesbib., D. MS. 157) was made in the 1590s. Facht's copy is the longest version, but in places he misunderstood, miscopied or intentionally changed Lechler's text. Düring also modified many of Lechler's spellings and expressions into Swiss German. The Karlsruhe copy is the most reliable of the three, but it contains only one-third of Lechler's text as found in Facht's copy.

Although Lechler mentioned that he would discuss military fortifications, the surviving copies of his booklet contain only techniques for designing the type of contemporary German aisled hall church with a single-cell choir. In separate places Lechler mentioned four principles pertaining to his design techniques. First, dimensions were to be commensurate with the quality of the stone: the better the stone, the smaller the dimensions. Second, dimensions were to be affected by the choice of scale: the 'old foot' used in former times, or the smaller 'new foot' generally preferred in his own day. Third, some design problems required decisions by the master mason for which no firm rules could be given. Fourth, the overriding concern in design was structural integrity; in Lechler's own words, 'an honourable work glorifies its master, if it stands up.'

Lechler's design technique can be described as modular and proportional. The width of the choir was used to provide the macro-module for determining other major measurements in the building, for example the length and height of the choir, the length, width and height of the nave, and the width of the side aisles. The width of the choir also determined the thickness of the choir walls by a ratio of 10:1 (if the choir was 30 feet wide, the walls should be 3 feet thick). This wall thickness then became a micro-module for determining the dimensions of the wall buttresses and the openings for the choir windows. This micro-module also provided proportional scaling for the window mullions and for the transverse ribs of the vault. The crossribs were in turn derived from the dimensions of the transverse ribs in a ratio of 5:7.

Although Lechler had no way of actually calculating structural forces, his principle of making the structural components proportional to the width and height of the choir was reasonable when used within the empirical evidence from other successful designs in churches of this type. Within the limits of his modular/proportional design principles there was enough flexibility for the designer to produce the variety that actually exists in the contemporary German hall churches of the type with which he was concerned.

*See also* MASONRY, §III and MASON (i), §IV.

BIBLIOGRAPHY

Thieme–Becker

A. Reichensperger: *Vermischte Schriften über christliche Kunst* (Leipzig, 1856), pp. 133–55 [the only edn of the Cologne copy of Lechler's 'Instructions', in a slightly transliterated version]

H. Rott: 'Oberrheinische Meister des 15. und 16. Jahrhunderts: Namen und Werke', *Oberrheinische Kst*, iii (1928), pp. 55–86

K. Menne: 'W. f⁰ 276*', *Mitt. Stadtarchv Köln*, x/1, pt 5 (1937), pp. 218–21

P. Anstett: 'Ein unbekanntes Baumeisterbildnis von Lorenz Lechler in der Dionysiuskirche zu Esslingen am Neckar', *Nachrbl. Dkmlpf. Baden-Württemberg*, vii (1964), pp. 97–100

A. Seeliger-Zeiss: *Lorenz Lechler von Heidelberg und sein Umkreis* (Heidelberg, 1967)

L. R. Shelby: 'Medieval Masons' Templates', *J. Soc. Archit. Hist.*, xxx (1971), pp. 140–54

L. R. Shelby and R. Mark: 'Late Gothic Structural Design in the "Instructions" of Lorenz Lechler', *Architectura* [Munich], ix (1979), pp. 113–31

A. Seeliger-Zeiss: 'Studien zum Steinmetzbuch des Lorenz Lechler von 1516: Ein bisher unbekannt gebliebenes Fragment im Besitz der Badischen Landesbibliothek Karlsruhe', *Architectura* [Munich], xii (1982), pp. 125–50 [contains analysis and transcription of the Karlsruhe copy of Lechler's 'Instructions']

LON R. SHELBY

**Lechner.** Hungarian family of architects.

**(1) Ödön** [Edmund] **Lechner** (*b* Pest [now Budapest], 27 Aug 1845; *d* Budapest, 10 June 1914). He came from a wealthy bourgeois Pest family with strong artistic connections. He studied (1865–6) at the József Applied Arts School, Pest, under Antal Szkalnitzky and then (1866–8) at the Königliche Akademie der Künste, Berlin. He went on to study for a year in Italy. On returning home to Pest he opened an architectural practice (1869–96) with Gyulá Pártos. Until the mid-1870s Lechner's work was typified by an eclecticism based on Italian Renaissance forms. He built blocks of flats, but the most interesting work of this period was a skating rink building (1875; destr. before 1896), City Park, Budapest. The three-storey building had two single-storey wings, Palladian windows and a façade composed of a graceful series of arcades facing the rink. Despite establishing a successful career, he felt hampered by the predominantly Germanic culture that had formed his education.

In 1875 Lechner travelled therefore to France, where he assisted in the rebuilding and restoring of châteaux undertaken by Clément Parent (1823–84). Lechner became interested in the origin of French Renaissance style, an amalgamation of French medieval and Italian Renaissance architecture. As an experiment he attempted mixing French Renaissance and Hungarian folk art forms to arrive at a deliberately original style. This resulted in the architecture of the Railways' Home (1881–4), Andrássy Street, and the Thonet House (1888–9), Váci Street, both in Budapest, the latter being the first building in the city to have overall ceramic tiles on the façades.

In 1889 Lechner went to England with Vilmos Zsolnay, who had been responsible for the decorated ceramic work on Lechner's buildings (*see* ZSOLNAY CERAMICS FACTORY). They studied the East Asian ceramic collections in the South Kensington (now Victoria and Albert) Museum, London, and Lechner discovered Anglo-Indian colonial architecture. On returning to Hungary he designed the Town Hall (1890), Kecskemét, which marks the transition from his early style to his mature, great work. The decoration of the ceramic facing, wonderfully coloured and of primarily Persian and Hindu influence, has the advantage of being ageless and immune to pollutants. In using Asian forms he stressed the origins of the Hungarian nation in that continent and found a basis for the creation of a Hungarian national style, which was his ultimate objective. He was also inspired by the Hungarian collector and writer Jószef Huszka (1854–1934), whose book *Magyar ornamentika* (1898) reflected similar concerns.

Between 1893 and 1902 Lechner built the three large projects on which his reputation rests: the Museum of Applied Arts, the Institute of Geology and the Postal Savings Bank, all in Budapest. The Museum of Applied Arts (1893–7), Üllői Street, is an extraordinary mixture of Hindu and Hungarian historicizing forms and modern construction. The main façade juts forward slightly in the middle as a semi-open porch, crowned by a cupola and decorated with coloured ceramics. The entrance hall is decorated with Indian palace motifs and lit by an iron-supported, glazed roof. The Institute of Geology (1899), Népstadion Street, has a tent-shaped roof covered with glazed tiles. The roof ridges, crests and plasterwork are decorated with coloured maiolica, and the façades and window bays with brick ornament imitating Hungarian embroidery motifs. The entrance halls, staircases and circular galleries employ undulating, soft forms that are entirely original.

The Postal Savings Bank (1899–1902; *see* HUNGARY, fig. 5), Rosenberg Street, Budapest, represents the peak of Lechner's career. It is simpler than the previous works in its handling of masses; on the façades it is the great decorative wall surfaces, rather than the details, that dominate. The five-storey block, with inner courtyard, prefigures the modern office building, with its unified window division and identical façades. Only the corners and the entrance are marked by the continuous narrow polygonal shafts, coupled windows and decorative friezes or gables. The brick decoration, again based on rich, appliqué folk embroidery, creates a restrained, harmonious effect. The maiolica ornamentation is richest on the steep roof. Inside, the columns, vaults, railings and interior elements are made up of luxuriant, biomorphic, Secessionist forms.

In the last decade of his life Lechner received fewer commissions, among them the Sipeki villa (1905–6) on May 1st Street, Budapest, and the St Elizabeth Church (1907–13), Poszony (now Bratislava, Slovakia). Inspired by a national cultural tradition, he created a forceful, individual architectural language that many Hungarian architects tried to follow and develop, among them his nephew (2) Jenő Lechner, BÉLA LAJTA, József and László VÁGÓ, Áladár Árkay (*see* ÁRKAY, (1)), GÉZA MÁRKUS, SÁNDOR BAUMGARTEN, and the Bálint & Jámbor and KOMOR & JAKAB partnerships.

BIBLIOGRAPHY
Thieme-Becker
F. Vámos: *Lechner Ödön*, 2 vols (Budapest, 1927)
J. Kismarty-Lechner: *Lechner Ödön* (Budapest, 1961)
T. Bakonyi and M. Kubinszky: *Lechner Ödön* (Budapest, 1981)

**(2) Jenő Lechner** [Kismarty-Lechner] (*b* Budapest, 23 Aug 1878; *d* Budapest, 24 Feb 1962). Nephew of (1) Ödön Lechner. In 1902 he received his degree in architecture, then in 1915 a doctorate from the Hungarian Imperial József Technical University, Budapest. His thorough grounding in historical styles formed his conservative approach. Like his uncle he wanted to create a style that expressed a Hungarian national identity, and his knowledge of Hungarian artistic traditions is evident in his early buildings, for instance the Teacher Training College (1909–12; with László Varga, 1878–1952), Sárospatak. It is an asymmetric building with a *cour d'honneur* and a dominant water-tower at the entrance; vernacular motifs are used for the carved and *sgraffito* decoration. His designs of the 1920s include the six-storey block of flats (1925) on the corner of Mester Street and Dandár Street, Budapest. This has a simplified façade, with grid-like window divisions and minimal ornament stressing the classicizing entrance piers.

The Votive Church (1928), Rezső Square, Budapest, is modelled on the centrally planned Esztergom Cathedral (1822–69; by József Hild and others). Lechner also designed the Heroes' Mausoleum (1932; with Pál Szontágh), Debrecen, an unornamented building with large, uniform vitrified brick surfaces, and the parish church (1940) at Remeteváros, Budapest. In the latter the closed masses, rectangular plan and flat ceiling indicate the influence of modernism, although a link with historicism is preserved in the three huge ogival arches of the entrance. His knowledge of architectural history was also applied in a series of restorations, including in 1927 the National Museum, Budapest.

### WRITINGS

*Tanulmányok a lengyelországi és felső-magyarországi reneszánsz építészetről* [Studies on Polish and northern Hungarian Renaissance architecture] (Budapest, 1913)
J. Kismarty-Lechner [J. Lechner]: *Lechner Ödön* (Budapest, 1961)
*Ödön Lechner, 1845–1914* (exh. cat., ed. L. Pusztai and A. Hadik; London, Heinz Gal., 1988)

### BIBLIOGRAPHY

*Jenő Lechner* (Geneva, 1930)

ÁKOS MORAVÁNSZKY,
KATALIN MORAVÁNSZKY-GYÖNGY

**Lechter, Melchior** (*b* Münster, 2 Oct 1865; *d* Raron, Switzerland, 8 Oct 1937). German designer and painter. After an apprenticeship in a stained-glass workshop, he studied painting at the Hochschule der Künste in Berlin (1894). An exhibition of his work at Fritz Gurlitt's gallery in Berlin established his reputation. His friendship with the German poet Stefan George led him to design books as works of art in their own right, for example an edition of Maurice Maeterlinck's *Der Schatz der Armen* (Leipzig, 1898) and George's *Teppich des Lebens* (Berlin, 1900). He was influenced in his book designs by the work of William Morris. In 1900 he won the Grand Prix at the Exposition Universelle, Paris, for his design of the Pallenberg Saal (Cologne, Kstgewmus.; mostly destr.), a reception room designed for the industrialist Jakob Pallenberg, in which ornaments and inscriptions filled walls and ceiling; the centrepiece was a painting *Consecration at the Mystic Well* (see Wissmann, p. 36). In 1909 he founded the Einhorn Presse in Berlin and published among others a luxurious *Tagebuch der indischen Reise* (Berlin, 1911) and editions of Thomas à Kempis, *Die vier Bücher von der Nachfolge Christi* (Berlin, 1914–22).

Lechter's stained-glass designs, including those for secular spaces, are characterized by their mystical church atmosphere, for example *Lumen de Lumine* (1907; Münster, Westfäl. Landesmus.); most of his designs were destroyed, as was his flat in Berlin for which he designed all the furniture and fittings. As a painter he was influenced by Pre-Raphaelite idealism: he attempted a spiritual harmony in which figures were ornamental and carried symbolic meanings, for example *Orpheus* (1896; Münster, Westfäl. Landesmus.).

### BIBLIOGRAPHY

F. Wolters: *Melchior Lechter* (Munich, 1911)
M. Hoffmann: *Mein Weg mit Melchior Lechter* (Amsterdam, 1966)
J. Wissmann: *Melchior Lechter* (Berlin, 1966)
W. Raub: *Melchior Lechter als Buchkünstler: Darstellung—Werkverzeichnis—Bibliographie* (Cologne, 1968)
B. Treffers and others: *Melchior Lechter: Der Meister des Buches, 1865–1937* (Amsterdam, 1987)

PETER W. GUENTHER

**Leck, Bart (Anthonij) van der** (*b* Utrecht, 26 Nov 1876; *d* Blaricum, 13 Nov 1958). Dutch painter and designer. He served his apprenticeship in several stained-glass studios in Utrecht (1891–9), after which he received a scholarship to study at the Nationaal school voor Kunstnijverheid, Amsterdam (1900–04). At the same time he attended evening classes at the Rijksakademie van Beeldende Kunsten, Amsterdam, under August Allebé. His earliest work reflected several stylistic sources. His paintings were influenced first by the Symbolists Anton Derkinderen and Jan Toorop and then by the Amsterdam Impressionists George Hendrik Breitner and Isaac Israëls, while his designs for a collector's edition of the *Song of Solomon*, which he produced in 1905 in collaboration with his close friend, the architect and furniture maker Piet Klaarhamer, showed an Egyptian influence. Following a brief and uninfluential visit to Paris in 1907, van der Leck spent the next nine years moving between Amsterdam, Utrecht, Amersfoort, The Hague and the province of Overijssel.

In keeping with other progressive artists of the time in the Netherlands, van der Leck developed an abiding interest in the way of life of the Dutch proletariat in his search for an authentic 20th-century social realism. He turned to the prosaic world of the washerwoman, the fishwife, the stallholder and the labourer as the starting-point for a simple, universally valid and comprehensible style that embraced the principle of 'unity in diversity', a theory augmented by his belief in the manipulation of humanity by forces beyond its control. The theme of textile workers in Overijssel returning home from the factory provided van der Leck with the first indications of a solution to his stylistic goal. The similarities in the appearance and behaviour of the employees prompted him to reduce the incidental details of form and subject-matter and led to his first significant painting, *Leaving the Factory* (1910; Rotterdam, Mus. Boymans–van Beuningen). While in Overijssel he met the teacher Bertha Teerink, whom he married in 1912.

Van der Leck signed his first contract with the art dealer and critic Hendricus Petrus Bremmer in 1912 and had his first one-man show at the Walrecht Gallery, The Hague, in 1913. Soon after, Bremmer introduced van der Leck to the collector Hélène Kröller-Müller, who became his most ardent supporter. Through Bremmer and Kröller-Müller, van der Leck received orders for a number of public and

Bart van der Leck: *Composition No. 4 (1916): The Mine Triptych*, oil on canvas, centre panel 1.10×1.10 m, side panels 1.10×0.55 m, 1916 (The Hague, Gemeentemuseum)

private commissions, including one for a large stained-glass window to decorate the head office of the Müller shipping and mining business in The Hague, *Window with Mine Scenes* (1916; Otterlo, Rijksmus. Kröller-Müller). On many of these commissions van der Leck collaborated with the architect H. P. Berlage, an arrangement neither party particularly welcomed.

Between 1912 and 1915, while striving towards a style that would extend figuration beyond the particular, van der Leck removed the last vestiges of representation from his work. The contours outlining the objects in his paintings were rendered schematically and the delineated areas coloured uniformly in subdued hues. With the introduction of a dominant white ground, the final illusion of naturalistic depth was denied. By 1916 van der Leck had arrived at his wholly idiosyncratic method of eliminating outlines altogether and of exclusively employing primary colours. In two paintings of 1916, *Work at the Docks* and especially *Storm* (both Otterlo, Rijksmus. Kröller-Müller), van der Leck achieved the desired synthesis of form and content.

It is more than likely that van der Leck was working on these two paintings when he first met Piet Mondrian in Laren in either April or May 1916. The impact of this meeting on the work of both artists became readily apparent. Mondrian's paintings showed a more open structure than that of his earlier 'plus and minus' style, and the colour that he reintroduced in his work was flat and emphatic. Under the older artist's influence, van der Leck began to number his paintings, calling them 'compositions', and arrived at an approach to picture-making that matched his demand for extreme objectification. Van der Leck derived an abstracted version of the motif composed of small planimetric stripes or blocks of primary colour set against a white ground by means of a laborious process of intermediate studies, the starting-point for which was often material from his previous realist period.

A fine example of this working method is *Composition No. 4 (1916): The Mine Triptych* (The Hague, Gemeentemus.; see fig.). Van der Leck developed this multi-panelled work from a sketch of 1914, made while he was on a study tour of the Müllers' mines in southern Spain and Algeria, by reducing the motifs of a mine entrance and miners at the coal-face to their most characteristic components. In adapting the format of an altarpiece for secular purposes, van der Leck was perhaps continuing a tradition begun in the late 19th century by the Belgian Realists, and by making formal analogies with ecclesiastical imagery, he invested his models with a degree of dignity that had previously been reserved for the ruling classes.

Van der Leck was briefly involved with DE STIJL. In 1917 he was a co-founder of its magazine, *De Stijl*, and was the first painter associated with the journal to use primary colours consistently in his work. His passionate quest for a contemporary synthesis of painting and architecture fostered the possibility of a new relationship between art and life and established the foundation for an important aspect of the theory of De Stijl. His activities during the first year of De Stijl's existence aimed at bringing about the reintegration of painting and architecture. In his only written contributions to the magazine, 'De plaats van het moderne schilderen in de architectuur' (i/1, 1917, pp. 6–7) and 'Over schilderen en bouwen' (i/4, 1918, pp. 37–8) he explained how a complete coordination of the two arts could be achieved. Van der Leck was allowed little opportunity during his career to put his theories on art and architecture into practice, since few patrons were prepared to employ him. Of the projects on which he was engaged, two have survived. Personal and theoretical disagreements with Theo van Doesburg, Mondrian and Vilmos Huszár, mainly over the role of architects on the magazine and the work of colleagues, precipitated van der Leck's disassociation from the journal after only a few months. He moved to the village of Blaricum, where he lived for the rest of his life. Convinced that painting addressed itself to the 'outward and visible plasticism of nature', van der Leck never fully relinquished his grasp on reality and continued to give abstract expression to motifs taken from the real world, principally birds, animals, flowers and members of the family group. Only in the last two years of his life did he begin to entertain notions of fully abstract painting of colour planes.

BIBLIOGRAPHY

W. C. Feltkamp: *B. A. van der Leck: Leven en werken* (Leiden, 1956)
F. Gribling: 'Het utopistische realisme van Bart van der Leck', *Mus. J.*, xxi/5 (1976), pp. 212–20
R. W. D. Oxenaar: *Bart van der Leck tot 1920: Een Primitief de nieuwe tijd* (diss., U. Utrecht, 1976) [with extensive bibliog.]
*Bart van der Leck, 1876–1958* (exh. cat., ed. P. Hefting and A. van der Woud; Otterlo, Rijksmus. Kröller-Müller; Amsterdam, Stedel. Mus.; 1976)
C. Hilhorst: 'Bart van der Leck', *De beginjaren van De Stijl, 1917–1922*, ed. C. Blotkamp (Utrecht, 1982; Eng. trans., London, 1986), pp. 155–85
P. Bonaventura: *Bart van der Leck: A Reflection of the New Age* (diss., U. London, 1984)

PAUL BONAVENTURA

**Leclerc.** French family of artists. Laurent Leclerc (1590–1695) was a goldsmith from Metz. The most prominent members of the Leclerc family were his son (1) Sébastien Leclerc (i) and Sébastien's son (2) Sébastien Leclerc (ii). Another son of Sébastien Leclerc (i), Louis-Auguste Leclerc (*b* Paris, 30 Nov 1699; *d* Copenhagen, 8 March 1771), was a sculptor and pupil of Antoine Coyzevox; from 1735 he worked in Denmark, becoming professor at the Kongelige Akademi for de Skønne Kunster in Copenhagen. His son and pupil Jacques-Sébastien Leclerc (*b* Paris, *c.* 1734; *d* Paris, 17 May 1785) became a painter, producing small-scale amorous scenes; from 1778 he taught at the Académie Royale de Peinture et de Sculpture in Paris.

**(1) Sébastien Leclerc (i)** (*b* Metz, *bapt* 26 Sept 1637; *d* Paris, 25 Oct 1714). Printmaker, draughtsman and military engineer. He probably learnt the rudiments of drawing and engraving from his father, and also from Claude Bouchard, a copper-plate printer; however, he soon abandoned line engraving for etching. Leclerc's earliest works that can be securely dated are from the years 1654–5. His first important series were the *Life of St Benedict* (1658–9; see Jombert, no. 57) and *Les Modes de Metz* (J 70), later republished in Paris. Having also studied geometry, perspective and mathematics, Leclerc became in 1660 a military engineer, working for Henri, Maréchal de La Ferté-Sénectère (1600–80), governor of Lorraine.

Around 1664–5 Leclerc moved to Paris, where he soon found a master and protector in Charles Le Brun. He entered the royal service and was granted lodgings in the Palais du Louvre. In 1668 he first appeared in the *Comptes des bâtiments du roi* as an engraver of zoological plates for the recently established Académie des Sciences. He was admitted (*reçu*) in 1672 to the Académie Royale de Peinture et de Sculpture, his *morceau de réception* being a plate of the *Funeral of Chancellor Pierre Séguier* (J 105), after a painting by Le Brun. Leclerc was also appointed professor of geometry and perspective. Jean-Baptiste Colbert made him teacher of drawing and mathematics to one of his sons, the Marquis de Blainville, for whom Leclerc engraved in 1679 a suite of 30 prints (J 150); in 1696 he also produced a suite (J 258) for another of his pupils, Louis, Duc de Bourgogne, grandson of Louis XIV. The numerous commissions he received enabled Leclerc to leave the King's service, to work on his own account; however, between 1680 and 1699 he was paid a modest retainer for teaching geometry and perspective at the Académie Royale. Moreover, from the end of 1691 he also taught at the Académie des Gobelins, which Pierre Mignard had recently founded.

In early 1693 Leclerc was appointed Graveur Ordinaire du Roi, filling a vacancy created by the death of Claude Mellan; he held the post until 1705. The following year the Nuncio Gualterio made him papal knight. By the end of his life he was laden with glory and honours; he had,

1. Sébastien Leclerc (i): *Battles of Alexander the Great*, engraving, 1696 (Paris, Bibliothèque Nationale)

2. Sébastien Leclerc (i): *Académie des sciences et des beaux-arts*, engraving, 1st state, 1698 (Paris, Bibliothèque Nationale)

however, rejected the attempts of Nicodemus Tessin the younger to entice him into the service of the Swedish crown.

Leclerc's engraved work is outstanding on two counts: because it extends to over 3100 items, the vast majority of them of his own invention, and because of its quality; the accuracy of his drawing, the intelligence of his compositions and the precision and neatness of his engraving leave him without equal in his own century, while in the succeeding one, only Nicolas Cochin the younger could claim to match him. As well as being abundantly inventive, he was also a most exact interpreter, as is shown by many of his works, such as the set of 150 medals in the Cabinet du Roi (J 176), or the tapestries of the *Great Conquests of Louis XIV* (J 212), after Le Brun. However, his masterpiece in this genre is undoubtedly his rendering in a much reduced format, also after Le Brun, of the *Battles of Alexander the Great* (1696; J 257; see fig. 1). Leclerc worked almost exclusively in small formats, except when circumstances required larger areas, as with the *Battle of Cassel* (c. 1677; J 145) or the astounding *Représentation des machines qui ont servi à élever les grandes pierres qui couvrent le fronton du Louvre* (c. 1677–9). The two major pieces in Leclerc's oeuvre were, however, original works: the *Académie des sciences et des beaux-arts* (1698; J 263; see fig. 2) and the *Entry of Alexander the Great into Babylon* (1704; J 285). The former work represents his testament as a graphic artist, for in it he scattered references to his own works. These two plates, which were copied several times, continued to be printed for a long time.

Because he worked in small formats, Leclerc was in demand as a book illustrator: more than half his output is devoted to this. Whether the work in question was one of religion, history or fiction, or about animal anatomy or geometry, he displayed there the same qualities of precision, elegance, imagination and discretion as in his individual compositions. In addition to his talents as a draughtsman and printmaker, Leclerc had pretensions to being a man of learning, to which he was to some extent entitled through his lasting association with the Académie des Sciences; most notably, he illustrated the *Mémoires pour servir à l'histoire naturelle des animaux* by Claude Perrault, published in 1671 by the Imprimerie Royale, and the same author's *Essais de physique* (1680–88). In his last, unfinished print he represented himself, in an ideal collector's room, filled with models of machines and curiosities (of which he was a collector), giving a physics demonstration to other men of learning. He also wrote a number of books, including *Discours touchant le point de vue* (1679) and a *Traité d'architecture* (1714).

For further illustration *see* PERRAULT, (2).

**(2) Sébastien Leclerc (ii)** (*b* Paris, 29 Sept 1676; *d* Paris, 29 June 1763). Painter, son of (1) Sébastien Leclerc (i). He was a pupil of Bon Boullogne; in 1704 he was admitted (*reçu*) to the Académie Royale de Peinture et de Sculpture with the *Deification of Aeneas* (Tours, Mus. B.-A.). He was appointed Peintre du Roi as well as assistant professor at the Académie des Gobelins in 1717, and professor of history, geometry and perspective in 1721. He is best known for his history paintings, such as the

*Death of Sapphira* (version Paris, Louvre); some of his works, such as the *Prodigal Son*, were engraved. Donat Nonotte painted his portrait (1741; Versailles, Château).

BIBLIOGRAPHY

Mariette; Thieme–Becker
C.-A. Jombert: *Catalogue raisonné de l'oeuvre de Sébastien Leclerc* (Paris, 1774) [I]
E. Meaume: *Sébastien Le Clerc et son oeuvre* (Paris, 1877)
C. Sibertin-Blanc: 'Remarques sur les dessins de Sébastien Le Clerc exposés a Metz', *Bull. Soc. Hist. A. Fr.* (1938), pp. 43–58
M. Préaud: *Inventaire du fonds français: Graveurs du dix-septième siècle*, Paris, Bib. N., Cab. Est. cat., viii and ix (Paris, 1980)
——: 'L'Académie des sciences et des beaux-arts: Le Testament graphique de Sébastien Leclerc', *Racar*, x (1983)

MAXIME PRÉAUD

**Leclerc [Le Clerc], Jean** (*b* Nancy, *c.* 1587; *d* Nancy, 20 Oct 1633). French painter and etcher. He was born into a family in the service of Duke Charles III of Lorraine (*reg* 1559–1608). He perhaps had his earliest training in the then independent duchy. He is said to have spent more than 20 years in Italy but is first recorded there in 1617, in the house in Rome of the Venetian painter Carlo Saraceni. His earliest known etching, a *Death of the Virgin* (see 1982 exh. cat., no. 5) after Saraceni, was published in Rome in 1619. In 1621 he signed the mural *Doge Enrico Dandolo Recruiting for the Crusade* in the Sala del Maggior Consiglio in the Doge's Palace in Venice. This work had been begun, or at least designed, by Saraceni before his death the previous year. As a reward Leclerc was made a knight of the Order of S Marco.

Leclerc had returned to Nancy by April 1622 and received many marks of favour from Duke Henry II (*reg* 1608–24). He was given commissions for easel paintings, including a group of portraits of the ducal family (untraced) sent to Italy in 1629, but he was not asked to undertake any large scale decorations, a genre monopolized at court by Claude Deruet, who had returned to Lorraine from Italy three years before Leclerc. His busy studio did, however, receive numerous commissions from the duke's brother François, Comte de Vaudémont (1572–1632), and also from the Jesuits in Nancy and at Chaumont-en-Bassigny.

The only certain surviving works by Leclerc are the two mentioned above and a large, documented though recently disputed (see 1992 exh. cat., p. 234) *St Francis Xavier Preaching*, painted for the Jesuits of Nancy in 1632 and now in the church of St Nicolas. A multi-figure night scene representing *St Peter Denying Christ* (Florence, Gal. Corsini; a version of the main episode, Stuttgart, Staatsgal.), once attributed to Saraceni, is now generally regarded as a work by Leclerc, as is a large and dramatic canvas of a *Shipwreck* (Piazzola sul Brenta, Villa Simes-Contarini; see 1982 exh. cat., no. 8), also once attributed to Saraceni. A *Nocturnal Concert* (Munich, Alte Pin.), a composition that also exists in the form of an etching (Vienna, Albertina) and in a number of versions or copies, was attributed to Leclerc by Longhi as early as 1935. It shows a party of musicians and singers gathered around a candlelit table in a darkened room. In its striking contrasts of light and shade this work bears witness to the indirect influence of Caravaggio on Leclerc's painting in the 1620s, indicating that it was through Leclerc that this stylistic current, absorbed from Saraceni, was introduced into Lorraine. Much debate turns on the degree to which Georges de La Tour might have been influenced by such nocturnes by Leclerc.

*See also* PENSIONANTE DEL SARACENI.

BIBLIOGRAPHY

R. Longhi: 'I pittori della realtà in Francia ovvero i caraveggeschi francesi del '600', *Italia Lett.* (10 Jan 1935); also in *Paragone*, xxiii/269 (1972), pp. 3–18
F. G. Pariset: 'Jean Le Clerc et l'*Adoration des bergers* du Musée de Langres', *Cah. Haut-Marnais*, xl (1955), pp. 56–60
N. Ivanoff: 'Jean Leclerc et Venise', *Actes du XIXe congrès international d'histoire de l'art: Paris, 1958*, pp. 390–94
F. G. Pariset: 'Note sur Jean Leclerc', *Rev. des A.*, 2 (1958), pp. 67–71
N. Ivanoff: 'Giovanni Le Clerc', *Crit. A.*, ix/53–4 (1962), pp. 62–76
H. Tanaka: 'Georges de La Tour dans ses rapports avec Le Clerc, Callot et Rembrandt', *Inf. Hist. A.*, xv/2 (1970), pp. 55–60
*Valentin et les caravagesques français* (exh. cat. by A. Brejon de Lavergnée and J. P. Cuzin, Rome, Acad. France; Paris, Grand Pal.; 1973–4), pp. 46–50
M. Sylvestre: 'Les Commandes faites en 1633 à Jean Leclerc par les Jésuites et les Carmélites de Chaumont', *La Haute-Marne et l'art: Peintres et sculpteurs du XVIe siècle à nos jours: 1982*, pp. 37–43
J. Thuillier: 'Jean Le Clerc', *Claude Lorrain e i pittori lorenesi in Italia nel XVII secolo* (exh. cat., Rome, Acad. France; Nancy, Mus. B.-A.; 1982), pp. 71–102
P. Choné: 'Jean Le Clerc, Claude Déruet et le Carmel de Chaumont', *Pays Lorrain*, lxv (1984), pp. 195–204
*L'Art en Lorraine au temps de Jacques Callot* (exh. cat. by C. Pétry and J. Thuillies, Nancy, Mus. B.-A., 1992), pp. 218–38, 278–81, 405–8 [incl. biog. by M. Sylvestre]

MICHEL SYLVESTRE

**Leclère, (Achille-)François-René** (*b* Paris, 29 Oct 1785; *d* Paris, 23 Dec 1853). French architect. He studied architecture first with Jean-Nicolas-Louis Durand and then with Charles Percier, under whose tutelage he became an ardent classicist. Leclère won the Prix de Rome in 1808 and spent the next six years in Italy. His studies culminated in his restoration drawings of the Pantheon (one set, London, RIBA), which were acclaimed for their precision. On his return to Paris in 1816 Leclère executed two designs for the rededication of the Madeleine, which was to be transformed from a Napoleonic temple into a church with royal chapel of atonement for the family of Louis XVI. Leclère's designs were grand in conception and reflected his affinity for ancient building types: his first scheme showed an immense Pantheon-like rotunda on a raised platform attached to the east end of a shortened Madeleine.

Though his efforts in official design were noticed, Leclère was not very active as a practising architect. He built a number of houses in the Rue Saint–Lazare (1819–20), Paris, and he also became known as a restorer of provincial châteaux. Of his executed designs, Leclère's tomb monuments for the Père–Lachaise cemetery in Paris most clearly display his archaeological interests; the tomb for the composer Luigi Cherubini (1760–1842) took the form of a Greek grave stele. Ultimately Leclère was known not for his buildings but for the products of his own atelier, which he conducted from 1815 until his death. He was responsible for training some of the architects who were most active in studying France's historic monuments, notably Viollet-le-Duc.

BIBLIOGRAPHY

C. Saunier: 'Deux projets d'Achille Leclère pour l'achèvement de la Madeleine', *Gaz. B.-A.*, n. s. 4, xiii (1917), pp. 349–60

L. Hautecoeur: *Architecture classique* (1943–57), vi, pp. 59, 124, 169–74; vii, pp. 119, 211, 304

R. Middleton and D. Watkin: *Neoclassical and 19th-century Architecture* (New York, 1980)

LISA B. REITZES

**Le Coeur, François** (*b* Paris, 1872; *d* Paris, 1934). French architect. The son of an architect, he was admitted to the Ecole Centrale des Arts et Manufactures, Paris, but left it to concentrate on architecture and was licensed by the government. As early as 1897 he won recognition for the hospital at Tournan, built in a rationalist spirit inherited from his teacher Anatole de Baudot, and for the use of new techniques in reinforced cement and brick, which he applied at an early stage in his career as architect of the postal administration; he held this post for most of his life, working in Paris and in the provinces. In his treatment of his functionalist buildings he broke with tradition. The new framework of the Post Office of La Cité Martignac (1907) in Paris had an unusual freedom in the plan and construction. Subsequently, Le Coeur provided further proof of his originality with, for example, the Bergère Telephone Exchange (1912) and the Temple Telephone Exchange (1920), the façade of which is in concrete. With the more classicist Hôtel des Postes (1920–27) in Reims Le Coeur introduced the concrete dome and harmoniously integrated his building into an old site. He also won fame with other public buildings, such as the Lycée Camille Sée (1934) in Paris, and several private residences, such as the Hôtel Fontaine (1913) and the Hôtel Estaunié (1922; destr.), both in Paris. Le Coeur's architecture is rarely decorated, but his bold structures reflect his understanding of the possibilities offered by concrete.

BIBLIOGRAPHY

R. Lemercier: *François Le Coeur architecte* (Paris, 1938)

R. Jullian: *Histoire de l'architecture moderne en France* (Paris, 1984), pp. 71–92

YAMILA TAHIER

**Le Coffre** [Coiffre], **Benoît** [Bendix] (*b* Copenhagen, 1671; *d* Copenhagen, 1722). Danish painter. He was the son of Claude Le Coffre, a French-born painter and sculptor, and went to France himself, presumably to study art, for in 1692 he won the Prix de Rome for *Abraham Repudiating Hagar and Ishmael*. In Paris he associated with Claude Gillot and Watteau. By 1696 he was back in Copenhagen, painting a portrait of *Princess Sophie Hedvig* (Copenhagen, Rosenborg Slot), the sister of the future Frederick IV, King of Denmark (*reg* 1699–1730). He continued to be a successful portrait painter but is best known for his decoration of ceilings in Frederick's newly renovated Rosenborg Castle, in Frederiksberg Castle (built 1703) and in the Finance Ministry (all in Copenhagen). In 1695 he became court painter. King Frederick's Italian travels had confirmed in him a love for dance, music and masked balls, themes that feature in Le Coffre's acclaimed *Masquerade* (1704), painted on the ceiling of an antechamber in Frederiksberg Palace. The festive scene represents 90 half-length masked and unmasked figures disporting themselves in an oval colonnaded space surmounted by an open balcony. Four portraits of *Frederick IV* by Le Coffre survive, the best known of which is probably the undated over life-size image of Frederick in coronation regalia (ex-Reventlow priv. col.), in which, following the manner of Hyacinthe Rigaud, Le Coffre depicts the slender regent as an absolute monarch, in flowing ermine-trimmed robes against a dramatically lit background of heavy draperies. Very different in style is the *Self-portrait* (*c.* 1720; Hillerød, Frederiksborg Slot), which shows the painter wigless and plainly dressed. Le Coffre's art owes much to Rigaud and to Poussin but nonetheless establishes a personal identity: a love of theatricality and an emphasis on colour and lustrous lighting effects, combined with whimsical touches, enliven his allegorical and mythological paintings.

BIBLIOGRAPHY

C. Elling: 'Bendix le Coffre', *Kstmus. Årsskr.*, xxiii (1936), pp. 1–25

G. Sutton: 'Scandinavian Painting in the Eighteenth Century', *Connoisseur*, cxxxv (1955), pp. 45–9

T. Colding: 'Benoît le Coffre, 1671–1722', *Dansk Kunst Historie Billedkunst og Skulptur: Rigets maend lader sig male 1500–1700* [Danish art history, painting and sculpture: Portraits of a statesman], ed. E. Lassen (Copenhagen, 1973) [excellent pls]

**Le Combel.** *See* PECH MERLE.

**Le Comte, Florent** (*b* ?1655; *d* ?1712). French writer. Little is known about his life; he described himself as a painter and sculptor, but none of his works has survived. He is now remembered only as the author of the *Cabinet des singularitez d'architecture, peinture, sculpture et graveure* (Paris, 1699–1700). This work, which was dedicated to Jules Hardouin Mansart, the Surintendant des Bâtiments du Roi, relies heavily on the publications of André Félibien and Roger de Piles, and on the works of various Classical and foreign authors. It was intended to be a complete history of art, combining history, biographical detail and information on technique. The most original sections of Le Comte's work are his catalogues of the works of the engravers Jean Marot, Robert Nanteuil, Claude Mellan, Antonio Tempesta, Jacques Callot and Stefano della Bella; it was, in fact, the earliest published manual for the print-collector. Also valuable is the information on artistic creativity and art collections in Paris at the end of the 17th century, such as the description of the Mays of Notre-Dame, and the Salon of 1699.

WRITINGS

*Cabinet des singularitez d'architecture, peinture, sculpture et graveure ou introduction à la connoisance des plus beaux arts figurés sur les tableaux, les statues & les estampes* (Paris, 1699–1700, rev. Brussels, 1702)

STÉPHANE LOIRE

**Lecomte, Georges** (*b* Mâcon, 9 July 1867; *d* Paris, 27 Aug 1958). French writer and critic. He studied law first in Dijon and from 1885 in Paris, where he worked first as a lawyer and then as a government official before devoting himself to literature. At the age of 15 he had already produced a journal called *La Salade* and in 1888 he became editor of the periodical *La Cravache*, which soon became an important forum for the Symbolists, with contributors such as Félix Fénéon, Joris-Karl Huysmans and Gustave Kahn. Paul Verlaine's poem *Parallèlement* first appeared in it and much space was devoted to art criticism. By the following year, however, Lecomte and the Symbolists moved to the periodical *La Vogue*. Despite his association with the Symbolist writers and poets, his own preferences in the visual arts were mainly for Impressionist and Neo-Impressionist works. In 1890 his friend Fénéon, who ran the biographical pamphlet series *Hommes d'aujourd'hui*, decided to devote some issues to Neo-Impressionism. Lecomte was asked to produce the first, which was on Camille Pissaro ('Camille Pissaro', *Hommes Aujourd'hui*, viii/366 (1890)); both men shared the same anarchist political beliefs. Lecomte's profile of Pissarro underplayed the role of Georges Seurat in the development of Neo-Impressionism, much to Seurat's dismay.

In 1891 Lecomte wrote and had performed the first of his plays, *La Meute*. The following year his book *L'Art impressioniste* appeared; based on the collection of Paul Durand-Ruel, it was a survey of the work of the major artists in the group. The last section, *L'Art de demain*, shows that Lecomte tended to see Impressionism from a Symbolist viewpoint. He described Impressionist work as representing 'the grandiose affirmation of the effort towards the Beautiful'; the contemporary Symbolist, mystic and decorative painters were less innovative, he thought, than they claimed to be. They were merely continuing, in a systematic and philosophical way, the exploration of 'the Idea' and 'the Dream' begun by the Impressionists. Durand-Ruel also published a periodical entitled *L'Art dans les deux mondes* from November 1890 to July 1891, and Lecomte contributed articles on Stanislas Lépine and Pissarro. He also wrote the preface for the catalogue (*Exposition Camille Pissarro*) of the Pissarro retrospective at the Galerie Durand-Ruel in January 1892. He stated that Pissarro's work reflected all the developments of Impressionism and absorbed that of two generations of artists and schools. Noting that Pissarro had long ceased to rely exclusively on nature, Lecomte saw his work of the 1890s as incorporating the decorative tendencies of contemporary art.

Lecomte's literary efforts were spread over a large number of journals, including the *Revue d'art*, the *Revue indépendante* and the *Revue bleue*. As well as writing art criticism, he also worked with Fénéon and Emile Pouget on anarchist periodicals. Later in life be began to produce a series of monographs in addition to novels and plays. In a monograph on Jean-François Raffaëlli he claimed that he was the artist closest to literary Naturalism, providing in painting what Emile Zola and others achieved in novels. Lecomte was elected to the Académie Française in 1924 and later became its permanent secretary, a post he held until his death.

### WRITINGS

*L'Art impressioniste d'après la collection privée de M. Durand-Ruel* (Paris, 1892)
*A. Delaherche* (Paris, 1922)
*Guillaumin* (Paris, 1926)
*Le Peintre Louis Charlot* (Paris, 1926)
*Raffaëlli* (Paris, 1927)
*La Vie heroïque et glorieuse de Carpeaux* (Paris, 1928)

### BIBLIOGRAPHY

J. L. Harlor: *Georges Lecomte* (Paris, 1935)
J. Rewald: *Post-Impressionism* (New York, 1956)
S. Monneret: *Impressionisme et son époque*, 4 vols (Paris, 1978), i, p. 323
R. E. Shikes and P. Harper: *Pissarro: His Life and Work* (New York, 1980)

□

**Lecomte, Hippolyte** (*b* Puiseaux, nr Fontainebleau, 28 Dec 1781; *d* Paris, 25 July 1857). French painter and lithographer. He was a pupil of Jean-Baptiste Regnault and Pierre-Antoine Mongin (1761–1827). He exhibited regularly at the Salon between 1804 and 1847 and received a first class medal as a genre painter in 1808. His reputation was based above all on his historical landscapes. Apart from a few contemporary subjects, for example the *View of Lake Garda* (exh. Salon 1806; Malmaison, Château N.), which shows the Empress Josephine abandoning her carriage in the face of enemy artillery, his subjects were taken from an idealized view of the Middle Ages. With Alexandre Millin-Duperreux (1764–1843) he formed a connection between historical landscape and the TROUBADOUR STYLE. His works combine landscape and contrived light effects with the trappings of chivalry fashionable under the Consulate and the Empire (e.g. *Joan of Arc Receiving a Sword from the Hands of Charles VII*, exh. Salon 1808; Blois, Mus. Mun.; *Squire Blondel Telling Marguerite of Flanders of King Richard's Exploits*, exh. Salon 1810; Paris, Louvre, on dep. Tokyo, Fr. Embassy). His reputation was enhanced by *Two Crusaders Leaving for the Holy Land* (exh. Salon 1804; untraced), which was bought by Josephine for the gallery at Malmaison. He was one of the first landscape painters to turn to medieval history, but unlike most painters of historical landscape he emphasized the setting and tried to raise landscape to the level of history painting. The tiny brushstrokes, the stiff elongated figures standing out in the icy, almost unreal light and the bright, acid colours, in their naivety and awkwardness, are tinged with poetry, and these early works contributed to the vogue for mythic medieval imagery, which began with the novels of the Comte de Tressan.

In 1819 Lecomte obtained a commission for the Galerie de Diane at the château of Fontainebleau, *Charlemagne Crossing the Alps* (*in situ*), which depicts horses and figures dramatically illuminated in an imaginary landscape. His fantastic vision of the Alps is characterized by the dramatic contrast of the brutal whiteness of the peak with the shadows of the mountain pass. He started work at the Musée Historique de Versailles in 1836, painting town views and 20 battles from the reigns of Louis XIV through to Napoleon, emphasizing their strategic aspects. The compositions of the Louis XIV paintings are inspired by Adam Frans van der Meulen (e.g. *Capture of Le Catelet* and *Capture of Landrecies*; both *in situ*). Most of these battle paintings are repetitive, lacking conviction or individuality, perhaps because of the overwhelming influence of his father-in-law Carle Vernet. There is, however, no definite proof that they ever collaborated on a picture. The town views can be stereotyped, as in the *Capture of Pignerol*, and the figures rather stiff, but they are more broadly painted than the highly coloured staffage of his Troubadour-style pictures. He also executed a number of historical paintings on contemporary themes, for example *Louis XVIII at Suze* (ex-Galerie de Diane, Fontainebleau, Château; Chambéry, Mus. B.-A.) and *English Prisoners Brought before Napoleon at Asthora* (Versailles, Château).

Lecomte also executed many lithographs showing his taste for picturesque detail and historical anecdote and costume, such as *Civilian and Military Costumes of the French Monarchy from 1200 to 1820* (380 lithographs) and

*Theatre Costumes between 1610 and 1820* (104 lithographs), as well as illustrations for the fables of Jean de La Fontaine, possibly in collaboration with Carle and Horace Vernet.

BIBLIOGRAPHY

P. Marmottan: *L'Ecole française de peinture, 1789–1830* (Paris, 1886), pp. 159–63
H. Béraldi: *Les Graveurs du XIXe siècle*, ix (Paris, 1889), pp. 74–5
A. Cox and A. Cox: 'Hippolyte Lecomte and the Rockingham Peasant Figures', *Connoisseur*, cxcv/785 (July 1977), pp. 195–200

MARIE-CLAUDE CHAUDONNERET

**Lecomte du Nouÿ, (Jules-)Jean(-Antoine)** (*b* Paris, 10 June 1842; *d* Paris, 19 Feb 1929). French painter and sculptor. He was born into a noble family of Piedmontese origin. He studied (1861–3) at the Ecole des Beaux-Arts in Paris under Charles Gleyre and Emile Signol. The major influence on his development, however, was Jean-Léon Gérôme, whose pupil he became in 1864. He was deeply affected by the polished realism of Gérôme's *Néo-grec* style. *Death of Jocasta* (1865; Arras, Mus. B.-A.) shows Lecomte du Nouÿ's taste for carefully detailed scenes, the subjects of which were drawn from antique sources. From 1863 he exhibited historical genre, religious paintings and portraits (e.g. *Adolphe Crémieux*, 1878; Paris, Mus. d'Orsay) at the annual Salons, but he did not receive official recognition until 1869, when *Bearers of Bad News* (Tunis, Min. Affaires Cult.) was acquired by the State. In 1872 he first visited Greece, Egypt, and Turkey, and on this and subsequent trips he executed sketches that would serve as the bases for his paintings. He was attracted to themes of eroticism, violence and oriental despotism and throughout his career successfully exhibited paintings of this sort at the Salon, such as the *Guard of the Seraglio: Souvenir of Cairo* (1876; Paris, priv. col., see 1984 exh. cat., no. 86) and the *White Slave* (1888; Nantes, Mus. B.-A.). He was also commissioned to provide paintings for various churches in Paris, including St Nicolas (1879) and the chapel of St Vincent-de-Paul (1879) in La Trinité, and later painted decorative cycles for such churches in Romania as Trei Ierarhi in Iaşi. In 1895 his first sculpture was exhibited at the Salon, and in 1901 he received an honorary mention for the sculpture *Death of Gavroche* (untraced). He also sculpted in Romania, producing such works as the bronze statue of *Prince Barbo Stirvey* in Craiova. His brother André Lecomte du Nouÿ (1844–1914) was an architect.

BIBLIOGRAPHY

G. de Montgailhard: *Lecomte du Nouÿ* (Paris, 1906)
V. Sisman: *Lecomte du Nouÿ* (diss., U. Paris X, 1981)
*The Orientalists: Delacroix to Matisse: European Painters in North Africa and the Near East* (exh. cat., ed. M. Stevens; London, RA, 1984)
*Tradition and Revolution in French Art, 1700–1880; Paintings and Drawings from Lille* (exh. cat., London, N.G., 1993)

JANE MUNRO

**Le Coq, Albert von** (*b* Darmstadt, 8 Sept 1860; *d* Berlin, 21 April 1930). German explorer and writer. After having attended Darmstadt grammar school, he left Germany and underwent commercial training in England and the USA (1881–7). He subsequently turned to medical studies, in which he received an American diploma. After his return to Darmstadt, he entered his father's firm A. LeCoq as partner. In 1900 he gave up business and moved to Berlin, where he started his academic career as an unpaid assistant in the African-Oceanic department of the Museum für Völkerkunde. A study of Arabic, Turkish and Persian followed. In 1902 he moved over to the Indian department and started to revise the Turkish Manichean texts from the finds of the first German expedition to TURFAN in Eastern Central Asia. In 1904 he took over the running of the second expedition to East Turkestan (now Xinjiang Autonomous Region, China), following the illness of ALBERT GRÜNWEDEL, who had led the first expedition and returned to lead the third. In 1913–14 Le Coq led the fourth and final expedition.

Le Coq's efforts were mainly responsible for the deposition of the Turfan finds in the Museum für Indische Kunst in Berlin, since he brought many of them back with him (*see* CENTRAL ASIA, §II, 7). Between 1907 and 1930 he published the scientific results of the expeditions. His best known works are *Manichaica* (3 vols), *Chotscho*, *Die buddhistische Spätantike in Mittelasien* (7 vols), *Bilderatlas* and the popular accounts of his journeys. In 1914 he was made Assistant Director of the Indian department of the Museum für Völkerkunde in Berlin, and in 1923 was named Director.

For fuller accounts of Le Coq's discoveries *see* BEZEKLIK; TUMSHUK; YARKHOTO; and CENTRAL ASIA, §II, 1(viii) and 2.

WRITINGS

'Bericht über Reisen und Arbeiten in Chinesisch-Turkistan', *Z. Ethnol.*, xxxix (1907), pp. 509–24
'A Short Account of the Origin, Journey, and Results of the First Royal Prussian (Second German) Expedition to Turfan in Chinese Turkistan', *J. Royal Asiat. Soc. GB & Ireland* (1909), no. 1, pp. 299–322
'Einige Fundstücke der zweiten Turfan-Expedition aus Idiqut-Schähri, Sängim Aghiz und Bäzäklik bei Murtuq (Oase von Turfan, Chinesisch-Turkistan)', *Amtl. Ber. Kön. Kstsamml.*, xxx (1909), pp. 302–7
*Türkische Manichaica aus Chotscho*, 3 vols (Berlin, 1912–22)
*Chotscho* (Berlin, 1913/*R* Graz, 1979)
'Die 4. deutsche Turfanexpedition', *Túrán Z. Osteuropä. Vorder- & Innerasiat. Stud.*, i (1918), pp. 7–24
*Die buddhistische Spätantike in Mittelasien*, 7 vols (Berlin, 1922–8)
*Bilderatlas zur Kunst- und Kulturgeschichte Mittel-Asiens* (Berlin, 1925)
*Auf Hellas Spuren in Ostturkistan: Berichte und Abenteuer der 2. und 3. Deutschen Turfan-Expedition* (Leipzig, 1926); Eng. trans. by A. Barwell (London, 1928)
*Von Land und Leuten in Ostturkistan: Berichte und Abenteuer der 4. Deutschen Turfanexpedition* (Leipzig, 1928)

BIBLIOGRAPHY

E. Haenisch: 'Zum Tode von F. W. K. Muller und A. von Le Coq', *Litt. Orient.*, xxxiii (1930), pp. 2–4; 'Werke und Abhandlungen von A. von Le Coq', pp. 5–7
O. Strauss: 'Albert von Le Coq', *Orient. Litztg.*, xxxiii/6 (1930), pp. 393–8
E. Waldschmidt: 'Albert von Le Coq', *Ostasiat. Z.*, n. s., vi (1930), pp. 145–9
P. Hopkirk: *Foreign Devils on the Silk Road* (London, 1980/*R* Oxford, 1984)

M. YALDIZ

**Lecoq de Boisbaudran, Horace** (*b* Paris, 24 June 1802; *d* Paris, 7 Aug 1897). French teacher and painter. Admitted to the Ecole des Beaux-Arts in Paris in 1819, he studied with Jacques Peyron and Guillaume Lethière. He made his début at the Salon of 1831 and regularly exhibited his work, mostly portraits and religious scenes, during the next decade. In 1841 he became an assistant professor at the Ecole Royale et Spéciale de Dessin et de Mathématique (a forerunner of the Ecole Nationale Supérieure des Arts Décoratifs, often referred to as the 'Petite Ecole'), where he developed his unique teaching method based on visual memory training. Lecoq first outlined this method in 1848 in a pamphlet entitled *L'Education de la mémoire pittoresque* and expanded on it in a second edition that appeared in 1862. He wrote two further works on the teaching of art, *Coup d'œil sur l'enseignement des beaux-arts* (1872) and *Lettres à un jeune professeur* (1876). In 1866 Lecoq became the director of the Petite Ecole, which he set out to reform according to his principles. Heavily attacked by the conservative faculty of the school, he felt compelled to resign three years later. After 1869 he taught at the Lycée Saint-Louis, the Ecole Spéciale d'Architecture and privately in his home.

Lecoq's teaching method was based on the principle that visual memory should and could be trained through a step-by-step curriculum in which students started by memorizing lines of given lengths, different angles and variously bent curves, and then moved on to memorize more complex models: line engravings, paintings, sculptures and scenes from life. Though initially his method was restricted to drawing, Lecoq later expanded it to include colour memorization, which he taught in the same graduated fashion. An innovative aspect of his teaching was the emphasis he placed on the study of models, clothed and nude, in outdoor settings, which anticipated Impressionist concerns. Lecoq taught many well-known painters, sculptors and craftsmen, including Georges Bellenger (1847–1915), Jean-Charles Cazin, Jules Dalou, Henri Fantin-Latour, Alphonse Legros, Léon Lhermitte, Auguste Rodin and the Régamey brothers—Guillaume (1837–75), Félix (1844–1907) and Frédéric (1849–1925). Others, such as Manet, Degas and Whistler, were indirectly influenced by Lecoq's ideas.

WRITINGS

*L'Education de la mémoire pittoresque* (Paris, 1848, rev. 1862/*R* 1913; Eng. trans., London, 1911)
*Coup d'œil sur l'enseignement des beaux-arts* (Paris, 1872)
*Lettres à un jeune professeur* (Paris, 1876)

BIBLIOGRAPHY

Félix Régamey: *Horace Lecoq de Boisbaudran et ses élèves: Notes et souvenirs* (Paris, 1903)
P. ten-Doesschate Chu: 'Lecoq de Boisbaudran and Memory Drawing: A Teaching Course between Idealism and Naturalism', *The European Realist Tradition*, ed. G. Weisberg (Bloomington, 1982), pp. 242–89

PETRA TEN-DOESSCHATE CHU

**Le Corbusier** [Jeanneret, Charles-Edouard] (*b* La Chaux de Fonds, 6 Oct 1887; *d* Roquebrune-Cap-Martin, Alps-Maritimes, France, 27 Aug 1965). Swiss architect, urban planner, painter, writer, designer and theorist, active mostly in France. In the range of his work and in his ability to enrage the establishment and surprise his followers, he was matched in the field of modern architecture perhaps only by Frank Lloyd Wright. He adopted the pseudonym Le Corbusier for his architectural work *c.* 1920 and for his paintings *c.* 1930. His visionary books, startling white houses and terrifying urban plans set him at the head of the MODERN MOVEMENT in the 1920s, while in the 1930s he became more of a complex and sceptical explorer of cultural and architectural possibilities. After World War II he frequently shifted position, serving as 'Old Master' of the establishment of modern architecture and as unpredictable and charismatic leader for the young. Most of his great ambitions (urban and housing projects) were never

fulfilled. However, the power of his designs to stimulate thought is the hallmark of his career. Before he died, he established the Fondation Le Corbusier in Paris to look after and make available to scholars his library, architectural drawings, sketches and paintings.

I. Life and work. II. Working methods and technique. III. Critical reception and posthumous reputation.

**I. Life and work.**

1. Architecture. 2. Paintings and drawings. 3. Decorative art designs. 4. Theoretical writings and urban plans.

1. ARCHITECTURE.

(i) La Chaux de Fonds, before 1917. (ii) Paris and Purism, 1917–*c.* 1928. (iii) The *Grands Projets, c.* 1928–39. (iv) War years, 1939–45. (v) Mature work, 1945–65.

*(i) La Chaux de Fonds, before 1917.*

*(a) Education and travels, before 1912.* He was the elder son of a watchcase designer and a music teacher. He enrolled at the Ecole d'Art in La Chaux de Fonds in 1902, intending to become a watch-engraver, but he came under the influence of the charismatic teacher Charles L'Eplattenier, who persuaded him to take up architecture instead. Jeanneret joined a group of students enthusiastically committed to the creation of a new regionalist Arts and Crafts style based on local flora, following the principles of John Ruskin, Charles Blanc, Owen Jones and Eugène-Samuel Grasset. When L'Eplattenier set up a new 'Cours spécial et supérieur de composition décorative' in 1905, Jeanneret was among the first to enrol, specializing in architectural decoration. Two years later the group collaborated on the decoration of a house for Louis-Edouard Fallet, a local jeweller and a director of the Ecole d'Art. Although René Chapallaz, a professional architect, submitted the drawings, it was Jeanneret who made the design.

In 1907 Jeanneret set off on the first of a series of travels, to Tuscany and Vienna. His watercolour sketches and letters show him obediently following the Baedeker route, with Ruskin's *Mornings in Florence* and Hippolyte Taine's *Voyage en Italie* accompanying him. In Vienna he spent much of his time designing the Jacquemet and Stotzer houses, both built in La Chaux de Fonds in 1908, the former supervised by Chapallaz. He made contact with Josef Hoffmann and was even offered a job, but in March 1908 he decided instead to go to Paris where he stayed for 18 months, working in the studio of the Perret brothers, Auguste and Gustave, in their revolutionary new concrete block of flats at 25 bis, Rue Franklin, and completing his historical, theoretical and technical education in the museums and in the Bibliothèque Nationale.

Jeanneret returned to La Chaux de Fonds for a few months and became involved in local building projects and the establishment of the Ateliers d'Art Réuni, an association of colleagues at the Ecole d'Art. He left again in 1910, this time for Germany, where he attended a Deutscher Werkbund conference and the Allgemeine Städtebau-Ausstellung in Berlin and worked in Peter Behrens's studio (October 1910–March 1911), shortly after Walter Gropius had left. Thus he came into contact with the leading ideas on architecture and urbanism in Europe. Early in 1911 he was commissioned by the Ecole d'Art to write a report on the organization of German design and teaching methods (published 1912). By May 1911 he had resumed his travels with an art-historian friend, August Klipstein. This became a journey of discovery down the Danube, through the Balkans to Istanbul, Mt Athos and Athens, and back through Italy. It marked the end of his apprenticeship and, as well as giving his drawing style its boldness and insight, provided the break that prepared the ground for a completely new approach to architecture. Fascination with the Arts and Crafts style was replaced by what he saw as the great challenge facing Europe: to combine the productive drive and rationalism of the Germans with the cultural tradition and taste of the French.

*(b) Early work, 1912–17.* On his return to La Chaux de Fonds in 1912, Jeanneret took up an appointment as professor in a newly instigated, but short-lived department of the Ecole d'Art, the Nouvelle Section: opposition closed it in 1914. A commission (1912) to build a new house for his parents at La Chaux de Fonds, however, enabled him to examine the theories of Alexandre Cingria Vaneyre (whose book he had read while in Germany), which associated Jura regionalism with Mediterranean classicism rather than with the Arts and Crafts style. The idea meshed perfectly with Jeanneret's new interest in stripped classicism, inspired by Behrens, Heinrich Tessenow and August Thiersch, and the design of the house for his parents marks a determined move towards an explicit, but sophisticated classicism.

With the outbreak of World War I, Jeanneret began the long series of experiments into low-cost concrete houses that he called 'Dom-Ino' (1914–15), in collaboration with the engineers Max Dubois and Juste Schneider. Housing 'cells' could be combined in terraced rows, courts or setbacks and treated architecturally in different ways. Each cell consisted of a structure supported by eight thin concrete stanchions, set back from the lateral walls but flush with the end walls; smooth floor slabs cast on

moveable and reusable steel shuttering were fixed to the stanchions. An application to patent this system was made in January 1916. The architectural designs (1915) did not seem to take advantage of the point-supports of the structure, which were normally hidden within internal partitions, and it was only gradually that Jeanneret distilled the architectural implications of separating structure from space-enclosing walls. Externally the houses look vaguely oriental, with bay windows similar to those of the wooden houses sketched in Istanbul in 1911. Comparisons have also been made with Tony Garnier's *Cité industrielle* (published in 1917 but prepared earlier): Jeanneret is known to have met Garnier in 1915 and possibly earlier.

In 1916 Jeanneret designed the Scala Cinema (destr.; rebuilt 1971) in La Chaux de Fonds, but it was the Villa Schwob (see fig. 1), also in his home town, that first enabled the young architect to bring together all the lessons of the previous five years. Its history is unclear, partly because Jeanneret left for Paris with the concrete building only half completed, under threat of legal proceedings. The house has a concrete frame and a double-height hall, with a window facing the garden. Facing the street is a huge blank wall, apparently intended for an Arts and Crafts mosaic or fresco, while the garden front is adorned with sculptural reliefs by Léon Perrin. A massively over-emphasized cornice, which doubles as a planter, adds to the sense of sculptural vigour and external brutalism, which accounts for the house's nickname, the 'Maison turque'. It combined the Arts and Crafts, the classical, the oriental and the new. If he had designed nothing else, he would have earned a place among his generation of mould-breaking young architects.

*(ii) Paris and Purism, 1917–c. 1928.* In October 1917 Jeanneret moved permanently to Paris and worked under contract (until January 1919) as consultant architect to Max Dubois's civil engineering firm, SABA, for which he designed industrial buildings and housing projects in concrete. He also invested in and ran a small brick factory in Alfortville (which went bankrupt), but he still relied heavily on his Swiss connections: for example for a Swiss watch manufacturer he built a group of workers' cottages (1917), in traditional materials and with pitched roofs, in the village of St Nicolas d'Aliermont outside Dieppe. In late December 1917 or early 1918 a key event changed his whole direction. He met the painter, critic and fashion expert AMÉDÉE OZENFANT, and within nine months they had put on an exhibition of paintings at the Galerie Thomas and published a booklet, *Après le Cubisme*, establishing the art movement PURISM (*see also* §2 below). Just over a year later, with the poet Paul Dermée, they founded the magazine *L'Esprit nouveau* (1920–25), and during this period Charles-Edouard Jeanneret, Arts and Crafts designer, became Le Corbusier, pioneer of the Modern Movement. (He first began to use the pseudonym Le Corbusier-Saugnier to sign articles on architecture in *L'Esprit nouveau*.) Supported by a number of wealthy Swiss bankers and industrialists, including Daniel Niestle and Raoul La Roche, *L'Esprit nouveau*, unlike other avant-garde magazines, aimed at convincing the new élite that modern art and architecture had a real future.

1. Le Corbusier: Villa Schwob, La Chaux de Fonds, 1916–17 (now altered)

In 1921 Le Corbusier took his younger cousin PIERRE JEANNERET into partnership, and it was Pierre who supervised (from 1923 until the partnership was dissolved in 1940) the day-to-day running of the studio established at 35, Rue de Sèvres, in a corridor off the courtyard of a monastery hidden away near the Bon Marché department store. Meanwhile Le Corbusier was beginning to evolve his language of modern architecture, keeping in touch with developments by Bruno Taut, Walter Gropius and Mies van der Rohe in Germany, and by J. J. P. Oud and Theo van Doesburg in the Netherlands. It is a measure of his reputation that even with so little realized work as yet to his credit, he was considered at the forefront of the Modern Movement in the *Haus am Horn* exhibition (1923) at the Weimar Bauhaus; his projects appeared in the *Bauhausbuch* commemorating it (W. Gropius: *Internationale Architektur*, Munich, 1925).

*(a) Unit housing.* One of Le Corbusier's first projects in his new studio was the development of the 'Dom-Ino' idea into the housing cells 'Maison Citrohan I' (1920) and 'Maison Citrohan II' (1922) for aggregation into large housing blocks. Instead of a constructional kit of parts, however, they were finished designs, which were exhibited as large plaster models, as modern works of art in their own right. Both versions incorporated double-height studio living-rooms, and 'Citrohan II' was elaborated into the 'Immeuble-Villa' cell (1922), designed for aggregation into large housing blocks. Each L-shaped unit was arranged around a double-height garden and was based on what Le Corbusier had seen on his visits (1907 and 1911) to the Certosa del Gallozzo (also known as di Val d'Ema), just outside Florence. Each Carthusian monk had a small dwelling unit on two levels opening off the cloister and also a small walled garden, in which to commune with nature without loss of privacy. Like the monastery, the 'Immeuble-Villa' blocks were to provide communal eating and recreation facilities while affording maximum privacy to individual families. An 'Immeuble-Villa' cell was actually built as the Pavillon de l'Esprit Nouveau at the Exposition des Arts Décoratifs et Industriels Modernes (1925), Paris, where, in a diorama attached to the pavilion, plans for his 'Ville contemporaine' (for 3 million inhabitants) of 1922 and a new plan for Paris, patronized by the Voisin aeroplane and car company, were exhibited on a monumental scale. The pavilion, as subsequently published, made an immense impression on architects throughout Europe, although few saw the actual building.

*(b) Industrial housing.* Le Corbusier made numerous designs for workers' housing, such as those for Troyes and Saint-Gobain (both 1919) and Grand-Couronne (1920). A plaster model of a Maison Ribot (exh. 1923), named after the author of the housing law of 1908, attracted the attention of Henri Frugès, an industrialist from Bordeaux for whom two schemes were completed, a small one at Lège (1924) and another at Pessac (1925–8), near Bordeaux. This last was a complete estate, planned to include 130 houses of which less than half were built. Frugès bought a cement cannon and set up a construction department to supervise the work. The scheme was fiercely opposed by local authorities: costs were much higher than expected, and there were numerous technical failures, but nevertheless the Pessac site was a key proving ground for reinforced-concrete architecture (*see* CONCRETE), and it allowed Le Corbusier and Pierre Jeanneret to develop details for windows, doors and concrete profiles, which became standards for the rest of their work in the 1920s. They also made their first experiment with polychromy. In 1927 Le Corbusier exhibited two houses at the Weissenhofsiedlung (extant), Stuttgart. One was a variant of 'Maison Citrohan II' in concrete; the other was a prototype for a steel-framed housing block.

*(c) Private houses.* Le Corbusier's private domestic clients during the Purist period divide roughly into impoverished artists and more wealthy patrons of the arts, often foreign. For the former group he built houses in Paris for Ozenfant (1923–4), Jacques Lipchitz and his sculptor friend Miestchaninoff (1923–5), the musician Paul Ternisien (1924–6) and the stone-carver Antoine Planeix (1924–7). Their openness to new ideas allowed Le Corbusier to take liberties with practical arrangements, and the results offer some dramatic images, such as Ozenfant's pristine glazed cube of a studio and the playful eccentricities of the house for Ternisien; but they tend to fall outside the main development of Le Corbusier's style, whereas houses for the second, wealthier group of clients contributed to its evolution. The house in Paris (1923–5) for his brother Albert Jeanneret, in which Purist colours were used to great effect, lies somewhere between the two groups: it is a tightly packed variant of the 'Maison Citrohan', with the living-room at the top, lit by a large bay window. It adjoins the Villa La Roche (1923–5), Paris, which was commissioned by the Swiss banker Raoul La Roche, whose brief also called for accommodating the splendid collection of Cubist and Purist paintings that Le Corbusier and Ozenfant had helped him to assemble. The house marks a radical departure in that it was more picturesque and spatially elaborate than its predecessors. Many of the most extraordinary features of the plan (e.g. an 'empty' hallway rising three storeys through the house, and a ramp in the gallery, which is in turn supported above an empty space by an exposed piloti) resulted directly from forced alterations. In the final stages of the design, forms and functions were literally moved around, and all the living functions of the house were placed in a vertical column at one end, in order to allow maximum freedom for a stunning 'promenade architecturale' (as Le Corbusier called it) through a display of Corbusian volumes and spaces. The house has been acclaimed as his first fully developed masterpiece.

Le Corbusier then designed three houses for the Americans William E. Cook, Michael and Sarah Stein, and Henry and Barbara Church, all of whom knew each other through Gertrude Stein. The house for Cook (1926), Boulogne-sur-Seine, Paris, marks the beginning of the codification of Le Corbusier's style. The ribbon windows and pilotis used in the Villa La Roche were now parts of a standard solution. The piloti, which had emerged there by accident, was made the focus of the design, starting from the centre of the ground-floor car parking space and rising up through the house. The notion of the free plan is accentuated with clever use of curving walls and double-height spaces to

2. Le Corbusier: Villa Stein–de Monzie, Garches, Paris, 1926–7 (now altered)

show how independent the form is of the structure. A Purist colour scheme was used internally to brilliant effect, and a roof garden formed the transition from interior to exterior space. The Villa Stein–de Monzie (now altered; see fig. 2), Garches, Paris, was begun for Mme Gabrielle de Monzie, who, together with her daughter, decided to live with the Steins. The design, which took 18 months, had thus to accommodate two families and the Steins' modern art collection. The eventual solution, based on an expanded version of the concept for the 'Immeuble-Villa', has been widely regarded as one of Le Corbusier's most sophisticated and enthralling compositions. An important part of the design intention was to show that truly noble spaces and a rich variety of experiences could be accommodated within a prismatically pure geometric frame. The villa has always appealed to architects for its abstruse conceits aimed primarily at the specialist. The three projects (1927–9; destr.) designed as extensions to the property then owned by the Church family at Ville d'Avray, Paris, were a free-standing guest-room building; a first-floor extension to a pavilion in the garden (library and study); and a proposed extension to the main villa that remained unexecuted. The library is one of the most successful interior designs of the period (see also §3 below). In 1928 Le Corbusier designed a house for the Tunisian industrialist Lucien Baizeau, in Carthage, Tunisia. He experimented with a complex section, allowing a free flow of air throughout the house. The finished design, however, reflected the client's insistence on more conventional floor-plans.

The classic domestic design of this period was the Villa Savoye (1929–31; see VILLA, fig. 10), built on an open grassy site overlooking the village of Poissy, near Versailles. The Olympian abstraction of the first design (October, 1928) is breathtaking: the ground-floor plan was determined by the turning circle of a motor car, and the transport analogy continued in the ramp, which rose through three storeys to the roof. The horizontal white box of the *piano nobile* floated above the ground on its pilotis and was crowned by a second-floor main bedroom suite, which appeared as a series of sculptural, curving screens. This design presented difficulties of size and cost, necessitating the removal of the rooms on the top floor.

The Villa Savoye has the pristine clarity and shocking simplicity to serve as a Modernist icon. It has often been misinterpreted as the ultimate expression of functionalism. In reality it is one of the most highly idealized and aestheticized conceptions of Le Corbusier's career.

*(d) Public housing.* In August 1928 Louis Loucheur was responsible for the legislation that finally made substantial sums of money available to support the Ribot housing law (1908), and this immediately led his friend Le Corbusier in a new direction. A political requirement of the 'Loi Loucheur' was that the buildings should provide employment for local masons in the regions: Le Corbusier's Maisons Loucheurs, therefore, were designed in prefabricated steel components to be attached to rough stone walls (450 mm thick). This extraordinary solution—half craft and half industrialized production—matched a schism that increasingly characterized his life and work.

In 1930 Le Corbusier married Yvonne Gallis, and the privacy of his domestic existence and the daily practice of painting that went with it lent Le Corbusier a strength of character and maturity, traces of which are to be found in his architecture of the 1930s, in the confident mixture of rectilinear and curvilinear plans, the use of mechanical and organic materials and an element of ironic self-parody in his work. Beginning with his vernacular experiments in private houses of *c.* 1928–9, he appeared to lose the single-minded clarity of his Modernist position, relinquishing the totalizing Purist view of the world that had marked the earlier *L'Esprit nouveau* ideology and his collaboration with Ozenfant. A project that exemplifies this development is the Villa de Mandrot (1929–31), Le Pradet, Toulon, for his old friend Hélène de Mandrot, who had hosted the first meeting of CIAM in her château at La Sarraz, Switzerland, the previous year. It follows closely on the move away from Purism to organic forms and figure studies in his paintings, and his political involvement with regional syndicalism and its celebration of tradition and craft skills. The first designs of the Villa de Mandrot combined elements of industrial prefabrication with local building techniques (like the Maisons Loucheurs), but ultimately only the main window walls were prefabricated in Paris, and the rest of the house was built of rustic materials by a local Italian builder. Indeed, to achieve the desired effect of rustic simplicity, Le Corbusier insisted on unrendered walls of local soft stone, which subsequently allowed the rain to penetrate with catastrophic results. In a design for a client in Chile, the Villa Errazuriz (1930), he experimented with timber and rough stone construction. He developed this simple rustic vocabulary in two other examples (both 1935): the Villa Félix ('Petite maison de weekend'), La Celle-Saint-Cloud, Paris, and the Maison aux Mathès, near Marennes. The former is deliberately 'organic', set low in the ground with concrete vaults and grass on the roof, its form much influenced by the undulating shell roof of a Gaudí building in the Sagrada Familia group at Barcelona; the latter is a simple holiday house built of rough stone and timber in a pine forest near the sea.

*(iii) The* Grands Projets, c. 1928–39. This was a period in which, for the first time, Le Corbusier earned enough

from a few large projects to buy time. In the main he used it to develop his urban-planning theories (*see* §4 below), to produce an endless stream of unexecuted urban plans for Paris and other cities worldwide, to participate in a number of *causes célèbres* and to undertake a punishing round of lectures and journalism.

(*a*) *The League of Nations competition.* The origins of Le Corbusier's ambitions as a world figure must be traced back to the competition in 1926–7 for headquarters for the League of Nations in Geneva. His designs were among the nine awarded first prize, out of 377 entries, but deadlock was reached because only Le Corbusier's proposal met the budget, and Le Corbusier and Siegfried Giedion whipped up an international outcry. After lengthy and difficult discussions, a committee of five diplomats gave the commission to the French academic architect Henri-Paul Nénot and his younger Swiss associate Flegenheimer, who were then instructed, with three of the other premiated competitors, to redesign an enlarged scheme on a different site. Le Corbusier immediately insisted that his plan had been expropriated and tried to sue the League for plagiarism. This outrageous ploy, coupled with a letter to the 'world élite', some well-judged exhibitions of the drawings and a book *Une Maison, un palais*, placed Le Corbusier firmly at the head of international Modernism in time to take a leading role in CIAM (founded 1928; *see* CIAM, fig. 11).

(*b*) *Hostels and flats.* For the French Salvation Army in Paris, Le Corbusier had already designed a white concrete

dormitory on stilts as an extension (1924–5) to an existing hostel in the Rue des Cordelières, and in 1928 he had adapted as a dormitory for them a concrete *péniche* (still moored on the Seine near the Pont d'Austerlitz). His third work for them was to design a new hostel on the Rue Cantagrel, originally envisaged as part of an ambitious housing and welfare complex accommodating 300 homeless families. Even as built, the hostel (1929–33), called the Cité de Refuge, constitutes a complete urban fragment, incorporating overnight accommodation for 680 people and a long-stay hostel for unmarried mothers, with a crèche, refectory, clubs and reading rooms. Le Corbusier's innovative but flawed system of environmental control by means of *murs neutralisants* (hermetically sealed, double-glazed walls with a shallow cavity into which hot or cold air could be pumped) was ultimately abandoned, but despite technical inadequacies the Cité de Refuge is a fascinating and rich building, full of fantasy and vision and yet surprisingly practical. The difficult site is exploited to the full with a circulation route through a monumental reception porch into a circular drum, which acts as a 'social condenser'. With its philosophy of strict discipline within an enclosed and protected working environment, the building expresses the bracing morality of William Booth and his French disciple Albin Peyron.

The Pavillon Suisse (see fig. 3), a hostel for 51 Swiss students in the Cité Universitaire, Paris, was Le Corbusier's only official Swiss commission. The main block, four storeys of hostel rooms on massive, sculpturally modelled concrete pilotis, is linked to a smaller single-storey service

3. Le Corbusier: Pavillon Suisse, Cité Universitaire, Paris, 1930–33

block with a sweeping concave wall to the north faced in rubble stonework housing the social functions of the hostel. This forms a marked contrast with the rest of the building, which is framed in steel, rectilinear and faced in concrete or glass. As a whole the building appeals to a cosmopolitan international Modernism and serves as a prototype mass-housing block in miniature.

The Maison Clarté (1931–3), Geneva, a lavish condominium block containing a range of sizes and types of flats, was built for his Swiss friend Edouard Wanner, an engineer with an interest in steel construction, for whom Le Corbusier had made a number of designs between 1928 and 1933. Wanner supervised the construction using state-of-the-art methods of welding and dry-assembly techniques. Glass walls, front and back, are protected from the sun by balconies with roller blinds. The flats have a cool, airy space and grandeur rare in Le Corbusier's executed work. The staircases, with their glass bricks, openwork stairs and exposed steel girders, offer one of the most evocative images of modernity in the tradition of iron and glass.

Le Corbusier's Porte Molitor condominium block (1931–4), overlooking the Parc des Princes, Paris, provided him with a home for the rest of his life, but due to a bank failure brought him close to bankruptcy. He invested in the project and contracted to buy the sixth and seventh floors, which he designed as a penthouse flat and studio for Yvonne and himself. The design comes from a free sketch made in 1929 labelled *Ma maison*, in which he used industrial shell vaults of a kind pioneered by Auguste Perret. The studio has concrete vaults and rubble masonry walls, and the bedroom has a rich, organic play of volumes and spaces.

*(c) Civic projects outside France.* Le Corbusier was already known to committed groups of modern Russian architects through his publications, notably his design for the headquarters for the League of Nations (*see* §(a) above). After a preliminary limited competition, in 1928 he was commissioned to design the headquarters of the Central Union of Consumer Operatives in Moscow, and with a team of devoted Russian colleagues produced the Tsentrosoyuz Building (1928–36), Kirova St (now Myasnitskaya St), Moscow. During construction its function was changed to that of the Ministry of Light Industry, however, and the design was seriously compromised. Though designed as a representational building, with great collective areas celebrating the strength of the Soviet proletariat, most of its planned spatial features were omitted, as was the intended air-conditioning system similar to the one projected for the Cité de Refuge. Nevertheless, despite his often turbulent interventions in Moscow's architectural politics, when the first competition for the Palace of the Soviets was announced in 1931, Le Corbusier was one of those invited to participate (along with Gropius, Erich Mendelsohn, Auguste Perret and Hans Poelzig). Due to changes in the political climate, however, decisions were delayed, and after two further competitions the scheme selected was in the neo-Baroque style of resurgent Stalinist architecture. The model submitted by Le Corbusier for this competition was exhibited at MOMA in New York and remains there.

It was also toward the end of this period that Le Corbusier was recalled to Rio de Janeiro (1936), which he had first visited in 1929, to act as a consultant to LÚCIO COSTA and his team for the design of the Brazilian Ministry of Education and Health (1937–45). In terms of the volume of work executed in Latin America in the following three decades by architects exposed to its design principles, this was perhaps the most influential of all modern buildings.

*(iv) War years, 1939–45.* Although he played a significant role in the anti-Fascist front at the Exposition Internationale des Arts et Techniques dans la Vie Moderne (1937), Paris, during World War II Le Corbusier found himself attracted to the desperate dreams of the Vichy government. It cost him the loyalty of Pierre Jeanneret and the designer Charlotte Perriand, who sided with the Resistance. After a frustrating period working on various urban and housing projects, he returned to occupied Paris in 1943 and founded the research collective ASCORAL (Assemblée des Constructeurs pour une Rénovation Architecturale), through which he aimed to provide the base of knowledge for post-war reconstruction. Over a hundred young planners, architects and engineers were drawn into the organization. Divided into specialist sectors, they studied many aspects of redevelopment from urban planning to aesthetics, from legislative reform to the standardization of building components for industrial production. ASCORAL also took up one of Le Corbusier's enduring preoccupations, the integration of architecture and engineering, and before the end of 1943 at least one of its members was at work on *Le Modulor*, the system of proportion developed by Le Corbusier to be 'universally applicable to architecture and mechanics'.

*(v) Mature work, 1945–65.*

*(a) Urban housing.* Le Corbusier made a number of plans for the rebuilding of devastated cities such as Saint-Dié and La Rochelle–La Pellice; these aroused interest, but no government reaction. He had a particular interest in Marseille, and when his friend Raoul Dautry was appointed Minister of Reconstruction in 1945 he allowed Le Corbusier to design a special block of flats there as a research prototype with a special allocation of funds (for illustration *see* BRUTALISM). This was in part a ploy to keep Le Corbusier away from the main reconstruction projects.

ATBAT was set up two years later under the leadership of Vladimir Bodiansky to prepare the engineering drawings for the Unité d'Habitation (1945–52), and when construction began André Wogensky (*b* 1916) was Le Corbusier's representative on site. The block, also called the Cité Radieuse, represents the coming together of two separate strands in Le Corbusier's work: the continuous research into the design of dwellings, which was related to his aspirations to produce unit housing on an urban scale, and the development of his urbanism. Here he envisaged a 'vertical garden city' based on the notion of self-supporting communities, like villages with their own services and schools. Like the 'Immeuble-Villa' projects, the Unité d'Habitation is based on autonomous two-storey 'houses', stacked together and linked by an internal street. Great care was taken to provide excellent sound insulation, and

4. Le Corbusier: Unité d'Habitation, Firminy-Vert, 1959–67

5. Le Corbusier: interior of house A, Maisons Jaoul, Neuilly-sur-Seine, 1951–5

the materials used (rough, textured concrete on the outside, varnished plywood and mahogany inside) were enlivened by colour. The project was opposed at both local and national level, and the finished block (referred to during construction as 'La Maison du Fada' or 'House of the loony') was not well received by the public, but the building has weathered relatively well and remained popular with its residents.

The Unité was meant to provide a prototype for other urban housing projects, and indeed versions of it were built at Rezé-lès-Nantes (1952–5), Charlottenburg in Berlin (1956–8) and Briey-en-Forêt (1957–9), but all were changed from Le Corbusier's ideal for reasons of cost or political compromise. The Unité at Firminy-Vert (see fig. 4) was built to the strict cost yardstick of HLM regulations and was one of several of his buildings in this coal-mining town near Lyon. He was commissioned by Eugène Claudius-Petit, who became mayor of Firminy in 1953, to design a central 'agora' including a sports stadium, cultural centre and church, as well as the Unité. The cultural centre (1963–6) was intended as part of the stadium (unexecuted) and preserves the characteristically steeply outward-sloping roof; the church remains a half-built ruin, and after the election of a Communist town council in 1971 even the highly successful Unité was threatened with closure.

(b) *Private houses.* Between 1951 and 1955 Le Corbusier designed two houses in Rue de Longchamp, Neuilly-sur-Seine, for the Jaoul family, one for his friend André Jaoul, a director of the Société d'Electro'Chimie (for whom he had already designed a house in 1937), and one for his son Michel (see fig. 5). Both have rough concrete vaults, as used in the Villa Félix in 1935 and later in a number of unrealized projects (including the 'self-build' Murondins housing, 1940; a house at Cherchel, Algeria; and the Roq and Rob housing, 1948, Cap-Martin, Alpes-Maritimes). Thus the Jaoul houses continued the recurrent allusion to the vernacular in Le Corbusier's rural buildings. The interiors are among his most successful, combining strength of lighting with warmth of colour and texture. The basic standards of construction (executed by cheap

Algerian labour), using roughly pointed bricks and rough shuttered concrete, made them deeply puzzling for the new generation of modern architects. Once the two houses were published, however, a whole movement in Britain, New Brutalism (*see* BRUTALISM), was based on their forms.

(c) *Ecclesiastical buildings.* Le Corbusier first became involved with church politics on behalf of his eccentric friend Edouard Trouin, whose plan to build an enormous underground church, dedicated to the Magdalene, at La Sainte-Baume mixed religious fervour and pagan animism (1946–8). It was, however, Père Couturier, the Franciscan editor of *L'Art sacré*, who proposed Le Corbusier as the architect to rebuild the pilgrimage chapel of Notre-Dame-du-Haut (see fig. 6) at Ronchamp, on the magnificent hilltop site near Besançon, overlooking one of the crossroads of history where French Catholicism confronted Swiss Calvinism. The design process, which extended over three years, drew in an astonishing range of sources from Istrian huts to the serapeum of Hadrian's Villa at Tivoli, from aeroplane wing sections to a crab's shell. The apparently free-form roof is a sophisticated piece of structural engineering, based on the design of concrete dams, and it serves also as a rainwater collector; the apparently informal interior has excellent acoustic properties, and the requirements for open-air celebration of mass have been carefully studied.

The design of the Dominican monastery of Ste Marie de La Tourette (1953–9), Eveux-sur-l'Arbresle, allowed Le Corbusier to return full circle to the principle of collective living, which had first inspired him at Ema in Italy in 1907. Partly a study in cheap housing (parallel to the Unités), it is also an investigation of the ideal of an enclosed, intellectual community. The steeply sloping site is used to dramatic effect, and Le Corbusier's interest in the power of light to generate emotion was given full rein in such features as the 'light cannons', which illuminate the crypt chapels. Completed in a régime of necessarily harsh economy, La Tourette demonstrates well the poignant contrast between the discipline of cheap materials and the grandeur of Le Corbusier's conception. The project architect, Iannis Xenakis (*b* 1922), put many of his own interests into the design, notably the subtle play of intervals in the concrete slat *ondulatoires*.

(d) *Civic projects outside France.* A master-plan for Chandigarh, the new capital of the Indian Punjab (*see* CHANDIGARH, §1), was commissioned from an American planner, Albert Mayer, soon after partition of the subcontinent in 1947. Working to Mayer's plan, Matthew Nowicki, who had worked with Le Corbusier at the Rue de Sèvres studio, was preparing preliminary designs for the city centre when he was killed in an air crash in 1950. P. L. Varma, the state engineer, and P. N. Thapar, an administrator with whom they had collaborated, immediately travelled to Europe and recruited E. Maxwell Fry and Jane Drew, who proposed that Le Corbusier should be appointed as consultant. He was joined by Pierre Jeanneret, who spent virtually the rest of his working life in Chandigarh, providing with Fry and Drew the continuity essential to its efficient execution. Le Corbusier rationalized the Mayer plan using the set scale of dimensions he called the 'Modulor' (*see* §4 below), but his main contribution was the design of the buildings that formed the Capitol: the

6. Le Corbusier: Notre-Dame-du-Haut, Ronchamp, 1950–55

7. Le Corbusier: Palace of Assembly, Chandigarh, 1964

High Court of Justice (1956), the Secretariat (1958), the Palace of Assembly (1964; see fig. 7) and the Governor's Palace (1952–4; unexecuted), which he grouped in a composition of monumental scale, symbolizing confidence in progress and the creation of harmony out of the turmoil of religious conflict and the partition riots. The buildings are in board-marked concrete; the High Court has a soaring parasol and interlacing ramps; the Secretariat's *brise-soleil* elevational treatment sets the pattern for the rest of the city's office buildings; and the Palace of Assembly features the huge truncated cone previously used for the church at Firminy, but here symbolizing the collective space used for democratic government. With these buildings Le Corbusier was concerned, as at Ronchamp and La Tourette, to find a semi-abstract decorative language resonant with a feeling for the sacred, without being limited to a specific iconography. Here also he designed a monumental version of his personal trademark, the *Open Hand* (not realized until 1990), a symbol that was originally derived from the opening pages of Nietzsche's *Also sprach Zarathustra*. The huge hand revolves on a stand in the wind, incorporating the form of a bird in flight and representing the sacrifice of the creator.

Le Corbusier's buildings in Ahmadabad, India, designed and built concurrently with Chandigarh, include the Millowners' Association Headquarters (1951–4) with its *brise-soleil* solution to the east and west façades, a cultural centre and museum (1951–8) and two houses (1951–6), which echo the Jaoul houses and the early projects (1928) for the Villa Baizeau in Tunisia. The concrete parasol of the latter was also the prototype for that used on the High Court in Chandigarh. Between 1954 and 1957 the buildings

at Ahmadabad were supervised by Balkrishna V. Doshi, who had gone to Paris in 1951 to work for Le Corbusier.

On the other side of the world, the Carpenter Center for the Visual Arts (1959–62), Harvard University, Cambridge, MA, was Le Corbusier's only North American commission. One of his erstwhile assistants in the Rue de Sèvres studio, Josep Lluís Sert, the new Dean of the Graduate School of Architecture at Harvard, called him in when a benefactor, St Vrain Carpenter, offered to fund a centre for the visual arts dedicated to learning by doing, in contrast (but adjacent) to the highly traditional Fogg Museum and Fine Arts Department. Le Corbusier declared as one of his reasons for accepting the commission that he wished to put on show in the USA the repertory of his 'inventions'. In fact, the building can be read as an inventory of his mature vocabulary: the *brise-soleil*, the *ondulatoires*, the *aérateurs*, as well as the older features such as the exposed piloti, the roof garden and the pedestrian ramp. An astonishing aspect, however, is that the building retains a freshness and dynamism that, on a confined site and in the presence of dignified red-brick campus classicism, takes the breath away. This was a case in which Le Corbusier's original sketch of 1 April 1960 survived all pragmatic alterations during the design and construction processes.

By contrast with the Carpenter Center, Le Corbusier's scheme for a new hospital in Venice shows his ability in later years to adopt completely fresh solutions. He responded to the delicate task with a hospital (1963–5) that is not a building in the conventional sense, but an extension of the cellular structure of the city, suspended over the water but kept low. The Venetian principle of the *campo* was used to organize a network of functions, with patients delivered and collected by water. Much of the design work was carried out by Guillermo Jullian de La Fuente, and the result is a model that has proved highly influential for architects such as Mario Botta, who worked on the hospital.

2. PAINTINGS AND DRAWINGS. Le Corbusier painted throughout his life, usually in the morning. He claimed towards the end of his life that this work, private and largely unrecognized, provided his architecture with its main moral and formal support. His early paintings and watercolours, made at La Chaux de Fonds, were influenced by Symbolism and Animism, but when he came under Ozenfant's influence, his approach to natural form changed dramatically. A major criticism of Cubism in *Après le Cubisme* and in the articles in *L'Esprit nouveau*, most of which were later grouped together in *La Peinture moderne* (1925), was that it lacked a serious attitude to iconography and was far too decorative. For the Purists, the task was to rediscover the laws of geometric order in nature, using 'rules' such as the golden section and reference to the so-called Phileban solids. They were aided in this by selecting as their subjects artefacts that themselves had these properties, typically the results of industrial production. An elaborate procedure for drawing and redrawing the appropriate glasses, carafes, plates and pipes was designed to discover the formal relationships. Paintings such as *Vertical Guitar* (second version, 1920; Paris, Fond. Le Corbusier) or *Still-life with a Pile of Plates* (versions, 1920; Basle, Kstmus., and New York, MOMA) show this approach very clearly. Colour was used according to strict rules: solid, sombre earth colours to express volume and more dynamic hues for emphasis.

As Le Corbusier became more confident and began to break away from Ozenfant's tutelage, his vocabulary became less restricted. A lighter tonality accompanied a more fluent juxtaposition of forms in such paintings as *Still-life: Léonce Rosenberg* (1922; for illustration *see* PURISM). In some of the later paintings, for example *Still-life with Numerous Objects* (Paris, Fond. Le Corbusier), the original references have been almost entirely occluded; there is an analogy here with his architecture, where forms that originally had specific meanings became 'transferred' during the design process to take on purely formal attributes.

Around 1927–8 Le Corbusier's paintings started to turn away from Purist iconography. He became increasingly interested in the female nude and the organic forms of bones, rocks and seaside objects, which he drew on his holidays at Le Piquey near Arcachon. The influence of Surrealism, both in theory and practice, can be discerned in paintings such as *Léa* (1931), where highly eroticized forms of mussel, bone and violin are used to represent the female figure. Le Corbusier's fascination with the exotic and the vernacular, always evident in travel sketches from 1911 onwards, now took centre-stage in his paintings. A long-running project to turn sketches and postcards of Algerian prostitutes into a new version of Delacroix's *Women of Algiers* preoccupied him throughout the 1930s, ending up as a *sgraffito* mural in the villa of his friend Eileen Gray at Roquebrune.

Throughout the post-war period Le Corbusier developed an iconographic language, which reinvested his work with a suitably momentous range of references. The high point of this attempt to create a set of universal modernist myths was the *Poem of the Right Angle*. Many of his later paintings, which tended to run in series with titles such as *Ozon*, *Ubu* and finally *The Bulls*, vary enormously in quality. An element of therapeutic labour, especially after his wife's death in 1957, characterized much of the later work. A lonely and occasionally bitter figure, Le Corbusier spent much of the year alone in a wooden hut, which he designed and built adjoining a fish restaurant near Cap-Martin. In an off-the-shelf garden hut a few yards away, he worked on the designs for the creative and liberated projects of his last years. When he died of a heart attack while taking his morning swim, he was living out a role created for himself as isolated hermit and marginalized hero.

3. DECORATIVE ART DESIGNS. Le Corbusier's training in the Arts and Crafts style predisposed him to consider every detail of the interior as part of the architect's province. In his period at La Chaux de Fonds, and in his first years in Paris, he earned valuable money as a decorator, often purchasing items for Swiss clients in shops in Paris. He also designed furniture, in a Biedermeier style, for houses and offices in La Chaux de Fonds. In the 1920s, however, he came under the influence of Adolf Loos, whose caustic attacks on the ludicrous pretensions of Arts and Crafts architects greatly impressed him. Not until 1928 did Le Corbusier design any significant pieces of furniture, preferring to follow Loos's advice and use established items of existing design. Most of his houses were thus furnished with Maples leather armchairs, the adjustable 'Morris' armchair and cheap Thonet bentwood chairs, with simple tribal rugs and white cotton curtains. Such items as metal tables or beds were constructed for him by whichever carpenter or worker was on site. Everything else was to be integrated into the 'architecture' as 'equipment': shelves, cupboards, lighting fixtures.

In 1928, however, as the villas for Le Corbusier's more wealthy clients neared completion, he decided that it was time to design his own 'modern furniture'. The stimulus for this came from the *Weissenhofsiedlungausstellung* (1927) in Stuttgart, where Mart Stam, Marcel Breuer and Mies van der Rohe showed tubular-steel furniture designs. These were conceived as 'standard' solutions, to be mass-produced, although the reality was that they remained expensive items of 'art furniture'. Le Corbusier took on the young avant-garde designer, CHARLOTTE PERRIAND, who had exhibited her own tubular-steel furniture in 1927. The three pieces of tubular-steel furniture that Le Corbusier, Pierre Jeanneret and Perriand designed were first put on show in the redesigned gallery of the Villa La Roche (1923–5), Paris, and in the library and study of the Villa Church (1928–9), Ville d'Avary, Paris. They were designed on quite different principles to the German and Dutch models. Each satisfied a distinct mode of sitting: active and purposeful (the 'chaise à dos basculant'), comfortable ('grand comfort') and total relaxation ('chaise longue'). The first was an adaptation of the office chair (inspired by the colonial officer's chair with leather straps known as a 'Safari' chair), the second was a tubular-steel version of the Maples club armchair, and the last was based on a patent pivoting chair known as the 'Surrepos', which Le Corbusier had seen in a magazine. After 1928 Le Corbusier's interventions in furniture design were spasmodic. Perriand played an important role in the fitting out of the Unité d'Habitation, introducing the warm textures and rich, sculptural details of the wooden fixtures.

Some of Le Corbusier's most interesting non-architectural designs were undertaken collaboratively in the 1950s. The sculptures he had made by the Italian cabinetmaker Jo Savina from 1944 were the products of a genuine partnership, the initiative coming alternately from both men. Le Corbusier worked with Pierre Baudoin on several tapestries during the 1950s, using papier collé sketches to work up designs, which were usually based on elements from his paintings. The enormous tapestries designed for the High Courts in Chandigarh were the most explicit attempt to use the vivid colours and warmth of tapestries on an architectural scale. A similar motivation lay behind the enamels with which he experimented. The enamelled doors for Notre-Dame-du-Haut, Ronchamp, and for the Palace of Assembly at Chandigarh play key roles in giving scale and meaning to these later works.

4. THEORETICAL WRITINGS AND URBAN PLANS. Le Corbusier was a prolific writer, who saw publishing as a tool for informing and moulding public opinion. From 1911 he produced a steady stream of articles and more than 50 books. Most of the first books, including *Vers une architecture* (1923), *Urbanisme* (1925), *L'Art décoratif d'aujourd'hui* (1925) and *L'Almanach de l'architecture moderne* (1925), began as collections of articles written for *L'Esprit nouveau*. The early books have in common an incisive style and creative use of images that owe much to their journalistic origins. Part of the power of *Vers une architecture*, for example, depends on its terse slogans, but the very effectiveness of its rhetoric has allowed unsympathetic critics to take its memorable phrases out of context. It is difficult to understand why it was ever seen as incorporating the doctrines of functionalism. The book is largely about the need to discover new principles of form, to rediscover the logic that is to be found in all great architecture of the past. The illustrations are selected as much for their formal qualities as for their mechanistic associations. If slogans such as 'A house is a machine for living in' can co-exist with 'Architecture is the masterly, correct and magnificent play of masses brought together in light', it is because Le Corbusier believed passionately in the power of architecture to resolve and transcend functional problems and achieve the status of great art. His historicism never overlaid his faith (and it verged on the religious) in the supra-historical status of great works of architecture such as the Greek Parthenon. Even more lively in its written form is the much-neglected book *Précisions sur un état présent de l'architecture et de l'urbanisme* (1930), a transcription of lectures given in Argentina in winter 1929, which gives precious insights into Le Corbusier's approach to design.

After World War II Le Corbusier's writings became more personal. Key projects were often written up by assistants (e.g. the Unité d'Habitation by André Wogensky). The most ambitious post-war books were *Le Modulor* (1950) and its sequel *Le Modulor 2, 1955*. They resulted from a research project begun at ASCORAL in 1943 and aimed at discovering some universal laws of harmonic proportion. The Modulor turned into a set scale of dimensions (in fact, two, a red and a blue scale), using the Fibonacci series (a whole number proportional series approximating to the golden section), intended to ensure that all dimensions in a project related to human proportions (*see* ARCHITECTURAL PROPORTION, fig. 8). Towards the end of his life, Le Corbusier also published several little books of brightly coloured sketches intended for students and schoolchildren.

Le Corbusier's worldwide influence stemmed as much from his publication and exhibition of urban-planning theories and projects as from his architecture and architectural theory. This urban theory developed in four main phases. The first grew from early interest in the Picturesque and was expressed in a manuscript treatise *La Construction des villes* (1910; unfinished) based on the garden-city movement and Camillo Sitte's work, which sought to avoid monotony and sterile geometric plans by advocating picturesque curving streets. In 1918 this gave way to a second, more radical and relentless theory of modern urbanism. Though developed from the manuscript of 1910, *Urbanisme* (1925) turns all the earlier tenets on their heads. Now only a superior intellectual order, rigid classification on a rectilinear grid, could solve the historic problems of urbanization. The 'Ville contemporaine' (1922) envisages a city centre peopled by tall office blocks (not residential as often claimed), outside of which the workers lived in garden suburbs. The application of these solutions to Paris in the 'Plan voisin' (see fig. 8), which would have involved the destruction of most of the Right Bank, achieved the intended effect of outraging even the most sympathetic planners. The extreme oversimplification of these two urban plans became a millstone from which Le Corbusier never escaped.

Le Corbusier's urban-planning theories were, however, modified over the years to accommodate his changing political allegiances. He tended to be attracted to maverick political opportunists, dissatisfied with the conventional left–right polarities. Many of his friends were involved with the Action Française, including Philippe Lamour, who became the leading figure in the magazine *Plans* (1930–31), to which Le Corbusier contributed the articles that were later republished as *La Ville radieuse* (1935), and Hubert Lagardelle, an exponent of regional syndicalism who became Vichy Secretary of State for Labour and encouraged Le Corbusier to join him. It was in this context that Le Corbusier developed the third phase of his urban theories of the 1930s: the 'ferme radieuse' (1933; a semi-industrialized agricultural collective) and the 'ville radieuse' (1930–33), which involved sweeping changes to property and planning legislation. In *La Ville radieuse* he stressed the need for responsiveness to topography, and, though making a case for high-density urbanization, the work advocates organic growth and cultural complexity rather than closed and abstracted diagrams.

Some of this re-thinking is already evident in the urban plans for Latin American cities, Rio de Janeiro, São Paulo and Buenos Aires among others, which date from 1929. At about the same time, he engaged in a major debate with urban planners in Moscow who favoured the linear

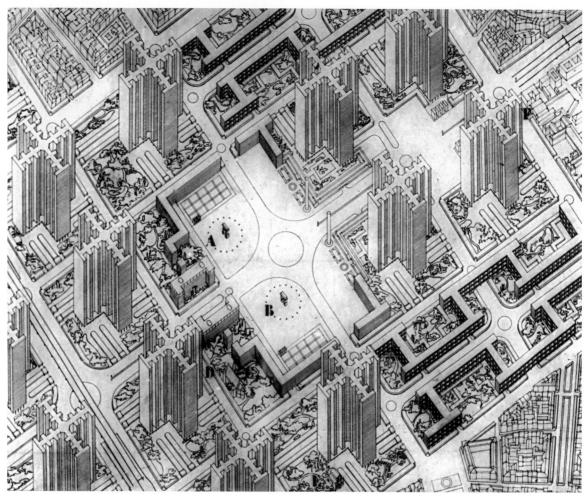

8. Le Corbusier: 'Plan voisin', urban plan for Paris, 1925; axonometric bird's-eye view

city, publishing in 1930 his 'Reply to Moscow', which formed the basis of the 'Ville radieuse' exhibited at CIAM III in Brussels. The Algiers projects (1931–42) also belong to this third phase: his first proposal, the 'Plan obus' (1932), features a spectacular building incorporating a road on its roof, which curves around the cliff-top contours like a whiplash. It was designed to relieve housing pressure along the coastal strip. The administrative centre of the western city was concentrated in one great building, variously placed in succeeding schemes, with the kasba left intact. A number of variants were proposed over the decade, but even his 'Plan directeur' (stripped of most of the original 'Plan obus' ideas), prepared under the Vichy administration in 1942, was rejected.

The final phase began during World War II when Le Corbusier rethought his whole approach to urbanism. He published *La Maison des hommes* (1942) and his version of the *Charte d'Athènes* (1943). In 1943 he also set out to re-establish himself in Paris, founding ASCORAL, which gave him the anonymity he needed to prepare for post-war reconstruction and a fresh theoretical start. Material produced by ASCORAL appeared in *Les Trois Etablissements humains* (1945) and *Manière de penser l'urbanisme*

(1946). Here it was proposed that 'fermes radieuses' (or 'usines vertes') would be linked to linear cities of 50–100 km in extent, which in turn connected the historic radial cities, which would be restricted in growth (to combat the flight from the countryside). In practice, however, Le Corbusier resigned himself to the realization that his urban interventions were likely to remain at the scale of the Unité d'Habitation rather than whole cities. It was left to others to carry out his ideas. Not until the Venice hospital proposals at the end of his working life was there a suggestion of a move towards a new and more culturally complex kind of urban intervention, but this phase was not fully developed.

## II. Working methods and technique.

1. COLLABORATION. Le Corbusier's career would have developed very differently without his collaboration with Pierre Jeanneret. It was Pierre who made the contact with August Perret in Paris in 1917, and it was Pierre who dealt with clients and administered the office at 35, Rue de Sèvres. Their collaboration was not simply one of *maître* and practical executant. Jeanneret's drawings often show

him originating ideas, which Le Corbusier would accept or modify, and if Jeanneret's independent work lacks his cousin's bold and sculptural imagination, the collaboration, which proceeded in erratic dialectical cycles, at its best was marked by a subtle blend of compliance and opposition never achieved with other later collaborators. While the partnership with Pierre lasted, other studio assistants played a decidedly subordinate role in the design process. During the late 1920s only Albert Frey and Ernst Weissmann were regularly paid, while others, such as Charlotte Perriand, were encouraged to keep their own practices going. Many architects with distinctive drawing styles and definite contributions to make passed through the studio, including Josep Lluís Sert and Kunio Maekawa.

After the war with the pressure of organizing major projects, the atelier experienced considerable stress. André Wogensky ran the studio until 1956, when he resigned. Thereafter Le Corbusier relied on loyal assistants such as Roggio Andreini, who looked after the day-to-day running of the office, and Fernand Gardien, who was his most frequent site architect in the 1950s. Le Corbusier's political estrangement from Pierre Jeanneret ended in 1950 when he invited him to renew their collaboration at Chandigarh. In 1956 the technical draughtsmen under Gardien were moved out of the Rue de Sèvres studio into the offices of Georges Presenté, a consultant engineer frequently used by Le Corbusier. Iannis Xenakis and Vladimir Bodiansky were both trained engineers who worked on the detailed drawings for the Unité d'Habitation at Marseille through ATBAT. Xenakis also played an important part in the extraordinary Philips Pavilion at the Exposition Universelle et Internationale in Brussels (1958) and supervised Ste Marie de La Tourette after Wogensky's departure; he was one of three designers who resigned in 1959 over demands to be allowed to sign their own drawings. Thereafter Guillermo Jullian de La Fuente was Le Corbusier's closest associate.

2. THE DESIGN PROCESS. Le Corbusier clearly set great store on the 'patient research' of architectural design: he preserved every scrap of drawing paper and made sure that his legacy would be preserved in the Fondation Le Corbusier. He carried a small sketchbook with him wherever he went, making sketches of details he observed and drafts of lectures. Most of these have been published. He often remarked that many of his best designs were never executed and called on others to vindicate him through research. Yet he seems to have agreed with Adolf Loos that the enemy of architectural invention is the drawing. He described his own creative process as a kind of mental fermentation, from which, in due course, a design would emerge fully formed, before a drawing had been made. Although many of his projects emerge on paper more or less fully defined, when the first idea did not work—due to the client's change of mind or pragmatic factors (cost, legal restrictions, structural difficulties)—Le Corbusier and Pierre Jeanneret would invariably cover many sheets of paper with revisions, often striking out in dramatically different directions. A fundamental tension within all of Le Corbusier's creative work is between the search for universal solutions ('standards') and the restless introduction of variety and invention. Designs often began in the universal mode but, as the work proceeded, developed more and more sophisticated complexities to fit particular circumstances.

Le Corbusier made thousands of rough sketches, but the real design work was carried out in plan, usually beginning with the ground-floor. Once the basic forms were established, overlays would be used to make modifications, tracing the outlines of the plan free-hand on to a roll of tracing paper, mounted to the side of each drawing-table. Le Corbusier often intervened on the drawings of his colleagues, with marginal sketches, written comments and, very commonly, three-dimensional projections or shadings to imagine the spatial dimension. As a project neared the point of being shown to the client, the assistants would produce an inked set of plans, elevations, sections and details, which were given stencilled numbers. These numbers were entered into a 'black book', still preserved, with the date and client's name and usually with the name of the draughtsman. One domestic account book preserves the full series, from 501 (Pessac, 29 February 1925) onwards. Other drawings were carried out in ink, for publication in the *Oeuvre complète*, while clients were presented with perspective views or beautifully coloured axonometrics in chalk (produced from *c.* 1927–8). Pierre Jeanneret specialized in a type of coloured spatter-rendering using a toothbrush. In 1920, 1922 and 1923 Le Corbusier had large white plaster models of his designs made for exhibition in the Salon d'Automne. He also made large models of the Palace of Soviets competition and his urban schemes ('Plan voisin' and the 'Ville radieuse'), which he also filmed.

After the war Le Corbusier's assistants made lightweight and insubstantial models of designs at particular points in the design process, only some of which have been preserved. These models sometimes played an active role in resolving formal or practical difficulties. During this period Le Corbusier also developed a symbolic use of colours, which he used systematically to represent circulation (yellow), outdoor space (green), indoor spaces (blue), vertical circulation (violet), as well as specific materials. He often drew his ideas out in rough chalk pencils on small pages of his sketchbooks, leaving it to his assistants to work up the measured drawings. Occasionally he would sign and date the measured drawings that best represented his intentions. All the members of the post-war studio were expected to use and understand the 'Modulor' system of proportions and measurements. Le Corbusier disapproved of other architectural scales, which occasionally led to difficulties with engineers and other specialists used as consultants.

### III. Critical reception and posthumous reputation.

Le Corbusier's reputation does not rest solely on his ability to produce dazzling demonstrations of architectural invention but also on the breadth of his interests and the fateful way in which he confronted many of the most important themes and problems of modern society. His charismatic leadership of the Modern Movement has led to his being held accountable, quite inaccurately, for the faults of modern architects and planners, which he spent his life contesting. Like Frank Lloyd Wright, he was acutely conscious of his position as a figurehead of modern architecture.

Of the many polemical debates in which Le Corbusier ensnared himself and others, a few examples help to explain his position in international Modernism. The Swiss critic Alexandre von Senger wrote *Le Cheval de Troie du bolchévisme* (1928 and 1930), accusing Le Corbusier of undermining Western society as part of a calculated subversion by the Comintern. There was a political engagement with the Beaux-Arts architect and academic Gustave Umbdenstock, who attacked him specifically in a lecture on 14 March 1932 and through a series of published conference papers over the following two or three years. Camille Mauclair, the art critic of *Le Figaro*, also launched an attack with a series of articles under the heading 'L'Architecture va-t-elle mourir?' in 1933. These presented Le Corbusier as a totalitarian, authoritarian figure trying to submerge national, racial and individual characteristics. His response was to publish *Croisade ou le crépuscule des académies* (1933), which was welcomed by architects of every persuasion. More significant, perhaps, was Le Corbusier's defence against an attack from the Left from his erstwhile Czech admirer Karel Teige, who charged him in 1929 with idealism and 'lofty speculation', with trying to replace functionalism with empty monumentality. His reply, 'Defence of Architecture, Reply to Karel Teige' (repr. in *Oppositions*, 1974, no. 4, pp. 93–108), addressed most of the important themes of 20th-century Modernism. It is the defence of architecture as an art, consistent in all his writings, however functionalist some of the rhetoric sounds, that is the most significant contribution that he made to the maturing of the Modern Movement. Perhaps his single greatest achievement was to reassert the primacy of lyricism and humanist values in architecture at a time when Modernism was in danger of becoming fixed within a reductive functionalist ideology.

## WRITINGS

Le Corbusier wrote over 50 books (reprinted and translated into many languages) and innumerable articles. The key texts are listed below.

*La Feuille d'avis de La Chaux de Fonds* (La Chaux de Fonds, 1911)
*Etude sur le mouvement d'art décoratif en Allemagne* (La Chaux de Fonds, 1912)
with A. Ozenfant: *Après le Cubisme* (Paris, 1918)
*Vers une architecture* (Paris, 1923, rev. 1924; Eng. trans., London, 1927)
*L'Almanach d'architecture moderne* (Paris, 1925, *R* Paris, 1990)
*L'Art décoratif d'aujourd'hui* (Paris, 1925, 2/1959; Eng. trans., London, 1987)
with A. Ozenfant: *La Peinture moderne* (Paris, 1925)
*Urbanisme* (Paris, 1925); Eng. trans. as *The City of Tomorrow and its Planning* (London, 1929)
*Une Maison, un palais* (Paris, 1929)
*Précisions sur un état présent de l'architecture et de l'urbanisme* (Paris, 1930; Eng. trans., 1991)
*Croisade ou le crépuscule des académies* (Paris, 1932)
*La Ville radieuse* (Paris, 1935; Eng. trans., London, 1967)
*Quand les cathédrales étaient blanches ou voyage au pays des timides* (Paris, 1937; Eng. trans., New York, 1947)
*Des Canons, des munitions? Merci, des logis SVP* (Paris, 1938)
*Destin de Paris* (Paris, 1941)
*Sur les quatre routes* (Paris, 1941; Eng. trans., London, 1947)
with F. de Pierrefeu: *La Maison des hommes* (Paris, 1942); Eng. trans. as *The Home of Man* (London, 1948)
*La Charte d'Athènes* (Paris, 1943, 2/1957; Eng. trans., London, 1948)
*Les Trois Etablissements humains* (Paris, 1945, rev. 2/1959)
*Manière de penser l'urbanisme* (Paris, 1946, Eng. trans., New York, 1971)
*Propos d'urbanisme* (Paris, 1947; Eng. trans., London, 1947)

*Le Modulor* (Paris, [1950]; Eng. trans., London, 1954)
*Le Modulor 2, 1955 (La Parole est aux usagers)* (Paris, 1955; Eng. trans., London, 1958)
*Ronchamp: Les Carnets de la recherche patiente* (Stuttgart, 1957)
*L'Atelier de la recherche patiente* (Paris, 1960); Eng. trans. as *Creation is a Patient Search* (New York, 1960)
*Textes et dessins pour Ronchamp* (Paris, 1965)
*Mise au point* (Paris, 1966)

### UNPUBLISHED SOURCES
Fondation Le Corbusier [33,000 archit. drgs; over 1000 boxes of docs; col. of photographs and slides; over 40 sketchbooks; Le Corbusier's lib. of bks, period. and misc. memorabilia]

### BIBLIOGRAPHY
The Fondation Le Corbusier has a full bibliographical card index.
*Le Corbusier: An Annotated Bibliography* (New York, 1985) by D. Brady [lists *c.* 1500 items but does not incl. the large quantity of pubns stimulated by the Centenary Year pubs (1987)]

#### PRIMARY SOURCES
W. Boesiger, ed.: *Oeuvre complète*, 8 vols (Zurich, 1930–70) [vol. i, ed. with O. Stonorov; vol. iii, ed. M. Bill]
*Le Corbusier Carnets: 1914–1964*, 4 vols (Paris, 1981–2; Eng. trans., New York, 1982)
H. A. Brooks, ed.: *The Le Corbusier Archive*, 32 vols (New York, London and Paris, 1982–4)

#### MONOGRAPHS
M. Besset: *Le Corbusier: To Live with the Light* (London, 1968, 2/1987)
C. Jencks: *Le Corbusier and the Tragic View of Architecture* (London and Cambridge, MA, 1973)
S. von Moos: *Le Corbusier: Elements of Synthesis* (Cambridge, MA, 1979)
G. H. Baker: *Le Corbusier: An Analysis of Form* (New York and London, 1983)
W. Curtis: *Le Corbusier: Ideas and Forms* (London, 1986)

#### SPECIALIST STUDIES

##### Early work
P. V. Turner: *The Education of Le Corbusier: A Study of the Development of Le Corbusier's Thought, 1900–1920* (New York and London, 1977)
M. P. M. Sekler: *The Early Drawings of Charles-Edouard Jeanneret (Le Corbusier), 1902–1908* (New York and London, 1978)
J. Gubler: 'Jeanneret et le régionalisme: Du sentiment à la raison', *Archithèse*, x/2 (1981), pp. 31–8
H. A. Brooks: 'Le Corbusier's Formative Years at La Chaux de Fonds', *The Le Corbusier Archive*, i (New York, 1982), pp. xv–xxv
L. M. Colli: *Arte, artigianato e tecnica nella poetica di Le Corbusier* (Bari, 1982)
M. Emery: 'Chapallaz versus Jeanneret', *Archithèse*, xiii/2 (1983), pp. 23–8 [part of a special issue]
G. Gresleri: *Le Corbusier viaggio in oriente* (Venice, 1984)
J. Gubler: 'La Chaux de Fonds', *Inventaire suisse d'architecture*, iii (Berne, 1984), pp. 127–217

##### Paris and Purism
C. Rowe: 'The Mathematics of the Ideal Villa', *Archit. Rev.* [London] (March 1947)
*Oppositions*, xv–xvi (Winter–Spring 1979) [special issue on Le Corbusier, 1905–33]
G. Gresleri and F. Alison: *L'Esprit nouveau* (Milan, 1979)
T. Benton: *Les Villas de Le Corbusier, 1920–1930* (Paris, 1984; Eng. trans., New Haven, 1987)
B. Reichlin: 'Für und wider das Langfenster: Die Kontroversie Perret—Le Corbusier', *Daidalos*, xiii (Sept 1984), pp. 65–78
I. Charollais and A. Ducret, eds: *Le Corbusier à Genève, 1922–32* (Lausanne, 1987)

##### 'Grands Projets'
S. F. Starr: 'Le Corbusier and the USSR: New Documentation', *Oppositions*, xxiii (Winter 1981), pp. 122–37
M. Mcleod: '"Architecture or Revolution": Taylorism, Technocracy and Social Change', *A. J.* [New York], xliii/2 (1983), pp. 132–47

##### Mature work
J. Stirling: 'Garches to Jaoul', *Archit. Rev.* [London], cxviii/705 (1955), pp. 145–51
*Oppositions*, xix–xx (Winter–Spring 1980) [special issue on Le Corbusier, 1933–60]

*Theoretical approaches*

R. Fishman: *Urban Utopias in the Twentieth Century* (Cambridge, MA, 1977, 2/1982)

R. Walden, ed.: *The Open Hand: Essays on Le Corbusier* (London and Cambridge, MA, 1977), pp. 216–43

T. Hilpert: *'Die funktionelle Stadt': Le Corbusier's Stadtvision* (Brunswick, 1978)

J. Guiton, ed.: *The Ideas of Le Corbusier on Architecture and Urban Planning* (New York, 1981) [useful col. of extracts of Le Corbusier's writings arranged by topic]

H. A. Brooks: 'Jeanneret and Sitte: Le Corbusier's Earliest Ideas on Urban Design', *In Search of Modern Architecture*, ed. H. Searing (Cambridge, MA, 1982), pp. 278–97

P. Eisenmann: 'Aspects du modernisme: La Maison Domino ou le signe autoréférentiel', *Cah. Rech. Archit.*, xii (1982), pp. 58–65

F. Passanti: 'Wolkenkratzer für die *Ville contemporaine*', *L'Esprit nouveau: Le Corbusier und die Industrie* (exh. cat., ed. S. von Moos; Zurich, Kstgewmus.; W. Berlin, Bauhaus-Archv; Strasbourg, Mus. A. Mod.; 1987)

*Design process*

A. Colquohon: 'Formal and Functional Interactions', *Archit. Des.*, xxxvi (May 1966), pp. 221–34

K. Frampton: 'The Humanist vs the Utilitarian Ideal', *Archit. Des.*, xxxviii (1968), pp. 134–6

J. Loach: 'Studio as Laboratory', *Archit. Rev.* [London], clxxxi/1079 (1987), pp. 73–7

*Critical reception*

*Le Corbusier im Brennpunkt* (Zurich, 1988) [debate on Le Corbusier's significance in the late 20th century]

INDIVIDUAL PROJECTS

J. Stirling: 'Ronchamp: Le Corbusier's Chapel and the Crisis of Rationalism', *Archit. Rev.* [London], cxix/711 (1956), pp. 155–61

A. Henz and B. Moosbrugger: *La Tourette, Le Corbusiers erster Klosterbau* (Starnberg, 1963)

S. von Moos: 'Wohnkollektiv, Hospiz und Dampfer', *Archithèse*, xii (1970), pp. 30–42

B. B. Taylor: *Le Corbusier et Pessac*, 2 vols (Paris, 1972)

R. Gabetti and C. Olmo: *Le Corbusier e 'L'Esprit nouveau'* (Turin, 1975)

M. Bernardi and others: *The Swiss Pavilion* (Paris, 1976)

J. Lowman: 'Le Corbusier as Structural Rationalist', *Archit. Rev.* [London], clx/953 (1976), pp. 229–33

W. Curtis and E. F. Sekler: *Le Corbusier at Work: The Genesis of the Carpenter Centre for the Visual Arts*, preface J. L. Sert (Cambridge, MA, and London, 1978)

M. Steinman: 'Der Völkerbundspalast: Eine *chronique scandaleuse*', *Werk-Archithèse*, xxiii–iv (1978), pp. 28–31

L. A. Anzivino and E. Godoli: *Ginevra, 1927: Il concorso per il Palazzo della Società delle Nazioni e il caso Le Corbusier* (Florence, 1979)

P. Boudon: *Lived-in Architecture: Le Corbusier's Pessac Revisited* (Cambridge, MA, 1979)

J.-L. Cohen: 'Cette mystique: L'URSS', *Archit., Movt, Cont.*, xlix (1979), pp. 75–84; expanded as 'Le Corbusier and the Mystique of the USSR', *Oppositions*, xxiii (Winter 1981), pp. 84–121

E. Gregh: 'The Domino Idea', *Oppositions*, xv–xvi (Winter–Spring 1979), pp. 61–87

G. Gresleri: *L'Esprit nouveau* (Milan, 1979)

C. Borngräber: 'Le Corbusier a Mosca', *Rassegna: Problemi di architettura dell'ambiente*, iv (1980), pp. 80–88

M. Mcleod: 'Le Corbusier and Algiers', *Oppositions*, xxiii (Winter–Spring 1980), pp. 184–201

D. Pauly: *Ronchamp: Lecture d'une architecture* (Paris, 1980)

B. B. Taylor: *Le Corbusier: La Cité de refuge* (Equerre, 1980)

W. J. R. Curtis: 'Ideas of Structure and the Structure of Ideas: Le Corbusier's Pavillon Suisse, 1930–1931', *J. Soc. Archit. Hist.*, xl/4 (1981), pp. 295–310

G. Gresleri and D. Matteoini: *La città mondiale* (Polis/Marisilio, 1982)

T. Benton: 'Le Corbusier and the Loi Loucheur', *AA Files*, 7 (Sept 1984), pp. 54–60

——: 'La Villa Mandrot i el lloc de la imaginaio', *Quad. Arquit. Urb.*, clxiii (Oct–Dec 1984), pp. 36–49

I. Xenakis: 'The Monastery of La Tourette', *The Le Corbusier Archive*, xxviii (New York, 1984), pp. ix–xxviii

F. Biot and F. Perrot: *Le Corbusier et l'art sacré, Sainte Marie de la Tourette Eveux* (Lyon, 1985)

D. Pauly: 'The Chapel of Ronchamp', *The Le Corbusier Archive*, xx (New York, 1985), pp. xiii–xxvi; repr. in *Archit. Des.*, lv/7–8 (1985), pp. 31–40 [part of issue on drgs by Le Corbusier in the Archv]

B. Reichlin: 'Le Corbusier vs de Stijl', *De Stijl et l'architecture en France* (Brussels, 1985)

H. de Soeten and T. Edelkoort: *La Tourette, Le Corbusier* (Delft, 1985)

T. Benton: 'Raoul La Roche Sammlung und Haus', *L'Esprit nouveau: Le Corbusier und die Industrie* (exh. cat., ed. S. von Moos; Zurich, Kstgewmus.; W. Berlin, Bauhaus-Archv; Strasbourg, Mus. A. Mod.; 1987)

B. Chiambretto: *Le Corbusier à Cap Martin* (Paris, 1987)

B. Reichlin: '"Cette belle pierre de Provence": La Villa de Mandrot', *Le Corbusier et la méditerranée* (exh. cat., Marseille, Mus. Marseille, 1987), pp. 131–41

J. Sbriglio: *Doctrines modernes et architectures du logement Marseille, 1945–1960* (Marseille, 1989)

C. Sumi: *Immeuble Clarté Genf 1932* (Zurich, 1990)

PAINTINGS AND SCULPTURES

K. E. Silver: 'Purism: Straightening up after the Great War', *Artforum*, xv/7 (1977), pp. 56–63

S. von Moos: 'Le Corbusier as Painter', *Oppositions*, xviii–xix (1980), pp. 87–107

F. de Franclieu: *Le Corbusier, Savina: Sculptures et dessins* (Paris, 1984)

C. Green: 'The Architect as Artist', *Le Corbusier: Architect of the Century* (exh. cat., ACGB, 1987), pp. 110–30

R. Ingersoll: *A Marriage of Contours* (Princeton, 1990)

DESIGN AND APPLIED ARTS

R. de Fusco: *Le Corbusier designer: I mobili del 1929* (Milan, 1976)

M. di Puolo, M. Fagiolo and M. L. Madonna: *'La Machine à s'asseoir': Le Corbusier/Charlotte Perriand/Pierre Jeanneret* (Rome, 1976)

C. Wilk: *Thonet: 150 Years of Furniture* (New York, 1980), pp. 151–67

C. Benton: 'L'Aventure du mobilier: Le Corbusier's Furniture Designs in the 1920s', *J. Dec. A. Soc.*, vi (1982), pp. 7–22

A. Ruegg: 'Charles Edouard Jeanneret, architecte–conseil pour toutes les questions de décoration intérieure . . .', *Archithèse*, xiii/2 (1983), pp. 39–44 [part of special issue]

C. Perriand: *Un Art de vivre* (Paris, 1985)

EXHIBITION CATALOGUES

*Le Corbusier: La ricerca paziente* (exh. cat., ed. S. Pagnamento and B. Reichlin; Lugano, 1980)

*Le Corbusier: Synthèse des Arts Aspekte des Spätwerks, 1945–1965* (exh. cat., ed. A. Vowinckel and T. Kesseler; Karlsruhe, Bad. Kstver., 1986)

*L'Esprit nouveau: Le Corbusier und die Industrie, 1920–25* (exh. cat., ed. S. von Moos; Zurich, Kstgewmus.; W. Berlin, Bauhaus-Archiv; Strasbourg, Mus. A. Mod.; 1987)

*Le Corbusier: Architect of the Century* (exh. cat., ed. M. Raeburn and V. Wilson; ACGB, 1987)

*Le Corbusier et la méditerranée* (exh. cat., Marseille, Cent. Vieille Charité, 1987)

*Le Corbusier: Une Encyclopédie* (exh. cat., ed. J. Lucan; Paris, Pompidou, 1987)

*Le Corbusier: Le Passé à réaction poétique* (exh. cat., Paris, Caisse N. Mnmts Hist. & Sites, 1987)

*Le Corbusier: Il viaggio in Toscana (1907)* (exh. cat., Venice, 1987)

TIM BENTON

**Lectionary.** *See under* SERVICE BOOK.

**Lecuona, Juan** (*b* Buenos Aires, 30 July 1956). Argentine painter. The geometric tension in his paintings reveals the forms that make up each structure, mobilizes them and tests their limits, but without breaking them. While operating with a perspective on abstraction, he retained simple elements (a course derived from informalism) and synthesized the principles of Neo-Geo (the new geometry). This is a type of dialectic—theoretical and practical—of forms retrieved from the past. It involves a rationalistic proposal executed with a careful technique. It is a deconstruction, a self-referential vision of existence and matter, expressed in images, that no other form would be capable of communicating.

BIBLIOGRAPHY
*Deconstrucción en la pintura* (exh. cat. by J. Glusberg, Rio de Janeiro, Mus.
   A. Mod., 1988), p. 4
                                                    JORGE GLUSBERG

**Lecurt, Juste.** *See* CORTE, JOSSE DE.

**Lederer, Hugo** (*b* Znaim, Moravia [now Znojmo, Czech
Republic], 16 Nov 1871; *d* Berlin, 1 Aug 1940). German
sculptor. At the age of 13 he entered the Fachschule für
Tonindustrie und Verwandte Gewerbe in Znaim. After
three years he completed his training with a certificate in
modelling and pottery. This craft training equipped him
with basic skills that served him well in his subsequent
training as a sculptor. He first worked as an assistant in
the studio of the craftsman A. Deutschmann in Erfurt
(1887–90), where he perfected his crafts skills. In nearby
Weimar he saw for the first time casts of works of
Michelangelo and prints of the works of Franz von Stuck.
Both made a strong impression on him.

The next stage of Lederer's career was in Dresden,
where he was accepted as an assistant at the workshop of
the renowned sculptor Johannes Schilling, like him a
follower of the tradition of Christian Daniel Rauch. He
achieved his first recognition for designs for the new
building of the Hochschule für Bildende Künste in Dresden (1891). The offer to transfer to the workshop of
Christian Behrens in Breslau (now Wrocław, Poland) was
certainly a distinction. Although he stayed for only a short
period with Behrens, he was strongly influenced by him.
Even in later years, Lederer repeatedly collaborated with
colleagues from his Moravian homeland or from the
Breslau studio.

In 1892 Lederer went to Berlin. He worked first in the
studio of Alexander Calandrelli, then for a longer period
with Robert Toberentz, whom he assisted in the monument to *Luther* for Berlin. After his mentor's death in
1895 he established himself independently, taking over
Toberentz's workshop. His first important early work was
the bronze relief *Homecoming (1812)* (Znojmo, S. Morav.
Mus.); in 1896 he produced the group *Fate* (Znojmo, S.
Morav. Mus.), which shows him still under the influence
of Reinhold Begas, whom he revered. His next work,
however, *Crouching Girl* (1897; Znojmo, S. Morav. Mus.),
shows tendencies that were to lead him into the orbit of
Begas's counterpart, Adolf von Hildebrand. The calm,
closed composition of the *Crouching Girl* fills the marble
block with inner tension: tectonic principles replace emotive pathos and picturesque effects. The bust of the
wrestler *Peruse* (1899–1904; priv. col., see Jochum-Bohrmann, pl. 42) had similar power. In these last two works
Lederer discovered the style that was to characterize his
work. His artistic breakthrough came, however, with the
monument to *Bismarck* in Elbhöhe, Hamburg (1901–2),
which he produced with the architect Emil Schaudt in a
collaboration of distinction. Dedicated in 1906, it marks
the beginning of a new, monumental conception of form
and content, which was to have great influence on future
monuments.

Another keypoint in Lederer's work was the figure of
the *Fencer* (1901–4) on the university fountain in Breslau.
His years of most intense and most successful work now
began. A monument to *Krupp* was produced for the

Margarethenhöhe, Essen (1905–7), and a *Wrestler* (1908)
by him was placed on the Heerstrasse in Berlin. He
produced a monument to *Emperor Frederick III* (1912)
on horseback for the Marktplatz, Aachen, as well as many
other works. He also produced significant works in the
fields of portrait sculpture (e.g. *Alfred Krupp* and *Friedrich
Alfred Krupp*, 1912; portrait bust of *Hindenburg*, 1916)
and funerary sculpture (e.g. *Jedlitzka* tomb, Berlin, 1902).
From 1913 he worked as a teacher at the Akademische
Hochschule in Berlin; in 1919 the Preussische Akademie
appointed him head of the sculpture studio as successor
to Louis Tuaillon. His pupils included Gustav Seitz. In his
later years he devoted himself increasingly to animal
sculptures, producing the Bear Fountain at the Wer-
derscher Markt, Berlin (1929; now a replica), the bear
group for the new Rathaus at Zehlendorf, Berlin (1930),
and a Fountain of Fertility with bulls for Arnswalder Platz,
Berlin (1927–34).

BIBLIOGRAPHY
H. Krey: *Hugo Lederer—Ein Meister der Plastik* (Berlin, 1931)
P. Bloch and W. Grzimek: *Das klassische Berlin* (Berlin, 1978)
*Abbilder—Leitbilder: Berliner Skulpturen von Schadow bis heute* (exh. cat.,
   W. Berlin, Neuer Berlin. Kstver., 1978)
P. Bloch and B. Hüfler: *Rheinland Westfalen und die Berliner Bildhauerschule
   des 19. Jahrhunderts* (Berlin, 1984)
E. Trier: 'Ein Denkmal der Arbeit von Hugo Lederer', *Walraff-Richartz-
   Jb.*, xlvii (1986), pp. 235–46
*Kunst in Berlin, 1648–1987* (exh. cat., E. Berlin, Altes Mus., 1987)
I. Jochum-Bohrmann: *Hugo Lederer: Ein deutsch-nationaler Bildhauer des
   20. Jahrhunderts* (diss., U. Heidelberg, 1988)
S. Einholz: 'Der gezwängte Mensch—Beobachtungen zu Berliner Grabre-
   liefs des frühen 20. Jahrhunderts', *Z. Dt. Ver. Kstwiss.*, xliii (1989),
   no. 2, pp. 80–93
                                                    SIBYLLE EINHOLZ

**Ledesma, Blas de** (*fl* Granada, 1602–14). Spanish
painter. He is known to have worked in Granada from
1602, and in 1614 he designed a stucco vault decoration
for the Alhambra. Archival sources testify to his renown
as a painter of decorative fresco grotesques (untraced)
and still-lifes. His activity as a still-life painter remains
debatable, partly because he has been confused with Blas
de Prado and also because of Torres Martín's controversial
attributions. Ledesma's only unanimously accepted autograph painting is *Still-life with Cherries and Flowers* (Atlanta,
GA, High Mus. A.), signed in Granada. A highly decorative
painting, it shows none of the sophistication of still-lifes
by Juan Sánchez Cotán, in Granada from 1603. It is
painted meticulously and drily. Depicting a severely drawn,
rather flat basket on a narrow ledge flanked by flowers
behind it, the rigorously symmetrical composition is relieved only by soft lighting and the studied disarray of
some fallen cherries. Two other unsigned and poorly
preserved still-lifes of analogous subject-matter have been
attributed to Ledesma (Madrid, Marqués de Deleitosa priv.
col., see Torres Martín, pls 24–5). Three very different
signed still-lifes depicting sweets, fruits and exotic birds
have also been tentatively accepted as autograph (priv.
cols, see exh. cat., pp. 66–7).

BIBLIOGRAPHY
R. Torres Martín: *Blas de Ledesma y el bodegón español* (Madrid, 1978)
*Spanish Still-life in the Golden Age, 1600–1650* (exh. cat. by W. B. Jordan,
   Fort Worth, TX, Kimbell A. Mus., 1985) [excellent pls]
                                                    PETER CHERRY

**Le Despenser**, 15th Baron. *See* DASHWOOD, FRANCIS.

**Lednice** [Ger. Eisgrub]. Town in southern Moravia, Czech Republic, known for its manor house and garden. Situated on the border with Lower Austria, about halfway between Brno and Vienna, the estate belonged to the Liechtenstein princes from the mid-13th century to 1945. Before 1588 Hartmann II, Landgrave of Feldberg, had commissioned a house and ornamental garden for use as the family's country seat. The house was modernized in the 17th century by Charles Eusebius, Prince of Liechtenstein, who employed, among others, the stuccoist Bernardo Bianchi, the masons Pietro Maderna, Pietro Tencalla and Francesco Caratti (1632) and the architects Giovanni Battista I Carlone (ii), Giovanni Giacomo Tencalla from Vienna and Andrea Erna from Brno (1638–41). Further modifications were made by Antonio Beduzzi in the 1730s, by Isidore Canevale in 1766–72 and by Joseph Kornhäusel, who gave the house a Neo-classical façade in 1815. The only part of the house to remain unaltered was the monumental riding school and its stables, designed in 1688 by Johann Bernhard Fischer von Erlach, who adorned them with Doric pilasters, changing to coupled columns and broken pediments at the gateways. Lednice acquired its present appearance during the period 1846–53. The architect Georg Wingelmüller (1810–48), who died before work was completed, used ideas from his tours of England, Scotland, Belgium and Switzerland to create a romantic Gothic Revival castle now noted primarily for its *boiserie*.

The plan to transform the grounds at Lednice into fashionably landscaped gardens was probably introduced by Canevale in the 1780s. His follower Josef Hardtmuth built the antique Sun Temple in 1794 (destr. 1838): the layout featured eight alleys leading radially from the temple each to a memorial or other building, of which only a minaret (1798) and the Monolith of Peace have survived. From 1805 to 1811 the architect Ercole Gaetano Fanti and the botanist van der Schott created naturalistic gardens that were later filled with statuary and innovative projects, including temples, an arcade, lodges, a pheasantry and waterworks in an Islamic style. The Lednice gardens, which have survived in this form, constitute a remarkable link with the tradition of the English landscape garden, while reflecting Viennese architectural taste of the early 19th century.

BIBLIOGRAPHY

V. Fleischer: *Fürst Karl Eusebius von Liechtenstein als Bauherr und Kunstsammler (1611–1684)* (Vienna, 1910)

E. Charvátová-Sedláčková and B. Štorm: *Lednice: Státní zámek* [Lednice: state castle] (Prague, 1958)

V. Richter and Z. Kudělka: 'Die Architektur des 17. und 18. Jahrhunderts in Mähren', *Sborn. Prac. Filoz. Fak. Brn. U.*, xvi (1972), pp. 91–130

H. Sedlmayr: *Johann Bernhard Fischer von Erlach* (Vienna, 1976)

G. Wilhelm: 'Die Fürsten von Liechtenstein und ihre Beziehungen zu Kunst und Wissenschaft', *Jb. Liechtenstein. Kstges.*, i (1979), pp. 9–179

JIŘÍ KROUPA

**Ledoux, Claude-Nicolas** (*b* Dormans, Champagne, 21 March 1736; *d* Paris, 19 Nov 1806). French architect and writer. He was one of the most successful and celebrated architects working in Paris at the end of the *ancien régime*. Grounded in the classical tradition, he gradually developed a highly imaginative architecture of simplified geometric forms and bold detailing, at the same time producing a large number of powerful visionary projects, for which he is perhaps best known.

1. Early work and private commissions, to *c.* 1780. 2. Saline de Chaux and public commissions, 1771 and after.

1. EARLY WORK AND PRIVATE COMMISSIONS, TO *c.* 1780. Ledoux studied first at the Collège de Dormans-Beauvais in Paris (1749–53) and then at the newly established Ecole des Arts of Jacques-François Blondel. From his classes in rhetoric he gained a lifelong love of the classics and a periphrastic literary style that pervaded his writings; from Blondel he derived his sense of the high professional role of the architect, his rudimentary understanding of architectural history, his taste for 17th-century classicism, his concepts of planning and aesthetic expression, and his vision of himself as an *architecte–philosophe*, heir to the reforming idealism of the mid-century. A contemporary friend and biographer, the architect Jacques Cellérier, noted that Ledoux worked as an engraver in order to pay his expenses. An echo of this early training is found in Ledoux's self-conscious emulation of the layout of the plates of the *Encyclopédie ou dictionnaire raisonné des sciences, des arts et des métiers* (Paris, 1750–76), by Denis Diderot and Jean le Rond d'Alembert, in the engraved presentation of his own projects. In 1764 Ledoux began to work for the Département des Eaux et Forêts in Burgundy and Franche-Comté; he prepared plans and estimates, decided on necessary repairs and designed new constructions for sacristies, presbyteries, school-houses, cemeteries, roads, river quays, wells, drinking fountains and washing-places, as well as larger structures such as bridges and churches (e.g. St Pierre-aux-liens, Rolampont; the church of the Assumption, Fouvent-le-Hau; St Didier, Roche-et-Raucourt; St Barthélémy, Cruzy-le-Châtel; all 1764–5). In their range these buildings must be seen as the foundation of Ledoux's growing preoccupation with the reform of rural architecture, and in their style they anticipate his later experiments in a reduced classicism suitable for public works.

Such work prepared Ledoux for a career that encompassed more than the traditional programmes of a society architect: the reform and maintenance of the forests, the social conditions of their population, the development of road and river transport, the construction of bridges and canals, the revolution of agrarian practices and the encouragement of rural industry all proved central to Ledoux's theory and design. From a practical point of view, his appointment to the Eaux et Forêts brought him into contact with a patronage circle that supported him throughout his career: the administrators of the Ferme Générale (General Tax Farm). These socially important connections were reinforced by Ledoux's marriage (1764) to the daughter of a prominent musician at the court, Joseph-Gaspard Bureau. From the mid-1760s Ledoux's connections at court, in the world of music, theatre and salons, increasingly supported a private practice that soon outstripped his administrative work, and he soon became the leading architect in Paris for private town houses for the wealthy (*see* HÔTEL PARTICULIER, §1). In 1766 he reconstructed a hôtel in the Marais district of Paris for Franz-Joseph d'Hallwyl, colonel of the Swiss Guard. D'Hallwyl himself was linked by business interests and proximity to the Swiss Protestant banking firm of Thélusson and Necker, his neighbours in the Rue Michel le Comte. Ledoux profited from these connections, both in the later commission for Madame Thélusson's hôtel in the Chaussée d'Antin (see below) and in his widening circle of friends in the arts, many of whom gathered in the salon of Madame Necker. Ledoux's position as architect to the nobility was finally confirmed by his introduction to one of the first families of France, the Montmorency-Luxembourgs; he built the Hôtel de Montmorency for the Prince and Princesse de Montmorency between 1769 and 1771.

The style of Ledoux's first Parisian hôtels has generally been identified with the movement, supported by Blondel and the Encyclopedists, that, beginning in the 1750s, turned away from the Rococo towards a new classicism. This was increasingly inflected by his personal version of a simplified neo-Palladianism, as exhibited in the pavilion (1765) for Gilles Hocquart, Fermier-Générale, the Hôtel de Montmorency and houses for Mademoiselle Saint-Germain and Pierre-René de Tabary, designed in the early 1770s. Commissions for country houses and châteaux were equally abundant between 1765 and 1770: at Montfermeil (1765) for Hocquart, at Maupertuis (1765) for the Marquis de Montesquieu and at Bénouville (1769–74) for the Marquis de Livry, Ledoux remodelled old family seats, extending the *corps de logis*, embellishing them with giant orders and porticos, adding service quarters and laying out new gardens.

In 1770 Ledoux's growing reputation as an architect of fashion was sealed by two commissions that were readily associated in the public imagination not only for the elegance of their design but also for the notoriety of their clients, two of the most celebrated courtesans of the day. The one, Mademoiselle Guimard, a dancer at the Opéra, under the protection of powerful admirers at the court, was, at 27, at the height of her career; for her Ledoux built a hôtel (1769–72) in the rapidly expanding quarter of the

Chaussée d'Antin, Paris, the gate-house of which housed a small but complete private theatre. The other client, Madame Du Barry, was the same age, and recently installed at Versailles as the favourite of the aging King Louis XV. Seeking to occupy herself as a patroness of the arts in the manner of her predecessor, Madame de Pompadour, she selected Ledoux, who was in competition with Charles de Wailly, to construct a pavilion on her new estate at Louveciennes as a retreat where she might receive the King in privacy (*see* DU BARRY). Construction on this celebrated Neo-classical project was begun at the end of 1770 and completed a year later, inaugurated by a reception in the presence of the King on 2 September 1771.

The Hôtel Thélusson (1778–81; destr.), Chaussée d'Antin, Paris, was the largest of Ledoux's private commissions to be realized, and it was certainly the most remarked— for its unorthodox composition and dramatic presentation to the street. A combination of pavilion and palace, it represented the late 18th-century *folie* at its most elaborate. At once a picturesque assemblage of set pieces derived from antique, Italian Renaissance and French classical architecture, welded into a neo-Palladian whole, it was also a huge and imposing building, set in a park that was equally picturesque, contrived with brilliant artifice as a miniature landscape garden, crossed by bridges, viaducts and tunnels, with separate public and private circulation inside. A virtual forum of antique fragments and quasi-Piranesian quotations in its parts, the hôtel was overtly theatrical in its composition, entered through a kind of proscenium formed by a wide half-sunken arch, the truncated proportions of which resembled some antique ruin depicted by Piranesi.

2. SALINE DE CHAUX AND PUBLIC COMMISSIONS, 1771 AND AFTER. Ledoux's two careers, private and public, came together on 20 September 1771, 18 days after the inaugural fête at Louveciennes, when he was appointed by order of the King (no doubt on the advice of Madame Du Barry) as Commissaire des Salines for Franche-Comté. In this capacity, acting for the Ferme Générale, Ledoux built the most celebrated of his commissions—the saltworks, Saline du Roi, at Arc-et-Senans, otherwise known as the Saline de Chaux after the nearby forest. Sited near Besançon, where Ledoux designed the new theatre (begun 1776; see below), the Saline, a complex of factory and living quarters, was laid out in the form of a semicircular ideal town. Its monumental form, accentuated by giant Doric and rusticated orders and carved stone motifs as in the Maison du Directeur (see fig. 1), immediately gave the architect a reputation for extravagance that overshadowed the careful disposition of functions, and an attention to the surveillance and social organization of labour that prefigured the ideas of the social reformer Jeremy Bentham. Constructed between 1774 and 1779, this small factory complex became an obsessive centre of Ledoux's architectural imagination until his death. He subsequently designed more ideal projects for its environs, proposing to expand it into an oval-plan town, Chaux, centred on the Saline but with economic and physical extensions into the surrounding provinces, and gradually assembling the elements of an entire Utopian city that illustrated the aspirations of the *ancien régime*. Although the town was

1. Claude-Nicolas Ledoux: Maison du Directeur, Saline de Chaux, 1774–9; engraving from his *L'Architecture considérée sous le rapport de l'art, des moeurs et de la législation*, i (Paris, 1804)

not executed, from 1775 Ledoux supervised the engraving of projects for its major public monuments and private houses, inventing institutions (e.g. the House of Unity or Brotherhood; the Pacifère, or House of Reconciliation; the Panaréthéon, or House of All Virtue; and the Oikéma, or ideal brothel; all probably designed between 1789 and 1799) and redesigning others (the church, the public baths, the stock exchange, and the cemetery; all *c.* 1784–5), such as to constitute a repertory of type-forms that would take their place beside the many prototype houses and multiple dwellings. This collection of engravings was first announced in 1784 and went through several iterations in Ledoux's mind until the final publication of a first volume in 1804 under the provocative title *L'Architecture considerée sous le rapport de l'art, des moeurs et de la législation.*

Between 1775 and 1789, from the laying of the foundation stone of the Saline de Chaux to the outbreak of the Revolution, Ledoux, despite numerous setbacks, real or imagined, developed one of the more brilliant and successful practices of the last years of the *ancien régime.* While continuing to expand his patronage for hôtels and housing in Paris and the provinces, he devoted equal attention to public commissions. Supported until the end by the Ferme Générale, he built a new salt-warehouse at Compiègne in 1775 and from 1783 began the construction of a large office building for the company's headquarters in Paris. Turning the friendship of Jean-Charles-Philibert Trudaine de Montigny, Intendant des Finances, to good account, he was introduced to provincial officials and recommended for public commissions. In 1775 the Intendant of Franche-Comté called him to Besançon to design the new theatre, finally completed in 1783 (for further discussion and illustration *see* THEATRE, §III, 3(ii)(a) and fig. 13). In 1776 he was asked by the Governor of Provence to prepare a report on the condition of the old Palais Comtale at Aix-en-Provence; this request led to a series of designs (1779–86) for the new prison and Palais de Justice at Aix (*see* LAW COURT, §2), the final versions of which were under construction by the start of the Revolution, although later modified. As a result of his work at Aix, Ledoux was able to negotiate with competing land speculators for the commission to build the new theatre at Marseille. In the circle of Mlle Guimard he was introduced to Frederick II, Landgrave of Hesse-Kassel, and in 1776 was invited to Kassel, where he designed a triumphal arch, redesigned the royal library and museum and projected grand plans for a royal palace. Another project outside France came some seven years later when he was asked to submit designs for the town hall of Neuchâtel in Switzerland. Other schemes included two designs for a discount bank, which he submitted to successive ministers of finance, Jacques Necker and Charles Alexandre de Calonne; he also proposed plans for a market development in the Rue Saint-Germain and a new cemetry for Paris.

From 1784 to 1789 Ledoux was engaged by Calonne and the Ferme to build a new tax-wall around Paris, together with attendant boulevards and toll-gates or *barrières.* These latter buildings Ledoux conceived as monumental entries to the city, for which he adopted simplified geometric forms and manipulated scale and classical elements to produce bold, imaginative designs; 40 were proposed, in many variations of a few prototypes, and

2. Claude-Nicolas Ledoux: project for the Maison des Gardes Agricoles, Maupertuis, *c.* 1785–7 (unexecuted); engraving from D. Ramée, ed.: *L'Architecture de C.-N. Ledoux,* ii (Paris, 1847), pl. 254

they were built very rapidly—almost all being completed in the four years before the Revolution—amid heated controversy and despite Ledoux's own dismissal from the work in 1789. The *barrières,* long a target of press criticism for their monumental scale and distorted motifs, were not unexpectedly the first recipients of that violence against monuments later called vandalism, and only four survived the 19th century: the Barrière d'Enfer, Barrière du Trône, Rotonde de la Villette and Rotonde de Monceau. The work at Aix was similarly suspended by the Revolution, but the idiosyncratic mix of geometrical purism and classical motifs, most apparent in the frowning 'physiognomy' of the prison at Aix, its entrances formed by solid semicircles resting on stubby Doric columns, marked Ledoux as a practitioner of what a later commentator (Léon Vaudoyer, 1852) termed *'architecture parlante',* or an architecture that would, in Ledoux's words, unambiguously 'speak to the eyes' about its function, role and emotional associations.

Such 'speaking architecture', while practised by a number of Ledoux's contemporaries (notably Etienne-Louis Boullée and the hermetic Jean-Jacques Lequeu) was in

Ledoux's own hands turned into a play of geometrical solids and associated functions. The engravings in *L'Architecture considérée* show a barrel-shaped workshop for barrel-makers; a cylindrical house with a stream flowing through it for river surveyors; and a spherical shelter for shepherds (see fig. 2). These became the almost caricatural leitmotifs of Ledoux's style for the later 19th century and the 20th, inspiring the view of Ledoux as the forerunner of modernist abstraction and social reform (see Kaufmann, 1933). However, at least with regard to his political affiliations, the classification of Ledoux as a 'revolutionary' architect was misleading. Without work after 1789, and imprisoned for a brief period under the Terror for his royalist sympathies, Ledoux spent the remainder of his life writing the text and completing the plates for his publication. He envisaged a five-volume work, but only succeeded in publishing the first before his death. Republished in 1847 by the historian Daniel Ramée, with the addition of several plates left out of the original, Ledoux's work was, so to speak, 'completed' by the discovery of 70 lost plates in Paris and their publication in 1991.

### WRITINGS

*L'Architecture considérée sous le rapport de l'art, des moeurs et de la législation*, i (Paris, 1804/*R* New York, 1980); ii, ed. D. Ramée (Paris, 1846)

D. Ramée, ed.: *L'Architecture de C.-N. Ledoux*, 2 vols (Paris, 1847/*R* Princeton, 1984)

M. Gallet, ed.: *Architecture de Ledoux: Inédits pour un tome III* (Paris, 1991)

### BIBLIOGRAPHY

J. C. [J. Cellérier]: *Notice rapide sur la vie et les ouvrages de Claude-Nicolas Ledoux* (Paris, 1806)

E. Kaufmann: *Von Ledoux bis Le Corbusier: Ursprung und Entwicklung der autonomen Architektur* (Vienna, 1933)

G. Levallet-Haug: *Claude-Nicolas Ledoux, 1736–1806* (Paris and Strasbourg, 1934)

M. Raval and J.-C. Moreux: *Claude-Nicolas Ledoux, 1736–1806* (Paris, 1945)

E. Kaufmann: 'Three Revolutionary Architects, Boullée, Ledoux and Lequeu', *Trans. Amer. Philos. Soc.*, n. s., xlii (1953), pp. 431–564

W. Herrmann: 'The Problem of Chronology in Claude-Nicolas Ledoux's Engraved Work', *A. Bull.*, xli (1960), pp. 191–210

M. Ozouf: 'L'Image de la ville chez Claude-Nicolas Ledoux', *An., Econ., Soc., Civilis.*, xxi (1966)

S. Conard: 'Aux sources de l'architecture parlante, l'archéologie mystique de C.-N. Ledoux', *Colloque Piranesi e la cultura antiquaria: Roma, 1976*

M. Gallet: *Claude-Nicolas Ledoux (1736–1806)* (Paris, 1980)

J.-J. Gloton and S. Conard: 'Aix-en-Provence dans l'oeuvre de Claude-Nicolas Ledoux', *Monuments et mémoires publiés par l'Académie des inscriptions et belles-lettres* (Vendôme, 1983)

A. Vidler: *The Writing of the Walls: Architectural Theory in the Late Enlightenment* (Princeton, 1987)

——: *Claude-Nicolas Ledoux: Architecture and Social Reform at the End of the Ancien Régime* (Cambridge, MA, 1990)

ANTHONY VIDLER

**Ledoux** [Ledoulx; Le Doux], **Louis** (*bapt* Mons, 2 Feb 1616; *d* Mons, 27 March 1667). Franco-Flemish sculptor and architect. He was a pupil of François Du Quesnoy in Rome. Thereafter he worked mainly in Mons. For the church of the Jesuits there he sculpted a monumental marble tomb of *Archbishop van der Burch* (1647–53; reclining figure of the Archbishop and life-size figures of *Hope* and *Charity* in Cambrai, Maison Ste Agnès; other fragments in Cambrai, Mus. Mun.). In 1664 he completed a sculpted marble enclosure for the chapel of St Barbara in Ste Waudru, Mons. Also in Ste Waudru are his statues of *St Peter* and *St Paul*. He is said to have executed a number of tombs at Brugelette. His statues of *St George*

and *St Quirinus* for the chapel of St George next to the town hall in Mons make use of marbling techniques. Ledoux's most famous work is the 87-m Baroque bell-tower in Mons (1662–74), in collaboration with the engineer Vincentius Anthony (*d* 1692), the only one still standing in Wallonia.

### BIBLIOGRAPHY

L. Devillers: *Le Passé artistique de la ville de Mons* (Mons, 1885)

E. Marchal: *La Sculpture et les chefs-d'oeuvre de l'orfèvrerie belges* (Brussels, 1895)

J. E. van Ackere: *Baroque and Classic Art in Belgium* (Brussels, 1972)

RENÉE VAN DER VLOODT

**Leduc, Fernand** (*b* Montreal, 4 July 1916). Canadian painter, tapestry designer and weaver. He studied at the Ecole des Beaux-Arts in Montreal. In 1941 he met Paul-Emile Borduas, who introduced him to Surrealism, and Leduc then experimented with automatism. He became one of LES AUTOMATISTES and his painting in the later 1940s became abstract and more gestural, as in *Napoleon's Last Campaign* (1946; artist's col., see 1970 exh. cat., pl. 6). In 1946 he exhibited at the first Automatistes show in the Rue Amherst and in 1947 at the second in the Rue Sherbrooke. He left Montreal for Paris that year and on his arrival had a two-man show with Jean-Paul Riopelle at the Galerie du Luxembourg. While in Paris he rebelled against the orthodox Surrealism centred on André Breton and sent a virulently critical letter to Breton. Towards the end of his stay in Paris he became influenced by Jean Bazaine and more conscious of order in his works.

After his return to Montreal in 1953 Leduc began to give greater structure to his paintings, as in *Untitled* (1954; Montreal, Mus. A. Contemp.). In the late 1950s they became more geometrical, under the influence of Mondrian, resulting in such works as *The Alpinist* (1957; Montreal, Mus. F.A.). Also in this period Leduc began to produce tapestries, using designs similar to those in his paintings, such as *Totemic Meeting at Chilkat* (1956; Montreal, Mus. F.A.). In 1959 he returned to live in France; from this time his paintings became curvaceous and less geometric. From 1964 to 1965 he produced a series of works using two colours only, such as *Green Binary Chromatism* (1964; Montreal, Mus. A. Contemp.). He continued in this style, using several colours and concentrating on the problem of light. In 1973 he produced a series of seven tapestries entitled *The 7 Days*.

### BIBLIOGRAPHY

*Fernand Leduc* (exh. cat. by G. Viau, Ottawa, N.G., 1970)

*Rétrospective Fernand Leduc* (exh. cat. by B. Teyssèdre, Montreal, Mus. A. Contemp., 1970)

*Tapisseries Les 7 Jours* (exh. cat. by J.-J. Lévêque, Paris, Cent. Cult. Can., 1973)

*Microchrome Gris Puissance 6: Fernand Leduc* (exh. cat. by R. Le Bihan, Paris, Cent. Cult. Can., 1977)

□

**Le Duc, Gabriel** (*b* Paris, 1623 or 1625; *d* Paris, 17 May 1696). French architect. He was the son of Gabriel Le Duc (*d* 1654), Master Mason of Paris, and Catherine Le Grand. He travelled in 1647 to Italy (a journey very much the fashion in Paris at the time), where he took notes on ancient and modern monuments, including Michelangelo's Porta Pia in Rome.

Back in Paris by 1649, Le Duc worked in collaboration with his father until he was engaged in 1654 to work on the construction of the abbey of Val-de-Grâce. There he supervised the construction of the church and its outbuildings, under the orders of Pierre Le Muet. His responsibilities were increased in 1664, when he was entrusted with some of the church fittings—choir stalls, cloister railings and possibly the railings of the baldacchino. This baldacchino was for a long time attributed to Gianlorenzo Bernini, but the legal documents name Le Muet and Le Duc without specifying which of the two was the maker of the work.

Le Duc worked at the Val-de-Grâce site until 1667 and also on other sites during the same period. In 1663 he succeeded Pierre Le Muet, Libéral Bruand and Robert Boudin as supervisor of the construction of the convent of the Discalced Augustinians, where he was responsible in particular for the design of the high altar (destr. 1739). This was situated in front of a small chapel decorated with openwork and was related to a type of high altar that first appeared in 1660. Le Duc also used the same design for St Denis-de-la-Chartre in 1665.

After the death of François Le Vau in 1676, Le Duc took over the construction of the church of St Louis-en-l'Ile, where he designed the roof timbering of the transept and of the bell-tower above it. During the same period he reconstructed the portal of the church of St Josse after the widening of the Rue Aubry-le-Boucher. He made evaluations for the administrators of the Hôtel-Dieu, who commissioned him in 1671 to construct a hôtel in Rue St Dominique (destr. 19th century), which is visible in two engravings by Jean Marot (Paris, Bib. N.). The hôtel was situated between a courtyard and garden, as was fashionable; there was also a portico forming the façade of the main building, an unusual element in French architecture at that time. There are similar porticos at the Hôtel Lambert (by Le Vau) and at the Hôtel Sagonne (by Jules Hardouin Mansart). With this feature Le Duc brought out the qualities of the façades while respecting the taste of his contemporaries for symmetry and regularity.

Although less distinguished than Le Vau and Mansart, Le Duc was no less respected by his contemporaries, as was demonstrated by his participation in the construction of Val-de-Grâce, second only to the Palais du Louvre in importance in Paris at that time. One of his sons, Guillaume Le Duc (b after 1672) was architect to Louis XIV.

BIBLIOGRAPHY

G. Brice: *Description de la ville de Paris et ce qu'elle contient de plus remarquable* (Paris, 1684, rev. 1752)

C. Mignot: 'L'Eglise du Val-de-Grâce au Faubourg Saint Jacques de Paris: Architecture et décor', *Bull. Soc. Hist. A. Fr.* (1975), pp. 101–36

R. M. Carpier: *L'Architecte parisien Gabriel Le Duc, XVIIe siècle* (diss., U. Paris IV, 1983)

R. M. CARPIER-BIENFAIT

**Leduc, Ozias** (*b* Saint-Hilaire, Qué., 8 Oct 1864; *d* Saint-Hyacinthe, Qué., 16 June 1955). Canadian painter. He worked on murals in various Québec churches as an assistant to Adolphe Rho (1839–1905) and Luigi Cappello (1843–1903). His first easel paintings were still-lifes made up of everyday objects taken from his surroundings (e.g. *Three Apples*, 1887; Montreal, Mus. F.A.) and portraits of family and friends that already show the intimate and calm quality that characterizes all his work. In 1897 he went for seven months to study in Paris, where he familiarized himself with the work of French muralists. In murals for 31 churches and chapels in Québec, Nova Scotia and New England, Leduc sought to reconcile a narrative and didactic treatment of religious iconography with a Symbolist interpretation of light and colour. His works after 1916—the church of St-Enfant-Jésus of Mile End, Montreal (*c.* 1916), the chapel of the Archbishop of Sherbrooke (1922–33), the baptistery of Notre-Dame of Montreal and the church of Notre-Dame de la Présentation, South Shawinigan—are integrated into their architectural surroundings and relate iconographically to their cultural and religious context.

Leduc's secular paintings, such as *Green Apples* (1914–15; Ottawa, N.G.), suggest a mystical interpretation of reality. In 1913 he began to paint a series of landscapes (e.g. *Mauve Twilight*, 1921; Montreal, Mus. F.A.), all of which suggest symbolic interpretations. Although Leduc was not an innovator, working outside contemporary artistic tendencies, his works bear witness to an independence of spirit and a wealth of ideas. He wrote a large number of essays and poems in which he pursued his theoretical reflections on the definition and functions of art, emphasizing its role as an intermediary between humanity and the divine. Leduc fostered the talent of Paul-Emile Borduas, who assisted him in church decoration from *c.* 1920 to 1932.

UNPUBLISHED SOURCES

Montreal, Archvs N. Qué. [corr., diaries, essays and poems]

BIBLIOGRAPHY

*Ozias Leduc: Symbolist and Religious Painting/Peinture symboliste et religieuse* (exh. cat. by J.-R. Ostiguy, Ottawa, N.G., 1974) [parallel text]

*Ozias Leduc, the Draughtsman* (exh. cat. by L. Lacroix and others, Montreal, Concordia U., 1978)

J. C. Stirling: *Ozias Leduc et la décoration intérieure de l'église de Saint-Hilaire* (Quebec, 1985)

*Contemplative Scenes: The Landscape of Ozias Leduc* (exh. cat. by L. Beaudry, Montreal, Mus. F.A., 1986)

LAURIER LACROIX

**Lee [Alee], John** (*fl c.* 1507–33). English architect. He is first mentioned at King's College, Cambridge, in May 1507 and was joint master mason for the chapel there with John Wastell from 1509 to 1515. He is recorded as having received payments and other rewards from August 1509 but not for design nor construction work. From February 1512 he was referred to as Mr Lee, and he signed the final account on 29 July 1515 as John Alee. In 1524 Lee designed the tomb of *Bishop John Fisher* and gave 'advice' on the chantry to contain it at St John's College, Cambridge, when he was called both 'Master Lee, the freemason' and 'Master Mason of Ely'. He was paid to construct the tomb in 1532–3 (destr. 1773). At Ely Cathedral, the chantry of Bishop West (1534) and the cloister campaign date from his time as master mason. The Fisher chantry (part destr.) was a Late Gothic monument, with mouldings drawn from the contemporary royal workshop style of Westminster Abbey, although the tomb itself was fully Renaissance in style, with 'antique' angle pilasters, egg-and-dart cornices, wreaths and Classical figures. The West chantry at Ely also freely combines Late Gothic designs and Renaissance motifs, with putti, urns and 'antique' inscriptions jumbled among Gothic canopies, tracery and a Late Gothic net vault. This vault is paralleled in one of the west front niches at King's College Chapel, added after Wastell's departure in July 1515. Lee was an early English exponent of the Renaissance style, which he mixed happily with florid Late Gothic motifs.

BIBLIOGRAPHY

Harvey

R. Willis: *The Architectural History of the University of Cambridge*, ed. J. W. Clark, 4 vols (Cambridge, 1886)

F. Woodman: *King's College Chapel, Cambridge* (London, 1986) [pls]

FRANCIS WOODMAN

**Lee, Sir Richard** (*b c.* 1513; *d* ?Sopwell, Herts, 1575). English engineer. It was probably as a mason that Lee was employed on the fortifications at Calais in 1533. In 1536, while still in his twenties, he was appointed Surveyor of the Works there and was responsible for a major programme of fortification designed to give the town the protection of artillery. In 1542 Lee left Calais with a considerable reputation both as a military engineer and as a man who enjoyed Henry VIII's confidence, and in 1544 he was appointed to the profitable office of General Receiver of the Court of Wards and Liveries. In the spring of that year he took part in the Scottish campaign, and he was knighted at Leith. From 1545 to 1547 he held the post of Surveyor of the King's Works, but he continued to be preoccupied with military rather than civil works, notably at Boulogne in 1544 and on the Scottish border, where he directed all the fortifications that maintained the English presence in Scotland from 1547 to 1550. In 1558 Lee initiated the greatest English military work of the 16th century, a line of bastions and ramparts enclosing the town of Berwick-upon-Tweed. Lee had acquired former monastic property at Sopwell near St Albans, Herts, in the 1540s. He was buried in St Peter's Church at St Albans.

Lee probably owed his successful career to his organizing ability as much as to his skill as a military architect. His earlier works at Calais, designed under the personal direction of Henry VIII, were of a rounded type similar to the new English coastal forts, and it was not until later that he learnt the principles of the Italian angle-bastion that he applied at Berwick.

BIBLIOGRAPHY

*DNB*; Harvey

H. M. Colvin, ed.: *History of the King's Works*, iii, iv (London, 1975, 1982)

HOWARD COLVIN

**Lee, Russell** (*b* Ottawa, IL, 21 July 1903; *d* Austin, TX, 28 Aug 1986). American photographer. He studied chemical engineering at Lehigh University, Bethlehem, PA, from 1917 to 1921. After marrying a painter, Doris Emrick, in 1927 he was inspired to enrol for a painting course at the California School of Fine Arts in San Francisco (1929–31). From 1931 to 1935 he attended classes run by John Sloan at the Art Students League, New York. He bought his first camera as an aid to his drawing but soon became more interested in the medium of photography. By 1935 he had sold some of his work to magazines.

Upon hearing about the project established by the Resettlement Administration (RA; later Farm Security Administration) to document the rural poverty caused by the Dust Bowl, Lee applied to join the photographic team and worked under Roy Stryker (1893–1975) from 1936 to 1942. He applied his frank, documentary approach in photographs such as *Spiro, Oklahoma* (1939; see Hurley, 1978, p. 76) of a mother and child bedded down on a dirty patchwork quilt in the open, and in many other images of migrant families, decrepit shacks and post-Depression deprivation.

Following his experience with the RA, Lee worked for the Office of War Information. Dissatisfaction with the nature of the work led him to leave in 1942 to take aerial photographs for the Air Transport Command (ATC) (1943–5). When World War II ended he left the ATC and became involved in a medical survey of the coal industry. His straight, clearcut style, necessary in a project such as this, resulted in such images as *Wyoming County, West Virginia* (1946; see Hurley, 1978, p. 124), which showed a long queue of miners, their serious faces looking suspiciously into the camera. From 1947 to 1965 Lee worked as an industrial and magazine photographer; publishers of his work included *The Lamp*, the journal of Standard Oil of New Jersey. Afterwards he became an independent photographer, also teaching in some universities.

PHOTOGRAPHIC PUBLICATIONS

J. T. Boone, ed.: *A Medical Survey of the Bituminous Coal Industry* (Washington, DC, 1947)

*Image of Italy* (Austin, 1966)

*Executive Order: The Internment of 110,000 Japanese Americans* (San Francisco, 1972)

BIBLIOGRAPHY

*Russell Lee: Retrospective Exhibition, 1934–1964* (exh. cat., Austin, U. TX, Huntington A.G.; San Antonio, TX, Witte Mus.; Washington, DC, Smithsonian Inst.; 1965)

F. J. Hurley: *Russell Lee: Photographer* (New York, 1978)

SAMANTHA ROBERTS

**Lee, Thomas Stirling** (*b* London, 16 March 1856; *d* London, 28 June 1916). English sculptor. He entered the Royal Academy Schools in 1875, won the Gold Medal in 1877 and, with the *Death of Abel* (untraced), won the travelling scholarship in 1879. He studied in Paris under Pierre-Jules Cavelier at the Ecole des Beaux-Arts in 1880–81, and in Rome in 1881–3. After a period in the studio of Birnie Philip he won the competition for reliefs for St George's Hall, Liverpool, with two series in marble, the *Story of Justice* and the *Story of Liverpool* (1886–94). Edmund Gosse criticized the *Dawn of Womanhood* (exh. RA 1893), which formed part of one of these series, for its 'crude realism', but Spielmann considered them 'the finest reliefs produced in the country', praising Lee's choice of materials and beautiful studies of the human form in narrative compositions. Other architectural work includes carved religious and allegorical figures in low relief on the Lindley clock tower (1902), Huddersfield, and bronze gates for the Adelphi Bank (1903), Liverpool.

With James Havard Thomas, Lee pioneered direct carving without assistants for marble work, following the example of the Greeks. His interest in technique led to his involvement with Alfred Gilbert in reviving the lost-wax process of bronze-casting, and he wrote papers on stone-carving (Architectural Association, 1895) and sculptors' methods (1892). He developed an idealizing style which he applied to allegorical subjects, such as the silver figure entitled the *Music of the Wind* (1907; Leeds, C.A.G.), and to portraits, such as *Margaret Clausen* (*c.* 1907; London, Tate), in which the fluidity of the figure belies the solidity of the marble. He was a founder-member of the New English Art Club (1886) and of the Royal Society of British Sculptors (1904), and a member of the Art Workers' Guild from 1889.

WRITINGS

'Sculpture and Sculptors' Methods on Relation to Architecture', *J. Proc. RIBA*, n. s., viii (1892), pp. 55–8
'Sculpture', *AA Notes*, xi/97 (1895), pp. 153–4

BIBLIOGRAPHY

E. Gosse: 'The New Sculpture', *A. J.* [London] (1894), pp. 200–02, 277
M. H. Spielmann: *British Sculpture and Sculptors of Today* (London, 1901), p. 66
B. Read: *Victorian Sculpture* (London, 1982)
S. Beattie: *The New Sculpture* (London, 1983)

FIONA PEARSON

**Lee, Vernon** [Paget, Violet] (*b* Château Saint-Leonard, nr Boulogne, 14 Oct 1856; *d* Villa Il Palmerino, nr Florence, 13 Feb 1935). English writer and art historian. Born of English parents, she was privately educated in Europe and was the childhood friend of John Singer Sargent. Her first published art-historical work, *Belcaro* (London, 1881), propounds the aesthetic primacy of form as combining intellectual conception and the physical embodiment of beauty, but with consideration also given to the demands of the materials employed. Viewing the artist as only part of the man, she opposed with great clarity Ruskin's equation of art with morality, holding that though art has no moral meaning, it has a moral value—the creation of happiness. In *Euphorion* (London, 1884), however, the partisan nature of her criticism obscures the scholarly insights of her essays on Renaissance art. The enthusiastic reception it nevertheless received was overturned with the publication of her novel, *Miss Brown* (Edinburgh, 1884), a savage and clumsy satire on the Pre-Raphaelites, whom she had met on her first visit to England in 1881 and among whom it caused much hostility.

*Juvenilia* (London, 1887), although often rambling, advocates the absorption of art into everyday life. The theme is developed in *Althea* (London, 1894), *Renaissance Fancies and Studies* (London, 1895) and *Laurus Nobilis* (London, 1909); in the second of these Lee also demonstrates a continuing awareness of the artist's relation to the materials and attitudes of his or her age. Her most controversial publications were two articles written with Clementine Anstruther-Thomson on 'Beauty and Ugliness' (*Contemporary Review*, lxxii, 1897; reprinted with other essays, London, 1912). They proposed a theory of psychological and physiological aesthetics, which suggested that there could be objective physical responses to aesthetic phenomena. The articles attracted some critical attention, especially in Germany, but elicited the (unfounded) charge of plagiarism from an erstwhile friend Bernard Berenson; Lee claimed that at the time neither of them was aware of Theodor Lipps's related theory of *Einfühlung* (empathy).

Lee's final work on aesthetics in art, *The Beautiful* (Cambridge, 1913), summarizes, cogently and concisely, her earlier views that it is 'shape' (form) that determines an appreciation of art, contemplated with 'attention', 'memory' and an 'empathetic movement'. Of her essays on gardening, the most measured and authoritative are in *Limbo* (London, 1897), where she outlines the history of the Italian garden and garden sculpture, contrasting the modern flower garden with the architectural garden of the 16th and 17th centuries. In *Hortus Vitae* (London, 1904) the concept of the garden was used for impressionistic and unhistorical musings, much along the lines of *Genius Loci* (London, 1899), travel writings that received, to her chagrin, greater acclaim than her more scholarly texts. Among her later publications are contributions to Anstruther-Thomson's *Art and Man* (London, 1924) and to a memorial of Sargent.

WRITINGS

*Beauty and Ugliness* (London, 1912)
Preface to C. Anstruther-Thomson: *Art and Man* (London, 1924), pp. 3–112
'John Singer Sargent *in memoriam*' in E. Charteris: *John Sargent* (London, 1927), pp. 233–55
I. Cooper Wills, ed.: *Letters* (London, 1937) [privately printed]

BIBLIOGRAPHY

P. Gunn: *Vernon Lee* (London, 1964)
V. Colby: The Singular Anomaly: *Women Novelists of the Nineteenth Century* (New York and London, 1970), pp. 235–304

EDWINA BURNESS

**Lee, Wesley Duke** (*b* São Paulo, 21 Dec 1931). Brazilian painter and draughtsman. In the 1950s he studied painting and printmaking in São Paulo, New York and Paris. His early work was influenced by Dada, especially Duchamp, and by Pop art, for example *The [red-light] District: Rosario Did Not Go Away. Why?* (1964; Nagaoka, Contemp. A. Mus.). At the João Sebastião Bar in São Paulo in 1963 he staged the first happening in Brazil. He was an influential promoter of new trends in São Paulo, especially in the 1960s and 1970s, for example through his creation of the Rex Gallery and the newspaper *Rex Time* in 1966–7. His espousal of mixed media led him to carry out a series of proposals for the synthesis of the arts from 1964 to 1968; the installation *Helicóptero*, a circular structure 4 m in diameter, painted on both sides and containing electrical components (1967; São Paulo, Mus. A. Assis Châteaubriand), was exhibited at the opening of the National Museum of Modern Art in Tokyo in 1969. He explored the aesthetic possibilities offered by new technology with characteristic irony and satire.

BIBLIOGRAPHY

*Report on the Art and Technology Program* (exh. cat. by M. Tuchman, Los Angeles, CA, Co. Mus. A., 1970)
C. Teixeira da Costa: *Wesley Duke Lee* (Rio de Janeiro, 1980)
A. Amaral: *Arte e meio artístico—entre a feijoada e o x-burguer* [Art and artistic milieu—between the bean stew and the x-burger] (São Paulo, 1983), pp. 249–53

ROBERTO PONTUAL

**Leech, John** (*b* Southwark, London, 29 Aug 1817; *d* London, 30 Oct 1864). English illustrator and caricaturist. He showed promise in drawing from an early age. He was educated at Charterhouse School, Surrey, and entered St Bartholomew's Hospital, London, to study medicine, where he showed aptitude in anatomical drawing. His family's bankruptcy in 1830 ended this career, and he was compelled to find work as an artist to support himself. Friendships with William Makepeace Thackeray at Charterhouse and with the comic writers Albert Smith and

Percival Leigh at St Bartholomew's gave him useful connections in illustration and journalism.

In 1836 Leech briefly studied at Versailles with an unidentified French caricaturist, being one of the few British artists to do so. Returning to Britain, he brought a new approach to social satire in the tradition of the French *comédie humaine*. His first productions in this style were a series of lithographs, published by W. Soffe as *Droll Doings* and *Funny Characters* (1836–8; e.g. see Houfe, p. 37), spirited exercises in a technique he shortly abandoned. With the revival of wood-engraving and the burgeoning of comic magazines in this medium, Leech learnt the art from the engraver Orrin Smith and joined the staff of *Bentley's Miscellany* in 1840. With the founding of *Punch* in 1841, Leech gradually established himself as the foremost artist of early Victorian pictorial satire in its pages. His work epitomizes the change in taste from the savagery of Regency caricature to the more gentle world of bourgeois domestic humour. He was less strong in draughtsmanship than some contemporaries, but his weekly *Punch* sketches provided a new freedom in execution and a vibrant view of the world that is an unerring barometer of Victorian trends and fashions.

From 1843 Leech shared the *Punch* cartoons with John Tenniel, completing 720 before 1864. He was at his best in political work, such as *Substance and Shadow* (*Punch*, v, 1843, p. 23), a biting attack on the government for favouring, in the decoration of the new Houses of Parliament, a genteel brand of High Art that singularly failed to address the pressing social issues of the time. (Leech's subtitle, 'Cartoon No. 1', was the first use of the word in its modern sense.) His most popular illustrations, however, were of sport, in particular the hunting field and the depiction of the follies of fashion. A wider public enjoyed his work through the pages of R. S. Surtees's novels, which he illustrated with wit and vigour between 1853 and 1864, immortalizing the characters of Soapy Sponge and Mr Jorrocks in *Mr Sponge's Sporting Tour* (London, 1853) and *Handley Cross* (London, 1854). Leech contributed illustrations to numerous novels, ballads, short stories and children's books between 1840 and his death, most notably for Charles Dickens in *A Christmas Carol* (London, 1843–4), *The Battle of Life* (London, 1846), *The Haunted Man* (London, 1847–8) and volumes by such other Victorian writers as Douglas Jerrold, Mark Lemon and R. H. Barham.

Leech contributed extensively to illustrated periodicals including *The New Monthly Magazine*, *The Illuminated Magazine*, *The Illustrated London News* and *The Field*. His circle included such leading artists as Sir John Everett Millais, William Powell Frith and Augustus Egg, who were influenced by his scenes of everyday life. From 1860 Leech experimented with a new process for producing oil sketches, using enlarged copies of his own *Punch* engravings printed on canvas that he tinted in oils. The series was exhibited at the Egyptian Hall, London, in 1862 and was well received. Despite continental cures, ill health and strain overtook him. A set of enlarged chromolithographs of his work, which remained popular for the rest of the 19th century, was published (London, 1865) by Agnew's.

PRINTS

*Droll Doings* (London, 1836–8)
*Funny Characters* (London, 1837–8)
*The Human Face Divine and De Vino* (London, 1837–8)

BIBLIOGRAPHY

*DNB*
W. M. Thackeray: 'John Leech's Pictures of Life and Character', *Q. Rev.* (1854), pp. 75–86
F. G. Kitton: *John Leech, Artist and Humorist: A Biographical Sketch* (London, 1883, rev. 1884)
W. P. Frith: *John Leech: His Life and Work*, 2 vols (London, 1891)
H. Silver: 'The Art Life of John Leech', *Mag. A.*, xvi (1893), pp. 115–20
——: 'The Home Life of John Leech', *Mag. A.*, xvi (1893), pp. 162–8
M. H. Spielmann: *The History of Punch* (London, 1895), pp. 170–77
J. R. Cohen: *Charles Dickens and his Original Illustrators* (Columbus, 1980), pp. 141–51
S. Houfe: *John Leech and the Victorian Scene* (Woodbridge, 1984) [complete list of published work]

SIMON HOUFE

**Leech, William John** (*b* Dublin, 10 April 1881; *d* Guildford, Surrey, 16 July 1968). Irish painter. The son of a law professor at Trinity College, Dublin, he studied at the Metropolitan School of Art and at the Royal Hibernian Academy (RHA) schools in Dublin (1899–1901), where he was taught by Walter Osborne. He exhibited at the RHA from 1900, becoming an Academician in 1910.

Leech went to Paris in 1901, studying at the Académie Julian, and lived at Concarneau in Brittany from *c.* 1903 to 1908. His Breton work varied between sombre interiors influenced by William Orpen such as *Interior of a Barber's Shop* (Cork, Crawford Mun. A. G.), pale sketches in the style of James Abbott McNeill Whistler and large 'Impressionistic' studies of figures in a landscape, for example *Convent Garden, Brittany* (Dublin, N.G.). His brightly coloured landscapes and garden scenes feature strong contrasts of sunlight and shadow, while his interiors show the influence of Pierre Bonnard and English contemporaries such as Walter Sickert and Gerald Kelly (*b* 1878). His work is characterized by an unusual perspective: an aerial viewpoint or asymmetrical composition. In 1910 Leech and his family moved to London, where in 1912 he held a one-man show of Swiss and Italian landscapes at the Goupil Gallery. Subsequently he exhibited at the Paris Salon in 1913–14, 1919 and 1920. He returned to France after the war, working at Concarneau from *c.* 1925 to 1933. He finally settled in Guildford, exhibiting at the RHA and the New English Art Club and holding three one-man shows at the Dawson Gallery, Dublin. Leech rarely dated his paintings, so it is difficult to establish an accurate chronology for them. His work can be seen in Dublin at the National Gallery and the Hugh Lane Municipal Gallery and in Belfast at the Ulster Museum.

BIBLIOGRAPHY
A. Denson: *An Irish Artist: W. J. Leech, R.H.A., 1881–1968*, 2 vols (Kendal, 1968–9)
——: 'W. J. Leech, R.H.A.: A Great Irish Artist (1881–1968)', *Capuchin Annu.* (1974), pp. 119–27
K. McContey: *A Free Spirit: Irish Art, 1860–1940* (London, 1990)
D. Ferran: *William Leech, 1881–1968* (Dublin, 1992)
——: 'W. J. Leech's Brittany', *Irish A. Rev.*, 1993, pp. 224–32
*William John Leech* (cxh. cat. by D. Ferran, Dublin, N.G.; Belfast, Ulster Mus., 1996)
*The Irish Impressionists* (exh. cat. by J. Campbell, Dublin, N.G., 1984), pp. 111–14, 259–65

JULIAN CAMPBELL

**Leeghwater, Jan Adriaensz.** (*b* De Rijp, 1575; *d* Amsterdam, 1650). Dutch architect and engineer. He was probably trained as a carpenter by his father, Adriaensz. Symonsz. While working as a millwright he discovered the possibility of using windmills to pump water from dammed lakes. His work on various land reclamation schemes north of Amsterdam, such as the Beemster (1607–12, involving 40 windmills) and the Purmer (from 1624), achieved great renown and he received various commissions from abroad. In 1630 he erected his only known building, the combined weigh-house and town hall in De Rijp. It is a small brick building of two storeys, free-standing on three sides. The façade is enlivened with striated brickwork, facing bricks and keystones in the relieving arches above the windows. The main elevation is surmounted by a gable with scrolled volutes in stone. The other elevations are surmounted by gables, crowned with a sphere on a segmental pediment. The town hall indicates that he was a provincial architect who continued to use the formal language of the Dutch Renaissance with a Mannerist strain even when it was no longer employed in the large cities.

BWN

BIBLIOGRAPHY
F. A. J. Vermeulen: *Handboek tot de geschiedenis der Nederlandsche bouwkunst*, [Handbook of the history of Dutch architecture] iii (The Hague, 1941)
J. J. F. W. van Agt: *De Nederlandse monumenten van geschiedenis en kunst*, viii (The Hague, 1953)

PAUL H. REM

**Lee-Johnson, Eric** (*b* Suva, Fiji, 8 Nov 1908; *d* Auckland, April 1993). New Zealand painter and photographer. He studied at the Elam School of Art, Auckland (1924–6). From 1930 to 1938 he worked in London, attending classes at the Central School of Art and Design. On his return to New Zealand he lived in various country towns in the Auckland and Northland districts, where he painted the scenes of provincial New Zealand on which his reputation rests (e.g. *Creamstand*, ink and watercolour, *c.* 1950; Wellington, Victoria U.). He interpreted the country towns and people of northern New Zealand in a romantic-realist style akin to the example of John Piper and Paul Nash. Lee-Johnson's talents lay in seizing on the typical and giving his imagery a symbolic force, as in his *Assaulted Landscape* series (1946–50). Most of his work is in watercolour; he was also active as a photographer.

BIBLIOGRAPHY
E. H. McCormick: *Eric Lee-Johnson* (Hamilton, 1956)

MICHAEL DUNN

**Lee Kang-so.** *See* KANG SO LEE.

**Leemput** [Lemmput; Lemput], **Remi van** [Remee; Remy] [Vallemput, Remigius; Vanlimpitt, Remigeus] (*bapt* Antwerp, 19 Dec 1607; *d* London, *bur* 9 Nov 1675). Flemish (possibly French) painter, copyist, collector and dealer, active in England. In 1635 he was living in the newly developed area of Covent Garden, London; at that time he was closely associated with Anthony van Dyck and presumably assisted in his studio. Through his varied activities, van Leemput became a leading figure in the London art world, and he assembled a major collection of paintings and drawings. He bought extensively when Charles I's collections were sold in 1649–51; his purchases included works attributed to Titian, Giorgione, Correggio and Andrea del Sarto. Later he acquired the great equestrian portrait by van Dyck of *Charles I with M. de St Antoine* (British Royal Col.), which he apparently attempted to sell in Antwerp but asked too high a price. It was still with him at the Restoration in 1660, when it was recovered from him for Charles II.

Although van Leemput painted original works, he was best known for his small-scale copies after van Dyck and others. A series of '14 . . . Ladies heads Copys by Remy' (described thus in Queen Anne's inventory) is in the Royal Collection, as is a copy after Sir Peter Lely's *Henry Hyde, Viscount Cornbury and Theodosia, Viscountess Cornbury*. In 1667 Charles II commissioned a small copy of Hans Holbein the younger's wall painting of *Henry VII, Elizabeth of York, Henry VIII and Jane Seymour* at Whitehall Palace, London, for which van Leemput was reputedly paid £150. This picture (British Royal Col.) and a further copy (Petworth House, W. Sussex, NT) that van Leemput painted in 1669 are the only records of Holbein's original composition, destroyed by fire in 1698.

Van Leemput is listed in various inventories simply as 'Remee', and there are many references to him as 'Old Remy'. His burial is registered under the name Remigeus Vanlimpitt. Of his several children, a son, Giovanni Remigio, became a copyist in Rome, and a daughter, Mary, also became a painter and married Thomas, son of Robert Streeter, the Serjeant-Painter.

BIBLIOGRAPHY
B. Buckeridge: 'An Essay towards an English School of Painters', *The Art of Painting* (London, 1706, 3/1754/R 1969), pp. 413–14 [Eng. trans. by J. Savage of R. de Piles: *Abrégé de la vie des peintres* (Paris, 1699)]
H. Walpole: *Anecdotes of Painting in England* (1762–71); ed. R. N. Wornum (1849), ii, pp. 432–3
'The Note-books of George Vertue', *Walpole Soc.*, xxviii (1930), xx (1932), xxiv (1936) [indexed in xxix (1947)], xxx (1955), p. 162
E. Croft-Murray: *Decorative Painting in England, 1537–1837*, i (London, 1962), pp. 19–20, 161, 228
O. Millar: *The Tudor, Stuart and Early Georgian Pictures in the Collection of Her Majesty The Queen* (London, 1963)
M. Edmond: 'Limners and Picturemakers', *Walpole Soc.*, xlvii (1980), pp. 187, 214

RICHARD JEFFREE

**Leemputten, van.** *See* VAN LEEMPUTTEN.

**Leeson, Joseph**, 1st Earl of Milltown (*b* ?Dublin, 11 March 1701; *d* Dublin, 2 Oct 1783). Irish politician, patron and collector. He was the heir to a Dublin brewery and sat in the Irish House of Commons from 1743 until 1756; he was created Viscount Russborough in the peerage of Ireland in 1760 and Earl of Milltown in 1763. The scale of the fortune Leeson inherited was matched by the distinction of Russborough, near Blessington, Co. Wicklow, the mansion built for him in 1742–55 by Richard Castle. It is unquestionably one of the finest Palladian houses in Ireland. Leeson's taste in architecture was complemented by that for pictures and was fortified by two visits to Italy, the first in 1744–5, the second, accompanied by his son Joseph Leeson (1730–1801; later 2nd Earl of Milltown) and nephew Joseph Henry of Straffan, in 1750–52. Among the paintings Leeson acquired were Lorenzo Lippi's *Angelica and Medoro* (*c.* 1645) and Giovanni Paolo Panini's *Campo Vaccino* and *The Colosseum* (1740; all Dublin, N.G.), but his importance in the history of Anglo-Irish taste owes more to his patronage of living artists than to his collecting activities. In 1744 he was the first Briton to sit to Pompeo Batoni (Dublin, N.G.) and on his second tour he secured landscapes by Joseph Vernet and scagliola table-tops from Pietro Belloni. He appears in Joshua Reynolds's *Parody of the School of Athens* (Dublin, N.G.), commissioned by his nephew Joseph Henry, and in other caricature groups by Reynolds. Most of the Milltown collection was presented to the National Gallery of Ireland in 1902, but a series of Vernets depicting *Morning*, *Noon*, *Evening* and *Night* is at Russborough.

BIBLIOGRAPHY

J. Cornforth: 'Russborough, Co. Wicklow', *Country Life*, cxxxiv (Dec 1963), pp. 1464–7, 1623–7, 1686–90

M. Wynne: 'The Milltowns as Patrons', *Apollo*, xcix (1974), pp. 104–11

FRANCIS RUSSELL

**Leest, Antonij van** (*b* Antwerp, *c.* 1545; *d* Antwerp, 1592). Flemish woodcutter and engraver. He entered the Guild of St Luke in Antwerp as a pupil of Bernard van de Putte (1528–80) in 1558–9 and is known primarily for the book illustrations that he executed while working for Christoph Plantin. Van Leest depicted a wide range of subjects in his woodcuts, including biblical themes in several editions of the New Testament (Flem. edns, 1571 and 1578; Fr. edn, 1573) and allegorical images such as those in J. B. Houwaert's *Declaratie van die triumphante incompst van den ... prince van Oraignien binnen die princelijke stadt van Brussele, 1578* ('Declaration of the triumphal entry of the ... Prince of Orange into the princely city of Brussels, 1578; Antwerp, 1579), which contains images alluding to contemporary politics. There are images of figures in exotic costume in Sluperius's *Omne fere gentium* (Antwerp, 1572) and in Nicolas de Nicolay's *Les Navigations pérégrinations et voyages faicts à la Turquie* (Antwerp, 1576) and vignettes with geometrical and allegorical figures in Cornelis Gemma's *De arte cyclognomica* (Antwerp, 1575–8). Van Leest also made medical vignettes to illustrate Gemma's *De naturis divinis ... spectaculis* (Antwerp, 1575). Finally, examples of botanical illustrations by the artist can be found in works by C. Clusius and R. Dodonaeus.

Van Leest is also known to have made engravings after Pieter van der Borcht and Pieter Huys and may also have made some original designs. It is possible that between 1572 and 1575 he may have visited Paris, where he might have copied designs for his illustrations for Sluperius. Van Leest signed his work 'A' or with the monogram 'AVL'. His style of engraving seems rather stiff and schematic and brings little depth to his images.

BIBLIOGRAPHY

Bénézit; Hollstein: *Dut. & Flem.*; Thieme–Becker

JETTY E. VAN DER STERRE

**Leeuw, Willem van der** (*b* Antwerp, *c.* 1603; *d* Antwerp, ?1665). Flemish etcher and engraver. He trained with Pieter Soutman, himself a pupil of Rubens, and engraved reproductions of paintings by Rubens, Rembrandt and Jan Lievens. His engravings after Rubens include *Lot and his Daughters* (Hollstein, no. 1), the *Martyrdom of St Catherine* (Hollstein, no. 7) and a few hunting scenes. Examples of his work after Rembrandt are *David Playing the Harp before Saul* (Hollstein, no. 2), *Tobias and his Wife* (Hollstein, no. 4) and a number of portraits of women (e.g. Hollstein, nos 15–16). Occasionally van der Leeuw managed to create an attractive chiaroscuro effect, as in *Daniel in the Lion's Den* (Hollstein, no. 3).

BIBLIOGRAPHY

Hollstein: *Dut. & Flem.*; Thieme–Becker

CHRISTIAN COPPENS

**Leeward Islands.** *See under* ANTILLES, LESSER.

**Le Fauconnier, Henri** (*b* Hesdin, Pas-de-Calais, 1881; *d* Paris, Jan 1946). French painter. He was the son of a physician and enrolled in 1900 at the Université de Paris to study law. After the death of his father, he attended the studio of Jean-Paul Laurens for a year, moving to the Académie Julian in 1902. In 1905 he exhibited for the first time at the Salon des Indépendants and shared an exhibition with the painter and printmaker Georges Le Meilleur (1861–1945), under the auspices of L'Independance Artistique (an association that exhibited at several venues in Paris). The following year Le Meilleur took Le Fauconnier on a painting trip to Brittany, where the wild, rocky shore around the fishing village of Ploumanac'h made an indelible impression. Until this trip Le Fauconnier was ranked, along with Braque, as a talented follower of Matisse, but by the Salon des Indépendants of 1908 he was separated from the younger Fauve painters for the boldness and simplification of his forms.

In 1907 Le Fauconnier met a Russian woman, Maroussia Baranikoff, with whom he eloped (they married in 1912) to Ploumanac'h, where they lived for about two years, with only occasional trips to Paris. From this period date his increasingly geometricized landscapes, the earliest of which, *Rocks at the Edge of the Sea: The Path of the Customs Officers* (1907; New York, Salander–O'Reilly Gals), is a dramatic but sober interpretation of the complex structure of huge boulders, painted in a Cubist style that Apollinaire in 1913 described as 'physical cubism'. Le Fauconnier, unaware of the developments of Braque and Picasso, explored this new style not only in landscapes but also in nudes and portraits such as *The Simpleton* (1908; Lyon, Mus. St Pierre A. Contemp.) and the portrait of the poet *Pierre-Jean Jouve* (1909; Paris, Pompidou). In 1910 Kandinsky asked him for an article as well as a painting for the second exhibition of the NEUE KÜNSTLERVEREINIGUNG MÜNCHEN. Le Fauconnier sent the painting *Abundance* (Stockholm, Mod. Mus.) and the preface 'Das Kunstwerk', which was printed in early September 1910, and which was the first written statement to articulate Cubist aesthetic principles. Both reflect Le Fauconnier's blend of cerebral and emotional elements, in which emphasis is placed on the mathematical ordering of the picture plane without sacrificing the sensuality of a bold attack with the brush. This combined approach particularly interested young painters, and in 1910 Le Fauconnier's Paris studio became a mecca for artists as diverse as Paul Klee, August Macke, the Scottish painter J. D. Fergusson, the Polish artist Tadeusz Makowski, the American Anne Estelle Rice (1879–1959), the Swede Georg Pauli (1855–1935), and especially the Dutch artists Conrad Kikkert (1882–1965), Lodewijk Schelfhout (1881–1943), Leo Gestel and Petrus Alma.

At the same time French artists such as Jean Metzinger, Fernand Léger, Robert Delaunay, Albert Gleizes, Apollinaire and André Salmon visited Le Fauconnier's studio in the Rue Visconti to watch the second, over-life-size version of the *Abundance* (The Hague, Gemeentemus.) brought to completion. In the Salon des Indépendants of 1911 this work was hung beside paintings by Delaunay, Gleizes, Metzinger, Léger and Marie Laurencin in the now famous room 41, provoking the public outcry about CUBISM that launched the movement. In order to effect this kind of block hanging at the Salon the artist-members had elected Le Fauconnier as chairman of the hanging committee. Perhaps even more important, however, as indicative of the relationships observed among artists who had not previously formed a group, was the article that Metzinger wrote in the journal *Pan* (Oct–Nov 1910), the 'Note sur la peinture', linking the work of Picasso, Braque, Delaunay and Le Fauconnier for concern with mobile perspective and simultaneity, which in Le Fauconnier's case included the junction of the present with the mythological past.

Le Fauconnier's reputation peaked in 1912–13. In 1912 he sent to the Salon d'Automne the enormous painting *Mountaineers Attacked by Bears* (New York, Salander–O'Reilly Gals, see 1989 exh. cat.), which the British art critic Raymond Drey characterized as 'the most remarkable and stimulating picture in the exhibition' (*Rhythm*, Dec 1912). He was represented by 27 recent works at the third Moderne Kunstkring exhibition in Amsterdam (1913) and selected by Mondrian, Jan Toorop and Kikkert to write the preface for the catalogue. The preface is a clear exposition of Cubist principles, though the word 'Cubism' never appears. When World War I began, Le Fauconnier was in Veere, Zeeland, on a painting trip with Mondrian and Toorop. He spent the next five years in the neutral Netherlands, where he became the decisive figure in the Bergen school of Dutch painters, as well as an important influence on a group of Belgian refugees living in Amsterdam, including Gustave De Smet, Frits Van den Berghe and André De Ridder. He participated in the pacifist movement Het Signal and painted a major series of four large works blending Cubism and Expressionism, called *The Vagabond* (1915–16; priv. col., see 1959 exh. cat.), in which he developed the motif of the eye with light bulb for retina. Returning to France, he never again enjoyed his previous level of fame. Nevertheless, he was the principal artist in the Parisian gallery of Joseph Billiet, a gathering-place for painters of the political left. In the 1930s Billiet's gallery, by then directed by Pierre Worms, continued to promote Le Fauconnier as the eldest of a group of artists of social conscience who eschewed both abstraction and Surrealism. Increasingly isolated from the world of art, he was cut off by World War II from his admirers in the northern countries and for the rest of his life he lived as a recluse in Paris.

WRITINGS

*Die Auffassung unserer Zeit und das Gemälde zur Ausstellung im Museum Folkwang, Hagen ... Dezember 1912, in Neue Kunst Hans Golz* (Munich, 1913)

BIBLIOGRAPHY

J. Metzinger: 'Note sur la peinture', *Pan* (Oct–Nov 1910), pp. 649–52
A. De Ridder: *Le Fauconnier* (Brussels, 1919)
J. Romains: *Le Fauconnier* (Amiens, 1921)
——: *Le Fauconnier* (Paris, 1927)
J. Golding: *Cubism, A History and an Analysis* (London, 1959/R 1988), pp. 151–60
*Le Fauconnier* (exh. cat. by A. De Ritter, Antwerp, Kon. Mus. S. Kst., 1959)
D. Cottington: 'Le Fauconnier's L'Abondance and its Literary Background', *Apollo*, cv/180 (Feb 1977), pp. 129–30
A. H. Murray: 'Le Fauconnier's Das Kunstwerk: An Early Statement of Cubist Aesthetic Theory', *A. Mag.*, 56 (Dec 1981), pp. 125–33
D. Robbins: 'Le Fauconnier and Cubism', *Cubism* (exh. cat., New York, James Goodman Gal., 1989)
*Henri Le Fauconnier: A Pioneer Cubist* (exh. cat., New York, Salander–O'Reilly Gals, 1990)

DANIEL ROBBINS

**Lefèbvre, Claude** (*b* Fontainebleau, *bapt* 12 Sept 1632; *d* Paris, 25 April 1675). French painter and engraver. He was the son of Jean Lefèbvre (1600–75), a painter, and joined the studio of Claude d'Hoey (1585–1660) at Fontainebleau. In 1654 he was a pupil of Eustache Le Sueur in Paris and in 1655 of Charles Le Brun. Under Le Brun's direction he seems to have assisted with the cartoons (untraced) for the series of tapestries illustrating the *History of the King* (Versailles, Château). He appears to have executed a *Nativity* (untraced) for Louis XIV, but Le Brun apparently considered his compositions weak and advised him to specialize in portraiture; in 1663 he was received (*reçu*) as a member by the Académie Royale de Peinture et de Sculpture with his portrait of *Jean-Baptiste Colbert* (Versailles, Château). He was an assistant professor at the Académie from 1664. At the height of his fame he exhibited ten pictures (nine of which were portraits) at the Salon of 1673. Apart from that of *Colbert*, Lefèbvre's painted portraits are now known only through the work of such engravers as Gérard Edelinck, Nicolas de Poilly and Pierre-Louis van Schuppen. Among works attributed to him on the basis of such evidence is the portrait of *Charles Couperin with the Artist's Daughter* (Versailles, Château). He was also a talented engraver, and examples of his work in this medium include a *Self-portrait* and a portrait of *Alexandre Boudan* (see Wildenstein, figs 1 and 2). He has sometimes been confused with Roland Lefèbvre, a portrait painter who died in London in 1677.

BIBLIOGRAPHY

A.-J. Dézallier d'Argenville: *Abrégé de la vie des plus fameux peintres* (1745–52, rev. 2/1762), iv, pp. 177–81 [also in Wildenstein]
G. Wildenstein: 'Claude Lefèbvre restitué par l'estampe', *Gaz. B.-A.*, 6th ser., lxii (1963), pp. 305–13 [with cat. of prts]

D. BRÊME

**Lefebvre, Jules(-Joseph)** (*b* Tournan, Seine-et-Marne, 14 March 1836; *d* Paris, 24 Feb 1911). French painter. He studied in Leon Cogniet's studio from 1852 and competed at the Ecole des Beaux-Arts in Paris from 1853 until he won the Prix de Rome in 1861. In Rome he was influenced by Mannerism and especially by Andrea del Sarto, whose works he copied. In his *Boy Painting a Tragic Mask* (1863; Auxerre, Mus. A. & Hist.) Lefebvre introduced the precise draughtsmanship, delicate colour and a lubricity characteristic of many of his later works. In 1866 he experienced a severe depression caused by the death of his parents and one of his sisters, and by criticism of the last major work he painted in Rome, *Cornelia, Mother of the Gracchi* (untraced). After these experiences he turned from history painting to portraits and nudes; he exhibited 72 portraits in Salons between 1855 and 1898 (e.g. *Julia Foster Ward*;

Hartford, CT, Wadsworth Atheneum), but little is known about them since nearly all remain in private collections. Although he occasionally finished large-scale, ambitious paintings (e.g. *Lady Godiva*, Amiens, Mus. Picardie; *Diana Surprised*, Buenos Aires, Mus. N. B.A.), he made his reputation with nudes such as *Reclining Woman* (exh. Salon 1868; untraced). Critics praised this painting and recognized its eroticism, yet there was no scandal as there had been with Manet's *Olympia* (1863; Paris, Mus. d'Orsay). Lefebvre avoided the signs of contemporary social reality, prostitution or the model's personality that characterized Manet's painting, focusing instead on the woman's beauty and stressing her passivity and availability.

Lefebvre became one of the best-known painters of the female nude, rivalled only by William Bouguereau. He was inspired by Ingres and the Fontainebleau school, notably in his stress on contour, graceful if exaggerated rhythms and smooth surfaces. Such works as *Truth* (1870; Paris, Mus. d'Orsay) earned Lefebvre a special niche among the contemporary painters of nudes, winning success at the Salon and spawning many imitators. He repeated this style and subject for the rest of his career. American collectors were avid fans of Lefebvre's work in the 1870s and 1880s as he satisfied their taste for simple, understandable paintings. Some contemporary critics wrote positively about his work (see Haller, 1899, pp. 213–38) but harsh judgements appeared in *La Presse* by 1875, and in the 1880s the newspaper *L'Intransigeant* expressed hostility towards his painting and to all academic art. Lefebvre sought to balance the rival claims of idealization, modernity, the study of nature and knowledge of the Old Masters in a way that revealed an original point of view, creating a modern ideal by combining art with recording physical reality.

Lefebvre was a professor at the Académie Julian in Paris from the 1870s until almost the end of his life; he was known for his sensitivity to precision in his students' life drawing despite the abstract idealism of the figures in his own paintings. His insistence on absolute accuracy in the rendering of nature was instilled in his students, who included Fernand Khnopff and Kenyon Cox, whether they ultimately decided to pursue some aspect of Realism or to rebel and enter the ranks of the avant-garde. He was a regular member of Salon juries from 1875. He won many awards and honours, becoming Commandeur of the Légion d'honneur in 1898 and a member of the Académie des Beaux-Arts of the Institut de France in 1891.

BIBLIOGRAPHY

F. Jahyer: 'Jules Lefebvre', *Gal. Contemp., Litt., A.*, iv b (1879) [unpaginated]

E. Strahan: *The Art Treasures of America* (Philadelphia, 1879)

J. Clarétie: 'Jules Lefebvre', *Grands peintres français et étrangers* (Paris, 1884), pp. 97–112

C. Vento: *Les Peintres de la femme* (Paris, 1888), pp. 299–333

F. Berteaux: *Les Artistes picards* (Paris, 1894)

G. Haller: *Nos grands peintres: Catalogue de leurs oeuvres et opinions de la presse* (Paris, 1899)

——: *Le Salon, dix ans de peinture* (Paris, 1902)

P. Grunchec: *Le Grand Prix de peinture* (Paris, 1983)

C. Fehrer: 'New Light on the Académie Julian and its Founder (Rodolphe Julian)', *Gaz. B.-A.*, 6th ser., ciii (1984), pp. 207–16

JULIUS KAPLAN

**Lefebvre, Pierre.** *See* FEVÈRE, PIETRO.

**Lefèvre, André** (*b* 21 May 1883; *d* 4 Aug 1963). French collector and stockbroker. From 1918 he systematically formed one of the finest collections of contemporary art in France. His initial guide was André Level (*c.* 1870–1946), the founder of the pre-war collecting club La Peau de l'Ours, who was a great admirer of Picasso and a pioneering advocate of African art. In 1921 Lefèvre, who was wealthier and less eclectic in his taste than Level, helped the latter set up and administer the Galerie Percier in Paris, devoted to contemporary art. He collected in depth the work of a fairly restricted number of living artists, most of them represented by Daniel-Henry Kahnweiler's Galerie Simon (later the Galerie Louise Leiris) in Paris. The core of his collection consisted of groups of pictures by André Beaudin, Juan Gris, Henri Laurens, Fernand Léger, Pablo Picasso and Suzanne Roger (*b* 1899). He collected African art but otherwise concentrated exclusively on 20th-century Western art; he purchased works by Paul Klee, André Masson and Joan Miró but otherwise excluded Surrealism (along with Expressionism, anecdotal or traditional paintings and the work of hedonistic painters such as Raoul Dufy and Henri Matisse) from his collection. The collection was therefore rather austere in character and was unusually homogeneous. Lefèvre and his wife donated a number of key works to the Musée National d'Art Moderne in Paris and to the Musée de Peinture et de Sculpture, Grenoble (now Musée de Grenoble). The bulk of the collection was sold at auction in Paris, after his death, at the Palais Galliéra (1 Dec 1964, 23–5 Nov 1965 and 29 Nov 1966) and at the Hôtel Drouot (24 Nov 1967).

BIBLIOGRAPHY

*La Collection André Lefèvre* (exh. cat.; Paris, Mus. N.A. Mod., 1964)

B. Dorival: 'La Donation André Lefèvre au Musée National d'Art Moderne', *Rev. Louvre*, xiv/1 (1964), pp. 23–41

——: 'La Préemption de l'Etat à la seconde vente André Lefèvre', *Rev. Louvre*, xvi/1 (1966), pp. 27–36; xvi/2 (1966), pp. 111–20

'Jérôme Peignot parle d'André Lefèvre', *Conn. A.*, clxviii (1966), pp. 41–3

MALCOLM GEE

**Lefèvre, Robert(-Jacques-François)** (*b* Bayeux, 24 Sept 1755; *d* Paris, 3 Oct 1830). French painter. He was the son of a Bayeux draper and originally worked as a law clerk before learning to paint, possibly in the studio of Pierre de Lesseline in Caen. Lefèvre quickly made a reputation for himself and established a sizeable practice in Normandy. About 1784 he went to Paris and entered the studio of Jean-Baptiste Regnault, where he formed a close friendship with the artist and critic Charles-Paul Landon.

Lefèvre's Salon début came at the open Salon of 1791, where he exhibited six paintings to great critical approval. At the 1795 Salon he showed a vibrant *Venus Disarming Love* in the style of Rubens (Fontainebleau, Château). The dislocation of patronage in the aftermath of the French Revolution forced Lefèvre to undertake some book illustration, but with the rise of Napoleon his career as a portrait painter took off, and he became a well-known and prolific painter of portraits of the imperial family. In 1801 he painted *The First Consul and General Berthier at the Battle of Marengo* (untraced; coloured stipple engraving by Anthony Cardon), for which Carle Vernet painted the landscape and JOSEPH BOZE attempted to steal the credit. In the same year Lefèvre painted his fellow artist *Pierre Guérin* (Orléans, Mus. B.-A.), whom he had met at Regnault's studio, presenting the frail and dandyish Guérin directly in an elegant portrait that shows the crispness and clarity of which he was capable. He excelled in rendering the textures of rich fabrics, and his contemporaries dubbed him 'the French van Dyck'. Such portraits of his friends and associates have an intensity and vigour that is often lacking in his official commissions.

In 1804 Lefèvre painted *Napoleon as First Consul* for the Hôtel de Ville at Dunkirk (destr. 1817). The unusually high quality of this painting briefly prompted speculation that it had been copied from a work by David. Enjoying the protection of Dominique Vivant-Denon, the Director-General of Museums, Lefèvre became Napoleon's official portrait painter. His best-known image of the Emperor is that showing *Napoleon in Coronation Robes* (1806 and later versions), of which no fewer than 37 replicas were requested. The portrait exists in two forms. The first depicts Napoleon bare-headed, with his left hand resting on his sword hilt (e.g. Paris, Mus. N. Légion d'Honneur). The second has Napoleon crowned and extending his left arm downwards (e.g. Versailles, Château). The Emperor evidently approved of these for their good likenesses, but Lefèvre insisted on executing all of the many replicas himself, resulting in progressive loss of quality. Lefèvre was also much in demand in society and portrayed many of the beautiful and fashionable women of his age, among them *Pauline Bonaparte, Princess Borghese* (version, London, Apsley House; see fig.). Here the Princess is shown elegant and relaxed, reclining on a cushion, a favourite device of Lefèvre's.

In 1814, in a bid to ingratiate himself with the restored Bourbon monarchy, Lefèvre painted a portrait of *Louis XVIII* 'done from memory'. This ploy worked, and in 1816 he was named Premier Peintre du Roi, in which capacity he was to execute many portraits of the royal family. In 1826 he painted *Charles X in Coronation Robes* (Paris, Louvre) in the traditional format of French royal portraits. In the 1820s Lefèvre resumed history painting with *The Baptism of the Duc de Bordeaux* (1821; destr.); also in 1821 he painted an *Assumption* for the church at Fontenay-Le-Comte, Vendée (*in situ*). At the 1827 Salon he exhibited a *Crucifixion*, commissioned by the Missionary Fathers of Mount Valerian but never delivered (now Caen, Mus. B.-A.). His last work was an *Apotheosis of St Louis* for the cathedral of La Rochelle (*in situ*). In 1830, worn out by pressure of work and possibly unsettled by the events of the revolution of that year, during which he lost his titles, he committed suicide.

### BIBLIOGRAPHY
Lady Morgan: *France in 1829–30*, i (London, 1830), pp. 334–54 [contains description of visit to Lefèvre's studio]
*Catalogue des tableaux et du cabinet de M. Robert Lefèvre* (Paris, 1831) [incl. 'Notice historique']
G. Lavelley: *Le Peintre Robert Lefèvre: Sa vie, son oeuvre* (Caen, [1902])
M. T. Folguera: *Robert Lefèvre, 1755–1830* (diss., U. Paris, 1976)

SIMON LEE

**Lefkandi.** Greek village between Chalkis and Eretria on the south-west coast of the island of Euboia. Nearby is the site of an important ancient Greek Bronze Age and

Robert Lefèvre: *Pauline Bonaparte, Princess Borghese*, oil on canvas, 806×630 mm, 1806 (London, Apsley House)

Dark Age settlement (occupied *c.* 2100–*c.* 700 BC). Excavations since the mid-1960s by the British School of Archaeology at Athens, joined later by the Greek Archaeological Service, have revealed a site comprising the settlement area of Xeropolis and five cemeteries, the most important of which is 1 km to the west on the hill of Toumba. Most of the finds, including those discussed here, are now in Eretria Archaeological Museum.

Xeropolis is a steep-sided plateau (*c.* 500×120 m), extending east–west along the outer edge of a broad coastal promontory. Although badly eroded, the site (especially in the north-west of the promontory) has retained habitation levels dating from the end of the Early Bronze Age to late Geometric times. The earliest occupation dates from around 2100 BC, with Early Helladic remains revealing west Anatolian affinities. Middle Helladic remains (*c.* 2050–*c.* 1600 BC) include a well and traces of a house with a pink plaster floor. Little survives from the LH I to LH IIIB levels, however, which were probably destroyed by the terracing and levelling that took place before the building of the larger LH IIIC settlement in the 12th century BC. The site was probably expanded to accommodate an influx of refugees fleeing the destruction of the Mycenaean palaces *c.* 1200 BC.

The LH IIIC site comprises three superimposed phases, each aligned differently and yielding distinct pottery styles. Excavation of Phase I uncovered the basements of two buildings separated by a passageway leading to a yard, and

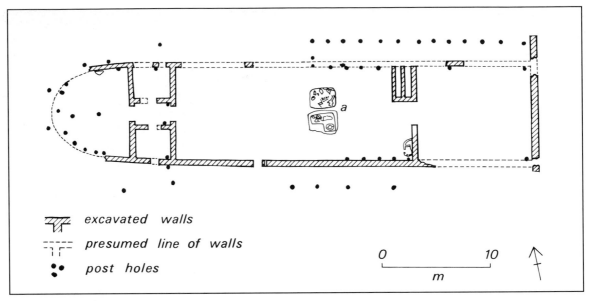

excavated  walls

presumed  line  of  walls

post  holes

0                    10
                   m

Lefkandi, plan of 'heroön', *c.* 1000–*c.* 950 BC; (a) burial shaft in central room

quantities of simply decorated pottery. The buildings' external walls were of pisé or mud-brick on stone socles. The main living rooms, which were of irregular shape and size, had mud-brick walls and were reached by a stairway. Phase I was destroyed by fire. The Phase II settlement, probably built by a new influx of Mycenaeans, consisted of carefully planned and well-constructed houses with stone walls carrying mud-brick superstructures. Associated pottery includes vases with figural scenes depicting humans and animals, both real and mythological. Such pictorial vases are rare in the LH IIIC period, and examples from Lefkandi provide important information on contemporary dress and armour. One of the finest vases is a tall alabastron showing two griffins feeding their young in a nest. Phase II, in its turn, was partly destroyed but was later repaired. The succeeding Phase III settlement fell into gradual abandonment and decline. A hiatus between the LH IIIC and Protogeometric settlement can only partially be filled by tomb evidence: continuity of occupation on the site is therefore unproven. No definite Protogeometric buildings have been found, but it appears that the settlement at this time was larger than those of either the Mycenaean or Geometric periods and, moreover, of a size and sophistication that is striking in a Greek Dark Age context. Settlement refuse pits included debris from a bronze workshop (*c.* 950–*c.* 900 BC) of high artistic and technological quality, and the grave goods found in nearby cemeteries are of a surprising richness and diversity.

Earlier indications of the importance of Protogeometric Lefkandi were reinforced by the discovery in 1980 of an extraordinary building at the cemetery area of Toumba. This structure, which may have been a 'heroön', dates from *c.* 1000–*c.* 950 BC. Measuring at least 45×10 m, it had a peristyle, an apse at its west end, probably a porch to the east and three intercommunicating sections (see fig.). The

walls had substantial stone socles and a mud-brick superstructure, and they were plastered inside. Parts are preserved to a height of *c.* 1.5 m. Internal and external post-holes indicate the use of timber supports. The floor was largely of clay laid directly on bedrock, and the roof was of reeds. In the central (main) room was a burial shaft (see fig. (a)) containing four sacrificed horses, a male cremation in a bronze cauldron and a female skeleton wearing rich gold jewellery. Almost immediately after its construction, or perhaps even before completion, the building was dismantled at both ends and filled in.

The sub-Protogeometric and Geometric settlements at Xeropolis (*c.* 900–*c.* 700 BC) have, despite stone robbing and erosion, revealed traces of a one-room house (8.5×5 m) orientated north–south. Nearby are the remains of three circular buildings (diam. *c.* 2 m), which were probably granaries, but which may have been olive or wine presses. Burials in the Lefkandi cemeteries ceased around 825 BC, and around 700 BC the settlement at Xeropolis was destroyed.

For illustration of a terracotta figurine from Lefkandi *see* GREECE, ANCIENT, fig. 48.

BIBLIOGRAPHY

M. R. Popham and L. H. Sackett: *Excavations at Lefkandi, Euboea, 1964–66* (London, 1968)

M. R. Popham and E. Milburn: 'The Late Helladic IIIC Pottery of Xeropolis (Lefkandi): A Summary', *Annu. Brit. Sch. Athens*, lxvi (1971), pp. 333–52

M. R. Popham, L. H. Sackett and P. G. Themelis, eds: *Lefkandi I: The Iron Age* (London, 1980)

P. G. Themelis: 'Die Nekropolen von Lefkandi Nord auf Euboea', *Griechenland, die Ägäis und die Levante während der 'Dark Ages': Vom 12. bis zum 9. Jh. v. Chr.: Akten des Symposions von Stift Zwettl (Niederösterreich): Zwettl, 1980*

R. H. Simpson: *Mycenaean Greece* (Park Ridge, NJ, 1981), p. 55

M. R. Popham, E. Touloupa and L. H. Sackett: 'The Hero of Lefkandi', *Antiquity*, lvi (1982), pp. 169–74

LOUISE SCHOFIELD

**Lefkas.** *See* LEUKAS.

**Lefler, Heinrich** (*b* Vienna, 7 Nov 1863; *d* Vienna, 14 March 1919). Austrian painter, decorative artist and printmaker. He was the son of the Bohemian painter Franz Lefler (1831–98), a member of the Künstlerhaus in Vienna. From 1880 to 1884 he studied in Vienna at the Akademie der Bildenden Künste under Christian Griepenkerl (1839–1916) and in Munich at the Akademie der Bildenden Künste under Nikolaos Gysis and Wilhelm von Diez (1839–1907). He first produced genre paintings, fairy-tale motifs and landscapes in the manner of Diez, but from 1895 (two years before the foundation of the Vienna Secession) his work showed *Jugendstil* tendencies. In 1891 he became a member of the Künstlerhaus in Vienna. As a printmaker he concentrated on commercial art; in the later 1890s he was one of the first Austrian artists to design posters for companies (e.g. *Auerlicht*, 1896–7; see Schweiger, p. 121), public events and periodicals (e.g. *Kunst und Kunsthandwerk*). In 1898–9, with his brother-in-law Joseph Urban, he produced the *Österreichischer Kalender* (Vienna, Hist. Mus.). Between 1896 and 1900 he contributed folios of prints (e.g. *Dancing*) to the folio series *Allegorien: Neue Folge*. He also designed menus, theatre programmes, the first publisher's mark and the standard title for music published by the famous Viennese firm Universal Edition (1901). With Urban he supplied designs for interior decoration (the Rathauskeller in Vienna, with frescoes from Viennese legends and history), furniture, folding screens, clocks, jewellery boxes, embroidery, fans, stage sets (he was chief scene painter for the Wiener Hofoper under Gustav Mahler in 1900–03) and festivals (e.g. the festive procession for the 60th jubilee of Emperor Francis Joseph I in 1908). In 1900 he founded the Hagenbund with Urban, acting as the first President in 1902 and a member until 1909. He produced posters for some exhibitions organized by the Hagenbund from 1902. From 1903 to 1910 he was a professor at the Akademie der Bildenden Künste in Vienna.

BIBLIOGRAPHY
P. Pauker: *Heinrich Lefler, sein Werk und seine Zeit* (diss., U. Vienna, 1962)
*Der Hagenbund* (exh. cat. by R. Waissenberger, Vienna, Hist. Mus., 1975)
W. J. Schweiger: *Meisterwerke der Wiener Werkstätte: Kunst und Kunsthandwerk* (Vienna, 1990)
SABINE KEHL-BAIERLE

**Le Fort du Plessy, Claude** (*d* Vienna, *c.* 1757). French architect and designer, active in Austria. He was involved in designing and furnishing the interior of Prince Eugene of Savoy's Stadtpalais in Vienna in 1707 and was mentioned in 1714 as Governor of the Arsenal. Two years later he was recorded in connection with work on a state bed for Empress Maria-Theresa. Between 1721 and 1728 he played a leading part in designing the interior of the imperial picture gallery in the upper floors of the Stallburg in the Hofburg (*see* VIENNA, §V, 5(i)). He is also believed to have designed the 'Goldkabinett' (before 1725), possibly Empress Maria-Theresa's bedroom, in the imperial summer palace, now the Theresianum. During the same period he was working on the interior of the Upper Belvedere; he is named as the designer of the interiors illustrated in the engraving (1731) by Salomon Kleiner,

where he is described as Kaiserlicher Rat und Obrist-Schiffamtsleutnand Claudius le Fort de Plessy. It is possible that the richly decorated galleries in the Hofbibliothek (1735; now the Nationalbibliothek), the interior furnishing of the Karlskirche (1730s) and the furnishing of the Savoysches Damenstift (*c.* 1740) were also designed by him.

BIBLIOGRAPHY
Thieme–Becker
B. Grimschitz: *Johann Lukas von Hildebrandt* (Vienna, 1932)
*Maria Theresia und ihre Zeit: Eine Darstellung der Epoche 1740–1780 aus Anlass der 200. Wiederkehr des Todestages der Kaiserin* (exh. cat., ed. W. Koschatzky; Schönbrunn, Schloss, 1980)
GABRIELE RAMSAUER

**Lefuel, Hector-Martin** (*b* Versailles, 14 Nov 1810; *d* Paris, 31 Dec 1880). French architect. He was Court Architect to Napoleon III during the Second Empire and is remembered chiefly for his additions to the Louvre and Tuileries palaces. His father Alexandre-Henri Lefuel (1782–1833) was a building contractor and Lefuel's first teacher. Lefuel entered the Ecole des Beaux-Arts in Paris in 1829 as a student of Jean-Nicolas Huyot and won second place in the Prix de Rome of 1833 before he left to take over his father's business. Re-entering the Ecole in 1838, Lefuel won the Prix de Rome of 1839 with his project for a Renaissance Revival hôtel de ville, and between 1840 and 1844 was a fellow at the Académie de France in Rome.

Upon his return to Paris Lefuel was appointed an Inspecteur des Travaux (1845–8) for the house of the president of the Chambre des Députés, and architect for the château of Meudon (1848), the Manufacture de Sèvres (1852) and the château of Fontainebleau (1853). Lefuel's work at Fontainebleau, where he rapidly built a new theatre in a Rococo style, caught the attention of Napoleon III, and early in 1854 the Emperor named him to succeed Louis-Tullius-Joachim Visconti as the architect of the Louvre and Tuileries palaces in Paris. Lefuel completed Visconti's New Louvre with such efficiency that he was made the Emperor's architect on 19 May 1855, and the new buildings were inaugurated on 14 August 1857, although their interiors were unfinished. Visconti's project for six pavilions extending west from the Old Louvre in two wings on either side of the Cour Napoléon had already been built up to the level of the second storey, but nevertheless Lefuel changed Visconti's design. Paraphrasing Jacques Le Mercier's Renaissance-style Pavillon de l'Horloge of 1624, for which Lefuel designed a new west façade, he transformed Visconti's restrained interpretation of Renaissance architecture through rich sculptural details, the addition of a narrow third storey and elaborately profiled silhouettes. Lefuel's design, although criticized (Vitet, 1866), was popular, and it established the widely imitated Second Empire style.

From 1861 to 1869 Lefuel rebuilt the Louvre's Grande Galerie along the Seine from the Guichets du Carrousel to the Pavillon de Flore. The Guichets are three broadly proportioned arches beneath the Salle des Etats, hemmed in by two pavilions and flanked by François Jouffroy's monumental sculptural groups *Marine Commerce* and *Naval Power* (1867–8); they have a formal power and originality that transcend their Renaissance Revival detailing. During the Third Republic Lefuel rebuilt (1871–6) the western half of the Louvre's Galerie Nord, ending at the Pavillon de Marsan, and he worked (1871–80) on an unexecuted project to rebuild the Tuileries, which had been gutted by fire in 1871 (destr. 1882). In his private practice Lefuel built the Hôtel Fould (1856; destr.) and the Hôtel Nieuwerkerke (1870) in Paris and the Schloss (1869–76) of Fürst Henkel von Donnersmarck, Neudeck bei Bethen in Silesia. Elected to the Académie des Beaux-Arts in 1855, Lefuel was appointed Inspecteur Général for the Conseil Général des Bâtiments Civils in 1866. Called a 'broad, correct, traditional and distinguished arranger' by Pascal in 1881, Lefuel remained a pragmatist rather than an innovator, preserving Neo-classicism by updating its forms with lush Renaissance Revival details.

### BIBLIOGRAPHY

Bauchal; Bellier de la Chavignerie–Auvray

L. Vitet: 'Le Nouveau Louvre et les nouvelles Tuileries', *Revue Deux Mondes*, xxxvi (1866), pp. 57–93

J.-L. Pascal: 'H. Lefuel', *Rev. Gén. Archit.*, xxxviii (1881), pp. 259–65

H. Delaborde: 'Notice sur la vie et les ouvrages de M. Lefuel', *Institut de France: Académie des Beaux-arts* (Paris, 1882), pp. 39–59; also as 'M. Lefuel, architecte: Sa vie et ses ouvrages', *Encyclopédie d'architecture*, 3rd ser., l (1882), pp. 83–8

L. Ginain: 'Notice sur M. Lefuel', *Institut de France: Académie des Beaux-arts* (Paris, 1882)

E. Delaire, D. de Penanrun and F. Roux: *Les Architectes 'élèves de l'Ecole des Beaux-arts'* (Paris, 1895, rev. 2/1907)

L. Hautecoeur: *Architecture classique*, vii (1957)

*The Second Empire: Art in France under Napoleon III* (exh. cat., Philadelphia, PA, Mus. A., 1978), pp. 59–61

J.-C. Daufresne: *Louvre et Tuileries: Architectures de papier* (Paris, 1987)

F. Hamon and C. MacCallum, eds: *Louis Visconti, 1791–1853* (Paris, 1991)

CHRISTOPHER MEAD

**Lega, Silvestro** (*b* Modigliana, nr Forlì, 8 Dec 1826; *d* Florence, 21 Sept 1895). Italian painter. From 1843 to 1847 he attended the Accademia di Belle Arti, Florence, studying drawing under Benedetto Servolini (1805–79) and Tommaso Gazzarini (1790–1853), then, briefly, painting under Giuseppe Bezzuoli. About 1847 he entered Luigi Mussini's school (*see* PURISMO), where the teaching emphasized the 15th-century Florentine principles of drawing and orderly construction. Then and for some years afterwards he continued to attend the Scuola del Nudo of the Accademia. After fighting in the military campaigns for Italian independence (1848–9) Lega resumed his training, this time under Antonio Ciseri, executing his first large-scale painting, *Doubting Thomas* (1850; Modigliana, Osp. Civ.). In 1852 he won the Concorso Trienniale dell'Accademia with *David Placating Saul* (1852; Florence, Accad.), a subject taken from Vittorio Alfieri's play *Saul* (1782).

About 1854–5 Lega began to pay occasional visits to the Caffè Michelangiolo, Florence, the gathering-place of progressive artists, and became exposed to the new tendencies advocated by the group of painters dubbed in 1862 the MACCHIAIOLI. About 1855–7 he went back to his native Modigliana, where he painted a number of portraits; he showed particular excellence in this genre, which comprises at least half his production. The portrait of his brother *Ettore Lega* (1855–7; Milan, priv. col., see 1988 exh. cat., pl. 2) testifies to Mussini's influence in the elegant outline and the simplicity of form, and it reflects a taste for the elongated forms and colouring of the Florentine Mannerists. The tenderness that is shown heralds the quality of intimacy that was to be characteristic of his art.

The transition in Lega's work from *Purismo* to Realism was slow. The Concorso Ricasoli of 1859—for paintings and sculptures on themes related to Italian independence—provided him with the stimulus to adopt the new style and to study nature. Like the *Macchiaioli*, he began to use outdoor settings depicting patriotic subjects, as in *Ambush of the Bersaglieri* (1860–61; Milan, priv. col., see Matteucci, ii, p. 86), integrating the figures in the landscape, which is rendered in a naturalistic manner. From 1861 Lega began to adopt the ideals of the *Macchiaioli*, sketching and painting out of doors at Piagentina, near Florence, where he was joined by Telemaco Signorini, Giuseppe Abbati (1836–68), Raffaello Sernesi (1838–66) and Odoardo Borrani (1831/3–1905).

The period between 1861 and 1870 was of fundamental importance in Lega's life and art. He established close friendships with members of the Batelli family, in particular Virginia Batelli, in whose home he spent the most serene and happy years of his life. The Batelli's villa was the subject of his first important large landscape, *View in Piagentina* (1863; Florence, priv. col., see Matteucci, ii, p. 126), which demonstrates the influence of Giovanni Costa in its breadth, subtle lighting and poetic interpretation of nature. He took as his subjects the women and children of the Batelli family, focusing on details of their everyday activities and elevating these to create timeless images, symbols of a way of life and an era. The originality of Lega's style lies in the way he adapted a contemporary use of colour, based on direct experience of the motif, to a traditional type of composition and carefully defined forms. This is illustrated by the *Singing of the Ballad* (1867; Florence, Pitti), which, together with *A Visit* (1868; Rome, G.N.A. Mod.) and *The Pergola* (see fig.), constitute the most important works of Lega's mature period and perhaps of his whole career. In the *Singing of the Ballad* the simplicity and balance of the composition, the transparency of the colours and rendering of atmosphere, the monumentality of the figures in profile and their pyramidal forms invest the scene with the solemnity of a painting by Piero della Francesca. *The Pergola* depicts the Batelli family out of doors, in the shade of an arbour. The composition is constructed by means of the tonal *macchia* technique, connecting the figures by the colours of the dresses and the contrasts of light and shade, as well as by subtle gestures and gazes. It is a meditated reality, the painting carefully finished in the studio.

Lega exhibited regularly and in 1870 won a silver medal at the prestigious Esposizione Italiana d'Arti Belle in Parma. About this time he suffered a series of misfortunes: Virginia Batelli, most of her family and three of his own brothers died. His style underwent a transformation, beginning to express strong emotions. He painted several landscapes, among them *In the Shade of the Villa* (1872–3; Milan, priv. col., see 1988 exh. cat., pl. 47), which convey deep emotional involvment. The ochres, browns and greens that he frequently used are loosely applied to define

Silvestro Lega: *The Pergola*, oil on canvas, 750×935 mm, 1868 (Milan, Pinacoteca di Brera)

intense summer light and cool shade, while figures, buildings and fields are reduced to abstract shapes of broadly brushed pigment. This freer style was due in part to the deteriorating condition of his eyesight. Lega suffered a crisis in 1874 and, apart from executing a few deeply melancholy landscapes, stopped painting until 1878.

Lega found renewed vigour and inspiration through other friends: the Cecchini and, later, the painter Adolfo Tommasi (1851–1933), at whose family villa at Bellariva he stayed from 1881 as painting instructor to Angiolo Tommasi (1858–1923) and Lodovico Tommasi (1866–1941). Women and children going about their daily lives, especially reading and doing homework, was a recurrent theme in his work, in, for example, *The Lesson* (*c.* 1880–81; Peschiera del Garda, Municipio). During this period Lega painted some fine portraits. As in *Eleonora Tommasi* (*c.* 1884–5; Milan, priv. col., see 1988 exh. cat., pl. 73), the sitters are usually set out of doors, often in profile—a Renaissance pictorial convention adopted because of his failing eyesight—flat against the greenery of a garden.

From 1886 Lega was a frequent guest of the Bandini family at their villa in Gabbro. It was a period of intense activity for Lega, by this time physically and emotionally ailing. He found the rugged landscape, village life and the people of Gabbro congenial to his state of mind, and, with the Bandini women, these became his principal subjects.

He was nearly blind, distinguishing only masses, not details, and the loose and emotionally heightened brushstrokes operate almost independently. Such of his late works as *Haystacks in the Sun* (*c.* 1890; Piacenza, Gal. A. Mod. Ricci Oddi) unintentionally possess an affinity with Impressionism that is unique among his Italian contemporaries.

During Lega's last years he concentrated on female portraits, painting on ceramic dishes and jars as well as on canvas. In his portrait of *Paolina Bandini* (1893; Livorno, priv. col., see Matteucci, i, p. 341) he combined elements of contemporary and 16th-century painting: the pose and elegance of the sitter may be seen as a reference to Bronzino, and the anxiety reflected in the intense turn of her face and clouded gaze as a reference to Pontormo. Lega's influence is seen in the work of, among others, Plinio Nomellini and Giuseppe Pellizza da Volpedo.

BIBLIOGRAPHY
D. Martelli: 'Silvestro Lega' (1895), *Scritti d'arte di Diego Martelli*, ed. A. Boschetto (Florence, 1952), pp. 240–43
M. Giardelli: *Silvestro Lega* (Milan, 1965)
*Silvestro Lega, 1826–1895* (exh. cat., ed. D. Durbè andC. Bonagura; Bologna, Mus. Civ., 1973)
G. Daddi: *Silvestro Lega: Spunti ed appunti* (Oggiono, 1978)
P. Dini: *Silvestro Lega: Gli anni di Piagentina* (Turin, 1984)
A. Marabottini: *Lega e la scuola di Piagentina* (Florence, 1984)
G. Matteucci: *Lega: L'opera completa*, 2 vols (Florence, 1987)
*Silvestro Lega: Dipinti* (exh. cat., ed. D. Durbè and others; Milan, Pal. Permanente; Florence, Pal. Strozzi; 1988)

EFREM GISELLA CALINGAERT

**Lega and related peoples.** Cluster of linguistically diverse Bantu-speaking peoples inhabiting east-central Zaïre. Although not immediately related, they exhibit common fundamental institutions and artistic achievements. In sharp contrast to the Hemba, Luba and Songye populations to the south, and the Nyanga, Hara, Hunde and Nande to the north, the Lega and related peoples have no centralized political systems. Their segmentary lineage organizations are overbridged by a unique, hierarchically graded, closed voluntary association called Bwami, Bukoto, Esambo or Lilura, with male and female membership. For initiation into the various grades of the association, the Lega and Bembe and, to some extent, other groups have created a unique type of sculpture. Lega sculpture in particular is widely represented in private collections and museums (e.g. Tervuren, Koninklijk Museum voor Midden-Afrika).

1. Cultural history. 2. Lega art. 3. Art of related peoples.

1. CULTURAL HISTORY. All of the various populations who immigrated into the area from different geographical regions were to some extent influenced by the culture of the pre-established Twa or Mbuti pygmies and other hunters, whom they thoroughly assimilated. Segments of these populations subsequently came into contact with one another; the contacts were followed by reciprocal exchanges of culture elements and to some extent also by partial or complete assimilation and incorporation. These factors account for the occurrence of select cultural similarities across ethnic boundaries and subtle cultural transitions. The core group of this cultural cluster are the Lega and their south-eastern neighbours, the Bembe. To the south and south-west are the Bangubangu, the Southern Binja (Zimba) and the Ngengele, some clans of which fit closely within the Lega cluster, while others are influenced by Hemba, Luba and Songye. To the north-west, most Songola (Northern Binja) clans exhibit features of Lega culture; to the north such small groups as the Kwami, Kanu, Konjo and Tembo show various degrees of affinity with the Lega, but they also exhibit northern influences from the Komo, Nyanga, Hunde, Havu and Shi. Further north-west, but not in immediate contact with the Lega, sub-groups of the Leka, Mitoko, Lengola, Mbole and Yela, although strongly influenced by the Komo and Mongo, present a certain cultural proximity to the Lega, particularly in their art-producing institutions.

Very few Lega artists have been observed by outsiders. One reason for this is the extreme secrecy in which they worked. More significantly, however, the associations that commissioned the art works were from early colonial times categorized as secret, subversive and immoral. Strong legal and police action against the membership of the associations contributed to the decline of at least the more external manifestations of their activities. Moreover, for the Lega and Bembe the emphasis was never on the makers, whose names are unknown, but on their owners and the cross-generational links among them. Initiates may quote several previous initiated owners of a particular art work, but not remember the sculptor responsible for its making.

Within the spectrum of the Lega style there are variations and differences that cannot be associated with any particular regional sub-grouping due to the merging of groups through ancient movements of kinship units and individuals. Patterns of initiation into the highest grades of Bwami also account for the distribution of objects across wide geographical areas. For centuries, until the rapid decline of Lega artistic traditions in the 1920s, sculptures travelled back and forth across Legaland with initiates settling with agnatic, cognatic and affinal relatives of their choice. Stylistic periods have not been convincingly

1. Lega figurine representing 'Wasakwa nyona', ivory, h. 185 mm, from Babene, Pangi, Zaïre, collected 1953 (Tervuren, Koninklijk Museum voor Midden-Afrika)

designated for Lega sculpture. On the one hand the documentation is too shallow in time; on the other hand the values of Bwami are structured on tradition and conservatism, preserving uniformity across time.

2. LEGA ART. The Lega have produced masks and masquettes as well as anthropomorphic and zoomorphic figurines in wood, ivory or bone. There are a few masks in elephant leather and figurines in stone, resin and tree marrow. The Lega also created such other carved objects as spoons, small daggers, dice, hammers, billhooks, axe blades, as well as stools in wood, ivory or bone. The sculptures are small: ivory and bone figurines are all less than 300 mm high, and the wooden ones are typically smaller than 400 mm. Most masks in wood, ivory or bone are between 100 and 190 mm high.

Lega sculptures are usually carved in a highly distinctive style, with a heart-shaped concave face with bulging forehead, a narrow nose-bridge, open slit eyes and open mouth. In both the figurines and the masks, however, there are deviations: some masks have flat or convex faces, while some figurines are angular and others rounded. The figurines are compact, with an emphasis on such body parts as short, bent legs on massive feet, or on such prototypical features as one arm, one leg, protuberant belly, multi-facedness or multi-headedness. Many figurines show no sex, and in general the male and female sexual parts are not emphasized. There are a number of other standard features. The faces of most wooden masks are rubbed with white clay, while perforations near the lower rim allow fibre beards to be attached to the chin and cheeks; few decorative designs (e.g. dotted lines) occur on wooden masks. Ivory and bone masks lack fibre beards, but some have circle–dot and dotted-line designs. The ivory and bone figurines (see fig. 1) are either full-bodied, but stylized with short arms and legs, or they are reduced to busts or sheer heads, or the upper part of the body ends in a blade or pole-shaped extension. Many of the ivory figurines are adorned with circle–dot designs or dotted lines, and while some have glued-on cowrie eyes, others have glued-on cowries on top of the head to signify the Bwami skull cap.

One of the most typical aspects of Lega sculpture, particularly of ivory and bone carvings, is the extraordinary patina achieved by the regular rubbing of these objects with castor oil and with hands imbued with camwood powder. When the relevant rituals begin the sculptures are removed from the shoulderbags in which they are kept and rubbed with oil 'to bring harmony among the heavy things of initiation'. The extreme secrecy of this rite is enhanced by the playing of such sacred instruments as mirlitons, bullroarers and blowpipes. Initiations are dramatic events that demand the participation of many male and female initiates of appropriate rank. During the initiations the sculptures are displayed obligatorily by all invited participants. They are danced with, placed in configurations and used in certain sequences, all to the accompaniment of sung aphorisms, drum and rattle music, dance, gestural movement and even light effects. Initiations also involve the transfer to the initiand of paraphernalia and art objects. Most actions unroll within a closed space, in early morning or late evening. Interpretations of

2. Lega *Lukwakongo* mask, wood and fibre, h. 173 mm, from Zaïre, collected 1950s (Tervuren, Koninklijk Museum voor Midden-Afrika)

the art are cryptic, often contradictory, and multi-layered to avoid divulgence. The poses, unusual features and gestures of the figurines, for example, can be understood only in terms of Bwami exegesis: a figurine with raised arms and hands is not imploring celestial powers for rain but imitating the typical gestures of the high initiate acting as an arbitrator of conflict. A figurine with one visible eye is not the image of an injured person or of one who is blind in one eye, but a symbol stressing the vigilance of an authority figure (feeble-minded persons think the elder is asleep, but in fact he is watching out of one semi-closed eye). Any one of the sculptures serves as a didactic tool in the elucidation of the Bwami value code.

Select sculptures are not owned individually by initiates, but are collectively held sacra. Some are temporarily entrusted to the most recent initiate in a socially and ritually defined group; others are kept by the most senior of all initiates within a clearly circumscribed community. These collectively held objects, also used as didactic devices, symbolize the unity and cohesion of distinctive ritual communities whose members act together for the purpose of initiation; their presence is a prerequisite for a socially sanctioned initiation to be held. The deep significance of the sculptures goes further in that such objects are not discarded when their owners die or move up to higher levels. They are symbols of interpersonal bonds across generations. A Yananio (member of the second highest Bwami grade) must obtain a wooden mask (see fig. 2), which will itself be replaced by an ivory or bone mask when the initiate ascends to the highest Kindi grade. Possession of the mask demonstrates legal membership in the highest levels of the association. Since different categories of art works, and of the materials from which they are fashioned, are linked with different grades, the sculptures are status symbols among the cognoscenti. They are also temporarily exposed on the tombs of their deceased owners, and they represent not merely pleasant memories of dead relatives but also, by association, powerful objects permeated with the 'forces' inherent in their previous owners. There is in them a transcendent power, beneficial to the rightful owner, lethal to offenders. The transcendent significance of the sculptures is most vividly illustrated by the fact that surface scrapings from the sculptures, especially from the ivory figurines, are administered to sick persons as ultimate remedies, when all others have failed.

3. ART OF RELATED PEOPLES. The Bembe are a less exclusive and less homogeneous ethnic group than the Lega. Profound influences of the pre-Bembe hunters (some of whom produced unique ancestral figures, whose style is linked with Tabwa, Hemba and other, unknown, styles) have moulded many ritual aspects of Bembe culture. This is manifest, for example, in the Alunga association of the Bembe, found only in some groups located near the shores of Lake Tanganyika. This association's activities centre on a spectacular bifrontal, bichrome, concave-faced, sometimes monoxyle, bell mask. The mask represents the bush spirit, Alunga. It is worn with a huge raffia costume and a large headdress of feathers and quills. In the performance context this otherwise carefully hidden mask comes out publicly to reinforce the rules of the Alunga association. Other, extremely rare, Bembe sculptures include a composite face mask used for social control by members of the Elanda association; small rudimentary figurines for the Mpunga association to protect members and inflict harm on antagonists; clay figurines for the earth spirit Iyangya; and polychrome wooden plankboard masks for the circumcision rites. Although of great socio-political and ritual importance, the Bwami association was never able to monopolize the artistic patrimony among the Bembe. Very few sculptures are known from the Bwami

association of the Bembe. The number of Bembe sculptures was never large, and the work was less diversified and mainly restricted to anthropomorphic figurines in ivory or bone, with some in wood, as well as some larger wooden face masks, wooden zoomorphic sculptures, awl-shaped pegs and miniature stools in bone and ivory, all used in the higher grades of Bwami, in ways similar to Lega practice.

Details on Zimba (Southern Binja) art are sparse, and some works ascribed to them are of Luba or Hemba type. The Batali (a Zimba sub-group) adhere to Bwami, and they are initiated among the neighbouring Lega (because of bonds of affinity) or organize their own initiation rites. For Bwami they have made or borrowed typical Lega figurines in wood and ivory. Some sub-units of the small, mixed ethnic groups called Kanu, Kwami and Konjo are in close contact with the northern Lega and have adopted some lower grade levels of Bwami. Except for a skull cult of important initiated men among the Kano and Konjo, no Bwami sculptures are known for any of them. Further north, the Nyanga, Hunde and Pere, who cannot in fact be included in the Lega cluster, have nevertheless produced for the Mbuntsu and Nsindi associations small figurines that have astonishing stylistic resemblances with some of the rarest Lega work in clay, resin and tree marrow.

The Leka are an extremely mixed group of peoples, showing some affiliations with the Enya and the Mitoko. Some wooden face masks with horns, close in style to the horned Kayamba masks of the Lega, were used in circumcision rites that were organized by members of a Bwami-like association. Little or nothing is known about such other members of the Lega cluster as the Songola, Babemo and Sengele. These groups have associations, called Nsubi and Esambo, that are patterned after the Bwami model, but are much less elaborate. Since distinctive paraphernalia and sacra are invariably linked with such associations, it is quite possible that some art works were made for initiation purposes.

The Mitoko, Lengola, Mbole and Yela have the Bukota and Lilwa associations, similar to Bwami. In those contexts they use wooden sculptures, mainly figurines, for initiation, social control and burial purposes. The figurines differ considerably in size and finish, but exhibit the facial features of Lega masks and figurines. This is not accidental, for there are strong historical links between the Lega and the Mitoko and much cultural borrowing across the region, mainly because of the secret networks of the initiations. All of them are structured on a common ideological and sociological pattern.

BIBLIOGRAPHY

D. P. Biebuyck: 'The *Kindi* Aristocrats and their Art among the Lega', *African Art and Leadership*, ed. D. Fraser and H. M. Cole (Madison, WI, 1972), pp. 7–20

——: *Lega Culture: Art, Initiation and Moral Philosophy among a Central African People* (Berkeley, 1973)

——: 'The Decline of Lega Sculptural Art', *Ethnic and Tourist Arts: Cultural Expressions from the Fourth World*, ed. N. H. H. Graburn (Berkeley, 1976), pp. 334–49

——: 'Schemata in Lega Art', *Form in Indigenous Art: Schematization in the Art of Aboriginal Australia and Prehistoric Europe*, ed. P. J. Ucko, Prehistory and Material Culture Series, 13 (Canberra and London, 1977), pp. 59–65

——: *Statuary from the Pre-Bembe Hunters: Issues in the Interpretation of Ancestral Figurines Ascribed to the Basikasingo–Bembe–Boyo: Statuary in*

the Collections of the Royal Museum of Central Africa, Tervuren, Belgium (Tervuren, 1981)
——: 'Lega Dress as Cultural Artefact', *Afr. A.*, xv/3 (1982), pp. 59–65, 92
S. Klopper: 'Speculations on Lega Figurines', *Afr. A.*, xix/1 (1985), pp. 64–9, 88
D. P. Biebuyck: *Eastern Zaïre: The Ritual and Artistic Context of Visual Associations*, ii of *The Arts of Zaïre* (Berkeley, 1985–6)
—— : *The Arts of Central Africa: An Annotated Bibliography*, Ref. Pubns A. Hist. (Boston, MA, 1987)

DANIEL P. BIEBUYCK

**Leganés**, 1st Marqués de. *See* GUZMÁN, (1).

**Legarda, Bernardo de** (*b* Quito, ?end of the 17th century; *d* Quito, 31 May 1773). Ecuadorian wood-carver and painter. He was a pupil of José Olmos, and he set up his workshop in Quito facing the Franciscan monastery for which he worked. A versatile artist, he was also active as a gold- and silversmith, printer and gunsmith. In 1736 Legarda carved his masterful *Virgin of the Apocalypse* or *Winged Virgin of Quito* (Quito, S Francisco), which was inspired by a painting by Miguel de Santiago. Legarda's fine work reflects the mystical fervour of the legend it depicts. The twisting figure of the Virgin, trampling the head of a dragon underfoot, is balanced by her outspread arms and wings. Her face reflects the beauty of the mestiza, the mixed-race woman of Quito. Elsewhere in Quito Legarda carved the Baroque altarpieces for the church of La Merced, the hospital and the churches of the Carmen Moderno and Cantuña, as well as the *Crucifixion* in this last church. In 1745 he gilded the high altar of the Jesuit church and decorated the dome of the Sagrario in Quito. His paintings include the *Nativity*, the *Adoration of the Magi*, the *Virgin of Sorrows* and the *Massacre of the Innocents*.

RICARDO DESCALZI

**Légaré.** French family of goldsmiths. Three presumed brothers, Laurent Légaré (*b* Chaumont-en-Bassigny, before 1610; *d* Paris, after 1658), Gilles Légaré (*b* Chaumont-en-Bassigny, *c*. 1610; *d* Paris, after 1685) and Gédéon Légaré (*b* Chaumont-en-Bassigny, *c*. 1611; *bur* Paris, 22 July 1676), worked together in Paris, probably in 1657–8. They were at that time established in the Rue Princesse in Saint-Germain-des-Prés. Another Laurent Légaré was active in the Rue de Harley in 1692; he was probably the son of Gédéon, although it is possible that he was one of the three brothers, in which case the Laurent Légaré who engraved a scene of a *Goldsmith's Shop* in 1625 would perhaps have been their father.

BIBLIOGRAPHY
Thieme–Becker
S. Leclerc and M. Préaud: *Inventaire du fonds français: Graveurs du XVIIe siècle*, 2 vols, Bib. N. Cab. Est. cat. (Paris, 1989)

MAXIME PRÉAUD

**Légaré, Joseph** (*b* Quebec City, 10 March 1795; *d* Quebec City, 21 June 1855). Canadian painter, collector and politician. After studying briefly at the Quebec Seminary, in 1812 he was apprenticed to the painter and glassmaker Moses Perce (*fl* 1806–48). The sale in Quebec City in 1817 of part of the collection of Louis-Joseph Desjardins (1766–1848), which comprised altogether about 200 European Old Master paintings, had a decisive effect on Légaré's career. He bought a number, which he cleaned

and restored himself, and, as an almost entirely self-taught artist, found them a valuable source of inspiration, technical example and income: many of his early commissions were for large copies of religious pictures from the collection. He painted about 100 religious works but in 1828 won an honorary medal for an original secular composition, the *Massacre of the Hurons by the Iroquois* (Quebec, Mus. Qué.).

Légaré's oeuvre (over 250 oils on canvas and on paper) was considerably more diverse and ambitious in subject-matter than that of such contemporaries as Jean-Baptiste Roy-Audy, Antoine Plamondon and Théophile Hamel, who favoured portraiture and religious painting. He was the first Canadian-born painter to specialize in landscapes, for example *Falls on the St Charles River* (*c*. 1840; Quebec, Mus. Qué.), the dark palette of which shows the influence of the discoloured European canvases in his collection. Légaré also recorded contemporary disasters in dramatic panoramic views, for example the cholera outbreak of 1832 (Ottawa, N.G.), the landslide at Cap-Diamant in 1841 (Quebec, Mus. Sémin.) and the fires of 1845 in the Saint-Roch and Saint-Jean districts of Quebec (Quebec, Mus. Qué.; Quebec, Mus. Sémin.; Toronto, A.G. Ont.). Among his most outstanding historical pictures were the *First Ursuline Convent in Quebec* (Quebec, Mus. Ursulines), *Recollections of the Jesuits of Nouvelle-France* (1843; Quebec, Vieille Maison Jesuites) and the *Battle of Sainte-Foy* (Ottawa, N.G.). Légaré also devoted a series of pictures to the customs of the North American Indians, the most famous being the portrait of *Josephte Ourné* (*c*. 1844; Ottawa, N.G.). His most important pupil was Antoine Plamondon, whom he took on as an apprentice in 1819.

Légaré did much to develop a taste for the fine arts among his countrymen. In 1833 he opened Canada's first art gallery in Quebec, where until 1835 he showed his personal collection of European paintings and engravings. He reopened the museum from 1838 to 1840 and again from 1852 to 1855; much of the collection is now in the Musée de l'Amérique Française, Université Laval, Quebec City. He was involved in many humanitarian, social and political activities in Quebec City, as a member of the first Conseil de Ville (1833–6) and one of the founder-members of the Société St Jean-Baptiste de Québec in 1834. He was arrested for taking part in the French-Canadian rebellion of 1837 and was made a member of the legislature in February 1855, a few months before his death.

BIBLIOGRAPHY
DCB
*The Works of Joseph Légaré, 1795–1855* (exh. cat. by J. R. Porter, Ottawa, N.G., 1978)
J. R. Porter: *Un Peintre et collectionneur québécois engagé dans son milieu: Joseph Légaré (1795–1855)* (diss., Montreal, U. Montréal, 1981)
——: 'Joseph Légaré', *Dictionnaire biographique du Canada*, viii (Quebec, 1985), pp. 547–52
D. Prioul: *Joseph Légaré, paysagiste* (diss., Quebec, U. Laval, 1993)

YVES LACASSE

**Legastelois, Jules(-Prosper)** (*b* Paris, 24 May 1885; *d* 1931). French sculptor and medallist. He studied sculpture with Emile Carlier (1849–1927) and medal making with Eugène Levasseur (*b* 1822) and Georges Tonnelier (*b* 1858). Legastelois's work included a number of plaquettes and medals for the Paris Mint, such as *Maternity* (1902),

*Work* (1908), *Horticulture* (1912) and *Georges Clemenceau* (1929). He also executed war memorials at Epinay, Eure, and Ermont, Val d'Oise.

BIBLIOGRAPHY

Edouard-Joseph
*Catalogue général des éditions de la Monnaie de Paris*, iii (Paris, 1979), pp. 232–7

MARK JONES

**Legeay** [Le Geay], **Jean-Laurent** (*b* Paris, *c.* 1710; *d* after 1786). French architect, draughtsman and teacher. He studied at the Ecole des Beaux-Arts, Paris, and won the Prix de Rome in 1732. His residence in Rome (1737–42) coincided with the arrival from Venice (1740) of Giovanni Battista Piranesi, who was considerably influenced by Legeay's dramatic engravings of the monuments of Roman antiquity. Legeay worked with Piranesi and other engravers on illustrations for guide books on Rome, including the *Varie vedute di Roma antica e moderna* (1745) by Fausto Amidei, and he was an important figure in the cross-currents of influence and ideas between Piranesi and the French scholars in Rome.

Legeay returned to Paris in 1742, and he was appointed professor at the Académie Royale d'Architecture, where his drawing methods and his teaching were enormously influential on such pupils as Charles de Wailly and Etienne-Louis Boullée. In 1745 Legeay went to Berlin, where he worked on plans for the Catholic church of St Hedwig, a circular design derived from the Pantheon in Rome, which was illustrated in six engravings published in 1747. The building was completed to a modified design in 1773, finally receiving the lantern and cross that he had intended in 1886–7. Legeay obtained appointments at the court of Mecklenburg-Schwerin from 1748 to the mid-1750s; he laid out the Schlossgarten at Schwerin in the style of André Le Nôtre in the early 1750s and designed the Saalanbau of the palace at Rostock. In 1756 he went to Potsdam, where he worked for Frederick II, King of Prussia, on the Neues Palais at Sanssouci, together with Johann Gottfried Buring, Karl Philipp Christian von Gontard and Heinrich Ludwig Manger (1728–89). His individual contribution is difficult to determine, and he fell out with the king and left in 1763 when construction work began. He is certainly responsible, however, for the Communs in Potsdam, a pair of Neo-classical palaces—the first in this style in Prussia—built to accommodate courtiers. These buildings face the Neues Palais across a broad square; they are fronted by imposing double-curved staircases and linked by a semicircular colonnade designed by von Gontard.

Legeay then travelled to England, where his presence is noted in 1766 and 1767. He was in contact with William Chambers, and he made a perspective drawing of Chambers's Casino at Marino, Dublin. He returned to France *c.* 1767 and worked on the publication of his various collections of engravings, including *Fontane* (1767), *Rovine* (1768), *Vasi* and *Tombeaux* (both published in Paris, 1770), all in the heavily monumental style that had so impressed Piranesi. Legeay is last recorded seeking a pension from the Duke of Mecklenburg in 1786 to enable him to spend his old age in Rome. His reputation is derived less from built works than from his drawings and projects, which inspired his French contemporaries in Rome (including Robert Le Lorrain, Nicolas-Marie Potain

and Jacques-Edmé Dumont) as well as his pupils at the Académie Royale with an enthusiasm for Neo-classical forms and ambitious scale that spelt the end of the Rococo and anticipated the era of French Revolutionary architecture.

BIBLIOGRAPHY

J. Harris: 'Le Geay, Piranesi and International Classicism in Rome, 1740–1750', *Essays in the History of Architecture Presented to Rudolf Wittkower*, ed. D. Fraser, H. Hibberd and M. J. Lemire (London, 1967), pp. 189–96
S. Eriksen: *Early Neo-classicism in France* (London, 1974)
*Piranèse et les Français, 1740–1790* (exh. cat., ed. A. Chastel and G. Brunel; Rome, Acad. France; Paris, Caisse N. Mnmts Hist. & Sites; 1976)
G. Erouart: *Jean-Laurent Legeay: Un Architecte français dans l'Europe des lumières* (Milan and Paris, 1982)

ALAN POWERS

**Legendre, Nicolas** (*b* Etampes, Essonne, 1619; *d* Paris, 30 Oct 1671). French sculptor. He began his career working principally as a sculptor in wood. His carvings for the doorcase of the Collège de la Marche, Paris (1650–55; destr. 1866), for the churchwarden's pew at St Paul, Paris (1655; destr. *c.* 1699), and for the rood screen at St Sépulchre, Paris (1655; after models by Philippe de Buyster; destr. after 1699), established his reputation. In 1658 he was commissioned by the Queen Mother, Anne of Austria, to carve a marble statue of *St Radegund* with her own features (Poitiers, Ste Radegonde). Legendre's friendship with Charles Le Brun led to commissions for decorative stuccowork for Nicolas Fouquet at the château of Vaux-le-Vicomte, Seine-et-Marne (1659; in collaboration with François Girardon), and for sculptures in wood, stone, stucco and marble at St Nicolas-du-Chardonnet, Paris (*c.* 1662; partly destr.).

As a member of the Académie de St Luc, Legendre was involved in the project to unite the institution with the Académie Royale de Peinture et de Sculpture, but, when this failed, he entered the Académie Royale in 1664, presenting a recumbent terracotta statuette of *Mary Magdalene* (untraced; bronze version, Washington, DC, N.G.A.). He later carved a stone pediment for the Collège Mazarin, Paris (1670; in situ), and was active on the royal works at the palaces of the Tuileries, the Louvre, Saint-Germain-en-Laye and Versailles. For the last, among other works, he executed with Laurent Magnier (1615–1700) a part of the lead decoration for the fountain of the *Bain des Nymphes* (1670; in situ) and, alone, statues of a *Water Nymph* and a *River God* for the attic storey of the north façade (stone, 1671; in situ). His subtle classicizing style made him one of the better sculptors of the first generation of artists assembled by Louis XIV to decorate his buildings and gardens.

BIBLIOGRAPHY

Lami; Souchal
Guillet de Saint-Georges [A. C. Guillet]: 'Mémoire historique des principaux ouvrages de sculpture de M. Legendre' (MS., Paris, Ecole N. Sup. B.-A., n. d.), in *Mémoires inédits . . . des membres de l'Académie Royale*, ed. L. Dussieux and others, i (Paris, 1854), pp. 408–14
J. Guiffrey: *Comptes des Bâtiments du Roi sous le règne de Louis XIV*, 5 vols (Paris, 1881–1901)

FRANÇOISE DE LA MOUREYRE

**Léger, Fernand** (*b* Argentan, Orne, 4 Feb 1881; *d* Gif-sur-Yvette, Seine-et-Oise, 17 Aug 1955). French painter, draughtsman, illustrator, printmaker, stage designer, film maker and ceramicist. Among the most prominent artists in Paris in the first half of the 20th century, he was prolific in many media and articulated a consistent position on the role of art in society in his many lectures and writings. His mature work underwent many changes, from a Cubist-derived abstraction in the 1910s to a distinctive realist imagery in the 1950s. Léger attracted numerous students to his various schools, and his ideas and philosophy were disseminated by modern artists throughout Europe and the Americas.

1. Life and work. 2. Working methods and technique.

### 1. LIFE AND WORK.

(i) Early years, to 1909. (ii) 1910–17. (iii) 1918–26. (iv) 1927–39. (v) 1940–49. (vi) 1950–55.

*(i) Early years, to 1909.* Born in rural Normandy, Léger often said that he was of 'peasant stock'. Although his father was a cattle merchant, Léger was sent by his family to Caen in 1897 to be an apprentice in an architect's office, where he remained until 1899. In 1900 he went to Paris and again worked in an architect's office as a draughtsman. After compulsory military service in 1902, when he was sent to Versailles with a corps of engineers, Léger was admitted in 1903 to the Ecole des Arts Décoratifs in Paris, but not to the more prestigious Ecole des Beaux-Arts. He studied under Jean-Léon Gérôme and Gabriel Ferrier (1847–1914) and began to visit the Académie Julian and the Musée du Louvre regularly, although he continued to work in an architect's office, earning additional money retouching photographs for a commercial photographer.

From 1904 to 1906 he shared a flat with a friend from Argentan, the designer and painter André Mare (1885–1932), with whom he would maintain a detailed correspondence until the early 1920s.

Between 1906 and 1908 Léger made four trips to Corsica, while also beginning to frequent avant-garde gatherings in Paris; by 1908 he was living at LA RUCHE, near Montparnasse, where he met many young artists, including Robert Delaunay, Marc Chagall, Chaïm Soutine, Henri Laurens and Jacques Lipchitz, as well as the poets Max Jacob, Guillaume Apollinaire, Pierre Reverdy, Maurice Raynal and Blaise Cendrars. His paintings of this period reveal the wide-ranging influences that Léger had absorbed and show a progression from early works, with a strongly impressionist flavour (e.g. *My Mother's Garden*, 1905; Biot, Mus. N. Fernand Léger), through brief Neo-Impressionist- and Fauve-inspired phases to an increasing concern with volumes and order, influenced by his visit and strong response to the memorial exhibition of Cézanne's work at the Salon d'Automne of 1907. Léger destroyed most of his work of pre-1910, and the examples that remain, comprising a few paintings (housed principally in the Musée National Fernand Léger, Biot) and a number of ink drawings, are characterized by a subdued impressionist palette in his painted landscapes, nudes and portraits and by a calligraphic quality in his drawings.

*(ii) 1910–17.* Although Léger had exhibited at the Salon d'Automne of 1909 with Constantin Brancusi, Marcel

1. Fernand Léger: *Nudes in a Forest*, 1911 (Otterlo, Rijksmuseum Kröller-Müller)

Duchamp, Roger de La Fresnaye, Albert Gleizes, Jean Metzinger and Francis Picabia, it was not until 1910 that his association with these avant-garde artists became marked and influential on his work. He joined Delaunay, Gleizes, Metzinger and Henri Le Fauconnier at meetings at Jacques Villon's studio in Puteaux, where the Section d'Or was founded. At this time Léger began to paint in a markedly Cubist style, distinguished from that of Picasso and Braque by its modelling of volumes and its slightly obscured but relatively accessible imagery. In 1910 he began the series *Smoke on the Roofs*, in which he concentrated on the value of volumetric contrasts with a minimum of chromatic variation, a preoccupation that lasted until the end of 1914. 'Contrast = dissonance', he wrote in an article of 1914 ('Les Révélations picturales actuelles', repr. in *Functions of Painting*, pp. 11–19), 'and hence a maximum expressive effect'. Referring to this series, he noted:

> I will take as an example a commonplace subject: the visual effect of curled and round puffs of smoke rising between houses. You want to convey their plastic value. Here you have the best example on which to apply research into multiplicative intensities. Concentrate your curves with the greatest possible variety without breaking up their mass; frame them by means of the hard, dry relationship of the surfaces of the houses, dead surfaces that will acquire movement by being coloured in contrast to the central mass and being opposed by live forms; you will obtain a maximum effect.

His large-scale paintings of *The Wedding* (2.57×2.06 m, 1910–11; Paris, Pompidou; *see* CUBISM, fig. 2) and *Nudes in a Forest* (1.2×1.7 m, 1911; Otterlo, Rijksmus. Kröller-Müller; see fig. 1) are culminations of this early research into contrasts.

In 1912 Léger participated in the Maison Cubiste, a part of the decorative arts section organized by his friend André Mare for the Salon d'Automne of 1912. Viewers entered the Maison Cubiste through a façade designed by Raymond Duchamp-Villon, leading to a domestic interior featuring the latest in contemporary design. Léger's *Level Crossing* (1912; Basle, Gal. Beyeler) was among the paintings by young artists associated with Cubism that graced the interior walls. His participation in this venture secured his position among the avant-garde of his generation. The following year Léger signed a three-year, exclusive contract with Daniel-Henry Kahnweiler, already established as the dealer of Picasso and Braque's work. Kahnweiler purchased all the paintings as well as 50 drawings from Léger's studio. By this time Léger was devoting himself fully to the issue of contrasts in his paintings in a series known as the *Contrasts of Forms*. His canvases were dominated by convex and concave volumes, accentuated by touches of primary and secondary colours. In a lecture of 1913 to the Académie Wassilieff (repr. in *Functions of Painting*, pp. 3–10) in Paris, he declared 'Pictorial contrasts used in their purest sense (complementary colours, lines and forms) are henceforth the structural basis of modern pictures'. Léger's fascination with contrasts emerged from his awareness that he was living in a vastly accelerated, dynamic world and that the rapid changes in contemporary life were jarring and unsettling to much of society; he sought to challenge the viewer and allow his art to conform to the pace of the world around him.

Léger's study of contrasts was interrupted by the outbreak of World War I. He was drafted in August 1914 and served in the Argonne until late 1915. Following a brief leave, during which he saw new films by Charlie Chaplin, accompanied by Guillaume Apollinaire, and also met his first wife, Jeanne Lohy, he returned to serve with the engineering corps at the Verdun and Fort Douaumont battlefields. While serving at Verdun in September 1916 Léger was gassed, and he was hospitalized at Villepinte, near Paris, until the end of 1917. Throughout Léger's service at the front and his subsequent hospitalization, he produced a considerable number of drawings, gouaches and several paintings. His *War Drawings*, made on every conceivable surface available to him, chronicle life at the front: the leisure activities of the soldiers, preparations for battle and the conditions in the trenches (e.g. *Soldiers in a Dugout*, 1915; priv. col., see Cassou and Leymarie, no. 39). He gained a new appreciation for the 'machine gun or the breech of a 75', which were 'more worth painting', Léger noted, 'than four apples on a table or a Saint-Cloud landscape'. The experience at the front transformed him; Léger felt he had finally encountered 'the people', and his art had to be accessible and relevant to them. In 1922 he decided that he would now model in pure and local colour, using large volumes, disdaining 'tasteful arrangements, delicate shading, and dead backgrounds'. Léger's *The Card Game* (1917; Otterlo, Rijksmus. Kröller-Müller), paying homage to his earliest hero, Cézanne, and suggestive of the changes to appear in his own subsequent work, fused the contrasts of his pre-war work with his post-war concern for the ordinary man. The painting is based on studies he made at the front of soldiers playing cards; in its style and content it marks a transition between Léger's early mature work of the 1910s and his machine-oriented pictures of the 1920s.

*(iii) 1918–26.* Léger's return to Paris coincided with a radical shift in his imagery. He produced a number of paintings on each of several specific themes, such as *The Discs*, *The Propellers* and *The Circus*. Machine-inspired imagery dominated; elements were densely packed and brightly coloured. For Léger the mechanical element was 'not a fixed position, an attitude, but a means of succeeding in conveying a feeling of strength and power.... It is necessary to retain what is useful in the subject and to extract from it the best part possible. I try to create *a beautiful object* with mechanical elements'. His mechanical elements were partly derived from his wartime experience and his awe at military hardware and its power. Léger graphically illustrated Blaise Cendrars's book *J'ai tué* (Paris, 1918) with tubular soldiers and sleek machines. His illustrations for Cendrars's prose-poem *La Fin du monde filmée par l'ange Notre-Dame* (Paris, 1919) prefigured his monumental painting of *The City* (1919; Philadelphia, PA, Mus. A.; see fig. 2). The artist's fascination with the dynamism of Paris and the visual landscape of advertising hoardings, kiosks and illuminated signs unite in this painting. Within a quasi-Cubist armature faceless cut-out figures hover amid intersecting planes of coloured walls, cropped signs and metal railings and towers. Colours were unmodulated and bold; in 1946 Léger reflected that in *The*

2. Fernand Léger: *The City*, oil on canvas, 2.30×2.98 m, 1919 (Philadelphia, PA, Museum of Art)

*City* pure colour had been incorporated into a geometric design to the greatest possible extent and that it was modern advertising that had first understood the importance of this new purity.

Léger's pre-war dealer, Kahnweiler, had been forced to abandon his gallery during the war years because of his German ancestry; his impressive collection of avant-garde art was sold during the 1920s at public sales in Paris. Like Kahnweiler's other artists, Léger sought a new dealer in the post-war years, and in July 1918 he signed a contract with Léonce Rosenberg, who showed Léger's work for the first time in a one-man exhibition at the new Galerie de l'Effort Moderne in 1919. In the same year Léger married Jeanne Lohy.

Although his work in the early 1920s continued the mechanical themes of the years immediately following the war, the figure also reappeared in Léger's work at this time. His paintings of *The Mechanic* (e.g. 1920; Ottawa, N.G.) depict a working man with what appear to be machine-made parts; in his paintings of women, especially in his paintings of 1921 devoted to *Le Grand Déjeuner* (final version in New York, MOMA), Léger invoked classicism in his quest to find monumental figures for his imagery. In pursuing this direction Léger's work very much paralleled Picasso's classicism of the same years. Building on themes of odalisques and languid nudes in

elaborate settings found in the works of David, Ingres and Puvis de Chavannes, Léger created more solid, less fleshy figures and situated them amid the objects and décor of a domestic bourgeois interior. Léger's interest in Classical subject-matter and his passion for medieval and Renaissance art took him to Venice and Ravenna with his dealer, Rosenberg, in 1924. A substantial number of paintings in Léger's work of the early 1920s were also devoted to the *Animated Landscape* (version 1921; Montreal, priv. col., see de Francia, pl. 18). These were depictions of the rural settings familiar to him from his childhood and of what he considered to be the welcome intrusion of contemporary life in them.

Léger's wartime experience encouraged him in the early 1920s to explore diverse media in order to reach the wide range of people that he had encountered during his years in the trenches. He became interested in printmaking around this time, although after a brief period of activity this interest waned, and also in book illustration as a vehicle to disseminate his ideas to wider audiences. Another means was the cinema, which Léger had particularly admired ever since he had first encountered Chaplin's films during the war. In 1920 he illustrated a book of poems devoted to Chaplin, Ivan Goll's *Die Chaplinade* (Dresden and Berlin, 1920). In the following year he assisted Blaise Cendrars, who was working for film maker

Abel Gance on *La Roue*. Léger appears to have participated in the creation, with Cendrars, of the fast-paced montage sections of the film, which received considerable attention in the press. Léger produced a promotional poster for the film and wrote an article in which he celebrated Gance's use of a mechanical object—the wheel of a train—as one of the principal characters in the film. Stimulated by his appreciation for Gance's achievement, Léger embarked on his own films. Initially he proposed several versions of an animated cartoon of *Charlot Cubiste* (*Cubist Chaplin*). Then he created sets for the laboratory section of Marcel L'Herbier's film *L'Inhumaine* (1923).

*Ballet mécanique* (1924) was the first film project realized principally by Léger. He was assisted technically by the American film maker Dudley Murphy, who at the suggestion of Ezra Pound had approached Léger with a proposal to make a film together. *Ballet mécanique* consisted of a rapid succession of mechanical images alternating with close-ups of faces, body parts, pots and pans, abstract shapes, and walking and swinging women. Léger wrote that in it he had set out to prove that it was possible to make a visually interesting film using only simple objects and fragments of objects, 'of a mechanical element, of rhythmic repetitions copied from certain objects of a commonplace nature and "artistic" in the least possible degree'. He was especially excited by the possibilities presented by montage. He also investigated current work on synchronization in the hope of marrying the American composer Georges Antheil's highly experimental score for the film with the images on the screen. Although synchronization was never successfully realized for the original version of the film, the nitrate version of which is now housed at the Anthology Film Archives, New York and which was first shown on the opening night of the Internationale Ausstellung Neuer Theatertechnik in Vienna in September 1924, the film was often screened with live performances of the score, and later versions feature it as a soundtrack. A fourth vehicle for Léger's exploration of diverse media was the stage. Léger was fascinated by performance and the possibilities inherent in the visual artist's collaboration with the choreographer, director, composer and writer. In 1922 his abstract geometric sets and costumes were essential components of the production by the Ballets Suédois of *Skating Rink*, based on Charlie Chaplin's film *The Rink* (1918). In 1923 Léger designed elaborate sets and costumes based on thorough studies of African sculpture for *La Création du monde*, a Ballets Suédois production based on Cendrars's collection of creation myths in his *Anthologie nègre* (1920).

Léger's collaborative projects culminated in the 1920s with his work for architectural settings. For the Exposition Internationale des Arts Décoratifs et Industriels Modernes (1925) in Paris Léger was commissioned with Robert Delaunay to produce murals and exhibit easel paintings as part of the décor of Robert Mallet-Stevens's Pavillon de Tourisme. For the same exhibition Léger exhibited his mural paintings (his most abstract works) along with canvases by Amédée Ozenfant in Le Corbusier's Pavillon de L'Esprit Nouveau; Léger subscribed in part to Le Corbusier's and Ozenfant's notion of PURISM and contributed to the journal *L'Esprit nouveau*, with which they were associated. These architecturally specific projects were part of Léger's overall interest in mural painting and his concern for the role of paintings in architecture, particularly in domestic settings. His views were no doubt influenced by his exposure to the ideas of De Stijl, particularly those conveyed through the exhibition of architectural work by this group at his dealer's Galerie de l'Effort Moderne in 1923. Léger advocated some type of agreement between the architect, the painter and the wall regarding colour, which he believed was a vital component in architecture and absent from much current work. Painters, he argued, could determine its place in architecture better than anyone else.

In 1924 Léger, with Ozenfant, founded the Académie de l'Art Moderne at Léger's studio at 86, Rue Notre-Dame-des-Champs in Montparnasse. Othon Friesz was the third member of the original teaching staff; later Alexandra Exter and Marie Laurencin joined the faculty. Ozenfant left the school in 1929, but Léger continued as its Director until 1939.

*(iv) 1927–39.* Léger's involvement with film in the early 1920s led him to place special emphasis on the close-up. 'The cinema', he observed in 1925, 'can become the gigantic microscope of things never before seen and never before felt.... This is the point of departure for a total renewal of the cinema and of the painted picture'. Léger's fascination with the isolated object increased in the late 1920s, when he embarked on a series of drawings and paintings in which single objects, ranging from a hand to leaves or a bunch of keys, were either seen at close range or were juxtaposed with other seemingly unrelated objects to create jarring contrasts. In drawings, usually made with pencil, these were rendered with great attention to modelling volumes. In paintings, objects were rendered flatly, with strong contours and filled-in colour set against simple decorative planes. Léger's cult of the object, the phase of his career that came closest to being Surrealist (although he denied any interest in Surrealism), culminated in 1934 with his exhibition *Objets* at the Galerie Vignon in Paris.

Increasingly in the early 1930s Léger advocated a realism that was more accessible to the people. His major paintings of the decade—*Mona Lisa with Keys* (1930), *Adam and Eve* (1935–9; both Biot, Mus. N. Fernand Léger) and *Composition with Two Parrots* (1935–9; Paris, Pompidou)—depict either instantly recognizable human images or monumental groups. Léger considered this imagery to correspond to a new realism that was appropriate for the masses and that acknowledged the power of contemporary media: film, radio, photography, advertising. Léger's idealistic views brought him into conflict in the mid-1930s with the more doctrinaire writer and poet Louis Aragon, a strong advocate of Socialist Realism. In the mid-1930s Léger supported the left-wing Popular Front, which came to power in France in 1936, and he attended meetings at the Maison de la Culture in Paris, site of the Association for Revolutionary Writers and Artists. Although he did not officially join the Communist Party until 1945, it is clear that he had been sympathetic to their aims for some time.

Léger's involvement with film and spectacle intensified in the 1930s. In the early part of the decade he corresponded extensively with the Soviet film maker Sergey

Eisenstein. In 1934 he spent several weeks in London preparing to design the sets for Alexander Korda's film *Things to Come* (1936); ultimately Korda rejected Léger's designs, preferring those of both his brother Vincent Korda (*b* 1897) and László Moholy-Nagy.

During his third trip to the USA in 1938–9, when he stayed with the architect Wallace K. Harrison (1895–1981) on Long Island, NY, and with the left-wing writer John Dos Passos in Provincetown, MA, Léger conceived an animated colour film to be projected within the entrance hall and visible from the escalators of the Rockefeller Center in New York. Projects for the stage also abounded in this period. Léger planned a spectacle on the subject of *The Death of Marat, Followed by his Funeral*, which he hoped would be executed in the spirit of the painter David; despite his extensive notes for the project and vigorous attempts in the 1930s, it remained unrealized, as did many of his other proposals for the theatre: *Le Jeu d'Adam*, *Parallèle* (a ballet) and *Le Vélo de fou*. In 1932 Léger had also begun a collaboration with the choreographer Léonide Massine for a ballet project that was never realized. Once again collaborating with the composer Darius Milhaud, with whom he had worked on *La Création du monde*, Léger

designed the sets and costumes for the choreographer Serge Lifar's play *David triomphant*, which opened in 1936 and was performed at the Paris Opéra in 1937. Also in 1937 Léger produced the décor for Jean Richard Bloch's *Naissance d'une cité* at the Vélodrome d'Hiver stadium. This production was among those celebrating the trade unions and was sponsored by the Maison de la Culture.

Léger's mural for the Palais de la Découverte at the Exposition Internationale des Arts et Techniques dans la Vie Moderne in Paris in 1937 was the most massive painting project he had undertaken so far. Entitled *Le Transport des Forces* (see Descargues, p. 119), the mural is a utopian vision, contrasting the mechanical world, as represented by structures resembling a power station and the forces emanating from it, and the natural world, as seen in the 'animated landscape', reminiscent of Léger's paintings of the 1920s. The mural was one of two realized by Léger for the exhibition; the other was designed for the pavilion of the Union des Artistes Modernes and is known only through an installation photograph. An interview in the magazine *Vu* revealed that Léger's ideas for the exhibition had been far more ambitious; he had envisaged 300,000 unemployed people cleaning the façades of all the buildings in Paris and coloured searchlights

3. Fernand Léger: *Adieu New York*, oil on canvas, 1.30×1.62 m, 1946 (Paris, Pompidou, Musée National d'Art Moderne)

4. Fernand Léger: *Leisure (Homage to Jacques-Louis David)*, oil on canvas, 1.54×1.85 m, 1948–9 (Paris, Pompidou, Musée National d'Art Moderne)

projecting from the Eiffel Tower at night as loudspeakers played music and aeroplanes hovered overhead.

*(v) 1940–49.* When the occupation of Paris during World War II became inevitable, Léger travelled first to his family farm in Lisores, Normandy, and then to Marseille and Lisbon, from where he left for the USA in October 1940. The first significant series of paintings Léger began was devoted to *Divers* and was inspired by the young people swimming off the docks in Marseille. In these paintings large swathes of liberated colour intersect the outlines of stylized figures (e.g. *Divers on a Yellow Ground*, 1941; Chicago, IL, A. Inst.). Léger sought to free colour from its traditional confines after seeing the effect of neon signs on the activity in the street on Broadway in New York. Work on the *Divers* theme occupied much of Léger's time in the early 1940s, and it was followed by his series devoted to *Acrobats* (e.g. *The Four Acrobats*, 1942–4; Paris, Pompidou), *Cyclists* (e.g. *The Four Cyclists*, 1943–8; Biot, Mus. N. Fernand Léger) and *Dancers*.

Léger's years in the USA were dominated by painting, fraternizing with many of the European exiles resident in New York, and teaching and travelling throughout the country. While he maintained a studio on W. 40th Street in New York, he taught at Yale University in New Haven, CT, shortly after his arrival in 1940, and at Mills College in Oakland, CA, in 1941. During the summers of 1943 and 1944 Léger lived near an abandoned farm in Rouses Point, NY, near the New York–Canada border. With French-speaking Montreal less than an hour away, Léger felt especially at home in the region, where he painted a sizeable number of landscapes and object-based paintings. The culmination of his wartime stay in the USA was *The Great Julie* (1945; New York, MOMA); the painting's theme is heroicized circus woman Julie, holding a flower in one hand and a twisted bicycle with juggler's hoops in the other. After completing more than 120 paintings during his exile, Léger returned to France in early 1946, observing that he had 'painted in America better than [he] had ever painted before' (see fig. 3).

After 1946 Léger began to participate vigorously in the activities of the Communist Party. Much of his involvement took place in concert with that of the poets Paul

Eluard and Louis Aragon; Léger became especially active in causes related to peace, including the first National Council of the World Peace Movement, of which he was a founder-member in 1948. His painting *Leisure (Homage to Jacques-Louis David)* (1948–9; Paris, Pompidou, see fig. 4) marked a resumption of Léger's interest in David's Neo-classicism combined with a large-scale depiction of the common man, from the French bourgeoisie to circus performers and acrobats. After World War II Léger also revived his academy. It reopened in January 1946 in Montrouge, a suburb of Paris, but moved a year later to a larger studio on the Boulevard Clichy in Paris. Nadia Khodassievitch, his student since 1924, directed the academy. Léger had numerous students after the war, including many American artists benefiting from the opportunities available to them under the post-war GI Bill, such as Sam Francis and Richard Stankiewicz. Léger also encouraged workers at the nearby Renault car factory to attend.

*(vi) 1950–55.* Léger's concern with the common man culminated in his series paintings of the 1950s: his *Builders, Campers* and *The Big Parade.* The *Builders* is perhaps the best-known series, inspired by Léger's view of electrical workers perched on poles. Léger made numerous drawings, prints and paintings related to the theme. Eager for these to be seen by ordinary working people, he temporarily installed several of the *Builders* paintings in the canteen at the Renault factory near Paris, where they met mixed reactions.

During the 1950s Léger also began to work in what were for him new media: stained glass, ceramics, mosaic and tapestry. His initial exposure to ceramics was through a former student, Roland Brice; Léger began to work with Brice during his stay in Biot, between Nice and Antibes on the Côte d'Azur, in 1949. Several of his commissioned works during these years—a mosaic (1949) for the church of Notre-Dame de Toute Grace at the plateau d'Assy in the Haute-Savoie, mosaics (1950) for the Catholic, Protestant and Jewish chapels of the American Memorial in Bastogne, Belgium, 10 stained-glass windows (1954) for the church at Courfaivre in Switzerland and a ceramic (1954) for the Gaz de France building in Alfortville, Val-de-Marne —were made possible by Léger's newly discovered interest in these techniques. The same was true with his designs for stained glass at the church at Audincourt (1951), Doubs, and at the University of Caracas (1954), Venezuela. Many of these commissions were the result of Léger's admiration for and friendship with the religious leader Père Couturier, whose friendship with many artists, including Braque and Matisse, resulted in several important post-war projects for churches throughout France. Léger channelled his efforts toward decidedly public presentations through large-scale, prominently placed works. He also continued his involvement with the theatre in his later years, collaborating again with Darius Milhaud on *Bolívar,* an opera that opened in Paris in May 1950. He designed all of the sets for the three-act opera as well as all 600 costumes. In 1952 he designed an innovative outdoor production of the ballet *Quatre gestes pour un génie* (music by Maurice Jarre), a homage to Leonardo da Vinci. Léger also became interested again in printmaking at about this time, producing *Le Cirque,* a series of 63 lithographs with text by the artist, for the publisher Tériade, who had published Matisse's *Jazz* in 1947.

Léger's first wife, Jeanne, died in 1950, and in 1952 he married his studio assistant Nadia Khodassievitch. He continued to produce at a prolific rate and to travel widely throughout Europe until his death.

2. WORKING METHODS AND TECHNIQUE. Throughout his career Léger's working practice was to produce groups of works (drawings, gouaches and even oil paintings) relating to specific themes, a method that encouraged the production of series from 1910. Although drawing represented his only artistic activity during World War I, it later became primarily important to him as a preliminary stage in his work and his teaching method. Careful preparatory drawings exist for works in virtually every medium, and selected versions were often then gridded for enlarging on canvas in a definitive version in oil. This was particularly true for his work after World War II, although some of his preparatory studies of 1923–4 are also remarkably finished. The preparatory drawings themselves would often evolve from loose sketches, but Léger was always careful to distinguish between the two. Some of his drawings from the 1940s, for example, show a freedom and boldness that suggest a renewed interest in draughtsmanship for its own sake about this time. The canvases emerged naturally from this process, with some themes being represented by several paintings as equally valid variations, while in other instances various treatments in oil, sometimes differing only in minute details, were seen only as part of the process of working towards a definitive image, as in the series leading to *Le Grand Déjeuner.* The essentially mechanical approach adopted by Léger towards his paintings is further demonstrated by his tendency to reuse certain standard elements, such as a pair of hands or lips, not just in treatments of related subjects but also in paintings and drawings on different themes.

Léger often used his students to paint his large-scale works. Academy pupils of the 1920s such as the Swedish artist Otto Carlsund recalled executing versions of Léger's paintings and several of his set designs. In the 1930s Léger used his students to help conceive and execute designs for *Naissance d'une cité* (1937) and to paint his mural for the Palais de la Découverte; among the students contributing to the latter was the Danish artist Asger Jorn. In the early 1950s Léger's students painted panels for the book festival of the 1953 Comité National d'Ecrivains. One of his former students, Bruce Gregory (*b* 1917), executed Léger's 1952 gouaches on a large scale as paintings for the east and west walls of the General Assembly of the United Nations in New York.

Léger's experiments with film, particularly the *Ballet mécanique,* reflect his enthusiasm with energetic, mechanized modernity. Although innovative, his films, like his response to the movements of the body in his designs for the ballet, were more concerned with formal aspects than with technical experiments. In his experiments with other media, his interest was again seldom purely technical. Indeed, in most cases his choice of a particular medium (mosaic, ceramics, stained glass) was based on its suitability for the monumental public display of his pre-conceived designs.

### WRITINGS

*Le Cirque* (Paris, 1950)
'Comment je conçois la figure', *La Figure dans l'oeuvre de Léger* (exh. cat., Paris, Louis Carré, 1952)
*Propos et présence* (Paris, 1959)
*La Ville* (Paris, 1959)
*Mes voyages* (Paris, 1960)
*Fonctions de la peinture* (Paris, 1965; Eng. trans. and rev. as *Functions of Painting*, New York, 1965)
C. Derouet, ed.: *Lettres à Simone*, intro. M. Jardot (Paris, 1987)
——: 'Une Correspondance de guerre à Louis Poughon, 1914–1918', *Cah. Mus. N. A. Mod.* (Paris, 1990)

### BIBLIOGRAPHY

#### MONOGRAPHS

M. Raynal: *Fernand Léger* (Paris, 1920)
W. George: *Fernand Léger* (Paris, 1929)
F. Elgar: *Léger: Peintures, 1911–1948* (Paris, 1948)
D. Cooper: *Fernand Léger et le nouvel espace* (Geneva, 1949)
P. Descargues: *Fernand Léger* (Paris, 1955)
L. Aragon: *Fernand Léger: Contrastes* (Paris, 1959)
R. Garaudy: *Pour un réalisme du XXe siècle: Dialogue posthume avec Fernand Léger* (Paris, 1968)
G. Le Noci: *Fernand Léger: Sa vie, son oeuvre, son rêve* (Milan, 1971)
J. Cassou and J. Leymarie: *Fernand Léger: Dessins et gouaches* (Paris, 1972)
J. Golding: *Fernand Léger: The Mechanic*, Masterpieces in the National Gallery of Canada, 6 (Ottawa, 1976)
C. Green: *Léger and the Avant-Garde* (New Haven and London, 1976)
L. Saphire: *Fernand Léger: The Complete Graphic Work* (New York, 1978) [cat. rais.]
C. Laugier and M. Richet: *Oeuvres de Fernand Léger*, (Paris, 1981)
P. de Francia: *Fernand Léger* (New Haven and London, 1983)
J. Freeman: 'Fernand Léger and the Ballets Suédois: The Pursuit of Collaborative Ideals in Performance', *Actes du 25ème Congrès International d'Histoire de l'Art: Vienne, 1984*
——: 'Bridging Purism and Surrealism: The Origins and Production of Fernand Léger's *Ballet Mécanique*', *Dada Surrealism*, xv (1986), pp. 28–45
G. Bauquier: *Fernand Léger: Vivre dans le vrai* (Paris, 1987)
G. Bauquier with N. Maillard: *Fernand Léger: Catalogue raisonné de l'oeuvre peint* (Paris, 1990)
G. Néret: *Léger* (Paris, 1990)

#### CATALOGUES

*Fernand Léger, 1881–1955* (exh. cat., ed. J. Cassou and F. Mathey; Paris, Mus. A. Déc., 1956) [the major memorial exh.]
*Fernand Léger: Five Themes and Variations* (exh. cat., ed. L. A. Svendsen; New York, Guggenheim, 1962)
*Léger and Purist Paris* (exh. cat., ed. J. Golding and C. Green; London, Tate, 1970–71) [focuses on work of late 1910s and 1920s in Purist Paris]
*Fernand Léger* (exh. cat., ed. J. Leymarie and M. Richet; Paris, Grand Pal., 1971–2)
*Théâtre de Fernand Léger* (exh. cat., Paris, Espace Pierre Cardin, 1971–2)
*Fernand Léger* (exh. cat., ed. D. Ruckhaberle; Berlin, Staatl. Ksthalle, 1980)
*Léger's 'Le Grand Déjeuner'* (exh. cat., ed. Robert L. Herbert; Minneapolis, MN, Inst. A., 1980)
*Fernand Léger: La Poésie de l'objet, 1928–34* (exh. cat., ed. C. Derouet; Paris, Pompidou, 1981)
*Fernand Léger* (exh. cat., ed. R. T. Buck, E. F. Fry and C. Kotik; Buffalo, NY, Albright–Knox A.G., 1982)
*Léger et l'esprit moderne; Une alternative d'avant-garde à l'art non-objectif* (exh. cat., ed. M.-O. Briot, G. Fabre and B. Rose; Paris, Mus. A. Mod. Ville Paris, 1982)
*Fernand Léger: Gouachen, Aquarellen, Zeichnungen* (exh. cat., ed. U. W. Schneede; Hamburg, Kstver., 1983)
*Fernand Léger: The Later Years* (exh. cat., ed. N. Serota; London, Whitechapel A.G., 1987–8)
*Fernand Léger: Rétrospective* (exh. cat., ed. A. Maeght; Saint-Paul-de-Vence, Fond. Maeght, 1988)
*Fernand Léger* (exh. cat., ed. H. Lassalle; Villeneuve d'Ascq, Mus. A. Mod., 1990)
*Fernand Léger: The Rhythm of Modern Life* (exh. cat., ed. D. Kosinski; Basle, Kstmus., 1994)

JUDI FREEMAN

**Leghorn.** *See* LIVORNO.

**Legorreta, Ricardo** (*b* Mexico City, 7 May 1931). Mexican architect, furniture designer and writer. He graduated from the Escuela Nacional de Arquitectura, Universidad Nacional Autónoma de México, Mexico City, in 1953. He began as a draughtsman in the studio of José Villagrán García, the leader of Mexican Functionalism, becoming his partner between 1955 and 1960. During this period he was a follower of the International Style, as seen in the Hotel María Isabel (1961–2; with Villagrán García and Juan Sordo Madaleno), Mexico City. In 1960 he set up in partnership with Noé Castro (*b* 1929) and Carlos Vargas (*b* 1938), specializing in the design of factories and office buildings, the most notable project of this period being the office building for Celanese Mexicana (1966–8; with Roberto Jean) in Mexico City, with its prismatic outline and technical brio in the use of the hanging structure. In the late 1960s, influenced by LUIS BARRAGÁN and MATHIAS GOERITZ and his own strong sense of Mexican identity, Legorreta embraced 'emotional architecture' (*see* MEXICO, §III, 2), which he developed into an important trend in late 20th-century Mexican architecture. His experience and technical mastery enabled him to combine functional solutions with variations on characteristic Mexican forms. This approach was applied to all types of buildings, including large-scale and complex projects. The first example was the Hotel Camino Real (1968) in Mexico City, where the idea of the tall building was replaced with a linear concept; in later examples, such as the Camino Real hotels in Cancún (1975) and Ixtapa (1981), the relationship of the buildings to their natural environment is stressed.

Legorreta was also active in the area of industrial architecture, designing such buildings as the IBM factory (1975), Guadalajara, and the Renault Engines factory (1983), Gómez Palacio, and in the design of bank buildings, for example the city-centre offices of the Banco de México (1982–5), Mexico City. He designed the Museo de Arte Contemporaneo, Monterrey, in 1991, one of Mexico's most lavish constructions, and in 1992 the new Cathedral in Managua, Nicaragua, with its multi-domed roof (*see* NICARAGUA, fig. 2). His private houses, for example the weekend house (1973) in Valle de Bravo, Mexico State, express vernacular influences more intensely, the whole being skilfully adapted to its surroundings, while his interior designs reflect his experience of creating furniture and accessories. Generally they follow a balance between austerity and opulence, using natural materials such as clay, wood and textiles, with decorations drawn from popular crafts.

### WRITINGS

*Muros de México* (Mexico City, 1978)
L. Noelle: *Ricardo Legorreta: Tradición y Modernidad* (Mexico City, 1989)
W. Attoe: *The Architecture of Ricardo Legorreta* (Austin, 1990)

LOUISE NOELLE

**Legot, Pablo** (*b* Marche, Luxembourg, 1598; *d* Cádiz, 1671). Spanish painter. Legot's parents moved from Luxembourg, then under Spanish rule, to Seville in 1610. It has long been believed that his first profession was that of embroiderer, and he appears as such in the registration of his marriage in 1619. In 1628 he is recorded as painter to the Archbishop of Seville, and in this capacity he undertook a large number of works, which he subcontracted to other painters. In 1635 he was appointed maritime customs official (Alguacil Fiscal del Real Almirantazgo) at Cádiz, and he continued to paint there until *c.* 1665, when ill-health forced him gradually to abandon painting.

Legot's work shows a clear orientation towards naturalism and a preference for tenebrist effects deriving from Ribera. His earliest work, the *Transfiguration* (1631) on the former main altarpiece in the church of El Salvador in Seville, is based on an engraving of Raphael's painting of the same subject (Rome, Pin. Vaticana). Legot also executed part of the *Adoration of the Shepherds* altarpiece in the church of Palacios in Seville, painted *c.* 1631. The most important paintings of the altarpiece in S María in Lebrija, near Seville, are Legot's *Adoration of the Shepherds* and *Adoration of the Magi* (both 1631–7). The same subject-matter is represented in his last works, dating from *c.* 1650 and depicting episodes related to the birth of Christ, in the reredos in the church of S María in Espera, Cádiz. Other important paintings by Legot are the *Adoration of the Magi* (1642) in Cádiz Cathedral and *St Jerome* in Seville Cathedral.

BIBLIOGRAPHY
E. Valdivieso and J. M. Serrera: *Pintura sevillana del primer tercio del siglo XVII* (Madrid, 1985), pp. 260–301
A. Pérez Sánchez: *Pintura barroca en España, 1600–1750* (Madrid, 1992), pp. 265–6

ENRIQUE VALDIVIESO

**Le Grain, Jean.** *See* ZIARNKO, JAN.

**Legrain, Pierre(-Emile)** (*b* Levallois-Perret, Hauts-de-Seine, 2 Oct 1889; *d* Paris, 17 July 1929). French designer. The son of a wealthy distiller, he studied drawing from a young age and from 1904 was trained at the Ecole des Arts Appliqués Germain Pilon. In 1908 Legrain joined the studio of the designer Paul Iribe (1883–1935), with whom he collaborated in 1912 on the apartment of the couturier and patron, JACQUES DOUCET. In 1917 Doucet commissioned Legrain to design bookbindings for his collection of manuscripts and first editions. The success of this commission and a disagreement with Doucet led Legrain to open his own bookbinding studio in 1919. The bindings that he designed were Cubist-inspired and invariably geometric in style and were instrumental in the revival of the art of bookbinding in the 1920s. He also framed pictures for Louis Marcoussis. By 1922 he was again working for Doucet, and in 1925 he was in charge of the decoration of Doucet's villa at Neuilly. Much of the furniture that Legrain designed for Doucet and others in the 1920s was inspired by African furniture (e.g. chaise longue, *c.* 1925; Paris, Mus. A. Déc.) and was executed in a variety of fashionable materials including exotic veneers, parchment and metal (*see* FRANCE, fig. 62).

BIBLIOGRAPHY
M. Dormoy and others: *Pierre Legrain, relieur* (Paris, 1965)
L. Thornton: 'Negro Art and the Furniture of Pierre-Emile Legrain', *Connoisseur*, clxxxi (1972), pp. 166–9

DONNA CORBIN

**Legrand, Jacques-Guillaume** (*b* Paris, 9 May 1743; *d* Saint-Denis, nr Paris, 9 Nov 1807). French architect and writer. He studied at the Académie Royale d'Architecture

and the Ecole des Ponts et Chaussées, Paris, as a pupil of Jacques-François Blondel and Jean-Rodolphe Perronet. In 1781 he was commissioned with Jacques Molinos to roof the courtyard of Nicolas Le Camus de Mézières's Halle au Blé, Paris, for which they designed an innovative light timber dome (subsequently replaced by a cast-iron dome by François-Joseph Bélanger). Thereafter they worked on many projects together (*see* MOLINOS, JACQUES); examples include the Halle aux Draps (1786), Théâtre Feydeau and Hôtel Marbeuf (both 1789) and a lecture theatre at the Jardin des Plantes, all in Paris, together with the Hôtel de Ville at Auteuil (1792). Legrand's most important independent works are two great houses in Paris. The Hôtel de Gallifet (1775–96) has a block-like appearance, with no end pavilions or side wings as became common in the 1770s; it is set off by colossal Ionic colonnades, engaged on the garden front and forming a portico on the entrance façade. Like most of his work, the interiors are designed in a style inspired by the Antique, which was then in vogue. Engaged columns articulate the walls, and in the Chambre de Parade they frame bays stuccoed with grotesques derived from Pompeii. The Hôtel de Jarnac (1783–7) has a courtyard front with an engaged colossal order supporting a straight entablature, similar to the garden elevation at Gallifet. The garden façade at Jarnac, however, is enlivened by a segmental pediment over its colossal order, here reduced to four columns. The Grand Salon features engaged Ionic columns, with false doors lined with mirrors reflecting the garden. Elsewhere in the room the walls are embellished with stucco arabesques. Legrand was also well known as a writer on architecture; he published several of his own works, and he provided the text for the second edition of the *Antiquités de la France* (1804) by his father-in-law, Charles-Louis Clérisseau.

WRITINGS
*Parallèle de l'architecture ancienne et moderne* (Paris, 1789)
with C.-L. Clérisseau: *Antiquités de la France* (2/Paris, 1804)
*Collection des chefs-d'oeuvres de l'architecture des différents peuples* (Paris, 1806)
with C. P. Landon: *Description de Paris et de ses édifices* (Paris, 1807)
with J.-N.-L. Durand: *Essai sur l'histoire générale de l'architecture* (Paris, 1809)

BIBLIOGRAPHY
J. Adhémar: 'La Coupole en charpente de la Halle au Blé et l'influence de Philibert Delorme au XVIIIème siècle', *Architecture*, xxxxvi (1933), pp. 249–52
H. Ottomeyer: 'Autobiographies d'architectes parisiens, 1759–1811', *Bull. Soc. Hist. Paris & Ile-de-France* xcviii (1971), pp. 141–206

GÉRARD ROUSSET-CHARNY

**Legrand, Louis(-Auguste-Mathieu)** (*b* Dijon, 23 Sept 1863; *d* Livry-Gargan, Picardy, 12 June 1951). French painter, printmaker and draughtsman. He trained at the Ecole des Beaux-Arts in Dijon and in 1884 moved to Paris, where he worked as a caricaturist and political satirist for *La Journée* and *Le Journal amusant* and from 1887 for the more influential *Courrier français*. He received a brief prison sentence for a mildly obscene satire in *Courrier français* on Emile Zola. About 1885 he met Félicien Rops, who taught him the techniques of etching. In 1891 he produced a series of watercolours for the magazine *Gil Blas*, depicting dancers warming up for the cancan. These proved so successful that he was asked to produce 11 etchings on a similar theme, *Danse, fin de siècle* (Paris, 1892). This success brought him to the attention of Gustave Pellet, one of the best print publishers of the period, who published his 15 lithographs, *Au Cap de la chèvre* (Paris, 1892). It was followed by a set of etchings depicting ballet rehearsals, *Les Petites de ballet* (Paris, 1893). He excelled in etchings of bars, cafés and other turn-of-the-century social scenes; later albums of these subjects included *La Petite Classe* (Paris, 1908) and *Les Bars* (Paris, 1909). He also produced landscapes such as *Les Bords de la Marne* (1905; Paris, Bib. N.). His work in other areas tended towards the sentimental, however, as in *Charles VI* (1909; Paris, Bib. N.).

Having established a reputation as a graphic artist, Legrand also turned to painting and pastels such as *The Serenade* (Cleveland, OH, Mus. A.). His paintings typically employ a thick impasto (*The Bath*, for illus. see Mauclair, p. 194); he worked more persistently in pastels. Throughout his graphic work, most notably in his illustrations for Edgar Allen Poe's *Quinze histoires* (Paris, 1897), there ran a strain of eroticism and the macabre, which he had perhaps inherited from Rops. After World War I his output decreased considerably. Amongst the numerous books he illustrated were Guy de Maupassant's *Cinq contes parisiens* (Paris, 1905), *Poèmes à l'eau-forte* (Paris, 1914) with poems by Baudelaire, Mallarmé, Rimbaud, Verlaine and others, and Francis Carco's *Quelques-unes* (Paris, 1931).

BIBLIOGRAPHY

E. Ramiro: *Louis Legrand* (Paris, 1896)
C. Mauclair: *Louis Legrand* (Paris, 1910)

**Le Gray, (Jean-Baptiste-)Gustave** (*b* Villiers-le-Bel, Seine-et-Oise, 30 Aug 1820; *d* Cairo, 30 July 1884). French photographer, painter and teacher. He studied painting with Paul Delaroche until 1843. A study trip to Switzerland and Italy, financed by his parents, followed, but it was cut short by an untimely marriage in 1844, his sudden return to his family's home and the subsequent birth of two children in 1845 and 1846. Skilled in painting as an experimenter with pigments, he was attracted to the experimental side of the new paper negative processes available in France after 1847 and plunged into photography, probably to finance the burdens of the family life newly thrust upon him. His treatise, *Traité pratique de photographie sur papier et sur verre* (1850), outlined his own variant of the dry waxed paper negative process using thinner paper, as well as a recipe for collodion on glass negatives rivalling that of the English inventor Frederick Scott Archer (*see* PHOTOGRAPHY, §I). A further modification to the waxed paper negative process was announced in 1851. Le Gray quickly gained a reputation as a brilliant and intuitive photography teacher and gave lessons from a factory building at the Barrière de Clichy in north-west Paris to many painters, including other students of Delaroche such as Henri Le Secq and Charles Nègre, and to countless amateurs who professed later that they could not remember anything Le Gray had taught them, except that they learnt to love photography.

Le Gray's teaching reinforced his view that to photograph was to practise an art with a set of rules that did not necessarily derive from painting. Nonetheless, in 1849 he was among the first photographers to follow the painters to the Forest of Fontainebleau and made mysteriously beautiful compositions of the 'black networks' of the trees (e.g. *In the Forest of Fontainebleau*, 1851, print after 1855; London, V&A) of the kind Victor Hugo characterized in his poetry. Le Gray's peregrinations in Fontainebleau were also part of the domestication of the forest initiated by its great connoisseurs, who since 1840 had been writing detailed guidebooks to the place as if it were a museum. Le Gray made at least one album of his trees but mainly sold the prints to artists; however, his public was probably envisaged as being the same as those who read the guidebooks.

Le Gray was a founder of the Société Héliographique in 1851 and of the Société Française de Photographie, and he served on many committees concerned to make photographs aesthetically pleasing as well as cheap and available. By 1851 he was an accomplished architectural photographer, and he took part in the Missions Héliographiques set up by the Commission des Monuments Historiques to record ancient monuments in France. Le Gray collaborated with his student O. Mestral (active 1850s), and both men's names appear on prints depicting the fortifications at Carcassonne, for example. Le Gray's work for the Missions has a highly romantic character. Burying his details in deepest shadow he was able to produce moonlight effects on the dreaming, silent cloister at Moissac (Paris, Mus. d'Orsay), for example, while photographing in broad daylight.

After the death of his father in 1855 and with the help of two financial backers, Le Gray established a commercial studio with sumptuously decorated rooms on the Boulevard des Capucines in Paris, where he concentrated on portraiture to guarantee an income. His depictions of living persons seem rather reticent regarding the force of human character, especially when compared with the work of his contemporary and rival Nadar. Le Gray was really more at home in open spaces and at this time began photographing seascapes from the Normandy coast (e.g. *Brig upon the Water*, 1856; New York, Met.; see fig.) and along the Mediterranean near Sète (e.g. *Broken Wave, Port de Sète*, 1856; London, V&A). Such works caused an immediate sensation and were widely exhibited and collected, initially by British collectors and amateurs. Le Gray was innovative in producing stunning effects of light and split-second effects of waves crashing on the shore with dynamic clouds overhead. He used the more sensitive collodion on glass process for this, to which he added his skills as a combination printer (using two different negatives for a single seascape in order to control sky and sea separately, a fact verified by the discovery of four different seascapes with exactly the same clouds). His work was an inspiration to the Impressionists, especially Claude Monet, whose work along the Normandy coast in the 1860s (e.g. *Terrace at Sainte-Adresse*, 1866; New York, Met.) reflects an awareness of certain Le Gray effects.

In 1857 Le Gray was commissioned by Napoleon III to record the principal scenes of the inauguration of a new instructional military site, the Camp de Châlons, and to produce a series of albums that the Emperor could present to his generals. Le Gray also used collodion on glass for

Gustave Le Gray: *Brig upon the Water*, albumen silver print from glass negative, 1856 (New York, Metropolitan Museum of Art)

this task, and, although he was unable to convey the fierce action of the manoeuvres celebrating the opening of the camp, he produced evocative symbols of military life in silent tableaux, for example *Souvenir of the Camp de Châlons, Addressed to General Decaën* (New York, MOMA). He used a similar approach back in Paris as he recorded along the Seine large views of urban architecture, which map out the city into topographies of bridges, domes and spires.

From the beginning Le Gray's career involved a terrible struggle to survive financially without compromising his artistic standards. Despite his renown as a teacher, experimenter and promoter of French photography's earliest aesthetic ideals, he was a feckless self-promoter who seems to have suffered gravely from little or no business acumen. In February 1860 he dissolved Le Gray and Company. By May he had boarded a yacht, the *Emma*, belonging to the writer Alexandre Dumas. With Dumas and several young passengers Le Gray headed for Egypt, abandoning his family, and, most significantly, his creditors in France. He never returned. For Le Gray the *Emma* was to be the perfect escape, a floating paradise moving toward a land of dreams. However, Dumas was detained in Sicily, where he met Garibaldi engaged in his struggle to unify Italy. Le Gray documented the aftermath of battles in Palermo and

made a portrait of *Garibaldi* himself. Of the score of images supposedly made, only a few survive (e.g. Paris, Bib. N., Cab. Est.). Wood-engravings of some, including the portrait of *Garibaldi*, were published in *Le Monde illustré* in July 1860. Dumas wanted to return to France to bring the General more arms. Le Gray refused to return, wanting instead to get to Egypt to experience, as Dumas put it, 'that voluptuous absence of will'. Le Gray remained in Egypt for the last 24 years of his life. In 1869 he was teaching drawing and painting at the Ecole Polytechnique of the viceroy in Cairo and still photographing.

WRITINGS
*Traité pratique de photographie sur papier et sur verre* (Paris, 1850; enlarged edn 1851, 1852, 1854)

BIBLIOGRAPHY
F. Tournachon: *Quand j'étais photographe* (Paris, 1900)
A. Jammes and E. P. Janis: *The Art of French Calotype, with a Critical Dictionary of Photographers, 1845–1870* (Princeton, 1983), pp. 33–8, 52–66, 200–05
E. P. Janis: *The Photography of Gustave Le Gray* (Chicago, 1987)

EUGENIA PARRY JANIS

**Legros.** French family of artists. (1) Pierre Legros (i) was a sculptor, who contributed to the decoration of the gardens of the château of Versailles. His elder son (2) Pierre Legros (ii) became one of the most successful monumental sculptors in early 18th-century Rome, his best-known work being the altar of St Ignatius in the church of Il Gesù. (3) Jean Legros, younger son of Pierre (i), was a portrait painter in the style of Hyacinthe Rigaud.

**(1) Pierre Legros (i)** (*b* Chartres, *bapt* 27 May 1629; *d* Paris, 10 May 1714). Sculptor. A pupil of Jacques Sarazin, he was received (*reçu*) in 1666 as a member of the Académie Royale, with a marble bas-relief of *St Peter* (Versailles, Notre-Dame). He was principally employed by the Bâtiments du Roi on the sculptural decoration of the château and gardens of Versailles. Within the constraints imposed by the designs and models supplied by Charles Le Brun and François Girardon, his numerous works of sculpture display a distinctive personality of sensual charm and high spirits. His earliest works for Versailles were six gilded lead fountains for the Allée d'Eau, consisting of exuberant groups of children, satyrs and tritons (1668–70, destr.; bronze replicas, 1688, *in situ*) composed with great sureness and freedom. He contributed similarly lively groups of children to the Demi-lune du Dragon (gilt lead, 1678–80, destr.; bronze replicas, 1688, *in situ*) and nymphs and children to the Parterre d'Eau (bronze, 1685–6; *in situ*). In addition he contributed lead bas-reliefs to the *Bain des nymphes* (1670; *in situ*) and a grotesque statue of *Aesop* and several animals from the *Fables* to the Labyrinthe (lead, 1672–6; Versailles, Château).

Pierre Legros's large marble statues for the gardens are successful examples of the classicism of Versailles and include an allegory of *Water* as a beautiful and melancholy woman from a series of the *Four Elements* based on designs by Le Brun (1674; *in situ*), as well as an allegory of *Daybreak* based on a model by Girardon (1686–96; *in situ*) and other works deriving from antique prototypes, such as his brilliant *Venus Leaving her Bath* (1685–9; *in situ*). His stone groups of *Cephalus and Procris* and *Vertumnus and Pomona* on the staircase of the Orangerie (1687; *in situ*), filled with passion, show a more Baroque tendency, reflecting a general movement towards a more animated style at Versailles in the 1680s. He also contributed statuary to the decoration of the façade of the château, including a statue of *Europa* for the balustrade of the Cour de Marbre (stone, 1679; in store), and to the decoration of the interior, including a number of elaborate gilt stucco cornices and reliefs for the Appartement de la Reine, the Grande Galerie and the Salon de la Paix (1679–84; *in situ*). From 1690 to 1700 he worked under Girardon's direction on the decoration of the church of the Invalides, Paris. He was also active at the royal châteaux of Trianon, Clagny (destr.), and Marly, Yvelines, and produced a large stone bas-relief of the *Conquest of Limburg* for the Porte St Martin, Paris (1675–7; *in situ*), and a stone group of *Christ Healing the Blind Man* for the choir of Chartres Cathedral (1682–3; *in situ*). Among his last commissions was a group of statues for the Elector Maximilian II Emanuel of Bavaria, which has been tentatively linked with four marble terms in the Louvre representing the *Seasons*, among which is the superbly dramatic figure of *Winter*.

**(2) Pierre Legros (ii)** (*b* Paris, 12 April 1666; *d* Rome, 3 May 1719). Sculptor. He was the son of (1) Pierre Legros (i) and his first wife, Jeanne, daughter of Gaspard Marsy.

He was trained by his father and between 1690 and 1695 was a *pensionnaire* at the Académie de France in Rome, where among other works he made a marble copy (1692–5; Paris, Jard. Tuileries) of the antique statue of *Vetturia*, then in the Villa Medici. In 1695 he was excluded from the Académie when he accepted an invitation from the Jesuit architect Father Andrea Pozzo to collaborate on the new altar for the chapel of S Ignazio at Il Gesù, Rome. For this vast Baroque ensemble he sculpted the large and dramatic four-figure marble group *Religion Overthrowing Heresy* (1695–9; *in situ*), and in 1697 he won the commission for the silver and bronze centrepiece of the altar, the statue of the *Apotheosis of St Ignatius of Loyola* (1697–8; *in situ*). His success brought him a flood of important commissions, and he rapidly became the most eminent sculptor in early 18th-century Rome, unanimously elected in 1700 as Accademico di Merito at the Accademia di S Luca. In 1697 Cardinal de Bouillon, the French Ambassador in Rome, commissioned sculptures for the ambitious family mausoleum that he intended to erect in the abbey of Cluny, Saône-et-Loire. Although never installed, such surviving fragments as the seated statues of *Frédéric-Maurice de la Tour d'Auvergne* and his wife and a bas-relief of a cavalry battle (all marble, 1697–before 1708; Cluny, Hôtel-Dieu) demonstrate Legros's lightness of touch and

Pierre Legros (ii): *Apotheosis of the Blessed Aloysius Gonzaga*, marble bas-relief, S Ignazio, Rome, 1698–9

dazzling virtuosity in the handling of marble. In 1698 he received another commission from the Jesuits, to produce the large bas-relief of the *Apotheosis of the Blessed Aloysius Gonzaga* (marble; 1698–9; *in situ*, see fig.) for the new altar in the Lancellotti chapel at S Ignazio, Rome, and in 1701 he executed a statue of *St Francis Xavier* for S Apollinare, Rome (marble; *in situ*), a work whose subtle contrapposto and rhythmically agitated draperies give it the appearance almost of weightlessness. Among Legros's other Jesuit commissions was the remarkably realistic polychrome marble statue of the *Death of the Blessed Stanislaus Kostka* (1702–3; Rome, S Andrea al Quirinale).

Legros also executed for the Dominicans in Rome, whose general, Père Antonin Cloche, was French, a number of important commissions. They included a gilt bronze sarcophagus relief of *St Pius V on his Deathbed* (1697–8; Rome, S Maria Maggiore), the bronze and coloured marble tomb of *Cardinal Girolamo Casanata* (1701–3; Rome, S Giovanni in Laterano), an animated and psychologically penetrating marble statue of the same *Cardinal Casanata* (1706–8; Rome, Bib. Casanatense) and an over life-size marble statue of *St Dominic* for a niche in the choir of St Peter's, Rome (1702; *in situ*).

Among his other projects, Legros sculpted from his own designs two of the twelve great marble statues of the *Apostles* for the nave of S Giovanni in Laterano, Rome: the vigorous and expressive *St Bartholomew* and *St Thomas* (1705–12; *in situ*). In 1708–10 he collaborated with the architect Filippo Juvarra on the Antamoro chapel at S Girolamo della Carità, Rome, where he carved the dynamic marble group (*in situ*) of *St Philip Neri in Glory*, silhouetted against an oval mandorla of light. In 1709–13 he was responsible for the grandiose funerary monument to *Pope Gregory XV and his Nephew Cardinal Ludovico Ludovisi* (marble and bronze; Rome, S Ignazio). By the time ill-health forced him to return to Paris in 1714, Legros had established himself as the most important sculptor at work in Rome since Bernini. He had developed late Baroque sculpture into a subtle and personal art form, charged with feeling and yet clearly expressing an inner spirituality. Much of his success in conveying such an atmosphere was due to his highly individual treatment of the surface of the marble, with its delicate interplay of light and shadow, a technique particularly apparent in such reliefs as *Tobit Lending Money to Gabael* (marble, 1702–5; Rome, Monte di Pietà).

In Paris Legros provided stucco decoration for the famous octagonal cabinet (1715; destr.) in the house in the Rue de Richelieu of the collector and patron Pierre Crozat, and also for the chapel (1715; destr.) of Crozat's country house at Montmorency. Legros was disappointed in the hope that his fame in Rome would gain him admission to the Académie Royale without the usual formalities; at the end of 1715 he returned to Rome, only to discover that his rival Camillo Rusconi had supplanted him in the work on the remaining Apostle statues for S Giovanni in Laterano. However, he received several new commissions, including a magnificent altar relief of *St Francis of Paola Imploring the Virgin* (marble, c. 1716; *in situ*) for S Giacomo degli Incurabili, Rome, and two statues for S Cristina, Turin: *St Christina*, in the classical manner

of Algardi, and *St Teresa*, with all Bernini's mysticism (both marble, 1716–17; now Turin, Cathedral).

Legros was primarily the undisputed master of religious compositions, who produced, in addition to his great permanent sculpture, a number of elaborate temporary decorations, such as those (1711; destr.) for the funeral service of the Dauphin at S Luigi dei Francesi, Rome. However, his terracotta *bozzetti* and his small and medium-sized works in marble and bronze, such as the numerous versions of *Marsyas* (e.g. bronze; Dresden, Skulpsamml.), were much sought after by the great collectors of the 18th century, including Crozat and Ange-Laurent La Live de Jully in France, and Augustus III of Poland. Both Crozat and Pierre-Jean Mariette owned drawings by Legros, whose inventory after death indicates that he had formed an extensive collection of Italian, Dutch and Flemish paintings of the 17th and 18th centuries.

(3) Jean Legros (*b* Paris, 3 Oct 1671; *d* Saint-Germain-en-Laye, 27 Jan 1741). Painter. He was the son of (1) Pierre Legros (i) by his second wife Marie, sister of Pierre Le Pautre. A pupil of Hyacinthe Rigaud, he practised as a portrait painter; his *morceau de réception* for admission to the Académie Royale, a formal portrait of the sculptor *Nicolas Coustou* (1722; Versailles, Château), gives a good indication of his rich style and reveals his teacher's influence.

BIBLIOGRAPHY
Lami; Mariette; Souchal; Thieme–Becker
N. Pio: 'Pietro Le Gros' (MS., Rome, Vatican, Bib. Apostolica, 1724); ed. E. Muntz, *Nouv. Archvs A. Fr.* (1874–5), pp. 199–201
Abbé L. Pascoli: *Vite de pittori, scultori ed architetti moderni*, i (1730), pp. 271–4
J. Guiffrey, ed.: *Comptes* (1881–1901)
A. de Montaiglon and J. Guiffrey, eds: *Correspondance des Directeurs de l'Académie de France à Rome avec les Surintendants des Bâtiments* (Paris, 1887–1908), i, ii, iv, v
P. d'Espezel: 'Notes historiques sur l'oeuvre et la vie de Pierre II Le Gros', *Gaz. B.-A.*, n. s. 5, xii (1934), pp. 5–16, 149–60
R. Enggass: *Early Eighteenth-century Sculpture in Rome*, 2 vols (1976), pp. 42–5, 49–51, 53–6, 124–48, pls 93–146
M. Conforti: 'P. Legros and the Role of Sculptors as Designers in Late Baroque Rome', *Burl. Mag.*, cxix (1977), pp. 556–60
M. Baker: 'That Most Rare Master Monsii Le Gros and his Marsyas', *Burl. Mag.*, cxxvii (1985), pp. 702–6
FRANÇOISE DE LA MOUREYRE

Legros, Alphonse (*b* Dijon, 8 May 1837; *d* Watford, 8 Dec 1911). British etcher, painter, sculptor and teacher of French birth. He is said to have been apprenticed at the age of 11 to a sign-painter, at which time he may also have attended classes at the Ecole des Beaux-Arts in Dijon. He was employed as assistant on a decorative scheme in Lyon Cathedral before moving in 1851 to Paris, where he worked initially for the theatre decorator C. A. Cambon (1802–75). He soon became a pupil of Horace Lecoq de Boisbaudran, whose methodical instruction and liberality in fostering individual talent proved of lasting benefit to Legros. In 1855 he enrolled at the Ecole des Beaux-Arts, Paris, attending irregularly until 1857. During this period Legros had a taste for early Netherlandish art and for French Romanticism, which was later superseded by his admiration for Claude, Poussin and Michelangelo. However, his devotion to Holbein proved constant and was apparent as early as his first Salon painting, *Portrait of the Artist's Father* (1857; Tours, Mus. B.-A.).

Legros began etching in 1855; he preferred this medium and produced over 600 plates. Many of his early works are deliberately rough in execution, yet Legros already valued the medium sufficiently to encourage the publisher Alphonse Cadart to establish the Société des Aquafortistes in 1862. Cadart had published Legros's portfolio *Esquisses à l'eau-forte* (1861), which was dedicated to Baudelaire, a reflection of the poet's important role as mentor and friend following his enthusiastic review of *Angelus* (ex-Lingard priv. col., Cheltenham) at the Salon of 1859.

In the same year Legros, Whistler and Henri Fantin-Latour, a fellow student at Lecoq's, dubbed themselves the Société des Trois: a union founded more on personal solidarity than on any artistic programme. With *Ex-voto* (Dijon, Mus. B.-A.), awarded an honourable mention at the Salon of 1860, Legros emerged as a leader of the younger generation of realists, notwithstanding his conspicuous dependence on Courbet. However, this critical success brought no financial security, and in 1863, with Whistler's encouragement, Legros visited London where he found admirers and patrons, notably the Ionides family, and was ardently promoted by the brothers Dante Gabriel Rossetti and William Michael Rossetti. Despite winning medals in the Salons of 1867 and 1868 and receiving the support of the critics Louis-Edmond Duranty and Philippe Burty in Paris, Legros resolved to remain in London. He was naturalized in 1880.

In 1876 Edward John Poynter recommended Legros to succeed him as Professor of Fine Art at the Slade School (*see* ENGLAND, §XV). Legros occupied this position until 1893 and introduced etching and modelling to the syllabus, a reflection of his own interests. He was a founder-member of the Society of Painter-Etchers in 1881 and of the Society of Medallists in 1885; the revival of the cast art medal was due almost entirely to his example. Particularly notable are his softly modelled portrait medallions of great Victorians, for instance *Alfred, Lord Tennyson* (bronze, *c.* 1882; Manchester, C.A.G.), which reveal his debt to Pisanello.

With its classically inspired economy of form and design, Legros's interpretation of his realist subject-matter exerted a decisive influence in England on the representation of peasant life in the 1880s, comparable with that of Jules Bastien-Lepage. He had a taste for the macabre, which endured from his illustrations of Edgar Allan Poe of 1861 to be absorbed into the Symbolism of the 1890s (as in the series *Triumph of Death*, begun 1894). In the etchings *Death of the Vagabond* and *Death and the Wood-cutter*, these themes coalesce in a stark blend of realism and fantasy which is simultaneously elevated and humane.

BIBLIOGRAPHY
L. Bénédite: 'Alphonse Legros', *The Studio*, xxix (1903), pp. 3–22
G. Soulier: *L'Oeuvre gravé et lithographié de Alphonse Legros* (Paris, 1904)
*A catalogue of Paintings, Drawings, Etchings and Lithographs by Professor Alphonse Legros (1837–1911) from the Collection of Frank E. Bliss* (exh. cat., London, Grosvenor Gal., 1922)
*A Catalogue of the Etchings, Drypoints and Lithographs by Professor Alphonse Legros (1837–1911) in the Collection of Frank E. Bliss* (London, 1923)
M. C. Salaman: *Alphonse Legros*, Modern Masters of Etching, ix (London, 1926)
G. P. Weisberg: 'Alphonse Legros and the Theme of Death and the Woodcutter', *Bull. Cleveland Mus. A.*, lxi (1974), pp. 128–35
A. Seltzer: *Alphonse Legros: The Development of an Archaic Visual Vocabulary in Nineteenth Century Art* (diss., Binghamton, SUNY, 1980)
T. J. Wilcox: *Alphonse Legros (1837–1911): Aspects of his Life and Work* (diss., U. London, 1981)
P. Attwood: 'The Medals of Alphonse Legros', *Medal*, ii (1983), pp. 7–23 [with list of sculptures]
*Alphonse Legros, 1837–1911* (exh. cat. by T. Wilcox, Dijon, Mus. B.-A., 1987)

TIMOTHY WILCOX

**Leh.** Capital of Ladakh, Jammu and Kashmir, India. Located near the River Indus on an ancient trade route between India, Tibet and China, Leh is notable for a Tibetan Buddhist monastery, known as the Tsemo Gompa, and the Lechen Pelkar palace and fort, all erected under the Namgyel rulers of the 16th–17th centuries. Among the buildings of the Tsemo Gompa is the Temple of the Guardian Deities, built by Tashi Namgyel in the 16th century, which contains images of the fierce protector Mahakala, Vaishravana (one of the four heavenly kings), the Great Goddess and another fierce guardian (yet to be identified). Also in the Tsemo Gompa, the Maitreya Temple contains a celebrated three-storey-high figure of the Future Buddha flanked by the *bodhisattva*s Avalokiteshvara and Manjushri; the shrine may date to the 16th century, but it has been extensively renovated in recent times. The palace is a ruined nine-storey structure set on a hill north-east of the town; founded by Senge Namgyel (*reg* 1590–1635), it has a façade with numerous overhanging projections and altimetric windows. To the south of the town are mani walls, almost 500 m long, with Tibetan inscriptions, which were erected from the 17th century as memorials to deceased nobles. The Soma Gompa Monastery, built below the fort in 1957, contains images of Shakyamuni, the historical Buddha, and other deities.

*See also* INDIAN SUBCONTINENT, §III, 7(ii)(e); MILITARY ARCHITECTURE AND FORTIFICATION, §VII, 1; and TIBET, §I, 5.

BIBLIOGRAPHY
L. Petech: *The Kingdom of Ladakh* (Rome, 1977)
D. L. Snellgrove and T. Skorupski: *The Cultural Heritage of Ladakh*, 2 vols (London, 1977–80)
C. Jest and J. Sanday: 'The Palace of Leh in Ladakh: An Example of Himalayan Architecture in Need of Conservation', *Monumentum*, xxv/3 (1982), pp. 179–98

KIRIT MANKODI

**Le Havre** [anc. Constantina Castra]. French city and port on the coast of Normandy, with a population of *c.* 200,000. On the site of modern Le Havre was the Roman camp of Constantina Castra, but little development took place there until the early 16th century. In 1517 Francis I decided to expand what was then only a small fishing village into an important port. This was given the name Havre-de-Grâce, after its chapel of Notre-Dame-de-Grâce. The rapid building programme, following a grid plan by Girolamo Bellarmato (1493–after 1554), was well advanced by 1520, when the King visited the port. The town became an important centre for commercial and military activity, depending on France's fluctuating relations with England. It was briefly held by the English under Ambrose Dudley, Earl of Warwick, from 1562 to 1563, after it had been handed over by the Huguenots. Under Cardinal Richelieu the town was further expanded, and from 1574 to 1638 the cathedral of Notre-Dame was built, following the design of Nicolas Duchemin (*d* 1598), in a mixture of styles. The main portal (1605–38) is in an elaborate late Renaissance style, while the earlier tower used an austere Gothic design. Louis XVI instigated large-scale projects that were later finished by Napoleon III, and under Napoleon I the port was further fortified. In 1868, as an indication of the port's significance, an international maritime exhibition was held in Le Havre, including a display of maritime art. Most of the important buildings in the city date from the 19th century. The grand Palais de Justice, for example, was inaugurated in 1876. Built in a Neo-classical style, it has statues by David d'Angers on either side of its entrance, one of the poet *Casimir Delavigne* and the other of the writer *Bernardin de Saint Pierre*, both natives of the city. Many of the most notable buildings built around the same time, however, were destroyed during World War II, when Le Havre was virtually flattened by British bombing in September 1944, after which it was reconstructed under the direction of Auguste Perret, absorbing the suburbs of Bléville and Sanvic and encroaching on nearby Sainte-Addresse and Harfleur. The neo-Byzantine church of St Joseph, for example, begun in 1871 and destroyed in the war, was replaced by a new church of the same name, inspired by a project of Perret and Raymond Audigier and executed by

George Brochard. This severely geometric church, with its tall central tower (h. 104 m) intended as a symbol of the resurrection of the city, was begun in 1951. Another significant building destroyed in the war was the town hall, inaugurated in 1859 and designed by Alfred-Louis Brunet-Debaines. Nicknamed the 'Petit Louvre', it contained an apartment reserved for Napoleon III. It was replaced by a building designed by Perret in the Place de l'Hôtel de Ville, with an imposing rectangular tower. After Perret's death in 1954, it was completed by Jacques Tournant and finished in 1959. The Neo-classical theatre of 1844, destroyed in the war, was replaced by the Maison de la Culture, a sweeping, curved building that emerges from below ground. Containing a theatre, cinema and other facilities, it is situated in L'Espace Oscar Niemeyer, named after its architect.

The undistinguished Musée des Beaux-Arts of 1845 was destroyed during World War II, but its excellent provincial collection was saved and is now housed in the new Musée des Beaux-Arts in the Boulevard J. F. Kennedy. Designed by Guy Lagneau and Audigier in collaboration with the curator Reynould Arnould, it was opened in 1961, and it is notable for its innovative use of glass, steel and aluminium. Outside is the large sculpture

*Le Havre: Le Bassin du Roy* by Othon Friesz, oil on canvas, 610×740 mm, *c.* 1903 (Le Havre, Musée des Beaux-Arts)

*Signal* by Henri-Georges Adam. The collection includes various works by such Old Masters as Bronzino, Caravaggio, Correggio, Murillo and Rubens, but more notable is its collection of modern art, reflecting the importance of the city to various painters of the early modern period, such as Eugène Boudin (who is particularly well represented), Edouard Manet, Claude Monet, Othon Friesz, Raoul Dufy and Georges Braque. Although born in Honfleur, Boudin spent most of his childhood and working life around Le Havre, while Monet, who was born in Paris, spent much of his childhood in the city and, having trained under Boudin, often returned to paint around the nearby coast. The area became particularly popular in the latter half of the 19th century for French and British visitors, thereby attracting other Impressionists and Manet as 'painters of modern life'. Dufy and Friesz were both born in Le Havre and depicted it many times in their paintings (see fig.). Georges Braque also spent his childhood in the city and was a member, with the sculptor Manolo and the critic Maurice Raynal, of the Cercle d'Art Moderne, founded in Le Havre in 1906. Braque, Dufy and Friesz trained together at the Ecole des Beaux-Arts, before becoming associated with Fauvism. Among more recent artists associated with Le Havre and represented in the museum is Jean Dubuffet, who was born in the city.

BIBLIOGRAPHY

A. E. Borély: *Histoire de la ville du Havre et de son ancien gouvernement*, 5 vols (Paris, 1880–85)
*Le Havre, Etretat-Fécamp*, Les Guides bleus illustrés (Paris, 1933)
J. Guillemard: *Esprit du Havre et ses aspects depuis ses origines* (Le Havre, 1951)
*De Corot à nos jours au Musée du Havre* (exh. cat. by B. Dorival, Paris, Mus. N. A. Mod., 1953–4)
J. Legoy and others: *Le Havre, 1516–1986: Du Havre d'autrefois à la métropole de la mer* (Rouen, 1986)
A. Corvisier, ed.: *Histoire du Havre et l'estuaire de la Seine* (Toulouse, 1987)

**Le Hay, Elisabeth-Sophie.** *See* CHÉRON, (2).

**Lehman.** American family of bankers and collectors. Philip Lehman (*b* New York, 9 Nov 1861; *d* New York, 21 March 1947) was director of Lehman Brothers, an investment banking firm, and initially began collecting early Italian Renaissance paintings. His purchases were particularly extensive between 1914 and 1920 when he bought Renaissance ceramics, furniture, tapestries and such paintings as Memling's *Annunciation* (1482; New York, Met.). Bernard Berenson numbered among his friends. Philip's son Robert Lehman (*b* New York, 29 Sept 1892; *d* New York, 9 Aug 1969) was already an enthusiastic collector while a student at Yale University, New Haven, CT (graduated 1913). In 1928 he published a catalogue of the paintings collected by his father and became head of Lehman Brothers investment bankers. He retained this post for over 40 years, turning the firm into one of the pillars of the economy and of American culture. Its headquarters were moved in 1928 to an Italian Renaissance style building in William Street, New York, which he decorated with works from his collection. As well as adding early works to the collection, from 1927 he began acquiring paintings by Cézanne, Degas, Renoir, Seurat and other modern artists, including Renoir's *Two Young Girls*

*at the Piano* (1892; New York, Met.). His interest in the Metropolitan Museum, New York, was fostered by the museum's Curator-in-Chief, Ted Rousseau, and Robert often allowed public exhibitions of the Lehman collection, such as those held at the Metropolitan Museum of Art in 1954 and at the Musée de l'Orangerie, Paris, in 1957. He was a member of the acquisitions committee of the Metropolitan Museum of Art, New York, and in 1967 he decided that after his death the family collection of over 1000 works would be donated to the museum. A specially built wing was added to the museum (opened 1975), which contains such world-famous works as Giovanni di Paolo's *Expulsion from Paradise* (*c.* 1445) and Petrus Christus's *St Elgius and the Lovers* (1449), both bought by Philip.

WRITINGS
R. Lehman: *The Philip Lehman Collection* (New York, 1928)

BIBLIOGRAPHY
G. Szabó: *The Robert Lehman Collection* (New York, 1975)
J. Pope-Hennessy: *Italian Paintings* (1987), i of *The Robert Lehman Collection*, ed. E. Haver Kamp-Begemann (New York, 1987–)

LAURENCE B. KANTER, PATRICK LE CHANU

**Lehmann (von Lewenwaldt), Caspar** (*b* Uelzen, *c.* 1563–5; *d* Prague, before 27 June 1623). German gem- and glass-engraver. He was trained as a gem-engraver in Munich under Duke William V of Bavaria (*reg* 1579–98), probably from 1583 or 1584. No work from his early career has been identified with certainty, although the carved depiction of *Ottavio Miseroni* on a large rock-crystal bowl (Vienna, Ksthist. Mus.) may be from this period. He seems to have first come into contact with the court of Rudolf II (*reg* 1576–1612) in Prague in about 1587; in 1590 he became a member of the imperial bodyguard, and in 1601 he was appointed gem-engraver of the imperial chamber, though he must have been active as a court craftsman before then; none of his engraved gems has been identified.

Lehmann is best known for introducing the technique of wheel-engraving on glass, a technique that was formerly used for cutting rock crystal and other hardstones. A prerequisite for this was high-quality Bohemian glass, and this was forthcoming from the glassworks established by the Emperor in 1598 at Bubenec outside Prague; the glass cut by Lehmann proved highly competitive with the expensive rock-crystal. Prominent in his ascribed output is a series of engraved-glass plaques with portraits of royal figures and mythological and religious scenes after works by such artists of the court of Rudolf II as Hans von Aachen and Bartholomeus Spranger. A plaque with *Jupiter and Juno* after Spranger (?before 1590; Dresden, Grünes Gewölbe) is ascribed to Lehmann, as is a glass plaque with a depiction of the *Adoration of the Shepherds*, after von Aachen or Jan Sadeler (i) (*c.* 1600; Dresden, Grünes Gewölbe). The only signed work—C. LEMAN. F.—is a tall glass beaker (1605; Prague, Mus. Dec. A.) with allegories of Power, Liberty and Nobility, after *Stradanus* by Jan Sadeler (i), and the arms of Wolfgang Sigmund von Losenstein and his wife Susanna von Rogendorf. Also ascribed to him from this period are plaques with portraits of *Rudolf II* (probably before 1606; Vienna, Ksthist.

Mus.), *Henry Julius, Duke of Brunswick–Wolfenbüttel* (Dresden, Grünes Gewölbe) and *Ludwig V, Landgrave of Hesse-Darmstadt* (Darmstadt, Hess. Landesmus.), as well as an engraved rock-crystal jug (*c.* 1605; Vienna, Ksthist. Mus.) mounted on a silver-gilt base and decorated with garnets. A plaque (London, V&A) with *Perseus and Andromeda*, commissioned by Rudolf II and made for Christian II, Elector of Saxony, and his wife Hedwig, was possibly made while Lehmann was at Prague. The model for this has repeatedly been ascribed to von Aachen but is certainly Cavaliere d'Arpino's painting on a slate of *Andromeda* (1602; Vienna, Ksthist. Mus.).

Falling out of imperial favour in 1605 through the intrigue of the Emperor's valet, Lehmann moved to the court of Christian II, Elector of Saxony, in Dresden. Produced at about this time was one of the most important pieces ascribed to him, a sumptuous covered goblet of rock crystal (*c.* 1606; Dresden, Grünes Gewölbe) with the *Bath of Diana* engraved on the sides and a depiction of *Actaeon* on the cover. Dating from 1607 is a plaque (Hamburg, Mus. Kst & Gew.) with an engraving of *Diana and Actaeon* after a scene from Ovid by Crispijn van de Passe (i). In Dresden there is a record of four clock-cases (untraced) carved by Lehmann, presumably worked in hardstones.

Lehmann remained in Dresden until 1608 when, restored to imperial favour, he returned to Prague. He received imperial privilege as a glass-engraver on 10 March 1609; in September 1612 he was granted a certificate of nobility by Emperor Matthias (*reg* 1612–19) with the title Lehmann von Lewenwaldt. Although he seems to have left court service *c.* 1614, he continued engraving glass (e.g. covered goblet, *c.* 1615; Munich, Bayer. Nmus.). A set of six engraved glass plaques with allegorical and emblematic subjects (framed together in the 19th century; now Corning, NY, Mus. Glass; Amsterdam, Rijksmus. and priv. cols) are ascribed to him. The depictions probably relate to leading political figures of the second decade of the 17th century, and the monogram CH indicates that three of these plaques were made for the Saxon court.

While in Prague, Lehmann worked with Valentin Drausch (or Trausch), whom he must have known from Munich, Daniel Creutz (later of Nuremberg) and Zacharias Peltzer (or Belzer), although none of their works is extant. Georg Schwanhardt the elder (1601–67) was a pupil of Lehmann's and became imperial glass-engraver in 1618.

BIBLIOGRAPHY
Thieme–Becker
W. Holzhausen: 'Dresden: Prager Glas- und Steinschnitt um 1600', *Neues Archv Sächs. Gesch. & Altertknd.*, lv (1934), pp. 86–91, 108–12
E. Meyer-Heisig: 'Caspar Lehmann: Ein Beitrag zur Frühgeschichte des deutschen Glasschnittes', *Anz. Ger. Nmus.* (1963), pp. 116–31
F. Röver: 'Caspar Lehmann aus Uelzen: Zur Biographie und Herkunft des ersten europäischen Glasschneiders der Neuzeit', *Niederdt. Beitr. Kstgesch.*, iv (1965), pp. 251–67 [with historical and genealogical tables]
E. Meyer-Heisig: 'Caspar Lehmann', *Kstjb. Stadt Linz* (1967), pp. 117–29
O. Drahotová: 'Comments on Caspar Lehmann: Central European Glass and Hard Stone Engraving', *J. Glass Stud.*, xxiii (1981), pp. 34–45
S. Minis: 'Caspar Lehmann: Glasgraveur aan het Hof van Rudolf II', *Leids Ksthist. Jb.*, i (1982), pp. 191–7
B. Bukovinská: 'Kunsthandwerk', *Die Kunst am Hofe Rudolfs II* (Prague, Vienna and Hanau, 1988), pp. 164–7
R. Distelberger: 'Die Kunstkammerstücke', *Prag um 1600: Kunst und Kultur am Hofe Rudolfs II*, 2 vols (exh. cat., Essen, Villa Hügel; Vienna, Ksthist. Mus.; 1988–9), i, pp. 478–9; ii, p. 258

S. Baumgärtner: Über Stein- und Glasschnitt: Zu einem unveröffentlichten Manuskript von Gustav E. Pazaurek', *Die Weltkunst*, xxiii (1993), pp. 3304–7; xxiv (1994), pp. 588–91, 2071–4
JÜRGEN ZIMMER

**Lehmann, (Charles-Ernest-Rodolphe-)Henri** [Karl Ernest Heinrich Salem before naturalization (1846)] (*b* Kiel, Holstein, 14 April 1814; *d* Paris, 30 March 1882). French painter and teacher of German origin. A pupil of his father, Leo Lehmann (1782–1859), and Ingres, whose studio he entered in 1831, Lehmann enjoyed a long and much honoured career. His work reflects his fervent admiration and emulation of Ingres, his respect for the art of the Nazarenes and his study of 17th-century Italian art. He exhibited regularly at the Salon from 1835, gaining first-class medals in 1840, 1848 and in 1855. He was represented by 20 works at the Exposition Universelle.

Lehmann's most celebrated large easel painting was the *Grief of the Oceanides at the Foot of the Rock where Prometheus Lies Enchained* (1851; Gap, Mus. Dépt.), which allowed him to exercise fully his talents for dramatic lighting and energetically posed nude figures. It was purchased by the State for 6000 francs. He was awarded many commissions for large-scale figure compositions including decorations for the newly enlarged Hôtel de Ville, Paris, in 1852 (destr. 1871), the church of Ste-Clotilde, Paris (1854), and the throne-room of the Palais du Luxembourg, Paris (1854–6). He produced portraits of many of the leading men and women of the period including Stendhal (1841; Grenoble, Mus. Stendhal), the Princess Belgiojoso (1844; ex-Marquis Franco del Pozzo d'Annone priv. col.) and his friend Franz Liszt (1840; Paris, Carnavalet), which is considered by many to be his most successful portrait. Lehmann concentrated on capturing Liszt's dramatic features and commanding gaze, isolating the composer's spare figure against a neutral background. He was also a prolific draughtsman.

Lehmann was awarded the Légion d'honneur in 1846 and was naturalized as a French citizen later that year. From 1875 until a year before his death, he taught at the Ecole des Beaux-Arts; his students included Camille Pissarro and Georges Seurat, who found his conservative regime unappealing.

BIBLIOGRAPHY
*Henri Lehmann* (exh. cat., ed. M.-M. Aubrun; Paris, Carnavalet, 1983)
M.-M. Aubrun: *Henri Lehmann, 1814–1882: Catalogue raisonné de l'oeuvre*, 2 vols (Paris, 1984)
MICHAEL HOWARD

**Lehmann** [Lehmann-Hartleben], **Karl** (*b* Rostock, 27 Sept 1894; *d* Basle, 17 Dec 1960). German art historian and archaeologist. He was educated at Tübingen, Göttingen and Munich, and in 1922 he received his PhD from Berlin and became a Fellow of the Deutsches Archäologisches Institut in Athens. He pursued his archaeological career first at Berlin and the Deutsches Archäologisches Institut in Rome (1922–5), then at Heidelberg. In 1929 he was appointed to the chair at Munster and served as the director of the university museum. Under pressure from the Nazi regime, Lehmann left to reside in Rome, subsequently joining the Institute of Fine Arts at New York University, then being developed as a premier research centre in archaeology and the history of art. By 1938

Lehmann had founded and was directing the Institute's Archaeological Research Fund, its primary objective being the study of ancient mystery cult and excavation of the Sanctuary of the Great Gods on Samothrace. His scholarship and teaching reflected the wide interests of a modern humanist, including, for example, the study of ancient buildings as represented by die-cutters for coins and the transformation of such ancient ship-fountains as the *Nike* of Samothrace into the Ship of the Christian Church. His studies of religious symbolism in the Bacchic cult (1942) and of celestial symbolism in domical structures (1945) are still fundamental. For his work on Samothrace, Lehmann was made an honorary citizen of the island, and in 1951 he was created a Knight Commander of the Royal Greek Order of the Phoenix. His work was informed by a lifelong interest in popular art, although he did not live to complete a book on vernacular monuments of antiquity.

### WRITINGS

*Die Trajanssäule: Ein römisches Kunstwerk zu Beginn der Spätantike*, 2 vols (Berlin and Leipzig, 1926)
with K. Kluge: *Die antiken Grossbronzen*, 3 vols (Berlin and Leipzig, 1927)
with E. C. Olsen: *Dionysiac Sarcophagi in Baltimore* (Baltimore, 1942)
'The Dome of Heaven', *A. Bull.*, xxvii (1945), pp. 1–27
*Thomas Jefferson: American Humanist* (New York, 1947)
with P. W. Lehmann: *Samothracian Reflections: Aspects of the Revival of the Antique* (New York, 1973)

### BIBLIOGRAPHY

L. F. Sandler, ed.: *Essays in Memory of Karl Lehmann* (New York, 1964) [incl. full list of writings]

PHYLLIS PRAY BOBER

**Lehmbruck, Wilhelm** (*b* Duisburg, 4 Jan 1881; *d* Berlin, 25 March 1919). German sculptor, painter and printmaker. He studied in Düsseldorf at the Kunstgewerbeschule from 1895 to 1901 and under Karl Janssen at the Kunstakademie from 1901 to 1906. His work was representative of established academic art. As well as making drawings of nudes and anatomical studies, he modelled works of typical contemporary subjects such as *Siegfried* and *Shotputter* (both clay, 1902; destr.); *Woman Bathing* (bronze, 1902; Duisburg, Lehmbruck-Mus.), however, displayed a new freedom and simplicity and one cast of it was bought by the Kunstakademie in Düsseldorf in 1904. Lehmbruck was inspired by works that he saw at the Deutsch-nationale Kunstausstellung (1902) and by the Internationale Kunstausstellung (1904), both held in Düsseldorf, particularly those by Jules Dalou, Constantin Meunier and Auguste Rodin. In September 1904 he travelled to the Netherlands and to Bournemouth and the south coast of England. After travelling in Italy (1905) he was heavily influenced by Michelangelo's work, and in particular the tombs of the Medici chapels in Florence.

On leaving the academy Lehmbruck worked as an independent artist in Düsseldorf. He exhibited for the first time at the Deutsche Kunstausstellung, in Cologne in 1906. During a trip to Paris in 1907 he saw the sculpture of Aristide Maillol. While there he joined the Société Nationale des Beaux-Arts, and in Germany the Vereinigung Düsseldorfer Künstler. At this time his work was still conventional, for example the plaster model for a *Monument to Work* (*c*. 1906; Duisburg, Lehmbruck-Mus.). At the *Ausstellung für Christliche Kunst* in Düsseldorf (1909) he and Wilhelm Kreis exhibited work as part of a

design for a cemetery. In the model for the Heine memorial (*c*. 1906), the drawings for reliefs of 1908–10 and the small bronze *Standing Female Nude* (375×95×75 mm, 1908; Duisburg, Lehmbruck-Mus.), however, an individual style of solid plasticity began to emerge, revealing a move away from the influences of Rodin and Meunier, and a new affinity with the sensual, rounded figures of Maillol.

Lehmbruck decided to live in Paris after visiting and exhibiting there, especially because he recognized that he had made great strides in his recent work. In 1910 he moved into the Rue de Vaugirard, Montparnasse, where he met Bernhard Hoetger; he also made contact with André Derain, Constantin Brancusi and Alexander Archipenko. In *Standing Female Figure* (bronze, 1965×540×400 mm, 1910; artist's estate, see 1979 exh. cat., no. 5) he combined the statuesque qualities of Hans von Marées's work and the plasticity of Maillol's; he also produced his first etchings and oil sketches at this time. Lehmbruck exhibited *Standing Female Figure* at the Salon d'Automne in Paris in 1910 with *Man* (plaster, 1909; Duisburg, Lehmbruck-Mus.), a sculpture in which the influence of Rodin was still marked. A radical change of style took place in 1911, however, embodied in the expressionistic *Woman Kneeling* (torso, stone cast, 1911; Berlin, Alte N.G.) in which clarity of form was balanced with an expressive, almost Gothic spirit. While the tectonics learnt from Marées and the mythical elements remained, the sensual curves of Maillol began to disappear; Theodor Däubler called the new work 'the preface to Expressionism in sculpture' (1916 exh. cat., intro.). Lehmbruck developed this tendency further in *Ascending Youth* (cast stone, 1913), a figure inspired by Nietzsche's *Also Sprach Zarathustra*.

In Paris Lehmbruck also came into contact with the avant-garde sculpture of Matisse, Modigliani, Derain and Archipenko. By this stage his own work was closer to that of Brancusi, although without the latter's subjective simplification of form and later geometric abstraction. In 1912 he exhibited in the Folkwang-Museum in Hagen, with Egon Schiele; Lehmbruck's existential figures shared great similarities with those of Schiele, while in their elongation, their tectonization and their clarity of form they were precursors of Max Beckmann's sculptural style of 1916–18. In contrast to the formal explorations by the avant-garde of Paris, the works of Schiele, Lehmbruck and Beckmann are characterized by their psychological depth and their Expressionism. In 1914 Lehmbruck had his first major one-man exhibition in the Galerie Levesque, Paris. With Ernst Barlach and Beckmann he became a director of the Berlin Free Secession.

Lehmbruck was forced to leave Paris at the outbreak of World War I, moving to Berlin, where he sought to avoid conscription as a soldier, and where he was assigned to the Hospital Corps. During the war years Lehmbruck received financial support from the manufacturer Sally Falk in Mannheim. Lehmbruck's work was included in the first German Kollektivausstellung, held in the Kunsthalle, Mannheim, in 1916. In the same year he exhibited a major example of Expressionist sculpture at the Berlin Secession, *Fallen Man* (1916; Berlin, Neue N.G.), portraying in the gesture of the fallen soldier reaching for the hilt of a sword the tragedy of the victims of war.

Wilhelm Lehmbruck: *Daphne*, artificial stone, h. 780 mm, 1918 (Duisburg, Wilhelm-Lehmbruck-Museum)

At the end of 1916 Lehmbruck emigrated to Switzerland. In Zurich he made contact with the Socialist L. Rubiner who collaborated on Franz Pfemfert's *Aktion*. He made portraits of friends such as *Theodor Däubler* (bust; destr.) and *Rubiner*. His second major work of the war years was *Seated Youth* (artificial stone cast, 1917; Frankfurt am Main, Städel. Kstinst.), also called *The Friend*, representing a naked youth mourning the victims of war. He planned further major works, including a Pietà for a war memorial and a kneeling youth, but he made only fragmentary sculptures, torsos such as *Daphne* (1918; see fig.) and the metaphorical self-portrait *Head of a Thinker* (1918; Duisburg, Lehmbruck-Mus.). Lehmbruck met a young actress, Elisabeth Bergner, and made models and drawings of her head. Among Lehmbruck's etchings (dating from 1910) are the later studies of the *Crucifixion* and of a kneeling youth (*Despair*), the prints and sketches for *Macbeth* and for a planned *Pietà*. In 1919 he was elected into the Prussian Kunstakademie, but shortly afterwards he committed suicide.

BIBLIOGRAPHY
C. Einstein: *Wilhelm Lehmbrucks graphisches Werk* (Berlin, 1913)
*Sonderkatalog der Kollektivausstellung: Wilhelm Lehmbruck* (exh. cat., intro. T. Däubler; Mannheim, Städt. Ksthalle, 1916)
K. Badt: 'Die Plastik Wilhelm Lehmbrucks', *Z. Bild. Kst*, xxxi (1920), pp. 69–82
W. Wolfradt: *Die neue Plastik* (Berlin, 1920)
F. von Unruh: 'Wilhelm Lehmbruck–Erinnerungen', *Berlin. Tagbl*. (23 March 1929)
E. Trier: *Lehmbruck: 'Die Kniende'* (Stuttgart, 1958)
E. Petermann: *Die Druckgraphik W. Lehmbrucks* (Stuttgart, 1964)
S. Salzmann and G. Roden: *Sieben Beiträge zum Gedenken seines 50. Todestag* (Duisburg, 1969)
*The Art of Wilhelm Lehmbruck* (exh. cat., Washington, DC, N.G.A.; Los Angeles, UCLA; San Francisco, CA, Mus. A.; Boston, MA, Mus. F.A.; 1972)
D. Schubert: 'Bildniszeichnungen expressionistischer Dichter von W. Lehmbruck', *Festschrift Wolfgang Braunfels* (Tübingen, 1977)
E. Bergner: *Bewundert viel und viel gescholten: Erinnerungen* (Munich, 1978)
E. G. Güse: *Lehmbruck und Italien* (Duisburg, 1979)
*Wilhelm Lehmbruck, 1881–1919* (exh. cat., intro. S. Salzmann; Edinburgh, N.G.; Dublin, Bank of Ireland Col.; Cardiff, N. Mus.; Sheffield, Mappin A.G.; 1979)
D. Schubert: 'Anmerkungen zur Kunst Lehmbrucks', *Pantheon*, xxxix/1 (1981), pp. 55–69
——: *Die Kunst Lehmbrucks* (Worms, 1981, rev. Dresden, 2/1990)
*Hommage à Lehmbruck: Lehmbruck in seiner Zeit* (exh. cat., Duisburg, Lehmbruck-Mus., 1981)
*Wilhelm Lehmbruck, 1881–1919* (exh. cat., Heilbronn, Deutschof-Mus.; Mainz, Landesmus. 1981–2)
*German Expressionist Sculpture* (exh. cat., ed. S. Barron; Los Angeles, CA, Co. Mus. A.; Cologne, Josef-Haubrich-Ksthalle; 1984)
G. Händler: *Wilhelm Lehmbruck: Die Zeichnungen der Reifezeit* (Stuttgart, 1985)
*Wilhelm Lehmbruck (1881–1919): Plastik, Malerei, Graphik* (exh. cat., Gotha, Mus. Nat.; E. Berlin, N.G.; Leipzig, Mus. Bild. Kst; 1987)
DIETRICH SCHUBERT

**Le Hongre, Etienne** (*b* Paris, 7 May 1628; *d* Paris, 28 April 1690). French sculptor. The son of a Parisian master joiner and wood-carver, he trained with Jacques Sarazin at the same time as Gaspard and Balthazar Marsy and Pierre Legros (i). They all later became members of the team of sculptors working for Louis XIV at the château of Versailles.

In 1653 Le Hongre went to Rome with a royal bursary. There it is likely that he knew Gianlorenzo Bernini, whose influence is noticeable in moderated form in his work. He returned to Paris in 1659, and he was approved (*agréé*) by the Académie Royale de Peinture et de Sculpture in 1663. He was received (*reçu*) as a full member of the Académie Royale in 1667 on presentation of an oval marble medallion of *Mary Magdalene* (Versailles, Notre-Dame). He subsequently had a successful career at the Académie Royale, rising through the hierarchy to become assistant rector in 1686. In that year he was granted lodgings in the Louvre by Louis XIV.

Between his return from Italy and 1670 Le Hongre worked for numerous private patrons in Paris: in 1661 he executed the monument for the *Heart of Louis-Timoléon de Cossé, Duc de Brissac* (marble; Paris, Louvre) and the tomb of *Louis Potier, Marquis de Gesvres* (marble, Paris, St Gervais), both originally in the church of the Célestins, Paris. In 1667 Jacques Souvré de Courtenvaux (*d* 1670), Grand Prior of the Order of the Knights of Malta, commissioned from him the carved stone façade decoration of his new Paris residence, the Hôtel de Souvré (destr. 1853), a work that made Le Hongre's reputation and brought him work from princely patrons including the Condé family and Anne-Marie-Louise d'Orléans, Duchesse de Montpensier (1627–93).

From 1663 Le Hongre was also active on the royal works of Louis XIV. In particular he contributed to the sculptural decoration of the château and gardens at VER-SAILLES. Among these works were two groups of dancing children (gilded lead, 1669–70, destr.; bronze versions, 1688, *in situ*) for the Allée d'Eau; naturalistic animals illustrating Aesop's *Fables* (painted lead, 1672–3; fragments, Versailles, Château) for the Labyrinthe; various decorative works for the Appartements Royaux (1674, 1675, 1678); a female allegorical statue representing *Air* (marble, 1680–84; *in situ*), his most famous work; as well as two reclining statues of nymphs and two similar statues representing the rivers *Marne* and *Seine* (all bronze, 1685–7; *in situ*) for the Parterre d'Eau. During this period Le Hongre was also employed on other royal projects. He provided decorative sculpture for the châteaux of Val, near Saint-Germain-en-Laye (1675–9; fragments *in situ*), Clagny, near Versailles (1675–82; destr.), and Marly, Yvelines (1681–3; destr.). Towards the end of his life he received two important non-royal commissions—that for a bronze equestrian statue of *Louis XIV* ordered by the Etats de Bourgogne for Dijon (1686–91; destr. 1792; a small bronze in Dijon, Mus. B.-A., may be a reduction) and that for a seated, marble statue of *Prudence* (1689–90) for the tomb of *Jules, Cardinal Mazarin* (Paris, Inst. France; for illustration *see* COYZEVOX, ANTOINE), a project executed in collaboration with Antoine Coyzevox and Jean Tuby.

Le Hongre's sculpture skilfully combines the influence of Sarazin with that of the Roman Baroque, tempering the austere realism of the former's work with an easy grace. This stylistic synthesis is particularly successful in his sculptures of women and children. Although Le Hongre, like the other sculptors working at Versailles, had to subordinate his invention to the classicizing designs of the Premier Peintre du Roi, Charles Le Brun, such works as the statue of *Air* express a personal style characterized by grace and harmony.

BIBLIOGRAPHY

Lami; Souchal

L. Dussieux and others, eds: *Mémoires inédits . . . des membres de l'Académie royale*, i (1854), pp. 363–82 [notice on Le Hongre by Guillet de Saint-Georges]

SIMONE HOOG

**Lehrs, Max** (*b* Berlin, 24 June 1855; *d* Dresden, 12 Nov 1938). German art historian and museum curator. Originally an art dealer, from 1880 he worked in the Schlesisches Museum in Breslau (now Wrocław, Poland) and from 1883 at the Kupferstichkabinett in Dresden, serving as Curator from 1896 to 1904. He was Curator of the Berlin Kupferstichkabinett (1905–8), before returning to Dresden to take charge of the Kupferstichkabinett until 1923. In Dresden he expanded the collection and undertook its systematic arrangement and conservation. As a result of his fundamental research into 15th-century copper-engraving he published a nine-volume history and critical catalogue, revealing great scholarship and knowledge. He also published studies on German monogrammists Wenzel von Olmütz (*fl* 1481), Alart du Hameel, Martin Schongauer and Albrecht Altdorfer, and on such contemporary artists as Arnold Böcklin, Jean-Louis Forain, Max Klinger and Käthe Kollwitz.

WRITINGS

*Die ältesten deutschen Spielkarten* (Dresden, 1885)

*Deutsche und niederländische Holzschnitte des XV. Jahrhunderts* (Berlin, 1908)

*Geschichte und kritischer Katalog des deutschen, niederländischen und französischen Kupferstichs im XV. Jahrhundert*, 9 vols (Vienna, 1908–34)

BIBLIOGRAPHY

A. Weixlgärtner: 'Nekrolog auf Max Lehrs', *Graph. Kst.*, n.s., 1, iii (1938–9), pp. 156–9

E. Braun: 'Der Briefwechsel zwischen Max Lehrs und Max Liebermann', *Jb. Staatl. Kstsamml. Dresden* (1989–90), pp. 81–106

CHRISTIAN DITTRICH

**Lehtinen, Kauko (Olavi)** (*b* Uusikaupunki, nr Turku, 1 Dec 1925). Finnish painter. He studied at the Drawing School of the Turku Art Association in 1943 and at the Académie de la Grande Chaumière in Paris in 1961. He later worked at various intervals in both Paris and Amsterdam for substantial periods. The earliest significant influence on his work was the modernist school in Turku, which during the 1920s and 1930s had concentrated particularly on Surrealism and abstract art. Lehtinen's paintings of the 1950s and early 1960s show his desire to create an individual atmosphere and his highly developed interest in the nature of different materials, as in *Head with Pink Background* (1962; Tampere, Hildén A. Mus.). It was only when he became fascinated by the experimentation of *Art informel*, Neo-Dada and Nouveau Réalisme, particularly the work of Robert Rauschenberg and Jean Tinguely, that his spontaneous fantasy world was released. During the 1960s he also began to use the linear motif, as in *The Green Earth* (1966; Turku, A. Mus.), which was to become the most essential feature of his style. Lehtinen's lines are filled with the freedom and mystery of the natural elements, and his images and motifs display a certain fluidity, seemingly accumulating gradually and each one fertilizing the next.

Lehtinen's work is based on the observation of reality, often a person or object, and he usually explored his subject through a series of paintings, examining transformations in theme and detail by a method of free association. This process of interpretation applied to the subject of the human head can produce a collection of bizarre creatures and textural compositions, as in *Fourteen Years of Friendship* (1970; Tampere, Hildén A. Mus.). Lehtinen also adapted paintings by well-known artists, such as the *Feast of Herod* (1968; Amsterdam, Stedel. Mus.) after Lucas Cranach I. He also reworked images by Picasso and Rembrandt. His redirection towards realism of the 1970s had a moderating effect on his fantastic imagery. He produced a number of relatively sparse compositions, for example *Oranges in a Bowl* (1974; Helsinki, Skop Col.), which reveal his highly cultivated and childishly candid delight in the smallest pleasures of life.

BIBLIOGRAPHY

J. B. Smith: *Modern Finnish Painting and Graphic Art* (London, 1970), pp. 38–9

*Teema ja toteus* [Theme and reality] (exh. cat., text K. Lehtinen; ed. S. Sarajas-Korte and S. Sinisalo; Helsinki, Acad. F.A., 1976), pp. 20–23

T. Vuorikoski, ed.: *Sara Hildén Art Museum: Finnish Paintings, Drawings and Sculpture* (Tampere, 1983), pp. 16–17, 50–51

*Kauko Lehtinen* (exh. cat., text R. Valorinta; Tampere, Hildén A. Mus., 1983) [retro.]

SOILI SINISALO

**Leibl, Wilhelm (Maria Hubertus)** (*b* Cologne, 23 Oct 1844; *d* Würzburg, 4 Dec 1900). German painter, draughtsman and etcher. In 1861 he abandoned his apprenticeship as a locksmith in order to train as a precision instrument maker, though a month or so later he decided to train as an artist, at first under the Cologne history painter and writer Hermann Becker (1817–85). In 1863 he moved to Munich; he studied there from March 1864, at the Akademie der Bildenden Künste, initially under Philipp von Foltz and Alexander Straehuber, drawing from plaster casts, and later in Hermann Anschütz's painting class. Here, Arthur von Ramberg (1819–75) stimulated Leibl's sensitivity to colour; and Karl Theodor von Piloty encouraged him to observe reality and incorporate its lessons boldly into compositions on historical themes. From the start, however, Leibl tended to think of his pictures in terms of form rather than content. While at the Akademie he first reached a standard of excellence with his draughtmanship, which is notable for its directness and objectivity. As an artist, Leibl's early works were not especially promising. However, as occurred throughout his career, a long period of mediocrity was crowned by an unexpected masterpiece, such as his portrait drawing of *Aunt Josepha* (*c.* 1864; Cologne, Wallraf-Richartz-Mus.). This is particularly striking for Leibl's use of the hands to add to the expression of the sitter's character and mood, a device he was to use frequently in later work. In Munich, Leibl supplemented the teaching of the Akademie by studying the works of the Old Masters in the Alte Pinakothek: he paid particular attention to painters of the Baroque period such as van Dyck, Cornelis de Vos and Rubens, and also to other great masters of portraiture such as Frans Hals and Velázquez. The presentation of the subject found in such works is reflected in Leibl's portrait of *Frau Gedon* (1869; Munich, Neue Pin.). When the work was shown at the Grossen Internationale Kunstausstellung in Munich in 1869 it was singled out as the best oil painting of the exhibition by Gustave Courbet and, as a result, Leibl was honoured with an invitation to Paris, where he arrived on 13 November 1869. Here, Leibl looked at the recent work of French painters, especially that of Courbet and Manet, and the influence of both of these and the Old Masters is to be found throughout the rest of his life. Leibl painted a number of captivating works at this time, including *Company at Table* (1872–3; Cologne, Wallraf-Richartz-Mus.) and two portraits of types rather than named individuals, the *Old Parisienne* and the *Cocotte* (both 1869–70; Cologne, Wallraf-Richartz-Mus.).

Leibl's stay in Paris was cut short by the start of the Franco-Prussian war in July 1870, but he maintained close contacts with the Parisian art world and continued to submit paintings to the Paris Salon. Back in Munich, he became the centre of a group of artists, including Carl Schuch, Johann Sperl and Wilhelm Trübner, that came to be known as the 'Leibl circle' and spoke of Leibl in terms of pure painting. They were united in the view that the work of art should convince solely through its formal qualities, and in their enthusiasm for art for art's sake. In the 1870s Leibl also experimented with etching, a medium for which his early skill suited him, producing works (e.g. the *Artist's Mother*, Berlin, 1879, and *Reading Woman*, Leipzig, 1878) that are comparable to the *Aunt Josepha*

portrait. He appears to have abandoned the medium after a few years. His drawings from this period onwards are important only as preliminary sketches for the oil paintings.

In 1873 Leibl left Munich and went to settle in Grasslfing near the village of Dachau in the country outside Munich, the first of many villages in Upper Bavaria in which he was to spend the rest of his life, including Berbling bei Aibling (1878–81), Bad Aibling (1881–92) and Kutterling (1892–1900). Here, he produced some successful portraits of simple country folk, as in the two *Women from Dachau* (1873–4, Berlin, N.G., and 1874–5, destr.; see Waldmann, 1930, pl. 37). In 1875–7 Leibl lived in Schondorf am Ammersee, and at this time a radical change occurred in his work. He set about trying to justify a comparison that a Parisian critic had drawn (though not literally) between Leibl's work and that of Hans Holbein the younger. Leibl was a meticulous worker; he often lost his overview of the work, and most of the works produced at this time are over-detailed, self-conscious imitations of German 16th-century painters. His emulation of Holbein was most successful in the painting for which Leibl is best known, *Three Women in Church* (1878–82; Hamburg, Ksthalle; see fig.). He also painted some less problematic, more immediately appealing pictures that are free of formalist constraints. His attempt at a similar work with male figures, *The Poachers* (1882–6; fragments in Berlin, Neue N.G.; Cologne, Wallraf-Richartz-Mus.; and priv.

Wilhelm Leibl: *Three Women in Church*, oil on wood, 1.13×0.77 m, 1878–82 (Hamburg, Kunsthalle)

cols), was unsuccessful, however. Intended as a dramatic genre painting, its style vacillates between pseudo-archaic and pictorialist tendencies, and Leibl cut it into several pieces when it proved unpopular on being shown in 1888 in Paris. After this, Leibl appears to have settled into a more relaxed style. Relinquishing grand gestures, he succeeded in recapturing the subtle pictorial qualities he had developed in the 1870s, and in giving his work the depth it had in earlier paintings such as *Frau Gedon*. Typical of this final phase are a number of group portraits (e.g. *Women Spinning*, 1892; Leipzig, Mus. Bld. Kst.) and intimate interiors with figures (e.g. *Woman at a Window*, 1899; Cologne, Wallraf-Richartz-Mus.). It culminated in one of Leibl's most expressive and beautifully painted female portraits, that of *Frau Rosner-Heine* (ex-Ksthalle, Bremen, destr. 1939–45; for illustration see Waldmann, 1914, no. 251). Leibl died shortly after completing this last work. Leibl's reputation largely depended on the French critics, since he sank into neglect in his homeland long before his reputation waned in France; he never gained the acknowledgement he deserved in Germany.

BIBLIOGRAPHY

*NDB*

G. Gronau: *Leibl* (Leipzig, 1901)

J. Mayr: *Wilhelm Leibl, sein Leben und sein Schaffen* (Berlin, 1907)

E. Waldmann: *Wilhelm Leibl: Eine Darstellung seiner Kunst* (Berlin, 1914/rev. 1930) [with cat. rais.]

H. Nasse: *Wilhelm Leibl* (Munich, 1923)

E. J. Wolf: *Leibl und sein Kreis* (Munich, 1923)

E. Hanfstaengl: *Leibl: Das bäuerliche Antlitz* (Burg, 1938)

E. Ruhmer: *Das Rein Malerische* (PhD diss., Halle U., 1940)

E. Waldmann: *Wilhelm Leibl als Zeichner* (Munich, 1943)

E. Ruhmer: 'Künstlerbildniss des Leibl-Kreises', *Kst & S. Heim*, lv (1959), pp. 121–5

A. Langer: *Wilhelm Leibl* (Leipzig, 1961/rev. Rosenheim, 1977)

*Wilhelm Leibl und sein Kreis* (exh. cat., Munich, Lenbachhaus, 1974)

E. Ruhmer: 'Wilhelm Leibl et ses amis, pour et contre l'Impressionisme', *Gaz. B.-A.*, xcv (1980), pp. 187–97

——: *Der Leibl-Kreis und die Reine Malerei* (Rosenheim, 1984)

——: 'Leibl als Vorbild', *Wilhelm Leibl zum 150 Gebürtstag* (exh. cat. Munich and Cologne, 1994)

EBERHARD RUHMER

**Leicester**, Earls of. *See under* COKE.

**Leicester**, 1st Earl of. *See* DUDLEY, (2).

**Leicester**, Sir **John Fleming**, Baron de Tabley (*b* Knutsford, Ches, 4 April 1762; *d* Knutsford, 18 June 1827). English politician, patron and collector. He was the most important collector of contemporary British art in the first quarter of the 19th century. He succeeded to the baronetcy in 1770, was educated at Trinity College, Cambridge, and travelled in France and Italy in 1785–6. Thereafter he settled comfortably into politics and was three times a Member of Parliament. A competent amateur artist, he was taught by Paul Sandby, among others, and made a small series of lithographs from his own drawings of fish, birds and landscapes.

Leicester's patronage of contemporary artists may have begun with the commission of at least nine portraits of his mistress, Emily St Clare, from various artists between 1801 and his marriage in 1810 to Georgiana Maria Cotten. The only extant portrait from this group is John Hoppner's full-length of *Miss St Clare as a Bacchante* (1806; Kansas City, MO, Nelson–Atkins Mus. A.). By 1806 Leicester was also purchasing landscapes and subject pictures, possibly on the advice of James Northcote. In 1808 he published the first of several catalogues of his collection, which at this date included Philippe Jacques de Loutherbourg's *The Avalanche* (London, Tate), Hoppner's *A Sleeping Nymph* (Petworth House, W. Sussex, NT), four subject pictures by John Opie, including *Damon and Musidora* (1788; Petworth), and at least eleven paintings by Northcote, including *Vulture and Snake* (1798; Tabley House, Ches). But his most prescient act of patronage was purchasing the six paintings by J. M. W. Turner that were in his collection by 1808, including *The Shipwreck* (London, Tate), later exchanged for the *Falls of the Rhine at Schaffhausen* (Boston, MA, Mus. F.A.) and the *Blacksmith's Forge* (London, Tate). The collection hung at Leicester's London house in Hill Street, Mayfair, and was open to artists and connoisseurs.

After 1810 Leicester began to acquire more paintings of historical subjects, among them works by Benjamin West (e.g. the *Flight of Lot*, 1810; Detroit, MI, Inst. A.), Johann Heinrich Füseli (e.g. *Friar Puck*, 1794–6; Tabley), William Hilton (e.g. the *Rape of Europa*, Petworth) and more by Northcote. He also bought additional landscapes by Turner: two views of the Leicester family's estate in Cheshire, *Tabley House* (Petworth and Tabley) and *Sun Rising through Vapour* (London, N.G.). He opened the gallery at his Mayfair home in 1818, 1819 and again in 1824, the only collection of modern British art that was accessible in this way. Catalogues were published in 1819 and 1821. Among the few later additions to his collection were West's the *Angel of the Revelation* (Minneapolis, MN, Inst. A.) and John Martin's *Pompeii (The Destruction of Herculaneum)* (Tabley).

Leicester was a tireless promoter of contemporary British art. He was one of the founders of the British Institution in 1805, the Royal Irish Institution *c.* 1823 and the Royal Manchester Institution in 1825. In 1823 he offered his entire collection as the foundation for a national gallery of British art, but it was refused. In 1826 he was raised to the peerage as Baron de Tabley. At a posthumous sale held at Christie's, London, on 7 July 1827, George Wyndham, 3rd Earl of Egremont, bought a number of Leicester's most important pictures and transferred them to Petworth House, W. Sussex.

BIBLIOGRAPHY

*DNB*

W. P. Carey: *A Descriptive Catalogue of a Collection of Paintings by British Artists in the Possession of Sir John Fleming Leicester, with Occasional Remarks, etc, by Sir Richard Colt Hoare* (London, 1819)

J. Young: *A Catalogue of Pictures by British Artists in the Possession of Sir John Fleming Leicester, Bart, with Etchings from the Whole Collection* (London, 1821)

W. P. Carey: *Some Memoirs of the Patronage and Progress of the Fine Arts in England and Ireland . . . with Anecdotes of Lord of Tabley, of Other Patrons, and of Eminent Artists, etc* (London, 1826)

D. Hall: 'The Tabley House Papers', *Walpole Soc.*, xxxviii (1960–62), pp. 59–122

S. Whittingham: 'A Most Liberal Patron: Sir John Fleming Leicester, Bart., 1st Baron de Tabley (1762–1827)', *Turner Stud.*, vi (1986), pp. 24–36

J. Wilson: 'Hoppner's "Tambourine Girl" Identified', *Burl. Mag.*, cxxx/10 (1988), pp. 763–7

P. Cannon-Brookes: *Paintings from Tabley* (exh. cat., London, Heim Gal., 1989)

JOHN WILSON

**Leickert, Charles (Henri Joseph)** (*b* Brussels, 22 Sept 1816; *d* Mainz, 5 Dec 1907). Dutch painter. He moved to The Hague as a child, studying drawing at the Koninklijke Academie van Beeldende Kunsten and painting with Bartholomeus Johannes van Hove, Wijnand Nuyen and Andreas Schelfhout. Nuyen's influence is discernible in Leickert's taste for picturesque townscapes enlivened by such details as drying laundry (*Townscape, c.* 1860; The Hague, Gemeentemus.). Many motifs in Leickert's winter scenes, such as *Winter View with a Distant Town* (1850; Amsterdam, Rijksmus.), are reminiscent of Schelfhout's work; however, Leickert often used light as a means of providing a structure for his compositions, which were not as tightly designed as Schelfhout's. Moreover, even his best paintings, such as *Winter View* (1867; Amsterdam, Rijksmus.), do not match up to Schelfhout's depiction of ice. Leickert was exceptionally prolific and consequently often repeated himself. The wintry townscapes now in Haastrecht (Mus. Sticht. Bisdom van Vliet) and Rotterdam (1871; Boymans–van Beuningen) are virtually identical. Leickert's sketches, sometimes in an almost impressionistic style, are much more original. He rarely produced finished drawings. He lived in Amsterdam between 1847 and 1887 and then settled in Mainz, where the Mittelrheinisches Landesmuseum holds his sketchbooks and drawings.

BIBLIOGRAPHY
Scheen
W. van der Laan: 'Charles Leickert "Kopieerlust des dagelijkschen levens?"' [The desire to copy everyday life?], *Tableau*, v (1982–3), pp. 390–95

ANNEMIEKE HOOGENBOOM

**Leiden** [formerly Leyden]. Dutch town in the province of South Holland, with a population of *c.* 105,000.

1. History and urban development. 2. Art life and organization.

1. HISTORY AND URBAN DEVELOPMENT. Leiden began as a settlement on a sand/clay bank and island at the confluence of two branches of the River Rhine. The two Roman *castella* in the neighbourhood of Leiden—Valkenburg several kilometres to the west and Matilo to the east—did not lead to urban settlements. In the 16th and 17th centuries there was a widespread belief that Leiden itself was a Roman town, to be identified with the Lugdunum on the Roman map *Tabula Peutingeriana*, hence the humanist place-name Lugdunum Batavorum. The availability of good inland waterways was important for Leiden's development. From Roman times until the second quarter of the 12th century, the main stream of the Rhine flowed into the sea near Katwijk. The island and a settlement on the north bank were originally called Leython, a Germanic word meaning 'at the streams'. The beginnings of Leiden date to the 10th century, when a mound with a palisade was built as a refuge on the west extremity of the island. Soon it became a 'burg' (stronghold) consisting of a high motte, with a massive circular wall on top (still surviving in its 12th-century form). The settlement had a mint in the mid-11th century. The so-called West Frisian Counts had their own *curtis* (manorial palace) near the south bank already in the 10th century. The village that developed between the *curtis* and the river adopted the name Leython, leaving the derivative Leytheridorp for the earlier settlement on the north bank.

When the power of the Counts began to increase from the early 12th century, Leiden became one of their main residences. Nevertheless the 'burg' remained the symbolic seat of a *castellanus* or burgrave, and it was in noble hands until it was bought by the town in 1651. In 1121 the Pieterskerk, built next to the *curtis* and probably on the site of an earlier chapel, was consecrated as the first parish church. At the same time a new government building, the Gravensteen, was constructed. (It was a house of correction from 1598, a penitentiary from 1655 and a court-house from 1671; designed by Willem van der Helm (1671), with sculpture by Pieter Xavery, it is now the Institute for the History of Law.) Leiden's temporary function as the counts' residence must have stimulated commercial, industrial and artistic activity, but development into a real town had made only a modest start by the mid-13th century.

In 1266 Leiden received urban charters, of which older versions, which are not preserved, probably date back to *c.* 1200. From this time the town developed rapidly, although in the second half of the 13th century the Counts of Holland chose The Hague as their primary residence. Between 1250 and 1350 the population grew from *c.* 1250 to *c.* 4500. Despite the immigration of more than 6000 people, there was only minor growth during the next 80 years, owing to the Black Death and its later visitations. Between 1430 and 1490 there was a sharp increase from 5000 to 14,000 inhabitants, connected with the first flourishing of the cloth industry, Leiden's main craft. The cultural aspirations of the patriciate and the requirements of the three Late Gothic parish churches and the many monasteries and convents generated important artistic activity. The Pieterskerk and the church of St Pancras or Hooglandse Kerk (see fig. 1) survive in their 15th-century form, except for the tower of the former, which collapsed in 1512 and was not rebuilt. Unfortunately, the medieval church fittings were destroyed during the Reformation (1566).

Before 1389 the town was enlarged several times by annexation of surrounding territory. This proved sufficient until the renewed growth of industry and population following the first stage of the Dutch Revolt. After two subsequent sieges (1573–4), Leiden was relieved by the Protestants on 3 October 1574. Within a quarter of a century the population grew to 25,000, swelled by refugees, mostly Calvinist textile-workers from the Flemish south. These immigrants contributed to the revival of the cloth industry by introducing lighter varieties such as serges. The former hospital of St James (originally for pilgrims to Santiago de Compostela; Roman Catholic again since 1809) was used as a serge-hall.

In 1575 the foundation of the first university in the liberated north made Leiden the educational centre of the northern Netherlands as well as for many students from the Protestant regions in the German Empire. The university was housed in former monasteries, of which the chapel of the White (Dominican) Nuns or Jacobinesses is still its central building. In 1599 the Latin School was rebuilt in the Dutch Renaissance style. At the end of the 16th century urban administration had expanded so much that a new town hall was required. The Flemish architect Lieven de Key, who served Haarlem as municipal architect,

1. Leiden, Hooglandse Kerk, 15th century

designed a new façade in 1594 (restored after a fire in 1929; *see* NETHERLANDS, THE, fig. 6). The dyke-reeve's offices also required more space, and the present building in the Breestraat was reconstructed in 1596 and 1663.

Three enlargements, in 1611, 1644 and 1659, determined the form that Leiden took until the end of the 19th century. In these new quarters were located the textile-workers and the new industries, including a series of fulling-mills. In 1639 Arentsz van 'sGravesande designed the new Lakenhal (Cloth-hall; now Stedel. Mus. Lakenhal). In the same year the Marekerk was built to his designs; it is an early example of an octagonal domed church. In 1657–9 a new Waag (Weigh-house) and Boterhuis (Butter-hall) were built to designs by Pieter Post, with sculpture by Rombout Verhulst. Two of the town gates, the Zijlpoort (1666; by van der Helm and Rombout Verhulst) and the Morschpoort (1669; by van der Helm) are still preserved. Many *hofjes* (almshouses) were founded in this period, and of the 35 that survive, 19 date from the 17th century.

Around 1670 Leiden attained its greatest size with *c.* 70,000 inhabitants; the last epidemic of plague (1669) and the immense socio-economic and political unrest in the so-called 'year of disaster' (1672) marked the end of the 'Golden Age'. After the French occupation (1795–1813), the population had fallen to 28,000, and many more almshouses were founded. Although the cloth industry waned in the 18th century, the patriciate continued building majestic houses, especially along the stately Rapenburg canal.

In 1807 the explosion of a gunpowder-ship destroyed a large part of the historic city centre, and most of the area lay vacant for 50 years. Only after 1850 did industrialization bring new opportunities, and several industries, including cotton-mills and canning factories, were located inside the old city. Soon houses were built outside the walls, at first for the élite, but later also for the working classes, especially after the demolition of the former fortifications allowed renewed urban expansion. Since the early 1960s the industries have left Leiden, and most factory buildings have been demolished or turned into apartments.

BIBLIOGRAPHY

*Leids jaarboekje: Jaarboekje voor de geschiedenis en oudheidkunde van Leiden en omstreken* (Leiden, 1902–)

N. W. Posthumus: *De geschiedenis van de Leidsche lakenindustrie*, 3 vols (The Hague, 1908–39)

P. J. Blok: *Geschiedenis eener Hollandsche stad*, 4 vols (The Hague, 1910–18)

R. E. O. Ekkart: *Athena Batavae: The University of Leiden, 1575–1975* (Leiden, 1975)

H. A. van Oerle: *Leiden binnen en buiten de stadsvesten: De geschiedenis van de stedebouwkundige ontwikkeling binnen het Leidse rechtsgebied tot aan het einde van de gouden eeuw*, 2 vols (Leiden, 1975)

H. Kleibrink and R. Spruit: *Hofjes in Leiden* (Leiden, 1979) [with Eng. summary]

S. A. Lamet: *Men in Government: The Patriciate of Leyden, 1550–1600* (Amherst, MA, 1979)

D. E. H. de Boer and others, eds: *Hutspot, haring en wittebrood: Tien eeuwen Leiden en de Leidenaars* (Zwolle and Leiden, 1980–81)

B. N. Leverland and J. D. Bangs: *The Pilgrims and Leiden, 1609–1620* (Leiden, 1984)

M. Prak: *Gezeten burgers: De elite in een Hollandse stad: Leiden, 1700–1780* (n.p., 1985) [with Eng. summary]

F. J. W. van Kan: *Sleutels tot de macht: De ontwikkeling van het Leidse patriciaat tot 1420* (Hilversum, 1988) [with Eng. summary]

2. ART LIFE AND ORGANIZATION. The documented history of Leiden as an art centre began *c.* 1450. A few goldsmiths, carvers and painters can be traced to the first half of the 15th century, but they and their work are hardly identifiable. The fact that around 1420 carved stones for the Pieterskerk were commissioned in The Hague from 'Joris de beeldesnijder' (*fl c.* 1410–35) indicates that the standard of the Leiden sculptors was not very high. Among the early painters Jacop Clementsz. (*fl c.* 1460–75) is best known. In 1462–5 he painted a *Last Judgement* and portraits of the Counts of Holland in the Stadhuis, and in 1467 a series of panels depicting the *Passion* and other biblical scenes for the chapel of the Jerusalem Almshouse (all destr.).

Manuscript illumination was particularly important, and it was produced mainly at the monastery of St Hieronymusdal, founded *c.* 1404 immediately outside the town walls. Around 1450 this workshop started to produce illuminated manuscripts and paintings for clients all over Holland. One of the painters trained there was Hugo Jacobsz., the father and teacher of Lucas van Leyden, the most famous Leiden painter and engraver of the late Middle Ages. Lucas probably also trained with Cornelis Engebrechtsz., whose two triptychs for the Augustinian convent of Marienpoel near Leiden—one with the *Lamentation* (*c.* 1508) and the other with the *Crucifixion* (*c.* 1517–22; for illustration *see* ENGEBRECHTSZ., CORNELIS)—as well as the van der Does–van Poelgeest panels (*c.* 1515) for the St Pieterskerk (all Leiden, Stedel. Mus. Lakenhal) are among the finest examples of late medieval paintings in the museum. Cornelis Engebrechtsz. might be linked as a designer with the rise of tapestry-weaving in Leiden, which attained its highest level after the arrival of Willem Andriesz. de Raedt (*d* ?1573) in 1540. The most talented of Cornelis's children was Pieter Cornelisz. Kunst (*fl* 1525–55), who designed the splendidly carved Renaissance pulpit in the Pieterskerk (*see* PULPIT, fig. 3).

Lucas van Leyden was commissioned by the heirs of a wood merchant to paint his famous triptych with the *Last Judgement* (1526–7; Leiden, Stedel. Mus. Lakenhal; *see* LUCAS VAN LEYDEN, fig. 4). The triptych was placed near the baptistery in the Pieterskerk, above the aldermen's bench, moved after the Iconoclasm of 1566 to the aldermen's room in the Stadhuis.

More than 50 painters worked in Leiden in the early 16th century, and most of them belonged to the Guild of St Luke. By the end of the century, however, painting had practically died out, and the Guild lost its significance. The most important painter in these days was Isaac Claesz. van Swanenburgh, who *c.* 1600 painted for the serge-hall (*see* §1 above) a series of large panels depicting the different stages of clothmaking (*The Old and the New Trade*; Leiden, Stedel. Mus. Lakenhal). The industrial boom of the first half of the 17th century, however, created new opportunities for artists. Dozens of painters had studios there, and although many of them later left for larger cities, Leiden remained an important art centre in this period. Van Swanenburgh and his son Jacob van Swanenburgh trained the new generation of Leiden painters (*see* NETHERLANDS,

THE, §III, 3). It was, however, Joris van Schooten (1587–1652), son of a Flemish immigrant, who most enthusiastically postulated the re-foundation of the Guild. He earned a reputation with his paintings of the civic guard (e.g. the *Civic Guard Company of Capt. Harman van Brosterhuyzen*, 1626; Leiden, Stedel. Mus. Lakenhal) and a series of religious panels in the Lutheran church (1640; *in situ*).

Among van Swanenburgh's famous pupils was Jan van Goyen, who had a studio in Leiden between 1618 and 1634, before moving to The Hague. The production of his studio must have amounted to thousands of drawings and paintings. From 1625 two young painters, Jan Lievens and Rembrandt, shared a studio in Leiden where they had many pupils, such as Gerrit Dou, son of a glasspainter. Unlike Lievens and Rembrandt, Dou stayed in the city and became the best known of the so-called Leidse fijnschilders (*see* LEIDEN 'FINE' PAINTERS), who between *c.* 1630 and *c.* 1760 produced very small paintings, often on copper, in an extremely meticulous and detailed style. Their works were already highly praised and priced in the 17th century. Of Dou's pupils and successors, Frans van Mieris the elder acquired most fame. One of van Mieris's friends was the outstanding genre painter Jan Steen, who was born in Leiden and taught by his father-in-law, Jan van Goyen. Another eminent genre painter, but more closely related to the 'Fine' painters, was their mutual friend Gabriel Metsu, who in 1648 was one of the founder-members of the new painters' guild, although after 1650 he worked mainly in Amsterdam.

2. Frans van Mieris the younger: *Three Generations*, oil on panel, 340×304 mm, 1742 (Leiden, Stedelijk Museum De Lakenhal); showing Frans van Mieris the elder, Willem van Mieris and Frans van Mieris the younger

In 1694 several 'Fine' painters founded the Leiden Tekeningenacademie, of which members of the van Mieris family (see fig. 2) were the directors until *c.* 1760. Then, with the death of Frans van Mieris the younger and Hieronymus van der Mij (1687–1761), the era of the 'Fine' painters ended. In 1799 the drawing academy was transformed into the Ars Aemula Naturae Society. During the 19th century this society encouraged high-standard amateur drawing and painting, thanks to the classes of such men as George Hendrik Breitner. Breitner's pupil Floris Verster became the most important Leiden painter of the early 20th century.

The most important art collector in 17th-century Leiden was Johan de Bye. His initiative in organizing public exhibitions of his collection looked forward to the emergence of museums in the 19th century. Leiden University assembled an excellent collection of drawings and engravings; of special importance is its gallery of many hundreds of professors' portraits, built up during the four centuries of its existence. Leiden is an outstanding museum town, with over a dozen state, municipal and private museums concentrated in a small area. The state museums were strongly supported in the first half of the 19th century by King William I, who wanted the Netherlands to have museums on a par with those abroad.

BIBLIOGRAPHY

R. E. O. Ekkart and others: *Leids Kunstlegaat: Kunst en historie rondom Ars Aemula Naturae* (Leiden, 1974)

R. E. O. Ekkart and M. F. van Kersen-Halbertsma: *Icones Leidenses: De portretverzameling van de Rijksuniversiteit te Leiden* (Leiden, 1975)

*Geschildert tot Leyden anno 1626: Schilderijen, tekeningen en prenten van Van Goyen, De Heem, Lievens, Porcellis, Rembrandt e.a.* (exh. cat. by R. E. O. Ekkart and M. L. Wurfbain, Leiden, Stedel. Mus. Lakenhal, 1977)

J. D. Bangs: *Cornelis Engebrechtsz.'s Leiden: Studies in Cultural History* (Assen, 1979)

T. H. Lunsingh Scheurleer, C. W. Fock and A. J. van Dissel: *Het Rapenburg: Geschiedenis van een Leidse gracht* (Leiden, 1986–)

*Leidse fijnschilders. Van Gerrit Dou tot Frans van Mieris de Jonge, 1630–1760* (exh. cat. by E. J. Sluijter; Leiden, Stedel Mus. Lakenhal, 1988) [with Eng. summary]

DICK E. H. DE BOER

**Leiden 'Fine' painters** [Leidse fijnschilders]. Name given to a number of Dutch painters, active in Leiden *c.* 1630 to *c.* 1760. They are known for their small paintings, principally genre scenes, full of minute detail and executed in a polished style. The most famous and influential practitioners of this school were GERRIT DOU and his pupil Frans van Mieris the elder (*see* MIERIS, VAN, (1)). Although the term was first used *c.* 1850, artists such as Dou, Frans van Mieris, Pieter van Slingeland (also a pupil of Dou), Frans's son Willem van Mieris and the latter's son Frans van Mieris the younger were apparently already being praised for those same qualities in their own time. Other contemporary sources suggest that the tradition of Dou's art was continued by Frans the elder and van Slingeland, that the art of Frans, in turn, lived on through the work of his sons Jan and Willem, and that Willem was imitated by Frans the younger. It may thus be assumed that they were, to some extent at least, aware of the fact that they resembled each other in style and subject-matter. From the beginning they were admired for their 'neat' and 'elaborate' manner of painting, and the general reaction was one of wonder

and amazement at the astonishing virtuosity and perfection of their small-scale paintings.

Already in his early paintings from the 1630s Dou applied himself continually to refining, with ever more detail, the manner of printing he learnt from the young Rembrandt, although from close up the brushstrokes can always be seen. That these paintings do not seem too meticulous is partly due to Dou's remarkably subtle use of chiaroscuro. Two of his most direct followers, Peter van Slingeland and Dominicus van Tol (after 1630–1676), were much less successful in this respect. Dou's most talented pupil, Frans van Mieris the elder, tried to conceal the effect of the brushstroke as much as possible. His highly polished paintings would probably seem rather stiff were it not for the lively handling of light. The same applies to the work of Arie de Vois. In van Mieris's later work, however, the enamel-like smoothness and the technical virtuosity became an end in themselves; his figures, too, became increasingly stylized. This tendency was continued in the work of his son Willem and that of his grandson Frans van Mieris the younger.

In the 1640s Dou began to develop what is known as the 'niche' format, which was to become virtually the hallmark of the Leiden 'Fine' painters. The stone window, usually framing a maidservant or old woman, is an entirely artificial motif (in the 17th century Dutch houses did not have such windows). It emphasizes the sense of illusion, although it is never possible to speak of an actual *trompe l'oeil*. The style and themes developed between *c.* 1640 and 1675 by Dou and van Mieris, were imitated, elaborated on and transformed by numerous painters for more than a century afterwards. With the third and fourth generations of Leiden 'Fine' painters, the colours are noticeably brighter, while the light is more even, and the figures are increasingly stereotyped, but essentially there were no stylistic or thematic innovations.

Dou, Frans van Mieris the elder and to a lesser degree van Slingeland and Willem van Mieris were among the most famous and best paid artists of their time, and their work was purchased not only by members of the Dutch bourgeoisie but also by foreign monarchs. In the course of the 19th century, however, appreciation of the Leiden 'Fine' painters dropped dramatically, reaching its lowest point at the beginning of the 20th century. It is only in the last few decades that their work has become acknowledged again as a highly important contribution to 17th-century Dutch genre painting.

Apart from the artists already mentioned, other Leiden artists commonly thought of as belonging to the group are Jacob van Spreeuwen (1609/10–after 1650), Johan Adriaensz van Staveren (1613/14–1669), Abraham de Pape (before 1621–1650), Adriaen van Gaesbeeck (1621–50), Johannes Cornelisz. van Swieten (?1635–61), Jacob Toorenvliet (1640–1719), Bartholomeus Maton (*c.* 1643–after 1682), Matthijs Naiveu, Abraham Snaphaen (1651–91), Karel de Moor, Jan van Mieris, Jacob van der Sluis (?1660–1732), Hieronymus van der Mij (1687–1761), Louis de Moni (1698–1771) and finally two rather weak artists, Pieter Cattel (1712–59) and Nicolaas Rijnenburg (1716–after 1776). Occasionally painters born or working in Leiden, such as Quiringh van Brekelenkam, Gabriel Metsu and Jan Steen, show the unmistakable influence of Dou and/or Frans van Mieris the elder. Outside Leiden the influence of the 'Fine' painters was also considerable on artists such as Jacob Ochtervelt, Godfried Schalcken, Eglon van der Neer, Caspar Netscher, Adriaen van der Werff, Arnold Boonen (1669–1729) and Philip van Dijk. Even in the 19th century there were artists, for example Machiel Versteegh (1756–1843) and George Gillis Haanen (1807–79), whose scenes hark back to works by Dou and his pupils.

### BIBLIOGRAPHY

S. van Leeuwen: *Korte besgrijving van het Lugdunum Batavorum nu Leyden* [A brief description of Lugdunum Batavorum, now Leyden] (Leiden, 1672), pp. 191–2

W. Martin: *Het leven en de werken van Gerrit Dou beschouwd in verband met het schildersleven van zijn tijd* [The life and works of Gerrit Dou in the context of contemporary painting] (Leiden, 1901; Eng. trans., abridged, London, 1902)

F. W. Robinson: 'Gerard Dou and his Circle of Influence', *Gabriel Metsu, 1629–1667: A Study of his Place in Dutch Genre Painting of the Golden Age* (New York, 1974), pp. 89–97

O. Naumann: *Frans van Mieris the Elder, 1635–1681*, 2 vols (Doornspijk, 1981)

*Masters of Seventeenth-century Dutch Genre Painting* (exh. cat., ed. P. Sutton; Philadelphia, PA, Mus. A.; Berlin, Gemäldegal.; London, RA; 1984), pp. xl–xliii

*Leidse fijnschilders: Van Gerrit Dou tot Frans van Mieris de Jonge, 1630–1760* (exh. cat., ed. E. J. Sluijter; Leiden, Stedel. Mus. Lakenhal, 1988) [with an extensive bibliog.]

*De Hollandse fijnschilders van Gerard Dou tot Adriaen van der Werff* (exh. cat. by Peter Hecht, Amsterdam, Rijksmus., 1989)

E. J. Sluijter: *De lof der schilderkunst: Over schilderijen van Gerrit Dou (1613–1675) en een traktaat van Philips Angel uit 1642* (Hilversum, 1993)

ERIC J. SLUIJTER

**Leighton, Frederic**, 1st Baron Leighton of Stretton (*b* Scarborough, 3 Dec 1830; *d* London, 25 Jan 1896). English painter and sculptor. He spent much of his youth travelling on the Continent with his family. This cosmopolitan background was of great importance to his development as an artist. After his father, a doctor, settled in Frankfurt am Main in 1846, Leighton enrolled at the Städelsches Kunstinstitut, where he studied under the Nazarene artist Edward von Steinle between 1850 and 1852. The style and subject-matter of such early works as the *Death of Brunelleschi* (1852; London, Leighton House A.G. & Mus.) show the influence of Nazarene art and suggest the growing importance of Italy as a source of inspiration. Leighton travelled to Rome in 1852 and became friendly with Giovanni Costa and George Heming Mason, who

later emerged as leading figures in the group of English and Italian artists known as the Etruscans. His first Royal Academy success, *Cimabue's Celebrated Madonna Is Carried in Procession through the Streets of Florence* (Brit. Royal Col.), was painted in Rome in 1855. This huge processional work, filled with incident and detail, takes its subject from Vasari's *Vite*. It was bought by Queen Victoria from the Royal Academy Summer Exhibition of 1855 and its success marked Leighton as one of the most promising artists of his generation.

Between 1855 and 1859 Leighton was based in Paris, where he aimed to perfect his technique and absorb the stimulating atmosphere of the studios. He met Jean-August-Dominique Ingres and Eugène Delacroix, but his art was chiefly influenced by such contemporaries as Ary Scheffer and Joseph Nicolas Robert-Fleury (1797–1890). The period marks the beginning of a transition in his work, from the exact draughtsmanship and historical detail of the Nazarenes to a broader synthesis of influences, embracing the painterly effects of Venetian art, the realistic landscapes of Jean-Baptiste-Camille Corot and Charles-François Daubigny and the classical subject-matter of Thomas Couture's followers.

The years 1859–64 were marked for Leighton by reverses and critical hostility. He returned to London in 1859 and for five years his contributions to the Royal Academy were systematically rejected or badly hung—a response indicative of the degree to which he was seen as a threatening and alien influence. A member of the Hogarth Club, he established close links with Dante Gabriel Rossetti, Edward Burne-Jones and others of the Pre-Raphaelite circle, and his work was championed by John Ruskin. In 1862 Leighton received a commission from *Cornhill Magazine* to illustrate George Eliot's *Romola*. These illustrations, together with such paintings as *Dante in Exile* (1864; British Rail Pension Fund, on loan to London, Leighton House A.G. & Mus.), are expressions of his renewed interest in Renaissance Italy. At the same time, he was increasingly preoccupied with the formal problems of academic painting. Though *Dante in Exile* is a full-blooded historical set piece, evoking the early Renaissance world of the Nazarenes, its structure owes more to Raphael and its painterly effects are indebted to the Venetian school. The *Syracusan Bride* (1865–6; priv. col.; see fig.) defines the areas of interest that Leighton

Frederic Leighton: *Syracusan Bride*, oil on canvas, 1.33×4.18 m, 1865–6 (private collection)

pursued with ever greater rigour for the rest of his life. Like *Cimabue*, it is a formal processional work. Its classically draped figures are inspired by the Parthenon sculptures (of which Leighton kept a cast in his studio) and its subject, drawn from lines in the second *Idyll* of Theokritos, is incidental to the artist's main intention: to represent idealized figures of artistic grace.

The psychological content of Leighton's work became increasingly complex in the late 1860s and the 1870s. Canvases of this period frequently show the confrontation between the forces of life and death, as in *Hercules Wrestling with Death for the Body of Alcestis* (1871; Hartford, CT, Wadsworth Atheneum). The struggling figures of Hercules and Death reflect the artist's desire to wrest beauty from the hold of decay. In catching the transience of ideal beauty, Leighton revealed himself to have been not only a classical painter but also a full-blooded aesthete.

Leighton made five trips to North Africa and the Near East (1857, 1867, 1868, 1873 and 1882), resulting in numerous oil sketches, which are striking for their direct, uncluttered depiction of the barren desert landscape (e.g. the *Temple of Philae (Looking up the Nile)*, 1868; Manchester, C.A.G.). After his stay in Damascus in 1873, he included decorative Eastern accessories in several paintings, though only a few—for instance *Portions of the Interior of the Grand Mosque of Damascus* (1873–5; Preston, Harris Mus. & A.G.)—were actually set in Damascus. A more notable result of this trip was the Arab Hall, designed by George Aitchison and added to Leighton's home (Leighton House, Holland Park, London) between 1877 and 1879. Leighton's own decorative schemes recall his early paintings in the Nazarene style. They include two frescoes (1878–83) for the South Kensington Museum (London, V&A) and the ceiling decoration (completed in 1886) commissioned by the American banker Henry Gurdon Marquand for the music room at his house in New York.

Leighton's interest in sculpture was a natural extension of his increasingly sculptural treatment of the painted canvas. While his paintings exploit to the full the expressive possibilities of drapery, his sculptures rely instead on the representation of idealized nude figures. His interest in Hellenic art and its revival brought him into sympathy with the sculptor Hamo Thornycroft, who was with Leighton one of the senior figures in the revival of sculpture known as NEW SCULPTURE. Leighton's *Athlete Wrestling with a Python* (exh. RA 1877; London, Tate) presents to the spectator both the physical and the psychological struggle for supremacy between man and snake. With its allusions to the *Laokoon* group (Rome, Vatican, Cortile Belvedere), the *Athlete* was a product of the complex eclecticism that was so important to Leighton's artistic development. Equally fine, though in striking contrast to this work, is the languid figure of *The Sluggard* (1884; London, Tate), which pays homage to Donatello.

After his election as President of the Royal Academy in 1878, Leighton was increasingly regarded as the leader of the Victorian art establishment. The themes already dominant in his art remained constant throughout the last 20 years of his life. In *Captive Andromache* (1888; Manchester, C.A.G), arguably his masterpiece, the confident academic underpinning of the composition enhances and enriches the palpable emotion of the subject. An austere figure, Leighton never married and such works as *Captive Andromache* provide indications of the extent to which he subordinated his own emotions to the demands of his art. Increasingly in his last years a note of melancholy entered his work. Mythological subjects, such as the *Return of Persephone* (1891; Leeds, C.A.G.) and *Clytie* (1895–6; India, priv. col., see L. Ormond and R. Ormond, pl. 192), manifest a yearning engendered by loss and sorrow that finds solace in sleep, as represented in the *Garden of the Hesperides* (c. 1892; Port Sunlight, Lady Lever A.G.) or *Flaming June* (c. 1895; Ponce, Mus. A.). These paintings, rich in colour and handling, are the final statement of the most intellectual and rigorous adherent of the Aesthetic Movement. The inclusion of two illustrations of Leighton's drawings in the first number of the *Yellow Book* (1894) indicates the extent to which a younger generation of artists led by Aubrey Beardsley, Charles Ricketts and Laurence Housman (*b* 1867) appreciated his generous encouragement of their efforts and recognized him as their spiritual antecedent. Leighton died exhausted by his battle with heart disease and the demands of his public role as President of the Royal Academy. He had already almost outlived his age, and it is significant that he left no school of pupils to continue a tradition that itself was almost exhausted.

### WRITINGS
*Addresses Delivered to the Students of the Royal Academy by the Late Lord Leighton* (London, 1896)

### BIBLIOGRAPHY
[Mrs A. Lang]: 'Sir Frederic Leighton, P.R.A.', *A. J.* [London] (1884), pp. 1–32 [suppl.]

E. Rhys: *Sir Frederic Leighton Bart., P.R.A.: An Illustrated Chronicle* (London, 1895) [with preface by F. G. Stephens]

A. Corkran: *Frederic Leighton* (London, 1904)

Mrs R. Barrington: *Life, Letters & Work of Frederic Leighton*, 2 vols (London, 1906)

J. E. Staley: *Lord Leighton of Stretton P.R.A.* (London, 1906)

L. Ormond and R. Ormond: *Lord Leighton* (London, 1975); review by J. Christian in *Burl. Mag.*, cxx (1978), pp. 684–9

R. Ormond: *Leighton's Frescoes in the Victoria and Albert Museum* (London, 1975)

R. G. Dorment: 'A Roman Lady by Frederick Leighton', *Bull. Philadelphia Mus. A.*, lxxiii (June 1977), pp. 2–11

*Victorian High Renaissance* (exh. cat., Minneapolis, Inst. A., 1978), pp. 95–127

I. Jenkins: 'Frederic Lord Leighton and Greek Vases', *Burl. Mag.*, cxxv (1983), pp. 597–605

STEPHEN JONES

**Leigudun** [Lei-ku-tun]. *See under* SUIZHOU.

**Leilan, Tell** [anc. Shekhna; Shubat Enlil]. Site on the Habur Plains of north-eastern Syria. It was one of a number of large cities in northern Mesopotamia in the mid-3rd and the early-2nd millennia BC. In the mid-3rd millennium the city was known as Shekhna, but its name was changed to Shubat Enlil by Shamshi-Adad I of Assyria (*reg* 1813–1782 BC) when he made the city one of the capitals of his north Mesopotamian empire. Archaeological data from Tell Leilan have contributed to the resolution of three problems of ancient Near Eastern art history.

The first concerns the apparent Sumerization of northern Mesopotamia in the mid-3rd millennium BC. Around 2600 BC the city states of southern Mesopotamia appear to have undergone a substantial reorganization of political and economic power. Palaces (i.e. administrative buildings clearly secular in nature) appear now for the first time as distinct from temples; they housed the ruling élites who controlled large teams of ration-paid agricultural labourers. At around the same time cities suddenly appeared in northern Mesopotamia, at Tell Leilan and other sites across the Assyrian plains. At Tell Leilan this change is documented as the transition from Ninevite 5 (Leilan III) culture to Leilan II culture during the period *c.* 2600–*c.* 2500 BC. Associated with this development in the north is the disappearance of the Ninevite 5 style of cylinder seal iconography and its sudden replacement with a Leilan IIId style, which is derived from southern Mesopotamian late Early Dynastic II–Early Dynastic III seal iconography, especially the typical banquet and contest scene motifs. The ruling élites of the nascent northern Mesopotamian cities appear to have legitimated their ruler through emulation of the administrative iconography of southern Mesopotamian polities.

A second question involves the temporal relationship between structural politico-economic change and ceramic style change. The transformation of northern Mesopotamian villages and towns into socially stratified cities, documented in the Leilan IIId period (*c.* 2600 BC) by the expansion of settlement from 15 to 90 ha and the construction on the acropolis of an administrative building with central grain stores, was not accompanied by a synchronous change in ceramic manufacture and style. Changes in pottery manufacture and styles from labour-intensive, highly decorated, individualized products to uniform

'mass-produced' wares did not occur until the succeeding Leilan II period, probably 100 years after Leilan urbanization and state formation.

Third, but perhaps most important, is the information Tell Leilan provides concerning the 'Babylonization' of northern Mesopotamia in the early 2nd millennium BC. Following the occupational hiatus of *c.* 2100–*c.* 1900 BC, northern Mesopotamia was reinhabited by a population bearing Hurrian and Amorite personal names. The cities and political structures of this period have few cultural links with those of the pre-hiatus period. Instead, cultural forms familiar from southern Mesopotamia were introduced into the region by Amorite rulers. This period's distinctive temple façades and cylinder seal iconography are documented at Tell Leilan and represent the introduction of southern, 'Babylonian' styles into northern Mesopotamia for the purpose of legitimating the reigns of the new Amorite rulers. Temple plans at Tell Leilan from the reign of Shamshi-Adad I are an innovation associated, for unknown reasons, with the 'Babylonizing' temple façades and administrative iconography.

The level 2–3 temples of the Leilan Acropolis Building are the earliest historic period examples of the architectural plan later typical of Assyrian temples of the 9th and 8th centuries BC, with direct access featuring the following room order: entrance; wideroom antecella; longroom cella. A temple of similar plan was constructed at Assur by Shamshi-Adad. Assyrian temples of the 16th–15th centuries BC follow the plan of the Leilan temple. The origins and functions of this plan, as opposed to the

Tell Leilan, Acropolis Building, level 2, north façade, *c.* 2000–1800 BC

'Babylonian' type plan with wideroom antecella, are un-known, but appear to be a Shamshi-Adad period innovation. The southern and northern façades of the Acropolis period I temples are decorated with mud-brick semi-engaged columns fashioned to resemble the trunks of trimmed palm trees. The columns are of five types: (1) plain-faced columns built as large spirals, twisting in alternate directions (Acropolis Building, level 2, north façade; see fig.); (2) plain-faced columns, twisted (level 3) or straight (level 2); (3) columns with mud-plaster sculpted into imbricated fronds with a smooth surface (level 2 south façade) or with surface vertical (pinnate) hatching (level 2, south façade); with step-like stages with surface vertical (pinnate) hatching and crosshatching (level 2, south façade); (4) column with mud-plaster diamond-shaped frond scars, surrounded by braided columns (level 3); (5) column with mud-plaster square, scale-like frond scars (level 2, south façade). Mud-brick columns fashioned to resemble palm trunks were a feature of southern Mesopotamian temples from as early as the Uruk period (*c.* 4000–*c.* 2900 BC). Mud-brick columns similar to those of the Leilan temples are known from Mari, Tell el-Rimah, Assur, Larsa, Ur and Tell Haddad.

Seventeen different seals were used to generate the corpus of 'Old Babylonian style' seal impressions retrieved from the Leilan Acropolis Building, level 'X', associated with officials of the royal family of Shamshi-Adad I, and the extant portions of the 18th-century BC Lower Town Palace, associated with local, post-Shamshi-Adad dynasts. The 'Old Babylonian' impressions are twice as numerous on the Acropolis as in the Lower Town Palace, where the 'Old Syrian mixed' and 'pure' styles dominate the seal impression assemblage.

BIBLIOGRAPHY

D. Parayre: 'Vers une définition de la culture des royaumes amorites de haute Mesopotamie: Les Particularités septentrionales de la glyptique de Tell Leilan a l'époque paléo-babylonienne', *Festschrift N. Ozguc* (n.d.)

H. Weiss: 'Tell Leilan in the Third and Second Millennia BC', *An. Archéol. Arabes Syr.*, xxxiii/1 (1983), pp. 47–73

——: 'Tell Leilan and Shubat Enlil', *Mari*, iv (1985), pp. 269–92

——: 'Tell Leilan on the Harbur Plains of Syria', *Bibl. Archaeologist*, xlviii/1 (1985), pp. 5–34

D. Parayre: 'Seals and Seal Impressions from Tell Leilan 1985', *Resurrecting the Past*, ed. M. van Loon, P. Matthiae and H. Weiss (Amsterdam, 1990)

H. Weiss: '"Civilizing" the Harbur Plains: Mid-third Millennium State Formation at Tell Leilan', *Resurrecting the Past*, ed. M. van Loon, P. Matthiae and H. Weiss (Amsterdam, 1990), pp. 387–407

——: 'Tell Leilan 1989: New Data for Mid-third Millennium Urbanization and State Formation', *Mitt. Dt. Orient-Ges.*, cxii (1990), pp. 193–218

H. Weiss and others: '1985 Excavations at Tell Leilan, Syria', *Amer. J. Archaeol.*, xciv (1990), pp. 529–42, 580–81

J.-C. Margueron: 'Troncs de palmiers et temples à haute terrasse de début du Bronze Moyen', *Orient Express Magazine*, 1 (1991), pp. 9–10

D. Parayre and H. Weiss: 'Cinq Campagnes de fouilles à Tell Leilan dans la Haute Jezireh, 1979–1987: Bilan et perspectives', *J. Sav.* (Jan–June 1991), pp. 3–16

HARVEY WEISS

**Leinberger, Hans** (*fl* 1511–30). German wood-carver and sculptor. He was the most eminent sculptor in Bavaria in the second and third decades of the 16th century. It is likely that he trained or was employed in the region of the Danube school, whether in Vienna (see Lill; Oettinger) or Regensburg (see Legner; Stange). There is also a possibility that he began his career in Nuremberg (see Liedke). His centre of activity was in Landshut, where his life is documented from 1510 until 1530. He paid tax in 1510 on a house there and between 1516 and 1530 received various payments from the court of Ludwig X (*reg* 1516–45), but none of his projects for the court is known to have survived. More than 50 individual or multi-partite sculptures (most of them listed by Lill) have been attributed to him. As a carver of figures for altarpieces, he worked mostly in lime-wood, but also produced sculpture in stone, bronze and fine-grained hardwoods, such as pear-wood and boxwood, selected according to the nature of the piece.

Leinberger's earliest documented work is the carved altarpiece for the former collegiate church of St Castulus in Moosburg (see fig. 1); probably commissioned in 1511 and completed in 1514, it remains *in situ* (although in an altered state). Sometimes likened to a gigantic monstrance, the altarpiece rises 14.4 m to the vaults of the church choir and contains ten large statues and a number of smaller ones. The shrine holds three over life-size statues: the *Virgin and Child*, flanked by *St Castulus* (whose relics had lain in Moosburg since the 8th century) and the *Emperor St Henry II*. On either side of the shrine, in the position of guardians, stand the slightly smaller figures of *St John*

1. Hans Leinberger: shrine of the *Virgin and Child* with *St Castulus* and *Emperor St Henry II*, lime-wood, 3.78×2.43 m, 1514 (Moosburg, St Castulus)

*the Baptist* and *St John Martyr of Rome*, the latter subsequently recast as *St John the Evangelist* (probably in the 18th century). A *Crucified Christ* appears at the apex of the altar crowning, flanked by the *Virgin* and *St John* one tier below. Just below them, left and right, stand *St Corbinian* and *St Sigismund.* Originally the altarpiece had the customary form of a triptych, with two shutters attached to either side of the shrine, but these had already been removed by 1856, the date of the lithograph of the altarpiece by Anton Harrer (*fl c.* 1846–56). The removal probably occurred in 1782, at which time the figures were also painted white. The present neo-Gothic polychromy dates from 1862, albeit considerably muted during a restoration of 1937–9. All that survives of the original shutters are four reliefs that portray the *Martyrdom of St Castulus*: completely stripped of their polychromy, they now hang on the wall of the choir behind the altarpiece. It is not certain whether the sculptures had originally been polychromed or left uncoloured (except for the tinting of lips and eyes). The predella, painted front and back by Hans Wertinger (1516) gives reason to think that the whole work had been polychromed: since there were paintings on the exterior of the predella, it is most likely that the exterior of the shutters had also had paintings, in which case one would expect the adjacent guardian saints to have also been polychromed, and the same would then presumably hold true for the figures and reliefs of the interior. The figures at Moosburg are striking for their sculptural energy. They are enveloped in deeply cut drapery, which is organized in massive folds that loop and swing over the bodies and produce strong contrasts of light and dark. Though still contained within the shallow space of the altarpiece, the saints turn or sway on their low, foliated pedestals. The *Virgin*, raised slightly higher than the other two figures in the corpus, appears to be ascending with the help of angels, whose heads protrude beneath the drapery at her feet. The hands and faces, the only flesh left uncovered, also appear quite mobile and present a naturalistic contrast to the abstract patterns of drapery.

Although Leinberger's sculpture does not lend itself to simple categories of period style, it does share certain qualities with the work of a number of other south German and Austrian wood-carvers of the same generation, especially the Master H. L. of Breisach and the carvers of the altarpiece at Mauer near Melk and that formerly at Zwettl (now Adamov near Brno). The plethora of drapery that swirls around figures individually or in groups, and other energized, curvilinear patterns of hair, beards or foliage that are found in the work of these artists, have invited descriptions such as Baroque, Gothic-Baroque or Mannerist. However, none of these terms serves to explain the phenomenon; nor is it known whether or how Leinberger might have had contact with these anonymous contemporaries. There is, however, a demonstrable connection between Leinberger's art and the pictorial models provided by Albrecht Altdorfer, and to a lesser degree, Lucas Cranach (i), both of whom were protagonists in the development of the Danube school.

Leinberger's relationship to Altdorfer appears not to have been one-sided. The *Virgin* in Moosburg anticipates by at least four years the earliest of Altdorfer's six versions of the *Schöne Maria*. Both artists replicated the type of image of the Virgin called the 'Madonna of St Luke' or *Hodegetria* ('Virgin who points the way'); a 13th-century Italo-Byzantine example of this can be seen in the Kollegiatstift Unserer Lieben Frau zur Alten Kapelle in Regensburg; yet when they composed the draped figure with a swinging movement, they consciously drew upon the form and expression of yet another source—the familiar image of the *Schöne Madonna* of *c.* 1400. The similarity between Altdorfer's drawing of the *Schöne Maria* (1518; Berlin, Kupferstichkab.) and Leinberger's bronze statuette of the same theme (Berlin, Gemäldegal.) defies coincidence, although the sequence of the two works remains uncertain. It is known, however, that between 1519 and 1521 Leinberger produced three statues (untraced) of the *Schöne Maria* for the former pilgrimage church of 'Zur schönen Maria', now the Protestant Neupfarrkirche, Regensburg.

The four relief panels at Moosburg reveal a highly expressive narrative style utilizing both vigorous sculptural corporeality and pictorial illusion. Leinberger spared no effort to make the carved wood carry as much information as possible: he used chisels and a large array of punches to describe texture and form of figures in different kinds of dress, architecture and landscape. The architecture and costumes, both contemporary and pseudo-antique, are clearly of Renaissance origin, and each scene is defined by architecture, although the space is largely a function of the scale and massing of figures. In the *Arrest of St Castulus*, for example, the saint and the arresting soldiers are massive in the left foreground, while the people to whom Castulus was preaching recede into space, but with exaggerated or inconsistent diminution of the figures. The effect is brutal and expressive of restless energy. The same can be said for *St Castulus before Diocletian*, and especially for the two martyrdom scenes, *St Castulus Beaten with Clubs*, in which he is suspended splayed and upside down, and *St Castulus Buried Alive*. In the foliage and some of the figures there are strong reminiscences to early drawings by Altdorfer, such as the *Wild Man* (London, BM) or *Two Soldiers and a Pair of Lovers* (Copenhagen, Stat. Mus. Kst), both dated 1508. Other indications that Leinberger had turned to graphic art in designing reliefs appear in three small, unpolychromed panels with scenes from the Passion. The *Crucifixion* (pear-wood, 220×150 mm; Munich, Bayer. Nmus.), monogrammed HL and dated [15]16, bears strong resemblance to Cranach's turbulent woodcut (1502) of the same subject. The *Descent from the Cross* (see fig. 2), like Altdorfer's version of the subject from his woodcut series of the *Fall and Redemption of Mankind* (*c.* 1513), portrays Christ pitching forward, while a man, leaning over the cross from above, strains to ease down the limp body. The third of these panels, the *Lamentation* (box-wood, 150×110 mm; Berlin, Skulpgal.) also bears the HL monogram. Behind the foreground cluster of strongly defined figures there lies a distant landscape carved in very low relief, suggestive of atmosphere as well as distance.

The Moosburg Altarpiece is evidently the work of an already mature artist. On the basis of resemblances to its sculptures, a small group of sculptural works have been suggested as early works by Leinberger: among these are two reliefs of lime-wood, the *Mass for the Dead* and *Two*

2. Hans Leinberger: *Descent from the Cross*, boxwood, 165×120 mm, *c.* 1520 (Berlin, Gemäldegalerie)

*Figures of Death Seizing a Bishop*, that may predate 1510, and a sandstone relief of an enthroned *Virgin and Child* of about the same time (all Berlin, Gemäldegal.); as well as a *Virgin and Child with St Anne* (Munich, Bayer. Nmus.), a lime-wood group that is carved with deep cavities and a suppleness that rivals terracotta. Of an altarpiece by Leinberger, commissioned in 1515 for the Johanneskirche in Moosberg, only two rounded lime-wood reliefs survive from the interior upper register of each wing: the *Baptism* (Berlin, Gemäldegal.), poly-chromed and monogrammed HL, and *St John the Baptist Preaching* (Freising, Diözmus.), probably executed by an assistant.

Another group of sculptures, mature works that pre-suppose the level of achievement already represented by the Moosburg Altarpiece, are thought to have been executed *c.* 1515–30. One of these is an over life-size, polychromed statue of the *Virgin and Child* (h. 2.20 m; Landshut, St Martin). It was formerly surrounded by a rosary in the manner of Veit Stoss's *Annunciation of the Rosary* (1517–18; Nuremberg, St Lorenz), and probably hung originally in the Dominican church of St Blasius, Landshut. Three medallions from the rosary, bearing reliefs of the *Virgin* are also extant (Aachen, Suermondt-Ludwig-Mus.; Frankfurt am Main, Städel. Kstinst. & Städt. Gal.; and priv. col.). The *Virgin and Child* is the very image of ascension, with the weight of the body nullified by the deeply cut drapery, the folds of which make high-velocity orbits about the body, and by the action of little angels, lifting it from below. These angels are nearly

identical to those supporting the *Virgin* at Moosburg; and they reappear beneath the *Enthroned Virgin* (1526–7; Polling, Pfarrkirche). This sculpture, the last known of Leinberger's monogrammed or documented works, is what remains from an altarpiece commissioned for the Liebfrauenkirche (destr.) in Polling near Weilheim.

However, the *Enthroned Virgin*, unlike the standing versions, gives no hint of soaring upwards, so that the angels just tumble out helter-skelter from beneath her robe. A seated figure of *St James the Greater*, now stripped of its polychromy (Munich, Bayer. Nmus.) displays a similar posture. He holds a large book, fingers keeping it open in several different places; from a point where the spine of the book rests on his knee, the pages radiate outwards in waves that are amplified by ridges and channels of drapery. The saint's face remains an island of serenity, surrounded by turbulent motion. Although Leinberger's sculpture speaks mainly through the medium of drapery, a nearly nude *Sorrowful Christ* (Berlin, Gemäldegal.) reveals the artist's capacity to give the body itself life and meaning. With its large feet and bulky physique, this seated figure seems much bigger than it is (h. 750 mm) and expresses the weight of an inner burden.

A large, armoured figure of *St George* standing on a lumpy, overturned dragon (Munich, Liebfrauenkirche) has generally been accepted as one of Leinberger's latest works; for most authorities this means the mid- to late 1520s. After 1530 he is no longer recorded in Landshut. According to a notice from 1535 in the records of the Stadtkammer in Munich (see Liedke), a sculptor identified as 'Hannsen pildschnitzer von Lanndsshut' paid a fee in order to gain citizenship there; there is no certainty that this refers to Leinberger, but the possibility remains that he moved to Munich and was still active in the 1530s.

BIBLIOGRAPHY

*Hans Leinberger, Hans Stethaimer* (exh. cat. by H. Buchheit and G. Lill, Landshut, 1932)

G. Lill: *Hans Leinberger: Der Bildschnitzer von Landshut* (Munich, 1942)

K. Oettinger: *Anton Pilgram und die Bildhauer von St Stephan* (Vienna, 1951)

T. Müller: *Die Bildwerke in Holz, Ton und Stein von der Mitte des XV. bis gegen Mitte des XVI. Jahrhunderts*, Kataloge des Bayerischen National-museums München, xiii (Munich, 1959), pp. 207–19

A. Legner: 'Plastik', *Die Kunst der Donauschule, 1490–1540* (exh. cat., Linz, Schlossmus. and Stift St Florian, 1965), pp. 235–56

A. Stange: 'Albrecht Altdorfer, Hans Leinberger und die bayerische Kunst ihrer Zeit', *Alte & Mod. Kst*, x (1965), pp. 14–19

A. Legner: 'Akzente der Donauplastik', *Werden und Wandlung: Studien zur Kunst der Donauschule* (Linz, 1967), pp. 148–57

G. von der Osten and H. Vey: *Painting and Sculpture in Germany and the Netherlands, 1500 to 1600*, Pelican Hist. A. (Harmondsworth, 1969), pp. 40–42, 252–3

V. Liedke: *Hans Leinberger: Marginalien zur künstlerischen und geneolo-gischen Herkunft des grossen Landshuter Bildschnitzers* (Munich, 1976)

A. Schädler: 'Zur künstlerischen Entwicklung Hans Leinbergers', *Münchn. Jb. Bild. Kst*, n. s. 2, xxviii (1977), pp. 59–90

H. Schindler: *Der Schnitzaltar* (Regensburg, 1978, rev. 2/1982), pp. 184–93

J. Taubert: *Farbige Skulpturen* (Munich, 1978), pp. 89–96

H. Thoma: *Hans Leinberger: Seine Stadt, seine Zeit, sein Werk* (Regensburg, 1979)

M. Baxandall: *The Limewood Sculptors of Renaissance Germany* (New Haven and London, 1980), pp. 202–16, 309–16

M. J. Liebmann: *Die deutsche Plastik, 1350–1550* (Leipzig, 1982)

C. Behle: 'Hans Leinberger', *Misc. Bavar. Monacensia*, cxxiv (1984)

B. Decker: *Das Ende des mittelalterlichen Kultbildes und die Plastik Hans Leinbergers*, Bamberg. Stud. Kstgesch. & Dkmlpf., iii (Bamberg, 1985)

O. Schmidt: 'Hans Leinberger oder Christian Jorham der Ältere? Überlegungen zum Moosburger Altar', xii, *Städel-Jb.* (1989), pp. 209–34

CHARLES TALBOT

**Leinberger, Simon.** *See* LAINBERGER, SIMON.

**Leiper, William** (*b* Glasgow, 21 May 1839; *d* Helensburgh, 27 May 1916). Scottish architect and painter. He was apprenticed to Charles Wilson's pupils James Boucher (1832–1906) and James Cousland (*c.* 1832–66) in 1855. In 1860 he went to London, where he worked in turn for J. L. Pearson and William White and entered the circle of William Burges, who in 1881 proposed him as an FRIBA. He returned to Scotland in 1862 to work for Andrew Heiton (1823–94) and then entered a short-lived partnership with Robert Grieve Melvin in 1864. Leiper's reputation was established when he won the competition for Downhill Church, Glasgow, in 1864. The spire was derived from Pearson's design for St Peter's (1863–4), Vauxhall, London, the 13th-century church spires of Rutland (now Leics) and examples illustrated in W. E. Nesfield's *Specimens of Medieval Architecture* (1862). The interior had a wide single-span roof, probably inspired by E. W. Godwin's Northampton Town Hall (1861–4), with stained glass and stencilled decoration by Daniel Cottier (1838–99). Leiper's designs (1865) for the richly sculptured Dumbarton Academy and Burgh Hall, Strathclyde, derived from Benjamin Woodward's University Museum (1854–60), Oxford, and Godwin's Congleton Town Hall (1865), Cheshire. Other works in an early French Gothic style include Kirktonhall House (1866; destr.), Dumbarton, Strathclyde, an extravagant design with a tower, and Cornhill (1871), Strathclyde, and The Elms (1864), Arbroath, Tayside, both smaller but more adroitly composed. In some of his less expensive early houses he adopted the low-pitched roofs and compositional methods of Alexander Thomson, notably at Bonnington (now Rhuarden; 1871), Helensburgh, Strathclyde, and in remodelling Castlepark (1880), Lanark, Strathclyde, which has an unusual combination of Swiss and Anglo-Japanese elements.

By 1869 Leiper was using his own version of Scottish Baronial, while still showing a French influence and featuring towers and turrets, for example at Colearn (now a hotel), Tayside. The house is compactly composed, with a high-quality woodwork influenced by the Aesthetic Movement, stained glass by Cottier and tiles by W. B. Simpson in an Anglo-Japanese style. Cairdhu (1871), Helensburgh, Strathclyde, similarly had a lavish Anglo-Japanese interior, although its exterior was an early example of François I Revival, as with his Partick Burgh Hall, Glasgow, the following year.

Leiper accepted both large and smaller domestic commissions. His preferred idiom was the Franco-Scottish style, evident, for example, at Kinlochmoidart (1884), Highland, but he also worked in turn in a range of other styles, from Neo-Jacobean to a half-timbered style derived from R. Norman Shaw, as at Piersland (1898), Strathclyde, and the Arts and Crafts style, occasionally with an American influence that became progressively more important. For his ecclesiastical commissions, Leiper adapted the French Gothic style to the requirements of the Presbyterian Church. Camphill Church (1875–81), Queen's Park, Glasgow, has galleries between masonry arcades but no chancel; its splendid tower and spire derive from examples in Normandy. The plan at Hyndland (1886), Glasgow, includes a chancel, but there were insufficient funds for the intended church tower and spire. The saddleback tower of his last church, St Columba's (1902–5), Kilmalcolm, Strathclyde, was also influenced by examples in Normandy, but by Flamboyant rather than early French Gothic. Leiper's commercial commissions were few but impressive. In 1889 he built the Templeton Carpet Factory, Glasgow Green, in a Venetian Gothic style, using polychrome red stone, brick and tile, and in 1893–4 the Sun Insurance Building, West George Street, Glasgow, in a François I style, which won a Silver Medal at the Exposition Universelle, Paris, in 1900.

Leiper was a skilful watercolourist, having interrupted his practice in 1878 to study in Paris at the Académie Julian and then at Robert Weir Allan's with Arthur Melville. (The painter Robert Weir Allan (1852–1942) was active in Glasgow and London.) Leiper designed the interior of Tsar Alexander II's yacht *Livadia* in 1880 and in 1898 he was commissioned to supervise the ambitious scheme of murals by the Glasgow Boys in the Banqueting Hall of the City Chambers, Glasgow. He was elected an associate of the Royal Scottish Academy in 1891 and a full member in 1896.

BIBLIOGRAPHY
'Men who Build: William Leiper RSA, FRIBA', *Bldr's J.*, vi (1898), pp. 487–8
William Hunter-McNab: Obituary, *RIBA J.*, n. s. 3, xxiii (1916), pp. 302–4
J. R. Hume: 'Hyndland Church, 1887–1987', *Hyndland News* (Glasgow, 1987) [special centenary edition]
S. Green: 'William Leiper's Houses in Helensburgh', *The Age of Mackintosh*, Architectural Heritage, iii, ed. I. Davidson and J. Lowrey (Edinburgh, 1992), pp. 32–41
J. R. Hume: 'The Scottish Houses of William Leiper', *Scottish Country Houses, 1600–1914*, ed. I. Gow and A. Rowan (Edinburgh, 1995), pp. 285–97, 337–43

DAVID WALKER

**Leipzig.** German city in Saxony on the east bank of the confluence of the Elster, Pleisse and Parthe rivers. It has a population of *c.* 500,000. Its medieval Easter and Michaelmas markets were the forerunners of the fairs for which the city is well known, notably the book fair. The University of Leipzig (founded 1409) is one of Germany's oldest centres of learning.

1. History and urban development. 2. Art life and organization.

1. HISTORY AND URBAN DEVELOPMENT. The town developed from a Slav settlement, Lipsk, at the crossing of the Via Regis and Via Imperii trade routes. In the 10th century a castle was built on the site of the first market place (now Richard-Wagner-Platz); in 1015 it is documented as 'Libzi'. The town developed to the north and north-east of this, and merchants settled along the Brühl. In the 12th century a second market was laid out to the south of the first, associated with a parish church, the predecessor of the Thomaskirche, and the village of St Petri and its church. The Markt became the centre of the town's grid plan.

About 1165 the city of 'Lipz' received its charter from Margraf Otto the Rich of Meissen (*reg* 1156–90), together with the right to hold markets within its precincts. The Neustadt subsequently developed, together with the Nikolaikirche (founded 1165) and a third market, the Neumarkt. Under Margraf Conrad of Meissen (*reg* 1123–56) the town was partially fortified: three fortresses were built in 1217. When the main castle was razed, the town was protected by Pleissenburg Castle. To the west the Augustinian priory of St Thomas was founded; the Thomaskirche was incorporated in it in 1213 and rebuilt in the 14th and 15th centuries. A Franciscan monastery was established on the site of the first castle, the Matthäikirchhof, and to the east, near the Grimma Gate, was the Dominican monastery of St Paul (occupied by the university from 1547). The Johannisspital was founded in the Grimma suburb in 1278.

From the 15th century Leipzig gained economic importance as a centre of international trade. The town was granted an additional New Year's market in 1453. In 1497 Emperor Maximilian I confirmed the market rights and conferred further rights in 1507. Trade in silver and copper proved highly lucrative. In 1477 the Gewandhaus and the Zeughaus were rebuilt on the Neumarkt. A new Rathaus was erected (*c.* 1480), and rebuilt by the mayor, Hieronymus Lotter (1497–1580), in 1556–7 and is now known as the Altes Rathaus (rest.; see fig. 1), housing the Museum für Geschichte der Stadt Leipzig. The Moritzbastei (1551–3; damaged) and Pleissenburg Castle (rebuilt 1550–67;

destr. 1897–8) were Lotter's contributions to the 15th- and 16th-century restoration of the fortifications; he also built the Alte Waage (1555). Many churches were remodelled into hall churches *c.* 1500: the Thomaskirche by Conrad Pflüger and Claus Röder (*fl* 1471–99); St Pauli (1485 and 1521); and in 1513–26 Benedikt Eisenberg rebuilt the Nikolaikirche.

After *c.* 1500 courtyards-cum-passages developed as trading areas, for example the oriel of the Goldenen Schlange House (1523; now part of Barthels Hof, 1748–50). The Handelshof (1530–38), commissioned by Dr Heinrich Stromer von Auerbach, occupied the site of the present Mädlerpassage (1912–14). After the Thirty Years War (1618–48), east–west trade gave rise to vigorous building activity: Christian Richter and Johann Georg Starcke built the Alte Börse (1678–87; rest.) on the Naschmarkt; Johann Gregor Fuchs (1650–1715) erected the Königshaus (1700) and the Romanushaus (1701–4; rebuilt; now Gal. Kstlergenoss.). In 1732 the Thomasschule was rebuilt, and in 1756 Friedrich Seltendorff (*d* 1778) built the Gohliser Schlösschen (from 1755) for Caspar Richter. In 1763 the fortifications were replaced with public parks. The city's musical heritage was reflected by the construction of a concert hall (1780) by Johann Friedrich Carl Dauthe (1749–1816) in the Zeughaus. The Nikolaikirche was classicized (1784–97) by Dauthe and Adam Friedrich Oeser, and some notable Neo-classical buildings were erected in the early 19th century, for example the theatre (1817) by Friedrich Weinbrenner and

1. Leipzig, Altes Rathaus, 1556–7; west façade

the main building (1831–6) of Leipzig University by Karl Friedrich Schinkel. From the mid-18th century Leipzig was the centre of German book production.

The city grew: in 1830 it had 41,000 inhabitants and by 1871 there were 107,000. Imposing buildings were put up in the centre, including the Bayerischer Bahnhof (1842), the Neues Theater (1867), the Gewandhaus (1882–4) and the former Reichsgericht (1887–95; now Mus. Bild. Kst.) by Ludwig Hoffmann and Peter Dybwad (1859–1921). Monuments to the victims of the Battle of Leipzig, or Battle of the Nations (1813), include that by Bruno Schmitz (1896–1913) and the Russian Gedächtniskirche (1911–13) by Vladimir Pokrovsky. HUGO LICHT was responsible for a large number of public buildings, the most important of which was the Neues Rathaus (1898–1905) on the site of Pleissenburg Castle. The development of the trade fairs after the turn of the century led to the building of such exhibition halls as the Brühlzentrum for fur, and the technical exhibition centre, Specks Hof (1908–9). By the late 20th century a number of publishers were still operating in Leipzig, and the city had the Deutsche Bücherei (1912–16). The main railway station, the Hauptbahnhof (1907–16), was built by William Lossow and Max Hans Kühne (1874–1942). German Bestelmeyer designed the high-rise Bankhaus Kroch (1927). Experimental housing schemes include Marienbrunn garden city (founded 1911), the Rundling development (1928) by Lössnig and the northern district of Gohlis (1929). The Curassi Museum (1925–7; now Mus. Vlkerknd.) by C. W. Zweck and H. Voigt stands on the site of the Johannisspital. The city suffered during World War II. Post-war additions include the 34-storey university building (1967–8), and the Neues Gewandhaus (1971–81) by R. Skoda.

2. ART LIFE AND ORGANIZATION. In the Middle Ages the religious orders provided considerable patronage in Leipzig. The city's prosperity was such that woodcarvers' and painters' workshops had to employ immigrant journeymen after 1470 to meet the demand. One 'Conrad aurifaber' was mentioned as early as 1368, and by 1452 the goldsmiths had their own guild rules. The 375 monstrances, reliquaries, altar crosses and other liturgical implements that were confiscated from local churches following the Reformation demonstrate their output. The goldsmiths' records also mention the presence of the embroiderers Hans Döring (1472); the embroiderer of Elector Frederick II of Brandenburg (*reg* 1440–71), Caspar Bernhardt (1488); and Hans Hegendorf, who obtained citizenship in 1489. A wood-carver, Master Hans, made a *Mount of Olives* and column-statues for Delitzsch in 1410. Heinrich Beyer (*fl* 1476–89) and Master Johannes (1492) are known by name, and the carved altar (*c.* 1500) of the monastery church of Schulpforta was signed by *Hans Topher Maler*. At that time Leipzig workshops were providing altars for places as far away as Mark Brandenburg (e.g. Lehninger Altar, Brandenburg Cathedral). The leading sculptor and wood-carver Stephan Hermsdorf (*fl* 1516–43) was granted citizenship, although he worked elsewhere after 1524.

There are records of 84 painters in the 15th and 16th centuries; in 1458 they combined with harnessmakers and saddlers to form a guild. Nikolaus Eisenberger, a Dominican who aroused the hostility of the guild, enrolled at the university in 1465 for protection, and between 1452 and 1484 he painted panels and decorated bells. Between 1500 and 1541 Heinrich Schmidt (*fl c.* 1470–1541) was named as a painter of altarpieces.

Book printing played an important role: in 1485 Kunz Kachelofen opened his printing press, followed by Martin Landsberg (1487–1523) and Melchior Lotter II (1494–1529). Georg Lemberger acquired citizenship (1523) and worked closely with printers. Between 1501 and 1536 2640 titles were published in Leipzig, and by 1600 the number came to 6400.

The Zeichnungs-Mahlerei und Architectur-Akademie was founded in 1764 to promote arts and crafts. ADAM FRIEDRICH OESER was its first director, and by 1767 it had over 100 pupils. Printing and art came together when the bookseller and publisher Philipp Erasmus Reich (1717–87; see fig. 2) commissioned Anton Graff to paint 31 portraits of eminent citizens of Leipzig.

In the 18th century Gottfried Winkler and Johann Thomas Richter assembled magnificent collections of art. A catalogue (1768) lists 638 oil paintings in the Winkler collection, and in 1783 it included 80,000 copper engravings and 2469 free-hand drawings, according to the auction catalogue of 1815. Works by Titian, Veronese, Reni, Rubens and Rembrandt were among over 400 paintings in the Richter collection, which also contained more than 1000 free-hand drawings and tens of thousands of engravings—Richter bought 14,000 engravings from the town library alone.

Societies flourished in the 19th century. The Leipziger Kunstverein, co-founded in 1837 by MAXIMILIAN SPECK

2. Anton Graff: *Philipp Erasmus Reich*, oil on canvas, 620×510 mm, 1774 (Leipzig, Universitätsbibliothek der Universität Leipzig)

VON STERNBURG, campaigned for a civic museum and held its first exhibition in 1848. Thanks to a donation from Adolf Heinrich Schletter, the museum (destr.) was built on the site now occupied by the Neues Gewandhaus; its collections are now in the Museum der Bildenden Künste. The Verein der Kunstfreunde was formed in 1848, the Leipziger Künstlerverein in 1858, and in 1860 the local branch of the Allgemeine Deutsche Kunstgenossenschaft was established.

In 1858 Ernst Arthur Seemann (1829–1904) founded his publishing firm, which provided commissions for both art historians and artists. The renown of the city's collections encouraged Anton Springer to accept the new chair of art history at Leipzig University in 1873. The Kunstgewerbemuseum opened in 1874, and the Künstlerhaus in 1899–1900. The academy became the Akademie für Graphische Künste und Buchgewerbe.

MAX KLINGER dominated art in the city from 1893; such artistic protest movements as the Leipzig Secession, founded in 1909 by Wilhelm Schulze-Rose (1872–1950), and the Expressionist Vereinigung für Neue Kunst, founded in 1918, failed to be as influential as Klinger. The Internationale Ausstellung für Buchgewerbe und Grafik achieved international significance from 1914, as did the Internationale Buchausstellung from 1927. Artists' associations in Leipzig were disbanded after 1933, while artists' representatives were either dismissed from office, as was Max Schwimmer (1895–1969), or, in the case of Alfred Frank (1884–1945), imprisoned and executed. After 1945 the newly founded Hochschule für Graphik und Buchkunst and the artists' association formed from the cultural alliance for the democratic renewal of Germany shaped artistic development until 1989–90. Max Schwimmer, Elisabeth Voigt (b 1898) and Walter Arnold (b 1909) all taught in Leipzig, training such artists as Bernhard Heisig, Ursula Mattheuer-Neustaedt (b 1926), Wolfgang Mattheuer and Werner Tübke, who, in turn, taught and directed this association. It had its own sales cooperative and regularly organized local art exhibitions and arranged for the participation of artists in exhibitions in Dresden.

After the reunification of Germany in 1990, the city's art life was reorganized. The Neuer Leipziger Kunstverein, which organizes its own exhibitions, was founded to promote art and support the Museum der Bildenden Künste. Besides the Museum der Bildenden Künste, Museum des Kunsthandwerkes and the Deutsches Buch und Schriftmuseum, the university, with its collections and exhibition centre for modern art, and the gallery of the Hochschule für Graphik und Buchkunst are the centres of the city's cultural life. Established commercial galleries include the Galerie am Sachsenplatz, Eigen+Art, Wort und Werk, Augen-Blick and the Galerie der Künstlergenossenschaft. Alternative art is found at such galleries as Stöck-Art, Am Kraftwerk, Zone and Pikanta e.V.

BIBLIOGRAPHY
C. Gurlitt: *Beschreibende Darstellung der älteren Bau- und Kunstdenkmäler des Königreichs Sachsen* (Dresden, 1896)
N. Pevsner: *Leipziger Barock: Die Baukunst der Barockzeit in Leipzig* (Dresden, 1928)
G. Dehio: *Handbuch der deutschen Kunstdenkmäler: Die Bezirke Dresden, Karl-Marx-Stadt, Leipzig*, ed. E. Lehmann (Berlin, 1965)
*Bibliographie zur Geschichte der Stadt Leipzig*, Historische Kommission der Sächsischen Akademie der Wissenschaften (Weimar, 1971–7)
G. Meissner: *Leipziger Künstler der Gegenwart* (Leipzig, 1977)
K. Czok: *Das alte Leipzig* (Leipzig, 1978)
W. Hocquel, ed.: *Leipzig* (Leipzig, 1983)
E. Ullman, ed.: *Kunst und Kunstgeschichte in Leipzig* (Leipzig, 1989)
ERNST ULLMANN

**Leistikow, Walter** (*b* Bromberg, 25 Oct 1865; *d* Schlachtensee, Berlin, 24 July 1908). German painter, decorative artist, etcher, exhibition organizer and writer. He studied painting briefly in 1883, at the Akademie in Berlin, but he was dismissed after six months as 'untalented'. From 1883 to 1885 he trained with the painter Hermann Eschke (1823–1900) and from 1885 to 1887 with the Norwegian painter Hans Fredrik Gude. Gude had a decisive influence on the style of Leistikow's early works, as is especially clear in Leistikow's light coastal landscapes with figures. His most significant work from this period, however, is *Brickworks near Eckernförde* (1887; ex-Gemäldegal. Neue Meister, Dresden). Leistikow's dismissal from the Akademie concentrated his attention on issues of artistic policy. When the German government decided not to send works for exhibition in the Exposition Universelle in Paris in 1889, Leistikow himself organized the dispatch of works to Paris. In 1892, under a pseudonym, he wrote articles on the outraged German reaction to the work of Edvard Munch, sharply attacking the Akademie and its director, Anton von Werner. In the same year, he was one of the founders of the Gruppe der Elf, out of which the Berlin Secession (*see* SECESSION, §2) developed in 1898. Leistikow also published a novel, *Auf der Schwelle* (1896), and remained in close contact with the Berlin literary world.

In the 1890s Leistikow's painting style moved away from realism towards greater stylization, and he concentrated on landscape painting (e.g. *Evening at Schlachtensee*, 1895; Berlin, Berlin Mus.; for illustration *see* SECESSION). He worked on a smaller scale and omitted figures altogether. Leistikow's pictures reflect the linear trend of *Jugendstil*, in particular as seen in the paintings of Ludwig von Hofmann (1861–after 1916). He favoured dark tones surrounded with fine outlines, and his works often convey a melancholy atmosphere, comparable to that invoked by the plays of Maurice Maeterlinck, which he greatly admired. Leistikow continued, however, to work from specific motifs, finding his subject-matter in the north German landscape and by lakes in the outskirts of Berlin (e.g. *Lake in Grunewald*, 1898; Berlin, Neue N.G.). Leistikow also made designs for carpets and wallpaper, and from 1896 he produced etchings. With the founding of the Berlin Secession in 1898, Leistikow worked wholeheartedly for the new association. Despite Leistikow's popularity in Germany, especially in Berlin, interest in his paintings waned after his death and he was much more widely remembered as an organizer of exhibitions than as an artist in his own right, even though the *Lake in Grunewald* went to the Nationalgalerie as a gift and was used by the director, Hugo von Tschudi, in a vain attempt to convince Emperor William II of the independent quality of modern German landscape painting.

BIBLIOGRAPHY
Thieme–Becker
L. Corinth: *Das Leben Walter Leistikows: Ein Stück Berliner Kulturgeschichte* (Berlin, 1910)

M. Bröhan: *Walter Leistikow (1865–1908): Maler der Berliner Landschaft* (Berlin, 1988)

ANDREAS BLÜHM

**Leistler, Carl** (*b* Vienna, 19 June 1805; *d* Kalksburg, nr Vienna, 25 Sept 1857). Austrian furniture-maker. In 1828 he took over the family furniture-making business, which had been established by his father, Matthias Leistler (1769–1836), in 1795, and in 1842 founded a parquet and furniture factory in Gumpendorf, Vienna. From 1843 until 1846 Leistler worked with Michael Thonet, under the direction of the English architect Peter Hubert Desvignes (1804–83), on the decoration of the 18th-century state rooms of the Palais Liechtenstein in Vienna (*see* AUSTRIA, fig. 27). The elaborate wall-decorations, parquet floors and furniture (*in situ*) were designed in the fashionable Rococo Revival style. In the 1850s Leistler continued to work in the service of John II, Prince of Liechtenstein, on the Gothic Revival furnishings (*in situ*) of the Bohemian castle of Lednice (Ger. Eisgrub), Czech Republic.

At the Great Exhibition of 1851 in London, Leistler, Thonet and August Kitschelt represented the Vienna furniture industry. Leistler showed several rooms designed by the architect Bernardo di Bernardis (1807–68), which used stylistic forms of the 16th and 17th centuries or naturalistic decoration. However, it was a monumental, Gothic Revival bookcase (London, V&A), with carvings by the Vienna sculptor Anton Dominik Fernkorn, that attracted particular attention; it was given by Francis Joseph I to Queen Victoria. After Leistler's death, the business continued under the name Gebrüder Leistler. At the International Exhibition of 1862 in London they displayed a prayer stool designed by the Vienna architect Carl Lösner (1804–69). The firm subsequently concentrated exclusively on the production of parquet and remained active until *c.* 1910.

BIBLIOGRAPHY
M. Zweig: *Das zweite Rokoko* (Vienna, 1924)
G. Himmelheber: *Die Kunst des deutschen Möbels: Klassizismus, Historismus, Jugendstil* (Munich, 1973), pp. 160–68
E. Aslin: 'A Victorian Gothic Bookcase', *V&A Mus. Yb.*, iv (1974), pp. 117–24

EVA B. OTTILLINGER

**Leitersdorfer, Béla.** *See* LAJTA, BÉLA.

**Leith, (George Esselmont) Gordon** (*b* Old Place, Knysna, Cape Province, 23 May 1886; *d* Johannesburg, 15 April 1965). South African architect. He studied art and music privately (1899–1902) and worked on the architectural staff of the South African Public Works Department (1903–5); he then enrolled at the Architectural Association School, London, qualified with distinction (1908) and rejoined the Public Works Department in South Africa, where he worked on a project (unexecuted) for a new parliament building in Pretoria. In 1910 he joined the office of Herbert Baker to work on the Union Buildings, Pretoria, and then became the first Herbert Baker Scholar at the British School in Rome (1911–13). Following active service in World War I, Leith worked under Baker and Edwin Lutyens for the Imperial War Graves Commission in France (1918–20).

In 1920 Leith returned to South Africa, establishing a private practice in Pretoria and later in Johannesburg, where he also became a teacher (1921) at the newly established School of Architecture, University of the Witwatersrand. In his early career he built mainly houses, tapping the same architectural sources as Herbert Baker before him: the classical architecture of Italy (columns, colonnades and the classical handling of form); the vernacular cottage architecture of England (stone rubble walls, broad shingled or slate roofs and prominent chimneys); and the 18th-century architecture of the Cape (white plastered walls, gables and timber sash windows with louvred shutters). He showed a consummate handling of materials and mastery of detail and design in all stylistic variations. Notable examples of his houses are those he built for Manley Anstey (destr.), Johannesburg, and Judge Curlewis, Pretoria, and Leith's own house, 'Harthill' in Johannesburg.

Leith also produced a large number of public and institutional buildings, particularly in Pretoria and Johannesburg, many of which were markedly influenced by Baker's work, particularly in the use of symmetrical ashlar-faced façades, Classical orders, pilasters and arched openings. Notable examples include the first Rand Water Board Building (1927; destr.), Johannesburg, the Technical College (1928; now Technikon), Pretoria, the Central Railway Station (1928; with Gerard Moerdijk), Johannesburg, the South African Reserve Bank (1933), Johannesburg, and town halls in Germiston (1935) and Bloemfontein (1936). The combination of ashlar with fair-faced brickwork, used in the Pretoria Technical College and Johannesburg Railway Station, is reminiscent of the contemporary architecture of the Public Works Department. The use of local stone, wood and clay products also gave an indigenous character to his buildings.

Although Leith was never part of the Modern Movement, for hospitals and offices he adopted a more functional approach reminiscent of early 20th-century Scandinavian architecture, as in the General Hospital (1935), Johannesburg, and Coronation Hospital (1942), Johannesburg. Occasionally vestiges of classical elements reappear in these works, such as the columns in the Union Corporation Building (1936), Johannesburg, and the Venetian palazzo form of the second Rand Water Board Building (1939), Johannesburg. Leith was a prolific architect and completed *c.* 500 buildings, including bank buildings throughout South Africa. He also worked in Northern Rhodesia (now Zambia), Portuguese East Africa (now Mozambique) and Nyasaland (now Malawi). In 1946 the University of the Witwatersrand, Johannesburg, conferred on him its first honorary Doctorate of Architecture in recognition of his reputation as one of the most distinguished South African architects of the day.

UNPUBLISHED SOURCES
Johannesburg, U. Witwatersrand [Leith papers]

BIBLIOGRAPHY
*DSAB*
'Dr. G. E. Gordon Leith, MC, RIBA, MIA', *S. Afr. Archit. Rec.*, xxxi/12 (1946), pp. 279–86
N. Eaton and K.F.E.G.: 'Gordon Leith: Tributes by Two Colleagues', *S. Afr. Archit. Rec.*, 1/5 (1965), pp. 12, 47

HERBERT PRINS

**Leiviskä, Juha** (*b* Helsinki, 1936). Finnish architect. He graduated from the Technical University in Helsinki in

1963 and thereafter practised independently as an architect in Helsinki. The original forms of Leiviskä's buildings are easily recognizable, not least because their basic shapes have stayed much the same over the years: with as few formal elements as possible he attempts to achieve great functional flexibility and lively massing. The effect of the buildings on their surroundings is derived from the juxtaposition of opposite motifs: while the public façade may be uncluttered and monumental, the more private parts of the building may be open and small-scale. Variation between high and low, light and dark is achieved by a rhythmical changing of the height and depth of the building mass and an exploitation of natural light. Leiviskä's architecture makes references to historical architecture and music, as well as De Stijl, whose influence reached Finland through the Modern Movement and, in particular, the teaching of Aulis Blomstedt. The town hall at Kouvola (1968; with Bertel Saarnio) has a square plan: the building is gathered around a central courtyard linked to a large marketplace laid out on coordinate systems based on different axes. Religious architecture, which dominates Leiviskä's work, began with the restoration of the 18th-century church at Lemi (1968). The light-filled atmosphere of its interior is echoed in his later commissions. The Old Student Union (1979; with Vilhelm Helander), Helsinki, is notable among his restoration projects. The small parish hall at Nakkila (1970), with its pale tile cladding, is a functionalist work, a low building designed to contrast with the massive church that dominates the flat surrounding landscape. St Thomas's Church (1975) in Oulu is conceived as part of the plan Leiviksä drew up for the Puolivälinkangas suburb (1971), a dense urban centre in which the scattered habitation was to be dominated by the church because of its siting. Here, as in many of his other designs, Leiviskä united two different systems, both originating in the site. The spatial variation in the church itself is achieved with different room heights, depending on function, and variations in lighting: there is a progression from low, shadowy rooms to higher, lighter ones. The interior spaces are white, with stucco or wood surfaces, while the outside walls have cladding of red brick, which dominates the entire centre. The façade of Kirkkonummi parish hall (1984) is white-painted clapboard; the interior, too, is white. The crafts and workshop building (1986) at the Niuvanniemi sanatorium in Kuopio is linked with its late 19th-century institutional neighbours. The stucco and brick surfaces of the new buildings are white and their sloping roofs are tin. In early 1987 Leiviskä won a restricted competition for the new West German Embassy in Helsinki. Leiviskä regularly designed lighting for his buildings, and many of his fittings went into commercial production.

BIBLIOGRAPHY
'Juha Leiviskä', *Process: Archit.*, 1 (1977), pp. 178–86, 256
'The Church of St Thomas, Oulu', *Architects' J.*, clxix/18 (1979), pp. 905–7
'Valon instrumentit' [Instruments of light], *Arkkitehti/Arkitekten*, lxxviii/2 (1981), pp. 26–33 [discussion with Leiviskä]
MARJA-RIITTA NORRI

**Lekanis** [lekane]. Ancient form of vessel, used to contain cosmetics, oils and perfumes (*see* GREECE, ANCIENT, fig. 71(v)h). ☐

**Lekuona, Nicolás de** (*b* Villafranca de Oricia, nr Guipúzcoa, 19 Dec 1913; *d* Fruniz, Viscaya, 11 June 1937). Spanish photographer and painter. A self-taught photographer, he first studied painting at the Escuela de Artes y Oficios in San Sebastian (1929–31) and at the Escuela de Aparejadores in Madrid (1932–5). He used photographic techniques, including photomontage, photocollage, *cliché-verre* and drawings on photographic paper. After his apprenticeship in his native town, he travelled to Madrid, where he came into contact with the artistic and literary world. His dynamic compositions and ability to organize apparent chaos into a harmonious and coherent space connect Lekuona's work with Futurism. In *Untitled* (photocollage, 1934) a runner advancing towards the picture plane, with a dancing woman at his shoulder, is enmeshed in a thread connected to a skull, with a suggestion of a 'dance of death'. Lekuona died on the Basque Front during the Spanish Civil War.

BIBLIOGRAPHY
*Nicolás de Lekuona: Obra fotográfica* (exh. cat. by A. Mayo, Bilbao, Mus. B.A., 1982)
*Nicolás de Lekuona: Pintura y dibujos* (exh. cat. by A. Mayo, Bilbao, Mus. B.A., 1982)
JOAN FONTCUBERTA

**Lekythos.** Ancient form of vessel, used to contain oil (*see* GREECE, ANCIENT, fig. 71(v)l,m). ☐

**Leland, John** (*b* London, *c.* 1503; *d* 1552). English topographer, antiquary and poet. He was educated at St Paul's School, London, Christ's College, Cambridge, and All Souls College, Oxford, completing his studies in Paris. A Classics scholar with some knowledge of French, Italian and Spanish, he became Library Keeper to Henry VIII and was appointed King's Antiquary. He was commissioned in 1533 to search monastic and college libraries for lost and forgotten records and English antiquities; his commission was extended to obtaining for the King's Library books and manuscripts from libraries despoiled at the Dissolution of the monasteries. Leland's itineraries, undertaken from 1534 to 1543, covered England and Wales from Carlisle and Berwick in the north to Caernarfon, St David's and Land's End in the south. Leland intended his notes to form the basis of a great work on the topography and antiquities of the nation. He had some talent as a Latin poet and his *Cygnae Canto* (1545) gives in 699 lines a swan's-eye view of the palaces on the River Thames between Oxford and Greenwich, with lengthy descriptions of those at Windsor and Greenwich. Although few of his works were published in his lifetime, William Camden, John Stow (?1525–1605), William Dugdale and others made use of his manuscripts.

UNPUBLISHED SOURCES
Oxford, Bodleian Lib., MSS Bodl. 3117–33

WRITINGS
*Cygnae Canto* (London, 1545)
T. Hearne, ed.: *Itinerary*, 9 vols (Oxford, 1710–12, 2/1745, rev. 3/1770)
——: *Collectanea*, 6 vols (Oxford, 1715, rev. as 5 vols, 1770, 3/1774)
L. Toulmin Smith, ed.: *The Itinerary of John Leland in or about the Years 1535–1543*, 5 vols (London, 1907–10)

*DNB*
BIBLIOGRAPHY
T. Kendrick: *British Antiquity* (London, 1959), pp. 45–64
JOHN HOPKINS

**Leleu, Jean-François** (*b* 1729; *d* Paris, 3 Sept 1807). French cabinetmaker. He trained in the workshop of Jean-François Oeben and on 19 September 1764 became a *maître-ébéniste*. He was one of the leading Parisian cabinet-makers during the last years of Louis XV and during the reign of Louis XVI. He was one of the most innovative craftsmen of his period, in the boldness of his constructions as well as in his concern for perfection. His highly architectural creations combined strength, restraint and vitality of line. Using few bronze mounts, he gave his furniture its form through mouldings, the arrangement of veneers and bold marquetry. He worked for such notable patrons as the Comtesse Du Barry, the Duc de Noailles, the Duc de Chaulnes and the Duc d'Uzès, the Comte d'Orsay, Baron d'Ivry, Mademoiselle Guimard and the financiers Randon de Boisset and François de Laborde de Méréville. He refurnished the Palais-Bourbon in Paris for Louis-François de Bourbon, Prince de Conti, even creating an astonishing new floor. Several of his creations for the Palais-Bourbon are extant, including a pair of small commodes (*c.* 1773; Versailles, Grand Trianon). His most notable extant works include roll-top desks (e.g. of 1767; San Marino, CA, Huntington A.G.) decorated with porcelain plaques from Sèvres and the desk (London, Wallace) and cartonnier (New York, Met.) decorated with porcelain plaques produced for J. B. Vandenyver. The most important illustration of Leleu's talent, however, is the trapezoid commode (ex-Wildenstein's, New York), decorated with a bronze mask and lyre of Apollo, which George Watson Taylor acquired at the beginning of the 19th century.

BIBLIOGRAPHY
F. de Salverte: *Les Ebénistes du XVIIIème siècle, leurs oeuvres et leurs marques* (Paris, 1923, rev. 5/1962)
J. Viaux: *Bibliographie du meuble (Mobilier civil français)*, 2 vols (Paris, 1966–88)
'Jean François Leleu', *L'Estampille*, ccxxviii (1989), pp. 66–75
JEAN-DOMINIQUE AUGARDE, JEAN NÉRÉE RONFORT

**Leleux.** French family of painters and printmakers. (1) Adolphe Leleux and his brother (2) Armand Leleux were both known mainly as painters of provincial rural life.

**(1) Adolphe Leleux** (*b* Paris, 15 Nov 1812; *d* Paris, 27 July 1891). Adolphe was 25 before he decided to become a painter. He received no formal schooling in art apart from an apprenticeship in engraving with the printer Alexandre Vincent Sixdeniers (1795–1846). Though brought up in Paris, he often painted rural scenes. In 1835 he exhibited scenes from Picardy at the Salon and in 1838 followed with genre scenes of the rural poor. Beginning in 1838 he turned to Brittany for inspiration. Salon critics such as Théophile Gautier found a sincerity in his work that made his scenes 'almost real'. Gautier praised *The Roadmenders* (exh. Salon 1844; untraced) as 'one of the major works of the realist school'.

Adolphe exhibited his Breton scenes, and occasionally a Spanish theme (after a trip to Spain in 1843), at the Salons from 1835 until 1881. He received third-class medals in 1842 and 1843, a second-class medal in 1848

and the Légion d'honneur in 1855. Adolphe fought in the revolution of 1848 and later painted pictures such as *The Password* (1848; Versailles, Château), inspired by his experience on the barricades. Many of these paintings were engraved, the products of which were widely distributed, gaining Leleux a broad following; his images of the 1848 revolution became icons that entered the national consciousness. Adolphe quickly became a favourite of Napoleon III and his canvas of the *Fairground of St Fargeau* (1855; untraced) was purchased by the state for 3000 francs. He received commissions for a number of works, was invited to official gatherings and enjoyed a profitable career. In later years his style softened, and it was criticized for its lack of definition and focus. Gautier unsuccessfully urged Adolphe to return to scenes in the realist tradition. By the time he died he had fallen into obscurity.

**(2) Armand Leleux** (*b* Paris, 1818 or 1820; *d* Paris, 1 June 1885). Brother of (1) Adolphe Leleux. He was trained by his brother. His early canvases also had Breton themes, although in his case the inspiration must have come from his brother, for he had never been to Brittany. Adolphe's official ties at court must have greatly assisted the development of Armand's career. In 1846 he was sent to Spain by the French government, probably in order to assess the state of the the arts there, to examine the collections and to study the people and customs of the country. In the same year he visited Switzerland; he returned there many times after his marriage to the Swiss painter Louise Emilie Giraud (1824–1885), who had studied in Paris at the atelier of Léon Cogniet, and he found many patrons and supporters of his work among her compatriots. In 1863 he also went to Italy. Like his brother, he became a favourite artist of Napoleon III and the court. His composition of *The Knitter* (1854; untraced) was purchased by Napoleon's wife, Empress Eugénie.

The locations of Armand's best-known canvases *The Clogmaker*, *Woman with a Lamp* and *The Forge* (all mid-1850s) were unknown by the 1990s, but they were frequently reproduced as engravings in periodicals of the time. These reproductions make clear that he was influenced by the realist painter François Bonvin and was capable of creating a direct, simple style that was easily understandable. This style, when it was used in the service of common work themes, led critics to regard him as an important contemporary realist. His scenes of rural Spain show a sensitivity to light and an exactitude very different from the frequently dour and dark tonality of his brother Adolphe's painting. Critics encouraged Armand to continue to paint in this mode, recognizing that he had a talent for depicting nature and the effects of sunlight in rich colours; but Armand preferred intimate scenes of family life, perhaps because they appealed to an upper middle-class market and afforded him a degree of financial security.

Armand first exhibited at the Salon in 1839, and his folklore scenes proved popular with the Salon jury. He was awarded a third-class medal in 1844, second-class medals in 1847 and 1848, a first-class medal in 1859 and the Légion d'honneur in 1850. This success generated numerous commissions for genre scenes both from patrons and from the French government. In 1867 Armand was selected for a committee studying popular costume for the Paris Exposition Universelle.

BIBLIOGRAPHY

L. Nochlin: *Gustave Courbet: A Study of Style and Society* (New York, 1976), pp. 115–17

*The Realist Tradition* (exh. cat., ed. G. P. Weisberg; Cleveland, OH, Mus. A., 1980)

G. P. Weisberg: 'The Leleux: Apostles of Proto-realism', *A. Mag.*, lvi (Sept 1981), pp. 128–30

GABRIEL P. WEISBERG

**Lelie, Adriaan de** (*b* Tilburg, 19 May 1755; *d* Amsterdam, 30 Nov 1820). Dutch painter. He was largely self-taught, although initially he received some training from his fellow townsman Cornelis van Spaendonck, whom he followed to Antwerp in 1773. There he worked with the wallpaper painter Peeters and later with Andreas Bernardus de Quertenmont (1750–1835), painting historical scenes and portraits. In Düsseldorf, de Lelie copied the work of Rubens and van Dyck. In 1784 he moved to Amsterdam having been urged to do so by the scholar Petrus Camper, whom he had met in Düsseldorf in 1782. In Amsterdam he became a portrait painter of enlightened and progressive citizens, in contrast to his close rival Charles Howard Hodges, who found his clients mostly among the aristocracy. De Lelie produced a remarkable set of four group portraits depicting the meetings of the Felix Meritis Society, of which he was himself a member (1792–1809; Amsterdam, Rijksmus. and Hist. Mus.). In addition he portrayed numerous figures from contemporary Dutch cultural life. With such outstanding paintings as the *Art Gallery of Jan Gildemeester* and the *Art Gallery of Josephus Brentano* (both Amsterdam, Rijksmus.), de Lelie set the tone for the early 19th-century Dutch conversation piece. He also painted genre scenes, which were mostly based on Dutch 17th-century examples (e.g. *Old Woman Making Pancakes*; Amsterdam, Rijksmus.). None of his documented allegorical works has yet been traced. Occasionally de Lelie worked in partnership with Egbert van Drielst who painted the scenery: for example *General W. H. Daendels Taking Leave of Lt-Col. C. R. T. Krayenhoff* (1795; Amsterdam, Rijksmus.).

BIBLIOGRAPHY

J. Knoef: *Tussen rococo en romantiek* [Between Rococo and Romanticism] (The Hague, 1943), pp. 38–62

A. Staring: *De Hollanders thuis* [The Dutch at home] (The Hague, 1956)

FRANS GRIJZENHOUT

**Leliman.** Dutch family of architects and writers. (1) Jan Leliman and his son (2) Willem Leliman worked separately but shared concerns in working-class housing, in functionally orientated rather than historicist design and in the organization of their profession. Jan Leliman was a pioneer in these fields and also a founder of Dutch basic technical schooling.

**(1) Jan** [Johannes] **(Hermanus) Leliman** (*b* Amsterdam, 26 June 1828; *d* Amsterdam, 1 Dec 1910). He trained (1843–7) in the carpenter's shop of Johan Frederik Metzelaar (1819–97), in Rotterdam, then studied between 1847 and 1850 with Martinus Gerardus Tetar van Elven (1803–83) at the Koninklijke Academie van Beeldende Kunsten, Amsterdam. After a period in Amsterdam as an apprentice in the offices of Izaäk Warnsinck (1811–57), he worked for various architects in Belgium, Germany and northern France, and then in the studio of Henri Labrouste in Paris. In addition to encountering Labrouste's highly unacademic and functionalist style of design, Jan also became acquainted with the possibilities of the comparatively new construction material, cast iron. While based in Paris he participated in three Dutch competitions: for a post office, a residential school for 200 children and a block of 60 workers' houses, winning prizes for all three entries. On his return to Amsterdam in 1853 he set up as an independent architect and designed several pioneering projects with a socially orientated character, such as the first bread factory in the Netherlands (1854–5; destr.), Vijzelgracht, Amsterdam, and the first 'modern' hospital in the Netherlands (1856; altered 1902), Prinsengracht, Amsterdam. From 1853 to 1873 he was employed as a permanent architect by the Salerno housing society. His housing block (1854) at Valckenierstraat 23–33, Amsterdam, for the latter, was the first such development in the Netherlands. He had a similar association with the Evangelical–Lutheran Congregation of Amsterdam. He was an eclectic architect with a clear preference for simple structure and good proportions and a formal language derived from the function of the building in question. His efforts to establish a sound and practical training for workers included founding the first Dutch technical school in Amsterdam in 1861, followed a few years later by a night drawing school for carpenters and a day drawing school for girls, both in Amsterdam. In addition he held several positions on the board of governors of the Maatschappij tot Bevordering der Bouwkunst (Society for the promotion of architecture) and was a founder member (1855) of the architects' society Architectura et Amicitia.

Leliman sought no commissions in later life and spent the years from 1877 writing articles, giving lectures, participating on governing bodies and designing houses, villas and country estates as a hobby.

UNPUBLISHED SOURCES

Delft, Tech. U., Fac. Archit. [plans, drawings]

WRITINGS

ed.: *Album: Verzameling van bouwkundige schetsen en ontwerpen*, 3 vols (Amsterdam, 1862–6)

*Nationaal monument, 1813–1863* (Amsterdam, 1863–5)

Regular contributions to *Architectura* [Amsterdam], *Bouwknd. Bijdr.*, *Bouwknd. Wkbld*, *De Opmerker*

BIBLIOGRAPHY

C. Schade: *Woningbouw voor arbeiders in het 19de-eeuwse Amsterdam* (Amsterdam, 1981), p. 78

M. Estourgie-Beyer: *J. H. Leliman, 1828–1910* (diss., Amsterdam, Vrije U., 1987)

**(2) (Johannes Hendrik) Willem Leliman** (*b* Amsterdam, 26 Aug 1878; *d* Baarn, 7 April 1921). Son of (1) Jan Leliman. He was spared the long and arduous training that his father underwent, enrolling in 1895 at the Polytechnische School (after 1905 called Technische Hogeschool), Delft. There he came under the influence of Eugen Gugel. Willem showed particular promise in architectural history and design and in the courses in free drawing from nature, but, like his fellow students, he had considerable trouble with the large quantities of mathematics included in the examination requirements: partly through his efforts this section of the examination was changed after 1901. He received his diploma in architectural engineering and architecture in 1899, and at the end of 1900 he participated in the first Dutch competition for the Prix de Rome in architecture. His design for a Palace of Justice was awarded the second prize. In 1901 he set up as an independent architect in Amsterdam, where his first major commission was the church of the Remonstrant Congregation (1903; destr. *c.* 1982) in Arnhem, the result of a competition. Shortly afterwards came a commission for a large villa (1904) in Aerdenhout, near Haarlem, the first of a long series of villas that formed the basis of his career. In his earlier years Willem was particularly influenced by English prototypes. Other important works included subsidized housing projects in Amsterdam and other parts of the Netherlands, in which he showed that it was possible to make intelligent use of requirements, such as the Woningwet (housing ordinance) of 1902, to produce workers' housing blocks with no more than two storeys under the roof; this example was emulated by other architects in later years. He also contributed a large number of utilitarian buildings, such as schools for higher and professional education, office blocks, hotels, a children's sanatorium, a garage and urban plans (1907–8) for Aalsmeer, Haarlemmermeer and Zandvoort. His efforts on behalf of the architectural profession include the founding of the periodical *De bouwwereld*, a 'weekly magazine for theory and practice', which he filled with his own writings, including a plea for a Netherlands Museum of Architecture. He was also an active participant in the Bond Heemschut, a society devoted to the 'protection of the beauty of the Netherlands', which he helped to found in 1911, and an important advocate for the development of garden suburbs in the Netherlands.

UNPUBLISHED SOURCES
Delft, Tech. U., Fac. Archit. [plans, drawings]
Rotterdam, Ned. Architectuurinst. [plans, drawings]

WRITINGS
*Graven en grafmonumenten* (Delft, 1900)
'De bouwkunst der laatste twintig jaren, 1880–1900', *Geschiedenis van de bouwstijlen in de hoofdtijdperken der architektuur* (Rotterdam, 3/1903)
'Een architectuurmuseum', *De Bouwwereld*, xi/44 (1912), pp. 345–7
*De ontsiering van stad en land en hare bestrijding* (Amsterdam, 1915)
with K. Sluyterman: *Het moderne landhuis in Nederland* (The Hague, 1916, rev. 1922)
*Het stadswoonhuis in Nederland gedurende de laatste 25 jaren* (The Hague, 1920)
Regular contributions to *Architectura* [Amsterdam], *Bouwknd. Wkbld*, *De Bouwwereld*, *Elsevier's Geïllus. Mdschr.*

BIBLIOGRAPHY
'Neue holländische Architektur: Bauten von J. H. W. Leliman, Dipl. Architekt in Amsterdam', *Arch. Rundschau*, 1 (1909), pp. 5–8
W. A. E. van Geuns: Obituary, *De Ingenieur*, xxxvi/30 (1921), pp. 567–9
A. Keppler: Obituary, *Tijdschr. Vlkshuisvest.*, ii/5 (1921), pp. 123–4
A. W. Weissman: Obituary, *De Bouwwereld*, xx/15 (1921), pp. 113–16
CHRIS SMEENK

**Lelli, Ercole** (*b* Bologna, 14 Sept 1702; *d* Bologna, 7 March 1766). Italian painter, draughtsman, sculptor, architect and coin-maker. His reputation is shadowed by the doubts that his contemporaries Luigi Crespi (ii) and Marcello Oretti cast on the authorship of many works to which he laid claim, and his many-sided career is difficult to reconstruct. He studied engraving with Giovanni Gioseffo dal Sole and then architecture with Ferdinando Galli-Bibiena. In 1727, favoured by his friend Giovan Pietro Zanotti, who was one of the judges, he won the Marsili prize offered by the Accademia Clementina of Bologna with his modest drawing of *Judith and Holofernes* (Bologna, Liceo A. & Accad. Clementina). This success enabled him to begin a career as a painter and sculptor. His paintings, few of which can be traced, include a *Self-portrait* (U. Bologna); a portrait of *Eustachio Manfredi* (U. Bologna, Ist. Scienze) is an example of his work as a sculptor.

In 1732 Lelli began to study anatomy, and in 1734 he signed and dated the two wooden statues that support the cathedra in the anatomical theatre of the Archiginnasio, Bologna. These *écorché* figures, called 'gli scuoiati' (flayed ones), however, were said by contemporaries to have been carved by Silvestro Giannotti (1680–1750). In the same year Lelli was appointed coin maker, although he delegated the work to Luigi Balugani. In 1742 he joined the Accademia Clementina, where he obtained important posts, including that of Principe (1746–7 and 1753–4). During these years he was commissioned to produce wax models for the Institute of Sciences (U. Bologna, Mus. Ist. Anatomia Umana Norm.). According to contemporary sources this work was also delegated to other artists, including Giovanni Manzolini (1700–55). Lelli was also active as a restorer, and was involved, for example, in the restoration of Giambologna's Neptune Fountain in Bologna.

BIBLIOGRAPHY
L. Crespi: *Vite de' pittori bolognese non descritte nella Felsina pittrice [di Malvasia]* (Bologna, 1769)
E. Riccomini: 'Scultura del settecento bolognese: Angelo Piò e altri problemi', *A. Ant. & Mod.*, xxi (1963), pp. 100–115
*Mostra della scultura bolognese del settecento* (exh. cat., ed. E. Riccomini; Bologna, Mus. Civ., 1966), pp. 104–9
*L'arte del settecento emiliano: La pittura* (exh. cat., ed. E. Emiliani and others; Bologna, Pal. Re Enzo, 1979), p. 236
FILIPPO PEDROCCO

**Le Lorrain, Charles.** *See* MELLIN, CHARLES.

**Le Lorrain, Louis-Joseph** (*b* Paris, 19 March 1715; *d* St Petersburg, 24 March 1759). French painter, furniture designer, architect and engraver. He studied with Jacques Dumont and won the Grand Prix de Peinture in 1739. He remained for eight years in Rome, where his architectural designs for the temporary centrepiece of the annual Chinea festival (1745, 1746 and 1747) are early examples of Neo-classicism, displaying a simple architectonic use of the orders that indicates his association with Giovanni Battista Piranesi in the circle of students of the Académie de France in Rome, who were highly influential in French architecture from the 1760s onwards. On his return to Paris in 1747, Le Lorrain enjoyed the patronage of the Comte de Caylus, for whom he executed engravings of ancient paintings and revived the technique of encaustic. Through de Caylus he obtained a commission from Count Carl Gustav Tessin to design *quadratura* representations of columns and niches for the dining-room walls of his country house at Åkerö, Sweden, in 1754. Le Lorrain also helped Julien-David Le Roy to prepare his drawings of ancient Greek monuments for engraving, published in *Les Ruines des plus beaux monuments de la Grèce* (1758).

Le Lorrain's most influential, if small-scale, achievement was the suite of ebony furniture (1756–8) designed for the collector and courtier Ange-Laurent de La Live de Jully, which marked the introduction of the Neo-classical style of ornament 'à la grecque' on items of furniture that are strongly architectural in form. The principal piece, a combined writing-table and cabinet, is in the Musée Condé, Chantilly, while the suite is depicted in a portrait of *La Live* by Jean-Baptiste Greuze (1759; Washington, DC, N.G.A.).

Early in 1758 Le Lorrain moved to Russia to become the first director of the new Academy of Arts at St Petersburg. His furniture, which was made to his own designs and intended to launch his career as a furniture designer in Russia, was seized by English pirates while in transit. Le Lorrain died in St Petersburg soon after his arrival.

Mariette

### BIBLIOGRAPHY

C.-N. Cochin: *Mémoirs inédits*, ed. C. Henry (Paris, 1880), pp. 142–3

S. Eriksen: 'Lalive de Jully's Furniture "à la grecque"', *Burl. Mag.*, ciii (1961), pp. 340–47

——: 'Om salen paa Åkerö og dens kunstner Louis-Joseph Le Lorrain' [On the hall at Åkerö and its artist Louis-Joseph Le Lorrain], *Ksthist. Tidskr.*, xxxii/3–4 (1963), pp. 94–120

J. Harris: 'Early Neo-classical Furniture', *J. Furn. Hist. Soc.*, ii (1966), pp. 1–6

S. Eriksen: *Early Neo-classicism in France* (London, 1974)

*Piranèse et les Français, 1740–1790* (exh. cat., ed. A. Chastel and G. Brunel; Rome, Acad. France; Paris, Caisse N. Mnmts Hist. & Sites; 1976)

ALAN POWERS

**Le Lorrain, Robert** (*b* Paris, 15 Nov 1666; *d* 1 June 1743). French sculptor. His family were functionaries associated with Nicolas Fouquet, Louis XIV's Minister of Finance, and were ruined by his disgrace. He trained first with the painter Pierre Mosnier, and in 1684 he entered the studio of François Girardon, where he worked under his orders on the execution of the tomb of *Cardinal Richelieu* (marble, *c.* 1683–9; Paris, Church of the Sorbonne). He later returned to help Girardon as the principal executant of Girardon's memorial to his wife, the flower painter *Catherine Duchemin* (marble, *c.* 1703–7; Paris, Ste Marguerite). In 1689 Le Lorrain was awarded the Prix de Rome for his relief of the *Drunkenness of Noah* (untraced) and arrived at the Académie de France in Rome in 1692. Financial constraints and Le Lorrain's difficult character led to the withdrawal of his grant two years later. He worked briefly as an assistant to the French sculptor Jean-Baptiste Théodon before returning to Paris. He left behind in Rome an unfinished marble medallion of *Christ in Benediction* (Rome, Pal. Montecitorio).

In Paris Le Lorrain executed a few copies after antique sculpture (e.g. marble statues of *Ceres* and *Pluto*, before 1697; untraced) and also collaborated with a marble mason specializing in carved chimney-pieces. Influential friends furnished him with several commissions, including the bronze *Andromeda* (before 1701; Paris, Louvre) executed for the collector Pierre Crozat. In 1701 Le Lorrain was received (*reçu*) as a member of the Académie Royale de Peinture et de Sculpture on presentation of a rather dryly elegant marble statuette of *Galatea* (Washington, DC, N.G.A.).

Employed as Sculpteur du Roi, Le Lorrain worked from 1702 at the royal châteaux of Versailles and nearby Marly. Little of his decorative garden sculpture for either site survives, with the exception of the Cascade or Buffet d'Eau (1702–4) at the Grand Trianon, Versailles, a collaborative effort in which Le Lorrain's own contribution is indistinguishable, and his marble statue of *Bacchus* (1710–12) near the Bassin d'Apollon, Versailles—a work of affected gracefulness inspired by Michelangelo's treatment of the same subject (Florence, Bargello). Le Lorrain's religious sculpture, a faithful reflection of the Counter-Reformation, included the ecstatic statue of *St Emilienne* in the church of the Invalides, Paris (plaster, 1705; destr.; see Beaulieu, fig. 27); the extant stone group of the *Virgin and Child* (*c.* 1706) in St Vigor-St Etienne at Marly-le-Roi, Yvelines; and the decorative stone relief sculpture and statues of virtues that he contributed to the chapel at Versailles (1707–10).

Neither of Le Lorrain's two independently executed funerary monuments survives. That of the *Laigue Family* (1705–9) for the church of the Jacobins in the Faubourg St Germain, Paris, was a marble wall tomb of striking austerity. It was designed by Gilles-Marie Oppenord, whose contract drawing (see Beaulieu, fig. 40) provides a record of its appearance. The more elaborate monument (*c.* 1720) to *Jacques-Joseph Benoist*, Director of the Orléans mint, formerly in St Pierre-le-Martroy, Orléans, was described by the artist's son and biographer, Father Le Lorrain, as a marble wall tomb with a standing child holding an hourglass in one hand and with the other pointing to a statue of *Christ* by Girardon. Of Le Lorrain's sixty decorative busts, a genre that seems to have been something of a speciality, only three are known to survive: they include the marble *Ceres* and *Head of a Young Girl* (both London, Wallace). In 1704 he exhibited three small-scale bronzes at the Salon: a *Bacchante* (best version Rennes, Mus. B.-A. & Archéol.) and the pendants *Vertumnus and Pomona* and *Venus and Adonis* (e.g. Paris, Pal. Elysée; St Petersburg, Hermitage; Honolulu, HI, Acad. A.). A terracotta statuette of a *River God* (exh. Salon 1737; Paris, Louvre) completed this series of small sculptures.

Much of Le Lorrain's most important work was executed for the princely Rohan family. In 1708 he supplied stone groups and a pedimental relief (destr. or substantially repaired; see Beaulieu, figs 65–72) for the façade of the Hôtel de Soubise, the Paris house of François de Rohan, Prince de Soubise, and from 1717 to 1723 he worked under the direction of Robert de Cotte on stone decoration (destr. 1779) for the Salon à Colonnes at the château of Saverne (Zabern), near Strasbourg, for Cardinal Armand-Gaston de Rohan. The sumptuous stone façade decoration (1735–8) of Cardinal de Rohan's episcopal palace at Strasbourg, the Palais Rohan, survives, though in a poor condition. The pediment and nine keystones over the ground-floor windows form part of a Universalist programme, while the entrance façade is animated by an elaborate allegorical programme relating to the episcopacy. It was also for Cardinal de Rohan that Le Lorrain carved his most famous work over the entrance to the stables of the Hôtel de Rohan, Paris—the virile and sensitive stone relief of the *Horses of Apollo* (1736–7; *in situ*)—which he completed before an attack of apoplexy cut short his career.

The work of Le Lorrain, the pupil of Girardon and the master of Jean-Baptiste Lemogne (ii) and Jean-Baptiste Pigalle, forms a vital link between the classicism of Versailles and the art of the Rococo. His portrait, painted by Hubert Drouais *c.* 1730, is in the Musée du Louvre, Paris.

BIBLIOGRAPHY

Souchal

M. Beaulieu: *Robert Le Lorrain, 1666–1743* (Paris, 1982) [cat. and extensive bibliog.]

**Lélu, Pierre** (*b* Paris, 13 Aug 1741; *d* Paris, 9 June 1810). French painter, draughtsman and engraver. He was a pupil of Boucher and of Gabriel-François Doyen. He travelled to Italy for the first time *c.* 1761, making copies of works by Raphael, Domenichino and other celebrated artists. Around 1775 he travelled to Spain and Portugal, then back to Italy. In 1777 he was in Marseille, where he was made a member of the academy. He then travelled to Paris, where he made the acquaintance of Michel-François Dandré-Bardon; in 1789 he made a third Italian journey.

At the 1793 Salon in Paris he exhibited a number of religious and historical scenes, including *Martha and Mary*, the *Entombment, Diomedes Wounding Venus, Pyrrhus Sacrificing Polyxena*, the *Death of Virginia* and *Cupid and Psyche*. He is known to have executed portraits of *Napoleon* and the *Marquis de Mirabeau*, among others, but did his finest work as an engraver, producing works such as *God Blessing the World* after Raphael (see Baudicour, no. 59) and *Virgin and Child* after Guercino (Baudicour, no. 67). On his death he left a large collection of works that was sold off in 1811; it included 460 drawings of Italian, French and Spanish monuments. He used pen and wash with verve and imagination, both to depict historical scenes, such as the *Vision of Abraham* (Orléans, Mus. B.-A.) and to record the appearance of interesting sites.

BIBLIOGRAPHY

Bellier de la Chavignerie–Auvray; Thieme–Becker

P. de Baudicour: *Le Peintre-graveur français*, i (Paris, 1859), pp. 231–86]

J. Guiffrey and P. Marcel: *Inventaire général des dessins du musée du Louvre et du musée de Versailles*, ix (Paris, 1921), pp. 15–16

*Autour de David: Dessins néo-classiques du musée des Beaux-Arts de Lille* (exh. cat. by A. Scottez, Lille, Mus. B.-A., 1983), p. 160

ANNIE SCOTTEZ-DE WAMBRECHIES

**Lely**, Sir **Peter** (*b* Soest, Westphalia, 14 Sept 1618; *d* London, 30 Nov 1680). Dutch painter, draughtsman and collector, active in England. By a combination of ability and good fortune, he rapidly established himself in mid-17th-century London as the natural successor in portrait painting to Anthony van Dyck. Between van Dyck's death in 1641 and the emergence of William Hogarth in the 1730s, Lely and his successor, Godfrey Kneller, were the leading portrait painters in England. After the restoration of the monarchy in 1660, Lely dominated the artistic scene, and his evocation of the court of Charles II is as potent and enduring as was van Dyck's of the halcyon days before the English Civil War. Although Lely's reputation was seriously damaged by portraits that came from his studio under his name but without much of his participation, his development of an efficient studio practice is of great importance in the history of British portrait painting. The collection of pictures, drawings, prints and sculpture he assembled was among the finest in 17th-century England after the dispersal of the legendary royal collections.

1. Life and work. 2. Working methods and technique. 3. Collection. 4. Critical reception and posthumous reputation.

1. LIFE AND WORK.

(i) Training in Holland and early years in England, before *c.* 1656. (ii) Maturity, late 1650s and after.

*(i) Training in Holland and early years in England, before c. 1656.* At the time of Lely's birth, his father, Johan van der Faes, was captain of an infantry company in a Dutch regiment serving the Elector of Brandenburg. His mother, Abigail van Vliet, came of a distinguished Utrecht family. The van der Faes family, perhaps originally from Antwerp, were people of substance in The Hague, where they had, since 1562, owned a house called *in de Lelye* because of the lily carved on its gable. From an early age Peter assumed the name of the house, a nickname by which he was always known. In 1637 he appeared as Pieter Lely in a list, in the minutes of the Guild of St Luke in Haarlem, of the pupils of Frans Pietersz. de Grebber (1573–1649).

Within ten years Lely had gone to London. There is no documentary evidence that he arrived there before van Dyck's death, and in stark contrast to the circumstances in which van Dyck had flourished, Lely built up his reputation and practice in a country torn by civil war and in a capital abandoned by the court. He was made freeman of the Painter-Stainers Company in London on 26 October 1647. By June 1650 he was established in a house on the Piazza in Covent Garden, a fashionable quarter where he lived for the rest of his life.

In the earliest printed account of Lely's career, published by Richard Graham in 1695, it is stated that when he arrived in England, he 'pursu'd the natural bent of his *Genius* in *Lantschapes* with *small Figures*, and *Historical Compositions*: but finding the practice of *Painting after the Life* generally more encourag'd, he apply'd himself to *Portraits*'. A small number of landscapes with figure subjects survive from the earliest period in Lely's career. Two small, very early canvases in the manner of Cornelis van Poelenburgh, *Diana and her Nymphs Bathing* (Nantes, Mus. B.-A.) and the *Finding of Moses* (Rennes, Mus. B.-A. & Archéol.), may have been painted before Lely left Holland. For all their obvious weaknesses, they already show a touch of poetry, a nostalgic mood in the landscape, an original richness of colour and an individual handling of light. In the colour in particular, and perhaps in the mood, there are reminiscences of the neo-Venetian qualities that painters such as Frans Wouters had evolved, partly from studying van Dyck. The poet Richard Lovelace, in his lines on 'Peinture', composed as a panegyric to his friend Lely, sympathized with him for the 'transalpine barbarous Neglect' with which such early pictures had been treated in England: an 'un-understanding land' where patrons were only interested in their 'varnish'd Idol-Mistresses' or 'their own dull counterfeits'.

After Lely began to concentrate on portraiture in London, it is unlikely that he painted more than a few subject pictures. His finest is the *Sleeping Nymphs by a*

1. Peter Lely: *Sleeping Nymphs by a Fountain*, oil on canvas, 1.28×1.44 m, *c.* ?1650, (London, Dulwich Picture Gallery)

*Fountain* (?*c.* 1650; London, Dulwich Pict. Gal.; see fig. 1): its composition and types are still fundamentally Dutch, but on a bigger scale than Poelenburgh's little pictures. It reveals an awareness of van Dyck; and, although awkwardly put together, the handling throughout is extremely sensuous, the colour rich and the lighting dramatic. These qualities are seen in the more individual and poetic *Concert* (London, Courtauld Inst. Gals), which contains obvious allusions to the painter's fondness for music (he liked to have music playing while he worked) and reminiscences of 16th-century *concerts champêtres* and of the Utrecht school which he admired. As late as 1654, he painted the *Music Lesson* (priv. col., see 1978 exh. cat., p. 48), van Dyckian in its treatment of the draperies, but akin to Gabriel Metsu in design and subject-matter. Lely's finest essays in this vein are the beautifully painted pictures of musicians (e.g. two in London, Tate), one of which perhaps represents the painter himself playing the lute (priv. col., see 1978 exh. cat., p. 42). Combining a Dutch spirit, a certain van Dyckian elegance and considerable tender charm, they are among Lely's most personal pictures and present him in an unusually appealing light.

Lely was fortunate, in his first years in London, that, after the death of William Dobson in 1648, there were no serious rivals in the field of portraiture. Lely secured the patronage of a group of rich and cultivated noblemen—the earls of Leicester, Salisbury, Pembroke and Northumberland—who had been prominent at court before the Civil War, but had remained in London during the conflict. Their collections were temporarily intact, and Northumberland and Pembroke had been important patrons of van Dyck, whose work Lely would have had the opportunity to study at leisure in their houses. Van Dyck's influence on him at this time is unequivocal, and it was to be the foundation of his style—of his sense of scale, his handling, his repertory of design and accessories, his marvellous ease or 'careless Romance'—until the end of his life. Northumberland commissioned portraits of members of his family to hang as sequels to the portraits van Dyck had painted for him some ten years earlier. Though van

Dyckian in pattern, the figures in Lely's early portraits are stiffly articulated and the draperies hang awkwardly; their relationship with the underlying forms are unclear and the designs have nothing of van Dyck's assurance. However, they have a charming freshness, the colour is subtle and individual, and the handling assured. In the latter two aspects of his craft Lely was already superior to any other painter in England, as can be seen in the most important pictures he painted for Northumberland: *Charles I with the Duke of York* (London, Syon House), for which Lely was paid £20 in 1648, and the *Children of Charles I* (Petworth House, W. Sussex, NT; see fig. 2), probably painted in 1647 and possibly originally a commission from the king. The implicit tragedy in the first is enhanced by the lack of the sinuous rhythms with which van Dyck would have handled such a composition; but the canvas displays the richness and spontaneity of Lely's touch at this period in such passages as the richly impasted silver lace on the Duke of York's warm grey doublet. The group of the royal children is to some extent a reworking of a group of the royal children painted by van Dyck in 1635 (a work Lely later briefly owned), but the creamy texture, strong lighting and romantic landscape are impressive

personal—essentially Dutch—qualities grafted on to the Flemish tradition of van Dyck. These qualities are also evident in two beautiful, slightly later, essays on an Arcadian theme, visual parallels to the pastoral verse of the period: the *Little Girl in Green* (Chatsworth, Derbys) and *Henry Sidney* (Penshurst Place, Kent), perhaps the finest portraits of children painted in England before the age of Reynolds and Gainsborough.

Lely continued to enjoy steady patronage throughout the Commonwealth (1649–60), not least from such royalist families as the Capels, Dormers and Somersets. He painted a series of three-quarter-length portraits (*c.* 1651) for Elizabeth Murray, Countess of Dysart, which still hang in the Long Gallery at Ham House, Surrey. (She was a friend of Oliver Cromwell, of whom Lely produced an official portrait in 1654 (Birmingham, Mus. & A.G.).) One of the portraits of Lady Dysart herself is closely based on a splendid portrait by van Dyck, *Henrietta of Lorraine* (London, Kenwood House), which had been in the collection of Charles I. In another portrait in the set, wrongly inscribed as representing the statesman Sir Henry Vane, Lely used a more sombre range of tones—rich

2. Peter Lely: *Children of Charles I*, oil on canvas, 1.98×2.33 m, 1647 (Petworth House, Egremont Collection)

blacks and whites against creamy flesh and a plain background—reminiscent of such Dutch artists as Bartholomeus van der Helst, Jacob van Loo or Jacob Adriaensz. Backer. In the portrait of a young man reasonably identified as *John Leslie, 7th Earl of Rothes* in the same collection, Lely's inability at this date to fit a head carefully painted from life on to a conventional posture is palpable, but the series as a whole makes a rich impression. In their fine Baroque frames the portraits foreshadow the sets of portraits that Lely was to paint after the Restoration.

At least two of the young men painted for Lady Dysart's gallery were active members of the ultra-royalist 'Sealed Knot'; and during a visit to Holland in the summer of 1656 with his friend, the royalist Hugh May, Lely may have made contact with the English court in exile. May was a lifelong friend and Lely later painted a *Self-portrait* in his company (*c.* 1675; priv. col., see 1978 exh. cat., p. 67). Earlier, in 1653, Lely had submitted to Parliament a scheme for an ambitious decorative scheme in the palace of Whitehall: a series of pictures commemorating the most memorable achievements of the Parliament; pictures of the principal battles and sieges of the Civil War; portraits of the leading commanders; and group portraits of the Council of State and the 'Assemblie of Parliament'.

*(ii) Maturity, late 1650s and after.* Lely's style did not attain complete maturity until the late 1650s, by which time he had achieved a satisfactory synthesis between his own,

essentially Dutch, abilities as a painter and a reinterpretation, albeit less refined, of the elegance he admired in van Dyck. On the eve of the Restoration he produced portraits of complete assurance and exceptional splendour; but the poetic element, so often a feature of his earlier pictures, tended to disappear under the increasing pressure of demands on his time and, probably, in the worldly atmosphere of the restored Stuart court. There are, for instance, fine passages in the group portrait of the *Perryer Family* (1655; Chequers, Bucks), but the elements of this sombre composition are clumsily assembled. By contrast, the splendid *Cotton Family* (1660; Manchester, C.A.G.) is brilliantly lit, and the individual members of the family, as well as the group as a whole, are handled with confidence. This increased self-confidence can also be sensed in the *Self-portrait* (London, N.P.G.) painted at this time. The most sumptuous portraits of this period are those of the *Duke of York* and his Duchess, *Anne Hyde* (both Edinburgh, N.P.G.; see fig. 3), painted soon after their marriage was made public in December 1660. Lely's handling was then at its most sensuous, his surface loaded with finely controlled liquid medium: the Duke in buff with a crimson sash, grey breeches with blue ribbons at his knee against rich golden-brown and brown-grey curtains; the Duchess in a deep yellow dress with a bright blue cloak against a deeper red-gold curtain. In the background of her portrait, and behind those of the Perryer and Cotton families, are examples of the elaborately carved pieces of Netherlandish Baroque sculpture that Lely often used to enrich his work.

In October 1661 Lely was granted by Charles II an annual pension, as Principal Painter, of £200, and in the summer of 1662 he was naturalized. Because Lely's portraits illustrate so blatantly the most familiar aspects of the court of Charles II, they have been cited in well-known descriptions of the atmosphere of that court: by Pope, for instance, in his *Imitations of Horace* ('In Days of Ease, . . ./Lely on animated Canvas stole/The sleepy Eye, that spoke the melting soul'). One early printed account of his career describes his sound drawing, fine colour, varied and graceful postures and flowing draperies; but also 'the languishing Air, long Eyes, and a Drowzy Sweetness peculiar to himself, for which they reckon him a *Mannerist*'. A contemporary wrote that after Lely had painted Barbara Villiers, Duchess of Cleveland, the most beautiful and notorious lady at court, 'he put something of Clevelands face or her Languishing eyes into every one Picture, so that all his pictures had an Air one of another, all the Eyes were Sleepy alike. So that Mr Walker ye Painter swore Lilly's Pictures was all Brothers & Sisters.' Such criticisms were probably prompted by the sets of female portraits (all including the Duchess) that Lely was producing at this period: the celebrated *Beauties* (London, Hampton Court, Royal Col.), painted for the Duke of York; the portraits commissioned by the Grand Duke of Tuscany (Florence, Uffizi); or the set compiled by Robert Spencer, 2nd Earl of Sunderland, for the gallery at Althorp House, Northants. Lely's assured draughtsmanship, fine colour and the flamboyant Baroque of his mature style are clearly seen in these sets. Moreover, van Dyck's continuing influence is evident, for instance, in the confident glance, swinging movement and fluttering drapery in Lely's *Duchess of Cleveland* at Althorp, almost certainly a reflection of

3. Peter Lely: *Anne Hyde, Duchess of York*, oil on canvas, 1.82×1.44 m, *c.* 1661–2 (Edinburgh, National Portrait Gallery)

van Dyck's portrait of *Mrs Endymion Porter* (London, Syon House), which Lely would have seen in Northumberland House.

In contrast to these perhaps over-familiar works, Lely produced portraits of a more serious nature. *Sir William Temple* (priv. col., see 1978 exh. cat., p. 56), for example, is distinguished by an air of good breeding which Reynolds would have been glad to achieve; and a portrait such as *John Maitland, 1st Duke of Lauderdale* (Edinburgh, N.P.G.) has a formidable presence and sheer power in execution that would have been difficult to surpass anywhere in Europe at that time. In Lely's sets of male portraits painted in the 1660s, likenesses of some of 'the most illustrious of our nation' commissioned by Edward Hyde, 1st Earl of Clarendon (now dispersed), or the famous portraits (London, N. Mar. Mus.) of the flag-officers who had served under the Duke of York in the Battle of Lowestoft, he produced a succession of interesting designs and, in the naval series, likenesses of these severe and puritanical seamen as formidably impressive as the portraits of their adversaries by van der Helst or Nicholas Maes. 'Very finely they are done indeed' was Samuel Pepys's comment.

In Lely's work of the late 1670s the colour is muted, there is less pigment on the canvas than hitherto and the paint is fused to achieve a softened, atmospheric quality across the composition. The sense of character is sensitive, occasionally surprisingly penetrating, but the articulation of the figures is sometimes more angular than in the richly composed portraits of the Restoration period. For instance, in such portraits as the *Duchess of Argyll* (Ham House, Surrey, NT) or the *Duchess of Portsmouth* (Malibu, CA, Getty Mus.) there is an artificial air that may reflect the influence of Simon Verelst or Henri Gascars. In the late full-length portraits, such as the pair depicting *Henry Howard, 6th Duke of Norfolk* and *Jane Bickerton, Duchess of Norfolk* (both 1677; Arundel Castle, W. Sussex), the elements of van Dyck's stagecraft are adapted to a new court style, which was to survive into the last years of the century. In the very late portrait of *Sir Richard Newdegate* (Arbury Hall, Warwicks) Lely's powers are still impressive: the characterization is vivid, the drawing crisp and fluent, the impasto applied with a masterly touch. The sitter is placed within a painted oval, a convention that Cornelis Jonson van Ceulen had first made popular in England; Lely himself had used it on many occasions, enriching it at this period by carving it into decorative scrolls and garlands. While established designs were produced in quantity in the studio, Lely continued to evolve new patterns to the end of his life. Outstanding portraits from his last years, all painted in subdued tones and with a restrained touch, are *Sir Thomas Isham* (late 1670s; Lamport Hall, Northants; see fig. 4), with its swinging sense of movement, *Sir Thomas Grosvenor* (priv. col., see 1978 exh. cat., p. 71), charming and well-bred, and the *3rd Earl of Dysart* (Weston Park, Salop), with the sitter's disillusioned air and relaxed, almost louche, posture. Two of these works are signed. Lely's signature, either the monogram *PL* or the full name with initials conjoined, occurs only on works of exceptional quality.

In January 1680 Lely was knighted. By then the success of Kneller was probably beginning to prey on his mind.

4. Peter Lely: *Sir Thomas Isham*, oil on canvas, 1.52×1.22 m, late 1670s (Lamport Hall, Northants)

Anxiety and the unrelenting pressure of work perhaps brought on the apopletic fit that struck Lely down at his easel. He was buried in St Paul's, Covent Garden, on 7 December 1680.

2. WORKING METHODS AND TECHNIQUE. From the time of the Restoration Lely was formidably busy. When Pepys called on him on 20 October 1662, Lely said he would not be at leisure for three weeks; and when Pepys visited him again on 18 July 1666 with Sir William Penn, who was to be included in the Duke of York's series, the painter could only offer an appointment six days later between 7.00 and 8.00 a.m. When the contents of Lely's studio were sold, his executors catalogued, as original works, over 70 three-quarter-lengths, more than 14 heads and 3 full-lengths; there were also more than 170 copies (including 12 portraits of the King, 10 of the Duke of York, 10 of his first Duchess and 12 of the Duchess of Cleveland): evidence of well-organized production and unbroken success.

*(i) Studio practice.* To cope with the enormous pressure of work, Lely had to rely on a body of apprentices or assistants, to whom he often entrusted the completion of a portrait after he had selected the design and painted the head. The young Robert Hooke was apprenticed to him for a short time in 1648. Thereafter the number of studio assistants must have increased. The most talented was probably John Greenhill. John Baptist Gaspars (*fl* 1641–92) and Gerrit Uylenburgh were among the assistants employed to paint drapery. Prosper Henry Lankrink and, for a short time, Nicolas de Largillierre were among specialist painters in Lely's studio. Mary Beale was a friend

and a close observer of Lely's method in the later part of his career; and her own work was much influenced by what she learnt under Lely's guidance.

Once a sitting had been arranged, the patron would be shown a rapid chalk drawing with a suggested pose, similar to those made by van Dyck. But Lely's drawings of this type are more richly worked; in one case (Paris, Fond. Custodia, Inst. Néer.), probably associated with a commission of 1661, part of the figure is painted in oil. Possibly to guide his assistants, Lely also sketched hands, a section of drapery or a piece of sculpture for use in a background. After the posture had been selected, sittings would take place. The head was painted from life, Lely at his easel six feet from the window of his studio, the light falling over his left shoulder, the sitter also six feet both from the light and the painter. While the sitter was still in the studio, Lely sketched the remainder of the composition on the canvas and laid in the colouring of hands and garments.

Some patrons were naturally apprehensive that commissions to Lely might be entrusted to assistants. In December 1677 the artist wrote to assure Sir Richard Newdegate that pictures he had ordered had been 'from Beginning to ye end drawne with my owne hands'. There are many portraits that Lely did indeed paint throughout himself, and he would always paint at least the prototype of a new pattern; but a *Study of the Head of the Duke of York* (London, N.P.G.) indicates the extent to which he was involved when under pressure: the face is completed, the hair and cravat only slightly suggested. In the finished works it is often possible to discern the point at which an assistant took over. The draperies and backgrounds in the Duke of York's portraits, for example, are competently drawn and painted but lack the freshness of touch that Lely himself would have given to the canvas, notably to the whites.

*(ii) Drawings.* Lely's distinction as a painter, and a reason for his continuing success, is partly the result of his sound draughtsmanship. Among the professional portrait painters in Stuart England, he was the finest draughtsman after van Dyck. Apart from drawings made in the course of carrying out a commissioned portrait, he produced a number of informal heads in black and red chalk, heightened with white, on brown or grey-brown paper. Good examples are the *Portrait of a Girl* or that of *Sir Charles Cotterell* (both London, BM); the finest is the youthful *Self-portrait* in the possession of Lely's descendants (see 1978 exh. cat., frontispiece). These drawings are frequently signed and were conceived as portraits in their own right, to be framed (usually in ebony) and hung in a small room. They reveal an unexpectedly charming side of Lely; and they helped to establish a tradition of small-scale portraiture subsequently developed in England by Greenhill, Ashfield and Lutterell. Lely also produced a series of drawings of figures from the procession of the Order of the Garter, executed in black chalk heightened with white on blue-grey paper (dispersed; 31 are known). They are not linked with any documented commission and may record an actual procession watched by Lely soon after the Restoration (all the figures move from right to left). Essentially Dutch in manner, they are perhaps the finest drawings of their kind to have been executed in England after the death of van Dyck.

OLIVER MILLAR

3. COLLECTION. From the time he arrived in London, Lely was acquiring paintings, prints, drawings and sculptures. He made purchases from the collections of Charles I, Thomas Howard, 2nd Earl of Arundel, Nicholas Lanier and van Dyck; it is likely that he also bought from agents based abroad. Lely's collection was strongest in 16th- and 17th-century Italian, Dutch and Flemish works, as were most English collections of this period, although some 16th-century German and 17th-century French artists were also represented. Bainbridge Buckridge, who believed that Lely's acquisitions were his substitute for foreign travel, considered them to be 'the best chosen Collection of any of his Time', adding that the benefit Lely gained from them 'may sufficiently appear by that wonderful stile of Painting which he acquired by his daily conversing with the works of those great men'. Following Lely's death and faced with a burden of nearly £9000 in debts and legacies, his executors organized the sale of his collection by auction. The pictures were valued by Parry Walton (*fl c.* 1660–1700) and John Baptist Gaspars, both of whom had been Lely's assistants. Copies of the descriptive catalogue written by one of the executors, the writer and lawyer Roger North, were sent to the Netherlands, France and Italy. The pictures and sculptures were placed on view at Lely's Covent Garden studio for 14 days before the sale, which opened on 18 April 1682. Besides Lely's own works, the paintings included works by or attributed to Veronese, Correggio, Hans Holbein the younger, van Dyck (e.g. *Lady Elizabeth Thimbleby and Dorothy, Viscountess Andover*, London, N.G.), Claude Lorrain, Pieter van Laer and Adriaen Brouwer; among the sculptures was Bernini's bust of *Mr Baker* (London, V&A). At the close of the four-day sale all works had been sold for over £6000.

Lely's collection of prints and drawings, one of the first to be formed in England by a painter–collector, was described by the artist Charles Beale as 'the best in Europe'; it included drawings by Leonardo da Vinci, Fra Bartolommeo, Raphael (e.g. *Constantine Addressing his Troops*, Chatsworth, Derbys; now considered a school work), Correggio, Giulio Romano, Polidoro da Caravaggio, Parmigianino (over 100 figurative and drapery studies), Veronese, Primaticcio, Federico Barocci, Taddeo and Federico Zuccaro, the Carracci, Rubens and van Dyck (including his Italian Sketchbook, London, BM). Here again, works by Italian, Dutch and Flemish artists predominated, although Lely did own a number of German drawings (e.g. by Hans Rottenhammer) and a few English drawings by Isaac Oliver and his son Peter. The prints and drawings (*c.* 10,000 items, each sheet marked by North with the distinctive PL stamp) were dispersed in two mixed sales on 11 April 1688 and 15 November 1694 and fetched over £2400.

DIANA DETHLOFF

4. CRITICAL RECEPTION AND POSTHUMOUS REPUTATION. Lely was a rich and successful man. At the end of his career he was charging £60 for a full-length portrait and £40 for a three-quarter-length. (For full-lengths at

this time Michael Wright and Gerard Soest probably charged £36 and £30 respectively; by 1691 Kneller was asking £50 for a full-length and only by 1706 was he asking £60. Van Dyck had usually received £30 for a three-quarter-length and £50 to £60 for a full-length.) Lely owned property in Surrey and Lincolnshire, as well as his share of the family's property in Holland. He lived in a grand way in Covent Garden: 'a mighty proud man, and full of state', in Pepys's well-known aside.

At the time Lely painted Cromwell in 1654, he was described as 'the best artist in England'. There were nevertheless occasional references to his failure to catch a satisfactory likeness. Dorothy Osborne reported to William Temple in October 1653 that Lely had been 'condemned for makeing the first hee drew for mee a little worse than I, and in makeing this better hee has made it as unlike as tother', and in 1655 Henry Osborne complained that in Lady Diana Rich's portrait 'one of the eyes was out, so I said onely that Mr Lilly should mend it'. Such criticisms persisted. Pepys, who saw him painting the Duchess of York on 24 March 1666, considered that even after two or three sittings the likeness eluded the painter. Dryden, in his preface to *Sylvae* (1685), wrote of 'the late noble painter . . . who drew many graceful pictures, but few of them were like. And this happened to him, because he always studied himself more than those who sat to him.' On the other hand, Sir Thomas Isham was assured in 1679 that Lely's portrait of him was 'extreme like'.

The burdens of the portrait practice and the demands of the leaders of society in Restoration London may have bred a vein of cynicism in Lely. Jonathan Richardson the elder, in his *Essay on the Theory of Painting* of 1715 (p. 228), recorded a conversation between the painter and a friend: 'For God's sake, Sir Peter, how came you to have so great a reputation? You know that I know you are no painter'. 'My Lord, I know I am not, but I am the best you have'. In fact Lely's best work, throughout his career, is fit to be set beside that of any portrait painter working in a comparable situation on the Continent. The finer qualities, of observation as well as of technique, in Lely's work have been obscured in the eyes of posterity by the seeming uniformity of his work and, even more, by the enormous number of inferior pictures with which his name, often unfairly, has been linked. Painters working early in the following century held his work in high esteem: Gerard de Lairesse, for example, called him 'the great *Lely*'. Later his work formed part of an inheritance of which van Dyck's achievement naturally formed the richest part; but in borrowings by Reynolds from that inheritance, Lely's legacy is often in evidence. Those later critics, from George Vertue to C. H. Collins Baker, who investigated his work in detail and with sympathy, never questioned his outstanding ability.

BIBLIOGRAPHY

J. von Sandrart: *Teutsche Academie* (1675–9); ed. A. R. Peltzer (1925), ii, pp. 354–5

R. Graham: 'Short Account of the Most Eminent Painters both Ancient and Modern', *De arte graphica/The Art of Painting*, C.-A. Dufresnoy (London, 1695), pp. 343–4 [bilingual text]

B. Buckeridge: 'Essay towards an English School of Painters', *The Art of Painting*, Eng. trans. by J. Savage of R. de Piles: *Abrégé de la vie des peintres* (London, 1706, 3/1754/R 1969), pp. 445–6

A. Houbraken: *De groote schouburgh* (1718–21), ii, pp. 33–8

C. H. Collins Baker: *Lely and the Stuart Portrait Painters*, 2 vols (London, 1912)

F. Lugt: *Marques* (1921), nos 2092–4

'Sir Peter Lely's Collection', *Burl. Mag.*, lxxxiii (1943), pp. 185–91 [sale cat. of Lely's pict. col.]

H. Ogden and M. Ogden: 'Sir Peter Lely's Collection: Further Notes', *Burl. Mag.*, lxxxiv (1944), p. 154

R. B. Beckett: *Lely* (London, 1951) [useful pls]

E. Waterhouse: *Painting in Britain, 1530–1790*, Pelican Hist. A. (London, 1953, rev. 4/1978), pp. 92–100

F. Lugt: *Marques*, suppl. (1956), no. 2091b

*Sir Peter Lely* (exh. cat. by O. Millar, London, N.P.G., 1978) [fully illus., up-to-date account, with full bibliog. and detailed refs to contemp. sources]

M. K. Talley: *Portrait Painting in England: Studies in the Technical Literature before 1700* (London, 1981) [important inf. on Lely's method, the org. of the sale and the dispersal of the contents of the artist's studio]

*Drawing in England from Hilliard to Hogarth* (exh. cat. by L. Stainton and C. White, London, BM, 1987), pp. 123–37

J. Foucart: 'Peter Lely: Dutch History Painter', *Hoogsteder-Naumann Mercury*, no. 8 (1989), pp. 17–26

J. Wood: 'Van Dyck and the Earl of Northumberland: Taste and Collecting in Stuart England', *Van Dyck 350*, ed. S. J. Barnes and A. K. Wheelock jr (Washington, DC, 1994), pp. 281–324

OLIVER MILLAR

**Lemaire, (Philippe-Joseph-)Henri** (*b* Valenciennes, 9 Jan 1798; *d* Paris, 2 Aug 1880). French sculptor. He was a pupil of François-Dominique-Aimé Milhomme, then of Pierre Cartellier, and won the Prix de Rome in 1821. Throughout his career he remained faithful to the Neoclassical style current in his youth and exemplified in the statues he made in Rome for the Paris Salon, such as *Virgil's Ploughman* (marble, 1826; Paris, Tuileries Gardens) and *Girl with a Butterfly* (1827; Valenciennes, Mus. B.-A.).

After his return to Paris in 1826 Lemaire was principally occupied with official and semi-official monumental sculpture for successive regimes. In 1829 he executed a statue of the *Duc de Bordeaux* for the Duchesse de Berry (marble; Valenciennes, Mus. B.-A.), and during the July Monarchy (1830–48) he worked on sculpture for the Galeries Historiques at the château of Versailles, the Arc de Triomphe, and the Colonne de la Grande-Armée in Boulogne, among other projects. He was also involved in the decoration of several Paris churches, his most important work being the monumental stone relief of the *Last Judgement* on the pediment of La Madeleine (1829–34). Its success earned him an invitation to St Petersburg, where he executed models for two pedimental reliefs of the *Resurrection* and *St Isaac* for the church of St Isaac (bronze, 1838–41).

He continued to contribute sculpture to the major Paris building projects of the Second Empire (1851–70), executing work for the Palais de Justice, the Gare du Nord and the Cour Carrée of the Louvre, while for Lille he made a statue of *Napoleon I* (bronze, 1854; Entrepôts municipaux) and for Valenciennes a monument to the chronicler *Froissart* (marble, 1856; Jardin Froissart). Many of his plaster and terracotta models are in the Musée des Beaux-Arts, Valenciennes, and many drawings are kept in the Musée des Beaux-Arts, Rouen.

BIBLIOGRAPHY

Lami

A. Le Normand: 'De Lemaire à Rodin: Dessins de sculpteurs du 19ème siècle', *Etudes de la Rev. Louvre*, i (1980), pp. 152–9

*De Carpeaux à Matisse: La Sculpture française de 1850 à 1914 dans les musées et les collections publiques du Nord de la France* (exh. cat., Calais,

Mus. B.-A.; Lille, Mus. B.-A.; Arras, Mus. B.-A.; and elsewhere; 1982–3), pp. 242–5
*La Sculpture française au XIXème siècle* (exh. cat., ed. P. Durey; Paris, Grand Pal., 1986)

ANTOINETTE LE NORMAND-ROMAIN

**Lemaire (de Belges), Jean** (*b* Bavay, Hainault, 1473; *d* after 1515). Franco-Flemish writer. He studied in Valenciennes with the poet and chronicler Jean Molinet and probably completed his education in Paris. In 1498 he was in Villefranche-sur-Saône, in the service of Peter II, Duke of Bourbon. In 1504 he went to Annecy to Margaret of Austria, then Duchess of Savoy, for whom he wrote *La Plaincte du désiré* (1503/4; pubd Lyon, 1509) on the death of her husband. In the poem, Lemaire discussed the art of painting—in particular the use of colour—and referred to several Italian Renaissance artists, as well as those of northern Europe. He also wrote the *Couronne Margaritique* (1504–5; pubd 1549) for the Duchess, a work in verse and prose in which he alluded to many contemporary painters, goldsmiths and sculptors. When Margaret became Governor of the Netherlands in 1507, Lemaire followed her to Mechelen and became her chronicler, occasionally acting as her diplomatic envoy in France and Italy. In Mechelen Lemaire began to work on the *Illustrations de Gaule et singularités de Troie*, a prose work influenced by Italian humanist culture explaining the ancestry of the princely families of the Rhineland, which was to inspire many tapestry designs. Margaret entrusted Lemaire with several assignments concerning the construction of the church at Bourg-en-Bresse to house the tomb of the Duke of Savoy. The tomb was to be executed by the sculptor Michel Colombe and painter Jean Perréal, the latter being a close friend of Lemaire. In 1512, Lemaire was in the service of the Queen of France, Anne of Brittany, then the wife of Louis XII. During this appointment, Lemaire published the *Concorde des deux langages* (1511) and various political writings and completed the *Illustrations* (1511–13).

BIBLIOGRAPHY

J. Stecher, ed.: *Oeuvres*, 4 vols (Leuven, 1882–91)
P. A. Becker: *Jean Lemaire, der erste humanistische Dichter Frankreichs* (Strasbourg, 1893)
G. Doutrepont: *Jean Lemaire de Belges et la Renaissance* (Brussels, 1934)
P. Jodogne: *Jean Lemaire de Belges, écrivain franco-bourguignon* (Brussels, 1972)

PIERRE JODOGNE

**Le Mans.** French city on the River Sarthe in the province of Maine. In the Iron Age it became the chief town of the Aulerici Cenomani, a Celtic tribe who constructed a promontory fort enclosing *c.* 10 ha. Gallo-Roman Suindinum became a provincial capital, and it expanded considerably during the 2nd and 3rd centuries AD: the remains of various buildings, including the arena and the military camp, have been discovered beyond the city walls. The 4th-century Gallo-Roman walls were erected in the wake of late 3rd-century barbarian attacks. They are well preserved and still include some towers on the river front. Their thick rubble core is faced with sandstone *petit appareil* traversed by brick courses and enlivened by patterns of different coloured stone. The christianization of Le Mans, supposedly effected by St Julien in the 1st century AD, probably occurred *c.* 300. Numerous religious establishments were founded during the Merovingian period (6th and 7th centuries), including the monasteries of St Victor and SS Peter and Paul, both located outside the walls, a church dedicated to St Julien and the cathedral. The town was attacked by the Vikings in the 9th century, and its most important religious foundations, the cathedral (*see* §1 below), Notre-Dame-du-Pré and Notre-Dame-de-la-Couture (*see* §2 below), were reconstructed between the 11th and 13th century. After being seized by William I of England, Le Mans fell into the hands of the Plantagenets in the mid-12th century. Among post-medieval buildings of interest in Le Mans is the 18th-century church of the Visitation, partly attributed to the nun Anne-Victoire Pillon. Le Mans is now an industrial centre, world-famous for its motor-race course.

BIBLIOGRAPHY

*Dict. Eglises France*
R. M. Butler: 'The Roman Walls of Le Mans', *J. Roman Stud.*, xlviii (1958), pp. 33–9

KATHRYN MORRISON

1. Cathedral. 2. Notre-Dame-de-la-Couture.

## 1. CATHEDRAL.

(i) Architecture. (ii) Sculpture. (iii) Stained glass.

*(i) Architecture.* The first cathedral of Le Mans, dedicated to the Virgin and St Peter, was founded at an uncertain date by Julien, first bishop of Le Mans. Gradually, SS Gervais, Protais and Julien were added to the dedicatees, and by the 13th century the latter was the principal tutelary saint. The history of the cathedral is unusually well documented. In particular, the *Acts of the Bishops of Le Mans* pays much attention to the building activities of successive bishops. The extant cathedral was partially rebuilt on various occasions between the late 11th century and the 15th and is a building of considerable archaeological complexity, but the pre-1080s cathedrals are known only from textual evidence. Julien's cathedral was rebuilt in the early 6th century with substantial transept arms: prominent transepts have remained a feature of the building. It was replaced by Bishop Aldric (*reg* 832–56). The *Acts* states unequivocally that the new choir, consecrated in 834, was surrounded by an ambulatory containing five altars. If this is true it is by far the earliest recorded ambulatory plan. The relics of St Julien were transferred to this church from their original resting place at Notre-Dame-du-Pré.

Bishop Vulgrin (*reg* 1053–65) began a new, larger church in the 1060s. His ambitious choir, built over a crypt and flanked by very high towers, soon collapsed. His successor, Arnaud (*reg* 1065–81), rebuilt it and laid the foundations for vast new transepts, with towers on the end of each arm, providing the plan of the present transepts. This is the first building campaign to have left any physical trace. The transept walls were built, and the choir paved, glazed and painted, by his successor Hoel (*reg* 1085–96). The *Acts* clearly describes a late 11th-century choir that was richly coloured, with columnar supports (and presumably, like its predecessor, an ambulatory) and with a wooden roof rather than a vault. It probably reflected Bishop Fulbert's cathedral at Chartres (*see* CHARTRES, §I, 1). Hoel built the nave aisle walls, the easternmost nave bay and probably the bulk of the west wall, with its enormous window and complex exterior decoration. Hoel's masonry is distinctive, using local limestone and red sandstone to produce polychromatic effects, especially in arch mouldings, which imitate the Gallo-Roman city wall. Hoel's nave was completed by Bishop Hildevert of Lavardin (*reg* 1096–1126). His architect was a monk called John from the abbey of La Trinité, Vendôme. The trace of this nave arcade is still clear along both north and south elevations, above the narrower later arcade arches. Hildevert's arcade was open and spacious, with the arches springing from simple, slender columns. The upper wall was very thin, and vaulting out of the question. The cathedral was finished and consecrated in 1120. The effects of the nave, with Hildevert's slender columnar arcade lit by Hoel's large windows, anticipated Abbot Suger's choir at Saint-Denis Abbey by some 20 years.

The cathedral was damaged in a city fire in 1134. In the late 1140s and 1150s a substantial refashioning was undertaken by Bishop Guillaume de Passavent (*reg* 1145–87). This was given a new impetus in 1151 when Geoffrey, Count of Anjou, was buried in the cathedral. It subsequently benefited from the generosity of his son, Henry II of England, who endowed a chapel for Geoffrey, from which survives Geoffrey's famous enamelled funerary plaque (Le Mans, Mus. Tessé), and provided lead for roofing. The refashioned building was consecrated in 1158. This campaign involved a recasing or rebuilding of the crossing and transept arms (the south-east crossing pier is inscribed 1145), and of the nave elevation, to allow both transepts and nave to be given rib vaults. The mid-12th-century masonry can be distinguished from earlier campaigns by the superb quality of the fine Jurassic limestone. Polychromy was rejected; 'Classical' effects were achieved instead by some of the finest acanthus capitals carved in 12th-century France.

The form of the vault dictates the design of the elevation below. The vaults are square in plan with a distinctly domed profile. In the nave (see fig. 1) they span double bays, and the nave elevation was redesigned with strong composite piers beneath the rib springings, and weak columns in between. The thin elevation was encased rather than rebuilt, although this involved underpinning Hildevert's arcade arches and wall with wooden supports while the piers were rebuilt. The openness of the old arcade was lost, but the domed square vaults spanning double bays created an impressive central space and were fireproof. Their deep lunettes allowed ample double lancet windows to light the clerestory. Flying buttresses, which were aligned with the strong piers, possibly gave extra support to the vaults. The design of the vaults is generally considered to depend on those in the nave of Angers Cathedral, which was rebuilt after 1149; but this type of vault was clearly intended at Le Mans in the work on the transepts as early as 1145, and Angers may reflect Le Mans. An elaborate south portal was added to the cathedral during this campaign.

In 1217 the chapter was given royal permission to breach the Gallo-Roman wall and build a new choir. This was finished, glazed and consecrated, and the relics of St Julien rehoused in new splendour, in 1254. The choir was built to an expansive design, with a double ambulatory and 13 separate and unusually deep radiating chapels. The

1. Le Mans Cathedral, interior looking east, rebuilt 1140s and 1150s

aisle elevations are stepped. The inner ambulatory has a three-level elevation, with triforium passage and clerestory windows: the main vessel elevation is reduced to two levels, with a massive arcade surmounted by a very high clerestory. The chapels are separated by triangular vault compartments, an arrangement that is reflected on the exterior of the building in the distinctive Y-shaped flying buttresses.

Three different architects, working in completely different styles, built the choir. The first architect established the plan and built the ambulatory chapels and the outer ambulatory wall. His formal repertory—of arch mouldings, beaked abaci, nibbed bosses, reduced buttress heads—together with the presence of an external passage running outside the chapel windows and through its buttresses, suggest that he came from Chartres. Some chapel capitals have naturalistic foliage and indicate that he had access to the most up-to-date sculptors from the Ile-de-France or Champagne areas.

The second architect introduced complex shaft and arch sections with deep concavities, rounded and polygonal abaci and Y-tracery with its sharply pointed lancets for window and triforium arches. Clearly, he came from Normandy. He was probably the architect of Bayeux Cathedral choir, built in the 1230s. He may have worked on both cathedrals concurrently. He imported Norman sculptors from the cloister at Mont-Saint-Michel for the virtuoso undercut ambulatory triforium spandrels.

The architect who finished the choir around 1250 came from the Paris area and worked in a Rayonnant style. His shafts are very attenuated; he used star-shaped abaci in straight bays; and his window tracery designs, with piled trilobes, derive from the Sainte-Chapelle. His training handling bar tracery made him the ideal architect for the vast clerestory.

Not until the early 14th century was there enough money to begin work on the transepts, and progress was very slow. The south transept was remodelled first, by the architect Mathieu Julien (*fl* early 14th century). It was finished by 1392, as is shown by a gift from Charles VI, specifically to bring the old north arm into line with the completed south arm. The first stone of the north transept remodelling was laid in 1403, and the work was finished around 1430. Two architects worked on it, Jean de Lescluze (*fl* 1420s) and Jean de Dammartin.

BIBLIOGRAPHY

R. J. F. Lotin, ed.: *Chartularium insignis ecclesiae Cenomanensis quod dicitur Liber Albus capituli* (Le Mans, 1869)

A. Ledru: *La Cathédrale du Mans* (Mamers, 1900)

G. Busson and A. Ledru, eds: *Actus pontificum Cenomannis in urbe degentium* [Acts of the bishops of Le Mans], Archives Historiques du Maine, ii (Le Mans, 1901)

F. Salet: 'La Cathédrale du Mans', *Congr. Archéol. France*, cxix (1961), pp. 18–58

J. Herschman: 'The Norman Ambulatory of Le Mans Cathedral, and the Chevet of the Cathedral of Coutances', *Gesta*, xx (1981), pp. 323–32

L. Grant: *Gothic Architecture in Normandy, 1150–1250* (diss., U. London, Courtauld Inst., 1986)

LINDY GRANT

*(ii) Sculpture.* The interior of Le Mans Cathedral contains three important series of capitals, corresponding to the principal architectural campaigns. The capitals of the nave aisles belong to the 11th-century building. They are carved in low relief with a variety of foliate, animal and figural motifs. The foliate capitals of the mid-12th-century nave range from austere simplicity to rich compositions in which heads, birds and beasts frequently appear among the leaves. Figures on the springers of the vault ribs also belong to this campaign. The most interesting sculpture in the 13th-century choir are the rib-statues and the triforium spandrels, which are decorated with openwork panels of naturalistic foliage.

The Early Gothic portal inserted into the fifth bay of the south aisle is the most notable sculptural element of the cathedral. The porch preceding the portal is stylistically associated with the mid-12th-century nave, which was rebuilt after fires in 1134 and 1137. It is presumed that both portal and porch were completed before the consecration of the nave in 1158. By its architectural design and sculptural programme the portal belongs to the series of Early Gothic doorways traditionally grouped with the Royal Portal of the west front of Chartres Cathedral. The absence of documentary evidence makes it difficult to establish the chronology of this series, but Le Mans retains archaic traits that suggest it is one of the earliest examples.

The focal point of the ensemble is the tympanum. There, as on the Royal Portal of Chartres, *Christ* is enthroned in a mandorla and is accompanied by the four

2. Le Mans Cathedral, tympanum and lintel of the portal in the south aisle, mid-12th century

*Evangelist Symbols* (see fig. 2). Below, on the lintel, the Twelve Apostles are seated under decorative arcading. As on the south portal of Bourges Cathedral, they are arranged in pairs, apparently engaged in conversation. The faces of the doorposts, like those of the Romanesque portal of St Pierre, Moissac, are carved with full-length figures representing, on the right, *St Peter* and, on the left, *St Paul*. The eight column-statues on the embrasures probably represent Old Testament characters: in 1841 the name 'Salomo' was still legible on the scroll held by the inner figure on the right. Though flatter, heavier and less undercut than their Chartres counterparts, the Le Mans statues display drapery conventions and facial types that reappear on the Royal Portal. Like the statues of the Chartres portal they stand on short, ornamented shafts. The plinths are plain except for the inner one on the right, which has simple fluting, another feature reminiscent of the Royal Portal. The Corinthian-derived capitals, carved with acanthus foliage, carry round arches. The inner archivolt is carved with ten standing, censing angels with, on the keystone, the Hand of God. On the remaining three archivolts, which show slight signs of trimming, scenes from the *Life of Christ* are arranged somewhat arbitrarily.

Several sculptors worked on the portal. Despite numerous analogies with the Royal Portal of Chartres this workshop was probably not employed there. Correspondences in composition and drapery suggest that the Chartres and Le Mans workshops consulted the same models for their tympana and column-statues. Other aspects of the Le Mans portal indicate limited, but perhaps more direct, relationships with other Early Gothic portals, particularly Ivry-la-Bataille (Eure). This supports a date of *c*. 1150.

BIBLIOGRAPHY

A. Lapeyre: *Des façades occidentales de Saint-Denis et de Chartres aux portails de Laon* (Paris, 1960), pp. 90–95

W. Sauerländer: *Gotische Skulptur in Frankreich, 1140–1270* (Munich, 1970; Eng. trans., London, 1972), p. 386

T. E. Polk II: 'The South Portal of the Cathedral at Le Mans: Its Place in the Development of Early Gothic Portal Composition', *Gesta*, xxiv/1 (1985), pp. 47–60

KATHRYN MORRISON

*(iii) Stained glass.* The nave of the cathedral boasts an important collection of Romanesque windows. Except for the great western window of the *Life of St Julien* (*c*. 1155–60), however, none of the 20 or so original stained glass cycles can be placed with certainty. The *Ascension* window, which Brisac dated as early as 1120, may be the oldest extant Romanesque glass in France, and its bold, expressive style occurs elsewhere in the region in Poitiers, Angers and a number of parish churches. Distinctive are the nested v-shaped folds of the drapery, enhancing the dramatic poses of the figures. Glazing continued in the cathedral throughout the 12th century, evidenced, for example, by fragments from a *Nativity* and a *Last Judgement*, *c*. 1150, the *Martyrdom of St Stephen* and a *Life of SS Gervais and Protais*, after 1160, and the *Discovery of the Relics of Gervais and Protais*, *c*. 1190.

In the 13th-century choir the extant glass is concentrated in the Lady chapel and upper levels. In the justly famous programme of the Lady chapel (*c*. 1240) the *Life and Passion of Christ* is relegated to the axial windows, and the side windows contain the *Virgin* as intercessor. The focal point of the choir programme of saints and apostles

(*c*. 1255–60) is provided by the axial lancets showing *Christ Displaying his Wounds* and the *Virgin and Child*. In most windows the donors are prominently displayed. Two appear to be guilds, the bakers and woodcutters, and others ecclesiastics or laypersons identified by coats of arms, for example Bishop Geoffrey of Loudun in the axial lancets. The triforium glazing (1250–55) constitutes the most intriguing of the entire ensemble. The 13 multi-lancet windows combine a number of saints' lives or biblical stories undoubtedly determined by stylistic and devotional tastes of the different donors.

The glass painting is somewhat heterogeneous in style. The Lady chapel exhibits a style typical of the measured cadences and narrative clarity of the ambulatory of Chartres Cathedral. Most of the choir windows appear to have been inspired by mid-13th-century Parisian formulae. The exceptions, however, are significant. A workshop presumably from western France displays in the *Flagellation of St Gervais* a powerful, extremely expressive style that exaggerates the angular contours of the features and drapery with abrupt, sometimes broken strokes. A third workshop, responsible for the lancet of the high priest *Aaron* among others, embodies a mannered style more typical of the late 13th century. In the triforium the window donated by Evron Abbey showing the founding of the abbey and Marian themes may be of a local Evron manufacture, and the axial window dedicated to the *Virgin* and *SS Gervais and Protais*, given by Rotrou V, Comte de Montfort, displays similarities to the style of the St Chéron Master of Chartres Cathedral. The glass was restored between 1858 and 1875.

BIBLIOGRAPHY

E. Hucher: *Calques des vitraux de la cathédrale du Mans* (Le Mans, 1855–62)

L. Grodecki: 'Les Vitraux de la cathédrale du Mans', *Congr. Archéol. France*, cxix (1961), pp. 59–99

A. Mussat, ed.: *La Cathédrale du Mans* (Paris, 1981), pp. 60–69, 103–26 [articles by C. Brisac; for plan of windows see pp. 182–4]

VIRGINIA CHIEFFO RAGUIN

2. NOTRE-DAME-DE-LA-COUTURE. The 12th-century rebuilding of the Benedictine abbey of Notre-Dame-de-la-Couture incorporated much of the 11th-century structure, including a series of carved capitals in the east end and, on the interior of the nave north wall, a pilaster carved with a figure of *Christ*. Rebuilding began after the middle of the 12th century with the upper parts of the choir. The springers of the vaulting ribs were carved with standing figures, which have been identified as *St Peter*, *St Paul*, (?)*St Lawrence* and *St Stephen*, *King David* and a *Queen*. This is one of the earliest series of rib-statues in western France. The rebuilding of La Couture, with its single-cell, dome-vaulted nave, continued into the second half of the 13th century. The west portal, sheltered by a porch and set between two square towers, carries a rich sculptural programme that can be dated *c*. 1250. The theme is the *Last Judgement*, following the iconography devised at Amiens Cathedral: the *Christ-Judge* on the tympanum is flanked by four kneeling figures—the *Virgin* and *St John* in their role as Intercessors and two angels carrying the Instruments of the Passion. The *Resurrection of the Dead* and the *Weighing of Souls* are represented on

the lintel. Angels and Elders occupy the three archivolts. Statues of six apostles stand against the oblique embrasures. Their feet are placed on crouching human figures, and the foliage capitals above their heads develop into broad architectural canopies. The trumeau, with its statue of *Christ*, has been destroyed.

The sculptural style of the embrasures and lintel is quite different from that of the tympanum and archivolts. The heavy-set column-statues are characterized by the Antique-inspired realism that originated in the Reims workshops of the 1230s. The portals of St Seurin, Bordeaux, and several churches in Burgundy appear to be closely related to this work. In contrast, the elegant tympanum and archivolt figures, with their elongated proportions and smooth draperies, are stylistically related to Parisian work of the mid-12th century (e.g. Notre-Dame, south transept portal). It is unlikely that the two stylistic trends represented at La Couture were separated by any significant time-lapse.

BIBLIOGRAPHY

F. Lesueur: 'L'Eglise de la Couture au Mans', *Congr. Archéol. France*, cxix (1961), pp. 119–37
A. Mussat: *Le Style gothique de l'ouest de la France* (Paris, 1963), pp. 110–14, 129–31
W. Sauerländer: *Gotische Skulptur in Frankreich, 1140–1270* (Munich, 1970; Eng. trans., London, 1972), p. 503

KATHRYN MORRISON

**Le Marchand, David** (*b* Dieppe, 12 Oct 1674; *d* London, 17 March 1726). French ivory-carver, active in Britain. He was the son of Guillaume Le Marchand, a painter, and was presumably trained in Dieppe, where ivory-carving was an important craft. Following the Revocation of the Edict of Nantes by Louis XIV in 1685, Le Marchand, a Huguenot, emigrated to Edinburgh, where in 1696 he opened a shop. The earliest medallion indubitably signed by him dates from that year. By 1705 he had moved to London, where he settled, becoming a member of the Huguenot community there; he became a naturalized citizen in 1709.

Portraiture became Le Marchand's speciality, although he also carved a few mythological or religious statuettes. His style initially reflected that of earlier carvers in Dieppe, such as Jean Mancel (*fl* 1681–1717), and that of Jean Cavalier, his gifted predecessor in London. His earliest portraits are in profile and in low relief on an oval plaque or medallion. However, he soon aspired to more ambitious kinds of portraiture, carving in 1697 a substantial and masterly bust in the round of the philosopher *John Locke* (untraced). Other busts in varying sizes followed: *Anne Churchill, Countess of Sunderland* (1699 or later; London, V&A); *Anne Nellthorpe* (1704), *John Vesey, Archbishop of Tuam* (1702) and *Francis Sambrooke* (1704; all three priv. col.); *John, 1st Baron Somers* (1706; Wimpole Hall, Cambs, NT); *Sir Isaac Newton* (1714, Melbourne, N.G. Victoria; 1718, London, BM); and *George I* (1716; London, V&A). The busts of *Locke* and *Newton* were much imitated contributions to the iconography of these famous men. Le Marchand's subjects also included *John Churchill, 1st Duke of Marlborough* (London, V&A), the Astronomer Royal *John Flamsteed* (Greenwich, Royal Observatory), *Christopher Wren* (London, BM; London, N.P.G.) and *Thomas Guy* (London, V&A), founder of Guy's Hospital

in London. His known oeuvre stands at some 70 pieces, nearly all of them signed and some dated; 10 of his works are in the British Museum, London, and 14 in the Victoria and Albert Museum, London.

As Le Marchand's fame increased, he also pioneered the use of much thicker plaques of ivory for his reliefs, so that the head and shoulders projected to almost half their natural depth (at the scale at which he was working). He probably made preliminary models from the life in wax, the ductile nature of which influenced the way he then carved the drapery in deeply scooped, sinuous folds. Flowing locks of hair and incisively chiselled facial features complete the brilliantly characterized portraits, which are among the most impressive ever carved in ivory. Le Marchand's comparatively few statuettes are as fine as the portraits; most intricate is *Time with Opportunity and Penitence* (London, V&A), a rendering on a miniature scale of a marble group of *Saturn Abducting Cybele* (1675–8) made by Thomas Regnaudin for the château of Versailles. Another work of his own invention, a *Crucified Christ* (London, V&A), demonstrates an aptitude for rendering anatomy and emotion.

BIBLIOGRAPHY

T. Hodgkinson: 'An Ingenious Man for Carving in Ivory', *V&A Mus. Bull.*, i (1965), pp. 29–32
S. R. Houfe: 'A Whig Artist in Ivory: David Le Marchand (1674–1726)', *Ant. Colr*, xlii (1971), pp. 66–70
*The Quiet Conquest: The Huguenots, 1685 to 1985* (exh. cat., London, Mus. London, 1985), pp. 208–12, nos 303–10
C. Avery: *Studies in European Sculpture*, ii (London, 1988), pp. 241–52

CHARLES AVERY

**Lemarchand, Louis-Edouard** (*b* Paris, 9 Oct 1795; *d* Paris, 1872). French cabinetmaker. He was the son of Charles-Joseph Lemarchand (1759–1826), a cabinetmaker of repute in Paris during the Empire period. He first studied architecture but in 1813 entered the military academy at Saint Cyr. He was a strong supporter of Napoleon and was later awarded the Légion d'honneur. After the Battle of Waterloo (1815) he returned to Paris to take over his father's firm. In 1846 he entered into a partnership with André Lemoyne and retired in 1852, although the firm continued under Lemoyne until 1893. Lemarchand became official cabinetmaker to both Charles X and Louis-Philippe, supplying furniture for at least five royal palaces. Furniture from these commissions includes bookcases in Boulle marquetry (Versailles, Château) and two consoles (1838; Versailles, Grand Trianon). He showed his wares at the Exposition des Produits de l'Industrie of 1844 in Paris but in general he seems to have shunned this method of publicity and to have dealt successfully with a large private clientele. He continued to produce his furniture in the Empire style, a taste that clearly accorded with his political preferences. The craftsmanship of his work remained high and dating can be difficult, although after 1820 a preference for lighter-coloured woods is evident. An album of his designs is in the Musée des Arts Décoratifs, Paris, and some of his designs were published by Pierre La Mésangère in *Collection de meubles et objets de goût* between 1802 and 1835. His most famous work was the ebony coffin (Paris, Invalides) ordered by the government in 1840 for the ashes of Napoleon when they were brought back from St Helena.

BIBLIOGRAPHY
D. Ledoux-Lebas: *Les Ebénistes du XIXe siècle* (Paris, 1989)

SARAH MEDLAM

**Lemba.** Village on the west coast of Cyprus, *c.* 5 km north of Paphos. An important Chalcolithic (*c.* 3800–*c.* 2300 BC) site 500 m west of the village at Lemba–Lakkous, which was excavated by E. J. Peltenburg in 1976–83. Though never a major site, it nonetheless exemplifies significant trends throughout the Chalcolithic period, at the end of which it was destroyed and abandoned; most excavated Chalcolithic sites cover shorter durations. Three main periods of occupation were discerned, Lemba I–III. Finds are housed in the District Archaeological Museum, Paphos.

Lemba I (*c.* 3500–3000 BC) consisted of small circular structures with pisé walls and central platform hearths; there were vestiges of Combed ware pottery like that of the Late Neolithic period (*see* CYPRUS, §II, 4(i)). Small, plain monochrome vessels characterize the finds of this period, although one piece with relief eyes like the well-known eye-jugs from Troy has been discovered.

Lemba II (*c.* 3400–2800 BC) comprises substantial circular buildings with paved floors, painted pottery including the earliest storage vessels or pithoi in Cyprus, and the earliest complete examples of cruciform-shaped picrolite figurines, which were worn as neck pendants (*see* CYPRUS, §II, 3(i)). On the floor of the destroyed Building 1 lay a fiddle-shaped limestone female statuette (h. nearly 400 mm), its subtle modelling and symmetrical incisions contrasting with later coarsely worked representations.

In Lemba III (*c.* 2700–2400 BC) the traditional circular buildings became more varied in size and function, coroplastic art declined, pottery decoration became mainly tonal and in relief, and seal-cutting appears for the first time in Cyprus. Necklaces (which had first appeared during the Middle Chalcolithic period, contemporary with Lemba II) continued to be made of clustered dentalium shells interspersed with picrolite pendants of various shapes (Paphos, Distr. Archeaol. Mus.). In general, the latest pottery reveals few features of the succeeding Early Bronze Age styles.

BIBLIOGRAPHY
E. J. Peltenburg and others: *Excavations at Lemba Lakkous, 1976–1983* (1985), i of *Lemba Archaeological Project* (Göteborg, 1985–)

E. J. PELTENBURG

**Lemberg.** *See* L'VIV.

**Lemberger, Georg** (*b* ?Nuremberg, *c.* 1490; *d* after 1537). German painter and woodcut designer. His main achievement was to introduce the painting principles of the Danube school to Middle Germany; he worked largely in Protestant contexts. Once thought to be a native of Landshut, he was probably the son of Simon Lainberger of Nuremberg, a painter and wood-carver, and brother of Hans Leinberger, a wood-carver in Landshut. A *Christ Bearing the Cross* (*c.* 1511–12; Moosburg, St Kastulus) on the reverse of the predella on a high altar carved by Hans Leinberger, with frontal paintings (1511–14) by the Landshut court painter Hans Wertinger, is ascribed to Lemberger. Despite this link with Wertinger, his method of working owes more to the restlessly creative style of his

supposed brother, which in turn shows the influence of Albrecht Altdorfer.

Between 1513 and 1515 Lemberger may have joined Altdorfer in Regensburg and collaborated on the miniatures in the *Triumphal Procession of Emperor Maximilian I* (Vienna, Albertina). Winzinger (1973) regarded him as Altdorfer's most important collaborator on this prestigious work, ascribing him some battle scenes as well as some especially fine cavalry and foot soldiers. He may also have visited Wolfgang Huber in Passau at that time, since, although his earliest identifiable pen drawings and a woodcut (1515) depict foot soldiers similar in style to those in the triumphal procession, they also betray some of Huber's characteristics in the line drawing. Lemberger is thought to have moved *c.* 1520 to Zeitz, near Leipzig, possibly summoned there by Prince-Bishop Philipp of Freising when he was appointed Bishop of Naumburg (1517); he was granted citizenship of Leipzig on 11 June 1523. At that period he worked mainly as a designer of woodcuts for printers in Leipzig and Wittenberg. After his expulsion from Leipzig in 1532 for taking part in a Lutheran service, there is evidence that he collaborated with the printer Michael Lotter (*d c.* 1555) in Magdeburg between 1532 and 1536, but he is last recorded back in Leipzig in 1537.

The few known paintings by Lemberger are clearly linked, in their luxuriant depiction of landscape, to the Danube school and show an unusual liking for decorative detail. The (unsigned) *Epitaph for Dr Heinrich Schmidburg and his Family* (1522; Leipzig, Mus. Bild. Kst.) dates from his time in Zeitz, as does a *Crucifixion* (1522; Lössen, nr Merseburg, Pfarrkirche), and there is also a *Battle Scene* (Merseburg Cathedral), possibly depicting the Turks fighting outside Vienna. A wide panel with the contrasting themes of the *Allegory of the Fall and Redemption* (1535; Nuremberg, German. Nmus.; see fig.) illustrates the Protestant concept of the complementary connection between the Old and New Testaments, with appropriate scenes set against a luxuriant landscape.

Lemberger's talents as a draughtsman, apparent in his paintings, are even more crucial in his woodcuts. In Leipzig and Magdeburg he became one of the most important book illustrators of his period, notably in his connection with Protestant printers. The title-page of the *Prague Missal* (Leipzig, 1522) was an outstanding early work in this field, with a depiction of the four national saints of Bohemia influenced by Matthias Grünewald's famous panels of *St Erasmus* and *St Mauritius*. His minor commissions included the full coat of arms of Cardinal Albrecht of Brandenburg (1525) and two woodcuts in the Emser New Testament (Dresden, 1527) of Duke George of Saxony, besides a series of illustrations for the octavo edition of Luther's Old and New Testaments printed by Melchior Lotter II (Wittenberg, 1522–5). His masterpiece comprised 125 woodcuts for the Old Testament, first published by Michael Lotter in Johannes Bugenhagen's Low German version of the Bible (Magdeburg, 1536). All these works were skilful and monumental compositions, distinguished by a wealth of architectural forms and luxuriant landscapes in which Lemberger's debt to the Danube school is obvious. He was inevitably influenced by Lucas Cranach I, and often woodcuts by both men

Georg Lemberger: *Allegory of the Fall and Redemption*, oil on panel, 680×890 mm, 1535 (Nuremberg, Germanisches Nationalmuseum)

appear in the same volumes. There are also small but perceptible borrowings from Albrecht Dürer's repertory of form and strong links with the monogrammist MS (*fl c.* 1530, Wittenberg), who was probably from the Danube area. Lemberger's contribution to the development of woodcut design in the early Renaissance in Germany is also reflected in a large number of anonymous imitators, notably the artist known as the Master of the Jacob's Ladder, who illustrated Luther's hymns (Wittenberg, 1544).

### BIBLIOGRAPHY

Hollstein: *Ger.*; *NDB*; Thieme–Becker
L. Grote: *Georg Lemberger* (Leipzig, 1933)
——: 'Die Tafelbilder Georg Lembergers', *Pantheon*, xiv (1934), pp. 198–203
F. Winzinger: 'Zum Werk Wolf Hubers, Georg Lembergers und des Meisters der Wunder von Mariazell', *Z. Kstgesch.*, xii (1958), pp. 71–94
——: 'Unbekannte Zeichnungen Georg Lembergers', *Z. Dt. Ver. Kstwiss.*, xviii (1964), pp. 81–90
H. Bleibrunner: '36 Holzschnitte von Georg Lemberger', *Beitr. Heimatknd. Niederbayern*, ii (1970), pp. 169–209
F. Winzinger: *Die Miniaturen zum Triumphzug Kaiser Maximilians I* (Graz, 1973)
V. Liedke: *Hans Leinberger: Marginalien zur künstlerischen und genealogischen Herkunft des grossen Landshuter Bildschnitzers* (Munich, 1976), pp. 7–9
*Albrecht Altdorfer et le réalisme fantastique dans l'art allemand* (exh. cat., ed. J. and M. Guillaud; Paris, Cent. Cult. Marais, 1984), pp. 432–7
*Albrecht Altdorfer, Zeichnungen, Deckfarbenmalerei, Druckgraphik* (exh. cat., ed. H. Mielke; Regensburg, Städt. Gal., 1988), pp. 310–11

JANEZ HÖFLER

**Lembessis, Polychronis** (*b* Salamis, 1848; *d* Athens, 1913). Greek painter. He studied at the School of Fine Arts in Athens (1866–70) and the Akademie der Bildenden Künste in Munich (1875–80). He produced genre paintings, landscapes, nudes and above all portraits, while in the last years of his life he turned to religious painting in order to make a living. His painting was of the academic realist school, but, in many works, especially in his portraits (e.g. *Brother of the Artist*, *Woman with a White Scarf* and *Old Woman*, all Athens, E. Koutlides priv. col., on loan to Athens, N.G.), he revealed an exceptional ability for characterization and traces of a personal style. He died in abject poverty.

### BIBLIOGRAPHY

N. Zias: 'Polychronis Lembessis', *E ellenes zographoi* [The Greek painters], ed. S. Lydakes and A. Karakatsane, i (Athens, 1974), pp. 302–35
C. Christou: *Greek Painting, 1832–1922* (Athens, 1981), pp. 60–62

N. Misigli: *Helliniki zographiki, 18os–19os aionas* [Greek painting, 18th–19th centuries] (Athens, 1993), pp. 122–3, 206

ALKIS CHARALAMPIDIS

**Le Mercier** [Lemercier], **Jacques** (*b* Pontoise, nr Paris, *c.*1585; *d* Paris, Jan 1654). French architect and engineer. Esteemed in his own time for his knowledge of antique and contemporary Roman architecture, he was largely responsible for introducing to France influences from early 17th-century Roman church design.

1. EARLY LIFE AND WORK, TO *c.* 1630. Le Mercier was a member of a family of master masons and architects from Pontoise and probably received his early training from his father, Nicolas Le Mercier (1541–1637), who worked at Pontoise and on the church of St Eustache in Paris. In 1607 he was in Rome, for in that year he signed and dated 'from Rome' an engraving of Michelangelo's final model for the Roman church of S Giovanni dei Fiorentini. Le Mercier made other engravings and drawings in Rome, including one of the Villa Farnese, Caprarola, and he designed a catafalque in honour of Henry IV, King of France (*d* 1610). He may also have studied in Rome with the architect Rosato Rosati. By 1612 he had returned to France and subsequently worked on various engineering projects, including some for canals and bridges in Toulouse (1613–14); he also received some relatively small architectural commissions, including a convent (1612; destr.) for the Minimes at Fublaines, near Meaux, and the first amphitheatre (1617; destr.) for the medical school in Paris.

In 1624 Le Mercier received a commission to build a Parisian town house, the Palais Cardinal (later Palais Royal), for Cardinal Richelieu (*see* RICHELIEU (ii), (1)), who thereafter remained his constant patron and for whom almost all his important work was done. Le Mercier worked on the Palais Cardinal until 1636; it was burnt down in 1763, and, apart from the vestige of a façade with high-relief sculpture, nothing of his work there survives, although both drawings and engravings exist. The building was partially constructed on the foundations of an earlier house, and Le Mercier does not seem to have been entirely successful in connecting the old and the new; the coherent handling of the whole was made more difficult by the piecemeal manner in which the site became available for building. The drawings show some elaborately decorated façades, many with high-relief sculptures of ships' prows and anchors that reflected Richelieu's command of the navy. The interior contained two celebrated long galleries and a theatre built by Le Mercier in 1639, the ancestor of the present theatre of the Comédie Française at the Palais Royal, Paris (*see* THEATRE, §III, 2 (ii) and fig. 6). From 1630 Le Mercier also enlarged the Hôtel de Liancourt (formerly the Hôtel de Bouillon), Paris, which had been begun in 1612 by Salomon de Brosse. This was later destroyed, but its plan and elevations were engraved by Jean Marot and show that in this case Le Mercier's additions were very successfully combined with the older buildings. He introduced an imposing staircase into one wing of the principal court, connected to a grand vestibule in the centre of the *corps-de-logis*. Such vestibules later became a feature of French domestic planning, and the triple-entrance motif of this example was much used in the plans of Louis Le Vau.

2. MATURE AND LATE WORK, AFTER *c.* 1630. In 1631 Richelieu commissioned Le Mercier to rebuild and vastly enlarge his family château (mostly destr. 19th century) at Richelieu, near Chinon (Indre-et-Loire). The designs were Le Mercier's own, but work on site was supervised by his brothers, initially by Pierre Le Mercier and then, after his death, by Nicolas Le Mercier. The elevations, extensively engraved by Jean Marot, show that the *corps-de-logis*, with its wings and pavilions grouped around the principal court, referred back to designs by Jacques Androuet Du Cerceau (i) and his circle. Far more original is the gate (heavily restored) in the entrance screen, which, on its inner side, recalls the type of Roman church façade of the period. A section drawn by Marot through the entrance staircase pavilion of the *corps-de-logis* shows a vestibule where, if Marot's rendering is true, Le Mercier achieved a truly Roman grandeur in the interior decoration.

The buildings of the large stable court (one altered pavilion remains) seem to have been more assured than those of the main château in their design and grouping (they are shown from various angles by Marot). Such a confident relationship between the château and the service buildings seems to anticipate that achieved later by Le Vau at Vaux-le-Vicomte. The two surviving grottoes in the former gardens are of impressive, rusticated design. One, forming part of a range of wine cellars, has a huge mask of Bacchus over the entrance; the other, perhaps originally connected with the ice-house, has a human mask of similar size and striking character, formed from icicles. The two buildings were originally linked by a semicircular screen with rectangular openings, which terminated the vista of the gardens from the château. In his planning of the complex at Richelieu, Le Mercier may have had in mind 16th-century precedents of châteaux on a vast scale, for example Charleval in Normandy, and possibly also Leonardo da Vinci's designs for Romorantin. The château itself has been criticized, perhaps unfairly, as being architecturally unworthy of so grand a scheme, but it brought great prestige to its architect.

Le Mercier also designed the town of Richelieu for the Cardinal (for a further discussion on both town and château *see* RICHELIEU (i)). The town declined after Richelieu's death (1642), as it was dependent on the château and was geographically and commercially ill-placed. Nevertheless it survives, enclosed within its original walls and with its grid system of streets and Le Mercier's church mostly intact. This was the first church to be commissioned from Le Mercier by the Cardinal. It has a severe rectangular plan and an equally severe interior, its arcades articulated by a giant order of Doric pilasters. The two-storey façade is similar to that of the Jesuit noviciate church (1630–42) in Paris by Etienne Martellange, itself a near copy of Giacomo della Porta's S Maria dei Monti (1580–88), Rome. Other commissions of this period for the Cardinal included a small château at Rueil, between Paris and Saint-Germain-en-Laye, and a façade for the nearby church (both 1631–6); Le Mercier also enlarged the gardens at Rueil, which, with their grottoes, fountains and garden buildings, became celebrated. The château, church and gardens were later all destroyed.

In addition to his projects for Richelieu, Le Mercier began work for King Louis XIII at the Louvre in Paris, starting in 1630 with alterations (modified in the 19th century) to the interior of Pierre Lescot's wing. In the late 1630s he took over the project for the continuation of the west wing of the Cour Carrée at the Louvre, begun by Lescot in 1546. This commission had been given to Clément Métézeau in 1624 but had not been executed. Le Mercier doubled Lescot's wing, repeating his design and constructing the Pavillon de l'Horloge (see fig. 1) to divide the old wing from the new. The Pavillon posed a problem for Le Mercier, as it rose one storey above the three-storey wings and no order could be introduced correctly above Lescot's Corinthian and Composite orders. Le Mercier therefore substituted twin caryatids, sculpted by Jacques Sarazin, to support the pediment; this was an unusual solution, but there were precedents in earlier French architecture as well as in antiquity. The tripartite pediment itself was probably derived from della Porta's façade for Il Gesù in Rome.

Roman influence is at its most concentrated in Le Mercier's church at the Sorbonne (1635–48), the University of Paris. This is one of his most important and successful works and is the only surviving building at the Sorbonne of several on which he had been working for Richelieu since 1626. The plan of the church is very similar indeed to Rosati's S Carlo ai Catinari (begun 1612), Rome, and shares with it the strict rectangularity already seen in

the church at Richelieu. The combination of a centralized plan and a longitudinal axis is typical of a group of churches, including S Alessandro in Milan as well as S Carlo ai Catinari, which were built for the Barnabites in Italy. The Sorbonne church differs from the Italian ones, however, by having two entrances, one from the street and one in the north transept from the university courtyard. Thus the longitudinal character of the church is stressed from one entrance and the centralized character from the other. Inside, a giant order of Corinthian pilasters was used for the arcades, as at S Carlo ai Catinari; here Le Mercier employed the order with greater assurance than in the church at Richelieu, and indeed the treatment of the whole, both internally and externally, is much more monumental than in the earlier work.

It would appear that Le Mercier knew all Rosati's designs for S Carlo ai Catinari. The design of this dome, its drum articulated by clustered Corinthian pilasters separating round-headed windows, had no parallel in contemporary Rome but was closely imitated by Le Mercier at the Sorbonne. Also unprecedented in Roman or French church architecture is the free-standing portico of ten Corinthian columns supporting a triangular pediment that precedes the courtyard façade (see fig. 2); it may derive from Michelangelo's design for the façade of St Peter's or from Andrea Palladio's villa porticos. The west front of the Sorbonne church is basically a repetition of the church façades of Richelieu and Rueil, but with the addition in the lower storey of three attached Corinthian columns on each side of the entrance door, which gives it more presence and greater depth.

In 1646 Le Mercier took charge of construction of the church of the Val-de-Grâce, Paris, after the dismissal of its architect, François Mansart. The completion of the church and the design of the dome have been attributed to Le Mercier, but it is now known that the work was virtually suspended from 1646 until 1655, a year after his death, and he is not now believed to have been responsible for the work. According to an inventory made after Le Mercier's death, he had in his substantial house a library of architectural books, a considerable collection of architectural drawings and engravings, including some of Roman buildings (among them St Peter's), 80 paintings and 'nine bronze heads'.

Since most of Le Mercier's buildings have disappeared, any assessment of his work and of his contributions to French architecture must be made with considerable reservations. In his Sorbonne church he introduced a completely assimilated Roman style based on one of the most interesting of contemporary Roman churches, while also introducing Italian-inspired innovations of his own. In his secular works, however, he seems to have been less assured and innovative. It is difficult to assess how he handled grand secular interiors, although Poussin complained bitterly (but perhaps unjustly) about his architectural decoration of the vault of the Long Gallery at the Louvre; but it is possible that these interiors may well have influenced both Mansart and Louis Le Vau. Nevertheless it is probable that even if more of his secular buildings had survived, they would not be considered as important as his churches. Contemporary appreciation of both his knowledge of Roman architecture and his inter-

1. Jacques Le Mercier: Pavillon de l'Horloge, Louvre, Paris, *c.* 1640

2. Jacques Le Mercier: church of the Sorbonne, Paris, courtyard façade, 1635–48

pretation of it was expressed by Henri Sauval, the historian of the city of Paris and a contemporary of Le Mercier, who described him as 'the Vitruvius of our times'.

### BIBLIOGRAPHY

J. Marot: *Recueil des plans, profils et élevations de plusiers palais, chasteaux, églises, sépultures, grotes et hostels bâtis dans Paris* (Paris, *c.* 1660–70/*R* Farnborough, 1969) ['*Petit Marot*']

——: *Architecture françoise* (Paris, *c.* 1670); rev. as vol. iv of P. J. Mariette: *L'Architecture françoise* (Paris, 1727/*R* 1970) ['*Grand Marot*'; together with the '*Petit Marot*' and a rare col. of engrs of the château of Richelieu, this is the principal source for Le Mercier's lost work]

H. Sauval: *Histoire et recherches des antiquités de Paris* (Paris, 1724)

A. Cramail: *Le Château de Rueil et ses jardins sous le Cardinal de Richelieu et sous la Duchesse d'Aiguillon* (Paris, 1888)

R. Blomfield: *History of French Architecture, 1499–1661* (London, 1911)

L. Batiffol: *Autour de Richelieu* (Paris, 1937), pp. 113–22 [correctly dates Sorbonne bldgs]

A. F. Blunt: *Art and Architecture in France, 1500–1700*, Pelican Hist. A. (Harmondsworth, 1953, rev. 4/1980/*R* 1982)

——: 'Two Unpublished Drawings by Lemercier for the Pavillon de l'Horloge', *Burl. Mag.*, cii/691 (1960), pp. 447–8

T. Sauvel: 'De l'Hôtel de Rambouillet au Palais Cardinal', *Bull. Mnmtl*, cxvii (1960), pp. 169–90

——: 'Le Palais royal de la mort de Richelieu à l'incendie en 1763', *Bull. Mnmtl*, cxx (1962), pp. 173–90

L. Hautecoeur: *Architecture classique* (1963–7) [the fullest account of Le Mercier's work; not entirely reliable]

M. Le Moel: 'Archives architecturales parisiennes en Suède', *L'Urbanisme de Paris et de l'Europe, 1600–1680* (Paris, 1969), p. 111 [court elevations of Sorbonne bldgs]

H. Wischermann: *Schloss Richelieu* (diss., U. Freiburg, 1971)

ROSALYS COOPE

**Le Mettay, Pierre-Charles** (*b* Fécamp, Seine-Maritime, *bapt* 19 July 1726; *d* Paris, 29 March 1759). French painter. From about 1742 he was a pupil of François Boucher and in 1748 won the Prix de Rome. He was at the Académie de France in Rome from 1749 to 1753, where, in addition to copies after the Old Masters and drawings of ancient monuments, he undertook private commissions, such as the two altarpieces of the *Resurrection of Lazarus* and the *Feast in the House of Simon* that he made for Notre-Dame-de-l'Assomption at Neuville-sur-Saône, near Lyon (*in situ*). His work at this period shows the strong influence of Jean-François de Troy, Director of the Académie de France in Rome.

Having tried unsuccessfully to prolong his stay in Rome, Le Mettay spent three years travelling in Italy, first to Naples and Bologna, and then in 1755–6 to Piedmont, where he made several altarpieces for churches around Turin. It was at this time that he began to produce marine paintings in the style of Joseph Vernet, such as *The Shipwreck* (Fécamp, Mus. Cent.-A.). On his return to Paris he was approved (*agréé*) in 1757 by the Académie Royale de Peinture et de Sculpture, and in the same year he showed his only Salon exhibit, the *Infant Bacchus Restored to the Nymphs* (Lons-le-Saunier, Mus. B.-A.), which, like much of his output, betrays the strong influence of Boucher. During the rest of his brief life Le Mettay painted a number of cabinet pictures, chiefly of genre and mythological subjects. He was also involved, with Louis-Joseph Le Lorrain, in providing drawings for Julien-David Le Roy's *Ruines des plus beaux monuments de la Grèce* (1758).

### BIBLIOGRAPHY

J. Hédou: *P.-C. Le Mettay: Peintre du Roy (1726–1759)* (Rouen, 1881)

G. Chomer: 'Le Peintre Pierre-Charles Le Mettay (1726–1759)', *Bull. Soc. Hist. A, Fr.* (1981), pp. 81–102

**Lemieux, Jean Paul** (*b* Quebec, 18 Nov 1904). Canadian painter. He lived as a child in Quebec but moved with his family to Montreal in 1917 after a year in California. From 1926 to 1929 he studied art in Montreal at the College Mont-Saint-Louis and the Ecole des Beaux-Arts, after which he spent a year in Paris, where he met Clarence Gagnon, before returning to Montreal to complete his studies at the Ecole des Beaux Arts from 1930 to 1934. He began teaching there in 1934 and from 1935 also at the Ecole de Meuble in Montreal. He began around this time to paint landscapes such as *Village* (1934; Windsor, Ont., A.G.), followed soon after by dream-like figure scenes on symbolic and religious themes, such as *Lazarus* (1941; Toronto, A.G. Ont.). His early tendency to a geometric and decorative approach led him to an ever greater simplification that was especially noticeable in a mural of the mid-1950s, *Medicine in Quebec City* (3×5.5 m; Quebec, U. Laval, Mus. B.-A.), in which a group of figures is displayed in a flattened manner against an architectural background.

In 1954 Lemieux went to France for a year on a Canada Council Grant, and on his return to Quebec he was inspired by his native landscape to treat one or more isolated figures within a bleak environment characterized by simple, almost empty compositions and sombre colours, as in *The Grown-ups* (1960; Montreal, Mus. F.A.). In

Johann Philipp Lemke: battle paintings of scenes from the wars of Karl X Gustav, 1683 (Stockholm, Drottningholm Slott)

a painting such as *Summer* (1959; London, Ont., Reg. A.G.), in which a single figure is shown against a sweeping expanse of open horizon, the relationship between the person and the stark landscape produces an effect of psychological rather than actual space. The somewhat dry and rough surfaces of the paintings, together with their slight awkwardness of touch, evoke intimate moods that synthesize the atmosphere of Surrealism with a simplified Cubist structure to create a powerful sense of French Canadian identity. In 1965 he retired with his wife, the painter Madeleine Derosiers, to the Ile-aux-Coudres on the Saint Lawrence River, where he continued to paint and to collect Canadian folk art, with which he felt a particular affinity.

BIBLIOGRAPHY

G. Robert: *Jean Paul Lemieux* (Quebec, 1968)

M. Champagne and D. Morency Dutil: *Le Silenciaire: Jean Paul Lemieux* (Montreal, 1980)

CELIA RABINOVITCH

**Le Mire, Noël** (*b* Rouen, 20 Nov 1724; *d* Paris, 20 March 1801). French engraver. He began his studies at the Ecole de Dessin in Rouen, which opened in 1740. Around 1746 he proceeded to Paris to continue his studies in the studio of Jacques-Philippe Lebas, becoming one of his best students; in 1750 he won the first prize for life drawing. He was admired both for the quality of his work and for his serious character and was made a member of several academies including those of Vienna, Rouen and Lille. He engraved many seascapes after Claude-Joseph Vernet, paintings by David Teniers (i) and a number of portraits. However, he was most important as an engraver of illustrations, and through his certainty of line and the beauty of his printing he contributed to the perfection of the vignette as an art form. He interpreted drawings by Charles Eisen, Charles Nicolas Cochin (ii), Hubert-François Gravelot and Jean-Michel Moreau. Among the more important works on which he collaborated are Boccaccio's *Decameron*, after drawings by Gravelot (Paris, 1757–60); Ovid's *Metamorphoses* (Paris, 1767–71) and Montesquieu's *Temple de Gnide* (Paris, 1772), after drawings by Eisen; and Jean-Jacques Rousseau's *Oeuvres complètes* (Paris, 1774), after designs by Moreau.

Le Mire was ruined by the French Revolution (1789–95) and was obliged to continue working for publishers well into old age, often on low-quality publications. He trained his brother Antoine-Louis (1727–57), who had a very brief career as an engraver of illustrations. One of his sisters was an engraver of letters.

BIBLIOGRAPHY

Portalis–Beraldi

J. Hédou: *Noël Le Mire et son oeuvre* (Paris, 1875) [with cat. of engrs by Antoine-Louis Le Mire]

R. Portalis and H. Béraldi: *Les Graveurs du dix-huitième siècle*, ii (Paris, 1881/*R* 1970), pp. 619–50

*Inventaire du fonds français: Graveurs du XVIIIe siècle*, Paris, Bib. N., Cab. Est. cat., xiv (Paris, 1977), pp. 91–233

MADELEINE BARBIN

**Lemke** [Lembke], **Johann Philipp** [Johan Philip] (*b* Nuremberg, 19 May 1631; *d* Stockholm, 13 April 1711). German painter, draughtsman and etcher, active in Italy and Sweden. His initial studies in Hamburg, Haarlem and Nuremberg were supplemented by several years of study in Italy, where he is known to have worked in Rome and Venice and where he was strongly influenced by the battle pictures of Jacques Courtois, for whom he may have been a copyist. Many of Lemke's drawings of the 1660s depict battles between Christians and Turks, suggesting that he accompanied the Venetian army serving against the Turks in Corfu. Although his graphic work has similarities with that of Dirck Stoop, his paintings capture the soft Mediterranean light of the Italian-based masters. In 1683 he was summoned to Sweden, where he executed large battle paintings in the lower and upper galleries in Drottningholm Slott (see fig.), depicting scenes from the wars of Karl X Gustav (*reg* 1654–60) and Karl XI (*reg* 1660–97), Kings of Sweden. These works are dominated by the flat, almost bird's-eye-view wide landscape of the battlefield; foregrounds are occupied by lively, skilfully executed figures. Lemke also worked with Erik Dahlbergh on numerous drawings of lively battle scenes (Stockholm, Nmus.; Göteborg, Kstmus.).

BIBLIOGRAPHY
C. Benedikt: 'J. P. Lembke, ein deutscher Malerradierer des 17. Jahrhunderts', *Der Cicerone*, xiv/13 (1922), pp. 731–5
W. Nisser: 'En skissbok av Johan Philip Lemke i Rydboholmssamlingen' [A sketchbook of Johan Philip Lemke in the Rydboholm collection], *Konstvetenskapliga essayer och studier tillägnade A. Hahr* [Art historical essays and studies dedicated to A. Hahr] (Stockholm, 1928)
B. Magnusson: 'Lemkes bataljmålningar på Drottningholm och deras förlagor' [Lemke's battle paintings at Drottningholm and their models], *Ksthist. Tidskr.*, xlix/3 (1980), pp. 121–31

TORBJÖRN FULTON

**Lemmen, Georges** (*b* Brussels, 26 Nov 1865; *d* Brussels, 5 July 1916). Belgian painter and decorative artist. He showed a precocious talent, first exhibiting in 1875. His only formal study was at a local school of drawing. Between 1884 and 1886 he showed at the Essor group in Brussels paintings that were based on Dürer and Holbein and closely related to those of Lemmen's contemporary, Khnopff. When Lemmen became a member of Les XX in 1888 his style developed quickly, influenced principally by French Neo-Impressionism and the English Arts and Crafts Movement. Lemmen adopted the pointillist technique following Seurat's first showing with Les XX in 1887. His best pointillist canvases include *The Carousel* (1890–91; Toulon, Mme Thevenin-Lemmen priv. col., see *Belgian Art, 1880–1914*, exh. cat., New York, Brooklyn Mus., 1980, p. 118, fig. 47) as well as portraits of *Julie* (1891; Chicago, IL, A. Inst.) and *Mme Lemmen* (1894–5; Paris, Mus. d'Orsay).

In the early 1890s Lemmen became a leader in the burgeoning decorative arts movement. In 1891 he wrote an important article in *Art Moderne* on Walter Crane and created his first catalogue cover for Les XX, a work of considerable stylistic influence in the development of Art Nouveau. He designed wallpaper, rugs, tiles, mosaics, books and bookplates. As his reputation grew, Lemmen was invited to work for two Parisian galleries, S. Bing's L'Art Nouveau and Julius Meier-Graefe's La Maison Moderne, and for the Keller & Reiner and Cassirer galleries

in Berlin. He contributed decorations and art criticism to the major avant-garde journals of the day, including *Art Moderne*, *Van nu en straks*, *The Savoy*, *Dekorative Kunst* and *Die Insel*. In 1899 he created the typeface for a monumental edition of Nietzsche's *Also sprach Zarathustra* (1908), decorated by Henry Van de Velde. Except for book designs, Lemmen abandoned the decorative arts after 1902.

Like many other pointillists, Lemmen had tired of the rigours of that style by 1900. His later work included intimist paintings of children or domestic interiors in a free, relaxed style incorporating rich colours and textures. He exhibited annually with Les XX between 1889 and 1893 and often with its successor, La Libre Esthétique. In Paris he showed nine times with the Indépendants between 1889 and 1908. Although Lemmen was plagued with poverty, one-man shows at the Galerie Druet in Paris in 1906 and 1908 brought a modest change of fortune. His one financially successful exhibition was in 1913 at the Galerie Giroux, Brussels.

BIBLIOGRAPHY
'Georges Lemmen', *A. Déc.*, 12 (Sept 1899), pp. 229–61
M. Nyns: *Georges Lemmen* (Antwerp, 1954)
*G. Lemmen* (exh. cat., ed. F. Aubry; Brussels, Mus. Horta, 1980)
J. Block: 'A Study in Belgian Neo-Impressionist Portraiture', *Mus. Stud.* [A. Inst. Chicago], xiii/1 (1987), pp. 36–51
——: 'A Neglected Collaboration: Van de Velde, Lemmen and the Diffusion of the Belgian Style', *The Documented Image: Visions in Art History* (Syracuse, 1987), pp. 147–64
R. Cardon: *Georges Lemmen (1865–1916)* (Antwerp, 1990)

JANE BLOCK

**Lemoine.** *See* LEMOYNE.

**Le Moiturier, Antoine** (*b* Avignon, *c.* 1425; *d* after 1495). French sculptor. He was the nephew and probably also the pupil of Jacques Morel, with whom he may have worked on the tomb of *Charles I, Duke of Bourbon and Agnes of Burgundy* (completed 1448–53) in St Pierre, Souvigny. In 1461 Le Moiturier was commissioned by Canon Jacques Oboli to execute an altarpiece for St Pierre, Avignon. Since this work remained unfinished at the time of the patron's death, a new contract was drawn up with the church canons in 1463 for a *Last Judgement* altarpiece, to be completed within two years. It was to include Christ as Judge, four angels, sixteen figures representing the resurrected, and statues of SS Peter and Paul. From this impressive stone monument (*c.* 7 m high; destr. 17th century), there survive two three-quarter life-size angels, one supporting emblems of the Passion, the other blowing the trumpet of judgement (see fig.).

In 1462 and 1463 Le Moiturier resided in Saint-Antoine-en-Viennois, probably in order to work on the local abbey church. In 1462 he was sent to Dijon on the recommendation of Agnes of Burgundy, who described him as 'one of the most notable and expert craftsmen'. In Dijon he agreed to complete the alabaster and black marble tomb of *Duke John the Fearless and Margaret of Bavaria*, begun by JUAN DE LA HUERTA for the Charterhouse of Champmol, which was based directly on that of John's father, *Philip the Bold* (both monuments now Dijon, Mus. B.-A.). Le Moiturier worked on this project from 1463 until 1469

Antoine Le Moiturier: two stone angels from the *Last Judgement* altarpiece, St Pierre, Avignon, *c.* 1463 (Avignon, Musée du Petit Palais)

Le Moiturier's work on the ducal tomb in Dijon, with which his name is primarily identified, contributes relatively little to our understanding of his style, because his life-size effigies of the Duke and Duchess were dismembered during the French Revolution (1789–95), and their surviving condition is essentially a 19th-century reconstruction. Only the heads and hands appear to be original, but they have been altered by modern polychromy and probably partially recarved. Documents show that Le Moiturier was also responsible for a series of tiny angel figures (lost; replaced by modern copies) and for at least some of the weepers decorating the base of the monument. The nine weepers at the head of the procession, now generally attributed to him, are rather uninspired and mechanical copies of their prescribed models on the tomb of Philip the Bold.

The two angels from the *Last Judgement* altarpiece reveal the hand of an important sculptor with a developed personal style, though showing less originality than Morel. Most distinctive is their adherence to simplified triangular forms that govern the overall design as well as the handling of detail. Unlike Morel's figures, with their restless intensity, the angels give a sense of calm both in their 'frozen' striding poses and in their serene facial expressions. The drapery, creased into a discontinuous pattern of triangular folds, which, in the trumpeting angel, break sharply against the base, represents a relatively early appearance of Late Gothic forms in this part of France. These two statues, 'rediscovered' in 1973, have enabled the artist's oeuvre to be reconstructed on a new basis. Works attributed to Le Moiturier by Quarré include a statue of *St Lawrence* in the chapel of Fleurey (Côte d'Or), a bishop and an angel, perhaps representing *St Michael* (Autun, Mus. Rolin), and a *St Peter* in the church of Remilly-en-Montagne, a fine example of the fully developed Late Gothic 'Hard style' in Burgundian sculpture. The moulded facial type and the unusually rigidified drapery of this latter figure recur in the *Entombment* group (1490) in Semur-en-Auxois, Burgundy, which has also been convincingly attributed to the artist. This stylistic evidence also lends support to Le Moiturier's authorship of the tomb of *Philippe Pot* (*c.* 1480–83; Paris, Louvre), long based solely on circumstantial documentary evidence. Other attributions are no longer tenable, including the archivolt angels and prophets of the abbey church of Saint-Antoine-en-Viennois and the votive statue of a kneeling man from Poligny (*c.* 1420; Paris, Louvre).

BIBLIOGRAPHY

Abbé Requin: 'Antoine le Moiturier', *Réun. Soc. B.-A. Dépt.*, xiv (1890), pp. 96–104

H. David: *De Sluter à Sambin* (Paris, 1933), vol. i, pp. 47–9, 103–8

G. Troescher: *Die burgundische Plastik des ausgehenden Mittelalters und ihre Wirkungen auf die europäische Kunst* (Frankfurt am Main, 1940), pp. 133–40

W. Forsyth: *The Entombment of Christ: French Sculptures of the Fifteenth and Sixteenth Centuries* (Cambridge, MA, 1970), pp. 76–9

*Antoine le Moiturier: Le Dernier des grands imagiers des ducs de Bourgogne* (exh. cat., Dijon, Mus. B.-A., 1973); review by A. Erlande-Brandenburg in *Bull. Mnmtl*, cxxxi (1973), pp. 379–80

P. Quarré: 'Le Tombeau du Chanoine Oboli et les anges du retable de Saint-Pierre d'Avignon par Antoine le Moiturier', *Bull. Soc. N. Antiqua. France* (1974), pp. 30–37

——: 'Une Statue de Saint Lazare sous les traits du cardinal Rolin par Jean de la Huerta', *Études d'art français offertes à Charles Sterling* (Paris, 1975), pp. 139–43

(formal contract 1466) and remained in Dijon after its completion, although he visited Avignon regularly. He is last mentioned in 1495, when he set out to seek further work in Paris.

——: 'Les Sculptures de la chapelle de Bourbon', *Mélanges d'histoire et d'archéologie offerts au professeur Kenneth John Conant par l'association splendide Bourgogne* (Mâcon, 1977), pp. 163–72
——: *La Sculpture en Bourgogne à la fin du moyen âge* (Freiburg, 1978), pp. 22–6

J. STEYAERT

**Lemos**, Conde de [Fernández de Castro Andrade y Portugal, Pedro; Marqués de Sarria] (*b* Monforte de Lemos, 1576; *d* Madrid, 19 Oct 1622). Spanish patron. The son of Fernando Ruiz de Castro, Viceroy of Naples (1599–1601), and Catalina Sandoval, he studied at the University of Salamanca. In 1598 he married Catalina Gómez de Sandoval y Rojas, daughter of the future Duque de Lerma, Francisco Gómez de Sandoval y Rojas, and in 1603 became President of the Council of Indies. Appointed Viceroy of Naples, he arrived there on 12 July 1610. Praised for his honesty and ability, he increased the Spanish cultural presence and promoted a variety of contacts with Spain in order to reinforce Spanish hegemony. Because he did not try to diminish the power of the Neapolitan nobility, he was able to realize important administrative and financial reforms. Under his presidency he formed an academy of poetry and encouraged writers from Spain including Bartolomé Juan Leonardo de Argensola (1562–1631), Francisco de Ortigosa, Antonio Mira de Mescua (1574/7–1644) and Gabriel de Barrionuevo. Promoting a new cultural policy in Naples, he encouraged the theatre and arranged visits from Spanish companies of players. He wrote a comedy that was recited before the Accademia degli Oziosi, an important literary institution founded in 1611, which he subsidized.

On 19 August 1610 the Conde de Lemos wrote to the Spanish authorities in Porto Ercole ordering them to send to Naples a painting by MICHELANGELO MERISI DA CARAVAGGIO, who had died there on 18 July. The painting of 'St John the Baptist' has not been positively identified, but it has been suggested that it was the late work *Salome Receives the Head of John the Baptist* (London, N.G.). Between 1611 and 1613 Lemos commissioned frescoes from Giovanni Battista Caracciolo, Belisario Corenzio and Giovanni Balducci to decorate the new Palazzo Reale, Naples; Caracciolo's frescoes are probably lost. In 1615 he initiated the reorganization of the University in Naples, taking as his model the statutes of the University of Salamanca, and it was inaugurated with a parade on 14 June of that year. The façade of the new building, a former barracks that had been converted by Giulio Fontana, was decorated with the royal coat of arms prominently flanked by those of the Viceroy, all carved by Cosimo Fanzago (all now Naples, Mus. N. S Martino).

The Conde de Lemos left Naples for Spain on 8 July 1616, where he became President of the Council of Italy, an office he had to leave when his father-in-law the Duque de Lerma fell from power in 1618. Exiled to Monforte in Galicia, he devoted himself to literature and poetry. In 1622 he was allowed back to Madrid but died soon afterwards. He was patron to the most famous writers of his age: Lope de Vega (*d* 1635) was his secretary in 1598, Quevedo (Francisco Gómez de Quevedo y Villegas, 1580–1645) called him the 'honra de nuestra edad' ('the honour of our age') and Miguel de Cervantes (*d* 1616) dedicated to him his *Novelas ejemplares* (1613), *Ocho comedias* (1615), the second part of *Don Quijote* (1615) and his last novel, *Los trabajos de Persiles y Sigismunda* (1616).

BIBLIOGRAPHY
G. Barrionuevo: *Panegyricus Ill.mo et Ex.mo dño Petro Fernández a Castro Lemensium et Andradae Comiti* (Naples, 1616)
D. A. Parrino: *Teatro erocio e politico de' governi de' viceré del Regno di Napoli* (Naples, 1770), i, pp. 311–32
A. Pardo Manuel de Villena, Marqués de Rafal: *Un mecenas español del siglo XVII: El Conde de Lemos* (Madrid, 1911)
A. Bulifon: *Giornali di Napoli dal MDXLVII al MDCCVI*; ed. N. Cortese (Naples, 1932), pp. 90–101
O. H. Green: 'The Literary Court of the Conde de Lemos at Naples, 1610–15', *Hispanic Review*, i (1933), pp. 290–308
G. Coniglio: *I viceré spagnoli di Napoli* (Naples, 1967), pp. 173–92
R. Longhi: *Caravaggio* (Rome, 1968), p. 46
R. Colapietra: 'Il governo spagnolo nell'Italia meridionale (Napoli dal 1580 al 1648)', *Storia di Napoli*, v (Cava de' Tirreni, 1972), pp. 195–9
*Painting in Naples, 1606–1705* (exh. cat., ed. C. Whitfield and J. Martineau; RA, London, 1982), pp. 133–5, n. 20
*Jusepe de Ribera, lo Spagnoletto* (exh. cat., ed. C. Felton and W. B. Jordan; Fort Worth, TX, Kimball A. Mus., 1982), p. 41
M. Cinotti and G. A. Dell'Acqua: 'Caravaggio', *I pittori bergamaschi: Il seicento*, i (Bergamo, 1983), pp. 501–2 n. 50, 559–60 n. 77, 574 n. 122
E. Nappi: 'I viceré e l'arte a Napoli', *Napoli Nob.*, xxii (1983), pp. 43–4
G. Cantone: *Napoli barocca e Cosimo Fanzago* (Naples, 1984), p. 39
V. Pacelli: 'Affreschi storici in Palazzo Reale', *Seicento napoletano* (exh. cat., Naples, Capodimonte, 1984), pp. 175–7
*Bernardo Cavallino of Naples* (exh. cat., ed. A. Percy and A. T. Lurie; Cleveland, OH, Mus. A.; Fort Worth, TX, Kimball A. Mus.; 1984), p. 20
*Pintura napolitana de Caravaggio a Giordano* (exh. cat., ed. A. E. Pérez Sánchez; Prado, Madrid, 1985), p. 48
M. Causa Picone: 'Battistello frescante nel Palazzo Reale di Napoli', *Paragone*, 443 (1987), p. 17
M. Marini: *Michelangelo Merisi da Caravaggio 'pictor praestantissimus'* (Rome, 1987), pp. 102 n. 495, 561–2 n. 103, 569 n. P–36

ANTONIO VANNUGLI

**Lemos, Duarte de**, 3rd Senhor de Trofa, Itales e Pampilhosa (*d* Trofa do Vouga, nr Aveiro, 27 June 1558). Portuguese soldier and patron. He was a kinsman of important noble families and had a distinguished military career in the Middle East and East Africa (1508–11) and later in Brazil. In 1534 he was responsible for the extensive rebuilding of the parish church of Trofa do Vouga, widening and restructuring the chapel, which he intended to become his family's mausoleum. The remodelling of the ceiling is attributed to Diogo de Castilho, who gave it ribbed star vaulting, the central boss of which bears the coat of arms of the Lemos family. The group of tombs by João de Ruão was carved in the local white limestone and is arranged along the sides in four arcosolia, those on the right separated by a Corinthian pilaster and those on the left by two double columns. The structures, resting on high bases and surmounted by entablatures, are carved in the early Renaissance style popular in Coimbra and are profusely decorated at the corners with grotesques and with medallions carved with heads. A large figure in the round (1535) depicting Lemos praying is carved on the cover with great realism and is attributed to Filipe Hodart. Ruão and Hodart collaborated in similar works, for example the figure of *Dom Luis da Silveira* (1530–35) in the parish church at Góis, which Lemos no doubt knew and wished to emulate.

BIBLIOGRAPHY
A. de Lacerda: *O panteom dos Lemos na Trofa do Vouga* (Oporto, 1928)
A. N. Gonçalves: *Inventário artístico de Portugal: Distrito de Aveiro, Zona Sul* (Lisbon, 1959)

P. Dias: *A arquitectura de Coimbra na transição do gótico para a renascença, 1490–1540* (Coimbra, 1982)

MIGUEL SOROMENHO

**Lemot, François-Frédéric, Baron** (*b* Lyon, 4 Nov 1772; *d* Paris, 6 May 1827). French sculptor. He studied drawing in Besançon before travelling to Paris, where he became a pupil of Claude Dejoux. In 1790 he was awarded the Prix de Rome with a low relief of the *Judgement of Solomon* (Paris, Ecole N. Sup. B.-A.), but his studies in Rome were terminated in 1793, when he was conscripted into the French Revolutionary armies on the Rhine. In 1795 he was recalled to Paris to take part in a competition to sculpt a colossal statue of the *French People*, a project initiated by the wood-carver Jean-Louis David (father of David d'Angers) that came to nothing. Lemot made his Salon debut in 1801 with a *Bacchante* (untraced), which had already been acquired by Napoleon. In 1808 he executed a gilt-lead *quadriga* to crown the Arc de Triomphe du Carrousel, Paris; the sculpture, which incorporated the Horses of St Mark's, looted from Venice, was removed in 1815. The figure of Napoleon that had originally been intended to form part of it, was never executed. Between 1808 and 1810 Lemot sculpted a pediment (*in situ*) for the colonnade of the Musée du Louvre, Paris. It represented *Minerva and the Muses Paying Homage to Napoleon*, but in 1815 the bust of *Napoleon* was replaced by one of *Louis XIV*. Under the Bourbon Restoration Lemot was principally employed in reconstructing two equestrian statues of monarchs that had been destroyed during the Revolution (1789–95). The first, *Henry IV* (1816–18), for the parapet of the Pont Neuf, Paris, was based on the original by Giambologna and Pietro Tacca. The second statue was of *Louis XIV* (1820–25), and replaced the original by Martin Desjardins in the Place Bellecour, Lyon. Shortly before his death Lemot was rewarded for his services to the restored monarchy by being created a baron.

Lami

BIBLIOGRAPHY

**Lemoyne** [Lemoine]. French family of sculptors.

**(1) Jean-Louis Lemoyne** (*b* Paris, 1665; *d* Paris, 31 May 1755). A pupil of Antoine Coyzevox, he won the Prix de Rome in 1687 with a low relief of the *Flood* (untraced), although he did not undertake the customary journey to Italy. Instead he entered the Ecole Académique at Bordeaux, presenting as his *morceau de réception* a portrait of *Louis XIV* (walnut, 1692; untraced). While in Bordeaux he modelled his bust of *Michel Du Plessis* (marble, 1694; Bordeaux, Mus. Aquitaine), one of the principal architects of the city. By 1697 he had returned to Paris and was received (*reçu*) as a member of the Académie Royale de Peinture et de Sculpture in 1703 on presentation of a magisterial, over life-size bust of *Jules Hardouin Mansart* (marble, h. 1.1 m; Paris, Louvre).

In the period 1703 to 1710 Lemoyne was involved in decorative work and garden sculpture for the royal châteaux of Versailles; for Marly, Yvelines; and for Meudon, Hauts-de-Seine, most of which has disappeared. However, a vase carved with the attributes of summer (marble, 1726–8; New York, Frick) and a statue representing a *Companion of Diana* (marble, 1710–24; Washington, DC,

N.G.A.), both from the château of La Muette, Seine-et-Oise, give an indication of the style of his work in these genres and show the influence of Coyzevox.

In the field of religious sculpture Lemoyne executed minor works for the church of Les Invalides, Paris (1702; destr.), and at Notre-Dame, Paris (1712–13; destr.), but his surviving work is confined to the chapel at Versailles, where from 1707 to 1709 he executed stone statues of *St Simon* and *St Thaddeus* for the exterior balustrade round the roof and a number of stone reliefs for the interior, including allegorical figures of *Piety* and *Obedience* in the spandrels of the nave arcades and two depictions of the *Carrying of the Cross*, one realistic and one allegorical, on a pillar and cornerstones of the nave arcades. In 1724 he executed the funerary monument of *François de Salignac de la Mothe-Fénelon, Archbishop of Cambrai* for Cambrai Cathedral; only the powerful portrait bust (marble; Cambrai, Mus. Mun.) survived the destruction of the Cathedral in 1794.

Jean-Louis Lemoyne's earlier works are heavily marked by the moderated Baroque style of Coyzevox, who was the subject of a realistic portrait (plaster; Paris, Ecole B.-A.), but at the same time Lemoyne had a baroque taste for the colossal, as exemplified by the bust of *Mansart*. He later moved towards a less formal and more spirited style that anticipates the Rococo. This is perfectly encaptured in the lighthearted marble group of a girl and a putto called *In Fear of Cupid's Darts* (marble, *c*. 1738–9; Washington, DC, N.G.A.), that was presented by Louis XV to the Marquis de Marigny for the gardens at the château of Ménars, Loir-et-Cher, and by the lively portrait bust of the architect *Jacques Gabriel* (V) (marble, 1736; Paris, Mus. Jacquemart-André). In the latter part of his career he collaborated on some of the major projects of his son (3) Jean-Baptiste Lemoyne (ii), including the equestrian statue of *Louis XV* for Bordeaux (bronze, 1731–43; destr. 1792).

**(2) Jean-Baptiste Lemoyne (i)** (*b* Paris, *bapt* 14 Sept 1679; *d* Paris, 20 Oct 1731). Brother of (1) Jean-Louis Lemoyne. He was approved (*agréé*) by the Académie Royale in 1710 on presentation of a plaster model of *Andromeda Chained to the Rock* (untraced, see Souchal, ii, p. 358) and was received (*reçu*) as a full member in 1715 with the statuette of the *Fall of Hippolytus* (marble; Paris, Louvre), an unusual subject probably inspired by Racine's play *Phèdre*). It is a bravura piece that demonstrates mastery of technique but no distinguishing personality. He later roughed out the marble statue of *St John the Baptist*, which was part of the group of the *Baptism of Christ* (Paris, St Roch) intended for the high altar of St Jean-en-Grève, Paris, and finished by his nephew (3) Jean-Baptiste Lemoyne (ii).

**(3) Jean-Baptiste Lemoyne (ii)** (*b* Paris, 19 Feb 1704; *d* Paris, 25 May 1778). Son of (1) Jean-Louis Lemoyne. He was trained by his father and from 1723 by Robert Le Lorrain, with additional advice from the portrait painters François de Troy and Nicolas de Largillierre; he won the Prix de Rome in 1725. However, his father's ill-health and financial misfortunes obliged him to forego the usual period of study at the Académie de France in Rome and to remain in Paris, a loss of which he was always conscious. In 1728 he was approved (*agréé*) by the Académie Royale on presentation of the marble group *Pyrrhus Immolating Polyxenes on the Tomb of Achilles* (untraced), and in 1738 he was received (*reçu*) as a full member with a marble statuette of a *Young Girl Leaving the Bath* (destr.). He had a successful academic career, eventually succeeding François Boucher as Rector of the Académie in 1768.

During the 1730s Lemoyne rapidly established himself as one of the most prominent decorative and monumental sculptors in France. He was also one of the outstanding portrait sculptors of the mid-18th century, leaving a remarkable series of portrait busts of his contemporaries in which he achieved a lively and alert sense of character through his virtuoso handling of terracotta and marble. However, although he enjoyed the king's patronage and received abundant commissions, he was always in straitened financial circumstances, burdened by the numerous children of his three marriages.

Lemoyne's monumental sculpture can be divided into two groups. From 1737 to 1740 he worked on the flamboyant lead group of *Oceanus with Sea Monsters* for the Bassin de Neptune at the château of Versailles (*in situ*) and on allegorical reliefs for the pendentives of the Salon Ovale at the Hôtel de Soubise, Paris (stucco, 1735; *in situ*). At the end of his career he was commissioned by Anges-Jacques Gabriel *c*. 1770 to provide reliefs for the main courtyard of the Ecole Militaire, Paris, but he only completed the models (untraced, reliefs executed posthumously). He also executed a series of free-standing works with mythological themes, including the marble fountain group *Venus and Cupid* (1744; Paris, priv. col., see Réau, pl. xvii), the stone group *Vertumnus and Pomona* (1760; Paris, Louvre), in which contemporaries detected an allusion to the liaison of Louis XV and Mme de Pompadour, and the outstanding marble statue of *Apollo* commissioned in 1765 by Frederick the Great (Potsdam, Schloss Sanssouci).

Lemoyne's religious works were almost entirely destroyed during the French Revolution (1789–95), but the marble group of the *Baptism of Christ* for the high altar of St Jean-en-Grève, Paris, begun by his uncle (2) Jean-Baptiste Lemoyne (i) but left unfinished at his death is still in existence. This early work (now Paris, St Roch), completed in 1731, has a highly theatrical quality that also characterized his other, no longer extant, religious sculptures such as the marble statues of *St Teresa* and *St Gregory*, commissioned in 1745 and 1746 respectively, for the church of Les Invalides, Paris. Lemoyne's earliest important funerary monument was that commissioned in 1735 for the painter Pierre Mignard by his daughter the Comtesse de Feuquières for the Jacobin church in the Rue Saint-Honoré, Paris (marble and lead, completed 1743, dismantled 1795, rebuilt in reduced form 1816; Paris, St Roch). In its original form it provided an elaborate late Baroque setting for a copy of Martin Desjardins's earlier bust of *Mignard* (Paris, Louvre), but all that remains of Lemoyne's work is the figure of the Comtesse weeping over the tomb of her father. By contrast the later monument to the dramatist *Prosper Crébillon* (marble, 1762–78; Dijon, Mus. B.-A.), which was unfinished at Lemoyne's death, is a masterpiece of sentimental Neo-classicism.

In 1731 Lemoyne, aged only 26, began work on his most ambitious project, the bronze equestrian monument to *Louis XV* for the Place Royale, Bordeaux (completed 1743, destr. 1792; bronze reduction, Bordeaux, Mus. Aquitaine). He also produced a statue of the King in Roman armour commissioned by the Duc d'Antin, Surintendant des Bâtiments du Roi, in 1737 (marble, completed posthumously; Rouen, Hôtel de Ville) and an over life-size bronze group of the King accompanied by *Hygeia* and a female personification of *Brittany* for a niche in the façade of the Hôtel de Ville at Rennes (1746–54; destr. 1790s; incomplete bronze reduction, Paris, Louvre). His unexecuted but very original project for a royal monument at Rouen rejected the usual antique references and instead showed the King supported on a shield held up by three kneeling warriors (before 1765; bronze reductions of 1766, Windsor Castle, Berks, Royal Col.; and 1772, Paris, Louvre).

Lemoyne's portrait busts reinvoke French society in the mid-18th century. Appointed portraitist to the King, he created an official image that he reproduced several times (1730–73; e.g. bronze, 1751, and marble, 1769; both Paris, Louvre). He also executed busts of other members of the royal family, producing two masterpieces: the bust of the King's daughter *Mme Adélaïde* (marble, 1767; priv. col., see Réau, pl. xxxv) and the bust of *Marie-Antoinette as Dauphine* (marble, 1772; Vienna, Ksthist. Mus.). The court is also brilliantly represented in his work: two contrasting examples are the rugged portrait of *Ulrich, Maréchal de Lowendal* (terracotta, exh. Salon 1750; Angers, Mus. B.-A.) and the svelte bust of the *Comtesse de Brionne* (marble, 1765; Stockholm, Nmus.). The worlds of science and medicine are represented by the lively, Rococo busts

Jean-Baptiste Lemoyne (ii): *Charles de Secondat, Baron de Montesquieu*, marble, h. 457 mm, 1767 (Bordeaux, Musée d'Aquitaine)

of *René-Antoine Ferchault de Réaumur* (terracotta, 1751; Paris, Louvre), and *François Gigot de La Peyronie* (marble, 1748; Paris, Faculté de Médecine), while the more classically conceived busts of *Charles de Secondat, Baron de Montesquieu* (marble, 1767; Bordeaux, Mus. Aquitaine; see fig.) and *Prosper Crébillon* (plaster, *c.* 1761; Dijon, Mus. B.-A.) represent the world of literature. Among Lemoyne's portraits of fellow artists is the extraordinary, lifelike head of *Noël-Nicolas Coypel* (terracotta, 1730; Paris, Louvre). The portrait of *Mlle Clairon as Melpomene* (marble, 1761; Paris, Mus. Comédie-Fr.) represents the acting profession; and finally the busts of *René-Nicolas de Maupeou* (marble, 1768; Paris, Mus. Jacquemart-André) and *Daniel-Charles Trudaine* (marble, 1767; Paris, Louvre) represent public office.

The warmth and vitality of Jean-Baptiste Lemoyne's art, combined with his remarkable technical expertise, attracted numerous pupils to his studio, most notably four of the greatest sculptors of 18th-century France: Etienne-Maurice Falconet, Jean-Baptiste Pigalle, Jean-Jacques Caffiéri and Augustin Pajou.

BIBLIOGRAPHY

Souchal [for Jean-Louis Lemoyne and Jean-Baptiste Lemoyne (i) only]
L. Réau: *Une Dynastie de sculpteurs au XVIIIe siècle: Les Lemoyne* (Paris, 1927)

**Lemoyne** [Lemoine; Le Moyne], **François** (*b* Paris, 1688; *d* Paris, 4 June 1737). French painter and draughtsman. He may have owed his vocation to his stepfather Robert Tournières, although he certainly did not receive any instruction from him. In 1701 he went to work in the studio of Louis Galloche, and he also studied at the Académie Royale de Peinture et de Sculpture, Paris, where Nicolas Lancret was a fellow student. In 1711 he won the Premier Prix but was not awarded the usual Rome scholarship. In 1716 he was approved (*agréé*) by the Académie Royale, and in the following year he received his first commission—a series of episodes from the *Life of Christ* (Sens Cathedral) for the Franciscan convent in Amiens. In 1718 Lemoyne was received (*reçu*) as a full member of the Académie Royale, a year after Antoine Watteau, on presentation of *Hercules and Cacus* (Paris, Ecole N. Sup. B.-A.). During the following years he painted a number of religious and mythological pictures as well as producing a scheme for the ceiling of the Banque Royale in Paris (drawing, Paris, Louvre; oil sketch, Paris, Mus. A. Déc.), a commission ultimately entrusted to Giovanni Antonio Pellegrini. In 1721 Lemoyne made the acquaintance of a financier, François Berger (1684–1747), who asked him to paint *Tancred and Clorinda* (Besançon, Mus. B.-A. & Archéol.) and invited the artist towards the end of 1723 to spend several months in Italy at his expense. Although Lemoyne's contemporaries believed they could detect the influence on his subsequent work of Veronese and Parmigianino and of Michelangelo and Pietro da Cortona, Watelet noted that this brief stay came too late in Lemoyne's career to result in any real change of style. It was in Italy that he painted *Hercules and Omphale* (Paris, Louvre) and the first version of *The Bather* (Dallas, TX, priv. col.), which was begun in Bologna,

continued in Venice and finished in Rome. Both these paintings were acquired by Berger.

On his return to France, Lemoyne exhibited in the Salon of 1725 and obtained commissions for works for the Hôtel du Grand Maître and for the church of St Louis, both at Versailles. In 1727 he was one of 12 painters chosen by the Duc d'Antin, Directeur des Bâtiments du Roi, to participate in a competition designed to promote history painting. For this he submitted the *Continence of Scipio* (Nancy, Mus. B.-A.), and he shared the prize with Jean-François de Troy. It was doubtless as compensation for this only partial victory that the King commissioned him in 1729 to produce for the Salon de la Paix at the château of Versailles a great allegory of *Louis XV Giving Peace to Europe* (*in situ*; see fig.). It was also at about this time that Lemoyne worked on the décor of the Hôtel Peyrenc de Moras, Paris, and he anticipated also doing that of the Hôtel Soubise, also in Paris. The latter commission was given eventually to his pupil Charles-Joseph Natoire.

Probably in 1728, Lemoyne received his most important commission, that for the ceiling of the Salon d'Hercule at Versailles, a vast, pyramidal composition representing the *Apotheosis of Hercules* (begun 1733) in an infinite sky. Painted on canvas glued to the ceiling, it contains 142 figures and is surrounded by feigned statues and garlands of flowers, perhaps painted by Charles-Gilles Dutillieu (1697–1738). When it was completed in 1736 the ceiling was warmly praised for its skilful distribution of light and shade and was considered to have the qualities of an epic

François Lemoyne: *Louis XV Giving Peace to Europe*, oil on canvas, 3.82×2.35 m, 1729 (Versailles, Musée National du Château de Versailles et de Trianon)

poem. It won for Lemoyne the position of Premier Peintre, which he had long been anticipating. Nevertheless it also aroused jealousy and criticism, which may have contributed to his suicide in a fit of depression while seemingly at the peak of his career.

Lemoyne was one of the major French artists of the first half of the 18th century, and, through his own example and through such outstanding pupils as Natoire and François Boucher, he helped to create a new school of painting in France. His achievement cannot be fully understood without reference to Watteau, whose drawings his own (e.g. *Backview Study of a Nude Woman*, Cambridge, MA, Fogg; *Bust of a Woman*, Paris, Louvre) so much resemble. In contrast to Lancret, however, who took from Watteau the subject-matter of the *fête galante*, Lemoyne took a certain kind of figure type and a Rubensian colouring, combining them with the influence of his Italian exemplars to become the painter of his time who best represented in France the grand style of Baroque painting. Watelet wrote that he had a thorough understanding of 'la machine pittoresque' and praised his precious colours, his refined palette, the naturalness and truth of his works and the grace of his compositions and figures. Lemoyne's premature death left the field clear for Natoire, whose early works closely resemble those of his master, and to Boucher, who gave a new life to his pictorial vocabulary. Lemoyne thus helped to give a new direction to decorative painting in France and was one of the creators of the Rococo style.

BIBLIOGRAPHY

C.-H. Watelet: *Dictionnaire des arts de peinture, sculpture et gravure* (Paris, 1792)
C. Saunier: 'Lemoine', *Les Peintres français du XVIIIe siècle*, ed. L. Dimier, i (Paris, 1928), pp. 61–91
J. Wilhelm: 'François Le Moyne and Antoine Watteau', *A. Q.* [Detroit], xiv (1951), pp. 216–30
J.-L. Bordeaux: *François Le Moyne and his Generation* (Paris, 1984)

MARIANNE ROLAND MICHEL

**Lemoyne, Paul** [Saint-Paul] (*b* Paris, 1783; *d* Bordeaux, 29 May 1873). French sculptor. Having failed to win the Prix de Rome, he went to Rome at his own expense in 1809 or 1810, remaining for 50 years. There he frequented the studio of Canova and the Académie de France, becoming friendly with Ingres and later with a succession of its directors from Pierre Guérin to Victor Schnetz. In Rome he worked on several commissions from French patrons, including a plaster statue of *St Julitta at the Stake* (1827) for St Leu-St Gilles, Paris. He also regularly sent works of a Neo-classical style to the Paris Salons, exhibiting, for example, a statue of *Hope* at the 1827 Salon (marble, 1826; Paris, Louvre). He ceased to do so, however, after the critical failure of his colossal, vehemently expressive group *Medea* (marble; untraced) at the 1837 Salon.

Among Lemoyne's works in Rome, principally memorials executed for the French colony, are the bust on the monument to *Nicolas Poussin* (marble, 1829; S Lorenzo in Lucina)—a work assigned to him by Chateaubriand—and the monuments to *Claude Lorrain* (marble, 1835–40), *Guérin* (marble, 1836) and the landscape painter *Didier Boguet* (marble, 1840), all in S Luigi dei Francesi. It seems he stopped working as a sculptor *c.* 1840.

BIBLIOGRAPHY

Lami
A. Le Normand: 'Paul Lemoyne: Un sculpteur français à Rome au XIXème siècle', *Rev. A.*, 36 (1977), pp. 27–41

ANTOINETTE LE NORMAND-ROMAIN

**Le Moyne de Morgues, Jacques** (*b* Dieppe, *c.* 1533; *d* London, before 1 June 1588). French painter, illustrator and explorer, also active in Florida and London. In April 1564 he sailed with René de Laudonnière as artist of the Huguenot expedition to Florida. In September 1565 the Spaniards overran the colony, but he escaped and returned to France. By *c.* 1580 he had settled in Blackfriars, London, 'for religion' and received letters of denization on 12 May 1581. He later came into contact with Sir Walter Ralegh and his colonizing circle and with John White, the artist of the first English colony of Virginia, with whom he exchanged ideas and perhaps collaborated. Ralegh commissioned him to illustrate the Florida enterprise, and Le Moyne produced an account *Brevis narratio eorum quae in Florida . . . acciderunt . . . auctore Iacobo le Moyne* with 42 illustrations and a map that Theodor de Bry published in Frankfurt au Main in 1591 as the second part of his *Collectiones periginationum in Indiam orientalem et occidentalem*. In 1586 Le Moyne produced a book of small woodcut designs, entitled *La Clef des champs, pour trouver plusieurs animaux, tant bestes qu'oyseaux, avec plusieurs fleurs et fruitz*, to serve as models for the artist and craftsman.

Though long known through the engravings of de Bry as the portrayer of the Timucua Indians of Florida, he has more recently established a reputation as one of the earliest and most gifted botanical painters. His surviving water-colours and miniatures (e.g. London, BM and V&A) show a surprising naturalism and a highly refined sense of colour and form. Apart from one miniature (New York, Pub. Lib.), his original Florida work is lost, and the de Bry engravings contain some ethnologically unacceptable details that suggest that he made his illustrations from memory and after a lapse of time. Two drawings of a Timucua man and woman that exist only in copies by John White (London, BM) reveal, however, how convincingly he could portray Amerindian subjects.

BIBLIOGRAPHY

P. Hulton: *The Work of Jacques Le Moyne de Morgues: A Huguenot Artist in France, Florida and England*, 2 vols (London, 1977) [good pls]
——: 'Images of the New World: Jacques Le Moyne de Morgues and John White', *The Westward Enterprise: English Activities in Ireland, the Atlantic and America, 1480–1650*, ed. K. R. Andrews, N. P. Canny and P. E. H. Hair (Liverpool, 1978), pp. 195–214

PAUL HULTON

**Lempereur, Jean-Denis, II** (*b* Paris, 1701; *d* Paris, 1779). French collector, goldsmith, draughtsman and engraver. He was a member of a Parisian family of goldsmiths. In 1756 he became an alderman of the city of Paris, an appointment that conferred nobility. He was a great connoisseur who numbered among his friends artists, art dealers and art lovers, including Edmé-François Gersaint, Jean-Georges Wille and Pierre-Jean Mariette, with whom he collaborated in publishing a work on Edme Bouchardon's equestrian statue of *Louis XV* (Paris, Place Louis XV; destr.). On Mariette's death, the King urged Lempereur to purchase for him the whole of his famous collection (*see* MARIETTE, (4)); the negotiations broke down, but

Lempereur did succeed in buying 1300 drawings (Paris, Louvre).

Lempereur himself also gathered together a superb collection of works of art (1218 items, sold 24 May 1773). The greater part of the drawings from Italy and the Netherlands (such as those by Raphael and Rembrandt) had come from the CROZAT collection. He also had a notable collection of drawings by French masters that included works by Nicolas Poussin, Claude Lorrain, François Lemoyne, Edme Bouchardon and François Boucher. The 1773 sale catalogue and a manuscript inventory (see Duits) record an equally distinguished collection of Old Master and modern paintings, formerly in the collection of the Comtesse de Verrue, JEANNE-BAPTISTE D'ALBERT DE LUYNES. A portrait medallion of *Jean-Denis Lempereur*, from a drawing by Nicolas Cochin *fils*, was engraved in 1764 by Pierre Gonord (*fl c.* 1760).

Lempereur was a noted jeweller at court and among artists in Paris. He made brooches, necklaces, chains and bracelets in the shape of flowers, in enamelled gold coloured with precious stones (all examples now dispersed, but for illustrations see Jean Henri Prosper Pouget: *Traité des pierres précieuses et de la manière de les employer en parure* (Paris, 1762, pls 75–9)). Lempereur was also enthusiastic about aquatint engraving and engraved after works in his collection, for example works by Cortona, B. Castiglione and van Dyck, as well as after his own drawings.

Lempereur's son, Jean-Baptiste-Denis Lempereur (1726–96), was likewise a draughtsman and engraver, but his work is difficult to distinguish from his father's. His oeuvre includes the *Banks of the Loiret near Orléans* and the *Landscape of Aulnay, near Sceaux* (Guiffrey and Marcel, nos 9112, 9113). He was the author of a *Dictionnaire général des artistes anciens et modernes* (Paris, 1795; MS. Paris, Bib. N.).

### BIBLIOGRAPHY
P. Mantz: 'Recherches sur l'histoire de l'orfèvrerie française: iii, Dix-huitième siècle', *Gaz. B.-A.*, xi (1861), pp. 110–34, 250–61
J. Guiffrey and P. Marcel: *Inventaire général des dessins du Musée du Louvre et du Musée de Versailles*, ix (Paris, 1921), nos 9112–13 [both drgs by Jean-Baptiste-Denis Lempereur]
F. Lugt: *Marques* (1921)
*Le Dessin français dans les collections du XVIIIème siècle* (exh. cat., ed. A. Rubinstein; Paris, Gal. B.-A., 1935)
C. Duits: 'Jean-Denis Lempereur (1701–1779): A Little-known Friend of Mariette', *A.Q.* [Detroit], (1965), pp. 10–16
Y. Sjöberg: *Inventaire du fonds français: Graveurs du dix-huitième siècle*, Paris, Bib. N., Cab. Est. cat., xiv (Paris, 1977), pp. 247–54

ANNE LECLAIR

**Lempereur, Louis-Simon.** (*b* Paris, 16 May 1728; *d* Paris, 6 April 1807). French engraver. He was a pupil of Pierre Aveline (ii). Having been appointed Graveur du Roi, he was approved (*agréé*) by the Académie Royale Peinture et de Sculpture in 1759 and received (*reçu*) in 1776. His oeuvre falls into three categories. He made individual prints, mostly after the works of contemporary painters, such as François Boucher, François de Troy, Pierre-Jacques Cazes, Carle Vanloo and Jean-Baptiste Marie Pierre. However, one of his most beautiful engravings was after Peter Paul Rubens: the *Garden of Love* (1769; Sjöberg, no. 128), 700 prints of which were sold on the day of publication. The pendant to it was the *Spanish Feast* after Anthonie Palamedesz (S 134).

Lempereur also engraved about 15 portraits, including one of *Marguerite Lecomte* after Claude-Henri Watelet (S 54) and one of *Etienne Jeaurat* after Alexander Roslin (1775; S 159) that was his *morceau de réception* for admission to the Académie Royale. Lempereur's work for publishers of illustrated books included illustrations for the *Works* of Giovanni Boccaccio (1757; S 58–91) and for the *Collected Plays* of Pierre Corneille (1764; S 119–20) after drawings by Gravelot. He also contributed to the *Histoire naturelle* of Buffon (Georges-Louis Leclerc, Comte de Buffon; S 28–38) and engraved 15 plates (S 30–53) for Jean de La Fontaine's *Fables* (1755–9) after Jean-Baptiste Oudry. The engraver Nicolas de Launay was among his pupils.

Lempereur's wife, Catherine-Elisabeth Cousinet (*b* Paris, 1726), was a talented engraver who worked in the studios of Laurent Cars and Etienne Fessard (1714–77). Her best engraving was the *Flemish Grace* after Louis Le Nain (S 10). She collaborated on the 1757 Boccaccio and the Oudry *Fables* of La Fontaine. She also made engravings after Giovanni Paolo Panini and Joseph Vernet.

### BIBLIOGRAPHY
Portalis–Beraldi
Y. Sjöberg: *Inventaire du fonds français: Graveurs du dix-huitième siècle*, Paris, Bib. N., Cab. Est. cat., xiv (Paris, 1977), pp. 243–337 [S]

MADELEINE BARBIN

**Lempicka, Tamara de.** *See* DE LEMPICKA, TAMARA.

**Lemput** [Lemmput], **Remi van.** *See* LEEMPUT, REMI VAN.

**Le Muet, Pierre** (*b* Dijon, 7 Oct 1591; *d* Paris, 28 Sept 1669). French architect, military engineer and writer. He was born of good Dijon stock ('*d'épée et de robe*')—his father Philippe was a provincial guardsman in the Burgundy artillery corps. He drew closer to his artisan and contractor contemporaries, Jacques Le Mercier, François Mansart and Louis Le Vau, when in 1631 he married Marie Autissier, daughter of one of the foremost building contractors of the time, Jean Autissier (*d* 1632).

Le Muet's career as 'Architecte Ordinaire du Roi et Commis aux fortifications de Picardie' falls into two contrasting stages. In 1616, as Architecte du Roi, he was paid for a model of the Palais du Luxembourg. From 1617 he was a military engineer, and it is in this capacity that he seems to have been preoccupied until 1637 (a collection of plans of the fortified places in Picardy, 1631, is in Paris, Bib. Arsenal, MS. 4517; there are works at Péronne and Corbie, Somme, 1635–8). Apart from the ground-plan of the church of Notre-Dame-des-Victoires (1629), where building was interrupted at an early stage, his architectural activity remained, as far as is known, that of a theorist and a publisher; he produced an anthology of models for town houses, *Manière de bastir pour toutes sortes de personnes* (1623); a French translation (1631–2), from the four-language Dutch edition of 1619, of Vignola's *Regola delle cinque ordini d'architettura*, which included ten unpublished designs for doors; and a French adaptation of the First Book of Palladio (1645), pre-dating the complete and faithful version by Fréart de Chambray (1650).

The publication of *Manière de bastir*, which was destined to make Le Muet's name, was underwritten by Louis XIII himself, as he received a yearly income of 600 livres (occasionally less) from 1618 to 1636 'so as to work at designs and elevations for houses'. Le Muet derived his initial inspiration from a method employed in the unpublished sixth book of Serlio's *Architettura, degli habitationi degli uomini*, which he may have consulted in manuscript form, and from the collections of designs published by Jacques Androuet Du Cerceau (i) in 1559 and 1582. *Manière de bastir* offered designs for urban dwellings fitted to eleven sites of increasing size, starting with the smallest house possible, and for two suburban houses, all of which reflect Parisian vernacular architectural practice more faithfully than the designs of either Serlio or Du Cerceau. Reprinted three times and translated into English in 1670, *Manière de bastir* was widely known, but by 1686 the Académie Royale d'Architecture in Paris considered its content somewhat out of date, and in 1720 Tiercelet published a collection called *Architecture moderne ou l'art de bien bastir pour toutes sortes de personnes*, which was designed to replace it.

The second stage of Le Muet's career began around 1637. He produced plans for three châteaux in quick succession: Chavigny (1637–45; mainly destr. 1833), at Lerné (Indre-et-Loire), for Claude Bouthillier, financial secretary and his son, Leon, 'M. de Chavigny', Secretary of State; Pont-sur-Seine (1638–44; destr. 1814), Aube, for Claude Bouthillier; and Tanlay (1642–5), Yonne, for Michel Particelli d'Hemery, financial secretary. At Chavigny, Le Muet kept a gallery from the original Henry II château as the basic motif for the central courtyard of the new building; at Tanlay, he completed in its original style a construction begun in the 16th century, but added a vestibule–atrium in the modern taste. Only Pont-sur-Seine was started from scratch on unbuilt land. These works belong to the traditional type of square château built round a central courtyard with outlying pavilions, brought up to date by the use of a central entrance hall treated as an atrium (at Tanlay and Pont), by staircases with an open well (at Chavigny and Pont) and by an impressive arrangement of forecourts. The design of the garden at Pont, with its terraces and its sizeable canal which faces the château, is an important link between the projects for Charleval and those for Vaux-le-Vicomte and Versailles.

Using his great experience in the theory of urban dwelling construction, Le Muet also built numerous large Parisian town houses. These were for paymaster Jacques Coquet, at 18, Rue Vivienne (1639; enlarged by Jacques Bruant); for paymaster Denis Marin de la Châtaigneraie, Rue des Francs-Bourgeois (1642; still extant, enlarged in the 18th century); and, in 1643, three almost identical houses for financial administrator Jacques Tubeuf, where the Rue des Petits-Champs meets the Rue Richelieu (1643; all three destr. to make way for the Bibliothèque Nationale). These houses appear to have been designed as variants on standard plans published in *Manière de bastir*, enriched with modern features, such as broken roofs as used by Mansart (of which Le Muet was to publish sections in his 1645 edition of Palladio), a cantilevered staircase spanning from the wing to the central block (a solution that Mansart had already used at Châteauneuf), rooms with alcoves etc.

In 1644 Le Muet built a large house at 71, Rue du Temple, Paris, for Claude d'Avaux, special ambassador and negotiator of the Treaty of Westphalia at Münster. With its courtyard punctuated with regularly spaced giant order pilasters and its garden façade copied from the Louvre, the Hôtel d'Avaux is probably the finest example of that aspiration to Roman grandeur and classical purism typical of the 1640s—rather like an architectural equivalent of the paintings of Le Sueur.

In 1646 Le Muet succeeded Mansart on the site of the Hôtel de Chevry-Tubeuf (1644), and presented designs for the main stable wing and for the library, which borders the Rue Richelieu. (This is now almost destroyed, but the joinery and panelling were removed and rebuilt in the Bibliothèque Mazarin of the Collège des Quatre Nations, Paris; drawing, Copenhagen Nmus.) After this, he built a new hôtel for Jacques Tubeuf at 16, Rue Vivienne (1648–54).

In 1655, with the support of Tubeuf, steward of Anne of Austria at the Val-de-Grâce site, Le Muet succeeded Le Mercier in charge of building, which he supervised until 1666, assisted by the young Gabriel Le Duc, who seems to have undertaken more responsible duties on site from 1663. Le Muet submitted a new design for the vault of the nave, the dome and the cupola, and completed the half-finished convent, increasing it by a storey and adding a pavilion to each of its four corners, one containing the Queen's apartments.

He designed at least six more town houses: three in the Rue Neuve St-Augustin, near the Palais Mazarin, for Martin de Bermond (1657; changed beyond recognition), for Nicholas Monnerot (1657; destr.) and for Jean-Baptiste Bermond (1660; destr.); two more on the Faubourg St-Germain, for the Marquis de Laigue at 18, Rue St-Guillaume (1659) and for the Duchesse de Chevreuse on the Rue St-Dominique (1660; destr. 1877 and 1900); and finally, one in the Rue Richelieu, near the Palais Royal (1664; destr. 1873), for Antoine Ratabon, superintendent of buildings.

In his later works Le Muet remained faithful to the principle of linear room arrangement, of which he had published examples in his youth. He was less inventive than Le Vau as regards planning his designs, for the hôtels for d'Avaux, Tubeuf and Ratabon reveal a classical style less original and subtle than François Mansart's, but more elegant and correct than Le Vau's, while the bareness of the Hôtel de Laigue anticipates the severe style of Pierre Bullet.

Following perhaps the example of Palladio, Le Muet was the first French architect to publish an anthology of his own works, *Nouveaux Bastimens faits en France par le sieur Le Muet*, which he added to the 1647 reprint of his *Manière de bastir*. In addition, Val-de-Grâce and four late town houses were published in Jean Marot's collections. For Henri Sauval (1724), he was the equal of Le Mercier or Mansart, 'one of the finest architects of his age'.

### WRITINGS

*Manière de bastir pour toutes sortes de personnes* (Paris, 1623); rev. with added section of 31 plates as *Nouveaux Bastimens faits en France par le sieur Le Muet* (Paris, 1647; 2/1663–4; 3/1681); Eng. trans. as *Art of Fair Building* (London, 1670); ed. C. Mignot (Aix-en-Provence, 1)
*Règles des cinq ordres d'architecture de Vignole reveue augmentées et reduites de grand en petit par le Muet* (Paris, 1631/2)
*Traité des cinq ordres d'architecture traduit du Palladio, augmenté de nouvelles inventions pour l'art de bien bastir par le sr Le Muet* (Paris, 1645, 2/1647);

Eng. trans. as *The First Book of Architecture by Andrea Palladio. . .with an Appendix Touching Doors and Windows by Pierre Le Muet* (London 1663) [there were 7 edns of the trans.]

BIBLIOGRAPHY

H. Sauval: *Histoire et recherches des antiquités de la ville de Paris* (Paris, 1724/R 1974)

J. Mauban: *Jean Marot* (Paris, 1944)

R. A. Weigert: 'Le Palais Mazarin, architectes et décorateurs', *A. France*, ii (1962), pp. 147–69

J. P. Babelon: 'L'Hôtel d'Assy, oeuvre de Pierre le Muet', *Mém. Féd. Soc. Paris & Ile-de-France* (1965–6), pp. 231–40

C. Mignot: 'L'Eglise du Val-de-Grâce: Nouveaux Documents, 1645–7', *Bull. Soc. Hist. A. Fr.* (1975), pp. 101–36

——: *Pierre le Muet, architecte (1591–1669)* (diss., A.N.R.T., U. Lille III, n.d.; microfilm)

——: *De Val-de-Grâce, l'ermitage d'une reine* (Paris, 1994)

CLAUDE MIGNOT

**Le Nain** [Lenain]. French family of painters. Antoine Le Nain (*b* ?Laon, *c.* 1600; *bur* Paris, 26 May 1648) and his brothers Louis Le Nain (*b* ?Laon, *c.* 1600; *bur* Paris, 24 May 1648) and Mathieu Le Nain (*b* Laon, *c.* 1607; *bur* Paris, 26 April 1677) lived together and shared a studio in Paris. Since the studio was headed by Antoine, he is assumed to have been older than Louis. The brothers' reputation rests on a number of paintings signed Le Nain, on the basis of which other paintings (but no drawings) have also been attributed to them. None of the signed paintings bears a Christian name, and there is no secure way of attributing works to the individual brothers, although many attempts have been made. Eighteenth-century sale catalogues, fearful of anonymity, effectively chose from the three names at random. Since the writings of Witt (1910) and Jamot (1922) in particular, it has been habitual to ascribe small paintings on copper to Antoine, and austere, larger peasant scenes to Louis. This division of hands will be found in almost all the subsequent literature on the artists, although it must be stressed that there is no evidence at all to support it. Great efforts have also been made to identify works by Mathieu, since he survived his brothers by nearly 30 years and presumably continued to paint after their deaths in 1648. However, no such activity after 1648 is securely documented, and none of the surviving works bears a date later than 1647; and the arguments for a separate Mathieu oeuvre, though cogent, should not be regarded as conclusive. The outstanding feature of the work of the Le Nain brothers, and the basis of their celebrity since the mid-19th century, is the artists' treatment of the poor.

1. Family history and signed works. 2. Style and subject-matter. 3. Posthumous reputation.

1. FAMILY HISTORY AND SIGNED WORKS. The little that is known about the lives of the Le Nain brothers

1. Le Nain brothers: *Peasants' Supper*, oil on canvas, 0.97×1.22 m, 1642 (Paris, Musée du Louvre)

2. Le Nain brothers: *Woman and Five Children*, oil on copper, 255×320 mm, 1642 (London, National Gallery)

comes predominantly from archival documents and an early 18th-century manuscript by Claude Leleu, a canon of Laon Cathedral. They were the sons of Jeanne Prévost and Isaac Le Nain (*d* 1636), Sergent Royal au Grenier à Sel in Laon. The family was modestly prosperous and, particularly after 1615, acquired vineyards and farms in and around the town. The brothers were taught by an 'artiste étranger', although it is not clear whether this means an artist from outside the town, or a foreigner: Claude Vignon has been tentatively proposed. No work by the brothers survives in Laon: in 1793, during the Revolution, every work of art in the churches in the town and the surrounding countryside was destroyed. The brothers moved to Paris before 1629, settling in Saint-Germain-des-Prés, presumably to circumvent burdensome guild regulations in Paris itself. The Le Nain studio received a number of commissions and took on apprentices. The brothers quickly established a solid reputation, especially for their portraits, which were praised by Du Bail in his novel of 1644, and Georges de Scudéry in his *Cabinet poétique* of 1646.

Louis is hardly mentioned individually in the documents. Antoine was admitted master in the Corporation of Painters in Saint-Germain-des-Prés on 16 May 1629, and in 1632 the Bureau de la Ville de Paris commissioned from him a large group portrait of the eight members of the municipality (untraced). There are more records of

Mathieu, who in 1633 was commissioned to paint the *Descent of the Holy Ghost*, the *Assumption of the Virgin* and the *Coronation of the Virgin* in the vaults of the Lady Chapel of St Germain-des-Prés (destr.), and, according to Leleu, was appointed painter to the city of Paris. Leleu also recorded that in the same year Mathieu became a lieutenant in a Parisian military company. In 1635 he was paid for cleaning and conservation work for the Bureau de la Ville de Paris. All three were present at the first meeting of the new Académie Royale de Peinture et de Sculpture on 1 March 1648, where they were admitted as founding members. Two months later Antoine and Louis were buried at St Sulpice. The following year Mathieu presented to the Académie a portrait of *Cardinal Mazarin* (untraced). He accumulated considerable property in Paris and Laon, and his growing social pretensions can be demonstrated by his styling himself in 1658 the Lord of La Jumelle, after the name of the small family farm not far from Laon. His status apparently rising rapidly, in 1662 he was given by the King the collar of the Order of St Michel, normally restricted to those of noble birth, and a remarkable honour for a painter; it has been suggested this was because of work as a military engineer. In 1663 he was struck from the Order and in 1666 imprisoned for continuing to wear its collar. This strange sequence of events remains unexplained but strongly suggests that

Mathieu had friends, and enemies, in very high places. In 1667 he was buried, like his brothers, at St Sulpice.

Of the sixteen signed works known (all in oils), ten are also legibly dated. *Venus at the Forge of Vulcan* (canvas, 1.50×1.17 m; Reims, Mus. St-Denis) and *The Cart* (canvas, 560×720 mm; Paris, Louvre) are dated 1641; *Return from the Baptism* (canvas, 610×780 mm; Paris, Louvre), *Peasants' Supper* (canvas, 0.97×1.22 m; Paris, Louvre; see fig. 1) and *Woman and Five Children* (copper, 255×320 mm; London, N.G.; see fig. 2) are dated 1642; *La Tabagie* (canvas, 1.17×1.37 m; Paris, Louvre), the *Young Card-players* (copper, 303×383 mm; Williamstown, MA, Clark A. Inst.) and *Children Dancing* (copper, 333×402 mm; Switzerland, priv. col.) are all dated 1643; the *Adoration of the Shepherds* (canvas, 590×670 mm; Dublin, N.G.) is dated 1644, but its authenticity has been doubted; *Portraits in an Interior* (copper, 270×375 mm; Paris, Louvre) is dated 1647. The other signed paintings, which are undated or do not have a legible date, are *Three Young Musicians* (panel, 273×343 mm; Los Angeles, CA, Co. Mus. A.), *Musical Gathering* (copper, 320×400 mm; Paris, Louvre), *Old Flageolet-player* (copper, 215×290 mm; Detroit, MI, Inst. A.), *The Victory* (canvas, 1.51×1.15 m; Paris, Louvre), *Soldiers Playing Cards* (canvas, 730×910 mm; Cardiff, N. Mus.) and the *Young Card-players* (canvas, 550×640 mm; London, Buckingham Gal.). The signature of the London *Young Card-players* was revealed during cleaning in September 1994. Although portraiture was the basis of the reputation of the Le Nain brothers among their contemporaries, the only known portrait of a single sitter—a life-size, full-length portrait of the *Marquis de Trevilles*, apparently signed and dated 1644—was sold at auction in 1950 and has not been traced thereafter. None of the works by the Le Nain brothers that are mentioned in the documents is known to survive.

2. STYLE AND SUBJECT-MATTER. Although there is no evidence that any of the Le Nain brothers visited Italy, an 18th-century source refers to Louis as 'le Romain', and a number of the works attributed to the brothers shows an awareness of contemporary Italian painting that would have been hard to acquire in France. Stylistic progression cannot be discerned among the surviving signed paintings, but it is possible to propose three groupings, which appear to be the work of different hands, and to which most of the generally accepted oeuvre can be allocated (leaving aside questions of joint authorship). Not included here are a number of paintings formerly attributed to the Le Nain brothers that in the 20th century were proposed as more likely to be by followers of the Le Nains. Thirteen of these were isolated by Cuzin, while others were isolated by Jamot and Thuillier (*see* MASTERS, ANONYMOUS, AND MONOGRAMMISTS, §I: MASTER OF THE GAMES and MASTER OF THE BÉGUINS, respectively). Although inevitably the subject of much debate, the following division, essentially Rosenberg's and Cuzin's, seems defensible.

The first is an easily identifiable group of small, multi-figure paintings, on copper or on wood. Of signed works these are the *Three Young Musicians*, *Musical Gathering*, *Portraits in an Interior*, *Old Flageolet-player*, *Woman and Five Children*, the Williamstown *Card-players* and *Children Dancing*. As well as their supports, all share an awkwardness of scale, particularly where both sitting and standing figures are shown; all have brilliant colours and a looseness

3. Le Nain brothers: *The Forge*, oil on canvas, 690×570 mm (Paris, Musée du Louvre)

of handling surprising for their small dimensions. Though apparently genre scenes, they have little animation of narrative. To this group may be added a number of other pictures of children on copper, and also the *Pontifical Mass* (copper; Paris, Louvre) and *Artists in a Studio* (panel, Great Britain, priv. col.). The works in this coherent group have little in common with other Le Nain paintings. Although there is nothing to justify the convention, they have habitually been ascribed to Antoine.

A second grouping is the animated pictures. Among the signed works, *The Victory*, *Soldiers Playing Cards* and the *Adoration of the Shepherds* (if authentic) share a number of distinguishing characteristics—a greater preponderance of diagonals in composition, a smoother, looser articulation of the human form and, in the latter two pictures, a heightened intensity of facial expression. This led Cuzin and Rosenberg to see them as the nucleus of a group that includes another *Adoration of the Shepherds* (London, N.G.), the *Pilgrims at Emmaus* (Paris, Louvre) and the *Last Supper* (Paris, Louvre), a picture emphatically rejected by Blunt. They would also include in this group the *Artist's Studio* (Poughkeepsie, NY, Vassar Coll. A.G.). The artist shown in this painting wears breeches of a sort that became fashionable in Paris only after 1652, and on this basis it and all the other pictures of the group would be ascribed to Mathieu, as the only brother still living at that date. The attribution of the *Artist's Studio* is, however, uncertain, and the construction of the group, as well as its authenticity, must remain tentative.

The third group distinguishable among the signed works contains the three celebrated peasant scenes in the Louvre—*The Cart*, the *Return from the Baptism* and the *Peasants' Supper*—alike subdued in both palette and emotional register, to which may credibly be added *Venus at* the *Forge of Vulcan*, *La Tabagie* and the London *Young Card-players*. The other works of the group include *The Forge* (Paris, Louvre; see fig. 3), the *Peasant Family* (Paris, Louvre), *Peasant Interior* (St Petersburg, Hermitage), another *Peasant Interior* (Fort Worth, TX, Kimbell A. Mus.) and the *Resting Cavalier* (London, V&A; see fig. 4). In most of these pictures a group of people calmly confronts the spectator, while action is suspended, and the figures, whatever their social origins, are neither idealized nor sentimentalized. These paintings have, again without any supporting evidence, frequently been ascribed to Louis.

As there are no known extant portraits of single sitters by the Le Nain brothers, it has not been possible to form a coherent view of the brothers' portrait oeuvre. X-rays of two paintings attributed to the brothers have, however, revealed portraits below: a bust-length portrait of a young man beneath the *Flageolet-player* (London, V&A), and an older man beneath *Four Figures at Table* (London, N.G.). Both figures wear costumes of the 1630s to 1640s, and there is no apparent reason why they should not be by the same hand as the paintings now visible above them—the *Flageolet-player* being ascribed by Rosenberg to Mathieu and *Four Figures at a Table* to Louis. A large (1.16×1.46 m) group portrait, known as *The Academy* (Paris, Louvre),

and given by Rosenberg to the 'Louis' group, has been very widely doubted; Blunt even suggested it was 'nearer to Abraham Bosse'.

While much effort has been made to distinguish an oeuvre for each brother, some paintings are almost certainly collaborative efforts. Sauval, writing, while Mathieu was still alive, of the St Germain chapel decorations (destr.), asserted that all three brothers painted heads in the *Assumption of the Virgin* and *Coronation of the Virgin*. Mariette said of Antoine and Louis that 'hardly a painting left their studio in which both had not had a hand', and this assertion of multiple authorship seems to be borne out by examination. Many pictures show extensive re-working: technical analysis of another *Peasant Family* in the Le Nain oeuvre (Petworth House, W. Sussex, NT) suggests two artists at work, with quite different palettes. Future analysis might reveal similar results in other paintings. Rosenberg argued convincingly that the *Birth of the Virgin* (Paris, Notre-Dame) has passages in two clearly distinguishable styles.

While in their religious and allegorical works there is little that cannot be paralleled in contemporary Flemish or Italian painting, it would be hard to find any other 17th-century European paintings in which farm-workers or

4. Le Nain brothers: *Resting Cavalier*, oil on canvas, 546×673 mm (London, Victoria and Albert Museum)

paupers are represented with such tranquil dignity and with so little hint of mockery or condescension as the work of the Le Nain brothers. The figures, who often look straight at the spectator, are frequently shown at table, with bread, wine and salt. Accordingly it has often been suggested that there may be an implied religious significance. Certainly, the *Peasants' Supper* has evident compositional echoes of depictions of the Supper at Emmaus. The representation of a well-dressed man in a prosperous room (there is an expensive bed with full hangings in the background) giving food and drink to a barefoot man in ragged clothes, would clearly fit a meditation on Christian charity. A similar mood, suffused with admiration for the quiet composure of the poor, pervades a number of the peasant scenes.

The proper treatment of the poor was a matter of intense debate across the whole of Europe in the mid-17th century, but it was a particular preoccupation of the pious Catholic movement in Paris and of the clergy of St Sulpice, the parish in which the three brothers lived, and where all were buried. The more evidently rural pictures, such as the *Resting Cavalier*, are no less particular. Figures, usually family groups, dressed in differing degrees of affluence or poverty, confront the viewer as they stand in landscapes to which they are often rather awkwardly related. The setting appears usually to be the countryside around Laon, where the brothers themselves owned land. In their austerity of mood, these works are far removed from any pastoral tradition in painting or literature. Like the indoor peasant pictures, their meaning and purpose remain uncertain. They may perhaps be connected with the emergence of middle-class urban landowners, who were exhorted in contemporary manuals to treat their farm-workers with the greatest respect. They may also be intended to depict the steadily deepening impoverishment during the period of the agricultural labour-force. Although the large number of copies of these pictures suggests that there was a substantial market for them, the genre found no resonance in the next generation of painters. While the surest guide to the significance of these paintings would be knowledge of their early owners, surprisingly for works by artists who were members of the Académie Royale, there is no such information available. The earliest provenance that can be established is not before 1740, when the St Petersburg *Peasant Interior* is mentioned in the inventory of Pierre Crozat. It must be assumed that the pictures quickly lost whatever meaning they may have had—certainly the religious and social preoccupations of the 1640s were rapidly superseded—or, more simply, they just went out of fashion.

3. POSTHUMOUS REPUTATION. Although disparaged by critics at the end of the 17th century—André Félibien wrote of their 'low and often ridiculous actions'—the Le Nain brothers never disappeared from view in the way that Georges de La Tour did. They figure in 18th-century sale catalogues and, not surprisingly, found increasing favour for their representations of simple country life in the years before the Revolution (1789–95). The turning-point in their reputation came with Champfleury's two studies of 1850 and 1862. In the context of the impassioned debates about Realism, he brought the brothers' work to

the attention of the public and of artists such as Manet, whose *Old Musician* (1862; Washington, DC, N.G.A.) clearly shows their influence. In the attempt to construct a view of the 17th century that went beyond Poussiniste classicism, Louis XIV and Versailles, the Le Nains were regarded as most significant. After their rehabilitation by Champfleury, the brothers were the subject of three major exhibitions: in London in 1910 (when Witt first distinguished and named three separate hands, see 1910 exh. cat.); in Paris in 1934, at the *Peintres de la réalité en France au XVIIe siècle*; and in Thuillier's monographic exhibition in Paris in 1978, the catalogue of which set a precedent for future discussion.

BIBLIOGRAPHY

Mariette
H. Sauval: *Histoire et recherches des antiquités de la ville de Paris* (Paris, 1724/*R* 1974)
Champfleury: *Essai sur la vie et l'oeuvre des Lenain, peintres laonnais* (Laon, 1850)
——: *Catalogues des tableaux des Le Nain* (Brussels, 1861)
——: *Les Peintres de la réalité sous Louis XIII: Les Frères Le Nain* (Paris, 1862)
*Catalogue of a Collection of Pictures, Including Examples of the Works of the Brothers Le Nain, and Other Works of Art* (exh. cat. by R. Witt, London, Burlington F.A. Club, 1910)
P. Jamot: 'Sur les frères Lenain', *Gaz. B.-A.*, n. s. 4, v (1922), pp. 129–36, 219–33, 293–308
——: *Les Le Nain* (Paris, 1929)
*Le Nain: Peintures, dessins etc* (exh. cat. by G. Barnaud, Paris, Petit Pal., 1934)
A. Blunt: *Art and Architecture in France, 1500–1700*, Pelican Hist. A. (Harmondsworth, 1954, rev. 3/1970)
J. Thuillier: 'Les Frères Le Nain: Une Nouvelle Oeuvre religieuse', *A. de France*, i (1961), pp. 327–8
V. Bloch: *Le Nain* (Paris, 1968)
J. P. Cuzin: 'A Hypothesis Concerning the Le Nain Brothers', *Burl. Mag.*, cxx (1978), pp. 875–6
*Les Frères Le Nain* (exh. cat. by J. Thuillier, Paris, Grand Pal., 1978) [with bibliog.]
A. Burnstock: 'Three Le Nain Paintings Re-examined', *Burl. Mag.*, cxxxv (1993), pp. 678–87
P. Rosenberg: *Tout l'oeuvre peint des Les Nain* (Paris, 1993) [with bibliog.]

NEIL MACGREGOR

**Lenbach, Franz von** (*b* Schrobenhausen, 13 Dec 1836; *d* Munich, 6 May 1904). German painter. The son of a master builder, he trained for his father's profession at the Königliche Landwirtschafts- und Gewerbeschule in Landshut, also working from 1851 in the sculpture studio of Anselm Sickinger (1807–73) in Munich. His elder brother, Karl August Lenbach (1828–47), had already become involved with painting, and it was through him that Franz Lenbach met Johann Baptist Hofner (1832–1913), an artist who had studied at the Akademie der Bildenden Künste in Munich. They went on sketching expeditions together, and Hofner introduced him to *plein-air* painting. After spending two semesters at the Polytechnische Schule in Augsburg (1852–3), and some months in the studio of Albert Gräfle (1807–89), a portrait painter in Munich, Lenbach entered the Akademie in Munich in 1854. In 1857 he attended the classes of Karl Theodor Piloty (later von Piloty), who was renowned for his history paintings. Lenbach produced his first important painting, the *Angel Appearing to Hagar in the Desert* (1858; destr.), while in this class, followed by *Peasants Trying to Take Shelter from a Thunderstorm in a Chapel* (1858; destr.; oil sketch, Schweinfurt, Samml. Schäfer). The sale of this

Franz von Lenbach: *The Artist with his Wife Lolo and his Daughters, Marion and Gabriele*, oil on pasteboard, 965×1220 mm, 1903 (Munich, Städtische Galerie im Lenbachhaus)

picture, together with a scholarship, enabled him to accompany Piloty on a journey to Rome with Ferdinand von Piloty (1828–95), Theodor Schüz (1830–1900) and Carl Ebert (1821–85). In Italy he made many oil and pencil sketches that inspired the *Arch of Titus* (1860; Budapest, Mus. F.A.) and the *Shepherd Boy* (1860; Munich, Schack-Gal.), both of which were finished after his return to Germany.

In 1860 Lenbach was offered a professorship at the newly founded Kunstschule in Weimar, on Piloty's recommendation. However he found that he did not enjoy teaching, and he returned to Munich early in 1862. He became acquainted with Adolph Friedrich Graf von Schack, who wanted to form a collection but could not afford Old Masters. Instead, he had such paintings copied by young artists, and he decided to employ Lenbach, whom he sent to Rome at the end of 1863. In Rome Lenbach met Anselm Feuerbach, Hans von Marées and Arnold Böcklin, who also produced copies for Schack. Lenbach's work pleased Schack, and he was sent to Florence in 1865, where he met the connoisseur Karl Eduard Baron von Liphart (1807–91), who introduced him to Florentine society. In Florence he painted numerous portraits, including *Ludwig I, King of Bavaria* (Munich, Wittelsbacher Ausgleichesfond) in 1866. In 1867 Lenbach

was awarded a gold medal at the Exposition Universelle in Paris, while he was on his way to Spain with the painter Ernst von Liphart (1847–1934). He continued to copy works for Schack, including Titian's *Charles V* (Munich, Schack-Gal.). In April 1868 Lenbach, Liphart and Schack travelled to Tangiers. This trip inspired Lenbach's last landscapes, such as the *Alhambra, Granada* (1868; Munich, Schack-Gal.).

Returning from Morocco in 1868, Lenbach began to spend increasing amounts of time in Vienna, where his friend Hans Makart lived. Contact with Richard Wagner, whom he painted several times (e.g. 1872; Bayreuth, Richard-Wagner-Mus.), helped him to succeed as a fashionable portrait painter in Vienna. In 1873 he painted *Emperor Francis Joseph I* (Vienna, Ksthist. Mus.), for which he was awarded a gold medal. In the summer of 1875 he travelled to Egypt with Makart, Adolf Gnauth (1840–77) and others. He produced only a few paintings on this short trip, among them *Portrait of an Arab* (1876; Munich, Lenbachhaus). On his return in 1876, he gave up his studio in Vienna and settled in Munich. In 1878 he painted his first portrait of Otto Fürst Bismarck, whom he was to paint about a hundred times, e.g. *Otto Fürst Bismarck* (1890; Munich, Lenbachhaus). From this point, Lenbach became the most celebrated contemporary German portrait painter, painting all the important men of the time, including the emperor *William I* (1886–7; Munich, Neue Pin.) and his family, *Field Marshal Helmut Graf Moltke* (1880; Bonn, Bundeskanzleramt) and the pope *Leo XIII* (1885; Munich, Neue Pin.).

In 1882 Lenbach was raised to the nobility. He bought an estate in Munich in 1886 and with his friend, the architect Gabriel von Seidl, he designed and built a Florentine villa, completed in 1891, which later became the Lenbachhaus museum. He was involved in a number of official projects, including the foundation of the Haus der Kunst and the Bayerisches Nationalmuseum in Munich. He married twice and had three daughters: Marion, Erica and Gabriele were frequently used as models, often in fancy dress, as in *Marion Lenbach Dressed in Armour* (1902; Munich, Lenbachhaus). His second wife, Charlotte (Lolo) Freiin von Hornstein (1861–1941), also appears in many of his pictures, in which his use of photography can be seen quite clearly (see fig.). His portraits are characterized by rich, Venetian colouring, vaguely historical costume and a glamorous allure that is especially apparent in such female portraits as *Fritzi Scheff with a Poodle* (1900; Munich, Lenbachhaus).

BIBLIOGRAPHY

*NDB*; Thieme–Becker
S. Wichmann: *Franz von Lenbach und seine Zeit* (Cologne, 1973)
S. Mehl: 'Franz von Lenbach', *Malerei der Gründerzeit*, München Gemälde Kataloge, vi (Munich, 1977), pp. 158–207
——: *Franz von Lenbach in der Städtischen Galerie im Lenbachhaus* (Munich, 1980)
S. von Baranow: *Franz von Lenbach: Leben und Werk* (Cologne, 1986)
——: 'Franz von Lenbach und die Fotografie', *Kst Alle: Mal., Plast., Graph., Archit.*, 12 (Dec 1986), pp. 912–17
——: *Das Lenbachmuseum Schrobenhausen* (Schrobenhausen, 1986)
W. Ranke: *Franz von Lenbach: Der Münchner Malerfürst* (Cologne, 1986)
*Franz von Lenbach, 1836–1904* (exh. cat., Munich, Lenbachhaus, 1987)

SONJA VON BARANOW

**Lencker** [Lenker], **Christoph** (*b* Ludwigsorget, *c.* 1556; *d* Augsburg, 1613). German goldsmith. He was the most outstanding goldsmith in Augsburg of the late 16th century. In 1583 he was licensed to practise as a master goldsmith in Augsburg, an increasingly important centre of goldsmithing (*see* AUGSBURG, §3(i)). His work represents the period of transition from the late Mannerist to the Baroque styles in goldsmiths' work from Augsburg, as that of Christoph Jamnitzer (*see* JAMNITZER, (2)) does in work from Nuremberg. Between 1585 and 1590 Lencker made one of three silver panels for the Reiche Kapelle in the Residenz, Munich: the framed psalm (Munich, Residenz) is held from behind by the statuette of *King David*. Like Christoph Jamnitzer, Lencker also worked for Emperor Rudolf II and for other German courts. The work that he completed in 1592 that formed part of the tribute to the Turks in that year is known only through documentary evidence. Further proof of Lencker's ability as a sculptor is the drinking vessel in the shape of a standard-bearer (Vienna, Ksthist. Mus.) that bears the initials of Archduke Ferdinand of Austria, Count of Tyrol (*reg* 1564–95), and was listed in 1596 in the inventory of Schloss Ambras, Innsbruck. In the same year Lencker was commissioned by Duke William V of Bavaria to make a silver altar for the church of the Holy Cross, Augsburg.

Lencker's most important work, a ewer and basin depicting the *Story of Europa* (ewer untraced; basin in Vienna, Ksthist. Mus.; *see* AUGSBURG, fig. 4), was also made before 1600. Several scenes from the myth, based on various engravings, are combined into one picture and arranged around a central boss on the basin. The prints used as models for this decorative feature cannot be identified with certainty. The similarity of this work to those of Adriaen de Vries and, particularly in the figural elements, to those of Hans von Aachen, who both worked for the Emperor, together with the fact that it came from the *Kunstkammer* in Prague, show that it was probably made for Rudolf II. It is not only a superb sculptural work, but it is also indicative of future stylistic developments: it is essentially Baroque in style, and its utilitarian function (shown by the incorporation of a central stand) is less important than its function as a pictorial relief framed by the flange. The ewer that accompanied it was in the form of a sculpture of *Europa and the Bull*. A version of it (1620; priv. col.) was made by Johannes Lencker I (1573–1637). A drawing (Nuremberg, Ger. Nmus.) of the bowl attributed to Johannes Lencker has a watercolour wash and therefore may be regarded as a presentation drawing rather than a preparatory design.

Other notable works made by Christoph Lencker between 1595 and 1600 include: a nautilus cup (Milan, Bib. Ambrosiana) with a figure of *Triton* forming the stem and surmounted by figures of *Venus* and *Cupid*; a ewer and basin (Nuremberg, Ger. Nmus.) with the imperial coat of arms in champlevé enamel; a tazza (Munich, Bayer. Nmus.) with the stem made of herm putti and two female herms with a coat of arms inside the bowl; and another tazza (Stuttgart, Württemberg. Landesmus.) with a relief depicting *Perseus and Andromeda*. From 1610 to 1612 Lencker held the office of Assaymaster and was a member of the Great Council of Nuremberg. From 1611 to 1613 he was recorded as an adviser, along with the painter Hans Rottenhammer I, on the so-called Pommerscher Kunstschrank (destr. 1945) that had been commissioned in Augsburg by the humanist Philipp Hainhofer.

BIBLIOGRAPHY

E. Krist: 'Goldschmiedearbeiten des Mittelalters, der Renaissance und des Barock', *Arbeiten in Gold und Silber*, v (Vienna, 1932)
H. Seling: *Die Kunst der Augsburger Goldschmiede, 1529–1868*, 3 vols (Munich, 1980)

FABIAN STEIN

**Lenckhardt, Adam** (*b* Würzburg, *bapt* 2 Sept 1610; *d* Vienna, 14 March 1661). German sculptor and ivory-carver. He was the son of Nikolaus Lenckhardt (*d* 1632), a sculptor, and first trained with his father (1622–4). He then set out on his journeyman's travels, visiting Italy in 1632. To this period of his career belongs an ivory panel representing the *Lamentation* (*c.* 1630; London, V&A). Its composition may have been based on an etching (1597) by Annibale Carracci, which was in turn indebted to Raphael. Rather more accomplished are two ivory panels of the *Lamentation* and the *Assumption of the Virgin* (both 1632; New York, Met.). Although Lenckhardt executed them while still a journeyman, they already display his complete mastery of his art. His first dated composition in the round is the group of the *Virgin and Child with St John* (1635; Vienna, Ksthist. Mus.), which bears the monogram AL. Again, the composition suggests that it was modelled on an Italian prototype. His *Cleopatra with the Asp* (Baltimore, MD, Walters A.G.), which probably belongs to the same period, may be traced back to the work of Rubens or his followers, which Lenckhardt probably knew from engravings.

In 1638 Lenckhardt was in Vienna, where he married. He was the most important ivory-carver, next to Matthias Steinl, at the imperial court in Vienna. From 1642 he worked for Charles Eusebius, Prince of Liechtenstein, being appointed court sculptor in September 1642. Lenckhardt worked chiefly in ivory and rhinoceros horn and probably also in wood and as a wax modeller. Some of his works from the period 1632 to 1653 are dated. He executed groups, reliefs and figures on religious, mythological or allegorical subjects; their style reveals his familiarity with Italian Early Baroque sculpture and with the Franconian sculptural tradition. His two figures of *St Jerome* (*c.* 1635–8) and the paired statuettes of *Vulcan* and *Venus* (*c.* 1640) appear calmer and more solid in their modelling than his earlier work, giving them a more naturalistic appearance in composition and detail. On 8 October 1646 he received a contract for a *Deposition* (1653; Cleveland, OH, Mus. A.) to be carved from one piece of ivory. The 1678 inventory of the Liechtenstein collection mentions 11 carved ivory vessels (untraced), received between 1647 and 1655.

Lenckhardt appears to have assimilated ideas from various sources, notably the work of such North Italian artists as Alessandro Vittoria. When executing works for the Prince of Liechtenstein he prepared *bozzetti* of his designs in various materials, such as wax or wood, before rendering them in costlier materials. His carvings were usually made to a scale suitable for ivory, and no large-scale work in stone, wood or bronze by him is extant. Theuerkauff (1965) has resolved an earlier problem of attribution by demonstrating that works signed *Adam Lenck* are the work of Lenckhardt.

Thieme–Becker
BIBLIOGRAPHY
E. von Philippovich: *Elfenbein: Ein Handbuch für Sammler und Liebhaber* (Brunswick, 1961, rev. Munich, 1982), pp. 195–8, 224, 333
C. Theuerkauff: 'Der Elfenbeinbildhauer Adam Lenckhardt', *Jb. Hamburg. Kstsamml.*, x (1965), pp. 27–70
——: *Die Bildwerke der Skulpturengalerie Berlin*, ii of *Nachmittelalterliche Elfenbeine* (Berlin, 1986), pp. 185–90

HANNELORE HÄGELE

**Lenehan, Andrew** (*b* Sligo, ?1805; *d* Sydney, 21 Feb 1886). Australian cabinetmaker of Irish birth. He arrived in Sydney a free settler in 1835 and started his own business in 1841 as a cabinetmaker, upholsterer and undertaker. His billhead, decorated with the royal coat of arms (indicative of vice-regal patronage), describes him as a 'Designer and Manufacturer of Superior Furniture'. His workshop was one of the most extensive mid-19th-century furniture manufactories in Sydney and attracted both official and private custom. In addition to being a prominent retailer of imported furniture, Lenehan produced a considerable amount of locally made furniture in both indigenous and imported woods. His designs drew heavily on contemporary British furniture pattern books and

catalogues. Apart from extant documented work at Government House, Sydney, examples can be found at Old Government House, Parramatta, NSW, identified by his impressed punch mark or one of several trade labels. Furniture from his workshop was exhibited in Sydney in 1854 and 1861 and at the International Exhibition of 1862 in London. Financial misadventure led to the disposal of the business by 1868, although Lenehan worked independently until his retirement *c.* 1875.

BIBLIOGRAPHY
K. Fahy: 'Andrew Lenehan: Sydney Cabinetmaker', *Australiana*, x/1 (1988), pp. 5–11

KEVIN FAHY

**Lenepveu, Jules-Eugène** (*b* Angers, 12 Dec 1819; *d* Paris, 16 Oct 1898). French painter. He began his artistic studies in 1834 with J.-M. Mercier (1786–1874), a former pupil of J.-B. Regnault, professor at the Angers drawing school and Director of Angers Museum. He obtained a municipal grant from Mercier to study at the Ecole des Beaux-Arts in Paris, and entered François-Edouard Picot's atelier in 1837. With his friend Léon Bénouville he decorated the Chapelle du Purgatoire of the church of Notre-Dame at Chantilly in 1841 and in 1842 and 1847 exhibited at the Salon with some success. In 1847 he won the Prix de Rome with the grisly *Death of Vitellius* (Paris, Ecole N. Sup. B.-A.). Before leaving for Rome, he finished a fresco for the church in Mareille (1847). He spent five years in Rome from 1848 to 1853, travelled across Italy and Sicily and copied not only the Antique but also Michelangelo, Veronese, Titian, Correggio and Raphael.

When Lenepveu returned to Paris in 1853, he produced a *Christ on the Cross* (1854) for the Palais de Justice and showed *Martyrs in the Catacombs* (Paris, Mus. d'Orsay) at the Exposition Universelle of 1855. Many of his pictures from this period drew on his memories of the Italian masters. In 1857 he showed *Venetian Wedding* (ex-E. Perreire Col.) which, wrote André Joubert, 'revealed the increasingly pronounced individuality of the artist'. His style was full of contrasting elements—an extremely academic classicism, occasionally a Baroque sensitivity and inspiration and a formal rigidity characteristic of the stylistic conventions of the period. He ceased exhibiting at the Salon in 1867.

Lenepveu was a remarkable portrait painter throughout his life: for example *Mercier* (1847; Angers, Mus. B.-A.), the *Five Joubert Ladies* (1872) and his brother *Prospère Lenepveu* (1884; both priv. cols). As a painter of religious scenes, he found his true form of expression in mural decoration. In 1857 he painted *Blessing the Hospice Chapel* for the chapel of the Hospice Général de Ste-Marie in Angers, to which he added ten scenes from the *Life of the Virgin and Christ* between 1858 and 1866. In 1859 Picot chose him to work up his sketches for the Chapelle de la Vierge in the church of Ste-Clothilde, Paris. Ten years later Lenepveu decorated the right transept with two scenes from the *Life of St Valerie*. In 1863 he painted the ceiling of the former Opéra in Rue Lepeltier, with G. Boulanger. In 1870, Lenepveu's friend, Charles Garnier, commissioned the ceiling of the new Opéra from him (obscured by Chagall's ceiling; sketch, Paris, Mus. d'Orsay). This painting, *The Muses and the Hours of Day and*

*Night*, depicted 63 figures on Mount Olympus. Painted in an elevated style and bright colours, it showed a compositional audacity reminiscent of Lanfranco and Giovanni Battista Tiepolo. From 1880 to 1890 Lenepveu did a series of cartoons for mosaics on the Daru staircase in the Louvre, on the theme of painting and antiquity (destr.). Finally, in 1889 he completed scenes from the *Life of Joan of Arc* in the Pantheon, Paris, which were used to illustrate history books for several generations.

Despite numerous honours, including election to the Institut in 1889 and the respect of his fellow artists, Lenepveu never gained a wide public reputation. The largest collection of his work is in the Musée des Beaux-Arts, Angers.

BIBLIOGRAPHY

A. Joubert: 'J. Lenepveu', *Rev. Anjou* (1881) [supernumerary issue]
F. Cormon: *Notice sur la vie et l'oeuvre de M. Jules Lenepveu* (Paris, 1899)
*Lenepveu, Dauban, Appert* (exh. cat., Angers, Soc. Amis A., 1929)
J. Foucart and L. A. Prat: *Les Peintures de l'Opéra de Paris de Baudry à Chagall* (Paris, 1980)

JEAN FOUACE

**Lenfant, Jean** (*b* Abbeville, *c.* 1620; *bur* Paris, 9 March 1674). French engraver. He was the son of a master embroiderer and learnt the trade of engraver in Paris (*c.* 1639–*c.* 1645) from his cousin Claude Mellan. After Lenfant had set up on his own in 1646, Herman Weyen published a set of his religious engravings, and Balthazar Moncornet published portraits by him; from 1657 Lenfant published his own engravings. In 1664 he married the daughter of Alexandre Boudan, printer and publisher, and in 1671 he was obliged to take over his deceased father-in-law's business, called the Image Saint-Maur, in Rue St Jacques. However, Lenfant himself died three years later, and in the same year his widow married the engraver Etienne Gantrel (1646–1706), who turned the Image Saint-Maur into a thriving print-publishing business.

Lenfant's engraved work is worthy of consideration: he produced *c.* 200 prints, 93 of them portraits; all were executed in a clear and very individual style that was both gentle and lively, showing the influences of Mellan, Charles-François Nanteuil and François de Poilly I. Most of his subjects were religious and included a *Virgin* after Claude François (1658; see Préaud, no. 3), *Virgin and Child* after Raphael (P 21) and *St Paul* after Poussin (P 49). Although Lenfant was primarily a reproductive engraver, he also drew 26 portraits from life, either in black chalk or in pastel. The only pupil to pass through Lenfant's studio was the Arlesian Jean-Louis Roullet (1645–99).

For a Lenfant engraving of an epitaph design by Nicolas Blasset *see* EPITAPH, fig. 2.

BIBLIOGRAPHY

C. Lamy-Lassalle: *Jean Lenfant: Graveur abbevillois* (1938)
M. Préaud: *Inventaire du fonds français: Graveurs du dix-septième siècle*, Paris, Bib. N., Dépt Est. cat., x (Paris, 1989) [P]

MAXIME PRÉAUD

**L'Enfant, Pierre-Charles** (*b* Paris, 2 Aug 1754; *d* Green Hill, MD, 14 June 1825). American urban planner and architect of French birth. He was born into an artistic family, members of which served the French court, and grew up in circumstances that imbued him with an appreciation for art, architecture, city planning and garden design (particularly the landscapes of André Le Nôtre at Versailles and elsewhere). In 1771 L'Enfant studied fine arts at the Académie Royale de Peinture et de Sculpture, Paris. Six years later, as a lieutenant in the French Army, he volunteered his services to the new American republic in its struggle with Great Britain. During the War of Independence (1775–81), he saw action at Valley Forge, PA, Charleston, SC, and Savannah, GA, and produced portraits and other illustrations in such quantity that he was referred to as the 'Artist of the American Revolution'. In 1782, at the request of General George Washington, L'Enfant designed a temporary pavilion (destr.) in Philadelphia for the celebration of the birth of Louis XVI's first son. In recognition of his services to the American nation, he was breveted a major in the Corps of Engineers in 1783. Soon after, L'Enfant designed the insignia and membership diploma for the newly formed Society of the Cincinnati, organized to perpetuate the ideals of the American Revolution. He returned to France in 1783 in order to work with experienced jewellery makers in casting the Society's medals. In 1784 he was in New York, where he practised architecture. Records of his commissions during this period are scarce; one project involved an addition to St Paul's Chapel (1787) to commemorate General Richard Montgomery.

From 1788 to 1789 L'Enfant was engaged on the redesigning of Federal Hall in New York (destr.) to provide a setting for the inauguration of President Washington. In 1789, as Congress took up the task of creating a new national capital city, L'Enfant approached Washington about providing the design. Washington approved of L'Enfant's appointment, and in March 1791 the designer arrived in the port city of Georgetown. By mid-1791 L'Enfant completed the design (for further discussion and illustration *see* WASHINGTON, DC, §I, 2 and fig. 1), which called for a system of radial avenues superimposed over a grid, with the conjunctions of the streets located on strategic topographical features and reinforced by the location of major public buildings and parks on them. The plan provided for a decentralized city, with growth occurring around major nodes spread throughout the city. Despite the brilliance of the plan, disagreements with the District Commissioners led to L'Enfant's dismissal in 1792. He was subsequently invited to prepare a city plan for Paterson, NJ; his design provided for radial avenues running to distant points, but it was never implemented.

From 1794 to 1796 L'Enfant designed and supervised the construction of Robert Morris's residence in Philadelphia, in a French Renaissance style with mansard roof and French windows. A grand building for its day, it was never completed and was demolished about 1800. He later drew designs for the reinforcement of Fort Mifflin, PA, and its Commandant's house. In 1800 he returned to Washington, DC, in an attempt to secure payment for his services in providing the plan for the city but to no avail. After the War of 1812, he designed and superintended the reconstruction of Fort Washington to the south of the capital, along the Potomac River.

L'Enfant was buried in Green Hill, MD, but in 1909 his remains were removed to the US Capitol to lie in state and were reinterred in Arlington National Cemetery. Around this time there was a new appreciation of his plan by the nation's leading architects and designers; when the McMillan Commission produced a new plan for the city in 1902, it cited its debt to the Neo-classical L'Enfant Plan.

BIBLIOGRAPHY

E. D. Kite, ed.: *L'Enfant and Washington, 1791–1792* (Baltimore, 1929)
H. P. Caemmerer: *The Life of Pierre Charles L'Enfant: Planner of the City Beautiful, the City of Washington* (Washington, DC, 1950)
J. Reps: *Monumental Washington: The Planning and Development of the Capital City* (Princeton, 1967)
P. D. Spreiregen, ed.: *On the Art of Designing Cities: Selected Essays of Elbert Peets* (Cambridge, MA, 1968)

ANTOINETTE J. LEE

**Lenica, Alfred** (*b* Pabianice, nr Łódź, 4 Aug 1899; *d* Warsaw, 15 June 1977). Polish painter. Between 1925 and 1928 he studied at the private studios of A. Hanytkiewicz and J. Kubowicz in Poznań. He defined his work as being the sum of influences from the ideologies of Expressionism, Surrealism and Communism (e.g. *Oil Rules the World*, 1940, and *When Youth is in the Wind*, 1948). Other paintings (e.g. *Workers*, 1932, *Illegal Executive*, 1940, and *Red Poster*, 1950) present programmatic themes in a simplified, classicizing and, regardless of scale, monumentalized form.

The problem of monumental painting allied to architecture and the urban environment was one of the theoretical slogans of the group 4F+R, which Lenica founded in Poznań in 1946. Experiments with new techniques (dripping, all-over painting, assemblage and collage), which he began in the 1950s, led him in the 1960s to devise his own technique: paint applied to the canvas in successive layers of increasingly dark colour was later removed with long, smooth, circular strokes of a spatula, revealing tones and hues hidden beneath the surface, as if sculpting the form of the painting. The turbulent, swirling compositions, often purely decorative in character, are seen as the expressive equivalents of freely interpreted psychic associations and states. Sometimes they contain allusions to figures and subjects, as in *Flowering Crystals* (1961) and *Meditations* (1967); they occasionally feature the unequivocal message of *Chile-Chile* (1973).

BIBLIOGRAPHY

B. Kowalska: *Polska awangarda malarska, 1945–1970* [Polish avant-garde painting, 1945–70] (Warsaw, 1975)
J. Bogucki: *Sztuka polski ludowej* [The art of the people's Poland] (Warsaw, 1983)

EWA MIKINA

**Lenin** [Ul'yanov], **V(ladimir) I(l'ich)** (*b* Simbirsk [later Ul'yanov], 22 April 1870; *d* Gorki [later Gorki-Leninskiye], nr Moscow, 21 Jan 1924). Russian politician and theorist. Although he had no particular interest in art and little knowledge of art history, he did make several incidental observations and appraisals that were interpreted as indisputable dogma and as a call to action, and that determined the policies of the Communist Party with regard to culture. As the initiator of the organization and literature of the party, in 1905 he proposed (in the essay 'Proletarian Organization and Proletarian Literature') the idea of the strict independence of the arts from politics and parties. In a series of articles on Lev Tolstoy he opposed universal moral codes in favour of proletarian ethics. After the October Revolution of 1917 he called for the destruction of the monuments of the old order and the realization of a utopian Monumental Propaganda Plan, for which sculptures of revolutionary and socialist figures were commissioned and created throughout Russia. (The decree 'On the Republic's Monuments' was published in *Pravda* and *Izvestiya* on 14 April 1918.) Soon afterwards he also signed a decree for the closure of the Academy of Arts in Petrograd (now St Petersburg), which was replaced in 1920 by VKHUTEMAS. He opposed Aleksandr Bogdanov's promotion of a special proletarian culture at the PROLETKUL'T, and as a result in 1920 he removed Bogdanov and curtailed the Prolet'kult's autonomous activity. In addition he denounced Futurism, with which he associated all modernist 20th-century tendencies. In his official speeches he proclaimed the idea of mastering the classical heritage. On the other hand, Lenin encouraged extreme nihilism in relation to this heritage. Subjected to official vandalism were both pre-revolutionary public monuments and churches (after Lenin's secret letter of 1922 stating the necessity of seizing church valuables, ostensibly to help those dying of starvation), whose artistic treasures were forcibly appropriated to help fill the state coffers. Basing his aesthetic ideas on those of N. G. Chernyshevsky and G. V. Plekhanov, Lenin considered the aim of art not to be the creation of élitist works but the education of the masses. He frequently repeated that art should be intelligible to the masses—a point of great importance for the Communist programme of art. He considered culture a political means and called for its conversion from an instrument of capitalism into an instrument of socialism, thereby combining the proletarian revolution and bourgeois culture.

WRITINGS

*Collected Works* (Moscow, 1964–80)
*V. I. Lenin i izobrazitel'noye iskusstvo. Dokumenty, pis'ma, vospominaniya* [V. I. Lenin and fine art. Documents, letters, reminiscences] (Moscow, 1977)

BIBLIOGRAPHY

B. Taylor: *Art and Literature under the Bolsheviks*, i (London, 1991)

SERGEY KUZNETSOV

**Leninabad.** *See* KHODZHENT.

**Leningrad.** *See* ST PETERSBURG.

**Lenk, (Kaspar-)Thomas** (*b* Berlin, 15 June 1933). German sculptor and printmaker. He studied briefly at the Staatliche Akademie der Bildenden Künste, Stuttgart (1950), before undertaking an apprenticeship as a stonemason. In the middle of the 1950s his early figurative works gave way to landscape themes, which were formally close to the predominant trend of *Art informel* (e.g. *Landscape 16: 'Scorched Earth VII'*, 1959; Stuttgart, Staatsgal.). He employed many different materials, including wood, lead, concrete, terracotta and stucco, sometimes used in combination, and his early work was clearly influenced by Giacometti. This period was followed at the beginning of the 1960s by his *Dialectical Objects* series (e.g. *Dialectical Object 13 (Bribri 1)*, 1962; priv. col., see 1976–7 exh. cat., p. 10), in which Lenk made conscious reference to Georg Wilhelm Friedrich Hegel's dialectical principle, that making art involves the intellect as well as a sensual response to the visual world. It confirmed Lenk's efforts to build a relationship between object and viewer.

In 1965, while toying with beermats, he discovered the variety of ordering possibilities within a flat, prefabricated module. He produced many sculptures based on this principle of 'layering', with contradictory spatial clues suggesting direction and movement as well as depth, but with flatness emphasized by the strong colours of the front element (e.g. *Layering 13b-Orakel, Cresta*, painted wood, 1964–5; Stuttgart, Staatsgal.). His *Inn Sculptures* series of the late 1960s (exh. Venice Biennale, 1970) were partially completed projects for large works designed to intervene in human living spaces, underlining Lenk's commitment to the social effectiveness of art. In the 1970s he made numerous large sculptures in public places, including *Stuttgart Gate* (1977) for Stuttgart. From the end of the 1970s he worked on possibilities of variation in the principle of the ruler (e.g. *ADGA 12*, 1979; Stuttgart, Staatsgal.). He was also a prolific printmaker and participated in many international print biennials.

BIBLIOGRAPHY
D. Honisch: *Lenk* (Stuttgart, 1976)
*Thomas Lenk* (exh. cat. by G. Inboden, Cologne, Kstver.; Stuttgart, Staatsgal.; 1976–7)
*Thomas Lenk: Serie ADGA* (exh. cat., Düsseldorf, Städt. Ksthalle; Tübingen, Ksthalle; Münster, Westfäl. Kstver.; 1980)
*Thomas Lenk: Skulpturen und Zeichnungen* (exh. cat., texts by H. Heissenbüttel and D. Honisch, Berlin, 1985)

EVA MEYER-HERMANN

**Lenné, Peter Joseph**, the younger (*b* Bonn, 29 Sept 1789; *d* Potsdam, 23 Jan 1866). German landscape designer and urban planner. He came from a family of horticulturists from Liège that had lived in Bonn since 1665, and he learnt botany and landscape design from his father, Peter Joseph Lenné the elder (1756–1821), in Bonn and Koblenz, and, until 1808, with his uncle Clemens Weyhe in Brühl. On visits to southern Germany in 1809 and 1812 he encountered gardens designed by Friedrich Ludwig von Sckell, and in Vienna he learnt about problems of urban planning. In Paris in 1811 he was influenced by the ideas of Gabriel Thouin (1747–1829), particularly Thouin's approach to drawing plans, use of geometrical curves and schemes for planting close to a main residence; Lenné also at this time studied architecture with Jean-Nicolas-Louis Durand. As imperial garden designer (1814–15) at Laxenburg, near Vienna, he designed the Schlosspark, most of which was executed. The following year he went to Potsdam as Gartengeselle, and in 1817 he became Gartenintendant, rising by 1854 to the rank of General Gartendirektor. Lenné's ideas, which were conceived on a grand scale (e.g. the plans for improving the Insel Potsdam, 1833 and 1842; or the plan for the Berlin Tiergarten, 1832–40, and zoo, 1833), were realized in stages and with limited resources. To alleviate the shortage of trees and trained gardeners, he founded a tree nursery and a gardeners' training institute in 1824. To encourage knowledge and interest in horticulture, he also founded the Verein zur Beförderung des Gartenbaues in den Königlich Preussischen Staaten (1822).

After laying out the Pfaueninsel (1818) and the park (1819) at Charlottenburg, Lenné produced a plan for an estate at Reichenbach in Pomerania in 1820. It was to be a model design for enhancing the beauty of the landscape and making economic improvements by growing plantations between the fields. On a visit to England in 1822 he was particularly impressed by the work of William Kent, while in the Volksgarten (1824) in Magdeburg he introduced Sckell's ideas to Prussia on a grand scale. Lenné collaborated closely with Karl Friedrich Schinkel (and later with Schinkel's pupils, who included Ludwig Persius, the designer of Lenné's house in Berlin) and with the Crown-Prince, later Frederick William IV, King of Prussia. The first and finest result of the collaboration was Charlottenhof, a southerly extension of Sanssouci, on which Lenné worked from 1825. Here, a geometrical garden attached to the house appears for the first time in the context of the reconstruction of antiquity. With variations on the basic forms of the mansion—the rectangle and the semicircle—Lenné produced a harmonious area (*c.* 1835) open to the landscaped park and leading to the 'Roman' Baths. All the subsequent gardens in and around Sanssouci (*see* POTSDAM, §2), from the Hippodrom (1835) to the Pfingstberg (1865), were conceived in relation to buildings or planned buildings and introduce a new historical element into the park design of the period.

A certain 'prettiness' in Lenné's early garden designs, derived from the 18th-century tradition and inherited from his father, gave way *c.* 1830 to a greater simplicity (compare his plans for the Tiergarten, Berlin, 1819 and 1833).

In 1840 Lenné began his urban planning work for Berlin (*see* BERLIN, §I, 3), with a project for the embellishment and demarcation of the city and its immediate surroundings. In it he tried to regulate the growth of the city and make it more human by means of squares and parks; but his urban planning schemes for such suburbs as Moabit and Tempelhof also included the provision of canals and railways. In the 1850s his advice on such problems was sought by a number of other German cities, including Munich, Leipzig and Dresden, but his plan (1858) for the Ringstrasse in Vienna was rejected as being inadequate and incapable of handling the anticipated volume of traffic. Lenné was also responsible for a large number of private gardens, particularly in Berlin, and for country houses in Prussia. A number of civic parks were also laid out to his designs. Lenné was unable to complete a projected textbook, but through his pupils, especially Gustav Meyer (1816–77), Gartendirektor in Berlin from 1871, and through his *Lehrbuch der schönen Gartenkunst*, his ideas remained influential until the late 19th century.

WRITINGS
Regular contributions to *Verhand. Ver. Beförd. Gtnbaues Kön. Preuss. Staaten* (1824–66)
*Über die Anlage eines Volksgartens bei der Stadt Magdeburg* (Berlin, 1825)
*Lehrbuch der schönen Gartenkunst* (Berlin, 1859)

BIBLIOGRAPHY
*ADB*; *NDB*; Thieme–Becker
G. A. Fintelmann: *Wegweiser auf der Pfauen-Insel* (Berlin, 1837/*R* 1986, with commentary by M. Seiler)
A. Kopisch: *Die königlichen Schlösser und Gärten zu Potsdam* (Berlin, 1845)
H. Wichmann: 'Peter Joseph Lenné hinter dem grünen Gitter', *Gesammelte Aufsätze* (Leipzig, 1887)
O. Hüttig: 'Der Park zu Babelsberg und seine Geschichte', *Der Bär*, xiv (1888), pp. 586–8
G. Sello: *Der Park von Sanssouci* (Breslau, 1889)
F. Meyer: *Der Berliner Tiergarten* (Berlin, 1892)
K. Kuhlow: *Das königliche Schloss Charlottenhof bei Potsdam* (Berlin, 1912)
H. Huth: *Der Park von Sanssouci* (Berlin, 1929)

G. Hinz: *Peter Joseph Lenné und seine bedeutendsten Schöpfungen in Berlin und Potsdam*, Kunstwissenschaftl. Studien, xxii (Berlin, 1938)

F. Bryk: *Lenné und Berlin* (Neubrandenburg, 1938)

G. Hinz: 'Peter Joseph Lennés märkische Parkanlagen', *Brandenburg. Jb.*, 14–15 (1939), pp. 68–100

A. Kutschmar: 'Berliner Städtebauprojekte von Peter Joseph Lenné', *Berlin. Heimat*, i (1961), pp. 12–18

K. K. Weber: 'Die "belebende Idee" des Glienicker Parkes', *Jb. Brandenburg. Gesch.*, xv (1964), pp. 50–59

D. Hennebo: 'Leben und Werk J. P. Lennés', *Beitr. Landespfl.*, iii (1967), pp. 1–17

G. Hinz: *Peter Joseph Lenné: Landschaftsgestalter und Städteplaner* (Göttingen, 1977) [contains a list of works]

H. Günther and S. Harksen: *Bestandskatalog der Lennépläne in der Plankammer der staatlichen Schlösser und Gärten Potsdam-Sanssouci*, 2 vols (Berlin, 1978–84, rev. 1989), iii (1990)

F. Wendland: *Berlins Gärten und Parke*, Das klassische Berlin (Frankfurt am Main and Vienna, 1979)

H. Günther: *Peter Joseph Lenné: Gärten, Parke, Landschaften* (Stuttgart, 1985)

C. A. Wimmer: *Die Gärten des Charlottenburger Schlosses* (Berlin, 1985)

M. Seiler: *Die Entwicklungsgeschichte des Landschaftsgartens Klein-Glienicke, 1796–1883* (diss., Hamburg, Hochsch. Bild. Kst., 1986)

F. von Buttlar, ed.: *Peter Joseph Lenné*, Berlin, Volkspark & Arkadien cat. (Berlin, 1989)

*6. Griefswalder Romantikkonferenz. Peter Joseph Lenné und die europäische Landschafts- und Gartenkunst im 19 Jh.: Griefswald, 1992*

H. Günther and S. Harksen: *Peter Joseph Lenné: Katalog der Zeichnungen* (Tübingen and Berlin, 1993)

EVA BÖRSCH-SUPAN

**Lennox.** English family of patrons and collectors. Charles Lennox, 1st Duke of Richmond and Lennox (1672–1723), was the natural son of Charles II, King of England and Scotland, and Louise de Keroualle, Duchess of Portsmouth. The considerable family estates, including the Jacobean house at Goodwood, W. Sussex (acquired 1697), passed in 1723 to his son (1) Charles Lennox, 2nd Duke of Richmond and Lennox, and in 1750 to his grandson (2) Charles Lennox, 3rd Duke of Richmond and Lennox. The latter was among those responsible for establishing a gallery (opened 1758) at Richmond House, Whitehall, London, the prime purpose of which was to serve as an academy providing free tuition in modelling and drawing. Goodwood remains the family's country seat and holds a substantial collection of paintings, many of which reflect the military careers and keen interest in hunting pursued by most generations of the family.

**(1) Charles Lennox**, 2nd Duke of Richmond and Lennox (*b* Goodwood, W. Sussex, 18 May 1701; *d* Godalming, 8 Aug 1750). He was Master of the Horse in 1734–5 and a Lord Justice on four occasions during the absence of King George II, becoming a prominent and popular member of the Whig oligarchy. His architectural tastes were predictably Palladian. Richard Boyle, 3rd Earl of Burlington, prepared designs for Richmond House, Whitehall (*c*. 1730; destr. 1791), and also for Foxhall (*c*. 1730), a banqueting house in the grounds of Goodwood, built for the Charlton Hunt, of which the Duke was the presiding spirit. Colen Campbell prepared a scheme for Goodwood itself, while a major folly, Carne's Seat (1743), is probably by Roger Morris: the Duchess and her daughters themselves decorated a celebrated shell grotto near by.

The Duke's equestrian interests led to his being a major patron of John Wootton, and an important group of his works remains at Goodwood, for example *Sheldon, a*

*Chestnut Hunter* (1746). His most important acquisition, documented by letters of 1726, was that of ten or more canvases from the series of allegorical paintings (now widely dispersed) commemorating *British Worthies*, which Owen McSwiny had commissioned in Italy from Giovanni Battista Piazzetta, Sebastiano Ricci and others. The connection with McSwiny led to the Duke's acquisition in 1727 of two small Venice *vedute* on copper by Canaletto (Goodwood House, W. Sussex), one of the painter's first English sales. Some twenty years later, again through the mediation of McSwiny, Canaletto was brought to the Duke's notice while in London: the result was the commission for *Whitehall and the Privy Garden from Richmond House* and the *River Thames and the City of London* (1746–7; Goodwood House, W. Sussex), a much celebrated pair of views of London from Richmond House. The Duke's interest in topographical painting was also reflected in his patronage of Antonio Joli, who painted decorative canvases at Richmond House (see Croft-Murray, ii).

UNPUBLISHED SOURCES

W. Sussex Rec. Office, Chichester [Goodwood MSS]

BIBLIOGRAPHY

Earl of March [C. Lennox, later 8th Duke of Richmond]: *A Duke and his Friends: The Life and Letters of the Second Duke of Richmond*, 2 vols (London, 1911)

W. G. Constable: *Canaletto, 1697–1768*, 2 vols (Oxford, 1962), rev. ed. J. G. Links (Oxford, 1976), i, pp. 11–17, 33; Appendix II, pp. 173–6

E. Croft-Murray: *Decorative Painting in England, 1714–1837*, 2 vols (London, 1970), ii, pp. 236, 241

G. Knox: ' "The Tombs of Famous Inglishmen" as Described in the Letters of Owen MacSwiny to the Duke of Richmond', *A. Ven.*, xxxvii (1983), pp. 228–35

FRANCIS RUSSELL

**(2) Charles Lennox**, 3rd Duke of Richmond and Lennox (*b* London, 22 Feb 1735; *d* Goodwood, W. Sussex, 29 Dec 1806). Son of (1) Charles Lennox. At 15 he inherited the family title and estates, which included Goodwood House, W. Sussex, and Richmond House, Whitehall, London. After graduating from Leiden University, he travelled in Europe with his tutor, making a five-month tour of Italy early in 1755 and returning to England late that year. In 1758 Horace Walpole wrote of a 'very grand seigneurial design', namely a gallery of plaster casts of famous statues formed at Richmond House, for the benefit of young artists and students. The idea for this 'academy', the first of its kind in England, must have come from Joseph Wilton, who advised on its formation. From November 1756 Lennox bought plaster statues from Matthew Brettingham (ii) and Wilton. Some two dozen fine statues, mostly casts from the Antique, and a number of busts, reliefs and fragments were in the gallery, which opened on 8 March 1758. Admission was free; on Saturdays Wilton and Giovanni Battista Cipriani were present to give instruction in modelling and drawing. Students included John Hamilton Mortimer, Richard Cosway, Joseph Nollekens, Joseph Farington, Thomas Jones, Tilly Kettle, Ozias Humphrey, George Earlom and George Romney. In 1763 William Parry (1742–91) exhibited a drawing (untraced) of the interior of the gallery at the Free Society of Artists, London.

The Society of Arts gave annual premiums for drawings and models made in the gallery. This continued until the spring of 1766, after which access seems to have become difficult. In his original advertisement Lennox had promised to award medals for merit, but he was soon called to his regiment, and medals were never awarded. J. T. Smith recorded misdemeanours by students, which caused Lennox to close the premises, but his account is vague as to when these events occurred; other sources suggest that students had damaged the casts. Wilton and Cipriani, who were not paid, ceased to attend after 1762, and the gallery subsequently declined. However, during its short existence, that is before the foundation of the Royal Academy in London, the Richmond House gallery had been of great benefit in encouraging 'a purer taste' in drawing. In 1770 the Incorporated Society of Artists once again obtained permission to make use of the gallery but did so only briefly. (Most of the plaster statues were sold at Christie's, London, on 19 July 1820.)

In 1758 Lennox became a member of the Society of Arts, of which he was appointed vice-president in 1761; he appears in James Barry's portrayal of the *Distribution of Premiums* (London, Royal Soc. A.). Apart from his gallery of casts, Lennox's disinterested patronage seems to have extended only to ordering marble copies (both untraced) of the *Apollo Belvedere* and Medici *Faun* from Wilton and assisting George Romney, whom he first noticed at work in his gallery, providing introductions in Rome and commissioning various portraits of his family.

In 1765–6, while serving as Ambassador to the court of Versailles, Lennox bought Gobelins tapestries, French furniture and Sèvres porcelain (Goodwood). Sir William Chambers built the stables there (1757–60) and a drawing by Chambers (1760) for the ceiling of the gallery at Richmond House survives at Sir John Soane's Museum, London, although it seems unlikely to have been executed. In 1782 Lennox employed James Wyatt to build a new river front at Richmond House, containing a fine staircase flanked by rooms; this involved removal of the gallery. Wyatt also redesigned Goodwood as a vast hollow octagon, of which only three sides were completed. Richmond House was destroyed entirely by fire in 1791, after which Lennox greatly reduced his patronage and expenditure.

BIBLIOGRAPHY
R. Dossie: *Memoirs of Agriculture*, iii (London, 1782), p. 444
E. Edwards: *Anecdotes of Painters* (London, 1808), pp. xvi–xix
J. T. Smith: *Nollekens and his Times*, ii (London, 1828), pp. 167–71
A. Graves: *The Society of Artists of Great Britain* (London, 1907), pp. 312–13
M. Whinney: *Sculpture in Britain, 1530–1830*, Pelican Hist. A. (London, 1964, rev. J. Physick, 2/1988), p. 136
M. M. Reese: *Goodwood's Oak: Life and Times of the Third Duke of Richmond, Lennox and Aubigny* (Addington, 1989)

JOHN KENWORTHY-BROWNE

**Lennox, E(dward) J(ames)** (*b* Toronto, 1855; *d* Toronto, 16 April 1933). Canadian architect. Apprenticed for five years with William Irving (1830–83) during the early 1870s, he then formed a partnership with William Frederick McGaw (*fl* 1876–82) from 1876 to 1881. During this period Lennox became thoroughly versed in the eclecticism of Victorian revival styles. Beginning with the impressive Broadway Tabernacle Church (1887–9; destr. 1930), Toronto, Lennox established his name by designing a series of masterful adaptations of H. H. Richardson's Romanesque Revival. He set a trend in the new Annex

District, Toronto's first middle- and professional-class suburb, laid out in 1887, with the Lewis Lukes House (1888–90), 37 Madison Avenue, a favourable blend of bold Romanesque forms and picturesque Queen Anne features. In this manner Lennox produced his masterpiece, Toronto's Old City Hall (its third) and Court-House (1889–99). Modelling it after Richardson's Allegheny County Court-House (1884–8), Pittsburgh, PA, Lennox enhanced his monumental, rock-faced building with polychrome stone and intricate carving.

After 1900 he designed in a range of styles with both authority and success. Indeed, Lennox was one of Toronto's most prominent and prolific architects around the turn of the century. In Toronto, notably, he contributed to the Renaissance Revival King Edward Hotel (1901–2), 37 King Street East, with the American architect Henry Ives Cobb, and to Casa Loma (*c.* 1908–14), 1 Austin Terrace, a pseudo-castle residence built for Sir Henry Pellatt.

BIBLIOGRAPHY
'E. J. Lennox': *Toronto Board of Trade Souvenir Book* (Toronto, 1893), p. 240
S. Beszedits: *Eminent Toronto Architects of the Past: Their Lives and Works* (Toronto, 1983), pp. 88–94

DAVID ROSE

**Leno** [Leni; de Lenis], **Giuliano** (*b* Rome, after 1467; *d* Rome, 12 Sept 1530). Italian building contractor and engineer. He was born into a minor but wealthy aristocratic family, whose members had made their careers in the papal service since the 14th century, mostly as lawyers or clerics. From the late 15th century Leno was engaged in a variety of agricultural and commercial activities, but his enterprises also included the management of numerous building projects, through which he was able to contribute to the realization of the major architectural creations of his friend Bramante. As the proprietor of quarries and lime-kilns and an owner of buffaloes, carts and barges for road and river transport, he was able to establish himself as an independent entrepreneur, supplying materials, tools and above all management and short-term funding for the papal building works. His knowledge of the workings and personalities within the administrations of both Rome and the papal court, his cordial rapport with the Roman aristocracy, to which he was closely related, and his control over the city gates, which he acquired under contract in the 1490s, placed him in a position of unrivalled commercial power as a contractor in the 1510s and 1520s and allowed him to accumulate great wealth, as well as a reputation for avarice.

In 1510–11 Leno was involved in the principal building projects of Pope Julius II (*reg* 1503–13): in 1510 at the Vatican Palace and the Palazzo dei Tribunali (in all probability from the inception of the works there) and in 1511 at St Peter's. On 17th June and 7 August 1510 he also undertook to construct two cloisters and a cistern at the church of S Pietro in Vincoli at the Pope's expense. Having established himself on the site of St Peter's under Pope Julius II, albeit with a limited range of tasks, Leno continued to undertake a steady flow of projects on behalf of Pope Leo X (*reg* 1513–21). These included works commissioned in association with the latter's coronation and the stables built from 1515 in the papal villa at

Magliana. On behalf of the Fabric of St Peter's he also drew up contracts with the stone-carvers who supplied capitals (1513–14, 1521), with the foremen for foundations (1514) and for the supply of quarried stone (1514). As well as a down payment, Leno gave the supplier the already established quarry, lent him props, picks and hammers for quarrying and guaranteed a fixed rate of payment in exchange for regular supplies over a period of time.

Subsequent papal projects in which Leno was involved include the construction of the Rocca di Civitavecchia, the seaport of Rome. During the years leading up to the Sack of Rome, Pope Clement VII (reg 1523–34) made use of Leno's organizational powers in a military context, sending him with Antonio da Sangallo (ii), Battista da Sangallo, Michele Sanmicheli, Antonio Labacco and others to inspect the fortifications of Parma and Piacenza. At the same time Leno also visited Modena, where he was consulted in relation to the alterations to the cathedral choir. In February 1527, as commissioner for the papal artillery, he was captured by the imperial forces of Charles V near Rome. He was subsequently empowered to cede Parma and Piacenza to the Emperor, after which he was sent to Perugia.

Leno's other building works were generally related indirectly to papal projects. In 1510, for example, he signed a contract for the construction of houses in the Planca Gardens, which had been opened up as a result of the opening of the Via Giulia. Further along the same road, adjacent to the abandoned site of the Palazzo dei Tribunali, he began in 1514 a building of his own (later the Palazzo Sacchetti), the only known instance of an independent project by Leno. The remains of Leno's building, comprising the ground floor and rows of shops on three sides of the plot, do not, however, demonstrate any architectural merit. When Antonio da Sangallo (ii) later resumed work on the site with a design of his own for the palazzo, he had to exercise particular ingenuity to incorporate a main staircase satisfactorily.

BIBLIOGRAPHY

Thieme–Becker
G. Vasari: *Vite* (1550, rev. 2/1568); ed. G. Milanesi (1878–85)
B. Niccolò and others, ed.: *I diarii di Marino Sanuto*, 2 vols (Venice, 1879)
R. Lanciani: *Storia degli scavi di Roma*, 4 vols (Rome, 1902–7)
K. Frey: 'Zur Baugeschichte des St Peter', *Jb. Preuss. Kstsamml.*, xxxi (1910), pp. 1–95
T. Amayden: *La storia delle famiglie romane*, ed. A. Bertini, ii (Rome, 1914), pp. 6–8
A. Mercati: *Le spese private di Leone X* (Roma, 1927), p. 108
C. L. Frommel: *Der römische Palastbau der Hochrenaissance*, ii (Tübingen, 1973), p. 300
——: 'Die Peterskirche unter Papst Julius II im Licht neuer Dokumente', *Röm. Jb. Kstgesch.*, xvi (1976), pp. 57–136
R. Pacciani: 'New Information on Raphael and Giuliano Leno in the Diplomatic Correspondence of Alphonso I d'Este', *A. Bull.*, lxvii/1 (1983), pp. 137–45
A. Bedon: 'I Maffei e il loro palazzo in via della Pigna', *Quad. Ist. Stor. Archit.*, n. s. i/12 (1988), pp. 45–64
C. L. Frommel: 'Il cantiere di S Pietro prima di Michelangelo', *Les Chantiers de la Renaissance* (Paris, 1991), pp. 175–90

PIER NICOLA PAGLIARA

**Lenoir.** French family of artists, writers and archaeologists. (1) Alexandre Lenoir was an undistinguished artist, but he created one of the first truly popular museums, the Musée des Antiquités et Monuments Français in Paris. His wife Adélaïde (née Binart; 1771–1832) was a painter,

who studied under Jean-Baptiste Regnault, and their son (2) Alexandre-Albert Lenoir became an architect and followed in his father's footsteps as a writer and archaeologist.
□

**(1) Alexandre(-Marie) Lenoir** (*b* Paris, 26 Dec 1761, *d* Paris, 11 June 1839). Museum official, writer and archaeologist. He began his career as a pupil of the painter Gabriel-François Doyen but is remembered as one of the most extraordinary figures of the French Revolution, devoted to saving the monuments of France's past from wholesale destruction.

Soon after the Church had been nationalized in November 1789, the religious houses of France were closed and their contents confiscated. In 1790 the Commission des Arts selected the Hôtel de Nesles and the convent of the Petits Augustins in Paris to house the paintings, statues and artefacts removed from the churches and noble houses. Doyen, who was a member of the Commission, was placed in charge of the Petits Augustins, and, with his help, Lenoir was appointed Garde du Dépôt des Petits Augustins on 6 June 1791. As such, he drew up inventories of paintings and statues entering the Dépôt. On 26 July 1791 the Comité d'Aliénation decreed that, of the seized booty, all the precious objects and sculptures should be sold, and the metal objects melted down; only the sculptures that did not find a buyer were to be retained. With the help of Doyen and the sculptor Daujon, Lenoir set about reconstructing and restoring the dismembered monuments; in 1791–2, for example, they rescued the tomb of *Louis de Lusignan*, Germain Pilon's *St Francis in Ecstasy* and Michelangelo's *Slaves* (Paris, Louvre; for an illustration of one of these sculptures see MICHELANGELO, fig. 3).

Revolutionary fervour intensified after the proclamation of the Republic in September 1792 and the abolition of Christianity a year later. Lenoir's role took on even greater importance therefore and he gathered the marble remains of the great royal tombs from Saint-Denis Abbey (see SAINT-DENIS ABBEY, §II, 2). Gradually all metal objects and paintings were returned to their original locations but it seems that even at this date Lenoir had plans to create a museum of monumental sculpture. This is confirmed by the publication in 1793 of a list of objects in the Dépôt Provisoire des Petits Augustins. The Commission Temporaire des Arts aided him in his desire to seize all that was historically or artistically significant, and his memoirs contain long and dramatic descriptions, some of which were undoubtedly true, of how he prevented revolutionary vandalism, despite his personal safety being in danger. The fruits of Lenoir's efforts were seen when, on 25 October 1795, the Commission des Arts appointed him 'conservateur', and a year later, on 1 September 1796, the Dépôt was opened to the public and officially became the Musée des Antiquités et Monuments Français. Shortly afterwards, Lenoir wrote to the Comité d'Instruction Publique requesting that, among other things, the tomb of *Francis I* be restored 'pour l'instruction de nos artistes à venir', and that, on a more general note, all statues from the Middle Ages relating to the chronology of French history be placed there. In planning the display of objects he was strongly influenced by the pattern of decline and fall in

Winckelmann's *Geschichte der Kunst des Alterthums* (Dresden, 1764), and arranged the exhibits chronologically, one evocatively decorated room per century (*see* DISPLAY OF ART, §III, 3(ii)). Thus the vault of the 13th-century room was painted blue with gold stars, with dim lighting.

In the following years Lenoir built up the collections by exchange and purchase. With official backing he was able to collect objects, mainly statues, not only from Paris but from all 83 départements of France. From 250 items (in 1793) the collection grew to several thousand items by 1814. The museum took on different functions: in 1799 Lenoir decided to bring together the remains of great figures from France's 'Golden Age'. The grounds of the convent were converted into a Jardin Elysée, filled with the tombs containing the remains of, among others, such illustrious writers as Molière, La Fontaine, Boileau and Mabillon, the military hero Turenne, and the historian Bernard de Montfaucon. The most popular tomb was that of *Abélard and Heloïse*, which was composed of disparate parts of the destroyed tombs. The Elysée became an important study centre for contemporary sculptors, and had a lasting effect on the historical accuracy and sentimental subjects of painters. Lenoir publicized his aims in the descriptive catalogues *Musée des monuments français* . . . and the *Description historique* . . ., which between them went through 16 editions between 1800 and 1816.

Lenoir's museum was not without its critics. Among the most articulate was Quatremère de Quincy, who became increasingly vociferous in his demand that objects be returned to their natural homes. FRANÇOIS-RENÉ CHATEAUBRIAND, although he admired the museum, lamented that the exhibited artefacts were deprived of interest to all except the art historian. There is little doubt that Lenoir had taken to 'saving' objects long after the threat of destruction had receded. The restoration of the monarchy in 1815 marked the official end of revolutionary danger, and thus of the ostensible raison d'être of Lenoir's collection. By a decree of 24 April 1816, Louis XVIII ordered that the contents of the Musée des Antiquités et Monuments Français be restored to their respective churches, and on 18 October the same year the buildings became the home of the Ecole Royale et Spéciale des Beaux-Arts. In the same year Quatremère de Quincy, by now Intendant Général des Arts et Monuments Publics, published his *Considérations morales* (Paris, 1815), a fierce attack on Lenoir and his activities. Although Lenoir's museum was perceived as an anachronism by the Restoration, its influence on artists and writers was inestimable. It also greatly influenced ALEXANDRE DU SOMMERARD, when in 1832 he organized the display of his collection in the Hôtel des Abbés de Cluny, Paris. In 1844 Lenoir's son (2) Alexandre-Albert Lenoir directed the establishment of the Musée de Cluny.

### WRITINGS

*Recueil de portraits inédits des hommes et des femmes qui ont illustré la France* (Paris, n.d.)
*Description historique et chronologique des monuments de sculpture réunis au Musée des monuments français*, 4 vols (Paris, 1795–1806)
*Musée des monuments français*, 5 vols (Paris, 1800–1805)
*Histoire de la peinture sur verre et description des vitraux anciens et modernes* (Paris, 1804)
*Nouvelles explications des hiéroglyphes*, 4 vols (Paris, 1809–22)

*Musée impérial des monuments français: Histoire des arts en France et description chronologique des statues en marbre et en bronze, bas-reliefs et tombeaux des hommes et des femmes célèbres, qui sont réunis dans ce musée* (Paris, 1810)
*Nouvelle collection d'arabesques* (Paris, 1810)
*Explication d'un monument égyptien* (Paris, 1813)
*La Francmaçonnerie rendue à sa véritable origine* (Paris, 1814)
*Mémoires sur les sépultures d'Héloïse et Abélard* (Paris, 1815)
*Considérations générales sur les sciences et les arts* (Paris, 1816)
*Atlas des monuments des arts libéraux, mécaniques et industriels de la France, depuis les Gaulois jusqu'à nos jours* (Paris, 1820)
*Description historique et critique des statues, bas-reliefs, bustes et inscriptions antiques en marbre et en bronze, des peintures et sculptures modernes du Musée royal*, 8 vols (Paris, 1820–22)
*Observations scientifiques et critiques sur le génie et les principales productions des peintures et autres artistes les plus célèbres de l'antiquité, du moyen âge et des temps modernes* (Paris, 1821, 2/1824)

### BIBLIOGRAPHY

Bellier de La Chavignerie–Auvray
L. Courajod: *Alexandre Lenoir: Son journal et le Musée des monuments français* (Paris, 1878)
'Ministère de l'instruction publique et des beaux-arts: Inventaire général des richesses d'art de la France', *Archives du Musée des monuments français*, i (1883); ii (1886); iii (1897)
P. Léon: *La Vie des monuments français: Destruction, restauration* (Paris, 1961), pp. 69–73, 81–6
B. Foucart: 'La Fortune critique d'Alexandre Lenoir et du premier Musée des monuments français', *Inf. Hist. A.*, xiv/5 (1969), pp. 223–32
S. Mellon: 'Alexandre Lenoir: The Museum Versus the Revolution', *Proceedings of the Consortium on Revolutionary Europe*, ix (1979), pp. 75–88
C. M. Greene: 'Alexandre Lenoir and the Musée des Monuments Français during the French Revolution', *Fr. Hist. Stud.* (1981), pp. 200–22
E. Kennedy: *A Cultural History of the French Revolution* (New Haven and London, 1989) [esp. chap. VIII, 'Vandalism and Conservation']
F. Haskell: *History and its Images: Art and the Interpretation of the Past* (New Haven and London, 1993), pp. 236–52

**(2) Alexandre-Albert Lenoir** (*b* Paris, 21 Oct 1801; *d* Paris, 17 Feb 1891). Architect, archaeologist and writer, son of (1) Alexandre Lenoir. He was trained as an architect by François Debret. From 1830 to 1831 Lenoir was in Italy, studying Etruscan architecture; he then travelled to various countries to study Greek and Byzantine monuments. The results of his work were published in the *Annales de l'Institut archéologique de Rome* in a series of articles such as 'Mémoires et dessins relatifs aux édifices grecs découverts en 1830 à Solunto' (1831). On his return to France he successfully submitted a plan for a museum to house the collection of the recently abolished Musée des Petits-Augustins. He proposed merging the buildings of the Palais des Thermes and the Hôtel de Cluny, and in 1844 the project was executed under his direction, establishing the Musée de Cluny.

Lenoir had a particular fondness for medieval architecture, which he thought unduly neglected in favour of its classical predecessors. His most important work, *Architecture monastique* (1852–6), was a detailed illustrated study of medieval religious architecture. In 1862 he became secretary of the Ecole des Beaux-Arts and in 1869 *membre libre* of the Académie des Beaux-Arts. In 1842, together with Nicolas-Marie-Joseph Chapuy (1790–1858), he produced a new edition of Palladio's works and through such populist writings as *Architecture et archéologie* (1848) he became well known to a broad public.

### WRITINGS

*Statistique monumentale de Paris depuis les Romains* (Paris, 1839)
*Architecture et archéologie: Instruction pour le peuple* (Paris, 1848)
*Architecture monastique: Documents inédits*, 2 vols (Paris, 1852–6)

BIBLIOGRAPHY
Hoefer
*La Grande Encyclopédie* (Paris, 1887–1902)
A. Soubies: *Les Membres de l'Académie des beaux-arts depuis la fondation de l'Institut*, 4 vols (Paris, 1904–13), iii, pp. 233–6

BIBLIOGRAPHY
M. Gallet: *Paris: Domestic Architecture of the 18th Century* (London, 1972)
P. Etienne: 'Le Grand Dessein de Samson-Nicolas Lenoir', *Le Faubourg Poissonnière: Architecture, élégance et décor*, Délégation à l'action artistique de la ville de Paris (Paris, 1986), pp. 154–85, 209–10

VALÉRIE-NOËLLE JOUFFRE

**Lenoir, Samson-Nicolas** [Le Romain] (*b* Saint-Germain-en-Laye, 3 July 1733; *d* Paris, 29 June 1810). French architect. He was a pupil of Jacques-François Blondel. Lenoir failed to win a prize in the Académie Royale d'Architecture competition in 1752, but he went to Rome independently in the following year with letters of recommendation from Abel-François Poisson de Vandières (later the Marquis de Marigny; *see* POISSON, (2)). On his return to France Lenoir settled in Burgundy, where he had family connections, and he became official architect to the *Intendance* (provincial administration) and to the Department of Water and Forests, dealing with such urban-planning matters as the construction of fountains and monumental gates in Beaunes, Dijon, Autun and other places. He also worked for the new aristocracy, including the speaker of Parliament, C.-P. Fyot de La Marche, for whom he restored the Hôtel Berbisey and made improvements to his estate at Montmusard near Dijon. Lenoir took part in the creation of the Ecole des Beaux-Arts at Dijon, but his main work in Dijon was the imposing hôtel of the Marquis Bénigne III Bouhier (1758; now the Préfecture de la Côte d'Or). In the same year Voltaire commissioned Lenoir to rebuild the church and château at Ferney.

From 1760 to 1767 Lenoir worked on plans for new buildings at CÎTEAUX ABBEY, completing a Neo-classical wing before the project was abandoned. He then returned to Paris, where he rebuilt the Abbaye Royale de Saint-Antoine-des-Champs (1763–70; now part of the Hôpital Saint-Antoine). Lenoir then came into contact with the world of speculative builders. Between 1771 and 1776 he built or restored private hôtels for such patrons as F. Benoît de Sainte-Paulle (Rue du Faubourg-Poissonnière), R. F. de Chestret (Château d'Orangis) and P. O. M. P. Giambone (Rue de Bondy; now Rue Taylor). In these works Lenoir asserted a style that gave rational interior planning an importance equal to the design of the façades. Lenoir was involved in speculative projects from 1775 until his death. He assisted in the creation of the Poissonnière district of Paris with C.-M. Goupy, F. Benoît de Sainte-Paulle, Denis-Pierre-Jean Papillon de la Ferté and his father-in-law, C.-H. Riboutté. He bought land and planned new streets and housing developments, building both for himself and for clients. Lenoir completed many public buildings, hôtels, investment properties, theatres and pleasure gardens, devising ingenious plans and decorations. However, the failure of other projects proved ruinous financially. In 1781 Lenoir erected a temporary Opéra on the Boulevard Saint-Martin (site of the present Théâtre de la Porte Saint-Martin) for the Académie Royale de Musique, after a fire at Pierre-Louis Moreau-Desproux's Palais-Royal Opéra; this was achieved in only 75 days. Lenoir had a long and productive career, and he holds an important place in the history of French Neo-classical architecture and the urban transformation of late 18th-century Paris.

**Lenoncourt, Gérard de.** *See* JACQUEMIN, GERARD.

**Le Normand** [Lenormant] **de Tournehem, Charles-François(-Paul)** (*b* Paris, 30 Dec 1684; *d* Paris, 19 Nov 1751). French administrator. He made an immense fortune as a fermier général (tax farmer); Louis XV's mistress, Madame de Pompadour, was his niece by marriage. In 1745 he succeeded the undistinguished Philibert Orry as Directeur-Général des Bâtiments du Roi. The task before him was staggering because of the bad state of the finances and the loss of moral prestige of the Académie Royale de Peinture et de Sculpture. Cautiously he initiated himself in matters of art, then revived the office of Premier Peintre du Roi, which had been in abeyance for 10 years, appointing Charles-Antoine Coypel, who was to remain his right-hand man. Assisted also by art critics who sought a return to the Grand Manner, such as Etienne Lafont de Saint-Yenne, Abbé Jean-Bernard Le Blanc and the Comte de Caylus, Tournehem and Coypel set about reorganizing, on a vast scale, the administration of the fine arts in France. To encourage history painting, Tournehem multiplied royal commissions to artists and established, on the model of the limited competition of 1727, the 1747 history painting competition for 11 officers of the Académie. He increased the prizes for history painting at the expense of portraits. Many other measures were taken to increase the neglected education of artists, particularly the opening in 1750 at the Palais du Luxembourg, Paris, of the Galerie de Marie de' Medici, with its famous series of paintings of the *Life of Marie de' Medici* by Peter Paul Rubens (now Paris, Louvre). Another innovation of Tournehem was the establishment of the Ecole Royale des Elèves Protégés (see PARIS, §VI, 1) for the winners of the Prix de Rome; this school's task was to prepare them adequately for their studies at the Académie de France in Rome.

Although Tournehem was also responsible for the maintenance and construction of royal houses, he did not leave his mark on architecture, in which the Premier Architecte du Roi, Anges-Jacques Gabriel, was all-powerful. Nevertheless, it was under his direction that Gabriel carried out his most important works, including the Ecole Militaire, Paris (1751). In a period of relative prosperity, Tournehem administered the Bâtiments' budget with vigour and impartiality, trying to restrain its expenditure. He resided at his château of Etiolles, but spent more time at his Paris house in the Rue de la Croix-des-Petits-Champs. Here he must have kept works of art: it is not, however, possible to know what they were, since his papers were burnt in 1871. A portrait by Louis Tocqué (Versailles, Château) captures the features of the man who so well prepared for the turning towards a new seriousness in French art during the term of the successor he had designated, Mme de Pompadour's brother, the Marquis de Marigny.

BIBLIOGRAPHY

L. Courajod, ed.: *Journal de Lazare-Duvaut* (Paris, 1873), i, p. cxlv

——: *L'Ecole royale des élèves protégés* (Paris, 1874)

J. Locquin: *La Peinture d'histoire en France de 1747 à 1785* (Paris, 1912)

L. Frank: *Lenormant de Tournehem et le mouvement des arts au milieu du XVIIIème siècle* (diss., Paris, Ecole Chartes, 1987), pp. 95–104

ANNE LECLAIR

**Le Nôtre** [Le Nostre], **André** (*b* Paris, 12 March 1613; *d* Paris, 15 Sept 1700). French garden designer and collector. He was outstanding in his time for his innovation and skill in garden design, particularly in his work at Vaux-le-Vicomte, Versailles and Chantilly, and his ardent disciples carried his gardening principles throughout France and beyond, so spreading his influence. Popular among contemporaries, he also enjoyed a special relationship with the traditionally aloof Louis XIV, who bestowed upon him the Order of St Lazare (later replaced by the even more prestigious Order of St Michel), a coat of arms and, on his retirement, a princely pension. Although the original spelling of his name was Le Nostre, by the late 20th century the form of Le Nôtre had gained most currency.

1. Training, early projects and Vaux-le-Vicomte. 2. Versailles and later projects.

1. TRAINING, EARLY PROJECTS AND VAUX-LE-VI-COMTE. His career was doubtless determined at an early age, since his grandfather, Pierre, and his father, Jean, were both royal gardeners, who worked principally at the Palais des Tuileries. He was thus initiated into gardening practice by his father and a coterie of distinguished gardeners that included Claude Mollet (i) (*c.* 1564–*c.* 1649) and Jacques

Boyceau. Following the proper training for gardeners recommended by Boyceau in his *Traité du jardinage* (1638), Le Nôtre studied painting and architecture with Simon Vouet and François Mansart respectively. During his apprenticeship with Mansart, he may have worked at the châteaux of Balleroy in Normandy, Blois in the Loire Valley, and Maisons-Lafitte outside Paris. His practical education was supplemented by treatises on gardening and theoretical works on optics that began to appear in France in the 1630s. The principles of optical illusion set down in Père Jean-François Niceron's *La Perspective curieuse* (1638) were soon to be applied to garden design.

In 1635 Le Nôtre was appointed gardener to Gaston, Duc d'Orléans, a post he held until the Duke's death (1660). Projects for the Duke included alterations to the parterres designed originally by Boyceau in the gardens of the Palais du Luxembourg. When his father retired in 1637, he was allowed by Louis XIII to pass on to his son his title of Premier Jardinier du Roi au Grand Jardin des Tuileries, so putting Le Nôtre into the employ of the King. Perhaps the earliest work for which Le Nôtre was solely responsible was the garden (1642–4) for Dominique Séguier, Bishop of Meaux. This set a precedent for executing gardens for prelates, since Le Nôtre later redesigned the gardens of the Archbishop of Paris at Conflans, near Paris. His future was assured, however, with the creation of VAUX-LE-VICOMTE (1656–61), the country residence of NICOLAS FOUQUET, the Minister of Finance under Louis XIV. This undertaking, a collaborative effort with the architect Louis Le Vau, resulted in a complex that became the wonder of the age (see fig. 1) and provided

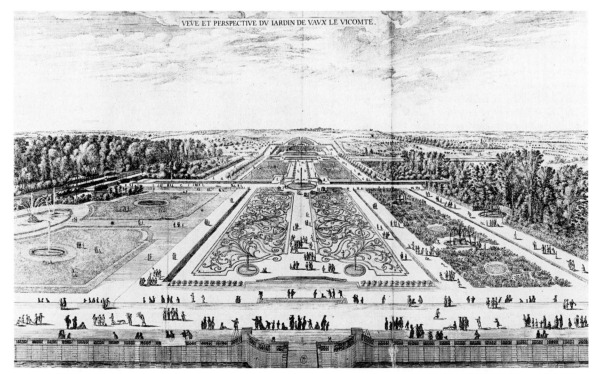

1. André Le Nôtre: gardens (1656–61) at Vaux-le-Vicomte, view from the château; from a print by Israel Silvestre (Paris, Bibliothèque Nationale)

Louis XIV with a perfect model for his own future schemes.

Le Nôtre insisted on an axial layout, the spine of which extended without deviation along the avenue of approach. Traversing a series of forecourts, it perfectly bisected Le Vau's symmetrically designed château, then continued outwards through the garden to the horizon. This central axis was bisected at intervals by transverse axes in the form of walks, pools and canals. Trees and other relief elements were established at some distance from the principal building, the former serving as enclosing walls of verdure along the sides and end of the garden. As a result the garden was suggested as both an enclosed space and as a logical continuation of the architectural space already encountered in the formal architecture of the main building. The château, closely surrounded by parterres, was thus laid bare; the parterres in front of the garden façade were planted with dwarf box, worked into intricately woven embroidery patterns, their clarity assured by the use of coloured materials—crushed brick and slate—placed in the intervals between the box.

At Vaux, as in Le Nôtre's gardens generally, the plan was conceived with two vantage points in mind: the vista of the garden as seen from the château, and the view from the foot of the garden. When standing before the garden façade, the visitor is struck by an all-pervasive sense of regularity and a perfect balance of parts; it is a flawless landscape based on a series of carefully considered geometric relationships, which together produce a strictly formal scheme. The sense of harmony, which so appealed to the 17th-century French rationalist mind, is in fact of a deceptive order, for underlying the apparent symmetry and visual balance are myriad surprises, the result of using optical foreshortening and emphasizing the constantly changing interplay of the garden components to produce countless perspective views. From the steps one descends to an area that had not appeared large when viewed from the château, but which is discovered to be immense. This results in part from the fact that the components of the garden—the paths, pools, fountains, sculptures—are all of a monumental scale. In addition, the promenader realizes that the garden, which had appeared relatively flat when viewed from the building, is in reality marked by a series of descending levels, which, once discovered, reveal hitherto concealed embellishments in the form of stairways, pools and sculptures. These many subtleties enliven Le Nôtre's awesomely grand and formal compositions and entice the visitor to continue and so to discover additional surprises underlying the layout of the gardens. Immediately following Vaux, Le Nôtre entered the service of the King, Louis XIV (*see* BOURBON, §I(8)), and modified the royal gardens at Fontainebleau (*see* GARDEN, §VIII, 4(ii)(b)), creating there the Grand Jardin du Roi, which at the time was unique in France for its huge scale (310×395 m).

2. VERSAILLES AND LATER PROJECTS. Simultaneously with Fontainebleau, Le Nôtre began work on his greatest project, Versailles (1661–87; *see* VERSAILLES, §2, and GARDEN, fig. 2), a collaborative effort first with Le Vau and later with Jules Hardouin Mansart. It was at Versailles that the ideas set forth by Le Nôtre at Vaux came to full fruition. The gardens were again laid out on

a single axis that bisected the château, an axis that was interrupted at intervals to provide transverse avenues leading to important focal points within the landscape. Visual harmony results from the interplay of carefully adjusted proportions and optical refinements. Like those of Vaux, the gardens were architectural extensions of the château itself, providing the ideal frame for the building.

The seemingly interminable axes were made tolerable for the intrepid visitor by the introduction of numerous 'surprises' in the form of hidden inclines, pools, fountains and sculptures, which revealed themselves only when the space was experienced by walking through it. Optical illusions were to be encountered at every turn, the result of foreshortening and the visual interaction of near and more distant objects within the landscape. These features provided the important leaven to Le Nôtre's otherwise formal design treatment. Scores of bosquets, secluded and decorated chambers carved out of the forested areas of the garden, afforded welcome refuge for the weary promenader. Of an extremely diverse nature, the bosquets presented the visitor with all manner of forms—labyrinths, elaborate trelliswork, marble colonnades and pavilions, topiary, fanciful sculpture and a great variety of water effects, including pools, cascades and fountains.

In addition to his designs for the principal gardens of the château, Le Nôtre created at Versailles the garden of the first Trianon, the Trianon de Porcelaine (1670); this he modified in 1687 when the Grand Trianon replaced it (*see* VERSAILLES, §3). The principle of '*forcer la nature*' governed every aspect of the Versailles gardens; at the nearby Grand Trianon, however, Le Nôtre's approach was somewhat different, for although the overall garden plan was equally formal, the flowers for which the site was justly famous were allowed to flourish in their own natural way without the intricate patterns used elsewhere at Versailles.

Le Nôtre's success, which put his services in great demand, led him to establish a workshop system, employing assistants for the refining of initial plans. In 1666 he was also given the title of Conseiller du Roi aux Conseils et Contrôleur Général des Bâtiments de Sa Majesté, which meant that he was required to inspect all newly constructed buildings. His architectural expertise was further confirmed by his listing in 1681 as a member of the Académie Royale d'Architecture.

Near to Versailles, Le Nôtre worked with Jules Hardouin Mansart on the château and gardens at Clagny (1674–6), a residence built for the royal mistress the Marquise de Montespan. With Le Nôtre's fame established, members of the royal family and the court vied with one another for a garden by him. Between 1665 and 1678 he landscaped SAINT-CLOUD (*see* GARDEN, fig. 46), the château of Philippe I, Duc d'Orléans, the King's brother. The Grand Condé, Louis II of Bourbon, a cousin of Louis XIV, also enlisted Le Nôtre's services in redesigning the 16th-century gardens of his château at Chantilly (1663–88; see fig. 2; *see also* CHANTILLY, §1(ii)); these were, by Le Nôtre's own admission, his favourite creation. In such projects to redesign pre-existing gardens, where the buildings and sites were of a highly irregular order, Le Nôtre strove to bring a sense of visual harmony to the project. His solutions were always of an imaginative,

2. André Le Nôtre: gardens (1663–88) at the château of Chantilly; aerial view from the south-west

inventive order, in which he brought his knowledge of optics into full play. At Chantilly the orientation of the 16th-century château precluded a principal axis abutting upon the entrance to the structure. Le Nôtre therefore created a vast raised terrace in front of the building, in the centre of which he placed a large equestrian figure of Anne, Duc de Montmorency and Constable of France. Upon this statue Le Nôtre drew his great axis, which was placed at right angles to the actual entrance of the Grand Condé's country residence. In the process of experiencing this axial progression, the visitor to the site encounters, as at Vaux, exciting optical illusions along the way, the result of subtle modifications to inclines and levels of ground.

Along with these demanding projects Le Nôtre designed the gardens for the château of Meudon (c. 1654 and 1679–82), Sceaux (1673–7) and the Palais Royal (1674) and those of numerous Parisian residences. He was also involved with smaller gardens at Maintenon (1675–8), Saint-Cyr (1685–7), Gaillon (1691–2) and Les Rochers (1689). Even after his official retirement from the King's service in 1693, Le Nôtre continued to practise, creating the splendid gardens of the château of Pontchartrain (1691–5). In addition to these documented works, there are scores of other gardens with which Le Nôtre's name has long been associated. With the exception of one trip to Italy (1679), it is doubtful that he ever left France, although he did provide plans for garden projects elsewhere, which in the case of the gardens at Greenwich Park (1662) and Windsor (1698) in England could be implemented by one of his emissaries, in the case of the latter his nephew, Claude Desgots.

Le Nôtre's professional success brought him moderate wealth. Much of his fortune was directed towards acquiring works of art, including paintings, sculptures and engraved stones, which he displayed in his residence in the Tuileries. His generosity to family and friends was legendary: even Louis XIV became a recipient of his largesse when Le Nôtre donated a significant part of his art collection to the King; the paintings acquired by Le Nôtre that later entered the royal collection included works by Nicolas Poussin, Claude Lorrain, Paul Bril, Jan Breugel I and Domenichino. With regard to his gardening principles, Le Nôtre himself never wrote them down, but they were soon reflected in A. J. Dézallier d'Argenville's *La Théorie et la pratique du jardinage* (1709). In addition to this, Le Nôtre's methods were widely disseminated by his pupils, making his influence felt as far afield as Russia, Spain, Portugal, Germany, Sweden and other parts of Europe. It was only with the advent of the so-called English garden that the French formal style was eclipsed.

BIBLIOGRAPHY

J. Guiffrey: *André Le Nostre* (Paris, 1912)
H. M. Fox: *André Le Nôtre, Garden Architect to Kings* (New York, 1962)
E. de Ganay: *André Le Nostre, 1613–1700* (Paris, 1962)
E. B. MacDougall and F. H. Hazlehurst, eds: *The French Formal Garden*, Dumbarton Oaks Ser. (Washington, DC, 1974)
W. H. Adams: *The French Garden, 1500–1800* (New York, 1979)
F. H. Hazlehurst: *Gardens of Illusion: The Genius of André Le Nostre* (Nashville, 1980)
K. Woodbridge: *Princely Gardens: The Origins and Development of the French Formal Style* (London, 1985)

F. HAMILTON HAZLEHURST

**Lenox, Walter Scott** (*b* Trenton, NJ, 29 March 1859; *d* Trenton, 11 Jan 1920). American pottery manufacturer and designer. He aspired to be an artist as a youth, and in 1875 he became interested in applying art to industry, learning to design pottery forms and decoration with

Elijah Tatler (1823–76) at the Trenton Pottery. In 1883 he became art director for Ott & Brewer, Trenton, and was instrumental in developing an American version of Irish Belleek that was highly decorated with coloured glazes and raised gold pastework. In 1887 he developed a similar line for the Willets Manufacturing Co. in Trenton. These two potteries made primarily ironstone dinner and toilet wares, but Lenox was determined to create a company completely devoted to art wares. With several partners he founded in 1889 the small Ceramic Art Co., Trenton, which made a delicate ivory porcelain elaborately decorated in high Victorian taste. About 1902 the firm began to experiment with tableware, making costly services for individual clients. In 1906 the manufacture of exclusively decorated table services was formally inaugurated, and the company's name changed to the Lenox China Co. In 1918 the firm produced the first American-made service for the White House, Washington, DC, during the presidency of Woodrow Wilson (1856–1924). The firm continued to provide china for the White House and to expand its share of the American fine dinnerware market. In the late 20th century Lenox was the largest producer of fine dinnerware in the USA.

BIBLIOGRAPHY

G. S. Holmes: *Lenox China: The Story of Walter Scott Lenox* (Trenton, 1924)

E. P. Denker: *Lenox China: Celebrating a Century of Quality, 1889–1989* (Trenton, 1989)

ELLEN PAUL DENKER

**Lens** [Lans; Lense; Lentz]. English family of artists. At least four generations of the family worked in a variety of (often overlapping) artistic occupations, including drawing instruction, printmaking, topographical work and painting in miniature. According to George Vertue ('Note-books', *Walpole Soc.*, xxvi (1938), p. 62), Bernard Lens (i) (*b* 1631; *d* 1708), who was probably born in the Netherlands, worked as a painter on enamel; he was also the author of several religious tracts. His son Bernard Lens (ii) (*b* 1659; *d* London, 28 April 1725), together with the copperplate engraver John Sturt (1658–1730), ran a drawing-school—one of the first in England—in St Paul's Churchyard, London, from 1697 until some time after 1710. In 1705 he was taken on at the nearby Christ's Hospital boys' charity school to provide instruction in the navigational drawing skills necessary for those destined for careers at sea or apprenticeships. Following his death, the position passed to one of his sons, Edward Lens (*b* 1685; *d* 1749). *A New and Compleat Drawing Book* (1750) has been attributed to another son, Bernard Lens (iii) (*b* 1681; *d* London, 24–30 Dec 1740), but it is probably a compilation of engravings made after drawings by his father and his brother Edward. Both texts and figural plates were adaptations made from earlier manuals by Gérard de Lairesse and Charles-Alfonse Dufresnoy, but the majority of the book's plates were coastal and fortress scenes made after drawings by various members of the family. Although there are washed pen-and-ink topographical views of the Islington area of London, Bath and elsewhere (examples London, BM; New Haven, CT, Yale Cent. Brit. A.) signed by Bernard Lens (ii), Bernard Lens (iii) and one of the latter's sons, Andrew Benjamin Lens (*b* c. 1713; *d* after

1779), their works are often hard to distinguish, in part since they frequently copied each other's work.

Bernard Lens (iii) was the most successful member of the family (for illustration *see* HERMITAGE). His earliest extant work, an accomplished miniature of *Dr Harris* (1707; New Haven, CT, Yale Cent. Brit. A.), suggests that he must have been painting miniatures for several years before then. Competition from foreign miniature painters working in England was strong, but he set his work apart by becoming the first English artist to shift from painting in watercolour on vellum to that of watercolour and gouache on ivory, a practice recently introduced by the Venetian artist Rosalba Carriera, whose work strongly influenced him. *Richard Whitmore* (1718) and *Katherine Whitmore* (1724; both London, V&A) are examples of his charming half-length miniatures of children. He was also a prolific copier in miniature of Old Master paintings on vellum. He was official limner to both George I and George II and one of the first fashionable drawing-masters. His pupils included Horace Walpole, later 4th Earl of Orford, Edward Harley, later 2nd Earl of Oxford, and Margaret Cavendish-Bentinck, later 2nd Duchess of Portland, as well as the children of the royal family, for whom he etched a drawing book in 1735 (London, BM). Two of his sons, Peter Paul Lens (*b* c. 1714; *d* after 1754) and the above-mentioned Andrew Benjamin Lens, were also painters in miniature (examples London, V&A) and topographical artists (examples London, BM). Another son, John Lens (*fl* c. 1750), who failed to win the position of drawing-master at Christ's Hospital in 1750, published a series of 12 etched landscapes.

BIBLIOGRAPHY

Thieme–Becker

I. Fleming-Williams: 'Drawing Masters', *Water-colour Painting in Britain*, ed. M. Hardie, iii (London, 1968), pp. 212–15

D. Foskett: *A Dictionary of British Miniature Painters*, 2 vols (London, 1972)

J. Murdoch and others: *The English Miniature* (London, 1981)

KIM SLOAN

**Lens, A(ndries) C(ornelis)** (*b* Antwerp, 31 March 1739; *d* Brussels, 30 March 1822). Flemish painter and writer. He was the son of the flower painter Cornelis Lens (*d* after 1766) and studied first under Charles Ykens II (1719–53) and then under Balthazar Beschey. In 1756 he was awarded first prize at the Academie of Antwerp and in 1763 was appointed to the staff on the strength of his decoration (destr.) of the refectory of the Alexians at Lier. He also came to the attention of Charles Alexandre, Duke of Lorraine and Bar, Governor-General of the Netherlands, who appointed him court painter in the following year.

Lens subsequently spent four years in Rome (1764–8), at a time when the theories of Johann Joachim Winckelmann were influential. Charles, Comte de Cobenzl, became his patron and introduced him to leading figures in Roman society, such as Cardinal Albani. Lens's sketchbooks and notes bear witness to his curiosity and fascination with finds from recent archaeological digs in the Campagna; from the moment he encountered these he devoted himself to the Antique. He also took a particular interest in the works of Raphael, Guido Reni and the Carracci. On his return to Antwerp in 1768, he attempted to alter

A. C. Lens: *Cornelia, Mother of the Gracchi*, oil on canvas, 1.42×1.14 m, (Brussels, private collection)

Schoenberg Castle with *Mars, Minerva and Venus* (Vienna, Ksthist. Mus.), as well as the Huis Walkiers in Laeken.

The arrival of French troops in the Netherlands in 1795 might have put his career in jeopardy, as French taste then favoured painters in the style of Jacques-Louis David, but Lens nevertheless retained his own faithful clientele. He continued with as much conviction as ever to seek the ideal of beauty he had been pursuing since his stay in Rome, in such works as *Samson and Delilah* (Brussels, Mus. A. Anc.) and *Cornelia, Mother of the Gracchi* (Brussels, priv. col.; see fig.). Lens's Neo-classical concept of ideal beauty was not understood, however, and in 1810 his *Annunciation* (Ghent, St Michielskerk) was rejected as immodest and irreverent. His graceful style, characterized by clear drawing, precise line and sober composition recalling that of Angelica Kauffman (with whom he is often confused), was abandoned by the new generation. Not until the beginning of the 19th century was his reputation revived and his contribution to the regeneration of Belgian painting acknowledged.

### BIBLIOGRAPHY
*BNB*

De Bast: *Annales du Salon de Gand* (Ghent, 1823)
F. B. Goethals: *A. C. Lens*, Histoire des lettres et des arts en Belgique, iii (Brussels, 1842)
L. Quarré-Reybourdon: *A. C. Lens et ses tableaux conservés à Lille* (Paris, 1902)
J. Dierckx: 'Kunstschilder A. C. Lens als theoreticus', *Gentse Bijdr. Kstgesch.*, viii (1941), pp. 173–4
D. Coekelberghs: *Les Peintres belges à Rome de 1700 à 1830* (Brussels and Rome, 1976), pp. 205–6
*1770–1830: Autour du néo-classicisme en Belgique* (exh. cat., Brussels, Mus. Ixelles, 1985–6), pp. 69–70
*A. C. Lens* (exh. cat., Antwerp, Kon. Mus. S. Kst., 1989)

ALAIN JACOBS

Flemish taste, which he considered decadent. He wrote two works—*Le Costume, ou essai sur les habillements et les usages de différents peuples de l'antiquité* (1776) and *Du bon goût* (1811)—in which his approach is close to that of Anton Raphael Mengs, like Winckelmann an enthusiastic champion of Neo-classical ideas. As director of the Antwerp Academie, he worked assiduously to introduce Neo-classical rules and to break up the Guild of St Luke (*see also* BELGIUM, §XV).

During this second period in Antwerp (1768–81), undoubtedly the most brilliant of his career, he decorated reception rooms for the bourgeoisie and the enlightened nobility (e.g. the Salon Stevens, Brussels, Mus. A. Anc.; and the Salon d'Orphée et d'Eurydice, Brussels, Gal. Arenberg). Dignitaries of the Austrian empire, such as Wenzel Anton, Prince of Kaunitz-Rietberg at Cobenzl, placed commissions with him, and there was demand for his talent from the English, Dutch and French businessmen passing through Antwerp, resulting in such works as *Jupiter Asleep in the Arms of Juno* (Vienna, Ksthist. Mus.); commissions from the Church included the *Life of St Rombaut* (1775; Mechelen, St-Rombaut); the *Presentation in the Temple* (Antwerp, St Andrieskerk); the series on the *Life of Mary Magdalene* (1778; Lille, La Madeleine). Lens's reputation grew enormously during this period, and pupils, including Joseph François, flocked to his studio. Emperor Joseph II offered him the directorship of the Vienna Akademie in 1781, but he refused and settled permanently in Brussels, where he decorated one of the halls of

**Lentulov, Aristarkh (Vasil'yevich)** (*b* Nizhny Lomov, Penza, 16 Jan 1882; *d* Moscow, 15 April 1943). Russian painter. He studied art in Penza (1897–1903), Kiev (1903–5), and in St Petersburg (1906) under Dmitry Kardovsky. He participated in major exhibitions, including *The Wreath* (1907–8), *The Link* (1908) and *Union of Russian Artists* (1910). He was a founder-member in 1910 of the avant-garde exhibiting society the JACK OF DIAMONDS and remained a leader of the group until its dissolution in 1916.

His painting style matured following a visit to Italy and France during 1911–12, when he worked with Henri Le Fauconnier in Paris. *Bathing* (1911–12; Moscow, Lentulova priv. col., see 1984 exh. cat., p. 183) was executed with a restricted palette and faceted in the manner of Fernand Léger. Later, the impact of Robert Delaunay and Umberto Boccioni is apparent in his masterpiece *Moscow* (1913; Moscow, Tret'yakov Gal.), a magnificent work spangled with fragments of colour precariously balanced one on the other, evoking the dynamism of the city. The series *At the Sea-side* (1915; Moscow, Lentulova priv. col., see 1984 exh. cat., p. 191) and other works of this period are treated in a more decorative manner, with rich applications of bronze, silver, lace and birch bark.

Following the 1917 Revolution Lentulov became a professor at Svomas (Free Art Studios). In 1925 he helped to organize the Society of Moscow Painters and in 1926 joined the ASSOCIATION OF ARTISTS OF REVOLUTIONARY

RUSSIA (AKhRR). In common with many artists of his generation, Lentulov's works of the late 1920s reverted to a more realistic style.

### WRITINGS
'Sokhranennoe pamyat'yu' [Preserved by memory], *Tvorchestvo* [Creative work], vii/272 (1979), pp. 16–19

### BIBLIOGRAPHY
*Aristarkh Lentulov* (exh. cat., Moscow, Un. Artists, 1968)
M. Lentulova: *Khudozhnik Aristarkh Lentulov: Vospominaniya* [The artist Aristarkh Lentulov: recollections] (Moscow, 1969)
*Sieben Moskauer Künstler/Seven Moscow artists 1910–1930* (exh. cat., Cologne, Gal. Gmurzynska, 1984) [good colour pls]
E. Murina: *Aristarkh Lentulov* (Milan, 1988)
E. B. Murina and S. G. Dzhafarova: *Aristarkh Lentulov* (Moscow, 1990)

ANTHONY PARTON

**Leo I** [Leo the Great], Pope (*b* ?Volterra, late 4th century AD; elected 29 Sept 440; *d* Rome, 10 Nov 461; *fd* 10 Nov, Western Church; 18 Feb, Eastern Church). Saint, pope, writer and patron. He was dedicated to maintaining the unity of the church against such heretics as the Pelagians, the Manichaeans and the Priscillianists, as is clear from his numerous sermons and letters (*see* CHRISTIANITY, §III, 3(i)). His reforms included maintaining strict ecclesiastical discipline at a time when barbarian culture threatened the stability of the Church in Rome. As an active patron of the arts, Leo funded the construction of a basilica over the grave of Pope Cornelius (251–3) on the Via Appia; he restored and redecorated S Paolo fuori le mura (395–408) after its roof collapsed in 441, even persuading GALLA PLACIDIA to pay for the mosaics (largely destr. 1823) on the Triumphal Arch; and he restored parts of Old St Peter's (*see* ROME, §V, 14(i)(a)). He encouraged the construction of S Stefano on the Via Latina, the ruins of which have been excavated.

### BIBLIOGRAPHY
T. Jalland: *The Life and Times of St Leo the Great* (London, 1941)
P. Stockmeier: *Leo I. des Grossen: Beurteilung der kaiserlichen Religionspolitik* (Munich, 1959)
W. Ullmann: 'Leo I and the Theme of Papal Primacy', *J. Theol. Stud.*, n. s., xi (1960), pp. 25–51
F. Paschoud: *Roma aeterna* (Rome, 1967)

SUSAN PINTO MADIGAN

**Leo III**, Pope (*b* Rome; elected 795; *d* Rome, 12 June 816; *can* 1673; *fd* 12 June). Saint, pope and patron. His pontificate was particularly important in the context of the Carolingian Renaissance, owing to his copious building activity and the impetus that he gave to the art of mosaic. His is the longest biography in the *Liber pontificalis*. His election as pope was disputed by factions of the Roman lay nobility. In 799 he sought the protection of Charlemagne at Paderborn, returning in triumph to Rome to crown him Emperor of the Romans in Old St Peter's on Christmas night 800.

The political implications of the coronation of Charlemagne as Emperor and the recently produced 'Donation of Constantine' (a forged document granting extensive papal powers in the Italian peninsula) were given figurative expression in the mosaic (destr.) over the central apse of the first *triclinium* (banqueting hall) built by Leo in the Lateran Palace. An 18th-century reproduction exists in the niche overlooking the Piazza di S Giovanni in Laterano, next to the Scala Santa. The *Missio apostolorum* is depicted in the semi-dome of the apse, and the arch bears two parallel groups of three figures: on the left, Christ hands the keys to St Peter and the labarum to Constantine, and on the right St Peter gives the pallium to Leo III and the 'patrician' standard to Charlemagne. The greatest religious and political authorities were, thus, placed on an equal level, each answerable to a higher power in his own sphere. The same theme was emphasized in the contemporary mosaic (destr.) in the church of S Susanna, where the images of Leo III and Charlemagne also appeared.

In the Lateran Palace Leo III also had an oratory constructed in honour of the Archangel Michael, rich in paintings and mosaics, and a second *triclinium*, larger than the first, with a terminal apse containing a mosaic and five frescoed conches on each side. The *triclinium*, later known as the Aula Concilii, could be reached either directly by a great stairway leading from the nearby basilica of the Saviour or from the main entrance of the Patriarchium, through a long corridor (the *macrona*). The oratory, the Aula Concilii, the *macrona* and much of the old papal residence were destroyed between 1586 and 1589 by Sixtus V (*reg* 1585–90) to make room for the new palace built by Domenico Fontana (iii).

Leo III favoured the urban development of the Vatican Borgo (*see* ROME, §II, 2), rebuilding the old papal palace and constructing a large *triclinium*, which perhaps resembled his first *triclinium* in the Lateran. He had a round bathhouse built near the obelisk on the south side of Old St Peter's, presumably for private use, and another bath for pilgrims and the poor. The planning of the ring of defensive walls around the Vatican Borgo is attributed to Leo III, although the walls were built only under Leo IV (*reg* 847–55).

As well as new constructions Leo sponsored much restoration work in the great basilicas, for example the Lateran basilica, Old St Peter's, where a new baptistery was built with columns of porphyry around the central basin, S Paolo fuori le mura, S Maria Maggiore and S Lorenzo fuori le mura. Building work and decoration were also carried out in such other Roman churches as S Anastasia, S Sabina (of which Leo had been the titular priest), S Susanna (where he had been ordained), SS Nereo ed Achilleo and S Pellegrino in Vaticano. Every Roman church received gifts: gold and silver liturgical vessels, vestments, veils, silver lamps and other objects. The list in the *Liber pontificalis* of his gifts to all the churches of the city in the year 807 is a historical and topographical document of exceptional interest. Leo was also responsible for rebuilding the roof and probably the apse mosaic in the church of S Apollinare in Classe, Ravenna (*see* RAVENNA, §2(v)).

### BIBLIOGRAPHY
A. Ciacconius: *Vitae et res gestae Pontificum Romanorum et S. R. E. Cardinalium ab initio nascentis Ecclesiae usque ad Clementem IX P. O. M.*, i (Rome, 1677), col. 562–78
*Liber pontificalis*, ed. L. Duchesne, ii (Paris, 1892), pp. 1–48
H. K. Mann: *The Lives of the Popes in the Early Middle Ages*, ii (London, 1906, 2/1925), pp. 1–110
H. Geertman: *More veterum: Il "Liber pontificalis" e gli edifici ecclesiastici di Roma nella tarda antichità e nell'alto medioevo* (Groningen, 1975)

MARIO D'ONOFRIO

**Leo VI.** *See* MACEDONIAN DYNASTY, (2).

**Leo X**, Pope. *See* MEDICI, DE', (7).

**Leo, Ludwig** (*b* Rostock, 2 Sept 1924). German architect. After studying architecture at the Hochschule für Bildende Künste in Berlin (1948–53), he worked in the office of Wassili and Hans Luckhardt until 1955 and then set up his own architectural practice in Berlin. His early works include the day-care centre (1958) in Charlottenburg, Berlin, built from prefabricated sections and constructed from building cubes of equal size; two-storey units are arranged round a central area linking sectors for various age groups and rest and play areas. Leo also built student residences at Eichkamp, Berlin, carried out in two phases (1959 and 1966–7; with Hans Müller and Georg Heinrichs). In the first phase independent *Punkthäuser* (focus houses) were sited at random in the extensive parkland site, each containing different types of rooms, with accommodation for 60 students. In the second phase the types of rooms were retained but built in larger rows of houses in line with the requirement for a more unified spatial composition.

Leo's concern with the expression of the individual functions of each building project is revealed in his Sporthalle (1962), Charlottenburg, Berlin, won in competition. His design clearly divides the functional areas from one another: the team rooms and playing areas are at ground-level and open on to the adjoining sports field, and the spectator areas and restaurant are located on the level above, reached via external staircases and ramps that also give access to the two stands. The concrete complex is spanned by a shallow barrel roof made from concrete struts arranged in a diamond pattern; by contrast the window frames, doors, preformed seating in the stands and handrails are picked out in colour. He also designed a residential complex and health-care building (1966–7) in the Märkisches Viertel, Berlin, planned in the early 1960s as a pioneering residential development for more than 40,000 people. He built 508 flats of varying size and type in buildings of different sizes, ranging from 5 to 17 storeys.

Two later buildings by Leo that develop his interest in the expression of function struck a very popular chord: first, the headquarters of the Deutsche Lebens-Rettungs-Gesellschaft (DLRG) (1969–71) and second, the Versuchsanstalt für Wasserbau und Schiffahrt (1975–6), both in Berlin. The significant form of these buildings is derived in both cases from the specific building task, the conditions of the site and the particular technical details. Using the technical structure of the buildings as their visual theme, he emphasized their function through the use of form and as a result created architecture with a strong visual impact and powerful symbolism. The DLRG Building (see fig.) combines the functions of headquarters, training and life-saving centre and maintenance and storage for the life-boats. It has a triangular profile formed by an inclined hoist at an angle of 45° on the lake frontage that carries the boats from a small branch canal up to one of the ten floors; the maintenance costs of this hoist are much lower than those for a traditional, vertically operated lift. This façade of the building, expressing the technology of the lift, steel stairs, doors, flaps, pipes and glass and metal cladding, combined with the tall transmitting mast, has a nautical flavour. By contrast, the landward side, with an

Ludwig Leo: DLRG Building, Spandau, Berlin, 1967–71

entrance for the rescue vehicles, consists of a simple, massive concrete tower with stair housings projecting at the side.

Like the DLRG station, the research institute for hydraulic engineering and shipping occupies an exposed site directly on the waterfront. Its technical nucleus is the circulation tank developed by the physicist and hydrodynamics specialist Christian Boës for flow experiments on models. Leo developed two building variants for two different locations: a horizontally installed tank, which is the usual form, and a vertical one that was constructed on the narrow site on the canal that used to form the frontier between West and East Berlin. The individual sections of the building, the concrete foundations, tanks, supports and laboratory building are openly shown as independent forms, differentiated from one another by the use of strong colours, white, pink, green and blue, in the spirit of Pop art. Both these buildings by Leo represent unique phenomena in architecture after World War II and, because of their multi-layered nature, they defy any attempt at categorization; they are most reminiscent perhaps of projects by the Soviet Constructivists. In 1975 Leo was appointed Professor of Project Planning at the Hochschule für Bildende Künste, Berlin.

BIBLIOGRAPHY

R. Rave and H.-J. Knöfel: *Bauen seit 1900 in Berlin* (Berlin, 1968)
U. Conrads: 'Zentrale der Deutschen Lebens-Rettungs-Gesellschaft an der Havel in Berlin', *Bauwelt*, lxiii/37 (1972), pp. 1461–4
H. and M. Bofinger, eds: *Architektur in Deutschland* (Stuttgart, 1979)
R. Rave, H.-J. Knöfel and J. Rave: *Bauen der 70er Jahre in Berlin* (Berlin, 1981)
P. Cook: 'Unappreciated Architects 3: Ludwig Leo: Berlin Mysteries', *Archit. Rev.* [London], clxix/1012 (1981), pp. 371–3
W. Pehnt: *Der Anfang der Bescheidenheit* (Munich, 1983)

M. Wörner and D. Mollenschott: *Architekturführer Berlin* (Berlin, 1989, rev. 1990)

ROLAND WOLFF

**Leo Bible.** The earliest surviving illustrated Byzantine Bible (Rome, Vatican, Bib. Apostolica, MS. Reg. gr. 1), produced in the 9th century AD or the first half of the 10th. It is named after the Byzantine official who commissioned it and is also known as the Bible of Queen Christina (of Sweden; *reg* 1626–89), from whose collection it passed to the Vatican Library. Leo, *patrikios*, *praepositos* (grand chamberlain and highest-ranking eunuch) and imperial *sakellarios* (treasurer), is identified in a metrical preface, and he had himself depicted in the first gathering of the manuscript, proffering his Bible to the Virgin. He is portrayed as white-haired and beardless, and it may be assumed that he was an elderly eunuch, a status eminently compatible with the office of *praepositos*.

Only one volume survives, containing the books from Genesis to Psalms. Both the preface and a contents page, however, testify that the original project comprised the whole of the Old and New Testaments. The volume (more than once trimmed and rebound) is distinguished by its unusually large format (410×270 mm). The full-page miniatures that preface selected books were inserted on separate leaves, which may imply that they were added after the completion of the text. There are also two dedicatory miniatures, one depicting Leo in the presence of the Virgin and Christ and the other his brother Constantine with Abbot Makar, kneeling before St Nicholas. All the miniatures are framed by verse inscriptions, which were apparently composed by Leo and, according to a contemporary note, were intended to serve as exegesis, although they are frequently more elliptical than illuminating. The miniatures include some uncommon iconography, such as the assembly of Samson, Gideon, Jephthah and Barak on a tribunal as the visual preface to the Book of Judges (see fig.) and a depiction of Judith and Holofernes, which is unique in Byzantine iconography. At least two and probably three artists were involved in the project.

The scale of the volume and the arrangement of its miniatures have provoked comparisons with 9th-century bibles from Tours, such as the Moutier-Grandval Bible (London, BL, Add. MS. 10546). Byzantinists, however, have generally preferred to compare its classicizing style with the PARIS PSALTER (Paris, Bib. N., MS. grec 139), with which it shares a common model for a number of miniatures, and have dated it *c.* 940 during the peak of the Macedonian Renaissance. The identity of the donor, Leo, has not been established beyond doubt; of the two possible candidates, one seems to have been an official in the first half of the 10th century and the other, though an old man, was in imperial service in the 840s.

BIBLIOGRAPHY
*Miniature della Bibbia Cod. Vat. Regin. gr. I e del Salterio Cod. Vat. Palat. gr. 381*, Collezione paleografica Vaticana, i (Milan, 1905) [facs.]
C. Mango: *The Date of Cod. Vat. Regin. Gr. I and the 'Macedonian Renaissance'*, Acta Archaeol. & A. Hist. Pertinentia, iv (1969), pp. 121–6
H. Kessler: *The Illustrated Bibles from Tours* (Princeton, 1977), p. 142

VALERIE NUNN

Leo Bible, miniature from the Book of Judges depicting Samson, Gideon, Jephthah and Barak on a tribunal, 410×270 mm, 9th century or first half of the 10th (Rome, Vatican, Biblioteca Apostolica, MS. Reg. gr. 1, fol. 206*r*)

**Leochares** (*b* ?Athens; *fl* later 4th century BC). Greek sculptor. One of the leading personalities in Attic sculpture of the 4th century BC, he may well have been an Athenian, as his original extant signatures are all from Athens. Leochares is explicitly described as an Athenian only in the inscription on the base of a lost imperial copy of his famous *Ganymede* (see below) from Rome (Florence, Uffizi; *Inscr. Gr./1*, xiv, 1253). According to Pliny (*Natural History* XXXIV.1), Leochares flourished in the 102nd Olympiad (372/1–368/7 BC), a date that seems too early given that he apparently collaborated with Lysippos on the lost bronze group of *Alexander's Lion-hunt*, a dedication by the general Krateros, who rescued the king during this event, erected at Delphi *c.* 320 BC (Plutarch: *Alexander* XL.iv). In fact, Leochares' career seems to have spanned the second half of the 4th century BC. One of his signatures is dated to 338/7 BC, but his career must have had an early phase a little before 355 BC, the year of the exile of the Athenian general Timotheos (411–354 BC), who had previously commissioned to Leochares a bronze portrait of the pro-Macedonian orator Isokrates (436–338 BC), which was erected in Eleusis (Plutarch: *Lives of Ten Orators: Isokrates* xxvii).

Leochares' bronze *Ganymede and the Eagle of Zeus* (see Pliny: XXXIV.79; Tatian: *Oration to the Greeks* XXXIV.3;

and the above inscription in Florence) can probably be identified with the marble group serving as a table foot (Rome, Vatican, Gal. Candelabri), in which the eagle is shown lifting the boy carefully by his cloak. Leochares is recorded as the sculptor of three statues of Zeus. His *Zeus Tonans* (Zeus with a thunderbolt) was erected under Augustus (*reg* 30 BC–AD 14) on the Capitol in Rome (Pliny: XXXIV.10 and 79). He also made a new statue of *Zeus Polieus* on the Athenian Acropolis and a sculptural group of *Zeus and Demos* at Peiraeus (Pausanias: *Guide to Greece* I.xxiv.4 and I.i.3 respectively). Attempts have been made to identify the type of *Zeus Tonans* on Roman coins of Augustan date as well as imperial copies.

Leochares is also credited with statues of Apollo. His *Apollo Diadematus* (Apollo with a fillet) is mentioned by Pliny (*Natural History* XXXIV.79), but the most famous *Apollo* of Leochares seems to have been the bronze statue of the god in the pronaos of the Temple of Apollo Patroos in the Athenian Agora (Pausanias: I.iii.4). This was probably erected during the Lykourgan period (338–322 BC) and is generally identified with the type represented by the *Apollo Belvedere* (Rome, Vatican, Mus. Pio-Clementino) and the so-called Steinhäuser head (Basle, Antikenmus.). The god is shown striding in a splendid epiphany, naked but for a cloak; the original influenced both Hellenistic sculpture (*Apollo* on the Gigantomachy frieze of the Pergamene Altar; Berlin, Pergamonmus.; *see* PERGAMON, fig. 5) and modern creations (*Perseus* by Antonio Canova; Rome, Vatican, Mus. Pio-Clementino). The identification is based mainly on the affinities between the *Apollo Belvedere* and the *Ganymede*, particularly the same elegant movement of the body. The slender proportions of the body and the diagonal movement of the *Apollo Belvedere* are repeated in the *Artemis* of Versailles type (Paris, Louvre), the bronze original of which has thus been assigned to Leochares.

Leochares is reported to have collaborated with Skopas, Timotheos and Bryaxis on the sculptural decoration of the Mausoleum at Halikarnassos (*c.* 360–350 BC; *see* HALIKARNASSOS, §2(i)), undertaking the west side of the monument (Pliny: XXXVI.30–31; Vitruvius: *On Architecture* VII. preface xii–xiii). Modern scholars, however, have attributed to Leochares slabs from the best-preserved Amazon frieze (e.g. London, BM, 1020–21 or 1013–15), as well as 1037 from the Chariot frieze, though inconclusively.

According to Bernard Ashmole, Leochares also worked later (*c.* 340 BC) on the marble statue of the enthroned mourning *Demeter* from Knidos (London, BM). This identification is due to the stylistic affinities between the head of the *Demeter* and the head of the youthful *Alexander* of the Erbach-Berlin type (Athens, Acropolis Mus.). The latter is accepted as a copy of the portrait of Alexander from the gold and ivory group of *King Philippos II of Macedonia and his Family* in the Philippeion at Olympia (Pausanias: V.xx.9), a commission given to Leochares after the battle of Chaironeia (338 BC). But the original might also have been an independent commission as a portrait for the Athenian Acropolis.

Leochares also worked with the sculptor Sthennis of Olynthos on a private family group on the Athenian Acropolis, and he made the statue of the pancratiast

Autolykos, who was assassinated by the Thirty Tyrants, erected in the prytaneion in the Athenian Agora. A possible attribution to Leochares is the type of the Lateran Sophocles (Rome, Vatican, Mus. Gregoriano Profano), which is thought to reflect one of the statues of the great Athenian tragic poets that were erected by Lykourgos at the theatre of Dionysos in Athens (338–322 BC). Modern scholars have credited Leochares with a preference for elegance as well as stark movement, expressed mainly by the outlines of his figures, slender proportions and a retrospective style.

BIBLIOGRAPHY
G. Lippold: *Griechische Plastik* (Munich, 1950), pp. 268–72
B. Ashmole: 'Demeter of Cnidus', *J. Hell. Stud.*, lxxi (1951), pp. 13–28
G. Donnay: 'La Chronologie de Léocharès', *Rev. Etud. Anc.*, lxi (1959), pp. 300–09
——: 'Un Sculpteur grec méconnu, Léocharès', *Gaz. B.-A.*, liii (1959), pp. 5–20
J. Charbonneaux: 'Le Zeus de Léocharès', *Mnmts Piot*, liii (1963), pp. 9–17
C. Picard: *La Sculpture: Période classique: IVe siècle*, iv/2 of *Manuels d'archéologie et d'histoire de l'art* (Paris, 1954–63), pp. 754–854
J. J. Pollitt: *The Art of Ancient Greece: Sources and Documents* (Englewood Cliffs, 1965, rev. Cambridge, MA, 2/1990), pp. 90–91, 100, 196, 198, 260
R. Tölle: 'Zum Apollon des Leochares', *Jb. Dt. Archäol. Inst.*, lxxxi (1966), pp. 142–72
I. Scheibler: 'Leochares in Halikarnassos: Zur Methode der Meisterforschung', *Wandlungen: Studien zur antiken und neuereren Kunst, Ernst Homann-Wedeking gewidmet* (Munich, 1975), pp. 152–62
L. Todisco: *Scultura greca del IV secolo: Maestri e scuole di statuaria tra classicità ed ellenismo* (Milan, 1993), pp. 103–7

I. LEVENTI

**León.** Spanish city and capital of the province of León, lying at the junction of the Bernesga and Torio rivers *c.* 90 km south of Oviedo and 250 km north-west of Madrid. The city's name reflects its Roman origin as the headquarters of the 7th Legion (Gemina), stationed there in AD 69 to guard the central Iberian plateau against incursions by the Astures from the Cantabrian Mountains to the north. Overrun during the 8th-century Moorish conquest of Iberia, the city was reconquered in AD 856, and it became the capital of the Christian kingdom of León from the early 10th century until the kingdom was finally unified with Castile in 1230.

I. History and urban development. II. Buildings.

### I. History and urban development.

The city's rectangular plan and the towered walls (probably dating from the 4th century AD) that survive on three sides are a reminder of its Roman past, but little is known of how this frontier town evolved into a city and Christian capital. Whether or not León was entirely deserted during the Muslim conquest, the chronicles confer the honour of its reoccupation in 856 on Ordoño I of Asturias (*reg* 850–66). Under his grandson Ordoño II (*reg* 914–25) León displaced Oviedo as the capital of the kingdom of Asturias–León.

The earliest Christian resettlement centred in the southern part of the walled area, along the major east–west axis that probably followed the *via principalis* of Roman León. According to the chronicle of Sampiro (*c.* 1040), Ordoño I converted the Roman baths in the south-east corner of the city into a residence (the discovery of a Roman mosaic under the cathedral in the 19th century confirmed the

Roman use of the site). When Ordoño II bestowed this palace on the bishop for a cathedral, the palatine complex was shifted towards the centre of the southern wall. Its church, S Salvador Palaz de Rey, built by Ramiro II (*reg* 931–51), survives, somewhat modified, as the oldest ecclesiastical building in León.

The city suffered destructive Muslim raids, but Alfonso V (*reg* 999–1028) 'repopulated and restored' it and issued the municipal charter (*fuero*) that was to govern the life of its citizens. He moved the palace to the northern sector of the city and adopted S Juan, later rededicated to St Isidore of Seville (*c.* AD 560–636), as the palatine church (*see* §II, 2 below). Under Alfonso the city became a true political and cultural heir to Oviedo, but it was under Ferdinand I of Castile (*reg* 1038–65) and his queen, Sancha, and their son Alfonso VI (*reg* 1065–1109) that imperial ambitions and contacts with France, typified by the alliance with Cluny Abbey, helped León to emerge as a centre for a new, Romanesque art. The city's role was enhanced by its situation on the pilgrimage route to Santiago de Compostela, and the consequent influx of pilgrims led to the opening of a new gate in the north-west corner by Ferdinand II (*reg* 1157–88) in 1168. International currents clearly explain the authentic French Gothic style of León Cathedral.

In the 16th century León benefited from the general prosperity accompanying Spain's conquest of the New World. The Order of the Knights of St James entrusted Pedro de Larrea (*fl* 1506–14) with the rebuilding of their hospital, the Convento de S Marcos, on the pilgrimage route just outside the city, and León gained a major monument. The hospital façade, executed in the 1530s under Martín de Villareal, is in the Plateresque style and is notable for the fine carving of figurative and ornamental details. A church (ded. 1541) in a Hispano-Flemish Gothic style was joined to the hospital; Guillelmus Donzel (*fl* 1537–47) signed the wooden stalls of the raised choir in 1542, having been assisted by Juan de Juní, and Juan de Badajoz the younger was responsible for the sacristy, executed in 1549.

The palace of the Guzman family was built from 1559 on the main east–west artery in a classicizing Renaissance style conceived, probably, by Rodrigo Gil de Hontañón. It is a building of some magnificence, the last in León with such a claim until Antonio Gaudí erected opposite it, in 1892–4, a block of flats (the Casa de los Botines) in his distinctive Art Nouveau style.

BIBLIOGRAPHY

M. Risco: *Historia de la ciudad y corte de León, y de sus reyes*, 2 vols (Madrid, 1792)

J. M. Quadrado: *Recuerdos y bellezas de España: Asturias y León* (Madrid, 1855), pp. 357–542

M. Gómez-Moreno: *Catálogo monumental de España: Provincia de León*, 2 vols (Madrid, 1925)

C. Sánchez-Albornoz: *Estampas de la vida en León hace mil años* (Madrid, 1926)

M. D. Berrueta: *León*, Guías artísticas de España, xii (Barcelona, 1953)

A. García Bellido: *Nueve estudios sobre la Legio VII Gemina y su campamento en León* (León, 1968)

A. Represa: 'Evolución urbana de León en los siglos XI–XIII', *León y su historia*, i (León, 1969), pp. 243–82

## II. Buildings.

1. Cathedral. 2. S Isidoro.

### 1. CATHEDRAL.

(i) Architecture. (ii) Sculpture. (iii) Stained glass.

*(i) Architecture.* The cathedral dedicated to S Maria de León is the purest reflection of French Gothic architecture in Spain, although its authenticity has been compromised by 15th- and 16th-century additions and several 19th-century restoration campaigns. The first cathedral was built on a site near the south-east corner of the walled city bestowed on the bishop by Ordoño II and previously occupied by Roman baths and the palace of Ordoño I. Chronicles record two subsequent reconstructions. The first resulted in a rededication in 1073 by Bishop Pelagio; Lucas of Tuy reported the second in his *Chronicon mundi* (*c.* 1236), in a passage attributing the foundation of a new cathedral to Bishop Manrique de Lara (1181–1205), who died before it was completed. Remains of this building, uncovered in 1886, showed that it was the same width (28 m) as the nave of the present cathedral and on the same axis. It had three semicircular eastern apses. The materials, brick and rubble, suggest links with Sahagún, home of a distinctive school of Romanesque brick architecture, and they illustrate the shortage of good stone that was to plague the final cathedral.

The provincialism implied by Manrique's cathedral was symptomatic of León's decline after the division of León–Castile from 1157 to 1230. With the accession of Alfonso X (the Learned) to the throne of Castile in 1252 and of Martín Fernández, royal notary, to the episcopal throne of León (1254–89), provincialism gave way to an ambitious scheme that left León with an important example of High Gothic architecture. In 1255 Alfonso granted financial privileges and access to a source of timber; three years later a council of the bishops of the realm granted indulgences to benefactors of the construction. Work began at the east end, which was laid out east of Manrique's church and required the removal of part of the city wall. By 1259 chaplains were appointed for two of the ambulatory chapels, and in 1302 Bishop Gonzalo Osorio was able to redirect rents from construction to the chapter because of the 'good state' of the church. In 1439, however, the Council of Basle granted new indulgences for construction, and work continued in each succeeding century, much of it devoted to reconstituting a fabric delicate in its conception and weakened by inferior stone. The new cathedral was thoroughly French Gothic in inspiration, with two western towers, three aisles, a transept located halfway between the east and west ends, an ambulatory with five radiating chapels, quadripartite rib vaulting, stained glass, including huge rose windows in each of the façades, and elaborately sculptured portals. Its highest vaults were 30 m above the floor, 2.7 times the width of the nave (see fig. 1).

Bishop Martín's Castilian background is evident in the choice of architects and sculptors for León. MASTER ENRIQUE, probably the second architect of the cathedral of Burgos, the capital of Castile, became the architect of León Cathedral. He is assumed to have been French by training. At his death in 1277 he was succeeded, at León

1. León Cathedral, interior looking west, begun *c.* 1258

and Burgos, by Johannes Petri (Juan Pérez) who died in 1296 or 1297. Enrique's campaign at Burgos included the erection of three façades inspired by Reims Cathedral, and it was from Reims, presumably through the agency of Enrique, that León derived its plan. The dimensions of León Cathedral represent a reduction of about a third, and the eight nave bays of Reims became four in León, but the plans coincided in the number of transept bays, including the intervention of a half bay between choir and ambulatory, and in the number of radiating chapels. Those of León are shallower than the Reims prototypes, and uniform, but their exterior elevations, the earliest work at León, are identical. The chief departure from the Reims plan is in the disposition of the west towers, which at León do not stand over the first bays of the nave, but beside them. Moreover, the porch of the west façade was inspired by the transept portals of Chartres Cathedral. The model for the elevation at León was Amiens Cathedral, although it was less conservatively followed. The substitution of areas of glass for stone was one motive for looking beyond Amiens to other French models, such as Saint-Denis Abbey Church; the whole triforium was opened and glazed, and extra, flanking lancets were squeezed into the triforium and clerestory levels. The building was also lightened visually at ground-level by the blind arcade that ran around the interior.

Owing to reconstructions, the original façades are lost, although the northern, apart from the gable of 1448, is closest to the primitive state. A giant relief of the *Annunciation* above the rose and a crowning gable with towers were added to the west façade *c.* 1570, possibly by Juan López (*d* 1571), but this part was redesigned in the 19th

century. The sober north-west tower (la Vieja) is essentially in its original form of the late 13th century and early 14th. The lower storey of the south-west tower (del Reloj) is also from this first campaign, but the upper half was designed, somewhat incoherently, by the Netherlander Joosken van Utrecht (*fl* 1429–67) in the third quarter of the 15th century. The south transept façade was razed and rebuilt, without care for its original form, in the 19th century.

The plan of the cloister, on the north side of the cathedral, seems also to depend on that of Burgos. Work began towards the end of the 13th century and continued into the 14th, but the elaborate vaults were not built until *c.* 1540 when Juan de Badajoz the younger was master of works. Unlike Burgos, however, León Cathedral was designed to be free-standing in the French manner; the cloister was joined to it only in the 14th century with the building of a series of large chapels in the intervening space along the façade of the north transept. A sacristy designed by Alfonso Ramos (*d* 1530) was annexed to the southernmost ambulatory chapel *c.* 1500, and, on the north side, a large library notable for its carved droleries was completed in 1505 by Juan de Badajoz the elder.

*See also* BADAJOZ, DE.

BIBLIOGRAPHY

G. E. Street: *An Account of Gothic Architecture in Spain* (London, 1865/*R* 1914), i, pp. 135–54

D. de los Rios y Serrano: *La catedral de León*, 2 vols (Madrid, 1895)

V. Lampérez y Romea: *Historia de la arquitectura cristiana española en la edad media* (Madrid, 1908), pp. 313–15

E. Lambert: *L'Art gothique en Espagne aux XIIe et XIIIe siècles* (Paris, 1931), pp. 238–50

L. Torres Balbás: *Arquitectura gótica*, A. Hisp., vii (Madrid, 1952), pp. 84–94

W. Merino Rubio: *Arquitectura hispano flamenca en León* (León, 1974), pp. 27–157

R. Cómez Ramos: *Las empresas artísticas de Alfonso X el Sabio* (Seville, 1979)

R. M. Esbert and others: *A Petrographic and Physical Study of the Building Stones from León Cathedral* (Bologna, 1981)

J. M. Villanueva Lázaro: *La ciudad de León: El gótico* (León, 1987)

H. Karge: *Die Kathedrale von Burgos und die spanische Architektur des 13. Jahrhunderts: Französische Hochgotik in Kastilien und León* (Berlin, 1989) [with Eng. summary]

*(ii) Sculpture.* The cathedral was designed to incorporate large assemblages of portal sculpture. The jamb statues—some of which are missing or are later replacements—portray apostles in the central portal and Old and New Testament figures in the north and south portals. The tympana, however, establish the essential iconographic programme. Like the architectural framework, the sculpture is thoroughly French in concept and style; it shows some resemblance to the portal sculpture of the cathedrals of Amiens, Paris and Reims, the influence of which may have come via Burgos Cathedral, and suggests that the sculpture at León dates from the last third of the 13th century. The tympanum of the central portal of the west façade at León has a *Last Judgement* resembling that in the north transept portal (Puerta de la Coronería) at Burgos, with scenes of Resurrection and Hell extending into the voussoirs of the enframing arches (see fig. 2). The tympanum of the south portal (Puerta de S Francisco) shows the *Coronation of the Virgin* and the *Death of the Virgin*, with the *Wise and Foolish Virgins* and the celestial hierarchy in the voussoirs, while that of the north portal (Puerta de

2. León Cathedral, *Last Judgement*, tympanum of the central portal of the west façade, *c.* 1275–80

S Juan) illustrates the *Infancy of Christ*, from the *Visitation* to the *Massacre of the Innocents*. The statue of the *Virgin and Child* on the trumeau of the central portal is the work of an unknown master who also carved most of the reliefs of the west façade. He has also been credited with three figures in the *Last Judgement* (the Virgin, St John and the angel to the right of Christ), the tympanum of the north portal, as well as two important tombs, in particular that of *Martín Fernández* in the south transept. This so-called Master of La Vírgen Blanca appears to have been influenced by the style of sculpture from Amiens, although his figures are distinguished by their modelled blockish forms. His hand has also been detected at Burgos in the sculpture of the Puerta de la Coronería (*c.* 1240).

The portal sculpture of the west façade at León is, however, dominated by the sculpture of the so-called Master of the Last Judgement, in particular by the representation of the *Saved* and the *Damned* on the lowest register of the central tympanum; the carvings are extraordinary in their detailed depiction of celebration and torture. This master's style is characterized by his attenuated, elegant and complex draperies, which appear to have their origins in the work of the Joseph Master at Reims.

The subject-matter of the tympanum of the south transept portal, with its *Apocalyptic Christ and the Evangelists*, a theme rarely depicted in the 13th century, closely resembles that of the south transept portal (Puerta del Sarmental) at Burgos, yet stylistically it combines the styles of the west façade. The jamb figures, however, are French in character, reminiscent of those at Amiens, Paris and Reims. Like those sites, León has a doorway devoted to the life of a local saint, S Froilán, patron of the diocese, on the right side of the south transept. The single door of the north transept seems to have been undertaken in the

last years of the 13th century. The theme of the central door of the south transept is repeated but with *Christ* standing in a mandorla. The *Virgin and Child* are depicted on the trumeau. The last great assemblage of sculpture was for the choir, and it comprised oak reliefs of biblical and hagiographic subjects begun in 1467 by two sculptors of Netherlandish origin, Juan de Malinas and Diego Copín The choir was separated from the crossing by an elaborate stone *trascoro* of Renaissance vocabulary completed by Juan Lopéz and Baltazar Gutiérrez in 1574. Shortly afterwards it was embellished with large alabaster reliefs of the *Life of the Virgin* by Esteban Jordán. In 1746 the choir and screen were moved westward into the nave.

For further illustration *see* GOTHIC, fig. 48.

BIBLIOGRAPHY
F. B. Deknatel: 'The Thirteenth-century Gothic Sculpture of the Cathedrals of Burgos and León', *A. Bull.*, xvii (1935), pp. 243–389 (322–89)
A. Durán Sanpere and J. Ainaud de Lasarte: *Escultura gótica*, A. Hisp., viii (Madrid, 1956), pp. 41–64
M. A. Franco Mata: *Escultura gótica en León* (León, 1976)

JOHN WILLIAMS

*(iii) Stained glass.* The great windows of León Cathedral were intended to be integral to the design. Under the influence of the Early Gothic of the Ile-de-France, the architect Enrique provided for three tiers of windows at clerestory, triforium and nave level, all tall, narrow and divided into two by a delicate mullion. Every window was eventually glazed, a total of 230, comprising more than 700 separate panels of glass making an area of 1800 sq. m. The earliest glass, in the nave clerestory and apse chapels, dates from the second half of the 13th century, the only surviving series of windows of this date in Spain. The two rose windows and most of the apse glass date from the 14th century, further nave aisle and clerestory windows

date from the 15th century, and work finished with the glass of the Santiago Chapel in the 16th century. Between 1936 and 1976 the artist C. J. F. Espino (*b* 1906) painted scaled-down cartoons of every window in the cathedral to aid future restoration.

The first windows date from 1260 to 1280 and are in three of the five radiating chapels at the east end, many in poor condition or much altered. They depict scenes from the *Life of Christ* and the *Lives of the Saints*; style and ornament can be compared to French glass of a generation earlier. Another series is in the upper apse, north nave and clerestory, pairs of patriarchs, prophets and Old Testament kings standing under canopies, with some purely ornamental panels in reds and blues. This is again in an archaic French style.

The north clerestory window in the fifth bay from the west is quite different. It is thought to have been moved from the palace of Alfonso X during the 14th century. The central panels of the four lights show a *Royal Hunt* (see fig. 3). A mounted king, presumed to be Alfonso himself, and horsemen bearing hawks and hunting-horns are accompanied by archers, hounds and other animals. One horseman carries a standard with the arms of Castile and León. Other panels show musical angels and the liberal arts: figures writing, painting, playing music and dancing. Such secular activities are unique in 13th-century glass; the designs are bold and lively and probably taken from contemporary manuscripts. It is ironic that the silver stain technique was not yet being used at León, although French glaziers had already learnt it from a treatise based on Moorish techniques compiled by Alfonso X.

3. León Cathedral, north clerestory, *Royal Hunt* window (detail), stained glass, third quarter of the 13th century

In the 14th century many of the apse windows were made to show two tiers of apostles under simple canopies. Their elongated figures are superbly designed to fit the narrow apertures and to be seen from a great distance. The exaggerated postures, powerful expressions and strong colours are evidence of a distinctively local style. Two of the rose windows also belong to this period. The west rose has the *Virgin and Child* in the centre surrounded by a ring of apostles and outer decorative panels. The colours are warm yellows and greens. The north rose, which was considerably reworked in the 15th century, has a central medallion of *Christ Enthroned*, surrounded by red and blue chequerwork, kings with musical instruments and plant scrolls. The south rose is a 19th-century copy of the north rose.

Many of the 15th-century windows illustrate the cosmopolitan nature of Spanish glass at this time. A French glazier, Jean d'Angers (*fl* 1420s), was known to have worked on the cathedral, as well as at Burgos. There were also workshops of Flemish glaziers, whose windows are in the west sides of the transepts and in the nave clerestories; they include Old Testament figures and the kings of Castile and León, and are characterized by the more muted colours and detailed drawing that were typical of Flemish glass. The Renaissance influence introduced by the Flemings can be seen in the 16th-century windows. The Santiago Chapel was glazed in 1524 by Diego de Santillana (*fl* 1497–1524) with a scheme of the *Virgin and Saints* with Old Testament kings, warriors and Fathers of the Church under canopies. The use of perspective, modelling of the flesh and architectural details is quite new. Other windows were installed in the central chapel of the ambulatory by Rodrigo de Herreras (*fl* 1560s) in 1565. These later windows show the distinctive style that was blended from the various foreign schools of the 15th century into a final flourishing of the craft.

### BIBLIOGRAPHY

J. Rosell de Torres: 'Las vidrieras pintadas en España y con especialidad las de la catedral de León', *Mus. Esp. Ant.*, ii (1873), pp. 285–301
C. H. Sherrill: *Stained Glass Tours in Spain and Flanders* (London, 1924)
J. Harvey: *The Cathedrals of Spain* (London, 1957)
J. Fernandez Arenas: *Las vidrieras de la catedral de León* (León, 1982)
L. Grodecki and C. Brisac: *Le Vitrail gothique au XIIIe siècle* (Fribourg, 1984); Eng. trans. as *Gothic Stained Glass, 1200–1300* (Ithaca and London, 1985)
C. Brisac: *Le Vitrail* (Paris, Tokyo and Milan, 1985); Eng. trans. as *A Thousand Years of Stained Glass* (London and New York, 1986)

CAROLA HICKS

### 2. S Isidoro.

(i) Church. (ii) Panteón de los Reyes.

#### (i) Church.

*(a) Architecture.* On 21 December 1063, after the translation of the relics of St Isidore from Seville to León, Ferdinand I (*reg* 1037–65) dedicated his new palatine church to the saint. The first church was a modest building (16.5×12 m), but already Romanesque in its ashlar masonry, a fragment of which, from the north-west corner, survives in the extant church. The plan and elevation of this three-aisled, barrel-vaulted basilica with squared apses were, however, Asturian (*see* ASTURIAN ARCHITECTURE). This, and the dedication, symbolized Ferdinand's assertion of the claims of the kings of Asturias–León to be the

legitimate successors of the Christian Visigothic kings of the peninsula.

Ferdinand's heirs, his son, Alfonso VI (*reg* 1065–1109), and granddaughter, Urraca (*reg* 1109–26), began a new church, probably in the 1090s: Urraca's epitaph credits her with an 'amplification'. Some foundations of this second, notably larger, basilica (26×19 m) were revealed under the transepts during restorations in 1908 and 1971. They showed that it had three aisles ending in semicircular apses, a plan conceived along the lines of the contemporary Aragonese cathedral of Jaca. Even before this new basilica was completed, a transept was introduced, probably after the completion of the transept at Santiago de Compostela (*c.* 1115): Santiago was the source of the sculptural style employed on the south transept portal at S Isidoro, and the masons' marks in this area, which differ from those of the adjacent aisle walls, are the same as the marks in the transept of Santiago. Barrel vaulting was also introduced. The rectangular shape of the crossing, which resulted from the change of plan, obviated the kind of domed crossing used at Jaca and Frómista. The great polylobed arches separating the transepts from the crossing are an extraordinary example of a motif that Romanesque architecture borrowed from Islamic buildings, here used on a uniquely large scale (see fig. 4). The use of the motif was precocious, if this area of S Isidoro was truly undertaken *c.* 1115–20. The small door connecting the nave with the Panteón de los Reyes (*see* §(ii)(a) below) also has a polylobed as well as a horseshoe arch. Recognition that a fabric originally prepared for a timber covering would not

sustain a stone vault led to the introduction of brick in the nave vault after a few courses of stone.

The epitaph on the tomb of Petrus Deustamben, known otherwise as a builder of bridges, honours him as the architect of the basilica of S Isidoro during the reign of Alfonso VII (*reg* 1126–57), but the church must have been essentially finished well before the dedication presided over by Alfonso in 1149, a ceremony that coincided with his coronation in the presence of dignitaries of the realm. Apart from the new chapter house built at the end of the north transept in the late 12th century, building stopped until the second quarter of the 15th, when a stone choir was built over the three westernmost bays of the nave. In 1513 the central apse was razed in order to erect a larger choir and sanctuary in a Hispano-Flemish Late Gothic style attributable to Juan de Badajoz I (*see* BADAJOZ, DE), architect of the library of León Cathedral.

BIBLIOGRAPHY
M. Gómez-Moreno: *El arte románico español: Esquema de un libro* (Madrid, 1934), pp. 102–6
W. M. Whitehill: *Spanish Romanesque Architecture of the Eleventh Century* (Oxford, 1941), pp. 143–54
J. Williams: 'San Isidoro in León: Evidence for a New History', *A. Bull.*, lv (1973), pp. 171–84
W. Merino Rubio: *Arquitectura hispano flamenca en León* (León, 1974), pp. 163–95

*(b) Sculpture.* There are two main ensembles of architectural sculpture at S Isidoro. The earlier of these is the capital sculpture of the Panteón de los Reyes (*see* §(ii)(b) below). The other comprises the portal sculpture of the basilica and more than 150 capitals on its exterior and interior. Owing to its proximity to the western wall of the city, public access to the church was through portals on its south side. The Puerta del Cordero, which opens into the south aisle (see fig. 5), takes its name from the relief on the tympanum (1.22×2.54 m), where the *Lamb of God*, in a medallion supported by angels, presides over a detailed depiction of the *Sacrifice of Isaac*. The figures of Abraham and Isaac are flanked by Sarah with Isaac on the right, and by Hagar, the 'mother of Arabs', and her son, Ishmael, on the left. It was an appropriate subject for the palatine church of the capital of a kingdom engaged in reconquering territories from the Muslims. The style employed in the *Sacrifice of Isaac* originated at S MARTÍN, FRÓMISTA and Jaca Cathedral (*see* JACA, §2). This is also true of the style of the *Signs of the Zodiac* and other reliefs of musicians and the *King David*, which appear below the cornice and in the spandrels of the arch, and of the capitals with squatting figures that flank the doorway. The two saints principally associated with the site flank the arches of the portals. On the left is *St Isidore*, who carries a crosier. He is identified by inscription, while the figure opposite is not; but the latter's almost feminine face identifies him as *St Pelagius*, the boy-martyr of Córdoba, dedicatee of the 10th-century church housing his relics that was eventually absorbed by Ferdinand I's S Isidoro. The style of these two figures is a synthesis of two major currents: that originating at S Martín de Frómista and that associated with St Sernin, Toulouse. The sculpture can be dated to the first campaign of construction in the early years of the 12th century, although some alterations to this portal may have taken place.

4. León, S Isidoro, interior of the nave and north transept, first quarter of the 12th century

5. León, S Isidoro, Puerta del Cordero, *c.* 1100–10

The south transept portal, traditionally known as the Puerta del Perdón, exhibits a different style, which is similar enough to that of figures on the transept façades at Santiago de Compostela that it may be attributed to the same workshop employed there in the second decade of the 12th century (*see* SANTIAGO DE COMPOSTELA, §1(ii)). The transept tympanum (1.10×1.72 m) features the *Descent from the Cross*, with the *Three Marys at the Tomb* to the right and on the left the *Ascension*. The representation of the *Ascension*, with Christ climbing upwards with the help of angels, must have been taken from the tympanum of the Porte Miègeville at St Sernin, Toulouse. It is likely that the choice of *St Peter* and *St Paul* to flank the portal was inspired by an admiration for the great portal at Cluny Abbey (destr.). Fragments of sculpture in the style of this transept portal are in the Museo-Biblioteca de la Real Colegiata de San Isidoro and the Museo Arqueológico Provincial, León.

The tympanum of the north transept doorway seems never to have been carved. One of the capitals, however, displays naked figures and serpents in a reprise of the style and motifs found at Jaca Cathedral. Motifs from Jaca and Compostela, and variations on them, especially themes related to courtly entertainment, informed most of the capital sculpture at S Isidoro. Their three-dimensional quality represents a new level of maturity, although, with the possible exception of those supporting the westernmost springers for arches of the nave vault, the capitals were probably carved in the early 12th century.

S Isidoro featured less and less in the plans of future rulers; little was added to its artistic treasure in the Gothic period, and thus its Romanesque sculpture survives relatively intact.

The Puerta del Cordero received its final embellishment in the mid-16th century, when an elaborate frontispiece displaying the imperial escutcheon of Charles V was raised over the portal bearing the *Lamb of God* relief. It depicts the legend of St Isidore aiding the army of Alfonso VII at Baeza—another icon of reconquest.

BIBLIOGRAPHY
G. Gaillard: *Les Débuts de la sculpture romane en Espagne* (Paris, 1938), pp. 40–86
A. Viñayo Gonzáles: *L'Ancien Royaume de León roman* (La Pierre-qui-vire, 1972)
S. Moralejo: 'Pour l'interprétation iconographique du portail de l'Agneau à Saint-Isidore de León: Les Signes du zodiaque', *Cah. Saint-Michel de Cuxa*, viii (1977), pp. 137–73
J. Williams: 'Generationes Abrahae: Reconquest Iconography in León', *Gesta*, xvi/2 (1977), pp. 3–14

*(ii) Panteón de los Reyes.*

*(a) Architecture.* The Panteón de los Reyes, to use a name that supplanted that of the chapel of S Catalina only in the 18th century, served as the cemetery of the kings of León. The Panteón proper is a groin-vaulted narthex (8×8 m) of six bays centred on the western portal of the first church of S Isidoro. The complex also included an aisle dividing the Panteón from the city wall, and a cloister gallery on its north side. On the second level it carries a large barrel-vaulted tribune, which originally provided communication between the palace and the church by means of a large arched window, and a tower, which is not quite on axis because it appropriated one of the towers of the city wall as its base.

The architecture of the Panteón, with its compound piers with half columns and figured capitals, represents a new, French style, sharply different from the Asturian style of the church to which it was attached. Although Ferdinand I chose S Isidoro as a dynastic cemetery, the Panteón itself must have been erected by his immediate heirs, Alfonso VI and Urraca, probably in the 1080s. Nevertheless, when it received a splendid set of frescoes of New Testament subjects early in the 12th century, the programme paid homage to Ferdinand and his queen, Sancha.

BIBLIOGRAPHY
M. Gómez-Moreno: *Arte románico español* (Madrid, 1934), pp. 58–62
G. Gaillard: *Les Débuts de la sculpture romane espagnole* (Paris, 1938), pp. 1–15

*(b) Sculpture.* The sculpture of the Panteón consists of some 40 limestone capitals distributed through the Panteón itself, the aisle separating it from the city wall, and the adjacent bays of the cloister gallery. The most important carvings are found in the Panteón proper (see fig. 6). The sculpture is generally homogeneous, but there is no distinct iconographic programme to explain all themes and locations, although some meanings may be deduced. Each of the two principal capitals (h 615 mm) that support the Panteón vaults rests on a section of a marble column, presumably reused from a local Roman building. The choice of supports was perhaps based on practical considerations, but the Corinthian capitals they carry are exceptional in their fidelity to a Classical prototype and may thereby have conveyed a sense of antiquity, and with it, of authority.

Of the remaining capitals, 15 are decorated exclusively with vegetal motifs, in particular pine-cones; 10 include animals, and 13 bear human figures. With their typical penitential themes, the *Raising of Lazarus* and the *Healing of the Leper*, the capitals flanking the doorway leading to the basilica are appropriate both to a cemetery and to the entrance to a church. The themes depicted on other

6. León, S Isidoro, Panteón de los Reyes, view towards south-west, begun c. 1080

capitals are appropriately redemptive. *Exodus*, an unusual subject for capital decoration, is an obvious example, as is *Daniel in the Lions' Den* and the *Sacrifice of Isaac*. The theme of deliverance may also be read into the three capitals on which are represented secular figures spearing lions, thereby combining a traditional hunting motif with the psalmodic plea for liberation from the mouth of the lion, as used in the Mass for the Dead. Salvation through the Eucharist is implied in three capitals that feature doves, peacocks and griffins drinking from chalices. Other capitals have ape-like creatures seated at the corners. These were damaged in the 16th-century reconstruction of the cloister gallery, and they are not clearly legible, but on one of them the creature seems to be ensnared by a serpentine form, possibly a metaphor for the state of Sin. The resemblance of another capital to that of the *Punishment of Dives* on the Porte des Comtes of S Sernin, Toulouse, may indicate that the sin of greed is represented. In two other undamaged capitals the reference to the Porte des Comtes is clearer: one shows a standing naked woman holding a pair of serpents aloft, while another pair fasten their mouths on her breasts, in the same way that Lust is depicted on the Toulouse door; and the other bears a motif—for which the capitals from the Porte des Comtes again offer parallels—of dragons menacing an orant. This capital is beside the window opening from the tribune to the church, and its companion opposite, partially obscured by the respond of the nave gallery of the new church,

seems to have displayed the themes of greed and luxury. The tribune was occupied by members of the royal family, presumably the audience for whom these lessons in personal morality were intended.

Some of the motifs used in the Panteón, such as the birds and chalices and the hunted lions, were traditional. Others, such as the animal heads emerging from floral scrolls and the addorsed lions, became common in the great ensembles of capital sculpture at S Martín, Frómista, Jaca Cathedral and Santiago de Compostela in the 1090s. Despite their technical simplicity, in their complex design and three-dimensional quality the capitals can be considered examples of a mature Romanesque style. Although some of the motifs can be compared to 10th-century Mozarabic capitals, such as those at S Miguel, Escalada, the echoes of the capitals of the Porte des Comtes and of the ball and pine-cone capitals in the church of S Sernin itself suggest Toulouse as the major source and indicate a date no earlier than the 1080s.

BIBLIOGRAPHY
D. Robb: 'The Capitals of the Panteón de los Reyes, San Isidoro de León', *A. Bull.*, xxvii (1945), pp. 165–74
D. Perrier: 'Das Verhältnis von Monumentalskulptur zur spanischen Kleinkunst des 11. Jahrhunderts', *Romanico padano, romanico europeo* (Parma, 1982), pp. 193–202
J. Williams: 'A Source for the Capital of the Offering of Abraham in the Pantheon of the Kings in León', *Scritti di storia dell'arte in onore di Roberto Salvini* (Florence, 1984), pp. 25–8

For further bibliography *see* §(a) above.

*(c) Painting.* The vaults and walls of the Panteón are decorated with 12 scenes of the *Life of Christ* and the *Second Coming.* The iconography is derived mainly from Byzantine sources, but specifically French are the portraits of SS Martin of Tours and Eligius, the depiction of St Martial of Limoges as a server at the *Last Supper* and the particular scheme employed for the *Labours of the Months.* Although the frescoes were presumably painted by a Spanish master, their style is also based on a French interpretation of Byzantine conventions, as seen, for example, in the crypt of Notre-Dame-la-Grande, Poitiers. The frescoes reflect the 'modernization' of Hispanic culture promoted by Alfonso VI, and they were probably carried out soon after his death in 1109. Homage was also paid to the founders, Ferdinand I and Sancha, who are represented kneeling in the *Crucifixion,* while the composition of the Apocalyptic scene in the vault above is based on two miniatures (fols 41*r*, 46*r*) in the Beatus Commentary commissioned by them in 1047 (Madrid, Bib. N., MS. Vit. 14–2). Restorations were undertaken in 1969.

BIBLIOGRAPHY
A. Viñayo González: *Pintura románica: Panteón real de San Isidoro* (León, 1971)
J. Williams: '*Marcialis Pincerna* and the Provincial in Spanish Medieval Art', *Hortus Imaginum: Essays in Western Art*, ed. R. Engass and M. Stokstad (Lawrence, KA, 1974), pp. 29–36
J. Wettstein: *La Fresque romane: La Route de Saint-Jacques, de Tours à León* (Geneva, 1978), pp. 109–26

JOHN WILLIAMS

**León, Fidelio Ponce de.** *See* PONCE DE LEÓN, FIDELIO.

**León, Juan van der Hamen y.** *See* HAMEN Y LEÓN, JUAN VAN DER.

**León, Teodoro González de.** *See* GONZÁLEZ DE LEÓN, TEODORO.

**Leonardi** [Leonardo; Lunardi], **Camillo** (*fl* Pesaro, late 15th century to early 16th). Italian scientist and writer. He is mentioned in 1480 as an astrologer with Costanzo Sforza in Pesaro. He published two works on astrology in 1496 and 1508. In 1502, in Venice, he published a *Speculum lapidum,* dedicated to Cesare Borgia. This volume enjoyed considerable popularity, partly because of the vernacular version that Lodovico Dolce printed in 1565 as his own work. Based largely on Aristotle and Albertus Magnus (*c.* 1190–1280), the *Speculum* is divided into three books, which deal respectively with the material aspect of stones, their virtue, and the magical figures that can be incised on them. Numerous passages in this treatise are of interest for the better understanding of contemporary artistic theory. For example, red, green and yellow are presented as the fundamental colours between black and white. The historical importance of the text, however, lies in the long list of contemporary artists which Leonardi gives in the second chapter of the third book. He turns his attention first to gem engravers such as Francesco Anichini and Jacopo Tagliacarne, but later he also mentions numerous painters, from Piero della Francesca and Melozzo da Forlì to Perugino and Mantegna. Leonardi's literary model is Pliny, who not only provided a direct precedent for incorporating art history within the context of a scientific treatise, but also gave precise critical formulae for the appreciation of artists.

BIBLIOGRAPHY
L. Thorndike: *A History of Magic and Experimental Science,* 8 vols (New York, 1923–58), iv, pp. 252, n. 22, 408–09; v, p. 218; vi, pp. 298–302, 313, 318–19; viii, p. 268
J. von Schlosser: *Die Kunstliteratur* (Vienna, 1924); 3rd Ital. ed. (Florence, 1964), pp. 109, 118, 711
E. Garin: 'Giudizi artistici di Camillo Lunardi', *Rinascimento,* ii (1951), pp. 191–2
C. Parkhurst: 'Camillo Leonardi and the Green-blue Shift in 16th-century Painting', *Intuition und Kunstwissenschaft: Festschrift Hanns Swarzenski* (Berlin, 1973), pp. 419–24

MARCO COLLARETA

**Leonardo, Benedetto di.** *See* MAIANO, DA, (2).

**Leonardo, Jusepe** [Chabacier, José] (*b* Calatayud, 1601; *d* Saragossa, before Sept 1653). Spanish painter. He was of Jewish ancestry and was baptized in the parish church of S Andrés, Calatayud, on 21 March 1601. Jusepe was the only child of Domingo Chabacier and Juana de Solimon; the surname Leonardo came from his paternal family. His mother died in 1611, his father remarried three months later, and Leonardo moved to Madrid in 1612. His initial training was probably under Vicente Carducho, but from 1616 until 1621 he studied under Pedro de las Cuevas. In February 1621 he married María de Cuellar, the widow of the painter Francisco del Moral (*d* 1615).

Leonardo's earliest known works, two paintings of the *Annunciation* (Toledo, parish church of Casarrubios del Monte, and Silos, S Domingo, Sacristy), both dated between 1621 and 1625, show the influence of Eugenio Cajés, with whom he had probably collaborated on a previous occasion. In six large paintings for the high altar of the church of Santiago, Cebreros, Ávila, a *Nativity, Adoration of the Magi, Miraculous Draught of Fishes, Martyrdom of St James, Last Supper* and *Ascension* (all 1625; *in situ*), Leonardo was concerned particularly with chiaroscuro, and the vivid colouring in them is reminiscent of El Greco.

In 1631 Leonardo bought a house in the street of Las Huertas, Madrid, and in 1635 he was recorded as a painter to the Archbishop of Toledo. He contributed to important series of paintings of victories commissioned from various artists for the Salón de Reinos in the palace of the Buen Retiro. His *Rendition of Juliers* and *Capture of Brisach* (both 1634; Madrid, Prado; see fig.) both combine fine colouring with excellent technique. Leonardo also collaborated on a series of portraits of *Ancient Kings* for the Buen Retiro; his signed portrait of *Alarico* (*c.* 1635; Madrid, Mus. Ejército), with its rich and original colouring, is one of the finest in the series. In 1638 he applied without success for one of the posts of Pintor del Rey to Philip IV, vacant after the deaths of Cajés and Carducho. Leonardo continued to work at court and between 1639 and 1640 painted two portraits of *Kings of Castile* for a series for the Salón Nuevo of the Alcázar, Madrid (four canvases of the series survived the fire of 1734; two of these were by Leonardo of unidentified *Kings*; Madrid, Prado).

Other works by Leonardo from this very active period include *St John the Baptist* (1630–35; Los Angeles, CA, Co. Mus. A.); the *Brazen Serpent* (1635–40; Madrid, Real

Jusepe Leonardo: *Capture of Brisach*, oil on canvas, 3.04×3.60 m, 1634 (Madrid, Museo del Prado)

Acad. S Fernando, Mus.), which shows his use of a daring foreshortening and the influence of Venetian painting; *St Sebastian* (*c*. 1635–40; Madrid, Prado), which was formerly attributed to Vicente Carducho; and the enchanting *Birth of the Virgin* (Madrid, Prado), which is reminiscent of Diego de Velázquez. His *Mary Magdalene at the Feet of Christ*, one of two canvases painted in 1639 for the high altar of the church of the Magdalena, Getafe, Madrid (*in situ*), combines intensity of feeling with beautiful colouring and luminosity.

In 1641 Jusepe Leonardo became a member of the Cofradía del Santisimo Sacramento de S Sebastián. In the same year he executed the wall paintings (subjects unknown; destr. 1734) for the Royal Chapel of the Alcázar, Madrid. His landscape paintings include *View of the Palace of Buen Retiro* (1636–7; Madrid, Pal. Real; formerly attributed to Juan Bautista Martínez del Mazo; *see* MADRID, fig. 7). He probably became ill and ceased painting around 1645, as traces of instability are evident in his last known work, the signed *St Jerome* (*c*. 1645; untraced). In 1648 Angelo Nardi claimed an advance payment for the work he was completing on the reliquary beneath the Royal Chapel in the Alcázar, Madrid, which Leonardo had left unfinished. Leonardo was moved to Saragossa and died in the asylum of the Hospital de Nuestra Señora de Gracia some time before September 1653.

Leonardo's style developed from Mannerism to a pre-Baroque naturalism. His compositions are well structured, although occasionally they show an instability that may have been due to Leonardo's illness. The elegance of his figures and their delicate poses and in particular his refined and original sense of colouring—very similar to that of Velázquez, by whom he was greatly influenced—make Leonardo one of the most gifted artists active in Madrid during the first half of the 17th century.

BIBLIOGRAPHY
M. L. Caturla: 'Los retratos de reyes del "Salón Dorado" en el antiguo Alcázar de Madrid', *Archv Esp. A.*, xx (1947)
M. S. Soria: 'José Leonardo, Velázquez's Best Disciple', *A. Q.*, xiii/4 (1950)
M. L. Caturla: 'Cartas de pago de los doce cuadros de batallas para el Salón de Reinos del Buen Retiro', *Archv Esp. A.* (1960)
M. A. Mazón de la Torre: 'La partida de bautismo de Jusepe Leonardo', *Archv Esp. A.* (1969), pp. 59–61
——: 'Jusepe Leonardo, el gran olvidado', *Goya*, 122 (1974), pp. 76–82
——: 'En torno a Jusepe Leonardo', *Archv Esp. A.* (1975)
——: *Jusepe Leonardo y su tiempo* (Saragossa, 1977)

D. Angulo Iñiguez and A. E. Pérez Sánchez: *Pintura madrileña del segundo tercio del siglo XVII* (Madrid, 1983)

M. A. MAZÓN DE LA TORRE

**Leonardo Aretino.** *See* BRUNI, LEONARDO.

**Leonardo (de' Molinari) da Besozzo** [Bissucio; Bisuccio] (*fl* 1421–81). Italian painter and illuminator. Son of the Lombard painter MICHELINO DA BESOZZO, he is documented in 1421 as his father's assistant in Milan Cathedral. Shortly afterwards he travelled south, arriving in Naples by 1438, when he painted the panel depicting *St Anthony of Padua* (Naples, S Lorenzo), of which only the crown of angels at the top remains. In S Giovanni a Carbonara (Naples), probably towards the end of the 1430s, he worked in the chapel of Sergianni Caracciolo, painting scenes from the *Life of the Virgin* and scenes of *Hermitic Life*, with the painter Perrinetto da Benevento and assistants. Leonardo can be credited with the *Nativity*, inscribed below with his name, the *Annunciation*, the *Coronation of the Virgin* and the last of the *Hermit* scenes. Probably later, in the same church, Leonardo also painted some figures of saints in the Mausoleum of King Ladislas. From 1454 Leonardo is documented as court painter to Alfonso of Aragon, King of Naples. In 1458 he frescoed the ceiling (destr.) of the Camera degli Angeli in the tower of Beverello at Castelnuovo, Naples.

Leonardo da Besozzo was also active as an illuminator; his paintings often resemble illuminated pages in their use of bright, *cangianti* (It.: 'changing'; 'shot', as in 'shot silk') colours and in the extreme Late Gothic refinement of the details. Between 1440 and 1446 he illuminated a *Cronaca universale* (Milan, Crespi Col.), a signed manuscript, which illustrates the traditional history of mankind through portraits of famous men and mythological narratives from the Creation to 1395, in 38 decorated pages with three tiers of illuminations.

Leonardo would have had the opportunity to return to Lombardy with Alfonso in 1459, when many artists were leaving Naples, and certain fresco cycles in Lombardy have been attributed to him on stylistic grounds. These include a detached fresco showing the *Virgin and Child with Two Saints* (Milan, S Calimero; ex-S Rocco, Milan) and a cycle of frescoes in the apse of the small church of S Margherita Casatenovo (Besana in Brianza), datable to 1463.

The painting of Leonardo da Besozzo unites the typical Lombard features of courtly Gothic with a firmer conception of space and a more pronounced realism. These formal qualities, which ultimately pointed towards humanism, were accessible to Leonardo through his direct knowledge of Tuscan art, especially that of Masolino da Panicale and of Neapolitan Netherlandish painting of the 15th century.

BIBLIOGRAPHY

G. Urbani: 'Leonardo da Besozzo e Perinetto da Benevento', *Boll. A.*, xxxviii (1953), pp. 297–306

A. Putaturo Murano: *Miniature napoletane del rinascimento* (Naples, 1973)

A. Cirillo Mastrocinque: 'Leonardo da Besozzo e Sergianni Caracciolo in San Giovanni a Carbonara', *Napoli Nob.*, xviii (1978), pp. 41–9

F. Navarro: 'La pittura a Napoli e nel Meridione nel quattrocento', *La pittura in Italia: Il quattrocento*, ii (Milan, 1988), pp. 446–73, 661–2

GIOVANNA CASSESE

**Leonardo da Vinci** (*b* Anchiano, nr Vinci, 15 April 1452; *d* Amboise, nr Tours, 2 May 1519). Italian painter, sculptor, architect, designer, theorist, engineer and scientist. He was the founding father of what is called the High Renaissance style and exercised an enormous influence on contemporary and later artists. His writings on art helped establish the ideals of representation and expression that were to dominate European academies for the next 400 years. The standards he set in figure draughtsmanship, handling of space, depiction of light and shade, representation of landscape, evocation of character and techniques of narrative radically transformed the range of art. A number of his inventions in architecture and in various fields of decoration entered the general currency of 16th-century design.

Although he brought relatively few works to completion, and even fewer have survived, Leonardo was responsible for some of the most influential images in the history of art. The '*Mona Lisa*' (Paris, Louvre; *see* DRESS, fig. 22) may fairly be described as the world's most famous painting. When the extent of his writings on many branches of science became increasingly apparent during the 19th century, he appeared to epitomize the idea of the universal genius and was hailed as one of the prophets of the modern era. More recent assessments of his intellectual achievements have recognized the medieval and Classical framework on which his theories were constructed but have done nothing to detract from the awesome range and intensity of his thought.

I. Life and works. II. Stylistic development and technique. III. Theory. IV. Character and personality. V. Influence and posthumous reputation.

### I. Life and works.

Leonardo's father, Ser Piero da Vinci (*d* 1504), came from a family of property owners and notaries in the Tuscan hill-town of Vinci. Leonardo was the illegitimate first child of Ser Piero and Caterina, who later married a local man. His father subsequently married four times. Tax returns and other references indicate that Leonardo was brought up in his paternal grandfather's house, as a member of an extended family, and enjoyed a particularly close relationship with his uncle Francesco da Vinci. His father pursued a successful career as a notary and from 1469 appears to have been more or less permanently based in Florence with a flourishing legal practice, including work for the Florentine government.

1. First Florentine period, 1472–*c*. 1482. 2. First Milanese period, *c*. 1482–99. 3. Second Florentine period, 1500–mid-1508. 4. Second Milanese period, mid-1508–1513. 5. Rome and France, after 1513.

1. FIRST FLORENTINE PERIOD, 1472–*c*. 1482. The first reference to Leonardo as an artist occurs in 1472, when he was required to pay his dues to the painters' Compagnia di S Luca in Florence. His apprenticeship in the studio of the sculptor Andrea Verrocchio is recorded by Vasari and confirmed by a reference in 1476 to his continued residence there, but the date at which this apprenticeship started is unknown. Verrocchio's workshop, which undertook a wide range of commissions, including sculpture in bronze, stone and terracotta, decorative work in metals and various stones, paintings and at

least one major feat of engineering (the orb on the top of the lantern of Florence Cathedral), provided a solid grounding for Leonardo's subsequent versatility. Verrocchio was himself an inventive artist, particularly in figure sculpture, in which he pioneered a freedom of movement and viewpoint.

The first dated indication of Leonardo's ability as an artist is a remarkable pen-and-ink drawing of a *Tuscan Landscape* dated 5 August 1473 (Florence, Uffizi), which already signals an exceptional talent and mind at work. The subsequent record of his activities before his move to Milan *c.* 1482 is sparse. In 1476 he was accused anonymously of sodomy, but no prosecution was sustained. His receipt of an official commission in January 1478 for an altarpiece in the chapel of S Bernardo in the Palazzo della Signoria indicates his growing reputation. The altarpiece was not executed by Leonardo and was eventually supplied by Filippino Lippi (Florence, Uffizi). The note on one of his drawings, the *Studies of Heads and Machines* (1478; Florence, Uffizi), saying that he 'began two Virgin Marys', probably refers to small panels rather than the altarpiece. A year later he made an annotated drawing of the *Hanged Body of Bernardo Baroncelli* (Bayonne, Mus. Bonnat), the murderer of Giuliano de' Medici, brother of Lorenzo the Magnificent, which may have been connected with a project to depict the traitors on the outside of the Palazzo del Podestà in the customary manner. The second recorded commission from this period was in March 1481 for an altarpiece in S Donato a Scopeto. Although the subject is not recorded, the unfinished panel of the *Adoration of the Magi* (Florence, Uffizi; see fig. 1) was almost certainly intended for this destination. Filippino Lippi subsequently provided a completed altarpiece of the same subject (Florence, Uffizi).

The visual record of Leonardo's work from this first Florentine period includes a remarkable group of inventive drawings for varied artistic projects. These, together with notes and an inventory of works completed just before or after his arrival in Milan (Milan, Bib. Ambrosiana, Cod. Atlantico, fol. 324r), also show the first signs of the broadening range of his interests. The surviving drawings illustrate machinery (including the precise gearing of scientific instruments), aspects of military engineering, as well as optical phenomena and geometry, and the inventory lists studies made from nature, detailed representations of surface anatomy, portrait and compositional drawings, together with 'some machines for ships' and 'some machines for water'. Besides the drawings there is a small body of paintings that can be attributed in whole or in part to him (*see* §II, 1 below).

2. FIRST MILANESE PERIOD, *c.* 1482–99. At some date after the last recorded payment from S Donato for the *Adoration of the Magi* (Sept 1481), Leonardo left Florence for Milan. He is not firmly documented there until April 1483, but it is likely that he moved during the course of 1482. In the draft of the letter in which he outlined his talents to Ludovico Sforza ('il Moro'), ruler of Milan and Duke of Bari, he concentrated on his capabilities as a military engineer, promising to 'apprise you of my secrets' (Cod. Atlantico, fol. 391r). He listed ten categories of military devices for use on land and sea,

1. Leonardo da Vinci: *Adoration of the Magi*, oil on panel, 2.43×2.46 m, *c.* 1481 (Florence, Galleria degli Uffizi)

ranging from bridges and tunnels to guns and mortars 'outside the common use'. Only at the end of the letter did he mention that he could 'undertake sculpture of marble, bronze and clay, similarly in painting whatever can be done, to bear comparison with anyone else, whoever he is'. He also mentions that 'work on the bronze horse may be taken on'. This refers to the long-standing scheme to erect an equestrian memorial to Francesco Sforza, Ludovico's father and the first Sforza Duke of Milan, a project for which initially Antonio Pollaiuolo appears to have been considered. The tone of the letter suggests that Leonardo hoped his move to Milan would provide greater opportunities to develop the full scope of his work than had been possible in Florence. It remained true throughout his life that his activities flourished better within a court and in receipt of a regular income than when he needed to make a living from the completion of commissioned works of art.

The first notice of Leonardo's activity in Milan occurs in a contract for work on an altarpiece. In company with the brothers Ambrogio and Evangelista de' Predis, he agreed to provide the painted decoration and panels for a large sculpted altarpiece by the wood-carver Giacomo di Damiano (*fl* 1469–1502) for the Confraternità dell' Immacolata Concezione in their chapel in S Francesco Grande, Milan. In addition to polychroming and gilding the wooden architecture and sculpture, the painters were expected to provide paintings of the Virgin, prophets and angels to be set in the frame. The subsequent history of this commission, which went through a series of protracted legal wrangles, involves some of the lengthiest and most confusing documentation for any Renaissance painting. The dispute centred on the confraternity's claims that the painters had failed to fulfil their obligations and the painters' assertion that the value of the panel of 'Our Lady done in oils' was far greater than the sum the confraternity was offering to pay. By the time a procurator was appointed in 1496 to settle the dispute, Ambrogio de' Predis and Leonardo had appealed to a higher authority, probably the Duke. By 1503 matters were still not resolved, by which time Leonardo had left Milan. In 1506 arbitrators stipulated that Leonardo had to complete the painting of 'the most glorious Virgin Mary' within two years at an agreed price. The painting was finished by August 1508, when Ambrogio, on Leonardo's behalf, was given permission to remove the painting from its frame to make a copy.

Of the two surviving versions of the painting, now known as the *Virgin of the Rocks*, one (London, N.G.; see fig. 2) is known to have come from the altarpiece in S Francesco Grande, while the early history of the other version (Paris, Louvre), stylistically the earlier of the two, is unclear. Attempts have been made to reconcile the written evidence and the two paintings, but none can be confirmed. The two most straightforward hypotheses are either that the Louvre painting was completed but withheld by the artists and sold privately elsewhere, while the London panel was a second version, made to fulfil the legal requirements; or that either the Louvre painting or some other part of the altarpiece was incomplete until 1508, and that the London version was the copy made in

that year and substituted for the original. The stylistic evidence marginally favours the former hypothesis, in that the Louvre *Virgin of the Rocks* appears to be wholly in the style of the 1480s, while the London version exhibits features of Leonardo's work from the mid-1490s, even if it is not wholly by him.

The nature of Leonardo's engagements at the Sforza court is unclear in the 1480s. His *Portrait of a Lady with an Ermine* (Kraków, Czartoryski Col.; see fig. 3), presumed to be the portrait of Ludovico Sforza's mistress *Cecilia Gallerani* that was celebrated in a Milanese poem, should be dated, on new evidence, to *c.* 1490–91. In 1487 Leonardo submitted a model for the scheme to design a *tiburio* (crossing tower) for Milan Cathedral, although he did not undertake the commission. It is also to this period that the Codex Trivulziano (Milan, Castello Sforzesco), the first of his surviving notebooks, can be dated. For the rest of his life he kept notebooks written in mirror handwriting and filled with drawings and diagrams that record various intellectual endeavours and scientific investigations in which he was involved. The Codex Trivulziano contains, among other things, studies for the *tiburio*, philosophical aphorisms and Latin word lists. A sheet in pen and ink, with *Two Studies of a Human Skull* (Windsor Castle, Royal Lib., 19059*r*), dated 1489, is one of a series of anatomical investigations concerned with the brain, nervous system and senses. Although there had been earlier signs of his interest in a range of scientific and technical matters, sustained explorations of questions lying outside his immediate professional involvements are fully documented only from the late 1480s.

During the 1490s Leonardo was involved with ceremonial activities at the Sforza court, with painting and sculpture and with his own intellectual pursuits in a growing range of natural, physical and mathematical sciences. Typical of his work as a court artist were his admired stage designs for the *Festa del paradiso*, a spectacle by Ludovico's leading court poet, Bernardo Bellincioni, composed in 1490 as a wedding celebration. The same year he resumed serious work on the equestrian monument to *Francesco Sforza*. In 1497 he is documented as nearing the completion of the *Last Supper*, begun *c.* 1495, in the refectory of S Maria delle Grazie, Milan (*in situ*), and in 1498 he was painting the mural decoration of the Sala delle Asse (Milan, Castello Sforzesco). His notebooks also suggest that he participated in various architectural and engineering projects, including the extensive schemes for canalization, urban planning and decoration in Vigevano, close to Ludovico's birthplace.

In his scientific work, Leonardo began to embrace a variety of concerns. Anatomy and optics were central among these (*see* ANATOMICAL STUDIES and SCIENCE AND ART), but he also embarked on detailed investigations of statics and dynamics, with an almost obsessional interest in the complex patterns of motion in water. His notebooks reflect a sustained campaign of self-education in the basic theoretical concepts of Classical and medieval science, and in the elements of mathematics. In this latter ambition he was greatly aided by the arrival of the mathematician Luca Pacioli at the court in 1496, and the following year they collaborated on the illustrations of geometrical bodies in

2. Leonardo da Vinci: *Virgin of the Rocks*, oil on panel, 1.89×1.20 m, mid-1490s (London, National Gallery)

3. Leonardo da Vinci: *Portrait of a Lady with an Ermine* (Cecilia Gallerani), oil on panel, 534×393 mm, *c.* 1490–91 (Kraków, Czartoryski Collection)

Pacioli's *De divina proportione*, which was eventually published in Venice in 1509.

The visual record of Leonardo's artistic products during the 1490s is disappointingly meagre. The project for the huge equestrian monument to *Francesco Sforza* progressed to the point at which the full-sized clay model could be exhibited in 1494, but the bronze was never cast, and the model seems not to have survived Ludovico's fall in 1499. The *Last Supper* was his major completed achievement. Early viewers testify to its extraordinary impact; however, the partly experimental technique led to the wall painting's rapid deterioration, and it exists today only as a fragmented ghost of its former presence. Although the Duke requested in 1497 that Leonardo start on 'the other wall' when he finished the *Last Supper*, no sign remains of other work by him in the refectory. The portraits of the *Duke and Duchess and their Children* added to Giovanni Donato da Montofano's *Crucifixion* on the opposite end wall are too damaged to permit a definite judgement, but the underdrawings appear too routine to be attributed confidently to Leonardo.

Leonardo's decorative painting in the Sala delle Asse, depicting trees intertwined as a great bower, also survives in an incomplete and heavily restored form. It seems likely that he was responsible for other work in the suite of rooms in the Castello Sforzesco, which Ludovico was transforming and extending, but no traces survive. Three portraits of more or less autograph quality—the *Portrait of a Musician* and the *Portrait of a Woman in Profile* (both

Milan, Bib. Ambriosiana) and the *Portrait of a Woman*, known as '*La Belle Ferronière*' (Paris, Louvre)—may also be assigned to his period at the Sforza court. When Ludovico fled Milan in 1499, in the face of the invading armies of the French king Louis XII, Leonardo sent money to Florence for safekeeping. Although he apparently entered into some kind of agreement with the King, he left Milan in December. He stayed briefly in Mantua, where he made a portrait drawing of *Isabella d'Este* (damaged version, Paris, Louvre; for illustration *see* ESTE (i), (6)), and in Venice, where he appears to have given some advice on hydraulic engineering. His visit to Mantua is not surprising in view of the close links between the Sforza and the Este families, and of Isabella's known interest in Leonardo's art.

3. SECOND FLORENTINE PERIOD, 1500–MID-1508. In April 1500 Leonardo returned to Florence, where he was faced with the prospect of re-establishing his career. During the next six years Isabella d'Este endeavoured to obtain a painting from him. She hoped that he would make a painting based on the portrait drawing and subsequently that he would provide a subject painting—at one point she suggested an image of Christ at the age of 12. The correspondence in which Isabella pursued her frustrating quest provides the best evidence for Leonardo's activities immediately after his return to Florence. Her plenipotentiary in Florence, the Carmelite Fra Pietro da Novellara, wrote to her on 3 and 14 April 1501, mentioning the painter's obsession with geometry and that his pupils were making copies of his paintings to which he occasionally put his hand. The letters also describe two works by Leonardo. One was a small panel painting for Florimond Robertet, the secretary to the French king, which showed the Virgin and Child contesting the possession of a yarnwinder. Later known as the *Madonna of the Yarnwinder*, the best versions of this much copied painting are in the Duke of Buccleuch's collection and a New York collection. The other work was a large-scale cartoon (untraced) of the *Virgin and Child with St Anne and a Lamb*, in which the life-sized figures were cunningly compressed into a compact group. The cartoon seems to have been drawn when Leonardo was involved with a commission for an altarpiece for SS Annunziata (later finished by Pietro Perugino), which was apparently ceded to him on his return to Florence by Filippino Lippi. Leonardo was provided with accommodation in the monastery of SS Annunziata, and it was there in 1501 that he exhibited his cartoon to large crowds, though it was probably not intended as the design for the altarpiece.

That Republican Florence did not provide the most appropriate arena for Leonardo's talents is perhaps indicated by the fact that in 1502 he accepted the appointment as Cesare Borgia's 'architect and general engineer', with responsibilities that took him to Urbino and other central Italian cities. The most spectacular product of his work for Cesare is the *Map of Imola* (Windsor Castle, Royal Lib., 12284). In 1503 he was again in Florence and appears to have been one of the engineers involved in Machiavelli's ill-fated plans to divert the River Arno around Pisa, when Florence was at war with the city.

Later in the same year Leonardo received the highly prestigious commission for a wall painting of the *Battle of*

*Anghiari* (destr.) in the Sala del Maggior Consiglio, the great new council hall in the Palazzo della Signoria, which the Republic had erected after the expulsion of the Medici in 1494. The subject was to commemorate a Florentine victory over the Milanese in 1440. Leonardo was provided with a room in S Maria Novella in which to make the huge cartoon (destr.), and work seems to have proceeded steadily, although it was interrupted during the autumn of 1504, when the Florentine authorities sent him to Piombino to advise on fortifications. Payments were made for materials during 1504, and one of his own notes (Madrid, Bib. N., MS. II, fol. 2*r*) provides evidence that he was actually painting on the wall in the summer of 1505. In 1504 Michelangelo received the commission to paint the *Battle of Cascina* (unexecuted) as a companion piece to the *Battle of Anghiari* and joined Leonardo as an apparently unsympathetic rival. However, there were growing signs that Leonardo might eventually fail to complete the commission. His characteristically experimental technique was running into trouble, and his notebooks testify that his diverse intellectual concerns were again coming to the fore, including studies of bird flight and geometry. Finally, in 1506 a train of events marked the abandonment of the project. In May he was granted leave of absence to work in Milan for three months, perhaps in response to the settlement of the litigation surrounding the *Virgin of the Rocks*. Although he returned to Florence briefly in March 1507, and for a longer period from September to the following spring, his residence in Florence was effectively at an end. The winter of 1506–7 was apparently occupied with the study of anatomy, bird flight and mathematics. The last of his substantial artistic involvements in Florence seems to have been the assistance he provided, according to Vasari, to Giovanni Francesco Rustici, who was making the bronze group of *St John the Baptist Preaching between a Pharisee and a Levite* (1506–11) for the exterior of the Florentine Baptistery (*in situ*).

It is difficult to assign a single, finished, wholly autograph painting to the years 1500 to 1508. It is reasonable to assume that the *Madonna of the Yarnwinder* was completed, but even that might not have been entirely by Leonardo. The incomplete and partly ruined painting of the *Battle of Anghiari* survived until the remodelling of the council hall in the 1560s, and, although strenuous efforts have been made to discover it under the later paintings by Vasari, it has not so far reappeared. A number of projects for compositions of the Virgin and Child can be dated to these years, as can an innovative design for a painting of an *Angel of the Annunciation* (untraced), which developed into the later composition of *St John the Baptist* (Paris, Louvre). He also began work on a composition of *Leda and the Swan* (see fig. 4), experimenting with a kneeling figure of Leda (reflected in versions by followers) and a standing version, the latter known to Raphael in Florence as a developed design, cartoon or unfinished painting. The final version of *Leda* (untraced) may not have been completed until after 1513.

The painting generally regarded as the central product of these years is the so-called '*Mona Lisa*' (Paris, Louvre), although even it presents some problems of dating. The identity of the sitter was for many years uncertain, but Vasari's claim that the lady in the portrait was 'M[ad]o[n]na

Lisa', the wife of Francesco del Giocondo (hence the alternative name of '*La Gioconda*' or '*La Giocondè*'), was confirmed in 1991 with the publication of the 1525 death inventory of Leonardo's assistant of 30 years, GIAN GIACOMO CAPROTTI, who seems to have been in possession of a number of his master's works, including this portrait (see Shell and Sironi). In 1495 Lisa Gherardini (*b* Florence, 1479) married Francesco del Giocondo, an important figure in the Republican government, whose portrait Leonardo is also thought to have painted. Earlier confusion over her identity arose, among other things, from what was previously thought to be the earliest reference to the portrait, written by Ambrogio de' Beatis on a visit to Leonardo in France in 1517; he described a portrait of 'a certain Florentine lady made from nature at the instigation of the late Magnificent Giuliano de' Medici' (the Duc de Nemours), who was Leonardo's patron in Rome after 1513, and it had long been assumed that he was referring to the '*Mona Lisa*'. (It is now thought likely that the work de' Beatis saw on this visit was the portrait of another Florentine woman.) According to Vasari, Leonardo began the portrait of *Lisa del Giocondo* between his arrival in Florence in 1500 and the commencement of his work on the *Battle of Anghiari* late in 1503; after four years, however, the work was still unfinished. The appearance of the picture lends support to the idea that it was painted over an extended period, since the craquelure of the face suggests that it was executed at a different time from the hands, which exhibit the thinness of his latest manner of painting.

4. Leonardo da Vinci: *Study for the Head of Leda* for *Leda and the Swan* (untraced), pen and ink over black chalk, 200×162 mm, 1500–08 (Windsor, Windsor Castle, Royal Library)

**4. SECOND MILANESE PERIOD, MID-1508–1513.**
From the summer of 1508 to September 1513 Leonardo was resident in or near Milan, working initially for the French rulers of the city under the direct supervision of the governor, Charles II d'Amboise, Comte de Chaumont. He appears to have taken up a range of duties broadly equivalent to those he had performed at the Sforza court, including providing designs for ephemeral items of courtly entertainment. He also embarked on designs for another equestrian monument, for Gian Giacomo Trivulzio, an Italian general who was serving the French. The scheme progressed as far as a detailed specification and costing of the life-size horse and rider, with a substantial base and secondary sculpture (Cod. Atlantico, fol. 179*ra*). The architectural work Leonardo is known to have undertaken for Charles d'Amboise is not clearly identifiable. Charles's project may have been for the kind of airy, colonnaded villa with which Leonardo had been experimenting since his first Milanese period (e.g. Cod. Atlantico, fol. 158*ra*). He may also have been involved in the plans for the church of S Maria alla Fontana, Milan, but the executant of the work is firmly documented as Giovanni Antonio Amadeo. After the reinstatement of the Sforza regime in 1512 under Ludovico's son Massimiliano, Leonardo remained in Lombardy for more than a year.

Among Leonardo's scientific endeavours during this second Milanese period is a series of outstanding anatomical drawings of human musculature and the skeletal system (for example *see* ANATOMICAL STUDIES, fig. 1). His exploration of certain geometrical questions, particularly problems of transformation of volume and area (e.g. the squaring of the circle), became increasingly obsessive, as did his investigation of the dynamics of fluids, whether in the guise of the motion of water or in such related forms as the turbulent flow of the blood in vessels of the human body.

The only documented painting completed on Leonardo's return to Milan was the *Virgin of the Rocks*: the style of the second version (London, N.G.) is consistent with its having been begun in the late 1490s and subsequently finished by Leonardo with studio assistants on his return to Milan. By contrast, the only autograph painting that can be wholly assigned with some confidence to this period is the *St John the Baptist* (Paris, Louvre), which developed from his Florentine *Angel of the Annunciation* and is reflected in pupils' drawings datable *c.* 1509. The Virgin and Child compositions on which he was working for Louis XII cannot be certainly identified with any of the surviving paintings, although it is highly likely that one of them was a variant of the theme of the Virgin and Child with St Anne. Two main types of this composition are known: the version that included the lamb, as in the lost cartoon of 1501 and a surviving painting (Paris, Louvre), and the type in which the young St John is integrated into the narrative, as in the Burlington House Cartoon (London, N.G.). The latter has sometimes been dated to 1490–1500, but the style of its draughtsmanship and of the closest preparatory drawing (pen and ink over black chalk; London, B.M.) is increasingly recognized as belonging to *c.* 1505–7. The Louvre *Virgin and Child with St Anne and a Lamb* (see fig. 5) is not clearly datable by reference to other paintings, but the related drawings (Windsor Castle,

5. Leonardo da Vinci: *Virgin and Child with St Anne and a Lamb*, oil on panel, 1.68×1.30 m, ?*c.* 1515 (Paris, Musée du Louvre)

Royal Lib., 12527, 12530, 12533), handling of colour and treatment of the landscape suggest a late date, perhaps *c.* 1515.

**5. ROME AND FRANCE, AFTER 1513.** In October 1513 Leonardo visited Florence on his way to Rome, where he was accommodated in the Belvedere under the patronage of Giuliano de' Medici, Duc de Nemours. He appears to have been involved with the military work that Giuliano was undertaking for the Medici pope, Leo X, and worked on the design and manufacture of burning mirrors that could have military and civil uses. The continued intensity and variety of his intellectual endeavours, particularly in anatomy (cardiology and embryology), optics and geometry, coupled with his travels in Giuliano's service, do much to explain the reported impatience of Pope Leo, who doubted whether Leonardo would ever finish anything.

It is possible that Leonardo was present at Bologna in 1515 at the meeting between Leo X and the new French king, Francis I. His elaborate red-chalk drawing of the *Allegory of the Wolf and Eagle* (Windsor Castle, Royal Lib., 12496) may well refer to the concordat between pope and king. In any event, Francis was as enthusiastic about Leonardo's work as his predecessor and succeeded in attracting Leonardo to France at some point between August 1516 and May 1517. For the rest of Leonardo's life, Francis seems to have acted as an ideal patron—actively promoting new projects and keen to exploit the range of Leonardo's talents, but also understanding of the artist's character as a natural philosopher or seer. Leonardo was clearly regarded as an ornament of the court and, as such, was visited by Cardinal Louis of Aragon's party on 10 October 1517, the occasion recorded by Ambrogio de' Beatis, who was the Cardinal's secretary. As 'first painter and engineer' to the King, Leonardo was provided with accommodation at the manor house of Clos-Lucé, Amboise.

Leonardo's final years have often been seen as dominated by his geometrical obsessions and a growing sense of pessimism, expressed most vividly in the visions of cataclysmic storms in his series of drawings of *A Deluge* (Windsor Castle, Royal Lib.; see fig. 6). His health was also apparently deteriorating. De' Beatis reported that some paralysis was affecting his right side, probably as the result of a stroke. However, a study of folios and notebooks datable to the period 1516–19 reveals a remarkable range of continuing activities. There are only occasional signs of physical frailty. His assistants, most prominent among whom was the well-born FRANCESCO MELZI from Lombardy, probably played an increasing role in the physical work, but his inventiveness appears undiminished.

As in his two Milanese periods, Leonardo furnished designs for courtly entertainments, including a revised version of his design for the *Festa del paradiso* of 1490. His most ambitious project was for a huge royal palace at Romorantin, with associated canalization. A scheme was devised for an extensive residence, translating French château design into the language of the Renaissance. Leonardo's concerns extended from the overall conception to such details as the design of toilet doors with counterweights. Although the project did not materialize, echoes of Leonardo's ideas can be seen in subsequent French château design.

The evidence of Leonardo's involvement with painting in France is equivocal, relying on secondary sources from later in the 16th century. It is virtually certain that the 'Mona Lisa', the *St John the Baptist*, the *Leda* and the *Virgin and Child with St Anne* were taken by Leonardo to France, where some may have been completed. He probably made an anamorphic painting for Francis I depicting a fight between a dragon and a lion in such a way that it made sense only when viewed from a shallow angle. A composition with a half-length female nude, known as the 'Monna Vanna', which exercised a notable influence on a series of erotic paintings from the school of Fontainebleau, may also have depended on a prototype by Leonardo

6. Leonardo da Vinci: *A Deluge*, black chalk, 163×210 mm, after 1513 (Windsor, Windsor Castle, Royal Library)

himself, possibly a drawing or cartoon (such as that in Chantilly, Mus. Condé). However, de' Beatis's testimony that illness had left Leonardo unable to undertake painting needs to be taken seriously, and it is unlikely that any wholly autograph paintings were initiated and completed in France.

On 23 April 1519 Leonardo drew up his will, bequeathing most of his drawn and written legacy to Melzi. Following Leonardo's death, Melzi wrote movingly to the painter's brothers in Florence, one of whom's son, PIERINO DA VINCI, became a sculptor. Several of Leonardo's paintings seem to have come into the hands of his assistant Caprotti, who had also travelled with his master to the French court. On 12 August 1519 Leonardo was buried in the church of St Florentin at Amboise, although his remains are thought later to have been transferred to the chapel of St Hubert at the Château of Amboise.

## II. Stylistic development and technique.

1. Paintings. 2. Drawings. 3. Sculpture. 4. Architecture. 5. Ephemeral designs.

1. PAINTINGS. Leonardo completed relatively few paintings, and no more than ten surviving works are generally accepted as being finished wholly by him. A further three autograph paintings remain unfinished, while a small group of works may be classified as studio products in which he played a greater or lesser role. Early sources, particularly Vasari and Giovanni Paolo Lomazzo, refer to a number of paintings now unknown, but there is often no way of telling if these works were indeed by Leonardo himself. Additionally, there is a host of Leonardesque paintings by followers, ranging from presumed copies of original works to free variations on Leonardo's compositions. Many of the Leonardesque paintings originated from Milan, where artists may have had access to originals brought back from France by Caprotti, whose own copies, as well as those by others, transmitted the conventional image of the 'Leonardesque' to later ages.

(i) First Florentine period, 1472–c. 1482. (ii) First Milanese period, c. 1482–99. (iii) Second Florentine period, 1500–mid-1508. (iv) Second Milanese period, mid-1508–1513. (v) Rome, c. 1515. (vi) 'Leonardesque' paintings and painters.

(i) *First Florentine period, 1472–c. 1482.* Besides the documented *Adoration of the Magi* (1481–2; Florence, Uffizi), left unfinished when Leonardo departed for Milan, there is a reasonable consensus of opinion on the attribution of other surviving paintings to this period, though less agreement about dating. Of the Virgin and Child paintings most closely associated with Leonardo in the 1470s (when, according to his own notes, he had begun 'two Madonnas'), the *Virgin and Child with a Vase of Flowers* (c. 1474–6; Munich, Alte Pin.) is the least fluent compositionally and stylistically the closest to works produced in Verrocchio's studio; the Benois *Madonna and Child* (c. 1479–81; St Petersburg, Hermitage) is close in conception to the *Adoration*, while the *Virgin and Child* known as the '*Madonna Litta*' (c. 1480–85; St Petersburg, Hermitage) gives a very awkward impression and can at best be seen as painted largely by another hand. Leonardo's inventory of 1481–2 refers to a Madonna 'in profile', but this has not been certainly identified.

Among the elements of the *Virgin and Child* in Munich recognizable as motifs common in Verrocchio's studio are the spiral knots of hair, the bunched drapery of the bodice held by a jewel, the precious gesture of the hand holding a carnation and the meticulous observation of the vase of flowers. The composition is assembled by adding one detail to another but is not conceived as a whole, and it is characteristic of such compositions produced in Florence at this period. However, Leonardo endeavoured to imbue the drapery and the motion of the Child with vigour and variety, and the flower buds are about to burst open, imparting a sense of superabundant vitality. The effects of atmospheric perspective in the strange, mountainous landscape are recognizably Leonardesque, and the puckered and wrinkled paint surface also bears witness to his experiments with the oil medium, even at this early date.

The Benois *Madonna*, by contrast, is a far more integrated composition. The figures are combined in such a way as to forge a new kind of formal and emotional interaction. This is achieved both through the interweaving of the motions and gestures and by the rhythmic interplay of curves in the composition. The emotional vitality of the Virgin reflects Leonardo's debt to 15th-century Florentine sculpture and may depend directly on the low-relief Madonnas traditionally attributed to Desiderio da Settignano. The light has an unprecedented directness and force, creating an almost exaggerated sense of relief, which is only partly disturbed by the blank (possibly overpainted) view through the window.

The arrangement of the '*Madonna Litta*' is characteristic of the ambitions that tended to strain Leonardo's compositions to breaking-point. The Virgin tenderly cradles the Child, who sucks from his mother's breast and twists restlessly to look at the spectator. It is not easy to recognize the handling of the figures as the work of Leonardo. The generalized surfaces and simplified contours suggest a laboured attempt to emulate Leonardo's style, though the graded recession of hills in the landscape is captured with a subtlety difficult to attribute to an assistant or follower.

Although the Munich Virgin is the earliest of these three compositions, it is not the earliest painting that can be attributed to Leonardo. The *Annunciation* (c. 1473; Florence, Uffizi), from the convent of Monte Oliveto, can be seen to an even greater degree as an assemblage of motifs from his earliest experiences of Florentine art. The influence of Verrocchio is paramount, particularly in the antique-style pedestal of the Virgin's reading-desk and emphatically sculptural draperies. The perspective of the house and tiled pavement on the right has been assembled in an almost mechanical manner over a series of geometrical lines incised in the gesso priming of the panel. The paint handling and conception of form are rather uneven, reflecting the young artist's search for appropriate ways of capturing a wide variety of natural effects. The depiction of the plants, including the Angel's lily, and the blue haze of the distant mountains indicate that Netherlandish art was already an important source of inspiration.

An attempt to combine the striking effects of surface naturalism in Netherlandish art with the formal values of the Florentine tradition is also apparent in the only surviving portrait from this period, that of *Ginevra de' Benci* (c. 1476; Washington, DC, N.G.A.). The sitter's name is indicated by the punning, heraldic device of the juniper bush (It. *ginepro*) behind her head, while the back of the panel is decorated with a wreath of palm and juniper and the motto *virtutem forma decorat* ('beauty adorns virtue') that appears to have been given to her by Bernardo Bembo. The decorative motif on the reverse confirms that the painting has been cut down by as much as a third at the bottom. It is likely that the sitter's hands were originally included, as in Verrocchio's marble bust of a *Woman Holding Flowers* (Florence, Bargello). (A silverpoint *Study of Arms and Hands* (*c.* 1476; Windsor Castle, Royal Lib., 12558) may indicate Leonardo's intentions.) The sense of brilliant striving for effects of light and texture in the painting is again reflected in Leonardo's technical experiments; he softened the modelling of the flesh by pressing his fingers into the wet paint. The wrinkled paint surface in the landscape results from his use of oily glazes to convey a nebulous atmospheric recession equivalent to that in his pen drawing of a *Tuscan Landscape* dated 1473 (Florence, Uffizi), though the painting probably dates from at least three years later.

A comparable quality can be seen in the landscape background on the left in Verrocchio's *Baptism* (Florence, Uffizi; see VERROCCHIO, fig. 5), originally from the monastic Church of S Salvi outside Florence. Leonardo's contributions to his master's picture may also be recognized in the angel on the far left (as testified by Albertini in 1510), in the water and probably in the glazes that model the face and body of Christ. Although it would be natural to assume that these contributions represent Leonardo's earliest known attempts at painting (i.e. *c.* 1470), the pose of the angel and delicately vivacious handling of paint suggest a technique at least as advanced as that of the portrait of *Ginevra de' Benci* and thus a date of *c.* 1476.

None of these examples of Leonardo's work, ambitious though they are, anticipates fully the extraordinary innovations revealed in the large-scale, unfinished *Adoration of the Magi* (see fig. 1 above). This was a popular subject for altarpieces in 15th-century Florence, not least as a reflection of the activities of the Compagnia de' Magi, a lay body responsible for organizing a great procession on the day of Epiphany. Florentine paintings of the subject, taking their cue particularly from Gentile da Fabriano's Strozzi Altarpiece (1423; Florence, Uffizi), had developed a rich, processional and even clamorous quality. Leonardo's preparatory studies, including the pen-and-ink compositional sketch (Paris, Louvre), show that he found his starting-point in this tradition. However, he invested every element in his composition with a fresh emotional charge, ranging from the contemplative absorption of the old man on the extreme right, through the intense reverence of the Magi, to the overt violence of the horsemen in the background. The emotional postures, gestures and faces are incorporated into a composition in which unprecedented dynamism is orchestrated within a rigorously controlled structure. The arc of adoring figures and the pyramidal disposition of the Virgin and kneeling Magi are given additional articulation by the trees, while the turbulence of the background takes place in some form of ruined architectural structure that was calculated with the highest degree of perspectival exactitude; this is also evident in the pen-and-ink study of the architectural background (Florence, Uffizi).

Reading the *Adoration* is not easy. It is not only unfinished in the conventional sense, but many of its forms are still in an emergent state. The fluidity of Leonardo's preliminary drawings is sustained into the underpainting itself, in a manner exceptional in a 15th-century painting. The identification of the background figures is particularly difficult, although the sense of turmoil and the destruction of the old order—symbolized also in the ruined architecture—are based on Florentine precedents. The retinue accompanying the Magi has been transformed into a series of urgently involved witnesses to the divine mystery, who are far removed from their traditionally supportive, decorative and anecdotal roles. The two flanking figures, one deeply pensive and the other youthfully romantic, may have been inspired by the framing figures on antique sarcophagi (also used by Donatello), but they play an unprecedented psychological role in the drama.

The rich tonal effects in the underpainting are also present in the panel of *St Jerome* (*c.* 1481–2; Rome, Vatican, Pin.), also unfinished, in which a foreshortened, contorted kneeling pose complements the sharply characterized expression of penitence in the saint's face. The physiognomy of the roaring lion, echoing St Jerome's torment, recalls the drawings in which Leonardo compared human and animal expressions (e.g. *Sheet of Studies with the Virgin and Child and Saints*, Windsor Castle, Royal Lib., 12276*r*), while the saint's sinewy neck must have been based on the kind of anatomical studies that were listed in his inventory of 1481–2.

The other strongest candidates for autograph paintings by Leonardo of this period are the *Virgin and Child*, called the Dreyfus *Madonna* (Washington, DC, N.G.A.), and the predella panel of the *Annunciation* (Paris, Louvre) from the altarpiece commissioned from Verrocchio but executed by Lorenzo di Credi and representing the *Virgin and Child Enthroned with SS John the Baptist and Donatus of Arezzo* (Pistoia Cathedral; see LORENZO DI CREDI, fig. 1). Both attributions have their supporters, but the Dreyfus *Madonna* may perhaps be better attributed to Verrocchio himself, while the *Annunciation* displays weaknesses in structure and handling that suggests that it is by another of Verrocchio's pupils.

*(ii) First Milanese period, c. 1482–99.* The troubled history of the commission in 1483 for the painted sections of the altarpiece of the Confraternity of the Immaculate Conception has led a few commentators to assume that the central image, the *Virgin of the Rocks* (Paris, Louvre), was not wholly completed during the first Milanese period. However, as far as can be judged beneath its layers of darkened varnish, the painting appears, in its delicate characterization of form and vitality of touch, to belong wholly to the 1480s. A devotional image of the Virgin has been translated into a scene of considerable formal, colouristic, iconographical and psychological complexity. The figures in the landscape setting depend distantly on Filippo Lippi's altarpiece of the *Virgin Adoring the Christ Child with SS Romuald and John the Baptist* (*c.* 1459; Berlin, Gemäldegal.), for the chapel in the Palazzo Medici, Florence, but

Filippo's image does not approach the subtle spatial interplays of glance, gesture and directional light. This is the most advanced expression to date of Leonardo's insistence on the dominance of tone over colour. Only the swathe of yellow lining of the Virgin's robe is allowed to assert itself independently of the tonal scheme, and even this merges into the substratum of shadow at the edges. The painting's complex iconography centres on an apocryphal narrative of the meeting of the Virgin and Child with St John and the Angel Uriel in the wilderness. The theme is underscored by botanical symbolism associated with Mary, while the rocky cavern in the distance may be drawn from the 'dove . . . in the clefts of rock' in the *Song of Songs* (ii.14) and refer to Mary's virginity. Whatever the intended meaning, the forms bear witness to Leonardo's intense scrutiny of nature and his recreation of natural forms in imaginative compounds that endow them with an aura of strangeness.

The formal and psychological suavity of the *Virgin of the Rocks* can also be recognized in the *Portrait of a Lady with an Ermine* (see fig. 3 above), thought to represent Cecilia Gallerani, one of Ludovico Sforza's mistresses. The animal in her arms appears to be a punning reference to her name (Gr. *galé=ermine*), as well as standing as an emblem of purity. The implied narrative of the sitter turning to look at an unseen companion gives the portrait an unprecedented freshness and permits a new kind of psychological communication in portraiture, only partly foreshadowed in Verrocchio's portrait busts. In spite of some inelegant overpainting of the background, which was originally grey, the portrait possesses a remarkable harmony of line, space, light and colour, without compromising the natural observation of forms and textures.

None of the other Milanese portraits associated with Leonardo achieves such a high level of complexity and innovation. Of these, the unfinished *Portrait of a Musician* (Milan, Bib. Ambrosiana) is the most widely accepted, the head possessing a sense of underlying structure and life characteristic of Leonardo's documented works. Moreover, the highlit spirals of hair share the febrile energy of Ginevra's curls. By comparison with the *Portrait of a Lady with an Ermine*, two unidentified female portraits associated with Leonardo appear superficially routine. Yet the head of the *Portrait of a Woman in Profile* (Milan, Bib. Ambrosiana) has a vibrancy of contour that escaped the best of his associates, and '*La Belle Ferronnière*' (Paris, Louvre) is more interesting than it might initially appear. Although the parapet in the latter prevents the figure from asserting its full presence, the motif of the glance, almost, but not quite, meeting the spectator's, is full of Leonardesque ingenuity. The painting of the accessories is more vital than most of the details in the Ambrosiana female portrait and may be substantially by Leonardo himself. The sitter has been tentatively identified as Ludovico's later mistress Lucrezia Crivelli, whose portrait by Leonardo is also described in a poem. If so, it would date from the mid-1490s, which is consistent with its style.

The most important painting of Leonardo's first Milanese period was the *Last Supper* on the end wall in the refectory of S Maria delle Grazie. Hailed originally as a triumph of illusionistic naturalism, it may now be described as the most famous wreck in the history of art. Leonardo's mediative methods of painting and his insistence on a full range of optical effects led him to seek an alternative to the true fresco technique. Analysis has revealed that he first primed the wall and then painted the mural in a manner resembling tempera painting on panel. Painting *a secco* (on dry plaster) was far from uncommon, but Leonardo's layered technique, which appears to have encouraged dampness to accumulate in the underlying plaster, resulted in imperfect adhesion. The restoration campaign begun in 1980, devoted to the removal of all later overpainting, has confirmed that in large areas only scattered flakes of original paint remain.

Even in its unhappy state, the grandeur and ingenuity of the conception of the *Last Supper* remain discernible. Leonardo created a compelling effect of a perspectival space opening off the refectory, but rendered the relationship between the illusionistic and real spaces deeply ambiguous at its margins. The ceiling passes upwards behind the lunettes to an imprecisely defined point, while the planes of the side walls do not precisely coincide with those of the refectory. The crowding and relative heights of the figures also subvert the requirements of strictly naturalistic logic for the sake of narrative effect. However, the restoration has revealed that many details were painted with consummate naturalistic skill and vibrant colour, including the still-life objects on the table—wine glasses, fruit, plates—and the folds of the cloth. The *Last Supper* is the supreme demonstration of Leonardo's belief that poses, gestures and facial expressions should reflect the 'notions of the mind' in a specific emotional context. Although it is anachronistic to read the painting as a 'frozen moment'—the gestures are meant to be read cumulatively, and successive moments in the biblical narrative are represented—the dominant intention is to convey the varieties of reaction to the central charge of Christ's impending betrayal. The theme of the Institution of the Eucharist, signalled by Christ's gestures towards the wine and bread, would also have been readily understood. The painting presents a rich series of themes for contemplation by the monks dining in the refectory.

The heavily restored remains of the decoration of the Sala delle Asse in the Castello Sforzesco, Milan, provide the most substantial visual indication of the inventiveness with which Leonardo performed his court duties. The motif of the regularly intertwined branches of the trees, interwoven with a meandering gold rope in one of his favourite knot patterns, succeeds superbly as decoration, without losing his characteristic sense of the natural vitality of living forms. The fragmentary underpainting on one of the walls, depicting roots insinuating themselves among rocks, suggests that the whole room was to be transformed into a bower. The heraldic shield of Ludovico Sforza and Beatrice d'Este in the central oculus and laudatory inscriptions make obvious dynastic references. The motif of interweaving may itself function as a kind of *impresa* (heraldic motif) of the union of Ludovico and his wife.

*(iii) Second Florentine period, 1500–mid-1508.* The two works on which Leonardo was most immediately engaged in Florence were the lost cartoon of 1501 representing the *Virgin and Child with St Anne and a Lamb* and the *Virgin of the Yarnwinder*, of which numerous versions and variants

are known. Examination of the versions belonging to the Duke of Buccleuch and another private collection have revealed comparable *pentimenti*, underdrawings and stylistic characteristics that suggest that Leonardo played a role in their design and perhaps also in their execution. They are probably studio realizations of Leonardo's invention. Fra Pietro da Novellara described the lost cartoon as showing St Anne rising from her seat to restrain the Virgin from separating the Child from the lamb. The best records of it may be a drawing (Geneva, priv. col., see Clark, 1939, rev. 1988, p. 33), which appears to imitate Leonardo's graphic style, and the rather wooden painting of the same subject attributed to Brescianino (Berlin, Bodemus.). The importance of these two works by Leonardo was that they demonstrated to the Florentines a dynamic new way of incorporating symbolism into an anecdotal type of Virgin and Child. The meaning of the symbols of the passion— the cross-shaped yarnwinder and the sacrificial lamb—is built in to the physical and psychological aspects of the interaction between the figures.

Documentary records confirm early accounts that Leonardo also used an experimental technique for the *Battle of Anghiari*, painting *a secco* on a sealed and primed wall surface, but on this occasion using oil as his chief binding medium. The sources further suggest that the paint proved reluctant to dry, but it is not known if the problems were sufficiently severe in themselves to lead to his abandonment of the project. The one section of his painting— apparently the central portion—that survived until the 1560s, albeit in an unfinished state, was recorded in paintings and drawings, and in an engraving by Lorenzo Zacchia. There are two painted copies of reasonable quality (Florence, Uffizi; Munich, G. Hoffman priv. col.), while the most artistically attractive of the graphic versions is the drawing that appears to have been reworked by Peter Paul Rubens (Paris, Louvre). Together with the preparatory drawings, the copies show that Leonardo's battle centred on a turbulent fight for a standard, in which rearing horses, elaborately armoured warriors and struggling foot soldiers were compressed into a tight knot of explosive action. Even in the copies the force and conviction of the contorted men and horses, together with their savagely bestial expressions, give an impression of unprecedented power. However, the detailed effects of dust, mingled with blood, rising in the air and the churned-up water in the river can only be envisaged through reading the descriptions in his notebooks. The fragmentary nature of the visual evidence works against a full-scale reconstruction of Leonardo's scheme for the whole wall and makes it difficult to read the narrative of the central group. However, Neri di Gino Capponi's manuscript account of the battle indicates that the capture of the Milanese standard was the crucial event, and it may therefore be possible to identify the horsemen to the left as Milanese struggling to retain their grip of the standard in the face of the Florentine assault from the right.

The remarkable power of Leonardo's second major invention of the period, the '*Mona Lisa*', results from his exceptional translation of an individual image into an archetype with deliberately universal connotations. None of the elements is unprecedented on its own: a portrait extending below the bust to include the hands had already been used by Verrocchio in his marble *Woman Holding Flowers* and by Leonardo in *Ginevra de' Benci*; the setting of a figure above a distant landscape had been exploited in Piero della Francesca's portraits of *Federigo da Montefeltro* and *Battista Sforza* (both Florence, Uffizi), and a comparable directness of expression, with the slight smile, had been developed in portraits by Antonello da Messina. But the effect of the ensemble has no parallel in earlier art. Yet the novelty of the '*Mona Lisa*' is partly a matter of form and technique. The monumental amplitude of the figure is emphasized by the sweeping contours of drapery and by the stabilizing devices of the wall behind the figure and framing columns. The form is modelled softly yet insistently in Leonardo's *sfumato* (It.: 'smoked') manner, in which the contours are rendered elusive under a veil of intervening atmosphere. More profound is the question of the implicit imagery in which woman and landscape together bear witness to the inner life of both human and earthly forms as reflections of cosmic motions. Leonardo was fascinated by the ancient idea of microcosm, in which the human body was regarded as a reflection on a reduced scale of the structures and processes of the world as a whole. In the '*Mona Lisa*', the analogy is underscored by parallels in the treatment of the curvaceous flow in the hair, draperies, embroidery patterns and rivers and valleys in the landscape. The subtle interplay between universal values and the particularity of the individual woman has been a crucial factor in the enduring fascination of Leonardo's image.

Leonardo seems to have started to work on his composition of *Leda and the Swan* at the same time he was planning the *Battle of Anghiari*. Initially he showed Leda in a complex kneeling pose, probably inspired by an antique statue of Venus, as in a pen drawing (Windsor Castle, Royal Lib., 12337*r*). Although this idea was taken up by his followers, he apparently abandoned it in favour of a standing Leda, in which a more mellifluous motion could be orchestrated. The basic pose, relying on the sinuous, triple turn of head, torso and hips around the central axis of her body, was established at least in a developed drawing or cartoon during this period in Florence. It was studied by Raphael and set new standards of figural complexity for the younger generation of Italian artists. The painting in its final form, with the four children bursting from the eggs, may not have reached completion until after 1513. The best variants (Florence, Pal. Vecchio; Wilton House, Wilts; London, Hyde col.) suggest that it contained rich allusions to the generative powers of nature as expressed in the human, animal and vegetable kingdoms.

The *Angel of the Annunciation* (best copy, Basle, Kstsamml.) is an unjustly neglected work. The Angel conveys the message of the Annunciation directly at the viewer, who becomes the privileged recipient standing in the place of the Virgin Annunciate. This remarkable conception may have arisen during Leonardo's involvement with Rustici's sculptural group of *St John the Baptist Preaching*, which exploits a comparably direct communication between saint and spectator. The original painting was recorded in the collection of Duke Cosimo I de' Medici in the 16th century, and a drawing (Windsor Castle, Royal Lib., 12328*r*) records Leonardo's initial idea.

*(iv) Second Milanese period, mid-1508–1513.* The best evidence of Leonardo's style during his second Milanese period is provided by the *St John the Baptist* (Paris, Louvre), which represents the extreme development of his ideas on the treatment of light and shade to achieve atmospheric effects and describe three dimensional objects. The figure emerges from a dark background, with the light, falling from above left, highlighting parts of the saint's head and shoulders and creating a sense of sculptural volume. The internal modelling and shaded contours are described with an extreme of ambiguous softness, even allowing for the yellowed varnish. The elusiveness of precise form corresponds to the conviction in Leonardo's optical writings that the mechanisms of vision result in complex ambiguities of space, form and colour. Leonardo also attempted to convey the inner motions of the character's mind. The saint's angelic smile had featured in earlier Florentine art, but Leonardo's exaggerated attempt to make the expression convey a sense of spiritual knowingness has resulted in a presence that many viewers have found enigmatically disturbing. The pointing gesture, here as elsewhere in his art, alludes to the other-worldly source and immaterial power of the creator of the world. A related project was for a painting of *St John the Baptist Seated in a Landscape.* A damaged but autograph drawing (ex-Mus. Baroffio, Varese; stolen 1973) shows the fully developed pose of the saint as it appears in a painted version (Paris, Louvre), in which, however, the figure has the attributes of Bacchus, perhaps as a result of a later intervention. Although demonstrably close to Leonardo in composition and spirit, the painting appears to be by an accomplished follower.

*(v) Rome,* c. *1515.* Although the *St John* was at one time assumed to be the last of Leonardo's surviving paintings, it now seems more likely that the *Virgin and Child with St Anne and a Lamb* (Paris, Louvre; see fig. 5 above) occupies this place. The forms of the draperies, rocks and landscape and the optical subtleties can best be aligned with his drawings and writings around 1515, when he was in Rome. The composition takes up the experiments of the lost cartoon of 1501; the integration of the three figures and the lamb is achieved by the shaping of their forms into a series of interlocking curves. The fluency of the motion disguises the physical improbability of the pyramidal group. Compared to the 1501 design described by Fra Pietro, St Anne no longer restrains the Christ Child from embracing the sacrificial lamb, but the underlying symbolism remains the same. The painting technique is characterized by the fluid use of translucent glazes of oil paint to create effects of softness, translucency and transparency. Typical of Leonardo's interests are the translucent veins of coloured minerals in the pebbles near St Anne's feet. There is a compelling sense of motion and flux, both in the physical forms of the natural world and in the infinite optical variables of mists, refractions and reflections.

*(vi) 'Leonardesque' paintings and painters.* No artist ever inspired more copies, variants and pastiches than Leonardo. Fra Pietro's testimony confirms that copying was practised in Leonardo's studio, and some of the best versions of his paintings, such as the *Angel* in Basle, may be studio products, often assumed to be autograph by later owners. The working of variations on Leonardo's favourite themes appears to have become something of an industry in Milan after his departure in 1513; the precise relationship of many of these pictures to Leonardo's own paintings and drawings is often obscure. There is a marked tendency among optimistic owners and art historians to hail the more convincing of the Leonardesque paintings as long-lost originals.

Variants that appear to reflect inventions by Leonardo himself include images of *Christ the Redeemer, Christ and the Doctors in the Temple, Christ Carrying the Cross,* the *Christ Child and the Infant St John at Play,* and the *Kneeling Virgin with the Christ Child and St John and a Lamb.* The firm attribution of the majority of the versions and variants of these and other Leonardesque paintings remains impossible, given the present state of knowledge of the minor artists who followed Leonardo. Only the personalities of the more independent masters, Andrea Solario and Bernadino Luini, have been satisfactorily defined. Among those in his immediate orbit, Giovanni Antonio Boltraffio, Giovanni Ambrogio de Predis and Cesare da Sesto painted in styles that can be characterized to greater or lesser degrees, but the full parameters of their styles have not been established securely, and other followers, including Francesco Melzi and Gian Giacomo Caprotti, remain shadowy, apart from the occasional signed or documented work.

7. Leonardo da Vinci: *Studies of a Standing Horse,* silverpoint on blue prepared paper, 214×160 mm, *c.* 1490 (Windsor, Windsor Castle, Royal Library)

2. DRAWINGS. Leonardo was one of the most innovative and fertile draughtsmen of any age. In his hands the practice of drawing became a flexible extension of creative thought, not only expressing a series of new ideas in teeming abundance but also becoming, through a rapid confusion of scribbled alternatives superimposed on each other, a way of permitting chance configurations to aid the inventive process. Drawing became a form of visual thinking rather than a merely functional means for the design of a picture.

At the beginning of his career Leonardo achieved mastery of the two most important drawing techniques of the period, metalpoint and pen and ink. The *Study of Arms and Hands* (Windsor Castle, Royal Lib., 12558) that may have served for the portrait of *Ginevra de' Benci* is drawn in silverpoint with white heightening on pink prepared paper and demonstrates a meticulous control of parallel hatching to suggest graded relief. One of the last instances in which Leonardo used this traditional medium, his *Studies of a Standing Horse*, seen from the side and front (*c.* 1490; Windsor Castle, Royal Lib.; see fig. 7), probably for the Sforza monument, may be regarded as having taken the potential of silverpoint to its limits.

Leonardo's work in pen exhibited from the first an exceptional vitality of touch, as in the *Tuscan Landscape* (1473; Florence, Uffizi), which is characterized by an extraordinary suggestion of life and atmosphere. In the drawings for the *Adoration of the Magi* and various Virgin and Child compositions of the 1480s and early 1490s he evolved a graphic style of unprecedented rapidity and suggestiveness. Other Renaissance draughtsmen, including Verrocchio, had used pen and ink for quick sketches, but no one had approached Leonardo's bold and dynamic method of 'brainstorming', in which alternative forms emerge from a tangled confusion of lines. The rapid pen studies of the *Virgin and Child with a Cat* (*c.* 1478–81; London, BM; see fig. 8) show the complex interweavings of bodies in motion that become possible with this approach. On the *verso* of this sheet, the design was traced through in reverse, becoming the starting-point for a further series of variations that were clarified by the addition of an ink wash. Such paintings as the Benois *Madonna* reflect the way in which complex motions can be orchestrated through this manner of sketching.

Throughout Leonardo's career, pen and ink remained the technique he most regularly used, not only for preliminary sketches but also for scientific illustrations and representations of machinery and architecture. During the late 1490s his system of shading with pen underwent an important and influential change: the use of diagonal parallel hatching, which moved from top left to bottom right (he was left-handed), was progressively replaced by curved pen strokes that follow the forms. The drawings for the *Leda* from 1506 onwards, such as the *Study for the Kneeling Leda* (pen and ink over black chalk; Chatsworth, Derbys) represent the extreme development of this graphic style.

For the study of the component parts of compositions, Leonardo often turned to other media. Early in his career he seems to have made studies of draperies arranged on lay figures using a fine brush and white heightening on linen (Paris, Louvre, and elsewhere) in the manner of his

8. Leonardo da Vinci: *Study of the Virgin and Child with a Cat*, pen and brown ink, 132×96 mm, *c.* 1478–81 (London, British Museum)

master, Verrocchio, and contemporaries such as Domenico Ghirlandaio, but he progressively used the softer and more flexible media of red and black chalk during the 1490s, above all in the studies for the *Last Supper*. The red-chalk drawings for Apostles' heads, sometimes on reddish prepared paper, such as the *Head of Judas* (Windsor Castle, Royal Lib., 12547), make subtle interplay between softly luminous shading, rhythmic contours and selective areas of dense shadow. The heads of shouting warriors for the *Battle of Anghiari* (e.g. Budapest, Mus. F.A.; see fig. 9) represent the high-point of this technique. The softer and grainier black chalk was particularly suited to creating effects of *sfumato* modelling. When combined with white heightening, as in a *Study of a Sleeve* for St Peter in the *Last Supper* (Windsor Castle, Royal Lib., 12546), or with heightening and wash, as in studies of drapery (Windsor Castle, Royal Lib., 12530; Paris, Louvre) for the Louvre *St Anne*, extraordinarily rich effects of light and shade could be attained. Comparable effects were achieved with charcoal and white heightening in the cartoon of the *Virgin and Child with SS Anne and John the Baptist* (London, N.G.), which retains a far greater degree of fluidity and lack of resolution than would have been normal in a full-scale drawing. Black chalk was also the favoured medium for his drawings of *A Deluge* (e.g. Windsor Castle, Royal Lib.; see fig. 6 above), where its sombre, atmospheric qualities were ideally suited to such dark expressions of cosmic violence.

Leonardo was also an innovator in the use of colour in drawings. His geographical studies use coloured washes to distinguish forms in flat maps according to a convention or colour code, and also for more naturalistically descriptive purposes, as in the *Bird's-eye View of Arezzo, Borgo San Sepolcro, Perugia, Chiusi and Siena* (1502; Windsor Castle, Royal Lib., 12680). His use of coloured pastels (*see* PASTEL, §1), mentioned in 16th-century sources, cannot be demonstrated in fully autograph drawings, but artists in his circle, most notably Giovanni Antonio Boltraffio, certainly exploited the technique.

In his scientific and technical drawing Leonardo experimented with many of the illustrative techniques used in later textbooks, including various forms of solid section, transparency of overlying parts and exploded diagrams of components. He pushed the descriptive potential of static drawing on a flat surface towards its ultimate limits.

3. SCULPTURE. That Leonardo practised as a sculptor is not in doubt, but attempts to attribute surviving sculpture to him have met with generally unsatisfactory results. Vasari was probably correct in saying that Leonardo made terracotta heads of women and children (perhaps of the infant Christ or the infant St John) early in his career, since such heads were part of the stock-in-trade of a sculptor's studio in the 1470s. When he advertised his services to Ludovico 'il Moro', he claimed proficiency in 'sculpture, in marble, bronze and clay', but the subsequent records of his sculptural activity suggest that he worked as a modeller rather than as a carver.

Leonardo's most substantial sculptural undertaking was the great equestrian monument to *Francesco Sforza* that was intended to be cast in bronze in Milan. The first record of his direct involvement occurs only in 1489, when the Duke expressed doubts about Leonardo's ability to complete the work. In April 1490 Leonardo himself noted that he 'restarted the horse' (Paris, Inst. France, MS. C, fol. 15*v*). By this time it is likely that he had set aside his technically impractical scheme for a rider on a rearing horse and reverted to the more traditional walking pose, as in Donatello's *Gattamelata* (*c.* 1447–53; Padua, Piazza del Santo; *see* DONATELLO, fig. 4) and Verrocchio's *Bartolommeo Colleoni* (1495; Venice, Campo SS Giovanni e Paolo), but on a scale of three times life size. In 1491 and 1492 he worked on the full-scale clay model, which made a great impact when it was shown as part of the marriage celebrations of Bianca Maria Sforza and Emperor Maximilian. The surviving records of Leonardo's project in his drawings and manuscripts are far from complete, but include beautiful studies of horses from life (e.g. fig. 7 above), proportional studies, for instance the silverpoint measured drawing of a *Horse in Profile to the Left* (Windsor Castle, Royal Lib., 12319) and elaborate schemes for the casting of the colossus mainly in the second Madrid codex (Madrid, Bib. N., MS. 8936). The drawings show his concern to capture the nervous vitality of a highly bred horse, both in its overall motion and in the rhythmic grace of individual parts. There is little indication of the intended pose of the rider, who may not even have been included in the clay model that was exhibited. The bronze was never cast, and the model was destroyed.

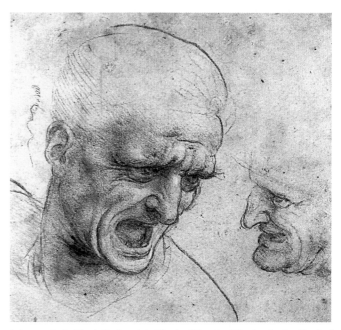

9. Leonardo da Vinci: *Studies of the Heads of Shouting Warriors* for the *Battle of Anghiari*, black and red chalk, 191×188 mm, *c.* 1504–5 (Budapest, Museum of Fine Arts)

Leonardo's plans for the equestrian monument to Gian Giacomo Trivulzio are recorded in a series of pen drawings (Windsor Castle, Royal Lib., 12353, 12355, 12356), which show that an energetically striding horse and gesturing rider were to have been mounted on an elaborate architectural base. The base was to have contained a recumbent image of Trivulzio on his sarcophagus, and a series of eight 'captives' (bound nude male figures) were to have been attached around its margins in a manner comparable to Michelangelo's projected scheme for the tomb of *Pope Julius II*. Leonardo's project was destined not to reach even the stage of a full-scale model, although some later drawings, such as the black-chalk study showing a fallen soldier trampled beneath his horse's hooves (Windsor Castle, Royal Lib., 12354) which may date from 1511, show that he continued to meditate on the possibility of reviving his earlier idea for a rearing horse.

The most tangible surviving evidence of Leonardo's qualities as a sculptor occurs in Rustici's bronze group of *St John the Baptist Preaching*. Although there is no direct documentation of Leonardo's involvement with this group, Vasari's account of Leonardo's participation is supported by the visual evidence. The complex yet monumentally graceful poses, the individual characterizations and contrasted expressions speak the language pioneered by Leonardo in the *Last Supper*, while the intricate communication between the figures and the spectator on the ground below can be seen as the realization of ideas with which Leonardo had long been experimenting. The precise roles of Rustici and Leonardo are impossible to disentangle, but it is clear that Leonardo's presence resulted in Rustici working on a higher plane than in any of his wholly independent works.

The high probability that Leonardo worked on smaller-scale sculpture in his studio, either in terracotta or wax, has encouraged a search for surviving examples or, more realistically, bronzes dependent on his models. The surviving terracotta that deserves the most serious consideration is a bust of the *Infant Christ* (ex-Galludt col.; see Pedretti, 1957, and Kemp, 1981), but, in the absence of any direct evidence of Leonardo's handling of terracotta, the attribution remains provisional. Among the bronzes that bear some resemblance to Leonardo's designs, the best contenders are a series of small-scale rearing horses with riders. Two versions (Budapest, N. Mus.; Louisville, KY, Speed A. Mus.), the latter probably representing *Marcus Curtius*, can be related to drawings of rearing horses of the *Battle of Anghiari* type, such as the sheet of studies of *Horses, a Cat and St George and the Dragon* (Windsor Castle, Royal Lib., 12331). However, the generalized anatomy of the Budapest horse suggests that it is at best a later variant of a Leonardo design, while the *Marcus Curtius* has an awkwardness in proportion and balance that points to a follower, possibly Rustici.

The topic of Leonardo and sculpture, if examined through the master's surviving work, is not encouraging, but it would be wrong to underestimate its importance. Sculptural values, particularly those of Verrocchio, exercised a notable impact on Leonardo's vision of form and communication in space, and some of his own ideas were absorbed into the sculptural tradition.

4. ARCHITECTURE. Discussion of Leonardo's contribution to architecture is as problematic as that of his contribution to sculpture. Although he may never have built anything, documents and drawings contain tantalizing glimpses of unrealized projects and brilliant inventions, and in his letter to Ludovico Sforza he claimed to be the equal of anyone in architecture, capable of designing public and private buildings. His architecture may be described as being in the spirit of Brunelleschi, combining a reverence for the proportional principles of antique buildings (as expounded by Vitruvius) with a relatively undogmatic use of the Classical vocabulary and an inventive ingenuity in matters of engineering.

Leonardo's architectural projects were of two kinds. The first were practical, completing or renovating extant buildings and working as a military architect; the second were theoretical and included schemes for ideal cities and plans for many types of building. It is possible that the designs in Codex B (Paris, Inst. France) were intended to initiate a treatise on architectural building types, while the first Madrid manuscript (Madrid, Bib. N.) deals with principles of construction. The treatment of churches in Codex B, consisting of illustrations with only a minimal commentary, may have influenced later writers on architecture, particularly Serlio. Leonardo's architectural drawings, together with those of Francesco di Giorgio Martini (one of whose architectural manuscripts Leonardo owned) and of Giuliano da Sangallo, are among the earliest known. Since no drawings of this date survive by Bramante (who worked in Milan as court architect alongside Leonardo for 19 years), they are crucial in illustrating the evolution of the High Renaissance style.

Leonardo's series of structural studies for the *tiburio* over the crossing of Milan Cathedral (1487–8; e.g. Cod. Atlantico, fol. 310*r*b; Cod. Trivulziano) show that he attempted to devise an architectural 'skeleton' that had more affinities with the principles of Gothic ribs than with Roman structures, while the shape of his dome pays obvious homage to Brunelleschi's at Florence Cathedral.

The fundamental principle behind Leonardo's schemes of urban planning, developed in connection with schemes for Milan and Vigevano, was to devise a functioning 'body' in which canals, roads and pavements would permit an efficient and healthy environment, with a highly organized stratification of social activities. The designs in Codex B (fols 16*r*, 37*v*) illustrate ideal schemes for raised pedestrian precincts and a subterranean canal system that had little hope of realization, but the planning undertaken by Ludovico Sforza at Vigevano in the 1490s appears to reflect the translation of Leonardo's ideas into reality.

The most impressive and coherent set of Leonardo's architectural drawings is the series of church designs in Codex B (fols 17*v*, 18*v*, 21*r*) and Ashburnham I (Paris, Inst. France, MS. B.N. 2037), which show his variations on centralized and Latin cross plans. Some represent free experiments with a variety of geometrical schemes, while a few (e.g. Ashburnham I, fol. 5*v*) depict relatively resolved structures in which complex aggregations of plastic form are erected over intricate geometrical ground-plans. The more compact of the centralized structures, relating to Brunelleschi's unfinished S Maria degli Angeli in Florence, may have been intended as a Sforza mausoleum on a limited scale rather than as a full-sized church.

Leonardo's inventiveness as a military architect was given full expression when he was in service with Cesare Borgia in 1502–3. His mission to Piombino on behalf of the Florentine government appears to have stimulated some remarkable schemes for fortified structures, ranging from projects for specific locations to great, ideal schemes for impregnable fortresses (e.g. Cod. Atlantico, fol. 41*v*a, 48*r*b). Massive, block-like structures, with curved or slanting profiles to deflect bombardments, are disposed around circular or polygonal plans, with elaborate passages for the internal circulation of forces. Although the grander schemes inevitably remained unrealized, it is reasonable to think that Leonardo's advice on modifications to existing structures were taken in hand by his patrons.

The grandest of Leonardo's plans for a residential structure dates from the last years of his career, when he was in France. His scheme for the château at Romorantin, involving a large rectangular palace block, formal gardens and a rectangular network of canals, has been reconstructed by Pedretti (1972) from a group of sketches (especially Cod. Atlantico, fol. 76*v*b; London, BL, MS. Arundel, fol. 270*r*). The style appears to marry indigenous French elements, such as the round corner towers, with Italian Renaissance elements in a way that is typical of Leonardo's undogmatic exploitation of Classical vocabulary. His sense of form and function ultimately took precedence over strict allegiance to Classical rules.

5. EPHEMERAL DESIGNS. A significant factor in Leonardo's value to his courtly patrons was his ability to

organize visual entertainments, particularly those connected with celebrations. His involvement with the design of courtly ephemera is relatively well documented, but the visual record is meagre. Only a few drawings in his surviving notebooks relate directly to known schemes. The most substantial autograph record relates to a pageant on the occasion of the weddings of Ludovico and Anna Sforza to Beatrice and Alfonso d'Este in 1491. A drawing of a richly caparisoned horse is accompanied by a note that explains an astonishingly rich series of symbolic allusions involving peacock feathers, a wheel of fortune and the Cardinal Virtues (MS. Arundel, fol. 250*r*). His drawings for allegorical compositions illustrating the Sforzas' reign show a comparable elaboration of arcane allusions, extreme even by Renaissance standards.

Leonardo was also involved in theatrical design, specializing in effects that required large-scale machinery. His drawings for 'Pluto's Paradise' (MS. Arundel, fol. 231*v*) show a scheme for the opening of a mountain to reveal Pluto and his attendants who play harsh percussion instruments. As a musician of some reputation himself (he played the *lira di braccio*), Leonardo was well placed to design effects that would work in concert with instrumental and vocal compositions. Contemporary accounts survive of his most famed design for Bellincioni's *Festa del paradiso*, which involved a great, glowing celestial hemisphere adorned with stars and planets. A slight drawing (Cod. Atlantico, fol. 385*v*b), apparently dating from this late period in Milan in the 1490s, suggests that he should also be credited with the invention of the shallow, perspectival stage set normally associated with Baldassare Peruzzi and illustrated in Sebastiano Serlio's treatise on architecture (1537–51).

Evidence of his more general work as a designer of courtly diversions is fragmentary. His notebooks contain designs for pictograms (picture writing), portable pavilions, festive architecture, automata, fountains and written outlines for amusing contrivances. Such employment was both advantageous and irksome for Leonardo: advantageous in that it helped to justify his salary at court, but irksome in that it occupied considerable amounts of time with no enduring result.

### III. Theory.

No one was ever more insistent than Leonardo on the intellectual nature of the visual arts. Painting was defined as 'the sole imitator of all the visible works of nature' and as 'a subtle invention which with subtle speculation considers the nature of all forms' (Rome, Vatican, Bib. Apostolica, MS. Urb. lat. fol. 4*v*). His aspiration was that the artist should be able to construct a created world on the basis of a comprehensive understanding of causes and effects in the natural world. Given his belief in painting as the ultimate end of science, it is impossible to draw any strict line between his art theory and his scientific work as a whole.

There is no rounded or fully coherent collection of Leonardo's views on painting. The so-called *Trattato della pittura* by Leonardo is a posthumous selection from his manuscripts (some surviving but the majority untraced) probably compiled by Francesco Melzi. Although it contains some sustained and relatively well-organized sections—most notably that concerning the *paragone*, the comparison of the arts—it is on the whole a patchy, repetitive and sometimes contradictory anthology of notes from various dates. Questions of LIGHT and COLOUR, motion, GESTURE and botany are relatively well represented, while his more mathematical concerns (particularly PERSPECTIVE) are treated in a misleadingly cursory manner, and the detailed science of human anatomy is not represented at all.

Leonardo's concerns in the earliest of his surviving theoretical writings are closely aligned with those of his Florentine predecessors. He believed that the artist should master the kind of disciplines recommended by Leon Battista Alberti and Lorenzo Ghiberti: orthodox perspective construction, anatomy, proportion (*see* HUMAN PROPORTION), the depiction of light and shade and the use of motion and gesture in narrative compositions. However, his exhaustive and inventive explorations not only led him to points of greater elaboration than his predecessors but also undermined the certainties on which Alberti's theory of imitation was founded. (For Leonardo's representation, after Vitruvius, of an ideally proportioned figure of a man inscribed within a circle and square, *see* HUMAN PROPORTION, fig. 1.)

Leonardo's optical researches, increasingly undertaken within the framework of the medieval geometry of vision, convinced him that the simple perspective used by painters corresponded only in a highly schematized manner to the way in which forms in space are actually seen by the eye. His investigation of the anomalies of orthodox perspective, particularly with respect to wide-angle vision, led him to consider methods of portrayal that involved lateral recession, but he did not develop a fully consistent alternative system. In his paintings following the *Last Supper*, he relied increasingly on creating effects of atmospheric perspective by means of deliberately blurring the clarity of detail and form in the distance, and progressively modifying colour. Although he became increasingly aware of the myriad variables and transitory effects of visual phenomena, he did not surrender his view that all the causes should be wholly codified and the full variety of effects mastered. The laborious and repetitive analyses of light and colour that survive in unfinished form in his notebooks testify to a heroic, if doomed, effort to construct a comprehensive visual science of painting.

Central to Leonardo's ambitions as an artist, as it had been to the Florentine tradition, was the portrayal of the human figure as a communicative vehicle of action, thought and emotion. His researches into the structure and functioning of the human body went far deeper than those of earlier artists, and indeed far deeper than those of Michelangelo in the next generation. To some extent this is a reflection of his fascination with anatomy and physiology in their own right, but it also relates to his conviction that the artist must understand the deepest causes of motion and emotion if he is to create figures that can function adequately as imitations of nature.

The most famous and sustained passages of art theory are contained in those earlier sections of the *Trattato* devoted to the PARAGONE. The general thrust of Leonardo's arguments is to demonstrate the superiority of painting over the arts of the ear, poetry and music, and over sculpture, the other major visual art. Since he seemed to identify poetry as a form of visual description, he had little difficulty in demonstrating the superior representational power of painting, and since he regarded the simultaneous perception of a harmonious composition as preferable to a sequential progression of effects, he was able to claim its superiority over music. His chief argument against sculpture was that it involved the mastery of only a limited number of visual variables with which the painter must grapple. The true end of his *paragone* is to prove that painting must be considered as a liberal art, indeed, the supreme liberal art, rather than as a manual craft.

Reading Leonardo's theory, it might be assumed that his own creations would appear more obviously naturalistic or 'photographic' in their representation of nature than they actually are. In his paintings and drawn compositions a sense of imagination and free invention is openly apparent, and not infrequently the effect involves elements of mystery, ambiguity and fantasy. His fascination with the demonic and grotesque, most notably expressed in his series of caricatured heads, for instance the pen drawing of *Five Grotesque Heads* (Windsor Castle, Royal Lib., 12495), stands in marked contrast to his rational search for the principles of beauty in nature. To some extent the fantastic properties in his creations can be explained in his own terms, in that he acknowledged the merits of the faculty of *fantasia* (imagination) and the necessity for *invenzione* in the creation of his own world of forms, but in the final analysis there were qualities in his imaginative life as expressed in his art that eluded his own rational definitions of the means and ends of painting.

## IV. Character and personality.

Contemporary accounts testify to the attractiveness of Leonardo and of the care with which he presented himself to the world. Together with the more personal aspects of the notebooks, they convey the picture of someone who was gentle, with a great respect for living things (he was probably a vegetarian), fastidious in personal habits, self-conscious in dress, gracious in manner, yet retaining a core of remoteness, reserve and impersonality. He fitted well into the courtly milieu of Milan under the Sforzas, appearing at ease within the court's ambience of snobbish refinement. Against this image of gentility must be set his continued involvement with the violent machinery of war, which appears to have fascinated him emotionally as well as presenting him with an irresistible series of technical challenges. Much has been made of his supposed homosexuality, and such evidence as is available suggests homosexual rather than heterosexual inclinations, but it is doubtful whether the notebooks and other documents provide sufficient material for a full-scale psychoanalysis in the Freudian manner.

Leonardo showed signs of secrecy and protectiveness towards his own inventions. He noted that he should test the wing of his flying machine out of sight of others, and he accused a German colleague in Rome of stealing one of his inventions. His notebooks are written in mirror writing, but this eccentricity may be explained in part by the fact that he was left-handed. The general impression is that he was ready to share his views with others, and that the organization of his studio facilitated the transmission of his ideas and inventions into a wider domain.

The traditional portrait image of Leonardo in old age, as a handsome, bearded and long-haired seer, originated at a time when people still recalled his appearance, but the so-called *Self-portrait* drawing in red chalk (Turin, Bib. Reale) cannot be taken unquestionably as representing the painter himself. Although the case for dismissing it as a forgery (Ost, 1980) is weak, it may have originated considerably earlier than its customary date of *c.* 1512 and could not therefore be a portrait of the artist himself as an aged man. None of the supposed portraits of the young Leonardo in his own works or those of others (such as Verrocchio's bronze statue of *David*; Florence, Bargello) possesses a secure foundation in fact.

## V. Influence and posthumous reputation.

There has never been a period in which Leonardo's greatness has not been acknowledged, though perceptions of the nature of his achievements have differed widely and have often not been founded on a secure sense of what he actually accomplished. Some of the most famous accounts, such as that by Walter Pater (1869), were based on an image of the Leonardesque rather than a clear conception of his actual oeuvre.

There was virtually no major aspect of the visual arts in 16th-century Italy (and to some degree in Europe) that remained untouched directly or indirectly by Leonardo's innovations. Each of his major narrative paintings made a significant contribution to the tradition of history painting. The complex orchestration of a crowd in his *Adoration of the Magi* was adopted in such works by Raphael as the *Disputa* and *School of Athens* (both Rome, Vatican, Stanza della Segnatura); the *Last Supper*, as much through engravings as the original, continued to influence artists as diverse as Rembrandt and Rubens; and the *Battle of Anghiari*, with Michelangelo's *Cascina* cartoon for its companion piece, became the 'school' for young artists who wished to achieve complex interlocking spatial patterns of figures in motion. The pyramidal yet fluent groups of his Virgin and Child compositions set the norm for younger artists, most notably Raphael. His portraits established the ambition to evoke the inner life of sitters, at the same time as setting new goals in formal sophistication for portrait painters such as Bronzino. A large number of his formal motifs were transmitted across Europe through copies, variants and pastiches of his compositions. Even major northern masters such as Quinten Metsys and Hans Holbein the younger proved susceptible to the seductiveness of Leonardo's inventions.

Leonardo's technique of making free sketches also exercised a profound influence on Italian creative methods, most radically those of the young Raphael, but also of Michelangelo. His revelation of the descriptive and evocative powers of red and black chalk inspired generations of figure draughtsmen in Italy, and, through them, in France and elsewhere. Although only a few of his drawings were directly engraved before the 18th century, a number of his characteristic obsessions, such as proportional studies and caricatured physiognomy, stimulated direct imitation.

None of Leonardo's major successors adopted his softly shadowed style of painting precisely, but his emphasis on tonal modelling and the principles of his *sfumato* ensured the passing of what Vasari regarded as the 'dry' manner of the Quattrocento. His technique has sometimes been credited with laying the foundations for the soft handling of form by Giorgione, but the Venetian colouristic blurring of contour is very different from Leonardo's shadow-based system. More obvious heirs may be seen in Antonio Correggio (particularly the early work) and Caravaggio at the end of the 16th century.

In sculpture, architecture and stage design Leonardo's influence is harder to define, in the absence of certainly autograph surviving works. His clearest impact was on the architecture of Donato Bramante, who responded to the complex spatial geometry of his colleague's schemes for centralized churches in his designs for the east end of S Maria della Grazie, Milan, and his plan for St Peter's in Rome. Contemporaries testify to the impact of Leonardo's various designs for theatrical spectacles and festivities, and it appears likely that he played a crucial role in the invention of the perspectival stage design.

The range, diversity and depth of Leonardo's scientific interests lay beyond most of his contemporaries and successors in the world of art, but his theories of art did seep into general circulation, although none was directly published before 1651. Perhaps the most significant impact was on Albrecht Dürer, whose ambitions in the theories of proportion and physiognomy come closest in spirit to those of Leonardo. The anthology of Leonardo's writings, the *Trattato della pittura*, circulated in various abridged manuscripts in the 16th century and the early 17th, particularly in Italian academic circles. The new generation of academically minded artists in early 17th-century Italy welcomed Leonardo's insistence on controlled expression in figure style and rational analysis of the forms of nature. One painter–theorist in the orbit of Domenichino, Matteo Zaccolini, compiled four manuscript treatises in a consciously Leonardesque vein, but they were never published, and their impact was limited.

Leonardo's enduring reputation as the founder of the High Renaissance was ensured by his position at the start of the third part of Vasari's *Vite*, and Vasari's portrait—including his reservations about the erratic variety of Leonardo's obsessions—dominated interpretations of Leonardo well into the 19th century. The earlier life by Paolo Giovio and the perceptive comments by Giovanni Paolo Lomazzo exercised less impact. The first serious attempt to come to terms with the range of Leonardo's legacy was undertaken by the great patron, antiquarian and arbiter of taste in 17th-century Rome, Cassiano dal Pozzo. Although Cassiano and his collaborator, Conte GALEAZZO ARCONATI, did not succeed in their aim of bringing Leonardo's manuscripts to publication, Cassiano was responsible for providing the manuscript, albeit abridged, of the *Trattato della pittura*, illustrated by Nicolas Poussin, that Paul Fréart Sieur de Chambray took to France and that was used in Raphael Trichet Du Fresne's first edition of the *Trattato* (1651). The treatise appeared in France at a crucial stage

in the development of the Académie Française and was welcomed by Charles Lebrun as providing an authentic pedigree for his ideas of rhetorical expression in academic painting.

Leonardo's reputation during the 17th and 18th centuries was not based on clearly defined knowledge of his actual oeuvre. Versions and pastiches were paraded as Leonardo's own work in the absence of a substantial body of surviving paintings by the master, although a few artists of the highest sensitivity, such as Antoine Watteau, do seem to have responded perceptively to the few autograph works available. By the late 18th century the situation was changing. The 'rediscovery' of the drawings in the British Royal Collection, some of which were subsequently engraved, gave a clearer idea of his draughtsmanship. Giovanni Battista Venturi's transcription of some of his notes on water and other matters evinced a renewed interest in his manuscripts, and Giuseppe Bossi's publication on the *Last Supper* in 1810, reviewed so tellingly by Goethe, represented a pioneering attempt to subject Leonardo's career to scholarly examination.

Great advances were made around 1900 in two main directions. First came the systematic scrutiny and publication of Leonardo's scattered and diminished (if still extensive) legacy of manuscripts. Jean Paul Richter's anthology, *The Literary Works of Leonardo da Vinci* (1883), is still a standard point of reference, particularly in conjunction with Carlo Pedretti's *Commentary* (1977). A wave of facsimiles, transcriptions and translations of the manuscripts in various European locations (most notably Milan and Paris), under the guidance of such scholars as Gerolamo Calvi, Giovanni Piumati and Charles Ravaisson-Mollien, brought the range of Leonardo's mind into the public domain. Gabriel Séailles (1892) and Paul Valéry (1895) made the first attempts to grapple with this new, 'universal' Leonardo. Second came the establishment of a firmly documented chronology for Leonardo's career. Eugene Müntz, Francesco Malaguzzi Valeri, Waldemar von Seidlitz, Giovanni Poggi and Paul Müller-Walde played significant roles, but the most lasting contribution was made by Luca Beltrami, whose *Documenti e memorie riguardanti la vita e le opere di Leonardo da Vinci* (1919) remains the basic source for Leonardo's biography. Calvi's book on the dating of the manuscripts was equally fundamental in laying down the groundwork for a chronological understanding of Leonardo's mind and graphic style.

Since the beginning of the 20th century an enormous body of literature on Leonardo has been published, much of it valueless, but a certain proportion contains material that has clarified his historical position and artistic stature. The study of the manuscripts has been substantially advanced by Edmondo Solmi's researches into the sources for Leonardo's opinions, while the more recent studies by Augusto Marinoni and Carlo Pedretti (the latter of whom has scrutinized Leonardo's legacy in considerable detail) have revealed that meticulous scholarship can still lead to new discoveries.

The greatest contribution to the picture of Leonardo as an artist was made by Kenneth Clark. His catalogue of Leonardo's artistic drawings at Windsor (1935) established an authoritative chronology, continuing the pioneer work of Anny Popp, and provided a compelling critical assessment of Leonardo as a draughtsman. He used this scholarly foundation as the basis for his relatively brief monograph (1939), which remains the most elegantly evocative account of the artist's creative personality.

Full-scale monographs continue to appear in large numbers. Among the most regularly cited in English are those by Ludwig Heydenreich (1954), Cecil Gould (1975), Carlo Pedretti (1973), Jack Wasserman (1975) and Martin Kemp (1981). Studies devoted to particular aspects of Leonardo's work include those by A. E. Popham on his drawings, Vasilij Zubov (particularly valuable on his scientific thought), E. H. Gombrich on his water studies, Kenneth Keele on anatomy, Pedretti on architecture, Pietro Marani on fortifications, Ladislao Reti on the Madrid manuscripts and Kim Veltman on perspective. The literature on Leonardo is now so discouragingly vast that it can only be mastered as a whole by a full-time 'Leonardista'.

## WRITINGS

P. Fréart, ed.: *Trattato della pittura* (Paris, 1651)
G. Venturi, ed.: *Fragments tirés des manuscrits de Léonard de Vinci* (Paris, 1797); and in G. B. de Toni: *Giambattista Venturi e la sua opera vinciana* (Rome, 1924)
C. Ravaisson-Mollien, ed.: *Les Manuscrits da Léonard de Vinci*, 6 vols (Paris, 1881–91)
H. Ludwig, ed.: *Leonardo da Vinci: Das Buch von der Malerei*, 2 vols (Vienna, 1882) [the Codex Urbinas in the Vatican, Rome; the standard critical edn of the *Trattato della pittura*]
J. P. Richter, ed.: *The Literary Works of Leonardo da Vinci*, 2 vols (London, 1883, rev. 1970); and in C. Pedretti: *The Literary Works of Leonardo da Vinci, edited by J. P. Richter: Commentary*, 2 vols (Oxford, 1977)
L. Beltrami, ed.: *Il codice di Leonardo da Vinci della Biblioteca del Principe Trivulzio in Milano* (Milan, 1891)
T. Sabachnikoff, G. Piumati and C. Ravaisson-Mollien, eds: *I manoscritti di Leonardo da Vinci: Codice sul volo degli uccelli e varie altre materie* (Paris, 1893)
G. Piumati, ed.: *Il Codice Atlantico di Leonardo da Vinci nella Biblioteca Ambrosiana di Milano*, 35 vols (Milan, 1894–1904)
T. Sachnikoff and G. Piumati, eds: *I manoscritti di Leonardo da Vinci della Biblioteca Reale di Windsor* (Paris, 1898)
G. Calvi, ed.: *Il codice di Leonardo da Vinci della Biblioteca di Lord Leicester in Holkham Hall* (Milan, 1909) [Codex Leicester, now called Codex Hammer]
D. C. L. Fonahn and H. Hopstock, eds: *Quaderni d'anatomia*, 6 vols (Kristiania, 1911–16)
*I manoscritti e i disegni di Leonardo da Vinci: Il Codice Arundel 263*, Reale Commissione Vinciana, 4 vols (Rome, 1923–30) [Arundel Codex, London, BM]
*Il Codice Forster I, etc*, Reale Commissione Vinciana, 5 vols (Rome, 1930–36) [Forster Codex, London, V&A]
*I manoscritti e i disegni di Leonardo da Vinci: Il Codice A*, Reale Commissione Vinciana (Rome, 1938)
E. MacCurdy, ed.: *The Notebooks of Leonardo da Vinci*, 2 vols (London, 1938)
*I manoscritti e i disegni di Leonardo da Vinci: Il Codice B*, Reale Commissione Vinciana (Rome, 1941)
A. M. Brizio, ed.: *Scritti scelti di Leonardo da Vinci* (Turin, 1952, rev. 2/1966)
A. Marinoni, ed.: *Leonardo da Vinci: Scritti letterari* (Milan, 1952, rev. 2/1974)
A. P. MacMahon, ed.: *Treatise on Painting by Leonardo da Vinci*, 2 vols (Princeton, 1956) [facs. and trans.]
C. Pedretti, ed.: *Leonardo da Vinci on Painting: A Lost Book (Libro A)* (London, 1965)
A. Courbeau and N. De Toni, eds: *The Manuscripts in the Bibliothèque de l'Institut de France, Paris* (Florence, 1972)
A. Marinoni, ed.: *Il Codice Atlantico di Leonardo da Vinci*, 24 vols (Florence, 1973–80)
L. Reti, ed.: *The Madrid Codices*, 5 vols (New York, 1974)
A. Marinoni, ed.: *Il codice sul volo degli uccelli di Leonardo da Vinci nella Biblioteca Reale di Torino* (Florence, 1976; Eng. trans., New York, 1982)

I. Richter, ed.: *Selections from the Notebooks of Leonardo da Vinci* (Oxford, 1977)
C. Pedretti, ed.: *The Codex Atlanticus: A Catalogue of its Newly-restored Sheets*, 2 vols (Los Angeles, 1978)
K. Keele and C. Pedretti, eds: *Leonardo da Vinci: Corpus of Anatomical Studies in the Collection of Her Majesty the Queen at Windsor Castle*, 3 vols (London, 1978–80)
A. Marinoni, ed.: *Il codice di Leonardo da Vinci nella Biblioteca Trivulziana di Milano* (Florence, 1980; Eng. trans., New York, 1982)
C. Pedretti, ed.: *The Codex Hammer of Leonardo da Vinci* (Florence, 1987)
M. Kemp and M. Walker, eds: *Leonardo on Painting: An Anthology of Writings by Leonardo da Vinci with a Selection of Documents Relating to his Career as an Artist* (London, 1989)
C. J. Farago, ed.: *Leonardo da Vinci's 'Paragone': A Critical Interpretation with a New Edition of the Text in the Codex Urbinus* (Leiden, 1992)
A. Marinoni, ed.: *I Codici Forster del Victoria and Albert Museum di Londra* (Florence, 1992)

## BIBLIOGRAPHY

### EARLY SOURCES

L. Pacioli: *De divina proportione* (Venice, 1509)
F. Albertini: *Memoriale di molte statue et picture che sono nella inclyta ciptà di Florentia* (Florence, 1510); ed. H. Horne (London, 1909); also in L. Beltrami: *Documenti e memorie riguardanti la vita e le opere di Leonardo da Vinci* (Milan, 1919)
P. Giovio: *Elogia virorum illustrum* (MS.; *c.* 1527); in *Gli elogi degli uomini illustri*, ed. R. Meregazzi (Rome, 1972), viii of *Pauli Iovii opera*, p. 229
*Il Codice Magliabechiano* (MS.; *c.* 1540); ed. C. Frey (Berlin, 1892), pp. 51–2; ed. C. Fabriszy as *Il codice dell'anonimo Gaddiano* (Florence, 1893), pp. 76–8
G. Vasari: *Vite* (1550, rev. 2/1568); ed. G. Milanesi (1878–85), iii, p. 371; iv, pp. 17–53; vi, pp. 136, 246, 600
M. Bandello: *Le novelle* (Lucca, 1554); ed. F. Picco (Milan, 1973) [dedication of no. lviii]
G. P. Lomazzo: *Trattato dell'arte della pittura, scultura ed architettura* (Milan, 1584); in *G. P. Lomazzo: Scritti sulle arti*, ed. R. P. Ciardi, 2 vols (Florence, 1973–4)
——: *Idea del tempio della pittura* (Milan, 1590); in *G. P. Lomazzo: Scritti sulle arti*, ed. R. P. Ciardi, 2 vols (Florence, 1973–4)

### MONOGRAPHIC STUDIES AND CATALOGUES RAISONNÉS

C. Amoretti: *Memorie storiche su la vita, gli studi e le opere di Leonardo da Vinci* (Milan, 1804)
W. Pater: 'Leonardo da Vinci' (1869), *Studies in the History of the Renaissance* (London, 1873)
G. Séailles: *Léonard de Vinci: L'Artiste et le savant* (Paris, 1892)
P. Valéry: 'Introduction à la méthode de Léonard de Vinci', *Nouv. Rev.* (15 Aug 1895); *Nouv. Rev. Fr.* (1919); Eng. trans. by T. McGreevy (London, 1929)
P. Müller-Walde: *Leonardo da Vinci: Lebensskizze und Forschungen über sein Verhältnis zur Florentiner Kunst und zu Rafael* (Munich, 1899)
E. Müntz: *Léonard de Vinci: L'Artiste, le penseur et le savant* (Paris, 1899)
E. Solmi: 'Le fonti dei manoscritti di Leonardo da Vinci', *G. Stor. Lett. It.*, suppl. (1908), 10–11, pp. 1–344
W. von Seidlitz: *Leonardo da Vinci, der Wendepunkt der Renaissance*, 2 vols (Berlin, 1909)
S. Freud: *Eine Kindheitserinnerung des Leonardo da Vinci* (Vienna, 1910; Eng. trans., London, 1957)
L. Beltrami: *Documenti e memorie riguardanti la vita e le opere di Leonardo da Vinci* (Milan, 1919)
G. Poggi: *Leonardo da Vinci: La 'Vita' di Giorgio Vasari, nuovamente commentata e illustrata con 200 tavole* (Florence, 1919)
G. Calvi: *I manoscritti di Leonardo da Vinci del punto di visto cronologico, storico e biografico* (Bologna, 1925)
H. Bodmer: *Leonardo: Des Meisters Gemälde und Zeichnungen*, Klass. Kst Gesamtausgaben (Stuttgart, 1931)
K. Clark: *Leonardo da Vinci: An Account of his Development as an Artist* (Cambridge, 1939, rev. Harmondsworth, 3/1967); rev. and ed. M. Kemp (1988)
L. Heydenreich: *Leonardo da Vinci*, 2 vols (Basle, 1954; Eng. trans., London, 1954)
C. Pedretti: *Studi vinciani* (Geneva, 1957)
V. P. Zubov: *Leonardo da Vinci* (Moscow, 1961; Eng. trans., Cambridge, MA, 1968)
C. D. O'Malley, ed.: *Leonardo's Legacy* (Los Angeles, 1969) [invaluable essays]
C. Pedretti: *Leonardo da Vinci: A Study in Chronology and Style* (London, 1973)

L. Reti, ed.: *The Unknown Leonardo* (London, 1974)
C. Gould: *Leonardo: The Artist and Non-artist* (London, 1975)
J. Wasserman: *Leonardo da Vinci* (New York, 1975)
A. Chastel: *The Genius of Leonardo da Vinci: Leonardo da Vinci and the Art of the Artist* (New York, 1981)
M. Kemp: *Leonardo da Vinci: The Marvellous Works of Nature and Man* (London, 1981, rev. 2/1988)
E. Belloni and P. Rossi, eds: *Leonardo e l'età della ragione* (Milan, 1982)
E. Winternitz: *Leonardo da Vinci as a Musician* (Milan, 1982)
L. D. Ettinger and A. Ottino della Chiesa: *The Complete Paintings of Leonardo da Vinci* (Harmondsworth, 1985)
P. Marani: *Leonardo: Catalogo completo* (Florence, 1989)
A. R. Turner: *Inventing Leonardo* (New York, 1993)

PERMANENT COLLECTION AND EXHIBITION CATALOGUES

K. Clark: *The Drawings of Leonardo da Vinci in the Collection of His Majesty the King* (London, 1935); rev. with C. Pedretti as *The Drawings of Leonardo da Vinci in the Collection of Her Majesty the Queen*, 2 vols (London, 1969)
A. E. Popham and P. Pouncey: *Italian Drawings: The Fourteenth and Fifteenth Centuries*, London, BM cat., 2 vols (London, 1950)
K. T. Parker: *The Catalogue of the Collection of Drawings in the Ashmolean Museum, II; The Italian Schools* (Oxford, 1956)
J. Byam Shaw: *Drawings by Old Masters at Christ Church, Oxford*, 2 vols (Oxford, 1976)
L. Cogliati Arano and A. Marinoni: *Disegni di Leonardo da Vinci e della sua cerchia alle Gallerie della Accademia di Venezia* (Milan, 1980)
——: *Disegni di Leonardo da Vinci e della sua cerchia alla Biblioteca Ambrosiana di Milano* (Milan, 1981)
C. Pedretti: *Landscapes, Plants and Water Studies in the Collection of Her Majesty the Queen at Windsor Castle* (London and New York, 1982)
C. Pedretti and G. Dalli Regoli: *I disegni di Leonardo da Vinci e della sua cerchia nel Gabinetto di Disegni e Stampe della Galleria degli Uffizi a Firenze* (Florence, 1985)
C. Pedretti: *Horses and Other Animals: Drawings by Leonardo da Vinci in the Collection of Her Majesty the Queen at Windsor Castle* (London and New York, 1987)
*Leonardo da Vinci: Engineer and Architect* (exh. cat., ed. P. Galuzzi; Montreal, Mus. F.A., 1987)
*Leonardo da Vinci* (exh. cat. by M. Kemp and J. Roberts, London, Hayward Gal., 1989)
C. Pedretti: *I disegni di Leonardo da Vinci e della sua cerchia nella Biblioteca Reale di Torino* (Florence, 1990)
C. Pedretti and P. Trutty Coohill: *The Drawings of Leonardo da Vinci and his Circle in the American Collections*, 2 vols (Florence, 1993)

SPECIALIST STUDIES

*Painting*

G. Bossi: *Del cenacolo di Leonardo da Vinci* (Milan, 1810); rev. by J. W. von Goethe in *Kst & Altert.*, I/iii (1817); Eng. trans. in *Goethe on Art*, ed. J. Gage (London, 1980)
F. Malaguzzi Valeri: *La corte di Ludovico il Moro, ii: Bramante e Leonardo* (Milan, 1915)
J. Wilde: 'The Hall of the Great Council of Florence', *J. Warb. & Court. Inst.*, vii (1944), pp. 65–81
E. Garin: 'La cultura fiorentina nell'età di Leonardo', *Medioevo e Rinascimento* (Florence, 1954, rev. 4/1980)
J. Shearman: 'Leonardo's Colour and Chiaroscuro', *Z. Kstgesch.*, xxv (1962), pp. 13–47
L. Steinberg: 'Leonardo's *Last Supper*', *A.Q.* [Detroit], xxxvi (1973), pp. 297–410
R. McMullen: *'Mona Lisa': The Picture and the Myth* (Boston, MA, 1975)
G. Sironi: *Nuovi documenti riguardanti la 'Vergine delle Rocce' di Leonardo da Vinci* (Milan, 1981)
H. T. Newton and J. Spencer: 'On the Location of Leonardo's *Battle of Anghiari*', *A. Bull.*, lxiv (1982), pp. 45–52
E. Winternitz: *Leonardo da Vinci as a Musician* (New Haven, 1982)
D. A. Brown: *Leonardo's 'Last Supper': The Restoration* (Washington, DC, 1983)
J. Shell and G. Sironi: 'Salai and Leonardo's Legacy', *Burl. Mag.*, cxxxiii/1055 (1991), pp. 95–108
C. Farago: 'Leonardo's *Battle of Anghiari*: A Study in the Exchange between Theory and Practice', *A. Bull.*, lxxvi (1994), pp. 301–30
M. Kemp: 'From Scientific Examination to the Renaissance Market: The Case of Leonardo da Vinci's *Madonna of the Yarnwinder*', *J. Med. & Ren. Stud.*, xxiv (1994), pp. 259–74

*Drawing*

A. E. Popp: *Leonardo da Vinci: Zeichnungen* (Munich, 1928)
A. E. Popham: *The Drawings of Leonardo da Vinci* (London, 1946, rev. 1994)
E. H. Gombrich: 'Leonardo's Methods of Working Out Compositions', *Norm and Form* (London, 1966)
H. Ost: *Das Leonardo-Porträt in der Königliche Bibliothek Turin und andere Falschungen des Giuseppe Bossi* (Berlin, 1980)

*Sculpture*

F. Malaguzzi-Valeri: *Leonardo da Vinci e la scultura* (Bologna, 1922)
W. R. Valentiner: 'Two Terracotta Reliefs by Leonardo', *Studies in Renaissance Sculpture* (London, 1950), pp. 178–92
M. V. Brugnoli: 'Documenti, notizie e ipotesi sulla scultura di Leonardo', *Leonardo, Saggi & Ric.* (Rome, 1954), pp. 359–89
V. Bush: 'Leonardo's Sforza Monument and Cinquecento Sculpture', *A. Lombarda*, l (1978), pp. 47–68
M. Agghazy: *Leonardo's Equestrian Statuette* (Budapest, 1989)
M. Kemp: 'Cristo Fanciullo', *Achad. Leonardi Vinci: J. Leonardo Stud. & Bibliog. Vinciana*, iv (1991), pp. 171–6

*Architecture and design*

K. T. Steinitz: 'Leonardo architetto teatrale e organizzatore di feste', *Lett. Vinc.*, ix (1969), pp. 5–21
C. Pedretti: *Leonardo da Vinci: The Royal Palace at Romorantin* (Cambridge, MA, 1972)
——: *Leonardo architetto* (Milan, 1978; Eng. trans., London, 1986)
P. Marani: *L'architettura fortificata negli studi di Leonardo da Vinci* (Florence, 1984)

*Science, anatomy and theory*

E. Solmi: 'Le fonti dei manoscritti di Leonardo da Vinci', *G. Stor. Lett. It.* (1908), suppl. 10–11, pp. 1–344; (1911), pp. 312–27
G. B. de Toni: *Le piante e gli animali di Leonardo da Vinci* (Bologna, 1922)
M. I. Hart: *The Mechanical Investigations of Leonardo da Vinci* (London, 1925, rev. Berkeley, 2/1963)
E. Panofsky: *The Codex Huygens and Leonardo da Vinci's Art Theory* (London, 1940)
C. D. O'Malley and J. B. de C. M. Saunders: *Leonardo da Vinci on the Human Body* (New York, 1952)
E. Garin: 'Il problema delle fonti del pensiero di Leonardo', *La cultura filosofica del rinascimento* (Florence, 1961), pp. 388–401
M. Kemp: 'Il concetto dell'anima in Leonardo's Early Skull Studies', *J. Warb. & Court. Inst.*, xxxiv (1971), pp. 115–34; rev. in 'From "Mimesis" to "Fantasia"', *Viator*, viii (1977), pp. 361–2, 379–81
E. H. Gombrich: 'Leonardo da Vinci's Method of Analysis and Permutation: The Grotesque Heads', *The Heritage of Apelles* (London, 1976), pp. 57–75
A. Marinoni: *Le matematica di Leonardo da Vinci* (Milan, 1982)
K. Keele: *Leonardo da Vinci's Elements of the Science of Man* (London, 1983)
K. Veltman: *Studies on Leonardo da Vinci, i: Linear Perspective and the Visual Dimensions of Science and Art* (Berlin, 1986)
W. Emboden: *Leonardo da Vinci on Plants and Gardens* (London, 1987)

*School*

W. Suida: *Leonardo und sein Kreis* (Munich, 1929)
P. Marani: *Leonardo e i Leonardeschi a Breva* (Florence, 1987)

SPECIALIST BIBLIOGRAPHIES

E. Verga: *Bibliografia vinciana, 1493–1930* (Bologna, 1931)
K. T. Steinitz: *Leonardo da Vinci's 'Trattato della pittura': A Bibliography* (Copenhagen, 1958)
A. Lorenzi and P. Marani: *Bibliografia vinciana, 1964–79* (Florence, 1982)
J. Ludmer: *Carlo Pedretti: A Bibliography of his Work on Leonardo da Vinci and the Renaissance* (Los Angeles, 1984)
M. Guerrini: *Biblioteca Leonardiana, 1493–1989*, (Vinci, 1991)

MARTIN KEMP

**Leonardo delle Notti.** *See* BRAMER, LEONARD.

**Leonardo di Ser Giovanni (da Firenze)** (*fl* 1358–71). Italian goldsmith. Trained in the workshop of the Florentine goldsmith Francesco di Niccolò, he matriculated in the goldsmiths' guild, the Arte della Seta, in 1358. In 1361 Francesco was commissioned to execute nine narrative reliefs of episodes from the *Old Testament* for the ante-pendium of the silver altar of S Jacopo in Pistoia (for further discussion of the altar *see* ANDREA DI JACOPO D'OGNABENE). Documents of 13 April 1363 and 30 June 1364 indicate that Leonardo assisted with this work, which was completed in 1364. The relief panels were originally to the left of the scenes on the main face of the antependium, to which they relate chronologically and iconographically: the altarpiece was dismantled in 1381, and the two lateral faces were transposed. Francesco was the principal author of the reliefs, but in the last two panels depicting the *Birth of the Virgin* and *Betrothal of the Virgin* a different hand has been identified, possibly that of Leonardo (Gai). On 16 January 1366 Leonardo and Betto di Geri (*fl* 1366–1402) received the prestigious commission from the Arte di Calimala to make a silver altar decorated with scenes from the *Life of St John the Baptist* (Florence, Mus. Opera Duomo) for the Florentine Baptistery. In 1367, while still working on some panels for the silver altar in Florence, Leonardo was commissioned to execute nine scenes from the *Life of St James the Greater* for the right side (now placed on the left) of the altar at Pistoia. This panel is inscribed DETTE OPERE SVB ANNO DOMINI MCCCLXXI PER ME LEONARDVM SER IOHANIS DE FRORENTIA AURIFICIS. It was because of this inscription that Vasari believed, incorrectly, that Leonardo had executed the entire altarpiece.

BIBLIOGRAPHY
L. Becherucci and G. Brunetti: *Il museo dell'opera del Duomo*, ii (Florence, 1971), pp. 215–28, pls 3–77
*Documenti toscani*, i (Arezzo, 1974), pp. 119–40, 141–62 [articles by P. Bacci]
L. Gai: *L'altare argento di San Jacopo nel Duomo di Pistoia* (Turin, 1984)

**Leonbruno** [de Leombeni; de Liombeni; Leombruno], **Lorenzo** (*b* Mantua, 1489; *d* ?Mantua, late 1537 or after). Italian painter. He was trained in the workshop of Andrea Mantegna and worked as an assistant to Pietro Perugino in Florence between 1504 and 1506. He also had formative contact with several Emilian artists, including Correggio and Dosso Dossi, whom he probably met in Mantua before going to Florence. In 1511 he briefly visited Venice and returned to Mantua the following year to work under Lorenzo Costa the elder on frescoes of Apollo and the nine Muses in the Palazzo di S Sebastiano, Mantua (destr.); he possibly assisted Costa on later commissions as well. Leonbruno worked under the patronage of Isabella d'Este, Marchioness of Mantua, and, later, of her son Federico II, 1st Duke of Mantua. In 1521, on the recommendation of Baldassare Castiglione, he went to Rome to study antique art and the work of Michelangelo and Raphael. On returning to Mantua he worked on the decoration of the Castello di Corte and the Palazzo Ducale, two projects that constituted a large proportion of his work as a court painter for Federico; in the Castello di Corte he painted two rooms with various decorations, paintings and grotesques. Between 1521 and 1523 Leonbruno produced various mythological scenes, decorative motifs and medallions for the lunettes and ceiling of the room known as Isabella d'Este's Schalcheria in the Grotta of the Palazzo Ducale. This project reveals the influence of Mantegna and Perugino, but its hunting motifs also make it reminiscent of Correggio's Camera di S Paolo in Parma. In 1524

he began designing the decorations for the Palazzo di Marmirolo (destr. 1798), Mantua, but his work there was suspended as a result of Giulio Romano's arrival. After working in Milan in 1531–2 as a military designer for Francesco Maria Sforza, Duke of Milan, he returned to Mantua, where he is last documented on the payroll of the court at the end of 1537. Besides his frescoes in various palaces he executed a number of panels with decorative and mythological subjects such as the *Calumny of Apelles* (*c.* 1525; Milan, Brera). Notwithstanding the interest of the Mantuan court in the Antique, Leonbruno also executed several religious works, among the most successful of which are the two examples of the *Nativity* (Worcester, MA, A. Mus.; London, ex-Christie's, 1977). Both paintings are datable to Leonbruno's middle period when he was under the influence of Costa. They are characterized by precise landscape details and brilliant colours, features that are also found in the mythological scenes of the Schalcheria, and represent Leonbruno at his best.

BIBLIOGRAPHY
G. B. Intra: 'Lorenzo Leombruno e Giulio Romano', *Archv Stor. Lombardo*, 2nd ser., ii (1887), pp. 569–73
C. Gamba: 'Lorenzo Leombruno', *Rass. A.*, v (1906), pp. 65–70
G. Fogolari: 'Un dipinto allegorico di Lorenzo Leombruno nel Museo di Verona', *Madonna Verona*, iii (1908), pp. 127–9
C. Gamba: 'Un nuovo dipinto del Leombruno', *Rass. A.*, ix (1909), pp. 30–31
P. K[risteller]: 'Ancora del Leombruno', *Rass. A.*, ix (1909), p. 186
E. Marani and C. Perina: *Mantova: Le arti*, II/i (Mantua, 1961), pp. 392–9
F. Russell: 'Saleroom Discoveries: A Nativity by Lorenzo Leonbruno', *Burl. Mag.*, cxix (1977), p. 601

**Leone, Andrea di.** *See* LIONE, ANDREA DI.

**Leonelli (da Crevalcore), Antonio.** *See* ANTONIO DA CREVALCORE.

**Leoni.** Italian family of sculptors, medallists and collectors. (1) Leone Leoni and his son (2) Pompeo Leoni gained their reputations in service to the Habsburg Holy Roman Emperor Charles V and his son Philip II, King of Spain. They are particularly noted for their bronze busts and portrait statues of the leading members of the Spanish Habsburgs. Leone was also one of the most outstanding medallists of the 16th century.

**(1) Leone Leoni** (*b* ?Menaggio, nr Como, *c.* 1509; *d* Milan, 22 July 1590). He was probably born in Menaggio on Lake Como, though his parents were from Arezzo, and throughout his life Leone referred to himself as Aretine. It is probable that his formative years were spent learning the trade of goldsmith, perhaps in Venice or Padua. The classicism and idealism of this school formed the basis of his style. Some time after 1533 he is recorded in Venice with his wife and infant son Pompeo, living under the protection of Pietro Aretino, to whom he was related. While in Venice, Leone worked as a goldsmith and made medals and statuettes (none of which can be identified). Leone's skill and connections secured him a position at the mint in Ferrara, although he was forced to abandon this when accused of counterfeiting, the first of several misadventures that were to plague his life. Through Pietro Aretino, Leone received an introduction to the poet

Pietro Bembo, and in 1537 he travelled to Padua to prepare Bembo's portrait medal (untraced).

By the autumn of 1537 Leone had moved to Rome, where he remained for the next three years working as an engraver in the papal mint. There he became acquainted with the major artists at the papal court, including Michelangelo and Baccio Bandinelli, who had a strong influence on his work. He also became familiar with the city's key works of ancient and contemporary art. The Roman sojourn was one not only of intense study but also of renewed controversy. In 1538 he was a prime witness against Benvenuto Cellini, who had been charged with stealing papal jewels during the Sack of Rome (1527). Later, according to Cellini, Leone had attempted to poison him while he was imprisoned in the Castel Sant'Angelo by sprinkling a ground diamond on his salad. Leone's fortunes took a turn for the worse early in 1540, when, in response to a personal affront, he attacked and maimed with a dagger Pellegrino di Leuti, the papal jeweller. Leone was sentenced to have his right hand cut off, and only the last-minute intervention of powerful friends spared him, although the new sentence might have been considered even worse: an indefinite period as a galley slave in the papal fleet. Leone was chained to an oar for about a year until he was unexpectedly released in Genoa through the intervention of Andrea Doria I, admiral of the imperial fleet.

Leone remained in Doria's service until early 1542, when he moved to Milan to begin work in the imperial mint. His career as a coiner and medallist flourished, and he produced impressive medals of *Daniele and Martin d'Anna* (1544–5; Milan, Castello Sforzesco), Flemish merchants residing in Venice, and of *Isabella of Portugal* (*c*. 1545; Vienna, Ksthist. Mus.), the late wife of Charles V, for Pietro Aretino. By 1546 he had been named master general of the mint of Parma and Piacenza and enjoyed a growing reputation for his medallic portraits.

Following Charles V's victory over the Protestant princes at Mühlberg in 1547, Leone proposed to erect an equestrian portrait to the Emperor in Milan. In 1548 he was invited by Charles V's adviser, Antoine Perrenot de Granville, Bishop of Arras, to discuss his proposal at the imperial court in Brussels, where he arrived in March 1549. After lengthy consultations with the Emperor, Leone received a commission for portrait busts and statues, the most important being an over life-size bronze, two-figured composition ultimately realized as *Charles V and Fury Restrained* (1549–55; Madrid, Prado; see fig. 1). The group is a sophisticated exercise in imperial propaganda, replete with Classical allusions celebrating the Emperor as Augustus, who, having chained Fury, initiates a new era of peace. Leone's bronze is both a technical and conceptual *tour de force*, as the suit of half armour can be removed to reveal Charles V in heroic nudity, a device never seen before in Western sculpture.

Leone's period at court resulted in additional commissions from the Emperor and his sister Mary of Hungary for medals, portrait busts and statues of members of the imperial family. The most notable of these are: the bronze bust of *Charles V Supported by an Eagle* (1551–5; Madrid, Prado; second version, Vienna Ksthist. Mus.); the bronze bust of *Mary, Queen of Hungary* (1550–53; Vienna, Ksthist.

Mus.; *see* METAL, colour pl. II, fig. 4); and the bronze statues of *Empress Isabella* (1555), *Mary, Queen of Hungary* (*c*. 1549–53) and *Prince Philip* (1549–51; all Madrid, Prado). In the sculpted portraits of the Emperor and Prince Philip, Leone developed an idealized style rooted in the classicism of his medallic training and related to the grand imperial portraits of Titian. His iconography is rich in references to Roman imperial art and celebrates Charles and Philip as the legitimate heirs of the Roman emperors. This imagery was conceived at the height of Habsburg power and at the moment when Charles was promoting Philip's claim to be his successor as Holy Roman Emperor.

In order to advance these projects, Charles V granted Leone a confiscated house near Milan Cathedral, ennobled him and made him an imperial knight, honours not lightly bestowed on an artist. Leone returned to Milan and worked on imperial commissions for the next seven years. In 1556 he accompanied his sculptures to Brussels, where the Emperor was residing on the eve of his retirement. Charles V asked the artist to travel with him to Spain, but Leone fell ill and sent Pompeo in his place. Many of the portrait bronzes were finished only in 1564, when Leone made a brief trip to Madrid. Indeed it appears that none was ever exhibited during the lifetime of Charles or Philip, as they are all recorded in an inventory of Pompeo's studio at his death.

The death of Charles V and his sister Mary in 1558 ended an important phase in Leone's career. His sources of patronage shifted away from Spain to Italy when in 1560 he received, on the recommendation of Michelangelo, a commission from Pope Pius IV to erect a tomb for the latter's brother Gian Giacomo de' Medici in Milan Cathedral. This project was completed in 1563 and is one of Leone's finest achievements. The life-size, bronze standing portrait statue of *Gian Giacomo de' Medici* dressed in armour and the two flanking seated bronze allegorical figures of *Peace* and *Military Virtue* are extraordinarily refined and reveal the stylistic influence of both Michelangelo and Sansovino.

In 1560 Leone also received a commission to erect a bronze monument to Ferrante Gonzaga (*d* 1557), the late governor of Milan in the Piazza Roma, Guastalla. *Ferrante Gonzaga Triumphant over Evil and Envy* was the artist's second two-figured group and shows Gonzaga standing over a hydra and prostrate satyr, who falls backwards off the base. Although Leone had seen Cellini's *Perseus and Medusa* in the Loggia dei Lanzi in Florence on his return to Milan from Rome in 1560, his group has none of the mannered elegance of Cellini's work. Leone's satyr is, in fact, a colossal version of one of Andrea Riccio's small bronzes, while the armed portrait of Gonzaga continues the classicized realism seen in his earlier busts and statues.

Between 1565 and 1567 Leone undertook the reconstruction of the house given to him in 1549 by Charles V. Now known as the Casa degli Omenoni ('House of the Big Men' in Milanese dialect), it is one of Milan's most distinctive architectural landmarks. Its unusual façade includes a frieze relief showing two lions attacking a satyr, two half-length caryatids flanking the central portal and six herms (double life-size barbarian prisoners, which gave the house its nickname; see fig. 2). Imposing figures of this kind had never been seen before on the façade of a

1. Leone Leoni: *Charles V and Fury Restrained*, bronze, h. 2.51 m, 1549–55 (Madrid, Museo del Prado)

2. Leone Leoni: façade of the Casa degli Omenoni, Milan, 1565–7

house or palazzo. According to Vasari, Leone dedicated his home to Marcus Aurelius, then considered the most virtuous of the ancient emperors. Thus the prisoners, each identified by an inscription as a tribe conquered by the emperor, together with a plaster cast of the Capitoline equestrian portrait of *Marcus Aurelius* in the centre of the courtyard, were part of a programme in which Leone presented himself to the public not as an artist but as a gentleman in the social milieu of the Habsburg empire.

Leone's last major commission from an Italian patron was from Vespasiano Gonzaga, Duke of Sabbioneta, for his portrait statue (Sabbioneta, church of the Incoronato). Probably executed between 1574 and 1577, the life-size seated bronze shows Vespasiano armed and extending his right arm outward in a gesture directly related to that in the *Marcus Aurelius*. The statue was erected in the central square of Sabbioneta in 1588 and served as the symbolic centrepiece of Gonzaga's ideal city. The last decade of Leone's life was occupied by his first major commission (1579) for the Habsburgs since the death of Charles V in 1558. This was for 15 colossal gilt-bronze statues for the high altar retable in the Capilla Mayor at the Escorial, near Madrid. Undertaken with Pompeo, this was the crowning achievement of his career. The majestic, broadly conceived statues convey the heroic vigour of the Counter-Reformation Church and are important prototypes for similar stylistic developments in Rome.

Leone was also known for his art collection. He had assembled a considerable number of plaster casts of both ancient and modern works, including, in addition to the equestrian portrait of *Marcus Aurelius*, Michelangelo's *Risen Christ* (Rome, S Maria sopra Minerva), the *Apollo*

*Belvedere* and the *Laokoon* (both Rome, Vatican, Mus. Pio-Clementino). These were complemented by his collection of paintings and sculptures, forming perhaps the first private gallery in Milan. The collection was displayed in an octagonal room on the *piano nobile* and included Correggio's *Jupiter and Io* (Vienna, Ksthist. Mus.) and *Jupiter and Danaë* (Rome, Gal. Borghese), two wax sculptures and drawings by Leonardo da Vinci, drawings by Michelangelo and paintings by Titian, Tintoretto and Parmigianino among others. His gallery rivalled those of many nobles and, along with the façade of his home, was additional evidence of his discernment, means and elevated social status.

**(2) Pompeo Leoni** (*b* ?Venice, *c.* 1533; *d* Madrid, 13 Oct 1608). Son of (1) Leone Leoni. He has long been overshadowed by his father, although he was an accomplished sculptor who produced an impressive body of work. This is partly due to their close working relationship, which continued until Leone's death. Pompeo was trained by Leone, assisted him with the commissions from Charles V and Mary, Queen of Hungary, and accompanied these works to Spain in 1556 on the retirement of Charles V. Soon after his arrival in Spain, Pompeo entered the service of the regent, Joanna of Austria. He produced several medals in 1557, but in 1558 work came to a halt when he was sentenced by the Inquisition to a year's confinement in a monastery because of his unorthodox opinions. In 1564 he helped to complete his father's bronzes, and in 1570 he designed a series of colossal, fictive bronze statues for the triumphal arches erected to celebrate the entry into Madrid of Anne of Austria, Philip II's new wife.

During the 1570s Pompeo received important commissions for marble sepulchral effigies: the kneeling figure of *Joanna of Austria* (1574) for her tomb in the convent of Las Descalzas Reales, Madrid; the sensitive and naturalistic portrait of the Inquisitor General, *Cardinal Diego de Espinosa* (1577), in the church of Martín Muñoz de las Posadas, Segovia; and the elaborate Italianate tomb of *Fernando de Valdés* (1576) at the collegiate church, Salas. However, all private work stopped in 1579 with the commission from Philip II for 15 bronze statues for the colossal retable of the Capilla Mayor at the Escorial, near Madrid. Pompeo travelled to Milan in 1582 to collaborate on the project with his father. He returned in 1589 and installed the statues in 1591. Pompeo's last great project was the commission from Philip II for the kneeling effigies of himself, Charles V and eight other members of the Habsburg family that now flank the high altar of the Capilla Mayor. These over life-size, gilt-bronze figures of extraordinary quality and detail kneel in perpetual veneration towards the Sacrament Tabernacle on the altar, pious expressions of Habsburg eucharistic devotion and dynastic supremacy. Like his father, Pompeo was also an avid art collector. He assembled an impressive number of works, including notebooks by Leonardo da Vinci (the *Atlantic Codex*, Milan, Bib. Ambrosiana; another at Windsor Castle, Berks, Royal Lib.).

BIBLIOGRAPHY

E. Plon: *Leone Leoni, sculpteur de Charles-Quint, et Pompeo Leoni, sculpteur de Philippe II* (Paris, 1887)

G. Proske: *Pompeo Leoni: Work in Marble and Alabaster in Relation to Spanish Sculpture* (New York, 1956)

M. Mezzatesta: 'The Façade of Leone Leoni's House in Milan, the Casa degli Omenoni: The Artist and the Public', *J. Soc. Archit. Hist.*, xliv (1985), pp. 233–49

J. Pope-Hennessy: *Italian High Renaissance and Baroque Sculpture* (New York, 1986)

MICHAEL P. MEZZATESTA

**Leoni, James** [Giacomo] (*b c.* 1686; *d* London, 8 June 1746). English architect of Italian origin. Apparently a Venetian, he was at the court of Elector Johann Wilhelm of the Palatinate at Düsseldorf from 1708. There he was influenced by the architect Count Matteo Alberti (?1660–1716), with whom he probably worked on the Elector's hunting-lodge, Schloss Bensburg, near Cologne. Alberti was an admirer of Inigo Jones, and it was Jones who also became Leoni's model; this is particularly evident in the earliest known designs made after his move to England *c.* 1714. These were proposals for rebuilding Wrest Park, Beds (prepared by July 1715), for Henry Grey, 1st Duke of Kent. The surviving proposal (Bedford, Rec. Office, Lucas and Dingwall MSS) shows a house with two internal courtyards divided by an axially placed hall, leading to a saloon at right angles to it on the garden front. The source appears to be John Webb's unexecuted project (1649) for Durham House, London, which Leoni probably mistook for one by Jones. Leoni made his name in 1715 with the publication of the first instalment of *The Architecture of A. Palladio* (1715–20), the first complete edition of Palladio's *I quattro libri dell'architettura* to appear in English. Although Leoni's engraved plates were bettered in some particulars in Isaac Ware's translation of the treatise (1738), Leoni's was the more successful, running to three editions, followed by a pirated one in 1735. He also produced *The Architecture of L. B. Alberti* (1726), a three-volume translation of Alberti's *De re aedificatoria*, illustrated by Leoni and with some of his own designs appended.

In 1721 Leoni's respect for Jones was still evident: 7 Burlington Gardens, which directly overlooked the garden of Richard Boyle, 3rd Earl of Burlington's own house (he approved the design), was Leoni's version of Jones's Queen's Gallery at Somerset House. By 1722, however, when Leoni designed his most original house, Carshalton Park, Surrey, for Thomas Scawen, his mentor appeared to be Colen Campbell. Carshalton's elevation is a version of Palladio's Palazzo Valmarana, but with some important differences taken from Campbell's own version of the Palazzo Valmarana in his *Vitruvius Britannicus*. In 1725 Leoni made designs for Peter Legh's Lyme Park, Ches, and between *c.* 1729 and 1735 he rebuilt the 16th-century house in progressive stages around its courtyard. Its pediment on the south elevation was raised above the roof-line (whereas Jones would have backed it with a raised attic or tall roof), but it crowns only three bays of a flat front (whereas Palladio would have reserved it for a projecting block). This combination of departures from currently accepted authorities had also been made by Campbell. Within Lyme Park is a staircase with vase-shaped balusters—probably a deliberate Caroline revival—an archaism also employed by Campbell (at Houghton) and his follower Roger Morris at Marble Hill. In 1728 Leoni began rebuilding another courtyard house in progressive stages: Moulsham Hall (destr.), Essex for Benjamin Mildmay, 1st Earl Fitzwalter. Its model seems to have been the elevation of Campbell's Newby Park, one that served (with some inventive variations) for two other designs: an unidentified country house dated 1727 (drawings at Cliveden, Bucks, NT) and, as late as 1743, Wortley Hall, S. Yorks, for Edward Wortley Montagu. For Peter Bold, Leoni built Bold Hall (destr.), Lancs, in the 1730s: its entire elevation, but particularly its high rusticated basement, is close to one Campbell drawing (London, RIBA). Burton Park (destr.), W. Sussex, built for Richard Biddulph in 1738, similarly had a high rusticated basement. Lathom House (*c.* 1740; destr.), Lancs, built for Sir Thomas Bootle, was again reminiscent of Campbell's Houghton, but without Houghton's corner domes.

Leoni's style lends little credence to his claim to be Venetian. Clandon Park (?1731–3), Surrey, for Thomas Onslow, 2nd Lord Onslow, slightly resembles the Villa Garzoni by Jacopo Sansovino, and it displays a panelled pediment, which could have been taken from Venetian examples. Yet Clandon Park also has chimney-pieces of a type peculiar to Campbell and Morris, in which the chimney-breast is not continued up to the cornice but breaks back to the wall plane at the top of the overmantel. Like Morris, then, Leoni would appear to be part of a Campbell school, a grouping of English neo-Palladian architects with a style different to that of Burlington, Kent and their followers. As Leoni was one of the few among them who could claim to have had direct contact with Palladio's own work, it is particularly remarkable that he should have chosen British architects for his models. Along with Alessandro Galilei and Nicolo Servandoni, Leoni is significant as one of the first Europeans to have been influenced by British architecture, instead of the other way round.

WRITINGS

ed.: *The Architecture of A. Palladio, Revis'd, Design'd and Publish'd by Giacomo Leoni, a Venetian; Architect to his Most Serene Highness, the Elector Palatine*, trans. N. Dubois (London, 1715, 3/1742)

trans.: *The Architecture of Leon Battista Alberti*, 3 vols (London, 1726, 3/1755); ed. J. Rykwert as *Ten Books in Architecture by Leone Battista Alberti* (London, 1955/*R* 1965)

BIBLIOGRAPHY

Colvin

R. Wittkower: 'Giacomo Leoni's Edition of Palladio's *Quattro libri dell'architettura*', *A. Veneta*, viii (1954), pp. 310–16

P. Collins: 'The McGill Leoni', *J. Royal Archit. Inst. Canada*, xxxiv (1957), pp. 3–4

——: 'New Light on Leoni', *Archit. Rev.*, cxxvii (1960), pp. 225–6

T. P. Hudson: 'Moor Park, Leoni, and Sir James Thornhill', *Burl. Mag.*, cxiii (1971), pp. 657–61

J. Cornforth: 'Lyme Park', *Country Life*, clvi (5, 12, 19, 26 Dec 1974), pp. 1724–7, 1858–61, 1930–33, 1998–2001

T. P. Hudson: *The Origins of English Palladianism* (diss., U. Cambridge, 1974)

R. Wittkower: 'English Neoclassicism and the Vicissitudes of Palladio's *Quattro libri*', *Palladio and English Palladianism* (London, 1974), pp. 88–90

T. Hudson: 'A Venetian Architect in England', *Country Life*, clvii (3 April 1975), p. 830

G. Jackson-Stops: 'The Cliveden Album: Drawings by Archer, Leoni and Gibbs for the 1st Earl of Orkney', *Archit. Hist.*, xix (1976), pp. 5–16

R. Hewlings: 'Wortley Hall', *Archaeol. J.*, cxxxvii (1980), p. 397

——: 'James Leoni', *The Architectural Outsiders*, ed. R. Brown (London, 1985), pp. 21–44

RICHARD HEWLINGS

**Leoni, Ottavio** [il Padovano] (*b* Rome, 1578; *d* Rome, 4 Sept 1630). Italian draughtsman, printmaker and painter. He was the son of the Paduan-born Ludovico Leoni

(1542–1612), a maker of medals and wax relief portraits. Although Ottavio was active entirely in Rome, where his father had also worked and died, he was often known as 'il Padovano' because of the family origins. In 1603 Ottavio was involved in a libel action against Caravaggio by the painter Giovanni Baglione, whose *vita* provides the best source of information on Leoni's life. One witness at the trial, Tommaso Salini, claimed he had received verses criticizing Baglione written by Orazio Gentileschi and 'Ottavio Padovano' (i.e. Leoni). Caravaggio testified that he knew Leoni without having ever spoken to him. The following year Leoni was admitted to the Accademia di S Luca in Rome and in 1614 became its principal. It was at this time, according to Baglione, that he painted two canvases, a *Martyrdom of St Martina* and an *Ascension* (both untraced). In 1621 Leoni became a member of the Accademia dei Virtuosi del Pantheon, the body to which he presented in 1628 an oil portrait of *Gregory XV* (*in situ*).

A portrait of the same pope (1621; London, BM; see fig.), drawn *à trois crayons*—that is in red, black and white chalk—on blue-grey paper, is typical of the many portrait drawings for which Leoni is best known. An important collection of such portrait drawings was assembled by Cardinal Scipione Borghese, Leoni's principal patron; their subjects represent not only leading Roman families but also artists, men of letters and ordinary citizens. According to Manilli (1650), the Borghese family also possessed many

oil portraits by Leoni. The famous 18th-century French connoisseur Pierre-Jean Mariette believed that the Borghese group constituted the sum total of Ottavio Leoni's drawn output. He said that he had seen, and still possessed, many artists' portraits from a collection of about 400 that was sold in 1747 on the death of Monsieur d'Aubigny, a group he confidently identified as that previously owned by the Borghese family. Some 27 of the drawn portraits were gathered into an album (Florence, Bib. Marucelliana), it is not known by whom, but the binding is 18th-century. Others were dispersed and are now in various public and private collections, the largest series being in Berlin (Kupferstichkab.), while other important sequences are in Genoa (Gal. Pal. Rosso). Many of the drawings are numbered and dated.

Leoni also practised printmaking, an activity that, according to Baglione, he pursued intensively during the second half of his life, so much so that his health was fatally damaged. Of the 40 portrait prints catalogued by Bartsch, 27 are of known sitters. Leoni's oeuvre as a painter remains little known. Baglione recorded that he painted an *Annunciation* in the church of S Eustachio (*in situ*), a canvas of the *Virgin and Child with St Hyacinth* in S Maria sopra Minerva (untraced), a canvas of *SS Charles, Francis and Nicholas* in S Urbano in Campo Carleo (destr.) and, lastly, fresco decorations in the chapel of the Palazzo Altemps, where Pope St Anicetus was buried. Restoration work at the Palazzo has revealed Leoni's hand in frescoes depicting the *Life of St Anicetus*, for which he was paid in 1618. Leoni's signature has also been found on a painting on copper of *Susanna and the Elders* (Detroit, MI, Inst. A.), previously attributed to Carlo Saraceni.

Ottavio's son Ippolito Leoni (*fl* 1627–73) was also a portraitist, some of whose drawings—which Mariette considered inferior to those of his father—were apparently included in the 1747 d'Aubigny sale. Baglione cited two portraits by Ippolito, one of his father and one of his grandfather, which he painted for the Accademia di S Luca (of which he was a member).

Ottavio Leoni: *Gregory XV*, black, red and white chalk on blue-grey paper, 230×158 mm, 1621 (London, British Museum)

## BIBLIOGRAPHY

Mariette

G. Baglione: *Vite* (1642); ed. V. Mariani (1935), pp. 145, 288, 321–2 [Ottavio]; p. 322 [Ippolito]

J. Manilli: *Villa Borghese fuori Porta Pinciana* (Rome, 1650), pp. 76–8

A. von Bartsch: *Le Peintre-graveur* (1803–21), xvii

M. Missirini: *Memorie per servire alla storia romana: Accademia di S Luca* (Rome, 1823), p. 92 [Ippolito]

F. A. F. Orbaan: 'Virtuosi al Pantheon: Archivalische Beiträge zur römischen Kunstgeschichte', *Repert. Kstwiss.*, xxxvii (1915), p. 255 [Ippolito]

G. Briganti: 'La fatica virtuosa di Ottavio Leoni', *Primato A. It.* (1942), pp. 111–12

R. Longhi: 'Volti della Roma caravaggesca', *Paragone*, xxi (1951), pp. 35–9

H. Kruft: 'Ein Album mit Porträtzeichnungen Ottavio Leonis', *Stor. A.*, iv (1969), pp. 447–58 [with good bibliog.]

R. Ward Bissel and A. P. Darr: 'A Rare Painting by Ottavio Leoni', *Bull. Detroit Inst. A.*, lviii/1 (1980), pp. 46–53

'Ottavio Leoni's Portraits *alla macchia*', *Baroque Portraiture in Italy: Works from North American Collections* (exh. cat. by J. T. Spike, Sarasota, FL, Ringling Mus. A.; Hartford, CT, Wadsworth Atheneum; 1984–5), pp. 12–19 [complete lists of known dated portrait drgs by Ottavio and Ippolito]

F. Scoppola, ed.: *Palazzo Altemps: Indagini per il restauro della fabbrica Riario, Soderini, Altemps* (Rome, 1987), pp. 48, 55, 228–9, 235, 301, 302

BERNARDINA SANI

**Leonidov, Ivan (Il'ich)** (*b* Vlasikh, nr Tver', 9 Feb 1902; *d* Moscow, 6 Nov 1959). Russian architect, urban planner, writer and teacher.

1. EARLY CAREER, TO 1930. His father was a farmer and woodsman on an isolated farmstead in the province of Tver'. From 1914 to 1917 Leonidov worked as a casual labourer on the docks of Petrograd (now St Petersburg). He then became an apprentice to an icon painter in Tver', who had noticed his drawing skills. His formal art studies began at the Svomas (Free art studios), Tver', and continued from 1921 to 1927 at the Vkhutemas (Higher (state) art and technical workshops), Moscow. While studying there under the painter and Constructivist architect Aleksandr Vesnin, Leonidov's attention shifted from painting to architecture. He entered several architectural competitions, producing designs for a model peasant cottage (1925), schemes for a block of flats (1926) in Ivanovo-Voznesensk, buildings (1926) for the Belorussian State University, Minsk, and prototypes for Workers' Clubs (1927). His diploma project (1927; unexecuted) for the Lenin Institute and Library, Moscow, brought him international recognition. The scheme was prominently displayed that year at the Exhibition of Contemporary Architecture, Moscow, and was published in the Constructivists' architectural journal *Sovremennaya arkhitektura*. Leonidov envisioned the institute as a technologically audacious ensemble of glass curtain-walled buildings on a vast scale. They include an auditorium in the form of a complete sphere supported on a single pylon, a science theatre with planetarium, and various research institutes. The buildings were to be connected by an elevated monorail and advanced telecommunication devices. A towering rectangular book repository that focuses the composition was intended to be a landmark in the Lenin Hills overlooking Moscow.

From 1927 to 1930 Leonidov taught at the Vkhutemas and edited *Sovremennaya arkhitektura*. His more notable designs of this period (all unexecuted) include those for the Sov-Kino Film Production Complex (1927), the Tsentrosoyuz Headquarters, Moscow, the Government Centre, Alma-Ata (both 1928), the monument to *Christopher Columbus* in Santo Domingo, Dominican Republic, and the House of Industry in Moscow (both 1929). His design for a Palace of Culture (1930; unexecuted) for the Proletarskii district, Moscow, like that for the Lenin Institute, used an extensive site and multiple buildings. In this instance the plan was to provide workers with comprehensive recreational facilities in a single utopian environment. During this period Leonidov was a staunch member of the Constructivist group OSA, although his work was not typical of the Constructivists. While the latter tended to conceive of buildings as dynamic interpenetrations of functionally and geometrically differentiated volumes, Leonidov separated the programmatic volumes into simplified, free-standing figures. The Constructivists also usually articulated structure and cladding to enliven their visually aggressive compositions, whereas Leonidov preferred to cover the structure under austere curtain walls. With the surfaces of the buidings thus neutralized, he provided visual interest in his laconic designs by contrasting the scale, geometry and orientation of the building volumes themselves.

2. LATER CAREER, FROM 1930. The planning solutions that Leonidov applied in the Palace of Culture project, particularly the fixing of the positions of buildings according to a matrix grid, were also applied by him in his design (1930; unexecuted) for Magnitogorsk, an entirely new industrial city in the Urals. Here, he conceived the idea of a linear city, extending from an industrial core into the countryside. The plan exhibits a broad residential ribbon that is flanked by parallel linear zones containing parks, recreational facilities, community services and a main highway. Streets perpendicular to this highway divide the city into a grid of square super-blocks containing the buildings and facilities appropriate to each zone. As the population grew, each sector was to be extended in discrete, linear increments further and further from the industrial core. Leonidov's proposal was part of the ongoing debate between the 'urbanists', representing traditional urban planning concepts, and the 'disurbanists', or supporters of the view that the traditional city must be replaced with new variants. At the same time the unrestrained originality and idealistic quality in Leonidov's work began to attract criticism, as the USSR prepared to abandon its association with modernist architecture. The official press began to pillory Leonidov and 'Leonidovism' became a term of abuse that was applied to any architect whose alleged failings included economic naivety and an exaggerated concern with aesthetics and utopianism.

The concerted criticism temporarily halted Leonidov's activity. He responded eventually, however, with the most sophisticated design of his career, the project for the headquarters (1934; unexecuted; see fig.) of the Ministry of Heavy Industry (Dom Narkomtyazhprom), Moscow. The projected location of the Ministry on Red Square was derived from Stalin's intentions for the centre of Moscow. A Palace of the Soviets, to be located to the Kremlin's south-west, was to commemorate the end of the first Five-Year Plan in 1932. The Ministry of Heavy Industry was to be the corresponding project to the north-east, marking the start of the second Five-Year Plan in 1933. Forming the north-east edge of Red Square, the Ministry's headquarters was to face the Kremlin and Lenin's Mausoleum. Thus, the Palace of the Soviets, together with the Ministry of Heavy Industry, would bracket the medieval Kremlin, a deliberate juxtaposition charged with political and symbolic overtones. The two complexes would celebrate and vindicate Stalin's achievements. Leonidov's memorable design comprises a low, elongated tribune of stepped terraces that form the new edge of Red Square. Three skyscrapers, differentiated through materials and form, surmount the terraced base. The tallest tower, facing Red Square, has an exposed skeleton frame and a crown of trussed radio antennas that enliven its rectangular form. A slender round tower of hyperbolic profile with prominent balconies stands directly behind. The third tower is Y-shaped, with flat end walls alternating against concave curtain walls. Bridges link the upper floors of three towers. At the northern end an auditorium with a low, multi-coloured drum matches the smaller scale of the adjacent Bol'shoy Theatre. Ultimately, however, all plans for the

Ivan Leonidov: design (1934) for the Ministry of Heavy Industry, Moscow (unexecuted); from A. Gozak and A. Leonidov: *Ivan Leonidov: Complete Known Works*, ed. C. Cooke (London and New York, 1988)

Ministry of Heavy Industry, together with those for the Palace of the Soviets, were cancelled.

From the early 1930s to the outbreak of World War II, Leonidov submitted various projects for sites on the Crimean coast under the leadership of Moisey Ginzburg. Only one scheme was built, the amphitheatre and ornamental staircase (1937) for the park of the Ordzhonikidze Sanatorium at Kislovodsk, which is one of his very few executed projects. After World War II he further developed his urban and architectural ideas with sketches for a City of the Sun, a grandiose project that remained fragmentary at his death. A revival of international interest in the work of Leonidov began in the 1970s.

WRITINGS

'Dom Narkomtyazhproma v Moskve: Proekt I. I. Leonidova: Poyasnitel'naya zapiska k proyektu' [The Ministry of Heavy Industry in Moscow: the project of I. I. Leonidov: explanatory notes about the project], *Arkhit. SSSR*, x (1934), pp. 14–15 [Eng. trans., 1988]
'Palitra arkhitektora' [The architect's palette], *Arkhit. SSSR*, iv (1934), pp. 32–3 [Eng. trans., 1988]
Regular contributions to *Sov Arkhit.* (1927–30)

BIBLIOGRAPHY

S. O. Khan-Magomedov: 'Ivan Leonidov', *Sov. Arkhit.*, xvi (1964), pp. 103–16
——: 'Kluby Leonidova' [Clubs by Leonidov], *Dek. Isk. SSSR*, xi (1967), pp. 17–22
P. A. Aleksandrov: 'I. I. Leonidov: Arkhitektor-novator' [I. I. Leonidov: architect and innovator], *Arkhit. SSSR*, 3 (1968), pp. 31–42
P. A. Aleksandrov and S. O. Khan-Magomedov: *Ivan Leonidov* (Moscow, 1971; It. trans., Milan, 1975)
*Mastera sovetskoy arkhitektury ob arkhitekture* [Masters of Soviet architecture on architecture], M. G. Barkhin ed. (Moscow, 1975), pp. 523–43
*Ivan Leonidov* (exh. cat., ed. G. Oorthuys; New York, Inst. Archit. & Urb. Stud., 1977)
S. O. Chan-Magomedov: *Pioniere der sowjetischen Architektur* (Dresden, 1983); Eng. trans. as S. O. Khan Magomedov: *Pioneers of Soviet Architecture* (London, 1987) [incl. Eng. trans. of some of Leonidov's writings]
R. Koolhaas: 'A Foundation of Amnesia', *Des. Q.*, cxxv (1984), pp. 4–9
A. Gozak and A. Leonidov: *Ivan Leonidov: Complete Known Works*, ed. C. Cooke (London and New York, 1988) [incl. Eng. trans. of Leonidov's contrib. to *Sovremennaya Arkhit.*]

K. PAUL ZYGAS

**Leonor of Viseu**, Queen of Portugal. *See* Aviz, (5).

**Leontopolis.** *See* YAHUDIYA, TELL EL-.

**Leo of Ostia** [Leone Marsicano; Leone Ostiense; Leone di Montecassino] (*b* ?1046; *d* ?1115). Italian illuminator and chronicler. Born into the noble family of de' Marsi, he joined the abbey of Montecassino (*see* MONTECASSINO, §2(i)) at the age of 14 and gained the trust and protection of the abbot Desiderius (later Pope Victor III). Montecassino excelled under Desiderius, who promoted artistic, religious and political splendour. Leo is one of the earliest recorded illuminators in Italy as well as one of the most accomplished. Among his works is the *Lives of SS Benedict, Maurus and Scholastica* (Rome, Vatican, Bib. Apostolica, MS. Vat. lat. 1202); its opening page shows Desiderius donating buildings and books to St Benedict. A book of *Homilies* (Montecassino Abbey, Lib., MS. 99), signed and dated 1072, shows Leo kneeling in front of St Benedict with the abbots Giovanni (914–43) and Desiderius standing on the bishop's right. Abbot Oderisius (1087–1105) commissioned him to write the life of Desiderius, which was enlarged into the *Chronica monasterii Casinensis*. Leo's account begins with the origins of the abbey and ends in 1075; it was based on documentation from the archives of Montecassino and on his own memory for events closer to him. He was created Cardinal of Ostia by Pope Paschal II (1099–1118).

WRITINGS

*Chronica monasterii Casinensis* (MS.; late 11th century); ed. H. Hoffmann, Mnmt Ger. Hist., Scriptores, xxxiv/3 (Hannover, 1980), pp. 358–457 [*Life of Desiderius*] [Lat. text]

BIBLIOGRAPHY

E. Berteaux: *L'Art dans l'Italie méridionale* (Paris, 1904), p. 193
P. d'Ancona: *La Miniature italienne du Xe au XVIe siècle* (Paris and Brussels, 1925)
F. Newton: 'The Desiderian Scriptorium at Monte Cassino: The *Chronicle* and Some Surviving Manuscripts', *Dumbarton Oaks Pap.*, xxx (1976), pp. 35–54

OLIMPIA THEODOLI

**Leopardi** [Liompardi], **Alessandro** (*fl* 1482–1522). Italian bronze-founder. Born into a well-known Venetian family, he is mentioned in 1482, first as a goldsmith and then as a jeweller, which suggests that he might have been carving hard stones. In 1484 he was employed at the Mint as an engraver of dies. Exiled in August 1487 for his part in an inheritance fraud, he was recalled from Ferrara in September 1488 to cast the equestrian statue of *Bartolomeo Colleoni* (*see* VERROCCHIO, ANDREA DEL, fig. 4) from the clay model left by Verrocchio at his death. He completed the casting, putting his signature on the girth strap

Alessandro Leopardi: bronze relief sculptures of nymphs and Tritons on standard base, Piazza S Marco, Venice, 1505–6

(ALEXANDER LEOPARDUS V.F. OPUS), and designed and executed the high pedestal with marble columns and bronze frieze himself. His execution of the pedestal clearly shows his familiarity with the Classical orders. The monument was erected in the Campo SS Giovanni e Paolo in 1494. He was employed again at the Mint in January 1496, working as master engraver of dies alongside Vittore Gambello, and he was still drawing a salary for this position in November 1521. He appears to have died early in the following year.

Leopardi's casting of the monument to *Colleoni* established his reputation as a founder. In January 1496 he was considered for a commission to cast bronze doors for the entrance of the Doge's Palace. In 1500 he cast pieces of artillery for the Venetian state. On 19 January 1504, in partnership with Antonio Lombardo, he undertook a project for a chapel in honour of Cardinal Giovanni Battista Zen in S Marco, Venice, which was to include three statues, a ciborium and a bronze tomb. However, though he was to have overseen the whole project, he immediately dissociated himself from the commission and was officially replaced by two other founders in May 1505. During this period he was engaged in casting three large bronze bases (see fig.) to carry the Venetian standards in front of S Marco. He was responsible for designing as well as casting these standard bases, which are decorated reliefs of marine processions, reminiscent of masked Venetian festival parades. The friezes of nymphs astride Tritons show the influence of Mantegna's engraving of the *Battle of the Sea Gods*. In the context of Venetian sculpture of the early 16th century Leopardi's standard bases are original and markedly different from the contemporary neo-classical works of the Lombardo family. The central one is dated August 1505 and the flanking pair must have been completed by July 1506. After this commission no further works in bronze by Leopardi are known.

On the basis of this very personal work attempts have been made to attribute various other statuettes and bronze reliefs to Leopardi, but these attributions have more often been based on similarities of subject-matter than on stylistic aspects. There is no evidence to suggest that his output was in any way comparable to that of the Paduan bronze founders. He seems, rather, to have created for himself a higher position in society, becoming a member of the group of Venetian humanists that included the philosopher Niccolò Leonico Tomeo and the scholar Marco Sanudo for whom he probably made scientific instruments. Leopardi was also active as an architect and civil engineer. He worked on the fortifications of Padua (1510) and Treviso (1511), and drew up plans for the rebuilding of the Scuola della Misericordia (1504–7) and the Fabbriche di Rialto (1514), both in Venice, but they were not adopted. He was appointed architect for the reconstruction of S Giustina in Padua in 1521 but was dismissed after a year.

BIBLIOGRAPHY

E. Cigogna: *Delle inscrizioni veneziane*, ii (Venice, 1827), pp. 297–301
M. Testolini: 'Ricerche attorno ad Alessandro Leopardi', *Archv Ven.*, iii (1872), pp. 246–50
W. Stedman Sheard: 'Note on the Proportions of the Base of the Colleoni Monument', in C. Seymour: *The Sculpture of Verrocchio* (London, 1971), pp. 182–4
B. Jestaz: 'Requiem pour Alessandro Leopardi', *Rev. A.*, lv (1982), pp. 23–34
G. Bonfiglio Dosio, ed.: *Il 'Capitolar dalle brocche' della Zecca di Venezia* (Padua, 1984)

BERTRAND JESTAZ

**Leopold I**, Holy Roman Emperor. *See* HABSBURG, §I(19).

**Leopold I**, King of Belgium. *See* COBURG, (1).

**Leopold II**, Holy Roman Emperor. *See* HABSBURG-LORRAINE, (1).

**Leopold II**, King of Belgium. *See* COBURG, (2).

**Leopoldstadt.** *See under* BUDAPEST, §I, 3.

**Leopold William**, Archduke of Austria. *See* HABSBURG, §I(18).

**Leopolski** [Leopoldski; Postel de Leopolski], **Wilhelm** (*b* Drohobycz, nr Lemberg [now Lviv, Ukraine], 5 May 1828; *d* Vienna, 29 Jan 1892). Polish painter. After completing law studies (1848–52) at the University of Lemberg, he trained (1853–6 and 1858–9) at the School of Fine Art, Kraków, under Wojciech Kornel Stattler (1800–75) and Władysław Łuszczkiewicz (1828–1900), and then (1860–61) at the Akademie der Bildenden Künste, Vienna, under Christian Ruben (1805–75), who encouraged him to work in a realistic style. In Vienna Leopolski also made a thorough study of the work of the Dutch and Venetian Old Masters. He then moved to the Munich Akademie and studied (1874–5) under Alexander Wagner (1838–1919). In 1878 he settled in Vienna. Leopolski's early work consisted of sentimental genre paintings based on motifs from Polish rural life. He also painted portraits of outstanding Polish personalities such as the dramatist *Aleksander Fredro* (Lviv, Pict. Gal.) and the poet and critic *Lucjan Siemieński* (Kraków, N. Mus.). His portraits were characterized by attentiveness to costume detail and the use of a neutral background. Leopolski painted with sweeping strokes laying paint on thickly and maintaining a balanced colour scheme, dominated by shades of bronze, olive green, grey and blue. In his portraits of women he generally used lighter colours enlivened with tones of red, blue and pink.

Leopolski also painted scenes from history: one of his most significant works was a large-scale composition, *The Death of Acerno* (1.85×2.30 m, 1867; Wrocław, N. Mus.), which shows the 16th-century poet Sebastian Klonowicz propped up on his deathbed under the watchful eye of his priest and his physician. The dying man gazes out at the viewer across a table cluttered with manuscripts and books. The room is lit by the moon and, despite the painting's essentially realistic style, Leopolski was able to convey the symbolic idea of death and to provide a fascinating psychological study of the main figure.

Leopolski's oeuvre also contains atmospheric landscapes, townscapes and interiors, painted in light and sometimes pastel tones. In Vienna he found support from many of those whose portraits he had painted, for instance *Count Wiktor Baworowski* and *Minister Florian Ziemiałkowski* (both Lviv, Pict. Gal.). Ziemiałkowski arranged for Leopolski to receive a commission to paint the portrait of the Austrian *Emperor Francis Joseph* (?Vienna). During the last years of his life Leopolski was troubled with advancing eye disease, and he abandoned painting.

BIBLIOGRAPHY

*PSB*; Thieme–Becker

*Wilhelm Leopolski*, Wrocław, N. Mus. cat. (Wrocław, 1964) [incl. article by E. Lisowa]

*Polnische Malerei von 1830 bis 1914* (exh. cat., Kiel, Christian-Albrechts U., Ksthalle; Stuttgart, Württemberg. Kstver.; Wuppertal, von der Heydt-Mus.; 1978–9)

ELŻBIETA CHARAZIŃSKA

**Lepakshi** [Lepākshi]. Town and temple site in Anantapur District, Andhra Pradesh, India. The Virabhadra temple at Lepakshi was constructed by two brothers who served as governors under Achyutadeva Raya (*reg* 1530–42) of the VIJAYANAGARA dynasty. The temple is built on an uneven outcrop of granite and is surrounded by two enclosures. The outer enclosure, lined by colonnades and carrying numerous inscriptions, is roughly rectangular in plan and has three entrances. The inner enclosure, laid out approximately in a square, is entered on the north and south through two *gopura*s, one with an incomplete superstructure of brick. Within is a medley of monuments. The open hall adjoining the north *gopura* has elaborately carved pillars with those on the central bays carrying large Shaiva images. The ceiling paintings are the principal examples surviving from the Vijayanagara period. The vividly coloured murals depict popular epic and Puranic legends, such as the boar hunt of Shiva. In addition there are donor portraits and processions of maidens attending upon Shiva and Parvati. The walls on the south contain narrative reliefs depicting Shaiva legends and the story of Arjuna's penance to obtain the bow of Shiva. The painted hall connects directly to the main temple, which consists of a closed hall and three shrines. The shrine of Virabhadra, containing a fierce life-size image of that god, is set axially with the entrance. To the west is a shrine of Vishnu and to the east a partially rock-cut shrine of Uma and Maheshvara. The hall ceiling has murals of Virabhadra, other aspects of Shiva and the temple donors. Externally, the building is plain except for the basement mouldings and pyramidal brick superstructures over the Virabhadra and Vishnu shrines. To the south of the main shrine (just inside the south *gopura*) is a granite boulder carved as the coils of a serpent. Its multi-hooded canopy shelters a polished Shiva *linga*. To the west of the boulder is an incomplete hall with piers sculptured with rearing animals in the 16th-century fashion. A short distance to the east of Lepakshi is a large image of the bull Nandi, also dating to the 16th century.

*See also* INDIAN SUBCONTINENT, §§IV, 7(vi)(d) and V, 4(vii).

BIBLIOGRAPHY

A. G. Rao: *Lepakshi* (Hyderabad, 1969)

V. Kameswara Rao: *Select Vijayanagara Temples of Rāyalaseema*, Govt Andhra Pradesh Archaeol. Ser., 47 (Hyderabad, 1976), pp. 77–84

R. Pachner: 'Paintings in the Temple of Virabhadra at Lepakshi', *Vijayanagara: City and Empire*, ed. A. L. Dallapiccola (Heidelberg, 1985), pp. 326–43

GEORGE MICHELL

**Le Parc, Julio** (*b* Mendoza, Argentina, 23 Sept 1928). Argentine kinetic artist. He was one of the most active members of the large group of South American artists who established themselves in Paris in the 1950s and played a major role in the launching of KINETIC ART in Europe in the next decade. He studied under Lucio Fontana at the Escuela Superior de Bellas Artes in Buenos Aires between 1942 and 1954, before going to Paris in 1958. There he visited Victor Vasarely's studio and met the gallery owner Denise René, who had already established herself as the leading Parisian sponsor of geometrical and kinetic art. In 1960 Le Parc joined 11 other artists, including Francisco Sobrino and his Argentine colleagues Hugo Demarco (*b* 1932) and Horacio García Rossi (*b* 1929), in founding the GROUPE DE RECHERCHE D'ART VISUEL. His reputation was founded on the theoretical stringency and active exhibiting policy of this group, but in 1966 he was awarded the Grand Prix for painting at the Venice Biennale. Ironically this acclaim was offered to a member of a group anxious to repudiate the notion of the celebrated individual artist.

Le Parc had begun working on two-dimensional compositions in colour and black and white as early as 1953, while he was still an art teacher in Buenos Aires. From 1960, however, he began to develop a series of distinctive works that made use of 'skimming' light: these objects, usually constructed with a lateral source of white light which was reflected and broken up by polished metal surfaces, combined a high degree of intensity with a subtle expression of continuous movement (e.g. *Light-continuum*, 1962; New Orleans, LA, Delgado Mus.; for illustration *see* KINETIC ART). At the *Kunst–Licht–Kunst* exhibition at the Stedelijk Van Abbemuseum, Eindhoven, in 1966, as at the Venice Biennale of the same year, Le Parc's individuality was rightly remarked on. Despite his commitment to the joint programme of the Groupe de Recherche d'Art Visuel, he was unable to resist the commercial and institutional pressures that singled him out from his colleagues.

BIBLIOGRAPHY

F. Popper: 'Le Parc and the Group Problem', *Form*, 2 (1966), pp. 5–9
——: *Origins and Development of Kinetic Art* (London, 1968)
*Soto, Vasarely, Le Parc* (exh. cat., Dublin, Hendriks Gal.; Belfast, Ulster Mus.; 1968)
E. Maurizi: *Le Parc: La modulazione della luce* (Macerata, 1980) [pubd at time of exhibition, by Macerata, Pin. & Mus. Com.]

STEPHEN BANN

**Le Pautre** [Le Paultre; Lepautre]. French family of artists. Adrien Le Pautre was a master joiner. Of his three notable sons (1) Jean Le Pautre was a designer and printmaker, whose published works, sold singly or in sets, were an important conduit for disseminating French architectural taste throughout Europe in the 17th century. Another son, also called Jean Le Pautre (1622–77), was active as a mason, but perhaps the most important member of the family was (2) Antoine Le Pautre, an architect whose Baroque style, manifested in his publication *Desseins de plusieurs palais*, found favour among members of the aristocracy and with King Louis XIV. Pierre I Le Pautre (*c.* 1648–1716), (3) Pierre II Le Pautre and Jacques Le Pautre (*c.* 1653–1684), an engraver, were sons of (1) Jean, while Antoine's sons included another Jean Le Pautre (1648–1735), a sculptor, and Claude Le Pautre (*b* 1649), an architect.

**(1) Jean Le Pautre** (*b* Paris, 1618; *d* Paris, 1682). Designer and engraver. He was active as a printmaker from 1643 but was most prolific in the 1660s. His output was prodigious, with 2348 prints having been recorded, and his range of subjects was extremely broad: interior decoration, including specific studies for bed alcoves, chimney-pieces (*see* CHIMNEY-PIECE, fig. 2), ceilings, wall-papers, furniture, friezes, vases, trophies, tapestry, garden ornament and grottoes were all explored in detail and executed with remarkable facility. He was equally at home delineating landscape and the human figure. Le Pautre's engravings are notable for their richness and their spirited and vivacious conception. Bernini held him in high respect, and clearly the admiration was returned. This is most evident in Le Pautre's set of engravings devoted to garden ornaments, which have elaborately ornamented borders that exhibit the same plasticity and movement found in Bernini's sculptures. Le Pautre's knowledge of Italian art was probably acquired second-hand: in 1645 he engraved a series of drawings of antique and Baroque ornament made by his teacher, Adam Philippon, in Italy. In 1670 he is recorded as being in the employ of the crown, and in 1677 he was elected to the Académie Française as a *dessignateur* and *graveur*. Many of his works were reprinted in 1751 by the publisher Jombert. According to Guilmard, Le Pautre was responsible for instigating the Louis XIV style, the grandiose and sumptuous character of which is evident in his prints. Examples of his work include *Vases ou burettes à la romaine* (Paris, [*c.* 1660]), published by Nicolas Langlois, the six plates depicting *L'Entrée triomphante de leurs majestez Louis XIV, roy de France, et Marie Thérèse d'Austriche son espouse, dans la ville de Paris* (Paris, 1662) and the series *Alcôves à l'italienne* (Paris, 1665) and *Alcôves à la romaine* (Paris, [*c.* 1670]) and *Vases à l'antique*

(Paris, [*c.* 1675]), all published by Pierre Mariette. A particularly splendid series is the group of five large engravings for the commemorative volume *Les Divertissements de Versailles, 1674* (Paris, 1676).

WRITINGS

*Oeuvres d'architecture*, 3 vols (Paris, 1751)

BIBLIOGRAPHY

D. Guilmard: *Les maîtres ornemanistes* (Paris, 1880), i, pp. 65–76
*Katalog der Ornamentstichsammlung der Staatlichen Kunstbibliothek Berlin* (Berlin and Leipzig, 1939), i and ii
R. Timm: *Staatliche Museen zu Berlin: Zauber des Ornaments* (Berlin, 1969), pp. 38, 64, 91, 93, 98, 122
S. Jervis: *The Penguin Dictionary of Design and Designers* (London, 1984), pp. 293–4
P. Jean-Richard: *Ornemanistes du XVe au XVIIe siècle au Musée du Louvre* (Paris, 1987)
M. Préaud: *Bibliothèque Nationale: Inventaire du fonds français, graveurs du XVII siècle*, xi (Paris, 1993), pp. 56–368

ELAINE EVANS DEE

**(2) Antoine** [Anthoine] **Le Pautre** (*b* Paris, 1621; *d* Paris, 1679). Architect, brother of (1) Jean Le Pautre.

1. LIFE AND WORK. He is said to have studied design and etching with his older brother (1) Jean Le Pautre, and probably learnt the rudiments of architecture from Etienne Martellange. A document of 1643 refers to him as mason and architect, and in 1644 he was called Architecte des Bâtiments du Roi, perhaps indicating that he had worked at a royal building site. His earliest patrons were the French Jansenists, to whom he became known through his father (or another relative), who had worked in 1639 in the Parisian hôtel of the Jansenist Anne de Rohan. In 1648 Le Pautre began the chapel of Port-Royal de Paris (completed 1648), the first Jansenist church, and the Hôtel de Fontenay-Mareuil, Paris (completed 1647; destr.), built for the French ambassador to Rome, whose mother was related to the Jansenist Arnauld family.

While at work on minor domestic commissions in Paris, at the end of 1652 or the beginning of 1653 Le Pautre published the *Desseins de plusieurs palais*, which contained engravings of his recently completed buildings as well as ideal designs for châteaux and hôtels, city gates, fountains, ceilings and ornamentation. In his preface Le Pautre stressed that the *Desseins* was not concerned with ancient architecture or theory but was simply a book of his own inventions. Significantly, it was dedicated to Cardinal Jules Mazarin, a powerful patron and advocate of contemporary Italian art, and the Baroque style of Le Pautre's ideal projects was intended to appeal to Mazarin and to aristocratic circles.

The book produced its desired result when, in 1654, Le Pautre was commissioned to build the Hôtel de Beauvais, Paris (completed 1660; see fig. 1) for Catherine Henriette Bellier, lady-in-waiting to the Queen Mother, Anne of Austria. That same year he remodelled the choir of his parish church, St Laurent, Paris, and in 1657 provided a design for the lateral façade of the church of the Jacobins, Lyon (completed 1687 or later; destr. 1816).

Le Pautre's success in constructing the Hôtel de Beauvais over medieval foundations on a highly irregular site, as well as the publication of imaginative projects in the *Desseins*, established him as a leading domestic designer. In 1659 he was appointed architect to Philippe I, Duc

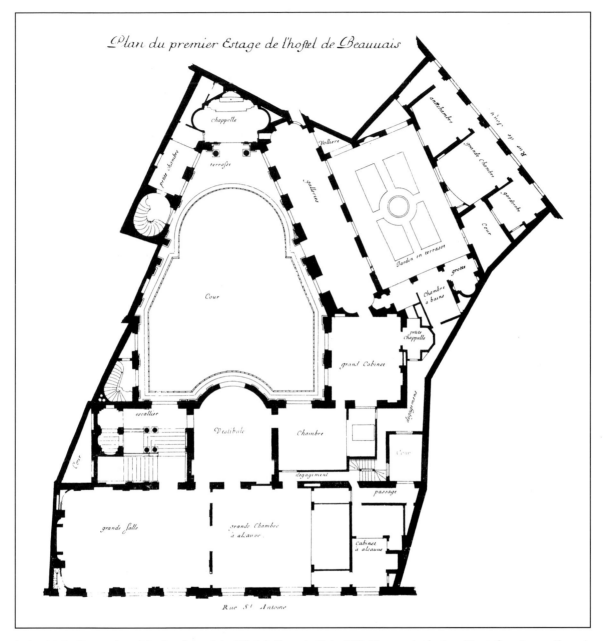

*Plan du premier Estage de l'hostel de Beauvais*

1. Antoine Le Pautre: plan of the first floor of the Hôtel de Beauvais, Paris, 1654–60; engraving by Jean Marot, from Jacques-François Blondel: *Architecture françoise*, ii (Paris, 1752)

d'Anjou (later Duc d'Orléans), and immediately set to work at Saint-Cloud, near Paris, Philippe's country residence.

At Saint-Cloud, Le Pautre added a dramatic architectural cascade (*c.* 1662–4) to the hydraulic attractions of the garden and completely refashioned the old Maison de Gondi into a free-standing block (*c.* 1660–68). It was decided *c.* 1669 to enlarge the château into a U-shaped plan, orientated towards the Seine, with the remodelled block incorporated as the left (south) wing. The right (north) wing, virtually a duplicate of the left one, was completed in or before 1677. In that year Le Pautre proposed a *corps-de-logis* linking the two wings, but his design was not adopted. Instead, a *corps-de-logis*, probably designed by Jean Girard, a mason working under Le Pautre, was constructed (*c.* 1677–80/81). (The wings of the château of Saint-Cloud were modified by Jules Hardouin Mansart beginning in the 1680s; the building was destroyed in 1870.) Another commission resulting from the connection with Philippe was the château of Seiglière de Boisfranc, Saint-Ouen (begun *c.* 1662; destr.), built for Philippe's treasurer.

Le Pautre also designed for Louis XIV. He provided plans (untraced) for the Louvre (1664) and Versailles (1669), but these were not adopted. In 1671 he was named a founder-member of the Académie Royale d'Architecture, and in 1674 he was commissioned by the King to design a château for Mme de Montespan and her children at Clagny, on the outskirts of Versailles. The building displeased Mme de Montespan, however; Le Pautre was dismissed and the following year the commission was handed to Jules Hardouin Mansart. Le Pautre's failure at Clagny, as well as the apparent reassignment of the Saint-Cloud *corps-de-logis* to Girard in 1677, indicate a serious downturn in Le Pautre's fortunes in the 1670s. When he died in 1679, however, he still bore the title of Contrôleur Général des Bâtiments du Monseigneur, Duc d'Orléans.

2. WORKING METHODS AND TECHNIQUE. Le Pautre's stylistic development falls into three phases. The initial period (1646–c. 1650) was shaped by the influence of Martellange and the patronage of the Jansenists. Martellange's Jesuit Novitiate, Paris (1630–42; destr.), was Le Pautre's model for the chapel of Port-Royal de Paris. The Novitiate was greatly admired by the classicist coterie recently formed around François Sublet de Noyers, Surintendant des Bâtiments du Roi, and Le Pautre had made accurate etchings of the building in 1640. The restrained style of the Novitiate was adapted by Le Pautre to serve as a suitable expression of Jansenist asceticism. The chapel forms a compact, longitudinal plan without a transept; texturally neutral, planar walls articulated by pilasters, and sober, small-scale ornament. These elements were also present in the Hôtel de Fontenay-Mareuil, where conventional square and rectangular rooms were loosely combined.

Le Pautre's second, Baroque, phase was inaugurated with the publication of his *Desseins* (1652/3). Although he did not visit Italy, he was influenced by the graphic style of his brother Jean, who had probably been there in the early 1640s and had formed his distinctive Italianate

Baroque style during that decade. Le Pautre was also keenly aware of the work of other French Baroque architects, especially that of Louis Le Vau. Le Pautre's new approach in the *Desseins* is found in his use of varied spatial units—including circular, oval, octagonal, trefoil, and apsidal-ended rooms—which are combined into graduated axial progressions, with the *salon à l'italienne* (a vaulted, two-storey, centrally planned room), often used as the climax. The elevations are distinguished by a marked emphasis on apparent weight, achieved by rustication, large scale, abundant decorative flourishes and complex, even bizarre, rooflines. The most remarkable example of such a roofline is the fourth design for an ideal château, which includes a new invention—the drum-without-dome—destined to have a long history in European architecture. This fourth design also features a colossal order and a movemented façade with concavities—two forms dear to the Baroque.

Le Pautre's new idiom, announced in the *Desseins*, was put into practice in the 1650s. At the Hôtel de Beauvais he created an ingenious plan on an irregular site, with varied room shapes and a courtyard formed by converging lateral walls and an apsidal termination. For the choir of St Laurent he used non-canonical architectural detailing and exuberant decoration to frame a sculptural tableau of the *Resurrection* (1657–8; destr.) by Gilles Guérin. His lateral façade of the church of the Jacobins—based on the façade of the Val-de-Grâce, Paris, by François Mansart and Jacques Le Mercier—was articulated by Le Pautre to conform closely to contemporary Roman Baroque taste.

Although Le Pautre was still in his Baroque period in the early 1660s, as shown by the cascade at Saint-Cloud (see fig. 2), with its dramatic and varied water display, at that time he shifted to a quieter vocabulary. The designs for the wings of the château of Saint-Cloud include traditional square and rectangular rooms. There, and at the château of Seiglière de Boisfranc, he used smooth, horizontally channelled masonry to create placid, uniform

2. Antoine Le Pautre: the cascade at Saint-Cloud, near Paris, c. 1662–4

elevations. The château of Clagny featured a long, low silhouette (intended to harmonize with buildings in the town of Versailles), with flat, untextured walls, sculpture rigorously confined within square panels, and a feeling of lightness, even delicacy, which seemed perhaps appropriate for the royal mistress and her children.

Le Pautre's final stylistic phase began before the accession of Jean-Baptiste Colbert as Surintendant des Bâtiments du Roi in 1664, and hence cannot simply be viewed as the architect's response to the new classicism favoured by Colbert: the tastes of Philippe d'Orléans and Boisfranc may have been crucial here. The radically new design for Clagny (1674), however, may have been derived from the Pavillon de l'Aurore at Colbert's country estate at Sceaux (early 1670s; possibly designed by Claude Perrault), and it is possible that the minister specifically proposed the Pavillon to Le Pautre as his model. The tripartite division of Le Pautre's stylistic evolution runs parallel to broad stylistic shifts in French 17th-century architecture. In the fourth design from the *Desseins de plusieurs palais*, the Hôtel de Beauvais, and the cascade at Saint-Cloud, Le Pautre produced designs of permanent value for French and European architecture.

WRITINGS

*Desseins de plusieurs palais* (Paris, [1652/3])

BIBLIOGRAPHY

[A. C. d'Aviler]: *Les Oeuvres d'architecture d'Anthoine Le Pautre* (Paris, [1681], R 1966)
L. Hautecoeur: *Histoire de l'architecture classique en France: Tome II, Le Règne de Louis XIV*, 2 vols (Paris, 1948)
R. W. Berger: 'Antoine Le Pautre and the Motif of the Drum-without-Dome', *J. Soc. Archit. Hist.*, xxv (1966), pp. 165–80
——: *Antoine Le Pautre: A French Architect of the Era of Louis XIV* (New York, 1969)
P. Reutersward: 'Autour de Saint-Ouen, Sceaux et Clagny (quelques dessins inédits)', *L'Urbanisme de Paris et l'Europe 1600–1680*, ed. P. Francastel (Paris, 1969), pp. 95–104
J. M. Thiveaud: 'Antoine Le Pautre (1621–1679)', *Ecole nationale des Chartes, Paris: Positions des thèses* (1970), pp. 215–23
——: *Antoine Le Pautre (1621–1679)* (diss., Ecole nationale des Chartes, Paris, 1970)
——: 'Antoine Le Pautre: Architecte de la Chapelle de Port-Royal de Paris', *Chroniques de Port-Royal; Bull. Soc. des Amis de Port-Royal*, no. 22–3 (1974), pp. 45–64

ROBERT W. BERGER

**(3) Pierre Le Pautre II** (*b* Paris, ?1659; *d* Paris, 22 Jan 1744). Sculptor, son of Jean Le Pautre (1622–76), a master mason and building contractor. In 1683 he won the Prix de Rome, and the following year he went to the Académie de France in Rome, where he was a talented and much praised student. Among his Roman works were two copies after the Antique executed for Louis XIV, the marble groups *Faun with a Kid* (1685–7; Paris, Louvre) and *Meleager* (1687–92; on loan to the Hôtel Matignon, Paris). He also executed two original works, the marble groups *Paetus and Arria* (1691–5; Paris, Louvre), from a model by Jean Théodon and started by him, and *Aeneas Carrying his Father Anchises* (1696–1718; Paris, Louvre), from a model by François Girardon. Both demonstrate his early mastery of complex Baroque compositional effects, and the popularity of the latter group is attested by numerous reductions in terracotta and bronze recorded in 18th- and 19th-century sales. He returned to Paris in 1701 and, although invited to become a member of the Académie

Royale, preferred instead to join the Académie de St Luc, of which he eventually became a Recteur for life.

Le Pautre was mostly employed by the Bâtiments du Roi, providing statuary and decorative sculpture for the royal building projects of the early 18th century. He provided an over life-size plaster statue of *St Marcelline* (*c.* 1702; destr.) for the church of the Invalides, Paris, and a running statue of *Atalanta* (marble, 1703–4; Paris, Louvre), based on an antique original, which was the first of a series of four 'runners' completed by Nicolas Coustou and Guillaume Coustou (i) for the gardens at the Château de Marly, Yvelines. He played an important role in the decoration of the chapel of Versailles where, between 1705 and 1710, he executed a number of decorative reliefs for the interior (stone; *in situ*) and bronze putti with animated drapery for two subsidiary altars (*in situ*), as well as statues of *St Ambrose* and *St Gregory* (stone; *in situ*) for the balustrade of the roof. In 1710 he carved a marble statue of a nymph (untraced) for the well-known series of *Companions of Diana* intended for Marly, and in 1712–13 he contributed to the decoration (destr.) of the choir of Notre Dame, Paris. In the years following the death of Louis XIV in 1715, during which major commissions from the Bâtiments du Roi were relatively rare, he undertook work for private patrons and in particular for the churches and religious communities of Paris. About 1716 he executed the monument in the church of St Merry, Paris, to *Jean Aubery, Marquis de Vastan* (marble; destr.), which consisted of a putto unveiling an oval portrait medallion of the deceased. His most important surviving religious work is the elaborate carved wooden churchwardens' pew at St Eustache, Paris. Executed *c.* 1720 to designs by Jean-Silvain Cartaud, it consists of a large portico supported by fluted Ionic columns on a semi-elliptical plan. The semi-elliptical pediment is surmounted by a cloud-borne statue of *St Agnes Surrounded by Putti*, and beneath it hangs a crucifix in an oval medallion supported by three angels. His last commission was a marble statue of *Clytie* (New York, priv. col., see Souchal, ii, p. 387), commissioned for Louis XV in 1730. In his maturity Le Pautre was one of the most consistent sculptors of the later part of the reign of Louis XIV and of the Régence period. His style, characterized by a balanced grace that did not exclude elegance or animation, drew on the lightly classicizing tendencies of the sculpture produced for Versailles at the end of the 17th century and on the decorative inventiveness of the emerging Rococo.

For an illustration of his work *see* URBAN PLANNING, fig. 6.

BIBLIOGRAPHY

Lami; Souchal
P. J. Mariette: 'Abecedario', *Archv. A. Fr.*, iii (1854–6), p. 190
A. Jal: *Dictionnaire critique de biographie et d'histoire* (Paris, 1872), pp. 773–5
J. Guiffrey: *Comptes des Bâtiments du Roi sous le règne de Louis XIV*, 5 vols (Paris, 1881–1901)
——: 'Scellés et inventaires d'artistes', *N. Archv. A. Fr.* (1884), p. 66
A. de Montaiglon: *Correspondance des directeurs de l'Académie de France à Rome*, i–iii (Paris, 1887–9)
M. Rambaud: *Documents du minutier central concernant l'histoire de l'art (1700–50)*, ii (Paris, 1971), pp. lxix, 475–81
*Sculptures des jardins du Louvre, du Carrousel et des Tuileries*, ii (Paris, 1986), pp. 264–76 [entries by G. Bresc-Bautier]

FRANÇOISE DE LA MOUREYRE

**Lepenski Vir.** Site in eastern Serbia, on the right bank of the River Danube above the Iron Gates. It was the centre of the complex and long-lived Mesolithic culture named after it, which flourished *c.* 6700–*c.* 5500 BC and produced the first monumental sculpture in Europe. Seven extensive, superimposed settlements of hunters, fishers and food-gatherers were discovered between 1965 and 1970 under an Early Neolithic settlement (Lepenski Vir III). They contained graves evidencing complex burial rites, an abundance of skilfully made stone, bone and antler implements, objects of personal adornment, as well as sanctuaries containing monumental stone sculptures.

The architecture of Lepenski Vir is distinguished by the absence of orthogonal bases and vertical walls. The earliest settlement (Proto-Lepenski Vir) was a seasonal camp, while settlements Lepenski Vir Ia–e and II were religious centres, presumably serving a broader area. They consisted of about 30 tentlike dwellings, all of which had a ground-plan in the form of a truncated segment of a circle with a steep roof resting directly on the base. Large stone blocks, forming a rectangular hearth, were embedded in the lime-plaster floor. Most dwellings contained sculptures (between one and three in each) and stone altars in the form of concave boulders or slabs, set near the hearth.

The sculptures from settlements Lepenski Vir I–II are made of large boulders and may be divided into three groups: figural sculptures; carvings of intricate arabesques; and abstract forms. The figural sculptures represent either humans or animals. The earliest show the human figure

full length and in a realistic way, while those from the later sanctuaries represent only the heads of humans, deer, fish or fish-like beings in the 'X-ray style'. A new development in the Lepenski Vir II settlement was the production of monumental human heads (see fig.). Certain facial features (eyes, eyebrows) were strongly emphasized, so that the earlier realistic treatment yielded to an expressionistic style. Sculptures of ornamental motifs display similar development. The ornaments on the earliest sculptures have a certain vitality and mobility, while those on the later sculptures are rigid and geometric. Iconographically the sculpture of the Lepenski Vir culture probably represents the origin myths of the hunter–gatherer communities of the central Danubian region in the 7th–6th millennia BC.

BIBLIOGRAPHY

D. Srejović: *Europe's First Monumental Sculpture: New Discoveries at Lepenski Vir* (London, 1972)
*Lepenski Vir: Menschenbilder einer frühen europäischen Kultur* (exh. cat. by D. Srejović, Cologne, Röm-Ger.-Mus., 1981)

DRAGOSLAV SREJOVIĆ

**Lepère, (Louis-)Auguste** (*b* Paris, 30 Nov 1849; *d* Domme, 20 Nov 1918). French printmaker and painter. From an early age he wanted to be a painter, but his father, the sculptor François Lepère (1829–71), stipulated that he also learn a craft that could provide him with a dependable livelihood. At 13 Lepère began an apprenticeship with Burn Smeeton (*fl* 1840–60), an English wood-engraver working in Paris. He began exhibiting paintings at the Paris Salon at the age of 20. In 1875 he showed a painting of the Commune at the Salon des Refusés, *Guardpost on the Rue des Rosiers* (Paris, Carnavalet), which won praise from Camille Pissarro and Armand Guillaumin. (Ten years later Lepère gave Pissarro's son, Lucien, his first lesson in wood-engraving.) From the early 1880s Lepère's wood-engraving business left him little time for painting. He only returned to it seriously after 1900, when success as a printmaker brought him a degree of financial security.

Lepère worked in many other media, including water-colour, ceramic decoration, etching, lithography and leather bookbinding; but it was as a woodcut artist that he made his greatest contribution. He played a major role in the transformation of the woodcut from a reproductive medium of illustration to an independent means of aesthetic expression. In 1875, when Lepère's first signed reproductive wood-engravings began appearing in illustrated periodicals, his name appeared as draughtsman as well as engraver. In 1877 he began publishing wood-engravings based on his own compositions. The first appeared in *Le Monde illustré* (12 May 1877)—five little wood-engravings of the construction of Sacré-Coeur signed 'after nature by M. Lepère'. This was unusual, given the strict division of labour prevalent in wood-engraving ateliers of the period. In the 1880s Lepère became known as an original wood-engraver through his contributions to cultural periodicals, particularly *La Revue illustrée*. He had, however, the more ambitious aim of establishing the woodcut as a medium that would be disseminated in the form of single-sheet prints, like etching and lithography. In 1888 he organized the Société de l'Estampe Originale, which published an album of ten original prints, including

Lepenski Vir II, monumental human head, *c.* 6700–*c.* 5500 BC (Lepenski Vir Museum)

Auguste Lepère: *The Convalescent*, colour woodcut, 406×299 mm, 1892 (London, Victoria and Albert Museum)

Lepère's work was disseminated in European and American collections. A complete set of these series is in the British Museum (*see* WOOD-ENGRAVING, fig. 2).

Lepère's favourite subject was the city of Paris and its inhabitants. His work in the medium of woodcut is characterized by two distinct styles. His wood-engravings for illustrated periodicals and books are notable for their expressive, etching-like style, unmatched for the atmospheric qualities achieved through the manipulation of fine black-and-white lines. His woodcuts of the 1890s, on the other hand, often still done on the endgrain, are much broader in approach. Again, one of their most notable attributes is their atmospheric quality, though achieved through different means; for example, in works such as *The Convalescent* subtle effects were achieved by inking the line blocks in brown, blue and grey, and by adding flat colour blocks inked with transparent, water-based pigments in imitation of the Japanese.

BIBLIOGRAPHY
R. Marx: 'Peintres-graveurs contemporains: L.-A. Lepère', *Gaz. B.-A.*, n.s. 3, xxxviii (1896), pp. 299–305; xxxix (1908), pp. 78–88, 394–402, 497–512; n.s. 4, iv (1910), pp. 66–70
A. Lotz-Brissonneau: *L'Oeuvre gravé de Auguste Lepère: Catalogue descriptif et analytique* (Paris, [1905])
C. Saunier: *Auguste Lepère, peintre et graveur, décorateur de livres* (Paris, 1931) [incl. G. M. Texier-Bernier's continuation of Lotz-Brissonneau's cat. rais.]
J. Baas: *Auguste Lepère and the Artistic Revival of the Woodcut in France, 1875–1895* (diss., Ann Arbor, U. MI, 1982)
*The Artistic Revival of the Woodcut in France, 1850–1900* (exh. cat. by J. Baas and R. S. Field, Ann Arbor, U. MI, Mus. A.; New Haven, CT, Yale U., A.G.; Baltimore, MD, Mus. A.; 1983–4), pp. 40–49

JACQUELYNN BAAS

four wood-engravings in May 1888. Further albums appeared in 1889 and 1891. The following year André Marty purchased the rights to the *L'Estampe originale* title and continued to include single-sheet woodcuts—a tribute to Lepère's campaign on behalf of the medium.

In 1889 Lepère broadened the expressive boundaries of the woodcut. He hand-coloured several of his earlier wood-engravings, produced a chiaroscuro woodcut (*Basketsellers*) and experimented with cutting and printing a colour woodcut from sidegrain pearwood with water-based colours in the manner of the Japanese (e.g. *Le Palais de Justice*). In March 1890 he contributed 23 woodcuts to the second Exposition des Peintres-Graveurs at Durand-Ruel's galleries. He continued to produce and exhibit colour woodcuts, his most important work in the medium being *The Convalescent* (1892; see fig.). His example may have encouraged Henri Rivière to produce woodcuts in the Japanese manner from 1889 and inspired experiments with the medium by Henri Guérard (1846–97) and Charles Maurin in 1890. Félix Vallotton, Maurice Denis, Aristide Maillol and Paul Gauguin took up the woodcut in the 1890s and by 1895 a full-scale revival of the medium was well underway.

In 1907 Auguste Desmoulins began publishing portfolios of three series of wood-engravings that Lepère had created for *La Revue illustrée* in the late 1880s. In 1913 the publisher-dealer Edmond Sagot produced an edition of the popular series *Rouen illustré*, originally made for the journal *L'Illustration* in 1888. Through these editions

**Lepic, Ludovic(-Napoléon)**, Vicomte (*b* Paris, 17 Sept 1839; *d* Paris, 27 Dec 1889). French printmaker, painter and sculptor. A member of a Napoleonic aristocratic family, Lepic was a man of many talents and interests: balletomane, dog breeder, amateur anthropologist and a gentleman jockey, as well as artist. Having abandoned a legal career to study under Charles Gleyre and Alexandre Cabanel, he exhibited at the Paris Salon from 1869.

Lepic became a founder-member of the Société des Aquafortistes in 1862 and by the mid-1870s had developed the idea of 'l'eau-forte mobile' (changeable etching). This technique consisted of using the original etching as a constant and employing various inking and wiping procedures to create different tonal effects. He claimed that he had reworked one of his plates, *View of the Banks of the Escaut*, 85 times, each time changing the light effects or introducing new details (19 impressions in Baltimore, MD, Mus. A.). He summarized his procedures in *Comment je devins graveur à l'eau-forte*, published by Alfred Cadart in 1876.

Lepic's role as a popularizer of a new expressive freedom in printmaking is of great importance, even if he was outstripped in virtuosity and intelligence by Degas, who took Lepic's basic ideas but abandoned the use of an etched line as the basis of the monotype to produce his masterpieces in the latter medium. The first monotype credited to Degas, *The Rehearsal* (*c.* 1874–5; Washington, DC, N.G.A.), bears the signatures of both men in the top left-hand corner. Probably because of his friendship with Degas, Lepic showed watercolours and etchings at the first two Impressionist exhibitions (1874, 1876). In 1872 he founded what is now the Musée Archéologique in Aix-les-Bains.

WRITINGS

*Comment je devins graveur à l'eau-forte* (Paris, 1876)

BIBLIOGRAPHY

H. Béraldi: *Les Graveurs du XIXe siècle*, ix (Paris, 1889), pp. 139–41, 143–5

L. Delteil: *Manuel de l'amateur d'estampes des XIXe et XXe siècles*, ii (Paris, 1925), p. 331

*Inventaire du fonds français après 1800*, Paris, Bib. N., Dépt. Est. cat., xiv (Paris, 1967)

J. Bailly-Herzberg: *L'Eau-forte de peintre au dix-neuvième siècle: La Société des Aquafortistes (1862–1867)*, ii (Paris, 1972), pp. 139–41

M. Melot: *L'Estampe impressionniste* (Paris, 1974), pp. 106–8

*The Painterly Print* (exh. cat., ed. J. P. O'Neill; New York, Met., 1980)

MICHAEL HOWARD

**Lépicié.** French family of artists. (1) Bernard Lépicié was an engraver who became secretary and historiographer of the Académie Royale de Peinture et de Sculpture (*see* PARIS, §VI, 1), in which capacity he compiled a catalogue of the paintings in the French royal collection and an important set of lives of the Premiers Peintres du Roi. His wife, Renée-Elisabeth Lépicié (née Marlie; 1714–73), was also an engraver, signing a number of plates after François Boucher, Jean-Siméon Chardin, Noël Hallé and other artists. Their son (2) Nicolas-Bernard Lépicié was a painter specializing in large historical and religious canvases, although he is perhaps best known for his charming small-scale genre scenes.

**(1) (François-)Bernard Lépicié** (*b* Paris, 6 Oct 1698; *d* Paris, 17 Jan 1755). Engraver, writer and administrator. He trained as an engraver under Jean Mariette and Gaspard Duchange and before 1724 visited London, where with Claude Dubosc (*fl* 1711–40) and Nicolas-Dauphin de Beauvais (1687–1763) he engraved the Raphael cartoons of the *Acts of the Apostles* at Hampton Court. In 1724 he returned to Paris, where he contributed to some major collections of engravings, including the famous *Recueil Crozat* (1729), but devoted himself mainly to interpreting the paintings of such contemporaries as Rosalba Carriera, Jean-Baptiste Pater, Jean-Marc Nattier and above all Charles-Antoine Coypel. Among his early prints are *Spring* after Rosalba and the *Coquettish Widow* after Coypel (Portalis–Beraldi, nos 26, 19). He was approved (*agréé*) at the Académie Royale in 1734, but he did not deliver his *morceau de réception*, a portrait of *Nicolas Bertin* (PB 28) after Jacques-François de Lyen (1684–1761), until 1740, when he was received (*reçu*) as a full member. It was the support of Coypel and of Philibert Orry, then Directeur-Général des Bâtiments du Roi, whose portrait after Hyacinthe Rigaud Lépicié engraved in 1737 (PB 38), that ensured his election as Secrétaire Historiographe (permanent secretary and official historian) to the Académie Royale on 26 April 1737.

After his appointment, Lépicié's output as an engraver diminished. He engraved a number of prints after Chardin (PB 4–13), from *The Governess* (1739) to *Grace* (1745)—perhaps his best-remembered works—but little else. In his capacity as Secrétaire Historiographe he became closely involved in the administration of the Académie Royale. In the late 1740s he took an active part in the reform of that institution and in the promotion of history painting undertaken by the Directeur-Général des Bâtiments du Roi, Charles-François Le Normand de Tournehem and Charles-Antoine Coypel, by then Premier Peintre du Roi. In 1749 he was made professor of history and geography at the Ecole Royale des Elèves Protégés (*see* FRANCE, §XV), and in 1752 Le Normand de Tournehem's successor, the Marquis de Marigny, appointed him to be his principal adviser on the arts. Both of Lépicié's books, the *Vies des premiers peintres du roi* (1752) and the *Catalogue raisonné des tableaux du roi* (1752–4), were directly related to his campaign of academic reform, and his *Catalogue raisonné* was begun at the behest of Coypel. Its purpose was threefold: to facilitate the opening (1750) of the picture gallery at the Palais du Luxembourg, Paris; to counter recent criticisms of the maintenance of the royal collection; and, in his own words, 'to acquaint Europe with the King's magnificent collection of paintings'. Separate volumes on the Italian, French and Northern schools of painting were planned, but only two dealing with the Italian school were completed. The *Vies des peintres* is a collection of lectures delivered to the Académie Royale by various speakers over many years and brought together by Lépicié in order to underline the French tradition in art and to stress the continuity between past and present at a time when contemporary painting in France was coming under increasing attack, most notably from Etienne La Font de Saint-Yenne in such works as the *Réflexions sur quelques causes de l'état présent de la peinture en France* (1747). At the time of his death he was collecting material for a comprehensive inventory of the royal collection.

WRITINGS

*Vies des premiers peintres du roi*, 2 vols (Paris, 1752)

*Catalogue raisonné des tableaux du roi*, 2 vols (Paris, 1752–4)

BIBLIOGRAPHY

Portalis–Beraldi [PB]; Thieme–Becker

M. Furcy-Raynaud: 'Correspondance de M. de Marigny avec Coypel, Lépicié et Cochin', *Nouv. Archvs A. Fr.*, xix (1903), pp. 84–6, 88–9, 97, 292, 360

A. Fontaine: *Les Doctrines d'art en France* (Paris, 1909), pp. 57, 160, 177, 179–80

J. Locquin: 'Bernard Lépicié à l'Ecole royale des élèves protégés', *Bull. Soc. Hist. A. Fr.* (1909), pp. 93–7

——: *La Peinture d'histoire en France de 1747 à 1785* (Paris, 1912)

W. McAllister Johnson: *French Royal Academy of Painting and Sculpture: Engraved Reception Pieces, 1672–1789* (Kingston, Ont., 1982), pp. 120–22

ANDREW McCLELLAN, with CHRISTIAN MICHEL

**(2) Nicolas-Bernard Lépicié** (*b* Paris, 16 June 1735; *d* Paris, 14 Sept 1784). Painter and draughtsman, son of (1) Bernard Lépicié. He was taught engraving by his father before entering the studio of the painter Carle Vanloo. In 1759 he won second prize in the Prix de Rome competition at the Académie Royale de Peinture et de Sculpture, but he never went to Rome. He was approved (*agréé*) by the Académie Royale in 1764 on presentation of a vast painting of the *Landing of William the Conqueror on the English Coast*, which is now in the Abbaye aux Hommes in Caen. He subsequently painted a series of pictures for the above foundation, including the *Baptism of Christ* (1765) and *Christ and the Little Children* (1767; both *in situ*), as well as a *Conversion of Saul* (1767; untraced). In 1769 he was received (*reçu*) as a full member by the Académie Royale on presentation of *Achilles and the Centaur Chiron* (Troyes,

Nicolas-Bernard Lépicié: *Fanchon Arising,* oil on canvas, 740×930 mm, exhibited at the Salon 1773 (Saint-Omer, Musée de l'Hôtel Sandelin)

Mus. B.-A. & Archéol.); he became an assistant professor in 1770 and a professor in 1777. His studio had a fine reputation, and several painters prominent in the Neoclassical generation trained there, including Carle Vernet, Jean-Baptiste Regnault, Jean-Joseph Taillasson and Henri-Pierre Danloux. His early success was doubtless facilitated by his father's reputation and by the friendship of Charles-Nicolas Cochin II, who had succeeded Bernard Lépicié as Secrétaire Perpétuel to the Académie Royale in 1755 and owned at least five of Nicolas-Bernard's works.

Lépicié was involved in major commissions for the Bâtiments du Roi, first under the Marquis de Marigny and then, from 1774, under Charles-Claude de Flahaut de la Billarderie, Comte d'Angiviller. For the Petit Trianon at Versailles he painted two works—*Adonis Changed into an Anemone by Venus* (exh. Salon 1769) and *Narcissus Changed into a Flower* (exh. Salon 1771; both *in situ*)— that recall the elegant, poetic style of Louis de Boullogne (ii). For the Ecole Militaire in Paris he depicted a subject from national history, *St Louis Dispensing Justice* (exh. Salon 1773; untraced). He was employed by Flahaut de la Billarderie to design large tapestry cartoons for the Gobelins, taking for his subjects scenes from ancient history. He also drew on ancient history in large-scale canvases such as the *Courage of Portia* (exh. Salon 1777; Lille, Mus.

B.-A.), an exaltation of heroic death inspired by Nicolas Poussin's *Death of Germanicus* (1628; Minneapolis, MN, Inst. A.); the *Departure of Regulus* (exh. Salon 1779; Carcassonne, Mus. B.-A.); the *Piety of Fabius Dorso* (exh. Salon 1781; Chartres, Mus. B.-A.); and the *Zeal of Matathias* (exh. Salon 1783; Tours, Mus. B.-A.). These paintings, which exemplify the moral virtues, reflect the character of a man who was, according to his contemporaries, both devout and scrupulous. Equally monumental were the numerous altarpieces he painted, including a *Visitation* for Bayonne Cathedral (1769) and a *Deposition* for Chalon-sur-Saône Cathedral (1779; both *in situ*).

Unlike most contemporary history painters, Lépicié also worked very successfully as a genre painter: his *Fanchon Arising* (Saint-Omer, Mus. Hôtel Sandelin; see fig.) won a chorus of praise at the Salon of 1773. The verisimilitude of his characters and the silvery tone of his colours, which led to comparisons with David Teniers (1610–90), were much admired. Lépicié's concern for realistic detail, precise drawing and delicate palette here take precedence over any obvious moral message: in the *Departure of the Poacher* (exh. Salon 1781; Roanne, Mus. Déchelelte) the allusion to the dubious virtue of the subject receives less consideration than the refinement of execution. In such scenes as the *Interior of a Customs House* (exh. Salon 1775;

Lugano, Col. Thyssen-Bornemisza) Lépicié's meticulous technique and his powers of observation recall the work of the Dutch masters of the 17th century, as well as that of contemporary Italian painters of *vedute*. Some of his portraits, for example *Emilie Vernet as a Child* (1769; Paris, Petit Pal.) and the *Young Draughtsman, or Carle Vernet as a Child* (exh. Salon 1779; Paris, Louvre), are genuine masterpieces—refined and subtle in their colouring yet quite without preciosity. The sensitive, serious character of the painter is apparent in two late self-portraits (exh. Salon 1777; Lisbon, Mus. Gulbenkian; Abbeville, Mus. Boucher-de-Perthes).

Despite his short life Lépicié left a large body of work: Gaston-Dreyfus included 562 paintings and drawings in his catalogue. The Musée du Louvre, Paris, among other French museums, has a large collection of his drawings, which range from studies for the history paintings to portrait heads (e.g. *Head of a Young Man*, red chalk; Grenoble, Mus. Grenoble) and genre scenes (e.g. *Young Girl Holding up her Apron*, sepia; Orléans, Mus. B.-A.).

BIBLIOGRAPHY

D. Diderot: *Salons* (1759–81), ed. J. Seznec and J. Adhémar, 4 vols (Oxford, 1957–67); rev. 3 vols (Oxford, 1975–83), i (1975), p. 13; ii (1979), pp. 6, 8–9, 41–2, 163, 181–6, 197; iii (1983), pp. 6, 8, 36, 274–5, 280, 318
P. Gaston-Dreyfus: *Catalogue raisonné de l'oeuvre peint et dessiné de Nicolas-Bernard Lépicié (1735–1784)* (Paris, 1923)
F. Ingersoll-Smouse: 'Nicolas-Bernard Lépicié', *Rev. A. Anc. & Mod.*, xliii (1923), pp. 39–43, 129–36, 364–78; xlvi (1924), pp. 122–30, 217–28
N. Volle: *Diderot et l'art de Boucher à David, les salons: 1759–1781* (exh. cat., Paris, Hôtel de la Monnaie, 1984–5), pp. 307–9

NATHALIE VOLLE

**Lépine, Stanislas(-Victor-Edouard)** (*b* Caen, 3 Oct 1835; *d* Paris, 28 Sept 1892). French painter. Originally self-taught, he became a student of Corot and an admirer of Johan Barthold Jongkind, who influenced him in his choice of ships as subject-matter. He also learnt from Jongkind not only how to paint ships accurately but also how to render the depth of the sky and the clarity of waves, as in *Sailing Boats in Caen Harbour* (priv. col., see Serullaz, p. 48). He produced a number of nocturnes of the port of Caen, including *Boats on the River, Moonlight* (Reims, Mus. St Denis) and *Port of Caen, Moonlight Effect* (*c.* 1859), the latter painting marking his début in 1859 at the Salon in Paris. He specialized in the depiction of the steep banks of the River Seine and the movement of the water, as in the *Seine at Bercy* (*c.* 1866–72; Edinburgh, N.G.). He also executed views of Paris and was particularly successful in reproducing the atmosphere of the city, especially its overcast days with cloudy skies, as in *Nuns and Schoolgirls Walking in the Tuileries Gardens, Paris* (*c.* 1871–83; London, N.G.). He also rendered such picturesque scenes in Paris as the old streets of Montmartre where he himself lived (e.g. *Rue Norvins at Montmartre*, 1878; Glasgow, A.G. & Mus.). In 1874 in Paris he exhibited *Banks of the Seine* (1869; Paris, Mus. d'Orsay) with the Société Anonyme des Artistes, Peintres, Sculpteurs, Graveurs etc, the first public showing outside the Salon by the Impressionist painters. Although his work can be said to anticipate the Impressionists' interest in light effects, his brushwork, as well as his depiction of light effects, is much more delicate and subtle than theirs.

BIBLIOGRAPHY

J. Couper: *Stanislas Lépine, 1835–1892: Sa vie, son oeuvre* (Paris, 1969)
M. Serullaz, ed.: *Phaidon Encyclopedia of Impressionism* (Oxford, 1978)
S. Monneret: *Impressionnisme et son époque: Dictionnaire international*, 4 vols (Paris, 1978–81)
P. Tucker: 'The First Impressionist Exhibition in Context', *The New Painting: Impressionism 1874–1886* (exh. cat., San Francisco, F. A. Museums; Washington, DC, N.G.A.; San Francisco, CA, de Young Mem. Mus.; 1986), p. 129
K. Adler: *Unknown Impressionists* (Oxford, 1988)

ATHENA S. E. LEOUSSI

**Lepoittevin** [Poidevin], **Eugène(-Modeste-Edmond)** (*b* Paris, 31 July 1806; *d* Paris, 6 Aug 1870). French painter and lithographer. A student of Louis Hersent and Auguste-Xavier Leprince, he was a prolific painter and lithographer and exhibited regularly in the Salons in Paris from 1831. He combined history, genre and landscape in his marine and pastoral narratives. The influence of Dutch painting is not only evident in his scale, topographical accuracy and attention to light and air but also in his choice of Dutch subjects, as in such works as *Van de Velde Painting the Effect of a Broadside Fired from the Ship of Admiral de Ruyter* (1846; see *Art-Union*, viii (1846), p. 100), the *Studio of Paul Potter* (1847; see *Art-Union*, ix (1847), p. 20) and the *Studio of van de Velde* (1854; see *A. J.* [London], vi (1854), p. 184). In these the Dutch painters are ironically depicted working in nature, not in their studios. Lepoittevin's primary figures are often at the apex of a pyramid composed of healthy women and children, faithful domestic animals and other elements in spacious, horizontal formats. While some paintings (e.g. *Shipwrecked*, 1839; *Frankish Women*, *c.* 1842; both Amiens, Mus. Picardie) suggest the violence of the Romantic Sublime, others, such as the *Fisherman's Return* (1848; see *Art-Union*, x (1848), p. 84), are more sentimental. Beraldi divided Lepoittevin's graphic work into categories entitled marines, patriotic souvenirs and, apparently his most popular, *Albums de diableries*. Lepoittevin travelled and sketched in England, the Netherlands, France and Italy; his work attracted a pan-European bourgeois audience interested in well-composed and carefully costumed romances on a human scale, borrowed from wide-ranging sources in history, art history and literature yet rooted in observed nature.

BIBLIOGRAPHY

Bénézit; Thieme–Becker
'The Living Artists of Europe, no. ix: Eugène Le Poittevin', *Art-Union*, viii (1846), pp. 100–01
H. Beraldi: *Les Graveurs du XIXe siècle*, ix (Paris, 1889), pp. 145–6
F. von Boetticher: *Malerwerke des neunzehnten Jahrhunderts*, ii (Dresden, 1895/R Leipzig, 1941), pp. 840–41
H. Mireur: *Dictionnaire des ventes d'art*, iv (Paris, 1911), p. 295
J. Robiquet: 'Pages d'albums de la Restauration', *La Renaissance*, xi (1928), pp. 386–8

NANCY DAVENPORT

**Le Prince.** French family of glass painters. They were the dominant stained-glass artists of the second quarter of the 16th century in Normandy and the diocese of Beauvais. One of the earliest securely dated works is the *Crucifixion* with the *Virgin of Pity and SS Hubert, Christopher, Francis and Louis* (1522) by Engrand Le Prince (*d* 1531) in Beauvais Cathedral. The *Tree of Jesse* in St Etienne, Beauvais, must also date *c.* 1522 and is signed by Engrand; the window of Notre-Dame-de-Lorette in St Etienne, however, dates from *c.* 1530 and shows the initials of Pierre Le Prince ( *fl* 1530s). At Rouen, Engrand collaborated with Jean Le Prince ( *fl* 1496–1555) in the *Triumph of the Virgin*, the *Life of John the Baptist* and the *Corporal Works of Mercy*, made for St Vincent (*c.* 1525; Rouen, St Jeanne d'Arc). Nicolas Le Prince ( *fl* 1531–51) appears to have created numerous windows with conservative compositions of small medallions, for example the *Legend of SS Crispin and Crispinian* in St Gervais, Gisors, inscribed VIVE NICOL and dated 1531. His monogram appears in the *Creation* and *History of Israelites* in the south transept rose of Beauvais Cathedral (1551).

The family's work is characterized by rich painterly effects, a delight in the torsion of the human form and brilliant colour contrasts, especially intense blues and reddish purples. Also characteristic is a meticulous yet seemingly spontaneous rendering of figure and landscape, for example the cathedral and bridge of Rouen in the window of the *Seven Deadly Sins* (1525; Rouen, Mus. Le Secq des Tournelles). The features are modelled by soft modulations of matt complemented by linear accents at points of transition, the mouth line, tip of the nose and the upper eye lid. The approach is highly painterly, with isolated touches of colour, mass and line coalescing into an undulating surface interplay.

BIBLIOGRAPHY

J. Lafond: 'La Renaissance', *Le Vitrail français*, ed. M. Aubert and others (Paris, 1958), pp. 220–34
F. Perrot: 'Les Vitraux de l'ancienne église de Saint-Vincent', *Bull. Amis Mnmts Rouen.* (1978–9) [special issue: *Le Vieux Marché de Rouen*], pp. 49–98 (52–3, 68–70, 75–9)

VIRGINIA CHIEFFO RAGUIN

**Leprince, Auguste-Xavier** (*b* Paris, 28 Aug 1799; *d* Nice, 24 Dec 1826). French painter and lithographer. He was the son and pupil of the painter and lithographer Anne-Pierre Leprince and the elder brother of the painters Robert-Léopold Leprince (1800–47) and Gustave Leprince (1810–37). Leprince received a medal at his first Salon of 1819 for one of six entries, five of which were landscapes of 17th-century Dutch inspiration, which came possibly via the work of Jean-Louis Demarne. Leprince quickly learnt to vary the contents of his paintings: at the Salon of 1822 his entries included three Paris street scenes, three portraits and two scenes on board a frigate. His numerous Paris street scenes usually depicted some well-known contemporary event, as in the *Restoration of the Barrière du Trône* (Paris, Carnavalet), which is one of a series. The *Embarkation of the Animals at the Port of Honfleur* (1823; Paris, Louvre) shows the successful application of Leprince's interest in R. P. Bonington, not only in its composition and content but also in its direct observation. The painting was purchased by Louis XVIII at the highly competitive Salon of 1824. Also reminiscent of Bonington is the small-scale contemporary history painting, *The Ordination* (1825; Angoulême, Mus. Mun.), again one of a series. In the last year of his short life Leprince showed himself to be a sensitive watercolour painter and lithographer, publishing a set of 12 lithographs entitled *Inconveniences of a Journey by Stage-coach*.

BIBLIOGRAPHY

H. Beraldi: *Les Graveurs du XIXe siècle: Guide de l'amateur d'estampes modernes* (Paris, 1885–92), ix, pp. 146–7

A. Michel: *L'Histoire de l'art depuis les premiers temps chrétiens jusqu'à nos jours*, VIII, i (Paris, 1925), p. 106
*Le Paysage français de Poussin à Corot* (exh. cat. by H. Lapauze, C. Goonkowski and A. Fauchier-Magnan, Paris, Petit Pal., 1925), pp. 146–7

LORRAINE PEAKE

**Le Prince, Jean-Baptiste** (*b* Metz, 17 Sept 1734; *d* Saint-Denis-du-Port, Seine-et-Marne, 30 Sept 1781). French painter, draughtsman and printmaker. Born to a family of ornamental sculptors and gilders, he became famous for creating a new kind of genre picture, based on the direct observation of Russian subjects, and also for perfecting aquatint technique. Sometime around 1750 he became a pupil of François Boucher, thanks to the protection of the Maréchal de Belle-Isle (1684–1761), governor of Metz. Boucher's saturated brushwork, highly finished surfaces and incisive drawing had a decisive impact upon the young artist, as did, perhaps, the diversity of his output. He was also inspired by 17th-century Dutch and Flemish genre and landscape painters.

Le Prince is said to have made a trip to Italy in 1754, fleeing from the much older wife whom he had married in 1752, but there is as much evidence against such a trip as for it. By July 1757 Le Prince had arrived in St Petersburg. Well received by the French envoy, the Marquis de l'Hôpital, he received more than 40 commissions to execute overdoors for the Empress Elizabeth in the newly constructed Winter Palace; he received more commissions from Peter III (1728–62). Le Prince is said to have travelled extensively in Russia, according to some as far as Siberia. His prints show a knowledge of the north-western and western Empire, but the number of imperial commissions that cover his entire sojourn from 1757 to 1762 makes it unlikely that he travelled as much as has been claimed. The drawings he made in Russia (e.g. Paris, Louvre) provided the basis for a considerable body of work that added to the general taste of the 18th century for exotica a specific one for *russeries*.

The years between 1763 and 1775 mark the summit of Le Prince's career and production. From 1764 to 1768 he was at work on drawings (Philadelphia, PA, Rosenbach Lib.) for the *Voyage en Sibérie* (Paris, 1768) of the Abbé Jean-Baptiste Chappe d'Auteroche (1728–69). In 1765 he was received (*reçu*) as a member of the Académie Royale de Peinture et de Sculpture with a painting representing a *Russian Baptism* (Paris, Louvre; see fig.) and showed 15 pictures at the Paris Salon, all of Russian subjects. In 1769 Denis Diderot severely criticized one of his Salon exhibits, *Le Cabak* (Stockholm, Nmus.), for its lack of finish; Diderot, however, also praised Le Prince for his refined mastery of aquatint technique (*Salons*, ed. J. Seznec and J. Adhémar, iv, Oxford, 1967, pp. 97–8). Between 1765 and 1768 Le Prince published several suites of etchings and aquatints on Russian themes, and he exhibited 29 sheets at the Salon of 1769. The popularity of his Russian subjects is also shown by his tapestry cartoons of *Russian Games* (fragments, Beauvais, Mus. Dépt. Oise), woven many times from 1769 at the Beauvais Manufactory (e.g. Paris, Jacquemart-André).

After 1770 ill-health caused Le Prince to retire to the Brie district near Paris. He then concentrated more on landscapes and pastoral subjects, such as *Landscape near*

Jean-Baptiste Le Prince: *Russian Baptism*, oil on canvas, 730×920 mm, 1765 (Paris, Musée du Louvre)

*Tobolsk* (Rouen, Mus. B.-A.) and the *Russian Festival* (1770; Angers, Mus. B.-A.). Working from sketches executed from life and using models and actual costumes brought back from his travels, Le Prince introduced an almost ethnographic concern and exacting accuracy into his rendition of exotic subjects. Although these Russian pictures constitute the best-known aspect of his output, he also produced Classical subjects, such as *Anacreon* (Lawrence, U. KS, Spencer Mus. A.), and gallant genre pictures, such as *Fear* (Toledo, OH, Mus. A.), as well as French landscapes.

### PRINTS

*Divers ajustements et usages de Russie* (Paris, 1764)
*Divers habillements des femmes de Moscovie* (Paris, 1764)
*Divers habillements des prêtres de Russie* (Paris, 1764)
*Première suite de cris et divers marchands de Pétersbourg et de Moscou* (Paris, 1765)
*Deuxième suite de divers cris de marchands de Russie* (Paris, 1765)
*Deuxième suite d'habillements des femmes de Moscovie* (Paris, 1768)

### BIBLIOGRAPHY

J. Hédou: *Jean Le Prince et son oeuvre* (Paris, 1879)
L. Réau: 'L'Exotisme russe dans l'oeuvre de J.-B. Le Prince', *Gaz. B.-A.*, n. s. 4, iii (1921), pp. 147–65
J. Proust: '*Le Joueur de flûte de Passy*: Diderot et l'image du paysannat russe', *Etud. 18ème Siècle*, iii (1976), pp. 223–33
F. Gardey and W. McAllister Johnson: 'Quelques archives de la gravure au 18ème siècle', *Nouv. Est.*, 45 (1979), pp. 8–34
M. E. Hellyer: *Recherches sur Jean-Baptiste Le Prince: 1734–1781* (diss., U. Paris-Sorbonne, 1982)
P. Grate: 'Le *Cabak* de Jean-Baptiste Le Prince', *Rev. A.*, 72 (1986), pp. 19–23
*Drawings by Jean-Baptiste Le Prince for the 'Voyage en Sibérie'* (exh. cat. by K. Rorschach, Philadelphia, PA, Rosenbach Mus.; Pittsburgh, PA, Frick A. Mus.; New York, Frick; 1986–7)
*La France et la Russie au siècle des lumières* (exh. cat., Paris, Grand Pal., 1986–7), nos 278–97, 496–7
*Jean-Baptiste Le Prince* (exh. cat., ed. M. Clermont-Joly; Metz, Mus. A. & Hist., 1988)

J. PATRICE MARANDEL

**Leptis Magna** [Lepcis Magna]. Roman site on the North African coast, 120 km east of Tripoli. Originally a Phoenician settlement, it was incorporated into the Roman Empire after Julius Caesar's victory at Thapsus in 46 BC. It flourished under Augustus (*reg* 27 BC–AD 14) and his successors, particularly Septimius Severus (*reg* AD 193–211) who was a native of the town. Its decline was accelerated by incursions of desert tribesmen, and, when it was reconquered by Justinian in AD 533, only a small area near the harbour was refortified. After the Arab conquest of AD 643, the site disappeared under sand dunes until the Italian excavations of the 1920s and 1930s.

1. ARCHITECTURE. Little has been uncovered of the original Punic settlement, but the adjacent Augustan forum

has been fully revealed. The planning of the square is neat and orderly apart from the oblique east side, which must have been dictated by a pre-existing Punic monument. On the north side of the square are three temples, the most important being the Temple of Liber Pater, the oldest building of the group, and the Temple of Rome and Augustus (AD 14–19). Both are approached frontally by high staircases in the Italian manner, and both have columns running around only three sides. Their high podia are joined together by a vaulted platform. Opposite them on the south side is the Basilica Vetus, whose entrance is on the short east side, although its long side faces the square. Built next to it in the early 2nd century AD, but on an oblique alignment, is the curia, a rectangular hall with two rows of tiered seats facing each other, enclosed by a colonnaded portico. The three temples on the west side are of later date. The limestone paving and colonnades were added in AD 53–4.

In the Augustan period Leptis Magna expanded rapidly along the main road that led south-west along the wadi Lebda (*see* ROME, ANCIENT, fig. 58), as can be seen in a number of firmly dated buildings, such as the market (9–8 BC), the theatre (AD 1–2) and the Chalcidicum (monumental portico; AD 11–12). The market (for illustration *see* MACELLUM) was built on similar lines to those at Pompeii and Puteoli and had a circular pavilion in the middle of a colonnaded enclosure, except that it has two circular pavilions, both surrounded by octagonal porticos, with stone counters between the columns. The surrounding enclosure with its internal porticos was added later (AD 31–7). The theatre, built by Annobal Rufus (according to an inscription over the south-eastern lateral exit from the *orchestra*), has an 88.5 m-wide *cavea* (auditorium) with the lowest part resting upon a natural slope, the middle part upon an earth embankment and the upper parts on annular and radial vaults. Externally the *cavea* wall is not articulated by arched openings as at Sabratha. Instead, six doorways give access to passageways that run up to the middle rows of seating. At the top of the *cavea* is a small temple

dedicated, according to an inscription, in AD 35–6 to Ceres Augusta. Originally the *orchestra* was floored in painted stucco, although this was replaced with marble in the 2nd century AD. Each of the three doorways in the *scaenae frons* is framed by a broad curved niche. Its three tiers of marble columns belong to the reign of Antoninus Pius (AD 138–61), as an inscription on the architrave records. Either side of the stage are large *versurae* (rooms used as foyers or for storage), and behind the stage is a courtyard with a temple in the middle dedicated to the Di Augusti, built by Iddibal Tapapius and dedicated in AD 43 by Q. Marcius Barea.

Until the time of Trajan (*reg* AD 98–117) the normal building material at Leptis was the local grey limestone. At the time of Hadrian (*reg* AD 117–38), however, white and coloured marbles from Greece and Asia Minor were introduced and soon transformed the appearance of the city. The first building to use marble veneer and columns was the great Hadrianic Baths built in AD 127 to the south of the main street near the wadi. They are orientated almost exactly north–south, so that they are almost diagonal to the main grid plan of the town. They are *thermae* (double-circulation baths; *see* BATH (ii), §1), although they are not completely symmetrical around the main north–south axis. Although they have the normal succession of *natatio, frigidarium, tepidarium* and *caldarium*, there are only two plunges in the *frigidarium* instead of the four that were common after the Baths of Titus in Rome (AD 80). They also lack the lateral palaestrae found in earlier Imperial baths such as the Baths of Trajan in Rome (AD 109), although a large palaestra was added to the north of the *natatio* in Antonine times.

The Hunting Baths (late 2nd century AD or early 3rd; see fig. 1) belong to the smaller type of Roman baths known as *balneae*. The simple succession of rectangular and octagonal rooms is laid out on the 'ring' system, with no attempt made to disguise the shape of the vaults from the outside. This transmission of interior shape to the exterior became common in some of the buildings of

1. Leptis Magna, Hunting Baths, late 2nd century AD or early 3rd

Hadrian's Villa at Tivoli, notably the Piazza d'Oro. As the excellent preservation of the Hunting Baths leaves no doubt as to their external appearance, there has been speculation as to whether other later Roman bath buildings had the pitched roofs covered with tiles often shown in reconstructions.

On the accession of Septimius Severus an extensive building programme began at Leptis. His major undertaking was a large forum–basilica complex (ded. AD 216) built in conjunction with a broad colonnaded street 400 m long leading past the Hadrianic Baths to the harbour. Since the Hadrianic Baths were built diagonally to the main grid of the town, the new street had to make a sharp change of direction after it had passed the baths. This problem was skilfully overcome by the siting of an ornate semicircular nymphaeum at the bend. This and other architectural and sculptural features of the complex suggest that Asiatic designers were involved in both the planning and execution of the project.

Along the north-east side of the street stands the forum, a large rectangular enclosure (100×60 m) surrounded by a high wall of severe, almost military, character. Indeed, the forum was converted into a fortress in Byzantine times. Around the inside of the enclosure ran an arcade supported on columns with lotus-and-acanthus capitals, with alternate Nereid and Medusa heads in the spandrels. Against the south-west wall dominating the forum stood a large temple dedicated to the Severan family. It was raised on a lofty podium and approached by a high spreading staircase. The red granite columns of the pronaos rested upon elaborately carved plinths (see §2 below). The column arrangement was tripteral at the front, and as the temple abutted against the rear wall of the forum there were no columns at the back. Opposite the temple and built transversely across the main axis of the forum was the Severan basilica (see fig. 2), a plan reminiscent of the Forum of Trajan in Rome. The basilica was a large twin-apsed structure with two-tiered rows of red granite columns dividing it into nave and aisles. Above the columns

were clerestory windows bringing the total height of the hall to over 30 m. A complicated arrangement of detached columns runs around each apse, with a pair of giant order columns in the middle and two tiers of smaller columns on each side, an odd feature that may have been caused by a change of plan. The building was roofed with a wooden ceiling that spanned 19 m. Each apse was flanked by two pairs of white marble pilasters, decorated with deeply undercut vine scrolls.

The colonnaded street led to the harbour, which Severus also improved. Along the two moles that enclosed the roughly circular harbour he built rows of warehouses with handsome porticos of Doric columns. Near the end of each mole close to the harbour mouth was a small temple. At the extreme end of the west mole, on an embankment that projects beyond the harbour mouth, are the remains of a rectangular lighthouse. He also enlarged the 2nd-century AD circus, which was situated near the seashore east of the harbour and adjacent to the amphitheatre. In gratitude for his generosity to the city the citizens of Leptis Magna erected a triumphal arch to Severus. It stood at a crossroads and was of the four-sided type (quadrifrons). Its wealth of ornament (see §2 below) once again links it stylistically with the East.

BIBLIOGRAPHY

P. Romanelli: *Leptis Magna* (Rome, 1925)
R. Bartoccini: *Le terme di Leptis* (Bergamo, 1929)
——: 'L'arco quadrifronte dei Severi a Lepcis', *Africa It.*, iv (1931), pp. 32–152
J. B. Ward-Perkins: 'Severan Art and Architecture at Leptis Magna', *J. Roman Stud.*, xxxviii (1948), pp. 59–80
J. B. Ward-Perkins and J. M. C. Toynbee: 'The Hunting Baths at Leptis Magna', *Archaeologia*, 93 (1949), pp. 165–95
N. Degrassi: 'Il mercato romano di Leptis Magna', *Quad. Archeol. Libia*, ii (1951), pp. 27–70
D. E. L. Haynes: *An Archaeological and Historical Guide to the Pre-Islamic Antiquities of Tripolitania* (Tripoli, 2/1955), pp. 71–106
L. Crema: *Enciclopedia classica*, III/xii/1: *L'architettura romana* (Turin, 1959)
R. Bartoccini: 'Il porto romano di Leptis Magna', *Boll. Cent. Stud. Stor. Archit.*, xiii (1960) [whole issue]
R. Bianchi Bandinelli, E. Vergara Caffarelli and G. Caputo: *Leptis Magna* (Rome, 1963)
R. G. Goodchild: 'The Unfinished "Imperial" Baths of Lepcis Magna', *Libya Ant.*, ii (1965), pp. 15–27
M. F. Squarciapino: *Leptis Magna* (Basle, 1966)
P. Romanelli: *Enciclopedia classica*, III/x/7: *Topografia e archeologia dell'Africa romana* (Turin, 1970)
J. H. Humphrey, F. B. Sear and M. B. Vickers: 'Aspects of the Circus at Lepcis Magna', *Libya Ant.*, ix–x (1972–3), pp. 25–97
O. Mahgiub, A. Chighione and R. Madaro: 'Nuove ricerche nell'anfiteatro di Leptis Magna', *Libya Ant.*, xiii–xiv (1976–7), pp. 21–36

2. SCULPTURE. The most notable sculpture from Leptis Magna occurs on buildings of Severan date (early 3rd century AD). It represented a shift away from the ideals of the Classical past, and many of its artists did not come from Rome. The four relief panels in the attic of the Arch of Septimius Severus (AD 203) are so remarkable that they are sometimes regarded as an officially inspired reaction against the pomposity of Antonine art. The scene (see fig. 3) is a marked departure from Hellenistic naturalism and contains a repetitious row of mainly frontal figures above which appear the heads of a second row of figures supposedly standing behind them. These features, along with the deep drilling that results in the loss of three-dimensionality, run counter to the normal conventions of

2. Leptis Magna, Severan basilica, dedicated AD 216

3. Leptis Magna, Arch of Septimius Severus, marble relief of a triumphal procession, dedicated AD 203

Classical art and anticipate the style of the late Empire and early Byzantine period. The corner pilasters with their richly ornamental acanthus scrolls are among the first extant works of a group of sculptors from Aphrodisias (*see* APHRODISIAS, §3) in Caria who were active in Leptis Magna at this period. Their style is characterized by heavy undercutting to produce strong black-and-white effects, and by a surface dissolved into a lace-like pattern of purely decorative forms. These features occur on the eight elaborately carved pilasters in the apses of the Severan basilica (AD 216), which are decorated with acanthus scrolls interspersed with figures from the Dionysiac cycle and the Labours of Hercules. Attic sculptors seem to have been responsible for the reliefs depicting the *Battle of the Gods and Giants* on the column plinths in the pronaos of the Temple of the Severan Family (AD 216). The Nereid and Medusa heads in the spandrels of the adjacent forum arcade are powerfully modelled, with a striking contrast between the smooth surface modelling and the deeply drilled eyes, mouths and hair.

BIBLIOGRAPHY

R. Bartoccini: 'L'arco quadrifronte dei Severi a Lepcis', *Africa It.*, iv (1931), pp. 32–152

M. F. Squarciapino: *La scuola di Afrodisia* (Rome, 1943)

J. B. Ward-Perkins: 'Severan Art and Architecture at Leptis Magna', *J. Roman Stud.*, xxxviii (1948), pp. 59–80

M. F. Squarciapino: *Sculture del foro severiano di Leptis Magna* (Rome, 1974)

D. E. Strong: *Roman Art*, Pelican Hist. A. (Harmondsworth, 1976), pp. 225–8

F. B. SEAR

**Le Puiset, Hugh of.** *See* HUGH OF LE PUISET.

**Le Puy.** French city in Haute-Loire. The production of Le Puy constitutes a circumscribed and highly idiosyncratic body of Romanesque sculpture. Surviving work of the Le Puy sculptors includes the cathedral of Notre-Dame with its baptistery and cloister, the chapels of St Clair and St Michel d'Aiguilhe and the church of St Martin, Polignac. The cathedral, an imposing structure with a rectangular choir, projecting transept and aisled nave of six bays, dominates the city. St Michel d'Aiguilhe, which stands on a volcanic peak near by, has a square core, with apses on three sides, that was enlarged in the Romanesque period with an irregularly shaped ambulatory and short nave. St Clair, located within the precinct of the former hospice of St Nicolas, in the same suburb, is an octagonal chapel with a semicircular eastern apse. The parish church of St Martin, Polignac, situated some 6 km north-west of Le Puy, was originally a dependency of Pébrac Abbey. Four bays of the Romanesque nave remain, terminated by a choir with triple apses. Fragments of sculpture found along the perimeter of the cathedral, which derive from other no longer identifiable structures, are preserved in the Musée Crozatier. The most common material is a local variety of soft-grained sandstone, which resists erosion poorly, with the occasional use of a local basalt. The study of the development of this sculpture is impeded by the virtual absence of secure documentary evidence and the substantial alterations to the appearance and fabric of the buildings made during the extensive 19th-century restorations.

The earliest known Romanesque sculpture in Le Puy is associated with the eastern parts of the cathedral: the choir and the lower tiers of the abutting steeple (the *clocher angélique*), the transept and the two eastern nave bays. It is assumed that the reconstruction of the cathedral was initiated in the second half of the 11th century and that the first building campaign was completed in the early years of the 12th. Nearly all the decorative sculpture in

Le Puy Cathedral, nave capital, second half of the 12th century

this part of the monument was replaced by modern copies during the restorations carried out by A. Mallay in the 1840s (originals now in the Musée Crozatier). The sculpture associated with the steeple forms a distinct group: the capitals are tapered, narrowly proportioned blocks on which stylized foliate motifs, as well as single figures of Virtues and simple scenic compositions, are displayed on a flat and undifferentiated ground. The capitals in the sanctuary and the eastern nave bays were executed by a different master or atelier; their shape is cubic, and the designs are free interpretations of Corinthian models. The sinuous tapestry of flattened foliage tendrils, punctuated by deep undercuts, results in effects that have been compared to lace or embroidery work. These capitals have also been used to illustrate the view that Islamic art had a pervasive impact on the Romanesque sculpture of Le Puy (Fikry), but more recent scholars have preferred to emphasize its participation in a broader renewal of sculptural form and technique, centred on the Corinthian capital, which can be observed in a large area around the Mediterranean during the 11th century.

This essentially aniconic architectural sculpture continues in the middle bays of the cathedral nave, the older parts of the cloister and the 12th-century enlargement of the chapel of St Michel d'Aiguilhe. In this series the leaves are frequently treated as blocky, undetailed masses, although a variety of designs was employed at all three sites. The cruder pieces at St Michel d'Aiguilhe are fairly literal imitations of Gallo-Roman models, probably furnished by

the monuments of Ruessio (Saint-Paulien) and ancient Anicium (Le Puy), from which there are appreciable remains, some of which were used in the construction of the Romanesque cathedral. The more refined and stylistically disparate sculpture of the cloister includes, besides the dominant Corinthian-derived vocabulary, examples of zoomorphic imagery and a few capitals with explicitly religious subjects. The formative influence of Gallo-Roman art seems in these carvings to be combined with reflections of the classicizing sculpture of contemporary monuments in Provence and the Rhône Valley.

The Late Romanesque phase is represented by the capitals of the two western bays of the cathedral nave and the Porche du For, the richly decorated entrance on its south-eastern side. It is probable that the major historiated doorways of Le Puy were executed in the same period, which now tends to be dated to the second half of the 12th century: the ornate, though much restored portal of St Michel d'Aiguilhe; the ruined tympanum and lintel of the Porte St Jean on the north-eastern side of the cathedral; and the fragments of a portal with column statues found in the Hôtel Dieu, now in the Musée Crozatier. The capitals of the final building campaign of the cathedral do not wholly depart from the aesthetic of the earlier phases, but figurative elements are introduced: the Lamb of God flanked by adoring angels, the four Evangelists and busts of saints in roundel-like hollows opened up in the foliage (see fig.). Capitals of the same type are found at St Martin, Polignac. The faintly exotic portal of St Michel d'Aiguilhe is the most spectacular realization of Romanesque art in Le Puy, combining marble and brick encrustation in different colours with figurative reliefs and framing elements of *ajouré* palmette foliage. Its theme is the Adoration of the 24 Elders of the Apocalypse, but by the end of the 20th century an explanation of certain aspects of the imagery and a persuasive interpretation of the entire composition had yet to be proposed.

*See also* GAUZFREDUS.

BIBLIOGRAPHY

N. Thiollier: *L'Architecture religieuse à l'époque romane dans l'ancien diocèse du Puy* (Paris, 1900/R 1979)
A. Fikry: *L'Art roman du Puy et les influences islamiques* (Paris, 1934)
G. Bandmann: 'Ein Fassadenprogramm des 12. Jahrhunderts und seine Stellung in der christlichen Ikonographie', *Das Münster*, v (1952), pp. 1–21
R. Gounot: *Collections lapidaires du Musée Crozatier du Puy-en-Velay* (Le Puy, 1957)
*Congr. Archéol. France*, cxxxiii (1976) [incl. various articles on the Romanesque monuments of Le Puy and its environs]
X. Barral i Altet: *Art roman en Auvergne* (Rennes, 1984), pp. 95–103
M. Durliat: 'Les Plus Anciens Chapiteaux de la cathédrale du Puy et leur place dans la sculpture du XIe siècle', *Cah. Archéol.*, xxxii (1984), pp. 63–88

WALTER CAHN

**Lequeu, Jean-Jacques** (*b* Rouen, 14 Sept 1757; *d* Paris, 28 March 1826). French architect and draughtsman. He was the son of a cabinetmaker and studied at the Ecole de Dessin in Rouen. In 1779 he was awarded a scholarship and went to Paris, where he attended the Académie Royale and worked in the office of Jacques-Germain Soufflot. Lequeu designed a *Style Gabriel* hôtel de ville (1779; unexecuted) for Rouen and several country houses in the form of ancient temples. He travelled to Italy in 1783, visiting Vicenza and its neighbourhood. During the French Revolution he worked as a draughtsman for the Fête de la Fédération (the celebration in 1791 of the fall of the Bastille) and then in the land survey department. From 1802 he served in the Bâtiments Civils, retiring in 1815. Lequeu is best known for his imaginative drawings and manuscripts (Paris, Bib. N.). These display a wide range of visionary projects in eclectic styles, executed with meticulous precision. Examples include a Gothic gallery for the château of Gaillon, with slender piers and large oblong windows that seem to foreshadow later constructions in cast iron. The façade he proposed for the 'Temple of Isis' of a masonic lodge in Rouen combined Gothic tracery and pinnacles, Ionic volutes, Baroque scrolls and an open belfry surmounted by a cross. A scheme for a Gothic dairy shows a structure flanked by a pair of columns that display cows' udders. A house for a gardener, inspired by one of William Chambers's Chinese designs, is a bungalow surmounted by a pavilion dedicated to Aurora. Like Etienne-Louis Boullée and Claude-Nicolas Ledoux, Lequeu also produced designs for spherical buildings: a palace of justice (1794), where the sphere motif is repeated inside as the base of a statue of *Justice*, and a Temple to Supreme Wisdom, the ceiling of which represents a starlit sky, as in Boullée's *Cenotaph to Newton*. Lequeu identified with the aims of the French Revolution: he designed a sixth architectural order where the upper half of the column shaft was carved to represent an aristocrat in chains.

UNPUBLISHED SOURCES
Paris, Bib. N., Cab. Est. [four vols on archit.; *Mécanique*; *Voyage en Italie*; *Précis méthodique pour apprendre à graver*; other works]

BIBLIOGRAPHY
E. Kaufmann: 'Jean Jacques Lequeu', *A. Bull.*, xxxi (1949), pp. 130–35
H. Rosenau: 'Architecture and the French Revolution: Jean Jacques Lequeu', *Archit. Rev.* [London], cvi (1949), pp. 111–16
——: 'Postscript on Lequeu', *Archit. Rev.* [London], cviii (1950), pp. 264–7
E. Kaufmann: *Three Revolutionary Architects: Boullée, Ledoux and Lequeu* (Philadelphia, 1952)
G. Metken: 'Jean-Jacques Lequeu ou l'architecture *rêvée*', *Gaz. B.-A.*, ser. 6, lxv (1965), pp. 213–30
A. Chastel: 'The Moralizing Architecture of Jean Jacques Lequeu', *ARTnews Annu.*, xxxii (1966), pp. 70–83
*Visionary Architects: Boullée, Ledoux, Lequeu* (exh. cat., Houston, U. St Thomas, 1967–8)
P. Duboy: *Lequeu: An Architectural Enigma* (London, 1986)

**Ler, de.** *See* ERRI.

**Lerambert, Louis, II** (*b* Paris, 1620; *d* Paris, 15 June 1670). French sculptor. He was a member of a gifted family of sculptors, painters and masons in the service of the kings of France who held the reversion of the title Garde des Antiques et des Marbres du Roi au Louvre. His great-grandfather Louis Lerambert I (*c.* 1538–1614) contributed to the decoration of the Valois Chapel at Saint-Denis Abbey; his great-uncle Henri Lerambert (1550–1609) was well-known for his tapestry cartoons; and his father Simon Lerambert (1577–1637) specialized in the engraving and carving of epitaphs for tombs. Louis Lerambert trained in the studio of Simon Vouet, where he met Jacques Sarazin. In 1637 he inherited the appointment of Garde des Antiques et des Marbres. Skilled as a poet, musician and dancer, he was received at court, where he earned numerous commissions for decorative sculpture, portrait busts and tombs. Among the few surviving examples of these works are the stucco decorations in the chapel at the château of Bonne-Chamarande, Essone, executed for Pierre Mérault *c.* 1660, and allegorical low reliefs from the tomb of *Jean Courtin and his Wife* (1660; Blois Cathedral). Lerambert was received (*reçu*) into the Académie Royale de Peinture et de Sculpture, Paris, with a terracotta bust of *Cardinal Mazarin* in 1664 (untraced; marble version, 1664–9; Paris, Bib. Mazarine). He was among the first generation of sculptors to work for Louis XIV on the embellishment of the gardens at the château of Versailles, executing twelve stone terms (1664; destr.), as well as stone statues of *Pan*, a *Faun*, a *Hamadryad* and a *Nymph*, dancing or holding musical instruments (1665; destr.; both series known from engravings by Simon Thomassin and Jean Le Pautre). Among his surviving works at Versailles are the well-known pair of marble *Sphinxes* on the Parterre des Fleurs (1667–8), carved in collaboration with Jacques Houzeau from a model by Sarazin, and six of the delightful fountains with playing children for the Allée d'Eau (originally gilt lead, 1669; recast in bronze, 1688). With their wit, vivacity and delicacy, these latter works show that Lerambert was one of the most gifted sculptors of the first generation at Versailles. Antoine Coyzevox was among his pupils.

Lami; Souchal

BIBLIOGRAPHY

Guillet de Saint-Georges [A. C. Guillet]: 'Mémoire historique des principaux ouvrages de sculpture de M. Lerambert' (MS.; Paris, Ecole N. Sup. B.-A.); ed. L. Dussieux and others, in *Mémoires inédits sur la vie des membres de l'Académie Royale de Peinture et de Sculpture publiés d'après les manuscrits conservés à l'Ecole Impériale des Beaux-Arts*, i (Paris, 1854), pp. 330–36 [written before 1693]
S. Thomassin: *Recueil des statues, groupes, fontaines, termes, vases et autre magnifiques ornements du château et du parc de Versailles, gravés d'après les originaux par Simon Thomassin* (The Hague, 1723), pp. 82, 114–15, 124
J. Guiffrey: *Comptes des Bâtiments du Roi sous le règne de Louis XIV*, 5 vols (Paris, 1881–1901)
R. Le Blant: 'Les Lerambert, maçons, peintres et sculpteurs aux XVIème et XVIIème siècles', *99ème Congrès national des sociétés savantes* (Saint-Etienne, 1973), pp. 479–97

FRANÇOISE DE LA MOUREYRE

**Lergaard(-Nielsen), Niels (Christian)** (*b* Vorup, nr Randers, 10 Feb 1893; *d* 1982). Danish painter. He trained as a house painter and spent a few years in Norway, where he became interested in Norwegian landscape painting. After his return to Denmark he studied at the Kunstakademi, Copenhagen (1917–20); he later taught there (1956–64). His early paintings were mostly figure compositions and landscapes that reveal an expressive interpretation of his surroundings. In the late 1920s, when he moved to the island of Bornholm in the Baltic, his compositions first achieved the disciplined construction that came to characterize his work. He often took a particular place, especially Bornholm (e.g. *Landscape, Gudhjem*, 1932; Humlebæk, Louisiana Mus.), as the point of departure for his pictures. He painted the sea, with a high horizon, the coast, figures with precisely constructed silhouettes, or Bornholm's steep cliffs. Lergaard clarified pictorial space with great concentration: he composed rhythmically the distribution of heavy and light masses on the picture plane and managed to achieve a tangible, material intimacy while concentrating on the formal elements of the composition. The dark colours he used in the 1930s, as in *People in an Interior* (1937; ex-priv. col., see Rabén & Sjögren: *Lexikon över modern skandinavisk konst*, Stockholm, 1958, p. 139), were gradually replaced by a lighter palette. He worked to release new expressive possibilities from oil colours and in this way further emphasized the luminous power and depth of the picture plane. Thus his landscapes display a deeply symbolic, transcendent power.

BIBLIOGRAPHY

J. Zibrandtsen: *Moderne dansk kunst* (Copenhagen, 1969), pp. 200–06
H. Bramsen: 'Niels Lergaard', *Vort eget århundrede* [Our own century] (Copenhagen, 1975), v of *Dansk Kunsthistorie*, pp. 170–71
R. Gregersen: *Niels Lergaard* (Århus, 1981)

RIGMOR LOVRING

**Lérida, Seo Antigua.** *See* LLEIDA, SEU VELLA.

**Lérins Monastery.** Island monastery on Saint-Honorat, *c.* 3 km south-east of Cannes, France. It was founded *c.* AD 410 by St Honoratus of Arles (*d* 429), a Roman who had left northern Europe at the collapse of the empire, and it combined the traditions of the educated Roman élite and the ascetic desert fathers to create a centre of monastic spirituality and theology, a training ground for bishops and holy men unique in 5th-century Europe. At its height there were some 3700 monks living in solitary cells scattered across all four islands in the group. The

Rule of St Benedict, introduced *c.* 661, brought a greater element of common life to Lérins and probably prompted the building of the cloisters. This golden age came to an end in 732 with the first Saracen invasion. Regular life was re-established at Lérins by the 11th century; the community accumulated vast estates and privileges, with some 60 dependent priories on the mainland. From 1070 onwards numerous building projects included a new monastery–fortress, the church of Notre-Dame (destr. 1876) and the restoration of the basilical church of St Honorat (destr. *c.* 1870). The latter was recorded in 1835 as having a nave divided by two rows of six columns supporting a 'Gothic' vault. A secular abbot was imposed in 1464 despite papal protection; in 1788 the monastery and its four monks were secularized. In 1870 Lérins was given to the Cistercian Order.

Seven small chapels (several in ruins) remain from pre-Benedictine Lérins. The chapel of the Trinity, with its trefoil apses, has a short nave of two bays and a sanctuary covered by an elongated cupola on pendentives. The original roof was covered with Roman flat and fluted tiles (*tegulae* and *imbrices*). The octagonal chapel of the Transfiguration has a semicircular apse and cupola covering the sanctuary. Both buildings have been stripped of all decoration, making it difficult to assign dates. A stone capital of Syrian or Coptic design is preserved in the island's museum.

BIBLIOGRAPHY

V. Barralis: *Chronologia sanctorum & aliorum virorum illustrium, ac abbatum sacrae insulae Lerinensis* (Lyon, 1613)
H. Moris: *L'Abbaye de Lérins, histoire et monuments* (Paris, 1909)
F. Benoit: 'Les Chapelles triconques paléochrétiennes de la Trinité de Lérins et de la Goyole', *Riv. Archaeol. Crist.*, xxv (1949), pp. 149–54
F. Prinz: *Frühes Mönchtum im Frankenreich: Kultur und Gesellschaft in Gallien, den Rheinlanden und Bayern am Beispiel der monastischen Entwicklung* (Munich and Vienna, 1965)

☐

**Lerma.** Spanish town on a hill overlooking the Arlanza River, *c.* 45 km south of Burgos. The central core of the town was founded in antiquity and, after it had been recaptured from the Moors, was walled in towards the end of the 9th century. In 1599 the 5th Marqués de Denia and 4th Conde de Lerma was created Duque de Lerma (*see* SANDOVAL Y ROJAS, (1)). In 1600 the new Duque made Lerma the capital of his estates and between 1601 and 1617 built there the most important urban–rural conglomerate of the 17th century in Spain, comparable to Valladolid (capital of the Spanish empire from 1601 to 1605), with its palace and gardens, and to the Aranjuez Palace. With the aid of the royal architect, Francisco de Mora (*see* MORA, DE, (1)), the Duque designed the estate's buildings, landscaping and environs, placing the town within woods and cultivated land and creating gardens and a park, making use of existing watercourses and building canals.

The Duque also transformed the town itself, converting the medieval castle into a ducal palace (1618), with corner towers by Juan Gómez de Mora, built round a central court. The palace faced the Plaza Ducal (see fig.), with arcades and porticos built in imitation of that before the Alcázar in Madrid, designed by Juan Bautista de Toledo. Reflecting the Counter-Reformation ethos of the Spanish nobility of the time, various religious foundations were

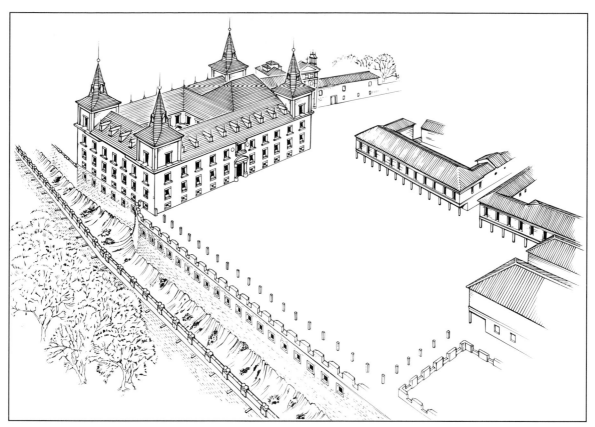

Lerma, Plaza Ducal, by Francisco de Mora, *c.* 1618; reconstruction drawing showing the Palacio Ducal and (in schematic form) porticos leading to conventual buildings

built around the square: the monasteries of S Blas, S Teresa, Asuención de Nuestro Señor, S Domingo, Nuestra Señora de S Vicente, S Francisco de los Reyes, Madre de Dios and the collegiate church of S Pedro (1606–16), most of which were connected to the palace by corridors. This scheme, which followed the architectural aesthetic principles expressed in the Escorial by Juan Bautista de Toledo and Juan de Herrera, was also the work of Francisco de Mora, together with his nephew Juan Gómez de Mora and the Carmelite Alberto de la Madre de Dios ( *fl* 1611).

As the King's chief minister, the Duque de Lerma was frequently the host of the royal family and members of the Spanish and foreign nobility, and it was in Lerma that Rubens painted his celebrated equestrian portrait of the *Duque de Lerma* (1603; Madrid, Prado). The town's heyday ended in 1618, when implication in a conspiracy caused the Duque to lose the King's favour and go into exile. Despite the sack of Lerma by the French during the War of Independence (or Peninsular War, 1808–13), the palace complex is relatively well preserved.

### BIBLIOGRAPHY

G. Kubler: *Arquitectura de los siglos XVII y XVIII*, A. Hisp. (1957)
F. J. Sánchez Cantón: 'La ciudad de Lerma', *Academia: Bol. Real Acad. B.A. San Fernando*, xx (1960)
L. Cervera Vera: *El conjunto palacial de la villa de Lerma* (Valencia, 1967)
*Resumen histórico del urbanismo en España* (Madrid, 1968)
L. Cervera Vera: *El núcleo urbano de Lerma desde sus orígenes al siglo XI* (Burgos, 1971)
——: *La iglesia colegial de San Pedro en Lerma* (Burgos, 1981)
——: *Lerma: Síntesis histórico-monumental* (Lerma, 1982)
J. Rivera: 'Catálogo', *Herrera y el clasicismo* (Valladolid, 1986)

JAVIER RIVERA

**Lerma**, Duque de. *See* SANDOVAL Y ROJAS, (1).

**Lermolieff, Ivan.** *See* MORELLI, GIOVANNI.

**Lerna.** Prehistoric coastal site in the Argolid, Greece, that flourished from the Neolithic period to the Late Bronze Age. It is located at the modern village of Myloi on the western shore of the Bay of Nauplion. North of the site, beside the stream Amymone, lie the Lernaian springs and marshes, mythical home of the Hydra, the many-headed monster slain by Herakles. Visible as a low mound of accumulated habitation debris, the site was noted as pre-Classical in the early 1900s. Excavations conducted from 1952 to 1958 by John L. Caskey, Director of the American School of Classical Studies at Athens, uncovered a prehistoric settlement of major importance. Lerna is significant because an undisturbed sequence of strata dating from Neolithic to Mycenaean times was preserved, enabling archaeologists to reconstruct a continuous picture of human life in prehistoric times on the mainland of Greece. Excavated material is housed in the Archaeological Museum of Argos. Architectural remains from each period have been preserved on the site for visitors.

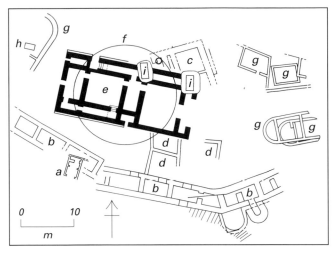

Lerna, *c.* 3600–*c.* 1500 BC, plan: (a) Neolithic house; (b) EH II fortification wall; (c) EH II monumental building; (d) EH II houses; (e) EH II House of the Tiles; (f) stone circle; (g) MH houses; (h) MH grave; (i) LH I shaft graves

During the three phases of Neolithic (to *c.* 3600 BC; Lerna periods I and II) the settlement was made up of houses with small rooms of rectangular plan (see fig.). An outstanding find among the pottery and other domestic objects of clay, stone and bone was a terracotta statuette (Lerna inventory no. L6.100), a remarkable example of naturalistic rendering of the female figure in Neolithic art. Without a break the site continued to be occupied in the Early Bronze Age. By Early Helladic (EH) II (*c.* 2900/2600–*c.* 2400 BC; Lerna period III) it had become a major political centre surrounded by a massive fortification wall. Built and rebuilt over a long period of time, the wall has partitions dividing the interior space into rooms, projecting towers, and a gateway entered by a road leading up from the sea. Among the small, ordinary houses of Lerna III was a series of monumental buildings that culminated in the House of the Tiles, one of the most imposing buildings known from prehistoric Greece. Named from the thousands of terracotta tiles used for the roof, the building (25×12 m) has been reconstructed as a two-storey structure of a type known as a 'corridor house', named after the narrow corridors on its long sides. Bronze was first used for tools and weapons in this period. The pottery is primarily monochrome: the most typical shapes are the 'sauceboat' and small saucer (*see* HELLADIC, §III, 2). A large number of clay lumps, burnt in a fire, had originally been used to close storage containers and were stamped with decorated seals (*see* HELLADIC, §X and fig. 23). These sealings, along with roller-impressed pithoi and hearths, potter's marks and monumental architecture, are evidence of a developed social and economic system.

Lerna III was destroyed by fire, and the debris of the House of the Tiles was heaped up and surrounded by a circle of stones. The immediately succeeding settlement of EH III (*c.* 2400–*c.* 2050 BC; Lerna period IV) marked the only drastic cultural break in the history of the site. Houses were small, of one or two rectangular rooms, some with rounded or apsidal ends. New ceramic technology, the potter's wheel and new wares, most notably Grey Minyan,

were introduced. The site may have lost the importance it had achieved in EH II but not its contacts with other areas of the Aegean: among other imports was a large jar from Troy (Lerna inventory no. L.22). The Middle Helladic settlement (*c.* 2050–*c.* 1600 BC; Lerna period V) directly followed from the preceding. The major change was in the pottery: Matt-painted and Lustrous-decorated wares replaced the earlier Patterned ware and many imports began to arrive from Crete, the Cyclades and Aigina. By the end of the period larger houses with more rooms and a drainage system were being built. The number of intramural burials with offerings of pottery and other objects increased. The early Mycenaean period (Lerna period VI) is best represented by two large shaft graves of the type well known from the grave circles at Mycenae. House walls and pottery demonstrate that the site continued to be occupied until Late Helladic IIIB (*c.* 1335–*c.* 1180 BC; Lerna period VII). Erosion of the mound has destroyed most of its later history, but there is evidence of human activity throughout antiquity.

BIBLIOGRAPHY

J. L. Caskey: 'Excavations at Lerna', *Hesperia*, xxiii (1954), pp. 3–30; xxiv (1955), pp. 25–49; xxv (1956), pp. 147–73; xxvi (1957), pp. 142–62; xxvii (1958), pp. 125–44

N.-G. Gejvall: *The Fauna* (1969), i of *Lerna* (Princeton, 1969–71)

J. L. Angel: *The People* (1971), ii of *Lerna* (Princeton, 1969–71)

CAROL ZERNER

**Lerner, Jaime** (*b* Curitiba, 17 Dec 1937). Brazilian urban planner. He graduated as an engineer (1960) and an architect (1964) from the Federal University of Paraná, Curitiba, and then developed an active career as an urban planner. He was Prefect of Curitiba in 1971–5, 1979–83 and from 1989, during which time a profound physical, cultural, economic and social transformation of the city was achieved. By giving priority to traffic problems, health and sanitation, leisure and industrialization, Lerner made Curitiba (pop. 1.5 million) a model of urban planning. His approach to planning was essentially humanist, concentrating on the need for citizens to identify with their urban environment through the development of cultural activities, to build at a human scale, to use infrastructure and service networks more efficiently, including the conservation and re-use of old buildings, and to mix functions, social classes and age groups. He also concentrated on the need for better management by the administrators of the city. Lerner subsequently prepared urban plans for most of the principal cities of Brazil including Recife (1975), Salvador (1976), Goiânia (1975), Campo Grande (1977), Aracajú (1976), João Pessoa (1978), Niterói (1978) and São Paulo (1975), as well as for Caracas, Venezuela (1975), and San Juan, Puerto Rico (1987). In 1983–6 he was Consultant to the State Government and Prefecture of Rio de Janeiro in implementing the programme Rio Ano 2000, starting with the improvement of mass transport and the revitalization of the historic centre of the old capital of the republic. Lerner taught urban and regional planning at the Federal University of Paraná and was a visiting professor at the University of California, Berkeley; he also acted as urban planning consultant to the United Nations and was appointed to the United Nations Environment Council in 1990.

WRITINGS

*Londrina: A situação 66* (1966)
*A cidade: Cenário do encontro* (1977)
*The City and Scala: One Turn Less of the Screw* (1982)

BIBLIOGRAPHY

*Brasil Post* (30 June 1991)
J. Maier jr: *Time* (14 Oct 1991), p. 44
M. Margolis: *Newsweek* (14 Oct 1991)

REGINA MARIA PROSPERI MEYER

**Leroi-Gourhan, André** (*b* Paris, 25 Aug 1911; *d* Paris, 19 Feb 1986). French social anthropologist, prehistorian and philosopher. He created the French school of 'cultural Technology' studies with his key concepts of *chaîne opératoire* and *tendance technique*. In *L'Homme et la matière* (1943–5) he analysed the relations between physical matter, technical constraints and style. In *Le Geste et la parole* (1964–5) he combined technology, physical anthropology, prehistory and philosophy into a 'programmatology' to describe the interrelationships between the physical evolution of mankind, the evolution of his cognitive abilities, the evolution of techniques in tool manufacture and the role played by style and symbolism. The excavation methods he applied to Upper Palaeolithic occupation levels have led to the formation of the school of 'prehistoric ethnology' dedicated to the reconstruction of prehistoric life and activities, as exemplified by the Magdalenian settlement of Pincevent (*see* PREHISTORIC EUROPE, §§I and II). His contribution to the study of prehistoric art represents a complete break with previous conceptions. Using a structuralist approach, he built a comprehensive theory including all Franco-Cantabrian Palaeolithic cave and portable art. After identifying several regional styles and four different chronological stylistic divisions (*see* PREHISTORIC EUROPE, fig. 9), he argued for the existence in painted caves of a general symbolic structure based on the opposition between groups of animal species associated with abstract signs symbolizing male and female principles. He considered caves to be sanctuaries, the topographic features of which also had a symbolic value that determined the type of animals or signs painted or engraved on the walls (*see* PREHISTORIC EUROPE, §II, 2(v)).

WRITINGS

*L'Homme et la matière*, 2 vols (Paris, 1943–5)
*Les Religions de la préhistoire* (Paris, 1964, rev. 3/1976)
*Le Geste et la parole*, 2 vols (Paris, 1964–5; Eng. trans., Cambridge, MA, 1993)
*Préhistoire de l'art occidental* (Paris, 1965); Eng. trans. as *Treasures of Prehistoric Art* (New York, 1967)
with others: *Fouilles de Pincevent: Essai d'analyse ethnographique d'un habitat magdalénien (la section 36)* (Paris, 1972)

FRANÇOISE AUDOUZE

**Le Roith, Harold (Hirsch)** (*b* 24 March 1905). South African architect. He was brought up in the Eastern Cape Province. He completed his architectural degree in 1934 at the University of the Witwatersrand, where he was one of the first generation of students to benefit from the revolution in architectural education initiated by Rex Martienssen. He began practice in Johannesburg in 1935. In his architecture he responded to the economic pressures of the market-place while successfully resisting their corrupting influence. In addition to some interesting industrial buildings, his work before World War II included two modern blocks of flats in Johannesburg of outstanding architectural merit, with strong plastic forms and a richer palette of materials than was customary in the rather purist avant-garde work of the period: Radoma Court (1937–8) and Illovo Mansions, Dunkeld (1937–9). Le Roith's most important assistant at this time, whose hand is felt in these designs, was the talented young Kurt Jonas, whose death in Jerusalem in 1942 put an end to a most promising career. Also of this early period was an elegant office block on a restricted city site, Washington House (1938), which combined a highly efficient plan with an interlocking street façade of great subtlety; and several fine private houses.

In the 1950s Le Roith's work expanded in range, scale and scope. One of his tall blocks of flats of this period, situated in the densely developed Hillbrow, a suburb of Johannesburg, was Groot Drakenstein (*c.* 1950): with its grid façade and recessed balconies, it is prototypical of the pervasive style of modern architecture that Nikolaus Pevsner was later to call the 'Johannesburg vernacular'. Le Roith's special contribution to the development of the Modern Movement in South Africa is best summed up in buildings such as this. His success lay in his popularization of modern architecture, translating it from an élitist movement to a broadly acceptable, and commercially viable, style.

BIBLIOGRAPHY

*Archit. Rev.*, 10 (1944) [special issue on South African architecture]
G. Herbert: *Martienssen and the International Style: The Modern Movement in South African Architecture* (Cape Town, 1975)

GILBERT HERBERT

**Lerolle, Henry** (*b* Paris, 3 Oct 1848; *d* Paris, 22 April 1929). French painter and collector. He was initially a pupil of Louis Lamothe (1822–69) in 1864 but never went to the École des Beaux-Arts. Independent in outlook, he began working in the Louvre, where he met Albert Besnard and Jean-Louis Forain, and made copies after Nicolas Poussin, Veronese and Peter Paul Rubens. He attended the Académie Suisse and exhibited at the Salon from 1868. Having briefly been influenced by Henri Regnault, Lerolle painted works that owed much to the scenes of contemporary life by Jules Bastien-Lepage, Henri Gervex, Alfred Roll and Jean Charles Cazin, who introduced the taste for naturalistic observation, bright colouring and *plein-air* painting to the official Salons. *At the Organ* (exh. Salon 1885; New York, Met.) and *At the Water's Edge* (1888; Boston, MA, Mus. F.A.) disseminated in more accessible terms the still controversial innovations of Edouard Manet and the Impressionists. Lerolle's concern for the structure of his compositions, in which the figures were sometimes off-centre, can be seen in his portraits, such as the *Artist's Mother* (exh. Salon 1895; Paris, Mus. d'Orsay), whose spare, austere realism is reminiscent of Henri Fantin-Latour and James Abbott McNeill Whistler.

Lerolle is known above all for his religious paintings: *Jacob in the House of Laban* (exh. Salon, 1879; Nice, Mus. B.-A.) and the *Adoration of the Shepherds* (1889; Carcassonne, Mus. B.-A.). He also executed many mural decorations in Paris, in which he combined allegory with contemporary dress: *Albert the Great* (1889; Sorbonne), *Christ Appearing to St Martin* (1890; St-Martin-des-Champs), the *Crowning of Science* and the *Teaching of Science*

(1889; both Hôtel de Ville). He decorated the salon of the composer Ernest Chausson (1855–99) at 22 Boulevard de Courcelles, Paris, in 18th-century taste, with airy figures and an animated sense of space. Lerolle was a founder-member of the Société Nationale des Beaux-Arts in 1890.

In 1883 Lerolle bought Puvis de Chavannes's *Prodigal Son* (1879; Zurich, Stift. Samml. Bührle) and two pastels by Edgar Degas. A knowledgeable collector, he owned works by Fantin-Latour, Albert Besnard, Jean-Baptiste-Camille Corot and Auguste Renoir. His wife was painted by Fantin-Latour (1882; Cleveland, OH, Mus. A.) and Renoir painted his daughters at the piano (1892; Paris, Mus. Orangerie). Lerolle's salon was attended by painters, poets and musicians, such as his biographer Maurice Denis, Stéphane Mallarmé, Octave Maus, Paul-Louis-Charles-Marie Claudel, André Gide, Claude Debussy, Degas and Renoir. Lerolle was a violinist and a pupil of Edouard Colonne (1838–1910). Through Ernest Chausson, who married his wife's sister, he discovered modern music, becoming an enthusiastic admirer of César Franck (1822–90).

BIBLIOGRAPHY

M. Denis: *Henry Lerolle et ses amis* (Paris, 1932)
*Le Triomphe des mairies* (exh. cat., Paris, Petit Pal., 1986), pp. 316–17

VALÉRIE M. C. BAJOU

**Leroulx-Delaville, Marie-Guillemine.** *See* BENOIST, MARIE-GUILLEMINE.

**Le Roux** [Leroux]. French family of architects. (1) Jacques Le Roux and his nephew, (2) Roulland Le Roux, were successive Masters of the Works of Rouen Cathedral. While the work of Jacques summarized the deeply rooted traditions of Flamboyant architecture in Rouen, Roulland introduced Renaissance style to the city in his design of secular buildings such as the Bureau des Finances.

**(1) Jacques** [Jacobus] **Le Roux** (*fl* 1489; *d* Rouen, before 24 March 1510). On 15 September 1489 he signed a contract with the abbot of La Trinité, Fécamp, to construct the axial Lady chapel. In 1496 he replaced Guillaume Pontis (*fl* 1443; *d* 1497) as Master of the Works at Rouen Cathedral. For the next 10 years he was occupied with finishing the south-west tower, the Tour de Beurre, begun by Pontis in 1487. Owing to lack of money and to the cathedral chapter's indecisiveness over the nature of the termination, work progressed slowly and the octagonal crown of the tower was not completed until 1507. Plans for a new central portal for the cathedral façade, signed by both Jacques and Roulland, were displayed in the Hôtel de Ville on 28 January 1508; shortly afterwards Jacques requested that Roulland replace him as Master of the Works. He was buried in the nave of the cathedral near the organ.

Jacques's name is associated with other Flamboyant works in Rouen. In 1492 he is documented as Master of the Works of the parish church of St Maclou, although his role there was probably supervisory. In an expertise ordered by the city councillors of Rouen on 12 September 1502 for the construction of the Salle des Pas-Perdus at the Palais de Justice, Jacques made recommendations for strengthening the southern terminal wall; his name has consequently often been associated with its design (*see*

ROUEN, fig. 2). Jacques's surviving works are characterized by the use of continuous prismatic mouldings and fillet bases, fluid double-curved cusped tracery, dense linear articulation with lush foliate bands of floral decoration executed with dazzling technical virtuosity. These features are typical of late 15th-century Flamboyant architecture in Rouen and are indistinguishable from those used by Pontis.

**(2) Roulland** [Roullant; Rouland; Roulant] **Le Roux** (*fl* 1508; *d* Rouen, ?1527). Nephew of (1) Jacques Le Roux. He succeeded Jacques as Master of the Works of Rouen Cathedral on 3 February 1510 and immediately undertook the reconstruction of the central portal of the west façade. Its gables and niches harmonize with the older Gothic work, and the design of the inner west wall is one of the masterpieces of late Flamboyant. Severe structural damage to the western nave vaults, rose window and portal was caused by the removal of the two lateral south nave walls when the chapel of St Etienne was built below the Tour de Beurre. After the crossing spire was destroyed by fire in 1514, Roulland reinforced the 13th-century tower base and built a new two-storey lantern.

As Master Mason to the City of Rouen and to the King of France, he was involved shortly after 1508 in the construction of the Grande Chambre du Parlement, attached to the Salle des Pas-Perdus, and between 1510 and 1512 he worked on the new Bureau des Finances; both schemes were under the patronage of Louis XII. The influence on Roulland of the Italian masons and sculptors brought to the Château de Gaillon in 1508 by the Archbishop of Rouen, Cardinal Georges I d'Amboise, is apparent in the new Renaissance forms, including medallions supported by putti, rinceaux reliefs and pilasters, used to articulate the façade of the Bureau des Finances. This new style is given full expression in Roulland's design of the large and elaborate tomb of Georges I d'Amboise in the Lady chapel of Rouen Cathedral, undertaken 10 years after the Cardinal's death in 1520, which bears no trace of Gothic motifs (for illustration *see* AMBOISE, (1)). The contrast in style between this tomb and the cathedral west portal demonstrates Roulland's versatility as an architect/designer of the Late Gothic and early Renaissance periods.

BIBLIOGRAPHY

A. Deville: *Revue des architectes de la cathédrale de Rouen jusqu'à la fin du XVIe siècle* (Rouen, 1848)
A. Lance: *Dictionnaire des architectes français*, 2 vols (Paris, 1872)
C. de Robillard de Beaurepaire: *Bull. Comm. Ant. Dépt Seine-Inférieure*, iv (1876–8), pp. 82–91 [publishes contract of Jacques Le Roux with La Trinité, Fécamp]
C. Bauchal: *Nouveau dictionnaire biographique et critique des architectes français* (Paris, 1887)
C. de Robillard de Beaurepaire: 'Notes sur les architectes de Rouen', *Bull. Amis Mnmts Rouen.* (1903), pp. 63–8 [1450–1500]; (1904–6), pp. 119–30 [1500–50]
Y. Bottineau-Fuchs: 'Maître d'oeuvre, maître d'ouvrage: Les Le Roux et le chapitre de la cathédrale de Rouen', *Colloque international associé du centre national de la recherche scientifique. Artistes, artisans et production artistique au moyen âge: Rennes, 1983*, i, pp. 183–95

For further bibliography, *see* ROUEN, §IV, 1(i).

L. E. NEAGLEY

**Leroux** [Le Roux], **(Louis) Hector** (*b* Verdun, 27 Dec 1829; *d* Angers, 11 Nov 1900). French painter. He trained and briefly worked as a wig-maker in Verdun while also following a drawing course at the local art college. His success in winning all the art prizes earned him a small bursary to continue his studies in Paris. He entered the Ecole des Beaux-Arts in 1849, working in the studio of François-Edouard Picot and supplementing his income by producing copies of museum works and illustrations. In 1857 he won the Deuxième Prix de Rome and spent the next 17 years based in Rome, travelling from there to the rest of Italy, to Greece, Asia Minor, Turkey and Egypt, with occasional visits to Paris. Soon after arriving in Rome he received a state commission to paint a copy of Titian's *Sacred and Profane Love* (*c.* 1515; Rome, Gal. Borghese) and also copied works for the Gobelins. His début at the Salon was made in 1863 with *A New Vestal Virgin* (1863; Verdun, Mus. Princerie). From this time he painted almost entirely classical subjects, for example *Roman Ladies at the Tomb of their Ancestors* (New York, Met.). In *Miracle of the Good Goddess* (1869; Ajaccio, Mus. Fesch), he treated a legend featuring a vestal virgin, one of his favourite themes. He occasionally painted biblical or historical subjects, which, as with all his work, were in an undistinguished academic style. His daughter Laura Leroux was also a painter.

BIBLIOGRAPHY

R. Ménard: *L'Art en Alsace-Lorraine* (Paris, 1876), pp. 441–3

E. Montrosier: *Les Artistes modernes*, i (Paris, 1881), pp. 105–8

**Le Roux, Jean-Baptiste** (*b c.* 1677; *d* 13 July 1746). French architect and designer. He was a pupil of François d'Orbay and had some early success as an interior designer and decorator, publishing with Jean Langlois before 1705 a series of six prints entitled *Nouveaux lambris de galeries, chambres et cabinets*. He also developed a thriving architectural practice in Paris. His earliest surviving town house is the Hôtel d'Avaray (85, Rue de Grenelle; now the Dutch Embassy), a restrained three-storey building. The garden façade has a slightly projecting central pavilion of three bays, with wide quoins and a pediment enclosing the owner's coat of arms. Le Roux employed the mason Charles Boscry to work on the house from 1720 to 1721; during the same period he built the Hôtel du Prat (1720; 60, Rue de Varenne).

In 1724 Le Roux obtained his first commission from the Maréchal de Roquelaure, who became an important client; this followed the death of the architect Pierre Lassurance I, when Le Roux was asked to complete the alterations to the Maréchal's town house at 244, Boulevard Saint-Germain (now the Ministère de l'Equipement). He carried out the entire interior decoration of the house in a restrained and orderly Rococo style (engraved; a small salon survives) and also designed the portal of the *cour d'honneur*. The Maréchal commissioned him to undertake further alterations to his town house in 1733, when Le Roux employed Nicolas Pineau to decorate the Maréchal's bedroom. The Maréchal also employed Le Roux at his château d'Athis (1736), near Paris, although there is no surviving evidence of the work undertaken. The decoration of the Hôtel Bonnier de la Mosson (1726–8; destr.), beside the Hôtel de Roquelaure, is also attributed to Le Roux, and in 1729 he received the commission for the Hôtel Bourgeois de Boines (3, Rue d'Antin; now the Banque de

Paris et des Pays-Bas; drawings, Paris, Archvs N.), in which the sculpted decoration is by Nicolas Pineau and Charles Bernard.

Le Roux appears from about 1730 to have passed on much of his decorative design work to ornamental sculptors, having by then firmly established himself as an architect, and he was one of a number of architects particularly enthusiastic about and supportive of the decorative sculptor Nicolas Pineau. As a result, however, he was accused by Jacques-François Blondel of not being able to design a proper decorative scheme. Le Roux's decorative masterpiece was created with the construction of the gallery (1731–3; destr. 19th century) added to the town house of the Maréchal de Villars in the Rue de Grenelle. In this gallery, however, the essential part of the overall effect came from the pier-glass with rich sculpted borders surmounted by paintings copied from famous masters. The gallery was engraved by Jacques-François Blondel in a collection published in 1746; surviving carved mirror surrounds and other ornamental features by Nicolas Pineau and Charles Bernard are preserved at Waddesdon Manor, Bucks (NT), and Mentmore Towers, Bucks (for illustration *see* PINEAU, NICOLAS). Another successful work, according to contemporaries, was commissioned by the Marquise de La Vrillière (later the Duchesse de Mazarin), for whom in 1736 he redesigned a town house at 61, Rue de Varenne (one wing survives, though altered), which had already been altered by Germain Boffrand. The interior was decorated by Pineau and the overdoors painted by François Boucher, Charles-Joseph Natoire and Jacques de Lajoüe. He also added an oval dining-room, housed in a rounded pavilion, to the Hôtel de Villeroy (78, Rue de Varenne); the decoration has been destroyed but is known from engravings. Le Roux's buildings, although often not very original, were nevertheless among the most pleasing of their time and were noted especially for their rich decoration, for which he chose the best among contemporary sculptors and decorators.

WRITINGS

*Divers dessins de cheminées de la composition du Sieur Le Roux, architecte* (Paris, n.d.)

PRINTS

*Nouveaux lambris de galeries, chambres et cabinets* (Paris, n.d.)

BIBLIOGRAPHY

S. de Groter: *L'Hôtel d'Avaray* (Paris, n.d.)

J.-F. Blondel: *L'Architecture française*, 8 vols (Paris, 1752–6/*R* 1904–5)

C.-A. Jombert: *Répertoire des artistes*, i (Paris, 1755), p. 11

J.-F. Blondel: *L'Homme du monde éclairé par les arts*, ii (Paris, 1774), p. 295

*La Rue de Varenne* (exh. cat., Paris, Mus. Rodin, 1981), pp. 40–45, 61–2

*La Rue Saint-Dominique, hôtels et amateurs* (exh. cat., Paris, Mus. Rodin, 1984), pp. 73, 151, 164–5

BRUNO PONS

**Leroy, Jules** (*b* Ablis, Dépt Yvelines, 10 April 1903; *d* Captelat, nr Limoges, 8 April 1979). French clergyman and art historian. In 1933 he obtained his degree in biblical studies from the Istituto Pontificio Biblico in Rome and in the following year moved to Paris where he taught until 1954. Meanwhile he attended lectures given by André Grabar at the Ecole Pratique des Hautes Etudes and studied illuminated Syriac manuscripts, first in Paris, then in Italy and Great Britain. From October 1954 to September 1956 Leroy travelled in Lebanon, Syria, Iraq and Turkey as a member of the Institut Français d'Archéologie de Beyrouth, studying and photographing illuminated Syriac manuscripts that he found in churches and monasteries from Tur 'Abdin to Sinai. The results of his considerable research appear in his major publication, *Les Manuscrits syriaques* (1964). Leroy became a researcher for the Centre National de la Recherche Scientifique in 1956, and later Director of the archaeological section of the Institut d'Etudes et de Recherches d'Ethiopie at Addis Ababa. He developed an interest in Ethiopian manuscript illumination and painting that resulted in a number of published studies. He subsequently devoted himself to Coptic art: mural paintings as well as illustrated manuscripts. He embarked on a complete survey of Coptic wall painting, although he was able to complete only two volumes, covering the Esna desert and Wādi'l-Natrun.

### WRITINGS
*Les Manuscrits syriaques à peintures conservés dans les bibliothèques d'Europe et d'Orient. Contribution à l'étude de l'iconographie des églises de langue syriaque*, 2 vols (Paris, 1964)
*Les Manuscrits coptes et coptes-arabes illustrés* (Paris, 1974)
*La Peinture murale chez les Coptes*, 2 vols (Cairo, 1975–82)

### BIBLIOGRAPHY
R. G. Coquin: Obituary, *Bull. Inst. Fr. Archéol. Orient.*, lxxx (1980), pp. 5–14 [with bibliog.]

A. N. PALMER, J. VAN GINKEL

**Le Roy** [Leroy], **Julien-David** (*b* Paris, 6 May 1724; *d* ?Paris, 27/28 Jan 1803). French architect and writer. He trained under Jacques-François Blondel and Jean-Laurent Legeay and won the Prix de Rome in 1750, having been placed second the preceding year (drawings, Paris, Ecole B.-A.). While in Rome (1751–4) he sketched the frescoes by Annibale Carracci in the Palazzo Farnese, and in 1754 he obtained permission to visit Athens. Travelling via Pula and Constantinople (now Istanbul) to Greece, he arrived only weeks after the departure of James Stuart and Nicholas Revett, both architects from the English community in Rome. After visiting Delos, he spent some months sketching and measuring in Athens. He also visited Corinth and Sparta, returning in 1755 via Rome to Paris. There, assisted by the Comte de Caylus and a team of draughtsmen and engravers that included Louis-Joseph Le Lorrain, Pierre-Charles Le Mettay and JEAN-FRANÇOIS DE NEUFFORGE, he began an intensive effort to prepare his book *Les Ruines des plus beaux monuments de la Grèce* (1758) for publication before a work on the same subject by Stuart and Revett. Le Roy's book comprises two sections, the first describing his travels in Greece, the second expounding his theories of Greek architecture, in which he suggests that the question of proportion might need to be re-examined in the light of his researches and that the judgement of Vitruvius was not impeccable, nor even followed by the Romans themselves on the evidence of surviving monuments. In addition, Le Roy's work gave his contemporaries a better understanding of the development of the Greek Doric order, which he classified into three phases, and he was the first to publish in detail the Greek Ionic order, which was quite different from that used in the 18th century. Le Roy's book influenced many contemporary architects, including Jacques-Denis Antoine, Jean-Arnaud Raymond, Alexandre-Théodore Brongniart and François-Joseph Bélanger. Soon after the publication of his book, Le Roy became a member of the

Académie Royale d'Architecture and was appointed assistant to Blondel, the professor. In 1762 Stuart and Revett published the first volume of their own *Antiquities of Athens*, in which they criticized a number of inaccuracies in Le Roy's work. He later defended himself in a booklet published in 1764 and in a second edition of the *Ruines* (1770).

Following the destruction of the municipal hospital (the Hôtel Dieu), Paris, in 1772, Le Roy submitted plans for its reconstruction, after those by Bernard Poyet, among others, had been rejected. He proposed a series of isolated buildings laid out in parallel lines, but the scheme was thwarted by the Revolution (1789–95). In 1774 he succeeded Blondel as professor at the Académie Royale d'Architecture. The following year he redesigned part of the park at the château of Chantilly in the style of an English landscape garden, emphasizing the complementary nature of Neo-classicism and Romanticism. In 1780 he submitted competition designs (unexecuted) to complete Ange-Jacques Gabriel's work at Versailles, and after 1789 he was a member of the commission supervising the new Musée d'Arts (now the Louvre). He continued to teach after the Académie was abolished in 1793 and was instrumental in the establishment of the Ecole Spéciale d'Architecture in 1795; he was a founder-member of the Institut de France.

### WRITINGS
*Les Ruines des plus beaux monuments de la Grèce* (Paris, 1758)
*Histoire des formes différentes que les chrétiens ont données à leurs temples* (Paris, 1764)
*Observations sur les édifices des anciens peuples* (Paris, 1767)

### BIBLIOGRAPHY
L. Hautecoeur: *Architecture classique*, iv (1952)
P. Collins: *Changing Ideals in Modern Architecture, 1750–1950* (London, 1965)
D. Wiebenson: *Sources of Greek Revival Architecture* (London, 1969)
A. Braham: *The Architecture of the French Enlightenment* (London, 1980, 2/1989)

GÉRARD ROUSSET CHARNY

**Leroy, Louis (Joseph)** (*b* Paris, 1812; *d* Paris, 1885). French critic and painter. He painted landscapes and showed at the Salon between 1835 and 1861. He exhibited mainly scenes of the Fontainebleau forest, an area made famous by the Barbizon school and also depicted by the Impressionists. In the 1860s he singled out Manet for attack, complaining that his work lacked the high finish and concern for detail that he admired in academic art. He is, however, remembered chiefly for his article of 25 April 1874 in the satirical magazine *Le Charivari*, which criticizes the first Impressionist exhibition, though his hostility to avant-garde art was already well established. His frequent punning use of the term 'impression' has led to his being credited with giving the movement its name, though it was in use by others. He dismissed Claude Monet's *Impression, Sunrise* (1873; Paris, Mus. Marmottan; *see* IMPRESSIONISM, fig. 1) as less finished than half-manufactured wallpaper and castigated the entire Impressionist group as 'hostile to good manners, to devotion to form, and respect for the masters'. Though much maligned for his aversion to Impressionism, his criticism is well informed, and the aspects he attacked indicate what was novel about the emerging style.

WRITINGS

'L'Exposition des Impressionnistes', *Le Charivari* (25 April 1874), pp. 2–3; abridged Eng. trans. in Rewald, pp. 256–61

BIBLIOGRAPHY

J. Rewald: *The History of Impressionism* (New York, 1946, rev. 4/1973)

G. H. Hamilton: *Manet and his Critics* (New Haven, 1954, New York, 2/1969)

S. Monneret: *L'Impressionnisme et son époque: Dictionnaire international*, 2 vols (Paris, 1978–9)

E. D. LILLEY

**Le Roy, Philibert** (*d* Paris, 1636). French architect and engineer. He was a noble gentleman and Lord of the Poterie, near Saint-Arnould (Seine-et-Oise), and was probably not related to the 'honourable' dynasty of Le Roy, master-masons (Jacques Le Roy, *d* 1599, and Marcel Le Roy, *d* 1647). In 1623 he was engineer to Charles d'Angoulême (1573–1650) and submitted a proposal (unexecuted) to dig a canal linking the rivers Marne and Seine in order to fill the Paris moats and create a port near the hospital of St Louis. In January 1626 he was appointed architect to Jean Baptiste Gaston, Duc d'Orléans (1608–60), and in November 1627 and March 1631 he was Architecte Ordinaire of the King's works. He was in charge of work at Versailles, under Louis XIII and built the Salle du Jeu de Paume there in 1629, as well as the second château (1631–6), consisting of three wings enclosing a quadrangle (the inner façades of the wings survive, somewhat altered, in the Cour de Marbre within the château). He revised the plans drawn up by Christophe Gamard (*d* 1649) for the church of St Sulpice, Paris (four drawings signed by Le Roy and dated 1636; Paris, Bib. N. Cab. Est.). In October 1639 he supervised various projects at the château of Wideville (Yvelines), including the construction of garden buildings, a gallery with aviaries and a boules court, and park walls. Le Roy was resident in Paris, at the Hôtel d'Angoulême, Rue Pavée, and, from 1631, in a house that he built for himself in the Rue Neuve Saint-Louis (now Rue de Turenne).

BIBLIOGRAPHY

L. Bariffol: 'Le Château de Versailles et son architecte Philibert Le Roy', *Gaz. B.-A.*, xi (1911), pp. 341–71

M. Dumolin: *Etudes de topographie parisienne* (Paris, 1929), i, p. 359; iii, pp. 176–7

M. Charageat: 'Actes divers concernant Wideville', *Bull. Soc. Hist. A. Fr.* (1936), pp. 172–8

CLAUDE MIGNOT

**Leroy** [Le Roy], **Pierre-François** (*b* Namur, 14 Jan 1739; *d* Brussels, 27 June 1812). Flemish sculptor. Travelling to Paris for the first time in 1753, he attended the courses at the Académie Royale de Peinture et de Sculpture and frequented the studio of Jacques Verberckt, who was at that time occupied on decorative sculpture at the château of Versailles. On returning to Namur, Leroy was made a master sculptor in 1755 and was entrusted with various works for religious buildings, such as a Crucifix for the church of the Confrères de la Miséricorde. He secured a scholarship from the Austrian government of the southern Netherlands to study with Laurent Delvaux for 18 months, acquiring from him the classicizing tendency in his art. In 1765–6 Leroy returned to Paris to resume his studies at the Académie Royale. There Charles-Antoine Bridan noticed him and invited him to collaborate with him on work at Metz, Le Havre and Chartres, such as the *Assumption of the Virgin* altar (Chartres Cathedral). Leroy also accompanied Bridan to Italy in connection with a commission for an *Assumption*. He was in Carrara in 1769, then in Florence in 1771 and Rome in 1772. On his return to Namur in 1773 Leroy sought to establish himself in the artistic circles of the southern Netherlands by working for the government and religious institutions. The French Revolution (1789–95) and political upheavals put an end to his output. Many of his works, often of modest size and delicate finish, are preserved in the Musée de l'Hôtel de Croix in Namur. Among them are the *Sleep of Innocence*, *Minerva*, *Profiles of Two Bearded Greeks*, *Lysimachus*, a bust of *Prince Stahremberg* and the *Emperor Joseph II*. These, though marked by the imprint of French plastic art of the 18th century, successfully combine the influence of antique sculpture with that of Flemish sculpture of the 17th century, particularly as exemplified in the classicizing work of François Du Quesnoy.

BIBLIOGRAPHY

M. Devigne: 'De la Parenté d'inspiration des artistes flamands du XVIIe et du XVIIIe siècle', *Mém. Acad. Royale Belgique: Cl. B.-A.*, n. s. 1, ii/1 (1928), pp. 20–33, 65–72

*1770–1830: Autour du Néo-classicisme en Belgique* (exh. cat., Brussels, Mus. Ixelles, 1985), pp. 61–4, 396–7

DOMINIQUE VAUTIER

**Leroy de Barde,** Vicomte **Alexandre-Isidore** [Le Chevalier de Barde] (*b* Montreuil, Pas-de-Calais, 15 Feb 1777; *d* Paris, 5 May 1828). French painter, active in England. An amateur virtuoso of still-life watercolour painting, Leroy de Barde appears to have been entirely self-taught. In 1792 he emigrated to England with his monarchist family to avoid the Revolution. The first mention of him as an artist is as an 'honorary' exhibitor at the Royal Academy exhibition of 1797 when he showed two watercolours, *Fruit* and *Grapes* (untraced). He styled himself 'Le Chevalier de Barde' and signed his works thus. He also exhibited in Royal Academy exhibitions in 1800, 1801 and 1802 with various flower paintings and a composition of *Moths and Butterflies*. The paintings exhibited in 1800 are still in the Royal Academy: *Double Narcissus and Lilies of the Valley*, *Lilac Branch* and *Green Oak*.

In 1803 Leroy de Barde began an extensive series of watercolours representing natural curiosities from the Bullock Museum in Piccadilly, London. The Bullock Museum catalogue of 1814 contains descriptions of, and engravings (by Thomas Bewick) after, several of Leroy de Barde's watercolours. The series was exhibited again at the Salon of 1817 and was bought by Louis XVIII. These large watercolours are vivid and meticulous renditions of animal, vegetable and mineral subjects and include *Shells* (1803), *Collection of Birds, Snakes, Shells, Minerals and Antique Vases, Royal Tiger Choked by a Boa* (both 1814) and *Exotic Birds Assembled in Different Cases* (1810; all Paris, Louvre). The last mentioned in particular shows his remarkable handling of *trompe l'oeil* effects.

Around 1804 Leroy de Barde joined the newly formed Society of Painters in Water-Colour, but after the Bourbon restoration in 1814 he returned to France and accompanied Louis XVIII to Ghent during the Hundred Days. In 1816 and 1817 he executed large watercolour landscapes as decorations for the Comte de Montbrun's Château de

Recques-sur-Course near Montreuil. Although Louis appointed him Premier Peintre d'Histoire Naturelle in 1816, these were probably the only major works he produced after 1815.

BIBLIOGRAPHY
*Catalogue of the Different Subjects Represented in the Large Watercolour Drawings by the Chevalier de Barde Now Exhibiting at Mr Bullock's Museum, the Egyptian Hall, Piccadilly, London* (London, 1814)
A. Braquehay: *Un Peintre d'histoire naturelle, Leroy de Barde et son temps (1777–1829)* (Abbeville, 1896)
*De David à Delacroix: La Peinture française de 1774 à 1830* (exh. cat., ed. P. Rosenberg; Paris, Grand Pal., 1974), pp. 528–31

STEPHANIE NEVISON BROWN

**Lerski, Helmar** [Schmuklerski, Israel] (*b* Strasbourg, 18 Feb 1871; *d* Zurich, 29 Nov 1956). Swiss photographer and film maker of Polish descent. He changed his name in 1896. After some years in the USA, he moved to Berlin in 1916, where he worked as a photographer and as a cameraman on various films, including Fritz Lang's *Metropolis* (1926). In 1931 he published *Köpfe des Alltags*, a collection of portraits of working-class figures, comparable to August Sander's *Antlitz der Zeit* (Munich, 1929). Lerski concentrated on archetypal characteristics rather than on individual features, favouring extreme close-ups and tight cropping, and he became renowned for his experiments with multiple light sources. From 1931 he worked as a photographer and film director in Palestine. In 1948 he settled in Zurich.

PHOTOGRAPHIC PUBLICATIONS
*Köpfe des Alltags* (Berlin, 1931)
*Verwandlungen durch Licht* (1936)
*Der Mensch: Mein Bruder*, ed. A. Lerski (Dresden, 1958)

BIBLIOGRAPHY
*Contemp. Phots*
U. Eskildsen, ed.: *Helmar Lerski: Verwandlungen durch Licht* (Freren, 1983)
J. Gross: 'I Write with Light', *Brit. J. Phot.*, 131 (Oct 1984), pp. 1054–8

☐

**Lery, Gaspard-Joseph Chaussegros de.** *See* CHAUSSEGROS DE LERY, GASPARD-JOSEPH.

**Lesbian art.** *See under* GAY AND LESBIAN ART.

**Lesbian cymatium.** *See under* CYMA.

**Lesbos** [Gr. Lésvos; now Mitilíni]. Large and mountainous Greek island off the coast of Turkey in the north-east Aegean, south of Lemnos and north of Chios. An important centre in the Early Bronze Age (*c.* 3600–*c.* 2000 BC), after *c.* 1000 BC it became a principal area of Aeolic Greek civilization. Somewhat neglected apart from a systematic German survey in the late 19th century, Lesbos numbers Mytilene (the capital), Methymna, Eressos, Pyrra, Antissa and Arisbe among its cities (see fig. ), but only at the first has much work been done.

The only Bronze Age site on the island excavated and published is Thermi, some 10 km north of Mytilene town on the south-east coast. British excavations in 1929–33 under Winifred Lamb uncovered an Early Bronze Age coastal settlement similar to TROY that passed through five stages before its abandonment, resettlement a thousand years later and final destruction by fire *c.* 1200 BC. Houses were of the typical megaron type with a long main room and porch, and streets were paved with pebbles; the

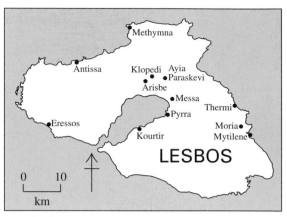

Map of Lesbos

final phase was fortified. Numerous clay figurines of mother goddess type were found. Other prehistoric settlements are known at Kourtir on the Gulf of Kalloni (partly submerged) and near Ayia Paraskevi in the centre of the island. Late Helladic III (*c.* 1390–*c.* 1050 BC) pottery has been found in small quantities, for example at Antissa and Methymna.

Some Protogeometric pottery (*c.* 1050–*c.* 900 BC) marks the first Greek settlement at Mytilene itself, while Geometric (*c.* 900–*c.* 700 BC) has appeared at Antissa and Methymna. Small Archaic (*c.* 700–*c.* 480 BC) apsidal buildings, possibly parts of sanctuaries, are known at Antissa, Pyrrha and Mytilene. More important is the large (37.5 m long) temple dating from the late 6th century BC at Klopedi near Ayia Paraskevi, a number of whose Aeolic capitals still survive; there is also a smaller temple near by. Other Aeolic capitals are known from Eressos and Mytilene. At Messa lie the remains of a major octostyle pseudodipteral Ionic temple, probably dating to early in the Hellenistic period (323–27 BC), and at Cape Vrysa are scanty remains of a Hellenistic Doric temple to Dionysus. At Mytilene are the remains of the only theatre visible on the island (another is known at Methymna under the school), a large structure seating about 10,000 with an orchestra 25 m across; dating from at least the Hellenistic period, it was rebuilt on several occasions and was converted for gladiatorial fights in the 2nd century AD. Plutarch claimed that it inspired Pompey to build the first stone theatre in Rome in 55 BC, but the relationship of the two structures is still unclear.

Other important ancient architectural remains at Mytilene include part of a long Hellenistic stoa near the North Harbour (whose ancient moles are still visible underwater), long stretches of the Late Archaic–early Classical (*c.* 550–475 BC) city walls in Lesbian-style masonry (curved joints fitted carefully together) west of the cemetery at Ayia Kyriaki, and a shorter stretch of the 4th century BC (mostly ashlar) on Nikomedia Street near the North Harbour, part of a bridge (perhaps Roman, i.e. 27 BC–AD 330) that linked the island part of the city to the mainland, a large 2nd-century AD Roman apsidal structure (possibly a nymphaeum) behind the cathedral, and a number of peristyle houses of the late 3rd century AD, including one, the

House of Menander in the Chorafa district, so-called because of the mosaic scenes from plays by him as well as the portrait of him that accompany a fine Orpheus mosaic. Vitruvius mentioned the orthogonal town plan disapprovingly (because it exposed the inhabitants to the force of the north and south winds); its existence and orientation were confirmed in 1988. At Moria and Lambrou Myloi are well-preserved stretches of arches from a major Roman aqueduct. Ancient marble quarries are known near Thermi and Moria. Canadian excavations since 1984 have revealed a modest Demeter/Cybele sanctuary on the Acropolis with at least five altars, including a hearth altar and prothysis altar, and evidence for a well-developed local ceramic and terracotta figurine industry from Archaic to early Roman times, including Archaic, Classical (the first known) and Hellenistic Grey wares, Hellenistic and early Roman Relief wares, a local imitation Sigillata and a fine Brown-gloss ware that may be from Tenedos. Fragments of late 6th century BC Ionic and Doric columns, possibly from a temple, and of an Aeolic capital also came from these excavations. Elsewhere fine figurines are known from graves at Pyrra. Roman sculpture includes some fine early imperial portraits and seven gladiatorial tomb relief scenes built into Mytilene's medieval castle walls along with remains of at least twenty ancient buildings, including a late 1st-century BC stoa tomb belonging to Prota, a local aristocrat. Numerous churches, mostly with nave and two aisles and sometimes with fine mosaics, are known from the 5th and 6th centuries AD throughout the island. Near the airport a major hoard of church silver plate and gold jewellery (now in Athens) of the early 7th century was found in 1954. A fine new museum with 15 galleries of material from the Bronze Age to the 4th century AD opened in Mytilene in the summer of 1991.

### BIBLIOGRAPHY

#### BRONZE AGE

W. Lamb: *Excavations at Thermi on Lesbos* (Cambridge, 1936)

#### LATER PERIODS

R. Koldewey and others: *Die antiken Baureste der Insel Lesbos* (Berlin, 1890)

E. Ledyard-Shields: *The Cults of Lesbos* (Baltimore, 1917)

E. Evangelides: 'Mytiline', *Archaiol. Deltion*, xi (1928), pp. 14–18

'Anaskaphai en to theatro tes Mytilenes' [Excavations in the theatre at Mytilene], *Praktika Athen. Archaiol. Etaireias* (1958), pp. 230–32

S. Charitonides: 'Palaiochristianiki topographia til Lesvou', *Archaiol. Deltion*, xxiii (1968), pp. 10–69

S. Charitonides, L. Kahil and R. Ginouves: 'Les Mosaïques de la Maison de Ménandre à Mytilène', *Ant. Kst* (1970) [suppl. vol. 6]

I. Kondis: *Lesviakon Polyptikon* (Athens, 1974) [good plans and photographs]

H. G. Buchholz: *Methymna* (Mainz, 1975)

I. Kondis: *Lesvos kai i mikrasiatiki periochi tis* [Lesbos and its lands in Asia Minor] (Athens, 1976) [good maps and plans]

P. Betancourt: *The Aeolic Style in Architecture* (Princeton, 1977)

C. Williams: 'Hellenistic and Roman Buildings in the Medieval Walls of Mytilene', *Phoenix*, xxxviii (1984), pp. 31–76

*Class. Views*, n. s., v– (1986–) [excav. rep. from Mytilene by C. Williams and H. Williams]

L. Acheilara: 'Thymese apo 4 monomakhous' [Memorials for four gladiators], *Lesviaka*, ix (1987), pp. 51–66

W. Schiering: 'Pyrrha auf Lesbos', *Archäol. Anz.* (1989), pp. 339–77

H. Williams: *The Greek Renaissance in the Roman Empire* (London, 1989), pp. 163–8

HECTOR WILLIAMS

**Lescaze, William Edmond** (*b* Geneva, 27 March 1896; *d* New York, 9 Feb 1969). American architect of Swiss birth. He studied architecture under Karl Moser at the Technische Hochschule in Zurich (MA, 1919) and worked in the Paris office of Henri Sauvage (1919–20). He emigrated to the USA in 1920 and after a brief stay in Cleveland, OH, set up his own practice in New York in 1923. Although his early commissions were small, he gained recognition for some unexecuted projects, such as 'The Future Country House', which was illustrated in the *Architectural Record* (November 1928). It was efficient, well-planned and insulated, with an adjacent aeroplane garage and runway.

In 1929 Lescaze was introduced to GEORGE HOWE. Wishing to break with the past and practise in the modern idiom, Howe joined with Lescaze; their partnership agreement stipulated that Lescaze would be the designer and that Howe would initiate business contacts. Howe's previous work for the Philadelphia Saving Fund Society led to the organization's commission for a £12.5 million highrise headquarters building (1929–33) on 12th and Filbert Streets, Philadelphia. A photograph of the incomplete building was included in the show *Modern Architecture: International Exhibition*, organized at MOMA, New York, in 1932 by Henry-Russell Hitchcock and Philip Johnson. Other works by Lescaze in the International Style displayed in the exhibition were the Capital Bus Terminal (1927), New York; the nursery building (1929) for the Oak Lane Country Day School, Philadelphia; the housing development (1931–2) at Chrystie-Forsyth Streets, New York, a project of 24 steel-frame buildings, each 10 storeys high; and the Hessian Hills School (1932–6), Mt Airy Road, Croton-on-Hudson, New York. After working with Lescaze on the nursery school, the headmaster, William Curry, moved to Dartington Hall, Devon, England, and introduced Lescaze to its owners, Leonard and Dorothy Elmhirst. This contact later led to commissions at Dartington for a headmaster's house (1931–2) for Curry, a gymnasium (1933–5), estate housing (1933–5), a house (1935) for the choreographer Kurt Jooss and a Central Office building (1935). All these buildings remain as part of the Elmhirsts' experiments in education, agriculture and local crafts.

After the dissolution of the firm of Howe & Lescaze in 1932, Lescaze used his share of the profits to purchase a row house at 211 East 48th Street in New York, a building he demolished and replaced with a modern house and office (1933–4) where he lived and worked until his death. Its most noticeable features were glass block ribbon windows running the width of the street façade at the 2nd and 3rd floor levels. He built numerous houses in both urban and rural settings, studios (1938) for the Columbia Broadcasting System, Hollywood, CA, and pavilions (e.g. the Aeronautics Pavilion) for several exhibitors at the World's Fair of 1939 in New York.

In 1942 Lescaze published *On Being an Architect*, which summed up his philosophy of architecture at a turning-point in his career, when he abandoned the clean, smooth, pure white and logical expression of the International Style in favour of glass curtain–wall construction. In the next 25 years Lescaze built his largest commissions, including two of the earliest high-rise buildings on Third Avenue, New York, numbers 711 (1954–6) and 777 (1962), a tower at One Oliver Plaza (1968), Pittsburgh, and Number One,

New York Plaza (1969), South and Broad Streets, New York, a 50-storey building in Manhattan. Although these buildings made Lescaze wealthy, they had none of the vitality of his innovative years from 1927 to 1942, when he perhaps ranked with Richard Neutra as one of the most significant American practitioners in the International Style.

### WRITINGS
*On Being an Architect* (New York, 1942)

### BIBLIOGRAPHY
H.-R. Hitchcock and P. Johnson: *The International Style: Architecture since 1922* (New York, 1932)
W. H. Jordy: 'PSFS: Its Development and its Significance in Modern Architecture', *J. Soc. Archit. Hist.*, xxi (May 1962), pp. 47–83
R. Stern: 'PSFS: Beaux-Arts, Theory and Rational Expressionism', *J. Soc. Archit. Hist.*, xxi (May 1962), pp. 84–95
L. Wodehouse: 'Lescaze at Dartington Hall', *Archit. Assoc. Q.*, viii (1976), no. 2, pp. 3–14
C. Hubert and L. S. Shapiro: *William Lescaze* (New York, 1982)
L. W. Lanmon: *William Lescaze, Architect* (Philadelphia, London and Toronto, 1987)

LAWRENCE WODEHOUSE

**Les Combarelles.** Cave site in France, in the Beune Valley 3 km from Les Eyzies, Dordogne. Like nearby FONT DE GAUME, it contains important examples of cave art of the Late Upper Palaeolithic period (*c.* 20,000–*c.* 10,000 BP) (*see also* PREHISTORIC EUROPE, §II, 1 and 2). The cave of Les Combarelles had long been known, but its engravings, dated *c.* 16,000–14,000 BP, were first discovered in 1901.

The cave takes the form of a narrow, winding gallery, just over 1 m wide and never more than 2 m in height; it is *c.* 240 m in length, with no side passages. When the art was found, some sections of the cave were extremely narrow, but many concretions have since been broken and the floor lowered to facilitate access. The French scholar Abbé HENRI BREUIL, writing in the 1920s, claimed that there were about 300 recognizable figures in the cave, as well as over 100 unidentifiable image fragments, and more figures have since been discovered. The figures—mostly engravings, although a few black drawings and a stencilled hand outline are also known—are often superimposed, making them difficult to decipher, and few are readily visible to the untrained eye. Their style is quite homogeneous, and they have been attributed to Style III (*c.* 20,000–*c.* 16,000 BP) and Style IV (*c.* 16,000–*c.* 11,000 BP) of the classification devised by ANDRÉ LEROI-GOURHAN (*see* PREHISTORIC EUROPE, fig. 9), ranging in date from the early Magdalenian period to the beginning of its late phase. The first known engravings are *c.* 70 m from the cave entrance; the first clear figures are found after *c.* 161 m and are fairly continuous thereafter. Drawn on both walls, though not on the ceiling, as its surface was unsuitable, they are grouped in panels separated by spaces. A rough guide to their content can be obtained from Breuil's list, comprising 116 horses, 37 bison, 7 cattle, 19 bears, 14 reindeer, 13 mammoths, 9 ibex, 9 deer, 5 lions, 1–4 canids, 1–3 rhinoceroses, 1 fox, 1 fish, 1 snake, 4 tectiform (hut-like) signs, 39 anthropomorphs and 4 sexual symbols. Some of these figures—in particular a bear, a mammoth with a curled trunk, a lion, a horse and a reindeer—are among the best-known in Palaeolithic art. The lines vary from deeply to finely engraved, and the animal outlines,

many up to 1 m in length, are often enhanced with extra detail, such as hatching to indicate hair.

The adjacent cave of Les Combarelles II, which contains only 33 figures, was discovered in 1909.

### BIBLIOGRAPHY
L. Capitan, H. Breuil and D. Peyrony: *Les Combarelles aux Eyzies (Dordogne)* (Paris, 1924)
M. Sarradet: *Les Combarelles* (Périgueux, 1971)
*Trav. Inst. A. Préhist. Toulouse*, xxiii–xxix (1981–7) [series of detailed studies by C. Barrière]
C. Barrière: 'Grotte des Combarelles I', *L'Art des cavernes* (Paris, 1984), pp. 109–13
M. Archambeau and C. Archambeau: *Les Combarelles* (Périgueux, 1989)

PAUL G. BAHN

**Lescot, Pierre** (*b* ?Paris, *c.* 1500–10; *d* Paris, 10 Sept 1578). French architect. He was born into a noble family of magistrates and inherited the title Seigneur de Clagny from his maternal ancestors. A poem by Pierre de Ronsard, entitled *Discours à Pierre Lescot* (1560), claims that, in his twenties, Lescot studied geometry, mathematics and architecture; indeed, together with Joachim Du Bellay, Ronsard praised Lescot's ability not only in these disciplines but also as a painter. According to François de La Croix du Maine (1552–92), writing in 1584, Lescot also illustrated manuscripts with numerous drawings. Lescot took minor orders, which enabled him to become a canon of Notre-Dame in Paris in 1554 and to be appointed Chaplain-in-Ordinary at court, although he was ordained as a priest only in 1570. He was well known at court and highly regarded by both Francis I and Henry II.

Two works can be attributed to Lescot with certainty: the rood screen (1541–4; destr. 1750) at St Germain-l'Auxerrois, Paris (*see* PARIS, §V, 4), and the new Palais du Louvre (1546–78; *see* PARIS, §V, 6(ii)), his major work, which was to be built on the site of Charles V's medieval castle. The general arrangement of the building, comprising three wings of the same height and corner pavilions, recalls the château at Ecouen (1531–63), but nothing is known of what the entrance to the courtyard would have been like as Lescot's project was completed on only two sides, the west (the main block) and the south (the wing overlooking the Seine). It is not known whether the doubling of the wings carried out in the 17th century was seriously considered in the mid-16th century; it is certain, however, that Lescot's courtyard façades (see fig.) were designed for an area of medium size and not for one as vast as the present Cour Carrée.

The external elevations (now incorporated into the 17th-century construction) borrowed many features from Antonio da Sangallo (ii)'s Palazzo Farnese (*see* SANGALLO, (4), fig. 2), Rome, including rusticated quoins, string courses separating storeys and windows of different forms on each level. The standard French arrangement, based on vertical bays, gave way to a composition in storeys; even dormer windows disappeared. The building produces a completely different effect from the Palazzo Farnese, however: the elongated wings contrast with the pavilion, which rises like a tower; the windows remain numerous, their proportions tall and slender.

On the courtyard façades Lescot created a highly complex composition, in a manner that was without any equivalent in Italy. He employed the orders but assigned

Pierre Lescot: west façade of the Cour Carrée (1546–56), Palais du Louvre, Paris

enormous importance to sculptural decoration, more and more abundant from the ground floor towards the attic; he clearly distinguished the storeys but introduced at the centre of the façades, and later (1549) at their extremities, projecting bays that supplied the vertical motifs that French taste preferred. Through subtle variations in the use of the orders and of decoration, he succeeded in accentuating the projecting bays while preserving the unity of the façade. The sculptural decoration of JEAN GOUJON and the architectural decoration, largely inspired by antique triumphal arches, celebrate the imperial character of the French monarchy.

Other works probably attributable to Lescot include the Hôtel Carnavalet (from 1546), built for a magistrate associated with the Lescot family, and the Fontaine des Innocents (1549; see GOUJON, JEAN and fig. 1), erected on the occasion of Henry II's entry into Paris. Both works have aspects in common with the Louvre, including the importance of the sculptural decoration by Jean Goujon and his collaborators, and the refined use of rustication and the orders. In addition, documents (Grodecki, 1985, pp. 144–5) prove that Lescot signed contracts in the name of the Maréchal de Saint-André concerning his town house (1549) in Paris and the château de Vallery (1555), Yonne, including the decoration of the pavilions and the garden gallery. Nothing is known of the town house, but the exceptional quality of the château, including the new use

of rustication and the subtle variation of window-frames from one storey to another, justifies its attribution to Pierre Lescot.

Lescot's genius, like that of Philibert de L'Orme, was to create a specifically French architecture inspired by antique and contemporary Roman buildings, possibly studied at first hand, but there is no proof that Lescot visited Rome. Three features characterize Lescot's style: a taste for ornament, which led him to treat the orders and rustication in a fashion more decorative than structural; a completely French sense of composition with vertical elements, which led him to design the projecting bays of the Louvre and the continuous superimposition of window architraves at Vallery; and a supreme skill in transitions and variations, which allowed him to link the projecting bays with the rest of the façade and to attenuate the contrasts between storeys. His work exercised an enormous influence, more lasting than that of de L'Orme. The rusticated jambs and quoins at Vallery and the projecting bays of the Louvre were immediately assimilated into French architecture, while the arrangement of the courtyard façade of the Louvre inspired the creators of 17th-century classicism, not least at the Palais du Luxembourg, Paris, and Versailles, where the influence of the Louvre, a cornerstone of modern French architecture, is to be found.

BIBLIOGRAPHY

F. Gebelin: *Les Châteaux de la Renaissance* (Paris, 1927), pp. 131–41, 177–8

L. Hautecoeur: 'Le Louvre de Pierre Lescot', *Gaz. B.-A.*, i (1927), pp. 199–218

L. Batiffol: 'Les Premières constructions de Pierre Lescot', *Gaz. B.-A.*, ii (1930), pp. 276–303

P. du Colombier: 'L'Enigme de Vallery', *Human. & Ren.*, iv (1937), pp. 7–15

L. Hautecoeur: *Architecture classique* (1943–57)

P. du Colombier: *Jean Goujon* (Paris, 1949)

A. Blunt: *Art and Architecture in France, 1500 to 1700*, Pelican Hist. A. (Harmondsworth, 1953, rev. 4/1982)

R. Planchenault: 'Les Châteaux de Vallery', *Bull. Mnmtl*, cxxi (1963), pp. 237–59

N. Miller: 'The Form and Meaning of the Fontaine des Innocents', *A. Bull.*, l (1968), pp. 270–77

J. P. Babelon: 'Du Grand Ferrare à Carnavalet: Naissance de l'hôtel classique', *Rev. A.*, xl–xli (1978), pp. 83–108

D. Thomson: 'A Note on Pierre Lescot, the Painter', *Burl. Mag.*, cxx (1978), pp. 666–7

V. Hoffmann: 'Le Louvre de Henri II: Un Palais impérial', *Bull. Soc. Hist. A. Fr.* (1982), pp. 7–15

J. M. Pérouse de Montclos: 'Du toit brisé et de quelques autres gallicismes de l'aile Lescot du Louvre', *Bull. Soc. Hist. A. Fr.* (1982), pp. 45–51

C. Grodecki: 'Les Marchés de construction pour l'aile Henri II du Louvre, 1546–1558, *Archvs A. Fr.*, xxvi (1984), pp. 19–38

D. Thomson: *Renaissance Paris* (London, 1984)

C. Grodecki: *Documents du minutier central des notaires de Paris: Histoire de l'art au XVIe siècle, 1540–1600*, i (Paris, 1985)

W. Prinz and R. G. Kecks: *Das französische Schloss der Renaissance* (Berlin, 1985), pp. 465–79

J. Guillaume et F.-C. James: 'L'Architecture savante, 1540–1560', *Le Château en France* (Paris, 1986), pp. 205–16

J.-P. Babelon: *Châteaux de France au siècle de la Renaissance* (Paris, 1989), pp. 410–17

G. Bresc-Bautier: 'La Sculpture de l'attique du Louvre par l'atelier de Jean Goujon', *Rev. Louvre*, ii (1989), pp. 97–111

J. M. Pérouse de Montclos: *Histoire de l'architecture française de la Renaissance à la Révolution* (Paris, 1989), pp. 98–103, 108–12

J. Guillaume: 'Les Français et les ordres, 1540–1550', *L'Emploi des ordres dans l'architecture de la Renaissance* (Paris, 1992), pp. 193–218 [esp. pp. 202–5]

H. Zerner: *L'art de la renaissance en France: L'invention du classicisme* (Paris, 1996)

JEAN GUILLAUME

**Lescuyer** [Lescuier], **Adenet** [Adam; Adenot; Admiet] (*fl* 1457–71). French illuminator. The earliest document relating to him is dated 1457, when he illuminated a manuscript for Joanna of Laval (m. 1454; *d* 1498), wife of René I, Duke of Anjou. In February 1457 the artist received 6 livres 17 sous 6 deniers of silver for producing 'ung ymaige et plusieurs lettres' for a copy of the *Miroir des dames* (untraced) for Joanna. In May the court moved to Provence and the *Miroir* was completed by another, unnamed, illuminator. In 1458 Adenet received payment from the chapter of Angers Cathedral for decorating a five-volume Gradual (untraced). He was paid the substantial sum of 42 sous 6 deniers for each of the 18 miniatures and was assisted by Gervaise Godelin. Although not officially attached to the court, Adenet was nevertheless described in this document as 'enlumineur de la reine de Sicile', possibly indicating the esteem in which he was held. The final record of his activities is on 19 May 1471, when he received 27 sous 1 denier for producing three miniatures for an Epistolary and an Evangeliary for the chapter of St Laud, Angers. No works by Adenet survive, although he has been tentatively identified (Durrieu, 1912), albeit unsuccessfully, with the Master of the Rohan Hours.

BIBLIOGRAPHY

C. Port: *Les Artistes–peintres angevins d'après les archives angevines* (Paris, 1881), pp. 192–3
P. Durrieu: *Les Heures à l'usage d'Angers* (Paris, 1912), pp. 22–3
——: 'Le Maître des *Grandes Heures de Rohan* et les Lescuier d'Angers', *Rev. A. Anc. & Mod.*, xxxii (1912), pp. 81–9, 161–3
C. Port: *Note complémentaire sur les artistes angevins* (Angers, 1915)

**Lesdiguières**, Ducs de. French family of soldiers, patrons and collectors.

**(1)** Duc **de Lesdiguières** [François de Bonne] (*b* Saint-Bonnet, Isère, 1 April 1543; *d* Valence, 21 Sept 1626). He was born into a family of Catholic notaries but converted to Protestantism at an early age. He had a brilliant military career and in 1598 was appointed Lieutenant-General of the Dauphiné; in 1609 he was made Maréchal de France, then duke in 1611. In 1622, his renunciation of Protestantism enabled him to receive the collar of the Order of the Saint-Esprit and become Constable of France. He amassed a great fortune that permitted him to become a lavish patron, particularly in the Dauphiné. Between 1611 and 1620 he rebuilt the château of Vizille, near Grenoble, where he employed numerous artists who were also responsible for the decoration of the palace of the Dauphins (now Palais de Justice) in Grenoble. These included painters such as Claude de Lavau (*d* before 1647), the Fleming Jean de Loanen (*fl c.* 1620) and the Brussels artist Antoine Schanaert (*fl* 1608–16). Eight battle scenes were painted by Schanaert in 1611 for the gallery of the château, of which two, the *Siege of Cavour* and the *Taking of the Village of Allemagne*, remain at Vizille. Among the sculptors working for Lesdiguières was Jacob Richier, who became one of his favourite artists. From 1612 he undertook numerous schemes for the Duke, including the tomb of his first wife *Claudine de Bérenger* (Gap, Mus. Dépt.), the equestrian statue of *Lesdiguières* over the main entrance to the château at Vizille, another statue of his patron in the guise of Hercules (Grenoble, Jardin de Ville), chimneys and fountains at Vizille and above all Lesdiguières's own funerary monument (Gap, Mus. Dépt.).

BIBLIOGRAPHY

J.-J.-A. Pilot: 'Sur les anciennes galeries de tableaux des Ducs de Lesdiguières à Grenoble et à Vizille', *Bull. Soc. Statistiques, Sci. Nat. & A. Indust. Dépt. Isère* (1878), pp. 420–31
E. Maignien: *Les Artistes grenoblois, architectes, armuriers, brodeurs, graveurs, musiciens, orfèvres, peintres, sculpteurs, tapissiers, tourneurs, etc . . . notes et documents inédits* (Grenoble, 1887)
E. Escallier: *Lesdiguières, dernier connétable de France* (Lyon, 1946/*R* Marseille, 1981)

**(2)** Duc **de Lesdiguières** [Charles de Blanchefort, Maréchal de Créquy] (*b* 1573; *d* Brema, 17 March 1638). Son-in-law of (1) François de Bonne, Duc de Lesdiguières. The siege of Laon in 1594 launched him on a brilliant military career that lasted until his death on the battlefield during Louis XIII's Italian campaign. He followed his father-in-law as Lieutenant-General of the Dauphiné in 1610. In 1621 he became Maréchal de France and in 1626 succeeded to the title of Duc de Lesdiguières and was appointed Lieutenant-General commanding the French army in Italy. In 1633 he was sent on a mission to Rome in order to win over the Pope to the French interest. It was mainly during his year-long stay in Rome that he built up his collection of paintings. His doubtless real love of art coincided with the political imperatives of ostentation necessary for his mission, and his collection included diplomatic gifts such as Poussin's *Destruction of the Temple in Jerusalem* (untraced). Créquy owned many paintings by 16th-century artists, especially non-Roman ones. Among them were Veronese's *Pilgrims at Emmaus* (Paris, Louvre), Innocenzo da Imola's *St John the Evangelist* (Versailles, Château), at that time attributed to Raphael, and pictures by Dosso Dossi, Garofalo, Bassano, Andrea del Sarto, Titian and even Bruegel. The collection also reflected the various strands of contemporary Roman art, with Guido Reni's *David with the Head of Goliath* (probably the work in the Louvre, Paris) and the *Flight into Egypt* (Brussels, Mus. A. Anc.); Annibale Carracci's *Adoration of the Shepherds* (Paris, Louvre); Leonello Spada's *Aeneas and Anchises* (Paris, Louvre), then attributed to Domenichino; Giovanni Lanfranco's *Angelica and Medoro* (Rio de Janeiro, Mus. N. B.A.); Caravaggio's *Concert of Youths* (New York, Met.); and further works by the Cavaliere d'Arpino, Antonio Tempesta, Francesco Albani, Ludovico Carracci, Guercino and others. Dutch artists such as Herman van Swanevelt and Cornelis van Poelenburch, Germans, including Joachim von Sandrart, and French painters, among them Claude Lorrain (probably two landscapes now in Duke of Buccleuch priv. col.), Simon Vouet and Jacques Stella, were represented by works very probably executed in Rome. The arrival in Paris of this rich collection of more than 150 works made a great stir. When it was broken up, probably after 1638, Cardinal Richelieu acquired the best pieces for himself.

BIBLIOGRAPHY

J. Humbert: *Le Maréchal de Créquy, gendre de Lesdiguières (1573–1638)* (Paris, 1962)
J.-C. Boyer and I. Wolf: 'Rome à Paris: Les Tableaux du Maréchal de Créquy (1638)', *Rev. A.* [Paris], 79 (1988), pp. 22–41

THIERRY BAJOU

**Lese, Benozzo di.** *See* GOZZOLI, BENOZZO.

**Le Secq (des Tournelles), Henri** (*b* Paris, 18 Aug 1818; *d* Paris, 26 Dec 1882). French photographer, painter, printmaker and collector. After studying with the sculptor James Pradier and the painters Jean-Pierre Granger (1779–1840) and Paul Delaroche, he made his début at the Salon of 1842, winning a third-class medal there in 1845. He turned to photography in the wave of self-enrichment preceding the 1848 Revolution. With Charles Nègre he experimented with the waxed paper negative process of Gustave Le Gray, from whom he probably received personal instruction before 1850. Unlike other photographers, who later adopted glass negatives, Le Secq continued to use paper, at first employing photographs as studies for his genre paintings.

By 1851 Le Secq excelled at rendering ancient and medieval monuments in a pictorial style that exploited the effects of light and shadow, turning architecture into symbolic fragments evoking a rapidly disappearing historical past, which Le Secq sought to save photographically. After helping found the Société Héliographique in 1851 he was engaged by the Commission des Monuments Historiques to record endangered buildings in Champagne, Alsace and Lorraine. He added the sculpture of Strasbourg, Amiens, Reims and Chartres to his original list, as well as other cathedrals and churches around Paris. He also documented the cathedral of Notre-Dame in Paris in 1852 and 1853 and changes in the design of the city (album in Paris, Carnavalet). In 1852 he photographed woods, fields and stone quarries in and around Montmirail (near Epernay) and sold the pictures to artists. The negatives are notable for their scale (from 520×380 mm to postcard size) and for stylistic affinities with Barbizon painting. The photography magazine *La Lumière* chronicled every phase of Le Secq's photographic career up to 1855, omitting only his still-lifes (*Fantaisies*), which probably originated in the late 1850s. Like the cathedrals, quarries and rubble of old Paris these are arrangements of piles of material facts, with surfaces deliberately eroded through manipulations of light and shade during extremely long exposures. The same interest in such sustained exposures led him around the same time to photograph boats at Dieppe beached in the harbour at low tide.

Le Secq's photographic career probably ended before 1860. The largest collection of his work is in the Bibliothèque des Arts Décoratifs, Paris, where it was deposited by his son Henry *c.* 1900. Le Secq continued to paint, exhibiting regularly at the Salon, and he participated in the French etching revival. He began collecting the work of major Impressionists as well as etchings by Jean-François Millet, Charles-François Daubigny, Charles Meryon and Rembrandt, among others. For nearly a century after his death Le Secq was known in France mainly for his important collection of forged iron, which he began soon after 1860 (now Rouen, Mus. Le Secq des Tournelles).

BIBLIOGRAPHY

C. Cromer: 'Un Photographe-artiste du milieu du XIX siècle, le peintre Henri Le Secq', *Bull. Soc. Fr. Phot.* (Oct 1930), no. 10, pp. 287–95
E. P. Janis: 'The Man on the Tower of Notre Dame: New Light on Henri Le Secq', *Image*, xix (Dec 1976), pp. 13–25
J. Buerger: 'Le Secq's Monuments and the Chartres Cathedral Portfolio', *Image*, xxiii (June 1980), pp. 1–5
A. Jammes and E. P. Janis: *The Art of French Calotype, with a Critical Dictionary of Photographers, 1845–1870* (Princeton, 1983), pp. 206–10
*Henri Le Secq, photographe de 1850 à 1860: Catalogue raisonné de la collection de la Bibliothèque des Arts Décoratifs*, essay E. P. Janis, cat. J. Sartre (Paris, 1986)
E. P. Janis: 'Demolition Picturesque: Photographs of Paris in 1852 and 1853 by Henri Le Secq', *Perspectives on Photography: Essays in Honor of Beaumont Newhall*, P. Walch and T. Barrow, eds (Albuquerque, 1986), pp. 33–66

EUGENIA PARRY JANIS

**Le Sidaner, Henri (Eugène Augustin)** (*b* Port-Louis, Mauritius, 7 Aug 1862; *d* Versailles, 1939). French painter and pastellist. He studied briefly under Alexandre Cabanel at the Ecole des Beaux-Arts in 1880, but his admiration for the Impressionists led him to reject this academic training and to work alone from 1882 to 1887 at Etaples in northern France. He first exhibited at the Salon des Artistes Français, where he won third prize in 1891, and later at the Salon de la Société Nationale. The subject-matter and smoothly painted surfaces of some of Le Sidaner's early paintings, such as *Sunday* (1898; Douai, Mus. Mun.), a picture of evanescent young girls in long white dresses against a very low horizon, caused him to be compared with the Pre-Raphaelite Brotherhood but also allied him with the Symbolists. From 1900, when he moved to Beauvais and later to Gerberoy, Oise, he began to paint urban landscapes and gardens, often in a deserted state. He began at that time to favour broken brushwork reminiscent of Georges Seurat, while working primarily from memory rather than from direct observation. After a stay in Venice in 1905 he painted a series of views, such as *Bridge of Sighs* (1906; Paris, Petit Pal.), that were hugely successful when exhibited in London and at the Salon de la Société Nationale in 1906.

BIBLIOGRAPHY

C. Mauclair: *Henri Le Sidaner* (Paris, 1928)
*French Symbolist Painters* (exh. cat. by P. Jullian, A. Bowness and G. Lacambre, London, Hayward Gal., 1972), pp. 65–6
*Henri Le Sidaner* (exh. cat., Dunkirk, Mus. B.-A., 1974)

VANINA COSTA

**Leslie, C(harles) R(obert)** (*b* Clerkenwell, London, 19 Oct 1794; *d* London, 5 May 1859). English painter and writer. The son of Robert Leslie, an American of Scottish descent who worked in London (1793–9), he received his earliest artistic training in Philadelphia, PA. At first he was self-taught, but in the course of a seven-year apprenticeship to the publishers Bradford & Inskeep (1808–15) he decided to become a professional artist. In March 1811 he achieved fame with a small sketch of the visiting English actor George Frederick Cooke as Shakespeare's character King Richard III. His talent was further recognized that year when the Pennsylvanian Academy of Fine Arts raised £100 to pay for him to study in Europe for two years. Leslie arrived in London in December 1811 with a letter of introduction to Benjamin West and immediately entered the circle of American history painters around West that included Washington Allston, Charles Bird King and Samuel F. B. Morse. From Allston in particular he learnt the colouristic and painterly skills that distinguish his mature work. These practical lessons complemented his studies at the Royal Academy Schools in London, which he entered in March 1813. For the next five years he worked as a history painter while painting portraits for a living. His best portraits from this period are those of *John*

C. R. Leslie: *Slender, with the Assistance of Shallow, Courting Anne Page: 'The Merry Wives of Windsor', Act 3, Scene iv*, oil on canvas, 677×775 mm, 1825 (New Haven, CT, Yale Center for British Art)

*Quincy Adams* and of his wife *Louisa Johnson Adams* (both 1816; Washington, DC, State Dept, see 1980 exh. cat., figs 135, 136), though ultimately the pose of the sitters and the warmth of the palette derive from Thomas Lawrence.

The *Murder of Rutland by Lord Clifford* (exh. RA 1816; Philadelphia, PA Acad. F.A.) is the largest surviving example of Leslie's history painting. Bearing affinities with the works for John Boydell's Shakespeare Gallery, it shows the influences of both Raphael and Reynolds, but also that of West in its historically correct costume. After this work he gradually changed direction, partly under the influence of David Wilkie's success as a painter of scenes from everyday life, but also because he acquired a taste for humorous literature through his friendship with Washington Irving. From this type of literature he found a style perfectly adapted to his own modest temperament and to public taste. His first important exercise in this manner was *Sancho Panza and the Duchess* (exh. 1824; Petworth House, W. Sussex, NT), inspired by Cervantes's *Don Quixote*. This was commissioned by George Wyndham,

3rd Earl of Egremont, and Leslie's achievement was that he avoided the use of caricature. Instead, gesture and accessories were all rendered from life in a painterly manner and with taste and affection. The artist found his prototypes for technique and scale in the works of Hogarth and De Hoogh, and Egremont rightly described Leslie as the 'Hogarth of elegant life'. The following year, he turned to Shakespeare's *The Merry Wives of Windsor* with the scene of *Slender, with the Assistance of Shallow, Courting Anne Page* (1825; New Haven, CT, Yale Cent. Brit. A.; see fig.). This richly conceived image of Elizabethan domestic manners uses scrupulously researched details of costume and decoration to convey a lively sense of the period. In 1826 Leslie was elected an RA, and for the rest of his career, with varying degrees of success, he repeated the formula for painting that he had by then established. Notable departures from his usual subject-matter were the royal commission *Queen Victoria Receiving the Sacrament at her Coronation* (1838–43; Brit. Royal Col.) and *Fairlop Fair* (1841; Arundel Castle, W. Sussex), a charming depiction of modern middle-class families at leisure.

During 1833–4 Leslie was drawing master at West Point Military Academy, NY, but family illness and other inconveniences caused him to return to London. Despite his work as an artist, Leslie is probably best known as the first biographer of John Constable, *Memoirs of the Life of John Constable* (1843) being the result of the friendship between the two painters. Relying very much on Constable's own correspondence and adhering to contemporary biographical conventions by toning down much of Constable's outspokenness, the *Memoirs* successfully dictated the way in which both scholars and public viewed Constable for more than a century. Leslie's other published writings include *A Handbook for Young Painters* (1854), based on lectures he gave while Professor of Painting at the Royal Academy (1847–52). At his death he left an unfinished biography of Reynolds that was completed by Tom Taylor and published in 1865 as *Life and Times of Sir Joshua Reynolds*. His sons Robert Charles Leslie (1826–1901) and George Dunlop Leslie (1835–1921) were also painters.

WRITINGS

*Memoirs of the Life of John Constable* (London, 1843, rev. 1951)
*A Handbook for Young Painters* (London, 1854)
T. Taylor, ed.: *Autobiographical Recollections*, 2 vols (London, 1860/*R* 1978)
with T. Taylor: *Life and Times of Sir Joshua Reynolds* (London, 1865)

BIBLIOGRAPHY

*Benjamin West and his American Students* (exh. cat. by D. Evans, Washington, DC, N.P.G., 1980), pp. 161–70, 177–80

ROBIN HAMLYN

**Lesotho** ['Muso o Lesotho; formerly Basutoland]. Country in southern Africa entirely surrounded by South Africa and consisting of a narrow band of fertile agricultural land and a larger mountainous region, suitable for rearing livestock. The total area is 30,355 sq. km and the total population 1,700,000 (UN estimate, 1989). The capital is Maseru. Lesotho has been independent since 1966.

SAN hunter-gatherers occupied the area for *c.* 20,000 years, before dying out at the beginning of the 20th century, and between 1400 and 1770 the South Sotho peoples settled here. At the end of the 20th century about half the South Sotho lived within Lesotho, where they comprise a large majority of the population. Under Moshoeshoe the Great (1786–1870) most of these peoples, along with significant numbers of Nguni-speakers, were united to form the Basotho. During wars in the 1850s and 1860s much of the country's arable land was lost to the Orange Free State, and, in the later 20th century, overcrowding led to a steady outflow of people seeking employment in South Africa. This entry covers the art produced in Lesotho since colonial times; for the art of earlier periods *see* AFRICA, §VII, 8.

Traditional art production is often organized by sex. Women produce decorated pottery, mats and woven materials, fertility dolls and some clothing, jewellery and musical instruments. Men make wooden implements (milking pails, large spoons), metal objects (jewellery, weapons, tools), large grain baskets, musical instruments and clothing from animal skins. Decoration often involves such symbols as circles—signifying wholeness, unity, cyclical patterns and seasons—or patterns suggesting such polarities of Sotho cosmology as male/female, individual/community, fast/slow and cool/hot. Both types of decoration continue to be evident in pottery and house decoration. Such totemic animal figures as lions, crocodiles and hippopotamuses are common on carved wooden objects. Both men and women continue to make such woven items as sleeping mats, baskets, beer strainers, ropes, jewellery and hats, including the cone-shaped *mokorotlo* hats that are now a national symbol.

Such Western crafts as knitting and tapestry-weaving were introduced by French Catholic missionaries at Roma in the 1860s, although the tapestries for which Lesotho is well known date from the 1930s and 1940s, when British aid schemes encouraged tapestry-weaving as an income-generating industry. Weaving has developed into the nation's largest craft industry. The production of woven mohair tapestries developed further in the late 1960s and early 1970s. Three workshops in particular have become well known. The Royal Lesotho Tapestry Weavers, Maseru (founded 1968) have specialized in geometric designs, drawing upon grass mat and mural designs. The Thabong Cooperative and TY (Teyateyaneng) Handicrafts Centre have specialized in figurative designs illustrating traditional village life. Earth colours were most common in early work from these workshops.

The traditional pottery of Lesotho includes clay dolls and animals made by children. Although pottery has been in decline since the 1850s, at such sites as Ha Tlebere and Ha Jublie some traditions are still maintained. In the late 20th century the Kolonyama Pottery Works were the largest in Lesotho, producing beautiful pots in foreign styles for tourists.

Traditional South Sotho architecture was found in villages built on ridges with large animal kraals surrounded by small dome-shaped houses of either reed and daga attached to a sapling frame planted in the ground or corbelled stone with secondary walling. Significant changes occurred during the early 19th century when cone-on-cylinder houses were introduced by such Sotho immigrants as the Taung and Rolong. At about the same time rectangular thatched structures typical of the Griqua and Boers were introduced. During the 19th century the corbelled stone house largely disappeared. Some housing maintained the reed-and-daga style, but a short stone wall base was added, and it ceased to function as an integral part of local architecture. In all of these various housing styles, decorative designs (*litema*), previously only used on interior walls and probably mirroring patterns seen on pottery, appeared on exterior walls. These designs were the preserve of women and are also used in modern beadwork, in braided hairstyles and in blankets. During the 19th century churches, missions and schools were built in French, Cape Dutch or English architectural styles, and small towns consisting of locally dressed sandstone buildings grew up around police camps and other colonial establishments. A rare attempt to incorporate traditional architectural motifs can be found in the Protestant church in Maseru (early 1950s). By the end of the 20th century building styles included thatched rondavels, rectangular buildings with corrugated iron roofs and European-style multi-level office complexes and shopping centres. In the peri-urban areas linear single- and double-roomed tenements (*malaene*) are common.

Until colonial times painting in Lesotho was restricted to the body. Later the graphic art of such missionaries as François Maeder (1811–88) and Frédéric Christol (1850–1933) received some recognition, and during the 20th century a number of local or locally resident painters emerged. Among these are Mpho Motsusi, Leetsang Ncheke, Meshu Mokitimi, Black Jesus, Martin Masoabi, James Dorothy, Earnest Ruch, Tony Hudson, Patrick Rorke and Ina-Maria Harris. By the 1990s their work had yet to be studied in detail.

There is little modern sculpture in Lesotho, although three men have gained recognition for their ceramic figures. Samuel Mokanyane (1905–44) began producing small figures (h. 150–200 mm) of animals in 1933, later producing figures of children and adults. He began working from pictures but later worked from life. One of his best-known figures is that of a mother and child, one example of which is inscribed with the words *Nyanya ngoana' ka, ke tsue ke u pepa* ('Suck, my child, so that I may carry you on my back'; see fig.). Some works were commissioned from Mokanyane for the British Empire Exhibition of 1936. Ts'itso Mohapi (*b* 1941) is less well known. He produced a wide variety of realistic figures of characters from traditional Sotho life. 'Mathabo Nthako produced biblical scenes.

An important collection of Basotho material culture is held by the Morija Museum and Archives, and there is a National Museum in Maseru. Exhibitions are sometimes staged at hotels, at the National University of Lesotho, Maseru, at the British Council, Maseru, at Machabeng High School and at Kolonyama Pottery. Traditionally, art education took place in the home, and there was little specialization. During the 19th century both missionary education and changing economic opportunities encouraged specialization. As cheap manufactured imports have replaced craft items and Western notions of art have been introduced, there has been a decline in traditional artistic practices. Since the advent of mass education following independence children have learnt less at home, while art education in schools has also declined. Efforts to start special art schools in Maseru had yet to succeed by the early 1990s, although some instruction was being given at Lerotholi Polytechnic and at some private schools.

BIBLIOGRAPHY

F. Christol: *L'Art dans l'Afrique australe* (Paris, 1911)
H. V. Meyerowitz: *A Report on the Possibilities of the Development of Village Crafts in Basutoland* (Morija, 1936)
C. G. Damant: *Samuel Makoanyane* (Morija, 1951)
J. Walton: *African Village* (Pretoria, 1956) [guidebook]
—: *Historic Buildings of Basutoland* (Morija, 1957)
*Expression* (1965–71) [irregular periodical]
N. S. Ndebele: 'Philemon Mpho Motsusi', *Expression*, ii/2 (1971), pp. 22–4
Sister Michel: 'The Teaching of Arts and Crafts at Mazenod Teachers College', *Educ. Botswana, Lesotho & Swaziland*, 10 (June 1975), pp. 18–20
R. Levinsohn: 'Lesotho Tapestry Weaving', *Afr. A.*, ix/4 (1976), pp. 52–5, 88
B. Mothibe: *Litema: Designs by the Students of the National Teacher Training College of Lesotho* (Maseru, 1976)
R. Levinsohn: 'Lesotho Silkscreens and Block Prints', *Afr. A.*, xiii/4 (1980), pp. 56–9
D. Costa and P. Des Ormeaux: *The Silent Language of Stone: On Maseru's Architectural Heritage* (Maseru, 1990)
*Morija Museum & Archives* (Morija, 1990)
D. Ambrose: *Maseru: An Illustrated History* (Morija, 1993)
G. Van Wyk: 'Through the Cosmic Flower: Secret Resistance in the Mural Art of Sotho-Tswana Women', *Secrecy: African Art that Conceals and Reveals*, ed. M. H. Nooter (New York and Munich, 1993), pp. 81–97
*Lesotho: Kingdom in the Sky* (exh. cat. by S. J. Gill and others; ed. J. A. M. Giesen; Berg en Dal, Afrika Mus., 1993)

STEPHEN J. GILL

**Lespingola [Spingola], François** (*b* Joinville, Meuse, 1644; *d* Paris, 16 July 1705). French sculptor. He was in Rome as a student at the Académie de France from 1665 to 1675 and in 1672 became a member of the Accademia di S Luca. During his years in Italy he may also have visited Florence. On his return to France he was received (*reçu*) as a member of the Académie Royale de Peinture et de Sculpture in 1676 on presentation of the low relief the *Union of the Académies of France and Rome* (untraced). He was principally employed on royal works at the château of Versailles and elsewhere. Among his works at Versailles are a charming, classicizing, stone statue of a woman representing *Altimetry* on the attic of the Aile du Midi (1681; *in situ*) and a number of decorative works executed in collaboration with Jacques Buirette (1631–99). These include models for trophies (1678–9 and 1682–3; destr.) subsequently cast in bronze for the Cabinets des Dômes in the park and for the Salon de la Guerre and the Grande Galerie (bronzes, Versailles, Château), as well as the lively group of *Three Children Playing with a Swan* (bronze, 1685–7; *in situ*) for the Parterre d'Eau.

Lespingola contributed two marble copies after the Antique to the gardens at Versailles: a statue of *Berenice* (1673; *in situ*), executed during his period in Rome, and a group of *Paetus and Arria* (1684–8; *in situ*). In 1688–9 he executed seven carved-wood overdoors representing vivacious putti with the attributes of the gods for the Grand

Figure of a woman and child by Samuel Mokanyane, pottery, h. 90 mm, *c.* 1940 (Morija, Morija Museum and Archives)

Trianon (six survive *in situ*). In the period 1690–1704 he was responsible for supplying models for sculpture for most of the important royal building projects, most notably the church of the Invalides, Paris, where he also carved a number of stone reliefs under the direction of François Girardon, including the *Pope Blessing St Louis and his Children* (1691–3; *in situ*), and where he designed the coloured marble pavement under the cupola. In 1699 he worked on decorative sculpture for the château of Meudon, Hauts-de-Seine (destr.), and the château of Marly, Yvelines (destr.).

The classicism of Lespingola's work is always accompanied by vivacity and ease of execution. The animated, Italianate group *Hercules Rescuing Prometheus*, a work of his own invention, was probably modelled *c.* 1695–1700; it is known in four bronze casts (e.g. that from the collection of Augustus, Elector of Saxony, h. 568 mm; Dresden, Grünes Gewölbe). This work is related to six other small bronze groups of a late Baroque character representing the *Labours of Hercules* (various cols; see Souchal, iv, pp. 169–73), for which the original models may also have been by Lespingola.

Lami; Souchal

BIBLIOGRAPHY

A. Jal: *Dictionnaire critique de biographie et d'histoire* (Paris, 1872), p. 779
J. Guiffrey: *Comptes des Bâtiments du Roi sous le règne de Louis XIV*, 5 vols (Paris, 1881–1901)
R. Gillet: 'Biographie et oeuvre de François Lespingola de Joinville', *Mém. Soc. Acad. Agric., Sci., A. & B.-Lett. Dép. Aube*, lxvii (1903), pp. 179–98
M. Rambaud: *Documents du minutier central concernant l'histoire de l'art (1700–50)*, ii (Paris, 1971), pp. lxxv, 483–5, 789, 1028
C. Avery: 'Hercules Delivering Prometheus', *Florentine Baroque Bronzes and Other Objects of Art* (exh. cat., Toronto, Royal Ont. Mus., 1975), pp. 73–5
*Highlights of the Untermyer Collection* (exh. cat. by J. Draper, New York, Met., 1977), no. 327

FRANÇOISE DE LA MOUREYRE

**Lespugue.** Cave site in France, in the Grotte des Rideaux, Haute Garonne. It has yielded important remains of Upper Palaeolithic date (*c.* 40,000–*c.* 10,000 BP; *see also* PREHISTORIC EUROPE, §II). The site was excavated by René de Saint-Périer from 1911 to 1914 and in 1922. A cave fauna, without artefacts, was found in the forward part of the cave, under levels disturbed in the Middle Ages. In the rear part, under 250 mm of vegetal zone, lay 1 m of ashes containing Upper Palaeolithic materials, with a loam (sand, silt and clay) deposit below it. The archaeological section drawing indicates that the rear part formed a depression more than 1 m deep. The fauna—including horse and reindeer (abundant), red deer (rare), a large bovid (possibly a bison), chamois and fox—contrasts with a poor stone tool industry of burins, a few end scrapers and some retouched blades, but no backed tools. The bone industry is characterized by cylindrical bone and antler points (the latter with longitudinal grooves), some polishers and decorated pieces (*see* PREHISTORIC EUROPE, fig. 13). Beads consist of perforated fox and red deer canines, and snails (one species from the Atlantic). This evidence suggests a site that was not intensively occupied, at least in the undisturbed back part where few artefacts were discarded.

On 9 August 1922 a female figurine, sculptured longitudinally from mammoth ivory, was discovered below a stone in the ashy level (see fig.). Missing parts at the front

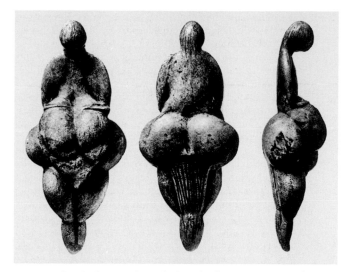

Lespugue, female figurine (front, back and side views), mammoth ivory, h. 147 mm, *c.* 25,000 BP (Paris, Musée de l'Homme)

are the result of damage by a pick during the excavation. On the small faceless head the hair is indicated by incised longitudinal lines. The upper part of the body is narrow, thin and slightly curved. The large breasts rest on the belly, where a portion of the once complete figurine is missing. The buttocks are wide and well pronounced on the hips, but the back is only moderately rounded. The thighs are separated by a deep groove, the lower legs very short and the feet indicated by a slight forward projection. The back is covered by a triangular loincloth composed of longitudinal incisions filled in their upper portions by short transverse lines. More generally, the thin upper part of the body is in contrast to the accentuated buttocks and hips. The thin arms are angled and rest on the breasts, and are separated from the upper body by small holes (*see also* PREHISTORIC EUROPE, §II, 3(i)).

BIBLIOGRAPHY
R. de Saint-Périer: 'Statuette de femme stéatopyge découverte à Lespugue (Haute-Garonne)', *L'Anthropologie*, xxxii (1922), pp. 361–81
H. Delporte: *L'Image de la femme dans l'art préhistorique* (Paris, 1979), pp. 32–6

JOACHIM HAHN

**Lesser Sunda islands.** *See under* INDONESIA.

**Lessing.** German family of artists.

**(1) Carl Friedrich Lessing** (*b* Breslau [now Wrocław, Poland], 15 Feb 1808; *d* Karlsruhe, 5 June 1880). Painter, great-nephew of GOTTHOLD EPHRAIM LESSING. He studied architecture in Berlin at the Königliche Bau-Akademie under Karl Friedrich Schinkel, before transferring to the Kunstakademie, where he became a pupil of Wilhelm Schadow in 1825. The next year Lessing followed Schadow to Düsseldorf, where the latter had been appointed Director of the Kunstakademie. Almost to the end of his career Lessing was to follow Schadow's rules for a standard series of procedures in the production of a finished work: compositional sketch, oil study, detailed model study, cartoon and underdrawing for the final painting. Without an official position, Lessing worked at the Düsseldorf

Akademie until 1858, when he was appointed Director of the Grossherzogliche Gemäldegalerie in Karlsruhe, a position he held until his death.

Lessing confirmed his commitment to landscape painting during a journey to the Baltic island of Rügen in 1822, and landscapes constitute most of his surviving oeuvre. In 1827, together with Johann Wilhelm Schirmer, he established an association of landscape painters, the Landschaftliche Componierverein. Lessing made many sketching trips to low German mountain ranges, such as the Harz Mountains; but, apart from a journey to Switzerland in 1866, he did not travel abroad. He made excellent, detailed drawings from nature, where he employed a purely objective approach to his subject. In his paintings, however, he strove for atmosphere and animated landscape settings with historical and narrative detail designed to spark certain associations, as in *Monastery Courtyard under Snow* (1830; Cologne, Wallraf-Richartz-Mus.) and *Castle on a Rock* (1828; Düsseldorf, Kstmus.). In such works Lessing followed in the landscape painting tradition of Caspar David Friedrich and Karl Friedrich Schinkel. Lessing's objective study of natural forms in his drawings did, however, contribute to the realistic depiction of the landscape settings he chose. A tendency to depict landscape more realistically is notable in works from the 1830s, as in *Eifel Landscape* (1834; Warsaw, N. Mus.).

Although Lessing produced relatively few history paintings, it was to works in this genre that he owed his renown during the 1830s and 1840s. Schadow and several of Lessing's friends had repeatedly encouraged him to treat historical themes, and Schadow helped Lessing secure a commission for frescoes in Heltorf Castle near Düsseldorf. Lessing, however, executed only one of these, as he had no liking for fresco painting. His *Grieving Royal Couple* (1830; St Petersburg, Hermitage) reveals an aptitude for history subjects of a calm and sentimental kind. Among Lessing's most important history paintings are those that deal with the lives of the 16th-century religious reformers Jan Hus and Martin Luther, for example *Hussite Sermon* (1836; Düsseldorf, Kstmus.; on loan Berlin, Neue N.G.), *Jan Hus on Trial in Constance* (1842; Frankfurt am Main, Städel. Kstinst. & Städt. Gal.) and *Martin Luther's Disputation with Johannes Eck in Leipzig, 1519* (1867; Karlsruhe, Staatl. Ksthalle), which was Lessing's last history painting. With these pictures, Lessing moved away from themes where sentiment was the main motivation and used events from the past to comment on the contemporary political situation, notably the tensions between Protestant Prussia and the traditionally Catholic Rhineland, which it had ruled since 1815. More generally, Lessing's pictures alluded to the struggle of the liberal German middle class for political independence. Lessing's history paintings made him one of the most celebrated and controversial painters of his age in Germany. Their impact owed most to the strong psychological characterization and the dramatic depiction of historical events. In these respects Lessing's pictures represented influential prototypes for the development of Realism in German painting.

BIBLIOGRAPHY

Thieme–Becker
W. Hütt: *Die Düsseldorfer Malerschule, 1819–1869* (Leipzig, 1964)
E. Scheyer: 'Carl Friedrich Lessing und die deutsche Landschaft', *Aurora: Eichendorff Alm.*, ed. K. Schodrok (Regensburg, 1965), pp. 49–64
I. Jenderko-Sichelschmidt: *Die Historienbilder Carl Friedrich Lessings* (diss., U. Cologne, 1973)
*Die Düsseldorfer Malerschule* (exh. cat., ed. W. von Kalnein; Düsseldorf, Kstmus.; Darmstadt, Ausstellhallen Mathildenhöhe; 1979), pp. 86–97
*Carl Friedrich Lessing, 1808–1880: Handzeichnungen aus dem Cincinnati Art Museum, Ohio/USA* (exh. cat., Karlsruhe, Staatl. Ksthalle, 1980)
V. Leuschner: *Carl Friedrich Lessing, 1808–1880: Die Handzeichnungen*, Dissertationen zur Kunstgeschichte, 14/II (Cologne and Vienna, 1982)

MARAIKE BUECKLING

**(2) Otto Lessing** (*b* Düsseldorf, 24 Feb 1846; *d* Berlin, 22 Nov 1912). Sculptor, writer and photographer, son of (1) Carl Friedrich Lessing. He studied drawing and then painting with his father and in 1863 went to the Akademie in Karlsruhe to study sculpture with C. J. Steinhäuser. Between 1865 and 1868 Lessing studied with the sculptor Albert Wolff at the Akademie in Berlin. In 1872 he settled in Berlin and opened his own studio, becoming established as one of the most favoured collaborators for Berlin architects. Buildings in Berlin to which Lessing contributed sculptural decoration include the Kunstgewerbemuseum (now the Gropiusbau), the Reichstag, the Technische Hochschule, the Deutsche (Neue) Kirche on the Gendarmenmarkt and the Deutsche Staatsbibliothek. Work outside Berlin included the Reichsgericht in Leipzig and the Schlesisches Museum in Breslau (now Muzeum Narodowe, Wrocław, Poland). In 1880 Lessing published *Ausgeführte Bauornamente Berlins* and in 1884 and 1890 the two volumes of *Bauornamente der Neuzeit*. After a visit to Paris in 1889, Lessing made a photographic study of Schloss Ansbach and subsequently published *Schloss Ansbach: Barock- und Roccoco-Dekorationen aus dem XVIII. Jahrhundert* (Berlin, [1892]).

After the rebuilding of the Königliches Schloss in Berlin in 1894, Lessing made reliefs of the *Great Elector* and of *Frederick the Great*, both shown on horseback, for the Weisse Saal, and of allegorical figures for the ceiling. For the royal stables he produced the figures of *Prometheus* and *Andromeda* and also a wall fountain. He also contributed work to the Siegesallee (dismantled after World War II) after the project began in 1895 (*see* GERMANY, §IV, 4). For the new cathedral, on the site of the Lustgarten, he made three bronze doors (*in situ*) and reliefs of the story of the apostles. Lessing also made sculptural monuments to *Emperor William I* (1900; Hildesheim), *Shakespeare* (1904; Weimar, Goethepark) and *Martin Luther* (1912; Hamburg). Other works include the marble Hercules Fountain for Lützowplatz in Berlin (1903; destr; see Bloch and Grzimek, p. 303), the bronze and stone Roland Fountain for Kemperplatz in Berlin (1902; destr; see Bloch and Grzimek, p. 306) and bronze reliefs for the Lessingbrücke in Moabit, Berlin (1903; destr.). With his overriding interest in past styles, Lessing achieved little stylistic development within his oeuvre.

BIBLIOGRAPHY

Bénézit; Thieme–Becker
E. Ingwersen: *Standbilder in Berlin*, Berlinische Reminiszenzen, 16 (Berlin, 1967)
P. Bloch and W. Grzimek: *Das klassische Berlin: Die Berliner Bildhauerschule im 19. Jahrhundert* (Berlin, 1978)
P. Bloch: 'Heroen der Kunst: Wissenschaft und Wirtschaft. Zierbrunnen und "freie" Kunst', *Kunst des 19. Jahrhunderts im Rheinland*, iv, *Plastik* (Düsseldorf, 1980), p. 507

*Berliner Kunst von 1770–1930: Studiensammlung Waldemar Grzimek* (exh. cat., W. Berlin, Berlin Mus., 1982)

BRIGITTE HÜFLER

**Lessing, Gotthold Ephraim** (*b* Kamenz, 21 Jan 1729; *d* Brunswick, 15 Feb 1781). German philosopher, critic and playwright. He was the leading representative of the German Enlightenment in the theatre and in criticism. Lessing studied theology at the University of Leipzig from 1746 to 1748, changing his faculty to medicine shortly before moving to Berlin. He was in Berlin intermittently until 1760, when he became secretary to the Prussian General von Tauentzien in Breslau (now Wrocław, Poland), remaining there until 1765. In 1767 he went to the liberal trading city of Hamburg in the hope of founding a German national theatre, and from 1770 until his death was the librarian to the Prince of Brunswick at Wolfenbüttel.

During Lessing's first stay in Berlin he contributed a series of brilliant articles to the *Vossische Zeitung*, a journal of popular philosophy dedicated to the propagation of Enlightenment ideas. His first major critical works were his contributions to *Briefe, die neueste Literatur betreffend* (1759–65), along with Moses Mendelssohn (1729–86), Christoph Friedrich Nicolai and other representatives of the Berlin Enlightenment. In these Lessing attacked Joachim Christoph Gottsched's legislation of the arts, seeing it with Johann Gottfried Herder (incorrectly) as an uninspired translation of French classicism. Lessing proposed in place of rules an emphasis on the genius and spontaneity of the artist. This theoretical position was reflected in his own writings, especially in his three great Enlightenment dramas: *Minna von Barnhelm oder das Soldatenglück* (1767), *Emilia Galotti* (1772) and *Nathan der Weise* (1779).

Lessing produced a large body of critical and philosophical works among which *Laokoon: Oder über die Grenzen der Malerei und Poesie* (Berlin, 1766), the *Hamburgische Dramaturgie* (Hamburg, 1767–9) and *Die Erziehung des Menschengeschlechts* (Berlin, 1780) were the most important and influential. In the *Hamburgische Dramaturgie* Lessing continued the campaign against the influence of Gottsched, seeking to establish a new, German drama. In the *Erziehung* Lessing offered a fine statement of the Enlightenment humanism that received dramatic expression in *Nathan der Weise*. The *Laokoon* is indisputably the most important work by Lessing concerning the visual arts: Lessing distinguished the modes of representation characteristic of painting and poetry, and argued that they should not be confused. It is a critical contribution to the UT PICTURA POESIS debate, dissenting from the view that poetry and painting are similar. The real objects of criticism were the contemporary tendencies towards the 'silent verse' of descriptive poetry and the 'speaking images' of allegorical painting.

One of the many peculiarities of the *Laokoon* is its choice of a sculpture—the *Laokoon* (Rome, Vatican, Mus. Pio-Clementino)—to determine the limits of painting and poetry. There are several reasons for this. The first, proposed by Lessing in his introduction, is a broad definition of painting that includes the plastic arts. This view, which was also Johann Joachim Winckelmann's, was vigorously disputed by Herder in his essay on sculpture.

The second is the polemical intent regarding Winckelmann's discussion of Greek sculpture in general, and of the *Laokoon* sculpture in particular. A third reason, perhaps underestimated, is that Lessing only knew the sculpture from engraved reproductions. The choice of the sculpture of Laokoon and his sons—then thought to be Greek but since recognized as a Roman copy—as the theme for distinguishing poetry and painting was determined by Winckelmann's comparison of the sculpture with Virgil's account of the death of Laokoon in the *Aeneid*. In *Gedanken über die Nachahmung der griechischen Werke in der Malerei und Bildhauer-Kunst*, Winckelmann claimed that Laokoon does not cry out, as Virgil says, but sighs. The sculpture is taken to exemplify his definition of Greek beauty as 'noble simplicity and quiet grandeur'.

Lessing agreed with the distinction between sculpture and poem, but insisted that it did not follow from the difference between Greek and Roman notions of beauty. The reason for the distinction lies in the distinct modes of imitation employed in the two arts. The distinction is set out in the crucial chapter XVI of the essay, where painting and poetry are said to employ different 'means or signs' in different ways. Painting disposes natural signs into simultaneous 'figures and colours in space', while poetry composes arbitrary signs into successive 'articulate sounds in time'. While painting represents in space at a given moment, poetry is a temporal medium; the one appeals to the eye, the other to the ear. (The idea of representation 'at a given moment' was later disputed as artificial by GEORG CHRISTOPH LICHTENBERG.) These distinctions were used as criteria for the judgement of poetry and painting and were critical both of Winckelmann's theory and of much contemporary art. In the case of Laokoon, Lessing argued, the sculptor cannot represent the figure as crying, since this would violate the limits of the art of painting. The cry, however, would be completely appropriate in a poem.

Lessing's clarification of the limits of poetry and painting, while not original, was immensely influential. It was reflected in his own dramatic practice in the innovative relationships that Lessing established between scenery and dialogue. The distinction of visual and audial art forms in terms of spatial and temporal modes of representation was so widely adopted that it became a commonplace. Fuseli, for example, cited Lessing's grounds for distinguishing between the two arts in his lectures. However, Lessing's distinction was criticized as early as 1778 by Herder, who objected that sculpture was a tactile and not a visual art. More recently, the *Laokoon* has again risen to prominence in the semiology of art by virtue of its distinction of natural and arbitrary signs.

WRITINGS

E. Bell, ed.: *Selected Prose Works of G. E. Lessing* (London, 1879)
K. Woelfel, ed.: *Lessings Werke*, 3 vols (Frankfurt, 1967)

BIBLIOGRAPHY

F. Mehring: *Die Lessing Legende* (Berlin, 1893)
J. G. Robertson: *Lessing's Dramatic Theory* (Cambridge, 1939)
E. H. Gombrich: 'Lessing', *Proc. Brit. Acad.*, xliii (1957)
E. M. Szarota: *Lessings 'Laokoon'* (Weimar, 1959)
M. Kommerell: *Lessing und Aristoteles* (Frankfurt am Main, 1960)
M. Allentuck: 'Henry Fuseli and Lessing', *Lessing Yb.*, 1 (1969), pp. 178–86
F. A. Brown: *Gotthold Ephraim Lessing* (New York, 1971)

E. Dvoretsky: *Lessing: Dokumente zur Wirkungsgeschichte, 1755-1968* (Munich, 1971)

D. Hildebrandt: *Lessing: Biographie einer Emanzipation* (Munich, 1979)

D. E. Wellbery: *Lessing's Laokoon: Semiotics and Aesthetics in the Age of Reason* (Cambridge, 1984)

A. Ugrinsky, ed.: *Lessing and the Enlightenment* (New York, 1986)

HOWARD CAYGILL

**Lessore** [née Brook], **Helen** (*b* London, 31 Oct 1907; *d* 6 May 1994). English painter and gallery director. She studied at the Slade School of Fine Art, London (1924–8). In 1931 she started working for the art dealer Frederick Lessore, who later became her husband. Financial and family responsibilities after his death in 1951 forced her to take over his West End gallery, the Beaux Arts Gallery in Bruton Place, London, whose director she remained until its closure in 1965. Nearly all the artists she promoted were graduates either of the Royal College of Art or of the Slade and were unknown at the time. Most—notably Craigie Aitchison (*b* 1926), Michael Andrews, Frank Auerbach, Francis Bacon, Leon Kossoff, Raymond Mason, Euan Uglow and the painters of the Kitchen Sink school—later gained considerable reputations, thus indicating in retrospect her determination to stand outside fashionable taste. All were unashamedly humanist in their approach, belonging to what Lessore has called the 'Great Tradition', in a period that saw the tail-end of Neo-Romanticism, the dominance of abstraction, the emergence of Pop art and the increasing commercialism of the art world. In 1958 she was made an OBE for her services to the fine arts.

Lessore's own work shared many of the qualities she looked for in her artists. She resumed painting in the early 1960s, using her family, friends and artists as her subject-matter. *Symposium I* (1974–7; London, Tate) and *Symposium II* (1974–83; artist's col.) show two versions of an informal gathering of her circle of artists. Her gauge of quality was always the figurative and technical example of Walter Sickert (whose third wife, Thérèse Lessore, was her sister-in-law). Her son, John Lessore (*b* 1939), is also a highly regarded painter working in the same tradition.

WRITINGS

*A Partial Testament: Essays on some Moderns in the Great Tradition* (London, 1986)

BIBLIOGRAPHY

*Helen Lessore and the Beaux Arts Gallery* (exh. cat. by A. Forge, London, Marlborough F.A., 1968)

*Paintings by Helen Lessore* (exh. cat. by M. Peppiatt, London, 12 Duke Street Gal., 1981)

*The Hard-won Image: Traditional Method and Subject in Recent British Art* (exh. cat. by R. Morphet, London, Tate, 1984)

*Helen Lessore* (exh. cat. by R. Morphet, London, F.A. Soc., 1987)

MONICA BOHM-DUCHEN

**Lester, Charles E(dwards)** (*b* Griswold, CT, 15 July 1815; *d* Detroit, MI, 29 Jan 1890). American writer. He qualified as a barrister in Natchez, MI, in 1838 after first studying for the ministry at Auburn Theological Seminary (1835–6). A period as a pastor in Liverpool, NY, was ended by ill health. He left the ministry and travelled to Britain in 1840. In 1842 he became the US Consul in Genoa, Italy (1842–7), and there began translating Italian autobiographies and histories and also wrote his major contribution to American art history, *The Artists of America: A Series of Biographical Sketches of American Artists with Portraits and Designs on Steel* (1846). In this he aimed to persuade the American public of the importance of their art and artists. Lengthy chapters cover the talents of such painters as Benjamin West, John Trumbull and Washington Allston; shorter chapters feature James de Vaux (1812–44), Thomas Crawford and Henry Inman, which Lester included to encourage interest in contemporary art. Two magazine articles on artists comprised the only other published writings by Lester concerning art.

UNPUBLISHED SOURCES

Detroit, Pub. Lib. [letters]

WRITINGS

*The Artists of America: A Series of Biographical Sketches of American Artists with Portraits and Designs on Steel* (New York, 1846)

BIBLIOGRAPHY

*Appletons Cyclo. of American Biography*

*National Cyclopedia of American Biography*

DARRYL PATRICK

**Le Sueur** [Lesueur], **Eustache** (*b* Paris, 19 Nov 1616; *d* Paris, 30 April 1655). French painter and draughtsman. He was one of the most important painters of historical, mythological and religious pictures in 17th-century France and one of the founders of French classicism. He was long considered the 'French Raphael' and the equal of Nicolas Poussin and Charles Le Brun. His reputation reached its zenith in the first half of the 19th century, but since then it has been in decline, largely as a result of the simplified and saccharine image of the man and his art created by Romantic writers and painters. Nevertheless, more recent recognition of the complexity of his art has resulted in a new interest in him and in his place in the evolution of French painting in the 17th century. Despite the almost total absence of signed and dated works, the chronology of Le Sueur's oeuvre can be established with the aid of a few surviving contracts, dated engravings after his paintings and the list of works published by Le Comte in 1700.

1. Life and work. 2. Critical reception and posthumous reputation.

1. LIFE AND WORK.

*(i) Early years and training, to c. 1645.* He was the son of Cathelin Le Sueur (*d* 1666), a wood-turner from Picardy, who had settled in Paris. Around 1632 Eustache's precocious talent and his family contacts gained him entry into the busiest and most famous studio in the capital, that of Simon Vouet, who had returned from Italy in 1627. Le Sueur remained there until about 1642, participated in Vouet's decorative projects and acquired something of his richness and breadth of touch as a decorative painter. During this period Le Sueur made use in his own work of his master's figure studies, arranging them into crowded compositions with little attention to organization or verisimilitude. The colouring of such early paintings as *Diana and Callisto* (*c.* 1638; Dijon, Mus. Magnin) is bright and agreeable and already shows considerable subtlety, while his facility and lyricism are apparent in his principal early works, the series of tapestry cartoons based on Francesco Colonna's romance *Hypnerotomachia Poliphili* (1499), of which five paintings survive (Malibu, CA, Getty Mus.; Le Mans, Mus. Tessé; Dijon, Mus. Magnin; Rouen, Mus. B.-A.; Salzburg, Residenzgal.). During the same period he also treated subjects from mythology, such as *Sleeping*

1. Eustache Le Sueur: *Gathering of Friends*, oil on canvas, 1.36×1.95 m, *c.* 1640 (Paris, Musée du Louvre)

*Venus Surprised by Cupid* (*c.* 1638; San Francisco, CA, Pal. Legion of Honor), from the Bible, including *Amnon and Tamar* (*c.* 1636; New York, Met.), and from ancient history, such as *Coriolanus* (*c.* 1638; Paris, Louvre). Le Sueur seems to have worked on the Polyphilus series over a period of several years and a development towards a greater sobriety and rigour of style is observable in the later pictures such as *Polyphilus before Queen Eleutherilida* (*c.* 1644; Rouen, Mus. B.-A.).

Between 1640 and 1645 Le Sueur produced a number of more modest works, whose variety indicates the beginning of a successful independent career: there were devotional paintings, such as the *Virgin and Child with the Infant St John* (Paris, Louvre), some of which were engraved by Pierre Daret and Michel Dorigny, as well as portraits, of which the most important is the *Gathering of Friends* (Paris, Louvre; see fig. 1), commissioned around 1640 by the enthusiastic amateur of music, Anne de Chambré. In these works he refined Vouet's style. There were also designs for engraved frontispieces for books. That of 1645, representing *David and Goliath*, for the thesis of Claude Bazin de Champigny, has a simplicity and solidity of composition new in Le Sueur's work.

*(ii) Early maturity and the 'Severe' style, c. 1645–52.* In 1644–5 Le Sueur was admitted as a master in the Paris painters' guild, with an ambitious work, *St Paul Exorcizing a Man Possessed of the Devil* (untraced, engraved). In 1645 he was commissioned to paint a cycle of 22 paintings depicting the *Life of St Bruno* (Paris, Louvre) for the small cloister of the charterhouse in Paris. He worked on this series for three years, moving away decisively from the style of Vouet (still evident in the first painting of the series, the *Sermon of Raymond Diocre*). He was absorbing the lessons of the art of Raphael (whose work he knew chiefly through prints) and of Poussin (who was in Paris from 1640 to 1642). The *Life of St Bruno* was much admired by Le Sueur's contemporaries. Around 1680 it was engraved by François Chauveau, and such was its reputation that the series was bought by Louis XVI in 1776. But Le Sueur, according to Félibien, was not satisfied with it, and certain scenes are slackly painted and may be attributable to assistants working from Le Sueur's drawings, the most important of which are in the so-called St Bruno Album (Paris, Louvre). During these years Le Sueur's work grew more serious, his style more austere and rigorous, though occasionally clumsy and uncertain. His compositions are carefully and rationally planned: he attached great importance to correct perspective and foreshortening in his ceiling paintings, such as the *Archangel Raphael Leaving the Family of Tobias* (1648; Grenoble, Mus. Peint. & Sculp.), which was part of a series illustrating the *Story of Tobias* (see below), and to the architectural settings of such works as the *Consecration of a Carthusian Church* (*c.* 1648; Paris, Louvre). His figures, with dignified drapery and gestures, have a stronger presence. His colouring, though less brilliant, is more expressive. He came to rely on his own drawings, both for

2. Eustache Le Sueur: *Birth of Love*, oil on panel, 1.82×1.25 m, *c.* 1646–7 (Paris, Musée du Louvre)

details and for overall compositions, as an essential part of the creative process. Large numbers of these survive (e.g. Paris, Louvre; Besançon, Mus. B.-A. & Archéol.; Chantilly, Mus. Condé; Montpellier, Mus. Fabre).

Despite difficult political and economic circumstances during the civil war of the Fronde, which virtually cancelled all royal and princely commissions during the late 1640s, Le Sueur continued to work uninterruptedly for a private clientele comprising chiefly members of the Paris Parlement, royal officials, wealthy merchants and financiers. At their request, he frequently painted subjects drawn from the Bible or ancient history, treating them in an austere and monumental style. Examples include the *Story of Tobias* (*c.* 1644–8; fragments Paris, Louvre; Grenoble, Mus. Peint. & Sculp.) for Gaspard de Fieubet; *Alexander and the Physician Philip* (*c.* 1648; untraced, engraved) for Jérôme de Nouveau; and *Darius Ordering the Tomb of Nitocris to be Opened* (1649; St Petersburg, Hermitage) for Vedeau de Grandmont. Le Sueur was also active as a decorator of chapels and private oratories, painting the monumental *Raising of Tabitha* (1647; Toronto, A.G. Ont.) for St Etienne-du-Mont, Paris, and the delicate *Annunciation* (1650; Toledo, OH, Mus. A.) for the Paris hôtel of Guillaume Brissonet.

In 1649 Le Sueur, appointed Peintre Ordinaire du Roi, was chosen to paint the May of Notre-Dame de Paris, the large painting presented annually to the cathedral of Notre-Dame by the guild of goldsmiths. With *St Paul at Ephesus*

(Paris, Louvre; oil sketches London, N.G., and Algiers, Mus. N. B.-A.), a large pyramidal composition, bold and bright, with no inessential details, he produced the crowning achievement of his Raphaelesque style. *St Paul at Ephesus*, like contemporary paintings by Charles Le Brun, Laurent de La Hyre and Sébastien Bourdon, who with Le Sueur were among the 12 'Anciens' appointed to teach at the Académie Royale de Peinture et de Sculpture founded the previous year (*see* PARIS, §VI, 1), defined a new stage in the development of the French classical style when judged against the more relaxed work of Vouet.

Le Sueur's talent also had a more charming, though unaffected, vein. Together with Giovanni Francesco Romanelli, Herman van Swanevelt and other painters, he decorated the Cabinet de l'Amour in the Hôtel Lambert, Paris (*c.* 1646–8 and 1652; most paintings Paris, Louvre). Among his pictures is the delightful *Birth of Love* (see fig. 2), the central section of the ceiling. The patron, the wealthy and fastidious financier Nicolas Lambert, was captivated by a painter who knew how to make the most of a relatively restricted space and who composed choice decorative schemes in which the richly ornamented setting displayed the freshly coloured paintings to advantage.

*(iii) Last works, 1652–55.* During the last years of his life, and especially after 1652, Le Sueur's art grew still more refined, combining decorative elegance with compositional severity. Line was more important than volume. He employed arabesque-like compositions and slender figures with clearly defined outlines. His paintings became surfaces divided by the play of curves and straight lines, and subjects were reduced to the basic essentials, as in the *Annunciation* (1652; Paris, Louvre) or the *Perfect Minister* (1653; Dunkirk, Mus. B.-A.).

In 1652 Le Sueur was again at work in the Hôtel Lambert, where he decorated the Chambre des Muses with five paintings depicting the nine *Muses* and a ceiling painting of *Phaeton Asking Apollo's Permission to Drive the Chariot of the Sun* (all Paris, Louvre). He also executed the ceiling of the Cabinet des Bains (*in situ*). In these intimate works, which combine figures and landscape, Le Sueur's subtle colour harmonies and blond light reached a level of perfection, and he seems at his most assured artistically. With the end of the Fronde, royal commissions were resumed: Le Sueur was commissioned to paint several political allegories for the Appartement des Bains of Anne of Austria at the Louvre, Paris. The only ones to survive are *Juno Hurling a Thunderbolt at Troy* and *Juno Distributing her Bounty over Carthage* (both 1653; Venice, Pin. Manfrediniana). He also provided allegorical paintings of the *French Monarchy Triumphing over its Enemies* (1654; untraced; drawings Paris, Louvre) and of *Royal Magnificence* (1654–5; Dayton, OH, A. Inst.) for the Louvre appartement of the young Louis XIV.

During the same period, commissioned by the church-wardens of St Gervais in Paris, Le Sueur executed the first cartoon for a series of six tapestries illustrating episodes from the *Lives of SS Gervase and Protase*. Only the *SS Gervase and Protase Led before Astasius* (1652–4; Paris, Louvre) was completed in Le Sueur's lifetime. A second cartoon, the *Martyrdom of St Gervase* (1654–5; Lyon, Mus.

B.-A.), was completed after his death by his brother-in-law Thomas Goussé (1627–58). In addition to these monumental cartoons with their strongly rhythmic compositions, other late works are the *Adoration of the Shepherds* painted for the Oratorians of La Rochelle (1653; La Rochelle, Mus. B.-A.) and four paintings executed in 1654 for the Benedictine abbey of Marmoutiers-les-Tours (Indre-et-Loire): *St Sebastian Tended by Irene and the Angels* and *St Louis Caring for the Poor* (both Tours, Mus. B.-A.) and the *Appearance of the Virgin to St Martin* and *St Martin's Mass* (both Paris, Louvre). In these works Le Sueur developed a restrained, concentrated, loftily conceived style, in which the narrative element diminished in importance with the action frozen, seemingly outside time.

Le Sueur's extremely industrious life was lacking in notable events; it was punctuated only by his marriage in 1644 to Geneviève Goussé, the daughter of a wealthy grocer, by whom he had seven children (none of whom became a painter). He worked with a small team of assistants drawn from his family: his brothers Pierre (*b* 1608), Antoine (*b* 1610) and Philippe (*b* 1613) Le Sueur, and his brother-in-law Thomas Goussé. His financial circumstances appear to have been comfortable but not affluent.

2. CRITICAL RECEPTION AND POSTHUMOUS REPUTATION. After his early death, caused by illness and overwork, a number of Le Sueur's paintings were finished by Goussé, but his pure and graceful style was soon overshadowed by the classicism of Charles Le Brun, who rapidly became the dominant figure in French art of the 1660s and 1670s. Nevertheless, in the 18th century, when Le Sueur was considered as the 'French Raphael', he came to be seen as one of the greatest figures in the history of art and a clear exemplar for history painters. In the 19th century a whole Romantic myth developed around him, turning him into an impoverished, persecuted painter, soft-hearted and pious, a kind of Parisian Fra Angelico. This ambiguous fame was based initially on the apocryphal tales of his self-styled descendant, the composer Jean-François Le Sueur (1760–1837), and embroidered by later writers including Théophile Gautier and his collaborators in *Les Dieux et demi-dieux de la peinture* (1864), as well as in a number of sentimental genre paintings such as Jean Vignaud's *Death of Le Sueur* (exh. Salon 1812; Versailles, Château). In reaction later writers began to charge him with academicism and sentimentality, especially since many of his works are badly preserved, and it is not always possible to distinguish between autograph originals, works painted with the help of assistants, copies and mere pastiches of more recent date. The full individuality and complexity of his art only began to be recognized in the second half of the 20th century; it is an art that is varied and often more powerful than has been admitted. On ground prepared by Vouet, Le Sueur developed his innovative, sometimes paradoxical, style, in which the strength of the final result is achieved by great economy of means.

### BIBLIOGRAPHY

Mariette

A. Félibien: *Entretiens sur les vies et les ouvrages des plus excellents peintres anciens et modernes*, v (Paris, 1688), pp. 23–44

G. Guillet [Guillet de Saint-Georges]: 'Mémoire historique des ouvrages de M. Le Sueur. . .lu à l'Académie le samedi 5 août 1690' (MS. 1690); ed. L. Dussieux and others, *Mémoires inédits sur la vie et les ouvrages des membres de l'Académie Royale*, i (Paris, 1854), pp. 147–73

F. Le Comte: *Cabinet des singularités d'architecture, peinture, sculpture et gravure* (Paris, 1699–1700), iii, pp. 93–100

A.-J. Dézallier d'Argenville: *Abrégé de la vie des plus fameux peintres* (1745–52, 2/1762), iv, pp. 105–17

L. Dussieux and A. de Montaiglon: 'Nouvelles recherches sur la vie et les ouvrages de Le Sueur', *Archvs A. Fr.*, iii (1852), pp. 1–121 [includes an attempt at a catalogue of works]

L. Vitet: *Eustache Le Sueur*, Etudes sur l'histoire de l'art (Paris, 1864), pp. 99–180

G. Rouchès: *Eustache Le Sueur* (Paris, 1923)

L. Dimier: *Histoire de la peinture française, du retour de Vouet à la mort de Le Brun*, ii (Paris and Brussels, 1927), pp. 1–28

*Le XVIIe Siècle français: Chefs-d'oeuvre des musées de province* (exh. cat. by M. Laclotte, Paris, Petit Pal., 1958), nos 96–101

J. Thuillier and A. Châtelet: *La Peinture française de Le Nain à Fragonard* (Geneva, 1964), pp. 83–9

C. Sterling: 'Eustache Le Sueur peintre de portraits', *Walter Friedlaender zum 90. Geburtstag: Eine Festgabe seiner europäischen Schüler, Freunde und Verehrer*, ed. G. Kaufman and W. Sauerländer (Berlin, 1965), pp. 181–4

P. Rosenberg: 'Dessins de Le Sueur à Budapest', *Bull. Mus. Hong. B.-A.*, 39 (1972), pp. 63–75

*Le Cabinet de l'Amour de l'Hôtel Lambert* (exh. cat. by J.-P. Babelon and others, Paris, Louvre, 1972)

*French Master Drawings of the XVIIth and XVIIIth Centuries in North American Collections* (exh. cat. by P. Rosenberg, Toronto, A.G. Ont.; Ottawa, N.G.; San Francisco, CA, Pal. Legion of Honor; New York, Cult. Cent.; 1972), nos 84–7

N. Rosenberg-Henderson: 'Le Sueur's Decorations for the Cabinet des Muses of the Hôtel Lambert', *A. Bull.*, lvi (1974), pp. 555–70

A. Mérot: 'La "Légende Dorée" d'un peintre: Eustache Le Sueur au XIXe siècle', *Bull. Soc. Hist. A. Fr.* (1982), pp. 107–18

——: 'La Renommée d'Eustache Le Sueur et l'estampe', *Rev. A.* [Paris], 55 (1982), pp. 57–65

*La Peinture française du XVIIe siècle dans les collections américaines* (exh. cat. by P. Rosenberg, Paris, Grand Pal.; New York, Met.; Chicago, IL, A. Inst.; 1982), nos 50–54

A. Mérot: 'Eustache Le Sueur et ses graveurs, 1635–1655', *Nouv. Est.*, 69 (1983), pp. 6–13

*Raphaël et l'art français* (exh. cat. by A. Mérot, Paris, Grand Pal., 1983), nos 154–9

*Simon Vouet–Eustache Le Sueur: Dessins du Musée de Besançon* (exh. cat. by B. Brejon de Lavergnée and A. Mérot, Besançon, Mus. B.-A. & Archéol.; Rennes, Mus. B.-A.; 1984), nos 35–46

A. Mérot: *Eustache Le Sueur* (Paris, 1987) [with cat. rais.]

ALAIN MÉROT

**Le Sueur, Hubert** (*b* Paris, *c.* 1590; *d* Paris, after 1658). French sculptor and bronze-founder, active also in England. He was the son of an armourer, Pierre Le Sueur (*d* 1616) and trained in Paris, where in 1614 he was appointed Sculpteur Ordinaire du Roi to Henry IV. Little survives from his early documented commissions for tombs and an equestrian monument of Henri de Montmorency, but several busts and some equestrian portrait statuettes of the King and the Dauphin (later Louis XIII; examples London, V&A) are attributed to him. In 1625, having been recruited as Court Sculptor by Charles I of England, he travelled to London. His first task was to model temporary statues to decorate the catafalque of *James I*; these are known from a drawing (Oxford, Worcester Coll.) by its designer, Inigo Jones. Though untraced, they are probably reflected in the bronze mourning caryatids that support the canopy of the tomb of *Ludovick Stuart, 2nd Duke of Lennox and 1st Duke of Richmond and his Duchess*, which had been established in Westminster Abbey by 1628. The effigies of the deceased are still and lifeless images, redeemed only by a laborious rendering of the pattern on armour and dress. The complex was crowned by an ambitious winged figure of *Fame*, recalling the bronze *Fame* (1597; Paris, Louvre) on Pierre Biart's tomb (destr.) of the *Duchesse d'Epernon* in Cadillac, Gironde. Le Sueur was also influenced by the neighbouring tomb of *Henry VII* (1512–18) by Pietro Torrigiano. In the 1630s Le Sueur contributed another great tomb to the abbey, that of *George Villiers, 1st Duke of Buckingham* (assassinated in 1628), and of *Katherine Manners*, his Duchess (*d* 1634). It included marble portrait statues of their children, as well as monumental bronze effigies and grand seated mourners. At the same period his practice extended also to public portraits: a statue of *William Herbert, 3rd Earl of Pembroke* (Oxford, Schools Quadrangle) for Wilton House, and the celebrated equestrian statue of *Charles I* (1633; London, Trafalgar Square), for Roehampton House. In both statues Le Sueur failed in his attempt to emulate Giambologna; however, he did succeed in introducing new portrait types into English art.

The first documented payment from the Crown to Le Sueur was in January 1631. Shortly afterwards he went to Italy, commissioned by the King to make moulds of famous ancient statues, in order to reproduce them in bronze, to decorate the gardens of St James's Palace. Four of these statues are now in the East Terrace Garden, Windsor Castle, and there is a set of busts of philosophers in the Orangery of Hampton Court Palace. Also in 1631 Le Sueur executed the earliest dated portrait bust of *Charles I* (marble; London, V&A). This northern-European, late Mannerist portrait is typical in being frontal, symmetrical and immobile, though successful in conveying the monarch's public image. It recalls the slightly earlier busts by Barthélemy Tremblay of Charles I's father-in-law *Henry IV* of France (marble, Paris, Louvre; bronze version, Paris, Mus. Jacquemart-André). Charles I owned three bronze busts of himself by Le Sueur, probably versions of the marble portrait of 1631, which may be presumed, on account of its material and lengthy inscription, to be the original. In one (Oxford, Bodleian Lib.) he is bare-headed; in another (Chichester, Council Chamber) he wears an ermine cape and the crown; in a third, unique, bust (Stourhead, Wilts, NT) he wears a helmet with a dragon crest, probably in reference to St George, patron of England, with whom the King consciously identified himself. All are equally hieratic, but stylistically long out of date. They were followed by stilted portrait statues of *Charles I* and *Queen Henrietta Maria* (1633; Oxford, St John's Coll.; for a version of 1636 *see* ENGLAND, fig. 28) and of *James I* (1638; Winchester Cathedral), as well as several busts or statues of courtiers, none of them imbued with much movement or vitality.

Le Sueur's greatest commission for mythological statuary was the Fountain of Arethusa, known as the Diana Fountain (Middlesex, Bushey Park), first erected in 1636 in the Thames-side garden of Somerset House, Henrietta Maria's residence. For it he again took as his model a work by Giambologna, the Fountain of Neptune (completed 1566; *see* FOUNTAIN, fig. 3) in Bologna, grossly paraphrasing its delightful nymphs and putti into a series of flaccid nude figures; the subjects and their scale may have impressed the English (and, indeed, offended some Puritans), but from an aesthetic standpoint they are disappointing.

With the arrival in England of a rival court sculptor, Francesco Fanelli, Le Sueur's days of fame were numbered, and the King rapidly tired of his outdated style and inflated bills. He was last paid by the Crown in 1639 and left London in 1641, his disgrace being cloaked by the outbreak of the Civil War. Back in Paris by June 1643, he was commissioned to make four casts of a bust of *Cardinal Richelieu* that had been modelled by Jean Warin (1643; version Paris, Bib. Mazarine). In 1648 he was commissioned to produce four casts after the Antique, two of *Diana* and two of *Commodus*, for the gardens of two prominent courtiers of the young Louis XIV. Thereafter Le Sueur's age and lack of stylistic innovation told against him in the Parisian ambience of younger, more imaginative court sculptors such as Jacques Sarazin and Simon Guillain, and the last documents mention no commissions.

### BIBLIOGRAPHY
M. D. Whinney and O. Millar: *English Art, 1625–1714* (Oxford, 1957), pp. 115–21
M. Whinney: *Sculpture in Britain, 1530 to 1830*, Pelican Hist. A. (Harmondsworth, 1964, rev. 1988), pp. 35–7
C. Avery: *Studies in European Sculpture*, 2 vols (London, 1981–8), i, pp. 189–204; ii, pp. 145–235
G. Bresc-Bautier: 'L'Activité parisienne d'Hubert le Sueur sculpteur du roi (connu de 1596 à 1658)', *Bull. Soc. Hist. A. Fr.* (1985), pp. 35–54
D. Howarth: 'Charles I, Sculpture and Sculptors', *The Late King's Goods*, ed. A. MacGregor (London, 1989), pp. 73–113

CHARLES AVERY

**Lesueur, Jean-Baptiste-Cicéron** (*b* Clairefontaine, 5 Oct 1794; *d* Paris, 25 Dec 1883). French architect, teacher and writer. He studied architecture from 1811 at the Ecole des Beaux-Arts, Paris, as a pupil of Charles Percier and Auguste Pierre Sainte-Marie Famin (1776–1859). He won various prizes there, including the competition (1819) for the Prix de Rome, won jointly with Félix-Emmanuel Callet (1791–1854), with a design for a cemetery. After his return from Rome in 1826 he built mansions in central Paris and the parish church at Vincennes (1826–30). In 1835 he and Etienne-Hippolyte Godde, chief architect to the city of Paris, were appointed jointly to design extensions to the Hôtel de Ville (1836–48; destr. 1871), the interior of which was completed by Victor Baltard. In 1841 Lesueur retired from commercial practice, having become an inspector in the Highways Commission. In 1852 he was elected professor of the theory of architecture at the Ecole des Beaux-Arts, a position he held until his death. He briefly practised again from 1854 to 1857, when he designed the conservatoire of music in Geneva. Lesueur was the author of books and papers on a wide range of subjects, including Egyptology and the buildings of Milan and Turin, and he was rewarded with the Légion d'Honneur in 1847, the year after he was elected an honorary member of the Royal Institute of British Architects, whose gold medal he received in 1861.

### WRITINGS
*L'Histoire et théorie de l'architecture*, (Paris, 1879)

### BIBLIOGRAPHY
Obituary, *The Builder*, xlvi (5 Jan 1884), pp. 5–6
R. Middleton, ed.: *The Beaux-Arts and Nineteenth-century French Architecture* (London, 1982)

L. el-Wakil: 'Genève: Sur les traces de deux prix de Rome d'architecture: F.-E. Callet (1791–1854) et J.-B.-C. Lesueur (1794–1883)', *Bull. Soc. Hist. A. Fr.* (April 1986), pp. 101–15

PHILIP MCEVANSONEYA

**Leszczyński, Stanislav I,** King of Poland. *See* STANISLAV I LESZCZYŃSKI.

**Letarouilly** [Le Tarouilly], **Paul-Marie** (*b* Coutances, 8 Oct 1795; *d* Paris, 25 Oct 1855). French architect. He belonged to the school of Charles Percier and Pierre-François Fontaine and continued their liberal doctrine of a classical tradition based on the Renaissance into the mid-19th century. In 1814, Letarouilly came to Paris, where he studied under Percier in 1816 and entered the Ecole des Beaux-Arts in 1817. He served as a supervisor of works in 1819 on the rebuilding of Charles de Wailly's and Marie-Joseph Peyre's Théâtre de l'Odéon in Paris (1779–82; destr. by fire for the second time in 1818) and similarly from 1825 to 1831 on the construction of François-Hippolyte Destailleur's Ministry of Finance (1822–32; destr. 1871), which was located on the section of the Rue de Rivoli in Paris designed by Percier and Fontaine. In 1832 he was appointed architect of the Collège de France in Paris and spent the rest of his life restoring and enlarging Jean-François-Thérèse Chalgrin's Neo-classical building (1780–84). Letarouilly was in Rome three times (1821–4, 1831–2 and 1844–5) preparing the illustrations for his great work, *Edifices de Rome moderne*. Its 355 plates in three volumes with accompanying text volume supported Percier and Fontaine's thesis that the Italian Renaissance was the best historical model for 19th-century architecture. Letarouilly left unfinished the intended sequel *Le Vatican et la basilique de Saint-Pierre de Rome*.

WRITINGS

*Edifices de Rome moderne, ou recueil des palais, maisons, églises, couvents et autres monuments publics et particuliers les plus remarquables de la ville de Rome*, 4 vols (Paris, 1840–57; Eng. trans., London 1944), rev. A. Morel (Paris, 1874) [incl. an extensive biog. of Letarouilly in the text vol., pp. xiii–xviii]
*Le Vatican et la basilique de Saint-Pierre de Rome*, 2 vols (Paris, 1878–82; Eng. trans., London, 1963)

BIBLIOGRAPHY

Bauchal; *MEA*
A. Lance: *Dictionnaire des architectes français*, 2 vols (Paris, 1872)

CHRISTOPHER MEAD

**Le Tavernier, Jean** [Jan de Tavernier] (*fl c.* 1434–60). South Netherlandish illuminator. He seems to have specialized in the illustration of chronicles and similar texts and to have undertaken commissions principally for the Burgundian ducal court. In 1434 Le Tavernier became a Master in Tournai, where he was still working in 1440 when he took on an apprentice. He contributed to the decorations for the 'banquet du faisan' organized in Lille in 1454 by Philip the Good, Duke of Burgundy, for which Le Tavernier's payment was higher than average. In the same year he was resident in Oudenaarde and received payment from Philip the Good for 230 grisailles and 2 full-colour miniatures in a Book of Hours belonging to the Duke, and for illuminating a 'Livre de Godeffroy de Buillon'. In 1460 Le Tavernier received a payment for 'certaines histoires de blanc et de noir' (grisailles executed in the first volume of a 'Livre de Charlemaigne') and an

advance payment for illustrations to be produced in the second volume of this work. The manuscript, the *Cronicques et conquestes de Charlemaine* (Brussels, Bib. Royale Albert 1er, MSS 9066–8), a text compiled and written by David Aubert, serves as a point of departure in defining Le Tavernier's style. It was originally in two volumes, the second of which is now divided (MSS 9067–8). The original patron was Jean de Créqui, as indicated in the colophon of the first volume; yet by the time of completion the work was intended for Philip the Good, who is named as the recipient in the colophon of the second volume. The date of completion is given in this volume as 1458, and the whole work is listed in the inventory of the Burgundian library of 1467: the payment of 1460 fits within this chronological framework. In the frontispiece of the first volume (fol. 11*r*), the presentation of the book to the Duke of Burgundy is shown only in a background scene and the Duke's coat of arms is incorporated almost furtively on a town-gate in the miniature: this is unusual for a high-quality manuscript of this type and may be connected with the change of patron.

As Hulin de Loo (*BNB*) and Winkler have emphasized, Le Tavernier's compositions draw significantly on panel painting of the 1430s and 1440s. He created wide picture areas, somewhat undisciplined in perspective, but generously proportioned. The interiors not only give ample space for the figures but also incorporate furniture and other decorative objects, which are depicted in the detailed style of early Netherlandish painting. In exterior scenes houses or landscape elements form planes, which are interlocked like stage scenery and populated with large numbers of small, very lively figures. This makes it possible for the painter to present several scenes simultaneously, thus facilitating the depiction of the, at times, complicated narratives. The figures often wear the 'robe courte' of 1440s Burgundian fashion; this sometimes results in unnatural movements and affected poses.

Le Tavernier specialized in grisaille painting, which he brought to an unprecedented level of refinement. The quality of his grisaille work is partly derived from the expressivity of the various graphic formulae that he developed, for different types of tree and plant, for example; this largely compensates for the loss of colour as a means of differentiation. In addition the range of grey tones, sometimes verging towards shades of brown or blue, was unsurpassed. Le Tavernier also skilfully allowed the warm parchment background to show through thinly applied paint or even to remain unpainted.

These characteristics make Le Tavernier's personal style so unmistakable that historians have been able to attribute a series of works to him. Perhaps the most beautiful of these is a Book of Hours for Philip the Good (The Hague, Kon. Bib., MS. 76.F.2), which contains 165 grisaille miniatures (some of which are later additions by the Master of the Prayer Books of *c.* 1500). In many of Le Tavernier's miniatures the Duke himself is included in the scene, kneeling before a prie-dieu. It is not certain, however, whether this manuscript can be identified as the Book of Hours recorded in 1454, as the latter contained 230 miniatures and the manuscript conserved in The Hague does not seem to be so seriously incomplete. Furthermore, the extraordinarily refined painting of The Hague's Book of Hours indicates that it belongs to a later phase of Le Tavernier's development. The evolution of Le Tavernier's style is shown very clearly by two manuscripts of the same text, the *Miracles de Nostre Dame*: the first volume (Paris, Bib. N., MS. fr. 9198) of one of these manuscripts was completed in The Hague in 1456, according to the colophon (the second volume is in Oxford, Bodleian Lib., MS. Douce 374; see fig.); the second volume (Paris, Bib. Nat., MS. fr. 9199) of another version of the same text is stylistically more subtle and more fully developed. If both volumes are from the same workshop, a stylistic progression and, therefore, a certain chronological interval between them must be assumed.

Le Tavernier also illuminated manuscripts with full-colour miniatures, including a two-volume Breviary (Brussels, Bib. Royale Albert 1er, MSS 9511 and 9026) for Philip the Good, probably produced in collaboration with Willem Vrelant, and, in particular, works translated by the Duke's secretary Jean Miélot, such as the *Traité sur l'oraison dominicale* (Brussels, Bib. Royal Albert 1er, MS. 9092). While this last manuscript is a high-quality work, decorated with three miniatures and borders painted in opaque colours, simple manuscripts on paper such as the 1455 translation by Miélot, the *Avis pour faire le passage d'outre-mer* (Brussels, Bib. Royale Albert 1er, MS. 9095), display another technique, that of tinted ink drawings. The portrait of the author of the *Avis*, the Dominican monk Brochard (fol. 1*r*), shows him composing his book and is executed in this technique using soft yellow, blue and pink tones

within a grey frame. The writer sits at a reading desk by an open window, in a light, sparsely furnished room. He is looking through the manuscript that lies on the desk, his pen raised, evidently ready to copy what he reads into his own manuscript, which is on his knee. Numerous books are scattered about the room, some of them still open, suggesting that they have been frequently consulted. The image is thus depicted with a strangely intense sensitivity.

BIBLIOGRAPHY

*BNB*

J. van den Gheyn: *Cronicques et conquestes de Charlemaine. Reproduction de 105 miniatures de Jean le Tavernier d'Audenarde* (Brussels, 1909)

F. Winkler: *Die flämische Buchmalerei* (Leipzig, 1925, 2/Amsterdam/R 1978), pp. 58–66

A. de Laborde: *Les Miracles de Nostre Dame*, 2 vols (Paris, 1929)

V. Leroquais: *Le Bréviaire de Philippe le Bon*, 2 vols (Paris, Brussels and New York, 1929)

*Le Siècle d'or de la miniature flamande* (exh. cat. by L. M. J. Delaissé, Brussels, Pal. B.-A.; Amsterdam, Rijksmus.; Paris, Bib. N.; 1959), pp. 92–8

P. Schatborn: '39 Grisailles in the Book of Hours of Philip the Good in The Hague: An Attribution to the "Gebetbuchmeister um 1500"', *Oud-Holland*, lxxxv (1970), pp. 45–8

*Miniaturen in Grisaille* (exh. cat., ed. P. Cockshaw; Brussels, Bib. Royal Albert 1er, 1986), pp. 20–23

G. Dogaer: *Flemish Miniature Painting in the 15th and 16th Centuries* (Amsterdam, 1987), pp. 70–76

BODO BRINKMANN

**Le Tellier, François Michel.** *See* LOUVOIS, Marquis de.

**Le Tellier, Pierre** (*b* Vernon, 28 Aug 1614; *d* Rouen, after 1680). French painter. He was the son of a stained-glass painter and was apprenticed for three years from 1628 to the painter and engraver Pierre Brébiette. His early biographers record that he travelled to Italy. In 1654 he became a master in the painters' guild in Rouen; inventories of the possessions of the clergy of Rouen drawn up at the time of the French Revolution (1789–95) indicate that he was a prolific producer of religious paintings, although only a small number of them survive (most now Rouen, Mus. B.-A.).

Le Tellier was not a particularly original painter, and his works tend to reflect the styles of the major painters of Paris, although he does not seem to have worked there himself. Thus, for instance, the influence of Philippe de Champaigne is apparent in *St Joseph Carrying the Infant Jesus* (1665), that of Laurent de La Hyre in *Rest on the Flight into Egypt* (1658) and that of Jacques Stella in the *Education of the Virgin* (all Rouen, Mus. B.-A.). His last known painting is the *Farewell of SS Peter and Paul* (1680; Rouen, Mus. B.-A.).

BIBLIOGRAPHY

M.-A. Dupuy: *La Peinture d'inspiration religieuse à Rouen au temps de Pierre Corneille, 1606–1684* (exh. cat., Rouen, St Ouen, 1984), pp. 131–46

THIERRY BAJOU

**Lethaby, W(illiam) R(ichard)** (*b* Barnstaple, 18 Jan 1857; *d* London, 17 July 1931). English architect, writer and designer. The son of a gilder who was a radical and lay preacher, in 1871 he was apprenticed to a local architect and painter, Alexander Lauder, who gave him a thorough training in the building crafts. In 1879 he was appointed chief clerk to RICHARD NORMAN SHAW, whose influence was already evident in Lethaby's architectural drawings.

Jean Le Tavernier: *Philip the Good Recommended by St Andrew to the Virgin and Child*, miniature from the *Miracles de Nostre Dame*, *c.* 1456 (Oxford, Bodleian Library, MS. Douce 374, fol. 1*r*)

He remained in this post for the next twelve years (the last two part-time), during which he became increasingly responsible for detailing Shaw's work, and in doing so made an important contribution to his style (e.g. a chimney-piece of 1883 for Cragside, Rothbury, Northumb.). Lethaby's independent design work up to the mid-1880s was in the Anglo-Dutch style of the 17th century, as for example in his unexecuted design for a silverware salad bowl, illustrated in *The Architect* (30 June 1883). About 1885 he began investigating the ways in which beliefs concerning the nature of the cosmos had influenced the forms of ancient architecture. This research resulted in a number of designs with complex and often esoteric iconography, such as his stained-glass window depicting the *Four Evangelists* (1885; Symondsbury, Dorset, St John), or the frontispiece of the *Architectural Association Sketchbook 1889*, as well as his first book, *Architecture, Mysticism and Myth* (1891), the first study of architectural symbolism.

Lethaby's distrust of historicism continued to grow after he had set up in practice in London in 1889, and his designs for Kenton & Co, a short-lived co-operative specializing in furniture (1890–92), founded with Ernest Gimson, Sidney Barnsley and others, were independent of any past style. He designed, and in some cases executed, highly original work in cast iron, silver, plaster, stone, stained glass, embroidery, book illustration and interior decoration; he was also an accomplished watercolourist.

Lethaby built little, and only up to the turn of the century; three examples of his buildings will serve to illustrate the development of his ideas. Avon Tyrrell, Ringwood, Hants (1891), a house for Lord Manners, was built of brick with stone trims; it was free from decoration save for the sills of the bays on the garden front, which were pargetted by Gimson (who also did the interior plasterwork); the façades are carefully considered formal compositions enriched with symbols, such as the peacocks (the emblem of the Manners family) on either side of the chimney-stack. By contrast, the façades of the Hurst, Sutton Coldfield, Warwicks (1894; destr.), which was also built of brick with stone trims and with interior plasterwork by Lethaby, simply expressed the function of the spaces within. For the third example, All Saints, Brockhampton, Hereford & Worcs (1901–2; see fig.), Lethaby used local materials such as thatch and rubble masonry; from the outside it appears to be a not untypical country church, but within it is very different: the aisleless nave is dominated by a steeply pointed tunnel vault, roughly cast in mass concrete and supported on stone arches that run directly into the imposts. Though there is nothing about the interior that is overtly medieval, the church is nonetheless intensely medieval in feeling and Expressionist in the modern sense of the term. After 1902 Lethaby ceased building; henceforward his ideas were to be expressed only through his writings.

Lethaby was influenced by John Ruskin, by Philip Webb, and most of all by William Morris. In turn he influenced many younger architects, who starting to practise in the 1930s, wanted a new architecture that would be a true product of modern life. He was a leading figure in the ARTS AND CRAFTS MOVEMENT, a founder of the ART

W. R. Lethaby: All Saints, Brockhampton, interior looking east, 1901–2

WORKERS' GUILD (1884) and the Arts and Crafts Exhibition Society (1888), with whom he was a frequent exhibitor. From 1894 to 1918 he was Art Inspector to the Technical Education Board of the nascent London County Council. He initiated art and craft education in the capital and helped found the Central School of Arts and Crafts (1896) of which he was Principal from 1902 to 1911. The chief innovations he introduced there were that teaching was to be performed by practising craftsmen and in specially equipped workshops. Such practices were quite the opposite in Government art schools, where design, thought to have little to do with either materials or the techniques of production, was taught by drawing-masters. Between 1901 and 1918 Lethaby was Professor of Design and Ornament at the Royal College of Art, and he was actively engaged in the organization of architectural education on a national scale from 1903. He was also one of the founders of the Design and Industries Association (1915) and a leading member of the Society for the Protection of Ancient Buildings (SPAB). The Surveyor of Westminster Abbey between 1906 and 1927, he introduced the Society's principles there, concentrating on cleaning and conserving the abbey's fabric instead of attempts at 'restoration'. His extensive writings made an important contribution to art and architectural history and methodology and included numerous articles in the art and architectural press. He was an inspiring teacher, arguing brilliantly that design and architecture were a matter of reason and not aesthetics. He advocated a functional, socially responsible architecture and one that was 'a developing structural art satisfying the special requirements of the time by experiment'. The essays in *Form in Civilization* contain the essence of his thought.

### WRITINGS

*Architecture, Mysticism and Myth* (London, 1891, 3/1975)
*Leadwork, Old and Ornamental and for the Most Part English* (London, 1893)
with H. Swainson: *The Church of Sancta Sophia, Constantinople: A Study of Byzantine Building* (London, 1894)
*London before the Conquest* (London, 1902)
*Medieval Art from the Peace of the Church to the Eve of the Renaissance* (London, 1904)

*Westminster Abbey & the Kings' Craftsmen: A Study of Medieval Building* (London, 1906)
*Westminster Abbey and the Antiquities of the Coronation* (London, 1911)
*Architecture: An Introduction to the History and Theory of the Art of Building* (London, 1912)
*Form in Civilization* (Oxford, 1922, 5/1957)
*Londinium Architecture and the Crafts* (London, 1923)
*Westminster Abbey Re-examined* (London, 1925)
*Philip Webb and his Work* (Oxford, 1935/R 1979)
*A National Architecture* (Coventry, 1984)
G. Rubens, ed.: *Essays on Architecture and Reason* (London, 1996)

BIBLIOGRAPHY
*W. R. Lethaby, 1857–1931* (exh. cat., ed. S. Backemeyer and T. Gronberg; London, Cent. Sch. A. & Crafts, 1984)
P. Kirkham: *Harry Peach* (London, 1986) [contains useful inf. on Lethaby]
G. Rubens: *William Richard Lethaby: His Life and Work, 1857–1931* (London, 1986)

GODFREY RUBENS

**Lethière** [Lethiers; Letiers], **Guillaume** [Guillon] (*b* Sainte-Anne, Guadeloupe, 10 Jan 1760; *d* Paris, 21 April 1832). French painter. He was the illegitimate son of a white government official and a freed black slave. Although his real name was Guillon, as the third child of the family he called himself Letiers, Lethiers and finally, from 1799, when recognized by his father, Lethière. While accompanying his father to France in 1774 Lethière entered the studio of Jean-Baptiste Descamps at the Académie in Rouen, where he won a drawing prize for an *académie* in 1776 (Rouen, Bib. Mun.). In 1777 he went to Paris and enrolled at the Académie Royale de Peinture et de Sculpture, studying under Gabriel-François Doyen and winning a first-class medal in July 1782. Lacking influential friends and patrons, before the Prix de Rome of 1784 Lethière attempted to attract support by writing to Mme de la Palum (related by marriage to the Minister of Foreign Affairs, Charles Gravier, Comte de Vergennes), asking her to intercede in his favour with the Premier Peintre du Roi, Jean-Baptiste Pierre (Paris, Archv. N., A.N. 1. O 1917 2, item 91). In the Prix, Lethière won second prize with the *Woman of Canaan at the Feet of Christ* (Angers, Mus. B.-A.). With its theatrical gestures and delicacy of form, the picture is reminiscent of the religious works of both Doyen and Joseph-Marie Vien. His entry for the Prix de Rome in 1785, *Horatius Killing his Sister* (Providence, RI, Sch. Des., Mus. A.), displays many changes from that of the previous year, and Lethière turned to a Neo-classical composition deriving from Pierre Peyron and David. He was again unsuccessful in the competition, probably due to some kind of plot or favouritism concerning the eventual winner, Frédéric Jean-Baptiste Desmarais (1756–1813). In 1786 no prizes at all were awarded because the Académie jury found a disturbing 'similarity of styles' between the entries due to the overwhelming influence of David. Lethière had gravitated towards the Davidian style, and the poet and critic Jean-Baptiste Publicola Chaussard (1766–1823), in his *Pausanias français* (1806), wrote that, 'Although M Le Thiers had begun by being the pupil of M Doyen, the school of David claimed him. Messieurs Le Thiers and Drouais were the first who walked with honour along the paths opened by this great master.' Lethière's painting for the Prix in 1786 is lost, but although he did not win, the diplomat and friend of Louis XVI, Armand-Marc, Comte de Montmorin, persuaded the Académie that he was worthy of the Roman *pension*. Lethière arrived in Rome

and while there painted a copy of Ribera's *Deposition* (Dijon, Mus. B.-A.). (He also became one of the few friends of the difficult Jean-Germain Drouais.)

In 1791 Lethière returned to Paris and opened a teaching studio in competition to that of David, though ironically his own painting style was greatly indebted to that of his rival. From 1793 until his death he exhibited irregularly at the Salon. A committed revolutionary, in 1799 he painted the *Homeland in Danger* (Vizille, Mus. Révolution Fr.), a patriotic image of departing conscripts swearing to defend the nation and a direct response to the military threat posed by the allies of the Second Coalition against France (1798). In 1801 he travelled to Spain as artistic adviser to Lucien Bonaparte, and an intimate relationship developed between Lethière's wife and Bonaparte, by whom she had an illegitimate son. Returning to Paris, the hot-tempered Lethière was involved in a fight with some soldiers. One was killed and another wounded, prompting the government to order Lethière's studio to be closed. Forced to quit Paris, Lethière and his family travelled in Europe until 1807, when, thanks to Lucien Bonaparte's influence, Lethière was appointed Director of the Académie de France in Rome. Ingres was one of his *pensionnaires* at the Académie, and the young artist produced a series of sympathetic pencil drawings of the family, for example *Mme Lethière and her Son* (New York, Met.). Removed from office at the Restoration, Lethière reopened his teaching studio in Paris, but his initial election to the Institut in 1816 was vetoed by Louis XVIII, either on the grounds of his attachment to the empire or because of some racial prejudice against the mulatto artist. In 1818 Lethière was finally elected and also awarded the Légion d'honneur. A year later he became a professor at the École des Beaux-Arts. His studio attracted numerous students from the French colonies, such as Jean-Baptiste Gibert (1802–89), Benjamin de Rolland (1777–1855) and Jean-Abel Lordon (*b* 1801).

Lethière had ambitious plans for a series of four pictures concerning the great eras of ancient Rome: *Brutus Condemning his Son to Death*, the *Death of Virginia* (both Paris, Louvre), the *Death of Caesar* and the *Defeat of Maxentius by Constantine*. Eventually only *Brutus* and the *Death of Virginia* (see fig.) were executed. Painted in Rome in 1811, *Brutus* was shown at the Salon of 1812 in Paris and again in London in 1817. Both this and the *Death of Virginia* show Lethière's stubborn attachment to the increasingly outmoded canons established by David, and consequently his works were the butt of much sarcastic criticism. The *Death of Virginia* had an abnormally long gestation period. The point of departure was a drawing presented to the Salon of 1795, and Lethière appears to have worked intermittently on the subject until the definitive picture was exhibited at the Salon in 1831. Of the two paintings, contemporaries preferred the more severe and static *Brutus* to the turbulent and rhetorical *Virginia*, which has a seemingly inextricable arrangement of hands and arms woven into the crowd scene. Lethière also produced historical landscapes, an increasingly popular genre at the time. In 1818 he painted *Dido and Aeneas* (Tourcoing, Mus. B.-A.), a commission from the Bâtiments du Roi, in which he borrowed from Poussin and Claude but added some dramatic meteorological effects. Some historical

Guillaume Lethière: *Death of Virginia*, oil on canvas, 4.58×7.78 m, exhibited at the Salon 1831 (Paris, Musée du Louvre)

landscapes were executed in collaboration with Jean-Joseph-Xavier Bidauld, with Bidauld painting the landscapes and Lethière adding the figures. Lethière also painted *St Louis Visiting the Plague-stricken of Carthage* (1822; Bagnères-de-Bigorre, Mus. A.), a medieval scene in the fashionable TROUBADOUR STYLE.

Lethière's interest in politics remained, and in 1822 he painted an allegory to celebrate the independence of Haiti, *The Oath of the Ancestors* (Port-au-Prince, Cathedral), in which the generals Alexandre Pétion and Jean-Jacques Dessalines are shown swearing the oath of union that led to the nation's freedom. Yet for all the diversity of his later years, Lethière's true vocation was to adhere fervently to Neo-classical principles. The critic Gustave Planche, in his review of the Salon of 1831, said that Lethière was bound 'to die impenitently', and this helps explain why the artist's work slipped so quickly into obscurity.

BIBLIOGRAPHY

F. Debret: *Funérailles de M. Guillon Lethière* (Paris, 1832)

T. Oriol: *Les Hommes célèbres de La Guadeloupe* (Basse-Terre, 1935), pp. 39–47

J. Patrice Marande: '*The Death of Camille*: Guillaume Lethière and the 1785 Prix de Rome', *Antol. B. A.*, iv/13–14 (1980), pp. 12–17

P. Bordes: '*La Patrie en danger* par Lethière et l'esprit militaire', *Rev. Louvre*, 4/5 (1986), pp. 301–6

B. Foucart, G. Capy and G. Flrent Laballe: *Guillaume Guillon Lethière* (Paris and Point-à-Pitre, 1991)

SIMON LEE

**Létin, Jacques de** (*b* Troyes, 1597; *d* 1661). French painter. He served an apprenticeship in Troyes before, like so many painters of his generation, leaving for Rome: he is known to have been there between 1622 and 1625. In Rome he met Simon Vouet, who was to influence him considerably without inhibiting the development of his individual talent. Back in Troyes in 1627 or 1628, Létin received numerous commissions for churches in the city and its district. Through contacts thus established he came to execute paintings for churches in other towns, such as Provins and Nevers and also found himself in demand in Paris. In 1636 he painted the May, the religious painting annually commissioned for the cathedral of Notre-Dame by the goldsmiths' corporation: the subject was *St Paul on Areopagus Converting St Denis and Others by his Preaching* (destr. in 1870; engraved by Abraham Bosse). For the Jesuits of St Paul–St Louis he painted the *Death of St Louis* (*in situ*) and also worked for the Jacobins of the Faubourg St Honoré. If the compositional rhythms, dramatic arrangement and figure types of his paintings reveal his debt to the pictorial language of Simon Vouet, his search for effects of light and colour and his freedom of handling show an independent personality, albeit one whose work is somewhat uneven. There exist about 40 pictures by Jacques de Létin, only three of which are of secular subjects: *Lycurgus Giving a Constitution to Sparta* and *Self-portrait* (both Troyes, Mus. B.-A. & Archéol.) and the *Death of Virginia* (Moscow, Pushkin Mus. F.A.). These three works show Jacques de Létin's true stature.

BIBLIOGRAPHY

*Jacques de Létin* (exh. cat. by J. Thuillier, J.-P. Sainte-Marie and D. Lavalle, Troyes, Mus. B.-A. & Archéol., 1976) [full bibliog.]

BARBARA BREJON DE LAVERGNÉE

**Letnitsa.** Archaeological site of the mid-4th century BC in north-central Bulgaria. A hoard of Thracian metalwork (Lovech, Hist. Mus.) found there contained 21 pieces of bridle equipment, including 12 silver gilt horse harness plaques; most are rectangular, measuring *c.* 50×40 mm, although some have an irregular outline following the form of the repoussé motif on them (*see* THRACIAN AND DACIAN ART). Some of the plaques are decorated with figural scenes that may belong to a heroic epic cycle. The finest shows a mounted hunter accompanied by his dog; the man wears an armoured greave of the AGIGHIOL type and is in the act of spearing a bear. Others show horsemen who, although their appearances differ (two are bearded, two are not), may represent a single figure known as the 'Thracian hero'. Behind one rider a disembodied horse's head and neck appear; another plaque shows a human head. On a third a marten-like animal is represented with a rider holding aloft a drinking cup in a pose reminiscent of images on signet rings from Brezovo and Gložene, also in Bulgaria. A remarkable sexual scene is often interpreted as representing a 'sacred marriage' (hierogamy), but it defies simple interpretation: a seated, mail-clad man is straddled by a long-robed woman, while a female attendant carrying an amphora-like vessel occludes the man's vision with a leafy branch so that he cannot see who is seducing him. Two other plaques depict a woman riding a horse-headed sea snake, and a similarly dressed but breastless figure holding a mirror and grasping a three-headed snake. The latter can be compared with androgynous figures on the GUNDESTRUP CAULDRON from Denmark (Copenhagen, Nmus.), and it may represent a transvestite diviner of the type recorded in Scythia by Herodotus in the 5th century BC.

BIBLIOGRAPHY

I. Venedikov and R. Popov: 'Sukrovishteto ot Letnitsa' [Treasure from Letnitsa], *Iskusstvo*, ix (1963)

R. Pittioni: 'Bemerkungen zur religionshistorischen Interpretation des Verwährfundes von Letniza, Bezirk Lovec, Bulgarien', *Anzo Österreich Akad. Wiss. Philos.-Hist. Kl. Sber.*, 321 (1977), pp. 1–39

T. Taylor: 'Flying Stags: Icons and Power in Thracian Art', *The Archaeology of Contextual Meanings*, ed. I. Hodder (Cambridge, 1987), pp. 117–32

TIMOTHY TAYLOR

**Leto, Pomponio** [Sanseverino, Giulio] (*b* Diano, Lucania, 1428; *d* Rome, 1498). Italian antiquarian. The illegitimate son of a noble Calabrese family, he moved to Rome around 1450 to study under Lorenzo Valla, whom he eventually succeeded as preceptor of rhetoric and Latin at the Studium Urbis. Around 1458 he headed the formation of the Roman Academy, a loosely organized group of scholars dedicated to the study of Classical philology and archaeology. Adopting the name of the ancient dramatist L. Pomponius, Leto took part in the first explorations of Early Christian catacombs (S Callisto, S Priscilla and later SS Marcellino e Pietro). His disciples, who included Alessandro Farnese (later Paul III) and Conrad Peutinger, similarly assumed Classical pseudonyms and referred to Leto as their Pontifex Maximus. In 1468 Paul II disbanded the Academy, perhaps in reaction to its pagan leanings, and several members were imprisoned, while Leto was recalled from Venice on charges of heresy. Following the election of Sixtus IV, however, the Academy was reconstituted as a 'sodalitas litteratorum' under the protection of Cardinal Domenico della Rovere (1478). During these years Leto produced authoritative editions and commentaries of Latin authors. Around 1484 he set to work on a guide to ancient Rome, the *De antiquitatibus urbis Romae libellus* (1510), of which only a fragment survives. Leto's lasting contribution to the study of Roman topography was an interpolated recension of the 4th-century AD regionary catalogues, first published in 1502/5 under the spurious authorship of Publius Victor (*see* ROME, §VII, 3). He also formed an extensive collection of Classical inscriptions, played a primary role in reviving ancient theatre and probably assisted Sulpizio da Veroli with his edition of Vitruvius' *On Architecture*; the two later collaborated on an edition of Frontinus' *De Aquaeductis*.

BIBLIOGRAPHY

Giovanni Battista De Rossi: 'L'accademia di Pomponio Leto e le sue memorie scritte sulle pareti delle catacombe', *Boll. Archeol. Crist. Roma*, i (1890), pp. 81–94

V. Zabughin: *Giulio Pomponio Leto: Saggio critico*, 2 vols (Rome, 1909–Grottaferrata, 1910)

P. Jacks: *The Antiquarian and the Myth of Antiquity. The Origin of Rome in Renaissance Thought* (Cambridge, 1993), pp. 143–57

PHILIP J. JACKS

**Letoön.** *See under* XANTHOS.

**Leu, Hans, II** (*b* Zurich, *c.* 1490; *d* Gubel, nr Zurich, 24 Oct 1531). Swiss painter and draughtsman. He probably served his apprenticeship in Zurich in the workshop of his father, Hans Leu I, who perhaps was one of the CARNATION MASTERS (*see* MASTERS, ANONYMOUS, AND MONOGRAMMISTS, §I). Travelling as a journeyman, soon after his father's death, Hans the younger apparently attached himself to Albrecht Dürer in Nuremberg. From the style of his free-hand drawings, it can be inferred that he also worked with Hans Baldung, perhaps in Strasbourg and no doubt, *c.* 1512–13, in Freiburg im Breisgau, where he may have painted the landscape backgrounds of Baldung's Schnewlin Altar in the cathedral. By 1514 Leu was active in Zurich, as is indicated mainly by his free-hand drawings. Lacking important commissions, he soon got into financial difficulties and, to improve his material position, served as a mercenary in the Duke of Württemberg's Italian campaigns of 1515 and 1519, although Dürer attested (1523) to having met Leu in Zurich in 1519. The increasing impact of the Reformation, which put a halt to church commissions, forced Leu to ally himself to the Catholic party. He was stabbed to death during a skirmish between religious factions in Zurich.

Although Leu was one of the most important Swiss painters of the period, he enjoyed purely local significance. His strength lay in free-hand drawing, and he was one of the first Swiss artists to apply this medium to the open landscape of the Alpine foothills. His spontaneous, romantically inclined draughtsmanship is shown in a series of chiaroscuro drawings, dating from 1513–14 onwards, including *Landscape with Mountains and Lake* (Basle, Kstmus.; see fig.) and *Landscape with a Moated Castle* (Nuremberg, Ger. Nmus., previously ascribed to Augustin Hirschvogel). Both the technique of these pen drawings, which are highlighted in white, and the natural forms are reminiscent of Albrecht Altdorfer, yet Leu's connection with this leading representative of the Danube school is still unclear. The influence of Albrecht Dürer's woodcuts can be seen in individual figural motifs in his drawings; however, Leu himself produced only four woodcuts (1516). In his panel paintings of *St Jerome* and *Orpheus* (1515 and 1519; both Basle, Kstmus.) the landscape typical

Hans Leu II: *Landscape with Mountains and Lake*, pen and brush and black ink, heightened with white, on dark green prepared paper, 277×210 mm, *c.* 1520 (Basle, Kupferstichkabinett)

of the Danube school dominates. These and other panel paintings (Zurich, Schweizer. Landesmus.; priv. cols) are traditional in concept, with somewhat awkward human figures. Leu also worked as a designer of stained glass.

BIBLIOGRAPHY

Hollstein: *Ger.*; *NDB*; Thieme–Becker

W. Hugelshofer: 'Das Werk des Zürcher Malers Hans Leu', *Anz. Schweiz. Altertknd*, n. s., xxvi (1924), pp. 28–42, 122–50; xxx (1928), pp. 163–79

H. Debrunner: *Der Zürcher Maler Hans Leu im Spiegel von Bild und Schrift* (Zurich, 1941)

D. Koepplin: 'Altdorfer und die Schweizer', *Alte & Mod. Kst*, xi (1966), no. 84, pp. 6–14

W. Hugelshofer: 'Überlegungen zu Hans Baldung', *Z. Schweiz. Archäol. & Kstgesch.*, xxxv (1978), pp. 263–75

*Albrecht Altdorfer und der fantastische Realismus in der deutschen Kunst* (exh. cat., ed. J. Guillaud and M. Guillaud; Paris, Cent. Cult. Marais, 1984), pp. 438–43

*Albrecht Altdorfer: Zeichnungen, Deckfarbenmalerei, Druckgraphik* (exh. cat., ed. H. Mielke; Regensburg, Museen Stadt, 1988), pp. 301–9

JANEZ HÖFLER

**Leu, Thomas de** (*b* Paris, *c.* 1555; *d* Paris, *c.* 1612). French engraver, publisher and print dealer. The son of a dealer in Audenarde, he worked first at Antwerp for Jean Ditmar (*c.* 1538–1603) and then went to Paris before 1580 to work for the painter and engraver Jean Rabel (1540/50–1603). He married first Marie, daughter of Antoine Caron, in 1583, and secondly, in 1605, Charlotte Bothereau. He skilfully moved from the side of the militant Catholic League in the Wars of Religion to that of Henry IV, and as a result made himself a fortune. He ran a busy workshop and published large numbers of prints by other hands. Among his apprentices were Jacques Honnervogt

(*fl* 1608–35) and Melchior Tavernier (*c.* 1564–1641). His first dated engraving is *Justice* (1579; Linzeler, no. 57), after Federico Zuccaro. He specialized mainly in portraiture (more than 300 plates), for example *Catherine de' Medici* (L 255), and in devotional engravings, such as *Christ in Blessing* (1598; L 7); he also made book illustrations. His work, the style of which is somewhat cold, is reminiscent of Flemish engravers of the 16th century, such as Cornelis Cort, the Sadelers and the Wierix.

BIBLIOGRAPHY

A. Linzeler and J. Adhémar: *Inventaire du fonds français: Graveurs du seizième siècle*, Paris, Bib. N., Cab. Est. cat. (Paris, 1932–8), i, pp. 461–546; ii, pp. 373–80 [L]

A. Jouan: *Thomas de Leu, graveur de portraits français du XVIe siècle* (diss., Paris, Ecole Louvre, 1955)

J. Ehrmann: 'La Vie de l'atelier du graveur Thomas de Leu gendre du peintre Antoine Caron', *Archvs A. Fr.*, 26 (1984), pp. 43–6

M. Grivel: *Le Commerce de l'estampe à Paris au XVIIe siècle* (Geneva, 1986)

——: *Dictionnaire des éditeurs d'estampes à Paris sous l'Ancien Régime* (Paris, 1987)

MARIANNE GRIVEL

**Leubus.** *See* LUBIĄŻ ABBEY.

**Leufert, Gerd** (*b* Klaipeda, Lithuania, 9 June 1914). Venezuelan graphic designer, printmaker, painter, sculptor, museum curator and photographer of Lithuanian birth. He studied at the High School of Design in Hannover, at the School of Arts and Crafts in Mainz, and at the Akademie der Bildenden Künste in Munich. He moved to Venezuela in 1951. In 1957 he was art director of the magazine *El Farol*, and in the following year he taught composition in the Faculty of Architecture and City Planning in the Universidad Central de Venezuela, Caracas, and graphic design in the Escuela de Artes Visuales 'Cristóbal Rojas', Caracas, becoming director of its graphic arts department. He also taught graphic design in the USA at the University of Iowa, Iowa City, and at the Pratt Institute, New York. On his return to Caracas in 1959, he became a curator at the Museo de Bellas Artes and artistic director of its magazine *Visual*. With M. F. Nedo, Leufert did much to revive the graphic arts in Venezuela, producing a series of prints in collaboration with Nedo and Alvaro Sotillo as a symbol of this revival. Leufert's best-known work includes *Marks*, a fusion of writing and graphic design, and *Funeral Songs*, monochrome works of heroic proportions in which sculpture, painting and graphic design are blended.

BIBLIOGRAPHY

A. Armas Alfonzo: *Diseño gráfico en Venezuela* (Caracas, 1985)

ANA TAPIAS

**Leukadia.** Village in western Macedonia, north Greece, near Naousa. Its ancient name may have been Mieza, where Aristotle taught. A number of Macedonian tombs, dating from the Hellenistic period, have been found here. The most interesting is a large tomb originally buried under a tumulus (probably 3rd century BC). The interior is simple, consisting of an anteroom and barrel-vaulted tomb chamber. The elaborate façade is built of limestone and covered with stucco, which was brightly painted. It has two orders, divided by a frieze showing a *Battle between Macedonians and Persians*. The lower consists of four Doric engaged columns and two antae (pilasters) at the angles. This order is surmounted by a smaller Ionic order (h. *c.* 1.5 m) with seven false doors between the engaged columns, and crowned by a pediment. The frieze of the lower order consisted of metopes and triglyphs; the metopes were not sculpted but painted in monochrome with a *Battle between the Lapiths and Centaurs*, probably imitating sculpture. Between the engaged Doric columns of the lower order runs a projecting moulding, above which there are four large painted figures. Those on the left of the entrance represent a *Warrior* (probably the dead man) next to *Hermes*, and those to the right show the judges of the dead, *Aeacus* (seated) and *Rhadamanthys* (leaning on his staff; *see* GREECE, ANCIENT, fig. 135). The last figure closely resembles an old man shown in the frescoes of the hall of a country house at Boscoreale, near Pompeii (probably 1st century BC), which suggests that the cycle from Boscoreale consists of a faithful copy after Greek originals.

BIBLIOGRAPHY

M. Petsas: *O taphos ton Lefkadion* [The grave at Leukadia] (Athens, 1966)
M. Robertson: *A History of Greek Art*, 2 vols (Cambridge, 1975), i, pp. 568–71

**Leukas.** Ionian island just off the western coast of central Greece. It was named after the high white cliffs at its southern end, where the lyric poet Sappho allegedly committed suicide. The German archaeologist W. Doerpfeld was so convinced that it was the true Homeric Ithaka that he dug numerous test trenches on the coastal plain of Nidhri, and the discovery in 1908 of rich burials seemed to confirm his belief. These, however, date to the Early Bronze Age (*c.* 2200 BC), and thus they cannot be linked to the *Odyssey*. The earliest graves were placed in circular stone platforms (diam. 3–10 m), each with a central burial, often richly furnished, and subsidiary burials, perhaps of relatives or retainers. The artefacts (Leukas, Archaeol. Col.) found reflect both the pottery traditions of mainland Greece and the copper metallurgy of the Cyclades. Items of gold and silver include spiral bracelets and decorated sheathing from dagger hilts. The burials represent the westernmost settlement in Early Bronze Age Greece and suggest that even at this early date there was trade in the Adriatic. By the Classical period (*c.* 480–323 BC) Leukas was wealthy enough to mint its own coins and to provide ships for a brief naval alliance against Athens, but there are few remains of the city itself.

BIBLIOGRAPHY

W. Doerpfeld: *Alt-Ithaka* (Munich, 1927)
K. Branigan: 'The Round Graves of Levkas Reconsidered', *Annu. Brit. Sch. Athens*, lxx (1975), pp. 37–50

K. A. WARDLE

**Leupenius, Johannes** (*b* Amsterdam, *bapt* 10 May 1643; *d* Amsterdam, *bur* 24 Dec 1693). Dutch draughtsman, etcher and surveyor. There is no documentation to confirm the 19th-century view that he studied under Rembrandt. In the late 1660s he drew picturesque landscapes in the strongly linear style of Gerbrandt van den Eeckhout, Philips Koninck and Jan Lievens. The earliest of these sheets, *Nijenrode Castle on the Vecht* (Amsterdam, Rijksmus.), is dated 1665; the latest, *Farm with Haystack on a Canal* (Lyon, Mus. B.-A.), is dated 1669. His interest in topography is also evident from panoramas drawn in 1666: *Nijmegen* (Arnhem, Gemeentemus.) and *Heemstede* (Haarlem, Gemeentearchf). The same strong graphic style is seen in etchings of views along the Vecht and the Amstel (1668–71).

Leupenius also made carefully executed portrait studies in black chalk on parchment. These are drawn in the style of Cornelis Visscher, although the execution is more naive, as in the *Shipbuilder van Ruyt and his Wife* (1670; Amsterdam, Kon. Oudhdknd. Genoot.). A presumed *Self-portrait* (Utrecht, H. van Leeuwen priv. col., see Sumowski, p. 3459) is signed *JLeupenius Landmeter* [surveyor]/*fecit 1669*, and on the van Ruyt portrait Leupenius designates himself mathematician. His artistic career ended in the 1670s. At the time of his marriage in 1677 he stated his profession as surveyor, and it was as a surveyor that he was mentioned in documents up to his death. Much of his cartographic work is in the Gemeente Archief, Amsterdam.

BIBLIOGRAPHY

Hollstein: *Dut. & Flem.*
W. Sumowski: *Drawings of the Rembrandt School*, vii (New York, 1983), pp. 3451–539

B. P. J. BROOS

**Leura Tjapaltjarri, Tim** (*b* Kooralia, N. Territory, ?1929–39; *d* Alice Springs, 1984). Australian Aboriginal painter and wood-carver. He was the initiated man of the Anmatyerre/Aranda language group. Leura grew up on Napperby station and worked as a stockman before moving to Papunya with his young family when the settlement was established in the late 1950s. There he worked as a carver of wooden snakes and goannas renowned in central Australia for their brilliant craftsmanship. When painting began at Papunya in 1971, he quickly joined the group and became the close friend and assistant of the art teacher Geoffrey Bardon (*b* 1940). He also enlisted his younger brother CLIFFORD POSSUM. In the mid-1970s the brothers' collaboration on a series of large topographical paintings incorporating several Dreaming stories in map-like configuration on one canvas was of considerable importance. It was one of the factors that gave the painting from Papunya a greater appeal to European sensibilities. Leura became custodian of the country known as Nurta on Napperby Creek, and painted the Possum, Yam, Fire, Blue Tongue Lizard, Sun, Moon and Morning Star Dreamings associated with this area. Always prolific, he had a delicacy of touch, and his translucent painterly effects are distinctive even in his earliest works. The sombreness of his work reflects a profound sadness at the loss of the old ways of life.

BIBLIOGRAPHY

*Dreamings: The Art of Aboriginal Australia* (exh. cat., ed. P. Sutton; New York, Asia Soc. Gals; U. Chicago, IL, Smart Mus.; Melbourne, Mus. Victoria; Adelaide, S. Austral. Mus.; 1988–90), pp. 107, 112–13, 122, 130–31, 237
G. Bardon: *Papunya Tula: Art of the Western Desert* (Ringwood, Victoria, 1991), pp. 117–24
*The Painted Dream* (exh. cat. by V. Johnson, Auckland, C.A.G., 1991), p. 19

VIVIEN JOHNSON

**Leusden, Willem van** (*b* Utrecht, 25 Sept 1886; *d* Maarssen, 8 March 1974). Dutch painter, printmaker and architect. He trained at the Kunstnijverheidschool in Utrecht from 1900 and until 1907 at the Koninklijke Academie voor Beeldende Kunsten in The Hague. During this period he worked mainly from nature. Until 1910 he attended the Rijksacademie in Amsterdam under Pieter Dupont who taught him etching and engraving techniques. Around 1915–16 traces of Cubism, Futurism and Expressionism can be seen in his work. Leusden met Gerrit Rietveld in 1918, through whom he came into contact with the views of the group centred around the magazine *De Stijl*. In 1923 he submitted three models to the exhibition *Les Architectes du Groupe De Stijl (Hollande)* at Galerie de l'Effort Moderne in Paris. In 1924 he redecorated his own house according to De Stijl principles, using for example his own furniture designs. His association with El Lissitzky led him to produce Constructivist work. After 1930, with Johannes Moesman and others he belonged to the Utrecht Surrealists. After World War II he developed an etching technique close to that of Hercules Segers.

BIBLIOGRAPHY

D. Adelaar, M. Roding and J. van Asperen: *Willem van Leusden: Essays over een verhard romanticus* (Utrecht, 1988)

JOHN STEEN

**Leuthner (von Grund), Abraham** (*b* Wildstein, nr Passau, *c*. 1640; *d* Prague, 12 Jan 1701). German architect, active in Bohemia. He arrived in Bohemia some time before 1665, in which year he became a citizen of Prague Neustadt. He worked as a builder on the Černín Palace (1669–76), Prague, which was designed by Francesco Caratti. His most significant work as an independent designer is the rebuilding of the Cistercian abbey church (1681–1704) at Waldsassen, in which he was assisted by his pupils Georg Dientzenhofer (1643–89) and Christoph Dientzenhofer. Leuthner introduced some of the concepts of the Bohemian Baroque in the church: it is an aisleless church in which the three bays of the nave were roofed with elliptical sail vaults treated as domes on pendentives, a design that had been used by Carlo Lurago in his rebuilding (1668) of Passau Cathedral. The side chapels have shallow oval domes, open in the centre in a typically Baroque instance of spatial interpenetration to reveal the ceiling of the gallery above and admit light from high-placed windows. Leuthner built the town hall (1682–5) at Loket, and he was responsible for the fortifications (1688–97) at Cheb, subsequently becoming surveyor-general for all fortification work in the kingdom of Bohemia. The treatise he published in 1677, written 'from a true German heart', includes engravings of his own work, and of centralized church plans, which influenced the Dientzenhofer brothers and Johann Bernhard Fischer von Erlach. Leuthner was the first builder of central European origin to break the hegemony of northern Italian architects in the Czech lands, while introducing some of their Baroque concepts into Franconia.

WRITINGS

*Gründliche Darstellung der Fünf Seulen* (1677; Prague, Acad. Applied A., inv. no. UPM 1.884–1.922)

BIBLIOGRAPHY

Thieme–Becker

V. Wachsmannová: 'Život a dílo Abrahama Lethnera' [Life and work of Abraham Leuthner], *Památky Archaeol.*, xlii (1946), pp. 15–60

E. Bachmann: 'Architektur', *Barock in Böhmen*, ed. K. M. Swoboda (Munich, 1964), pp. 20–24

V. Naňková: 'Abraham Leuthner', *Encyklopedie českého výtvarného umění* [Encyclopedia of Czech art], (Prague, 1975), p. 265

——: 'Barokní architektura v západních Čechách' [Baroque architecture in western Bohemia], *Umění*, xxviii (1980), pp. 22, 46

JIŘÍ T. KOTALÍK

**Leutschau.** *See* LEVOČA.

**Leutze, Emanuel (Gottlieb)** (*b* Schwäbisch Gmünd, Baden-Württemberg, 24 May 1816; *d* Washington, DC, 18 July 1868). American painter of German birth. When he was nine, Leutze's family emigrated to America and settled in Philadelphia. In 1834 he began to study art with the draughtsman John Rubens Smith (1775–1849). Leutze developed his skills as a portrait painter by taking likenesses to be engraved for publication in the *National Portrait Gallery of Distinguished Americans* and then working as an itinerant painter. He also experimented with imaginative compositions, such as the *Poet's Dream* (Philadelphia, PA Acad. F.A.). Philadelphia patrons sponsored his study in Europe, and in 1841 he enrolled at the Königliche Kunstakademie in Düsseldorf. Although attempts at history painting won approval in Germany and in the USA, Leutze left the academy in 1843. He travelled for two years in Germany and Italy, during which time he became convinced of the importance of freedom and liberty, which he believed to be fundamental institutions of the American political system.

Leutze returned to Düsseldorf, where he married and became one of the city's most prolific painters and active liberals in the period preceding the March 1848 Revolution. As president of the Verein Düsseldorfer Künstler and co-founder of the Malkasten (an artists' club based on democratic principles), Leutze led the independent artists' community and was friend, adviser and financial backer to numerous American painters, such as Eastman Johnson, Worthington Whittredge and Albert Bierstadt, who were studying in Düsseldorf.

Leutze's fame grew steadily as a result of the success of his history paintings, especially those devoted to Christopher Columbus. His most popular painting was *Washington Crossing the Delaware* (1851; New York, Met.), and in 1851 Leutze travelled to the USA to exhibit it and to petition Congress to commission another version and a pendant, *Washington Rallying the Troops at Monmouth* (1854; Berkeley, U. CA, A. Mus.). He lived in Düsseldorf until 1859 when he became discouraged by the political situation in Germany and a decline in commissions and so settled once more in the USA. Several important undertakings ensued, including the 1862 mural *Westward the Course of Empire Takes its Way* for the Capitol. After the Civil War he painted portraits of Abraham Lincoln and various Union army officers. Leutze was working on the cartoon for a mural depicting the *Emancipation of the Slaves* when he died.

Leutze was a talented portraitist but is usually regarded as an artist of ambitious, large-scale history pieces, although the quality of his history paintings is inconsistent. He painted figures well but occasionally slipped into melodrama. His announced intention to paint 'a long cycle from the first dawnings of free institutions in the middle ages. . .to the Revolution and Declaration of Independence' resulted in some handsome paintings (e.g. *Hohenstaufen, Württemberg*, *c.* 1854; New York, Century Assoc.) and culminated in several canvases devoted to George Washington: the 1851 version of *Washington Crossing the Delaware* became an icon of American history and patriotism. There were two other versions of this painting; an earlier one, originally in Bremen, was destroyed by fire during World War II; a third, smaller replica, painted with Eastman Johnson, was the model in 1853 for the engraving by Paul Girardet (1821–93) published by Goupil, Vibert & Co., the distribution of which enhanced the painting's already considerable renown.

BIBLIOGRAPHY

J. Herring and J. Barton: *National Portrait Gallery of Distinguished Americans*, 4 vols (New York, 1834–9)

H. Tuckerman: *Book of the Artists: American Artist Life* (New York, 1867), pp. 333–45

F. von Boetticher: *Malerwerke des neunzehnten Jahrhunderts*, 2 vols (Leipzig, 1891–1901), i, pp. 857–8

*Emanuel Leutze, 1816–1868* (exh. cat. by E. Kratz, Schwäbisch Gmünd, Städt. Mus., 1968)

R. L. Stehle: *Life and Works of Emanuel Leutze* (Washington, DC, 1972)

*Emanuel Leutze, 1816–1868: Freedom Is the Only King* (exh. cat. by B. S. Groseclose, Washington, DC, N. Col. F.A., 1975)

BARBARA GROSECLOSE

**Leuven** [Fr. Louvain; Ger. Löwen]. Belgian town with a population of *c.* 85,000. It was the Carolingian capital of the county of the same name, and from 1106 the capital of the duchy of Brabant. In the 9th century Arnold of Carinthia (*reg* AD 887–99) defeated the Vikings who occupied the area and built a castle on the site of the present Groot Begijnhof. The St Pieterskerk was built in Mosan style around 1100, and the town expanded after the first ramparts were built (*c.* 1150; mostly destr.). The St Michielskerk (destr.) was built over one of the town gates in 1165. The Romanesque St Kwintenskerk (*c.* 1200) and St Jacobskerk (1220–30) each have a tower over the first bay of their naves. The portals of the Gasthuis (*c.* 1220) and the west door of the St Jacobskerk (*c.* 1230) bear the oldest traces of sculptural decoration. Around 1250 the population of Leuven grew rapidly because of the booming linen industry, and the Gothic style was used in the Dominican church (1255–76), which was decorated before 1300 with wall and glass paintings. The St Jacobskerk, the former abbey church of St Geertrui (1298–1453) and the church (1305) of the Groot Begijnhof use a characteristic local Gothic style. Leuven architects built the Lakenhal (Linen Hall) in 1317, and the second set of ramparts was begun in 1357. Goldsmiths and wood-carvers formed guilds in 1360, followed (1388) by tapestry-weavers who had been active since the beginning of the 14th century.

Although the ducal residence moved to Brussels in the 15th century, Leuven maintained a significant position in Brabant. The St Pieterskerk was rebuilt in Brabantine Gothic style (*c.* 1410–1541; damaged in the world wars) by Sulpitius van Vorst (*d* 1439), Jan Keldermans II and Matheus de Layens, who also built the Stadhuis (1439–69; *see* TOWN HALL, fig. 2). From 1425 the university laid out buildings overlooking the town. Jan van Ruysbroeck enriched St Geertrui with an openwork spire (*c.* 1452–3; rest.). Although such sculptors as Joes Beyaert (*d* 1488) and Hendrik Roesen (*fl* second half 15th century–early

16th) were famous, wood-carvers from Brussels worked on the St Pieterskerk and the Stadhuis, and Matthys de Waeyer (*fl c.* 1529–43) of Brussels made the pews (*c.* 1540) of St Geertrui.

Painters and glass painters formed the Brotherhood of St Luke in 1495. Dieric Bouts I (*see* BOUTS, (1)) came to Leuven from Haarlem; his sons, especially Albrecht Bouts, and such painters from Leuven as Jan Rombouts (*d* 1535), Jan Vanden Berge (*fl c.* 1498–1531) and Jan Vander Cautheren (*fl c.* 1522–8) continued the Bouts tradition for decades. Quinten Metsys's move to Antwerp in 1491 was a symptom of Leuven's decline. Glass painting flourished during the second half of the 15th century with such practitioners as Hendrik van Diependale (*d* 1509), Rombout Keldermans I (*fl* 1455–75) and Hendrik Scoenenberghe (*fl c.* 1487–92). Tapestry production declined around 1550.

The Renaissance developed slowly in Leuven. Renaissance characteristics appear in the work of Jan Willems (*d* 1548), town painter from 1527 to 1548, and Jan van Rillaer the elder (*d* 1568). In the late 16th century art in Leuven suffered from the departure of several painters, for example Geldorp Goltzius (*d* 1616) to Antwerp in 1570 and Jan van Rillaer the younger (*d* 1592) to Denmark in 1580. Baroque architecture includes the St Michielskerk (1650–66; rest.) by WILLEM HESIUS and the chapel of Onze-Lieve-Vrouw-ter-Koorts (1651–1733). Among notable painters of the period were Joos Vander Baeren (*fl c.* 1572–1612), Hendrik de Smet (*fl c.* 1575–1639), who was town painter in 1627, Theodoor van Loon and Martinus Blendeff (*c.* 1650–1710). The leading glass painter was Jean de Caumont (*d* 1659). Economic prosperity during the 18th century led to the rebuilding of various university buildings and teaching institutions, such as Pope Adrian VI College (1776–8) by Louis Montoyer and other premises of the university by Laurent-Benoît Dewez. The Rubéniste painter Pierre-Joseph Verhagen worked for churches and monasteries in Leuven and influenced Antoon Clevenbergh (1755–1810). Goldsmithing flourished once more.

In the 19th century the Gothic Revival changed the town's appearance, with the restoration of the Stadhuis (1824–41) and the architecture of Joris Helleputte (e.g. the Anatomy Theatre, 1877, of the Catholic University) and his followers. Leuven was an international centre of Gothic Revival sculpture until the beginning of the 20th century, with a number of studios. The Charlier studios (1890–1964) were known for restoration and imitation of old stained glass. Professor Armand Thiéry (1868–1955) built and restored numerous complexes in the Gothic Revival spirit and revived the production of glass, ceramics and tapestries using old techniques and models. The founding of the Akademie voor Schone Kunsten in 1800 attracted such teachers as Constantin Meunier and Alfred N. Delaunois (*b* 1876), who became director in 1920. After World War I parts of the town were rebuilt in Renaissance Revival and Baroque Revival styles. The university library (1921–8) was built by Whitney Warren (1864–1943) of Warren & Wetmore. Henry Van de Velde, René Braem and Mark Dessauvage (1931–84) all worked in the town. The famous Leuven bell-foundries were active until the mid-20th century. In 1970 a francophone university was set up at Louvain-la-Neuve. The town has several museums.

BIBLIOGRAPHY

E. van Even: *L'Ancienne Ecole de peinture de Louvain* (Brussels and Leuven, 1860)
——: *Louvain dans le passé et dans le présent* (Leuven, 1895)
*Oude Kunst C.O.O. Leuven* (exh. cat., Leuven, Mus. Vander Kelen-Mertens, 1970)
R. Lemaire, ed.: *Bouwen door de eeuwen heen. Inventaris van het cultuurbezit in Vlaanderen: Architectuur*, I/i (Leuven, 1971)
M. Smeyers: 'Aspecten van de schilderkunst te Leuven tijdens de laatgotische periode', *Aspecten van de laat-gotiek in Brabant* (exh. cat., Leuven, Mus. Vander Kelen-Mertens, 1971), pp. 180–240
*Leuvense kunst van de XXe eeuw* (exh. cat., Leuven, Mus. Vander Kelen-Mertens, 1971)
*Arca Lovan.* (1972–) [period. containing various relevant articles]
*Dirk Bouts en zijn tijd* (exh. cat., Leuven, St Pieterskerk, 1975)
J. Crab: *Het Brabants beeldsnijcentrum Leuven* (Leuven, 1977)
*Het laatgotische beeldsnijcentrum Leuven* (exh. cat., Leuven, Mus. Vander Kelen-Mertens, 1979)
R. van Uytven, ed.: *Leuven 'de beste stad van Brabant'* (Leuven, 1980)
M. Bols, G. Huybens and L. Verpoest: *Het stedelijk kunstonderwijs te Leuven* (Leuven, 1985)
P. Uyttenhove and J. Celis: *De wederopbouw van Leuven na 1914* (Leuven, 1991)

M. SMEYERS

**Leux, Frans.** *See* LUYCKX, FRANS.

**Levantine rock art.** *See* SPANISH LEVANTINE ROCK ART.

**Levasseur.** Canadian family of artists, of French origin. Jean Levasseur (1622–86) and his brother Pierre Levasseur (1629–*c*. 1681) trained in France as master joiners, before settling in Quebec. From the mid-17th century they and their numerous descendants executed ornamental interiors for civil and ecclesiastical buildings, greatly contributing to the richness of French-influenced architectural decoration in churches throughout Quebec. Records in public archives show contracts and receipts for major new projects, repairs, restoration, statues, crucifixes, candlesticks, coats of arms and boat-carving undertaken by family members, many of whom remain unidentified. The most notable member of the family was the architectural sculptor Noël Levasseur (1680–1740), who worked with his two sons François-Noël Levasseur (1703–94) and Jean-Baptiste-Antoine Levasseur (1717–75), also both sculptors, and with his brother Pierre Levasseur (1684–1744), who was a master joiner. Noël Levasseur is credited with introducing the open-balustraded tabernacle or baldacchino to Canada in the chapel (1721–2) of the Hôpital-Général, Quebec (*in situ*), and in the Huron church (*c*. 1722) of Jeune-Lorette, Loretteville (*in situ*). He and his assistants also did extensive work in the cathedral of Notre-Dame, Quebec, between 1722 and 1743. Eight stone capitals carved with swags and ornaments and 19.5 m of carved-stone frieze (*c*. 1730) are also attributed to him, and he executed many religious statues (e.g. *St Joseph*, *c*. 1730; La Pocatière, Mus. Coll. Ste-Anne), notable for their sense of calm, classical grandeur.

Noël's cousin Pierre-Louis-Noël Levasseur (1690–1770) was the finest Baroque architectural sculptor of his day, designing entire interiors. With Nöel and François-Nöel Levasseur, Pierre-Louis-Nöel executed the magnificently carved wooden pulpit and retable (1726–36), with its robust figures of saints and angels, preserved in the

chapel of the convent of the Ursulines, Quebec. The statues of *St Peter* and *St Paul* (1742–3) in the church of St Charles Borromée, Charlesbourg, with their riffling hair and drapery, are also by him. François-Noël Levasseur worked in the Louis XV style favoured by the next generation. In his church decoration he sought extravagant overall effects that belied the subtlety of his sculptured figures. During a career that spanned over 40 years he executed numerous canopies, altar tables, statues, reliefs, crucifixes and reliquaries, frequently assisted by his brother Jean-Baptiste-Antoine. A notable example is the tabernacle (*c*. 1773–5) in the church of Montmagny.

BIBLIOGRAPHY
A. J. H. Richardson and others: *Quebec City: Architects, Artisans and Builders* (Ottawa, 1984), pp. 355–68

**Levasseur, Etienne** (*b* 1721; *d* Paris, 8 Dec 1798). French cabinetmaker. He was an independent workman before becoming a *maître-ébéniste* on 2 April 1767. His known works are all in the Neo-classical style, in both its architectural and arabesque forms. He specialized in Boulle marquetry. Under the direction of the *marchand-mercier* Claude-François Julliot, he produced such rare masterpieces using brass and tortoiseshell as the Comte de Luc's *secrétaire* (Windsor Castle, Berks, Royal Col.) and the commode (Versailles, Château) for the Comte d'Artois. He repaired many pieces of furniture by André Charles Boulle, and made several pieces in the same style, sometimes using designs by the cabinetmaker Alexandre Jean Oppenord (1639–1715) and Boulle (e.g. book-cabinet; London, Wallace). During the reign of Louis XVI he produced some beautiful works decorated with lacquer and in veneers of mahogany and citrus-wood, many of which were acquired, through the *marchand-merciers* Darnault and Dominique Daguerre, by the Garde Meuble de la Couronne and by Mesdames Adelaïde and Victoire, daughters of Louis XV.

BIBLIOGRAPHY
F. de Salverte: *Les Ebénistes du XVIIIème siècle, leurs oeuvres et leurs marques* (Paris, 1923, rev. 5/1962)
J. Viaux: *Bibliographie du meuble (Mobilier civil français)*, 2 vols (Paris, 1966–88)

JEAN-DOMINIQUE AUGARDE,
JEAN NÉRÉE RONFORT

**Le Vasseur, Jean-Charles** (*b* Abbeville, 21 Oct 1734; *d* Paris, 29 Nov 1816). French printmaker. He studied drawing and engraving in Abbeville with Philippe-Auguste Lefébure (*fl c.* 1770); he then moved to Paris, where he worked first in Jacques-Firmin Beauvarlet's studio and then in that of Jean Daullé. On 29 July 1769 he was approved (*agréé*) by the Académie Royale and was received (*reçu*) on 26 February 1771, on presentation of *Diana and Endymion* after Jean-Baptiste van Loo. He was also a member of the Akademie of Vienna and the Accademia di S Luca in Venice. He was a reproductive engraver tackling a great variety of subjects, particularly the works of contemporary French artists, such as François Boucher, Carle Vanloo, Jean-Baptiste Greuze, Jean Restout II, Nicolas-Bernard Lépicié and François Lemoyne. His oeuvre consists of almost 170 prints, mostly etchings, half of which are large. They display delicate modelling, a sure touch, an exuberant style and a steady hand, but, overall, the quality of his work is uneven. He engraved his own portrait by Greuze (Abbeville, Mus. Boucher-de-Perthes).

BIBLIOGRAPHY

E. Delignières: *Catalogue raisonné de l'oeuvre gravé de Jean-Charles Le Vasseur d'Abbeville, précédé d'une notice sur sa vie et ses ouvrages* (Paris, 1865)

*French Royal Academy of Painting and Sculpture: Engraved Reception Pieces, 1672–1789/Les Morceaux de réception gravés de l'Académie Royale de Peinture et de Sculpture: 1672–1789* (exh. cat. by W. McAllister Johnson, Kingston, Ont., Queen's U., Agnes Etherington A. Cent.; Montreal, Mus. F.A.; London, U. W. Ont., McIntosh A.G.; and elsewhere; 1982–3), pp. 152–3

VÉRONIQUE MEYER

**Le Vau** [Le Veau]. French family of architects and building contractors. Louis Le Veau (*d* Feb 1661), a mason active in Paris, had two sons who became architects: (1) Louis Le Vau and (2) François Le Vau. The family worked together in the 1630s and 1640s, but both Louis and François subsequently changed the spelling of their name in order to lose the plebeian taint of 'Le Veau' ('the calf') and to promote their social and professional careers designing houses and châteaux for royal officials, members of the nobility and, ultimately, working for Louis XIV himself on the principal commissions of his reign: the Palais du Louvre and the château of Versailles.

**(1) Louis Le Vau** (*b* ?1612–13; *d* Paris, 11 Oct 1670). For the 20 years following the death of Louis XIII in 1643—a period roughly coinciding with the ministerial rule of Cardinal Mazarin under the young Louis XIV—Le Vau was the most successful and, with François Mansart, the most important architect in France. He designed a large number of houses and châteaux in and around Paris, endowing their architectural masses and spaces with individuality by varying their decorative treatment, form and placing; and by grouping them in ingenious combinations around a dominant spatial feature he created a new, freer organization of space that was fundamental to the LOUIS XIV STYLE and subsequently to the design of palaces all over Europe.

1. Early career, to *c*. 1638. 2. The Hôtel Lambert and Le Vau's personal style, *c*. 1638–53. 3. Mature work, 1654–63. 4. Le Vau under Colbert, after 1663.

1. EARLY CAREER, TO *c*. 1638. It is not known with whom Le Vau studied, or how he acquired the reputation that gained him his first important commission, the Hôtel de Bautru (1634–7; destr.), when he was still so young. It has been assumed that he was taught by his father, Louis Le Veau, but this cannot be so since the latter was a mason who did not even become a master of his trade until *c*. 1635 and whose business flourished only when he was working with his son on the Ile Saint-Louis. Le Vau probably derived his early ideas from Michel Villedo, contractor for the Hôtel de Bautru, who continued to be the most important source of his major private commissions for many years. The style in which the Hôtel de Bautru was built does at least cast some light on Le Vau's artistic sources. His vocabulary of forms was conspicuously indebted to Salomon de Brosse and Clément Metezeau II; but his formal language was also indebted to a second building tradition, one ingrained in the brick and stone architecture of his day. He dispensed with architectural decoration set off in a sculptural, generally classically organized context against a plain supporting wall. Instead he deployed strip-like, shallowly recessed compositions, which tended to integrate window surrounds, cornices, architraves and pilasters into a system of similar panels whose homogeneity needed no special differentiation through the use of mouldings. Three-dimensional effects were not applied to the outer surfaces of walls but were always displayed as 'internal' parts of them. Even the usual massive apparatus of external balconies was transformed into a light and slender structure through the use of thin platforms and metal brackets and balustrades. Alongside this innovative architectural approach, another notable feature of the Hôtel de Bautru was the design of its private *appartements*; these were conceived with comfort in mind and—perhaps for the first time—incorporated alcoves right from the start. It was probably these interiors that led to Le Vau's employment in 1639 on François Mansart's Hôtel de La Vrillière (begun 1635; see MANSART, (1)), specifically to insert another private suite including an alcove (1639; destr.) into the design.

Very early in his career, Le Vau sought to combine his fiduciary role as an architect with various entrepreneurial activities as a contractor, promoting his own speculative interests by acting as an undeclared partner in building projects. This began in 1635, when he worked with his father on houses on the Ile Saint-Louis, and continued throughout his career (*see also* §4 below).

2. THE HÔTEL LAMBERT AND LE VAU'S PERSONAL STYLE, *c*. 1638–53. Commissions from senior officials such as Bautru and La Vrillière were unusual for Le Vau before the 1650s. In 1638 he was appointed an Architecte Ordinaire des Bâtiments du Roi, but he mostly worked for artisan tradesmen, for lower- and middle-grade officials and, above all, for the upwardly mobile and newly affluent class that enjoyed the lucrative combination of a post in the royal finance administration and a private business that had dealings with the crown. To make himself indispensable to them, he set out to become an expert purveyor of the architecture that was their principal means of self-display; and once he had made himself socially acceptable he aspired to join their ranks. After changing the spelling of his name in 1638, he married the daughter of a provincial official in 1639; the dowry, and his growing income, enabled him to purchase the office of a Conseiller et Secrétaire du Roi, Maison et Couronne de France et de ses Finances in 1644. This gave him the basic privileges of nobility, to which he was later to add the territorial dignity of lord (seigneur) of Beaumont in 1665.

Until *c*. 1653 Le Vau's major buildings were almost exclusively designed for members of this class of financiers, who were both the tools and the protégés of Mazarin; among the clients for whom he built large town houses and châteaux at this time were Jean-Baptiste Lambert, Louis Hesselin, Jacques Bordier, Jean Tambonneau and at least a dozen others (*see* HÔTEL PARTICULIER, §1). His association with these men, whose entrepreneurial instincts had much in common with his own, was a decisive factor in his career. When the civil uprisings of the Fronde (1648–53) pitted financiers against civil servants and the

Parlement—and ultimately the higher nobility against Mazarin and the King—Le Vau found himself architect to a party within a polarized society. Even when he did have clients from outside the world of the financiers, such as Marshals Gramont, Aumont and Villeroy, these were the 'King's men' and thus allies of Mazarin: he never compromised himself by working for the Frondeurs.

The Hôtel Lambert (begun 1639; see fig. 1) on the Ile Saint-Louis was Le Vau's masterpiece among his early town houses, revealing his personal style in fully developed form (see also LAMBERT, (1)). The spatial entity that the wall surfaces, with their shallow relief, serve to delineate is not that of the mass of the building itself but that of the space that abuts upon it. This appears best in the fronts on the terraced garden. The three-storey façade system of the corps de logis (see fig. 2) is continued along the adjoining gallery by buckling at right angles the colossal pilaster, entablature and attic pilaster where they meet at the extremities of the two walls. At the other end of the façade these buckled forms are repeated at full height like a monumental hinge, to join only a low garden wall, so that instead of enclosing the solid mass of the house and defining its corner, the hinge demarcates the corner of the garden. The form created is the shell of the garden. Le Vau shows the viewer the disposition and decoration of a space that is immediately visible and actually penetrable but says nothing about features of the solid structure behind, which can be seen only piecemeal and can be experienced as a whole only in imagination.

Interested in complete, empirically presented entities, Le Vau could dispense with high, steep roofs that revealed a building as a three-dimensional form; with the flat or complex pitched roofs of the Hôtel Lambert, there was nothing to convey the volume behind the façade. He made the main and garden fronts of the Hôtel Lambert so utterly

different from one another that there were no means of establishing the identity and homogeneity of the building by making the levels of basement and eaves, and the sequence and decorative treatment of storeys, recognizably the same from all viewpoints.

The fact that Le Vau's façades refer to a new spatial entity, which is always the surrounding space that the beholder sees, had far-reaching consequences for his conception of the hôtel particulier. Freed from the formula of a linear structure one room deep, he was able to compose houses from apparently freely arranged ensembles of pavilions interspersed with internal light wells and courts, as he did, for example, at the Hôtel Hesselin (begun 1641; destr.). At the same time he also avoided the conventional tripartite structure of the central corps de logis flanked by wings. In his endeavour to make the courtyard space the formal focus of the house, he displaced the corps de logis from its prominent position on the main axis of the court and moved it out to take the place of the wings. In the Hôtel Lambert only, the staircase remained at the centre of the back wall of the court; the Hôtel Hesselin's court opened directly into the garden. This idea of marking the major axis of a building by an architecturally defined open space or series of spaces and not by a solid structure is an original contribution on Le Vau's part to contemporary French architecture. He employed it both for small town houses, such as the Hôtel Boyer (1645; destr.) and for large ones, such as the Hôtel Fouquet (begun 1654; destr.), and, perhaps to greatest effect, for the châteaux of Saint-Mandé (begun 1655; destr.) and Vincennes (1658; see §3 below), and later in 1668 in the remodelling and 'envelope' treatment of Versailles (see §4 below).

In his interiors Le Vau again gave autonomy to the beholder's space by releasing it from the traditional reference to unifying features, in this case the system of

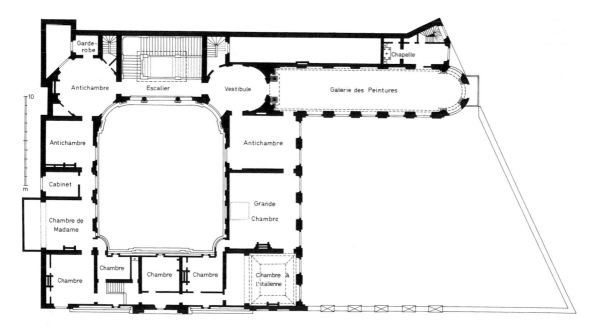

1. Louis Le Vau: plan of the second principal storey of the Hôtel Lambert, Paris, begun 1639; reconstruction

2. Louis Le Vau: main courtyard façade of the Hôtel Lambert, Paris, begun 1639

consistent wall and ceiling alignments. He designed manifold, staggered spatial entities whose walls and ceilings broke through, curved round and kinked. In 1639 he began to insert a high-vaulted *chambre à l'italienne* into the sequence of rooms with flat ceilings that makes up a French *appartement*; he did this both in single-storey versions (hôtels de la Vrillière and Lambert) and in two-storey ones (château of Chantemesle, near Corbeil; destr.). He used this same individual spatial formula for the château of Le Raincy, which he began in 1643 (destr.) for Jacques Bordier. Now an interior space became the dominant organizing feature, not only of an enfilade of rooms within but of the external elevation as well. The result was his most celebrated and influential creation, the central salon: a vaulted room derived from reconstructions of the palaces of antiquity, two storeys high, equipped with a classical order of pilasters and, at Le Raincy, with two convex exedrae standing proud of its façades. These central salons monumentalize the intersection of the two most important spatial sequences in a château by introducing a third, vertical sequence, sometimes continued into external space through a wide oculus in the vault. The salons commonly adopted a rounded form, which Le Vau also used at the château of Meudon (work begun 1656; destr.) and in his grand design for the château of Vaux-le-Vicomte (begun 1656; *see* §3 below). As a formal link between sequences of rooms, the salon probably owes less to Italian precedents than has been supposed. As it spread through Europe it was quite rightly described as a French invention. Le Vau's later version of the salon—

one combined with a gallery and terrace, as at the château of Fontainebleau (1654; destr.)—was also widely followed.

Le Vau succeeded in presenting unencumbered spaces even in stairwells filled with the then fashionable type of stairs, which had straight flights with landings round a central void. He solved the problem simply by not revealing the overall form, which would have been seen as obstructed. The stairway of the Hôtel Lambert gives no indication of the vertical alignments of the stairwell. Each flight is closed in below to divide the staircase into four separate spaces bounded by walls and, in part, by ceilings of their own, and in these spaces even the stairs surprise the beholder by appearing in an unconventional form. This creative reinterpretation of the staircase as a sequence of discrete spatial entities establishes Le Vau's work as a landmark in European staircase design. Its maturest form appears once more in the 1650s: the double staircase at Meudon, which led the visitor up through five successive spaces, each of which was wider, higher and lighter than the preceding one and had its own ceiling, and finally up a last, boldly cantilevered, flight of stairs into an even wider, higher and lighter salon.

Le Vau's supreme virtue as an architect lay in his capacity for the dynamic structuring of a sequence of ingenious individual spaces. In the upper storey of the Hôtel Lambert, for example, the elongated form of the landing seems to 'stretch' the oval of the following vestibule to produce the spatial form of the gallery next in order. As with all Le Vau's spaces, the shape of the gallery cannot be ascertained before it is reached, but when encountered it can be seen, when considered with the spaces that have gone before, as a stage in an idiosyncratic but perfectly logical spatial development. These coherent spatial sequences, empirically arranged right down to the details of their decorative treatment, were ultimately impossible to imitate. Antoine Le Pautre was probably the first architect partially to grasp the new freedom of Le Vau's spatial conceptions, but his spatial configurations are arbitrary in their eccentricity and remain ineffective.

3. MATURE WORK, 1654–63. With the triumph of Mazarin's party over the Frondeurs in 1653, Le Vau's star was in the ascendant, and when he succeeded Jacques Le Mercier as Premier Architecte (1654) and later became Intendant des Bâtiments du Roi, his architecture attained the supreme social status of being the chosen form through which the image of a king was to be transmitted to posterity. His other clients were thenceforth drawn only from the uppermost reaches of Mazarin's party, a small, powerful ministerial team of financiers and diplomats. This included Barthélemy Hervart, Abel Servien and NICOLAS FOUQUET, Le Vau's greatest patron, who with Guillaume de Lamoignon also controlled the Parlement; others were Hugues de Lionne and Mazarin himself, who with his Intendant, Colbert, also acted for the King in architectural matters. Le Vau's previous, less illustrious, clientele was handed over, almost without exception, to other architects.

For a decade Le Vau held an unchallenged position in which he could realize the most ambitious projects; and of course this brought him up against the problem of large-scale form. The pavilions for the King and Queen that Le Vau designed at Vincennes (*see* VINCENNES, §1; begun 1654) must have revealed to him that the spatial compositions of the 1640s could not be used to achieve an effect of monumental power: they lacked the necessary massiveness and sculptural quality. On the other hand, walls that did have such qualities could hardly be used to define a void, but losing the reference to this spatial entity would turn them into mere theatrical flats. Le Vau therefore concentrated on the centres of the façades; he opened them up to receive the full force of the building's overriding axial focus, and they thereupon retreat and draw the adjoining walls back into a curve. This can be seen at Vaux-le-Vicomte and at the Collège des Quatre Nations (Collège Mazarin; now the Institut de France), which was endowed by the Cardinal and which Le Vau began in 1662 (see fig. 3). In these buildings, in a way otherwise unknown in France, the axial impact on the centre is marked dramatically, and in typically Baroque fashion, by massive groups of columns that advance from the façade to form pedimented or statue-crowned *avant-corps*; sometimes assembled from superimposed triple arcades or together with an attic storey, they enfold a pavilion like a cuff, as in the south front of the Palais du Louvre (1661; destr. 1669), then the principal royal residence in Paris. Only after 1663, in designs for an east façade for the Louvre, fronted along its entire length by a colossal order of detached columns, did Le Vau reveal a tendency towards the autonomous monumental display wall; in this and other late works (*see* §4 below) the progressive simplification of the basic volume reveals once more the impulse to produce the effect of flat walls, even

when they are given a free rhythmic articulation by columned *avant-corps*, as at Versailles (1668).

Three characteristics mark Le Vau's work between 1654 and 1663. The first was his withdrawal from his role as an interior designer, the capacity in which he had first worked for the King, while Le Mercier was still alive, in the Louvre's Appartement du Conseil (1653; destr.). After 1655, when the interior design function was taken over by Giovanni Francesco Romanelli (who was succeeded by Charles Errard *le fils* and Charles Le Brun), the evidence suggests that Le Vau involved himself only in the most general of decisions on matters of decoration and fixtures (as at the Collège des Quatres Nations). The second was the continuing importance of his work as a garden architect, designing not only staircases, grottoes and waterfalls but whole gardens, as in the châteaux of Saint-Cloud (begun 1655), Basville (1660) and Fontainebleau (Parterre du Tibre, 1662). This makes it hard to distinguish Le Vau's contribution from that of André Le Nôtre where they worked together, as they did in the late 1640s (at Le Raincy) and after, sometimes negotiating together with clients. Their joint masterpiece was VAUX-LE-VICOMTE (see fig. 4) for Nicolas Fouquet, the most splendid château and garden to be found in France at that time. Garden space and interior space were equivalent in principle; Le Vau's system of creating shallow spatial shells to demarcate volumes was equally applicable to the garden architecture of his contemporary Le Nôtre. It may well be that Le Vau's mature style, which crystallized remarkably early in his career, had more influence on Le Nôtre than has hitherto been supposed. Finally, Le Vau was indubitably

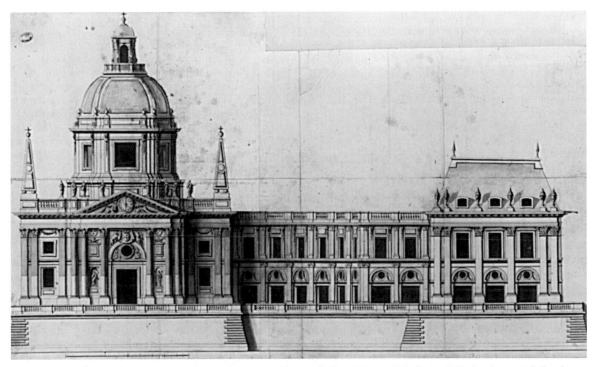

3. Louis Le Vau: partial front elevation of the Collège des Quatre Nations (Collège Mazarin), Paris, begun 1662, showing central chapel, west wing and pavilion; pen and black ink, 438×845 mm (Paris, Archives Nationales)

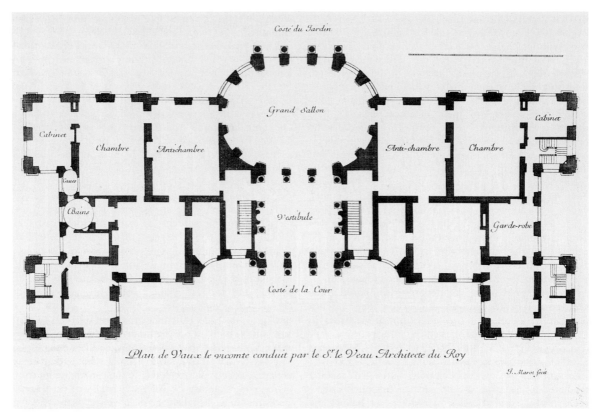

*Coste du Jardin*

*Grand Sallon*

*Cabinet*

*Chambre*    *Antichambre*

*Anti-chambre*    *Chambre*

*Cabinet*

*Caues*

*Bains*

*Vestibule*

*Garde-robe*

*Coste de la Cour*

*Plan de Vaux le vicomte conduit par le Sʳ le Veau Architecte du Roy*

*J. Marot fecit*

4. Louis Le Vau: plan of the first floor of the château of Vaux-le-Vicomte, begun 1657; engraving from Jean Marot: *L'Architecture française* (1670)

the most talented urban planner of his day. In extensive projects to open out and connect the sites of the Louvre and the Collège des Quatre Nations and, similarly, the châteaux of Vincennes and Saint-Germain-en-Laye, and in his later plans for the town of Versailles, there appeared a number of ideas that in some cases remained influential until well into the 19th century. The best of these is perhaps the principle (which was to be so fruitful in the evolution of the Paris townscape) of aligning buildings across the Seine and linking them by spatial axes or bridges (as with the bridge between the Louvre and a structure on the site of the Collège des Quatre Nations, 1660).

4. LE VAU UNDER COLBERT, AFTER 1663. Fouquet's arrest (1661) and conviction for treason (1664) unleashed a wave of prosecutions that shook the Mazarin party to the core and instantly damped its enthusiasm for building. From 1663 onwards Le Vau could expect new commissions only from the King (*see* BOURBON, §I(9)). But Fouquet's fall was only the beginning of Colbert's campaign to put an end to the disruptive private entrepreneurial activities of the King's officials. Le Vau's promotion of his own speculative interests had continued in 1643 in partnership with his brothers-in-law, especially Charles Thoison, in an enterprise involving the building of embankments there and a new bridge, the Pont de la Tournelle, and the placing of 86 houses on the existing Pont Marie and its approaches. Some years later in 1665,

when Le Vau was involved in building the Collège des Quatre Nations (*see* §3 above), his speculation in site values came to light, but Jean-Baptiste Colbert, who in January 1664 had become the King's Surintendant des Bâtiments, hushed up the scandal in the interests of the royal building programme as a whole. Also in 1665, following earlier experiments, Le Vau started a factory, with the official support of Colbert, to produce tinplate as a cheaper substitute for lead on roofs and, later, also weapons, at Beaumont-la-Ferrière, Nièvre. But for various reasons the enterprise did not prosper, increasing his debts at his death to over half a million livres.

After Colbert became Surintendant des Bâtiments du Roi, he deprived Le Vau, the Premier Architecte, of much of his power by dividing his role into separate, rationally defined and, where possible, controllable functions. Even his *de facto* monopoly of designing buildings for the King was taken away from him. The all-embracing organizational and artistic control that Le Vau had exercised over the building process, and which had made him so powerful, was now in the hands of a bureaucratic authority to which he as an official was answerable (*see* COLBERT, (1)).

The story of the east façade of the Louvre, for which Le Vau produced a number of designs, illustrates this process. In 1664, when the building had already risen above foundation level, work was stopped, and public criticism of Le Vau's project (his fifth) was encouraged in a way that was tantamount to a request for new designs.

Colbert, who disliked Le Vau himself and his style of management as much as he did his project, looked to Rome for a new design for what was at the time the most important architectural commission in France, and he approached Bernini (*see* BERNINI, (2), §I, 3(iii)). However, Bernini's visit to Paris in 1665 was doomed to failure; not least because, in his supreme self-confidence, he insisted on dealing direct with the King. Le Vau was then appointed, together with Charles Le Brun and Claude Perrault, to a committee or *petit conseil* (1667), which was to elaborate a joint project so that, according to the minutes, 'none might claim to be its author in preference to the others'. Rather than a competition winner, Colbert wanted a group of 'advisers' who would make it necessary for Colbert himself to present a synthesis to the King and give him alternatives from which to choose. Although authorship of the design, much disputed, is often attributed to Perrault (*see* PERRAULT, (2)), it is clear, at least, that the basic idea of the Louvre colonnade—a line of columns detached from, and parallel to, the wall—had long been familiar to the Le Vau brothers; that François Le Vau had proposed it in a project for the Louvre in 1664 (*see* (2) below); that the colonnade, as begun in 1667, is worked out in a succession of autograph drawings by Louis Le Vau (mainly Paris, Archvs N.; Bib.N., Cab. Est.; Louvre, Cab. Dessins); and that the change of plan in 1668, too, may have been initiated by the Le Vau brothers. Even so, the colonnade, as built, underwent a functional and stylistic transformation that freed it from the structural requirements initially laid down; it is a collective achievement incorporating the deliberations of the *petit conseil* as filtered by the ministerially prescribed process of mutual recrimination within that body. This was a process in which, by 1668, the voice of doctrinaire academicism could only grow in authority the longer the debate dragged on. (For further discussion of the Louvre project *see* PARIS, §V, 6(ii).)

One factor that makes it even harder to determine the extent of Le Vau's contribution to the projects of the 1660s is the problematic role of his draughtsman, FRANÇOIS D'ORBAY, who had worked for him since about 1658. It can safely be assumed that Le Vau was only too glad to adopt d'Orbay's suggestions in so far as they might further his own success, but this cannot have been happening before 1661, up to which date there is documentary proof of d'Orbay's lack of technical competence. There is some reason to doubt whether he ever did make any creative contribution, both because of the unoriginality of the few buildings he built on his own account and because he was not present at any of the planning committee meetings at which, during Colbert's first decade in power, architectural projects were hammered out. D'Orbay's influence cannot have been significant before the stage of the finished drawings, when he was responsible for the design of details; and these were then normally commented on, or corrected, by Le Vau.

After 1667 other, rival architects began to contribute to major royal building projects; Claude Perrault's designs, for example, for the Observatoire and triumphal arch at the Porte Saint-Antoine were largely adopted. Le Vau's last triumph came with a late masterpiece at Versailles (*see* VERSAILLES, §1), where he had carried out some previous work for the King. Work on his so-called *enveloppe* (1668), which enfolded the old château on the garden side in a U-shaped structure incorporating two lateral courtyards, was halted in 1669; this was followed by a competition, which Le Vau won, for a design for the complete rebuilding of the whole château. In the same year, however, work started again on his initial design, largely unmodified. Le Vau's very first studies for the *enveloppe* at Versailles already incorporated the pivotal idea, first used at the Hôtel Lambert, of carrying the ascending line of Le Nôtre's terraced garden right into the building by way of an unseen flat roof and an additional terrace with orange trees and fountain on the level of the principal storey of the château. Seldom has a large building been so perfectly integrated with a sympathetic environment as here.

Le Vau was a pioneer in the art of spatial effects; but his essentially practical, empirical talent, hard to reconcile with anything so rigid as a programme, and his disinclination to acknowledge norms, let alone feature them in his architecture, stood in the way of the establishment of a lasting reputation, particularly after the cultural policy of Colbert brought a standardized, theoretically based architecture back into favour. To a classically trained observer, Le Vau's startling discontinuities of decorative treatment, and his violations of conventions, looked like dissonances, barbarisms or just plain mistakes. Jacques-François Blondel, however, could at least identify the problem: an expert, he was able to detect 'an ingenious variety. . .a cunning, within this near-disorder, which seems to compensate for all these liberties', without, however, being able to find a rational definition for this 'cunning' (*sçavoir*). Blondel the teacher therefore had no choice but to regard Le Vau as an unsuitable model for students to follow and to warn his readers against imitating the architect in his rule-breaking because 'it requires merit, to discern where it is possible to follow, and great experience and skill, to dare to make use of these examples' (*L'Architecture françoise*, ii (Paris, 1752), p. 127).

**(2) François Le Vau** (*b* ?1624; *d* Paris, 4 July 1676). Brother of (1) Louis Le Vau. His teacher was his revered brother, who was his elder by more than ten years and with whom he parted company only in his twenties, during the civil wars of the Fronde (1648–53), when he became Architecte des Bâtiments du Roi et de Son Altesse Royale Mademoiselle. As the favourite architect of Anne Marie Louise d'Orléans, Duchesse de Montpensier, a leading participant in the events of the Fronde, he designed her *appartements* at the Tuileries in Paris (before 1652; destr.), her residence in exile, the château of Saint-Fargeau, Yonne (1652–7), and her later residence in the Palais du Luxembourg (1662; destr.). He was also employed by other members of the upper nobility and their adherents; all were Frondeurs, supporters of the losing side who were slipping into political obscurity. He designed *appartements* for the town houses of Maximilien-François de Béthune, Duc de Sully (1651), and Louis de la Rivière (1652), and for that of Charles Armand de la Porte, Duc de la Meilleraye (later Duc de Mazarin), in the Arsenal (begun 1654; destr.). He worked on the château of Rambouillet (begun 1659) for Charles Montausier, Duc de Saint-Maure, the Montpipaux project for Louis de Rochechouart and the château of Bercy (begun 1658; destr.) for Charles Henry de Malon. His clients very occasionally included financiers, passed on to him by his brother Louis, such as Hierosme de Nouveau (château of Lignières, Cher, 1654–60) and Nicolas Lambert (château of Sucy-en-Brie, begun 1660; *see* LAMBERT, (2)). Louis Le Vau also seems to have ceded to his brother the further construction work on Saint-Louis-en-l'Ile after 1656.

In 1662 Colbert appointed François Le Vau to an official post as supervisor of highway and bridge maintenance, mainly in the Loire area, and inspector of crown building works. Thereafter, apart from occasional major building projects such as Colbert's own château de Seignelay, Yonne (destr.), Sainte-Croix, Orléans (1665; unexecuted), and the citadel and town of Rochefort, Charente (1671–3), his work seems to have been mainly routine, technical and administrative. But he published engravings of his architectural designs and in 1671 became a founder-member of the Académie d'Architecture; he enjoyed an established position as an architect and was a respected and increasingly affluent figure. The most interesting of his surviving buildings illustrates his dependence on his brother's example. The vestibule at Sucy simplifies the ingenious vestibule space at Le Raincy; and the original idea of replacing the round-headed arcades in the most sharply curved sections of the *anse-de-panier* apse of Saint-Louis-en-l'Ile with two rectangular openings seems to be derived from Louis Le Vau's initial plan. The lack of a sense of inevitability in his disposition of architectural mass and space, in his use of concave sections of façades and in the decorative elements that, in his work, seem merely applied to the surface reveal his inferiority as an artist. But his individual way of conceiving wide horizontal masses that maintain their horizontal orientation right up to the roof area and articulating them by means of narrow vertical strip compositions that tie the storeys together—and which often turn into pier-like units consisting of pedestals surmounted by paired pilasters or columns—did lead him to create one major work: the design for the Louvre colonnade, which he prepared for Colbert in 1662–4 and which embodies essentials of the solution that was eventually adopted.

### BIBLIOGRAPHY

P. Clément, ed.: *Lettres, instructions et mémoires de Colbert*, v (Paris, 1868)
J. Guiffrey, ed.: *Comptes des bâtiments du roi sous le règne de Louis XIV*, i (Paris, 1881)
P. de Nolhac: *La Création de Versailles d'après les sources inédites* (Versailles, 1901)
H. Lemonnier: *Le Collège Mazarin et le Palais de l'Institut* (Paris, 1921)
J. Cordey: *Vaux-le-Vicomte* (Paris, 1924)
L. Hautecoeur: *Le Louvre et les Tuileries de Louis XIV* (Paris and Brussels, 1927)
M. Dumolin: *Etudes de topographie parisienne* (Paris, 1931), ii, pp. 111–400; iii, pp. 1–288
J. Cordey: 'Colbert, Le Vau et la construction du château de Vincennes au XVIIe siècle', *Gaz. B.-A.*, lxxv (1933), pp. 273–93
N. Bourdel: 'Nouveaux documents sur Louis Le Vau premier architecte de Louis XIV', *Paris et Ile-de-France*, viii (1956), pp. 213–35
C. Tooth: 'The Early Private Houses of Louis Le Vau', *Burl. Mag.*, cix (1957), pp. 510–18 [with notes by P. Smith]
A. Laprade: *François d'Orbay architecte de Louis XIV* (Paris, 1960)
M. Whiteley and A. Braham: 'Louis Le Vau's Projects for the Louvre and the Colonnade', *Gaz. B.-A.*, lxiv (1964), pp. 285–96, 347–62
A. Erlande-Brandenburg: 'Les Fouilles du Louvre et les projets de Le Vau', *Vie Urb.* (1964), pp. 241–63; (1965), pp. 12–32
A. Marie: *Naissance de Versailles*, 2 vols (Paris, 1968)
M. Whiteley and A. Braham: 'Les Soubassements de l'aile orientale du Louvre', *Rev. A.* [Paris], i/4 (1969), pp. 30–43
G. Mabille: 'La Ménagerie de Versailles', *Gaz. B.-A.*, lxxxiii (1974), pp. 5–36
J.-P. Babelon: 'Le Château de Sucy-en-Brie: Oeuvre de François Le Vau', *Bull. Soc. Hist. Paris & Ile-de-France*, ci–cii (1974–5), pp. 83–102
D. Feldmann: *Maison Lambert, Maison Hesselin und andere Bauten von Louis Le Vau (1612/13–1670) auf der Ile Saint-Louis in Paris* (Hamburg, 1976)
R. W. Berger: 'The Chronology of the Enveloppe of Versailles', *Archit.: Z. Gesch. Archit.*, x (1980), pp. 105–33
M. Rambaud: 'Nouvelles recherches sur Saint-Louis-en-l'Ile', *Commission du vieux Paris* (2 March 1981), pp. 6–14, 18–34 [suppl. to *Bull. Mun. Officiel Ville Paris*, lii (1982)]
D. Feldmann: 'Das Hôtel de La Vrillière und die Räume *à l'italienne* bei Louis Le Vau', *Z. Kstgesch.*, xlv (1982), pp. 395–422
J. C. Le Guillou: 'Le Château-neuf ou enveloppe de Versailles: Conception et évolution du premier projet', *Gaz. B.-A.*, cii (1983), pp. 193–207

DIETRICH FELDMANN

**Le Veau, Jean-Jacques(-André)** (*b* Rouen, 9 Jan 1729; *d* Paris, April 1786). French engraver. In his youth he was ill with scrofula, and it was during a stay in hospital, when he was 16 or 17, that a copy he made of a painting was brought to the attention of Jean-Baptiste Descamps, founder and director of the free school of drawing in Rouen, who gave him his earliest lessons in drawing. Descamps succeeded in placing him in the Paris studio of Jacques-Philippe Lebas, who signed two of Le Veau's earliest engravings (Hédou 41, 43). Le Veau then collaborated with Noël Le Mire, himself a former pupil of Descamps in Rouen, who involved him in the production of the sumptuous edition by Pierre-François Basan and Le Mire of Ovid's *Metamorphoses* (1767–71); Le Veau contributed 16 pieces (H 189–204), including a fine engraving of *Spring* (H 189) after Charles Eisen and the *Birth of Bacchus* (H 195) and *Vertumnus and Pomona* (H 204), both after François Boucher. Le Veau engraved for other important luxury editions as well, such as that of La Fontaine's *Contes et nouvelles* (1762), known as the edition of the 'Fermiers généraux' (H 154–60). Hédou considered Le Veau's personal style to have developed *c.* 1770, and that *The Guardroom* after Jean-Baptiste Le Prince (1778; Paris, Bib. N., H 29) was his masterpiece. In 1775 Le Veau became an associate of the Académie de Rouen. Of his two children his daughter, Victoire-Geneviève-Louise (*b* 1766), also became an engraver.

### BIBLIOGRAPHY

J. Hédou: *J.-J.-A. Le Veau: Sa Vie et son oeuvre (1729–1786)* (Paris, 1903) [H]

M.-E. HELLYER

**Leveilly** [Leveillé], **Michel** (*fl* 1714; *d* Bonn, 23 Jan 1762). French architect and designer, active in Germany. He was a pupil in Paris of Robert de Cotte and Jacques-François Blondel. On the recommendation of de Cotte, he entered the service of Joseph Clemens, Elector of Cologne, in 1714, continuing with his successor, Clemens August, in 1719. Leveilly worked initially under the direction of Benoît de Fortier and then of Guillaume de Hauberat. From 1729 to 1740 he supervised the construction of Falkenlust, a hunting-lodge near Brühl, to the designs of François de Cuvilliés I. His own built work includes, most notably, the Rathaus (1737–8) in Bonn. Its main façade on the market-place is articulated in seven bays by a giant order of pilasters over a plinth storey. At *piano nobile* level, the window heads are adorned with Rococo shell motifs under the blind arches of a minor order, while the wider central bay accommodates the entrance, reached from the square via an open double stair. An ornate clock flanked by bearers replaces the regular upper-floor fenestration in this bay, and a coat of arms rests on the cornice above it in front of a mansard roof. Leveilly is also credited with the design of St Michael's Gate (1751), Bonn, and the Arff House (1750), Worringen. His main achievement, however, lies in the design of stuccowork, in which he introduced, for example, scenes of the chase in the main pavilion of Johann Conrad Schlaun's hunting-lodge at Clemenswerth, near Münster, and, with equal facility, cherubs sliding down clouds for its chapel. Besides Clemenswerth and Falkenlust, Leveilly's stucco designs, generally executed by Carlo Pietro Morsegno (*d* 1754) and the brothers Carlo and Domenico Castelli, formed part of the décor at the castles of Brühl (*see* BRÜHL, SCHLOSS), Paderborn, Nordkirchen (the ceiling of the Red Room) and Poppelsdorf. As he was cut off from the latest developments in Paris, however, Leveilly's style became outmoded, and from 1740 he was gradually superseded by Balthasar Neumann.

BIBLIOGRAPHY

E. Renard: 'Die Bauten des Kurfürsten Joseph Clemens und Clemens August von Köln', *Bonn. Jb.*, xcix (1895), pp. 165–240; c (1896), pp. 1–102

P. du Colombier: *L'Art français dans les cours rhénanes* (Paris, 1930)

H. Kinsky: 'Studien zur Ausstrahlung kurkölnischer Hofkunst des 18. Jahrhunderts am Niederrhein (I)', *An. Hist. Ver. Niederrhein, Alte Erzbistum Köln* (1965), pp. 106–23

W. Borchers: 'Das Jagdschloss Clemenswerth im Hümmling', *Schlaunstudie I*, ed. K. Bussmann (Münster, 1973), pp. 80–103

K. Bussmann: 'Die Entwürfe Schlauns, Leveillys u.a. für das Jagdschloss Clemenswerth', *Schlaunstudie I*, ed. K. Bussmann (Münster, 1973), pp. 104–24

**Levêque, Auguste** (*b* Nivelles, 12 March 1866; *d* Brussels, 22 Feb 1921). Belgian painter and sculptor. From 1878 to 1884 he attended the academy in Nivelles; he then studied at the Académie Royale des Beaux-Arts in Brussels until 1889. In May 1889 he submitted *Job* (Brussels, Mus. Ixelles), a strikingly Realist work, for the Prix de Rome. His profound disappointment at failing to win caused him to withdraw and seek consolation in dreams and the exaltation of an ideal beauty. In 1893 he set up his studio in Brussels and devoted himself to a gloomy and tormented art. He read philosophy and poetry, especially the work of Dante, and sought to become a literary painter. He allied himself with Jean Delville, who founded the Salons d'Art Idéaliste in 1896, and, with Delville's followers Emile Fabry, Constant Montald and Emile Motte (1860–1931), Levêque practised a style of painting inspired by the theories of Joséphin Péladan and Idealist art. However, he did not exhibit with the followers of these tendencies due to an ideological quarrel with Delville in 1896. For health reasons he settled in Nice from 1895 to 1898. The sunnier climate of the south of France encouraged him to abandon his former pessimistic outlook, together with Idealist art, and he underwent a personal artistic rebirth. He also became a writer and polemicist, attacking what he had previously venerated.

On his return to Belgium, Levêque settled in Brussels and exhibited regularly with growing success, notably at the Salons in Antwerp (1898), Ghent (1899) and Brussels (1900). The works shown were more serene and sometimes bore witness to the social concerns explored by Constantin Meunier and Eugène Laermans, for example the *Triumph of Death* (Antwerp, Kon. Mus. S. Kst.), *Balzac* (Nivelles, Mus. Com. Archéol.), *The Parcae* (Tournai, Mus. B.-A.) and the triptych the *Tragic Workers* (Brussels, Musées Royaux B.-A., destr. 1940). He also executed sculptures, in which he evoked human vigour and the sensuality of life, as in the *Triumph of the Vine* (Liège, Mus. B.-A.). In 1914 Levêque's career was crowned by a retrospective exhibition in the Salle Aeolian in Brussels. He retained to the end of his life his taste for allegory, concern for the human condition and an immaculately finished drawing style, in which line always predominated over colour.

BIBLIOGRAPHY

C. Lemonnier: *L'Ecole belge de peinture, 1830–1905* (Brussels, 1906)

G. Vanzype: *L'Art belge au XIXe siècle* (Brussels, 1923)

E. de Lalieux: 'L'Idéaliste Auguste Levêque', *Rif Tout Dju* [Nivelles] (1967), 107–9, 112–14; (1968), 116, 118–19; (1969), 125, 127–8, 131, 133; (1970), 135–6, 141, 143; (1971), 145, 147, 149; (1972), 155

GISÈLE OLLINGER-ZINQUE

**Lever, William Hesketh**, 1st Viscount Leverhulme (*b* Bolton, Lancs, 19 Sept 1851; *d* Hampstead, London, 7 May 1925). English industrialist, patron and collector. The son of a prosperous Bolton Congregational wholesale grocer, Lever entered the family firm at the age of 16; he diversified into soap-making, first at Warrington in 1885 and later at Port Sunlight (nr Liverpool) in 1889. His firm, Lever Brothers, was immediately successful; by 1897 his annual income was about £92,000 and had risen to £242,000 in 1912. He started collecting contemporary paintings seriously around 1889. Following the example of Thomas James Barratt, another soap manufacturer, he began to incorporate these works into his soap advertisements. Just as Barratt had quarrelled with John Everett Millais over the use of his *Bubbles* (1886; London, A. & F. Pears Ltd) in an advertisement, so Lever antagonized William Powell Frith by the similar exploitation of his *New Frock* (exh. RA 1889; Port Sunlight, Lady Lever A.G.).

The works that Lever collected for commercial purposes were by artists specializing in contemporary subjects and were thus relatively experimental. However, Lever was also assembling a private collection of a more conservative nature for his country house, Thornton Manor (nr Port Sunlight); for example, the classical works of Frederic Leighton were strongly represented. Lever adhered to the well-established tradition among successful northern industrialists for collecting contemporary art until *c.* 1897, when he started buying the newly fashionable 18th-century British portraits (and to a smaller extent landscape and genre paintings). Lever generally relied on his dealers for advice about acquisitions, but this new interest in earlier British art was probably encouraged by his friendship with the collector, painter and polemicist James Orrock (1829–1913). Between 1896 and 1913 Lever bought a vast number of paintings (as well as some furniture and porcelain) from Orrock; these acquisitions included many works by Constable, Gainsborough, Richard Wilson and George Morland (as well as a considerable number of forgeries and imitations). Lever was a major purchaser at the sale of the George McCulloch collection of grand late Victorian paintings (Christie's, London, 23–30 May 1913) and his collection is best known for such pictures, notably the later works of Leighton, Luke Fildes, William Holman Hunt, Millais and William Quiller Orchardson.

Lever was also an architectural patron, with a significant involvement in town planning. Port Sunlight village (1889–1938) was inspired both by low-density suburban developments, such as Bedford Park near London (begun 1875), and by the 'improved' housing estates provided by some philanthropic industrialists and progressive agriculturalists for their workers. The result was a model village created by numerous architects in a broadly vernacular or Old English style, adjoining the huge soap factory and comprising about 890 houses on 56.7 ha by 1925. The village also included many open spaces and public buildings, most notably the Lady Lever Art Gallery, intended to improve the villagers' quality of life. The gallery contains Lever's pictures and about half of his large collection of sculpture, tapestries, embroideries, porcelain, Wedgwood pottery, furniture and ethnographica; the remainder was sold in 1925–6 by his executors. The furniture is best known for the late 18th-century English commodes and the porcelain for the 17th- and 18th-century Chinese blue-and-white and *famille verte* vases.

UNPUBLISHED SOURCES

Port Sunlight, Lady Lever A.G. [corr. and inventories]

BIBLIOGRAPHY

*DNB*

Viscount Leverhulme: *Viscount Leverhulme* (London, 1927) [a biography by his son]

*A Record of the Collection in the Lady Lever Art Gallery, Port Sunlight:* R. R. Tatlock: *English Painting of the 18th–20th Centuries*; R. L. Hobson: *Chinese Porcelain and Wedgwood Pottery*; P. Macquoid: *English Furniture, Tapestry and Needlework of the 16th–19th Centuries* (London, 1928)

*Lord Leverhulme* (exh. cat., ed. E. Morris and others; London, RA, 1980)

E. Morris and M. Evans: *Catalogue of Foreign Paintings, Drawings, Miniatures, Tapestries, Post-classical Sculpture and Prints, Lady Lever Art Gallery, Port Sunlight* (Liverpool, 1983)

E. Hubbard and M. Shippobottom: *A Guide to Port Sunlight* (Liverpool, 1988)

EDWARD MORRIS

**Leverton, Thomas** (*b* Woodford, Essex, *bapt* Waltham Abbey, 11 June 1743; *d* London, 29 Sept 1824). English architect. He was the son of a builder, Lancelot Leverton of Woodford in Essex, from whom he learnt the building business before turning to architecture. Leverton exhibited 34 designs for villas, country houses, town houses, business premises, 'penitentiary houses' and other buildings at the Royal Academy in London between 1771 and 1803. His extant works in London include 65 Lincoln's Inn Fields (1772) for Henry Kendall, the interior of 13 Bedford Square (1775) for himself and the layout of Hamilton Place (1806), Piccadilly, for the Crown. He may have planned Bedford Square and designed some of the other houses. Outside London, extant works include Boyles Court (1776), Great Warley, Essex, Watton Wood Hall (1772–82; now Woodhall Place Preparatory School), Herts, for Sir Thomas Rumbold, in a Neo-classical style reminiscent of Robert Adam, and a triumphal arch to commemorate the War of American Independence (1781–

3) at Parlington House, W. Yorks, for Sir Thomas Gascoigne. He also carried out the remodelling of Scampston House (1803), N. Yorks, for W. T. St Quintin and the remodelling in a Gothic style of Herringston (*c.* 1803), Winterborn Herringston, Dorset, for Edward Williams. It is very likely that Leverton designed Plaistow Lodge (1777–80; now Quernmore Secondary School), Bromley, London. Leverton was one of the first architects to take up the Adam style, best seen in the exquisite Neo-classical interiors of Walton Wood Hall (with its domed Etruscan-style saloon) and Plaistow Lodge. Each is composed of a central block linked by curved wings to pedimented pavilions with large Venetian windows. It is not possible to characterize his later work, since most of it has been destroyed. Leverton's niece Jane married his pupil James Donaldson (*c.* 1756–1843), and they were the parents of the architect T. L. DONALDSON.

BIBLIOGRAPHY

Colvin; *DNB*; Papworth

JILL LEVER

**Leveson-Gower.** English family.

**(1) George Granville Leveson-Gower**, Earl Gower, 2nd Marquess of Stafford and 1st Duke of Sutherland (*b* London, 9 Jan 1758; *d* Dunrobin Castle, Sutherland, 19 July 1833). Patron and collector. He travelled extensively on the Continent (1780–6), served as a Liberal MP for Newcastle under Lyme (1778 and 1780) and for Staffordshire (1787–98), and was ambassador to Paris (1790–92) and joint postmaster-general (1799–1810). He acquired the greater part of Sutherlandshire (now Highland) through his marriage to Elizabeth (1765–1839), Countess of Sutherland, and inherited substantially on the deaths of his uncle, Francis Egerton, 3rd Duke of Bridgewater (*see* EGERTON, (1)), and his father, the 1st Marquess of Stafford. In 1807 he retired from politics and devoted himself to the improvement of his estates and the patronage of art. In 1798 he, his uncle and Frederick Howard, 5th Earl of Carlisle, jointly acquired the Italian and French paintings from the Orléans collection, and he added his uncle's collection to his own when he inherited the Bridgewater estates. He played an important part in the movement towards a national art museum, which culminated in the opening of the Dulwich Gallery (1814) and the National Gallery (1824). He was a founding member, Vice-President (1810–20) and President (1820–5) of the British Institution for Promoting the Fine Arts in the United Kingdom (1805–67), a body of aristocratic connoisseurs that offered to British artists additional selling space in the form of an annual exhibition, as well as more direct patronage in premiums, commissions and purchases of exhibited works, and a repository of examples to be studied in the annual loan exhibitions of Old Masters. To the first such exhibition in 1806, he lent Anthony van Dyck's portrait of *Thomas Howard, 2nd Earl of Arundel* (1620–21; Malibu, CA, Getty Mus.). He continued the reconstruction of Cleveland House and its picture gallery, added to and re-arranged the collection, and in 1806 opened the collection to a ticket-holding audience every Wednesday for several months, an example followed by other owners of private collections. In 1807 he bought 15 works from the British Institution's contemporary exhibition, among them paintings by John Opie, Richard Westall, William Beechey, Martin Archer Shee, and a painting of *Flowers* by James Hewlett. In 1828, he presented to the National Gallery, London, Rubens's celebrated *Minerva Protects Pax from Mars* ('*Peace and War*'; *c.* 1629–30), which he had acquired from the Doria collection. After his death, part of the family collection was bequeathed to his second son, Francis Egerton, 1st Earl of Ellesmere (*see* EGERTON, (2)).

### BIBLIOGRAPHY

*DNB*
W. Buchanan: *Memoirs of Painting with a Chronological History of the Importation of Pictures by the Great Masters into England since the French Revolution*, 2 vols (London, 1824)
G. F. Waagen: *Treasures of Art in Great Britain*, (London, 1854), iii
W. Whitley: *Art in England, 1800–1820* (Cambridge, 1921)
P. Fullerton: *Some Aspects of the Early Years of the British Institution for Promoting the Fine Arts in the United Kingdom, 1805–25* (MA thesis, U. London, Courtauld Inst., 1979)

**(2) Lord Ronald (Charles) (Sutherland-Leveson-) Gower** (*b* 2 Aug 1845; *d* 9 March 1916). Sculptor and writer, grandson of (1) George Granville Leveson-Gower. As a young man he sat for seven years as a Liberal MP for Sutherland. After relinquishing his seat in 1874, he began to make lengthy visits to Paris, studying sculpture in the workshop of Albert-Ernest Carrier-Belleuse. He eventually took a studio of his own in Paris and, assisted by the Italian Luca Madrassi (*fl c.* 1869–1914), produced a series of statues and statuettes, exhibiting them in London at the Royal Academy and the Grosvenor Gallery and in Paris at the Salon. A lively illustrative effect, a quality unusual in British sculpture of the period, is to be found in *Marie-Antoinette Leaving the Conciergerie* (marble; Eaton Hall, Ches) and the *Old Guard* (bronzed plaster; Windsor Castle, Berks, Royal Col.), both of which were exhibited at the Royal Academy in 1877. Gower's most ambitious work was the *Shakespeare* monument (bronze; Stratford-on-Avon, Bancroft Gdns), inaugurated in 1888. It comprises a seated figure of the poet and four characters from his plays. Gower was one of a number of late 19th-century amateur sculptors who successfully exploited the semi-industrial methods of production devised by the sculptors of the Second Empire in France. His literary endeavours include the catalogue of his collection of engraved portraits of Marie-Antoinette.

### WRITINGS

*Iconographie de la reine Marie-Antoinette: Catalogue descriptif et raisonné de la collection de portraits . . . formée par Lord Ronald Gower* (Paris, 1883)
*My Reminiscences*, 2 vols (London, 1883, 5/1895)

### BIBLIOGRAPHY

P. Ward-Jackson: 'Lord Ronald Gower, Gustave Doré and the Genesis of the Shakespeare Memorial at Stratford-on-Avon', *J. Warb. & Court. Inst.*, l (1987), pp. 160–70
M. Kimberley: *Lord Ronald Gower's Monument to Shakespeare*, Stratford-upon-Avon Pap., iii (Stratford-upon-Avon, 1989)

PHILIP WARD-JACKSON

**Levi, Juan de.** *See* JUAN DE LEVI.

**Levi, Rino** (*b* São Paulo, 31 Dec 1901; *d* São Paulo, 29 Sept 1965). Brazilian architect. He studied at the Academy of Fine Arts in Milan (1921–2) and the School of Architecture, Rome (Dip. Arch., 1926). In 1927 he established his own office in São Paulo, at that time still a provincial city with hardly more than a million inhabitants. His first projects show a variety of influences including Italian Rationalism and Art Deco, but he then designed the first modern block of flats in São Paulo, the Columbus Building, completed in 1932. His design had a considerable impact on the still largely horizontal urban landscape and contrasted strongly with the eclecticism of most of the larger houses in the city, winning him an immediate reputation as a modernist architect. Another important work of the 1930s was the design of a large new cinema for São Paulo. Opened in 1936, the UFA Palace, with 3100 seats, was an entirely new concept in cinema design: it had no boxes, but the whole audience was seated in the great auditorium and balcony in perfect viewing and acoustic conditions. The work received enormous critical and public acclaim and won him commissions for further cinemas including the Ipiranga (1919 seats) in São Paulo, designed in 1941. This was a more complex project incorporating the 200-room Hotel Excelsior on the narrow site; the result was an outstanding synthesis of technology, function and aesthetics.

At the end of World War II Brazil entered a phase of intense industrialization and rapid urbanization. These were very productive years for Levi, whose practice extended to include as partners Roberto Cerqueira Cesar (*b* 1917) in 1941 and Luiz Roberto Carvalho Franco (*b* 1926) in 1951, and undertook a series of large-scale buildings. The first stemmed from a prize-winning project for the University of São Paulo Maternity Hospital in 1945. Despite being unexecuted, the design impressed technical experts by the clarity with which the various functions were integrated. It led to Levi's association with a group of doctors who were interested in the rationalization of hospital design and administration, and to a series of important designs for hospitals: the Central Cancer Hospital (1947), the Children's Hospital for the Pro-Infancia Crusade (1950) and the Albert Einstein General Hospital (1958), all in São Paulo. All of these hospitals were planned as a group of separate but interlinked buildings accommodating different activities, and they all provided highly practical solutions to technical and functional problems. In 1959 Levi's office won a contract from the Venezuelan government to advise local architects on a national network of 17 hospitals, many of which were subsequently built.

In 1957 Levi and his team received third prize for their competition entry for the new federal capital, Brasília, which was a radical proposal based on a limited number of very high density blocks. Although the design would have been impossible to achieve with the technology available in Brazil at the time, it remained a topic of discussion and argument. Levi's last major work, and his largest, was the Civic Centre of Santo André, won in competition in 1965. Comprising three different buildings, a Town Hall, Council Chamber and Cultural Centre planned around a pedestrian walkway, the design had an exposed concrete structure, with a grid reinforced by *brise-soleils*, and distinguishes between the functions of each building as Levi had done in his hospital designs. The centre was subsequently completed with gardens and works of art by Roberto Burle Marx.

Levi made an important contribution to the introduction of modern architecture to Brazil, not only through his buildings but also in his teaching roles at the University of São Paulo (1954–9) and the University of Caracas (1959), and through his professional activities as founder and President of the Institute of Architects of Brazil and member of CIAM. After his death, on completion of the Civic Centre project, his practice continued and developed, remaining one of the most important in Brazil. Working under the name Rino Levi Architects Associates, and including Paulo J. V. Bruna (*b* 1941) as a partner from 1971, it carried out a long series of important industrial and educational buildings in the 1970s and 1980s.

BIBLIOGRAPHY

'L'Architecture est un art et une science', *Archit. Aujourd'hui*, 27 (1949), p. 50

H. R. Hitchcock: *Latin American Architecture since 1945* (New York, 1955)

H. E. Mindlin: *Modern Architecture in Brazil* (Rio de Janeiro, 1956)

'Hospital in São Paulo, Brazil', *Archit. Rev.* [London], cxxvi/751 (1959), pp. 109–12

'Rapporto Brasile', *Zodiac*, 6 (1960), pp. 84–95

*Rino Levi*, intro. R. Burle Marx and N. Goulart (Milan, 1974)

PAULO J. V. BRUNA

**Levieux** [Le Vieux; Levieux de Languedoc], **Reynaud** [Renaud] (*b* Nîmes, 1613; *d* ?Rome, after 1694). French painter. The son of a Protestant glass painter who had settled in Nîmes, Levieux went to Rome in 1640, meeting Nicolas Poussin there in 1642. In Rome he executed copies of works by Raphael intended as tapestry cartoons to be woven in France. He returned to Nîmes in 1644, moving to Montpellier five years later; there he worked on the decoration of the hôtel of the Baron de Vauvert and executed tapestry cartoons (untraced) on the theme of the *Life of Moses*. Around 1651 Levieux was in Avignon, where he painted a *Holy Family* (Villeneuve-les-Avignon, Notre-Dame) for the Carthusians, from whom numerous further commissions followed. In 1654 he painted the *Purification of the Virgin* for Notre-Dame-des-Doms, Avignon, and in 1659 he joined the Confrérie des Pénitents Noirs in that city, for whom he painted the *Beheading of St John the Baptist* (Nîmes, Mus. B.-A.). As well as large paintings for churches and private houses in Avignon, Levieux painted still-lifes and portraits and supplied designs to local wood-carvers and sculptors. After his chief rivals Nicolas Mignard and Jean Daret left for Paris, Levieux was able to establish himself as the foremost painter in Provence, dividing his time between Avignon (e.g. the decoration of the chapel of the Pénitents Noirs in 1665) and Aix (e.g. *St Bruno*, 1665; St Jean).

In 1669 Levieux returned to Rome, accompanied by his pupils. There he executed commissions received from Provence, for example his *Assumption* (Isle-sur-la-Sorgue, parish church), while local commissions include the *St Denis* and *Miracle of the Blind Man* painted for S Luigi dei Francesi, Rome. He is recorded *c.* 1690 among those artists in the circle of Pope Alexander VIII; there is no further trace of his activities after this date, and he may have spent his final years as a Carthusian monk.

Levieux's art—a form of classicism in the tradition of Raphael—is refined in both colouring and execution; his compositions are formally dignified, and the features of his saints and others are austere. These aspects are typical of the 17th-century classical movement, which dominated painting in southern France, and have led to Levieux being called a French Sassoferrato. Wytenhove's research has done much to restore the reputation of this hitherto neglected artist.

BIBLIOGRAPHY

P. de Chennevières: *Recherches sur la vie et les ouvrages de quelques peintres provinciaux de l'ancienne France*, i (Paris, 1847), pp. 71–92

J. Boyer: 'La Peinture et la gravure à Aix-en-Provence aux XVIe, XVIIe et XVIIIe siècles', *Gaz. B.-A.*, n. s. 5, lxxviii (1971), pp. 5–187

*La Peinture en Provence au XVIIe siècle* (exh. cat. by H. Wytenhove, Marseille, Mus. B.-A., 1978)

*La Peinture française du XVIIe siècle dans les collections américaines* (exh. cat. by P. Rosenberg, Paris, Grand Pal.; New York, Met.; Chicago, IL, A. Inst.; 1982), pp. 274–5

LAURENCE GUILMARD GEDDES

**Levine, Jack** (*b* Boston, MA, 3 Jan 1915). American painter, printmaker and draughtsman. He studied drawing at the Community Center, Roxbury, MA (1924–31) and painting at Harvard University, Cambridge, MA (1929–33). Levine had a precocious talent for drawing, as is shown by the delicate and meticulous *At the Watering Place* (1931; Cambridge, MA, Fogg). From 1935 to 1940 he was intermittently employed by the Works Progress Administration's Federal Art Project in Boston. He established his reputation with *The Feast of Pure Reason* (1937; New York, MOMA), whose title comes from James Joyce's novel *Ulysses*. The work shows a politician, policeman and capitalist engaged in disreputable collusion, revealing Levine's interest in socially committed art. By the late 1930s he employed exaggeration and distortion to enhance the satire or pathos in his works, as in *Neighbourhood Physician* (1939; Minneapolis, MN, Walker A. Cent.), in which he characteristically enlarged the head and used broader, looser brushstrokes. In 1939 he had his first one-man show at the Downtown Gallery in New York, and from 1942 to 1945 he served in the US Army. A trip to Europe in 1947 deepened his understanding of the Old Masters whose works he preferred to those of 20th-century artists. He often used their techniques, styles and subjects, as in *Magic for the Millions* (1948; Seattle, WA, A. Mus.), in which he adopted El Greco's Mannerist forms in a satire on religious mysticism. In the 1950s he adopted a tighter, more strongly modelled style and treated numerous biblical subjects, such as *King Asa* (1953; Cambridge, MA, Fogg). He also painted satires of contemporary society, such as *Election Night* (1954; New York, MOMA), a tawdry night scene populated with dissipated, lifeless figures. Similar works appeared in the 1960s, such as *The Last Waltz* (1962; Washington, DC, Hirshhorn). After earlier experiments in the 1940s, in the 1960s he also turned to printmaking, producing such powerful works as the aquatint *The Prisoner* (1963; Chicago, IL, A. Inst.). His later painting included the huge diptych *Panethnikon* (1978; priv. col., see Frankel, pp. 122–3), depicting a gathering of world leaders. He painted several biblical works in the 1980s, such as *David and Saul* (1987–9; artist's col., see Frankel, p. 135).

BIBLIOGRAPHY

*Jack Levine* (exh. cat. by K. W. Prescott, New York, Jew. Mus. and elsewhere, 1978–80)

K. W. Prescott and E.-S. Prescott: *The Complete Graphic Work of Jack Levine* (New York, 1986)

S. R. Frankel, ed.: *Jack Levine* (New York, 1989)

**Levine, Les(lie Leopold)** (*b* Dublin, 6 Oct 1935). Canadian sculptor and video maker of Irish birth. He studied art at the Central School of Arts and Crafts in London before emigrating to Canada in 1958. In 1964 he moved permanently to New York. An important precursor of conceptual art and a self-styled 'media sculptor', he became known in the 1960s for his environments and for his 'Disposables': cheap, vacuum-formed plastic reliefs of commonplace objects produced in multiples. His most notable environment was *Slipcover* (1966), a silvery, reflective plastic slipcover for an entire gallery at the Art Gallery of Ontario, Toronto, which also incorporated delayed playback sound and a constantly changing play of light and images. Works like these, using the techniques and materials of modern technology, earned him the nickname 'Plastic man', but his concerns were more with processes than materials. His interest in communications and with the art world as a system led to ironic commentaries that took such varied forms as a consulting service for artists, an underground newspaper and a closed-circuit TV sculpture that recorded its viewers.

Levine was one of the first artists to recognize the potential of television as an art medium. His videotapes serve as a link between his earlier parodies of the art world and his later sociological studies such as *The Troubles* (1973), a multi-media documentary of the people of war-torn Northern Ireland. In the 1980s he used television commercials, billboards and the New York subway system for his mildly subversive messages, using the media to comment on itself as the pervasive environment of our time.

WRITINGS

*Media: The Bio-tech Rehearsal for Leaving the Body* (exh. cat., Calgary, Alta Coll., A.G., 1979)

BIBLIOGRAPHY

P. Russell: 'Les Levine's *Slipcover*', *Artscanada*, xxiv (Feb 1967), pp. 18–19

J. Perrault: 'Plastic Man Strikes', *ARTnews*, lxvii (March 1968), pp. 36–7, 72–3

J. Burnham: 'Les Levine and *The Troubles*', *A. Mag.*, xlvii (April, 1973), pp. 56–9

*Les Levine: Language+Emotion+Syntax=Message* (exh. cat., Vancouver, U. BC, F.A. Gal., 1976)

DIANA NEMIROFF

**Levine, Sherrie** (*b* Hazelton, PA, 17 April 1947). American photographer and conceptual artist. She studied at the University of Wisconsin, Madison (BA 1969, MFA 1973). Biographical information on Levine is limited, since she has refused to participate in 'myth-making' associated with art production. She first gained critical attention in the early 1980s, when she was associated with Cindy Sherman, Robert Longo, David Salle and others known as 'Appropriationists' for drawing on existing imagery from 'high' and 'low' culture. Her works have been interpreted as a commentary on the death of Modernism and its ideals, notions of artistic originality, the authenticity and autonomy of the art object and its status as a commodity. In *Untitled (after Walker Evans)* (10×8 photograph, 1981) Levine re-photographed a reproduction of a photograph by Evans. Such works articulated her fascination with the photographic process and its reproduction, while raising post-structuralist discourses on authorship, originality and history, from which they partly derive. Levine's theoretical rigour was complemented by a delicate, timid, if not remote, handling of materials, adding a sensuous dimension to an otherwise academic pursuit.

BIBLIOGRAPHY

G. Marzorati: 'Sherrie Levine: "Art in the (Re)Making"', *ARTnews*, lxxxv/5 (1986), pp. 90–99

D. Deitcher: 'Sherrie Levine: Rules of the Game', *Sherrie Levine* (exh. cat., Zurich, Ksthalle; Münster, Westfäl. Landesmus.; Malmö, Rooseum; Paris, Hôtel A.; 1991), pp. 7–13

**Levinson, Yevgeny (Adol'fovich)** (*b* Odessa, 19 Oct 1894; *d* Leningrad [now St Petersburg], 21 March 1968). Russian architect, urban planner and teacher of Ukrainian birth. He studied at the Academy of Arts (1923–7), St Petersburg, under Ivan Fomin and Vladimir Shchuko. During this period he also experimented with stage design and book illustration, which influenced his approach to architecture. His diploma design (1927) for the monument to the leaders of the October Revolution paid tribute to academic traditions, but Levinson was subsequently influenced more by Constructivism. His severely geometrical Palace of Culture (1930) on Kirov [now Kamenoostrovsky] Prospect was followed by the residential block (1931–5; with Igor' Fomin) on the embankment of the River Karpovka, both in Leningrad. The latter is a monumental and picturesque building combining elements of Russian Neo-classicism with the Constructivist influences of its reinforced-concrete construction and stepped composition. In 1933 Levinson and Fomin headed the architectural workshop of the Lenproyekt Trust, where they designed an extensive scheme in Shchemilovka, a new residential district. Their buildings there, notably the local Soviet of People's Deputies (1935), the multi-storey residential buildings (1937) on Moskovsky Prospect and the buildings (from 1936) on Ivanovskaya Street, combine innovation with tradition. The classicist element became increasingly dominant in Levinson's work, for example in the residential building (1931–9) on Petrovskaya Embankment, the façade of which has a giant order colonnade echoing the architectural panorama on the River Neva.

Levinson's most significant buildings immediately after World War II are the residential blocks and railway station (1944–50) at Pushkin. The Neo-classical architecture of the station brilliantly expresses his intention of evoking the world of Aleksandr Pushkin as visitors arrive at the city. The illusion is continued in the interiors, for which he used lavish classicist decorations, in stucco, of his own design. The work of Levinson's later career is characterized by a rejection of classical traditions, in common with other Soviet architects, in favour of the flat Modernist forms associated with industrial methods of building. Examples are the Hotel Sovetskaya (1961; with Anatoly I. Pribul'sky (*b* 1916)), on the embankment of the River Fontanka, and the Lenin Palace of Culture (1963–4; with Boris A. Grigor'yev (*b* 1917)), both in Leningrad. He also produced some notable monuments, including those to the

Ukrainian poet *Taras Shevchenko* (1938–9; with the sculptor Matvey Manizer), Kiev and Kaniv, and the Piskaryovskoye Cemetery Ensemble (1945–60; with Alexandr V. Vasil'yev (1913–76)), Leningrad, where the mass graves of the victims of the Siege of Leningrad are commemorated in a solemn conjunction of architectural form, sculpture and epitaph. Levinson was a professor (1946–68) in the architectural faculty of the I. E. Repin Institute for Painting, Sculpture and Architecture, Leningrad.

BIBLIOGRAPHY

S. B. Speransky: 'Vsegda v tvorchestvom poiske' [Always involved in a creative search], *Stroitel'stvo & Arkhit. Leningrada* (1965), no. 1, pp. 26–8

Ya. O. Svirsky: 'Tvorchestvo Ye. A. Levinsona' [The creative work of Ye. A. Levinson], *Arkhit. SSSR*, iv (1965), pp. 51–54

*Evgeny Adol'fovich Levinson: Postroyki, proyekty, grafika* [Construction, design and graphic art] (Leningrad, 1965)

G. A. Ol' and Ye. Ye. Levinson: *Ye. Levinson* (Leningrad, 1976)

YE. YE. LEVINSON, G. A. OL'

**Levinson-Lessing, Vladimir (Frantsevich)** (*b* Yur'yev [now Tartu, Estonia], 2 March 1893; *d* Leningrad [now St Petersburg], 27 June 1972). Russian art historian. A history graduate of Petrograd (St Petersburg) University, he began his museum career in 1918 when he joined the Commission for the Preservation of Monuments of Art and Antiquity (subsequently the State Museum Foundation). He then worked at the Russian Museum (1919–23) before joining Alexandre Benois's staff in the reorganization of the Hermitage's picture gallery. Appointed head of western European art there in 1936 and vice-director of scientific work in 1956, his influence was most pronounced in the organization of exhibitions and in research, although it was also felt in the museum's collecting and conservation policies. One of his most significant contributions lay in the cataloguing of the Hermitage's collections. To this end he edited the two-volume catalogue of western European painting (1958). Although he published comparatively little, his specializations were very broad, ranging from the Renaissance to van Eyck, Dürer and Rembrandt as well as museum studies, all of which served as subjects for courses he taught at the Repin Institute for Painting, Sculpture and Architecture and at Leningrad University. He conducted research into Dutch and Flemish art of the 17th century and the history of collecting in Russia. Of great significance were his articles on Peter I's approach to collecting, on the appraisal of Italian art by Denis Fonvizin (1744/5–92) and the historical development of the Hermitage's collection (all in *Istoriya kartinnoy galerei Ermitazha*, 1986). His comprehensive study of the Hermitage picture gallery, its formation and context in Russian and European cultural life, although not fully published, remains the primary account of one of the world's greatest collections of art.

WRITINGS

*Sneyders i flamandskiy natyurmort* [Snyders and Flemish still-life] (Leningrad, 1926)

ed.: *Gosudarstvennyy Ermitazh: Otdel zapadnoyevropeyskogo iskusstva: Katalog zhivopisi* [The State Hermitage: department of western European art: catalogue of the paintings], 2 vols (Leningrad, 1958, rev. 1976 81)

*Istoriya kartinnoy galerei Ermitazha (1764–1917)* [A history of the Hermitage picture gallery (1764–1917)] (Leningrad, 1986)

BIBLIOGRAPHY

Y. Rusakov: 'Vladimir Frantsevich Levinson-Lessing (1893–1972)', *Sov. Isk.*, lxx/1 (1978), pp. 272–91

JEREMY HOWARD

**Leviny, Ernest** (*b* Georgenberg, Hungary, 1818; *d* Castlemaine, Victoria, March 1905). Australian silversmith and jeweller. He probably trained as a gold- and silversmith in Vienna. He moved to Paris in the early 1840s and then to London, where, in partnership with Frederick Boocke, he operated between 1851 and 1852 as a jeweller at 86 Newman Street. In 1853 he sailed for Australia, where he attempted to establish a mining enterprise on the goldfields at Castlemaine in Victoria. When this failed, he commenced business in Castlemaine as a watchmaker and jeweller, retiring by the mid-1860s. Only a few pieces are recorded to have been made by him, but the ambitious nature of their design and manufacture and the incorporation of Australian imagery are significant. Two of his most important works are a gold inkstand (*c.* 1858; untraced), which was exhibited at the International Exhibition of 1862 in London, and the silver standing cup presented to C. A. Saint in 1863 (*c.* 1860; Melbourne, N.G. Victoria; *see* AUSTRALIA, fig. 21). Some of Leviny's designs for jewellery survive (Castlemaine, Buda).

BIBLIOGRAPHY

J. B. Hawkins: *Nineteenth Century Australian Silver*, i (Woodbridge, 1990)

JUDITH O'CALLAGHAN

**Levis** [Levi], **Giuseppe** [Joseph] **de** (*b* Verona, 1552; *d* Verona, 1611–14). Italian sculptor and bronze-founder. He was the outstanding member of a dynasty of bronzefoundrymen specializing in ornamental artefacts such as church- and table-bells, mortars, inkstands, door-knockers, firedogs etc. His works have been identified from the signature that he customarily cast on to his products: IOSEPH DE LEVIS IN VERONA MI FECE. As well as his signature, he often added a date on his works (as was traditional with bells), which has enabled a substantial dated oeuvre of some 30 items to be built up. The idea that he might have been Jewish, on account of the suggestive form of his name as he gave it in signatures, *Joseph Levi*, now has to be discounted in view of Rognini's discovery that the family came from the village of Levo (Benjamin, p. 415). The Latinized form of the name is pure snobbery, normal at the time in people who had pretensions to a position in society even when they were not of noble birth.

De Levis was capable of modelling small figurines for the handles of his bells etc., but for more significant figures he collaborated with the sculptor Angelo de Rossi: each signed one of the notable pair of bronze statuettes of *St John the Baptist* and *St George* that crown the holy water stoups in the church of S Giorgio in Braida, Verona; while both names are cast inside an inkstand with the *Three Graces* (1599; New York, Met.). All these figures are in the late Mannerist idiom current in the Veneto. De Levis alone signed an impressive bust of *A Man* (Liverpool, Walker A. G.) and a highly decorated pair of firedogs (London, V&A). Towards the end of the 16th century, the names of Giuseppe's sons Paolo (1572–1635) and Francesco (1573–1630), as well as those of his nephews

Servo (1570–1616/27), Giovanni Battista (1572–1628) and Ottavio (1574–1613/14), appear on typical products from the de Levis workshop. Probably from well into the 17th century date two mortars with Hebrew inscriptions and symbols, signed by Servo and Paolo respectively (Jerusalem, Israel Mus., and priv. col.).

### BIBLIOGRAPHY

*Fonditori di campane a Verona dal XI al XX secolo* (exh. cat., ed. L. Franzoni; Verona, Castelvecchio, 1979), p. 71, no. 21

C. Avery: *Studies in European Sculpture* (London, 1981) [reprints a series of articles first published in *The Connoisseur*]

C. Benjamin: *The Stieglitz Collection: Masterpieces of Jewish Art*, Jerusalem, Israel Mus. cat. (Jerusalem, 1987), pp. 415–19, nos 279, 280

*Gardens and Ghettos: The Art of Jewish Life in Italy* (exh. cat., ed. V. Mann; New York, Jew. Mus., 1989), nos 170–76

C. Avery: 'Giuseppe de Levis and his Relatives in the Bronze-casting Industry in Verona', *Verona Illust.*, v (1992), pp. 45–52, pls 15–33

CHARLES AVERY

**Lévi-Strauss, Claude** (*b* Brussels, 28 Nov 1908). French social anthropologist. The son of an artist and graduate in philosophy at the University of Paris, he was associated with the intellectual circle around JEAN-PAUL SARTRE in the early 1930s. After teaching in a school for two years, he worked as a professor of sociology in the University of São Paulo, Brazil (1934–7), and then conducted fieldwork in the Brazilian interior. During World War II he was a member of the Surrealist circle exiled in New York and taught at the New School for Social Research. He was made Director of Studies at the Ecole Pratique des Hautes Etudes in Paris in 1950, and in 1959 he became the first ever Professor of Social Anthropology at the Collège de France.

In order to bring order and precision to social anthropology, Lévi-Strauss propounded his own particular, highly influential brand of STRUCTURALISM, which has had a profound influence on the study of anthropology and art history. Drawing on cybernetics, information theory and the structural linguistics of his friend Ramon Jakobson, he treated cultures as systems of communication. Cultures, organized like languages, were the product of the unconscious structures of human thought. Focusing on the relations between the constituent elements of these structures rather than on their culturally constituted content, he believed that the comparative study of these relations in different societies throughout the world would lead to the discovery of innate, universal mechanisms of the human mind. Emphasizing the importance of structure also resolved the debate between form and content.

The cerebral mechanisms for processing speech and music may be represented in two dimensions as a rectangular mould that can be scanned horizontally or vertically. To Lévi-Strauss, the processing of a message within one culture could be similarly represented: metaphor, the harmonic of the mould, was likened to parts of speech (such as nouns or verbs), and metonym, the melody, to sentences or syntax. Metaphor is based on the recognition of similarity and metonym on the recognition of contiguity. The cultural logic constructed within this system depends not on formal contrasts of abstract ideas but on the observed contrasts in the sensory qualities of concrete objects, such as the differences between wet and dry, male and female, left and right. The perception of such related

differences in nature is used to produce cultural differences that have the same structure of relations. Thus relations between different types of food can be homologous to the relations between categories of people, especially on ceremonial occasions. Lévi-Strauss sited the fundamental distinction between nature and culture in the cooking of food: the basic transformation of a biological necessity into a cultural product.

This non-rational logic of the concrete can be most easily uncovered by analysing the rituals or myths of a culture. While each myth contains only a few cultural messages, the corpus of myths in any one society redundantly transmits all the messages of that society. In his study of South American myths, Lévi-Strauss demonstrated that sets of social relations can be represented as relations between different kinds of animals; between categories of food; between animals and plants; between categories of smell and taste (such as pleasant/unpleasant, sweet/sour); between categories of sound and silence (whether animal cries or music); or between combinations of any of these sets of relations. All these transformations follow the same set of logical rules.

Lévi-Strauss stressed the highly sophisticated classificatory ability of 'primitive' man. Totemic species, for instance, are valued not because they are 'goods to eat' but because they are 'goods to think with', culturally valuable categories that can represent the differences between social groups. Lévi-Strauss likened a 'primitive' thinker to a *bricoleur* (handyman). *Bricoleurs* do odd jobs with a limited set of tools. When confronted with a new kind of task, they do not invent new tools but adapt their present ones to the novel situation. Similarly, 'primitive' thinkers do not create new concepts when presented with a new type of problem. Instead they reorder existing concrete elements into a configuration that accommodates the new set of circumstances.

Despite his pretensions to scientific objectivity, Lévi-Strauss's poetically inspired (if not at times Surrealist) style and his repeated refusal to consider ethnographic examples that contradict his grand generalizations have prompted some to suggest that his theories reveal not structures of the human mind, but forms of aesthetic perception.

### WRITINGS

*Les Structures élémentaires de la parenté* (Paris, 1949; Eng. trans., London, 1968)

*Tristes tropiques* (Paris, 1955); Eng. trans. as *A World on the Wane* (London, 1961); rev. as *Tristes Tropiques* (London, 1973)

*Anthropologie structurale* (Paris, 1958; Eng. trans., London and New York, 1963)

*La Pensée sauvage* (Paris, 1962; Eng. trans., London, 1966)

*Le Totémisme aujourd'hui* (Paris, 1962; Eng. trans., London, 1964)

*Mythologiques*, 4 vols (Paris, 1964–71; Eng. trans., 1969–81)

*Anthropologie structurale*, ii (Paris, 1973; Eng. trans., New York, 1976)

*La Voie des masques* (Geneva, 1975; Eng. trans., Seattle, 1983)

### BIBLIOGRAPHY

N. E. Hayes and T. Hayes, eds: *Claude Lévi-Strauss: The Anthropologist as Hero* (Cambridge, MA, 1970)

E. Leach: *Lévi-Strauss* (London, 1970)

J. Boon: *From Symbolism to Structuralism: Lévi-Strauss in a Literary Tradition* (New York, 1972)

D. Pace: *Claude Lévi-Strauss: The Bearer of Ashes* (New York, 1983)

JEREMY MacCLANCY

**Levitan, Isaak (Il'ich)** (*b* Kibarta, near Verzhbolovo Station, Suvalksk province [now Kibartay, Lithuania], 30

Aug 1860; *d* Moscow, 4 Aug 1900). Russian painter of Lithuanian birth. He largely painted landscapes (including pastel sketches), which are noted for their emotive or symbolic resonance. His 'landscapes of mood' had a profound influence on Russian landscape painting, to which he introduced a sense of the unity of humankind and nature, and of the spiritual power of the Russian countryside.

1. EARLY CAREER, LATE 1870S TO 1889. Levitan came from a poor Jewish village but was able to study (1873–5) at the Moscow School of Painting, Sculpture and Architecture, where he showed outstanding talent for landscape painting. He was taught by Vasily Perov, Aleksey Savrasov and Vasily Polenov. The influence of the last two on Levitan's work was particularly significant. His earliest surviving paintings date from the later 1870s: they show simple, modest landscape motifs with a measure of lyricism, in the manner of Savrasov. By 1879, however, in the picture an *Autumn Day* (Moscow, Tret'yakov Gal.), Levitan's individuality is apparent: the picture shows a path in the park near Moscow with the lone figure of a walking woman presented so as to achieve a unity of nature and humanity previously unknown in Russian art. The picture was enthusiastically received on its exhibition and was immediately acquired by Pavel Tret'yakov.

During the early 1880s Levitan turned to examples of work by both Russian and European landscape painters, for example Ivan Shishkin and Jean-Baptiste-Camille Co-rot. His own experiments with light and colour drew him to those of Polenov. Levitan's paintings from the mid-1880s, such as the *First Shoots: May* (1883–8), the *Little Bridge: Savvinskaya* (1884) and the *Birch Grove* (1885–9; all Moscow, Tret'yakov Gal.), were conceived or executed under the influence of Polenov. They mark a new stage in Levitan's developing style with their use of bright, satu-rated colours and bolder contrasts of light and shade. One may also note a parallel to the search for poetic effects in the early Valentin Serov and other young painters of the 1880s.

In 1883 or 1884 Levitan came to know the writer Anton Chekhov, whose brother had been Levitan's contemporary at the Moscow School of Painting. A close friendship developed between Levitan and Chekhov, and this lasted, with short intervals, until the ends of their lives. In 1884 Levitan began to frequent a sketching club in the home of Savva Mamontov, and also took part in the activities of the Abramtsevo artistic circle organized by Mamontov, executing stage designs for a series of productions (e.g. Dargomizhsky's *Rusalka*, and Glinka's *A Life for the Tsar*, for which he painted the watercolour the *Ipat'yev Monas-tery*, now in Moscow, Bakhrushkin Cent. Theat. Mus., and published in Suirkina) in Mamontov's Private Russian Opera in Moscow. In the summer of 1884 Levitan worked with other artists in the village of Savvinskaya, near Zvenigorod. In the spring of 1886 he made his first trip to the Crimea, and in 1887 to the Volga. His Crimean scenes (e.g. *In the Crimean Mountains*, Moscow, Tret'yakov Gal.) capture the bright sun and the heat of the region, but with the Volga paintings Levitan was able to convey the poetry he found in the landscape. Between 1887 and 1890 he spent several months each summer in small towns along the Volga such as Ples and Vasil'sursk, and here he was deeply moved by the sense of distance and the grandeur in such settings.

In the first small picture of the Volga series, the austere *Evening on the Volga* (1887–8; Moscow, Tret'yakov Gal.), there are intimations that the artist regards the visible as a starting-point for contemplation of the invisible, for thoughts of the nation and its destiny. In his next works, *Evening: Golden Ples* (1889) and *After the Rain: Ples* (1889; both Moscow, Tret'yakov Gal.), both more detailed and more seductive in colouring, a coherent and deeply poetic image of Russian life emerges, with a strong sense of the indissoluble connection between nature and man. In these paintings Levitan uses a complex spatial arrangement with confidence, and his brushwork suggests spontaneity backed by firmness of purpose. The palette is more varied, with subtle tones used to obtain specific effects. Levitan painted the Volga in various weather and light conditions, using these to convey a wide range of associated moods. The Volga series established Levitan as the painter of the 'landscape of mood', which was for many years the established style of Moscow landscape painting.

2. ARTISTIC MATURITY, 1890–1900. During the 1890s Levitan reached artistic maturity. He travelled for the first time to countries in western Europe, including visits to Berlin, Paris, Nice, Bordighera, Menton, Venice and Florence. He sketched and painted the landscapes of Italy, and in Paris he became familiar with recent move-ments in French art, being especially interested in the work of the Impressionists because of his own experience of working *en plein air*. In 1890 Levitan was elected a member of the WANDERERS (Peredvizhniki) though he had in fact exhibited with them since 1884.

Professional success, however, was to some degree offset by social difficulties in a time of growing anti-Semitism: in September 1892, in connection with the eviction of Jews from Moscow, Levitan was forced to go to the village of Boldino in Vladimir province, only being permitted to return, after a few months, through the intervention of artist friends. Levitan was prone to ex-tremes of emotion, and given to long periods of intro-spection and melancholy. The development of a heart condition increased his propensity to depression, and he made several attempts at suicide.

Levitan's hopes and disappointments are reflected in a series of large paintings from the early 1890s. *By the Pond* (1892; Moscow, Tret'yakov Gal.) allows a sense of enigma and melancholy to dominate a realistically presented motif through the treatment of the evening light. The contem-porary, more overtly poetic approach of the Abramtsevo artists, who often looked to the forms of folk art as well as of Symbolism, may possibly have influenced another of Levitan's works from this time, *At Eternal Rest* (1894; Moscow, Tret'yakov Gal.; see fig.). Here the natural grandeur of the setting takes on the character of a symbol of the elemental might of the universe, revealing, by contrast, the transience of man's life: the great sweep of the water surface, the expanse of empty land all around and the huge, swirling clouds contrast with an old wooden church sheltering in the foreground, with a faint light in the window, and a half-forgotten country churchyard. The

Isaak Levitan: *At Eternal Rest*, oil on canvas, 1.50×2.06 m, 1894 (Moscow, Tret'yakov Gallery)

picture also has a strong decorative aspect in the emphatic flatness and the element of silhouette in the composition, and in the harmony of the colouring. Levitan considered this picture his most important work. In another painting from this period, *Vladimirka* (1892; Moscow, Tret'yakov Gal.) a symbolic image has a more precise meaning: the road running under a low grey sky through fields and woods, and eventually disappearing in the distance is the Vladimir road leading to Siberia, the road taken by political exiles.

In the mid- and later 1890s Levitan produced a number of works in which the beauty of the Russian landscape in various seasons is more directly appreciated: bright sun on snow in *March* (1895), a dazzle of warm yellow and orange tones in *Golden Autumn* (1895) and a subtle study of light, water and delicate plant forms in *Spring–the Large Pool* (1897; all Moscow, Tret'yakov Gal.). In these works Levitan's brushstroke is freer and more varied; there is less concern with traditional finish; but the rougher quality is itself decorative.

The work of Levitan's last years suggests two distinct aims: firstly, utmost simplicity of motif and expression to convey the greatest poignancy. Works such as *Dusk: A Hayrick* (1899; Moscow, Tret'yakov Gal.) achieve their effect by these means. Levitan also sought, however, motifs of a certain monumentality in their own right, in order to find an image to synthesize many impressions, thoughts and emotions. Levitan's last large picture, *The*

*Lake* (1899–1900; St Petersburg, Rus. Mus.) is an example. Levitan also called the picture *Rus'*, suggesting his interpretation of the motif as the embodiment of Russia, its landscape, its people and its history.

Levitan's early death cut short a career of national, as well as international, promise: in 1897 he had been made a full member of the Munich Secession, in whose exhibitions he had taken part in 1898 and 1899. In the same years he had begun to show his work in St Petersburg in the exhibitions organized by the editors of the journal *Mir iskusstva* (*see* WORLD OF ART), with whom he felt much sympathy. In 1898 Levitan had been given the title of Academician by the St Petersburg Academy of Art; and he had then begun to teach at the Moscow School of Painting, Sculpture and Architecture, where he taught Nikolay Sapunov, among others.

The small Levitan house museum in Plyos on the River Volga (Ivanovo Region) has a very modest selection of his works, certainly not the most famous. But its situation in a small, old, picturesque town gives us an excellent impression of the historical and ecological conditions in which he produced his work.

For further illustration *see* RUSSIA, fig. 25.

### WRITINGS
Pis'ma. Dokumenty. Vospominaniya. [Letters. Documents. Reminiscences.] (Moscow, 1956)

BIBLIOGRAPHY
F. Y. Suirkina: *Russkoye teatral'no-dekoratsionnaye iskusstvo vtoroy poloviny XIX veka. Ocherki* [Russian stage art in the second half of the nineteenth century. Sketches] (Moscow, 1956), pp. 208, 253
A. A. Fedorov-Davydov: *Isaak Il'ich Levitan: Zhizn' i tvorchestvo* [Isaak Il'ich Levitan: life and work], 2 vols (Moscow, 1966)
——: *Isaak Il'ich Levitan: Zhizn' i tvorchestvo, 1860–1900* [Isaak Il'ich Levitan: life and work, 1860–1900] (Moscow, 1976) [with summary in Eng., Ger. and Fr.]
T. V. Yurova, ed.: *Levitan: Al'bom* [Levitan: art book] (Leningrad, 1987)
L. I. IOVLEVA

**Levitsky, Dmitry (Grigor'yevich)** (*b* Kiev, ?May 1735; *d* St Petersburg, 16 April 1822). Russian painter of Ukrainian birth. Together with Fyodor Rokotov and Vladimir Borovikovsky, he ranks foremost among 18th-century Russian portrait painters. He received his first lessons in painting from his father, Grigory Levitsky-Nos (1697–1769), a priest, engraver and painter. He also studied under Aleksey Antropov, who had come to Kiev to decorate St Andrew's church (1752–5). In the late 1750s Levitsky went with Antropov to St Petersburg, where he stayed until 1764; he continued with lessons from Antropov to whom, it appears, he owed the objectivity that was to characterize his work. It is probable that he also studied at the St Petersburg Academy of Arts, attending classes under Louis Lagrenée. Levitsky worked with Antropov on the decoration of triumphal arches in Moscow for Catherine II's coronation in 1762. His first known portraits are rather formal, for example that of the architect *Aleksandr Kokorinov* (1769; St Petersburg, Rus. Mus.), which won Levitsky the title of Academician in 1770. In such works he made successful use of a compositional structure typical of formal European portrait painting, intended to emphasize the importance of the sitter. (Kokorinov was the first director of the Academy of Arts and had also designed its building.) Levitsky used a restrained yet dignified colour scheme, based on a combination of golden brown and olive tints.

Levitsky was most productive during the 1770s and 1780s, when he painted many ceremonial and informal portraits, and also portrait pictures intended to tell a story. His models were drawn from several social classes and presented in a wide range of contexts; Levitsky also adopted a great number of different compositional devices. Among the first works from this period was a series of seven decorative portraits of pupils from the Smol'ny Institute for Young Ladies of the Nobility. The portraits of *Nataliya Borshchova, Yekaterina Nelidova, Aleksandra Molchanova* (all 1772–6; St Petersburg, Rus. Mus.) and others are uniform in conception, and they may have been intended as decoration for one of the imperial palaces. The young ladies are all portrayed full-length, either in their school uniform or in theatrical costume on the occasion of a school celebration; dancing, acting or playing an instrument. The colouring in each case is designed to reflect the sitter's character. These portraits reveal Levitsky's brilliance as a portrait painter. The texture of the various materials is admirably rendered; the poses are unaffected and lively. The portraits are a celebration of youthful charm and the unalloyed pleasure of living. The portrait of *Prokofy Demidov* (1773; Moscow, Tret'yakov Gal.) is formal, yet it has intimate touches, and it can be regarded as a portrait with a certain narrative element. The sitter was a rich mine-owner, well educated and known for the idiosyncrasy of his tastes and interests. He is shown in a bright red dressing-gown and a nightcap against a background of columns and drapery; he leans on a watering-can and points down at two potted plants, thus indicating his interest in gardening. Every detail in the picture suggests his tastes and character. A later portrait of the same type is that of *Catherine II as Lawgiver* (1783; St Petersburg, Rus. Mus.; *see* ST PETERSBURG, fig. 6). The Empress is depicted in the Temple of the Goddess of Justice, burning poppies on the altar to symbolize her sacrifice of private rest for the public good. Despite its artificiality in conception, Levitsky's work is a magnificent pictorial ode and presents an ideal picture of the enlightened ruler as she was seen by the progressive element in Russian society. The painting was very well received, and Levitsky made several versions of it.

In addition to large 'public' works Levitsky painted many portraits of a more intimate type, concentrating attention on the sitters' features and attempting to convey their thoughts and character. The portrait of the French philosopher *Denis Diderot* (1773; Geneva, Mus. A. & Hist.), painted during his stay in St Petersburg, shows him in a dressing-gown. Focusing attention on the face, Levitsky attempted to convey a sense of Diderot's noble and penetrating mind. Levitsky's endeavour to enhance the emotional appeal of his pictures through the use of colour and chiaroscuro is evident in many portraits of the 1770s, in particular the *Old Man*, thought to be the artist's father (1779; St Petersburg, Rus. Mus.). There are no accessories, only the affectionate record of the sitter's self-absorbed expression against a dark background. It is a work of great depth and force.

Levitsky painted a number of portraits of his friends, invariably with emphasis on their depth and richness of spirit. Among these are the portrait of his wife *Nastas'ya Levitskaya* (1780s; St Petersburg, Rus. Mus.) and three portraits of his friend of many years, the architect, poet and composer *Nikolay L'vov*. The first and most accomplished of these (late 1770s; Moscow, Lit. Mus.) admirably reflects the sitter's keenness of mind and his youthful sincerity, friendliness and enthusiasm. The portrait of L'vov's future wife, *Mariya D'yakova* (1778; see fig.) is one of Levitsky's most poetic works, full of sympathy for this charming and attractive sitter. In the 1780s Levitsky's portraits became more austere and solemn and the characterization more sober and detached. Many of his paintings were executed for the court and aristocracy, and he began to repeat compositional devices and arrangements of figures. His methods, however, always varied according to the sitter's character: this is seen, for instance, in the different treatment of the diplomat *Pyotr Bakunin* and of his wife *Yekaterina* (both 1782; Moscow, Tret'yakov Gal.). In the former, cold grey tones predominate, emphasizing the subject's character as an official, rational man of business. The portrait of Bakunin's wife is predominantly grey and white, but the bright colours of the face and of some details help us to see in her a somewhat eccentric, cheerful person.

In portraits of the aristocracy Levitsky was often constrained to limit the force of his characterization; he thus devoted great attention to the role of pictorial values.

Dmitry Levitsky: *Mariya D'yakova*, oil on canvas, 610×500 mm, 1778 (Moscow, Tret'yakov Gallery)

BIBLIOGRAPHY
N. M. Gerschenzon-Chegodayeva: *D. G. Levitsky* (Moscow, 1964)
N. M. Voronina: *Levitsky* (Moscow, 1968)
N. M. Moleva: *D. G. Levitsky* (Moscow, 1980)
*Dmitry Grigor'yevich Levitsky, 1735–1822* (exh. cat., Leningrad, Rus. Mus., 1987)

G. KOMELOVA

**Levitsky, Sergey (L'vovich)** (*b* Moscow, 1819; *d* St Petersburg, 22 June 1898). Russian photographer, writer and critic. He began taking daguerreotypes in 1839 as soon as the process became known. After graduating from the faculty of law of Moscow University he entered the office of the Ministry of the Interior in St Petersburg. In 1843 he was sent on a government survey of mineral water in the Caucasus, where he took 25 daguerreotypes of Piatigorsk, Kislovodsk, Mount Meshuk and Beshtan (untraced). Five of these reached the lensmaker Charles Chevalier (1804–59) in Paris, who displayed two in his shop window. As a result of his success Levitsky decided to become a full-time daguerreotypist in 1844 and travelled to Vienna, Rome, Paris and London in order to study art, chemistry and physics. In 1845 he made his pioneering daguerreotype group portrait of *N. V. Gogol' among a Group of Russian Artists in Rome* (see Morozov, 1986, p. 23), the first of a number of group portraits and portraits of writers and artists, which became his speciality. In Paris in 1845 Levitsky met Louis Daguerre, and he also worked with William E. Kilburn (*fl* 1846–62) in London. He constructed his own camera in 1847.

Levitsky returned to St Petersburg in 1849 and opened a daguerreotype studio by Kazan' Cathedral in 1850. After ten years he opened a studio in Paris, returning to St Petersburg and working with his son Lev from 1867. Levitsky was an innovative practitioner, constantly searching for ways to improve photographic portraiture. He initiated the use of decorative backgrounds in portrait daguerreotypes, and his large daguerreotype portrait groups won a gold medal at the Exposition Universelle in Paris in 1851. His portraits of groups and of individuals, especially writers, made him famous; they are always sensitively lit and posed and convey a thoughtfulness rare at the time, as in his portrait of the writers *Goncharov, Turgenev, Tolstoy, Grigorovich, Druzhinin and Ostrovsky* (1856; see Morozov, 1977, fig. 1) and his portrait of *A. I. Gertsen* (1860s; see Morozov, 1977, fig. 2).

Although Levitsky later adopted the wet collodion process, he continued to experiment, in particular with electric lighting. He had attempted to make daguerreotype portraits by artificial lighting as early as the 1840s, but it was only in 1879 that he made his first successful portrait by electric light. In 1880 he converted his studio to electric lighting and began to make portraits combining natural and electric light in 1882. He also developed the art of retouching the negative, which was proposed in the 1860s. He was later compelled, however, to denounce its abuse in flattering the sitters in portraits, and he criticised the conferment of awards on photographers who retouched portrait negatives.

Levitsky was prolific as a writer and critic concerning photography. A founder-member of the first Russian Photographic Society in 1872, he wrote many articles for their journal *Fotograf* in the early 1880s. He was an admirer,

A good example is the portrait of the haughty *Countess Ursula Mniszek* (1782; Moscow, Tret'yakov Gal.). The picture is distinguished by its refined composition and delicate colour scheme; but Levitsky does not fail to convey his rather negative impression of the sitter's character in her pose. Another case is the portrait of the Italian singer *Anna Daviya Bernuzzi* (1782; Moscow, Tret'yakov Gal.): she is shown as a *belle jardinière*, but one whose surface amiability fails to conceal the calculating nature of her smile. Among Levitsky's last works from the 1780s and 1790s are portraits of the Vorontsov family. The sybaritic *Count Artemy Vorontsov* (late 1780s; St Petersburg, Rus. Mus.) is shown in a careless pose, with his shirt collar unbuttoned; the portraits of his four daughters (late 1780s or early 1790s; St Petersburg, Rus. Mus.) represent admirably the character of each but, above all, make clear their directness of manner, poetic charm and youthful purity, qualities to which Levitsky returned repeatedly throughout his career. One of Levitsky's finest portraits from this time is that of the writer and social reformist *Nikolay Novikov* (1790s; known only from replicas, one in Moscow, Tret'yakov Gal.). The painting, in restrained colours, emphasizes the sitter's simple and natural disposition as well as his importance in society. At the end of the 1790s Levitsky's work began to deteriorate, and during his last years he scarcely painted at all, owing to increasing difficulties with his eyesight.

Levitsky played a significant role as a teacher. From 1771 to 1786 he directed the portrait-painting class of the St Petersburg Academy of Arts, where he trained, among others, Stepan Shchukin (1762–1826), Pyotr Drozhdin (1762–1805) and Leonty Miropolsky (1749–1819).

in particular, of the work of Henry Peach Robinson. He worked tirelessly to promote photography and served on numerous juries for international exhibitions.

WRITINGS

'Pis'mo k redaktoru' [Letter to the editor], *Fotograf*, 9–10 (1865), p. 215

'Obzor uspekhov fotografii na Parizhskoy vsemirnoy vystavke 1878–goda' [Survey of the progress of photography in the Paris Exposition Universelle of 1878], *Zapiski Rus. Tekh. Obshchestva*, 2 (1879), pp. 95, 107

'Kak ya sdelalsya fotografom' [How I became a photographer], *Fotolyubitel'* (1896)

BIBLIOGRAPHY

G. Boltyansky: *Ocherki po istorii fotografii v SSSR* [Studies in the history of photography in the USSR] (Moscow, 1939), pp. 15–20

S. Morozov: *Pervye russkiye fotografy-khudozhniki* [The first Russian photographer-artists] (Moscow, 1952)

——: 'Early Photography in Eastern Europe: Russia', *Hist. Phot.*, i/4 (1977), pp. 327–47

——: *Tvorcheskaya fotografiya* [Creative photography] (Moscow, 1986)

KEVIN HALLIWELL

**Levitt, Helen** (*b* New York, 31 Aug 1913). American photographer. She studied at the Art Students League in New York. After seeing photographs by Henri Cartier-Bresson, Levitt decided to become a photographer and, using a Leica, began to photograph poor sections of New York. She studied with Walker Evans in 1938–9, working with him in the subways. Levitt worked on several projects whose themes promoted humanist causes. She began to photograph children in the inner city in the 1940s, bringing to her black-and-white photographs a characteristic warmth and humanity. She showed at MOMA, New York, in 1941 and with the encouragement of James Agee (1909–55) began to make 16 mm films. They produced *The Quiet One* together in 1948. In 1965 she published her first book, *A Way of Seeing*, with Agee. In 1970 Levitt began to work in colour. One of the first street photographers to do so, Levitt set colourfully clothed figures against the drab backgrounds of tenements and city streets to make photographs that both describe personalities and present archetypal figures (e.g. *New York City*, 1972; New York, Brooklyn Mus.).

PHOTOGRAPHIC PUBLICATIONS

with J. Agee: *A Way of Seeing* (New York, 1965)

BIBLIOGRAPHY

*Helen Levitt* (exh. cat., Washington, DC, Corcoran Gal. A., 1980)

SHERYL CONKELTON

**Levkas.** *See* LEUKAS.

**Levni** [Levnī; 'Abd al-Jalil Čelebi; Abdülcelil Çelebi] (*fl* 1700–1720s; *d* 1732). Ottoman painter. Better known by his pen name Levni, he was the foremost court painter during the Tulip Period, the second classical age of Ottoman art in the first quarter of the 18th century. The artist revived the classical tradition of the 16th century and was the last great illustrator of manuscripts in the Islamic world (*see* ISLAMIC ART, §III, 4(vi)(e)). His works reflect the last flowering of the genre of historical painting, while avoiding European features adopted by his contemporaries. Levni is first mentioned by Demetrius Cantemir, prince of Moldavia, as the sultan's portraitist (*musavvir*) responsible for the portraits that Cantemir copied in his book, *The History of the Growth and Decay of the Ottoman Empire* (1734–5). According to the Ottoman biographer

Ayvansaraylı (*d* 1787), Levni came from Edirne to Istanbul where he began as an apprentice decorator–painter (*nakkaş*) and then rose to the rank of master, excelling in gilding and the *Saz* style. He eventually mastered the art of portraiture, becoming the most famous practitioner of the age. He also wrote poetry in classical and folk genres.

Levni's most outstanding illustrations appear in the *Sūrnāma-i Vehbī* (Istanbul, Topkapı Pal. Lib., A. 3593), the court poet Vehbi's account of the circumcision festival that Ahmed III arranged for his four sons in 1720. Levni's signature appears on 2 of the 137 paintings: on the stool beneath the sultan's feet in a reception scene (fol. 20*v*) and below a courtly rider in a parade, possibly intended as a self-portrait (fol. 171*r*), but the paintings show such a consistent style that all must have been executed under his close supervision. A superb draughtsman and colourist, Levni excelled in composing highly structured scenes, some of which include more than 100 figures (*see* ISLAMIC ART, fig. 195). The narrative cycle is independent of the text and reads like a documentary film strip of the festival with each episode and figure clearly identified. A second copy of the *Sūrnāma-i Vehbī* (Istanbul, Topkapı Pal. Lib., A. 3594), based on Levni's copy, was produced by other court artists, perhaps for the grand vizier IBRAHIM PAHA.

Levni also painted portraits of the Ottoman sultans in several copies of the *Silsilanāma*, a genealogy of the Ottoman house. The 22 portraits in a lost copy painted *c.* 1700 are known from engraved copies by Cantemir, and Levni did 22 of 29 portraits in another copy (*c.* 1700–18; Istanbul, Topkapı Pal. Lib., A. 3109). He also painted single studies of court figures which were bound into albums. He signed 43 of 46 studies of men and women in an album (*c.* 1710–20; Istanbul, Topkapı Pal. Lib., H. 2164) and a portrait of a lady (*c.* 1710–20; Paris, Bib. N., MS. arabe 6076, fol. 56*r*). Several other copies of the *Silsilanāma* and single-figure paintings incorporated into albums are attributed to his studio.

BIBLIOGRAPHY

A. S. Ünver: *Ressam Levnī: Hayatı ve eserleri* [The painter Levni: his life and works] (Istanbul, 1939)

——: *Levnī* (Istanbul, 1957)

E. Atıl: *Surname-i Vehbi: An Eighteenth Century Ottoman Book of Festivals* (diss., Ann Arbor, U. MI, 1969)

ESIN ATIL

**Levoča** [formerly Ger. Leutschau; Hung. Lőcse]. Slovak town, capital of the Spiš region at the foot of the High Tatra Mountains. On account of its location the region was a natural buffer zone protecting the northern border of Hungary since the early Middle Ages. It was crossed by major trade routes, the most important of which, the Magna Via, linked the Balkans with the Baltic area. Levoča grew out of a Slav settlement that existed at the intersection of these routes and that constantly suffered Tatar invasions, with great destruction being caused in 1241. In subsequent years there was a wave of German colonization, and the town grew and began to prosper. A privilege was granted by King Stephen V (*reg* 1270–72) in 1271, giving rise to a commonwealth of 24 towns within the Spiš region, headed by Levoča. Levoča's status as a

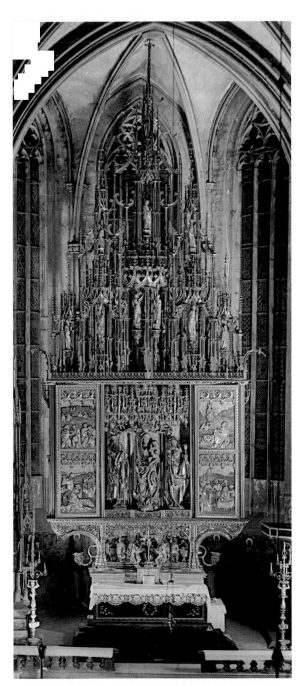

Levoča, St James, altarpiece by Pavel of Levoča showing the *Virgin and Child*, *St John the Baptist* and *St James*, polychromed wood, 1508–17

Franciscan friary was established close to the bulwarks. Both churches can be ascribed to the same builders. The development of Levoča set an example for other towns within the Spiš region, and the influence of the Spiš builders is reflected in a remarkable series of twin-nave churches erected before the first quarter of the 15th century in Spiš. Around the second quarter of the 15th century several painting and sculpture workshops were established in Levoča, and some of their works, especially Late Gothic winged altarpieces combining painting and sculpture, were of a particularly high standard. These developments culminated in the work of Pavel of Levoča (*fl* first quarter of the 16th century), whose great achievement was the main altarpiece (1508–17) in St James (see fig.). This elaborate structure is the highest Late Gothic altarpiece ever constructed; it shows the *Virgin and Child* flanked by *St John the Baptist* and *St James*, with narrative scenes on the inner and outer faces of the wings. Pavel's later work reflects the Renaissance style. His superb craftsmanship influenced a large circle of artists in the Spiš region and beyond.

The period between the 1480s and the mid-17th century was marked by a new wave of architectural activity, with a great number of burghers' houses being built. The finest examples, many of which are in the main square, typically feature arcaded courtyards and decorated façades. The town hall, which had been destroyed in a fire, was replaced in the 1550s by a fine Renaissance building with arcades and gables. The Baroque style was introduced to Spiš relatively late, on account of the region's Protestantism. The most prominent examples in Levoča are the church of the Holy Spirit, built after a fire in 1747 and incorporating typically regional features, and the reconstruction (*c.* 1675), by Olaf Engelholm, of the interior of the Franciscan church. Neo-classicism emerged as the dominant architectural style in the late 18th century, and notable structures include the Evangelical church (1823–7) and the Great Komitat House, built in the first half of the 19th century by Anton Povolny. In the late 18th century and the early 19th a number of natives of Levoča made a significant contribution to the revival of the Slovak language and Slovak literature and arts. The portraitists Jan Stunder (1759–1811) and Josef Czauczik (1780–1857) were the most notable exponents of this movement in the field of painting. The town's importance diminished steadily from the mid-19th century, particularly since it did not participate in the process of industrialization, and its decline continued into the 20th century. On account of its well-preserved historic core it was declared an area of architectural conservation.

BIBLIOGRAPHY
V. Kotrba and F. Kotrba: *Levočský oltár majstra Pavla* [The Levoča altar of Master Pavel] (Bratislava, 1955)
R. Felber: *Levoča* (Košice, 1964)
L. Hromadová: *Levoča* (Bratislava, 1970)
M. Suchý: *Dejiny Levoče* [The history of Levoča], 2 vols (Košice, 1974–5)
L. Šášky: *Kunstdenkmäler der Slovakei* (Bratislava, 1988)

JAROMÍR HOMOLKA

**Levrac-Tournières.** *See* TOURNIÈRES, ROBERT.

**Lévy.** French collectors and patrons. Pierre Lévy (*b* Guebwiller, Haut-Rhin, 11 April 1907), an industrialist

political, economic and cultural centre was further enhanced when, maintaining contacts with regions of Germany, Silesia, Poland and areas along the Danube (present-day Austria), it became a Royal Free Town.

During the 14th century the town was built on a regular grid plan and surrounded by fortifications. A parish church (1332–42) dedicated to St James and a town hall were built in the middle of the rectangular market-place, and a specializing in textiles, and his wife Denise Lévy (née Lièvre) donated in 1976 a substantial part of their collection of *c.* 4000 works of art and *objets d'art* to the Musées Nationaux de France. Housed in the Musée d'Art Moderne, Troyes, in the old bishop's residence, the gift includes 337 paintings, 1277 drawings, 104 sculptures, 1 print, another 157 works of art and 81 pieces of African art. The Lévys collected over a period of 40 years, acquiring many works directly from artists with whom they were friends as much as patrons. In addition to works of art, they also collected artists' letters. The collection focuses on French art from *c.* 1880 to the mid–1970s; it is particularly strong on the work of the Fauves, although it also includes work by Cubist artists and works from the mid-19th century. The collection includes four bronzes by Degas, three works by Seurat, Honoré Daumier's *Bathing*, four works by Chaïm Soutine, as well as works by Aristide Maillol, Wols, Nicolas de Staël and Balthus. The Lévys consciously collected groups of works by individual artists, seeking to create study collections for artists and to resurrect neglected artists from obscurity. While there are 14 paintings by Roger de La Fresnaye, works by Derain, a personal friend, represent the largest group, with over 80 paintings, including the *Port of Collioure* and *Hyde Park*, 53 drawings and watercolours, and a complete series of 77 bronzes, cast posthumously under the direction of Pierre Lévy and the artist's widow. The collection also includes 43 works in glass by Maurice Marinot. The Lévys exhibited their paintings, ceramics, sculpture, together with a Matisse tapestry and African art, in their home and offices in Troyes. Their interest in African and Oceanic art was inspired by that of the contemporary artists they collected and from whom they purchased many of the pieces.

### WRITINGS
P. Lévy: *L'Art ou l'argent* (Paris, 1982)

### BIBLIOGRAPHY
*Donation Pierre Lévy* (exh. cat. by A. Fay-Halle and others, Paris, Mus. Orangerie, 1978)
P. Chabert: *Donation Pierre et Denise Lévy: Musée d'art moderne, Troyes*, 2 vols (Troyes, 1982)

□

**Lévy, Emile** (*b* Paris, 29 Aug 1826; *d* Passy, 4 Aug 1890). French painter, illustrator and pastellist. He was a pupil of Alexandre Abel de Pujol and François-Edouard Picot at the Ecole des Beaux-Arts in Paris and made his début at the Salon of 1848. In 1854 he won the Prix de Rome with *Abraham Washing the Feet of the Angels* (Paris, Ecole N. Sup. B.-A.). In 1855 he sent *Noah Cursing Canaan* (Aurillac, Mus. Parieu) from Rome for exhibition at the Exposition Universelle in Paris, and the work was bought by the French government. He specialized in classical and biblical subjects executed with the soft colouring, linear precision, prettiness and graceful poses of the Neoclassical style. He became particularly famous for his antique pastoral love scenes, such as *The Bowl: Idyll* (Pau, Mus. B.-A.), which were much appreciated by such contemporary critics as Jules Claretie (1840–1913). However, he also depicted moments of violence and drama such as the *Death of Orpheus* (1866; ex-Mus. Luxembourg, Paris) and the *Judgement of Midas* (1870; Montpellier, Mus. Fabre). His Jewish background led him to choose subjects

from the Old Testament in such works as *Ruth and Naomi* (1859; Rouen, Mus. B.-A.) and to describe Jewish rituals in such others as the *Feast of Tabernacles as Celebrated by a Jewish Family in the Middle Ages*. He made a few attempts to treat modern subjects in the manner of Carolus-Duran, depicting fashionable and worldly ladies in low-cut dresses using brilliant and contrasting colours, as in the interior scene *Letter*.

Lévy received a number of commissions for decorative paintings for both public and private buildings in Paris, such as the chapel of the Virgin in the Trinité, the register office of the Mairie of the seventh *arrondissement* and a café in the Boulevard des Capucines. He also produced illustrations for such books of classical literature as *Poésies de l'Anacréon* (1885). The most successful of his illustrations were those etched by Léopold Flameng (1831–1911) for *Longus: Daphnis et Chloé* (1872). He also illustrated an edition of La Fontaine's *Fables* (1880) and made one etching, *Le Masque*, for *Sonnets et eaux-fortes* (n.d.).

### BIBLIOGRAPHY
Bénézit
G. Vapereau: *Dictionnaire universel des contemporains* (Paris, 1858, 5/1880), p. 1162
J. Claretie: *Peintres et sculpteurs contemporains* (Paris, 1873, 2/1874)
*Encyclopaedia Judaica* (Berlin, 1928–34), x

ATHENA S. E. LEOUSSI

**Lévy, Henri Léopold** (*b* Nancy, 23 Sept 1840; *d* Paris, 30 Dec 1904). French painter. He trained at the Ecole des Beaux-Arts in Paris from 1856, where he studied first under François-Edouard Picot and Alexandre Cabanel, then with Eugène Fromentin. He made his début at the Salon in 1865 with *Hecuba Finding her Son Polydorus by the Sea* (1865; Roubaix, Mus. B.-A.) and continued to exhibit there until the year of his death. His reputation was established with *Jesus in the Tomb* (Reims, Mus. St Denis), exhibited at the 1873 Salon; contemporary critics admired it as a modern treatment of a traditional subject that stayed faithful to biblical accounts.

Lévy's work mostly consists of historical, allegorical or mythological subjects executed in an undistinguished academic style. In 1878 he painted four large canvases depicting scenes from the *Life of St Denis* for the church of St Merri in Paris. These were exhibited at the Exposition Universelle of 1878 in Paris, and he was awarded a first-class medal. His public commissions included the mural the *Crowning of Charlemagne* for the Panthéon in Paris. Amongst other private commissions, he painted ten decorative panels depicting mythological subjects for Adrien Chevallier's house in Paris. He also decorated the ceiling of the Bon Marché department store in Paris with 15 panels, including scenes depicting *Industry*, *Commerce* and *Mercury*. Some later works, such as *Oedipus Going into Exile* (1892; Paris, Louvre), show the influence of Symbolism. Lévy won medals at the Salons of 1865, 1867 and 1869, and he was decorated with the Légion d'honneur in 1872.

### BIBLIOGRAPHY
G. Vapereau: *Dictionnaire universel des contemporains* (Paris, 1858, 5/1880)
R. Ménard: *L'Art en Alsace-Lorraine* (Paris, 1876)
G. Desandrouin: 'Dix compositions décoratives de Henri Lévy', *L'Art*, xviii (1907), pp. 115–26

□

**Levy, Rudolf** (*b* Stettin, Pomerania [now Szczecin, Poland], 15 July 1875; *d* Italy, after 13 Jan 1944). German painter. After training as a carpenter, he attended the Kunstgewerbeschule at Karlsruhe (1895). In 1897 he moved to Munich, studying painting at the Kunstakademie with Nicolas Gyzis in 1899, at the private painting school of Heinrich Knirr (1862–1944) in 1900 and in the *plein-air* studio of Heinrich von Zügel (1850–1941) in 1901–3. In 1903 he went to Paris, where he had a central role in the artists' circle at the Café du Dôme. The contact with Impressionism and Post-Impressionism had a lasting influence on his artistic development. From *c.* 1905 to 1914 Levy's study of Paul Cézanne's art dominated his work, for example *Houses by the Cliff* (1914; Feldafing, Lothar-Günther Buchheim priv. coll.; see 1988 exh. cat., no. 48). At the same time Henri Matisse became model and teacher to a group of young painters who attended Matisse's school from 1908 to 1912. With Oskar Moll and Hans Purrmann, Levy was among Matisse's most important German pupils.

Cézanne and Matisse represented a process of stylistic searching that ended abruptly with the outbreak of World War I in 1914. From 1914 to 1918 Levy fought as a German soldier in France. From 1921 to 1933 he lived in Berlin, where Alfred Flechtheim organized his first one-man exhibition in 1922. In his work, for example *Studio Still-life with Begonias* (1922; Darmstadt, Hess. Landesmus.), Levy resumed a dialogue with Matisse's art, particularly that of the post-Fauvist period (1907–12). During the 1920s Levy's post-Fauvist style was clarified and consolidated. His paintings show a consistent respect for objective reality combined with a magical evocation of natural impressions through a heightened and luminous use of colour applied to weighty forms. About 1930 a colouristic, expressive realism was predominant, with a simplification of objects.

In 1933 Levy began a bitter period of emigration, staying in France, Spain, the USA, Yugoslavia and Italy. His life threatened, he suffered the fate of a homeless emigrant. In 1941–3 he went underground in Florence, where he was arrested by Gestapo agents disguised as art dealers. He died on the way to a concentration camp. Many landscapes, portraits and still-lifes survive from his late period, 1933–43, showing an increasingly condensed colourism and an expressive power heightened to a metaphysical intensity. The serious portraits such as *Self-portrait IV* (1943; Kaiserslautern, Pfalzgal.) speak of the sorrow of a man marked by exile. Levy found his way to Expressionism via Paris. He was not an avant-garde artist but a latecomer in the epoch of painting ushered in by Cézanne and Matisse. Between the two World Wars Levy was one of the important mediators of French traditions in Germany.

BIBLIOGRAPHY

*NDB*

S. Thesing: *Der Maler Rudolf Levy (1875–1944): Monographie und Werkverzeichnis* (diss., U. Munich, 1979)

——: '"Und lass uns wieder von Cézanne reden": Der Maler Rudolf Levy', *Matisse und seine deutschen Schüler* (exh. cat., Kaiserslautern, Pfalzgal., 1988) pp. 75–82

SUSANNE THESING

**Lévy-Dhurmer, Lucien** (*b* Algiers, 30 Sept 1865; *d* Le Vésinet, 24 Sept 1953). French painter and potter. From 1879 he studied at the Ecole Supérieure de Dessin et de Sculpture in Paris. In his first exhibition at the Salon in 1882 he showed a small porcelain plaque depicting the *Birth of Venus* in the style of Alexandre Cabanel and he continued to exhibit there regularly. From 1886 to 1895 he worked as a decorator of earthenware and then as artistic director of the studio of Clément Massier (*c.* 1845–1917) at Golfe Juan, near Cannes. Around 1892 he signed his first pieces of earthenware inspired by Islamic ceramics and made a name for himself primarily as a potter at the Salon des Artistes Français in 1895. An innovator in ceramic shapes, techniques and glazes, he participated in the revival of the decorative arts at the end of the 19th century. During this period he spent some time in Italy, notably in Venice where he familiarized himself with 15th-century Italian art. In 1896 he exhibited for the first time at the Galerie Georges Petit: about twenty pastels and paintings were displayed, revealing his individual style and gifts as a portrait painter. The female form, influenced by the art of Leonardo and the Pre-Raphaelites became, with landscape, one of his favoured themes and was invested with mystery, using a technique at once full-bodied and refined (e.g. *Eve*, 1896; Paris, Mus. d'Orsay). In the 20th century he gradually departed from Symbolism except in some representations of women illustrating the music of Ludwig van Beethoven, Gabriel Fauré and Claude Debussy and in some landscapes (e.g. *Winter, Petit Trianon*, 1929; Paris, Petit Pal.).

BIBLIOGRAPHY

*Autour de Lévy-Dhurmer: Visionnaires et intimistes en 1900* (exh. cat., Paris, Grand Pal., 1973)

G. Lacambre: 'Lucien Lévy-Dhurmer', *Rev. Louvre*, xxiii (1973), pp. 27–34

THALIE GOETZ

**Lewerentz, Sigurd** (*b* Sandö, Bjärtrå 29 July 1885; *d* Lund, Scania, 29 Dec 1975). Swedish architect. He studied at Chalmers Tekniska Högskola in Göteborg (1905–8) and then practised for two years in Berlin and Munich in the offices of Bruno Möhring, Theodor Fischer and Richard Riemerschmid. He also visited Italy. After a term at the Kungliga Akademi för de fria Konsterna he left to join the group opposed to academic training who gathered in a free studio in 1910–11, with Ivar Tengbom and Ragnar Östberg among the instructors. After this he ran his own practice, from 1911 in Stockholm, and from 1933 in Eskilstuna where he directed a steel-window manufacturing enterprise. His early production included urban planning and housing schemes with references to Heinrich Tessenow and to Östberg. Contacts with the crematory movement were crucial for his career. He made a model for a crematorium in Helsingborg, which was exhibited at the Baltic Exposition in Malmö in 1914. In this project he expressed symbolistic and ritual ideas, which replaced the hygienics-based crematory ideology. This resulted in his lasting involvement in crematorium and cemetery projects, and the first practical result was his association with Gunnar Asplund in a winning entry in the competition of 1914–15 for the Stockholm South (Woodland) Cemetery. In the development of this project (1915–35), the Woodland Cemetery emerged as the joint production of two

Sigurd Lewerentz: Chapel of the Resurrection, Woodland Cemetery, Stockholm, 1926–8

architects with strong artistic integrity. The integration of landscape and architecture, and the ideas about the ritual arrangement of the chapels, however, bear the imprint of Lewerentz's radical but subtle approach to the task. Both architects drew inspiration from Italy and Mediterranean culture as well as from the ideals of 18th-century Scandinavian Neo-classicism.

The Chapel of the Resurrection (1926–8; see fig.) in the Woodland Cemetery is the most sophisticated expression of these ideals. It has a peristylar portico facing a rectilinear clearing through the forest. The chapel, a tall, narrow rectangular building with pedimented gables, is set at a very slight angle to the portico and turns its only window, with an aedicule frame, to the south. The vocabulary is strictly classical, bearing affinities to Karl Friedrich Schinkel's work. Lewerentz's project for the Eastern Cemetery (1916), Malmö, developed the same ideas, in which classical themes were increasingly refined from National Romantic influences. Lewerentz joined the move from neo-classicism towards Functionalism c. 1930. The National Insurance Building (1930–32) in Stockholm is a rational, modern office block, although it retains a classical symmetry and geometricity in the cubic volume with an oval courtyard, and the fenestration of the street-façade makes reference to Asplund's City Library. Lewerentz designed the symbol and posters for the Stockholm Exhibition of 1930, where he also presented model housing projects. His major work of the 1930s is the Malmö City Theatre, which he was obliged to design in collaboration with Erik Lallerstedt and David Helldén. For the next 20 years he devoted most of his effort to the steel-window factory IDESTA, but he also designed such radically modernist houses as Villa Edstrand (1935) at Falsterbo. He completed Malmö Cemetery with two crematory chapels in 1943–5. From 1956 Lewerentz lived and worked in Skanör and Lund in Scania, near Malmö. As a result of his involvement in restoration projects for Uppsala Cathedral and contact with the young architect Peter Celsing, he returned to religious architecture with a

competition project for a suburban church in Stockholm, St Mark's (1956–60) at Björkhagen. This low church reposes in a grove of birch trees and attains a homogeneous exterior and interior character from the brickwork, which is laid with thick mortar. The transverse vaulting rests on iron girders of varying heights. The window panes have no frames, which creates the effect of clear openings through the walls; another characteristic feature of Lewerentz's practicality is the simple device for running off rain water. The same simplicity of design was employed in Lewerentz's last work, St Peter's (1962–6) at Klippan in Scania. The straight vaulting rests on a cross of steel girders in the centre of the rectangular church, and the floor slopes gently towards the altar at the centre of one long side. Roof, floor and walls all display the same dark brownish-purple brick, which is also used for other parish facilities. No complete drawings preceded the building, and many design problems were solved by the architect on the site during construction.

BIBLIOGRAPHY
'Swedish Grace: Modern Classicism in Stockholm', Int. Archit., i/8 (1982) [whole issue]
Nordisk klassicism/Nordic Classicism, 1910–1930 (exh. cat., ed. S. Paavilainen; Helsinki, Mus. Fin. Archit., 1982)
J. Ahlin: Sigurd Lewerentz, arkitekt (Stockholm, 1985)
H. O. Andersson and F. Bedoire: Swedish Architecture (Stockholm, 1986)
□

**Lewers, Darani.** See under LARSEN AND LEWERS.

**Lewis (i).** English family of painters and printmakers. Frederick Christian Lewis the elder (b London, 14 March 1779; d Enfield, London, 18 Dec 1856) was a student of Joseph Constantine Stadler (fl 1780–1812) and of the Royal Academy Schools, London, who became an eminent reproductive engraver and landscape painter. He made aquatints after Thomas Girtin's Twenty of the Most Picturesque Views in Paris and its Environs (London, 1803) and produced one plate—Bridge and Goats—for Turner's Liber Studiorum (London, 1807) before collaboration collapsed after a financial disagreement. He worked extensively in reproducing master drawings in various intaglio techniques, especially for William Young Ottley's 3-volume The Italian School of Design (London, 1808–23), and was Engraver of Drawings to Princess Charlotte, Prince Leopold, George IV, William IV and Queen Victoria. He executed engravings after many contemporary painters' works, particularly Thomas Lawrence's portrait drawings, and, under the patronage of John Russell, 6th Duke of Bedford, and other landowners and connoisseurs, etched or aquatinted published series of topographical views of Devon and Cornwall. He consistently exhibited somewhat conventional landscapes in oil and watercolour at the Royal Academy (1802–53), the British Institution (1817–53), the Society of British Artists (1824–46) and the Old Water-Colour Society. These were painted in a soft, loose and flat manner reminiscent of Girtin and were often well-reviewed by critics, although subsequently overshadowed by his engraved oeuvre. He had two brothers who were also active as artists. George Robert Lewis (b London, 27 March 1782; d London, 15 May 1871) was a pupil of Fuseli and became a portrait and landscape painter and an engraver of a variety of topographical, scientific and antiquarian illustrations. William Lewis (fl 1804–38) was an amateur landscape painter who nevertheless exhibited over 200 works between the years 1804 and 1838. Another brother, Charles Lewis (*b* London, 1786; *d* London, 8 Jan 1836), was a distinguished bookbinder in London. Frederick Christian Lewis the elder's sons were (1) John Frederick Lewis and Charles George Lewis (*b* Enfield, London, 13 June 1808; *d* Felpham, W. Sussex, 16 June 1880). Charles George Lewis was taught by his father and became a prominent reproductive engraver in etching, stipple and mezzotint after such popular contemporary painters and Academicians as Edwin Landseer and Rosa Bonheur. A third son, Frederick Christian Lewis the younger (*b* London, 1813; *d* Genoa, 26 May 1875), was a pupil of Lawrence and painted watercolours of ethnographic subjects. He depicted state and ceremonial events for local potentates in India during his numerous visits to that country (1839–49, 1851–6, 1863–7 and 1874–5), acquiring the name 'Indian Lewis'. He also travelled in Europe and the USA and visited Malta, Constantinople, Baghdad and Persia, as well as the Far East (1856–63). He in turn trained his son John Hardwicke Lewis (*b* Hyderabad, 1840; *d* Veytaux, Vaud, 1927), who worked with Thomas Couture in Paris as a portrait painter and in California as an illustrator (1875–85); he is best remembered, however, for his later suave, polished watercolours of mountain views in France and Switzerland. George Robert Lewis's son Lennard Lewis (*b* London, 18 March 1826; *d* 1913) was a writer and a painter of watercolour landscapes who exhibited from 1848 to 1898.

BIBLIOGRAPHY
*DNB*; Thieme–Becker

**(1) John Frederick Lewis** (*b* London, ?14 ?July 1805; *d* Walton-on-Thames, 15 Aug 1876). He developed his precocious talents as draughtsman and etcher within the family circle. In 1820 he entered Thomas Lawrence's studio as a draughtsman of animals, which, in close association with his childhood neighbour Edwin Landseer, he had studied from live specimens and dissected cadavers. Lewis made six intaglio prints after his drawings of the larger felines (published 1825), while domesticated beasts figured more prominently in the twelve etchings of *Domestic Subjects* published in 1826. His work as a sporting and wildlife painter culminated in *Buck-shooting in Windsor Great Park* (1825; London, Tate) and his one contemporary, royal commission, *John Clark with the Animals at Sandpit Gate, Windsor Great Park* (Windsor Castle, Berks, Royal Col.).

By 1827 Lewis had turned to watercolours, concentrating on landscape and topographical views and picturesque genre subjects. He rapidly developed an accomplished technique of increasing intricacy, with extensive use of gouache. Initially working under the stylistic influences of Richard Parkes Bonington and David Wilkie, he began to travel in search of motifs, starting with an extensive sketching tour on the Continent in 1827. In 1829 he became a full member of the Old Water-Colour Society and visited Devon and Scotland. These trips inspired watercolours of increasingly ambitious composition and meticulous finish (e.g. *Highland Hospitality*, 1829; New Haven, CT, Yale Cent. Brit. A.). More important was his tour of Spain and Morocco between 1832 and 1834. After his return to England he elaborated his sketches and

drawings into a sequence of richly flamboyant watercolours, which earned him the sobriquet 'Spanish Lewis'. A typical example is *Spanish Fiesta* (1836; U. Manchester, Whitworth A.G.), with its brilliant colour and acutely observed local types and incidents. Drawings made *in situ* were reproduced as lithographs either by himself or by others for *Sketches and Drawings of the Alhambra, made during a Residence in Granada in the Years 1833–4* (1835) and *Lewis's Sketches of Spain and Spanish Character* (1836).

In 1837 Lewis left England for a prolonged tour of Europe and the Near East. After travelling through Italy and Greece he reached Constantinople (now Istanbul) by October 1840 and made numerous evocative studies of the city and its environs before sailing for Egypt in November 1841. He rented a large Mamluk mansion in the Azbakiyyah quarter of Cairo, and Thackeray, the most notable of his English visitors, published an amusing account of Lewis's lifestyle in *Notes of a Journey from Cornhill to Grand Cairo* (London, 1846). Lewis married Marian Harper in Alexandria on 8 May 1847. In 1849 he completed *The Hhareem* (Japan, priv. col.; partial replica, London, V&A), an intricately wrought fantasy based on Cairene models, dress and setting that received widespread critical acclaim at the Old Water-Colour Society in 1850 and established the pattern for all future production.

In 1851 Lewis and his wife returned to London, and they settled in Walton-on-Thames, Surrey, in 1854. Although he had been elected President of the Old Water-Colour Society by 1855, Lewis returned to oil painting for financial reasons, with minimal modification of handling and none of style. He continued to produce highly polished portrayals of Eastern markets, bazaars and mosques, imaginary desert encounters and fictive harem incidents, derived from life studies and a limited repertory of images: *Intercepted Correspondence, Cairo* (1869; priv. col.) is a free variation of *The Hhareem*. For all their insistent polychromy, obsessive detail and anecdotal embellishments, his Orientalist paintings (e.g. *Frank Encampment in the Desert of Mt Sinai, 1842, the Convent of St Catherine in the Distance*, 1856; New Haven, CT, Yale Cent. Brit. A.; for illustration *see* ORIENTALISM) remain the most sumptuously explicit and comprehensively documented of those of the Victorian Orientalists.

PRINTS
*Domestic Subjects* (London, 1826)

WRITINGS
*Sketches and Drawings of the Alhambra, made during a Residence in Granada in the Years 1833–34* (London, 1835)
*Lewis's Sketches of Spain and Spanish Character* (London, 1836)

BIBLIOGRAPHY
'British Artists: Their Style and Character, xxxii: John Frederick Lewis', *A.J.* [London], iv (1858), pp. 41–3
R. Davies and B. S. Long: 'John Frederick Lewis, RA (1805–76)', *Old Wtrcol. Soc. Club*, iii (1925–6), pp. 31–50
H. Stokes: 'John Frederick Lewis, RA (1805–1876)', *Walker's Q.*, xxviii (1929) [whole issue]
*John Frederick Lewis, RA, 1805–1876* (exh. cat., Newcastle upon Tyne, Laing A.G., 1971)
M. Lewis: *John Frederick Lewis, RA, 1805–1876* (Leigh-on-Sea, 1978)
H. H. Preston: *J. F. Lewis, 1805–1876* (in preparation)

HARLEY PRESTON

**Lewis (ii).** American patrons and collectors. Sydney Lewis (*b* Richmond, VA, 24 Oct 1919) and his wife Frances

Lewis (*b* Brooklyn, NY, 27 June 1922) began collecting in the early 1960s by acquiring works by leading Pop artists, to which they added major works by other contemporary American and European artists. In the late 1960s they also began to collect turn-of-the-century decorative art, beginning with Art Nouveau and later including Art Deco and products of the Arts and Crafts Movement; these collections were donated in 1985 to the Virginia Museum of Fine Arts in Richmond, VA, together with funds to help build an extensive wing to house them. The Lewises also acted as patrons both as individuals and through their company, Best Products Co., Inc., supporting younger artists, sponsoring museum exhibitions and commissioning innovative architectural projects throughout the USA; among the architects and firms employed to design their striking buildings, which quickly became a trademark of the company, were SITE; Venturi, Rauch & Scott Brown; and Hardy Holzman Pfeiffer Associates.

BIBLIOGRAPHY

F. Brandt: 'Building a Collection for the Twentieth Century: The Sydney and Frances Lewis Collection of Late Twentieth-century American Art', *Apollo*, cxxii/286 (1985), pp. 484–7
——: *Late 19th and Early 20th-century Decorative Arts: The Sydney and Frances Lewis Collection in the Virginia Museum of Fine Arts*, Richmond, VA Mus. F.A. cat. (Richmond, VA, 1985)
——: *Late 20th-century Art: Selections from the Sydney and Frances Lewis Collection in the Virginia Museum of Fine Arts*, Richmond, VA Mus. F.A. cat. (Richmond, VA, 1985)

FREDERICK R. BRANDT

**Lewis, (Mary) Edmonia** [Wildfire] (*b* New York, 1845; *d* after 1911). American sculptor. Born to an African-American father and a Native American mother, she was the first Black American sculptor to achieve national prominence. During her early childhood she travelled with her family in the Chippewa tribe, by whom she was known as Wildfire. At 12 she attended school at Albany, NY (1857–9), then a liberal arts course at Oberlin College, OH (1860–63). Lewis then went to Boston (1863) to study with Edward Brackett (1818–1908) and Anne Whitney. Her medallion of the abolitionist *John Browne* and a bust of the Civil War hero *Col. Robert Shaw* were exhibited at the Soldiers' Relief Fair (1864), Boston; the latter sold over 100 plaster copies, enabling Lewis to travel to Rome (1865). There she was introduced to the White Marmorean Flock, a group of women sculptors, including Harriet Hosmer and Emma Stebbins, who worked in a Neoclassical style. Examples of Lewis's own work include *Forever Free* (1867; Washington, DC, Howard U., Gal. A.), a depiction of a slave breaking his bonds and several sculptures evoking her Native American heritage, inspired by the *Song of Hiawatha* by Henry Wadsworth Longfellow, such as *Minnehaha* (1867; Detroit, MI, Inst. A.). Notably successful was *Hagar* (1875; Washington, DC, N. Mus. Amer. A.; *see* AFRICAN AMERICAN ART, fig. 1), portraying the servant of Abraham cast into the wilderness by his wife, Sarah. Many of her works are in the National Museum of American Art, Washington, DC.

BIBLIOGRAPHY

*The White Marmorean Flock: 19th-century American Neo-classical Sculpture* (exh. cat., ed. W. H. Gerdts jr; Poughkeepsie, NY, Vassar Coll. A.G., 1972)
*Two Centuries of Black American Art* (exh. cat. by D. Driskoll, Los Angeles, CA, Co. Mus. A., 1976)

P. Dunford: *A Biographical Dictionary of Women Artists in Europe and America since 1850* (Philadelphia, PA, 1989; 2/Hemel Hempstead, 1990)
C. S. Rubinstein: *American Women Sculptors* (Boston, MA, 1990)

**Lewis, Ion.** *See under* WHIDDEN & LEWIS.

**Lewis, Lucy M(artin)** (*b* Acoma Pueblo, NM, *c*. 1895; *d* 12 March 1992). Native American potter. As a child she made and sold Acoma polychrome pottery, which by 1900 had deteriorated into tourist wares such as vases and ashtrays, but in the 1930s she began working in the Acoma pottery tradition of the 19th century, making jars with a red-slip base and white-slip body that were decorated with the bird and flower motifs that had been common from *c*. 1880. In the 1940s she adapted designs from prehistoric ceramics: non-figurative motifs from Hohokam and Anasazi wares (5th–13th centuries) and figurative designs from Mimbres wares (10th–13th centuries). From the former she adopted repetitive fine-line patterning that covered the entire body of the vessel (e.g. 1959, Santa Fe, NM, Sch. Amer. Res., 2780) as well as 'negative' patterns in white slip against a black painted background with occasional orange accents (e.g. late 1940s, Santa Fe, NM, Sch. Amer. Res., 2979). Working in the coil-and-scrape method with the dense grey clay of the Acoma area tempered with ground potsherds, Lewis produced miniature pots, seed jars, bowls, animal effigies and water jars, all rarely more than 250 mm in height. Several coats of white slip were applied, and each coat was polished with a wet stone until the slip was opaque. Paints made from ground minerals with a binder of boiled vegetal matter were applied with a chewed yucca-leaf brush. The vessels were then fired outdoors using dried cow dung. Lewis printed 'Acoma N.M.' on the bottom of pieces made before 1950 and 'Lucy M. Lewis, Acoma N.M.' on pieces made after that date. Until her death she continued to work at her home in McCartys, NM, assisted by her daughters.

*See also* NATIVE NORTH AMERICAN ART, §V, 1(ii).

BIBLIOGRAPHY

R. Dillingham: 'The Pottery of Acoma Pueblo', *Amer. Ind. A.*, ii/4 (1977), pp. 44–51
F. Harlow: *Modern Pueblo Pottery* (Flagstaff, 1977)
S. Peterson: *Lucy M. Lewis: American Indian Potter* (Tokyo, 1984)

BARBARA KRAMER

**Lewis, Mortimer (William)** (*b* London, 1796; *d* Sydney, 9 March 1879). Australian architect of English birth. His early experience was in London as a military surveyor and draughtsman in government service and then in private practice. He arrived in Sydney in March 1840 as an assistant surveyor in the office of the Surveyor-General of New South Wales, Thomas L. Mitchell. Under Mitchell he was appointed town surveyor in Sydney, becoming Colonial Architect of New South Wales in 1835. He is particularly admired for his designs for government buildings in the Greek Revival idiom, of which one is extant, though extended, the Darlinghurst Court House (1837). Another surviving government building is the Maitland Gaol (1847–50), New South Wales. As Colonial Architect he is credited as the chief designer of government buildings, although evidence suggests that capable subordinate clerks of works such as James Rattenbury ( *fl* 1839–45) and Henry Ginn ( *fl* 1846–51) also had that duty for projects remote from Sydney. Other surviving designs attributed to Lewis are the Berrima Court House and the Hartley Court House, both in rural New South Wales. He also supervised the construction of the Tudor Gothic Government House in Sydney (begun 1837) to the design (1834) of Edward Blore.

As Mitchell's protégé Lewis shared his patron's interest in romantic and picturesque design and was a follower of John Claudius Loudon, making use of his *Encyclopaedia of Cottage, Farm and Villa Architecture* (London, 1833). This was reflected in domestic architecture including designs for his own residences, in particular the position and layout of Bronte Villa and Richmond Villa (1849), Sydney, the latter also deriving features from Decimus Burton's villas in Regent's Park, London. An admired Gothic work is the design for St John's (1840–49) at Camden, New South Wales, and an unusual one is the Legislative Assembly building (1843), Melbourne, which has a Gothick interior and an Italianate exterior. His career as a public official ended with his resignation in 1849 after an official enquiry expressed dissatisfaction over his role in the construction of the Australian Museum (*c.* 1847–50).

## BIBLIOGRAPHY

*AUDB*

M. Herman: *The Early Australian Architects and their Work* (Sydney, 1954, rev. 1970), pp. 190–206

J. Kerr and J. Broadbent: *Gothick Taste in the Colony of New South Wales* (Sydney, 1980)

GEORGE TIBBITS

**Lewis, Roberto (Gerónimo)** (*b* Panama City, 30 Sept 1874; *d* Panama City, 22 Sept 1949). Panamanian painter. He studied painting in Paris at the Académie des Beaux-Arts and in the studio of Léon Bonnat, combining the influence of academic and Post-Impressionist art. On his return to Panama in 1912 he was commissioned to paint the interiors of several new public buildings, among them the Teatro Nacional and the Palacio de Gobierno, which he decorated in the official Neo-classical style. He was an accomplished portraitist and numbered among his sitters many political figures, including numerous Panamanian governors and all the presidents of Panama from 1904 to 1948 (Panama City, Pal. Presidencial).

Lewis was a pioneer of modern art in his country. While his official portraits were academic in style, his landscapes were painted with a Post-Impressionist spontaneity. His murals *Tamarinds of Taboga* (1936; Panama City, Pal. Presidencial), which are among his best-known works, depict bucolic scenes that combine allegory and classical and symbolist elements with the lively brushwork, bright colours and luminosity of late 19th-century European *plein-air* painting. Lewis was also a dedicated teacher, and as founder (1913) and first director (1913–38) of the Academia Nacional de Pintura (now Escuela Nacional de Artes Plásticas) in Panama City he was responsible for training an entire generation of Panamanian artists.

## BIBLIOGRAPHY

R. Miró: 'Lewis, Amador, Ivaldi', *Rev. Lotería*, 219 (1974), pp. 72–80

*Exposición Maestros-maestros* (exh. cat. by P. Prados, Panama City, U. Panamá, 1987), pp. 15–17

MONICA E. KUPFER

**Lewis, (Percy) Wyndham** (*b* Amherst, NS, 18 Nov 1882; *d* London, 7 March 1957). British painter and writer. He attended Rugby School and then studied painting at the Slade School of Art, London (1898–1901), where he earned a reputation both as a draughtsman and as a poet. His early artistic and intellectual mentors were Augustus John and Thomas Sturge Moore. From 1902 to 1908 Lewis travelled widely in Europe and studied in many of the major museums. He was one of the first British artists to be aware of, and interested in, Cubism and Expressionism, though little of his work before 1909 survives as evidence of his early development. In late 1908 Lewis settled in London and as well as painting began to publish satirical short stories that take a mechanistic view of human social behaviour, evident in the deliberately clumsy and grotesque figures in his art of the period 1909 to 1912. By 1910 he was including Cubist elements in his watercolour drawings (his preferred medium), and by 1912 he had developed his own linear vocabulary of forms, indebted to Cubist, Futurist and Expressionist forms, which gives an often ironic visual dimension to the themes of his fiction. Another important influence on his art was that of Japanese woodblock prints, as seen in the watercolour drawing later called *The Vorticist* (1912; Southampton, C.A.G.). By 1913 he was popularly seen as the leading British avant-garde artist.

A brief period spent working for Roger Fry's Omega Workshops in 1913 was followed by a public dispute with Fry and the founding of the rival but unsuccessful REBEL ART CENTRE. Along with Edward Wadsworth, Henri Gaudier-Brzeska and others, Lewis began to produce a geometrical and semi-abstract art based on machine and architectural forms. This was termed 'VORTICISM' and led to the publication in July 1914 of the magazine *Blast*, in which Lewis's play *Enemy of the Stars* attempted to introduce the stark imagery and style of the new art into a complex poetic prose. One of Lewis's few surviving large Vorticist canvases, *The Crowd* (1914–15; London, Tate), shows how he incorporated literary and intellectual interests into his art. The work appears to have been based on a sociological study of Gustave Le Bon, entitled *The Crowd: A Study of the Popular Mind* (1913), and shows blocks of revolutionary figures moving like automata across a bleakly modern urban landscape. From this period onwards Lewis became obsessed with politics and its implications for art.

During World War I Lewis fought as an artillery officer in France and obtained a commission to paint pictures of the front from the Canadian Government. This work, for example *A Battery Shelled* (1918; London, Imp. War Mus.), marks a return to a more representational style, albeit with a distinctly angular, Vorticist look. From 1919 until about 1922 Lewis made many drawings from the figure, such as *L'Ingénue* (1919; Manchester, C.A.G.); these use bold, sharp lines and are among his most impressive works.

After the war Lewis tried to keep the pre-war avant-garde alive with two ventures—the GROUP X exhibition at Heal's Gallery in 1920 and a magazine, *The Tyro*, of which only two issues appeared, in 1921 and 1922. In the latter, and in related paintings and ink drawings, Lewis created a breed of grinning, naive creatures called 'tyros', which were eventually to become transformed into the absurd characters of his huge satirical novel, *The Apes of God* (1930). Throughout the 1920s, in deliberate secession from the rest of British 'high-brow' culture, Lewis, posing as the 'enemy', produced a bewildering quantity and range of work. Major books of criticism on philosophy, politics and literature as well as the extraordinary afterworld fantasy *Childermass* (1928) were written at the same time that Lewis was painting striking portraits, for example *Edith Sitwell* (1923–35; London, Tate), and highly sophisticated variants on Dadaist, Surrealist and Constructivist art forms. This imaginative work constitutes the most original body of avant-garde art produced in Britain during the 1920s. Complex, often totemic compositions bring together human, insect and mechanical forms into richly suggestive combinations. These works are closely related to the ink designs with which Lewis decorated many of his books.

During the 1930s Lewis ran into widespread opposition to his political views, which, although far more intricate and liberal than is usually allowed, have to be described as authoritarian. A series of books on contemporary political issues which gave qualified support to fascist regimes made Lewis appear in public eyes what W. H. Auden dubbed 'that lonely old volcano of the right'. In spite of this and serious illness throughout the 1930s, Lewis managed to paint a series of portraits and imaginative works. His portraits of *T. S. Eliot* (1938; Durban, A. Mus.) and *Ezra Pound* (1938–9; London, Tate) are remarkable tributes to close friends, the former causing a public storm when it was rejected by the Royal Academy in 1938. Lewis's one-man show at the Leicester Galleries in December 1937 was a commercial failure but contained some important works in oil. Paintings such as *Inca and*

*the Birds* (1933; AC Eng; see fig.) are evocative figure groups in surreal landscapes which have a suggested narrative often derived from Lewis's literary and historical interests and his own satirical themes. Many younger artists, such as Henry Moore, acknowledged a debt to Lewis's work at this time.

Lewis sailed to North America in 1939 in search of work. He lived in New York and later moved to Toronto and Windsor, eking out a living by painting, writing and lecturing. The tragedy of this exile and its impact on Lewis are the subject of his novel *Self-condemned* (1954). His most important visual work of this period is a series of delicate watercolour drawings made between 1941 and 1943 dealing with themes of myth, fantasy and creativity. Lewis returned to London in 1945. A malignant tumour was crushing his optic nerve, and he eventually went blind in 1951, having painted little since the war. He had continued to write, however, and from 1946 to 1951 was art critic for *The Listener*, where he supported the work of young British figurative artists such as Francis Bacon and Robert Colquhoun. His impatience with extreme abstraction is voiced in *The Demon of Progress in the Arts* (1954).

### WRITINGS
W. Michel and C. J. Fox, eds: *Wyndham Lewis on Art: Collected Writings, 1913–1956* (London, 1969)

### BIBLIOGRAPHY
W. Michel: *Wyndham Lewis: Paintings and Drawings* (London, 1971) [complete cat., incl. preface by H. Kenner]
B. Morrow and B. Lafourcade, eds: *A Bibliography of the Writings of Wyndham Lewis* (Santa Barbara, 1978)
J. Meyers: *The Enemy: A Biography of Wyndham Lewis* (London, 1980)
*Wyndham Lewis* (exh. cat. by J. Farington, Manchester, C.A.G., 1980)

RICHARD HUMPHREYS

**LeWitt, Sol** (*b* Hartford, CT, 9 Sept 1928). American sculptor, printmaker and draughtsman. He studied at Syracuse University, NY, from 1945 to 1949, and between 1951 and 1952 he served in the US Army in Japan and Korea, where he was able to visit oriental shrines, temples and gardens. In 1953 he moved to New York, where he attended the Cartoonists and Illustrators School. From 1955 to 1956 he worked as a graphic designer for the architect I. M. Pei, and he began to make paintings while continuing to work as a graphic designer. He abandoned painting in 1962 and began to make abstract black-and-white reliefs, followed in 1963 by relief constructions with nested enclosures projecting into space, and box- and table-like constructions. He first made serial and modular works, for which he is best known, in 1965. Initially these were wall and floor structures, but in 1968 LeWitt made his first wall drawing in pencil on plaster, at the Paula Cooper Gallery, New York (see 1978 exh. cat., p. 92). From that time he continued to make structures, wall drawings and drawings on paper as well as prints, which he first made in 1971.

LeWitt's work, like that of other Minimalist and conceptual artists, stressed idea over execution. For each work a system was worked out in advance, which could then be executed by an assistant as easily as by the artist. In some cases systems were not based on theory or logic but were randomly selected in defiance of logic so that the results could not be foreseen. Establishing a system was like devising the rules of a game, the results of which could

Wyndham Lewis: *Inca and the Birds*, oil on canvas, 673×546 mm, 1933 (London, Arts Council of Great Britain)

Sol LeWitt: *Cube Structures Based on Five Modules*, white enamel paint on wood, 620×980×620 mm, 1971 (Edinburgh, National Gallery of Modern Art)

not be predicted. LeWitt stated that his art was 'not theoretical or illustrative of theories; it is intuitive, it is involved with all types of mental processes and it is purposeless' (LeWitt, 1967, p. 80). His art appealed to the intellect rather than to the emotions. To this end he employed materials that were abstract and neutral. His sculptures were often made of white baked enamel, for example *Large Modular Cube* (0.6×0.6×0.6 m, 1969; Basle, Kstmus.), or white painted wood, for example *Cube Structures Based on Five Modules* (1971; see fig.); in drawings he used hard pencils, and in coloured drawings and prints he restricted himself to the use of the four basic colours used in mass-production colour printing: red, yellow, blue and black. Any other colours had to be arrived at by superimposition.

The shapes drawn or constructed by LeWitt are basic geometric forms: the quadrilateral, triangle and sphere or variations on them. A structure might consist of a cube or series of cubes, or a combination of all three forms in their various manifestations. LeWitt's desire was to create a grammar for all his works in which the basic unit becomes

> deliberately uninteresting so that it may more easily become an intrinsic part of the entire work. Using complex basic forms only disrupts the unity of the whole. Using a simple form repeatedly narrows the field of the work and concentrates the intensity to the arrangement of the form. The arrangement becomes the end while the form becomes the means. (LeWitt, 1967, p. 80)

LeWitt's methods have often been compared to those of an architect or a composer, particularly in his use of a basic syntax of forms for the production of variations on a theme. However, his grammatical concerns, his view of

the work of art as a system and the methods he employed reveal an affinity with linguistic theory, in particular of the structuralist concerns of Ferdinand de Saussure and Roland Barthes. In this way LeWitt subjected the basic elements and structures of his visual language to a rigorous examination.

WRITINGS
'Paragraphs on Conceptual Art', *Artforum*, v/10 (1967), pp. 79–83
'Sentences on Conceptual Art', *Art Language*, i/1 (1969), p. 11

BIBLIOGRAPHY
*Sol LeWitt* (exh. cat., ed. A. Legg; New York, MOMA, 1978)
*Sol LeWitt Wall Drawings* (exh. cat., ed. S. Singer; Amsterdam, Stedel. Mus.; Eindhoven, Stedel. Van Abbemus.; Hartford, CT, Wadsworth Atheneum; 1984)
*Sol LeWitt Prints, 1970–86* (exh. cat., ed. J. Lewison; London, Tate, 1986)
*Sol LeWitt Wall Drawings 1984–1988* (exh. cat., ed. S. Singer; Berne, Ksthalle, 1989)
*Sol LeWitt Drawings 1958–1992* (exh. cat., ed. S. Singer; The Hague, Gemeentemus, 1992)

JEREMY LEWISON

**Lewyn, John** (*fl* 1364–98). English architect. Called 'Bishop's mason' *c*. 1368–9, he was the principal mason of Durham Cathedral priory and also a royal mason-contractor. He worked on monasteries dependent on Durham, including Coldingham Priory (Borders; ruined), in 1364, and Finchale Priory (Durham; part destr.) in the 1390s. Lewyn built the great kitchen at Durham and began the present cloisters. The octagonal kitchen is vaulted with intersecting ribs, which leave the centre free for a lantern. This vault has been compared to the timber Octagon at Ely Cathedral and several Islamic designs. The severe, unvaulted cloisters have simple intersecting tracery with no decorative cusping.

Lewyn clearly specialized in secular building. The bishops and the local nobility were responsible for the defence of the north against the Scots, and Lewyn probably rebuilt the keep of Durham Castle (*c.* 1365; reconstructed) for Bishop Thomas of Hatfield (*reg* 1345–81). His work for the Crown included Bamburgh Castle (1368–72), Northumb., but in 1375 his financial management became the subject of an official inquiry. In 1378 he received a Crown contract for work on the castles of Carlisle (Cumbria) and Roxburgh (Borders), each requiring several new towers, with a gate and barbican at Carlisle. Lewyn also built towers and a gateway at Bolton Castle (N. Yorks) for Richard le Scrope, 1st Baron Scrope of Bolton (? 1327–1403), and a 'mantelet', or protective wooden screen, at Dunstanburgh Castle (ruined), Northumb., for John of Gaunt, Duke of Lancaster (1340–99), in 1380. He and his son Walter rebuilt roads at Brancepeth (Durham) for Ralph, 6th Baron Neville (1364–1425), and possibly worked on his castle at Raby (Cumbria).

BIBLIOGRAPHY
Harvey
S. Toy: *The Castles of Great Britain* (London, 1953, rev. 3/1963)
J. Harvey: *The Perpendicular Style* (London, 1978)

FRANCIS WOODMAN

**Leyden.** *See* LEIDEN.

**Leyden, Aertgen van.** *See* AERTGEN VAN LEYDEN.

**Leyden, Lucas van.** *See* LUCAS VAN LEYDEN.

**Leygebe, Gottfried Christian** (*b* Freystadt, Lower Silesia, 1630; *d* Berlin, 1683). German die-cutter, medallist and sculptor. In 1645 he travelled to Nuremberg to train as an armourer with Albrecht Liechtmann. He specialized in engraving on iron, made contact with Georg Pfründt, an artist experienced in this technique, and developed into one of the best medallists and die-cutters of his time. In 1653 he had his own workshop as a sculptor and medallist. Sandrart praised Leygebe's art as something extraordinary, probably on account of his claim to be able to carve statuettes from an iron block; in reality, however, the three surviving examples of Leygebe's iron statuettes are cast. In 1659–60 he produced an equestrian statuette of *Leopold I* (Copenhagen, Rosenborg Slot). It was followed *c.* 1660–62 by an equestrian statuette of *Charles II* (Dresden, Grünes Gewölbe), occasioned by the restoration of the English monarchy. A portrayal of *Frederick William, the Great Elector, as Bellerophon on Pegasus Vanquishing the Chimera* (before 1672) is untraced; there is also a statuette of the same prince portrayed as *St George Killing the Dragon* (1680; Berlin, Skulpgal.).

In 1668 Leygebe was summoned by Frederick William, Elector of Brandenburg, to Berlin, where he became court die-cutter, medallist and sculptor. His most important field of activity was the production of coins and medals, mainly for the ruling house, but also for private persons. He also carved seals and signets, supplied moulds for the glass factory of Johann Kunckel (?1630–1703) and was called on for tasks such as designing flags and triumphal arches. Although his portraits in wax have been lost, of his bronze works there survives a portrait relief of the *Great Elector* (1671; Potsdam, Schloss Sanssouci); it clearly reveals the Nuremberg origins of Leygebe's Baroque style.

BIBLIOGRAPHY
J. von Sandrart: *Teutsche Academie* (1675–9); ed. A. R. Peltzer (1925)
F. Nicolai: *Nachricht von den Baumeistern, Bildhauern, Malern, Stukkaturern, und anderen Künstlern welche vom dreyzehnten Jahrhunderte bis jetzt in und um Berlin sich aufgehalten haben* (Berlin and Stettin, 1786)
*Die Brandenburgisch-preussische Kunstkammer* (exh. cat., Berlin, Gropiusbau, 1981)
C. Theuerkauff: 'Zur Geschichte der Bildhauerkunst in Berlin und Potsdam von der Mitte des 16. bis zum späten 18. Jahrhunderts', *Ethos und Pathos: Die Berliner Bildhauerschule, 1786–1914: Beiträge* (exh. cat. by P. Bloch and others, Berlin, Hamburg. Bahnhof, 1990), pp. 13–36

HELMUT BÖRSCH-SUPAN

**Leygonier y Haubert, Francisco de** (*b* ?Seville, 1812; *d* ?Seville, 1882). Photographer active in Spain. He is particularly known for his calotypes, mainly views of Seville. The city boasted a large number of photographers using the calotype process, of whom he was one of the most notable. By 1851, a decade after he announced his 'heliographic' views (as he called these early calotypes), he was making daguerreotypes and wet-collodion glass-plate negatives, as well as calotype positives. Almost as soon as stereoscopic glass plates were devised, Leygonier announced that he had an assortment of these. Even with all his innovative modern methods, he continued to practise the calotype process at least until 1859. Examples of his calotypes include two views of the *Patio de las Doncellas in the Alcázar of Seville* (Austin, U. TX, Ransom Humanities Res. Cent.). Also active as a teacher of photography, his forte was his rapid assimilation and commercial diffusion of the newest photographic media.

BIBLIOGRAPHY
L. Fontanella: *La historia de la fotografía en España desde sus orígenes hasta 1900* (Madrid, 1981)
*Photography in Spain in the Nineteenth Century* (exh. cat. by L. Fontanella, Dallas, TX, Delahunty & Fraenkel Gals, 1984)

LEE FONTANELLA

**Leyland, F(rederick) R(ichard)** (*b* Liverpool, 1831; *d* London, 4 Jan 1892). English shipping magnate and collector. Hired as an apprentice by the Liverpool shipping firm of Bibby, Sons & Co., he rose rapidly through the ranks, buying out the firm in 1872. He became a major patron of Dante Gabriel Rossetti, buying from 1867 such works as *Lady Lilith* (1868; Wilmington, DE A. Mus.) and *La Pia de' Tolomei* (1868–80; Lawrence, U. KS, Spencer Mus. A.). Leyland liked musical subjects and he ensured that his purchases accorded in mood and size with one another or with his existing decorative scheme. Under Rossetti's guidance he built up an extraordinary collection of Italian Renaissance pictures, including works by Giovanni Bellini, Giorgione, Sandro Botticelli (the *Casa Pucci* series; Madrid, Prado) and Carlo Crivelli. He also bought such works by Edward Burne-Jones as the *Wine of Circe* (1863–9; priv. col., see *The Pre-Raphaelites*, exh. cat., London, Tate, 1984, p. 304).

Rossetti introduced Leyland to James Abbott McNeill Whistler in 1864. After starting the *Six Projects*, a series of decorative paintings, for Leyland, Whistler painted *Arrangement in Black: Portrait of F. R. Leyland* (1870–73; Washington, DC, Freer) and *Symphony in Flesh Colour and Pink: Mrs Frances Leyland* (1871–3; New York, Frisk), at their home, Speke Hall, near Liverpool. In 1876 Whistler was given permission to make modest alterations to the dining-room of Leyland's house at 49 Prince's Gate, London. Instead, he created *Harmony in Blue and Gold: The Peacock Room* (Washington, DC, Freer) by painting the magnificent Spanish leather wallhangings blue, superimposing a gold wave and scale pattern and placing golden peacocks on the backs of the shutters. Outraged by the artist's impudence, his growing intimacy with Mrs Leyland and the size of his bill, Leyland refused to pay. Whistler retaliated by painting fighting peacocks on the end wall, which he called *L'Art et l'argent* (or *The Story of the Room*). In 1879 Leyland precipitated Whistler's bankruptcy, and Mrs Leyland filed for separation. The *Peacock Room* episode is said to have shortened Leyland's life. His collection was sold at Christie's, London, on 28 May 1892.

UNPUBLISHED SOURCES

Glasgow, U. Lib. [Whistler Papers; Whistler–Leyland corr.]

BIBLIOGRAPHY

T. Child: 'A Pre-Raphaelite Mansion', *Harper's Mthly*, lxxxii (1890), pp. 81–98

V. C. Prinsep: 'A Collector's Correspondence', *A.J.* [London] (1892), pp. 249–52

L. Robinson: 'The Private Collections of London: The Late Mr. Frederick Leyland's in Prince's Gate', *A.J.* [London] (1892), pp. 129–38

*The Whistler Peacock Room*, Washington, DC, Freer (Washington, DC, 1972)

F. L. Fennell, ed.: *The Rossetti-Leyland Letters* (Athens, OH, 1978)

M. S. Duval: 'F. R. Leyland: A Maecenas from Liverpool', *Apollo*, cxxiv (1986), pp. 110–15

KATHARINE A. LOCHNAN

**Leys, Henri** [Hendrik], Baron (*b* Antwerp, 18 Feb 1815; *d* Antwerp, 26 Aug 1869). Belgian painter. He trained with Mathieu Ignace Van Brée at the Koninklijke Academie voor Schone Kunsten in Antwerp and then with Ferdinand De Braekeleer. His earliest pictures drew on the Romantic works of Gustaf Wappers, with whom he painted a *Spanish Battle Scene* (1832–6; Brussels, Mus. A. Mod.). He subseqently treated other typically Romantic subjects, ranging from heroic scenes of war and brigandage to scenes of daily life such as weddings and country festivals. The influence of Paul Delaroche, whom he met in Paris in 1835, is occasionally evident. From 1839 he distanced himself from the Romantic school, whose authority in Antwerp was diminishing. His painting *Flemish Nuptials in the 17th Century* (1839; Antwerp, Kon. Mus. S. Kst.) seems to herald a more sober style, an approach that more accurately reflected the national heritage. From that time onwards the desire for historical and psychological truthfulness replaced the tendency towards pathos and sentimental anecdote. In his reconstructions of 16th-century Antwerp, Leys sought to convey the spirit and atmosphere of the time. These compositions, whether of historical events—for example the *Re-establishment of Worship in the Church of Onze Lieuwe Vrouwe in Antwerp* (1845; Brussels, Mus. A. Mod.) and the *Thirty-day Mass of Berthal de Haze* (1854; see fig.)—or scenes of everyday life, for instance, *The Archers* (1863) and *Leaving Mass* (1866; both Antwerp, Kon. Mus. S. Kst.), are disconcertingly realistic, enriched by scrupulous observation of contemporary life in the old quarters of Antwerp. It seems likely that in moving away from Romanticism Leys was influenced by the French Realists Gustave Courbet and Jean-François Millet. On the other hand, his study of 16th-century

Henri Leys: *Thirty-day Mass of Berthal de Haze*, oil on panel, 900×1335 mm, 1854 (Brussels, Musée d'Art Moderne)

Flemish and German painters also contributed to the development of his personal style, which mingled archaistic rigidity with realistic observation.

Even though in his preoccupation with the past Leys continued to be dependent on the Romantic aesthetic, his evolution towards Realism made him one of its forerunners in Belgium. When Nicaise De Keyser succeeded Wappers as the head of the Antwerp Academie (1853), progressive artists were disappointed, seeing Leys as their leader. By contrast, official circles responded unenthusiastically to his increasingly innovative work; meanwhile in Paris he was recognized as an artist of the first rank, and his participation in the Exposition Universelle (1855) was acclaimed. Some of his most important works remain in Antwerp, including the frescoes from his own house depicting *Christmas in the 16th Century* (1855; *in situ*) and a series of murals (1863–9; studies in the Antwerp Stadhuis). His portraits strongly convey the stifling atmosphere of bourgeois life, untempered by idealism, as in the portrait of his daughter *Lucie Leys* (1865) and of *Mme H. Leys-Van Haren* (1866; both Antwerp, Kon. Mus. S. Kst.). Each detail of the physiognomy of his model is carefully rendered, again revealing Ley's powers of observation. As a teacher he influenced many young artists. Some, such as Joseph Lies, Frans Vinck (1827–1903) and Karel Ooms (1845–1900), were content to plagiarize his work; others, among them Henri De Braekeleer and Jan Stobbaerts were more original.

BIBLIOGRAPHY

C. Lemonnier: *L'Ecole belge de peinture, 1830–1905* (Brussels, 1906), pp. 63–71

L. Delteil: *Henri Leys, Henri de Braekeleer, James Engor* (1925), xix of *Le Peintre-graveur illustré*, 31 vols (Paris, 1906–26/*R* New York, 1969)

G. Van Zype: *Henri Leys* (Brussels, 1934)

*Schilderkunst in Belgie ten tijde van H. Leys (1815–69)* (exh. cat., ed. J. F. Buyck and A. A. Moerman; Antwerp, Kon. Mus. S. Kst., 1969)

*Quelques maîtres romantiques belges de Gustaf Wappers à Henri Leys* (exh. cat., ed. A. A. Moerman; Brussels, Musées Royaux B.-A., 1973)

R. Kerremans: 'Middeleeuwen en collectieve verbeelding in de Belgische schilder- en beeldhouwkunst van de 19de eeuw', *Neo-gotiek in België* (exh. cat., Ghent, 1994), p. 37

SIBYLLE VALCKE

**Leyster, Judith** (*b* Haarlem, *bapt* 28 July 1609; *d* Heemstede, *bur* 10 Feb 1660). Dutch painter. She painted genre scenes, portraits and still-lifes, and she may also have made small etchings; no drawings by her are known. She specialized in small intimate genre scenes, usually with women seated by candlelight, and single half-length figures set against a neutral background. She was influenced by both the UTRECHT CARAVAGGISTI and Frans Hals.

Leyster may have worked in Hals's shop (*c.* 1626–8 and *c.* 1629–33), where she copied and adapted several of his paintings, although the nature of her work in his shop has been disputed. These possible works include *The Jester* (Amsterdam, Rijksmus.), a copy after Hals's *Lute Player* (Paris, Louvre), and the *Rommel-pot Player* (Chicago, IL, A. Inst.), after Hals's lost work. However, it is also possible that her early career began in the shop of the Haarlem portrait painter Frans Pietersz. de Grebber, with whom she is mentioned in Samuel Ampzing's poem about Haarlem of 1627/8. This would also explain the somewhat passé nature of her few known later portraits, for example *Portrait of a Woman* (1635; Haarlem, Frans Halsmus.), the

shallow space of which seems to push the woman forward on to the picture plane.

In 1628 Leyster's family moved to Vreeland, near Utrecht, where, it is assumed, she came under the direct influence of the Utrecht Caravaggisti Hendrick Terbrugghen and Gerrit van Honthorst. The influence of the Caravaggisti can be seen in subsequent night-scenes, including those executed in Haarlem, such as *The Serenade* (1629; Amsterdam, Rijksmus.), which depicts a lute player illuminated by flickering yet unseen candlelight. The broad brushstrokes of the costume and the face also show the influence of Hals and give an illusion of monumentality to this small painting (455×350m). The upward glance of the lute player is a typical device of Leyster's.

Leyster is credited with introducing a visible light source to nocturnal painting in Haarlem, for example the lit candle between a drinker and a smoker in the *Last Drop* (*c.* 1629; Philadelphia, PA, John G. Johnson priv. col.) and the lit lamp in *The Proposition* (1631; The Hague, Mauritshuis; see fig.). In this painting, the lamplight illuminates the scene of a man offering money to a woman for her sexual favours, a style and subject common among the Caravaggisti; but Leyster's woman does not appear to be a courtesan, nor is she encouraging this overture, unlike a copy of the work (ex-Amédée Provost priv. col.; sold Brussels, 20 June 1928, lot 56) where such additional motifs as a wine-glass and a map over the woman's head imply that she is a *vrouwe-wereld* (Dut.: 'woman of the world'). In adapting this common theme, Leyster seems to have questioned the usual assumption of the woman as temptress.

Judith Leyster: *The Proposition*, oil on panel, 309×242 mm, 1631 (The Hague, Mauritshuis)

By 1633 Leyster had become a member of the Haarlem Guild of St Luke. As her admission piece she may have submitted her *Self-portrait* (Washington, DC, N.G.A.), which shows her seated at her easel in formal dress, wielding a palette and 18 brushes and painting a fiddler; this fiddler reappears in her *Merry Company* (The Netherlands, priv. col.). On 1 June 1636 she married the Haarlem genre and portrait painter JAN MIENSE MOLENAER; they lived in Amsterdam until October 1648, when they moved to Heemstede. They also owned several properties in Amsterdam and Haarlem, which they seem to have rented out for additional income. They had five children between 1637 and 1650, but only two survived their parents. Leyster's *Tulip* pages (1643; Haarlem, Frans Halsmus.), possibly part of a tulip-bulb catalogue and executed in watercolour and silverpoint on vellum, suggest a scale and change of medium and subject that may have been more adaptable to her new domestic situation. Many paintings by Leyster are recorded in the inventory of Molenaer's possessions after his death in 1668. Included are several other still-lifes as well as many works now lost. Leyster's output after her marriage and after her children were born seems greatly reduced, although it cannot be discounted that she may have collaborated with her husband.

In 1647–8 she was praised by Theodore Schrevel in his book on Haarlem, in which he makes a pun on her name, calling her Ley/sterr (Dut.: 'lodestar'), a 'leading star' in art. Leyster also used this pun in her monogram, formed by her conjoined initials and a star shooting out to the right. Despite praise from her contemporaries, she was not mentioned in other early sources, such as Cornelis de Bie's *Het gulden cabinet*, published only a year after her death, and Arnold Houbraken's *Groote schouburgh* of 1718–21. By the end of the 19th century she was virtually unknown, so much so that no works were ascribed to her. Her monogram was thought either indecipherable or, as in a court case in 1892 involving her painting the *Carousing Couple* (1630; Paris, Louvre), was said to contain all the letters of Hals's name. This painting of a vivid, buoyant couple drinking, smoking and making music in a canopied arbour, marks the turning-point in Leyster's reputation. Discoveries of other paintings by her followed, many previously ascribed to Hals; others, such as her masterpiece of light and still-life elements, the *Young Flute Player* (Stockholm, Nmus.), were once attributed to Jan de Bray. Leyster's paintings of mothers and children and women with their lovers may have served as prototypes for genre painters of the second half of the 17th century, such as Gerard ter Borch II, Gabriel Metsu and Pieter de Hooch. Also, 18th-century artists such as Alexis Grimou based some of their single half-length figures on her work.

Three students are recorded in Leyster's shop: Willem Woutersz. in 1634, Davidt de Burry and Hendrick Jacobs. Although no works by them are known, it is assumed that they made many copies of her paintings. Woutersz. was also the subject of a dispute between Leyster and Hals when the latter accepted him as a student, without permission of the Guild, and when he was already in Leyster's shop.

BIBLIOGRAPHY

S. Ampzing: *Beschryvinge ende lof der stad Haerlem* [Description and praise of the town of Haarlem] (Haarlem, 1628/*R* Amsterdam, 1974), p. 370

T. Schrevel: *Harlemum* (Haarlem, 1647), p. 292; Dut. trans. as *Harlemias* (Haarlem, 1648), p. 445

C. Hofstede de Groot: 'Judith Leyster', *Jb. Preuss. Kstsamml.*, xiv (1893), pp. 190–98, 232

A. Bredius: 'Een conflict tusschen Frans Hals en Judith Leyster', *Oud-Holland*, xxxix (1917), pp. 71–3

A. von Schneider: 'Gerard Honthorst and Judith Leyster', *Oud-Holland*, xl (1922), pp. 169–73

J. Harms: 'Judith Leyster: Ihr Leben und ihr Werk', *Oud-Holland*, xlix (1927), pp. 88–96, 113–26, 145–54, 221–42, 275–9

H. F. Wijnman: 'Het geboortejaar van Judith Leyster', *Oud-Holland*, xlix (1932), pp. 62–5

F. F. Hofrichter: 'Judith Leyster's *Proposition*: Between Virtue and Vice', *Fem. A. J.*, iv (1975), pp. 22–6; repr. in *Feminism and Art History: Questioning the Litany*, ed. N. Broude and M. D. Garrard (New York, 1982), pp. 173–82

*Women Artists, 1550–1950* (exh. cat. by A. S. Harris and L. Nochlin, Los Angeles, Co. Mus. A., 1976)

F. F. Hofrichter: 'Judith Leyster's *Self-portrait*: *Ut pictura poesis*', *Essays in Northern European Art Presented to Egbert Haverkamp-Begemann on his 60th Birthday* (Doornspijk, 1983), pp. 106–9

*Masters of Seventeenth-century Dutch Genre Painting* (exh. cat. by P. Sutton and others, Philadelphia, Mus. A.; W. Berlin, Gemäldegal.; London, RA; 1984)

F. F. Hofrichter: 'Games People Play: Judith Leyster's *A Game of Trictrac*', Worcester A. Mus., vii (1985), pp. 19–27

——: *Judith Leyster: A Woman Painter in Holland's Golden Age* (Doornspijk, 1989)

*Judith Leyster: A Dutch Master and her World* (exh. cat. by J. A. Welu and others, Haarlem, Frans Halsmus.; Worcester, MA, A. Mus.; 1993)

FRIMA FOX HOFRICHTER

**Lhasa.** Capital of the Tibetan Autonomous Region of China and seat of Tibet's religious and civil authority. It is situated on the northern bank of the Lhasa River, a branch of the Kyichu (Chin. Quxu) River in the ancient Ü Province, central Tibet. It was established in the 7th century AD during the reign of King Songtsen Gampo (*reg c.* 620–49) as the capital of the Yarlung dynasty. The city was originally the site of a lake or marsh, which the king ordered to be filled in as the foundation of the Jokhang Temple. Lhasa was greatly expanded by Trisong Detsen (*reg* 755–*c.* 794), under whom Tibet became a major military power in Central Asia. When the Yarlung dynasty ended with the collapse of centralized authority in the middle of the 9th century AD, Lhasa still continued to function as a major city, even though religious and political power had by then become dispersed. Only in the mid-17th century did Lhasa regain its status as the capital of Tibet and the seat of the government. The majority of the historical sites and cultural relics to be seen in Lhasa date back no further than the city's second flowering.

The Jokhang Temple, located in the centre of the old city, the Barkor, was the first Buddhist institution in the country and remains one of the most important (see fig.). It was established by Songtsen Gampo to house a statue of Akshobhya Buddha that his Nepalese queen, Bhrikuti, had brought with her from Nepal. A statue of Shakyamuni, the historical Buddha (the so-called Jowo image originally housed in the Ramoche Temple), presented by the king's Chinese queen, Wencheng, was later installed in the Jokhang, and the Akshobhya statue was moved to the Ramoche instead.

At the side of the entrance to the monastery are three inscriptions, one of which contains the text of the treaty

Lhasa, Jokhang Temple, founded *c.* AD 640

between Tibet and China from AD 821. The Jokhang itself is a huge, two-storey series of buildings containing several hundred shrine-rooms, chapels and rooms that serve as living quarters. Access is through a front courtyard, a main doorway and a corridor, which opens on to a large inner courtyard. The main building, which can be circumambulated by means of a long corridor with wall paintings, is directly in front of the entrance across the courtyard and houses on the ground floor the shrines of Tsong Khapa (1357–1419), founder of the Gelugpa sect, and his main disciples. The Eight Medicine Buddhas, the Thousand-armed Compassionate Avalokiteshvara, Maitreya, the future Buddha, and Amitabha, among others, also have shrines here. The most important shrine-room is that devoted to the Jowo Shakyamuni, a large bronze statue covered with precious stones and textiles. Other images in this central building include those of Tsong Khapa, the monk Atisha (982–1054) and two of the Dalai Lamas. Its upper floor contains shrine-rooms and chapels dedicated to Songtsen Gampo, the *siddha* Padmasambhava, the guardian deity Samvara and the female protector Palden Lhamo. In the building opposite the entrance to the main shrine-room is the shrine devoted to the female deity, the Green Tara. Behind her are seated images of the Twenty-one Taras, other manifestations of the goddess. At the back of the principal shrine is a small meditation chamber with wall paintings of the wrathful protectors of the Gelugpa school. The roof of the main shrine is particularly fine (*see* TIBET, §V, 6).

The Potala (*see* TIBET, fig. 5) was built in AD 1645 by the fifth Dalai Lama (1617–82). The palace takes its name from the holy mountain of the *bodhisattva* Avalokiteshvara, in southern India (*see* BUDDHISM, §III, 6). It is built on top of a small rocky outcrop and is reached via stairs that zigzag up the hill. The greater part is occupied by the White Palace, a building of 13 storeys that originally housed the monks' living quarters, libraries and school rooms. From the inner courtyard of the White Palace, the Red Palace, the central building of the complex, is entered through a flight of stairs in its right side. Completed in 1694, it has four storeys. On the roof are the large Reception Hall, containing one of the Dalai Lama's thrones, and the Dalai Lama's private rooms and audience chamber, where bronze images of various Tantric deities including Ushnishavijaya, goddess of longevity, Manjushri, *bodhisattva* of wisdom, and the great Sages or *mahāsiddhas* are on view. On the upper floor are several shrine-rooms, including one dedicated to Maitreya and filled with art treasures and religious relics related to the Dalai Lamas. Other sanctuaries include the shrine of the Three-dimensional *Maṇḍala*s, the shrine of Immortal Bliss and the tomb of the thirteenth Dalai Lama. The upper middle floor has shrines dedicated to the worship of Kalachakra, identified with the wheel of time, Shakyamuni and Amitayus, the Buddha of longevity. The first of these has a large, three-dimensional *maṇḍala* made of gold and copper. With a diameter of nearly 4 m and a height of slightly less than 3 m, it presents images of all the deities relating to the *Kalachakra Tantra*. The bottom floor contains the large assembly hall as well as four additional shrines, one of which houses the golden stupa containing the relics of the fifth Dalai Lama. Wall paintings depicting important religious incidents in the history of Tibet, as well as scrolls (*tangka*s) with Buddhist figures and deities, are found throughout the Potala.

Norbulingka, a large park and the Dalai Lamas' Summer Palace, is situated some 4 km west of Lhasa. The site was used by the seventh Dalai Lama (1708–57), and buildings were first erected there by his successor (1758–1805). It was the scene of heavy Tibetan resistance against the Chinese in 1959, and several of the old buildings were damaged or destroyed. Most of what can be seen in Norbulingka today, including the majority of the palace buildings, does not predate the 20th century.

*See also* TIBET, fig. 16.

BIBLIOGRAPHY
S. C. Das: *Journey to Lhasa and Central Tibet* (London, 1902/*R* New Delhi, 1970)
S. Hummel: 'Die Kathedrale von Lhasa', *Antaios*, vii/3 (1965), pp. 280–90
D. L. Snellgrove and H. E. Richardson: *A Cultural History of Tibet* (Boulder, 1980)
M. Henss: *Tibet: Die Kulturdenkmäler* (Zurich, 1981), pp. 45–106
*The Potala Palace of Tibet*, The Cultural Relics Administration Committee (Hong Kong, 1982)
S. Batchelor: *The Tibet Guide* (London, 1987), pp. 71–123
K. Dowman: *The Power-places of Central Tibet: A Pilgrim's Guide* (London and New York, 1988), pp. 38–72
Liu Lizhong: *Buddhist Art of the Tibetan Plateau* (Hong Kong, 1988)
R. Vitali: *Early Temples of Central Tibet* (London, 1990)

HENRIK H. SØRENSEN

**Lhermitte, Léon(-Augustin)** (*b* Mont Saint-Père, Aisne, 31 July 1844; *d* Paris, 27 July 1925). French draughtsman, printmaker, painter and illustrator. He was the only son of a village schoolmaster and his precocious drawing skill won him an annual grant from the state. In 1863 he went to Paris and became a student at the Petite Ecole, where one of his teachers was Horace Lecoq de Boisbaudran, famed for his method of training the visual memory. Jean-Charles Cazin, a fellow pupil, became a lifelong friend and Lhermitte later got to know Alphonse Legros, Henri Fantin-Latour, Jules Dalou and Rodin, who had all studied at the school. In 1864 his charcoal drawing the *Banks of the Marne near Alfort* (untraced) was exhibited at the Salon. By inclination and by training a meticulous draughtsman, he continued to exhibit his drawings at the Salon until 1889.

In 1866 his first oil painting, *Violets in a Glass, Shells, Screen* (untraced), was exhibited at the Salon, and he produced his first etching, for his friend Frédéric Henriet's book *Paysagiste aux champs* (Paris, 1876). He also did illustrations for a book on insects and for furniture-makers and designed boxes for sweets. In 1869 he made his first visit to London, where he met Legros. On his second visit in 1871 Legros recommended him as an illustrator for *Works of Art in the Collections of England Drawn by E. Lièvre* and introduced him to the dealer Durand-Ruel, who agreed to sell several of his drawings. In 1873 Durand-Ruel sent some of Lhermitte's works to the Dudley Gallery for the first of the annual Black and White exhibitions and Lhermitte subsequently became a regular participant. Prints after Lhermitte's works, which were published in

Léon Lhermitte: *Harvesters' Payday*, oil on canvas, 2.15×2.72 m, 1882 (Paris, Musée d'Orsay)

the Galerie Durand-Ruel's *Recueil d'estampes gravées à l'eau-forte* (1873), contributed to his growing reputation.

Lhermitte won a third-class medal in the Salon of 1874 for his painting *The Harvest* (Carcassonne, Mus. B.-A.), which was bought by the state. In 1879 Degas noted in a sketchbook his intention to invite Lhermitte to exhibit with the Impressionists, but Lhermitte never participated in any of their shows. *The Tavern* (priv. col., see Le Pelley Fonteny, 1987), exhibited in the Salon of 1881, initiated the monumental series of paintings on the life of the agricultural worker that came closest to justifying van Gogh's admiring appellation 'Millet the Second'. The next in the series, *Harvesters' Payday* (1882; Paris, Mus. d'Orsay; see fig.), was bought for the state and became the artist's best-known work. *The Harvest* (1883; St Louis, MO, Washington U., Gal. A.), third in the series, was included with ten charcoal drawings in the Exposition Nationale in 1883. Lhermitte received the Légion d'honneur in 1884 when he exhibited the fourth monumental composition the *Grape Harvest* (New York, Met.), where the shift in emphasis from physical toil to the emotional rapport between a peasant woman and small boy is indicative of the increased sentimentality of his later work.

Lhermitte was commissioned in 1886 to do two large portrait groups to decorate the Sorbonne. The first, *Claude Bernard in his Laboratory at the Collège de France* (Paris, Acad. N. Médec.), was shown in the Salon of 1889. In 1888 André Theuriet asked him to illustrate *La Vie rustique* (1888), a major commission for which Lhermitte used the many drawings of peasant life he had already executed. Lhermitte was a founder-member of the Société Nationale des Beaux-Arts in 1890. In 1894 he was made an officer of the Légion d'honneur while working on the enormous painting *Les Halles* (4.0×6.3 m; Paris, Petit Pal.), commissioned by the city of Paris to decorate the Hôtel de Ville. This huge, opulent panorama depicting workers at the market dwarfs Ford Madox Brown's *Work* (Manchester, C.A.G.) as an image of labour. Lhermitte was elected to fill Jacques Henner's chair in painting at the Institut in 1905. He continued to exhibit in the first decades of the 20th century, when he was generally seen as a relic of a bygone era, although his style later had an influence on Socialist Realism. Increasingly he worked in pastel, his draughtsman's skill ever in evidence, producing some sensitive portraits and peasant scenes reminiscent of the earlier and more powerful depictions that van Gogh had cited as 'an ideal'.

BIBLIOGRAPHY

F. Henriet: *Les Eaux-fortes de Léon Lhermitte* (Paris, 1905)
E. Ménard: *Notice sur la vie et les travaux de L. Lhermitte* (Paris, 1927)
E. Friant: *Discours prononcé à l'occasion de l'inauguration du monument élevé à la mémoire de Léon Lhermitte à Mont Saint Père le 29 juillet 1928* (Paris, 1928)
J. Lhermitte: 'Un Peintre champenois: Léon Lhermitte', *Vie Campagne*, xlvii (1957), p. 26
M. Le Pelley Fonteny: *La Vie domestique dans l'oeuvre de Léon Lhermitte* (Paris, 1971)
——: 'Léon Lhermitte', *A. & Curiosité*, xlv (1973), pp. 4–10
M. M. Hamel: *A French Artist: Léon Lhermitte (1844–1925)* (diss., St Louis, MO, Washington U., 1974)
*Léon Lhermitte* (exh. cat. by M. M. Hamel, Oshkosh, WI, Paine A. Cent., 1974)
*The Realist Tradition: French Painting and Drawing, 1830–1900* (exh. cat., ed. G. P. Weisberg; Cleveland, OH, Mus. A.; New York, Brooklyn Mus.; St Louis, MO, A. Mus.; Glasgow, A.G. & Mus.; 1980), pp. 301–2
M. Le Pelley Fonteny: *Léon-Augustin Lhermitte: Sa vie, son oeuvre: Catalogue des peintures, pastels, dessins et gravures* (diss., U. Paris IV, 1987)

JAMES P. W. THOMPSON

**Lheureux, Louis-Ernest** (*b* Fontainebleau, 15 July 1827; *d* 17 Dec 1898). French architect. He studied under Henri Labrouste and in 1856 entered the service of the city of Paris as Chief Architect of the 5th arrondissement. In this role he carried out work on the municipal bonded warehouse for wine, then on the Quai St Bernard, and was involved in the building of the two churches of St Francis Xavier (1861–75), under François Uchard (1809–91), and St Augustin (1862–8), under Victor Baltard. He subsequently became Chief Architect of the third section of the city of Paris, comprising the 4th and 12th arrondissements. In 1878 he was put in charge of rebuilding a bonded warehouse at Bercy to replace that on the Quai St Bernard; however, he executed only part of the planned work, notably the two small restaurants located on the wharf. On the Ile St Louis he built a school (L'Ecole Elémentaire du Quartier) for boys, for which approval for construction was granted in 1886. Lheureux appears also to have designed numerous private mansions and town houses (mostly destr.), including his own small house, with a tower and vaulted ceilings, in the Rue Largillière, Passy.

Lheureux's two most important undertakings were a preparatory school, the Collège Ste Barbe (before 1878), and the enlargement of the Faculté de Droit, both in the Latin Quarter, Paris. The Collège Ste Barbe comprised a day school with a classroom and study-room, and a boarding-school with a dormitory and refectory. The disposition of the rooms and, above all, the circulation were extremely well worked out, and the whole was both airy and functional, demonstrating a masterly use of such 'modern' materials as iron and glass. The enlargement of the Faculté de Droit (1893–8) involved the creation of a 400-seat lecture theatre, a large conference hall, examination rooms, a reading-room and studies for the professors. The lecture theatre was the masterpiece of the entire scheme. Lheureux set it against the wall of the library and, in order to accommodate the 400 places, he created a mezzanine gallery with two rows of seats, each student having his own desk and chair. The large halls were covered by a vast iron skeleton with polychrome brick vaults and a few touches of mosaic. The remainder of the construction was in stone and rusticated ashlar. Again, careful attention was paid to circulation within the building.

Lheureux was a medal-winner in the competitions organized for the reconstruction of the Hotel de Ville (1873), Paris, and for the new Sorbonne (1878), and he received the Special Jury Prize at the Exposition Universelle, Paris, in 1889 for his monument (unexecuted) to the glory of the French Revolution. It was designed as a kind of pyramid, inspired by the architecture of the Far East, to be located on the site of the Tuileries Palace. Like his master Labrouste, Lheureux was a rationalist. He appears, however, never to have been militantly in favour of any particular movement, unlike Viollet-le-Duc or Anatole de Boudot, who nevertheless held the same views. His contemporaries praised the clarity of his solutions to problems and his masterly use of materials, particularly iron, the malleability of which he turned to advantage.

Thieme–Becker                  BIBLIOGRAPHY
                                FRANÇOISE BERCÉ

**Lhote, André** (*b* Bordeaux, 5 July 1885; *d* Paris, 25 Jan 1962). French painter, critic and teacher. From the age of 12 he was apprenticed by his father to a maker of wood-carvings. He followed the course in decorative arts at the Ecole des Beaux-Arts in Bordeaux and did not definitively abandon ornamental sculpture for painting until 1905. Perhaps as a consequence, Lhote was one of the few 20th-century artists and theoreticians who not only accepted the term 'decorative' in connection with art but also exalted it, finding in mural painting the highest public realization of his ambitions. Like Albert Gleizes and Fernand Léger, he welcomed the limitations of wall painting because its conditions insisted on flatness as integral to a large plane surface.

The first paintings shown by Lhote to a large public in Paris, at the Salon d'Automne of 1907, were characterized by vigorous brushstrokes and bright colours. While they had affinities with Fauvism, they were already disciplined by his admiration for Cézanne, visible in the break-up of surfaces into smaller planes. These early works were mostly landscapes; a few larger religious paintings from as late as 1910 (the year in which he held his first one-man exhibition, at the Galerie Druet in Paris) betray Lhote's initial enthusiasm for Gauguin, to whose work he had been introduced in 1906 by an influential collector from Bordeaux, Gabriel Frizeau. Through Frizeau, Lhote began a long friendship with the young writers Jacques Rivière (1886–1925) and Henri Alain Fournier. Another collector and amateur art critic, deputy attorney general Joseph Granie, secured a year's scholarship for him in 1909 at the Villa Médicis Libre, founded by Georges Bonjean in Orgeville, Eure, for non-academic married artists. Raoul Dufy, a fellow at the same time as Lhote, was instrumental in introducing him to advanced poets and artists. He became aware of the work of Robert Delaunay, Jean Metzinger, Henri Le Fauconnier, Fernand Léger and Albert Gleizes; in 1911, thanks to the radical decision of the hanging committee of the Salon des Indépendants to group artists by stylistic tendency, his work, along with that of Roger de la Fresnaye and André Dunoyer de Segonzac, was placed in the room adjacent to the notorious Salle 41, where Cubism was first shown in force. According to Gleizes's later recollections, friendship among a number of these artists began in the spring of 1911 as they became aware for the first time of the extent of their common interests. This shared identity was further exploited by the arrangement of room 8 at the Salon d'Automne in 1911, where paintings by Gleizes, Metzinger and Léger were adjacent to Lhote's *Port of Bordeaux* and works by Jacques Villon, Marcel Duchamp, de la Fresnaye and Luc-Albert Moreau. Thus began Lhote's identification with Cubism, taken further in 1912 with his inclusion in the *Salon de la Section d'Or* (*see* SECTION D'OR (ii)). Not only the port of Bordeaux but also that of Marseille continued to furnish Lhote with his most common subjects, for example in his illustrations to Jean Cocteau's *Escales* (Paris, 1920); he

André Lhote: *Rugby*, oil on canvas, 1.28×1.33 m, 1917 (Paris, Pompidou, Musée National d'Art Moderne)

combined variations of port and port amusements in many paintings throughout his life, for example in *Entry to the Floating Dock in Bordeaux* (1912; Bordeaux, Mus. B.-A.).

For medical reasons Lhote served in the army for only a year, and from 1915 to 1919 he divided his time between Arcachon and Paris, where he was active among the wartime Cubist group that included Juan Gris, Metzinger, Gino Severini, Maria Blanchard, Jacques Lipchitz and Diego Rivera. Already it was clear that Lhote championed a version of Cubism in which a certain coefficient of realism was not only tolerated but encouraged, as in *Rugby* (1917; Paris, Pompidou; see fig.), in which stylized but clearly delineated representations of sportsmen contribute to the decorative and dynamic surface design. His début as art critic for the *Nouvelle revue française*, a post he filled until 1940, took place in 1917 when he developed the idea of painting as a 'plastic metaphor ... pushed to the limit of resemblance'. Lhote welcomed the role of teacher and theoretician. From 1918 he taught painting in Paris, first at the Académie Notre-Dame des Champs and from 1922 at his own Académie André Lhote. In an important article published in 1919, 'De la nécessité des théories' (*Nouv. Rev. Fr.*, 75, Dec 1919), he made a careful distinction between a priori ideas and those that proceeded from experience. He maintained that the most dangerous trap for painting was to remain content with old formulae, but he also insisted that for an artist not to profit from the accumulated wisdom of his own experience was a travesty of historical understanding, a foolish downgrading of the importance of tradition. His theory of art and his sophisticated understanding of Cubism led him to reject the general view that Cézanne's accomplishment was a reaction against Impressionism or that Cubism was a radical departure. He believed that for all great painting, concern for 'material' reality, for representation, was of no importance; what counted was the interior reality that the artist imposed in his vision of the world. For Lhote greatness consisted in the pictorial invention of wider and more ideal generalizations that created an equivalence between emotion and visual sensation, as in the work of Cézanne. Painting, he explained, consisted of certain constant elements that he called 'plastic invariables'.

Lhote's ability to reconcile pre-war experimentation (demonstrated in his bright palette and formal manifestations) and inter-war figuration in his work made him particularly influential. This blend of subdued modernism and a self-consciously French subject-matter, already suggested in his *Homage to Watteau* (1918; Geneva, Petit Pal.), was epitomized in works such as *14th July at Avignon* (1923; Pau, Mus. B.-A.). In the 1930s his personal form of Cubist-influenced figurative painting was further distilled in large compositions such as *Bathers* (1.33×2.15 m, 1935; Bordeaux, Mus. B.-A.), culminating in his mural the *Derivatives of Carbon* for the Exposition Internationale des Arts et Techniques dans la Vie Moderne in Paris (1937). Although often seen primarily in the context of French art, Lhote was highly influential on an international level, especially during the 1920s and 1930s; as late as the 1950s he lectured widely outside France and attracted students as well as readers from all over the world. In the 1940s and 1950s the earlier severity gave way to a more lyrical style, fired by intense colour combinations and concentrating increasingly on idyllic landscapes (e.g. *Pines at Arcachon*, 1948; Bordeaux, Mus. B.-A.). His three-panel painting the *Glory of Bordeaux* (1955), a large work painted for the Faculté de Médecine at the Université de Bordeaux II, won him the Grand Prix National de Peinture.

WRITINGS

*Traité du paysage* (Paris, 1939)
*Traité de la figure* (Paris, 1950)
*Peinture libérée* (Paris, 1956)
*Traités du paysage et de la figure* (Paris, 1958) [new edn of two prev. treatises]

BIBLIOGRAPHY

A. Jakovsky: *André Lhote* (Paris, 1947)
Jean Cassou, ed.: *André Lhote: Les Invariants plastiques* (Paris, 1967)
*Hommage à André Lhote* (exh. cat., preface G. Martin-Méry; Bordeaux, Mus. B.-A., 1967)
*André Lhote, 1885–1962: Cubism* (exh. cat., preface J. Cassou, essay D. Robbins; New York, Leonard Hutton Gals, 1976)
*André Lhote* (exh. cat. by B. Dorival, Paris, Artcurial, 1981)
*La Peinture, le coeur et l'esprit: Catalogue des oeuvres d'André Lhote* (exh. cat. by F. Garcia, Bordeaux, Mus. B.-A., 1986)

DANIEL ROBBINS

**Li (i).** Chinese family of painters. They were descended on the paternal side from Gaozu (*reg* 618–26), the first emperor of the Tang dynasty. (1) Li Sixun and his son, (2) Li Zhaodao, are acknowledged as the foremost exponents of the Tang-period (AD 618–907) Blue-and-green (*qinglü*) manner of landscape painting, sometimes called the Gold-and-green (*jinbi*) style because of the gold highlights used together with azurite blue and malachite green; traditional Chinese texts further credit them with the invention of the technique (*see also* CHINA, §V, 3(iv)(b)). Their finely detailed paintings were executed in delicate brushwork with 'iron-wire' strokes (*tiexian miao*) and 'small axe-cut' texture strokes (*xiao fupi cun*), a technique consistent with the literalism of the palace style. The Blue-and-green tradition was an aspect of the NORTHERN SCHOOL of professional artists, as distinct from the SOUTHERN SCHOOL of literati painters. In the late 16th century and early 17th Dong Qichang defined it as one of the major characterisitics of antiquity, and its colour formula was used to re-create the spirit of the Tang period.

MARY S. LAWTON

**(1) Li Sixun** [Li Ssu-hsün; *ming* Jianjian] (*b c.* AD 653; *d* 718). He was a member of the imperial family of the Tang dynasty and held various civil and military government positions, including Great General of the Left Militant Guard (*c.* 713), earning the nickname Great General Li (Da Li Jiangjun).

The period during which Li was active was one of the most flourishing in the cultural and artistic history of China. Figure painting reached its peak with the famous 8th-century AD artist WU DAOZI, while landscape was established as a major independent category. During this formative stage, Li Sixun was regarded as one of the most influential landscape painters. In his *Lidai minghua ji* ('Record of famous painters of successive generations', preface AD 847) Zhang Yanyuan records that the transformation of landscape painting began with Wu Daozi and was perfected by Li Sixun and (2) Li Zhaodao. Although this is impossible as Li Sixun probably died before Wu started his career, it indicates the esteem in which he was held. Writing *c.* AD 840 in the *Tangchao minghua lu* ('Record of famous painters of the Tang period'), Zhu Jingxuan classified painters according to their ability and placed Li in the lower grade of the 'inspired class'. Zhu also related that Emperor Xuanzong (*reg* 712–56) was extremely impressed by landscapes that Li had painted on some palace screens and walls: he said he could hear the sound of water from them and that Li was the foremost painter of the Tang dynasty. An alternative version tells how Wu Daozi and Li were invited to paint landscapes in a hall in Datong (now in Sichuan Province). While commending them both on their magnificent attainments, the emperor noted 'Li Sixun's achievement of many months and Wu Daozi's work of a single day', contrasting Li's meticulous craftsmanship with the inspired spontaneous technique of Wu. This fictitious anecdote would have been forgotten had it not been for the influence it exerted on later critics of Li's style.

Written sources are the only reliable testimony for Li's work. His paintings were copied at an early date, and no extant paintings fully represent his style. The unsigned hanging scroll *Pavilions and River with Sails* (*Jiangfan louge tu*; Taipei, N. Pal. Mus.) was first attributed to Li by the Qing-period (1644–1911) collector An Qi, and although this landscape is undoubtedly early, it is impossible to substantiate the attribution. A cluster of paintings centering on the unsigned handscroll (*Emperor Minghuang's Journey to Shu*; see fig.) is usually regarded as typical of his style. The painting has been claimed to depict Emperor Xuanzong's flight to Sichuan after the rebellion of An Lushan in AD 756. A painting of this motif was attributed to Li Sixun by Su Shi—anachronistically, as Sixun died almost 40 years before the revolt. Later scholars have reattributed the composition to Li Zhaodao. Certain

Li Sixun (attrib.): *Emperor Minghuang's Journey to Shu*, handscroll, *c.* AD 700 (Taipei, National Palace Museum)

features indicate that the Taipei version illustrated was based on a Tang-period original. The structure of the rocks is reminiscent of wall paintings in the tombs of the princes Yide and Zhanghuai at QIAN XIAN, in Shaanxi Province, executed by court painters during the early 8th century; so too is the manner of rendering distance by showing figures half-hidden by hills and promontories. The swirling clouds fit the descriptions of the way in which Li painted clouds and mists, and the narrative richness is also typical of early Chinese landscape painting. The brushwork is, however, of much later date. Finally, the pleasant atmosphere of the composition is not in keeping with the subject-matter of the title, and it is doubtful whether any member of the imperial house would depict such a humiliating event.

While no Tang source describes Li's paintings as especially decorative, he was later renowned for colourful and painstaking landscapes executed in the Gold-and-green manner. In the 13th century the connoisseur Zhao Xigu was the first to connect this manner with the two Li, specifically with Li Zhaodao. The 14th-century writer Tang Hou, on the other hand, considered Li Sixun to be the first exponent of the technique. When the influential artist and theorist Dong Qichang developed his theories of the Northern and Southern schools in painting, in the 16th and 17th centuries, he selected Li Sixun as the grand ancestor of the Northern school, chiefly for the elaborate and decorative paintings that were said to be preferred by the court and the merchant class.

BIBLIOGRAPHY

Jin Weinuo: 'Li Sixun fuzi' [Li Sixun and his son], *Wenwu* (1961), no. 6, pp. 13–15

Li Lin-ts'an: 'A Study of the Masterpiece *Tang Ming-huang's Journey to Shu*', *A. Orient.*, iv (1961), pp. 315–21

Fu Xinian: 'Guanyu Zhan Ziqian *Youchun tu* niandai de tantao' [An investigation of the date of *Travelling in Spring* by Zhan Ziqian], *Wenwu* (1978), no. 11, pp. 40–52

Zhang Boju: 'Guanyu Zhan Ziqian *Youchun tu* niandai de yi dian qianjian' [Some shallow reflections regarding the date of *Travelling in Spring* by Zhan Ziqian], *Wenwu* (1979), no. 4, pp. 83–4

M. Sullivan: *Chinese Landscape Painting in the Sui and Tang Dynasties* (Berkeley, 1980), pp. 46–50

Fu Xinian: 'Lun ji fu zhuan wei Li Sixun huapai jinbi shanshui de huizhi shidai' [A discussion of the date of some landscapes in the *jinbi* mode, traditionally attributed to the school of Li Sixun], *Wenwu* (1983), no. 11, pp. 77–86

METTE SIGGSTEDT

**(2) Li Zhaodao** [Li Chao-tao] (*b c.* AD 675; *d* 730). Son of (1) Li Sixun. He was appointed to the position of vice-president of the Right Grand Secretariat of the crown prince, but little else is known of his life. Whether he actually served in the army cannot be confirmed, but he came to be called Xiao Li Jiangjun (Little General Li) to distinguish him from his father, (1) Li Sixun, called Da Li Jiangjun (Great General Li). Later art critics preferred now one, now the other; but it has become impossible to differentiate between the two from the extant copies of their works available for study.

Two extant works are usually suggested to be copies of paintings by Li Zhaodao as they have come to be closely identified with his traditions. The *Picture of the Winding*

*River* (*Ch'u Chiang T'u*; hanging scroll, colours on silk, h. 1712 mm, w. 1113 mm; Taipei, N. Pal. Mus.) is a faithful re-creation of the 8th-century landscape style, with a strongly linear design developed by folded and fissured mountain forms. The more frequently reproduced *Emperor Minghuang's Journey to Shu* (Philadelphia, U. PA Mus.; for illustration *see* §(1) above) depicts an event that took place in 756, after Li Zhaodao's death. There are two other copies of the same composition, one in Taipei (N. Pal. Mus.) and one in Philadelphia (U. PA Mus.).

BIBLIOGRAPHY

L. Sickman and A. Soper: *The Art and Architecture of China*, Pelican Hist. A. (Harmondsworth, 1956, rev. 3/1968/*R* 1984)
O. Sirén: *Chinese Painting: Leading Masters and Principles* (London and New York, 1956–8), i, pp. 103–8
M. Loehr: *Three Great Painters of China* (New York, 1980), pp. 64–72
*Eight Dynasties of Chinese Painting: The Collections of the Nelson–Atkins Museum of Art, Kansas City, and the Cleveland Museum of Art* (exh. cat. by Wai-kam Ho and others, Kansas City, MO, Nelson–Atkins Mus. A., Cleveland, OH, Mus. A. and Tokyo, N. Mus., 1980–81), no. 136
T. Miyagawa, ed.: *Chinese Painting* (Tokyo, 1983), pp. 116–17

MARY S. LAWTON

**Li (ii).** *See* ITSUNEN SHŌYŪ.

**Liagno, Teodor de.** *See* NAPOLETANO, FILIPPO.

**Liancourt,** Duc de [Plessis, Roger du] (*b* 1598; *d* 5 Jan 1674). French patron and collector. He owned the celebrated Hôtel de Liancourt, 14–18 Rue de Seine, Paris, rebuilt (1610–13) by Salomon de Brosse, for the Duc de Bouillon and enlarged for Liancourt by Jacques Le Mercier in 1623. Although demolished in the 19th century, it is recorded in engraved views by Israel Silvestre (i), and its influential design, which successfully concealed from the visitor the fact that the front and rear façades were on different axes, was engraved by Jean Marot I for the '*Petit Marot*'. Liancourt also owned a late-16th-century château with fine gardens in Oise (destr.). The English virtuoso John Evelyn visited the Hôtel de Liancourt in 1644, where he admired the art collection and the garden, which contained a miniature theatre, ingenious waterworks and an illusionistic painted perspective depicting an extensive river landscape. Some of Evelyn's attributions of paintings are doubtful (he identified in one bedchamber a portrait of *Cardinal de Liancourt* as by Raphael, when chronology shows this to have been impossible), but Liancourt certainly owned Caravaggio's *Alof de Wignacourt* (Paris, Louvre). In 1644 he commissioned the *Seaport with Ulysses returning Chryseis to her Father* and its pendant *Landscape with Paris and Oenone* (both Paris, Louvre) from Claude Lorrain in Rome, ordered through the French ambassador there, François du Val, Marquis de Fontenay-Mareuil (*c.* 1594–1665). Liancourt also owned a portrait of *Gaston de Foix, Duc de Nemours*, then attributed to Giorgione, which inspired Philippe de Champaigne's *Gaston de Foix* (1635; Versailles, Château), for the series in the Galerie des Hommes Illustres at the Palais Cardinal, Paris, of Armand-Jean du Plessis, Cardinal de Richelieu. The Hôtel de Liancourt and most of the art collection that was contained within it passed at Liancourt's death to his granddaughter, who in 1659 had married François, Duc de la Rochefoucauld.

BIBLIOGRAPHY

J. Marot: *Recueil des plans, profils et élévations de plusieurs palais, chasteaux, églises, sépultures, grotes et hostels bâtis dans Paris* (Paris, *c.* 1660–70/*R* 1970)
G. Brice: *Description nouvelle de la ville de Paris* (Paris, 1713), ii, pp. 272
E. Bonnaffé: *Dictionnaire des amateurs français au XVIIe siècle* (Paris, 1884), pp. 185–6
A. Blunt: *Art and Architecture in France, 1500–1700*, Pelican Hist. A. (Harmondsworth, 1953, rev. 4/1980/*R* 1982), p. 199
J. Evelyn: *The Diary of John Evelyn*, ed. E. S. de Beer (Oxford, 1955), ii, pp. 112–14

ANNE THACKRAY

**Liang-chu.** *See* LIANGZHU.

**Liang Kai** [Liang K'ai; *zi* Boliang; *hao* Fengzi] (*b* Dongping, Shandong Province, late 12th century; *d* ?Lin-an after ?1246). Chinese painter. Although he originally painted in traditional styles, his later work became both more spontaneous in execution and more conceptual, in a manner that can be associated with the southern Chan (Jap. Zen) Buddhist approach to enlightenment (*see* BUDDHISM, §III, 8). Together with Muqi he became one of the best known painters of Chan subjects (*see* CHINA, §V, 3(ii)(b)) of the late Southern Song period (1127–1279).

According to the *Tuhui baojian* ('Precious mirror for examining painting') by Xia Wenyan (preface dated 1365), which is the basic source for all later references, Liang was a follower of Jia Shigu (*fl* 1130–60), an official from Bianliang (now Kaifeng, Henan Province), who served in the imperial painting academy at Lin'an (now Hangzhou, Zhejiang Province) during the Shaoxing period (1131–61) of the reign of Gaozong (*reg* 1127–62). Liang was also a member of the Academy and between 1201 and 1204 held the rank of painter in attendance (*daizhao*). Although he was awarded the *jindai* ('golden belt'), the highest honour given to members of the Academy, he appears to have subsequently resigned his official position. After leaving the court he went to live in Liutong si, a temple near Lin'an that was a centre of Chan painting. He did not go there for religious reasons but probably in protest against the bureaucracy and mainstream Chinese painting. Whatever the reason, his new painting style was far removed from his earlier Academic conservatism. All of his extant work, with the exception of two possible attributions, is to be found in Japan, where he exerted great influence on Zen painting (*see also* JAPAN, §VI, 4(vii)).

Liang Kai's retirement from official life marked a radical change in his artistic style. His early works are painted in the plain-line drawing (*baimiao*) traditions of LI GONGLIN as interpreted by Jia Shigu. His subjects included ghosts and celestial deities as well as Confucian and Daoist themes. An example of Liang's early style may be seen in the *Scholar of the Eastern Fence* (Taipei, N. Pal. Mus.), which depicts the great poet Tao Yuanming (AD 365–427) in a conventional setting associated with the compositional techniques of Ma Yuan and Xia Gui. Liang was also proficient in the monumental landscape style of the Northern Song period (960–1279; *see* CHINA, §V, 3(iv)(a)). His retreat from the capital marked the introduction of the use of spontaneous reduced brush (*jianbi*) technique, which is associated with Chan painting. He studied this new approach with a Chan master Wuzhun (1177–1249), a mediocre painter but a good calligrapher.

Liang Kai: *Huineng, the Sixth Chan Patriarch, Chopping Bamboo at the Moment of Enlightenment*, hanging scroll, ink on paper, 730×320 mm, probably after 1246 (Tokyo, National Museum)

Liang's later work reveals a strong calligraphic influence in the total control of the ink tones and the flexibility of the brush. In the brevity and descriptiveness of his brushstrokes he exploits the properties of the ink and the brush to the full. Such brushwork is also related to literati painting traditions. A poem by the Chan monk Beijian (*d* 1246) relates Liang's approach to painting: 'Liang Kai treasured his ink as if it were gold. But when he got drunk [the valued drops of ink] could suddenly become a

downpour' (*Encyclopedia of World Art*, ix, p. 240). Such a release of inhibitions through alcohol provides yet another explanation for the radical change in his style.

Liang Kai painted with strong brushstrokes, but he also utilized the wet 'boneless' technique (*mogu*), in which washes of graded ink tones define shape and form without lines, especially in the new genre referred to as pictures of Chan enlightenment (*Chan ji tu*). His painting of *A Sage* (Taipei, N. Pal. Mus.) is the only example of such a spontaneous style in the collection. It is an imaginary portrait executed in the 'splashed-ink' (*pomo*) technique, with scratchy, wet strokes that flow into washes or wet areas in a process that is only partially controlled. The broad washes composing the Sage's body contrast with the wispy lines that define the facial features. The *Nan Song yuan hua lu* ('Record of the Southern Song Academy', 1721), compiled by the poet and scholar Li O (1692–1752), notes that Liang Kai painted with wedge-like strokes (*piena*). This technique is especially obvious in *Huineng, the Sixth Chan Patriarch, Chopping Bamboo at the Moment of Enlightenment* (see fig.). Liang Kai painted a variety of traditional Buddhist themes, but none was as specifically connected with the Chan sect as this composition and another entitled *Huineng, the Sixth Chan Patriarch, Tearing up a Sutra* (Tokyo, T. Mitsui priv. col.), with which it is usually paired. Both paintings were apparently brought to Japan fairly soon after their completion but were later separated. In the first painting, which is largely conceptual in character, space is suggested by a single dry brushstroke that indicates the ground-plane and a fragmented tree trunk that establishes recession in the composition. The angular figure of the patriarch is created through a series of equally angular choplike 'stake-head' (*juetou*) strokes. Washes in graded ink tones give an impression of three dimensions. The energetic definition of the strong brushstrokes contrasts with the more delicate wispy hair and tightly defined features of the man's face shown in profile consistent in style with the technique of *A Sage*.

*EWA*

BIBLIOGRAPHY

Xia Wenyan: *Tuhui baojian* [Precious mirror for examining painting] (preface dated 1365), *Hua shi congshu* [Collected works on painting history], ed. Yu Anlan (Shanghai, 1962)

S. Shimada and Y. Yonezawa: *Painting of the Sung and Yuan Dynasties* (Tokyo, 1951)

O. Sirén: *Chinese Painting: Leading Masters and Principles* (London, 1956–8), ii, pp. 133–8

*Liang Kai* (Kyoto, 1957)

J. Cahill: *Chinese Painting* (Geneva and New York, 1960)

M. Loehr: *The Great Painters of China* (New York, 1980)

T. Miyagawa, ed.: *Chugoku no bijutsu: Kaiga* (Kyoto, 1982); Eng. trans., ed. T. Miyagawa as *Chinese Painting* (Tokyo, 1983), p. 182

MARY S. LAWTON

**Liang Sicheng** [Liang Ssu-ch'eng] (*b* Tokyo, 20 April 1901; *d* Beijing, 9 Jan 1972). Chinese architect and architectural historian. Son of the political reformer Liang Qichao, Liang Sicheng was born in Tokyo, where his family was exiled from 1898 to 1912. They were forced to leave China after Liang Qichao's participation in the unsuccessful reform movement of 1898. After returning to China, Liang Sicheng left in 1924 to attend the School of Architecture at the University of Pennsylvania, greatly inspired by his fiancée and fellow student, Lin Huiyin, who became his wife and collaborator until her death in 1955. At the University of Pennsylvania he became interested in the history of architecture, a subject until then unknown to him. In 1927 he received his M.A. in architecture, and in 1928 he and Lin Huiyin married on their way back to China. Liang became a teacher of architecture at the University of Mukden (Shenyang) in Manchuria between 1928 and 1931, when the Japanese invaded.

Back in Beijing he was made Director of the Society, later Institute, for Research in Chinese Architecture, which had been established with the reprint in 1925 of the *Yingzao fashi* (*see* CHINA, §II, 2(v)), a building manual dating to 1100, which aroused worldwide interest in ancient Chinese architecture. The Society studied the few existing texts on Chinese building but made little progress, as the terminology was unknown. Liang introduced a new approach, interviewing the artisans in charge of maintaining the Imperial Palace in Beijing and measuring and describing ancient buildings. The results were published in the *Zhongguo yingzao xueshe huikan* [Bulletin of the society for research in Chinese architecture]. Conscious of the threat of impending war with Japan, the members of the society measured and photographed as many old buildings as they could identify, most of them situated on remote and isolated mountains; they published the results of their fieldwork between 1931 and 1936.

During the Japanese occupation most intellectuals, among them the members of the Society, migrated to the western parts of China. Liang Sicheng wrote his main works at Lichuang in Sichuan Province: *Zhongguo jianzhu shi* [History of Chinese architecture] and an annotated edition of the *Yingzao fashi*, with corrected drawings. After 1949 Liang became Professor of Architecture at Qinghua University in Beijing. He was forced to go through a series of self-criticism sessions during the Cultural Revolution (1966–76). After his death, his main work was published by his collaborators and students.

### WRITINGS

*Song Yingzhao fashi tuzhu* [Drawings for the *Yingzao fashi* of the Song] (Beijing, n.d.)
*Qingshi yingzao suanli ji zeli* [Building regulations of the Qing dynasty] (Beijing, 1934/*R* 1981)
*Yingzao fashi zhushi, juan shang* [Commentaries to the *Yingzao fashi*], i (Beijing, 1980)

ELSE GLAHN

**Liang Ssu-ch'eng.** *See* LIANG SICHENG.

**Liangzhu** [Liang-chu]. Chinese late Neolithic culture of the area of Shanghai, southern Jiangsu Province and northern Zhejiang Province. The type site is near Hangzhou in Zhejiang Province. The Liangzhu culture was discovered in the 1930s. Excavations of major Liangzhu habitation and burial sites have produced a series of radiocarbon dates of between 3300 BC and 2200 BC; they show that the culture developed out of the Majiabang (*c.* 5500–*c.* 3000 BC) and Songze (*c.* 3900–*c.* 3300 BC) cultures, which occupied a similar geographical area.

Favourable soil conditions at Liangzhu sites have preserved organic remains, including plaited bamboo mats and baskets, wooden boats and oars, houses built of wattle and daub over timber, and a variety of wooden tools and utensils. Pottery from Liangzhu graves is characteristically of fine paste and grey or black. The finer vessels, probably ceremonial in function, were wheelmade and highly burnished; some examples have elaborate incised designs. Vessel shapes, many of which are also found in the classic Longshan culture of Shandong Province and other late Neolithic, Longshan-type, east-coast cultures, include a variety of *ding* tripods, lug-handled jars, tall pedestalled cups and shallow plates and bowls. Legs and ring feet are sometimes pierced or incised with geometric patterns, and the rims of several vessels are incised with as yet indecipherable characters or signs.

The jade industry of the Liangzhu culture was particularly highly developed. Excavations of richly furnished graves at Caoxieshan, Zhanglingshan and Sidun in Jiangsu Province, Fanshan and Yaoshan in Zhejiang Province, Fuquanshan in Shanghai Municipality and other Liangzhu sites have yielded large numbers of carefully carved and polished jade axes, beads, arc-shaped rings, bracelets, *bi* discs, and square *cong* tubes. While the exact function of these is unknown, their prevalence in certain graves suggests they were important as indicators of status and power (*see also* CHINA, §VIII, 1 and fig. 234). The ritual function of the *cong* is suggested by the recurring animal-mask designs that straddle the corners of many of the tubes, often in multiple tiers. Although usually composed of two simple ring eyes and a bar nose, several of these faces are more detailed, showing what some scholars believe are shamanistic scenes of human–animal transformation. It is possible that the animal-masks found on *cong* tubes are related to incipient *taotie* designs on early Shang bronze vessels (*see* CHINA, §VI, 3(ii)(a)).

### BIBLIOGRAPHY

'Jiangsu Wu xian Caoxieshan yizhi' [The site of Caoxieshan, Wu xian, Jiangsu], *Wenwu Ziliao Congkan* (1980), no. 3, pp. 1–24
'1982 nian Jiangsu Changzhou Wujin Sidun yizhi de fajue' [The 1982 excavation of the site of Wujin Sidun, Changzhou, Jiangsu], *Kaogu* (1984), no. 2, pp. 109–29
'Yuhang Yaoshan Liangzhu wenhua jitan yizhi fajue jianbao' [Report on the excavation of the altar remains of the Liangzhu culture at Yaoshan, Yuhang], *Wenwu* (1988), no. 1, pp. 32–51
'Zhejiang Yuhang Fanshan Liangzhu mudi fajue jianbao' [Report on the excavation of the Liangzhu cemetery at Fanshan, Yuhang, Zhejiang], *Wenwu* (1988), no. 1, pp. 1–31
K. C. Chang: 'An Essay on *cong*', *Orientations*, xx/6 (1989), pp. 37–43
Xuan-Pei Huang and others: *Liangzhu wenhua yüqi* [Jades of the Liangzhu culture] (Beijing and Hong Kong, 1989) [excellent pls]

ROBERT E. MUROWCHICK

**Liani** [Liano; Llano], **Francesco** (*b* ?Borgo San Donnino, nr Parma; *fl* Naples, ?1759–77). Italian painter. He had left Parma and established himself at the court of Ferdinand IV of Naples (*reg* 1751–1825) by 1765, and may have been working in Naples before this date since he made large equestrian portraits of Ferdinand's parents, *Charles III Bourbon* and *Maria Amalia of Saxony* (both Naples, Capodimonte), who left the city for Madrid in 1759. Liani's set of portraits of Charles and Maria Amalia's eight children (Capua, Mus. Prov. Campano) may also date from *c.* 1759. The series of religious narrative canvases, *Christ Falling under the Cross*, *Christ Falls a Second Time* and *Christ Stripped of his Robes* (Capua Cathedral) seem likely to have been painted around the same time as the royal portraits.

They show Liani to have been a refined decorator rather than a painter who could convey emotions. In the cycle of canvases showing scenes from the *Life of Christ* and *Life of the Virgin* (*c.* 1760–65; Capua, Mus. Prov. Campano) the expressions of the figures are again restrained. The paintings are also characterized by precious chromatic effects achieved by touches of pure colour, which are indebted to the work of Domenico Mondo and Giovanni Battista Rossi. Liani's mature portraits appear to have been exclusively of members of the Neapolitan court. He was commissioned to paint a portrait of *King Ferdinand IV* (1765; Copenhagen, Amalienborg) for the government of Denmark. In works such as his two portraits entitled *Gentleman in Armour* (Florence, priv. col., see Gregori, figs 36–7) Liani was clearly influenced by Anton Raphael Mengs's style of portrait painting.

BIBLIOGRAPHY

M. Gregori: 'Liani, rittrattista d'eccezione', *Paragone*, xxvi/309 (1975), pp. 103–8

N. Spinosa: 'Francesco Liani, pittore emiliano al servizio della corte di Napoli', *Paragone*, xxvi/309 (1975), pp. 38–53

**Liaño, Felipe de** (*b c.* 1560–70; *d c.* 1603). Spanish painter. He specialized in portraits and miniatures, although there are no works that can be securely attributed to him. He was unanimously praised by contemporaries, including Félix Lope de Vega, who, in his *Rimas humanas* (Madrid, 1604), included an epitaph following the early death of Liaño. He may have trained under Alonso Sánchez Coello, and his style must have been based on the European court portrait, especially on the two styles that existed at the court of Philip II: the Flemish represented by Anthonis Mor and the Venetian of Titian. Evidence of his relationship with Sánchez Coello is given in a document of 22 October 1584, when Liaño was a witness at the wedding of Jerónimo Sánchez (1531–after 1600), painter and stepbrother of Sánchez Coello, to Antonia de Liaño, probably a sister of Felipe de Liaño. The fame of Liaño as a portrait painter was exalted in literature. The military figure Cristobal Mosquera de Figueroa praised a portrait of *Alvaro de Bazán, 1st Marqués de Santa Cruz* (1584; untraced), made to be sent to Emperor Rudolf II. A drawing included in the *Descripción de verdaderos retratos de ilustres y memorables varones* (MS., Madrid, Mus. Lázaro Galdiano) by Francisco Pacheco shows a copy of one that Liaño had made of the same Mosquera de Figueroa and that Pacheco had taken from Mosquera de Figueroa's letters-patent of nobility. Narciso Sentenach (1856–1925) reproduced in *La colección Lázaro* (Madrid, 1922) an oval miniature of *Prince Philip*, from an old collection of José Lázaro, inscribed on the reverse *9 Felipe Vo, principe, F Liaño fecit*. In 1617 a self-portrait is mentioned as being owned by Diego Valentín Díaz in Valladolid. Liaño has also been connected with a portrait identified as that of the poet *Alonso de Ercilla* (Budapest, Mus. F.A.), and Lassalle suggested that Liaño painted the portrait of *Isabel Clara Eugenia and the Dwarf Magdalena Ruíz* (Madrid, Prado), so reviving an old attribution that had been unanimously rejected.

BIBLIOGRAPHY

C. Lassalle: 'Felipe de Liaño: El pequeño Tiziano', *Bol. Inst. & Mus. 'Camón Aznar'*, ii–iii (1981), pp. 51–84

ISMAEL GUTIÉRREZ PASTOR

**Liao dynasty.** Northern Chinese dynasty founded by the proto-Mongolian Khitan (Qidan) people, dating to 907–1125. It ruled an area of China north of the Great Wall that included modern Beijing and most of modern Inner Mongolia. There were five capitals, based on the Buddhist idea of the five-fold structure of the universe as illustrated in Tantric *maṇḍala*s, and dual prime ministers, Chinese and Khitan. Yanzhou (modern Beijing) was the southern capital. The Liao period was contemporary with that of the Five Dynasties (907–60) and Northern Song (960–1127; *see* SONG DYNASTY) further south, with whom the Liao traded and from whom they received payment to keep the peace.

The Khitan were a nomadic people with little artistic tradition of their own; they were influenced by Tang (AD 618–907) forms, techniques and decoration. Liao architecture reflects both Tang influence and an adherence to Buddhism, with pagoda shafts having Buddhist group relief decoration of cosmological significance. Liao buildings that remain include the Bai ta (White Pagoda) at Balin, Inner Mongolia, a whitewashed, wide and gently stepped pagoda, typical of Mongolian style; the library for the Bhagavad *sūtra*s (*c.* 1038) of Huayan Lower Temple, DATONG, Shanxi Province, which contains 32 original Liao statues and wooden scripture cabinets in pavilion form; and the Mu ta (Timber Pagoda) in Ying xian (Ying County), Shanxi Province, the oldest surviving Chinese timber pagoda (*see also* CHINA, §II, 2(vi)).

Tang influence is also visible in Liao ceramics, although tomb finds show that Song and other wares were imported. Typical Liao shapes include pilgrim flasks based on nomadic, leather prototypes or imitating metalwork (*see* CHINA, §VII, 3(iv)(a) and fig. 195). Gold and silver wares were also produced using Tang and Song metalworking and gilding techniques. Literary sources and archaeology reveal that Liao burials included such items of metalwork as death masks (*see* CHINA, §X, 1(iv)).

The assimilation of Chinese wealth and culture, combined with Buddhist pacificism, undermined the Khitan's martial spirit. A series of natural disasters and dissension within the ruling family resulted in defeat by the invading Jin (1115–1234), who then went on to overthrow the Northern Song. Remnants of the Liao survived as the Western Liao (1125–1211) in an area around the Tian shan range. These were eventually defeated by the Mongols under Genghis Khan in 1211.

BIBLIOGRAPHY

Fu Lo-huan: *'Nat Pat' and 'Ordos' (Camps and Tents): A Study of the Way of Life and Military Organization of the Khitan Emperors and their People* (London, 1950)

*Liao ci xuanji* [Selection of Liao-period ceramics], Jinzhou, Liaoning Prov. Mus. cat. (Beijing, 1961)

R. Paine: 'A Crown of the Liao Dynasty', *Boston Mus. Bull.*, lxii (1964), no. 328, pp. 44–7

Y. Mino: *Ceramics in the Liao Dynasty North and South of the Great Wall* (New York, 1973)

W. Watson: *Tang and Liao Ceramics* (London, 1984)

*Imperial Gold from Ancient China* (exh. cat. by C. Deydier; London, Orient. Bronzes Ltd, 1990)

CAROL MICHAELSON

**Liautaud, Georges** (*b* Croix des Bouquets, nr Port-au-Prince, 1899; *d* 1991). Haitian sculptor. He lived all his life in the dusty crossroads village where he was born. He was discovered in 1955 by the American watercolourist Dewitt Peters (1901–66) and Antonio Joseph, who had noticed some unusual forged iron crosses in the town cemetery. Inquiring about the maker of these unique crosses, they were directed to a local blacksmith's shop. Liautaud had worked as a mechanic on the sugar railroad. He explained the crosses as belonging to the graves of Vodounists and offered to make some for his visitors. It was the beginning of a long personal career as well as an entire genre of cut and forged metal sculpture in Haiti. He began to include representational elements in his work, cutting forms out of old oil drums or scrap with a hand chisel or hacksaw, as in *Crucifixion* (1959; Washington, DC, Mus. Mod. A. Latin America). The technique demanded physical force and produced a roughly contoured shape whose edges were then filed and smoothed. Liautaud also forged elements, heating and hammering the metal to the desired shape; some details were rounded by hammering over forms or bent so that they extended into space. He often took the loa (spirits) of Vodoun as his subjects, transforming them into personal metaphors suggesting the darker side of Vodoun. His figures have attenuated and often contorted limbs. Crosses symbolic of Legba (spirit guardian of the crossroads) or of Baron Samedi (lord of the cemetery and the realm of the dead) recur in his work. La Sirène, the mermaid, was his favourite subject, which he loved to adorn with trinkets to accent her sensuality.

BIBLIOGRAPHY
S. Rodman: *Where Art is Joy* (New York, 1988), pp. 123–38
*Haïti: Art naïf—art vaudou* (exh. cat., Paris, Grand Pal., 1988)
*Black Art: Ancestral Legacy* (exh. cat., Dallas, TX, Mus. A., 1989)
DOLORES M. YONKER

**Libbey Glass Co.** American glass factory founded by William L. Libbey (1827–83), who had owned the New England Glass Co. in Cambridge, MA, since 1872. In 1888 his son Edward Drummond Libbey (1854–1925) decided to close the factory during a long strike and to take advantage of the natural gas available in the Midwest. When the firm again made glass in 1888, it was as the W. L. Libbey & Son Co. of Toledo, OH; in 1892 it became the Libbey Glass Co. The succes of the Libbey Glass Co. enabled Edward Drummond Libbey to help found the Toledo Museum of Art, OH, in 1901 and to bequeath to it his collection of European paintings, supplemented by a trust provided by his estate.

Many fashionable cut-glass patterns were produced at Libbey during the so-called 'Brilliant Period' between 1880 and 1915, and Libbey produced some magnificent exhibition pieces, including a cut-glass table 813 mm high and a cut-glass floor lamp nearly 1.5 m high. The firm's major product was a more popular line of goods made from blanks; these had previously been pressed in a metal mould in the pattern to be cut, thus avoiding the expense of mould-blowing blanks and marking them for cutting. As one of the most important American cut-glass factories at the time, the firm erected a large crystal palace for the World's Columbian Exposition of 1893 in Chicago. In the exhibition factory glass-blowing and cutting were demonstrated, as were the new methods of spinning and weaving glass fibres for upholstery, drapery and lamp shades.

Libbey became a major force in developing industrial products of glass. The superintendent of the factory, Michael Joseph Owens (1859–1923), developed machinery for producing light bulbs mechanically (*c.* 1892), for moulding tumblers (1895) and for making bottles automatically (1903), which resulted in the establishment of the Owens Bottle Machine Co. In 1929 it merged with the Illinois Glass Co. to become Owens-Illinois Inc. Owens's method of mass production was adopted by the Corning Glass Works in 1916 for its 'Pyrex' line of heat-resistant ovenware. In 1916 Owens developed sheet glass manufacture with Libbey's help, forming a company subsequently called Libbey-Owens-Ford. In 1936 Libbey Glass became a division of Owens-Illinois Inc. In the late 20th century it was producing informal table glass.

BIBLIOGRAPHY
A. C. Revi: *American Cut and Engraved Glass* (New York, 1965)
*Libbey Glass: A Tradition of 150 Years, 1818–1968* (exh. cat. by J. W. Keefe, Toledo, OH, Mus. A., 1968)
ELLEN PAUL DENKER

**Libellus.** *See under* SAINTS' LIVES.

**Libera, Adalberto** (*b* Villa Lagarina, Upper Adige, 1903; *d* Rome, 1963). Italian architect. At the outbreak of World War I his family moved to Parma, where he attended the Scuola Superiore, receiving his architecture degree in 1928. As early as 1926 he was active in the GRUPPO 7, and he is said to have been influential in that group's early writings. He replaced Ubaldo Castagnoli as a fully-fledged member of the group in 1927 and in 1928 he helped to set up the Movimento dell'Architettura Razionale (MAR) and, in 1930, the Movimento Italiano per l'Architettura Razionale (MIAR). In 1928 he began to practise in Rome. With other members of the Milanese and Roman Rationalists, Libera participated in the Weissenhofsiedlung Exhibition in Stuttgart in 1927, where he showed a project for a hotel in the mountains. In 1928 (with Gaetano Minnucci) he organized the first Esposizione dell' Architettura Razionale in Rome and helped organize the second, held in Pier Maria Bardi's gallery in Via Veneto in Rome (1931), which contained Bardi's famous 'Table of Horrors' (*la tavola degli orrori*, caricatures of the Academic architecture of the period) shown to Mussolini. This show prompted the more reactionary architects to form Raggruppimento degli Architetti Moderni Italiani (RAMI) supported by Marcello Piacentini, a force that soon caused the dissolution of MIAR.

Libera continued to design for the regime, however. In 1932 he was selected to design (with Mario De Renzi) the temporary façade for the Tenth Anniversary Exhibit of the Fascist Revolution, held in the Palazzo delle Esposizioni, also in Rome, which became one of the emblems of Italian Modernist (and Fascist) architecture, with its 'Art Deco' stylized *fasci littori* in riveted steel. Libera was to use the same motif on later exhibitions during the 1930s. In 1934 he submitted a project in the competition for the National Fascist Party Headquarters, the Palazzo Littorio:

Adalberto Libera: Palazzo de Ricevimenti e Congressi (Palazzo delle Esposizione), Città Giardino EUR, near Rome, 1937–40

his proposal consisted of an enormous concave wall of building set behind a huge *fascio littorio.* As the winner of another competition he also designed and built the Post Office in the Quartiere Aventino (completed 1934), which has an interior of great subtlety and quality, and remains one of the emblems of Italian Rationalist architecture.

Two buildings of the late 1930s are considered to be Libera's masterpieces. One is the Villa Malaparte, built for Curzio Malaparte on the island of Capri in 1938, an enigmatic design of a block of a house-cum-stair. The second is the winning competition entry for the Palazzo de Ricevimenti e Congressi (Palazzo delle Esposizioni; 1937–40; *see* fig.) in the Città Giardino EUR outside Rome. This building is possibly the finest example of a great interior space in the architecture of 20th-century Italy and is considerably larger than Giuseppe Terragni's interior atrium in the Casa del Fascio (now Casa del Popolo) in Como. The building also portrays the problems of a Fascist and a Modernist architecture. The rear façade is composed of a great curtain wall, braced by elegant vertical bow-trusses, covered by a wide overhanging concrete slab, while at the front vaguely Doric columns support the slab, thus presenting a 'Roman' face to the city.

Libera participated in the planning of E '42, the exposition planned by Mussolini for 1942, but cancelled because of World War II. His 50 m high semicircular arched gateway was copied by Eero Saarinen for his winning entry in the Gateway to the West, St Louis, MO, competition of 1954. Libera and his family threatened Saarinen with a lawsuit. Libera spent almost three years in self-imposed isolation in northern Italy after the war but emerged in 1947 to take up practice in Rome. His post-war buildings are fairly routine and consist mainly of housing. He became director of INA-Casa, the great insurance cooperative housing company: the buildings included most of the development in the Tuscolano housing quarter of Rome (1954). He was responsible for the Olympic Village (with Luigi Moretti, Pier Luigi Nervi and others), Rome (1959–60). From 1953 to 1962 he was Professor of Architecture at the University of Rome.

*See also* RATIONALISM (ii).

BIBLIOGRAPHY
B. Zevi: *Storia dell'architettura moderna* (Turin, 1953)
C. de Seta: *La cultura architettonica in Italia tra le due guerre* (Bari, 1972)
G. C. Argan: *Adalberto Libera* (Rome, 1976)
A. Batey: 'Villa Malaparte', *Archetype*, i/4 (1980), pp. 23–9

THOMAS L. SCHUMACHER

**Liberale (Bonfanti) da Verona** [Liberale di Jacopo dalla Biava] (*b* Verona, *c.* 1445; *d* Verona, 1527–9). Italian illuminator, painter and woodcut designer. His father, the baker Jacopo, came from Monza; his mother, Jacoba, was the daughter of the Veronese painter Zeno Solimani (*fl c.* 1438) and sister of the painter Nicolò Solimani (*fl c.* 1462–1493). The latter, according to Vasari, was Liberale's teacher (but mistakenly called Vincenzo di Stefano in the *Vite*). Liberale is documented in Verona in 1455 and 1465, but works from this period are not known. His career thereafter may be divided into two periods: as a young artist he was based in Siena, where his work on a group of choir-books for the cathedral demonstrates his originality as an illuminator; in or soon after 1476 he returned to Verona, where he established himself as one of the city's major painters. During both periods he travelled and worked in other centres.

1. Siena, *c.* 1467–76. 2. Verona, *c.* 1476 and after.

1. SIENA, *c.* 1467–76. Called to Siena before 1467 by the Olivetans, Liberale illuminated four choir-books (Chiusi, Mus. Cattedrale, Cods A, Q, R and Y) for the

abbey of Monte Oliveto Maggiore. The miniatures show a mixture of styles: Sienese influences, especially the Late Gothic ornament of Sano di Pietro, are combined with such stylistic components from the Veneto and Emilia as sculpturally modelled, animated draperies, expressive physiognomies and tense, nervous gestures. Liberale worked as an illuminator for Siena Cathedral from 1467. After a trial piece (*Christ in Majesty*, U. Birmingham, Barber Inst.), until 1476 he painted miniatures for 16 choir-books and a Missal. He was the first important and most prolific illuminator of this well-preserved series of liturgical books (all Siena, Bib. Piccolomini), and this well-documented nine-year period was the most creative phase of his artistic activity.

The imaginative early miniatures of Graduals 24.9, 20.5 and 25.10 reflect great artistic freedom. Executed between 1467 and autumn 1470, the scenes, full of fresh liveliness, testify to a rapid development and heightening of Liberale's capacity for figural expression and dramatic action in increasingly daring compositions. High points are such brilliant illustrations as the eloquent, ingeniously composed double scene with the *Parable of the Mote and the Beam* and the *Blind Leading the Blind* (1468; Gradual 24.9, fol. 1*r*), or the boldly drawn, furious *North Wind* (1470; Gradual 20.5, fol. 36*v*). Florentine influence was transmitted in part by Liberale's colleague Francesco Rosselli. Alongside these works he executed devotional images, cassoni and a predella, which reveal the influence of Sienese painting shifting from the work of Sano to that of Francesco di Giorgio Martini and Neroccio de' Landi. When GIROLAMO DA CREMONA illuminated three folios of Gradual 28.12 in Siena in early 1470, no noticeable stylistic exchange with Liberale took place. The situation changed abruptly in December 1470. For the most part autonomous up to that point, Liberale received the unfinished gradual with the three miniatures by Girolamo and the commission to decorate further folios after his model. These works, paid for in March 1471, reveal a radical stylistic change in Liberale's ornament: antique scrolls, Ferrarese-influenced fleurons with filigree backgrounds and pearl decoration in the style of Girolamo. Liberale thus abandoned his usual repertory with its Gothic elements and its integration of studies from nature, since this pleased his patrons less than that of the Cremonese artist. On the other hand, Liberale's illustrative style, full of ebullience and charged with tension, remained hardly influenced and, in the expressive dynamism of the *St Michael* (fol. 80*v*), underwent further intensification. The *Crucifixion* (fol. 181*v*) of the Missal (Siena, Bib. Com. Intronati, MS. X.*II*.3), completed in April 1471 for the cathedral, also shows Liberale's typical figures in an orientalizing framework of decorative elements that he derived from Girolamo.

In the following year Liberale executed for Viterbo Cathedral his most inspired painting, the altarpiece of the *Salvator mundi with Four Saints* (*in situ*), dated 1472. After the resumption of his Sienese work in August 1472, Liberale found in the elder Girolamo da Cremona, who for the first time was contemporaneously engaged on the choir-book project, an artistic equal, albeit a more experienced one, and a highly influential colleague. They competed with each other and in the following months spurred

Liberale da Verona: *Angel of the Last Judgement*; historiated initial from an Antiphonal, 1474 (Siena, Biblioteca Piccolomini, 1.A, fol. 133*r*)

each other on to exceptional achievements. Liberale's work was at its peak in the illustration of Gradual 21.6, where spectacular spiritual tension and dramatic intensity is displayed in the *Christ Healing the Possessed* (fol. 2*r*) and in the turbulent *Christ Driven from the Temple* (fol. 74*v*). Under the direct influence of the contemporary masterpieces in Gradual 23.8 by Girolamo, Liberale enlivened the extensive ornamental parts with imaginative antique motifs executed with exceptional care. He adopted the darker, intensely glowing palette of his colleague in the process and began to loosen up the expression and gestures of his figures, as is clear in the *Miracle of the Loaves and Fishes* (fol. 39*r*). Girolamo, for his part, was briefly inspired to livelier representations and more animated draperies. Despite the quality of Liberale's work, the more experienced and efficient Girolamo was for the most part better paid.

The recognition that he had lost his position as dominant illuminator for the Opera del Duomo led to an artistic crisis and explains Liberale's pronouncedly mannered style of illumination from 1473: his settings lost their spontaneity and vitality; resigned melancholy and frustrated indifference overpower the physiognomies of his figures, with their tired, schematic gestures. In 1473 Liberale worked on Graduals 23.8, 16.1, 19.4, 18.3 as well as on parts of 17.2 and 22.7 in close contact with Girolamo. Despite their technical impeccability, his scenes lack artistic engagement, and his figures the inner motivation found in his works up to 1472. The hypothesis of a division of labour (design by Liberale, painting by Girolamo) has been disproved and the contrary documented: after the completion of Graduals 17.2 and 22.7, Liberale completed four miniatures in Antiphonal 10.L during September 1474, which Girolamo had left unfinished after his departure from Siena in early 1474. After that Liberale illuminated the historiated folios of Antiphonal 1.A (see fig.). All these works, carried out with reference to Girolamo, are identical in style to those created before the latter's departure.

Evidence of private commissions is provided by three miniatures from a Book of Hours from the Piccolomini family (Philadelphia, PA, Free Lib., Lewis MS. 118), as well as cassone panels (e.g. New York, Met.) and devotional paintings. Between November 1474 and June 1475 Liberale painted an altarpiece of the *Virgin and Child with Two Saints* (*in situ*) for the Olivetan church of S Francesca Romana in Rome.

Again in Siena, a final, ten-month phase of work on the liturgical books followed, in collaboration with the Milanese artist Venturino Mercati (*fl c.* 1473–9), who executed only ornamental initials. After completion of Antiphonal 10.L, they illuminated the Antiphonals 13.O, 3.C and 12.N, with Liberale consistently working on the front section. The financial crisis of the Opera del Duomo, which led to a five-year interruption in the refurbishing of the choir-books, was one of the reasons for Liberale's return to north Italy.

2. VERONA, c. 1476 AND AFTER. Free from external constraints, Liberale's narrative talent and brio was revealed in the witty pictorial ideas of a printed *Aesop* (Verona, 1479). The masterful inventions of its 68 woodcuts were iconographically influential for decades. Although artistically superior to other local painters, Liberale was again forced to seek work outside Verona. In 1481 he was contracted, together with his uncle Nicolò Solimani, who lived in Mantua, to decorate a chapel in the church of the Annunziata, Rovato, with an extensive pictorial programme. The lost frescoes are his earliest documented wall paintings.

Two paintings for altars dedicated to St Sebastian testify to a later sojourn in Venice: the winged altarpiece probably created for Verona (ex-Albarelli priv. col., Verona; centre panel, Berlin, Kaiser-Friedrich Mus., destr.) and the *St Sebastian* panel (Milan, Brera), originally in Ancona. Both versions are formally based on Venetian models by Antonio Rizzo and Antonello da Messina. The version in Milan, with its Venetian canal view, shows a single-point perspective construction, exceptional in Liberale's oeuvre, which was inspired by paintings of Jacopo Bellini and his school. Still in Venice in 1487, where he was also influenced by Bartolomeo Vivarini, Liberale returned to Verona, probably in 1488, and was married in 1489. The Olivetan *Virgin with Four Saints* (Berlin, Gemäldegal.) and the predella painted for a sculptural altar of the Virgin for Verona Cathedral (Verona, Pal. Vescovile) both date from 1489. Grouped with these paintings, which are characterized by feverish theatricality and sculptural, metallic drapery style, are two major works, the emotional *Pietà* (Munich, Alte Pin.), and the richly coloured composition of unusual iconography, the *Adoration of the Magi* (Verona

Cathedral), in which Liberale interpreted his home town as a *minor Ierusalem*.

Liberale was, with Domenico Morone, the most active painter in Verona. He influenced the style of the Veronese artists Cristoforo Scacco (*fl c.* 1493–1500), Giovanni Maria Falconetto, Francesco Dai Libri and the exuberant protomannerist Francesco di Bettino (*fl c.* 1495), who was deeply impressed by Bernardino Butinone. His closest followers were Nicola Giolfino, Gian Francesco Caroto, Giovanni Caroto, Antonio da Vendri (*fl c.* 1485–1545) and Francesco Torbido. His professional success around 1490 reflected his personal happiness as demonstrated by the intimate pen drawing of the *Nursing Mother* (Vienna, Albertina), probably of his first wife, Ginevra, with one of their daughters. The virtuoso drawing of *Musicmaking Angels* (London, BM) is a sketch for the frescoes of the Bonaveri Chapel in S Anastasia, which, together with the altarpiece of the *Assumption of St Mary Magdalene* (*in situ*), were his main accomplishments of the early 1490s. The figures—some vital and lively and some inexpressive and hastily painted—show variations in quality. These signs of failing creative ability are corroborated by the fact that the Olivetans of S Maria in Organo commissioned the 50-year-old painter as an illuminator of subordinate status to Francesco and Girolamo Dai Libri.

During the last 30 years of his life, Liberale's work became conservative, although he continued to find customers, not only for numerous devotional paintings, but also for large public altarpieces and frescoes (lower church, S Fermo Maggiore). A Breviary (Treviso, Bib. Com., MS. 888) documents Liberale's late attempt to modernize his formal repertory as an illuminator. His will of 1527 indicates that he was at work on an *Assumption of the Virgin* for Verona Cathedral.

BIBLIOGRAPHY

G. Vasari: *Vite* (1550, rev. 2/1568); ed. G. Milanesi (1878–85), pp. 274–80

R. Brenzoni: *Liberale da Verona* (Milan, 1930)

E. Carli: *Miniature di Liberale da Verona dai corali per il Duomo di Siena* (Milan, 1953)

C. Del Bravo: *Liberale da Verona* (Florence, 1967) [with earlier bibliog.]

B. Berenson: *Central and North Italian Schools* (1968), pp. 209–14

H.-J. Eberhardt: 'Das Testament des Liberale da Verona', *Mitt. Ksthist. Inst. Florenz*, xv (1971), pp. 219–25

R. Brenzoni: *Dizionario di artisti veneti* (Florence, 1972), pp. 172–8

M. G. Ciardi Dupré: *I corali del Duomo di Siena* (Milan, 1972)

F. Bisogni: 'Liberale o Girolamo?', *A. Illus.*, vi (1973), pp. 400–08

G. Mardersteig and L. Magagnato: *Liberale ritrovato nell'Esopo veronese del 1479* (Verona, 1973)

H.-J. Eberhardt: 'Liberale da Verona', *Maestri della pittura veronese*, ed. P. Brugnoli (Verona, 1974), pp. 101–12

L. Menegazzi: 'Il *Breviarium Cartusianum* di Treviso', *Crit. A.*, n.s., xliii (1978), nos 160–62, pp. 67–78

M. T. Cuppini: 'L'arte a Verona tra XV e XVI secolo', *Verona e il suo territorio*, IV/i (Verona, 1981), pp. 241–522

H.-J. Eberhardt: 'Sull'attività senese di Liberale da Verona, Girolamo da Cremona, Venturino da Milano, Giovanni da Udine e Prete Carlo da Venezia', *La miniatura italiana tra Gotico e Rinascimento: Atti del II congresso di storia della miniatura italiana: Cortona, 1982*, i, pp. 415–34

*Codici liturgici miniati dei Benedettini in Toscana* (exh. cat., ed. M. G. Ciardi Dupré Dal Poggetto; Florence, Certosa del Galluzzo, Pin., 1982)

H.-J. Eberhardt: *Die Miniaturen von Liberale da Verona: Girolamo da Cremona und Venturino da Milano in den Chorbüchern des Doms von Siena* (Munich, 1983)

G. Mariani Canova: 'Miniatura rinascimentale veronese', *A. Ven.*, xl (1986), pp. 278–84

*Miniatura veronese del Rinascimento* (exh. cat., ed. G. Castiglioni and S. Marinelli; Verona, Castelvecchio, 1986)

A. De Marchi: 'Liberale da Verona', *La pittura in Italia: Il quattrocento*, 2 vols, ed. F. Zeri (Milan, 1986, rev. 2/1987), ii, pp. 664f

L. Rognini: 'Per la genealogia di Liberale da Verona: I Solimani pittori', *Civiltà Veron.*, ii/6 (1986), pp. 13–20

*Paintings in Renaissance Siena, 1420–1500* (exh. cat., ed. K. Christiansen, L. B. Kanter and C. B. Strehlke; New York, Met., 1988–9) [entries by K. Christiansen; bibliog.]

*Francesco di Giorgio e il Rinascimento a Siena, 1450–1500* (exh. cat., ed. L. Bellosi; Siena, S. Agostino, 1993) [entries by L. Bellosi and A. De Marchi]

*The Painted Page: Italian Renaissance Book Illumination, 1450–1550* (exh. cat., ed. J. J. G. Alexander; London, RA, 1994)

HANS-JOACHIM EBERHARDT

**Liberatore, Niccolò di.** *See* NICCOLÒ DA FOLIGNO.

**Libergier, Hugues** (*fl* 1231; *d* Reims, 1263). French architect. He was master mason of the Benedictine abbey church of St Nicaise, Reims, begun in 1231 (destr.; *see* REIMS, §IV, 2). Libergier probably established the plan of the entire church and directed construction work on the nave and the extraordinary west front. In certain respects the plan was influenced by Cistercian buildings, but the treatment of the three-storey elevation, in which the relatively large clerestory was linked to the triforium by continuous mullions, was new. The magnificent twin-towered west façade was probably begun some time after the start of work (perhaps towards 1250). Its seven gables were arranged in a rhythmic composition across the front surface of the four buttresses, creating shallow pockets of space for the porches; the entire central bay of the façade was unified by tracery.

The image of Hugues Libergier engraved in his tomb slab, originally in the nave of St Nicaise but now in Reims Cathedral, expresses most forcefully the elevated status of the Gothic master mason. Dressed in an elegant robe and cape, holding his measuring cane in the left hand and a model of the church that he had designed in the right, the master is flanked by the instruments of his profession, square and compass, and enclosed in a gabled, cusped arch above which are two censing angels. The inscription around the frame reads: CY GIST MAISTRE HUES LIBER-GIERS QUI COMENSA CESTE EGLISE AN [EN] LAN DE LINCARNATION MCC ET XXIX *[sic]* LE MARDI DE PAQUES ET TRESPASSA LAN DE LINCARNATION MCCLXIII LE SE-MEDI APRES PAQUES POUR D[I]EU P[R]IEZ PO[U]R LUI ('Here lies Master Hues Libergier who began this church in 1229 AD [sic], the Tuesday of Easter, and died the Saturday after Easter in 1263 AD. Pray for him to God').

BIBLIOGRAPHY

C. Giverlet: *L'Eglise et l'abbaye de Saint-Nicaise de Reims: Notice historique et archéologique sur l'architecture depuis leurs origines jusqu'à leur destruction* (Reims, 1897)

H. Deneux: 'L'Ancienne Eglise Saint-Nicaise de Reims', *Bull. Mnmtl*, lxxxv (1926), pp. 117–52

P. du Columbier: *Les Chantiers des cathédrales* (Paris, 1953)

R. Branner: *Saint Louis and the Court Style in Gothic Architecture* (London, 1965)

K. Bauch: *Das mittelalterliche Grabbild: Figürliche Grabmäler des 11. bis 15. Jahrhunderts in Europa* (Berlin and New York, 1976)

M. Bideault and C. Lautier: 'Saint-Nicaise de Reims: Chronologie et nouvelles remarques sur l'architecture', *Bull. Mnmtl*, cxxxv (1977), pp. 295–330

STEPHEN MURRAY

**Liberi, Pietro** (*b* Padua, 1605; *d* Venice, 8 Oct 1687). Italian painter. He moved to Venice at an early age and studied with Alessandro Varotari (il Padovanino). Travels from 1628 to 1638 took him to Constantinople, Tunis and several European countries. In Rome from 1638 to 1640, he copied the frescoes of Michelangelo and Raphael, studied the works of the Carracci, Pietro da Cortona and Guido Reni, and also came under the prevailing influence of Gianlorenzo Bernini. His earliest known work, the *Rape of the Sabines* (1641; Siena, Pin. N.), richly reflects this experience of Rome. On his return journey to Venice (*c.* 1643) he stopped in Bologna and may have seen works by Emilian artists, from Correggio to Reni, in Parma.

Liberi did not receive his first official commission in Venice until 1650, when he painted his *Mary Magdalene at the Foot of the Cross* (Venice, SS Giovanni e Paolo). Like *St Anthony Interceding on Behalf of Venice* (1652; Venice, S Maria della Salute), it unites a decidedly Baroque composition and dramatic intensity with light tonalities inherited from Veronese. In the same period he executed the fresco decoration of the Villa Minelli at Ponzano Veneto, where spirited female figures, which look back to 16th-century Venice, move within a Baroque architectural setting. This work established Liberi as a mediator between Venetian tradition and the Baroque of central Italy.

The frescoes in the Villa Negrelli at Stra, executed in collaboration with the *quadraturista* Domenico Bruni (?1591–1666), date from 1652. The two main scenes, *Allegory of the Arts and Sciences* and *Allegory of War and Peace*, demonstrate the increasing originality of Liberi's style, and are early examples of an interest in sensual and erotic 'libertine' subjects that made for his success with collectors. By now a painter of considerable renown (in 1653 he was made a Cavaliere di S Marco), between 1650 and 1670 he executed many mythological and allegorical paintings, such as *Venus* (Vercelli, Mus. Civ. Borgogna), *Allegory* (Venice, Gal. Querini–Stampalia) and the *Toilet of Bathsheba* (Munich, Alte Pin.), all of which are distinguished Baroque reinterpretations of 16th-century subjects. In 1658 he made a journey through Austria, Hungary and Bohemia, where he created numerous works for the Holy Roman Emperor Leopold I (who made him a Count Palatine) and for private collectors. Shortly after his return to Venice in 1659 he painted the *Brazen Serpent* for the cathedral of S Pietro di Castello in Venice, a vast canvas characterized by swirling brushwork and an unprecedented dramatic power, emphasized by his free and bold handling. His celebratory canvas depicting the *Venetian Victory at the Dardanelles* (1660–64; see fig.), painted for the Sala dello Scrutinio in the Palazzo Ducale, is even more unrestrained.

Liberi continued to produce an uninterrupted flow of secular subjects; outstanding works of the 1670s include *Venus and the Graces* (Venice, Pal. Albrizzi), *Diana* (Berlin, Gemäldegal.) and *Medorus and Angelica* (Schleissheim, Neues Schloss). The latter work suggests an awareness of the compositional techniques of Sebastiano Mazzoni, a friend of Liberi, who designed for him the Florentine Palazzo Moro-Lin on the Grand Canal (built 1671–3).

With the help of his son Marco (*b c.* 1644) Liberi completed the fresco decoration of the sacristy vault in the basilica of S Antonio (il Santo) in Padua with the

Pietro Liberi: *Venetian Victory at the Dardanelles*, oil on canvas, 1660–64 (Venice, Doge's Palace)

*Virgin Appearing to St Anthony* (1665); here his feeling for colour is secondary to the dramatic intensity. A little later he decorated a few rooms in the Palazzo Ferro Fini on the Grand Canal, where he painted a series of canvases of *Allegories of the Virtues and Vices*. His later works are characterized by increasing chiaroscuro: his *Vision of Augustus* (Vicenza, S Maria del Aracoeli) and *Ecstasy of St Gertrude* (1676–8; Padua, S Giustina) are elegant works in this vein. This development reached its height in the *Marriage of St Catherine* (1676–82; Vicenza, S Caterina), a rich, virtuoso display of brilliant colour, in sharp contrast to the sombre works of the tenebrists.

BIBLIOGRAPHY

G. G. Priorato: *Vite del Cavaliere Pietro Liberi pittore padovano scritta lui vivente* (1664), ed. L. Trissino (1818)
F. d'Arcais: 'La formazione di Pietro Liberi', *Crit. A.*, lxxxviii (1967), pp. 58–68
——: *Gli affreschi nelle ville venete dal seicento all'ottocento* (Venice, 1978)
R. Pallucchini: *La pittura veneziana del seicento*, 2 vols (Milan, 1981), i, pp. 196–206
V. Sgarbi: 'Sacro e profano nella pittura di Pietro Liberi', *Le ricche minere della pittura veneziana* (Rome, 1982), pp. 105–17
M. Gregori and E. Schleier, eds: *La pittura in Italia: Il seicento*, 2 vols (Milan, 1989), p. 786 [with full bibliog.]

FILIPPO PEDROCCO

**Liberia**, Republic of. Country on the west coast of Africa, bordered by Sierra Leone to the north-west, Guinea to the north-east and Côte d'Ivoire to the east. Liberia has a total area of about 111,369 sq. km and a population of 2,508,000 (UN estimate, 1989). The capital is Monrovia and the official language English. Liberia lies in a region of tropical rain-forests. The staple food crop is rice and the primary exports rubber, iron ore and timber. The Liberian State was established by repatriated slaves and freedmen from the USA, commonly referred to as Americo-Liberians. The settlers, who began arriving on the coast in 1822, declared their independence in 1847, thereby establishing Africa's first republic. Since 1990 the nation has been convulsed by civil war affecting all aspects of civil and cultural life. This entry covers the art produced in Liberia since the foundation of the Liberian State; for the art of the area in earlier times, *see* AFRICA, §VII, 4. *See also* DAN; KISSI; and MENDE.

1. CONTINUING TRADITIONS. Historically, the Americo-Liberian community has been concentrated in a few urban coastal centres. The community has continued to preserve many of its aesthetic traditions, including quilting, music, dance and architecture, brought to Liberia from the southern USA. In addition to the Americo-Liberian community, 16 other ethnic groups with their own aesthetic traditions are recognized officially. These ethnic groups can be clustered into three larger units based on similarities of artistic style and shared cultural institutions. These larger units fall into three geographic regions.

The first region is the western part of the country where the Vai, Gola, Mende and De produce closely related mask forms, the most important type being the wooden helmet masks of the Sande secret society for women. Such masks, known as Sowo or Sowei among the Vai and Mende, and Zogbe among the Gola and De, uniquely in Africa are worn and owned by women. The masks play an extremely important role in Sande ritual, embodying the spirit-force that protects and empowers the women's society.

The second region is in the north-western area, where the Loma, Bande and Kissi live. There the use of all mask types is very restricted. Although some can be seen by anyone, others can only be seen by initiates of the Poro, the men's secret society.

The third region is eastern Liberia, best known for the wooden masks and sculptures of the Dan and We peoples (both of whom are also found in Côte d'Ivoire). The range of mask types is exceptionally wide here. Many variations on specific mask types are found within ethnic groups as well as across ethnic boundaries.

2. ARCHITECTURE. Traditionally almost all architecture was domestic. Although there was a wide range of house types, most were circular wattle-and-daub construction with conical thatched roofs. The men's and women's secret societies continue to build meeting-houses as well as ritual fences on the outskirts of their villages. The women's structures remain unpainted, but the men's are commonly decorated with elaborate painted designs.

In their coastal settlements Americo-Liberians built houses patterned after early 19th-century types found in tidewater areas of Virginia and the Carolinas. In 1847 the first government buildings were built in Georgian style. The most prominent of these was the National Legislative Hall (1862; converted to the National Museum in 1987) in Monrovia. Most 19th-century churches and a number of private residences built in southern American styles still stand; but many buildings, particularly private residences, were demolished in the late 20th century. Afro-Brazilian styles, used primarily for domestic buildings but occasionally for commercial ones, were popular in the 1920s. Many buildings from that era remain intact.

During an economic boom in the 1950s and 1960s a number of government buildings, including the Executive Mansion, the Capitol and the Supreme Court (all Monrovia), were constructed in modern international styles, by firms from Italy and the USA. During the same period the True Whig Party Headquarters was built in the same style by the most prominent Liberian architectural firm, Milton and Richards.

3. PAINTING, GRAPHIC ARTS AND SCULPTURE. Traditionally painting and graphic arts were limited almost exclusively to decorating the exteriors of private dwellings and the walls of the men's secret society houses. Women decorated private dwellings with geometric designs, while figurative representations, whether on dwellings or on men's society houses, were painted by men. Until the mid-20th century the Americo-Liberian community produced almost no painting, graphic arts or sculpture. What was produced was primarily Christian-orientated religious art.

In the 1960s, however, a group of artists began to emerge. Some had been trained abroad. The number of artists increased in the 1970s and 1980s, and a number of exhibitions were held. Unfortunately, the outbreak of the civil war in 1990 devastated the artistic community. Two of Liberia's most important artists, Vanjah Richards, a sculptor, and Jallah Kollie, a painter and graphic artist,

were killed, and Liberia's most prominent painter, Cietta Mensah, went to live in exile in the USA, where she had received her formal art education. Mensah's work is abstract expressionist, executed in acrylic on canvas. Before the war she taught art at the University of Liberia. Liberia's other major abstract expressionist painter, Winston Richards, is also acclaimed as an architect.

Wantue Major, a graphic artist active in Liberia, produced early works depicting scenes from daily life and the architecture of Americo-Liberian settlements. His later works focused increasingly on political and social commentary, particularly in response to the horrors of the war. The painter Omar Al Shabu also received international attention for his colourful canvases (Kennedy, pp. 93–4).

4. PATRONAGE AND ART INSTITUTIONS. Modern Liberian artists have had few patrons. By far the most successful modern sculptor was Vanjah Richards, who received major commissions to produce interior screens at the Ducor Palace Hotel and Hotel Africa and also for exterior work on the True Whig Party Headquarters (all Monrovia). For these works Richards sculpted representational scenes from Liberian history and folklore. Until the beginning of the civil war in 1990, Liberia had thriving antiquities and tourist art markets. These were almost exclusively in the hands of Manding dealers from Guinea, who were forced out of the country during the war.

Before the civil war there were five museums in Liberia. Of these, the William V. S. Tubman Museum in Harper and the Tubman Center for African Culture in Robertsport were essentially libraries that also housed small art and ethnographic collections. The National Museum, fully restored and refurbished in 1986, was looted during the civil war, and only a handful of objects and photographs remain.

The Africana Museum at Cuttington University College houses the largest and by far the most important art collection in Liberia. It contains more than 2000 items including a full range of traditional art objects from all parts of the country. The focus is on masks and figurative sculpture, but the museum also contains an important group of ceramics and archaeological materials.

Before the civil war art education was a significant part of the work of the National Museum, which conducted tours and outreach programmes for students in schools in Monrovia. Although a number of private schools had art education programmes, none existed in government schools. Both the University of Liberia and Cuttington University College offered non-degree courses in art history and studio art.

BIBLIOGRAPHY

*Liberia: Arts and Crafts* (Monrovia, n.d.)

G. Schwab and G. W. Harley: *Tribes of the Liberian Hinterland*, Pap. Peabody Mus. Archaeol. & Ethnol., xxxi (Cambridge, MA, 1947)

G. W. Harley: *Masks as Agents of Social Control in North-east Liberia*, Pap. Peabody Mus. Archaeol. & Ethnol., xxxii/2 (Cambridge, MA, 1950/R New York, 1975)

K. Zetterström: *House and Settlement in Liberia* (Robertsport, 1970)

B. W. Robinson: 'The African Art Trade in Monrovia', *Liber. Stud. J.*, vi/1 (1975), pp. 73–9

*Rock of the Ancestors: Ngamoa Koni* (exh. cat. by W. Siegmann and C. Schmidt, Suakoko, Cuttington Coll. Mus., 1977)

*Ethnol. Z. Zürich*, i (1980) [special issue on initiation and masking traditions in Liberia, Sierra Leone and Côte d'Ivoire]

*Liberia-Forum* (1985–)

M. Belcher, S. E. Holsoe and B. L. Herman: *A Land and Life Remembered: Americo-Liberian Folk Architecture* (Athens, GA, 1988)

S. Peters and others, eds: *Directory of Museums in Africa/Répertoire des musées en Afrique* (London and New York, 1990)

J. Kennedy: *New Currents, Ancient Rivers: Contemporary African Artists in a Generation of Change* (Washington, DC, and London, 1992)

WILLIAM C. SIEGMANN

**Liberty**, Sir **Arthur Lasenby** (*b* Chesham, Bucks, 13 Aug 1843; *d* The Lee, Bucks, 11 May 1917). English merchant. In 1862 he joined Farmer & Rogers's Oriental Warehouse in Regent Street, London. In 1875 he left to set up on his own and on 15 May 1875 he opened his first shop, East India House, at 218A Regent Street, London, which was an immediate success. His imported coloured Eastern silks were an important element in the Aesthetic Movement and their weaves and dyes were later produced for him in 'Liberty colours' by English textile converters. He imported a wide range of furnishings from Japan and the Far East, soon supplemented by the products of the ARTS AND CRAFTS MOVEMENT. In 1884 he opened a dress department managed by E. W. Godwin, a crusader for dress reform, and Liberty gowns soon became high fashion. The Paris branch, set up in 1890, helped to introduce the English version of the Art Nouveau style to the Continent. Liberty's became a public company in 1894, and by the 1890s Arthur Liberty had become a public figure, credited with having created an entirely new taste in fabrics, dress and interior decoration. His friendship with Christopher Dresser, and his own idea of combining the elements of Celtic design and ornament with those of Art Nouveau, led in 1899 to the launch of the Cymric collection of silver and jewellery, followed in 1903 by Tudric domestic pewterware. Both ranges were very successful, and their designs, together with those of Liberty fabrics and wall hangings, are the best examples of English Art Nouveau.

From the early 1900s an increasing amount of Liberty's time was taken up by his large estate in Buckinghamshire. In 1913 he was knighted and the following year he retired from the company. Early in his career Liberty was described as having brought art to the tea table. He was an outstanding shopkeeper who always kept in touch with popular taste, realized the need to stay slightly ahead of changes in such taste and relied almost entirely on the artistic judgement of others. He wanted to produce objects that were useful and beautiful at a reasonable price, and designs were modified so that they could be mass-produced by mechanical means. This entailed diluting the ideals of the Arts and Crafts Movement in order to make their products more affordable: the Cymric and Tudric ranges, for example, although described as 'hand finished' were, in the main, machine-made (*see* MASS PRODUCTION). Liberty commissioned work from many well-known designers (including W. R. Lethaby, ARCHIBALD KNOX, the Silver Studio), but as a matter of company policy work was never attributed.

BIBLIOGRAPHY

J. Laver: *The Liberty Story* (London, 1959)

A. Adburgham: *Liberty's: A Biography of a Shop* (London, 1975)

JOHN MAWER

**Library.** Building for storage of and access to texts. Over time the format of texts has changed, from papyrus rolls and cuneiform tablets, to codices, to printed books, to microforms, and the technology of storage and the notion of 'access' have also changed significantly. Library buildings in turn have evolved.

Libraries have often hosted other activities, including lectures and the display of art and artefacts. These roles extend back to the Hellenistic period (323–31 BC), were revived in the Renaissance and Baroque libraries of Europe, and have found new emphasis in the 20th century.

Libraries also have performed important symbolic roles: they preserve knowledge, inspire scholars, and measure cultural achievement for institutions or entire nations; they also provide an opportunity for enlightened patronage. These symbolic functions have been expressed in various furnishings: for example, gates and chains protect medieval bookcases; allegorical motifs or emblems serve to glorify the arts and sciences; authors' portraits may inspire readers; and donors' portraits immortalize their dedication to literature.

I. Ancient and Classical world. II. Later development.

*I. Ancient and Classical world.*

1. ANCIENT NEAR EAST. The cuneiform system of writing on clay tablets was developed in southern Mesopotamia (now Iraq) before 3000 BC (*see* ANCIENT NEAR EAST, §I, 3), and during the next three millennia it spread throughout the Ancient Near East. Tablets have survived in numerous temple, palace and private archives that were primarily administrative in purpose (e.g. MARI; EBLA; and NUZI). They were stored in baskets, bags, jars and on wooden shelves. The Assyrian king Assurbanipal (*reg* 668–627 BC) sent scribes to collect and copy ancient texts in archives throughout Mesopotamia and built up a library of some 26,000 tablets that was housed in NINEVEH in his own palace and in that of his predecessor Sennacherib (*reg* 704–681 BC). These tablets are now in the British Museum in London, but their ancient method of storage was not recorded when they were excavated in the late 19th century.

In the Neo-Babylonian (6th century BC) temple library at SIPPAR, the tablets were set on edge in small niches arranged in horizontal rows on three sides of a room. Other systems of writing, on perishable materials, also existed; among them was the Phoenician script that gradually replaced cuneiform from the 8th century BC onwards. Such documents rarely survive, and their methods of storage are not known.

2. GREECE AND ROME. Ancient Greek and Roman libraries were located in palaces, municipal buildings and temples, and some were open to the public. Written sources are not very specific about their architectural form, and Vitruvius's few comments on libraries, describing their eastwards orientation, are found in his discussion of domestic architecture rather than public buildings (*On Architecture*, VI.iv.1 and vii.3). Libraries are difficult to identify archaeologically, as their wooden furnishings have perished.

*(i) Buildings.* The earliest library buildings about which much is known are Hellenistic, although these were preceded by the renowned collections of Peisistratos and Aristotle in Classical Athens. The most famous Hellenistic library was the collection begun by Ptolemy I Soter (*reg c.* 305–282 BC) in the early 3rd century BC in Alexandria as part of the Mouseion, an academy on the palace grounds. A smaller collection in the Serapeion became the main Alexandrian library after the Mouseion was destroyed by fire. The Attalid rulers of Pergamon entered into notorious bibliographic competition with Alexandria after King Eumenes II established a library *c.* 175 BC. Excavations suggest that the Pergamene library was located in the north stoa of the Sanctuary of Athena. In the Roman period a library was also established in the Asklepieion.

The Flemish classicist Justus Lipsius observed in 1602 that of the twenty-nine institutional libraries recorded in Constantinian Rome, tantalizingly brief descriptions of only seven remained. The earliest was the public library erected by C. Asinius Pollio in the Atrium Libertatis (*c.* 39–33 BC). Augustus built a pair of Greek and Latin libraries near the portico of the Temple of Apollo on the Palatine, and sponsored the restoration of the Porticus Octaviae, which included Greek and Latin libraries. Tiberius installed a library in his Palatine residence. The Flavian Templum Pacis is thought to have housed a library, although it may simply have been a records office. At the Forum Traiani important Greek and Roman libraries stood adjacent to the Basilica Ulpia. Exedrae in the Baths of Trajan and Caracalla have been proposed as libraries, although they may simply have been lecture rooms.

In the 2nd century AD library-building activity shifted to the provincial capitals, including the Library of Celsus at Ephesos (*c.* AD 110–15; *see* ROME, ANCIENT, fig. 46), the Rogatinus Library at Timgad (Thamugadi) and the library at Nysa. Athens had no notable library building until the Roman era, when Pantainos erected one in a colonnade next to the Stoa of Attalos. Hadrian's beneficence to Athens included the richly decorated library at one end of a large peristyle court (*see* ROME, ANCIENT, fig. 43). Pausanias described its columns of Phrygian stone as 'most splendid of all' the Athenian structures of that era (*Guide to Greece*, I.xviii.9).

*(ii) Internal features.* Features thought to characterize Hellenistic library interiors include a main lecture room (*oikos*) lined with podia and a statue niche or pedestal; and separate book storage rooms. They were usually part of larger building complexes, opening on to stoas. They may have evolved from the exedral rooms of the gymnasium, or palaestra as described by Vitruvius (*On Architecture*, V.xi.2). Roman libraries combined book storage and reading space: elevated rectangular niches apparently held bookcases, with podia providing limited access; colonnaded galleries were sometimes included; insulating corridors often provided protection from dampness. Roman libraries also exhibited greater independence from surrounding porticos, and a dominant lengthwise axis in contrast to the short-axis orientation of Greek libraries. Later Roman provincial libraries tended to fuse Greek and Roman traits. For instance, reconstructions show the Library of Celsus at Ephesos on a free-standing podium,

but with a short-axis orientation culminating in an apsidal niche. The niche surmounted Celsus's crypt, providing an unusual secondary function as sepulchral monument. The library had a gallery and insulating corridor.

Roman writers provide glimpses of richly decorated library interiors. Many details, however, remain unclear, including whether bookcases had doors, and how they were mounted on plinths or in wall niches. Papyrus rolls were stacked with their decorated edges and labels showing (Cicero: *Letters to Atticus*, IV.viii), and wooden bookcases were ornamented with precious inlays (Seneca: *De tranquillate animi*, IX). Portrait busts inspired readers (Pliny: *Natural History*, XXXV.ii.9–10). The Library of Hadrian at Athens displayed gilded ceilings, walls lined with alabaster, statues and paintings (Pausanias: *Guide to Greece*, I.viii.9).

BIBLIOGRAPHY
Pauly–Wissowa: 'Bibliotheken'
C. Callmer: 'Antike Bibliotheken', *Opuscula Archaeol.*, iii (1944), pp. 145–93
C. Wendel: 'Die bauliche Entwicklung der antiken Bibliothek', *Centbl. Bibwsn*, lxiii (1949), pp. 407–28
——: 'Antike Bibliotheken', *Handbuch der Bibliothekswissenschaft*, ed. G. Leyh (Stuttgart, 1955), iii, pp. 51–145
E. Makowiecka: *The Origin and Evolution of the Architectural Form of the Roman Library*, Studia Antiqua (Warsaw, 1978)
V. M. Strocka: 'Römische Bibliotheken', *Gymnasium*, lxxxviii (1981), pp. 298–329
K. R. Veenhof, ed.: *Cuneiform Archives and Libraries* (Leiden, 1986)

## II. Later development.

1. Before the 19th century. 2. 19th century. 3. 20th century.

### 1. BEFORE THE 19TH CENTURY.

(i) Europe. (ii) Islamic lands. (iii) East Asia.

*(i) Europe.*

(a) Medieval. (b) Renaissance and Baroque. (c) Rococo. (d) Neo-classical.

*(a) Medieval.* After the destruction or dissolution of ancient libraries, written literature in Europe survived in tiny monastic collections rarely numbering over 100 volumes. Parchment codices had replaced papyrus rolls by the 5th century AD, but the ancient practice of storing texts in *armaria* or wooden cupboards continued. Often these were still set in recessed niches, in the cloister wall outside the transept entrance to abbey churches. Serious readers had to be content with a seat in the cloister; in fact, study carrels (enclosed wooden desks) were installed in cloister bays at Gloucester and Canterbury cathedrals. In time various small vaulted rooms off the cloisters housed book chests and treasuries. Guidelines for book collecting were established by the founders of various orders, especially St Benedict, and under Charlemagne, but reading was often secondary to manuscript production (*see* CAROLINGIAN ART, §IV, 3). The plan for St Gall Abbey (*c.* 820; for illustration *see* ST GALL ABBEY) showed an ideal library, a two-storey, free-standing building with the essential SCRIPTORIUM on the ground floor.

In the late 13th century and 14th the fully equipped 'monastic' library room finally developed in response to the broader educational role of clerics, especially at newly founded universities. While books were still distributed from chests, reference collections intended for prolonged consultation had to accommodate a greater number and variety of readers. The typical library building was a long narrow room furnished with rows of lectern desks having slanted reading surfaces and attached benches, low windows between the projecting desks, and a central aisle. An important early model was the Sorbonne in Paris, where an extraordinary collection numbering over 1000 volumes in 1289 was housed on 28 lecterns. Chains connecting heavy bound folios to metal rods on the desks provided the security required for increased 'public' access. Libraries were generally elevated above the ground floor for security and protection against dampness; they were undistinguished from the exterior in cloister ranges except for evenly spaced windows ideally found on both of the long walls.

During the 15th century there occurred an architectural maturation of the monastic library, which nevertheless remained medieval in spirit. In England most of the colleges at Oxford and Cambridge received their own library rooms, and Humphrey, Duke of Gloucester (1391–1447) bequeathed a collection that was housed in a library with tall pointed windows over the Divinity School at Oxford (1488), restored in the early 17th century by Sir Thomas Bodley (1545–1613). Patrons' crests and emblems of learning decorated carved ends of lecterns, the truss ceiling in Duke Humphrey's library, and stained window quarries. In northern Europe libraries occupied rooms having a variety of vaulting and pier supports at Troyes Cathedral (1477–9), Rouen Cathedral (1477–9) and Noyon Cathedral (1507). In early Renaissance Italy a basilical form was adapted to the monastic aisled library. In the monastery of S Marco in Florence (1441), Cosimo de' Medici had Michelozzo di Bartolomeo design a library neatly organizing lecterns in cross-vaulted aisles flanking a taller barrel-vaulted passage supported by a simple Ionic order. At Cesena, Novello Malatesta asked Matteo Nuti to erect a similar library in 1452; it echoes the calm green walls of the Libreria Marciana in Venice (following guidelines laid down by Isidore of Seville), but the surviving lecterns indicate the dark medieval atmosphere, despite composite heraldic columns and an aedicular entrance. Even the Vatican collections, revived under Nicholas V and grown to 2500 volumes under Sixtus IV, are depicted on narrow lecterns in a view by Melozzo da Forlì (1475).

In the 16th century political uncertainties in northern Europe probably fostered the conservatism that persisted in institutional libraries. In Zutphen at the church of SS Peter and Walburga, a faithful interpretation of a Gothic library was built as late as 1561–4, with two aisles (no central passage here), octagonal piers and ribbed vaulting. At Oxford and Cambridge stall shelving was widely applied at the end of the century in order to accommodate collections beginning to expand beyond the typical 500 volumes. Extra shelves were simply added above the lecterns, shelving books vertically in a much more economical use of space. Academic conservatism retained book-chains at Oxford into the mid-18th century, and it has preserved many collegiate 'monastic' libraries to the present day, creating the impression of a distinctive architectural type. Forms of stall shelving also appeared on the Continent, however, as noted in a view dated 1610 of the University of Leiden library.

*(b) Renaissance and Baroque.* In the early Renaissance private library collections began to grow, inspired by the revival of humanistic literature, and the emergence of a commercial trade in manuscripts and fine printing. In well-stocked private cabinets books were supplemented by maps, globes, coins and artefacts. Humanist scholars inspired bibliophiles to emulate ancient Roman liberality by opening private collections to scholars.

Palace libraries achieved a new monumentality in 16th-century Italy and Spain, where commissions were given to important architects who experimented with new forms of shelving to provide a greater storage capacity in a unified design. In 1523 Clement VII asked Michelangelo to house the Medici collection over the cloisters of S Lorenzo in Florence. When the Biblioteca Laurenziana was finally completed in 1571, its rows of carved lectern desks seemed archaic, but the rhythmic repetition of a Classical architectural order in an uninterrupted span was influential (see fig. 1 and MICHELANGELO, fig. 10). The Laurenziana also formalized a type of room sequence that underwent various modifications in the next two centuries: a large staircase, an anteroom (here combined with the stair in unsettling Mannerist proportions), the long hall for display of books, and a more secluded area housing special collections. In Venice the Libreria Marciana's *c.* 27 m long *salone* and vestibule occupied just half of the Procuratia begun in 1536 under Jacopo Sansovino, and completed in 1581–3 by Vincenzo Scamozzi (see VENICE, §IV, 7). The superimposed arcades of this civic structure impressed Palladio, who considered it the 'richest and most adorned edifice' since the Romans. Sixtus V chose a dramatic site for the new Biblioteca Vaticana, bisecting the Belvedere courtyard. The rather fussy arcaded exterior by Domenico Fontana (1587–8) was proudly illustrated in his *Della trasportatione dell'obelisco Vaticano* (1590). The room wavered between monastic seclusion and Baroque grandeur. Manuscripts were enclosed in cupboards in a room divided by piers, but made splendid by frescos depicting the history of writing.

In Spain the erudite collections of King Philip II were housed in the monastic Escorial palace, in an enormous room *c.* 64 m long with a frescoed barrel vault extending to a height of *c.* 11 m. Juan de Herrera designed the room (*c.* 1567) where for the first time wall shelving appeared unified by an engaged Doric order.

In the 17th century scholars and bibliophiles were highly conscious of the 'golden era' of libraries, the Hellenistic and Roman periods. Justus Lipsius carefully described ancient library buildings from literary sources in *De bibliothecis syntagma*. Gabriel Naudé (1600–53) composed a brief but influential manual, *Advis pour dresser une bibliothèque*, frequently citing Roman examples. Renaissance library buildings were also gaining attention in guidebooks and surveys of library history.

Public access to libraries, not in the modern sense but as a *noblesse oblige* in support of learning, was important for both private collections and newly established academic institutions. In Milan the Biblioteca Ambrosiana (1603–9), founded by Cardinal Federigo Borromeo, was cited by Naudé as one of the few 'public' libraries in Europe. As part of an academy enriched by the Pinacoteca, the Ambrosiana recalled the Alexandrian Mouseion of the

1. Biblioteca Laurenziana, S Lorenzo, Florence, by Michelangelo, 1523–71

Hellenistic period. The library's interior suggested its institutional role: industrious Counter-Reformational scholarship was served by an expansive but tidily organized room in which galleried wall shelving rose nearly to the breaking of the barrel vault below portraits of the church fathers.

In northern Europe palace library collections rivalled one another in Konigsberg (now Kaliningrad), Heidelberg, Wolfenbüttel, Munich and Vienna. A number of endowed municipal libraries also developed in the Protestant north, including Augsburg, Hamburg, Nuremberg and Berne. Universities, reorganized on a post-monastic basis, began to expand their libraries. Distinctive architectural types failed to emerge at first, however, since many collections were housed in old monastic buidings, chapels, schools or town halls.

Libraries in Baroque Rome were not as large or externally prominent as the great Renaissance libraries, but they were richly furnished with manuscripts, portraits and delicately tailored bookcases. The library in the Palazzo Barberini (1633) was accessible to scholars by a special entrance. Borromini created a similar ambience in the remodelled Biblioteca Vallicelliana (1642–4). It too had reading desks set into book presses, with a gallery reached by hidden corner stairs and supported by balusters instead of wooden columns. Borromini was also responsible for the remodelling of the Angelica library (1660–61) and the University of Rome's Biblioteca Alessandrina in the Sapienza (1661–6).

On the eve of the Enlightenment many European libraries had grown tremendously, aided by the spread of printed books and the eclectic tastes of generous donors. Wall shelving and galleries were widely used. Instead of seeming wasteful, the open spaces and panorama of books encircling the reader may have suggested the expanded spectrum of knowledge, just as monastic bookcases had encased the known world in a more static scheme.

In Britain Christopher Wren's design for the new library at Trinity College, Cambridge (1676–95; see fig. 2) transformed the furnishings of British collegiate libraries. Projecting bookcases were converted into alcoves forming giant Serlian bays with arched windows corresponding to the articulation of the c. 60 m-long façade, masking the discrepancy between library floor level and exterior entablature. At Oxford, Cambridge and Trinity College in Dublin a period of ambitious rebuilding began, with library façades as the focal points of classicized Baroque quadrangles. The culmination was the Radcliffe Camera at Oxford, planned by Nicholas Hawksmoor (1712–35) and finally executed by James Gibbs (1737–46; see GIBBS, JAMES, fig. 2). This domed rotunda is often viewed as a symbolic

2. Library of Trinity College, Cambridge, by Christopher Wren, 1676–95

mausoleum for Dr Radcliffe, whose full-length statue surveys the interior.

Late Baroque libraries on the Continent simply enlarged and regularized themes already established. In Paris Cardinal Mazarin's extensive collection was bequeathed to the Collège des Quatre Nations in 1661, and incorporated into the building by Louis Le Vau. Shelving from Mazarin's palace inspired a room over 65 m long, where tall Corinthian columns neatly organized wall cases and a narrow gallery. In Rome two library interiors, the Casanatense at S Maria sopra Minerva (founded 1700; enlarged 1719–29), and the Angelica (remodelled by Vanvitelli 1753–68), expanded the Ambrosiana model, with sheer walls of books reaching to austere undecorated vaulting. The library of the Duke of Brunswick-Wolfenbüttel at Wolfenbüttel received an innovative free-standing building (1706–10) by Hermann Korb: a tall oval rotunda within a rectangular 'Palladian' façade.

While palace collections were transferred to institutions, libraries had become palatial. Renaissance picture galleries probably inspired the long narrow spaces and alternation of ample fenestration with wall cabinets. Taller library salons with projecting galleries suggested noble reception rooms. Where libraries gained status as independent buildings, they reflected the block plans of Renaissance palaces, first in the Vatican library and Marciana, then achieving a special library idiom in the British Baroque libraries. Even the arcades, which became a dominant façade motif for libraries raised above the ground floor, expressed the Classical proportions of palace courtyards, rather than humbler origins in monastic cloisters. Ancient porticos and stoas were probably also evoked by the use of Classical orders inside and out. Expanded library interiors borrowed from a number of other indigenous building types, notably hall-type chapels, which provided a broad, uninterrupted span and tall windows casting light down on enlarged bookcases. The flow of light on to walls of books was a dominant theme, with ingenious solutions often required, such as clerestories, lunettes or skylights.

In many libraries, especially in England, interiors were ornamented simply by the array of books framed by architectonic elements. The interest in ancient libraries also revived the custom of inspiring the reader with authors' portraits. At first illustrated in robust vernacular, such as the frieze in the Bodleian, portrait busts became part of the classicized vocabulary of Baroque libraries. Renaissance humanism inspired the decoration of libraries with allegorical personifications or emblems of the divisions of learning, developed to the greatest degree in murals at the Escorial, the Marciana and the Vatican.

*(c) Rococo.* In the 18th century the most vigorous library-building activity took place in central Europe, where monasteries reasserted their wealth and influence by rebuilding in a princely Rococo style. Most of these libraries were designed by the 1730s, although the last of them, the Philosophical Hall in Strahov Monastery, Prague, was not erected until 1783–93. Their form is the hall type developed in earlier Baroque libraries. They are distinguished by an exuberant *Gesamtkunstwerk*, combining richly carved bookcases, allegorical murals, multiple light sources and complex vaulting in an emotional tribute to humanistic learning and divine wisdom. Their antecedents are the mural-lined Escorial and Vatican libraries, and they are related to the Portuguese libraries at Coimbra University (begun 1716) and Mafra palace (begun 1717), where rocaille encrustations overshadow the bookcases in an encompassing visual spectacle.

The earliest Rococo libraries had fairly low ceilings, which were flat at Neresheim (1695–1700) and Kremsmünster; modified barrel vaulting with transverse arches was introduced in the Theological Hall (1671, 1721–7), Strahov Monastery, Prague, Waldsassen (1704–26) and Vorau (1731). The predominant wall shelving was soon expanded in taller rooms with galleries, which either projected over elaborated brackets, as at Waldsassen and Melk (1731–2), or were supported by columns dictating the architectural theme. Ottobeuren Abbey (1721–4) had paired *faux-marbre* columns (see fig. 3); the Clementinum (1728) in Prague alternated a twisted and plain Corinthian order; the imperial collections in the Hofbibliothek (1723–

6) in the Hofburg, Vienna, were framed by tapered pilasters and giant Corinthian columns designed by Johann Bernhard Fischer von Erlach.

Ultimately, monastic libraries echoed the complex spatial divisions of Rococo churches. Domes or shallow vaults created cross-axes and sequential spaces in the Clementinum, the Hofbibliothek, and Admont (1774). Galleries receded and projected rhythmically at the abbeys of St Gall, Admont and Einsiedeln (1740).

In addition to gilded rocaille ornament, these libraries were decorated with painted ceilings. Some simply displayed painted panels framed by stucco; illusionistic scenes opened up the vaulted ceilings at the Hofbibliothek, Strahov Monastery and the Clementinum in Prague, and Admont. The most memorable motifs are the carved personifications, such as the colourful atlantids representing book production at Waldsassen, or the *Four Last Things* (*c.* 1774) by Josef Thaddäus Stammel in the crossing at Admont.

*(d) Neo-classical.* The few libraries built in the rest of Europe in the late 18th century grappled with the increasing difficulty of fitting burgeoning collections into the wall-shelving formula. Alcoves were reintroduced, expanded by galleries, as in the monastic library at Amorbach (1799). Etienne-Louis Boullée's futuristic proposals for the Bibliothèque du Roi (nationalized after the Revolution) extended the library hall to its limits in a pansophic stack of galleries ascending to a vast coffered barrel vault. The predominant mode was Neo-classical, delicately refined in the many private libraries by Robert Adam in England (*see* ADAM (i), (3), fig. 3). In larger institutions the hall-type reading room had nearly exhausted its options, and awaited the development of the 19th-century stack library (*see* §2 below).

*(ii) Islamic lands.* Libraries and books were important in the Islamic world because of the primacy accorded the written word in Islam (*see* ISLAMIC ART, §III). Islam inherited its tradition of libraries from Late Antiquity and Byzantium, and public and private libraries were built throughout the Islamic lands. Most were incorporated into such other institutions as mosques and madrasas, but separate structures were also known. The library of the Buyid ruler 'Adud al-Dawla (*reg* 949–83) at Shiraz, for example, consisted of a long vaulted building with 360 domed rooms on 2 storeys along its 3 sides. The walls of the central and side rooms were lined with cases of carved wood three cubits high and wide, closed with doors let down from the top. In the 11th-century library of the Fatimids at Cairo there were bookcases (Arab. *rufūf*) divided by partitions into separate compartments (Arab. *hājiz*) with hinged doors that could be locked. Books were normally stacked on shelves, explaining the common practice of writing a short title on the book's upper and lower edges. A unique representation of a medieval Islamic library is preserved in the copy (Paris, Bib. N., MS. arabe 5847, fol. 5*v*) of al-Hariri's *Maqāmāt* ('Assemblies'), painted by Yahya al-Wasiti in 1237. It shows books stacked flat on shelves within niches whose arched profile recalls those found decorating the walls of 9th-century residences at Samarra in Iraq. Books were also stored underneath

3. Library of Ottobeuren Abbey, attributed to J. M. Fischer, 1721–4

wooden minbars or stepped pulpits, found in congregational mosques, and another piece of wooden furniture associated with books is the folding lectern (Arab. and Pers. *kursi, rahl*; Turk. *rahle*). Charitable foundations erected by the Ottoman sultans after the conquest of Constantinople (now Istanbul) in 1453 often included a library. The mosque complex of Mehmed II (*reg* 1463–70), for example, had a small domed library or book-store near the north gate.

*(iii) East Asia.* Japan has a long tradition of libraries. Aristocratic and warrior families gathered clan records, religious materials and literary texts in storehouses called *bunko*. This practice predates the Nara period (AD 710–94), although great libraries were not formed until later centuries. A good example of the aristocratic library (*kuge bunko*) is the Yōmei Bunko, Kyoto, of the Konoe family, which houses more than 10,000 books and printed records in addition to *c.* 10,000 manuscripts and art objects. The pre-eminent warrior library (*buke bunko*) is the Kanazawa Bunko, founded in 1275 in what is now Kanagawa Prefecture. Although many of these collections were strictly private, others were open to scholars, samurai or educated family retainers.

Buddhist temples also included special buildings for storing *sūtra*s, temple records and other written materials. The Yumedono (Dream Hall) at Hōryūji (late 7th century AD) is probably the oldest of these *sūtra* repositories (*kyōzō* or *kyōrō*). Often octagonal in shape, these repositories frequently housed huge revolving *sūtra* cases with pigeonholes for hundreds of *sūtra*s. Beginning in the 15th century, temple residences and élite houses featured a study or 'book room' (*shoin*). Although not used for the storage of books, the *shoin* was the favoured location for reading, writing and literary gatherings. There is also a tradition of government-sponsored libraries. In AD 701 the imperial court established the Bureau of Books (*zushoryō*). Later, shogunal houses built libraries to store government documents and their collections of books.

In China, the fostering of scholarship and connoisseurship under the Ming dynasty (1368–1644) also entailed a flourishing of private libraries. The important role of palace libraries can be seen in the suite of library rooms in the inner palace of the Forbidden City in Beijing, which was complemented by a printing house.

### BIBLIOGRAPHY

*Enc. Islam/2*: 'Maktaba'
J. Lipsius: *De bibliothecis syntagma* (Antwerp, 1602, 2/1607); Eng. trans. by J. C. Dunn as *Brief Outline of the History of Libraries* (Chicago, 1907/*R* 1967)
G. Naudé: *Advis pour dresser une bibliothèque* (Paris, 1627, rev. 2/1644); Eng. trans. by John Evelyn as *Instructions Concerning Erecting of a Library* (1661/*R* 1903); and as *Advice on Establishing a Library*, intro. A. Taylor (Berkeley, CA, and Los Angeles, 1950)
P. Le Gallois: *Traitté des plus belles bibliothèques de l'Europe* (Paris, 1680, 2/1685)
L. C. F. Petit-Radel: *Recherches sur les bibliothèques anciennes et modernes* (Paris, 1819)
E. Edwards: *Memoirs of Libraries*, 2 vols (London, 1859, rev. 2/1901)
A. Franklin: *Les Anciennes Bibliothèques de Paris*, 3 vols (Paris, 1867–73)
J. W. Clark: *The Care of Books* (Cambridge, 1901, 2/1902)
A. Hessel: *Geschichte der Bibliotheken* (Göttingen, 1925; Eng. trans. by R. Peiss as *A History of Libraries*, New Brunswick, NJ, 1950, 2/1955)
W. Schürmayer: *Bibliotheksräume aus fünf Jahrhunderten* (Frankfurt am Main, 1929)
B. H. Streeter: *The Chained Library* (London, 1931)

F. Milkau and G. Leyh: *Handbuch der Bibliothekswissenschaft*, 3 vols (Leipzig, 1931–40, rev. Stuttgart, 1950–)
G. Adriani: *Die Klosterbibliotheken des Spätbarock in Österreich und Süddeutschland* (Graz, 1935)
J. W. Thompson, ed.: *The Medieval Library* (Chicago, 1939/*R* 1957)
E. Lehmann: *Die Bibliotheksräume der deutschen Klöster im Mittelalter* (Berlin, 1957)
F. Wormald and C. E. Wright, eds: *The English Library before 1700* (London, 1958)
M. Baur-Heinhold: *Schöne alte Bibliotheken* (Munich, 1972)
A. Masson: *Le Décor des bibliothèques* (Geneva, 1972)
J. F. O'Gorman: *The Architecture of the Monastic Libraries in Italy, 1300–1600* (New York, 1972)
W. Löschburg: *Historic Libraries of Europe* (Leipzig, 1974)
N. Pevsner: 'Libraries', *A History of Building Types* (London and Princeton, 1976), pp. 91–110
A. Masson: *The Pictorial Catalogue, Mural Decoration in Libraries* (Oxford, 1981)
E. Bottasso: *Storia della biblioteca in Italia* (Milan, 1984)
H. Ben Aicha: 'Mosques as Libraries in Islamic Civilization, 700–1400 AD', *Journal of Library History, Philosophy & Comparative Librarianship*, xxi (1986), pp. 362–75

VIRGINIA M. KERR

## 2. 19TH CENTURY.

*(i) c. 1800–c. 1850.* Two changes that occurred during the 18th century affected the creation of library buildings in Europe. Movements for secularizing church property and, later, the French Revolution (1789–95), both led directly to the creation of national libraries, either by the sequestering or the presentation of royal or religious house collections. This was most important in France, where the collections formed the basis of several important new libraries. Less directly it led towards libraries for the general populace, and in the second half of the 19th century this became the public library movement. The second change came from technological advances that provided new materials and new methods of construction, especially the use of cast or wrought iron, making possible less weighty structures and the opportunity to bring natural light into reading rooms. The development of the iron press and later the steam press also brought changes by increasing book production.

The problem of accommodating hundreds of thousands of books and of making them available to large numbers of people called for a new relationship between books and readers. As both of these became more numerous there were additional problems in lighting and ventilating large reading rooms before the development of gas or electric power. Design tended to be conditioned by this and by the problem of handling the large upper space over an open room. In the early 19th century a number of buildings were erected on the older pattern; most of these were national or state libraries in the Germanic kingdoms, an example being the Bayerische Staatsbibliothek in Munich by Friedrich von Gärtner, erected 1832–40. This building was planned in blocks, each with a large hall lined with books; its façade is said to have been based on the Palazzo Strozzi in Florence.

The first of the new libraries was the Bibliothèque Ste Geneviève (1844–50) in Paris. This library, which is now part of the University of Paris, was designed with a frontage that was plain (for its time) and a reading room 91.4 m long with large windows on one side, most of the book-stack being in surrounding rooms. The architect was Henri Labrouste (*see* LABROUSTE, HENRI, figs 1–2), who also

4. Reading room of the original British Library, London, by Sir Robert Smirke, 1854–7

designed the Bibliothèque Nationale, which opened in 1854. There the reading room had slender iron columns with Corinthian capitals supporting a metal roof divided into nine equal compartments, each with a saucer dome of glass and iron that illuminated the whole square reading room below.

In England the library of the British Museum had been receiving donations of royal collections and was becoming the *de facto* national library, although its stocks were much smaller than those of the Bodleian in Oxford. Its new library building (built 1854–7, though planned earlier) was in fact an addition, constructed in a courtyard of the classical museum building, but was extremely influential because of the way it handled the relationship between large numbers of books and readers. The domed reading room (see fig. 4) was iron-framed, with windows between the main ribs, and had a roof formed into two separate and concentric air-chambers to equalize the temperature. Seating radiated from a central counter; some books were shelved around the walls, but most of the book-stack was in surrounding rooms. The library's architect was Sir Robert Smirke (*see* SMIRKE, (2), fig. 2) but much of the credit for the layout is due to the librarian, Sir Anthony Panizzi (1797–1879). (The reading room is scheduled for a change of function once the British Library moves from its current premises in the British Museum to its new site near St Pancras Station, London.)

*(ii)* c. *1850–c. 1900.* Up to the mid-19th century European nations, and in particular the states of Germany, had been the most prolific builders of libraries, chiefly heavy Renaissance-style buildings with ornate and pompous exteriors. No library in North America, except perhaps Harvard's at Cambridge, MA, held a tenth of the books of the major German universities. Although some older university libraries of Britain, France and Germany were extended or rebuilt at this time, it was the creation of libraries of a new kind that caused the second half of the 19th century to be known as the 'golden age of library building'. Further attempts were made to produce better relationships between books and readers, an extreme example being the Peabody Library (1857) in Baltimore by E. J. Lind (1829–1909), with its seven tiers of iron galleries surrounding a largely wasted open space below.

Domes were commonly used, as in the Picton Library (1879), Liverpool, by Cornelius Sherlock (*d* 1888) and in particular the highly acclaimed and influential Library of Congress (1897), Washington, DC, by SMITHMEYER & PELZ. This library was planned to hold four and a half million volumes; at the time this was thought to allow for a century of expansion, but two annexes have since been added.

Classical forms had been used early in the 19th century. In 1840 CARL LUDWIG ENGEL built a library in Helsinki, but heavy Renaissance-style buildings with highly decorated fronts remained common for university libraries. The Bibliothèque National et Universitaire (1889–94), Strasbourg, by Hartel & Neckelmann and Universitaatsbibliothek (1888–91), Leipzig, by Arwed Rossbach are important examples. Elsewhere the Gothic Revival came into use, from the red brick of Copenhagen University (1861) to the Victorian Gothic of the Guildhall Library (1872), London, designed by Sir HORACE JONES. In North America the small Romanesque-style libraries of H. H. RICHARDSON, mainly in Massachusetts, had various imitators.

At this time most libraries with separate buildings were either royal (or ex-royal), national, university or a combination of these, according to a country's political structure. An exception was the Surgeon-General's Library in Washington, DC (later the Army Medical Library), built in 1887. Around the mid-19th century, however, social pressures led to the development of the public library, and this soon became the greatest of all creators of library buildings. Although at various times libraries had been called 'public', and limited efforts towards libraries open to all had been made in a number of countries, the public library in its modern form came into being almost simultaneously in several Western countries. Norway was perhaps the first to give direct government backing, but the greatest development took place in Britain and North America. From the beginning the intention had been to engage the charity of private benefactors, but this was more successful in the USA than in Britain, where most of the many buildings erected were small, the undistinguished architecture reflecting the lack of priority and shortage of funds. In the USA some were very large, notably McKim, Mead & White's Cinquecento-style building for the Boston Public Library (1888; *see* MCKIM, MEAD & WHITE, fig. 2). Probably based on the Bibliothèque Ste Geneviève of Paris, this was a showpiece with internal features designed as exact copies of Italian Renaissance buildings. This library and the parallel fashion for massive Neo-classical monuments set the tone for major American public library buildings well into the next century. In Japan in the late 19th century, educators such as Fukuzawa Yukichi (1835–1901) advocated the construction of public libraries on the Western model.

A basic functional change now began to affect the interior planning of libraries. Most libraries of the past had been places where a reader could find books and a place to study. The public library provided this, but it also loaned books for use off the premises. Readers looked in the catalogue and asked for the books they wanted; these were sought and handed over by members of staff. Towards the end of the 19th century the system of 'open access' began, whereby readers themselves were allowed to search for books, and this revolutionized layouts in two ways. First, bookcases had to be both low enough and far enough apart for readers to use. Second, there had to be a control to prevent book theft, and this was the bottleneck counter across exit doors that became almost universal in public libraries for most of the 20th century. Academic libraries adopted this system but at different speeds in different countries. Britain and the USA used it almost exclusively, but some European countries were in effect 'closed access' until late into the 20th century.

### BIBLIOGRAPHY

E. Edwards: *Memoirs of Libraries*, 2 vols (London, 1859)
G. Barwick: *The Reading Room of the British Museum* (London, 1929)
C. Moore: *The Life and Times of Charles Follen McKim* (Boston, 1929)
G. Leyh: 'Das Haus und seine Einrichtung', *Handbuch der Bibliothekswissenschaft*, ed. F. Milkau and G. Leyh (Leipzig, 1931–40), ii
A. Esdaile: *National Libraries of the World* (London, 1935)
M. Burton: *Famous Libraries of the World: Their History, Collections and Administration* (London, 1937)
A. Predeek: *A History of Libraries in Great Britain and North America* (Chicago, 1947)
H. R. Hitchcock: *The Architecture of H. H. Richardson and his Times* (Hamden, CT, 1961)
H. M. Crass: *Bibliotheksbauten des 19. Jahrhunderts in Deutschland: Kunsthistorische und architektonische* (Munich, 1976) [with Eng. summary]
N. Pevsner: *A History of Building Types* (London and Princeton, 1976), pp. 103–8
A. W. Ball: *The Public Libraries of Greater London: A Pictorial History, 1856–1914* (London, 1977)

### 3. 20TH CENTURY.

(i) Before World War II. (ii) After World War II.

*(i) Before World War II.* External changes affected all the categories of libraries likely to have independent buildings. Political polarization meant larger but fewer national libraries. State libraries arose in federal countries; private benefactions, particularly in the USA, established many special research libraries, including rare book libraries such as the Henry Huntington Library (1919–28), in San Marino, CA, by Myron Hunt and Elmer Grey, and the Folger Shakespeare Library (1932) in Washington, DC, by PAUL CRET. College libraries became large enough to need their own buildings, but it was the public library sector that produced most new buildings (for illustration of Providence Public Library *see* PROVIDENCE).

The outstanding influence here was the series of grants from ANDREW CARNEGIE and later from the Carnegie Foundation that he set up. They began in Dunfermline, Scotland, in 1885, but most came in the first two decades of the 20th century. More than 2500 such libraries were built: 1681 in the United States, 125 in Canada and 660 in Great Britain and Ireland.

There were other benefactors at this time, but the sheer number of the Carnegie grants made his the most important contribution. His staff inspected and criticized proposed plans; the advice they gave directed attention to function rather than ornament and above all to economy of staffing. The buildings so created, chiefly small and economical, seldom attracted distinguished architects, and the styles range from Italian Renaissance, Mannerist, Neo-classical and Victorian Gothic to Arts and Crafts Movement, and some show, at least in their façades, the influence of Art Nouveau. More than 20 still exist in London, although some are no longer used as libraries. In the USA numerous small public libraries were built, but there were also large library buildings with massive façades in the Neo-classical manner. Of these the most notable is the New York Public Library (1911; *see* NEW YORK, fig. 3) by CARRÈRE & HASTINGS. It opened with more than two million books, and, despite the Neo-classical exterior, it was carefully planned to meet users' needs, the main reading room for 800 readers being sited above the book stacks and with excellent natural light. Most buildings of this type either had the reading room at the front and the stacks at the rear, or had the stacks below the reading room; a major change was inaugurated with the beginning of subject departmentalization, in which the USA led the way.

At this period it was also in the USA that university library building growth was most striking. The styles were varied: Harvard's Widener Memorial Library (1915), Cambridge, MA, is a large Georgian-style building by HORACE TRUMBAUER; Yale's Sterling Memorial Library (1930), New Haven, CT, by JAMES GAMBLE ROGERS is neo-Gothic to match the surrounding buildings, with a stack tower designed to take three and a half million books on its sixteen floors.

Neo-classical styles lingered: Philadelphia Public Library (1927) by Horace Trumbauer; both Stockholm (1927) and Fredericksberg (1935) public libraries; and the National Library of Wales, designed in 1914 but not completed until 1937 (by Sidney K. Greenslade, succeeded in 1933 by Charles Holden). Manchester Central Library (1934) by Vincent Harris, and the Lenin State Library (1938) in Moscow both had Neo-classical façades but were well thought out. The latter, by V. A. Shchuko & V. G. Gelfrein, probably then the largest library in the world, had a book-stack behind the reading rooms to hold six million books, with a further three million in adjacent storage.

These were exceptions. Library design generally followed the less monumental styles of the 1920s. The Swiss National Library (1931) at Berne, by Olshger, Kaufmann & Hostettler consisted of plain blocks with a nine-storey book-stack close to the main reading room. Similarly, new universities in Britain usually had plain, brick-faced libraries. The new Cambridge University Library (1934) by Sir Giles Gilbert Scott (*see* SCOTT (ii), (4)) was in four blocks with a nine-storey tower holding free-standing book-stacks. The extension (1939) to the Bodleian Library at Oxford, by the same architect, faced the old buildings, and it was connected to them by an underground tunnel, which housed, among other things, an electric book conveyor.

In the field of public libraries the Finnish architect ALVAR AALTO designed a fairly small library in Viipuri, which was in fact a complex of public services. Aalto used a variation of floor levels to provide both good book access and economical staff supervision. Though designed in 1927, it was not built until 1935 and was destroyed in the war, but it had great influence in Scandinavia, Germany and Great Britain after World War II.

The trend towards lighter and plainer buildings continued, and many public libraries were built in the 1930s in contemporary styles. In England they were often neo-Georgian or small, polite versions of the current office buildings. In North America they ranged from Colonial to Western Ranch style. One of the last libraries to be built in Europe before World War II was the Centrale Bibliotheek der Rijksuniversiteit te Gent, Belgium: another plain building to hold one and a half million books and with a twenty-six-storey reinforced-concrete book-stack. The building was begun in 1935 but was not finished until 1940; the architect, HENRY VAN DE VELDE, was a leader of the Modern Movement.

*(ii) After World War II.* Library building began again all over the world, and not only was the demand great (following the population and education explosions), but also book production soon grew enormously. As library book stocks increased, the separation of reader and book-stack, even in open-access conditions, became a major consideration. Many university libraries in the Modernist style now resembled glass-walled office blocks. The book-stack formed the core of the building, readers being seated around the perimeter with the advantage of natural light. Although these buildings with their modular construction gave much more functional flexibility, they were seldom attractive. It was unfortunate that this style predominated at the time when many of the newly independent 'Third World' countries acquired their first major libraries. In

5. Metro Toronto Reference Library, Toronto, by Raymond Moriyama, 1976–7

Japan there was a boom in the construction of libraries, ranging from the National Diet Library in Tokyo, to university libraries, prefectural libraries and local community libraries. As befits their important social role, libraries are often designed by leading architects. Best known is the municipal library in Kita-Kyushu, Fukuoka Prefecture, by ARATA ISOZAKI. The architect Kita Asuza, a specialist in library design, has built a number of fine libraries across Japan.

For the largest universities it was no longer a question of a single library but of numerous subject-orientated buildings, the architecture being that of the libraries that enclosed them. Cooperative book storage was developed, the best known example being that of the Midwest Interlibrary Center in Chicago. A further step was the building erected at Boston Spa for the Lending Division of the British Library, a factory for the storage and rapid delivery of books on request.

At Harvard the Lamont Library was built in 1949 by Coolidge, Shepley, Bulfinch & Abbott entirely for the 14,000 undergraduates. At Yale the Beinecke Rare Book Library was built in 1971 to hold 800,000 rare books and over a million manuscripts in a steel-framed building of thin white marble, translucent and striking in its contrast to the sober buildings around it.

As fashion changed, the all-glass libraries were challenged by heavier concrete buildings, although few fell under the influence of Brutalism. The lessons learnt from the use of modular construction were applied, so that by the 1970s large libraries could be functionally effective without being necessarily rectangular in plan. This was especially noticeable in a number of new West German university libraries.

Public libraries, on the other hand, needed glass to induce readers to notice them. Birmingham's Victorian Renaissance Central Library was replaced in 1975 by a building whose separate elements frame a central piazza (by John Madin Design Group). Rotterdam has a glass-and-metal-skinned Central Library by Bakema & Weeber, with an escalator diagonally crossing an open interior. Even more striking internally is the Metro Toronto Reference Library (1976–7) by RAYMOND MORIYAMA with its full atrium with balcony subject areas (see fig. 5). The Alexander Building by Cameron, Chisholm & Nicol of the State Library at Perth, Western Australia, serves also as the headquarters of the public libraries of the state. With a floor area of more than 30,000 sq. m., it seems to obtain many of the advantages of the atrium without its disadvantages. Glass is the predominant element of the façades of the central public libraries of Michigan City and New Orleans.

Professional awareness of the problems to be faced from the ever-growing book stocks led to miniaturization, with microfilm becoming widespread by the 1950s. Later came the use of computers, accessible with increasing facility by staff and readers. This new step has had a dramatic influence on interior design and layout, because a major feature of all large libraries so far—the great catalogue hall near the entrance—is already disappearing, being superseded by numerous small terminals throughout the building.

Building solutions to pressure on space led to more stack towers and to underground libraries, of which the Sedgewick Library (1970) of the University of British Columbia, by Rhone and Iredale, is perhaps the most praised. In some countries the economic recession and the fuel crisis of the 1970s has had an effect. In the Netherlands the building of libraries was suspended for a time, while in Britain the deliberations of the Atkinson Committee in 1976 made it apparent that continuous expansion could not continue indefinitely. This led to the concept of the 'self-renewing library' (that is, a library with a set size of bookstock, any additions being balanced by a similar number of withdrawals). Many critics, however, believe that the deliberate search for economy, especially in Britain, has produced better-designed university libraries than those in countries where there appears to be no limit to the funds available.

Despite economic limits, the creation of libraries continues apace; the total number in the former Soviet Union was reported to be over half a million. In the USA in the 1970s and 1980s there were reported to be 16 new university libraries built each year. Libraries continue to get bigger. The Robarts Library (1973) of the University of Toronto, by Warner, Burns, Toan & Lunde has bookstacks on floors 9 to 13 of the 14-storey triangular building; its 100,000 sq. m. of floor space make it much the largest university library in the world. Successive extensions to the Library of Congress in 1938 and 1980 brought the total length of shelving to 858 km and the book stock to well over 20 million.

In London a replacement for Panizzi's reading room at the British Library was planned by Sir Leslie Martin and Colin St. John Wilson for the adjacent Bloomsbury area, but the effect on the environment would have been so damaging that the pressure of public opinion forced a reconsideration. The new building (begun 1982) for the reference division of the British Library, by COLIN ST JOHN WILSON is close to Sir George Gilbert Scott's St Pancras Station. Because of height limitations by surrounding buildings, the bulk of its stack occupies seven basements. In these conditions the library is not a striking piece of architecture, and its long delayed opening, due to technical problems, has caused considerable criticism. On the other hand, it is specifically designed to serve readers and appears to do this effectively.

By contrast, the new Bibliothèque de France by Dominique Perrault (b 1953) is a striking contribution to the landscape of east central Paris. Standing on the banks of the Seine, it has 4 L-shaped 20-storey towers, described as looking like open books. Due to open in 1995 with capacity for 15 million books and 5000 readers, it remains to be seen whether its successful image will compensate for the inefficiency in reader service already anticipated by experts.

Where space is plentiful (for example in the richer countries of the Middle East and South-east Asia), predominant influences are more likely to be national in character and are well illustrated by the new library of the University of Qatar at Doha, by K. El Kafrawi. An earlier example of the trend towards the expression of folk history was shown in the Central Library (1948–50; for illustration see JUAN O'GORMAN) of the Autonomous University of Mexico, where an almost cubic building without windows was used to demonstrate Mexican history in the mosaics of architect Juan O'Gorman.

Although no major library has yet been designed specifically for computer information systems, that time must come. Already many libraries are moving from storage to an access policy. As the contents of libraries worldwide can be accessed from terminals, not necessarily within a library, the need for large book holdings in individual libraries must be seriously questioned, and a completely new approach to library design may be possible.

BIBLIOGRAPHY

J. Wheeler and A. M. Githens: *The American Public Library Building* (Chicago, 1941)
A. Whittick: *European Architecture in the 20th Century*, 2 vols (London, 1950)
J. Les Cain: *Transformations de la Bibliothèque Nationale de 1936 à 1959* (Paris, 1959)
G. S. Bobinski: *Carnegie Libraries: Their History and Impact on American Public Library Development* (Chicago, 1969)
M. Brawne: *Libraries: Architecture and Equipment* (New York and London, 1970), pp. 15–20
N. Pevsner: *A History of Building Types* (London and Princeton, 1976), pp. 108–10
A. W. Ball: *The Public Libraries of Greater London: A Pictorial History, 1856–1914* (London, 1977)

GODFREY THOMPSON

**Libre Esthétique.** Belgian avant-garde exhibition society sponsoring art exhibitions, concerts and lectures, 1894–1914. A direct outgrowth of Les XX, it abandoned the earlier group's government by consensus and was administered solely by Octave Maus. Maus founded the Libre Esthétique in order to run the group more freely and avoid the problems of Les XX, which included argumentative artist-members and charges of exclusivity. Ostensibly dedicated to the struggle for new, evolving and progressive art from all countries, it focused on French and Belgian work continuing Les XX's practice of showing the decorative arts, which helped to make Belgium the European centre for such works in the 1890s. In its first decade, Symbolist and Impressionist artists, poets and musicians prevailed. Former Les XX members such as Constantin Meunier and Félicien Rops were included in shows and were frequently represented by many pieces. In its second decade, the exhibitions gradually lost their avant-garde edge, except that they introduced all the Fauve artists. During this period, Maus often chose a thematic approach for group shows, organizing exhibitions around subjects such as Impressionism (1903), landscape (1910) or the south of France (1913). He acted as curator, installer and packer for the exhibitions, assisted when necessary by Paul Dubois (ii), Gisbert Combaz (1869–1941) and Théo Van Rysselberghe, and he organized all the lectures. Eugène Ysaye (1858–1931) continued to take charge of the concerts that accompanied the exhibitions, as he had done for Les XX, but Maus contributed to the planning and at times even performed on the piano. The exhibitions were increasingly successful with the public; the State bought works from them, and the King and Queen always visited. The lectures became less popular and were cancelled after 1906. Despite the loss of revolutionary focus, Maus planned to continue the exhibitions after the forced hiatus caused by World War I, but his death marked the end of the Libre Esthétique.

BIBLIOGRAPHY

M. O. Maus: *Trente années de lutte pour l'art* (Brussels, 1926) [primary archival and anecdotal source written by wife of organizer]

J. Block: *Les XX and Belgian Avant-Gardism, 1868–1894* (Ann Arbor, 1984), pp. 74–8

JULIUS KAPLAN

**Libri, dai.** Italian family of artists. The best-known member of the family is (2) Girolamo dai Libri, the son of (1) Francesco dai Libri and grandson of Stefano 'a Libris' (*b* before 1433; *d* after 1473), who was also an illuminator. They were principally active in Verona.

**(1) Francesco dai Libri** (*b* *c*. 1450; *d* after 1503). Illuminator. He was known only from documents and references in Giorgio Vasari's *Vite* until the discovery of an illuminated initial signed by him in the *Liber perfectionis vitae* (1503; Padua, Bib. Semin., MS. 432, fol. 1*r*). Works now attributed to Francesco are the miniatures in the style of Andrea Mantegna in a Greek and Latin Psalter (Milan, Castello Sforzesco, MS. 2161), those in the *Statuta et ordinamenta domus mercatorum* (Verona, Castelvecchio) and fragments depicting the *Adoration of the Magi* (Paris, Mus. Marmottan, 56), the *Entombment* (U. London, Courtauld Inst. Gals) and the *Pietà* (Cleveland, OH, Mus. A., 51.394). Although Mantegna was the dominant influence on his style, Francesco was still open to ideas from Paduan and Ferrarese illuminators inspired by Girolamo da Cremona and Liberale da Verona. He preferred the portrayal of a pleasant, ordinary ambience to the idealized, classical world of Mantegna, and his illuminations are robustly drawn and brilliantly coloured.

**(2) Girolamo dai Libri** (*b* ?Verona, 1474–5; *d* ?Verona, ?2 July 1555). Illuminator and painter, son of (1) Francesco dai Libri. He was evidently trained by his father, but he received commissions for altarpieces as well as manuscripts. Documents indicate that he lived in Verona all his life, but an early miniature of the *Nativity* (Brescia, Pin. Civ. Tosio-Martinengo, MS. II, B.I.3, fol. 5*r*), the only work by him in a series of choir-books almost certainly painted in Ferrara, suggests that he may have spent some time there. Vasari's record that he worked as an illuminator in the monastery of S Salvatore in Candiana (Padua) may be true, as some of Girolamo's surviving miniatures were executed for the abbey. The only record of Girolamo's views on his art occurs in a register of 1544: 'a good and worthy painter must know how to imitate nature well and to feign that which nature makes, and he must be universal in depicting landscapes, figures of every kind, animals and scenes and houses and in general all the things that nature produces' (Brenzoni).

Many of Girolamo's early miniatures, almost all detached leaves from choir-books, show that the hard, archaeological style of Mantegna, learnt from his father, was moderated by a particular sweetness. In various miniatures of the *Nativity* painted in the 1490s, for example, the scene is depicted as a domestic idyll set in a peaceful landscape (Brescia, Pin. Civ. Tosio-Martinengo, MS. II, B.I.3, fol. 5*r*; Cleveland, OH, Mus. A., 53.281; Verona, Castelvecchio, 4468 (1769); New Haven, CT, Yale U. A.G).

According to Vasari, the altarpiece of the *Deposition* (2.7×1.5 m) in the parish church of Malcesine, near Verona, was painted when Girolamo was only 16. The apparent influence of Bartolommeo Montagna's fresco of the *Pietà* (1500; Vicenza, Santuario di Monte Berico) suggests, however, that it was painted in the early 16th century. Paintings dating from the first decade of the 16th century, such as the *Nativity with Rabbits* (Verona, Castelvecchio), the *Virgin and Child with SS Bartholomew and Zeno* (Berlin, Bodemus.) and the altarpiece of *SS Roch, Job and Sebastian* (Verona, S Tomaso Cantuariense), the last probably painted at the time of the plague of 1510, demonstrate Girolamo's evolution from a style based on precise draughtsmanship and minute, naturalistic detail typical of late 15th-century taste towards a softer more mellow manner.

From his years of collaboration with Francesco Morone (particularly in the second decade of the 16th century) Girolamo acquired a more delicate and softer way of painting and a passing interest in Vittore Carpaccio. Morone and Girolamo both preferred a discreet, unemphatic painting style that focused on the everyday quality of figures and objects. They collaborated on the organ doors (1515–16) of S Maria in Organo (now in the parish church of Marcellise, nr Verona). The allocation of work is disputed, but Vasari's attribution to Girolamo of the *Nativity* and *SS Catherine and Mary Magdalene* is probably correct. They are stylistically comparable with the *Virgin and Child with Saints* (New York, Met.) and the *Virgin and Child with St Anne* (1518; London N.G.). The *Christ with the Woman of Samaria* (1.5×1.8 m) in the parish church of Monteforte near Verona combines a broad, airy landscape typical of Girolamo with a background cavalcade that is more characteristic of Morone, whose style is especially apparent in the figure of Christ.

Although Girolamo received numerous commissions for illuminating manuscripts, for example a series of choir-books for the Olivetan monastery at S Maria in Organo in 1519–20, this activity as a book illustrator can now be traced only in scattered works, under other names, in various museums and libraries. Works now identified include the *Miserere* (New York, Met., 12.56.3), *Pentecost* (Stockholm, Nmus., B 1386), *David the Musician* (Budapest, Mus. F.A., 3131) and the *Ascension* (Cincinnati, OH, A. Mus., 1950.34).

The predella with scenes from the *Lives of SS Blaise and Juliana* (Verona, SS Nazaro e Celso) and the *Virgin and Child with SS Lorenzo Giustiniani and Zeno* (oil on canvas; Verona, S Giorgio in Braida; see fig.), both painted in 1526, illustrate the essential conservatism yet high quality of Girolamo's art; he was not greatly influenced by the new developments in Rome, Florence and Venice, even when these were adopted by other Veronese painters. The so-called *Baptism of Christ with Ibis* (Verona, Castelvecchio), restored after much 19th-century repainting, is now dated to the end of the 1520s. In the *Virgin and Child of the Parasol* (1530; Verona, Castelvecchio), Girolamo's landscape painting, with the use of vivid greens and deep perspective, reaches its culmination. The *Virgin and Child of the Oak Tree* (Verona, Castelvecchio), perhaps his finest work, with its measured distribution of volumes and fine colour scheme, must have been painted after 1533: its

Girolamo Dai Libri e Liberale', pp. 101–51; and U. Bauer-Eberhardt: 'Aggiunte a Girolamo Dai Libri', pp. 153–61]

GINO CASTIGLIONI

Girolamo dai Libri: *Virgin and Child with SS Lorenzo Giustiniani and Zeno*, oil on canvas, 1526 (Verona, S Giorgio in Braida)

composition and low viewpoint are similar to an altarpiece by Giovanni Girolamo Savoldo, which was installed that year in S Maria in Organo, Verona.

Only manuscript illumination survives from Girolamo's later years: psalters and hymnals for the Benedictine abbey of San Benedetto in Polirone (1554 and 1555; Mantua, Mus. Diocesano, MSS S1, 6T, 3). Although they may lack invention, they still show a lively and spirited use of colour. Vasari's record that Girolamo trained Giulio Clovio in S Salvatore in Candiana is perhaps illustrated by the beautiful initial page of a Psalter (Paris, Mus. Marmottan, 90) produced there, which combines Girolamo's style with a rich margin decoration of allegorical figures and cameos characteristic of Clovio.

BIBLIOGRAPHY

*DBI*; Thieme–Becker

G. Vasari: *Vite* (1550, rev. 2/1568); ed. G. Milanesi (1878–85), v, pp. 327–31

B. Dal Pozzo: *Le vite dei pittori, degli scultori et architetti veronesi* (Verona, 1718)

L. Di Canossa: 'La famiglia Dai Libri', *Atti & Mem. Accad. Agric., Sci. & Lett. Verona*, xii (1912), pp. 85–124

R. Wittkower: 'Studien zur Geschichte der Malerei in Verona', *Jb. Kstwiss.*, iv (1927), pp. 185–222

E. Calabi: 'I corali, miniati del convento di S. Francesco a Brescia', *Crit. A.*, iii (1938), pp. 57–67

M. Levi D'Ancona: 'A Masterpiece by Girolamo Dai Libri', *V&A Mus. Yb.*, i (1969), pp. 16–26

R. Brenzoni: *Dizionario di artisti veneti* (Florence, 1972), pp. 102–4

H. J. Eberhardt: 'Girolamo dai Libri', *Maestri della pittura veronese*, ed. P. Brugnoli (Verona, 1974), pp. 141–52

*Miniatura veronese del rinascimento* (exh. cat., ed. G. Castiglioni and S. Marinelli; Verona, Castelvecchio, 1986) [contains essays by G. Castiglioni: 'Un secolo di miniature veronese, 1450–1550', pp. 45–99, 239–76; H. J. Eberhardt: 'Nuovi studi su Domenico Morone,

**Libya** [Great Socialist People's Libyan Arab Jamahiriyya; Arab. Al-Jamāhīriyyah al-'Arabiyyah al-Lībiyyah al-Sha'biyyah al-Ishtirākiyyah al-'Uẓmā]. Country in North Africa with its capital at Tripoli. Libya has an area of *c.* 1,760,000 sq. km, extending from the south shore of the Mediterranean Sea into the Sahara; it is bordered by Tunisia and Algeria to the west, Niger and Chad to the south, and Sudan and Egypt to the east. Apart from two narrow coastal strips and the oases of Fezzan in the south-west, most of Libya is desert. The people (3,955,000, 1986 est.) are mainly Arabs, with Berber tribes in the west and aboriginal tribes in the Fezzan. The majority are Sunni Muslim; most of the old-established Jewish population and 20th-century Italian settlers left in the decades after World War II. Oil was discovered in the south in 1959, which, together with gas, is Libya's main export. Oil wealth and the military coup of 1969 created radical change; in the 1980s the economy began to decline and large numbers of foreign workers left or were expelled.

Prehistoric rock art depicting people and animals was found by an Italian expedition in the Sahara in the Acacus caves east of Ghat. Tripolitania, a Phoenician colony in the 1st millennium BC, became a Roman province after the destruction of Carthage in 146 BC; its main cities were Oea (modern Tripoli; the few Roman remains include the arch of Marcus Aurelius, erected in AD 163), SABRATHA and LEPTIS MAGNA. Cyrenaica was colonized by the Greeks, then ruled by the Ptolemeys before being taken over by the Romans. Three of its major cities were CYRENE, APOLLONIA and PTOLEMAIS. Byzantine remains are also found, dating from the brief period before the arrival of the Arabs in the 7th century AD. There are important medieval Islamic ruins in Ajdabiya, south of Benghazi, which was prosperous in the Fatimid period. (For more on Libya's early history *see* AFRICA, §VII, 1; BERBER; ISLAMIC ART; MILITARY ARCHITECTURE AND FORTIFICATION, fig. 7 and ROME, ANCIENT. This article covers the art produced in the 20th century.)

In 1835 the Ottoman empire attempted to re-establish its authority over Libya after a period of autonomy, but as a result of the Italo–Turkish war of 1911–12 ceded Libya to Italy. Resistance (initially from the Sanusi, a religious movement founded in 1837) thwarted full colonial control until the early 1930s, when large numbers of Italians settled in the north. Libya, until then a geographical expression, became the official name of the Italian colony. In 1942–3 Libya came under British and Free French administration; the three Libyan provinces were administered separately: Tripolitania (north-western Libya) and Cyrenaica (eastern Libya) by the British, the Fezzan (south-western Libya) by the French. In 1951 Libya was the first independent state to be created by the United Nations. It became a federal monarchy under Muhammad Idris al-Sanusi I, Amir of Cyrenaica and leader of the Sanusi since 1918, who became King Idris (*reg* 1951–69). In 1963 the federal system was abolished and Libya became a unitary state. Sudden oil wealth, social dislocation caused by rural migration to the towns and Arab nationalism (particularly the example of President Nasser in Egypt) prompted the coup in 1969 by a group of young army officers, led by Colonel Mu'ammar al-Qadhafi, and Libya was declared a republic. In 1973 Qadhafi announced a cultural revolution to destroy all anti-Islamic and anti-Arab elements. In 1977 direct popular democracy was proclaimed, expressed through the *jamāhīriyya* (the 'State of the masses'), although power was in effect held by Qadhafi and a small group linked by personal ties or kinship. Relations with the West deteriorated further from the 1980s when Libya's alleged involvement in international terrorism brought military and economic reprisals by Western powers.

The vernacular architecture of Libya can be divided according to geographical regions: the coastal strip, the Jabal Nafusa in the north-west and the southern oases. Much of the coastal vernacular has disappeared with modern development. Surviving buildings on the coast and in the Jabal area are made of stone, or rubble and mortar, or mud-brick, together with wood and plaster. Many of the buildings in the Jabal are set low into the ground or are completely underground. Those in the Fezzan have a design similar to buildings in southern Algeria, with low crenellated walls cornered by towers. At Ghadames, near the borders with Tunisia and Algeria, the old town was divided into two levels to ensure the separation of men from women. The street level was reserved for men, and there were pathways on the rooftops for women. After bombardment by the Italians and French, it fell into disrepair; a new town was built for the inhabitants, with air-conditioned housing and running water.

There has been much modern development in Tripoli and Benghazi, the former joint capital, which was badly damaged in World War II, as were other towns and villages in Cyrenaica. One outstanding new building is the University of Garyounis at Benghazi (1966–77), designed by JAMES CUBITT. The medina in Tripoli is in a bad state of disrepair but has not substantially changed in plan since the 17th century; some renovation has taken place. It has Ottoman courtyard houses and many Italianate buildings, such as the grandiose cathedral of the Sacred Heart of Jesus, designed by Panteri (opened 1928). Most churches have been converted into mosques.

Modern art in the Western sense never gained a foothold in Libya, as it did in other countries in North Africa, and artistic activities were carried on through individual artists rather than through movements. Among early artists were Mahmoud al-Arnaouti (*b* 1904), who studied at the School of Islamic Arts and Decoration in Tripoli and later took up painting in a primitive, detailed style, and Awad Ubeid (*b* 1923), who trained in Benghazi with an Italian painter called Fray, in a classical photographic manner. In the 1950s a number of Libyan artists, including Ali Gana (*b* 1925), Taher al-Maghribi (*b* 1949) and Ali al-Bani (*b* 1948), were trained at the Accademia di Belle Arte in Rome and the College of Fine Arts in Cairo. The most prominent Libyan painter is Ali Omer Ermes (*b* 1945), who won a scholarship to the Plymouth School of Architecture and Design, graduating in 1970. His work is based on the modern calligraphic school, using Arabic letters as a graphic and literary language by which he

identifies with his culture and beliefs (e.g. *Tah*, 1980; Amman, N. G. F.A.).

Both al-Fatih University in Tripoli and Garyounis University in Benghazi have courses in art, and art classes are included in secondary-school curricula. After 1980, when the General Association of Arab Artists held its Third Arab Biennale in Tripoli, cultural contacts between Libya and the outside world were severed as a consequence of government policy. The Fine Arts Section of the General Directorate of Culture, at the Ministry of Information, however, concerns itself with official artistic activities; meanwhile, there is also the Union of Libyan Artists, embracing visual artists, writers, poets, actors and musicians, which is supervised by the government.

Traditional handicrafts, which included carpets, embroidery, metalwork, pottery, basketware, woodwork and leather, have declined because of the competition from imported goods; silks and silver jewellery, however, have been more successful. Decoration is usually non-figural. The textiles of Libya have a strong family resemblance to those of other countries of the Maghreb, although under the Italian occupation the domestic production of textiles suffered when forced to compete with the manufacture of cheap machine-made goods. It was at this time also that Venetian glass became popular among the leading families.

Archaeological, ethnographical and natural history museums were set up by the Italians in 1934 at the citadel in Tripoli. A modern national museum, the Libyan Arab Jamahiriyya Museum, designed by a British architect and funded largely by UNESCO, was built on this site in 1982–8. There are also archaeological museums at the various sites, all of which are supervised by the Department of Antiquities.

BIBLIOGRAPHY

A. M. Ramadan: *Reflections upon Islamic Architecture in Libya* (Tripoli, 1975) [Eng., Fr. and Arab. texts; good pls]

*Islamic Art and Architecture in Libya* (exh. cat. by A. Hutt and others, London, Archit. Assoc., 1976)

S. A. Hamid: *Al-ma'ālim al-islāmiyya bi'l-mathaf al-islāmī bi-madīna Ṭarābulus* [The treasures of the Islamic Museum in Tripoli] (Tripoli, 1978)

*Qasamāt wa-malāmih al-tanmiyat al-thaqāfiya fī al-jamāhīriyya* [On the development of cultural institutions in Libya] (Tripoli, 1979)

A. Bahnassi: *Ruwwad al-fann al-hadith fi'l-bilad al-'arabiyah* [Pioneers of modern art in the Arab countries] (Beirut, 1985)

M. M. Buru, S. M. Ghanem and K. S. McLachlan, eds: *Planning and Change in Modern Libya* (London, 1985)

E. Braun: *The New Tripoli* (1986)

W. Ali, ed.: *Contemporary Art from the Islamic World* (London, 1989)

E. L. Peters: *The Bedouin of Cyrenaica: Studies in Personal and Corporate Power* (Cambridge, 1990)

W. Ali: *A Survey of Modern Painting in the Islamic World and the Development of the Contemporary Calligraphic School* (diss., U. London, SOAS, 1993)

N. Danziger: *Danziger's Adventures* (London, 1993), pp. 226–38

*Ali Omar Ermes: Art and Ideas* (exh. cat., Kuala Lumpur, Maybank A.G., 1993)

**Ličenoski, Lazar** (*b* Galičnik, nr Debar, 26 March 1901; *d* Skopje, 10 April 1964). Macedonian painter. He graduated in 1925 from the Art School in Belgrade, where he had studied under Milan Milovanović (1876–1946), Ljubomir Ivanović (1882–1945) and Petar Dobrović (1890–1942), and in 1927 he began specializing in techniques of wall painting in Paris. There he attended the Ecole des Arts et Métiers (1927–9) and frequented the studio of

André Lhote. In 1929 he returned to Belgrade and became a member of the group Oblik. In the 1930s he gradually abandoned portraiture and social issues as subject-matter in favour of painting the Macedonian landscape, which he rendered with somewhat crude brushwork and thick layers of intense colour. During that decade he decorated ecclesiastical and other buildings and worked on the monument *Albanian Golgotha* (1940) for the Serbian soldiers' cemetery on the island of Vido (Greece). He moved to Skopje in 1945 and became a professor at the newly established School of Applied Arts. Ličenoski exhibited at several one-man and group shows at home and abroad. His style had developed in the context of the Ecole de Paris, which contrasted with the narrative models he had inherited from the Post-Byzantine tradition. In his mature work he introduced the idiom of Expressionism into modern Macedonian art.

BIBLIOGRAPHY

B. Petkovski: 'Lazar Ličenoski', *Otkrivanja* [Discoveries] (Skopje, 1977), pp. 63–70

*Lazar Ličenoski, Macedonian Landscape* (exh. cat. by B. Koneski, Skopje, Macedon. Acad. A. & Sci., 1979)

BOJAN IVANOV

**Li Chao-tao.** *See* LI (i), (2).

**Li Cheng** [Li Ch'eng; *zi* Xianxi; *hao* Yingqiu] (*b* AD 919; *d* 967). Chinese painter. His ancestors, members of the imperial clan, were natives of Chang'an (now Xi'an, Shaanxi Province), the Tang-dynasty (AD 618–907) capital. During disturbances at the end of the 9th century the clan split into two branches. Li's grandfather, who settled in Qingzhou (now Shandong), and his father both held official posts. From 956 to 958 Li was in government service in Bianliang (now Kaifeng), at the invitation of his friend Wang Pu, then Commissioner of Military Affairs for Emperor Shizong (*reg* 944–54). Li came to know many important scholar–officials, but, despondent after the death of Wang, took to poetry, music, painting and drink. His paintings became sought after, but he remained at first socially aloof. Later he became a habitual wanderer, until, some time after 964, he accepted an invitation to live in Huaiyang (Henan Province), where he died of overindulgence in wine.

Li Cheng exemplifies the Chinese phenomenon of a profoundly admired artist whose true style was, within a century of his death, obscured by unreliable attributions, the relationships of which to the original can no longer be determined. His fame was established early in the Northern Song period (960–1127), when critics considered his brushwork to have 'captured the miracle of creation [and] Li to have become the master of a hundred generations'. The *Xuanhe huapu* ('Xuanhe collection of painting', catalogue of the collection of Emperor Huizong (*reg* 1101–25); preface dated 1120) states, 'When it comes to landscapes, Li Cheng remains unmatched in history or in the present day'. The outspoken artist and critic Mi Fu was ambivalent in his assessment of Li, whom he decried as having 'vulgar airs...with much skilful artifice but little natural spirit'. At the same time, Mi described Li's painting methods in meticulous detail, thereby revealing how attentively he had studied them. In the *Hua shi* ('History

of painting'; *c.* 1100), Mi claimed to have seen 300 imitations and only two genuine works, a four-scroll set of landscapes and another of pines and rocks; he was thus rejecting the authenticity of 159 attributions to Li in the *Xuanhe huapu*.

The *Xuanhe* compiler had admired in particular Li's brush-power (*bili*) and quoted Li's alleged self-appraisal, 'I am a Confucian scholar who paints only for my own pleasure. How could people summon me to deploy pigments in their homes and to be treated as a professional painter!' Li Cheng was one of the earliest of the upper-class Chinese scholars who regarded painting as a private spiritual activity (a cast of mind and pursuit known as *shidai fu hua*). He took great pains to depict in detail rugged mountains, generally with a massive peak or cliff dominating the picture (see fig.). The critic Guo Ruoxu (11th century) ranked Li Cheng and FAN KUAN, a student of Li's work, as the absolute masters of landscape painting, and it was to them that two major schools of painting, differing in overall style and specifically in ink techniques, traced their origins (*see* DONG YUAN).

After Li Cheng's death, the scarcity of his works, combined with the admiration in which they came to be

Li Cheng: *Fishing on the River in Winter*, ink on silk, mid-10th century (Taipei, National Palace Museum)

held, spawned energetic and continuous production of forgeries. In the 13th century these specimens had become so common and so inferior as almost to obliterate Li's reputation as the finest landscapist of his time. Critics such as Yuan Haowen (1190–1257), writing in 1234, lamented (inappropriately, for he was misled by imitations) that Li's brush spirit was 'fragmented and confused, exuding an aura of the professional hack'. Nevertheless, Li Cheng's iconic status among collectors and writers has remained relatively undiminished throughout the history of Chinese painting criticism. During the Southern Song period (1127–1279) the Li–Guo style (named after Li Cheng and his late 11th-century follower GUO XI) became an established stream in painting. During the first two decades of the 14th century, the Li–Guo style in its Yuan-period (1279–1368) transformation was introduced to Korea, where it became a foundation for Chosŏn-period (1392–1910) academic painting (see KOREA, §IV, 2(i)(d)); its reverberations are also found as far west as Persia in the landscape elements of miniature painting. In the 14th century Li Cheng ceded celebrity to Guo Xi, whose landscapes feature convoluted mountain shapes. However, the restlessness and turbulence associated until modern times with the Li–Guo school are probably wrongly attributed in view of the copious retouchings and inventive accretions inflicted on the works in the Yuan and early Ming (1368–1644) periods.

The earliest observers did not mention the air of agitation that Li Cheng's paintings reputedly exuded. Mi Fu wrote:

Extraordinarily elegant and moist, the pine trunk is sinuous and straight, the branches and leaves create shade, the small woods and brambles show no redundant brushwork and do not coil like dragons, snakes or goblin spirits. . . . When making a tree knot, [Li] does not draw an ink circle but deposits a huge wet blob, then draws across the gap with a brush of thoroughly pale ink, looking as if made in heaven. Across are modelled rocks rising out of the water round and moist. From the peak the brushstroke plunges straight down to be level with the foot of the rock. . .there is a rock in the water, below which pale ink wash is deployed for reflection, creating gravel that sinks straight down in the water. This is unlike common imitations with their [confused] straight and oblique strokes that reveal no ground at the bottom, nor any water dynamics, [where things] float as if in mid-air, so that those who have not seen real autographs criticise Li Cheng works as having no feet.

Mi stressed the sparing use of ink, the simplicity of brushwork and the straightness of forms typical of genuine Li Cheng examples. He also noted the insubstantiality and the excessive curlicues that were emerging among late 11th-century forgeries.

Among surviving attributions, none is of the period. The vertical landscape *Solitary Temple amid Clearing Peaks* (Kansas City, MO, Nelson–Atkins Mus. A.; see CONFUCIANISM, fig. 1) represents what may be considered an anonymous late 11th-century view of the Jing Hao–Fan Kuan style. All other works in Li Cheng's style depict gnarled, wintry trees or are landscapes inspired by Guo Xi. The rendition of earthen banks and desolate trees in the left upper section of Guo Xi's *Early Spring* (Taipei, N.

Pal. Mus.; for illustration *see* GUO XI), painted in 1072, fully a century after Li's death, offers an indirect glimpse into Li's manner, specifically the claim that he 'used ink sparingly as if it were gold' (*see also* CHINA, fig. 121).

Li's son, Li Jue (AD 948–93), who passed the national civil service examination to become a *jinshi*, in 988 invited fellow historiographer Song Bai to write his father's official tomb biography (*muzhi ming*). Li Jue and his son Li You both became well-known Confucian scholars and did not wish the family to be associated with the craft of painting, which had not yet acquired its respectability as a form of literati self-expression. Li You therefore paid high prices to buy back paintings attributed to Li Cheng, although many of them were probably imitations by his fellow townsman of Yingqiu (now Linzi, Shandong Province), the musician Cui Yuanshen, who had successfully mastered the Li Cheng manner.

*See also* CHINA, §V, 1(ii); 3(iv)(a) and (b); and 4(ii).

### BIBLIOGRAPHY
Pei Xiaoyuan: *Zhenguan gongsi huashi* [Record of paintings in public and private collections in the Zhenguan era [AD 627–50]] (preface AD 639); *R* in *Huapin congshu* [Collected evaluations of painting], ed. Yu Anlan (Shanghai, 1982), pp. 23–43
Liu Daoshun: *Shengchao minghua ping* [Critique of famous painters of the present [Song] dynasty] (1059)
Guo Ruoxu: *Tuhua jianwen zhi* [Experiences in painting] (preface 1075); Eng. trans. by A. C. Soper as *Kuo Jo-hsü's 'Experiences in Painting' (T'u-hua chien-wen chih)* (Washington, DC, 1951/*R* 1971)
Mi Fu: *Hua shi* [History of painting] (*c.* 1100)
*Xuanhe huapu* [Xuanhe collection of painting] (preface 1120), *juan* 13
Deng Chun: *Hua ji* [Painting continued] (preface *c.* 1167)
Tuotuo, ed.: *Song shi* [Standard history of the Song] (Yuan period, 1279–1368)
Zhou Mi: *Yunyan guoyan lu* [Yuan-period catalogue of paintings and calligraphies] (*c.* late 13th century)
Wai-kam Ho: 'Li Cheng luezhuan: Li Cheng yu Bei Song shanshuihua zhi zhuliu' [A biography of Li Cheng: Li Cheng and the mainstreams of Northern Song painting, Part I], *Gugong Jikan*, v/3 (1971–2), pp. 33–61
Yu Jianhua, ed.: *Zhongguo meishujia renming cidian* [Dictionary of Chinese artists] (Shanghai, 1981)
Chen Gaohua: *Song Liao Jin huajia shiliao* [Historical materials on painters of the Song, Liao and Jin periods] (Tianjin, 1984), pp. 154–77

JOAN STANLEY-BAKER

**Li Chi** [Li Ji] (*b* Zhongxiang, Hebei Province, 1896; *d* Taipei, 1 Aug 1979). Chinese anthropologist and archaeologist. He studied psychology, sociology and anthropology at Harvard University from 1918 to 1923 and wrote a doctoral dissertation on the origins of the Chinese people. In 1923 he returned to China to teach anthropology and in 1928 was appointed director of the excavations of Shang-period (*c.* 1600–*c.* 1050 BC) ANYANG, Henan Province, conducted by the Academia Sinica. Owing to the turbulence of the Chinese civil war and the Japanese invasion of north China, excavations at Anyang and plans for a central museum organized by Li were abandoned in 1937. The Academia Sinica and Li followed the Guomindang (KMT, Nationalist Party) government to Taiwan in 1949 where, eventually, the National Palace Museum was established in Taipei. Li became head of the Department of Archaeology and Anthropology at the National Taiwan University in 1950, and from 1955 to 1973 he was head of the Institute of History and Philology. Li published around 150 titles during his career and travelled all over the world giving lectures on the Chinese past. Li's archaeological work helped establish the existence of the Shang dynasty as a historical fact. In the history of Chinese art his chief contributions lie in the areas of terminology and classification, for example of bronze vessels.

WRITINGS

*Anyang fajue baoguo* [Reports of the excavations at Anyang], 4 vols (Beijing, 1929–31)
'Ji Xiaotun chutu de qingtongqi' [Studies of bronzes from Xiaotun], *Zhongguo kaogu xuebao*, iii (1948), pp. 1–100; iv (1949), pp. 1–70
*Xiaotun taoqi* [Pottery from Xiaotun] (Taipei, 1956)

BIBLIOGRAPHY

K. C. Chang: 'Li Chi (1896–1979)', *Artibus Asiae*, xlii/2–3 (1980), pp. 221–2
——: 'Obituary: Li Chi (1896–1979)', *J. Asian Stud.*, xl (1980), pp. 218–19
Cho-yun Hsü: 'Obituary: Li Chi (1896–1979)' *J. Asian Stud.*, xl (1980), pp. 217–18

BENT NIELSEN

**Licht, Hugo** (*b* Nieder Zeidlitz, Posen [now Poznań, Poland], 21 Feb 1841; *d* Leipzig, 28 Feb 1923). German architect and writer. He began his training in the firm of Ende & Böckmann, Berlin, in 1862. He continued his studies at the Bauakademie, Berlin, under Friedrich Adler, and later worked under Richard Lucae and in Vienna under Heinrich von Ferstel. He worked as a private architect in Berlin between 1871 and 1879, but his most important work dates from the period 1879 to 1906, when he was director of municipal building administration in Leipzig. In this official capacity he built a large number of public buildings, including a music conservatoire (1885–7), the police headquarters (1889–90), a market hall (1889–91) and the Johanniskirche, which he rebuilt (1894–7; destr.), incorporating the existing tower; together these buildings formed the architectural character of the city. His main work was the new Rathaus (1898–1905). The monumental design, incorporating the tower of a former castle on the site, liberally used German Renaissance and Baroque forms, but not without references to the local architecture of Leipzig. From the 1880s Licht began to develop a massive masonry style using Romanesque elements and motifs, seen particularly in the competition design (1891; unexecuted) for the Kaiser-Wilhelm Museum, Krefeld, influenced by the work of the American architect H. H. Richardson. Licht was widely acclaimed in Germany for his versatility and his design skills. He also made an important contribution to architectural journalism as the editor of two influential periodicals, *Die Architektur des XX. Jahrhunderts: Zeitschrift für moderne Baukunst* (1901–14) and *Profanbau* (1906–22). Produced in conjunction with the publishing house of Wasmuth in Berlin, these journals propagated contemporary architecture through lavish photography and publicized new designs and building types.

WRITINGS

ed.: *Die Architektur Deutschlands*, 2 vols (Berlin, 1879–82)
ed.: *Die Architektur der Gegenwart*, 5 vols (Berlin, 1886–1900)

BIBLIOGRAPHY

*Macmillan Enc. Architects*; *NDB*; Wasmuth
C. Kranz-Michaelis: *Rathäuser der deutschen Kaiserzeit, 1871–1918*, Materialien zur Kunst des 19. Jahrhunderts, xxiii (Munich, 1976)

**Lichtenberg, Georg Christoph** (*b* Oberramstadt, nr Darmstadt, 1 July 1742; *d* Göttingen, 24 Feb 1799). German writer and physicist. He studied mathematics, physics and astronomy at the University of Göttingen between 1763 and 1767. During this time he kept his famous 'scribble books', in which he jotted the thoughts on various subjects that were edited and published posthumously as his *Aphorisms*. In 1770 he made his first short visit to England and returned for a longer stay in 1774–5. From his experiences there he wrote *Briefe aus England* (published in *Deutsches Museum*, 1776, nos 6, 11; 1778, nos 1, 5), an exercise in the description of English manners that he later exploited in *Ausführliche Erklärungen der Hogarth'schen Kupferstiche*, first published in *Göttingen Taschenkalender* (1784–96), a publication he edited from 1777 until his death. In the early issues he commissioned engravings from Daniel Chodowiecki, to which he added commentaries; later he turned his attention to Hogarth. At the same time Lichtenberg pursued a successful career as Professor of Physics at the University of Göttingen.

Lichtenberg's philosophical reputation rests upon his inimitable *Aphorisms*, which were appreciated for their style and ideas by Johann Wolfgang von Goethe, Friedrich Nietzsche and Ludwig Wittgenstein, among others. The *Erklärungen*, however, secured him most recognition as a writer during his lifetime. Lichtenberg described himself as an 'interpreter' of Hogarth's engravings, a role he fulfilled with great forensic skill and shrewd enthusiasm. His method consisted in applying the knowledge he gained from his visits to England to interpreting the details of the engravings. By relating the contents of an artwork to the structure of manners of the time in which it was produced, Lichtenberg's *Erklärungen* anticipated the content analysis of the sociology of art, although the virtuoso character of his performance ensured that his method of interpretation had few imitators. However, it is important not to underestimate the subtlety of the theoretical position underlying the welter of description and digression. The *Erklärungen* represent a critique of Gotthold Ephraim Lessing's distinction between painting as the representation of objects in space and poetry as the representation of actions over time. Lichtenberg disputed the difference by an appeal to mathematical calculus, which allowed him to think of the moment represented by painting as a 'differential': 'the painter of the living and the moving...ought to present only an infinitely small moment of time' (1966, p. 135). Hogarth's engravings are thus regarded as showing frozen moments from a continuous action, and their interpretation consists in plotting the progress of the action either side of what is seen. In this way painting has its temporal narrative character restored.

WRITINGS

*Commentaries on Hogarth's Engravings* (London, 1966)
W. Promies, ed.: *Schriften und Briefe*, 4 vols (Munich 1967–72)

BIBLIOGRAPHY

J. P. Stern: *Lichtenberg: A Doctrine of Scattered Occasions* (Bloomington, 1959, *R* London, 1963)
P. Requadt: *Lichtenberg* (Stuttgart, 1964)
F. H. Mauthner: *Lichtenberg: Geschichte seines Geistes* (Berlin, 1968)

HOWARD CAYGILL

**Lichtenstein, Roy** (*b* New York, 28 Oct 1923; *d* New York, 29 Sept 1997). American painter, sculptor, print-

Roy Lichtenstein: *Hopeless*, acrylic on canvas, 1.12×1.12 m, 1963 (Basle, Kunstmuseum)

maker and decorative artist. His paintings based on the motifs and procedures of comic strips and advertisements made him one of the central figures of American POP ART.

He first studied under Reginald Marsh in a summer course at the Art Students League, New York, in 1939, continuing from 1940 to 1943 at Ohio State University in Columbus. He was particularly influenced by the teaching of Hoyt L. Sherman, a late Fauvist painter, designer and architect who introduced his students to modernism in a period dominated by American Scene painting. Sherman was interested in the psychology of perception and problems of pictorial representation. In his teaching he insisted that the act of representation should be separated from everyday experience and considered solely for its formal qualities, as an 'abstraction'.

After military service in Europe in World War II Lichtenstein returned to Columbus in 1946, completing his Master of Fine Arts in 1949. The subject-matter of his early works became apparent *c.* 1949–50. Drawing on the biomorphic abstraction and heroic themes of Abstract Expressionism, Lichtenstein painted such subjects as anthropomorphic plants, beautiful women in gardens, and wild animals, as well as romantic medieval subjects of knights and battles. All this was painted with a subtle tongue-in-cheek irony, and stylistically oriented towards such European modernists as Picasso, Klee, Kandinsky and Miró. In 1951 Lichtenstein devised his first major theme: American history and the conquest of the 'Wild West' as in *Inside Fort Laramie* (1955; priv. col., see Alloway, p. 14). He borrowed subjects treated by 19th-century artists, first using such well-known models as Emanuel Gottlieb Leutze's *Washington Crossing the Delaware* (1851; New York, Met.) and early paintings of American Indians by artists such as Carl Wimar and Carl Bodmer, and then turning to anonymous illustrations. The

source material on which he based his pictures was selected for its wealth of authentic detail and for its dependence on pictorial conventions; another critical factor was that he was working not from original works but from reproductions. He adopted a series of different artistic languages, first approximating Picasso's style of the 1940s, in 1956 turning to a more ornamental idiom and then to Rococo motifs, and finally turning to abstraction in 1958 in a late variation of Action painting.

Lichtenstein taught from 1946 to 1951 at Ohio State University, then from 1957 at the State University of New York at Oswego, and from 1960 to 1963 at Douglass College, Rutgers University in New Brunswick, NJ, where he met Allan Kaprow and other artists associated with Happenings (*see* PERFORMANCE ART). These contacts encouraged his interest in cartoon imagery, stemming initially from small-scale 19th-century illustrations and from an anthropomorphic treatment of animals in the work of such modern artists as Miró. Lichtenstein recognized that devices favoured by cartoonists were very similar to those employed by such painters as Picasso and Klee, whom he had studied so intensively.

In 1961 Lichtenstein made the final break with his early work. Whereas he had previously translated his source materials into personal variants of Cubism or Constructivism, he now appropriated from comic strips not only the subject-matter but also the style. In these Pop paintings he favoured highly simplified colour schemes and procedures that mimicked commercial printing techniques, representing tonal variations with patterns of coloured circles that imitated the half-tone screens of Ben Day dots used in newspaper printing, and surrounding these with black outlines similar to those used to conceal imperfections in cheap newsprint. He applied these techniques to paintings based on small advertisements, as in *Spray* (1962; Stuttgart, Staatsgal.); war comics, for example *Whaam!* (1963; London, Tate) or *As I Opened Fire* (1964; Amsterdam, Stedel. Mus.); and comic strips on themes of love and romance, such as *Hopeless* (1963; Basle, Kstmus.; see fig.) or *We Rose up Slowly* (1964; Frankfurt am Main, Mus. Mod. Kst).

Having established this apparently anonymous style as, paradoxically, his personal style, Lichtenstein began to apply it also to paintings based on familiar works by other artists. *Man with Folded Arms* (1962; Milan, G. Panza di Biumo priv. col.) was based on a diagram found in a book on Cézanne's composition, while *Femme au chapeau* (1962; Meriden, CT, B. Tremaine priv. col.) and *Non-objective I* (1964; Darmstadt, Hess. Landesmus.) were pastiches, rather than direct copies, after Picasso and Mondrian respectively.

The essence of Lichtenstein's procedure lay in the enlargement and unification of his source material, whether its original purpose was to tell a story or sell a consumer product, on the basis of strict artistic principles. This involved a strengthening of the formal aspects of the composition, a stylization of the motif and a 'freezing' of both emotion and action. At its most extreme, for example in *Tension* (1964; Paris, M. Boulois priv. col.), the process of formalization, combined with one's awareness that the motif is only a segment of a larger narrative, transforms the image into a virtual abstraction. By such means

Lichtenstein emphasized that comic strips and advertisements were not realist, as is often assumed, but highly artificial pictures that convey their messages with a sparing use of pictorial conventions. A constant if restrained irony and a gentle sense of humour contribute just as much to the cheerful lightness of Lichtenstein's work as the balanced, completely harmonious composition.

By enlarging his source material, Lichtenstein emphasized the banality and emptiness of his motifs as an equivalent to the impersonal, mechanized style of drawing. This led to speculation as to his intended criticism of modern industrial America. The formalization and irony could be taken to support such a theory, but Lichtenstein ultimately would appear to accept the environment as revealed by his reference material as part of American capitalist industrial culture.

In 1962, the year in which he held his first one-man exhibition at the Leo Castelli gallery, New York, Lichtenstein made his first Pop prints, such as *Foot and Hand* (1962; see Waldman, 1969, p. 216), in which the association with comic books was strengthened by his choice of a technique generally used for commercial printing: offset lithography. In 1964 he made the first of his screen prints, *Sandwich and Soda* (see Waldman, 1969, p. 218), exploiting the inherent impersonality of the medium still further in works printed on synthetic materials, as in *Seascape* (1965; see Waldman, 1969, p. 222). The subtelty and technical inventiveness of his work as a printmaker, combined with his exquisite draughtsmanship, contributed greatly to his growing reputation.

The principle that Lichtenstein had created of basing each painting on a specific source was broken in 1964 with a series of imaginary landscapes. These were followed by paintings such as *Yellow and Green Brushstrokes* (1966; Darmstadt, Hess. Landesmus.), which parodied the broad brushwork of Abstract Expressionism in his usual comic-strip style. In such works Lichtenstein began to devise his own compositions, sometimes taking specific motifs from his own or other artists' work as found objects or quotations. His pastiches of the brushstrokes of Action painting gave way in the later 1960s to paintings and sculptures based on the 'rational' geometry of Art Deco, such as the *Modular* series of canvases, and in the 1970s to parodies of such 20th-century styles as Cubism, Purism, Futurism, Surrealism and Expressionism, always processed into the same dispassionate comic-strip style. Over the years his palette became richer and more varied, and in addition to the dots he incorporated other textures such as imitation wood-graining and cross-hatching.

Lichtenstein also periodically produced groups of sculptures. Some of the earliest of these were wood sculptures from pieces of furniture in the early 1950s; later followed glazed ceramics, including female busts such as *Blonde* (1965; Cologne, Mus. Ludwig) and a 1965 series, *Ceramic Sculptures*, which consisted of stacked cups and saucers (see 1977 exh. cat., pp. 7–26). These were followed by the *Modern Sculpture* series of 1967–8 (see Alloway, pp. 58–9), which made reference to motifs from Art Deco architecture. In his painted bronzes of the mid-1970s (see Cowart, pp. 149–59) Lichtenstein made punning use of linear devices from his paintings to produce three-dimensional but flat-looking representations of familiar objects. In the

late 1970s and during the 1980s, Lichtenstein received major commissions for works in public places: the sculptures *Mermaid* (6.4×7.2×3.4 m, 1979; Miami Beach, FL, Theat. Perf. A.) and *Brushstrokes in Flight* (1984; Columbus, OH, Port Columbus Int. Airport), and the five-storey high *Mural with Blue Brushstrokes* (1986; New York, Equitable Cent.).

The theme basic to all of Lichtenstein's work was succinctly stated in his *Mirrors* series of 1970–72, such as the oval *Mirror No. 2* (Philadelphia, PA, Kardon priv. col., see Alloway, p. 67), which explicitly questioned the assumption that the function of representational art was to reflect reality. Throughout his work in all media, he continued to affirm that the arrangement of forms and colours obeyed pictorial rules independent of the subject portrayed. The succession of styles alluded to in his art, rather than being taken for granted as a self-perpetuating system, thus becomes an instrument for understanding art as the expression of an ideal state.

For illustration of *Still-life with Crystal Bowl* (1973) *see* STILL-LIFE, fig. 9.

### BIBLIOGRAPHY

*Roy Lichtenstein* (exh. cat. by W. A. L. Beeren, Amsterdam, Stedel. Mus., 1967)
*Roy Lichtenstein* (exh. cat. by R. Morphet, London, Tate, 1968)
*Roy Lichtenstein* (exh. cat. by J. C. Amman and W. A. L. Beeren, Berne, Ksthalle, 1968)
*Roy Lichtenstein* (exh. cat. by W. Schmied, Hannover, Kestner-Ges.,1968)
D. Waldman: *Roy Lichtenstein: Drawings and Prints* (New York, 1969)
——: *Roy Lichtenstein* (London, 1971)
J. Coplans, ed.: *Roy Lichtenstein* (New York, 1972)
D. B. Kuspit: 'Pop Art: A Reactionary Realism', *A. J.* [New York], xxxvi/1 (1976), pp. 31–8
*Roy Lichtenstein: Ceramic Sculpture* (exh. cat. by C. W. Glenn, Long Beach, CA State U., A. Gals, 1977)
J. Lipman and R. Marshall: *Art about Art* (New York, 1978)
J. Cowart: *Roy Lichtenstein, 1970–1980* (New York, 1981)
L. Alloway: *Roy Lichtenstein* (New York, 1983)
C. Tomkins and B. Adelman: *Roy Lichtenstein; Mural with Blue Brushstrokes* (New York, 1987)
*The Drawings of Roy Lichtenstein* (exh. cat. by B. Rose, New York, MOMA, 1987)
E. A. Busche: *Roy Lichtenstein: Das Frühwerk, 1942–1960* (Berlin, 1988)
For further bibliography *see* POP ART.

ERNST A. BUSCHE

**Licini, Osvaldo** (*b* Monte Vidon Corrado, nr Ascoli Piceno, 22 March 1894; *d* Monte Vidon Corrado, 11 Oct 1958). Italian painter. From 1911 he trained at the Accademia di Belle Arti in Bologna (with Giorgio Morandi) and from 1914 to 1916 at the Accademia di Belle Arti in Florence. From 1917 to 1926 he lived on the Côte d'Azur, where he devoted himself to landscape painting, and in Paris, where he had contacts with such artists of the Ecole de Paris as Modigliani, Picasso and Kisling, and with avant-garde poets and literati, including Jean Cocteau and Blaise Cendrars. He developed a brightly coloured naturalistic style, influenced by Matisse and Raoul Dufy, and in 1923 and 1924 he exhibited at the Salon des Indépendants in Paris. In 1926 he returned to Italy and took part in the first exhibition of the Novecento Italiano in Milan.

In about 1930, when he participated in exhibitions of Italian modern art in Berne and Basle, there was a decisive stylistic change in Licini's painting towards an abstraction that was initially geometric and Constructivist, for example in his *Bird* (1931; Turin, Gal. Civ. A. Mod.). The results of this new direction were presented in an exhibition in Milan in the Galleria Il Milione and in the *Prima mostra collettiva d'arte astratta italiana* in the studio of Felice and Enrico Paulucci in Turin, both in 1935. In the same year he joined the Abstraction–Création group. In 1938 he signed Marinetti's manifesto *La linea italiana dell'arte* and, in 1941, the manifesto of the Gruppo Primordiale Futurista. His art became gradually more lyrical and fantastic, marked by a return to archetypal and highly personal figurative elements (e.g. *Amalassunta 2*, 1950; Rome, G.N.A. Mod.). In 1958 he was awarded the international painting prize at the Venice Biennale.

WRITINGS

G. Baratta, F. Bartoli and Z. Birolli, eds: *Errante, erotico, eretico: Gli scritti letterari e tutte le lettere* (Milan, 1974)

BIBLIOGRAPHY

G. Marchiori: *Licini* (Ivrea, 1958)
*Osvaldo Licini* (exh. cat., ed. Z. Birolli and F. Passoni; Turin, Gal. Civ. A. Mod., 1968)

ANTONELLO NEGRI

**Licinio.** Italian family of painters.

**(1) Bernardino Licinio** (*b* Venice, *c.* 1490; *d* Venice, after 1549). Born in Venice of Bergamese descent, he was trained within the tradition of Giovanni Bellini, possibly in his workshop, and followed a successful career in the city. His own workshop produced half-length panels of the Virgin and Child, altarpieces and numerous individual and group portraits. Although not an innovator, Bernardino remained open to developments in contemporary Venetian painting. Whereas his early paintings, such as the *Adoration of the Shepherds* (Brescia, Pin. Civ. Tosio-Martinengo) and the *Portrait of a Courtesan* (ex-Dal Vecchio priv. col., Genoa), are close in mood to Giorgione, the religious paintings from the 1520s and 1530s frequently reflect the work of Titian. For example, the signed and dated triptych of the *Resurrection* (1528; Lonato, S Giovanni Battista) was influenced by Titian's polyptych of the same subject (1522; Brescia, SS Nazzaro e Celso). Increasing workshop intervention occurs in the paintings from the 1530s onwards and the workshop paintings frequently repeat established formal models. Bernardino's signed and dated *Virgin and Child Enthroned with Saints* (1535; Venice, S Maria Gloriosa dei Frari) recalls Titian's work in the pose and expression of the saints but, in contrast to Titian's innovative treatment of altarpiece conventions, Bernardino adheres to the traditional figurative scheme, arranging the saints symmetrically around the central figures of the enthroned Virgin and Child.

Bernardino was active as a portrait painter and his rather conservative skills are perhaps best represented in this genre. Here too he looked to the work of his Venetian contemporaries. Two signed and dated works, the *Portrait of a Man Holding a Missal* (1524; York, C.A.G.) and the portrait of *Stefano Nani* (1528; London, N.G.), are indebted to Lorenzo Lotto and Titian respectively. Bernardino also painted a number of group portraits. These include the *Family Group* (London, Hampton Court, Royal Col.), the *Portrait of a Sculptor with Five Apprentices* (Alnwick Castle, Northumb.) and the portrait of *Arrigo Licinio and his Family* (Rome, Gal. Borghese). The last

represents the family of Bernardino's elder brother, also recorded as a painter and includes a portrait of (2) Giulio Licinio offering his mother a bowl of roses. The work was possibly a collaborative effort, with certain passages painted by Giulio, who worked in his uncle's shop.

Vasari confused Bernardino with his contemporary Pordenone. This error persisted until the early 20th century. In the 19th century many of his works were attributed to Pordenone, although Bernardino's work is in marked contrast to Pordenone's Mannerist innovations. While accommodating the taste for central Italian and Roman art in his work from the 1530s onwards, Bernardino remained a painter within the mainstream of the Venetian tradition.

**(2) Giulio Licinio** (*b* Venice, *c.* 1527; *d* ?Venice, after 1584). He was the son of the painter Arrigo and younger brother of Fabio Licinio, who was trained as a goldsmith and practised as an etcher. Giulio was trained in the workshop of his uncle (1) Bernardino Licinio and worked as his assistant. In 1556 he was among the painters competing for the commission to furnish the ceiling tondi for the Biblioteca Marciana, Venice. The artists were invited to provide three paintings each, their work to be judged by Titian and Sansovino. Giulio was awarded the commission to paint three allegorical compositions, *Vigilance and Patience* and *Glory and Beatitude* (Venice, Bib. N. Marciana) and the *Virtuous Acts*. The first two conform to the central Italian Mannerist style common to the painters involved in the decorative project, among them Andrea Schiavone, Giuseppe Salviati and Paolo Veronese. In 1559 Giulio left Venice to work in Augsburg. In the 1570s and 1580s he was recorded as again resident in Venice. Other works by Giulio include the signed *Pietà* (Graz Cathedral) and the signed altarpiece in the parish church of Lonno in Val Serianna.

BIBLIOGRAPHY

A. Venturi: *Storia* (1901–40)
L. Vertova: 'Bernardino Licinio', *I pittori bergamaschi: Il cinquecento*, i (Bergamo, 1975)
*The Genius of Venice* (exh. cat., ed. C. Hope and J. Martineau; London, R.A., 1983), pp. 174–5

**Li Di** [Li Ti] (*b* Qiantang, near Hangzhou, Zhejiang Province, *c.* 1125; *d c.* 1200). Chinese painter. He was probably born around the time of the fall of the Northern Song dynasty (960–1127), after which the Song court moved to Lin'an (modern Hangzhou). Li Di's activity as a court painter is documented in a small number of dated works from the period 1174–97. According to the *Huaji buyi* ('Supplement to the succession of painters'; 1298), attributed to Zhuang Su (*fl* late 13th century), he worked in the imperial painting academy under three emperors from 1163 until his death and is said to have served as the assistant director (*fushi*). Although he is known primarily for his paintings of flowers, bamboo and various animals, including birds, he also painted landscapes with figures in the style of the Northern Song academy. Surviving works ascribed to him include a number of album leaves as well as some painted fans; his favoured media were ink and colours on silk.

Li Di: *Herdboys and Buffaloes in a Rainstorm*, hanging scroll, ink and colours on silk, 1.20×1.02 m, 1174 (Taipei, National Palace Museum)

Li Di's paintings of animals, most of which are in the form of album leaves, show the painter's predilection for minute details and a preoccupation with precise rendering of his topics. His paintings are naturalistic but at the same time rather static. He followed the style established at the Imperial Painting Academy under Emperor Huizong (*reg* 1101–25), in particular that of the early Northern Song painter ZHAO CHANG. His landscape paintings are executed with the same care and detail as his close-view renderings of animals: they do not show sweeping vistas of mountains and rivers shrouded in mist but are more concerned with intimate scenes of country life, notably the popular theme of cowherds and water-buffaloes.

The brushwork of Li Di is extremely fine and, although it cannot be considered very original, it certainly shows a high degree of technical skill. Flowers and bamboo are usually rendered in the outline manner (*baimiao*). In the album leaf *Two Chicks* (Shanghai Mus.), the birds are depicted against a plain background with the utmost attention to individual details, the down rendered in a most delicate manner. Li's landscapes show the influence of the style of painters such as Fan Kuan and Li Tang. In his celebrated landscape painting *Herdboys and Buffaloes in a Rainstorm* (see fig.), two water-buffaloes with their herdboys perched on their backs are making their way home through a violent storm. The buffaloes are painted in the outline manner, filled out with washes in various shades of ink. The tree trunks are painted with heavy, blunt strokes in deep shades of ink. In the far left of the painting the river bank and some rocks are depicted in slightly modified axe-cut strokes (*fupi cun*).

In his style as well as his choice of subject-matter Li Di is very close to another Southern Song painter, Lin Chun (*fl* 12th–13th century), who also came from Qiantang near Hangzhou and who also served in the imperial painting academy.

Franke: '*Li Ti*'    BIBLIOGRAPHY
O. Sirén: *Chinese Painting: Leading Masters and Principles* (London and New York, 1956–8), ii, p. 247
J. Cahill: *An Index of Early Chinese Painters and Paintings* (Berkeley, 1980), pp. 125–7

HENRIK H. SØRENSEN

**Lido.** Open-air swimming-pool or bathing beach, with such added amenities as changing booths and cafés. The term came into use in the 20th century and is derived from the Venetian island of Lido, the most fashionable seaside resort in Italy for nearly 60 years from *c.* 1900. The original concept of communal bathing as a social and physical activity was developed in antiquity, in Greek gymnasia and Roman baths, as well as in several Asian countries (*see* BATH (ii), §1). The popularity of the lido in Europe, however, can be dated to the early 20th century, when there was a significant increase in the leisure time of the working population. Swimming and bathing, primarily sanitary measures in the 19th century, became popular forms of recreation, and medical experts advocated the beneficial health effects of the sun, with swimming facilities featuring greatly in civic health and physical fitness programmes, particularly in Germany. For the emerging Modern Movement, preoccupied with air and light, the public lido became an important area for experimentation with modern design. Prominent Modernist designers of lidos included Paul Bonatz (e.g. Inselbad Untertürkheim, Stuttgart, 1928–9) and Bruno Taut (e.g. Seebad Rangsdorf, Berlin, 1929). Situated on lakes, rivers or inland 'garden baths', the most prominent building at the lido was the restaurant or café, which was adjacent to rows of changing booths (sometimes with sunbathing terraces). There were also spacious areas of grass or sand for sunbathing. European lidos were mostly built to modern designs in white, rendered concrete, often with elaborate, cantilevered diving towers. In Britain, however, some lidos were still being built in a Neo-classical style in the 1920s (e.g. Blackpool, *c.* 1923; destr.), until the 1930s, when modern streamlined styles became prominent (e.g. Ruislip Lido, 1936; Showboat Lido, part of a roadhouse complex, Birkenhead, 1933). The London County Council designed a large number of brick lidos influenced by the designs of W. M. Dudok (e.g. Brockwell Park, 1937, rest. 1994;

Parliament Hill Fields, 1938). The Art Deco style was also popular in Britain, and lidos possibly modelled on the Art Deco Piscine Molitor (1929), Paris, included Tinside Lido (1935), Plymouth, and Portobello Pool (1936; destr.), Edinburgh.

BIBLIOGRAPHY
E. J. Margold, ed.: *Bauten der Volkserziehung und Volksgesundheit* (Berlin, *c.* 1930), pp. 162–83
*Taking the Plunge: the Architecture of Bathing* (exh. cat. by M. Binney, H. Laing and A. Laing, London, RIBA, Heinz Gal., 1982)
A. Powers, ed.: *Farewell my Lido* (London, 1991) [Thirties Society report]

**Lidval', Fyodor (Ivanovich)** [Lidval, Johann-Friedrich] (*b* St Petersburg, 1 June 1870; *d* Stockholm, 14 March 1945). Swedish architect, active in Russia. He studied at the Academy of Arts, St Petersburg, from 1890 to 1896, where he spent his final years in the studio of Leonty Benois. He subsequently established a reputation as one of the most important architects in St Petersburg in the early 20th century. In his early works there he created an original version of northern European Art Nouveau (Rus. *modern*), related to Swedish and Finnish National Romantic architecture but distinguished by its strict restraint and elegant forms. In the block of flats on Kamennoostrovsky Prospect 1–3 that belonged to his mother (1899–1904), he used a deep *cour d'honneur* to form a spacious nucleus to the well-equipped and comfortable complex. The sophisticated plastic quality of the buildings, which are of various heights, the free design and textural variety of the façades and the stylized motifs of flora and fauna all distinguish this as northern *modern*, of which this was the first example built in St Petersburg. Nuances of the style recur variously in the residential blocks of the Swedish Church on Bol'shoy Prospect, on Vasil'yevsky Island, and on B. Konyushennaya Street, all 1904–5. A. F. Tsimmerman's block of flats (1906–7), Kamennoostrovsky Prospect, is distinguished by the sculptural quality of its mass, its expressive silhouette and the brilliant polychromy of the facing.

After *c.* 1905 Lidval' began to adopt a modernized classicism that reflected the wider revival of the classical traditions of St Petersburg architecture. His interpretation of historic styles is highly individual, reflecting the influence of *modern* style and allowing new methods of construction and new materials to determine form; at the same time the decorative possibilities of natural stone emerged. These features occur particularly in Lidval''s designs for banks, which with residential buildings are a large component of his work. In the buildings for the Second Mutual Credit Society (1907–8) on Sadovaya Street, and the Azov–Don Bank (1907–9; 1912–13) on Bol'shaya Morskaya' Street the Neo-classical façades, which employ the architectural orders and are faced with granite, conceal spacious, bright 'atrium-halls' with open-frame structures and glazed roofs. Lidval' was also commissioned around this time by the Swedish industrialist Emmanuel Nobel to execute a number of works, including an administrative building (1909), on Griboyedov Canal, and a block of flats (1910–12), on the Lesnoy Prospect, which combines traits of the Renaissance Revival and traditional Swedish architecture and is among the most accomplished and original of his creations. Stylized Neo-classical forms also abound in the interiors (1908–10) of the Yevropeyskaya Hotel (Hotel Europa), Mikhailovskaya Street, and throughout the Astoriya Hotel (1911–12) on Isaac's Square. The latter combined reinforced-concrete construction with façades in pink granite. The residential complexes of the 1910s are marked by a free interpretation of classical devices and the novelty of their solutions to city building. In the block of flats of Count M. P. Tolstoy (1910–12) on the Fontanka Embankment, most attention is devoted to the organization, the linking and layout of the three interior courtyards.

From 1910 to 1917 Lidval' taught at the Women's Polytechnical Institute, St Petersburg. From December 1918 he lived and worked in Sweden, where he built a residential complex on Eriksdalsområdet in Stockholm that approaches the principles of Functionalism. Other buildings, including banks and office blocks, exemplify the late phase of National Romanticism and the influence of Neo-classicism, largely a continuation of his work in St Petersburg.

BIBLIOGRAPHY

[A. Ol']: *F. Lidval'* (St Petersburg, 1914)

B. L. Vasil'yev and B. M. Kirikov: 'Tvorcheskiye svyazi finskikh i Peter-burgskikh zodchikh v nachale XX veka: *Arkhitektura 'severnogo moderna'* [Creative links between Finnish and St Petersburg architects at the beginning of the 20th century: northern Art Nouveau architecture], *Skandinavskiy sbornik XXVI* [Scandinavian collection XXVI], ed. H. Piirimär (Tallinn, 1981), pp. 190–94

V. G. Isachenko and G. A. Ol': *Fyodor Lidval'* (Leningrad, 1987)

S. G. FYODOROV, B. M. KIRIKOV

**Lieb, Mihály.** *See* MUNKÁCSY, MIHÁLY.

**Liebermann, Max** (*b* Berlin, 20 July 1847; *d* Berlin, 8 Feb 1935). German painter, draughtsman, printmaker and collector. He dominated the German art world from the 1890s to the 1930s. Although at first a highly controversial figure, after the turn of the century he was showered with honours. His Naturalist and Impressionist works have been consistently admired, despite being banned during the Nazi period. Liebermann's approach was that of a liberal cosmopolitan, and his work is distinguished by its honesty and commitment to social reform. Influenced by Dutch and French painting, he led the modernist movement in Germany away from the literary art of the 19th century.

1. Life and work. 2. Working methods and technique. 3. Public life.

### 1. LIFE AND WORK.

(i) Training, travels and early work, to 1883. (ii) Mature work, 1884 and after.

*(i) Training, travels and early work, to 1883.* The son of a Jewish businessman from Berlin, Liebermann initially studied philosophy, but in 1866 he became a pupil of Carl Steffeck, who had given him occasional drawing tuition. In 1868–72 he studied under Ferdinand Wilhelm Pauwels (1830–1904), Charles Verlat and Paul Thumann (1834–1908) at the Kunsthochschule in Weimar. In 1871, with Theodor Hagen (1842–1919), he visited Mihály Munkácsy in Düsseldorf; impressed by his painting *Lint-makers* (1872) Liebermann painted *Goose Pluckers* (1871–2; Berlin, Alte N.G.), his first important picture and the first in a series on the subject of work. When the painting was exhibited in Berlin, it brought him immediate notoriety: he was branded an 'apostle of ugliness' and a 'painter of filth'. Undeterred by this criticism, Liebermann continued to work on similar subjects, becoming the leading figure of the anti-establishment Naturalist movement in the 1880s and 1890s.

In 1872 Liebermann travelled to Paris, where he was inspired by the works of Courbet and Jean-François Millet. On a visit to the Netherlands he planned *Women Preparing Conserves* (1872; Winterthur, priv. col., see Pauli, 1911, pl. 8), which he exhibited with success at the salon in Antwerp. He lived in Paris between 1874 and 1878. After visits to Barbizon in 1874 and 1875 he produced *Potato Harvest* (1875; Düsseldorf, Kstmus.) and *Workers in the Turnip Field* (1876; Hannover, Niedersächs. Landesmus.), both paintings still in Munkácsy's brownish tones and with subjects influenced by Millet. In all these depictions of country labourers occupied in heavy and monotonous work, Liebermann was concerned to show the dignity of labour and to enhance the image of those classes that were socially and politically marginalized. His conception of society was not revolutionary, as some German critics suspected, but reformist. The pictures also reveal an element of utopianism concerning the power of rural collective labour to foster a sense of community.

After 1875 Liebermann spent nearly every summer in the Netherlands, until 1913. Here, he found not only a wealth of new subjects but also a tradition of Realist art. In studies from nature he designed the majority of his large-scale exhibition pictures. In the Dutch light his palette became brighter. He learnt tonal painting and free brushwork from the work of Frans Hals, which he copied intensively. He was also attracted by what seemed to be a social system of free and responsible citizens and independent farmers, living in harmony with nature. He began to use schools, orphanages and old men's homes in which he initiated a popular genre as subjects, in such paintings as *Sewing School in the Amsterdam Orphanage* (1876–7; Wuppertal, von der Heydt-Mus.) and studies (1876; Bremen, Ksthalle) for *Recreation Time in the Amsterdam Orphanage* and *Old Men's Home in Amsterdam* (1880; Schweinfurt, Samml. Schäfer). In these pictures the artist discovered light: with a subdued *contre-jour* to emphasize the concentration and order in *Sewing School* and bright patches of light amidst the calm of *Old Men's Home*.

On the advice of Franz von Lenbach, Liebermann moved to Munich in 1878. However, whereas he had exhibited frequently and with success in Paris and Amsterdam, Munich was a disaster. The painting *Christ in the Temple* (1879; Hamburg, Ksthalle) provoked a scandal. The naturalistic style and lack of idealization were condemned as blasphemous; there was even a debate in the state parliament. His works from the Munich period reveal the influence of Wilhelm Leibl, one of the few colleagues who acknowledged Liebermann during these years. The paintings *Recreation Time in the Amsterdam Orphanage* (1881; Frankfurt am Main, Städel. Kstinst. & Städt. Gal.), *Eva* (1882; Hamburg, Ksthalle) and also the *Bleaching Field* (1882–3; Cologne, Wallraf-Richartz-Mus.) show a use of flat areas of colour with a heightened formal precision similar to Leibl's work.

*(ii) Mature work, 1884 and after.* In 1884 Liebermann settled in Berlin. His tendency towards the anecdotal, already apparent in Munich (e.g. *Munich Beer Garden*, 1884; Munich, Neue Pin.), persisted initially, as in *Dutch Village Street* (1885; Hannover, Niedersächs. Landesmus.), but the impressions left by visits to the Netherlands in 1886 and 1887 led to a renewed concentration on truth to reality. In this effort Liebermann drew on earlier work, such as the *Shoemaker's Workshop* (1881; Berlin, Alte N.G.), a masterly study in *contre-jour*. The painting *Flax Barn at Laren* (1887; Berlin, Alte N.G.; see fig. 1) became an emblem for Naturalism and a homage to the work ethic of the rural collective. In a low barn flooded with sunlight, women stand with long flax threads in their hands; children sitting along the opposite wall turn large flywheels to wind the thread on spools. In this semi-mechanical mode of production, the women are degraded to mere appendages of the flax thread. They nonetheless dominate the scene, which is harmoniously blended by the sunlight.

From the late 1880s, Liebermann became more interested in painting the natural world in a variety of moods. The melancholy landscape of the Dutch coast forms a foil for working people in such works as *Net Weavers* (1889; Hamburg, Ksthalle), which reflects the atmospheric painting of Jozef Israëls, a friend of Liebermann. The numerous pictures of farmers no longer bear witness to a harmonious exchange between man and nature; they show fruitless toil, isolation and dissonance, as in *Woman with Goats* (1890; Munich, Neue Pin.). One of his last naturalistic works, the over-life-size *Walking Farmer* (1894; destr. World War II, see Pauli, 1911, pl. 110), which was painted entirely from nature, shows that Liebermann had already abandoned this attempt to find truth in the observation of everyday life.

After 1895 Liebermann turned to an Impressionist style of painting. At the same time he became one of the most successful modernist artists in Germany. Exhibitions, purchases, medals and other honours became increasingly frequent; 31 of his works were shown in the Grosse Berliner Kunstausstellung in 1897 and he was made a professor of the Königlicher Akademie der Künste but never took up the post. Liebermann had been interested in the French Impressionist painters since the mid-1880s. He was one of the first to collect pictures by Degas, Monet and Cézanne; in 1900 he owned the largest collection of Manet's works in Germany. His stylistic proximity to the French artists, with his predilection for fleeting movements, vivid colours and strong brushwork, could be seen from 1884 in the first of a series of market scenes and in his many paintings of the Judengasse in Amsterdam. However, as is clear in *Parrot Man* (1902; Essen, Mus. Flkwang), Liebermann's works differ significantly from those of contemporary French Impressionist painters: they are characterized by strong local colours, solid volumes, pools of light and a heavy impasto, rather than by diffuse colour, flatness and a pointillist style. Liebermann by this time was only concerned with 'pure' painting, with movement and light in nature. The subject of pictures became relatively unimportant; he painted many versions of boys bathing, of riders on the beach, of polo players, of spa visitors and of people strolling. He painted sunlit beach cafés and restaurants in the Netherlands and Hamburg, and, when World War I restricted travel, he painted the beer gardens on the Wannsee in Berlin.

Liebermann's portraits set new standards in Germany. His earliest official commission, *Burgomaster Carl Petersen* (1891; Hamburg, Ksthalle), is characteristic of later works. Despite the pompous official uniform, the human being

1. Max Liebermann: *Flax Barn at Laren*, oil on canvas, 1.35×2.32 m, 1887 (Berlin, Alte Nationalgalerie)

who wears it can be seen, a fragile old man surrounded by the trappings of power. After indignant reactions to this picture, Liebermann painted mainly literary figures and scientists such as *Georg Brandes* (1902; Bremen, Ksthalle), *Wilhelm von Bode* (1904; Berlin, Alte N.G.) and *Richard Dehmel* (1909; Hamburg, Ksthalle). During the Weimar Republic he became the most sought-after portrait painter in Germany. With the exception of his wife and daughter, he painted women infrequently; only the portraits of *Lola Leder* (1921; Berlin, priv. col., see Meissner, no. 105) reveal a more sensuous approach.

Liebermann painted a large number of self-portraits from 1902. In *Self-portrait with Cap* (1925; Berlin, Neue N.G.; see fig. 2) the old, tired painter pauses before the canvas, an attentive observer reassuring himself of his craft. The clear composition dispels the effect of the dark colours.

In the last 20 years of his life, Liebermann confined himself (apart from portrait commissions) to self-portraits, pictures of his granddaughter at play and of the garden of his summer villa on the Wannsee. Little of the political upheaval of the outside world penetrated this private sphere. Liebermann painted his garden from many angles: bordered and obscured by trees or opening up in the distance; nature cultivated or almost untouched, painted with powerful gestures and strong colours or with gentle brushstrokes and in light colours. The paintings give an impression of freedom or security, rather than emptiness or constriction, as in *Garden Bench* (1916; Berlin, Neue N.G.), which is surrounded by dense but light green.

Liebermann's move towards Impressionism increased his interest in etching. The cold-needle technique, which

2. Max Liebermann: *Self-portrait with Cap*, oil on canvas, 1120×890 mm, 1925 (Berlin, Neue Nationalgalerie)

he used in an unconventional way, was particularly suited to the depiction of fleeting movement in light and air. Between 1914 and 1916 he produced 27 lithographs for the magazine *Kriegszeit, Künstlerflugblätter* (Berlin, 1914–16), a patriotic magazine of German art; however, he soon distanced himself from this enthusiasm for the war. His prints also included portraits, for example *Albert Einstein* (1925; Berlin, Kupferstichkab.), as well as illustrations to the works of Goethe, Heinrich von Kleist, Heinrich Heine and Theodor Fontane.

2. WORKING METHODS AND TECHNIQUE. Liebermann always painted directly from nature and never simply from his imagination. During the summer he accumulated *plein-air* studies, which he developed in his studio during the winter. He experimented with the gestural and heavy application of colour, which culminated in a frenzied palette knife technique, as in *Stevenstift in Leyden* (1889; Berlin, Neue N.G.). Later he also used the palette knife with thickly applied paint; in these paintings, although the form is largely dissolved, the connection between colour and subject is always preserved. By the late 1890s the difference between the sketch and the final execution of a picture became less distinct. While in the 1880s he had held the spontaneous gesture to be the hallmark of art, from 1900 he extended this principle to the fleeting, sketch-like execution of the painting as a whole. He described the direct transposition of an impression of nature into the medium of painting as *Phantasie in der Malerei*, which was also the title of an essay written in 1904 and published in *Gesammelte Schriften* (Berlin, 1922).

Liebermann was one of the most important draughtsmen of the period. He considered drawing of fundamental importance: the imagination, intuition and personality of the artist are preserved in the fleeting sketch, whereas they are often lost in the process of working on a painting. He collected the drawings of other artists, including Adolph von Menzel, Honoré Daumier and Degas, and left thousands of his own drawings at his death. These were sketches, subject studies or fully developed designs (e.g. Dresden, Kupferstichkab.) executed in pencil, charcoal or chalk and mainly intended as preparation for paintings. In the late 1880s he renounced precise linearity in favour of a swift, softly drawn overview; light and atmosphere were captured in the finest variations of tonal values. From the mid-1890s he filled sheets of sketches with spontaneous studies of movement, with the aim of further simplifying form. After 1900, pastels became more important as a medium which lent itself well to the Impressionist style.

3. PUBLIC LIFE. After he had become an established artist, Liebermann committed himself to encouraging public recognition of Impressionist and Post-Impressionist art. He held a number of important official positions in the cultural world of Berlin after 1900, leading the Secession from its foundation in 1898, until 1911, when his reluctance to accept the young Expressionists led to crises, division and eventually his resignation. In 1903 he was elected President of the Deutscher Künstlerbund, which had been formed in opposition to the artistic dictatorship exercised by Emperor William II. From 1920 he was President of the Prussian Akademie der Künste,

the highest artistic institution of the Weimar Republic, a position which he held with integrity and broad-mindedness. In 1932, after the Nazi attacks on him intensified, he resigned the office. He died three years later. In 1943 his wife took poison to avoid deportation by the Gestapo.

### WRITINGS
*Gesammelte Schriften* (Berlin, 1922)
G. Busch, ed.: *Die Phantasie in der Malerei: Schriften und Reden* (Frankfurt am Main, 1978)

### BIBLIOGRAPHY
H. Rosenhagen: *Max Liebermann* (Bielefeld and Leipzig, 1900, 2/1927)
G. Schiefler: *Das graphische Werk von Max Liebermann* (Berlin, 1902–14, 2/1923)
G. Pauli: *Max Liebermann: Des Meisters Gemälde*, xix of *Klassiker der Kunst* (Stuttgart and Leipzig, 1911–22)
E. Hancke: *Max Liebermann: Sein Leben und seine Werke* (Berlin, 1914, 2/1923)
R. Göres: 'Max Liebermanns Handzeichnungen in der Nationalgalerie', *Forsch. & Ber.: Staatl. Mus. Berlin*, xi (1968), pp. 105–14
——: *Die Handzeichnungen Max Liebermanns: Ihr Verhältnis zu seiner Malerei, ihr Beitrag zum Realismus* (diss., E. Berlin, Humboldt-U., 1971)
S. Achenbach: *Die Druckgraphik Max Liebermanns* (diss., Heidelberg, Ruprecht-Karls-U., 1974)
G. Meissner: *Max Liebermann* (Leipzig, 1974)
*Max Liebermann in seiner Zeit* (exh. cat., W. Berlin, N.G., 1979; Munich, Hauskst., 1979–80)
M. F. Desmukh: 'Max Liebermann: Observations on the Politics of Painting in Imperial Germany, 1870–1914', *Ger. Stud. Rev.*, iii (1980)
——: 'German Impressionist Painters and World War I', *A. Hist.*, iv (1981), pp. 66–79
*Für Max Liebermann: 1874–1935* (exh. cat., E. Berlin, Altes Mus., 1985)
G. Busch: *Max Liebermann: Maler, Zeichner, Graphiker* (Frankfurt am Main, 1986)
C. Lenz: *Max Liebermann: 'Münchener Biergarten'* (exh. cat., Munich, 1986)
M. Bunge: *Max Liebermann als Künstler der Farbe: Eine Untersuchung zum Wesen seiner Kunst* (Berlin, 1990)
*Max Liebermann in Hamburg: Landschaften zwischen Alster und Elbe, 1890–1910* (exh. cat., ed. J. E. Howoldt and A. Baur; Hamburg, Ksthalle, 1994)
M. Eberle: *Max Liebermann: Werkverzeichnis der Gemälde* (Munich, 1995)

BETTINA BRAND

**Liechtenstein**, House of. Austrian dynasty of rulers, patrons and collectors. They derived their name from their castle near Mödling, south of Vienna, and it was applied to their estates on the Upper Rhine after those estates became an imperial principality in 1719 (*see* LIECHTENSTEIN, Principality of, below); the hereditary rank of prince, however, dates from 1608, when (1) Charles I was given the title. Since 1921 the principality has been a constitutional monarchy. The family resided in Vienna until 1938, when they moved into Schloss Vaduz in Liechtenstein. Since 1989 the ruler has been John-Adam II, Prince of Liechtenstein (*b* 1945).

### BIBLIOGRAPHY
J. von Falke: *Geschichte des fürstlichen Hauses Liechtenstein*, 3 vols (Vienna, 1868–82/*R* Vaduz, 1984)
*Meisterwerke aus den Sammlungen des Fürsten von Liechtenstein* (exh. cat., Lucerne, Kstmus., 1948)
N. Jansen: *Franz Josef II., Fürst von und zu Liechtenstein: Ein Porträt, mit einer kurzgefassten Geschichte des Landes und des Hauses Liechtenstein* (Vaduz, 1978)
V. Press: 'Die Entstehung des Fürstentums Liechtenstein', *Das Fürstentum Liechtenstein: Ein landeskundliches Porträt*, ed. W. Müller, Veröffentlichung des Alemannischen Instituts Freiburg im Breisgau, 50 (Bühl and Baden, 1981), pp. 63–92
*Liechtenstein: The Princely Collections* (exh. cat., New York, Met., 1985)
V. Press and D. Willoweit, eds: *Liechtenstein, Fürstliches Haus und staatliche Ordnung: Geschichtliche Grundlagen und moderne Perspektiven* (Vaduz, Munich and Vienna, 1987)
E. Oberhammer, ed.: *Der ganzen Welt ein Lob und Spiegel: Das Fürstenhaus Liechtenstein in der frühen Neuzeit* (Vienna and Munich, 1990)
P. Vogt: *Brücken zur Vergangenheit* (Vaduz, 1990), pp. 39–70

NORBERT W. HASLER

**(1) Charles** [Karl] **I**, Prince of Liechtenstein (*b* Feldsberg [now Valtice, Czech Republic], ?30 June 1569; *reg* 1608–27; *d* Prague, 12 Feb 1627). The founder of the princely house of Liechtenstein, he was brought up in the Protestant faith but converted to Catholicism in 1599. A year later the Holy Roman Emperor Rudolf II summoned him as head steward to his court in Prague, where he remained with interruptions until 1607. He was raised to the rank of prince in 1608, became governor and viceroy of Bohemia in 1620 and received the Order of the Golden Fleece in 1622. Through the lands he acquired and held in Bohemia, Silesia and Moravia, he created the material basis for his descendants. He had the family palaces at Eisgrub (now Lednice, Czech Republic) and Feldsberg enlarged as residences and founded the Liechtenstein stud-farm. Impressed by the art cabinet of Rudolf II, the inventory of which he had had drawn up in 1607, Charles began collecting, primarily examples of the arts of goldsmithing and gem-carving. In 1607 he awarded Adriaen de Vries the commission for the over life-size bronze sculpture *Christ as Man of Sorrows* (Vaduz, Samml. Liechtenstein), dedicated to the Capuchin monastery in Prague. In 1627 the Holy Roman Emperor Ferdinand II praised him as a man 'who took a special delight in artistic matters'.

### BIBLIOGRAPHY
H. Haupt: *Fürst Karl I. von Liechtenstein, Obersthofmeister Kaiser Rudolfs II. und Vizekönig von Böhmen: Hofstaat und Sammeltätigkeit*, 2 vols, Quellen und Studien zur Geschichte des Fürstenhauses Liechtenstein (Vienna, Cologne and Graz, 1983)

**(2) Charles** [Karl]**-Eusebius**, Prince of Liechtenstein (*b* Prague, 11 April 1611; *reg* 1627–84; *d* Schwarzkosteletz, 3 Feb 1684). Son of (1) Charles I. His long period of rule coincided with the devastation of the Thirty Years War (1618-48), plague and the threat of Turkish invasion. Nevertheless, he was the founder of the Liechtenstein picture gallery. He prized paintings highly and was an avid buyer. The Prince preferred Italian painting, and the record of the many dealers and agents who inundated him with offers bear witness to the intensity and passion with which he set about making his purchases; his agents included the art-loving imperial *valet de chambre* Wolf Wilhelm Prämer, the imperial inspector of galleries Christoph Lauch (1618–1702), the glass painter Gerhard Janssen and the brothers Alexander and Wilhelm Forchoudt. At the end of his life the Prince had so many paintings that he turned down works offered to him, on the grounds that he did not know where to put them.

The parish church at Feldsberg (now Valtice, Czech Republic), founded by the Prince in 1631, is one of the decisive achievements of central European architecture of the time. The work of the north Italian architect and master builder Giovanni Giacomo Tencalla, it was consecrated in 1671, after a protracted period of construction rich in mishaps. The extension of the princely summer residence at Eisgrub (Lednice, Czech Republic) occupied Charles-Eusebius throughout his life, and its pleasure garden became one of the most opulent in Europe. His treatise *Instruction über die Gebäuder* (1671) is regarded as one of the most significant works of architectural theory of the 17th century, its theme being the ennobling power of architecture, which secures imperishable renown for the patron. The aesthetic ideals expressed by Charles-Eusebius in this work provided the basis for the initiative of his son and successor, (3) John Adam, in rebuilding Schloss Plumenau (Plumlov, Czech Republic) in the 1680s.

The stud-farm that Charles-Eusebius built up systematically and with great technical knowledge was regarded as the best in Europe, and his writings, on a wide range of subjects, include treatises on harness and stud-farm rules, equine medication and the rules of hunting. He was also convinced of the scientific value and practical use of alchemy.

BIBLIOGRAPHY

V. Fleisher: *Fürst Karl Eusebius von Liechtenstein als Bauherr und Kunstsammler (1611–1684)* (Vienna and Leipzig, 1910)
G. Wilhelm: 'Die Fürsten von Liechtenstein und ihre Beziehungen zu Kunst und Wissenschaft', *Jb. Liechtenstein. Kstges.*, i (1976), pp. 11–179
B. von Götz-Mohr: 'Gedächtnis und Curiosität: Der Fürst als dilettierender Architekt und Sammler', *Die Bronzen der fürstlichen Sammlung Liechtenstein* (exh. cat., Frankfurt am Main, Schirn Ksthalle, 1986), pp. 67–75

**(3) John [Johann]-Adam-Andreas**, Prince of Liechtenstein (*b* Brünn, 30 Nov 1657; *reg* 1684–1712; *d* Vienna, 16 June 1712). Son of (2) Charles-Eusebius. Adept management of his estates made the Prince rich and enabled him frequently to lend money to the imperial house. In 1687 the Holy Roman Emperor Leopold I appointed him a privy councillor, and in 1693 he was awarded the Order of the Golden Fleece. From 1703 to 1705 he served as head of the newly founded imperial bank. With the purchase of estates at Schellenberg in 1699 and Vaduz in 1712, he became the founder of the present-day principality of Liechtenstein.

John-Adam-Andreas's wealth and his excellent art education enabled him to purchase paintings of the highest artistic standard. His correspondence (1691–1709) with the Bolognese painter Marcantonio Franceschini shows how well informed he was about the painting both of earlier times and of his own. His especial predilection for the works of Peter Paul Rubens and Anthony van Dyck led him to have them sought throughout Europe, and he thus acquired, for example, in 1696, the eight paintings making up Rubens's *Decius Mus* series (1616–18; Vaduz, Samml. Liechtenstein). The Prince attached importance to mounting paintings in frames of the best quality, calling on highly paid Italian sculptors and frame-carvers for this purpose. From the 1690s he was in frequent contact with the imperial inspector of galleries Christoph Lauch (1618–1702) and the imperial court painter and engraver Jakob Männl (*c.* 1654–1712). In 1695 Lauch drew up an inventory of the paintings kept in the palaces of Feldsberg (Valtice, Czech Republic) and Eisgrub (Lednice, Czech Republic) and produced a first manuscript catalogue.

Prince John-Adam-Andreas was also one of the most important architectural patrons of his time. After Schloss Plumenau (Plumlov, Czech Republic), built from 1680 according to his father's plan and instructions, and the stables at Eisgrub (begun 1688), the Prince devoted himself to his palace buildings, taking an active part in their design. The summer palace in Rossau, designed by Domenico Martinelli and completed in 1702, and the Stadtpalais in Bankgasse, Vienna, completed in 1711, designed by Martinelli and finished by Gabriel de' Gabrieli, are outstanding examples of Baroque palace architecture. The picture gallery established in the Stadtpalais was entrusted to the curatorship of Männl.

The Prince's interest in sculpture prompted him several times to contact the sculptor Mathias Rauchmiller. Massimiliano Soldani produced bronze casts after ancient sculptures and after designs by Michelangelo and Bernini for the Prince, but also supplied bronze reliefs of his own design (Vaduz, Samml. Liechtenstein). Later, the Bolognese sculptor Giuseppe Mazza supplied the Prince with wax models, clay *bozzetti* and powerful marble busts (Vaduz, Samml. Liechtenstein).

BIBLIOGRAPHY

H. Lorenz: *Liechtenstein Palaces in Vienna from the Age of the Baroque* (New York, 1985)
H. Haupt: 'Rara sunt cara: Kulturelle Schwerpunkte fürstlichen Lebensstils', *Der ganzen Welt ein Lob und Spiegel: Das Fürstenhaus Liechtenstein in der frühen Neuzeit*, ed. E. Oberhammer (Vienna and Munich, 1990), pp. 115–37
D. C. Miller: *Marcantonio Franceschini and the Liechtensteins: Prince Johann Adam Andreas and the Decoration of the Garden Palace at Rossau-Vienna* (Cambridge, 1991)

**(4) (Joseph-)Wenceslas [Wenzel] (-Lorenz)**, Prince of Liechtenstein (*b* Prague, 9 Aug 1696; *reg* 1748–72; *d* Vienna, 10 Feb 1772). Cousin of (3) John-Adam-Andreas. His military career began in the war against the Turks in 1716, and from the 1730s he was employed in diplomatic missions, mainly in France and Germany. He increased his family's collection of paintings by purchases he made at the sites of his military and diplomatic activity. The portraits of *Frederick II, King of Prussia* by Amédée van Loo (e.g. London, Royal Coll. A.), for example, originated from his period in Berlin, from 1735. After his return from the Prussian court Wenceslas was twice painted by Pietro van Roy, accompanied by the court Moor, Angelo Soliman (1630–1716). In Paris (1737–41) Wenceslas acquired genre paintings by Jean-Siméon Chardin and a series of Limoges enamels with scenes from the Trojan War (Vaduz, Samml. Liechtenstein). Of the five carriages built for his arrival in splendour as ambassador to the court in Versailles in December 1738, one, the 'Golden Coach', survives (Vaduz, Samml. Liechtenstein). During the campaign in Italy that he led in 1745–6, Wenceslas acquired works of art for the Holy Roman Empress Maria Theresa; in 1757, as an expression of thanks for his services to the Austrian artillery, she commissioned a gilt-bronze bust of the Prince from Balthasar Ferdinand Moll in collaboration with Johann Georg Dorfmeister (Vienna, Belvedere, Österreich. Barockmus.). In return, in 1760, the Prince commissioned Franz Xaver Messerschmidt to produce busts of the Empress and Emperor (Vienna, Belvedere), which were displayed in the Zeughaus in Vienna. The court painter Martin van Meytens (1695–1770) painted portraits of the Prince, his wife and members of his family *c.* 1770.

Prince Wenceslas's private picture collection, the main part of which, a total of 632 paintings, was formed by the legacy of Prince John-Adam-Andreas, was kept in his house in the Herrengasse, Vienna; the Majoratsgalerie, the main Liechtenstein gallery, remained in the Stadtpalais, also in Vienna. The catalogue of the Majoratsgalerie, compiled by Vincent Anton Joseph Fanti (1719–76) and published in 1767, is the first surviving complete list of the Liechtenstein gallery and was also the first gallery catalogue to have been printed in Vienna. Prince Wenceslas's predilection for *veduta* painting is unmistakable. He commissioned Bernardo Bellotto to paint a view of the summer palace at Rossau with its large Baroque garden (1759–60; Vaduz, Samml. Liechtenstein) and acquired several Venetian *vedute* from Canaletto (two examples Vaduz, Samml. Liechtenstein; one example Lugano, Col. Thyssen-Bornemisza). The Prince had Rubens's large *Assumption of the Virgin* (1635; Vaduz, Samml. Liechtenstein) brought from the parish church at Feldsberg (Valtice, Czech Republic) to the Viennese gallery in 1764.

BIBLIOGRAPHY

*Der goldene Wagen des Fürsten Joseph Wenzel von Liechtenstein* (exh. cat., Vienna, Schloss Schönbrunn, 1977)

*Joseph Wenzel von Liechtenstein: Fürst und Diplomat im Europa des 18. Jahrhunderts* (exh. cat., Vaduz, Samml. Liechtenstein, 1990)

H. HAUPT

**(5) Francis-Joseph** [Franz Josef] **I**, Prince of Liechtenstein (*b* Milan, 19 Nov 1726; *reg* 1772–81; *d* Metz, 18 Aug 1781). Nephew of (4) Wenceslas. He strengthened the House of Liechtenstein through administrative and economic reforms, and it was further enriched by inheritance from his kinswoman Maria Theresa, Duchess of Savoy (1694–1772). In Vienna, Francis-Joseph combined the Majoratsgalerie in the Stadtpalais and the former private gallery of Prince Wenceslas in the palace on the Herrengasse, both of which were supplemented with purchases of his own. The gallery catalogue annotated by the superintendent Johann Dallinger von Dalling (1741–1806) in 1780 lists 713 pictures and 138 sculptures. Among the 183 paintings the Prince rehoused in the Majoratsgalerie were such masterpieces as the *Sacrifice of Abraham* (1531) by Lucas Cranach I, the *Road to Market* (1604) by Jan Breughel I and the *King's Drink* (*c.* 1637; all Vaduz, Samml. Liechtenstein) by Jan Miense Molenaer; from Schloss Feldsberg (now Valtice, Czech Republic) the Prince brought, among other works, animal paintings by Frans Snyders. According to contemporary reports, the pictures he bought included works by Poussin, Perugino, Tintoretto, Tiepolo, Correggio, Jan van Huysum and Jacob Jordaens. All the works by old German masters in the collection are also said to have been acquired by Francis-Joseph. Eight portraits of the Prince and his family were painted by Friedrich Ölenhainz (1745–1804) in 1776, and the Swede Alexandre Roslin painted a half-length portrait of the Prince (both Vaduz, Samml. Liechtenstein) in 1778.

BIBLIOGRAPHY

J. Dallinger: *Katalog der Galerie Liechtenstein in Wien* (Vienna, 1780)

G. Wilhelm: *Die Fürsten von Liechtenstein und ihre Beziehungen zu Kunst und Wissenschaft* (Schaan, 1976), pp. 11–179, esp. 131–3

**(6) Alois(-Joseph** [Josef]**) I**, Prince of Liechtenstein (*b* 14 May 1759; *reg* 1781–1805; *d* Vienna, 24 March 1805). Son of (5) Francis-Joseph I. He concentrated on the administration and modernization of the family's possessions and built several palace theatres. He enlarged the Liechtenstein family Kupferstichkabinett with the acquisition of the collection of engravings of Baron Gundel in 1783 and expanded the family library, building for it a new room in his palace on the Herrengasse in Vienna in 1793.

The Prince moved the family's picture collections, scattered over several palaces, into the Majoratsgalerie in Vienna, together with new acquisitions of his own, and sold minor works at auctions in 1799 and 1800. The gallery's catalogue, compiled in 1805 by Johann Dallinger von Dalling (1741–1806), includes *c.* 800 works. Among Prince Alois's 306 purchases was the oil painting *Leopards Attacking a Lion* (1665–7; Vaduz, Samml. Liechtenstein) by Carl Borromäus Andreas Ruthart, purchased from the collection of Freiherr von Bartholotti von Barthenfeld in Vienna in 1786 (see 1985 exh. cat., p. 248). In 1794 Eduard Ströhling painted the Prince's portrait, and, according to the Prince's records, Elisabeth-Louise Vigée Le Brun that (untraced) of his wife. Prince Alois's predilection for architecture and botany culminated in the grandiose remodelling (from 1790) of the park of Schloss Eisgrub in Moravia (now Lednice, Czech Republic) as an English landscape garden with various Romantic buildings, ponds and exotic copses. His architect was Joseph Hardtmuth (1758–1816).

**(7) John** [Johann] **(-Joseph** [Josef]**) I**, Prince of Liechtenstein (*b* Vienna, 27 June 1760; *reg* 1805–36; *d* Vienna, 20 April 1836). Brother of (6) Alois I. The principality of Liechtenstein attained full sovereignty in 1806 during his reign, and the Prince strengthened the family possessions by administrative reforms and by a skilful purchasing policy. He increased the gallery's holding from 840 to 1613 pictures: there was hardly an auction in Vienna at which he did not buy paintings. The Prince admired atmospheric Dutch landscapes of the 17th century, such as *Hilly Landscape* (1666; Vaduz, Samml. Liechtenstein) by Jan Wijnants. In 1810 he had the picture gallery moved from Vienna to the summer palace or Gartenpalais in der Rossau, creating a 'museum in the landscape'.

Prince John I built numerous palaces in the early Romantic spirit, restored castles and was a devotee of English gardens and ruins. Joseph Hardtmuth (1758–1816), Joseph Kornhüsel and Franz Engel (*d* 1827) worked for him as architects. His castles are depicted in paintings (1813–14; Vaduz, Samml. Liechtenstein) by Ferdinand Runk (1764–1834). To the landscape garden around Schloss Eisgrub (Lednice, Czech Republic) begun by his brother Alois I, he added an artificial neo-Gothic ruin, the Hansenburg (1807). A new historic awareness induced John I to buy and restore (along with many other ruins) the Liechtenstein family's original castle near Mödling, south of Vienna. The Prince's portrait was painted in 1816 by Johann Baptist Lampi (i), and his wife's by Angelica Kauffman (both Vaduz, Samml. Liechtenstein).

BIBLIOGRAPHY

O. Criste: *Feldmarschall Johannes, Fürst von Liechtenstein* (Vienna, 1905)

G. Schmidt: 'Fürst Johann I. (1760–1836): "Souveränität und Modernisierung" Liechtensteins', *Liechtenstein, fürstliches Haus und staatliche Ordnung: Geschichtliche Grundlagen und moderne Perspektiven*, ed. V. Press and D. Willoweit (Vaduz, Munich and Vienna, 1987), pp. 382–418

**(8) Alois (-Joseph** [Josef]**) II**, Prince of Liechtenstein (*b* Vienna, 25 May 1796; *reg* 1836–58; *d* Eisgrub [Lednice, Czech Republic], 12 Nov 1858). Son of (7) John I. With a programme of conservative reforms and early industrial enterprises the Prince guided his family successfully into the modern era, using Britain as his model. In 1842 he became the first prince of Liechtenstein to visit the principality.

Alois II did not modify the structure of the Liechtenstein gallery, then at Rossau, but tended and preserved it. He favoured the Viennese Biedermeier style and bought paintings by such contemporary Austrian painters as Ferdinand Georg Waldmüller, Friedrich von Amerling, Johann Ranftl (1805–54), Peter Fendi, Joseph Kriehuber (1800–76) and Friedrich Gauermann. The Viennese painter Josef Höger (1801–77), who executed watercolours of many Liechtenstein family castles and palaces (examples Vaduz, Samml. Liechtenstein), was drawing teacher to the Prince's children. Rudolf Alt was commissioned by the Prince to execute paintings (Vaduz, Samml. Liechtenstein) of the interiors of the Viennese palaces and those in Feldsberg (Valtice, Czech Republic), Eisgrub (Lednice, Czech Republic) and Seebenstein. Von Amerling also painted a portrait of the Prince, who was depicted dressed in the robes of the Order of the Golden Fleece (Vaduz, Samml. Liechtenstein).

Alois II was a significant architectural patron, his architects including Georg Wingelmüller (1810–48) and the Englishman Peter Hubert Desvignes. Among his most important projects was the elegant remodelling c. 1840 of the Majoratspalast (now Palais Liechtenstein) at Bankgasse 9 (formerly Schenkenstrassenpalast) in Vienna, in the style of the 'Second Rococo' (*see* AUSTRIA, fig. 27). He had Schloss Eisgrub rebuilt (1845–58) in the English Tudor Gothic style, making it the most important neo-Gothic palace in Moravia. Its winter garden, designed by Desvignes, was completed by 1845, before the London Crystal Palace by Joseph Paxton, and soon became famous as the first large glass and iron structure in the Habsburg empire; its glasshouse still exists. The restoration of the Moravian Schloss Lundenburg (Břeclav, Czech Republic), also indebted to English Gothic, and the interior decoration of Burg Seebenstein with a medieval armoury are notable examples of mid-19th-century historicism. The Prince decided to enlarge the semi-derelict Schloss Vaduz in the principality of Liechtenstein in the 1840s, for which Martin Kink (1800–77) made designs (1842; Bregenz, Vorarlberg. Landesmus., MS. 243/25), but the project was not executed until a generation later.

BIBLIOGRAPHY

H. Recht: *Eisgrub in graphischen Bilddarstellungen des 18. und 19. Jahrhunderts* (Vienna, 1979)

E. Castellani Zahir: *Die Wiederherstellung von Schloss Vaduz, 1904 bis 1914: Burgendenkmalpflege zwischen Historismus und Moderne*, 2 vols (Vaduz, 1993)

**(9) John** [Johann] **II**, Prince of Liechtenstein (*b* Eisgrub [Lednice, Czech Republic], 5 Oct 1840; *reg* 1858–1929; *d* Feldsberg [Valtice, Czech Republic], 11 Feb 1929). Son of (8) Alois II. In his reign Liechtenstein was transformed into a constitutional monarchy and turned, politically and economically, away from Austria and towards Switzerland. However, the Prince was rarely in Liechtenstein, preferring Vienna, Eisgrub and Feldsberg. An enthusiastic collector of antiquities, often acquiring them on his travels, he enriched the gallery in the Gartenpalace in der Rossau with an important collection of works of art and crafts. New 'epoch rooms', with pictures and examples of the decorative arts, were arranged in a cosy, atmospheric manner.

After John II had subjected the family's collection to rigorous scrutiny, some pictures were sent to other Liechtenstein palaces, and some were auctioned in Paris; the gallery catalogue of 1885 lists only 839 works, compared with 1451 works 12 years before. As a collector, the Prince sought to complement the existing works and to represent each artistic epoch by its most important artists. He acquired many Italian Renaissance and early Dutch paintings, including, for example, *Rich Cuisine* (?before 1651; Vaduz, Samml. Liechtenstein) by Jan Steen. The Prince took advice from the art historian Wilhelm Bode, who systematized the collection. John II also made generous donations to museums and public collections, notably in Vienna, and financed archaeological research and art-historical publications, including *Österreichische Burgen* (Vienna, 1902–10) by Otto Piper (1841–1921), *Die Markgrafschaft Mähren in kunstgeschichtlicher Beziehung* (Vienna, 1904) by August Prokop and Max Lehrs's *Der deutsche, niederländische und französische Kupferstich des 15. Jahrhunderts* (Vienna, 1908).

John II's highly developed historical understanding gave rise to numerous restorations of castles, including the Feste Liechtenstein near Mödling (1884–1903), the ancestral castle in Lower Austria, then Burg Fischhorn (1862–7) in the Salzburg region, Schloss Sternberg (1885–1913) in Moravia (now Šternberk, Czech Republic) and Schloss Vaduz (1904–14) in the principality of Liechtenstein. John II initiated architectural projects in both the ecclesiastical and secular spheres, notably the neo-Gothic parish church in Vaduz (1869–73) by Friedrich von Schmidt and buildings by Gustav von Neumann (1856–1928), Ignaz Banko (1839–97) and the Vaduz architect Egon Rheinberger (1839–97).

BIBLIOGRAPHY

F. Kraetzl: *Das Fürstentum Liechtenstein und der gesamte Fürst Johann von und zu Liechtenstein'sche Güterbesitz* (Brünn, 1898, rev. 8/1914/*R* 1984)

K. Höss: *Fürst Johann II von Liechtenstein und die bildende Kunst* (Vienna, 1908)

E. Castellani Zahir: *Die Wiederherstellung von Schloss Vaduz, 1904 bis 1914: Burgendenkmalpflege zwischen Historismus und Moderne*, 2 vols (Vaduz and Stuttgart, 1993)

E. CASTELLANI ZAHIR

**Liechtenstein**, Principality of. Country in Europe, bordered to the south and west by Switzerland and to the east by Austria. It has an area of *c.* 160 sq. km and a population of *c.* 33,000. The capital is Vaduz. In 1719 the Holy Roman Emperor Charles VI elevated the Lordship of Schellenberg and the county of Vaduz to the rank of the imperial principality of Liechtenstein. It is the only state of the Holy Roman Empire (dissolved 1806), the Rhenish Confederation (dissolved 1815) and the German Confederation (dissolved 1866) that exists in its original form. In 1921 the principality was given the constitution that is still in use today, whereby democratic and parliamentary rights were integrated with hereditary monarchy; the ruling family is the House of Liechtenstein (*see* LIECHTENSTEIN, House of, above), of Austrian origin. In 1923 Liechtenstein formed a customs union with Switzerland, and in 1990 its sovereignty was confirmed by its acceptance as a member state of the United Nations.

NORBERT W. HASLER

**Liédet, Loyset** (*b* ?Hesdin, *c.* 1420; *d* Bruges, 1479). South Netherlandish illuminator. His earliest work is a two-volume copy of Jean Mansel's *Fleur des histoires* (Paris, Bib. Arsenal, MSS 5087–8), which, according to the colophon, was completed in Hesdin in 1454. A bill dated 29 March 1460 refers to this manuscript, stating that Liédet, who was then in Hesdin, was paid for 'cinquante cinq histoires, vignettes, grosses lettres et paraffes' in a *Fleur des histoires* for Philip the Good, Duke of Burgundy. The influence of SIMON MARMION is very clear on Liédet's best miniatures in the first volume. In the second volume there is stylistic evidence that Liédet collaborated with the Master of Amiens 200, named after a Book of Hours (Amiens, Bib. Mun., MS. 200), who originated from Marmion's circle.

There are no further references to Liédet until 1468, when he was in Bruges, becoming a member of the Bruges guild the following year. A large number of commissions is recorded for 1468: in July he was paid for 51 miniatures in the first volume of a four-volume copy of *Renaud de Montauban* (Paris, Bib. Arsenal, MSS 5072–5), for 20 miniatures in a *Bible moralisée* and for 20 more in a copy of the *Vengeance de Nostre Seigneur* (Chatsworth, Derbys., no. 7310; see fig.). In November he was paid for 22 miniatures in the third volume of *Chroniques de Hainaut* (Brussels, Bib. Royale Albert 1er, MSS 9242–4; for illustration *see* BURGUNDY, (3)), the frontispiece of the first volume of which is attributed to Rogier van der Weyden. The second volume of the *Renaud de Montauban* followed in December, with the third and fourth volumes being completed in June and August 1469. In January 1470 Liédet was paid for a fifth volume (Munich, Bayer.

Loyset Liédet: *Maître Alphonse on his Sick-bed*, miniature from the *Vengeance de Nostre Seigneur*, 1468 (Chatsworth, Derbyshire, no. 7310, fol. 4*r*)

Staatsbib., Cod. gall. 7). A bill dated February 1470 records payments for seven miniatures in a copy of Jean Froissart's *Chronique de France*, which can perhaps be identified with the Breslau copy (Berlin, Staatsbib. Preuss. Kultbes., MS. Dep. Breslau I), and for three more in a copy of Philippe de Mezières's *Songe du vieil pelerin* (Paris, Bib. N., MSS fr. 9200–1). In November 1470 Liédet was paid for 86 miniatures in a copy of the *Faits et gestes d'Alexandre*, translated from the original of Quintus Curtius Rufus (Paris, Bib. N., MS. fr. 22547). Authentication for Liédet's largest work, the *Chausons de Charles Martel* (Brussels, Bib. Royale Albert 1er, MSS 6–9), is provided by a bill of 31 March 1472, and by a signature on one of the miniatures (MS. 9, fol. 7*r*). The signature *Loysit* appears in another manuscript (New York, Pierpont Morgan Lib., MS. M. 672, fol. 88*r*).

Liédet sometimes worked wholly or partly in grisaille (e.g. the Breslau Froissart), but most of his work is distinguished by its gaudy, artificial colouring, dominated on the one hand by contrasting tones of russet, orange and pink, and on the other by a rich, bright blue. The latter was used not only on garments, where it is shaded with black to create convincing lustre effects, but also for roofs and landscape backgrounds, and even for hair and beards. Bilious green and a liberal use of gold add variety to the palette. A strong, dark brown is often used for the roof tops, as well as blue; and the bricks of town-walls, for example, are painted in a striking pink. The buildings that border these colourful scenes are grey, often tending towards green, blue or violet tones. The lighting can be very bright and harsh, with an almost complete absence of shadows. Dogaer has observed that the miniatures in the works produced in Hesdin are surrounded by borders, whereas those of the Bruges period are framed only by a simple gold bar, without the border decoration customary in other Bruges manuscripts, a simplification possibly determined by economic factors.

Liédet's figures have long, awkwardly jointed limbs, and stiff poses. The men almost always stand with their legs apart and their knees bent, a stance that looks curiously awkward and unstable. The garments are of coarse material, which falls in wide folds, with intricately pleated, tubular folds standing out sharply from the smoother sections. As a result, the fabric often appears mannered. The faces are all of the same type, with distinctive long, straight noses and large, sleepy-looking black eyes, the eyelids drawn in an elongated curve. The head of a young man with long, bushy black curls appears in almost every work. The men's faces are so heavily modelled with black or brownish shading that they look unshaven, and the dark tone in which their cheeks are painted stands out sharply against the lighter flesh colour of the rest of the face. The naso-labial fold is always a sharp black line. The female faces by contrast look empty and dull. A typical motif in Liédet's landscapes is a type of poplar with a thin, stakelike trunk and a crown like candy-floss, while his views of towns show many dormer windows on the roof tops. The picture planes are constructed with views into alleys or houses, opened like arcades, through town gates or into gardens, but Liédet's control of foreshortening and the perspectival scaling down of figures is rarely successful.

Liédet's painting gives the impression that he was attempting to imitate models of a higher quality, with increasing success. He was clearly not among the leading artists of his period, yet his work is worthy of attention on several counts. He seems to have been the most active illuminator at the Burgundian court *c.* 1470, producing over 400 miniatures in two years for Charles the Bold. This places him among the last representatives of the generation of illuminators who worked to commission rather than speculatively for the open market. The variety of subjects he illustrated poses questions concerning his methods of design and the sources of his models. Liédet also provides an opportunity to examine the way in which such an evidently efficient illuminator's workshop was organized: for example, the Master of Amiens 200 must have been a member of Liédet's workshop *c.* 1454–60, although he is not mentioned in any documents, while an illuminator called Pol Fruit is recorded as having been paid separately for painting the initials in the *Chansons de Charles Martel.*

BIBLIOGRAPHY

J. van den Gheyn: *Histoire de Charles-Martel: Reproduction des 102 miniatures de Loyset Liedet, 1470* (Brussels and Paris, 1910)

F. Winkler: 'Loyset Liédet, der Meister des goldenen Vliesses und der Breslauer Froissart', *Repert. Kstwiss.*, xxxiv (1911), pp. 224–31

H. Martin: *Les Histoires romaines de Jean Mansel, illustrées par Loyset Liédet* (Paris, 1914)

P. Durrieu: *La Miniature flamande au temps de la cour de Bourgogne, 1415–1530* (Brussels and Paris, 1921)

F. Winkler: *Die flämische Buchmalerei* (Leipzig, 1925/R Amsterdam, 1978), pp. 75–8

*Le Siècle d'or de la miniature flamande* (exh. cat. by L. M. J. Delaissé, Brussels, Pal. B.-A.; Amsterdam, Rijksmus.; Paris, Bib. N.; 1959), pp. 69–75, 101, 123–30

P. Cockshaw: *Les Miniatures des Chroniques de Hainaut* (Mons, 1979), pp. 10–13, 214–57

G. Dogaer: *Flemish Miniature Painting in the 15th and 16th Centuries* (Amsterdam, 1987), pp. 106–12

BODO BRINKMANN

**Lieferinxe** [Lifferin; Lifferinxe], **Josse** [Master of St Sebastian] (*fl* 1493–1505; *d* before 16 Oct 1508). South Netherlandish painter, active in France. A native of Hainaut, in the diocese of Cambrai, he may have come from Lieferinge near Enghien (Claessens). He is documented in Marseille and Aix-en-Provence from 1493 to 1505, often being described as a 'Picard painter'. In 1503 he married Michelle, one of the daughters of Jean Changenet, the most prominent painter of the time in Avignon, with whom he may have trained. The last great representative of the 'School of Avignon', Lieferinxe appears to have concentrated on the production of altarpieces.

In 1493 Lieferinxe was working on behalf of a Marseille painter, Philippon Mauroux, on an altarpiece of the *Madonna of Mercy* (untraced) for the Hôpital St Lazare in Marseille. On 14 June 1497 Guillaume Tiénard, a carpenter of Marseille, entrusted Lieferinxe with the painting of an altarpiece of the *Virgin and Child with SS John and Peter* that he had made (untraced); this contract describes Lieferinxe as a painter, citizen and inhabitant of Marseille. At this time Lieferinxe was associated with a Piedmontese painter, Bernardino Simondi (mentioned in Die, Aix and Marseille 1496–8). On 11 July 1497 Lieferinxe and Simondi were commissioned by the confraternity of St Sebastian to paint their chapel (destr.) in Notre-Dame-des-Accoules,

1. Josse Lieferinxe: *St Irene Ministers to St Sebastian*, panel, 800× 500 mm, 1497–8 (Philadelphia, PA, Museum of Art)

Marseille, and to provide a new altarpiece that was to depict a nude, martyred *St Sebastian with SS Anthony and Roche* and scenes from the *Life of St Sebastian* on the eight side panels; the predella was to include a *Pietà*. After Simondi's death Lieferinxe signed a new contract on 6 August 1498 agreeing to honour this commission, and in the same year he undertook to finish an altarpiece barely begun by Simondi for Barthélémy Capeau, a Marseille merchant, agreeing also to paint Capeau's portrait and those of his family. In his will filed in Aix on 12 May 1498 Simondi bequeathed to Lieferinxe a sketchbook of original drawings.

Lieferinxe was also commissioned to paint a number of works now untraced: an altarpiece representing *St Crispin between SS Louis and Crispinian* for the Confrérie des Cordonniers for the Chapelle St Crépin in the Augustinian church in Aix (11 Aug 1499); an altarpiece of *St Anthony of Padua* for the Confrérie de St Antoine de Padoue for the Franciscan church in Aix (30 Oct 1499; replacing a previous contract dated 30 Dec 1498); a painting for the mariner Raphaël Rostang of the *Virgin Suckling the Christ Child* (with a man and woman praying at her feet) flanked by scenes of the *Adoration of the Magi* and the *Flight into Egypt*, for the Chapelle Notre-Dame-de-Bethléem in the Franciscan church in Marseille, on the model of that of the *Transfiguration* in the same church (1 Feb 1500); and

2. Josse Lieferinxe (attrib.): *Annunciation*, tempera on panel, 780×570 mm, element from a triptych, *c.* 1500 (Avignon, Musée du Petit Palais)

an altarpiece of the *Visitation*, the background and woodwork of which were to be in burnished gold, for the mother and widow of Jacques Rabasten (13 July 1503). Lieferinxe died between 5 February 1505 and 16 October 1508, the date on which his cousin and heir Hans Clemer gave a receipt for an unfinished altarpiece of *St Mary Magdalene* for the Dominicans of St Maximin.

Four panels illustrating scenes from the *Life of St Sebastian* (*St Sebastian Destroying Idols*; *Martyrdom of St Sebastian*; *St Irene Ministers to St Sebastian* (see fig. 1); *St Sebastian Whipped to Death*; all 800×500 mm; Philadelphia, PA, Mus. A.) have been associated (Sterling, 1941) with the side panels of the altarpiece painted in 1497–8 by Lieferinxe and Simondi for Notre-Dame-des-Accoules, Marseille. Three other panels from the same series have also been recovered subsequently: *St Sebastian before Diocletian and Maximilian* (St Petersburg, Hermitage), *St Sebastian Intervenes during the Plague in Rome* (Baltimore, MD, Walters A.G.) and *Pilgrims before the Tomb of St Sebastian* (Rome, Pal. Barberini). The identification of these panels with the contract of 1497 seems confirmed both by the depiction of several scenes of the Life of St Sebastian, which is very rare for altarpieces, and by the blend of northern, chiefly Dutch characteristics (the technique, figure types and poses are derived from Geertgen tot Sint Jans) with Piedmontese elements (showing affiliations to works by Giovanni Martini Spanzotti), which ties in with the origins of Lieferinxe and Simondi. The

panels also show links with the mid-15th-century Provençal style (e.g. Enguerrand Quarton), however, in the clearly defined compositions—the figures noble and reserved despite their quality of pathos—and in the energetic use of light with strong contrasts, emphasizing volumes. Although it is difficult to determine precisely the contribution of each painter, the premature death of Simondi tends to suggest that Lieferinxe was responsible for at least the final effects of these scenes, their lighting and range of colours. It has also been proposed that a *Pietà* (Antwerp, Kon. Mus. S. Kst.) formed the central element of the predella, but this seems unlikely.

Other works have been attributed to Lieferinxe on the basis of style. These comprise five scenes from the *Life of the Virgin*, probably from a large triptych with movable wings: a *Marriage of the Virgin* (800×600 mm; Brussels, Pal. B.-A.), an *Annunciation* (see fig. 2) with *St Michael* on the reverse, a *Visitation* (Paris, Louvre), a *Circumcision* with *St Catherine* (780×580 mm) on the reverse (both Avignon, Mus. Petit Pal.) and two fragmentary panels, an *Adoration of the Christ Child* with the lower part of the figure of a bishop on the back (390×590 mm; Paris, Louvre) and a *Visitation* with a figure of *St Lucy* on the back (385×475 mm); it has sometimes been suggested that a monumental *Calvary* (1.70×1.26 m; Paris, Louvre) could have formed the central panel of the altarpiece. These paintings, marked by a greater serenity than the *St Sebastian* series, and showing even clearer influence of Enguerrand Quarton, are probably later, like the *Calvary* in the Louvre, the *Pietà* in Antwerp, the fragmentary painting of *Abraham and the Three Angels* (460×670 mm; Denver, CO, A. Mus.), inspired by a composition by Antonello da Messina (Reggio Calabria, Mus. N.) and an important *Ecce homo*. An *Adoration of the Magi* (2.27×2.03 m; Carpentras, Mus. Duplessis) of fairly dry workmanship may be a replica of a lost panel by Lieferinxe.

BIBLIOGRAPHY

Abbé J. H. Albanès: 'Josse Lifferin, peintre marseillais du XVe siècle', *Bull. Archéol. Cté Trav. Hist. & Sci.* (1884), pp. 240–58

L. H. Labande: *Les Primitifs français: Peintres et peintres-verriers de la Provence occidentale* (Marseille, 1932), pp. 129–31, 140

C. Sterling: *La Peinture française: Les Peintres du moyen âge* (Paris, 1941), pp. 54–5; XVe siècle suppl. A, pp. 34–8

——: 'Two XV-century Provençal Painters Revived (II): The Master of St Sebastian (Josse Lieferinxe?)', *Gaz. B.-A.*, xxii (1942), pp. 135–48

——: 'Josse Lieferinxe, peintre provençal', *Rev. Louvre*, xiv/1 (1964), pp. 1–22

M. Laclotte and D. Thiébaut: *L'Ecole d'Avignon* (Paris, 1983), pp. 104–13, 255–64

H. Claessens: 'Le Maître de Saint Sébastien alias Josse Lieferinxe', *L'Oeil*, 377 (1986), pp. 40–43

D. Thiébaut: 'Josse Lieferinxe et son influence en Provence', *Homage à Michel Laclotte* (Milan and Paris, 1994), pp. 194–214

DOMINIQUE THIÉBAUT

**Liefrinck.** Netherlandish family of artists. There are at least two families of printmakers with this surname, and it is unclear whether or not or exactly how they were related. Willem Liefrinck (*b* Augsburg, 1490; *d* Antwerp, 1542) was a woodcutter, who worked in Augsburg in 1516 and 1518 on book illustrations for Emperor Maximilian. His son Hans Liefrinck I (*b* ?Augsburg, ?1518; *d* Antwerp, *bur* 28 Feb 1573) was active in Antwerp as a print publisher, engraver, woodcutter and etcher from 1538 until his death. Among the prints attributed to him are portrait engravings of the nobility and clergy, and a series of 44 woodcut portraits of *Princes and Princesses* (Hollstein, nos 92–135) after Cornelis Anthonisz. Hans I's daughter Mynken [Wilhelmine] Liefrinck (*fl* Antwerp, *c.* 1567–82) was a printer, illuminator and woodcutter, who worked mainly for Christoph Plantin in Antwerp, printing and hand-colouring maps and engraved book illustrations; she was also responsible for a woodcut *Map of Greece* (1578; Hollstein, no. 1) after Hubertus Goltzius.

Cornelis Liefrinck I (*b* Antwerp; *d* before 1545) was also active in the print workshop of Emperor Maximilian in Augsburg; from 1510 to 1518 he worked on the same imperial projects as Hans I (who was perhaps a brother or cousin). Cornelis I's son Hans Liefrinck II (*fl* Leiden, from 1567; *d* Leiden, 1599) seems to have worked exclusively in Leiden, where he drew mostly maps and plans. On 22 August 1580 he was honoured by the Leiden magistrates for his plan and view of Leiden, which featured in Guicciardini's *Descrittione. . .di tutti Paesi Bassi* (published by Plantin, Antwerp, 1581). In 1584 Hans II provided a cartoon with an allegorical representation of the *Liberation of Leiden*, which included a plan of the town, for a tapestry woven in 1587 by Joost Jansz. Lanckaert (Leiden, Stadhuis). The only print by him catalogued by Hollstein is a woodcut *Vignette with the Coat of Arms of Leiden* (1575; Hollstein, no. 1), which appeared in J. J. Orlers's *Beschryvinge der stad Leyden* (Leiden, 1614). (It is unlikely that the Hans Liefrinck II enrolled in the Antwerp Guild of St Luke in 1581 as the son of a master was the same artist, despite the connection made by Bénézit; he is more likely to be an as yet unidentified son of Hans I.) Hans II of Leiden had a son Cornelis Johannesz. Liefrinck (*b* Leiden, *c.* 1581; *d* after 1640), who was a painter and engraver in Leiden until 1626, when he served as a paintings assessor along with Jan van Goyen.

BIBLIOGRAPHY

Bénézit; Hollstein: *Dut. & Flem.*; Thieme–Becker

*Bull. Rijksmus.*, xxix (1981), p. 33 [list of recent acquisitions]

JETTY E. VAN DER STERRE

**Liège** [Flem. Luik; Ger. Lüttich]. Belgian city on the River Meuse and capital of Liège province, Wallonia, with a population of *c.* 202,000.

1. History and urban development. 2. Art life and organization. 3. Centre of production. 4. St Jacques.

1. HISTORY AND URBAN DEVELOPMENT.

The fertile Meuse Valley was among the earliest agricultural settlements in Europe. Liège became prominent when St Hubert, Bishop of Maastricht (*d* AD 727), transferred his see to the city in AD 721. A period of rapid economic expansion transformed the rural bishopric into a prosperous settlement with progressive land clearing and abundant production of corn, wool, linen and metalwork. The principality took shape with the annexation of 184 *villae*, Theux Forest and important local abbeys with their estates. Situated within the heartland of the Carolingian empire in the 9th century, Liège became the capital of a large principality. In 972 Holy Roman Emperor Otto I elevated Notger (*reg* 972–1008) to the see. Notger vigorously pursued a policy of aggrandizement, extending territory and commerce and fortifying the city. He adopted the title of

Prince-Bishop in 980. The prince-bishops wielded substantial political and economic power until their fall from power during the French Revolution. They endowed hundreds of churches, patronized scholars and musicians, and presided over the Mosan school of ivory-, gold- and silverwork (*see* §3(ii) below) as well as sculpture and architecture. The cathedral of St Lambert (ded. 1050; destr. 1794), a prototype of Mosan architecture, showed Carolingian influence in its double-ended choir, two towers, squared apse and vaults on columns. Some 240 churches survive from the 10th–12th centuries, including St Denis (founded 987), with polygonal choir and tower at the west end, St Jean (*c.* 998), modelled on the octagonal Palatine chapel at Aachen, and the Mosan Romanesque St Barthélemy (1010–15), with its flat chevet, external crypt and transept with radiating apsidal chapels. The cathedral school became a centre of learning in Latin Christendom, and Liégeois merchants and artisans could be found in the new towns of central Europe.

Although Liège continued to expand—from 25 to 196 ha—the 12th century brought important changes. The Papacy and the French Crown were growing more powerful, and the influence of the university of Paris, and of the architecture of the Ile-de-France, Burgundy and Champagne, eclipsed that of entrenched Liégeois scholars and artists. The cathedral was rebuilt in Gothic style over four campaigns, adding two choirs and transepts, and radiating apsidal chapels (1189 to mid-14th century). The Gothic style persisted in the churches of St Paul (1232 to the beginning of the 15th century), St Jacques (11th–15th centuries; *see* §4 below) and St Nicholas and St Hubert (both 16th century).

In a region of small towns, only Liège and Tournai had a population exceeding 10,000 in 1400. Not only was Liège a capital city, it was also an industrial town; coal had been mined there since the 12th century and much of its wealth derived from metallurgical industries. As with most European cities of the time, there were fierce clashes between the bourgeoisie and the nobility, but neither could withstand the power of Charles the Bold, 4th Duke of Burgundy, who punished Liégeois resistance to his authority by razing the city in 1468. The accession of Prince-Bishop Erard de la Marck (*reg* 1506–38) brought renewed prosperity as coal and iron mining expanded and Liège became the armaments manufacturer to all of Europe. An energetic defender of Liège's independence, Erard maintained a political and religious neutrality that kept the principality out of the 16th-century Wars of Religion. He was also a generous patron of the arts. The Italianate Renaissance Palais des Prince-Evêques was begun under Arnould van Mulken (*fl* 1513–40) in 1526. The first of its two courtyards is surrounded with 60 columns, the capital of each carved with a grotesque inspired by images of the New World and by Desiderius Erasmus's *Praise of Folly* (1511).

From the 16th to the 18th century the Bavarian prince-bishops pursued a policy of neutrality and capitalism, and the profits of industrial growth financed *c.* 30 new convents, chapels and hospitals. The interiors of St Barthélemy, St Denis and St Lambert were renovated in 18th-century Rococo style, and a classical façade was added to the Palais. Jean de Corte, supplier of munitions to the king of Spain, had a mansion (now Musée Curtius) built *c.* 1600. The red-brick Renaissance house with high-pitched roof and tower cost about one million gold francs. The brick house (early 18th century) of Liège banker Michel Willems had 21 windows in its façade; the internal furnishings were entirely of solid carved oak without any painting and gilding, but the ceilings were ornate Rococo stucco.

Liège elected a National Assembly in 1793 and union with France was decreed in 1795. The cathedral, loathed symbol of princely power, was torn down, its stone subsequently quarried for building in the 19th century. The Théâtre Royal, built in 1818, incorporates carved columns taken from the city's charterhouse. In 1831, Liège became part of the newly created independent state of Belgium. Most of medieval Liège has disappeared: walls, towers, churches and frescoes are gone; bridges were destroyed in World War II; little survives of the workers' quarters; and in the 1960s houses were destroyed in the course of further urban development.

For an illustration of the fort at Liège *see* MILITARY ARCHITECTURE AND FORTIFICATION, fig. 22.

BIBLIOGRAPHY
*Dict. Eglises France*
J. Lejeune: *Liège et son pays: Naissance d'une patrie* (Paris and Liège, 1948)
L.-F. Genicot: *Les Eglises romanes du pays mosan* (Celles, 1970)
J. van Ackere: *Belgique baroque et classique* (Brussels, 1972)
L.-F. Genicot, ed.: *Histoire de la Wallonie* (Toulouse, 1973)

2. ART LIFE AND ORGANIZATION. Notger, the first Prince-Bishop (*reg* 972–1008), was the earliest major patron in Liège. From that period, the principality was the main centre for Mosan art, which was produced in the area around the River Meuse. During the 12th century the Liège region was one of the most brilliant artistic centres of western Europe, noted for its manuscript painting, sculpture and, above all, metalwork, especially enamelwork (*see* ROMANESQUE, §VII, and BELGIUM, fig. 22). It lost this status during the 13th century, when artists rejected local traditions in favour of French Gothic. The Gothic art of Liège remains relatively unknown, largely because much was destroyed during the sack of Liège ordered by Charles the Bold, 4th Duke of Burgundy, in 1468. However, a new artistic vigour emerged during the reign of Prince-Bishop Erard de la Marck (*reg* 1506–38). It was then that Gothic art reached its apogee in Liège, and the precepts of the Renaissance began to be introduced. The leading exponent of Renaissance ideas in Liège was the humanist artist LAMBERT LOMBARD, who founded *c.* 1538 the first northern academy of art in the city, said to have been modelled on that supposedly run by Baccio Bandinelli in Florence. Lombard's workshop trained some of the great Flemish artists of that time.

In the 17th century a new school of painting was developed by such artists as GÉRARD DOUFFET, BERTHO-LET FLÉMAL, Jean-Guillaume Carlier and Gérard de Lairesse. This was influenced more by Italy and France than by Flanders. The leading sculptor was JEAN DELCOUR, a founder of the Liège Baroque school, which lasted until the end of the 18th century. During this period the guilds in Liège retained their rigid organization, and no distinction was made between artists and artisans. Painters wishing to work had to register with the goldsmiths' guild and sculptors were likewise members of the carpenters' guild. Throughout the 17th and 18th centuries artists attempted to break free from the guilds.

Painters officially obtained their autonomy in 1769. Two years later proposals were put forward for a school of drawing. The Prince-Bishop François-Charles de Velbruck (*reg* 1772–84) agreed to the project; a school of architecture followed in 1774, and in 1775 the Académie de Peinture, de Sculpture et de Gravure was founded, which survived only until the French Revolution. Léonard Defrance, a founder and director of Velbruck's Académie and a painter of genre scenes, was the only painter of note in Liège during the 18th century. However, the decorative arts flourished, especially goldsmiths' work and the production of distinctive furniture. After the Revolution, the early 19th century was marked by rather provincial interpretations of Neo-classicism, Romanticism and historicism. From the mid-19th century most of Liège's best artists were trained either at the Académie des Beaux-Arts (founded in 1835) or at the Ecole St Luc (founded in 1880).

BIBLIOGRAPHY
J. Helbig and J. Brassinne: *L'Art mosan depuis l'introduction du christianisme jusqu'à la fin du XVIIIe siècle*, 2 vols (Brussels, 1906–11)
T. Gobert: 'Les Débuts de l'enseignement des beaux-arts à Liège', *Bull. Inst. Archéol. Liég.*, xliii (1913), pp. 13–87
J. Bosmant: *La Peinture et la sculpture au pays de Liège de 1793 à nos jours* (Liège, 1930)
L. Tollanaere: *La Sculpture sur pierre de l'ancien diocèse de Liège à l'époque romane* (Gembloux, 1957)
J. J. M. Timmers: *De kunst van het Maasland*, 2 vols (Assen, 1971–80)
R. Lejeune and J. Stiennon, eds: *La Wallonie, le pays et les hommes: Lettres, arts, culture*, 4 vols (Brussels, 1977–80)

PIERRE-YVES KAIRIS

3. CENTRE OF PRODUCTION.

(i) *Furniture.* So-called 'Liège' furniture denotes the luxury pieces produced in Wallonia during the 18th century. With a few exceptions, these highly decorative items were made in the major French Louis XIV to Louis XVI styles, oak being the preferred timber for massive carved work. The most popular categories included storage cabinets, the well-known longcase and cartel clocks, frames for mirrors, barometer cases and beautifully worked doors, panelling and wainscoting for private houses as well as churches. Fine marquetry commodes and secretaires, buffets, corner-cupboards, and library bookcases survive in large numbers, while seat furniture included elaborately ornamented chairs, settees and couches. Local furniture-makers also produced all kinds of tables and stands.

With a few exceptions, furniture made in Liège was rarely signed or dated, although many furniture-makers have been identified through archival research and some official commissions are also well documented. Sources included the engravings and pattern books published in France by Jean Berain I, Daniel Marot, J. Ch. Weigeles, J. G. Hertel and François de Neufforge. Liège pieces in the Louis XIV style can be dated approximately between 1715 and 1740. The asymmetrical Rococo style was in fashion between about 1740 and 1765, after which the more restrained Louis XVI style was introduced. To a lesser degree marquetry furniture was also made in Liège, as well as partly painted and gilded storage cabinets. Nearly all this furniture is preserved either in monasteries in Liège or in various Wallonian museums and private collections. Authenticity can be problematic: in the middle of the 19th century local furniture-makers sometimes produced detailed copies that are difficult to distinguish from original 18th-century pieces. Liège-style furniture was also made in the region of Verviers, Aachen and Namur (although this last centre developed its own distinctive idiom) and is sometimes wrongly attributed to France.

BIBLIOGRAPHY

E. Nemery: *Le Meuble namurois au XVIIIe siècle* (Gembloux, 1970)
J. Philippe: *Le Meuble liégeois à son âge d'or (XVIIIe siècle)* (Liège, 1990)

STÉPHANE VANDENBERGHE

*(ii) Gold and silver.* The goldsmiths of Liège, who were members of the Corporation de St Eloi, had already formed an organized body in the 14th century. Their craft was more important politically than was the case in the cities of the Spanish, later the Austrian, Netherlands. The assaying system of Liège is different from that used elsewhere in Belgium. A hallmark was recorded during the rule of Prince-Bishop Adolf de la Marck (1313–44). From the 15th century a two-headed eagle was used as a hallmark, indicating that Liège was part of the Holy Roman Empire. In the 17th century the year number or letter was stamped in the lower part of this mark. In addition to this *millésime* (eagle stamp with year), the arms of the reigning prince-bishop and the maker's mark, silver made in Liège usually carries a clearly evident assaying scratch, the so-called *strich*. During the 18th century three grades of silver were permitted: the *argent de poinçon*, the silver content of which was the same as that of the local currency; the higher *argent de louis* or *argent de France*, based on the French *écus d'argent* or *louis blancs,* and the *argent de bavière,* the lower silver content of which was the same as that of the local coinage struck by the Prince-Bishops Ernest and Ferdinand de Barrière.

*See also* BELGIUM, §IX, 1(i) and (ii).

BIBLIOGRAPHY

J. Brassinne: *L'Orfèvrerie civile liégeoise,* 4 vols (Liège, 1935–48)
P. Colman: *L'Orfèvrerie religieuse liégeoise du 15e siècle à la Révolution,* 2 vols (Liège, 1966)
D. de Schaetzen and P. Colman: *Orfèvreries liégeoises* (Antwerp, 1976)
——: *Orfèvreries liégeoises: Recueil complémentaire* (Liège, 1979)
——: *Orfèvreries liégeoises: Deuxième recueil complémentaire* (Liège, 1983)
*L'Orfèvrerie civile ancienne du pays de Liège* (exh. cat. by D. de Schaetzen and P. Colman, Liège, Mus. A. Wallon, 1991)

LEO DE REN

4. ST JACQUES. The former Benedictine abbey was founded in AD 1015 by Baldéric II, the Prince-Bishop of Liège, and the church was transformed into a collegiate church in the 18th century and into a parish church in 1803. In 1107 the abbey numbered 23 monks. The present building combines a 12th-century façade block from the Romanesque church, consecrated in 1030, with a Gothic building started in the 15th century. It comprises an aisled nave of six bays, a transept, which does not project except for its annexes, and a sanctuary with two straight bays and an apse. The choir proper has aisles, and five equal, hexagonal radiating chapels opening directly on to the apse, a rare arrangement also found in the contemporary Notre-Dame at Hal. The Romanesque building had a crypt, consecrated in 1016, where the founder was buried; it survived at least until 1551.

The façade block was a western choir, built of sandstone under Abbot Drogon (1153–73), with two square towers (destr. after 1651) framing an octagonal central tower. The interior comprises a groin-vaulted hall choir with spiral staircases in the corners giving access to the upper storey, which is given over to a single large ceilinged chamber. The exterior is articulated by a corbel table and blind arcades. The rebuilding of the eastern choir, begun in the 15th century, halted *c.* 1436, to be resumed in 1513 during the episcopate of Erard de la Marck (*reg* 1506–38), and continued until 1538. The work was directed by Arnould van Mulken (*fl* 1513–40), who combined Renaissance and Late Gothic motifs in the abundant decoration.

Although the choir elevation is of two storeys, resembling Brabantine churches derived from Antwerp Cathedral, its great decorative wealth is more closely related to aspects of German Late Gothic. The relatively low sanctuary arcades are surmounted by a tall clerestory set above a wall passage fronted by a balustrade. Statues crowned by canopies support the vault springers, as at St Martin, Ypres, and Notre-Dame, Hal. There are Italian elements in the style of the stained glass. In the straight bays there are quasi-galleries below the clerestory windows, with an openwork balustrade below their lobed and subcusped arches.

The nave is just as richly ornamented, but its proportions differ. The arcades are much higher, with a double row of trilobed cusps along the intrados; relief heads set in medallions amid delicate arabesques decorate the spandrels. There is a false triforium consisting of two niches set in the back wall of each bay, fronted by an elaborately traceried balustrade. Above the niches are six blind cusped arches divided into two groups by a central mullion to correspond with the clerestory window lights. As in some other churches in Belgium and the Netherlands, the upper elevation is set on a different plane from the arcade. The shallow vault has a lozenge pattern and is decoratively and structurally analogous to English Decorated vaults. The division into bays is completely blurred in the vaults, whereas in elevation it is clearly affirmed. There are numerous bosses, and the vault is highly coloured. The aisles have a Rémois passage with a balustrade, reflecting the persistence of Champenois 13th-century traditions. On the exterior, under a cornice, an openwork gallery runs around the whole building over the clerestory windows.

The portal, built between 1558 and 1568 and attributed to Lambert Lombard, is one of the first manifestations of a classical style in present-day Belgium. This frontispiece, which completely masks a Gothic porch, has three storeys, separated by robust entablatures, and three bays. The lateral bays are narrow and demarcated by Corinthian columns framing niches crowned by rounded broken pediments. In the centre is a large round-arched doorway, and the middle storey is decorated with a large medallion sculpted in low relief, representing the *Dream of Jacob* and framed by Victories and small rectangular panels. The top has two rectangular panels, which must once have been carved, flanking a narrow niche bordered by S-shaped volutes in its upper part and crowned by a rounded broken pediment.

BIBLIOGRAPHY
Abbé L. Hendrix: *L'Eglise Saint-Jacques à Liège* (Liège, 1928)
L. Gothier: 'L'Eglise Saint-Jacques à Liège, *Soc. Royale Vieux Liège: Feuil. Archéol.* (1955)

JACQUES THIEBAUT

**Liège, Jean de.** *See* JEAN DE LIÈGE (i) and (ii).

**Liegeois, Paul** (*fl* Paris, mid-17th century). French painter. He belonged to the circle of Protestant still-life painters working in the Saint-Germain-des-Prés district of Paris in the 17th century, and he was clearly acquainted with the work of Louise Moillon, Jacques Linard and Lubin Baugin. The fluency of his technique owes a debt to Flemish prototypes, yet the sturdy realism of his work is peculiarly French. Unlike contemporary still-life painters, he preferred not to display his fruits in dishes but scattered them as if at random across a table. *Peaches* (Besançon, Mus. B.-A. & Archéol.), which has the fruit with the leaves still attached as if just plucked from a tree, is the opposite of a conventional 'dessert piece'; even Liegeois's customary cloth has been omitted from the simple composition, and the space is ill-defined. Similarly, the small *Plums and Pears on a Table Top* (Dijon, Mus. B.-A.) resembles more a study of fruit than a finished painting. Faré identified Liegeois as an important link between the 'masters of Reality' such as Linard and Moillon and the decorative tradition of French still-life painters of the 18th century.

BIBLIOGRAPHY
M. Faré: *La Nature morte en France* (Geneva, 1962)
——: *Le Grand Siècle de la nature morte en France* (Fribourg, 1974)

LESLEY STEVENSON

**Liemaecker** [Liemaker; Liermacker; Roose], **Nicolaas** [Nicolas; Niklaas] **de** (*b* Ghent, 1600–01; *d* Ghent, 28 Oct 1646). Flemish painter. His father was Jacques de Liemaecker (*fl* 1597–*c*. 1630), a painter in Ghent, where Nicolaas joined the painters' guild in 1624. Nicolaas must have been regarded as one of Ghent's leading artists, judging from the many works known to have been commissioned from him. These were mostly religious subjects and intended for the decoration of churches and cloisters in and around Ghent. De Liemaecker also played an important part in the execution of the mythological compositions made on the occasion of the Joyous Entry into the city of Cardinal-Infante Ferdinand in 1635, undoubtedly the most important official commission placed in Ghent during the 17th century. De Liemaecker has an easily recognizable style, with a preference for mannered effects in composition, movement and facial expression. His early work, of before *c*. 1640, shows a strong sense of modelling, a preference for local colour and the influence of the work of Rubens and Gaspar de Crayer (e.g. *Alexander and Diogenes*, *c*. 1630–35; Ghent, Oudhdknd. Mus. Bijloke). In the work executed after *c*. 1640, mainly altarpieces and devotional subjects (e.g. the *Presentation in the Temple*, Ghent, Klein Beginhof Church), the sense of pathos is stronger, the colours are brighter and there is a sharper contrast between light and dark areas. The later paintings tend to have a flat, decorative structure as opposed to the three-dimensionality of the early works.

BIBLIOGRAPHY
Thieme–Becker
G. Celis: *Een Gentsche schilder Nicolaas de Liemacker* (Ghent, 1910)
C. Van de Velde and H. Vlieghe: *Stadsversieringen te Gent in 1635 voor de Blijde Intrede van de Kardinaal-Infant* (Ghent, 1969)

HANS VLIEGHE

**Lienau, Detlef** (*b* Ütersen, Holstein, 17 Feb 1818; *d* New York, 29 Aug 1887). American architect of Danish origin. He was educated in Stettin and Berlin, where he was trained in carpentry. He pursued further study at the Königliche Baugewerksschule in Munich and by 1842 had moved to Paris, where he spent five years in the atelier of Pierre-François Henri Labrouste. Late in 1848 Lienau arrived in New York and by 1850 he had established an extensive practice, designing both private and public buildings. His first important commission was Grace Church (1850–53), Jersey City, NJ, in a modified Gothic Revival style. Meanwhile Lienau began to receive important commissions from wealthy merchants, beginning with a city residence (1850–52; destr.) for German-born Hart M. Shiff, the first building in the city to incorporate the mansard roof. Lienau used this French Second Empire style, which quickly became highly fashionable in New York, in several subsequent urban residences, most notably the adjoining mansions for the wealthy brothers William Schermerhorn and Edmund H. Schermerhorn (1853–9 and 1867–9 respectively).

After the Civil War Lienau completed a sumptuous mansion (1864–8) for LeGrand Lockwood at 295 West Avenue, South Norwalk, CT, as well as designing a number of multiple dwelling residences in New York, beginning with the eight attached townhouses (1868–70; destr.) for Rebecca Colford Jones, a long block articulated at roof level by a succession of mansards of differing pitch over the individual house units. In New York Lienau also built a number of apartment hotels, such as the Schermerhorn Apartments (1870–71; destr.), and designed a model tenement block of flats for the poor (1879; destr.) on Elm Street. In the mid-1870s Lienau continued to use his by now old-fashioned French mansard idiom for collegiate buildings, such as Suydam Hall (1871–3) and the Sage Library (1873–5), both at the General Theological Seminary, New Brunswick, NJ.

Although sometimes viewed as a stylist, Lienau was also concerned with rational and functional planning, a practice learnt from Labrouste. This is evident not only in the conveniences he incorporated in his blocks of flats, but even more in the structural solutions and the materials used in his fireproof Hodgson Hall and the Public Library (1873–6), both in Savannah, GA. Even better was his highly functional design for the Matthiessen and Weichers Sugar Refinery complex (1862–70), Jersey City, NJ, whose layout abandoned artificial symmetry and was determined strictly by internal operations based around the new centrifugal separation machines. These buildings served as models for the sugar refining industry for many years. Lienau's extended influence was felt not only through his buildings, which introduced a new urban character to New York, but also through the work of the young men trained in his office, most notably Paul J. Pelz (1841–1918) and Henry Janeway Hardenbergh.

BIBLIOGRAPHY

*DAB*; *Macmillan Enc. Architects*

M. Schuyler: 'Works of Henry J. Hardenbergh', *Archit. Rec.*, vi (1897), pp. 335–6

S. Hartmann: 'A Conversation with Henry Janeway Hardenbergh', *Archit. Rec.*, xix (1906), pp. 376–80

E. W. Kramer: 'Detlef Lienau: An Architect of the Brown Decades', *J. Soc. Archit. Hist.*, xiv (1955), pp. 18–25

——: *The Domestic Architecture of Detlef Lienau, a Conservative Victorian* (diss., New York U., 1958)

M. D. Schaak: 'The Lockwood-Mathews Mansion', *Interior Des.*, xxxviii (1967), pp. 155–63

LELAND M. ROTH

**Liender, Paulus van** (*b* Utrecht, 25 Sept 1731; *d* Utrecht, 26 May 1797). Dutch timber merchant, draughtsman, engraver and collector. He made drawings, engravings and watercolours of townscapes, landscapes and buildings. His elder brother Pieter Jan van Liender (1727–79) was also a draughtsman, and he was first taught by his uncle Jacobus (1696–1759). In Amsterdam, where Paulus went to learn the commercial trade, he studied under Cornelis Pronk. There he became friends with a fellow student, Jan de Beyer, with whom he went on a study trip to Germany. Their work was stylistically very similar, and together they created a series of topographical prints, which were included in *Het verheerlykt Nederland of kabinet van hedendaagsche gezigten* ('The glorious Netherlands or cabinet of modern views'; Amsterdam, 1745–7). Van Liender also became known for his contributions to other topographical atlases, such as that of the city of Amersfoort (1760). About 1760 he settled in Haarlem and became a timber merchant, and from 1779 to 1794 he worked as a first collector of wine taxes. Increasingly, he favoured drawing the landscape around Haarlem. No paintings by him are known.

Van Liender was treasurer of the board of the Haarlem city drawing academy. For reasons of health, in 1794 he returned to Utrecht, where he lived with his brother Pieter Jan van Liender. Paulus, who like his brothers stayed unmarried, was buried in the family grave in the Geertekerk in Utrecht. His collection of paintings, drawings and prints was auctioned in Haarlem on 14 March and 30 October 1798.

BIBLIOGRAPHY

P. Knolle: 'De drie van Lienders: Utrechtse tekenaars uit de 18de eeuw', *Mdbl. Oud-Utrecht* (1978), pp. 93–6

*Jacobus van Liender, Pieter Jan van Liender, Paulus van Liender en de stad Utrecht: Topografische tekenaars uit de 18de eeuw* (exh. cat. by I. J. Soer, Utrecht, Gemeente Archf, 1978)

P. KNOLLE

**Lies, Joseph (Hubert)** (*b* Antwerp, 14 June 1821; *d* Antwerp, 3 Jan 1865). Belgian painter and etcher. A pupil of Nicaise De Keyser at the Antwerp Academie, he swiftly became successful. From his very first works (e.g. *Alms*, 1838; untraced), he determinedly allied himself with his friend Henri Leys in attempting to restore the traditional values of Flemish painting. In 1849 he was appointed Secretary of the Vereniging van Antwerpse Kunsternaars.

Lies's vast knowledge of literature and philosophy emerges strongly in his work, characterized by warm and vigorous colours. A Romantic painter, he produced history paintings (e.g. *Albrecht Dürer going down the Rhine*, 1855; Antwerp, Kon. Mus. S. Kst.), imaginative genre scenes (e.g. *The Landing Stage*; Brussels, Mus. A. Mod.) and

portraits (e.g. *Baroness Henri Leys*; Antwerp, Kon. Mus. S. Kst.). In 1859–60 a lung disease forced him to travel south, giving him the opportunity to visit France, Italy, Switzerland and the Rhine. He was subsequently appointed Professor at the Antwerp Academie, where his pupils included Charles Verlat. At the end of his life he gave up Romantic subjects for landscape; he was certainly more at ease in this field, painting spirited and charming scenes of the Flemish countryside (e.g. Antwerp, Kon. Mus. S. Kst.).

BIBLIOGRAPHY

E. Lefèvre: *Joseph Lies: Sa Vie, ses oeuvres, ses écrits et ses juges* (Antwerp, 1888)

ALAIN JACOBS

**Lieven de Vogeleer.** *See* VOGHELARIUS, LIVINUS.

**Lievens** [Lievensz.]**, Jan** (*b* Leiden, 24 Oct 1607; *d* Amsterdam, 4 June 1674). Dutch painter, draughtsman and printmaker. His work has often suffered by comparison with that of Rembrandt, with whom he was closely associated from 1625 to 1631. Yet Lievens's early work is equal to that of Rembrandt, although in later years he turned more towards a somewhat facile rendering of the international Baroque style favoured by his noble patrons, thus never fully realizing his early promise. Nonetheless, he became a renowned portrait painter and draughtsman, and his drawings include some of the finest examples of 17th-century Dutch portraiture in the medium.

1. Jan Lievens: *Samson and Delilah*, oil on canvas, 1.31×1.10 m, *c*. 1628 (Amsterdam, Rijksmuseum)

1. LEIDEN, 1607–31. He was, the son of Lieven Hendricxz. [De Rechte] (*bur* Leiden, 8 May 1612), an embroiderer, hatmaker and hatseller in Leiden, and his wife, Machteld Jansdr. van Noortsant (*bur* Leiden, 6 March 1622). According to Orlers, at the age of eight Jan became a pupil of the Leiden painter Joris van Schooten (*c.* 1587–*c.* 1653) and *c.* 1617–19 studied in Amsterdam with the history painter Pieter Lastman. The latter's influence is evident in Lievens's earliest known works, *c.* 1625. Lievens returned to Leiden and settled there as an independent master. Orlers recorded that Lievens's work after his return (e.g. a portrait of his mother, 1621; untraced) won him general admiration. From 1625 to 1631 Lievens worked closely with his fellow townsman REMBRANDT VAN RIJN, possibly sharing a studio with him. The rivalry between the two young painters is revealed in their earliest works, which show mutual borrowings of composition and subject. The two used such a similar painting technique that it is extremely difficult to ascribe their unsigned works of this period correctly. Rembrandt began his training *c.* 1620, much later than Lievens, who therefore had the initial advantage. From 1628, however, Rembrandt overtook Lievens. In these first Leiden years, Lievens and Rembrandt repeatedly painted portraits of each other.

Apart from Lastman, the clearest influence on Lievens's earliest paintings was the work produced by the Utrecht Caravaggisti, particularly Gerrit van Honthorst. This is evident in Lievens's preference at that time (one shared by Rembrandt) for half-length figures and for strong chiaroscuro effects from artificial light sources (e.g. the *Allegory of Smell*, Warsaw, N. Mus.). Around 1625 both Lievens and Rembrandt made their first prints, which were published by the Haarlem publisher Jan Pietersz. Berendrecht.

After 1628 Lievens's technique changed. His use of colours tended to be more monochromatic, moving away from Lastman's early influence, with an increasing use of impasto to define form, as in the grisaille oil sketch of *Samson and Delilah* (*c.* 1628; Amsterdam, Rijksmus.). In the same year Lievens began to achieve recognition from outside Leiden and supplied various paintings to Stadholder Frederick Henry and his wife Amalia van Solms, including *The Oriental* (Potsdam, Bildergal.) and another version, in oil on canvas, of *Samson and Delilah* (Amsterdam, Rijksmus.; see fig. 1). Orlers said that Lievens also executed a life-size painting of a *Man Reading by a Fire* (untraced), which won him such praise that the Stadholder ordered the picture to be bought for the English ambassador Sir Robert Kerr, 1st Earl of Ancram (1578–1654), who, in turn, gave it to Charles I of England.

Constantijn Huygens the elder, the Stadholder's secretary, was the first to write about the duo of Lievens and Rembrandt. In his autobiography, written between 1629 and 1631, Huygens praised the two young painters highly and compared their talents. He wrote that Lievens was better than Rembrandt because his magnificent invention and daring subjects and designs were greater, while Rembrandt, in his view, exceeded Lievens in precision and vitality of emotions. Huygens also praised Lievens for his strength of mind and very mature, sharp and profound sense of judgement. The portrait of himself (Douai, Mus. Mun.; on loan Amsterdam, Rijksmus.) that Huygens

2. Jan Lievens: *Job on the Dung-hill*, oil on canvas, 1.29×1.30 m, 1631 (Ottawa, National Gallery of Canada)

commissioned from Lievens and described in his autobiography was probably executed during the winter of 1629–30.

In his last two years in Leiden, Lievens executed a number of works that can be regarded as the highpoints of his oeuvre, including three from 1631: *Job on the Dung-hill* (Ottawa, N.G.; see fig. 2), the *Raising of Lazarus* (Brighton, A.G. & Mus.) and *Eli and Samuel* (Malibu, CA, Getty Mus.). From 1628 the collaboration with Rembrandt became less close, and in late 1631 Rembrandt moved to Amsterdam.

2. ENGLAND AND AMSTERDAM, 1632–43. Although Orlers claimed that Lievens went to England in 1631, a document signed by Lievens in Leiden on 2 February 1632 suggests that he left Leiden just after that date. He remained in England until 1635, during which time it seems that he was less productive than in Leiden; scarcely any dated works are known from his English period. From a poem written by Huygens in 1633, it is known that Lievens painted portraits of members of the English royal family and court; however, none has survived. In London, Lievens met Anthony van Dyck, who painted his portrait (untraced; known only through the engraving by Lucas Vorsterman), for van Dyck's *Iconography* (*c.* 1632–44). During this time Lievens's style was influenced by van Dyck, and his modified use of colour suggests he was able to study Italian paintings in English collections.

In 1635 Lievens was registered as a member of the Guild of St Luke in Antwerp. There he eliminated the last remnants of his Leiden style from his work and adopted completely the Flemish Baroque style of van Dyck and

Rubens, in paintings such as his large altarpiece (*in situ*) of the *Holy Family with the Young Baptist* for the Jesuit church of S Carlo Borromeo in Antwerp. On 1 May 1636 Lievens took on Hans van den Wijngaard (1614–79) as his pupil. Jan Davidsz. de Heem and Adriaen Brouwer, both painters active in Antwerp, were involved in the contract, and it is also known that Lievens collaborated with the Antwerp still-life painter Jan van der Hecke (1620–84). In 1638, still in Antwerp, Lievens married Susanna de Nole, daughter of the sculptor Andries Colyn de Nole. Lievens interrupted his stay in Antwerp once to visit Leiden, probably *c.* 1639–40, when he painted an overmantel for the Leiden Stadhuis depicting the *Justice of Scipio Africanus* (destr. 1929) and etched the portrait of *Daniel Heinsius*, who was a professor in Leiden.

In his painted, drawn and etched portraits Lievens sought to emulate the international style of van Dyck and in his portrait drawings and prints, in particular, he occasionally achieved a level rarely equalled by his contemporaries. In his landscape drawings and paintings, a genre Lievens probably first attempted in England, he produced high-quality works characterized by a very subtle use of colour in the paintings (e.g. *Landscape with Pollarded Willows*, *c.* 1640; Paris, Fond. Custodia, Inst. Néer.) and a boldly hatched linear approach in the pen-and-ink drawings (e.g. *Wooded Landscape with an Angler*; Haarlem, Teylers Mus.). Several of his painted landscapes were long taken to be by Adriaen Brouwer or one of Brouwer's followers, and the attribution of a few is still controversial. Despite Lievens's many commissions, he still had financial problems and on 3 October 1643 his property in Antwerp was seized. He decided to leave the city, moving to Amsterdam in 1644, shortly after the baptism of his son Jan Andrea (*b* Antwerp, *bapt* 20 Jan 1644; *d* Amsterdam, *bur* 30 Jan 1680), who became an artist after training with his father. Susanna de Nole probably died soon after the birth of her son.

3. AMSTERDAM, 1644–74. Lievens lived in Amsterdam for the rest of his life, although he visited The Hague (1650 and again in 1670), Berlin (*c.* 1653–5), Cleves (1664) and Leiden (1670–72). On 2 August 1648 he married Cornelia de Bray, daughter of the Haarlem painter Jan de Bray. Altogether Lievens had nine children from his two marriages, three of whom died young. On his return to the northern Netherlands, Lievens received many important commissions and was able to achieve an important position through his readiness to adapt to the prevailing classicizing taste. In 1650 he was commissioned by Amalia van Solms, by then widow of the Stadholder, to collaborate on the decoration of the Oranjezaal in the Huis ten Bosch (*see* THE HAGUE, §V, 3). The large figures in the *Five Muses* (*in situ*) are closely in keeping with the classicizing Flemish style Lievens had developed in Antwerp. This style also brought him international acclaim; in 1653–4 he worked in Berlin for Amalia van Solms's daughter Louisa Henrietta and her husband Frederick William, Elector of Brandenburg, who commissioned *Mars and Venus* (1653; Berlin, Jagdschloss Grunewald) and *Diana with her Nymphs* (1654; Potsdam, Bildergal.). Sir Robert Kerr, then in exile in Amsterdam, who had his portrait painted by Lievens shortly before the artist's trip to Berlin (*c.* 1653;

Edinburgh, N.P.G.), called Lievens 'the Duke of Brandenburg's painter', in a letter of 1654 to his son in Scotland, adding that Lievens had such a high opinion of himself that he thought no painter in the northern and southern Netherlands or Germany could match him.

Back in Amsterdam, Lievens was commissioned to paint an overmantel in the Burgomaster's room in the new Stadhuis (now Royal Palace) on the Dam. This large picture (1656; *in situ*) shows the Roman consul Suessa commanding his father Quintus Fabius Maximus to dismount from his horse before he speaks to him. Lievens received a second commission for the same building in January 1661. This belongs to the Claudius Civilis series in the Great Gallery on the theme of the Batavians' uprising against the Romans and shows *Brinio Promoted to General* (1661; *in situ*). The colossal piece (5.46×5.38 m) was painted in great haste, and he received his payment in March of the same year. Lievens executed two paintings for the Rijnlandshuis, Leiden: *The Mathematician* (1668; *in situ*), which was completed to his design by his son Jan Andrea, and the allegorical overmantel *Justice Receiving the Body of the Law from Time* (1670; *in situ*), which was almost entirely overpainted by the Leiden painter Karel de Moor during restoration.

Lievens also obtained various important portrait commissions during his Amsterdam years. He painted the portrait of *Adriaan Trip* (1644; The Hague, S. Laman Trip priv. col., for illustration see Sumowski, *Gemälde der Rembrandt-Schüler*, 1983, p. 1929), some years later a

3. Jan Lievens: *Joost van den Vondel*, etching, 322×246 mm, *c.* 1644–50 (Amsterdam, Rijksmuseum)

posthumous portrait of the *Vice-Admiral Maerten Harpertzs. Tromp* and his wife *Cornelia Teding van Berkhout* (both after 1653; Amsterdam, Rijksmus.) and the poet and artist *Anna Maria Schuurman* (1649; London, N.G.). The black chalk portrait drawing of the lawyer *Johannes Wtenbogaert* (1650; Amsterdam, Hist. Mus.) and the etching of the poet *Joost van den Vondel* (*c.* 1644–50; Hollstein, no. 21; see fig. 3) are particularly successful. Lievens was also responsible for the design of a number of woodcuts (an unusual medium in the 17th century); those of figures and heads were probably cut by a professional woodcutter, while one of a *Landscape with Trees* (Hollstein, no. 100) is so close to the style of his landscape drawings that it has been suggested that Lievens cut the block himself.

### BIBLIOGRAPHY

Hollstein: *Dut. & Flem.*

J. J. Orlers: *Beschrijvinge der Stadt Leyden* [Description of the town of Leyden] (Leiden, 1641), pp. 375–7 [Eng. trans. in Vogelaer, ed., 1991, pp. 138–9]

J. W. Worp: 'Constantijn Huygens over de schilders van zijn tijd' [Constantijn Huygens on the painters on his time], *Oud-Holland*, ix (1891), pp. 106–36 [first Dut. trans. of Huygens's remarks on Rembrandt and Lievens in his biography, 1629–31; for Eng. version see Vogelaer, pp. 132–4]

E. W. Moes: 'Jan Lievens', *Leids Jb.*, iv (1907), pp. 136–64

A. Bredius: *Künstler-Inventare: Urkunden zur Geschichte der holländische Kunst des XVIten, XVIIten and XVIIIten Jahrhunderts*, i (The Hague, 1915), pp. 186–227

H. Schneider: *Jan Lievens: sein Leben und seine Werken* (Haarlem, 1932); rev. with suppl. by R. E. O. Ekkart (Amsterdam, 1973)

K. Bauch: 'Rembrandt und Lievens', *Wallraf-Richartz-Jb.*, xi (1939), pp. 239–68

——: *Der frühe Rembrandt und seine Zeit: Studien zur geschichtlichen Bedeutung seines Frühstils* (Berlin, 1960)

E. Larsen: 'Brouwer ou Lievens: Etude d'un problème dans le paysage flamande', *Rev. Belge Archéol. & Hist. A.*, xxix (1960), pp. 37–48

*Jan Lievens: Ein Maler im Schatten Rembrandts* (exh. cat., ed. R. Klessmann; Brunswick, Herzog Anton Ulrich-Mus., 1979)

W. Sumowski: *Drawings of the Rembrandt School*, vii (New York, 1983), pp. 3143–708

——: *Gemälde der Rembrandt-Schüler*, iii (Landau-Pfalz, 1983), pp. 1764–950

*Jan Lievens, 1607–1674: Prenten & tekeningen/Prints & Drawings* (exh. cat. by P. Schatborn, Amsterdam, Rembrandthuis, 1988–9)

C. Vogelaer, ed.: *Rembrandt & Lievens in Leiden* (Zwolle and Leiden, 1991) [pubd. to coincide with exh. at Leiden, Stedel. Mus. Lakenhal, 1991–2]

ERIC DOMELA NIEUWENHUIS

**Lieven van Lathem** [Laethem] (*fl* 1454; *d* Antwerp, before 14 March 1493). South Netherlandish illuminator. He became a master of the Ghent painters' guild on 30 October 1454. Between 1457 and 1459 he was in the service of Philip the Good, Duke of Burgundy. In 1462 he enrolled in the Antwerp Guild of St Luke, to which he belonged until his death. He was also active for short periods outside Antwerp: in 1468, for example, he contributed to extensive preparations in Bruges for the assembly of the Order of the Golden Fleece and for the marriage of Charles the Bold to Margaret of York.

This artist was first recognized by De Schryver, who attributed to him a small prayerbook (the 'Little Hours') with the Office of the Passion, commissioned by Charles the Bold in 1469 (Larrivière, Charnacé priv. col.). By comparison with the style of this manuscript, most of the miniatures in the Hours of Mary of Burgundy (Vienna, Österreich. Nbib., Cod. 1857; see fig.), previously considered as works of Philippe de Mazerolles, can be attributed to Lieven van Lathem (*see* MASTERS, ANONYMOUS, AND MONOGRAMMISTS, §I: MASTER OF MARY OF BURGUNDY). As a result of this, the section of Philippe de Mazerolles's oeuvre that had been grouped around the Vienna miniatures naturally also falls to Lieven van Lathem. Among these works are a prayerbook illuminated for Philip the Good (Paris, Bib. N., MS. nouv. acq. fr. 16428) and a *Roman de Gilles de Trazegnies* by David Aubert, dated 1464, for Louis de Gruuthuse (Chatsworth, Derbys, MS. 7535).

The miniatures by Lieven van Lathem are distinguished above all by their radiant colour. All the pictures convey the atmosphere of a summer's day, with light-blue, lightly clouded sky, a strong effect of aerial perspective through the blue tones of the background, and a clear, almost harsh light. Bright blue and red dominate the artist's palette; yellow is often prominent too, shaded with orange. The grotesque figures in the borders are of a remarkably high quality. Lieven van Lathem's style takes up that of the Master of the Girart de Roussillon, who was the other most important contributor to the Paris prayerbook of Philip the Good. The relationship of these two artists calls for close examination.

Lieven van Lathem's brother Jacob or Jacques (*fl* 1493–1522) was also an artist. Court painter to Philip the Fair, he has been tentatively identified with the MASTER OF THE JOSEPH SEQUENCE (see MASTERS, ANONYMOUS, AND MONOGRAMMISTS, §I).

Lieven van Lathem: *Crown of Thorns*, 225×163 mm; miniature from the Hours of Mary of Burgundy, 1466–77 (Vienna, Österreichische Nationalbibliothek, Cod. 1857, fol. 84*v*)

BIBLIOGRAPHY

P. Durrieu: 'Livre de prières peint pour Charles le Téméraire par son enlumineur en titre Philippe de Mazerolles (le Maître de la Conquête de la Toison d'Or)', *Mnmts Piot*, xxii (1916), pp. 71–130

F. Winkler: *Die flämische Buchmalerei* (Leipzig, 1925/*R* Amsterdam, 1978), pp. 88–93

A. De Schryver: 'Lieven van Lathem, een onbekende grootmeester van de Vlaamse miniatuurschilderkunst', *Handelingen van het XXe Vlaams Filologencongres* (Ghent, 1957), pp. 338–42

A. De Schryver and F. Unterkircher: *Gebetbuch Karls des Kühnen vel potius Stundenbuch der Maria von Burgund* (Graz, 1969) [facs. edn]

A. H. van Buren: 'The Master of Mary of Burgundy and his Colleagues: The State of Research and Questions of Method', *Z. Kstgesch.*, xxxviii (1975), pp. 286–309

M. Thomas: 'Le Livre de prières de Philippe le Bon: Premier bilan d'une découverte', *Doss. Archéol.*, xvi (1976), pp. 84–95

J. Harthan: *Books of Hours and their Owners* (London, 1977), pp. 106–13

G. Dogaer: *Flemish Miniature Painting in the 15th and 16th Centuries* (Amsterdam, 1987), pp. 132–6

*Flämische Buchmalerei: Handschriftenschätze aus dem Burgunderreich* (exh. cat. by D. Thoss, Vienna, Österreich. Nbib., 1987), pp. 52–6

BODO BRINKMANN

**Liezen-Mayer, Sándor** (*b* Győr, 24 Jan 1839; *d* Munich, 19 Feb 1898). Hungarian painter and illustrator, active in Germany. He studied at the Akademie der Bildenden Künste first in Vienna in 1855 and then in Munich in 1856; in 1862 he became a pupil of Karl Theodor von Piloty. He spent most of his life in Germany, only visiting Hungary occasionally. In 1865 he won the Munich Akademie prize for *St Elizabeth Blessing Hungary*, only sketches of which survive (Budapest, N.G.). For the rest of his career he was preoccupied with two themes: St Elizabeth of Hungary and Margarete from Goethe's *Faust*. He liked drawing beautiful, harmonious, benign female figures and in general sought subjects that did not demand too many figures and objects in order to concentrate on these ideal women (e.g. *St Elizabeth of Hungary*, 1882; *Faust and Margarete*, 1875; both Budapest, N.G.). He was also attracted to remote historical events, as in the dramatic *Queen Elizabeth I Signing Mary Stuart's Death Sentence* (1873; Cologne, Stadtmus.), and he often illustrated editions of Shakespeare, Goethe and Schiller. In 1880 Liezen-Mayer became the Director of the Staatliche Akademie der Bildenden Künste in Stuttgart, but three years later he returned to Munich to become a teacher at the Akademie, a post he held until his death. In 1900 a retrospective exhibition was held of his work in the Art Hall, Budapest. Although his balanced, uniform work was based on academic principles, his lyrical compositions were not as conventional. His colours were unusual and almost pastel-like in their softness, and the slightly static quality of his figures gave his work its distinctive style.

BIBLIOGRAPHY

N. Gyöngyösi: 'Sándor Liezen-Mayer', *Képzőművészet* (1930), pp. 3–10

T. Dénes: *Sándor Liezen-Mayer* (Győr, 1932)

J. Jajczay: 'Sándor Liezen-Mayer', *Szépművészet*, iv (1943), pp. 205–8

MÁRIA SZOBOR-BERNÁTH

**Lifferin** [Lifferinxe], **Josse.** *See* LIEFERINXE, JOSSE.

**Lift.** *See under* SKYSCRAPER, §1.

**Lift-ground etching.** *See* ETCHING, LIFT-GROUND.

**Li Futang** [Fu-t'ang]. *See* LI SHAN.

**Light.** The external agent responsible for vision, which takes place as receptors on the retina of the eye respond to that portion of the spectrum of wave energy that is called visible light. It is discussed here in its role as a factor always present when looking at paintings, and as a central feature and source of meaning in the history of Western pictorial representation.

1. Introduction. 2. Pictorial representation of light. 3. Elements of pictorial light. 4. History of light in Western painting. 5. Light symbolism.

1. INTRODUCTION. Light is a form of electromagnetic radiation directly emitted from luminous sources (sun, lamps, candles), absorbed and reflected by opaque surfaces and refracted through transparent surfaces. Light travels in straight lines, and its strength or intensity, measured in milliamberts by instruments known as photometers, diminishes as the distance from the light source increases. The visual characteristics of surfaces are distinguished by their response to light. All surfaces either absorb, reflect or refract light, or perform these actions jointly, to some degree. Surfaces that absorb most of the light are described as opaque; reflective surfaces appear shiny, and refractive surfaces are distinguished as transparent or translucent.

Some works of art use colour, surface texture and materials with the specific aim of reflecting a high proportion of the ambient light; this is a characteristic of paintings that employ gold and other precious metals, including Byzantine painting and mosaic, Romanesque illuminated manuscripts and Italian panel paintings from the 13th to 14th centuries. Other works create an illusion of the presence of light within the picture by arranging colours in combinations that reflect the distribution of light and shadow values in nature. Most Western representational painting from the Renaissance to the present creates pictorial light by colour juxtapositions. The illusion of pictorial light is created through the interaction of the painting surface with the light that strikes it (the 'incident light'). Therefore, the history of light in painting is inseparable from the study of display, whether paintings were exhibited in dimly lit churches or light-filled galleries (*see* DISPLAY OF ART, §I). Since 'light' is perceived in contrast to 'less light' or shadow, the painter must use colour to create variations in the amount of light returned to the eye over the surface of the picture. The history of painting technique is an important factor because the properties of pigments, binding media, grounds and glazes alter the luminance of pictorial surfaces. Conservation studies help to determine how ageing and condition have affected the lightness, hue and opacity of the materials. This article, however, limits discussion to the way that painters manipulate colour relationships to create luminance differences; these differences produce the illusion of pictorial light to the extent that they imitate the distribution of light in nature and create a similar perceptual response.

2. PICTORIAL REPRESENTATION OF LIGHT. Paintings, like other surfaces, are visible because part of the incident light is reflected back to the eye, and their appearance varies according to three aspects of that reflected light. The wavelength of this reflected light determines what colour hues are seen (*see* COLOUR, §I).

The total amount of light reflected to the observer is called 'luminance' and accounts for the overall level of brightness of a surface. Objects illuminated by bright sunlight will have a higher luminance than those in partial light. Extremes of luminance affect the perception of pictorial light because colour relationships vary at very high and very low levels; luminance is also an important factor in paintings that use gold and other highly reflective materials. Any perception of light relies heavily on comparative judgement. The impression of lightness and darkness, of black, white and various shades of grey, depends on the 'reflectance' of surfaces, which is the percentage of ambient light reflected. Pale colours (e.g. white and yellow) have a high reflectance and will look light regardless of the total illumination as long as a dark surface (of lower reflectance) is seen at the same time. Strong contrasts of light and dark create perceptual effects of enhanced brightness or darkness, especially at edges; hue and saturation contrasts may create perceptual effects of vividness and vibration associated with scintillating light. Light objects on dark grounds often seem to spread light beyond their confines, an effect known as 'irradiation'.

The imitation of light in paint is complicated by the fact that the optical array of light gives the mind information not just about light and colour but also about such fixed properties in the environment as shape and space. Surfaces facing the light are brighter than those placed obliquely to it; gradations in the intensity of light give information about rounded surfaces; abrupt shifts indicate angular or discontinuous surfaces. The painter has to use the same variations in colour, tone and technique to create both the illusion of surface illumination and that of solid three-dimensionality (imitating both the variant and the invariant properties of the optical array).

Tonal modelling is the most commonly used practice to create the illusion of three-dimensional relief. It depends on gradations of lighter and darker tones of the same colour, which describe the variations in light intensity over the surface of a form. In addition to mixing colours to get these variations, tonal modelling has also been accomplished by layering translucent colour over gradated underpaintings, and by the juxtaposition of small colour areas to create optical mixing. Scholars have identified different approaches to tonal modelling, including the use of pure colour in the shadows mixed with white to create lighter tones (described by Cennino Cennini and used in Italian painting *c.* 1290–1450); the use of saturated colour in the mid-tones with light and dark additives to create CHIAROSCURO (described by Leon Battista Alberti and used in Italian painting from *c.* 1440); the use of saturated colour in the highlights with gradual darkening to create shadows through tonal underpainting (used by Leonardo da Vinci in the *Virgin of the Rocks*, 1485; Paris, Louvre; and other works); and hue-based modelling known as *cangianti*, in which a lighter hue such as yellow represents illuminated portions of drapery, while a darker hue such as violet represents shadowed portions (used by Michelangelo in the lunettes on the vault of the Sistine Chapel, 1508–12, in Rome). Jan van Eyck's luminous effects depend less on modelling than on the density of the paint surface, which permits light to pass through and reflect back from the white underpainting. In his *Giovanni*

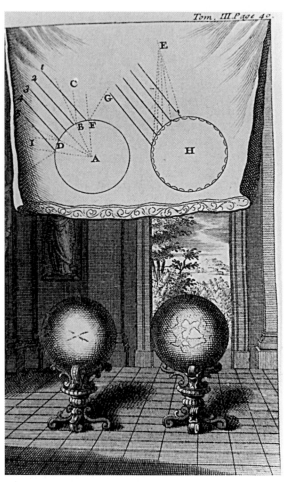

Light reflected on smooth and matt surfaces; from André Félibien: *Entretiens sur les vies et les ouvrages des plus excellens peintres anciens et modernes* (Paris, 1666–88), iii, p. 40

*Arnolfini and Giovanna Cenami* (1434; London, N.G.; *see* EYCK, VAN (2), fig. 3), the build-up of many coloured glazes creates opaque areas that the light does not penetrate and that represent shadows.

Consistency of modelling is an important factor in creating the illusion of pictorial light. The regular diminution of colour in the shadows is more important than equivalence of value in the highlights, since luminance patterns in nature reveal a narrower range in low light than in bright light. The illusion of light is most convincing when the tonal highlights are more saturated than the shadows and half-shadows.

The pattern of reflections and highlights gives information about the sheen of surfaces and contributes to the illusion of pictorial light. Shiny surfaces such as flesh, glass and metal have distinct reflections called lustres. The lustre appears at the point where the incident light is reflected straight to the eye. Because light follows the geometric principle that the angle of incidence is equal to the angle of reflection, the location of the lustre changes with the observer's position. Hence the placement of lustres is a cue to the viewer's position and the location of the light source. Matt surfaces scatter the light so there are no lustres, only tonal highlights where the quantity of light is greatest (see fig.).

Colour juxtapositions contribute to the illusion of pictorial light, because the perceived brightness of an object depends on its relationship to other brightness values in the total visual field (*see* COLOUR INTERACTION). Contrasts of light with dark result in the light looking brighter and the dark, darker. Since saturated colours are perceived as more vivid and brighter than greyed colours, the use of saturated colours or the juxtaposition of saturated with greyed colours can enhance the illusion of brightness. Contrasts of complementary colours mutually intensify the perceived saturation of each colour and, when juxtaposed, may create luminous, scintillating perceptual effects. Pictorial light has a more limited tonal range than light in most natural conditions; therefore, painters frequently use bold contrasts to create enhanced perceptual effects. Frequently white as a local colour is toned down so that pure white, juxtaposed with darks, serves to imitate the intensity of lustres.

3. ELEMENTS OF PICTORIAL LIGHT. The pattern of light and shadow follows optical principles that give information about the location and quality of the light. Surfaces close to the source of light appear to be brighter than those which are remote. Shadows vary in darkness, shape, colour and clarity of edges according to their distance from the light, their orientation to the light source and their relation to other reflective surfaces. The description of pictorial light should take into account the following elements: the type of light represented, whether natural (daylight), artificial (lamps, candles, torches), supernatural or a combination; the quality of light, whether direct and focused or indirect and diffused; the level of illumination; the direction of light, whether frontal, lateral, cross light, backlight, overhead or from below; the colour of the light; and the relationship between the pictorial light and the actual light.

The direction of the light source is indicated by the size, shape and position of shadows and highlights. When the light source is high, as at midday, cast shadows will be short; when the light is low, as at twilight, cast shadows are long. Cast shadows are projected according to the laws of linear perspective and are shown as foreshortened if seen at an oblique angle. If the light source is smaller than the object, the cast shadows will diverge and gradually lessen in intensity; sources larger than the object cause the cast shadows to converge to a point and lighten rapidly. Sunlight results in cast shadows that are parallel because of the great distance of the sun from the earth.

The quality of light is indicated both by colour and design: high or strong contrasts indicate an intense light, while low contrasts indicate a weak light. Crisp edges on forms and cast shadows indicate a focused light, while soft, blurred edges and penumbra suggest diffused light. Bright light reveals colour at its most saturated; dazzling light makes colour appear washed-out; colours in dim light appear greyed or pale. Incandescent illumination has a warm, reddish-yellow colour; daylight and fluorescent light have a cool, bluish tonality. In moderate conditions, reflected light is particularly evident; the light reflected into shadows makes them appear lighter and more transparent, enabling us to see the contours, details and colour of the shaded object. Reflected light picks up the colours of adjacent surfaces and transforms the colour of objects.

Both direction and quality have been manipulated by Western artists for their expressive possibilities. The most typical placement of the light in Western European painting is frontal–lateral from above—at about a 45° angle—which illuminates about three-quarters of the surface of objects and seems most natural. Frontal lighting tends to give bold, direct effects; Edouard Manet used this to great advantage in *Le Déjeuner sur l'herbe* (1863; Paris, Mus. d'Orsay) and the *Bar at the Folies-Bergère* (1882; U. London, Courtauld Inst. Gals; *see* MANET, EDOUARD, figs 1 and 3). Backlighting (also known as *contre-jour*) creates dramatic effects, as in Rembrandt's *Blinding of Samson* (1638; Frankfurt am Main, Städel Kstinst.), *Supper at Emmaus* (1628–9; Paris, Mus. Jacquemart-André) and other works from his early years. Lateral lighting produces alternating zones of light and shadow, which were exploited for spatial effects by such Baroque landscape artists as Claude Lorrain. Cross-lighting (two or more sources) was used by Domenichino (e.g. the *Last Communion of St Jerome*, 1614; Rome, Vatican Mus.; *see* DOMENICHINO, fig. 1) to mitigate the obscurity of shadows, rendering shadowed forms visible without disregarding the laws of nature. Light from below was frequently used by Georges de La Tour, Gerrit van Honthorst and other tenebrist painters for its eerie, disturbing quality.

Western painters have frequently tried to match the direction of light in the picture to the ambient illumination. Treatise writers from the Renaissance, beginning with Cennini, recommended matching the direction of pictorial light to the actual light in the church or chapel, which Gould has shown was common in Renaissance Italy. Many other solutions coexisted in 16th-century Italy: where there were two or more windows, painters tended to choose lighting from the stronger, south exposure; altarpieces on the side walls of naves showed the source of lighting as coming from the closest end wall; to avoid the unpleasing effects of illumination from below, vault and ceiling paintings showed the light as coming from above, often from the direction of the altar; and paintings on window walls often had fictive illumination.

4. HISTORY OF LIGHT IN WESTERN PAINTING.

*(i) 13th–16th centuries.* Italian 13th-century and 14th-century fresco painters and mosaicists revived the Classical practice of creating an illusion of pictorial light. In the mosaics at S Maria in Trastevere, Rome, Pietro Cavallini introduced tonal modelling and rejected outlines that tended to interfere with the illusion of light (*see* CAVALLINI, PIETRO, fig. 4). In the Arena Chapel frescoes, Padua, Giotto showed how to imitate diffuse overhead illumination by indicating shadows cast by overhanging roofs, how to distinguish flat surfaces from curved surfaces by the absence or presence of gradients, and how to distinguish the orientation of flat surfaces by three tones: lightest for horizontal surfaces, medium for frontal vertical surfaces, darkest for receding vertical surfaces (*see* GIOTTO, §I, 3(i)

and figs 1–5). In such a work as the *Annunciation to the Shepherds* (Florence, Santa Croce, Baroncelli Chapel), Taddeo Gaddi represented divine light in a night scene with yellow–violet contrasts, a visible light source and a rapid drop in the pattern of light distribution characteristic of point light sources.

This interest in the illusion of natural light continued to develop throughout the Italian Renaissance. Gentile da Fabriano distinguished natural, artificial and supernatural light sources in the predella panels of the *Adoration of the Magi* (1423; Florence, Uffizi; *see* GENTILE DA FABRIANO, fig. 3) and integrated gold leaf and *sgraffito* techniques with tonal modelling to create the illusion of light. Masaccio represented bright, focused light coming from specific directions in the *Virgin and Child with Angels* (1426; London, N.G.; *see* MASACCIO, fig. 1) by depicting cast shadows on the throne of the Virgin. Leonardo da Vinci showed how the subtle indirect light of a loggia could lend softness and relief to faces in the portrait of '*Mona Lisa*' (1503–8; Paris, Louvre; *see* DRESS, fig. 22). Raphael represented dramatic effects of night light in the *Deliverance of St Peter* (*c.* 1512–13; Rome, Vatican, Stanza d'Eliodoro). Titian painted coloured light in sunset in *Charles V on Horseback* (1548; Madrid, Prado), broke up local colour and focused on the flickering effect of light on surfaces in the *Crowning with Thorns* (1570; Munich, Alte Pin.).

In the Netherlands, Jan and Hubert van Eyck and the Master of Flémalle were particularly accomplished at distinguishing the play of light on surfaces of differing textures and sheen, at imitating the reflections of light on mirrors and metallic surfaces and at representing the lustrous quality of coloured gems (e.g. The Master of Flémalle's Mérode Triptych, 1425–8; New York, Cloisters; Hubert van Eyck's Ghent Altarpiece, 1432; Ghent, S Bavo (for illustration *see* EYCK, (1)); and Jan van Eyck's *Virgin and Child with Canon van der Paele*, 1436; Bruges, Groeningemus.). They frequently represented daylight and artificial light in the same paintings. Hugo van der Goes represented cross-lighting on the fictive statues on the outside of the Portinari Altarpiece (*c.* 1476; Florence, Uffizi).

The Renaissance also witnessed the rise of a literature devoted to the painting of light. Alberti (*De pictura*) identified the reception of light as one of the three parts of painting. Leonardo wrote two books on light and shade, MS. C (Paris, Bib. France) and the lost Libro W, and substantial parts of his *Treatise on Painting* are devoted to the scientific study of light. Albrecht Dürer published a mathematical procedure for determining the projection of shadows cast by objects illuminated by light radiating from a point source, such as candlelight. Giovanni Paolo Lomazzo devoted the fourth book of his *Trattato* (1584) to light, transforming Neo-Platonic light metaphysics into the language of art by ordering light in descending orders of brightness from primary sunlight, divine light and such artificial lights as torchlight, to the weaker secondary light reflected by illuminated bodies.

*(ii) 17th–18th centuries.* In the 17th century light became the object of scientific investigations by Johannes Kepler (1571–1630), Francesco Maria Grimaldi (1618–63), Isaac Newton (1642–1727), Christian Huygens (1629–95) and Robert Boyle (1627–91). Art treatises from the 17th century to the present have described the physical appearance of light and the principles of geometric optics to which light is subject in order to help artists represent light accurately. Many treatises on perspective contained sections on reflections and on shadow projection, and in the late 18th and early 19th centuries many specialized treatises on shadow projection were published. A particular concern of Roger de Piles and such 18th-century writers as Claude-Henri Watelet and Francesco Algarotti was the distribution of light and shadow, which was said to be most pleasing when one principal area of highest light was juxtaposed to the area of darkest shadow, and the lesser lights and shadows were grouped together. This massing avoids the scattering of many small lights which William Hogarth in his *Analysis of Beauty* (1753) compared to the disturbing effect of several voices talking at once. A frequently recommended method of studying lighting was that of making small models which were placed in the positions of the figures, often in a box; this method, employed by Jacopo Tintoretto, was explored by Nicolas Poussin for its potential for natural and varied light effects. The decorum of light was also a widely discussed issue: Caravaggio's tenebrous lighting and Guido Reni's sweet, clear lighting were regarded as the two extremes: the forceful style versus the sweet style.

The representation of natural light became a focus of 17th-century painting, and painters began to show preferences for different types of lighting. Vermeer is praised for his great skill in representing bright daylight and diffused interior light; in the *Woman with a Water Pitcher* (*c.* 1660; Amsterdam, Rijksmus.; *see* VERMEER, JOHANNES, fig. 2), he used small white, grey and ochre dots to suggest the scintillation of light on lustrous surfaces. Rembrandt is renowned for his dramatic and expressive light, created by bold contrasts held together with colour built up in complex layers with glazes that allow light to permeate his flesh tones and reflect back from the white underpainting. Poussin revealed his interest in the scientific optics of light in paintings of the Seven Sacraments executed for Cassiano dal Pozzo and Paul Fréart de Chantelou (e.g. *Extreme Unction*, 1647; Duke of Sutherland, on loan to Edinburgh, N.G.; *see* POUSSIN, NICOLAS, fig. 3), as did Pietro Testa in his etching, the *Suicide of Cato* (1648). Many other artists explored the effects of artificial illumination by candlelight or torchlight, the quality of light in different types of weather and the reflections of light on glass, water and shiny surfaces.

In the 18th century Rococo artists tended to prefer evenly illuminated scenes in bright daylight, or colourful sunrises and sunsets. Giambattista Tiepolo's light-filled celestial visions, created with high-value pastels and broken colours, decorated the walls and ceilings of churches and palaces (e.g. *Apollo Conducting Beatrice of Burgundy to Emperor Frederick Barbarossa*, 1752; Würzburg, Residenz; *see* TIEPOLO, (1), fig. 3). Renewed interest in strong contrasts at the end of the 18th century in France has been related by Whiteley to the growth of the Neo-classicism of David and to academic programmes in which pupils were encouraged to copy Guercino, Moïse Valentin (*c.* 1591–1632) and Caravaggio and to draw by artificial light. These practices went out of fashion by the 1830s in favour of a diffused daylight.

*(iii) 19th–20th centuries.* In the early 19th century Corot and the Barbizon school took to painting out of doors (*en plein air*) in order to capture the shifting quality of natural light. Related to this were John Constable's concerns with conditions of sky, light and atmosphere; in *Stoke-by-Nayland* (1836; Chicago, IL, A. Inst.), he sprinkled dabs of white paint—known as 'Constable's snow'—on foliage to simulate the impression of dazzling light. J. M. W. Turner equated light with colour and tried to create a natural symbolism based on the role of colour in nature; he created paintings based on the antithesis of light and dark with a dominant tonality, as in the *Slave Ship* (1840; Boston, MA, Mus. F.A.), in which he introduced spectacular expressive effects of light and colour. Such sublime natural light effects as sunsets and storms particularly interested German Romantic painters (e.g. Caspar David Friedrich's *Polar Sea*, 1824; and Philip Otto Runge's *Morning*, 1809; both Hamburg, Ksthalle), while, later in the century, the American landscape painters known as the Luminists captured subtle nuances of sunlight and moonlight, creating moods of stillness and tranquillity.

The Impressionists devoted attention to the momentary effects of light and atmosphere, executing small landscapes and scenes of middle-class leisure activities with pure colours and juxtaposed brushstrokes. Moving away from black and earth tones, they produced effects of sunlight without strong value contrasts by exploiting effects of hue contrast, as in Renoir's *Ball at the Moulin de la Galette* (1876; Paris, Mus. d'Orsay; *see* RENOIR, AUGUSTE, fig. 1). The Impressionists also studied subtle shifts of perception due to changes in light (e.g. Monet's series depicting Rouen Cathedral in shifting light, including *Rouen Cathedral: The Façade in Sunlight*, 1894, Williamstown, MA, Clark A. Inst.; *see* MONET, CLAUDE, fig. 3), reflections on water and on human forms and coloured shadows.

Georges Seurat created strong light effects in such Conté crayon drawings as the *Black Bow* (Paris, Mus. d'Orsay), but he is best known for his Chromo-Luminarism, a style called Neo Impressionism (also practised by his follower Paul Signac; *see* DIVISIONISM), in which he attempted to capture both the brilliance of sunlight, as in *Sunday Afternoon on the Island of La Grande Jatte* (1884–6; Chicago, IL, A. Inst.; *see* SEURAT, GEORGES, fig. 1) and the glare of gas jets at night in *Le Chahut* (1889–90; Otterlo, Rijksmus. Kröller-Müller) and *The Parade* (1889; New York, Met.). He employed the technique of pointillism, which consists of applying small dots of pure colour that mix optically according to the laws of colour vision proposed by Michel-Eugène Chevreul, Ogden Rood, Charles Henry, and other colour scientists.

By the early 20th century the size of the patches or strokes of colour representing the effects of light or shadow grew as the scale of the works increased. Important scientific studies on the nature of light as a form of electromagnetic radiation by Max Planck and Albert Einstein coincided with such developments as Orphism and Futurism, in which light became symbolic of the energy and dynamism of the modern world. In the 1960s Op artists explored chromatic and achromatic contrast

effects that produced the illusion of both luminous areas, and even movement, in painting. Light became a medium in its own right, used, for example, by László Moholy Nagy in *Light-Space Modulator* (1930; Cambridge, MA, Busch-Reisinger Mus.), in the experiments of the Groupe de Recherche d'Art Visuel, in Dan Flavin's arrangements of neon tubes and fluorescent light fixtures and in Charles Ross's work with prisms. Multi media images include light through reflective surfaces such as mirrors, water and highly polished steel. Laser light is used to make a three-dimensional image in the HOLOGRAM.

5. LIGHT SYMBOLISM.

*(i) The literature of light symbolism.* Light has been associated with truth, faith, wisdom, virtue, grace, knowledge, sanctity and divinity. In the Old Testament, light is part of the figurative language used to describe God; it is a SYMBOL of God's presence and a metaphor for God's nature (Exodus 13:21; 1 Samuel 3:3; 2 Chronicles 4:7, 13:11; Isaiah 10:17, 60:19; Psalms 35:10; Wisdom of Solomon 7:26). The presence of light signifies divine favour or divine protection (Numbers 6:25; Psalms 4:7, 26:1, 88:16; Job 22:28; Micah 7:8). This language is continued in the New Testament, where Christ is presented as the light-bringer and the light of the world (Luke 1:79, 2:32; Acts 26:23; 2 Corinthians 4:6; John 8:12, 9:5, 12:46). Those who believe in him become the children of light opposed to the children of darkness, which signifies ignorance, error, death and evil (Matthew 5:14–16; Luke 16:8; John 3:19, 5:35, 12:36; Acts 13:47).

For Aristotle, light was not substance but the actualization of the transparency inherent in media such as air and water; it is incorporeal but participates in corporeality because it is the state of a corporeal substance. Plato regarded light as a central feature of the world, at once transcendent and physical; from these ideas the Neo-Platonist Plotinus (AD 205–70) developed a metaphysical system based on the principle of emanation from God, in which light is especially important because it is the emanation most accessible to the senses, the visible image of the invisible. He rejected the idea that light requires a transparent medium but saw it as a form of all corporeal substance, which goes forth from the luminous body, leaps across space and actualizes a suitable recipient, bringing forth either colour or a mirror image.

A metaphysics of light developed in Europe and the Islamic world in the Middle Ages, combining Greek and Judeo-Christian ideas. Philosophers, starting with Avicenna (Ibn Sina, 980–1037), distinguished two kinds of light: *lux*, designated the primary light or light source, or, alternatively, the internal psychic awareness of light; and *lumen*, used to designate the light seen by the eye, which flows from the source through a physical medium. St Augustine (354–430) combined Plotinus' teaching with the Platonic distinction between sensible and spiritual light, in which the enlightenment of the mind was compared to the sun's illumination of the earth but considered more trustworthy. Pseudo-Dionysius (*c.* 500) identified God as the source of all radiation, and physical light as a symbol of divine immanence and transcendence. His *Hierarchia caelestia* was the handbook of Christian light symbolism until the end of the 17th century, and it inspired Abbot Suger's design of the abbey church of Saint-Denis (1140–44), Paris, especially his use of stained glass in the windows, which reflected the harmony and radiance of God on earth (*see also* LIGHTING, §1(i)). Robert Grosseteste (1168–1253) developed an elaborate light metaphysics, which synthesized Christian theology with scientific optics based on the Arabic concept of light (expounded by Ibn al-Haytham, or Alhazen, 965–1039) as an external agent conveying images and the Euclidean concept of light as rays. Light was seen as subject to the principles of geometry—of straight lines and angles—thus providing the framework for a mathematical structure of the universe. His theory had a decisive influence on natural philosophers at the universities of Oxford and Paris, especially Roger Bacon (*c.* 1214–92), and on the Polish writer Witelo (Erazm Ciołek, *c.* 1210–*c.* 1273). The metaphysics of light combined with Christian theology continued to dominate Western thought throughout the Renaissance. St Bonaventura (1221–74), Duns Scotus (*c.* 1265–1308), Hildegard of Bingen, Bernard Sylvestris, Meister Eckhart (*c.* 1260–1327) and Nicholas of Cusa also made significant contributions to the theology and metaphysics of light.

*(ii) Medieval light symbolism.* The importance of light in Christian theology and metaphysics assured its representation throughout the history of Western painting. In Early Christian and Byzantine painting, the supernatural light denoting the holiness of saints and the divinity was represented schematically in the form of haloes, mandorlas and circles of light. Mosaics became the preferred form of church decoration, although their expense limited their numbers; since glass tesserae reflect and scatter light, mosaics are more luminous than painting, thereby conferring a spiritual, immaterial quality to the images. At Hagia Sophia, Hosios Loukas and Dafni, optical devices increase the quantity of light within the mosaics, aided by the curved surfaces and uneven setting bed of the tesserae. Effects of radiance and splendour were also achieved in panel paintings and manuscripts (*see* EARLY CHRISTIAN AND BYZANTINE ART, §§VI, 1, and V, 2(i)) by applying gold leaf to increase luminance and create lustres. Gold tesserae were used as the ground in mosaic panels, and yellow paint, imitating gold tesserae, was used as the ground for paintings, so that the interiors of Byzantine churches became bathed in light, the embodiment of God; and gold ornament was also used prolifically, such as the 30 gold crowns hanging before the altar of Hagia Sophia (*see* EARLY CHRISTIAN AND BYZANTINE ART, §III).

Some medieval texts of the 12th to 14th centuries have been interpreted by modern scholars to mean that Gothic stained glass was intended to reflect the Neo-Platonic aesthetic of light as actualizing colour by embodying light in colour. Irregularities in the glass break up the sun's rays and make vibrating light; coloured spots on the walls dematerialize the masses of masonry. Abbot Suger at Saint-Denis Abbey wrote about light as a conjunction of 'the material with the immaterial, the corporeal with the spiritual'. Divine light was associated with coloured light, and luminosity was considered one of the principal characteristics of beauty. Liturgical objects (altars, chalices, crosses) were covered with reflective metals embedded with brightly coloured stones to reflect divine light, thereby transforming substance into immaterial spirit (*see* STAINED GLASS, §II, 1).

*(iii) 15th- and 16th-century light symbolism.* Abundant literary sources testify to the significance of light and of windows as symbols of divine revelation, which became a common theme in 15th-century Netherlandish panel painting. In Jan van Eyck's *Annunciation in a Church* (*c.* 1435–47; Washington, DC, N.G.A.), seven gold rays denoting the seven gifts of the Holy Spirit with which Christ was endowed are shown to pass through a clerestory window and terminate at the womb of the Virgin, thus creating a visual metaphor for the Incarnation. Because everyday household objects were considered metaphors for things spiritual, prominence was given to luminous and reflective objects such as candles, brass ewers and mirrors; sunlight suffuses domestic interiors through doors and windows, elevating the mundane to the transcendental, as in Robert Campin's *Mérode Altarpiece* (1425–8; New York, Met.) and van Eyck's *Giovanni Arnolfini and Giovanna Cenami* (1434; London, N.G.).

Italian painters of the 14th and 15th centuries represented supernatural light in night scenes to indicate the presence of miracles (e.g. Taddeo Gaddi, *Annunciation to the Shepherds*, Florence, Santa Croce; Gentile da Fabriano's *Stigmatization of St Francis*, 1420; priv. col., see Hills (1986), p. 119). Painters in the 16th century represented brilliant supernatural lighting to dramatize miraculous events; Geertgen tot Sint Jans was one of the earliest painters to represent the Nativity as a night scene, with light emanating from the Christ Child and selectively illuminating the faces of the Virgin and admiring child angels (e.g. *Night Nativity*, 1480–85; London, N.G.). In the *Resurrected Christ* from the Isenheim Altarpiece (*c.* 1510–15; Colmar, Mus. Unterlinden), Grünewald exploited the effects of simultaneous brightness contrast to make the gloriole emanating from Christ appear to glow. In Titian's *Annunciation* (1564; Venice, S Salvatore) the boundaries between natural and supernatural are blurred, as the Holy Spirit represented by light streams down from the sky like a beam of sunlight breaking through the clouds.

*(iv) 17th- and 18th-century light symbolism.* In the 17th century paintings by artists as diverse as Caravaggio and Rembrandt explored the idea of light as a metaphor of grace and its action against evil. In Caravaggio's *Calling of St Matthew* (1600; Rome, S Luigi dei Francesi; *see* CARAVAGGIO, MICHELANGELO MERISI DA, fig. 4), a focused beam of light travels along the line of Christ's forceful gesture until it reaches Matthew, and in his *Conversion of St Paul* (1601; Rome, S Maria del Popolo), light conveys the miraculous meaning of Saul's temporary blindness. In Rembrandt's *Danäe* (1636; St Petersburg, Hermitage) Jupiter's appearance is shown by golden light flooding the room as the servant pulls aside the bed curtain. Beginning with the pictorial ensembles of Gianlorenzo Bernini, rays of light from hidden windows became particularly associated with themes of ecstasy, in the *St Bibiana* (1624–6; Rome, S Bibiana), the *Ecstasy of St Teresa* (1645–52; Rome, S Maria della Vittoria) and the *Death of the Blessed Ludovica Albertoni* (1674; Rome, S Francesco a Ripa). Sedlmayr

(1960) has shown that sun symbolism was a central theme in the palace and garden of Versailles (*see* VERSAILLES, §1), expounding the metaphor of Louis XIV as the Sun King through the signs of a sun disc with rays, such numerous luminous and reflecting materials as mirrors, gold and water in the palace and gardens, and Apollo–Helios themes in the decoration.

Although mystical theories of light were promulgated by William Law (1681–1761) in 1752 and John Hutchinson (1674–1737), collected in *The Philosophical and Theological Works of the Late Truly Learned John Hutchinson, Esq.* (London, 1748–9), the late 18th century witnessed the demise of 'transcendental' or 'divine' light as mechanistic, rational hypotheses gained support. Light symbolism became transformed into secular themes, where light was used to indicate understanding, awakening, rebirth and goodness, and was opposed to ignorance, death and evil.

## BIBLIOGRAPHY

### EARLY SOURCES

Ibn al-Haytham [Alhazen]: *The Optics of Ibn al-Haytham*; Eng. trans., ed. A. I. Sabra, Stud. Warb. Inst., xl (1989)

—— 'Le "Discours de la lumière" d'Ibn al-Haytham', *Rev. Hist. Sci. & Applic.*, xxi (1968), pp. 197–224

Bartholomaeus Anglicus: *De proprietatibus rerum; On the Properties of Things*; Eng. trans. by John of Trevisa, ed. M. C. Seymour (Oxford, 1975)

R. Grosseteste: *On Light*; Eng. trans., ed. C. Riedel (Milwaukee, 1942)

R. Bacon: *Roger Bacon's Philosophy of Nature: A Critical Edition, with English Translation, Introduction and Notes, of 'De multiplicatione specierum' and 'De speculis comburentibus'*; Eng. trans., ed. D. Lindberg (Oxford, 1983)

Witelo: 'Perspectiva', in *Witelo: Ein Philosoph und Naturforscher des XIII. Jahrhunderts*, ed. C. Baumker (Münster, 1908)

N. Oresme: *Nicole Oresme on Light, Color and the Rainbow: An Edition and Translation, with Introduction and Critical Notes, of Part of Book Three of his 'Questiones super quatuor libros Meteororum'*; Eng. trans., ed. S. C. McCluskey jr (diss., U. Wisconsin, 1974)

D. Scotus: *Medieval Light Theory and Optics and Duns Scotus' Treatment of Light in D. 13 of Book II of his 'Commentary on the Sentences'*, ed. E. R. McCarthy (diss., New York, City U., 1976)

O. Lehmann-Brockhaus: *Lateinische Schriftquellen zur Kunst in England, Wales und Schottland vom Jahre 901 bis zum Jahre 1308*, 3 vols (Munich, 1955–60)

L. B. Alberti: *On Painting and On Sculpture: The Latin Texts of 'De pictura' and 'De statua'*; ed. C. Grayson (London, 1972)

D. Strong: *Leonardo on the Eye: An English Translation and Critical Commentary of MS. D in the Bibliothèque Nationale, Paris, with Studies on Leonardo's Methodology and Theories on Optics* (New York, 1979)

Leonardo da Vinci: *Treatise on Painting*; Eng. trans., ed. P. McMahon (Princeton, 1956) [with facs. of MS. Vat. Cod. Urbina 1270]

A. Dürer: *Underweysung der Messung* (Nuremburg, 1525); Eng. trans. by W. Strauss as *The Painter's Manual* (New York, 1977), pp. 373–87

G. P. Lomazzo: *Trattato dell'arte de la pittura, scoltura et architettura* (Milan, 1584); Eng. trans. by R. Haydocke as *A Tracte Containing the Artes of Curious Paintinge Carvinge and Buildinge* (Oxford, 1598)

——: *Idea del tempio della pittura* (Milan, 1590); repr. with the *Trattato* in *Scritti sulle arti*, ed. R. Ciardi, i (Florence, 1973), pp. 242–373; ii (Florence, 1974)

J. Kepler: *Les Fondements de l'optique moderne: Paralipomènes à Vitellion [Ad Vitellionem Parlipomena]*; Fr. trans. by C. Chevalley (Paris, 1980) [Theory of optics pubd in Prague in 1604]

F. Junius: *The Painting of the Ancients, in Three Bookes* (London, 1638); rev. and trans. by P. Fehl (London, 1992)

M. Cureau de la Chambre: *La Lumière* (Paris, 1657)

F. Grimaldi: *Physico-mathesis de lumine coloribus et iride* (Berne, 1665/R London, 1966)

A. Félibien: *Entretiens sur les vies et les ouvrages des plus excellens peintres anciens et modernes*, 10 vols (Paris, 1666–88, rev. Trévoux, 1725/R London, 1967)

J. Richardson: *An Account of the Statues, Bas-reliefs, Drawings and Pictures in Italy, France & with Remarks* (London, 1722)

L. Dupain: *La Science des ombres par rapport au dessin* (Paris, 1750)

E. S. Jeurat: *Traité de perspective à l'usage des artistes* (Paris, 1750)

D. Diderot: *Encyclopédie, ou dictionnaire raisonné des sciences, des arts, et des métiers* (Paris, 1751) [entries on light by C. Watelet]

M. Lacombe: *Dictionnaire portatif des beaux-arts* (Paris, 1752)

F. Algarotti: *Saggio sopra la pittura* (Venice, 1756); repr. as *Saggi*, ed. G. da Pozzo, ccvi of *Scrittori d'Italia* (Bari, 1963)

J. H. Lambert: *Photometrie sive de mensure et gradibus luminis, colorum et umbrae* (Augsburg, 1760)

C. Watelet: *L'Art de peindre: Poëme avec des réflexions sur les différentes parties de la peinture* (Paris, 1760; rev. Amsterdam, 1761)

J. H. Lambert: 'Mémoire sur la partie photométrique de l'art du peintre', *Mém. Acad. Royale Sci. & B.-Lett.* [Berlin], xxiv (1768), pp. 80–108

M. Rossi: *Saggio intorno alla determinazione delle ombre* (Florence, 1805)

H. Richter: *Day-light: A Recent Discovery in the Art of Painting with Hints on the Philosophy of the Fine Arts and on that of the Human Mind as First Dissected by Emmanual Kant* (London, 1817)

C. Amati: *Regole del chiaro-oscuro* (Milan, 1840)

A. Parronchi: *Studi su la dolce prospettiva* (Milan, 1964)

### SCIENTIFIC AND PHILOSOPHICAL STUDIES

V. Ronchi: *The Nature of Light* (Bologna, 1939); Eng. trans. by V. Barocas (London, 1970)

M. Minnaert: *Light and Colour in the Open Air*, Eng. trans. by H. M. Kremer-Preist (London, 1940); R as *The Nature of Light and Colour in the Open Air* (New York, 1959)

A. Wood and F. Oldham: *Thomas Young: Natural Philosopher, 1773–1829* (Cambridge, 1954)

P. A. Pav: *Eighteenth-century Optics: The Age of Unenlightenment* (diss., Bloomington, IN U., 1964)

V. Ronchi: 'Light', *New Catholic Encyclopedia*, viii (1967), pp. 747–9

A. I. Sabra: *Theories of Light from Descartes to Newton* (London, 1967)

T. Cornsweet: *Visual Perception* (New York, 1970)

D. Lindberg: *Theories of Vision from al-Kiudi to Kepler* (Chicago, 1976)

J. McEvoy: 'The Metaphysics of Light in the Middle Ages', *Philos. Stud.*, xxvi (1979), pp. 125–43

R. Osborne: *Lights and Pigments: Colour Principles for Artists* (New York, 1980)

P. Marshall: 'Nicole Oresme on the Nature, Reflection, and Speed of Light', *Isis*, lxxii (1981), pp. 357–74

J. McEvoy: *The Philosophy of Robert Grosseteste* (Oxford, 1982)

B. Wheaton: 'Light', *Dictionary of the History of Science*, ed. W. F. Bynum, E. J. Browne and R. Porter (London, 1983), pp. 235–7

G. Cantor: 'Light and Enlightenment: An Exploration of Mid-eighteenth-century Modes of Discourse', *The Discourse of Light from the Middle Ages to the Enlightenment* (Los Angeles, 1985), pp. 69–104

D. Lindberg: 'Laying the Foundations of Geometrical Optics: Maurolico, Kepler, and the Medieval Tradition', *The Discourse of Light from the Middle Ages to the Enlightenment* (Los Angeles, 1985), pp. 3–65

——: 'The Genesis of Kepler's Theory of Light: Light Metaphysics from Plotinus to Kepler', *Osiris*, 2nd ser., ii (1986), pp. 5–42

### GENERAL

R. Rood: *Color and Light in Painting* (New York, 1941)

R. Arnheim: *Art and Visual Perception* (Berkeley, 1954/R 1974), pp. 303–29

W. Schöne: *Über das Licht in der Malerei* (Berlin, 1954) [classic study]; review by A. Neumeyer in *A. Bull.*, xxxvii (1955), pp. 301–4

E. Gombrich: *Art and Illusion* (London, 1962/R 1969, 5/1977)

T. Hess and J. Ashbery, eds: *Light: From Aten to Laser*, ART news Annu., xxxv (New York, 1969) [articles on Byz., Gothic, Ren. and Mod. periods]

R. Weale: *Theories of Light and Colour in Relation to the History of Painting* (MPhil thesis, U. London, 1973)

D. Bremer: 'Licht als universales Darstellungsmedium: Materialen und Bibliographie', *Archv Begriffsgesch.*, xviii (1974), pp. 185–206

D. Jameson and L. Hurvich: 'From Contrast to Assimilation: In Art and in the Eye', *Leonardo*, viii (1975), pp. 125–31; also in *Vision and Artifact*, ed. M. Henle (New York, 1976), pp. 49–64

T. Kaufmann: 'The Perspective of Shadows: The History of the Theory of Shadow Projection', *J. Warb. & Court. Inst.*, xxxvii (1975), pp. 258–87

E. Gombrich: 'The Heritage of Apelles' and 'Light, Form and Texture', *The Heritage of Apelles* (Oxford, 1976), pp. 1–35

V. Nieto Alcaide: *La luz, simbolo y sistema visual: El espacio y la luz en el arte gotico y del renacimiento* (Madrid, 1978)

R. Verbraeken: *Clair-obscur: Histoire d'un mot* (Nogent-le-Roi, 1979)

T. Jacobs: *Light for the Artists* (New York, 1988)

J. Steer: 'Art History and Direct Perception: A General View', *A. Hist.*, xii (1989), pp. 93–107

LIGHT SYMBOLISM

J. A. Notopoulos: 'The Symbolism of the Sun and Light in the Republic of Plato', *Class. Philol.*, xxxix (1944), pp. 163–72, 223–40

M. Meiss: 'Light as Form and Symbol in some Fifteenth-century Paintings', *A. Bull.*, xxvii (1945), pp. 43–68; also in M. Meiss: *The Painter's Choice: Problems in the Interpretation of Renaissance Art* (New York, 1976), pp. 3–18

R. Bultmann: 'Zur Geschichte der Lichtsymbolik im Altertum', *Philologus*, xcvii (1948), pp. 1–36

E. Panofsky: *Early Netherlandish Painting* (New York, 1953/*R* 1971)

D. G. Carter: 'Reflections in Armor in the *Canon van der Paele Madonna*', *A. Bull.*, xxxvi/1 (1954), pp. 60–62

G. Mensching: 'Die Lichtsymbolik in der Religionsgeschichte', *Stud. Gen.*, x (1957), pp. 422–31

J. Koch: 'Über die Lichtsymbolik im Bereich der Philosophie und der Mystik des Mittelalters', *Stud. Gen.*, xiii (1960), pp. 653–70

H. Sedlmayr: 'Das Licht in seinen künstlerischen Manifestationen', *Stud. Gen.*, xiii (1960), pp. 313–24; also in H. Sedlmayr: *Das Licht in seinen künstlerischen Manifestationen* (Mittenwald, 1979)

D. Tarrant: 'Greek Metaphors of Light', *Class. Q.*, liv (1960), pp. 181–7

J. Białostocki: 'Ars auro prior', *Mélanges de littérature comparée et de philologie offerts à Mieczyslaw Brahmer* (Warsaw, 1967), pp. 55–63

B. I. Mullahy: 'Liturgical Use of Light', *New Catholic Encyclopedia*, viii (1967), pp. 751–5

C. E. Schützinger: 'Light', *New Catholic Encyclopedia*, viii (1967), pp. 749–50

J. Białostocki: 'The Eye and the Window: Realism and Symbolism of Light—Reflections in the Art of Albrecht Dürer and his Predecessors', *Festschrift für Gert von der Osten* (Cologne, 1970), pp. 159–76; also in J. Białostocki: *The Message of Images: Studies in the History of Art* (Vienna, 1988), pp. 77–92; see also pp. 93–107

D. Rosand: 'Titian's Light as Form and Symbol', *A. Bull.*, lvii (1975), pp. 58–64

H. R. Schmid: *Lux incorporata: Zur ontologischen Begrundung einer Systematik des farbigen Aufbaus in der Malerei* (Hildesheim, 1975)

J. Białostocki: 'Man and Mirror in Painting: Reality and Transience', *Studies in Late Medieval and Renaissance Painting in Honor of Millard Meiss*, ed. I. Lavin and J. Plummer (New York, 1978), pp. 61–72

K. Murawska: 'Milton's Tower: From the Symbol of Divine Guidance to that of Secret Wisdom', *Bull. Mus. N. Varsovie/Biul. Muz. N. Warsaw*, xxiii (1982), pp. 44–55

C. Del Bravo: 'Sul significato della luce nel Caravaggio e in Gianlorenzo Bernini', *Artibus & Hist.*, iv (1983), pp. 69–77; also in *Le risposte dell'arte*, ed. C. Del Bravo (Florence, 1985)

D. Davies: 'El Greco and the Spiritual Reform Movements in Spain', *El Greco: Italy and Spain*, ed. J. Brown and M. Pita Andrade, Studies in the History of Art, xiii (Washington, DC, 1984), pp. 57–74

F. Hartt: 'Lo specchio urbinate', *Studi su Raffaello: Atti del congresso internazionale di studi: Urbino, 1984*, pp. 441–53 [on mirrors in Raphael and Piero della Francesca]

P. Reuterswärd: 'Windows of Divine Light', *Interpretazioni veneziane: Studi di storia dell'arte in onore di Michelangelo Muraro*, ed. D. Rosand (Venice, 1984), pp. 77–84; also in *The Visible and the Invisible in Art*, ed. P. Reuterswärd (Vienna, 1991) [incl. 'What Colour is Divine Light?']

J. Miller: 'Symbolic Light in Giotto and the Early Quattrocento in Florence', *Source*, v (1985), pp. 7–13

L. Schneider: 'Shadow Metaphors and Piero della Francesca's Arezzo *Annunciation*', *Source*, v (1985), pp. 18–22

J. Schultze: 'Das Bestimmte und das Unbestimmte: Zu Rodins Hell-Dunkel-Strukturen', *Niederd. Beitr. Kstgesch.*, xxiv (1985), pp. 201–08

P. Rotondi: 'La grande luce di Michelangelo nella volta della Cappella Sistina', *A. Crist.*, lxxv (1987), pp. 263–70

L. Steinberg and S. Edgerton: 'How Shall This Be?: Reflections on Filippo Lippi's *Annunciation* in London', *Artibus & Hist.*, viii (1987), pp. 25–53

SPECIALIST STUDIES
*Classical and medieval*

A. Rumpf: 'Classical and Post-Classical Greek Painting', *J. Hell. Stud.*, lxvii (1947)

M. Meiss: 'Some Remarkably Early Shadows in a Rare Type of Threnos', *Festschrift Ulrich Middledorf* (Berlin, 1968), pp. 112–18

H. B. Maginnis: 'Cast Shadows in Pietro Lorenzetti's Assisi Cycle', *Gaz. B.-A.*, n.s. 6, lxxvii (1971), pp. 63–4

V. Bruno: *Form and Color in Greek Painting* (New York, 1977)

J. Gage: 'Colour in History: Relative and Absolute', *A. Hist.*, i (1978), pp. 104–30 [colour and light values in med. glass]

E. Panofsky, ed.: *Abbot Suger on the Abbey Church of St Denis and its Art Treasures* (Princeton, 1979)

J. Gage: 'Gothic Glass: Two Aspects of a Dionysian Aesthetic', *A. Hist.*, v (1982), pp. 36–58

*Renaissance*

H. Siebenhühner: *Über den Kolorismus der Frührenaissance vornehmlich dargestellt in dem 'Trattato della pittura' des L. B. Alberti* (diss., U. Leipzig, 1935)

T. Hetzer: *Titian: Geschichte seiner Farbe* (Frankfurt am Main, 1948)

A. Bovi: 'Il periodo milanese di Leonardo: La nuova prospettiva di luce e di ombra', *A. Lombarda*, vii (1962), pp. 43–8

M. Rzepinska: 'Light and Shadow in the Late Writings of Leonardo da Vinci', *Rac. Vinc.*, xix (1962), pp. 259–66

J. Białostocki: 'Puer Sufflans Egnes', *Arte in Europa: Scritti di storia dell'arte in onore di Edoardo Arslan* (Pavia, 1966), pp. 591–5; also in J. Białostocki: *The Message of Images: Studies in the History of Art* (Vienna, 1988), pp. 139–44

M. Rzepinska: 'Teoria koloru i światło w pismach Gian Paolo Lomazzo' [Theory of colour and light in the works of Gian Paolo Lomazzo], *Stud. Estet.*, vi (1969), pp. 187–99

M. Calvesi: 'Caravaggio o la ricerca della salvazione', *Stor. A.*, ix–x (1971), pp. 93–142

K. Weil-Garris Posner: *Leonardo and Central Italian Art, 1515–1550* (New York, 1974)

Z. Filipczak: 'New Light on Mona Lisa: Leonardo's Optical Knowledge and his Choice of Lighting', *A. Bull.*, lvix (1977), pp. 518–23

R. Le Molle: 'Significato di luce e di lume nelle *Vite* del Vasari', *Vasari storiografo e artista* (Florence, 1977), pp. 163–77

J. Ackerman: 'Alberti's Light', *Studies in Late Medieval and Renaissance Painting in Honor of Millard Meiss*, ed. I. Lavin and J. Plummer (New York, 1978), pp. 1–28

M. Barasch: *Light and Color in the Italian Renaissance Theory of Art* (New York, 1978)

C. Brandi: 'L'ombra in Giorgione', *A. Ven.*, xxxii (1978), pp. 85–7

G. Brucher: *Farbe und Licht in Albrecht Altdorfers Sebastiansalter in St Florian* (Graz, 1978)

G. Kouskoff: 'Quelques réflexions sur la théorie des couleurs dans le *De subtilitate* de Jérôme Cardan et sa critique par Jules-César Scaliger', *Acta conventus neo-latini amstelodamensis: Proceedings of the Second International Congress of Neo-Latin Studies: Munich, 1979*, pp. 620–34

H. Miedema and B. Meijer: 'The Introduction of Coloured Ground in Painting, and its Influence on Stylistic Development, with Particular Respect to Sixteenth-century Netherlandish Art', *Stor. A.*, xxxv (1979), pp. 79–93

C. H. Smyth: 'Venice and the Emergence of the High Renaissance in Florence: Observations and Questions', *Florence and Venice: Comparisons and Relations*, ed. S. Bertelli, N. Rubenstein and C. H. Smyth, i (Florence, 1979), pp. 209–49

C. Maltese: 'Il colore per Leonardo dalla pittura alla scienza', *Leonardo e l'età della ragione*, ed. E. Bellone and P. Rossi (Milan, 1982), pp. 171–83

J. Ruda: *Filippo Lippi Studies: Naturalism, Style and Iconography in Early Renaissance Art* (New York, 1982)

K. Keele: *Leonardo da Vinci's Elements of the Science of Man* (New York, 1983)

C. Maltese: 'Leonardo e la teoria dei colori', *Röm. Jb. Kstgesch.*, xx (1983), pp. 209–19

——: 'Come illuminò veramente Leonardo il proprio studio?', *Fra Rinascimento, Manierismo e realtà. Scritti di storia dell'arte in memoria di Anna Maria Brizio* (Florence, 1984), pp. 31–40

E. Olszewski: 'Distortions, Shadows and Conventions in Sixteenth-century Italian Art', *Artibus & Hist.*, vi (1985), pp. 101–24

P. Hills: *The Light of Early Italian Painting* (New Haven and London, 1986)

K. H. Veltman with K. D. Keele: *Studies on Leonardo da Vinci I: Linear Perspective and the Visual Dimensions of Science and Art* (Munich, 1986)

C. Maltese: 'Raffaello e la cultura scientifica e tecnologica del suo tempo', *Studi su Raffaello*, ed. M. H. Hamoud and M. L. Strochi (Urbino, 1987), pp. 441–53

C. Parkhurst: 'Leon Battista Alberti's Place in the History of Color Theories', *Color and Technique in Renaissance Painting*, ed. M. Hall (Locust Valley, 1987), pp. 161–204

D. Summers: 'The Stylistics of Color', *Color and Technique in Renaissance Painting*, ed. M. Hall (Locust Valley, 1987)

*1700–1900*

E. Heuck: *Die Farbe in der französischen Kunsttheorie des 17. Jahrhunderts* (Strasbourg, 1929)

J. R. Johnson: 'The Stained-glass Theories of Viollet-le-Duc', *A. Bull.*, xlv (1963), pp. 121–34

J. Gage: *Colour in Turner: Poetry and Truth* (London, 1969)

J. Whiteley: 'Light and Shade in French Neo-classicism', *Burl. Mag.*, cxvii (1975), pp. 768–73

J. Martin: *Baroque* (New York, 1977) [incl. chap. on light]

J. Muller: 'Rubens' Museum of Antique Sculpture: An Introduction', *A. Bull.*, lvix (1977), pp. 571–82

B. Nicolson: *The International Caravaggesque Movement* (Oxford, 1979), rev. as *Caravaggism in Europe*, ed. L. Vertova (Turin, 1990)

A. Wheelock: *Vermeer* (New York, 1981)

P. Schweizer: 'John Constable, Rainbow Science and English Color Theory', *A. Bull.*, xliv (1982), pp. 424–45

*Northern Light: Realism and Symbolism in Scandinavian Painting* (exh. cat., ed. K. Varnedoe; Washington, DC, Corcoran Gal.; New York, Brooklyn Mus.; Minneapolis, MN, Inst. A.; 1982–3)

E. Cropper: *The Ideal of Painting: Pietro Testa's Düsseldorf Notebook* (Princeton, 1984)

R. Jouy: 'George Inness's Swedenborgian Dimension', *SECAC Rev.*, xi (1986), pp. 14–22

R. Rzepinska: 'Tenebrism in Baroque Painting and its Ideological Background', *Artibus & Hist.*, vii (1986), pp. 91–112

B. Birbaumer: 'Die Lichttechnik ab Ausdrucksträger der Ölmalerei des 17. Jahrhunderts am Beispiel Neapels', *Wien. Jb. Kstgesch.*, xl (1987), pp. 45–55

S. Bordini: 'Luce e pittura: Il *Daylight* di Henry Richter (1817)', *Ric. Stor. A.*, xxxiii (1987), pp. 71–85

B. W. Keyser: *Science and Sensibility: The Victorian Way to Modern Art* (diss., U. Toronto, 1992)

*20th century*

W. Homer: *Seurat and the Science of Painting* (Cambridge, 1964)

*Laser Light: A New Visual Art* (exh. cat., Cincinnati, OH, A. Mus., 1969)

*Charles Ross: The Substance of Light* (exh. cat. by Charles Ross, La Jolla, CA, Mus. Contemp. A., 1976)

*Elektronische Kunst, kybernetische Objekte* (exh. cat., ed. B. Holeczek; Brunswick, Kunstver., 1977–8)

G. Levin, ed.: *Edward Hopper: The Art and the Artist* (New York, 1981)

*Light Vista, Light Visions* (exh. cat., U. Notre Dame, IN, Snite Mus. A., 1983) [holography exh.]

A. Lipp and P. Zec: *More Light: Artists' Holograms and Light Objects* (Hamburg, 1985)

For further bibliography *see* CHIAROSCURO.

JANIS CALLEN BELL

**Lightbown, Aspinall** & Co. English wallpaper manufacturing company founded in 1854 in Bredbury, Lancs, by Henry Lightbown (1819–99), who had worked for POTTER & Co. By 1847, he was in business with his brother-in-law William Aspinall and Doctor Graham, a partner in Potter's, as wallpaper merchants and block printers in Manchester. In 1854 Henry Lightbown, his brother James Lightbown and William Aspinall set up a new factory, Hayfield Mills, at Bredbury, where they became one of the largest producers of cheap machine-printed wallpapers in 19th-century Britain.

In the early 1880s the firm introduced a range of medium-priced papers printed with an embossed finish called the Early English Style. In 1884 the company succeeded in printing multi-coloured 'sanitary' papers (previously only available in a single colour); these were printed with copper rollers etched with intaglio designs using spirit or oil-based colours that could be varnished to produce washable papers. In the 1890s the Cordovan Leathers range of embossed wallpapers imitating gilded leathers was introduced, as were patterns by such freelance designers as A. F. Brophy (1846–1912), Christopher Dresser, Sidney Haward (*fl c.* 1882–1940) and the Silver

Studio. In the early 1900s damask and flock designs were added to the sanitary range, possibly inspired by the designer G. F. Jackson, who is also credited with introducing *c.* 1905 the 'Crown' decoration that incorporated filling paper and frieze in a single design. The company also produced stencilled friezes (printed by aerograph from 1900) and in 1920 acquired the firm of David Walker of Middleton.

After the firm was absorbed into the Wall Paper Manufacturers Ltd *c.* 1900 production continued at Bredbury. Under the directorship of R. V. M. Busby (1908–90) the mill printed papers for the group's Lancastria ranges during the late 1940s and early 1950s. From 1952 Busby introduced high-quality modern design into cheap machine prints with notable success in the screen-printed Palladio collections (1955–63); the *Architects' Book*, issued from 1952 onwards, which contained 100 contemporary papers; and in the Modus and Magnus ranges, produced in the early 1960s, that were also primarily for architects.

BIBLIOGRAPHY

A. V. Sugden and J. L. Edmondson: *A History of English Wallpaper, 1509–1914* (London, 1926)

C. C. Oman and J. Hamilton: *Wallpapers: A History and Illustrated Catalogue of the Collection of the Victoria and Albert Museum* (London, 1982)

*A Popular Art: British Wallpapers, 1930–1960* (exh. cat. by L. Hoskins, M. Pinney and M. Turner, London, Middx Poly., Silver Studio Col., 1990)

CLARE TAYLOR

**Lightfoot, Maxwell Gordon** (*b* Liverpool, 19 July 1886; *d* London, 27 Sept 1911). English painter and draughtsman. He studied at Chester Art School from *c.* 1901 until *c.* 1905. Between 1905 and 1907 he was apprenticed as a chromolithographer and attended evening classes at the Sandon Terrace Studios, Liverpool, under Herbert McNair (1865–1955) and Gerard Chowne (1875–1911), whose flower paintings influenced Lightfoot's earliest works. On Chowne's advice he studied at the Slade School in London from 1907 until 1909 where he won several prizes, including the Melville Nettleship prize for figure drawing with *Interior of a Barn with Resting Labourers* (1909–10; London, U. Coll., Slade Sch. F.A.).

During 1910 Lightfoot worked in many media and styles. He drew and painted stylized panoramic landscapes in Wales in which he deliberately simplified colour and form; he produced a series of pen, ink and wash figure drawings, their highly charged emotional content suggesting literary derivations; and he began to study isolated animal and figure subjects, using heavy simplified outlines and flat areas of colour or tone which represent the amalgam of his response to the art of the Pont-Aven School, Jean-François Millet and Pierre Puvis de Chavannes. In 1910 he also exhibited with the New English Art Club in London.

In February 1911 Lightfoot contributed four drawings, including *The Stonebreaker* (Liverpool, Walker A.G.), to an exhibition of work by members of the FRIDAY CLUB. He was invited to join the CAMDEN TOWN GROUP and contributed two drawings and two tender figure paintings, *Mother and Child* and *Boy with a Hoop, Frank* (both priv. col., see Baron, pp. 262–3), to the first exhibition in June 1911. Lightfoot's work was totally different in mood, style and ideal from that of his fellow exhibitors. His inspiration for these paintings was not the French Post-Impressionists as it was for the core of the Camden Town Group; in *Frank* he looked back to Whistler and Velázquez, and in the tondo *Mother and Child* (a theme he explored in 1911) he recalled Italian Renaissance models. His work was acclaimed by the critics who were surprised at his association with the Camden Town Group. The artist himself regretted his membership and resigned. Three months later he killed himself.

BIBLIOGRAPHY

*Maxwell Gordon Lightfoot* (exh. cat. by G. Engert, Liverpool, Walker A.G., 1972)

W. Baron: *The Camden Town Group* (London, 1979)

WENDY BARON

**Lightfoot Runner.** *See* WEST, RICHARD.

**Lighthouse.** Structure built on a coast or on a rock in the open sea that exhibits a powerful light to aid navigation and warn of hazards to shipping. The most renowned lighthouse of antiquity—one of the seven wonders of the ancient world—was built *c.* 280 BC on the island of Pharos at Alexandria. Constructed of stone in three storeys (h. *c.* 137 m), the lower storey was 30 m square, the second octagonal and the top circular, with a wood fire on its roof. From this structure (destr. 13th or 14th century) the word 'pharos' came to be generally adopted as denoting a beacon, although not necessarily one bearing a light. The Romans built numerous lighthouses: the pharos at the entrance to Ostia harbour, completed by Emperor Claudius *c.* AD 50, was similar in form to the one at Alexandria but only a quarter its height. At least 30 lighthouses existed before AD 400, including surviving examples at Dover and La Coruña (refurbished late 18th century).

Lighthouses were built in several areas of the Islamic world along navigable rivers and coastlines, for example

the cylindrical tower (AD 821) at Sousse on the Tunisian coast, which, as indicated by its Koranic inscription, was used to guide ships into harbour. In Europe lighthouse construction recommenced from *c.* 1100. An outstanding example is the Lanterna at Genoa, built before 1161 and reconstructed in its present form in 1544; it comprises two pillars, 9.1 m and 7 m square respectively, each over 30 m in height, set one upon the other on a rocky eminence. Cordouan Lighthouse, a notable French example, was designed in 1581 by the engineer–architect Louis de Foix to replace an existing structure; built on an islet in the estuary of the River Gironde, it was the first lighthouse since Roman times to be entirely surrounded by water. The barrel-shaped building (upper part replaced 1788–90) contained two vaulted rooms: a great hall (diam. 15.8 m) and a spacious chapel above. The principal dome carried an open lantern crowned by a turret, which enclosed the fire, with a tapering chimney above. Externally the lighthouse was profusely decorated with parapets and pilasters, which disguised the building's unattractive form. It was not until 1610 that work was sufficiently advanced to allow a navigation fire to be shown. The principal unforeseen difficulty was erosion by the sea, and an encircling wall and parapet (begun 1595; subsequently enlarged) saved the lighthouse from destruction.

The first lighthouse to be completely exposed to the sea was built in 1696–8 on the wave-swept Eddystone Rock in the English Channel, *c.* 22 km from Plymouth, by Henry Winstanley (1644–1703); it was subsequently rebuilt and enlarged (1699; destr. 1703). Both were extraordinarily ornate designs (see fig.). The third Eddystone Lighthouse was a simple, conical tower (1706–8) built by John Rudyerd (*d* 1713); sheathed with caulked planking like a ship, it was destroyed by a fire that started in its timber lantern in 1755. The fourth Eddystone tower (1756–9) by JOHN SMEATON revolutionized lighthouse design. It was

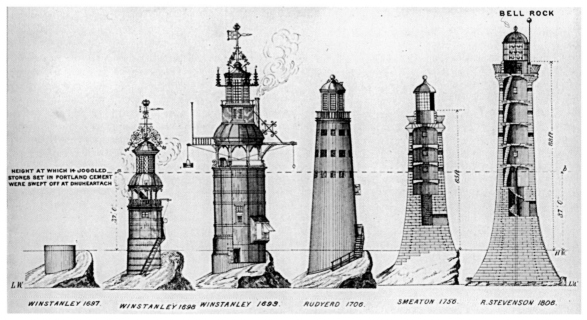

British lighthouses, 1697–1806; from T. Stevenson: *Lighthouse Construction and Illumination* (London, 1881), pl. 1

built entirely of stone with concentric courses of interlocking dovetailed blocks secured vertically by stone cubes to prevent sliding. To combat the destructive effect of wave action on traditional lime mortar he developed a hydraulic mortar using Italian pozzolana, a natural volcanic ash (*see* CONCRETE, §II, 1(iii)). This achieved a homogeneous structure with greater weight, strength and durability, which was enhanced by the wide-based, tapering form of the tower, inspired by the shape of the bole and trunk of an oak tree (see fig.). The light at its summit was provided by a chandelier of candles.

Smeaton's structure was highly influential on lighthouse design throughout the world for the next 150 years, as seen in two outstanding wave-swept lighthouses off the Scottish coast, Bell Rock (1807–11; see fig.) by Robert Stevenson and Skerryvore (1838–43) by his son Alan Stevenson (1807–65), both of which, when built, were the largest of the type. A new, much larger Eddystone Lighthouse, also built of interlocking masonry, was later constructed (1882) on a different rock due to erosion of the first; it was designed by James Douglass (1826–98), who also built the second Bishop's Rock Lighthouse (1852–8; enlarged 1882–8), Scilly Isles, and Wolf Rock Lighthouse (1862–9) off Land's End. The upper part of Smeaton's tower was re-erected as a monument on Plymouth Hoe. The Fastnet Rock Lighthouse (completed 1904), by Douglass's son William Tregarthen Douglass, also followed Smeaton's concept.

Important developments in lighting and optical technology for lighthouses took place in the 18th and 19th centuries. In 1782 the Swiss scientist Aimé Argand invented an oil lamp that gave a steady, smokeless flame, providing a major improvement in illumination. Argand lamps remained the standard form of lighthouse illumination until the late 19th century, although gas-mantle and pressurized-kerosene lamps were also developed in the late 19th century and early 20th. The first optical system designed to concentrate and focus the light was the catoptric system, in which light is distributed by metallic reflectors in the form of a parabolic curve. It was introduced at Liverpool by William Hutchinson, dockmaster in 1763. Revolving catoptric lights were first used at Carlsten Lighthouse by the Swedish engineer Jonal Norberg in 1781. Early independently designed revolving catoptric systems were installed in the new upper tower at Cordouan (1788–90) and in St Agnes Lighthouse, Scilly Isles, in 1790. Robert Stevenson introduced improved parabolic reflectors, developed intermittent and flashing lights and in 1810 designed a double light for the Isle of May Lighthouse. The dioptric system, using concentric prisms of glass around a lens to refract the light into a narrow, horizontal beam, was invented in 1822 by the physicist Augustin Fresnel (1788–1827). He also initiated the catadioptric system, with combined refracting and reflecting prisms. Alan Stevenson and Thomas Stevenson (1818–87) developed Fresnel's work. The invention by Thomas Stevenson in 1849–50 of holophotal systems, which combined the whole spectrum of rays diverging from a light source into a single beam of parallel rays, marked a major improvement in lighthouse illumination that came into universal use for about a century. In 1890 a method was invented to reduce friction in revolving lights by floating the apparatus on a bath of mercury, and this allowed the frequency of rotation to be increased.

In the 20th century the development of reinforced-concrete and steel construction, electric lighting, electronic communications and the use of helicopters for construction and servicing have all facilitated lighthouse provision and operation. Prefabricated reinforced-concrete construction techniques for lighthouses resulted in the telescopic method of erection using caissons that was established in the late 1950s, while Ve Skerries Lighthouse (1979), West Shetland, designed by Robert MacKay (*b* 1929) has a tower (h. 15.7 m) built of prestressed, post-tensioned concrete shafts anchored into the rock. In the 1960s US Coastguard towers were built off Texas in the Bay of Mexico with open frames of braced steelwork resembling oil rigs. Incandescent electric lamps became the standard form of illumination in lighthouses from the 1920s, but later developments included sophisticated arc lamps and lights powered by solar cells and sealed-beam lamp arrays; radio and radar beacons are also used for navigational purposes. Such developments resulted in manned lighthouses gradually being automated or superseded by automatic lights, which are continuously monitored from a central headquarters. A new automatic lighthouse was built to MacKay's design at North Rona (1984), off Cape Wrath on the Scottish coast; the last manned lighthouses in the USA were automated in the late 1980s and in Britain automation is planned for completion in 1998.

BIBLIOGRAPHY

'Lighthouse', *Encyclopedia Britannica* (London, 1768–71, rev. 15/1974), x, pp. 952–7
J. Smeaton: *Narrative of the Building and Description of the Construction of the Edystone Lighthouse* (London, 1791, rev. 3/1813)
R. Stevenson: *An Account of the Bell Rock Lighthouse* (Edinburgh, 1824); ed. A. F. Collins as *The Bell Rock Lighthouse* (Cambridge, 1931)
A. Stevenson: *Account of the Skerryvore Lighthouse with Notes on the Illumination of Lighthouses* (Edinburgh, 1848)
——: *A Rudimentary Treatise on the History, Construction and Illumination of Lighthouses* (London, 1850)
T. Stevenson: *Lighthouse Construction and Illumination* (London, 1881)
D. A. Stevenson: *The World's Lighthouses before 1820* (Oxford, 1959)
J. Guillaume: 'Le Phare de Cordouan', *Rev. A.*, viii/8 (1970), pp. 33–52
P. Beaver: *A History of Lighthouses* (London, 1971)
D. B. Hague and R. Christie: *Lighthouses: Their Architecture, History and Archaeology* (Llandysul, 1975)
R. J. Mackay: 'Ve Skerries', *X Conference of the International Association of Lighthouse Authorities: Tokyo, 1980* [paper 2.4.8]
——: 'Construction of a Major Automatic Offshore Lighthouse', *XI Conference of the International Association of Lighthouse Authorities: Brighton, 1985* [paper 2.5.1]
K. Sutton-Jones: *Pharos: The Lighthouse Yesterday, Today and Tomorrow* (Salisbury) 1985)

ROLAND PAXTON

**Lighting.** Architectural use of natural and artificial light. The lighting of buildings has two aspects: functional, in which interiors need to be efficiently lit by both daylight and artificial light to enable human activities to take place over an extended period of time, and aesthetic, in which the qualities of light and its form-giving potential can be used to achieve effects of great beauty, on both the exteriors of buildings and their interiors. For thousands of years the production of artificial light depended on combustion and the brightness of a flame, initially by fire and then by burning fats and oils. During this period, most detailed human activities were confined to the hours between sunrise and sunset, and the design of natural lighting was of paramount importance. New sources of artificial light, which were developed in the 19th century as an integral part of the Industrial Revolution, led to remarkable improvements in lighting technology and its architectural application. The combination of natural and artificial lighting in different environments subsequently became both an art and an exact science, accompanied by a series of regulatory measures that attempted to balance the environmental factors involved, including thermal and acoustic performance and energy conservation as well as illumination (*see also* ENVIRONMENTAL DESIGN).

1. Before *c.* 1800. 2. After *c.* 1800.

### 1. BEFORE *c.* 1800.

*(i) Natural lighting.* From the earliest times, light has played a special role in places of worship. The sun was revered as one of the most powerful manifestations of Nature, symbolizing the cycle of life, while light, the manifestation of divinity, symbolized intelligence, enlightenment and reason, with the power to dispel the forces of darkness. Such concepts were celebrated in all ancient cultures and their buildings. The form-giving qualities of light were also appreciated, as in the rhythm of shadows in the colonnades of ancient Greek temples and the fine detail of column fluting and entablature mouldings, which are thrown into sharp relief by the strong light available in the warm climate. In ancient Rome, the toplighting of interiors was introduced, as seen in the Pantheon (*c.* AD 118–25), a circular temple lit by an oculus in the centre of the dome (*see* ROME, §V, 8, and fig. 26).

Perhaps the most expressive use of light in religious buildings was embodied in Christian churches. The Byzantine church of Hagia Sophia (AD 532–62) at Constantinople (now Istanbul) gave Procopius the impression of being 'so singularly full of light and sunshine it appears not so much to be lit from the sun without as from heavenly light within'. With major structural supports located on the outside, the interior is opened up and flooded with light from windows on all sides. The building is covered by a great dome pierced by 40 windows so that, in the words of a contemporary, 'it seemed…to cover the place beneath as though it was suspended from heaven by a golden chain' (see fig. 1). The walls of Hagia Sophia were originally covered in shimmering glass mosaics that reflected the light (*see* MOSAIC, §I), thus dematerialising the images and imparting a spiritual quality to them; such mosaics often incorporated metallic foil or were set in a gold background that increased their luminosity in dark interiors, for example in the 6th-century AD churches of S Apollinare Nuovo and S Vitale in Ravenna (*see* RAVENNA, §2).

The Christian symbolism of heavenly light (*see* LIGHT, §5) was fundamental to the development of the Gothic style, in which the stone structure of churches was progressively opened up to incorporate large windows of stained glass: as the physical light pervaded the glass to reveal the story painted on it, so Divine Light was intended to enlighten and illuminate the human intellect (*see* STAINED GLASS, §II, 1). The use of such large windows

was an appropriate development in the darker climates of northern Europe, where church interiors were irradiated with deep, glowing, coloured light (e.g. La Sainte Chapelle, begun 1239–43, completed 1248; *see* PARIS, fig. 34). More light was admitted with the use of GRISAILLE in the late 13th century and the 14th, and as the window area increased, the walls appeared as shimmering tapestries of light. The soft, diffuse daylight of northern Europe was also a factor in the development of intricate, deeply sculpted, pinnacled exteriors of churches there in contrast to the simpler, geometric forms of Italian architecture, echoing those of antiquity.

Natural light was manipulated in a particularly dramatic way in Baroque churches. Windows, often concealed, were placed deliberately to produce complex, theatrical lighting effects, with architectural elements and sculpture strongly modelled by side lighting. This can be seen, for example, in the diaphanous, perforated domes of the chapel of SS Sindone, Turin Cathedral, and S Lorenzo, Turin (both begun 1668; *see* GUARINI, GUARINO, fig. 1; *see also* ITALY, fig. 20). Light was also used to induce movement—as in the alternation of dark spaces with light—and to highlight such important elements as the altar, as, for example, at the Benedictine monastery church of Weltenburg an der Donau (see fig. 2). The main dome of this church, frescoed by Cosmas Damian Asam, is lit in such a way that it appears to float (for illustration *see* ASAM, §I(2)).

In secular buildings, the use of natural light in the West has historically been related to climate, the need for security and the cost and availability of glass. The value of daylight to buildings was recognized under Roman Law in the 1st century AD, which penalized infringement of light, but glass for windows was scarce and expensive, and houses were generally designed around an open court or atrium that admitted light to the surrounding rooms. Internal courtyards were also a feature of large houses in the late medieval and early Renaissance periods, providing security as well as light. Meanwhile, as window glass became more widely available for secular architecture in the 15th and 16th centuries, the size of windows progressively increased (for further discussion *see* GLASS, §IV, 2). The effect of climate on the daylighting of buildings can be seen in the generally smaller windows of southern Europe, where arcades and loggias were often built to shade interiors from intense sunlight and heat, compared to those in northern Europe, where windows often incorporated oriels or projecting bays to maximize interior light (e.g. Longleat House, Wilts, from 1568). Large windows providing even daylighting, and with glazing bars moulded to reduce glare, became characteristic of secular architecture in the West in the 17th century and after, the lighting effect often enhanced and reflected by the use of mirrors. At Versailles, such effects, including the use of gold and water as well as mirrors, were related to the sun symbolism associated with Louis XIV. In other parts of the world, interiors might be shaded from intense sunlight by verandahs—common in colonial architecture in India and, later, Australia—while the use of carved screens in such Islamic countries as North Africa filtered sunlight and produced intricate patterns of light and shade. In East Asia, the use of paper to cover openings resulted in the admission of very soft, diffuse daylight.

1. Lighting of the dome of Hagia Sophia, Istanbul, AD 532–62

2. Concealed lighting of the altar in the Benedictine monastery church of Weltenburg an der Donau by Cosmas Damian Asam and Egid Quirin Asam, 1716–21

(ii) *Artificial lighting.* The principal forms of artificial lighting before the 19th century were rushlights, candles and oil lamps that burnt vegetable or fish oil. Rushlights were made by dipping a rush stem repeatedly in hot tallow (animal fat) until a thick layer was built up. Candles with fibre wicks were used in antiquity, and Pliny described the manufacture of both tallow and beeswax candles in the first century AD. The CANDLESTICK was a portable, personal light source, carried from room to room, while branched and ornamented candelabra provided more light in larger houses and became a highly developed art form in the ancient world (*see* CANDELABRUM). By the 13th century candlemaking (chandlering) was a recognized craft, separately organized for tallow and wax candles. Materials were often scarce, and many medieval monasteries had a large apiary to provide beeswax candles for the church, especially for the celebration of Candlemas, symbolizing the presentation of Christ, the 'light of the world'. Candlesticks, increasingly ornate and produced in precious metals, were made adjustable in the 17th century, so that the height of the flame above the surface remained constant. Fixed lighting sources were provided by wall sconces backed by reflective metal (*see* SCONCE) and, later, by ornate brass or crystal chandeliers hung from ceilings (*see* CHANDELIER); the latter greatly increased lighting

levels in large buildings, including theatres, with mirrors or reflective surfaces again emphasizing their effect. Improvements in chandlering appeared in the 18th and 19th centuries, when whale spermaceti and paraffin wax were introduced, together with plaited wicks to overcome uneven burning, and candle-making machines were invented. Candles became cheap and reliable, and they gave their name to the first standard unit of illumination, the foot-candle (the amount of illumination on a surface one foot away from a common candle).

Oil lamps were also used in antiquity: tall floor lamps were found in Crete from the Minoan civilization, and precious replicas of shell lamps, which contained a natural wick channel and may have burnt mineral oil, were found in the royal tombs at Ur (*c.* 2500 BC). The basic type of oil lamp, an open saucer, was improved in ancient Greece by the addition of a handle and the turning of the wick channel inwards to form a lip; this was gradually extended to cover the top of the saucer, and a recess was formed in the base so that it could be placed on a spike (*see* GREECE, ANCIENT, §X, 8, and fig. 171). Multiple-wick pottery oil lamps were mass produced in ancient Rome, where they were common in the houses of the wealthy and in military barracks (*see* ROME, ANCIENT, §X, 6, and fig. 122). The simple, open-saucer type was most commonly used in the centuries after the fall of Rome, while an oil lamp with a 'bird-fountain' feed to maintain a constant oil level was known in AD 200 and reinvented in the 16th century. The value of a chimney placed above the flame to induce an updraught was discovered in the 16th century, and glass chimneys were commonly used from the 17th century. More curious were oil lamps formed from the oil-rich bodies of petrels, threaded with a wick, which were used in the Shetland Isles. A major improvement in oil lamps came in 1783, when the Swiss scientist Aimé Argand invented the Argand lamp that gave a steady, smokeless flame; it had a tubular wick and glass chimney, with air drawn up through a tube inside the wick to aerate the centre of the flame, greatly increasing illumination. Until the late 19th century, Argand lamps were the principal form of illumination for lighthouses, where techniques were developed to concentrate and focus the light (*see* LIGHTHOUSE).

### 2. AFTER *c.* 1800.

(i) Natural lighting. (ii) Artificial lighting.

(i) *Natural lighting.* With the advent of the Industrial Revolution, the lighting requirements of a new range of large, secular buildings to serve the needs of industry and commerce became of paramount importance. During the 19th century, protection of daylight to habitable rooms (usually in dwellings but also in small offices and workrooms) was provided in many countries, for example under the Prescription Act (1832) in Britain, in which a right to light was acquired after 20 years' uninterrupted enjoyment. The working environment in particular is fundamentally geared to seeing, and new industrial and technical processes involving intricate tasks required much higher levels of lighting. The provision of natural light and ventilation determined the courtyard plans and light wells of large buildings throughout the 19th century and into

3. Natural lighting in the pilgrimage chapel of Notre-Dame-du-Haut, Ronchamp, by Le Corbusier, 1950–55

the first half of the 20th (e.g. the Wainwright Building, St Louis, MO, 1890 91, and Guaranty Building, Buffalo, NY, 1894–6; both by Louis Sullivan and Dankmar Adler). At the same time, the development of new iron and glass structural techniques permitted much larger areas of glazing and the use of glazed roofs, as seen in commercial exchanges (for illustration *see* EXCHANGE; *see also* IRON AND STEEL, fig. 3), shopping arcades (for illustration *see* MENGONI, GIUSEPPE) and factories. More complex structural daylighting was provided by such buildings as the Jahrhunderthalle (1913), Breslau (now Wrocław; for illustration *see* BERG, MAX), and the Esders Clothing Factory (1919; by Auguste and Gustave Perret), Paris (*see* CONCRETE, fig. 3). By the early 20th century, the development of fully framed structures, both of steel and reinforced concrete, allowed the use of fully glazed infill walls, leading to the glass curtain wall that came to dominate large-scale commercial architecture after World War II (for further discussion *see* GLASS, §IV, 2(ii) and (iii)). In domestic architecture, a variety of window designs (e.g. vertical or horizontal, high-level or low-level) and types of glass (e.g. diffuse, patterned or concentrated) allowed much greater modulation of daylight and hence rendering of form.

The lighting requirements of museums and art galleries differ from most other building types: in art galleries the surfaces to be lit are usually vertical, with a consequent need to avoid glare, while in both museums and galleries the objects on display are subject to damage from ultraviolet light. Before the late 19th century, museums were largely dependent on natural light, initially provided by side lighting and, from about 1800, more frequently by high-level clerestory windows and rooflights (*see* DISPLAY OF ART, §I; *see also* MUSEUM, fig. 5). Concealed daylighting was later used to great effect in modern museums and art galleries, such as the Kimbell Art Museum (1966–72), Fort Worth, TX (for illustration *see* KAHN, LOUIS I.), and special light-scoops became a feature of many museum designs, for example at the Fondation Maeght (1959–64), Saint-Paul-de-Vence (for illustration *see* SERT, JOSEP LLUÍS). A similar concern for controlled daylighting is seen in library design, as at Kahn's Phillips Exeter Academy Library (1966–72), Exeter, NH. Kahn, who thought of structure as 'the giver of light', was, with Le Corbusier ('Architecture is the masterly, correct and magnificent play of masses brought together in light'), one of the most influential modern thinkers about the quality of natural light in architecture.

Meanwhile, natural light continued to be used expressively in churches, evoking the works of the Gothic builders. Notable 20th-century examples include Notre-Dame-du-Raincy (1922–3; by the Perret brothers), Paris (*see* PERRET, fig. 1), with walls of precast-concrete elements filled with coloured glass; and Notre-Dame-du-Haut (1950–55; by Le Corbusier), Ronchamp, which celebrates natural light both inside, with small, jewel-like stained-glass windows set in deep embrasures (see fig. 3), and outside, the rough, textured surface of the curvilinear form reflecting the play of sunlight and shadow (*see* LE CORBUSIER, fig. 6). Other churches are flooded with direct light, for example Brasília Cathedral (1958–87; by Oscar Niemeyer; *see* GLASS, fig. 8), which has a flower-like structure of curved concrete elements filled with glass; and the Crystal Cathedral (1980; Garden Grove, CA) by Philip Johnson and John Burgee (*see* IRON AND STEEL, fig. 5), a huge glass envelope supported on a steel space frame.

Despite the use of extensive window and roof glazing (including modern atrium designs), however, it is impossible to provide adequate illumination in most large modern buildings by daylight alone. Extensive glazing can also have environmental problems (e.g. thermal performance and glare), and the variability of natural light may disrupt work processes. Although the visual comfort of daylighting and the therapeutic and psychological importance of sunlight and views through windows cannot be overestimated, the development of cheap, efficient artificial lighting was crucial to the provision of effective illumination for modern industry and commerce: it was a major factor in the development of such buildings as skyscrapers and in the revolution in the workplace that led to the 24-hour working day.

### (ii) Artificial lighting.

*(a) Types.* Rapid improvements in lighting technology after 1800 included the introduction of new fuels for oil lamps, notably paraffin (kerosene), first distilled from crude petroleum oil in the mid-19th century in the USA to produce a suitable lamp oil. Within a few years, lamp oil was being produced cheaply and in large quantities, with easily adjustable lamps burning steadily and requiring little attention. In the meantime, the first experiments in the use of coal gas for large-scale lighting had been made in 1792 by the Scottish mechanic William Murdoch, who installed a multiple-burner gas system in the Philips and Lee Cotton Mill (by James Watt and Matthew Boulton), Salford, Lancs, in 1806. The early burners were simply open tubes; these were later closed at the end and pierced by small holes to spread the flame. Gas lighting gradually came into general use for the lighting of buildings and streets; by 1815, for example, London had 42 km of gas line supplying street lamps and a few houses. In 1820 the improved fishtail burner was developed, but the light produced by all gas burners depended on the brightness of the flame itself, and although there was a huge increase in the number of lighting outlets in the second half of the century, they were not significantly more effective than oil lamps; both also created considerable problems with pollution and soot deposits. A dramatic improvement came with the invention of the incandescent mantle in 1885 by the Viennese chemist Carl Auer, Baron von Welsbach. When placed over a flame (gas or oil), the Welsbach mantle—a gauze fabric impregnated with thorium and cerium oxides—burns with an intense brightness proportional to the heat of the flame. The Welsbach mantle was, however, soon superseded in general use by the invention of incandescent electric lamps.

The earliest form of electric lighting was the arc lamp (first demonstrated in London in 1810), in which an electric current arcing between two carbon electrodes produces an intensely bright light. Arc lighting was first used in 1844 at the Paris Opéra, when it was powered by batteries; in 1858 it was installed in the South Foreland Lighthouse, Kent, England, powered by one of the first electricity generators. Arc lamps were used commercially for street lighting and public buildings, but they required constant maintenance; furthermore, the light was too bright for domestic use, and it could not be subdivided. These problems were overcome by the invention of practical incandescent filament electric lamps, developed independently by Joseph Swan in England (1878) and by

Thomas Edison in the USA (1879). The lamps consisted of carbon filaments placed in a vacuum in a glass tube and heated by an electric current until they glowed. Their development was dependent on the invention of the Sprengel air pump (1875), which made possible a sufficiently high degree of vacuum to minimize oxidation. Swan and Edison installed the first central power stations (driven by steam engines) in London and New York in the 1880s, and these were rapidly followed by many others, inaugurating the modern era of clean, efficient artificial lighting. Improvements to the incandescent lamp were made in 1906 and in 1909, when tungsten metal was drawn into a wire, its increased length formed into a cage, which made possible a lamp with a greater luminous efficiency. At such higher temperatures, however, the filament evaporated in the vacuum and blackened the glass, a tendency partially resolved by replacing the vacuum with an inert gas (such as nitrogen or argon) and by coiling the filament to prevent heat loss. The coiled filament, established in the manufacture of incandescent lamps in 1934, increased the efficiency of the smaller domestic lamps by up to 20%.

Incandescent lamps produce considerable heat, however, and their efficiency is greatly outweighed by that of electric discharge tubes, in which an electric current passing between two electrodes in a glass tube creates light by ionizing metal vapour in the tube. The colour of the light is determined by the vapour: sodium lamps, widely used for street lighting, produce a bright yellow light, mercury vapour lamps a greenish-blue light, and neon a reddish glow. The first practicable tubes were developed at the end of the 19th century, but they used high voltages, making them unsuitable for most purposes. Neon tubes were used for advertising purposes from about 1910. Hot cathode discharge tubes use tungsten filaments heated to incandescence to excite the electrons, allowing them to be used with mains electric current. The most successful and widely used discharge tube is the fluorescent lamp, known since the 1860s but first practically developed in 1938; this converts the ultraviolet radiation from mercury vapour into a wide spectrum of visible light by a coating of fluorescent powder on the inner surface of the tube. It is economical in its use of electricity and has a greatly diminished heat output. By about 1950, fluorescent lighting had largely replaced incandescent lamps in schools, offices, hospitals, shops and factories, although the latter remained common for domestic and individual applications. In 1959 a new range of efficient electric lamps was developed by the addition of a halogen, such as iodine, to the gas filling of a lamp having a compact quartz envelope, kept above 250°C. This type of light was increasingly used for recessed ceiling fittings and, particularly, for display purposes. In the 1980s the compact single-ended fluorescent lamp was developed, its phosphor coating approximating the warm colour of incandescent lamps but with greatly increased luminous efficiency, making it suitable for domestic lighting.

*(b) Uses.* Fixed lighting in dwellings and other buildings became a necessity with the advent of piped gas and then electric lighting, which initially used existing gas fixtures on walls or in the centre of the ceiling. The central ceiling fixture remained for many years the standard form of

lighting in rooms, although inefficient as a source of lighting for such tasks as reading. Concealed lighting was also used by many architects, for example in Le Corbusier's Villa Savoye (1929–31), Poissy, where lighting from a long, suspended trough was directed at the ceiling, using it as a reflector. Small portable lamps, providing more flexible, effective lighting, subsequently became widespread for individual tasks and domestic use. The design of lamps and light fittings came to play an important role in the work of designers and architects, who often produced extraordinary effects for special purposes, such as the concealed, coved lighting and sculpted light columns designed by Hans Poelzig for the Grosses Schauspielhaus (1919, Berlin; *see* EXPRESSIONISM, fig. 3).

With the advent of cheap, efficient electric light, the lighting systems designed for office buildings and other workplaces were aimed at providing plentiful, uniform illumination, with lighting levels (the amount of illumination on a work surface) calculated in accordance with continually increasing recommendations. One of the most creative applications of ceiling illumination in the first half of the 20th century was designed for the Johnson Wax Administration Building (1936–8), Racine, WI, by Frank Lloyd Wright—a master of concealed lighting; there the central, windowless typing room is covered by a ceiling of glass tubes, supported by a forest of tapering mushroom columns and illuminated from above (for illustration *see* OFFICE BUILDING). The same building also demonstrates the use of tube lighting to emphasize architectural form (see fig. 4). However, the introduction of fluorescent lighting, the tubes encased in diffusers and employed in continuous grids over office ceilings, confirmed the general tendency to uniformity and monotony. Obviating the need for light wells, fluorescent lighting was a principal factor— together with the introduction of air conditioning—in the development of the 'full-floor' rectangular plan for large buildings. This change coincided with the growing dominance of the International Style, resulting in the slab skyscrapers of the late 1940s and after. The deep floor plans of such buildings subsequently led to the concept of permanent supplementary artificial lighting for areas distant from the glazed walls.

In the 1970s and after, however, an increased concern with energy conservation led to the growing use of localized lighting design in large buildings, with reduced levels for non-critical areas and with special lighting (such as uplighters) for spaces where self-luminous visual display units (VDUs) are extensively used. Late 20th-century office buildings employ a variety of light fittings: the Lloyds Building (1977–86; by Richard Rogers), London, for example, has circular fluorescent lamps in air-handling luminaires incorporating sprinkler heads, with quartz-halogen lamps in special areas, and the Broadgate Building (Phase 3, 1989), London, has a mixture of fluorescent downlighters, low-voltage spotlights and metal-halide uplighters to minimize reflections on VDU screens.

In factories, lighting levels are varied according to the type of operation undertaken: some tasks that are self-luminous, such as glass-blowing, are more difficult if lighting levels are too high, while disturbing or confusing flicker and stroboscopic effects—more marked with fluorescent lighting—must be avoided. In museums and art

4. Glass-tube lighting at the Johnson Wax Administration Building, Racine, Wisconsin, by Frank Lloyd Wright, 1936–8

galleries, artificial lighting, which is easier to control than daylight, is designed largely around display methods and the need to protect exhibits from ultraviolet radiation, usually achieved by the use of filters and controlling the intensity of light. Metal-halide lamps are increasingly used in museums, where their compact size and brilliant light offer an advantage in highlighting exhibits. Unwanted reflections are avoided by careful design of lighting (both natural and artificial) and disposition of the exhibits.

Meanwhile, with the recognition that the design of good lighting systems involves far more than the provision of sufficient illumination for tasks, some extraordinarily creative lighting schemes were developed. Many of these recognized the psychological effect of light and the ability of lighting to produce a cheerful environment or a gloomy one and to reveal or distort colours. Light can also be used to model objects or flatten them, and to model spaces, creating focal points and highlighting objects or architectural elements, particularly curved ceilings, walls or balconies, for example in theatres and cinemas (see fig. 5). Such lighting often constitutes the principal means of interior decoration in theatres, where stage lighting has also become a highly technical science.

The exterior lighting of façades can be achieved by the skilful use of lights and illuminated lettering (e.g. Bioscoop Vreeburg Cinema, Utrecht, 1936, by Gerrit Rietveld); by neon strip lighting, which can create an entire outdoor environment of coloured light (for illustration *see* LAS VEGAS); and by floodlighting, usually by high-pressure sodium discharge lamps or metal-halide lamps, which can achieve an extremely subtle modelling of architectural form (e.g. on the curved shells of Sydney Opera House, completed 1973, by Jørn Utzon). Equally dramatic exterior lighting effects can be produced with fully glazed structures whose interiors are exposed at night by a blaze of artificial

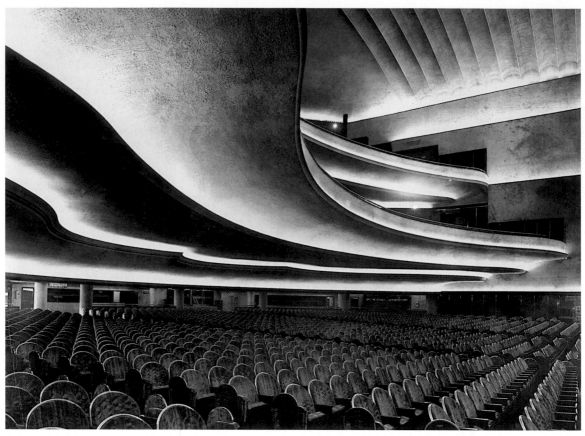

5. Auditorium lighting at the Gaumont Film Palace, Paris, by M. Belloc, 1931

lights shining through a curtain of glass (for illustration *see* CURTAIN WALL (ii)); in such buildings, light is used to invert the traditional concept of solid structure.

BIBLIOGRAPHY

R. Sheppard and H. Wright: *Building for Daylight* (London, 1948)
W. T. O'Dea: *A Short History of Lighting* (London, 1958)
W. Kohler and W. Luckhardt: *Lighting in Architecture* (New York, 1959)
P. R. Banham: *The Architecture of the Well-tempered Environment* (London and Chicago, 1969)
L. C. Kalff: *Creative Light* (London, 1971)
S. Wells: *Period Lighting* (London, 1975)
S. T. Henderson: *Daylight and its Spectrum* (Bristol, 1977)
R. N. Helms: *Illumination Engineering for Energy Efficient Luminous Environments* (Englewood Cliffs, NJ, 1980)
B. E. Evans: *Daylight in Architecture* (New York, 1981)
P. C. Sorcar: *Energy Saving Lighting Systems* (New York, 1982)
M. D. Egan: *Concepts in Architectural Lighting* (New York, 1983)
F. Moore: *Concepts and Practice of Architectural Daylighting* (New York, 1985)
J. B. Murdoch: *Illumination Engineering: From Edison's Lamp to the Laser* (New York, 1985)
D. Sudjic: *The Lighting Book: A Complete Guide to Lighting Your Home* (London, 1985)
W. M. C. Lam: *Sunlighting as Formgiver for Architecture* (New York, 1986)
C. L. Robbins: *Daylighting: Design and Analysis* (New York, 1986)
*Lighting Handbook*, Illuminating Engineering Society (New York, 1986)
JAMES LONGMORE

**Lightning Brothers.** Site of Aboriginal culture at Delamere Station, *c.* 380 km south of Darwin, Northern Territory, Australia. It consists of several galleries of paintings and engravings in rock shelters around and near the base of a monolithic sandstone outcrop. Painted motifs include birds, echidnas, kangaroos, a dingo, a Rainbow snake, lizards, a turtle, human figures, hafted stone axes and a European with firearms and cattle. Most of the paintings are silhouettes, either monochrome or outlined with a contrasting colour. Some have additional elaboration, such as internal dividing lines or simple X-ray features. The paintings are probably less than 1000 years old, since the Delamere sandstone is relatively soft. The engravings are abraded, most being randomly orientated, parallel grooves, with some bird and animal tracks and circular pits. These abraded motifs are also unlikely to be very old.

The name derives from the huge and highly elaborate painted figures of the two Lightning Brothers, which dominate the major gallery. According to Aboriginal mythology, the Lightning Brothers originated in the Warlpiri language area of the Tanami Desert and travelled to the land of the Wardaman speakers at Delamere Station and then far to the north-west, leaving along their route many signs of their passing at sites still significant to contemporary Aborigines. The bodies and limbs of the figures at Delamere Station are outlined in white pigment and infilled with parallel red and yellow stripes. The larger figure (h. more than 4 m) has a tall headdress of vertical red and black stripes. Ears, armpits, eyes, joints and internal divisions are picked out with black and white pigments (*see* ABORIGINAL AUSTRALIA, §II, 2(ii)(b)). Between the legs of each figure there is a deep abraded groove, infilled with red ochre, which represents a subincised penis. According to the Wardaman-speaking custodians, the painted stone axes near the figures are those used by the Brothers to create thunder and to split trees where lightning strikes. The abraded grooves are said to represent falling rain, and they were probably created during rain-making ceremonies at the site.

Some researchers have suggested that there is a stylistic link with the painted Wandjina figures of the Kimberley region of Western Australia (*see* ABORIGINAL AUSTRALIA, §III, 3), but this has not been demonstrated conclusively. The presence of some X-ray style features indicates a degree of stylistic influence from Western Arnhem Land (*see* ABORIGINAL AUSTRALIA, §III, 4), to which it is closest geographically, although it seems more likely that the figures of the two Lightning Brothers and other very elaborate paintings in the Wardaman language area are part of a distinctive local tradition.

DARRELL LEWIS

### BIBLIOGRAPHY
G. Chaloupka: 'Endangered Sites: A Famous Example', *Conservation of Rock Art*, ed. C. Pearson, Institute for the Conservation of Cultural Material (Canberra, 1978), pp. 81–8

**Ligne, Prince Charles-Joseph-Emmanuel de** (*b* Vienna, 7 Sept 1759; *d* Argonne, 13 Sept 1792). French soldier, publisher and collector. With his father, Prince Charles-Joseph de Ligne (1735–1814), he operated an important publishing house at the Château de Belœil, Haincourt (now in Belgium), though he was also an officer in the engineering corps and in fact died in battle. Described by Adam von Bartsch as one of the finest connoisseurs of his time, de Ligne assembled a collection of over 2587 Old Master and contemporary drawings, many of which had derived from the collections of Giorgio Vasari, Pierre Crozat, Jean Mariette and Jean de Jullienne. These works included 48 by Raphael, 11 by Michelangelo, 8 by Leonardo, 11 by Dürer, 26 by Rembrandt and 15 by Poussin but relatively few by 18th-century French and English masters. To complement his collection of drawings, de Ligne acquired over 13,500 prints, especially original etchings and facsimiles of drawings. Bartsch's illustrated catalogue of de Ligne's drawings collection includes etchings made by de Ligne himself, after drawings; 35 of his etchings (primarily after Italian drawings) were published as a collection. According to the terms of his will, his collection was sold (Vienna, 29 April 1793; 4 Nov 1794) for the benefit of his natural daughter and a Turkish child he had saved during the sack of Istanbul. His father had a monument (dedication date 1791; *in situ*) built to his memory in the park of Belœil.

### BIBLIOGRAPHY
A. von Bartsch: *Catalogue raisonné des dessins originaux des plus grands maîtres anciens et modernes qui faisaient partie du cabinet de feu le Prince Charles de Ligne* (Vienna, 1794)
F. Lugt: *Marques* (Amsterdam, 1921), p. 106
G.-M. Englebert: *Le Prince de Ligne et son temps* (Belœil, 1982)

**Li Gonglin** [Li Kung-lin; *zi* Boshi; *hao* Longmian, Longmian Jushi; Li Lung-mien] (*b* Shucheng County, Anhui Province, *c.* 1047; *d* 1106). Chinese painter and collector. He was from a family of scholar-officials, possibly related to the Li clan who were rulers of the Southern Tang (AD 937–75). In 1070 he passed the national civil-service examinations to gain the title of *jinshi*, which in the Song period (960–1279) was the culmination of scholarly achievement and means to the highest official careers. Li Gonglin, however, began by retiring to his native district.

Little is known of Li's life during the 1070s. He was joined by friends in the mountains, and around 1076 went to Nanjing to visit the reformer Wang Anshi (1021–86). In early 1078, Li bought land in Mt Longmian, south-west of Shucheng, and began building a villa that he later depicted in a handscroll painting. A surviving copy of this painting is *Shanzhuang tu* ('Longmian mountain villa'; Taipei, N. Pal. Mus.), one scene of which, 'Hall of Ink Meditation', alludes to Li's practice of calligraphy and painting as a means to enlightenment; there are also other versions (Beijing, Pal. Mus. and Florence, I Tatti). In 1079 Li left his mountain home to serve as an examination official in the capital Bianliang (modern Kaifeng, Henan Province) and shortly after was transferred to Nanchang, Jiangxi Province, and Zhangyuan, Hunan Province, where he may have met the artists Mi Fu and Huang Tingjian. By early 1086, Li had returned to Kaifeng and was promoted to a post in the Secretariat Chancellery. During his decade in the capital, Li renewed old friendships and cultivated new ones, becoming acquainted with Su Shi and his brother, with Wang Shen, Zhang Lei (1052–1112) and others.

As collector, antiquarian and connoisseur, Li left his imprint on many aspects of art. The numerous extant paintings bearing his name demonstrate his versatility; in the genres of figure painting, horse painting and landscape, Li set a standard that remained exemplary.

Among the paintings of horses attributed to Li, two are arguably genuine. *Five Tribute Horses* (see fig.) has no artist's signature or seals, but the two colophons dated 1090 and 1131, written respectively by Huang Tingjian and Zeng (1073–1135), confirm its authenticity. The painting, following a type familiar in the Tang period (AD 618–907) but executed in *baimiao* or ink outline, a medium associated with the 4th-century painter Gu Haizhi and in which Li was the acknowledged master, depicts five horses sent as tribute from West Asia, each led by a groom from a different country. One of the horses has been identified as having been sent to the Song court in 1088, when Li would have been aged 40 to 42. The painting disappeared in World War II. *Pasturing Horses, after Wei Yan of the Tang Dynasty* (handscroll, ink and colour on silk; Beijing, Pal. Mus.) was executed, according to the artist's inscription, by imperial order after a lost Tang painting. A triumph of organization, it marshalls over 1200 horses and more than 100 human figures in an expanse of pasture. A comparison with the hunting scene from the Tang tomb of Prince Zhanghuai (*d* 682; reburied 702) at Qian xian, Shaanxi Province, shows how the painting corresponds to the processional paintings that were presumably common in the Tang period.

Paintings attributed to Li referring to the classics and history include the *Classic of Filial Piety* (New York, Met.). This originally consisted of 18 sections, of which 15

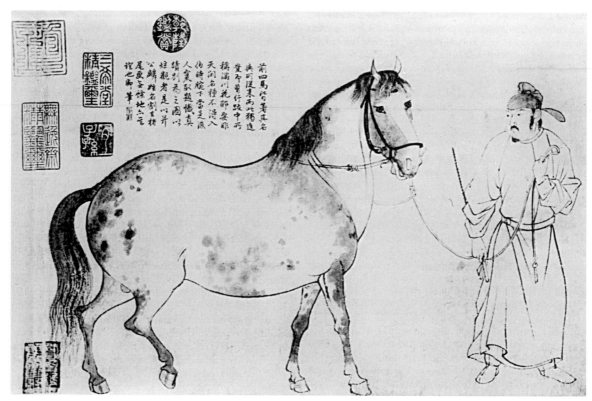

Li Gonglin: *Five Tribute Horses* (detail), handscroll, ink on paper, 0.3×*c*. 1.8 m, *c*. 1088 (untraced)

remain, each with an illustration and a transcription from the Confucian *Xiaojing* ('Classic of filial piety'), written in the old-fashioned style of the calligrapher Zhong You (AD 151–230). Though also executed in *baimiao*, the brushwork is less confident than that of *Five Tribute Horses*; it has been suggested that the painting 'has the look of a first draft', but a mistake in the prescribed number of bells for Confucian rites in one scene, which Li surely would not have made, suggests that this is in fact an early copy after Li. A *Classic of Filial Piety* (Shanghai Mus.) in five scenes with text in seal script (*zhuanshu*) is dated to the Yuan period (1279–1368) and is very similar in style to the scroll in the Metropolitan Museum. Even as imitations, these paintings are valuable as revivals of the archetype Li established. Li's renderings in *baimiao* of other literary subjects, such as Tao Yuanming's *Returning Home* and Qu Yuan's *Nine Songs*, were also frequently imitated.

Li also painted Buddhist and Daoist subjects, though none of these have survived in the original: a painting of Vimalakirti depicting the layman attended by a *devi* holding a flower is generally considered to be a Southern Song (1127–1279) painting (Tokyo, N. Mus.), and a long handscroll of Buddhist and Daoist figures (London, BM) with a colophon by the Yuan connoisseur Yu Ji (1272–1348) is imitative of Li's style. Li Gonglin established a canon of classical styles, based on the achievements of some of the greatest figure, landscape and animal painters of the Tang and pre-Tang period (see Barnhart). He is considered a master of the highest order: his classical learning informed every aspect of his painting.

BIBLIOGRAPHY

R. M. Barnhart: 'Li Kung-lin's Use of Past Styles', *Artists and Traditions: Uses of the Past in Chinese Culture*, ed. C. F. Murck (Princeton, 1976)

*Zhongguo meishujia renming cidian* [Biographical dictionary of Chinese artists] (Shanghai, 1985), p. 347

R. E. Harrist jr: 'A Biography of Li Kung-lin', *Li Kung-lin's Classic of Filial Piety*, ed. R. M. Barnhart (New York, 1993)

Hui-liang J. Chu: 'The Calligraphy of Li Kung-lin', *Li kung-lin's Classic of Filial Piety*, ed. R. M. Barnhart (New York, 1993)

RODERICK WHITFIELD

**Ligorio, Pirro** (*b* Naples, *c*. 1513; *d* Ferrara, 26 Oct 1583). Italian architect, painter, draughtsman and antiquary. He is best known for his designs for the Casino of Pius IV in the Vatican and his gardens for the Villa d'Este at Tivoli, which greatly influenced Renaissance garden design. His work reflects his interest in the reconstruction of Classical antiquity, although this was sometimes based on fragmentary information, and his painting and architecture are closely dependent on classicism with a richness of detail associated with Roman Imperial art.

1. Early activity. 2. Papal service. 3. Tivoli and Ferrara.

1. EARLY ACTIVITY. He was presumably born into a noble family and probably moved to Rome in 1534. At first he was active producing decorative paintings for palaces: Giovanni Baglione recorded numerous houses in Rome with façades frescoed by Ligorio in a distinctive yellow monochrome in the manner of Polidoro da Caravaggio or Baldassare Peruzzi. The only extant example of his figurative painting is a fresco depicting the *Dance of*

*Salome* (*c*. 1544; Rome, Oratory of S Giovanni Decollato). In 1546 he agreed to paint a processional banner (untraced) for the Confraternity of S Maria at Rieti. Two years later he was proposed for membership in the Confraternity of the Virtuosi al Pantheon, a fraternity of artists.

At least as early as the 1540s Ligorio was also pursuing archaeological investigations, noting, for example, the discovery in 1546 of the remains of the Arch of Augustus in the Forum Romanum. In 1549 he entered the service of Cardinal Ippolito II d'Este of Ferrara as court archaeologist; he was also employed as a painter, being paid for the decoration of the salon in the Cardinal's newly acquired palace of Monte Giordano in Rome. Ligorio is first mentioned in the Vatican records on 23 November 1549 upon his appointment as overseer of the fountain in the square of St Peter's.

Ligorio's major publications, especially those regarding Roman archaeology, date from the 1550s. Between 1552 and 1561 he published three maps of the city of Rome, of which two (1553 and 1561) were archaeological reconstructions. *Delle antichità di Roma* (Venice, 1553) is concerned with the ancient theatres and circuses; its copyright notice also covered some engraved reconstructions of antiquities. Seven engravings were issued separately between 1552 and 1558, including reconstructions of the Circus Maximus and the Aviary of Varro. The Venetian humanist Daniele Barbaro and Andrea Palladio met Ligorio during their visit to Rome in 1554, probably drawn by his renown in archaeology.

2. PAPAL SERVICE. Ligorio's entry into papal service was eased in 1555 by the election of a fellow Neapolitan as Pope Paul IV. In April 1557 Ligorio was recorded on the papal roll as 'designator' and in January 1558 he was appointed architect of the Vatican Palace, while his predecessor Sallustio Peruzzi remained at his original (and lesser) salary. Ligorio's first appointment may have been occasioned by the commission to design a reliquary for the chapel that Peruzzi had begun for the new papal apartment in the Belvedere Court. The reliquary was later cast in bronze and sent to Milan, where it was altered by Pellegrino Tibaldi and installed in the cathedral. Ligorio worked on the chapel until September 1558, including painting two angels (destr.). He was also given an ill-advised commission to improve the lighting of the Sala di Costantino, but the project was abandoned before too much damage was done to the existing decoration. At this time he began to prepare illustrations for *Fabulae centum ex antiquis auctoribus* (Rome, 1563) by his friend Gabriele Faerno (*d* 1561).

As papal architect Ligorio's main project was to design a new casino in the Vatican gardens as an afternoon retreat for the Pope. Work on the structure, which began in May 1558, stopped in November but was resumed in May 1560 after the accession of Pius IV, who was determined to complete many of his predecessor's architectural projects. The casino complex is one of the most charming secluded retreats ever built (see fig. 1). It faces a separate free-standing loggia across an oval courtyard, with a pair of entrance arches at the two narrow ends. The arrangement appears to be based upon reconstructions of naumachias, as depicted on Roman coins. The courtyard is bordered by benches and has a fountain at the centre. Another fountain is placed on the garden side of the loggia. The exterior walls are encrusted with lavish stuccowork, presenting a decorative repertory closely modelled on motifs from ancient tombs. The figural reliefs celebrate Pius IV, after whom the casino came to be named. The design of the ground floor facing the courtyard faintly recalls Baldassare Peruzzi's Palazzo Massimo alle Colonne, Rome. The casino, with its asymmetrically placed belvedere tower, is reminiscent of earlier villa buildings. The interiors are lavishly decorated with paintings and stuccowork by Federico Barocci, Federico Zuccaro and others.

Ligorio also undertook extensive work on the repair and redecoration of the Vatican Palace. In July 1560 the Loggia della Cosmografia, the uppermost of Bramante's tier of loggias attached to the east side of the palace, was being repaired and decorated with frescoed maps, and in September the rooms of the Borgia Apartment were being redecorated, especially the Sala dei Pontefici. By November the major building campaign was under way with Ligorio's design to revise and complete the monumental Belvedere Court. As well as completing the long western side, he added a curved auditorium in the lower court, backing on to the Vatican Palace, and vaulted the semicircular exedra at the north end, thus converting it into a huge niche. In 1560 he was made an honorary citizen of Rome in recognition of his contributions to the city and the papal court.

1. Pirro Ligorio: façade of the Casino of Pius IV, Vatican, Rome, 1558–62

A drawing by Ligorio of the route of the Acqua Vergine (Florence, Uffizi, cat. no. 4236A) would appear to confirm his claim that he suggested a plan to improve Rome's water supply by repairing the ancient aqueduct. Another papal commission was the Palazzina of Pius IV (1561–4), set above the public fountain that had been built for Julius III on the Via Flaminia. In 1563 Ligorio began to erect a building to house papal conclaves at the Vatican, but this was soon converted into a papal archive. In the following year he undertook several important commissions outside the Vatican Palace, including refurbishing the north transept façade of S Giovanni in Laterano. Work also began on his design for a new court for the Palazzo della Sapienza, but was interrupted in September 1565. He received his most prestigious commission in August 1564 when he was appointed to succeed Michelangelo as architect of St Peter's. Little was accomplished under Ligorio's direction, however, except work on the entablature of the dome's drum and the cutting of some capitals for the chapels.

On 31 July 1565 Ligorio was accused of financial larceny and imprisoned in the Torre di Nona for 22 days. He was apparently cleared of the charge and by October was supervising repairs to the Sistine Chapel. He remained in papal service for a short time after the election of Pius V in 1566: with Sallustio Peruzzi's assistance he was in charge of the decorations for the papal coronation. He

was commissioned to design a lavish tomb for *Pope Paul IV* (1566; Rome, S Maria sopra Minerva). This is set against a wall within a strong architectural frame and employs a rich variety of polychromatic marbles; above the sarcophagus is a rectangular niche containing a seated figure of the pope by Giacomo Cassignola (*d* 1588). Between 1566 and 1569 a new Palace of the Inquisition (now the Palazzo del S Uffizio) was built to the plans of Ligorio and Peruzzi. Early in 1567, as if foreseeing a change in his career, Ligorio sold to Cardinal Alessandro Farnese his collection of ancient medals and his first manuscript encyclopedia of antiquities, the *Libri dell' antichità di Roma* (Naples, Bib. N.); by at least June he had been succeeded as architect of the Vatican Palace by Nanni di Baccio Bigio.

3. TIVOLI AND FERRARA. In 1550 Cardinal Ippolito II d'Este bought some land at Tivoli on the hillside below the governor's palace, which was housed in the monastery of S Maria Maggiore, as the setting for a magnificent villa and gardens (*see* TIVOLI, §3). In the following years, in his capacity as court archaeologist, Ligorio explored the antiquities of Hadrian's nearby villa and helped lay out the gardens of the Villa d'Este, devising an elaborate iconographic programme in honour of the Cardinal. The latter was exiled between 1555 and 1559, however, and little was achieved until 1560. After Ligorio left papal service, he

2. Pirro Ligorio: Fountain of Rometta (1567–8) at the Villa d'Este, Tivoli (1550–72)

resided in Tivoli during the summers of 1567 and 1568, in which years he produced the designs for statues of nymphs for the great Fountain of Tivoli in the gardens and the figure of *Roma* for the Fountain of Rometta (see fig. 2).

At the end of 1568 Ligorio was appointed court antiquary to Alfonso II d'Este, Duke of Ferrara, where his varied duties principally involved the organization of the ducal collection of antiquities. He was also appointed a Lector at the University of Ferrara and collaborated with Cornelio Bentivoglio I on the designs (1569; Ferrara, Civ. Bib. Ariostea) of the theatrical apparatus for an allegorical tournament or naumachia entitled *L'isola beata*. In November 1569 he completed a number of drawings of the *Story of Hippolytus* (New York, Pierpont Morgan Lib., MS. M. A. 542), which were probably intended for an unexecuted series of tapestries, presumably for the Villa d'Este at Tivoli.

Much of Ferrara was severely damaged in an earthquake in 1570 and Ligorio's diary (Turin, Archv Stato, MS. J.a.II, 15) records the further shocks in the following months. In 1571, while repairing the Castello Estense, he took the opportunity to design and build a library and museum for antiquities, decorated with a large map of Rome. He was commissioned to design the tomb of *Ludovico Ariosto* (1573; Ferrara, S Benedetto, destr.); this was replaced in 1612 by a more sumptuous monument (now Ferrara, Civ. Bib. Ariostea), which retained two of Ligorio's allegorical figures, *Poetry* and *Glory*. At this time he also prepared many of the illustrations for the second edition of *De arte gymnastica* (Venice, 1573) by Girolamo Mercuriale (1530–1606). In 1574 Ligorio designed six richly decorated, temporary triumphal arches for the procession through Ferrara of Henry III of France. As propaganda in the fight between Florence and Ferrara over precedence in court ceremonies, Ligorio made drawings illustrating the genealogy of the Este family for a series of frescoes to decorate the courtyard of the Castello Estense; these were completed in 1577 by Bartolommeo Faccini (1532–77) and Girolamo Faccini (1547–before 1616). At about the same time the frescoes by Sebastiano Filippi II in the two Sale dei Giocchi and the Sala dell'Aurora in the Castello Estense probably also followed Ligorio's designs. He was made an honorary citizen of Ferrara in 1580, enabling him to claim that he was a 'patrician' of Naples and a citizen of both Rome and Ferrara.

Ligorio left a substantial body of manuscript writings in addition to his *Libri dell'antichità di Roma*. The most notable collection (Turin, Archv Stato) comprises some 30 volumes, most of which belong to another encyclopedia of antiquities. During the 19th century much of his antiquarian information, which he had reconstructed from fragmentary inscriptions and archaeological sites, was considered suspect, but this view has been reconsidered. His reconstructions are now believed to be reasonably accurate, given the level of archaeological information then available, and many of the inscriptions formerly labelled as forgeries have been recognized as genuine.

#### UNPUBLISHED SOURCES
Ligorio's copious manuscript writings are held by several libraries, including the following:

Eton, Berks, Coll. Lib., Topham Coll., Bn 10, fol. 53

Ferrara, Civ. Bib. Ariostea, MS.I, 217 and MS.II, 384

Naples, Bib. N., MSS XIII.B, 1–10 (*Libri dell'antichità di Roma*)

Oxford, Bodleian Lib., MS. Canon. ital. 138 (*c.* 1545–9)

Paris, Bib. N., MS. ital. 1129

Turin, Archv Stato, MSS J.a.II, 1–16; J.a.III, 3–16 (including *Libri dell'antichità*)

#### WRITINGS
*Libro di M. Pyrrho Ligori napolitano, delle antichità di Roma, nel quale si tratta de' circhi, theatri, & anfitheatri* (Venice, 1553)

*Fragmento d'istoria dell'antichità della nobilissima città di Ferrara* (Venice, 1676)

*Descriptio superbae et magnificentissimae villae Tiburtinae Hadrianeae* (MS.; Paris, Bib. N., MS. ital. 1129); ed. J. G. Graevius, *Thesaurus antiquitatum et historiarum Italiae*, viii/4 (Leiden, 1723)

#### BIBLIOGRAPHY
G. Baglione: *Vite* (1642); ed. V. Mariani (1935), pp. 9–11

F. Cerasoli: 'Il monumento di Paolo IV nella chiesa della Minerva', *Stud. & Doc. Stor. & Dir.*, xv (1894), pp. 131–4

R. Ancel: 'Le Vatican sous Paul IV: Contribution à l'histoire du palais pontifical', *Rev. Bénédictine*, xxv (1908), pp. 48–71

W. Friedländer: *Das Kasino Pius des Vierten* (Leipzig, 1912)

P. Tomei: 'Gli architetti del Palazzo della Sapienza', *Palladio*, v (1941), pp. 270–82

J. S. Ackerman: *The Cortile del Belvedere*, Stud. & Doc. Stor. Pal. Apostol. Vatic., iii (Rome, 1954)

D. R. Coffin: 'Pirro Ligorio and Decoration of the Late Sixteenth Century at Ferrara', *A. Bull.*, xxxvii (1955), pp. 167–85

H. Thelen: *Der Palazzo della Sapienza in Rom*, Röm. Forsch. Bib. Hertziana, xvi (1961), pp. 285–307

E. Mandowsky and C. Mitchell, eds: *Pirro Ligorio's Roman Antiquities: The Drawings in MS. XIII.B.7 in the National Library in Naples*, Stud. Warb. Inst., xxviii (London, 1963)

D. R. Coffin: 'Pirro Ligorio on the Nobility of the Arts', *J. Warb. & Court. Inst.*, xxvii (1964), pp. 191–210

J. Wasserman: 'Giacomo della Porta's Church of the Sapienza in Rome and Other Matters Relating to the Palace', *A. Bull.*, xlvi (1964), pp. 501–10

J. A. Gere: 'Some Early Drawings by Pirro Ligorio', *Master Drgs*, ix (1971), pp. 239–50

M. Fagiolo and M. L. Madonna: 'La Casina di Pio IV in Vaticano: Pirro Ligorio e l'architettura come geroglifico', *Stor. A.*, xv–xvi (1972), pp. 237–81

——: 'La "Roma di Pio IV": La "Civitas Pia", La "Salus Medica", La "Custodita Angelica"', *A. Illus.*, 51 (1972), pp. 383–402

P. Barocchi: *Scritti d'arte del cinquecento* (1973), xxxii of *La letteratura italiana: Storia e testi* (Milan and Naples, 1971–7)

R. E. Keller: *Das Oratorium von San Giovanni Decollato in Rom: Eine Studie seiner Fresken* (Rome, 1976)

G. Smith: *The Casino of Pius IV* (Princeton, 1977)

S. Benedetti: 'Un'aggiunta a Pirro Ligorio: Il tabernacolo di Pio IV nel Duomo di Milano', *Palladio*, xxvii (1978), pp. 45–64

M. L. Madonna: 'L'"Enciclopedia del mondo antico" di Pirro Ligorio', *Primo congresso nazionale di storia dell'arte: Roma, 1978*, pp. 257–71

D. R. Coffin: *The Villa in the Life of Renaissance Rome* (Princeton, 1979)

M. Fagiolo: 'Il significato dell'acqua e la dialettica del giardino: Pirro Ligorio e la "filosofia" della villa cinquecentesca', *Natura e artificio*, ed. M. Fagiolo (Rome, 1979), pp. 176–89

J. S. Weisz: *Pittura e misericordia: The Oratory of S Giovanni Decollato in Rome* (diss., Cambridge, MA, Harvard U., 1982)

J. Bentini and L. Spezzaferro, eds: *L'impresa di Alfonso II* (Bologna, 1987)

R. W. Gaston, ed.: *Pirro Ligorio: Artist and Antiquarian* (Florence, 1988)

For further bibliography *see* TIVOLI, §3

DAVID R. COFFIN

**Ligozzi, Jacopo** (*b* Verona, 1547; *d* Florence, 26 March 1627). Italian painter, draughtsman, miniaturist and printmaker. He was one of the most productive artists in 17th-century Florence, although in the context of the Florentine Baroque, with its pageantry and decorative form, Ligozzi remained as much a foreigner in terms of his precise drawing, veristic figures and expressive content, as he was by birth. He was the son of the painter Giovanni Ermanno Ligozzi (*fl* 1572–88; *d* before 1605) and came from a

Veronese family of painters and designers of armour, tapestries and embroidery on silk. Other members of the family who were painters (Fumagalli in 1986 exh. cat.) were Jacopo's brother Francesco (*d* before 1635), whose career seems to have been in Verona, his cousin Francesco di Mercurio, who worked for the Medici in Florence in 1590–91, and his son Francesco (active Florence, 1585; *d* Florence, 1641).

Around 1576 Ligozzi went to Florence to work for Grand Duke Francesco I and began his lifelong service to the Medici Guardaroba. The Grand Duke, impressed by his detailed draughtsmanship and abilities as a miniaturist, employed him as a scientific draughtsman, and his activity in this field is documented from 1577 to 1591. Francesco exchanged both specimens and drawings, in watercolour and tempera, of birds, fish, plants and animals (Florence, Uffizi) with the Bolognese naturalist ULISSE ALDROVANDI. Ligozzi matriculated in the Accademia del Disegno in 1578 and is often documented in official roles. In 1584 he contributed to the decoration of the loggia, Tribuna and rooms that became the Uffizi gallery (Berti; Bacci in 1986 exh. cat.). With the accession of Grand Duke Ferdinand I in 1587, Ligozzi became court painter and had his workshop in the Casino Mediceo, where he produced works of many different types. He made drawings of plants, animals and people in varied costumes for the Medici (Florence, Uffizi), some of which were copied by his cousin, Francesco, in 1590–91 (untraced; Fumagalli). He made designs to be rendered in pietra dura, for objects in glass (Heikamp) and for festival decorations (1969 exh. cat., no. 73). Ligozzi also made many drawings of allegories and religious scenes (Bacci and Viatte), which show a concern for detail and expressive content that is typical of northern European art. Often these were intended as independent works of art, and they are highly finished, delicately executed in pen and brown wash, on coloured paper, and highlighted with touches of gold that recall his training as a miniaturist. In 1587 he made a series of pen drawings illustrating Dante's *Divine Comedy* (Oxford, Christchurch; Vienna, Albertina; Paris, Louvre), probably for an unrealized project of prints and relating to similar studies by Johannes Stradanus and Lodovico Cigoli (Bacci and Chapel in 1986 exh. cat.).

In the 1590s Ligozzi became more active as a painter and produced both altarpieces and frescoes for Florentine churches; his religious art conveys the austere spirituality of the Florentine Counter-Reformation. His first public commissions were the *Deposition* (1591; San Gimignano, Santo Spirito) and the two large-scale paintings of historical scenes in the Salone del Cinquecento in the Palazzo Vecchio, Florence: the *Coronation of Cosimo I* and *Pope Boniface VIII Receiving the Florentine Ambassadors* (1591), works that reveal his debt to the art of the Veneto, particularly to Paolo Veronese. In 1591–2 he visited Verona and Mantua to paint portraits of Duke Vincenzo and his sons (untraced); in 1593 he visited Mantua and Ferrara and received employment from the Gonzaga court until 1602. Ligozzi continued to produce works on all scales, from his altarpiece of *St Jerome Supported by an Angel* (1593; Florence, S Giovannino degli Scolopi), with its vignettes of still-life elements, and his ambitious frescoed lunettes of the *Life of St Francis* (begun 1599–1600;

Florence, Ognissanti) to the small and ornate portable altar of *Christ on the Mount of Olives* (1608; Oberlin Coll., OH, Allen Mem. A. Mus.; see fig.). He also continued to design for pietra dura, of which his great table (1618; Florence, Uffizi; *see* HARDSTONES, colour pl. I, fig. 1) is an important example.

Several of Ligozzi's most remarkable drawings have been dated to the last years of his career. A series of allegorical drawings about the power of death, which may be dated to *c*. 1625, includes *Lovers Surprised by Death* (New York, Pierpont Morgan Lib.) and *Death Trapping the Hunters* (Paris, Louvre); the macabre element, which runs through much of Ligozzi's art, is here clearly indebted to German chiaroscuro woodcuts of the 16th century, such as those by Hans Baldung and Hans Burgkmair the elder. His late paintings, however, such as the *Apotheosis of St Giulia* (1623; Livorno Cathedral), remain indebted to Veronese. Among Ligozzi's pupils were his son, Francesco Ligozzi, Donato Mascagni (1569–1636) and Mario Balassi (1604–67).

Jacopo Ligozzi: portable altar, wood, inlaid with pietra dura, 584×337 mm, and a painting of *Christ on the Mount of Olives*, oil on copper, 267×159 mm, 1608 (Oberlin, OH, Oberlin College, Allen Memorial Art Museum)

BIBLIOGRAPHY

Thieme–Becker

*Mostra di disegni di Jacopo Ligozzi* (exh. cat. by M. Bacci and A. Forlani Tempesti, Florence, Uffizi, 1961)

M. Bacci: 'Jacopo Ligozzi e la sua posizione nella pittura fiorentina', *Proporzioni*, iv (1963), pp. 46–84 [with bibliog.]

L. Berti: *Il principe dello studiolo* (Florence, 1967)

*Feste e apparati medicei da Cosimo I a Cosimo II* (exh. cat. by G. Bertelà and A. M. Petrioli Tofani, Florence, Uffizi, 1969), p. 124, n. 73

*Il primato del disegno* (exh. cat., Florence, Pal. Strozzi, 1980), pp. 134–6, nn. 273–85

*Il seicento fiorentino: Arte a Firenze da Ferdinando I a Cosimo III*, 3 vols (exh. cat., Florence, Pal. Strozzi, 1986), i, pp. 91–5; ii, pp. 73–82, 126; iii, pp. 103–7

D. Heikamp: 'Studien zur mediceischen Glaskunst: Archivalien Entwurfszeichnungen, Gläser und Scherben', *Mit. Ksthist. Inst. Florenz*, xxx/1–2 (1986), pp. 1–423

F. Viatte: *Dessins italiens du Musée du Louvre: Dessins toscans, XVIe–XVIIIe siècles* (Paris, 1988), i, pp. 133–50, nn. 235–67

L. Conigliello: 'L'intervento di Jacopo Ligozzi e il completamento del ciclo' and 'Gli affreschi', *Il Chiostro di Ognissanti a Firenze: Gli affreschi del ciclo francescano*, A. Paolucci and others (Florence, 1990), pp. 31–65

——: 'Alcune note su Jacopo Ligozzi e sui dipinti del 1594', *Paragone*, xli/485 (1990), pp. 21–41

MILES L. CHAPPELL

**Li Ji.** *See* LI CHI.

**Li Kan** [*zi* Zhongbin; *hao* Xizhai Daoren] (*b* Beijing, 1244; *d* Yangzhou, Zhejiang province, 1320). Chinese painter and government official. He was born in northern China after the Mongols had taken over that area from the Jürchen Jin dynasty (1115–1234) but before they had conquered southern China. As a result he spent his life serving under the Mongol Yuan dynasty, which ruled China from 1279 to 1368. From a modest family, he began as a petty official and was gradually promoted to become one of the highest officials at court. As a boy he had studied the paintings of Wang Danyou and his father Wang Tingyun, the greatest painter of bamboo during the Jin period. Their work led him to study that of Wen Tong, the originator of the literati tradition of bamboo painting during the Northern Song period (960–1127). Absorbing these examples, Li developed his own style and came to be recognized as the great bamboo painter of the early Yuan period. In his wide travels in southern China and in Annam (now Vietnam), where he acted as an envoy, he studied the many different species of bamboo and in 1307 completed *Zhupu xianglu* ('Bamboo manual'). Combining the study of paintings of the old masters as models with observation of bamboo in its natural habitat, he was able to achieve a new synthesis in this genre.

Li Kan first travelled to Yangzhou on the River Yangzi in southern Jiangsu Province around 1281. Having grown up in the north, he became completely taken with the contrasting culture of the south, which still retained the cultural and artistic brilliance that had been developed during the Southern Song period (1127–1279), especially in Lin'an (Hangzhou), the old dynastic capital. He was particularly interested in the literati painting tradition and, with such northern artists as Gao Kegong and Xianyu Shu (?1257–1302), became an admirer of the southern tradition. He befriended many southern scholars and painters, especially Zhao Mengfu, and took up residence in Yangzhou, where he eventually died after having returned to the capital, Dadu (Khanbalik, now Beijing), for some years to serve at court.

Among his surviving works are two handscrolls that were originally one, but which were probably separated during the Ming period (1368–1644): *Bamboo* (ink on paper; Kansas City, MO, Nelson–Atkins Mus. A.), which depicts two clumps of bamboo; and *The Four Purities* (ink on paper, 1307; Beijing, Pal. Mus.), which portrays bamboos, orchids, *wutong* trees and rocks. These scrolls represent the full range of techniques employed by Li when depicting bamboo in monochrome ink and his keen eye for the subtleties that differentiate the species. Many of his bamboo compositions, mounted as hanging scrolls and mostly executed in ink on silk, are now in the collections of the Palace Museum, Beijing, the Nanjing Museum, the Guangdong Provincial Museum, Guangzhou, the National Palace Museum, Taipei, the Imperial Household Collection, Tokyo, and the Metropolitan Museum, New York. Some show his technique of drawing the plants and leaves in outline and others exemplify his calligraphic technique, whereby such elements as leaves and stem segments are executed in a single stroke. Both types combine realism with the symbolic expression of literati feeling and aspirations, as do his paintings of tall pines (e.g. Taipei, N. Pal. Mus.; Indianapolis, IN, Mus. A.). Li Kan's contribution to the history of bamboo painting lies in his revival of an interest in the literati tradition of Wen Tong and Su Shi in the early Yuan period and in his combination of the northern and southern traditions in bamboo to form a new tradition, which became established as one of the mainstreams of bamboo painting.

BIBLIOGRAPHY

J. Cahill: *Hills beyond a River: Chinese Painting of the Yuan Dynasty, 1279–1368* (New York and Tokyo, 1976), pp. 159–60

Chang Kuang-pin: 'Li K'an and the Revival of Bamboo Painting in the Style of Wen T'ung', *N. Pal. Mus. Bull.*, xiii/5 (1978), pp. 1–13

Arthur Mu-sen Kao: *Li K'an: Bamboo Painter of the Yuan Dynasty* (diss., Lawrence, U. KS, 1979)

Chen Gaohua: *Yuan dai huajia shiliao* [Historical material on Yuan period painters] (Shanghai, 1980), pp. 100–21

CHU-TSING LI

**Li Keran** [Li K'o-jan] (*b* Xuzhou, Jiangsu Province, 26 March 1907; *d* Beijing, 5 Dec 1989). Chinese painter. The son of a poor peasant family, Li studied painting under Pan Tianshou in 1923 at the Shanghai Academy of Fine Art, then in 1929 enrolled in graduate studies in oil painting and drawing at the National Academy of Art in Hangzhou, Jiangsu Province. The director of the Academy, LIN FENGMIAN, was a modernist who helped to introduce Western art techniques to China. While in Hangzhou, Li Keran practised Chinese painting and studied art theory on his own. As a political activist he also joined the Eighteen Society, a progressive art group inspired by Lu Xun. In 1932 he returned to Xuzhou to teach in a private art school.

When war broke out with Japan in 1937, Li moved first to Wuhan, Hubei Province, and then, after the death of his wife, Su E, to Chongqing, Sichuan Province, where he organized groups of artists to participate in anti-Japanese activities. It was in Chongqing that he developed his own style based on traditional Chinese painting. His familiar renditions of herd boys and water buffaloes date from this period. *Softness of Twilight* (Chang, p. 101) shows an inky buffalo tethered in the foreground and two boys in the background perched on a tree, playing flutes. The traditional subject is playfully rendered, with a mastery of suffused and modelled ink that Li later transferred to landscapes.

In 1943 Li married Zhou Peizhu and taught Chinese painting at the Chongqing National Art College. In 1946, he accepted Xu Beihong's invitation to teach at the Beiping [Beijing] Academy of Art and moved to Beijing, where he studied with Qi Baishi and Huang Binhong. When the Central Academy of Fine Arts was founded in 1950, he was appointed Professor of Chinese painting, a post that he held until his death in 1989.

During the 1950s Li Keran took a number of government-sponsored trips to various provinces in China and began to paint landscapes such as *Road to Shu* (Chang, p. 103). The government policy of sponsoring Chinese artists' travel was meant to foster Socialist Realism, but Li resisted the pressure to paint in that style and held to the traditional Chinese theory that individual interpretation is more important than form. He wrote that 'it is idiotic to imitate nature slavishly in the style of those who tend toward naturalism. It should be noted that the artist paints not only what he sees, but what he knows … [He] relies not only on his senses … but what is more important, on thought.' (Li K'o-jan, 1959, p. 146). In an article published in *Chinese Literature* in 1961 Li also protested against the idea that peasants and workers could become painters simply because their ideology was sound, pointing out that consistent and long-term training was needed to become a professional artist.

In the early 1960s Li finally succumbed to political pressure. In *Ten Thousand Crimson Hills* (1964; see Mayching Kao, pl. 2) the monumental mountain is presented in a traditional composition, but the foliage is ablaze with red, the colour of revolutionary fervour, and the title is an obvious allusion to one of Mao's poems. In 1964 Li also wrote a favourable review of the People's Liberation Army exhibition in Beijing, probably under pressure to atone for his earlier criticism.

Despite his efforts to appear politically correct, during the Cultural Revolution (1966–76) Li was not allowed to paint but performed manual labour in the countryside along with his colleagues from the Central Academy. When Zhou Enlai commissioned artists in late 1971 to decorate Beijing's hotels and state buildings with traditional Chinese paintings, Li Keran briefly came back into political favour, painting such works for the government as a large painting of the Li River for the Minzu Hotel. His paintings from the early 1970s are full, rich mountain landscapes built up through layers of saturated ink. Many of them are political, such as *Marching through Loushan Pass at Sunset* (see Cohen, pl. 343), which shows an episode from the Long March and illustrates a poem by Mao. However, in 1974 Jiang Qing mounted another attack on traditional Chinese painters, and Li Keran was castigated as a 'black painter'. His work *Mountain Village after Rain* (see Laing, pl. 13), a masterful contrast of subtly modelled ink wash, mountains and misty water with neat white houses and bright pink cherry blossoms, was censured as nothing but black ink and black water.

In the early 1980s Li returned to the spontaneous and warmly humorous style of non-political figure painting he had used in the 1940s. *Playfulness in the Autumn* (1982; see Lim, pl. 22) shows two herd boys playing while their water buffaloes sleep. *Laughing Monk* (1983; see Lim, pl. 21) shows a fat, jovial monk laughing at the cares of the world. Later in the decade he painted more of the dark, full, richly coloured landscapes that he had first begun to experiment with in the 1950s, bringing them at last to full fruition.

### WRITINGS

*Li Keran shuimo fengjing xiesheng huaji* [Collection of Li Keran's watercolours of landscapes and still-lifes] (Tianjin, 1956)

Li K'o-jan [Li Keran]: 'Some Thoughts on Chinese Painting', *Chin. Lit.* (1959), no. 8, pp. 139–46; *R* in *E. Horizon*, i/4 (Oct 1960), pp. 32–8

Li K'o-jan [Li Keran]: 'Art Is Achieved by Hard Work', *Chin. Lit.* (1961), no. 7, pp. 120–25

### BIBLIOGRAPHY

A. Chang: *Painting in the People's Republic of China: The Politics of Style* (Boulder, 1980), pp. 57–63, 101–9

J. L. Cohen: *China Today* (New York, 1980)

L. Lim: *Contemporary Chinese Painting* (San Francisco, 1983)

J. L. Cohen: *The New Chinese Painting, 1949–1986* (New York, 1987)

Ch'en Po'chueh:: *Li Keran hualun yu huihua zhi yanjiu* [A study of Li Keran's painting and theory of painting] (MA thesis, Taiwan Chin. Cult. & A. Res. Inst., 1988)

Mayching Kao: *Twentieth-century Chinese Painting* (Hong Kong, 1988)

E. Laing: *The Winking Owl: Art in the People's Republic of China* (Berkeley, 1988)

'Jinian Li Keran xiansheng' [In commemoration of Mr Li Keran], *Meishu*, 267 (March 1990), pp. 4–35

ANN BARROTT WICKS

**Likhachov, Dmitry (Sergeyevich)** (*b* St Petersburg, 28 Nov 1906). Russian cultural historian. He graduated from Leningrad (now St Petersburg) University in 1928, then spent over six years in the Solovetsky prison camp and in forced labour on the White Sea Canal. After his return to Leningrad, he began work at the Institute of Russian Literature (Pushkin House), his intellectual home for the next 50 years. He was in charge of the Old Russian literature section from 1954, where his specialist study of medieval Russian manuscripts established him as the Soviet Union's foremost scholar in the field. The correlation of word and image in the manuscripts led him to the study of the broader social and historical context of their creation, as in his books on the 'song of Igor's campaign' (1978) and on the 'laughing world' of Old Rus' (1976). This study of the parallel processes in literature and visual art is also developed in the anthology he edited on the interrelations of Old Russian literature and fine art (1985). In addition, he proposed that the Russian culture of the 14th–16th centuries was essentially pre-Renaissance and that it further developed directly into the Baroque, thereby bypassing the Renaissance of western Europe. Likhachov considered his role to be that of a 'cultural ecologist': the defender and champion of the most valuable in Russian culture. To this end he attempted to restrain all that was damaging to that culture, be it the destruction of churches, towns, parks, libraries or moral values. At the same time he advanced the synthesis of human knowledge and eternal nature that he saw in the parks of Tsarskoye Selo (now Pushkin) and Pavlovsk as a supreme example for poetical and literary inspiration. This stance led to his appointment as President of the new Soviet Culture Fund in 1986, a national foundation of the perestroika era that sought to protect the Russian cultural heritage.

WRITINGS

'*Smekhovoy mir*' *Drevney Rusi* [The 'laughing world' of Old Rus'] (Leningrad, 1976)

'*Slovo o polku Igoreve*' *i kul'tura yego vremeni* [The 'song of Igor's campaign' and the culture of its times] (Leningrad, 1978)

ed.: *Vzaimodeystviye drevnerusskoy literatury i izobrazitel'nogo iskusstva* [The interrelations of Old Russian literature and fine art] (Leningrad, 1985)

*Reflections on Russia* (Boulder, 1991)

*Russkoye iskusstvo ot drevnosti do avangarda* [Russian art from antiquity to the avant-garde] (Moscow, 1993)

BIBLIOGRAPHY

V. Adrianova-Peretts, M. Salmina and G. Finashina: *Dmitry Sergeyevich Likhachov* (Moscow, 1977)

D. Obolensky: *The Byzantine Inheritance of Eastern Europe* (London, 1982), pp. 1–16

F. Lesourd: 'Une Expression nouvelle de l'idée nationale russe: Dmitri Lihacev', *Cah. Monde Rus. & Sov.*, xxviii/3–4 (1987), pp. 323–46

JEREMY HOWARD, SERGEY KUZNETSOV

**Li K'o-jan.** *See* LI KERAN.

**Li Kuchan** [K'u-ch'an] (*b* Gaotang County, Shandong Province, 11 Jan 1899; *d* Beijing, 11 June 1983). Chinese painter, calligrapher and art educator. Coming from a poor peasant family, Li took up hard labour to earn his way through art school in Beijing. He also studied with Xu Beihong and Qi Baishi; the latter considered Li his best student. Li was active as an art teacher in Beijing from 1926, notably at the Central Academy of Fine Arts from 1949 until his death in 1983. He specialized in bird-and-flower painting in the free and spontaneous *xieyi* ('sketching the idea') style that captures the spirit of the subjects through expressive calligraphic brushwork and simplified forms. He was known for his depiction of birds of prey throughout his career, but the works of his later years are particularly free and bold. The phrase 'Pan of the south and Li of the north' was coined in recognition of the similarity of Li's style with that of PAN TIANSHOU.

WRITINGS

*Huaniao renwu hufen* [Section on flowers, birds and figures] (1987), xvii of *Rongbao zhai huapu* [Rongbao zhai painting manual] (Beijing, 1984–)

BIBLIOGRAPHY

Fan Zeng: 'Li Kuchan, Painter of Flowers and Birds', *Chin. Lit.* (1979), no. 4, pp. 101–5

MAYCHING KAO

**Li Kung-lin.** *See* LI GONGLIN.

**Lilienfeld Abbey.** Cistercian abbey in southern Lower Austria. The abbey was founded by Duke Leopold VI of Austria (*reg* 1198–1230) in 1202 and settled with monks from Heiligenkreuz Abbey in 1206. The first building campaign ended in 1217, when Bishop Ulrich of Passau consecrated four altars. Leopold VI was present at this consecration; he wished to see for himself the building of his monastery before he set off on crusade to Egypt. On his return he presented a large relic of the True Cross from the Holy Land to Lilienfeld.

Construction began with the choir. At first this was based on an ambulatory scheme with radiating chapels, as at the abbeys of Cîteaux and Ebrach, and it is assumed that Cistercian builders were responsible for the earliest work. In the course of this campaign there was a change

of plan with the result that the radiating chapels were united into a hall ambulatory (see fig.). The vault of the polygonal chevet is supported by flying buttresses over the ambulatory. The polygonal piers of the ambulatory stand on unusually tall pedestals, which may perhaps be the remains of the chapel walls, and they have lily capitals with unconventional details comparable to the capitals in the chapter house of the Cistercian abbey of Bebenhausen. The ambulatory has piers along the middle axis (cf. Cîteaux, Morimond), while the polygonal end of the choir is open to the ambulatory, but the conflict is resolved by means of three radiating ribs in the ambulatory vaulting. Several features made their first appearance in Austria at Lilienfeld: the hall choir, which occurs most frequently in the second third of the 13th century in the Přemyslid architecture of Bohemia and Moravia; the plan of the choir (five sides of a decagon), which predates the consecration of the Speciosa Chapel at Klosterneuburg (1222); and the flying buttresses, which were used later at Ardagger (from 1225). The choice of a hall ambulatory choir at Lilienfeld began a development that was continued at the Cistercian abbeys of Heiligenkreuz, Neuberg and Zwettl and that was also an important influence on non-monastic church architecture.

The second building campaign included the transept and the first bay of the nave adjoining it to the west. Eastern chapels were apparently originally planned for the transept, as at Cîteaux, but these were later integrated into the hall area of the choir ambulatory. More archaic details

Lilienfeld Abbey, view of choir ambulatory from the north transept, *c.* 1217

are found in both the south transept (flat strips as vaulting ribs) and the portal leading into the cloister than in the north transept. The easternmost bay of the nave has a hall cross-section. Oettinger considered that the transept and first nave bay were complete at the time of the church's consecration in 1230 by Archbishop Eberhard of Salzburg and the bishops of Passau and Chiemsee. On that occasion the body of the founder Leopold VI, who had died a few months previously, was buried before the high altar.

The consecration of 1230 also seems to have included the cloister south of the church, a square of c. 42 m with 30 quadripartite rib-vaulted bays and 660 red marble colonnettes, originally the most richly decorated of a group of stylistically related cloisters (cf. Zwettl, Heiligenkreuz). The cloister arcades were restored in simplified form after a fire in 1810. As at Zwettl and Heiligenkreuz, the stylistic development of the Early Gothic capitals and rib mouldings indicates that construction began with the north side and continued through the east and south to the west. The lavatorium in the middle of the south side was completely rebuilt (1886) by Dominik Avanzo (1845–1910) in an Early Gothic style based on the original and on the lavatorium at Zwettl Abbey. Of the monastic buildings surrounding the cloister there survives the chapter house, a hall divided into three aisles and three bays by sturdy round piers, the details of which suggest a dating even earlier than 1217. The day room, a three-aisled hall at the south-east of the cloister, and the dormitory in the upper storey of the east range were destroyed in 1810, as was the refectory on the south side. The cellarium and the lay brothers' dormitory above it are divided into two aisles, and they have pointed vaulting built up over shuttering; they probably date from shortly before 1230. Under Přemysl Ottakar II, King of Bohemia, the construction of the nave of the abbey church continued from east to west. The type of pier established before 1230 continued to be used, and the width of the nave remained the same, but the next six bays were built with a basilican cross-section. Last came the west façade with a splayed, richly articulated, pointed portal. The consecration of the completed building took place in 1263. The church is 82.3 m long internally and 24.5 m high; the medieval structures were built of limestone and sandstone.

Lilienfeld seems to have influenced the ecclesiastical architecture of Bohemia and Moravia: the Cistercian church built under Ottakar II at Hradiště nad Jizerou was a stereotyped copy of the ground-plan that had evolved gradually at Lilienfeld, and the cloister of the Cistercian nunnery at Tišnov follows the same basic concepts as Lilienfeld and Heiligenkreuz. The Baroque monastic buildings to the east and west of the medieval monastery were built between 1638 and 1674 by Domenico Sciassia; the west tower of the abbey church was erected before 1716. Daniel Gran and Martino Altomonte collaborated on the Baroque decoration of the church. The monastery library contains 226 medieval manuscripts, including the *Concordia caritatis* (MS. 151), a compendium of traditional picture types dating from the 14th century.

BIBLIOGRAPHY

P. Tobner: *Lilienfeld, 1202–1902* (Vienna, 1902)
——: 'Lilienfeld', *Topographie von Niederösterreich*, v (Vienna, 1907), pp. 843–995
M. Riesenhuber: *Die kirchlichen Kunstdenkmäler des Bistums St Pölten* (St Pölten, 1923), pp. 167–77
K. Oettinger: 'Kirche und Stift Lilienfeld', *Stift Lilienfeld* (Vienna, 1952), pp. 11–39
——: 'Die Entstehung von Lilienfeld', *Festschrift zum 800. Jahrgedächtnis des Todes Bernhards von Clairvaux* (Vienna, 1953), pp. 232–59
R. Wagner-Rieger: 'Architektur', *Gotik in Österreich* (exh. cat., Krems, Hist. Mus., 1967), pp. 332–3, 369–70, no. 338
F. Vongrey: 'Kreuzgang', 'Kapitelsaal', 'Durchgang', 'Stiftskirche', 'Cellarium', 'Konversendormitorium', *1000 Jahre Babenberger in Österreich* (exh. cat., Lilienfeld Abbey, 1976), pp. 167–70, 237, 308, 328–34, 445, 522
M. Schwarz: *Studien zur Klosterbaukunst in Österreich unter den letzten Babenbergern* (diss., U. Vienna, 1981), pp. 118–21, 124–5, 129–30

MARIO SCHWARZ

**Li Liufang** [Li Liu-fang; *zi* Maozai, Changheng; *hao* Tanyuan, Xianghai, Paoan, Shenyu Jushi] (*b* She xian, Anhui Province, 1575; *d* 1629). Chinese painter and poet. His family moved to Jiading, now part of Shanghai, where he spent most of his life. Li received his *juren* degree in 1606 and twice attempted the higher examinations, failing the first and arriving late for the second, which disqualified him. Having the means, he chose to abandon pursuit of a government career to lead a cultured life of leisure. He built a house and garden in Nanxiang, near Jiading, called Tan yuan (Sandalwood Garden) after the sandalwood trees that grew there, using the garden's name thereafter as one of his *hao* names. He is classed, along with Tang Shisheng (1551–1636), Lou Jian (*d* 1631) and Cheng Jiasu (1565–1644), as one of the Four Gentlemen of Jiading. All were well-known poets, and Li and Cheng were painters. Li is not known as a calligrapher, although he had an adequately trained hand in a style based on that of Su Shi. In seal-carving, contemporaries praised him as the rival of He Shen (*fl c.* 1573–1620). However, while He Shen turned to Han-period (206 BC–AD 220) seals as models (*see* CHINA, §XIII, 22), carving intaglio and deliberately wrecking surfaces to give an antique flavour, Li typically carved in relief, in the more conservative style used by Zhao Mengfu of the 13th and 14th centuries and Wen Peng of the 16th. Li also enjoyed carving bamboo.

In painting Li is best known as a landscapist. Almost 100 of his works are recorded, and his dated paintings, according to Guo Weichu (1908–71), range from 1614 to 1628. His acknowledged model was the Yuan (1279–1368) master WU ZHEN. One landscape, *Thin Forest and Distant Mountains* (Cleveland, OH, Mus. A.), is typical of his style. Although, like Wu Zhen, Li favoured a brush loaded with wet wash, his schematic composition, with its abbreviation and repetition of elements, was far closer to the work of Dong Qichang, the most influential painter of the period. In a vertical format, a few meagre trees, rooted in a small island of rocks, stretch up over the expanse of water behind to overlap a distant mountain. The viewer's gaze is drawn straight up the picture. Black dabs of ink in the foreground foliage, repeated on the surface of the mountain, reinforce the vertical line. The result is a compact, tightly knit work. Although Li's paintings had a limited range of style and composition and lacked the weight and intricacy of line and texture found in artists of greater talent, he was capable of producing work of fresh, nonchalant elegance. His son, Li Hangzhi (*d* 1644), painted in a similar style.

BIBLIOGRAPHY
*DMB*: 'Li Liu-fang'
Guo Weichu: *Sung Yuan Ming Qing shuhua nianbiao* [Historical table of Song, Yuan, Ming and Qing calligraphy and painting] (Beijing, 1958), pp. 197, 214
Yu Jianhua, ed.: *Zhongguo huajia da zidian* [Dictionary of Chinese painters] (Shanghai, 1981), p. 377
*Guangdong sheng bowuguan canghua ji* [Collection of paintings from the Guangdong Provincial Art Museum] (Beijing, 1986), no. 81

ELIZABETH F. BENNETT

**Liljefors, Bruno (Andreas)** (*b* Uppsala, 14 May 1860; *d* Uppsala, 18 Dec 1939). Swedish painter. He studied at the Konstakademi in Stockholm (1879–82). During a trip abroad in 1882–3 he attended lectures by the German animal painter Carl Friedrich Deiker (*d* 1892) in Düsseldorf, where he also made animal studies at the city zoo, one of the largest in Europe. He concluded his travels by visiting France in 1883–4 and again in 1886. For a while he was a member of the Scandinavian artists' colony in Grez-sur-Loing and he exhibited at the Salon in Paris in 1884. The influence of both French *plein-air* painting and Japanese woodcuts is apparent in his first important work, *Hawk and Black Game* (1884; Stockholm, Nmus.; see fig.), a 'close-up' of nature that fills the whole picture surface. The birds' struggle in the centre of the painting is depicted with detailed precision, and the animals' lightning movements at the moment of attack are accurately caught. The surroundings are smoothly sketched in pale grey tones.

The *Mating of the Capercaillies* (1885; Göteborg, Kstmus.) prefigures the change that occurred in Liljefors's painting at the end of the 1880s and the beginning of the 1890s in line with a contemporary northern trend towards synthetism. The picture space widens to show the depths of a forest, with daylight giving way to twilight. The brushstrokes become broader, the forms more summary. In a number of paintings of the first half of the 1890s, Liljefors showed people instead of animals; in some pictures, even if they did not appear, he made clear their proximity. *The Poacher* (1894; Stockholm, Nmus.) conveys a sense of enclosed mystery in the forest and suggests the presence of the eager hunter awaiting his prey in the twilight; it shows how Liljefors's work often touched upon the mystical effects of nature. After a visit to the archipelago off the east coast of Sweden in 1894, Liljefors was inspired by a new subject: the sea with its rich birdlife. *Morning Mood by the Sea* (1896; Stockholm, Thielska Gal.) is painted in a technique approaching pointillism: the sky fills almost half the canvas and gleams gold and lilac above the glinting surface of the waves. In the foreground is a rock with a small flock of eider just taking to the water.

Despite his reputation and the favourable critical reception at home and abroad, Liljefors's work sold badly and his financial situation was poor. The financier and patron Ernest Thiel came to his aid, however, and from 1900 to 1907 supported him. Liljefors was thus able to regain the peace and confidence he felt he needed to continue working. He was now able to return to the subject of bird flight. In the enormous canvas *Soaring Eiders* (1901; Stockholm, Thielska Gal.) he succeeded in conveying, in a boldly impressionistic technique, the birds' rapid flight

Bruno Liljefors: *Hawk and Black Game*, oil on canvas, 1.43×2.03 m, 1884 (Stockholm, Nationalmuseum)

close to the choppy water surface, their wings beating in unison.

From an early age Liljefors had been fascinated by the relationship between animals and their habitat; animal and bird camouflage was a theme to which he often returned. In *Snipes* (1906; Stockholm, Thielska Gal.) a bird appears to be growing out of the grass and in *Curlew* (1907; Stockholm, Nmus.) the speckled plumage is like a reduced version of the marsh landscape the bird inhabits. During Liljefors's last decades his work changed very little and it suffered sometimes because of the large number of commissions he received. It did, however, become much more widely known through the books he published and illustrated, such as *Ute i markerna* ('Out on the land'; Stockholm, 1912) and *Det vildas rike* ('The wilderness's riches'; Stockholm, 1934).

### BIBLIOGRAPHY

T. Hedberg: *Bruno Liljefors: En studie* [Bruno Liljefors: a study] (Stockholm, 1902)
K. E. Russow: *Bruno Liljefors: En studie* [Bruno Liljefors: a study] (Stockholm, 1929)
B. Lindwall and L. Liljefors: *Bruno Liljefors* (Stockholm, 1960)
*Brujo Liljefors i det vildas rike: Målningar, teckningar, dokument* [Bruno Liljefors in the wilderness's riches: paintings, drawings and documents] (exh. cat., Södertälje, Ksthall, 1978)
M. Hill: 'Liljefors of Sweden: The Peerless Eye', *Audubon*, lxxx/5 (1978), pp. 70–104
A. Ellenius: *Bruno Liljefors* (Uppsala, 1981) [excellent pls]
J. Tersmeden: *Bruno Liljefors: Konst och person inför svensk och utländsk allmänhet, 1890–97* (diss., U. Umeå, 1985)

BRITA LINDE

**Lille.** French city and capital of the Nord département, 10 km from the Belgian border.

1. History and urban development. 2. Art life and organization. 3. Centre of production.

1. HISTORY AND URBAN DEVELOPMENT. Little is known of Lille's origins before the 11th century AD due to lack of documentation, although it is generally thought to have become the seat of the County of Flanders by the 9th century. The River Deûle crossed the earliest site of the present city via numerous rivulets, dividing it into a cluster of small villages; hence the city's name, which derives from the Latin *insula* and the late Latin *lisle*.

Lille began to take shape around the Palais Comtal and the collegiate church of St Pierre (1055). It flourished during the next three centuries, when three new parishes were created, and eventually became the capital of Flanders, chosen for the fertility of that region and its position on routes between northern Europe and the British Isles on the one hand and Champagne and Italy on the other. The site of one of five great fairs, the Lille fair drew large numbers of Spanish, Italian and British merchants, attracted by the prosperous trade in wool and woollen cloth. This privileged strategic and commercial position was envied by King Philip II of France (*reg* 1180–1223), who successfully attacked Lille at the Battle of Bouvines (1214). Joanna of Flanders governed the county until 1244, founding a large number of charitable institutions including the Hospice Comtesse (1237). Social problems affected Lille's prosperity in the late 13th century, however, and King Philip IV annexed the town in 1297.

After the marriage of Marguerite de Mâle to Philip the Bold, Duke of Burgundy, in 1369, the ducal family often stayed in Lille, and they contributed to the town's splendour. One of the few buildings remaining from this early period is the church of S Maurice (14th–15th century; remodelled 1872), which has five aisles. The Palais de Rihour (1453–73) is notable for its Gothic chapel, stair-turret and guard-room. Flanders came under Habsburg control in 1477, and in the 16th century Lille became the capital of the southern Netherlands under Charles V, Holy Roman Emperor; there followed, however, another period of political and religious unrest.

The 17th century was a golden age for Lille, earning it the nickname of 'Paris of the Netherlands'; the region underwent an economic recovery and a religious revival, and the population also increased. The Flemish Renaissance style of the period was exemplified by such buildings as the Ancienne Bourse (1652) by Julien Destré. Lille was annexed to France when Louis XIV took the town in 1667 after a brief siege. He expanded the town and made it the administrative capital of the northern provinces, and the royal engineer Sébastien Leprestre de Vauban was commissioned to build the impregnable pentagonal Citadel (1667–70); Vauban also built the royal quarter. The Porte de Paris arch was erected in 1682 (see fig. 1) by Simon Vollant (1622–94) to commemorate Louis XIV's victory, and the town began to acquire a French classical appearance.

During the War of the Spanish Succession (1701–14) the Dutch took control of the town (1708); it was finally restored to France under the Treaty of Utrecht (1713–14). Lille suffered considerable upheaval during the French Revolution (1789), and a large number of buildings, including St Pierre, were sacked. In September 1792 the town resisted an Austrian siege. In the same year François Verly began drawing up his plans for the reconstruction of the town, but these were never executed. Napoleon passed through Lille in 1803; impressed by the town, he made it a Departmental Prefecture. A new age of industrial and commercial prosperity developed during the 19th

1. Lille, Porte de Paris (1682) by Simon Vollant

century. The cathedral, Notre-Dame-de-la-Treille, was designed (1854–6) by Henry Clutton and William Burges, although it was never completed. The population doubled, and in 1858 the city began to undergo expansion; the first rail link between Lille and Paris was built in 1864.

A significant architect in Lille in the early 20th century was Louis Marie Cordonnier (1859–1940), who designed the Théâtre (1914). The town was occupied during World War I and suffered heavy bombardment during World War II, but by the 1980s it was a regional capital and formed the centre of a conurbation of over a million inhabitants. The construction of two new transport routes, the Channel Tunnel and the TGV Nord, stood to reinforce Lille's natural position at the heart of northern Europe. A project was launched in 1982 to refurbish old factories for use as housing with funding from local government (e.g. the refurbishment of Usine Le Blan).

BIBLIOGRAPHY

P. Pierrard: *Lille: Dix Siècles d'histoire* (La Madeleine, 1972)

L. Trenard and others: *Histoire d'une métropole: Lille, Roubaix, Tourcoing* (Toulouse, 1977)

L. Grenier: 'L'Eclatement de la métropole lilloise', *Mnmts Hist. France*, 102 (April 1979), pp. 42–5

M.-T. Gérard: 'A Lille, du XIXe au XXe siècle: De l'usine au logement social, une volonté de réhabilitation', *Sites & Mnmts*, 95 (July–Sept 1981), pp. 26–30

H. Oursel and others: *Histoire de Lille: De Charles-Quint à la conquête française, 1500–1715* (Toulouse, 1981)

2. ART LIFE AND ORGANIZATION. Save for a short visit (1426–8) by Jan van Eyck, painting in Lille was generally not outstanding before the early 17th century, when painters from Antwerp such as Rubens, van Dyck and Jordaens received numerous commissions for religious buildings, including the four *Apostles* by Jordaens (Lille, Mus. B.-A.). This northern tendency was continued by such artists as JEAN-BAPTISTE MONNOYER, who painted floral compositions, and WALLERANT VAILLANT and his brother Bernard Vaillant (1632–98), who produced portraits. Tapestry-weavers also continued the Flemish tradition, as did goldsmiths, who numbered no less than 80 in the early 18th century (e.g. the *Stappaert Monstrance*, 17th century; Lille, Mus. B.-A.).

Unity with France in 1667 stabilized political life in Lille, creating a favourable environment for the arts, and the town established itself as a principal artistic centre comparable with Valenciennes and Arras. An original artistic style emerged as French influence took hold, and this was continually stimulated by both French and Flemish trends. ARNOULD DE VUEZ, who came to Lille *c*. 1680, was the first artist to attempt a synthesis of Dutch, French and Italian masters in his paintings for religious institutions (e.g. *Presentation of the Virgin in the Temple*, 1692). The painter Bernard Joseph Wamps (1689–1750) increased his closeness by using a French style coloured with the freedom and grace of the pre-Rococo.

De Vuez created the open-access Ecole de Dessin; this was shortly followed by an architecture course, and together they made up the Ecoles Académiques of Lille, which did much to encourage local artistic talent. The first Salon d'Art was held in 1773 at the suggestion of Louis Watteau (*see* WATTEAU, (2)). Watteau directed the Ecole de Dessin (1778–98) and was succeeded by his son François (*see* WATTEAU, (3)), who held the position until

2. Carolus-Duran: *The Kiss*, oil on canvas, 1868 (Lille, Musée des Beaux-Arts)

his death. The family was also closely involved with founding the Musée des Beaux-Arts in 1801. The Académie des Arts was founded in 1775, based on the Parisian example. Notable artists that emerged from the Ecole and the Académie included PHILIPPE-LAURENT ROLAND, the visionary architect FRANÇOIS VERLY and JEAN-BAPTISTE WICAR, who bequeathed a collection of drawings to the Société des Sciences et des Arts de Lille; the collection was finally moved to the Musée des Beaux-Arts. He also founded the Wicar prize to fund studies in Italy for artists from Lille.

Artistic achievement in Lille reached its height in the 19th century with the development of the school of Lille, which favoured a traditional academic approach and encouraged close relations with Parisian artists. Notable artists of the period included AMAND GAUTIER, VICTOR MOTTEZ (e.g. *Melitus Accusing Socrates*, exh. Salon 1857; Lille, Mus. B.-A.) and CAROLUS-DURAN, whose realist style showed Spanish influence in *The Kiss* (see fig. 2).

In 1891 work was completed on the Palais des Beaux-Arts, to which various collectors bequeathed their collections, including Maurice Masson, who donated Impressionist works. The academic schools in Lille became the Ecole Régionale d'Art in 1897, but the artistic profile of the city declined in the 20th century. A few artists achieved renown, including the abstract painters AUGUSTE HERBIN and JEAN DEWASNE, and the sculptor EUGÈNE DODEIGNE (e.g. *Stone*, 1957; Lille, Mus. B.-A.). A collection formed by Jean Masurel and his wife, which included over 200 works by such artists as Picasso, Modigliani and Léger, led to the construction (1978–83) of a new museum, the Musée d'Art Moderne du Nord, at Villeneuve-d'Ascq, Lille-Est, designed by Roland Simounet.

BIBLIOGRAPHY
*Bi-centenaire de l'Ecole des Beaux-Arts de Lille, 1755–1955* (exh. cat., ed. M. Thibault and M. Borrewater; Lille, Mus. B.-A., 1955)

P. Pietresson de Saint-Aubin: 'Notice historique sur Lille', *Mus. Lille, Bull. Amis*, xxiv (June 1960)

L. Grenier and H. Wieser-Benedetti: *Le Siècle de l'éclectisme: Lille, 1830–1930* (Paris and Brussels, 1979)

*Donation Geneviève et Jean Masurel à la communauté urbaine de Lille* (exh. cat. by P. Chaigneau and F. Berthier, Paris, Mus. Luxembourg, 1980)

*De Matisse à nos jours: Tendances de l'art dans la Région Nord-Pas-de-Calais depuis 1945* (exh. cat. by A. Cordonnier, Lille, Mus. B.-A., 1982–3)

*Tradition and Revolution in French Art, 1700–1880: Paintings and Drawings from Lille* (exh. cat., London, N.G., 1993)

### 3. CENTRE OF PRODUCTION.

*(i) Ceramics.* The first faience factory in Lille was founded in 1696 by Jacques Febvrier (*d* 1729) from Tournai and the painter Jean Bossut from Gand. Febvrier successfully directed the factory from 1700 until his death, with the assistance of experienced workers from Ghent, Rouen, Nevers and the northern Netherlands. He was succeeded first by his son-in-law Joseph-François Boussemart, then by his widow and finally Philippe-Auguste Petit until 1802. In 1711 Barthélémy Dorez and his nephew Pierre Pélissier established a second factory to produce both faience and porcelain. The skill of Pélissier, who had learnt to make this type of porcelain from 1691 at the factory in Saint-Cloud, enabled the factory to produce soft-paste porcelain from 1711 to 1730. Decoration often took the form of blue lambrequins, a form of ornamentation taken from Saint-Cloud and Rouen. From 1729 the widow Dorez and her eldest son concentrated production mainly on faience. They were succeeded by Michel Herreng in 1750, then by his widow and finally by Lefebvre until the factory closed in 1817. In 1740 Jean-Baptiste Wamps, a former employee of Febvrier, opened the third faience factory, which specialized in tiles. In 1755 his successor Masquelier diversified production, and the operation was continued by his family until 1820. The second porcelain factory, founded by Leperre-Durot in 1784, produced hard-paste porcelain in the style of wares from Sèvres. In 1785 it was styled the Manufacture de Monseigneur le Dauphin and adopted the crowned head of a dauphin as its mark. Wares were directly inspired by Parisian factories and were decorated in polychrome with gold bouquets (e.g. basin, *c.* 1790; Sèvres, Mus. N. Cér.). Due to a two-year stay in Paris, however, Leperre-Durot's business was ruined, and he was forced to close. The factory was reopened in 1790 by Gaboria and continued by Roger, Graindorge and Renault.

BIBLIOGRAPHY

J. Houdoy: *Histoire de la céramique lilloise* (Paris, 1869)

ANNIE SCOTTEZ-DE WAMBRECHIES

*(ii) Tapestry.* Archival documents confirm that high-warp weavers worked in Lille from the end of the 14th century. The first was probably Robert Poisson (*fl c.* 1375–*c.* 1400), who became a burgher of Lille in 1398 and who had been previously associated with the merchant and master weaver Nicolas Bataille on the *Apocalypse* series (1373–82; Angers, Château, Col. Tap.). References to weavers proliferate at the beginning of the 15th century, and many of these weavers seem to have come from the Arras region. The first commission (pieces bearing the coat of arms of Lille) authenticated as woven in Lille is dated 1424 (destr.).

Towards the mid-15th century the reputation of the Lille workshops grew, and they received important commissions from such patrons as Philip the Good, 3rd Duke of Burgundy, who commissioned Jean Lecoq (*fl* mid-15th century) in 1458 for a *Baptism of Clovis*, which has often been putatively suggested as the tapestry now in Reims Cathedral. In 1466 the Duke also commissioned a large tapestry with his coats of arms on a *millefleurs* background (Berne, Kstmus.) from Jean de Haze (*fl* final third quarter of 15th century), who also held municipal office in Lille between 1462 and 1469. At the same time other master weavers were active in Lille, among them Camus Dugardin (*fl* third quarter of 15th century). He also received commissions from the Duke of Burgundy, and from the Abbot of Saint-Vaast in Arras. Dugardin's son Pierre Dugardin (*fl* final third of 15th century) continued his father's workshop for many more years. The most illustrious of these master weavers was Pierre de Los, an entrepreneur in the manner of Pasquier Grenier (*d* 1493) from Tournai. De Los was in contact with colleagues at other major centres of tapestry production, owned a depot in Bruges and had an international clientele. Between 1453 and 1462 he delivered numerous sets of hangings (all destr.) to Giovanni de' Medici and Piero de' Medici, including the *Story of Samson*, six *Triumphs* after drawings sent to him from Florence, and a series of *verdures*, with seated characters and coats of arms. Gasparo, Count of Vimercato and Governor of Genoa in 1464, also commissioned from Pierre de Los five sets of tapestries for the considerable sum of 2234 livres. Although there followed a decline, weavers in Lille continued working up to the mid-16th century: in 1538 there were still 22 master weavers in Lille, and the town was mentioned as one of the main centres of production in an ordinance of Emperor Charles V in 1544.

In 1625 Vincent van Quilkerberghe (*fl* second quarter of 17th century) established a workshop that continued producing tapestries up to the mid-17th century. Following the French conquest of 1667, there were various initiatives aimed at re-establishing tapestry weaving in Lille, although it was never to achieve the level reached during the medieval period. In 1684 François and André Pannemaker, master high-warp weavers from Brussels, established a workshop in Lille that was prosperous for over 50 years, specializing in *verdures* in the manner of OUDENAARDE tapestries, which were very popular at the time. In 1688 another tapestry weaver from Brussels, Jean de Melter, set up a workshop in Lille and acquired an international reputation; he was succeeded by his son-in-law Guillaume Werniers (pseud. Wenier; *d* 1738). Favourite subjects were genre scenes after David Teniers the younger, many examples of which have survived (e.g. Château de la Vigne, Bondues, Nord département). The workshop also produced such literary themes as the *Story of Don Quixote*, probably after Charles-Antoine Coypel (Houdoy, p. 112), religious scenes and historical scenes such as *Jeanne of Constantinople, Countess of Flanders, between her Two Husbands* (1703; Lille, Mus. Hosp. Comtesse). In 1749 Jean-François Bouché (*fl* 1749–*c.* 1775) set up a workshop staffed by weavers from the Gobelins, but production ceased *c.* 1775. The only surviving hanging that can be attributed to Bouché is the *Story of Psyche* (fragments, Arras, Mus. B.-A.).

BIBLIOGRAPHY

J. Houdoy: *Les Tapisseries de haute lisse: Histoire de la fabrication lilloise du XIVe au XVIIIe siècle* (Lille, 1871)

J. Lestocquoy: 'Deux siècles de l'histoire de la tapisserie (1300–1500): Paris, Arras, Lille, Tournai, Bruxelles', *Mémoires de la Commission départementale des monuments historiques du Pas-de-Calais*, xix (1978)

H. Oursel: 'Les Arts avant la conquête française', 'Les Arts sous Louis XIV', *Histoire de Lille*, ii (Toulouse, 1981), pp. 270–72, 402–4

——: 'Les Arts sous Louis XV et Louis XVI', *Histoire de Lille*, iii (Toulouse, 1991), pp. 184–5

HERVÉ OURSEL

**Lilli, (Giovanni) Andrea** [d'Ancona; Lilio, Andrea] (*b* Ancona, *c.* 1570; *d* ?Ascoli Piceno, after 1635). Italian painter and draughtsman. He arrived in Rome during the papacy of Sixtus V (1585–90) and is documented there as a member in 1601 of the Accademia di S Luca and Segretario dell'Accademia in 1602. He worked principally with Giovanni Guerra and Cesare Nebbia. With these and other artists, including Francesco Vanni, Ventura Salimbeni, Ferraú Fenzone (1562–1645) and Antonio Viviani, he participated in many of the painting projects commissioned by Sixtus V, for example frescoes in the Salone Sistino of the Biblioteca Apostolica Vaticana, the Scala Santa and the Sistine Chapel, S Maria Maggiore. His presence in Rome was not unbroken; he returned several times to the Marches, where many of his paintings remain.

Examples of Lilli's altarpieces include the panel depicting the *Death of Ananias and Sapphira* (Rome, Ospedale di Santo Spirito in Sassia), which reveals a direct link with early Tuscan Mannerism, especially Pontormo, to whom the panel was for a long time attributed, and the signed and dated *Road to Calvary* (1589; Oggiono, parish church), which is quite different with a more strongly accentuated chiaroscuro contrast and a more personal style. His altarpieces reveal a less easily definable stylistic development than the somewhat predictable Mannerism of such frescoes as the *Birth of the Virgin*, the *Adoration of the Shepherds* and the *Anastasis* (all 1591–3; Rome, S Maria Maggiore). One of his most successful paintings is the panel representing the *Miraculous Draught of Fishes* (Rome, S Giovanni in Laterano), where the formal energy is held in check within a remarkably restrained composition. The still-life of the fish in the net and the shimmering marine landscape in the background are particularly skilfully executed.

Between 1597 and 1601 Lilli was in Ancona, where he painted the *Virgin Crowning St Nicholas of Tolentino* (ex-Pin. Com., Ancona), a series of small panels depicting scenes from the *Life of St Nicholas of Tolentino* (see fig.) and *Four Saints in Ecstasy* (all Ancona, Pin. Com.). These clearly define the various aspects of his style, namely figures in contorted poses, acid and discordant colours, a heightened expressionism and extravagant draperies, all in an atmosphere of mystical spirituality. Among his most impressive works, executed after he returned to Rome, is the canvas *Saints in Glory* (1604) for the high altar of the Nolfi Chapel, Fano Cathedral. The *Miracles of St Anthony of Padua* (Barcelona, Mus. A. Catalunya) and the *Virgin with Angels and Saints* (Apiro, collegiate church) belong to this period, but the number of commissions offered to Lilli began to drop drastically. Around this time, however, he began to produce designs for engravings. His last work, signed and dated 1631, is the *Crucifixion with SS Charles*

Andrea Lilli: scene from the *Life of St Nicolas of Tolentino*, oil on panel, 530×930 mm, *c.* 1597–1601 (Ancona, Pinacoteca Comunale)

*and Ubaldus* (Ancona, S Giovanni Battista). Lilli was documented living in Rome in 1635; he reportedly died while working on frescoes depicting the *Life of St Benedict* in the cloisters of the convent of S Angelo Magno, Ascoli Piceno.

Lilli's reputation increased in the later 20th century; he was formerly, and erroneously, regarded as a follower of Federico Barocci. His early works reveal affinities with early Sienese Mannerism, with which he became acquainted through Francesco Vanni and Ventura Salimbeni. Although undoubtedly eclectic, his style indicates a certain intellectual curiosity as seen, for example, in his interest in Caravaggio, from whom he took certain formal features that he grafted on to his own strictly Mannerist background.

BIBLIOGRAPHY

*Andrea Lilli nella pittura delle Marche tra cinquecento e seicento* (exh. cat., ed. L. Arcangeli and P. Zampetti; Ancona, Pin. Com., 1985) [with full bibliog.]

FIORENZA RANGONI

**Lilly, Edmund** (*b* ?Norfolk, *fl* from *c*. 1695; *d* Richmond, Surrey, *bur* 25 May 1716). English painter. He was extensively patronized by Queen Anne both before and after her accession in 1702. Anne commissioned full-length state portraits of herself and her family from him in preference to either Godfrey Kneller or Michael Dahl. The portrait of *William, Duke of Gloucester* (Windsor Castle, Berks, Royal Col.), Anne's short-lived son, is a signed example of these. The Queen sat for Lilly at least twice after her accession: the full-length *Queen Anne* (1703; Blenheim Pal., Oxon), afterwards engraved by Jean (or John) Simon (1675–1751), is the most grandiose of all her state portraits and shows the influence of John Closterman at his most Baroque. Many versions of this portrait and others by Lilly were made for leading nobles. Other works by Lilly include the strongly characterized *Dr Edward Tyson* (London, Royal Coll. Physicians) in his academic robes. Lilly's last known works (both signed and dated 1707) are *Sir Whitmore Acton* and *Lady Acton* (sold London, Christie's, 26 April 1929), both reminiscent of Johann Kerseboom's manner. No examples are known of the still-lifes and history pieces Lilly is said to have painted.

BIBLIOGRAPHY

Waterhouse: *18th C.*

M. Whinney and O. Millar: *English Art, 1625–1714*, Oxford Hist. Eng. A. (Oxford, 1957), p. 92, n. 3

*Manners and Morals: Hogarth and British Painting, 1700–1760* (exh. cat., ed. E. Einberg; London, Tate, 1988), p. 31

RICHARD JEFFREE

**Li Longmian.** *See* LI GONGLIN.

**Li Lung-mien.** *See* LI GONGLIN.

**Lim, William S(iew) W(ai)** (*b* Hong Kong, 19 July 1932). Singaporean architect, urban planner and writer. He studied at the Architectural Association School, London, graduating in 1955; he worked for the London County Council for a year and then was a Fulbright Fellow in the Department of City and Regional Planning at Harvard University, Cambridge, MA (1956–7). After 1957 he worked exclusively in Singapore and Malaysia as partner in a number of practices, and as principal of Design Partnership (DP). Working in a modernist style, he concentrated on residential and commerical works within an urban or historic framework, with a particular interest in the improvement of the urban environment. He built several large-scale shopping complexes in Singapore and Kuala Lumpur, the first being the People's Park (1973; with Tay Kheng Soon), Singapore; this multi-level centre, with innovative atrium spaces and a mix of large and small shops, became a model for much subsequent commercial development in the city. Other important projects in Singapore included the Golden Mile Shopping Centre (1972) and the Tanglin Shopping Centre (1971 and 1980), which also explored similar themes. Non-commercial buildings include St Andrew's Junior College (1978) and a striking, curved and pink-tiled luxury block of flats, Unit 8 (1984). He also built some low-cost housing projects in Malaysia. In the 1980s Lim began to work on projects related to conservation and revitalization: for example, the Central Market (1985; with Chen Voon Fee) in Kuala Lumpur was changed from a wet market into a shopping, eating and entertainment centre in the heart of the old city, similar in nature to Covent Garden in London, and the Church of Our Saviour (1987), Singapore, was converted from an early 1960s cinema into a place of worship. Several other later buildings reveal his experimentation with the Post-modernist idiom, while some of his houses, such as the Reuter's House (1990), Singapore, explore themes of South-east Asian tradition and identity. In 1986 he set up an independent practice, William Lim Associates, working with a group of younger designers. His work continued to evolve in a lively dialogue with current architectural theories, stimulated by his emphasis on group working methods to generate creativity. He sat on various planning and transport committees, was a director of several companies and taught at the University of Singapore and as a visiting faculty member at other universities around the world. He initiated AA Asia (1992), for graduates and teachers of the Architectural Association, to discuss design directions in Asia. A founder-member of the Singapore Heritage Society, he sat on the board of advisers of a number of international journals including *Habitat International, Mimar: Architecture in Development* and *Solidarity*.

WRITINGS

*Equity and Urban Environment in the Third World* (Singapore, 1975)
*An Alternative Urban Strategy* (Singapore, 1980)
*Cities for People: Reflections of a Southeast Asian Architect* (Singapore, 1990)

BIBLIOGRAPHY

U. Kultermann: *Architecture in the Seventies* (London, 1980), pp. 126–8
R. Khosla: 'Hotels in Asia: 5-star Lifestyle', *Mimar: Archit. Dev.*, 11 (1984), pp. 26–7
U. Kultermann: 'Architecture in South-east Asia 3: Singapore', *Mimar: Archit. Dev.*, 23 (1987), pp. 45–55
R. Powell: *Innovative Architecture* (Singapore, 1989)
——: *Asian House* (Singapore, 1993)

HASAN-UDDIN KHAN

**Lima.** Capital of Peru and of the department of Lima, in the Rímac, Chillón and Lurín valleys, with a population of *c.* 8,000,000 (1993). It was a Pre-Hispanic regional capital, and then capital of the Viceroyalty of Peru, which included all Spanish territory in South America. Its Pacific port, Callao, is *c.* 6 km to the west.

1. Pre-Columbian. 2. Colonial. 3. Republican.

1. PRE-COLUMBIAN. The first settlements were established in the Pre-Ceramic period (before *c.* 1800 BC) in three valleys (*see* SOUTH AMERICA, PRE-COLUMBIAN, §III, 1(ii)(b)). There are a number of later Pre-Ceramic sites near the modern city, for example El Paraíso, Tablada de Lurín, Chilca and Asia. Communities grew, and by the Pre-Ceramic period VI (*c.* 2500–*c.* 1800 BC) there were sizeable ceremonial centres with accompanying settlements (e.g. El Paraíso). Settlements were later founded further inland, usually near or in the watershed of the River Rímac. At Garagay there are exceptional examples of wall painting (*c.* 1200 BC) at the U-shaped temple. Anthropomorphic heads and monstrous figures with feline attributes are depicted in glowing red, pink, blue, purple and yellow on a high-relief frieze modelled in clay. During the Early Intermediate period (*c.* 200 BC–*c.* AD 600) the population probably expanded throughout all three valleys. A series of elegant smaller pyramids and platform mounds were built, mainly in the Rímac Valley, using adobe bricks that are much smaller than those used earlier or later. The Playa Grande (or Interlocking) style was used for wall paintings, pottery and textiles (e.g. fragments, Lima, Mus. Arqueol. & Etnol.); its characteristics include smaller angular interlocking units portraying polychrome geometricized snakes, double- and multiple-headed snakes, fish, cats and birds, usually in yellow, black, cream, brown, purple, orange and red. With population expansion came changes in architecture and art, including the Maranga (or Proto-Lima) style. A new, black pottery and the use of geometric designs in white on a red or orange background were introduced. Architecture was still based on the stepped pyramid. About AD 700 the area was affected by a series of developments in southern Peru, particularly at such sites as Pachacamac, for which the people of the Huari culture were probably responsible. Settlements used variations of grid plans increasingly, as at Cajamarquilla. Pottery also became more formalized, featuring geometric polychrome anthropomorphic figures. After the decline of the Huari empire *c.* AD 800 a series of small city states developed *c.* AD 1200. Located within Lima, and in the Chillón, Canta and Chancay valleys, they were often based around fortified hill-forts within rectangular walls. Nevertheless, under Inca Yupanqui (*reg c.* 1471–93) the Incas conquered much of the coast.

2. COLONIAL. On 1 February 1533 Europeans arrived in the Rímac Valley. Francisco Pizarro knew he would need towns on the Pacific coast of Peru, and Lima and its port, Callao, were established in January 1535. The symbolic foundation stones of the future cathedral were laid, and the central square was marked out; the blocks (*cuadras* or *manzanas*) forming the grid plan radiated from it. Each was split into four plots (*solares*), on which individuals were encouraged to build, preferably using 'noble' materials, such as stone. Suitable stone was not readily available, however, nor was it an appropriate building material for an earthquake-sensitive region; therefore such traditional materials as adobe, *quincha* (clay or plaster wattle) and cane were used. The materials were also suitable for the dry climate. Consequently, buildings appeared to have a

strength and monumentality, particularly where stone portals were incorporated. The National University of S Marcos was founded in 1551. Earthquakes in 1656, 1687 and 1746 severely damaged the city, which nevertheless grew; by 1786 it had 350 streets and 8222 houses. Such anti-seismic measures as the use of light building materials were applied to a variety of buildings within the Cercado, or walled area. From 1586 the Viceroy, Conde del Villar, forced the original inhabitants to move to satellite settlements outside the Cercado. The Puente de Piedra (1610), which spans the Rímac, is a rare, early stone structure; it was built under Viceroy Juan de Mendoza y Luna, Marqués de Montesclaros.

Architecture in Lima generally reflected European developments, though with a delay of *c.* 10 to 20 years. Some of these developments subsequently flowed from the capital to the provinces, creating greater anachronisms. During the early colonial period until the 17th century architecture was Gothic or Renaissance in style. Diego Maroto surveyed Lima after the earthquake of 1687. Expressions of the Plateresque (e.g. S Marcelo) were short-lived. Baroque architecture is well represented; the forms of Rococo dominated, largely due to Viceroy José Antonio Manso de Velasco's enthusiastic rebuilding of the city after the devastating earthquake of 1746. Neo-classicism was fashionable at the end of the 18th century and remained so until *c.* 1821. Lima's colonial architecture reflected its status as the political and administrative centre of the Viceroyalty of Peru. The city had a thriving import–export trade directly with Spain, and building materials were imported, for example wood from Costa Rica, stone from Panama, and ironwork, glazed tiles (*azulejos*), glass and textiles (e.g. brocade) from Spain.

Surviving colonial ecclesiastical architecture in Lima includes the cathedral (begun 1598) by FRANCISCO BECERRA (*see* PERU, §III, 1 and fig. 4); S Pedro, or La Compañía (1568; rebuilt 1624–38); the Baroque churches of La Merced (1541–2; altered) and S Agustín (from 1574; rest.); S Domingo (1540–52), with its Rococo-cum-Neoclassical façade; and S Francisco, which has a church and cloister (1657–74; rebuilt) by CONSTANTINO DE VASCONCELOS. MATEO PÉREZ DE ALESIO executed a variety of commissions in Lima's churches. In the 18th century Spanish tradition began to give way to French and Austrian architecture, as at Las Nazarenas (1766–71; rebuilt 1835) and Los Huérfanos (completed 1758–66). The smaller churches of Jesús Maria (1722), La Magdalena Vieja (1557; rebuilt 1931), Nuestra Señora de Patrocinio (1734), Trinitarias (inaugurated 1722), S Carlos (in Cocharcas), S Rosa de las Monjas (1704–8), Santiago de Surco, and S Teresa (rebuilt after 1746; destr. 1946) preserve in varying degrees a somewhat formulaic Baroque. Some of the city's churches are richly furnished (*see* PERU, §IV, 1).

Lima's gradual expansion caused the destruction of much colonial domestic and administrative architecture. The grid plan and a few domestic structures survive, however: for example the Palacio de Torre Tagle (completed 1735; now part of the Ministerio de Asuntos Exteriores), with its distinctive Moorish and *Mudéjar* elements (see fig. 1); the portal of the Casa de Pilatos (first half of 17th century); the wooden balconies on buildings near S Domingo; the Casa de Rada; the Quinta Presa

1. Lima, façade of the Palacio de Torre Tagle, completed 1735, now part of the Ministerio de Asuntos Exteriores

(1766–7; rest.; now Museo del Vîrreinato); the Casa de Oquendo; and the Casa de Osma. While residential architecture did not follow a set formula or style, houses were typically of one storey with large bay windows with decorative wrought-iron grilles; two-storey dwellings usually had flat roofs, wooden balconies and a two-colonnaded inner patio.

In the final years of the colonial period a number of schools and higher-education centres were established, including a school of art, the Seminario de S Toribio, S Tomás, with its magnificent circular cloister (c. 1750; see PERU, fig. 4), and the Court of the Inquisition (c. 1569; now Museo del Tribunal de la Santa Inquisición). French-influenced gardens and pedestrian areas, such as the Alameda de los Descalzos and the Paseo de Aguas (begun 1770; formerly La Navona), were inspired by Viceroy MANUEL AMAT.

All that survives of the city's defensive walls (1685; destr. 1869) is a section at the Cuartel de S Catalina. At Callao is the Real Felipe Fort (completed 1774; now Museo Histórico Militar), a substantial stone fortification estimated to contain several million egg whites in its mortar; it was built to defend the port and city after the attacks (1624) of the Dutch pirate Jacques Ermite, and to replace earlier structures destroyed in the earthquake of 1746.

3. REPUBLICAN. The Proclamation of Independence (July 1821) by José de San Martín in Lima heralded many architectural changes; the rejection of Hispanic traditions led to the destruction and replacement of colonial structures with buildings initially based on French and Italian models. Locally developed architecture, suited to the environment, was phased out because it was considered Spanish and unrepublican; at first, it was not understood that colonial architecture was not purely Spanish, but rather a distinctly Peruvian manifestation of Peninsular traditions. In some ways, however, most noticeably in domestic architecture, there was little perceptible change for a considerable period.

The rejection of the colonial past was expressed in the adornment of façades with such Neo-classical elements as long, Ionic columns with Doric capitals, and cornices with Ionic and Corinthian features. The change was thus confined to exteriors and did not affect interior planning. The inner patio system, balconies with Classical detailing, and the large main portal remained in use. Lima's population in 1821 was 64,000; the city could not sustain major architectural projects. The innovative Lima Penitenciería was built, however, employing panoptic radial design; it was designed by Maximiliano Mimey and built by Mariano Felipe Paz-Soldán y Ureta (1821–86) in stone, brick and *quincha*. Administrative and commercial buildings were erected for overseas companies. New materials (e.g. cast iron and glass) and methods of construction were used, as at the Palacio de la Exposición (1875; now Museo de Arte) built by Antonio Leonard and Manuel Anastasio Fuentes (1820–89). The Puente de Hierro (now Puente Balta) and a series of ornamental and functional piers were put up on the coast. The development of railways under José Balta (President, 1868–72) indirectly affected architecture in Lima, its suburbs and further afield, as people came from both the provinces and the industrialized nations, bringing with them the latest European architectural and engineering techniques. For example, the Hospital Dos de Mayo (1868–75; now Museo Hospital Dos de Mayo; partly rebuilt) by Mateo Graziani has radial colonnaded (Doric) galleries around a central octagonal garden of Italian inspiration. The growth of trade that followed the Dreyfuss Contract (1869) concerning the sale of guano to Europe financed the transformation of such areas as Callao.

Fashionable French academic Neo-classicism was promoted by the architects who came from France and Italy. There were several art schools in Lima with a series of distinguished directors (see PERU, §IV, 2). Urban planning regained its early colonial importance and was applied in such areas as Rímac and the Barrios Altos. Parks and squares, for example the Plaza Bolívar with the equestrian monument to *Simón Bolívar* (1859) by Adamo Tadolini, were laid out by such planners as Jacob Wrey Mould. After 1870 a moderate, Italian Neo-classicism was widely applied and adapted to local needs. The Chilean invasion (1881) halted many building projects, which remained in abeyance well into the early 20th century. The period immediately after the War of the Pacific (1879–83) has been seen as eclectic and characterized by mediocre architectural projects that debased the remnants of Neo-classicism through over-use and an uncomfortable combination with Art Nouveau. Around the Plaza Dos de Mayo (1866) and the circular Plaza Bolognesi long, wide avenues recalling

Parisian boulevards were laid out, flanked by buildings of the *petit-hôtel* type. On the outskirts of Lima, at Miraflores and Chosica, the first Mock Tudor English houses were built. Traditional architecture had been almost totally abandoned. Such public buildings as the Casa de Correos (1895), built during the government of Nicolás de Piérola, were typically large, spacious and strong, and could be adapted to a variety of uses.

After 1914 new materials and building techniques, together with increasingly accessible information on architectural trends, became available. A school of architecture was established in Lima, and an interest rekindled in establishing a suitable, identifiably Peruvian architecture. Early experimental styles included some absurd interpretations of earlier forms, for example the replication of adobe walls in brick and concrete and an injudicious overuse of colonial elements. The concurrent influence of international Modernism is evident in a number of houses, schools and hospitals, such as the Hospital del Obrero (1938) built during the presidency of Oscar R. Benavides Larrea. The Paseo de la República (1935; now Vía Expresa or Zanjón), linking central Lima and Miraflores, was planned and built by Ricardo Malachowski the elder; it is now flanked by late 20th-century buildings.

In the 1930s a Peruvian Colonial Revival style arose, which is particularly evident in the early work of Rafael Marquina y Bueno (1884–1964), Malachowski the elder and Claudio Salurt. They also explored technological developments in such materials as glass, aluminium and plastics. Their earlier work is represented by the Palacio Arzobispal (1916), the Palacio de Gobierno (1921–38; see fig. 2), the Hotel Bolívar, Plaza S Martín and the Avenida Nicolás de Piérola (or Colmena), as well as numerous houses. The Palacio Arzobispal has been considered by some as excessively florid, tasteless and anachronistic, a criticism that may also be levelled at the numerous

exaggerated Colonial Revival-style houses. By contrast, in the 1920s sporadic attempts were made to impose an Inca-derived style, as in the Museo Nacional de la Cultura Peruana (founded 1945; formerly the Museo Víctor Larco Herrera, founded 1919; *see* PERU, §X). This style did not find acceptance, and only such individual elements as polygonal-stone or modelled wall cladding were retained on some residential buildings. As with other art forms, a division emerged between the nationalist Hispanists or Traditionalists and the socialist Indigenists, the latter aligning themselves with the socially responsive theories of Le Corbusier, Mies van der Rohe, Frank Lloyd Wright and Walter Gropius.

The Agrupación Espacio was established in 1947 to provide a platform for the discussion of issues raised by Piqueras Cotolí, and subsequently explored by such eminent architects as Benavides, Emilio Harth-terré (1899–1983) and José Alvarez Calderón. Harth-terré and his group were instrumental in creating and promoting the Escuela Nacional de Ingeniería, the Sociedad de Arquitectos (founded 1937), and the Consejo Nacional para la Restauración y Conservación de Monumentos Históricos (*see* PERU, §III, 2). Despite strenuous efforts by such individuals as Bruno Roselli to preserve colonial and early republican buildings in Lima numerous *casonas* (mansions) were demolished in favour of new road schemes and building projects.

Fernando Belaúnde Terry (*b* 1912) explored the use of shapes, blocks and masses at Limatambo Airport (1945–8) and later at Jorge Chávez Airport (1965). Luis Miró Quesada Garland (*b* 1915) designed such experimental housing developments as the Residencial Palomino, and Henri Ciriani designed the Residencial S Felipe, which provides low-cost housing for a high-density population, similar to social housing schemes in Cuba. Functionalist

2. Lima, façade of the Palacio de Gobierno, 1921–38

architecture with Neo-classical undertones is found in various housing areas, ministries (e.g. Ministry of Work and Ministry of Public Health) and hospitals (e.g. Hospital del Empleado, 1950–56). In the 1950s and 1960s a massive, largely undocumented building boom on the outskirts of the city took place in El Agustino and Comas. Such areas, known as *barriadas* or *pueblos jóvenes*, developed at an unprecedented, unpredictable rate, sometimes unplanned. By the late 20th century *c.* 60% of Lima's population occupied these areas, where architecture ranges from the rudimentary (e.g. at Villa El Salvador) to the substantial (e.g. at S Martín de Porres). Housing needs have led to the emergence of self-made architects, surveyors and engineers, who combine native forms, modern technology and materials. Examples of buildings from the 1970s and 1980s include the Centro Cívico y Comercial (1971) by Córdoba, Crousse, José García Bryce, Málaga, Núñez, Páez, Ortiz and others. With its volumetric masses of grey cement and stressed concrete, it refers to Pre-Columbian traditions of walled compounds. Adjacent is the Sheraton Hotel (*c.* 1970) by Ricardo Malachowski the younger, who also built the Hospital de la Fuerza Aérea del Perú. Both buildings are 15–20 storeys high and are substantial structures of reinforced concrete, aluminium and glass, set on wide, horizontal platforms. Some buildings combine glass with vast expanses of concrete or curtain walls, for instance Miguel Rodrigo's Banco Central Hipotecario de Peru (1977) and housing developments (1971–2) in Callao. In the 1980s the search for indigenous roots was abandoned in favour of the use of tinted glass, coloured tiling and various textures, for example in the Banco Continental (1983) and the Centro Comercial Camino Real.

BIBLIOGRAPHY

H. Velarde: *Arquitectura peruana* (Mexico City, 1946)
J. Jijón y Caamaño: *Maranga: Contribución al conocimiento de los aborígenes del Rímac* (Quito, 1949)
H. E. Wethey: *Colonial Architecture and Sculpture in Peru* (Cambridge, MA, 1949)
P. Keleman: *Baroque and Rococo in Latin America* (New York, 1951)
A. Kroeber: 'Proto Lima: A Middle Period Culture of Peru', *Fieldiana Anthropol.*, xliv (1954) [whole issue]
F. Engel: 'A Preceramic Settlement on the Central Coast of Peru: Asia, Unit 1', *Trans. Amer. Philos. Soc.*, liii/3 (1963) [whole issue]
E. Tabío: *Excavaciones en la costa central del Perú (1955–1958)* (Havana, 1965)
J. M. Ugarte Elespurú: *Lima y lo limeño* (Lima, 1966)
H. Velarde: *Itinerarios de Lima: Guía de monumentos y lugares históricos* (Lima [1971]); Eng. trans. as *Guide to Lima: Historical Monuments and Sites* (Lima, 1972)
R. Ramírez Villar: *San Francisco de Lima* (Lima, 1974)
E. Harth-Terré: *Perú: Monumentos históricos y arqueologicos* (Mexico City, 1975)
R. Ravines and W. H. Isbell: 'Garagay: Sitio ceremonial temprano en el Valle de Lima', *Rev. Mus. N.*, xli (1975), pp. 253–75
M. Rostworowski de Diez Canseco: *Señoríos indígenas de Lima y Canta* (Lima, 1978)
P. Lloyd: *The 'Young Towns' of Lima: Aspects of Urbanization in Peru* (Cambridge, 1980)
S. A. Calvo: *Lima prehispánica* (Lima, 1984)
*Inventario de monumentos arqueológicos del Perú, Lima metropolitana* (Lima, 1985)
J. B. Ballesteros: *Historia del arte hispanoamericano: Siglos XVI a XVIII*, ii (Madrid, 1987)
L. Castedo: *Historia del arte iberoamericano*, ii (Madrid, 1988), pp. 31–4, 208–14
V. Fraser: *The Architecture of Conquest: Building in the Viceroyalty of Peru, 1535–1635* (Cambridge, 1990)
M. Ibáñez Sanchez: 'Problemas de geografía urbana en Lima metropolitana al año 2010', *Bol. Lima*, xiii (1991), pp. 65–90
R. Ravines: 'La conservación y restauración de edificios históricos en los centros urbanos', *Bol. Lima*, xiv (1992), pp. 15–18

W. IAIN MACKAY

**Lima, João Filgueiras.** *See* FILGUEIRAS LIMA, JOÃO.

**Lima, Santos Pacheco de.** *See* SANTOS PACHECO.

**Lima, Victor Meirelles de.** *See* MEIRELLES DE LIMA, VICTOR.

**Lima Corrêa, Attilio.** *See* CORRÊA LIMA, ATTILIO.

**Limbourg, de** [Limbourc; Maelwael, Malouel, Manuel] North Netherlandish family of illuminators, active in France. The three brothers, Pol de Limbourg [Paul, Paulequin, Polequin], Jean de Limbourg [Hannequin, Janequin, Jannechin, Jehanequin, Jehannequin, Jennekin] and Herman de Limbourg, came to Paris from Nijmegen around the beginning of the 15th century and are particularly renowned for the illumination of two manuscripts for Jean, Duc de Berry (*see* VALOIS, (3)): the Belles Heures and the Très Riches Heures (*see* §1(i) below), both of which are outstanding examples of the Late Gothic style. With the notable exception of Meiss, most art historians agree that it is impossible to distinguish adequately the artistic personality and style of each of the three brothers and that their oeuvre is more appropriately treated as a single entity, with Pol de Limbourg the acknowledged master of the group.

1. Family history and works. 2. Working methods and techniques. 3. Critical reception and posthumous reputation.

### 1. FAMILY HISTORY AND WORKS.

(i) Attributions and chronology. (ii) Stylistic influences. (iii) Illumination of Books of Hours.

*(i) Attributions and chronology.* The brothers' father, Arnold Limbourg, was a sculptor whose family came from the small duchy of Limburg, near Aachen, but they are also referred to in some of the documents by their mother's name, Malouel (with various spellings). Their mother's brother, JEAN MALOUEL, was a painter active in Paris and later Valet de Chambre at the court of Philip the Bold, Duke of Burgundy, in Dijon in 1397. The first mention of two brothers Maleuel/Malauel in Paris is problematic. Philip the Bold is recorded on 2 May 1400 as paying the ransom for two young boys 'Hermant and Jacquemin or Gillequin Maleuel' who had been taken prisoner in Brussels on their way back to their native Guelders. The boys, nephews of Jean Malouel, had been apprenticed to a Parisian goldsmith, Alebret de Bolure, but were sent home when an epidemic broke out in the city. Philip came to the aid of the goldsmiths and painters of Brussels when, out of respect for their fellow artist, Jean Malouel, they decided to try to arrange the ransom sum. The account contains a reference to the mother of the boys as being a widow and very poor at the time. Meiss (*French Painting*, 1974) interpreted this document as a reference to the two young Limbourgs, Herman and Jean, who entered the service of Philip the Bold as illuminators in Paris two years later. Cazelles (in Cazelles and Rathofer, 1988), on the other hand, unwilling to accept the names Jacquemin or Gillequin as alternatives for Jean, also claimed that there was a

discrepancy between the description of the mother of the young apprentice goldsmiths as 'very poor' and another reference in a document ten years later to the consignment of property in Nijmegen by Herman and Jean de Limbourg to their mother, Mechtilde. Such property, he argued, must have been left to the boys by their father, who would have also provided for the widow; thus, according to Cazelles, the young apprentice goldsmiths, while also nephews of Jean Malouel, must have belonged to another branch of the family. Though possible, therefore, it is not certain that two of the Limbourgs began as goldsmiths in Paris before specializing in illumination.

The accounts of Philip the Bold record that early in 1402, through his physician Jean Durant who lived in Paris, the Duke engaged the illuminators Polequin and Jehannequin Manuel to work solely for him for the next four years on the illumination of a 'very fine and notable bible'. Durant was advanced two years' wages for the illuminators. Entries for the following year note payment to Durant for the purchase of six ounces of a 'fine blue' for the illumination of certain books, and to Jean and Pol for their clothing while working for the Duke and resident with Durant. A further advance to the physician for the illuminators' wages and for costs related to the production of the Bible was made in January 1404. Philip died only a few months later, on 27 April, and there is no further mention of the project. Meiss (*French Painting*, 1974) has identified a *Bible moralisée* (Paris, Bib. N., MS. fr. 166) with this commission (and specifically the 384 miniatures of the first three gatherings). He argued that, although the book bears no marks of ownership, its extensive illustrative programme was modelled on that of a mid-14th-century copy (Paris, Bib. N., MS. fr. 167), known to have been in the Duke's collection and therefore accessible to his artists. Moreover, the style of the illumination of the first three gatherings is closely related to that of the Belles Heures, a manuscript of Jean de Berry. The Belles Heures, described in the inventory of Robinet d'Etampes as 'Unes Belles Heures, tres bien et richement historiees . . .', was identified by Delisle (1884) with a Book of Hours (New York, Cloisters) once owned by the French branch of the Rothschild family. Although the entry states only that the book was illuminated by the Duc's 'ouvriers', this manuscript has been accepted as the work of the Limbourgs, as its illumination compares closely with that of the Très Riches Heures (Durrieu, 1906; see below).

Although earlier writers, including Durrieu (1904) and Porcher (1953), also observed the similarity between the *Bible moralisée* and the Belles Heures, they were not persuaded that it was the Bible referred to in the accounts of Philip the Bold. Meiss met one of their substantial reservations by demonstrating, through further research on the inventories of Jean de Berry, that the Belles Heures, previously thought to have been completed *c.* 1413, that is some nine years after work on the Bible for Philip the Bold, was in fact finished in 1408 or by early 1409 at the latest. He argued that the Limbourgs were, therefore, engaged in the illumination of the Belles Heures from *c.* 1405–8. This would account for its close stylistic relationship with the first three gatherings of the *Bible moralisée*, which were illuminated, according to this argument, *c.* 1402–4. There is general agreement that the first

1. Limbourg brothers: scenes from *Exodus*, 400×295 mm; illustrations from the *Bible moralisée*, *c.* 1402–4 (Paris, Bibliothèque Nationale, MS. fr. 166, fol. 19r)

part of this *Bible moralisée* contains the earliest known illumination of the Limbourg brothers and that the distinctive qualities of their style are already evident in the miniatures (see fig. 1).

In this manuscript the artists' expert use of colour, with figures modelled in light and colour rather than in line, is already evident. The restricted palette presents the figures predominantly in shades of off-white, with blue, pale rose, red, orange and brown largely reserved for the undergarments, contrasting details or less prominent figures. Despite the small dimensions of the miniatures (eight scenes per page), the figures assume an almost monumental quality in the most successful compositions; already showing a propensity for elongated proportions, they occupy the foreground plane and when standing take up most of the vertical space of the miniature. Olive-green landscapes with curved and jagged conventionalized mountains, ultimately derived from Byzantine models, thrust the palely robed luminous figures into relief as they twist and turn in dramatic action, or with magnified gestures express a range of emotional reactions to the events taking place. Whether two or three of the brothers were involved in the book's production must depend to some extent on whether or not it is to be identified with the 1402–4 commission of Philip the Bold, which involved only Pol and Jean. While most scholars have distinguished variations of quality and differing characteristics over the three gatherings, Meiss used these miniatures as the basis for the construction of an individual artistic style and persona for Pol and Jean, a process that he developed in his analysis of the Belles Heures and the Très Riches Heures and extended to include Herman as well.

During the period *c*. 1405–15 Pol and his two brothers are mentioned several times in the inventories of Jean de Berry. The Duc's pleasure is expressed in gifts of gold coins and precious jewels, especially to Pol but also on occasion to Herman and Jean. The familiar and favoured position that the artists enjoyed in the Duc's household is also attested to by the fact that they in turn gave presents to him. The simulated book presented to Jean de Berry by the Limbourgs on 1 January 1411 was described and recorded in the Duc's inventory, alongside his most precious possessions. In 1413 Pol, by this time a Valet de Chambre of the Duc, was made a gift of 100 écus 'in consideration of the good and welcome services he has rendered, renders each day, and it is hoped, will render in the future, and also to clothe himself and to be more honourably in the Duke's service, notwithstanding other gifts given by the Duke . . .', and in 1415 the Duc gave the three brothers, all of whom were listed as Valets de Chambre, a gold ring with a small fine ruby as security for the large sum of 1000 écus he owed them. Pol was also given a spacious house in Bourges, after its recovery from the Duc's treasurer on 22 June 1411. The reference in a document of 1434 concerning this property to a 'painter of the Duke's called Pol, a native of Germany', raises the possibility that Pol de Limbourg was the 'German painter' recorded as working for Jean de Berry at his residence in Bicêtre on the outskirts of Paris in 1408, a reference that may indicate that he was a painter of panels and frescoes as well as manuscripts. In the same year the Duc attempted by forceful methods to procure an eight-year-old girl, Gilette la Mercière, daughter of a wealthy merchant of Bruges, as wife for this German painter. After the intervention of Charles VI it was resolved that they marry when she turned 12; the marriage took place in 1411 or shortly afterwards.

It was during this period, starting in 1411 or 1413, that work on the TRÈS RICHES HEURES (Chantilly, Mus. Condé, MS. 65) was begun by the Limbourg brothers and their assistants, as is testified in an inventory (1416) of the Duc de Berry, 'several gatherings of a very rich Book of Hours, richly historiated and illuminated, that Pol and his brothers made'. By 9 March 1416 Jean de Limbourg was dead, and by September/October in the same year the other two Limbourgs had died, leaving the Très Riches Heures unfinished. Referred to as youths in 1402, they must have been still relatively young at the time of their deaths, and it has been suggested that they fell prey to the plague or an epidemic of some kind. Other works that are generally acknowledged, on the basis of stylistic comparisons, to be by the Limbourgs are the three added miniatures in the Très Belles Heures de Notre-Dame (*c*. 1405–9; Paris, Bib. N., MS. nouv. acq. lat. 3093, pp. 225, 240 and a lithograph copy), the frontispiece to a copy of Valerius Maximus' *De*

*dictis factisque mirabilibus* (*c*. 1410; Rome, Vatican, Bib. Apostolica, MS. Reg. lat. 939, fol. 1) and the added miniature in the Petites Heures (*c*. 1412; Paris, Bib. N., MS. lat. 18014, fol. 288*v*). Meiss has also attributed to the brothers the introductory historiated initial of the charter (1405) for the Sainte-Chapelle, Bourges, which survives in a 19th-century copy.

*(ii) Stylistic influences.* The Limbourgs' preference for modelling in pale colours, their consummate rendering of the play of light on forms and their preoccupation with landscape stem from their native Netherlandish tradition; and affinities and links have been identified between their early work and that of such other artists who came to Paris from the Netherlands around the turn of the 15th century as the Master of the Coronation of the Virgin, who was responsible for a depiction of that theme in a manuscript of Voragine's *Golden Legend* (*c*. 1402; Paris, Bib. N., MS. fr. 242). On the other hand, the articulation of figures, the planar organization of space and the dramatic, psychological emphasis that characterizes several of the miniatures in the *Bible moralisée* reveal that even at this early stage, the Limbourgs had absorbed many of the principles of Italian art, probably through contact with artists and illuminators at the courts of Philip the Bold and Jean de Berry. Both dukes spent a considerable time in Paris in each other's company while Pol and Jean were working on the *Bible moralisée*, and it would not have been difficult to arrange for the illuminators to meet with court artists or to see their work. Early contacts are especially discernible with artists resident at the Burgundian court, including Jean de Beaumetz and his successor, the Limbourgs' uncle, Jean Malouel. Acquaintance with the style of the illuminator Jacquemart de Hesdin may have been made through the Très Belles Heures (Brussels, Bib. Royale Albert 1er, MSS 11060–61), which Jean de Berry gave to his brother, possibly around this time. Set apart by the conditions of their employment, the Limbourgs seem to have made only sporadic contact with the large Parisian ateliers throughout their career, although they reveal a continuing knowledge of the work of the Boucicaut Master, with whom they shared similar preoccupations.

In their later work, the Très Riches Heures, the landscapes of the calendar miniatures (see fig. 2; for further illustration *see* VALOIS, (3)) provide a strong contrast to many of the more conventionalized backgrounds of the Limbourgs' earlier illustrations. Panoramic views showing sloping fields, meadows and streams, or architectural vistas with identifiable buildings were new to French art; Pächt (1950) and other scholars have discerned here the influence of north Italian nature studies and 14th-century Tuscan painters such as Pietro and Ambrogio Lorenzetti. The Limbourgs filled their expansive calendar landscapes with a blend of conventional, ritualized activities and such keenly observed naturalistic detail as the breath of a peasant visible in the icy air of *February* or the distorted shape of swimmers, glimpsed through rippling water in *August*. Their work, however, is always within the idiom of the international courtly style. The more advanced elements in the miniatures for *October* and *December* and in parts of *March* and *June*, such as cast shadows, individualized facial expressions and more boldly modelled figures and buildings, have been convincingly attributed by Bellosi and others to a mid-15th century illuminator.

Scholars have produced a number of examples of motifs and compositions that reveal the Limbourgs' knowledge of Italian art, particularly of 14th-century Tuscan artists such as Simone Martini, Taddeo Gaddi and the Lorenzetti brothers. Italian art was, however, more than a source for discrete borrowings for the Limbourgs; it acted as a catalyst for their own creative expression. Lombard art and culture, in particular, seems to have had a pervasive presence in Jean de Berry's court: the border and initial decoration of the Limbourgs and their collaborator, the Master of the Breviary of Jean sans Peur, is unthinkable without reference to such artists as Giovannino de Grassi and Michelino da Besozzo; the alterations to the layout and the shape of certain miniatures in the Belles Heures and the Très Riches Heures reflect Lombard models; the unusually full Mass section in the latter invites textual comparisons with a north Italian Missal–Hours (c. 1385–90; Paris, Bib. N., MS. lat. 757); and for their illustration of the *Te Deum* in the Très Riches Heures, the brothers adopted a Milanese theme, the *Baptism of St Augustine by St Ambrose*.

The Limbourgs' interest in the Antique, revealed in such figures as that of Adam in *The Fall* in the Très Riches Heures, or the foreshortened fallen warriors in the *Agony in the Garden*, was fostered by exposure to works in the Duc's collections, as well as by their knowledge of Italian art. The artists' knowledge of the Antique seems also to have been mediated through such medieval or contemporary copies as, for example, the medals *all'antica* purchased by the Duc c. 1401–3, showing portraits of the emperors *Constantine* and *Heraclius*; several aspects of these were reflected in the artists' compositions.

*(iii) Illumination of Books of Hours.* When the Limbourgs entered the service of Jean de Berry, their natural talents and professional expertise were greatly stimulated. It is not known how much of their time was spent in Paris or in Bourges, how often they travelled with the Duc between his several residences in the Champagne and the Berry, and whether or not one or more of the brothers journeyed to Italy. There is no doubt, however, that the Belles Heures and the Très Riches Heures are works produced in the context of greatly enlarged cultural perspectives. As a personal prayerbook, the Book of Hours was less subject to canonical prescriptions than liturgical books and provided far more scope for the Limbourgs; Jean de Berry's court particularly favoured the development of this genre. The Duc's religious education and commitment to private and public prayer ensured a continuing need for such books, and their use was built into the daily life of his court. Chaplains, confessors and clerical advisers provided fresh compilations of texts and played an important role in the overall planning of manuals in which the images were seen to be intimately connected with the prayers. Both the designers and illuminators of new Books of Hours for the Duc were able to refer to earlier exemplars in his possession and to those belonging to his relatives and friends, while other books in his library provided further ideas for enriching textual and visual elements.

2. Limbourg brothers: *April*, 290×210 mm; calendar miniature from the Très Riches Heures, *c.* 1411/13–16 (Chantilly, Musée Condé, Château de Chantilly, MS. 65, fol. 4*v*)

Several unusual miniatures and cycles of illustrations in the Belles Heures reveal the Limbourgs developing new compositions with special reference to the interests of their patron. The prayer for a safe journey, for example, seems to have been incorporated into the Belles Heures expressly for the Duc; it was also added to two of his earlier prayerbooks. The Limbourgs, charged with illustrating the prayer in all three manuscripts, devised three different compositions that depict Jean de Berry's own arrivals and departures. The Belles Heures contains eight pictorial cycles representing the *Lives of the Saints*, the *Legend of the Finding of the True Cross* and the *Institution of the Greater Litanies*. The text for these cycles, based on the popular *Golden Legend*, is normally reduced to four lines per page beneath large miniatures, which combine narrative and dramatic elements with those more directed to encourage contemplation. Among these cycles, the rare account of the *Life of St Bruno* and his founding of the Carthusians and the *Lives of SS Paul and Anthony*, the desert fathers, reflect the Duc's interest in the eremitical tradition fostered especially by the Carthusians at this time. They may also reflect the court's contact with Lombardy, since similar influences helped to shape the work of the Lombard illuminators, Michelino da Besozzo and Giovannino de Grassi, with whom the Limbourgs had strong stylistic affiliations at this time. The striking rendering of the *Institution of the Greater Litanies* (see fig. 3) in the Belles Heures is also based on a text from the *Golden Legend*. Visually, it combines the drama of the plague with allusions to contemporary groups of flagellants and the more formal prayer of the Church through the theme of procession, a theme that is adopted in the Très Riches Heures for another rarely illustrated text, that of the litanies themselves.

Very different from these large narrative pictures, but no less unusual, are the small miniatures that illustrate each of the penitential Psalms in the Belles Heures. These draw on an ancient tradition of psalm illustration, rarely featured in Books of Hours. It is further developed, however, in the Très Riches Heures, where nearly all the psalms and canticles are so illustrated, thus forming an abbreviated Psalter as a 'sub-text' to the book's various offices and other devotions. Some of the Limbourgs' most sensitively executed paintings were produced for the Hours of the Virgin and the Hours of the Passion in both Books of Hours: two facing miniatures, instead of one for each Hour, develop a contemplative emphasis on Christ's Passion, and in the Très Riches Heures this expansion of visual material in relation to the text occurs also in parts of the Hours of the Virgin. The theme of the *Adoration of the Magi*, for example, which introduces the Hour of Sext, is expressed in a double-page opening that encompasses the *Meeting of the Magi* (see fig. 4) on their way to Bethlehem, as well as the *Adoration* itself (*see* FRANCE, fig. 19).

Codicological studies have shown that the original plans for both Books of Hours were altered and expanded during their execution and that the large extensive picture cycles of the Belles Heures, as well as the eight full-page miniatures painted on separate folios or bi-folios in the Très Riches Heures, belong to the expanded plans. While the alterations also involved additional textual material and adjustments to the existing text, there is no doubt that they resulted in an overall increased visual emphasis, which may well reflect the Limbourgs' influence on the development of Books of Hours. Since the additional visual material maintains close links with the contemplative or instructional function of the Très Riches Heures, it is reasonable to conclude that the alterations proceeded collaboratively with the involvement of both the patron and his learned adviser, as well as of the Limbourgs.

2. WORKING METHODS AND TECHNIQUES. As illuminators the Limbourgs were required to work in close collaboration with the scribe and the designer responsible for the layout of text and decoration of a particular book. For the detailed visual programmes commissioned by the dukes of Burgundy and Berry, this also meant working to the written instructions of a learned adviser, as well as referring to other books as models and to their own store of patterns. Collaboration was a key element, and one that was expanded to include the contribution of assistants, especially for decorated initials and borders.

Since several of the miniatures of the Très Riches Heures were completed by Jean Colombe in a quite different style many years later (*c.* 1485–6; for illustration *see* TRÈS RICHES HEURES), scholars have been able to discern progressive stages in their illumination. First the composition was drawn in ink within the space ruled up for the miniature. Then the sky, landscape or architectural backgrounds were painted, followed by the foreground and figures, with heads and faces left until last. Given the controlling underdrawing, and the minute detailing required of some areas, it is understandable that sometimes one illuminator worked on similar sections of several miniatures, before he or another member of the team returned to complete a particular painting. Work was also shared out by folios or gatherings. Stylistic variations, therefore, within the Limbourgs' work, especially in a large commission, may be due to a number of factors. These include authorship of the underdrawing, its relationship to earlier models and the control it exercised over the whole composition, as well as the degree of collaboration within a particular miniature, folio or gathering. Patterns of individual stylistic development, moreover, were no doubt affected by the illuminators working so closely together. The large detailed projects undertaken by the Limbourgs from the earliest known stages of their career promoted both the development of specialist skills and the conscious integration of discrete elements in the final composition.

3. Limbourg brothers: *Great Litany Procession*, 238×170 mm;, miniature from the Belles Heures, *c.* 1405–8 (New York, The Cloisters, fol. 73*v*)

3. CRITICAL RECEPTION AND POSTHUMOUS REPU-TATION. Evaluation of the Limbourgs' influence on their immediate contemporaries has been affected by changing attributions. The Breviary of Jean sans Peur (1413–19; London, BL, Add. MS. 35311 and Harley MS. 2897), for example, was formerly considered to be by the Limbourgs themselves; but the Master of the Breviary of Jean sans Peur has now been acknowledged as a distinct artistic personality (Meiss, 1970, and *French Painting*, 1974). Displaying particular talents for innovative border deco-ration, this artist worked closely with the Limbourgs on the Très Riches Heures and later produced compositions in the Breviary, based on those of the brothers. The later work of the Master of the Rohan Hours, active *c.* 1410–40, also reflects the Limbourgs' influence, and copies of compositions in the Très Riches Heures were made by French illuminators, perhaps from drawings, up to 1435. Meiss (*French Painting*, 1974) provided a number of examples by the Master of St Jerome (who, he suggested, may have been Arnold, the youngest of the Limbourg family), by the Master of the Harvard Hannibal and by the Bedford Master workshop. In a more general sense, mid-15th-century French artists such as Jean Fouquet continued the Limbourgs' innovative approach to the rendering of landscape and contemporary architectural settings in devotional pictures. Meiss also demonstrated that the contact with Italy was not one-way, arguing that Pisanello, for example, may well have been influenced by the Limbourgs' work. Scholars such as Panofsky and Meiss saw the Limbourgs as forerunners of Jan van Eyck; but this view has been challenged by the research of Bellosi, who has convincingly demonstrated by an analysis based on the history of dress, in the first instance, that features of some of the calendar miniatures previously identified as pre-Eyckian are the result of an intermediate phase of illumination between the Limbourgs and Jean Colombe, carried out possibly by Barthélemy d'Eyck, a mid-15th-century artist of Netherlandish origins who worked at the court of René of Anjou. By the early 16th century all the calendar illustrations of the Très Riches Heures, including those by the Limbourgs, were known in the Netherlands, and several versions by south Netherlandish artists were produced, notably in the Grimiani Breviary. The Lim-bourgs continue to occupy an important part in the history of Western art because of their achievements as manuscript illuminators and as exponents of the Late Gothic courtly style.

4. Limbourg brothers: *Meeting of the Magi*, 290×210 mm; miniature from the Très Riches Heures, *c.* 1411/13–16 (Chantilly, Musée Condé, Château de Chantilly, MS. 65, fol. 51*v*)

BIBLIOGRAPHY

L. Delisle: *Mélanges de paléographie et de bibliographie* (Paris, 1880)
——: 'Les Livres d'Heures du duc de Berry', *Gaz. B.-A.*, xxix (1884), pp. 97–110, 281–92, 391–405
A. de Champeaux and P. Gauchery: *Les Travaux d'art executés pour Jean de France, duc de Berry, avec une étude biographique sur les artistes employés par ce prince* (Paris, 1894)
J. Guiffrey: *Inventaires de Jean duc de Berry, 1401–1416*, 2 vols (Paris, 1894–6)
P. Durrieu: *Les Très Riches Heures de Jean de France, duc de Berry* (Paris, 1904)
——: 'Les "Belles Heures" de Jean de France duc de Berry', *Gaz. B.-A.*, xxxv (1906), pp. 21–35
O. Pächt: 'Early Italian Nature Studies and the Early Calendar Landscape', *J. Warb. & Court. Inst.*, xiii (1950), pp. 13–47
J. Porcher: *Les Belles Heures de Jean de France, duc de Berry* (Paris, 1953)
F. Gorissen: 'Jan Maelwael und die Brüder Limburg', *Gelre*, liv (1954), pp. 153–221

J. Porcher: *L'Enluminure française* (Paris, 1959; Eng. trans., New York, 1959)
M. Meiss: *French Painting in the Time of Jean de Berry: The Late XIV Century and the Patronage of the Duke*, 2 vols (London and New York, 1967, rev. 1969)
M. Meiss with K. Morand and E. W. Kirsch: *French Painting in the Time of Jean de Berry: The Boucicaut Master* (London and New York, 1968)
J. Longman and R. Cazelles with M. Meiss: *Les Très Riches Heures du Duc de Berry* (London, 1969)
M. Meiss: 'The Master of the Breviary of Jean sans Peur and the Limbourgs', *Proc. Brit. Acad.*, lvi (1970), pp. 111–29; as booklet (London, 1971)
M. Meiss with S. Off: 'The Bookkeeping of Robinet d'Estampes and the Chronology of Jean de Berry's Manuscripts', *A. Bull.*, liii (1971), pp. 225–35
M. Meiss with S. O. Smith and E. H. Beatson: *French Painting in the Time of Jean de Berry: The Limbourgs and their Contemporaries*, 2 vols (New York and London, 1974) [includes article by J. Plummer, pp. 334–6]
*The Belles Heures of Jean, Duke of Berry* (exh. cat. by M. Meiss and E. H. Beatson, New York, Cloisters, 1974)
J. Plummer: 'A Blank Page in the Belles Heures', *Gatherings in Honor of Dorothy E. Miner*, ed. U. E. McCracken, L. C. Randall and R. H. Randall jr (Baltimore, 1974), pp. 193–202
F. Avril: 'La Peinture française au temps de Jean de Berry', *Rev. A.* [Paris], xxviii (1975), pp. 40–52
L. Bellosi: 'I Limbourg precursori di Van Eyck? Nuove osservazioni sui *Mesi* di Chantilly', *Prospettiva*, i (1975), pp. 24–34
E. König: 'Le Peintre de l'Octobre des *Très Riches Heures* du duc de Berry', *Doss. Archéol.*, xvi (1976), pp. 96–123
M. Jones: 'The First Cast Medals and the Limbourgs: The Iconography and Attribution of the Constantine and Heraclius Medals', *A. Hist.*, ii (1979), pp. 35–44
M. Thomas: *The Golden Age: Manuscript Painting at the Time of Jean, Duke of Berry* (New York, 1979)

J. J. G. Alexander: 'The Limbourg Brothers and Italian Art: A New Source', *Z. Kstgesch.*, xlvi (1983), pp. 425–35

D. Byrne: 'Manuscript Ruling and Pictorial Design in the Work of the Limbourgs, the Bedford Master, and the Boucicaut Master', *A. Bull.*, lxvi (1984), pp. 118–35

R. Cazelles and J. Rathofer: *Les Très Riches Heures du Duc de Berry*, 2 vols (New York, 1984) [facs. and commentary]

M. Bath: 'Imperial *renovatio symbolism* in the Très Riches Heures', *Simiolus*, xvii (1987), no. 1, pp. 5–22

R. Cazelles and J. Rathofer: *Illuminations of Heaven and Earth: The Glories of the Très Riches Heures du Duc de Berry* (New York, 1988)

J. J. G. Alexander: 'Labeur and Paresse: Ideological Images of Medieval Peasant Labour', *A. Bull.*, lxxii (1990), pp. 437–8

——: *Medieval Illuminators and their Methods of Work* (New Haven, 1992), pp. 139–43

J. Plummer: 'The Beginnings of the *Belles Heures*', *The Cloisters: Studies in Honor of the Fiftieth Anniversary*, ed. E. C. Parker with M. B. Shepard (New York, 1992), pp. 421–39

*Les Manuscrits en France, 1440–1520* (exh. cat., ed. F. Avril and N. Reynaud; Paris, 1992–3), p. 2

MARGARET M. MANION

**Limburg auf der Haardt Abbey.** Former Benedictine abbey in the Rhineland-Palatinate, Germany, *c.* 4 km west of Bad Dürkheim. It was founded as a family monastery by Conrad II (*reg* 1024–39) on the site of his old dynastic castle, the Lintburg, in gratitude for his recent election as German King and as a demonstration of the Salian dynasty's newly won power. The crypt was consecrated in the presence of the founder in 1035, and the church was dedicated in 1042, although it was not completed until 1045. The church was destroyed in 1504 by supporters of Graf von Leiningen. The monastery was closed in 1574.

The church was a three-aisled, flat-ceilinged basilica with columns, with eleven bays in the nave and an isolated crossing, above which rose an octagonal crossing tower on squinches. The sanctuary is straight-ended, and beneath it is a three-aisled, groin-vaulted hall-crypt. The westwork presumably consisted of two square towers separated by a porch with a gallery above, possibly the royal oratory. The towers were each flanked by a round stair-turret reaching to the level of the ridge of the nave roof. The westwork was preceded by a paradise bounded by a wall with small arcades. The omission of a western apse, which had been a common feature in the Ottonian period, resulted in an axial alignment and made the church appear more elongated. The emphasis on the west entrance (paradise, porch, twin towers and stair-turrets) is counterbalanced by the rich ensemble at the east end formed by the sanctuary, choir, transept with apses and the crossing tower. The pilaster strips and round-headed blind arches that articulate the lower windows of the transept and sanctuary inside the church (*see* ROMANESQUE, fig. 4) and the clerestory outside are particularly majestic. The church is notable throughout for its tall proportions.

Poppo of Stablo (978–1048), the first abbot, was a close confidant of Conrad II and a keen advocate of monastic reform: he had previously reformed twelve monasteries in Lotharingia and four royal abbeys within the Holy Roman Empire. This explains many of the church's peculiarities, the roots of which may be sought in Burgundy and the Cluniac reform movement (*see* CLUNIAC ORDER, §I). These elements, including the paradise in front of the west door, the porch between the west towers, the marked axial alignment, the use of columns supporting the arcade in the nave and the flat ceiling, foreshadow the architecture of the German reformed monasteries, especially those associated with the Hirsau congregation, for example at Alpirsbach, which has similar proportions. The wall articulation at the east end, the large hall-crypt and the crossing tower, however, anticipate Conrad's other great foundation, Speyer Cathedral (*c.* 1030–61; *see* SPEYER, §1). After he selected the latter as the burial-place for his royal dynasty and changed his policy towards the reformed monasteries, which he had initially supported, Limburg auf der Haardt Abbey lost much of its importance. Even so, it can be seen as a forerunner of what would be so superbly fulfilled in the imperial cathedral at Speyer.

BIBLIOGRAPHY

W. Manchot: *Kloster Limburg a.d. Haardt* (Mannheim, 1892)

H. Kunze: 'Die Klosterkirche in Limburg a.d.H. und die Frage der Doppelturmfassade am Oberrhein', *Oberrhein. Kst*, x (1942), pp. 5–38

E. Gall: *Dome und Klosterkirchen am Rhein* (Munich, 1956; Eng. trans., London, 1963)

ERNST ULLMANN

**Limerick.** Irish city and seat of the county of the same name, known for its production of gold and silver. Archaeological evidence shows that goldsmiths were active in Co. Limerick about 700 BC, as demonstrated by the find of magnificent gold gorgets (Dublin, N. Mus.). The earliest dated piece made in silver is probably the Askeaton Chalice (Askeaton parish), inscribed with the date 1663. A large quantity of silver was manufactured in Limerick from the mid-17th century until *c.* 1820. From 1637, under Royal Charter, all silver was required to be sent to Dublin for assaying and hallmarking (*see* DUBLIN, §III, 1); however, very little Limerick silver actually reached Dublin because of the long distance. During the 17th century silversmiths in Limerick stamped a maker's mark, a castle gate and a star on their wares, and, like silversmiths in Cork, they adopted the 'Sterling' mark *c.* 1710. Silversmiths active in Limerick during the 18th century included Collins Brehon (*d* 1768), Jonathan Buck II (*d* 1762), Joseph Johns (*d* 1775) and Samuel Johns (*d* 1795).

BIBLIOGRAPHY

D. Bennett: *Irish Georgian Silver* (London, 1972)

D. Bennett and R. Folliott: 'The Silvermakers of Limerick', *Irish Ancestor*, x/2 (1978), pp. 99–115

D. Bennett: *Collecting Irish Silver* (London, 1984)

——: *The Silver Collection, Trinity College Dublin* (Dublin, 1988)

DOUGLAS BENNETT

**Lime secco.** Wall painting technique that is a variant of FRESCO. The painting is executed with fresco pigments that have been mixed into a paste with water and lime. On drying they develop a characteristically pale tonality. In preparation for painting, the wall should be absolutely dry and the surface smoothed with pumice stone. It is then washed with limewater. When the wall has again dried out, it is dampened with plain water, and the design is transferred from a cartoon by pouncing.

The origins of lime secco are ancient, and it was much used in the Romanesque and Gothic periods as well as in 18th-century decorative painting. In the late Roman period and in the 16th century a hybrid technique related to fresco painting was used, particularly for paintings with a white background. The dry *intonaco* was faced with a thick layer of lime, on to which the design was transferred by pouncing. As the lime dried it formed a transparent, vitreous layer of calcium carbonate on its surface, into which the pigments became fixed. If the artist wished to exploit this property, he painted while the lime was still damp, using fresco colours bound in water with a small quantity of adhesive. If a large area had to be painted, the work was carried out on dry lime with pigments bound in limewater and milk.

The conservation of lime secco is problematic, since the thick, inflexible layer of lime on which the painting is executed often becomes detached from the *intonaco* as the masonry of the wall gradually settles. It then forms ridge-like protrusions that may run the length of the painting in an almost geometrical fashion.

BIBLIOGRAPHY

G. Ronchetti: *Pittura murale* (Milan, 1983)

GIANLUIGI COLALUCCI

**Limited edition.** Term applied to sets of both two- and three-dimensional works. The limitation of the number produced indicates controlled production of a replicated image or model from the matrix of an original work of art and adds value to the works themselves, since the purchaser thereby has an implicit guarantee of exclusivity.

1. PRINTS. It has been cogently stated that 'To be unlimited is actually a physical impossibility in printing' (Gilmour), since any run of prints is finite, because the matrix (copper plate, stone, roller) or the work (incised or raised lines etc) made on that matrix will eventually wear out. The notion of limitation is, however, intricately bound up with the aesthetic merits and values of printmaking and the appreciation and commercial value of prints. The origins of the limited edition lie partly in the endeavours of artists to produce unique, special proofs of their prints, exceptional from the points of view of printing, colour of ink and type of paper. Such endeavours reach back to the early years of printmaking (e.g. Mantegna) but probably achieved their consummation in the work of Rembrandt. The Etching Revival in France and Britain in the 1860s–1880s (*see* ETCHING, §V) drew on these achievements and codified them, in that artists increasingly attached their names first to outstanding impressions (e.g. Whistler, who charged double for signed impressions), then to designate different states and numbers of proofs within each state (e.g. Pissarro). Parallel to this essentially fine art practice was the procedure of commercial reproductive printmakers whose work accounted for the bulk of 19th-century output. In 1847 the Printsellers' Association was founded in Britain with the intention of controlling the quality of reproductions. In 1880 the Association distinguished between four categories of prints (artist's proofs (A.P.), proofs before letters, lettered proofs and prints) and decreed that all proofs of prints approved by the Association were to be produced in limited editions, with each impression of the artist's proofs and proofs before letters marked with a combination of letters in the margins. The practice of fractional numbering of the impressions in an edition (e.g. '3/50' or third impression of an edition of fifty) began *c.* 1900.

The modern principle of the limited edition is straightforward. A run of prints is limited (by agreement between the artist, publisher and printer) to a certain number of impressions, commonly 50, 75, 100 or 500 but rarely more than 1000. Usually each impression is numbered in pencil or pen in the lower margin, sometimes by the artist, sometimes by someone in the printer's studio, and then signed by the artist. In addition to the numbered edition, a few extra impressions are generally printed in the form of artist's proofs and printer's proofs and are lettered and sometimes numbered accordingly. Impressions specifically designated as outside the edition (lettered 'H.C.', Fr. *hors commerce*) may also be available and are sometimes numbered. The inclusion of information on edition sizes (including how many H.C. and A.P. proofs were produced) in modern catalogues raisonnés of printmakers reinforces the system of exclusivity.

*See also* PRINTS, §IV, 2.

BIBLIOGRAPHY

P. Gilmour: *Understanding Prints: A Contemporary Guide* (London, 1979), p. 62

M. Melot and others: *Prints: History of an Art* (Geneva, 1981)

S. Lambert: *The Image Multiplied: Five Centuries of Printed Reproductions of Paintings and Drawings* (London, 1987)

LAURA SUFFIELD

2. SCULPTURE. The application of the concept of the limited edition to sculpture developed from the rapid expansion of its markets during the 19th century. In response to the growing public demand, highly productive foundries were established from the 1830s across Europe to enable the broad-based manufacture of popular works. Conventional techniques of modelling were superseded by the Collas Machine, invented by Achille Collas in 1836, which allowed the reduction of statues in the round. Thereafter miniature versions of celebrated masterworks or noted exhibits in the annual Salons were produced in thousands for general distribution. Auguste Rodin released his works in variable quantities according to public response, although he gave undertakings to certain collectors, such as Antony Roux in 1891, to destroy the plaster original to ensure the unique value of a bronze cast. The process of production was formalized in 1900 in a sole agreement with the Alexis Rudier foundry in Paris. Thereafter Rodin's bronze sculptures bore the particular mark of the foundry, date of casting and, in cases, the number and limit of the edition inscribed in the surface.

In the 20th century artists employed new technologies to replicate their work in limited editions. César, for example, cast parts of the body, then used a pantograph to enlarge the scale of the original for various models in metal and plastic. In 1955 the term 'multiples' was used by Yaacov Agam and Jean Tinguely to describe the practice of producing series of art works in limited and non-limited editions. The idea was eventually implemented in 1962 with the release of strictly limited series of works, often miniature versions of typical examples of an artist's handwork. In the Pop art era of the 1960s artists experimented with a variety of industrial manufacturing techniques. Eduardo Paolozzi entered an artist–industry relationship with a foundry and pattern-makers, W. L. Shepherd of London, making sculptures to a prefabricated design. During a period of vigorously expanding markets in fashion and entertainment some artists held ambitions to distribute editions of objects and artefacts through retail networks, such as supermarket chains. Richard Hamilton made multiple vacuum-formed plastic replicas of the Solomon R. Guggenheim Museum, New York, which were sold in the museum's shop. Joseph Beuys released both multiple and limited editions of his work, which ranged from natural assemblages to sets of boxed recordings, considered as sculptures in their own right. The efforts of artists to reach a mass audience with works of specialized and intellectual appeal raised the dichotomy of the unique status of original art, protected by levels of high investment that ensured the successful continuity of a collector's market. For this reason, and the need to maintain individual reputations within the gallery and museum system, by the late 1970s the multiples strategy was largely abandoned.

### BIBLIOGRAPHY

*Multiples: The First Decade* (exh. cat., Philadelphia, PA, Mus. A., 1971)
*New Multiple Art* (exh. cat., London, Whitechapel A.G., 1971)
D. Britt, ed.: *Modern Art: Impressionism to Post-modernism* (London, 1989), pp. 334–5
J. A. Walker: *Glossary of Art, Architecture & Design since 1945* (London, 1992), no. 427

**Limning.** Term for the painting of portrait miniatures in watercolour, a technique that was popular from the 17th to the 19th century (*see* MINIATURE, §II). The term has also been applied to manuscript illumination, and in the USA self-taught naive portrait painters were described as limners until the early 19th century.

RUPERT FEATHERSTONE

**Limoges.** Capital city of the Haute-Vienne département in south central France and an important centre for the production of enamel and porcelain.

1. CENTRE OF ENAMEL PRODUCTION. During the early 12th century there was a distinct movement towards the production of champlevé enamelling on copper or bronze, which afforded larger areas to be decorated than was previously possible with gold cloisonné enamelling (*see* ENAMEL, §2(i)). By the mid-12th century Limoges workshops had become highly commercial, manufacturing enamelled goods in the Romanesque style for civil and religious purposes, and exporting them throughout Europe and beyond until the late 14th century (*see* GOTHIC, §VI and fig. 93). There was a demand for such items as reliquaries and shrines, which served as the 'canvas' for the superb enamel embellishments, and most church treasures included an ecclesiastical object enamelled in Limoges. Towards the end of the 13th century, however, there were signs that the manufacture was in decline. The craft of champlevé enamelling was brought to an end by the sacking of Limoges (1371) during the early stages of the Hundred Years War (1337–1453).

By 1470 painted enamels on copper were being made in Limoges, and by the early 16th century Limoges was again the main centre of enamel production. Metal divisions used in the earlier techniques were replaced by a network of drawn lines screening off areas for underpainting and subsequent application of colours. Nevertheless, the tradition that classified enamellers as goldsmiths continued. The enamels of this period are based on copper

plaques, which could be assembled in metal-framed sets to form polyptychs. The decoration on these early pieces was usually religious with stained glass as a major source of inspiration, both in subject-matter and style, which gave rise to a technique known as grisaille. This technique of underpainting, introduced *c.* 1535, is part of the Limoges school method.

Nardon PÉNICAUD was one of the earliest masters to exercise a style that contrasted dramatically with the vivid colours employed in the earlier champlevé period. Enamels painted in Limoges were dark and sombre, reflecting the pessimism prevalent during the Reformation. Late 15th-century enamellers included the Pénicaud family and an anonymous enameller or enamellers known as the Monvaërni. Paintings and prints by contemporary painters and engravers were frequently copied or adapted by enamellers, and many specially commissioned pieces bore family crests. Limoges enamels retained an almost exclusively religious character until the Italian Renaissance encouraged the portrayal of mythological compositions; pagan and Christian subjects were, however, also produced.

LÉONARD LIMOSIN excelled at enamelled portraits and in 1548 was appointed Emailleur du Roi by Henry II. More than 1000 enamels were produced in his workshop, including functional and decorative pieces (see ENAMEL, colour pl. IV, fig. 1). The Bishop of Limoges, Jean de Langeac, was Limosin's first patron and probably introduced him to the court of Francis I at Fontainebleau, where the craft of the Limoges enamellers won international recognition. The Limosin family occupied the same house in Rue Manigne, the enamellers' quarter in Limoges, for over a hundred years.

Pierre Raymond (1513–*c.* 1584) was a notable Limoges enameller who headed a workshop specializing in enamelled tableware mainly commissioned by wealthy German families. He is also known for his iconographical plaques, including a series of 16 illustrating the Life and Passion of Christ. His compositions are taken almost entirely from designs by 16th-century European engravers. During the 16th century three notable enamellers emerged from the Court family: Jean Court, *dit* Vigier (*b c.* 1545), Jean de Court (*fl* 1541–64) and the only known female Limoges enameller Suzanne de Court (see fig.), whose polychrome style achieved an interesting 'counter-reformation' in the early 17th century. During the same period Pierre Courteys (*b c.* 1520) executed large, decorative plaques and enamelled wares in the style of Pierre Raymond, but in a more vigorous and colourful manner. However, Courteys's two sons left Limoges to become painters and goldsmiths at court due to the decline in demand for Limoges painted enamels towards the end of the 16th century.

Limoges remained identified with Renaissance designs until the beginning of the 20th century, when enamellers responded to mainstream contemporary art. At the Exposition Internationale des Arts Décoratifs et Industriels Modernes in 1925 in Paris the work of such Limoges enamellers as Léon Jouhaud (1874–1950) and his contemporaries Paul Bonnard, Camille Fauré, Jean-Baptiste Issanchou, Alexandre Marty, Charles Peltant, Jules Sarlandie and Jeanne Soubourou was exhibited. In 1972 a first Biennale was held in Limoges to show the work of contemporary leading international enamellers, and this once again established Limoges as an important centre for enamelling. Limoges enamellers who have gained international reputations in the late 20th century include Christian Christel (*b* 1925), Alain Dubain (*b* 1951), Anny Dhelomme (*b c.* 1950), Dominique Gilbert (*b* 1953) and Michèle Gilbert (*b* 1955).

BIBLIOGRAPHY

P. Verdier: *Painted Enamels of the Renaissance* (Baltimore, 1967)
R. Pinkham: *Limoges Painted Enamels* (London, 1974)
P. Verdier: 'Limoges Painted Enamels of the Sixteenth and Seventeenth Centuries', *Enamels, Rugs and Silver in the Frick Collection*, New York, Frick cat., viii (New York, 1977), pp. 5–243
S. Benjamin: *Enamels* (Washington, DC, 1983)
M. Campbell: *Medieval Enamels* (London, 1983)
*L'Art de l'émail* (exh. cat., ed. M. Kiener; Limoges, Chapelle du Lycée Gay-Lussac, 1986)
*Emaux de Léon Jouhaud* (exh. cat., ed. B. Lachaniette; Limoges Dir. Rég. Affaires Cult. Limousin, 1988)
S. L. Caroselli: *The Painted Enamels of Limoges* (Los Angeles, 1993)
*Enamels of Limoges* (exh. cat., New York, Met., 1996)

G. H. BYROM

2. CENTRE OF PORCELAIN PRODUCTION. Kaolin (china clay) deposits were discovered at Saint-Yrieix, near Limoges, in 1765. In 1771 Joseph Massié, whose father André Massié (*d* 1763) had set up a faience factory in Limoges in 1736, went into partnership with Nicolas Fournérat, a chemist and member of the Académie des Sciences in Paris, and the merchants Pierre Grellet (*d* 1774) and Gabriel Grellet, producing hard-paste porcelain (e.g. bouillon cup and cover, *c.* 1771–3; Limoges, Mus. N. Adrien-Dubouché). The factory received the support of the Comte d'Artois and produced wares decorated mainly with naturalistic flowers. After financial difficulties, it was purchased by Louis XVI in 1784 for the production of plain white wares to be decorated at Sèvres. From this period Limoges became internationally famous, especially during the 19th century, for supplying increasingly refined white paste; the technical improvements were principally carried out by François Allaud (1739–99), a director of the Manufacture Royale between 1788 and 1791, and François Pouyat (1754–1835). The Limoges paste was sent to porcelain factories in Paris (*see* PARIS, §IV, 2) and the rest of France and exported throughout Europe. Decoration at the Manufacture Royale, which operated until 1792, was strongly influenced by Sèvres (e.g. *écuelle* and platter, *c.* 1788–93; Sèvres, Mus. N. Cér.).

Other important porcelain factories operating in Limoges during the 18th century were those of La Seynie and Baignol. La Seynie was founded in 1774 by Jean-Baptiste-Joseph du Gareau de la Seynie (1735–98), after china clay and china stone deposits were discovered on his land. The wares were noted for being extremely white and were decorated in a style that was influenced by Sèvres (e.g. sauceboat and platter; Limoges, Mus. N. Adrien-Dubouché). La Seynie was taken over in 1789 by Etienne Baignol (1750–1822), who had previously been first modeller at the Manufacture Royale. Baignol left in 1797 to start his own factory in the Couvent des Augustins, producing wares that reflected the current Neo-classical style in form and decoration (e.g. sugar bowl, cover and platter; Limoges, Mus. N. Adrien-Dubouché).

During the 19th century the number of factories in Limoges increased; many of them were associated with

Limoges tazza by Suzanne de Court showing *Melchizedek Welcoming Abraham*, diam. 255 mm, painted enamel, late 16th century (Oxford, Ashmolean Museum)

Parisian porcelain factories and decorating workshops. The Allauad family continued to produce useful wares and such ornamental vases as the Vases Medici. In 1858 the factory passed through marriage to Haviland Brothers & Co., the American firm of porcelain retailers established in Limoges in 1838. The Limoges branch was started by David Haviland (1814–79), who acted for the New York retailing business before he opened a decorating workshop in 1847 and produced porcelain from 1855. The firm continued in many forms, run by various members of the Haviland family, throughout the 19th and 20th centuries. From the beginning Haviland Brothers & Co. (1838–65) and Haviland & Co. (1864–1930) concentrated on producing domestic wares principally for the American market, even supplying the White House in Washington, DC, with services. They also produced more ornamental pieces and services, winning the gold medal at the 1853–4 Exhibition of the Industry of All Nations in New York and a silver medal at the 1867 Exposition Universelle in Paris, where they showed a 'Gothique' sugar bowl. Haviland & Co. started a decorating workshop in Auteuil (1873–82), run by Félix Bracquemond, in order to achieve more artistic production. Bracquemond was influenced by Japanese prints and East Asian ceramics. The designer Albert-Louis Dammouse (1848–1926) also worked at the Haviland workshop, as did Ernest Chaplet after 1875.

From the 18th century the firm of Pouyat (1837–1912) continued to be operated by members of the family of that name and became known for the moulded decoration and sculptural qualities of the brilliant, marble-like white wares. Louis Dammouse designed the 'Grains de riz' service of 1878, which was decorated with elaborate, pierced work filled with translucent enamel. Other notable

Limoges factories were the Tharaud Factory, which operated at intervals between 1822 and 1968 and was known in the 20th century for decoration using high-temperature colours; the Ruaud Factory (1829–69), which produced blue-and-white as well as ornamental wares; and the Ardent Factory (1854–90), which specialized in biscuit porcelain and employed the sculptor Albert-Ernest Carrier-Belleuse. The sculptor Edouard Marcel Sandoz, the painter and engraver Jean Dufy (1888–1964) and painter Georges de Feure (1868–1943) were among the principal artists and designers who worked for a number of Limoges factories producing Art Deco style work.

BIBLIOGRAPHY

*Cah. Cer., Verre & A. Feu*, xiii (1959) [whole issue]
J. d'Albis and C. Romanet: *La Porcelaine de Limoges* (Paris, 1980)

BET MCLEOD

**Limosin** [Limousin], **Léonard** (*b* Limoges, *c.* 1505; *d* Limoges, 1575/7). French enameller, etcher, painter and miniature painter. He was the best-known enameller of Renaissance France and may have learnt that trade in the Pécinaud workshop in Limoges. Encouraged by the Bishop of Limoges, Jean de Langeac, who probably put him in touch with the court of Francis I, Limosin produced painted enamels on copper in all forms, including plates and plaques with mythological and religious subjects, tableware and caskets. His chief speciality was the interpretation in enamels of portrait drawings by artists of the school of Jean and François Clouet, such as that of *Anne de Montmorency* (Paris, Louvre; see ENAMEL, colour pl. IV, fig. 1).

Limosin's earliest enamels were inspired by German engravings; in 1532 he copied Albrecht Dürer's *Small Passion* series (Paris, Mus. Cluny). From 1535, however, he turned more towards Italian art and that of the FONTAINEBLEAU SCHOOL, using, for instance, motifs from Raphael's *Legend of Psyche*, engraved by the Master of the Die, for a large plate (Paris, priv. col., see Lavedan, p. 85) enamelled with the *Feast of the Gods*, which was probably made for Anne de Montmorency. It is possible that Limosin went to Fontainebleau and that he tried his hand at printmaking there; eight etchings by him are known (Zerner, nos 1–8), all on the theme of the *Life of Christ* and all signed either with his full name or with the initials L.L. (e.g. Paris, Bib. N.; Brussels, Bib. Royale Albert 1er). Five are dated 1544, and their unity of style as well as theme suggests that they are all of the same period. While *Christ Dismissed by Herod* (Z 7) is Limosin's own invention, the *Resurrection* (Z 8) is a reworking of a composition by Rosso Fiorentino. These works, excessively angular in form and rather clumsily extravagant, were little more than an experiment; in 1557 they provided Limosin with a model for 12 enamelled plaques illustrating the *Passion* (Paris, Mus. Cluny).

In 1545 Francis I commissioned Limosin to produce a suite of 12 large enamelled plaques of the *Apostles* (Chartres, Mus. B.-A.), using painted models by Michel Rochetel (*fl* 1540s) after designs by Francesco Primaticcio. In 1548 he was appointed Valet de Chambre and Emailleur du Roi, and in 1553 he received a commission from Henry II for two enamel altarpieces (Paris, Louvre), more than 1 m in height and representing the *Crucifixion* and the *Resurrection* for the Sainte-Chapelle, Paris. These are perhaps his most ambitious and best-known works. He was also a somewhat mediocre painter, as may be seen from his *Incredulity of St Thomas* (Limoges, Mus. Mun.), which is signed and dated 1551. Limosin also assisted in the decorations for Charles IX's and Catherine de' Medici's entry into Bordeaux in 1564. He stayed in Limoges for irregular periods and became a consul there in 1572. Though a mediocre draughtsman and engraver, Limosin was an original enameller by virtue of his choice of subjects, the skill of his compositions and his sense of colour. Even if the scale of production in his workshop (more than 1000 pieces between 1533 and 1574) sometimes detracted from the quality of his output, the success of this aspect of his career attests to the importance of painted enamels in the diffusion of the Renaissance style in France.

BIBLIOGRAPHY

L. Bourdery: *Léonard Limosin et son oeuvre* (Limoges, 1895)
L. Bourdery and E. Lachenaud: *Léonard Limosin: Peintre de portraits* (Paris, 1897)
A. Demartial: 'Léonard Limosin: Emailleur et graveur', *Rev. A. Chrét.*, lxii (1912), pp. 18–28
P. Lavedan: *Léonard Limosin et les émailleurs français* (Paris, 1913)
J. Adhémar: *Inventaire du fond français: Graveurs du seizième siècle*, Paris, Bib. N., Cab. Est. cat., ii (Paris, 1938), pp. 1–3
O. Raggio: 'Decorative Portraits by Léonard Limousin', *Bull. Met.*, x (1951), pp. 96–105
H. Zerner: *Ecole de Fontainebleau: Gravures* (Paris, 1969) [z]
*L'Ecole de Fontainebleau* (exh. cat., Paris, Grand Pal., 1972), pp. 291, 444–7

MARIANNE GRIVEL

**Lin, Maya** (*b* Athens, OH, 5 Oct 1959). American sculptor and architect. She studied at Yale University (1977–81), New Haven, CT, graduating with an MFA in Architecture. Her best-known work is the Vietnam Veterans' Memorial (1981–83) on the National Mall in Washington, DC. While she was still a student (in 1981), her design was selected from 1421 final entries to a competition initiated by the Vietnam Veterans' Memorial Fund for a memorial to be built in the capital. Its purpose was to commemorate those who fought and died in the War and to help reconcile some of the differences that the War had provoked among the American public, government leaders and war veterans. Lin's design created a new paradigm for memorials. The monument both serves its complex and particular purpose and re-evaluates completely the traditional form of the public monument. It is a low V-shaped black granite wall partially submerged in the manner of ancient burial sites; the names of all those who died or went missing are inscribed on it. Its reflective surface means that those who view it and read the roll-call of names become immediate participants in the experience of remembering the dead. Names of servicemen and women are recorded in the order in which they perished, from 1959–1975, giving the memorial a sense of real time in history. The viewer recognizes the singularity of each name, while also having a clear sense of the huge number of names making up the whole list. The memorial's Minimalist design aroused controversy and provoked profound feelings about grief and the Vietnam War in general. On 11 Nov 1984 a more traditional memorial by Frederick Hart, showing three American servicemen, was dedicated near by. Lin also designed the Civil Rights Memorial, a granite fountain, in Montgomery, AL, dedicated in November 1989, and in 1991 worked on an outdoor sculpture for Yale University, New Haven, CT, honouring the women of that institution.

WRITINGS
'On Nationality: 13 Artists', *A. America*, lxxix (1991), pp. 127–8

BIBLIOGRAPHY
S. N. Blum: 'The National Vietnam War Memorial', *Arts* [New York], lix (1984), pp. 124–8

□

**Lin'an.** *See* HANGZHOU.

**Linar, Rochus Quirinus**, Graf zu. *See* LYNAR, ROCHUS QUIRINUS.

**Linard, Jacques** (*b c.* 1600; *d* Paris, 1645). French painter. He was in Paris by 1626, and his first securely attributed still-life work is dated the following year. He lived in the Saint-Germain-des-Prés district, where a number of French still-life painters such as Louise Moillon and Lubin Baugin worked alongside Flemish artists specializing in this genre. In 1631 he was created Peintre et Valet de Chambre du Roi, a post that guaranteed him a degree of financial independence. Linard's works of 1627–44 were mainly of fruit and flowers; with Louise Moillon, however, he was among the first French artists to combine successfully the female form with still-life elements, as, for example, in *Woman with Flowers* and *Woman with Fruit* (both Paris, priv. col., see Faré, 1974, pp. 22–3). A painting such as *Basket of Flowers* (Paris, Louvre) owes something to Flemish prototypes in the anachronistic grouping of flowers that span several months. Patiently recording the flowers as they bloomed, and working on the picture from a series of drawings and sketches, Linard demonstrated his commitment to working from nature. However, this work also has a distinctively French elegance and economy of composition.

The works of Linard's maturity are more allegorical. The *Five Senses* (1638; Strasbourg, Mus. B.-A.) depicts a book of music (hearing); a Chinese bowl full of apples, grapes and a fig (taste); a vase of roses (smell); a set of playing-cards and a purse of coins (touch); and a small mirror and a landscape painting (sight). The painting is also a *memento mori*—the passing of time is symbolized by perishable objects (the fruit and flowers) and the transience of worldly goods by the purse of money. A remarkable delicacy of execution coupled with a well-planned composition led Georges de Scudéry to link Linard with his contemporary still-life painters Moillon and Pierre Boucle, whom he thought not unworthy of comparison with Michelangelo, Veronese and Titian.

BIBLIOGRAPHY
M. Faré: *La Nature morte en France* (Geneva, 1962)
J. Lauts: *Stilleben alter Meister, II: Franzosen* (Karlsruhe, 1970)
M. Faré: *Le Grand Siècle de la nature morte en France* (Fribourg, 1974)
*La Peinture française du XVIIe siècle dans les collections américaines* (exh. cat. by P. Rosenberg, Paris, Grand Pal.; New York, Met.; Chicago, IL, A. Inst.; 1982)

LESLEY STEVENSON

**Linati (de Prevost), Claudio** (*b* Parma, 1790; *d* Tampico, 11 Dec 1832). Italian lithographer, active in Mexico. In 1809 he completed his studies in Paris but, after returning to Italy, he was sentenced to death in 1824 for revolutionary activities. He went to Mexico with his colleague Gaspar Franchini in 1825, apparently attracted by the idea of putting his revolutionary ideas into practice. He took a lithographic press with him and set up the first lithographic workshop in Mexico City. In addition to teaching, he printed a weekly periodical, *El Iris,* from February to August 1826, featuring lithographs of fashion models and portraits of such heroes of Mexican independence as Miguel Hidalgo y Costilla. Under this innocent guise, that of printers of a publication intended for women, he and his collaborators gave expression to political comment that led to the periodical's closure, and in September 1826 he was forced to leave Mexico. In 1828 in Brussels he published *Costumes civils, militaires et religieux du Mexique,* one of the first albums to depict different types of Mexicans in costume.

PRINTS
*Costumes civils, militaires et religieux du Mexique* (Brussels, 1828)

BIBLIOGRAPHY
L. M. Schneider, ed.: *'El Iris': Periódico crítico literario por Linati, Galli y Heredia: Primera revista literaria del México independiente*, intro. by C. Ruiz Castañeda, 2 vols (Mexico City, 1826/R 1986)
J. Fernández: *Claudio Linati: Trajes civiles, militares y religiosos de México*, intro. by M. Toussaint (Mexico City, 1956)

MÓNICA MARTÍ COTARELO

**Linck, Jean-Antoine** (*b* Geneva, 14 Dec 1766; *d* Geneva, 20 Sept 1843). Swiss painter and printmaker. He was trained by his father, the engraver Johann Konrad Linck (1735–95). Jean-Antoine used a method of engraving perfected in 1766 by Johann Ludwig Aberli. The lines of the drawing were engraved (with a soft cutting edge) on to a copper plate; the print thus obtained was then coloured by hand. Engravings such as *View of the Waterfall at Pissevache* (Geneva, Mus. Ethnog.) or *View of the Waterfall at Arpenaz* (Annecy, Paul Payot priv. col.) had a similar effect to that of a watercolour. In 1789 Linck took part in the first exhibition of painting and sculpture in Geneva, and the gouaches that he showed, for example *View of Nant d'Arpennaz*, immediately established his reputation. He dedicated himself from that time solely to landscape painting, particularly to mountain landscapes. His preferred technique was gouache; he made up his own colours and often used a fig-juice fixative of his own invention. In 1802 he married Jeanne-Pernette Bouvier, whose family had considerable influence and successfully advanced his work. Among Linck's distinguished patrons were the Empress Josephine Bonaparte (who bought his gouaches for the Château de Malmaison, near Paris), Lucien Bonaparte, Joseph Fesch and Catherine II, Empress of Russia.

In 1809 Linck bought a small estate near Geneva where he installed his studio. As the demand for his gouaches, watercolours and drawings was very great, his brother Jean-Philippe Linck (1770–1812) and his friend Carl Hackert (1740–96) helped him to satisfy popular demand by producing prints of them. Linck showed his works at exhibitions in Geneva in 1816, 1820, 1823 and 1826; in 1820 he was accepted as a member of the Société des Arts. He produced a considerable body of work; his major innovation was a new type of view influenced by the prints of geologists such as Horace Bénédicte de Saussure, in which he depicted the mountains at close quarters from high vantage points, as in *Mont Blanc Seen from the Summit of the Brévert* (Geneva, Mus. A. & Hist.).

BIBLIOGRAPHY

H. Friederich: 'Les Linck', *Page A*. (Jan 1925), pp. 45–56
M. Sandoz: 'Essai sur l'évolution du paysage de montagne consécutive à la "découverte" des "glacières" du Faucigny du milieu du dix-huitième au milieu du dix-neuvième siècle', *Genava*, n. s., xix (1971), pp. 214–29
B. Weber, ed.: *Die Alpen in der Malerei* (Rosenheim, 1981)
*Jean-Antoine Linck, peintre genevois, paysages de Savoie au XVIIIe siècle* (exh. cat., Annecy, Conserv. A. & Hist. Haute-Savoie, 1990)

ANNE PASTORI ZUMBACH

**Lincoln** [Lat. Lindum]. English city, county town of Lincolnshire and the seat of a bishopric since 1070. It is situated at the Witham Gap, a natural break in the Jurassic limestone ridge known locally as Lincoln Edge. The city was strategically important in Roman times as it straddles Ermine Street, the major north–south Roman road. From the top of the hill on which it partly sits the city commands a view over the valley of the River Witham and the large expanse of land between the River Trent and Lincoln Edge; both rivers are navigable and are linked by a canal, the Foss Dyke, which is thought to date back to the Roman period and was certainly in existence by the early 12th century.

Lincoln was probably not a major pre-Roman settlement, despite bearing a British name derived from the early name for Brayford Pool, a natural lake that, together with the River Witham and the Foss Dyke, still dominates the topography of the city. Before the 19th century Lincoln could be divided into four main areas: the upper city, the Bail, which was originally a Roman fortress, then became a colonia and subsequently the location of the cathedral, castle and castle bailey; the lower city, an undefended extension of the colonia, which was walled in the late 2nd century AD or the early 3rd and became the commercial heart of the city in the 10th century; Wigford, an extensive ribbon development along Ermine Street south of the Witham; and the suburbs of Newport (to the north), Newland (to the west of the lower city), Butwerk (to the east of the lower city) and the Close (to the east of the upper city).

1. History and urban development. 2. Cathedral.

1. HISTORY AND URBAN DEVELOPMENT. The colonia was founded by *c.* AD 96 using the walls and principal streets of the legionary fortress, which appears to have been built in the reign of Nero (*reg* AD 54–68). By the early 2nd century AD the walls had been rebuilt in stone, mainly the local limestone, which is the source for most of the building stone used in the city. A stone forum–basilica complex had been built in the centre of the old fortress and occupation had extended outside the walls, especially to the south on the site of the lower city and across the Witham in Wigford. Late in the 2nd century, or early in the 3rd, a stone wall and earth rampart was built around the lower city suburb. At about the same time stone interval towers were added to the original colonia defences; the foundations of one such tower have been preserved at East Bight. In the 4th century Lincoln became one of the four provincial capitals of Britannia and may then have

had a bishopric that disappeared in the Anglo-Saxon invasions. The town defences were renovated during the 4th century, and occupation of some sort continued into the early 5th. The principal surviving monuments of Roman Lincoln are its gates, of which Newport Arch, the north gate of the original colonia, is still in use, and parts of the forum–basilica complex. The latter includes part of the north wall of the basilica, known as the Mint Wall, the foundations of the east range of the forum, excavated in 1984, and parts of the eastern roadside colonnade. The main street in the upper city, Bailgate, veers away from the Roman alignment, and the line of the colonnade is marked by stones set in the middle of the modern street.

By the 7th century AD Lincoln was again an important centre in the Anglo-Saxon kingdom of Lindsey. The only evidence for activity within the area at this time comes from the excavation of St Paul-in-the-Bail church, which revealed what may be a late Roman or British timber church, consisting of an aisle-less nave and semicircular apse, which was replaced by a Christian inhumation cemetery. A late cist grave, subsequently robbed, was surrounded by a rectangular timber, later stone, structure and accompanied by an enamelled hanging bowl, probably of early 7th-century date, now in the cathedral treasury.

In the late 9th century Lincoln became one of the Five Boroughs of the Danelaw, and probably by *c.* 900 new streets had been laid out, along which timber buildings were erected. During the later 10th century, and especially in the 11th, numerous churches were built. At least one, St Mark's, Wigford, was built first in timber but rebuilt in stone. Most of the 47 medieval churches have been demolished or entirely rebuilt. Two mid- to late 11th-century western towers survive, at St Mary-le-Wigford and St Peter-at-Gowts, while two further examples are known from excavations at St Mark's and St Peter Stanthaket (at the north end of Hungate).

Two years after the Norman Conquest of 1066 the castle was erected in the south-west corner of the upper city. The Roman west gate was buried under its rampart; it was exposed in 1836 but collapsed soon after. Little remains of the medieval castle except for the Norman west gate, the later east gate, two mottes on which stand the Lucy Tower and the Observatory, both of which contain much renovated medieval masonry, and the curtain wall. When it became expedient to shift the centre of the midland diocese northwards from Dorchester-on-Thames, the memory of the Roman bishopric seems to have surfaced, and the see was established at Lincoln in 1070 under the Norman bishop Remigius (*d* 1092). Building work for the new cathedral started soon after that of the castle, in 1073. The cathedral (*see* §2(i) below) and its associated buildings originally occupied the whole of the south-east quarter of the upper city. Immediately south of the cathedral stands the remains of the Bishop's Palace, which was begun around the middle of the 12th century, although the earliest surviving structure is the early 13th-century east hall. Renovations by Bishop Alnwick (1436–49) included modification to the west hall, a new north range and the Alnwick Tower. Two late 12th-century stone houses survive in the lower city: Jews House in the Strait, and the Norman House at the corner of Christ's Hospital Terrace and Steep Hill. Popular mythology states that these houses belonged to the Jewish community, who needed stone houses owing to the risk of arson that they faced; but, although both houses lie in the centre of the medieval Jewry and were probably built for Jews, excavation has shown that similar stone houses were quite common in the late 12th and 13th centuries.

During the 13th century the suburb outside and to the south-east of the upper city's east gate came into the hands of the Dean and Chapter: many of the buildings within the close, for example Deloraine Court and the Cantilupe Chantry, have substantial medieval remains. In the late 13th century and the 14th this suburb was enclosed within the Close Wall. The wall incorporated an earlier hall, now known as the Priory, and two of the Close Wall turrets, and two gates, the Pottergate arch and Exchequergate, survive. At the same time work started on the Vicars Court, built for the Vicars Choral south-east of the cathedral. The south and west ranges are the earliest surviving parts of the complex, including two large garderobe blocks, acting as buttresses on the south side. Vicars Court was completed in the 15th century, the date of the main gateway and the 'Tithe Barn', which was probably originally a service range, incorporating storerooms and the kitchen.

In the early 13th century the city council met in a hall in the south-east corner of the lower city. This hall was subsequently given to the Franciscans: the sole surviving building from their friary now houses the City and County Museum. As compensation the council was given use of a chamber above the Stonebow, the southern gateway to the lower city. The present structure, though much restored, dates to the 16th century. A much larger stone hall on the east side of the High Street in Wigford once held St Mary's Guild, a socio-religious guild to which belonged the élite of medieval Lincoln. The hall (see fig. 1), constructed in the mid-12th century directly on to the metalled surface of Ermine Street, is the only physical reminder of Wigford's prominence in the Middle Ages. Many wealthy Lincolnshire families had houses there, but the association of the suburb in popular legend with John of Gaunt, Duke of Lancaster, apparently has no validity. The northern range of St Mary's Guildhall, known alternatively as John of Gaunt's Stables and the Norman House, has been dated to the 16th or 17th century. A late 14th-century oriel window, now in the east gateway of the castle, originally came from the so-called John of Gaunt's House (destr.), which used to stand opposite St Mary's Guildhall.

Signs of decline are detectable in Lincoln as early as the mid-13th century, when the city seems to have ceased to be an international port and its merchants gradually shifted their interests to Boston at the mouth of the Witham. Lincoln also lost its position on the main route north from London, following the development of the alternative route diverting at Newark through Doncaster to York. By the mid-14th century several parishes are recorded as having fewer than ten parishioners. The suburbs of Butwerk and Newland were deserted during the 14th and 15th centuries, as were some intra-mural streets such as Beaumont Fee, just inside the western defences. Despite this decline, the city continued to be an important centre owing to the presence of the cathedral and the castle, which was the administrative centre for the shire. A theme

1. Lincoln, St Mary's Guildhall, Wigford, *c.* 1150–70

running through the later medieval history of Lincoln is the conflict between the city, the bail and the close, all three of which were vying to control a dwindling amount of trade. Seventeenth-century Lincoln has been described as 'a market town existing in the ruins of a city' and by the early 18th Lincoln consisted essentially of a single street running north from St Botolph's church to the Newport suburb.

The development of Brayford Pool as an inland port in the late 18th century led to economic revival and some of the churches were rebuilt at this period. The coming of the railways in the 1840s was a further factor in the moderate growth experienced by the city in the 19th century, especially from the 1880s to *c.* 1900.

BIBLIOGRAPHY

J. W. F. Hill: *Medieval Lincoln* (Cambridge, 1948)
——: *Tudor and Stuart Lincoln* (Cambridge, 1956)
——: *Georgian Lincoln* (Cambridge, 1966)
——: *Victorian Lincoln* (Cambridge, 1974)
H. Chapman and others: *Excavations at the Bishop's Palace, Lincoln, 1968–72*, Society for Lincolnshire History and Archaeology, Occasional Papers, i (Sleaford, 1975)
M. J. Jones and others: *The Defences of the Upper Roman Enclosure*, Archaeology of Lincoln, vii/1 (London, 1980)
B. J. J. Gilmour and D. A. Stocker: *St Mark's Church and Cemetery*, Lincoln Archaeological Trust Monographs, xiii/1 (London, 1986)
S. Jones and others: *Survey of Ancient Houses in Lincoln*, Lincoln Civic Trust, 3 vols (Lincoln, 1989–90)
D. M. Short: *A Bibliography of Printed Items Relating to the City of Lincoln*, Lincoln Record Society, lxxix (Woodbridge, 1990)
D. A. Stocker: *St Mary's Guildhall: The Archeology of Lincoln* (Lincoln, 1991)
ALAN VINCE

2. CATHEDRAL.

(i) Architecture. (ii) Sculpture. (iii) Stained glass.

*(i) Architecture.*

*(a) Anglo-Norman Cathedral.* The first medieval cathedral, dedicated to St Mary and built between 1073 and 1092, was the work of Bishop Remigius (*d* 1092). It was built of local limestone akin to Barnack. Traces of the plan have been recovered and suggest that the east end and

transept were modelled on Archbishop Lanfranc's cathedral at Canterbury (*see* CANTERBURY, §III, 1); this, however, was not the model for the surviving portion. Embedded in the present west façade are three colossal arches with a simple type of machicolation, both forms with specifically Roman connotations. It is uncertain whether they also had serious military purposes: other explanations are possible, among them the desire to draw attention to the Roman origins of the bishopric.

During the 12th century Remigius's cathedral was extensively remodelled. According to Gerald of Wales, Bishop Alexander (1123–48) was 'the first to give the cathedral a stone roof', that is, a vault. Traces of it survive between the western towers. The vaulting might have been built either after a fire *c.* 1123, or after the sack following the Battle of Lincoln in 1141. Modern opinion generally favours the later date; but Gerald, who was in a position to know, implies the earlier. If he was right, Lincoln probably preceded Durham Cathedral (*see* DURHAM, §1(i)) in being the first English cathedral to be completely vaulted. Other 12th-century works, most of which survive, included the lower parts of the western towers, its sculptured portals and a frieze of reliefs across the façade (*see* §(ii)(a) below).

*(b) St Hugh's choir, the nave and chapter house.* In 1185 part of the Romanesque cathedral collapsed, and the present church was created in a series of campaigns. It now comprises the east (Angel) choir of five bays (*see* §(c) below) and the west (St Hugh's) choir of four bays, separated by an eastern transept. The main transept, west of St Hugh's choir, leads to the seven-bay nave. The internal length is 147 m. All the building campaigns were characterized by extravagance and innovations, and the first bears the mark of an architect of genius. He was responsible for St Hugh's choir, which takes its name from Hugh of Avalon (*d* 1200), who was Bishop when the rebuilding began in 1192. The model was the recently completed third choir of Canterbury Cathedral (*see* CANTERBURY, §III, 1): it had the same kind of three-storey elevation, complex structural and buttressing system, and clerestory wall passage. Mannerisms were freely imposed on both plan and elevation, however, and, although these idiosyncrasies were never copied elsewhere, they gave English Gothic a distinctive twist and defined the terms within which it was practised for most of the 13th century.

St Hugh's choir (*see* GOTHIC, fig. 8) terminated, not in a straightforward polygon, but in a wedge-shaped apse, organized around an octagon with one of its corners on the main axis. This curiosity disappeared when the Angel choir was built, but enough traces survive under the pavement for its geometry to be elucidated. The second major mannerism was in the vaults, which survive in the choir itself. Instead of arches intersecting one another at a single keystone in the centre of each bay, these vaults are made up of separate ribs that meet at oblique angles at two keystones. Each keystone has three ribs arranged asymmetrically, as well as a ridge-rib, the discords being resolved within each pair. In a notable departure from Canterbury, where sexpartite vaults are set over double bays, all the vaults in both transepts are sexpartite over single bays. The evidence suggests that sexpartite vaults

were intended to be used throughout the eastern limb, and that the modification was introduced in the main part of the building during the course of construction. The intention may have been to improve the lighting of St Hugh's choir, which it does by making room for a third lancet in each bay of the clerestory, or to meet the exigencies of the peculiar apse, which was incompatible with ordinary vault patterns.

The purpose of the choir plan was to provide a spacious choir for the canons and to include a large chapel at the east end, which, on the analogy of Canterbury, should have been intended for a reliquary. In due course St Hugh himself came to be buried in this part of the cathedral; but in 1192 Hugh was still only a bishop, and presumably he and the Chapter had someone else in mind. The most likely candidate was the founder, Remigius, whose saintly life and alleged miracles were being written by Gerald of Wales at the time. In the event Remigius was never canonized, and within 60 years the cult of St Hugh had reached such a pitch that the apse was swept away and replaced by the Angel choir. The imaginative touch, borrowed from actual reliquaries, of evoking busts of angels out of the double arcading along the choir aisle walls, is a reminder that the reliquary function was there from the start. Although St Hugh's choir was in many ways an experimental structure, it admirably fulfilled its

2. Lincoln Cathedral, north side of the nave, *c.* 1220–*c.* 1237

3. Lincoln Cathedral, chapter house looking east through the vestibule, c. 1220–50

primary function of providing a grand setting for cult and liturgy. Shafts of ornamental marble, much of it from the Alwalton quarry near Peterborough, were lavishly used to enhance the opulence. The choir was meant to make a sharp contrast with the Romanesque nave; and even the main transept, which was laid out at the same time with a two-storey GALILEE porch off the south arm, was built in a distinctly different style.

The decisive event in the evolution of the Gothic cathedral was the extension of operations to the nave. The decision to rebuild it must have been taken around 1220, the year Bishop Hugh was canonized, although his cult, spontaneous and popular with the laity, had flourished since his death. It offered the prospect of turning the cathedral into a pilgrimage church, and the immediate consequence was the renewal of the nave, the laity's part of the cathedral, and the reversal of all the presuppositions that had guided the work so far.

The nave (see fig. 2) was altogether grander than the eastern limb. It occupied the same site as the Romanesque nave, but instead of ten bays there were only seven. These Gothic bays, c. 8 m, are among the longest ever built. The section was designed ad quadratum, whereas the choir was ad triangulum. The elevation, in three stages that roughly correspond to St Hugh's choir, is loftier, more spacious and more ornate. Advantage was taken of the enlarged scale to fulfil and intensify all the experimental tendencies of the earlier work. This was particularly true of the vaults.

There are signs in the south gallery that the nave, like the transepts, was originally intended to have sexpartite vaults over single bays. If this intention had been carried out, the 'crazy vaults' of St Hugh's choir would have been no more than a pragmatic oddity, but in the end the designer of the nave took the 'crazy vaults' as his starting point. There are now three keystones in each bay along the ridge, and two more in subsidiary positions at the sides, with seven ribs springing from each *tas-de-charge* between the bays. These are veritable, if incomplete, cones and opened the way to a whole range of further developments.

On either side of the nave at the west end are two spacious chapels: the Morning Chapel (north) and the Consistory Court (south; formerly the chapel of St Giles), which have the effect of turning the west front into an extended screen. In the Morning Chapel there is a completely free-standing cone of eight ribs, which anticipates the magnificent cone with twenty ribs that is the principal feature of the chapter house (begun c. 1220; see fig. 3). Conversely, the ribs in the Consistory Court are no more than a pattern on the surface of the vault, which is in fact part of a dome. These experiments with vaults were emancipating: not only do they anticipate many of the visual effects of later Gothic, but they imply an intuitive grasp of the behaviour of shell structures (*see* MASONRY, §III, 3(iii)), allowing Late Gothic architects to get away from the French tendency to think of vaults in terms of arches. In this sense Lincoln Cathedral was of European significance. At home, however, the aesthetics probably left a deeper impression than the structural theory. The uniform density of pattern appealed to English taste. It was achieved largely by means of shafts, ribs and mouldings, which required great resources of skilled and unskilled labour and were prodigal with expensive materials (for further discussion *see* EARLY ENGLISH).

*(c) The Angel choir.* The nave must have been finished before the central tower collapsed (1237 or 1239). The new tower has close stylistic links with the west front. Shortly afterwards attention returned to the east end. Although a reliquary chapel had featured in the 1192 design, the arrangements were unable to cope with the numbers of visitors seeking access to St Hugh's tomb, and the Chapter's privacy and seclusion were threatened. By the 1250s they decided to replace the existing east end with a proper setting for a major saint, one that would at the same time leave them in peace.

Although it had to match the smaller dimensions of St Hugh's choir, the Angel choir is the architectural climax of the cathedral. It is a rectangular five-bay extension of the main body of the church. All the decorative resources of the nave are present, if anything concentrated by the reduced scale. In addition there are the carved angels in the spandrels of the triforium, from which the choir derives its name, and the geometric bar tracery, which not only fills the windows but is repeated as a free-standing screen on the inner plane of the clerestory wall. This culminates in the huge eight-light composition occupying the whole east wall, the earliest and largest surviving window of its type in England. On the west front there is the frame of an earlier window, which this was no doubt intended to surpass. For pilgrims to the shrine there was a special entrance on the south side, the Judgement portal, and a discreet exit opposite. The design of the Angel choir managed to reconcile with effortless ease every type of ornament currently available. It represents the end of a tradition as well as its high point.

In 1280, when the Angel choir was consecrated, the cathedral was substantially complete, and the pace of building work slackened. Many of the subsequent additions did not materially alter the building's character; these include the cloister, the choir screen, the flowing traceried rose window (the Bishop's Eye) in the south-west transept and furnishings at the east end, including the tombs, chantries and choir-stalls (*see* CHOIR-STALLS, fig. 1). The three towers were another matter. They were all additional storeys to existing towers, the central one dating from 1306 and the two western towers from the third quarter of the 14th century. In accordance with the prevailing fashion in later medieval England, they turned a building that had hitherto been long and low into one with emphatic vertical accents. Originally all three were surmounted by spires (that on the central tower allegedly rising more than 150 m), but these had to be dismantled in 1548 and 1807. The south-west tower was restored by W. H. Barlow in 1875–7.

### BIBLIOGRAPHY

Gerald of Wales: *Opera* (12th century); ed. J. F. Dimock, Rolls Ser., xxi (1877), vii, p. 33

E. Venables: 'Some Account of the Recent Discovery of the Foundations of the Eastern Termination of Lincoln Minster as Erected by St Hugh', *Archaeol. J.*, xliv (1887), pp. 194–202

J. Bilson: 'Lincoln Cathedral: The New Reading', *RIBA J.*, n. s. 2, xviii/13 (1911), pp. 464–75, 551–5

——: 'The Plan of the First Cathedral Church of Lincoln', *Archaeologia*, lxii (1911), pp. 543–64

F. Saxl: 'Lincoln Cathedral: The Eleventh-century Design for the West Front', *Archaeol. J.*, ciii (1946), pp. 106–18

P. Frankl: 'The "Crazy" Vaults of Lincoln Cathedral', *A. Bull.*, xxxv (1953), pp. 95–108

F. Nordström: 'Peterborough, Lincoln and the Science of Robert Grosseteste: A Study in Thirteenth-century Architecture and Iconography', *A. Bull.*, xxxvii/4 (1955), pp. 241–72

P. Frankl: 'Lincoln Cathedral', *A. Bull.*, xliv/1 (1962), pp. 29–37

*British Archaeological Association Conference Transactions: Medieval Art and Architecture at Lincoln Cathedral: Lincoln, 1982*

PETER KIDSON

*(ii) Sculpture.* There are two main programmes of sculpture at Lincoln Cathedral: the two phases of the west façade and the Judgement portal and interior sculptures of the Angel choir. The tombs and the wooden bosses of the cloister are also noteworthy.

*(a) West façade.* The west façade is the piecemeal result of the building campaigns of bishops Remigius, from *c.* 1075, and Alexander, after the fire of 1141. The sculpture of the first phase is austere, limited to simple geometric ornament and rudimentary Corinthian capitals of the type current in 11th-century Normandy, perhaps reflecting Remigius's time as a monk of Fécamp Abbey. Bishop Alexander was a nephew of the powerful Bishop Roger of Salisbury and an active and astute patron. He provided the three richly sculpted doorways and large-scale narrative frieze. The doorways are encrusted with bands of geometric ornament. The large central portal has six orders, the flanking side doorways four. All were heavily restored by

J. C. Buckler (1770–1851), who appears to have based his restoration on original pieces that had been removed by his predecessor, JAMES ESSEX. The side doorways have chevron ornament, beakhead and, on the north, a keeled moulding flanked by dogtooth ornament. All three doorways have large label stops in the form of dragon heads. All these features are typically Anglo-Norman. Similarly bold geometric ornament was used across the country, although particularly close stylistic connections have been observed with the castles and churches erected by Roger of Salisbury. Most of the capitals are scallop-shaped, but some on the north door have refined acanthus, for which parallels can be found in the Ile-de-France. The supple coils of foliage inhabited by small, nude figures on the columns of the central portal are so similar to a shaft from Saint-Denis Abbey (now Paris, Mus. Cluny) that they may be a direct imitation. This relationship is confirmed by Zarnecki's discovery that the central doorway was originally fitted with a pair of column statues. As the first use of column statues was at Saint-Denis (1140), the west front of Lincoln manifests an early interest in contemporary French developments.

The monumental narrative frieze is set high on the façade. Old Testament scenes are represented on the south side of the main doorway, New Testament on the north side. The Old Testament scenes are: the *Expulsion*, *Adam and Cain Receiving Seeds from the Hand of God*, the *Birth of Abel* and *Eve Spinning*, *God Speaking to Noah*, *Noah Building the Ark*, *Daniel in the Lions' Den*, *Noah and his Family Leaving the Ark* and *God's Covenant with Noah*. The New Testament scenes are: *Dives and Lazarus*, the *Death of Dives and of Lazarus* (see fig. 4), the *Soul of Lazarus in Abraham's Bosom*, the *Blessed in Heaven*, the *Harrowing of Hell* and the *Torments of the Damned*. One

4. Lincoln Cathedral, west front, detail of the *Death of Dives and of Lazarus*, 1140s

unfinished panel showing the *Deluge* was set inside the south-west tower. When during the 13th century the large window was inserted in the middle of the façade, various carvings contemporary with the frieze were displaced, including part of a *Jesse Tree*, the figure of *Christ in Majesty* and a figure of *St Paul*. It was presumably also at this time that the plaque with *Daniel in the Lions' Den* was moved to its current position as part of the narrative frieze. At least two sculptors were involved. All the Old Testament scenes are by a single artist, but the group of the *Blessed in Heaven* and the *Torments of the Damned* are by a different craftsman, whose forms are more deeply modelled and more dynamic. The limbs of some of the nude figures in the Hell scene are carved nearly in the round; they are anatomically more correct than the doll-like figures of the Old Testament scenes. Yet despite the involvement of two sculptors, the panels form a unified group; the figures are set against plain backgrounds in compositions that appear crowded even where there are only two figures.

The disposition of the sculpture on the Lincoln façade is exceptional in England, where narrative carving was usually confined to tympana. There is, however, evidence that a similar frieze existed at Bury St Edmunds Abbey and the 11th-century frieze relief from the Old Minster at Winchester (Winchester, City Mus.) indicates that there was a long tradition of narrative frieze sculpture in England. Nevertheless, Lincoln is the only cathedral church in England to preserve lavish Romanesque decoration of the highest quality.

BIBLIOGRAPHY
*English Romanesque Art, 1066–1200* (exh. cat., ed. G. Zarnecki; London, Hayward Gal., 1984), p. 180
G. Zarnecki: *Romanesque Sculpture at Lincoln Cathedral*, Lincoln Minster Pamphlet (Lincoln, 1988)

DEBORAH KAHN

(*b*) *Later sculpture.* The south door to the Angel choir (the Judgement portal) was made from *c.* 1270, and is one of the few surviving monumental sculpture compositions of 13th-century England. It is usually compared to the earlier sculptures of Wells Cathedral and Westminster Abbey. The iconography is influenced by France, but the style and arrangement are English. There is a sculptured tympanum, with two rows of archivolt figures and four statues on the door jambs (two of which are identifiable as *Church* and *Synagogue*), with three others on adjacent buttresses. The *Virgin* on the trumeau is a 19th-century invention, and there is much 19th-century restoration (a pre-restoration cast of the tympanum is in the Victoria and Albert Museum, London). In English fashion the tympanum is penetrated by the pointed arches of the door, and its design is centred on a large quatrefoil with relief sculptures of *Christ the Judge* and two angels. The remaining space is filled by angels, the *Resurrection, Mouth of Hell* and *Torture of the Damned*. The archivolts have deeply cut, entwined stiff-leaf foliage, the setting for figures of the *Wise and Foolish Virgins* (see fig. 5), Apostles and saints.

The design is based on that of the destroyed north transept portal of Westminster Abbey, and Roberts has suggested that the unusual iconography of Christ gesturing to the wound in his side is also derived from there. For *Church* and *Synagogue* stylistic comparisons have been made with the west front of Wells Cathedral (Brieger) and

5. Lincoln Cathedral, detail of the Judgement portal, *c.* 1270s

the *Annunciation* of Westminster Abbey chapter house (Stone), whence derive the archivolt figures in foliage settings. The linear, softly looped draperies reflect these earlier styles, but the flatter handling of the buttress figures anticipates work of *c.* 1300, as exemplified at Lincoln in the crisp, broad style of the wooden bosses of the cloister vault and the sleeping soldiers on the stone *Tomb of Christ* in the choir (both *c.* 1296; for further discussion *see* EASTER SEPULCHRE).

The theme of the Judgement portal is reflected in the attributes carried by some of the triforium angels of the Angel choir, which may also have connotations of the reliquary symbolism of the choir itself. They are more crudely carved, but their smiling faces set a type that remained popular until the end of the 13th century.

BIBLIOGRAPHY
L. Stone: *Sculpture in Britain: The Middle Ages*, Pelican Hist. A. (Harmondsworth, 1955, 2/1972), pp. 125–7, 130–33
P. Brieger: *English Art, 1216–1307* (Oxford, 1957/R 1968), pp. 191–3
V. Glenn: 'The Sculpture of the Angel Choir at Lincoln', *British Archaeological Association Conference Transactions: Medieval Art and Architecture at Lincoln Cathedral: Lincoln, 1982*, pp. 102–8

M. E. Roberts: 'The Relic of the Holy Blood and the Iconography of the Thirteenth-century North Transept Portal of Westminster Abbey', *Proceedings of the 1984 Harlaxton Symposium: England in the Thirteenth Century: Harlaxton, 1984*, pp. 129–42, 132–5

*Age of Chivalry: Art in Plantagenet England, 1200–1400* (exh. cat., ed. J. Alexander and P. Binski; London, RA, 1987), p. 102

T. A. Heslop: 'The Iconography of the Angel Choir at Lincoln', *Medieval Architecture and its Intellectual Context: Studies in Honour of Peter Kidson*, ed. E. Fernie and P. Crossley (London, 1990), pp. 151–8

*Romanesque Stone Sculpture from Medieval England* (exh. cat. by B. Heywood and others, Leeds, Henry Moore Inst., 1993)

□

*(iii) Stained glass.* The stained glass of Lincoln Cathedral is second only to that of Canterbury Cathedral (*see* CANTERBURY, §III, 3) in its importance for the earliest period of surviving work in England. Most of the medieval glass at Lincoln is of *c.* 1200–50, but some in the south rose (the Bishop's Eye) is of *c.* 1325–50, and ornamental glass at the top of the west window is of *c.* 1370–80. The dating of the glass has been proposed in relation to the dates of completion of the various parts of the building on the assumption that the windows were glazed shortly after. The north rose (the Dean's Eye), depicting the *Last Judgement*, is the only complete window *in situ*. The south rose contains some of its original glass, also of the *Last Judgement*, but it is mostly rearranged and interspersed with glass from elsewhere in the cathedral. The remaining glass was gathered together from various windows in the late 18th century and placed in four locations: the two eastern windows of the choir aisles, and in the two groups of lancet windows below each of the rose windows of the main transept. The 18th-century glaziers effected this rearrangement with complete disregard for the original subject-matter of the figure panels. Old and New Testament scenes were intermingled with scenes from the lives of the saints, and panels of such subjects were even inserted into the *Last Judgement* of the north rose where its original glazing had been lost. Similarly, ornamental borders and sections of grisaille of various periods were juxtaposed within the same window and rearranged into ornamental patterns designed by the 18th-century glazier.

In spite of the confusion caused by this rearrangement, the majority of the subjects of the panels can be identified, and the main themes of the original windows reconstructed. They included Old Testament subjects of the lives of *Noah*, *Moses* and *David*, probably once paralleled with New Testament scenes in typological windows. There were windows of the *Miracles of the Virgin* (see fig. 6) and the lives of SS *John the Evangelist*, *Nicholas*, *Denis* and *Hugh of Lincoln*. These windows were probably in the chapels of the dedicatory saints. Among the latest in date of the figure panels are a group of standing apostles and prophets (*c.* 1250). In style this 13th-century glass at Lincoln differs from Canterbury and comes closest to some of the glass at Beverley Minster. The fragments of the figure glazing of the south rose show a stylistic connection with the west window of York Minster (1338).

The ornamental glass of Lincoln shows a great range of decorative border and grisaille designs. The latter can be reconstructed from sections of the patterns randomly set in the 18th-century rearrangement, and from the substantial survival of grisaille windows in the lancets below the north rose. These are probably not *in situ* but were placed

6. Lincoln Cathedral, stained-glass window of the *Legend of Theophilus*, one of the *Miracles of the Virgin*, north choir aisle, *c.* 1200–35

there in the 18th century or early 19th. This grisaille is the earliest surviving in England except for a few fragments in parish churches. It predates the grisaille at Salisbury Cathedral of *c.* 1235–50. The 19th-century glass is mainly by Ward & Hughes and Clayton & Bell.

BIBLIOGRAPHY

C. Winston: *Memoirs Illustrative of the Art of Glass Painting* (London, 1865); pp. 77–105, 222–30

C. Woodforde: *A Guide to the Medieval Glass in Lincoln Cathedral* (London, 1933)

J. Lafond: 'The Stained Glass Decoration of Lincoln Cathedral in the Thirteenth Century', *Archaeol. J.*, ciii (1946), pp. 119–56

P. B. G. Binnall: *The Nineteenth Century Stained Glass in Lincoln Minster*, Lincoln Minster Pamphlets, n. s., iii (Lincoln, 1966)

D. J. King: 'The Glazing of the South Rose of Lincoln Cathedral', *British Archaeological Association Conference Transactions: Medieval Art and Architecture at Lincoln Cathedral: Lincoln, 1982*, pp. 132–45

N. J. Morgan: *The Medieval Painted Glass of Lincoln Cathedral* (London, 1983)

**Lincoln**, 1st Earl of. *See* CLINTON, EDWARD FIENNES DE.

**Lindblom, Andreas (Adolf Frederik)** (*b* Askeby, Östergotland, 8 Feb 1889; *d* Stockholm, 22 March 1977). Swedish art historian and museum official. He began his career as an assistant curator (1909–16) at the Statens Historiska Museum, Stockholm, during which time he published his first book (1916), which presented the first fully documented history of 13th- and 14th-century Scandinavian painting and remains a standard text. From 1917–19 he worked at the Nationalmuseum, Stockholm. After a period as art critic for *Stockholms Dagblad* he was professor of art history at the Högskola (1921–5) and at the Konsthögskola (1925–9), both in Stockholm. In 1929 he was appointed as the director of the Nordiska Museum och Skansen, a post that he held until his retirement in 1955. Lindblom's many publications in Swedish cover a variety of aspects of medieval Swedish painting and sculpture, Vadstena Abbey, St Bridget (*c.* 1303–73; *can* 1391) and general Swedish art history.

### WRITINGS

*La Peinture gothique en Suède et en Norvège* (Stockholm, 1916)
*Den heliga Birgitta: Bildverk i skulptur och maleri från Sveriges medeltid* [St Bridget: imagery in sculpture and painting from the Middle Ages in Sweden] (Stockholm, 1918)
*Sveriges konsthistoria* [Swedish art history], 3 vols (Stockholm, 1944)
*Svensk konst: Från stenåldern till rymdåldern* [Swedish art: from the stone age to the space age] (Stockholm, 1960)
*Krucifixmästarna i Linköping: Bildhuggare på Birgittas tid* [The crucifix masters in Linköping: sculptors in Bridget's time] (Vadstena, 1976)
*Madonnabilder från svensk medeltid* [Swedish medieval depictions of the Virgin] (Vadstena, 1978)

### BIBLIOGRAPHY

*SBL* [bibliog. from 1955]
K. Ehrnborg: *Andreas Lindbloms tryckta skrifter under femtio år 1906–1955* [Andreas Lindblom's published writings over 50 years, 1906–1955] (Stockholm, 1957) [bibliog. up to 1955]

NIGEL J. MORGAN

**Lindegren, Yrjö (Lorenzo)** (*b* Tampere, 13 Aug 1900; *d* Helsinki, 13 Nov 1952). Finnish architect. He was an important exponent of functionalism in Finland. In 1937 he won the Grand Prix at the Exposition Internationale des Arts et Techniques dans la Vie Moderne, held in Paris. His best-known works include the Olympic Stadium (1940–52) in Helsinki, which he designed with Toivo Jäntti. From time to time he collaborated with Alvar Aalto. Lindegren designed many sports centres in Finland, including those at Pori, Riihimäki (1949–50) and Varkaus. The last, the Kanavasaari Sports Centre, won him the gold medal in the Art Competition of the Olympic Games in 1948. After World War II he designed a general plan for central Helsinki (with Erik Krakström), on which Alvar Aalto's later plan is largely based. Other outstanding designs include the Vaalijala Central Institute for the Mentally Handicapped in Pieksämäki, which comprises *c.* 30 pavilion-like buildings linked by covered service corridors, thus avoiding the problems of one large, integrated institutional building. One of the last of Lindegren's executed works is the Serpentine flats (1951), a living complex in Helsinki: all the dwellings are situated in a curving mass so that each has an unbroken view of the forest beyond and the gently rolling countryside. During his lifetime Lindegren had a considerable influence on his architectural colleagues, and he was chairman of the Finnish Architects' Association several times.

### BIBLIOGRAPHY

'Yrjö Lindegren arkitekt', *Arkitekten* (1950), pp. 137–63 [includes summaries in English; text partly by Lindegren]
A. Blomstedt: Obituary, *Arkkitehti/Arkitekten* (1952), pp. 171–4 [includes notes in English, French and German]

PETRI BLOMSTEDT

**Lindenast, Sebastian**, the elder (*b* Nuremberg, *c.* 1460; *d* Nuremberg, 1526). German metalworker. He was the most prominent member of a family that held the right to produce gilt and silvered copperwork in Nuremberg between *c.* 1450 and 1550. He probably became a master coppersmith *c.* 1490. His manner of working copper using the intricate techniques found on goldsmiths' work was unusual for the period. He successfully resisted repeated attempts by the goldsmiths' guild of Nuremberg to suppress this competition and in 1513 obtained a privilege from Emperor Maximilian I permitting him to produce this type of copperwork. An inventory of Lindenast's goods illustrates the wide range of his work, which included silvered and gilt half-length figures (probably reliquaries), relief panels depicting religious subjects, vessels in the manner of goldsmiths' work, for example tankards, bowls for sweetmeats, dishes, plates, goblets, monstrances, patens and altar candlesticks; and such smaller works as book- and beltclasps and jewellery. Among the few surviving pieces is a fantastically shaped gilt and painted dish with a lid (1480–1500; London, V&A). Its general form follows that of the 'Vestner Tower', an emblem of the city of Nuremberg; miniature medieval buildings are featured on the lid. The technical virtuosity of this piece suggests that it may have been his masterpiece. The influence of the work of Peter Vischer and Adam Kraft, with whom Lindenast was acquainted, can be discerned in a relic statuette of *St James* (1490–1500; Nuremberg, Ger. Nmus.). From 1506 to 1509 he produced many figures for the *Männleinlaufen,* a mechanical display on the Frauenkirche in Nuremberg (*in situ*) representing homage being paid to Emperor Charles IV. Book mounts produced by Lindenast for the council of Nuremberg in 1519 show the transition to an early Renaissance style in his late work.

### BIBLIOGRAPHY

H. Kohlhaussen: *Nürnberger Goldschmiedekunst des Mittelalters und der Dürerzeit, 1240–1540* (Berlin, 1968), pp. 108, 111, 286ff

FABIAN STEIN

**Lindgren, Armas (Eliel)** (*b* Hämeenlinna, 28 Nov 1874; *d* Copenhagen, 3 Oct 1929). Finnish architect. He graduated from the Helsinki Polytechnic in 1897 and subsequently spent his career both in the study of historical architecture and art and in original design work. Between 1896 and 1902 he accompanied the art historical study trips arranged by the Finnish Antiquarian Society as artist and photographer. He undertook other trips, too, for the Finnish Archaeological Bureau. In 1896 Lindgren formed a partnership with Eliel Saarinen and Herman Gesellius (*see* GESELLIUS, LINDGREN, SAARINEN). They designed a block of flats at Fabianinkatu 17 (1900–01) and three blocks of flats in the Katajanokka area of Helsinki: the Tallberg House (1897–8) at Luotsikatu 11, Satamakatu 7; the Olofsborg (1900–02) at Kauppiaankatu 7; and Eol (1901–3) at Luotsikatu. From the interiors to the lively design and ornamentation of the exteriors, the style of these buildings with their free-formed layouts combines motifs from Finnish and international history with elements from the new European tendencies. In the façade of the Pohjola Insurance Company building (1899–1901), influenced by H. H. Richardson's work, figures from Finnish mythology, flora and fauna adorn the soapstone. Gesellius, Lindgren & Saarinen had first attracted international attention with the design for the Finnish Pavilion at the Exposition Universelle in Paris in 1900. Hvitträsk, the studio-complex in which all three also lived with their families, bears evidence to the living ideals of the time, despite fire damage and restoration work. The grand country house (1901–3; destr.) of Suur-Merijoki in Viipuri province (now in Russia) similarly fulfilled the idea of a total harmony in living environment. In 1902 Lindgren was appointed artistic director of the Central School of Applied Arts and in 1905 he left the partnership. The only work of the firm with which he remained involved was the winning competition entry for the Finnish National Museum (completed in 1916). The competition for the museum, whose design was based on the modern pavilion principle, was to a large extent the result of Lindgren's own enthusiasm.

From 1905, alongside his work at the Central School of Applied Arts, Lindgren had his own office. Among its most important achievements are the new Students' Union building (1910) in Helsinki and the Estonia Theatre and Concert hall (1913) in Tallinn on which he collaborated with Wivi Lönn. These are generously proportioned buildings. In the office building for the Kaleva insurance company (1914) in Helsinki, built as an extension to the students' union, the granite façades wrap tightly around a corner site, with a uniform crenellation binding the upper edge of the volume in a new but tranquil way. The Suomi insurance company building (1911) in Helsinki, for which Lindgren, after winning the competition, designed the façades, marks the peak of a new monumental phase. The composition stems from a classic, disciplined perspective. The many subjects, materials and colours of the ornamentation and the plentiful ornamental sculpture (by Gunnar Finne, 1886–1952) make up a rich whole that is nevertheless characterized by a calm dignity. Otto Wagner and Josef Hoffman appear to have influenced Lindgren during this phase in both architecture and interior design.

In 1912 Lindgren gave up his position at the School, but remained chairman of the Applied Arts Association. In housing Lindgren was instrumental in changing the Vallila area of Helsinki from an area of small houses to low-rise blocks of flats grouped around large, open courtyards when he designed workers' accommodation (built 1917–29) for Kone ja Silta Oy (Machine and Bridge Ltd) as a fortress-like whole around a large open space. This idea came from Denmark via Sweden (Göteborg in particular) through the work of Otto-Iivari Meurman. As part of the first phases of building the suburb of Kulosaari, Lindgren had designed some small villas in addition to his own house (1913). The central work of the second phase of building was the Ribbingshof terrace houses (1917). In 1919 he was appointed Professor of Architecture at the Technical University. Many of the early exponents of functionalism and other students, including Alvar Aalto, have praised his enthusiastic teaching. Also in 1919 Lindgren set up an office with Bertel Liljequist (1885–1954). In the 1920s the restoration of churches became an important part of Lindgren's work, in addition to the design of new ones. He was the leader of restoration work in Turku Cathedral. Connections with industrial firms provided support for Säynätsalo Church (1926), Kuusankoski Church (1929) and Noormarkku Church (1933). Lindgren's ecclesiastical buildings exhibit a synthesis of the elements of his architecture: the historical features, universal themes and details become starting points for a personal and artistic process of creation. Lindgren was often called a romantic, and this is witnessed by the devout atmosphere of the church buildings: colour is softly graded, materials and decoration used with a carefully considered generosity.

BIBLIOGRAPHY

R. Nikula: *Yhtenäinen kaupunkikuva, 1900–1930* [The harmonious townscape, 1900–1930], Bidrag till kännedom av Finlands natur och folk, cxxvii (Helsinki, 1981)

——: *Armas Lindgren och den historiska arkitekturen* [Armas Lindgren and the history of architecture], Taidehistoriallisia tutkimuksia [Studies in the history of art], ix (Helsinki, 1986)

R. Nikula and H. Grönlund: *Armas Lingren, 1874–1929: Arkkitehti/ Architect* (Helsinki, 1988)

RIITTA NIKULA

**Lindholm, Berndt (Adolf)** (*b* Loviisa, 20 Aug 1841; *d* Göteborg, 15 May 1914). Finnish painter. He received his initial art education at the School of Drawing in Turku between 1856 and 1861. He was prompted to take up a career as an artist by his admiration for Werner Holmberg, whose example he followed by studying in Düsseldorf. He was disappointed by the city's Kunstakademie, however, where Holmberg's instructor, Hans Fredrik Gude, no longer taught. Lindholm studied under Gude in Karlsuhe in 1865–6. He was inspired by the French landscape paintings he saw there to travel to Paris. He subsequently worked and studied in Paris from 1868 to 1870 and from 1873 to 1876 (in 1873–4 under the direction of Léon Bonnat). Lindholm became a fervent adherent of French art, particularly the Barbizon school, and of emphasizing colour. Charles-François Daubigny and Jean-Baptiste-Camille Corot were his most important influences.

The small landscapes that Lindholm painted in France in the first half of the 1870s were relatively modern for Finnish art. At the same time he also persisted with Realism for his larger portrayals of Finnish landscapes, as in *Vallinkoski Rapids* (1872; Helsinki, N.G., Banqueting Hall). His representation of forest settings is particularly noteworthy; in 1874 he achieved great success at the Paris Salon with *Finnish Forest* (Liverpool, Walker A.G.). However, he felt that the French current in his work was not sufficiently appreciated in Finland, and in his vexation he moved to Göteborg, Sweden, in 1876. Here he was nominated custodian of the Konstmuseum. Although Lindholm remained in Sweden until his death, he always considered himself a Finnish artist and participated in Finnish exhibitions. He was elected a member of the Konstakademi in Stockholm in 1881.

In Sweden Lindholm's style soon became more deliberate and Realist; the light, pictorial quality of his earlier work gradually disappeared. Sweden's rocky shorelines and crashing waves became his central theme (e.g. *Kattegat in a Storm*, 1894; Helsinki, Athenaeum A. Mus.). In his later years he also travelled to Norway to paint in the summertime. As an artist he grew increasingly conservative, and Gude's influence began to resurface at the expense of the Parisian style he had favoured as a young man.

BIBLIOGRAPHY

V. Loos: *Friluftsmåleriets genombrott i svensk konst, 1860–1885* [The emergence of *plein-air* painting in Swedish art, 1860–1885] (Stockholm, 1945)

A. Hedvall: *Bohuslän i konsten* [Bohuslän in art] (Stockholm, 1956)

AIMO REITALA

**Lindisfarne Gospels.** Manuscript of the four Gospels, in Latin, written and illuminated on vellum in the Northumbrian island monastery of Lindisfarne at the end of the 7th century AD (London, BL, Cotton MS. Nero D. IV). It is the most complete and best documented of all the Insular Gospel books of its period.

The names of the craftsmen responsible for this magnificent book are preserved in a colophon that was added during the third quarter of the 10th century. This records that the manuscript was produced in honour of God and of St Cuthbert, Bishop of Lindisfarne (*d* 687). The scribe was Eadfrith, who became Bishop of Lindisfarne himself in May 698. The original binding (destr.) was provided soon after 698 by Ethelwald, Prior of Melrose and Eadfrith's successor in 721. Ornaments of jewels and precious metals were added to the covers by Billfrith the Anchorite, probably later in the 8th century. Both Eadfrith and Ethelwald had been members of the Lindisfarne monastic community during Cuthbert's lifetime. It is likely that the book was made to honour the translation of the saint's relics in 698. The colophon itself was written by the priest Aldred, afterwards Provost of Chester-le-Street, probably soon after the middle of the 10th century. Aldred added an interlinear translation of the Gospels into Anglo-Saxon, the earliest surviving version of this text in any form of the English language.

With the exception of a few very minor details Eadfrith was entirely responsible for the design and execution of the decoration as well as the text. His script is a stately insular majuscule typical of the Lindisfarne scriptorium. The volume opens with a 'carpet' page of pure decoration based on the form of the cross and a major initial page, introducing the letter of St Jerome to Pope Damasus I (*reg* 366–83). There are 16 pages of arcaded canon tables in which panels of pure interlace alternate with panels of zoomorphic ornament. Each Gospel is prefaced by a portrait of the appropriate Evangelist (*see* BOOK, fig. 3), a carpet page and a decorated initial page. An additional major initial introduces the Christmas narrative in Matthew. The material preceding each of the Gospels is punctuated by smaller decorated initials.

Sources are many and varied. The Evangelist miniatures are based on Mediterranean models, possibly obtained through the neighbouring community of Monkwearmouth–Jarrow, which had strong links with Italy. The pages of pure decoration include motifs familiar from metalwork and jewellery alongside bird and animal ornament that, while ultimately dependent upon the zoomorphic ornament of the Migration period, seems to be coloured by first-hand observation of local wildlife. This is exemplified in Eadfrith's portrayal of a bewhiskered cat in the margin of the initial page to Luke (fol. 139*r*; see fig.). A very large and subtle range of colours is employed. They are variously derived from animal, vegetable and mineral sources, some available locally and others imported from as far afield as the Mediterranean and, in the unique case of lapis lazuli, from the Himalayas.

The Lindisfarne Gospels manuscript shared the history and wanderings of the relics of St Cuthbert, with which it was preserved, reaching Durham via Chester-le-Street in 995. The manuscript was separated from the shrine in 1539, when Durham Cathedral Priory was dissolved by

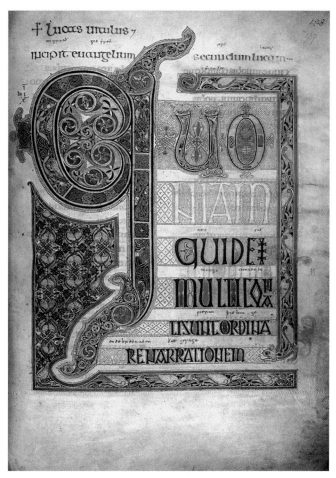

Lindisfarne Gospels, initial page of St Luke's Gospel, body colour on vellum, 340×250 mm, *c.* AD 698 (London, British Library, Cotton MS. Nero D. IV, fol. 139*r*)

Henry VIII's commissioners. Early in the 17th century it passed into the hands of Sir Robert Cotton, and in 1753, as part of the Cotton collection, it was incorporated into the newly founded British Museum.

BIBLIOGRAPHY
*Evangelium Quattuor Codex Lindisfarnensis*, 2 vols (Lausanne, 1956–60) [complete facsimile edition with contributions by T. D. Kendrick and others]
J. J. G. Alexander: *Insular Manuscripts, 6th to the 9th Century*, Survey of Manuscripts Illuminated in the British Isles, i (London, 1978), no. 9 [comprehensive bibliography]
J. Backhouse: *The Lindisfarne Gospels* (Oxford, 1981)

JANET BACKHOUSE

**Lindner, Richard** (*b* Hamburg, 11 Nov 1901; *d* New York, 16 April 1978). American painter of German birth. He grew up in a bourgeois Jewish household in Nuremberg; the city's fairy-tale appearance and atmosphere, its reputation as the toy capital of Europe and as the home of the Iron Maiden and its suffocating smugness were all later cited by him as influences on his work. Lindner's early studies were in music and he seemed destined for a career as a concert pianist, but his growing interest in art led him to study at the Kunstakademie in Munich from

Richard Lindner: *The Meeting*, oil on canvas, 1.52×1.83 m, 1953 (New York, Museum of Modern Art)

1925 to 1927. He lived in Berlin from 1927 to 1928 and returned to Munich in 1929 as art director at the large publishing house of Knorr & Hirth. Lindner's politics were Social Democratic and on Hitler's ascent to power in 1933 Lindner hurriedly left Germany just as he was about to be arrested by the Nazis. He went to Paris, where he continued to work in graphic design until 1939, when he was interned as an alien; shortly thereafter he joined the French army. In March 1941 he arrived in New York, where he quickly became a highly successful illustrator for such magazines as *Fortune*, *Harper's Bazaar* and *Vogue*.

Almost nothing remains of the work Lindner produced in Germany and France or indeed of a modest production of paintings and objects made in New York during the 1940s. Extant examples of his early work include broadly painted figure studies influenced by Cubism and Expressionism, for example a portrait of *Marcel Proust* (1950; New York, Mr and Mrs Arne H. Ekstrom priv. col., see Ashton, pl. 42), and a few small, primitivistic fetish objects embellished in bright colours; he later recalled the impact on his art of a visit he had made in 1925 to the remarkable collection of works by psychotics assembled by the art

historian and psychiatrist Hans Prinzhorn (1886–1933) at the psychiatric clinic at the University of Heidelberg (*see* PSYCHOTIC ART). The expressive force of this work remained vivid for Lindner throughout his career and may be sensed as an underlying influence on his later preference for unsettling images.

Lindner's mature production began unusually late. In 1952, determined to devote his time entirely to his art, he abandoned his commercial work and concentrated his efforts on drawing and painting as well as teaching at the Pratt Institute in Brooklyn. In his work of the 1950s he used precise and refined draughtsmanship, pastel colours and tonal nuance. Images such as the *Child's Dream* (1952; New York, Whitney) characteristically evoke childhood and early adolescence, evidently a turbulent period for the artist, with intimations of sexuality and seduction in late Victorian settings. The mood of such scenes is often one of poignant fantasy and nostalgia, as if recalled in memory. One of Lindner's major early works, *The Meeting* (1953; New York, MOMA; see fig.), is an autobiographical group portrait including the artist Saul Steinberg, Lindner's aunt, his sister in a childishly seductive pose and Lindner himself as a child; it also pays homage to imaginary companions and friends. To the left is a resplendent King Ludwig II of Bavaria, whose extravagant and creative madness fascinated the artist; in the centre is a corseted woman seen from behind, personifying Lindner's belief in the strength and imaginative powers of women. In other work of the 1950s he depicted child prodigies playing symbolic games, sometimes joined with complex mechanical structures, as in *Boy with Machine* (1954; New York, Stephen Mazoh, see 1974 exh. cat., no. 7).

Lindner regarded his work of the 1950s as European, a recollection of his past, and his later art as American and as specifically rooted in New York. This Americanization of his work in paintings such as *New York City Life IV* (1964; Washington, DC, Hirshhorn) coincided with the emergence of Pop art, but it had very different and unrelated origins. In contrast to his preceding manner, in the 1960s Lindner composed his designs with flat, brilliantly coloured planes that resemble cut-outs; modelling, when it occurs, defines form volumetrically, giving it a mechanical aspect recalling the work of Léger. Representational elements are mixed with abstract shapes, signs and typography. Lindner's imagery is of extravagantly attired men and women— gangsters, pimps and whores— drawn from the bizarre types and raucous ambience around Times Square, New York; a typical example is *East 69th Street* (1972; Rotterdam, Mus. Boymans–van Beuningen), a full-frontal portrait of a handcuffed man dressed in a gaudy suit and tie. Canvases such as *The Street* (1963; Düsseldorf, Kstsamml. Nordrhein-Westfalen) evoke a bigger-and-brighter-than-life vision of a glitzy underworld that is ultimately more a reflection of a German fantasy about Al Capone's Chicago than of the sleazy neon-lit Times Square. Lindner was a passionate collector of toys; his gangsters in their zoot suits with their brassy, sexy Valkyrie molls are marionettes decked out in the symbolic dress of the underworld.

In 1973 Lindner began to spend nearly half of each year in Paris, his second wife's home, and from this changed personal life came a fusion of American and European experiences and a compromise between his styles of the 1950s and 1960s. This new manner was particularly evident in a series of large-scale compositions such as *Solitaire* (oil on canvas, 2×1.8 m, 1973; Geneva, Gal. Jeanneret). He returned to the autobiographical image of the adolescent boy and to themes of sexual initiation but introduced a boldness and great adroitness of pictorial organization, a preference for larger areas of flat colour and darker and more subdued tonalities appropriate to the more ambiguous scenarios narrated. Lindner's richly individual paintings continued to exist outside the mainstream and to synthesize a broad range of artistic devices and references, for example to Expressionism and popular culture. Taken as a whole his art is a brilliant exploration of personal obsession.

BIBLIOGRAPHY

D. Ashton: *Richard Lindner* (New York, 1969)

R.-G. Dienst: *Richard Lindner* (New York, 1969)

*Richard Lindner* (exh. cat., intro. J.-H. Martin; Paris, Mus. N. A. Mod., 1974)

H. Kramer: *Richard Lindner* (London, 1975) [with cat. of ptgs and wtrcols, 1968–74]

'A Conversation with Richard Lindner and Stephen Prokopoff', *Richard Lindner: A Retrospective Exhibition* (exh. cat., Chicago, IL, Mus. Contemp. A., 1977)

W. Spies: *Lindner* (Paris, 1980)

STEPHEN S. PROKOPOFF

**Lindos.** *See under* RHODES.

**Lindqvist, Selim (Arvid)** (*b* Helsinki, 19 May 1867; *d* Helsinki, 17 May 1939). Finnish architect. He studied architecture (1884–8) at the Polytechnic Institute, Helsinki, and with F. A. Sjöström (1840–85), an architect who designed several important Neo-classical buildings in Helsinki and elsewhere in Finland. Sjöström's influence is clearly evident in Lindqvist's student projects and early independent designs. His first important work, the Merkurius Building (1888–90), 33 Pohjoisesplanadi, Helsinki, was designed when he was 21. The façade of this building, a residential block with shops and offices on the ground and mezzanine floors, demonstrates Lindqvist's assured handling of Neo-classical forms. It is also notable for the use of modern construction techniques, whereby the upper storeys are supported on cast-iron pillars that allow the office storeys below to be fronted with large plate-glass windows. It is not clear whether this innovation, which represented a completely new approach in Finnish architecture, was the work of Lindqvist or the master builder Elia Heikel (1852–1917), with whom he collaborated on this and other projects in Helsinki until 1900. Heikel was responsible for the plans and structure of all these projects, with Lindqvist designing the façades, and it is probable that Heikel had become acquainted with new building techniques and taught their use to his younger partner. Their final collaboration was the Lundqvist Building (1900; altered 1981), 13 Aleksanterinkatu, Helsinki, one of the first office blocks in the city. This building reflects construction techniques in use in the USA at the time, with interior floors supported by rows of cast-iron columns allowing a flexible arrangement of the working space, while the load-bearing brick façades are eclectic in style, in this case Gothic Revival.

At the end of the 1890s there was in Finland, as elsewhere, a move away from the eclecticism that dominated the 19th century, with such architects as Eliel Saarinen and Lars Sonck favouring a National Romantic style of architecture. Lindqvist, however, was more interested in international trends, particularly Viennese *Jugendstil*, and the rationalist basis of his architecture became stronger. His early interest in new building techniques continued and he is regarded as one of the pioneers of concrete construction in Finland, which he introduced in 1900 (spool factory in Kaukaa), only a few years after its development in continental Europe. He remained almost alone among his contemporaries in his enthusiasm for the new technique, which became intense. Inspired by *Jugendstil* and the work of Josef Hoffmann, he designed a series of villas that included the Villa Johanna (1906), 25 Laivurinkatu, and Villa Ensi (1910–11), 23 Merikatu, both in Helsinki. The latter bears comparison to Hoffman's Palais Stoclet (1910), Brussels, both in structure and detailing. A major work of this period, the Suvilahti steam power station (completed 1908), Helsinki, secures Lindqvist's place among the international pioneers of concrete design. In this building, also influenced by the Viennese Secession and with *Jugendstil* ornament, the reinforced-concrete structure is clearly expressed and given an aesthetic role of its own in the same way as Auguste Perret's well-known garage in Paris, designed three years earlier. Lindqvist also designed a large number of technical buildings for the city of Helsinki, including electricity board buildings (the first of which was Kasarmikatu 32, Helsinki) and tram sheds, in which his rationalist concrete architecture came into its own; and they remained impressive elements in the cityscape of Helsinki.

Lindqvist's active work as an architect ended in the 1920s. He later designed only occasional buildings, the last and most interesting being his own house (1932; Konalantie 17–Selim Lindqvistintie 2) in Helsinki in which he was able to show how a disciplined understanding of structure in itself led to a 'modern' result. Externally it is reminiscent of the modernist buildings of the time, particularly the architecture of Adolf Loos, which developed from the same starting points of rationalism and the sympathetic use of concrete. Lindqvist was an important architect, pioneering international styles and construction techniques in the first decades of the 20th century and producing some of the finest buildings in Finland. However, he worked apart from the mainstream of stylistic development in Finland, and his works were not publicized there to the same extent as those of the leaders of National Romanticism. Little was written on Lindqvist throughout the 20th century, and thus he remained almost unknown internationally.

BIBLIOGRAPHY

J. M. Richards: *800 Years of Finnish Architecture* (London, 1978), pp. 117–18, 122, 128

'Raportti Suvilahdesta', *Arkkitehti/Arkitekten*, lxxviii/8 (1981), pp. 22–5

A. Ilonen: *Helsinki: An Architectural Guide* (Helsinki, 1990) [with photographs of Lindqvist's major buildings]

ASKO SALOKORPI

**Lindsay, Alexander (William Crawford)**, 25th Earl of Crawford and 8th Earl of Balcarres (*b* Muncaster Castle, Cumbria, 16 Oct 1812; *d* Florence, 13 Dec 1880). English writer and collector. He was educated at Eton College and in 1827 entered Trinity College, Cambridge. In 1829 he wrote a history of the Lindsay family based on the papers at Haigh Hall, near Wigan, Lancs, the house to which the family had moved. This was rewritten ten years later and published as *Lives of the Lindsays* (1840). His travels to Palestine, Egypt and elsewhere in 1836–7 provided the basis for *Letters on Egypt, Edom and the Holy Land* (1838). In 1836 he also went with his cousin COUTTS LINDSAY to Italy, where on further visits he gathered material for the three-volume *Sketches of the History of Christian Art* (1847). The first volume opens with a discussion of 'The Ideal', in which Lindsay claimed that there were three aspects of man 'Sense, Intellect and Spirit' and three stages of artistic development corresponding to man's ascent to the state of the Spirit. The monumental and massive architecture of ancient Egypt expressed the ideal of Sense or Matter, while 'the Sculpture of [ancient] Greece is the voice of Intellect and Thought, communing with itself in solitude, feeding on beauty and yearning for truth' (p. xiv). Later, however, came the 'Painting of Christendom', which was the voice 'of an immortal Spirit conversing with its

God' (p. xiv). Intertwined with this progress was a development in each of the branches of art: whereas the Egyptians had excelled only in architecture and the Greeks in sculpture and architecture, the Christian era brought equal 'stature and perfection' to painting, sculpture and architecture. After this tendentious preface Lindsay moved on to a discussion of Christian 'mythology', followed by a roughly chronological survey of Christian art itself. His three volumes in fact cover only Period 1 of the complex classification he provided in the first volume (pp. ccix–ccxlviii), treating art from the Roman Empire up to the early 16th century. The survey is notably selective towards the end, including, for example, Dürer and Hans Holbein the younger but not Raphael, Leonardo or Michelangelo, who were assigned to other periods. The book closes with a call for a renewed study of the Renaissance so that contemporary artists could produce works of a similar quality. Although Lindsay had intended to continue the work up to his own time, no further volumes were written. In its artistic appraisals the book reflects his belief that works of art should be judged by their moral and spiritual qualities, an attitude that led him to favour 14th-century Italian art.

In 1834 Lindsay received a substantial legacy from a distant relation, and this allowed him to indulge his passion for collecting art and books. He initially collected 14th-century Italian art, but his tastes later widened. His purchases of the 1840s were rather indiscriminate and lacking in quality. In a letter of 1849 he expressed his desire to create a gallery that would illustrate the whole development of European art, indicating his increasing eclecticism. In Florence about 1856 he met the dealer and artist William Blundell Spence, through whom he began to buy works of a greater quality and wider range. In 1858 he bought Guido Reni's *Flight into Egypt* (Bradford, Cartwright Hall), although his most important purchases were made between about 1864 and 1875. During this period he acquired such works as the *Virgin and Child Enthroned* (London, N.G.) attributed to Domenico Veneziano, a huge terracotta altarpiece then thought to be by Giovanni della Robbia but now attributed to the workshop of Benedetto Buglioni (priv. col., on loan to Edinburgh, Royal Mus. Scotland), an altarpiece by Lorenzo di Bicci (London, Westminster Abbey) and Luca Signorelli's altarpiece *Madonna and Child with Saints* (Washington, DC, N.G.A.).

Lindsay was an avid book collector and greatly expanded the family collection, the Bibliotheca Lindesiana, kept at Haigh Hall. By the time of his death it contained over 50,000 volumes and formed the greatest private library of its time. When he died Lindsay was constructing a new building for it at Dunecht, Grampian. Many of the books were sold in two sales in 1887 and 1889, the first including 2149 items and the second 1105. In the more important first sale there was a rare copy of Cristoforo Landino's *Comento sopra la Comedia di Danthe* (1481), with 19 engravings by Baccio Baldini after designs by Sandro Botticelli. In addition there were various sets of prints, such as 20 engravings by Dürer depicting the *Life of the Virgin*, 17 of them from 1504 and the rest from 1509–11, and a copy of the first French edition of Holbein's *Les Simulacres et historiques faces de la mort* (Lyon, 1538), illustrated with woodcuts. The rest of the Bibliotheca Lindesiana remained in the family's possession, and parts were either expanded or sold.

### WRITINGS
*Letters on Egypt, Edom and the Holy Land*, 2 vols (London, 1838)
*Lives of the Lindsays*, 4 vols (Wigan, 1840)
*Sketches of the History of Christian Art*, 3 vols (London, 1847)
*Etruscan Inscriptions* (London, 1872)
*The Creed of Japhet* (London, 1891)

### BIBLIOGRAPHY
*DNB*
D. A. R. Lindsay: *The Bibliotheca Lindesiana* (Manchester, 1946)
——: *Alexander Lindsay, 25th Earl of Crawford and the Bibliotheca Lindesiana* (New York, 1957)
H. Brigstocke: *Lord Lindsay and James Dennistoun: Two Scottish Art Historians and Collectors of Early Italian Art* (diss., U. Edinburgh, 1976)
N. Barker: *Bibliotheca Lindesiana* (London, 1977)
H. Brigstocke: 'Lord Lindsay and the *Sketches of the History of Christian Art', Bull. John Rylands Lib.*, lxiv (1981–2), pp. 27–60
——: 'Lord Lindsay as a Collector', *Bull. John Rylands Lib.*, lxiv (1981–2), pp. 287–333

**Lindsay**, Sir **Coutts**, Bart (*b* Balcarres, Fife, 2 Feb 1824; *d* London, 7 May 1913). Scottish painter and gallery owner. He was a grandson of the banker Sir Coutts Trotter and the son of James and Anne Lindsay of Balcarres. In 1838 he visited Italy for the first time, with his cousin Alexander, Lord Lindsay (who, in 1847, dedicated his *Sketches of the History of Christian Art* to him). As a young man Lindsay had a passionate interest in the arts. He experimented with fresco painting and took drawing lessons. In 1854, in Rome, Lindsay met Mrs Adelaide Sartoris, who introduced him to a circle of English painters, probably including Frederic Leighton, George Heming Mason and Edward John Poynter. In London he joined the Little Holland House circle and numbered many painters among his friends.

Lindsay's most important early work was a fresco (1875) for Dorchester House, London (destr.), the mansion of his brother-in-law Robert Staynor Holford. Between 1862 and 1875 he occasionally submitted portraits and figurative subjects to the Royal Academy, but his works were often rejected. His dissatisfaction with the organization of the Academy and low opinion of much of the work shown there caused him in 1875 to contemplate starting a private gallery, where works by his many painter friends and others of standing might be shown. Having failed to find an existing gallery he spent about £120,000 constructing the Grosvenor Gallery at 135–7 New Bond Street, which opened in 1877.

Satirized by W. S. Gilbert as the 'Greenery-Yallery Grosvenor Gallery', it was a stupendous success and immediately became the forum where paintings of the Aesthetic Movement were shown. Edward Burne-Jones, who had not exhibited since 1873, made a vast impact; in 1877 his exhibits included *The Mirror of Venus* (1873–7; Lisbon, Mus. Gulbenkian) and *The Beguiling of Merlin* (1872–7; Port Sunlight, Lady Lever A.G.). Whistler showed *Nocturne in Black and Gold: The Falling Rocket* (*c.* 1874; Detroit, MI, Inst. A.), the spark for the famous libel case against Ruskin. Other prominent exhibitors were G. F. Watts (who in 1877 showed *Love and Death*; London, Tate), Lawrence Alma-Tadema and Poynter. Leighton also accepted the invitation to exhibit but sent

nothing of importance. The Grosvenor differed from all existing galleries in that artists were personally invited to exhibit in the summer shows. Once invited they might show any work as long as it had not been previously submitted to the Royal Academy. Thus Lindsay forestalled accusations that the Grosvenor was an easy alternative to the Academy. Some but not all Grosvenor pictures were for sale, but efforts were made to keep the commercial aspect discreet. Great care was taken with the arrangement of the galleries and the sympathetic and symmetrical hanging of the pictures. Furniture and works of art were combined to create a rich and highly decorative effect. It was one of the first galleries to be lit by electricity, from 1883. Lindsay was assisted in running the gallery by Charles Hallé (1846–1914) and J. Comyns-Carr (1849–1916). In 1882 Lindsay's marriage to Blanche Fitzroy, a talented musician and painter and Rothschild heiress, broke down. Her consequent withdrawal from the gallery caused mounting financial strain. Lindsay sought to make more money from the gallery and introduced various commercial sidelines. Hallé and Comyns-Carr were replaced by business managers and, in 1887, resigned to form the New Gallery, taking with them many leading painters including Burne-Jones; the New Gallery quickly overtook the Grosvenor as the avant-garde exhibition space of the period. The Grosvenor finally closed in 1890, and Lindsay withdrew from artistic life.

### BIBLIOGRAPHY
B. Bullen: 'The Palace of Art: Sir Coutts Lindsay and the Grosvenor Gallery', *Apollo*, cii (1975), pp. 352–7

CHRISTOPHER NEWALL

**Lindsay, Norman (Alfred Williams)** (*b* Creswick, Victoria, 23 Feb 1879; *d* Sydney, NSW, 21 Nov 1969). Australian draughtsman, painter and writer. Born into a family that produced fine artists, his early skill in drawing and reading was encouraged by relatives. He received his only formal training in 1897 at the art colony run by Walter Withers at 'Charterisville' in Heidelberg. In 1899 he moved to Sydney, married in 1900, and began a lifelong association with the *Bulletin*. He was best known for exquisite pen drawings whose dark areas were enlivened by minute traces of white. In 1906 he began producing wash drawings; during World War I he designed government posters, and after the war he took up watercolour painting. From 1918 to 1938 he concentrated on etchings, which were printed by his second wife, Rose Soady (*b c.* 1885), whom he married in 1920. She collected the drawings and proofs for his over two hundred published etchings, which are now in the Mitchell Library, Sydney. In 1927 he founded the Fanfrolico Press with his son Jack. His home at Springwood, NSW, is now a gallery and museum.

Lindsay's belief that the artist exists outside the visible world led him to fill his works with beings from myth and fantasy. His lush imagery of ribald satyrs and fleshy nymphs was generally in a Rococo style, executed with great technical skill. He was also a prolific writer, producing poetry, novels, criticism and children's stories.

### WRITINGS
*Creative Effort* (Sydney, 1920, rev. London, 1924)

BIBLIOGRAPHY

J. Heatherington: *Norman Lindsay: The Embattled Olympian* (Melbourne, 1973)

L. Bloomfield, ed.: *The World of Norman Lindsay* (Melbourne, 1979)

ROSEMARY T. SMITH

**Lindsay**, Major **Robert**. *See under* LOYD, SAMUEL JONES.

**Lindtmayer** [Lindtmeyer]. Swiss family of artists. The family was typical of 16th-century families of artisans, passing trade from father to son. During this period Swiss glass painting underwent a radical shift from predominantly architectural commissions to the *Kabinettscheibe* (independent panel), which was mostly commissioned by lay donors for insertion in secular settings. The record of the Lindtmayers shows the increasing importance of the designer (the *Risser*) who furnished drawings for execution by the glass painter, often for a variety of workshops. Presumably the son of Baschion Lindtmayer (*d* 1519), an itinerant glass painter who settled in Schaffhausen, Felix Lindtmayer I (*d* Schaffhausen, *c.* 1543), also a glass painter, is credited with panels from the monastery of St George (Schaffhausen, Mus. Allerheiligen) and a panel of a corporation (Zurich, Schweizer. Landesmus.).

(1) **Felix Lindtmayer II** (*b* ?1523/4; *d* Schaffhausen, 5 Oct 1574). Glass painter and draughtsman. He was the son of Felix Lindtmayer I. His work was of great technical brilliance, both in the handling of the sketch and in the selection of colour and exploitation of painterly effect in the medium of glass. A drawing of *Two Standard-bearers with the Banner of Schaffhausen* (Boston, MA, Mus. F.A., 44.828) shows great facility in the handling of outline and shading using variegated neutral washes. His own coat of arms was found on a panel painted in 1552 showing the standing figures of Lindtmayer and Galle Jäger over their respective shields (Schaffhausen, Dr Bernhard Peyer, priv. col.).

(2) **Daniel Lindtmayer II** (*b* Schaffhausen, 1552; *d* Lucerne, 1602–7). Glass painter, draughtsman and engraver, son of (1) Felix Lindtmayer II. He learnt his trade in the workshop of his father but was also influenced by the painter and engraver Tobias Stimmer, a resident of Schaffhausen who transferred his workshop to Basle. Daniel also moved to Basle and by 1574/5 is documented as a designer for local glass painters. In 1588 he married the widow of Werner Kübler (1555–86). Basle was an important and cosmopolitan city, linked with the upper Rhine as well as with Switzerland, where artists were likely to receive ideas, influences and commissions from many other regions. Daniel's work was far more complicated and 'literary' than his father's. His designs for *Kabinettscheiben* are deeply influenced by developments in the representation of linear perspective in contemporary prints. The images are far more elaborate and incorporate Renaissance strapwork, Classical elements in the architectural frames and volumetric rendering of the human figure, including the allegorical nude—for example in the image of *Fortuna with the Shield of Nussbaum* (Zurich, Schweizer. Landesmus.; see fig.). A signed drawing with the arms of Falkner and Obermeyer (1574; Darmstadt, Hess. Landesmus.) shows a wealth of classical figures in the upper panel

Daniel Lindtmayer II: *Fortuna with the Shield of Nussbaum*, pen and black ink and grey wash, 415×310 mm, 1580 (Zurich, Schweizerisches Landesmuseum)

and an architectural frame populated by putti and allegorical figures, similar to Stimmer's *Bilderbibel* (illustrated Bible) formats. Daniel Lindtmayer led a turbulent life and in 1595 apparently attempted to murder a goldsmith named Stülz in Konstanz; he escaped punishment on the grounds of insanity.

BIBLIOGRAPHY

P. Ganz: *Die Basler Glasmaler der Spätrenaissance und der Barockzeit* (Basle, 1966), pp. 42–5

F. Thöne: *Daniel Lindtmayer, 1552–1606/7: Die Schaffhauser Künstlerfamilie Lindtmayer* (Zurich, 1975)

VIRGINIA CHIEFFO RAGUIN

**Line, John**, & Sons Ltd. English wallpaper manufacturing company founded *c.* 1880 by John Line. He was originally a cabinetmaker in Bath and in 1874 acquired a furniture business in Reading that was then run by Line's three sons. The company had a London agent by 1880, when it began trading from Reading as a wallpaper wholesaler. Later it branched out into private design production, then block-printing and stencilling. The firm's first pattern book (London, V&A, see Oman and Hamilton, no. 701) offered cheap machine prints, whose patterns showed the influence of design reformers, together with a few original blocked and stencilled patterns, many of which were designed for the firm by F. G. Froggatt. In 1892 the company moved to London and in 1905 issued a small collection, the success of which led to the building of a block-printing factory at Southall in 1906. By the same year complete decorative schemes could be printed to customers' specifications. Designers who worked for Line included Christopher Dresser, the Silver Studio, C. F. A. Voysey and William J. Neatby (1860–1910), who was the firm's chief designer from 1907 to 1910. The firm became well known for its flock wallpapers that were produced into the 1950s. In the 1930s the firm played an important role in the revival of interest in scenic papers, featuring modernist motifs as well as romantic landscapes.

In 1951 Line issued the first British set of screenprinted papers, an influential and successful collection called Limited Editions. Each design was stamped with the name of the pattern and the designer, among whom were such artists as John Minton, who designed 'Tuscany', and Lucienne Day (b 1917), who designed 'Provence' (both 1951; London, V&A; for illustration of the latter see WALLPAPER, colour pl. V, fig. 3). Also in 1951, W. J. Odell, then a staff member and later chief designer, produced a set of designs based on atomic structures for the Festival Pattern Group (London, V&A). In 1953 the firm opened a new showroom in Tottenham Court Road, launching the Contemporary Backgrounds collection and also introducing complementary wallpapers consisting of a large-scale, bold-patterned paper with a quieter, coordinated design. After merger with SHAND KYDD Ltd in 1958 the Line brand continued to be used for certain collections, in particular the Folio range.

BIBLIOGRAPHY

A. V. Sugden and J. L. Edmondson: *A History of English Wallpaper, 1509–1914* (London, 1926)

C. C. Oman and J. Hamilton: *Wallpapers: A History and Illustrated Catalogue of the Collection of the Victoria and Albert Museum* (London, 1982)

*A Popular Art: British Wallpapers, 1930–1960* (exh. cat. by L. Hoskins, M. Pinney and M. Turner, London, Middx Poly., Silver Studio Col., 1990)

CLARE TAYLOR

**Linear perspective.** *See* PERSPECTIVE, §II.

**Linen diaper and damask.** Self-patterned, fine white linen that has been used in western Europe since the 15th century for tablecloths, napkins and handtowels. Initially, these figured linens were described in various ways, but in England by the mid-16th century they were classed, notably in probate inventories, as either 'diaper' or 'damask'. This classification was descriptive rather than technical, 'diaper' and 'damask' being differentiated solely on the complexity of the pattern: small repeat patterns, often of a geometrical form, were described as 'diaper' and figurative patterns with longer repeats as 'damasks'.

1. Techniques. 2. Patterns. 3. Centres of production.

1. TECHNIQUES. Diaper and damask are both 'float' or 'self-patterned' weaves, and it is the warp or weft threads 'floating' unbound over two or more weft or warp threads that catch the light and reveal the figure. The three basic binding systems, tabby, twill and satin (*see* TEXTILE, §II, 1(ii)), were all used for float weaves. A few figured linens with tabby bindings survive, probably what were described in the 17th century as 'huckaback-diaper'. The diapers with patterns that match such inventory descriptions as 'losinge', 'cross diamondes' and 'birdes eyes' have twill bindings. Some, particularly those of fine quality

1. Linen-damask tablecloth (detail) with 'tables' depicting *Abraham and Isaac* and *Samson and the Lion*, 2.27×1.96 m, from Kortrijk, Flanders, early 16th century (London, Victoria and Albert Museum)

woven in the Dutch Republic from the 17th century, have satin bindings.

Unlike diapers, which exhibit all three binding systems, damasks normally have only satin bindings. Of the many possible satin bindings, just three have been used in the weaving of linen damasks: satin of 5, 7 and 8. Before 1700 most damasks were of satin of 5. Nevertheless, there is a small group of very beautiful damasks (see fig. 1) woven between 1515 and 1530 in satin of 7. They have unbalanced weaves with weft counts often double that of the warp. From the mid-16th century balanced weaves were normally used, with point repeats (see fig. 2), in which successive units of pattern are mirror images of each other. Around 1710 Saxon weavers began to use satin of 8, with comber repeats (see fig. 3), a practice followed later in the century in several other centres, and in which there is a horizontal repetition of units of pattern without variation.

The production of linen thread from flax and the finishing processes, including bleaching, were similar for all fine linens (*see* TEXTILE, §I, 1); it was the weaving process that set diapers and damasks apart. Diapers were mostly woven on a shaft loom. Damasks were always woven on the much more complicated draw loom.

For weaving diapers with twill bindings, a loom with four shafts was used for the many small-repeat patterns, but considerably more shafts were required for some of the patterns with longer repeats. Diapers with satin of 5 bindings were woven on a loom with either five shafts or a double harness of ten. Knowledge of weaving practice is sketchy, but in the 19th century diaper patterns with satin of 8 bindings were woven on looms with 16 shafts.

The draw loom was first used to weave linen damask in the Low Countries during the 15th century. Certain modifications were made to the loom in the 18th century, and early in the 19th century Joseph-Marie Jacquard

3. Linen-damask napkin with bizarre silk pattern, 655×635 mm, from Silesia or Saxony, *c*. 1708 (London, Victoria and Albert Museum)

replaced the leashes and drawboy with a punched-card mechanism. By 1840 Jacquard looms were widely used for weaving linen damasks. Soon afterwards power looms were developed. These technological changes had considerable cost benefits, and damasks, which in the early 16th century were found only in the houses of the great, now graced the tables of the middle classes.

Three types of cloth were woven in diaper and damask: tabling, napkining and towelling. They were made in a series of standard widths based on the local ell. In Kortrijk and Haarlem this was *c*. 700 mm, while in Silesia and Saxony it was *c*. 670 mm. In the Low Countries most damask tablecloths were 3 or 4 ells wide, and napkins 1 ell or 5 quarters of an ell wide. Before the widespread use of forks (which in several countries did not occur until *c*. 1700), towels were used at table for the washing of hands. In the 18th century new beverages and a changed pattern of meals required smaller cloths for supper and napkins for tea.

2. PATTERNS. These can be grouped in three categories: first, those woven for stock for the general market (typically, these were biblical stories, hunting scenes and commemorative and floral designs); second, stock designs personalized by the addition of coats of arms or inscriptions (see fig. 2); third, unique designs to fulfil a personal order.

Initially, the patterns were designed by the weavers, who took ideas from a variety of sources. Engravings were fertile ground (see fig. 1): in two pieces (London, V&A; Amsterdam, Rijksmus.) a portrait of Elizabeth I was taken

2. Linen-damask handtowel with scene of *Orpheus Charming the Animals with his Music*, 1.68×0.73 m, from Haarlem, 1645 (Amsterdam, Rijksmuseum)

from an engraving of 1559, possibly by Frans Huys; several early 17th-century biblical scenes were derived from illustrations by Jean de Tournes (1504–64) and Jost Amman (for illustration see van Ysselsteyn, 1962, figs vii and viii, cat. nos 92 and 98); and in the 18th century engravings after Antoine Watteau, Daniel Marot I and P. P. Bacqueville (*fl* 1720) were used by Saxon weavers (Kortrijk, Mus. S. Kst.). The influence of other woven textiles was also pervasive: several early 16th-century linen damasks have fields of the foliate designs used in the 15th century for silk damasks and velvets (fig. 1); in the first decade of the 18th century bizarre silk designs occurred on German table-linen (fig. 3); a group of finely woven damasks, dating from the 1760s, has patterns of undulating lacy ribbons strewn with posies of flowers similar to those widely produced in silk, typically by L. Galy Gallien & Cie in Lyon. Both these sources can be seen in the engravings by Paul Androuet Du Cerceau, *Feuillage et fleures propres aux peintres, brodeurs et ouvriers en soye* (Paris, *c*. 1670); there are Dutch napkins from the 1660s (for illustration see J. D. Hunt, ed.: 'The Anglo-Dutch Garden in the Age of William and Mary', *J. Gdn Hist.*, April–Sept 1988) with designs that reflect this work.

It seems that the weavers prepared the point paper plans, from which the loom was set up, from their own preliminary sketches until the mid-18th century, when specialists were commissioned to prepare the designs. In Scotland, for example, the Board of Trustees not only commissioned local artists to design patterns for manufacturers but also sponsored annual design competitions. Between 1818 and 1838 prizes were awarded to 25 designers in these competitions, including the painter Joseph Noël Paton, who was to become the most famous Scottish damask designer in the middle of the century. Designs were subsequently produced by such celebrated artists as Walter Crane in England and Chris Lebeau in Holland.

Before 1550 three types of composition can be distinguished. The simplest has single motifs with modest horizontal and vertical repeats, often within a decorative lattice, but without any borders; inventory entries seem to describe such designs as 'knotts [with] roses in them', 'roses and Eagles' and 'flower de luces crowned'. A second type has individual scenes treated as elaborately framed 'tables' or pictures. These occupy the whole of a napkin and for a tablecloth are typically set against a 'pomegranate' ground (see fig. 1). They have unbalanced weaves of satin of seven. The third type has up to seven horizontal registers woven in point repeat. These illustrate scenes that tell a story in a complete vertical repeat, which may be as long as 3 m.

This final compositional idea was the most widely used between 1550 and 1750. Initially some pieces were borderless, but after 1600 most tablecloths and napkins had two distinct components, a central field and either two or four borders. The finest work always had four borders, but the cheaper damasks even into the 18th century sported only side borders. As linen damask was woven in a continuous piece *c*. 33 m long, it was easier to weave it without regular top and bottom borders. Further, there was more flexibility for the merchant and his customer, who could cut the piece into any desired lengths.

As with such similar bordered items as tapestries, the two design elements were initially treated quite separately. Even if similar subjects were used, for example a commemorative design of a siege with military trophies in the borders, the two elements were separated not only by their scale and graphic treatment but also physically by lines between the border and field. For tapestries it was early in the 17th century, but for damasks rather later, that the strict differentiation between the border and the field began to break down, and border motifs began to overflow into the field. By the Rococo period the differentiation had disappeared completely. The Neo-classical revival reinstated the strict hierarchy of the border, but with the difference that the border motifs and the urns and swags of the corner transitions were closely related to those of the field to form a coherent whole.

There were also attempts to break out of the episodic strait-jacket of horizontal registers. An illusion of three dimensions was created by gradations in the vertical scale and by the use of dropped point repeats. One such attempt is the series of patterns of 1680–1740 of an elegant couple by a fountain in a palace garden with the vista closed by a hunting-lodge in the deer-park beyond, most probably woven in Kortrijk (London, V&A; Kortrijk, Mus. S. Kst.).

A great number of subjects were depicted on linen damask, but they broadly fall into five groups: armorial, biblical and mythological, floral, commemorative and topographical. Although these were made in all the major production centres, the proportion associated with each type obviously varied with time and place. A significant number of the pieces dominated by coats of arms and heraldic badges were bespoke designs. However, there were stock designs marking the coronations and marriages of princes, often woven for a particular national market.

Biblical subjects from both the Old and New Testaments were made in considerable variety and number in the Low Countries in the 16th and 17th centuries. The early designs included several versions of the Annunciation and the Glorification of the Virgin Mary; later the popular Old Testament stories predominated, although the New Testament was also represented, notably by the parables of the Prodigal Son and the Good Samaritan. This changing emphasis was probably associated with the Reformation, as Haarlem's markets were mostly Protestant and Kortrijk's partly so. Mythological subjects were also made but in much smaller numbers.

Floral designs occurred in profusion and variety, reflecting the current fashion in flowers: gillyflowers and pine-cones from Kortrijk in the 16th century; exuberant Baroque tulips and crown-imperials from Haarlem in the 1670s; wide borders of tendrilled passion-flowers from Ireland *c*. 1800; and Art Nouveau arum lilies from the end of the 19th century. Commemorative patterns were also woven in each period, although the largest number were made during the War of Spanish Succession (1701–13). As most of these were woven in Kortrijk, the particular victories that were celebrated depended on the fortunes of war, for the town changed hands between the Grand Alliance and France several times. The speed of production, as one siege followed hard on the heels of another, meant that many horizontal registers and borders were

simply reused with different inscriptions. The topographical patterns were principally views of European cities.
There were splendid napkins of London and Venice from
the Low Countries, although the majority of pieces in this
group were woven in Germany in the early 18th century.
In the 19th century, views were woven in Sweden of the
factory at Vadstena and in Russia of the elegant panoramas
of the city of Yaroslavl'.

It is difficult to establish the numbers that were woven
in each group, as it is only the most treasured or fortunate
pieces that survive. It seems likely that a higher proportion
of stock floral patterns were made than have survived,
particularly in view of the comment by the London linen-
draper quoted above. This supposition is reinforced by a
study of 16th-century English inventories that suggests
that more than half the patterns were floral. Most damask
patterns made now are still of flowers, but they tend to be
pale reflections of their former glory.

3. CENTRES OF PRODUCTION. Diaper, woven on the
widely distributed shaft loom, was produced in many
places, while linen damasks woven on the rarer draw loom
were confined to a few specialized centres. Diaper was
made in Italy, Germany and the Low Countries from at
least the 14th century and subsequently in many other
parts of Europe. Linen damask was first woven in the
southern Netherlands during the 15th century (see NETH-
ERLANDS, THE, §XI, 3) and was established at Kortrijk in
Flanders by 1496, when the Guild of St Catherine promulgated detailed statues for its production. Although some
damask was woven at Caen in Normandy during the 16th
century, Kortrijk remained the only important centre until,
following the Dutch Revolt, certain weavers moved to
Haarlem c. 1585. One of the weavers who moved north
was Passchier Lamertijn (1563–1620). He established a
considerable enterprise in Haarlem supplying table-linen
to the town council and the States-General of the United
Provinces as gifts for foreign princes and visiting dignitaries. In 1607 he moved to Alkmaar and after 1619 to
Copenhagen, where until his death he worked for Christian
IV. Several splendid examples of his work survive (Amsterdam, Rijksmus.; London, V&A; Edinburgh, Royal
Mus. Scotland).

Both Kortrijk and Haarlem exported some damask,
whereas the Flemish weavers relied heavily on their
overseas markets. In the 16th and 17th centuries these
were very dependent on the political situation: France, for
example, was an important market, which at certain periods
was closed to Flemish goods.

Around 1600 Flemish weavers also moved to Schleswig-
Holstein and Silesia, where the production of damask
table-linen was established by the middle of the century.
Apart from a few dated pieces from the first half of the
17th century, there are modest entries of 'Sletia' damask
in the customs books for the Port of London from 1611.
It appears that the first manufacture of linen damask in
Saxony was established at Gross Schonau, near Zittau, in
1666 by Friedrich Lange and Christian Lange. Towards
the end of the century very large quantities of both diaper
and damask were produced in Saxony and Silesia. It was
not of such good quality as that from the Low Countries,

but it was less expensive. In 1695 a London linen-draper
wrote (J. F., 1696):

> It [sleasie-damask] is not so fine nor of such curious works
> as the former [Holland-Damask], it being usually wrought all
> in Flowers, and with this farther difference, that it will not
> wear white after washed, as the Holland-Damask doth . . .
> but it is always bought much cheaper.

From c. 1710 the quality of both design and manufacture
improved dramatically, showing a vitality, a desire for
experiment and a rapid response to changing fashion. This
reflected the contemporary burgeoning of another Saxon
industry, that of porcelain at Meissen. Exports were
buoyant, putting pressure on the Low Countries' trade.

In France diaper was produced at several centres from
the 15th century, and by the mid-17th century considerable
quantities were woven in Normandy. In the 1670s imports
to England of French diaper were more than double those
from the Low Countries. Damask was produced by the
Graindorge family in Caen at the end of the 16th century.
It seems that there was a decline from c. 1640, although
some damask was shipped from Caen in the 1670s. During
Jean-Baptiste Colbert's ministry there were attempts to
encourage a native industry, and in the 18th century several
manufactures were established in French Flanders, but
none of them prospered for very long. In the 19th century
several factories were built, including those at Panissières
(Loire) and Pau-en-Béarn (Pyrénées-Atlantiques).

In Russia, Sweden and Britain there were also attempts
to set up a native industry on the basis of the sort of
import-substitution familiar in the case of other commodities. Peter the Great established a large factory at Yaroslavl' in 1722. Although the original factory closed in 1856,
other factories continued to weave damask at the end of
the 20th century. In Sweden damask was produced briefly
in Stockholm at the start of the 18th century and then at
the Flors factory in Hälsingland. In 1753 a mill was
founded by the state at Vadstena, although it quickly
passed into private hands. It closed in 1843.

The British government's first attempt to improve the
linen industries was in Ireland, where William III granted
a patent in 1698 to a Huguenot, Louis Crommelin, to set
up a fine-linen manufacture in Lisburn. As in similar
ventures in Saxony, Russia and Sweden, specialists from
Holland or Flanders were initially employed. The industry
prospered, helped by the establishment in 1711 of the
Irish Linen Board, which concentrated on improving the
quality of plain linens.

In 1737 Lionel Cranfield Sackville, the 1st Duke of
Dorset, who had served as Lord Lieutenant in Ireland,
ordered considerable quantities of Irish damask and diaper
for the royal household, where he was Lord Steward to
George II. From this date the English Crown no longer
bought damask and diaper from the Low Countries but
switched entirely to Irish production. However, only a few
identified examples of Irish damask (London, V&A)
survive from before the late 18th century; many of these
were produced by the I. W. W. Coulson factory established
at Lisburn in 1765. Factories were also established in
Belfast, and some of these continued to operate into the
20th century.

In Scotland the existing linen industry was similarly encouraged by the Scottish Board of Trustees, formed in 1727. Although both diaper and damask had been woven in the 17th century, the concentration, as in Ireland, was on plain linens. Nevertheless, determined efforts were made in the middle of the century to improve the quality of diaper by 'means of the fforeigner some years brought overhere' (Campbell, 1964, p. 82). The only damasks produced in any quantity were bespoke napkins, often woven with the year and the names of husband and wife. It was only from *c*. 1800 that Scottish stock patterns were able to compete with Continental designs. In the 19th century production expanded considerably, and Dunfermline became a major centre of production.

Both Scotland and Ireland not only satisfied the British market but also exported large quantities of table-linen to the USA and to the expanding British empire. In the 20th century all the manufacturing centres in Britain and Continental Europe experienced a severe decline.

### BIBLIOGRAPHY

J. F.: *The Merchant's Warehouse Laid Open, or The Plain Dealing Linnen-Draper* (London, 1696)

E. Kumsch: *Leinendamastmuster des XVII und XVIII Jahrhunderts* (Dresden, 1891)

A. F. Gryaznov: *Yaroslavskaya bol'shaya manufatture* [The great Yaroslavl' manufactory] (Moscow, 1910)

*Linnedamast* (Stockholm, 1931)

M. Braun-Ronsdorf: *Alte Tafeldamaste* (Darmstadt, 1955)

C. A. Burgers: *Damast* ('s Hertogenbosch, 1959)

——: 'De Friese wapens tussen andere wapen inwerikngen in Haarlemse linnen Tafeldamasten mit de 17c aeeuw', *Vrije Fries*, xliv (1960), pp. 123–48 [Frisian armorials]

G. T. van Ysselsteyn: *White Figurated Linen Damask* (The Hague, 1962) [bibliog. incl. pioneering works by J. Six and J. de Bethune]

A. S. Cavallo: 'Joseph Neil Paton: Designer of Damasks', *Connoisseur*, cliii (1963), pp. 59–64

——: 'To Set a Smart Board', *Bus. Hist. Rev.*, xxxvii (1963), pp. 49–58

C. A. Burgers: *Antiek damast modern geulvks* [Antique damask in modern table settings] (Enschede, 1964)

R. H. Campbell, ed.: *States of the Annual Progress of the Linen Manufacture, 1727–54* (Edinburgh, 1964), p. 82

C. A. Burgers: 'Nogmaals Passchier Lammertijn', *Oud-Holland*, lxxx (1965), pp. 139–68

A. S. Cavallo: 'Continental Sources of Early Damask Patterns in Scotland', *Burl. Mag.*, cvii (1965), pp. 559–63

A. Bugge and S. Haugstoga: *Damaskveving på bondegården* [Damask weaving on farms] (Oslo, 1968)

R. Jacques: *Gebilddamast* (Krefeld, 1968)

C. A. Burgers: 'De verovering van Boeda-Pest' [The capture of Budapest], *Bull. Rijksmus.*, xvii (1969), pp. 126–34

E. László: 'Gebilddamaste aus Sachsen und Schlesien', *A. Dec.*, iv (1976), pp. 69–87

C. A. Burgers: 'Bizarre patronen in linnen damast', *Ned. Ksthist. Jb.*, xxxi (1980), pp. 289–98

——: 'Dutch Damasks for Denmark', *Documenta Textilia*, ed. M. Flury-Lemberg and K. Stolleis (1981), pp. 251–60

M. Prinet: *Le Damas de lin historié* (Berne, 1982)

A.-S. Topelius: *Damastduktyg, och verksamheten vid Vadstena fabrik, 1753–1843* [Damask tablecloths and the products of the Vadstena factory, 1753–1843] (Stockholm, 1985) [bibliog. incl. 19 important works by E. Thorman, 1933–51]

A. G. Pauwels and I. Bauwens-de Jaegere: *Damast* (Kortrijk, 1986)

C. A. Burgers: 'Some Notes on Western European Table Linen', *Upholstery in America and Europe* (New York, 1987), pp. 149–61

D. M. Mitchell: 'By your Leave my Masters', *Textile Hist.*, xx (1989), pp. 49–77

C. Paludan and B. Wieth-Knudsen, eds: *Damask og drejl* [Damask and drill] (Copenhagen, 1989)

D. M. MITCHELL

**Lin Fengmian** [Lin Feng-mien; Lin Fengmin] (*b* Mei xian, Guangdong Province, 1900; *d* 1991). Chinese art educator and painter. His grandfather was a carver of tombstones, as was his father, who also learnt to paint. He began carving and painting as a child, often copying from the *Jiezi yuan huazhuan* ('Mustard-seed Garden painting manual'; 1679 and 1701). He sold his first painting at the age of nine. In 1918 he moved to Shanghai, where he saw an advertisement for a work-study programme in France. That winter he began work in France as a signboard painter, after which he spent some months studying French at Fontainebleau and elsewhere. One school had a collection of plaster casts, which he began to draw in his spare time. In the spring of 1920 he entered the Dijon National Academy of Fine Arts and began to draw figures in charcoal. Within six months he had been recommended by the head of the school, a relief sculptor, to the Ecole Nationale Supérieure des Beaux-Arts in Paris. He also studied drawing and oil painting at the Cormon art studio in Paris and learnt much from the collections of the Louvre and the Musée Guimet. In 1922 his oil painting *Autumn* was exhibited at the Salon d'Automne. He spent 1923 in Berlin, where his limited funds would extend further and where he was introduced to northern European movements in painting. In 1924 he contributed over 40 oil paintings and Chinese-media paintings (executed using water-based ink and natural pigments on paper or silk) to an exhibition of ancient and modern Chinese art in Strasbourg, organized by the Chinese government; these revealed his interest in combining Eastern and Western concepts in his painting. Two large oil paintings were accepted for the 1924 Salon d'Automne. The following year Lin exhibited in the Chinese section of the Exposition Internationale des Arts Décoratifs.

He returned to China in the winter of 1925, with his French second wife, to become principal of the Beiping [Beijing] Academy of Art, but resigned two years later because of political instability in northern China. In Nanjing, as chairman of an art education committee under the government's University Council, he prepared the first all-China art exhibition in 1928 and planned the new Hangzhou National Academy of Arts, of which he served as principal until 1938, when the Beiping Academy was merged with the Hangzhou Academy, and he became chairman of its administrative committee. The eruption of student unrest at the time contributed to his decision to become an independent painter in Shanghai. In 1939 the Sino-Japanese War (1937–45) forced Lin to leave for unoccupied territory. During the war he served the government in various capacities, and afterwards taught intermittently until 1952, when deteriorating health caused him to move to Shanghai. In 1956 his wife and daughter moved to Brazil. From 1966 to 1976 Lin suffered persecution during the Cultural Revolution and in 1977 he left mainland China to make his home in Hong Kong.

Lin Fengmian had major one-man exhibitions in Beijing, Shanghai and Hong Kong from 1926 onwards. His paintings were also shown at the Musée Guimet and the Jeu de Paume in Paris in 1946, 1953, 1955 and 1979. The National Gallery in Prague owns some of his works. The large oil paintings of Lin Fengmian's early Paris period no longer survive, but their titles, such as *Desire to Live* and

*Search* suggest Fauvist influence. His Chinese-style water-colour paintings of flowers and birds from that time reveal elements of the late works of Cézanne and of the Expressionists, in the breaking up of contours and the use of strong colours. During the war, he developed a personal style in landscapes and paintings of female beauties, simplifying form and line in an apparently naive manner derived from Chinese folk art and early representational works, especially of the Han period (206 BC–AD 220). His study of painting on ceramics in Paris at the Museum of Porcelain and Pottery prompted him to strive for effects of clarity and transparency in his use of colour. In later years his subject-matter increasingly embraced Chinese themes, ranging from Peking Opera to New Year woodblock prints. His figural works, especially of women, nevertheless retained stylizations derived from Matisse and Modigliani, and his use of Chinese traditional media was modfied by his knowledge of Western watercolour, oil-painting and pastel techniques. He also showed a preference for the easel format rather than Chinese scroll compositions. Through these and other innovations, Lin Fengmian sought to release Chinese painting from the sterility he perceived in the literati painting tradition.

### WRITINGS
*Zhongguo huihua xinlun* [New theories of Chinese painting] (Beijing, 1929)

### BIBLIOGRAPHY
De-jinn Shiy: *Contemporary Chinese Painter: Lin Feng-mien* (Taipei, 1979)

HSIO-YEN SHIH

**Lingelbach, Johannes** [Jan] (*b* Frankfurt am Main, *bapt* 10 Oct 1622; *d* Amsterdam, Nov 1674). German painter, active in the Netherlands and Italy. By 1634 his family had settled in Amsterdam, where presumably Lingelbach trained as a painter. According to Houbraken, he visited France in 1642 and arrived in Italy two years later. However, he is not mentioned in any document of 1644, although he is recorded in Rome from 1647 to 1649. The artist left Rome in 1650 and by 1653 was back in Amsterdam, where he remained until his death. Lingelbach is perhaps the only one of the Dutch Italianates with a catalogue of numerous signed and dated works to document his artistic development. The first two signed works are *The Blacksmith* (1650; Rome, Melmeluzzi priv. col., see Briganti, Trezzani and Laureati, fig. 10.1) and *Self-portrait with Violin* (1650; Zurich, Ksthaus). Unfortunately no certain works survive from the previous years. Kren (1982) attributed a series of works depicting Roman trades, some formerly ascribed to Pieter van Laer, to Lingelbach's early career. The original group consisted of three small paintings: the *Acquavita-seller*, the *Cake-seller* and *The Tobacconist* (all Rome, Pal. Corsini). While these paintings have some striking points in common with the Melmeluzzi

Johannes Lingelbach: *Market in the Piazza del Popolo*, oil on canvas, 870×1175 mm, 1664 (Vienna, Akademie der Bildenden Künste)

*Blacksmith* of 1650 and the signed *Dentist on Horseback* (1651; Amsterdam, Rijksmus.), it is still uncertain whether they belong to Lingelbach's pre-1650 work or are by another hand (sometimes called the Master of the Trades). In the Melmeluzzi *Blacksmith* the forms are drawn with a dry, incisive line that gives the figures an almost caricature-like air, whereas in the Roman *Trades* the volumes are given body by a dense, intense and mellow style of painting.

In the next few years Lingelbach painted large compositions that are his best-known works: the great *Market in the Piazza Navona* (Frankfurt am Main, Städel. Kstinst.) and the *Carnival* (Vienna, Ksthist. Mus.). These fancifully painted Roman piazzas are crowded and busy; the settings evoke a feeling of space and distance, fading more and more into memory. By comparison with the Amsterdam *Dentist on Horseback*, the *Market in the Piazza del Popolo* (1664; Vienna, Akad. Bild. Kst.; see fig.) is Dutch in its language and in the figure types depicted. Northern collectors wanted an 'impression' of Rome, not a historically correct reconstruction of the city. Thus Lingelbach developed the 'Italianate' genre that was imitated by Dutch artists who had never been to Italy. Lingelbach also produced paintings of port scenes populated by a great variety of types: Turks, merchants, gamblers and pedlars.

BIBLIOGRAPHY

A. Houbraken: *De groote schouburgh* (1718–21)
A.-N. Dézallier d'Argenville: *Abrégé de la vie des plus fameux peintres* (1745–52, 2/1762)
A. Busiri Vici: 'Fantasie romane di Johannes Lingelbach', *Stud. Romani*, vii (1950), pp. 42–53
A. M. Clark: 'J. Lingelbach, "Piazza del Popolo"', *Minneapolis Inst. A. Bull.*, li (1962), pp. 53–4
C. Burger Wegener: *Johannes Lingelbach, 1622–1674* (Schwerin, 1976)
T. Kren: 'Johannes Lingelbach in Rome', *Getty Mus. J.*, x (1982), pp. 42–62
G. Briganti, L. Trezzani and L. Laureati: *The Bamboccianti* (Rome, 1983), pp. 250–85
*Civiltà del seicento a Napoli* (exh. cat., Naples, Capodimonte, 1984), pp. 155–8
*Masters of Seventeenth-century Dutch Genre Painting* (exh. cat. by P. Sutton, Philadelphia, PA, Mus. A.; Berlin, Gemäldegal.; London, RA; 1984), pp. 235–7
*Die Niederländer in Italien: Italianisante Niederländer des 17. Jahrhunderts* (exh. cat., ed. R. Trnek; Salzburg, Residenzgal.; Vienna, Akad. Bild. Kst.; 1986), pp. 123–34
*I Bamboccianti: Niederländische Malerrebellen im Rom des Barock* (exh. cat., ed. D. A. Levine and E. Mai; Cologne, Wallraf-Richartz-Mus.; Utrecht, Cent. Mus.; 1991–2), pp. 212–34

LAURA LAUREATI

**Lingeri, Pietro** (*b* Tremezzo, 25 Jan 1894; *d* Tremezzo, 15 May 1968). Italian architect. He graduated from the Accademia di Belle Arti, Milan, in 1926. A member of the Italian Rationalist movement, he was particularly active in the group from Como that participated alongside the GRUPPO 7 and MIAR in the struggles to assert the values of Modernist architecture in Italy. His design for the headquarters of the Club Motonautico A.M.I.L.A. (1926), Tremezzo, was among the first projects of Italian Rationalism to be built and was publicized by Giuseppe Pagano in the magazine *Casabella*. Lingeri also redesigned (1930) the Galleria Il Milione in Milan, which was at that time the centre of the Milanese avant-garde. Between 1926 and 1940 he collaborated regularly with the leading Rationalist Giuseppe Terragni on a number of important works, including a war memorial project (1926) in Como, the Novocomum block of flats (1927–8), Como, and five blocks in Milan. Of the latter the Rustici House (1935), Corso Sempione 36, is the most important, expressing a radical attempt to revise the conventional formulae for rented housing through innovations in volume and distribution of space. In collaboration with Terragni and with others, including the painter Mario Sironi, Lingeri also worked on unexecuted projects commissioned by the Fascist government, such as the Palazzo del Littorio (1937), in the Fori Imperiali, Rome, the reception building (1937) intended for the Esposizione Universale di Roma (1942; cancelled) and the Danteum (1938), Rome. After World War II he designed a tall housing block (1951) in the QT8 quarter of Milan and was head of a group responsible for planning the working-class housing developments of Vialba (1958), Milan, and Sagnino (1959), Como.

BIBLIOGRAPHY

E. Mantero: *Giuseppe Terragni e la città del razionalismo italiano* (Bari, 1983)
E. Mantero, ed.: *Il razionalismo italiano* (Bologna, 1984)

MATILDE BAFFA RIVOLTA

**Lingnan school.** Term used to refer to a style and movement established by a small group of painters in Guangdong Province who studied in Japan in the early 20th century. Lingnan (Chin.: 'south of the mountains') is often used less properly for all artists from Guangdong.

The main figures of the school were GAO JIANFU, his brother Gao Qifeng (1889–1935) and their compatriot Chen Shuren (1883–1949). All three came from Panyu County near Guangzhou [Canton] and learnt the foundations of traditional Chinese painting from the Guangdong master Ju Lian (1828–1904), who specialized in bird-and-flower subjects. Ju Lian painted in the 'boneless' (*mogu*) style practised by the 17th-century master Yun Shouping. However, he also pioneered or perfected new colouring and ink-spreading techniques that were to influence Lingnan school artists, among them 'splashed water' (*zhuang shui*) and 'sprinkled powder' (*zhuang fen*). In the latter, white powder was sprinkled on to the coloured areas, especially flower petals, to produce a bright, somewhat glossy surface. In the former, the 'boneless' technique for painting leaves was extended by carefully controlling the flow of dripped water to form the borders. All of Ju Lian's followers, most notably Chen Shuren, mastered the style of combining such techniques with meticulous attention to naturalistic detail, which imparted a freshness to studies of small birds and insects. This type of painting (e.g. Hong Kong, Chin. U., A.G.) is usually in album leaf or fan painting format; large hanging scrolls were painted only occasionally, as in an impressive undated work by Ju Lian, *Rocks, Insects and Flowers* (Guangzhou, Guangdong Prov. Mus.).

Exposure to new intellectual, political and artistic currents in late Meiji Japan (1868–1912) transformed Chen and the two Gaos from apprentices in a provincial style to major innovators in modern Chinese painting. Gao Jianfu first went to Tokyo in 1905, bringing his brother two years later; Chen Shuren studied in Kyoto from 1906 to 1911. Caught in the highly charged atmosphere of Chinese student politics, they quickly joined their fellow Cantonese Sun Yat-sen's revolutionary Alliance Society

(Tongmeng hui) and participated in underground revolutionary work. The same ideals of national rejuvenation and selective borrowing of modern Western values that made these artists political revolutionaries also informed their art, and although they seldom painted overtly political subjects, the fusing of political and artistic ideals was central to the character of the Lingnan school and its role in the history of 20th-century China.

The Japanese groups that most influenced the Lingnan painters were the Tokyo-based school of new Japanese painting, *Nihonga*, under the leadership of Tenshin Okakura (*see* JAPAN, §VI, 5(iii)) and the Kyoto-centred Maruyama-Shijo school (*see* JAPAN, §VI, 4(viii)), particularly its last great protagonist, Takeuchi Seiho. By the late Meiji period both these schools had assimilated certain techniques from Western painting, notably fixed-point perspective and a modified chiaroscuro, in order to give ink painting greater realism and dramatic impact without detracting from its strong national character. This was exactly what the young Chinese revolutionaries were looking for—a style of painting that was bold, new and apparently modern but that did not merely copy Western conventions. It appealed to their nationalism and their desire for change and became the basis for the Lingnan school's distinctively eclectic style, as is evident in the abrupt changes of style and subject-matter after the artists returned to China. Though elements of the Ju Lian tradition remained, the small bird-and-flower studies were replaced by boldly romantic landscapes and dramatic pictures of lions, tigers, monkeys, hawks and eagles. Techniques derived from Western art are obvious, including the use of perspective, shading and strong atmospheric effects. Most striking, however, is the change from a spirit of intimate communion with nature and restrained aesthetic sensibility, typical of traditional Chinese bird-and-flower painting, to strongly romantic yet realistic visions of storms, struggle and heroic exertion. Gao Qifeng's *Autumn Eagle* (see fig.), painted soon after his return from Japan, is typical of the heroic bird-and-animal painting in which he excelled. The hunched wings, aggressive pose and prominent claws and beak are influenced by the Japanese Kanō school. The combination of realistic detail in the drawing of the bird contrasted with a much looser handling of the background—in this case derived from the late Maruyama–Shijo school (*see* JAPAN, §XI, 4(xiii))—became a hallmark of the new Lingnan style.

Gao Jianfu produced similar pictures in the 1910s and early 1920s, but he became better known for landscapes, in which he often used fixed-point perspective and dramatic effects of light and shade to achieve a comparable combination of realism and romanticism with the emphasis on grandeur. Typical of this type is *Himalayan Snow Scene* (hanging scroll, 2400×950 mm, 1933; Hong Kong, Chin. U., A.G.). The verticality and internal movement within the composition is heightened by the contrast between the detailed realism of a jagged series of receding mountain ridges in the top half of the painting and the loose washes used for the foreground slopes. An abandoned Buddhist stupa adds a note of romantic melancholy. Exotic locations, vigorous brushwork and emotional impact were characteristic of the elder Gao's early landscape style.

Lingnan school painting by Gao Qifeng: *Autumn Eagle*, ink and colour on paper, 1645×670 mm, after 1924 (Guangzhou, Guangdong Provincial Museum)

Although Chen Shuren painted both heroic animals and dramatic landscapes, he is best remembered for his more intimate, serene and cheerful flower-and-bird paintings, especially his numerous studies of the red-flowering kapok tree. A typical example of this subject is *Lingnan Spring Colour* (860×510 mm, 1946; Croizier, 1988, p. 1), where he combines animated renderings of small birds with brightly coloured flowers in a composition carefully balanced by the strong diagonal formed by a tree trunk. This decorative side of the Lingnan school grew stronger in Chen Shuren and Gao Qifeng's later works, but in their early period all three artists tried to inject a stronger emotional tone into Chinese painting in an attempt to stimulate the spirit of nationalism.

After the revolution of 1911 the Gao brothers tried unsuccessfully to popularize their new art in Shanghai, through ventures such as an illustrated magazine, the *Zhenxiang huabao*/*The True Record*, and an art publishing house. By 1920 they had returned to Guangzhou, where they established the Lingnan school on a secure regional base. This was partly due to the successful cultivation of followers by the Gao brothers, and partly the result of the revival of Sun Yat-sen's revolutionary movement and his Nationalist Party in Guangzhou. The Gao brothers did not return to politics, but Gao Qifeng demonstrated his support in three symbolic paintings of a sea eagle, a white horse and a roaring lion for the Sun Yat-sen Memorial Hall in Guangzhou, and Gao Jianfu illustrated Sun Yat-sen's slogan, 'Aviation to save the nation', with a room full of paintings of aeroplanes. This combination of new subject-matter in traditional landscapes was not always successful. *Flying in the Rain* (460×350 mm, 1923; Hong Kong, Chin. U., A.G.) shows a straggling formation of seven biplanes, looking more like the insects of Ju Lian's small nature studies than modern engines of war as they pass over a misty landscape complete with pagoda. The loose ink washes and dreamy effect contradict somewhat the message of modernization. As political art, his brother's allegorical animal studies were more effective.

By the end of the 1920s the Lingnan school had established a national reputation. Nevertheless despite its members' successful exhibitions, government honours and favourable critical response in the new art journals, this Japanese-derived 'New Chinese-style Painting' (*Xin guohua*), based on a fusion of Eastern and Western techniques, remained distinctly regional. It seems that while the Lingnan artists offended conservative taste by emphasizing new techniques at the expense of traditional line and brushwork, they were not sufficiently radical, either artistically or politically, for the new generation. Despite some explicitly anti-Japanese art by Gao Jianfu and his followers at the outbreak of the Sino-Japanese War in 1937, most works displayed unmistakable signs of Japanese stylistic influence, which aroused the ire of patriots as well as artistic conservatives.

After the Communist revolution of 1949, the Lingnan school as an organized movement ceased to exist in China. Continuity of the school's style has been strongest in Hong Kong, where Zhao Shaoang (*b* 1905) and Yang Shanshen (*b* 1912) have maintained, respectively, the Gao Qifeng and Gao Jianfu traditions. Zhao was the foremost exponent of the more decorative aspect of the Lingnan style, whereas Yang Shanshen veered towards a less spectacular but more diversified approach. Both trained many students, but it has been Zhao Shaoang's numerous protégés, working in a remarkably uniform style, who have extended the influence of the Lingnan school to Taiwan and overseas Chinese centres in South-east Asia and North America. Until the late 1970s it was impolitic to advertise a Lingnan school identification in China because of the school's close association with the Nationalist government. In the 1980s this stigma was removed, and artists such as Guan Shangue (*b* 1912) and Li Xiongcai (*b* 1911), both

former students of Gao Jianfu, received greater recognition.

BIBLIOGRAPHY
Gao Jianfu: *Wo de xiandai guohua guan* [My views on contemporary Chinese-style painting] (Shanghai, 1936)
*The Art of Kao Chien-Fu* (exh. cat., ed. G. C. C. Tsang; Hong Kong, Mus. A., 1978)
*The Art of Chen Shuren* (exh. cat., ed. L. C. S. Tam; Hong Kong, Mus. A., 1980)
*The Art of Gao Qifeng* (exh. cat., ed. C. Chu; Hong Kong, Mus. A., 1981)
Chi Ke: 'The Three Founders of the Lingnan School', *Chin. Lit.* (1982), no. 7, pp. 75–84
Wang Lipu: *Lingnan hua pai* [The Lingnan school of painting] (Taipei, 1983)
R. Croizier: 'Reverse Current: Early 20th-century Japanese Influence on Chinese Painting', *Sino-Japanese Cultural Interchange: Aspects of Archaeology and Art History*, ed. Y. H. Tam (Hong Kong, 1985), pp. 169–97
——: *Art and Revolution in Modern China: The Lingnan (Cantonese) School of Painting* (Berkeley, 1988)

RALPH CROIZIER

**Linhart, Evžen** (*b* Kouřim, Bohemia [now Czech Republic], 20 March 1898; *d* Prague, 29 Dec 1949). Czech architect. He studied architecture at the Czech Technical University, Prague, and together with his fellow-students Karel Honzík, Jaroslav Fragner and Vít Obrtel (1901–88), he formed the Four Purists; he also became a member of Devětsil, the avant-garde group centred on Karel Teige. After graduating Linhart spent his entire career working as an architect in the construction office of the city of Prague. His first designs followed the principles of Czech Cubism but in the early 1920s he gradually simplified the three-dimensional Cubist façades to smooth, clean, Purist volumes. He sought inspiration for his formal vocabulary in the early work of Le Corbusier, whose aesthetic principles he applied in his own house (1926–8) in Dejvice, Prague. He thus produced the first family house in Prague in the spirit of the International Style, and he followed the same principles in the construction of a secondary school (1935), also in Dejvice. After World War II, in collaboration with Václav Hilský, he won the competition for a communal dwelling (1946–51) in Litvínov, in which the idea of collective living was expressed in maisonette flats with all necessary services centrally supplied. This form of housing had been the main concern of the architectural section of the Left Front in Prague in the late 1920s and early 1930s.

BIBLIOGRAPHY
F. R. S. Yorke: *The Modern House* (London, 1934), pp. 100–01
M. Benešová: 'Dvacátá léta v díle Evžena Linharta' [The twenties and the work of Evžen Linhart], *Archit. ČSR*, xxxvii/4 (1978), pp. 54–5
*Devětsil: Czech Avant-Garde Art, Architecture and Design of the 1920s and 1930s* (exh. cat., ed. R. Švácha; Oxford, MOMA; London, Des. Mus.; 1990)

VLADIMÍR ŠLAPETA

**Lining.** *See* RELINING.

**Link, O(gle) Winston** (*b* Brooklyn, NY, 1911). American photographer. He worked as an advertising and public relations photographer, but from 1955, spurred by his obsessive interest in steam trains, he devoted himself to photographing the trains and workers of the Norfolk and Western Railway, situated mostly in Virginia. He worked generally at night using vast banks of simultaneously triggered flash-bulbs, so allowing him to manipulate the images as desired. The Norfolk and Western was the last railway to change to diesel, and he thus recorded the last days of the steam era in America through a series of striking black-and-white photographs. They were first published in the 1980s.

PHOTOGRAPHIC PUBLICATIONS
O. W. Link: *America's Last Steam Railroad: Steam, Steel and Stars* (New York, 1987) [with texts by T. Hensley and T. H. Garver]

BIBLIOGRAPHY
*Ghost Trains: Railroad Photographs of the 1950s by O. Winston Link* (exh. cat. by C. K. Carr, Akron, OH, A. Mus.; New York, Int. Cent. Phot.; Norfolk, VA, Chrysler Mus.; 1983)

☐

**Linked Ring**, Brotherhood of the. Association of photographers that flourished in Britain between 1892 and 1909. The association was founded by a group of artistic photographers (mainly Pictorialist) who were disenchanted with the attitudes and activities of the council members of the Photographic Society of Great Britain, the majority of whom were photographic scientists and technologists (*see* PICTORIAL PHOTOGRAPHY). The lecture and exhibition programmes were directed to their interests. Alfred Maskell and George Davison were instrumental in bringing together on 27 May 1892 the 15 British photographers who were the founders of the Linked Ring: Bernard Alfieri, Tom Bright, Arthur Burchett (1875–1913), Henry Hay Cameron (1856–1911, son of Julia Margaret Cameron), Lyonel Clark, Francis Cobb, Henry E. Davis, Alfred Horsley Hinton (1863–1906), Henry Peach Robinson and his son Ralph W. Robinson (1862–1942), Francis Seyton Scott, Henry Van der Weyde and William Willis (1841–1923). All were either distinguished photographers or closely involved in the medium. The name was chosen to symbolize the unity of the members linked together in a spiritual and aesthetic band of brothers. The association was constituted 'as a means of bringing together those who are interested in the development of the highest form of Art of which Photography is capable' and those only were eligible who admitted the artistic capabilities in photography.

In order to carry out the principal aim of the Linked Ring (the promotion of the art of photography), the Links (members) added to their numbers many of the most distinguished photographers of the period at an international level, including Gertrude Käsebier, Clarence H. White, James Craig Annan, Edward J. Steichen, Heinrich Kuehn, Alvin Langdon Coburn, F. Holland Day, Hugo Henneberg and Hans Watzek. There was no differentiation between amateur and professional. Several worked in a range of media, although the dominating interest for most was photography. Those Links able to do so met once a month to discuss matters of mutual interest and make decisions on admission of new members. The major activity was the annual exhibition known as the Photographic Salon, which set new standards in photographic art. Initially it was held in the Dudley Gallery in Piccadilly, London. Other exhibitions (usually loans of members' work) were also organized. Although the Links did not publish a magazine, the *Linked Ring Papers* were printed privately for circulation among members only. Copies of these are rarely seen.

In aesthetic matters considerable variety is to be found in the work of the Links, from what had become unfashionable realism, as in the work of Joseph Gale (*c.* 1835–1906), through naturalistic and impressionistic work to Pictorial photography (at which time it reached its peak of artistry and popular appeal). The latter explored mood and atmosphere, which were achieved by various means, such as *contre-jour* lighting, soft-focus lenses and special printing processes. The Pictorialists produced a wonderfully rich range of prints, employing such processes as platinum, carbon, gum and oil prints, and combinations such as gum platinum and bromoil (*see* PHOTOGRAPHY, §I).

Monochromatic colours ranged from etching black to red chalk. Workers who used carbon printing sometimes produced prints in blues and greens (for appropriate subjects). When the major objective had apparently been achieved (the promotion of photography as a visual art) internal dissensions occurred within the Linked Ring, and the association was disbanded, with considerable reluctance, on 24 November 1909.

BIBLIOGRAPHY
M. F. Harker: *The Linked Ring: The Secession Movement in Photography in Britain, 1892–1910* (London, 1979)

For further bibliography *see* PICTORIAL PHOTOGRAPHY.

MARGARET HARKER

**Linköping.** Swedish city in Östergötland. It is referred to as an episcopal residence in 1120, and the importance of the city and the diocese is shown by the choice of Linköping for the meeting between the papal legate, Cardinal Nicolaus of Albano, and the clerical and secular magnates in 1153. Towards the end of the 15th century the bishop's palace near the cathedral was extended and rebuilt as a magnificent ring-wall castle. Following the edicts of the Reformation Parliament in 1527, Gustav I (*reg* 1523–60) took over the palace, and it was rebuilt in a Renaissance style but has since been further altered. Most of the medieval buildings in the area around the cathedral have been identified in excavations.

After the Reformation, the bishop probably lived in the (preserved) medieval stone house north-east of the cathedral, which later became the deanery. It is now used by the County Museum for exhibitions concerning the cathedral. In 1733–4 a new bishop's palace was built north of the cathedral on the site of a Franciscan monastery founded by Magnus III (*reg* 1275–90) and the bishop in 1278. Some walling from the 14th-century cathedral school is preserved in the parish hall south of the cathedral.

The cathedral is now surrounded by a park, largely corresponding to the former churchyard, which was enclosed by a strong wall forming a limit to the castle and its garden to the west. A detached bell-tower was erected in front of the sacristy in the south-eastern corner of the churchyard. The parish church of St Lars, dating from the 12th century and situated directly east of the cathedral, has been much rebuilt, but remains of the earliest walls survive under the present choir. Linköping became an important cultural centre for the province through the grammar school founded in 1627, and it has retained its character as an educational and cultural centre; the university was founded in 1970.

1. CATHEDRAL. One of Scandinavia's best-preserved and most richly decorated medieval cathedrals, the cathedral of SS Peter and Paul is central to the architectural history of north-western Europe. The medieval building history covers nearly 300 years, from *c.* 1230 to 1500. The west tower, however, which is a characteristic feature of the exterior, was built only in the 1880s.

The diocese of Linköping is mentioned in the so-called Florence list (Florence, Bib. Medicea-Laurenziana) of *c.* 1120, and the predecessor to the present building was probably constructed at this time. The foundations of this significantly smaller building have been excavated under the floor of the present nave. It had a three-aisled nave, a transept with small eastern apses and a strikingly large choir and main apse. There was a massive western tower with two narrower side chapels. The arrangement of the west end was to characterize several Romanesque churches in the area with episcopal or royal connections.

Work on a new and larger cathedral was in progress in 1232. The building, which was of limestone, had an elaborate and expensive design. In the first campaign a new choir and transept were joined to the existing transept and nave. This stage was probably completed by 1251 when a coronation took place there. The choir was replaced again in the late Middle Ages. Surviving traces show that the 13th-century choir had an ambulatory with an eastern chapel. Small bays were added to both the east and west sides of the transept, with chapels on the ground storey and towers above.

The combination of a choir with ambulatory and transept with corner towers is very unusual and may derive from Limburg an der Lahn Cathedral in the Rhineland, which was built from 1215 to 1235. Only the north and south walls and the north portal survive in the present transept. The capital sculptures and design of the north portal also show influences from the Rhineland and Westphalia, which may have been partly due to the influence of stonemasons from St Mary's, VISBY. In the transept, however, English influence also becomes apparent in, for instance, the groups of triple-lancet windows, which are typical of Early English design.

A similar combination of influences can be seen in work of the second campaign, from 1250 to 1296. Owing to lack of funds, progress was slow. A three-aisled hall nave with four bays and a west tower (destr.) was added: it was joined into the west bay of the transept, and the corner towers were demolished. The nave design is related to the German hall church, which also had an offshoot in St Mary's, Visby. The interior walls were decorated with blind arcades, which, with some of the capitals, show English influence.

Owing to the poor economy and troubled times, the third building campaign was also very protracted, lasting from 1308 to 1360. The west tower was demolished, the nave was lengthened by two bays and the two south portals were renovated. German and English influences again predominate. The Early English style is apparent in the transept portal, built *c.* 1310, and in the lower part of the large door of the nave. The upper part of the tympanum, however, with its rich figurative reliefs, completed in the mid-1320s, shows German influence, as does the rich capital sculpture on the interior. The blind arcades, dating from the early 1320s, were finished with human heads, figures and mythical beasts. Here, again, English influence is very clear. (English coins were discovered in the ends of the blind arcades during excavations.)

The present choir with ambulatory and three chapels (see fig.) was built in two phases, *c.* 1408–20 and 1487–1500. A memorial tablet establishes that the architect, Gierlach, came from Cologne. Craftsmen from Cologne and the surrounding area were also called in for the second campaign, and the choir design reflects these Rhenish connections. The choir was also richly decorated. The capitals have a wide variety of ornament, and in the ambulatory there are consoles decorated with figures with partly preserved original colouring. The rib vaults have heraldic bosses. The vault in the south chapel is decorated with the *Arma Christi*—shields showing the Instruments of the Passion—by ADAM VAN DÜREN, the only mason in the last phase to be known by name. His mason's mark appears on a boss, a capital and some mouldings. The two elaborate limestone aumbries in the upper choir were executed at the same time. The sculptor appears from his mason's mark to be responsible also for the figurative consoles in the ambulatory: they are portraits of craftsmen and probably depict some of the masons active in the masons' lodge.

From 1849 to 1870 the cathedral was comprehensively restored. Window frames and mullions, mouldings and portals were badly damaged through weathering and had to be largely replaced. All three portals are now accurate copies. Some of the original reliefs from the south portal of the nave survive in the chancel. The western section was, as mentioned above, rebuilt in the Gothic Revival

Linköping Cathedral, ambulatory and chapels, *c.* 1408–20 and 1487–1500

style in the 1880s. These changes involved demolishing the medieval west front and its three doorways. During the restoration in the 1960s *c.* 6000 masons' marks in the cathedral were recorded: covering the years 1280–1500 they represent 172 masons and clearly show the four different building phases as well as the varying intensity of the campaigns.

BIBLIOGRAPHY

B. Cnattingius and others: *Linköpings domkyrka*, Sveriges Kyrkor, cc–cci (Stockholm, 1987) [with full bibliog., Eng. summary and captions]

MARIAN ULLÉN

**Lin Liang** [*zi* Yishan] (*b* Nanhai, Guangdong Province, *c.* 1416; *d c.* 1480). Chinese painter. He became a provincial administrator and was referred to the court during the reign of the Tianshun emperor (1457–64). He was later promoted to the Imperial Guard under the system of titles given to court painters in the early Ming period (1368–1644). His surviving works feature large subjects in monochrome ink, although he is recorded as having also been proficient in colours. He has been seen as chiefly influenced by Bian Wenjin (*c.* 1400–40), with whom he painted *Cranes* (hanging scroll, ink on silk, 1.74×0.87 m; Guangzhou, Guangdong Prov. Mus.). He is thought of as one of the foremost protagonists of the ZHE SCHOOL, painting boldly in ink on silk, with no more than a signature inscribed on his works. Lin Liang also painted magpies, peacocks, pheasants and magnificent eagles, many of them almost filling his hanging scrolls.

*Birds Assembling in a Thicket* (handscroll, ink on paper, 0.34×12.11 m; Beijing, Pal. Mus.) is the finest example of Lin Liang's lively brushwork. The composition begins with sparrows flying towards the upper branches of a flowering plum in which orioles are singing, then moves deep into the midst of the thicket. Bamboo and a venerable pine dominate in the left half of the scroll, with a final bankside section depicting wading birds beneath rushes. Over 70 birds are shown in all attitudes, from sparrows and kingfishers to a single eagle in the branches of the pine tree. *Geese and Reeds* (hanging scroll, ink on silk, 1.88×0.99 m; London, BM) exemplifies his work in ink and wash on silk. It shows four geese in the foreground by a swiftly flowing stream. In the stream are small boulders or rocks edged with thick black ink; reeds grow in a dense tangle with a few blades of long grass on the bank, obscuring the view into the middle and far distance. Since the focus is on the foreground, the subjects are large—the two geese in the front are close to full size—yet the painting is not cluttered, owing to the unifying effect of the ink washes and lines.

BIBLIOGRAPHY

Mu Yiqin: *Ming dai gongting yu Zhe pai huihua xuanji* [Selection of Ming-dynasty court paintings and Zhe school paintings] (Beijing, 1983), col. pl. v, pls. 31–5

Xu Bangda, ed.: *Zhongguo huihua shi tulu* [Illustrated record of the history of Chinese painting] (Shanghai, 1984), ii, pp. 515–24, pls. 316–19

Sung Hou-mei: 'Lin Liang and his Eagle Paintings', *Archvs Asian A.*, xliv (1991), pp. 95–102

*Painters of the Great Ming: The Imperial Court and the Zhe School* (exh. cat. by R. M. Barnhart, New York, Met., Dallas, TX, Mus. A., 1993), pp. 195–205, nos 51–5

RODERICK WHITFIELD

**Linnell, John (i)** (*b* London, 1729; *d* 1796). English designer and cabinetmaker. He was the son of the cabinetmaker William Linnell (*c.* 1703–63) and studied drawing at the St Martin's Lane Academy, London, before beginning work as a designer for his father's firm in Long Acre, Covent Garden. In 1754 the firm was moved to new premises at 28 Berkeley Square, and both their workshops and clientele were expanded. Furniture was produced in a variety of styles, including 'Chinese Chippendale' (*see* CHINOISERIE, fig. 2). In 1758 Linnell became a freeman of the Joiners' Company and after his father's death he took over the firm and its clients. A skilled draughtsman, he executed hundreds of designs for furniture in pen-and-ink and coloured washes (London, V&A). For Nathaniel Curzon, 1st Baron Scarsdale, he designed two pairs of sofas elaborately carved with mermen and mermaids, dolphins, nymphs and tritons for the State Drawing-room at Kedleston Hall (*in situ*). As well as making furniture to his own designs for clients, Linnell also made furniture to designs by Robert Adam for Robert Child (1739–82) at Osterley Park House, London, and for Kedleston Hall. The firm closed after Linnell's death in 1796.

BIBLIOGRAPHY

H. Hayward and P. Kirkham: *William and John Linnell: Eighteenth Century Furniture Makers*, 2 vols (London, 1980)

G. Beard and C. Gilbert, eds: *Dictionary of English Furniture Makers, 1660–1840* (Leeds, 1986)

JULIA H. M. SMITH

**Linnell, John (ii)** (*b* London, 16 June 1792; *d* Redhill, Surrey, 20 Jan 1882). English painter. The son of a framemaker, he came to the notice of connoisseurs and artists at an early age: he visited Benjamin West *c.* 1804; and Joseph Farington (*Diary*, 14 Nov 1806) mentioned Sir George Beaumont's interest in Linnell's sketches. In 1805 he entered the Royal Academy Schools and became a pupil of John Varley. He participated in the naturalist movement of the early 19th century, making oil sketches from nature along the Thames (e.g. *Study of Buildings—Study from Nature*, 1806; London, Tate), in the company of William Henry Hunt and William Mulready. His friendship with Cornelius Varley led in 1811–12 to his entry into the Baptist church and a more intense interest in humble landscapes, often including labourers at work (e.g. *Kensington Gravel Pits*, 1812; London, Tate; see fig.). In the following decade he made several sketching tours, including a trip to north Wales with George Robert Lewis (1782–1871) in 1813, and produced remarkably fresh watercolour sketches. He exhibited his oils at the Society of Painters in Oil and Water-Colours in 1813–20. With his marriage in 1817 and the onset of family responsibilities, he turned his attention to portraiture. He acquired royal and aristo-cratic patronage and executed a miniature of *Princess Sophia Matilda* (1821; Brit. Royal Col.), the daughter of William Henry, Duke of Gloucester. Large-scale portraits in oil, such as *Lady Torrens and her Family* (1820; New York, Mrs Richard Selle priv. col.), show the influence of Sir Thomas Lawrence.

Linnell played an important part in the last years of William Blake's life (from 1818), commissioning the engravings for the *Book of Job* (1826) in 1823 and the watercolours for Dante's *Divine Comedy* (1827) in 1824,

John Linnell (ii): *Kensington Gravel Pits*, oil on canvas, 711×1067 mm, 1812 (London, Tate Gallery)

and giving Blake a regular income in his old age. Linnell introduced Samuel Palmer to Blake in 1824, having already encouraged Palmer, since meeting him in 1822, to study early Renaissance art and to make intensive studies from nature. Linnell and Palmer became close friends, and Linnell made several visits to Palmer's house in Shoreham, Kent. He has often been blamed for Palmer's move away from visionary landscape, but in the 1820s he was a fruitful influence on Palmer, and the two men shared many of the same ideals, including a belief that landscape painting could be a form of religious art. From the time of Palmer's marriage to Linnell's daughter Hannah in 1837 the relationship deteriorated, owing mainly to political and religious differences (Linnell was a radical Nonconformist, Palmer a High Church Tory). Linnell became more extreme in his views and eccentric in his habits. His eccentricity led to rifts with other artists, including Constable, and may account for his failure to be elected to the Royal Academy, despite repeated applications from 1821 to *c.* 1843. He wrote a pamphlet calling for the reform of the Academy in 1869.

In the mid-1840s Linnell's increasing prosperity enabled him to give up portraiture, and from 1851, when he settled at Redhill, Surrey, he specialized in rural landscapes, which found a ready market, through dealers such as William Agnew, among merchants and manufacturers in the northern cities. One such painting, sold through Agnew, was the *Mid-day Rest (Windsor Forest)* (1863; Manchester, C.A.G.). Linnell's real ambition was to paint biblical subjects (e.g. *Noah: The Eve of the Deluge*, 1848; Cleveland,

OH, Mus. A.), which was purchased by Joseph Gillott for £1000. His patrons, however, preferred pastorals, which Linnell was able to see as 'poetical' by giving them religious significance: a harvest, for example, could illustrate God's benevolence to man. Linnell, in contrast to Palmer, enjoyed great worldly success, and his later landscapes—which became increasingly sketchy and repetitive—sold for high prices. His reputation declined after his death, but his work began to be reassessed in the 1970s, with the emphasis being placed on the more inspired, sometimes visionary, early landscapes.

UNPUBLISHED SOURCES

Artist's estate [Journals (1811, 1817–79), unfinished autobiography (1863) and account books]
London, BM, 1976–1–31–6/7 [*Landscape and Portrait Sketchbooks*, which contain a record of most of his paintings]

WRITINGS

*Michelangelo's Frescoes in the Sistine Chapel* (London, 1834)
*The Royal Gallery of Pictures* (London, 1840)
'Dialogue upon Art: Painter and Friend', *The Bouquet*, 25 (1853)
'Dialogue upon Art: Collector and Painter', *The Bouquet*, 33 (1854)
*Diatheeke, Covenant not Testament* (Redhill, 1856)
*Burnt-offering not in the Hebrew Bible: Shown by a Revised Version of the First Part of Leviticus* (Redhill, 1864)
*The Royal Academy, a National Institution* (London, 1869)

BIBLIOGRAPHY

A. T. Story: *The Life of John Linnell*, 2 vols (London, 1892)
E. R. Firestone: *John Linnell, English Artist: Works, Patrons and Dealers* (diss., Madison, U. WI, 1971)
——: 'John Linnell and the Picture Merchants', *Connoisseur*, clxxxii (1973), pp. 124–31
*A Loan Exhibition of Drawings, Watercolours and Paintings by John Linnell and his Circle* (exh. cat., London, Colnaghi's, 1973)

E. R. Firestone: 'John Linnell: *The Eve of the Deluge*', *Bull. Cleveland Mus. A.*, lxii/4 (1975), pp. 131–9

C. Knowles: *John Linnell: His Early Landscapes to 1830* (MA thesis, U. London, Courtauld Inst., 1980)

C. Payne: 'John Linnell and Samuel Palmer in the 1820s', *Burl. Mag.*, cxxix (1982), pp. 131–6

*John Linnell: A Centennial Exhibition* (exh. cat., ed. K. Crouan; Cambridge, Fitzwilliam, 1982)

*John Linnell: Truth to Nature (a Centennial Exhibition)* (exh. cat., ed. K. Crouan; London, Martyn Gregory, 1982)

D. Linnell: *Blake, Palmer, Linnell and Co.: The Life of John Linnell* (Lewes, 1994)

CHRISTIANA PAYNE

**Linnqvist, Hilding** (*b* Stockholm, 20 April 1891; *d* Stockholm, 30 Sept 1984). Swedish painter and designer. He studied at the Konsthögskola in Stockholm from 1910 to 1912 and then became influenced by Edvard Munch and Ernst Josephson, as shown by *Self-portrait* (1913; Göteborg, Kstmus.), executed in swift, loose brushstrokes. At the same time he experimented with a type of Cubism, as in the angular, stylized *Mountain Landscape* (1913; Lidingö, Stift. Hilding Linnqvists Kst), which was influenced by the work of André Lhote. In 1917 he painted a mural for the Tekniska Högskola in Stockholm and the same year was a founder-member of a Swedish painters' group that included Victor Axelson (1883–1954), Alf Munthe (1892–1971), Fritiof Sçüldt (*d* 1891) and Axel Nilsson (*b* 1889), which was active until 1923. From 1920 to 1923 he travelled in Italy, England and France. Having been influenced from the 1910s by the Swedish folk art tradition, he developed a naive painting style, as in *Market Scene: Small French Town (Chinon)* (1921–5; Stockholm, Mod. Mus.). In 1928 he painted murals for the Stadsbibliotek in Stockholm and in the same period visited Spain and Morocco. In 1934 he became a member of the FÄRG OCH FORM group and in 1937–8 travelled in Greece. During the 1930s Linnqvist became influenced by the work of Cézanne: his painting lost its earlier naive style and was executed in firm, broad brushstrokes, as in *Chapel in the Wilderness: Scene from Greece* (1938; Stockholm, Mod. Mus.). He was a professor at the Konsthögskola in 1939–41 and in 1946–7 travelled in Egypt, producing such brightly coloured works as *Pasha'a Island* (1947; priv. col., see exh. cat., p. 50). In 1948 he executed a fresco for Sofia Church in Stockholm and in 1956 designed the décor for a performance of Mozart's *Die Zauberflöte* at the Kungliga Teater in Stockholm. In the late 1950s and early 1960s he collaborated with the Aubusson firm in designing various tapestries, such as the *Dream of Disa* (1959) for Nytorps Skola in Stockholm. His paintings of the 1950s and 1960s were strongly outlined and firmly brushed, as in *Villa Entrance at Gardasjön* (1968; Stockholm, Mod. Mus.), showing an increasing debt to Cézanne. He continued painting and executing decorative commissions; his later works include the watercolour *Gardone* (1979; priv. col., see exh. cat., p. 59). In 1982 he established the Hilding Linnqvist Foundation which has exhibited frequently in Sweden and in 1991 at the Villa Reale in Milan. The foundation, now controlled by the State, holds an important collection by Linnqvist.

BIBLIOGRAPHY

*Hilding Linnqvist* (exh. cat. by U. Linde, Stockholm, Mod. Mus.; Göteborg, Kstmus.; 1986–7)

□

**Lino, Raul** (*b* Lisbon, 21 Nov 1879; *d* Lisbon, 13 July 1974). Portuguese architect, graphic artist and writer. He was educated in England and then studied architecture (1893–7) at the Technische Hochschule, Hannover, under Albrecht Haupt. His grounding in Anglo-Saxon and German culture was unusual among Portuguese artists of the time, who tended to be orientated towards French influences, and it directed him to a search for the deeper and more spiritual roots of Portuguese architecture. From 1898 to 1901 he spent time travelling and drawing in southern Portugal and Morocco, observing the persistence of local traditions in Mozarabic and Islamic architectural forms and spatial planning. Some of these he later adopted in his designs for domestic buildings, particularly the use of the patio as a nucleus for rooms and the use of decorative elements (such as bricks, tiles and whitewash). He thus participated in the nationalist *Casa Portuguesa* style, but he also sought to modernize this tradition, integrating it with the innovative European currents of Art Nouveau; such houses as the Casa Roque Gameiro (1898), Venteira, Amadora, with Islamic turrets, Casa Monsalvat (1901) and Casa Silva Gomes (1902), both at Monte Estoril, together constitute the most significant contribution to this approach, with their innovative plans and treatment of mass. In his own house (1912) at Cipreste, S Pedro de Sintra, Lino exploited the dramatic site at an old stone quarry in a romantic way, creating an inimitable building in which a curved corridor leads from a cloistered patio to an atrium decorated with Art Nouveau *azulejos* (glazed tiles), with views across the landscape towards the 16th-century Palácio Nacional and Palácio de Pena in the mountains beyond. Lino's city buildings, all in Lisbon, are less innovative: they include a house (1906; destr., see 1970 exh. cat., p. 175) in Avenida Fontes Pereira de Melo; Casa Elisa Vaz (1912; destr., see 1970 exh. cat., p. 167), Avenida da República; the neo-classical Tivoli Cinema (1924), Avenida da Liberdade; and Casa António Sérgio (1925; rebuilt), Travessa do Moinho de Vento.

Lino was a man of wide cultural interests and maintained links with the other arts. He illustrated books of poems (1912 and 1916) by Affonso Lopes Vieira (1878–1946) and designed stage scenery and costumes, for example for a production of Oscar Wilde's *Salome* in 1925 at the Politeama, Lisbon. He also wrote extensively on the theory of architecture and such books as *A casa Portuguesa* (1929) secured his reputation as a leading exponent of the *Casa Portuguesa* style. In the 1930s, estranged from modernism, his style became dry and austere and he tended to conservatism, particularly in his official commissions for the government. Examples of his work at this time include Loja das Meias (1938; altered, see 1970 exh. cat., p. 173), Rossio; his own house (1939), Rua Feio Terenas; and the Brazilian Pavilion (1940; destr., see 1970 exh. cat., p. 181), Exposição do Mundo Português, all in Lisbon. The last had a remarkable portico system with modulated pillars representing a palm-tree image and supporting a light, tropical-style roof. His important works ended with the Portuguese Embassy (1941; destr. World War II) in Berlin. Thereafter he confined himself to theory, becoming increasingly out of sympathy with the world of modernism, but he lived to see a retrospective exhibition of his work at the Museu Calouste Gulbenkian, Lisbon, in 1970.

WRITINGS

*A nossa casa* (Lisbon, 1918)
*A casa Portuguesa* (Seville, 1929)
*Casas Portuguesas* (Lisbon, 1933)

BIBLIOGRAPHY

J.-A. França: *A arte em Portugal no século XIX*, ii (Lisbon, 1966), pp. 149–55
*Raul Lino* (exh. cat., ed. F. C. Gulbenkian; Lisbon, Fund. Gulbenkian, 1970)
'Raul Lino', *Belas A.*, xxviii–xxix (1975), pp. 5–29 [various articles]

JOSÉ MANUEL FERNANDES

**Linocut** [linoleum cut, linoleum block print; Fr. *linogravure*, Ger. *Linolschnitt*, It. *linografia*, Sp. *grabado en linóleo*]. Type of relief print in which linoleum is used as the printing surface. Using gouges and knives, the artist cuts the design into linoleum, a man-made sheet flooring composed primarily of oxidized linseed oil and ground cork. Battleship linoleum, a variety *c.* 6 mm thick, is frequently recommended, as is Desk-top, a thinner sheet. With the advent of synthetic floorings, linoleum became less easily available. In the late 20th century it was no longer produced in the USA but was manufactured in Scotland and commonly sold only in artists' shops. For printmaking, linoleum may be mounted on to plywood, to produce a block that can be printed mechanically. The linocut can also be printed in a simple screw or lever press or by hand, by rubbing the paper against the inked block with a spoon, rolling pin or *baren* (a slightly concave disc sheathed in bamboo), or by laying the inked linoleum on to the paper and hammering the back of the block. These hand-printing methods can also be used to print on to textiles, or the inked block can be turned on to fabric stretched on the floor and trodden on by the printer.

Either water- or oil-based inks are used, the former often preferred for their ease of cleaning. Waterfast inks are essential for textile printing. Any paper suitable for relief painting, damp or dry, can be used with linoleum blocks, depending on its texture and on the printing method. Type-high linoleum blocks can easily be printed with type and have been used in book illustration. Because sheet linoleum weighs relatively little and can be printed by hand, it has been used for exceptionally large printed images. Because linocuts are so easily printed by hand, they have been favoured by many artists who personally produce very small editions, although mechanically printed editions of as many as 25,000 are reported (Yeaton, p. 21). Since linoleum lends itself to broad effects, it is particularly adapted to multicolour printing, usually with a separate block for each colour. Linocut manuals commonly prescribe the offsetting of an impression of the key block, which establishes the composition, on to additional blocks in order to guarantee correct registration of colour areas. Likewise, in printing, a jig or other registration device is recommended to locate the paper precisely on each inked block.

Linocuts resemble woodcuts, although the softness and lack of grain of linoleum, which permit the artist to cut fluently in every direction, deprive cuts of the vigour and bias often seen in woodcuts. As fine networks of printing lines tend to crumble in linoleum, broader effects are usually sought. As the surface of linoleum is smooth, unless specially treated, it will not print with a texture that is visible in some woodcuts. The slickness of linoleum can produce a distinctive curdled effect in broadly inked areas, as seen in the *Frog Queen* (1905; see fig.) by Erich Heckel; in this print linoleum's lack of grain bias is evident in the perpendicular clusters of gouge strokes.

Although linoleum was invented in the early 1860s, it was first used for printing only in 1890 in Germany for the manufacture of wallpaper. By the early 20th century it had been popularized for artists' prints, largely through the efforts of Franz Cižek, an Austrian artist and teacher who recognized the medium's potential to instruct children in colour and design: it was cheap, easily worked with simple tools, adaptable to water-based inks, and versatile. Cižek toured Europe and North America with examples by his pupils and influenced art education worldwide. The earliest linocut by Heckel, the first major artist to adopt the medium, is dated 1903. He and the other artists of Die Brücke regularly used linocut through the next dozen years.

Such major artists as Henri Matisse and Pablo Picasso worked in linoleum. Matisse executed 70 linocuts between 1938 and 1952, in a fluent white-line technique, taking evident advantage of the smooth passage of the knife through the soft material. Picasso, after using linoleum for popular posters in the early 1950s, began a series of innovative colour linocuts in 1959. He developed a method of printing in different colours progressive states cut on a single block, so that the finished print comprises layered impressions of all the states.

Linocut gained particular favour in poorer cultures that were less inhibited by a tradition of fine printing. In

Colour linocut by Erich Heckel: *Frog Queen*, 237×191 mm, 1905 (Berlin, Kupferstichkabinett)

revolutionary Russia important linocuts were produced by Luubov' Popova *c.* 1918. In Canada in the 1920s and 1930s the linocut was more common than the woodcut. The most important British advocate of the linocut was Claude Flight (1881–1955), who taught linocut from 1925 at the Grosvenor School of Modern Art in London and emphasized its accessibility to the proletariat. This attitude was later demonstrated by such prints as *Smokers* (1982) by the Australian artist Richard Bosman (*b* 1944), which was printed by the artist and his wife in an edition of two rolls of paper towels. Prejudice grew up against linoleum block printing, as suitable only for children, amateurs and the uncultured. The linocut's popularity also fell with the rise of commercial collaboration between printmaker and publisher, which encouraged more technically complex media.

BIBLIOGRAPHY
C. Flight: *Lino-cuts* (London, 1927)
L. B. Yeaton: *Linoleum Block Printing for the Amateur* (New York, 1931)
F. J. Kafka: *Linoleum Block Printing* (New York, 1955)
J. Erickson: *Block Printing on Textiles* (New York, 1961)
M. Rothenstein: *Linocuts and Woodcuts* (New York, *c.* 1962)
P. Ainslie: *Images of the Land* (Calgary, 1984)
W. S. Liebermann and L. D. McVinney: *Picasso Linoleum Cuts* (New York, 1985)

M. B. COHN

**Linstow, Hans Ditlev Franciscus** (*b* Hørsholm, Denmark, 4 March 1787; *d* Christiania [now Oslo], 10 July 1851). Norwegian architect of Danish birth. He was educated as a mining engineer and officer in Copenhagen, where he also attended drawing, painting and possibly architectural classes at the Royal Danish Academy of Fine Arts, and in Kongsberg, Norway, from 1812 to 1815. He began teaching drawing at Christiania's Royal School of Design in 1819 and taught architecture there from 1822 to 1840. Despite his relative lack of formal architectural education, Linstow's works are distinguished by artistic ability and solid historical knowledge. Numerous churches throughout Norway were built after Neo-classical pattern drawings prepared by him (1838–41). His major project, the Royal Palace in Oslo (1823–48), is a reduced version of a much larger original project, with Baroque details inspired by Nicodemus Tessin the younger's Royal Palace in Stockholm. The Palladian building, facing Karl Johans Gate and the city, is dominated by a central pavilion with giant Ionic columns of Norwegian marble. The interiors, like those of C. F. Hansen's contemporary Christiansborg Palace in Copenhagen, were influenced by the classicism of Karl Friedrich Schinkel, whom Linstow visited while in Germany in 1836–7. A visit to Munich on the same trip prompted Linstow's plan (1838) for the regulation of Karl Johans Gate and surrounding streets. Although this street layout was carried through, however, with the exception of Christian Heinrich Grosch's University building the buildings that Linstow planned for it were not realized. Linstow was also responsible for introducing to Norway the wooden 'Swiss' or 'Chalet' style. In the 1840s, in his smaller wooden houses in Christiania in this style (including his own), Linstow began a long and rich development in Norwegian wooden architecture. A characteristic example is the guardhouse (1848) in the Palace park, with vertical board cladding and exposed posts, braces and tie-beams supporting the projection of the roof at the front.

Linstow's last work (1851) was a model project for a worker's house, which he described as 'simply Norwegian'.

*NKL*
BIBLIOGRAPHY
S. T. Madsen: *To kongeslott* [Two royal palaces] (Oslo, 1952)
G. Kavli and G. Hjelde: *Slottet i Oslo* [The palace in Oslo] (Oslo, 1973)

CHRISTIAN NORBERG-SCHULZ

**Lint, Pieter** [Pierre] **van** (*b* Antwerp, 28 June 1609; *d* Antwerp, 25 Sept 1690). Flemish painter and draughtsman, active also in Italy. Before becoming master of the Antwerp Guild of St Luke in 1632, van Lint worked for several years with Artus Wolffort; he recorded their collaboration in his diary (Paris, Fond. Custodia, Inst. Néer.). During these years he frequently copied the more famous paintings in Antwerp's churches, not only those by Peter Paul Rubens, but also works by older masters such as Marten de Vos and the Francken brothers. His earliest known painting, an *Adoration of the Shepherds* (1632; Vienna, Salesianerinnenkirche), shows a clear indebtedness to Wolffort's style, which was in the pre-Rubensian, academic manner of Otto van Veen.

Between 1633 and 1640 van Lint was in Rome, in the service of the Cibo family and Cardinal Ginnasio, among others. He painted a series of frescoes representing the medieval legend of the *History of the True Cross* for the Cibo Chapel in S Maria del Popolo in Rome. Here his style was Classical in inspiration, in the academic Roman Baroque manner. His copies after the Antique, studies (e.g. Paris, Fond. Custodia, Inst. Néer.) after the *Venus de' Medici* (Florence, Uffizi), for instance, confirm this preference. During his years in Rome, he also drew acutely characterized scenes from Roman street life in the vein of the BAMBOCCIANTI (e.g. *Five Travellers in a Boat*; U. Würzburg, Wagner-Mus.).

After his return to Antwerp, van Lint continued to paint in a classicizing style, influenced by Wolffort as well as by Roman examples, and he produced several altarpieces in this manner. His main efforts, however, went into the production, often in series, of relatively small and especially devotional pictures for the Spanish and South American markets. He often received commissions from such leading art dealers as Matthijs Musson and Forchondt.

BIBLIOGRAPHY
M. D. Padron: 'La obra de Pierre van Lint en España', *Goya* (1978), pp. 2–19
E. Valdino: 'Nuevas obras de Pieter van Lint', *Bol. Mus. Prov. B.A. Valladolid* (1979), pp. 469–79
H. Vlieghe: 'De leerpraktijk van een jonge schilder: Het notitieboekje van Pieter van Lint in het Institut Néerlandais te Parijs', *Jb.: Kon. Mus. S. Kst.* (1979), pp. 249–79
A. Busiri Vici: *Peter, Hendrik e Giovanni van Lint* (Rome, 1987)
M. Plomp: 'Opere sconosciute di Pieter van Lint (1609–1690)', *Bol. Mus. Civ. Genovesi* (1991), pp. 65–71

HANS VLIEGHE

**Lintel.** Term for the horizontal beam of wood or stone placed across an opening (e.g. a door, window or space between columns or piers) to support the wall above.

☐

**Linton, J(ames) W(alter) R(obert)** (*b* London, 14 June 1869; *d* Perth, 29 Aug 1947). Australian silversmith, jeweller, woodworker and painter of English birth. His father was the watercolourist Sir James Dromgole Linton

(1840–1916). Having trained as a painter and architect in London, he travelled to Western Australia in 1896 and began practising metalwork after settling in Perth; he was appointed head of the art department of Perth Technical School in 1902. Following a trip to London in 1907, when he attended classes at the Sir John Cass Technical Institute under Harold Stabler, he concentrated on producing metalwork. Working in partnership with Arthur Cross, William Andrews and his own son Jamie Linton (1904–80), he produced ecclesiastical and domestic wares, presentation pieces and jewellery. His designs were influenced by British Arts and Crafts metalwork and were bold and simple, with decoration generally confined to hammered surfaces, twisted wire, hardstones and enamels. A highly influential figure in Perth's artistic community and an energetic teacher, Linton played an important role in the promotion of crafts in Western Australia.

BIBLIOGRAPHY

A. Gray: *Line, Light and Shadow, James W. R. Linton: Painter, Craftsman, Teacher* (Freemantle, 1986)

JUDITH O'CALLAGHAN

**Linton, William James** (*b* London, 7 Dec 1812; *d* New Haven, CT, 1 Jan 1898). English wood-engraver. On completion of a six-year apprenticeship (1828–34) to the London wood-engraver George Wilmot Bonner (1796–1836), Linton worked as a journeyman engraver with some of the most notable reproductive wood-engravers of the period. In 1842, in partnership with John Orrin Smith (1799–1843), he engraved for the innovative *Illustrated London News* in addition to working for the publishers of illustrated books. In 1866 Linton left for the USA, where his reputation as an engraver of exceptional skill had preceded him and where he came quickly to enjoy both critical and financial success. However, his polemical campaign to allow the engraver a measure of artistic freedom in interpreting the work of others brought him into conflict with the 'new school' of engravers led by TIMOTHY COLE, who were more concerned to reproduce as faithfully as possible the subtleties of oil painting.

Linton was a restless man who crammed much into a long life: he was not only a wood-engraver, but also wrote poetry and political tracts. He was in turn an editor, art director and publisher of illustrated journals and he was active as a Chartist. He wrote much about engraving on wood and his books, together with his journal articles, constitute an important source of information and insight into the theory and practice of the process during the 19th century. His brother Henry Duff Linton (1816–99) was also a wood-engraver and occasionally assisted him.

WRITINGS

*Some Practical Hints on Wood Engraving* (Boston, 1879)
*A History of Wood Engraving in America* (Boston, 1882)
*Masters of Wood Engraving* (New Haven, 1889)
*Memories* (London, 1895)

BIBLIOGRAPHY

F. G. Kitton: 'William James Linton: Engraver, Poet and Political Writer', *Eng. Illus. Mag.*, viii (1891), pp. 490–500
F. B. Smith: *Radical Artisan: William James Linton, 1812–1897* (Manchester, 1973)

LEO JOHN DE FREITAS

**Lintong** [Lin-t'ung]. County and city in Shaanxi Province, China, north-east of Xi'an, and site of the mausoleum complex of Qin Shi Huangdi (*reg* 221–210 BC), the 'First Emperor of Qin', who unified the Chinese territories in 221 BC. The mausoleum lies near modern Lintong city, east of the site of the Qin capital at Xianyang; the pits associated with it contain the world-renowned life-size terracotta army.

The unexcavated tomb of Qin Shi Huangdi is marked by an imposing stepped pyramidal mound (h. *c.* 45 m) surrounded by a square, gated inner wall and an oblong outer wall *c.* 6.4 km in circumference. The Han-period (206 BC–AD 220) historian Sima Qian (*c.* 145–*c.* 90 BC) wrote about the tomb in the *Shiji* ('Records of the historian'), recording its construction and noting that it had already been pillaged and burnt in 206 BC by Xiang Yu, a rival of the first Han emperor. The Qin emperor began the mausoleum while he was still only king of the state of Qin and not yet emperor of China. The tomb thus contains a microcosm, an ideal model of the realm over which he had ruled and intended to continue to rule after his death. Some 700,000 people were reputedly conscripted to build it, and it was protected from robbers by devices such as ingenious automatic crossbows and rivers of mercury. The emperor's childless wives and the workmen who built the mausoleum are supposedly buried with him.

Over the years before 1974 a variety of remains were discovered outside the outer enclosure, including human and animal sacrifical burials, masonry workshops and a few isolated terracotta figures. Only in 1974, during the sinking of a well 1.5 km east of the mausoleum, was the discovery of the life-size terracotta figures made. Subsequent archaeological excavations revealed a total of four pits, ancillary to the emperor's main mausoleum. Three of these contained an army and its accoutrements of horses, chariots (*see* CHINA, §VI, 3(v)) and arms. Although the terracotta warriors had been broken and crushed, the majority were in restorable condition; they had fallen where they stood so that their relative positions could be ascertained. Pit 2, found in 1976, is about 20 m north of Pit 1, and Pit 3, the smallest of the three, is north-west of Pit 1. Pit 4, about one acre sq., situated between pits 2 and 3, is empty, possibly because work on the army was abandoned when rebellions against the Qin began soon after the first emperor's death.

Pit 1 is an underground structure of wood and masonry measuring 210 m east–west, 60 m north–south and 5 m deep; a museum has been constructed over it. It contains eleven parallel corridors and has two galleries, one at each of the eastern and western ends, running north–south and approached by earthen ramps. The main chamber has a wooden, cross-beamed roof and a brick floor. Many of the items in this pit had been destroyed by fire, but there were originally about 6400 terracotta soldiers. Armoured and unarmoured infantry stand in battle formation, facing eastwards (see fig.), with a vanguard of unarmoured archers, 200 sharpshooters and 6 wooden, four-horse chariots, 2 equipped with bells and drums to sound the retreat or advance. Guards at the front and rear face outwards. The soldiers' average height is *c.* 1.8 m, and the horses' *c.* 1.74 m. Bronze weapons are real.

Pit 2 is *c.* 600 sq. m in area and contains *c.* 1400 soldiers. These include armoured and unarmoured infantry, both

Lintong, mausoleum complex of Qin Shi Huangdi, Pit 1, life-size terracotta figures of infantry soldiers, Qin period, 221–206 BC (Lintong, Shaanxi Province, Museum of Emperor Qin Shi Huangdi's Tomb)

standing and kneeling, armoured archers, cavalry and charioteers in wooden chariots drawn by horses, all in military formation and divided into four groups; unit commanders wear distinctive mail coats. The prominence of war chariots suggests that they were still significant in Qin warfare. Pit 3 is *c*. 500 sq. m in area and appears to represent the commander-in-chief's headquarters. It contains *c*. 68 soldiers in protective positions guarding the commander, whose four-horse chariot has a painted canopy indicating his rank. The layout of this pit resembles a garrison headquarters, with a main hall and a room for stables and chariots.

The soldiers appear to have individual facial features, some of which reflect the diverse ethnic mix of the newly formed empire; however, a closer inspection reveals that most of the faces conform to an idealized type and variations are effected by the application of different hairstyles or of such details as moustaches or beards (*see also* CHINA, §VII, 3(ii)(b)). As such, they are unique for their time. Officers wear caps, display badges of rank and generally wear armour. The sharpshooters' clothing is of light material suited to mobility. Common soldiers wear knee-length tunics, either over high-collared inner garments and tied with belts, or beneath armoured jackets. They wear square-toed sandals, and hair in chignons. Charioteers wear in addition leggings and caps, and cavalrymen have short battle vests and boots. The commanders in Pit 3 are dressed in battle tunics with armoured aprons.

The high-fired terracotta figures and horses are made with coarse, grey clay from nearby Mt Li. Figures were made individually, with limbs, heads and ears constructed separately, then joined by clay strips before being fired. Detail was not incorporated in moulds, despite the large numbers of figures involved. Instead, features such as armour and hairstyles were modelled in the wet clay. Most warriors are posed at attention or in action, depending on their weaponry or military role. The horses have hollow bodies and solid legs; holes were made in their stomachs to prevent explosion during firing, and then plugs inserted to hide these. Tails and forelocks were fired separately and joined later. All pieces were painted in various colours, faded over time, including green, black, purple, yellow, white and red. Some armoured infantrymen sported different colours, presumably for identification purposes.

Thousands of weapons and parts of weapons have been recovered from the pits: swords, spears, halberds, bows, crossbows and arrowheads. Most are of bronze and some of iron; many were plundered soon after entombment. Shields have not been found, but seven different types of protective mail tunic have been identified (*see also* CHINA, §§II, 2(ii) and 6(i) (c), and XIII, 1 and fig. 281b).

BIBLIOGRAPHY
B. Watson: *Records of the Grand Historian of China: Translated from the Shih Chi of Ssu-ma Ch'ien* (New York and London, 1961), pp. 13–69
M. K. Hearn: 'The Terracotta Army of the First Emperor of Qin (221–206)', *The Great Bronze Age of China: An Exhibition from the People's Republic of China* (exh. cat. by W. Fong, New York, Met., 1980), pp. 353–73
A. Cotterell: *The First Emperor of China* (London, 1981)

Li Xueqin: *Eastern Zhou and Qin Civilizations* (New Haven and London, 1985), pp. 251–61

*The Emperor's Warriors: Catalogue of the Exhibition of the Terracotta Figures of Warriors and Horses of the Qin Dynasty of China* (exh. cat., Edinburgh, City A. Cent., 1985)

Yuan Zhongyi: 'Qin Shihuangling kaogu jiyao', *Kaogu Yu Wenwu*, 5/6 (1988), pp. 133–46

*Jenseits der grossen Mauer: Der erste Kaiser von China und seine terrakotta Armee* (exh. cat. by L. Ledderose and A. Schlombs, Dortmund, Mus. Ostwall, 1990)

CAROL MICHAELSON

**Lin-t'ung.** *See* LINTONG.

**Linz.** Austrian city and capital of the federal state of Upper Austria. Situated on the right bank of the River Danube, it has a population of *c.* 200,000. A settlement existed on the site in the Palaeolithic period. The Celts, who gave the place its original name (Lentia), fortified the Freinberg hill, and the Romans subsequently held Lentia for several centuries, installing a garrison during the late Empire. The first documentary reference to a castle and church there is in a Carolingian source of AD 799. Both buildings still exist, although in a much altered form. At the Martinskirche, excavation and restoration have re-created the original character of the Carolingian hall with three arches in each wall of the nave, opening into rectilinear niches; it is one of the earliest surviving medieval buildings in Austria.

The urban development of Linz began after *c.* 1190, when it passed to Leopold V of Babenberg (*reg* 1177–94). The layout of the Hauptplatz, enclosed by walls and a moat (destr. after the great fire of 1800), was decisive for further expansion. Linz was the provincial capital from 1490 and became the residence of the Diet of Upper Austria. As such it developed, especially in the 17th and 18th centuries, a modest but steady economic and cultural prosperity (*see* AUSTRIA, §XI, 1(ii) and 2). As a conscious display of the town's local and national status, the Rathaus and the Landhaus were erected soon after the appropriate rights had been granted. Only an octagonal bay window survives of the original Gothic structure of the Rathaus, which was rebuilt and enlarged in 1658–9. The Landhaus (begun 1564), a vast complex grouped around three courtyards, was largely destroyed by fire in 1800 and was rebuilt thereafter in Neo-classical style. The surviving original courtyard (1568–74) has three-storey, superposed arcades of fine proportions and severe but delicate decoration. It contains an octagonal fountain, the Planetenbrunnen (1581), with bronze statuettes of the *Seven Planets*. The north façade of the Landhaus still has its late Renaissance marble portal (*c.* 1570), an elaborate ensemble with a round-headed archway flanked by Tuscan half columns. Superposed above the entablature and a relief with putti and Austrian heraldic emblems, it has a triple window-arcade on Ionic columns.

The Schloss was completely rebuilt between 1599 and 1607 by order of Emperor Rudolf II. The huge, plain structure dominates the town from the slopes of the Freinberg hill and, like many buildings in Linz, was partly destroyed by fire (1800). It was the residence of the governor but has been a museum since 1966.

During the Counter-Reformation many of the reformed orders (among them the Jesuits, Ursulines, Capuchins and

Linz, view of Landstrasse with (left to right) the Jesuit, Ursuline and Carmelite churches

Carmelites) were invited to Linz by the emperor to confront the traditionally strong Protestant groups of the Upper Austrian nobility and bourgeoisie. They settled in the suburbs and subsequently displayed an industrious interest in church-building (see fig.), the most notable example being the Jesuit church of St Ignatius (1669–78) by Peter Franz Carlone (ii). It became the cathedral in 1785, when the diocese of Linz was established to replace that of Passau, but was returned to the Jesuits in 1900. The exterior has two tall façade towers and a steep roof. The interior follows the pattern of Il Gesù in Rome (*see* ROME, §V, 16); the hall nave has three bays, flanked by side chapels and galleries above, and a stuccoed barrel vault resting on massive piers.

The most important Baroque building in the city is the former Deutschordenskirche (1717–25), now the Seminarkirche, which was designed by Johann Lukas von Hildebrandt. Erected on a centralized elliptical ground-plan, the small church has a gently curved façade, linked by volutes to a richly sculptured tower over the entrance bay, surmounted by a mushroom-shaped cupola. The perfect architectural and decorative unity of the interior, which has a stuccoed dome over the crossing, is typical of Hildebrandt's art. Jakob Prandtauer designed the bishop's palace (1719–26), formerly (until 1785) the palace of Kremsmünster Abbey.

In the 19th century Linz entered a new stage of urban and architectural development. Between 1830 and 1836 a new fortification was constructed at the behest of Archduke Maximilian Joseph of Austria (1782–1863). This vast ring of 32 circular towers surrounded the town, with the main fort situated on the Pöstlingberg hill. In 1864 the Neustadt, laid out on a rectangular grid, was begun east of the old centre. The huge, neo-Gothic cathedral (1862–86, consecrated 1924) by VINCENZ STATZ represents the spiritual and architectural achievement of 19th-century historicism. After the Votivkirche in Vienna (1853), it is the most ambitious and accomplished work of its kind in Austria. Based on the classic French cathedral scheme of a basilica with transept and chevet, the building, with its west tower rising to a height of 135 m, competes in scale with the Stephansdom in Vienna. Another representative piece of 19th-century architecture is the Landesmuseum (1886–92) by Bruno Schmitz, a neo-Renaissance cubic building with a huge external marble frieze and a monumental staircase illuminated by a glass dome.

In the 20th century Linz developed into Austria's most important industrial city. Leading architects who worked in Linz included Peter Behrens, who, with Alexander Popp (1891–1945), designed the tobacco factory (1936) and the Friedenskirche (1933); and Clemens Holzmeister, who designed the Kreuzschwesternschule (1926), the Kammerspiele theatre (1955–6) and the reconstructed Landestheater auditorium (1957–8). The church of St Theresia in Keferfeld (1957–62) by Rudolf Schwarz is a bold concrete construction on an elliptical ground-plan. A new cultural tradition was established in 1974 with the opening of the Brucknerhaus (festival hall; 1969–74), a circular glass structure designed by Heikki and Kaija Sirén (see SIRÉN, (2)).

BIBLIOGRAPHY

E. Haiwisch: *Oberösterreich*, Dehio-Handbuch (Vienna, 1958), pp. 159–87
K. Oettinger, ed.: *Kunstführer Österreich*, i (Stuttgart, 1961, rev. 2/1968), pp. 244–70
J. Schmidt: *Neues Linz* (Munich, 1961)
W. Frodl, ed.: *Die kirchlichen Kunstdenkmäler der Stadt Linz*, Österreichische Kunsttopographie, xxxvi (Vienna, 1964)
G. Wacha: 'Die Kunst in Linz um 1600' *Kstjb. Stadt Linz* (1967), pp. 5–54
T. Melicher: 'Die städtebauliche Entwicklung von Linz im 19. Jahrhundert', *Kstjb. Stadt Linz* (1968), pp. 5–44
E. Frodl-Kraft, ed.: *Die profanen Bau- und Kunstdenkmäler der Stadt Linz*, Österreichische Kunsttopographie, xlii (Vienna, 1977)
F. Achleitner: *Österreichische Architektur im 20. Jahrhundert*, i (Vienna, 1980)
F. Mayrhofer: *Linz* (Vienna and Munich, 1984)

SUSANNE KRONBICHLER-SKACHA

**Liombeni, Lorenzo de.** *See* LEONBRUNO, LORENZO.

**Liompardi, Alessandro.** *See* LEOPARDI, ALESSANDRO.

**Lion Cachet, C(arel) A(dolph)** (*b* Amsterdam, 28 Nov 1864; *d* Vreeland, 20 May 1945). Dutch decorative artist and designer. He first trained as an art teacher at the Rijksnormaalschool in Amsterdam between 1887 and 1891, but afterwards he devoted himself almost exclusively to decorative art and design. His designs included furniture, batiks, upholstery fabrics and carpets. Because of their imaginative, often capricious, decorations they occupied a special place within the Nieuwe Kunst movement.

From 1889 until 1906, with T. W. Nieuwenhuis and Gerrit Willem Dijsselhof, he worked for the furniture workshop E. J. Wisselingh & Co. in Amsterdam (*see* NETHERLANDS, THE, §VI, 5). In addition, from 1901 he ran his own Atelier voor Versieringskunst (Studio for Decorative Art) in Vreeland. He collaborated with Nieuwenhuis on the sumptuous interiors designed *c.* 1901–12 for the lawyer G. T. Dentz van Schaick in Amsterdam; each artist was responsible for the design of his own room. The panelling and furniture are richly decorated with low-relief carving and are inlaid with oak and ivory. The woollen carpets and the gilded leather and parchment ceiling were also designed by Lion Cachet. A reconstruction of the interior can be seen at the Centraal Museum, Utrecht.

Around 1890 Lion Cachet started to experiment with the technique of batik, specializing in batik on parchment, used, for example, for certificates and bindings. Between 1906 and 1940 he designed a great number of interiors for luxury ocean liners. The purpose-designed carpets, made by the Koninklijke Verenigde Tapijtfabrieken in Rotterdam and Deventer, and the mock velvet upholstery fabrics, produced by Schellens & Marto in Eindhoven, were more in line with the style of the Amsterdam school rather than Nieuwe Kunst because of their lively, expressive style.

BIBLIOGRAPHY

B. W. Wierink: *C. A. Lion Cachet* (Gronigen, 1931)
L. Gans: *Nieuwe Kunst: De Nederlandse bijdrage tot de Art Nouveau: Dekoratieve kunst, kunstnijverheid en architektuur omstreeks 1900* [Nieuwe Kunst: the Dutch contribution to Art Nouveau: decorative art, applied arts and architecture *c.* 1900] (Utrecht, 1966), pp. 96–9
*C. A. Lion Cachet 1864–1945* (exh. cat., Rotterdam, Mus. Boymans–van Beuningen, 1994)

M. W. F. SIMON THOMAS

**Lione, Andrea di** [Lione, Andrea de; Leone, Andrea di] (*b* Naples, 8 Sept 1610; *d* Naples 12 Feb 1685). Italian painter. An eclectic and varied artist, he painted scenes from the Old and New Testaments, Roman history and mythology as well as still-lifes. He studied in Naples with the late Mannerist artist Belisario Corenzio, with whom he collaborated on frescoes of battle scenes for the Palazzo Reale in Naples (*in situ*). Then, attracted by the battle paintings of Aniello Falcone, he entered Falcone's studio, and his red chalk studies of the nude (e.g. *Male Nude*, Philadelphia, PA, Mus. A.) and of parts of the body reflect the rigorous academic training that he received there. He became known as a painter of battles himself, and his works in this genre include two signed paintings, the *Battle between the Hebrews and the Amalekites* and the *Combat between David and Goliath* (both Naples, Capodimonte), and the signed and dated *Battle against the Turks* (1641; Paris, Louvre). In these works Lione moved away from the rather static compositions of Falcone and created more dramatic scenes, with richer colour and looser brushwork. Between 1637 and 1644 he was patronized by Ramiro Nuñez de Guzman, Duque de Medina de las Torres (Viceroy of Naples between 1637 and 1644), who commissioned works from him and from other Neapolitan painters to decorate the palace of the Buen Retiro, just outside Madrid; Lione's contributions included the *Elephants in a Roman Circus* (Madrid, Prado).

Lione's art was deeply influenced by that of Giovanni Benedetto Castiglione, whom he may have met during

Castiglione's visit to Naples in 1635, and whom he probably met again in Rome in the 1640s; the relationship between their art was both complex and long lasting. The *Voyage of Jacob* by Castiglione (1633; New York, priv. col., see Brigstocke, fig. 1) inspired a group of works by Lione, particularly his signed *Voyage of Jacob* (1635–40; Vienna, Ksthist. Mus.), an elegant and romantic rendering of an Old Testament scene, enriched by animals, still-life and genre details, and set in a warmly coloured and softly atmospheric landscape. This and other works suggest so strong a debt to both Castiglione and the Venetianizing elements in Nicolas Poussin's early work, to which Castiglione himself responded, that it has been suggested that Lione travelled to Rome (Blunt) and became one of the circle of artists who gathered around Poussin and Pietro Testa. The date of the visit is unclear, but it may have been in the mid-1630s, or between 1642 and 1644. In 1647 Lione produced a signed and dated portrait of the rebel leader *Masaniello* (Rome, Nicolo Castellino priv. col.) and after Masaniello's revolt he left Naples for a period (de Dominici) and may have visited Rome.

Other works, while still indebted to Castiglione, show the influence of Poussin's more classical style and reveal an awareness of other French artists working in Rome, such as Sébastien Bourdon and Charles Mellin. Outstanding among these is *Tobit Burying the Dead* (early 1640s; New York, Met.), related to which are a group of drawings (e.g. U. London, Courtauld Inst. Gals; Cleveland, OH, Mus. A.) and a print by Castiglione, and four drawings by Lione (Berlin, Kupferstichkab.; London, V&A; Naples, Capodimonte; Sacramento, CA, Crocker A. Mus.), which suggest a complex relationship between the two artists. Yet the final picture, in which the figures are arranged in a frieze-like group before an architectural landscape, is more austere than Castiglione and closer to the ordered compositions of Poussin.

Lione's later works probably include *Venus and Adonis* (mid-1650s; New York, Mario Lan priv. col., see 1982 exh. cat., p. 107), a romantic and very freely painted work, which echoes the poetry of Poussin's most lyrical mythological scenes, and *Jacob's Journey* (1666; Madrid, Prado), again dependent on Castiglione. Five frescoes of scenes from the *Life of St Athanasius*, signed and dated 1677 (Naples Cathedral, Cappella Galeota), survive in a ruinous condition. Lione was also a still-life painter, and his works in this genre include a signed *Still-life* (Geneva, priv. col.) and two *Still-lifes with Fruit* (Pau, Mus. B.-A.).

Mariette

BIBLIOGRAPHY

B. de Dominici: *Vite* (1742–5), p. 113

A. Blunt: 'A Poussin-Castiglione Problem: Classicism and the Picturesque in 17th-century Rome', *J. Warb. & Court. Inst.*, iii (1939–40), pp. 142–7

M. S. Soria: 'Andrea di Leone: A Master of the Bucolic Scene', *A.Q.* [Detroit], xxiii (1960), pp. 23–35

M. Newcome: 'A Castiglione–Leone Problem', *Master Drgs*, xvi/2 (1978), pp. 163–72

H. Brigstocke: 'Castiglione: Two Recently Discovered Paintings', *Burl. Mag.*, cxxii (1980), pp. 292–8

*Painting in Naples: From Caravaggio to Giordano* (exh. cat., ed. C. Whitfield and J. Martineau; London, R.A.; Washington, DC, N.G.A.; 1982), pp. 106–8

A. Brejon de Lavergnée: 'Nouvelles toiles d'Andrea di Lione: Essai de catalogue', *Scritti di storia dell'arte in onore di Federico Zeri*, ed. F. Porzio, ii (Milan, 1984), pp. 656–80

F. Zeri: 'Andrea de Lione e la natura morta', *Scritti in onore di Raffaello Causa* (Naples, 1988), pp. 203–8

F. Porzio, ed.: *La natura morta in Italia*, ii (Milan, 1989), pp. 862, 871

**Liotard, Jean-Etienne** (*b* Geneva, 22 Dec 1702; *d* Geneva, 12 June 1789). Swiss pastellist, painter, printmaker and writer. He was born to French Protestant parents, who had fled to Switzerland after the Revocation of the Edict of Nantes. Having studied with the miniature painter Daniel Gardelle in Geneva, in 1723 he travelled to Paris, where until 1726 he was a pupil of Jean-Baptiste Massé. In 1734 he submitted his only known history painting, *King David and the High Priest Abimelech in the Tabernacle* (untraced, see Humbert, Revilliod and Tilanus, no. 110), for the painting prize of the Académie Royale de Peinture et de Sculpture, but it was rejected. He subsequently travelled to Naples and then to Rome, where he executed a portrait of *Pope Clement XII* (untraced). In Florence he met Sir William Ponsonby (1704–93), later 2nd Earl of Bessborough, whom he accompanied to the Levant in 1738, breaking the journey in Capri, Messina, Syracuse, Malta and the Greek islands; there, seduced by the beauty of Eastern dress, he made a large number of acute and charming drawings in black and red chalks (Paris, Louvre; Paris, Bib. N.).

Liotard then spent 1738–42 in Constantinople (now Istanbul), during which time he painted pastel portraits of members of the British colony, including the full-length portrait of *Richard Pococke in Turkish Costume* (Geneva, Mus. A. & Hist; see fig. 1). He himself acquired the habit of wearing Turkish dress and grew a long beard; his eccentric appearance contributed not a little to his celebrity on his return to Europe.

From 1743 to 1745 Liotard was in Vienna, where he found favour at court and painted the *Empress Maria-Theresa* (version, Weimar, Schlossmus.) as well as executing his most famous pastel, a full-length figure of a chambermaid carrying a tray with a cup of chocolate, *La Belle Chocolatière* (Dresden, Staatl. Kstsammlungen; *see* SWITZERLAND, fig. 7). He then visited Venice and was in Geneva in 1746, leaving again for Paris two years later. While in Lyon on this journey, he painted his niece Mlle Lavergne, a charming half-length portrait known as *La Belle Liseuse* (versions, Amsterdam, Rijksmus.; Dresden, Staatl. Kstsammlungen). Among the several works he produced in Paris is the exotic portrait of *?Maria Gunning, Countess of Coventry* (versions, Geneva, Mus. A. & Hist.; Amsterdam, Rijksmus.; see fig. 2). Introduced at court in 1749 by Maurice, Maréchal de Saxe (1696–1750), he received an important commission for portraits of *Louis XV* and of his five daughters (all Stupinigi, Pal. Mauriziana).

Despite his success in France and abroad, the Académie Royale refused to admit Liotard as a member, and he instead joined the Académie de St Luc, exhibiting works at its exhibitions in 1751 and 1752. In 1755 he travelled to London, where he enjoyed a warm welcome and executed pastel portraits of *Augusta, Princess of Wales* and of her nine children (all Windsor Castle, Berks, Royal Col.). He then moved on to Amsterdam and The Hague and in 1757 settled in Geneva, where he depicted the local

1. Jean-Etienne Liotard: *Richard Pococke in Turkish Costume*, oil on canvas, 2.02×1.34 m, 1738–9 (Geneva, Musée d'Art et d'Histoire)

bourgeoisie with an accomplished and rigorous mastery. His most remarkable portraits of this period are those of the family and friends of François Tronchin, a notable collector, including *François Tronchin Looking at a Painting by Rembrandt* (1757; Geneva, Givaudan priv. col., HRT 78) and *Mme d'Epinay* (Geneva, Mus. A. & Hist.), which is considered his masterpiece.

Liotard continued to travel until near the end of his life: in 1762 he returned to Vienna and in 1771–2 was in Paris, where he painted *Marie-Antoinette* and *Louis XVI* (both Stupinigi, Pal. Mauriziana). From 1773 to 1775 he was in London, where he exhibited five portraits at the Royal Academy, including one of *John, Viscount Mount Stuart* (London, priv. col., HRT 62). In Vienna, where he stayed again in 1777–8, he executed some of his most beautiful drawings *aux trois crayons*, including those of the 11 children of the Empress Maria-Theresa (all Geneva, Mus. A. & Hist.).

Throughout his career Liotard made self-portraits, both as self-examination and as self-advertisement, in order to keep up the image that had earnt him the nickname of 'the Turkish painter'. Some 15 are known, including oils, pastels, miniatures and engravings, the first of which dates from 1727 (Geneva, Salmanowitz priv. col.). Towards the end of his life he painted an increasing number, among which his *Self-portrait as an Old Man with Chin in Hand*

(Geneva, Mus. A. & Hist.) is a masterly work of great emotional content.

At the end of his career, out of fashion and short of commissions, Liotard began to paint pastel still-lifes of flowers and fruit (e.g. Geneva, Mus. A. & Hist.; Winterthur, Samml. Oskar Reinhart). These astonishingly modern still-lifes, many of which date from after 1783, owe a good deal to the work of Jean-Siméon Chardin but are yet more austere. One pastel landscape by Liotard is known, a *View of Geneva Looking towards the Mountain* (Amsterdam, Rijksmus.).

Liotard also worked occasionally in media other than pastel and oil; thus early in his career he painted enamel miniatures, and he later experimented with painting on glass and porcelain. He made a number of etchings (*see* ETCHING, SOFT GROUND, §2), including the *Self-portrait in the Artist's Studio* (e.g. Vienna, Albertina), and he experimented with colour printing as a means of disseminating his pastel portraits.

At the age of almost 80, Liotard published the *Traité des principes et des règles de la peinture*, in which he explained his concept of painting as a mirror of nature, using this to justify a violent attack on the method of applying paint in touches or dabs: a deceitful artifice, in his opinion, because non-existent in nature. The book also contains high praise for the still-life painter Jan van Huysum, several of whose paintings he had collected.

As a portrait painter, Liotard remained faithful all his life to a style that owed little to other artists or to the conventions of fashionable salon art. Whether his sitters

2. Jean-Etienne Liotard: *?Maria Gunning, Countess of Coventry*, pastel, 930×730 mm (Amsterdam, Rijksmuseum)

came from the nobility, the bourgeoisie or the world of artists, he treated them all with startling directness. His models are depicted firmly against a plain background (usually grey-brown), simply lit and set in a space with little depth. He never sought to embellish his subjects nor to flatter them by means of the pose selected, and he used no ornaments, drapery or symbols of rank or office to distract the eye. Liotard's success as a portrait painter rested on the care he took to achieve a close likeness, his unreserved submission to the real, his sober and incisive style and the simplicity of the composition of his works.

Liotard's twin brother, Jean-Michel Liotard (1702–96), was an etcher and engraver. After training in Paris he worked for Joseph Smith, British consul in Venice from 1735, for whom he engraved works by Carlo Cignani and Sebastiano Ricci (published Venice, 1743). After his return to Paris he was principally engaged in reproducing works by Antoine Watteau and Eustache Le Sueur. He later settled in Geneva, to be near Jean-Etienne.

WRITINGS

*Traité des principes et des règles de la peinture* (Geneva, 1781)

BIBLIOGRAPHY

E. D. Humbert, A. Revilliod and J. W. Tilanus: *La Vie et les oeuvres de Jean-Etienne Liotard* (Amsterdam, 1897) [HRT]

L. Grelly, ed.: 'La Biographie de Jean-Etienne Liotard, écrite par son fils', *Geneva: Bull. Mus. A. & Hist. Genève Mus. Ariana & Soc. Aux. Mus., Bib. Pub. & U.*, xi (1933), pp. 190–200

F. Fosca: *La Vie, les voyages et les oeuvres de Jean-Etienne Liotard, citoyen de Genève, dit le peintre turc* (Lausanne and Paris, 1956)

R. Loche and M. Roethlisberger: *L'opera completa di Liotard* (Milan, 1978)

*Les Portraits de Liotard* (exh. cat., ed. F. Baumann and R. Storrer; Zurich, Ksthaus, 1978)

*Dessins de Liotard* (exh. cat. by A. de Herdt, Geneva, Mus. A. & Hist., Paris, Louvre; 1992)

NICOLE PARMANTIER-LALLEMENT

**Lipchitz, Jacques** [Chaïm Jacob] (*b* Druskieniki, Lithuania, 22 Aug 1891; *d* Capri, 26 May 1973). French sculptor of Russian birth active in the USA. Lipchitz grew up in Druskieniki. His father, a Jewish building contractor, opposed his son's desire to become a sculptor, but his mother was sympathetic and arranged for him to go to Paris in 1909. He arrived with no formal academic training and studied briefly at the Ecole des Beaux-Arts before transferring to the Académie Julian. Mornings were spent drawing and modelling from life; during the rest of the day he visited museums. Lipchitz's early nudes and portraits of 1910–12 have much in common with the classicism of Maillol and Charles Despiau, although he himself suggested that they had a common source in Greek and medieval art. On a visit to St Petersburg in 1911, he became particularly interested in the Scythian sculpture collection in the Hermitage. Lipchitz remained fascinated with the sculpture of the great non-European traditions throughout his life, and was an ardent collector of non-Western (especially African) art.

On his return to Paris in 1912, Lipchitz moved into a studio next to Constantin Brancusi in Montparnasse. During these early years in Paris he met many of the most prominent artists and poets of the day: Chaïm Soutine, Amedeo Modigliani, Alexander Archipenko and Max Jacob. In 1913, through his friend Diego Rivera, he met Picasso; the encounter had far-reaching implications in the development of Lipchitz's work. He intuitively understood the sculptural possibilities of Picasso's Cubist paintings and soon abandoned the naturalist, Art Nouveau style of his previous work in favour of a more simplified, geometric style. *Mother and Child* (bronze, 1913–14: priv. col., see Lipchitz and Arnason, 1972, p. 22) is representative of Lipchitz's proto-Cubist works. It reflects his assimilation of bold, simplified Cubist forms, as well as a confluence of other influences: Egyptian and African sculpture and the work of Brancusi and Modigliani.

Lipchitz's first purely Cubist sculptures were executed in 1915–16; they represent the most abstract phase of his development. *Head* (bronze, 1915; London, Tate) is composed of abstract, interlocking planes and curved edges but retains such features as the nose, which make the subject legible. This sculpture was almost certainly inspired by such works by Picasso as *Head of a Woman* (bronze; New York, MOMA). Also in 1915 Lipchitz made several sculptures in wood and began a number of totemic sculptures that had only the most obscure references to

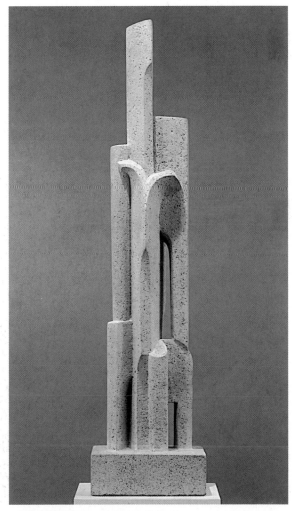

Jacques Lipchitz: *Standing Personage*, limestone, h. 1.06 m, 1916 (New York, Solomon R. Guggenheim Museum)

the human figure. He later compared the stone *Standing Personage* (1916; New York, Guggenheim; see fig.) to a cluster of skyscraper towers, and indeed the work seems closer to architecture than to the human figure. Lipchitz appears to have borrowed freely from various phases of Picasso's Cubism, in this case, from such paintings as *Man Leaning on a Table* (1916). Lipchitz's Cubist sculptures were made in clay or plaster. Some were transferred into stone in Paris under his supervision; but most of the works were not cast in bronze until the 1960s, when the sculptor was living in the USA.

In 1916 Lipchitz met Juan Gris, and they soon became close friends. He also signed a contract with the dealer Léonce Rosenberg (who also represented Picasso, Braque, Gris and Rivera), producing for him a series of stone figures (e.g. *Sculpture*, 1915–16; London, Tate), which the dealer exhibited at his gallery in Paris in 1920. Lipchitz was concerned that some of his sculpture was too abstract, that he had almost lost the sense of the subject, of its humanity. In 1917–18 he abandoned the austere purity that had characterized much of his recent work and created clearly legible Cubist subjects: bathers, musicians, harlequins and still-lifes. In *Seated Man with Guitar* (bronze, 1918; Dallas, Mr and Mrs A. H. Meadows priv. col., see Hammacher, 1975, pl. 77) the guitar and simplified anatomical forms are clearly defined. The sculpture also reflects Lipchitz's renewed interest in frontality, an aspect of Egyptian and archaic sculpture that he greatly admired.

By the 1920s Lipchitz's work was becoming more widely known and admired. In 1922 the American collector Dr Albert C. Barnes acquired a number of sculptures from the artist and commissioned relief sculptures for the Barnes Foundation at Merion Station, PA.

In 1925 Lipchitz began experimenting with a radical approach to three-dimensional form. In his small 'transparents', as he called them, he found himself 'playing with space, with a kind of open, lyrical construction that was a revelation to me' (Lipchitz and Arnason, 1972, p. 86). These skeletal figures, bronzes cast from constructions in wax and cardboard, represented a hitherto unexplored juxtaposition of solids and voids; their fragile forms presented new technical problems in terms of casting. Lipchitz described *Acrobat on a Ball* (bronze, 1926; priv. col., see 1954 exh. cat., p. 43), composed of thin, twisting, interlocking forms, as a kind of drawing in space. Lipchitz's 'transparents' were among the most innovative works of his career, and they influenced Picasso and Julio González's metal constructions of 1928.

Until the mid-1920s almost all Lipchitz's sculptures were modest in scale (between 500 mm and 1000 mm high). The large *Figure* (bronze, 1926–30; New York, MOMA) was among the first of many commissioned monumental sculptures. During the late 1920s and 1930s Lipchitz created a number of highly personal works relating at times to events in his own life. The theme of *Joy of Life* (bronze, priv. col., see Hammacher, 1975, pl. 38), commissioned in 1927, was chosen to cheer up his sister, who was ill in hospital. Much of Lipchitz's work from the late 1920s until his death combines the formal language of Cubism with the open, lyrical quality of his transparents. Mythological, biblical and sexual themes came to dominate his work: for instance in *The Cry (The*

*Couple)* (bronze, 1928–9; Otterlo, Rijksmus. Kröller-Müller) and the *Return of the Prodigal Son* (bronze, 1930; priv. col., see Lipchitz and Arnason, 1972, p. 121). *Prometheus Strangling the Vulture* (plaster; 1936–7; destr.) was conceived as an attack on Nazism by Lipchitz, with Prometheus symbolizing democracy. It was commissioned by the (Socialist) French Government for the Exposition Internationale des Arts et Techniques dans la Vie Moderne in 1937 in Paris, but was destroyed afterwards following a virulent press campaign against it. A preliminary plaster model and a study (ink and gouache on paper) are in the Tate Gallery, London.

Upon the German invasion of France (1940), Lipchitz and his wife fled to Toulouse; the following year they emigrated to New York. His sculpture became more directly autobiographical, in such works as *Flight* (bronze, 1940; priv. col., see 1954 exh. cat., p. 65) and *Arrival* (bronze, 1941; see 1973 exh. cat., p. 19). In *Mother and Child* (bronze, 1941–5; Toronto, A.G. Ont.) Lipchitz's horror of war is expressed in the anguished despair of the mother, whose stump-like arms and truncated body create a poignant image of mutilation.

Lipchitz exhibited at Curt Valentin's influential Buchholz Galleries, New York, in 1942 and returned to Paris in 1946. In 1947 he was commissioned to carve a Madonna for the church of Notre-Dame-de-Liesse (*in situ*) in Assy, near Chamonix, a project not completed until 1955. On his return to the USA in 1947 he moved to Hastings-on-Hudson, New York. During the early 1950s he received other important commissions: *Birth of the Muses* (bas-relief; Rockefeller priv. col., see 1973 exh. cat.) for Mrs John D. Rockefeller and the *Spirit of Enterprise* (bronze) for Fairmount Park, Philadelphia. In 1955 Lipchitz began experimenting with 'semi-automatics', in which he would splash or squeeze warm wax in a basin of water and let it harden. The haphazard method suggested many different images that could be developed. In 1958 Lipchitz worked with the architect Philip Johnson on the gateway for the Roofless Church, New Harmony, IN.

During the 1960s and early 1970s there were major exhibitions of Lipchitz's work in the USA, Europe and Israel. Many of his large bronzes were cast at the Tommasi foundry at Pietrasanta, Italy, where Lipchitz worked during the summers. *Peace on Earth* (bronze, 1967–9; Los Angeles, CA, Music Cent.) was one of his last monumental projects. It is an enlargement of the Virgin at Assy, and its open, transparent structure and powerful baroque rhythms make it a summation and resolution of the varied stylistic currents that informed his work for more than half a century. Lipchitz had become acutely conscious of the Jewish cause during the 1940s. *Our Tree of Life* (bronze), commissioned by the Hadassah University Hospital of Jerusalem in 1967, was intended as a Jewish counterpart of the Virgin Mary at Assy and included a series of subjects showing the growth of Judaism. The final version (made from Lipchitz's last maquette) was installed on Mount Scopus in 1978. Lipchitz regarded Israel as his spiritual home, and was buried there.

### WRITINGS
*Amedeo Modigliani* (Paris, 1954)
with H. H. Arnason: *My Life in Sculpture* (London, 1972)

BIBLIOGRAPHY

M. Raynal: *Lipchitz* (Paris, 1920)

R. Vitrac: *Jacques Lipchitz* (Paris, 1929)

*Jacques Lipchitz* (exh. cat. by E. Faure, New York, Brummer Gal., 1935)

*The Drawings of Jacques Lipchitz* (exh. cat., New York, Buchholz Gals, 1944)

M. Raynal: *Jacques Lipchitz* (Paris, 1947)

*The Sculpture of Jacques Lipchitz* (exh. cat. by H. R. Hope, New York, MOMA; Minneapolis, Walker A. Center; Cleveland, Mus. A.; 1954)

A. E. Elsen: 'The Humanism of Rodin and Lipchitz', *Coll. A. J.*, xvii/3 (1958), pp. 247–65

*Sculptures by Jacques Lipchitz* (exh. cat. by B. Dorival, London, Tate, 1959)

A. M. Hammacher: *Jacques Lipchitz: His Sculpture* (New York, 1960, rev. 1975) [by a close friend of Lipchitz; incl. introductory statement by the artist and an extensive bibliog.]

I. Patai: *Encounters: The Life of Jacques Lipchitz* (New York, 1960)

*The Lipchitz Collection* (exh. cat. by R. Goldwater and J. Lipchitz, New York, Mus. Primitive A., 1960) [small but important selection of Lipchitz's extensive col. of primitive art]

*Lipchitz: The Cubist Period* (exh. cat. by A. Werner, New York, Marlborough–Gerson Gal., 1968)

A. A. Arnason: *Jacques Lipchitz: Sketches in Bronze* (New York, 1969) [foreword by Lipchitz]

*The Partial Figure in Modern Sculpture from Rodin to 1969* (exh. cat. by A. E. Elsen, Baltimore, MD, Mus. A., 1969), pp. 45–6

*The Cubist Epoch* (exh. cat. by D. Cooper, Los Angeles, CA, Co. Mus. A.; New York, Met., 1971), pp. 249–53

*A Tribute to Jacques Lipchitz: Lipchitz in America, 1941–1973* (exh. cat. by A. M. Hammacher, New York, Marlborough Gal., 1973)

A. M. Hammacher: *Lipchitz in Otterlo*, Otterlo, Rijksmus. Kröller-Müller cat. (Otterlo, 1977)

N. Barbier: *Lipchitz: Oeuvres de Jacques Lipchitz (1891–1973) dans les collections du Musée National d'Art Moderne* (Paris, 1978)

*The Essential Cubism: Braque, Picasso and their Friends, 1907–1920* (exh. cat. by D. Cooper and G. Tinterow; London, Tate, 1983), pp. 402–19

A. G. Wilkinson: 'Paris and London: Modigliani, Lipchitz, Epstein, and Gaudier-Brzeska', *'Primitivism' in 20th Century Art: Affinity of the Tribal and the Modern*, 2 vols (exh. cat., ed. W. S. Rubin; New York, MOMA, 1984), ii, pp. 417–50

*Jacques Lipchitz: Selected Sculpture, Reliefs and Drawings, 1911–1972* (exh. cat., New York, Marlborough Gal., 1985)

*The Lipchitz Gift: Models for Sculpture* (exh. cat. by D. Fraser Jenkins and D. Pullen, London, Tate, 1986) [incl. the 57 photos and terracottas given to the Tate by the Lipchitz Foundation: invaluable study of Lipchitz's working method]

ALAN G. WILKINSON

**Lipman.** American collectors. Howard W. Lipman (*b* Albany, NY, 11 July 1905) and his wife, the art historian Jean Lipman, formed a major American folk art collection, which was acquired in 1950 by the Museum of New York State Historical Association, Cooperstown, NY. They also assembled an important collection of American sculpture of the 1960s, notably the work of Alexander Calder and Louise Nevelson, which they later donated to the Whitney Museum of American Art, New York, through the Howard and Jean Lipman Foundation.

Howard W. Lipman became a trustee of the Whitney in 1967, and, after serving as its President (1974–7), he was made Chairman of its board in 1977. He was also a trustee of the Art Museum in Phoenix, AZ, from 1972 to 1974. Jean Lipman built her reputation as an art historian on the study of American folk art, which she had undertaken from the 1930s. In 1974, with Alice Winchester, she wrote *The Flowering of American Folk Art, 1776–1876*, the catalogue for a major exhibition at the Whitney and the first publication to survey the entire range of American folk art. As editor of *Art in America* (1940–70) and later editor of publications at the Whitney, she wrote 15 books and more than 100 articles on American art.

WRITINGS

J. Lipman: *American Folk Art in Wood, Metal and Stone* (New York, 1948/*R* 1972)

*The Flowering of American Folk Art, 1776–1876* (exh. cat. by J. Lipman and A. Winchester, New York, Whitney, 1974)

J. Lipman: *Calder's Universe* (New York, 1976)

——: *Nevelson's World* (New York, 1983)

BIBLIOGRAPHY

A. I. Furman, ed.: *Who's Who in American Art, 1991–1992: 19th Edition* (New York, 1990)

EDWARD BRYANT

**Lipótváros.** *See under* BUDAPEST, §I, 3.

**Lippert, Philipp Daniel** (*b* Dresden, 29 Sept 1702; *d* Dresden, 28 March 1785). German draughtsman and antiquarian. After an apprenticeship as a glazier and classes at the Dresden school of drawing, he served an apprenticeship at the Meissen porcelain factory, where he was recorded in 1726 as an artist. With the support of the Dresden architect Friedrich August Krubsacius, he obtained commissions from the court, and in 1735 he was appointed a drawing master at its Pagenakademie. Lippert began the study of antique gems and collected impressions of them from all over Europe. After the invention of a new substance for taking impressions, he edited his *Dactyliotheca* (1755–6) in three booklike boxes, with notes in Latin by well-known scholars; he later produced a selection with his own German text. His collection of impressions considerably furthered both the study of Classical antiquity during the Enlightenment and the classicist tendencies in art. It became a model for the collections of impressions of gems that remained popular in the 19th century.

COLLECTED EDITIONS

*Dactyliotheca universalis*, i, ii (Leipzig and Dresden, 1755–6; text by J. F. Christ), iii (Leipzig and Dresden, 1762; text by C. G. Heyne)

*Dactyliothec . . . in zwey tausend Abdrücken ediret* (Leipzig and Dresden, 1767; suppl., 1776)

BIBLIOGRAPHY

C. Justi: *Winckelmann*, iii (Leipzig, 1923), pp. 389–403

G. Heres: 'Daktyliotheken der Goethezeit', *Forsch. & Ber.: Staatl. Mus. Berlin*, xiii (1971), pp. 59–74

P. Zazoff: *Gemmensammler und Gemmenforscher* (Munich, 1983), pp. 153–61

GERALD HERES

**Lippi.** Italian family of painters and draughtsmen. (1) Fra Filippo Lippi, a Carmelite monk who was one of the leading Florentine painters of the mid-15th century, had a son by Lucrezia Buti, the nun he abducted in 1456. This son, (2) Filippino Lippi, became in turn one of the leading Florentine painters of the late 15th century.

BIBLIOGRAPHY

G. Vasari: *Vite* (1550, rev. 2/1568); ed. G. Milanesi (1878–85), ii, pp. 611–46, iii, pp. 461–92

I. B. Supino: *Les Deux Lippi* (Florence, 1904)

U. Mengin: *Les Deux Lippi* (Paris, 1932)

B. Berenson: *Florentine School* (1963), pp. 111–14

**(1)** Fra **Filippo (di Tommaso) Lippi** (*b* Florence, *c.* 1406; *d* Spoleto, 9 Oct 1469). He was one of the leading painters in Renaissance Florence in the generation following Masaccio. Influenced by him in his youth, Filippo developed a linear, expressive style, which anticipated the achievements of his pupil Botticelli. Lippi was among the earliest painters indebted to Donatello. His mature works are some of the first Italian paintings to be inspired by the realistic technique (and occasionally by the compositions) of Netherlandish pioneers such as Rogier van der Weyden and Jan van Eyck. Beginning work in the late 1430s, Lippi won several important commissions for large-scale altarpieces, and in his later years he produced two fresco cycles that (as Vasari noted) had a decisive impact on 16th-century cycles. He produced some of the earliest autonomous portrait paintings of the Renaissance, and his smaller-scale *Virgin and Child* compositions are among the most personal and expressive of that era. Throughout most of his career he was patronized by the powerful Medici family and allied clans. The operation of his workshop remains a matter of conjecture.

1. Life and work. 2. Working methods and technique. 3. Workshop organization.

### 1. LIFE AND WORK.

(i) Before 1437. (ii) 1437–52. (iii) 1452–69.

*(i) Before 1437.* Lippi is first documented on 18 June 1421, when he took vows at the Carmelite monastery of S Maria del Carmine in Florence. Since the minimum age for entering the order was 15, he was probably born *c.* 1406. He appears in the annual records of the monastery from 1422 to 1432. On 7 November 1428 he was given permission to spend the following year at the Carmelite monastery in Siena. Here he may have come into contact with Domenico di Bartolo, who, according to Vasari, painted the high altar of S Maria del Carmine in Florence. In Siena, Lippi could have seen sculptural works such as the font in the baptistery with relief panels by Jacopo della Quercia, Lorenzo Ghiberti, Donatello and others, as well as polychromed wooden statues by della Quercia and Domenico di Niccolò de' Cori.

There are no records relating to Lippi's training and no surviving documented paintings by his hand from before 1437. As a monk he was apparently exempt from membership of the Arte dei Medici e Speziali or the Compagnia di S Luca. He is first referred to as a painter in 1430 in the accounts of S Maria del Carmine. Vasari, who is almost the only source for Lippi's early career, stated that his style was formed on Masaccio's Brancacci Chapel frescoes in S Maria del Carmine (*see* MASACCIO, fig. 6) and that his reputation was established by a fresco of *St Martial* (destr. 1568) in the same church. Only one of Lippi's frescoes described by Vasari in the Carmine precincts has survived: the *Reform of the Carmelite Rule* shows Albert of Avogadro, the patriarch of Jerusalem, conferring the rule on the Mount Carmel hermits, an event that took place between 1206 and 1214. While the perspective is awkward and the treatment of anatomy crude, Masaccio's influence is apparent in the facial types and in the simple, unadorned style. The fresco has been convincingly dated to *c.* 1428–30. A gable with the *Madonna of Humility with Three Carmelite Saints and Angels* (Milan, Castello Sforzesco) is very close in style to the Carmine fresco and may have come from there. Indeed an altar dedicated to two of the Carmelite saints, SS Angelo and Albert of Sicily, once formed part of the *tramezzo* of this church. Like the fresco, the gable shows a special concern for expression at the expense of a rational depiction of space. This work should probably be considered an independent work of art rather than a fragment (Christiansen, 1985).

Two small autograph panels survive from the early 1430s: an abraded *Pietà* (Milan, Mus. Poldi Pezzoli) and a *Mourning St John the Evangelist* (priv. col., see Christiansen, 1985), part of an altarpiece that probably included a *Dead Christ* and *Mourning Virgin* (both untraced). The brilliant linear design and the intense colour range of these works show that Lippi had developed beyond Masaccio's interest in form and anticipate his own mature, highly original style. On 3 May 1431 Lippi paid dues to the Compagnia di S Maria delle Laude e di S Agnese, a confraternity based in the Carmine, of which Bicci di Lorenzo and Masolino were also members. By 1434 he was in Padua, where on 1 July he was paid for some ultramarine for the reliquary cupboard in the basilica of S Antonio. On 15 October he and Francesco Squarcione evaluated some work by two local painters. Marcantonio Michiel recorded that he decorated the chapel of the Palazzo del Podestà in Padua and parts of a fresco called the 'Madonna del Pilastro', also in S Antonio (all destr.). Lippi must have spent about two years in Padua, but his whereabouts after this are unknown. It has been suggested (Ames-Lewis, 1979) that he may have made a trip to the southern Netherlands.

*(ii) 1437–52.* Lippi was a naturally curious artist, open to influence from every quarter, yet highly original and often innovative. Both the setting and the arrangement of the figures in the Tarquinia *Virgin and Child* (1437; Rome, Pal. Barberini; named from its former location at Tarquinia) seem to have been inspired by a lost *Virgin and Child* by Rogier van der Weyden, and the rendering of light, shadow and texture is profoundly indebted to Netherlandish practice. Possibly for the first time in Italian art, the Virgin is depicted in a domestic setting. Neither she nor the Christ Child has a halo, and the date is inscribed on a *trompe l'oeil cartellino*—a device that later became common but was unknown in Italian painting before this date.

In a letter of 1 April 1438 to Piero di Cosimo de' Medici, Domenico Veneziano reported that Filippo Lippi and Fra Angelico had established themselves as the two most sought-after painters in Florence. He added that Lippi had begun a painting for Santo Spirito that would take years to complete. This was the *Virgin and Child with SS Frediano and Augustine* (Paris, Louvre; see fig. 1), first recorded in a payment of 8 March 1437. Despite Domenico Veneziano's misgivings, the Barbadori Altarpiece, as it was called after its donor, Gherardo di Bartolommeo Barbadori (*d* 1429), was completed before the end of 1439. Vasari described it as 'a work of rare excellence which has ever been held in the highest esteem by men versed in our arts'. The painting's central vertical axis is stressed by the standing Virgin and Child, reminiscent of Donatello, and by the two columns that relate ambiguously to the arched frame. The two saints kneeling at the Virgin's feet are rigorously modelled and form the base of a stable, pyramidal composition. Both this and the combination of stances were inspired by Masaccio's *Trinity* in S Maria Novella, Florence (*see* MASACCIO, fig. 5). The Christ Child probably influenced the same figure in Michelangelo's *Madonna and Child* (Bruges, Notre-Dame). The setting of the Barbadori Altarpiece recalls a church choir, and balustrades and steps

1. Filippo Lippi: *Virgin and Child with SS Frediano and Augustine* (the Barbadori Altarpiece), tempera on panel, 2.08×2.40 m, *c.* 1437–9 (Paris, Musée du Louvre)

in the foreground imply further levels and rooms beyond the frame. Such imaginative spatial design, matched previously in Florence only by the Masaccio *Trinity*, may ultimately derive, like the harmonic relationship between figure and setting, from Lippi's study of frescoes by Altichiero and Guariento during his time in Padua. Contemporary with the Barbadori Altarpiece is the (undocumented) *Annunciation* in S Lorenzo, Florence. The cringeing Virgin is loosely based on that of Donatello's *Annunciation* tabernacle (Florence, Santa Croce), while the richly coloured vestments of the three angels and the illusionistic crystal vase in the foreground are evidence of Lippi's fascination with Netherlandish painting.

Another large-scale commission of this period was the *Coronation of the Virgin* for the high altar of S Ambrogio in Florence (Florence, Uffizi). Funding for this began in 1439, but payments were irregular so that work on it lasted until 9 June 1447. It was one of the costliest altarpieces of the 15th century—Lippi alone received 1716 lire. Of the predella, which was paid for in August 1458, all that remains is the *Miracle of St Ambrose* (Berlin, Gemäldegal.;

for documentation see Borsook, 1981). The Gothic-style frame (destr.) was apparently designed by Lorenzo Ghiberti, one of the donor's three executors.

Critics have found the composition of the *Coronation* unfocused and additive, probably because of the underplaying of the architectural elements. However, cleaning in 1957–71 revealed a subtly modulated play of light and shade and luminous colours, dependent on Netherlandish qualities of light and colour, which, together with a few beautifully rendered key figures, form guides by which the painting's crowded composition is organized. Vasari recorded the *Coronation*'s immediate critical success and added that it won for Lippi the friendship of Cosimo (il vecchio) de' Medici. A later Medici commission was the *Virgin and Child with SS Francis, Damian, Cosmas and Anthony of Padua* (*c.* 1445; Florence, Uffizi) for the Novitiates' Chapel in Santa Croce. The draperies of the figures at the sides are less convincing than in earlier paintings, and the perspective is eccentric. The idea of placing the figures against an architectural backdrop reminiscent of Michelozzo's designs may have come from Fra

2. Filippo Lippi: *Annunciation*, tempera on panel, 203×186 mm, *c.* 1450 (Munich, Alte Pinakothek)

Branca claimed that a painting he had commissioned from Lippi was not the master's own work. The outcome of the case is not known, but since Lippi later received payment for materials, he seems to have won it. On another occasion Lorenzo Manetti accused him of grossly overcharging for an unidentified picture of St Jerome. The case appeared before the Vicario Arcivescovile, who ordered the return of the painting and Manetti's advance payment. Lippi's misconduct was deemed so serious that the arbiter considered excommunication. On 19 May 1455 Lippi was stripped of his Legnaia benefice, as well as the post of chaplain at the convent church of S Niccolò ai Fieri, Florence, and on 3 January 1456 he was transferred to the chaplaincy of the Augustinian nuns at S Margherita, Prato.

The influence of Fra Angelico is increasingly apparent in Lippi's work from the mid-1440s. The *Adoration of the Magi*, known as the Cook Tondo (Washington, DC, N.G.A.), which Fra Angelico had almost finished by the time he left for Rome in late 1445, was completed by Lippi, who added the foreground figures (with the exception of the Christ Child), most of the Virgin and the figure of the young Magus. There is an obvious attempt to harmonize his style with that of Fra Angelico, the extent of whose influence can be gauged in Lippi's *Annunciation* (*c.* 1450; Munich, Alte Pin.; see fig. 2), executed for the Benedictine nuns' convent of Le Murate, near Florence. Here the features of the Virgin and angel appear more generalized and the figures more elongated and refined, while the localized colours of Lippi's work in the 1430s have yielded to more pervasively bright hues, in keeping with Fra Angelico's luminous palette.

*(iii) 1452–69.* By 1452 Lippi had moved to Prato. Efforts to engage Fra Angelico to fresco the choir of the local Pieve (later the cathedral) had failed, and on 6 May 1452 Lippi was solicited for this task. Two months later he had begun, but the frescoes were not completed until January 1466. Besides being the most expensive fresco cycle of the 15th century in Tuscany, the Prato frescoes are the most completely documented (see Borsook, 1975). Evidence shows that the long delays are attributable not just to Lippi's lack of application or to his other artistic commitments, but to gross mismanagement and lack of funds.

The vault of the choir is decorated with frescoes of the seated *Evangelists*. Scenes from the *Life of St Stephen*, the titular saint of the cathedral, are painted in three registers on the north wall, while on the south wall is the *Life of St John the Baptist*. The scenes of the *Stoning of St Stephen* and the *Beheading of St John the Baptist* are painted outside chronological sequence across the corners of the altar wall and the north and south walls. In this way they could be seen by the priest while celebrating the Mass, as reminders of Christ's sacrifice. The exact order of execution of the Prato frescoes is unknown, although the two *Nativity* scenes in the lunettes were the first to be painted. The 'doll's house' architectural settings are traditional but also show similarities of detail with Ghiberti's recently completed bronze reliefs for the Gates of Paradise of the Florentine Baptistery. The relationship of figures with their setting and the abrupt transitions between foreground and background recall Altichiero's frescoes in Padua,

Angelico's altarpiece for Bosco ai Frati (Florence, S Marco).

Lippi was also a dedicated portrait painter. His interest in individual likenesses must have been stimulated by a knowledge of Netherlandish portraiture. Lifelike portraits appear in altarpieces such as the Barbadori Altarpiece and the *Coronation*, in both of which Lippi included his own likeness. Two independent portraits by Lippi survive and are among the earliest examples of this genre in Italian Renaissance art. The first, the *Portrait of a Man and a Woman at a Casement* (*c.* 1440; New York, Met.), shows the woman in an interior setting with a landscape viewed through the window behind her profile; her suitor appears through the window. (The sitter in the second, much later example, a *Portrait of a Woman* (?*c.* 1455; Berlin, Gemäldegal.), is also in profile and in an interior setting, but without a landscape view.)

Lippi is last recorded at the Carmine on 8 October 1441. On 27 February 1442 he took up the post of rector at S Quirico a Legnaia, just outside Florence. On 16 May 1447 he was paid for a painting of the Virgin and St Bernard for the Palazzo della Signoria in Florence, which can probably be identified as the *Vision of St Bernard* (London, N.G.), attributed to Lippi's workshop. In 1450 the painter Giovanni di Francesco accused Lippi of not paying him for the restoration of a painting by Giotto, which he had carried out on Filippo's behalf in 1442. Litigation lasted until 1455 when torture on the rack forced Lippi to confess to having forged a receipt for the payment. The two men's association appears to have continued nevertheless. Documents reveal that Lippi was brought to court on more than one occasion: in 1451 Antonio del which Lippi had seen in 1434. Both middle registers contain landscapes, rendered in rich shades of light green and rusty orange, whose softly modulated tones and mysterious rock formations convey a deeply romantic response to nature. By contrast, the bottom two scenes are primarily architectural compositions. The *Celebration of St Stephen's Relics* takes place in a monumental nave, and the rows of over life-size portrait figures (including *Pius II*, *Carlo de' Medici* and a self-portrait) are arranged parallel to the picture plane in the foreground and anticipate Ghirlandaio's murals in Santa Trinita, Florence. The dancing Salome in the *Feast of Herod*, is a masterpiece of linear design, which looks forward to the art of Lippi's pupil Botticelli.

During his 14 years at Prato, Lippi also painted many panels. On 8 August 1452 he promised to complete a tondo for Leonardo di Bartolommeo Bartolini by 8 December, but it was still unfinished by 16 April 1453. This is identifiable with the *Virgin and Child with Scenes from the Life of the Virgin* (Florence, Pitti). It is the first image of the Virgin in Florentine art to appear on a tondo, a form hitherto associated with the decorative trays known as *deschi da parto*. The background composition recalls Ghiberti's *Jacob and Esau* panel from the Gates of Paradise. Probably dating from the same period as this tondo and the two *Nativity* lunettes at Prato is the *Virgin and Child in a Niche* (Florence, Pal. Medici–Riccardi). Its design resembles contemporary sculpted reliefs of the Virgin, but its appeal depends largely on painterly effects such as the rich, warmly coloured materials, the tender expressions of the two figures and the play of light on the Christ Child's face. From the 1450s Lippi developed the theme of the Virgin adoring the Christ Child in a woodland setting. His earliest altarpiece with this subject was probably the *Adoration of the Christ Child* (Florence, Uffizi; see fig. 3), painted for the Annalena convent in Florence just after its establishment in 1453. As in the *Virgin and Child* tondo, the principal figures are brought close to the foreground plane, while the romantic wooded setting with its high horizon line recalls the landscapes in the Prato frescoes.

The adoration of the Christ Child was the subject of the central panel of a triptych sent to Alfonso of Aragon as a diplomatic present from Giovanni di Cosimo de' Medici early in 1458. Only the side panels, representing *St Anthony Abbot* and *St Michael*, survive (both Cleveland, OH, Mus. A.). Lippi made a sketch of the proposed triptych at the bottom of a letter of 20 July 1457 to Giovanni de' Medici, in which he discusses the materials to be used for this painting. Another Medici commission was the *Adoration of the Christ Child with St Romuald and the Infant John the Baptist* (*c.* 1459; Berlin, Gemäldegal.), intended for the altar of the chapel in the Palazzo Medici, Florence, but later replaced by a copy. Its complicated iconography is perhaps expressive of the pietism of Piero de' Medici and his wife, Lucrezia Tornabuoni.

During the mid-1450s Lippi was engaged on a variety of work. In 1454 he restored Agnolo Gaddi's frescoes of the *Legend of the Holy Girdle* at the Pieve in Prato, and on 10 July 1457 he and Domenico Veneziano appraised Pesellino's unfinished *Trinity with Saints* (London, N.G.) for a confraternity in Pistoia. In 1458, after Pesellino's

3. Filippo Lippi: *Adoration of the Christ Child*, tempera on panel, 1.37×1.34 m, *c.* 1453 (Florence, Galleria degli Uffizi)

death, Lippi accepted an offer to complete it; by early June 1459 he had finished the main panel. The predella was executed by his workshop. On 1 May 1456 Lippi abducted Lucrezia Buti, a nun in the Augustinian convent of S Margherita, Prato, where he was chaplain. She was soon living with him, to be joined later by her sister and the three remaining nuns from the convent. At first Lippi was not penalized, but on 8 May 1461 a public denouncement of him mentioned a son, namely (2) Filippino Lippi. By 1465 Filippo had been stripped of all his benefices, although, according to Vasari, he was permitted to continue living with Lucrezia. In the same year she bore him a second child, a daughter named Alessandra.

Lippi's last works include the *Virgin and Child with Two Angels* (Florence, Uffizi) and frescoes of the *Life of the Virgin* in the apse of Spoleto Cathedral, begun in May 1466. At the end of 1468, some scaffolding was dismantled, suggesting that the upper scene of the *Coronation of the Virgin* (see fig. 4) was complete. The combination of bold compositional design and rich technique, together with the brilliant illusion of distance, including sunset views over the Umbrian hills, suggests that this scene is Lippi's own work. From this date onwards, however, recurring ill-health must have prevented him from working, and the later frescoes, especially the *Nativity*, show the intervention of assistants. After Lippi's death, Fra Diamante took over, completing the cycle by 23 December 1469. For this he received about a fifth of the total fee of 697 ducats.

On the whole, Lippi enjoyed the steady support of loyal and accommodating patrons. Most of his known commissions derived from the Medici and allied families such as the Martelli, Alessandri, Benci and Inghirami. Some of his works served the cause of diplomacy, being sent as gifts

4. Filippo Lippi: *Coronation of the Virgin* (1466–8), fresco, diam. 10.95 m, Spoleto Cathedral

to Pope Eugenius IV, Cardinal Marco Barbo and Alfonso V, King of Sicily and Naples. Notwithstanding Lippi's known delays, the Medici remained loyal patrons. Although his early works were for the Carmelite Order, he later worked for other orders and congregations.

2. WORKING METHODS AND TECHNIQUE. Lippi worked both in tempera on panel and in fresco. In early panel paintings such as the *Mourning St John the Evangelist* (priv. col., see Christiansen, 1985) he showed a penchant for finely applied glazes, often placing contrasting hues over each other, as in the figure of Gabriel in the *Annunciation* (Munich, Alte Pin.). Details of clothing and landscape are exquisitely wrought. This attention to technique and use of line must have led to the interest in Netherlandish painting evident in his Tarquinia *Virgin and Child*. The Barbadori Altarpiece depends on sculpture as a source of new pictorial ideas. It was usual for Lippi to experiment continually with his compositions until the desired result had been obtained, and the dramatic spatial effects in the foreground of the Barbadori Altarpiece were apparently a late revision. In the Uffizi *Coronation of the Virgin*, details were suppressed as the painting neared completion, while others were added. X-ray examination of a late *Virgin and Child* (Munich, Alte Pin.) has revealed that the Christ Child was originally placed higher up, in the same pose as that of the Uffizi *Virgin and Child with Two Angels*. In the Prato frescoes black *pastiglia* outlining is used to emphasize the protagonists of each story, and the landscapes are full of the sort of rich detail more often

found in panel paintings. In the *Feast of Herod*, Lippi made extensive use of *a secco* technique.

Lippi's only documented drawing is the sketch for an altarpiece made on a letter to Giovanni Cosimo de' Medici of 1457. The drawing of a *Crucifixion with Saints* (early to mid-1440s; London, BM, 1936–10–10–9) is executed in a similarly rapid, impressionistic manner. Neither this nor the two figures on a double-sided sheet (late 1430s–early 1440s; London, BM, 1895–9–15–442) can be associated with any known paintings by Lippi. The double-sided sheet contains a standing female saint on the *recto* (probably a Virgin for a projected Crucifixion scene) and a clerical figure on the *verso*. They are executed in metalpoint and black chalk and heightened with white lead, rich in chiaroscuro effects and with vivid emotional expression. A new addition to the small corpus of autograph drawings by Lippi is a copy after Masaccio's figure of *St Peter Baptizing the Neophytes* in the Brancacci Chapel, executed in black chalk and pen and brown ink and heightened with white (Florence, Uffizi, 65). This work eloquently illustrates Vasari's claim that on Masaccio's death his spirit passed into the body of his follower Fra Filippo Lippi.

3. WORKSHOP ORGANIZATION. Vasari reported that Botticelli, Pesellino and Jacopo del Sellaio were among Lippi's pupils, and although there is no documentary evidence, it seems that this statement is true. Botticelli in his earliest years reworked several of Lippi's compositions and is believed to have taught Filippino Lippi. Filippo probably hired Pesellino for specialized work such as

painting small-scale narrative scenes, at which he excelled. This was probably the case with the predella (divided between Paris, Louvre, and Florence, Uffizi) that he painted for Lippi's *Virgin and Child with SS Francis, Damian, Cosmas and Anthony of Padua* in the mid-1440s. Motifs from the oeuvre of each of these painters were plagiarized by the anonymous artist (or workshop) dubbed the PSEUDO-PIER FRANCESCO FIORENTINO (*see* MASTERS, ANONYMOUS, AND MONOGRAMMISTS, §I). Jacopo del Sellaio's earliest documented work is modelled on Botticelli rather than Lippi.

From *c.* 1440, when Lippi began work on the Uffizi *Coronation*, he appears to have made regular use of assistants. In 1445 and 1446 small payments were made to Fra Carnevale (described as Lippi's pupil), who may have worked on certain portions of the *Coronation* as well as on others of Lippi's commissions. On 17 July 1447 a 'Fra Diamante di Fra Filippo' received payment for gilding the altarpiece's temporary predella. Two other artists worked as partners in a very minor capacity. At Prato, Lippi was assisted by two *garzoni* named Jacopo and Domenico, the latter perhaps identifiable as Domenico Ghirlandaio. In Spoleto, Piermatteo d'Amelia (*c.* 1450– *c.* 1505) is named as a studio hand. The exact nature of the work assigned to such assistants is unknown, as is the manner of Lippi's workshop organization. Since he was not a member of the painters' guild, he probably had more flexibility in subcontracting or working in partnership. Like Pesellino, Giovanni di Francesco may also have worked with Lippi on a subcontractual basis. As Lippi's reputation grew, commissions of lesser importance were inevitably delegated to assistants, who were trained to counterfeit their master's style. From the mid-1440s, therefore, the quality of pictures produced in Lippi's workshop began to vary, and many of them require critical reappraisal. Those that Berenson assigned to an 'Angelican phase', for instance, may owe their character more to the handiwork of assistants than to the influence of Fra Angelico.

### BIBLIOGRAPHY

F. Baldinucci: *Notizie* (1681–1728); ed. F. Ranalli (1845–7), i, pp. 507–13
I. B. Supino: *Fra Filippo Lippi* (Florence, 1902)
H. Mendelson: *Fra Filippo Lippi* (Berlin, 1909) [most of the essential Lippi docs are reproduced]
B. Berenson: 'Fra Angelico, Fra Filippo e la cronologia', *Boll. A.*, xxvi (1932–3), pp. 1–22, 49–66; Eng. trans. in *Homeless Paintings of the Renaissance* (Bloomington, IN, 1969), pp. 199–233 [fundamental for Lippi's chronology]
G. Poggi: 'Sulla data dell'affresco di Fra Filippo Lippi', *Riv. A.*, xviii (1936), pp. 95–106 [documentation for years at the Carmine]
G. Pudelko: 'Per la datazione delle opere di Fra Filippo Lippi', *Riv. A.*, xviii (1936), pp. 45–76
R. Oertel: *Fra Filippo Lippi* (Vienna, 1942) [good on patronage]
M. Pittaluga: *Filippo Lippi* (Florence, 1949) [cat., chronology and extensive illus.]
C. de Tolnay: 'The Autobiographic Aspect of Fra Filippo Lippi's Virgins', *Gaz. B.-A.*, xxxix (1952), pp. 253–64
M. A. Lavin: 'Giovannino Battista: A Study in Renaissance Religious Symbolism', *A. Bull.*, xxxvii (1955), pp. 85–101
M. Meiss: 'Jan van Eyck and the Italian Renaissance', *Atti del XVIII congresso internazionale di storia dell'arte, Venezia e l'Europa: 1955*, pp. 58–69
J. White: *The Birth and Rebirth of Pictorial Space* (London, 1957, rev. 2/1967/R New York, 1972), pp. 170–88
P. Caioli: 'Un altro sguardo sulla vita di Fra Filippo Lippi', *Carmelus*, v (1958), i, pp. 30–72
E. Borsook: 'Fra Filippo Lippi and the Murals for Prato Cathedral', *Mitt. Ksthist. Inst. Florenz*, xix (1975), pp. 1–148
G. Marchini: 'Una curiosità sul Lippi', *Archv. Stor. Prat.*, li (1975), ii, pp. 171–5
——: *Filippo Lippi* (Milan, 1975)
J. Ruda: 'The National Gallery Tondo of the *Adoration of the Magi* and the Early Style of Filippo Lippi', *Stud. Hist. A.*, vii (1975), pp. 6–39
A. Sabatini, ed.: *Atti dei capitoli provinciali dei Carmelitani, 1375–1491* (Rome, 1975), p. 173
M. Boskovits: 'Appunti sull'Angelico', *Paragone*, 313 (1976), pp 30–54 (45–7)
L. De Angelis and A. Conti: 'Un libro antico della sagrestia di Sant'Ambrogio', *An. Scu. Norm. Sup. Pisa*, ser. 3, vi/1 (1976), pp. 97–109
F. Ames-Lewis: 'Fra Filippo Lippi and Flanders', *Z. Kstgesch.*, xlii (1979), pp. 255–73
E. Borsook: 'Cults and Imagery at Sant'Ambrogio in Florence', *Mitt. Ksthist. Inst. Florenz*, xxv (1981), pp. 147–202
J. Ruda: *Filippo Lippi Studies: Naturalism, Style and Iconography in Early Renaissance Art* (New York, 1982)
E. W. Rowlands: *Filippo Lippi's Stay in Padua and its Impact on his Art* (diss., New Brunswick, NJ, Rutgers U., 1983)
K. Christiansen: 'New Light on the Early Work of Filippo Lippi', *Apollo*, cxxii (1985), pp. 338–43
*Disegni italiani del tempo di Donatello* (exh. cat. by A. Angelini, Florence, Uffizi, 1986), pp. 40–53
J. Ruda: *Fra Filippo Lippi: Life & Work with a Complete Catalogue* (London, 1993)

ELIOT W. ROWLANDS

**(2) Filippino Lippi** (*b* Prato, *c.* 1457; *d* Florence, 18 April 1504). Son of (1) Filippo Lippi. He was a painter of altarpieces, *cassone* panels and frescoes and also an exceptional draughtsman. His success lay in his ability to absorb, without slavishly following, the most popular trends in contemporary painting. He worked in Florence and Rome at a time when patrons were beginning to intermingle personal, religious, social and political ideals in their ambitions for palaces and chapels: with the support of wealthy and erudite patrons, such as Lorenzo de' Medici ('il Magnifico') and Filippo Strozzi, he won important civic and private commissions. Lippi's most distinguished achievement was the decoration of the Strozzi Chapel in S Maria Novella, Florence.

1. Life and work. 2. Working methods and technique.

### 1. LIFE AND WORK.

(i) Training and early work in Florence and Lucca, before *c.* 1485. (ii) Early maturity, *c.* 1485–7. (iii) Carafa Chapel, Rome, and other contemporary work, 1488–93. (iv) Late work, 1494 and after.

*(i) Training and early work in Florence and Lucca, before c. 1485.* Filippino received his first training from his father. He was in Spoleto between 1467 and 1469, when Filippo Lippi was painting the cathedral choir, and there received his earliest technical training in fresco work. His father died in October 1469, and Filippino left Spoleto in 1470, probably with his appointed guardian, Fra Diamante, Filippo's assistant. Around 1472 Filippino was apprenticed to Sandro Botticelli; in 1472 and 1473 his name appears in the ledger of the Florentine Compagnia di S Luca, linked with that of Botticelli.

Several paintings have been assigned to Filippino's early career (1475–81), yet this period remains the most problematic to reconstruct. Not one painting is signed, dated or unquestionably connected to a patron, and each was once attributed to another painter: to a Fra Filippo follower; to Botticelli or a follower; to Ghirlandaio; and most often to 'Amico di Sandro', an entity Berenson fabricated (1899) to identify a painter influenced by, but distinct from, Botticelli and Filippino. Berenson later reassigned Amico's works to Filippino (1932), a judgement with which most scholars concur. Included in the works that have been dated before 1482 are several small, devotional panels and narrative scenes: the *Virgin and Child with the Infant St John the Baptist* (London, N.G.); the *Virgin and Child* (Florence, Uffizi); the *Virgin and Child* (ex-Kaiser-Friedrich Mus., Berlin, destr.); *Tobias and the Angel* (Washington, DC, N.G.A.); the *Adoration of the Christ Child* (St Petersburg, Hermitage); and the *Adoration of the Magi* (London, N.G.). These panels are influenced in various ways by aspects of the art of Fra Filippo, Botticelli and Verrocchio and reveal a burgeoning interest in the kind of landscape enriched with monasteries, castles, bridges, lakes and the activities of people and animals that is present in Filippino's later paintings. Also often assigned to Filippino's early period are paintings that were once furniture (*cassone*) panels. Among these are five panels showing the *Story of Esther* (one each Paris, Louvre; Chantilly, Mus. Condé; Florence, Mus. Horne; and two panels Ottawa, N.G.); one oblong panel of the *Story of Virginia* (Paris, Louvre) and one oblong panel of the *Story of Lucretia* (Florence, Pitti). All of the panels reflect characteristics of Fra Filippo's figures and architecture, filtered through Botticelli. Fra Filippo's indoor arcades, open-air loggias, piers penetrated with long, rectilinear slots, and multilevel stages appear in the scenes of *Esther*, *Virginia* and *Lucretia*, but with a greater unity between the paved, urban foreground and the distant countryside. The architecture serves to unify a series of events and to convey the development of the narratives, in which theatrical figures enact desperate events. The panels are not, however, stylistically homogeneous: they should be dated nearer to the 1490s.

In 1481, when Botticelli was called to Rome to decorate the Sistine Chapel in the Vatican, Filippino was probably in Lucca. His *SS Roch, Sebastian, Jerome and Helena* (Lucca, S Michele), in which four saints stand together in a single setting, is one of the earliest paintings securely attributable to him. The panel seems cut at the top and sides and lacks the focal-point that an additional panel or panels would provide. Two panels, one with *SS Bernard and Apollonia* and the other with *SS Paul and Frediano* (Los Angeles, CA, Norton Simon Found.), have been identified (Meiss, 1973) as the tabernacle wings of a single altarpiece in S Ponziano, Lucca, that was described by Vasari. All three panels contain contemplative, lanky figures linked through the proximity of their arms and hands, with twisted fingers and exaggerated joints and veins that reveal Filippino's debt to Botticelli, although gesture and expression are subtler and softer than in Botticelli's art. The saints of these two panels look forward to the physically and psychologically refined and integrated figures that Filippino produced *c.* 1485. His increasing success was marked, in 1482, by his being selected to replace Perugino in the execution of a fresco in the Palazzo della Signoria (now the Palazzo Vecchio), Florence. His earliest recorded commission for the Strozzi family, for a wall hanging in their family chapel in S Maria Novella, Florence, dates from the same year.

*(ii) Early maturity, c. 1485–7.* Around 1485 Filippino was asked to complete a cycle of frescoes on the *Life of St Peter* in the Brancacci Chapel, S Maria del Carmine, which Masolino and Masaccio had left unfinished nearly 60 years before. Filippino began by completing Masaccio's unfinished scene of the *Raising of the Son of the Prefect of Antioch* on the lower-left wall register. More than half the wall had already been painted, and Filippino harmonized his work with Masaccio's; yet his preference for leaner and less volumetric figures and for breaking solid areas of colour is apparent. Vasari singled out several recognizable portraits, including that of Piero del Pugliese (third from far left), one of the artist's patrons. The composition is enlivened by rhythmic gestures; Filippino's aristocratic figures are restrained and elegant, and the collars, hems and loose-fitting sleeves of their garments delicately trimmed with white. He applied the pigment like thread, tacking bodies together and snapping life into sombre colour combinations. The opposite wall, where Filippino painted the entire register, is considerably more open and lively. He placed three events within one register: *Peter and Simon Magus before Nero, Peter Led to Execution* and the *Crucifixion of Peter*. A hallmark of his style is evident here in the animated effect obtained by amalgamating ornamental and human forms: the soldiers, for instance, are intertwined through gestures, drapery folds, inclined heads, colours of similar hue and value and similar body types.

On 20 February 1486 Filippino completed the *Virgin Enthroned with SS John the Baptist, Victor, Bernard and Zenobius* (Florence, Uffizi; see fig. 1) for one of the governing bodies of Florence, the Otto di Pratica, who had commissioned the altarpiece for a new altar in the council chamber of the Palazzo della Signoria. The prestigious commission marks a critical point in Filippino's career. In this innovative work he replaced the remote and still images of the traditional *sacra conversazione* with life-size, emotive figures, who participate in a developing drama. Nothing is static: Filippino created the dynamism of an unfolding moment by activating nearly every painted inch of the panel and by compressing the figures into a shallow room almost too small to contain them. The walls of this room are reduced to a series of quickly receding, stepped planes that are laden with organic and geometric patterns. The solid forms seem almost to flex under the pressure of the ornate embellishments. There is a clear debt, as often in his career, to sculpture, in particular to the late works of Donatello and to works by Verrocchio; Filippino's figure of John the Baptist is closely modelled on that of Thomas in Verrocchio's group *St Thomas* (1483; Florence, Orsanmichele; *see* VERROCCHIO, ANDREA DEL, fig. 1).

Around 1485–7 Filippino painted one of his most renowned works, the *Virgin Appearing to St Bernard* (Florence, Badia Fiorentina; see fig. 2), for the family chapel of Piero del Pugliese in the monastery church of Le Campora at Marignolle near Florence. Pugliese appears at the lower right, near Bernard, who sits outdoors at a writing desk. Filippino showed Bernard as a scholar absorbed in a mystical vision of the Virgin descending to earth, accompanied by angels and offering him spiritual nourishment. Touching her breast with one hand and the

1. Filippino Lippi: *Virgin Enthroned with SS John the Baptist, Victor, Bernard and Zenobius*, oil on panel, 3.55×2.25 m, 1486 (Florence, Galleria degli Uffizi)

page with the other, she enlivens Bernard's text with the milk of wisdom. For the image of Bernard, Filippino looked to Botticelli's archetypal mystic, *St Augustine* (Florence, Ognissanti), whose miraculous revelation is materialized by his vibrating body. Yet whereas Botticelli painted a moment suspended in time, Filippino created a temporal and fleeting instant. To this end, he bestirred and particularized every detail of nature. Knowledge of Leonardo's seamless integration of human forms in nature and of his light, with its warm, life-giving qualities, helped Filippino to integrate the things of heaven and earth; the sky still glows after Mary and the angels' descent. They are welcomed on earth by a flourishing nature that bristles with energy. Filippino learnt from Hugo van der Goes's Portinari Altarpiece (*c.* 1473–9; Florence, Uffizi; *see* GOES, HUGO VAN DER, fig. 1), which entered Florence in May 1483, how to describe seasonal changes in nature and how to populate a hillside with anecdotal information. His landscape backgrounds were also influenced by Antonio del Pollaiuolo and by Hans Memling's *Virgin and Child with Angels* (Florence, Uffizi). By 1487 Filippino had become a reputable and popular painter, and it was probably in this year that he began fresco decorations in the Villa Spedaletto (destr.) for Lorenzo de' Medici.

*(iii) Carafa Chapel, Rome, and other contemporary work, 1488–93.* In 1488 Filippino went to Rome on Lorenzo de' Medici's recommendation and accepted a commission from the Neapolitan cardinal Oliviero Carafa (2 Sept 1488) to decorate a burial chapel in the Dominican church of S Maria sopra Minerva. Before starting work, he returned to Florence twice: to make the first of two wills (21 Sept 1488) and in the following year to work on the fresco decoration in the Strozzi Chapel in S Maria Novella, for which he had signed a contract with the wealthy banker Filippo Strozzi on 21 April 1487, in which it was stipulated that the work would be completed by 1 March 1490. Filippino probably also went to Venice, fulfilling another stipulation in the Strozzi contract. He was back in Rome shortly afterwards and, apart from a design submitted to a competition for the Florence Cathedral façade in 1491 (perhaps sent from Rome), is not recorded in Florence again until 1494. Work ended in the Carafa Chapel either by 25 March 1493, when Pope Alexander VI visited it on the Annunciation feast day, or two months later, when he granted indulgences to worshippers at the chapel.

The chapel was dedicated to the Virgin of the Annunciation and to St Thomas Aquinas. On the vault Filippino painted four sibyls—the Cumaean, the Delphic, the Tiburtine and the Hellespontine—each of whom appears with angels, texts, scrolls and plaques. On the altar wall he painted the *Assumption of the Virgin*, surrounding a frescoed altarpiece framed by marble, depicting the *Annunciation with St Thomas Aquinas Presenting Cardinal Carafa to the Virgin*. In the lunette of the west wall he painted a *Miracle of St Thomas* and, beneath this, the *Triumph of St Thomas*. No frescoes remain on the east wall; they were destroyed when a marble wall tomb was made for the Cardinal's nephew, Pope Paul IV, in the later 16th century. Vasari described allegories of Virtues conquering Vices, and these may be the subjects of the lost frescoes. On the stuccoed barrel vault of an oblong chamber behind the east wall are *Stories of Virginia* and allegorical figures designed by Filippino and painted by Raffaellino del Garbo.

Filippino's unique talent was his ability to translate erudite Dominican doctrine into lively tangible forms and to give immediacy and life to the abstract ideas of ancient history. Each sibyl covers more area of the quadrant than earlier vault figures had done, and each prophetess seemingly reaches out to initiate the chain of events on the walls below. The altar wall is most prominently connected with the patron. Filippino painted Carafa inside the very room of the Annunciation, where his presence serves to emphasize the Virgin's role as mediator between heaven and earth. The Virgin ascending to heaven dominates the wall, her figure seeming to increase in volume as she is lifted upwards. Filippino accomplished this illusion by greatly amplifying the drapery that envelops her, thereby drawing attention to the entry of the Virgin's incorruptible body into heaven, where she became a mediator for humanity. Mary is confirmed in her new role as she looks downward from heaven towards the kneeling Carafa. This *Assumption* seems indebted to Mantegna's in the Ovetari Chapel in the church of the Eremitani, Padua, which Filippino may have studied on his way to Venice. In the frescoes of the *Life of St Thomas*, Filippino gave life to the

2. Filippino Lippi: *Virgin Appearing to St Bernard*, oil on panel, 2.10×1.95 m, *c.* 1485–7 (Florence, Badia Fiorentina)

drama by varying the size and location of the figures. The largest figure in the *Triumph of St Thomas* is a hulking Dominican, a type derived from Fra Filippo and Donatello, which Filippino positioned at the chapel's entrance to introduce and to link the walls of the chapel; the figure probably represents Friar Joachim Torriani, Master General of the Order. In these frescoes Filippino was responding to the relics of the Roman Classical world; there is a wealth of detailed information that includes Roman monuments, descriptive reliefs on giant pilasters, inscribed texts, plaques and scrolls. He must have exchanged ideas with Mantegna and other painters, including Pinturicchio,

whose illusionistic architectural constructions in the Bufalini Chapel in S Maria in Aracoeli, Rome, influenced many painters.

*(iv) Late works, 1494 and after.* Filippino was again in Florence in 1494. He designed a window in Santo Spirito for the Tanai de' Nerli family chapel, depicting *St Martin and the Beggar* (untraced), and painted an altarpiece of the *Virgin and Child and SS Catherine and Martin with Tanai and his Wife*, works that functioned in concert. A presentation drawing (Florence, Uffizi; see fig. 3) for the window shows Filippino's mastery in disposing the figures within a narrow, vertical format: the telescoped niche, the fluidly

3. Filippino Lippi: *St Martin and the Beggar*, pen and brown ink and brown wash, over traces of black chalk, 382×76 mm, 1494 (Florence, Galleria degli Uffizi)

figures in the altarpiece of 1486, painted for the Palazzo della Signoria, these figures are solid, three-dimensional types with identifiable temperaments. Tanai and Nanna with age-etched faces are portrayed as pious, beseeching people kneeling before the Virgin, yet in the background they stand proudly by their palazzo with one of their children. Filippino subtly inserted anecdotal details about the family where information about saints would normally be expected. The realistic handling of details in this altarpiece reflects an increased interest in Netherlandish art, as well as the influence of Piero di Cosimo's work.

Probably completed after the Nerli altarpiece are the *Annunciation* tondi for the San Gimignano town hall: two large round panels, one showing the *Angel Gabriel* and the other the *Virgin Mary* (both San Gimignano, Mus. Civ.). Filippino understood the subtleties of the drama in Leonardo's *Annunciation* (Florence, Uffizi), particularly the visual significance of Leonardo's low horizontal wall, which simultaneously separates and connects the Virgin and Gabriel. The solemn drama unfolds in two distinct moments, on two panels with independent perspectives intended for separate inspection. It is the Virgin's chamber that holds the attention longer, with its emphasis on the unseen miracle taking place in her body. The use of diagonals and lighting to this end is similar to the use of angles of the architecture in Leonardo's *Annunciation*. Yet Filippino gave greater immediacy to the drama by giving the Virgin a massive body that glows with light and bends forward, seemingly pulled by the unyielding weight of her cloak. Leonardo's influence is again present in the *Adoration of the Magi* (Florence, Uffizi) completed on 29 March 1496 (signed and dated on the back) for S Donato a Scopeto, outside Florence. This painting was commissioned to replace one begun by Leonardo (1472–82; Florence, Uffizi; *see* LEONARDO DA VINCI, fig. 1) but left unfinished on his departure for Milan. Filippino organized figures around a pyramidal structure with the Virgin and Child at the apex (similar to Leonardo's unfinished work) and orchestrated a range of movements, emotions and physiognomic types (including several portraits) that animate the event with whirling activity.

In 1498 Filippino made a second will, after marrying Maddalena di Pietro Paolo Monti the year before; he also received a prestigious commission for the main council chamber of the Palazzo della Signoria (it was never executed), and he was asked to give advice on repairing the dome of Florence Cathedral. The largest painting he completed that year (dated on the painting) was an outdoor frescoed tabernacle of the *Virgin and Child with SS Stephen, Catherine, Anthony Abbot and Margaret* (Prato, Mus. Com.). Here Filippino once again gave tangibility and immediacy to the mystical presence of the Virgin and Child in a *sacra conversazione*. A three-dimensional niche with side walls positioned at 90° angles afforded him a way to bring the flanking saints into intimate contact with the Virgin and Child, while simultaneously isolating them. Though the saints' figures ostensibly break through the boundaries of the side wall-frames, the honoured positions of the Virgin, weightless and looming as the Queen of Heaven, and of the Infant Jesus as the *Salvator mundi* (Saviour of the World, blessing with his right hand and holding an orb in his left) are manifestly clear. The

interlocked figures of Martin, horse and beggar, and the antique elements above and below the group are all bound into one animated and majestic element. Two tritons ceremoniously display the Nerli family crest, and members of the family itself appear prominently in the altarpiece, placed directly below the stained glass. Compared with significance of the Virgin and Child for all time is revealed in the central panel, where sphinxes, the ancient guardians of religious mysteries, support the sacrificial altar table at the Virgin's feet, and plump seraphim, heaven's guardians, encircle the regal couple.

While these and other works were in progress, Filippino continued to paint the Strozzi Chapel, probably completing most of the decoration between 1497 and 1500. The scene of the *Raising of Drusiana* is signed and dated 1502, and the stained-glass window was put in place in 1503. Filippo Strozzi's will had stipulated that the chapel (commissioned in 1487) was to be completed by 1493, and in 1497 Filippino's slow progress led to a court case, after which his fee was increased. Payments to Filippino are documented, but precisely what scenes were completed when is not recorded. On the vault quadrants are the Old Testament patriarchs: *Abraham, Adam, Noah* and *Jacob*. Beneath *Abraham*, on the east wall, are scenes from the *Life of St Philip*, Strozzi's patron saint: the *Crucifixion of St Philip* (lunette) and, below, *St Philip Exorcizing a Demon*. The chapel is dedicated to St John the Evangelist, scenes from whose life are painted on the west wall, below *Noah*: *St John Boiled in Oil* (lunette) and below, the *Raising of Drusiana* (fig. 4). These scenes, enriched with exuberant ornament, much of it derived from antiquity, culminate on the altar wall with a *tour de force* of illusionistic

architecture: a Classical triumphal arch, painted in grisaille with touches of colour, surrounding the arched recess that holds Filippo Strozzi's basanite tomb (1491–5) by Benedetto da Maiano. Above the tomb is the great stained-glass window (designed by Filippino before 1497), depicting the *Virgin and Child with SS Philip and John the Evangelist*, with fictive mouldings and grotesque decoration lining the window embrasure. Above the tomb recess are winged genii attending to bones and skulls. Personifications of Virtues, Muses, and Music occupy the lower zone while angels of mythic size stand atop projecting entablatures supporting inscribed plaques, brandishing banners and holding shields bearing the Strozzi arms by their sides. The Strozzi frescoes are the culminating point of Filippino's quest for illusionism and for unity—not a quiet or inert unity, but the fusion of many richly embellished and interactive parts.

Filippino's late works reflect an interest in volumetric figures, sombre colours and solid, monumental forms arranged formally in open-air settings. In 1501 he painted the *Mystic Marriage of St Catherine, Attended by SS Joseph, John the Baptist, Peter, Paul and Sebastian* for the Isolani family chapel in S Domenico, Bologna, inscribing his name and the date on a stone fragment in the right foreground. His stately Virgin and Child are surrounded by saints who theatrically call attention to their attributes (Peter's keys,

4. Filippino Lippi: *Raising of Drusiana* (1502), fresco, Strozzi Chapel, S Maria Novella, Florence

Catherine's wheel, Paul's sword, and Sebastian's arrows), and the painting sets up a hierarchy between heaven and earth through the placing of the figures of heaven (God and angels) so far away from the spectator that the saints, who are nearer but elevated to an inaccessible level, seem to occupy a plateau midway between heaven and earth.

So renowned was Filippino in his lifetime that shops in the Via dei Servi, Florence, closed on the day of his burial in S Michele Visdomini, Florence. Early in his career (c. 1492–4) the agent of Ludovico Sforza, Duke of Milan, had commented that it would be difficult to choose the foremost among the painters working at Lorenzo de' Medici's Villa Spedaletto, adding that Filippino's art was sweeter, yet less artful, than that of Botticelli. In his *Summa de arithmetica* (Venice, 1494) Fra Luca Pacioli praised Filippino and Botticelli as masters of perspective. In the early 16th century Paolo Cortese, in *De cardinalatu* (1510), recommended that the ideal imagery for a cardinal's chapel could be seen in the Carafa Chapel in S Maria sopra Minerva. Certainly Filippino's knowledge of illusionistic devices and antique ornaments would have interested Pope Julius II (the dedicatee of Cortese's book), Raphael and Michelangelo. Yet later in the 16th century his fame diminished quite rapidly, and, although he may have influenced 16th- and 17th-century art, he remains in the shadow of Botticelli and Leonardo.

2. WORKING METHODS AND TECHNIQUE. Filippino was a prolific draughtsman, who prepared his panel paintings and frescoes through a series of drawings that included rapid sketches in which he recorded his first ideas; finished composition and presentation drawings; figure drawings; and studies of individual details, such as head and drapery. More drawings have been attributed to him than to any other 15th-century Florentine painter apart from Leonardo, and this may be due to the nature of his training and to his complex iconographical programmes. His compositional drawings are generally in pen and ink, with some wash, on white paper; the first sketches were begun in black chalk, which he later went over with pen and ink. For figure drawings he used metalpoint on coloured prepared paper, enlivened with white lead highlights. His early drawings are not connected with specific paintings, but a study for the figure of *St Bernard* (Florence, Uffizi) in the *Virgin Appearing to St Bernard* (c. 1485–7) survives, and after this date drawings associated with known paintings increase. In the drawing Filippino conceived the ledge beneath St Bernard as a flat and immobile plank, but in the picture it is tilted. This is characteristic of his tendency to transform the settings in his final works, a tendency confirmed by the exceptionally spirited compositional drawing in pen, brown ink and brown wash (London, BM), for the fresco of the *Triumph of St Thomas* in the Carafa Chapel. In the drawing the figures move freely in space, while in the final composition they are more severely contained by the architecture. These changes satisfied the demands of the patron and also enabled Filippino to include a richer display of ornament. His late metalpoint studies, among which are a *Study for the Head of Piero del Pugliese* (Milan, Ambrosiana) in the Uffizi *Adoration* and the *Head of a Man* (c. 1495; Windsor Castle, Berks, Royal Lib.), executed on blue-grey prepared paper with blue heightening, are distinguished by an increasingly expressive use of the medium.

The decoration of the Strozzi Chapel reveals Filippino's confidence and experience as a fresco painter. The contract stipulated that he alone was to execute the murals, in true fresco, and using the most expensive colours, especially lapis lazuli, and gold leaf for the haloes and highlights of the jewellery. The large size of the *giornate* indicates that he worked quickly; no *sinopie* have been found, and he used cartoons for the minor figures and ornament (Borsook, 1970). Several drawings give an idea of the changes in direction that he took while making preliminary studies. The ideas in a preliminary drawing for the *Raising of Drusiana* (Florence, Uffizi), begun in black chalk and gone over in pen and ink with a light use of wash, showing Filippino's interest in the dynamic relationships between figures and architecture, are taken much further in the fresco, where figures nearly explode the parameters of shallow spaces. An abundance of descriptive detail in clothing and in physiognomy interlocks figures into an excited animation. The architecture is no longer central but placed off balance; planes tilt to intensify the rapid movements of the concentrated masses of people. At least two drawings were done for the patriarchs, showing a change in Filippino's plan for the ceiling figures. One of the two (Florence, Uffizi, 134E) describes calmer, seated figures, while the other, the *Study of Four Seated Nude Men* (Lille, Mus. B.A., 290), defines more active, twisted and volumetric forms that are closer to the complex movements of the painted figures: Adam twists around Seth as the serpent Eve coils about the tree, and Abraham's billowing garments envelop and expand his body nearly to the width of the frame. Filippino enlivened Abraham with light, bright colour changes that are similar to the way patches of light define the muscle tissue of the figures in the Lille drawing. His knowledge of Pollaiuolo's figures for the tomb of *Sixtus IV* and of antique sculpture, such as the personification of the River Nile in Monte Cavallo in Rome, is apparent. Yet he never laboriously copied sources. His drawn studies of antique ornaments (e.g. Florence, Uffizi, 1636E; 6333–6335E) capture the lively essence of the decoration rather than record archaeological detail.

BIBLIOGRAPHY

G. B. Cavalcaselle and J. A. Crowe: *History of Painting in Italy* (London, 1864)
B. Berenson: 'Amico di Sandro', *Gaz. B.-A.*, xxi (1899), pp. 459–71; xxii (1899), pp. 21–36
——: *The Study and Criticism of Italian Art* (London, 1902)
——: *Drawings of the Florentine Painters*, 3 vols (London, 1903/R Chicago, 1938; rev. N. Mariano and L. V. Nicolson, Milan, 1961)
A. Scharf: *Filippino Lippi* (Vienna, 1935)
K. Neilson: *Filippino Lippi* (Cambridge, MA, 1938)
A. Scharf: *Filippino Lippi* (Vienna, 1950)
*Mostra di disegni di Filippino Lippi e Piero di Cosimo* (exh. cat. by M. Fossi-Todorrow, Florence, Uffizi, 1955)
L. Berti and U. Baldini: *Filippino Lippi* (Florence, 1957)
F. Gamba: *Filippino Lippi nella storia della critica* (Florence, 1958)
E. Borsook: *The Mural Painters of Tuscany: From Cimabue to Andrea del Sarto* (London, 1960, rev. Oxford, 1980)
S. Sandström: *Levels of Unreality* (Uppsala, 1963)
C. Bertelli: 'Il restauro della Cappella Carafa in S Maria sopra Minerva a Roma', *Boll. Ist. Cent. Rest.*, xlii (1965), pp. 145–95
E. Winternitz: *Musical Instruments and their Symbolism in Western Art* (New York, 1967), pp. 166–84

E. Borsook: 'Documents for Filippo Strozzi's Chapel in S Maria Novella and Other Related Papers - I', *Burl. Mag.*, 112 (1970), pp. 737–45

——: 'Documents for Filippo Strozzi's Chapel in S Maria Novella and Other Related Papers - II', *Burl. Mag.*, 112 (1970), pp. 800–04

D. Friedman: 'The Burial Chapel of Filippo Strozzi in Maria Novella in Florence', *L'Arte*, ix (1970), pp. 108–31

M. Meiss: 'A New Monumental Painting by Filippino Lippi', *A. Bull.*, lv (1973), pp. 479–93

I. H. Shoemaker: *Filippino Lippi as a Draughtsman* (London, 1977)

R. Sale: *Filippino Lippi's Strozzi Chapel in Santa Maria Novella* (New York, 1979)

M. Lavin: *The Place of Narrative* (Chicago, 1990)

MARILYN BRADSHAW

**Lippi, Giovanni.** *See* BIGIO, NANNI DI BACCIO.

**Lippi, Lorenzo** (*b* Florence, 3 May 1606; *d* Florence, 15 April 1665). Italian painter and poet. He was trained by Matteo Rosselli, with whom he worked for many years in close partnership. His collaboration was sometimes anonymous but is documented from 1622, when they decorated the ceiling of the Sala della Stufa (Florence, Pitti), to 1631–2, when they worked together on lunettes portraying *St Francis Adoring the Child* and *St Catherine in Prison* (Florence, S Gaetano). In 1630 Lippi was enrolled in the Accademia del Disegno but appears not to have had his own workshop until after 1634, although he worked independently before then. The earliest paintings attributable to him are, both in facial types and in the soft, rich folds of the drapery, close in style to the work of Rosselli. Examples include canvases of the Apostles *James*, *John* and *Matthew*, and *Christ Blessing* (all 1628; Vaglia, S Pietro), and the *Virgin Handing the Child to St Francis* (1629; Florence, S Salvatore di Camaldoli). In the 1630s Lippi painted decorative and theatrical compositions, mainly on literary and biblical themes, which remained

indebted to Rosselli, for example *Samson and Delilah* (1632; Stockholm, Nmus.) and the *Virgin in Glory with Saints* (1634; Ronta, nr Barberino di Mugello, S Michele). Shortly afterwards he produced works (e.g. the *Sacrifice of Isaac* and *Hagar and the Angel*; both San Miniato, Mus. Dioc. A. Sacra), which, in their use of *sfumato* as a means of heightening the feeling of pathos, are reminiscent of the work of Francesco Furini.

The simpler composition and more concentrated light of Lippi's *Martyrdom of St Andrew* (1639; Florence, S Agata) introduced a more marked change of direction. In the 1640s, in such works as the *Flight into Egypt* (1642; Massa Maríttima, S Agostino), he developed his own strictly purist figurative language, inspired by Santi di Tito and intended to revive the style of such great 16th-century masters as Andrea del Sarto and Fra Bartolommeo. After a journey to Austria in 1643–4 in the entourage of Claudia de' Medici (1604–1648), for whom he painted portraits and the classical *Christ and the Woman of Samaria* (see fig.), he painted his great *Crucifixion* (1647; Florence, Mus. S Marco), the most austere and deeply devotional of his religious works. A series of moralizing half-length allegorical figures, among them *Pretence* (Angers, Mus. B.-A.) and *Innocence* (Oxford, Ashmolean), dates from the mid-1640s.

In the 1650s and 1660s Lippi painted many altarpieces (e.g. the *Madonna of the Rosary*, 1652; Foiano della Chiana, nr Arezzo, S Domenico; and *St Thomas Giving Alms*, 1662; Prato, S Agostino), which are executed in the simplified style he developed in the 1640s. He also painted works intended for private collectors, on Old Testament and literary subjects, such as the *Triumph of David* (1656; Florence, priv. col., see exh. cat., 1986, *Pittura*, p. 347) and *Erminia among the Shepherds* (*c.* 1658; Pistoia, Rospigliosi Museo Clemente; see exh. cat., 1986, *Pittura*, p. 345). These always adhere closely to their texts and are characterized by clearly defined shapes and direct and unambiguous gesture and expression.

The extreme clarity and purity of Lippi's art reflected his desire for a moral and didactic style of painting, which was attuned to his literary and philosophical interests. He frequented Florence's religious companies and literary academies and was a friend of Salvator Rosa (in Florence, 1640–49), with whom he shared an interest in philosophical and elevating subjects. He also knew Filippo Baldinucci, who was the inspiration for parts of his mock heroic poem, *Il malmantile racquistato* (1649; published posthumously). Baldinucci recorded Lippi's life but was an admirer of his poetry rather than of his painting. He could not understand or sympathize with Lippi's refined simplicity and criticized him for excessive naturalism and lack of invention and richness.

WRITINGS

P. Zipoli [L. Lippi]: *Il malmantile racquistato* (Finaro, 1676) [incl. 'Vita dell'autore' by G. Cinelli]

BIBLIOGRAPHY

F. Baldinucci: *Notizie* (1681–1728); ed. F. Ranalli (1845–7), v, pp. 261–78

A. Alterocca: *La vita e l'opera poetica e pittorica di Lorenzo Lippi* (Catania, 1914)

F. Sricchia: 'Lorenzo Lippi nello svolgimento della pittura fiorentina della prima metà del seicento', *Proporzioni*, iv (1963), pp. 254–70

C. d'Afflitto: 'Precisazioni sulla fase giovanile di Lorenzo Lippi', *Paragone*, xxx/353 (1979), pp. 61–76

Lorenzo Lippi: *Christ and the Woman of Samaria*, oil on canvas, 1.85×1.75 m, 1644 (Vienna, Kunsthistorisches Museum)

——: 'La "conversione" di Lorenzo Lippi', *Paradigma*, iv (1982), pp. 111–38

R. Spinelli: 'Domenico Pugliani e Lorenzo Lippi alla Compagnia della Madonna della Neve di Vaglia', *Paragone*, xxxvii/437 (1986), pp. 35–52

*Il seicento fiorentino*, 3 vols (exh. cat., Florence, Pal. Strozzi, 1986), i, *Pittura*, pp. 339–48; ii, *Disegno*, pp. 305–6; iii, *Biografie*, pp. 107–9

*Pitture fiorentine del seicento* (exh. cat., Florence, Pal. Ridolfi, 1987), pp. 80, 82–4

CHIARA D'AFFLITTO

**Lippincott, Roy (Alston)** (*b* Harrisburg, PA, 1 July 1885; *d* Santa Barbara, CA, 28 April 1969). American architect, active in Australia and New Zealand. He studied architecture (1905–9) at Cornell University, Ithaca, NY, and on graduation worked for the firms of Von Holst and Fyfe (1909–11) and Spencer and Powers (1912), both in Chicago. In 1913 Lippincott became chief draughtsman to Walter Burley Griffin, becoming a junior partner and moving to Australia with Griffin in 1914, when he also married Griffin's sister, Genevieve. Lippincott participated in planning the new capital of Canberra and managed the firm's Melbourne office. It is difficult to distinguish his designs from those of Griffin, and Lippincott's own house (1917), 21 Glenard Drive, Heidelberg, Victoria, clearly reveals the influence of the Prairie school. In 1920, in partnership with Edward Billson, who also worked in Griffin's office, he won the competition for the Arts Building (1921–6; for illustration *see* AUCKLAND), University of Auckland, and in 1921 he moved to New Zealand to supervise the construction of this abstracted Gothic-style design. Their entry to the *Chicago Tribune* Tower competition (1922), also with severely abstracted Gothic-style elements, received honourable mention. Lippincott established an independent practice in Auckland in 1925. His commercial works, notably additions (1927–9) to Smith and Caughey's Department Store, Elliot Street, houses, including the Lippincott House (1927), Remuera Road, and Scott House (1935), Paratai Drive, all in Auckland, and educational buildings, for example the Biology Building (1937–9), University of Auckland, became valuable models of Chicago school design for the architectural profession in New Zealand, which was still conservative. Lippincott vigorously advocated university training for architects in New Zealand and also advised on methods of earthquake-resistant construction. On the outbreak of World War II he returned to the USA and practised in Los Angeles and Santa Barbara. His work of this period, which included the house for Donald K. Lippincott (1948) in Orinda, CA, was less influential than that of the years he spent in New Zealand when he helped counteract the insularity of architecture there by providing a direct link with a key phase of 20th-century American architecture.

WRITINGS

'The Development of Concrete as an Artistic Architectural Material', *NZ Inst. Architects J.*, vii/2 (1928), pp. 22–31

'Present Day Difficulties of Architectural Education in New Zealand', *NZ Inst. Architects J.*, ix/2 (1930), pp. 25–37

BIBLIOGRAPHY

D. L. Johnson: *Australian Architecture, 1901–1951: Sources of Modernism* (Sydney, 1980)

M. A. Bruce: *Roy Alston Lippincott: An American Connection* (diss., U. Auckland, 1985)

IAN J. LOCHHEAD

**Lippo di Benivieni** (*fl* Florence, 1296–1320). Italian painter. The earliest documentary reference to the artist records the apprenticeship of a certain Nerio di Binduccio to him in 1296, which suggests that Lippo was an established figure by this date. He is further recorded as a member of the Arte dei Medici e Speziali in Florence from 1312 to 1320. No documented works by him are known, however, and a reconstruction of his career was first suggested by Offner. The documented dates make Lippo a contemporary of Giotto, but the works attributed to him show a much stronger response to Sienese rather than Florentine painting, particularly that of the followers of Duccio. The *Mocking of Christ* (Strasbourg, Mus. B.-A.) shows their influence very clearly in its characteristic emotional content and the rhythmic element in its composition. Panels from two dismembered altarpieces of the *Virgin and Child with Saints* (Florence, Acton priv. col.; Florence, Uffizi, formerly Alessandri priv. col.; see Fremantle, figs 49, 54, 59) now attributed to Lippo di Benivieni were once assigned on stylistic grounds, and on the basis of the signatures LIPPUS ME FECIT that they bear, to the Sienese painter Lippo Memmi. Although the authenticity of the signatures is now questioned, the attribution to Lippo di Benivieni remains. The large dossal of a *Lamentation* (Pistoia, Mus. Civ.), with its intense characterization and emotional impact, is probably the artist's finest work and shows him to have been one of the most original Florentine painters of his time. Other attributions to Lippi are still debated but should surely include the portable altar in Memphis (Memphis, TN, Brooks Mus. A.).

BIBLIOGRAPHY

R. Offner and K. Steinweg: *Corpus* (1930–79), III/vi, pp. iii–ix, 29–45

C. Volpe: 'Frammenti di Lippo di Benivieni', *Paragone*, xxiii/261 (1972), pp. 3–13

R. Fremantle: *Florentine Gothic Painters* (London, 1975)

M. Boskovits: *Corpus* (1984)

A. Tartuferi: 'Corpus of Florentine Painting: Nouveautés sur le trecento', *Rev. A.*, lxxi (1986), pp. 43–6

ANGELO TARTUFERI

**Lippo di Dalmasio** [Lippo delle Madonne] (*d c.* 1410). Italian painter. First recorded in Bologna, he was probably trained by his father DALMASIO SCANNABECCHI and his uncle Simone dei Crocefissi. In 1377 he was a Bolognese citizen resident in Pistoia. He is recorded in both Bologna and Pistoia in 1385 but returned finally to Bologna in 1389. This phase of Lippo's career is represented by a fresco of the *Madonna of Humility with SS Dominic and Catherine* (Pistoia, S Domenico), striking for its expressive triangular faces appealing to the spectator, and for the pavilion over the Virgin, a feature probably invented by Vitale da Bologna and much copied by his followers. The linear simplification of form combined with simple areas of boldly contrasted colour and the choice of the Madonna of Humility as the subject remain typical of his work. Later he appears to have been influenced by the Florentine art of Andrea di Cione and his brothers.

Between 1391 and 1410 Lippo lived in Bologna, where he painted the numerous renderings of the Virgin and Child as well as altarpieces, frequently signed, that in the 16th century earned him a reputation as a pious artist and the sobriquet 'Lippo delle Madonne'. Three dated works, the *Coronation of the Virgin* (1394; Bologna, Pin. N.), the

Lippo Memmi: *Virgin and Child*, tempera on panel, 780×510 mm, *c.* 1335 (Siena, S Maria dei Servi)

*Madonna of Mercy* (1397; Bologna, S Maria della Misericordia) and the *Virgin and Child* (1409; Norton Hall, Glos, P. Pollen priv. col.) show a steady evolution towards a heavier style and a change in the signature from *lippus dalmassi pinxit* to *lipus dalmaxii pinsit*. Lippo's most complete work, the altarpiece of the *Virgin and Child Enthroned with Saints* (Bologna, Pii Ist. Educ., on dep. Pin. N.) shows Florentine influence most clearly in its forms and light sharp colours. His finest work, despite retouching, is perhaps the earlier *Madonna of Humility* (London, N.G.). A fresco of the *Virgin and Child* dated 1407 (Pistoia, Pal. Pub.), if really by Lippo, represents a very different style for a different public. Lippo served as the notary in charge of the public records of Bologna, and as a judge and court officer—a remarkably distinguished political career for an artist of this period.

BIBLIOGRAPHY

F. Filippini and G. Zucchini: *Miniatori e pittori a Bologna: Documenti dei secoli XIII e XIV* (Florence, 1947), pp. 57–61, 153–61
L. Bellosi: *Buffalmacco e il Trionfo della Morte* (Turin, 1974), p. 84
M. Boskovits: *Pittura fiorentina alla vigilia del rinascimento* (Florence, 1975)
F. Arcangeli: *Pittura bolognese del '300* (Bologna, 1978), pp. 96–105, 228–33 [notes by M. Ferretti and P. G. Castagnoli]
R. Gibbs: 'Two Families of Painters at Bologna in the Later Fourteenth Century', *Burl. Mag.*, cxxi (1979), pp. 560–68
D. Benati: *Jacopo Avanzi* (Bologna, 1992), pp. 120–29

ROBERT GIBBS

**Lippold, Richard** (*b* Milwaukee, WI, 3 May 1915). American sculptor. He studied industrial design in Chicago, at the University and at the School of the Art Institute (1933–7). He began making sculptures *c.* 1942 and achieved major recognition following his one-man show at the Willard Gallery, New York (1947). His sculptures reveal a concern for the space that they occupy, and for movement, real and apparent. They are often made of fragmented metal, wire or rods, sometimes giving an impression of weightlessness.

Lippold's reputation was assured by the purchase in 1950 of *Variation No. 7: Full Moon* (1949–50) by the Museum of Modern Art in New York. A larger, but similar construction in metal wire, *Variation within a Sphere, No. 10: The Sun* (6.6×1.5 m, 1953–6), was commissioned by the Metropolitan Museum of Art. A diaphanous web of gold-filled wire, anchored to the ceiling, floor, and walls by thin steel wires, the sculpture is illuminated by specially arranged lights. Among his other commissions, which he preferred to speculative work, were *Radiant I* (gold, stainless steel and enamelled copper, 3.9×4.57×7.31 m, 1957) for the Inland Steel Building in Chicago, *Orpheus and Apollo* (brass sheeting suspended from stainless steel wires, 1962) for the Philharmonic Hall in the Lincoln Center in New York and sculptures for the Harvard University Graduate Law School (1950) and Seagram Building in New York (1982). Lippold's work is rare in commissioned art in attracting general public approval, especially of its suitability to the site.

BIBLIOGRAPHY

L. Campbell: 'Lippold Makes a Construction', *ARTnews*, lv/6 (1956), pp. 30–33, 63–4
*200 Years of American Sculpture* (exh. cat., ed. T. Armstrong; New York, Whitney, 1976), pp. 181, 184, 288
W. Craven: *Sculpture in America* (Newark, DE, 1984), pp. 645, 649–50, 668

DAVID M. SOKOL

**Lippo Memmi** (*fl* 1317–*c.* 1350). Italian painter. He was the son of MEMMO DI FILIPPUCCIO, the brother of Tederigho (also spelt Federigo) Memmi and, after 1324, brother-in-law of Simone and Donato Martini, all of whom were painters. He is known through signed works, documentary references and early secondary sources. In 1317 he signed and dated a frescoed *Virgin and Child Enthroned with Saints* ('Maestà') in the Palazzo del Popolo, San Gimignano (*see* DRESS, fig. 18). Commissioned by the *podestà*, Nello di Mino de' Tolomei of Siena, the work is an adaptation of Simone Martini's fresco of the *Maestà* in the Sala del Mappamondo of the Palazzo Pubblico, Siena. A diptych of the *Virgin and Child* and *St John the Baptist*, originally in Pisa (Berlin, Gemäldegal., and New York, W. B. Golovin priv. col.), is signed and dated 1333. In the same year Lippo and Simone Martini signed and dated the altarpiece of the *Annunciation* (Florence, Uffizi), originally from the altar of St Ansanus in Siena Cathedral. The precise nature and extent of Lippo's participation in this work are disputed by scholars. A fragmentary fresco of the *Virgin and Child Enthroned with SS Peter and Paul and Two Angels* (Siena, Pin. N.) from the cloister of S Domenico, Siena, once bore a signature and, perhaps, a partial date of MCCCL. . . . In S Maria dei Servi, Siena, there is a signed but undated half-length *Virgin and Child* (see fig.). A *Virgin and Child Enthroned* (Altenburg, Staatl. Lindenau-Mus.) carries what is apparently an original inscription (LIPPUS MEMMI DE SENIS ME PINXIT), but its style bears little resemblance to that of Lippo Memmi's other known works. A *Madonna of Mercy* in Orvieto Cathedral is signed LIPPUS DE SENA, but there is much disagreement over attempts to identify this artist with Lippo Memmi.

Documents relating to Lippo Memmi between 1317 and 1348 include references to lost works of art: a figure of *St Ansanus* (1326/7) for the office of the Gabella dei Contratti in the Palazzo Pubblico, Siena; an unspecified and perhaps uncompleted project (1341) executed in collaboration with Lippo's brother Tederigho for the tower of the Palazzo Pubblico; and a triptych (1344), executed jointly with his brother, for the hospital of S Maria della Scala, Siena, though apparently sent outside the city by that institution. Documents also survive relating to the Uffizi *Annunciation*. Early secondary sources record the existence of a signed polyptych in S Paolo a Ripa d'Arno, Pisa, and a signed altarpiece on the high altar of S Francesco, Pistoia, but attempts to associate surviving panels with these works have not been generally accepted. There was once an altarpiece signed by Lippo and his brother and dated 1347 in the Franciscan church in Avignon.

Few early Sienese painters have posed as many problems or generated such scholarly disagreement as Lippo Memmi. The visual evidence of the signed works and his collaboration on the Uffizi *Annunciation* indicate his close association with Simone Martini. Documents and early sources testify to his collaboration with his brother Tederigho, but no signed or securely documented work by the latter is known. Moreover, it is generally acknowledged that Lippo was part of a much larger group of painters surrounding and profoundly influenced by Simone Martini. The complex interconnections among painters of this group have led to a tendency to treat the material as a stylistic block (Bagnoli and Bellosi in exh. cat., Martindale), but the successes of this approach are limited. An attempt has also been made to identify Lippo as the author of the *New Testament* cycle in the Collegiata of San Gimignano, traditionally attributed to BARNA DA SIENA.

On the basis of the signed works, many panels and some frescoes have been attributed to Lippo Memmi. The most widely accepted attributions include a half-length *Virgin and Child* (Siena, Pin. N.), once part of an altarpiece with panels of *St John the Evangelist* and *St Peter* (both untraced); a half-length *Virgin and Child with Donor* (Washington, DC, N.G.A.); a half-length *Virgin and Child with Saints* (Boston, MA, Isabella Stewart Gardner Mus.); a *Virgin and Child* (Berlin, Gemäldegal.); a series of saints from a polyptych: *St Paul* (New York, Met.), *St Louis of Toulouse* and *St Francis* (Siena, Pin. N.), *St Peter* (Paris, Louvre), *St John the Evangelist* (New Haven, CT, Yale U. A.G.) and *St John the Baptist* (Washington, DC, N.G.A.); a polyptych of the *Virgin and Child with SS John the Evangelist, Paul, Stephen and Thomas Aquinas*, originally from Pisa Cathedral and now in S Niccolò, Casciana Alta (Pisa); and a half-length *Virgin and Child* (Kansas City, MO, Nelson–Atkins Mus. A.). Many of these works show

the intervention of assistants, but the group as a whole, with the signed works, constitutes a basis against which a wide range of controversial attributions can be tested.

Because of the debate surrounding Lippo Memmi's oeuvre, any estimation of the artist must be tentative. The generally accepted and signed works reveal a painter of high technical competence and considerable charm but of limited invention. His technique and figure style were inspired by Simone Martini, even before the two were related by marriage. After Simone Martini's departure from Siena in 1336, however, Lippo seems to have received only one major civic commission (work in the new tower of the Palazzo Pubblico), suggesting that contemporary assessment of his work accorded with that of modern critics.

## BIBLIOGRAPHY

Thieme–Becker
P. Bacci: *Fonti e commenti per la storia dell'arte senese* (Siena, 1944)
B. A. Bennett: *Lippo Memmi, Simone Martini's 'Fratello in Arte': The Image Revealed by his Documented Works* (diss., U. Pittsburgh, 1977)
*Simone Martini e 'chompagni'* (exh. cat., ed. A. Bagnoli and L. Bellosi; Siena, Pin. N., 1985)
A. Martindale: *Simone Martini: Complete Edition* (Oxford, 1988)
H. B. J. Maginnis: 'Chiarimenti documentari: Simone Martini, i Memmi e Ambrogio Lorenzetti', *Riv. A.*, 4th ser., v (1989), pp. 3–23

H. B. J. MAGINNIS

**Lippo (di) Vanni** (*b* ?Siena; *fl c.* 1340–75). Italian painter and illuminator. He is documented as a painter and illuminator in Siena between 1344 and 1375, and in 1360 and 1373 he took part in the General Council of Siena. The earliest work attributed to him is the illumination of the choirbooks for the Collegiata at San Gimignano (*c.* 1340–42; San Gimignano, Mus. A. Sacra, MS. LXVIII.5, 6 and 7), in which the supple movement and individuality of figures and scenes already show the expressive quality characteristic of Lippo's later documented work. In these illuminations the decorated initial is conceived as an aperture and not a framing device, and even principal figures are often only partially visible. Lippo treated the historiated initial in different ways in each major series of illuminations. In a Gradual for the Collegiata at Casole d'Elsa, near Siena, bold and brilliant colour contrasts and harmonies unify the letter and its historiation; architectural details are more complex and are used to create an impression of greater depth. This spatial effect is undoubtedly a response to the art of Pietro Lorenzetti, as is the treatment of form; the figures, although often dynamic, are more compact and solid, and their faces are distinctly modelled.

The only documented illuminations by Lippo are the first five historiated initials in a Gradual of 1344–5 (Siena, Mus. Opera Duomo, MS. 98/4), which was commissioned by the hospital of S Maria della Scala, Siena. In these even more complex and ambitious designs, Lippo assimilated other features from the work of both Ambrogio and Pietro Lorenzetti, and the figures inhabit more fully realized interiors. Lippo, however, was never content simply to borrow, and his own designs are adaptations of the work of Lorenzetti: for example the *Presentation in the Temple* (fol. 27*r*; see fig.) is a reworking of Ambrogio's panel of 1342 (Florence, Uffizi). The figures have been regrouped, the high priest and his assistants enclosed within the inner sanctuary, while Mary, Joseph and Simeon listen attentively

Lippo Vanni: *Presentation in the Temple*, detail from a Gradual, 1344–5 (Siena, Museo dell'Opera del Duomo, MS. 98/4, fol. 27*r*)

to Anna's prophecy, and a heightened sense of the revelation replaces the meditative quality of Ambrogio's vision. A choirbook of *c*. 1363 (Florence, S Lorenzo, Archv Capitolare, choirbook E), probably a Florentine commission, shows the extraordinary technical virtuosity of Lippo's mature style. In the *Nativity* (fol. 42*v*) he has captured perfectly the contrasting moods of Mary and Joseph.

Commissions of the kind that Lippo received after the mid-14th century suggest that he was seen by patrons as the major talent in Siena, and in 1356 he was mentioned at the head of a list of painters there. In 1352 he completed a fresco of the *Coronation of the Virgin* in the Palazzo Pubblico (now entirely repainted), and in 1363 his workshop began work on the frescoes of the *Battle of the Val di Chiana* and *St Paul Surrounded by Virtues* in the Sala del Mappamondo in the same building (*see* SIENA, fig. 10). His only surviving signed and dated altarpiece is a triptych of the *Virgin and Child with Saints*, with scenes from the *Life of St Aurea* on the side panels (1358; Rome, SS Domenico and Sisto), which was executed five years earlier.

The frescoes in the choir of the hermitage at San Leonardo al Lago, near Siena (*c.* 1360–70), include scenes from the *Life of Mary*, which reveal Lippo's concern to create elegant and elaborate architectural settings for his narrative scenes. The developed illusionism of the *Annunciation* is particularly effective, the angel and Virgin shown in small rooms on either side of the central window of the choir. The colour scheme is characteristic of Lippo's adventurous approach, and the unusual shades of dull yellow, deep burgundy, purple and green unite the murals of the vaults and the inner walls of the choir.

BIBLIOGRAPHY

G. C. Dini: 'Lippo di Vanni', *Il gotico a Siena: Miniature, pitture, oreficere, oggetti d'arte* (exh. cat., Siena, Pal. Pub., 1982), p. 255

V. Wainwright: 'Late Illuminations by Lippo di Vanni and his Workshop', *Pantheon*, 46 (1988), pp. 26–36

VALERIE WAINWRIGHT

**Lipps, Theodor** (*b* Wallhalben, Bavaria, 28 July 1851; *d* Munich, 17 Oct 1914). German psychologist and philosopher. After studying theology at the universities of Tübingen (1867–71) and Utrecht (1871–2), he turned to philosophy and natural sciences. Following his research at Bonn University (1874–7), he taught there from 1877 to 1890, becoming a professor in 1884. He then held academic posts at the universities of Breslau (1890–94) and Munich (1894–1914). His importance to art lies in his aesthetic theories, set out in most detail in his book *Ästhetik* (1903–06). His system is centred on the notion of *Einfühlung* or empathy, a term first used by the writer Robert Vischer (1847–1933) in *Über das optische Formgefühl* (Leipzig, 1873), though in spirit it can be traced back to Johann Gottfried Herder and the German Romantics. Lipps divides empathy into four main types: general empathy (*allgemeine Einfühlung*), by which forms and outlines are animated; empirical or natural empathy (*Empirische- oder Natureinfühlung*), by which surrounding natural objects are animated, such that, for example, a tree might be said to groan; mood empathy (*Stimmungseinfühlung*), in which, for example, colours acquire character and music is imbued with expressive power; and empathy through which the physical appearance of a fellow human is seen as suggestive of an inner life. In the field of art he asserted that aesthetic pleasure is self-enjoyment, the individual projecting himself into an art object by empathy and so dissolving the distinction between subject and object. While empathizing the self becomes aware of its own energy and activity. If the empathy demanded by the object can be given without opposition by the individual then the empathy is positive and the object beautiful. If, on the contrary, internal opposition is caused between the natural striving for self-activation and that demanded by the object, the empathy is negative and the object ugly. Negative empathy can afford no aesthetic pleasure and so is unconnected to art.

The fusion between self and object that occurs in the act of empathy in aesthetic situations does not involve the practical or ordinary self with its concomitant sensations, ideas, thoughts and feelings; rather it is the ideal self that, though no less real than the practical self, exists only in the contemplation of the object. The aesthetic self-enjoyment experienced in positive empathy is thus possible even in the presence of ostensibly unpleasant or disturbing works of art, because the experience is attached to the ideal, not practical, self. This aspect of his theory undermines any suggestion that the process of empathy is merely a pleasurable association of ideas caused by the object because, since the ideal self has no ideas and thoughts, association cannot take place. Furthermore the lack of personal features in the ideal self implies that positive empathy can only be explained by reference to the qualities of the object, not of the individual, thus giving works of art an objective footing. The advantages of his theory are gained at a price however: the concept of the ideal self, which lacks any empirical basis, could be seen as a convenient solution to certain problems. Lipps applied this basic theory in greater detail to the various arts and in *Raumästhetik* (1897) discussed empathy in relation to spatial forms, also covering various optical illusions. The empathy theory had numerous adherents, notably such writers as Johannes Volkeit and Karl Groos in Germany, Victor Basch in France and VERNON LEE in England, and enjoyed great popularity in the early 20th century. Lipps's ideas had considerable influence on *Abstraktion und Einfühlung* (Munich, 1908), the book by Wilhelm Worringer that played an important role in German Expressionism.

WRITINGS

*Raumästhetik und geometrischoptische Täuschungen* (Leipzig, 1897)
*Ästhetik*, 2 vols (Leipzig, 1903–06)

BIBLIOGRAPHY

*NDB*
E. F. Carritt: *The Theory of Beauty* (London, 1914)
Earl of Listowel: *A Critical History of Modern Aesthetics* (London, 1939)
M. Rader, ed.: *A Modern Book of Esthetics* (New York, 1979)

□

**Lipsius, (Johann Wilhelm) Constantin** (*b* Leipzig, 20 Oct 1832; *d* Dresden, 11 April 1894). German architect and teacher. He trained under Albert Geutebrück (1800–68) at the Leipzig Baugewerkeschule and studied at the Dresden Kunstakademie with Georg Hermann Nicolai (1851–4). After study visits to Berlin, Venice and Paris, where he saw the office of Jacques-Ignace Hittorff, he set up as an architect in Leipzig, becoming a State building adviser (1872), director of the Leipzig Baugewerkeschule (1876) and Professor of Architecture at the Dresdner Akademie (1881). An eclectic, showing little independent style of his own, his models were French medieval architecture, the Baroque and the work of contemporary French architects. His first work was the funerary chapel (1855) for Baronesse von Eberstein at Schönfeld, near Leipzig. In restoring (1866–8) the Stadtkirche at Borna he employed a pure French Gothic style. The Johannishospital (1870–71) in Leipzig was also built in medieval French idiom. In his purist restoration (1878–89) of the Leipzig Thomaskirche, which was given a Gothic Revival west front, Lipsius removed the Baroque decoration. His principal work was the Akademie- und Kunstvereinsgebäude (1886–93; destr. 1945) on the Brühlsche Terrasse in Dresden. This huge complex was primarily influenced by Charles Garnier's Mannerist style. Lipsius also rebuilt Schloss Püchau (1888), near Wurzen. Both his creative and teaching work exemplify the change of stylistic models in Dresden architecture. The temperate Italian High Renaissance gave way to a luxuriant French neo-Baroque, a transition in which the individuality of Dresden architecture after Gottfried Semper and Nicolai was lost.

BIBLIOGRAPHY

*ADB*
*Leipzig und seine Bauten* (Leipzig, 1892)
Obituary, *Dt. Bauztg* (1894), p. 28
V. Helas: *Architektur in Dresden, 1800–1900* (Brunswick, 1985), p. 197

VOLKER HELAS

**Lipsius, Justus** [Lips, Joest] (*b* Overijse, 18 Oct 1547; *d* Leuven, 23 March 1606). Flemish humanist and philosopher. After studying at Leuven and travelling to Italy, Lipsius taught at Lutheran Jena, Calvinist Leiden and Catholic Leuven, changing his religious affiliation accordingly. As well as his editions of Tacitus and Seneca, his treatises on Stoic philosophy and his influential works on politics, he produced a series of antiquarian tracts, including *De amphitheatro* (1584) and *Admiranda, sive de magnitudine romana* (1598), the third book of which is devoted to the topography of ancient Rome. He published and substantially augmented Martinus Smetius's collection of ancient inscriptions (1588) and also wrote *De cruce* (1593), in which he traced the origins of the cross as a Christian symbol. The most famous portrait of him is in the *Four Philosophers* (Florence, Pitti) by Peter Paul Rubens, who also designed title-pages for some of Lipsius's works (for another portrait *see also* DE JODE, (4)).

BIBLIOGRAPHY

G. Oestreich: 'Justus Lipsius als Universalgelehrter zwischen Renaissance und Barock', *Leiden University in the Seventeenth Century: An Exchange of Learning* (Leiden, 1975), pp. 177–201
J. R. Judson and C. van de Velde: *Book Illustrations and Title-pages*, Corpus Rubenianum Ludwig Burchard, xxi/1–2 (London, 1978)
H. Vlieghe: *Rubens' Portraits of Identified Sitters Painted in Antwerp*, Corpus Rubenianum Ludwig Burchard, xix/2 (London, 1987), pp. 129–32 (cat. no. 117)
M. Morford: *Stoics and Neostoics: Rubens and the Circle of Lipsius* (Princeton, 1991)

JILL KRAYE

**Lipton, Seymour** (*b* New York, 6 Nov 1903; *d* 15 Dec 1986). American sculptor. One of the few native New Yorkers in the New York School. He graduated as a doctor of dental surgery in 1927, his serious work as an artist beginning only in 1932. He first exhibited in 1933–4, and his first one-man exhibition, mainly of woodcarvings dealing with themes of social concern, was in 1938. From the early 1940s until 1958 he taught sculpture at various colleges in the New York area and was a visiting critic at Yale University. By the mid-1940s he was working in lead and then bronze. During this technical evolution his formal vocabulary also changed from more or less figurative images, such as *Imprisoned Figure* (lead and wood, 1948; New York, MOMA), to gaunt, Surrealistic constructions in several materials, such as *Sea King* (nickel-silver on Monel metal, 1955; Buffalo, NY, Albright–Knox). Eventually he developed unique and influential techniques.

Lipton sketched constantly, copying forms from a wide variety of objects. He also worked from photographs. When satisfied with a design, he would convert it to a small maquette assembled from metal sheets that he cut and spot-brazed. These he then altered, sometimes combining two or more themes or ideas, to make a new formal arrangement, from which a full-size version was produced. In the tradition of Constructivist sculpture, Lipton assembled sheets of metal, but he did not weld the sheets as did, for example, Julio Gonzalez and then David Smith; instead he brazed different alloys, using a hard solder, on to sheets of cut Monel metal. The stable, non-ferrous Monel metal provided a non-corrosive platform for the alloys (usually bronze or nickel-silver) melted on to it. These sheets, covered with an irregularly applied coating of a second metal, were cut and bent into the desired shapes before being joined at their edges. This technique allowed Lipton to experiment with a wide variety of forms, especially those that did not respond to a geometric or mechanical interpretation, for example *Ancestor* (nickel-silver on Monel metal, 1959; Washington, priv. col.).

Lipton's organic and abstract sculpture, such as *Defender* (nickel-silver on Monel metal, 1962; Washington, DC, N. Mus. Amer. Art), has a textured, hand-made surface. His technique was conducive to the development of both small- and large-scale works that could combine vegetative lushness, demonic ferocity and solidity of form. From the 1950s to the 1970s Lipton produced a series of works distinguished by a great degree of formal variation and invention. His forms could suggest human anatomy, or machines, animals or plants, but often all these elements combined in synthesis with disturbing, mythic connotations. He made a major contribution to post-War Abstract-Expressionist sculpture, which could evoke massive forms with a great economy of means. His work was recognized and displayed in many different contexts. It demonstrates the possibility of working as intuitively in sculpture as in painting.

BIBLIOGRAPHY

J. Burnham: *Beyond Modern Sculpture* (New York, 1968)
A. Elsen: *Seymour Lipton* (New York [1970])
H. Rand: *Seymour Lipton: Aspects of Sculpture* (Washington, DC, 1979)

HARRY RAND

**Lira, Pedro** (*b* Santiago, 2 March 1845; *d* Santiago, 20 April 1912). Chilean painter and writer. He began his studies in 1862 at the Academia de Pintura in Santiago, simultaneously studying law at the Universidad de Chile in Santiago but abandoning that profession after qualifying in 1867. His solid intellectual grounding, his social standing and his strong personality enabled him both to organize art exhibitions and to write about art in newspapers and magazines. With government support he initiated plans to establish a venue for permanent exhibitions in Santiago, the Edificio El Partenón in the Quinta Normal district, which opened in 1886. He also taught and from 1892 to 1907 served as director of the Academia de Bellas Artes in Santiago.

Up to the time of his first trip to Europe in 1873, Lira worked in a Neo-classical style influenced by the work of Raymond Monvoisin (1809–70), the most important French painter to have reached Chile during the 19th century. Living in Paris until 1882, apart from a brief visit home, he borrowed elements from Neo-classicism, Romanticism and Realism but was particularly sympathetic to the academic style favoured in the official salons, demonstrating his technical facility for accurate portrayals in works such as *Philip II and the Grand Inquisitor* (1880; Santiago, Mus. N. B.A.). Lira remained an eclectic painter after his return to Chile in 1882, both in historical works such as *The Foundation of Santiago* (1883; Santiago, Congr. N.) and in works on Realist or Romantic themes, as in *The Letter* (Santiago, Mus. N. B.A.).

Lira also painted portraits and landscapes, finding in the latter subject the stimulus for his most important and individual works after 1900. In paintings such as *In the Quinta Normal* (1908; Santiago, Mus. N. B.A.) he began to dissolve forms, using more spontaneous brushwork, and above all to emphasize the pictorial qualities of his subject-matter.

WRITINGS
*Diccionario biográfico de pintores* (Santiago, 1902)

BIBLIOGRAPHY
*Pedro Lira y su obra* (exh. cat. by A. Romera, Santiago, 1974)

MILAN IVELIĆ

**Lironi, Giuseppe** (*b* 1679 or 1689; *d* Rome, 1749). Italian sculptor. He was probably a member of a family of sculptors from Vacallo in the Canton of Ticino (Switzerland). From 1720 onwards he was recorded in Rome, where he became a member of the Accademia di S Luca (4 January 1733) and subsequently an examiner of sculpture for the same institution. The only work sent outside of Rome was a statue of *St Joseph*, commissioned in 1732 by Cardinal Annibale Albani and donated to the oratorio of S Giuseppe, Urbino. The artist was active on a number of important 18th-century projects in Rome, including several commissions for St Peter's, where he worked as a sculptor, decorator and stuccoist. His statues of *Prudence* and *Hope* (both 1728) were executed for the portico of the basilica. A *bozzetto* in terracotta (Frankfurt am Main, Liebieghaus) survives for the statue of *Prudence*. Lironi also sculpted a *Putto* supporting one of the two holy water stoups, as well as various stucco works for the choir chapel (*c.* 1736). For Padre d'Evora, the Portuguese ambassador in Rome, he executed the relief of the *Virgin and Child with St Antony* for the pediment of the basilica at Mafra (*in situ*) based on a modello by José de Almeida, and the statue of *St Bruno* (terracotta, *bozzetto*; both Mafra Mus.). In 1734–6 he was involved with decorations for the Corsini Chapel, for which he sculpted his *Justice with Two Putti* (Rome, S Giovanni in Laterano). Two reliefs in stucco illustrating scenes from the *Life of St Theresa* (1734–45) were commissioned from Lironi by the Carmelite Fathers for the altar dedicated to the saint in S Maria della Scala, Rome. For the restored façade of S Maria Maggiore in Rome the sculptor produced a *Virgin and Child* (1741–2) and the relief illustrating the *Exarch Olimpius and Pope Martin I* for the portico (*c.* 1743).

BIBLIOGRAPHY
G. Roisecco, ed.: *Roma antica e moderna* (Rome, 1750), i, pp. 171–2; ii, pp. 442, 529–31
U. Schlegel: 'Beiträge zur romischen Plastik des 18. Jahrhunderts', *Mitt. Ksthist. Inst. Florenz*, x (1963), pp. 253–71
R. Enggass: *Early Eighteenth-century Sculpture in Rome: An Illustrated Catalogue Raisonné* (University Park, PA, 1976), pp. 171–5
A. Nava Cellini: *La scultura del settecento* (Turin, 1982), p. 37

*Roma lusitana: Lisbona romana* (exh. cat. by Sandra Vasco Rocca, Gabriele Borghini and Paola Ferraris, Rome, S Michele a Ripa, 1990), pp. 56, 125

DONATELLA GERMANÒ SIRACUSA

**Lisboa.** Portuguese family of artists, active in Brazil. The architect (1) Manoel Francisco Lisboa often appears in the history of Brazilian art only as the father of (2) Antônio Francisco Lisboa. He was, however, the leading architect in the gold-mining province of Minas Gerais in the mid-18th century and was responsible for most of the secular and ecclesiastical buildings that give Ouro Prêto (formerly Vila Rica) its present individual appearance. His brother, the carpenter and master mason Antônio Francisco Pombal (*fl* 1720–45), probably accompanied him on his emigration to Brazil *c.* 1720. Although there are few documentary references to Pombal, he won fame for his decoration (1736–45) of the nave of the parish church of Pilar in Vila Rica. In a move that was revolutionary for the time, he transformed the traditional rectangular interior of the church into a ten-sided polygon. The architect and sculptor (2) Antônio Francisco Lisboa was the leading Brazilian artist of the colonial period. He became highly influential for the ingenious and original way in which he developed the Rococo religious style that reached Brazil in the mid-18th century.

BIBLIOGRAPHY
J. Martins: *Dicionário de artistas e artífices dos séculos XVIII e XIX em Minas Gerais*, ii (Rio de Janeiro, 1974)

**(1) Manoel Francisco Lisboa** (*b* Lisbon; *fl c.* 1720; *d* Vila Rica [now Ouro Prêto], Brazil, before 8 Aug 1767). Architect. Probably together with his brother, Antônio Francisco Pombal, he was in the first wave of Portuguese artists to emigrate to Brazil, attracted by the exceptional working conditions offered by the gold-mining region, where from the second decade of the 18th century economic prosperity and population growth led to intensive construction work. He is documented continuously from 1721, when his name first appears in connection with the payment of the 'royal fifths' (*reais quintos*; taxes related to mining), until his death.

Lisboa's first major commission was in 1727, when he planned and directed the building of one of the most important churches in Vila Rica: Nossa Senhora da Conceição, the parish church of Antônio Dias (completed 1742), with its altars and impressive arches designed according to the precepts of Jacopo Vignola. Lisboa also gave practical lessons in architecture and between 1729 and 1759 combined this with his appointment as assessor of his profession (*juíz de ofício*), in which capacity he had to examine and issue licences to practise; all this activity suggests a professional prestige that was rare among contemporary artists. In addition, he frequently provided valuations, giving expert technical and artistic opinion of the work of other artists. In 1753 he was appointed Master of the Royal Works and Appraiser of the Royal Property and in that year was sent by the governor to the city of Mariana in the gold-mining province to prepare an estimate for the building of the episcopal palace. In 1760 he provided estimates and laid down conditions of tender for improvements to Mariana Cathedral.

Manoel Francisco Lisboa: S Efigênia, Ouro Prêto, Brazil, 1743–9

Lisboa was responsible for other principal buildings that today dominate Ouro Prêto, such as the Casa dos Contas (1734), Governor's Palace (1741–53), S Efigênia (1743–9; see fig.) and various chapels, bridges and fountains. He was equally significant as a teacher, helping to train the first generation of Brazilian-born architects and masons, who in the second half of the 18th century were fundamental to the development of a regional style independent of the Portuguese motherland.

BIBLIOGRAPHY
J. Martins: 'Subsídios para a biografia de Manoel Francisco Lisboa', *Rev. SPAHN*, 4 (1940), pp. 121–53
A. J. R. Russell-Wood: *Manuel Francisco Lisboa* (Belo Horizonte, 1968)

**(2) Antônio Francisco Lisboa** [O Aleijadinho] (*b* Vila Rica [now Ouro Prêto], Minas Gerais, *c.* 1738; *d* Vila Rica, 18 Nov 1814). Architect and sculptor, son of (1) Manoel Francisco Lisboa. An illegitimate son by an African slave, he had a training that was essentially practical, acquired in association with his father and other artists, such as the draughtsman João Gomes Batista (*d* 1788), a former official of the Casa da Moeda in Lisbon, who was appointed in 1751 to the Casa de Fundicão in Vila Rica. Lisboa, also known as Aleijadinho, never left Brazil and, as far as is known, visited the capital Rio de Janeiro only once or twice. His knowledge of contemporary European styles and particularly of elaborate Rococo forms came from ornamental engravings and publications of architectural theory. His sculpture and decorative work shows the influence of southern German prints, particularly those by the KLAUBER brothers, who were active in Augsburg in the mid-18th century and specialized in religious subjects. From 1777 Aleijadinho was stricken by an unidentified disease that led to a progressive deformation of his limbs, including the loss of some of his fingers and toes, hence his nickname 'O Aleijadinho', the little cripple. Nevertheless, he continued to work until the end of his life, and it is remarkable that the greater part of his documented work dates from after the onset of the disease. He died in great poverty and physical suffering, never having accumulated wealth or achieved social prominence commensurate with his talent.

Aleijadinho's extensive work as an architect and sculptor is entirely confined to the province of Minas Gerais in cities such as Ouro Prêto, São João del Rei and Sabará, which were prosperous centres in the 18th century. Other centres of Minas Gerais, such as Mariana, Santa Rita Durão, Catas Altas, Carté and Tiradentes, contain works that he designed or executed. Individual statues are in Brazilian museums (Ouro Prêto, Mus. Inconfidência; São Paulo, Mus. A. Sacra), religious and civic institutions and in private collections.

Aleijadinho's first important commission was probably to design S Francisco de Assis (1766–94), Ouro Prêto, a church for the Ordem Terceira de S Francisco. This is the outstanding example of his highly original architectural style in which, in the ground-plan, sections of curved lines are combined harmoniously as contrasting elements with straight lines. Essentially, this is a compromise between a rectangular Portuguese plan in the Mannerist tradition and a curvilinear plan after Francesco Borromini. Also for S Francisco he designed and carved an extensive series of works, including two pulpits (1771–2), ornamentation of the cupola over the chancel (1773–4), sculptured reliefs on the portal (begun 1774), the lavatorium in the sacristy (1777–9) and the principal retable (1778–94). His splendid decoration of the chancel is considered the finest example of Rococo decoration in Portuguese Brazil.

The principal retable of S Francisco is typical of Aleijadinho's novel altar designs, which had a great influence in the region. The main characteristic is the simplification of the structure, which is stripped of such ornamentation as the canopies and entablatures usual in Portuguese and Brazilian altars at this date and decorated with only a central composition on which all attention is concentrated. In those retables carved by the artist himself, such as that at S Francisco, this central feature expands into a majestic sculptural representation of the Trinity, above the Immaculate Conception, in a lozenge-shaped composition, the effect of which owes much to his outstanding skill as a sculptor. In almost all of his altars, pulpits and fountains the remarkable figurative reliefs of subjects from both the Old and New Testaments have certain medieval traits (Bazin, 1963), such as the Gothic formalism of the figures and the composition of the scenes, which are depicted without regard for perspective.

At the same time as his work at S Francisco, Ouro Prêto, Aleijadinho carried out the external and internal decoration of the churches of the Ordem Terceira do Carmo at Ouro Prêto (portal, sacristy lavatorium and retables of the nave, 1771–1809) and at Sabará (portal, pulpits, choir, nave balustrade and statues of *St Simão Stock* and *St John of the Cross*, 1771–82). In 1774 he

Antônio Francisco Lisboa: sculpture complex for the atrium and great staircase of the pilgrimage sanctuary of Bom Jesus de Matozinhos, Congonhas do Campo, 1800–05

designed S Francisco de Assis, São João del Rei, another church for the Ordem Terceira de S Francisco, which was intended to rival that at Ouro Prêto. Considerably modified in execution, this plan, of which the drawing for the façade exists (Ouro Prêto, Mus. Inconfidência), represents an important development in the adoption of German Rococo forms, principally in the design of the lateral towers. His other works in this church are the sculptured reliefs of the portal and some of the retables (dates uncertain; *see* RETABLE, fig. 5).

The most effective and surprising elements in Aleijadinho's work as an architect are in his façades. The design of the cylindrical towers with their bulbous crowns (as at S Francisco de Assis, Ouro Prêto) are almost without precedent in contemporary European architecture, and the decorative stone reliefs at the centres display, out of doors, all the complexity and delicacy of Rococo motifs previously confined to internal church decoration. Although all these forms, with the exception of the cylindrical towers, can be related to prototypes in Portuguese art, Aleijadinho's use of them, and the graceful and harmonious way he created new combinations, is totally original. His adoption and popularization of the local steatite or soapstone, which is easy to carve, enabled lace-work effects that are impossible with any other kind of stone.

The finest example of Aleijadinho's work as a sculptor is the exceptional ensemble of the pilgrimage church of Bom Jesus de Matozinhos, Congonhas do Campo. The Brazilian version of the Italian *sacro monte*, it has important Portuguese precedents, including the stairways at Lamego (1750–60) and Bom Jesus (1781–1811), Braga. Using assistants from his workshop who are named in receipts

(and whose participation can be recognized on stylistic grounds), between 1796 and 1799 Aleijadinho carried out the first part of the commission, consisting of 64 life size wooden statues for the chapels of the Passos (episodes of the Passion), or via Sacra, in front of the church, arranged in 7 groups: the *Last Supper*, *Agony in the Garden*, *Betrayal*, *Flagellation*, *Crowning with Thorns*, *Road to Calvary* and *Crucifixion*. Between 1800 and 1805 he carved 12 monumental statues of Old Testament prophets for the atrium of the church and the great staircase leading up to it (see fig.). The ensemble of statues is best viewed from one place, but as the worshipper climbs the stairway and sees them from different angles they are so disposed in different groupings that, in the best medieval tradition, he participates in a deeply expressive staging of the sacred drama. Starting from the prophets, whose predictions prefigured the Redemption, the pilgrim passes all the stages of the Passion of Christ, who is represented in seven magnificent images that synthesize all the nuances of human suffering. In these figures Aleijadinho, in final expression of the Baroque, transcended the stylistic models of his time and breathed new spiritual life into religious sculpture at a moment when in European art, in the Age of Enlightenment, the emphasis was predominantly secular.

BIBLIOGRAPHY
J. Bury: 'The Twelve Prophets at Congonhas do Campo', *The Month*, ii/3 (Sept 1949), pp. 152–71
——: 'The Little Cripple', *World Rev.*, n. s., 25 (March 1951), pp. 29–37
——: '"Estilo" Aleijadinho and the Churches of 18th-century Brazil', *Archit. Rev.* [London], cxi (1952), pp. 93–100
——: 'The "Borrominesque" Churches of Colonial Brazil', *A. Bull.*, xxxvii/1 (1955), pp. 26–53
G. Bazin: *L'Architecture religieuse baroque au Brésil*, 2 vols (Paris, 1956–8) [catalogue raisonné]

R. J. F. Brêtas: 'Traços biográficos relativos ao finado Antônio Francisco Lisboa', *Correio Oficial Minas*, 169–70 (1958) [basic biography]

G. Bazin: *Aleijadinho et la sculpture baroque au Brésil* (Paris, 1963)

R. C. Smith: *Congonhas do Campo* (Rio de Janeiro, 1973) [in Port. & Eng.]

S. de Vasconcellos: *Vida e obra de Antônio Francisco Lisboa, o Aleijadinho* (São Paulo, 1979)

M. A. Ribeiro de Oliveira: *O Santuário de Congonhas e a arte do Aleijadinho* (Belo Horizonte, 1981) [in Port., Fr. & Eng.]

F. Jorge: *O Aleijadinho: Sua vida, sua obra, seu gênio* (São Paulo, 1984)

M. A. Ribeiro de Oliveira: *Passos da Paixão: Antônio Francisco Lisboa, o Aleijadinho* (Rio de Janeiro, 1984) [in Port. & Eng.]

MYRIAM A. RIBEIRO DE OLIVEIRA

**Lisbon** [Lisboa]. Capital city of Portugal and a major Atlantic port. Almost 1 million people live within the municipal boundaries, and the metropolitan area of Greater Lisbon probably has more than 2 million inhabitants. The city is situated halfway between Portugal's south coast and its northern frontier with Spain, on the north bank of the Tagus estuary, facing south across a bay and spreading along the shore and inland over hills and valleys. There are many legends concerning the city's foundation, and its name is often interpreted as deriving from Phoenician *Alis Ubbo* ('pleasant bay') or Greek *Olissipo* ('city of Ulysses'). It was established as an important port in Roman times, but, after periods of Visigothic domination (409–714) and Moorish occupation (714–1147), it flourished particularly between the 16th and 18th centuries, when Portugal was at the height of its international influence, and when most of its important buildings were erected. Since the late 18th century it has also been an important centre for the production of ceramics. The city has experienced a number of natural disasters, the most notable being a major earthquake in 1755.

1. History, urban development and art life. 2. Centre of ceramics production. 3. Palacio das Necessidades.

### 1. HISTORY, URBAN DEVELOPMENT AND ART LIFE.

(i) Before *c.* 1500. (ii) *c.* 1500–*c.* 1800. (iii) *c.* 1800 and after.

*(i) Before* c. *1500.* Lisbon was occupied by the Romans in 205 BC and given the status of *municipio*, subject to the *conventus* of Scalabis (now Santarém) further inland. During the Roman period Lisbon probably consisted of a fortified *castrum* and a lower waterside area, although the ruins of a theatre (AD 57) and traces of baths, foundations and buildings on the slopes of the castle hill towards the river provide the only evidence of a centre or forum. The maritime function of the lower part of the town is confirmed, however, by the remains of quays, a network of tunnels (the Rua da Conceição Baths of the reign of Tiberias) and of salting-troughs discovered in 1983 along the former shore-line. To the Visigothic period probably belongs the complex of walls known as the Cerca Moura (Moorish Ring), which were later used or rebuilt by the Moors. These clearly define the position at the summit of the central hill occupied by the Moorish Alcáçova (now the castle of St George) and mark the residential and commercial nucleus areas descending towards the southwest. The urbanized area of Roman times may have contracted by the Moorish period, however, as happened in other towns, since some Roman ruins lie outside the Moorish walls. The principal mosque probably stood on the site of the present Romanesque cathedral (see fig. 1)

1. Lisbon Cathedral by Roberto, mid-12th century; largely rebuilt 1337–47

and near Nero's theatre, confirming the continuity of a central area for civic and religious purposes (forum or equivalent) on this slope.

Roads developed along the east–west axes of the hillside. Possibly to the Roman, but more probably to the Moorish phase belong those from the Porta do Sol to the Porta de Alfofa, near the Alcáçova; from the Porta do Sol to the Porta do Ferro, near the principal mosque; and from the Porta de S Pedro to the Porta do Ferro (commercial sector). To the east a road from Porta de S Pedro entered the Alfama, while another climbed from the Porta do Sol to S Tome and Graça; to the west along the former river-beds from the Porta do Ferro via S Nicolau were the northern extensions towards S Antão and Largo Martim Moniz. From Alfofa a road converged on Martim Moniz via S Cristóvão. In this phase the town probably had no more than 15,000 inhabitants.

After the Reconquest, and especially after Alfonso III established his court in Lisbon in 1256, the suburbs formed during the final stages of the Moorish period were expanded and consolidated; north of the castle was the Mouraria or Moorish quarter; to the east was the Alfama, where Christians and Muslims mixed and where Jews settled; but the greatest growth took place in the area between the Porta do Ferro and the present Baixa, spreading up along the slope of S Catarina and S Francisco, where there was more free ground for commercial building and direct access to the river and port. At the turn of the 13th century, with the reign of King Diniz (*reg* 1279–1325), the importance of the Baixa area was emphasized by the care given to its development. The new Rua Nova dos Ferros was a broad east–west development spreading towards the slope of S Francisco. The northern Santana slope, between the S Antão and Martim Moniz axes, was planned with some symmetry, as later was that of Rua S Catarina (the future Chiado). The Rua Nova running along the line of the coast, and the Rua S Catarina, following the high line of the ridge and turning with the slope away from the shore, were the two new arms of urban expansion parallel to the river, extending the growth of the city out to Santos, Alcântara and Belém.

Simultaneously with this came a more organic growth. Consolidation and further new building followed the creation of parishes and the settlement of monastic orders, which developed land granted to them and attracted religious foundations. Franciscans, Carmelites and Trinitarians erected conventual buildings on the slopes to the west of the developed urban area, while the Augustinian Order of S Vicente, the Mónicas and the Graça Convent settled to the east of the city. Following the example of the Paço Real (14th century), built in the Alcáçova, the nobility began to build prestigious residences, usually sited close to the gates or on the outskirts of the city; examples include the Palácio da Rosa (16th century; near the Mouraria), the Palacio dos Almadas (1467; on the way to S Antão) and the palace of the Marquês de Alegrete (c. 1694; on the way to Martim Moniz). Most houses of the late medieval and Renaissance periods, however, were of two or three storeys, with very low ceilings (1.9 m). A few examples have survived from the 15th and 16th centuries; they are usually rather crudely built (as in the districts of S Tome or Encarnação) and with projecting floors overhanging the street (Alfama, Mouraria) or with pitched roofs meeting in a point over the front (Santana). *Rossios* and *largos*, respectively larger and smaller open spaces, provided room for movement and congregation and were sited by gateways in the city walls or beside public buildings such as churches and hospitals. The most important of these squares was near the S Antão gates, the site of both the large Misericórdia Hospital and a food market, used as a fairground and for festivities and public celebrations. It marked the clearly defined frontier between city and countryside.

The boundaries of the city in the last third of the 14th century were defined by an important new ring of fortifications erected between 1373 and 1375 by King Ferdinand I (*reg* 1367–83) to defend the city in the war between Portugal and Castile. These walls indicate clearly how Lisbon, which now had nearly 40,000 inhabitants and had far outgrown its limits of two centuries earlier, had expanded along the river, more towards the west than to the east. The plan shows two areas fanning out from the old Cerca Moura, making the total perimeter c. 5400 m, the west side containing about twice the area of the east. The Cerca Fernandina (Fernandine Ring), as the new fortifications came to be called, protected the convents, churches and palaces, excluded the Mouraria area to the north and the shipyards to the south, and clearly restated the 'sacred' and enclosed conception of the medieval town.

*(ii) c. 1500–c. 1800.* The most interesting and innovative period in Lisbon's development came between the beginning of the 16th century and the end of the 18th. This was the result not only of the city's status as a centre of overseas trade in the wake of a period of maritime expansion but also of reconstruction necessitated by various natural catastrophes, of which the earthquake of 1755 was the greatest. The population passed 100,000 during the 16th century, making Lisbon the largest city in the Iberian peninsula and one of the largest in Europe. However, due to the annexation of Portugal by Spain (1580–1640) and the absence of the court during those years, and also to the decline of Portuguese overseas trade and the loss of human life through disasters, population growth stabilized and did not exceed 180,000 until the end of the 18th century.

After almost a century of maritime exploration by the Portuguese, beginning in 1415, in 1497 Vasco da Gama opened up the sea route to India. The continuous stream of exotic spices that subsequently arrived in the city meant that the effective centre shifted to the waterside area of the Ribeira, outside the city walls. Many foreign artists, especially from the Netherlands, settled in Lisbon around this time. There a new and vast square was built, the Terreiro do Paço, including the Alfândegas (customs houses), the Casa da India and the royal residence, which was transferred here from the walled town. It complemented and rivalled in importance as an urban centre the Rossio with the Misericórdia Hospital to the north; its activity was directed towards the sea, while the Rossio related to the agricultural, food-producing hinterland. Both provided space for great celebrations: bull-fights, receptions, festivities and later the *autos-da-fé* of the Inquisition (established in 1536).

Development was also taking place at Belém, a village to the west near the river bar and the sea, where King Manuel I (*see* AVIZ, (6)) carried out an elaborate programme of buildings that symbolized the new era. Most significant were the Hieronymite monastery (1501–5; *see* PORTUGAL, fig. 3) and the elegant military defensive tower on the shore, Belém Tower (1515–20; *see also* BELÉM (i)). These two buildings heralded the new style of architecture which, in transition from Gothic to Renaissance, was symbolic of the Portuguese discoveries: the MANUELINE STYLE, exuberant and decorative but also original and assertive in its mass.

From the first quarter of the 16th century there spread along the west shore of the estuary, outside the gates of the Cerca Fernandina, the Vila Nova de Andrade, now known as the Bairro Alto (High Quarter), at first built close to the river, then rising to the top of the hill. It is possible that building in this new area was begun or at least accelerated as a result of a serious earth tremor in 1531. Built at a time when the attraction of trade with 'the Indies' was bringing more people to the city, leading to increased pressure for modernization (straighter roads, more regular blocks and larger plots for patios, gardens and *quintas* or manor houses), the Bairro Alto can be called the planning equivalent of the Manueline style in architecture. It was developed as a privileged area for dwellings of the new classes, from sea-pilots to merchants, directly concerned with the expansion. Subsequently, however, its network of streets became denser and its inhabitants more working-class, a process that continued until the 19th century. Among painters active in Lisbon in the late 16th century, Italian influence became evident, notably in the work of GASPAR DIAS, DIOGO TEIXEIRA and the Spaniard FRANCISCO VENEGAS. In the early 17th century many of the most important artists were members of the Irmandade de S Lucas, a society formed in 1602 and centred on the Anunciada Church (see PORTUGAL, §III).

Two transformations in the 16th century changed the enclosed atmosphere of the medieval city into the openness of a more modern city involved in international and trans-oceanic activities. These were the occupation of reclaimed land outside the walls for facilities required by the overseas expansion and for the palatial dwellings of the leading merchants (as well as for the king and many prominent nobles) and the development planned for the new middle class connected with commerce and maritime trade. Although expansion into the countryside did not continue at the same rate in the 17th century, due to limitations imposed by the annexation by Spain of the Portuguese crown, nevertheless the nobility and the classes enriched by maritime trade settled on the outskirts all round the city, creating *quintas* and building houses in the austere and restrained style that has been described as *Arquitectura Chã* (or Plain Style; see also PORTUGAL, §II, 2(ii)). This lasted into the 18th century and was characteristically Portuguese in its traditionalism. This phase of Lisbon's consolidation could be described as a kind of de-urbanization, a mixing of urban and rural development; it took place above all along the routes radiating from the old walled city northwards and along the shore. Planning was irregular, with large sectors of the city still engaged in rural activities but surrounded by other, more urban areas; this state of affairs persisted until well into the 19th century.

Lisbon did not progress to a commercial and pre-industrial economy in the 17th century; instead, it gradually moved away from the European model then developing in Vienna, Paris and London and settled into an *ancien régime* that was only disturbed a century later. On the other hand its originality strongly influenced many cities in Portuguese territories overseas, combining in a unique and imaginative way with a series of exotic environments to create such cities as Rio de Janeiro, Goa and Luanda. A recurrent and dominant feature was the dichotomy of a 'high' residential quarter and a 'low' commercial and maritime quarter, always set against the background of a 'pleasant bay', of the kind that the Phoenicians had found at Lisbon. In painting, Lisbon was the centre of the Portuguese Baroque, with such artists as ANDRÉ REINOSO and JOSÉ DE AVELAR REBELO both producing important works for the church of S Roque (see PORTUGAL, §III).

At the beginning of the 18th century the impetus for overseas exploration was reinforced by the discovery of precious metals in Ouro Preto, Brazil. Reaction in Lisbon took the form of a new style of building, coinciding with the diffusion of the Baroque in Portugal, the installation of modern supply infrastructures in the new planned extensions to the city and modernization by rebuilding. The reign of King John V (1706–50) brought the construction of many splendid palaces and gardens in the immediate neighbourhood of the city, culminating in the palace-convent of Mafra (1717–35; for illustration see MAFRA and LUDOVICE, JOÃO FREDERICO). Many large town houses

were also built within the city, and the monumental aqueduct of Águas Livres was completed (1729–48) by MANUEL DA MAIA and CUSTÓDIO VIEIRA. Its 14 pointed arches running north-west across the Alcântara Valley were impressive enough for the aqueduct to be compared with Roman construction and helped supply the city with the piped water it needed for fountains and public water-spouts. These were all magnificent works, but the reign of John V lacked overall vision. This was provided, however, under his successor in a time of emergency.

The earthquake and fire of November 1755 destroyed practically all the Baixa area, the centre of Lisbon, and made possible a planned action led by the group of military engineers who had been active since the previous reign. Working under King Joseph's minister, the future 1st Marquês de POMBAL, and within a rigid and coherent scheme of blocks, squares and buildings for the rebuilt areas, Manuel da Maia, EUGÉNIO DOS SANTOS and Carlos Mardel were able to introduce the much-needed functional modernization of Lisbon (see fig. 2). The rebuilding of Lisbon was a typical example of Enlightenment urban planning. There was wise exploitation of the traditional elements of the city; the Rossio (Praça Dom Pedro IV) and the Terreiro do Paço (now renamed Praça do Comércio; see fig. 3) were more precisely defined and rebuilt in the same locations, as were also the Rua Nova dos Ferros (now Rua do Comércio) and a series of former cross streets. Religious buildings were rebuilt (some of them with new decoration by PEDRO ALEXANDRINO CARVALHO) and realigned to fit the new urban network and away from their former orientation towards the east. Indeed, despite an apparent respect for the former structure, the axis of the city as a whole changed from its previous east–west alignment to become largely north–south in direction; the most important of the new streets built in the grid system were the Rua do Ouro, Rua da Prata and Rua Augusta running north–south between the Rossio and the new Praça do Comércio.

The style of the new Pombaline buildings was derived in part from the austere, standardized constructions of the Plain style, which combined classicizing and regional characteristics (their form defined by pilasters and cornices, with large gently sloped tiled roofs). They acquired a new individuality, however, from the prefabricated and anti-seismic systems they incorporated and the new scale and dimension of the buildings, comprising apartment blocks of four or five storeys plus a mansard attic (see also POMBALINE STYLE).

*(iii) c. 1800 and after.* The end of the 18th century and the first half of the 19th constituted a period of crisis and paralysis in the city's urban growth. Fundamental was the fact that Lisbon was definitely only a minor European capital, the centre of a poor country on the periphery of industrialization; other factors included the transfer of the court to Brazil following the Napoleonic invasion in 1807 and prolonged civil strife between Conservatives and Liberals. The rebuilding of the city centre that had taken place during the second half of the previous century continued at a slower pace and was accompanied by decentralization to the Baixa, where the Chiado (the area of the old Rua S Catarina, to the west) had acquired

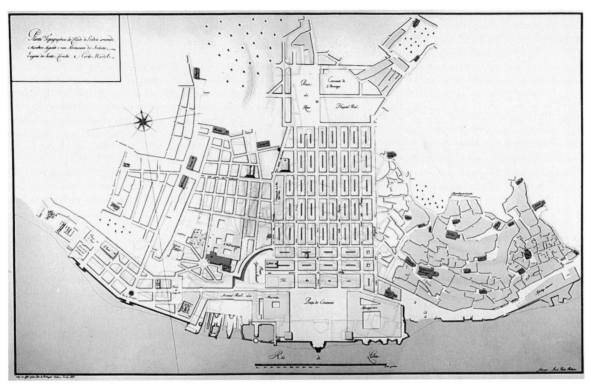

2. Lisbon, plan by Eugénio dos Santos for the rebuilding of the central Baixa area after the earthquake of 1755, 610×890 mm (Lisbon, Museu da Cidade)

3. Lisbon, Terreiro do Paço (now Praça do Comércio), with the bronze equestrian statue of *Joseph, King of Portugal*, by Joaquim Machado de Castro, erected 1755

residential and cultural prestige with the new Opera House (the Teatro S Carlos, 1792) and the Grémio Literario (Literary Guild; founded 1846). The gardens and parks near the city centre also assumed importance, especially the promenade called the Passeio Público (1763), conceived during the Pombaline period and favoured by the court. These projects indicated the new direction of development towards the north, beyond Valverde, and the sloping terraces of the S Pedro de Alcântara gardens to the west or those of Torel to the east show the persistence of old Lisbon's image as a city of hills. Following the earthquake and the destruction of the royal palace (Palacio da Ribeira), and so as to avoid the frequent epidemics, the site of the royal residence was moved from the riverside to the western edge of the city, to the palaces of Ajuda (built from 1802) and Necessidades (1743–50; *see* §3 below).

An important event in the art life of Lisbon in the first half of the 19th century was the foundation there of the Academia de Belas-Artes in 1836. A parallel academy was also opened in Oporto at the same time, helping to focus artistic activity on these two cities, but only with a new era of relative political stability after 1852 was there a new phase of expansion in Lisbon. An important figure at this time was the French architect PIERRE JOSEPH PEZERAT, who was appointed Engineer and Architect to Lisbon Municipality in 1852. The move towards industrialization gradually gained strength, railway lines were laid down to encircle the city and link it with the provinces (1885), and the urban area increased with the construction of a new ring-road (1852–64). This network of infrastructures had the effect of reaffirming the basic roots and symmetry of the city: the two valleys, Alcântara to the west and Chelas to the east, served both the railway and the encircling road. The two valleys, abundant in water, became the twin poles of the burgeoning industry, comprising dormitory towns (*vilas*) for the new working class and the two cemeteries (Prazeres to the west and Alto de S João to the east). Development on previously reclaimed land was also extended and the area replanned, with the improvement of the embankment between Alcântara and the centre (continuing the old dynamic of growth towards the west) and to a lesser extent of the area from the centre to Chelas. In 1887 the plan for the new port, its technology dependent on new industrial processes, was awarded to a Frenchman, LOUIS HERSENT. A new industrial dynamic was brought to the city's development by this decision, which coincided with the northward thrust of the broad residential avenues (1879–85), involving zoning of industrial, commercial and residential properties, and a model of radial (and multidirectional) growth was evolved. The northward expansion to the north of the city that had been anticipated by the axes of the Pombaline development was thus finally realized.

French influence at this time was evident in all the arts: in painting, the naturalism of the Barbizon school, for example, made a particular impact on ANTONIO SILVA PORTO and other members of the Grupo do Leão, which held its first exhibition in Lisbon in 1881 (for illustration of the group's members *see* BORDALO PINHEIRO, (2)). In urban planning the first great boulevard to be built on the French model was the Avenida da Liberdade (1879), which took the place of the Passeio Público. Its construction marked the success of private investment in residential development carried out by a new capitalist bourgeoisie. On the east side of the Avenida, the Bairro Camões, named to honour the tricentenary of the death of Portugal's greatest poet, was begun in 1880, and on the other side rose the Barata Salgeiro estate. A large park, called the Parque Eduardo VII, terminated the upper end of the Avenida da Liberdade, curving north-east towards the high land beyond. At the same time and on a humbler scale the future Avenida Almirante Reis was begun to the east, which reinforced the traditional Lisbon contrast of the principal and prestigious west and the secondary and less well-off east. Another phase of residential expansion completed in 1910 (designed by RESSANO GARCIA) was known as the Avenidas Novas and provided a continuation on the same axis as the Avenida da Liberdade of the extensive new Avenida da República.

This development, although based on the reconstruction of Paris, was entirely distinctive in Lisbon, since the *rotundas* (circuses), tree-lined avenues and generously proportioned quarters, with large town houses alternating with apartment blocks, were built in a rural area, rather than elements in the renovation of an existing urban structure. The new areas were served by amenities constructed in iron, such as markets, garages, the many bridges and viaducts needed on the hilly ground to supplement the old network of roads, and tunnels, which emerged in the Largo das Palmeiras, in Avenida Duque de Ávila and in Rua António A. Aguiar. A modern network of electric trams along the principal arteries connected them to the old centre, and public funiculars were used to overcome steep alterations in level. Land reclaimed from the river, which became the site of industries, port warehouses and workshops, was also inevitably developed into new residential areas for the middle class who wanted to settle farther inland to the north of the old coastal suburb. The city thus lost some of its traditional character as it was modernized in accordance with contemporary European models. Some noteworthy individual buildings were, however, designed by VENTURA TERRA and others.

By 1910, the year of the Republican revolution, the population of Lisbon, which in 1871 had been only 200,000, had risen to 450,000. The period after the revolution, however, was one of crisis, which halted expansion. The more radical modernist currents, which broke with tradition throughout Europe between World War I and 1925, had little effect upon Portuguese literature and the arts, although Surrealism had a number of adherents later in the century, after World War II (*see* PORTUGAL, §III, 3). Since the state was bankrupt and the political situation unstable, urbanism was confined to utopian plans for public parks, the beginnings of some 'Bairros Sociais' (social quarters) for the poor that were never completed, and the continuation of outmoded 19th-century architecture, though without the quality and building materials of 19th-century construction. Building in the port areas and along the Avenidas continued slowly and with enormous difficulty.

The Estado Novo, the authoritarian regime established by António de Oliveira Salazar (1889–1970) between 1926 and 1968, sought to promote a new image of Lisbon as capital of an empire but depended on the exploitation of the African colonies, the weakness of the politically divided middle class and the creation of an image of a contented rural population. Lisbon resumed the rapid rhythm of growth of the late 19th century, based on a policy of public works that took advantage of cheap labour and the desire for stability. New institutions, such as the university, were begun, telephone and radio systems were introduced and an airport and motorways were built, all contributing to the city's adaptation to the 20th century. In charge of these efforts was Duarte Pacheco (1900–43), who was president of the Lisbon Municipality and the Ministerio das Obras Públicas. Pacheco initiated a vast programme of public housing, based on extensive compulsory purchase schemes, and contributed, after a phase of accepting the most innovative purist forms of modernism and the use of reinforced concrete (1930–38), to the creation of a more national architectural style, *Português Suave*. This was a mixture of classicizing and neo-18th-century vocabulary, which was used on an urban scale in prestigious works such as the Praça do Areeiro (1938–48) by LUIS CRISTINO DA SILVA. The most important project of this period, however, was the Plano de Urbanização de Lisboa, carried out between 1938 and 1948, under which a system of circular and radial roads divided up the whole city, with areas set aside for schools, green spaces and social and industrial purposes in an approach still influenced by French academic urbanism. The scheme was drawn up by the urban planner De Gröer (*b*1882). Another influential planner of this period was Faria da Costa (1906–71), who in such plans as those for Restelo (1940) and Alvalade (1948) combined traditional conceptions of neighbourhood units with more advanced ideas, based on the Athens Charter, the 'manifesto' of the Modern Movement. These included 'open blocks', pedestrian zones and the provision of small gardens between residential blocks.

In the 1950s, parallel with the decline of the Salazar regime, urban growth became increasingly uncontrolled and rapidly deteriorated into suburban sprawl, with substandard dwellings devoid of architectural quality being built on land previously occupied by *quintas*, and new suburbs springing up. By the 1960s the population of Lisbon's metropolitan area, which in the 1940s had been *c.* 700,000, had doubled. Public resources for the extra housing needed were inadequate, and the isolated high-rise blocks in the green belt (Olivais, for 60,000 persons, by Carlos Duarte (*b*1926) and José Rafael Botelho (*b*1923) and later Chelas and Telheiras) were the only large areas of planned housing.

At the end of the 20th century Lisbon's growth continued to be guided by the Plano Director (1967), which renewed the ideas of the Plano de Urbanização de Lisboa but without any appreciation of the change in scale. Planning and administration were inadequate to deal with the accelerated industrial and residential growth between the 1950s and 1970s, and, as a result, the suburban structure had virtually disintegrated by the time of the revolution of 1974 that led to political democracy. In the following decade there was an unparalleled increase in unauthorized construction, in buildings of insufficient dimensions and lacking adequate infrastructures, problems that were aggravated by the settlement of many repatriates

from the African ex-colonies. The metropolitan underground network also proved inadequate to the problems caused by this uncontrolled development. Restoration works were undertaken in the historic city centre, but a more pressing need continued to be the reorganization and control of the now vast and diffuse metropolitan area, recognized by the appointment of a planning director in 1993.

### BIBLIOGRAPHY

R. Proença: *Guia de Portugal: I Lisboa e arredores* (Lisbon, 1924)
A. Vieira da Silva: *A cerca moura de Lisboa* (Lisbon, 1939)
——: *A cerca fernandina de Lisboa* (Lisbon, 1948)
M. da Conceição Oliveira Marques: 'Introdução ao estudo do desenvolvimento urbano de Lisboa, 1879–1938', *Rev. Arquit.* [Lisbon], 112 (1969), pp. 266–75; 113 (1970), pp. 5–7; 119 (1971), pp. 34–9; 120 (1971), pp. 72–7; 124 (1971–2), pp. 38–40; 125 (1972), pp. 74–8
R. Soeiro de Brito: *Lisboa: Esboço geográfico* (Lisbon, 1976)
J.-A. França: *Lisboa pombalina e o iluminismo* (Lisbon, 1977)
M. J. Madeira Rodrigues: *Tradição, transição e mudança: A produção do Espaço urbano na Lisboa oitocentista* (Lisbon, 1978)
*Guia urbanístico e arquitectónico de Lisboa* (Lisbon, 1987)
F. Santana and E. Sucena: *Dicionário da história de Lisboa* (Lisbon, 1994)
I. Molta: *O livro de Lisboa* (Lisbon, 1994)

JOSÉ MANUEL FERNANDES

2. CENTRE OF CERAMICS PRODUCTION. The first important faience factory to be established in Lisbon was the REAL FÁBRICA DO RATO in 1767. Under the directorship of TOMÁS BRUNETTO and his successor SEBASTIÃO INÁCIO DE ALMEIDA, a distinctive body of wares was produced, including tureens shaped into hens, roebucks' heads and geese (see fig. 4) and blue-and-white tableware. In the late 18th century the Real Fábrica da Bica do Sapato was founded; it was also known as the Fábrica do Capitão-Mor due to its location on the site of that name. There is extant only one oval dish marked with the name of this factory. Other pieces attributed to the Bica do Sapato are characterized by their high technical standard and their unmistakable colour scheme of dark olive-green, yellow, orange, blue and manganese-purple. Decorative schemes include land- and seascapes within panels and medallions in bold, single brushstrokes, which were probably inspired by contemporary engravings and by works by the French artist JEAN PILLEMENT who was in Portugal in 1780. There are stylistic similarities with the ware produced at the Real Fábrica de Custodio Ferreira Braga, Lisbon, during the same period. In 1835 the Real Fábrica do Rato was auctioned due to increasing financial and administrative difficulties.

The Fábrica de Cerâmica Constância was founded in 1836 under the trade name Companhia Fabril de Louça and was administered by Inácio Augusto da Silva Lisboa. The factory was renamed the Companhia Constância when it was taken over by a new company in 1842 and was also known as the Fábrica dos Marianos and the Fábrica das Janelas Verdes. In 1849 the Fábrica Cerâmica Viúva Lamego Lda. was founded by António da Costa Lamego (*d*1876). Initially it produced ordinary, red earthenwares, but in 1863 it began to successfully manufacture faience, and by 1876 the factory had 5 kilns and nearly 80 workers. A steam-engine was installed in 1878. In addition to red-clay pottery, painted and white household ware and artistic faience, production also included tiles and industrial construction material, all of which were exported to Africa and Brazil.

4. Faience tureen in the shape of a goose with the coat of arms of the Marquês de Pombal, h. 340 mm, monogrammed by Tomás Brunetto, Real Fábrica do Rato, Lisbon, 18th century (Lisbon, Museu Nacional de Arte Antiga)

The Fábrica de Cerâmica Constância has been particularly associated with the Bohemian artist Venceslas Cifka (d 1883) who worked there in 1876–7. His delicately executed polychrome wares often featured neo-classical subjects. Of particular note is an elaborately decorated blue violin featuring medallion portraits of the Italian composers Alessandro Scarlatti (1660–1725) and Arcangelo Corelli (1653–1713), the royal coat of arms and neoclassical figures (Lisbon, Mus. N. A. Ant.). Both creamware and black basalts were also manufactured during the late 19th century. At the beginning of the 20th century faience and tiles were painted by José António Jorge Pinto (1876–1945). Artists at the Fábrica Cerâmica Viúva Lamego Lda. working at the beginning of the 20th century included José Maria Pereira jr (1841–1921). Jorge Nicholson Moore Barradas (1894–1971) worked there from the late 1920s until 1970. In the late 20th century artists associated with the factory included Querubim Lapa (b 1925), JÚLIO POMAR and VIEIRA DA SILVA. Artists at the Fábrica de Cerâmica Constância in the 1920s included Viriato Silva (b 1874) and the Italian Leopaldi Baptista. In 1963 the factory was rejuvenated by Francisco d'Almeida, and artists working there subsequently have included Rafael Salinas Calado, João Charters de Almeida e Silva (b 1935), Joaquim da Costa Rebocho (b 1912) and Nuno José de Siqueira (b 1929), producing both wares and tiles.

BIBLIOGRAPHY
J. Queirós: Cerâmica portuguesa (Lisbon, 1907, rev. in 2 vols, 1948/R 1987)
R. dos Santos: Oito séculos de arte portuguesa: História e espírito, iii (Lisbon, 1970)
A. de Sandão: Faiança portuguesa, séculos XVIII, XIX (Oporto, 1976)
                                        BERNADETTE NELSON

3. PALACIO DAS NECESSIDADES. The original plan for the palace, built on the site of a chapel dedicated to Nossa Senhora das Necessidades, was probably by the Portuguese architect Custódio Vieira, although it has been attributed variously to the Italian Giovanni Servandoni, to Eugenio dos Santos and to Caetano Tomás de Sousa (fl 1718–64). The Palacio first served as the residence of the brothers of King John V (reg 1706–50) but was later used to house visiting dignitaries, such as the Prince of Wales (the future George IV of Great Britain and Ireland) and his brother the Duke of Sussex. The Duke of Wellington also inhabited the Palacio after 1808 as Commander-in-Chief of the Anglo-Portuguese army.

In 1833 Pedro, Duke of Braganza, undertook the first major alterations, replacing the tiled floors of the bedrooms and reception rooms with wooden boards. The palace became the home of the Duke's daughter, Maria II (reg 1826 and 1834–53), both with her first husband, Auguste de Beauharnais, Duke of Leuchtenberg, and after his death with her second husband, Ferdinand of Saxe-Coburg-Gotha (Ferdinand II of Portugal, see BRAGANZA, (13). In 1844–6 improvements and alterations were made by the royal architect, POSSIDÓNIO DA SILVA, and Giuseppe Cinatti, the Italian scenographer at the Teatro S Carlos, took charge of the decoration, including the stuccowork and the carving. António Manuel da Fonseca, who had studied in Rome, was commissioned to paint the interior: the Etruscan Room in the Pompeian style, the dining room, with its hunting and fishing scenes, and the ceiling of the Red Room are good examples of his work. The most beautiful paintings, however, are in the Renaissance Room and are by Cinatti, who painted buildings of different architectural styles over the doors and in medallions on the ceiling; these include views of the Palacio de Pena, Sintra, before the enlargements made by Ferdinand, its façade and its Manueline cloister. Local craftsmen were commissioned to provide furniture for the state rooms (see PORTUGAL, §VI).

Following the death of Maria in 1853, further restoration was carried out by King Peter V (reg 1853–61), and more furniture, plate and objets d'art were acquired in Lisbon and Paris in preparation for the King's marriage to Estephania of Hohenzollern-Sigmaringen. The Queen lived there only briefly before her death in 1859, however, and her husband died in 1861. His brother Luís, who succeeded him (reg 1861–89), occupied the Palacio de Ajuda, and it was only in 1889 that the Palacio das Necessidades became a royal residence again with the accession of Charles (reg 1889–1908). Further improvements and redecorations were planned, including a gallery leading to the reception rooms (completed 1905) and a new banqueting hall (1903–8), by Francisco Vilaça, but these decorations were left incomplete in 1910, when the monarchy fell from power. The palace's contents were dispersed among museums, including the Museu de Arte Antiga in Lisbon. The building subsequently served as the headquarters of the Lisbon army and as the Ministry of Foreign Affairs.

BIBLIOGRAPHY

M. Côrte-Real: *O Palácio das Necessidades* (Lisbon, 1983)

MANUEL CÔRTE-REAL

**Lisch, Jean-Juste-Gustave** (*b* Alençon, Orne, 10 June 1828; *d* Paris, 1910). French architect. His prolific and eclectic oeuvre was unified by a lifelong desire to resolve the various theoretical strains of his training. He was a student of Henri Labrouste and Léon Vaudoyer at the Ecole des Beaux-Arts, Paris, and of Eugène-Emmanuel Viollet-le-Duc, under whose influence he worked in the Commission des Monuments Historiques in the late 1850s. Lisch restored the churches of St Benoît sur Loire (1865) and St Germain des Prés (1868–71), both near Orléans, and was named Diocesan Architect for Luçon in 1857, Amiens in 1874 and Angoulême in 1880; for Luçon he designed the seminary and the Gothic Revival bishop's palace (both 1872). While his chapel for the Couvent des Oiseaux in Paris (designed 1865; built 1873–6) synthesized classical and Byzantine elements in the manner of Vaudoyer, his designs for the Exposition Universelle of 1889 and railway stations, including the new Gare Saint-Lazare (1886–9), take up Viollet-le-Duc's challenge to incorporate new materials, especially iron and glass. In his small station on the Champs de Mars (1875–7) and his Ecole Commerciale in the Rue Trudaine, Paris (1862), Lisch embellished the system of rectilinear framing with glazed brick and ceramic tile infill propagated by Pierre Chabat's *La Brique et la terre-cuite* (Paris, 1881); in the small stations for the Exposition Universelle of 1900, notably the Gare des Invalides, this system is masked by the monumental classical decoration of the exhibition's main buildings. An important collection of original Lisch material is in Musée d'Orsay, Paris.

BIBLIOGRAPHY

C. Daly: 'Ecole des Beaux-Arts de Paris: Concours mensuel de 2e classe', *Rev. Gén. Archit.*, x (1852), cols 42–3, 146–7, pl. 9

R. Lisch: 'Les Gares de Paris et Juste Lisch', *Les Grandes Gares parisiennes du XIXe siècle*, ed. K. Bowle (Paris, 1987), pp. 159–69

J.-M. Leniaud: *Les cathédrales au XIXe siècle* (Paris, 1993), p. 737

BARRY BERGDOLL

**Li Shan** [*zi* Zongyang; *hao* Futang, Fu-t'ang; Aodaoren; Momoren] (*b* Xinghua, Jiangsu Province, 1686; *d* Yangzhou, 1760). Chinese painter. He was born into a wealthy family and received a sound classical education. Wei Lingchang, his first painting instructor, taught him landscape in the style of the ORTHODOX SCHOOL, and with Wang Yuan, a female relative and painter from Gaoyou, Jiangsu Province, he studied flower-and-bird painting. At the age of 22 he passed the provincial civil service examinations and two years later he was granted an audience with the Kangxi emperor (*reg* 1662–1723) after having presented a poem at the latter's 60th birthday. Chosen as an attendant at the Nan shufang ('Southern imperial study'; a literary advisory body to the emperor), he studied the style of Huang Quan and Xu Xi from Jiang Tingxi (1669–1732), a major scholar–painter of the court.

Several years later Li Shan left Beijing and returned to Xinhua, where he remained politically inactive for the next 20 years and concentrated on painting. He returned to the capital once, ostensibly to study painting with GAO QIPEI, who was best known for finger painting, before moving to Yangzhou where he was impressed by the works of DAOJI. It appears to have been during this phase that his idiosyncratic style, with its expressive brushwork, evolved, and at the same time he began to move in Yangzhou's artistic circles. In Yangzhou, Li Shan's works were forged even during his lifetime, and he displayed strong displeasure at the practice, worried that his reputation would be spoilt by inferior forgeries. His acquaintances in Yangzhou included wealthy merchants and patrons, such as Wang Xiwen and He Wucun; seal-carvers, including Shen Feng; and painters of such calibre as Zheng Xie, Huang Shen and Li Fangying (1695–1754).

In 1736 Li Shan returned to Beijing, this time probably to take the *jinshi* examination. Despite failing, he was made magistrate of Linzi, Shandong Province, in 1737, and in the following year he was transferred to Teng xian, also in Shandong Province. In 1740 he was dismissed and returned to Xinhua, where he constructed the Fuou guan

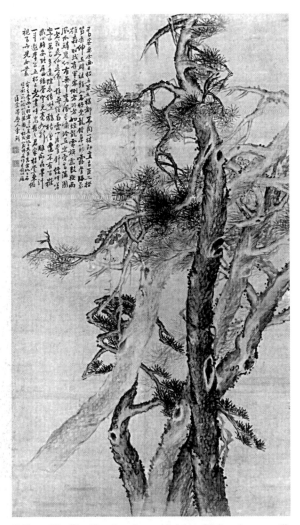

Li Shan: *Five Pine Trees*, hanging scroll, ink and light colours on silk, 1602×890 mm, 18th century (Tokyo, National Museum)

(Floating Lodge) in the south of the city. By the winter of 1745 it was recorded that Li Shan had returned to Yangzhou, selling paintings to make a living.

Li Shan's painting style is intensely vibrant, if also casual. Equally bold is his calligraphy in the *Xingcao* (running cursive) script, a fitting complement to the painted images. In painting, his skilful use of colour washes was probably influenced by Jian Tingxi. However, it was his early departure from the court that left him free to explore a more vigorous approach to painting inspired by the uninhibited style of such artists as Daoji, ZHU DA and Gao Qipei. Gao Qipei's finger painting did not appear to find favour with Li, although it appears that he experimented with this technique even before his discipleship. Of Li Shan's paintings, *Five Pines* (see fig.), which was acclaimed by his contemporaries, is perhaps the best known; several versions are extant. A number of albums dealing with flowers, plants and other miscellaneous subjects also bear his signature. Li's artistic heritage was continued by his disciples, Chen Fu and Dai Li.

*See also* YANGZHOU SCHOOL.

BIBLIOGRAPHY

Li Dou: *Yangzhou huafang lu* [A record of the painted pleasure boats of Yangzhou] (*c.* 1795/*R* Taipei, 1969)
Jiang Biaolin: *Molin jinhua* [Comments on contemporary painters] (Shanghai, 1852/*R* Taipei, 1975)
*Li Futang huahui pingtiao* [The painting of Li Shan] (Wuxi, 1928)
Gu Linwen: *Yangzhou bajia shiliao* [Historical materials on the eight eccentrics of Yangzhou] (Shanghai, 1962)
Chang Wan-li and Hu Jen-mou: *The Selected Painting and Calligraphy of the Eight Eccentrics of Yangchow* (Hong Kong, 1969)
*Hachidai sanjin Yoshu hakkei* [Bada Shanren and the eight eccentrics of Yangzhou] (1978), xi of *Suiboku bijutsu daiklan* [Survey of ink painting] (Tokyo, 1975–8)
Yang Xin: *Yangzhou baguai* [The eight eccentrics of Yangzhou] (Beijing, 1981)
*Li Shan huahui ce* [Catalogue of paintings by Li Shan], Sichuan Prov. Mus. cat. (Shanghai, 1984)
*Paintings by Yangzhou Artists of the Qing Dynasty from the Palace Museum* (exh. cat., ed. Mayching Kao; Hong Kong, Chin. U., A.G., 1984–5)
Ju-hsi Chou and C. Brown: *The Elegant Brush: Chinese Painting under the Qianlong Emperor, 1735–1795* (Phoenix, 1985)
Lin Xiuwei: *Yangzhou huapai/The Yang-chou School of Painting* (Taipei, 1985) [Chin., with Eng. captions]

JU-HSI CHOU, WAI FONG ANITA SIU

**Li Shida** [Li Shih-ta; *zi* Yanghuai] (*b* Suzhou, Jiangsu Province; *fl c.* 1580–1620). Chinese painter. He earned his living by painting both landscapes and figures and was heir to the late WU SCHOOL painting tradition. His paintings display an impressive range of styles and subjects from literati themes, as in *Gazing Out from a Pavilion in the Mountains* (ink and colour on paper; 1618; Tokyo, Seikadō Bunko), to more careful and conservative compositions of figures in landscapes, such as *Tao Yuanming Appreciating Chrysanthemums* (ink and colour on silk; 1619; Ann Arbor, U. MI, Mus. A.). The former demonstrate a subtle and accomplished handling of brush and ink with minimal use of colour, capturing the naturalistic aspects of mountain scenery. The latter are tightly constructed parodies of inherited conventions. Usually, the composition is divided into three sections from bottom to top with an exaggerated middle ground of water, a practice that dates back to the Yuan period (1279–1368). In the Ann Arbor painting, the water is delineated by the archaic fishnet pattern that originated in the Tang period

(AD 618–907). A decorative effect is achieved through the repetition of the waves and the repeated application of twisting hemp-fibre texture strokes (*pima cun*) to describe the rock surfaces. The elongated proportions of the scroll and use of attenuated pine trees reflect the influence of Wu School artists Wen Zhengming and Qiu Ying. The painting depicts the famous poet–statesman Tao Yuanming (AD 365–427), who became the archetypal literatus, idealized because he retired early from his government position to pursue his own interests of writing and growing chrysanthemums. The figures are drawn in fine lines and colours with mannered and distorted features and proportions. The heads appear strangely flattened; the figures are portly and humorous. Li's bizarre figure style influenced his contemporary Sheng Maoye.

BIBLIOGRAPHY

*DMB*: 'Li Shih-ta'
J. Cahill: *The Distant Mountains: Chinese Painting of the Late Ming Dynasty, 1570–1644* (New York and Tokyo, 1982)
*Deities, Emperors, Ladies and Literati: Figure Painting of the Ming and Qing Dynasties* (exh. cat. by A. R. M. Hyland, Birmingham, AL, Mus. A., 1987)

ALICE R. M. HYLAND

**Li Shih-ta.** *See* LI SHIDA.

**Lisht, El-.** Ancient Egyptian site on the west bank of the Nile, 56 km south of Cairo. Although it was settled from the Predynastic Period (*c.* 3500 BC), the area first became important during the Middle Kingdom (*c.* 2008–*c.* 1630 BC), when Ammenemes I (*reg c.* 1938–*c.* 1908 BC) moved the capital there from Thebes early in his reign. However, the actual site of the town, named Itjtawy, has never been satisfactorily identified: it may lie under the modern village of Bamha. El-Lisht is therefore chiefly of interest because of its necropolis containing the pyramid complexes of Ammenemes I and his son Sesostris I (*reg c.* 1918–*c.* 1875 BC). The complex of Ammenemes, now badly ruined, is of similar design to those at Giza, with a pyramid, mortuary temple and associated subsidiary burials set inside an enclosure wall and connected by a causeway to a valley temple. The pyramid of Sesostris I, which originally stood about 60 m high on a terrace overlooking the mortuary temple, was of innovative construction: the solid mass is divided diagonally and crosswise by stone walls into 16 compartments filled with sand and rubble. Within its enclosure are nine subsidiary pyramids with mortuary chapels. The causeway leading from the valley temple (destr.) was lined with Osirid statues of the King, and the mortuary temple has yielded some of the finest known Middle Kingdom statuary and reliefs (see EGYPT, ANCIENT, §IX, 3(v)(b)), the latter exemplified by a superb carving of the goddess Seshat recording foreign tribute (New York, Met., 52.129). Ten life-size seated statues of Sesostris I from the temple court (Cairo, Egyp. Mus., CG 411–420) are reminiscent of Old Kingdom statuary. Both pyramids make considerable use of high-quality limestone blocks quarried from Old Kingdom monuments, including funerary buildings of Cheops and Chephren (e.g. New York, Met., 22.123). Noteworthy private burials at el-Lisht include the 12th Dynasty (*c.* 1938–*c.* 1756 BC) tomb of Senebtisi, which was discovered intact, yielding a collection of jewellery and personal objects (New York, Met.), and the tomb of Senusertankh, whose burial chamber was carved with some of the Pyramid Texts, funerary inscriptions normally associated with royal burials. The mastaba of the priest Imhotep contained fine wooden statuettes of Sesostris I wearing the crowns of Upper and Lower Egypt (Cairo, Egyp. Mus., JE 44951 and New York, Met., 14.3.17).

BIBLIOGRAPHY

W. C. Hayes: *Texts in the Mastaba of S'en-wosret'ankh at Lisht* (New York, 1937)
I. E. S. Edwards: *The Pyramids of Egypt* (London, 1947, rev. 2/1972)
W. K. Simpson: *The Pyramid of Amen-em-het I at Lisht: The Twelfth Dynasty Pyramid Complex and Mastabas* (diss., New Haven, CT, Yale U., 1954)
H. Goedicke: *Re-used Blocks from the Pyramid of Amenemhet at Lisht* (New York, 1971)

DOMINIC MONTSERRAT

**Lisiewska, Anna Dorothea.** *See* THERBUSCH, ANNA DOROTHEA.

**Li Sixun.** *See* LI (i), (1).

**Lismer, Arthur** (*b* Sheffield, S Yorks, 27 June 1885; *d* Montreal, 23 March 1969). Canadian painter, draughtsman and teacher. He studied at the Sheffield School of Art (1898–1905) and at the Académie des Beaux-Arts in Antwerp (1906–7). In 1911 he emigrated to Canada, where he worked as a commercial artist for Grip Ltd, Toronto. In 1916 he began a long and distinguished career as a teacher, during which he held a number of influential posts, including that of principal of the Victoria School (now Nova Scotia College) of Art and Design (1916–19) and principal of the School of Art and Design at the Montreal Museum of Fine Arts (1942–67). He had a profound interest in the teaching of art to children, and was influenced in this by Franz Cižek and by John Dewey. Lismer's belief in the importance of a child's imaginative growth and self-expression led to him founding the Children's Art Centre at the Art Gallery of Toronto (1933) and at the Montreal Museum of Fine Arts (1946).

Lismer was primarily a landscape artist. As one of the founding members of the GROUP OF SEVEN he wished to express an indigenous vision of the Canadian landscape. Although he depicted scenes of Ontario, British Columbia, Quebec, the Maritimes and the Rockies, as in *Rock, Pine and Sunlight* (1920; Toronto, A.G.), he is best known for studies of Georgian Bay, Ontario: *A September Gale, Georgian Bay* (1921; Ottawa, N.G.) shows a centred, close-up view of an isolated tree in the grip of a storm.

BIBLIOGRAPHY

E. Tolmatch: *L'Esthétique du paysage chez Arthur Lismer* (MA thesis, U. Montreal, 1979)
*Canadian Jungle: The Later Works of Arthur Lismer* (exh. cat. by D. Reid, Toronto, A.G., 1985)
For further bibliography *see* GROUP OF SEVEN.

ELAINE TOLMATCH

**Liss** [Lys], **Johann** (*b* Oldenburg, *c*. 1595–1600; *d* Verona, 5 Dec 1631). German painter, draughtsman and print-maker, active in Italy. He was one of the few painters working in Venice in the 17th century to achieve European significance. In less than 15 years of artistic activity, he showed exceptional promise, always responding to new inspirations and incorporating them in his own style.

Having had his early training in the Netherlands, he brought new vigour to the rich tradition of Venetian painting that had ended with Tintoretto.

1. LIFE AND WORK.

*(i) Background and training in the north, c. 1615–c. 1620.* According to Joachim von Sandrart, who knew Liss well, the artist came from the most northerly part of Germany, the Oldenburg region north of Lübeck. His father may have been a painter in the service of the Dukes of Holstein: a painter also named Johann Liss is recorded at Schleswig, where the Dukes resided, and was commissioned by this court to decorate standards (1622, 1649). His wife, Anna Liss (*b* 1576–7; *d* after 1651), also worked as a painter at the court. Their son Johann could have obtained his first training in their studio before setting out on the journey to the Netherlands customary for north German artists.

In 1615–19 the younger Johann was apparently in Haarlem, Amsterdam and Antwerp and, according to Sandrart, was a follower of Hendrick Goltzius; no paintings survive from his Netherlandish period, but the few drawings in his hand reveal the influence of Haarlem Mannerism and reflect the style of Willem Buytewech and Dirk Hals as well as Goltzius. His wash drawing of a *Peasants' Brawl* (*c*.1615–20; Hamburg, Ksthalle) could have been inspired by Karel van Mander I. A signed etching, the *Fool as Matchmaker* (Hollstein, no. 3), the only one from the Netherlandish years, points to an artist with an original turn of mind but as yet unskilled in technique.

Liss travelled south *c*.1620 via Antwerp and Paris to Venice. At Antwerp, in works by Rubens, Abraham Janssen and Jacob Jordaens, he first encountered the new realism derived from Caravaggio and his successors. Study of the style of his Flemish contemporaries stimulated him to work on the large figural compositions that character-ized his development in the Italian years.

*(ii) Venice, c. 1620–c. 1622.* Only a few paintings, small in format and composed of small figures, can be associated with Liss's first stay in Venice. The *Morra Game* (*c*.1621; Kassel, Gemäldegal.), the *Gallant Couple* (*c*.1620; Pommersfelden, Schloss Weissenstein) and the *Prodigal Son* (*c*.1621; Vienna, Akad. Bild. Kst.) recall his Haarlem sources but are more especially indicative of his contact with Domenico Fetti, who was then working in Venice. While formally following Fetti's style, both in compostion and in the bright tones of his palette, he nevertheless imparted a new note to Venetian painting with his integra-tion of Dutch subjects.

*(iii) Rome, c. 1622–c. 1625.* Liss's move to Rome in the early 1620s brought him into contact with the city's leading artists. His paintings at this time show that he declined to be associated with only one school. The large-scale *Prodigal Son Feasting with Harlots* (Nuremberg, Ger. Nmus.), which betrays the influence of Bartolomeo Manfredi and Nicolas Régnier, shows him seeking a link with the followers of Caravaggio. This painting, the erotic honesty of which far exceeded the accepted norms, is believed to have brought him the derisive nickname 'Pan' with which he was registered as a member of the Schildersbent, a society of northern artists formed in Rome *c*. 1623. Also bearing the

1. Johann Liss: *Judith*, oil on canvas, 1.28×1.04 m, *c.* 1622–3 (London, National Gallery)

Caravaggio stamp and Roman in character are two half-length history paintings, *Judith* (*c.* 1623; London, N.G.; see fig. 1) and the *Death of Cleopatra* (*c.* 1624; Munich, Alte Pin.) and the allegorial work *Amor vincit* (*c.* 1623; Cleveland, OH, Mus. A.). At the same time these works hark back to Liss's Flemish experience, being reminiscent of comparable compositions by Rubens and Abraham Janssen. The *Satyr and the Peasants* (Washington, DC, N.G.A.) imitates Jordaens not only in theme but also in personal style.

Alongside these examples of Flemish–Roman realism Liss produced a group of quite different paintings while in Rome. These are mainly of mythological subjects, with nude figures in southern landscapes, as in works by Annibale Carracci and his circle. The *Toilet of Venus* (*c.* 1624; Pommersfelden, Schloss Weissenstein), his only work painted on panel, is comparable in inventiveness to works by Goltzius, though in the modelling of the bodies and in its brushwork more redolent of Jacob Jordaens; yet these Dutch and Flemish elements are secondary to the Italian character and the inspiration of Annibale. Liss's preoccupation with landscape is also to be seen in works of the Roman period, such as the *Fall of Phaëthon* (*c.* 1624; Sir Denis Mahon priv. col.; see 1975 exh. cat., pl. 26). The surprising glimpse here of nature from the Roman Campagna recalls the style of Cornelis van Poelenburch, as do *Venus and Adonis* (*c.* 1624; Karlsruhe, Staatl. Ksthalle)

and the *Flaying of Marsyas* (*c.* 1624; Moscow, Pushkin Mus. F.A.), both painted on copper.

This characteristic symbiosis of ideal figures in a southern setting with Netherlandish sharpness of observation is also found in a pen-and-ink and wash drawing representing an *Allegory of Christian Faith* (*c.* 1622; Cleveland, OH, Mus. A.). Taken from an *album amicorum*, this is the only work by Liss that he confirmed as originating in Rome. The style of the drawing exactly corresponds to his second etching, *Cephalus and Procris* (*c.* 1624; see 1975 exh. cat., pl. 54), and proves that he tried his hand at printmaking while in Rome.

*(iv) Second stay in Venice, c. 1625–30.* Liss left Rome for Venice *c.* 1625. He was evidently seen as the artistic successor to Domenico Fetti who had recently died. His *Dream of St Paul* (*c.* 1627; Berlin, Gemäldegal.; see fig. 2) was painted as a companion piece to an untraced *St Peter* by Fetti. In it St Paul sits surrounded by books while an angel draws aside a curtain. The apostle looks up aghast at the opening expanse of the heavens, with the angels making music and the Trinity in the distance. The colours range from the dark violet of St Paul's cloak through the green of the curtain to the delicate yellow, blue and pink hues of the clouds. With its light, manifold wealth of colour, the painting represents a highpoint in Liss's oeuvre, anticipating Venetian painting of the 18th century. It is possible that the *Dream of St Paul* led to his being commissioned to deliver a large altarpiece, the *Inspiration of St Jerome* (*c.* 1628; Venice, S Nicolò da Tolentino), the only official commission that he is known to have received

2. Johann Liss: *Dream of St Paul*, oil on canvas, 800×585 mm, *c.* 1627 (Berlin, Gemäldegalerie)

and the largest sacred painting he ever produced. The Church Father appears as a hermit and teacher, sitting naked on a rock, pen in hand, looking expectantly at an angel. Characteristically for a painter schooled in the Netherlands, realistic narration reasserts itself, even if the theme is supernatural. No other painting by Liss has been so frequently copied, especially by 18th-century painters, who recognized him as a spiritual ancestor.

The paintings Liss produced in his final years reveal that unrestrained flocculent syle that characterizes all Venetian painting since Titian, warranting Sandrart's observation that Liss followed the style of Titian, Tintoretto, Veronese and Fetti. The influence of the last is also clearly felt in such late paintings as *Hercules at the Crossroads* (*c.* 1628; Dresden, Gemäldegal. Alte Meister). In contending that Liss's small pictures were superior in quality to the others, Sandrart may have had in mind *Adam and Eve Mourning Abel's Death* (Venice, Accad.), with its red evening sky echoing the lamentation for the dead man, or perhaps the small copper panel *Agony in the Garden* (priv. col., see 1975 exh. cat., pl. 41), the only painting signed by the artist.

2. CRITICAL RECEPTION AND POSTHUMOUS REPU-TATION. The name Johann Liss with the addition of 'Flemish' was first recorded in 1629, in the lists of the brotherhood of Venetian painters. In that year Sandrart visited the city and stayed with the painter, and his is the only detailed account of the artist's life and working methods. Sandrart emphasized the many-sided talents of the painter who had mastered both the 'ancient' and the 'modern' styles and acquired 'an entirely different style' in Rome. In his large-scale *Prodigal Son Feasting with Harlots* Liss successfully adopted the new style that Sandrart called the 'Manfrediana methodus' and employed Caravaggio's style to make sketches for two further group paintings (The Hague, Mus. Bredius; Honolulu, HI, Acad. A.). But even in Rome he did not abandon the 'antique manner' that he had brought with him from Holland, learnt in the circle of Goltzius. The whirling group of nymphs clinging to each other in the *Fall of Phaëthon* remains indebted to Haarlem Mannerism, as do the nude figures in the *Toilet of Venus*. The artist's skill in depicting naked bodies points to the studies from nude models customary in Haarlem, which he continued in Venice. Sandrart specifically emphasized drawing from life, since Liss made no use of his studies of the Antique. He is thought to have painted without a studio or pupils in the traditional sense. His near frenzied method of working on his pictures was precisely described by Sandrart and not uncritically. Shortly after his death in Verona, where he had fled from the plague which had broken out in Venice, various of his works found their way to Holland, including the *Prodigal Son Feasting with Harlots* and *Dream of St Paul*, subsequently in the collection of the businessman Gerrit Reynst. These helped considerably to spread Liss's reputation in northern Europe.

BIBLIOGRAPHY

Hollstein: *Ger.*; *NDB*

J. von Sandrart: *Teutsche Academie* (1675–9); ed. A. R. Peltzer (1925), pp. 187–8, 402, 422

K. Steinbart: *Johann Liss, der Maler aus Holstein* (Berlin, 1940)

V. Bloch: 'Lissiana', *Oud-Holland*, lxi (1946), pp. 122–9

K. Steinbart: *Johann Liss* (Vienna, 1946)

A. Welcker: 'Bijdrage tot Lissiana 1' [Contributions to Lissiana 1], *Oud-Holland*, lxii (1947), pp. 135–7

V. Bloch: 'Liss and his Fall of Phaeton', *Burl. Mag.*, xcii (1950), pp. 278–82

O. Benesch: 'Liss's Temptation of St Anthony', *Burl. Mag.*, xciii (1951), pp. 376–9

E. Schilling: 'Betrachtungen zu Zeichnungen von Johan Liss', *Festschrift für Karl Lohmeyer* (Saarbrücken, 1954), pp. 30–38

V. Bloch: 'Addenda to Liss', *Burl. Mag.*, xcvi (1955), pp. 323ff

K. Steinbart: 'Das Werk des Johann Liss in alter und neuer Sicht', *Saggi & Mem. Stor. A.*, ii (1959), pp. 157–206

R. Klessmann: 'Ein neues Werk des Johann Liss in der Berliner Gemäldegalerie', *Nordelbingen*, xxxiv (1965), pp. 82–7

*Deutsche Maler und Zeichner des 17. Jahrhunderts* (exh. cat. ed. by R. Klessmann; E. Berlin, Staatl. Museen, 1966), pp. 47–55, 120–4, 157ff [bibliog.]

C. Donzelli and G. M. Pilo: *I pittori del seicento veneto* (Florence, 1967), pp. 240–43 [bibliog.]

R. Klessmann: *Schleswig-Holsteinisches biographisches Lexikon*, i (Neumünster, 1970), pp. 185ff

——: 'Johann Liss: Zum Werk der vorvenezianischen Zeit', *Kunstchronik*, xxiii (1970), pp. 292–3

E. Antoniazzi: 'Addenda: La data di morte di Johann Liss', *A. Ven.*, xxix (1975), pp. 306

R. Klessmann: 'Johann Liss: Leben und Werk', *Johann Liss* (exh. cat., ed. B. Bushart; Augsburg, Städt. Kstsammlungen; Cleveland, OH, Mus. A., 1975)

J. Rowlands: 'Johann Liss at Augsburg', *Burl. Mag.*, cxvii (1975), pp. 832–6

E. A. Safarik: 'La mostra di Johann Liss', *A. Ven.*, xxix (1975), pp. 297–306

A. Tzeutschler Lurie: 'Liss and the God of Love', *Bull. Cleveland Mus. A.*, lxii (1975), pp. 283–90

J. Bean: 'Johann Liss (and Paolo Pagani)', *Master Drgs*, xiv (1976), pp. 64–6

R. E. Spear: 'Johann Liss Reconsidered', *A. Bull.*, lviii (1976), pp. 582–93

W. Wegner: 'Eine frühe Zeichnung von Johann Liss in Berlin', *Pantheon*, xxxvi (1978), pp. 142–3

P. Amelung: 'Die Stammbücher des 16./17. Jahrhunderts als Quelle der Kultur- und Kunstgeschichte', *Zeichnung in Deutschland: Deutsche Zeichner 1540–1640*, ii (exh. cat.; Stuttgart, Staatsgal., 1979), p. 221

R. Pallucchini: *La pittura veneziana del seicento*, ii (Venice, 1981), pp. 141–8

R. Klessmann: 'Addenda to Johann Liss', *Burl. Mag.*, cxxviii (1986), pp. 191–4

——: 'Gartenfeste und Gelage: Ein bevorzugtes Bildthema von Johann Liss', *Kst & Ant.*, 9 (1992), pp. 27–31

RÜDIGER KLESSMANN

**Lissandrino.** *See* MAGNASCO, (2).

**Lisse, Dirck van der** (*b* Breda; *d* The Hague, *bur* 31 Jan 1669). Dutch painter and draughtsman. He was a pupil of Cornelis van Poelenburch *c.* 1630. In 1635 the Stadholder, Prince Frederik Hendrik of Orange Nassau, commissioned him, along with van Poelenburch, Abraham Bloemaert and Herman Saftleven, to paint a cycle of scenes based on Giovanni Battista Guarini's *Il pastor fido* for the restored hunting castle at Honselaarsdijk. In 1639 van der Lisse moved to The Hague, where he was a founder–member of the painters' confraternity Pictura in 1656; he became Burgomaster of the city in 1660.

Van der Lisse painted landscapes with mythological and biblical figures, close in style and subject-matter to the work of van Poelenburch, whose paintings he sometimes copied directly. His use of colour, however, is distinctive. In *Sleeping Nymphs Harassed by Satyrs* (Innsbruck, Tirol. Landesmus.), for example, there is a striking and characteristic use of unmixed yellows and oranges. He seems to have been the most talented of van Poelenburch's many pupils, but unlike others, such as Johan van Haensbergen (1642–1705) and Daniel Vertangen (*c.* 1598–1681/4), who mainly tried to imitate van Poelenburch's later polished style, he drew his inspiration especially from his master's early work. There are several preparatory chalk studies of nude figures by van der Lisse and also some signed and finished watercolours intended for sale.

BIBLIOGRAPHY

*Nederlandse 17e eeuwse Italianiserende landschapschilders* (exh. cat. by A. Blankert, Utrecht, Centraal Mus., 1965); rev. and trans. as *Dutch 17th-century Italianate Landscape Painters* (Soest, 1978), pp. 108–9

W. Bernt: *Die niederländische Maler und Zeichner des 17. Jahrhunderts* (Munich, 1980), ii, p. 35, pl. 743; v, pls 370–71

*Die Niederländer in Italien: Italianisante Niederländer des 17. Jahrhunderts aus österreichischem Besitz* (exh. cat., ed. R. Trnek; Salzburg, Residenzgal.; Vienna, Gemäldegal. Akad. Bild. Kst.; 1986), pp. 134–6

L. J. WASSINK

**Lissitzky** [Lissitsky], **El** [Lisitsky, El'; Lisitsky, Lazar' (Markovich)] (*b* Pochinok, Smolensk province, 23 Nov 1890; *d* Moscow, 30 Dec 1941). Russian draughtsman, architect, printmaker, painter, illustrator, designer, photographer, teacher and theorist.

1. Study and early graphic work, 1890–1918. 2. Vitebsk, Suprematism and the *Proun* works, 1919–21. 3. Moscow, Constructivism and later work, 1921–41.

1. STUDY AND EARLY GRAPHIC WORK, 1890–1918. After attending school in Smolensk, he enrolled in 1909 at the Technische Hochschule, Darmstadt, to study architecture and engineering. He also travelled extensively in Europe, however, and he made a tour of Italy to study art and architecture. He frequently made drawings of the architectural monuments he encountered on his travels. These early graphic works were executed in a restrained, decorative style reminiscent of Russian Art Nouveau book illustration. His drawings of Vitebsk and Smolensk (1910; Eindhoven, Stedel. Van Abbemus.), for example, show a professional interest in recording specific architectural structures and motifs, but they are simultaneously decorative graphic works in their own right and highly suitable for publication. This innate awareness of the importance of controlling the design of the page was to remain a feature of Lissitzky's work throughout radical stylistic transformations. He also recorded buildings in Ravenna, Venice and elsewhere in Italy in 1913. These works, using line and colour wash, retain an informative structural description while also allowing a more atmospheric evocation of place. The early architectural drawings as a whole show him using his talents as a graphic artist from the beginning of his career to analyse architecture in particular and show the synthesis of artistic and architectural interests that were to define much of his mature work. He graduated in architecture from the Technological Institute of Riga (evacuated to Moscow) in 1915 and to a substantial degree remained an architect throughout his career.

Lissitzky first exhibited with the Artists' Union in St Petersburg in 1912 and later with the World of Art and Jack of Diamonds groups in 1916–17. Architecture was not, however, the only theme of his early graphic work. Lissitzky was Jewish, and he made watercolour illustrations of the Passover story *Khad Gadya* ('One billy goat', 1914;

Moscow, Tret'yakov Gal.). These illustrations were executed in a looser, more calligraphic style appropriate to the swift-moving narrative. A revised sequence of illustrations to *Khad Gadya* (*see* JEWISH ART, fig. 21) was published as lithographs in Kiev in 1919. These works reveal Lissitzky illustrating Jewish themes with a sense of wit and fantasy that encouraged a dynamic and unrealistic handling of the picture space. The lithographic technique required separate printing of the colours, which disciplined the drawing and also demanded exact colour registration. The resultant combination of imagination and discipline was a fruitful discovery. Figures fly through the air, and unity of scale is disrupted so that animals are bigger than houses, for example, just as they frequently are in the work of Marc Chagall. The experience of working with lithography was in itself an important part of Lissitzky's technical education: it led him away from architecture towards the manipulation of graphic and reproductive printing processes.

2. VITEBSK, SUPREMATISM AND THE 'PROUN' WORKS, 1919–21. During the formative period of his development, the Russian Revolution of 1917 had involved Lissitzky in early Soviet attempts to formulate an art appropriate to Communism. His recent and direct involvement in Jewish culture attracted him to Chagall's work, and in 1919 he moved to Vitebsk to work with Chagall at the newly reorganized art school as Professor of Graphic Art and Architecture. Chagall's influence is evident in Lissitzky's book illustrations from 1919. But there was relatively little in the work of either Chagall or Lissitzky that was overtly Communist at this time, although the early years of the Revolution did witness a revival of Jewish culture to which they both made significant contributions. Lissitzky's involvement with revolutionary art was instigated by the arrival in Vitebsk of Kazimir Malevich. By 1919 Malevich's geometric system, SUPREMATISM, was at its most influential. While Lissitzky was not among the exhibitors at important Suprematist exhibitions in Petrograd (now St Petersburg) or Moscow, he learnt about Suprematism from Malevich in person and became a complete convert to its systematic and geometric procedures. Malevich was invited to teach at Vitebsk in 1919. He had published important essays on Suprematism and in Vitebsk he became an active and committed teacher. In his essay *O novykh sistemakh v isskustve* ('On new systems in art'; Vitebsk, 1919) he declared: 'There came to art a pure comprehension of the value of texture as such, without any need for the linear, architectural building of houses.' Suprematism was fundamentally concerned to define the underlying general principles of creativity, which were only subsequently applicable to specific professional activities and projects.

Working with Malevich transformed Lissitzky's attitudes and designs permanently. By 1919 he was fully aware of the range and potential of Suprematism. He exhibited, for example, at the *Pervaya gosudarstvennaya vystavka kartin mestnykh i moskovskikh khudozhnikov* ('First state exhibition of paintings by local and Moscow artists') in Vitebsk in 1919, which included work by Malevich, Ivan Klyun, Aleksandr Rodchenko and Alexandra Exter, as well as Chagall, Kandinsky and others. During the next year

Lissitzky applied the dynamics of Suprematism to the political demands of the day. The most celebrated instance of this shows his complete adoption of the new means: *Beat the Whites with the Red Wedge* (1919–20; repr. 1966; Eindhoven, Stedel. Van Abbemus.; see fig. 1) was designed as a lithographic poster in red and black on white utilizing the geometric motif of a red triangle cutting into a white circle to make a propaganda poster for the Civil War effort. Lissitzky was immediately concerned with adapting Suprematist visual language into a politically committed means of communication. Malevich had been thought unintelligible to the masses, but Lissitzky used Malevich's innovations to construct a visual analogy that gave the dynamics of Suprematism a specific, public and Communist purpose. This indicates both his debt to Malevich and his independence. The poster also contained formal innovations: it incorporated lettering, and in a few of its forms it suggested three-dimensional geometric objects, a device that Lissitzky was to develop into a spatial system of subtlety and sophistication during the next few years. In this respect he developed potential avenues of enquiry that Malevich himself had only begun to explore. Lissitzky's realization of the generative and fundamental

nature of Suprematism was immediate. By implying the existence of three-dimensional geometric objects within the framework of a Suprematist picture space, he could suggest construction; in other words a basic language of architectural form could be developed.

From the point of view of Lissitzky's interests and established abilities, this was a development full of potential. It brought together architecture, painting, printing and graphics into a new synthesis, and these were all areas of activity to which he was already committed. In 1919 he coined the new word *proun* to signify this innovative form of creative work, part painterly, part architectural and part graphic, and capable of application in any of these fields of activity. Lissitzky had extended the vocabulary of Suprematism so that the triangles, trapezia and circles of Malevich took on depth, solidity and textures suggestive of various materials. Inherent in this is the concept of an underlying unity beneath the apparent diversity of creative activity. Lissitzky was well placed to explore this possibility. He collaborated at Vitebsk with the Suprematist group Unovis, contributing his knowledge of engineering, architectural and graphic skills, including axonometric drawing,

1. El Lissitzky: *Beat the Whites with the Red Wedge*, lithographic poster, 483×584 mm, 1919–20 (Eindhoven, Stedelijk Van Abbemuseum)

which he used in a deliberately contradictory and inconsistent way to imply construction without undermining the floating pictorial space that Malevich had first evolved. Lissitzky made Suprematism applicable in design. The *Proun* projects of 1919–24 were the source of Lissitzky's inventiveness: they formed the basis of his subsequent typography and even photography, as well as his book, exhibition and poster design. *Proun 1E: The Town* (Moscow, Tret'yakov Gal.), a lithograph from a portfolio of 1919–20, exemplifies this potential: a white circle dominates a grainy rectangle and is crossed diagonally by planes that meet in a square upon and around which rectangular blocks assemble like buildings in the central square of a future city. Such a design was not site-specific but represented an organizational solution that was complete at a generative stage, capable of development and application as the basis of architecture, urban planning or even a poster. In 1920, for example, the Unovis collective devised a plan to support a series of platforms upon a girder diagonally rising from a red cube. Once the concept was defined in graphic terms it could be developed as a practical proposition, which is how Lissitzky evolved the *Lenin Podium* project of 1924 (design, Moscow, Tret'yakov Gal.).

If *Proun* designs approached practical feasibility, they also embraced political rhetoric. Tatlin's *Monument to the Third International* had done this in 1919–20 (*see* TATLIN, VLADIMIR). Lissitzky was well aware of this utopian project and referred to it in a collage of 1921–2, *Tatlin Working on the Monument* (London, Estorick priv. col., see 1990–91 exh. cat., no. 11). This collage was used as an illustration to Il'ya Ehrenburg's book *Shest' povestey o lyogkikh kontsakh* ('Six stories about easy endings'; Moscow and Berlin, 1922). The figure of Tatlin is drawn from a photograph and reveals that depiction of the figure is not incompatible with the geometry of the *Proun* designs as long as it is in some way one kind of object among others in the construction. The introduction of pasted photographic fragments is also possible in this way and occurs at the top of the work. Photomontage and the seamless blending of photographic images were later to extend this technique. Here, however, Tatlin appears surrounded by geometric forms; his eyes have become dividers that measure the universe. It is an image of the constructor and visionary, relevant to Lissitzky's own concerns.

3. MOSCOW, CONSTRUCTIVISM AND LATER WORK, 1921–41. Lissitzky's move to Moscow in 1921 as a professor of architecture at VKHUTEMAS coincided with the emergence of Constructivism (*see* CONSTRUCTIVISM, §2). Distinct from, but inspired by, the achievements of Tatlin, Constructivists sought to define creative activity in material and mathematical terms, replacing intuitive self-expression with conscious experimental investigation designed ultimately to reorganize society along materialist and Communist lines. In 1921 they renounced easel painting in favour of politically committed or directly utilitarian design. Lissitzky's position was similar but distinct: he did become a prolific designer of the most diverse projects, and his output was increasingly public in concept, but he also made an astonishing number of contacts with Western artists in an attempt to establish an international network of compatible creative talents. He

travelled widely in Western Europe from 1922, when he was involved in designing the exhibition space at the *Erste russische Kunstausstellung* at the Van Diemen Galerie in Berlin. During his travels he contacted or collaborated with Hans Arp, Kurt Schwitters and Man Ray, as well as J. J. P. Oud, Mart Stam, Gerrit Rietveld, Piet Mondrian and Theo van Doesburg from the group De Stijl. He published a multilingual periodical *Veshch—Objet—Gegenstand* with the writer Il'ya Ehrenburg in Berlin in 1922, a copy of the periodical *Merz* with Schwitters (No. 8/9, 1924), the periodical *Broom* in Berlin in 1923, a *Proun* cover for the Dutch periodical *Wendingen* (No. 11, 1922), and his geometric book for children, *Suprematisticheskiy skaz pro dva kvadrata v 6ti postroykakh* ('The Suprematist story of two squares in six constructions'; Berlin, 1922; repr. De Stijl, 11/12, 1922). With Arp he published the trilingual book *Die Kunstismen—Les Ismes de l'art—The Isms of Art* (1925) to survey contemporary trends, and he became an immensely original graphic designer in the process. The entire project for Lissitzky was an application of the principles evolved in his first *Proun* works, now manifest not only in paintings (see fig. 2) but, more importantly, in books, posters and portfolios of lithographs. The books were no longer simply illustrated but wholly redesigned and incorporated spectacular Suprematist typography. Mayakovsky's book *Dlya golosa* ('For the voice'; Moscow and Berlin, 1923) is an example in which the pages are cut to form a visual index of the poems, which are themselves laid out in a red and black graphic version that responds to their imagery and sound.

2. El Lissitzky: *Proun 12E*, oil on canvas, 571×427 mm, *c.* 1920 (Cambridge, MA, Busch-Reisinger Museum)

Pervading all of this was the sense of construction that had guided Lissitzky's interests from his early professional training and had been evident in his early architectural drawings. While this was never fully realized in actual buildings, architecture remained a major part of his activities. His largest executed projects were exhibition designs, in which he was an influential innovator. In 1924 he exhibited his first Constructivist environment, the *Proun* space, at the Grosse Berliner Kunstausstellung. He returned to Russia in 1925, but two of his most inventive projects were later executed in Germany, and both were devised as settings for collections of contemporary art. In 1926 he built the *Room for Constructive Art* at the Internationale Kunstausstellung in Dresden (destr., see 1990–91 exh. cat., nos 119–21). While this display incorporated works by Lissitzky, it was also necessary to incorporate paintings by Mondrian, László Moholy-Nagy, Francis Picabia and other artists, as well as a construction by Naum Gabo. The sculpture was placed centrally on a constructed plinth, which reveals Lissitzky's awareness of the Moscow Constructivists' structures of five years earlier, but in two other respects Lissitzky was wholly original: the walls of the room were lined with strips of wood painted white one side and black the other so that, as the spectator moved, the room appeared to change and shift its appearance in an optical haze of black, white and grey. More provocative still was the inclusion of sliding panels of perforated metal, which the spectator could move to cover or reveal particular exhibits. Similar devices were recreated in the *Abstract Cabinet* for the Provinzialmuseum, Hannover, in 1930 (original design; Hannover, Niedersächs. Landesmus., reconstruction, 1969; now Hannover, Sprengel Mus.).

After 1926 Lissitzky was increasingly engaged in international trade exhibitions promoting a positive image of Soviet achievements. To do this he employed the full range of his experience with architectural form, geometric structure, photography, photomontage and graphic display. Among these trade exhibitions the Soviet pavilion at the exhibition *Pressa: Internationale Presse Ausstellung* in Cologne in 1928 was among the most dynamic and original, establishing a busy use of every surface, including the floor and ceiling, and integrating three-dimensional display structures with photomontage and lettering. Comparable devices were used at the Soviet pavilions of the Internationale Hygiene Ausstellung in Dresden in 1930 (original ground-plan, Moscow, Tret'yakov Gal.). While Lissitzky here subordinated his talents to the requirements of politically sensitive displays that are ostensibly unconnected with art, investigation of the plans and organization of these displays immediately reveals their Suprematist and Constructivist roots, which now perform an underlying role in the dynamics of the display. This is an interesting achievement in times of changing ideology, but it would be to underestimate the scope of Lissitzky's work to assume that these designs were a rejection of his earlier priorities. His *Proun* concept had been applied to varied projects from books to posters since its inception in 1919, and it is significant that his work provides no clear frontier between art and design. The hand-painted *Proun* leads to the print, which leads to the book and poster or feeds into planning and architecture. His exhibition design was no less his own, whether displaying the work of other artists or newspapers and furs. For Lissitzky there was no ultimate distinction between his art work and his design work.

Ambitious architectural projects included one of Lissitzky's most celebrated designs, the unrealized Wolkenbügel (Cloudprop) skyscraper for Moscow (designs, Moscow, Tret'yakov Gal.). This three-legged skyscraper, surmounted and joined together by horizontal, cantilevered and massive accommodation blocks, was to be repeated at various points in the city. At the furthest edge of feasibility, it was an inspiring and utopian vision of the future city that defied gravity in its buildings just as the painted forms of Suprematism achieved in painting. He published his architectural ideas in *Russland: Die Rekonstruktion der Architektur in der Sowjetunion* (1930). In addition, Lissitzky was innovative in his use of photography, experimenting with 'cameraless images' (photograms), superimposition, photomontage and photocollage, which he employed in his book, exhibition and poster designs. He worked on the design and layout of the photojournalist periodical *USSR im Bau (SSR na stroyke)*. He also designed furniture. His entire and remarkable range of production was characterized by extensive planning and a minute precision of execution. He was inventive and influential internationally in a wide range of art and design practices because of his conviction that an underlying unity existed beneath them all.

### WRITINGS

with H. Arp, ed.: *Die Kunstismen—Les Ismes de l'art—The Isms of Art* (Zurich, 1925/*R* New York, 1968, Baden, 1990)
*Russland: Die Rekonstruktion der Architektur in der Sowjetunion* (Vienna, 1930; Eng. trans., London and Cambridge, MA, 1970)

### BIBLIOGRAPHY

H. Richter: *El Lissitzky—Sieg über die Sonne: Zur Kunst des Konstruktivismus* (Cologne, 1958)
C. Abramsky: 'El Lissitzky as Jewish Illustrator and Typographer', *Studio Int.*, clxxii/882 (1966), pp. 182–5
S. Lissitzky-Küppers: *El Lissitzky—Maler, Architekt, Typograf: Erinnerungen, Briefe, Schriften* (Dresden, 1967, rev. 2/Leipzig, 1976); Eng. trans. by H. Aldwinkle and M. Whittal as *El Lissitzky: Life, Letters, Texts* (London and Greenwich, CT., 1968, rev. 2/1980)
A. Birnholz: *El Lissitzky* (diss., Yale U., 1973; microfilm, Ann Arbor, 1978)
——: 'El Lissitzky and the Jewish Tradition', *Studio Int.*, clxxxvi/959 (1973), pp. 130–36
Y.-A. Bois: 'El Lissitzky: Didactiques de lecture', *Sov. Un./Un. Sov.*, iii/2 (1976), pp. 233–52
P. Larson: 'El Lissitzky's "Victory over the Sun"', *Prt Colr Newslett.* (March-April 1976), pp. 10–11
*El Lissitzky* (exh. cat., Cologne, Gal. Gmurzynska, 1976)
*El Lissitzky, 1890–1941: Retrospektive* (exh. cat., Hannover, Sprengel Mus.; Halle, Staatl. Gal. Moritzburg; 1988)
*L. M. Lisitsky, 1890–1941* (exh. cat., Moscow, Tret'yakov Gal., 1990)
*El Lissitzky, 1890–1941: Architect, Painter, Photographer, Typographer* (exh. cat., ed. J. Debbaut and others; Eindhoven, Stedel. Van Abbemus.; Madrid, Fund. Caja Pensiones; Paris, Mus. A. Mod. Ville Paris; 1990–91) [Eng. edn]

JOHN MILNER

**Li Ssu-hsün.** *See* LI, (1).

**List, Herbert** (*b* Hamburg, 7 Oct 1903; *d* Munich, 4 April 1975). German photographer and collector. He was a self-taught photographer but was given some support by his friend Andreas Feininger. For a long time he worked at various jobs and for the family coffee importing business. He fled from Germany in 1936 and went first to London and then to Paris, where he became a professional photographer and enjoyed a great success with publications in *Vogue*, *Life Magazine*, *Harper's Bazaar*, *Arts et Métiers graphiques* and *The Studio*.

At this time List's work was already characterized as mysterious, magical and surreal. In 1937 a photograph of the *Lykabettos* (see Metken, no. 22), one of his most characteristic and best-known works, appeared in the *Arts et Métiers graphiques* yearbook; it depicted a woman draped in white, holding a mirror in front of her head in which she reflects her own outstretched hand. List saw photography as one of the fine arts and referred to the influence of artistic circles on his work. As a result his photographs are close both to Pittura Metafisica (e.g. *Ostsee*, 1933; see Metken, no. 14) and to Surrealism, with its principle of chance encounter, the juxtaposition of apparently unconnected objects that develop their own poetic force, as in *Santorini* (1937; see Metken, no. 17).

In Munich between 1945 and 1966 List worked mostly for the magazine *Du* and also for some time as the editor of the magazine *Heute*. From 1960 he completely abandoned his work as a photographer to devote himself to his collection, which he had begun after World War II. It first comprised Flemish, French and German artists' work, mainly from the 16th to 18th centuries. Later he concentrated on Italian artists, including Tiepolo, Piranesi, Francesco Zuccarelli, Bellini and many others. On List's death over 700 Italian drawings were acquired by the Ratjen Foundation, Munich.

#### PHOTOGRAPHIC PUBLICATIONS
*Licht über Hellas—Eine Symphonie in Bildern von Herbert List* (Munich, 1953)
*Dom, Bilder und Eindrücke* (Biberach, 1960)

#### BIBLIOGRAPHY
G. Metken: *Herbert List: Photographien, 1930–1970* (Munich, 1976/R New York, 1981)
*Italienische Zeichnungen des 16.–18. Jahrhunderts* (Munich, 1977) [cat. of Ratjen Foundation collection]
M. Scheler, ed.: *Herbert List: Portraits, Kunst und Geist um die Jahrhundertmitte* (Hamburg, 1977)
——: *Herbert List: Fotografia Metafisica* (Munich, 1980)
*Herbert List: Photographies, 1930–1960* (exh. cat., Paris, Mus. A. Mod. Ville Paris, 1983)

REINHOLD MISSELBECK

**Li Tang** [Li T'ang; *zi* Xigu] (*b* Heyang, Henan Province, 1050s; *d* after 1130). Chinese painter. Li was the oldest and most influential painter to make the transition from the Painting Academy of the Northern Song (960–1127) emperor Huizong (*reg* 1101–26) in Bianliang (now Kaifeng, Henan Province) to the Southern Song (1127–1279) court in Lin'an (now Hangzhou, Zhejiang Province). It was there, while in his 80s, that he introduced an entirely new approach that became the basis for the influential traditions of Southern Song landscape painting (*see* CHINA, §V, 3(iv)).

Li Tang apparently occupied no official position in Bianliang, although he was very highly regarded and held the rank of painter in attendance (*daizhao*) in the Imperial Painting Academy. In 1126 the Song court was forced to flee south from the invading Jürchen nomads, who ruled northern China during the Jin period (1115–1234). Before his arrival at the Southern Song court of the emperor Gaozong (*reg* 1127–63) Li took refuge from the fighting

in the woods, where he met his future pupil, the robber Xiao Zhao. According to Deng Chun's *Hua ji* ('Painting continued'; preface dated 1167), Li was already 80 years old when he left Bianliang for Lin'an. There he was appointed head of the Southern Song Painting Academy and was awarded its highest honour, the *jindai* ('golden belt').

Li Tang did not merely transmit the official style of the Northern Song Academy. He was an independent genius who continued to develop stylistically as well as technically throughout his career. Later critics claimed that he attained full artistic freedom only at the end of his life. The bulk of his work appears to have been completed in Bianliang, but he exerted a major influence on the new style of landscape painting developed at the new Academy, later referred to as the Ma–Xia school after its two most prominent representatives, Ma Yuan and Xia Gui. Li's influence was twofold: his innovative use of monochrome ink in graded washes was especially influential for Ma Yuan, who modelled his rock and cliff structures after those of the older master; he also introduced a compositional format that reinterpreted conceptual space by presenting an oblique view of the landscape. This projected a diagonal thrust into the compositional distance in a daring, new, simplified organization of pictorial elements. In his *Hua shanshui jue* ('Secrets of painting landscape'; preface dated 1221), the painter Li Chengsou (*c.* 1150–after 1221) stated that the essential element of Li Tang's 'change of style' was the way in which he rendered space through the balance of emptiness and fullness. Recognizing the importance of Li's work, he went on to say that 'many men of ancient and modern times have reached a high standard as landscape painters . . . Each one established his own style . . . Many later men have followed after, but only Li Tang and Xiao Zhao have transformed their styles and in one swoop surpassed all modern and ancient men by their terse, light and swift manner of painting. They are, indeed, of the divine [*shen*] class' (Sirén, pp. 92–3).

Li Tang's creative versatility was readily apparent throughout his long career. While he is said to have painted in the more decorative and professionally orientated blue-and-green technique in his early years, there is no evidence of this in his later landscapes, except possibly in his somewhat mannered textural brushwork. However, as a mark of his favour the emperor Gaozong gave the artist the name Tang Li, implying that he was comparable to the Tang (618–907) painter LI SIXUN, the foremost practitioner of the blue-and-green manner. The graded washes that dominated his later style mark a sharp contrast with such earlier tight rendering. He is best known as a landscape painter, but he was also commended for his ability to paint other subjects. Ming (1368–1644) critics such as Zhang Chou equated the quality of his figure painting with that of his landscapes. Zhang wrote in the *[Qinghe] shuhua fang* ('The Qinghe boat-studio of painting and calligraphy'; preface dated 1616) that 'Li Tang was a good painter of human figures and landscapes . . . he excelled even more in painting oxen, following in this the manner of Dai Song' (Sirén, p. 95). In the *Shu hua ji* ('Record of calligraphy and paintings'; completed by Wu Qizhen *c.* 1677) Li's scroll depicting a scholar playing the *qin* (lute) is described as having a rendering so vivid that one 'could hear the sound of the water as well as that of the *qin*' (Sirén, p. 95). Li was consistently praised for his ability to paint rustic scenes as well as buffalo, both of which were popular themes during the Southern Song period. Unfortunately, the weakness of execution of some extant paintings of these subjects suggests that these may be later copies.

Two of Li's paintings are in the Kōtōin (Kyoto, Daitokuji). They are undated and only one is signed. The paintings were probably cut down, which has altered the proportion of the original compositions, but the brushwork and asymmetrical composition suggest that they belong to the last phase of Li's development. The signed and dated *Wind in the Pines amid Myriad Ravines* (see fig.) was painted in Bianliang and may be said to mark a middle stage in his stylistic development. In composition it reflects a derivation from the traditions of FAN KUAN in a revival of the heroic style, combined with influences from the traditions of Northern Song monumental landscape painting and the introduction of a new and more intimate portrayal of nature. Moreover, Fan's tradition of brushwork had been hardened into mannered patterns painted in *fupi cun* ('axe-cut texture stroke') with a relatively stiff brush from which the ink has been squeezed out, known as *cabi*, which leaves the impression of diagonal stratification. While the earlier focus on a centralized axis is retained, it nevertheless indicates the direction of future developments.

Li Tang: *Wind in the Pines amid Myriad Ravines*, hanging scroll, ink and light colour on silk, 1.89×1.40 m, 1124 (Taipei, National Palace Museum)

Li's influence on the painting of the Southern Song did not continue into the Yuan period (1279–1368). However, his use of ink and compositional devices—as treated by the Ma–Xia school—again came into prominence with the development of the Zhe school during the Ming period. Zhou Chen and Tang Yin are among the leading Ming artists whose works reveal the depth of this revival of Li's style.

BIBLIOGRAPHY
S. Shimada: 'Kōtōin shozō no sansuiga ni tsuite' [On the landscape paintings in the Kōtōin], *Bijutsu kenkyū*, clxv (1951)
O. Sirén: *Chinese Painting: Leading Masters and Principles* (London, 1956–8), ii, pp. 92–8
M. Loehr: *The Great Painters of China* (New York, 1980), pp. 168–70
T. Miyagawa, ed.: *Chinese Painting* (Tokyo, 1983), p. 130

MARY S. LAWTON

**Lithares.** *See under* THEBES (ii), §1.

**Lithography** [Fr. *Lithographie*, Ger. *Steindruckerei, chemische Druckerei*]. Planographic printmaking technique based on the antipathy of grease and water, and the attraction of these two substances to others of a similar nature and to a prepared surface of porous limestone or grained metal (*see* PRINTS, §III, 3). The term was first used in French on a music cover *c.* 1803; however, its Prague-born inventor, J. N. F. ALOIS SENEFELDER, preferred the term 'chemical printing' for the technique he developed in Munich between 1796 and 1799. In Britain it was called 'polyautography', until H. Bankes entitled the first English treatise: *Lithography; or, The Art of Making Drawings on Stone, for the Purpose of Being Multiplied by Printing* (Bath, 1813). Adaptations of Senefelder's technique are still called lithography, although stone has long been commercially superseded. Senefelder himself discussed metal and composition plates in his 1801 patent and 1818 treatise. Recently, micro-layered plates with two metals—one receptive to grease, another to water—have been devised, as has waterless litho, where different substances within the plate attract or reject the ink. Manual or photomechanical images generated on translucent film can also be transferred by light to continuous tone alloy plates. The link between traditional and contemporary practice is a surface with ink-accepting and ink-rejecting areas in the same plane.

GENERAL BIBLIOGRAPHY
J. Pennell and E. R. Pennell: *Lithography and Lithographers: Some Chapters in the History of the Art* (London, 1898, 2/1915)
C. Kampmann: *Die Literatur der Lithographie von 1798–1898* (Vienna, 1899)
C. Wagner: *Die Geschichte der Lithographie* (Leipzig, 1914)
M. J. Friedländer: *Die Lithographie* (Berlin, 1922)
J. Adhémar: *L'Estampe française: La Lithographie française au XIXe siècle* (Paris, 1944)
L. Lang and J. E. Bersier: *La Lithographie en France*, 3 vols (Mulhouse, 1946–52)
*One Hundred and Fifty Years of Lithography* (exh. cat. by G. von Groschwitz, Cincinnati, OH, A. Mus., 1948)
*Bild von Stein: Die Entwicklung der Lithographie von Senefelder bis heute* (exh. cat., Munich, Staatl. Graph. Samml., 1961)
W. Weber: *Saxa loquuntur, Steine reden: Geschichte der Lithographie* (Heidelberg and Berlin, 1961); Eng. trans. as *A History of Lithography* (London, 1966; Fr. trans., Paris, 1967)
F. H. Man: *Artists' Lithographs: A World History from Senefelder to the Present Day* (London and New York, 1970)
M. Twyman: *Lithography, 1800–1850: The Techniques of Drawing on Stone in England and France and their Application in Works of Topography*

(London, New York and Toronto, 1970) [the most thorough and reliable account in Eng.]

M. Knigin and M. Zimiles: *The Contemporary Lithographic Workshop around the World* (New York, 1974)

*Tamarind Technical Papers* (Albuquerque, 1974–8); *Tamarind Papers* (Albuquerque, 1978–) [hist., crit. & tech. articles on prts, esp. lithog.]

*La Pierre parle: Lithography in France, 1848–1900* (exh. cat. by D. Druick and P. Zegers, Ottawa, N.G., 1981)

D. Porzio, ed.: *La Litografia: Duecento anni di storia, arte e tecnica* (Milan, 1982, 2/1983; Fr. and Eng. trans., both 1983)

*La Lithographie en France des origines à nos jours* (exh. cat. by B. Bouret and C. Bouret; Paris, Fond. N. A. Graph. & Plast., [1984])

P. Gilmour, ed.: *Lasting Impressions: Lithography as Art* (London, Philadelphia and Canberra, 1988) [comprehensive bibliography; new research on C. Hullmandel & A. Clot; essays on Ger., Fr., Amer. & Austral. lithog.]

I. Materials and techniques. II. History.

## I. Materials and techniques.

Artists in the 19th century customarily employed a drawing medium of carbon pigment, binders and fatty substances, including soap, applied to a slab of porous limestone. Although artists have utilized the most recent discoveries, many still value stone for its fidelity to every nuance of the hand. To make a lithograph on stone, the surface is ground with abrasives to prepare a grease-free surface, which can be smooth or coarse, to suit the intended image. The drawing medium comes in solid sticks of various consistencies or as tusche (Ger.: 'ink'), which is diluted with distilled water or more volatile solvents for application by pen or brush. When the drawn stone has been treated with a mixture of acid and gum arabic (called 'the etch' but not related to intaglio printing), adsorption bonds the greasy constituents to the stone, creating insoluble particles so integral to its surface that it can be reused only when they have been ground away. The 'etch' also creates a water-loving barrier to resist grease, thus establishing image and non-image area simultaneously. After a solvent has removed the pigment in the image to leave only the grease, impressions are made by sponging the stone with water, then inking the image with a roller bearing oil-based printing ink. Drawn areas repel water and attract ink, undrawn areas retain water and repel ink. Lithographs from zinc—sometimes called zincographs—are made in a similar way.

To draw a pen lithograph the stone must be polished, whereas for crayon work the stone is roughened. A granular effect imparted by the 'tooth' of a stone or plate is therefore natural to chalk or crayon and can be mistaken for the intaglio 'crayon manner'. In the 19th century burin engraving was imitated by needling the image through a water-soluble ground to admit grease selectively to the stone. A mezzotint manner (Fr. *manière noire*), perfected in the 1830s, entailed modifying a coating of drawing medium with tools or abrasives. From *c*. 1840 lithotint simulated watercolour with diluted tusche—a procedure so tricky that wash (Fr. *lavis*) was often imitated by rubbing crayon. For Senefelder's sprinkled manner (Fr. *crachis*), a shower of liquid medium was spattered by passing a knife across a loaded brush and controlling the random halftone by stencil or gum stop-out; airbrushing is a later variant. Artists have also harnessed the effects of oxidation on zinc, known as *peau-de-crapaud* (Fr.: 'toadskin').

Senefelder devised a way of writing with a special liquid on prepared paper and transferring it to stone by damping it and passing it, face down, through the press. Chalk drawings too can be transferred, as can inked impressions from relief blocks, intaglio plates or 'mother stones' replicated for the speedier delivery of large editions. Whereas a direct drawing reverses when printed and must be conceived back-to-front, transferred images are returned to their original orientation by double reversal. Senefelder believed this 'the principal and most important part' of his discovery.

Lithographs can be crudely printed by placing paper over an inked image and rubbing it from the back, but Senefelder built an upright pole press with a hardwood scraper-bar pulled under pressure across a greased tympan holding the sheet of paper against the inked stone. Professor Hermann Joseph Mitterer (1764–1821) of Munich designed the 'star wheel' or cylinder press *c*. 1805, keeping the scraper-bar stationary and moving the stone; this was forerunner to the French Brisset press, which dominated the Continent by the mid-19th century. In the late 20th century similar presses were still used by some printers and artists continuing the craft of hand-printing.

A separate stone or plate is normally used to print each colour, but small rollers can localize many colours on one surface, and skilful printers can seamlessly blend a number of inks on the roller—a technique called 'rainbow roll' or iris printing. The grey scale in monochrome lithography is unparalleled. Traditional lithographs look soft and flat, with veils of ink rather than palpable deposits. While thousands of impressions can be taken from robust crayon work, delicate washes wear more rapidly. No clue as obvious as an intaglio platemark betrays the process, but as the scraper-bar smooths the paper it may leave a trace of the stone's rounded corners or the metal plate's sharper perimeter.

After 1850 commercial and 'artistic' or fine art lithography began to diverge as a result of mechanical and photochemical developments. Senefelder foresaw automated damping and inking, but the Sigl press, patented in Austria and France in 1851, was the first successful powered machine. It produced up to 1000 sheets an hour—some ten times faster than manual presses. Such speeds could only be attained by using highly polished stones. As the flood of commercial colour printing increased during the second half of the 19th century, armies of chromolithographers, so skilful that they were able to make colour separations by eye, had to render tonal values by pen stippling. In 1879, Benjamin Day (1836–1916) marketed labour-saving 'shading mediums' to facilitate the task, and by 1887 chromolithographic draughtsmen could choose from many different patterns embossed on to flexible sheets to be inked and transferred to the stones. As a result of this increasing mechanization, the word 'chromolithograph'—which simply means a lithograph in colour—became a pejorative term, particularly as it was usually applied to reproductive rather than to 'original' printmaking.

The first photolithographs were made in France, *c*. 1852, by the printer Rosé-Joseph Lemercier (1803–87), helped by an optician and two chemists. Stones coated with light-sensitive asphaltum were exposed under paper negatives for a set of architectural subjects called *Lithophotographie; ou, Impressions obtenues sur pierre à l'aide de la photographie* (Paris, 1853). In 1855 Alphonse-Louis Poitevin patented an alternative, using chromates on a mixture of albumen and gelatin. Lemercier bought the rights in 1857, but both methods proved commercially uneconomic. Line photolithographs were developed for cartography in 1859 by Eduard Asser in the Netherlands and J. W. Osborne (1828–1902) in Australia. Osborne transferred images on photosensitized paper to stone. Col. Henry James (1803–77), Director of Ordnance Survey in England, adapted the method to zinc in 1860. Despite many experiments, such as a patent of November 1865 to copy photos on to sensitized transfer paper impressed with an aquatint grain, photolithography lacked commercially viable half-tones. 'Ink photos' from reticulated gelatine provided tonal transfers in the mid-1880s, but half-tone screens were satisfactorily combined with the process only in the early 20th century.

Offset lithography—an extension of the principle of double reversal previously achieved by transfer paper—was first used on tin in 1875. The inked image was transferred to rubberized cloth, thence to metal. By 1904 Ira Rubel of New Jersey had built the first practical offset press for paper. One cylinder carried a curved metal printing plate automatically inked and dampened, the second a rubberized 'blanket' to relay the image, the third a sheet of paper to be printed. By 1910 speeds reached 5000–6000 sheets an hour. When photomechanical and photochemical techniques were combined with web-fed paper, simultaneously printed on both sides, offset outstripped most other mass-production methods.

Transparent plastic plates, used for mapmaking during World War II, were developed for artists after 1945, notably by W. S. Cowell. Photocomposition and electronic scanners able to convert transparencies into trichromatic half-tones appeared in the 1950s. Screenless or continuous tone lithography became viable *c.* 1960, when hand-drawn or photo positives on translucent film could be transferred by ultra-violet light to sensitized polymer-coated anodized aluminium plates.

Despite the fact that offset plates can also be hand-drawn, the technique's association with photomechanical production and supposed lack of 'originality' rendered it suspect for 'art', especially in the USA *c.* 1960. By the early 1970s this prejudice had been largely overcome and offset proofing presses increasingly adopted by artists' printers. Offset impressions are lighter than those from a direct press; the image suffers less wear, and many colours can be superimposed with precision. These characteristics make it an attractive process for the painter.

### BIBLIOGRAPHY

W. D. Richmond: *The Grammar of Lithography: A Practical Guide for the Artist and Printer in Commercial and Artistic Lithography and Chromolithography, Zincography, Photo-lithography and Lithographic Machine Printing* (London, 1878, 2/1880, 12/*c.* 1901); Ger. trans. by C. A. Franke (Leipzig, 1880)

J. Schnauss: *Der Lichtdruck und die Photolithographie* (Düsseldorf, 1879, 3/1886); Eng. trans. as *Collotype and Photo-lithography Practically Elaborated* ([?London], 1889)

W. T. Wilkinson: *Photo-mechanical Processes: A Practical Guide to Photo-zincography, Photo-lithography and Collotype* (London, 1892, 2/1897)

D. Cumming: *Handbook of Lithography: A Practical Treatise* (London, 1904, 2/1919, 3/1932)

E. de Crauzat: *Handbook of Lithography* (London, 1905/*R* 1919; rev. 1932)

B. Brown: *Lithography* (New York, 1923)

O. Kruger: *Die lithographischen Verfahren und der Offsetdruck* (Leipzig, 1929)

B. Brown: *Lithography for Artists* (Chicago, [1930])

C. A. Seward: *Metal Plate Lithography for Artists and Draftsmen* (New York, 1931)

A. S. Hartrick: *Lithography as a Fine Art* (London, 1932)

S. Wengenroth: *Making a Lithograph* (London, 1936)

W. Söderstrom: *The Lithographer's Manual* (New York, 1937)

L. Barrett: *Techniques of Stone Preparation* (Colorado Springs, 1940)

G. Arnold: *Creative Lithography and How to Do it* (New York, 1941)

T. E. Griffits: *The Technique of Colour Printing by Lithography* (London, [1944])

A. Dehn and L. Barrett: *How to Draw and Print Lithographs* (New York, 1950)

P. J. Hartsuch: *Chemistry of Lithography* (New York, 1952)

L. E. Lawson: *Offset Lithography* (London, 1963)

H. Cliffe: *Lithography* (New York, 1965)

M. Twyman: 'The Tinted Lithograph', *J. Prtg Hist. Soc.*, i (1965), pp. 39–56

P. Weaver: *The Technique of Lithography* (New York, 1965)

E. Weddige: *Lithography* (Scranton, NJ, 1966)

M. Twyman: 'The Lithographic Hand Press, 1796–1850', *J. Prtg Hist. Soc.*, iii (1967), pp. 3–50

——: 'Lithographic Stone and the Printing Trade in the Nineteenth Century', *J. Prtg Hist. Soc.*, viii (1972), pp. 1–41

R. Vicary: *The Thames & Hudson Manual of Advanced Lithography* (London, 1976)

M. Hunter: *The New Lithography: A Complete Guide for Artists and Printers in the Use of Modern Translucent Materials for the Creation of Hand-drawn Original Fine-art Lithographic Prints* (New York, 1984)

## II. History.

1. Invention and incunabula, before *c.* 1818. 2. Developments after *c.* 1818.

1. INVENTION AND INCUNABULA, BEFORE *c.* 1818. Senefelder seems to have been confused about the exact nature of his invention, for his various writings date it to 1796, 1798 and 1799. A dramatist, hoping to circulate his plays cheaply, he experimented from the mid-1790s with stereotyping and reversed writing on intaglio plates. A limestone slab used for mixing ink and the composition of wax, soap and lampblack devised for his writing experiments led to his discovery. In an oft-quoted passage, he related that having no paper handy, he jotted his mother's laundry list on to the limestone slab, using his new composition. In July 1796 he bit the stone with dilute acid and printed from the lettering, 'elevated about . . . 1/120th part of an inch' (0.2 mm), by inking it with a board covered in fine cloth. 'Thus', he explained, 'was the new art invented'. While the inking-board and acid-resistant composition were innovative, relief-etched stone was not. It was at least two years before Senefelder perfected the planographic method, after experiments had convinced him that gum arabic was essential to the interaction of the ingredients. The earliest legal documents relating to lithography were a 15-year privilege dated 3 September 1799 giving Senefelder exclusive rights in Bavaria; a contract signed 25 days later allowing the music publisher Johann Anton André (1775–1842) of Offenbach to exploit the process as Senefelder's partner; and British patents granted on 19 June 1801 for Scotland and a day later for England and Wales. By 1820 the process had spread through Europe, as well as to Russia and the USA.

*(i) German-speaking states.* Senefelder's first publication from relief-etched stone was *12 Neue Lieder für's Klavier*

1. Pen lithograph by Konrad Gessner: *Cavalry Charging*, image size: 230×316 mm, 1801 (Canberra, National Gallery of Australia); from *Specimens of Polyautography* (London, 1803), printed by J.N.F. Alois Senefelder

(Munich, 1796) by his friend Franz Gleissner (1760–*c.* 1820). The title-page of the same composer's *Eine Symphonie von vier obligaten Stimmen* (Munich, 1799) pioneered true lithography, but in the 'engraved manner'. By then capable of pictorial motifs, the inventor had sufficient business at his Munich press to employ his brothers, Georg Senefelder (1778–1827) and Theobald Senefelder (1777–1846), plus two apprentices. André paid Alois Senefelder 2000 florins for rights to exploit the process and to help to convert his own business to 'chemical printing'. On 10 August 1801 he paid a further 3000 florins for British patents, but a quarrel ended the partnership a day later.

Thereafter, André promoted lithography without Senefelder's help. André's cousin, François Johannot of Offenbach, produced a chalk landscape for Matthias Koch as early as 1802 and in 1803 gave assistance to Christoph Wilhelm Reuter of Berlin. In the next few years Reuter, who made some 130 lithographs himself, encouraged Johann Gottfried Schadow, Carl Friedrich Hampe (1772–1848) and Johann Gottfried Niedlich (1766–1837) to contribute to *Polyautographische Zeichnungen vorzüglicher Berliner Künstler* (Berlin, 1804–8). The first German masterpiece, however, was Karl Friedrich Schinkel's pen lithograph of a *Gothic Church behind an Oak Grove* (1810).

From 1801 to 1806 Senefelder printed music in Vienna and explored lithography's potential on calico, but his business capital and acumen did not equal his inventiveness. In October 1806 he set up his second Munich press with Baron Christoph von Aretin (1773–1824). He printed music, maps and, in 1808, a facsimile edition of Dürer's drawings in the *Book of Hours of the Emperor Maximilian I* (Munich, Bayer. Staatsbib.) and 24 specimens entitled *Musterbuch über alle lithographischen Kunstmanieren.* Despite Senefelder's 'exclusive rights', several other Bavarian presses were operating. From 1804 Mitterer produced figures and plants as teaching aids at the Feiertagsschule für Künstler und Techniker in Munich, followed by *Lithographische Kunstprodukte*, which appeared from October 1805 to December 1807 in 26 monthly parts, totalling 156 lithographs by local artists, including Max Wagenbauer (1774–1829) and Simon Petrus Klotz. In October 1809 Senefelder became an inspector at a Munich press engaged in land survey for tax assessment; this sinecure allowed him time to refine his discovery and to complete the treatise he published in 1818. His own press passed to Johann Christian von Mannlich in 1810. As court painter and director of the imperial museums, von Mannlich initiated two publications reproducing 600 paintings in tinted (two-tone) lithography by Johann Nepomuk Strixner, Ferdinand Piloty (1786–1844) and others.

*(ii) Britain.* Senefelder was in London from late 1800 to mid-1801, helping André's brother Philipp to establish the

first press outside the German-speaking states. He gave Philipp André instruction and helped the Swiss artist Konrad Gessner to produce some of the earliest artists' lithographs (see fig. 1). Felix H. Man recorded that by 1810, 165 lithographs had been produced in England.

The process was regarded as a way of multiplying drawings, and André published 12 *Specimens of Polyautography* on 30 April 1803. Works in pen were made by Benjamin West, President of the Royal Academy, and by Royal Academicians James Barry, Henry Fuseli and Thomas Stothard. In 1803 André also printed *Twelve Views of Scotland Delineated by a Lady*, technically precocious but aesthetically timid chalk drawings by Miss F. Waring ( *fl* 1802–26). From 1806 G. J. Vollweiler of Offenbach completed 36 *Specimens of Polyautography* as a series. Discouraged by poor sales, he returned to Germany in August 1807, after printing William Blake's pen drawing and frescoes in a Stratford-upon-Avon chapel recorded by the antiquary Thomas Fisher (1782–1836) of Hoxton.

Under licence from Vollweiler, the Quarter-Master-General's Office produced circulars and maps with the help of the English press's former assistant, D. J. Redman. In 1812 or 1813 Redman opened the first independent lithographic workshop in Bath. His principal client was Thomas Barker, who in 1813 drew *Forty Lithographic Impressions of Rustic Figures* and in 1814 the remarkable *Thirty-two Lithographic Impressions from Pen Drawings of Landscape Scenery*. But Redman was technically limited; lithography was to progress only when, in 1819, Rudolph Ackermann published Senefelder's treatise in English, and the artist–printer Charles Joseph Hullmandel set up his own press.

*(iii) France.* Peter Friedrich [Frédéric] André was granted a *brevet d'importation* on 11 February 1802, but inexperience and the Napoleonic Wars hindered his development. He sold licences to other printers and produced music at Charenton until *c.* May 1804; then he worked until early 1806 in the Rue Saint-Sébastien, Paris. After a hiatus in 1807, he opened a third press in the Rue du Pont-aux-Choux, which he abandoned in 1809. Several early French music covers were embellished by Pierre-Nolasque Bergeret, whose 1804 vignette of *Mercury* advertising André's 'imprimerie lithographique' was once wrongly thought to be the earliest lithograph made in France. In fact, Bergeret began reproducing paintings in the Louvre for an English publisher in 1803, but, due to renewed hostilities, only a prospectus, and pen lithographs after Rubens and Giulio Romano, were completed. Coterminous with these abortive attempts to establish the process, several influential Frenchmen learnt of it in Munich. Two of Napoleon's officers and his brother tried it between 1805 and 1807. Baron Dominique Vivant Denon, director general of the imperial museums, became an enthusiast after visiting von Mannlich's press in 1809. In 1812 and 1814 respectively, Charles-Philibert de Lasteyrie (1759–1849) and Godefroy Engelmann took instruction and became France's first successful printers.

From late 1815 Lasteyrie produced routine commercial work at the Ministère de l'Intérieur; his second press at 54, Rue du Four, Saint-Germain, Paris, published prints, illustration and caricature by Carle and Horace Vernet,

Jean-Baptiste Isabey, Baron Antoine-Jean Gros and Vivant Denon. Engelmann experimented with the process from 1813 after reading *Das Geheimniss des Steindrucks* (Tübingen, 1810) by Heinrich Rapp (1761–1832). Engelmann's first press was in Mulhouse, his second opened at 18, Rue Cassette, Paris, on 15 June 1816. On 3 August he sent prints to the Académie Royale des Beaux-Arts, which appointed a commission to study lithography; 23 days later he deposited *Le Chien de l'aveugle* by Pierre-Antoine Mongin (1761–1827) at the *dépôt légal* (Paris, Bib. N.). France's supremacy sprang largely from Engelmann's improvements, and the process came of age on 8 October 1817, when it was subjected to the same regulations as other graphic media.

BIBLIOGRAPHY

H. Bankes: *Lithography; or, The Art of Making Drawings on Stone, for the Purpose of Being Multiplied by Printing* (Bath, 1813/*R* 1816, 2/1816); ed. M. Twyman as *Henry Bankes's Treatise on Lithography* (London, 1976)

[G. Engelmann]: *Rapport de la lithographie, et particulièrement sur un recueil de dessins lithographies par M. Engelmann* (Paris, 1816)

[F.] M[airet]: *Notice sur la lithographie, ou L'art d'imprimer sur pierre* (Dijon, 1818)

A. Senefelder: *Vollständiges Lehrbuch der Steindruckerey enthaltend eine richtige und deutliche Anweisung zu den verschiedenen Manipulations-Arten derselben in allen ihren Zweigen und Manieren, belegt mit den nöthigen Musterblättern, nebst einer vorangehenden ausführlichen Geschichte dieser Kunst von ihrem Entstehen bis auf die gegenwärtige Zeit*, 2 vols (Munich and Vienna, 1818, 2/1821, 3/1827); Eng. trans. as *A Complete Course of Lithography* (London, 1819); Fr. trans. as *L'Art de la lithographie* (Paris, 1819)

G. P[eignot]: *Essai historique sur la lithographie* (Paris, 1819)

A. Raucourt (de Charleville): *Mémoire sur les expériences lithographiques faites à l'Ecole Royale des Ponts et Chaussées de France; ou Manuel théorique et pratique de dessinateur et de l'imprimeur lithographes* (Toulon, 1819; Eng. trans. by C. Hullmandel as *Manual of Lithography: Memoir on the Lithographic Experiments Made in Paris at the Royal School of the Roads and Bridges* (London, 1820, 2/1821))

F. M. Ferchl: 'Übersicht der einzig bestehenden, vollständigen Incunabeln-Sammlung der Lithographie und der übrigen Senefelder'schen Erfindungen als Metallographie, Papyrographie, Papierstereotypen und Volgemälde-Druck (ohne Presse)', *Oberbayer. Archv Vaterländ. Gesch.*, xvi (1856), pp. 115–203

——: *Geschichte der Errichtung der ersten lithographischen Kunstanstalt bei der Feiertagsschule für Künstler und Techniker in München* (Munich, 1862)

W. Gräff: *Die Einführung der Lithographie in Frankreich: Eine kunstgeschichtliche Untersuchung* (Heidelberg, 1906)

E. Bouvy: 'L'Imprimeur Gaulon et les origines de la lithographie à Bordeaux', *Rev. Philom. Bordeaux & Sud-Ouest* (1917), pp. 241–55

H. Schwarz: *Die Anfänge der Lithographie in Österreich* (Vienna, 1921); rev. and ed. E. Herrmann-Fichtenau (Vienna, 1988)

L. Dussler: *Die Incunabeln der deutschen Lithographie (1796–1821)* (Berlin, 1925, 2/1955)

G. Fumagalli: *Incunabuli della litografia d'Italia* (Rome, 1937)

H. Menz: *Die Frühzeit der Lithographie in Deutschland* (Dresden, 1955)

F. H. Man: 'Lithography in England, 1801–1810', *Prints: Thirteen Illustrated Essays on the Art of the Print, Selected for the Print Council of America*, ed. C. Zigrosser (New York and London, 1962), pp. 97–130

L. Lang: 'Les Premiers Essais de G. Engelmann: Catalogue des incunables de la lithographie française, 1814–1815', *Nouv. Est.* (1972), pp. 11–19

——: 'Le Catalogue par A. Winkler des premières lithographies allemandes', *Nouv. Est.* (1975), pp. 10–12

'L'Arrivée de la lithographie en France (1802): Un document inédit', *Nouv. Est.* (1975), pp. 12–13

R. A. Winkler: *Die Frühzeit der deutschen Lithographie: Katalog der Bilddrücke von 1796–1821* (Munich, 1975)

M. Twyman: 'Thomas Barker's Lithographic Stones', *J. Prtg Hist. Soc.*, xiii–xiv (1977–8), pp. 1–32

R. Butler: 'Australia's First Lithographs', *Austral. Connoisseur & Colr*, iii (1982), pp. 94–9, 130 [Augustus Earle]

R. P. Hargreaves: 'The First New Zealand Lithographs', *A. NZ* (1982), pp. 50–51

M. Twyman: *Rudolf Ackermann and Lithography* (Reading, 1983)

T. Szrajber: 'Orlowski and the Beginnings of Russian Lithography', *Prt Q.*, ix (1992), pp. 371–9

P. Wrightson: 'Benjamin West, Thomas Rowlandson and William Combe', *Prt Q.*, ix (1992), pp. 361–8

## 2. DEVELOPMENTS AFTER *c.* 1818.

(i) Commercial. (ii) Fine art.

*(i) Commercial.* Since its inception, the use of lithography has been primarily commercial—for maps, music, books, picture reproduction and jobbing printing. Naturalists recorded species: the Frenchman Charles-Alexandre Lesueur (1778–1846) made some of America's earliest lithographs in 1821–2 when he depicted fish in the *Journal of the Academy of Natural Sciences*; Edward Lear's plates for an important study of parrots (*see* BOOK ILLUSTRATION, fig. 6) date from a decade later. Topography dominated during the 1820s, when newly explored lands and the European 'Grand Tour' were recorded. Baron Taylor's *Voyages pittoresques et romantiques dans l'ancienne France* (Paris, 1820–78), in some 20 volumes, was the most ambitious project. J. D. Harding, who produced several lithographic drawing manuals, pioneered may of Hullmandel's discoveries, notably lithotint in *The Park and the Forest* (London, 1841). John Cooke Bourne brought poetry to his lithographic record of Britain's railways. Intaglio dominated art reproduction, but some French artists lithographed their own paintings or had them

3. Colour lithograph by Francis Bedford (after drawing by J. Sliegh): *Ornamental Gun Stand from Tunis*, page size: 470×314 mm (Canberra, National Gallery of Australia); pl. 34 from vol. i (1853) of M. Digby Wyatt: *Industrial Arts of the Nineteenth Century at the Great Exhbition (MDCCCLI)*, 3 vols (London, 1851–3), printed in February 1852 by Day & Son

2. Colour lithograph by Thomas Shotter Boys: *Belfry, Ghent*, image size: 384×263 mm (Canberra, National Gallery of Australia); pl. 3 from *Picturesque Architecture in Paris, Ghent, Antwerp, Rouen &c* (London, 1839), printed by Charles Hullmandel, published by the artist's cousin Thomas Boys

professionally reproduced. The process was ideal for facsimiles of drawings, as in Richard James Lane's *Studies of Figures by Gainsborough* (London, 1825) and those drawn in the 1860s after Delacroix by A.-E. Robaut (1830–1909). Albert Concanen (1835–86) specialized in music covers, but famous painters also decorated song-sheets.

The caricaturist 'H. B.' [John Doyle] drew *Political Sketches* for 20 years from 1827. Social and political ideas were conveyed through thousands of superb lithographs by Paul Gavarni and Honoré Daumier (for an illustration by the latter *see* SATIRE, fig. 2), published in Charles Philipon's *Le Charivari*, founded in 1832, and other journals. The Swiss Roldolphe Töpffer, father of the comic strip, originated his picture satires on transfer paper. Famous figures were drawn for *Vanity Fair* by 'Ape' [Carlo Pellegrini] from 1865 and by 'Spy' [Leslie Ward] from 1873. But whereas 'H. B.', Daumier, Gavarni and Töpffer drew their own prints, those for *Vanity Fair* were reproduced by chromolithographers.

Notable early attempts at colour included two nine-stone lithographs of 1820 by Joseph Lanzedelly (1774–1832) of Vienna, but Engelmann's *Album chromolithographique* (Paris and Leipzig, 1837) introduced the standard trichromatic procedure, as well as the terminology for commercial colour. Hullmandel, who, as early as 1835, had colour-printed George Alexander Hoskins's *Travels in Ethiopia* (London), produced *Picturesque Architecture in Paris, Ghent, Antwerp, Rouen &c* (London, 1839) for Thomas Shotter Boys (see fig. 2), using sophisticated tint stones. These different approaches mark the separation of art from commerce and the reproductive chromolithographer from the 'original' artist. The Great Exhibition (London, 1851; *see* PUGIN, fig. 3) and two Expositions Universelles (Paris, 1867 and 1878) consolidated the

4. Six-colour lithographic poster designed by Oskar Kokoschka: *Woman Picking Cotton*, paper size: 940×625 mm, 1908 (London, Victoria and Albert Museum); produced and printed by Albert Berger, Vienna, for the Internationale Kunstschau

chromolithographic era, ushering in popular 'estampes' and a flood of cheap ephemera, including labels, calendars, playing and greetings cards, postcards, fans and even 'diaphanies' imitating stained glass. But chromolithographers also produced memorable work after designs by others, as in such Victorian books as *Illuminated Books of the Middle Ages* (London, 1844–9) by H. Noel Humphrey (1810–79), lithographed by Owen Jones; Jones's own *Grammar of Ornament* (London, 1856), lithographed by Francis Bedford; and the *Industrial Arts of the Nineteenth Century at the Great Exhibition (MDCCCLI)* (London, 1851–3) by Matthew Digby Wyatt (see fig. 3), for which three lithographers put 160 images by 20 artists on to 1069 stones, entailing 1,300,000 press runs. In North America the reproduction of paintings democratized culture: 60 firms employing 800 people in 1860 had expanded to 700 firms employing 8000 people by 1890 (see Marzio). From 1834 Nathaniel Currier (later partnered by James Merritt Ives) produced over 7000 popular, often hand-coloured, prints. The most important were by the English emigrant Frances Palmer. From 1865 Louis Prang popularized the American wilderness in chromolithographs after paintings by Thomas Moran, Albert Bierstadt and others. Britain's Arundel Society, formed in 1848, published nearly 200 chromolithographs of Italian frescoes and paintings; 123 London printers listed in 1852 had grown to 474 by 1893. Commerce and art coincided in the colour posters of Jules Chéret (for illustrations *see* CHÉRET, JULES and POSTER, fig. 1), which were part of the 'original print' market by the 1880s. In England between the wars, particularly at the Curwen and Baynard presses, painters were encouraged to emulate the French, with autographic pattern papers, posters for Shell UK Ltd and London Transport, popular prints and King Penguin books. Like Kokoschka in 1908, however, most artists involved in poster-making tended to make designs in other media, which were translated into lithographic posters by their chromistes (or lithographic draughtsmen; see fig. 4).

### BIBLIOGRAPHY

G. Engelmann: *Manuel du dessinateur lithographe: Description des meilleurs moyens à employer pour faire des dessins sur pierre dans tous les genres connus* (Paris, 1822, 2/1824, 3/1830); Ger. trans. by K. Dielitz as *Godefroy Engelmanns Handbuch für Steinzeichner* (Berlin, 1833)

C. Hullmandel: *The Art of Drawing on Stone* (London, 1824, 2/1833, 3/1835)

——: *On Some Improvements in Lithographic Printing* (London, 1827)

P. B. Watts: 'The Rise and Progress of Lithography in Britain', *Brit. Lithographer*, i (1892), no. 2, pp. 21–3; no. 3, pp. 13–17; no. 4, pp. 22–5; no. 5, pp. 29–31

R. Graul and F. Dornhoffer, eds: *Die Lithographie* (Vienna, 1903), iv of *Die vervielfältigende Kunst der Gegenwart*

R. M. Burch: *Colour Printing and Colour Printers* (London, 1910, 2/1910, rev. 1983)

O. Kruger: *Die lithographischen Verfahren und der Offsetdruck* (Leipzig, 1929)

H. T. Peters: *America on Stone* (New York, 1931)

R. V. Tooley: *English Books with Coloured Plates, 1790 to 1860: A Bibliographic Account of the Most Important Books Illustrated by English Artists in Colour Aquatint and Colour Lithography* (London, 1935, 2/1954, rev. 1979)

J. R. Abbey: *Scenery of Great Britain and Ireland in Aquatint and Lithography, 1770–1860* (London, 1952)

——: *Life in England in Aquatint and Lithography, 1770–1860* (London, 1953)

——: *Travel in Aquatint and Lithography, 1770–1860*, 2 vols (London, 1956–7)

L. E. Lawson: *Offset Lithography* (London, 1963)

5. Chalk lithograph by Carle Vernet: *Delpech's Print Shop*, 1st state (before letters), image size: 170×244 mm, *c.* 1818 (Canberra, National Gallery of Australia); printed by François Delpech

F. A. Conningham and C. Simkin: *Currier and Ives Prints: An Illustrated Check List* (New York, 1970)

J. Schurre: *Currier and Ives Prints: A Check List of Unrecorded Prints Produced by Currier and Ives, N. Currier and C. Currier* (New York, 1970)

*Art and Commerce: American Prints of the 19th Century: Boston, 1975*

M. Twyman: 'A Directory of London Lithographic Printers', *J. Prtg Hist. Soc.*, x (1974–5), pp. 1–55; repr. as monograph (London, 1976)

*Artists at Curwen* (exh. cat. by P. Gilmour, London, Tate, 1977)

R. Cooper: 'The Popularization of Renaissance Art in Victorian England: The Arundel Society', *A. Hist.*, i (1978), pp. 263–92

*Color Printing in England, 1486–1870* (exh. cat. by J. M. Friedman, New Haven, CT, Yale Cent. Brit. A., 1978)

P. C. Marzio: *The Democratic Art: Pictures for a 19th-century America, Chromolithography, 1840–1900* (Boston, 1979)

B. Gascoigne: 'The Earliest English Chromolithographs', *J. Prtg Hist. Soc.*, xvii (1982–3), pp. 63–71

*Charles Hullmandel and James Duffield Harding: A Study of the English Art of Drawing on Stone, 1818–1850* (exh. cat. by C. Swenson, Northampton, MA, Smith Coll. Mus. A., 1982)

P. J. Weimerskirch: 'Naturalists and the Beginnings of Lithography in America', *From Linnaeus to Darwin: Commentaries on the History of Biology and Geology* (London, 1985)

J. Rosen: 'The Printed Photograph and the Logic of Progress in Nineteenth-century France', *A. J.* [New York], xlvi (1987), pp. 305–11

M. Twyman: *Early Lithographed Books: A Study of the Design and Production of Improper Books in the Age of the Hand Press* (London, 1990) [incl. cat.]

*(ii) Fine art.*

(a) 1818–89. (b) The 1890s. (c) 20th century.

*(a) 1818–89.* During the first half of the 19th century the German-speaking states produced such competent portrait lithographers as Franz Krüger of Berlin and Josef Kriehuber (1800–76) of Vienna. But few masterpieces emerged between the reverent landscapes of Salzburg and Berchtesgaden completed by the Nazarene Ferdinand Olivier in 1822 and the six exquisite *Experiments on Stone with Brush and Scraper* of 1851 by the painter Adolph Menzel, son of a lithographer.

Artists of high calibre gave France a decisive lead by the end of the second decade, because they were able to call on very competent printers. Vernet's lithograph of *c.* 1818 (see fig. 5) shows the shop of his printer, François Delpech, with customers viewing albums while a boy carries off a stone to an artist on his head. There were at least 18 Parisian and 26 provincial French presses by the 1820s (see Twyman, 1970 in general bibliography), including Gaulon in Bordeaux, who in 1825 printed four superb bullfights for the exiled Goya.

Romantic lithographers helped keep the Napoleonic legend alive. The ardent Bonapartists Carle and Horace Vernet depicted everyday army scenes, while Nicolas-Toussaint Charlet, who had made over 1000 prints by the 1850s, dramatized the soldier–hero. By the 1830s, Auguste Raffet was rendering Napoleonic campaigns like epic film sets, with soldiers crossing battlefields in waves. Lithography was also used by the greatest French artists of the era, Théodore Gericault and Eugène Delacroix. When Gericault visited London in 1820 to show the *Raft of the Medusa* (1819; Paris, Louvre), Hullmandel printed his

*Various Subjects Drawn from Life and on Stone*, 11 of which depicted horses. Gericault continued to draw lithographs of horses (see fig. 6) until his premature death in 1824, and he inspired James Ward to make his own equestrian suite of lithographs.

The theme of ungovernable animals was taken up by Delacroix, who also brilliantly interpreted literature in lithographs, tackling *Macbeth* (1825), *Faust* (1827; *see* DELACROIX, EUGÈNE, fig. 2) and *Hamlet* (1834–43). The public disapproved of his expressive wildness, however, preferring academic finish, as in the *Danaë* (1824) by Hyacinthe-Aubrey Lecomte (1797–1858): carefully stippled after Anne-Louis Girodet's painting (1798; Leipzig, Mus. Bild. Kst.), it sold some 600 copies in only two days. Animals provided subject-matter for lithographs by the sculptor Antoine-Louis Barye and the celebrated female artist Rosa Bonheur. The chaste *Venus Anadyomène* (1839) was Théodore Chassériau's lithographic masterpiece. Jean Gigoux and Achille Devéria produced incisive lithographic portraits of celebrated contemporaries, and Devéria made some 3000 works on stone, including accomplished costume studies.

Richard Parkes Bonington and Eugène Isabey worked on Baron Taylor's *Voyages pittoresques*; English-born Bonington was renowned for his exquisite lithographic townscapes, while Isabey excelled at moody seascapes and tone poems inspired by the Auvergne. Landscapes anticipating the Barbizon school were drawn on stone by the Petits maîtres Paul Huet and Jules Dupré. Published in *L'Artiste* in the 1830s, Dupré reappeared in *Souvenirs d'artistes* (1860–76), a publication reviving earlier masters at a time when lithography, eclipsed by etching, was at a low ebb.

When Alphonse Cadart's Société des Aquafortistes published intaglio prints in 1862, Cadart also attempted to revitalize lithography, by sending stones to Edouard Manet, Henri Fantin-Latour, Alphonse Legros, Félix Bracquemond and Théodule Ribot. But the printer Lemercier declined to edition them. His protest that Fantin-Latour's work was 'detestable, insane, barbaric' probably caused Cadart to abandon publication. The initiative bore indirect fruit, however: Fantin-Latour drew on stone again a decade later and by 1889 had made 90 imaginative evocations of the Romantic composers Berlioz, Schumann, Brahms and Wagner. Establishing essentials on transfer paper placed

6. Chalk lithograph, with stop-out, by Théodore Gericault: *Shoeing the Horse*, image size: 138×170 mm (Canberra, National Gallery of Australia); from the *Suite de sept petites pièces* (Paris, 1823), printed by Villain

over textured surfaces, he later reworked the stone with crayon and scraper. Odilon Redon adopted Fantin-Latour's method in 1879; in blacks as powerful as his charcoal drawings, he took lithography into the 1890s, with such albums as *Dans le rêve* (1879), *Les Origines* (1883), *La Nuit* (1886) and *Le Juré* (1887)

Rodolphe Bresdin's pen lithograph of the *Good Samaritan* (1861; for illustration *see* BRESDIN, RODOLPHE) achieved 1000 impressions in all, and in 1873 Lemercier transferred several Bresdin etchings to stone to make the editions easier to print. Transfer paper improved in the 1870s; Corot's breezy landscapes of 1871 revived the idea of 'multiplied drawing' inspiring Camille Pissarro to take up the method three years later, although his proofs were never published. Indeed, lithography was often an experimental, even private, activity. Manet published a caricature, a song-sheet and a book placard in the 1860s, but his other lithographs were not seen (or even processed) until after his death in 1883. *The Races* (*see* MANET, EDOUARD, fig. 4), one of five prints so delayed, acclaimed for the modernity of its expressive scribbles, may have been a rough sketch on a handy stone to resolve a related painting. The innovative *Balloon* for Cadart was only proofed; Manet's indictment of Napoleon III for abandoning Emperor Maximilian (1832–67) in Mexico was censored, as was the print showing reprisals against Communards (1871) and the political caricature *Polichinelle* (1874). But his masterly brush drawings ('autographies', possibly photomechanically derived) transformed Mallarmé's translation of *The Raven* (Paris, 1875) into the first modern artist's book (*see* LIVRE D'ARTISTE). Manet also influenced Edgar Degas to generate prints by tracing reduced photos of works in other media. During the late 1870s, with his aborted journal *Jour et nuit* in mind, Degas worked on transferred monotypes to depict the café concert; proofs survive, but no edition was printed.

Zinc, which was light, cheap, pliable and ideal for large-scale work, was perfected as an alternative to stone in the 1870s; by the 1880s Paris had succumbed to poster mania. In 1886 Henri Beraldi catalogued posters by Chéret in *Les Graveurs du XIXe siècle* (Paris). The same year Ernest Maindron published his major study, *Les Affiches illustrées*, and in 1889 organized the first extensive poster exhibition. There were few colour prints apart from posters; those by John-Lewis Brown from 1883 and Théâtre Libre programmes by Adolph Willette and Paul Signac in 1888 are isolated examples. Nevertheless, a lithography revival was under way. In 1881 the dealer Edmond Sagot (*fl* 1864–91) became the first to specialize in graphic art. In 1884 the Société des Artistes Lithographes Français, which was pledged 'to perpetuate the art of lithography', raised its profile in the Salon. In 1888 J. D. Maillard's Société de l'Estampe Originale marked a shift to 'original' printmaking, publishing two lithographs by Henri-Patrice Dillon (1851–1909) in a somewhat unsuccessful monochrome album. The lithographs van Gogh made in Nuenen in the early 1880s inspired Paul Gauguin and Emile Bernard to try Synthetism on zinc; their albums, with unusual washes, were available on demand in 1889 at the Volpini Café during the Exposition Universelle. The same year the Société des Peintres-graveurs staged its first original print exhibition.

BIBLIOGRAPHY
A. Bry: *L'Imprimeur lithographe* (Paris, 1835)
*French Lithography: The Restoration Salons, 1817–1824* (exh. cat. by W. McAllister Johnson, Kingston, Ont., Queen's U., Agnes Etherington A. Cent., 1977)
B. Farwell: *French Popular Lithographic Imagery, 1815–1870*, 2 vols (Chicago and London, 1981–2)
*All the Banners Wave: Art and War in the Romantic Era, 1792–1852* (exh. cat., Providence, RI, Brown U., 1982)

*(b) The 1890s.* The use of colour in lithography in the 1890s was stimulated not only by posters (for Klimt's colour poster of the First Secession Exhibition of 1898 *see* VIENNA, fig. 11) but also by the Impressionist palette, colour illustration in journals and the Japanese colour woodcuts printed in water-based inks that were shown in depth at the Ecole des Beaux Arts in 1890. In April of the following year the Société des Artistes Lithographes Français charted lithography's history with 1000 prints and launched *Les Peintres-lithographes*, which published 70 prints by 60 artists. Raffet was shown in 1892, Charlet in 1893, followed in 1895 by the centennial exhibition of the invention. These events were nationalistic: the French knew very well that true lithography post-dated 1795, but by jumping the gun they stole a march on the Germans and demonstrated their superiority.

In England the intaglio printer Frederick Goulding (1842–1909) introduced transfer paper to several artists, whose first (and sometimes only) lithographs represented Britain in Paris. The American expatriate James McNeill Whistler, whose exquisite London lithotints were made in the 1870s with the printer T. R. Way (1861–1913), also exhibited with the 'English school'. Having failed to complete a set of colour prints in Paris in 1892, due to the bankruptcy of the printer Belfond, Whistler resumed monochrome transfers with Way by post. He inspired William Rothenstein's portraits of 1897, some 50 tender figure studies by Charles Shannon and the dedication of fellow American Joseph Pennell, who became his disciple. When Sickert called Pennell's transfer lithographs 'reproductions' in the *Saturday Review* in 1896, the artist, backed by Whistler, sued for libel and won.

Lithography's vitality stemmed from its ability to extend downmarket to popular images and upmarket to rarefied proofs. Posters from the hoardings were printed for collectors on good paper and without letters. Zincographs that had appeared in serials such as *L'Escaramouche* were also marketed as signed prints. Literary journals, among them *La Revue blanche* and *La Plume*, produced posters and albums for their readers, and *La Plume* ran the Salon des Cent to exhibit them. 'Original prints' reached the public as limited editions and as low-priced song-sheets or theatre programmes. In 1893, 60 costly proofs of Henri de Toulouse-Lautrec's *Miss Loïe Fuller* (*see* PRINTS, fig. 13) were iris-inked, dusted with metallic powders and sold in gold-embellished mounts, yet his equally lavish eight-colour *Bust of Marcelle Lender* (1895) was circulated free to 1200 subscribers of the German journal *Pan*.

André Mellerio, publisher of *L'Estampe et l'affiche*, wrote the decade's most influential book on the subject, *La Lithographie originale en couleurs* (Paris, 1898). Describing the infrastructure for graphic art, he declared colour lithography 'the distinctive art form of our time' and found 40 artists worthy of special mention. Chief among them

7. Chalk and wash lithograph by Edvard Munch: *Lovers in the Waves*, image size: 358×470 mm, 1896 (courtesy Pat Gilmour); printed in an edition of *c.* 50 by Auguste Clot, Paris

were Toulouse-Lautrec and four of the Nabis—Pierre Bonnard, Edouard Vuillard, Maurice Denis and Ker-Xavier Roussel. Each produced a justly celebrated suite with up to 12 prints: Toulouse-Lautrec's *Elles* (1896) revealed the domestic life of prostitutes; Bonnard's *Quelques aspects de la vie de Paris* (1895–9) showed the city from unusual vantage points; Vuillard's *Paysages et intérieurs* (1898–9) featured bourgeois settings; and Denis's *Amour* (1897–9) recalled his betrothal. Roussel's poetic landscapes, proofed *c.* 1899, were sold as single prints. Ambroise Vollard commissioned the Nabis; *Elles* was published by Gustave Pellet (1859–1919), who in 1897–8 also issued colour suites by Maximilien Luce, Alexandre Lunois (1863–1916) and Signac.

Mellerio also noticed three printers: Henry Stern, who was with Edward Ancourt (*fl* 1860s–1890s) before working exclusively for Toulouse-Lautrec; Edouard Dûchatel (*fl* 1880s–1930s), famed for subtle work with Eugène Carrière and author of an important treatise; and the remarkable Lemercier chromiste, Auguste Clot (1858–1936), who opened his own workshop *c.* 1895. As printer to Vollard and Pellet, Clot worked with the most famous artists of the lithography revival. He reproduced Degas's pastel for *Germinal* in 1899 and printed final states for three of the artist's *After the bath* prints, begun *c.* 1891. Edvard Munch of Norway worked on 23 stones in Clot's

shop in 1896–7 (see fig. 7), as well as the woodcut *Moonlight*, part of which may have been transferred to stone. While praising Clot's intelligence, Mellerio, a purist concerned to distinguish 'original prints' from chromolithographs, took him to task for helping artists too much. Dûchatel's treatise made clear, however, that colour washes often needed professional retouching; even for an artist of Toulouse-Lautrec's distinction, colours were drawn or corrected by his printers. Letters prove that many colour prints were partly (even entirely) drawn by Clot. He added colour to Paul Cézanne's black keystone for the *Large Bathers*. Auguste Renoir's *Child with Biscuit*, *Bather*, *Children Playing Ball* and *Pinned Hat* were evolved by Clot from pastels, as were Alfred Sisley's *By the River (Geese)* and Redon's *Béatrice*. Even in André Marty's *L'Estampe originale*—a series greatly approved by Mellerio—Signac's print was from a watercolour copied at Ancourt's workshop, while *Le Jeu* by Puvis de Chavannes was a photolithographed drawing.

Nevertheless, Marty's *L'Estampe originale* succeeded where Maillard had failed. Between March 1893 and March 1895, 94 prints were issued in quarterly instalments, and of 60 lithographs, almost half were in colour. Advanced tendencies were represented by the British artists already named above, and by Puvis de Chavannes, Signac and fellow Pointillist Luce, Fantin-Latour and Redon, Toulouse-Lautrec and the Nabis, Chéret and Eugène-Samuel Grasset, Gauguin, Carrière, Lunois, Henri-Gabriel Ibels, Henri Rivière, Camille Pissarro, Georges de Feure, Hermann-Paul and Charles-Marie Dulac. Paul and Dulac each made two important lithographic suites.

From December 1894 *L'Epreuve*, published by Maurice Dumont (1870–99), numbered 79 lithographs among its 120 monochrome prints. Vollard's group albums—'an encyclopaedia of colour'—came out in 1896 and 1897, with another intended for 1898 released as 11 separate prints; 52 from a total of 64 prints were lithographs, 44 in colour. Two unrelated portfolios were both called *L'Estampe moderne*; the first was published from November 1895 to March 1896 by Loys-Henri Delteil, with five sets each of six prints; the other, by Masson and Piazza, came out in 24 monthly parts, each of four prints, from May 1897 to April 1899. Delteil's series included 17 lithographs; of the later group, 60 were colour lithographs, the rest photolithographs or collotypes after drawings. Most albums were in 100 to 200 copies, but *L'Estampe moderne* of 1897 was in an edition of 2000. Mellerio described the prints as banal chromolithographs, but several reproductions were superb, and although, in general, the set reflected middle-brow taste, there were fine prints by Henri Evenepoel, Edmond Aman-Jean, Louis John Rhead and Richard Ranft, and four silk panels for subscribers— *The Arts* by Alphonse Mucha—printed in colour and metallic inks. Such decorative panels, together with *estampes murales* and prints for schools—notably *Winter* (1896) and the series *Aspects of Nature* (1897–9) by Rivière—bridged the size between posters and albums. Lithography also served the vogue for 'le beau dans l'utile', being used to print wallpaper, lampshades, fans and stationery designed by artists. Bonnard's magnificent four-panel screen *Nannies Promenade* (Molines, 1896) exemplifies this development. The Salon had banned colour in 1891, arguing that prints were essentially 'an art of black and white'. Ironically, by 1899, when it relented, the colour explosion was very largely over.

BIBLIOGRAPHY

L. Monrocq: *Manuel pratique de lithographie sur zinc* (Paris, 1891)
E. Dûchatel: *Traité de lithographie artistique* (Paris, [1893], repr. 1907)
H. Bouchot: *La Lithographie* (Paris, 1895)
*La Centenaire de la lithographie* (exh. cat., Paris, Acad. B.-A., 1895)
A. Lemercier: *La Lithographie française de 1796 à 1896: Et les arts qui s'y rattachent s'adressant aux artistes et aux imprimeurs* (Paris, [1896–8])
P. Leprieur: 'Le Centenaire de la lithographie', *Gaz. B.-A.*, n.s. 2, xv (1896), pp. 45–57; xvi (1896), pp. 147–62
J. Pennell and E. R. Pennell: 'The Centenary of Lithography', *Fortnightly Rev.*, lxx (1898), pp. 968–83
U. E. Johnson: *Ambroise Vollard, éditeur: Prints, Books, Bronzes* (New York, 1944, rev. 1977)
D. M. Stein and D. H. Karshan: *L'Estampe originale: A Catalogue Raisonné* (New York, 1970)
A. M. Fern and D. R. Rubinstein: *The Avant-garde in Theatre and Art: French Playbills of the 1890s* (Washington, DC, 1972)
*From Manet to Toulouse-Lautrec: French Lithographs, 1860–1900* (exh. cat. by F. Carey and A. Griffiths, London, BM, 1978)
*The Color Revolution: Color Lithography in France, 1890–1900* (exh. cat. by P. D. Cate and S. Hitchings; New Brunswick, NJ, Rutgers U., Zimmerli A. Mus.; Baltimore, U. MD Mus. A.; Boston, MA, Pub. Lib., 1978–9) [with Eng. trans. of A. Mellerio: *La Lithographie originale en couleurs* (Paris, 1898)]
P. D. Cate: 'La Plume and its Salon des Cent: Promoter of Posters and Prints in the 1890s', *Prt Rev.* (1978), pp. 61–8
F. Chapon: 'Ambroise Vollard éditeur', *Gaz. B. A.* (1979), pp. 33–47; (1980), pp. 25–38
*The Print in Germany, 1880–1933* (exh. cat. by F. Carey and A. Griffiths, London, BM, 1984)
*The Artists of 'La Revue Blanche'* (exh. cat. by B. Waller and G. Seiberling; U. Rochester, NY, Mem. A.G., 1984)

*(c) 20th century.* Colour did not instantly disappear, nor did luxury publication cease at the turn of the century. In Paris in 1902 Vollard published *Parallèlement* (for illustration *see* LIVRE D'ARTISTE) and *Daphnis et Chloë*, with some 250 prints by Bonnard, and *Le Jardin des Supplices*, by Clot after Auguste Rodin's drawings. The same year Rivière's book *36 vues de la Tour Eiffel* (Paris) appeared, with lithographs based on Japanese colour woodcuts (for illustration *see* JAPONISME). In 1903 Fantin-Latour interpreted the *Poems of André Chénier* (Paris). Lunois reported his travels in superb washes, both in black and white (see fig. 8) and in lucid colour. Colour survived in posters; in 1907 Denis even drew a colour *Nativity*, which was printed in 1500 copies for the *Gazette des Beaux-Arts*. But gradually cheaper monochrome became the norm, for humourists and for those recording the 'humanity of the streets', among them Charles-Lucien Léandre, Jean Véber (1864–1928), Adolphe Willette and Théophile-Alexandre Steinlen.

From 1908 Paul Cassirer published 'stone drawings' by the Berlin Impressionists Lovis Corinth, Max Slevogt and Max Liebermann. His publishing house, Pan-presse, also supported the Expressionists Ernst Barlach and Oskar

8. Chalk and wash lithograph by Alexandre Lunois: *Guitar-player*, image size: 235×173 mm; from *La Revue de l'art ancien et moderne*, ix (1901), printed by Auguste Clot, Paris

Kokoschka, who, like Ludwig Meidner, illustrated literature, including their own writings. Pungent suites by Max Beckmann—*Hell* (1919) and *Berlin Journey* (1922)—pictured the post-war collapse of society, as did the savage photolithographs for which George Grosz was often fined. Käthe Kollwitz used her broadside chalk to support humane causes. Karl Schmidt-Rottluff had introduced lithography to the Dresden group Die Brücke in 1906; he, Erich Heckel, Max Pechstein, Ernst Luwig Kirchner and Otto Mueller made some 1500 lithographs. Dispersing their drawings with turpentine washes before applying unconventional 'etches', they inked the stone's edge to emphasize its characteristics. Keystones were reused to add colour, limiting output to monoprints or a few proofs. Even their associate Emil Nolde, whose brush lithos of 1913 and 1926 were professionally printed, permutated one subject in 69 colour variants, further undermining the standard edition. Lithographs comprised two thirds of the Bauhaus albums (1921–4). Paul Klee's monotype transfers and Kurt Schwitters's Dada scribbles were autographic, but those by Vasily Kandinsky, Oskar Schlemmer and Willi Baumeister suggested technical drawing. Styles ranging from Cubo-Futurism to Suprematism occurred in some 50 Russian *livres d'artiste*, drawn from 1912 to 1916 by David and Vladimir Burlyuk, Mikhail Larionov, Natal'ya Goncharova, Ol'ga Rozanova and Kazimir Malevich. In 1923 three remarkable Constructivist suites appeared in Hannover: El Lissitzky's *Victory over the Sun*, six impersonal *Constructions* by László Moholy-Nagy and Schwitters's collage prints of inked half-tones, rectangles and letters, 'Merzd by hand on to the stone'.

Inflation had largely killed the German market by 1923, but activity in France survived the 1929 crash. In concentrated bouts of printmaking from 1906 Matisse ranged between arabesques and densely modelled figure studies. Luc-Albert Moreau became a devotee after working for one of Frapier's two albums (1924–6). The Fauve artist Raoul Dufy made a colour suite of lithographs featuring the sea (1925). Robert Delaunay illustrated *Allo! Paris!* in 1926. Georges Rouault concluded 60 masterly prints with the lithograph *Autumn* in 1933; Aristide Maillol illustrated Ovid in 1935. Maurice Utrillo and Maurice de Vlaminck discovered the workshop of Fernand Mourlot (1895–1988): already famed for its museum posters, it dominated lithography after World War II.

Paris was a magnet even before the war, but after 1945 its network of galleries, workshops, publishers such as the Guilde de la Gravure and L'Oeuvre Gravé, and Aimé Maeght's serial publication *Derrière le miroir*, surpassed the infrastructure of the 1890s. Print biennials in Ljubljana, Kraków, Bradford, Tokyo and Fredrikstad offered world-wide exposure. Among foreigners who made lithographs in Paris were Karel Appel, Pierre Alechinsky, Corneille and Asger Jorn of Cobra; André Masson, Raoul Ubac, Henri Michaux and Bram van Velde from the Low Countries; Alexander Archipenko, André Lanskoy, Serge Poliakoff and Ossip Zadkine from Russia; Max Ernst, Hans Hartung, Ernst Wilhelm Nay and Paul Wunderlich from Germany; Antoni Clavé, Antonio Saura and Antoni Tàpies from Spain; Afro, Massimo Campigli, Giuseppe Capogrossi, Alberto Magnelli, Marino Marini, Giuseppe Santomaso, Emilio Vedova and Zoran Anton Music from

Italy; John Piper and Graham Sutherland from England; Ralston Crawford, Federico Castellón (1914–71) and Alexander Calder of the USA; Alberto Giacometti and Kurt Seligmann from Switzerland; Wifredo Lam from Cuba; Jean-Paul Riopelle from Canada; Kumi Sugai from Japan; and Zao Wou-Ki from China. Among the French, Jean-Michel Atlan, Roger Bissière, Maurice Estève, Alfred Manessier, Jean Le Moal (*b* 1909) and Gustave Singier—in some cases influenced by stained glass—revelled in the potential for colour. The book *1c Life* (1964) by Walasse Ting (*b* 1929), containing 62 lithos by 28 European and American artists, was also realized in Paris.

The best-known painters were highly productive: Braque's masterpiece was *Leaves, Colour, Light* (1954; see fig. 9); Léger celebrated the circus; Miró's enormous output ranged from his austere *Barcelona* series (1939; *see* MIRÓ, JOAN, fig. 3) to large and playful pictographs; Chagall used lithography to make some 700 posters, prints and illustrations. In 1958 Dubuffet and his printer Serge Lozingot (*b* 1935) embarked on the extraordinary *Phénomènes*—24 albums with 350 poetically titled transfers from such unlikely surfaces as fruit and human skin. But it was Picasso who convinced the world that lithography was a

9. Colour lithograph by Georges Braque: *Leaves, Colour, Light*, image size: 972×605 mm, 1953 (courtesy Pat Gilmour); printed in an edition of 75 by H. Deschamps at Mourlot Frères, Paris

major art form. Mourlot's proofer, Père Tutin, disliked Picasso's work so much that he tore up a gift of his famous dove. Yet from 1945 the old craftsman faithfully processed tusche-covered collages, Rorschach blots, gouache drawings over grease and incredible mutations in up to 30 states of such lithographs as *The Bull*, *Two Nude Women*, *David and Bathsheba* and *Armchair Woman*.

England's Senefelder Club, formed in 1908 by Joseph Pennell, F. E. Jackson (1872–1945), Archibald Standish Hartrick (1864–1950) and others, had toured 45 shows by 1914. Christopher Nevinson and Paul Nash memorably recorded the war, while David Bomberg's abstract colour booklet *Russian Ballet* (London, 1919) and Robert Bevan's studies of horses were landmarks in 1919–20. But English prints tended to be programmatic: *Contemporary Lithographs* (1937–8) and *School Prints* (1946–51) were aimed at children; the left-wing Artists' International Association produced 52 *Everyman Prints* by 1940, and 18 *1951 Lithographs* for the Festival of Britain; Edwin La Dell (1914–70) organized the *Coronation* series at the Royal College of Art in 1953. Lithographs for Lyons's tea-rooms were made in 1955, and for the *Guinness Book of Records* in 1957. In 1958 Curwen opened a studio on French lines, run by the artist Stanley Jones (*b* 1933). Paris-trained, he pioneered continuous tone work from 1960, printing for Piper, Robert MacBryde, Robert Colquhoun, Ceri Richards, Alan Davie, Allen Jones, Reg Butler, William Scott, Barbara Hepworth and Henry Moore, as well as two of the eight *Europäische Graphik* portfolios (1963–72), edited by the lithographic historian Felix H. Man.

In New York during World War I George Miller (1894–1965) was persuaded to print for artists by Albert Sterner (1863–1946), whose own work inspired the artist Bolton Brown (1865–1936) to study litho in London. Brown later printed for himself and others, notably George Bellows. In the post-war period the Modernists Adolf Dehn (1895–1968), Stuart Davis, Yasuo Kuniyoshi, Louis Lozowick (1892–1973) and Benton Spruance (1904–67) worked in Europe. At home the Realists campaigned for social change, emulating the Mexicans Diego Rivera, José Clemente Orozco and David Alfaro Siqueiros. Grant Wood, John Steuart Curry, Thomas Hart Benton and Raphael Soyer (*b* 1899) were among many artists making $5 populist prints for the American Artists' Association. Jean Charlot's autographic colour *Picture Book* (Los Angeles, 1933), printed by offset, encouraged Lynton Kistler (1897–1993), its Los Angeles printer, to open an artists' workshop, which also offered stone. Charlot continued offset work in New York with Albert Carman (1899–1949), who, in 1937 as an independent printer, produced a 50¢ album of 30 prints for the American Abstract Artists; he also colour-printed Chagall's wartime illustrations for *The Arabian Nights* (New York, 1945).

Black artist Robert Blackburn (*b* 1920) learnt lithography on Harlem's Federal Art Project (FAP); helped by Will Barnet (*b* 1911), he opened a New York access workshop in 1949. Margaret Lowengrund (1902–57), first to use colour at New York FAP (1936–43), promoted lithography through her gallery–workshop, The Contemporaries, from 1952. FAP supervisor Gustave von Groschwitz (1906–91) ran five colour biennials in Cincinnati (1950–58). Proselytizing for 'original prints' from 1956,

the Print Council of America (PCA) toured two exhibitions called *American Prints Today* in 1958 and 1962; only 13 prints shown in 1962 were lithographs, but *Coat Hanger* by Jasper Johns and *Skies of Venice* by Adja Yunkers heralded radical change. The print by Johns was published by Universal Limited Art Editions (ULAE), founded *c.*1957 by Maurice Grosman (1900–76) and Tatyana Grosman (1904–82). Blackburn helped the Grosmans to introduce lithography to members of the US avant-garde, among them Robert Rauschenberg, whose lithograph *Accident* (1963), printed from a broken stone, took Ljubljana's grand prize before Venice recognized his painting.

Yunkers's superb washes came from the Tamarind Lithography Workshop; an initiative of the artist June Wayne, it transformed the ecology for printmaking. When Kistler gave up stone in 1958, Wayne, who had worked with him for a decade, travelled to Paris for a printer. Afraid stone was dying out, she persuaded the Ford Foundation to grant £2 million to resuscitate it, by opening a workshop where artists of varied aesthetics could collaborate with printers. Wayne ran Tamarind in Los Angeles from 1960 until 1970, when her early associate, the artist Clinton Adams, continued it as the self-supporting Tamarind Institute at the University of New Mexico, Albuquerque. Tamarind set ethical documentation standards and ended trade secrecy, sharing extensive research through the *Tamarind Book of Lithography* (New York, 1971), written by Adams and Garo Antreasian (*b* 1922), the shop's first master printer. By 1984 Tamarind had worked with over 480 artists and trained 120 printers; in that year, a journal listed 164 artists' workshops across 25 American states.

Among Tamarind artists toured in 1985 were Josef Albers, Judy Chicago, José Luis Cuevas, Richard Diebenkorn, Sam Francis, Philip Guston, George McNeil (*b* 1908), George Miyasaki (*b* 1935), Louise Nevelson, Nathan Oliveira (*b* 1928), Philip Pearlstein, Rufino Tamayo and Emerson Woelffer (*b* 1914). Many Tamarind printers became publishers. In New York from 1964 Irwin Hollander (*b* 1927) published artists from Willem de Kooning to Shikō Munakata. In 1966 Kenneth E. Tyler (*b* 1931) launched Gemini GEL in Los Angeles with Albers's *White Line Squares*; within three years Gemini had published Frank Stella's *Stars of Persia* (1967), Roy Lichtenstein's *Cathedrals* (1969), Rauschenberg's 2.25 m *Sky Garden* (1969) from the *Stoned Moon Series* celebrating the moon landing and Johns's *Colour Numerals* (1967), one of which sold for £250,000 in 1989. Jean Milant (*b* 1943) opened Cirrus Editions in 1970, focusing on the Californians Edward Ruscha, Joe Goode (*b* 1937), Kenneth Price (*b* 1935) and Ed Moses (*b* 1926). Christo, Nancy Graves (*d* 1995), Sol LeWitt and William Wiley (*b* 1937) worked at Chicago's Landfall Press, begun in 1971 by Jack Lemon (*b* 1936). In 1975 the first Tamarind-trained woman, Judith Solodkin (*b* 1945), opened Solo Press in New York, where she worked with Howard Hodgkin, Robert Kushner (*b* 1949), Françoise Gilot (*b* 1921) and Joyce Kozloff. Maurice Sanchez (*b* 1945) started Derrière l'Etoile in New York in 1978 after printing James Rosenquist's 7.5 m *F.111* for London's Petersburg Press. Tamarind skills also spread through education: for example, in the 1970s Paul Clinton (*b* 1942), Charles

Ringness (*b* 1946) and Julio Juristo (*b* 1927) printed superb suites for Jim Dine, Rosenquist and Arakawa at GraphicStudio, the research institute at the University of South Florida, Tampa, established by Donald Saff (*b* 1937).

Offset lithography, even photo-offset, gradually infiltrated art. A pioneer of the 1950s, Eugene Feldman (1921–75) of Philadelphia, played with his commercial press after a day's work. At London's Royal College 24 artists legitimated the process in the series *Wapping to Windsor* (1960); by 1968 *Life Class* by Allen Jones and the *Critic Laughs* by Richard Hamilton were wittily contrasting hand and camera. Offset also served Photorealist or conceptual artists as diverse as Richard Long, Joseph Beuys, Hanne Darboven, Gerhard Richter, Sigmar Polke, Dieter Roth, John Clem Clarke (*b* 1937) and John Salt (*b* 1937) and proved ideal for inexpensive artists' books, typified by Ruscha's *26 Gasoline Stations* (1962). But it was Johns's *Decoy* (1971) for ULAE and Stella's mutilcoloured mazes (1972–3) for London's Petersburg Press that eventually confirmed offset's respectability and overcame the PCA's post-war resistance.

Another tendency of the 1970s was the multimedia print, which combined lithography with other processes, including custom-made paper. Tyler, who left Los Angeles to found a New York workshop in 1973, played a central role in this development. Honouring him at Tamarind's 30th birthday in 1990, Adams noted that the Lithography Workshop in 1960 had been closer to the world of Brown and Bellows than to the *Welcome to the Water Planet* series that Tyler had just completed for Rosenquist, combining lithographic collage with coloured paperworks 'of unimagined scale and complexity'. But although such multimedia works and 48-colour offset prints by David Hockney may characterize Tyler's recent output, traditional lithography has also survived. The first print Robert Motherwell drew at Tyler Graphics in 1974—a print the artist entitled *The Stoneness of the Stone* (see fig. 10)—featured two dramatic wash gestures on a sheet exactly the size and colour of the surface on which they were drawn.

For further illustrations of lithographs *see* FONTANESI, ANTONIO, fig. 1; KUBIN, ALFRED; LISSITSKY, EL, fig. 1; and MARSEILLE, fig. 3.

10. Wash lithograph on duplex paper in two greys made by Twinrocker by Robert Motherwell: *The Stoneness of the Stone*, paper size: 1041×762 mm, 1974 (courtesy Tyler Graphics Ltd); printed in an edition of 75 by Kenneth E. Tyler, published by Tyler Graphics Ltd, New York

### BIBLIOGRAPHY

*The Neolith* (1907–8) [quarterly produced by F. E. Jackson at the Central School of Arts and Crafts with text and illustration entirely lithographic]
J. Pennell: 'The Senefelder Club and the Revival of Artistic Lithography', *The Studio*, lxi (1914), pp. 3–17
C. Dodgson and J. Pennell: *The Senefelder Club* (London, 1922)
F. E. Jackson: 'Modern Lithography', *Prt Colr Q.*, xi (1924), pp. 205–26
A. S. Hartrick: 'Lithography and the Senefelder Club', *Apollo*, ii (1925), pp. 203–10
L. Kistler: *How to Make a Lithograph* (Los Angeles, 1950)
*International Biennial of Contemporary Color Lithography* (exh. cats, ed. G. von Groschwitz; Cincinnati, OH, A. Mus., 1950–58) [5 vols]
*The Artist and the Book (1860–1960) in Western Europe and the United States* (exh. cat., Boston, MA, Mus. F.A., 1961, 2/1972)
*The Senefelder Group, 1910–1960* (exh. cat. by H. Trivick, London, ACGB, 1961)
S. Jones: *Lithography for Artists* (London, 1967)
C. Adams and G. Z. Antreasian: *The Tamarind Book of Lithography: Art and Techniques* (New York, 1971)
*Technics and Creativity: Gemini G.E.L.* (exh. cat. by R. Castleman, New York, MOMA, 1971)
F. Mourlot: *Souvenirs et portraits d'artistes* (Paris, 1973)
*Offset Lithography* (exh. cat. by L. Sperling and R. S. Field, Middletown, CT, Wesleyan U., Davison A. Cent., 1973)

F. Woimant and M. Elgrishi: 'Répertoire des imprimeurs lithographes en France (1975)', *Nouv. Est.*, xxiv (1975), pp. 19–28
C. Tomkins: 'Profiles: The Moods of a Stone, Tatyana Grosman', *New Yorker* (7 June 1976), pp. 42–76
F. Mourlot: *Gravés dans ma mémoire: Cinquante ans de lithographie avec Picasso, Matisse, Chagall, Braque, Miró* (Paris, 1979)
*Tamarind Lithographs: A Complete Catalogue of Lithographs Printed at Tamarind Institute, 1970–79* (Albuquerque, 1980)
C. Adams: *American Lithographers, 1900–1960: The Artists and their Printers* (Albuquerque, 1983)
*Art and Technology: Offset Prints* (exh. cat. by H. Davies and H. Murata, Bethlehem, PA, Lehigh U., Ralph Wilson Gal., 1983)
L. Peters: 'Print Workshops U.S.A.—A Listing', *Prt Colr Newslett.*, xiii (1983), pp. 201–6
C. Adams: 'Margaret Lowengrund and the Contemporaries', *Tamarind Pap.*, vii (1984), pp. 17–23
*The Print in Germany, 1880–1933: The Age of Expressionism* (exh. cat. by F. Carey and A. Griffiths, London, BM, 1984)
*Gemini G.E.L.: Art and Collaboration* (exh. cat. by R. E. Fine, Washington, DC, N.G.A., 1984)
*Tamarind: From Los Angeles to Albuquerque* (exh. cat., ed. L. Gedeon; Los Angeles, UCLA, Grunwald Cent. Graph. A., 1985)
*Ken Tyler: Master Printer and the American Print Renaissance* (exh. cat. by P. Gilmour, Canberra, N.G., 1986)
P. Delaney: 'F. Ernest Jackson: Draughtsman and Lithographer', *Apollo*, cxxv (1987), pp. 338–43
M. Friedman and others: *Tyler Graphics: The Extended Image* (Minneapolis, 1987)
K. Tyler: *Tyler Graphics: Catalogue Raisonné, 1974–1985* (New York, 1987)
E. Sparks: *Universal Limited Art Editions: A History and Catalogue, the First Twenty-five Years* (Chicago, 1989)
*Tamarind Lithography Workshop Inc: Catalogue Raisonné, 1960–1970* (Albuquerque, 1989)

*Graphicstudio: Contemporary Art from the Collaborative Workshop at the University of South Florida* (exh. cat. by R. Fine and M. L. Corlett, Washington, DC, N.G.A., 1991)

PAT GILMOUR

**Lithuania** [Lith. Lietuva, Rus. Litva]. Country in north-eastern Europe. It is bounded on the north by Latvia, on the west by the Baltic Sea, on the east by Belarus' and on the south-west by Poland and the Kaliningrad province of the Russian Federation (see fig. 1). Its principal river is the Neman, and its area, *c.* 62,250 sq. km, is predominantly a gently rolling plain. Its population is *c.* 3.4 million; Lithuanians, who are mainly Roman Catholic, form 80% of the total, with small minorities of Poles and Russians. The capital is VILNIUS.

Trade links with the Scandinavians, Germans, Slavs and the Byzantine empire had already been established by the feudal period (9th–12th centuries AD). Lithuania developed as a powerful medieval state in the 13th century, while neighbouring Latvia and Estonia came under the control of the German Knights of the Sword. Grand Duke Mindaugas (*reg c.* 1235–63) adopted Christianity in 1250–51, but the country reverted to paganism in the late 13th century, providing a pretext for Crusader attacks (*see* TEUTONIC ORDER, §1). The Grand Duchy expanded eastwards, incorporating the region now known as BELARUS' and reaching its maximum size in the 14th century, when it annexed several East Slavonic principalities seeking protection from Tatar–Mongol incursions. The German threat prompted a union with Poland, which was formed in 1386 when Vladislav II Jagiellon (*reg* Lithuania, 1382–92; *reg* Poland, 1386–1434) married Jadwiga of Poland (*reg* 1382–95). Christianity was reintroduced into Lithuania at this time. Grand Duke Vytautas (*reg* 1392–1430) was victorious against the Teutonic Order in 1422, and after brief attempts in the 15th century to separate from Poland, the dual state experienced a long, comparatively peaceful period. The region passed to Russian rule in 1795 as a result of the Third Partition of Poland. After the Russian Revolution of 1917, Lithuania proclaimed its independence, which was recognized by the USSR in 1920. In 1940, however, Lithuania was incorporated into the USSR as a Soviet republic; it was occupied by Nazi Germany for three years from June 1941. In 1991, with the break-up of the USSR, Lithuania became an independent republic.

This article covers the art of Lithuania from the feudal period onwards; for the earliest art of the region *see* PREHISTORIC EUROPE. Because the borders of Lithuania have changed often during its history, it is not always possible to make a firm distinction between Lithuanian art and that of neighbouring regions; moreover, the names of individual sites and artists are often cited in the literature

1. Map of Lithuania; those sites with separate entries in this dictionary are distinguished by CROSS-REFERENCE TYPE

in Polish and Belarusian forms (in particular) as well as the Lithuanian ones used in this article.

I. Before *c.* 1530. II. *c.* 1530–*c.* 1780. III. After *c.* 1780.

### I. Before c. 1530.

During the early feudal period, Lithuanian castles were built of wood and have not survived. Timber long remained the principal building material, as suitable stone was rare. The technique of making clay bricks was brought to the country from Kievan Rus, who settled in the eastern Lithuanian lands in the 11th–12th centuries. Grand Duke Mindaugas, who united Lithuanian lands, built the first masonry cathedral in Lithuania; its foundations have been found under the present Vilnius Cathedral. Its brickwork is similar to that of 13th-century buildings in Riga, Latvia, while the plan of the building, remnants of the glazed floor-tiles and of relief panels are in a style that marks the transition from Romanesque to Gothic.

Towns expanded in the 14th century. Although Grand Duke Gediminas (*reg* 1316–41), was a pagan, he maintained contacts with Roman Catholic and Orthodox leaders and invited artisans and merchants from western Europe. Western and Byzantine influences mingled, but after Lithuania adopted Catholic Christianity, Western forms became dominant. In painting, however, Byzantine influence lasted until the 16th century. A Gothic cathedral (completed 1387; destr. 1419) was erected by Vladislav II Jagiellon on the site of the 13th-century cathedral in Vilnius. This cathedral had octagonal pillars and a roof of glazed tiles. Fragments of wall paintings have survived: a wall painting in Byzantine style in the south crypt of the nave is the earliest wall painting in Lithuania.

By the 14th century there were brick castles at Krėva, Lyda, Medininkai, Naugardukas, KAUNAS, Vilnius and Trakai. Flat, deeper Gothic bricks (known in East Slavonic principalities as Lithuanian bricks), laid in Flemish bond, were introduced. Grand Duke Vytautas built and restored many castles, with the help of German craftsmen: existing castles were equipped with tall Gothic towers and walls supported by buttresses, as at Naugardukas and Vilnius Upper Castle, while castellated buildings were built in Gothic style on the plains. Among the castles defended by water were Trakai Castle on the island in Lake Galvė and Kaunas Castle (rebuilt 1404–9) on the River Neris. Trakai Castle, which is comparatively well preserved, consists of the castle building with a seven-storey gate-tower and a ward with five round towers of the Flemish type. Fifteenth-century wall paintings depicting life in the castle survive *in situ*.

Early Gothic ecclesiastical architecture of the Vytautas period includes remains of St Anne's, Vilnius, the first churches of the Franciscan missions and the chapels of the German traders invited to Vilnius. Gothic parish churches built or begun in the Vytautas period survive in Vilnius, Kaunas, Trakai and Merkinė. The Franciscan monasteries in Vilnius and Kaunas and the Benedictine monastery in Trakai were also built in Gothic style in this period, as were brick houses in Vilnius and Kaunas. The brick Gothic style dominant in the early 15th century in Lithuania was based on the vertical organization of masses and planes and a modified geometric ornamentation.

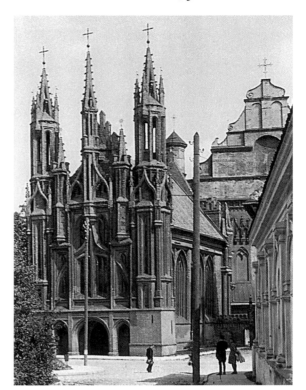

2. Vilnius, St Anne, west front, completed 1581

These features have survived in the church of St Nicholas in Vilnius, which was restored in the 16th century in the spirit of Late Gothic. The churches of that period are mostly of a hall church type, with pointed window and door arches, angular choir, octagonal towers and pillars, ribbed vaults and massive buttresses (*see* BRICK, §II, 3(i)(g)).

Late Gothic buildings of the 16th century include the Cistercian churches with their cellular vaults in Vilnius and Kaunas, some of which have survived. Such vaults can also be found in 16th-century houses in Vilnius. The reticulated and star vaults of an irregular rib construction in the St Nicholas churches in Vilnius and Kaunas also date to the 16th century. Walls are decorated with rhythmical reliefs, as in the bell-tower of the Cistercian church in Vilnius, or with niches, as in the church of St Jonas in Zapyškis or Murius Castle. The church of St Anne in Vilnius (completed 1581; see fig. 2), a masterpiece of brick Late Gothic, is close in its modelling to Flemish brick Gothic.

### II. c. 1530–c. 1780.

The Renaissance is linked in Lithuania with the reigns of Sigismund I (*reg* 1506–48) and Sigismund II Augustus (*reg* 1548–72; *see* JAGIELLON, (2) and (4)). The palace of the grand dukes in Vilnius became an important centre of science and art, although few examples of Renaissance architecture have survived in Vilnius. Most of the city wall with nine gates (1503–22) was destroyed in 1799–1805, but portions of wall with houses attached remain, together with the Medininkai (now the Dawn [Aušros]) Gate with an adjoining chapel housing the *Madonna of the Dawn Gate.* After a fire in Vilnius Cathedral in 1530, its restoration and the extension of the Lower Castle was entrusted to the Italians BERNARDO ZANOBI DE GIANOTIS, Giovanni Cini (*fl* 1519–65) and Filippo da Fiesole (*d* 1540), although the traditions of the still dominant local Gothic were taken into account in the reconstruction. The palace of the grand dukes (destr.) incorporated many features of the Italian Renaissance, with a stress on horizontality in the disposition of the voids and a square courtyard in the centre, with surrounding galleries. Italian craftsmen created altars, portals and monuments in Vilnius: Giovanni Maria Mosca Padovano, for example, created the monument to the first wife of Sigismund II Augustus, *Elizabeth of Habsburg* (1546; destr.), and Bernardino Zanobi de Gianotis constructed the *Goštautas* monument (Vilnius cathedral). Little of their work survived the Russian invasion of 1655 and the destruction of the interiors of many churches and palaces.

Byzantine traditions in painting lasted until the 16th century, since a portrait of *Vytautas* (destr.), executed after the cathedral fire of 1530, was painted using Byzantine techniques. Portraits of a more Western type, however, for example the 'three-handed' *St Casimir* (Vilnius, Lith. A. Mus.), were executed in Lithuania as early as the 15th century. Among foreign painters working at the court of Sigismund I was the German Georg Helwig. Several Italians worked for Sigismund II Augustus (*see* JAGIELLON, (4)), including the Venetian Giovanni dal Monte.

The Reformation reached Lithuania *c.* 1530, but it spread only after the death of Sigismund I in 1548, fostered by influential noblemen. Sigismund II Augustus remained a Roman Catholic but sympathized with Reformation ideas. The Calvinists built many brick churches, which

either did not survive or were converted into Catholic churches. One of the earliest is a small church in Rykantai (*c.* 1555). A late expression of the Renaissance is the Calvinist church built by Janusz Radziwiłł (1612–55) in Kėdainiai in 1627–54. The influence of the Reformation in Lithuania was brief, however. The nobility returned to Catholicism, while the Jesuits, who arrived in Lithuania in 1569, began consolidating the position of the Church of Rome. They inspired the early flowering of Italian Baroque in Lithuania, which dominated the 17th century and most of the 18th, acquiring several local features.

The first Baroque building in Lithuania is the Jesuit church (1586–99), founded by Mikalaj Krzysztof Radziwiłł (1549–1616) at Nieśwież (now Nesvizh, Belarus'; *see* RADZIWIŁŁ). Its architect was the Italian Giovanni Maria Bernardoni (1541–1605). The first purely Baroque church in Vilnius is the Jesuit church of St Casimir (1604–16), inspired by Il Gesù, Rome. The chapel of St Casimir (1634–6) in Vilnius Cathedral, built in the early Baroque style and abundantly decorated with marble, porphyry and silver, was designed by Constante Tencalla (*see* TENCALLA, (1)), who had previously worked in Rome. The church of St Teresa in Vilnius, built in 1638–58 for the Discalced Carmelites, is also by Tencalla.

After the grand duke's court moved in the 17th century to Poland, cultural life in Lithuania was concentrated on monasteries and on the estates of influential nobility such as the Radziwiłł, Sapieha, Chodkiewicz, Tyszkiewicz and Ogiński families. The Radziwiłł family built new fortified palaces at Nieśwież (begun 1583) and Biržai (before 1655). The Sapieha family built a palace in Vilnius (1691); the Pac family built palaces in Kaunas and Jieznas. The Lithuanian nobility employed foreign painters such as BARTHOLOMÄUS STROBEL II and DANIEL SCHULTZ II. Michelangelo Palloni (1637–1705/14) and Abraham van Westervelt (*d* 1692) both worked in Lithuania for Janusz Radziwiłł. Peter Danckerts de Rij was court painter to Vladislav IV Vasa (*see* VASA, (3)). Many 17th-century portraits were painted by local artists, whose work does not constitute an identifiable school, although it differs from contemporary Polish or Ukrainian portraiture and shows both Byzantine and Renaissance influences.

By the 16th century Vilnius had become an important publishing centre in eastern Europe. The Lithuanian Statute (1588) and the title page (1563) of the Radziwiłł Lithuanian Brest Bible, with its complex Renaissance composition, are examples of original 16th-century embellishment (both Vilnius, Hist. & Ethnog. Mus.). Several engravers were at work in Vilnius in the 17th century, including Conradt Götke (*fl* 1635–52), Aleksander Tarasewicz (*d c.* 1672), Leon Tarasewicz (*d c.* 1700) and the cartographer Tomasz Makowski.

In the 17th century the Lithuanian–Polish state was involved in two disastrous wars—with Russia (1654–67) and Sweden (1655–60). Vilnius was devastated and plundered by the Russians in 1655, and many art treasures were destroyed; but in spite of this, the Baroque reached an unprecedented level of development in Lithuania at the end of the 17th century. The powerful Pac family founded the best-known Baroque building in Lithuania, the Camaldolese monastery (1667–74; completed 1726) in Pažaislis, near Kaunas, built by Gian Battista Frediani

3. Vilnius, SS Peter and Paul, interior; stucco decoration by Pietro Peretti, Giovanni Maria Galli and others, 1668–76

(*fl* 1672–95), Carlo Putini and Pietro Putini. Pažaislis is also known for its wall paintings, which are close to the Venetian school; they are by Delbenė (vestibule and chapels), Michelangelo Palloni (choir) and Fernando della Croce (ceiling of the chapter house). The stuccos are by J. Merli and other Lombard stuccoists. Another remarkable Baroque building is the church of SS Peter and Paul in Vilnius (1668–76; by Jan Zaor and Fernando da Lucca), with its numerous reliefs and over 2000 stucco sculptures by Pietro Peretti and Giovanni Maria Galli from Milan and also by local craftsmen (see fig. 3). Wall paintings in the nave and the vestry are by Martino Altomonte.

Almost a third of Lithuania's population died during the 1709–11 famine and plague. The economic and political power of the Lithuanian–Polish state was undermined by deadlock in the assemblies of the nobility and by the interference of Russia and Prussia. Even in this unfavourable situation, however, a local school of architecture was set up (architecture had been taught by the Jesuits and the Dominicans), rich libraries were established and numerous churches built. After fires in 1726, 1738 and 1748 many secular buildings in Vilnius were renovated in late Baroque style, which in Lithuania was moderate; elements of French Rococo, which was spreading in western Europe, are evident only in some interiors.

One of the distinctive features of 18th-century churches—slender twin-tower façades, Gothic in their proportions—emerged in Vilnius when existing towers were rebuilt: for example the façade of the Benedictine church of St Catherine (1741–2; by JAN KRZYSTOF GLAUBITZ). The type of twin-tower Baroque façade spread through Lithuania, and the façades of existing churches were raised, as in the Jesuit church, Kaunas, and the Dominican churches at Jieznas, Seinai and Virbalis. The towerless façade of the church of St Jonas in Vilnius, attributed to Francesco Placidi (*d* after 1768), is especially notable. A further characteristic of Lithuanian late Baroque developed in the mid-18th century: elements of ornamentation and wall structure were organized into a unified undulating mass, as in the interior of the Dominican church of the Holy Spirit in Vilnius by Ludwik Hryncewicz, the façade of the church at Berezwecz (1753–63) and the Basil Gate (1761; by Glaubitz) in Vilnius.

There are many surviving 18th-century church interiors including altars with Rococo decoration, sculptures, woodcarvings and furniture, as in the high altar in St Jonas's and the interior of St Catherine's (by Glaubitz and J. Herdegen) in Vilnius. Unfortunately, the wood-carvings in the Cistercian church in Vilnius were almost completely destroyed after World War II. Wall paintings with illusionistic elements elevating the central nave have survived in the Calvary Church in Vilnius. Painters in the 18th century included artists who had studied abroad, such as FRANCISZEK SMUGLEWICZ, local artists influenced by them, and foreigners such as Augustyn de Mirys and Jakub Wessel. There were also monastic artists (e.g. Jokubas Breceris). Eighteenth-century engravers included Jozeph Perli and Ipolit Perli, J. E. Beling and Ignatas Karega (1764–95).

### III. After *c.* 1780.

Neo-classicism began to emerge in Lithuania at the end of the 18th century. The Jesuit academy in Vilnius,

reorganized at the end of the century into the Principal School of Lithuania (Vilnius University from 1803), included among its teachers one of the forerunners of Lithuanian Neo-classicism, M. Knakfus (*d* 1794), architect of the Verkiai Palace ensemble, the façade of the University Observatory and the Wittinghof House. His talented pupil WAWRZYNIEC GUCIEWICZ supervised the reconstruction of Vilnius Cathedral from 1783 and rebuilt Vilnius Town Hall (1781–6). Karolis Podčasinskis (1790–1860), professor of architecture in Vilnius in the early 19th century, built the Jašiunai Palace and the Vilnius Evangelical Reform church (1830–35). The Neo-classical style was also used in the construction of Catholic churches (e.g. at Nedzingė and Taujėnai). The most impressive rotunda church is at Sudervė (1802–11; by L. Bortkevičius). The Neo-classical style is mainly evident, however, in palaces and manor houses. It is also seen in buildings constructed during the Russian colonization of Lithuania, although many of these buildings remained alien to the Lithuanian context, as did the numerous Russian churches of little architectural merit built to spread Orthodoxy in Lithuania.

Besides architecture (1793), departments of painting (1797) and later of sculpture and engraving (1805) were set up within the Principal School of Lithuania, and these became known later as the Vilnius School of Arts. The department of painting was headed by Franciszek Smuglewicz, who produced many paintings for Vilnius Cathedral and other churches and who decorated the aula of Vilnius University. Together with JONAS RUSTEMAS, he trained a whole generation of painters; including WALENTY WAŃKOWICZ and KANUTAS RUSECKAS. The aesthetics of classicism and Romanticism were fostered at the school, and certain rudiments of realism were reflected in the work of pupils of Jonas Rustemas in the first half of the 19th century, including Karol Ripinski (1808–92) and Aleksander Slendzinski (?1803–?76). The Vilnius School of Arts was also attended by the engravers Joseph Saunders (1773–1845) and Bogumil Kisling (1790–?1846). The department of sculpture, headed by André-Jean Lebrun (1737–1811) and Kazimierz Jelski (1782–1867), was not as influential as the department of painting.

Vilnius University set up the first museum collection at the end of the 18th century, and collections of paintings and drawings, medals and coins, together with botanical and mineralogical items, increased substantially at the beginning of the 19th century and were accessible to researchers and the public. In 1812 some Lithuanian aristocrats took Napoleon's side in the war against the Russians, and after their defeat their estates and collections were confiscated; paintings from Nieświez belonging to Dominik Radziwiłł were taken to Russia while less important portraits remained in Nieświez.

After the 1831 uprising the collections of the rebels were taken to various Russian museums and sometimes destroyed. Vilnius University, including the Vilnius School of Arts, was closed in 1832 and the collections distributed among the universities of Kiev, Tartu and Khar'kov. Kanutas Ruseckas almost alone continued the traditions of the Vilnius School of Arts, producing several academicist paintings for churches and idealized images of peasants. His studio, and the workshops of Vincentas Dmachauskas (1807–62) and Karolis Ripinskis, became art centres in Vilnius. Mykolas Elviras Andriolis (1836–93), who studied in St Petersburg, Rome and Paris, executed 11 paintings for Kaunas Cathedral, illustrations for works by the poet Adam Mickiewicz, and history paintings. Romantic paintings on Lithuanian history were executed by Kazimieras Alchimavičius (1840–1916), who lived in Warsaw. Also painting at this time were Adomas Šemešys (?1808–64), Karolis Rafalavičius (1831–61) and Jonas Zenkevičius (1825–88).

Many painters were also printmakers, including the lithographers Kazimieras Bachmatavičius (1808–37), Konstantinas Kukevičius (1810–?40) and Karolis Račinskis (1802–89). The *Vilnius Album* (1848–60), published by Jonas Kazimieras Vilčinskis (1806–62), comprised work by Ruseckas, Mykolas Kulieša (1800–63), Albertas Žametas-Žemaitis (1819–76) and Andriolis, among others. Juzef Ozemblowski (1804–78) produced lithographs of historical sites in Lithuania, while woodcuts by Vincentas Smakauskas (1779–1876) published in J. Kraševskis's *Vitoli's Lament* (Vilnius, 1846) are of particular note.

On the basis of the collection of E. Tyszkiewicz, a museum of antiquities was set up in 1855 in the aula of the closed Vilnius University. The initial collection of medals, old atlases, drawings and portraits and the library consisting of 3000 volumes was supplemented by history paintings donated by Smuglewicz, Rustemas, Jonas Damelis (1780–1840), Juozapas Oleškevičius (1777–1830), Juozapas Peška (1767–1831) and Tommaso Dolabella. Attempts were made to acquire for the museum collections confiscated after the 1831 uprising, but after the 1863 uprising the museum was broken up, and only the Vilnius Public Library remained. All art treasures linked with Lithuanian history were taken to the Rumyantsev Museum in Moscow, mainly portraits, history paintings, drawings and examples of applied art. (A collection of 150 drawings was returned to Lithuania from the Pushkin Museum of Fine Arts, Moscow, in 1966, and some paintings were returned in 1962.) The distribution of folk woodcuts with Lithuanian inscriptions was banned, as was the building or repairing of traditional wooden crosses and chapels. Many well-known artists took part in the 1863 uprising, including Andriolis and Alchimavičius. Some of them perished, some were exiled, some emigrated. Between 1866 and 1914 there was only one art school in Vilnius training painters and draughtsmen.

The post-uprising repressions could not halt the national regeneration, expressed above all in the fostering of the Lithuanian language and history and later in an interest in folk art (textiles, vernacular architecture, wooden sculpture etc). Attempts were made to unite Lithuanian artists in diaspora. After the lifting of the prohibition on the Lithuanian press in 1904 and under the influence of the Russian revolution of 1905 and the Vilnius Seimas (parliament), cultural life revived.

The sculptor PETRAS RIMŠA was one of the organizers of the first Lithuanian art exhibition, which took place in 1907 in Vilnius. Participants in the exhibition included the painters M. K. ČIURLIONIS (see fig. 4), ANTANAS ŽMUIDZINAVIČIUS, PETRAS KALPOKAS and Kajctonas Šklėrius (1876–1932), the sculptors Petras Rimša, Juozas Zikaras (1881–1944) and Jonas Danauskas (1861–1937) and the architects Kazimieras Gabrėnas, Ipolitas Januška, besides

4. M. K. Čiurlionis: *Sonata No 6 (Sonata of the Stars)*, tempera on paper, 722×614 mm, 1908 (Kaunus, M. K. Čiurlionis Art Museum)

folk artists. Artists who returned from western Europe brought with them the influence of Post-Impressionism, while those who had lived in Russia had been influenced by Russian realism. The Lithuanian Art Society was set up in 1907 and organized eight exhibitions before World War I. Additional participants included Adomas Varnas (1879–1979), Antanas Vivulskis (architect; 1877–1919), Kazimieras Ulianskas, Adalbertas Staneika, Jonas Mackevičius (1872–1954), Jonas Šileika, Tadas Daugirdas, the graphic artist Paulius Galaunė (1890–1989) and Justinas Vienožinskis (1886–1960).

The 1911 posthumous Čiurlionis exhibition, also held in St Petersburg and Moscow, enjoyed great success. The artist's symbolic, intuitive visions corresponded with the spiritual and aesthetic mood of the time, but there were no followers of this trend in Lithuania. Čiurlionis had some influence on Kazys Šimonis (1887–1978), but the impact of Expressionism and Constructivism is more pronounced in Šimonis's work.

Lithuania gained independence in 1918, and the Lithuanian Art Society was revived in 1920, in Kaunas, because Vilnius was occupied by the Poles. A Society of Artists, with sections for the theatre, music, literature and fine arts, already existed in Kaunas, and an exhibition organized by both societies was held in 1920. The Society of Artists, which in 1922 became the Lithuanian School of Art, established painting courses led by Vienožinskis. Painting was taught by Kalpokas, sculpture by Zikaras, drawing by Adomas Galdikas (1893–1969), wall painting and mosaic by Juozas Mikėnas (1901–64) and Stasys Ušinskas (1905–74), decorative arts by Vladas Didžiokas (1889–1942), ceramics by Pranas Brazdžius (1895–1982). Grants were awarded to more talented students to train in western European art centres.

The archaeological commission was entrusted with collecting and preserving works of art in Lithuania. The M. K. Čiurlionis State Art Museum in Kaunas houses the collections of artists' societies and the Čiurlionis heritage. It acquired its own building in 1925, with Paulius Galaunė as its Director. Its role included the collecting of folk art as well as fine arts, the supervision of privately owned works of art, which, not protected by law, were liable to be removed from Lithuania, the preservation of architectural monuments and the negotiation of the return of works taken to Russia before World War I.

In the early 20th century and during the period of Lithuanian independence, architecture, limited by lack of finance, was biased towards Functionalism but retained an aesthetic dimension, as in the work of Vladas Dubeneckis (1888–1932), MIKOLAS SONGAYLA and Vytantas Landsbergis-Žemkalnis (1893–1994). The first graduates of the School of Art in Kaunas were active from 1930. The Society of Independent Artists was set up and included Adolfas Valeška, Antanas Samuolis (1899–1942), Viktoras Vizgirda (1904–93), Leonardas Kazokas (1905–81) and Antanas Rugštelė. They opposed academicism, naturalism and dilettantism but at the same time were not attracted to Modernism. Because of the society's lack of a defined programme, in 1932 some members, among them Samuolis and Vizgirda, joined a new group, ARS, which included Adomas Galdikas, Antanas Gudaitis (1904–90), Vytautas Kazimieras Jonynas (*b* 1907), Telesforas Kulakauskas (1907–77), Juozas Mikėnas and J. Stepanavičius. Its programme was to revive the style of the epoch of national regeneration, based on folk art traditions. A pro-Marxist society of artists was set up in the same year. It adopted the principles of SOCIALIST REALISM, which were later imposed on all other artists during the Soviet occupation. A joint union of Lithuanian artists was formed in 1935 and organized large exhibitions. The Soviet stranglehold on art was less extreme after Stalin's death in 1953, but it still prevented artistic independence. Art education and museum work, especially the collecting of modern art, were subjected to the criteria and interests of the totalitarian system. Almost the entire staff of the Vilnius School of Arts was replaced.

In 1944, during the Russian advance on Lithuania, many talented artists left for the West, including Galdikas, Jonynas and Vizgirda. While working in difficult conditions in refugee camps in 1946–9, on the initiative of Jonynas they set up an Institute of Applied Arts in Freiburg, Germany, which was attended by such artists as Romas Viesulas (*b* 1918) and Vytautas Ignas (*b* 1924), who had grown up in emigration. Exhibitions of Lithuanian art soon moved from the refugee camps to German galleries and museums. Galdikas, Jonynas and Vytautas Kasiulis (1918–95) held an exhibition in Paris, and Viktoras Petravičius (1906–89), Jonynas and the Estonian Eduard Viiralt held a joint exhibition of prints in Rome. Numerous illustrated books of poetry and albums of reproductions were published.

About 1950, many Lithuanian artists moved to the USA; some moved to Australia and Canada, while others remained in Paris (Galdikas, V. Kasiulis and Antanas Mončys (1921–93)); the sculptor Elena Gaputytė (1927–92) stayed in Britain. Lithuanian art in emigration ranged from representational, often Expressionist work to pure abstraction. An émigré generation educated in the USA and Europe emerged in the 1960s and 1970s; some of them gained international recognition, including the graphic artist Romas Viesulas, the painter Keytutis Zapkus (*b* 1938) and the sculptor Antanas Brazdys (*b* 1939), all of whom produced abstract art.

Among the few artists of the older generation who remained in Lithuania yet retained their artistic individuality were the sculptors Robertas Antinis (1898–1981), Juozas Mikėnas and Bronius Pundzius (1907–59), the painters Antanas Gudaitis, Justinas Vienožinskis, Stasys Ušinskas, the graphic artist Telesforas Kulakauskas and the stage designer Liudas Truikys (1904–87), who was almost completely excluded from public life. GEDIMINAS JAKUBONIS developed the ideas of Lithuanian sculptors of the 1930s, such as Vincas Grybas.

The generation that emerged in Lithuania in the 1960s and 1970s restored the artificially interrupted links between the generations and put an end to the country's isolation from art life in the West. These artists, including the painters Augustinas Savickas (*b* 1919) and Vincas Kisarauskas (1934–88) and the sculptors Teodoras Kazimieras Valaitis (1934–74) and Vladas Vildžiunas (*b* 1932; see

5. Vladas Vildžiunas: *Ecce homo*, marble, 1971, Villány, Hungary

fig. 5), did not attempt to follow Western trends for their own sake, however, seeking their inspiration instead in the Lithuanian heritage. Their work is dominated by representational elements and reflects complex spiritual realities. The painters Kazimiera Zimblytė (*b* 1933) and Linas Katinas (*b* 1941) and the draughtsman Vlaclas Žilius (*b*?1933) favoured abstraction. In the 1980s sculpture developed in different stylistic directions, in the work of Gediminas Karalius (*b* 1942), Stanislovas Kuzma (*b* 1947), Petras Mazuras (*b* 1949), Mindaugas Navakas (*b* 1952), Ksenija Jaroševaitė (*b* 1953) and Vladas Urbanavičius (*b* 1951), and marked the end of ideological influence in Lithuania's art life. Works previously unknown to the public began to be exhibited. Western influences, such as Expressionism and Surrealism, could be seen in the work of such painters as Rimantas Šlizys (*b* 1952), Šarūnas Šauka (*b* 1958) and Vaidas Žukas (*b* 1956) and the draughtsman Mikas Vilutis (*b* 1944).

BIBLIOGRAPHY

V. Maciūnas, ed.: *Lietuva* [Lithuania], xv (Boston, 1968, rev. Vilnius, 2/1990)
I. Korsakaitė, ed.: *XX a. Lietuviu, dailės istorija* [20th-century Lithuanian art history], 2 vols (Vilnius, 1982–3)
M. Matušaitė: *Portretas XVI–XVIII a. Lietuvoje* [The portrait in Lithuania in the 16th–18th centuries] (Vilnius, 1984)
N. Kitkauskas and P. Ališanka: 'Apie viduramžiu Vilniaus katedra' [About Vilnius cathedral in the middle ages], *Kult. Barai*, 4–7 (1986)
Z. Žemaitytė: *Paulius Galaunė* (Vilnius, 1988)
B. Kulnytė, ed.: *Lietuvos istorijos paminklai iš Lietuvos istorijos ir etnografijos muziejaus rinkiniu* [Relics of Lithuanian history from the collections of the Lithuanian Historical and Ethnographical Museum] (Vilnius, 1990)

LIUDVIKA VILDŽIŪNAITĖ-POCIŪNIENĖ

**Li Ti.** *See* LI DI.

**Litomyšl Castle.** Renaissance palace in Litomyšl, 57 km south-east of Hradec Králové in the Czech Republic. The 16th-century building is one of the best examples of Czech Renaissance architecture. There was a fortified Slav settlement on the site, then a castle (first mentioned in AD 981) and from 1344 a bishop's residence. In 1567 it was acquired by the Bohemian Chancellor, Vratislav of Pernštejn, who decided to build a luxurious and imposing family residence there. He summoned from Prague the court architect Giovanni Battista Aostalli, who was in charge of the project from 1568 to 1575. The house was completed by Ulrico Aostalli in 1581. Its plan comprises a massive three-storey block in four wings around two internal courtyards, with the chapel of St Michael in the south-east corner. The older medieval buildings were incorporated into the Renaissance complex in parts of the west and north wings. The main exterior façades are not architecturally articulated except for a loggia opened to both sides on the second floor of the south wing. After 1580 the façades were faced with *sgraffito* rustication by Simon Vlach. The corner pavilions of the building are topped by gables, articulated with pilasters over which horizontal cornices run.

Three sides of the square courtyard have arcades, supported on the ground floor by banded piers and on the upper floors by Tuscan and Ionic columns. The main façade of the north wing is rusticated on the ground floor; on the upper floors it is decorated with figurative *sgraffiti* depicting the *Battle of the Milvian Bridge* after the painting (before 1524) by Giulio Romano in the Sala di Costantino,

Vatican, and scenes from the story of Samson (in the areas between the windows), inspired by the drawings of Maarten van Heemskerck, both sets mediated through engravings. The house was damaged by fire in 1775 and repaired during the 1790s, when the theatre was also constructed (1796–7); this has a painted curtain and decorations by the Viennese court painter Josef Platzer (1751–1806), and it is one of the oldest theatres preserved in a European great house. In 1950 the town of Litomyšl and the house were made a national conservation area; the building now houses the Museum of Czech Music.

BIBLIOGRAPHY

E. Šamánková: *Architektura české renesance* [Bohemian Renaissance architecture] (Prague, 1961)
K. Reichertová: *Litomyšl* (Prague, 1977)
J. Hořejší: 'Litomyšl', *Umělecké památky Čech* [Artistic monuments of Bohemia], ii (Prague, 1978), pp. 290–300
J. Krčálová: 'The Palace and the Château', *Renaissance Art in Bohemia* (London, 1979), pp. 101–2

JIŘINA HOŘEJŠÍ

**Li Tsai.** *See* LI ZAI.

**Little, Arthur** (*b* Boston, MA, 29 Nov 1852; *d* Wenham, MA, 28 March 1925). American architect. He was an important member of the group of Boston architects who, during the last quarter of the 19th century, were responsible for reviving interest in colonial buildings (*see* COLONIAL REVIVAL). He trained at the Massachusetts Institute of Technology, Cambridge, in 1871–5. In 1876 he studied architecture there while also apprenticed in the firm of Peabody & Stearns. Robert Swain Peabody, the principal designer of the firm, was an enthusiast of 18th- and early 19th-century architecture and probably encouraged Little to publish *Early New England Interiors* (1878), which reproduces Little's sketches of colonial buildings in Boston, New Hampshire and Maine. Little established an independent practice in 1878, and one of his first works was Cliffs (1879), Manchester-by-the-Sea, MA, a private house with details such as balustrades and pedimented dormers that derive from Federal-style houses in New England. Between 1880 and 1882 he built a number of summer residences for members of his family at Swampscott, MA, including Shingleside (1880–81) and Grasshead (1882). Both houses are typical of the Shingle style, responding to their seaside sites with natural materials such as roughly textured wood shingles. The plans of the houses allow living spaces to flow into one another, thus reflecting their use as seasonal retreats by affluent clients. Little formed a partnership with Herbert Browne (1860–1946) around 1890; the two continued to design elaborate residences such as the Larz Anderson House (1902–5), in the north-west part of Washington, DC, which demonstrates Little's interest in Italian Renaissance palaces.

WRITINGS

*Early New England Interiors: Sketches in Salem, Marblehead, Portsmouth and Kittery* (Boston, 1878)

BIBLIOGRAPHY

V. J. Scully jr: *The Shingle Style and the Stick Style* (New Haven, 1955, rev. 1971)
W. K. Sturges: 'Arthur Little and the Colonial Revival', *J. Soc. Archt. Historians*, xxxii (1973), pp. 147–63

KEVIN D. MURPHY

**Little Masters** [Fr. *Petits maîtres*; Ger. *Kleinmeister*]. Term that refers in the broadest sense to northern European artists who made small-format prints (almost exclusively engravings) during the first half of the 16th century. As early as 1679 Joachim von Sandrart referred to the '*kleine Meister*', and John Evelyn's reference of 1662 to 'the Polite Masters' is probably a confusion with the French *Petits maîtres*. The term has most frequently been applied exclusively to three artists in the generation immediately following Albrecht Dürer in Nuremberg: Sebald Beham, his brother Barthel Beham and Georg Pencz. The phrase 'Nuremberg Little Masters' is often used to make this clarification, although only Pencz pursued his entire career in Nuremberg. In addition to their preference for a small engraving format, these three shared an association with Dürer (for whom Pencz probably worked) and the distinction of having been evicted from Nuremberg in January 1525 (at the culmination of the German Peasant Revolt) for their agnostic and anarchistic convictions. Because of their radical political and religious views, they were also known as the 'three godless painters'. When the term is used in a broader sense, Little Masters may include other engravers who favoured a minute format, such as Jakob Binck, Master I.B. and Heinrich Aldegrever in Germany and Allaert Claesz. and Dirk Vellert in the Low Countries.

Although not generally considered to be a Little Master himself, Albrecht Altdorfer's small engravings (in part inspired by Italian niello engravings) strongly influenced the Little Masters. The rise in popularity of small engravings could be due to several factors: the custom of collecting them in folders and books, their applications in the decorative arts and a growing interest in miniature objects that was not to find its full expression until later in the century with the evolution of the *Kunstkammer*. The size of the Little Masters' engravings, excepting portraits and friezes, rarely exceeds that of Dürer's *Engraved Passion* series (about 117×75 mm). Their smallest works are about the size of a postage stamp.

The engravings by this group of artists encompass a wide range of Renaissance concerns, including allegory, antiquity, biblical themes, secular themes and decorative designs. Although their compositions often derive from Dürer and his contemporaries, such as the Italian Marcantonio Raimondi, the Little Masters were particularly inventive when dealing with the themes of sexuality, mortality and scenes of soldiers and peasants. The Nuremberg Little Masters fully explored these secular themes in their large woodcuts as well.

Barthel Beham may be singled out as the most gifted and inventive of the Little Masters. His first dated engravings, for example *Foot Soldier in front of a Tree* (1520; see Pauli, no. 50), done at the age of 18, display a considerable virtuosity and a preference for complex figural compositions. In 1547 Johann Neudörfer remarked that the Beham brothers and Pencz were famous for their paintings, drawings and prints and that their prints, including Sebald's entire graphic output, were still abundantly available (Neudörfer, p. 138). When Karel van Mander wrote his *Schilderboeck* 57 years later, however, the artists had fallen into obscurity.

BIBLIOGRAPHY
J. Neudörfer: *Des Johann Neudörfer Schreib- und Rechenmeisters zu Nürnberg Nachrichten von Künstlern und Werkleuten daselbst aus dem Jahre 1547*, ed. G. W. K. Lochner (Vienna, 1875)
W. B. Scott: *The Little Masters* (New York and London, 1879)
H. W. Singer: *Die Kleinmeister*, Künstler-Monographien, xcii (Bielefeld and Leipzig, 1908)
E. Waldmann: *Die Nürnberger Kleinmeister*, Meister der Graphik, v (Leipzig, 1910)
G. Pauli: *Barthel Beham: Ein kritisches Verzeichnis seiner Kupferstiche* (Strasburg, 1911)
H. Zschelletzschky: *Die 'drei gottlosen Maler' von Nürnberg, Sebald Beham, Barthel Beham, und Georg Pencz: Historische Grundlagen und ikonologische Probleme ihrer Graphik zu Reformations- und Bauernkriegszeit* (Leipzig, 1975)
G. Vogler: *Nürnberg, 1524/25: Studien zur Geschichte der reformatorischen und sozialen Bewegung in der Reichsstadt* (Berlin, 1982)
*The World in Miniature: Engravings by the German Little Masters, 1500–1550* (exh. cat. by S. H. Goddard and others, Lawrence, U. KS, Spencer Mus. A., 1988)
K. Moxey and others: 'The Graphic Art of the Godless Painters of Nuremberg', *Register* [Lawrence, U. KS], viii/6 (1989)
STEPHEN H. GODDARD

**Littleton, Harvey K.** (*b* Corning, NY, 1922). American glassmaker, potter and teacher. He was introduced to glass science and technology by his father, Jesse Littleton, director of research for the Corning Glass Works, and had an academic art education under the sculptor Enfred Anderson at the Corning Free Academy. He studied industrial design at the University of Michigan (1947) and then sculpture and ceramics at the Cranbrook Academy of Art, Bloomfield Hills, MI. During summer vacations he worked at Corning. Despite some early experiments in glass casting from ceramic models, Littleton worked primarily in ceramics from 1946 until the late 1950s, when he gradually realized that glassblowing could be carried out in small art studios and did not need to be confined to factory production. In 1962 in his workshop at the Toledo Museum of Art, OH, he demonstrated this idea to young artists with Dominick Labino (1910–87). He thus provided the foundation for forming studio glass courses in American universities; the first was set up in 1963 at the University of Wisconsin at Madison, where he taught. Before this most studio glass was made by casting sculpture or laminating sheet glass for two-dimensional works.

Littleton's studio glass in the 1960s was vessel-orientated, but he was able to free his work from this formal constraint in the late 1960s when he began to work in a mature sculptural style, with geometric forms, usually columns or tubes, defined by the colour of multiple cased overlays (*see* GLASS, colour pl. VII, fig. 2). In 1976 Littleton left the University of Wisconsin to pursue his own work in North Carolina.

BIBLIOGRAPHY
*Harvey K. Littleton: A Retrospective Exhibition* (exh. cat. by J. F. Byrd, Atlanta, GA, High Mus. A., 1984)
ELLEN PAUL DENKER

**Littmann, Max** (*b* Chemnitz, 3 Jan 1862; *d* Munich, 20 Sept 1931). German architect. After an apprenticeship as a mason in Chemnitz, he studied architecture (1880–85) at the Dresden Akademie before moving to Munich where his first buildings (1888–92) were large residential blocks in a Baroque Revival style. As a partner in the building firm of Heilmann & Littmann, founded with his father-in-law in 1892, he was involved in a large number of diverse buildings in Munich, and it is not always possible to determine Littmann's exact contribution to a design. Apart from numerous residential buildings (over 100 survive), the firm built in Munich his most popular building, the Hofbräuhaus (1897), making use of the South German Renaissance idiom typical of the time; the Schauspielhaus (1900–01), one of the outstanding examples of German *Jugendstil* architecture; and the Prinzregententheater (1900–01), closely modelled on the concept of the Richard-Wagner-Festspielhaus in Bayreuth, with a steep amphitheatre without tiers.

Other work included the department stores of Hermann Tietz and Oberpollinger (1903), the publishing house of the *Süddeutsche Zeitung* (1904–5) and one of the first buildings using exposed reinforced concrete, the bare, undecorated Bau der Anatomie (1905–8). This was one of the most modern utilitarian buildings of its time, its façade, which was extensively glazed, reflecting the uses of the interior space.

On account of the success of his Kurhaus at Bad Reichenhall (1898–1900), Littmann was commissioned (1908) by the Bavarian regional government to construct extensive health resort buildings at Bad Kissingen, where he had built the Kurtheater in 1904–5. About this time he detached himself increasingly from the firm of Heilmann & Littmann to allow more scope for his own artistic work. He had evolved a special interest in theatre design, building the Schillertheater (1905–6; *see* THEATRE, §III, 4(ii)(a)), Berlin, the Hoftheater (1906–7), Weimar, the Künstlertheater (1908; destr. 1945), Munich, and the Stadttheater (1908–9; destr. 1945), Hildesheim. In addition, he took part in many theatre competitions (1901–12). The pinnacle of his work is undoubtedly the Stuttgart Hoftheater (1909–12). Two theatres of different sizes, the 'Kleines Haus' (destr. 1944) and the 'Grosses Haus' (rest. 1983–4), were linked by administrative and storage wings to form an extensive complex. Before his death Littmann was able to complete two further theatres, at Bozen (now Bolzano, Italy; 1913–18) and Neustrelitz (1926–8).

BIBLIOGRAPHY

Thieme–Becker; Wasmuth

G. J. Wolf: *Max Littmann, 1862–1931* (Munich, 1931)

D. Weiss-Vossenkuhl: *Das Opernhaus in Stuttgart von Max Littmann, 1910–1912* (Stuttgart, 1983)

H. Habel: *Denkmäler in Bayern* (1985), I/i of Landeshauptstadt München (Munich, 1985–6)

B. P. Schaul: *Das Prinzregententheater in München und die Reform des Theaterbaus um 1900: Max Littmann als Theaterarchitekt* (Munich, 1987)

DIETRICH NEUMANN

**Liu Chüeh.** *See* LIU JUE.

**Liudprand** (*b* Pavia, *c.* AD 920; *d c.* 970–73). Frankish historian, diplomat and Bishop of Cremona. His two unusually informative accounts of missions to Constantinople are of great art-historical interest. The *Antapodosis* (Book of Revenge) enthusiastically describes the union of art, culture and ceremonial he observed on a visit to the court of Constantine VII in 949, introducing Western readers to Byzantine self-representation. The *Legatio* (Embassy) chronicled his failed mission for Emperor Otto I to Nicephorus II Phocas in 968, and mirrored the diplomatic difficulties between the two emperors as well as depicting the more sober atmosphere of Nicephoran Constantinople. In this work Liudprand fiercely attacked anything Byzantine, repeating old prejudices against the 'treacherous and effeminate' Greeks and emphasizing religious differences.

Although emotional and egocentric, these two accounts use accurately observed detail to justify their contradictory verdicts upon Byzantine culture. *Antapodosis* VI.5 is famous for its description of the mechanized artefacts of the imperial audience hall, where gilded lions roared with opened mouths and quivering tongues while their tails beat the floor, gilded bronze songbirds warbled from a similar tree and the throne could be raised to the ceiling. Sections VI.7–10 detail the topography of the palace, the ceremonial and entertainments during banquets, and such ceremonies as the Feast of the Nineteen Couches. The *Legatio* continuously makes disparaging but informative references to daily life, meals, ceremonies and even customs regulations.

WRITINGS

F. A. Wright, ed.: *Works of Liudprand of Cremona* (London, 1930)

B. Scott, ed. and trans.: *Liudprand: Relatio de legatione Constantinopolitana* (Bristol, 1993)

F. A. Wright, trans.: *Liudprand: The Embassy to Constantinople and Other Writings*, ed. J. J. Norwich (London and Rutland, VT, 1993)

BIBLIOGRAPHY

J. Koder and M. Weber: *Liutprand von Cremona in Konstantinopel* (Vienna, 1980)

M. Rentschler: *Liudprand von Cremona: Eine Studie zum ost-westlichen Kulturgefälle im Mittelalter* (Frankfurt, 1981)

CONSTANZE M. SCHUMMER

**Liu Guosong.** *See* LIU KUO-SONG.

**Liu Haisu** [Liu Hai-su; *ming* Pan; *zi* Jifang; *hao* Haiweng] (*b* Changzhou, Jiangsu Province, 1896; *d* Shanghai, 6 Aug 1994). Chinese art educator and painter. He came from a merchant family that had supported the Taiping Rebellion (1850–64). He began to learn painting at the age of six by studying line drawings in the style of YUN SHOUPING. At the age of 13 he went to Shanghai, hoping to study Western painting. He did not find any established art school there but discovered the works of Velázquez and Goya, which he copied to learn Western oil and watercolour techniques. In 1912 he established the Shanghai Academy of Painting, predecessor of the Shanghai Academy of Fine Arts, with Wu Shiguang, Zhang Yuguang (1885–1968) and others. He also worked with a teacher who had studied Western painting in Japan and briefly attended Aurora University, which was run by French Catholic missionaries.

Liu Haisu held many progressive ideas about art education: he introduced mixed-sex education, started a summer school and correspondence courses in art, instituted public exhibitions of works by members of the academy and took students on trips to learn to sketch from life. In 1914 he began to use live models in drawing classes, probably the first instance of this practice in China. This caused such a furore that in 1926 the academy was ordered to be closed and Liu Haisu to be arrested. The threat was only averted by the intervention of many progressive intellectuals, notably the then president of Peking University, Cai Yuanpei (1876–1940).

Liu made a number of trips abroad, including visits to Japan in 1919, 1920 and 1927. On his first tour of Europe, between 1929 and 1931, he met such artists as Matisse and Picasso, and he exhibited works in the Salon d'Automne (see PARIS, §III, 3). On his second tour, between 1933 and 1935, he introduced modern Chinese painting to a European audience in exhibitions and lectures held in Germany, the Netherlands, Switzerland, France and Britain. Although Liu Haisu continued to paint in Western media throughout his life, his trips abroad usually stimulated him to return to Chinese painting techniques. While his early works are marked by Impressionist and Post-Impressionist influences, especially that of Van Gogh, after his return from his second European tour Liu's oil paintings often included such Chinese devices as the use of floating clouds to suggest space, unpainted areas to convey the vastness of nature, and calligraphic brushwork to enliven the pictorial surfaces. At the same time, his Chinese paintings were enriched with a typically European use of colour, light and shade, and definition of forms. He is also known for his traditional Chinese paintings of tigers, lions and eagles together with pine trees, symbols of China's strength and endurance.

In 1952 Liu Haisu was made Principal of the East China Academy of Fine Arts, and in 1979 he became Principal of the Nanjing Academy of Fine Arts. In 1981 he was designated honorary fellow of the Italian Academy of Fine Arts, and in 1988 the French Ministry of Culture awarded him the honorary title 'Commandeur de l'ordre des arts et des lettres'.

WRITINGS

Zhongguo huihua shang de liufa lun [On the six principles of Chinese painting] (Shanghai, 1957)

BIBLIOGRAPHY

V. Wu: Contemporary Chinese Painters, i (Hong Kong, 1982)
Mayching Kao, ed.: Twentieth-century Chinese Painting (New York, 1988)
Obituary, The Times (20 Sept 1994)

HSIO-YEN SHIH

**Liu Jue** [Liu Chüeh; zi Tingmei; hao Wan'an] (b Suzhou, Jiangsu Province, 1410; d Suzhou, 1472). Chinese painter, calligrapher, poet and government official. He mainly painted landscapes inspired by the great painters of the Yuan period (1279–1368). Having obtained the juren provincial degree in 1438, he served at the imperial court in Beijing until he was 50 years old, when he retired to his native city. There he built a house and a garden, in which he held meetings and parties with his learned friends. Shen Zhou, the founder of the Wu school and Liu's younger contemporary, was greatly influenced by him. In Liu's later years they often met and travelled together.

Liu successfully blended the styles of the Four Masters of the Yuan period—Ni Zan, Huang Gongwang, Wu Zhen and Wang Meng. Such works were usually executed in ink on paper, often with sparingly applied washes. He did not seek merely to imitate former masterpieces but rather to grasp their mood and incorporate their spirit into his own works. He created a more formal structure in the compositions executed to be mounted in the hanging scroll format than his Yuan predecessors did, by stressing a firm

foreground and a closer relationship between the background and foreground. The towering cliffs in the background rise upwards close to the middle ground in a high, massive group with accompanying lower cliffs to the sides. In the mountains, small, rounded boulders are densely covered with ink dots of dark moss and grasses that convey the impression of wild nature. The middle ground is separated from the foreground by an inlet of water, while the trees growing on the rocky ground in the front reach across the water to unite them. By combining thick, dry brushstrokes with wetter strokes in the dotting and finer details, he obtained a rhythmic movement in a bold expressionistic fashion. An example of this is Pure and Plain Pavilion, a painting of his own retreat and the garden just behind the low buildings (hanging scroll, ink on paper, 972×354 mm, 1458; Taipei, N. Pal. Mus.).

In small paintings he depicted close-up views of landscapes by placing darker ink dots and strokes among lighter strokes in graduated ink tones in a dynamic interplay of mass and space. The dramatic contrast between long and short strokes, sometimes in winding and crossing lines, together with the dots gives an impression of excitement, as seen in Landscape (handscroll, ink on paper, 336×578 mm, 1471; Washington, DC, Freer). Like other painters, he inscribed his paintings, and famous contemporaries as well as later well-known people added poems and notes on them.

BIBLIOGRAPHY

J. Cahill: Parting at the Shore: Chinese Painting of the Early and Middle Ming Dynasty, 1368–1580 (New York and Tokyo, 1978), pp. 79–82

BENT L. PEDERSEN

**Liu Kuo-song** [Liu Guosong] (b Yidu, Shandong Province, 1932). Chinese painter. The son of an army officer who died early in the Sino-Japanese War (1937–45), Liu Kuo-song spent his childhood as a refugee in central China. He arrived in Taiwan in 1949 and was admitted to the Art Department of the National Normal University in 1951, graduating in 1956, the same year that he and fellow students founded the Wuyue huahui (Fifth Moon Painting Group). Although he was trained in both traditional Chinese and Western techniques, Liu was most interested in modern and contemporary movements in the West: Cézanne, Matisse, Picasso and Klee were among the first important influences on his painting. More important, however, was the impact made by ABSTRACT EXPRESSIONISM in the late 1950s. Liu and his colleagues recognized theoretical and stylistic similarities between this American art movement and Chinese literati (wenren hua) painting: Willem de Kooning, Mark Rothko, Franz Kline and Jackson Pollock became their inspiration. Liu and his group became the second generation of Chinese painters to interpret Chinese traditions with modern Western techniques and images. Unlike Xu Beihong, Lin Fengmian and Liu Haisu, who had all received training abroad, these young painters learnt of developments in America and Europe from books and had little exposure to original works.

In 1961 Liu Kuo-song abandoned two years of experiments using oil mixed with plaster and other media and returned to Chinese ink painting. His use of traditional materials included such techniques as collage, frottage and indirect application of ink. By 1963 he had achieved a distinctive personal style in which he applied ink boldly with a large brush and made subtle use of light colours to contrast with the whiteness and coarse texture of the long-fibred paper, evoking mountains, rocks, mists and clouds. While he had already participated in the Young Asian Artists exhibition in Tokyo as early as 1957, and in both the São Paolo and Paris biennales from 1959, it was his work in this new and individual style that was shown in his first one-man exhibition at the National Taiwan Art Gallery in Taipei in 1965. This event attracted his first notices in English and the attention of a number of Chinese art historians based in the USA. The following year Liu visited the USA, and his works were among the exhibits in the New Chinese Landscape exhibition.

The international success of Liu's paintings and the publication in 1965 of his book of essays, *Zhongguo xiandaihua de lu* ('Whither Chinese painting?'), made him the most prominent of his generation of artists from Taiwan. He wrote numerous newspaper and journal articles on issues in contemporary Chinese art, as well as a second book, *Linmo, xiesheng, chuangzao* ('Copying, drawing, creating') published in 1966. Liu continued to explore the possiblities of abstraction in Chinese media, but between 1967 and 1972 he produced works in mixed media, often ink and acrylic on paper, including a series called *Which is Earth?*, inspired by photographs of the first landing on the moon. He taught at various art schools in Taiwan, the USA and Hong Kong. Since 1971 he has lectured in the Department of Fine Arts at the Chinese University of Hong Kong.

WRITINGS

*Zhongguo xiandaihua de lu* [Whither Chinese painting?] (Taipei, 1965)
*Linmo, xiesheng, chuangzao* [Copying, drawing, creating] (Taipei, 1966)

BIBLIOGRAPHY

Chu-tsing Li: *Liu Kuo-sung: The Growth of a Modern Chinese Artist* (Taipei, 1969)
——: *Trends in Modern Chinese Painting* (Ascona, 1979), pp. 186–93

**Liu Songnian** [Liu Sung-nien] (*b* Qiantang [modern Hangzhou], Zhejiang Province; *fl* 1170s–early 13th century). Chinese painter. There is a lack of information about Liu since, as a member of the imperial painting academy, he was disdained by the Southern Song (1127–1279) literati, who considered professionals barely superior to artisans. It is known that he resided at a gate called the Qingpo men or An men in Hangzhou. He was appointed *huayuan xueshi* ('scholar of the painting academy') between 1174 and 1189 and became a *daizhao* (painter in attendance) between 1190 and 1194. The Emperor Ningzong (*reg* 1195–1224) awarded him the *jindai* ('golden belt') in 1195.

Liu studied painting with Zhang Dunli, a native of Bianliang (modern Kaifeng), Henan Province, and son-in-law of the Northern Song (960–1127) emperor Zhezong (*reg* 1086–1100). Unlike Zhang, who specialized in a Six Dynasties (AD 222–589) style of figure painting, Liu was better known for his landscape painting. Liu's style referred back to the Northern Song, with elaborately composed ascending forms in receding planes (see CHINA, §V,

3(iv)(a)), which were imitated in the 15th century by Dai Jin, leading exponent of the Zhe school. Liu described trees with trunks consisting of two lines drawn with a vertical brush and foliage built up in successive layers, later interpreted by Wu Zhen and Wen Zhengming. The complexity and refinement of this technique sometimes required years of work on a single painting, and Liu was, consequently, not a prolific artist: by the 17th century, connoisseurs knew of only some ten works by him.

Works earlier attributed to Liu Songnian bore titles indicating the dominance of landscape over figural elements (see Franke), but the reverse is true of extant attributions. *A Cottage by a River in Autumn* (Boston,

Liu Songnian: *Friendly Conversation in a Pavilion by a Stream*, hanging scroll, ink and colour on silk, early 13th century (Taipei, National Palace Museum)

MA, Mus. F.A.) and *Reading the 'Yijing' by a Window in Autumn* (Shenyang, Liaoning Prov. Mus.), two round fan paintings, recall Northern Song precedents in their use of straight texture strokes, although both are composed with a diagonal emphasis more typical of the 12th century. *Reading the 'Yijing' by a Window* can be compared to the hanging scroll *Friendly Conversation in a Pavilion by a Stream* (see fig.), similarly constructed with use of *pifu cun* (small axe texture strokes). A long handscroll showing changing scenery in the four seasons (Beijing, Pal. Mus.) is very close in style to *Friendly Conversation* and is also executed in ink and colours on silk. The best known extant attributions to Liu are three paintings of *Luohan* (Skt *arhat*: 'enlightened beings') on silk (1207; Taipei, N. Pal. Mus.). The large sala tree in one of these paintings confirms Wen Zhengming's indebtedness to Liu Songnian's style.

BIBLIOGRAPHY

Franke: 'Liu Sung-nien'

HSIO-YEN SHIH

**Liu Sung-nien.** *See* LIU SONGNIAN.

**Liu Yong** [Liu Yung; *hao* Shi'an] (*b* Zhucheng, Shandong Province, 1720; *d* Beijing, 1805). Chinese calligrapher and scholar–official. The son of a Grand Secretary, he passed the civil-service examination to become a *jinshi* in 1751, then progressed from one official post to the next, working his way up through the ranks of government administration. Although there are no works extant from his early years, most texts report that Liu studied the works of Zhao Mengfu first, and then, in middle age, those of DONG QICHANG and Su Shi. As a follower of Zhao and Dong, the standard models of the day, Liu is often categorized as a calligrapher of the Copybook (*tie*) school (*see* CHINA, §IV, 2(vii)).

Liu spoke out courageously against Heshen (1750–99), the corrupt guardsman who from about 1775 held sway over the Qianlong emperor and so abused his power that the Qing court slid into decline. Liu is thus traditionally respected as a figure of honesty and integrity, and some critics say that these qualities are reflected in his calligraphy. His best works, generally in small regular script (*xiao kaishu*) or running script (*xingshu*), convey a remarkable clarity, precision and depth. Indeed, Bao Shichen ranked his small regular script as 'immortal'.

Liu was influenced in later years, as Bao and others report, by calligraphy of the Wei (AD 220–65) and Jin (AD 265–316) periods and in his seventies by the stelae of the Northern Wei (AD 386–534). Liu's interest in stelae may be reflected in his shift in the last ten years of his life away from rich, soft ink effects towards an increased strength and tautness of character formation. After periods of being out of imperial favour, Liu was eventually made Grand Secretary in 1797. After his death, his work, which Qianlong had much admired, was inscribed on stone and reproduced in the volume *Qing'ai tang shike* ('Inscriptions from Qing'ai Studio') at the order of the Jiaqing emperor (*reg* 1796–1820).

BIBLIOGRAPHY

Hummel: 'Liu Yung'

K. Shimonaka, ed.: *Shodō zenshū* [Complete collection of calligraphy], xxi (Tokyo, 2/1961), pp. 168–70, 185, pls 82–9

Uno Yukimura: *Chūgoku shodōshi* [History of Chinese calligraphy], ii (Tokyo, 1962), pp. 275–8

Yu Jianhua: *Zhongguo meishujia renming cidian* [Dictionary of Chinese artists] (Shanghai, 1981), p. 1327

ELIZABETH F. BENNETT

**Liu Yung.** *See* LIU YONG.

**Live art.** *See* PERFORMANCE ART.

**Liverpool.** Major English city and port in the metropolitan district of Merseyside. On the north-west coast of England, it is on the north-east bank of the River Mersey, where the estuary narrows before opening out to the sea. Originally a fishing village, it received a royal charter in 1207 and was dominated from the early 13th century by a powerful castle (destr. 1720). With the development of transatlantic trade in the late 17th century and the 18th, Liverpool grew quickly, until in the 19th century it became rich and the second port after London to a vast empire. With an efficient network of canals and railways, it served a large industrial hinterland. Prosperity created an adventurous, dynamic and sometimes prestigious architecture. Since 1945 changing patterns of shipping and industry have brought severe economic decline. With a population of about half a million (1981), Liverpool is the seat of two universities, the older of which started as University College in 1881, a Roman Catholic cathedral (diocese founded in 1850) and an Anglican cathedral (diocese founded in 1880).

1. History and urban development. 2. Art life and organization. 3. Centre of ceramics production.

1. HISTORY AND URBAN DEVELOPMENT. Liverpool's growth in the 18th century was marked by early buildings, such as the large Bluecoat School (1716–17), School Lane, and the Town Hall (1749–54), by John Wood the elder and modified (1789–92) by James Wyatt and from 1796 by John Foster the elder (*see* FOSTER, (1)); city merchants developed Georgian squares and terraces, such as Rodney Street, Mornington Terrace and Gambier Terrace (1830–*c.* 1837) on the hills encircling the city centre. The Greek Revival style was influential here among such local architects as Thomas Harrison, who designed the Lyceum Club (1802), Bold Street, and John Foster the younger, who had studied in Greece and whose Mortuary Chapel at St James's Cemetery (1823–4) epitomized the style. The design of St George's Hall, the finest Neo-classical building in Britain, was won in competition in 1839 by Harvey Lonsdale Elmes, then in his early 20s. It was intended to serve as a concert hall with attached assize courts and after Elmes's death in 1847 was completed (1856) by Charles Robert Cockerell. The adjacent public buildings included the William Brown Library and Museum (1859), designed by Thomas Allom (1804–72) and John Grey Weightman (1801–72); the Wellington column (1863) by G. A. Lawson; the Walker Art Gallery (1874–7) by Cornelius Sherlock (*d* 1888) and H. H. Vale (1830–75); and the circular Picton Reading Room (1875–9) by Sherlock.

Less inhibited than those in London, engineers and architects developed advanced methods of design and construction. Structural cast iron was used in 1774 to support the galleries of St James's Church, Toxteth.

1. Liverpool, view of the Pierhead (from left to right): the Royal Liver Building by Walter Aubrey Thomas, 1908–11; the Cunard Building by W. E. Willink and P. C. Thickness, 1914–16; and the Mersey Docks and Harbour Board Offices by Arnold Thornely, 1907

Thomas Rickman, who was based in Liverpool during 1807–18 and whose lectures there around 1812 on the origin of Gothic affected the revival of that style, produced prefabricated cast-iron churches at St George's (1812), Everton, and at St Michael-in-the-Hamlet (1814), Toxteth. Jesse Hartley (1780–1860), who was Liverpool dock engineer between 1824 and 1860, created an enclosed warehouse system in the Albert Dock (1839–45; for illustration see DOCK), where the fire-proof buildings in iron, brick and stone rise sheer from the dock walls. Within Albert Dock stands the dock Traffic Office (1846–7), designed by Philip Hardwick, with a cast-iron Tuscan portico. In a style similar to those of the Albert Dock, Hartley built warehouses at Wapping Dock (opened 1856) and Stanley Dock (1852–6) and the impressive crenellated clock tower at Salisbury Dock (1845–8). The designs and construction of the Liverpool to Manchester railway (opened 1830), the world's first passenger railway system, and the extension of the line through deep cuttings to Lime Street Station (completed 1836), were both innovative. The third and present station was finished in 1879. By William Baker (1817–78) and C. R. Stevenson, it is formed of two fine, slightly curved iron and glass spans. Its monumental hotel (1868–71) was built by Alfred Waterhouse.

Along with London, Liverpool was the birthplace in Britain of the office as a building type, and early examples were in the Italianate style. C. R. Cockerell experimented with methods to improve interior daylighting in Bank Chambers (1849; destr.), Cook Street, and designed (1844) and built the impressive Branch Bank of England, Castle Street, probably his masterpiece, with imaginative Greek detail. Peter Ellis (1804–84) was the first to use large sheets of plate glass, in Oriel Chambers (1864), Water Street, and at 16 Cook Street (1866); in their courtyards he also provided a very early use of cladding with glass and thin stone panels. Waterhouse built the Prudential Assurance Office (1885), Dale Street, in red pressed brick and the Victoria University buildings (1887–92) in red brick. Towards the end of the century buildings became taller and grander with Richard Norman Shaw's White Star Line Offices (1895–8), James Street (see SHAW, RICHARD NORMAN, fig. 2), and the Royal Insurance Building (1896–1903), Dale Street, by J. Francis Doyle (1840–1913),

where, helped by Shaw, Doyle produced an early steel-framed structure, stone clad, with a frieze carved by Charles J. Allen (1862–1956), all topped by a gilded dome.

The greatest expression of Liverpool's commercial power came with the building of the Pierhead group of offices facing the River Mersey (see fig. 1). First came the Mersey Docks and Harbour Board Offices (1907) by Arnold Thornely (1870–1953), an impressive pile of Portland stone, the base Italian, the superstructure a giant neo-classical church dome supported by a cluster of lesser domes. Walter Aubrey Thomas (d 1912) designed the Royal Liver Building (1908–11), tall, bulky (the first large multi-storey reinforced concrete building in the world) and clad in granite. From it rise two massive towers, surmounted by the mythical Liver birds. Between these offices stands the Cunard Building (1914–16) by W. E. Willink (1856–1924) and P. C. Thickness (1860–1920), a Renaissance Revival building with Greek details. These three buildings, intended to be seen from approaching Atlantic liners, have become the leitmotif of Liverpool. In the inter-war years further large offices were built: in Water Street the India Buildings (1924–32) and Martins Bank (1927–32), both by Herbert J. Rowse (1887–1963), who also designed the architecture associated with the Mersey Tunnel (1925–35) and in Hope Street, under the influence of W. M. Dudok, the Philharmonic Hall (1937–9).

There are many fine Victorian churches in Liverpool, but the swan-song of Gothic must be the Anglican cathedral by Giles Gilbert Scott, won in competition in 1903 (for illustration of James M. Hay's unsuccessful entry see ECLECTICISM). Scott modified (1909–10) his competition design to the present plan, where the central tower rises between double transepts. Sir Edwin Lutyens began to build (1933) his monumental Roman Catholic cathedral in Hope Street, but, owing to World War II and a shortage of money, the project was abandoned after the crypt had been built, and in 1960 Frederick Gibberd designed a smaller, circular cathedral (consecrated 1967; for illustration see GIBBERD, FREDERICK). In the inter-war years, Liverpool, like London, carried out a large-scale policy of building corporation flats. Much influenced by Dutch architecture, they were designed by Director of Housing and later City Architect, Lancelot Keay (1883–1960), and his senior assistant, John Hughes (1903–77). Keay also designed the many fine neo-Georgian housing estates built beyond the ring road of the city, for example those in Walton, to the north.

BIBLIOGRAPHY

J. A. Picton: *Memorials of Liverpool*, 2 vols (London, 1873, rev. 1907)
C. H. Reilly: *Some Liverpool Streets and Buildings* (Liverpool, 1921)
Q. Hughes: *Seaport* (London, 1964/R 1969)
——: *Liverpool* (London, 1969)
N. Pevsner: *South Lancashire*, Bldgs England (Harmondsworth, 1969)
*Buildings of Liverpool*, Liverpool Heritage Bureau (Liverpool, 1978)
N. Ritchie-Noakes: *Liverpool's Historic Waterfront* (London, 1984)

QUENTIN HUGHES

2. ART LIFE AND ORGANIZATION. The fine arts were less quick than the ceramic industry (*see* §3 below) to take root in Liverpool. The outstanding early patron in Liverpool was WILLIAM ROSCOE, who encouraged and helped John Gibson (i). The sculptor spent his childhood in Liverpool and is perhaps the most eminent artist to have come from there. In 1769, a year after the foundation of the Royal Academy in London, the Society of Artists was founded in Liverpool with a membership of 22, but it was dissolved soon afterwards. In 1773 the Society for the Encouragement of Designing, Drawing and Painting was founded with 59 members and with Roscoe as its driving force, but it was defunct by 1775, to be succeeded in 1783 by the Society for Promoting the Arts in Liverpool, of which Roscoe was Vice-President and Treasurer. An exhibition was held by the Society in 1784 with 206 works on show, including canvases by Reynolds, Fuseli and Joseph Wright. In addition there were works by such local artists as the portrait painter Richard Caddick (*c.* 1750–1823) and the portrait and landscape painter Thomas Chubbard (1739–1809). By 1794 this society also had been dissolved.

In 1810 the Liverpool Academy of Arts was founded to encourage the arts and to provide lectures and life classes for students. The first president was the furniture-maker and sculptor George Bullock, with Roscoe as Treasurer. Its first exhibition (1810) included works by the London artists William Etty, Turner and James Ward, as well as by such Liverpool painters as Thomas Hargreaves (1773–1847), John Williamson (1751–1818) and his son Samuel Williamson (1792–1840). Among the works exhibited in 1840 was *Grouse Shooting: Luncheon on the Moors* (1840; Liverpool, Walker A.G.) by the Liverpool artist Richard Ansdell. This was typical of the numerous sporting and landscape pictures produced by local artists at that time. The Liverpool Academy was the only official body in Britain to support the Pre-Raphaelites, by awarding prizes to such members of the group as John Everett Millais (1857) and Ford Madox Brown (1858). Most notable among the supporters of the Pre-Raphaelites was WILLIAM LINDSAY WINDUS, whose own work was much influenced by the Brotherhood, as is shown by his painting *Burd Helen* (1856; Liverpool, Walker A.G.; see fig. 2), exhibited in 1864. The leader of the faction opposed to the Pre-Raphaelites was the topographical painter William Gawin Herdman (1805–82). Internal and external pressures forced the Academy to cease its exhibitions in 1867, and they were not resumed until 1897.

The first public museum to open was the Walker Art Gallery in 1877, endowed by Andrew Barclay Walker

2. William Lindsay Windus: *Burd Helen*, oil on canvas, 845×667 mm, 1856 (Liverpool, Walker Art Gallery)

(1824–93). This contains paintings from all countries and periods, but it is especially strong in 19th-century British works. It also contains important early Italian and Netherlandish works from Roscoe's collection and foreign and British works from the past and present. The gallery also holds regular temporary exhibitions. The annual autumn exhibition, started in 1871 and organized by the Corporation of Liverpool, has been held at the Walker Art Gallery since 1877, as, since 1951, have the exhibitions of the Liverpool Academy. In 1957 the biennial John Moores Liverpool Exhibition, designed to bring contemporary British painting to Liverpool, was begun and held at the Walker. In 1971 the biennial Peter Moores Liverpool Project was first held, also at the Walker; this consists of exhibitions concentrating on a narrow aspect of contemporary or European art. Many of the works from both of these events have been purchased and donated to the Walker by the founders, John and Peter Moores; exhibiting artists have included R. B. Kitaj, Allen Jones and the Liverpool painter Sam Walsh (1934–89).

Other museums include the Liverpool Museum, which opened as a natural history museum in 1853 and was subsequently expanded in size and content by a number of bequests in the 19th century. It holds notable collections of Anglo-Saxon art, medieval ivories and Classical sculpture. Sudley Art Gallery, which contains the collection of British art formed by George Holt (1825–96), a member of a prominent shipping family, was bequeathed to Liverpool in 1944. The University of Liverpool Art Gallery, founded in 1977, is particularly strong in works by Turner, English watercolours from 1750 to 1850 and English porcelain. Much of the collection was bequeathed by Sir Sydney Jones (1872–1947). In 1988 the Tate Gallery, Liverpool, was opened to display works from the permanent collection of the Tate Gallery in London and to hold temporary exhibitions. To sustain Liverpool's art life, in 1976 the Bridewell Studios were opened for the use of independent artists and craftworkers. Since 1980 these have been the location for the artists-in-residence scheme funded by the Arts Council of Great Britain.

BIBLIOGRAPHY

H. C. Marillier: *The Liverpool School of Painters* (London, 1904)
J. Touzeau: *The Rise and Progress of Liverpool, 1551–1835*, 2 vols (Liverpool, 1910)
J. Willett: *Art in a City* (London, 1967)
M. Bennett: *Merseyside Painters, People and Places*, Liverpool, Walker A.G. cat., 2 vols (Liverpool, 1978)
*A Guide to Pictures in the Walker Art Gallery, Liverpool* (Liverpool, 1980)
P. Curtis, ed.: *Patronage and Practice: Sculpture on Merseyside* (Liverpool, 1989)

PHILIP COOPER

3. CENTRE OF CERAMICS PRODUCTION. During the 18th century and early 19th virtually every type of ceramic was made in Liverpool, from coarse wares, utilitarian stonewares and creamwares to English delftwares and porcelains. Liverpool was also an important centre for the export of ceramic wares to the colonies. Production of tin-glazed earthenwares started *c.* 1710. Specialities of the many Liverpool delftware potteries were tiles, puzzle jugs and punch-bowls painted with ships on the interiors. By 1760 there were about eight delftware potteries in the area, producing wares sometimes decorated with chinoiseries. A rare product was the so-called tin-glazed stoneware used for some tea and coffee wares. About 1755 William Reid & Co. (1755–61) built the first Liverpool porcelain factory on Brownlow Hill, and the small delftware potteries of Richard Chaffers & Co. (1755–65) and Samuel Gilbody (*c.* 1755–60) also started to make porcelain. Although vases and some figures were produced, these factories concentrated mainly on good-quality tea and coffee services. Later Liverpool porcelain factories produced considerable quantities of more routine wares, much of it transfer-printed with underglaze-blue decoration. Liverpool was an important centre for the decoration of ceramics with overglaze transfer-printing. John Sadler (1720–89), a pioneer of this technique, and his partner Guy Green (1729–1803) started printing Liverpool delftware tiles *c.* 1756. Enamels, porcelains and creamwares were also printed, but not always on locally produced materials; Josiah Wedgwood, for example, sent wares to be transfer-printed at the firm of Sadler & Green. The last Liverpool pottery was taken over in 1796 by Worthington, Humble & Holland and renamed the Herculaneum. The factory was strongly influenced by the Staffordshire potteries and employed many Staffordshire potters. It produced a wide variety of earthenwares, stonewares and bone chinas. It closed in 1840.

BIBLIOGRAPHY

F. H. Garner: *English Delftware* (London, 1948, rev. 2/1972)
K. Boney: *Liverpool Porcelain of the Eighteenth Century and its Makers* (London, 1957/*R* 1989)
A. Smith: *The Illustrated Guide to Liverpool Herculaneum Pottery* (London, 1970)
*Herculaneum: The Last Liverpool Pottery* (exh. cat., Warrington, Mus. & A.G., 1983)
M. Hillis: *The Liverpool Porcelains*, Northern Ceramic Society occasional paper, 1 (Hanley, 1985)
*Made in Liverpool: Liverpool Pottery and Porcelain, 1700–1850* (exh. cat., ed. E. M. Brown and T. A. Lockett; Liverpool, Walker A.G., 1993)

MAURICE HILLIS

**Liverseege, Henry** (*b* Manchester, 4 Sept 1803; *d* Manchester, 13 Jan 1832). English painter. The son of a mechanic, he was brought up from the age of 13 by his uncle, a wealthy mill-owner who encouraged his nephew's talent for sketching and his love of literature and amateur dramatics. Sickly from birth, he was slight of frame with deformed shoulders and diseased lungs which led to his early death. As a young man he painted inn signs, silhouettes, miniatures and portraits, but in 1827 he showed at the Royal Manchester Institution three small pictures (untraced) of bandits; in the following five years he painted many cabinet-sized genre and literary subjects, mainly from Scott, Shakespeare and Cervantes. In 1828 he went to London, where he studied the Old Masters, but failed to gain entry to the Royal Academy Schools; he was in London again from 1829 to 1831.

Liverseege was much influenced by David Teniers II and David Wilkie, as seen in *The Recruit* (exh. RA 1832; Manchester, Whitworth A.G.). His more dramatic subjects are often weak, but his shadowy interiors, relieved by rich handling and sparkling highlights, are akin to the work of R. P. Bonington, though less refined or inventive; an example is the humorously characterized *A Touch of the Spasms* (n.d.; Manchester, C.A.G). Liverseege seems to have painted replicas of many of his works, though one of his best-known compositions, the *Weekly Register* (exh. British Inst. 1830; untraced), was much copied by others. His pictures were bought by many northern patrons including the Bolton engineer Benjamin Hick, Thomas Egerton, 2nd Earl of Wilton and William Cavendish, 6th Duke of Devonshire, who purchased *Sir Piercie Shafton and Mysie Happer* (exh. RA 1831; Chatsworth, Derbys).

BIBLIOGRAPHY

*Engravings from the works of Henry Liverseege* (London, 1835; rev. with a memoir by G. Richardson, 1875)
C. Swain: *Memoir of Henry Liverseege* (Manchester, 1864)
R. Edwards: 'The Pictures of Henry Liverseege (1803–1832)', *Apollo*, xx (1934), pp. 25–9

JULIAN TREUHERZ

**Livery hall.** Building that houses the headquarters of a livery company or guild, or association of merchants, craftsmen or traders, so named from the trade's distinctive ceremonial livery. Houses or buildings belonging to late medieval guilds or fraternities of merchants survive in several cities (e.g. York, Merchant Taylors' Hall, interior *c.* 1400, and Merchant Adventurers' Hall, *c.* 1580), but the livery companies and their halls are specifically associated with the City of London, emerging in the 15th century with the development of guilds and lay fraternities. The late medieval type of large hall with ancillary rooms persisted in City livery halls, despite their almost complete rebuilding after the Great Fire of London in 1666. All but three were destroyed in World War II.

The livery hall is not a seat of government or of active trade: it houses the administration, business meetings, charity-dispensing and social gatherings of the company

Fishmongers' Hall, London, by Henry Roberts, interior of the banqueting hall, 1831; from an engraving in the *Illustrated London News* (23 November 1861)

members. While there is no exact equivalent elsewhere, the activities of the livery companies may loosely be compared with those of the Venetian Scuole (*see* VENICE, §V). The hall was originally sited near but not in its own market-place, and it had no facilities for storing or selling goods, except in revenue-producing space let out to tenants. Accommodation generally consists of a dining hall and a council chamber or courtroom, with subsidiary rooms for social and committee use; and an office, formerly with living quarters, for the chief clerk or administrator and his staff, with space for company records not only of trade supervision but also of the management of much landed property and the charities subsidized from it. Medieval accommodation often included almshouses.

Although at first the City livery companies met in local inns or in the house of a leading member, by the late 14th century many were acquiring property for their use. The Merchant Taylors bought a house in 1339 and had built their hall (30 Threadneedle Street) by 1375 (damaged World War II; undercroft survives). The Mercers' Company met at the Hospital of St Thomas Acon, Cheapside, building a chapel and hall next door in 1517, before acquiring the whole property after the Reformation in 1542 (hall destr. 1666; rebuilt twice). The medieval fishmongers, who were organized in several distinct groups, met in different places until they united at the 14th-century merchants' house and wharf on Thames Street, which was rebuilt piecemeal in the 16th century and forms part of the present site of Fishmongers' Hall.

The style and planning of the livery halls may be traced directly to their medieval antecedents: courtyard houses with attached halls, which formed the nucleus of adaptations and enlargements made by the companies. Owing to the need for a large, central hall, the type of open-roofed hall (seen also at the Inns of Court), which elsewhere became obsolete, survived into the 17th century, with later rebuilding or even new buildings adhering to the general medieval layout. The present Fishmongers' Hall, largely a Greek Revival building designed in 1831 by Henry Roberts (1803–76) to suit the style and levels of the newly rebuilt London Bridge, demonstrates the persistence of the livery hall type: above wharfside warehouse space intended for commercial tenants, the hall proper, entered from the bridge approach, is mainly two-storey, with administrative offices and courtroom on the entrance floor, from which a grand staircase rises to the social core of the building, the great banqueting hall (see fig.) and attendant reception rooms.

Most 17th-century livery halls were characterized by the Artisan Mannerism practised by City surveyors and craftsmen such as Edward Jerman (*d* 1668) and Peter Mills. Some, however, were more sophisticated, for example the hip-roofed, red-brick Goldsmiths' Hall, Foster Lane, of 1635 (destr. 1829), reflecting the Dutch training of its architect, Nicholas Stone; the courtroom and anatomical theatre added in 1636 to the Barber Surgeons' Hall, Monkwell Street, by Inigo Jones; and the Fishmongers' new riverside block, a design of 1669 (destr. 1827) in Sir

Roger Pratt's domestic style. In the early 19th century the Roman giant order fronting Philip Hardwick's rebuilt Goldsmiths' Hall (1835) continued the full-blooded spirit of, for example, the Mansion House by George Dance sr. Halls rebuilt after World War II tended towards conservatism.

The woodwork of some medieval halls survived the Great Fire or was installed shortly afterwards, notably such classicizing pieces as the 'reredos' of 1669–71 in the Apothecaries' Hall, Blackfriars Lane; the fireplace of 1670 in the Skinners' Hall, Dowgate Hill; and the grand staircase in the Vintners' Hall, Upper Thames Street (1671). Decoration tended to reflect that of the private merchants' houses from which the halls developed. Before 1666 the company arms and patron saints might be painted on an end wall above the panelling or tapestries behind the head table: the Merchant Taylors had a carved and painted figure of St John the Baptist (destr.), and a 16th-century stone figure of Christ was discovered in the foundations of the Mercers' Hall, Ironmonger Lane (London, Mercers' Hall).

Among prized company possessions in the late Middle Ages were the embroidered funeral palls to cover the coffins of members as they lay in state: those of the Brewers, Aldermanbury Square, and the Saddlers, Gutter Lane (London, Brewers' Hall; London, Saddlers' Hall), both dating from c. 1490–1538, have the company arms and appropriate decorative motifs. Although Crown demands for money in the 16th century and early 17th forced many livery companies to sell their plate, they built up their collections again along with other more sophisticated company ornaments, including the Fishmongers' Coade stone figure of *Charity* (untraced). Relations with royalty having improved after 1688, most paintings subsequently commissioned by the livery companies were royal portraits. The only group portrait known to have been commissioned for a London livery hall was that by Hans Holbein (ii) for the Barber Surgeons (London, Barber Surgeons' Hall), showing Henry VIII granting them their charter in 1541, a picture prized more as a documentary record than as a work of art.

UNPUBLISHED SOURCES

London, Guildhall Lib. [*Guide to the Archives of the City Livery Companies* (1982)]

BIBLIOGRAPHY

J. Stow: *Survey of London* (London 1598, 2/1603); ed. C. L. Kingsford, 2 vols (Oxford, 1908/*R* 1971)
P. Metcalf: *The Hall of the Fishmongers* (London, 1977)
B. Weinreb and C. Hibbert, eds: *The London Encyclopaedia* (London, 1983)
J. Schofield: *The Building of London from the Conquest to the Great Fire* (London, 1984)
'Medieval Art, Architecture and Archaeology in London', *Brit. Archaeol. Assoc. Confer. Trans.*, x (1984) [articles by J. Schofield and P. Wallis]
D. Keene and V. Harding: *Historical Gazetteer of London before the Great Fire*, i (London, 1987) [Cheapside: Mercers' Hall]

PRISCILLA METCALF

**Living painting.** *See* PERFORMANCE ART.

**Livinus Voghelarius.** *See* VOGHELARIUS, LIVINUS.

**Livois**, Marquis de [Eveillard, Pierre-Louis] (*b* Angers, 6 Sept 1736; *d* Angers, 2 Dec 1790). French patron and collector. From an established family in Brittany and Anjou, he assembled an important collection of French 18th-century and Old Master paintings while living in a hôtel in the Rue St Michel, Angers, which he probably had built for himself. Much of his collection now forms the nucleus of the Musée des Beaux-Arts, Angers (all works cited below are there unless otherwise stated). Livois is known to have travelled in Flanders and Holland and to have been an amateur artist himself, working in both oil and pastel. He painted and commissioned copies of paintings, referring to his taste for painting as 'notre belle maîtresse' and admitting that pleasure had always been his best doctor. Among the paintings he collected are Antoine Watteau's *Le Concert champêtre* or *La Déclaration attendue*, the attribution of which is occasionally disputed, and four paintings and one pastel by François Boucher, of which only the *Shepherd and Shepherdess Reposing* (1761; London, Wallace) can be securely identified. Livois's favourite painter appears to have been Jean-Siméon Chardin, numerically the most frequently represented artist in the collection, which included *Basket of Grapes with Three Lady-apples, a Pear and Two Marzipans* (1764). Next is Jean-Honoré Fragonard, represented by such paintings as *Boy as Pierrot* (London, Wallace) and a very early version of his *morceau de réception* at the Académie Royale, *Coresus and Callirhoë*. Livois also owned Jean-Baptiste Greuze's masterpiece *Young Woman with a Spaniel* or *Portrait of Mme de Porcin* and works by almost all the major painters of the reign of Louis XV. The rest of the collection consisted of Italian and northern paintings, in particular more than 80 Dutch pictures, including a landscape by Jacob van Ruisdael. A strong taste for landscape characterizes the collection as a whole. Livois would appear to have formed his collection in a random rather than a systematic way. In 1781, for instance, he acquired 75 paintings of unequal quality for 14,000 livres from the equerry Jean-Jacques Lenoir; occasionally, however, he would try to achieve a more even standard by taking the advice of the painter Louis Watteau. He was also a patron of Watteau's son François-Louis-Joseph.

The attributions of many works in the collection have been altered, but the catalogue written after Livois's death by the Anjou painter Pierre Sentout remains the only important contemporary source for the collection, which comprised c. 400 paintings, 250 of them by contemporary French painters. Because of the turbulence caused by the French Revolution the sale for which Sentout wrote the catalogue did not take place, and in 1793 the paintings were sequestered by the local authorities. In 1799 the collection was divided in two, half going to Livois's Republican heirs (part of this reappeared in the Bartolommeo Gamba sale of 17–18 Dec 1811) and half to his émigré heirs; it was the latter half that was confiscated by the state and forms the basis of the museum in Angers. The estate was finally settled in 1842.

BIBLIOGRAPHY

P. Sentout: *Catalogue raisonné d'une très belle collection de tableaux, des écoles d'Italie, de Flandres, de Hollande et de France; Pastels, miniatures, gouaches, dessins qui composoient le cabinet de feu M. de Livois à Angers* (Angers, 1791)
R. Planchenault: 'L'Art français dans la collection du marquis de Livois', *Bull. Soc. Hist. A. Fr.* (1933), pp. 149–58 [incl. letters from Louis-Joseph Watteau de Lille and François-Louis-Joseph Watteau]

——: 'La Collection du marquis de Livois', *Gaz. B.-A.*, 6th ser., x (1933), pp. 14–30, 220–37

——: 'La Dispersion de la collection du marquis de Livois', *Prov. Anjou*, 49 (1934), pp. 249–65

V. Huchard: *Musée d'Angers* (Angers, 1982) [contains 27 repr. of works from the Livois col.]

M.-E. HELLYER

**Livonia.** *See under* ESTONIA and LATVIA.

**Livorno** [Leghorn]. Italian city, the capital of Livorno province in Tuscany and an important port on the Ligurian Sea. The city (population *c.* 176,000) is located on the ancient Roman Aurelian Way, *c.* 20 km south of Pisa and *c.* 80 km south-west of Florence. Originally a fishing village that was ruled successively by Pisa, Milan and Genoa, Livorno was purchased by Florence in 1421 with the intention of developing it as a seaport. The Fortezza Vecchia, overlooking the sea and incorporating the remains of an earlier fort and 11th-century tower, was built there in the early 16th century by Antonio da Sangallo the elder. In accordance with plans drawn up in 1576 by Bernardo Buontalenti under Grand Duke Francesco I, a new town was then laid out on a grid set within a fortified pentagonal perimeter (see fig.), the village and pre-existing fortifications being incorporated into the new town and its defences. Through his work for Grand Duke Cosimo I, Buontalenti had known some of the leading military architects of the period, when urban planning was heavily dependent on fortification theory. Livorno's plan, deceptively simple, was a testing ground for new ideas.

Building work within the town was begun after 1590 under Grand Duke Ferdinando I (*see* MEDICI, DE', (17)). New architects were brought to the project, including Ferdinando's half-brother, Giovanni de' Medici, who soon replaced Buontalenti. Two modifications were made to the plan: the construction of the moated Fortezza Nuova from one of the newly built bastions on the north side of the city, and the creation of a central piazza (Piazza Grande). Lined by loggias, the piazza became an important military rallying point as well as being the site of the cathedral of S Francesco (begun 1594; rest. 1950s), designed by Buontalenti and completed by Alessandro Pieroni (1550–1607); it too has an arcaded loggia. Modest but dignified houses lined the main street, the Via Ferdinanda (now Via Grande), which passed through the piazza to connect the two city gates leading to the mainland and the port. The narrow streets perpendicular to the Via Ferdinanda were lined with two-storey terraced houses containing shops on the ground floor, following a building type found in Florence. Small industries were located in peripheral areas, and warehouses and a prison were built near the port. The façades of even the most modest dwellings were covered with *sgraffito* or fresco decoration

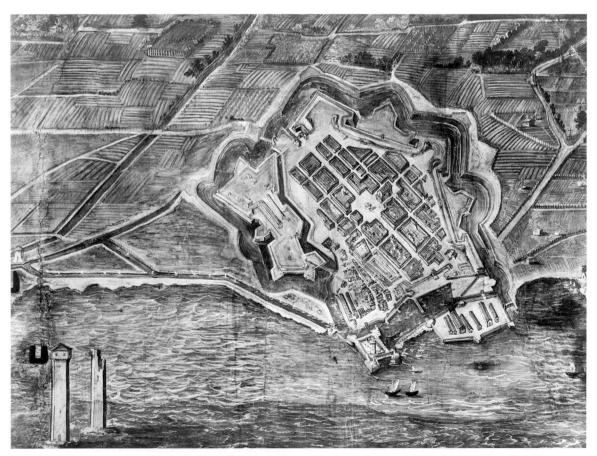

*Livorno*, detail from *Deeds of the First Medici Grand Dukes* (*c.* 1608), fresco by Bernardino Poccetti, Sala di Bona, Palazzo Pitti, Florence

depicting Florentine festivals, the naval exploits of the Knights of St Stephen and scenes of life in the port, reflecting the practice of such port cities as Venice, Genoa and Pesaro. Directly facing the port in Piazza Micheli is Giovanni Bandini's statue of *Ferdinando I de' Medici* (begun 1595); Pietro Tacca (*see* TACCA, (1)) designed the *Four Slaves* (1621–6) at its base as well as two fountains (now in Florence, Piazza SS Annunziata).

Due to its increased size, its reputation as a safe harbour and a series of proclamations issued by Ferdinando in 1593 which encouraged trade and political and religious freedom, by the end of the 16th century Livorno had become the second most important port in the Mediterranean, frequented by many nationalities. Population increases led to further need for housing, and canals and construction techniques imported from Venice and Holland characterized the new neighbourhood of Venezia Nuova that was built in two stages: in 1630 on some land near the port, and in 1696 in an area of Fortezza Nuova, by then partially dismantled. Further modernizations were carried out on the fortifications until 1838, when it was decided to extend the free trade area of the city. This meant that a new set of walls had to be built, and consequently the old walls were torn down. Luigi de Cambray-Digny, Alessandro Manetti (1787–1865) and Pasquale Poccianti submitted proposals: Manetti's was accepted, and the new walls were largely completed by 1840. At this time the canal that had surrounded the 16th-century town was partially straightened, and a section of it to the east was built over by the new Piazza del Voltone (now Piazza della Repubblica); this provided a link between the old town and its suburbs, which had grown up over the years outside the old walls. A new aqueduct and related buildings were constructed, including the Cisternino and Cisternone (1829–42), clearly inspired by Neoclassicism (for further discussion and illustration *see* POCCIANTI, PASQUALE). Livorno became a popular seaside resort in the 19th century, and the Viale Italia, skirting the suburbs along the shore, is lined with elegant houses and hotels. A canal completed in 1938 connects Livorno with Pisa. Little of the 16th-century nucleus of the city survived the 20th century, however, due to destruction in World War II and subsequent rebuilding. Livorno was the birthplace of Giovanni Fattori and Amedeo Modigliani, and the SCUOLA LABRONICA, a group of naturalist painters, was founded there in 1920. The city's principal museum, the Museo Civico Giovanni Fattori, situated in the park of the Villa Fabbricotti, has a good collection of works by the 19th-century *Macchiaioli* painters.

BIBLIOGRAPHY

G. Nudi: *Storia urbanistica di Livorno: Dalle origini al secolo XVI* (Venice, 1959)
L. Bortolotti: *Livorno dal 1748 al 1958: Profilo storico-urbanistico* (Florence, 1970)
*Livorno: Progetto e storia di una città tra il 1500 e il 1600* (exh. cat., Livorno, Bottini Olio, 1980)
D. Matteoni: *Livorno: La città nella storia d'Italia* (Bari, 1985, 2/1988)
C. Danielson: *Livorno: A Study in 16th Century Town Planning in Italy* (diss., New York, Columbia U., 1986)

CORNELIA DANIELSON

**Livre d'artiste** [Fr.: 'artist's book']. Term used to define a variety of illustrated book that originated in France in the early 20th century. The essential feature of the *livre d'artiste* is that each illustration is an original work executed by the artist directly on the support (stone, wood, metal, linoleum etc) from which it is printed. Its originator was the dealer Ambroise Vollard, who commissioned Pierre Bonnard to illustrate with lithographs *Parallèlement*, poems by Paul Verlaine, published in Paris in 1900 (see fig.).

Subsequently Vollard enlisted the services of other painters and sculptors, including Auguste Rodin, Maurice Denis, Picasso, Aristide Maillol, Georges Braque and Georges Rouault. Three of his most successful matchings of artist to text are: Balzac's *Le Chef-d'oeuvre inconnu* (Paris, 1931), with etchings by Picasso; *Les Réincarnations du Père Ubu* (Paris, 1932), Vollard's own text, with aquatint full-page illustrations by Rouault; and, with etchings in colour by the same artist, *Passion*, which Vollard published in Paris shortly before his death in 1939. Vollard completed 27 *livres d'artiste* and left 24 in progress.

Vollard's example inspired other publishers. In 1909 Daniel-Henri Kahnweiler published *L'Enchanteur pourrissant* (Paris) by Guillaume Apollinaire with wood-engravings by André Derain. In 1911 Deplanche published *Le Bestiaire, ou le cortège d'Orphée* (Paris) by Apollinaire, with white-line wood-engravings by Raoul Dufy. In 1932 Albert Skira published Stéphane Mallarmé's *Poésies* (Lausanne), with etchings by Henri Matisse, and in 1936 Vergil's *Les Bucoliques* (Paris), with etchings by André Beaudin. Even during the German Occupation of France (1940–44) production did not halt. Martin Fabiani published Georges-Louis-Leclerc, Comte de Buffon's *Histoire naturelle* (Paris, 1942), with sugar aquatints by Picasso, and *Pasiphaé, chants de Minos* (Paris, 1944) by Henri de Montherlant, with linocuts by Matisse. Skira published Rabelais's *Pantagruel* (Paris, 1946), with coloured intaglio wood-engravings by Derain. Major *livres d'artiste* that followed include Vergil's *Les Géorgiques* (Paris, 1947), with etchings by André Dunoyer de Segonzac, himself the publisher, and Shakespeare's *Macbeth* (Paris, 1958), with etchings by Marcel Gromaire. Bibliophile societies commissioned many notable *livres d'artiste*: Les Bibliophiles de Provence produced Rabelais's *Gargantua* (Paris, 1955), with colour lithographs by Antoni Clavé; Les Impénitents produced *Chiméra* (Paris, 1955; B. Citroën's trans. of Lewis Carroll's *Misadventures of a Photographer*), with etchings by Mario Avati (*b* 1921). Abram Krol (*b* 1919), a leading engraver, executed and published cut-out copper engravings for Oscar Wilde's *The Ballad of Reading Gaol* (Paris, 1962), published by the artist.

In the mid-1950s Pierre Lecuire came to prominence, publishing his prose-poem texts (28 completed by 1989) in collaboration with the famous artists of his time; for example Nicolas de Staël did etchings for *Ballets-minute* (Paris, 1954), André Lanskoy did paper-cuts for *Cortège* (Paris, 1959), the sculptor Etienne Hajdu did *estampilles* (uninked relief designs) for *Règnes* (Paris, 1961) and Pierre Tal-Coat did mixed-etchings for *Bestiaire* (Paris, 1985), a worthy successor to other treatments of the theme.

Two important and unusual books were produced in the 1980s by Paris galleries: from Aimé Maeght, *Sang* (Paris, 1980) by Jacques Dupin with text as well as lithographic illustrations drawn by Valerio Adami; and from Sylvie Galanis, *Autour de la montagne* (Paris, 1981) by André Frénaud with slate engravings by the sculptor Raoul Ubac, printed on Misumi paper.

Although the *livre d'artiste* is primarily a French phenomenon, the term is sometimes applied more loosely to similar works produced elsewhere. Notable examples include David Hockney's etchings for *Illustrations for Fourteen Poems from C. P. Cavafy* (London, 1966) and for Wallace Stevens's *The Blue Guitar* (London and New York, 1977), Tom Phillips's lithographs and silk-screen prints for *A Humument* (London, 1970–73), Patrick Caulfield's screenprints for *Some Poems of Jules Laforgue* (London, 1973), Jasper Johns's 33 etchings for Samuel Beckett's *Foirades/Fizzles* (London, 1975–6) and Francesco Clemente's lithographs for *The Departure of the Argonauts* (New York and London, 1986).

The production of *livres d'artiste* requires specialized printers. Among the best-known presses for the texts, which can also deal with wood-engraving, are the Imprimerie Nationale, Imprimerie Fequet & Baudier, R. Blanchet & Fils and François Da Ros. Metal-processes are dealt with by *taille-douciers*, who can print engravings, etchings and aquatints; famous ateliers specializing in this work include Lacourière & Frélaut, G. Leblanc and Rigal. Equally renowned for lithography are Mourlot Frères and Desjobert. The names of such workshops figure on the *achevé d'imprimer* or *justification du tirage* (colophon) on each copy of the book, as well as the names of the author, illustrator and publisher. The number of copies is also recorded, as is the smaller number of *exemplaires de tête* (special copies), usually printed on a different paper and often with a suite of separate, sometimes supplementary, illustrations.

Editions of *livres d'artiste* usually vary from 20 to 300 copies, and they are published *en feuilles* (unsewn sheets). This practice has several advantages. First, it permits individual *reliures* (original bindings). Secondly, illustrations can extend, uninterrupted, across two facing pages. An example is *Le Petit Ami* (Société Normande du Livre, Paris, 1960) by P. Léautaud, which contains 25 double-spread lithographs by André Minaux. Thirdly, it allows eccentricity of folding, as in *Poèmes du dimanche* (Editions Sic, Paris, 1977; 30 copies signed by author and artist) by Pierre Albert-Birot, in which five concertina-folded sheets of hand-made Moulin Larroque Auvergne paper carry the text and impressed colour engravings by Ania Staritsky (1908–81). The final and most important advantage is that *livres d'artiste* can be dismantled for representative displays.

The paper used for *livres d'artiste* is either a *vélin* (wove; e.g. *vélin d'Arches*) or a *vergé* (laid; e.g. *vergé de Montval*); the former is better for fine, engraved lines. A good example is *L'Ecclésiaste* (Michel de Romilly, Paris, 1950) translated by the artist Roger Vieillard (*b* 1907), whose 14 copper engravings were printed on Arches (110 copies), Montval (32) and van Gelder (18). Bindings are an unnecessary luxury, since all *livres d'artiste* are well-presented and protected, first by the *emboîtage* (box), then the *étui* (slip-case). Features special to the genre are *lettrines* (original initial letters), *bandeaux* (illustrations at the head of the page) and *culs-de-lampe* (tailpieces). Typefaces in frequent use include Garamond, Caslon, sanserif Univers,

*Livre d'artiste* lithograph by Pierre Bonnard, illustrating a poem by Paul Verlaine; from *Parallèlement*, commissioned by Ambroise Vollard (Paris, 1900)

Ile-de-France and the classic Romain du Roi, an Imprimerie Nationale monopoly. Garamond italic was used for Vollard's edition of *Parallèlement*; Romain du Roi was used for Vollard's second book, *Daphnis et Chloé* (Paris, 1902) and for Gide's edition of Goethe's *Prométhée* (Paris, 1951), illustrated with colour lithographs by Henry Moore. Like *Parallèlement*, *Daphnis et Chloé* is illustrated with lithographs by Bonnard; both books incorporate all the features that characterize the hundreds of *livres d'artiste* produced subsequently.

BIBLIOGRAPHY

A. Skira: *Anthologie du livre illustré par les peintres et sculpteurs de l'Ecole de Paris* (Geneva, 1946)

*Modern Painters and Sculptors as Illustrators* (exh. cat., intro. M. Wheeler; New York, MOMA, 1947)

A. Léjard, ed.: *The Art of the French Book* (London, 1949)

G. A. Dassonville: *Les Livres illustrés par Avati* (Paris, 1964)

R. Ranc: *Henri Jonquières, éditeur, typographe* (Paris, 1964)

W. J. Strachan: *The Artist and the Book in France* (London, 1969)

——: 'Modern French Bestiaries', *Priv. Lib.*, n. s. 1, iii/4 (1970), pp. 171–92

——: 'Sculptors as Book-illustrators', *Connoisseur*, clxxiii (1970), pp. 153–61

——: 'The Books of Pierre Lecuire', *Connoisseur*, clxxxii (1973), p. 65

——: 'The Livre d'artiste, 1967–80', *Priv. Lib.*, n. s. 2, iv/1 (1981), pp. 3–48

——: 'Recent livres d'artiste', *Priv. Lib.*, n. s. 2, vii/3 (1984), pp. 135–40

*From Manet to Hockney: Modern Artists' Illustrated Books* (exh. cat. by C. Hogburn and R. Watson, London, V&A, 1985–6)

F. Chapon: *Le Peintre et le livre; 1870–1970* (Paris, 1987)

W. J. Strachan: 'A New Bestiaire', *Priv. Lib.*, n. s. 2, x/2 (1987), pp. 85–90

*Le Livre d'artiste: A Catalogue of the W. J. Strachan Gift to the Taylor Institution* (exh. cat. by W. J. Strachan, Oxford, Ashmolean, 1987)

W. J. STRACHAN

**Liwan.** *See* IWAN.

**Liyu** [Li-yü]. Site in Hunyuan County, northern Shanxi Province, China. A tomb or hoard of Eastern Zhou (771–256 BC) bronzes was discovered at the site in 1923. The bronzes (mainly Shanghai, Shanghai Mus.; Paris, Mus. Guimet; Washington, DC, Freer; New York, Met.) include one vessel decorated in copper inlay with a turbulent hunting scene and another textured with a repetitive pattern of tiny interlocked dragons in rectangular units. The majority, however, are decorated in low or high relief with horizontal bands of large-scale dragon interlace and are often further embellished with intaglio sketches or modelled figures of such creatures as fish, ducks and water buffalo. In Western writings about Chinese bronzes the name of the site has been attached to designs of this last type. A large bronze *pan* (Beijing, Pal. Mus.), though not from the Liyu group, is a dazzling example of the so-called Liyu style. The style probably spanned the late 6th century BC and the 5th; a pair of *hu* vessels (London, BM), the only Liyu-style bronzes that can be dated by their inscriptions, were cast in or shortly after 482 BC. Since 1923 Liyu-style bronzes have been unearthed at many places in northern China, notably at Hui xian in Henan Province and at Taiyuan, Changzhi and Houma in Shanxi Province. The style was firmly connected with the early Eastern Zhou state of Jin by the discovery of clay mould fragments bearing its characteristic designs at a foundry site excavated in the 1960s at HOUMA, where the Jin capital was located between 585 and 453 BC. In the light of these discoveries the geographic emphasis of the term 'Liyu style' has come to seem misplaced: the designs flourished in the heart of the Jin state and apparently had no special connection with the remote border area where the first examples were found. Moreover, what was once thought to be a sharply defined style, easily distinguished from its contemporaries, seems increasingly to belong to a broad continuum of Eastern Zhou dragon designs whose regional and temporal variations have yet to be clarified. Even a restricted definition such as 'dragon interlace designs represented in the Houma foundry debris' might not represent a helpful category for historical study, and it might be best either to regard the term as only an imprecise convenience or to avoid it altogether.

*See also* CHINA, §VI, 3(iv)(a).

BIBLIOGRAPHY

Shang Chengzuo: *Hunyuan yiqi tu* [Bronzes from Hunyuan] (Nanjing, 1936)

S. Umehara: *Sengoku-shiki dōki no kenkyū/Etude des bronzes des royaumes combattants* (Kyoto, 1936) [Fr. summary]

G. W. Weber: *The Ornaments of Late Chou Bronzes* (New Brunswick, 1973)

*The Great Bronze Age of China: An Exhibition from the People's Republic of China* (exh. cat., ed. Wen Fong; New York, Met.; Los Angeles, CA, Co. Mus. A.; 1980–81), entries 68–70

ROBERT W. BAGLEY

**Li Zai** [Li Tsai; *zi* Yizheng] (*b* Putian, Fujian Province; *d* 1431). Chinese painter. He became one of the leading court painters in the reign of the Xuande emperor (*reg* 1426–35) and one of the forerunners of the ZHE SCHOOL. The Japanese monk–painter Tōyō Sesshū, who visited China in 1468, called him one of the most important masters of the period. Together with Xia Zhi, a student of DAI JIN, and Ma Shi, he painted a long handscroll in 11 scenes (see fig.) that illustrated couplets from a famous poem by Tao Yuanming, showing the elegant figure of the poet at various stages on his return to his native village. Each scene presents a vignette rather than a complete landscape, with quite large figures and landscape details, both exhibiting a brilliant command of the brush in the style of the Southern Song (1127–1279) academy. Li Zai's monumental landscape style, based on the imposing compositions of the Northern Song period (960–1127), admirably exemplified Ming-period (1368–1644) aspirations to emulate painting of that period. *Landscape* (Tokyo, N. Mus.) may be compared with Guo Xi's famous *Early Spring* of 1072 (Taipei, N. Pal. Mus.; for illustration *see* GUO XI). A pair of great pine trees stand at the centre of the painting, against a backdrop of tall peaks; the latter, however, are flattened and silhouetted in a way that differs markedly from the complex organization of Guo Xi's painting.

In 1982 two of Li Zai's paintings, as well as paintings by Xia Chang, were found during the excavation in Huaian

Li Zai, with Xia Zhi and Ma Shi: *Illustrations to the Homecoming Ode of Tao Yuanming* (detail), ink on paper, 280×830 mm, 1424 (Jinzhou, Liaoning Provincial Museum)

County, Jiangsu Province, of the tomb of Wang Zhen (1424–96). Both are album leaves: one depicts misty hills and rivers in the amorphous style of Mi Youren (*see* MI, (2)), while the other, somewhat different in style from his other works, shows a day-lily. The paintings, now in the Premier Zhou Enlai Museum, Huaian, Jiangsu Province, reveal a greater range in Li Zai's style than was hitherto known.

BIBLIOGRAPHY

J. Cahill: *Parting at the Shore: Chinese Painting of the Early and Middle Ming Dynasty, 1368–1580* (New York and Tokyo, 1978)

Yu Jianhua, ed.: *Zhongguo meishujia renming cidian* [Dictionary of Chinese artists] (Shanghai, 1981), p. 357

*Ming dai gongting yu Zhe pai huihua xuanji* [A selection of Ming-dynasty court paintings and Zhe-school paintings] (Beijing, 1983), pls 18–19

L. Ledderose: *Im Schatten hoher Bäumen* (Baden-Baden, 1985)

Mu Yiqin, ed.: *Ming dai yuanti Zhe pai shiliao* [Historical sources on the courtly style in the Zhe school of the Ming period] (Shanghai, 1985), pp. 31, 230–31

Xu Bangda: 'Huai'an Ming mu chutu shuhua jianxi' [Notes on the paintings and calligraphies found in the Ming tomb at Huai'an], *Wenwu* (1987), no. 3, pp. 16–18

*The Wang Zen Tomb of the Ming Dynasty at Huai'an* (Huai'an, 1988)

*Ming dai huihua* [Ming-dynasty painting], Zhongguo meishu quanji: huihua bian [Encyclopedia of Chinese art: painting] (Beijing and Shanghai, 1984–9), pls 21–4, 26–7

Yang Renkai, ed.: *Zhongguo huihua* [Chinese painting] (Shanghai, 1992), p. 410

RODERICK WHITFIELD

**Lizard.** English family of painters of French descent. Nicholas Lizard was born in France, but he entered the service of Henry VIII probably in the late 1520s or early 1530s and may have been the 'Master Nykolas' who worked with Holbein at Greenwich Palace in 1527. He succeeded Antonio Toto del Nunziata as SERJEANT PAINTER in 1554. Lizard did much decorative work for royal funerals and coronations. In 1556 he presented Queen Mary with a New Year gift of a panel 'painted with the Maundy', and in 1558 he gave Queen Elizabeth a panel representing the 'history of Ahasuerus'. He was buried at St Martin-in-the-Fields, London, on 5 April 1571.

Four of Lizard's five sons were decorative painters, and they were employed at various times by the Office of the Revels, which was responsible for producing stage scenery painted on canvas, stage properties, banners, coats of arms and other decorative work. William headed the team (including Robert Peake and John Bettes the younger) employed during the Christmas season of 1578–9. John Lizard settled in the parish of St Alban, Wood Street, where he died in 1574. Another John, Yeoman Painter to Her Majesty and probably a cousin, was buried at St Dunstan-in-the-West, Fleet Street, in 1565. Nicholas the younger was at Eastwood, Notts, in 1574. Lewes was employed by the Office of the Works in the 1580s: he did some work at Richmond Palace; in 1583–4 he and the Serjeant Painter George Gower worked on the Exchequer windows, and Lewes and his 'Companie of painters' decorated the ceiling of the Banqueting House in the original Whitehall Palace.

BIBLIOGRAPHY

E. Auerbach: *Tudor Artists* (London, 1954), pp. 51–2, 59, 91–4, 107, 111–12, 116–18, 145–6, 174–5

M. Edmond: 'Limners and Picturemakers', *Walpole Soc.*, xlvii (London, 1980), pp. 178–9, 212

MARY EDMOND

**Lizars, William Home** (*b* Edinburgh, 1788; *d* Jedburgh, 30 March 1859). Scottish painter and engraver. He was taught to engrave by his father, Daniel Lizars (*d* 1812), but he also studied painting at the Trustees' Academy in Edinburgh under John Graham (1754–1817) between 1802 and 1805; he was a contemporary there of David Wilkie. His earliest exhibited paintings were portraits, the most ambitious being the *Earl of Buchan Presenting Henry Gattie with a Medal* (exh. Edinburgh, 1808). In 1811 he exhibited two genre works in Edinburgh, *Reading the Will* and the *Scotch Wedding* (both Edinburgh, N.G.), which clearly reveal the influence of Wilkie, though they predate the latter's treatment of the same subjects. The unfinished *Interior of a Church* (Edinburgh, Royal Scot. Acad.) suggests that Lizars might have developed into a genre artist of some originality, but after the death of his father in 1812 he concentrated increasingly on engraving, though he continued to exhibit sporadically until 1830. His first important engraving, the *Landing of Mary Queen of Scots* after W. C. Sheriff (1786–1805), was published in 1807. In his early career he also engraved banknotes and quickly established himself as the leading engraver in Edinburgh. In cooperation with his brother, the surgeon John Lizars, he produced a *System of Anatomical Plates of the Human Body* (Edinburgh, 1822). He was also the engraver chosen by J. J. Audubon for his *Birds of America*, on which he worked between 1826 and 1830. (He subsequently surrendered the contract, and his plates were recut.) He also produced topographical engravings in cooperation with various artists, including 16 engravings after Alexander Nasmyth for Sir Walter Scott's *Provincial and Border Antiquities of Scotland* (1821).

Lizars experimented with new techniques of printmaking and in 1821 published in the *Gentleman's Magazine* an account of a new method of engraving in 'alto relievo'. It involved printing under low pressure from the reserved rather than the etched surface of a copperplate, thus combining the advantages of wood-engraving with those of etching on copper. He also experimented with lithography. In a series of lithographs recording the aftermath of the great fire in Edinburgh in 1824, he exploited to great effect the capacity of the new medium to capture the spontaneity of drawing, giving a hitherto unprecedented immediacy to visual reporting. Lizars took an active part in the art life of Edinburgh. As an associate engraver, he was a founder-member of the Scottish Academy and became an Honorary Academician in 1834.

WRITINGS

*Gent. Mag.* (1821)

BIBLIOGRAPHY

R. Brydall: *History of Art in Scotland* (Edinburgh, 1889), pp. 209–11

J. Caw: *Scottish Painting, 1620–1908* (London, 1908), pp. 104–5

D. and F. Irwin: *Scottish Painters at Home and Abroad* (London, 1975), pp. 191–2

*Painting in Scotland: The Golden Age* (exh. cat. by D. Macmillan, Edinburgh, N.G., 1986), p. 173

DUNCAN MACMILLAN

**Li Zhaodao.** *See* LI (i), (2).

**Ljubljana** [Lat. Emona; formerly Ger. Laibach]. Capital and largest city of the Republic of Slovenia. It was the former capital of the Duchy of Carniola (1364–1918), of the Illyrian Provinces (1809–13) and of the former Slovenian part of Yugoslavia (1918–41, 1945–91). Located on the River Ljubljanica between Castle Hill to the east and Šišenski Hill to the west, the city is strategically placed at the Ljubljana Gate, formerly an economic and cultural passage from the Roman province of Pannonia to the Adriatic Sea. A late Neolithic (Copper Age) and Bronze Age settlement was established south of the present city on the Ljubljana Marsh. Tombs from the Urnfield culture (*c.* 1000–*c.* 700 BC) and from the Hallstatt period (*c.* 750–*c.* 450 BC), as well as Celtic silver coins of the La Tène period (*c.* 450–*c.* 50 BC), have been found in the centre of Ljubljana. An Illyrian town occupied the site until it became a Roman military camp in the 1st century BC. Emperor Augustus then enlarged it into a fortified town, Emona, built on a square plan with surrounding walls dating from AD 14–15, parts of which have been preserved. The Roman town originally had towers, gates, a forum and a port area. The square-shaped Early Christian baptistery and its mosaics date from the beginning of the 5th century. The city was invaded and destroyed at the time of the great migrations of people westwards and their advances towards Italy in the 5th and 6th centuries. The city was slowly rebuilt by the Slavs, whose first excavated findings date from the 9th century.

In the 12th century Ljubljana (known as Laibach 1144–1918) was part of the holdings of the Frankish-Carinthian Dukes of Spanheim, whose seat of power was Ljubljana Castle. A mint was established in the city by Bernhard Spanheim, and it was due to Spanheim that the part of the city called Mesto (City) was the first to be surrounded by walls (*c.* 1220). Medieval Ljubljana was dominated by its castle, and its town plan was dictated by the course of the river on one side and the foot of Castle Hill on the other. In Mesto the principal buildings are the City Hall (Magistrat), begun in 1481 and rebuilt in 1718 by Gregor Maček (1682–1745), and St Nicholas Cathedral, a Romanesque structure enlarged and rebuilt in the Gothic style and again redesigned from 1701 to 1708 after plans by Andrea Pozzo. Its interior contains frescoes by Giulio Quaglio II (1688–1751) and Baroque sculpture by Angelo Pozzo (*fl* 1699–1716), Jacopo Contieri (*fl* 1720–21) and FRANCESCO ROBBA. The Old Quarter (Stari trg), another part of the original medieval city, comprises the area from the Shoemakers' (Čevljarski) Bridge to St Jacob, a medieval church, rebuilt (1613–15) as a Jesuit church and with a late 19th-century exterior. The Baroque altarpieces in the interior are by Contieri (dating from 1720), Angelo Pozzo, Robba (dating from 1732) and Franz Rottman (*c.* 1710–88); the octagonal chapel of St Francis Xavier has remarkable stuccowork of 1666–9. The New Quarter (Novi trg) is also medieval, although it is on the opposite bank of the river. Principal buildings here include Križanke, a medieval monastery (now a school) built by the Teutonic Knights of the Cross, and its church, which was rebuilt (1714–15), probably by Domenico Rossi (1657–1737).

From 1335 to 1918 Ljubljana was under the rule of the Habsburgs. Ljubljana's period of strongest Italian influence was from 1693 to *c.* 1726, when the members of the Accademia Operosorum, in an attempt to transform the city into a 'second Rome', brought in many Italian artists. At this time several major Baroque structures were built,

including the Ursuline church (1718–26) by Giovanni Frigmelica (1653–1732) with its marble high altar (1744) by Robba, and the seminary (begun 1708) by Carlo Martinuzzi (1674–after 1720) containing the first public library (opened 1725) with frescoes (1721) by G. Quaglio and his workshop. The Gruber Palace (1773) by Gabriel Gruber (1740–1805), with paintings by Martin Johann Schmidt, is a later Baroque building. During the Napoleonic period (1809–13) Ljubljana was capital of the Illyrian Provinces, and it was at this time that the Jewish population, who had been settled in the city until the end of the 15th century, returned. One of the major buildings erected in the city during the second half of the 19th century was the National Museum (1885), constructed in a Renaissance Revival style by Wilhelm Treo (1845–1926) and containing archaeological material and items from Slovenia's cultural history.

After a major earthquake in 1895, Ljubljana was rebuilt. A new square (Sodnijski trg) was designed, and many houses in *Sezessionstil* were built, among them the Bamberg House (1907) by MAX FABIANI and the Čuden House (1901) by Ciril Metod Koch (1867–1932). After World War I JOŽE PLEČNIK redesigned many parts of the city, building the Tromostovje Bridge (1931) and several churches, monuments and private dwellings, and IVAN VURNIK became a pioneer of modern architecture. Edo Ravnikar (1907–93), Edo Mihevc (1911–85) and their pupils contributed to the redevelopment of Ljubljana after World War II. Three of the more important museums are the National Gallery, which has a collection of Slovene and European art from the Middle Ages to 1918; the Municipal Museum, with archaeological and numismatic displays, collections of historic furniture and decorative arts and open-air reconstructions of Roman and Early Christian settlements; and the Gallery of Modern Art, which houses modern Slovene art and has hosted from 1955 the International Biennale of Graphic Art.

BIBLIOGRAPHY
M. Kos: *Srednjeveška Ljubljana* [Medieval Ljubljana] (Ljubljana, 1955)
N. Šumi: *Ljubljana* (Belgrade and Florence, 1975)
*Rešena arheološka dediščina Ljubljane* [The archaeological heritage of Ljubljana] (exh. cat. by L. Plesničar-Gec and others, Ljubljana, Mun. Mus., 1979)
*Zgodovina Ljubljane: Prispevki za monografijo* [The history of Ljubljana: contributions to a monograph] (Ljubljana, 1984)
KSENIJA ROZMAN

**Ljubljana, Johannes of.** *See* JOHANNES OF LJUBLJANA.

**Llano, Francesco.** *See* LIANI, FRANCESCO.

**Llano, Teodor de.** *See* NAPOLETANO, FILIPPO.

**Llanos and Yañez.** Spanish painters. Fernando Llanos (*b* ?Castella la Nueva; *fl* 1506–16) and Fernando Yañez [Yañez de la Almedina] (*b* Almedina, Ciudad Real; *fl* 1506–31) are first recorded in Valencia around 1506, painting in a style originating in Florentine art and the work of Leonardo da Vinci, although it is also recorded that in 1505 a Fernando Spagnuolo was receiving payment for work on the cartoon for Leonardo's *Battle of Anghiari* (1503–8; destr.; copy, Florence, Uffizi). Although there is no documentary evidence to show that the two trained in Italy, it seems likely in the light of the innovations that they brought to Renaissance Valencian painting, including models derived from Leonardo, and a preference for scenes with monumental architecture in which figures are symmetrically arranged in parallel planes in the Italian manner. It is difficult to distinguish between the styles of the two artists, as the differences in their work are slight, although it seems that Yañez was the more gifted. He conceived his figures with greater monumentality, and his work was more classical and serene, painted with a greater clarity and breadth of composition than that of his colleague. The figures painted by Llanos are smaller and more restless and are sometimes unusually proportioned.

One of the first important contracts gained by Llanos and Yañez was for the high altar of Valencia Cathedral, dated 1507. The paintings attributed to Yañez for this commission are the *Meeting of St Joachim and St Anne*, the *Presentation of the Virgin*, the *Visitation*, the *Adoration of the Shepherds*, *Pentecost* and the *Death of the Virgin*; those attributed to Llanos are the *Purification*, the *Birth of the Virgin*, the *Flight into Egypt* and the *Adoration of the Kings*. The two artists received final payment for the works in 1510, and from this date on there exists no documentation of joint work. In 1513 they were sharing the same house in Valencia. They probably continued to live together, but the many commissions they received from this date, both in and away from Valencia, had to be attended to separately, although they may have worked jointly on the layout and plans for these.

Llanos continued to work in Valencia Cathedral in 1513 and 1515. He was in Murcia from 1516, where he worked in the cathedral and painted the *Betrothal* and the *Nativity* (both *c.* 1516; Murcia Cathedral). The *Stations of the Cross* (1516; Caravaca, parish church) is of the same period.

In 1515 Yañez was working in Barcelona and in 1526 in Cuenca, where he stayed until 1531. Works attributed to him in the period *c.* 1520–26 are the splendid *St Catherine* (Madrid, Prado), considered by Tormo (1915) to be the most beautiful Spanish painting of the 16th century, the *Pietà* (Valencia Cathedral), *St Anne* and the *Virgin and Child* (both Valencia, S Nicolás) and the *Annunciation* (Valencia, Colegio del Patriarca). The influence of both Leonardo and Raphael is evident in the compositions of Yañez's *Epiphany* and *Pietà* (1526–31; Cuenca Cathedral). At this time he also painted two altarpieces of the *Nativity* and the *Crucifixion* (1526–31; Cuenca Cathedral). Closely related to the style of these panels are the *Last Judgement* (*c.* 1530; Palma de Mallorca, Col. March) and a late and very beautiful work, influenced by an engraving of the same subject by Dürer, the *Holy Family* (*c.* 1530; Madrid, Prado).

Llanos and Yañez created a school in Valencia that extended through Murcia, Cuenca and Albacete. Among their direct followers were Martín Gómez the elder ( *fl* 1552), the Master of Grifo, the Master of Alcira, Miguel Esteve ( *fl* 1513–20) and the Master of Albacete.

*See also* SPAIN, fig. 13.

BIBLIOGRAPHY

E. Tormo: 'Yañez de la Almedina, il más exquisito pintor del renacimiento en España', *Bol. Soc. Esp. Excurs.*, xxiii (1915), pp. 198–205
——: 'Obras conocidas y desconocidas de Yañez de la Almedina', *Bol. Soc. Esp. Excurs.*, xxxii (1924), pp. 32–9
C. R. Post: *A History of Spanish Painting*, xi (Cambridge, 1953), pp. 175–244
D. Angulo Iñiguez: *Pintura del renacimiento*, A. Hisp., xii (Madrid, 1954), pp. 41–57
F. Garin Ortiz de Taranco: *Yañez de la Almedina* (Valencia, 1954)
J. Camón Aznar: 'La pintura española del siglo xvi', *Summa A.*, xxiv (1979), pp. 43–61
L. Rokiski: 'Sobre Hernando Yañez en Cuenca', *Archv Esp. A.*, lix (1986), pp. 106–7
X. Company i Climent: *La pintura del renaixement* (Valencia, 1987), pp. 43–9

ISABEL MATEO GOMEZ

**Llanos (y) Valdés, Sebastián de** (*b* Seville, ?1605; *d* Seville, 1677). Spanish painter. He belonged to the lesser nobility and must have possessed means sufficient for him not to have depended on income from his painting. He trained with Francisco de (i) Herrera and had his own workshop from 1630. He was receptive to current pictorial tendencies, and his style was influenced successively by Herrera, Zurbarán, Murillo and Juan de Valdés Leal. This range of influences is reflected in his work, which is varied and uneven: while a few paintings show a careful technique, others are badly executed and of poor quality. In his early works Llanos y Valdés showed an interest in tenebrist effects, with strongly lit figures set against a dark background. The earliest of his known works is the signed *Magdalene* (1658; Seville, Casa de Pilatos), in which the dramatic presentation and strong chiaroscuro are clearly derived from Ribera. The *Virgin of the Rosary* (1664; Seville Cathedral) perfectly exemplifies the artist's style; the figures are sweet and meditative but somewhat inexpressive. The *Immaculate Child* (1665; Seville, Gómez Barreda priv. col., see Angulo Iñiguez, 1946, fig. 1) echoes the work of Zurbarán, as does the *Crucifixion* (1666; Seville Cathedral, sacristy). In the *Pietà* (1666; Seville Cathedral) Llanos y Valdés succeeded in portraying a convincing group of mourning figures around the body of Christ. His best works are probably the *Calling of St Matthew* and *St John the Baptist before the Sanhedrin*, both of 1668 and located on the outer wall of the main altar in Seville Cathedral. In these Llanos y Valdés depicts ordinary figures with contrasting characterization and psychological insight. One of his frequent subjects was the severed heads of saints, the best examples being the *Head of John the Baptist* and the *Head of St Paul*, both signed and dated 1670 and located in the church of El Salvador in Seville.

BIBLIOGRAPHY

D. Angulo Iñiguez: 'Sebastián de Llanos Valdés', *Archv. Esp. A.*, xix (1946), p. 309–18
J. Guerrero Lovillo: 'Obras inéditas de Don Sebastián de Llanos Valdés', *Archv. Esp. A.*, xx (1947), p. 329–32
D. Angulo Iñiguez: *Pintura del siglo XVII*, A. Hisp., xv (Madrid, 1971), p. 258
V. Lleo Canal: 'El pintor Don Sebastián de Llanos Valdés', *Rev. A. Sevill.*, 1 (1982), p. 21–33
E. Valdivieso: *Historia de la pintura sevillana* (Seville, 1986), p. 194
A. E. Pérez Sánchez: *Pintura barroca española* (Madrid, 1992), p. 266

ENRIQUE VALDIVIESO

**Lleida, Seu Vella** [Sp. Lérida, Seo Antigua]. Former cathedral in the city of Lleida in Catalonia, Spain. It was built on an elevated site that housed a mosque and an Arab fortress, the Zuda. The mosque, which was probably built on the site of an older, perhaps Visigothic, cathedral, was consecrated as the cathedral of S María in Sede on 30

October 1149, six days after the expulsion of the Arabs. In June 1193 Pedro de Coma (Decumba) was appointed master of the works of a new cathedral, which was to be built on or near the site of the mosque. The foundation stone was laid on 22 July 1203, and the perimeter walls were probably determined and much of the east end constructed by the time of Pedro de Coma's death (1220). The new building had an aisled, three-bay nave and five apses in echelon opening from a projecting transept. Master Pedro de Pennafreita (*d* 1286) is credited with the design of the elegant, double-shell octagonal cupola, with the completion of the nave vaulting and with the beginning of the east and north wings of the cloister. The cloister, largely constructed in the 14th century, is situated to the west of the cathedral and functions as an atrium, with an entrance, the Porta dels Apòstols, on its western side. The openings to the cloister garth contain very fine tracery (rest.). Its location was determined by site constraints. Alterations to the cathedral have included the renovation of the two southern apses in the 14th century and the destruction of the northernmost apse by an explosion in 1812. The building suffered heavily during the War of Succession (1701–14), and it was converted into a barracks in 1707. Some of the sculpture, especially from the Porta dels Apòstols, was smashed during the Civil War (1936–9). Restorations were begun in 1949.

The earliest sculpture studio began work shortly before 1210, and it was responsible for work in the eastern apses, the transept and the portals. The capitals display great variety and include Corinthian forms, inhabited foliage, warriors fighting fantastic monsters and everyday, hagiographic and biblical scenes. The finest carvings have been attributed to a sculptor who had worked under Benedetto Antelami at the baptistery of Parma, but there are also clear indications of the influence of sculpture at Toulouse, particularly from La Daurade and St Etienne (*see* TOULOUSE, §2(ii) and (iii)).

The north transept Portal of S Berenguer, the simplest and the earliest of the portals, has a fine chrismon, as does the south transept portal of the Annunciata. The latter also has a range of corbels framing decorative relief plaques and supporting a *rinceau* cornice. A running inscription relates the angel Gabriel's salutation to the Virgin. The archivolts are composed of a rounded torus, and bands of floral decoration and the capitals form a continuous frieze. The niches on either side of the portals originally contained an *Annunciation* group. The figures of the angel Gabriel and the Virgin (Lleida, Mus. Catedralici) have been compared with sculpture in Toulouse, Tarragona and Solsona. A *terminus ante quem* of 1215, based on a funerary inscription, is generally accepted for the portal.

The south aisle Porta dels Fillols (now covered by a late 14th-century porch) bears archivolts composed of a ringed torus, zigzags, overlapping arches and a capital frieze of foliage and inhabited vines, giving a rich, decorative effect. Corbels, plaques with inhabited vine-scrolls and a *rinceau* cornice crown the façade. The sculpture of the west façade, now darkened by the cloister, is part of the same decorative programme. The portal sculpture at Lleida has been seen as the source for a number of provincial works, including S María, Agramunt, and its influence extended as far as Valencia.

The vault bosses of the late 14th-century Requesens Chapel are decorated with escutcheons and with a Virgin, at whose feet kneels a bishop, undoubtedly the patron Guerrau de Requesens. Carved bosses also appear in the chapel of S Juan Bautista and in the chapel of Cescomes (or Jesús), completed in 1334 by an architect sent by King Edward II of England (*reg* 1307–27) to King James II (*reg* 1291–1327), Reinard des Fonoll, who also worked at the Cistercian abbeys of Santes Creus and Poblet and at Tarragona Cathedral. From 1360 to 1380 Bartomeu Robió worked on a marble and alabaster high altar, of which only fragments survive, probably including a *Virgin* now in S Llorenç, Lleida. The late 14th-century Porta dels Apòstols by Guillermo Solivella (*fl* 1392) at the cloister entrance bears a tympanum with *Christ in Judgement* flanked by angels and surrounded by Apostles and representations of the saved and damned. The *Virgin del Blau* from the trumeau is now in the Catedral Nueva.

BIBLIOGRAPHY

V. Lampérez y Romeo: 'La Catedral Vieja de Lérida', *Bol. Real Acad. Hist.*, xviii (1918), pp. 473–80
J. Bergos: *La Catedral Vella de Lleida* (Barcelona, 1928)
——: *L'escultura a la Seu Vella de Lleida* (Barcelona, 1935)
M. Herrera y Ges: *La Catedral Antigua de Lérida* (Lleida, 2/1948)
E. Lambert: 'La Cathédrale de Lérida', *Congr. Archéol. France*, cxvii (1959), pp. 136–46
J. Lladonosa Pujol: *Visita a la Catedral Antigua de Lérida* (Lleida, 1965, 2/1980)
J. Vives i Miret: *Reinard des Fonoll, mestre britànic, renovador de l'art gòtic a Catalunya (1321–1362)* (Barcelona, 1969)
J. Lladonosa Pujol: 'Santa Maria l'Antigua y la primitiva canonjia de Lleida (1149–1278)', *Miscellania històrica catalana: Homenatge al P. Jaume Finestres, historiador de Poblet* (Poblet, 1970), pp. 85–136
J. Sarrate Forga: *Las portadas románicas de la Seo de Lérida* (Lleida, 1972)
J. Lacoste: 'Découvertes dans la cathédrale romane de Lérida', *Bull. Mnmtl*, cxxxii (1974), pp. 231–4
——: 'La Cathédrale de Lérida: Les Débuts de la sculpture', *Cah. Saint-Michel de Cuxa*, vi (1975), pp. 275–98
G. Alonso García: *Los maestros de la Seu Vella de Lleida y sus colaboradores* (Lérida, 1976)
F. Español i Bertran: 'El mestre del frontal de Santa Tecla i l'escultura romànica tardana a la Catalunya Nova', *Quad. Estud. Med.*, iv (1988), pp. 81–103

DAVID L. SIMON

**Llewelyn, John Dillwyn** (*b* Swansea, 12 Jan 1810; *d* Swansea, 24 Aug 1882). Welsh photographer and chemist. He typified the scientific gentleman amateur who embraced the new art of photography. From its earliest days he experimented with the daguerreotype alongside Antoine Claudet. Most of his early photography documents facets of life on his estate of Penllergare in West Glamorgan. It was in the 1850s that Llewelyn's influence in the British photographic community fully emerged. He was an accomplished landscape photographer himself, and through his oxymel process he addressed the problems peculiar to field photography. Oxymel (a pharmacist's mixture of honey and vinegar) produced a stable photographic plate that circumvented the need to carry a laboratory into the field. Llewelyn was a pioneer of instantaneous photography and a founder-member of the Photographic Society of London (later the Royal Photographic Society).

Llewelyn's work benefited from significant family connections. His wife, Emma Thomasina (née Talbot, 1808–81), was a cousin of William Henry Fox Talbot. His daughter Thereza Mary (1834–1926) married Nevil Story-Maskelyne (1823–1911), a pioneering photographic researcher. While John Dillwyn Llewelyn mastered the art of making negatives, Emma proved more expert at the challenging task of producing the print. She was one of the few practitioners of Talbot's Photoglyphic Engraving (a photomechanical process). As a young girl Thereza had sat for daguerreotype experiments, and she became an accomplished photographer herself. Throughout her life she arranged and stored the family's photographic corpus and thereby preserved a significant legacy of early photographic history.

BIBLIOGRAPHY
*John Dillwyn Llewelyn, 1810–1882* (exh. cat., ed. R. Morris; ACGB, 1980)
C. Titterington: 'Llewelyn and Instantaneity', *V&A Mus. Album*, iv (1985), pp. 138–45
L. J. Schaaf, ed.: *Sun Pictures, Catalogue Two: Llewelyn, Maskelyne, Talbot—a Family Circle* (New York, 1986)

L. J. SCHAAF

**Llewelyn-Davies, Richard** (*b* London, 24 Dec 1912; *d* London, 27 Oct 1981). English architect and planner. He studied engineering at Trinity College, Cambridge, graduating in 1933. The social and political commitment then shared by many Cambridge scientists appealed to him and shaped his early career. Turning to architecture, he studied at the Architectural Association School, London (1934–8), where he was a covert but powerful influence on the student rebellion against outmoded, Beaux-Arts teaching methods. With Peter Moro (*b* 1911) he helped design a large Modernist house, Harbour Meadow at Birdham, W. Sussex (1939–40). During the early part of World War II Llewelyn-Davies joined W. G. Holford's large collaborative team constructing munitions factories and housing He then joined Leslie Martin in the Architect's Development Group of the London, Midland and Scottish Railway. This group concerned itself particularly with developing flexible techniques of design for the mass production of industrial building, notably through the use of coordinated dimensions. The group's work concentrated on 'unit stations'; few of these were built (one example survives at Queen's Park, London), but its thinking profoundly influenced post-war British architectural methodology.

Llewelyn-Davies affirmed his commitment to architectural research and method as the director of a team, funded by the Nuffield Foundation, studying design problems in hospitals and related buildings (1948–60). Few new British hospitals were designed in these years, but Llewelyn-Davies's conclusions deeply affected the National Health Service's buildings of the 1960s. He also ran his own practice, at first on a small scale in partnership with his long-time colleague John Weeks, which later expanded to become the interdisciplinary team of Llewelyn-Davies, Weeks, Robert Forestier-Walker and Walter Bor (*b* 1916). Hospitals were naturally among the firm's specialities, but the planned groups of village housing built for Lord Rothschild at Rushbrooke, Suffolk (1956–60), earned much early praise.

In 1960 Llewelyn-Davies became professor at the Bartlett School of Architecture, University College, London, where a version of Beaux-Arts teaching had lasted into the 1950s. He set out to transform the school into an interdisciplinary centre for 'environmental' skills and research and brought in new blood. For the students, his was mainly a distant presence, but his impact on the school as a whole was immense. He also inaugurated the Centre for Environmental Studies, London, in 1967 and became Professor of Urban Planning at University College (1969–75). By then his expanding practice, strengthened by the arrival of Bor, was much taken up with urban planning. In 1965–6 the firm provided the master-plan for Washington New Town, County Durham (now Tyne & Wear), which unlike earlier British new towns had a plan articulated by a two-level grid of roads. This approach was developed in more sophisticated form in the master-plan for Milton Keynes, undertaken in 1969–70. Milton Keynes, conceived with a target population of 250,000, was the culmination of the British new town tradition, but it also drew on a range of international thinking, notably on American theories that too rigid a physical plan limited individual freedom and could cause economic damage to a city. Llewelyn-Davies's strategic gifts, breadth of approach and personal learning allowed this point of view to be integrated successfully with well-tried, native assumptions about urban planning. Though his firm built little at Milton Keynes, it became one of the most successful modern planned communities in the world due to the scrupulous intelligence of the original plan.

For an illustration of his work *see* HOSPITAL, fig. 4.

WRITINGS
with D. J. Petty: *Building Elements* (London, 1956, 3/1969)
with A. M. C. Macaulay: *Hospital Planning and Administration* (Geneva, 1966)
'The Tuscan Artist: Thought and Action in Design', *RIBA J.*, lxxxiii/8 (1976), pp. 350–53 [Harvard lecture]
'Planning Health Facilities in Developing Countries', *World Hosp.*, xll/3 (1976), pp. 159–63

BIBLIOGRAPHY
*Contemp. Architects*
S. Braybrooke: 'Llewelyn-Davies: A Profile of his Professional Philosophy', *Urb. Des. Int.*, i/2 (1980), pp. 34–9
Obituary, *RIBA J.*, lxxxviii/4 (1981), p. 28

☐

**Llorens Artigas, Josep.** *See* ARTIGAS.

**Llorenz Saragozza.** *See* LORENZO ZARAGOZA.

**Lloyd, Mrs Hugh.** *See* MOSER (i), (2).

**Lloyd, Seton (Howard Frederick)** (*b* Edgbaston, Birmingham, 30 May 1902; *d* Oxford, 7 Jan 1996). English excavator, architect, writer and teacher. He qualified as an architect (RIBA) 1926, working for two years for Sir Edwin Lutyens before setting up his own practice. His employment as architect during the 1929 excavations at Tell el-Amarna led to a change in career, and until 1937 he worked for the Oriental Institute of the University of Chicago excavations in the Diyala region of Iraq, northeast of Baghdad, at Khorsabad in northern Iraq and on the aqueduct built by the Assyrian king Sennacherib (*reg* 704–681 BC) at Jerwan; Lloyd helped perfect techniques for tracing mud-brick architecture and made innovative use of kite photography. Between 1937 and 1939 he excavated with Sir John Garstang at Mersin in southern

Turkey and carried out a key survey of sites in the Sinjar district of northern Iraq. Between 1939 and 1948, while working as Adviser to the Directorate General of Antiquities in Baghdad, he excavated Hassuna, Tell Uqair, Tell Harmal and Eridu. In 1949 Lloyd became the first Director of the British Institute of Archaeology in Ankara. He established archaeological sequences for the centre (Polatli) and west (Beycesultan) of the Anatolian plateau and worked at Harran, Sultantepe and Alanya in the south.

In 1962 Lloyd succeeded Max Mallowan as professor at the Institute of Archaeology of the University of London (Emeritus 1969) and, in 1965, directed excavations at Kayalidere in Urartu (eastern Turkey). All his excavations were carefully selected to answer specific problems, and their prompt and meticulous publication, illustrated by his beautiful plans and drawings and those of his wife Hydie—an artist and sculptor—ensured that the results were swiftly available. Lloyd was also a successful popularizer, writing many books and articles.

### WRITINGS

*Twin Rivers: A Brief History of Iraq from the Earliest Times to the Present Day* (Oxford and Bombay, 1943; 2/1943; 3/1961; Rus. trans., 1974)
*Foundations in the Dust: A Story of Mesopotamian Exploration* (Oxford, 1947; 2/1949; Harmondsworth, 1955; rev. and enlarged, London, 1980)
*The Art of the Ancient Near East* (London, 1961; later edns trans. into Ger., Dut., Sp., It. and Rus.)
*Mounds of the Near East* (Edinburgh, 1963)
*The Archaeology of Mesopotamia* (London, 1978)
*Iraq*, xliv (1982), pp. 221–4 [complete bibliog. to date]
*The Interval: A Life in Near Eastern Archaeology* (Faringdon, 1986) [autobiography, with updated bibliog., p. 179]
*Ancient Turkey: A Traveller's History of Anatolia* (London, 1989, 2/1992)

For further bibliography *see* excavation reports under individual entries for sites mentioned in above text.

DOMINIQUE COLLON

Loarre Castle, interior view of castle church, *c.* 1073–97

**Loarre Castle.** Fortress in Huesca province, Aragon, Spain. It commands a magnificent situation in the foothills of the Pyrenees overlooking the vast plains of Sotonera south to Huesca and beyond. The complex was built largely during the 11th and 12th centuries, when its position on the frontier between Christian and Muslim lands gave it its strategic importance. The first of the two major building programmes began *c.* 1020, when Sancho el Mayor (*reg* 1063–94) reconquered the surrounding lands from the Muslims. At least three towers, two of which survive, the Torre del Homenaje and the Torre de la Reina, as well as a chapel dedicated to S María de Valverde and connecting walls are attributed to this campaign. The Torre del Homenaje was built in an isolated position in front of the fortifications, to which it was connected by a wooden bridge. It contained a basement and five floors. The Torre de la Reina, comprising a basement and three floors, is particularly noteworthy for three sets of twin-arched windows, with columns of exaggerated entasis and trapezoidal capitals that have been related to both Lombard and Mozarabic architectural forms. The chapel is composed of a single-cell nave with an eastern apse covered by a semicircular vault. The original timber roof of the nave was replaced by a vault at the end of the 11th century.

After 1070 Loarre became increasingly important. In 1073 King Sancho installed a community of Augustinian canons, and it was from Loarre that he prepared for the conquest of Huesca in 1094. In 1097, however, his successor, Peter I (*reg* 1094–1104), donated all the goods of Loarre to a new royal monastery at Montearagon. This evidence suggests that the second major construction programme was undertaken between 1073 and 1097, and much building evidently does date from this period. By comparison with other monuments, however, it is also clear that the building and decorative programme continued into the 12th century.

The outermost walls of the castle and their eight towers were erected in the 13th or 14th century. The church and castle have been the subject of numerous restorations, a major one in 1913 and subsequent ones, particularly during the 1970s, have resulted in the rebuilding of many walls and towers that had fallen into disrepair.

1. CASTLE CHURCH. The most impressive monument of the second building campaign is the castle church, built to the east of the chapel and dedicated to the Saviour and St Peter. It was built over and it defines a new entrance to the castle complex, and it has a fortified appearance, with walls rising dramatically to the level of the fortifications. On the south a portal provides access to an impressive barrel-vaulted stairway that runs under the width of the church, leading to a doorway in its north flank. To the left of this long passage is a chamber, probably a guards' room, and to the right, the crypt of the church. The crypt is vaulted and is decorated by a wall arcade supported on columns with carved capitals. Two stairways give direct access to the church.

The church is composed of a single-cell nave of two bays, one barrel-vaulted and the other covered by a cupola rising above double squinches (see fig.). The impression of great height is accentuated by the addition of four oculi placed above the arches supporting the dome. There is little evidence to suggest that the unique double squinches are not an original feature, and their only purpose seems to be a means of increasing the sensation of height, although some scholars have interpreted their architectural form as a reflection of the elaborate vaulted and domed coverings of the Muslim architecture of Spain. The vaulted apse is decorated with arcading: an upper row of five arches and a lower of thirteen. The decorative repertory of the church, in the general use of the torus around doors and windows articulated with billet bands, suggests a connection to Jaca Cathedral, a link that is confirmed by such sculptural details as the use of a feathered projection on the edges of some capitals; there is also a clear parallel between an impost block of the apse arcade and one from the chapter house of Jaca. The sculpture of Loarre may also be seen in the context of a general current that spread along the north of Christian Spain, particularly in León and Fromista, but there is also a strong relationship to French sculpture, particularly to that of Moissac and St Sernin, Toulouse.

BIBLIOGRAPHY

R. del Arco: 'El castillo-abadía de Loarre', *Semin. A. Aragon.*, xiii–xv (1968), pp. 5–36

F. Iñiguez Almech: 'Las empresas constructivas de Sancho el Mayor: El castillo de Loarre', *Archv Esp. A.*, xliii (1970), pp. 363–73

A. Canellas-López and A. San Vicente: *Aragon roman*, Nuit Temps (La Pierre-qui-vire, 1971)

A. Duran Gudiol: *El castillo de Loarre* (Saragossa, 1971)

J. F. Esteban Lorente, F. Galtier Martí and M. García Guatas: *El nacimiento del arte románico en Aragón: Arquitectura*, Investigaciones de Arte Aragonés (Saragossa, 1982)

J. E. Mann: *San Pedro at the Castle of Loarre: A Study in the Relation of Cultural Forces to the Design, Decoration and Construction of a Romanesque Church* (diss., New York, Columbia U., 1991)

DAVID L. SIMON

**Loarte, Alejandro de** (*b* ?1595–1600; *d* Toledo, 12 Dec 1626). Spanish painter. The son of a painter, he was married in Madrid in 1619 but later lived and worked in Toledo, where he enjoyed a wide-ranging but short-lived career. His few extant religious paintings are mediocre, although his large, multi-figured *Miracle of the Loaves and Fishes* (1622; see 1995 exh. cat., fig. 39) is ambitious and accomplished. His best works are still-lifes, all dating from the last four years of his life. These compositions portray objects suspended and arranged within a window-frame or on a shelf and broadly follow the format of works by Juan Sánchez Cotán and Juan van der Hamen y León, but they lack the same spatial clarity or refined sense of interval. In Loarte's *Still-life with Fruit and Game* (1623; Madrid, Fund. Santamarca) the restrained palette and awkward drawing of the central basket are consistent with his diffident handling of pictorial space, and the composition reveals his predilection for symmetry. The foodstuffs, however, are realistically painted, with a fresh, sensuous touch, and the control of light and dark is skilful. His last painting, the *Poultry Vendor* (1626; priv. col., see 1985 exh. cat., pl. 11, p. 101), depicts a Toledan market scene, in which the discrepancy between the dryly modelled and stilted figures and the richly painted fowl betrays his artistic immaturity.

BIBLIOGRAPHY

A. Méndez Casal: 'El pintor Alejandro de Loarte', *Rev. Esp. A.*, xii (1934), pp. 187–202 [docs only]

*Spanish Still-life in the Golden Age, 1600–50* (exh. cat. by W. B. Jordan, Fort Worth, TX, Kimbell A. Mus., 1985) [excellent pls]

*Spanish Still-life from Velázquez to Goya* (exh. cat. by W. B. Jordan and P. Cherry, London, N.G., 1995), pp. 56–61

PETER CHERRY

**Lobi.** Voltaic-speaking people numbering *c.* 120,000 and inhabiting south-western Burkina Faso and north-eastern Côte d'Ivoire. The Lobi are bordered to the north by the Dagari and the Bobo, to the west and south by the Senufo and to the east by the Bwa. They grow millet, sorghum and maize and herd some cattle, goats and sheep. They are thought to have migrated to their present region from northern Ghana *c.* 1770. The Lobi are best known for their figure sculpture, although they also have a distinctive architecture and produce a range of other arts. Lobi sculpture has been widely collected, in part because the figures display the sort of strength of form that is admired by collectors of African art, and in part because the Lobi are very prolific artists and much of their art has been available on the market. A major exhibition of works from European collections, both public and private, was held at the Museum Rietberg, Zurich, in 1981. The accompanying exhibition catalogue (see bibliography) is the standard reference work for Lobi art.

1. FIGURE SCULPTURE. Lobi artists produce figures to represent nature spirits (*thila*), mostly in wood, but also in brass, clay, ivory and other materials. Most Lobi figures are naturalistic, with fully rounded arms and legs carved free from the body and large spherical heads with detailed hairstyles. Ornaments and decorative scarification patterns may also be represented. In contrast, some Lobi figures are quite stylized and angular. Because each Lobi male considers himself potentially an artist, a great variety of styles have appeared, ranging from very abstract, rather rough and stylized to very naturalistic and polished. Indeed, Lobi artists are so independent that they feel few constraints to conform to a particular style that might be identified as 'Lobi'. The figures are called *boteba* and may be placed on shrines to make the spirits visible. The particular character or ability of the spirit that the figure represents may be expressed through specific gestures. It is, indeed, essential to understand Lobi gesture in order to understand Lobi sculpture. A figure with its head bowed and its hands clasped behind its back is mourning on its owner's behalf the death of a loved one. A figure with one arm stretched out to the side blocks the entrance of malevolent spirits into the family home. In addition to their major talents *boteba* can perform such temporary tasks as finding lost items, helping women conceive children, preventing illness or curing disease.

Many Lobi figures have multiple arms, legs or heads. These represent exceptional beings or *ti bala*. These are *thila* that are exceptionally strong or powerful. They are particularly unhuman. The more unhuman the spirit the more powerful it is. Thus a figure with more than one head is doubly perceptive and quick to act against malevolent forces. These and the other *thila* are controlled by men, known as *thildara*, who may possess as many as 50 and who have become famous because they can, for a fee, provide the protection of any of their spirits to strangers. The shrines over which such men preside may include

Lobi shrine, Gaoua, Burkina Faso, 1984

dozens of carved figures in a variety of poses, each ready to deal with a specific concern or threat (see fig.).

2. ARCHITECTURE. Among the characteristic forms of Lobi architecture are expansive single-storey houses of puddled mud, with walls built up in 0.6–1.0 m layers or courses to a height of 2–3 m. The walls have few openings, whether doors or windows. The plan is very organic, with external circular walls enclosing an interior space that expands or contracts with the changing needs of the extended family. The clay for the walls is dug from the interior of the house, so that one has to step down into the house on entering it. The exterior walls, in consequence, give little indication of the actual height of the ceilings. The latter are supported by a lattice of logs and brush. Insects are kept from damaging the wooden supports by the smoke of cooking fires that quickly blackens the beams. The flat roofs are used for drying grain and for sleeping during the hot season. Access is by ladders carved from forking tree branches into which steps are cut. Shrines to nature spirits are frequently constructed on the roof, or in very small internal chambers.

3. OTHER ARTS. As well as wooden figures Lobi men carve beautiful three-legged stools, sometimes decorated with animal heads. These are carried in the evenings and make handy weapons when fights break out. Large quantities of cast-brass jewellery are also produced, including such items as pendants in the form of snakes. Among the most beautiful of Lobi objects are stylized pendants carved of ivory. Called *thungbubiel*, they represent small whistles. These elegant carvings are often rubbed with palm oil and range in colour from almost pure white when new to a translucent reddish-orange when old. Very old pieces are almost black.

BIBLIOGRAPHY

H. Labouret: *Les Tribus du rameau lobi* (Paris, 1931)
——: *Nouvelles Notes sur les tribus du rameau lobi* (Dakar, 1958)
J. Goody: *Death, Property and the Ancestors* (Stanford, 1962)
G. Savonnet: 'Interrogatoire d'une défunte chez les Lobi de Pora', *Notes Afr.*, cviii (1962), pp. 119–24
G. Antongini and T. Spini: *Il cammino degli antenati: I Lobi dell'Alto Volta* (Rome, 1981)
*Kunst und Religion der Lobi* (exh. cat. by P. Meyer, Zurich, Mus. Rietberg, 1981)
K. Schneider: *Handwerk und materialisierte Kultur der Lobi in Burkina Faso*, Studien zur Kulturkunde, 94 (Stuttgart, 1990)
G. F. Scanzi: *L'Art traditionnel lobi/Lobi Traditional Art* (Abidjan and Bergamo, 1993) [Eng. and Fr. text]

CHRISTOPHER D. ROY

**Lobkowitz, Juan Caramuel de.** *See* CARAMUEL DE LOBKOWITZ, JUAN.

**Lobmeyr, J. & L.** Austrian glass company. It was founded in Vienna in 1823 by Josef Lobmeyr (*b* Grieskirchen, 1792; *d* Vienna, 1855). Glass for the firm was made mainly at the Harrachhütte glassworks in Neuwelt and the Vetterhütte glassworks in Parchen. In 1835 the first large table service was delivered to Emperor Ferdinand (Vienna, Hofburg-Schauräume; Vienna, J. & L. Lobmeyr). In 1848 the firm was commissioned by Emperor Francis Joseph for the banqueting service for his coronation, which was designed by Josef Lobmeyr's son, Ludwig Lobmeyr (*b* Vienna, 1829; *d* Vienna, 1917). In 1851 the firm established a studio in Polevsko for cutting, painting and engraving blanks. In 1855 Josef Lobmeyr's son, Josef Lobmeyr jr (*b* Vienna, 1828; *d* Vienna, 1864), became director and began exporting chandeliers to countries such as India, Egypt, Turkey and America. After Josef's death Ludwig Lobmeyr became director. He was a great patron of the arts in Vienna and did much to foster working relations with Bohemian glass factories. Architects who designed for the company included Theophilus Hansen, Josef von Storck and Friedrich von Schmidt. Such new techniques as lustering and painting with platinum were developed in conjunction with the LÖTZ WITWE glassworks in Klostermühle, and wares were produced in the *Jugendstil* style. In 1902 Stefan Rath (*b* Vienna, 1876; *d* Vienna, 1960), a nephew of Ludwig, who had studied under Josef Hoffmann at the Kunstgewerbeschule in Vienna, began designing work for the firm. Hoffmann later designed for the firm and was responsible for a style of decoration known as 'Bronzit', in which geometrical designs were painted in matt-black on frosted glass (see fig.). After World War I a branch factory was founded in Kamenicky Šenov in northern Bohemia. Such designers as Rath's daughter Marianne Rath (*b* Vienna, 1904; *d* Vienna, 1985), Lotte Fink, Adolf Loos and Jaroslav Horejc (1886–1971) were then designing for the company. The firm was particularly successful at the Exposition Internationale des Arts Décoratifs et Industriels Modernes of 1925 in Paris. In 1938 Hans Harald Rath (*b* Vienna, 1904; *d* Vienna, 1968) became director, and Stefan Rath moved to Kamenicky Šenov where he was director until 1951. Many works with *Hochschnitt* decoration were produced during this period for the Third Reich, Czechoslovakia and finally for the communist nationalized industries. Crystal chandeliers were produced for castles in Kraków and Poznań; after World War II chandeliers were also produced for the

Glass service with 'Bronzit' decoration, designed by Josef Hoffmann in 1914 (from left to right): water beaker, h. 105 mm, series 'B'; decanter, h. 220 mm, and wine-glass, h. 135 mm, series 'A'; made at J. & L. Lobmeyr (Vienna, J. & L. Lobmeyr)

Vienna State Opera House (1955) and the Metropolitan Opera House (1966), New York. After Hans Harald Rath's death in 1968 his three sons Harald Rath (*b* Limpsfield, 1938), Peter Rath (*b* Vienna, 1939) and Stefan Rath jr (*b* Vienna, 1943) took over the firm, and further chandeliers were made for the J. F. Kennedy Center of the Performing Arts (1970), Washington, DC, and for the Presidium of the Supreme Soviet (1971) in the Kremlin, Moscow. In 1973 the firm started a studio glass furnace in Stoob with Zdenek Stahlavsky (*b* 1926) and Jindra Beranek (*b* 1927).

Lobmeyr and the American Jack Ink (*b* 1944) established a studio in Baden, which produced studio glass and was sold in 1989. At the end of the twentieth century, the company was involved with the contemporary art glass movement, the World Crafts Council, which is affiliated to UNESCO, and the Austrian Design Centre in Vienna.

BIBLIOGRAPHY
R. Schmidt: *100 Jahre österreichischer Glaskunst* (Vienna, 1925)
M. Despot: 'Josef Lobmeyr and his Glassworks in Slavonia', *J. Glass Stud.*, iv (1962), pp. 103–7
S. Rath: *Lobmeyr* (Vienna, 1962)
*150 Jahre österreichischer Glaskunst: Lobmeyr, 1823–1973* (exh. cat., Vienna, J. & L. Lobmeyr, 1973)
L. Lobmeyr: *Die Glasindustrie* (Stuttgart, 1974)

PETER RATH

**Lobo, António** (*d* 1719). Portuguese painter. The chief follower of Vicenzo Baccarelli (1682–1745), who introduced the Italian tradition of *trompe l'oeil* architectural perspectives to ceiling painting in Portugal, he absorbed Italian Baroque models and passed them on to his own pupils, creating a school that continued into the 19th century. Lobo's only certainly attributable work, the ceiling (after 1705) of the church of Nossa Senhora da Pena in Lisbon, is closely related to late Italian Baroque fresco cycles. It represents an architectural interior of three storeys, with columns, entablatures and balconies with balustrades, filled with small fluttering angels and surmounted by an open sky in which the Coronation of the Virgin is taking place, drawing on a strictly architectural composition. He did not reach the standard of his master in drawing figures but succeeded in giving them a kind of airy lightness, especially the small angels, the only ones that overlie the architectonic elements. Lobo's pupils, who kept alive the influence of Italian perspective in Portuguese painting, included his son, Francisco Xavier Lobo, who painted the ceiling (*c.* 1750) of the nave in the church of S Paulo, Lisbon, António Simões Ribeiro, who was responsible for the ceilings (1722–4) of the library of the University of Coimbra, and António Pimenta Rolim.

BIBLIOGRAPHY
R. dos Santos: 'A pintura dos tectos no século XVIII em Portugal', *Belas A.*, n. s., xviii (1962), pp. 13–22
N. Correia Borges: *Do barroco ao rococó*, Hist. A. Portugal, ix (Lisbon, 1986)
*Dicionário de arte barroca em Portugal* (Lisbon, 1989)
N. Saldanha: *A pintura na Igreja da N. Sra. da Pena em Lisboa* (Lisbon, 1989)

LUISA ARRUDA

**Lobo, Baltasar** (*b* Cerecinos de Campos, Zamora, 22 Feb 1910; *d* Oct 1993). Spanish sculptor, active in France. When he was 12 years old he worked at a workshop in Valladolid making religious images, while also attending evening classes at the Escuela de Artes y Oficios. In 1927 he held an exhibition that helped him obtain a grant to study at the Escuela de Bellas Artes in Madrid, but, after three months, bored with the academic teaching, he left the school to continue his studies informally: these consisted largely of enthusiastic visits to the Museo Arqueológico Nacional in Madrid and a growing interest in Iberian sculpture. His career was interrupted in 1936 by the outbreak of the Civil War, and in 1939 he went into permanent exile in Paris. There he formed friendships with Picasso, Jacques Lipchitz and in particular with Henri Laurens, who offered him a place in his workshop, and whose influence was to prove decisive in his future development and his subsequent involvement in the Ecole de Paris. After his participation in the exhibition *Maîtres contemporains* at the Galerie Vendôme in Paris in 1945, he had exhibitions in Oslo, Brussels, Zurich, Luxembourg and Tokyo. He had his first exhibition in Spain in 1960 and in 1984 received the Premio Nacional de Artes Plásticas. Lobo's work, for example the monument *To the Spaniards who Died for Liberty* (1948; Annecy) or *Fontana* (bronze, h. 1.3 m, 1971; Madrid, Cent. Reina Sofía), contains elements of the primitive Iberian tradition, crude, simple and robust, combined with the elegance of a classical, Mediterranean spirit, in the style of Aristide Maillol; it also shows a debt to the Cubism of Laurens and the abstraction of Brancusi and Arp. His works often depict the female figure and images of motherhood, as in *Motherhood* (1953; Caracas, U. Cent. Venezuela, Ciudad U.); although they never lose touch with reality, they verge on abstraction in their reduction of form to a compact, minimal shape with rounded, sensual curves and outlines emphasized by the softness of the carving, usually in marble, and the perfectly polished surface of the stone.

BIBLIOGRAPHY

A. Lanskoy: *Baltasar Lobo* (Zurich, 1976)

J. Roy Dolcet: 'La escultura como forma de ser. Baltasar Lobo', *Escultura ibérica contemporánea* (exh. cat., ed. J. L. Coomonte; Zamora, Mus. Zamora, 1986), pp. 37–44

JOSEFINA ALIX TRUEBA

**Lobo, Filipe** (*fl* Lisbon, 1650–73). Portuguese painter. He was active in the Irmandade de S Lucas, the guild of painters of Lisbon, where he occupied various posts. He may have been a follower of Dirk Stoop, who worked in Portugal between 1659 and 1662. His only surviving signed work is the *View of Belém Abbey* (1650; Lisbon, Mus. N. A. Ant.), which reveals him as a landscape painter of some merit, especially in his concern with minute detail. Dos Santos noted that, like Stoop, Lobo used tones of creamy beige and grey in the Dutch manner, although he displayed some awkwardness in the depiction of groups of people.

BIBLIOGRAPHY

G. Teixeira: *A Irmandade de S Lucas corporação de artistas* (Lisbon, 1931), pp. 119, 123

R. dos Santos: 'A pintura da segunda metade do século XVI ao final do século XVII', *Arte portuguesa*, ed. J. Barreira (Lisbon, 1951), pp. 300–01

VITOR SERRÃO

**Lobo, Silvestre de Faria** (*b* Lisbon, *bapt* 7 Jan 1725; *d* Lisbon, 11 April 1786). Portuguese carver and sculptor. He was the leading wood-carver at the court of Joseph I (*reg* 1750–77) and was a pupil of João Frederico Ludovice. In 1766 he was appointed judge of carving in the guild of cabinetmakers. He began work around 1752 as a master carver at the royal palace of Queluz, near Lisbon (begun 1746), where he worked until *c*. 1777 and supervised a team of craftsmen. He played an important role in carrying out the carved decoration in the palace, notably in the Room of the Ambassadors, or Hall of Mirrors, where he carved the door pelmets. In the music-room he worked on the beautiful ceiling, which shows the influence of central European decoration. In the former throne-room, completed *c*. 1768 and built during the second phase of construction of the palace that started in 1758, he was assisted among others by the French decorator Antoine Collin; the curved white-and-gold ceiling is strewn with delicate French Rococo tendril motifs.

Between about 1750 and 1760 Lobo worked on the interior of the royal chapel at Queluz and on the main retable, which was completed in July 1752. This shows his use of Rococo ornament, composed of shells, garlands, angels and scrolls, on the altarpiece, decoration that also covers the whole interior of the chapel giving a delicate sense of movement. This interior, and in particular the refinement of Lobo's technique, was an important influence on wood-carving in the Lisbon region. At Queluz he also worked on the marble statues for the garden; attributed to him is the frame of the Rococo painted coach (*c*. 1750; Lisbon, Mus. N. Coches) used by the Meninos de Palhavã, illegitimate sons of John V.

In 1768 Lobo executed the carving in the chancel, lateral chapels, choir rails and pulpit in the church of Nossa Senhora de Monserrate, Amoreiras, Lisbon. In 1782 he collaborated on the mausoleum of Dona Mariana Vitória (1718–81) in the church of S Francisco de Paula, Lisbon. Works attributed to him are the retables of S Cristo, do Espírito Santo and Nossa Senhora da Conceição, in the church of S António da Sé, Lisbon, begun after the 1755 earthquake.

BIBLIOGRAPHY

N. B. Correia Guedes: *O palácio dos senhores do infantado em Queluz* (Lisbon, 1971)

NATÁLIA MARINHO FERREIRA ALVES

**Lobovikov, Sergey (Aleksandrovich)** (*b* Belskoye, Vyatka province, 1870; *d* Leningrad [now St Petersburg], 1942). Russian photographer. The son of a deacon, he learnt the techniques of photography as a boy. During the 1890s he worked chiefly in landscape, receiving a prize for his efforts at the 1899 St Petersburg Concours. Shortly thereafter his interests turned to PICTORIAL PHOTOGRAPHY, using gum bichromate, platinum and other refined printing techniques that were gaining popularity at the time (*see* PHOTOGRAPHY, §I). He was a founder-member of the Vyatka (later Kirov) Museum of History and Arts and an adjunct member of the Dresden Photographic Society and of the Société Française de Photographie. Lobovikov was also the recipient of several awards for his photography at the international exhibitions in Paris (1905), Dresden, (1909), Budapest (1911) and Kiev (1911). In the late 1930s he was a scientific photographer for the Soviet Academy of Sciences (Leningrad).

BIBLIOGRAPHY

D. Elliott: *Photography in Russia, 1840–1940* (London, 1992)

JAMES CRUMP

**Locatelli, Andrea** (*b* Rome, 19 Dec 1695; *d* Rome, 19 Feb 1741). Italian painter. He received his first artistic training from his father, Giovanni Francesco Locatelli (*b* Florence, *c*. 1660; *d* Rome, 1741), a little-known painter who settled in the district of Trastevere in Rome *c*. 1699. He then studied with Monsù Alto (*d c*. 1712), a painter of coastal views, few of whose works are known. After Alto's death he moved to the studio of Bernardino Fergioni (1674–*c*. 1738) and, lastly, to that of Biagio Puccini. His study of the human figure in the latter's studio laid the foundations of his later success as a painter of *bambocciate*. In 1715 he was commissioned to decorate a room in the Palazzo Ruspoli in Rome with marine scenes in gouache; he apparently painted only the figures himself and was already being paid at the rate customary for a master painter. He also decorated Prince Antonio Ottoboni's apartments in the Palazzo della Cancelleria, Rome, with landscapes (untraced), which were highly praised by Pio (1724). His most distinguished commissions were from Filippo Juvarra on behalf of Victor-Amadeus II of Savoy for two views of the unfinished castello of Rivoli in Turin, in which Locatelli interpreted Juvarra's plans and designs (1723–5; Racconigi, Castello). In 1735, again through Juvarra, he received a commission from King Philip V of Spain for two overdoors for La Granja, which show *Christ in the Desert* and *Christ and the Woman of Samaria* (both *in situ*). In 1738 he decorated two doors in the Palazzo Corsini, Rome (both *in situ*), each with four decorative panels of landscapes.

However, Locatelli was primarily a painter of easel pictures, which were sought after by an international clientele, and he was supported by distinguished Roman patrons, including Cardinal Alessandro Albani and Cardinal Pietro Ottoboni. In 1783 the Colonna family owned 80 of his pictures. Throughout his career he experimented with many genres and his art developed from a realism close to that of his 17th-century sources to an increasingly graceful idealization. He first specialized in river and coastal scenes, influenced by the marine pictures of Salvator Rosa. The *Landscape with a Group of Figures on the Shores of a Lake* (Rome, Gal. Pallavicini), in which the emphasis is on a distant view of the sea, is one example. Also from his earliest period is a group of works that show landscapes with ancient ruins, such as the *Three Figures at the Ruins of the Temple of Vespasian* (Rome, Francisci priv. col., see Busiri Vici, fig. 5). His interest in this genre was brief, although he established himself as a brilliant imitator of Giovanni Paolo Panini. Later he painted idyllic views of the Roman Campagna, influenced by Gaspard Dughet, reinterpreted through the lighter, clearer pictures of Jan Frans van Bloemen, such as the *Landscape in Latium with Two Shepherds* (see fig.). Other works set mythological scenes in Arcadian landscapes (three, St Petersburg, Hermitage; four, Wörlitz, Schloss), seven surviving from a series devoted to the *Legends of Diana* (21 were once in the Barberini collection).

Locatelli painted few realistic *vedute*, although the *View of the Piazza Navona with a Market* (1733; Vienna, Gemäldegal. Akad. Bild. Kst.) is an exceptional work, which concentrates less on the monumental beauty of the square than on the vitality and vivid colours of the market-day crowd. He also painted *bambocciate* with, in the late

years, elegant and graceful figures, as in the *Gypsy Scene with a Fortune-teller* (Rome, priv col., see Busiri Vici, fig. 211); yet in other pictures the figures were painted by professional specialists, including Giuseppe Tommasi, Pierre Subleyras and Pompeo Batoni. Locatelli died, after a dissolute life, in poverty and unlamented, his widow renouncing all claim to an estate that was crippled with debts.

BIBLIOGRAPHY
N. Pio: *Vite* (1724); ed. C. Enggass and R. Enggass (1977)
R. E. Spear: *Renaissance and Baroque Paintings from the Sciarra and Fiano Collections* (Rome, 1972)
A. Busiri Vici: *Andrea Locatelli e il paesaggio romano del settecento* (Rome, 1976)
G. Michel and O. Michel: 'La Décoration du palais Ruspoli en 1715 et la redécouverte de "Monsù Francesco Borgognone"', *Mél. Ecole Fr. Rome: Moyen Age, Temps Mod.*, lxxxix (1977), pp. 265–340
J. Urrea Fernández: *La pintura italiana del siglo XVIII en España* (Valladolid, 1977)
T. Busmina: 'Some New Data on the Art of Andrea Locatelli and Three of his Pictures in the Hermitage Collection', *Soobshcheniya Gosudarstvennogo Ermitazha*, xlviii (1983), pp. 10–12, 44–5
E. Borsellino: 'Le decorazioni settecentesche di palazzo Corsini alla Lungara', *Ville e palazzi, illusione scenica e miti archeologici*, Studi sul settecento romano, iii (Rome, 1987), pp. 181–211
OLIVIER MICHEL

**Lo Chen-yü.** *See* LUO ZHENYU.

**Löcherer, Alois** (*b* Munich, 14 Aug 1815; *d* Munich, 15 July 1862). German photographer. He studied chemistry and pharmacology in Munich from 1837 before becoming a pharmacist. He learnt to take daguerreotypes in 1840, possibly from the Swiss photographer Johann Baptist Isenring (1796–1860), who travelled through the area.

Between 1845 and 1850 Löcherer photographed the making, transport and installation of Ludwig von Schwanthaler's bronze statue of *Bavaria*, using paper negatives; this series is one of the earliest examples of photographic reportage (Cologne, Mus. Ludwig; Munich, Fotomus.). From around 1850 he also photographed celebrities (including the chemist Justus von Liebig and the painter Wilhelm von Kaulbach), publishing their portraits in his *Photographisches Album der Zeitgenossen* (Munich). He used various processes including daguerreotypes and calotypes, improving them by experiment and publishing his formulae.

BIBLIOGRAPHY
W. Baier: *Quellendarstellungen zur Geschichte der Fotografie* (Halle, 1964)
H. Gebhardt: *Königlich bayerische Photographie, 1838–1918* (Munich, 1978)
HANS CHRISTIAN ADAM

**Loches.** Town in Indre-et-Loire, western France. According to Gregory of Tours, Loches was a *vicus* when Eustache, one of his predecessors in the bishopric, founded the parish towards the middle of the 5th century AD. The site was probably already fortified at this time, as it was when St Ours settled there in the last quarter of the 6th century. A frontier town of the Visigothic and then Aquitainian states on the border with the kingdom of the Franks, it was destroyed by Pepin the Short in 742. Towards the third quarter of the 9th century, Emperor Charles the Bald gave it to one of his local chiefs, Allaud. On the marriage of the latter's granddaughter Roussille to Fulk the Red, Count of Anjou (*c.* 900), the town passed to the Angevin dynasty. Between 963 and 985 Geoffrey I,

Andrea Locatelli: *Landscape in Latium with Two Shepherds*, tempera on canvas, 1355×986 mm (Rome, Galleria Pallavicini)

Count of Anjou (*reg* 958–87), founded a college in honour of the Virgin (now St Ours). About 1004 a later count, Fulk III Nerra (*reg* 987–1040), founded an abbey dedicated to the Trinity in the newly established suburb of Beaulieu-lès-Loches, on the opposite bank of the Indre. The town and borough did not return to the French Crown until Philip Augustus finally managed to capture them in 1205. Initially given to Dreu of Mello, who had led the siege, the town was bought back by Louis IX in 1249, who installed a royal governor. While it served no essential military role in the Hundred Years War (1337–1453), the castle became one of the favourite residences of the French kings Charles VII and his son, the future Louis XI, and then Louis XII. From the time of Francis I and the Wars of Religion in the 16th century, it was relegated to an occasional royal stopping-off point and from then until the Revolution took on the less elegant role of a royal prison. The fortified site was established on a promontory (450 m long) over-looking the River Indre. It can be divided into two parts: the defensive works to the south and the ecclesiastical and later residential works to the north.

1. CASTLE AND WALLS. The citadel is dominated to the south by a rectangular donjon, 25×13 m in plan and 37 m high, with an entrance tower rising to 25 m on its north face. This was undoubtedly incorporated into the initial building campaign in the 11th century. The walls, 2.80 m thick, are revetted in ashlar (*moyen appareil*). The faces and angles are articulated with half shafts on pilasters. Originally the keep was divided by wooden floors into a ground-floor cellar and three upper levels, which were lit by round-headed windows. A stairway in the tower provided access to the first floor of the keep; from here, ramps and spiral staircases within the walls served the upper floors as well as the cellar. An apsidal chapel (St Salleboeuf) was situated in the tower above the stairway. Chimney remains pose the question of the introduction of this feature into castle architecture. The building phases of the donjon, and their chronology, are disputed. The lower half of the west wall seems to belong to an earlier construction, probably one dating from the time of Fulk III Nerra, while comparisons with La Trinité, Beaulieu-lès-Loches, suggest that the main building campaign may well have been started under his son, Geoffrey II Martel (*reg* 1040–60). Loches, with Amboise and Chinon, was among the most important castles in the Touraine, and there is no reason for it to be seen as the culmination of a typological series of increasingly larger and more compli-cated donjons in the Loire Valley (e.g. Montbazon, Mont-richard etc, Langeais being a *domicilium*), which would place it at the end of the 11th century or beginning of the 12th. However, it is possible that, because of the nearly identical construction of the two parts in question, the first donjon for which there is archaeological evidence was never completed, and that building was carried out in a single campaign beginning perhaps as early as the 1030s and continuing, with several modifications, throughout the rest of the 11th century.

Initially isolated on a motte, the donjon became asso-ciated with three different types of wall. A linear defensive wall that continued the south wall of the donjon to the east and west, blocking off the small southern section of the promontory, may have been built as early as the first quarter of the 12th century. Soon afterwards, however, an enclosure wall was raised that left only the eastern wall of the keep and tower and the northern wall of the tower exposed. Finally an enormous curtain wall with a moat and single gate (the Porte Royale) was built all around the promontory, encircling not only the recent enclosure wall but also the college of Notre-Dame (now St Ours) and the palace at the far end of the site. The southern section of this wall was reinforced during the 13th century with three large towers *à bec*. The Porte Royale was rebuilt and a round tower was erected to protect the exposed eastern face of the keep. At the northern end of the promontory the old palace was replaced by a new *logis* (the 'Logis du Roy') built in two campaigns, one at the end of the 14th century (the 'Vieux Logis'), the other at the end of the 15th century and beginning of the 16th (the 'Nouveau Logis'). While the fortification of the inner borough of St Ours probably dates from before the 14th century, the lower town may not have been walled before the 15th.

In the 15th century, outbuildings forming an entrance block with a new donjon (the Tour Neuve or Ronde) were constructed along the outside of the northern face of the enclosure wall. They were probably designed as part of a new outer enclosure, of which only the north-eastern barbican (La Marche) seems to have been completed. A new structure was built over the old 13th-century Porte Royale. Another new tower (Le Martelet) with dungeons was inserted between the enclosure and curtain walls, and a new wall between these created two new enclosures to the west and south.

2. ST OURS. Geoffrey I, Count of Anjou, founded a college in honour of the Virgin (now St Ours) between 963 and 985 on the site of a ruined church dedicated to St Mary Magdalene. This was to the north of the promontory, to the south of his palace and immediately west of the church of St Ours. The early Romanesque collegiate church was largely rebuilt in its present form during the 12th century by one of its priors, Thomas Pactius (*c*. 1130–68), notary and chaplain to Fulk the younger. Only the late 11th-century tower porch of the Romanesque building was preserved. Thomas started by building a vaulted chevet with three apses in echelon to the east of the old projecting transept, which he rebuilt on existing foundations. As the new dome-covered crossing was narrower than the old single-aisled nave, he was obliged to construct an arcade with flanking passages between the two. He then vaulted the nave with two extraordinary pyramids, called 'dubes' in a contemporary document, and added an upper storey to the tower porch, making it as high as the crossing tower. Although planned, it is not certain that the side aisles were built at this time. With its two octagonal spired towers and two nave cones, his church presents a unique silhouette (see fig.). A vaulted porch with an inner portal sculptured with animal and plant motifs in a radical arrangement was added to the west of the tower porch after his death, towards the end of the 12th century. An *Adoration of the Magi* and several standing figures were mortised into the wall of the tower porch around the portal.

Loches, view showing St Ours (founded 963–85; rebuilt mid-12th century) on the left and the 'Vieux Logis' (late 14th century) and 'Nouveau Logis' (late 15th century–early 16th) on the right

3. LA TRINITÉ, BEAULIEU-LÈS-LOCHES. Although the first abbey church of La Trinité, founded by Fulk III about 1004, was consecrated in 1007, there seems to be no trace of a building going back to this time. An enormous Romanesque church, substantial parts of which can still be seen, was probably built by Geoffrey II towards the middle of the 11th century. It comprised a choir with ambulatory and radiating chapels, an almost continuous projecting transept with crossing tower and a huge single-cell nave. This first Romanesque structure, wooden-roofed except for the choir, was modified from around the turn of the 12th century. The transept arms were vaulted and the single-cell nave transformed into a ten-bay, three-aisled barrel-vaulted structure with cruciform piers. This style of church, with a blind nave and indirect lighting from large windows in the side aisles, was also being developed in Poitou at this time. The sculpture on the north transept gable could be earlier. A very tall bell-tower was subsequently added to the north-west of the façade, which may well have had a narthex originally. Severely damaged during the Hundred Years War, the church was largely remodelled in the 15th century (new choir, vaulting of the 'crossing' and the four eastern bays of the nave). The six western bays of the nave were definitively abandoned after the Wars of Religion later in the 16th century.

BIBLIOGRAPHY

J. Vallery-Radot: *Loches* (Paris, 1926)
——: 'Loches', *Congr. Archéol. France*, cvi (1948), pp. 111–25
'Actes du colloque médiéval de Loches (1973)', *Mém. Soc. Archéol. Touraine*, 4th ser., ix (1975) [congress title]
M. Deyres: 'Le Premier Projet pour la construction du donjon de Loches', *Gaz. B.-A.* (1974), pp. 41–8
C. Lelong: *Touraine romane*, Nuit Temps (La Pierre-qui-vire, 1977), pp. 237–48
J. Ottaway: *Beaulieu-lès-Loches: Une Eglise princière de l'ouest de la France aux alentours de l'an mil*, 5 vols (diss., Poitiers, CESCM, 1986)
N. Faucherre, J. Ottaway and J.-M. Pérouse de Montclos: *Architectures en région centre*, Le Guide du Patrimoine (Paris, 1987), pp. 409–21
P. Héliot and M. Deyres: 'Le Château de Loches', *Bull. Mnmtl*, cxlv (1987), pp. 15–85
J. Ottaway: 'Liberté, ordre et révolte d'après la charte dite de fondation de l'abbaye de Beaulieu-lès-Loches', *Violence et contestation au moyen âge: Actes du 114e congrès national des sociétés savantes, section d'histoire médiévale et de philologie: Paris, 1989*, pp. 19–46

JOHN OTTAWAY

**Lochner, Stefan** (*fl* Cologne, *c.* 1440–? after 1453). German painter. The paintings traditionally associated with this name constitute the most significant and influential contribution to the 'school of Cologne', but the identity of the artist is now uncertain (though the name is retained here for convenience).

1. Identity. 2. Work.

1. IDENTITY. His name derives from a misreading of an entry in Dürer's travel expense accounts, which record that during a stay in Cologne in October 1520 Dürer paid '2 weißpfennig' to have an altarpiece, painted by a master Stefan of Cologne, opened for his inspection. There is no additional information, and the complete name of the master, as well as the location and age of the altarpiece, must remain the subject of conjecture. Nonetheless, Böhmer (1823) felt able to identify the altarpiece as the *Dombild* or triptych of the *Patron Saints of Cologne* (originally placed in the Cologne Council Chapel, which

was built in 1426 but deconsecrated in 1794; the altarpiece was subsequently moved to the cathedral *c.* 1809), since he judged this to be the finest and most significant altarpiece in the town. Consequently, Merlo (1852) linked the altarpiece with the only painter 'Stefan' still documented in Cologne, the prominent and prosperous master Stefan Lochner, an immigrant from the Konstanz area, who appears in the city records between 1442 and 1451. This hypothesis was accepted as fact until Wolfson (1986) pointed out that while it was reasonable to assume that Dürer would have wished to see the famous altarpiece in the Council Chapel during his extended visit to Cologne, he may well have visited it on another day, unrecorded in his accounts if there were no expense involved. Furthermore, he would have found the altarpiece of the *Patron Saints of Cologne* already opened, as he visited during the period of the feast of the patron saint Ursula.

The documented Stefan Lochner died in 1451, and the painter of the *Dombild* has been plausibly linked with a Book of Hours (Darmstadt, Hess. Landes- & Hochschbib., MS. Hs. 70) that bears the date 1453 and certainly connected with a lost altarpiece, of which the surviving wing panels (London, N.G., and Cologne, Wallraf-Richartz-Mus.) have been dated by dendrochronological examination to 1454. Until further evidence emerges, the identity of the painter conventionally called Stefan Lochner remains uncertain. Conclusions concerning his career and his oeuvre must rely solely on the visual, technical and iconographic evidence provided by the impressive altarpiece in Cologne Cathedral, the *Dombild* (see fig. 1). However, profound differences in technique and style between works by the painter of the *Dombild* and those from the Bohemian-influenced workshops in the Konstanz area demonstrate that the painter traditionally called Lochner did not learn his trade in that part of southern Germany; his precursors are more likely to be found in Cologne or Westphalia (see Konrad, 1993).

2. WORK. The Cologne master's knowledge of Westphalian painting, whether by direct experience or though intermediaries, is particularly apparent in the *Dombild*, a triptych usually dated on stylistic grounds to *c.* 1440–45. In composition, style and subject-matter, its central panel reflects another altarpiece from a council church, the Dortmund Altarpiece by the Westphalian painter Conrad von Soest (*c.* 1420; Dortmund, Marienkirche; for central panel, *see* CONRAD VON SOEST, fig. 3). In both altarpieces, the *Adoration of the Magi* is depicted in a symmetrical composition, against a gold ground. Both masters show the adored Virgin enthroned, placed in a shallow meadow setting, without further narrative or architectural motifs. The courtly style of the protagonists, the naturalistic description of flowers and brocades, the realism of the features of the kneeling kings and the punchwork all reflect the work of the Westphalian master. Single motifs that derive from Conrad's autograph works include the brocade patterns, the slit gown allowing the royal leg to protrude, the unusual pose of the Child, the unicorn brooch of the Virgin, the floating angels and the figure of the inward-facing courtier. Some of these designs had already been introduced into Cologne by the Master of St Veronica, who appears to have worked as a journeyman in the workshop of Conrad von Soest (see Corley, 1996). However, the *Dombild* artist's subtle application of painterly hues and his sensitivity to the dramatic effect of light and shade show that he responded to Conrad's art with a profound understanding never achieved by the St Veronica Master. The carved canopy in the Cologne *Adoration*, for instance, shelters and shades the third king in a manner derived from the effect of the painted canopy in the left wing of Conrad's Niederwildungen Altarpiece (1403; Bad Wildungen, Stadtkirche; *see* CONRAD VON SOEST, fig. 1); the copied pose of the king confirms the direct reference. The method of indicating recession in space through

1. Stefan Lochner: *Dombild* (triptych with the *Patron Saints of Cologne*), oil and tempera on panel, 2.6×5.7 m (open), *c.* 1440–45 (Cologne Cathedral)

diminishing colour values and through shading was introduced into northern Germany by Conrad and into Cologne by the artist known as Lochner.

The subject of the Adoration of the Magi was particularly suitable for an altarpiece of the *Patron Saints of Cologne*, since the Magi had been adopted as city patrons in 1322 when their relic shrine was placed in Cologne Cathedral. Their retinue in this triptych—which is conceived as a single narrative scene—also includes the two other patron saints, adopted because they were said to have been martyred in the city (in AD 304). St Ursula, accompanied by her prince and her maidens, is shown leading the procession in the left wing, and St Gereon and his attendants are depicted in the right wing. In narrative concept, monumental figure style, drapery patterns and in the description of glistening jewels, the retinue groups on the two wings are considerably indebted to the Ghent Altarpiece by Hubert and Jan van Eyck (1432; Ghent, St Bavo), and it is generally accepted that Lochner had studied the work of the van Eyck brothers in the Netherlands. The notion of a sojourn in the workshop of the Master of Flémalle, however, has been discredited by Faries (1993). Her examination by infra-red reflectography revealed that the *St Jerome* (Raleigh, NC, Mus. A.), usually cited as principal evidence for such a connection, was neither designed nor painted by Lochner.

In contrast to the dominant Eyckian influence in wing panels of the *Dombild*, the *Annunciation*, depicted on the reverse side of the wings, again develops elements found in the work of Conrad von Soest. The interior setting, suggesting a curtained-off prayer space, and the desk can be found in the Niederwildungen Altarpiece, in which the Virgin adopts an identical pose and the angel also approaches from the right side. The bench behind the Virgin, however, occurred first in the Dortmund *Annunciation*. Yet in spatial conception and in monumental drapery patterns, the *Annunciation* on the reverse sides of the wings of the *Dombild* again acknowledges a close study of the Ghent Altarpiece, which also features the Annunciation scene across both closed wings. In fact, the retardataire tendencies expressed in Lochner's use of gold grounds, elaborate punch- and framework, tapestry meadows and other characteristics of the International Courtly style may reflect donor preferences, which the artist balanced with perceptive characterization, innovative spatial constructions and an intelligent response to recent stylistic developments in the Netherlands.

The facial features of the Virgin and the Child in the *Dombild* are of Cologne provenance and develop the pattern notable in the St Veronica Master's *Virgin with the Sweet Pea Blossom* (Cologne, Wallraf-Richartz-Mus.). Lochner had already perfected the idealized features with small mouths, straight noses, hooded eyes and strongly lit foreheads in the *Virgin of the Rose Bower* (Cologne, Wallraf-Richartz-Mus.; see fig. 2), a small devotional panel depicting the Madonna of Humility, which in subject-matter and courtly style appears entirely indebted to the Cologne/Westphalian precursors. The rounded folds in the drapery here relate to designs in Lochner's large *Last Judgement* (Cologne, Wallraf-Richartz-Mus.), which is considered an early work (*c.* 1435) owing to the still elongated

2. Stefan Lochner: *Virgin of the Rose Bower*, oil on panel, 505×399 mm, *c.* 1435–40 (Cologne, Wallraf-Richartz-Museum)

forms. The drapery style and the fact that the dendrochronological date of the small panel showing the *Virgin of the Rose Bower* is 1398 permit a reassessment of its date: 1435–40 appears more plausible than the formerly proposed date of 1450.

The underdrawing style and surface characteristics confirm that the *Last Judgement* is the work of the painter of the *Dombild*. In it the main protagonists are depicted in monumental size silhouetted against a gold ground. Christ is described as the active recipient of intercessional prayers from the Virgin and St John, both kneeling on earth. Below, angels and devils struggle to separate the saved and the damned, all shown in smaller scale. Heaven is presented as a Gothic portal at which St Peter and musicmaking angels welcome the resurrected; hell offers fire and monsters to receive the sinners. A curious scene outside the gate of the burning city illustrates a then popular text by Caesarius von Heisterbach (*c.* 1200). At a later date coats of arms were added to the panel. Although the whole composition has certainly a Netherlandish flavour (cf. the wing panels of the *Crucifixion* and *Last Judgement* attrib. to Jan van Eyck, *c.* 1425–30; New York, Met.), especially also in the realistic description of nudes and the gallery of musician angels, the iconography and certain individual motifs, including the facial types of some of the angels and the devil pulling the reluctant sinner into hell's mouth, derive from Cologne prototypes (e.g. a painting of *c.* 1410–20; Cologne, Wallraf-Richartz-Mus., 389). The application of translucent layers of pigments, which usually contain some oil, creates a glowing surface of rich colours.

The provenance of the *Last Judgement* remains disputed (see Zehnder). The painting is seen either as a justice panel from the former town hall or as part of a triptych from the church of St Laurenz (deconsecrated 1803). The wing panels from St Laurenz were separated; the obverse sides (Frankfurt am Main, Städel. Kstinst. & Städt. Gal.) are decorated with 12 lively scenes from the *Martyrdom of Apostles* (see Lukatis); the reverse sides (Munich, Alte Pin.) show three standing saints and a small unidentified male donor figure in each wing (see Goldberg and Scheffler). Examination by infra-red reflectography has confirmed that the wing paintings are by the so-called Lochner hand. However, stylistic discrepancies perceived by Wolfson, among others, led him to suggest that the wing panels belonged to another, later triptych.

The three standing saints represented on the reverse sides of the wings in Munich, with their weighty drapery, display a monumental figure style that is comparable to that of the *Virgin with the Violet* (Cologne, Erzbischöf. Diöz.-Mus.), in which the life-size Virgin holding the Child in her arm and a violet in her hand stands in a flowery meadow. The luminous sky reveals the other figures of the Trinity balanced by three angels, all holding scrolls. Two angels on earth display a golden cloth of honour behind the Virgin, thus deliberately negating the space created by the naturalistic light and shade enveloping figures and nature. The surface pattern of the brocade is echoed by decorative patches of the lining in the drapery. The painting seems indebted to the Master of St Veronica's *Virgin with the Pea Blossom* (*c*. 1410–15; Nuremberg, Ger. Nmus.), especially in the facial features and in the surface pattern created by coloured cloak linings, yet its iconography and setting and the weighty and voluminous drapery appear directly derived from Jan van Eyck's *Virgin at the Fountain* (Antwerp, Kon. Mus. S. Kst.). Lochner combined the Cologne tradition with Eyckian iconography and naturalism into a harmonious personal style. The small donor figure is identified by her coats of arms; Elisabeth von Reichenstein became abbess of St Cäcilien in Cologne in 1433. Here still dressed as a nun, she must have commissioned the panel just before her appointment.

The only dated work with an undisputed attribution to the artist known as Lochner is the *Presentation in the Temple* (Darmstadt, Hess. Landesmus.; *see* GERMANY, fig. 16). The date 1447 is inscribed in the scroll held by an attendant Knight of the Teutonic Order, who, according to a description of 1818, formerly sheltered a three-dimensional cruciform reliquary in his right hand. The scroll states that the relic it contained was that of 'the righteous' St Simeon. In the painting Simeon is shown displaying the Child on the altar to the Virgin and to an attending crowd, led by children carrying candles. An image of Moses on the painted altar refers to the ancient law here enacted by Simeon. This late work by Lochner still displays a gold ground on which God the Father is depicted in a circle of angels in the Westphalian tradition. A preference for hierarchical scales for saintly protagonists, already noted in the *Last Judgement*, persists, but the tendency towards elongation has been abandoned. Moreover, the monumental, almost sturdy figures, derived from Eyckian models, occupy a plausible space in a realistic manner. This space is outlined by framing pillars and limited by a cloth of honour behind the painted altar. Receding tiles define the depth of the space, and diminishing colour values and the strong light and shade that envelop forms confirm its reality. The painting is again devoid of all unnecessary architectural embellishment. The variety of hues in the glowing colours is impressive. Only the central panel survives from this altarpiece, which was originally from St Katharina, the church of the Teutonic Order in Cologne. However, the iconographic programme of the wings, containing scenes from the *Life of the Virgin*, is known from later copies. A *Presentation in the Temple* by Johann Koerbecke (Münster, Westfäl. Landesmus.), usually dated to *c*. 1457, also contains the otherwise unusual group of candle-carrying youths. The painting is, however, so different in all other respects that a mutual Westphalian source for the design cannot be excluded.

The painter of the *Dombild* achieved a complete harmony of content and form in his late *Presentation*, with its unique blend of elements from the International Courtly style dominant in Cologne and the new empirical realism of the Netherlandish panel painters. His work found imitators not only in the workshops of Cologne (see 1993 *Lochner* exh. cat.); Rogier van der Weyden appears to have made changes in the design of the Columba Triptych (*c*. 1455; Munich, Alte Pin.; *see* WEYDEN, VAN DER, (1), fig. 3) after seeing the *Dombild* (see Dijkstra), and examination by infra-red reflectography apparently confirms that Memling's *Last Judgement* (?1467; Gdańsk, N. Mus.; *see* MEMLING, HANS, fig. 1) is partially indebted to Lochner's design (see 1993 *Lochner* exh. cat., p. 276).

BIBLIOGRAPHY
J. F. Böhmer: 'Meister Stephan, Maler zu Cöln', *Kunstblatt*, viii (1823), pp. 31–2
O. H. Förster: *Stefan Lochner: Ein Maler zu Köln* (Frankfurt am Main, 1938)
G. Goldberg and G. Scheffler: *Katalog der Alten Pinakothek München: Altdeutsche Gemälde, Köln und Nordwestdeutschland* (Munich, 1972), p. 109
J. Dijkstra: 'Interpretatie van de infrarood reflectografie van het Columba altaarstuk: Een hypothese over het ontstaan van het triptiek', *Le Dessin sous-jacent dans la peinture, Colloque V: Louvain-La-Neuve, 1983*
M. Wolfson: 'Hat Dürer das *Dombild* gesehen? Ein Beitrag zur Lochner Forschung', *Z. Kstgesch.*, xlix (1986), pp. 229–35
R. Lauer, C. Schulze-Senger and W. Hansmann: 'Der *Altar der Stadtpatrone* im Kölner Dom', *Köln. Dombl.*, lii (1987), pp. 9–80
F. G. Zehnder: *Katalog der Altkölner Malerei*, Cologne, Wallraf-Richartz-Mus. cat., xi (Cologne, 1990)
B. Corley: *Conrad von Soest: His Altarpieces, his Workshop and his Place in European Art* (diss., U. London, Courtauld Inst. and Birkbeck Coll., 1991)
C. Lukatis: 'Die Apostelmartyrien Stefan Lochners', *Städel-Jb.*, n.s., xiv (1993)
*Seeschwäbische Malerei von 1400 bis 1450 und ihre Beziehungen zu Köln* (exh. cat. by B. Konrad, Cologne, Wallraf-Richartz-Mus., 1993), pp. 31–4
*Stefan Lochner, Meister zu Köln: Herkunft—Werke—Wirkung* (exh. cat., Cologne, Wallraf-Richartz-Mus., 1993)
B. Corley: *Conrad von Soest: Painter among Merchant Princes* (London, 1996)
——: *A Plausible Provenance for Stefan Lochner*, suppl. to 1993 exh. cat. *Stefan Lochner, Meister zu Köln: Herkunft—Werke—Wirkung* (in preparation)
BRIGITTE CORLEY

**Lock, Matthias** [Mathias] (*b* London, *c*. 1710; *bur* London, 22 Dec 1765). English furniture designer and carver. The earliest record of Matthias Lock is his apprenticeship in London to his father, Matthias, joiner, and to Richard Goldsaddle, carver, in 1724. As the usual age to begin an apprenticeship was 14, he was presumably born *c.* 1710. He married Mary Lee at St Paul's, Covent Garden, London, in July 1734. Between 1742 and 1744 he executed work for the 2nd Earl Poulett of Hinton House, Somerset; annotated sketches in his own hand survive from this commission, which include a side-table, pier-glass and candle stands. A pier-glass and table from the Tapestry Room of Hinton House are now at the Victoria and Albert Museum, London, which also owns a large collection of Lock's drawings.

Lock is most famous for designing pieces in the Rococo style, with a fluency and grace not hitherto achieved in England. In 1744 he published *Six Sconces.* There followed *Six Tables* two years later, when he was living at Nottingham Corner, Castle Street, near Long Acre, London. *A Book of Ornaments* appeared in 1747, and in 1752, in collaboration with Henry Copland (*c.* 1706–53), an engraver and designer of trade cards, Lock brought out *A New Book of Ornaments*, on 12 leaves, which includes side-tables, *torchères*, clocks, frames, pier-glasses and fireplaces, very much in the Rococo idiom but also including such chinoiserie motifs as ho-ho birds and oriental figures.

In 1752 Lock's address was given as 'near the Swan Tottenham Court Road'. In the Lock Collection (London, V&A), sheets from his diary for this year indicate furniture carved for the 4th Earl of Holderness, the 2nd Earl of Northumberland and a Mr Bradshaw. The collection also contains a design for a chair that the painter Richard Cosway acquired for his studio. Lock is not recorded in Mortimer's *Universal Director* of 1763, and it has been suggested that he had retired by then.

Roger Sayer reissued Lock's engravings posthumously in 1768, describing him as 'the famous Mr Matt Lock recently deceased who was reputed the best Draftsman in that way that had ever been in England'. It is now thought that the Mathias Lock who issued *A New Book of Pier Frame's, Oval's, Gerandole's, Table's &c* in 1769 was most likely to have been his son.

### WRITINGS
*A New Drawing Book of Ornaments* (London, 1740)
*Six Sconces* (London, 1744)
*Six Tables* (London, 1746)
*A Book of Ornaments* (London, 1747)
with H. Copland: *A New Book of Ornaments* (London, 1752)

### BIBLIOGRAPHY
J. F. Hayward: 'Furniture Designed and Carved by Mathias Lock for Hinton House, Somerset', *Connoisseur*, cxlvii (Jan 1961), pp. 284–6
H. Hayward: 'A Unique Rococo Chair by Matthias Lock', *Apollo*, cviii (1973), pp. 268–71
M. Heckscher: 'Lock and Copland: A Catalogue of the Engraved Ornament', *Furn. Hist.*, xv (1979), pp. 1–23
G. Beard and C. Gilbert, eds: *Dictionary of English Furniture Makers, 1660–1840* (Leeds, 1986)

JAMES YORKE

**Locke [Lock], William** (*b* 1732; *d* Norbury Park, Surrey, 5 Oct 1810). English collector and patron. His wealthy family claimed kinship with the philosopher John Locke. After a classical education, he undertook a Grand Tour, in the course of which he accompanied Richard Wilson in 1751 on a journey from Venice to Rome, and purchased Wilson's drawings recording the journey, including the *Cascade of Terni* (New Haven, CT, Yale Cent. Brit. A.); he also bought some portrait and caricature sketches, such as

*Signora Felice Bocca Stretto* (Oxford, Ashmolean), drawn in Rome in 1752–3. During his time in Rome Locke acquired some antique sculpture through the dealer Thomas Jenkins, and he continued to do so, through various agents, on his return to England. Although less important than the collections of Charles Townley or Henry Blundell, Locke's collection included a *Discobolus* (Duncombe Park, N. Yorks) bought from the Italian sculptor and dealer Bartolomeo Cavaceppi and a much admired cast of the *Venus de' Medici*, taken from the original, not from a copy. Locke also bought Old Master paintings, including Claude Lorrain's *Seaport with the Embarkation of St Ursula* (London, N.G.), which he sold in 1774, possibly to help him purchase an estate at Norbury, near Mickleham, Surrey, where he employed George Barret and Bartolomeo Cipriani to decorate his new house.

Locke played an important role in the early career of Thomas Lawrence by buying some of his works, including a portrait of himself (exh. RA 1790; Boston, MA, Mus. F.A.), and by introducing him to John Julius Angerstein, whose son married Locke's daughter, and to the Baring family. Lawrence, to whom Locke also advanced money, considered him to be one of his greatest friends.

### BIBLIOGRAPHY
*DNB*
J. Dallaway: *Anecdotes of the Arts in England; or, Comparative Remarks on Architecture, Sculpture, and Painting, Chiefly Illustrated by Specimens at Oxford* (London, 1800)
F. Burney: *The Diary and Letters of Madame d'Arblay*, 7 vols (London, 1842–6)
Vittoria, Duchess of Sermoneta: *The Locks of Norbury* (London, 1940)
K. Garlick: *Sir Thomas Lawrence* (London, 1989)

DAVID RODGERS

**Lockey, Rowland** (*b* ?1565–7; *d* London, March 1616). English painter and goldsmith. Son of a crossbow maker of the parish of St Bride's, London, he was probably aged between 14 and 16 in 1581, when he began his eight-year apprenticeship to the miniature painter and goldsmith Nicholas Hilliard, but he seems to have absorbed relatively little of Hilliard's talent.

Lockey was working independently by 1590, when he painted a series of group portraits of the *Family of Sir Thomas More*, deriving largely from Hans Holbein the younger's composition of the same sitters (destr.; sketch, Basle, Kstmus.). The large-scale oil paintings (e.g. London, N.P.G.) and the miniature (London, V&A) of this subject show a worthy, if pedestrian, technique. Similarly his signed and dated portrait of *Margaret Beaufort* (1598; Cambridge, St John's Coll.), a copy of a much earlier work, is a routine piece of decorative painting typical of an ancestor-obsessed age. In 1592 Hilliard introduced him to Elizabeth, Countess of Shrewsbury, the redoubtable Bess of Hardwick, from whom he received 40s. for two paintings (untraced). From 1608 to 1613 her son, William Cavendish, 1st Earl of Devonshire (*d* 1626), commissioned many pictures from Lockey for Hardwick Hall, including a portrait of *Mary, Queen of Scots* (Hardwick Hall, Derbys, NT), copied from an earlier painting. Despite the lack of signed or documented miniatures by Lockey, scholars consistently ascribe to him a moderate talent and a sub-Hilliard style. This judgement may need to be revised, since Lockey was famous in his day. Both Francis Meres in his *Palladis Tamia* (London, 1598) and Richard Haydocke in his translation (1598) of G. P. Lomazzo's *Trattato dell'arte della pittura* refer to him as among the better English painters, and the poet John Davies of Hereford wrote a flattering epigram about 'the rare painter, my approved friend. . .Mr. Row. Locky'. The antiquary William Burton referred in 1593 to Lockey as 'Hilliard's expert scholar. . .skillful in limning, oil-works and perspectives'.

Lockey's brother Nicholas Lockey (*fl c.* 1600–20) was apprenticed to him as a goldsmith in 1600. In his will Rowland left to his brother 'all my Italian prints', implying an acquaintance with Italian Renaissance models that is scarcely suggested by his known work.

BIBLIOGRAPHY
O. Kurz: 'Rowland Lockey', *Burl. Mag.*, xcix (1957), pp. 13–16
E. Auerbach: *Nicholas Hilliard* (London, 1961), pp. 254–62
R. Strong: *The English Icon: Elizabethan and Jacobean Portraiture* (London, 1969), pp. 255–8
*The English Miniature* (exh. cat. by R. Strong and others, New Haven, CT, Yale Cent. Brit. A.; Toronto, A.G. Ont.; Fort Worth, TX, Kimbell A. Mus.; 1981–2), pp. 59–62
*Artists of the Tudor Court: The Portrait Miniature Rediscovered, 1520–1620* (exh. cat., ed. R. Strong and V. J. Murrell; London, V&A, 1983)
CHRISTOPHER FOLEY

**Locri Epizephyrii.** *See* LOKROI EPIZEPHYRIOI.

**Lőcse.** *See* LEVOČA.

**Lodewijk van Gruuthuse.** *See* LOUIS DE GRUUTHUSE.

**Lodgebook.** Book containing regulations for the masons' craft (*see* MASON (i), §I). With the increasing literacy of masons in their own vernacular languages in late medieval Europe, books played a more prominent role in the craft. Well-known examples of books of regulations, 'Articles and Points', were developed by English and German masons, based on 'customs of the masons' that had been maintained in earlier centuries through oral traditions rather than in writing. Two English versions of the 'Articles and Points of Masonry' have survived from the beginning of the 15th century (London, BL, Bibl. Reg. 17 A1; London, BL, Add. MS. 23198), but these were not the first such written 'custumals', for the second version (the Cooke MS.) refers to 'old books of masonry' and 'the book of charges' that had been 'written in Latin and in French both'.

The English Articles and Points do not stipulate that these written regulations were to be kept in a book in the masons' lodges, as did the regulations drawn up at a gathering of German masons in Regensburg in 1459. This meeting produced a codification of the 'law and customs' of local building lodges into an 'Ordinance' containing numerous 'Points and Articles'. The Ordinance was compiled into 'the Book' (*das Buch*), copies of which were distributed to the masons' lodges on major building projects. These books may be properly referred to as the masons' lodgebooks, and in the following decades German-speaking masons in other regions developed their own versions based on the Regensburg Ordinance. No direct copy of the Ordinance of 1459 has survived, unfortunately, and German scholars have tried to reconstruct its content from these later versions.

There were both many similarities and some important differences between the English and German Articles and Points of Masonry. Both shared great concern for the training and certification of masons in the craft. Primary responsibility for the teaching of apprentices fell to the master mason, but all journeymen were enjoined to assist those who were not yet fully skilled in the craft. Since masons were itinerant craftsmen, the need to certify the level of skill of a mason who wandered on to a site was particularly important. Both the English and German Articles and Points devoted attention to this certification process, with the German procedures being somewhat more elaborate. There was a common interest in assuring building patrons and clients that a man who called himself a master mason was indeed worthy of that title. German masons sought this assurance by certifying a master through the promotion process known in the German lodgebooks as the *Fürdrung* (mod. Ger. *Förderung*), which occurred within the local building lodges.

One of the major differences between the English and German Articles and Points was the attempt to establish an organization for the craft above the level of the local building lodge. The English documents proposed a regional assembly or congregation of masons that would certify that the masters and journeymen were upholding in the local lodges the particulars of the Articles and Points. After careful study of the records pertaining to medieval English masons, however, Knoop and Jones concluded that these assemblies were seldom, if ever, held. Although the German model of craft organization that emerged from the Regensburg meeting called for four pre-eminent building lodges (Strasbourg, Cologne, Vienna and Berne) to have jurisdictional authority over other building lodges within their region, it seems to have been no more effective than the English model in establishing an official authority of masons above the local building lodges.

Other types of book were collected and kept in the building lodges of German masons, although it is highly questionable whether these should be called lodgebooks. This practice was given authoritative endorsement by Hahnloser when he entitled the Portfolio of VILLARD DE HONNECOURT a *Bauhüttenbuch*. Villard's Portfolio is unique in the history of medieval French masons, but several books of technical design and construction drawings by 15th-century German master masons have survived, and it is evident that these were sometimes kept in building lodges after the departure or death of the master masons who had produced them. Similarly in the late 15th century a small literature of technical 'how-to-do-it' booklets were written by masons and, in some cases, published in the new technology of printing (*see* RORICZER, (3)). These booklets were probably also prized by those lodges that obtained copies, but they should also be thought of as books preserved in the lodge, rather than as lodgebooks.

BIBLIOGRAPHY
D. Knoop and G. P. Jones: *The Mediaeval Mason* (Manchester, 1933, 3/1967)
H. R. Hahnloser: *Villard de Honnecourt: Kritische Gesamtausgabe des Bauhüttenbuches Ms. Fr. 19093 der Pariser Nationalbibliothek* (Vienna, 1935, rev. Graz, 2/1972)
D. Knoop, G. P. Jones and D. Hamer, eds: *The Two Earliest Masonic MSS: The Regius Ms. (B. M. Bibl. Reg. 17 A1): The Cooke Ms. (B. M.*

*Add. Ms. 23198)*, Publications of the University of Manchester, 259 (Manchester, 1938)

L. R. Shelby: 'The "Secret" of the Medieval Masons', *On Pre-modern Technology and Science: Studies in Honor of Lynn White, Jr.*, ed. B. S. Hall and D. C. West, Humana Civilitas: Sources and Studies Relating to the Middle Ages and the Renaissance, 1 (Malibu, 1976), pp. 217–18, no. 50

——: *The Fifteenth-century Design Booklets of Mathes Roriczer and Hanns Schmuttermayer* (Carbondale, 1977) [full bibliog.]

U. Coenen: *Die spätgotischen Werkmeisterbücher in Deutschland als Beitrag zur mittelalterlichen Architekturtheorie: Untersuchung und Edition der Lehrschriften fur Entwurf und Ausfuhrung von Sakralbauten* (Aachen, 1989) [full bibliog.]

LON R. SHELBY

**Lodgebook of Wolfgang Rixner and Jerg Reitner.** *See* VIENNA SKETCHBOOK.

**Lodi** [Lodī]. Dynasty of Afghans that ruled portions of northern India from 1451 to 1526. It was founded by Buhlul Lodi, an ambitious Afghan governor who captured the throne of Delhi as the SAYYID house disintegrated. Buhlul (*reg* 1451–89) was preoccupied for most of his reign with subduing the Sharqi rulers of Jaunpur. His tomb, a modest square structure, is in Delhi. Buhlul's successor Sikandar (*reg* 1489–1517) continued to reassert sultanate authority and to regain lost territory. Sikandar's campaigns focused on Malwa and Gwalior, where he had a protracted conflict with the Tomar Rajputs. Sikandar constructed a number of buildings in Agra, where the suburb of Sikandara bears his name. His tomb in Delhi is contained in a walled garden with a mosque (*see* DELHI, §III). It exemplifies the octagonal mausolea that appeared in the time of the Sayyids and, like much Lodi architecture, has features that anticipate developments under the Sur (*see* SUR (ii)) and MUGHAL dynasties. Ibrahim Lodi (*reg* 1517–26) became embroiled in conflicts with his nobles, and Daulat Khan Lodi, governor of Lahore, was so disaffected that he invited Babur, who was at that time ruling Kabul, to attack. In 1526, Babur killed Ibrahim Lodi in the Battle of Panipat and established the Mughal dynasty.

*See also* INDIAN SUBCONTINENT, §III, 6(ii)(b).

BIBLIOGRAPHY

Ni'amatu'llah al-Harawi: *Tārīkh-i Khān Jahānī u Makhzān-i Afghānī* [History of Khan Jahani and the Afghan legacy] (1613); ed. S. M. Imamuddin (Dhaka, 1962); Eng. trans. by B. Dorn (London, 1829–36)

H. Elliot and J. Dowson: *History of India as Told by its Own Historians (The Muhammedan Period)*, 8 vols (London, 1866–77/R Allahabad, 1964)

R. C. Majumdar, ed.: *The Delhi Sultanate*, vi of *The History and Culture of the Indian People* (Bombay, 1960/R 1967)

Abdullah: *Tārīkh-i Dāudī* [History of Daud], ed. S. A. Rashid (Aligarh, 1969)

K. S. Lal: *Twilight of the Sultanate* (Bombay, 1973, rev. New Delhi, 1980)

A. Halim: *History of the Lodi Sultans of Delhi and Agra* (Delhi, 1974)

R. NATH

**Lodi, Callisto da.** *See* PIAZZA, (1).

**Lodi, Fortunato** (*b* Lisbon, 1812; *fl* Lisbon, 1840s). Portuguese architect and stage designer of Italian descent. He was a son of Francisco Lodi, the impresario of the Teatro S Carlos, Lisbon. Nothing is known of his academic training, and his importance to the architecture of 19th-century Lisbon is largely due to his design of the Teatro Nacional Dona Maria II (1842–6), Praça do Rossio, Lisbon. When a public competition for the design of the theatre was proclaimed in 1841 none of the entries submitted was chosen, but the Conde de Farrobo, a powerful capitalist and the principal financial backer of the theatre, ensured the presentation and acceptance of the designs of Lodi, who was his brother-in-law. In spite of the unusual way in which Lodi was appointed to build the theatre, over the heads of more highly reputed and experienced architects and academics, the result was nevertheless a satisfactory one. The theatre was built swiftly and became a landmark in one of the most important squares in the city. Of Neo-classical derivation with Palladian elements, the design of the building is notable for the erudition of its central portico of six Ionic columns, which elegantly emphasizes the comparative austerity of the wings, and for its balanced proportions, which blend into the overall context of the city. The building became one of the most familiar sights of Lisbon. Lodi also designed the Teatro da Quinta das Laranjeiras (1842–3; destr. 1862), Lisbon, a property owned by Farrobo, and he may have been involved in the reconstruction of the Palácio Corte-Real (1841), 138 Rua da Junqueira, Belém. However, it is with the Teatro Nacional that his name is most closely associated.

BIBLIOGRAPHY

J.-A. França: *A arte em Portugal no século XIX*, i (Lisbon, 1966)

RAQUEL HENRIQUES DA SILVA

**Lodi, Giovanni Agostino da.** *See* GIOVANNI AGOSTINO DA LODI.

**Lodi, Giovanni di Domenico da.** *See* BATTAGGIO, GIOVANNI DI DOMENICO.

**Lodoli, Carlo (Cristoforo Ignazio Antonio)** (*b* Venice, *bapt* 28 Nov 1690; *d* Padua, 27 Oct 1761). Italian architectural theorist, teacher and writer. He was one of the most original Italian theorists of the 18th century, his ideas on functionalism later being viewed as precursors of Modernist principles. He came from a family who had close connections with the Venetian Arsenal and military engineering. After completing his initial studies at the monastery of S Francesco della Vigna, Venice, in 1706 he became an Observant Friar Minor in Dalmatia. In 1709 he was transferred to the monastery of S Maria in Aracoeli in Rome, where he continued his studies in philosophy, science, theology, Greek and French. He remained in Rome for about four years, during which time he developed his interest in art and architecture; he was then transferred to the monastery of S Biagio in Forlì. From 1715 to 1720 he lived in Verona, where he began teaching astronomy, physics and mathematics to Veronese noblemen, and philosophy to the novices of the monastery of S Bernardino. Also in Verona he contributed to an edition of the works of the French humanist Marc-Antoine Muretus (1526–85) and began his friendship with the writer Angelo Calogerà (1699–1768) and Scipione Maffei. During this period he probably also visited Tuscany, including Florence, acquiring a profound knowledge of the art of the region. In 1720 Lodoli was transferred to Venice to teach theology and was immediately at the centre of the city's cultural life. Also during the 1720s Lodoli was engaged in the extension and reorganization of the library

Carlo Lodoli: window trim, *c.* 1740, cloisters of S Francesco della Vigna, Venice

of S Francesco della Vigna and acted as historian of the Franciscan Order and its writers.

In the 1730s Lodoli began to teach the sons of Venetian noblemen. Architecture was included in the course of study, and in the garden of S Francesco della Vigna he assembled a collection of architectural fragments for teaching purposes. From 1739 to 1751 Lodoli held the office of Padre Generale Commissario di Terra Santa in Venice, and he also devoted himself to the restoration (1739–43) of the pilgrim's hospice attached to the monastery. Here, with few resources, he put his architectural theories into practice, designing such features as doors and windows (see fig.) according to his own particular rules of function and form. His idea was to replace traditional architectural elements with others conforming to a new architectural system that was rational, functional and consistent in the use of materials. Similar doors and windows were later built by two of his pupils, Francesco Venier (*b* 1700), at an unidentified villa outside Dolo, near Venice, and Andrea Memmo, at his own house in Venice and at the residence of the Venetian ambassador in Constantinople. An example of a door by Lodoli was illustrated in the second volume of *L'architettura di Jacopo Barozzi da Vignola ridotta a facile metodo* (Venice, 1748), which Jacopo Ziborghi dedicated to Lodoli. Over the entrance to the hospice Lodoli also placed a low relief of great simplicity and immediacy representing Giacomo Piceno, the protector of the Frati di Gerusalemme. According to Lodoli, this was an example of an appropriate application of ornament, being applied to an architectural structure in a purely decorative manner.

This project, the only one Lodoli executed, encapsulates the essence of his architectural theories as set out in the only surviving original source: two draft outlines of his unpublished treatise on architecture (untraced), which appeared in the second volume of Andrea Memmo's *Elementi d'architettura lodoliana* (*see* MEMMO, ANDREA; *see*

*also* TREATISE, §I). In these two draft outlines, Lodoli's functionalism and rationalism are expressed in condensed form. According to Memmo, Lodoli wanted to find in architecture the same scientific principles that Galileo Galilei had discovered in physics; his architecture thus assumed the character of a science based on certain principles and static rules. It also concerned the search for structural truth, expressed in terms of a building's solidity, which involved the honest use of materials, especially stone. This concept reflected the military engineering environment of the Venetian Arsenal and the rationalist and anti-Baroque tendencies present in Venice in the early 18th century. Lodoli argued that proper function and form were the only final, scientific aims of civil architecture, and that nothing should be put on show that is not a working part of the structure. The different architectural systems of antiquity were set out, but Vitruvius' five orders of architecture were criticized as being inappropriate to stone because they were originally based on timber structures. Following an original classification, the treatise deals with the primary integral elements of architecture, solidity and proportion, as well as with the secondary integral elements, convenience and ornament. Lodoli admitted ornament, except mosaic, and in order to overcome the monotony of continuous imitation of the same forms he encouraged the invention of new ones or the selection from ancient and modern architectural styles, including Gothic and Moorish, of ornament that suited the characteristics of stone. According to Memmo, Lodoli also admitted those elements of the Classical orders that corresponded to a structure's function and suited the characteristics of stone: columns, bases, capitals, pedestals, triglyphs, metopes and consoles. He particularly favoured ground-floor rustication and included drawings of 16 different types in his treatise. His taste for Doric and Tuscan capitals probably arose from the fact that to him, as later to his friend Piranesi, these represented examples of primitive Italic architecture, the origin of the art.

Lodoli was interested in garden design, particularly of English landscape gardens, and he was also interested in the design of carriages and furniture, which he termed 'organic architecture'. He designed a functional chair, fitted to the contours of the human body, and admired the Venetian gondola as a synthesis of form and function and as an example of the rational use of materials. Passionately keen on painting and sculpture, he was one of the first connoisseurs of medieval art, and his own collection, which included relics of Hellenistic and Byzantine painting as well as primitive and modern works, was arranged in such a way as to illustrate the development of art.

The critical reception of Lodoli's ideas has had a rather complex history, partly because, with the loss of his original writings, they are known only indirectly through the works of others. Girolamo Zanetti reported that in 1754, after 20 years, Lodoli finally completed his treatise on architecture, but that he refused to publish it. After an unsuccessful attempt by Federico Foscari, at Memmo's invitation Francesco Algarotti undertook to publicize Lodoli's theories in an essay entitled *Saggio sopra l'architettura* (Venice, 1757). Fearing, however, that Lodoli's ideas might lead to the destruction of the whole architectural tradition, Algarotti modified them, adapting them to his own, more orthodox way of thinking, which was closer to current notions of imitation in architecture. It was Memmo who finally tried to restore Lodoli's original ideas, although he was influenced by the theoretical developments of the second half of the 18th century, especially the syncretism of Francesco Milizia, who had by then expounded some of Lodoli's ideas without mentioning their source. The first volume of Memmo's work, *Elementi d'architettura lodoliana*, was published anonymously in Rome in April 1786. In the following year Lodoli's *Apologhi* appeared: these were short educational tales in a satirical and paradoxical style, which had been transmitted orally among his friends and pupils. When the complete edition of Memmo's *Elementi* was finally published in 1834, Lodoli's polemical thought assumed a new relevance. Memmo's version of Lodoli in fact formed the basis of every attempt made by Italian architectural critics in the first half of the 19th century to contest the ruling classicist and academic culture. Lodoli's ideas were revived around 1930, when critics saw them as the forerunner of contemporary architectural rationalism.

WRITINGS
*Apologhi immaginati* (Bassano, 1787)

BIBLIOGRAPHY
*Macmillan Enc. Architects*
S. Maffei: *Verona illustrata*, vi (Verona, 1731), p. 67
G. Zanetti and A. Calogerà: *Memorie per servire all'istoria letteraria*, iii (1754), pp. 65–6; v (1755), pp. 40–46
A. Memmo: *Elementi d'architettura lodoliana*, 2 vols (Zara, 1834)
M. L. Gengaro: 'Il valore dell'architettura nella teoria settecentesca del padre Carlo Lodoli', *L'Arte*, xl (1937), pp. 313–17
E. Kaufmann: 'At an Eighteenth-century Crossroads: Algarotti versus Lodoli', *J. Amer. Soc. Archit. Hist.*, iv (1944), pp. 23–9
A. Gabrielli: 'La teoria architettonica di Carlo Lodoli', *A. Figurative*, iii (1945), pp. 123–36
E. Kaufmann: 'Piranesi, Algarotti and Lodoli: A Controversy in XVIII Century Venice', *Gaz. B.-A.*, ii (1955), pp. 21–8
M. De Benedetti: 'La teoria dell'architettura funzionale del Lodoli e la pratica dell'architettura in Italia', *Atti del V convegno nazionale di storia dell'architettura: Firenze, 1957*, pp. 157–63
F. Haskell: *Patrons and Painters: A Study in the Relations between Italian Art and Society in the Age of the Baroque* (London, 1963, rev. 2/1980)
G. Torcellan: *Una figura della Venezia settecentesca: Andrea Memmo* (Venice, 1963)
E. Kaufmann jr: 'Memmo's Lodoli', *A. Bull.*, xlvi (1964), pp. 159–75
A. Cavallari Murat: 'Congetture sul trattato di architettura progettato dal Lodoli', *Atti e rassegna tecnica della società degli ingegneri e degli architetti di Torino: Torino, 1966*, vii, pp. 3–12
E. Concina: 'Architettura militare e scienza: Prospettive di indagine sulla formazione veneziana di padre Carlo Lodoli', *Stor. Archit.*, iii (1975), pp. 19–22
——: 'Per padre Carlo Lodoli, Giovambattista Lodoli, ingegnere militare', *A. Ven.*, xxx (1976), p. 240
J. Rykwert: 'Lodoli on Function and Representation', *Archit. Rev.* [London], clx (1976), pp. 21–6
F. Bernabei: 'Mito, ragione e architettura: Vico e Lodoli', *Vico e Venezia* (Florence, 1982), pp. 223–43
S. P. Caligaris: 'Fra Carlo Lodoli', *A. Crist.*, lxx (1982), no. 684, pp. 1–5; no. 691, pp. 231–4; no. 692, pp. 265–8
J. Rykwert: *The First Moderns: The Architects of the Eighteenth Century* (Cambridge, MA, and London, 1983), pp. 288–337
S. P. Caligaris: 'Fra Carlo Lodoli: La ristrutturazione dell'Ospizio di Terrasanta presso il Convento di S Francesco della Vigna in Venezia: Tra realtà e ipotesi', *A. Crist.*, lxxviii/736 (1990), pp. 31–42

VALERIA FARINATI

**Lods, Marcel** (*b* Paris, 16 Aug 1891; *d* Paris, 9 Sept 1978). French architect. He studied at the Ecole Nationale des Arts Décoratifs and the Ecole Nationale des Beaux-Arts in Paris (Dip. Arch., 1923). During both World Wars he served in the French army, where he developed an enduring passion for aeronautics. From 1928 to 1940 Lods was in partnership with EUGÈNE BEAUDOUIN, bringing to the team his energy and his fascination for the world of modern industry. As a devotee of modern industry and aeronautics in particular, he was always seeking to introduce new methods of production on his building sites, based on prefabrication and the simplification of assemblies. On the Champ des Oiseaux estate (1930) in Bagneux and the Cité de la Muette (1932–4; destr.; see *Le Métier d'architecte*) in Drancy, Lods was responsible for the detailed design of the housing units and in particular the development of the dry-assembly principle of the construction components. He was responsible for the team's move towards ever lighter buildings, ranging from the open-air school (1934) at Suresnes with its mobile external walls, to the Maison du Peuple (1936–9) in Clichy, executed with Vladimir Bodiansky and Jean Prouvé. This ideal of an architecture tending towards immateriality is illustrated by the Roland Garros airport club house (1935) in Buc and the huge unexecuted glass and steel Palais des Expositions planned at La Défense (1935), Paris, which was to have a metallic roof accessible to cars via ramps running through glass façades.

During the Occupation Lods worked with Le Corbusier. A major turning-point in his thinking on construction came during a visit to the USA shortly after the war. He returned with a great fascination for the building sites of the Tennessee Valley Authority and for the light architecture of Richard Neutra. From 1946 to 1955 he was in charge of the reconstruction of Sotteville-lès-Rouen where he drew up the town plan and built large slabs spaced at generous intervals for the working-class population. His most ambitious undertaking in the immediate post-war period was an attempt, with Gerald Hanning (1919–80) and the German urban planner Adolf Bayer (*b* 1909), to implement a radical functionalist plan for the reconstruction of the German town of Mainz (1946–8). Faced with the fierce resistance of a section of the German authorities, Lods lost the support of the French military officials and was unable to realize his plans which supported the functionalist principles of the Charte d'Athènes. Throughout this period, at large public conferences he preached continuously in favour of town and country planning. He had greater success in North and West Africa, where from the 1950s he carried out numerous building projects with Xavier Arsène-Henry (*b* 1919) and Luc Arsène-Henry (*b* 1923). Deeply committed to lightweight metallic prefabrication and concerned with the problems of construction and assembly, he built mainly university complexes and large housing developments, such as the 1500 housing units of Les Grandes Terres (1958) in Marly, the Meaux ZUP (zone designated for priority housing development) and the Grande Mare development in Rouen, where he put into practice the Groupe d'Etudes pour l'Architecture Industrialisée (GEAI) industrialized process based on the use of floors made up of three-dimensional metal latticework. Among his last works the Maison des Sciences de l'Homme (1967; with Paul Depondt, Henri Beauclair and André Malizard), Paris, remains a late and mature homage to metal, used both in the framework and in the façades with their folding shutters, the surface of which reflects ironically the diversity of the architecture on the Boulevard Raspail.

WRITINGS

with H. Le Boterf: *Le Métier d'architecte* (Paris, 1976)
*Marcel Lods 1891–1978: Photographies d'architecte* (Paris, 1991) [pubd posth., with contributions by others]

BIBLIOGRAPHY
'Marcel Lods, 1891–1978', *Tech. & Archit.*, 321 (Oct 1978)

JEAN-LOUIS COHEN

**Łódź.** Polish city in Wielkopolska (Greater Poland), south-east of Warsaw, with a population of *c.* 900,000. It is noted for its 19th-century architecture and, in the 20th century, for its role as an important centre of modern art and of the film and music industry. Łódź received municipal rights in 1423 but remained small and insignificant until the 19th century. The rapid growth of Łódź as a centre of the textile industry began in 1821, when the government of the Congress Kingdom of Poland decreed it a factory town and developed the production of cotton and linen fabric; growth was further boosted after trade barriers with Russia were lifted in 1850 and 1877. The population grew dramatically following these decisions, and building activity developed on a great scale. Separate districts for cotton and linen weavers and other textile manufacturers were built on a regular grid either side of a north–south axis (now Piotrkowska Street) that led out of the old town. Most of the buildings of this period were timber and have not survived, but interesting brick examples include the Neo-classical Weaving Mill (1835–7) at 280–82 Piotrkowska Street, built for the industrialist Ludwik Geyer and now housing the Central Museum of Textiles.

The industrial boom of the 1870s and 1880s resulted in a rapidly growing number of large industrial estates that usually combined the residence of the industrialist, factory buildings and workers' tenements, as, for example, in Karol Wilhelm Scheibler's estate built at Książęcy Młyn after 1877. In 1872 Hilary Majewski (1838–92) was appointed chief architect of the city. Educated in St Petersburg and in Florence, he contributed to the major development of residential, industrial and public buildings and created a type of multi-storey industrial brick building that had no direct counterpart outside Łódź. The five-storey cotton mill at 15 Ogrodowa Street, built in 1878 for Izrael Kalmanowicz Poznański, is a good example of this type (see fig.). Poznański's palace (1902–3), adjacent to the mill, has a monumental dome, and its neo-Baroque façade has an attic crowned with free-standing statues. It is typical of the palaces and villas that Majewski and other architects designed for the newly emerging class of rich industrialists: they were usually eclectic in style, inspired by Renaissance and Baroque architecture. In 1879 Majewski built an Italianate villa surrounded by a park

Łódź, former cotton mill (1878; left) and palace (1902–3; right) of Izrael Kalmanowicz Poznański

(Przędzalniana Street) for Edward Herbst, and his other works include a bank (77 Piotrkowska Street) and an Orthodox church (1880; Kiliński Street).

By the end of the 19th century Łódź had become one of the largest textile centres in the world and was dubbed the 'Polish Manchester'. The population surged from *c.* 50,000 in 1870 to *c.* 314,000 in 1897, creating a great demand for housing. Four- and five-storey terraced tenement blocks were built in different historical styles, and they became city landmarks. Apart from numerous neo-Gothic and neo-Renaissance examples, fine Art Nouveau houses were built, for example the house at 31–3 Wólczańska Street (1903), designed by Gustaw Landau-Gutenberger (*c.* 1870–1917). Most of the industrial and residential estates survived World War II undamaged. In the 1930s Łódź became an important centre of modern art, and the A.R. GROUP, a literary and artistic movement founded by Poland's leading Constructivist artists, was established there between 1929 and 1936. In 1931, at the initiative of Władysław Strzemiński and other members of the a.r. group, the Art Museum was formed. It comprised the art collection bequeathed (1928) to the city by Kazimierz Bartoszewicz (1852–1930), a historian and writer, as well as works of art from other sources. It was one of the first museums of modern art in Europe, and it functions as a leading institution promoting modern art in Poland.

BIBLIOGRAPHY

I. Popławska: 'Architektura Łodzi około 1900r.' [Architecture in Łódź around 1900], *Sztuka około 1900* [Art *c.* 1900] (Warsaw, 1969), pp. 113–28

S. Lorentz: *Przewodnik po muzeach i zbiorach w Polsce* [Guide to museums and collections in Poland] (Warsaw, 1971), pp. 154–64

H. Jaworowski: 'Łódź', *Zabytki urbanistyki i architektury w Polsce: Miasta historyczne* [Monuments of architecture and urban planning in Poland: historic towns], ed. W. Zin (Warsaw, 1986), pp. 307–28

K. Stefański: 'Berliner Architektur in Lodz zu Beginn des 20. Jahrhunderts', *Architectura*, xxi/2 (1991), pp. 164–76

ANNA BENTKOWSKA

**Loeb, Pierre** (*b* Paris, 1897; *d* 1964). French art dealer. He became interested in modern art through a collector friend, Dr Tzanck, who knew Jules Pascin and André Derain, while working for his father's lace business just after World War I. In 1924 he opened the Galerie Pierre at 13, Rue Bonaparte in Paris, near Derain's home, and featured Pascin's work in the first exhibition. In 1926 Loeb moved his gallery to 2, Rue Bonaparte, in the same year meeting Picasso, who became a close friend and whose work he showed in 1929. Loeb also became a staunch supporter of Surrealist painting, the subject of his gallery's most memorable exhibition (1925), which marked the group's first public appearance, bringing together Arp, De Chirico, Ernst, Klee, Masson, Miró, Man Ray and Picasso; he was particularly devoted to the work of Miró, which he featured in 11 one-man exhibitions from 1927 to 1939.

The Galerie Pierre remained associated above all with Surrealism and related trends; in 1934, for example, it was host to Balthus's first one-man exhibition. Loeb's eclectic and ever-changing interests, however, led him to mount remarkable displays not only of contemporary art but of recent work that was already entering into art history, including sculptures by Matisse (1930), Picasso's Cubist papiers collés (1935) and Braque's Fauvist landscapes

(1938). Loeb was in Cuba from 1941 to the end of World War II, marking his return to Paris with an extraordinary exhibition of drawings by Antonin Artaud (1947), followed by an emphasis on abstract art by the Cobra group and by artists of the Ecole de Paris such as Vieira da Silva, Zao Wou-Ki and Camille Bryen.

WRITINGS

*Voyages à travers la peinture* (Dole-du-Jura, 1946)

ISABELLE MONOD-FONTAINE

**Loeber, Lou** [Louise Marie] (*b* Amsterdam, 3 May 1894; *d* Blaricum, 1 Feb 1983). Dutch painter. She trained at the Rijksacademie in Amsterdam (1915–18). She discovered Cubism, especially that of Albert Gleizes, the work of De Stijl and of Le Corbusier in 1919. During 1920–21 the form in her work became more rigid and the colour more sober. She came into contact with works by Piet Mondrian in the Salomon Bernard Slijper (1884–1971) collection (now at the Gemeentemuseum, The Hague), in particular *Evolution* (1910–11) and *Red Windmill* (1910). In 1927 she travelled to the Bauhaus at Dessau and to Berlin. She favoured subjects taken from industry and technology and stylized reality using the diagonal, as well as the horizontal and vertical line. A link with visible reality was maintained, however.

BIBLIOGRAPHY

'Herinneringen door Lou Loeber' [Lou Loeber's memories], *Cent. Mus. Utrecht Meded.*, 28–9 (1980) [incl. bibliog.]

JOHN STEEN

**Loedewich, Master.** *See* JUPAN, LUDWIG.

**Loehr, Max** (*b* Chemnitz, 4 Dec 1903; *d* Nashua, NH, 16 Sept 1988). German art historian. After schooling broken by the death of his father in 1920, Loehr enrolled in 1931 at the University of Munich, where he studied Classical archaeology, art history, Sanskrit and Chinese. His PhD, a study of the earliest styles of Chinese bronzes, was awarded in 1936, after which he worked as an assistant at the Staatliches Museum für Völkerkunde in Munich. He quickly established himself as one of the foremost authorities on Chinese bronzes, displaying a preference for stylistic analyses. A further interest was in Chinese painting. In 1940 he went to Beijing to study at the Sino–German Institute, of which he was Director from 1941 to 1945. From 1947 to 1948 he served as Associate Professor at Qinghua University in Beijing. On his return to Munich, he worked from 1949 to 1951 as Curator of Oriental Art at the Staatliches Museum and lectured at the University of Munich. From 1951 to 1974 he held professorial posts in East Asian art and archaeology at the universities of Michigan and Harvard in the USA and served as Curator of Oriental Art at the Fogg Art Museum in Cambridge, MA.

Most of Loehr's publications were catalogues of objects in museums or private collections, in the main Chinese bronzes, weapons, jades and paintings. He also wrote on theory and methodology, including art theory in China. Although in his studies of Chinese bronzes he examined archaeological and inscriptional evidence, his arguments were based ultimately on stylistic analyses. His article 'The Bronze Styles of the Anyang Period (1300–1028 BC)', for example, laid out a clear sequence of styles, which were largely confirmed by subsequent excavations. Although somewhat modified, Loehr's pattern of stylistic development continued to underlie studies of the subject into the late 20th century.

### WRITINGS
'The Bronze Styles of the Anyang Period (1300–1028 B.C.)', *Archvs Chin. A. Soc. America*, vii (1953), pp. 42–53
*Chinese Bronze Age Weapons: The Werner Jannings Collection in the Chinese National Palace Museum, Peking* (Ann Arbor and London, 1956)
*Relics of Ancient China from the Collection of Dr. Paul Singer* (exh. cat., New York, Asia House Gals, 1965)
*Ritual Vessels of Bronze Age China* (exh. cat., New York, Asia House Gals, 1968)
*The Great Painters of China* (Oxford, 1980)

### BIBLIOGRAPHY
J. Cahill: 'Max Loehr at Seventy', *A. Orient.*, x (1975), pp. 1–10 [incl. bibliography of writings]
S. Bush: Obituary, *Orient. A.*, n. s., xxxv/1 (1989), pp. 69–70
J. Cahill: Obituary, *J. Asian Stud.*, xlviii/1 (1989), p. 240

S. J. VERNOIT

**Loeser, Charles Alexander** (*b* Brooklyn, 1864; *d* New York, 18 March 1928). American art historian, critic and collector. The son of Frederick Loeser, a department store owner and early donor of 19th-century European paintings to the Metropolitan Museum, New York, he studied at Harvard, earning a master's degree in philosophy in 1887. He continued his study of philosophy in Berlin the following winter and in 1890 moved to Florence, where he lived in Villa Gattaia, furnished with old and modern furniture and works of art. Influenced by Giovanni Morelli, he was a pioneer connoisseur of drawings and built a major private collection, primarily Italian and representing the history of draughtsmanship, with a new emphasis on Baroque and Mannerist works. He contributed two volumes (Titian and Tintoretto, and Filippino Lippi) to the annotated facsimile publication of drawings from the Uffizi and wrote critical essays on Old Master drawings in various collections. He was an adviser to the Fogg Museum at Harvard University and to the Brooklyn Museum. He bequeathed 262 Old Master drawings (including works by Michelangelo, Pontormo, Guardi and Rembrandt) as a study collection to Harvard University, 8 paintings by Cézanne to the White House, Washington, DC, and 30 sculptures and paintings to the Palazzo Vecchio, Florence. He left other works to his wife, Olga Kaufmann Lebert, and a daughter. Sotheby's sold the family's collection in London and Florence in 1959–60 and 1974.

### WRITINGS
'Die Handzeichnungen der königlichen Bibliothek in Turin, mit besonderer Berücksichtigung der italienischen Meister', *Repert. Kstwiss.*, xxii/1 (1889), pp. 13–21
'La Collection Beckerath au cabinet des estampes de Berlin', *Gaz. B.-A.*, xxviii (1902), pp. 471–82
'Über einige italienische Handzeichnungen des Berliner Kupferstichkabinetts', *Repert. Kstwiss.*, xxv/5 (1902), pp. 348–59
'L'Art italien au Musée des arts décoratifs', *Gaz. B.-A.*, xl (1908), pp. 402–16
with P. N. Ferri and C. Gambe: *Mostra di disegni e stampe di scuola veneziana dei secoli XV e XVI* (exh. cat., Florence, Uffizi, n.d.)

### BIBLIOGRAPHY
Obituary, *ARTnews* (24 March 1928)
A. Mongan: 'The Loeser Collection of Drawings', *Bull. Fogg A. Mus.*, xii/2 (1933), pp. 22–4
M. Tinti: 'La collezione Loeser in Palazzo Vecchio', *Illus. Tosc.*, xii (1934)

K. Oberhuber: 'Charles Loeser as a Collector of Drawings', *Apollo*, cvii (1978), pp. 477–9
K. Oberhuber, ed.: *Old Master Drawings: Selections from the Charles A. Loeser Bequest*, Cambridge, MA, Fogg Handbooks (Cambridge, MA, 1979)

☐

**Loew, Elias.** *See* LOWE, ELIAS AVERY.

**Loewy, Raymond (Fernand)** (*b* Paris, 5 Nov 1893; *d* Monaco, 14 July 1986). American industrial designer of French birth. He studied (1918) for a degree in engineering at the Ecole de Lanneau in Paris, before serving in the French Army. In 1919 he emigrated to the USA (naturalized 1938). After a brief period as a window-dresser he worked as a freelance fashion illustrator for *Harper's Bazaar* and *Vogue* (e.g. *Metropolis* advertisement for Saks Fifth Avenue from *Vogue*, 15 March 1927; see Wilson, Pilgrim and Tashjian, p. 86). Working in advertising design steered him towards industrial design. His disappointment with the quality and vulgarity of American products led him in 1929 to design and re-style radios for Westinghouse and duplicating machines for Gestetner. In 1934 he designed the Coldspot refrigerator for Sears Roebuck. Loewy's success was based on his rehousing of American products in streamlined forms in the 1930s. From the 1940s to the 1970s he worked on a number of commissions, such as the corporate logos of many major businesses, including British Petroleum and Shell Oil. Other successful projects were the designs for the S-I locomotive (1937) for the Pennsylvania Railroad Company, styling for Studebaker cars (including the Avanti) from 1937 to 1962, the Dole Coca Cola dispenser (*c*. 1948), architectural designs for International Harvester dealer showrooms and interiors of NASA's Saturn–Apollo and Skylab projects (1967–73). He had offices in many American and foreign cities and enjoyed great success until the 1980s, when financial pressure led to the contraction of his business.

### WRITINGS
*Never Leave Well Enough Alone* (New York, 1951)
*Industrial Design, Raymond Loewy* (Woodstock, 1979)

### BIBLIOGRAPHY
'Designer Raymond Loewy: He Streamlines the Sales Curve', *Time*, liv/18 (1949), pp. 68–74 & cover
L. F. Brand: *The Designs of Raymond Loewy* (Washington, DC, 1975)
D. Bush: *The Streamlined Decade* (New York, 1975)
J. L. Meikle: *Twentieth Century Limited: Industrial Design in America, 1925–1939* (Philadelphia, 1979)
A. Pulos: *American Design Ethic: A History of Industrial Design to 1940* (Cambridge, MA, 1983), pp. 274, 276, 322–3, 354, 358, 402
R. G. Wilson, D. Pilgrim and D. Tashjian: *The Machine Age in America, 1918–1941* (New York, 1986), pp. 25, 43, 57, 60–61, 67–8, 83–8, 125, 135, 140–42, 147, 283, 308

RICHARD GUY WILSON

**Löffler, Bertold** (*b* Liberec, Bohemia [now in Czech Republic], 28 Sept 1874; *d* Vienna, 23 March 1960). Austrian painter, printmaker, designer and ceramicist. After being taught to draw at the Gewerbemuseum in Reichenberg, from 1890 to 1900 he studied drawing at the Kunstgewerbeschule in Vienna (now the Hochschule für Angewandte Kunst) under the Austrian Franz von Matsch (1861–1942). In 1909 he was appointed a teacher at the Kunststickereischule in Vienna, and from 1909 to 1935 he was a professor at the Kunstgewerbeschule. In 1906 he founded Wiener Keramik with Michael Powolny. The firm contributed tiles for Josef Hoffmann's Palais Stoclet in Brussels (1905–11). From 1907 the Wiener Werkstätte took over the distribution and sale of their vases, figurines, boxes and tiles, selling them also in Germany from 1908. In 1913 Wiener Keramik merged with the Künstlerische Werkstätte Franz und Emilie Schleiss in Gmunden to form the Vereinigte Wiener und Gmundner Keramik. In collaborative works by Löffler and Powolny it is often very difficult to establish who did different aspects. Löffler preferred to provide the often fanciful designs, leaving the modelling to other assistants, for example in the figurines *Lady in a Stylized Crinoline* (Vienna, Hist. Mus.) and *Putto with Horns of Plenty* (*c.* 1912; priv. col., see 1964 exh. cat., pl. 15). In 1907 he collaborated on the decoration and furnishing of Kabarett Fledermaus, his contribution including a poster, illustrations for the first programme sheet, the entrance ticket and a fan (Vienna, Hist. Mus.). He also provided designs for pieces of jewellery and postcards for the Wiener Werkstätte and designed the posters for the *Kunstschau* of 1908 and the *Internationale Kunstschau* of 1909 in Vienna (Vienna, Hist. Mus.). He produced much graphic work involving books, especially for Wiener Verlag (e.g. the wrapper, title page and design for Arthur Schnitzler's *Reigen*, 1903), ex-libris plates, different types of printing and designs for banknotes, securities and postage stamps. His work in other media included a fresco of *St Florian* (1930; Dürnstein, Gasthof Thiry) and the altarpiece *Salvator Mundi* (1923; Vienna, Am Schüttel church). From 1921 he was a member of the Künstlerhaus in Vienna; he was awarded its 'Goldener Lorbeer' in 1954.

BIBLIOGRAPHY
*Wien um 1900* (exh. cat. by F. Novotny, Vienna, Sezession, Kstlerhaus and Hist. Mus., 1964)
*Bertold Löffler (1874–1960)* (exh. cat., Vienna, Hochsch. Angewandte Kst, 1978)
E. Frottier: *Michael Powolny, Keramik und Glas aus Wien, 1900 bis 1950: Monographie und Werkverzeichnis* (Vienna, 1990), pp. 29, 30, 35–7, 39–44, 48, 65, 66, 101–2
SABINE KEHL-BAIERLE

**Logelain, Henri** (*b* Brussels, 11 Feb 1889; *d* Brussels, 12 Jan 1968). Belgian watercolourist, draughtsman and painter. He began to study at the Ecole des Arts Décoratifs in Ixelles at the age of 12, moving later to the Académie des Beaux-Arts in Brussels. For several years he earned his living in his uncle's industrial painting workshop, where he learnt to imitate wood and marble. His first exhibition took place in 1911 in the Salle Boute in Brussels, and from 1912 he exhibited regularly in the triennial Salon at Liège. At this time he worked exclusively in watercolour, with lavish use of washes and mixtures of tones (e.g. *Maternity with Bathtub*, 1913; priv. col., see 1970 exh. cat., no. 147). He was concerned above all with effects of light and generally produced still-lifes and landscapes of the outskirts of Brussels.

Between 1916 and 1918 Logelain made many nude studies in pencil, ink and charcoal, the majority of which are in private collections. His simplification of the human form by cautious recourse to geometry and the solidity of his figures reappear later in his portraits and in such works as *Large Nude* (1940; priv. col., see 1970 exh. cat., no. 40); while these were initially related to contemporary Cubist

work, and Logelain was influenced by some avant-garde movements, he remained largely faithful to figuration and to the academic tradition. In the late 1910s Logelain worked with the group L'Effort, which included Auguste Oleffe, who became his friend and adviser. Logelain's first retrospective exhibition took place in 1921 at the Cercle Artistique et Littéraire of Brussels; it was a success, and Logelain became a member of the Société Royale Belge des Aquarellistes.

By the early 1920s Logelain started to paint in oils, producing open-air studies in which he effectively captured the rain-filled Belgian skies, as in *Quartier Léopold, Brussels* (1927; priv. col., see 1970 exh. cat., no. 3). He also produced portraits, including several of his daughter Bietje (e.g. *Portrait of a Young Girl*, 1934; Brussels, Mus. A. Mod.), and still-lifes composed with great care to balance the bold colours and simple forms that he favoured (e.g. *Mushrooms and Artichokes on a Blue Dish*, 1931; Charleroi, Mus. Com. B.-A.). During the 1930s he continued to produce such views of Brussels as *Le Palais de Justice* (1930; Brussels, Mus. A. Mod.).

In 1938 Logelain travelled to Africa, visiting Dakar and staying in the Congo. He brought back works depicting landscapes and the everyday life of the former Belgian colony (e.g. *Market in Léopoldville*, 1938; priv. col., see 1970 exh. cat., no. 243), subjects admirably suited to his habitual use of bold colours and forms. In 1946 his work was exhibited in Elisabethville (now Lubumbashi), and other exhibitions in the Congo followed. In 1948 he stayed at the Académie Belge in Rome, where he painted such townscapes as *Piazza del Popolo* (1948; priv. col., see 1970 exh. cat., no. 67), which show a new development in his technique; the large coloured areas of his earlier paintings were replaced by small, free brushstrokes. He continued to paint in this style until the end of his career.

BIBLIOGRAPHY
S. Pierron: 'Le Peintre Henri Logelain', *Savoir & Beauté* (1927), pp. 204–10
R. Dupierreux: 'Henri Logelain', *A. Belge* (Dec 1936) [Christmas issue]
*Rétrospective Henri Logelain* (exh. cat., Brussels, Mus. Ixelles, 1970)
RICHARD KERREMANS

**Loggan, David** (*b* Danzig [now Gdańsk], *bapt* 27 Aug 1634; *d* London, *bur* 1 Aug 1692). British engraver, draughtsman and painter. Descended from an Anglo-Scottish family, he first studied in Danzig under Willem Hondius (?1600–58) and then in Amsterdam under Crispijn van de Passe II, before coming to London *c.* 1656–8. Although his training was in engraving, which remained his principal activity, from the late 1650s onwards he also produced a large number of miniature portrait drawings in black lead (graphite) on parchment, for example *Thomas Barlow, Bishop of Lincoln* (*c.* 1672; London, BM). In 1662 he engraved the title-page for the folio *Book of Common Prayer*. He married in 1663 and moved two years later to Nuffield, Oxon, to avoid the plague. He was living in Oxford by 1669, when he was appointed 'public sculptor' to the university. He then proceeded to draw and engrave all the Oxford colleges in bird's-eye views for his famous folio *Oxonia illustrata* (*see* COLLEGE, fig. 1), published in 1675, the year that he was made a British citizen. That year he once again settled in London, living in Leicester

Fields, where he let rooms to aristocratic patrons, notably Sir Thomas Isham, and acted as their agent in the acquisition of works of art. From 1676 he was involved in preparing the folio *Cantabrigia illustrata*, and in 1690, the year it was published, he was made engraver to Cambridge University.

Loggan employed several assistants on his two university surveys, and pupils included Robert White, who also worked in graphite. He maintained contacts with artists in the Low Countries, and he was instrumental in bringing Abraham Blooteling (1632–98) and Gerard Valck to London. He was one of the last significant line-engravers to work in England, and many of his plates were based on portraits after his own *ad vivum* drawings; examples are *John Wallis* (London, N.P.G.) and *James Butler, 1st Duke of Ormonde* (London, BM). His drawings in graphite are among the earliest and most distinguished in this medium, also known as plumbago. The many examples in public collections include the poets *Edmund Waller* (1685; London, N.P.G.) and *John Wilmot, 2nd Earl of Rochester* (1671; London, BM), in which Rochester's face is gently tinted with wash. Loggan's few oil portraits do not approach this calibre.

#### PRINTS
*Oxonia illustrata* (Oxford, 1675)
*Cantabrigia illustrata* (Cambridge, 1690); ed. J. W. Clark (Cambridge, 1905)

#### BIBLIOGRAPHY
J. von Sandrart: *Teutsche Academie* (1675–9); ed. A. R. Peltzer (1925)
C. F. Bell and R. L. Poole: 'English Seventeenth-century Portrait Drawings in Oxford Collections: Part II', *Walpole Soc.*, xiv (1926), pp. 55–64, pl. xxxix
M. Whinney and O. Millar: *English Art, 1625–1714* (Oxford, 1957), pp. 101–3, 270
E. Croft-Murray and P. Hulton: *XVI and XVII Centuries* (1960), i of *British Museum Catalogue of British Drawings* (London, 1960–), pp. 428–34
G. Isham: 'The Correspondence of David Loggan with Sir Thomas Isham', *Connoisseur*, clii (1963), pp. 231–6; cliv (1963), pp. 84–91
*Drawing in England from Hilliard to Hogarth* (exh. cat. by L. Stainton and C. White, London, BM, 1987), p. 167

RICHARD JEFFREE

**Loggia.** External roofed gallery with open arches on one or both sides. □

**Loghem, Johannes Bernardus van** (*b* Haarlem, 19 Oct 1881; *d* Haarlem, 26 Feb 1940). Dutch architect. He studied architecture at the Technische Hogeschool in Delft (1905–9) and established a practice in Haarlem. His first projects, such as his own house (1912) in Haarlem, were fairly traditional designs, but by 1916 the influence of Frank Lloyd Wright was already apparent in a small banking office and residence in Hoofddorp. In 1917 he began work on the first of a series of housing complexes in Haarlem, including Rosenhage (1919–22). He evolved a plain, flat-roofed brick style that used no ornament but only modelling of building volume to great effect; in Tuinwijk Zuid (1920–22) the rows of housing are complex compositions in which units are manipulated in all three dimensions to form roof terraces, entrance setbacks, window bays and portals leading into the small park at the centre of the U-shaped block. In 1922–3 he built the Patria housing complex in north Haarlem; it has a brick ground storey, but the upper storey is one of the first built manifestations of the International style: flat, orthogonal, white stucco with square windows and glazed corners. He was able to complete this stylistic breakthrough completely in another commission, the two-storey rows (1922–3), built as part of Amsterdam's Betondorp concrete village.

Van Loghem's architecture was from the beginning animated by his commitment to socialism. In 1926–7 he visited the USSR; adapting to primitive circumstances, he built a school and housing blocks in Kemerovo, Siberia, using log construction and brick. Such pragmatism continued to be characteristic of his work after his return to the Netherlands. He settled in Rotterdam and became a member of DE OPBOUW; his was one of the influences that made this architects' group increasingly radical; he also became a member of CIAM.

Although van Loghem built one of Europe's finest International style buildings, the Blauwvoet Rest Home (1930), Driebergen, his work in the 1930s also continued to develop the more modelled brick version of Functionalism that he had begun in the 1920s. His largest and best-known building, the Sports Fund Swimming-baths (1932–5) in Haarlem, is basically a metal shed enclosing the pool area, but the ancillary rooms are placed in a varied composition of lower tan brick volumes. His two books, *Bouwen* (1932) and *Acoustisch en thermaal bouwen* (1936), were both significant manifestations of idealistic pre-war Functionalism in the Netherlands.

#### WRITINGS
*Bouwen/Bauen/Bâtir/Building* (Amsterdam, 1932; *R* Nijmegen, 1988)
*Acoustisch en thermaal bouwen* (Amsterdam, 1936)

#### BIBLIOGRAPHY
G. Fanelli: *Architettura moderna* (1968)
*Plan*, 12 (1971) [whole issue]
B. Colenbrander: 'J. B. van Loghem, een strijdbaar architect' [J. B. van Loghem, a combative architect], *Het Nieuwe Bouwen: Voorgeschiedenis* (Delft, 1982), pp. 121–34
B. Rebel: *Het Nieuwe Bouwen* (The Hague, 1983)

J. P. BAETEN

**Logteren, van.** Dutch family of sculptors. Coming after Hendrick de Keyser and Artus Quellinus (i), the van Logterens formed the third and final high-point in the late Baroque sculpture of the northern Netherlands, developing in Amsterdam a remarkable and individual late Louis XIV style.

**(1) Ignatius van Logteren** (*b* Amsterdam, *bapt* 7 June 1685; *d* Amsterdam, *bur* 4 Nov 1732). He was the son of a painter, Jan van Logteren ( *fl c.* 1685–c. 1709), and trained with his father and possibly with Johannes Blommendael; he submitted his masterpiece in 1709. He worked in marble, sandstone, stucco, terracotta, palmwood and oak and was primarily known as 'statuarius', executing sculptures for country houses and gardens in the neighbourhood of Amsterdam. He also produced a considerable amount of architectural sculpture and made decoration for interiors, collaborating with the architects Daniel Marot I and Coulon. His style developed from that of Artus Quellinus (i) and Rombout Verhulst but was also influenced by some of the more recent developments in Italy, France and Flanders; it is characterized by classicism, combined with a strongly personal and harmonious lyricism. Van

Logteren's works in Amsterdam include the sandstone fountain at the Frankendaal house (1714); the façade (1717) of Herengracht 539; and the cornice and staircase (1731) of Herengracht 476. He also executed the exterior and interior of 'Beeckestijn' (1718) in Velsen, near Haarlem. His statue of *Flora* (marble, 1717) is in the Rijksmuseum, Amsterdam.

**(2) Jan van Logteren** (*b* Amsterdam, *bapt* 9 March 1709; *d* Amsterdam, *bur* 11 Oct 1745). Son of (1) Ignatius van Logteren. He was his father's pupil and assistant and perpetuated his style. He worked mostly in Amsterdam and Haarlem. His sensitive style can be distinguished from that of his father by the incorporation of Régence, Rocaille and even early Romantic elements. His works in Amsterdam include the interior stucco decoration (1733) of Herengracht 168 and the exterior and interior work (1736) at Herengracht 475. In Haarlem Jan van Logteren executed the organ of the Grote Kerk and the exterior and interior of Kruisweg 45 (both 1735-8). In Loenen, near Utrecht, he was responsible for the interior stucco decoration of 'Nieuwerhoek'. He also made garden statues for 'Oostermeer' in Oudekerk, near Amsterdam, and for 'Manpad' in Bennebroek, near Haarlem (both 1734; Amsterdam, Rijksmus.).

BIBLIOGRAPHY
J. Knoef: 'I. en J. van Logteren', *Oud-Holland*, xliii (1926), pp. 153–61
P. M. Fischer: 'Eighteenth-century Dutch Sculpture', *Apollo*, xcvi (1972), pp. 396–405
C. C. G. Quarles van Ufford: *Catalogus van overwegend Amsterdamse architectuur- en decoratieontwerpen* [Catalogue of architectural and decorative designs, principally in Amsterdam] (diss., Rijksuniv. Utrecht, 1972)
P. M. Fischer: 'Flora en Bacchus en de beeldhouwers van Logteren', *Bull. Rijksmus.*, xxxi (1982), pp. 3–6
——: 'De beeldhouwers van Logteren en het Amsterdamse gevelornament' [The van Logteren sculptors and Amsterdam gable decoration], *De Lamp*, xvii (1983), pp. 29–31
——: 'Die fontein van Frankendaal', *Ons Amsterdam*, xxxvii (1985), pp. 42–7
                                      PIETER M. FISCHER

**Lohse, Richard Paul** (*b* Zurich, 13 Sept 1902; *d* Zurich, 1988). Swiss painter, draughtsman, printmaker and writer. He studied at the Kunstgewerbeschule in Zurich from 1920 to 1924 while also working in an advertising studio from 1922 to 1927. He began painting landscapes and still-lifes under the influence of late Cubism in 1925–6 and in 1940 produced his first drawings of diagonal, vertical and horizontal structures. These led to paintings such as *Transformation of Four Identical Figures* (1942; Basle, Kstmus.), which were influenced by Constructivism in their use of diagonals and groups of shapes ranged on a flatly painted background. During this period Lohse was very active as a poster designer and as a vigorous promoter of the avant-garde: in 1933 he met Paul Klee and a number of other leading artists; in 1937 he co-founded the Allianz Vereinigung Moderner Schweizer Künstler with Leo Leuppi (1893–1972); he joined the Schweizerischer Werkbund in 1942; and he contributed to the *Abstrakt/Konkret* review in 1944–5.

From 1943 Lohse based his work exclusively on horizontal and vertical elements, in response to the art of Mondrian, Bart van der Leck and Theo van Doesburg and to the work produced by Josef Albers at the Bauhaus. The paintings that he began producing during this period, such as *Elements in Rows Concentrated in Rhythmic Groups* (oil on canvas, 900×900 mm, 1946–56; Aarau, Aargauer Ksthaus), demonstrate his rigorous approach to geometric abstraction; he preferred the term 'systemic art' to Concrete art. Lohse thought that everything in a painting could and should be controlled, from its initial development to its completion, with the aim of eliminating all signs of individuality or subjectivity.

Lohse's formal vocabulary consisted of neutral, anonymous and easily readable forms such as lines, squares and multiples of squares, arranged as a flat design in order to define the total field of the picture as an orthogonal structure without creating motifs or indulging in figure–ground relationships. He chose colours on strict principles and applied them without visible signs of brushwork. Composition was entirely programmed, with colours and shapes numbered and deployed in measurable quantities; the size of a picture was dictated by a multiple of the basic unit chosen as the point of departure.

By such means Lohse's paintings became visual illustrations of a system, as indicated by his use of titles such as *Twelve Vertical Progressions and Twelve Horizontal Progressions* (see fig.). The 12 vertical bands of different width and colour in this picture are arranged in relation to spaces that increase in size along the horizontal on a mathematical principle, while each of the lines is divided from top to bottom into 12 different coloured segments, the lengths of which are determined on the same principle. The 12 colours are used in equal quantities but always in a new position on the vertical line or horizontal row.

All of Lohse's later work was devoted to the systematic exploration of themes based on two categories, which he himself called modular orders and serial orders. He intended to create a series of extremely varied compositions based on the symmetry of one or more axes, rotation,

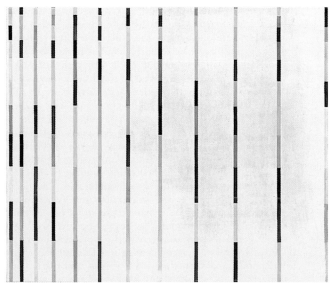

Richard Paul Lohse: *Twelve Vertical Progressions and Twelve Horizontal Progressions*, oil on canvas, 780×900 mm, 1943–4 (Zurich, Richard Paul Lohse Stiftung)

asymmetry, equality of colour and shape, and a limited or unlimited number of structures. This approach, which involved the precise planning of each painting in the form of a drawing, led Lohse to a philosophical system that he applied not only to typography and poster art, but also to architecture and interior environments, for example in his *Wall Arrangement in Rows of Complementary Colours* (1982; see Albrecht and others, 1984, pp. 294–5) for the Staatsarchiv des Kantons Zürich, designed by the architect Jakob Schilling. His ideas on such matters were propagated in his writings, notably for the review *Bauen+Wohnen*, of which he was co-editor from 1947 to 1955; he was also joint editor of *Neue Grafik* from 1959. Since he regarded his serial compositions as models of democratic organization, in so far as all their elements were interdependent but equal, Lohse also took an active interest in the artist's political engagement with society and in this way formed part of the tradition of Constructivism exemplified by artists such as van Doesburg, El Lissitzky and Moholy-Nagy. Lohse made a strong case for an extrovert, rational art with a universal appeal, and he exercised a profound influence on artists in Switzerland and in Europe at large.

*See also* COLD ART.

### BIBLIOGRAPHY

H. Neuberg and others: *Richard P. Lohse* (Teufen, 1962)
*Richard Paul Lohse* (exh. cat., Berne, Ksthalle, 1970)
E. Gomringer and others: *Richard Paul Lohse: Modulare und serielle Ordnungen* (Cologne, 1973)
H. J. Albrecht and others: *Richard Paul Lohse: Modulare und serielle Ordnungen, 1943–84/Modular and Serial Orders, 1943–84* (Zurich, 1984) [Ger., Fr. and Eng. text]
H.-P. Riese and F. W. Heckmanns: *Richard Paul Lohse: Drawings, 1935–1985*, foreword D. Bachmann (New York, 1986)
*Richard Paul Lohse* (exh. cat. by S. Lemoine, Grenoble, Mus. Grenoble, 1988)

SERGE LEMOINE

**Lohuizen-de Leeuw, Johanna Engelberta van** (*b* Amsterdam, 1919; *d* Amsterdam, 8 Dec 1983). Dutch historian. After spending her early years in the USA, which led to early proficiency in English, she studied Indian and Indo-Javanese subjects at the Rijksuniversiteit, Leiden, under Jean Philippe Vogel and Nicholaas Johannes Krom and learned Sanskrit and Pali. When the university was closed during World War II, she was briefly librarian at the Kern Institute in Leiden and then went to the Rijksuniversiteit te Utrecht, Utrecht, where she studied under Jan Gonda. Her dissertation—a study of art in north India from the 1st century BC to 3rd century AD—was published as *The 'Scythian' Period* in 1949. She was appointed lecturer at Cambridge University in 1951 and the same year went on her first visit to South Asia. In 1959 she was appointed Professor of South and South-east Asian Archaeology at the Universiteit van Amsterdam, Amsterdam, where she remained for most of her later career, founding the Institute of South Asian Archaeology. In 1977 she was elected Research Fellow at Cambridge University and was instrumental in establishing the Ancient India and Iran Trust (founded 1979, in Cambridge). Her published writings, which are mainly in English, embrace many topics, including the architecture and arts of Afghanistan, Pakistan, India, Sri Lanka and South-east Asia, whether Hindu, Buddhist or Jaina, and ranging from prehistoric to modern times. Her most notable achievement was her work on the Kushana art of Mathura and Gandhara, and she made important contributions to subjects as diverse as the stupa in Indonesia, pre-Islamic antiquities in Sind, Indian ivories, Rajput sculptures and the temples of Borobudur. She also produced a descriptive catalogue of the Indian sculptures in the Eduard von der Heydt collection.

### WRITINGS

*The 'Scythian' Period: An Approach to the History, Art, Epigraphy and Palaeography of North India from the 1st Century B.C. to the 3rd Century A.D.* (Leiden, 1949)
*Indische Skulpturen der Sammlung Eduard von der Heydt: Beschreibender Katalog* (Zurich, n.d. [1964])
'Gandhāra and Mathurā: Their Cultural Relationship', *Aspects of Indian Art: Papers Presented in a Symposium at the Los Angeles County Museum of Art: Los Angeles, 1970*, pp. 27–43

### BIBLIOGRAPHY

J. M. Rosenfield: Obituary, *Archvs Asian A.*, xxxvii (1984), pp. 109–10
D. M. Srinivasan: Obituary, *Artibus Asiae*, xlvi (1985), pp. 149–53
J. Boisselier: Obituary, *A. Asiatiques*, xlii (1987), pp. 102–4 [incl. bibliog. of writings]

S. J. VERNOIT

**Loir.** French family of artists.

**(1) Nicolas-Pierre Loir** (*b* Paris, 1624; *d* Paris, 6 May 1679). Painter and engraver. He was the son of a goldsmith and studied with Simon Vouet and Sébastien Bourdon. He was most influenced, however, by Nicolas Poussin during a visit to Italy (1647–9) and is said to have made copies of his work. On his return to France he was commissioned in 1650 to paint the May of Notre-Dame, a painting annually presented by the goldsmiths' guild, on a subject from the Acts of the Apostles. Loir's painting (*in situ*) was *St Paul Striking Blind the Sorcerer Elymas*: it was strongly influenced by Raphael. Working for Parisian collectors, he painted altarpieces for churches, such as *St Mary of Egypt* (Marseille, Mus. B.-A.), and decorations for town houses, such as the Hôtel de Vigny and the Hôtel de La Ferté-Senneterre (destr.). He executed several paintings in the tradition of Poussin on biblical subjects; these included *Eliezer and Rebecca* (Angers, Mus. B.-A.). He also painted a number of versions of the *Holy Family*, which he himself engraved several times. In 1663 he was admitted (*reçu*) by the Académie Royale de Peinture et de Sculpture on the recommendation of Charles Le Brun and Louis XIV himself, but did not submit his *morceau de réception* until 1666. This painting, the *Allegory of the Progress of the Arts* (Versailles, Château), shows the influence of both Le Brun and Poussin. From 1668 he received a regular pension from the King and was mostly employed on royal building projects: he worked at the Gobelins, Saint-Germain-en-Laye, and particularly at the Tuileries, Paris (destr.), and at Versailles, for which he painted seven pictures (1671–9) for the Appartement de la Reine, of which one survives (Bourg-en-Bresse, Mus. Ain.). Three were exhibited at the Salon of 1673. Loir was a skilful and inventive painter but lacked inspiration. He helped to propagate Poussin's academic classicism in the age of Louis XIV.

### BIBLIOGRAPHY

H. Jouin, ed.: *Conférences de l'Académie royale de peinture et de sculpture* (Paris, 1883), pp. 100–03
G. Wildenstein: 'Les Vierges de Nicolas Loir: Contribution à l'histoire de l'académisme', *Gaz. B.-A.*, n. s. 5, liii (1959), pp. 145–52

A. Schnapper: 'De Nicolas Loir à Jean Jouvenet: Quelques traces de Poussin dans le troisième tiers du XVIIe siècle', *Rev. Louvre*, 3 (1962), pp. 115–22

N. Reynaud and J. Vilain: 'Fragments retrouvés de la décoration du grand appartement de la reine Marie-Thérèse à Versailles', *Rev. Louvre*, 4–5 (1970), pp. 231–8

*Le Classicisme français: Masterpieces of Seventeenth-century Painting* (exh. cat. by S. Laveissière, Dublin, N.G., 1985), pp. 44–5

STÉPHANE LOIRE

**(2) Alexis Loir I** (*b* Paris, 1640; *d* Paris, 14 or 15 Jan 1713). Silversmith and engraver, brother of (1) Nicolas-Pierre Loir. He probably became a master in the silversmiths' guild before 1666, when he was described as having completed work in silver. He made furniture and large ornamental silver pieces for Louis XIV between 1666 and 1686, including vases for orange trees (1666), basins (by 1684) and chandeliers (1686), as well as a balustrade (1681–2) for the king's bedchamber made in collaboration with Claude de Villers (*d* 1678). No example of Loir's silver has survived, but the solid, sculptural character of his work is illustrated in his engravings, for example *Desseins de brasiers dont les ornements peuvent servir aux cuvettes, tables, et autres ouvrages d'orfèvrerie inventés et gravés par A. Loir* (n.d.). On 5 March 1678 Loir was accepted as an amateur member of the Académie Royale following his presentation of an engraving after a painting by Nicolas Poussin. Loir was appointed an honorary councillor of the Académie Royale in 1686 and served as warden (1697), senior warden (1698) and consul (1699) of the silversmiths' guild. He had retired by 1702 when he was listed as one of the silversmiths in Paris without a shop.

BIBLIOGRAPHY

H. Nocq: *Le Poinçon de Paris* (Paris, 1926–31), iii, pp. 150–52

CLARE LE CORBEILLER

**(3) Alexis Loir III** (*b* Paris, 1712; *d* Paris, 18 Aug 1785). Pastellist and sculptor, probably great-nephew of (2) Alexis Loir I. He was first recorded in Rome in 1739, when Pier Leone Ghezzi drew his portrait (Rome, Vatican, Biblioteca Apostolica). In 1746 he was approved (*agréé*) by the Académie Royale de Peinture et de Sculpture in Paris, presenting pastel portraits and two sculptures—a bust of *Carle Vanloo* (untraced) and a terracotta statuette of *Marsyas* (Paris, Louvre). He exhibited pastel portraits at the Salons of 1747, 1748 and 1759 but did not again exhibit sculpture until 1785, when he sent to the Salon a bust of *Jean de Jullienne* (1746; untraced). That Alexis Loir III counted so celebrated a collector and connoisseur as Jullienne among his patrons suggests that he was highly thought of by his contemporaries. The fact that so little is known of his life and work is in part explained by the long periods he spent outside Paris. In 1753 he visited England and in 1763 went to Russia, where he apparently stayed until *c.* 1769. In 1772 he settled for several years in Béarn in south-west France. A delicate, classicizing terracotta relief of *Vestals Sacrificing* (exh. London, Heim Gal., 1979, no. 25; untraced) dated that year is evidence of Loir's continuing activity as a sculptor. In 1779 he was finally received (*reçu*) as a member of the Académie Royale with a pastel portrait of the painter *Clément Belle* (Paris, Louvre) as his *morceau de réception*. The austere composition and sombre colours of this large, ambitious work, and the severe face of the sitter suggest a deliberate avoidance of Rococo grace. In 1783 Loir became a councillor at the Académie Royale.

BIBLIOGRAPHY

Thieme–Becker

E. Dacier and P. Ratouis de Limay: *Pastels français des XVIIe et XVIIIe siècles* (Paris, 1927), p. 27 and pl. 86

EMMA BARKER

**(4) Marianne Loir** (*fl* second half of 18th century). Painter, sister of (3) Alexis Loir. Little is known about her life, but there is documentary evidence of her presence in Paris during the second half of the 18th century. She is traditionally thought to have studied in Rome under Jean-François de Troy, who was Director of the Académie de France in 1738; this is very plausible, because there is no mention of her presence in Paris between 1738 and 1746. Possibly because it was difficult for her to enter the Academy and establish a reputation in Paris, she left the city after 1760 to build up a clientele in the provinces. She worked as a portrait painter in the south of France, as she became a member of the Marseille Academy in 1762 and executed commissions in both Pau and Toulouse. Only ten of her portraits are known, dated between 1745 and 1769. The majority of her subjects were women from well-off or aristocratic backgrounds. Her handsomely executed works display a technique and predominantly grey-blue colouring similar to those of Louis Tocqué and Jean-Marc Nattier, with whose oeuvre her paintings are sometimes confused, for example *Portrait of ?Marchioness du Châtelet* (Bordeaux, Mus. B.-A.).

BIBLIOGRAPHY

*Women Artists* (exh. cat., ed. A. Sutherland Harris and L. Nochlin; Los Angeles, CA, Co. Mus. A.; 1976), pp. 167–8

PHILIPPE NUSBAUMER

**Lois** [Loys], **Jacob** (*fl* 1634; *d* Rotterdam, 31 Aug 1676). Dutch architect. He probably received no formal training in architecture but taught himself the principles: he is known to have possessed the most important architectural books of his time. The only building attributable to him is the former Gemeenlandshuis of Sliedrecht, or 'Schielands-huis', in Rotterdam (1662), a monumental free-standing structure clad entirely in sandstone. Its façade consists of a low ground floor above which are two storeys, articulated by superimposed tiers of pilasters. The central projection of the façade has free-standing columns at the angles and extends upwards to a large attic, which is crowned by a pediment containing sculpture. The entrance has a perron and is hooded over with an opulently decorated balcony on coupled free-standing columns. This imposing building was erected in the classical style of Pieter Post (whose advice may have been solicited), but the façade exhibits a robust, Baroque appearance. The Schielandshuis became the home of the Museum Boymans (1849–1958), though gutted by fire in 1864. It was subsequently rebuilt, retaining the old façades, and now houses the Historisch Museum of Rotterdam. In 1986 the building was thoroughly restored.

BIBLIOGRAPHY

Thieme–Becker

F. A. J. Vermeulen: *Handboek tot de geschiedenis der Nederlandsche bouwkunst* [History of Dutch architecture], iii (The Hague, 1941)

S. J. Fockema Andreae and others: *Duizend jaar bouwen in Nederland* [One thousand years of Dutch architecture], ii (Amsterdam, 1957)

PAUL H. REM

**Loiseau, Gustave** (*b* Paris, 3 Oct 1865; *d* Paris, 10 Oct 1935). French painter. He was apprenticed first to a butcher and in 1880 to a house painter. It was not until 1887, when he received a small inheritance, that he was able to devote himself to painting. He spent a year studying modelling and design at the Ecole des Arts Décoratifs in Paris and then entered the studio of the French landscape painter Fernand Just Quignon (*b* 1854) for six months in 1889. After settling in 1890 in Pont-Aven in Brittany, where he met the painters Maxime Maufra and Henri Moret (1856–1913), he produced such carefully executed works as the *Green Rocks* (1893; Geneva, Petit Pal.). It was not until 1894, however, that he met Gauguin on the latter's return from Tahiti, and though he did not accept Gauguin's synthetist ideas the encounter led to a stronger structure and freer brushstrokes in his subsequent work.

Loiseau first exhibited his work at the Salon des Indépendants in Paris in 1893, showing also at the Salon de la Société Nationale in 1895 and from 1903 to 1930 at the Salon d'Automne. The contract he received in 1897 from Paul Durand-Ruel gave him the freedom to travel through northern France and the Channel coast, in particular through the valleys of the Oise, the Seine and the Eure, with Pont-Aven as his base in the summers. This led to such works as *Snowstorm* (1899) and *Dieppe* (1905; both Geneva, Petit Pal.), which, though using an Impressionist brushstroke, appear less spontaneous than Impressionist works. Just before World War I Loiseau turned to subjects from the Ile de France, such as *Village in the Snow (Ile de France)* (1913; priv. col., see exh. cat., pl. 17). Although he continued to travel in the north from the 1920s until his death, he specialized during this period in subjects from the Seine Valley and Paris and also ventured down to the Dordogne region. In his later works he used careful, cross-hatched brushstrokes and a more restrained palette, as in *Avenue de Friedland, Paris* (1925; Geneva, Petit Pal.).

BIBLIOGRAPHY

Thiébault-Sisson: *Gustave Loiseau* (Paris, 1930)
*Gustave Loiseau* (exh. cat. by M.-D. Baranger, Paris, Didier Imbert F.A., 1985)

**Loisel, Robert** (*fl* 1383–1408). French sculptor. He is first mentioned in a document of 1383 recording payment for the mausoleum of *Isabelle of France*, daughter of Philip VI (*reg* 1328–50) and wife of Peter I, Duke of Bourbon (*reg* 1341–56), which was located in the church of the Cordeliers (destr.), Paris. As the pupil and successor of the sculptor Jean de Liège (i), Loisel received payment in 1384 for the liquidation of works remaining in the workshop after the death of his master. Among these, the double tomb of *Blanche, Duchess of Orléans* (Saint-Denis Abbey) and *Marie of France* (bust, New York, Met.; for illustration *see* JEAN DE LIÈGE (i)), daughters of Charles IV (*reg* 1322–8), was probably virtually complete; Loisel seems to have carved the base and installed the ensemble at Saint-Denis Abbey. Between 1389 and 1397 he collaborated with Thomas Privé on the execution of the tomb of the Constable of France *Bertrand du Guesclin* (*d* 1380), which was installed at Saint-Denis in the chapel where Charles V and his queen were also interred. The tomb is described (Vitry and Brière) as having an alabaster gisant, which rested on a base of black marble. The effigy (*in situ*), wearing armour, is notable for the realistic portrayal of du Guesclin's unattractive appearance. In 1392 Loisel is listed among those employed by Philip the Bold, Duke of Burgundy, at his capital in Dijon. He is last documented in a contract of 1408 with the sacristan of St Martin-du-Champs for the execution of a lectern with an eagle (untraced).

BIBLIOGRAPHY

Lami; Thieme–Becker
P. Vitry and G. Brière: *L'Eglise abbatiale de Saint-Denis et ses tombeaux* (Paris, 1925), p. 157
*Les Fastes du gothique: Le Siècle de Charles V* (exh. cat., Paris, Grand Pal., 1981–2), no. 78

DOROTHY GILLERMAN

**Lojze, Aloysius.** *See* SPAZZAPAN, LUIGI.

**Lokroi Epizephyrioi** [Lat. Locri Epizephyrii]. Greek colony founded from Lokris in the first half of the 7th century BC on the narrow coastal plain of eastern Calabria, Italy, about 80 km from Rhegion. The site had been inhabited since the 9th century BC by Italiote tribesmen, and it was of great importance because it was on the ancient coast road, and it constituted the last mainland port for ships bound for Sicily. Two important temples were found on the site. That of Marasà was built in the 7th century BC and enlarged in the 6th century BC. It was rebuilt in the late 5th century BC as a larger Ionic structure, fronted by a great altar and surmounted by a marble acroterion representing a Nereid flanked by the Dioscuroi on horseback supported by Tritons (Reggio Calabria, Mus. N.). The temple of Casa Marafioti, perhaps dedicated to Olympian Zeus, dates to the 5th century BC and is in the Doric order with some Ionic features. It was also surmounted by elaborate acroteria, this time of terracotta, consisting of men riding horses supported by sphinxes (Reggio Calabria, Mus. N.). Near by is a well-preserved theatre (3rd century BC), close to which were found 37 bronze tablets that relate to the administration and public buildings of the city (Reggio Calabria, Mus. N.). Much of the 7-km-long city wall, dating to the 4th century BC, can still be traced, and some streets and houses are visible in the Centocamere area.

The Sanctuary of Persephone outside the city walls contained hundreds of *pinakes*, votive terracotta tablets dating to the first half of the 5th century BC (Reggio Calabria, Mus. N., and Taranto, Mus. N.). They are rectangular and carry brightly painted relief scenes of the cult of Persephone. Lokroi was also famous for the production and export of bronze mirrors with handles in the shape of human figures and may have produced two masterpieces of Early Classical sculpture: the Ludovisi Throne (*c*. 460 BC; Rome, Mus. N. Romano) and the Boston Throne (?*c*. 460 BC; Boston, MA, Mus. F.A.).

BIBLIOGRAPHY

*Enc. A. Ant.*: 'Locri Epizefiri'
A. De Franciscis: *Ricerche sulla topografia e i monumenti di Locri Epizefiri*, i (Naples, 1971)
——: *Stato e società in Locri Epizefiri* (Naples, 1972)

M. Guido: *Southern Italy: An Archaeological Guide* (London, 1972), pp. 170–76, 180–82

S. Moscati: *Italia archeologica*, i (Novara, 1973), pp. 52–8

*Le tavole di Locri: Atti del colloquio: Napoli, 1977*

A. De Franciscis: *Il santuario di Marasà in Locri Epizefiri*, Monumenti antichi della Magna Grecia (Naples, 1979)

F. B. SEAR

**Loma Negra.** *See* VICÚS.

**Lomazzo, Giovanni Paolo** [Gianpaolo] (*b* Milan, 26 April 1538; *d* Milan, 13 Feb 1600). Italian writer, painter and draughtsman. He is best known for his writings, which include metaphysical discussions of the philosophy of artistic creation at levels of complexity to rival those from any period. He was a conspicuous figure in artistic and intellectual circles in northern Italy and a painter of some reputation beyond Milan, but those of his works that survive do not suggest a talent of a higher order than that of a skilled late Mannerist working in an eclectic version of the Lombard style.

1. Early career: paintings and literary activities, 1560–71. 2. Later career: theoretical writings, 1571–91.

1. EARLY CAREER: PAINTINGS AND LITERARY AC-TIVITIES, 1560–71. Born to a family of some social status, Lomazzo appears to have received a better education than most painters. Early indications of his artistic abilities led to his studying with the little-known Giovanni Battista della Cerva (*fl* ?1540–48), an assistant of Gaudenzio Ferrari (whom Lomazzo appears to have regarded as his real master). Lomazzo's autobiography, published with his *Rime* in 1587, indicates that he received a steady stream of commissions for murals and altarpieces, once he became an independent master. His many connections, among whom was Giuliano Goselini (1525–87), secretary to successive dukes of Milan and a poet of some note, helped to ensure that he was also asked to supply numerous portraits of friends and aristocratic patrons.

He moved at ease within literary circles in Milan and became closely involved in an extraordinary burlesque 'academy' of letters. The Accademiglia dra Vall d'Bregn, founded in 1560, was dedicated to a contrived dialect, which purported to be the ancient language of Swiss wine porters working in Lombardy. The 160 members of the 'academy' were devoted both to social pleasures and to the promotion of a body of serio-comic literature in their deliberately arcane dialect.

In 1562 his frescoed copy (destr.) of Leonardo's *Last Supper* (Milan, S Maria delle Grazie) made for the refectory of the convent of S Maria della Pace, Milan, met with a hostile reception, and Lomazzo left Milan to travel within Italy and perhaps to Flanders, avidly observing a wide range of art. The formative influences on Lomazzo's style were the painters whose works he had seen in Milan, including, besides Leonardo, the Lombard Mannerists such as Aurelio Luini (1530–93) and Gaudenzio Ferrari, and the Bolognese Pellegrino Tibaldi. In these travels he developed a profound admiration for the draughtsmanship of Raphael and Michelangelo (whose 'serpentine' figure style he especially praised), while looking towards the Venetian masters for the handling of colour. By his own testimony he was also affected by the inventiveness of

Albrecht Dürer, whom he called 'the great Druid'. The resulting eclecticism of his style is typical of academic Mannerism in northern Italy in the later part of the 16th century.

On his return to Milan in 1565, he undertook many religious and secular works, most of which have been lost or destroyed or remain unidentified. His major surviving cycle of religious paintings (1565) is in the Foppa Chapel of S Marco, Milan. The relatively sober altarpiece of the *Virgin and SS Peter, Paul and Augustine* is dated 1571. The cupola is decorated with grandiloquent images of the *Prophets and Sibyls*, and the apsidal semi-dome with a tumultuous vision of the angelic *Paradise*. The narratives on the walls depict the *Conversion of Saul* (almost obliter-ated) and the *Fall of Simon Magus*, who plunges headlong into the space of the mural in abrupt perspective. In his figure style Lomazzo strove to combine monumentality and complexity, exploiting rhetorical gestures to convey meaning. The vault figures are strongly foreshortened, and a preparatory drawing (Princeton U., NJ, A. Mus.; see fig.) shows that he used the *quadratura* technique of schema-tizing the figure into a series of box-like components to facilitate the placing of limbs in perspective.

Giovanni Paolo Lomazzo: *Figure Study*, pen and brown ink with black and red chalk, 190×120 mm, *c.* 1565 (Princeton, NJ, Princeton University, Art Museum); for the prophet in the vault fresco (1565), Foppa Chapel, S Marco, Milan

In 1568 Lomazzo became 'Abbot' or '*Nabad*' of the Accademiglia, and a collection of his own literary compositions was published in 1589 as *Rabisch dra Accademiglia dor compà Zavargna, Nabad dra Vall d'Bregn*. It is in this role that Lomazzo (or 'Zavargna', to give him his dialect name) appears in his *Self-portrait as Abbot of the Accademiglia* (1568; Milan, Brera). This iconographically complex work, painted in a chiaroscuro style that owes as much to Giorgione or Dosso Dossi as to Leonardo or his fellow Milanese artists, is his masterpiece as a painter of secular subjects. The image makes clear allusions to Bacchus as protector of the 'academy' and is loaded with other symbolic references. For instance, the robe signifies the weighty problems of his office, while the straw hat evokes humility. The compasses obviously refer to his insistence on mathematical precision, but, in conjunction with his riveting stare, may also allude to the Michelangelesque dictum that the painter should possess compasses in his eyes rather than his hands.

Lomazzo's dated pictures include: a massive *Quadragesimal Supper* ('Lenten Supper'; 1567; Piacenza, S Agostino; destr. but known through photographs and preparatory drawings in Windsor Castle, Royal Lib., and Oxford, Christ Church); a *Madonna di S Michele* (1570; Busto Arsizio, S Maria di Piazza) for S Romano, Lodi, and a *Crucifixion with the Virgin, St John and Mary Magdalene* (1571; Milan, Brera, on dep. Milan, Semin. Vescovile) for S Giovanni in Conca, Milan. His burgeoning career as a painter was cut short from 1571 by the progressive loss of his sight, and he subsequently devoted himself to his writings in art theory and other literary genres. His work as a painter has not been fully studied, and most of his activity as a portrait painter remains obscure. His leading pupil was Ambrogio Figino, who shared his academic instincts.

2. LATER CAREER: THEORETICAL WRITINGS, 1571–91. In 1584 Lomazzo published his *Trattato dell'arte de la pittura* and in 1590 his *Idea del tempio della pittura*, which contain his main body of writing on the visual arts. In addition to his *Rime* (1587) and *Rabisch* (1589), he also wrote a treatise on the Muses, intended to instruct painters and sculptors (*Della forma delle Muse*, 1591), and a manuscript of dreams and dialogues, *Gli sogni e ragionamento di Giovan Paolo Lomazzo milanese, con le figure de gli spiriti che li racontano* (London, BL).

In the *Trattato* and *Idea* Lomazzo aspired to create a great, unified theory for the philosophy and practice of art within the context of an elaborate cosmological scheme, which was strongly coloured by Neo-Platonism and astrology, although he also drew on a number of Aristotelian scholastic sources, including St Thomas Aquinas (*see* AESTHETICS, §II, 2). His statements on the divine origins and spiritual transmission of beauty in the *Idea* were paraphrased from the commentary *De amore* (1469) on Plato's *Symposium* by the Renaissance philosopher MARSILIO FICINO. His fusion of astrological metaphysics with late medieval science owed much to Henricus Cornelius Agrippa's *De occulta philosophia* (pubd 1533), while the direct source for his seven-part 'temple of painting' was Giulio Camillo's *L'idea del teatro* (pubd 1550). He was not unfailingly successful in welding the ideas from his various

sources into a consistent unity, and the editing of his texts reflects the problems caused by his blindness, but the whole enterprise is impressive in scope and achievement.

The *Trattato*, the longer, more rambling and scholastic of these two works, is presented in seven books. The first deals with natural and artificial proportions as the harmonic foundations for art. In an elaboration of Albrecht Dürer's theories of proportion (*see* DÜRER, (1)), expressed in the *Vier Bücher von menschlicher Proportion* (pubd 1528), Lomazzo outlined a number of systems of human proportion based on lengths both of face and of head and subsequently dealt with the proportions of children, horses and architecture. The second book is devoted to actions and gestures, establishing the principles of decorum and expression. The basic types of human nature are expounded through the four temperaments—choleric, sanguine, phlegmatic and melancholic—and in terms of the astrological influences of the seven planets. The attributes of Mars, for example, will be reflected by a fiery temperament and ruddy colouring, whereas the Sun will incline man in a majestic and 'Apollonian' direction. In Book 3 a scale of seven colours adapted from Aristotelian colour science—white, *palido* (pale or light violet), yellow, red, purple, green and black—is associated with the planets in such a way that the expressive qualities of each colour are identified with the characters of the deities. In his discussion of light in Book 4 he is predisposed to adopt the old and largely discredited notion from the Platonic tradition that seeing rays are emitted from the eye, although his system of classification for light and its behaviour is largely derived from medieval optical science, particularly that of Erasmus Witelo (*c.* 1233–*c.* 1278), whose treatise on optics, *Perspectiva*, dates from the early 1270s (*see* AESTHETICS, §II, 2). His obsession with classifying and naming categories on the basis of book learning did not prevent Lomazzo here as elsewhere from making a series of sharply perceptive observations of actual phenomena. The spiritual power of light finds practical expression in art in the science of perspective, which he treated theoretically in Book 5 and practically in Book 6. Dealing with perspective constructions wholly in words, with no diagrams, causes virtually insuperable problems in understanding his techniques, but his emphasis on the need to undertake meticulous mathematical construction rather than relying on judgement by eye emerges clearly. His insistence is underlined by his devotion to the perspectival tradition of his Milanese predecessors, above all Bramantino, whose lost writings he quoted. The long sixth and seventh books show how the theories should be put into practice in actual compositions and within various categories of subject. Citing a welter of literary and visual sources, he demonstrated how secular and religious narratives should be depicted and how the painter's cast of characters, such as the saints and planetary gods, should be portrayed.

His *Idea* is dedicated to the exposition of a temple, whose architectural components signify the seven parts of painting. The temple is round in plan and capped by a dome and lantern, rather in the manner of Donato Bramante's *Tempietto* (1499–1502) in the courtyard of S Pietro in Montorio, Rome. The role of the peristyle columns is performed by caryatid statues of each of the seven 'governors' of art—Michelangelo, Gaudenzio Ferrari, Polidoro da Caravaggio, Leonardo, Raphael, Andrea Mantegna and Titian. The walls of the temple are built, in ascending order, from proportion, motion, colour, light and perspective (the five 'theories' of painting), while the dome and lantern signify composition and *forma* (the two parts of 'practice'). *Forma* embodies 'all that may be occasioned in the imagination and may be seen by the eye'. Each of the governors corresponds to a planet—Michelangelo to Saturn, Gaudenzio to Jupiter, Polidoro to Mars, Leonardo to the Sun, Raphael to Venus, Mantegna to Mercury and Titian to the Moon. These painters are associated with a series of corresponding attributes, including the elements, the seasons, seven metals and seven animals. The artistic temperament of each artist mirrors that of his planetary deity in such a way as to exercise a characteristic influence over his mastery of each of the seven parts of painting. Although each governor is not precisely associated with a particular part of painting, the artists do show special excellence in certain fields. Raphael is particularly commended for proportion, as is Michelangelo, while a high command of motion is demonstrated by Raphael, Gaudenzio, Polidoro, Michelangelo and Leonardo. Titian, not surprisingly, is accorded particular praise for his handling of colour and shares mastery of light with Leonardo and Raphael.

Although there has been a tendency to dismiss Lomazzo's system as an elaborate piece of astrological nonsense, there is something heroic in his ability to relate the broadest of cosmologies to carefully observed details of the practice of art. His was the first developed and coherent attempt both to demonstrate the universal rules of art as reflections of a single source of divine beauty and to explain how it was possible for different artists to possess different styles of equal merit. His treatises were supreme representatives of the often arcane complexities of late Mannerist art and thought. They proved to be highly vulnerable to any change of taste towards simpler systems, whether naturalistic or idealizing, such as occurred around 1600 in early Baroque theories and practice. Neither treatise was to appear in a second Italian edition until over 200 years later. An English translation by Richard Haydocke of the greater part of the first five books of the *Trattato* was published in 1598, and a French translation of the first book appeared in 1649. Both translations used illustrations based on Dürer's *Vier Bücher*. The modern editions of his writings by Robert Klein and Roberto Ciardi present an opportunity to resurrect Lomazzo from the unjustified neglect into which he fell after his death.

### WRITINGS

*Trattato dell'arte de la pittura* (Milan, 1584); Eng. trans. by R. Haydocke as *A Tracte Containing the Artes of Curious Paintinge, Carvinge & Buildinge* (Oxford, 1598/R 1971)
*Rime . . . divise in sette libri, nelle quali ad imitatione de' grotteschi usati da' pittori, ha cantato le lodi di Dio . . . con la vita dell'autore* (Milan, 1587)
*Rabisch dra Accademiglia dor compà Zavargna, Nabad dra Vall d'Bregn* (Milan, 1589)
*Idea del tempio della pittura* (Milan, 1590); ed. R. Klein, 2 vols (Florence, 1974)
*Della forma delle muse cavate dagli antichi autori greci e latini: Opera utilissima a' pittori e scultori* (Milan, 1591)
R. Ciardi, ed.: *Scritti sull'arte*, 2 vols (Florence, 1974)

### BIBLIOGRAPHY

E. Panofsky: *Idea: Ein Beitrag zur Begriffsgeschichte der älteren Kunsttheorie* (1924); Eng. trans. by J. J. S. Peake (Columbia, SC, 1968/R New York, 1974), pp. 95–9
E. Spina Barelli: 'Il Lomazzo e il ruolo delle personalità psicologiche nella estetica dell'ultimo manierismo Lombardo', *A. Lombarda*, iii (1958), pp. 119–24
J. Lynch: 'Giovanni Paolo Lomazzo's Self-portrait in the Brera', *Gaz. B.-A.*, 6th ser., lxiv (1964), pp. 189–97
R. Ciardi: 'Struttura e significato delle opere teoriche del Lomazzo', *Crit. A.*, xii (1965), pp. 20–30; xiii (1966), pp. 37–44
J. Lynch: 'Lomazzo and the Accademia della Valle Bregno', *A. Bull.*, xliii (1966), pp. 210–11
G. Ackerman: 'Lomazzo's Treatise on Painting', *A. Bull.*, xlix (1967), pp. 317–26
R. Klein: *La Forme et l'intelligible: Ecrits sur la Renaissance et l'art moderne* (Paris, 1970); Eng. trans. by M. Jay and L. Wieseltier (New York, 1979), pp. 43–61, 62–88, 161–9
M. Kemp: '"Equal Excellences": Lomazzo and the Explanation of Individual Style in the Visual Arts', *Ren. Stud.*, i (1987), pp. 1–26
P. Marani: *Leonardo e i Leonardeschi a Brera* (Milan, 1988), pp. 242–5
M. Kemp: *The Science of Art: Optical Themes in Western Art from Brunelleschi to Seurat* (London and New Haven, 1990), pp. 72–3, 83–4, 269–73

MARTIN KEMP

**Lombard, Lambert** (*b* Liège, 1505; *d* Liège, Aug 1566). Flemish painter, draughtsman, architect, humanist and numismatist. He belonged to the generation of artists who sought to revive Flemish painting by turning to the art of antiquity and the Italian Renaissance. However, because of his northern training, he assimilated his models with difficulty and produced a hesitant form of art, one that was academic and cold. He was nonetheless an important innovator in the Low Countries through his investigation of the forms and compositions of Classical art. He also founded the first academy of art in the Low Countries and was influential through the prime role he accorded to scholarship in the training of the artist.

After his apprenticeship in Antwerp with Jan or Arnold de Beer, Lombard continued his training in Liège and Middelburg. He was especially influenced by the Romanist painters Jan Gossart and Jan van Scorel. From 1532 Lombard is mentioned in accounts as a painter appointed to Erard de la Marck, Prince-bishop of Liège. In August 1537 Lombard left for Rome in the retinue of the English humanist Cardinal Reginald Pole (1500–58), whose circle, known for its deep religiosity and searching humanist studies, must have strongly impressed Lombard. For Cardinal Pole the painter executed a painting representing a *Tabula cebetis* (untraced). In the Eternal City Lombard studied antique and contemporary works and came into contact with Francesco Salviati and Baccio Bandinelli. On returning to Liège in 1538 or 1539, he founded his academy of art along Italian lines; among the students were Frans Floris, Willem Key, Lambert Suavius, Hubertus Goltzius and Pierre Furnius (*c.* 1549–1626). In 1557 Lombard travelled to Germany, where he copied the low reliefs on the grave monument (*c.* AD 250) at Igel (drawing, Liège, Cab. Est. & Dessins), as well as the medieval wall paintings at Schwarzrheindorf near Bonn (drawing, Rome, Gab. N. Stampe). He remained in the service of the prince-bishops of Liège until his death.

Most of Lombard's paintings have disappeared. The earliest four that can be attributed to him represent scenes from the *Life of St Denis* (?1533; now dispersed between Liège, Mus. A. Wallon and St Denis, and Brussels, Mus.

A. Anc.; *see* BELGIUM, fig. 13), which originally formed part of the predella of the altarpiece in St Denis, Liège. There are numerous motifs borrowed from Italian prints, but the forms, technique and taste for anecdote still derive from Antwerp Mannerism. In the paintings done after his Roman journey, for instance the *Rejection of Joachim's Offering* (Liège, Mus. A. Wallon; see fig.) from a series depicting the *Story of Joachim*, and the *Judith*, *Esther*, *Claudia Quinta* and the *Tiburtine Sibyl* (all Stokrooie, nr Hasselt, St Amand), the influence of antique statuary and Raphael's cartoons of the *Acts of the Apostles* is more profound and the compositions more classicizing.

Despite the scarcity of surviving paintings by Lombard, it is possible to document, better than for any other contemporary Flemish artist, his artistic and humanist interests. Nearly 500 drawings from his hand have been preserved, as well as nearly 80 engravings of his designs and a letter on art that he wrote to Vasari in 1565. Moreover, comments about him are found in the works of Goltzius, Abraham Ortelius and Jean Vivianus (*c.* 1530–98). The best source of information, however, is the biography of Lombard by his disciple Domenicus Lampsonius (1532–98), published in 1565. This text, written in the spirit of Vasari's *Vite*, is the first art-historical commentary published in the Low Countries. In it Lampsonius described his master's unbounded admiration for antiquity, his taste for Mantegna, Raphael, Michelangelo, Bandinelli and Titian, as well as for medieval works; Lampsonius

also explained Lombard's artistic theories and the significance he placed on scholarship in the training of an artist.

Lampsonius's account is confirmed by Lombard's many surviving drawings. Of these, 400 form part of the Arenberg Album (Liège, Cab. Est. & Dessins), in which there are studies done in Rome after antique statuary, as well as copies of Gallo-Roman and medieval works. Many sketches are interpretations of Italian, German, Flemish and French engravings of the 15th and 16th centuries. The Arenberg Album also includes drapery studies intended to serve as models in the academy. These reveal Lombard's desire to revive figure representation through the rational study of proportion, movement and expression. To do this, he reconstructed in a schematic fashion the classicizing figures of Raphael and his school. Such figures, cold and intellectualized, people his painted and engraved compositions. Lombard's humanist tendencies are further demonstrated by his choice of scholarly subjects: ancient history, mythography, archaeology, ancient religions, emblems and hieroglyphs. Lombard also collected and drew Roman coins, and his pupil Hubertus Goltzius wrote one of the most important numismatic treatises of the 16th century.

The 80 engravings after Lombard's designs, generally published in Antwerp by Hieronymus Cock, also illustrate humanist and allegorical subjects. Yet, sensitive to the religious problems of the age and the importance accorded to the rereading of the Bible, Lombard also took up many themes derived from the New Testament.

Lombard's architectural work remains problematic. The various town houses he built in Liège in the style of the Italian Renaissance have undergone much damage and alteration.

BIBLIOGRAPHY

Hollstein: *Dut. & Flem.*
D. Lampsonius: *Lamberti Lombardi apud Eburones pictoris celeberrimi vita* (Bruges, 1565)
J. Helbig: *Lambert Lombard: Peintre et architecte* (Brussels, 1893)
A. Goldschmidt: 'Lambert Lombard', *Jb. Preuss. Kstsamml.*, xlii (1919), pp. 206–40
J. Yernaux: 'Lambert Lombard', *Bull. Inst. Archéol. Liège.*, lxxii (1957–8), pp. 267–377
N. Dacos: *Les Peintres belges à Rome au XVIe siècle* (Brussels and Rome, 1964)
*Lambert Lombard et son temps* (exh. cat., Liège, Mus. A. Wallon, 1966)
E. Kemp and W. Kemp: 'Lambert Lombards antiquarische Theorie und Praxis', *Z. Kstgesch.*, xxxvi (1973), pp. 122–52
W. Krönig: 'Lambert Lombard', *Wallraf-Richartz-Jb.*, xxxvi (1974), pp. 105–58
*The Age of Bruegel: Netherlandish Drawings in the Sixteenth Century* (exh. cat. by J. O. Hand and others, Washington, DC, N.G.A.; New York, Pierpont Morgan Lib.; 1986–7), pp. 206–9
G. Denhaene: 'Lambert Lombard: Oeuvres peintes', *Bull. Inst. Hist. Belge Rome*, lvii (1987), pp. 71–110
——: 'L'Album d'Arenberg', *Stud. Warburg Inst.* (in preparation)

G. DENHAENE

Lambert Lombard: *Rejection of Joachim's Offering*, oil on panel, 1.12×0.80 m, after 1538 or 1539 (Liège, Musée de l'Art Wallon)

**Lombard art.** Term in general use until the mid-20th century to indicate the art forms of the Italian peninsula from AD 568 to 774 under the political control of the Lombards (*see also* MIGRATION PERIOD).

1. INTRODUCTION. Since at least the Renaissance, Lombard art had been viewed with distaste, its purported poor quality attributed to the inferior nature of the Lombard stock, physically degenerate, mentally deficient,

morally corrupt and non-Christian. It was assumed that this barbarian people caused the disintegration of the classical Early Christian tradition by introducing elements antithetical to it. Rather than the Early Christian preference for symmetry, primary colours and presentation of the world through a style of visual realism, including three-dimensional representation, Lombard art forms exploited asymmetry, colours such as orange, green and purple, and flat abstraction.

Little Lombard art has survived: unsettled conditions at the time may have deterred potential patrons from commissioning works, and most of the movable artefacts have perished. What survives, however, has been shown to represent several artistic traditions that appeared simultaneously in different centres. Rome remained the focus of traditional Early Christian forms in art and architecture, while some Irish influence came through the monastery of Bobbio, founded in 612 by the Irish monk Columban (*c.* 543–615) at the request of the Lombard King Agilulf (*reg* 590–615). Other centres of production, or at least subject to Lombard political domination, were Cividale del Friuli, the capital of the first Lombard duchy in Italy, Brescia, Pavia (the political capital) and Monza.

It is difficult to interpret the objects of this period in terms of traditional scholarly divisions. An example is the gold Gospels cover (Monza, Mus. Serpero Tesoro) given by Pope Gregory I in 603 to Queen Theodolinde (*d* 625). It is lavishly set with cloisonné garnets and Classical cameos bordering a jewelled cross on the obverse and reverse. It was an appropriate gift since the Queen was instrumental in bringing her subjects from the Arian heresy to Roman Catholicism. The object was presumably made in Rome, but the origin of the craftsmen is unknown. It has long been believed that the use of garnets in cloisonné work was introduced by the barbarians. The stones themselves had come to Europe from their source in India via the area north of the Black Sea, where they were worked by local peoples. The Gospels cover does not belong to the sedate Early Christian aesthetic: even though the design of the piece is totally symmetrical, the technique and shimmering appearance are or were associated with barbarian work. It is easier to consider both this and other objects as products of the early 7th century and to avoid the terms Lombard or barbarian, until they can be used without pejorative connotations. Another extraordinary object associated with Theodolinde is a silver-gilt platter with a hen and seven chicks (Monza, Mus. Serpero Tesoro), shown pecking at the ground. This was possibly didactic in purpose, representing Mother Church caring for the faithful. It too might have been made at Rome or possibly by metalsmiths at the Lombard court.

2. MANUSCRIPTS. Manuscript production of the Lombard period developed at the scriptorium of Bobbio. Irish in inspiration (*see* INSULAR ART, §3), its associated manuscripts are the earliest surviving to have illuminated initials, a crucial invention for the Middle Ages. Bobbio sent manuscripts north to another of Columban's foundations at Luxeuil (founded 590; destr.; Haute-Saône). These were presumably responsible for the stylistic development of the scriptorium at Luxeuil. The initial 'T' of the word '*tempore*' in one of the earliest examples (Paris, Bib. N.,

MS. lat. 9427 fol. 144) stretches the height of the page, decorating the left margin of the text. The crossbar is made up of fish, struck by a compass; two birds drawn in the same manner support the bar from the central staff. The decorative motifs are in red and green on a yellow ground.

A related manuscript, the Valerianus Gospels (*c.* 675; Munich, Bayer. Staatsbib., Clm. 6224), was written in north-east Italy and may be considered an example of the Lombard style. It displays all the basic elements of the decorated initial letters eventually used by Merovingian scriptoria north of the Alps. Its coloured inks are predominantly orange, green and deep red. Neither manuscript has historiated initials or historiated scenes using the human figure; for its portrayal in Lombard art it is necessary to turn to relief sculpture.

3. SCULPTURE. Relief sculpture provides the best instances of what has been considered as Lombard art. Beautiful examples are to be found at Bobbio, Brescia, Rome, Pavia, Cividale, on the Istrian peninsula and on the northern islands of the Adriatic. The relief sculptures were normally carved on marble closure slabs 900–1500 mm long, about 900 mm high and 75–125 mm thick, and were used for choir enclosures, gallery balustrades, pulpit facings and for tomb monuments. This size, however, made them liable to be moved and hence difficult to date.

The only relief that may be dated with any security comprises four slabs (Pavia, Pin. Malaspina) that formed part of the tomb of *Theodota* (*d*?720), Abbess of the convent of S Maria, Pavia. On one of the long sides of the tomb, within a broad border of vine leaves, two peacocks drink from a kantharos, a stylized chalice or cup used for communion, surmounted by a cross (see fig. 1). The background is filled by rosettes, palmettes, lilies and rope twists. This is iconographically a very traditional scene, but, although the visual strength of the peacock motif gives the composition apparent symmetry, the motif has been moved off-centre to the left to provide room for the crossed lily stems. This cannot have been accidental: on none of the remaining panels is the design symmetrical. The sculptor was playing with asymmetry by placing it in a context of apparent symmetry. This anti-Classical approach to design and representation is found in most Lombard work in Italy outside Rome. The Roman preference for Classicism, however, also had adherents throughout the peninsula, as is seen in the extraordinary illusionistic wall paintings (?8th century) in S Maria Foris Portas, Castelseprio.

The Lombard tendency towards non-Classical modes of expression could develop into representations of positive brutality, as on the Altar of Duke Ratchis (*c.* 737; Cividale del Friuli, Mus. Crist. & Tesoro Duomo). On the narrow sides are the *Visitation* and the *Adoration of the Magi* (see fig. 2); on the front is a *Christ in Majesty* and on the back a small door for access. All three scenes are bordered by bands of rope twists or inscriptions; inside this border runs a bead and reel moulding. All elements within the fields have been reduced to a linear composition: physical reality is rendered in graphic surface lines that describe the motifs just sufficiently for a star, body, chair or rosette to be recognizable. Even relative scale is

1. Lombard closure slab representing two peacocks drinking from a kantharos, marble, 660×1760 mm, from the tomb of *Abbess Theodota*, *c.* AD 720 (Pavia, Pinacoteca Malaspina)

grossly abused, for example in the half rosettes, above which float the tiny feet of the Magi and on which the throne of the Virgin is precariously balanced. Even the ciborium over the Virgin and Child is unbalanced and unfinished as it ends abruptly over Christ's head. Most extraordinary is the avoidance of any semblance of traditional beauty for the Virgin's face, a squashed apelike visage (*see also* ITALY, §IV, 2(iii)).

The Tempietto Longobardo (or S Maria della Valle) at Cividale is essentially one room, two storeys high, with a screen across the east end making a sanctuary. Against the west wall is an aggregation of sculpture in stucco, once a common medium (*see* STUCCO AND PLASTERWORK, §III, 2) but subsequently almost all destroyed. Above the entrance, which is decorated in abstract motifs, are six life-size female saints flanking a central arched niche. The beautiful carving has sharp cuts and linear qualities, while the vine trails and interlace are precise. Both the vine trails and the female saints carefully follow Early Christian prototypes, except for the figures' peculiar elongation. These stuccos and their accompanying wall paintings have been dated variously between the 8th and the 11th centuries. There are no obvious close stylistic parallels, and they may reflect the conservative aspects of Lombard taste.

Equally associated with the Lombard name are many marble plaques decorated with interlace. It was once thought that interlace, the weaving together of several strands, was brought to Italy by the Lombards through their brilliant jewellery. The development of interlace and the gradual introduction of animal forms, fish, birds and quadrupeds, for example on the ciborium over the font in the Cividale baptistery (*c.* 712–*c.* 743; now in Cividale del Friuli, Mus. Crist & Tesoro Duomo), can, however, be traced in Italy, disproving the idea of barbarian interference with Early Christian traditions. In Italy, in particular, motifs of interlace and interlace with knots were widespread. Almost all the 7th- and 8th-century relief slabs with this type of motif are designed asymmetrically in a traditional context. The carving is very vigorous. In inscriptions the letters refuse to stay in line or in scale, so that even the epigraphy, as with scripts in books, obeys the same laws of diversity in the context of tradition.

### BIBLIOGRAPHY
R. Cattaneo: *L'architettura in Italia dal secolo VI al mille circa* (Venice, 1889)

N. Åberg: *Lombard Italy* (1945), ii of *The Occident and the Orient in the Art of the Seventh Century* (Stockholm, 1943–7)

A. Grabar and C. Nordenfalk: *Early Medieval Painting: From the 4th to the 11th Century* (Geneva, 1957)

H. Roth: *Die Ornamentik der Langobarden in Italien: Eine Untersuchung zur Stilentwicklung anhand der Grabfunde* (Bonn, 1973)

H. P. L'Orange and H. Torp: *Il Tempietto Longobardo di Cividale*, Acta Archaeol. & A. Hist. Pertinentia, 3 vols (Rome, 1977–9)

*Longobardi e la Lombardia: Saggi: Milano, 1978*

*Cultura in Italia fra tardo antico e alto medioevo: Atti del convegno di consiglio nazionale dalle ricerche: Roma, 1979*, pp. 837–66, 933–46 [articles by M. Rotili]

R. Kutzli: *Langobardische Kunst: Die Sprache der Flechtbänder* (Stuttgart, 1981)

M. G. Arcamone and others: *Magistra barbaritas: I barbari in Italia* (Milan, 1984)

2. Lombard relief of the *Adoration of the Magi*, marble, 800×900 mm, from the Altar of Duke Ratchis, *c.* AD 737 (Cividale del Friuli, Museo Cristiano e Tesoro del Duomo)

*Adelchi: Dai Longobardi ai Carolingi* (exh. cat., ed. C. Calderini; Milan, Castello Szforzesco, 1984)

W. Menghin: *Die Langobarden: Archäologie und Geschichte* (Stuttgart, 1985)

*I Longobardi* (exh. cat., ed. G. C. Menis; Cividale del Friuli, Pal. Provveditori Veneti; Passariano, Villa Manin, 1990); review by D. Kidd in *Burl. Mag.*, cxxxiii (1991), pp. 197–8

CARL D. SHEPPARD

**Lombardi, Alfonso** (*b* Ferrara, *c*. 1497; *d* Bologna, 1 Dec 1537). Italian sculptor and medallist. He began his career at the court of Alfonso I d'Este, Duke of Ferrara, where he executed portraits (in stucco, wax and clay) and medals (e.g. London, BM; Weimar, Goethe-Nmus. Frauenplan). In 1516 he moved to Bologna, where he soon established a reputation. His terracotta group of *Hercules and the Hydra*, which was completed on 3 July 1519, was placed in the great hall of the Palazzo Pubblico (now Pal. Com.) there. On 2 December of that year he signed a contract, with his father Niccolò, for a *Death of the Virgin* (Bologna, S Maria della Vita), a group of 14 terracotta figures, over life-size, for which he was paid on 15 June 1522. The fame of this work brought him commissions at Faenza (*Virgin and Child with Saints*, Pin. Com.) and Castelbolognese (*Crucifixion*, S Petronio). Between 1522 and 1524 he executed other works in terracotta: *St Bartholomew* (Bologna, S Maria della Pioggia) and the group of the *Virgin and Child with SS John the Evangelist and John the Baptist* (Ferrara, Pin. Com.). The latter shows Venetian influence, probably absorbed in Ferrara from Antonio Lombardo, who worked there from 1506 to 1516. This work had a strong influence on Emilian sculptors, especially Antonio Begarelli. Lombardi's four terracotta statues of the *Patron Saints* (SS Proclus, Petronius, Dominic and Francis) were erected in the Torre dell'Arengo of the Palazzo del Podestà, Bologna, in August 1525. The following month he began carving sculptures in marble for the façade of S Petronio, Bologna, including the lunette of the *Resurrection* (1527) and the side doors with the *Annunciation* and *Adam and Eve* (1526–32; all *in situ*). These works, executed with his shop, show a change in style, influenced by the school of Sansovino.

While working on S Petronio Lombardi returned to funerary sculpture, a genre in which he had worked earlier (tomb of *Ercole Buttrigari*, 1522; Bologna, Certosa), executing the tomb of *Amarciotto de' Ramazzotti* (Bologna, S Michele in Bosco). He resumed the terracotta technique for the triumphal arch erected for the coronation in Bologna of Charles V as Holy Roman Emperor in 1530. That year he went to Carrara to get marble for a series of busts for Federico II Gonzaga, 1st Duke of Mantua. These are untraced but are documented in numerous letters. On 20 November 1532 he was commissioned to execute the marble relief of scenes from the *Life of St Dominic* for the saint's tomb (Bologna, S Domenico). This work, finished the following year, was signed *Alphonsus de Lombardis Ferrariensis F.* Shortly afterwards he went in the service of Cardinal Ippolito de' Medici to Rome, where he carved busts of *Clement VII* and *Giuliano de' Medici* (both Florence, Pal. Vecchio, Sala di Leone X). In this period he received the commission for the tomb of Clement VII, for which, according to Vasari, he produced a wax model based on sketches by Michelangelo. After the death of

Cardinal Ippolito in 1535, however, the commission was transferred to Baccio Bandinelli, and Lombardi left Rome. On his return to Bologna he stopped in Florence, where he presented a marble bust of *Charles V* to the Duke, Alessandro de' Medici. Documents indicate that he produced four marble busts of Charles V, though only one is identified (Paris, Mus. Jacquemart-André).

BIBLIOGRAPHY
A. Venturi: *Storia* (1901–40), X/i, pp. 575–601
M. Fanti: 'Il San Procolo della Fabbriceria di San Petronio in Bologna', *A. Ant. Mod.*, II/6 (1959), pp. 183–90
A. Parronchi: 'Il San Sebastiano ligneo di S Maria del Baraccano', *Atti Mem. Accad. Clementina Bologna*, xi (1974), pp. 59–65
F. Bergonzoni: 'I quattro santi protettori di Bologna: Vicende e restauri del voltone del Podestà', *Strenna Stor. Bologn.*, xxvi (1976), pp. 43–70
U. Middeldorf: 'Zu einigen Medaillen der italienischen Renaissance', *Festschrift Wolfgang Braufels* (Tübingen, 1977), pp. 263–5
N. Gramaccini: *Alfonso Lombardi* (Frankfurt am Main, 1980)

CHIARA STEFANI

**Lombardo** [Lombardi]. Italian family of artists. (1) Pietro Lombardo and his sons, (2) Tullio Lombardo and (3) Antonio Lombardo, were dominant figures in Venetian sculpture and architecture from *c*. 1465 until the death of Tullio in 1532. Because Pietro was born in Carona, the place of origin of the Solari, a famous family of stone-carvers, it is assumed that he was a member of that family. For this reason members of the Lombardi family are sometimes referred to by the name of Solari, although only Antonio's sons used the name themselves. Pietro transformed Tuscan Renaissance prototypes into a Venetian style, as seen in his earliest projects, the chancel of S Giobbe, Venice, and the tomb of *Antonio Roselli* in S Antonio (Il Santo), Padua, and that of *Doge Pasquale Malipiero* in SS Giovanni e Paolo, Venice. The typical features of this style, a simple, planar architecture covered with beautifully carved low-relief ornament, were so widely imitated that the designation Lombardesque was coined to characterize it as a Venetian phenomenon of the late 15th century and early 16th.

I. Introduction. II. Family members.

### I. Introduction.

The specific roles of Tullio and Antonio in the family workshop cannot be identified before the late 1480s, although such reliable sources as Matteo Collaccio (1486) and Francesco Sansovino (1581) attest to their participation in the mid-1470s. Presumably they worked alongside other assistants on less important aspects of tombs and architectural projects under Pietro's supervision. The *Bishop Zanetti* tomb in Treviso Cathedral of the late 1480s is probably the first project in which the individual contributions of Tullio and Antonio can be convincingly distinguished. The division of labour, with all three Lombardi working on different sculptures from Pietro's design, gives a fascinating picture of their close collaboration (Munman, 1977). Pietro's correspondence in the 1490s with Francesco Gonzaga, 4th Marchese of Mantua, which reveals that he intended to execute Mantuan commissions in Venice with the help of 25 assistants, is the only documented indication of the size of the workshop, which was evidently very large at that date.

By the 1490s Tullio and Antonio had assumed the dominant role in family commissions, and an increasingly classicizing style is evident in such projects as the tomb of *Doge Andrea Vendramin* (Venice, SS Giovanni e Paolo) of the early 1490s. The brothers' deep-seated classicism derived from the collection and study of Greco-Roman works of art. Marcantonio Michiel recorded that Tullio once owned an antique headless marble statue of a woman that he reproduced many times in his own sculpture, and he apparently also restored antique sculpture (Pincus, 1979). According to Pomponius Gauricus, Tullio was the greatest Venetian marble sculptor, and his classicizing works would have appealed greatly to contemporary humanists. Pietro's appointment as Protomagister of the rebuilding of the Doge's Palace, Venice, in 1498 absorbed most of his time, and thereafter his continued collaboration with his sons seems to have been primarily as an adviser. Yet even when the younger Lombardi were well established in the early 16th century, their cooperation with their father was close, and all three collaborated in the execution of the funerary chapel of Cardinal Zen in S Marco, Venice (Jestaz, 1986).

Antonio's departure for Ferrara in 1506 left Tullio as the *de facto* head of the family workshop. Tullio's architecture made a break from that of his father. Perhaps as early as the 1490s he eschewed the exquisite low-relief ornamentation that had been the Lombardo hallmark and planned buildings that were more classicizing, volumetric and austere than Pietro's. Tullio's death in 1532 occurred just after Jacopo Sansovino's arrival in Venice and marked the end of the Lombardo era, although Antonio's sons, (4) Aurelio Lombardo, (5) Girolamo Lombardo and Ludovico Lombardo [Solari; Ludovico da Ferrara] (1507/8–75), worked as sculptors. The brothers inscribed their most important work, the bronze tabernacle that Pius IV commissioned for the high altar of Milan Cathedral, *Aurelius, Hieronymus et Ludov. Frs. [fratres] Solari Lombardi F.* (Thieme–Becker). Tullio's son, (6) Sante Lombardo, practised as an architect. Girolamo's three sons, Antonio Lombardo (*d* between 4 June 1608 and 14 April 1610), Pietro Lombardo (*d* before 1608) and Paolo Lombardo, were sculptors. Sante's two sons, Tullio Lombardo and Giovanni Girolamo Lombardo, became architects of minor note. More research needs to be done to clarify the details of the careers of the later generations of the Lombardi.

## BIBLIOGRAPHY

### EARLY SOURCES

M. Collaccio: *Philologica opuscola* (Venice, 1486)
P. Gauricus: *De sculptura* (1504), ed. and trans. A. Chastel and R. Klein (Geneva and Paris, 1969)
Vitruvius: *De architectura*, ed. C. Cesariano (Como, 1521)
M. Michiel: *Notizie d'opera del disegno* (MS. before 1552); ed. T. Frimmel as *Der Anonimo Morelliano* (Vienna, 1888)
F. Sansovino: *Venetia: Città nobilissima et singolare* (Venice, 1581); ed. G. Martinioni (Venice, 1663/*R* New York, 1968)
T. Temanza: *Vite dei più celebri architetti e scultori veneziani che fiorirono nel secolo decimosesto* (Venice, 1778)

### GENERAL WORKS

Thieme–Becker
P. Paoletti: *L'architettura e la scultura del rinascimento in Venezia: Ricerche storico-artistiche*, ii (Venice, 1893), pp. 110–13, 135, 238–255
L. Planiscig: *Venezianische Bildhauer der Renaissance* (Vienna, 1921)
L. Coletti: *Catalogo delle cose d'arte e di antichità d'Italia: Treviso* (Rome, 1935), pp. 152–3, 395–9

J. Pope-Hennessy: *Italian Renaissance Sculpture* (London, 1963, rev. Oxford, 3/1985)
C. Seymour jr: *Sculpture in Italy, 1400–1500*, Pelican Hist. A. (Harmondsworth, 1966)
L. Heydenreich and W. Lotz: *Architecture in Italy, 1400 to 1600*, Pelican Hist. A. (Harmondsworth, 1974)
S. M. Connell: *The Employment of Sculptors and Stone Masons in Venice in the Fifteenth Century* (diss., U. London, Warburg Inst., 1976)
J. McAndrew: *Venetian Architecture of the Early Renaissance* (Cambridge, MA, 1980)
R. Lieberman: *Renaissance Architecture in Venice, 1450–1540* (New York, 1982)
N. Huse and W. Wolters: *The Art of Renaissance Venice: Architecture, Sculpture and Painting, 1460–1540* (Chicago, 1990)

### SPECIALIST STUDIES

G. Boni: 'Santa Maria dei Miracoli in Venezia', *Archv Ven.*, xxxiii (1887), pp. 236–74
G. Biscaro: 'Pietro Lombardo e la cattedrale di Treviso', *Archv Stor. A.*, 2nd ser., iii (1897), pp. 142–54
——: 'Note storico-artistiche sulla cattedrale di Treviso', *Nuovo Archv Ven.*, xvii (1899), pp. 135–94
——: 'I Solari da Carona', *Boll. Stor. Svizzera It.*, xxxiv/1–7 (1912), pp. 61–77
P. Paoletti: *La scuola grande di San Marco* (Venice, 1929)
L. Planiscig: 'Pietro, Tullio und Antonio Lombardo: Neue Beiträge zu ihrem Werk', *Jb. Ksthist. Samml. Wien*, xi (1937), pp. 87–115
N. Gallimberti: 'La tradizione architettonica religiosa tra Venezia e Padova', *Boll. Mus. Civ. Padova*, lii (1963), pp. 115–92
C. Semenzato: 'Pietro e Tullio Lombardo, architetti', *Boll. Cent. Int. Stud. Archit. Andrea Palladio*, vi/2 (1964), pp. 262–70
F. Zava Boccazzi: *I Lombardi*, I maestri della scultura, lxxii (Milan, 1966)
R. Munman: *Venetian Renaissance Tomb Monuments* (diss., Cambridge, MA, Harvard U., 1968)
J. McAndrew: 'Sant'Andrea della Certosa', *A. Bull.*, li (1969), pp. 15–28
A. Crivelli: *Artisti ticinesi in Italia* (Locarno and Lugano, 1971)
R. Lieberman: *The Church of Santa Maria dei Miracoli in Venice* (diss., New York U., 1972)
A. Markham Schulz: 'The Giustiniani Chapel and the Art of the Lombardo', *Ant. Viva*, xvi/27 (1977), pp. 27–44
R. Munman: 'The Lombardo Family and the Tomb of Giovanni Zanetti', *A. Bull.*, lix (1977), pp. 28–38
E. Ruhmer: 'Paduaner Quattrocento-Plastiken als Bildquellen der Hochrenaissance', *A. Ven.*, xxxii (1978), pp. 61–7
D. Pincus: 'Tullio Lombardo as a Restorer of Antiquities: An Aspect of Fifteenth-century Venetian Antiquarianism', *A. Ven.*, xxxiii (1979), pp. 29–42
P. Sohm: *The Scuola Grande di San Marco, 1437–1550: The Architecture of a Venetian Lay Confraternity* (New York, 1982)
D. Lewis: 'The Sculptures in the Chapel of the Villa Giustinian at Roncade, and their Relation to those in the Giustinian Chapel at San Francesco della Vigna', *Mitt. Ksthist. Inst. Florenz*, xxvii (1983), pp. 307–52
P. Dittmar: 'Die dekorative Skulptur der venezianischen Frührenaissance', *Z. Kstgesch.*, xlvii (1984), pp. 158–85
B. Jestaz: *La Chapelle Zen à Saint-Marc de Venise d'Antonio à Tullio Lombardo* (Stuttgart, 1986)
S. B. McHam: *The Chapel of St Anthony at the Santo and the Development of Venetian Renaissance Sculpture* (Cambridge, 1993)

## II. Family members.

**(1) Pietro Lombardo** [Pietro Solari] (*b* Carona, Lombardy, *c.* 1435; *d* Venice, June 1515). Sculptor and architect.

1. SCULPTURE. He is first documented in Bologna, where he rented a workshop at S Petronio between July 1462 and May 1463, presumably to work on some commission for the cathedral, perhaps the Rossi Chapel chancel (Beck, 1968). By 1464 he and his family had moved to Padua, where his most important work was the wall tomb of *Doge Antonio Roselli* in S Antonio (Il Santo), which he designed in early 1464 and finished by 8 April 1467 (Moschetti, 1913, 1914). The *Roselli* tomb introduced the 15th-century Florentine humanist tomb type into the

region and marks the beginning of true Renaissance sculpture in the Veneto. Its derivation from the *Carlo Marsuppini* monument in Santa Croce, Florence, by Desiderio da Settignano suggests that Pietro visited Florence during his sojourn in Bologna. Pietro interpreted the Florentine model in a way that became characteristic of later Venetian tombs. He transformed it into a more heavily decorated and imposing tomb through the addition of a high base, monumental flanking pilasters, long decorative relief swags and an ornate cornice. At this date he also completed some architectural projects in Padua and Vicenza.

Pietro and his family are first documented in Venice on 11 August 1474, but it seems likely that they arrived soon after 1467. Pietro's first tomb in Venice, that of *Doge Pasquale Malipiero* in SS Giovanni e Paolo, which probably dates from the late 1460s, is also derived from Florentine wall tombs, but by omitting the elaborate enframing architecture of the *Roselli* tomb, Pietro transformed the Florentine prototype into a Venetian type, the pensile wall tomb embellished by a tent-like baldacchino hanging around the doge's sarcophagus.

Pietro's next project, the tomb of *Doge Pietro Mocenigo* (*d* 1476; *see* TOMB, fig. 13), also in SS Giovanni e Paolo, is his grandest funerary monument. Francesco Sansovino (1581) indicated that both Tullio and Antonio worked on it with Pietro, but their contribution is difficult to isolate. The tomb dates from between 1476 and 1481. The vast wall tomb, arranged in the form of a triumphal arch, fills nearly one-third of the interior façade of the church and originally included 17 figures. The Doge stands on top of his sarcophagus, which is supported by three warriors, in the centre of the arch. This is flanked by three storeys of niches containing figures of warriors and pages on each side. The base is decorated with reliefs of the Labours of Hercules and Roman trophy designs. The standing figure of the Doge in armour, the reliefs of his military victories on the sarcophagus, the absence of a recumbent effigy, the triumphal arch format and allusions to trophies and Hercules all proclaim the triumphant and secular character of the monument. The only religious elements, a relief of the *Three Marys at the Tomb* and the figure of the *Standing Christ* (originally flanked by *St Mark* and *St Theodore*, now transferred to the contiguous *Alvise Mocenigo* monument), are placed at the summit of the monument, so far distant from the spectator as to seem secondary. Originally the tomb must have been even more spectacular since it was gilded and polychromed, traces of which can be discerned in the niches and figures. The grandeur and format of the *Mocenigo* tomb probably influenced Antonio Rizzo's tomb of *Doge Niccolò Tron* in S Maria dei Frari, Venice, which is almost exactly contemporary, and certainly determined the appearance of a later Lombardo commission, that of the tomb of *Doge Andrea Vendramin* (Venice, SS Giovanni e Paolo), originally in S Maria dei Servi, Venice, in which Pietro's son Tullio played the major role.

During the 1480s the Lombardo shop was very busy with a series of tomb commissions in and around Venice, including the tomb of *Jacopo Marcello* (*d* 1484; Venice, S Maria dei Frari), the tomb of *Lodovico Foscarini* (*d* 1480; ex-S Maria dei Frari, Venice; destr., fragments in south

transept wall) and the tomb of *Giovanni Zanetti, Archbishop of Thebes and Bishop of Treviso* (*d* 1484; Treviso Cathedral). These are all pensile wall tombs of modest scale, in which the sarcophagi and commemorative plaques are framed by oval cornices. This format derives from the arrangement of the central section of the *Pietro Mocenigo* tomb, isolated and reshaped as an oval.

The *Niccolò Marcello* monument (*c.* 1481–5; Venice, constructed in S Marina; later moved to SS Giovanni e Paolo), the other major tomb commission probably executed in the 1480s, is a more tightly organized variant of the triumphal arch type that Pietro used first in the *Pietro Mocenigo* monument. Of much smaller scale, it holds only four figures in addition to the recumbent figure of the Doge. The central portion of the tomb is built forward, which emphasizes the effigy, sarcophagus and lunette relief, unlike the sprawling, flat structure of the *Pietro Mocenigo* monument.

2. ARCHITECTURE. In the early 1470s, on the commission of Doge Cristoforo Moro, Pietro supervised the building of the church of S Giobbe, Venice, which had been started by Gambello in the 1450s, and designed the architecture and decoration of its chancel. A letter of 1485 written by Matteo Collaccio establishes the *terminus ante quem* for the completion of the chancel. Although it specifies only that the figure sculpture was carved by Pietro, it is generally agreed that he was responsible for the architecture as well. Pietro created the first Renaissance-style interior in Venice. The chancel's dome supported on pendentives, the articulation of grey *pietra serena* against white plaster and the four tondo reliefs of the *Evangelists* in the spandrels all derive from Brunelleschi's Old Sacristy in S Lorenzo or from the Pazzi Chapel, both in Florence. The small full-length angels that support the roundels resemble putti carved by Antonio Rossellino, further corroborating Pietro's preoccupation with Florentine models early in his career.

Pietro next supervised the building of the Cappella Maggiore and its cupola for Treviso Cathedral, begun by 1485 or 1486 (Biscaro, 1897, 1899). When the dome collapsed in 1486, Pietro promised to entrust its rebuilding to a capable architect, who in an agreement of 1488 was identified as his son Tullio.

Pietro's other architectural commissions were for major Venetian buildings: S Maria dei Miracoli (see fig.) and the Scuola Grande di S Marco (*see* VENICE, §V, 3 and fig. 27). Because of increased popular devotion to a miracle-working image of the Virgin and Child housed there, a competition was held in 1480 to design a new building for the Miracoli. Initially Pietro Lombardo was hired to supervise the construction of a simple votive chapel and told to follow the chosen model (the designer's name is not recorded); however, so much money was collected that in 1485 a new contract was drawn up. It expressly named Pietro as the architect and stipulated that the structure, now apparently regarded as a convent church rather than a chapel, should be vaulted and have a chancel.

Pietro's solution for the revised project was ingenious: he elevated the chancel and placed the sacristy in the crypt-like space below it, connecting it to the altar area with a spiral stair in the bell-tower at the left of the chancel. The

Pietro Lombardo: S Maria dei Miracoli, Venice, 1485–9

architectural elements of the chancel are exquisitely carved with fanciful floral ornaments and mythological marine creatures. The interior and exterior walls of the Miracoli are veneered with coloured marbles, evidently procured from surplus supplies at S Marco. The Miracoli is the only Venetian church other than S Marco so decorated; its simple, aisleless, barrel-vaulted form and lavish incrustation make it seem a bejewelled reliquary casket, an appropriate setting for the miracle-working image it houses. To some extent, this system of marble incrustation was inspired by the Cappella del Perdono in the Palazzo Ducale, Urbino; a Montefeltro emblem is reused at the Miracoli, indicating close connections between the two projects (Lieberman, 1972).

In 1489 Pietro was hired to supervise construction at the Scuola Grande di S Marco, Venice, which had been destroyed by fire in 1485. He designed the lower part of the façade in conjunction with Giovanni di Antonio Buora before they were replaced by Antonio Rizzo and Mauro Codussi in 1490. Francesco Sansovino wrote that Tullio executed the reliefs flanking the two portals of the Scuola. These extremely pictorial reliefs complement the ostentatiously decorated façade, which has been called the most picturesque architectural concept of the 15th century. Its coloured marble veneer, asymmetry, use of statues and pictorial reliefs and non-classical organization of proportions have come to epitomize Venetian taste for extravagance and colour in architecture. In fact, the lobes of its upper façade were probably intended to recall the domes of S Marco, its namesake, and the apparently unorthodox organization of the façade has been shown to reflect the organization and functions of the Scuola's interior (Sohm, 1982).

After serving as Antonio Rizzo's assistant for several years, Pietro became Protomagister of the Doge's Palace in 1498 when Rizzo was accused of embezzlement and fled from Venice. This position engaged most of Pietro's energies for the rest of his working career (he withdrew in 1511). He supervised the completion of most of the northern part of the courtyard façade of the eastern wing of the palace, but probably was not responsible for its design, which has been attributed either to Rizzo or Codussi.

In 1495 Pietro was commissioned to carve an elaborate altarpiece for the Cappella della Madonna in the Duomo, Mantua, for which neither drawings nor model seem to have survived. In 1502 he worked on a new dome for Cividale Cathedral. In 1509 he submitted a model (untraced) for the new building of the Scuola Grande della Misericordia in Venice. Otherwise in his last years Pietro seems to have been active mainly in conjunction with his sons on commissions in which they were the principals. He helped to supervise the construction of the chapel of the Holy Sacrament, designed by Antonio, in Treviso Cathedral, and that by Tullio at S Salvatore in Venice; he played a more limited role in Antonio's work on the Zen Chapel in S Marco. In 1514 Pietro served as the head of the stonemasons' guild in Venice, an indication of the pre-eminent position he held in Venetian architecture even in his last years.

BIBLIOGRAPHY

G. B. Lorenzi: *Monumenti per servire alla storia del palazzo ducale di Venezia* (Venice, 1868), pp. 121–55
A. Moschetti: 'Un quadriennio di Pietro Lombardo a Padova (1464–1467) con una appendice sulla data di nascita e di morte di Bartolomeo Bellano', *Boll. Mus. Civ. Padova*, xvi (1913), pp. 1–99; xvii (1914), pp. 1–43
——: 'Pietro e altri lapidici a Bellano', *Atti Ist. Ven. Sci., Lett. & A.*, lxxxvii/2 (1927–8), p. 1481–1515
L. Planiscig: 'Pietro Lombardi ed alcuni bassirilievi veneziani del 400', *Dedalo*, x (1929–30), pp. 461–81
——: 'Deux reliefs en marbre de Pietro Lombardi', *Gaz. B.-A.*, 6th ser., iv (1930), pp. 1–10
G. Mariacher: 'Pietro Lombardo a Venezia', *A. Ven.*, ix (1955), pp. 36–52
G. Zorzi: 'Architetti e scultori dei laghi di Lugano e di Como a Vicenza nel secolo XV', *Arte e artisti dei laghi lombardi*, ed. E. Arslan, i (Como, 1959), pp. 343–71
E. Bandelloni: 'Pietro Lombardo architetto nella critica d'arte', *Boll. Mus. Civ. Padova*, li/2 (1962), pp. 25–56
A. Meli: 'Cappella Colleoni: I tre santi dell'ancona', *Bergomum*, xxxix/1 (1965), pp. 3–46
J. Beck: 'A Notice for the Early Career of Pietro Lombardo', *Mitt. Ksthist. Inst. Florenz*, xiii (1968), pp. 189–92
C. M. Brown: 'Little Known and Unpublished Documents Concerning . . . Pietro Lombardo . . . II', *L'Arte*, vii–viii (1969), pp. 182–214
R. Munman: 'Giovanni Buora: The "Missing" Sculpture', *A. Ven.*, xxv (1976), pp. 41–61
H. G. Brand: *Die Grabmonumente Pietro Lombardos: Studien zum venezianischen Wandgrabmal des späten Quattrocento* (diss., U. Augsburg, 1977)
R. Munman: 'The Sculpture of Giovanni Buora: A Supplement', *A. Ven.*, xxxiii (1979), pp. 19–28
A. Markham Schulz: 'Pietro Lombardo's Barbarigo Tomb in the Venetian Church of S Maria della Carità', *Art the Ape of Nature: Studies in Honor of H. W. Janson*, ed. M. Barasch, L. F. Sandler and P. Egan (New York, 1981), pp. 171–92
T. Hirthe: 'Mauro Codussi als Architekt des Dogenpalastes', *A. Ven.*, xxxvi (1982), pp. 31–44

A. Markham Schulz: 'Giovanni Buora lapicida', *A. Lombarda*, lxv/2 (1983), pp. 49–72

**(2) Tullio Lombardo** (*b* ?*c.* 1455; *d* Venice, 17 Nov 1532). Sculptor and architect, son of (1) Pietro Lombardo.

1. Sculpture. 2. Architecture.

1. SCULPTURE. Tullio, together with his brother Antonio, is first mentioned in a letter of 1475 written by Matteo Collaccio that has been traditionally construed to mean that by the mid-1470s the brothers were active in their father's workshop, contributing to secondary aspects of commissions. Maek-Gérard (1974, 1980), however, argued that Tullio and Antonio were born in Padua in the 1460s, about ten years later than is usually assumed. The later birthdates would explain the difficulty of distinguishing their role in the family workshop before the late 1480s. It would also mean that, since they were born in Padua, both were citizens of the Venetian Empire, which, Maek-Gérard contended, explained their continued receipt of important Venetian commissions in the early 16th century after the Venetian sculptors' guild had curtailed the rights of non-Venetian sculptors.

Tullio's earliest signed sculptures seem to be the figures of four kneeling angels (Venice, S Martino), carved for the shrine of the Holy Sepulchre in S Sepolcro, Venice. Although not finished until 1511 the shrine itself is inscribed 1484, and most historians (except Mariacher, 1954; Jestaz, 1986) date the angels to *c.* 1484. Pomponius Gauricus (1504), a close friend of Tullio's, provided specific information about Tullio's role in the next major sculptural commission awarded to the family workshop. He described the purportedly envious reaction of Antonio Rizzo, a rival sculptor, to the beautiful ornament that Tullio carved for the tomb of *Bishop Zanetti* in Treviso Cathedral in the late 1480s. Tullio is also recorded by Francesco Sansovino as having sculpted marble statues (destr.) for the chancel of S Maria dei Miracoli, Venice, which Pietro had constructed in 1485–9. Details of the elaborate decorative carving of the socle of the chancel arch and pilasters can also be attributed to Tullio.

Sansovino made it clear that Tullio was responsible for the two reliefs of *St Mark Baptizing Anianus* and *St Mark Healing Anianus* flanking the portals on the façade of the Scuola Grande di S Marco, Venice, which must have been sculpted in 1489–90 when his father Pietro designed the façade's lower portion. They are the earliest relief sculptures definitely by Tullio and establish certain principles that can be traced in his later narrative reliefs. The figures are large and are arranged in an isocephalic frieze. They stand crowded together on a projecting ledge before an architectural setting shown in perspective that creates the unprecedented illusion of receding architectural space on a real architectural façade. The reliefs combine a classicism of form and organization that Tullio might have learnt from such triumphal arch reliefs as the *Adlocution of Hadrian* (Rome, Pal. Conserv.) with the theatrical immediacy of *tableaux vivants*. The vaulted architecture shown in perspective may be derived ultimately from Bramante's S Maria presso S Satiro, Milan (Sheard, 1984, both publications).

In the 1490s Tullio and Antonio assumed the major role in sculptural commissions awarded to the family shop. The most important project of this decade was the tomb of *Doge Andrea Vendramin* (Venice, SS Giovanni e Paolo; see fig. 1), originally in S Maria dei Servi in Venice. The design of the tomb and a large part of its figure sculpture are usually credited to Tullio. Following the death of Andrea del Verrocchio, who had provided the first project for the tomb, Tullio began work after 1488 and had almost finished it *c.* 1493–4.

The tomb is the earliest Venetian Renaissance wall tomb to be so grandly classical. Its architectural structure transforms the pagan triumphal arch type into a Gate of Paradise, before which were originally positioned the nude figures *Adam* (New York, Met.) and *Eve* (untraced) and the recumbent effigy of the Doge. The 18 figures that once decorated the tomb, more than on any other Venetian funerary monument of the period, have antique prototypes (Sheard, 1971, 1977, 1978). The figure of *Adam*, signed by Tullio, is the tomb's masterpiece and serves as a paradigm of Tullio's style in figure sculpture. The idealized male nude type derives from antique statues of Apollo, although its unstable contrapposto, unclassical proportions and abstract description of skin surfaces also suggest the influence of Late Antique ivory sculpture (Wilk, 1978).

Tullio's only monumental relief altarpiece, a *Coronation of the Virgin*, for the Bernabò Chapel in S Giovanni Crisostomo, Venice, can be dated *c.* 1500–02. The chapel

1. Tullio Lombardo: tomb of *Doge Andrea Vendramin*, marble, 10.8×7.8 m at widest part of the base, *c.* 1488–94 (Venice, SS Giovanni e Paolo)

was redecorated as part of the neo-Byzantine reconstruction of the church as a domed quincunx by Mauro Codussi, and the relief altarpiece adheres to the same stylistic standards. It breaks with conventional iconography of the subject; the isocephalic frieze of Christ, the Apostles and the kneeling Virgin derives from a relief of the *Traditio legis* (Venice, Tesoro S Marco) then considered to be antique but now believed to be a 13th-century copy of an Early Christian prototype (Wilk, 1978).

The next major project in which Tullio was involved was the redecoration of the Cappella dell'Arca di S Antonio in Il Santo, Padua (see fig. 2). The chapel, in which the relics of St Anthony are entombed, was elaborately refurbished with a series of nine monumental marble reliefs illustrating the *Miracles of St Anthony* carved from *c.* 1500

to 1577. Tullio was commissioned to sculpt five of these reliefs, although he completed only two of them, the *Miracle of the Reattached Leg*, begun in 1500, largely finished in 1501 and delivered in 1504, and the *Miracle of the Miser's Heart* (installed in 1525), the commission for which was transferred from Antonio Lombardo to Tullio in 1520.

It seems likely that Tullio was also largely responsible for the design of the chapel's architecture and sculpture, which has previously been attributed to either Andrea Riccio or Giovanni d'Antonio Minelli Bardi (*c.* 1460–1527), a minor Paduan sculptor. Tullio and Antonio were the first artists selected to carve reliefs for the chapel; Tullio was the leading artist associated with the chapel's redecoration from *c.* 1500 until his death in 1532, and he was chosen to carve more reliefs than any other artist. It

2. Tullio Lombardo (attrib.): Cappella dell'Arca di S Antonio in Il Santo, Padua, design, *c.* 1500; with marble reliefs of the *Miracle of the Reattached Leg* (begun 1500) and the *Miracle of the Miser's Heart* (1520–25), both by Tullio Lombardo, and the *Miracle of the Newborn Babe* (1500–04) by Antonio Lombardo

3. Tullio Lombardo: *Bacchus and Ariadne*, marble relief, 560×715 mm, *c.* 1500 (Vienna, Kunsthistorisches Museum)

can be argued that the whole complex must have been planned in detail from the outset, given the chapel's carefully coordinated perspectival illusionism, in which the fictive vaulted architecture of the rear wall reliefs is seen through the real arches of its front wall, and the similar compositional arrangement of all the reliefs. Many aspects of the composition of the reliefs and their perspectival illusionism correspond closely to such documented sculptures by Tullio as the reliefs on the Scuola Grande di S Marco or his *Coronation of the Virgin* altarpiece (Wilk, 1984).

While working on the Paduan project, Tullio must have also executed the tomb of *Doge Giovanni Mocenigo* in SS Giovanni e Paolo, Venice. The Doge died in 1485, but his funerary monument was not erected before 1522, although its sculpture is generally presumed on stylistic grounds to have been carved in the first decade of the 16th century. The bold, undecorated simplicity of the tomb's heavy classical architecture makes a striking contrast to the comparatively two-dimensional structure and profusion of carved ornament of the *Vendramin* tomb of the early 1490s. Tullio seems to have abjured the decorative carving that was the hallmark of Pietro's and his own earlier production; the elegance of the *Mocenigo* tomb depends

on its proportions and the beautiful white, grey and caramel-coloured marbles of its austere architecture.

Tullio was selected to carve two more monumental reliefs for the Cappella dell'Arca in the 1520s, but neither was executed. His only other major sculptural commission in this decade was for the funerary chapel of Guidarello Guidarelli in S Francesco, Ravenna, which probably dates to *c.* 1520–25. Only the effigy of the dead soldier in full armour (Ravenna, Mus. N.) and the architectural details of the chapel are extant (see Wilk, 1978). Tullio's last sculptural commissions were probably largely executed by assistants. The tomb for *Matteo Bellati* in Feltre Cathedral, signed and dated 1528, is a simpler version of a well-known Lombardo tomb type, and the carving is of indifferent quality. The *Pietà* that Tullio designed for Rovigo Cathedral in the late 1520s falls into the same category.

Tullio also carved several reliefs of bust-length portraits of young couples that convey an intense poetic mood. They would seem to have been inspired by Roman double-portrait reliefs, but their purpose is uncertain. The relief known as *Bacchus and Ariadne* (*c.* 1500; Vienna, Ksthist. Mus.; see fig. 3) may in fact be a portrait of a youthful couple. It has been suggested that the relief in the Cà d'Oro, Venice, is a portrait of the artist and his wife (Luchs, 1989).

2. ARCHITECTURE. Tullio made his début as an architect rebuilding the Cappella Maggiore and its dome in Treviso Cathedral. Tullio ratified the 1488 agreement to reconstruct the dome, which had collapsed in 1486 after its remodelling by his father. He may well have supervised the reconstruction from 1486, and the interior's restrained decoration and volumetric organization may reflect a design of Pietro's from which Tullio worked. The next architectural commission usually assigned to Tullio is the church of the Benedictine abbey at Praglia, near Padua, its cloister and some of the contiguous monastic complex (c. 1490). The attribution rests on the style of the architecture and local tradition. Tullio is also thought to have assumed the reconstruction of Cividale Cathedral, which Pietro had originally undertaken in May 1502. Pietro then became Protomagister at the Doge's Palace and probably had no time for projects outside Venice (Paoletti, 1893–7). The reconstruction of Cividale Cathedral dragged on past 1535, after the deaths of both Pietro and Tullio, but the interior organization and simplicity of the architecture again suggest that Tullio was interpreting his father's plan.

It has been argued that the Villa Giustinian at Roncade, the earliest surviving villa in the Veneto, should also be attributed to Tullio and dated c. 1495–1510 (Lewis, 1977). Lewis pointed out that the villa, traditionally attributed to an anonymous follower of Mauro Codussi, shows instead features characteristic of the Lombardi and displays a classicism more austere than that of Codussi but connected with other projects attributed to Tullio in these years.

In 1507 Tullio was named as the architect for the rebuilding of S Salvatore in Venice, with Pietro working as his associate. Tullio's role seems to have been to execute Giorgio Spavento's design, which had been approved in 1506 and already begun. Tullio apparently remained the architect in charge of S Salvatore until his death. The church, the most important building in Venice with which Tullio was associated, is a bold extension of the nine cell square plan that creates fascinating spatial plays through its longitudinal and lateral alternation of wide and narrow bays. By 1511 the eastern end, including the transepts and dome piers, had been erected up to the first major cornice. The vaulting of the Cappella Maggiore and apse were not completed until at least 1518, but by 1529 when Doge Andrea Gritti visited it, the major construction was almost finished (McAndrew, 1980; Tafuri, 1983; Burns, 1986).

In 1509 Tullio and Pietro were jointly named the Protos of a new building for the Scuola Grande della Misericordia in Venice, but in 1515 the Scuola was negotiating with Alessandro Leopardi over his model for the building; nothing is known to survive of the Lombardo plans for this commission. Tullio took over the supervision of the Zen Chapel in S Marco in 1512, when work recommenced after interruptions caused by Antonio's departure for Ferrara in 1506 and by the War of the League of Cambrai, and made significant modifications to its architecture (Jestaz, 1986). In 1506 he had carved two of its column socles. Tullio also worked on the Cappella dell'Argento (destr.) in Ravenna Cathedral in 1515. In 1517 he was paid for a model for the reconstruction of Belluno Cathedral;

the building is similar to Treviso Cathedral, the abbey church at Praglia and Cividale Cathedral, so it seems likely that Tullio's plans were executed. Around 1521 Tullio provided plans for the reconstruction of S Giorgio Maggiore, Venice, and its conventual buildings (unexecuted; drawings, Venice, Archv Stato). In 1523 and 1527 he provided door frames and other decorative architectural elements for the Gonzaga family of Mantua.

BIBLIOGRAPHY

C. Ricci: *La statua di Guidarello* (Ravenna, 1897)
A. Moschetti: 'Il monastero di Praglia', *L'Arte*, vii (1904), pp. 324–5
S. Bernicoli: 'Arte e artisti in Ravenna (continuazione)', *Felix Ravenna*, xiii (1914), pp. 551–66
L. Baldass: 'Eine Reliefbüste von Tullio Lombardo', *Jb. Preuss. Kstsamml.*, xlvii (1929), pp. 109–11
L. Planiscig: 'Per il quarto centenario della morte di Tullio Lombardo e di Andrea Riccio', *Dedalo*, xii/3 (1932), pp. 901–24
——: 'Del Giorgionismo nella scultura veneziana all'inizio del cinquecento', *Boll. A.*, 3rd ser., xxviii (1934–5), pp. 146–55
G. Mariacher: 'Problemi di scultura veneziana (II): 3. L'Eva Vendramin', *A. Ven.*, iv (1950), pp. 107–9
——: 'Tullio Lombardo Studies', *Burl. Mag.*, xcvi (1954), pp. 366–74
W. S. Sheard: *The Tomb of Doge Andrea Vendramin in Venice by Tullio Lombardo* (diss., New Haven, Yale U., 1971)
L. Puppi: 'Per Tullio Lombardo', *A. Lombarda*, xvii/1 (1972), pp. 100–03
R. Stone: 'Tullio Lombardo's Adam from the Vendramin Tomb: A New Terminus ante quem', *Marsyas*, xvi (1972–3), pp. 87–8
S. B. Wilk: 'Tullio Lombardo's "Double-portrait" Reliefs', *Marsyas*, xvi (1972–3), pp. 67–86
M. Maek-Gérard: *Tullio Lombardo: Ein Beitrag zur Problematik der venezianischen Werkstatt bis zu den Auswirkungen des Krieges gegen die Liga von Cambrai* (diss., U. Frankfurt am Main, 1974)
C. K. Lewis: *The Villa Giustinian at Roncade* (New York, 1977)
W. S. Sheard: 'Sanudo's List of Notable Things in Venetian Churches and the Date of the Vendramin Tomb', *Yale It. Stud.*, i (1977), pp. 219–68
——: '"Asa Adorna": The Prehistory of the Vendramin Tomb', *Jb. Berlin. Mus.*, 2nd ser., xx (1978), pp. 117–56
S. B. Wilk: *The Sculpture of Tullio Lombardo: Studies in Sources and Meaning* (New York, 1978)
D. Pincus: 'Tullio Lombardo as a Restorer of Antiquities: An Aspect of Fifteenth-century Venetian Antiquarianism', *A. Ven.*, xxxiii (1979), pp. 29–42
W. S. Sheard: 'Giorgione and Tullio Lombardo', *Giorgione: Atti del convegno internazionale di studio per il 5 centenario della nascita: Castelfranco Veneto, 1979*, pp. 201–11
M. Maek-Gérard: 'Die "Milanexi" in Venedig: Ein Beitrag zur Entwicklungsgeschichte der Lombardi Werkstatt', *Wallraf-Richartz-Jb.*, xli (1980), pp. 105–30
D. Pincus: 'An Antique Fragment as Workshop Model: Classicism in the Andrea Vendramin Tomb', *Burl. Mag.*, cxxiii (1981), pp. 342–7
P. Stepan: *Die Reliefs der Cappella del Santo in Padua: Quellenstudien und Untersuchungen zu ihrer Ikonographie* (diss., Munich, Ludwig-Maximilians-U., 1982)
M. Tafuri: '"Pietà" repubblicana, neobizantinismo e umanesimo: Giorgio Spavento e Tullio Lombardo nella chiesa di San Salvador', *Ric. Stor. A.*, xix (1983), pp. 5–36
S. B. Wilk: 'Titian's Paduan Experience and its Influence on his Style', *A. Bull.*, lxv (1983), pp. 51–61
*The Genius of Venice* (exh. cat., ed. J. Martineau and C. Hope; London, RA, 1983), pp. 365–7
W. S. Sheard: 'The Birth of the Monumental Classicising Relief in Venice on the Façade of the Scuola di San Marco', *Interpretazioni veneziane: Studi di storia dell'arte in onore di Michelangelo Muraro*, ed. D. Rosand (Venice, 1984), pp. 149–74
——: 'Bramante e i Lombardo: Ipotesi su una connessione', *Venezia–Milano* (Milan, 1984), pp. 25–56
S. B. Wilk: 'La decorazione cinquecentesca della cappella dell'Arca di S Antonio', *Le sculture del Santo di Padova*, ed. G. Lorenzoni (Vicenza, 1984), pp. 109–72
C. Carpanese and S. Trolese: *L'abbazia di Santa Maria di Praglia* (Milan, 1985)
A. M. Odenthal: *Die Kirche San Giovanni Crisostomo in Venedig: Ein Beitrag zur venezianischen Sakralarchitektur des späten 15. Jahrhunderts* (diss., Bonn, Rhein. Friedrich-Wilhelms-U., 1985)

P. Stepan: 'Die Reliefs der Cappella del Santo in Padua', *Das Münster*, xxxviii (1985), pp. 55–6

C. E. Burns: *San Salvatore and Venetian Church Architecture, 1490–1530* (diss., New York U., 1986)

A. Luchs: 'Tullio Lombardo's Cà d'Oro Relief: A Self-portrait with the Artist's Wife?', *A. Bull.*, lxxi (1989), pp. 230–36

C. M. Brown: 'Tullio Lombardo and Mantua . . .', *A. Ven.*, lxiii (1989–90), pp. 121–30

M. T. Fiorio: 'Between Milan and Venice: The Role of Sculpture', *Leonardo and Venice* (Milan, 1992), pp. 137–54, 388–95

**(3) Antonio Lombardo** (*b* ?*c*. 1458; *d* Ferrara, ?1516). Sculptor, son of (1) Pietro Lombardo. Unlike Pietro and his brother Tullio, he practised sculpture exclusively, and he worked in bronze as well as marble. He was trained in his father's workshop, but his specific role is difficult to discern before the funerary monument to *Bishop Zanetti* in Treviso Cathedral in the late 1480s. He has been convincingly credited with the carving of the extremely realistic portrait of the deceased bishop and with the eagle and some of the decorative carving on the sarcophagus (Munman, 1977). Much of the decorative carving on the base of the *Vendramin* tomb (Venice, SS Giovanni e Paolo) has also been attributed to Antonio (Sheard, 1971), as has the relief of the *Baptism* on the *Giovanni Mocenigo* monument (Venice, SS Giovanni e Paolo).

Antonio's first signed and documented sculpture is his monumental relief of the *Miracle of the Newborn Babe* for the Cappella dell'Arca in Il Santo, Padua. The relief was commissioned in 1500 and finished in 1504. Antonio's sculpture met with such favour that in 1501 he was hired to carve the *Miracle of the Miser's Heart*. Although he never executed the relief (Tullio replaced him in 1520), Antonio must have worked out a basic composition because a drawing of the subject (England, priv. col., see 1980 exh. cat.) reflects Antonio's style in the *Newborn Babe* relief.

The executed relief of the *Miracle of the Newborn Babe* has been characterized as an antique scene into which two friars have strayed (Pope-Hennessy, 1963). Together with Tullio's contemporary relief of the *Miracle of the Reattached Leg*, it set the standard for the remaining seven reliefs in the chapel. Nevertheless, there are distinctions between Antonio's and Tullio's interpretation of the set compositional formula: Antonio's figures are understated in their emotional reaction, more three-dimensional, full-bodied, softly sensuous and languid, whereas Tullio's are tense and melodramatic.

Antonio's other major commission, the funerary chapel of Cardinal Zen in the narthex of S Marco, Venice, was begun in late 1503 in collaboration with Alessandro Leopardi. By May 1505 Leopardi had withdrawn from the project leaving Antonio in charge with Tullio helping him. Before Antonio went to Ferrara in 1506, he had finished the over-life-size bronze of the *Virgin and Child*, known as the *Madonna della Scarpa*, on the chapel's altar and the altar baldacchino with the relief of *God the Father and Angels*. Between 1512 and its completion in 1521, Tullio took charge of the project. The Cardinal's sarcophagus and altar antependium were executed by Paolo Savin, but the elaborate description of the chapel in the Cardinal's will (1501) makes it likely that the ensemble was planned before his death (Jestaz, 1986).

In 1506 Antonio was called to Ferrara by Alfonso I d'Este, Duke of Ferrara, to work on his private apartments in the Castello. He was involved with this commission until his death. For it he carved a number of mythological and decorative reliefs in marble, of which 30 survive (St Petersburg, Hermitage; Florence, Bargello). Of the 28 reliefs in St Petersburg, 2 are larger and illustrate mythological themes, traditionally identified as the *Forge of Vulcan* and the *Contest between Minerva and Neptune*, although their precise subjects are uncertain. The 2 reliefs in Florence depict ?*Venus* and *Apollo*. The assumption that Antonio's reliefs complemented the bacchanals by Titian and other painters in Alfonso's Camerino di alabastro has been challenged by indications that the sculptures were intended for another room in the palace. It has also been suggested that these themes, which are unusual in Renaissance art, were inspired by Pausanias' description of the sculptures by Phidias at the Parthenon, Athens. Although the text of Pausanias was not published until 1516, it was known to Pomponius Gauricus, a friend of the Lombardi, who alluded to it in his own treatise published in 1504. Not only the subjects of the reliefs but their many quotations from ancient art bespeak Antonio's conscious emulation of the Greco-Roman past (Hope, 1971; Goodgal, 1978).

BIBLIOGRAPHY

J. von Schlosser: 'Aus der Bildnerwerkstatt der Renaissance, III: Eine Reliefserie des Antonio Lombardo', *Jb. Ksthist. Samml. Allhöch. Ksrhaus.*, xxxi (1913/14), pp. 87–100

G. de Nicola: 'Notes on the Museo Nazionale of Florence—IV', *Burl. Mag.*, xxxi (1917), pp. 174–7

W. Stechow: 'The Authorship of the Walters "Lucretia"', *J. Walters A. G.*, xxiii (1960), pp. 72–85

J. Pope-Hennessy: *Catalogue of Italian Sculpture in the Victoria and Albert Museum*, i (London, 1964), pp. 353–7

C. Hope: 'The "Camerini d'alabastro" of Alfonso d'Este', *Burl. Mag.*, cxiii (1971), pp. 641–50, 712–21

W. S. Sheard: *The Tomb of Doge Andrea Vendramin in Venice by Tullio Lombardo* (diss., New Haven, Yale U., 1971)

E. Ruhmer: 'Antonio Lombardo: Versuch einer Charakteristik', *A. Ven.*, xxviii (1974), pp. 39–73

J. Biscontin: 'Une Frise de marbre d'Antonio Lombardo au Musée du Louvre', *Rev. Louvre*, xxv/4 (1975), pp. 234–6

D. Goodgal: 'The Camerino of Alfonso I d'Este', *A. Hist.*, i (1978), pp. 162–90

D. Lewis: 'The Washington Relief of *Peace* and its Pendant: A Commission of Alfonso d'Este to Antonio Lombardo in 1512', *Collaboration in Italian Renaissance Art*, ed. J. Paoletti and W. S. Sheard (New Haven, 1978), pp. 233–44

*Disegni veneti di collezioni inglesi* (exh. cat., ed. J. Stock; Venice, Fond. Cini, 1980), p. 24, cat. no. 3

*The Genius of Venice, 1500–1600* (exh. cat., ed. J. Martineau and C. Hope; London, RA, 1983), pp. 363–5

U. Schlegel: 'Mars, Venus und Amor: Ein Relief von Antonio Lombardi', *Mitt. Ksthist. Inst. Florenz*, xxviii (1984), pp. 65–76

B. Jestaz: *La Chapelle Zen à Saint-Marc de Venise d'Antonio à Tullio Lombardo* (Stuttgart, 1986)

W. S. Sheard: 'Antonio Lombardo's Reliefs for Alfonso d'Este's Studio di Marmi . . .', *Titian 500*, ed. J. Manca, *Stud. Hist. A.*, xlv (1994)

SARAH BLAKE MCHAM

**(4) Aurelio Lombardo** (*b* Venice, *c*. 1501; *d* Recanati, 9 Sept 1563). Sculptor and bronze-caster, son of (3) Antonio Lombardo. He is first documented in Ferrara, in 1524 and 1529. From 1539 he was in Loreto, where he and his brother (5) Girolamo Lombardo made a series of marble statues of *Prophets* for the Santa Casa in the basilica (*in situ*; see LORETO, §II, 1(ii)). The precise contribution of each brother is still debated. Aurelio also worked in bronze, and for the chapel of the Holy Sacrament in the basilica he made a bronze cornucopia candleholder (1547–8) and a chandelier (1547–50) with *all'antica* motifs of cornucopias and putti. In 1550 he was in Recanati, where he and his brothers Girolamo and Ludovico Lombardo (1507/8–75) established a bronze foundry. With them he executed for Pope Pius IV a bronze cylindrical tabernacle with reliefs of scenes from the *Life of Christ* (1560) for Milan Cathedral (*in situ*). His work was stylistically similar to that of (2) Tullio Lombardo and Antonio, as is seen in the door of a marble tabernacle, with two angels and a figure of God the Father (Loreto, Pal. Apostolico) also made for the chapel of the Holy Sacrament.

BIBLIOGRAPHY

Thieme–Becker

G. Vasari: *Vite* (1550, rev. 2/1568); ed. G. Milanesi (1878–85), iv, p. 520; vi, p. 480; ix, p. 88

F. Grimaldi: *Loreto: Basilica della Santa Casa* (Bologna, 1975)

F. Grimaldi and K. Sordi: *Scultori a Loreto: Fratelli Lombardi, Antonio Calcagni e Tiburzio Vergelli: Documenti* (Ancona, 1987)

**(5) Girolamo Lombardo** (*b* Ferrara, *c.* 1505–10; *d* Loreto, between 17 Jan 1584 and 12 June 1589). Sculptor and bronze-caster, son of (3) Antonio Lombardo. According to Vasari, he was a pupil of JACOPO SANSOVINO and worked with Tiziano Minio and Danese Cattaneo on the decorative sculpture for Sansovino's Loggetta (*c.* 1537–42) in the Piazza S Marco, Venice (*in situ*). His precise contribution is debated, but he may have executed marble reliefs of mythological subjects. Vasari also mentioned that he worked in *mezzo rilievo* on the decoration of Sansovino's Libreria Marciana (1532–48) in Venice with Cattaneo, Bartolomeo Ammannati and Tommaso Lombardo. He may have executed the relief panels of garlands and putti for the soffits of the Library. In 1543 he left Venice for Loreto, where he and his brother (4) Aurelio Lombardo executed a series of marble statues of *Prophets* for the Santa Casa in the basilica (*in situ*). From 1550 he lived in Recanati. In Rome *c.* 1560 he and Aurelio were commissioned by Pope Pius IV to make a bronze tabernacle for Milan Cathedral (*in situ*), with reliefs of scenes from the *Life of Christ* (1560). From 1568 to 1576 he worked on the bronze doors on the north and south sides of the Santa Casa at Loreto with his brother Ludovico Lombardo (1507/8–75), Tiburzio Vergelli and Antonio Calcagni. The doors were decorated with narrative scenes from the *Life of Christ*. In 1570 he made a bronze tabernacle for the chapel of the Holy Sacrament in Fermo Cathedral (*in situ*). After 1572 he worked as a papal bronze-caster. He executed a bronze statue of *Pope Gregory XIII* (1575; destr.) for Ascoli Piceno. Girolamo also produced another statue of a prophet, *Amos*, for the Santa Casa, Loreto (1578–9; *in situ*; see fig.). In 1581 he made a bronze cornucopia candleholder to match one made earlier by Aurelio for the chapel of the Holy Sacrament in Loreto. In 1583 he completed the bronze statue of the *Virgin and Child* above the main portico of the Santa Casa at Loreto (*in situ*), executed with his son Antonio Lombardo (*d* between 4 June 1608 and 14 April 1610).

BIBLIOGRAPHY

Thieme–Becker

Vasari: *Vite* (1550, rev. 2/1568); ed. G. Milanesi (1878–85), iv, pp. 514, 519; vi, pp. 479ff

F. Grimaldi: *Loreto: Basilica della Santa Casa* (Bologna, 1975)

Girolamo Lombardo: *Amos*, marble, 1578–9 (Loreto, S Maria di Loreto, Santa Casa)

F. Grimaldi and K. Sordi: *Scultori a Loreto: Fratelli Lombardi, Antonio Calcagni e Tiburzio Vergelli: Documenti* (Ancona, 1987)

**(6) Sante Lombardo** (*b* Venice, 1504; *d* Venice, 1560). Architect, son of (2) Tullio Lombardo. He had a career of limited importance as an architect in Venice. He was Protomagister at the Scuola Grande di S Rocco between 1524 and 1527, executing a model apparently designed by his predecessor, Pietro Bon; Tullio served as the responsible architect because Sante was only 20 years old when he became Proto. Sante evidently made little progress before his replacement by Antonio Scarpagnino, who completed the building.

Sante is also credited with the design of S Giorgio dei Greci, the Greek national church in Venice. Construction was begun in 1539, but was finished in 1561 by Giovanni Antonio Chiona. Sante was one of the architects involved in the Palazzo Malipicro-Trevisan, one of the most striking Lombardesque private buildings in Venice, but his role there is unclear. The rebuilding of S Felice, Venice, in 1551–6 in the form of a neo-Byzantine domed quincunx in imitation of Codussi's S Giovanni Crisostomo has also been attributed to Sante. Sante's two sons also became architects of minor note, but more research needs to be done to clarify the details of their careers.

BIBLIOGRAPHY

R. v. d. Malsburg: *Die Architektur der Scuola Grande di San Rocco in Venedig* (diss., Heidelberg, Ruprecht-Karls-U., 1976)

V. Willmes: *Studien zur Scuola di San Rocco in Venedig* (Munich, 1985)

SARAH BLAKE McHAM

**Lombardo, Costanzo.** *See* COSTANZO DA FERRARA.

**Lombardo, Cristoforo** [il Lombardino] (*b* Milan, ?1480–90; *d* Milan, Oct 1555). Italian sculptor and architect. He first trained as a mason, probably in the workshop of Milan Cathedral, but then dedicated himself to sculpture and is first recorded as a sculptor in a payment made to him by the Veneranda Fabbrica in 1510. In 1513–14 he went to Rome and on his return to Milan was readmitted among the sculptors at the cathedral. He collaborated on commissions accepted by BAMBAIA, including the funerary monument of *Lancino Curzio* in 1515 (Milan, Castello Sforzesco) and, in the following years, the monument to *Gaston de Foix* (dismembered; fragment in Milan, Ambrosiana).

Lombardo also practised architecture in the cathedral workshop and was commissioned in 1518 to build a pinnacle and two rainwater ducts beneath the lantern staircase. In 1526, due to his experience as a sculptor and architect, he succeeded Andrea da Fusina as engineer of the Fabbrica del Duomo (cathedral works), a position that he held until his death. He developed a perfect understanding of the Gothic structure, which he respected, although he isolated the loadbearing structure from the decorative elements. From 1538 he was engaged on plans for the north portal (on the site of the present altar of the *Madonna dell'albero*). For this he prepared a number of drawings and at least two models, arriving at a solution embodying a three-arched opening with a clear distinction between architectural structure and sculpted reliefs, as can be seen in the great wooden model of the cathedral (Milan, Mus. Duomo). He himself executed one of the reliefs intended for the door, depicting the *Presentation of the Virgin*; this is now positioned, with the others executed at the same time by other artists, on the left pier at the entrance to the Lady Chapel.

Lombardo's work for Milan Cathedral also included designs for some of the religious furnishings, often in collaboration with Bambaia. He was certainly responsible for the architectural design of altars and tombs, including the *Caracciolo* monument (1538–48) in black stone with a Doric order in the ambulatory, and the altar of the Presentation (1543) in the right transept. In both of these works the architectural elements are treated quite autonomously and serve to coordinate the areas intended for reliefs and statues. For the altar of the Presentation Lombardo also executed the statue of *St Catherine*.

In his capacity as engineer of the cathedral works, Lombardo was often called on to supervise and advise on other religious buildings in Milan. From 1530 he worked at Bramante's S Maria presso S Celso, overseeing the completion of the aisles and their marble facing, and also the coffering of the ceiling, a job that took 20 years to complete. From 1532 he was occupied with the marble floor of S Satiro, which was still being executed 20 years later: further drawings and designs were requested from him in 1551. In 1532 he assessed the value of the work on the marble font of S Stefano in Brolo, and he remained in the service of the Maintenance Committee of this church for a number of years, working on the choir (destr.) in 1538. From 1537 he worked on the church of S Eustorgio. He also worked (from 1534) for Massimiliano Stampa (*d* 1552), restructuring the latter's city houses into a palace, the Palazzo Stampa di Soncino (altered in the 19th and 20th centuries). He endowed the entrance with a lofty tower, articulated with features inflected as coupled columns at ground-floor level, as pilasters on the next two floors, and thereafter as lesene framing, the whole crowned with a double eagle on two tall columns with the motto 'plus ultra', the emblem of Charles V. Subsequent architectural projects include the construction of the church of S Caterina della Chiusa (destr.), which is known through 19th-century reliefs by Luigi Cagnola. The façade features superimposed orders with strict classical detailing and delicate mouldings around the voids. Similar skill in the disposition of wall spaces can be found in the interior of the centrally planned chapel of S Caterina presso S Nazaro (1541–2), which is attributed to Lombardo. Around 1542 he submitted a design for the completion of the Certosa di Pavia (a trace of which remains in a drawing in Milan, Castello Sforzesco; Bianconi Col.), which was subsequently executed under his supervision. Between 1545 and 1547 Lombardo is recorded as active at the sanctuary of the *Madonna dei Miracoli* (1498), Saronno, and from 1547 he worked on the completion of the Trivulzio Chapel in S Nazaro.

As Architect to Milan Cathedral, Lombardo was also often concerned with matters relating to the cathedral square, especially on such festive occasions as the entry of Emperor Charles V in 1541 and that of King Philip II of Spain in 1548. In 1541 the floats and displays were designed by Giulio Romano, who was also asked for an opinion on the north transept door of the cathedral. Through Giulio's intervention, Lombardo was called to Bologna in 1545 to provide a drawing for the façade of S Petronio in collaboration with Giulio, and Giulio's influence can be seen in Lombardo's later works, for example the octagonal lantern of the church of S Maria della Passione, which he worked on in 1550–51. Inside, the half columns at the angles between the chapels are projected upwards above the entablature as wall strips and then into the vault as ribs, giving a marked vertical thrust. From 1552 Lombardo suffered increasingly from gout, forcing him to delegate part of the site-work in all his commissions to his collaborator Vincenzo Seregni.

BIBLIOGRAPHY

*Annali della fabbrica del Duomo di Milano dall'origine fino al presente*, iii (Milan, 1880)

C. Baroni: *Documenti per la storia dell'architettura a Milano nel rinascimento e nel barocco*, i (Florence, 1940); ii (Rome, 1968)

P. Mezzanotte: 'S Caterina alla Chiusa e Cristoforo Lombardo', *Palladio*, vii (1943), pp. 23–6

G. Treccani degli Alfieri, ed.: *Storia di Milano*, viii (Milan, 1957)

G. Struffolino Krüger: 'Qualità, valore, armonia nell'architettura della chiesa di S Caterina presso S Nazaro', *A. Lombarda*, xii (1967), pp. 37–48

M. G. Albertini Ottolenghi, R. Bossaglia and F. R. Pesenti: *La Certosa di Pavia* (Milan, 1968)

R. Bossaglia: 'La scultura', *Il Duomo di Milano*, ii (Milan, 1973), pp. 65–176
H. Heydenreich and W. Lotz: *Art and Architecture in Italy 1400–1600*, Pelican Hist. A. (Harmondsworth, 1974)
*Omaggio a Tiziano: La cultura artistica milanese nell'età di Carlo V* (exh. cat., ed. G. Bologna; Milan, Pal. Reale, 1977), pp. 97–131
A. Scotti and others: *S Maria della Passione e il Conservatorio G. Verdi a Milano* (Milan, 1982)
*Giulio Romano* (exh. cat., intro. E. Gombrich; Mantua, Pal. Te and Pal. Ducale, 1982) [incl. prev. unpubd designs for S Petronio façade, 1545]

AURORA SCOTTI TOSINI

**Lombardo, il.** *See* RAGGI, ANTONIO.

**Lombardo, Tommaso** [da Lugano] (*fl c.* 1536–50). Italian sculptor. He is first recorded as an assistant of Jacopo Sansovino in Venice from 1536 to 1546. He may have trained previously with Sansovino since his role during these years was that of factotum who carried out Sansovino's ideas efficiently and faithfully. With Luca Lancia he blocked out the marble *Virgin, Child and Angels* (Venice, Doge's Pal., chapel), and he also worked on the first of the marble *pergoli* (balconies) designed by Sansovino for the choir of S Marco (1536–7). At the same time he supervised the production of the bronze reliefs for the first *pergolo*. In 1542–4, he was in charge of another set of bronze reliefs for the second *pergolo*, and he also oversaw the early stages in the production of Sansovino's bronze sacristy door for S Marco (1546).

Vasari, who was unusually well informed about Sansovino's followers, ascribed to Tommaso unspecified carved figures for the Library of S Marco, probably some of the river gods and victories on the spandrels. He also stated that Tommaso left Sansovino's workshop just before the creation of one of his major surviving works, the marble altarpiece of the *Virgin, Child and Infant Baptist* (*c.* 1546–7; Venice, S Sebastiano). Tommaso's other known statue, a marble *St Jerome* (?before 1547), was for the chapel of Hieronimo Priuli in S Salvatore, Venice. Vasari also mentioned a lost bust of the Emperor Charles V and stucco decorations (unidentified).

Tommaso's critical reputation has never been high: Francesco Sansovino observed that the altarpiece in S Sebastiano was a copy of a group by his father, Jacopo, in the Loggetta in Venice, and the *St Jerome* and its relief of *God the Father* invite comparison with motifs from other works by Jacopo Sansovino. They reveal a craftsman of good technical ability though devoid of imagination. It was this that made Lombardo, with his self-effacing personality, a valued collaborator of Sansovino.

BIBLIOGRAPHY
G. Vasari: *Vite* (1550, rev. 2/1568); ed. G. Milanesi (1878–85), vii, p. 520
A. Venturi: *Storia* (1901–40), x/3, pp. 58–63
E. Ybl: 'Tommaso Lombardos Altarstatuen in Bissone', *Z. Schweiz. Archäol. & Kstgesch.*, viii (1946), pp. 53–6
B Boucher: 'Jacopo Sansovino and the Choir of St Mark's', *Burl. Mag.*, cxviii/881 (1976), pp. 552–66
——: 'Jacopo Sansovino and the Choir of St Mark's', *Burl. Mag.*, cxxi/912 (1979), pp. 155–68
For further bibliography *see* SANSOVINO, (1).

BRUCE BOUCHER

**Lombart** [Lombard], **Pierre** (*b c.* 1613; *d* Paris, 30 Dec 1682). French engraver. Although he was apparently trained in France, he worked from 1649 until *c.* 1662 in London. Some of the prints that he made there were mediocre, such as the *Seven Liberal Arts* after Louis Richer (*fl c.* 1658) and his engravings after Francis Cleyn for John Ogilby's translation of the works of Virgil (1654); others were of high quality (e.g. the *Twelve Countesses* after van Dyck). After returning to France in 1663 Lombart made interpretations of religious subjects after Nicolas Poussin, Annibale Carracci, Philippe de Champaigne and Jean Lefèbvre (1600–75), and portraits after Wallerant Vaillant, Florent de la Mare-Richart (*c.* 1630–1718) and Antoine Dieu, which in 1673 gained him a place in the Académie Royale. One of his most curious pieces is the equestrian portrait engraved after van Dyck, in which the heads of Charles I of England, Oliver Cromwell and Louis XIV of France appear in the successive states.

BIBLIOGRAPHY
O'Donoghue; Thieme–Becker

MAXIME PRÉAUD

**Lome** [le Home], **Jehan** [Lomme, Janin] (*b* ?Tournai; *fl* 1411; *d* Viana, 1449). Netherlandish sculptor, active in Spain. He was probably trained in Paris. He came to Navarre in 1411 to work on the tomb of *Charles III and Eleanor* and settled there for the rest of his life; he is documented in the royal service at Olite, Sangüesa, Tafalla, Pamplona and Viana. The double tomb of Charles and Eleanor, situated in the nave of Pamplona Cathedral, was executed between 1413 and 1419 by Lome and his assistants, and it is one of the best examples of Late Gothic funerary sculpture in the Iberian Peninsula. The form of the monument, a free-standing tomb chest with arcaded sides sheltering cloaked weepers and the recumbent effigies of the sovereigns on top, follows Franco-Flemish traditions. Lome's courtly style can be identified in other contemporary works in Navarre, for example the *Coronation of the Virgin* portal on the north transept of Pamplona Cathedral; the figures of *Queen Blanche of Navarre* and the *Virgin and Child* at the entrance to the atrium of S María, Olite; and the niche-tomb of *Bishop Sancho Sánchez de Oteiza* (1420–25) in the chapel of S Juan Evangelista in Pamplona Cathedral. Through the work of his followers, Lome's influence was felt in Navarre until the second half of the 15th century.

BIBLIOGRAPHY
E. Bertaux: 'Le Mausolée de Charles le Noble à Pampelune et l'art franco-flamand en Navarre', *Gaz. B.-A.*, 3rd ser., xl/2 (1908), pp. 89–112
R. S. Janke: *Jehan Lome y la escultura gótica posterior en Navarra* (Pamplona, 1977)

M. C. LACARRA DUCAY

**Loménie, Louis-Henri de.** *See* BRIENNE, Comte de.

**Lomonosov** [formerly Oranienbaum]. Imperial summer residence and adjacent town, 41 km west of St Petersburg, Russia, on the southern shore of the Gulf of Finland. The monumental Great Palace was built in the 1710s and 1720s on the estate of Prince Menshikov (*c.* 1660–1729), a favourite of Peter I (*reg* 1682–1725). Erected on a sea embankment, its four-storey central block is connected to the lofty domed pavilions by three-storey galleries. A canal led from the palace to the sea, and in front of it a regular park was laid out with low ornamental parterres. The estate was one of the most luxurious of the period. The first architect was Giovanni Maria Fontana, and Gottfried Schädel was employed from 1716. Five days after the celebration to mark the completion of the palace in 1729, Prince Menshikov was exiled, and the estate passed to the Crown. In 1743 Elizabeth I (*reg* 1741–61) gave Oranienbaum to her nephew from Holstein, Pyotr Fyodorovich, the future Emperor Peter III (*reg* 1761–2). In the 1740s and 1750s Bartolomeo-Francesco Rastrelli restored the old palace and redecorated the interiors. In 1756 the Italian architect ANTONIO RINALDI began to erect for the militaristic Peter the distinctive Peterstadt complex (destr.), comprising a small pentagonal fortress complete with cannon and housing a regular complement of soldiers from Holstein. The fortress contained a diminutive Rococo palace, an arsenal, a hospital and barracks.

After deposing Peter in 1762, Catherine II (*reg* 1762–96) commissioned Rinaldi to build a dacha ensemble for her at Oranienbaum. This incorporated a garden in a Rococo style. The modest, single-storey Chinese Palace (1762–8) had a Neo-classical façade and contained remarkable chinoiserie interiors, richly decorated mainly by Italian artists. A park was laid out, consisting of both regular, intricately patterned and more ornamental and picturesque areas. Over a score of pavilions in Chinese style, partly borrowed from the pattern books of William Halfpenny (1752 and 1755), were erected, including the famous Katal'naya Gorka ('Sliding hillock', 1762–74), with a pavilion from which visitors could descend a long artificial ramp (destr.), in specially designed trolleys in summer and sleighs in winter. When work was completed at Oranienbaum in the 1770s, Catherine II had lost interest in the estate (she rarely stayed there), and no further work was done until the end of the 19th century, when the architects Lyudvig Bonshtedt and Harald Julius Bosse built a number of small buildings. During the 19th and 20th centuries the Great Palace was the home of several grand dukes and later housed government offices. In the Soviet period the town was renamed in honour of the famous Russian poet and scientist, Mikhail Lomonosov (1711–65). The palaces and park were badly damaged by German artillery during World War II, but restoration began in the late 20th century.

BIBLIOGRAPHY

A. Uspensky: *Imperatorskiye dvortsy: Dvorets Petra III v Oranienbaume* [Imperial palaces: Peter III's palace at Oranienbaum] (St Petersburg, 1913)

V. Kennett and A. Kennett: *The Palaces of Leningrad* (London, 1973)

A. Raskin: *Gorod Lomonosov* [The town of Lomonosov] (Leningrad, 1979)

A. N. Petrov and others: *Pamyatniki arkhitektury prigorodov Leningrada* [Architectural monuments of the Leningrad suburbs] (Leningrad, 1983)

D. Kyuchariants: *Antonio Rinal'di* (Leningrad, 1984)

——: *Khudozhestvennyye pamyatniki gorod Lomonosova* [Art monuments of the town of Lomonosov] (Leningrad, 1985)

D. O. SHVIDKOVSKY

**Lomonosov, Mikhail (Vasil'yevich)** (*b* Denisovka, Arkhangel province, 19 Nov 1711; *d* St Petersburg, 15 April 1765). Russian scientist, writer, entrepreneur and administrator. Born into a relatively humble family in the far north of Russia, he was sent to Moscow in 1731 to study at the Slavo-Graeco-Latin Academy, and he transferred to the Academy University in St Petersburg in 1735. The following year he went to Germany (until 1741), studying principally in Marburg and Freiburg. In 1745 he was appointed Professor of Chemistry at the Academy University, the first Russian to hold such a post. One of the most brilliant scholars in Europe, he is chiefly renowned for his achievements in the natural sciences; he also worked on Russian history, his *Rossiyskaya grammatika* ('Russian grammar'; St Petersburg, 1757) was of paramount significance in the standardization of the Russian literary language, and he was also influential as a writer of verse. He was the driving force behind the foundation of Moscow University by his patron Count Ivan Shuvalov in 1755, and he constantly pressed for the reform of the Academy of Sciences, including the separation from it of the arts and crafts sections. This, however, was not achieved until 1766, even though an Academy of Arts had been inaugurated in St Petersburg in 1757.

Lomonosov's involvement in the imperial firework displays in the 1750s was probably due more to his skill as a chemist than as a designer, and his other major involvement in the arts also grew out of his work in natural science. Dissatisfied with the coloured glass available for his work on optics, he used his scientific knowledge to devise an improved method of production. His proposal of 1751 for a state glass factory was turned down, and in 1752 he decided to open his own, receiving, through Shuvalov's influence, a site and a state loan of 4,000 roubles in 1753. In 1754 the factory began to produce decorative glass and mosaics, but it proved unprofitable, not least because of a lack of orders for the costly mosaics. To save the situation Lomonosov produced a project for a monument at the tomb of *Peter I* in the cathedral of SS Peter and Paul in St Petersburg, accompanied by a cycle of mosaics celebrating his deeds. This was steered through the Senate within a few months in 1757 by the prominent politician and industrialist Count Pyotr Shuvalov, but final approval was obtained only in 1761, and the only part of it ever to be realized was the mosaic *Battle of Poltava* (1762–4), after a specially commissioned picture by Karl Ludwig Christinek (*c.* 1733–93). Though the picture contains a number of anachronisms and some of the likenesses are questionable, it is admired for the intensity of its colours, due to the quality of Lomonosov's glass and his practice of working with relatively large pieces. Lomonosov's factory, never profitable, was closed shortly after his death.

BIBLIOGRAPHY

V. K. Makarov: *Khudozhestvennoye naslediye M. V. Lomonosova: Mozaiki* [M. V. Lomonosov's artistic heritage: the mosaics] (Moscow and Leningrad, 1950)

Ye. I. Gavrilova: 'Lomonosov i osnovaniye Akademii khudozhestv' [Lomonosov and the foundation of the Academy of Arts], *Russkoye iskusstvo XVIII veka: Materialy i issledovaniya*, ed. T. V. Alekseyeva (Moscow, 1973), pp. 66–75

B. A. Kosolapov: 'O proyektakh monumenta Petru I v Petropavlovskom sobore i rabote nad mozaichnoy kartinoy *Poltavskaya bataliya*' [On the projects for a monument to Peter I in the cathedral of SS Peter and Paul and the work on the mosaic *Battle of Poltava*], *Sov. Isk.* (1984), no. 1, pp. 266–82

R. M. CLEMINSON

**Lomp.** *See* LAMPI.

**Londerseel, Johannes** [Ioannes; Jan] **van** (*b* Antwerp, 25 Jan 1578; *d* Rotterdam, before 7 Jan 1625). Flemish engraver, etcher and print publisher. He apparently trained in Antwerp, where he may have worked in the workshop of Abraham de Bruyn, father of his brother-in-law Nicolaes de Bruyn. About 1600 he followed his brother A(ha)ssuerus van Londerseel (*bapt* Antwerp, 30 March 1572; *d* before 21 May 1649), also an engraver and print publisher, to Rotterdam. He seems to have been active there between 1610 and 1625; in 1614 he was living in Delft.

Londerseel's reproductive engravings after landscapes by David Vinckboons, Gillis d'Hondecoetre and others are large and have a standard composition, with trees on either side, a high horizon and hills, rivers and villages. The landscapes, unlike the figures in them, are engraved with great virtuosity and reveal a preference for picturesque detail, such as gnarled trees. These engravings are characterized by their mixture of emphatic contrasts between black and white in the foreground (e.g. on the leaves) and pale, lightly etched backgrounds. One fine example is the *Landscape with Susanna and the Elders* (Hollstein, no. 7; original drawing by Vinckboons, New York, Pierpont Morgan Lib.). Londerseel seems to have been strongly influenced by Nicolaes de Bruyn in these prints. His reproductive engravings after Marten de Vos, which are presumably early, and the fine *Interior of the Church of S Giovanni in Laterano, Rome* (H 75) after Hendrick Aerts are exceptional in an oeuvre otherwise dominated by landscape subjects. Another remarkable piece is the *View of The Hague* (H 74), a huge engraving on two sheets, made in collaboration with Nicolaus de Clerck in 1614. Londerseel's estate inventory shows that he printed and published his own work. Later editions of many of his engravings were produced by Claes Jansz. Visscher. Londerseel had at least one son, Johannes van Londerseel the younger, by whom only one rather clumsy engraving is known (1654; H 16).

BIBLIOGRAPHY

Hollstein: *Dut. & Flem.* [H]; *NKL*; Thieme–Becker
F. G. Waller: *Biographisch woordenboek van noord-Nederlandsche graveurs* (The Hague, 1938), p. 205
D. Freedberg: *Dutch Landscape Prints of the Seventeenth Century* (London, 1980), p. 23

MANFRED SELLINK

**London** [anc. Rom. Londinium]. Capital of the United Kingdom, situated in south-east England in the middle Thames Valley *c.* 64 km from the estuary of the River Thames. Greater London extends into the counties of Essex, Middlesex, Hertfordshire, Buckinghamshire, Surrey and Kent, covering an area of 1580 sq. km, and is the largest conurbation in Europe, with a population of about eight million. London grew up round two historic nuclei, the commercial centre comprising the City of London on the north (left) bank of the Thames with Southwark on the opposite bank, and the seat of administration and government at Westminster (*see* §V, 3 below) on the left bank *c.* 3 km upstream. The foremost commercial, financial and cultural city in the United Kingdom, London is a leading centre of art education and the international art market. Some of the most important public art collections in the world are located there. This article discusses mainly central London, that is, the City of London, Docklands and inner residential suburbs.

*See also* CHISWICK HOUSE, GREENWICH, HAMPTON COURT PALACE, KEW, ROYAL BOTANIC GARDENS OF and NONSUCH PALACE.

I. History. II. Urban development. III. Art life and organization. IV. Centre of production. V. Buildings and gardens. VI. Royal Academy of Arts.

## I. History.

The name London is possibly derived from the Celtic Iron Age name Londonion. The region has been inhabited continuously since some time after 5000 BC, but the city's documented history begins with the Roman foundation of Londinium, probably *c.* AD 50 (*see* §II, 1 below), as the fledgling commercial centre was sacked by the Iceni under Boudicca in AD 61. London was the administrative centre of the Roman province of Britannia, and it remained an important place after the end of rule from Rome in the early 5th century. Christianity was established with the foundation of St Paul's Cathedral (*see* §V, 1 below) in 604; Westminster Abbey (*see* §V, 2 below) may also have been founded in the 7th century. London was raided by the Vikings several times from 842 and occupied by them in 879, but it was retaken by Alfred, King of Wessex, in 886 and thereafter its prosperity increased. The city received its first charter after the Norman Conquest of 1066 under William I (*reg* 1066–89), who also built the White Tower (now Tower of London; *see* §§II, 2 and V, 4 below).

London was already the largest town and port in the kingdom in medieval times, with a population before the Black Death of 1348–9 of perhaps 80,000. The Palace of Westminster (*see* §V, 3 below), which had been founded by King Edward the Confessor (*reg* 1042–66), gradually became the seat of government administration, and Henry III established the abbey as the coronation church. Whitehall Palace (*see* §V, 5 below) was developed from the 1530s as the main royal residence, and from the mid-16th century Westminster became the permanent seat of the Houses of Parliament. London reached new levels of prosperity under Elizabeth I, but outbreaks of plague in the 17th century were followed by the Great Fire of 1666 (see fig. 4 below). London expanded greatly, with new residential areas westwards, from the 18th century, and with the excavation of the docks in the 19th it was able to maintain its position as the leading port of the kingdom until the docks declined irretrievably in the 1970s. University College, London, was founded in 1826, and the University of London was incorporated in 1836.

From 1888, while the Corporation of the City of London retained responsibility for administering the City of London itself, the newly founded London County Council administered the County of London, including much of Middlesex. The LCC was replaced in 1963 by the Greater London Council, which was itself abolished in 1986. The government of Greater London is now run by the 32 individual borough councils.

BIBLIOGRAPHY

*Survey of London* (London, 1900–) [a detailed account of London, district by district, in over 40 volumes to date]
*London*, Royal Comm. Anc. & Hist. Mnmts & Constr. England, iii–v (London, 1928–30)
S. E. Rasmussen: *London: The Unique City* (Copenhagen, 1934, rev. Cambridge, MA, 1982)
N. Pevsner: *London 1: The Cities of London and Westminster*, Bldgs England (Harmondsworth, 1957, rev. B. Cherry, 3/1973)
P. Glanville: *London in Maps* (London, 1972)
C. Hibbert: *London: The Biography of a City* (London, 1977)

B. Cherry and N. Pevsner: *London 2: South*, Bldgs England (Harmondsworth, 1983/*R* 1990)

B. Weinreb and C. Hibbert, eds: *The London Encyclopaedia* (London, 1983/*R* 1992)

F. Barker and P. Jackson, eds: *The History of London in Maps* (London, 1990)

B. Cherry and N. Pevsner: *London 3: North West*, Bldgs England (Harmondsworth, 1991)

——: *London 4: North and North East* (in preparation)

## II. Urban development.

London as it is today is the survivor of two devastating destructions: much of the city was burnt in the Great Fire of 1666; and bomb damage inflicted in World War II destroyed many buildings not only in the city but also in outer London. Inner London, however, still consists of an amalgamation of distinct districts, different quarters retaining their own characters. The former docks lie east of the City, and the Inns of Court and the theatre district west of it. The main shopping streets are around Oxford St, Regent St and Bond St, while Mayfair and Belgravia are the most central residential areas. Parliament and government are at Westminster and Whitehall, with the royal residence at Buckingham Palace. The latter is set between St James's Park and Green Park, which, with the contiguous Hyde Park and Kensington Gardens, create a large open space in the middle of the West End, with Regent's Park northwards and Battersea Park south of the Thames opposite Chelsea. Since 1935 a green belt, designed to prevent further urban sprawl, has surrounded Greater London.

1. Before 1066. 2. 1066–1665. 3. 1666–1799. 4. 1800–88. 5. 1889–1945. 6. After 1945.

1. BEFORE 1066. Evidence of Palaeolithic habitation has been found in the London area, and settlement seems to have begun in the 5th millennium BC. Settlements dated *c.* 2500 BC have been excavated on both sides of the Thames at Southwark, Lambeth and Westminster, but the London Basin declined in the Early Bronze Age, to revive *c.* 1300 BC, with both settlement and cult sites in what is now central London from *c.* 1000 BC. Timber buildings and pottery (London, Mus. London) have been excavated at Westminster, Southwark and Whitehall. A quantity of fine bronze swords, axes and spearheads (London, Mus. London) recovered from the Thames suggests that death rituals were associated with the river, and that these continued into the Iron Age is indicated by a shield and helmet (both London, BM) dated to the 1st century BC or the early 1st century AD and also found near the river (*see* CELTIC ART, §II, 5). The Thames may already have been bridged at this time.

The traditional view that London was established as a military supply base after the Roman invasion in AD 43 has been modified: groups of Roman pottery predating AD 60 are uncommon, indicating a date of AD 50 for the start of the settlement, a conclusion supported by the date of construction of roads in Southwark converging on the crossing-point of the River Thames. Civilian settlement, suggested by Tacitus, has been confirmed by archaeological excavation: evidence of streets, and of buildings of timber and clay, occasionally with mosaics and decorated

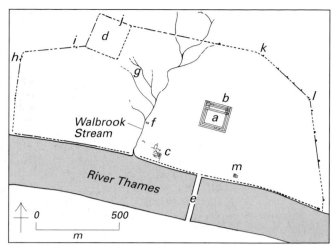

1. London, plan of the Roman city, 3rd century AD: (a) forum; (b) basilica; (c) governor's palace; (d) Cripplegate fort; (e) bridge; (f) Mithraeum; (g) amphitheatre; (h) Ludgate; (i) Newgate; (j) Aldersgate; (k) Bishopsgate; (l) Aldgate; (m) Billingsgate bathhouse

wall plaster, has been found on various sites spread over two low hills divided by the Walbrook Stream.

London's increasing status was emphasized by the construction in the late 1st century AD of the first forum and basilica on Cornhill, and of a provincial governor's palace south of Cannon Street (see fig. 1); during the early 2nd century a stone-walled fort, probably for the governor's bodyguard and staff, was established at Cripplegate to the north-west (extant fragments include west gate, London Wall), with an amphitheatre to its south-east. A second, much larger, forum and basilica replaced the first in the 120s. The Romans built a bridge with timber piers across the Thames from *c.* AD 70 to link the north bank with the northernmost of the gravel islands on which Southwark developed. On the north bank were artificial terraces supporting buildings, including warehouses and other port installations. The waterfront expanded several times to its limit immediately south of the present Thames Street (up to 80 m behind the present water-line) in 225–45.

In the early 3rd century AD the city was first walled in stone, although some of the gates (destr. mid-18th century) may have pre-existed it as boundary markers; the wall is visible at several points, for example at Tower Hill and Noble Street. The city was also enhanced by new or rebuilt temples, as is testified by the 53 sculptured blocks from a monumental arch and a *Screen of Gods* (London, Mus. London) built into a late 3rd-century section of the riverside city wall (*see* §III, 1 below). In the 240s a fine residence in the Walbrook Valley had a private Mithraeum added (reconstructed at 11 Queen Victoria Street in 1954). By contrast to the bustling port of the 1st and 2nd centuries, late Roman London (*c.* 200–400) was probably a city of fewer, widely spaced buildings of grand proportions, given over to government and its associated ceremonial functions. On many sites the slighter buildings of the 1st and 2nd centuries are overlaid by a homogeneous stratum of featureless 'dark earth' indicating large, open spaces. But the city was still evidently worth defending; a string of interval towers was added to the eastern wall, and the 1.5 km-long riverside closed off either with a wall, or by strengthening previous disparate embankment walls. Defensive works at the south-east corner of the city (now the site of the Tower of London) were being undertaken as late as the closing decade of the 4th century.

The city was chosen as a centre of the Christian mission in AD 604, when St Paul's Cathedral was founded, implying London's importance and perhaps the size of its population. Tradition, and inference from later documents, suggest a royal palace of Offa, King of Mercia (*reg* 757–96), within the walls of the Cripplegate fort, with St Alban's (datable only to the Saxon period generally; rebuilt by Wren; destr. World War II), Wood Street, as its chapel. In the 730s Bede (673–735) referred to London in his *Ecclesiastical History of the English Nation* (II.3) as 'a market of many nations, coming to it by land and sea'. An assessment of finds from building sites (Vince, 1990) suggests that this trading area lay not within the walls but immediately west of the city on both sides of the Strand. Signs of mid-Saxon habitation (650–850) have since been found in the Covent Garden area. This settlement, perhaps seasonal, may be the 'Lundentunes hythe' of the 8th-century charters (London, BM) that granted tolls of London to church dignitaries.

Two land grants issued by Alfred after he retook London from the Vikings in AD 886 refer to an area north of Queenhithe, strongly suggesting that London was being restored, like Winchester, by laying out streets, and, like Worcester, by granting commercial privileges to bishops (*see* ANGLO-SAXON ART, §II). Timber buildings from the mid-10th century can be traced along streets, and an embankment was constructed upstream of Billingsgate, which was first mentioned as a landing-place for imports *c.* 1000. By this date London was the largest town in England. Extant fragments of buildings include the results of archaeological excavation, as well as an arch and quoin of reused Roman tiles at All Hallows Barking (founded *c.* 660–70), Great Tower Street, and foundations at St Bride, off Fleet Street.

2. 1066–1665. London had three Norman castles: the White Tower (*c.* 1077–*c.* 1100) in the Tower of London (*see* §V, 4 below) in the east, and two smaller fortifications in the west, the sites of which are only approximately known: Baynard's Castle I (probably built by 1087; destr. *c.* 1275) and Montfichet's Tower (by 1136; destr. *c.* 1275), both near the present Blackfriars Station. St Paul's Cathedral was rebuilt from 1087, although engravings indicate that much of the nave dated from after the serious fire of 1135 (*see* §V, 1(i)(a) below). There were large-scale monastic buildings at St Mary Overie (founded 1106; rebuilt 13th–15th centuries; rest. 19th century; now Southwark Cathedral), Southwark, Holy Trinity Priory (1108; mostly destr.), Aldgate, and St Bartholomew's Hospital and Priory (founded 1123; substantial remains of the 12th-century choir survive). Hospitals, nunneries and houses of the crusading orders followed: the Knights Templar began *c.* 1128 in Holborn, moving to New Temple, Fleet Street, in 1161; of their church, the round nave and porch (*c.* 1160–85) and chancel (*c.* 1220), both restored, survive. The Knights Hospitaller were established at the priory of

St John of Jerusalem, Clerkenwell, *c.* 1144. Also founded were the nunnery of St Mary (*c.* 1145), Clerkenwell, the hospital of St Katharine by the Tower (1148; destr. 1825), the hospital of St Mary without Bishopsgate (also known as St Mary Spital; founded 1197), the Benedictine nunnery of St Helen (before 1216), Bishopsgate, the hospital of St Thomas of Acre (early 13th century; destr.), Cheapside, the hospital of St Mary of Bethlehem (1247; destr.) and Elsing Spital (1329; destr.). The Cistercian abbey of St Mary Graces (destr.) was founded east of the city in 1346 by Edward III.

The city was entirely contained by the early 3rd-century Roman wall, except for a late 13th-century enlargement enclosing the Blackfriars precinct, and successive enlargements of the Tower fortifications. A series of interval towers was added in the 13th and 14th centuries from the Walbrook head-water to Ludgate; the Blackfriars extension was also towered. Northern sections of the wall were repaired in brick in 1477 and strengthened, perhaps against cannon. The city also provided a water-supply (from 1237) and covered markets (e.g. the Stocks, 1282; rebuilt 1410; destr. 1666); the main landing-places for goods imported by river were at Billingsgate and Queenhithe (the installations are known mainly from 16th-century panoramas). London Bridge was rebuilt from 1176 to 1209 (destr. 1831) with 19 arches and a drawbridge; a chapel on the bridge was rebuilt by Henry Yevele in 1384–97. North of Cheapside from the 12th century lay the Guildhall (rest. by George Dance (ii) in 1788, and by Giles Gilbert Scott after World War II), which was rebuilt on a stone undercroft *c.* 1270 and enlarged in 1411–40 (see fig. 2) with imposing perpendicular windows to the designs of John Croxton (*fl* 1411–47). The complex included various civic offices and a chapel. About 1440 the Leadenhall (destr. 19th century), a large quadrangular market and granary surrounded by a ground-floor arcade, with its own chapel, was built in Cornhill (now Leadenhall Street).

The main mendicant orders had large houses (all destr.) in London: the Dominicans (Blackfriars) from 1221 (moved site 1275), the Franciscans (Greyfriars) from 1222, the Carmelites (Whitefriars) from 1247, the Augustinian Friars from 1253 and the Crutched Friars before 1269, as well as several minor orders (e.g. the Poor Clares (Minoresses), *c.* 1293–4). By 1300 London had 106 parish churches, many of which must have had pre-Conquest origins as chapels for individual estates or for such groups as traders and craftsmen. St Mary-le-Bow (rebuilt 1678–80 by Christopher Wren) retains its late 11th-century crypt, and 12th-century work can be seen at St Helen, Bishopsgate; there was 14th- and 15th-century work at St Ethelburga (partly destr. 1993), Bishopsgate, and St Andrew Undershaft, Leadenhall Street, was comprehensively rebuilt in 1520–32. The great majority of London's medieval parish churches, however, were either destroyed in the Great Fire of 1666 (some later rebuilt by Wren) or badly damaged in World War II.

Property plots dating from the 10th century can be traced on certain streets and on the river bank above Billingsgate. London had developed building regulations by 1200, designed to improve construction and prevent fires; traces of Norman stone houses have been found in the City and Southwark. Parts of more prestigious houses,

2. London, Guildhall, founded 12th century, enlarged by John Croxton, 1411–40; from a reconstruction by Terry Ball of its appearance in the mid-15th century (private collection)

for instance towers and undercrofts, were built in stone; Kentish ragstone was commonly used for external walling, and softer Reigate stone for carved details and mouldings. Most domestic buildings, however, were of timber. There were jettied buildings of two and probably three storeys by 1300; by 1600 some houses reached five storeys with garrets. Brick was introduced during the first half of the 15th century, as at Drapers' Hall, St Swithin's Lane (1425; destr. 1666), and the rebuilt west end of St Mary Overie (1469; rebuilt 1890–97), but few buildings were made entirely of brick even by 1600.

The number of town houses, or inns, of church dignitaries was notable; at least 48 are known, for example the chapel of the inn of the Bishop of Ely (now St Etheldreda (c. 1284; rest.), Ely Place) and the hall of the Bishop of Chichester (now the hall of Lincoln's Inn (1493), Chancery Lane). Secular lords or civic leaders also had town houses (e.g. Crosby Place (1466; hall removed to Chelsea, 1908), Bishopsgate). Some of these houses, often built around a courtyard, became company halls for guilds from the mid-14th century (Merchant Taylors' Hall (14th century; rest.), 30 Threadneedle Street; see LIVERY HALL); when John Stow (?1525–1605) wrote *A Survey of London* (1598) 46 were scattered through the city. Gardens were probably common in the early medieval city, but by 1600 they were restricted to major houses and livery halls, except in the suburbs.

The waterfront area south of Thames Street expanded by means of piecemeal land reclamation, especially around the nodal commercial centres of Queenhithe, Dowgate and Billingsgate. Expansion occurred at the greatest rate between c. 1100 and c. 1300, after which it decreased; previous timber revetments were replaced, usually with stone walls, which did not need so much repair. In the late medieval period the waterfront took on the character of an industrial suburb, with dyers and brewers (see fig. 3); Baynard's Castle II (destr.) was also built here, on the site of a previous noble's house, by Henry VII in 1501. The line of the riverfront at this time is marked on the site (now City of London Boys' School, Queen Victoria Street). Near by, on the west side of the increasingly noxious Fleet Valley, Henry VIII's Bridewell Palace (destr. 1863–4) was built in 1515–23, comprising two courtyards, a long gallery and Thames-side range, royal apartments and probably the first staircase in England designed for state occasions. (The palace was given to the city by Edward VI (reg 1547–53); it was damaged in the Great Fire, but is partly known from 18th-century engravings and modern excavations.)

The western suburb along Holborn and Fleet Street developed as a legal quarter during the late 14th century and the 15th (e.g. hall of Barnard's Inn (c. 1420), Holborn). The surviving Inns of Court and Chancery buildings, however, date largely from the mid-16th century: for example, the halls of Gray's Inn (1556–70), Gray's Inn Road, Middle Temple (1573), Fleet Street, and Staple Inn (1590), Holborn (all rest. after war damage 1939–45).

The effects of the Dissolution of the Monasteries (1536–40) were wide-ranging. Holy Trinity Priory, Aldgate, was

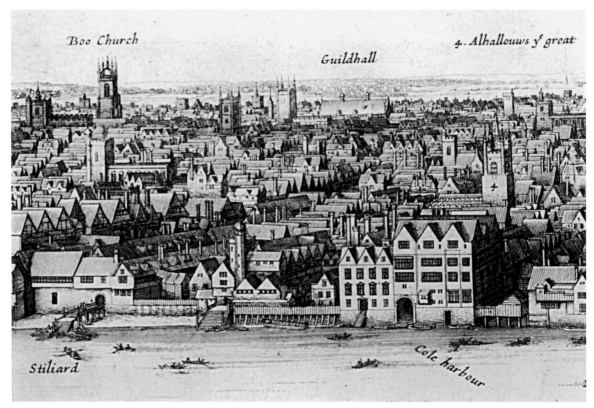

Boo Church

Guildhall

4. Alhallouws yᵉ great

Stiliard

Cole harbour

3. London, Hanseatic Steelyard and waterfront buildings (destroyed 1666; now site of Cannon Street Station); detail from Wenzel Hollar's panorama, engraved 1647 (London, British Museum)

already dissolved in 1532 and given to Thomas Audley (1488–1544), who rebuilt it as a large town house. Similar fates befell most of the religious house precincts; St Bartholomew's Priory (now St Bartholomew the Great, Smithfield) was given to Sir Richard Rich (?1496–1567) and Charterhouse (mostly destr.) to Edward North (?1496–1564). Much urban property, previously monastic or chantry lands, came into secular ownership. This coincided with an influx of immigrants, especially refugees from the Netherlands. Contemporary observers bemoaned the fact that gardens were being built over, along with the sudden spread of housing beyond the suburbs, and the alarming increase of population in inadequate housing. Surveys of London houses (c. 1612) by Ralph Treswell (c. 1540–1616) illustrate the congestion and predominant use of timber-framing. Even parish churches sold strips of land adjacent to churches or on the edges of cemeteries for building; many shops were built.

In the 16th century first THOMAS WOLSEY and then Henry VIII created palaces both in the city (St James's Palace and Whitehall Palace; see §V, 5 below) and near London (e.g. NONSUCH PALACE and Hampton Court). There were few Elizabethan buildings of note inside the city walls, however. Thomas Gresham (?1519–79) built the Royal Exchange (1566; destr. 1666) and a large brick house (destr.) in Netherlandish style in Broad Street; both buildings were designed by Hans Henryk van Passe. James I was determined to have it said of himself 'that we had

found our Citie and suburbs of London of stickes, and left them of bricke' (Larkin and Hughes, p. 346). Proclamations from 1605 demanded brick and stone buildings, but were soon amended and frequently avoided, although brick houses with curved gables were noted in Holborn in 1619.

The development of such villages as Kensington and Hampstead, which would eventually become inner suburbs, began in the early 17th century with the building of substantial Italianate villas for merchants and noblemen (see VILLA, §II, 4). Closer in, Inigo Jones laid out Covent Garden (1630) with St Paul's Church (1631–3; see RUSSELL, (2)); Lincoln's Inn Fields and perhaps the design for Lindsey House there (both c. 1640); and he worked on St Paul's Cathedral (see §V, 1(i)(c) below and JONES, INIGO, §1(i)). Despite stylistic innovations by Jones and Nicholas Stone (see STONE (ii), (1)), the intramural city remained little affected by contemporary architectural fashion. After London was taken by the Parliamentarians in 1641 a line of defences c. 18 km long with forts and batteries was built around the urban area on both sides of the river, but they were thoroughly dismantled after 1647. At the Restoration of the monarchy in 1660 London was much as it had been in Tudor and Stuart times. Commercial life went on in the walled medieval town, while government was centred at Westminster. Along the Thames between these two points ran the Strand, flanked by the palaces of the nobility. Farmland and market gardens extended to the edge of the town and among the outlying houses. The City Corporation and guilds controlled trade within the walls, and jealously guarded their power and privilege, attempting to prevent the development of rival business centres in the suburbs.

### BIBLIOGRAPHY

J. Stow: *Survey of London* (London, 1598, 2/1603), ed. C. L. Kingsford, 2 vols (London, 1908/*R* 1971)
A. Clapham and W. Godfrey: *Some Famous Buildings and Their Story* (London, 1913)
E. A. Webb: *The Records of St Bartholomew's Priory*, 2 vols (London, 1922)
R. E. M. Wheeler: *London and the Vikings* (London, 1927)
N. G. Brett-James: *The Growth of Stuart London* (London, 1935)
D. Knowles and W. F. Grimes: *Charterhouse: The Medieval Foundation in the Light of Recent Discoveries* (London, 1954)
R. Merrifield: *The Roman City of London* (London, 1965)
W. F. Grimes: *The Excavation of Roman and Medieval London* (London, 1968)
J. F. Larkin and P. L. Hughes: *King James I, 1603–1625* (1973), i of *Stuart Royal Proclamations* (Oxford, 1973–)
C. Barron: *The Medieval Guildhall of London* (London, 1974)
C. N. L. Brooke and G. Keir: *London, 800–1216: The Shaping of a City* (Berkeley, CA, 1975)
A. Prockter and R. Taylor: *The A to Z of Elizabethan London* (London, 1979)
J. Schofield and T. Dyson, eds: *Archaeology of the City of London* (London, 1980)
P. Marsden: *Roman London* (London, 1981)
R. Merrifield: *London: City of the Romans* (London, 1983)
T. Dyson and J. Schofield: 'Saxon London', *Anglo-Saxon Towns in Southern England*, ed. J. Haslam (Chichester, 1984), pp. 285–314
J. Schofield: *The Building of London from the Conquest to the Great Fire* (London, 1984)
D. Keene and V. Harding: *A Survey of Documentary Sources for Property Holding in London Before the Great Fire*, London Record Society, xxii (London, 1985)
G. Milne: *The Port of Roman London* (London, 1985)
*Archive Catalogue*, London, Mus. London (London, rev. 3/1987)
J. Schofield: *The London Surveys of Ralph Treswell*, London Topographical Society, cxxxv (London, 1987)
M. Lobel, ed.: *The City of London from Prehistoric Times to c. 1520*, iii of *British Atlas of Historic Towns* (Oxford, 1990)
A. Vince: *Saxon London* (London, 1990)

For further bibliography *see* §I above.

JOHN SCHOFIELD

### 3. 1666–1799.

*(i) 1666–1712.* In September 1666 the Great Fire of London destroyed 13,200 houses and most of the city's public buildings, including Old St Paul's Cathedral (see fig. 4). Not only was the fabric of the town destroyed, but the power of the City Corporation was weakened. After the Great Fire Charles II received a number of town plans that proposed radically rebuilding the city on formal lines (*see* URBAN PLANNING, §II, 2 and fig. 5). Christopher Wren was first, with a scheme that would isolate such buildings as St Paul's Cathedral (*see* §V, 1(ii)(a) below) and the Royal Exchange on open sites and link them with wide, straight avenues. John Evelyn suggested that the ground should be levelled and excess rubble used to extend and straighten the shoreline of the Thames, which would then form an impressive river front for public buildings. ROBERT HOOKE planned a utilitarian grid. In the event, lack of funds and jealousy over established property boundaries prevented the implementation of any of these schemes, but St Paul's itself was rebuilt to designs by Wren, who also designed 47 parish churches (many destr. World War II) to replace those lost in the fire (*see* WREN, CHRISTOPHER). The city silhouette was thus much altered, and further profound change resulted from new legislation on domestic building. In February 1667 *An Act for the Rebuilding of the City of London* laid down that all new houses were to be built in brick or stone, and that the size of the houses should correspond to the width and

4. London, the Great Fire of 1666; from a contemporary engraving (London, Guildhall Library, Print Room)

importance of the streets. Four categories, which ranged from two-storey terraced houses to four-storey detached houses, were laid down, and tables detailed the thickness of walls, height from floor to ceiling, depth of cellars and sufficiency of party walls. Building workers from around the country were given the freedom of the city for seven years because the legislators foresaw that the guilds would attempt to stop them practising their trade within the city.

It has been calculated that 80,000 people left London after the fire; 20,000 had not returned by 1672, and 3420 new houses were unoccupied. Tradesmen could operate in the suburbs immediately abutting the old walls free from the restrictions imposed within the city; the growing suburban population provided sufficient business without the need to become freemen of the city. The City Corporation was so alarmed at the decrease in population and thus their revenue that they had asked the King to make a proclamation in 1671 forbidding new building in the suburbs except by licence. The westward spread of London had, however, begun.

The pattern of development in the West End was established during the 1670s and 1680s when such developers as Nicholas Barbon (d 1698) began to buy old aristocratic mansions, gardens and nearby farmland, which were then subdivided into lots with narrow frontages. Barbon was active in the Strand, Red Lion Square and Holborn. Further west Henry Jermyn, 1st Earl of St Albans (d 1684), began leasing plots in St James's Square and Jermyn Street, while Thomas Neale (d 1699) was active near St Giles, where he obtained a licence to build Seven Dials in 1693. Barbon and the other developers often got into difficulties when their building schemes ran ahead of their ability to secure the necessary investment. In order to attract builders and ultimately house-buyers,

they had to lay out roads and arrange drainage, and in a primitive money market it was difficult to borrow capital. As a result, schemes were started, but rarely completed as intended.

*(ii) 1713–99.* The Treaty of Utrecht in 1713 brought a boost to building in the form of a period of financial stability. Nicholas Hawksmoor (*see* HAWKSMOOR, NICHOLAS and fig. 3) and JAMES GIBBS were involved with the project to build 50 new churches in the suburbs, as well as with other buildings in London. Richard Lumley, 1st Earl of Scarborough (?1650–1721), acquired two freehold acres on which Hanover Square and adjacent streets were built in 1717–19. Just south of this development in 1717 Richard Boyle, 3rd Earl of Burlington, received permission to grant leases on land behind Burlington House (*see* BOYLE, (2), fig. 1); many such Palladian architects as COLEN CAMPBELL, WILLIAM KENT and HENRY FLITCROFT acquired lots in Old Burlington Street, Savile Row and Sackville Street.

Although there was no coordinating plan for these developments, many of them depended on a square for their centrepiece. This urban form had been introduced to London by Thomas Wriothesley, 4th Earl of Southampton (d 1667), when he built his mansion in Bloomsbury and a square of houses in front of it in 1661. In 1721 the Grosvenor family introduced in Grosvenor Square the idea of treating the façade of each side of the square as one grand mansion, with a large pedimented house in the centre of the row (see fig. 5). Although uniformity was achieved only on the east side, its degree of unity influenced later developments. The development north of Oxford Street in 1717 on the Cavendish–Harley estate in Marylebone Fields had Cavendish Square as its centrepiece. The

5. London, Grosvenor Square, view from the south; engraving by Thomas Bowles, 1751

estate was intended to provide town houses for the Tory nobility, but they were not inclined to invest in their town houses, preferring the standard terraced houses of speculative builders to the mansions planned for the square. The impressive houses on the north side of the square were not built until a later building boom in the 1770s.

Building slowed during the 1730s, and the next 30 years was a period of consolidation in London; rebuilding went on in areas that had first been built immediately after the Great Fire, such as St James's Square. Development began again after the Treaty of Paris in 1763 and continued into the 1770s. Public buildings included the Mansion House (1739–53) by George Dance (i), Newgate Gaol (1768–75; destr. 1902; see DANCE, (1); for illustration see DANCE, (3)) by George Dance (ii) and the Bank of England (1788–1833; rebuilt 1921–37) by JOHN SOANE. The Pantheon (1769–72; destr. 1937) in Oxford Street by Samuel Wyatt and James Wyatt (see WYATT, (1) and (2)) was an influential building. Other architects, such as HENRY HOLLAND, undertook individual commissions, but this was essentially the period when the great London estates began to be built on an unprecedented scale.

In 1768 Robert Adam (see ADAM (i), (3)) and his brothers built the Adelphi (begun 1772; rebuilt 1936–8) on leased land between the Strand and the Thames. Their scheme was to embank the river and to build vaulted warehouses for rent by the Ordnance under the houses (destr. 1936) of Royal Terrace, which would thus be raised to the level of the Strand. Unfortunately the Ordnance did not rent the warehouses and the houses did not sell. The brothers were able to stave off financial disaster only by organizing a lottery; their difficulties highlight the problems of launching large-scale developments at this time. The Adam family was also involved in the construction of Portland Place (1776–c. 1780) and Fitzroy Square (1790–94), among other London buildings.

All these schemes depended on previous development. Since it was difficult to entice prospective residents beyond the built-up areas, every developer endeavoured to link his streets with those of the adjacent estate. Bloomsbury, just beyond the estates in Holborn and the Strand, could already boast Great Russell Street and Lord Southampton's square of 1661. In 1775 Gertrude, Dowager Duchess of Bedford (d 1794), decided to go ahead with the scheme of her late husband, John Russell, 4th Duke of Bedford (1710–71), to build Bedford Square further west. In 1776 building agreements were drawn up; the resulting square represents the mature Georgian square, which, while not regular in every detail, endeavoured to appear so by marking the four sides with a pedimented central house, rendered in stucco. The other houses are of exposed brown brick, their façades distinguished only by the

6. London, Doughty Street, east side, 1792–1810

vermiculated voussoirs and keystones around the doors made from Coade stone. Bedford Square formed the nucleus of a network of streets of different status and was the reference point for the rest of the Bedford estate in Bloomsbury.

By the end of the 18th century the development westward had resulted in the establishment of a substantial area of fine residences and fashionable shops that did not depend on the City of London. The areas on the other boundaries of the City were far more dependent on its economy for their welfare. In the 17th century the only north–south road link across the Thames was London Bridge, and to the south of it in Southwark there was a well-established settlement. Here, outside the jurisdiction of the city, theatres, inns and pleasure gardens (*see* §V, 6 below) catered for the inhabitants of the city. The second crossing, Westminster Bridge, was begun only in 1739 (rebuilt 1862), and the resulting traffic brought further development south of the river. Blackfriars Bridge was built from 1760 to 1769 (rebuilt 1862–4 and 1884–6).

To the east was Stepney, which became a largely working-class area. After the revocation of the Edict of Nantes in 1685 Huguenot refugees came to Spitalfields in Stepney, where many of them established silk-weaving businesses in the streets around Christ Church. They were the first of many immigrants to occupy this area. Directly north of the city the parishes of Clerkenwell and St Luke's expanded during the 18th century, when artisans found that they could live outside the confines of the city without jeopardizing business. The jewellery and clockmaking trades became associated with Clerkenwell, and seamstresses, milliners and hosiers moved to the Strand.

In a largely pedestrian city it was important for those dependent on the city for their work to live within walking distance; the introduction of regular coach services, however, made it possible for those who could afford it to commute. The coaches led to a demand for thoroughfares permitting through-traffic. In the 1750s the New Road (renamed Euston Road, 1857) was completed from Paddington to Islington, and by 1768 a regular coach service allowed middle-class businessmen to live in the West End of London while maintaining their businesses in the city. Where main thoroughfares were built development was not long far behind. Henry Holland was involved in the development of Chelsea, and around 1773 Henry Penton began building streets of modest brick terraces north of the New Road for the clerks who were increasingly in demand as such commercial activities as banking and insurance began to dominate the nearby city.

Thus at the end of the 18th century the pattern for the further development of London was established. What had been suburban hamlets were soon covered in streets (see fig. 6) and squares of brick terraced houses that imitated those in the fashionable West End. Although in no sense could London be described as a planned city, the consensus at the beginning of its period of greatest growth, embodied in the London Building Act of 1774, meant that nonetheless a homogeneous urban form was achieved.

### BIBLIOGRAPHY
N. G. Brett-Jones: *The Growth of Stuart London* (London, 1935)
T. F. Reddaway: *The Rebuilding of London after the Great Fire* (London, 1940)
J. Summerson: *Georgian London* (London, 1945, rev. 1988)
D. J. Olsen: *Town Planning in London* (New Haven, 1964, rev. 2/1982)
H. Philips: *Mid-Georgian London* (London, 1964)
J. E. N. Hearsey: *London and the Great Fire* (London, 1965)
F. M. L. Thompson: *Hampstead: Building a Borough, 1650–1964* (London, 1974)
G. E. Mingay: *Georgian London* (London, 1975)
A. Byrne: *Bedford Square: An Architectural Study* (London, 1990)
D. Cruikshank: *Life in the Georgian City* (London, 1990)

TANIS HINCHCLIFFE

4. 1800–88. In its size and pace of growth London held a unique position throughout the 19th century. In 1801 its population was just under one million, more than eleven times that of Liverpool, its nearest British rival. It held its lead in the decades that followed, reaching over two million by 1850 and four million by 1890. On a world scale, only Paris and New York could compete in terms of size. Contemporaries found the scale of London and the speed of its expansion bewildering and awesome. Furthermore, the fragmentation of local government within the city and the diversity of its economy meant that its civic life and architecture seemed to lack the order and focus that characterized other great urban centres. Until the mid-19th century its government was divided between a host of institutions—parish vestries, sewer commissions and improvement trusts, as well as the City Corporation, which had jurisdiction over the square mile at its heart. A partial rationalization was achieved in 1855 when an indirectly elected body, the Metropolitan Board of Works, was established for 'the better management of sewerage and drainage and the paving, cleansing, lighting and improvement thereof' (Metropolis Local Management Act, 1855). The Board accomplished much that was expected of it, principally the construction of a new drainage system to prevent sewage from being discharged into urban sections of the Thames and the building of handsome stretches of river embankment; but it was denied sufficient income and power to develop new initiatives once its preliminary tasks had been completed. It was succeeded in 1889 by the London County Council, the city's first elected body capable of carrying out a programme of effective reforms.

Economically, after 1800 London was indisputably an industrial city, albeit an unrepresentative one. There were some large-scale industries—for instance, brewing, engineering and gas-works—but most of its industry took the form of small-scale, workshop trades. These multiplied and expanded in response to the development of London as a consumer centre. Furniture-making (*see* §IV, 1 below), clothing and footwear, printing, jewellery (*see* §IV, 5 below) and precision manufacture were concentrated as near to city-centre outlets as possible and grew by spawning more small units or by adding outworkers. In 1851 86% of London employers had fewer than ten employees each. London's rise to the status of an international centre of commerce, finance and administration, however, brought a large increase in white-collar workers. In 1800 about a fifth of its population could be defined as middle class, ranging from small-scale employers and shopkeepers to merchants and professionals, and that proportion rose in subsequent decades. The presence of a relatively large and wealthy middle class compared to that in other cities had

7. London, Regent Street, the Quadrant (1818–20), by John Nash, showing the removal of the colonnades in 1848

important consequences for the city's social and cultural life.

As a result of its subdivided government and its lack of large-scale industries, London was without the conventional symbols of civic pride and productivity, such as an ostentatious town hall and overbearing factories, which marked many industrial cities, although it did have buildings and structures appropriate to its position as a hub of commerce and government. The enclosed docks that developed along the Thames from the turn of the century were regarded as patriotic enterprises: the works (1800) of the London Dock Co. were, it was said, 'conceived on a scale to support the dignity of a nation'. The last of the first generation of docks was St Katharine's Dock by Thomas Telford and Philip Hardwick (see HARDWICK, (2)), largely completed by 1828. Its brick warehouses, partly supported on cast-iron Doric columns, were sited directly on the quayside to facilitate cargo handling.

After the 1820s the commercial prominence of the City of London brought about rebuilding to provide accommodation for the banks, insurance companies, discount houses and hundreds of smaller firms that traded there. Such specially commissioned buildings as the Sun Fire and Life Assurance Office (1841–3; destr. 1970) by C. R. Cockerell (see COCKERELL, (2)) and the palazzo (1849; destr. c. 1960) by JOHN GIBSON (ii) for the Imperial Assurance Co. (both in Threadneedle Street) attracted most attention; but speculatively built blocks intended for multiple letting were as significant in this great transformation. Further west were offices of another kind, namely the government buildings along Whitehall (see GOVERNMENT BUILDING, fig. 1) in the shadow of the rebuilt Palace of Westminster (begun 1847; see §V, 3(iii) below; see also BARRY, (1) and PUGIN, (2)). The best-known of the former, the Foreign and India Offices, were erected in 1863–8 after an absurd series of events in which George Gilbert Scott I (see SCOTT (ii), (1)) altered his designs from Gothic to Byzantine Revival style, and finally to Neo-classical. Elsewhere in Westminster, and further west in Kensington, were the citadels of consumption and enlightenment. Despite their splendour, most London shops were quite modest in size, and even department stores (e.g. Harrods, Brompton Road, 1894, 1902–3) hid their true extent behind façades built in stages: there was nothing until the end of the century to match the architectural coherence of the Bon Marché (1876) by Gustave Eiffel and Louis-Charles Boileau in Paris. Museums and galleries, however, were appropriately monumental, despite grudging state finance (see MUSEUM, §II). With the British Museum (1823–48; see ENGLAND, fig. 8) by Robert Smirke (ii) (see SMIRKE, (2)) and the National Gallery (1832–8) by WILLIAM WILKINS, London made its mark as a centre of self-improving consumption (see ENGLAND, §XIV). The development of the museums enclave (e.g. the Natural History Museum, 1872–81; see WATERHOUSE, ALFRED and fig; and the Victoria and Albert Museum, 1864; see TERRACOTTA, fig. 10) in Kensington, just south of the Hyde Park location of the Crystal Palace (moved to Sydenham 1852–4; destr. 1936; see INTERNATIONAL EXHIBITION and fig. 1; see also PAXTON, JOSEPH and fig.), was a beneficial by-product of the immensely successful Great Exhibition in 1851.

The amount of rebuilding and new building was such that the largest employer was the building industry. Like the rest of the London economy, the building world was one of small companies, undercapitalization and insecure employment. The hold that such builders as Thomas Cubitt, George Myers (1803–75) and the brothers Charles Thomas Lucas (1820–95) and Thomas Lucas (1822–1902) had over major projects concealed the fact that most work was undertaken by lesser men. Among the 739 London builders recorded in the census of 1851 only 57 employed 50 men or more. In particular, suburban house-building was dominated by small companies that built a few houses at a time. For such companies the standard design of the terraced house and the customary methods of estate development inherited from the 18th century had the attraction of familiarity; and in contrast to the continental (and Scottish) traditions of flat construction, preliminary large-scale investment was not necessary. Several organizations built tenements in the 1880s, notably the East End Dwellings Co. (founded by Samuel Augustus Barnett (1844–1913) and Henrietta Barnett (1851–1936); *see* §5 below), the Four Per Cent Industrial Dwellings Co. (founded by the Rothschild family) and the Guinness Trust.

The suburbs of low-density terraced housing, such as those in Camberwell and Acton, that encircled London for a radius of *c.* 16 km succeeded because they met an expanding middle-class demand for an appropriately secluded setting for family life, providing protection from the turmoil and amorality of city-centre streets. Predictably, however, the enforced communalism of the terraced house led to its fall from favour. From quiet beginnings in St John's Wood in 1795 the idea of the detached or semi-detached villa gradually gained in popularity to become the norm in wealthier suburbs by the late 19th century. Cubitt built detached villas in Clapham, and although Bedford Park in west London, started in 1876, was promoted as being the epitome of the new suburban ideal, apart from the employment of such distinguished architects as E. W. Godwin and RICHARD NORMAN SHAW, it was simply following an acknowledged trend.

The devotion of successful Londoners to their domestic arrangements was in some respects at the expense of the city's public life. The boldest restructuring attempted was the layout of Regent Street (see fig. 7) and Regent's Park, which JOHN NASH master-minded from 1812 (*see also* BURTON, DECIMUS and ZOO), together with the west Strand improvements completed in 1831. Charles Barry

8. London, Victoria Embankment (1864–70), by Joseph Bazalgette, looking north from Westminster Pier towards Charing Cross Station (1863; since rebuilt) and Hungerford Bridge (1863), both by John Hawkshaw; from a photograph of *c.* 1900

laid out Trafalgar Square in the 1830s, and JAMES PEN-NETHORNE took over Nash's practice in 1834, but nothing so bold was permitted again. The governmental Office of Works, and later the Metropolitan Board of Works, used new streets (e.g. Shaftesbury Avenue, 1877–86) to clear or isolate slums, thus remaining true to the social engineering element of Nash's schemes, but lacking his architectural bravado. In the absence of another Nash, or of an authority with his power and imagination, the shaping of the city was left largely to private interests, guided only by sanitary and building regulations. The greatest powers of planning and development lay with major landowners and the railway companies. Railways were forbidden to penetrate the central area, and so established their termini in a ring round its fringe (e.g. Paddington Station (1851–4; see RAILWAY STATION, fig. 2), by Isambard Kingdom Brunel and Matthew Digby Wyatt); many of them were linked by the underground railway that was first opened in 1863. The erection of such stations as Euston (1836–7; rebuilt 1963–8) and St Pancras (1863–8) by W. H. BARLOW (hotel (1866–76) by George Gilbert Scott I), appallingly disruptive but with spectacular architectural results, came closer than any other projects to sustaining the scale and impact of the Regency improvements. Various projects altered the appearance of urban stretches of the Thames. JOHN RENNIE built a number of bridges (all destr. or no longer in situ) over it, and JOSEPH BAZALGETTE built the Victoria Embankment (1864–70; see fig. 8) between Westminster Bridge (rebuilt 1862) and Blackfriars Bridge (rebuilt 1865–9) on the north bank.

London in the 1880s was a healthier and better-serviced city than it had ever been; the cholera epidemic of 1866 was the last, but clean water and improved drainage were insufficient palliatives for the poor. The riots of the unemployed in 1886 and 1887 were a forceful reminder that, despite signs of progress in the suburbs or the city centre, the necessities of a decent urban life were still far from the reach of many Londoners.

### BIBLIOGRAPHY

H. J. Dyos: *Victorian Suburb: A Study in the Growth of Camberwell* (Leicester, 1961)
A. Briggs: *Victorian Cities* (London, 1963)
J. T. Coppock and H. T. Prince, eds: *Greater London* (London, 1964)
F. Sheppard: *London, 1808–1870: The Infernal Wen* (London, 1971)
H. J. Dyos and M. Wolff, eds: *The Victorian City: Images and Realities*, 2 vols (London, 1973)
J. Summerson: *The London Building World of the Eighteen-sixties* (London, 1973)
R. Hyde: *The Printed Maps of Victorian London, 1851–1900* (Folkestone, 1975)
D. J. Olsen: *The Growth of Victorian London* (London, 1976)
J. Summerson: *The Architecture of Victorian London* (Charlottesville, 1976)
——: 'The Victorian Rebuilding of the City of London', *London J.*, iii (1977), pp. 163–85
A. S. Wohl: *The Eternal Slum: Housing and Social Policy in Victorian London* (London, 1977)
F. Sheppard, V. Belcher and P. Cottrell: 'The Middlesex and Yorkshire Deeds Registers and the Study of Building Fluctuations', *London J.*, v (1979), pp. 176–217
G. Stamp and C. Amery: *Victorian Buildings of London* (London, 1980)
D. Cannadine and D. Reeder, eds: *Exploring the Urban Past: Essays in Urban History by H. J. Dyos* (Cambridge, 1982)
D. Owen: *The Government of Victorian London, 1855–1889* (Cambridge, MA, 1982)
F. M. L. Thompson, ed.: *The Rise of Suburbia* (Leicester, 1982)
G. Tyack: *Sir James Pennethorne and the Making of Victorian London* (Cambridge, 1992)
G. C. Clifton: *Professionalism, Patronage and Public Service in Victorian London: The Staff of the Metropolitan Board of Works, 1856–1889* (London, 1993)
*London, World City, 1800–1840* (exh. cat., ed. C. Fox; Essen, Villa Hügel, 1993)

5. 1889–1945. The residential population of inner London reached its peak in 1900, and thereafter the major increases were in the outer areas as the population shifted from the centre to the suburbs. The development of low-density suburbs had the effect of doubling the area of London between 1918 and 1939. The importance of London was reinforced by its status as the centre of an expanding empire, and by its increasing hold over national communications. From the 1890s London newspapers were increasingly read throughout the country, and later the development of radio broadcasting was London-based. Thus independent provincial cultures that had flourished in the 19th century were gradually superseded by the centralizing influence of London as capital city.

To many people London remained as disturbing and incomprehensible as it had been in the mid-19th century, yet in two respects it acquired a more orderly identity. First, in 1889 the inaugural elections were held for the London County Council (LCC), the first democratic strategic government the city had known, and ten years later local government was also reorganized. The powers of the LCC were not as extensive as those of some of its European counterparts: it never gained control of the city's water-supply or its electricity industry, and its transport powers were confined to running the trams. Yet in housing, education and public welfare, its interventions were highly significant and were marked by the erection of buildings designed by its own architectural department. The establishment by the LCC of a green belt of safeguarded open space around London from 1935 was the most significant planning decision of the period. The second unifying factor was transport. In 1890 the first deep-level underground railway, using electric traction, was opened. Its success engendered a series of similar schemes that were completed during the next 20 years, forming the main network of the London Underground system. For over 30 years the development of the Underground was guided by Frank Pick (1878–1941), whose belief in a combination of management and good design helped to create a unified system. Pick commissioned CHARLES HOLDEN to design a series of distinctive Underground stations (e.g. Northern line, Clapham to Morden (1924)), and in 1933 he introduced the diagrammatic Underground map (designed by Henry C. Beck (1901–74)), which remains one of the most familiar and comprehensible maps of London.

Transport improvements eventually helped to alleviate the inner London housing problem, but not before unprecedented official efforts had been made to rehouse slum-dwellers in the areas where they lived. After 1890 the LCC, and later the local boroughs, embarked on a campaign of house-building, concentrating at first on five-storey blocks of flats. The first major LCC estate at Boundary Street (1895–1900), Bethnal Green, had 23 blocks arranged on streets radiating from a central circus. Yet as these projects were completed, a suburban solution to inner city problems was being advocated by, among others, Henrietta Barnett, who from 1905 directed the development of Hampstead Garden Suburb, a socially mixed community in north London linked to a new Underground station. Her chief planner, Raymond Unwin, used the project to test his ideal low-density cottage-style layout (*see* PARKER & UNWIN and fig.). Under his promotion, this style subsequently became the standard for publicly subsidized housing throughout the country. After 1918 the LCC concentrated on building municipal versions (e.g. Roehampton estate (1921–7), Wandsworth) of Barnett's scheme, but without the latter's prescribed facilities and mix of households. Only after 1928 did attention revert to slum clearance projects in the inner areas.

Housing estates built by the LCC and the boroughs dominated certain parts of London, but formed a smaller proportion of new housing than elsewhere in England. From 1920 to 1938 75% of houses were built speculatively for sale. House-builders, operating on a larger scale than their 19th-century predecessors, built what first-time buyers could afford: two- or three-bedroom semi-detached houses in such areas as Wembley and Bexley, with such features as bay windows to distinguish them from local authority housing. These houses had such modern facilities as electricity, but few revealed any signs of architectural Modernism. New factories were as much a feature of some London suburbs as new homes. London benefited from the restructuring of the national economy because the main growth industries were those based on the domestic consumer market, for instance the electrical industry, food processing and vehicle manufacturing. Suburban industrial areas, especially in outer west London, attracted firms from inner London as well as newly established companies. Instead of small workshops they had large, self-contained factories, usually with an office-block fronting the manufacturing shed, as at the Hoover Factory (1931–5) at Perivale. No attempt was made to coordinate factory development and housing provision.

Compared to the pace of suburban development, new building in central London was intermittent and patchy.

Office buildings and department stores increased in size, although before 1945 their height was still restricted by the 100 ft (30.48 m) limit imposed by London Building Acts. The introduction of the steel frame in the 1900s (at e.g. Selfridge's Department Store (1906) by the practice of Daniel H. Burnham) accelerated and simplified construction without having any marked effect on architectural appearance. Selfridge's has a self-supporting stone facing in the Ionic Order, and such facings continued at, for example, Unilever House (1930–31), Blackfriars. It was not until the mid-1930s that the idea of hanging the exterior wall from the frame was adopted, as at the Peter Jones Department Store (1932–7; see fig. 9) in Sloane Square, Chelsea. Other major new landmarks in central London were the products of either local government or the leisure industry. County Hall (1912–33), the headquarters of the LCC, gradually rose on the south bank to the designs of Ralph Knott (1871–1929). On a smaller scale municipal action was exemplified by the erection of schools (e.g. Cassland Road School (1902), Hackney), fire stations (e.g. Hammersmith (1913–14)) and town halls (e.g. Lambeth (1906–8)) for the local boroughs. The architectural sobriety of these buildings was quite distinct from the ostentation of the numerous pubs (e.g. King's Head (1897), Tooting) and theatres (e.g. Richmond Theatre (1899) by FRANK MATCHAM) built in the 1880s and 1890s; many were in exotic contrast to their surroundings. The same exaggerated quality was evident in their subsequent rivals, the super cinemas of the inter-war years (e.g. Gaumont State (1937), Kilburn; *see* CINEMA).

During the late 19th century Londoners became acutely aware of the need to record and cherish the city's historic architecture. The *Survey of London* (London, 1900–) was set up by C. R. ASHBEE for that purpose. Nevertheless, many major landmarks were subsequently demolished, including Newgate Gaol (destr. 1902) and the Bank of England (rebuilt 1921–37), as well as the 19th-century Waterloo Bridge (rebuilt 1934–46 by Giles Gilbert Scott; *see* SCOTT (ii), (4)). The effects of bombing during World Wars I and II were even more devastating to the fabric of London. Among the buildings bombed during World War II were sixteen churches by Christopher Wren, all but three of the city livery halls and the Commons Chamber in the Palace of Westminster (*see* §V, 3(iii) below). From the experience of war came a new determination to plan for the future of London and at the same time to protect the best of the past. The Planning Act of 1944 established the means to achieve both ends.

### BIBLIOGRAPHY

H. P. Clunn: *London Rebuilt, 1897–1927* (London, 1927)
G. Gibbon and R. W. Bell: *History of the London County Council* (London, 1939)
W. Kent: *The Lost Treasures of London* (London, 1947)
C. H. Holden and W. G. Holford: *The City of London: A Record of Destruction and Survival* (London, 1951) [rep. 1947]
P. G. Hall: *The Industries of London since 1861* (London, 1962)
T. C. Barker and M. Robbins: *A History of London Transport*, 2 vols (London, 1963–74)
R. Glass, ed.: *London: Aspects of Change* (London, 1964)
D. Thomas: *London's Green Belt* (London, 1970)
M. Girouard: *Victorian Pubs* (London, 1973)
A. A. Jackson: *Semi-detached London* (London, 1973)
G. Stamp, ed.: 'London (1900)', *Archit. Des.*, xlviii (1978), pp. 302–94
S. M. Beattie: *A Revolution in London Housing* (London, 1980)

9. London, Sloane Square, Peter Jones Department Store, 1932–7; view from the east

S. Pepper: 'Ossulton Street: Early L.C.C. Experiments in High-rise Housing (1925–9)', *London J.*, vii (1981), pp. 46–64

K. Young and P. Garside: *Metropolitan London: Politics and Urban Change, 1837–1981* (London, 1982)

A. Saint, ed.: *Politics and the People of London: The London County Council, 1889–1965* (London, 1989)

ROBERT THORNE

6. AFTER 1945. The vast tracts of London that were laid waste during World War II provided the opportunity to restructure London and redistribute its population. Initial policy formulation had taken place during the war in a series of seminal plans that reflected contemporary radical planning theories, notably the Greater London Plan (1944) by PATRICK ABERCROMBIE. The aim was to disaggregate the metropolis into largely self-sufficient 'neighbourhood units', separated by a concentric web of arterial roads. First F. J. Forty, and then Charles Holden and WILLIAM HOLFORD, drew up parallel proposals to zone London's historic centre—by now largely given over to commerce and retail—into architecturally distinct and functionally homogeneous urban 'precincts'. Surplus population was to be decanted to a ring of satellite 'new towns', of which only Stevenage (Herts) and Harlow (Essex) have been fully realized, or to existing designated provincial towns near London. Industry was to be expelled from the capital into new greenfield industrial parks, such as Slough, Park Royal, Hendon and Elstree, that were isolated from the metropolis by the green belt. The implementation of these proposals had two major phases. The first phase in the 1950s and 1960s reflected the immediate post-war need for housing and took the form of social and welfare planning on an heroic scale. It was spearheaded by the LCC (known as Greater London Council (GLC) from 1963; abolished 1986), using compulsory purchase, relocation of non-residential institutions, wholesale demolition and comprehensive redevelopment of housing estates. These were rarely supported by the range of community facilities envisaged in the original neighbourhood unit concept, although the Lansbury Estate (1951), Poplar, which was opened in time for the Festival of Britain (1951) as the showpiece for the new model communities, was a notable exception. The influence of international architectural movements on social housing was short-lived and superficial. In the first wave of post-war reconstruction, distinctive 'mixed developments' of high-rise slabs and tower blocks, interspersed with two- to four-storey housing (e.g. Alton East (1952–5), Roehampton, and Thamesmead), were built throughout the capital.

The structuring of central London into precincts was partially realized in the city during the 1950s as the war-damaged areas were redeveloped with modern office blocks (e.g. William Holford's scheme (1961) for St Paul's precinct), but urban design on a public scale was largely abandoned in the subsequent period of speculative building of offices and hotels. A notable commercial development of this period in the West End is the Economist Building (1964; for illustration *see* SMITHSON), two blocks rising from a small plaza adjacent to St James's Street. In the late 1960s and early 1970s some of London's first high-rise office buildings, notably the Centre Point Tower (1966), New Oxford Street, by RICHARD SEIFERT, were also produced.

Shopping, leisure and cultural activities in London were increasingly concentrated in indoor centres that were conceived as self-contained complexes, divorced from the surrounding urban fabric, for example the South Bank arts centre, built on the site of the Festival of Britain, when the Royal Festival Hall (1948–51, see fig. 10) by Leslie Martin and the LCC was opened. The Queen Elizabeth Hall and Hayward Gallery (1967–8; by Hubert Bennett)

10. London, Royal Festival Hall, by Leslie Martin and the LCC, 1948–51

and the National Theatre (1967–76; *see* LASDUN, DENYS and fig.) were later additions. Another large arts complex is contained in the mixed-use Barbican Centre (1966–81; *see* CHAMBERLIN, POWELL & BON and fig.) in the City.

By the early 1970s previous confidence in the ability to forecast demographic trends accurately and to engineer community formation by design was widely believed to have been misplaced. There followed a more modest, permissive collaboration between private enterprise, market forces, public planning and environmental pressure groups to regenerate decaying areas. In this second phase, the dominant form of social housing was the low-rise, high-density urban village of family dwellings, which attempted to articulate an urban vernacular for London, for example the brick-built Lillington Gardens Estate (1964–72), Pimlico, designed around a series of gardens by DARBOURNE & DARKE, or the stepped concrete terraces of the Brunswick Centre (1959–72), Bloomsbury, by PATRICK HODGKINSON, with shops and a cinema. This produced small-scale, enclosed, often labyrinthine, housing estates, which were quite unlike previous urban patterns. Elsewhere, housing rehabilitation superseded wholesale clearance.

Adaptation and reuse of historic commercial buildings became popular from the late 1960s, as in Coutts Bank, the Strand, by Frederick Gibberd, where a modern office building was constructed (1969) behind a Neo-classical façade by John Nash, to which it is connected by a dramatic glazed atrium, the first of its kind in London. At the same time, comprehensive redevelopment was abandoned in the 1970s, initially in favour of conservation schemes to preserve such historic areas as Covent Garden and St Katharine's Dock, which were both transformed into leisure retail complexes, and later, of enterprise zones, which combined relaxed planning controls with tax incentives in areas where new building was deemed appropriate. As a by-product of the former policy, development on major sites in central London was radically modified, as at Coin Street, South Bank, where traditional streets of social housing were built, rather than a large, commercial arcade. Although development in enterprise zones was coupled with the provision of local housing stocks and amenities, the extent to which this benefited existing local communities in the Docklands, the largest such project, was questioned. The Docklands redevelopment, on 2226 ha of derelict waterfront land, is dominated by the Canary Wharf scheme on the Isle of Dogs, where a total of 26 commercial buildings is planned; Canary Wharf Tower by Cesar Pelli was the tallest building in Britain on its completion (1988–91; h. 240 m; *see* PELLI, CESAR and fig.). The wave of commercial development that took place in the 1980s also produced several individual landmark buildings, notably the National Westminster Bank Tower (1981) by Seifert and the Lloyd's of London Headquarters (1979–87; for illustration *see* ROGERS, RICHARD), both in the City, and Embankment Place (1987–90; see fig. 11) by Terry Farrell, which is suspended above Charing Cross Station on a striking arched structure.

Some of the policies that shaped London after 1945 were later reversed. The attempt to create an arterial road network for Greater London ceased with the completion in the 1980s of the M25 motorway, which links motorways

11. London, Charing Cross, Embankment Place, by Terry Farrell, 1987–90

converging on London in a ring outside the built-up area. Such strategies as the improvement of public transport and the discouragement of unnecessary road use were employed to reduce congestion. Urban densification and integration with the surrounding fabric replaced disaggregation and fragmentation as means of structuring both residential and commercial urban localities, as in plans for the redevelopment of the King's Cross area by Sir Norman Foster of Foster Associates, and the Broadgate office development around Liverpool Street Station (completed 1991) by Arup Associates and Skidmore, Owings & Merrill, which contains three urban plazas.

BIBLIOGRAPHY

J. H. Forshaw and P. Abercrombie: *County of London Plan* (London, 1943)
F. J. Forty: *The City of London Plan* (London, 1944)
P. Abercrombie: *Greater London Plan, 1944* (London, 1945)
*An Introduction to Housing Layout*, Greater London Council (London, 1978)
J. C. Kirschenmann and C. Muschalek: *Residential Districts* (London, Toronto and New York, 1980), p. 191
S. Andresen and U. Noehr: *Storbyers byfornyelse: En kommenteret tidsskriftbibliografi om Danmark, Holland, Sverige, Storbritanien og Vesttyskland* [Urban renewal of big cities: an annotated bibliography of periodicals on Denmark, Holland, Sweden, Great Britain and West Germany] (Copenhagen, 1984)
G. Cullen: 'A Tale of Two Cities', *Archit. Rev.*, clxxix (1986), pp. 47–52
L. Krier: 'God Save the Prince!', *Mod. Painters*, i (1988), pp. 23–5
P. Barker: 'Is This What We Want?', *Country Life*, clxxxiii (6 April 1989), pp. 116–17
Y. Marin: 'La "Gentrification" de Londres', *Etud. Angl.*, xlii (1989), pp. 313–32
K. Powell: 'Facing the New', *Country Life*, clxxxiii (27 July 1989), p. 143

JULIENNE HANSON

### III. Art life and organization.

This article discusses mainly the development of London as a centre for the art market, and of art education and exhibitions. For public monuments and open-air sculpture *see* OVE ARUP, BACON, (1), JOSEPH EDGAR BOEHM, THOMAS BROCK, FRANCIS CHANTREY, CAIUS GABRIEL CIBBER, JACOB EPSTEIN, GRINLING GIBBONS, ALFRED GILBERT, HUBERT LE SUEUR, EDWIN LUTYENS, BERTRAM MACKENNAL, CARLO MAROCCHETTI, MATTHEW NOBLE, HAMO THORNYCROFT, WESTMACOTT, (2), and WYATT, (5).

1. Before 1066. 2. 1066–1535. 3. 1536–1659. 4. 1660–1768. 5. 1769–1850. 6. 1851–1909. 7. After 1909.

1. BEFORE 1066. Although there is evidence of prehistoric settlement in the area of London well before the arrival of the Romans in AD 43 (*see* §II, 1 above), the only art dating to this early period is that which embellishes arms and armour found in the River Thames well upstream from the later City of London, for example at Waterloo, Battersea, Wandsworth and Brentford, and dating from the late Bronze Age and late Iron Age (e.g. London, Mus. London; London, BM). The Roman historian Tacitus described London by AD 60 as 'an important centre for businessmen and merchandise' (*Annals* XIV.xxxiii). It was also clearly a place of manufacture, and there is evidence of a *gemmarius* in Eastcheap at this time and of a goldsmith's workshop in the area of Cannon Street some 20 years later. As the administrative centre of Britannia, London was a magnet for artists. Little is known of the décor of the enormous basilica on Cornhill or of the governor's palace at Cannon Street. However, the quality of early 2nd-century wall painting at its best can be appreciated from a fresco of illusionistic architecture (London, Mus. London), which employs expensive imported cinnabar and gold leaf and was discovered in the excavation of a bath building on the site of Winchester Palace, Southwark. There must have been many imperial statues, but the over life-size bronze head of *Hadrian* (London, BM) from London Bridge is the only recognizable portrait that survives. Immigrant craftsmen laid mosaic floors in London in the 1st century, but in the late 2nd century there was a workshop in the city, one of whose finest products is the geometric Bucklersbury pavement (London, Mus. London). Sculpture in oolitic limestone can be ascribed to sculptors from the Cotswold region or from further north in Northamptonshire and includes those blocks from an arch and screen that incorporate depictions of various deities, which were reused in the late 3rd-century riverside wall (London, Mus. London). There is also British limestone sculpture from the Walbrook mithraeum, but the most valuable works here, including the head of *Mithras* (London, Mus. London; see fig. 12), are imports of Italian marble.

During the late Roman period London seems to have declined (except as an administrative centre), and after the collapse of Imperial authority in the early 5th century there was no artistic life until the 7th-century revival (*see* §II, 1 above). The first St Paul's Cathedral (604) was presumably well endowed from the first with sculpture and painting. All that survives, however, are the much later tombstones, one of which (11th century; London, Mus. London) is a masterpiece depicting a dragon in RINGERIKE style. A number of very fine objects of later Saxon date have been found in London, including an 8th-century silver-gilt

12. Head of *Mithras* from the Walbrook Mithraeum, marble (probably Carrara), h. 369 mm, late 2nd century AD–early 3rd (London, Museum of London)

sword-hilt from Fetter Lane, the enamelled, gold filigree Dowgate Hill brooch of the 9th or 10th century and, from the Strand settlement, the gold filigree Garrick Street ring, probably of the 8th or 9th century (all London, BM). There is no clue as to where any of these prestige objects were made, although a cache of early 11th-century pewter trinkets (London, Mus. London) from Cheapside is clearly a jeweller's stock-in-trade.

BIBLIOGRAPHY
R. Merrifield: *London: City of the Romans* (London, 1983)
D. M. Wilson: *Anglo-Saxon Art* (London, 1984)
J. M. C. Toynbee: *The Roman Art Treasures from the Temple of Mithras*, London and Middlesex Archaeological Society Special Papers, 7 (London, 1986)
A. Vince: *Saxon London: An Archaeological Investigation* (London, 1990)
T. Murdoch, ed.: *Treasures and Trinkets: Jewellery in London from Pre-Roman Times to the 1930s* (London, 1991)
L. Webster and J. Backhouse, eds: *The Making of England: Anglo-Saxon Art and Culture, AD 600–900* (London, 1991)
M. Henig: *The Art of Roman Britain* (in preparation)

MARTIN HENIG

2. 1066–1535. Thanks to the presence of the court, with its patrons, and the royal mint at the Tower, London

13. Wax seal of the 'barons' (i.e. citizens) of London: *St Paul, Patron Saint of London, Standing on the Tower of St Paul's Cathedral* (obverse), diam. 72 mm, *c.* 1219 (London, Public Record Office, E 329/428)

for their patrons and was at the centre of the country's road system.

Masons and painters were organized into guilds late in the Middle Ages, and then not very wholeheartedly. This was partly as a result of the peripatetic nature of much of

14. Monumental brass of *Sir Robert de Bures*, set in Purbeck marble, l. 2.02 m, made in London, *c.* 1331 (Acton, Suffolk, All Saints)

was always the predominant English centre for goldwork (*see* §IV, 2 and 5 below). The engravers who produced dies for the coinage were concentrated in London by the time of the Conquest. In the 12th and 13th centuries the organization of traders and craftsmen into guilds was a development that was paralleled in other English cities, but it was a structuring of society that became particularly complicated in London because the population was so large and its activities so various. A guild of weavers in London is first mentioned in a tax record of 1129–30. A guild might defer for many years the purchase of a royal charter of incorporation, a meeting hall or a grant of arms; for example, a guild of goldsmiths existed by 1179–80, but it acquired a royal charter only in 1327. The chronicler and ecclesiastic Giraldus Cambrensis [Gerald of Wales] visited London *c.* 1200 and marvelled at the abundance of gold and gilt rings, gold belts adorned with ivory, earrings of gold and filigree, and signet rings. Shrines throughout England—at Beverley Minster, Hereford and Lincoln cathedrals, for instance—were made or repaired by London goldsmiths in the 13th and 14th centuries. There were also craftsmen in related fields, for example sealmakers (see fig. 13), jewellers and spanglers (makers of the spangles sewn on to clothing), as well as goldbeaters, goldwire drawers, burnishers and gilders.

The increasing amount of time spent by the court at Westminster both reflected and enhanced London's importance as the principal city of the kingdom. The marblers, who produced MONUMENTAL BRASSES, generally set in Purbeck marble slabs (see fig. 14), established themselves in the early 14th century near Old St Paul's Cathedral, doubtless because it was conveniently located their employment and partly because of the predominance of the Crown as the greatest patron of building activity. The royal Palace of Westminster was outside the area of the City of London's jurisdiction, and craftsmen engaged by the Crown had no need to be freemen since they were not plying a trade in the city. Groups of craftsmen came from the country, as did Michael of Canterbury and other masons from Kent in the early 1290s, or the East Anglian painters who worked on the decoration (mid-14th century) of St Stephen's Chapel in the Palace of Westminster; and it was natural for them to look for work in London when they left the Crown's service. The population of medieval London was constantly being replenished from without, and it cannot have been difficult for established artists and craftsmen to secure admission to the city's freedom. Court styles and fashions could percolate through to London-based patrons, and thus to the provinces. In the early 14th century London began to emerge as a major centre of book production. In 1331 Queen Philippa at Westminster paid Richard of Oxford for illuminating two small Books of Hours of the Virgin for her; he had perhaps come from Oxford and settled in London or Westminster. In the course of the 14th century the bookbinders, scriveners and illuminators became numerous, but many of the scriveners were writers of court hand, practising primarily in a legal context. The limners, whose guild is first mentioned in 1389, merged in 1403 with the text writers (or writers of text hand), but London was never a major centre for book decoration to be compared with, say, Ghent or Bruges. The goldsmiths had a particularly close relationship with the Crown because they controlled the exchange of old coin and plate for new coin and produced coinage (see fig. 15). A list of 1421–2 names 111 different crafts, not all of which were necessarily formally organized into guilds.

Guilds were set up because practitioners of a particular craft or trade wished to regulate it, setting standards of production and of personal conduct to protect their reputation. Once established, each guild naturally claimed monopoly powers in its own field of activity, and so it gradually came to be part of the machinery of city government: citizenship was gained through admission to the membership of a professional guild, and the guilds' leading members came to form the oligarchy of mayor and aldermen that controlled the city. Foreigners could not easily enter a guild and therefore had to practise their craft outside the city, although some guilds even tried to extend their power outside London. The goldsmiths' hallmarking arrangements were applied throughout England, while the horners and embroiderers claimed rights specifically over certain country fairs, which were an important outlet for the sale of many goods.

London's significance as a centre of bookselling (both second-hand and new) rather than of book production is reflected in the rise of the stationers, or booksellers, within the Limners' and Text Writers' Company, which was known from the mid-15th century as the Stationers' Company. Aliens, or those born outside the English royal dominions and who had not taken out letters of naturalization, were prominent in the late medieval book trade, especially after a liberalizing statute of 1484. They could not trade within the city unless they were made free of the Stationers' Company, but they set up businesses both in the western suburbs beyond Temple bar and in Southwark. They met with some hostility: the French printer Richard Pynson was assaulted in 1500 and said that his workmen had been terrorized into leaving his service by constant attacks.

In the second half of the 15th century there seem to have been increasing numbers of alien goldsmiths practising near London; plate and jewellery made by foreigners were more fashionable, as London craftsmen were slow to adopt the Renaissance style. The Goldsmiths' Company was more tolerant of foreigners than most of the guilds and allowed some aliens to join, perhaps because many goldsmiths had become merchants rather than craftsmen.

15. Noble of Edward III, gold, 118.3 grains (*c.* 7.65 g), struck in London, 1351 (London, British Museum)

London's primacy in England's art life is unquestionable, but its artists' talents went into producing works that were purchased perhaps more outside London than by other Londoners. London was a centre of production rather than a source of demand, and its richest inhabitants were not its artists or craftsmen but the merchants who traded in the wool and cloth produced in other parts of England.

BIBLIOGRAPHY

G. Unwin: *The Gilds & Companies of London* (London, 1904, 4/1963)
G. Pollard: 'The Company of Stationers before 1557', *The Library*, 4th ser., xviii (1937–8), pp. 1–38
L. Stone: *Sculpture in Britain: The Middle Ages*, Pelican Hist. A. (Harmondsworth, 1955, 2/1972)
R. Allen Brown, H. M. Colvin and A. J. Taylor: *History of the King's Works*, i (London, 1963)
G. A. Williams: *Medieval London: From Commune to Capital* (London, 1963, rev. 1970)
A. E. J. Hollaender and W. Kellaway, eds: *Studies in London History Presented to Philip Edmund Jones* (London, 1969)
R. Emmerson: 'Monumental Brasses: London Design (*c.* 1420–85)', *J. Brit. Archaeol. Assoc.*, cxxxi (1978), pp. 50–78
J. Blair: 'Henry Lakenham, Marbler of London, and a Tomb Contract of 1376', *Antiqua. J.*, lx (1980), pp. 66–74
*Medieval Art, Architecture and Archaeology in London. British Archaeological Association Conference Transactions: London, 1984*
N. L. Ramsay: 'Artists, Craftsmen and Design in England, 1200–1400', *Age of Chivalry: Art in Plantagenet England, 1200–1400* (exh. cat., ed. J. Alexander and P. Binski; London, RA, 1987), pp. 49–54
M. A. Michael: 'Oxford, Cambridge and London: Towards a Theory for "Grouping" Manuscripts', *Burl. Mag.*, cxxx (1988), pp. 107–15
W. J. Blair and N. L. Ramsay, eds: *English Medieval Industries, Craftsmen, Techniques, Products* (London, 1991)

NIGEL RAMSAY

3. 1536–1659. The courts of Henry VIII at the beginning of this period and Charles I towards its end generated much artistic activity. Royal and noble patronage was extended to painters, sculptors and miniaturists and to goldsmiths, jewellers, weavers and masque devisers, many of them immigrants who invigorated the art world. The period was characterized by a new appetite for secular art and by flamboyant royal display, by the amassing of collections and the destruction and dispersal of others: the accumulated religious treasures of three centuries were seized at the Dissolution of the Monasteries (from 1536), and later royal holdings were sold to meet the debts of the Crown. During the Civil War (1642–9) and until the Restoration artistic activity in the city was greatly subdued.

Official visitors to the palaces at Whitehall (*see* §V, 5 below) and Greenwich were taken to the Presence Chamber through rooms dressed to dazzle and to impress. At the Tower of London historic arms and armour, curiosities and tapestries were on general show, while the Jewel House store of outstanding goldsmiths' work was opened up for privileged visitors. The monuments and royal effigies in Westminster Abbey (*see* §V, 2(ii)(b) below) and St Paul's Cathedral could be viewed. Periodically the streets were enlivened by elaborate civic pageants, such as triumphal entries of monarchs, and the annual Lord Mayor's procession, with emblematic painted floats and river barges. The urban élite expressed their increasing wealth by beautifying civic and domestic structures as the focus of expenditure shifted from cathedrals and chantries after the Dissolution. The interior courtyard of the Royal Exchange (1566–9) was adorned with statues of English monarchs, of which that of *Elizabeth I* (London, Guildhall

A.G.) is the only survivor; the city gates also carried statues.

Compared to Antwerp, London's art market was primitive. The first art dealers were the peripatetic Flemish agents supplying the courts of Henry VIII and Edward VI, such as Peter van de Walle, who imported tapestries from Brussels, sets of chased cups from Antwerp and such elaborate interior fixtures as fireplaces. They were followed by the 17th-century agent–collectors Balthazar Gerbier, Endymion Porter and Nicholas Lanier. There was no market for the sale of new pictures in the modern sense, as much work was produced on commission. Pictures were estimated to be considerably less valuable than tapestries, large decorated pieces of furniture, goldsmiths' work or clothing in expensive materials. A flourishing second-hand market facilitated the creation and dispersal of collections. At the sales of goods seized from churches that took place in the 1550s, pursemakers and other dealers in fashionable accessories purchased Late Gothic altar frontals and vestments for refashioning. Auctions of art emerged only in the early 17th century and were then largely confined to East Indian goods. Printsellers sold popular portraits, inexpensive and somewhat crudely produced local maps and views, costume series and *Cries of London* as well as imported engravings of ornament, which were a practical source of design ideas for artisans. The sales (1649–51) of Charles I's goods (see below) to pay his debts produced a sudden glut of artistic masterpieces on the London market. Huge profits were made by London syndicates selling on to the European collectors.

After the death of Henry VIII in 1547, substantial royal patronage did not re-emerge until the time of Henry, Prince of Wales. He established the first gallery in St James's Palace to house royal pictures and bronzes. His younger brother, Charles I, an avid and discriminating collector, resumed royal patronage and attracted foreign artists to court. During Charles I's reign there was an unprecedented concentration of works of art in London. Certain chambers at the palaces of Whitehall and St James held semi-public displays of paintings and works of art, as did others in the London mansions of the nobility along the Strand and at Charing Cross. Charles I's most prized paintings by Titian hung in the Privy Lodging Rooms at Whitehall, and a large collection of fine pictures was displayed in the Banqueting House with its ceiling paintings by Rubens. Charles I's purchase of the collection of antique and Renaissance sculpture of Vincenzo II Gonzaga, 7th Duke of Mantua, provided inspiration for his sculptors, such as Nicholas Stone (i) the elder and the immigré Hubert Le Sueur. The London house of Thomas Howard, 2nd Earl of Arundel, contained a remarkable collection of drawings, paintings, Limoges enamels and antique marbles (see fig. 16) and, like the collection of Sir Walter Cope (*c.* 1552–1614) in the 1590s, included a Cabinet of Curiosities. Informed collectors and artists were allowed access, but Arundel's house and garden were not formally open to the public, whereas John Tradescant the elder's collection of exotica and curios at Lambeth was set out as a public attraction.

Painting and other crafts had a much lower status than mathematics or architecture. Painting, whether of pageant

16. Daniel Mijtens I: *Thomas Howard, 2nd Earl of Arundel*, oil on canvas, 2.07×1.27 m, *c.* 1618 (London, National Portrait Gallery, on dep. Arundel Castle, W. Sussex); in the background is the Sculpture Gallery of Arundel House, London

floats, wall hangings, funeral monuments, shop signs or portraits, was the business of the Painter–Stainers', a livery company formed in 1502 from the amalgamation of the Painters, who traditionally worked on cloth, with the Stainers, who worked on wood and metal. The Painter–Stainers' provided training, the nearest thing to an academy at that time. Alien artists bringing credentials, such as Peter Lely, were normally admitted to the Company.

From the 1540s successive waves of foreign artists and craftsmen with special skills from goldsmithing to silk-weaving (*see* HUGUENOTS) flooded across the Channel, some at the invitation of the monarch, and they dominated the luxury trades. In 1635 there were several hundred, running workshops and employing outworkers. A general condition of domicile was that their skills should be taught to English craftsmen. Typical was the Westminster workshop of Christiaen van Vianen, employing 11 journeymen both native and Dutch. In order to protect its members from competition all the livery companies concerned with luxury crafts imposed inordinate controls on alien workers. Netherlandish sculptor-masons such as Garat Johnson were established in workshops, where apprentices also

trained, in Southwark, beyond the city boundaries and jurisdiction. Southwark and Aldgate, and later Lambeth, also housed potteries, producing tin-glazed earthenware and English delftware.

As yet, London had no formal drawing academy, and skilled apprentices learnt in their masters' workshops, although the tight-knit community of foreign artists and craftsmen in Clerkenwell and Blackfriars and, from the late 1630s, in Covent Garden included drawing masters and specialist instructors in the arts of engraving, cartography and calligraphy. Sixteenth-century debates on image-making dictated the preference for commissioned portraiture both at court and in the institutional collections of the city, resulting in such works as Hans Holbein the younger's portrait of *King Henry VIII* (London, Barber-Surgeons' Hall), commissioned in 1541. In the 17th century topographical views of London by such artists as Claude de Jongh, Cornelis Boel and Wenzel Hollar (see fig. 3 above) proliferated.

BIBLIOGRAPHY
N. G. Brett-James: *The Growth of Stuart London* (London, 1935)
C. Williams, ed.: *Thomas Platter's Travels in England, 1599* (London, 1937)
H. B. Walters: *London Churches before the Reformation* (London, 1939)
O. Millar, ed.: 'The Inventories and Valuations of the King's Goods, 1649–51', *Walpole Soc.*, xliii (1970) [whole issue]
D. M. Bergeron: *English Civic Pageantry, 1558–1642* (London, 1971)
I. Scouladi: 'Return of Strangers in the Metropolis, 1593–1639', *Huguenot Society Proceedings*, Quarto [London], lvii (London, 1985)
A. MacGregor, ed.: *The Late King's Goods* (London and Oxford, 1989)

For further bibliography *see* §II, 2 above.

PHILIPPA GLANVILLE

4. 1660–1768. The most notable feature of this period was the rise of art schools, auction-houses, public exhibitions, museums and artists' clubs (see fig. 17). Many of these institutions were initiated by the artists themselves to counteract the deficiencies of patronage, and, as a whole, they gradually came to form an interacting if differentiated system. This system paralleled the rise of an English school of artists conscious of their national identity, the gradual institutionalization of sections of private patronage, the organization of the art market and the growth of a large, anonymous audience characteristic of mature bourgeois societies.

Early educational institutions included the academy attended by William Gandy (*c.* 1655–1729) *c.* 1673, the school advertised by its master, Jacques d'Agar, in the *London Gazette* in 1681 and the academy recommended by Marshall Smith to the readers of his *Art of Painting* (1692). Also in 1692 Edward Millington opened the earliest auction-house documented in London, and a drawing-class in the capital was initiated at Christ's Hospital (a charitable school founded in 1553). This class, which aimed to educate technical draughtsmen and designers, was established on a permanent basis in 1705, when Bernard Lens (ii) was appointed its drawing-master. In 1697 Lens, together with John Sturt (1658–1730), had opened a drawing school in St Paul's Churchyard, which combined the functions of a preparatory academy with those of a school of design. These early institutions constituted the embryo from which developed an institutional system for the arts. Its growth was favoured initially

17. Gawen Hamilton: *A Conversation of Virtuosis at the Kings Armes (A Club of Artists)*, oil on canvas, 876×1125 mm, 1735 (London, National Portrait Gallery)

by clubs of artists, amateurs, collectors and connoisseurs, such as the Virtuosi of St Luke (1689–1743) and the Rose and Crown Club (*c.* 1704–45). The Virtuosi (*c.* 57 members) were involved in the earliest scheme for the establishment of a royal academy of art (in 1698), and they contributed to the dissemination of a taste for the arts among the educated classes. The Rose and Crown, a less selective club, played an important role in promoting the cause of English art. Its membership (around 85 persons) often crossed with those of the Academy in Great Queen Street (1711–20), with *c.* 97 subscribers, and the first St Martin's Lane Academy (1720–24) with *c.* 36 subscribers. Drawing from life was the principal aim of these and of later classes meeting in the evening. At Great Queen Street (under the successive governorships of Sir Godfrey Kneller and Sir James Thornhill) artists drew after male models, while in St Martin's Lane (under the directorship of Louis Chéron and John Vanderbank) both male and female models were used. In 1724 Thornhill opened a free academy attached to his house in Covent Garden, and in 1729–31 he prepared drawings (London, V&A) of details of Raphael's cartoons of the *Acts of the Apostles* (London, V&A) then at Hampton Court Palace for the (unrealized) publication of a set designed for the use of art students.

By the early 1730s the art world in London had grown remarkably, as the gathering in William Hogarth's *An Auction of Pictures* (*c.* 1730; see fig. 18) suggests. Old Master paintings were in great demand. About 1726 Christopher Cock had opened the earliest, long-lasting establishment for the auction of works of art. New opportunities of employment were offered to living artists by printsellers, publishers, theatre managers and by the demand for instructors in copying and drawing. All this could hardly take an English school to the artistic fore, however, or create a market for contemporary English art. The change took place in 1735, when the Engravers Copyright Act became law and the second Academy in St Martin's Lane was established. Hogarth was the principal instigator of both events. The Engravers Copyright Act protected original (but not reproductive) engravers from unauthorized copies of their works for a period of 14 years from the date inscribed on each print. (It was revised in 1767 to extend protection over a period of 28 years.) The Act, an early attempt at modifying prices in favour of living artists, was the precondition for the establishment of the second St Martin's Lane Academy, with around 83 subscribers. This lasted until 1768, the year the Royal Academy of Arts was founded. It was the subscribing artists to this academy and the larger community meeting at Slaughter's coffee-house near by who made the greatest efforts. They explored new market channels and marketing techniques, promoted public exhibitions of works by living artists, established exhibiting societies, made use of illustrated books as a sort of surrogate art gallery, and used advertisements published in the press, pamphlets and other printed statements in ways that anticipated the art press. Moreover, it was these same artists who, to the disappointment and with the disagreement of Hogarth, elaborated plans for the establishment of a public or royal academy in 1749 and again in 1755.

Artists of the St Martin's Lane circle, such as Louis-François Roubiliac, Francis Hayman and George Michael Moser (i), took an active part in the Rococo decorations for Vauxhall Gardens (c. 1736–60; see §V, 6 below). This first meeting with a large and anonymous audience was followed in 1746 by the attempt to transform the Foundling Hospital (a charitable institution founded in 1739) into a museum of contemporary art. While artists were busy with initiatives such as these, which might win them the attention of the public, a group of patrons and Grand Tourists who had organized themselves into the Society of Dilettanti (1732) offered encouragement in February 1749 to schemes for the establishment of an academy. Following this John Gwynn, a St Martin's Lane artist, published his *Essay on Design* (1749), which included a project for an artist-dominated academy to be established by public subscription until such time as a royal institution were created by George II (*reg* 1727–60). Frederick, Prince

of Wales, reacted immediately, commissioning George Vertue to plan an academy to be created under Frederick's patronage. Although no public or royal academy was established as a result, a web of institutions developed in London in the 1750s. William Shipley's Drawing School (1753–68) was a preparatory academy and a school of design. The academy (1758–c. 1768) attached to the sculpture gallery at Richmond House, Whitehall, owned by Charles Lennox, 3rd Duke of Richmond and Lennox, was a school for the study of the Antique. Joseph Wilton and Giovanni Battista Cipriani instructed students there until c. 1762, and more advanced courses were held in St Martin's Lane. From 1755 premiums were offered to the young by the Society for the Encouragement of Arts, Manufactures and Commerce (founded 1754; later the Royal Society of Arts). The study and visual documentation of the antiquities of Britain were the care of the Society of Antiquaries of London (founded 1586; re-established 1717). The documentation of the antiquities of Rome, Greece and Asia Minor was promoted by the Society of Dilettanti. The establishment of an academy for the study of the Antique in Rome (1752–8), supported by James Caulfeild, 1st Earl of Charlemont, rekindled the Society of Dilettanti's desire for an educational institution as prestigious as the British Museum (founded 1753) to be established in London. Reacting promptly to the Society's moves in this direction, the St Martin's Lane artists appointed a Select Committee (Oct 1753) charged with the plan for an academy, which they eventually produced in January 1755 and submitted to the Dilettanti

18. William Hogarth: *An Auction of Pictures*, oil on canvas, 438×749 mm, c. 1730 (private collection); unfinished sketch

and Society of Arts the following month. Following the failure of this second attempt, the St Martin's Lane artists concentrated on initiatives designed to win them the favour of the public and to force George II to support their cause.

The earliest large-scale exhibition was held in the Great Room of the Society of Arts, Denmark Court, the Strand, from 21 April to 3 May 1760. There were 130 exhibits from 69 exhibitors; 6582 catalogues were sold and over 12,000 visitors attended. From 1761 annual exhibitions were organized by the newly founded Society of Artists of Great Britain (incorporated by Royal Charter in 1765 to become the Incorporated Society of Artists, it dissolved in 1791) and the Free Society of Artists (1761–83). Annual exhibitions and their success with the public created the conditions for the establishment of the Royal Academy of Arts in 1768 (*see* §VI below). The 1760s represent a turning-point. There were changes in government attitudes towards the arts following the accession of George III: the rise of a public style that paralleled annual exhibitions and the publication of proper reviews in the press; the growing involvement of artists in politics and of politicians in the arts; the separation of fine artists from engravers and designers; the divorce of the academy from the school of design; and the expansion of the art market. (The auction-house Christie's was established in 1766; Sotheby's, established in 1734, did not sell paintings until early in the 19th century.) In the event, Joshua Reynolds's notion of a regulated academy of art prevailed over that of the unregulated art school, an attitude that went back to the age of Hogarth and was still current in 1755.

BIBLIOGRAPHY

J. Pye: *Patronage of British Art* (London, 1845)
W. T. Whitley: *Artists and their Friends in England, 1700–1790*, 2 vols (London, 1928)
'The Note-books of George Vertue', *Walpole Soc.*, xviii (1930), xx (1932), xxii (1934), xxiv (1936), xxix (1942), xxx (1950)
I. Bignamini: 'Art Institutions in London, 1689–1768', *Walpole Soc.*, liv (1988), pp. 19–148
*The Artist's Model: Its Role in British Art from Lely to Etty* (exh. cat. by I. Bignamini and M. Postle, Nottingham; London, Kenwood House, 1991)

ILARIA BIGNAMINI

5. 1769–1850. This period was dominated by the influence of the Royal Academy (*see* §VI and fig. 42 below), which stimulated public interest in contemporary art but monopolized training and exhibitions, despite challenges from other institutions. Until the end of the 18th century, such fashionable artists as Reynolds had large studios, usually in the West End, where the public could view their paintings; by 1850 artists were moving further out to Hampstead, Kensington and St John's Wood. Through the formation of galleries, the public had more access to works of art, and a larger potential buying population increased the market for both Old Masters and, later, contemporary paintings. These changes, as well as greater attention to art in newspapers and periodicals, helped to raise the status of artists, who could command high prices and prestigious patronage. The interest in foreign art declined as the market encouraged the development of a national school.

The Royal Academy, founded in 1768 and opened on 2 January 1769 with Joshua Reynolds as the first president,

sponsored a school and an annual exhibition, which from 1780 was held in the Great Room in Somerset House (see fig. 19; *see also* EXHIBITION, fig. 3). The 40 Academicians formed an élite circle to which many aspired: Joseph Farington's *Diaries*, covering the period 1793–1821, record much canvassing for election and other 'business' conducted outside official meetings and at annual Academy dinners. Royal support encouraged artists to exhibit at the Academy or to seek membership, and other exhibition institutions suffered as a result. The Incorporated Society of Artists (founded 1761, incorporated 1765) took charge of Charles Lennox, 3rd Duke of Richmond's Gallery from 1770, and opened its own gallery in 1772, but lack of support led to its eventual demise in 1791, preceded by the close of the Free Society in 1783. The monopoly of the Royal Academy was challenged by Robert Strange in his *Inquiry into the Rise of the Royal Academy of Arts* (London, 1775) and by John Pye, whose *Patronage of British Art* (London, 1845) saw the Academy as an élitist institution fostering hardship among non-member artists. A Royal Commission enquiry into the affairs of the Royal Academy (1853) highlighted these grievances but did nothing to change its policies. Artists continued to seek membership, which enhanced their status and respectability, gave them an annual opportunity to exhibit their work before an increasingly attentive public and allowed them to command higher prices for their paintings.

Challenges to the Royal Academy monopoly included the formation of complementary institutions and more competitive efforts by individuals. The short-lived British School (1802–3) was an exhibition society sponsored by George, Prince of Wales (later George IV), and the more successful British Institution (1805–67) aimed 'to encourage and reward' artists, particularly those who had gained recognition through the Royal Academy exhibitions. The annual exhibitions of the British Institution helped to secure buyers for many works shown previously at the Royal Academy. The British Institution also included exhibitions of Old Master paintings and of works by deceased British artists in British private collections, such as those of Reynolds (1813) and Hogarth, Wilson, Gainsborough and Zoffany (1814). These shows created a platform for the display of riches in British private collections and gave artists an opportunity to view and copy paintings.

Other gaps were filled by the Society of Painters in Watercolours (formed 1805) and the Associated Artists in Watercolours (formed 1808), which gave watercolour painters the chance to exhibit works together, rather than in comparison with oil paintings, as was done at the Royal Academy. The Artist's Benevolent Fund (formed 1809, incorporated 1827) created a mutual assurance society for artists who were not members of the Royal Academy.

Individuals discovered the commercial and practical benefits of exhibiting their works privately; profits were gained from admission fees, and the works could be seen without interference. John Singleton Copley showed his sensational *Death of the Earl of Chatham* (1779–81; London, Tate) at Spring Gardens in 1781, drawing crowds away from the Royal Academy exhibition. His later *Siege of Gibraltar* (1783–91; London, Guildhall A.G.) was so large that a tent had to be erected in Green Park to show

19. Thomas Rowlandson and A. C. Pugin: *The Great Room, Somerset House*, engraving, 1808 (London, Royal Academy of Arts)

it. Likewise Benjamin Robert Haydon, who felt unfairly excluded from the privileges of the Royal Academy, exhibited his *Judgement of Solomon* (1812–14; J. B. Gold priv. col.) at the Spring Gardens gallery (1814), and his *Christ's Entry into Jerusalem* (1814–20; Cincinnati, OH, St George's Semin.) at the Egyptian Hall in Piccadilly (1820). The populist nature of such exhibitions was derided by Royal Academicians who feared the challenge to their commercial ascendency, although they, too, often found private exhibition an advantage. Turner, for example, had a 'gallery' of his work at Queen Anne Street West, for show by invitation only.

The trade in Old Master paintings increased in the 1790s when the French Revolution and subsequent up-heavals in Europe brought large numbers of paintings into the London art market. These works were either sold in London or passed through London on their way to country houses. Sales were engineered by picture dealers, such as Noel Desanfans and Benjamin Vandergucht, and auction-eers, such as Skinner and Dyke and James Christie (*see* CHRISTIE'S). The major sales of the period included that of Louis-Philippe-Joseph, Duc d'Orléans from 1792, part of whose collection was bought by Francis Egerton, 3rd Duke of Bridgewater, Frederick Howard, 5th Earl of Carlisle, and George Granville Leveson-Gower, 2nd Duke of Sutherland. Some of these works were re-sold, but all

were shown at Bryan's the picture dealer's (Pall Mall and the Strand): the Dutch and Flemish pictures in 1793 and the Italian ones in 1798. These exhibitions were beneficial to artists who had little previous access to European painting and inspired public interest in Old Masters. Other sales included those of the collections of Charles Alexandre de Calonne, the French Ambassador (1793–5), and of Joshua Reynolds (1794–8). The sale and re-sale of pictures flooded the market, and the Napoleonic Wars—which had earlier helped establish London as a 'safe' marketplace—stopped the flow of pictures from Europe.

During the early part of the 19th century market interest turned to the productions of contemporary artists, such as David Wilkie. Patrons (particularly those of the indus-trial middle class) were discouraged by stories of Old Master faking and found modern works not only more accessible but also a more certain investment. The popu-larity of contemporary art was fuelled by the growing attention of newspapers and journals. The reviews of the vitriolic 'Anthony Pasquin' (John Williams) in the *Morning Post* during the 1790s, and of William Hazlitt during the 1810s and 1820s, were followed by the foundation of journals devoted solely to art, such as the *Annals of the Fine Arts* (1819–24) and the *Art-Union* (formed 1839), later called the *Art Journal*, which championed new painters over Old Masters and helped change the focus of market interest.

Exhibitions offered an opportunity for only a temporary display of art, but during this period various attempts were made to create more permanent settings. Several Royal Academicians (including Reynolds and James Barry) offered to decorate the interior of St Paul's Cathedral in 1773, but this was vetoed by the Bishop of London; a commission to decorate the Great Room of the Society for the Encouragement of Arts, Manufactures and Commerce was likewise abortive at first, but Barry took over the project in 1777. Equally ill-judged was the Shakespeare Gallery, initiated by the printseller John Boydell in 1786. The Gallery opened in Pall Mall in 1789 with paintings of scenes from Shakespeare's plays by eminent Royal Academicians, and for a time it was a fashionable, if controversial, part of London art life. But the international market for the gallery engravings was cut off by war with France, and this and other problems led Boydell to declare bankruptcy, selling the gallery by lottery in 1805. A similar fate ended other gallery projects, such as Henry Fuseli's Milton Gallery, Thomas Macklin's Poet's Gallery and Robert Bowyer's Historic and Biblical Galleries.

The commercial, contemporary and ultimately ephemeral nature of these galleries contrasted with the success of the Dulwich Picture Gallery and the National Gallery, both of which were formed from private collections of Old Master paintings. The Dulwich Picture Gallery, housed in a building designed by Sir John Soane, opened in 1814 to display the picture collection bequeathed by Peter Francis Bourgeois (and left to him by Desanfans). By contrast, the National Gallery was formed from three collections. When the House of Commons voted to purchase John Julius Angerstein's collection (which included his house at 100 Pall Mall) in 1824, George Beaumont offered his collection to the nation, while that of William Howell Carr was bequeathed a few years later. The National Gallery opened in May 1824 in its cramped accommodation in Pall Mall, but although it proved an invaluable source for artists, the public was at first relatively indifferent. In April 1838 it moved to the new building in Trafalgar Square designed by William Wilkins. It shared the building with the Royal Academy (until 1869), leading to furious public debate about the relative worth of the two institutions. William Seguier was the gallery's first keeper, followed by Charles Lock Eastlake in 1843, who became the first director in 1855. Soane's own collection, displayed in his house (reconstructed 1792) in Lincoln's Inn Fields, was established as Sir John Soane's Museum in 1837 (see ARTIST'S HOUSE, fig. 5 and SOANE, JOHN, fig. 3).

BIBLIOGRAPHY

J. Pye: *Patronage of British Art* (London, 1845)
C. Holmes and C. H. Collins Baker: *The Making of the National Gallery* (London, 1924)
W. T. Whitley: *Artists and their Friends in England, 1700–1799*, 2 vols (London, 1928)
——: *Art in England, 1800–1820* (Cambridge, 1928)
S. Hutchinson: *The History of the Royal Academy, 1768–1968* (London, 1968)
W. Friedman: *Boydell's Shakespeare Gallery* (New York, 1976)
K. Garlick and A. MacIntyre, eds: *The Diary of Joseph Farington*, 6 vols (London, 1978)
D. Sutton: 'Aspects of British Collecting, Part III: A Wealth of Pictures', *Apollo*, cxix/267 (1984), pp. 346–56
——: 'The Orléans Collection', *Apollo*, cxix/267 (1984), pp. 357–72
*London: World City, 1800–1840* (exh. cat., ed. C. Fox; Essen, Villa Hügel, 1992)

SHEARER WEST

6. 1851–1909. In the 1850s the Royal Academy continued to be the city's main exhibition venue (see fig. 20) and was the centre of the Pre-Raphaelite Brotherhood (see PRE-RAPHAELITISM). Of this group, in the 1860s John Everett Millais alone kept his eye on official honours and eventually became President of the Royal Academy in 1896. After the Royal Academy moved to Burlington House, Piccadilly, in 1869 resentment grew against its members, who monopolized this prime exhibition space. Artists such as William Powell Frith, a Royal Academician, also courted public attention by showing at a dealer's gallery. The *Railway Station* (1862; Egham, U. London, Royal Holloway & Bedford New Coll.) attracted huge crowds, and many engravings of it were sold, which was a common practice undertaken by such dealers as Ernest Gambart and Louis Victor Flatow.

The Aesthetic Movement, devoted to the principle of Art for Art's Sake, with Dante Gabriel Rossetti, JAMES McNEILL WHISTLER, Edward Burne-Jones, Algernon Charles Swinburne and G. F. Watts among its members, emerged in the 1860s. Watts lived at Little Holland House, Kensington, home of Henry Thoby Prinsep (1792–1878), where a number of artists gathered. Rossetti ignored the Royal Academy and sold his paintings to such private patrons as James Leathart. Others in his circle shared his disdain for Royal Academy success. When the Grosvenor Gallery, run by Sir Coutts Lindsay and others, held its first exhibition in 1877, it was welcomed as an alternative to the Royal Academy. The works of Burne-Jones and Whistler, both of whom had not showed at the Royal Academy for some time, and those of Albert Joseph Moore, a close associate of Whistler, attracted much notice. Whistler's *Nocturne in Black and Gold: The Falling Rocket* (1875; Detroit, MI, Inst. A.), shown at the Grosvenor Gallery in 1877, outraged John Ruskin, which resulted in Whistler's famous libel lawsuit (1878). The Grosvenor Gallery flourished in the 1880s, showing the work of, among others, French-trained British artists, and its exhibitions were considered a real threat to the Royal Academy.

The Royal Academy, however, was invigorated under the presidency (1878–96) of Frederic Leighton, who introduced many reforms. The winter exhibitions of Old Master paintings were popular and attendances soared. As president, Leighton arranged the election of some of his old Art for Art's Sake associates, including Burne-Jones. He also encouraged new young artists to join, for example Stanhope Forbes and George Clausen, both of whom were early members of the NEW ENGLISH ART CLUB (NEAC), founded in 1886 by French-inspired artists who felt neglected by the Royal Academy. Henry Herbert La Thangue, William Holman Hunt and Walter Crane were also members of this group. In 1884 the ART WORKERS' GUILD was formed.

As new groups and splinter groups emerged in the 1880s, artists looked for alternative exhibition venues. Whistler, for instance, arranged a number of one-man exhibitions at such venues as the Flemish Gallery, the Fine Art Society and William Dowdeswell's gallery. In 1886 he became President of the Society of British Artists, which

20. Charles West Cope: *Council of the Royal Academy Selecting Pictures for the Exhibition*, oil on canvas, 1.45×2.20 m, 1876 (London, Royal Academy of Arts)

had premises on Pall Mall and was granted a Royal Charter in 1887. Whistler's ambitious plans to reform the Society were, however, poorly received, and he was forced to resign in 1888. He took a large group of followers with him, some of whom formed an Impressionist clique, taking control of the NEAC from 1888. Headed by Walter Richard Sickert, the group included Frances Bate, Frederick Brown, Francis James (1849–1920), Paul Maitland (1869–1909), Théodore Roussel, Sidney Starr (1857–1925), Philip Wilson Steer, George Thomson and Bernhard Sickert (1862–1932). They exhibited as the 'London Impressionists' at the Goupil Galleries in December 1889 and in Sickert's Chelsea studio. Two new periodicals, the *Whirlwind* and the *Art Weekly*, supported them.

Twenty paintings by Claude Monet were shown at the Goupil Galleries in 1889 in one of several exhibitions of French Impressionists organized by dealers in England between 1870 and 1905. The Society of French Artists acquired some works by Monet, Camille Pissarro and Edgar Degas. The dealer Paul Durand-Ruel also brought Impressionist works to England. At Whistler's invitation, Monet sent four pictures to the Royal Society of British Artists in 1887. The NEAC showed works by Degas, Monet and Berthe Morisot. In the 1890s, a new exhibiting group, the International Society of Sculptors, Painters and Gravers, with first Whistler (from 1898) and then Auguste Rodin as president, was set up to encourage links with artists abroad. The most notorious show was of Degas's *Absinthe Drinker* (1875–6; Paris, Mus. d'Orsay) at the

Grafton Gallery in 1893, which prompted a heated debate led by George Moore, Dugald Sutherland MacColl and Elisabeth Pennell. In addition, the Tate Gallery was opened in 1897.

Just as there were alternatives to the RA exhibitions, so too were there alternatives to its schools. Many artists went abroad to study in the 1880s and 1890s, but after Frederick Brown was appointed professor of the Slade School of Fine Art in 1893, teaching based on drawing and painting nudes, as in Europe, was available in London. Brown brought his friends Steer and Henry Tonks to teach there, and its students, including many women, were the liveliest of their generation. Among them were Augustus John, Gwen John and Spencer Gore.

BIBLIOGRAPHY
R. Pickvance: '*L'Absinthe* in England', *Apollo*, lxxvii (1963), pp. 395–8
D. Farr: *English Art, 1870–1940* (Oxford, 1978)
*Great Victorian Pictures: Their Paths to Fame* (exh. cat. by R. Treble, London, RA, 1978)
K. Flint: *Impressionists in England: The Critical Reception* (London, 1984)
*The Pre-Raphaelites* (exh. cat., ed. L. Parris; London, Tate, 1984)
A. Robins: 'Feuds and Factions at the New English Art Club', *The New English Art Club Centenary Exhibition* (exh. cat. by A. Robins, London, Christie's, 1986), pp. 1–13
J. Stokes: *In the Nineties* (Hemel Hempstead, 1989)
A. Gruetzner Robins: *British Impressionism: The Magic and Poetry of Life around Them*, World Impressionism (New York, 1990)

ANNA GRUETZNER ROBINS

7. AFTER 1909. With his exhibitions in 1910–11 and 1912 of Post-Impressionism at the Grafton Galleries (see fig. 21) Roger Fry introduced a reluctant London to

21. Roger Fry: *A Room at the Second Post-Impressionist Exhibition*, oil on panel, 514×629 mm, 1912 (Paris, Musée d'Orsay)

modern art. Following Samuel Courtauld's donation (1931) of the foundation collection to the Courtauld Institute Galleries, Fry's own collection was bequeathed in 1934. Both collections betray a strong French bias, which was also reflected in the teaching of the modern period at that institute under the directorship (1947–74) of Anthony Blunt. Since 1926 the Tate Gallery (originally the National Gallery of British Art) has displayed foreign art as well as British art from the 16th century onwards. However, at this time it was obstinately insular in its collecting and missed many opportunities to acquire innovative continental art. With the Royal Academy also pursuing a trenchantly conservative policy for most of the 20th century, avant-garde artists had to look to other government agencies, private patrons or the marketplace for support. Gradually, attitudes towards modernism changed in both institutions: at the Tate marginalized modernists of the 1930s (e.g. Barbara Hepworth) were appointed trustees in the 1950s and 1960s, and in the 1980s the gallery formed a close association with the private collector Charles Saatchi, who maintained and opened to the public his international collection of contemporary art in north London. By the late 1980s Pop artists such as Peter Blake ranked as senior Academicians, marking a late conversion at the Royal Academy.

The American patron Peggy Guggenheim and the critic Herbert Read made tentative efforts in 1938 to establish a museum of modern art in London but were thwarted by the advent of World War II. Their efforts, however, paved the way for the creation of the Institute of Contemporary Arts in 1947 as a meeting-place for experimental artists. The INDEPENDENT GROUP (which included Nigel Henderson, Richard Hamilton and Eduardo Paolozzi) was formed by young artists who met at the ICA from 1952 to 1955.

The Contemporary Art Society (founded 1910), which purchased works for public collections, was an alternative to the conservative Chantrey Bequest, administered by the Royal Academy. During both World Wars, the War Office provided much needed commissions to artists, while two government bodies that were to prove instrumental in British (and London) art life in the post-war period owe their existence to World War II. These were the Arts Council of Great Britain, which evolved out of the Council for the Encouragement of the Arts and Music set up in 1942 to preserve artistic heritage in a time of crisis, and the British Council, established initially to counter Nazi propaganda in the 1930s, which ensured representation of British artists abroad, thus playing an important role in the internationalization of London as an art capital.

Besides official institutions, artists—especially those seeking to challenge the status quo—formed their own groupings and associations. From 1912 a stylistically diverse group that included Charles Ginner, Spencer Gore, Wyndham Lewis and Jacob Epstein gathered around Madame Frida Strindberg's cabaret club, the Cave of the Golden Calf in Soho. This was a rare instance of London artists attempting to compensate for their city's lack of cafés, essential props in continental art life. In the first half of the 20th century several associations were started by artists who felt excluded from the Royal Academy (whose Summer Exhibition was a lucrative outlet to the general public) or who wanted to stay away from that sort of atmosphere. The New English Art Club, from the last century, had itself become a staid and exclusive exhibiting society by the time the CAMDEN TOWN GROUP formed itself around Walter Richard Sickert in 1911. The LONDON GROUP, founded in 1913, absorbed many members from the latter and remained a significant influence on British art into the 1930s. The short-lived UNIT ONE, formed in 1934 and dissolved soon after, typifies the isolated position of avant-garde art in Britain between the wars, as artists from opposing Surrealist and abstract tendencies felt the need to join together with a vague, almost apologetic manifesto (in contrast to the belligerent stance of the Vorticists two decades earlier). In post-war years groups were often established by artists who had just left art school and were eager to assert the novelty and youthfulness of their style. This was the case with SITUATION, the hard-edged abstract group formed in 1960 by Harold Cohen (b 1928), Bernard Cohen and Robyn Denny (b 1930), among others.

London has never had artist quarters of the concentration of Montparnasse in Paris or Greenwich Village in New York, but several areas have lent their name to a group or phase in British art, of which the most significant is Bloomsbury. The BLOOMSBURY GROUP, active in the first three decades of the century, was moulded by the personalities of Leonard Woolf (1880–1969) and Virginia Woolf (1882–1941), the painters Vanessa Bell and Duncan Grant, and the critics Roger Fry and Clive Bell. From before it was even founded, members of the Camden Town Group lived around Fitzroy Street, in particular gathering at the large rented studio at number 19 (for illustration *see* CAMDEN TOWN GROUP), and they continued to do so after the decline of the official group. In the 1930s a number of younger artists and critics gravitated towards Hampstead: the group included Herbert Read, Henry Moore, Ben Nicholson and Barbara Hepworth, with Paul Nash, Roland Penrose and Adrian Stokes near by. Several European emigrés moved to the area immediately before the War, including Mondrian and Gropius. During and after World War II, Fitzroy Square, next to Fitzroy Street, lent its name to Fitzrovia, which along with Soho was a milieu of NEO-ROMANTICISM, and also to those realists associated with William Coldstream's art school on the Euston Road and later the nearby Slade School of Art, where he was director (*see* EUSTON ROAD SCHOOL). By the 1960s artists were dispersed around London, but the 1970s and 1980s marked a significant migration towards the East End, where vacant factories and warehouses provided cheap workspaces in the style of New York's lofts. Several artist-run associations such as SPACE, AIR and ACME were formed to manage and let such studios, the latter two also running galleries for a while.

London's art schools have always played a vital role in the art life of the capital, not least for the employment they have offered to artists, so enabling their contact with its cultural activity. They also provide a barometer of trends and tendencies, and student friendships often form the nucleus of new groups. The Slade was the training place of most of the luminaries of the 1920s and 1930s: Nicholson, Nash, David Bomberg, Mark Gertler, Wyndham Lewis—all pupils of the legendary drawing instructor Henry Tonks. The students entering in one remarkable year at the Royal College of Art in 1959 included the core Pop artists: David Hockney, R. B. Kitaj, Derek Boshier, Allen Jones and Patrick Caulfield. In the 1960s the sculpture department at St Martin's School of Art, where Anthony Caro was the main influence, produced several innovative and radical sculptors: Phillip King, David Annesly, Richard Long, and Gilbert and George. In the early 1990s Goldsmith's College graduates nurtured by Michael Craig-Martin and Jon Thompson, such as Julian Opie, Caroline Russell, Damien Hirst and Simon Linke (b 1958), achieved prominence for their neo-conceptual work. Although the 1980s were marked by a government policy of cuts in the art schools and art funding bodies as well as the closure of numerous galleries, the wealth of London's museums, commercial galleries, printmaking facilities and specialist art libraries constitutes a sign of London's continued vitality as an art capital. New buildings were opened at the Tate Gallery (Clore Gallery, 1980–85, by James Stirling) and the National Gallery (extension 1987–91, by Venturi, Rauch & Scott Brown), and in 1989 the Courtauld Institute and Gallery moved to Somerset House.

## BIBLIOGRAPHY

W. R. Sickert: *A Free House, or the Artist as Craftsman* (London, 1947)
R. Cork: *Vorticism and Abstract Art in the First Machine Age*, 2 vols (London, 1976)
D. Farr: *English Art, 1870–1940* (Oxford, 1978)
C. Harrison: *English Art and Modernism, 1900–1939* (London and Bloomington, 1981)
F. Spalding: *British Art since 1900* (London, 1986)
*British Art in the 20th Century: The Modern Movement* (exh. cat., ed. S. Compton; London, RA, 1987)
B. Ford, ed.: *Since the Second World War*, ix of *The Cambridge Guide to the Arts in Britain* (Cambridge, 1988/R as *Modern Britain*, ix of *Cambridge Cultural History of Britain*, 1992)
M. Yorke: *The Spirit of Place: Nine Neo-Romantic Artists and their Times* (London, 1988)
M. R. D. Foot: *Art and War: Twentieth Century Warfare as Depicted by War Artists* (London, 1990)
A. Bowness and others: *British Contemporary Art, 1910–1990* (London, 1991)
L. Gillick and A. Renton, eds: *Technique Anglaise: Current Trends in British Art* (London, 1991)
B. Sewell: 'Nicholas Serota and the Tate Gallery', *Modern Painters* (Summer 1992), pp. 66–9

DAVID COHEN

## IV. Centre of production.

1. Furniture. 2. Metalwork. 3. Ceramics. 4. Glass. 5. Objects of vertu. 6. Tapestry.

1. FURNITURE. Carpenters, joiners, coffer-makers, turners as well as upholders played a role in furniture

production, and by the late 14th century in London separate guilds were emerging for all these crafts, though charters formally recognizing their rights and privileges were not obtained until a century or more later. The guilds had powers to regulate admission to their crafts, the number of journeymen that a master could employ and powers of search to detect substandard workmanship. At times demarcation disputes arose, for example that between the Carpenters' Company and the Joiners' Company in 1632, when the Court of Aldermen of the City of London laid down that work involving mortice or dovetail joints was rightly the province of the joiners, leaving only furniture of a simpler nature to the carpenters. City companies were, however, united against the competition of foreign craftsmen. The Joiners' Company forbade them from practising their crafts except as journeymen and hunted down 'foreigners' from other English towns or other countries. In a search carried out in April 1583, 99 unlicensed joiners and carvers were discovered. Foreign craftsmen exercised their skills in areas outside the control of the city companies, and in the late 16th century German workers were active in Southwark producing 'Nonsuch' chests and other items of furniture inlaid with intarsia.

Rising wealth in the 17th century coupled with the adoption of French court styles and skills from the Netherlands produced great advances both in construction and finish. The court circle that patronized such architects and designers as INIGO JONES and FRANCIS CLEYN initiated the change in furnishings, but it was not to be properly established until the reign of Charles II and coincided with the building programmes of the late Stuart monarchs at Hampton Court, Greenwich Hospital and Kensington Palace, and the rebuilding of the City of London after the fire of 1666. To be near city patronage and accessible to imported timber supplies, furniture-makers in the main worked within the city boundaries, with St Paul's Churchyard the most popular location. The arts of cabinetmaking, veneering and marquetry owed much to the craft skills imported from the Continent, but it was in upholstery that the greatest influence, from the court style of the French king, Louis XIV, was to be seen. Those of foreign extraction who supplied the royal family included John Casbert (fl1660–76), Philip Guibert (fl1692–1739), John Pelletier (fl1690–1710) and GERRIT JENSEN. Cane chairmaking became important in the London furniture trade, and in 1689 the Upholders' Company petitioned Parliament to prohibit their manufacture as such chairs were ousting those covered with English 'Turkey work'. The London trade faced up to the competition from Japanese and Chinese lacquer by practising the art of japanning, and in 1700 the Joiners' Company petitioned for restriction on these imports.

The development of the squares and terraces of Soho and the West End provided opportunities for furniture-makers catering for the fashionable trade to move their business premises. The areas surrounding St Martin's Lane and Long Acre were chosen by Thomas Chippendale the elder (see CHIPPENDALE, (1)), WILLIAM VILE, JOHN CHANNON, JOHN COBB and William Haltett (c. 1709–81), while William Linnell (c. 1703–63) and JOHN LINNELL (i) traded from premises at 28 Berkeley Square.

At the beginning of the 18th century businessmen had concentrated on one aspect of the trade—upholstery, cabinetmaking, chair-making or carving—but by the mid-18th century many of the leading London furniture-makers had expanded the size of the businesses to provide a comprehensive service. To undertake the complete furnishing of a residence it was necessary to employ 40 to 50 craftsmen, and Chippendale's business appears to have been of this size; an exception was the firm of George Seddon (see SEDDON, (1)), which was employing 400 journeymen in 1783. By the first decade of the 19th century such firms employed on average 100 to 150 craftsmen. There were still some specialist firms, and in the Regency period there was a considerable trade in patent and multi-purpose furniture. The making of this centred on Catherine Street, the Strand, where Morgan & Sanders (fl1801–20; see fig. 22) and Thomas Butler (fl1787–1814) were active rivals. Such small fancy cabinet wares as writing-desks, dressing-cases and tea-caddies were the speciality of other firms (see also MARQUETRY, colour pl. VIII, fig. 1). Many of their showrooms were in the Strand, while the workshops were in and around Clerkenwell and Aldersgate.

Visitors to London on parliamentary, legal and other business would often visit furniture-makers to place their orders, and many country houses built in the Georgian period were wholly or partly furnished from London. The makers would arrange for the carriage and installation of the furniture, and the decoration of the rooms as well. The export trade was also of importance, with much of the furniture made in London finding its way to the American colonies and the West Indies. There were also European markets in the Netherlands and Germany, and GILES GRENDEY had an active trade that included japanned furniture with Spain and Portugal in the first half of the 18th century.

In the Victorian period there were two main developments, one of which was the expansion of the comprehensive firm. The census of 1851 records that HOLLAND & SONS were employing 350 persons (Kirkham, 1988, p. 78), and by the 1870s Jackson & Graham's workforce had reached 600–1000. Such firms began to decline in the 1870s, however, when the property values in the West End became too high for the maintenance of large factories there. West End firms were also badly injured by a second development, the rise of the furniture trade in the East End, which had started early in the century and acquired the means for national marketing through easier access both to the docks and railway goods yards. By the end of the 19th century the furniture was often sold to wholesale warehouses in Curtain Road, Great Eastern Street and City Road, and manufacturers and wholesalers from the area supplied retail furnishers and department stores in the West End. By the beginning of the 20th century Tottenham Court Road was gaining a reputation as an important centre of retail furnishing. The East End trade produced a wide range of furniture, from such high-class reproductions as those produced by S. Hille & Co. from its works in Old Street to cheap pieces 'in the white'.

The furniture-making industry remained active in the East End until World War II. Increasing congestion, the lack of materials and labour during the War and bomb

22. Furniture showrooms of Morgan & Sanders, Catherine Street, the Strand, London; engraving from Rudolph Ackermann: *The Repository of Arts*, ii (London, 1809), pl. 10

damage had their effect. The firms best able to take advantage of the post-war demand were those in the provinces with room for expansion and the automation of manufacturing processes. A reduced furniture industry continues to exist in London, mainly in the form of specialist firms and manufacturers of reproduction furniture.

BIBLIOGRAPHY
R. Edwards and M. Jourdain: *Georgian Cabinet-makers* (London, 1944, rev. 3/1955)
A. Heal: *The London Furniture Makers: From the Restoration to the Victorian Era, 1660–1840* (London, 1953/R New York, 1959)
G. Beard and C. Gilbert, eds: *Dictionary of English Furniture Makers, 1660–1840* (London and Leeds, 1986)
P. Kirkham, R. Mace and J. Porter: *Furnishing the World: The East London Furniture Trade, 1830–1980* (London, 1987)
P. Kirkham: *The London Furniture Trade, 1700–1870* (London, 1988)
BRIAN AUSTEN

## 2. METALWORK.

*(i) Gold and silver.* From the 12th century there was an organized body of goldsmiths in London, which was the centre of the English trade, supported by ecclesiastical and civic patronage and royal commissions (e.g. the effigies of *Henry III* and *Eleanor of Castile*, both 1291, in Westminster Abbey, by William Torel). Aspects of goldsmiths' work included seals (see fig. 13 above), coins and jewellery, and specializations existed from the 13th century. The Worshipful Company of Goldsmiths received its first charter in 1327; it maintained the sterling standard of silver, assayed and marked silverwork and curbed foreign competition. Royal patronage was exercised through the Master of the Jewel House and the Royal Goldsmiths, who were often selected more for their financial skills than for their craftsmanship, and who frequently acted as agents for other goldsmiths. In 1544 Henry VIII set up the London Assay Office.

Artisans and retailers made up the trade in the 18th century. The 22 retailers in Westminster in 1749 were reliant on a network of specialist suppliers and outworkers. There were also a number of women smiths (*see* SILVER, fig. 1). The use of marriage to reinforce business connections, already discernible in the late 15th century, characterized some of the most successful 18th-century firms. There was a seven-year apprenticeship to enter the trade, which was regarded as the most 'genteel' of the 'mechanical trades'. In the 17th and 18th centuries a number of foreign gold- and silversmiths worked in London, including Christiaen van Vianen, Philip Rollos and Charles Kandler. The 18th-century influx of such Huguenot craftsmen as Peter Archambo, Nicholas Sprimont, Pierre Harache, Pierre Platel, PAUL DE LAMERIE (see fig. 23), David Willaume, David Tanqueray and Paul Crespin had a major impact. Their skills and style influenced local smiths, for example George Wickes and Thomas Heming.

In the late 18th century industrialization and competition from Birmingham and Sheffield threatened London's supremacy. The introduction of new technology that enabled mass production by such firms as the Bateman workshop (*see* BATEMAN, HESTER) brought extensive production of thin-gauge silverwares. As a result, many small workers and small firms specialized or were subsumed into larger businesses. Trade organizations, for example RUNDELL, BRIDGE & RUNDELL, set an example

23. Silver sideboard dish by Paul de Lamerie, diam. 788 mm, made in London for the Goldsmiths' Company and showing its arms, 1741 (London, Goldsmiths' Company)

that was followed by such firms as Garrard & Co. Ltd (*see* GARRARD), Hunt & Roskell (*see* ENGLAND, fig. 80) and Edward Barnard & Sons. The need for formal art training led to the establishment of the London School of Design in 1837. The Museum of Manufactures (now London, V&A), set up to improve taste and offer examples to designers, contained silverware purchased from the Great Exhibition of 1851. Henry Cole, its first director, also launched the Felix Summerly's Art-Manufacturer's scheme in 1847 for the manufacture of well-designed articles. Followers of the Arts and Crafts Movement, such as Henry Wilson and C. R. Ashbee and his School and Guild of Handicraft (est. 1888), rejected commercial practices, revived old techniques and brought craftsmen together in small workshops. Liberty & Co. employed such London-based designers as Archibald Knox, Omar Ramsden and Jessie M. King to design pewter- and silverware, which was mass-produced in Birmingham for the shop in Regent Street.

In the 20th century formal college-based courses virtually eliminated the traditional apprentice system. The artist–craftsman who sought creative freedom pursued his craft in isolation (e.g. Harold Stabler), while the more conservative, industrialized manufacturers served a larger, safer market. From the 1960s many old manufacturing and retail firms were replaced by such bulk market chains as Ratners and H. Samuel, which concentrated on inexpensive silver, silverplate and jewellery. Such firms as Garrard & Co. Ltd and Asprey & Co. supplied more expensive items and had their own design studios, as well as buying in from different suppliers. The Goldsmiths' Company helped to revive creativity and traditional skills with competitions, exhibitions, debate, a consistent policy

of commissioning from such established and emerging silversmiths as Robert Welch and David Mellor and by encouraging patronage.

*(ii) Base metals.* Pewterers were recognized as a specialist group from the early 14th century, and for over four centuries London was a focal point of the English pewter industry. Pewter was England's second largest export. In 1456–7 there were 193 craftsmen and 43 workshops in London. The largest workshop was Thomas Daunton's, which employed 7 journeymen and 11 apprentices. Large groups of pewterers were located in Billingsgate, Bishopsgate and Newgate. In 1474 the craft was incorporated into a company with a hall in Lime Street (1496; destr.; rebuilt 1959–60 in Oat Lane). It controlled prices and the quality of alloys and workmanship, and it restricted numbers and competition among its members. Subcontracting was prevalent, and since materials and equipment were costly many craftsmen did piece-work using hired or shared moulds and materials. Pewterwares were sold at market stalls in Eastcheap, at fairs and through chapmen and hawkers, but in the later 17th century there were attempts to restrict sales to shops. The industry expanded sevenfold between the early 16th century and the mid-17th, despite the shortage of tin, but by the late 18th century competition from other materials brought London's dominance of the trade to an end.

Potters (founders of copper alloy pots etc), braziers, coppersmiths and latteners were involved in the working of copper and brass in the Middle Ages. Little is known about their workshops and product distribution. Trade controls attempted to restrict noise levels and such dishonest practices as alloying with so much lead that pots melted when placed over a fire. The import of dinanderie was restricted. Brass items that did not require a fully equipped brazier's workshop were made by lorimers and girdlemakers and larger, heavier objects by braziers and founders. In 1532 the Worshipful Company of Founders, which included many brass founders, erected its first hall. At workshops in Rotherhithe and Isleworth brass sheet was hammered into latten and passed on to small groups of outworkers. Nevertheless, until the 18th century large-scale import of brass continued.

The economic disruption of the 1630s and the Civil War (1642–51) nearly stopped brassmaking in London. The plague and the Great Fire killed many craftsmen and merchandise was destroyed. Any subsequent brasswork was carried out east of the Tower of London, where imported brass was unloaded. From 1720 Birmingham became the principal English brassmaking centre, although there was an attempted revival of brass- and copperwares in London in the late 19th century, which was promoted by the Guild of Handicraft and the designs for mass production of Christopher Dresser and W. A. S. BENSON.

In 1298 sixteen 'masters of the trade of smiths' attempted to form a fraternity, and by 1376 six ironworking guilds existed for smiths, ironmongers, cutlers, armourers, spurriers and lorimers. Foundry workers included moulders, founders and probably patternmakers. Qualified provincial craftsmen came to London to buy their freedom and set up in business, but restrictive measures against outsiders were introduced in the mid-15th century. There were frequent initiatives to improve standards, such as the gradual introduction of makers' marks. In 1372 freemen wishing to sell their goods outside a shop were allowed to trade at certain points in Gracechurch Street and Cornhill. Women were taken into the membership of the guild when their husbands or fathers became masters, and they could be business partners and responsible for apprentices. In 1346 one smith's wife took over the forge at the Tower in her husband's absence.

Elizabeth I, alarmed at the industry's consumption of timber, prohibited its use for a time and forbade new ironworks within 35.2 km of London. The smiths and blacksmiths were incorporated into a company in 1578; a year later Elizabeth suppressed the Hanseatic Steelyard (see fig. 3 above) and restricted its iron-importing privileges. London was supplied by a number of regional ironmaking centres. Under Charles II foundries were established in Southwark and Wandsworth. The ironmongers spilled from Ironmonger Lane into Old Jewry and Thames Street. Such architects as Nicholas Hawksmoor and Christopher Wren employed such metalworkers as JEAN TIJOU to make wrought-iron railings, gates and balconies. In the 18th and 19th centuries London iron foundries supplied cast-iron architectural embellishments in standard patterns. Despite a general decline in the popularity of iron in the 20th century, particularly for domestic use, some foundries remained, together with a few forges that produced architectural features, sculpture and jewellery.

See also ENGLAND, §IX and MARKS, §4.

### BIBLIOGRAPHY
J. Starkie Gardner: *Ironwork*, 3 vols (London, 1922, rev. 4/1978)
R. Lister: *Decorative Cast Ironwork in Great Britain* (London, 1960)
T. F. Reddaway: 'Elizabethan London: Goldsmiths' Row in Cheapside (1558–1645)', *Guildhall Misc.*, ii/5 (1963), pp. 181–206
S. Bury: 'The Lengthening Shadow of Rundells', *Connoisseur*, clxi (1966), pp. 79–85, 152–8, 218–22
J. Hatcher and T. C. Barker: *A History of British Pewter* (London, 1974)
J. Bannister: 'Identity Parade: The Barnard Ledgers', *Proc. Soc. Silver Colrs*, ii (1974–6), 9/10 (1980)
R. Gentle and R. Feild: *English Domestic Brass* (London, 1975)
T. F. Reddaway and L. E. M. Walker: *The Early History of the Goldsmiths' Company, 1327–1509* (London, 1975)
A. Grimwade: *London Goldsmiths, 1697–1837: Their Marks and Lives* (London, 1976, rev. 3/1990)
J. Culme: *Nineteenth-century Silver* (London, 1977)
*Touching Gold and Silver: 500 Years of Hallmarks* (exh. cat. by S. Hare, London, Goldsmiths' Co., 1978)
E. Barr: *George Wickes, 1698–1761, Royal Goldsmith* (London, 1980)
C. Blair, ed.: *The History of Silver* (London, 1987)
P. Hornsby: *Collecting Antique Copper and Brass* (Ashbourne, 1989)
*Paul de Lamerie: The Work of England's Master Goldsmith* (exh. cat. by S. Hare, London, Goldsmiths' Co., 1990)
J. Blair and N. Ramsay, eds: *English Medieval Industries* (London, 1991)
J. P. Fallon: *Marks of London Goldsmiths and Silversmiths, 1836–1914* (London, 1992)

PHILIPPA GLANVILLE

3. CERAMICS. Tin-glazed earthenware was first made in London from *c*. 1571 by Jacob Janson (*d* 1593) at Aldgate and then by various 17th- and 18th-century potteries that were mostly based in Southwark. Fine salt-glazed stonewares were made by JOHN DWIGHT at Fulham in the late 17th century. The British porcelain industry began in London, when the two major factories of Bow (*see* BOW PORCELAIN FACTORY) and Chelsea (*see* CHELSEA PORCELAIN FACTORY) were both founded *c*. 1744.

THOMAS FRYE at Bow and NICHOLAS SPRIMONT at Chelsea were the dominant artistic figures. The production of brown and art stonewares by Doulton & Co (*see* DOULTON CERAMIC FACTORY) in Lambeth and the MARTIN (ii) brothers in their studio in Fulham, alongside others making useful stonewares in London, continued throughout the 19th century and into the 20th.

### BIBLIOGRAPHY
E. Adams and D. Redstone: *Bow Porcelain* (London, 1981, 2/1991)
E. Adams: *Chelsea Porcelain* (London, 1987)
F. Britton: *London Delftware* (London, 1987)

4. GLASS. London became an important glassmaking centre when the Venetian glassmaker Giacomo Verzelini (1522–1616) obtained a monopoly from Elizabeth I in 1574 to make soda glass. In 1674, after Sir Robert Mansell (1573–1656) had succeeded in organizing the glass industry on a national scale, GEORGE RAVENSCROFT was employed by the Worshipful Company of Glass Sellers of London to improve soda-lime glass. His experiments at the Savoy Glasshouse and at Henley-on-Thames, Oxon, led to the creation of English lead glass (*see* ENGLAND, fig. 69). A number of glasshouses were situated near the City of London by the late 17th century including the Whitefriars Glassworks (1680) situated between Fleet Street and the Thames, the Cockpit and Ratcliff glasshouses owned by John Bowles (1640–1709) in Southwark and the glasshouse in Vauxhall (*c*. 1663) that produced plate glass. These London factories largely continued throughout the 18th century, though Bristol and the Midlands were developing greater importance. About 1790 Apsley Pellatt I of the Falcon Glasshouse, Southwark, founded a firm, which continued on the site until 1878 and at New Cross until 1895. Apsley Pellatt II (1791–1863) some time after 1810 introduced the famous incrusted glass cameos for which the company is best known, alongside its staple production of cut glass, which differed little from contemporary work in Ireland and in other parts of England. From the mid-19th century James Powell & Son of Whitefriars rose to be one of the most important firms of London glassmakers, much influenced by the work of William Morris and his followers in the later 19th century and the early 20th. London afterwards declined as a centre of glassmaking, though the manufacture of bottles continued until the 1960s.

### BIBLIOGRAPHY
W. A. Thorpe: *English Glass* (London, 1955, rev. 3/1961)

ELIZABETH ADAMS

5. OBJECTS OF VERTU. From the late medieval period the production of jewellery and objects of vertu in precious metals was under the jurisdiction of the Goldsmiths' Company, and jewellery-making was recognized as an independent profession by the late 14th century. Efforts were made to restrict sales to goldsmiths' shops although jewellery was also sold by mercers, haberdashers, upholders and at such fairs as the St Bartholomew's fair, where the Company's wardens exacted penalties for such malpractices as the use of counterfeit stones and below-standard precious metals. Immigrant craftsmen, particularly, tended to be blamed for such offences. There was strong competition from abroad, and monarchs bought

from the many itinerant foreign merchants. Some employed foreign jewellers as well as commissioning work from their royal jewellers and buying on the open market via agents. Mass-produced items in such cheaper materials as pewter, copper, brass and tin-plated iron were made by craftsmen in the areas of Cheapside and Blackfriars. In the 16th century jewellers supplied pomanders, girdle prayer books, comfit boxes, toothpicks, earpicks, bodkins etc as well as, during and after her reign, cameo portraits of Elizabeth I for inclusion in jewels.

From 1680 to 1760 over 40 Huguenot jewellers worked in London, mainly in Soho, Covent Garden and St James's in the West End, and attracted an aristocratic clientele. Some worked as merchant jewellers. London firms imported jewellery and snuff-boxes and exported their work to the Continent and America. The luxury crafts flourished in 18th-century London, and such items as memorial jewellery, tweezer cases, toothpick cases, enamelled snuff-boxes, watches, chains and enamel dials for clocks and watches were extensively produced. Cheaper substitutes for precious metals, for example pinchbeck and cut steel, came into use for chatelaines, étuis and watch cases. Many gold boxes were made by the same craftsmen who made jewellery, watchcases and objects of vertu, and they usually combined the skills of a team of artists: enameller, gem setter, chaser, engraver, turner etc. George Michael Moser and James Morisset (*fl* 1767–1806) were two of the most distinguished of such specialist craftsmen in this period (Blair, 1972). Like snuff-boxes and watches, presentation swords were seen as masculine jewellery and were supplied to such retailers as James Shrapnell, Parker & Wakelin and the entrepreneurial James Cox (*fl* 1749–72; *d c.* 1791). The proprietor of a museum of automata opened at Charing Cross in February 1772, Cox described himself as a jeweller and a merchant and dealt in watches, nécessaires, scent bottles, boxes, jewellery etc. From 1753 to 1756 enamelled toys (miniaturized practical objects and novelties, originally of modest value) were produced at York House, Battersea, where the invention of transfer-printing made mass production possible (*see* ENGLAND, §X, 2). At the CHELSEA PORCELAIN FACTORY boxes, scent flasks, cane handles, toothpick cases and *bonbonnières* appear to have been made from 1758 to 1770.

In the 19th century the term jeweller was extended to such subdivisions as chainmakers, diamond-cutters, polishers and lapidaries; they were located in Soho and increasingly in Clerkenwell. In 1861 there were 764 goldsmiths and jewellers and 232 in related trades working there, supplying the city and West End retailers. E. Gray & Sons of Clerkenwell Green supplied machine-made gold and silver sheet, wire and stamped ornament for the jewellery trade, and there were steam-powered diamond-cutting and lapidary works. Major West End firms such as the Goldsmiths & Silversmiths Co. and Hunt & Roskell operated large manufactories in and around Clerkenwell alongside the clock and watchmaking trades. By the early 1880s there were at least 900 jewellery shops in London and a large number of wholesalers, some at Hatton Garden and Holborn Circus.

The craftsmen of the ARTS AND CRAFTS MOVEMENT, eschewing commercialism, worked by hand in small groups emulating medieval guilds, for example the Guild of Handicraft and the Artificers' Guild. In 1899 Liberty & Co. in Regent Street launched the 'Cymric' range of jewellery, largely mass-produced in Birmingham, but much of it designed in London. Between 1906 and 1917 the Russian firm of Fabergé maintained a shop in London. In the 20th century such old-established firms as Garrard & Co. Ltd, Asprey & Co. and Wartski Ltd provided luxury items, while the cheaper bulk manufacturers, for example H. Samuel, supplied the high street jewellers and stores. In the late 20th century a lively trade in second-hand jewellery and related objects flourished in salerooms and antique markets, and the West End shop Halcyon Days contributed to the revival of the production of enamelled and porcelain toys. At the same time arose the innovative artist–jeweller, art school-trained, working alone and nurtured by Goldsmiths' Hall, the Crafts Council and others.

### BIBLIOGRAPHY

R. Campbell: *The London Tradesman* (London, 1747)
J. Evans: *Jewellery* (London, 1953, rev. 1970)
P. J. Shears: 'Huguenot Connections with the Clockmaking Trade in England', *Proc. Huguenot Soc. London*, xx/2 (1959–60)
C. Le Corbeiller: *European and American Snuff Boxes, 1730–1830* (London, 1966)
K. Snowman: *Eighteenth Century Gold Boxes of Europe* (London, 1966, rev. 1990)
C. Le Corbeiller: 'James Cox: A Biographical Review', *Burl. Mag.*, cxii (1970), pp. 350–58
H. Ricketts: *Objects of Vertu* (London, 1971)
C. Blair: *Three Presentation Swords* (London, 1972)
S. Benjamin: *English Enamel Boxes* (London, 1978)
*Princely Magnificence: Court Jewels of the Renaissance, 1500–1630* (exh. cat. by A. Somers Cocks, London, V&A, 1980)
A. von Solodkoff: 'Fabergé's London Branch', *Connoisseur*, ccix (1982), pp. 105–8
L. Weiss: *Watchmaking in England, 1760–1820* (London, 1982)
S. Bury: *Jewellery, 1789–1910: The International Era* (Woodbridge, 1991)
R. Lightbown: *Medieval European Jewellery* (London, 1992)

6. TAPESTRY. Tapestry-weaving in London began in 1620 when Sir Francis Crane (*c.* 1579–1636) established a workshop at Mortlake on the River Thames. The chief designer at the factory was FRANCIS CLEYN. About 1670 William Benood (*fl* 1645–75), a weaver from Mortlake, established a workshop in Lambeth where Mortlake and Gobelins designs were reworked. Other competition to Mortlake was provided by the Great Wardrobe in Hatton Garden, which was responsible for the repair, maintenance and creation of the royal tapestries. In 1689 the Wardrobe moved to Great Queen Street in Soho; it closed in 1782. Other independent workshops, including that of Joshua Morris (*fl c.* 1720–28) in Frith Street, were established in Soho during the early 18th century, and the production of these workshops gave rise to the term 'Soho' tapestries. By the late 18th century, tapestry production in London had virtually ceased. In 1881 WILLIAM MORRIS founded the Merton Abbey Tapestry Workshop in Surrey, where tapestries were manufactured until the factory closed in 1940 (*see* ENGLAND, §XI, 1).

DIANA FOWLE

## V. Buildings and gardens.

1. St Paul's Cathedral. 2. Westminster Abbey. 3. Palace of Westminster. 4. Tower of London. 5. Whitehall Palace. 6. Vauxhall Gardens.

*See also* CHISWICK HOUSE; GREENWICH; HAMPTON COURT PALACE; KEW, ROYAL BOTANIC GARDENS OF; and NONSUCH PALACE.

1. St Paul's Cathedral. The cathedral was founded in AD 604, but the Anglo-Saxon building was replaced by the huge Romanesque and Gothic basilica known as Old St Paul's (*see* §(i) below). This was burnt in the Great Fire of London in 1666, and the present cathedral was built by Christopher Wren from 1675 (*see* §(ii) below).

(i) Old St Paul's. (ii) St Paul's.

*(i) Old St Paul's.* Christopher Wren's cathedral now occupies most of the site of Old St Paul's, though on a slightly different axis. Evidence for the appearance and development of the old cathedral is thus derived mainly from the mid-17th-century views by Wenzel Hollar published by William Dugdale (see fig. 24), some drawings by Wren and information recorded from lost documents, notably by Dugdale and John Stow. None of these sources is entirely satisfactory; in particular they reveal nothing about the form of the Saxon buildings. The first cathedral on this site, near the west gate of the Roman city, was founded in 604 by Bishop Mellitus (*d* 624) and dedicated to St Paul. The parish church of St Gregory, which adjoined the south-west corner of the medieval cathedral, was also pre-Conquest in origin.

*(a) Romanesque.* In 1087 a new Romanesque cathedral was begun, after a fire had seriously damaged its Saxon predecessor. The eastern parts were ready for use by 1148, when a new shrine containing the relics of the Saxon bishop St Erkenwald (*d* 693) was translated to a site behind the high altar. Such slow progress is hard to explain, even allowing for another fire in 1135 and for the exceptional size of the church. Of the Romanesque elevation only that of the nave is known, because it survived until the 17th century; but the west bays shown by Hollar were judged by Wren to be additions, and therefore may not be entirely representative. It consisted typically of three stages: tall arcade, large gallery without sub-arches and a clerestory (presumably with a passage).

Plain blank arcading decorated the aisle walls (as in Ely Cathedral, nave), with responds of three shafts each for groin or rib vaulting. The main arcade and gallery arches were of three moulded orders with rich abstract decoration springing from cushion capitals (as at Durham Cathedral, nave, *c.* 1100–28). The arcade consisted of 12-shafted compound piers without alternation, each 3.75 m thick. Hollar shows three Romanesque shafts rising to clerestory level to support a quadripartite rib vault, which is clearly 13th century but may represent the original intention. Winchester Cathedral (from 1079) has been cited as the closest parallel to the plan of the eastern parts, but much is supposition. There were probably four bays east of the crossing plus a semicircular ambulatory, with a crypt beneath. Illustrations of the 17th century show impressive transept arms with east and west aisles, like Winchester and great continental pilgrimage churches, but it is uncertain whether this represents the original scheme of 1087; in their final form, the eastern aisles look substantially of the late 13th century. The 12-bay nave extended *c.* 101.5 m, one of the longest in Europe.

*(b) Gothic.* At the west end, Hollar shows two low towers standing outside the aisles, but of uncertain date. The main tower was at the crossing, and a detached bell-tower stood to the south-east. The crossing tower was completed in 1221/2, originally capped by a timber spire, which, when rebuilt in 1314/15, made the steeple the tallest in Britain (estimated h. 147–161 m). The spire was destroyed by fire in 1561, and the prominent exterior buttresses testify to the structural problems created by the great height of the tower. The tower was evidently part of a wider scheme to modernize the liturgical choir by partly remaking the crossing arches and Romanesque east end in the Early Gothic style, completed by 1241 (when there was a new dedication of the church). Hollar's views, however, indicate that the tracery and vaults of these bays were rebuilt again in the early 14th century. Also in the Early Gothic period quadripartite rib vaults and new

24. London, Old St Paul's Cathedral, 12th–13th centuries, view from the south showing the partial recasing by Inigo Jones; engraving after Wenzel Hollar from Sir William Dugdale: *The History of St Paul's Cathedral in London* (London, 1658); reproduced in W. Benham: *Old St Paul's Cathedral* (London, 1902), pl. I (London, British Library); the parish church of St Gregory is at the extreme left

clerestory windows were apparently inserted in the nave and transept, perhaps not finished until *c.* 1255.

The most significant Gothic addition was the 'New Work', a vast extension of eight bays to the east end to provide the grandest setting for St Erkenwald's shrine. The general inspiration probably derived from the rebuilding of Westminster Abbey around St Edward's shrine (from 1245), but the closest prototype was Bishop Northwold's new extension at Ely Cathedral (completed 1252), with tierceron vaults running the whole length of the eastern arm and a terminal wall filled with glazing. The campaign at St Paul's opened probably in 1258 with the new crypt of St Faith, which ran under the whole extension, and at about the same time the transept east aisles received new windows, according to Stow. Parts of the south-east corner of the crypt survive below ground and prove the general accuracy of Hollar's recording of architectural detail. Dugdale's inference that most of the New Work was finished by *c.* 1280 is incorrect, as Lethaby noted: the main work on the aisles and arcades began only *c.* 1265–70. The triforium and clerestory levels were not begun until *c.* 1280. The high vaults were executed mainly or entirely in the early 14th century. The old bays were updated *c.* 1310–25, and the whole east end of 12 bays was officially entered only in 1327. The elevation followed the tripartite division of the Romanesque church, though with a larger clerestory. Although it is generally regarded as a conservative English design, a full awareness of French Rayonnant is revealed in the pinnacled array of flying buttresses, in the vertical linkage of the vault shafts and, especially, in the window tracery. St Paul's was the first major display in England of such recent French motifs as the impaled trefoil in the aisle windows, and the pointed trefoil and small curved triangle in the triforium and clerestory: these were all copied in English churches in the following decades, such as at Exeter Cathedral (*see* EXETER, §1(i)). The great traceried east window was the forerunner of the spectacular examples at Gloucester and York Minster, and the rose in its head may have incorporated the first prominent usage of the ogee arch in English tracery (*c.* 1290). The designer of the New Work is anonymous, but MICHAEL OF CANTERBURY and Robert of Beverley (*fl* 1253–85) have been associated with it. In 1332 WILLIAM RAMSEY is documented working on the new octagonal chapter house, set unusually between the nave and the south transept within a two-storey cloister garth (finished *c.* 1349; see fig. 24). Surviving stonework and Hollar's illustration show that in their detail these were key pioneer works for the Perpendicular style. Old St Paul's was the greatest cathedral of medieval Britain: its steeple was taller than Salisbury's, its length greater than Winchester's and its eastern arm as large as York Minster's.

UNPUBLISHED SOURCES

Oxford, All Souls Coll., Codrington Lib., Wren Drawings, ii, nos 4, 6, 7 [pre-fire design drawings for Old St Paul's Cathedral by C. Wren]

BIBLIOGRAPHY

J. Stow: *Survey of London* (London, 1598, 2/1603; ed. H. B. Wheatly, London, 1955)
W. Dugdale: *The History of St Paul's Cathedral in London* (London, 1658)
F. C. Penrose: 'On the Recent Discoveries of Portions of Old St Paul's Cathedral', *Archaeologia*, xlvii (1883), pp. 381–92
W. R. Lethaby: 'Old St Paul's', *Builder*, cxxxviii (Jan–June 1930), pp. 671–3, 862–4, 1091–3; cxxxix (July–Dec 1930), pp. 24–6, 193–5, 234–6, 393–5, 613–15, 791–3, 1005–7, 1088–90
R. H. C. Finch: 'Old St Paul's: A Reconstruction', *Builder*, cxlviii (April 1935), pp. 728–30, 772–3, 778–9
G. H. Cook: *Old St Paul's Cathedral* (London 1955)
J. H. Harvey: 'The Origin of the Perpendicular Style', *Studies in Building History*, ed. E. M. Jope (London, 1961), pp. 139–41
C. Wilson: *The Origins of the Perpendicular Style and its Development to c. 1360* (diss., U. London, 1980) [for the chapter house and cloister]
*British Archaeological Association Conference Transactions*, x: *Medieval Art and Architecture in the City of London: London, 1984*

R. K. MORRIS

*(c) Restoration.* Following three Stuart enquiries into the physical state of Old St Paul's, work finally began in 1633 with Inigo Jones (*see* JONES, INIGO, §1(i)) as surveyor to the works and John Webb (i) as his 'Clerk engrosser'. On the exterior, the choir was merely repaired, while the nave was encased with a new skin of antique ornament, as were the west transept walls and their north and south façades, with the east transept walls, like the choir, repaired. Interior work involved repair, not resurfacing, but included a new choir-screen. At the west end Jones added a portico (destr.), the height of which, at *c.* 17 m, rivalled the Pantheon as the largest surviving free-standing Corinthian portico since antiquity. It is recorded in engravings by Wenzel Hollar for William Dugdale (*see* §(a) and fig. 24 above). Jones's resurfacing testifies to the symbolic importance that the Stuart monarchy attached to Old St Paul's as the spiritual centre of the reformed faith; its restoration formed part of their plan to monumentalize London in rivalry with Rome through, in particular, their projected palace in Whitehall. Work came to a halt in September 1642 owing to the outbreak of the Civil War, and although Jones's portico survived the Great Fire of 1666, much of the old cathedral was destroyed. Demolition began in 1668 to make way for Christopher Wren's Baroque masterpiece (*see* §(ii)(a) below).

BIBLIOGRAPHY

J. Summerson: 'Inigo Jones: Covent Garden and the Restoration of St Paul's Cathedral', *The Unromantic Castle* (London, 1990), pp. 41–62
V. Hart: *Art and Magic in the Court of the Stuarts* (London, 1994)

*(ii) St Paul's.*

*(a) Architecture.* The centrepiece of the plan drawn up by Sir Christopher Wren to remodel London after the Great Fire was his new, domed St Paul's Cathedral. It was at first planned to incorporate Inigo Jones's surviving portico of the old cathedral into a new design, but this was abandoned and in November 1673 Charles II issued a long Commission for rebuilding St Paul's based on a design by Wren for a cathedral with a Greek-cross plan (*see* WREN, CHRISTOPHER). A subsequent giant model of this was made, which survives (London, St Paul's Cathedral; *see* WREN, CHRISTOPHER, fig. 2) and is an important record of this early design, said to be Wren's favourite. He was, however, forced to abandon it by the clergy, who favoured instead the traditional, medieval Latin-cross form, which gave a larger choir, of utility for separate worship. This led to a new scheme, the 'Warrant' design (Oxford, All Souls Coll.), so-called after the royal approval granted it on 14 May 1675. It is evident from the drawings that this design, complete with twin domes surmounted by a tall steeple, was only the first stage in the evolution

of the final building, for during the construction Wren made full use of the King's permission to 'make variations, rather ornamental than essential, as from time to time he should see proper'. The foundation-stone was laid at the south-east corner of the new cathedral on 25 June 1675. Portland stone was used for all the exterior work, the most durable in London's smoky conditions. While the Royal Warrant had clearly intended that the cathedral be built in parts, with the choir first, as early as March 1676 contracts were signed for the south-west and north-west 'Peer or Legg of the Dome', and in 1678 work began on the exterior of the south transept. By 1684 work was underway on the north side of the nave, while a contract to carve the great cornice inside the choir was issued the following year. Work began on the west end in August 1688. In a change from the Warrant plan, the nave was reduced from five bays to three, thereby balancing the three bays of the choir and reflecting the earlier, centrally planned model. By October 1694 the masonry of the choir was finished, but the internal fittings had yet to be installed; JEAN TIJOU supplied various wrought-iron work, including the sanctuary screen, Bernard Smith made the organ, while Grinling Gibbons carved the bishop's throne, choir-stalls and screens to the rear facing the aisles. Gibbons also carved the external panels below the great round-headed windows, and FRANCIS BIRD carved the relief depicting the *Conversion of St Paul* in the pediment surmounting the giant, two-tier portico on the west front (see fig. 25). The choir was opened on 2 December 1697, and the cathedral was itself finished in 1711 following the completion of the three skins forming the dome (*see* MASONRY, fig. 5), some 36 years after building work had begun. Through its Baroque ornamentation and geometric forms, Wren's St Paul's represented an attempt to find an architectural style suitable for Protestant worship, with the subsequent illustrations in Colen Campbell's *Vitruvius Britannicus* (1715–17) not surprisingly proclaiming the cathedral to be a rival to St Peter's in Rome.

*See also* ILLUSIONISM, colour pl. V.

BIBLIOGRAPHY
M. Whinney: *Wren*, World A. (London, 1971/*R* 1987)
P. Burman: *St Paul's Cathedral*, New Bell's Cathedral Guides (London, 1987)
K. Downes: *Sir Christopher Wren: The Design of St Paul's Cathedral* (London, 1988)
V. Hart: *St Paul's Cathedral: Sir Christopher Wren*, Architecture in Detail (in preparation)
VAUGHAN HART

(b) *Sculpture*. The Great Fire (1666) destroyed most of the monuments in Old St Paul's. Nicholas Stone the elder's innovative shrouded figure of *Dr John Donne* (1631–2; for illustration *see* STONE (ii), (1)) survives virtually unscathed; a few mutilated earlier fragments are in the crypt, along with a Baroque marble monument to *John Martin* (*d* 1680) and *Mary Martin*, his wife, by an unidentified sculptor. The cathedral itself was deliberately kept clear of monuments until almost the end of the 18th century, when the Royal Academy asked the dean for permission for memorials to be erected. This was refused because of the opposition of the Bishop of London, Richard Terrick, but a standing figure of *John Howard* (marble, 1796) by John Bacon (i) was allowed in 1796.

25. London, St Paul's Cathedral by Christopher Wren, west front, 1675–1711

In the same year Parliament voted money to pay for monuments to naval and military heroes killed in engagements against the French, provided that the sculpture was approved by the Royal Academy. In 1802 the Treasury, unhappy that large sums of money were under the control of artists and sculptors, appointed what was popularly known as the Committee of Taste under the chairmanship of Charles Long. This committee, which included Charles Townley, Thomas Hope and Sir George Beaumont, was responsible until about 1823 for selecting designs and sculptors, and for the position of monuments. Several designs by Francis Chantrey, John Bacon (i), JOHN CHARLES FELIX ROSSI and Richard Westmacott (ii) survive (London, PRO). All the sculpture approved was Neoclassical, with much male nudity; the most notorious for the brevity of its drapery was the monument to *Captain Burgess* (marble, 1802) by Thomas Banks. Among other large contemporary works are the marble monuments to *Earl Howe* (1803–11) and *Horatio, Viscount Nelson* by John Flaxman, Richard Westmacott's *Gen. Sir Ralph Abercromby* (1803–9; *see* WESTMACOTT, (2) and fig.) and *Sir John Moore* (1810–15) by John Bacon (ii). As available floor space was filled, smaller relief panels were placed high on the walls (e.g. Chantrey's to *Gen. Bernard Foord Bowes* (marble, *c.* 1812)).

The cathedral's largest monument, however, is that to *Arthur Wellesley, 1st Duke of Wellington* (marble and bronze, h. 12 m; see fig. 26). The government's open

26. London, St Paul's Cathedral, monument to *Arthur Wellesley, 1st Duke of Wellington*, by Alfred Stevens (ii), completed by John Tweed, marble and bronze, h. 12 m, 1857–1912

competition for a national Wellington Memorial resulted in the commission being given to ALFRED STEVENS in 1857. It was completed only in 1912, after Stevens's death, by the addition of his equestrian statue cast in bronze by John Tweed. During the 19th century St Paul's Cathedral became another national Valhalla, like Westminster Abbey, but with an emphasis on military figures, writers and artists. The sarcophagus (black marble, *c.* 1524–36) originally made for Thomas Wolsey by Benedetto da Rovezzano was given by George III to contain the body of Horatio, Viscount Nelson, in 1805. Some of the later

sculpture is as banal as that approved by the Committee of Taste. The cathedral's 'New Sculpture' provides a contrast to this earlier work and includes the monuments to *Frederic Leighton* (bronze and marble, 1900–02) by Thomas Brock and to *Randolph Caldecott* (bronze, 1885–7; crypt) by Alfred Gilbert. Also in the crypt are several works by Edward Hodges Baily, Rossi and Westmacott and the bronze bust of *Sir Stafford Cripps* (1953) by Jacob Epstein. As in Westminster Abbey, later 20th-century monuments are mainly inscribed wall tablets.

BIBLIOGRAPHY

M. D. Whinney: *Sculpture in Britain, 1530–1830*, Pelican Hist. A. (Harmondsworth, 1964, rev. 2/1988)

F. A. Whiting: 'The Committee of Taste', *Apollo*, lxxxii (1965), pp. 326–30

J. Physick: *The Wellington Monument* (London, 1970)

N. Pevsner and P. Metcalf, eds: *The Cathedrals of England*, ii (London, 1985)

P. Burman: *St Paul's Cathedral*, New Bell's Cathedral Guides (London, 1987)

JOHN PHYSICK

2. WESTMINSTER ABBEY. The abbey of St Peter, the royal palace (*see* §3 below) and the adjacent town of Westminster have always been distinct from the City of London, situated about 3 km downstream. The abbey may have been founded in the early 7th century. It certainly existed by the late 8th, although its architectural history is unknown before the rebuilding undertaken by King Edward the Confessor (*reg* 1042–66; *can* 1161), probably in the late 1040s, when he apparently also began the palace. The former Benedictine, now collegiate, church contains an immense quantity of monumental sculpture from the Middle Ages onwards, as well as important medieval paintings.

(i) Architecture. (ii) Sculpture. (iii) Painting.

*(i) Architecture.* The anonymous life of St Edward the Confessor, written 1065–7 (Cambridge, Corpus Christi Coll., MS. 161; Barlow, 1962), gives a long description of the parts of the abbey that existed when Edward died in January 1066. This, together with evidence from small-scale 19th- and early 20th-century excavations, permits a reconstruction of the completed church as a near-double of the church of Notre-Dame, JUMIÈGES ABBEY, in Normandy, although Westminster Abbey was longer than any French church of the period. Edward's upbringing in Normandy helps explain the urge to embark on a total rebuilding as well as the use of the Norman Romanesque style (*see* ROMANESQUE, §II), not previously employed in England. The appointment of Robert Champart, the builder and Abbot of Jumièges, as Bishop of London (*reg* 1044–51), and later as Archbishop of Canterbury (*reg* 1051–2), may account for the choice of architectural model. Edward's work included an apsed and vaulted chapter house, but the extant parts of the 11th-century monastic offices to the south are probably post-Conquest. The most notable survivals are the groin-vaulted dormitory undercroft, parts of the refectory, faced externally with *opus reticulatum* formed of red tiles, tufa and freestone, and several sculptured capitals dated by an inscription on one now lost to the reign of William II (*reg* 1087–1100). The ruined Late Romanesque infirmary chapel of St Katharine (*c.* 1160) is the only important 12th-century survival *in situ*.

Henry III's practical interest in the buildings of the abbey started in 1240 when he took over most of the funding of the Lady Chapel, which had been begun east of the 11th-century apse in 1220. This chapel, later replaced by Henry VII's Chapel, was self-contained and did not represent a first phase of the completely new building begun in 1246, yet it may well have sparked the idea of rebuilding in the King's mind. The aim of Henry III's unique assumption of sole responsibility for the construction of a great cathedral-like church is explicitly stated only by Matthew Paris (*Monachi Sancti Albani: Chronica majora*, ed. H. R. Luard, Rolls Ser., iv (1877), p. 427), who specifies Henry's devotion to St Edward the Confessor. Pious imitation of the saint's patronage may indeed have been the single greatest influence on the decision to rebuild, and it could even account for the requirement that the new church be of French rather than English format, for it seems to have been generally realized that the Confessor's church had been the first example of Norman Romanesque in England. Emulation of the French Crown must also have been a factor; otherwise it is almost impossible to account for the heavy indebtedness to the out-dated architecture of Reims Cathedral, the French coronation church. Ultimately the most important reason for the rebuilding must be Henry III's extreme and well-attested piety. Westminster is the most sumptuously finished church of the 13th century, and it was probably also the most costly. The total of *c.* £42,000 spent was around 1.2 times the average annual revenues of the English Crown.

The 13th-century church has a polygonal apse with an ambulatory and five chapels (the axial chapel was the Lady Chapel (begun 1220), replaced from 1503 by Henry VII's Chapel). The transepts have four bays with east and west aisles, and the nave has eleven bays including the west towers. Thanks to Henry III's establishment of a special financial department to administer the works, the church is among the earliest major medieval building projects for which detailed accounts have survived. A consequence of this survival is that the names of the three successive architects are known. Of these, Henry of Reyns (*fl* 1243–*c.* 1253) was the most important, since his designs were adhered to by his successors John of Gloucester (*fl c.* 1245–60) and Robert of Beverley, who made only comparatively minor changes. The precise significance of Henry's toponymic (the standard 13th-century spelling of Reims) is unclear, but arguments about his nationality are of little relevance since his English training and lack of familiarity with some aspects of French practice are revealed in details too inconspicuous to be the result of the patron's intervention, yet too significant to have been left to the executant masons, who were certainly nearly all English. No important 13th century French churches have radiating chapels so irregularly set out and so large relative to the main apse, main vessels with such thick walls (see fig. 27), high vaults with ridge ribs, or vault shafts that are thinner than those within the bays they define. Two other major instances of deviation from French Gothic practice, the richness of the Lincoln-inspired gallery openings and the smallness of the clerestory windows, both ensure that the clerestory is not, as it almost invariably is in French Gothic churches, the climax of the main vessels and hence

28. London, Westminster Abbey, interior of north transept and presbytery looking north-east from the muniment room, from 1246

a complement to the verticality of their articulation. The lowness of Westminster relative to the most ambitious 13th-century French churches (h. 31 m as compared to 42 m at Amiens Cathedral) can also be explained in terms of adhering to English usage, for the crossing carries the beginnings of a great lantern-tower, a feature long favoured in England but sacrificed by the French to their pursuit of ever-higher main vessels.

The large-scale French ideas embodied in Henry III's Westminster Abbey—the polygonal chevet, tall proportions, flying buttresses, cavernous north portals, rose windows of the transept façades—are complemented by touches that show a knowledge of the fine details of French Gothic buildings, often surprisingly recent works. In this category are practically all the tracery designs apart from the 35-year-old Reims-derived pattern used throughout the clerestory and aisles. The gallery windows, for instance, are curious convex-sided triangles derived from the lower chapel of the Sainte-Chapelle in Paris, begun 1239–43. The 'glass cage' Gothic ideal, perfected in the upper chapel of the Sainte-Chapelle, is realized completely in the chapter house (structurally complete by 1253), despite the fact that this building belongs to the purely English tradition of centralized chapter houses. This is probably the only part of Henry of Reyns's work where a fusion, as opposed to a mingling, of French and English concepts can be seen.

28. London, Westminster Abbey, the vault of the south aisle of Henry VII's Chapel, 1503–9

Many minor modifications were made to the design in the course of building, even by Henry of Reyns. The most conspicuous changes were John of Gloucester's introduction in the easternmost nave bays (the ritual choir) of eight-shaft piers and tierceron vaulting instead of the four-shaft piers and quadripartite vaults used further east. From 1376 to 1506 the remaining seven nave bays were built slowly, with a fluctuating level of royal support. The western parts of the nave are a notable but by no means extreme late medieval instance of the suppression of the normal desire for modernity in the interests of maintaining the unity of an out-dated design. However, the moulding profiles, a vehicle for so much expression in English Gothic, are of their time rather than pastiche. The second architect of the nave continuation, Henry Yevele (master mason at the abbey 1375–1400), was probably responsible for the design of the west front. Its 'welcoming porch' is very like the one that Yevele built around the same time at Westminster Hall, but the dominant feature of the front, which was abandoned incomplete in 1534, is the palisade-like miniature buttresses that clad the four main structural buttresses and rise sheer with no reduction of their mass.

The west gable (1735) and towers (1734–45) are by Nicholas Hawksmoor.

In 1503–9 the early 13th-century Lady Chapel was replaced by a new chapel intended to contain the shrine of the canonized Henry VI together with the tombs of his mother, Catherine of Valois (1401–37), Henry VII, his wife, Elizabeth of York (d 1503), and his mother, Margaret Beaufort (see §(ii)(b) below). The campaign for Henry VI's canonization languished, and his body remained buried in St George's Chapel, Windsor Castle. The internal elevations of the Westminster chapel were conceived as an enriched version of those of St George's, whereas the apse and radiating chapels consciously echo the setting of Westminster's existing royal saint. The pendant vault over the main vessel is the technical and aesthetic culmination of 150 years of Perpendicular vaulting design. It is the only large-scale example of fan vaulting constructed in the classic ashlar shell technique, and more than any other fan vault it gives the impression of consisting entirely of tracery (see fig. 28). The transverse arches intersecting the pendants and the openwork tracery at the sides are clear debts to the vault (c. 1479–83) of the Oxford Divinity School. The most original part of the chapel is the exterior of the aisles, where the forms of Gothic church architecture are displaced by borrowings from the repertory of palatial architecture: bay windows of complex and varied plan (as at Henry VII's Tower, Windsor Castle) and polygonal turrets (such as occur on numerous Tudor collegiate and palace gate-houses). The building accounts are lost, and opinion is divided as to whether the architect was Robert Vertue I (see VERTUE, (1)) or Robert Janyns (see JANYNS, (3)).

Apart from the chapter house, the main surviving late medieval monastic building is the cloister. The north part of the east walk was under construction in 1253 together with the west aisle of the south transept, into which it has to obtrude for want of space on the east–west axis. The tracery here (three trefoils over three lights) is very advanced even by mid-13th-century Parisian standards. Most of the north walk is by John of Gloucester and Robert of Beverley, and its tracery (three circles over three lights) is probably the earliest example of the design most favoured in England c. 1260–80. The south part of the east walk dates from c. 1300 and has what may be the oldest ogee reticulated tracery, which was the commonest kind of flowing tracery in early 14th-century England. Opposite the chapter house entrance is one of the most spectacular of Gothic tracery designs, a reticulated pattern formed of different types of Kentish tracery. The style is that of Michael of Canterbury. The south walk, started in 1344, is an almost exact enlargement of the earliest work of Perpendicular Gothic in London, the cloister (destr.) of Old St Paul's Cathedral, built from 1332 by WILLIAM RAMSEY. In the west walk, completed in 1366, the tracery is a squatter, four-light version of this, typical of late 14th-century south-eastern Perpendicular in its close adherence to Ramsey's manner. Of the abbot's house, transformed c. 1367–86 by Abbot Nicholas Litlyngton, the most notable parts extant are the Great Hall and adjoining Great Chamber (Jerusalem Chamber).

See also STONE, colour pl. XII.

BIBLIOGRAPHY

G. G. Scott and others: *Gleanings from Westminster Abbey* (Oxford, 1861, rev. 2/1863)

W. R. Lethaby: *Westminster Abbey and the King's Craftsmen* (London, 1906)

R. B. Rackham: 'The Nave of Westminster', *Proc. Brit. Acad.*, iv (1909–10), pp. 1–64

——: 'Building at Westminster Abbey from the Great Fire (1298) to the Great Plague (1348)', *Archaeol. J.*, lxvii (1910), pp. 259–78

*Westminster Abbey*, Royal Comm. Anc. & Hist. Mnmts & Constr. England (London, 1924)

W. R. Lethaby: *Westminster Abbey Re-examined* (London, 1925)

J. Perkins: *Westminster Abbey: Its Worship and Ornaments*, Alcuin Club Collections, 3 vols (Oxford, 1938–52)

G. Webb: 'The Decorative Character of Westminster Abbey', *J. Warb. & Court. Inst.*, xii (1949), pp. 15–20

J. H. Harvey: 'The Masons of Westminster Abbey', *Archaeol. J.*, cxiii (1951), pp. 82–101

F. Barlow, ed.: *The Life of King Edward who Rests at Westminster* (London, 1962, 2/1992), pp. 68–71

H. M. Colvin, ed.: *The History of the King's Works* (London, 1963–82), pp. 130–59; iii, pp. 206–22

R. Branner: 'Westminster Abbey and the French Court Style', *J. Soc. Archit. Hist.*, xxiii (1964), pp. 3–18

H. M. Colvin, ed.: *Building Accounts of King Henry III* (Oxford, 1971), pp. 190–247, 388–439

R. D. H. Gem: 'The Romanesque Rebuilding of Westminster Abbey (with a Reconstruction by W. T. Ball)', *Proceedings of the Battle Conference on Anglo-Norman Studies: Battle, 1980*, iii, pp. 33–60

W. C. Leedy: *Fan Vaulting: A Study of Form, Technology and Meaning* (London, 1980), pp. 214–17

C. Wilson and others: *Westminster Abbey*, New Bell's Cathedral Guides (London, 1986), pp. 6–89

CHRISTOPHER WILSON

*(ii) Sculpture.* The sculpture of Westminster Abbey can be broadly divided into the architectural sculpture mostly contemporary with the building, and tombs and monuments dating from the 13th century onwards.

(a) Before 1511. (b) 1511 and later

### (a) Before 1511.

*Architectural sculpture.* All the architectural sculpture in the building dates from before 1511. It includes not only work associated with the 13th-century campaign but also the sculpture of Henry VII's Chapel (see fig. 28). There are also important fragments from the Romanesque church, notably the figurative and foliate capitals assigned to the cloister and datable *c.* 1087–1100.

The lavish sculptural programme of Henry III's abbey accounts for a major element in the huge building cost and helps to differentiate the church from its French sources. The three main areas with large-scale figure sculpture are the north transept portals, the interior elevations of the north and south transepts, and the chapter house.

The north transept portals, probably completed in 1253, have lost all their original imagery with the exception of one vault boss. The arrangement of the figure sculpture markedly departed from that on French buildings. The deployment of the statuary over much of the wall surface represents a mingling of French and English arrangements. The archivolts and tympana were also differently treated from French models. The central portal appears to have contained a number of small traceried compartments below a central quatrefoil. There is good evidence that Purbeck marble was employed for carved capitals and moulded abaci, and for shafts and bases, an indication that the traditional English taste for polychrome masonry appeared. The central portal is likely to have shown the *Last Judgement.* There are documentary references to images of the Virgin and St Peter, and St Edward the Confessor would undoubtedly also have featured; there is doubtful evidence for images of the Apostles. (One entrance doorway in the east wall of the north transept still survives, albeit in very deteriorated condition.)

The other surviving large-scale figures of major importance are the groups below the transept rose windows. In the south transept triforium spandrels is a pair of *Angels* swinging censers (see fig. 29), flanking a central group usually identified as *St Edward the Confessor and the Pilgrim* (partly destr.; *see* ODERISIO, PIETRO DI). Although the flanking relief angels on the north transept are preserved, the central figures have been lost; they may have shown SS Edward and John, depicting an episode from the *Life of St Edward the Confessor.* The *Angels* in the south transept are of higher quality than those in the north, which have less complex draperies, more clumsily executed feet and hands and thinner, flatter hair. All these images retain considerable traces of medieval paint. Further relief sculpture decorated the north transept interior: small figures generally identified as *Henry III* and *St Edward the Confessor* in the jambs of the north transept lancet windows flank a set of 24 small bust-size angels carved in the soffits of the window arches in medallions or roundels decorated with stiff-leaf foliage.

29. London, Westminster Abbey, south transept triforium spandrel, censing *Angel*, mid-13th century

Much of the copious small-scale sculpture in the abbey is of extremely high quality, and some is possibly by the same sculptor responsible for the censing *Angels* of the south transept. He or his assistants may be responsible for a large amount of imagery, including bosses in the muniment room (originally a royal gallery in which the king could attend services), in the eastern chapels, the *Annunciation* boss in the west aisle of the north transept, and the corbels of St Faith's Chapel and elsewhere. The wall arcades throughout the east end of the building are decorated with sculpture of varying quality and carved from differing stones: subjects include *St Margaret*, *Christ the Judge* and what is probably *Adam Naming the Animals*. Some of the apse triforium heads have a marked tendency towards caricature. The foliage sculpture includes some of the earliest naturalistic foliage in English Gothic sculpture. In the nave bays heraldic shields appear, an early instance of a form of decoration that later became extremely popular (*see* HERALDRY, §IV).

In the chapter house there is a clear emphasis on imagery of the Virgin and the genealogy of Christ. The two well-preserved figures (h. *c.* 1.9 m) from the *Annunciation* group (1253) by William Yxwerth are the first significant pieces of English Gothic figure sculpture that can be securely attributed. *Gabriel* (*see* ENGLAND, fig. 25) has powerfully pleated draperies, carried over the left hand, and an angular pose originally complemented by wooden wings, for which a wide groove in the back and a slot in the shoulder remain. The verticality of the *Virgin's* dress is tempered by the handling of the cloak, with its long looping folds. In their angularity and drapery style, the Westminster figures sharply diverge from French models, such as those at Amiens Cathedral, and are more closely related to English sculptures of *c.* 1220–40, for example those on the west front of Wells Cathedral. Pairs of small censing *Angels* occupy sunk trefoils set against rosette diaper, flanking the *Annunciation* group's niches. The central space in the doorway, now filled by a double-sided image of *Christ* supplied during the restoration of 1866–72 by George Gilbert I Scott (ii), was originally an open cusped circle lighting the vestibule staircase. Fine stiff-leaf foliage carved in Purbeck marble (the original capital on the south side depicts a trio of small lions) ornaments the capitals supporting the superarch; a few other original sculpted capitals (including some of Purbeck marble from the eastern recess) survive. The voussoir features *Prophets* housed in deeply undercut foliage. The same treatment of the voussoir is exhibited on the vestibule side. Flanking the shafts on the south side only are two jambs containing more seated figures, including *Moses*, the *Virgin* and *Christ*, housed in foliage. The chapter house entrance from the cloisters is very decayed. A central image (destr.) of the *Virgin and Child* was flanked by angels, set against a foliate background. The outer voussoir depicts the *Tree of Jesse* and the decayed inner one appears to have been foliate.

Apart from William Yxwerth, very few sculptors are mentioned in the accounts. JOHN OF ST ALBANS has been tentatively identified as the master of the south transept *Angels* and head of a sculptural workshop at Westminster. The origins of Henry III's sculptors were undoubtedly varied, but some were definitely drawn from London.

Later architectural sculpture is concentrated in the chantry chapels of Henry V and Henry VII, and the high altar screen. The screen, completed in 1441, contains narrative scenes from the *Life of St Edward*. Henry V's Chapel, largely built in the 1440s (rest. from 1809 by James Wyatt), spans the ambulatory to the east of the shrine. Access to the first-floor chapel is through octagonal turrets adorned with large statuary; richly encrusted with smaller statues, narrative reliefs and heraldry, the chapel marks the high point of mid-century sculpture. The fine statuary of the reredos, including figures of *St George* and *St Denis*, shows clearly the influence of Flemish art (*see* GOTHIC, §III, 1(i)(d) and fig. 33).

Netherlandish sculptors were probably employed to provide statuary for the huge programme of imagery for Henry VII's Chapel, *c.* 1503–9. This is the central monument of early 16th-century sculpture. Of the original 107 internal statues, 95 survive, although the external sculpture was removed in the early 18th century. The quality is very variable. Statues are of two sizes: *c.* 1 m in the niches at triforium level and *c.* 1.5 m in the aisles and lateral chapels. There is some repetition in the iconography (e.g. *Martyrdom of St Sebastian*), which concentrates the most important figures in the east chapel and apse of the triforium. The latter has *Christ*, flanked by the *Annunciation*, SS *Peter* and *Paul*, the *Apostles*, and female saints; the former has SS *Thomas Becket*, *Nicholas*, *Edward the Confessor*, *Peter* and *Edmund*, and included a *Henry VI* (lost).

*Effigial sculpture.* Until the Reformation burials and monuments in Westminster Abbey were confined to sovereigns, their relatives, abbots and occasionally members of the royal household (e.g. Geoffrey Chaucer (*d* 1400)). The abbey church contains the most important medieval effigial sculptures in England. Among them must be numbered three early high-relief effigies of abbots in the south walk of the cloister, the gilt-bronze effigies of *Henry III* and *Eleanor of Castile* (from 1291, by WILLIAM TOREL; *see also* PLANTAGENET, (3)), *Edward III* (?1380s, possibly by John Orchard), and *Richard II* and *Anne of Bohemia* (*c.* 1394–8; *see* PLANTAGENET, (6)). The silver-gilt and silver effigy of *Henry V* (1415–31; rest. 1971) is now reduced to its wooden core, but the Limoges effigy of *William de Valence* (*d* 1296), of chased and enamelled copper over an oak core, survives. Marble or freestone effigies include those of three early abbots in the south walk of the cloister. *Aveline, Countess of Lancaster* (see fig. 30), *Edmund Crouchback, Earl of Lancaster* (*c.* 1300) and *Aymer de Valence* (*c.* 1325) are all housed within canopied tombs; Edmund's tomb has been compared to the work of Alexander of Abingdon and Michael of Canterbury. Later effigies include those of *Archbishop Simon Langham* (*d* 1376; alabaster), *Sir Bernard Brocas* (*d* 1395), *Abbot William of Colchester* (*d* 1420) and *Philippa, Duchess of York* (*d* 1431; all freestone). In addition, the alabaster effigy of *John of Eltham, Earl of Cornwall* (*c.* 1340), with its weepers set against a black ground, and the small alabaster figures of *William of Windsor* and *Blanche de la Tour* (both *c.* 1376), children of Edward III, should be mentioned. There is a white marble effigy of *Philippa of Hainault* (1367, by JEAN DE LIÈGE (i)); a marble angel, once thought to be from the tomb—which

R. P. Howgrave-Graham: 'Various Bosses, Capitals, and Corbels of the Thirteenth Century', *J. Brit. Archaeol. Assoc.*, viii (1943), pp. 1–4

A. Gardner: *English Medieval Sculpture* (Cambridge, 1951, rev. New York, 1973)

J. D. Tanner: 'Tombs of Royal Babies in Westminster Abbey', *J. Brit. Archaeol. Assoc.*, 3rd ser., xvi (1953), pp. 25–40

L. Stone: *Sculpture in Britain: The Middle Ages*, Pelican Hist. A. (Harmondsworth, 1955, rev. 2/1972)

D. Carpenter: 'Westminster Abbey: Some Characteristics of its Sculpture', *J. Brit. Archaeol. Assoc.*, 3rd ser., xxxv (1972), pp. 1–14

S. E. Rigold: *The Chapter House and the Pyx Chamber* (London, 1976)

M. E. Roberts: 'The Relic of the Holy Blood and the Iconography of the Thirteenth-century North Transept Portal of Westminster Abbey', *England in the Thirteenth century*, ed. W. M. Ormrod (Nottingham, 1985), pp. 129–42

*Age of Chivalry: Art in Plantagenet England, 1200–1400* (exh. cat., ed. J. Alexander and P. Binski; London, RA, 1987)

P. Williamson: 'The Westminster Abbey Chapter House Annunciation Group', *Burl. Mag.*, cxxx (1988), pp. 123–4

——: letter in *Burl. Mag.*, cxxx (1988), p. 928

P. Lindley: '"Una grande opera al mio re": Gilt-bronze Effigies in England from the Middle Ages to the Renaissance', *J. Brit. Archaeol. Assoc.*, cxliii (1990), pp. 112–30

——: 'Westminster and London as Sculptural Centres in the Thirteenth Century', *Skulptur des 12. und 13. Jahrhunderts*, ed. H. Beck and K. Hengevoss-Dürkop (Frankfurt am Main, 1994), pp. 231–50

For further bibliography *see* §(i) above.

□

**(b) 1511 and later.** During the 16th century, as all the eastern chapels around Edward the Confessor's shrine in Westminster Abbey had become redundant, they began quickly to be filled with monuments; the abbey now houses work by almost every major sculptor working in England, and it has become, in effect, the national museum of sculpture. It is the only building where a complete survey of sculpture can be seen from the 16th century to the beginning of the 20th. Oliver Cromwell seems to have been the first to express the idea that the building could be a national Valhalla. (The existence of a monument does not necessarily imply interment in the church.)

The monument by Pietro Torrigiani to *Margaret Beaufort* (from 1511) is still recognizably Gothic, although of gilt-bronze with much painted colour (now vestigial). The influence of the Renaissance became apparent only with a monument to *Henry VII and Elizabeth of York* (gilt-bronze and white and black marble, from 1512; *see* TORRIGIANI, PIETRO and fig. 1). Late 16th-century monuments by the Southwark school (*see* ENGLAND, §IV, 2) reflect the Elizabethan love of symbolism, and heraldry is used lavishly to establish the claims of the new bourgeois aristocracy. In the absence of contracts or designs attributions cannot be made to individual workshops. The largest Southwark school monument in the abbey is that to *Henry Carey, 1st Baron Hunsdon* (*d* 1596; alabaster and touch, h. *c.* 13 m), which is without figures. Early in the 17th century a chasteness appeared in the Southwark work with the monuments to *Elizabeth I* (black and white marble, 1605–7) by MAXIMILIAN COLT and *Mary, Queen of Scots* (marble, 1605–*c.* 1613) by Cornelius Cure and William Cure (ii). Nicholas Stone the elder was the first to introduce new and varied forms, and he demonstrated a clearer understanding of Renaissance detail (e.g. *Francis Holles, d* 1622; alabaster on a stone pedestal). He worked in alabaster at first but soon almost exclusively used black and white marble. Contemporary work includes that by

30. London, Westminster Abbey, presbytery, tomb of *Aveline, Countess of Lancaster*, early 1290s

was later adorned with six copper angels (1376, by John Orchard)—has recently been rediscovered. Important brasses include those of *Bishop John de Waltham of Salisbury* (*d* 1395), *Archbishop Robert Waldeby of York* (*d* 1397), *Eleanor Bohun, Duchess of Gloucester* (*d* 1399), *Sir John Harpenden* (*d* 1457), *Sir Thomas Vaughan* (*d* 1483), and *Abbot John Estney* (*d* 1498).

BIBLIOGRAPHY
J. T. Micklethwaite: 'Notes on the Imagery of Henry the Seventh's Chapel, Westminster', *Archaeologia*, xlvii (1883), pp. 361–80

E. S. Prior and A. Gardner: *Medieval Figure-sculpture in England* (Cambridge, 1912)

W. H. St J. Hope: 'The Funeral, Monument and Chantry Chapel of King Henry the Fifth', *Archaeologia*, lxv (1914), pp. 130–86

J. G. Noppen: 'Further Sculptures of the Westminster School', *Burl. Mag.*, liii (1928), pp. 74–8

C. J. P. Cave and L. E. Tanner: 'A Thirteenth-century Choir of Angels in the North Transept of Westminster Abbey and the Adjacent Figures of Two Kings', *Archaeologia*, lxxxiv (1935), pp. 63–7

Hubert Le Sueur (e.g. *George Villiers, 1st Duke of Buckingham, d* 1628; bronze and marble) and Francesco Fanelli (e.g. *Francis Cottington, 1st Baron Cottington,* marble, *c.* 1679). Baroque cartouches and monuments with architectural frames, by such mason–sculptors as William Stanton, were placed in the west portion of the building during the second half of the 17th century, together with work by Grinling Gibbons, Artus Quellinus (iii), John Bushnell and Francis Bird (*see* BIRD, FRANCIS and fig.), most with reclining figures and large, architectural backgrounds. In the 18th century architects and sculptors began to collaborate: James Gibbs with Francis Bird, Giovanni Battista Guelfi and Michael Rysbrack (*see* RYSBRACK, (2)); William Kent with Rysbrack and Peter Scheemakers (ii) (*see* SCHEEMAKERS, (2) and fig.; *see also* ENGLAND, §IV, 3). Rysbrack, Scheemakers and Laurent Delvaux also designed monuments themselves. The mid-18th century is lavishly represented by the brilliant, Rococo dramatic sculptures of Louis-François Roubiliac (*see* ROUBILIAC, LOUIS-FRANÇOIS and figs 1 and 2). Henry Cheere (see fig. 31), who produced some large works, is best represented by his smaller, delicate Rococo monuments, which complement the abbey's architecture without damaging its fabric, as had happened throughout the century.

The visual damage caused by the towering Baroque monument to *John Holles, 1st Duke of Newcastle* (marble, 1721) by JAMES GIBBS in the north transept, at a height of *c.* 13 m rivalling the Hunsdon Monument, became only too apparent when overpowering official Neo-classical memorials, funded by Parliament, were installed towards the end of the 18th century. These were the work of RAs such as Joseph Nollekens, John Bacon (i), John Flaxman and Francis Chantrey. Fortunately, it was decided to place most of the monuments to those who fell in the wars with France in St Paul's Cathedral (*see* §1(ii)(b) above). With the 19th century came the realization that there was little space left for memorials, and a greater control was exercised by the dean and chapter. Consideration was given to the idea of using an additional building to house memorials. Subsequent memorials have been restricted to standing figures, busts, small works (e.g. *Henry Fawcett* (bronze, 1888) by Alfred Gilbert) and even smaller tablets. Except for the large marble and bronze monuments to *Robert Cecil, 3rd Marquess of Salisbury* (1909) by William Goscombe John and to *Sir Henry Campbell-Bannerman* (*d* 1908) by Paul Montford (1868–1938), during most of the 20th century there has been little sculptural work. Nevertheless, some of the tablets, for example *Sir Frederick Bridge* (*d* 1924; stone) by Eric Gill and *Sir Winston Churchill* (*d* 1965; green marble) by Reynolds Stone (1909–79), have fine lettering. Breaking with tradition, the slate tablet in the cloisters to *Edmund Halley* (1986) by Richard Kindersley is in the form of a stylized comet.

### BIBLIOGRAPHY

A. Higgins: 'On the Work of the Florentine Sculptors in England in the Early Part of the Sixteenth Century', *Archaeol. J.*, li (1894), pp. 129–220

R. F. Scott: 'On the Contracts for the Tomb of Lady Margaret Beaufort', *Archaeologia*, lxvi (1915), pp. 365–76

M. D. Whinney: *Sculpture in Britain, 1530–1830*, Pelican Hist. A. (Harmondsworth, 1964, rev. 2/1988)

31. London, Westminster Abbey, nave monument to *Admiral Sir Thomas Hardy* by Henry Cheere, marble, *c.* 1738

A. P. Darr: 'The Sculptures of Torrigiano: The Westminster Abbey Tombs', *Connoisseur*, cc (1979), pp. 177–84

N. Pevsner and P. Metcalf: *The Cathedrals of England*, ii (London, 1985)

A. White: 'Westminster Abbey in the Seventeenth Century: A Powerhouse of Ideas', *Ch. Mnmt.*, iv (1989), pp. 16–53

J. Whitlock Blundell and J. Physick: *Westminster Abbey: The Monuments* (London, 1989) [phot. of details of the sculp.]

JOHN PHYSICK

*(iii) Painting.* Westminster Abbey possesses some of the most important 13th- and 14th-century panel and wall paintings in north Europe. The earliest work is the finest, namely the Westminster Retable, a damaged rectangular panel painting executed on oak measuring 3.34×0.96 m.

Nothing certain is known about the date or function of this unique survival. Its construction is that of an altarpiece, probably a dossal or retable rather than a frontal. It combines standing figures under tabernacles with small narrative scenes set in eight-pointed medallions. The choice of themes is exceptional. Under a central, portal-like, gabled tabernacle stands Christ holding a globe (*Salvator mundi*), with the *Virgin* and *St John* holding palms; three *Miracles of Christ* remain in the medallions (*see* GOTHIC, fig. 71); and *St Peter* stands as witness in the left tabernacle. Evidently St Peter, the patron saint of the abbey, has opened the gates of Paradise to show Christ as saviour; Christ's works in the world are the subject of the medallions. A representation of *St Paul* is lost.

The decoration of the retable's frame is complex, combining exquisite micro-architectural design with polychromy, decorative glass and painted enamel ornamentation reminiscent of the interior decoration of the Sainte-Chapelle in Paris (*see* GOTHIC, fig. 67). This combination of glassware and paint anticipates the *verre églomisé* techniques of 14th-century Italian panel painting. The style of the remaining paintings has taxed the understanding of art historians for over a century. They are executed in a delicate, lustrous oil technique surpassing in skill comparable surviving panels in Italy or Norway. The principal stylistic analogies are court works such as the Douce Apocalypse (*c.* 1270; Oxford, Bodleian Lib., MS. Douce 180; *see* GOTHIC, fig. 73) and the wall paintings (destr. 1834; copies (1819) London, Soc. Antiqua.) in the Painted Chamber in the Palace of Westminster executed in the second half of the 13th century (*see* §3(i)(b) below). Comparisons may also be made with later 13th-century English and French miniature painting, such as that in the Alphonso Psalter (*c.* 1284; London, BL, Add. MS. 24686; *see* HERALDRY, fig. 20) and works from the circle of Master Honoré in Paris of the 1290s. Although undated, the retable provides key evidence for the links between French and English painting in the period *c.* 1270–90.

Three wall paintings depicting *St Faith* (chapel of St Faith), *St Thomas* and *St Christopher* (both south transept), and paintings on the sedilia in the sanctuary form a group dating probably to *c.* 1300–10. The large wall paintings are executed in oil on a thin, lead white ground. The oak sedilia (panels h. 2–4 m, 1307–8) are richly coloured and adorned in the manner of the painted tomb of *Edmund Crouchback, Earl of Lancaster* (*c.* 1300; *see* §(ii)(a) above), which is also in the sanctuary. The fragmentary images of kings, saints and the *Annunciation* are closely related to the work of the Madonna Master in the Psalter of Robert de Lisle (*c.* 1310 and before 1339; London, BL, Arundel MS. 83, pt II). The painted oak Coronation Chair (1299–1301) of Edward I by Walter of Durham (*fl c.* 1265–1300) is decorated in the same tradition (*see* THRONE, §II, 1(ii)).

The chapter house has late 14th-century wall paintings. These include a fragmentary *Apocalypse* executed in a style close to that of Master Bertram, but almost certainly based on an English recension. Other paintings depict *Christ the Judge* and winged cherubim devoted to the theme of penance, reflecting the monastic function of the chapter house; they were thus monastic commissions, executed in an Italianate style similar to court wall paintings (1350–63; mostly destr. 1800 and 1834; fragments London, BM)

formerly in St Stephen's Chapel (partly destr.), Palace of Westminster. Roughly contemporary with the chapter house paintings is a rectangular portrait of *Richard II* (1394–5; see fig. 32; *see also* PLANTAGENET, (6)), executed on oak with a lavish gesso ground (now mostly erased); the King is shown seated in state and represented in a style controversially linked to Bohemian painting of the period.

BIBLIOGRAPHY

W. R. Lethaby: 'Medieval Paintings at Westminster', *Proc. Brit. Acad.*, xiii (1927), pp. 123–51

F. Wormald: 'Paintings in Westminster Abbey and Contemporary Paintings', *Proc. Brit. Acad.*, xxxv (1949), pp. 161–76

E. W. Tristram: *English Medieval Wall Painting: The Thirteenth Century*, 2 vols (Oxford, 1950), i, pp. 127–48

——: *English Wall Painting of the Fourteenth Century* (London, 1955)

B. Turner: 'The Patronage of John of Northampton', *J. Brit. Archaeol. Assoc.*, cxxxviii (1985), pp. 89–100

32. London, Westminster Abbey, *Richard II*, panel, 2.14×1.10 m, 1394–5

P. Binski: 'What Was the Westminster Retable?', *J. Brit. Archaeol. Assoc.*, cxl (1987), pp. 152–74

*Making and Meaning: The Wilton Diptych* (exh. cat. by D. Gordon and others, London, N.G., 1993)

PAUL BINSKI

3. PALACE OF WESTMINSTER. Situated by the River Thames, directly east of Westminster Abbey (*see* §2 above), the Palace of Westminster was first built in the mid-11th century. Increasingly established as the centre of government administration and, later, as the Houses of Parliament, the medieval palace (see fig. 33) burnt down on 16 October 1834, to be replaced by the present building. Westminster Hall, the lower chapel (St Mary) of St Stephen's, the cloisters and Jewel Tower are the only buildings to have survived the fire.

(i) *c.* 1059–1547. (ii) 1548–1834. (iii) After 1834.

### (i) c. 1059–1547.

(a) Architecture. (b) Painting.

*(a) Architecture.* Edward the Confessor died in 1066 in the palace that he had probably established about the time of his refoundation of Westminster Abbey (*see* §2 above). William I carried out stone building works there but their

scope is unknown. The hall of William II (*reg* 1087–1100), Westminster Hall, was, at *c.* 73 m long, the largest in western Europe (33f); its completion in 1099 assured the architectural and ceremonial pre-eminence of Westminster among the English kings' residences. The hall was remodelled in the 14th century but the design of its long side walls is recoverable: plain walling to a height of about 6.5 m (presumably to facilitate the use of decorative hangings), with an upper windowed zone that incorporated wall passages screened by arches much as in the clerestory of a great Anglo-Norman Romanesque church. Ten capitals carved with secular subjects (London, Mus. London, and Pal. Westminster, Jewel Tower) probably come from the north front, which contained the main entrance, as it still does. It faced a great court (now New Palace Yard; 33a), which could be approached from the City of London by river or via King Street (now Whitehall). From the first, great feasts and the dispensation of royal justice would have taken place in the hall, but by the early 12th century the regular needs of the royal household were met by the Lesser, New or White Hall, a room of more conventional dimensions standing a little to the south (33b). Thus there existed from an early date the distinction, formalized only

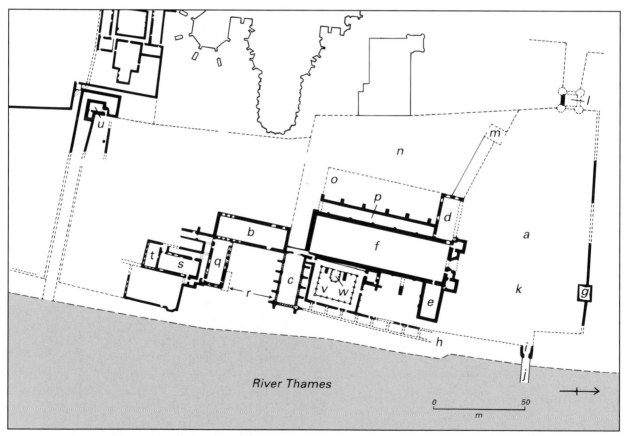

33. London, Palace of Westminster, plan of the medieval buildings: (a) great court; (b) Lesser, New or White Hall; (c) St Stephen's Chapel (subsequently House of Commons); (d) Exchequer; (e) Receipt of the Exchequer; (f) great hall; (g) clock-tower; (h) Star Chamber; (i) water-gate; (j) King's Bridge; (k) great conduit; (l) main gate-house; (m) inner gate; (n) base-court; (o) kitchen; (p) chamber built for King's household knights; (q) Painted Chamber; (r) approx. site of gallery; (s) Queen's Chamber (subsequently House of Lords); (t) Queen's Chapel; (u) Jewel Tower; (v) St Stephen's Cloister; (w) chapter house

in the 14th century, between the public Great Palace, and the Privy Palace to the south, where the royal household lived and worked. The principal chapel, St Stephen's, stood at the boundary of these two spheres (33c).

*The Great Palace.* During Henry II's reign the Exchequer was detached from the itinerant household and established at Westminster. In the late 12th century the Receipt of the Exchequer, where the accounts were drawn up, occupied a stone building (33d) east of the main north entrance to the great hall, but by 1243 it had been transferred to a spacious new office on the west side of the hall, which had tall, transomed, plate-traceried windows (33df). During the early 13th century the Court of Common Pleas was more or less permanently established in the hall, but its accommodation was always utilitarian, wooden and removable to make way for ceremonies. From 1367 the Court's proceedings were regulated by a clock in a plainly treated tower facing the hall across the great court (33g). A new royal council chamber, known as the Star Chamber because of its ceiling decoration, was built on the east side of the court in 1349 (33h). After being rebuilt *c.* 1456–61, it was remodelled and extended northwards in 1517 to produce a fine timber-framed range of offices, which contained some elegant Late Gothic ceilings. This range figures prominently in the oldest extant view of the palace (see fig. 34). The water-gate, which stood at the north end of this range, was rebuilt in the late 15th century (33i). In 1502 its landing-stage (the King's Bridge; 33j) bore large polychrome wooden figures of *Guy of Warwick*, *Colbrand the Dane* and Henry VII's heraldic beasts. In the centre of the court stood the great conduit (33k). Emergency excavation of the site (1972–4) yielded fragments of late 12th-century Purbeck marble basins of complex polylobed design, decorated with stiff-leaf foliage. The canopy over the conduit shown in Wenzel Hollar's engraving of 1647 had a Tudor onion dome but was probably still basically the one made in 1443.

The four-turreted main gate-house linking the great court and King Street was begun in 1397, abandoned in 1399 and continued in 1411 (33l). On the south side of the court an inner gate (1244–5; 33m) led to a long narrow court (in 1502 called the base-court; 33n) surrounded by timber-framed offices: the offices on the north pertained to the adjoining Exchequer; those on the north part of the east side included the Office of the Clerk of the King's Works (*see* CLERK OF WORKS) with its various drawing offices and store-houses for materials; and to the south of this the remainder mostly pertained to the kitchen. Behind the kitchen (33o), against the west side of Westminster Hall, was the two-storey chamber built in 1244 for the King's household knights (33p). The offices on the north side of the base-court were replaced in 1536–42 by the Court of Augmentations, a three-storey range in diapered brick. The almonry stood, appropriately, by the entrance to the Privy Palace at the south end of the court.

Richard II remodelled Westminster Hall from 1394. By common consent, the roof of the hall ranks as the supreme achievement of the distinctively English late medieval genre of virtuoso timber architecture (*see* TIMBER STRUCTURE, fig. 6). The designer, Hugh Herland, inherited a century-old tradition of ingeniously designed roofs covering single spans; however, the scale of the work and the concept of achieving lateral and longitudinal rigidity through the interlocking of hammerbeams, hammerposts, arched braces and longitudinally braced collar purlins are without known precedent. The ornamentation is equally impressive: great shield-bearing angels swooping inwards from puffs of cloud impaled by the hammerbeams, two spired louvres treated internally as miniature versions of the octagon of Ely Cathedral, and harpstring-like Perpendicular screenwork over the arched braces and hammerbeams (compare Windsor Castle great hall roof (*c.* 1362–5; destr.)). Below the armorial corbels for the roof principals, Henry Yevele's stonework is plain, as in the 11th-century hall. On the south wall (restored by Charles Barry) are six canopied niches housing *Kings* (1385) carved by Thomas Canon and painted by Nicholas Tryer for the old hall.

Yevele's north front is unique, for its twin towers, huge window, image screen and 'welcoming porch' are all forms proper to major church architecture. The provision for 31

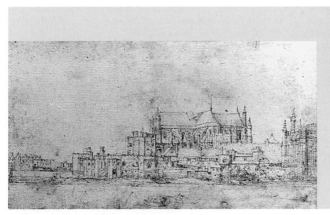 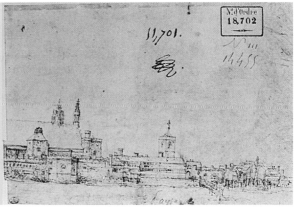

34. London, Palace of Westminster, possibly parts of a single drawing, ink on paper, ?Netherlandish, ?first half of the 16th century: (left) Westminster Abbey with the south wall and half the east end of St Stephen's Chapel, 100×175 mm (London, Victoria and Albert Museum); (right) the roof of Westminster Hall and the clock-tower, 115×163 mm (Paris, Musée du Louvre)

enriched *Kings* and *Queens* (destr.) is likewise unprecedented in English secular art, and although their identities are lost, the intention to emulate the longer series (destr.) of French kings installed by Philip IV of France inside the analogous hall (destr.) in the Palais de la Cité in Paris seems clear.

*Privy Palace.* The Lesser Hall, the most northerly of the earlier Privy Palace buildings, retained some chevron-decorated ground-floor windows (*c.* 1125–50) until its destruction in the 19th century. Some of these windows in the east wall were blocked by the Painted Chamber (34q; *see* §(b) below). By the 1230s this grandest of bedsitters housed an elaborate state bed connected visually by a round window to an oratory projecting from the north-east corner. In the 1320s the oratory was linked to the upper chapel of St Stephen's by an early example of a raised gallery (33r), giving not only access to but views of nearby gardens. The Queen's Chamber (1237–8; 33s), slightly shorter than the king's, but with similar plate-tracery windows, was designed by the Cistercian lay brother John of Waverley (*fl* 1226–51). Structurally integral with its south wall was the contemporary lanceted Queen's Chapel (33t).

In the mid-14th century, when the king's and queen's chambers became the usual meeting-places of parliament, the south extremity of the precinct began to develop as a more genuinely private residence for the royal family. The one building to survive from this sector is the Jewel Tower (1365–6; 33u), a depository for a variety of valuables, designed by Henry Yevele and built on land purloined from Westminster Abbey, presumably to avoid impinging on the adjacent king's garden. The topography of the southern Privy Palace is vague because it was gutted by fire in 1512 and mostly demolished from 1532 to provide materials for building Whitehall Palace (*see* §5 below). The fire of 1512 probably also destroyed the adjoining palace of the Princes of Wales, which stood against the boundary with the abbey, roughly opposite the Queen's Chamber. After 1512 Westminster Palace ceased to be a royal residence.

*St Stephen's Chapel.* The date of the first chapel, redecorated in the 1230s and 1250s by Henry III, is unknown, but it stood on the same site as the great chapel begun in 1292. Why Edward I initiated this work then is unclear, but it is certain that the intention was to equal the Sainte-Chapelle in the Palais de la Cité in Paris. Work was abandoned because of the Scottish wars in 1297, and it was structurally completed only in 1348 after six further campaigns. The two-storey format and the overall dimensions are all that St Stephen's owed to the Sainte-Chapelle. In the upper chapel (destr.) the architect of St Stephen's, Michael of Canterbury, set himself the strange task of transforming by means of rich decoration a comparatively humble building type, namely the wooden roofed chapel with high east window (e.g. Merton College Chapel Choir (*c.* 1289–97), Oxford, or St Etheldreda's (*c.* 1284), London). The considerable areas of plain wall available between the windows on account of the lack of vault responds were filled with miniature canopy work based on French Rayonnant portal architecture. These canopy-encrusted walls, along with many other aspects of St Stephen's, influenced

a whole generation of English architects. For example, the lower chapel has the earliest English example of lierne vaulting and the earliest window tracery incorporating the ogee, and the free-standing mullions that screen the exterior of the lower chapel windows were a major source for the south transept (*c.* 1331–6) of Gloucester Abbey (now Cathedral), the earliest example of Perpendicular architecture. Although such individual innovations were enormously influential in England, comparatively few architects grasped the radical philosophy underlying the starkly different treatments of the two interiors and the exterior: the abandonment of the self-consistent, systematic character of Gothic in favour of individualistic, proto-picturesque diversity.

From 1326 the formal coherence of the chapel was compromised by the addition of a clerestory and vault, and in the mid-1340s a west porch was added by William Ramsey. The porch, which was of a sumptuousness clearly intended to complement the by then out-dated style of the chapel proper, was a frequently raided treasury of ornamental Perpendicular architecture for over a century. The founding of a college in 1348 initiated a very protracted process of providing collegiate buildings between Westminster Hall and the Thames. The most notable of these buildings was also the latest, the two-storey cloister (*c.* 1526–9), possibly designed by William Vertue. The fan-vaulted lower cloister and chapter house are among the most accomplished products of almost two centuries of Perpendicular architecture in London (33v–w).

BIBLIOGRAPHY

J. Topham and H. C. Engelfield: *Some Account of the Collegiate of St Stephen, Westminster* (London, 1795–1811)

J. T. Smith: *Antiquities of Westminster* (London, 1807/*R* 1809)

'Notes and Remarks by the Late Mr William Capon, to Accompany his Plan of the Ancient Palace of Westminster', *Vetusta Monumenta*, v (London, 1835), pl. xlvii, pp. 1–7

E. W. Brayley and J. Britton: *The History of the Ancient Palace and Late Houses of Parliament at Westminster* (London, 1836)

F. Mackenzie: *The Architectural Antiquities of the Collegiate Chapel of St Stephen, Westminster* (London, 1844)

C. L. Kingsford: 'Our Lady of the Pew: The King's Oratory or Closet in the Palace of Westminster', *Archaeologia*, lxviii (1916), pp. 1–20

M. Hastings: *St Stephen's Chapel and its Place in the Development of Perpendicular Style in England* (Cambridge, 1955)

H. M. Colvin: 'Four 14th-century Building Contracts', *Archit. Hist.*, ii (1959), pp. 19–25

J. H. Harvey: 'The Origin of the Perpendicular Style', *Studies in Building History: Essays in Recognition of the Work of B. H. St J. O'Neill*, ed. E. M. Jope (London, 1961), pp. 134–65

H. M. Colvin, ed.: *The History of the King's Works* (London, 1963–82), i–vi

——: 'Views of the Old Palace of Westminster', *Archit. Hist.*, ix (1966), pp. 23–184

W. C. Leedy: *Fan Vaulting: A Study of Form, Technology and Meaning* (London, 1980), pp. 217–8

L. T. Courtenay: 'The Westminster Hall Roof and its 14th-century Sources', *J. Soc. Archit. Historians*, xliii (1984), pp. 295–309

A. Saunders: 'Westminster Hall: A 16th-century Drawing?' *London J.*, xii (1986), pp. 29–35

V. Horsman and B. Davison: 'The New Palace Yard and its Fountains: Excavations in the Palace of Westminster, 1972–4', *Antiqua. J.*, lxix (1989), pp. 279–97

P. Binski: *Westminster Abbey and the Plantagenets: Kingship and the Representation of Power, 1200–1400* (New Haven, CT, and London, 1995)

C. Wilson: 'The Designer of Henry VII's Chapel, Westminster Abbey', *The Reign of Henry VII*, ed. B. Thompson, Harlaxton Medieval Studies, 5 (Stamford, 1995), pp. 133–56

CHRISTOPHER  WILSON

*(b) Painting.* The medieval Palace of Westminster was decorated with two wall painting schemes of outstanding importance, known either through copies or fragmentary survivals now *ex situ*. The first of these was in the aptly named Painted Chamber, a first-floor apartment of substantial size (24.5×9.7×7.9 m) that acted in the 13th century as the king's bedroom. Fragments of its wall paintings were uncovered in the early 19th century and copied in watercolour in 1819 by Charles Alfred Stothard and Edward Crocker (*c.* 1757–1836); they were completely destroyed in the fire of 1834.

The Painted Chamber copies (London, Soc. Antiqua.) provide rare evidence of the sort of wall paintings that decorated aristocratic residences in the Middle Ages. So far as the dates of the originals are concerned, the watercolours corroborate the remarkably full documentary evidence, but there is a measure of uncertainty owing to reports at the time of their discovery that they had been repainted. What was copied in 1819 dated mainly from the second half of the 13th century and seems to have been the subject of campaigns of wall painting recorded in the 1260s and 1290s under Henry III and Edward I. Walter of Durham (*fl c.* 1265–1300) supervised. Scenes depicted included a large *Coronation of St Edward the Confessor* (see fig. 35), images of *St Edward* and *Virtues and Vices* (both h. 370 mm) on the window splays, and an exceptionally full and unorthodox series of Old Testament narratives in registers around the room. The numerous inscriptions were in French. The *Coronation* was behind the king's bed; a payment in 1267 for paintings around the bed probably refers to it, among other works. It demonstrates the popularity at court of St Edward as a subject around the time of the saint's translation to his new shrine in Westminster Abbey in 1269. The *Virtues* and *Vices* may also have belonged to this phase of work since the Virtues were shown being crowned, presumably representing the virtuous kingship of St Edward inaugurated at his coronation. As copied, the style of the *Coronation* resembles that of the Westminster Retable (London, Westminster Abbey; *see* §2(iii) above) and of the Douce Apocalypse (Oxford, Bodleian Lib., MS. Douce 180), made *c.* 1270 for Edward I or Eleanor of Castile, indicating the importance of court patronage in formulating the French-influenced painting styles found in the period 1260–80.

The Old Testament pictures must have post-dated the *Coronation*, since they incorporated architectural motifs and compositions of a late 13th-century character, indicating a date in the 1290s. If this is so, then they reveal the accretion of imagery in the room that converted it from a chamber with wall paintings to a formal, Painted Chamber; it is significant that the term 'painted chamber' was applied to the room only under Edward II (*reg* 1307–27), and that 'histories' are first mentioned there only in 1307–8. A description of the room by two Irish friars in 1323 notes that it contained 'all the warlike stories of the whole Bible', which indicates how striking the biblical battle scenes in the room were, especially the unprecedented number of illustrations from 1 Maccabees in the topmost registers. The pictures were not exclusively military, however, since the downfall of bad kings was a major theme of other illustrations drawn from 2 Kings and Judges, echoing the preoccupation of much earlier cycles, for example the one depicting the downfall of bad pagans that is believed to have adorned the Carolingian Palace at Ingelheim (*see* CAROLINGIAN, §IV, 1(i)). Some of the

35. London, Palace of Westminster, *Coronation of St Edward the Confessor* by Charles Alfred Stothard, watercolour with raised gilt detail, 183×330 mm, 1819 (London, Society of Antiquaries of London); copy of a late 13th-century wall painting in the Painted Chamber (destr. 1834)

models for the pictures were French—Old Testament warfare is a major theme of the mid-13th-century French Macejowski Bible (New York, Pierpont Morgan Lib., MS. M.638), and illustrated Maccabees romances were in vogue in France by the 1280s—but using these particular biblical exempla, and the choice of the Maccabees, lacked true precedent in France. In general the Painted Chamber shows that full narrative mural decoration was not the sole preserve of Italy in this period. In 1993 two panels from the original ceiling of the Painted Chamber, showing a cherub and a prophet, were discovered; the panels are allied in style to the Bodleian and Douce apocalypses respectively and appear to date from the mid-1260s.

The British Museum houses fragments of the second scheme in the palace, formerly in the upper chapel of St Stephen, which is also known from copies. The paintings were torn out in 1800, and the chapel was gutted along with the Painted Chamber in the fire of 1834. The style of St Stephen's was not ideally suited to figurative mural decoration; the decision to decorate it with oil-based paintings and gilt-embossed work—techniques anticipated in the Painted Chamber—was not taken until 1350–63, when painters were impressed into Edward III's service for the task. The surviving fragments, evidently inserted after a change of plan into the lower half of the chapel's side windows, are small in size (h. 0.18–1.18 m) and are based on Job, with inscriptions in Latin. The scheme also included the *Life of Tobias* from the book of Tobit, perhaps indicating contact with the 13th-century glazing of the Sainte-Chapelle in Paris, although, as in the Painted Chamber, an idiosyncratic exemplary use of the Bible may have occurred. The *Job* wall paintings are in an Italianate style, like that of the *Angels* (copy; London, Soc. Antiqua.) holding cloths of honour painted on the dossals of the stalls. They indicate acquaintance with central or northern Italian painting styles, which are also reflected in the chapter house wall paintings of Westminster Abbey (*see* §V, 2(iii) above and GOTHIC, §IV, 5(ix)).

Other paintings included figures of military saints and a composition (copy (*c.* 1800) by Richard Smirke; London, Soc. Antiqua.) on the east wall showing the royal family and St George kneeling beneath the Nativity, doubtless once accompanied by a painted altarpiece, and iconographically reflecting the popularity of the Virgin and St George at the time of the foundation of the Order of the Garter (1348). The decorations were rich and complex, reviving on a grand scale the polychromy and composite applied techniques inaugurated in England on the Westminster Retable (*see* §2(iii) above) in the previous century. Both St Stephen's and the Painted Chamber featured armorial decoration (*see* HERALDRY, §IV).

*See also* JOHN OF ST ALBANS.

BIBLIOGRAPHY

J. Gage Rokewode: 'A Memoir on the Painted Chamber in the Palace of Westminster', *Vetusta Monumenta*, vi (London, 1885), pls xxvi–xxxix, pp. 1–37
E. W. Tristram: *English Wall Painting of the Fourteenth Century* (London, 1955), pp. 48–54, 57–8, 206–19
H. M. Colvin, ed.: *The History of the King's Works*, i (London, 1963), pp. 518–19
P. Binski: *The Painted Chamber at Westminster*, Soc. Antiqua. London, Occas. Pap., n. s. ix (London, 1986)

PAUL BINSKI

*(ii) 1548–1834.* Soon after the suppression in 1547 of religious collegiate foundations, which included the college of St Stephen, Parliament began to use regularly the substantial empty buildings on the site, the Commons the upper chapel of St Stephen, and the Lords a large room further south, which originally was used by the court of medieval queens and remained substantially unaltered until 1801. For the House of Commons St Stephen's Chapel was divided into an outer lobby and the chamber. In 1692 a major alteration to the chamber took place under the supervision of Christopher Wren, with the removal of the 14th-century clerestory and roof. The interior was also reconstructed and made more comfortable. Wren replaced the medieval windows with sash windows and introduced wainscoting and north and south galleries. In 1707 the need to accommodate 45 Scottish members led to the widening of the galleries.

Westminster Hall had been home to the Courts of Justice since medieval times. The courts of Chancery and King's Bench were housed in makeshift wooden enclosures at the south end, and from time to time the hall was fitted up to accommodate such state trials as those of Sir Thomas More (1535) and Charles I (1649). In 1739 William Kent placed an elegant Gothic screen, pierced with ogee windows and articulated with buttresses and pinnacles, in front of the courts. In 1755 the screen was raised in height, and ceilings were inserted over these courts.

In 1733 the inconvenience of the House of Commons led to a proposal for a new parliament house. Between 1733 and 1739 William Kent made designs for a great rectangular building standing immediately south of Westminster Hall (*see* KENT, WILLIAM, §2(ii)), but the project was dropped following the outbreak of war with Spain, and then the costly War of the Austrian Succession (1741–8). In place of this grand classical building some minor additions were made in the late 18th century; between 1755 and 1760 the central block of a new building, known as the Stone Building (destr. 1883), was constructed on the west side of Westminster Hall. It was designed by John Vardy and was of standard Palladian composition, with a pedimented central block flanked by lower wings terminating in pavilions. The south wing was added between 1766 and 1769. The building was then continued eastwards across Old Palace Yard between 1768 and 1770 to form the new main entrance to the House of Commons.

The inadequate facilities of the Houses of Parliament worsened and were vividly described in a report of 1789 (*Commons J.*, xliv (1788–9), pp. 548–9). In 1794 JOHN SOANE, who had longed for the opportunity, was asked by a House of Lords committee to consider schemes for improving their accommodation. His final design (1796) consisted of an imposing Neo-classical building with two main façades, one east, the other west, with terminal domes and giant Corinthian colonnades. The great mass of Westminster Hall balanced this new building, and the Painted Chamber and St Stephen's Chapel were both to be restored, but Soane's scheme was defeated by a mixture of government parsimony and the influence of James Wyatt.

The influx of Irish members following the Act of Union (1800), however, made action imperative and between

1800 and 1812 Wyatt was responsible for substantial piecemeal additions and alterations. The House of Commons was enlarged and refurbished, and the House of Lords moved into the Court of Requests (the medieval White Hall). A new royal entrance and new offices were erected in Old Palace Yard fronting the Court of Requests, and the Speaker's House was rebuilt and extended into St Stephen's Cloister. Wyatt's work, which was hidden behind two plain battlemented façades, one to the River Thames and one to Old Palace Yard, attracted much criticism.

Following Wyatt's death in 1813 and the reforms of the OFFICE OF WORKS in 1814–15, Soane was appointed Attached Architect with responsibility for the Palace of Westminster, and in this capacity he was finally able to produce some major work there. First came the rebuilding in 1819 of the north front of Westminster Hall, together with the insertion of dormer windows in the roof and the renewal of the lantern. Then followed the construction of the new Law Courts (1822–5) against the west wall of Westminster Hall, ingeniously fitted into the complicated site, which included the completion of the Stone Building by its north wing. Simultaneously on the south side of the palace Soane provided a new royal entrance and a Scala Regia (see fig. 36) in a characteristic, grand Neo-classical manner, a royal gallery, committee rooms and libraries (1822–7; destr. c. 1845). In the course of this work the medieval buildings of the old House of Lords and the

Prince's Chamber were demolished. In the centre of the site, however, the old buildings (especially the House of Commons), hallowed by tradition but unsuitable for their purpose, remained, until completely gutted in the fire of 1834. Apart from the medieval architecture, the greatest works of art to be lost were the *Armada* tapestries (1592–5), designed by Hendrick Vroom (see VROOM, (1)), which hung in the House of Lords.

*(iii) After 1834.* For temporary accommodation Robert Smirke (ii) fitted out the former House of Lords for the Commons and the Painted Chamber for the Lords. It was, however, decided that there should be a comprehensive rebuilding with the architect chosen in a competition that stipulated that the entries should be in either Gothic or Elizabethan Revival style. At the end of January 1836 CHARLES BARRY was declared the winner, deservedly because of his well-organized plan. He was, however, greatly helped by the splendid draughtsmanship of his entry (lost), which was the work of his young assistant, A. W. N. PUGIN, who helped him on the project from 1835 until 1837. Much time was taken up by committees, adaptations to the plan and elevations, choosing the stone, building a coffer dam in the Thames and laying the foundations, before the first stone was laid at the north-east corner of the river front in 1840.

The essential elements of Barry's plan as executed remained unaltered from his competition entry, particularly his integration into it of the surviving medieval buildings, and the location of all the principal rooms on one unified floor, with the House of Commons in the northern half and the House of Lords in the southern. It was a building of unprecedented size and complexity, which covered 3.6 ha (see ENGLAND, fig. 9). The range to the river contained the more private areas of the palace, including the libraries and refreshment rooms, and at either end splendid residencies, to the north the Speaker's House, and to the south accommodation for officials in the House of Lords. The central range included both chambers and their lobbies on either side of an octagonal central lobby. Further south Barry designed a great processional route of Robing Room, Royal Gallery and Prince's Chamber for the monarch's entrance to the House of Lords. The entrance façade has the Clock Tower to the north, and the Victoria Tower, designed and still used as a repository for the records of Parliament, to the south. Barry made the main public entrance through St Stephen's Porch in the centre of the building, but on this façade he never achieved his plan for enclosing New Palace Yard and giving a new front to Soane's Law Courts.

Barry took immense trouble with his external elevations, which were designed in a Perpendicular style to harmonize with Henry VII's Chapel in Westminster Abbey. There was much sculptural decoration, which was supervised by John Thomas (ii) (see THOMAS, (2)). Barry was a perfectionist and realized that he would need help with the Gothic Revival interiors. Thus in September 1844 he invited Pugin to design the fittings for the House of Lords, and the two men worked together until Pugin's death in 1852. They made a most successful partnership, with Barry refining Pugin's ceaseless stream of designs. Their masterpiece is the House of Lords (see fig. 37), which was called

36. London, Palace of Westminster, view of the Scala Regia, by John Soane, 1820s; engraving from John Soane: *Designs for Public and Private Buildings* (London, 1828), pl. 21

37. London, Palace of Westminster, interior of the House of Lords by Charles Barry and A. W. N. Pugin, opened 1847; view from the Bar looking towards the Throne and Woolsack; from a photograph by Benjamin Stone, 1897

at its opening in 1847 'the finest specimen of Gothic architecture in Europe' (*Illus. London News*, 17 April 1847, p. 245). Barry enabled Pugin to employ his colleagues: John Hardman (1811–67) for the stained glass (largely destr. in World War II) and metalwork, Herbert Minton (1793–1858) for the encaustic tiles, and John Gregory Crace for wallpapers, textiles, gilding and decorative painting. These items and the woodwork, carried out by the Thames Bank workshops, and furniture, made by several firms, are splendid examples of Pugin's vivid and inventive designs, which draw their inspiration from his profound understanding of medieval prototypes.

The rebuilding of the Houses of Parliament was seen as a great opportunity for the promotion of the fine arts, and in 1841 a commission was set up with Prince Albert as its president, which resulted in a major scheme of state patronage, most importantly of wall painting. The commissioners organized competitions for cartoons in 1843 and 1845 (*see* ENGLAND, §III, 4), and on the basis of these WILLIAM DYCE, DANIEL MACLISE, Charles West Cope and John Callcott Horsley were chosen to paint the six arched spaces in the north and south walls of the House of Lords. This first work was completed in 1846–9. The subjects for the paintings were determined by the commissioners, and the next major scheme (1849–54) to be

completed was for the Upper Waiting Hall. With its themes taken from English poetry it became known as the Poets' Hall. The artists were Cope, J. R. Herbert, G. F. Watts, Horsley, John Tenniel and Edward Armitage. Cope painted the Peers' Corridor with pictures (1856–66) illustrating the fight between Charles I and Parliament, and from 1857 to 1868 E. M. Ward continued with scenes from later 17th-century history on the Commons' Corridor. Daniel Maclise painted his two splendid history pieces, the *Meeting of Wellington and Blücher* (1861) and the *Death of Nelson* (1865), in the Royal Gallery. They represented, however, only a fragment of the original scheme, and this was also true of the scenes from the *Morte d'Arthur* (1848–63) by William Dyce in the Robing Room, and of Herbert's work (1858–64 and 1880) in the Peers' Robing Room (now the Moses Room) on the subject of justice. The commissioners frequently found it difficult to get the artists to work; fresco painting was not generally understood, different techniques were tried, the results were uneven, and much restoration work has subsequently been carried out. Sculpture was also commissioned, the most significant pieces being the marble statues of *Queen Victoria* flanked by *Justice* and *Mercy* (1850–55) by John Gibson (i), and bronze low-relief panels (1852–9) by William Theed III, both in the Prince's Chamber. The commission was dissolved in 1863. It represented a typical 19th-century view of the hierarchy of the arts, with the fine arts taking precedence over the decorative arts, and in some cases failed to respect Barry's carefully planned interiors.

Meanwhile in 1852 the House of Commons was opened, Barry received his knighthood, and the work continued. The Speaker's House was fitted up in the late 1850s. The bell, Big Ben, was delivered to the Clock Tower in 1858, and the Victoria Tower was nearly complete at the time of Barry's death in 1860. His son, E. M. Barry, was then appointed architect and was responsible for most of the final work, executed in a rich, colourful high Victorian Gothic Revival style. This is seen particularly in the redecoration (1860–70) of the chapel of St Mary Undercroft and New Palace Yard arcade (1864). After the new Royal Courts of Justice were opened in the Strand in 1882 Soane's Law Courts were demolished. The west side of Westminster Hall was then restored (1882–8) by J. L. Pearson, who at the same time added the Grand Committee Room at the north-west corner.

A substantial picture collection, mostly of portraits and topographical views of Westminster, was gradually built up, and from the turn of the century there was a revival of interest in decorating the building, with paintings (1908–10) in the East Corridor, mosaics (1923–5) in the Central Lobby and St Stephen's Hall, and paintings (finished 1927) in St Stephen's Hall. During World War II the building was damaged a number of times, and in May 1941 the chamber of the House of Commons was destroyed. In 1943 a select committee for rebuilding was appointed, which chose Sir Giles Gilbert Scott (ii) (see SCOTT (4)) as architect. Work started in 1945, and the new chamber was opened in 1950. Its proportions are similar to those of its predecessor, but the Gothic style used is more angular, paler and less ornate. Since 1963 much additional accommodation has been provided by infilling on the original site, but in 1983 it was decided to redevelop the area to the north of Bridge Street for future parliamentary use.

UNPUBLISHED SOURCES

London, Pal. Westminster [R. J. B. Walker: *A Catalogue of Paintings, Drawings, Sculpture and Engravings in the Palace of Westminster*, 4 vols, typescript (1988)]

BIBLIOGRAPHY

H. Ryde: *Illustrations of the New Palace of Westminster*, 1st series (London, 1849)

E. N. Holmes: *Illustrations of the New Palace of Westminster*, 2nd series (London, 1865)

A. Barry: *The Life and Works of Sir Charles Barry* (London, 1867, 2/1870/R New York, 1973)

A. Wright and P. Smith: *Parliament Past and Present* (London, 1903)

B. H. Fell and K. R. Mackenzie: *The Houses of Parliament: A Guide to the Palace of Westminster* (London, 1930, rev. 14/1988)

P. Stanton: *Pugin* (London, 1971)

M. H. Port, ed.: *The Houses of Parliament* (London and New Haven, 1976)

A. Wedgwood: *The Pugin Family: Catalogue of the Drawings Collection of the R.I.B.A.* (Farnborough, 1977)

A. Wedgwood: 'The Throne in the House of Lords and its Setting', *Archit. Hist.*, xxvii (1984), pp. 59–73

——: *Pugin and the Pugin Family: Catalogue of Architectural Drawings in the Victoria & Albert Museum* (London, 1985)

For further bibliography see §(i)(a) above.

ALEXANDRA WEDGWOOD

**4. TOWER OF LONDON.** The castle was founded by William I immediately after the Norman Conquest (1066). It was strategically sited in the south-east angle of the Roman city wall, just downstream from Old London Bridge, commanding open countryside to the east, the Thames and the bridge to the south, and the city to the north and west. By the end of the 13th century the outer wall enclosed an area of *c.* 7 ha, which is roughly the present size of the castle (see fig. 38).

The castle first consisted of a small quadrilateral enclosure defended to the east and south by the existing Roman city walls and to the north and west by ditches and a palisaded bank. The huge stone donjon, later known as the White Tower (38a), which was henceforth to dominate the castle, was begun shortly after 1077 by William I and completed *c.* 1100 by William II (*reg* 1087–1100), the works being entrusted to Gundulf, Bishop of Rochester. It was built of Kentish ragstone and local mudstone, with Caen limestone dressings. The donjon was almost square (36.0×32.5 m) and 27.5 m high, and its only rival was the contemporary donjon at Colchester, which also had a projecting chapel apse. The donjon at the Tower of London consisted of three floors, each divided into three compartments; the upper and grandest storey was of double height with galleries and contained the chapel of St John (see fig. 39), which has a round-columned nave and a triforium gallery passage. Designed as a palace as well as a stronghold, the donjon had fireplaces and latrines on both upper floors.

Although William II may have enclosed the castle with a masonry wall to the north and west, there is little evidence of important building works until the end of the 12th century when, in the reigns of Richard I (*reg* 1189–99) and John (*reg* 1199–1216), a major extension was built that ran west to the site of the present Beauchamp Tower (38m), thence south to the Bell Tower (38i) and back along the river. Of these buildings, only the Bell Tower, a strong two-storey angle tower containing a radiating rib vault, and the south curtain wall running to the gateway beneath the Bloody Tower (38g) remain.

Henry III greatly enlarged the castle. The original bailey was refortified with the twin-towered Coldharbour Gate (*c.* 1225; destr.), linked by a heavily defended curtain wall to the massive, circular Wakefield Tower (38f) to the south. The latter controlled a new water-gate to the east and a postern to the west. Its vaulted upper chamber, with a small oratory originally decorated with mural paintings, is the only element of the richly appointed palace built during the reign of Henry III to survive; the great hall nearby, visible in early illustrations, was destroyed in the late 18th century. In the mid-13th century the outer defences were extended northwards from a main outer gate (destr.), on the site of the present Beauchamp Tower, to the Devereux Tower (38o), and thence, breaking through the Roman wall, eastwards to the Martin Tower (38b) and south to the Salt Tower (38c), rejoining the earlier defences at the Lanthorn Tower (38e). St Peter ad Vincula, previously a parish church outside the walls, became a chapel (38n) within the castle precincts.

The full development of the Tower of London was achieved during the reign of Edward I, when Henry III's enceinte was completely enclosed by an outer curtain wall

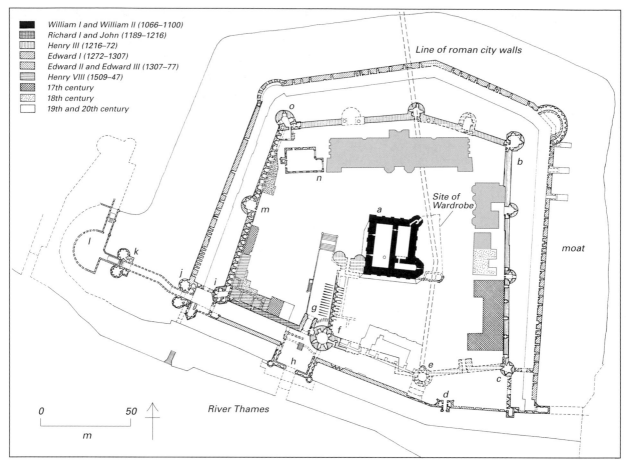

William I and William II (1066–1100)
Richard I and John (1189–1216)
Henry III (1216–72)
Edward I (1272–1307)
Edward II and Edward III (1307–77)
Henry VIII (1509–47)
17th century
18th century
19th and 20th century

Line of roman city walls

Site of
Wardrobe

moat

River Thames

0    50

m

38. London, plan of the Tower of London: (a) White Tower; (b) Martin Tower; (c) Salt Tower; (d) Cradle Tower; (e) Lanthorn Tower; (f) Wakefield Tower; (g) Bloody Tower; (h) St Thomas's Tower; (i) Bell Tower; (j) Byward Tower; (k) Middle Tower; (l) Lion Tower; (m) Beauchamp Tower; (n) chapel of St Peter ad Vincula; (o) Devereux Tower

fronted on the landward sides by a vast moat, transforming it into one of the largest and most powerful of concentric castles. The main land gate was moved from the middle of the west curtain wall to the south-west angle and was replaced by the Beauchamp Tower. The new entrance was defended successively by a fortified causeway, a huge semicircular barbican (the Lion Tower; 38l) and, after a right-angled turn, by two strong gate-houses (the Byward and Middle Towers; 38j–k). In addition, the narrow space between the two curtain walls was controlled by cross walls that have largely disappeared. To the south, Henry III's water-gate became the new land entrance to the inner ward and an enormous new water-gate, St Thomas's Tower (38h), was built, possibly derived from that at the Louvre in Paris. St Thomas's Tower contained state lodgings on the upper floor, linked by a bridge to the Wakefield Tower and the palace.

The outlines of the Tower were subsequently little altered but the building remained the object of constant expenditure. In the reign of Edward III new works included a secondary water-gate (the Cradle Tower; 38d)), the vault of the Bloody Tower gateway and a postern at the Byward Tower, all with ribbed vaults and enriched

bosses. In the late 14th century the main beam of the upper gate hall of the Byward Tower was painted with birds, lions and fleurs-de-lys. The south wall also bears a finely executed but damaged painting of *Christ in Majesty* (*c.* 1390–1400). Post-medieval demolition has left no trace of the many recorded alterations and additions made to the palace and buildings around the White Tower. Throughout the Middle Ages the Tower of London was used as a fortress, palace, arsenal, mint, royal menagerie and prison. John II, King of France (*reg* 1332–56), taken prisoner at the Battle of Poitiers (1356), and Charles, Duke of Orléans, imprisoned after Agincourt (1415), were both lodged royally in the Tower; a famous illustration (London, BL, Royal MS. 16. F. 11, fol. 73) shows the latter writing poetry in a spacious chamber in the White Tower. From Henry VIII's reign the Tower's use as a royal residence declined. Surviving from this period is the chapel of St Peter ad Vincula, rebuilt in 1519 after a fire; it consists of nave, chancel and a wide north aisle, all with tie-beam roofs and large windows. James Nedeham, who built the roof of St Peter's, rebuilt the timber lodging at St Thomas's Tower in 1532. In 1540 he reconstructed the Queen's House (before *c.* 1880 better known as the Lieutenant's

Lodgings) with an ogee-braced timber frame and open first-floor hall, which was floored in 1607 to form an upper great chamber; in 1608 the extraordinary marble monument commemorating the failure of the Gunpowder Plot was installed here.

Between the Restoration (1660) and the mid-19th century numerous buildings were provided for the storage and manufacture of ordnance; in the 1680s the fortifications were improved to mount 90 guns. Significant remains include the New Armouries (1664), the upper part of Legge's Mount Battery (1682) and the fine carved pediment of the Great Storehouse (1692). The Waterloo Barracks (1845) replaced the Great Storehouse itself, which was destroyed by fire in 1841. In the later 19th century most of the ordnance buildings were removed, and the Tower was restored, first by ANTHONY SALVIN (1853–68) and subsequently by architects of the Office of Works, giving it the medieval appearance it bears today.

### BIBLIOGRAPHY
*London*, Royal Comm. Anc. & Hist. Mnmts & Constr. England, v (London, 1930), pp. 74–95
H. M. Colvin, ed.: *The History of the King's Works*, 6 vols (London, 1963–82) [esp. ii, pp. 706–29]
J. Charlton, ed.: *The Tower of London: Its Buildings and Institutions* (London, 1978) [contains an extensive bibliog.]
R. Allen Brown and P. E. Curnow: *Tower of London* (London, 1984)
G. Parnell: *The Tower of London* (London, 1993)

P. E. CURNOW

5. WHITEHALL PALACE. A former royal palace in the City of Westminster, London, between its rise in the 1530s and its destruction by fire in 1698 it was for much of its existence the largest of the English sovereign's residences. It covered a greater area than the château of Versailles, but unlike its rationally planned French counterpart, the sequential manner of building over the decades without a master-plan gave Whitehall Palace a random appearance. Although externally the palace might have lacked grandeur, its interior was considered sumptuous. At its architectural peak in the 1680s, the palace consisted of a series of long galleries, living-quarters, state rooms, banqueting rooms, chapels, grand entrance-gates, gardens, a great number of different types of entertainment buildings, courtyards and support buildings, all lying between the capital's principal transportation route, the River Thames, and the royal pleasure grounds of St James's Park (see fig. 40).

The nucleus of Whitehall Palace was York Place, which for three centuries had been the London residence of the archbishops of York. In 1529 Cardinal Thomas Wolsey, who had rebuilt the house on a magnificent scale, was forced, on his fall from favour with Henry VIII, to relinquish it to the King. When Henry bought neighbouring property and embarked on an ambitious building programme, London's new palace acquired the name Whitehall. The core of Wolsey's mansion, the Great Hall (1528), was retained and became the principal setting for banquets and plays during the Tudor period. Henry VIII also inherited the Chapel Royal, which adjoined the Great Hall on the river side, and the vaulted wine cellars, which are the oldest surviving remains.

The palace was divided, physically and functionally, into two distinct sections: on the east or river side lay the main buildings, while on the west or park side were the

39. London, Tower of London, interior of St John's Chapel, *c.* 1077–*c.* 1100

entertainment buildings. Through the centre of the palace ran a public road called the Street, later known simply as Whitehall. At either end Henry ordered the construction of two monumental gatehouses. The Holbein Gate (*c.* 1530; destr. 1759) to the north was a three-storey structure in a chequered pattern of stone and flint, adorned with portrait medallions probably by Giovanni da Maiano (*see* MAIANO, (3)). In contrast to this portal's distinctly Tudor-style profile was the contemporary King Street Gate to the south (destr. 1723), the pilasters and pediments of which illustrated the increasing influence of the Italian Renaissance. The principal approach to Whitehall Palace, however, was by water. The public used the simple wooden steps of Whitehall Stairs; dignitaries entered by the Privy Stairs, a double-tiered pier extending into the Thames. This wharf was demolished in 1691 to make way for Mary II's riverside terrace, an ornamental garden designed by Christopher Wren (*see* WREN, CHRISTOPHER).

To the south lay the Privy Garden, divided into 16 grassed sections, each containing a statue, except for one that contained a complex sundial designed by the mathematician Edmund Gunter. Two sides of the garden were lined by long gallery buildings and apartments. The ceiling of the eastern gallery, known as the Long or Matted Gallery, was painted by Hans Holbein (i), who was also responsible for the most famous Tudor portrait from the palace, the wall painting (1537; destr. 1698) in the Privy Chamber representing Henry VIII and Jane Seymour flanked by the King's parents, Henry VII and Elizabeth of York (cartoon fragment, London, N.P.G.; *see* ENGLAND, fig. 15). During the reign of Charles I the Long Gallery served as the picture gallery, in which were displayed the many fine paintings acquired by Charles and his brother Henry Frederick, Prince of Wales (1594–1612).

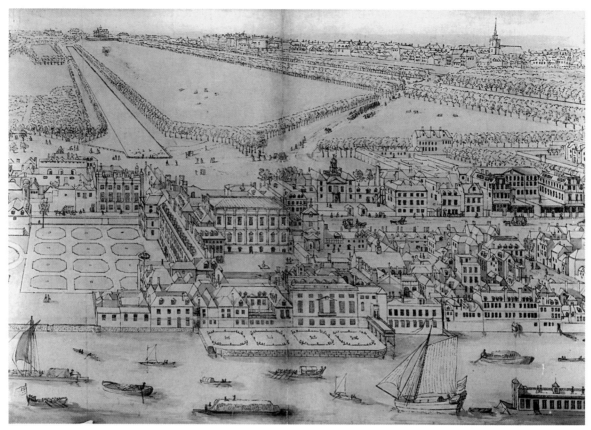

40. London, Whitehall Palace; from a drawing attributed to Leonard Knijff, pen and ink and wash, 541×787 mm, *c.* 1695 (London, City of Westminster Archives Centre)

The lodgings for the king and queen both looked out on to the river and were separated by the Volary Garden. Nearby was the Great Court, divided from the Pebble Court by a terrace. Further to the north were several large courtyards, all confusingly called Scotland Yard.

Various entertainment buildings were situated near the park. Throughout the history of the palace there existed several tennis courts, some enclosed, others open-air; the walls of one survive, incorporated in Charles Barry's Privy Council Building (1846). There was a tiltyard, a long enclosure used for jousts, military exercises and bear-baiting, alongside which ran a gallery that served as a royal box for watching events below and as the main passage leading between Holbein Gate and the staircase descending into the park. The Cockpit (completed 1534), with brick walls and a tall pyramidal roof, at first was used for cockfights, but in 1629–30 it was converted by Inigo Jones into a playhouse (*see* THEATRE, §III, 2(iii)(a)), frequently mentioned by the diarist Samuel Pepys.

The finest building at Whitehall Palace and almost the only one to survive the fire of 1698 was the Banqueting House (1619–22) by Inigo Jones, the first completed Renaissance building in England (*see* ENGLAND, §II, 3). The two-storey façade of seven bays divided by columns and pilasters encloses one large, double-cube room, which was used for a variety of court festivities, entertainments

and masques. Rubens's nine great ceiling canvases depicting, in allegorical terms, the achievements of James I were installed in 1635, when the hall became reserved for royal audiences; a new room for masques (1637–8; destr. 1645), constructed of timber, was built alongside. The Civil War and execution of Charles I destroyed any chances of success for the scheme proposed by John Webb (i) in the late 1630s and 1640s for rebuilding a vast new Whitehall Palace on an amplified theme of Jones's Banqueting House.

BIBLIOGRAPHY
*Survey of London*, xiii–xiv (London, 1930–31)
P. Palme: *Triumph of Peace: A Study of the Whitehall Banqueting House* (Stockholm, 1956)
H. M. Colvin, ed.: *The History of the King's Works*, iii–v (London, 1975–82)

NEIL R. BINGHAM

**6. VAUXHALL GARDENS.** They were the most celebrated and long-lived of the pleasure gardens that were established throughout London in the 17th and 18th centuries after the Restoration (1660) to provide secure places for public entertainment. The gardens were situated on the south bank of the River Thames opposite Westminster in Lambeth, near the present Vauxhall Bridge, and were reached by boats stopping at Vauxhall Steps, which greatly enhanced their attraction. John Evelyn mentioned the gardens, until 1785 known as New Spring Gardens, in his diary entry for 2 July 1661. In 1728 the gardens were leased by Jonathan Tyers (1702–67), who by 1758 had become the owner; under his management they were at their height of popularity. Tyers relaunched the gardens in spectacular fashion in June 1732, with a *Ridotto al' fresco* for which the artistic guidance was provided by William Hogarth. The gardens became a major feature of London social life: Frederick, Prince of Wales, had a private pavilion there, and the clientele was satirized in the work of Thomas Rowlandson (for illustration *see* ROWLANDSON, THOMAS). The gardens were recorded in contemporary prints by such engravers as Johann Sebastian Müller (1715–*c.* 1785; see fig. 41) after paintings by SAMUEL WALE. Antonio Canaletto depicted various views, notably *Vauxhall Gardens, the Grand Walk* (*c.* 1751; priv. col.). The gardens were laid out as a 5-ha rectangle divided by four avenues, each *c.* 275 m long: the Grand Walk, from the entrance, the South Walk with triumphal arches, and two smaller lateral avenues, all of which were transversed by the Grand Cross Walk. At the end of the walks, *trompe l'oeil* paintings extended the vistas. The area bounded by the Grand, South and Grand Cross walks was known as the Grove; an orchestra occupied the centre, and semicircular rows of supper-boxes, decorated with large paintings (*c.* 1741–2; five in London, V&A), mostly by FRANCIS HAYMAN, surrounded it on three sides. A statue of *George Frideric Handel* (1738; London, V&A) by Louis-François Roubiliac was the most important work of art in the gardens. The buildings were in various exotic styles, and the garden structures were of wood covered with painted canvas. The Rotunda, behind the north row, was a ballroom with a lavish Rococo interior. The gardens were primarily a place of evening entertainment; the numerous lamps and such animated scenery as the Cascade lent them a theatrical character.

The gardens changed little until the 19th century when there were minor changes and additions, which may be seen in a survey of 1826 (Southworth). Their character gradually changed to that of an amusement park with circus performances, and contemporary writers, including Charles Dickens in *Sketches by Boz* (London, 1836), recorded their decline. The gardens were finally dismantled in 1859. A model (1984) of Vauxhall Gardens, based on Wale's *General Prospect* (*c.* 1751; London, Mus. London), is in the Victoria and Albert Museum, London.

BIBLIOGRAPHY
W. Worth: *The London Pleasure Gardens of the Eighteenth Century* (London, 1896)
J. G. Southworth: *Vauxhall Gardens: A Chapter in the Social History of London* (New York, 1941)
*Vauxhall Gardens* (exh. cat., ed. T. J. Edelstein; New Haven, CT, Yale Cent. Brit. A., 1983)
D. Coke: 'Vauxhall Gardens', *Rococo Art and Design in Hogarth's England* (exh. cat., ed. M. Snodin; London, V&A, 1984), pp. 74–98
J. D. Hunt: *Vauxhall and London's Garden Theatre* (London, 1985)

## VI. Royal Academy of Arts.

The principal activities of the Academy, founded in 1768 during the reign of George III, were at first centred on art education in its Schools (*see also* ENGLAND, §XV) and on

41. *Vauxhall Gardens, the Grand Walk*, engraving and etching by Johann Sebastian Müller after Samuel Wale, 315×442 mm, *c.* 1751 (London, Museum of London)

arranging annual exhibitions of contemporary art; today, loan and retrospective exhibitions are its principal features.

1. ORIGINS AND DEVELOPMENT. By the time the Academy was established in 1768, a modern system for the organization of the arts had already developed in London. Private academies, art clubs, auction-houses and print-shops had existed in the capital for almost a century (see §III, 4 above). Attempts to establish a public or royal academy of art had been made in 1698 during the reign of William III and in 1749 and 1755 during the reign of George II. The Royal Academy's Instrument of Foundation was signed by George III on 10 December 1768. It consisted of 27 articles designed for the good government of the institution, and the founder-members included Sir Joshua Reynolds and Benjamin West, the first (1768–92) and second (1792–1805, 1806–20) presidents of the Academy (PRA) respectively, and Sir William Chambers, its first Treasurer (1768–96). One of the last academies of art to be formed in Europe, the Royal Academy was, however, the first of its type to establish itself as a truly modern institution, which was run by artists who were virtually independent of the monarch, government or private patronage, and which supported itself through annual exhibitions. These were designed to show and sell works of art executed by all the artists active in Britain, not by members and students only. The Academy's membership originally consisted of 40 Royal Academicians (RA), each of whom was a professional painter, sculptor or architect. The membership diploma (see DIPLOMA WORK) was etched by Francesco Bartolozzi on the Academy's foundation (for illustration see BARTOLOZZI, (1)). A few engravers were admitted as Associates (ARA) after 1769 when this new class was devised, and from 1853 they became eligible for election as Academicians. Two women, Angelica Kauffman and Mary Moser (i), were among the founder-members, but they held no appointment. No other female name was recorded in the Schools until the 1860s, and the first woman ARA (Annie Louisa Swynnerton) was not elected until 1922. The numbers of both Academicians and Associates changed during the Academy's history. From 1972 there were 50 Academicians and 25 Associates, but in 1992 the category of ARA was abolished altogether. Also, from 1918 any RAs and ARAs who reached the age of 75 automatically became Senior Academicians or Senior Associates and had reduced duties and privileges.

The Academy was democratically governed by its Academicians, who were organized into two bodies: a Council (formed by the elected President and eight Academicians), which framed new laws and regulations, and a General Assembly (formed by all the Academicians), which ratified Council decisions. After 1769 Academicians were chosen from among the Associates and these, in their turn, were chosen from among the exhibitors at the Annual Exhibition. The President, initially a practising painter (Reynolds and West were followed by Thomas Lawrence), stood at the head of a body consisting of a Keeper, Treasurer, Secretary and Librarian; professors of painting, sculpture

42. *Life Class at the Royal Academy* by Johan Zoffany, oil on canvas, 1.00×1.47 m, 1771–2 (Windsor Castle, Berks, Royal Collection)

(from 1810), architecture, perspective, anatomy and chemistry (from 1871); and honorary members including, after 1770, readers of ancient history and literature. For the first 11 years (1768–79) the Academy's premises were on the south side of Pall Mall, although its Schools moved into Old Somerset House (destr.) on the Strand in 1771. Johan Zoffany's group portrait *Life Class at the Royal Academy* (1771–2; Windsor Castle, Berks, Royal Col.; see fig. 42) celebrates George III's generosity in making these premises available to the Schools. In 1780 the Academy itself moved into premises in the Strand: the new Somerset House, designed by Chambers. It remained there until 1836. From 1837 to 1868 the Academy occupied the eastern half of a new building in Trafalgar Square, sharing its entrance with the National Gallery. This dual-purpose building was commissioned from William Wilkins by the government in 1832, expressly for the purpose of housing both the Academy and the National Gallery in one place. In 1869 the Academy moved into its present leasehold premises at Burlington House, Piccadilly (once the home of Richard Boyle, 3rd Earl of Burlington and 4th Earl of Cork), which the government purchased on the Academy's behalf.

Until the end of the 19th century the Royal Academy held a central position in British art both as an arbiter of taste and as the institution to which aspiring artists looked for acceptance. However, by the end of the 19th century and particularly from the beginning of the 20th it came increasingly under attack for its conservative attitudes, as reflected in its membership and in the selection of works for its Summer Exhibition. The election of a series of largely unadventurous presidents in the first half of the 20th century was crowned by that of Alfred Munnings, who held the post from 1944 to 1949. His hostility to modern art was unconcealed, and in 1949 at the Annual Dinner he railed against what he thought were the excesses of modernism, selecting Matisse and Picasso for particular criticism. Dissatisfaction with the Academy's apparent indifference towards modern art variously resulted in the spectacular resignations of several of the more avant-garde Academicians in this period: Stanley Spencer and Walter Richard Sickert resigned in 1935 and Augustus John in 1938. After Munnings's presidency concerted efforts were made by his successors, such as Gerald Kelly (PRA 1949–54) and W. T. Monnington (PRA 1966–76), to liberalize the Academy's outlook. Although it recovered some of its former prestige, it never recaptured the crucial position it once enjoyed.

2. EDUCATION. The Royal Academy Schools, the responsibility of the Keeper, consisted of an Antique or Plaster Academy, an Academy of Living Models and a Painting School (opened in 1815, after the privilege of borrowing pictures from the Dulwich Picture Gallery was given). Students first had to serve a probationary period before they were formally admitted—a rule that had developed gradually, as had the rule that students had to spend a term in the Antique Academy before being allowed to work after the living model. In the life class female as well as male models were used, in continuation of a tradition established in London as early as 1720 (*see* §III, 4 above). Education at the Schools was free (until 1977).

The term of studentship was six years; this was extended to seven in 1792 and to ten in 1800, but many students did not complete the course. Gold and silver medals were awarded annually from 1769 and every two years from 1772. On the occasion of each prize-giving, a discourse was delivered by the President before his colleagues and students: Reynolds's 15 *Discourses*, given between 1769 and 1790, were a public statement of the Academy's policy for the arts (*see* REYNOLDS, JOSHUA, §III, 2). The Schools had no serious rival until the Royal College of Art (founded in 1837 as the Government School of Design) and the Slade School of Fine Arts (1871), both in London, challenged their position. Criticism was, however, raised earlier by such artists as James Barry, William Blake and Benjamin Robert Haydon, and alternative educational institutions were established in and outside London during the 19th century. Teaching at the Schools was mainly carried out by visiting artists, drawn from the ranks of the RAs and ARAs, who spent two or three months in this capacity. In 1927 this was changed and a small permanent staff was employed as well as visiting artists. The latter were, however, no longer taken exclusively from the Academy and were obliged to teach on a more regular basis than before. By the 1990s the students were all postgraduate, and the old academic system of teaching was abandoned in favour of a much more liberal, loosely structured one.

3. EXHIBITIONS. The Academy's Annual Exhibition of contemporary art (first held in 1769) was the financial core of the institution and for many years the foremost artistic event in London. Until 1779 the financial deficit these exhibitions incurred was reimbursed from the Privy purse. From 1780, when works were exhibited for the first time in the Great Room at Somerset House (see fig. 19 above; *see also* EXHIBITION, fig. 3), the Annual Exhibition increased in size and began to make a profit. This enabled the Academy to become a fully independent institution, running a charitable fund for the relief of impoverished or destitute artists and their families. Public exhibitions held by other organizations (*see* §III, 5 above) did not undermine the success of the Academy exhibitions or its leading role in the arts until the second half of the 19th century. At this time commercial art galleries fully developed, exhibiting societies increased in number, and the conservative taste of the Academy's Selection and Hanging Committees (see fig. 20 above), was challenged by avant-garde bodies, such as the New English Art Club founded in 1886. The Academy's Annual, or Summer, Exhibition did not lose so much in popularity as in prestige.

In addition to the Summer Exhibition, since 1870 the Royal Academy has held loan exhibitions. Initially there was one a year, the Winter Exhibition, which consisted of works by Old Masters or living artists, lent from British collections. The turning-point came in 1920–21 when an exhibition of Spanish art was held that included many works from abroad. Rapidly expanding in scale, in 1930 a loan exhibition of Italian art from 1200 to 1900 was organized that contained an unprecedented number of masterpieces, from Italy and elsewhere. In keeping with the general conservatism of the Academy in that period, in the first half of the 20th century these exhibitions were primarily historical. Thereafter they became more eclectic and included contemporary art as well. Gradually their frequency increased (there were 15 in 1978), and they came to form a dominant part of the Academy's activity.

BIBLIOGRAPHY

J. Reynolds: *Discourses on Art* (London, 1778); ed. R. R. Wark (San Marino, CA, 1959/*R* New Haven and London, 1975)

R. Wornum, ed.: *Lectures on Painting by Royal Academicians* (London, 1847)

A. Graves: *The Royal Academy of Arts: A Complete Dictionary of Contributors and their Work from its Foundation in 1769 to 1904*, 8 vols (London, 1905–6/*R* in 4 vols, Bath, 1970)

W. R. M. Lamb: *The Royal Academy: A Short History of its Foundation and Development* (London, 1951)

S. C. Hutchison: 'The Royal Academy Schools, 1768–1830', *Walpole Soc.*, xxxviii (1960–62), pp. 123–91

H. C. Morgan: *A History of the Organization and Growth of the Royal Academy Schools from the Beginning of the Academy to 1836* (diss., U. Leeds, 1964)

S. C. Hutchison: *The History of the Royal Academy, 1768–1968* (London, 1968, rev. 2/1986)

H. C. Morgan: 'The Lost Opportunity of the Royal Academy: An Assessment of its Position in the Nineteenth Century', *J. Warb. & Court. Inst.*, xxxii (1969), pp. 410–20

——: 'The Schools of the Royal Academy', *Brit. J. Educ. Stud.*, xxi/1 (1973), pp. 88–103

T. P. Cowdell: *The Role of the Royal Academy in English Art, 1918–30* (diss., U. Leeds, 1980)

E. Shanes: *The Genius of the Royal Academy* (London, 1981)

*The Edwardians and After: The Royal Academy, 1900–50* (exh. cat., ed. M. A. Stevens; New York, IBM Gal. Sci. & A.; Washington, DC, Meridian House Int.; Memphis, TN, Dixon Gal.; Newport, RI, A. Mus. & A. Assoc.; 1988–9)

*The Artist's Model: Its Role in British Art from Lely to Etty* (exh. cat. by I. Bignamini and M. Postel, Nottingham; London, Kenwood House, 1991)

ILARIA BIGNAMINI

**London, George** (*d* Edgware [now in London], 12 Jan 1714). English garden designer. He probably first trained at St James's Palace, and he was subsequently Bishop Henry Compton's gardener at Fulham Palace. In 1681 he co-founded Brompton Park nursery; by 1687 HENRY WISE had joined, soon becoming London's sole business partner and co-translator of their two gardening directories.

At William III's accession in 1688 London's political connections secured him the post of Master Gardener and Deputy Superintendent of the Royal Gardens. William spent large sums on his palace grounds, and London and Wise brought new designs, with stock supplied from Brompton, to Kensington, Hampton Court and elsewhere. Through his contacts in architectural and aristocratic circles, London strove further to expand his business; with Wise left in charge at Brompton, London travelled ceaselessly and gradually received commissions from the provinces. He served an aristocracy demanding productive yet ostentatious gardens, and his numerous layouts were mostly developed through the 1690s and beyond. At Chatsworth (Derbys), Longleat (Wilts), Wimpole Hall (Cambs), Staunton Harold (Leics) and elsewhere he conjured up a variety of designs from his wide geometrical and horticultural repertory. Such was his stamina, Stephen Switzer recalled with some amazement, that 'this one person actually saw and gave directions once or twice a year in most of the gentlemen's gardens in England'.

Around each house London invariably laid out numerous compartments, walled or delineated by low box hedging. Some were grass plots ornamented with statues and tubs of orange and bay, basins of water or squares and diamonds of dwarf evergreens; others were embroidered flourishes of bedded plants in colourful Baroque arabesques of 'C' and 'S' scrollwork. Further out from each house were kitchen gardens, orchards of exotic fruits (espaliered or planted in quincunx) and bosky mazes through which meandering paths were sculpted out. These vaguely Franco-Dutch jigsaws were linked by gravel paths, ramps and balustraded staircases. Invariably a wooded deer park lay beyond, also geometrically figured. Although unrealized, London's design (*c.* 1699; London, V&A, E434–1951) for the park at Castle Howard, N. Yorks, with its vast avenues, ridings, wheels and stars, is typical: a sizeable capital investment in timber could be decoratively planted out for a later generation to fell profitably.

Although almost all London's gardens have since been obliterated, many were recorded in engraved suites of bird's-eye views popular at the time, such as Leonard Knyff's and Johannes Kip's *Britannia illustrata* (1707). After 1706, London travelled infrequently but about that year began two massive, if short-lived, gardens: Wanstead in Essex and, for James Bridges, 1st Duke of Chandos, the extravagant Canons, near Edgware.

WRITINGS

ed., with H. Wise: *The Compleat Gard'ner* (London, 1699); trans. of J. de la Quintinie: *Instructions pour les jardins fruitiers et potagers* (Paris, 1690) [abridged edn of J. Evelyn's trans., 1693]

ed., with H. Wise: *The Retir'd Gard'ner*, 2 vols (London, 1706); trans. of F. Gentil: *Le Jardinier solitaire*, i (Paris, 1704), and L. Liger: *Le Jardinier fleuriste et historiographe*, ii (Paris, 1704)

BIBLIOGRAPHY

S. Switzer: *The Nobleman, Gentleman, and Gardener's Recreation* (London, 1715), pp. 59–62

J. Harvey: *Early Nurserymen* (London, 1974)

J. Harris: *William Talman: Maverick Architect* (London, 1982), pp. 43–5

S. R. Jeffery: 'John James and George London at Herriard: Architectural Drawings in the Jervoise of Herriard Collection', *Archit. Hist.*, xxviii (1985), pp. 40–70

ROBERT WILLIAMS

**London Group.** English exhibiting society founded in November 1913. On its foundation it absorbed many members of the CAMDEN TOWN GROUP and also incorporated the more avant-garde artists influenced by Cubism and Futurism, some of whom afterwards joined the Vorticist movement. Among the founder-members were David Bomberg, Henri Gaudier-Brzeska, Jacob Epstein, Harold Gilman (the group's first president until his death in 1919), Charles Ginner, Spencer Gore, Percy Wyndham Lewis, John Nash, Christopher Nevinson and Edward Wadsworth. The group was organized in opposition to the conservatism of the Royal Academy and the stagnation of the formerly radical New English Art Club. Though, as can be judged from the names of its founders, it had no homogeneous style or aesthetic, it acted as a focal point for the more progressive elements in British art at that time.

The first unofficial manifestation of the London Group was an exhibition held in Brighton (Dec 1913–Jan 1914) under the auspices of the Camden Town Group. Its subtitle, however, 'An Exhibition of the Work of English Post-Impressionists, Cubists and Others', revealed a greater breadth of style than that associated with the

Camden Town Group. Sickert, though he did not exhibit with the London Group until 1916, made a speech at the opening arguing for the need to keep the group free from attachment to specific styles or factions. Despite this call for independence the London Group was most interesting and influential when under the sway of a particular, more homogeneous element of its membership. In 1914 it was officially named the London Group on the suggestion of Epstein and that year held its first exhibition under this name at the Goupil Galleries in London from March to April; the works were selected by a hanging committee elected from the membership. The following year two exhibitions were held, as was the practice until 1930 when they became annual. At an early stage non-members were also encouraged to exhibit and this remained the policy thereafter.

During World War I the Vorticists Wyndham Lewis and Wadsworth as well as Epstein were among those who left the group. Gore and Gaudier-Brzeska died during the war and Gilman soon afterwards. With the acceptance of Roger Fry into the group in 1917, followed in 1919 by Vanessa Bell and Duncan Grant (who was also listed as a founder-member), the Bloomsbury Group became the most influential circle within the group. Other artists, including Frank Dobson, Mark Gertler and Matthew Smith, were also important figures in the 1920s. In 1928 a retrospective of the first 15 years of the group's existence was held at the New Burlington Galleries in London.

In 1930 Henry Moore, Barbara Hepworth, Maurice Lambert (1901–64) and John Skeaping (1901–80) became members of the group, so introducing a strong faction of progressive sculptors. The participation of Moore and Hepworth was short-lived, however, as they found the group too eclectic; other avant-garde artists of the time, notably Ben Nicholson, remained outside altogether. In the later 1930s the London Group was an important forum for the Euston Road School. The London Group was at its most vital from the 1910s to the 1930s, after which its position as a significant force in British art began to decline.

### BIBLIOGRAPHY

G. S. Whittet: 'Groups and Guerrillas: London Commentary', *The Studio*, clxviii (Sept 1964), no. 857, pp. 134–5

*London Group: 1914–64 Jubilee Exhibition: Fifty Years of British Art at the Tate Gallery* (exh. cat. by A. Forge, A. Bowness and D. Farr, London, Tate, 1964)

S. Watney: *English Post-Impressionism* (London, 1980), pp. 109–17

C. Harrison: *English Art and Modernism 1900–1939* (London and Bloomington, 1981)

**London Miscellany.** Volume of a large selection of texts, from the Hebrew Bible to 13th-century Jewish writings, copied from *c.* 1280 to 1290, the first part of which was lavishly illuminated in the late 13th century; some miniatures were added to the end in the second decade of the 14th century (London, BL, MS. Add. 11639). Although of modest size (binding 170×130×85 mm), it contains an enormous variety of texts, 55 copied in the justification of the leaves and 29 copied in the margins, and a veritable treasury of images. The leaves, of very fine parchment, are numbered to 746, but there are in fact 749: 5–739 from the 13th century, 740–45 from the 14th century and folios 739A and 744–6 added in the 15th.

The Miscellany contains a complete set of the Books of the Bible except for Chronicles (although Prophets is represented only by the readings of the annual cycle), including even the Books of Judith and Tobit from the Apocrypha, a very unusual feature. It also has the prayers and hymns for all the festivals together with their Bible readings, the HAGGADAH (Passover ritual), blessings for marriage, burial and every other occasion of note, the 613 *mitzvot* (commandments), a code of religious law (the recently completed (1277–8) *Sefer Mitzvot Katan* by Isaac of Corbeil (*d* 1280)), the rules of *shehitah* (ritual slaughter), the formulae for deeds and Jewish laws, collections of rabbinical judgements, the *tiqqun soferim* (rules for copying the Torah), treatises on vocalization and accents, calendars, commentaries on the hymns, the lists of rabbis from the Talmud, *gematriot* (hermeneutical rules applicable to the Bible, based on numerical values of letters) and religious and secular poems. Other inclusions, unrelated to the original contents but valuable for their historical significance, are loan certificates, deeds of sale and death certificates.

The script of the main text and almost all the marginal texts is of high quality and very consistent, and may be attributed to a single copyist, about whom only his first name, Benjamin, is known; this manuscript is his only extant work. It appears that he lived in Paris, a pupil of Yehiel of Paris, at the latest in the years before 1260, when Yehiel left for Palestine. A religious elegy signed with Benjamin's name suggests that he was a poet. The contents of the volume show him to have been well versed in the Law and the ritual, while, nevertheless, not shunning secular poetry. Since he has not mentioned any patron in his colophons, it seems likely that Benjamin created this little portable library (begun *c.* 1280) for his own use and had the book decorated on his own initiative. The he had himself some aesthetic inclination is emphasised by the way he laid out one of the texts, the *tiqqun soferim*, in decorative patterns, first as a crenelated line framing the main text, then, near its end, in labyrinths (fol. 143*r* and 158*v*) and in concentric lines between the four spokes, shaped as human legs (fol. 159*r*), of a wheel. But obviously professional, and most likely Christian, illuminators, among the best in the trade in Parisian workshops, were commissioned for the painted decoration, mostly of initial words, as was also the case for the added full-page illustrations.

A striking feature of the book is the way the copying and decorating were carried out alternately; only a small number of the marginal texts was copied when three successive series of ornaments were inserted in the pages, at times overflowing the margins, so that the remaining marginal texts had to stop at or go round the decorations, in their turn putting a restraint on the following series of ornaments. Moreover the various series do not simply follow each other, but are imbricated one within the other. This complex interplay between text and decoration was concluded when the latter was abandoned, after the fol. 452. Nevertheless the codex is enriched with some 736 decorations, probably completed *c.* 1290, in the text. Besides a handful of minute illustrations (e.g. for the Haggadah) executed at the same time as one of the first series of decorations, the codex comprises an impressive

*London Miscellany*, from miniature of the *Judgement of Soloman*, 168×122mm, Paris, 14th century (London, British Library, MS. Add. 11639 fol. 518*r*)

set of 40 full-page biblical illustrations (see fig.) that appear to have been created independently of the process of copying and decorating. Of various hands and periods, they have been executed in three phases, the first (19 images) not later than 1290, the second (15 images) before the end of the 13th century and the third (6 images) between 1317 and 1322. These series of full-page miniatures are also imbricated one in the other, as the meaning of the original, mostly narrative, cycle was enriched by more complex and far-reaching meanings, giving visual dimension to the particular plight and hopes of the Jews of those times. The richness and beauty of its decoration and particularly the very high quality of the full-page miniatures of the last decade of the 13th century and the mystery of their patronship, the Christian and Parisian artists' participation and the Jewish purpose of the whole, make the London Miscellany a very rare monument to the art of illumination.

*See also* JEWISH ART, §V, 1.

BIBLIOGRAPHY

J. Leveen: *The Bible in Art* (London, 1944), pp. 72–84, pls xxv–xxviii
M. Metzger: 'Les Illustrations bibliques d'un manuscrit hébreu du nord de la France (1278–1340 environ)', *Mélanges offerts à René Crozet* (Poitiers, 1966), ii, pp. 1237–53
B. Narkiss: *Hebrew Illuminated Manuscripts* (Jerusalem, 1969, 3/1978; Hebr. trans. rev. and enlarged, 1984), pp. 28, 86 and pl. 23
Z. Ameisenowa: 'Die hebräische Sammelhandschrift Add. 11639 des British Museum', *Wien. Jb. Kstgesch.*, xxiv (1971), pp. 10–48
M. Metzger: *La Haggada enluminée* (Leyde, 1973), i, p. 139, n. 2; p. 231, n. 2, 5, 8
J. Gutmann: *Hebrew Manuscript Painting* (New York, 1978), pp. 78–81
T. Metzger and M. Metzger: *La Vie juive au moyen âge, illustrée par les manuscrits hébraïques enluminés du XIIIe au XVIe siècle* (Fribourg and Paris, 1982), chaps i, iii, iv and vi, p. 307, no. 90 [23 figs]
G. Sed-Rajna: 'The Paintings of the London Miscellany, British Library, Add. Ms. 11639', *J. Jew. A.*, ix (1982), pp. 18–30
W. C. Jordan: 'A Jewish Atelier for Illuminated Hebrew Manuscripts at Amiens?', *Wien. Jb. Kstgesch.*, xxxvii (1984), pp. 155–6
T. Metzger and M. Metzger: 'Les Enluminures du Ms. Add. 11639 de la British Library, un manuscrit hébreu du nord de la France (fin du XIIIe siècle–premier quart du XIVe siècle)', *Wien. Jb. Kstgesch.*, xxxviii (1985), pp. 59–113, 281–90
——: 'A propos de la date du décès de Yehiel de Paris et de la copie du Ms. Add. 11639 de la British Library', *Wien. Jb. Kstgesch.*, xxxix (1986), p. 221
C. Sirat: 'Le Plus beau manuscipt écrit en France', *Mise en page et mise en texte du livre manuscrit*, ed. H.-J. Martin and J. Vezin, preface J. Monfrin ([Paris], 1990), pp. 101–104 [on London, BL, MS. Add 11639]

THÉRÈSE METZGER, MENDEL METZGER

**Long.** English family. (1) Charles Long was a collector; his wife, (2) Amelia Long, was a noted watercolourist.

**(1) Charles Long**, 1st Baron Farnborough (*b* 1760; *d* Bromley Hill, Kent, 17 Jan 1838). Politician and collector. He was appointed Secretary of State for Ireland (1806) and Paymaster General (1810) and was created Baron Farnborough on his retirement from politics in 1826. As a connoisseur he favoured established masters. In 1798 he was a purchaser from the Orléans collection, and in 1799 he displayed in his house in Lincoln's Inn Fields, London, the two paintings by Claude from the Palazzo Altieri, Rome (now in Anglesey Abbey, Cambs, NT), after their arrival in England and before their purchase by William Beckford. In 1806 he was an organizer of the first exhibition of the British Institution, London, of which he became Deputy President. As a lender to the exhibitions of 1815 and 1816, he shared with Sir George Beaumont the criticisms levelled at connoisseurs by artists of the Royal Academy, London. He acted as adviser to George IV, encouraging the King in his own fondness for Dutch and Flemish pictures, and assisted in the decoration of the royal palaces. He was a trustee of the British Museum, London, from 1812 and as an early proponent of a separate national gallery was instrumental in the purchase of John Julius Angerstein's pictures in 1823 and the presentation of Sir George Beaumont's collection. In 1824 he was nominated a member of the committee to superintend the gallery and, as a trustee, set out its purchasing policy as being to 'obtain the best works of any considerable master', naming especially Raphael, Correggio and Titian. In 1827 he gave the National Gallery Gainsborough's *Watering Place* (exh. R.A. 1777) and on his death bequeathed pictures by Canaletto, Rubens, Gaspard Dughet, Willem van de Velde the younger and Nicolaes Maes.

*DNB*

BIBLIOGRAPHY

G. F. Waagen: *Treasures of Art in Great Britain*, i (London, 1854)

DAVID BLAYNEY BROWN

**(2) Amelia Long** [née Hume], Lady Farnborough (*b* London, 29 Jan 1772; *d* Bromley Hill, Kent, 15 Jan 1837). Watercolourist and garden designer, wife of (1) Charles Long. The daughter of Sir ABRAHAM HUME, she completed her formal classical education with a visit to Italy, before marrying in 1793. The couple acquired Bromley Hill Place in Kent, and Amelia designed the celebrated Italianate grounds that subsequently became the main source for her sketches in watercolour, pencil, charcoal with chalk and soft-ground etching of *Views of Bromley Hill* (1805; London, BM). She was reputed to be the favourite pupil of Thomas Girtin, and her early work is distinguished by a broad topographical style. Her *View of St Paul's from the Thames* (1805; Edinburgh, N.G.) is one of several accomplished copies after Girtin. In her later work she concentrated on the picturesque elements of architecture, natural foliage and country scenery under the influence of Henry Edridge and Dr Thomas Monro. Apart from three trips to France and Holland between 1815 and 1819, surviving sketchbooks (London, V&A, and Perth, Tayside, Mus. & A.G.) indicate that her travels were mostly concentrated in the south of England. She produced only a small number of oil paintings, including *Tour de Fête at St Cloud with the British Troops on Duty* (1815; Anglesey Abbey, Cambs, NT) and *Landscape with an Old Woman* (*c.* 1817; London, V&A), which is reminiscent of Corot. She was respected by professional artists, and she gained honorary status at the Royal Academy (1807–22) and the British Institution (1825).

BIBLIOGRAPHY
*Amelia Long, Lady Farnborough, 1772–1837* (exh. cat., ed. T. Sidey; Dundee, McManus Gals, 1979)

TESSA SIDEY

**Long, Edwin (Longsden)** (*b* Bath, 12 July 1829; *d* Hampstead, London, 15 May 1891). English painter. He was taught by John 'Spanish' Phillip and began his career painting portraits and Spanish subjects, such as *Dialogus diversus* (1873; priv. col., see Quick, p. 10). However, he became successful and rich with very large historical and biblical subjects such as the *Babylonian Marriage Market* (1875; Egham, U. London, Royal Holloway & Bedford New Coll.), which changed hands in his lifetime for immense sums. His choice of subject-matter was indebted to the example of Sir Lawrence Alma-Tadema, while his style closely resembles that of Edward Armitage. His success enabled him to commission two houses (1878 and 1887), both in Hampstead, from Richard Norman Shaw. He was elected ARA in 1876 and RA in 1881. The largest collection of his work is in the Russell-Cotes Art Gallery, Bournemouth.

BIBLIOGRAPHY
R. Quick: *The Life and Works of Edwin Long, RA* (Bournemouth, 1931, rev. 2/1970)
J. Chapel: *Victorian Taste* (London, 1982), pp. 107–9

ROBIN SIMON

**Long, Richard** (*b* Bristol, 2 June 1945). English sculptor, photographer and painter. He studied at West of England College of Art in Bristol (1962–5) and from 1966 to 1968 at St Martin's School of Art, London, where his fellow students included other artists who were redefining the terms of sculpture in England, among them Hamish Fulton, Jan Dibbets, Gilbert and George and John Hilliard. Within a year of his departure from St Martin's, Long was closely associated with the emergence of a new art form, LAND ART, having already produced such works as *A Line Made by Walking* (1967; London, Tate), a photograph of the trail left in the grass by walking back and forth in a straight line; another work, *England* (1968; London, Tate), consists of an X shape made by cutting off the heads of flowers in a field, again presented in the form of a photograph.

Long made his international reputation during the 1970s with sculptures made as the result of epic walks, sometimes

Richard Long: *Slate Circle*, 214 pieces of slate, diam. *c.* 6.6 m, 1979 (London, Tate Gallery)

lasting many days, to remote parts of the world, including desert regions of Africa as well as Australia, Canada, Japan, Switzerland and Norway. Guided by a great respect for nature and by the formal structure of basic shapes, especially circles, he never allowed facile exotic connotations to intrude into his work, although some of his sculptures evoked the mysterious connotations of ancient stone circles and other such monuments. Different modes of presentation, sometimes combined, were used to bring his experience of nature back into the museum or gallery. These included, above all, photographs documenting the sculptures left behind in their original setting, such as *A Somerset Beach, England* (1968), made by shifting stones, or *Walking a Line in Peru* (1972), composed of crushed grass; works combining photographs, maps and emblematic drawings recording a particular journey (e.g. *Cerne Abbas Walk*, 1975; London, Tate); works consisting simply of handwritten or printed texts as fragments of an experience of nature; and installations, often in the form of lines, circles or spirals, made from materials gathered together in specific environments (such as wood, mud, slate and other kinds of stone), as in *River Avon Driftwood* (1976; London, Tate) and *Slate Circle* (1979; London, Tate; see fig.). From 1981 he also alluded to the terms of painting by applying mud in a very liquid state by hand to a wall in similar configurations, establishing a dialogue between the primal gesture of the hand-print and the formal elegance of its display. He stressed that the meaning of his work lay in the visibility of his actions rather than in the representation of a particular landscape.

Like other land artists, Long broke with traditional sculptural methods both by conceiving his works outside of the studio, in nature itself, and by rejecting the fetishization of the object through his use of photography, which was still questioned as an artistic medium, and large installations, which were difficult to exploit as commercial commodities. Long distinguished himself from American land artists by the lightness of his interventions on the ground; he saw this both as an ethical principle, in refusing to despoil or exploit the landscape, and as an aesthetic one. Although critics frequently emphasized the continuity between his practice and the English landscape tradition, his work helped establish a new conception of sculpture. It points up the most elementary relations between people and their environment: thus, in order to re-establish and experience again the raw reality of nature, he would trace on a map the geometric figure of his proposed journey over the land, without sparing himself difficulties by taking existing roads. The idea of the walk itself related to certain traditional notions about sculpture, such as stability or the relation to the ground, but with an emphasis on horizontality rather than on the verticality of traditional statuary; the spectator, moreover, is confronted not with the artist's experience itself but with the indirect evidence of it. Long represented Great Britain at the Venice Biennale in 1976 and was the recipient of the Turner Prize, awarded by the Tate Gallery in London, in 1989.

### WRITINGS

*Five, Six, Pick Up Sticks* (exh. cat., London, Anthony d'Offay Gal., 1980)
*Richard Long: In Conversation: Bristol 19.11.1985* (Noordwijk, n.d.) [transcription of tape recordings with M. Giezen]

### BIBLIOGRAPHY

*Richard Long* (exh. cat., Bordeaux, Cent. A. Plast. Contemp., 1981)
*Richard Long* (exh. cat. by A. Wildemuth, Basle, Gal. Buchmann, 1985)
R. Fuchs: *Richard Long* (London, 1986)
*Piedras: Richard Long* (exh. cat. by A. Seymour, Madrid, Pal. Cristal, 1986)
*Richard Long* (exh. cat., St Gall, Kstver., 1989)

VANINA COSTA

**Long, Robert Cary**, jr (*b* Baltimore, MD, *c.* 1810; *d* New York, 9 May 1849). American architect and writer. He was the son of the Baltimore architect Robert Cary Long sr (1770–1833), who designed the Baltimore Museum and Gallery of the Fine Arts (1814; now Peale Museum) and other Greek Revival buildings in and around Baltimore. Long jr went to New York in 1826 for further architectural training with Martin E. Thompson (1787–1877). In 1833 he returned to Baltimore and set up his own practice, which he relocated to New York in 1848. A romantic architect influenced by Ithiel Town, Alexander Jackson Davis and William Strickland, Long was eclectic in his choice of style. His State Institution for the Deaf, Dumb and Blind (1839–44), Staunton, VA, is Grecian in style. For the Greenmount Cemetery, Baltimore, he proposed an Egyptian gateway in 1838, later changed to a Gothic Revival design and built in 1840. He specialized in designing churches, some severely Grecian and others Gothic. Among his classical designs the best is perhaps the Roman Catholic church of St Peter the Apostle (1843–4), Poppleton Street, Baltimore. His most elaborate Gothic Revival design, also Roman Catholic, was St Alphonsus (1842–*c.* 1844), Baltimore. Long was an active writer and lecturer, and on his move to New York contributed regularly to *The Literary World* (1848–9), including a series of articles entitled 'Architectonics'.

### WRITINGS

'On the Development of the Semi-Arch with the Future Advancement of Architectural Art', *Civ. Engin. & Architect's J.*, v (1842), pp. 370–72
'On the Alleged Degeneracy of Modern Architecture', *J. Franklin Inst.*, n. s. 2, ii (1843), pp. 346–9
'Gothic Architecture—New Church', *US Cath. Mag.*, ii/5 (1843), pp. 297–304
*The Ancient Architecture of America* (New York, 1849)

### BIBLIOGRAPHY

*Macmillan Enc. Architects*
T. B. Ghequiere: 'The Messrs. Long, Architects', *Amer. Architect & Bldg News*, i (1876), p. 207
R. H. Howland and E. Spencer: *The Architecture of Baltimore* (Baltimore, 1953)
W. H. Hunter: 'Robert Cary Long, jr., and the Battle of the Styles', *J. Soc. Archit. Hist.*, xvi (1957), pp. 28–30
P. B. Stanton: *The Gothic Revival and American Church Architecture* (Baltimore, 1968)

LELAND M. ROTH

**Long, Sydney** [Sid] (*b* Goulburn, NSW, 20 Aug 1871; *d* London, 25 Jan 1955). Australian painter and printmaker. In the early 1890s, while studying art part-time at the Art Society of New South Wales at Sydney, he attracted the attention of Julian Rossi Ashton, then head teacher. In 1894 his first major painting, *By Tranquil Waters* (1894), a river-bathing scene in a self-conscious Impressionist style, was purchased by the National Art Gallery of New South Wales. In the next 15 years he painted increasingly decorative works, emphasizing the flatness of the pictureplane and adopting a narrow tonal range of moody blues and grey–greens. In his subject-matter he tried to create a specifically Australian myth. His most important painting, *Spirit of the Plains* (1897; Brisbane, Queensland A.G.), shows a female bush spirit leading her brolgas in a dance. His favourite painting, *Pan* (1898; Sydney, A.G. NSW), transposes European mythology to an Australian setting of rhythmically decorative gum trees. His distinctive use of decorative vegetation remained the principal characteristic of his style.

Despite his at times strident nationalism, Long yearned for international fame and in September 1910 left for England. Although he visited Bruges and Paris, he spent most of the years from 1910 to 1921 in London, where he enrolled at the Kennington Art School and the City Guild Art School. In 1918, after hearing that fellow Australian artist Lionel Lindsay (1874–1961) had based an aquatint on one of his paintings, Long turned to printmaking, studying at the Central School of Arts and Crafts. He falsified the dates of his earliest prints, however, so that they would appear to pre-date Lindsay's. Although he tried to emulate the British academic etchers of his generation and made many landscape etchings and drypoints in their crisp style, his most successful prints were aquatint reinterpretations of *Pan* (see Mendelssohn, p. 128) and *Spirit of the Plains* (see Mendelssohn, p. 142).

In 1920 Long was elected ARE and in 1921 returned to Sydney, where he attempted to use his newly established status in claiming to be Australia's most important printmaker. In 1925 he settled in Sydney, where he taught etching in his studio and painted gently lyrical landscapes of the suburban countryside. His later years were characterized by a bitterness towards more successful Australian artists and an unrelenting hostility to modern art. In 1952 he realized that his health was failing and returned to London.

BIBLIOGRAPHY

D. Paul: *The Etched Work of Sydney Long* (Sydney, 1928)
*Sydney Long Memorial Exhibition* (exh. cat., Sydney, N.A.G. NSW, 1955)
J. Mendelssohn: *The Life and Work of Sydney Long* (Sydney, 1979)

JOANNA MENDELSSOHN

**Longhena, Baldassare** (*b* Venice, 1596; *d* Venice, 17 Feb 1682). Italian architect. He was by far the most important native architect of the city of Venice and one of the principal masters of Italian High Baroque classicism, the stylistic pre-eminence of which he helped to assure. Longhena is also important as one of the first fully professional architects of modern times to devote himself exclusively to building. His pioneering of modern workshop practice in part paralleled that of Francesco Borromini, especially because he used the newer medium of pencil for his designs, while retaining traditional pen and ink for presentation drawings. He was the principal state architect in Venice for 45 years, a prestigious role that helped bring him a constant stream of private commissions. An officer of his professional association (the stonemasons' guild), he was in demand throughout his life for consultations and expert testimony. He was also skilled as an engineer, his grasp of statics and strength of materials so advanced that even in the difficult environment of Venice his buildings are conspicuous by their technical soundness.

1. Training and early work, to c. 1630. 2. S Maria della Salute and other works, c. 1630–c. 1648. 3. Mature works, c. 1648–c. 1660. 4. Late works, after c. 1660.

1. TRAINING AND EARLY WORK, TO c. 1630. Longhena's family came from Brescia, and his father, Melchisedech Longhena (1566–1616), was a Venetian marbleworker and importer who carried out important commissions in Venice. Longhena's earliest biographer, Tommaso Temanza, named as his teacher Vincenzo Scamozzi, a tradition that came to Temanza from the descendant of a Scamozzi patron, who had been a friend of Longhena. Longhena inherited the personal favour of Scamozzi's last patrons, the Contarini family, who commissioned Longhena's first work—a villa (1616–19; destr. 1810–28) for Pietro Contarini at Mira—immediately after Scamozzi's death. Its debt to that master was indicated in such details as isolated corner pilasters and square-headed windows forming vestigial Serlianas.

Longhena was also greatly influenced by Alessandro Vittoria and Girolamo Campagna, who transmitted to the 17th century the architectural tradition of Jacopo Sansovino, Michele Sanmicheli and Palladio. The association of Melchisedech Longhena and Vittoria is documented on at least two works: Vittoria's altars of S Saba at S Antonino and the Rosary at S Domenico, both in Venice, executed by Melchisedech respectively in 1591 and 1600. Campagna and Scamozzi had collaborated in 1601–4, so Baldassare Longhena would have known the former from an early age; Campagna's last masterwork was an enormous high altar (1615–17) as an interior screen wall at S Lorenzo, Venice, for another member of the Contarini family. An indication of Longhena's debt to Campagna is afforded by the latter's *Bragadin* monument (1615–16) for Santo Sepolcro, Venice: it was precisely reflected in Longhena's first documented work, his monument to *Archbishop Gabriele Seviros* (1619) in the nearby S Giorgio dei Greci, Venice. This commission evidently resulted from Melchisedech Longhena's collaboration with Vittoria on the altar of S Saba (jointly officiated at S Antonino by the Roman Catholic and Greek Orthodox clergy), which in turn had precipitated the elder Longhena's high altar (1604; now in the Scuola dei Greci, Venice) at S Giorgio for the same Greek community.

This circle was also responsible for Baldassare Longhena's astonishingly prominent early commission on the Grand Canal in Venice: a palace (1619–23) for an émigré branch of the Lolin family who had been friends of Seviros and patrons of Scamozzi. Known after 1624 as the Palazzo Giustinian-Lolin, this, too, in the manner of the Villa Contarini, has features that recall the work of Scamozzi. Such influences, however, were sequentially purged from the Palazzo Lolin's immediate successors in Venice: a horizontally stretched and elaborated palace project for Procurator Giovanni da Lezze and his son Senator Andrea da Lezze at the Misericordia (1623–40s); the garden façade (1626) and canal façade (1627) for the Palazzo Basadonna at S Trovaso; and, especially, the Palazzo Serotti (1627–9; after 1633 Palazzo Widmann) at S Canciano, Venice, at which for the first time appeared a Longhena motif derived through his father from Vittoria: massive scrolled brackets, here enlarged to support a dramatically extruded central balcony.

A striking instance of Longhena's revolutionary reworking of 16th-century prototypes is his superb revival of Palladian models in the magnificent cathedral of S Maria (1627–47) at Chioggia on the Venetian lagoon, a prestigious first public commission secured for him in 1624 by the nephew of Scamozzi's principal patron, the Venetian governor of Chioggia, Alvise Duodo. It helped Longhena obtain two significant tomb commissions in Venice: of *Captain Bartolomeo Orsini d'Alviano* in the church of S Stefano (1629–33), and the vast interior façade monument (1629–53) of *Procurator Paolo Parutaital, Provveditore Andrea Paruta and Counsellor Marco Paruta* in the church of the Spirito Santo.

2. S MARIA DELLA SALUTE AND OTHER WORKS, *c.* 1630–*c.* 1648. Longhena's greatest opportunity came with the Venetian Senate's decision in 1630 to offer a new church to the Queen of Heaven in thanksgiving for the state's deliverance from plague. Longhena's project was selected in 1631 by the senatorial commissioners (including the distinguished Scamozzi patron Procurator Girolamo Cornaro). The resulting domed church of S Maria della Salute (see fig. 1), built at the junction of the Giudecca and Grand canals at the focal point of the city of Venice, occupied Longhena for more than 50 years and was consecrated after his death on 9 November 1687. Its governing concept—an octagonal space surrounded by an ambulatory (*see* ITALY, fig. 19)—appeared in Italy in Early

1. Baldassare Longhena: S Maria della Salute, Venice, 1631–87

Christian and Byzantine architecture but also in the monumental sanctuary (1528–61) by Diego de Siloe for Granada Cathedral in Spain, an engraving of which was produced in 1612–14 by Francisco Heylan. Its sculptural exterior characterized by massive scrolls buttressing the dome, Longhena's Salute incorporates subtle scenographic effects and is one of the most important buildings of the early Italian Baroque (for further discussion *see* VENICE, §IV, 5).

S Maria della Salute was imitated all over Europe: Longhena himself apparently sent plans (1676–7) for its replica in the church of the Immaculate Conception (1677–98, 1718–80) at Gostyn, Poland; Carlo Fontana reintroduced its design into Spain in the church (1681–1738) of the Jesuit College at Loyola; while the great hall (begun 1752) of the Royal Palace at Caserta by Luigi Vanvitelli is perhaps the most splendid tribute to its continuing appeal.

Longhena's winning of this commission, the largest of the 17th century in Venice, soon led to his official public appointment as consultant (1634), adjutant (1638) and, finally, supervising architect (or *proto*; 1640–81) to the Procuratori di S Marco—a large office with a busy practice that brought him into daily contact with the most influential men in the Republic. His most visible commission from this body, in 1638, was the completion (1640–*c.* 1660) of the Procuratie Nuove, the first ten bays of which had been designed and built by Scamozzi and which eventually closed the south and west sides of the Piazza S Marco, connecting Jacopo Sansovino's Library of St Mark with the church of S Geminiano. Such public prominence brought new commissions, including monuments to *Doge Domenico Michiel* (1635–7) and *Pietro Civran* (1638) at Palladio's church of S Giorgio Maggiore, Venice; these were progressive derivations from Campagna's *Cicogna* monument in the Crociferi, Venice. Longhena, at that time, began to add the full sculptural elaboration that, from this first association with the sculptor Giovanni Battista Paliari (?1595–1645) for the *Michiel* monument, became a dominant feature of his work. He unveiled his own volumetric, plastically elaborated style in collaboration with the sculptor Clemente Molli (*fl* 1635–63) in the Widmann family chapel of S Massimo (1635–9) at S Canciano and the church façade of S Giustina, Venice (1633–8; altered 1638–40 to include Molli's Soranzo family monuments; high altar chapel 1639–40).

Longhena's tombs at S Giorgio Maggiore, although officially sponsored by the government, brought him into close collaboration with the Benedictine Order there. From its chapter he received several capital commissions (*see* VENICE, §IV, 2): the new monastic library (1641–53); a loggia (1640s) between the two cloisters beneath it; and the great stair (1643–5) from the first cloister to the abbatical and ducal apartments, an innovative design with an initial centre flight, intermediate landing and double-branched flights along the back and side walls of a vaulted staircase hall. The ensemble was a prototype for the Escalier des Ambassadeurs (1670s) at Versailles by Louis Le Vau.

3. MATURE WORKS, *c.* 1648–*c.* 1660. The late 1640s opened a prolific period for Longhena, beginning with one of his most beautiful and influential palaces, the

Palazzo Belloni (1648–*c*. 1655; after 1664 Palazzo Belloni-Battagia) on the Grand Canal, Venice, a commission probably due to connections with the Widmann family; its courtyard even reproduces the otherwise unique rusticated Tuscan order of Palazzo Widmann. The brilliantly syncopated rhythms of Palazzo Belloni's façade afford space between the central frontispiece and outermost windows for huge shields of arms, massive sculptural accents directly emulated from Vittoria. This splendid advertisement for High Baroque classicism in domestic palace design evidently acted as a catalyst for Longhena's two commissions on the Grand Canal that produced the Venetian paradigms of the type: Palazzo Bon (façade block 1649–62; rear block and great stair 1666–82; completed as Ca' Rezzonico, 1750–58, by Giorgio Massari); and Palazzo Pesaro (begun 1652–9; completed 1682–1710 by Antonio Gaspari). These masterworks were challenging not only by their huge size; they were also stunning demonstrations of Longhena's genius for fully three-dimensional modelling of exceptionally bold masses, their façade planes dissolved into powerful sculptural projections between almost continuous windows, with richly concatenated systems of rooms, stairs and courts of exhilarating spatial variety (for illustration of Ca' Rezzonico *see* VENICE, fig. 5).

Longhena wrote on 22 April 1649 in a letter (Vicenza, Mus. Civ. A. & Stor.) that three of his noble clients were urgently requesting his attention that week: Procurator (later Doge) Giovanni Pesaro, for his villa (1649–52; completed 1682–1710s by Gaspari) at Este; Procurator Alvise Morosini and Patriarch Gianfrancesco Morosini, for their sumptuous Palazzo dal Giardino, connecting independent Rio and Campo blocks (respectively 1644–9 and *c*. 1660–65; destr. *c*. 1840) at SS Apostoli, Venice; and Count Gian Luigi Valmarana, for a loggia (1649–54) in the Giardino Valmarana, Vicenza. Simultaneously he was working at the Venetian cathedral church, S Pietro di Castello (high altar design 1646–51; revised 1662), as well as on the Carmelite monastery of the Scalzi (1649–59), Venice. For the latter order he designed one of his most important churches, S Maria di Nazareth (1656–73) on the Grand Canal, reproducing the wide, shallow-vaulted hall, deep chancel and correspondingly arched centre nave chapels from the church of S Lazzaro dei Mendicanti, Venice, executed in 1634–8 by Tommaso Contin (*fl* 1600–38) and Francesco Contin (*fl* 1618–59), partly on the basis of models supplied in 1601 by Scamozzi. The same scheme was repeated with even greater clarity in an almost unknown work of great beauty, Longhena's church of S Maria Assunta (1658–76) at Loreo, near Chioggia, a commission secured through Marco Contarini, governor of Chioggia. The high altar at Loreo, closely reflecting Campagna's altar at S Lorenzo, supports an enormous tabernacle *alla romana*, a type that became a Longhena speciality.

Other projects by Longhena in the Veneto included the design (1655) for the brick campanile of Beata Vergine del Soccorso at Rovigo (executed by local masons, 1650s and 1769–93); and the design (1656) for the provincial prisons at Vicenza (executed 1656–64 by Antonio Pizzocaro; destr. 1886). His most celebrated regional work of this period was the magnificent Villa Lezze (1656–60;

remodelled *c*. 1687 by Gaspari; destr. 1813–25) at Rovarè (near Treviso), the plan, elevation, and rusticated columnar frontispiece of which were pioneered at the villa of Procurator Alvise Priuli (*c*. 1648–56; destr. *c*. 1820s) at Treville (near Castelfranco Veneto). These villas were direct formal prototypes for the surviving, later Villa Rezzonico at Bassano, which exactly reproduces their plan and details as well as the angle-towered silhouette of Gaspari's remodelling of Villa Lezze. Aurelio Rezzonico was a documented associate of Longhena's for two works of the mid-1670s at S Lazzaro in Venice, and thus the splendid Villa Rezzonico is most likely to have been a project begun by Longhena in 1675–82 and completed 1682–1712 by Gaspari. A similarly undocumented attribution to Longhena is the Spanish Synagogue (Scuola Spagnola; *c*. 1655–60), Venice. Details, especially of its ark, recall his altars dated to these years.

4. LATE WORKS, AFTER *c*. 1660. One of Longhena's most beautifully designed and perfectly resolved works, the Cappella Vendramin at the church of S Pietro di Castello, Venice, was probably begun *c*. 1658 as the frame for an extensive cycle of figural sculptures (*c*. 1662–7) by Michael Fabris Ongaro (1644–84). The rich but controlled colours of variegated marbles in the main space are set off by white stucco vaults and the brilliantly lit altar (see fig. 2), providing a dramatic scenographic focus for its painting of the *Madonna delle Grazie* (1667) by Luca Giordano. The effect is of a festive but restrained *Gesamtkunstwerk*, an exuberant shaping of architectonic space by sculptural and even painterly means. Longhena's Morosini altar (1641–54) and high altar for the same church became similar frameworks for figural sculpture.

2. Baldassare Longhena: Cappella Vendramin, S Pietro di Castello, Venice, *c*. 1658–62

On these Longhena worked with Clemente Molli, Francesco Cavrioli ( *fl* 1632–66), Melchior Barthel, Bernardo Falcone and Claude Perreau ( *fl c.* 1640s–*c.* 1660s), all under the collaborative supervision of Josse de Corte.

The best known of Longhena's sculptural extravaganzas is his vast monument (1659–69) to *Doge Giovanni Pesaro* in S Maria Gloriosa dei Frari, Venice. The size of a considerable church façade, its lower storey presents bronze skeletons holding inscriptions between colossal, naturalistically draped, black and white marble Moors supporting a heavy entablature; the huge upper storey is a trabeated triumphal arch in black marble, with the Doge enthroned in life above his casket, borne by dragons and surrounded with allegorical figures and groups by Josse de Corte's standard sculptural team. An exactly analogous exterior façade was erected immediately afterwards in the course of Longhena's extensive work at the Ospedaletto of S Maria dei Derelitti, Venice (conventual buildings 1667–78; church 1670–78; façade 1670–72, with telamon figures by de Corte). Longhena's nearby work for the Ospedale di S Lazzaro (second cloister *c.* 1656; stair to oratory 1658), and the monastery of S Domenico, attached to the church of SS Giovanni e Paolo, produced a conspicuously less extroverted catalogue: a tabernacle *alla romana* (*c.* 1659–63) for the high altar of the church; a modestly decorated double-ramp stair (1664–6), prefiguring those at Palazzo Bon and the Somaschian Priory of the 1670s; an altar and monumental door casings (1666–74) for the access halls of the dormitories; and a richly panelled library (1674–81; woodwork by Giacomo Piazzetta). These soberly professional works are paralleled by a fine but quiet canal façade for Palazzo Zane (1665–77) at S Agostin, Venice, and by the chaste but majestic monument to *Procurator Lorenzo Venier* (1667) in S Giorgio Maggiore.

Longhena's more exuberant late style characterizes his temporary catafalque (1669; engraved by Antonio Bosio) for the state funeral at S Marco, Venice, of François de Beaufort, Duc de Vendôme. Its vigorous telamonic and allegorical figures on two tall octagonal registers, crowned by a dome bearing a celestial visitant, were all precisely replicated in stone on his and de Corte's colossal high altar tabernacle for S Nicolò da Tolentino, Venice (contract 1661; executed 1670–72). The two lower zones of the latter are repeated almost identically on the high altar (1670) of S Maria della Salute, also with a sculptural tableau by de Corte. These free-standing examples developed from Longhena's wall altars of the Crucifixion (1658–64; destr.) in S Ternità, Venice, and S Maria del Carmine (1669–70) at S Francesco, Zadar—the latter exactly copying his high altar (1662–3; destr.) for S Daniele, Venice. A splendidly pictorial variant is Longhena's and de Corte's triumphal monument to *Captain Cattarino Cornaro* (1672–4) in S Antonio, Padua. Its thorough documentation permits a confident ascription to Longhena of the similar compositions in the Morosini chapel (1676–8) at S Clemente in Isola, Venice, as well as the Crucifixion altar (1676–80) for the Cappella del Capitolo in the same church.

A calm, balanced classicism suffuses Longhena's valedictory façade (1671–8) for his church of S Basso on the Piazza S Marco, Venice: its monumentalized Palladian order purifies and ennobles the model of his S Giustina façade of 40 years earlier. His most appealing late projects, the Collegio Flangini (1678–82) and Scuola di S Nicolò (1678–88), picturesquely composed in the churchyard of S Giorgio dei Greci, Venice, where his metropolitan career had begun, were executed by Alessandro Tremignon. His last years were devoted to a resumption of his father's maritime trade in Istrian stone and modest public enterprises in Venice: a series of rental houses (*c.* 1680) at S Fantin and a design (1681–2) for the pious institution of the Ospizio delle Muneghette. His last dated project (26 August 1681) arranged for one of the finishing touches to his life's work: the paving of the campo and water steps at S Maria della Salute, Venice. Longhena's principal follower, Antonio Gaspari, completed his outstanding works in a style imaginatively combining Venetian classicism with the spatial and decorative elaboration of the Roman Baroque.

## BIBLIOGRAPHY

*Macmillan Enc. Architects*: 'Gaspari, Antonio'

T. Temanza: *Zibaldon de' memorie storiche* (1738–78); ed. N. Ivanoff (Venice, 1963), pp. 33–7

C. Semenzato: *L'architettura di Baldassare Longhena* (diss., U. Padua, 1954)

E. Bassi: *L'architettura del sei e settecento a Venezia* (Naples, 1962), pp. 83–183

G. Cristinelli: *Baldassare Longhena* (Padua, 1972, 2/1978); review by D. Lewis in *A. Ven.*, xxvii (1973), pp. 328–30

D. Lewis: 'Una decina di documenti del Longhena', *A. Ven.*, xxvii (1973), pp. 309–17

R. Wittkower: 'S Maria della Salute: Scenographic Architecture and the Venetian Baroque', *Studies in the Italian Baroque* (London, 1975), pp. 125–52

S. Mason Rinaldi: 'Il libro dei conti della famiglia Tiepolo per la cappella di S Saba in S Antonin', *Atti Ist. Ven. Sci. Lett. & A.*, cxxxv (1976–7), pp. 194–212

G. Vio: 'I "mistri" della chiesa di S Fantin in Venezia', *A. Ven.*, xxxi (1977), pp. 225–31

D. Howard: *The Architectural History of Venice* (London, 1981)

G. Vio: 'L'altare di S Lorenzo Giustiniani in S Pietro di Castello', *A. Ven.*, xxxv (1981), pp. 209–17

*Longhena* (exh. cat., ed. O. Selvafolta; Lugano, Villa Malpensata, 1982) [cat. entries by S. Biadene]

L. Puppi: 'Nuovi documenti sul Longhena', *Not. Pal. Albani*, xii (1983), pp. 181–8

——: 'La vera origine della famiglia Longhena e Melchisedec "tagliapiera"', *Studi in onore di Gino Barbieri*, iii (Pisa, 1983), pp. 1269–89

——: 'Le case, e il testamento, di Baldassare Longhena', *Interpretazioni veneziane: Studi di storia dell'arte in onore di Michelangelo Muraro* (Venice, 1984), pp. 387–91

C. H. Krinsky: *Synagogues of Europe* (Cambridge, MA, 1985), pp. 381–6

F. Nacamulli: 'Michael Fabris Ongaro', *A. Ven.*, xxxix (1985), pp. 87–100

G. Vio: 'Nella cerchia dei Longhena', *A. Ven.*, xl (1986), pp. 225–9

L. Puppi: 'Pietre di Venezia perdute', *Opere d'arte di Venezia in Friuli*, ed. G. Ganzer (Udine, 1987), pp. 37–53

P. Rossi: 'L'altare di Francesco Morosini di S Pietro di Castello', *A. Ven.*, xlii (1988), pp. 163–9

F. Magani: 'Il collezionismo e la committenza artistica della famiglia Widmann', *Mem. Ist. Ven. Sci. Lett. & A.*, xli/3 (1989), pp. 7–119

P. Rossi: 'Appunti sull'attività veneziana di Clemente Molli', *Venezia A.*, iii (1989), pp. 61–8

R. Pellegriti: 'La chiesa dell'ospedale di S Lazzaro dei Mendicanti', *A. Ven.*, xliii (1989–90), pp. 152–65

M. Frank: 'Baldassare Longhena e il palazzo Basadonna a S Trovaso', *Annali di architettura: Rivista del centro internazionale di studi di architettura Andrea Palladio*, ii (1990), pp. 121–5

P. Rossi: 'I "marmi loquaci" del monumento Pesaro ai Frari', *Venezia A.*, iv (1990), pp. 84–93

——: 'Bernardo Falcone collaboratore del Longhena negli altari dei SS Giovanni e Paolo e di S Pietro in Castello', *Studi in onore di Elena Bassi* (Venice, 1991)

D. Lewis: *Longhena and his Patrons: The Creation of the Venetian Baroque* (in preparation)

DOUGLAS LEWIS

**Longhi** [Lunghi] **(i).** Italian family of painters. They flourished during the 16th century and the early 17th. The Mannerist painter (1) Luca Longhi, who produced mainly religious paintings and portraits, trained two of his children, (2) Francesco Longhi and (3) Barbara Longhi. They collaborated with him on several of his later works, including the *Marriage of Cana* (1579–80; Ravenna, Bib. Com. Classense), which incorporates portraits of Barbara and Francesco Longhi.

**(1) Luca Longhi** (*b* Ravenna, 10 Jan 1507; *d* Ravenna, 12 Aug 1580). His earliest works, such as the *Marriage of St Catherine* (1529–32; Ravenna, Pin. Com.), show the influence of Baldassare Carrari ( *fl* 1489–1516), Francesco Zaganelli and Niccolò Rondinelli, but he also learnt from the works of mainstream painters, in particular Giorgio Vasari, as is evident in his *Circumcision* (1561; ex-S Benedetto, Ferrara; Ferrara, Pin. N.), in which he introduced portraits of Dante Alighieri, Michelangelo and Titian among the spectators. Vasari claimed that Luca Longhi never left Ravenna, and this isolation no doubt contributed to his limitations. However, he was a skilled portrait painter, his subjects being local dignitaries, patricians and professional men, such as *Girolamo Rossi, Raffaele Rasponi* and *Giovanni Arrigoni* (all 1567; all Ravenna, Accad. B.A.).

BIBLIOGRAPHY
G. Vasari: *Vite* (1550; rev. 2/1568); ed. G. Milanesi, vii (1881), p. 420
A. Pigler: 'Zur Bildniskunst von Luca Longhi', *Pantheon*, xv (1935), pp. 120–24
*Luca Longhi e la pittura su tavola in Romagna nel cinquecento* (exh. cat., ed. J. Bentini; Ravenna, Loggetta Lombard., 1982), pp. 13–78

**(2) Francesco Longhi** (*b* Ravenna, 10 Feb 1544; *d* Ravenna, 1618). Son of (1) Luca Longhi. He received his early training in his father's workshop and was influenced by the works of Giorgio Vasari and Marcello Venusti; elements from their paintings can be seen in the figure of Christ in his *Crucifixion with the Virgin and SS John, Apollinare and Vitale* (Ravenna, Pin. Com.). He also looked to the works of Federico Zuccaro, Correggio and, above all, Gian Francesco Modigliani ( *fl* 1598–?1609). Like his father, Francesco Longhi executed mainly altarpieces for local churches (1586, 1604, Ravenna, S Giovanni Battista; 1605, Ravenna, S Maria in Porto).

BIBLIOGRAPHY
*Luca Longhi e la pittura su tavola in Romagna nel cinquecento* (exh. cat., ed. J. Bentini; Ravenna, Loggetta Lombard., 1982), pp. 169–77

**(3) Barbara Longhi** (*b* Ravenna, 1552; *d c.* 1638). Daughter of (1) Luca Longhi. She assisted her father with large altarpieces and copied many of his works. Her own work often resembles his but is on a smaller scale. She was also indebted to contemporary Florentine and Bolognese painters. Of her 15 known works (Cheney), 12 are small *Virgin and Child* compositions, which Vasari praised for their 'purity of line and soft brilliance of colour' (Vasari, 1568; Cheney, p. 16). Her early works are simple compositions, using a limited palette and emphasizing linearity over modelling. *St Catherine of Alexandria* (1589; Ravenna, Pin. Com.) was painted for the monastery of Classe in Ravenna and is probably a self-portrait of the artist. After 1590 Longhi's colour became more brilliant, and her figures attained a certain monumentality. She also began to employ the device of a curtain draped around a column (taken from such painters as Correggio and Parmigianino) and of an area opening out onto a landscape or sky in the background of her compositions, as in *Virgin and Child with St John the Baptist* (*c.* 1595–1600; Dresden, Gemäldegal. Alte Meister). The *sfumato* technique and the pyramidal composition are reminiscent of Leonardo and of Raphael's Florentine works (1506–8). After 1600 she seems to have abandoned full-figure compositions in architectural settings in preference for simple pious images. The *Virgin with Sleeping Child* (*c.* 1600–05; Baltimore, MD, Walters A.G.), one of her most devotional paintings, avoids narrative or Mannerist pictorial riddles and concentrates on the viewer's intimate relation to the figures depicted. As with most of her work, it reflects the intense religious ideals of the Counter-Reformation.

BIBLIOGRAPHY
L. D. Cheney: 'Barbara Longhi of Ravenna', *Woman's A.J.*, ix (1988), pp. 16–20

**Longhi** [Longo; Lunghi; Lungo] **(ii).** Italian family of architects and masons. They were originally from Viggiù on the Lombard–Swiss border, but the three most prominent members of the family, the architects (1) Martino Longhi I, (2) Onorio Longhi and (3) Martino Longhi II, were active in Rome from the late 16th century until the first half of the 17th. Their careers reflect the changes that took place in Italian architecture from the period of the late Renaissance to the High Baroque.

BIBLIOGRAPHY
*I. Longhi: Una famiglia di architetti tra manierismo e barocco* (exh. cat., ed. L. Patetta; Viggiù, Mus. Enrico Butti; Rome, Accad. N. S Luca, 1980)
*La Roma dei Longhi: Papi e architetti tra manierismo e barocco* (exh. cat., ed. M. Fagiolo dell'Arco; Rome, Accad. N. S Luca, 1982)

**(1) Martino Longhi I** [the elder] (*b* Viggiù, *c.* 1534; *d* Rome, *c.* 1591). He seems to have begun his career in the masonry trade in Viggiù. The first records of his architectural activity date from 1562–7, when he was involved in the planning of Schloss Hohenems, near Bregenz, for the family of Cardinal Marcus Sitticus Altemps, and of Santa Croce (1566–72), Bosco Marengo, which was commissioned directly by Pope Pius V for his home town. Influenced no doubt by his Austrian patron, as well as by his contacts with the architect Jacopo Vignola, Longhi settled in Rome *c.* 1569 and remained there for the rest of his life.

Longhi's first Roman commission of consequence was the Villa Mondragone in FRASCATI, begun in 1573 for Cardinal Altemps. Longhi's design of the villa and Altemps's close friendship with the newly elected Pope Gregory XIII led to his appointment as papal architect. In this capacity he oversaw the expansion (1575) of the Cortile di S Damaso in the Vatican Palace and remodelled part of the Baths of Diocletian in order to turn it into a granary (plans, Rome, Accad. N. S Luca). His career continued to flourish even after he was replaced as papal architect by Ottaviano Mascherino in 1577. Longhi built the handsome two-tiered bell-tower (1578) on the Palazzo

Senatorio and was soon actively involved in the construction of the Palazzo Cesi (now Palazzo Mellini; plans, Rome, Accad. N. S Luca, MS. 2401; rebuilt mid-19th century), the Palazzo Altemps and the Palazzo Deza (now Palazzo Borghese). The latter, situated near the Tiber, brought Longhi his greatest fame. He was responsible for the wing facing the Via di Monte d'Oro, which is the longest palazzo elevation in Rome and is clearly divided into three storeys, with three deep mezzanine levels. Its relative decorative plainness is compensated for by its impressive scale. He was probably also responsible for the courtyard, which was later completed by Flaminio Ponzio. As a designer of churches, Longhi remodelled the interior and built the lower storey of the façade of S Maria della Consolazione (after 1581). In 1584 Cardinal Altemps commissioned the Altemps Chapel in S Maria in Trastevere, which was frescoed by Pasquale Cati (*c.* 1550–*c.* 1620) with figures and themes associated with the Altemps family. Longhi continued the construction of S Maria in Vallicella (1586–90; plans, Rome, Archv Congregazione Oratorio) and designed the façade of S Girolamo degli Schiavoni (1587–90).

Throughout his career Martino the elder seldom broke from the prevailing architectural conventions of Vignola, his presumed mentor. His work, like that of his contemporaries Domenico Fontana (iii), Mascherino and Francesco da Volterra, is characterized by a bland conformity that hardly anticipates the vitality and inventiveness of the coming Baroque. Longhi's façade of S Girolamo degli Schiavoni gives the clearest idea of his personal style, since he was in complete control of the construction from beginning to end; it typifies in both its flatness and its reliance on earlier Roman models (e.g. Vignola's Il Gesù) the timidity and unadventurous attitude of its age. Only in the courtyard of the Palazzo Deza—if indeed it may be attributed to him—did Longhi introduce new vocabulary and syntax into the grammar of Roman Late Mannerism.

BIBLIOGRAPHY
G. Baglione: *Vite* (1642); ed. V. Mariani (1935), pp. 68–9
H. Hibbard: 'The Architecture of the Palazzo Borghese', *Mem. Amer. Acad. Rome*, xxvii (1962), pp. 83–93
G. Koksa: *S. Girolamo degli Schiavoni* (Rome, 1971)
C. Bertsch: 'Brief und Pläne von Martino Longhi d. Ä. aus dem Palastarchiv zu Hohenems', *Röm. Jb. Kstgesch.*, xxvi (1990), pp. 171–84

**(2) Onorio Longhi** (*b* Viggiù, 12 Oct 1568; *d* Rome, 13 Dec 1619). Son of (1) Martino Longhi I. On his father's death *c.* 1591, Onorio inherited a few of his architectural commissions, such as the Orsini Chapel in S Maria d'Aracoeli, but his career proceeded slowly and was marked by discontinuity. His early biographers described him as an eccentric and quarrelsome personality, and his frequent clashes with the law are documented in the Roman police records (Bertolotti). In 1606 he was forced, together with Caravaggio, to flee the Papal States owing to involvement in a homicide, and for the next five years Onorio pursued his career in Lombardy without much success. His abortive plans included schemes for the façades of Milan Cathedral (?1607; Milan, Castello Sforzesco) and S Alessandro, Milan (Milan, Bib. Ambrosiana). In 1611 he received a papal pardon permitting him to return to Rome, where his executed work reveals his shifting allegiance to Lombard and Roman architectural practices.

Onorio's most important commission came in 1612 when the Lombard confraternity in Rome asked him to design the vast longitudinal church of SS Ambrogio e Carlo al Corso (choir plans, Rome, Vatican, Bib. Apostolica). It is chiefly remarkable for introducing such north Italian features as the continuous ambulatory—reminiscent of Milan Cathedral—into the mainstream of Roman architecture. Although it was not built according to his plans as depicted on a medal of 1612, later engraved by Claude Du Molinet in *Historia summorum pontificum* (Paris, 1679), Onorio's intended use of detached columns to articulate the façade follows the Lombard tradition.

Few of Onorio's works are securely dated, and the stylistic evolution of his buildings is not easily characterized. His designs for a number of altars and chapels in Roman churches—of which the chapel of S Filippo Neri (1600–02) in S Maria in Vallicella is the best known—demonstrate his fondness for lavish surface decoration. In other instances, such as the façade of S Maria Liberatrice (1617; destr. 1901) in the Forum Romanum, he adopted the flat, austere conventions of the late 1500s, reworking the outdated formulae of Counter-Reformation churches, such as his father's S Girolamo degli Schiavoni (1587–90). In what was perhaps his most successful building, the Villa Altemps (*c.* 1600; destr.), outside the Porta del Popolo, he resolved the conflict to a considerable extent. Its façade, which was rebuilt next to the Palazzo Senatorio on the Capitoline Hill in 1927, combines restraint with a few rich architectural and sculptural embellishments.

BIBLIOGRAPHY
G. Baglione: *Vite* (1642); ed. V. Mariani (1935), p. 156
A. Bertolotti: *Artisti lombardi a Roma nei secoli XV, XVI, e XVII: Studi e ricerche negli archivi romani*, ii (Milan, 1881), pp. 17–22

**(3) Martino Longhi II** [the younger] (*b* Rome, 18 March 1602; *d* Viggiù, 15 Dec 1660). Son of (2) Onorio Longhi. He was active mainly in Rome. He trained as an architect with his father, from whom he inherited an eccentric and contentious personality. As an architect he was the most daringly original of his family and was at his most innovative when designing church façades. His architectural work was never doctrinaire, and he was consistently guided by progressive principles. While he never received a significant papal commission, as did his contemporaries Gianlorenzo Bernini, Pietro da Cortona and Carlo Rainaldi, he introduced a number of innovations into the repertory of Roman Baroque architecture, such as the rich treatment of diagonal elements on façades.

Passeri claimed that Martino the younger assumed the direction of the building works at SS Ambrogio e Carlo al Corso after his father's death in 1619, although building records do not attest to his presence on the site until 1634. His first securely documented commission is the rebuilding of S Antonio dei Portoghesi (begun *c.* 1629) for the Portuguese community in Rome. The Latin-cross interior, completed by Carlo Rainaldi and Christoph Schor, is less remarkable than the handsome façade, which is a development of the standard two-storey elevation that was standard among Roman Counter-Reformation churches—including those designed by his father and grandfather—and is dramatically enlivened by emphasizing planar

1. Martino Longhi II: façade of SS Vincenzo ed Anastasio, Rome, 1646–50

viewers approaching the church on the diagonal, made their first appearance on a Roman church façade. The expressive effects of these devices were not lost on other contemporary architects, such as Pietro da Cortona and Rainaldi, who employed similar features at the churches of S Maria della Pace (1656–7) and S Maria in Campitelli (1663), respectively.

In 1653 Longhi undertook the remodelling of S Adriano al Foro Romano (the ancient Roman Curia). Given the predetermined ground-plan, he was limited to vaulting the simple six-bay nave and building some additional chapels. Rather than erecting a barrel vault over the full length of the nave (there was no transept), he constructed a five-bay vault with an oval cupola over the sixth bay. In creating the effect of a crossing dome, Longhi transformed the movement of the interior space without violating the nave arcade. To support the small cupola, he erected two free-standing, fluted Corinthian columns between the fifth and sixth bays, which effectively divided the nave and chancel. The scenographic effect thus achieved was new to Roman architecture and may have served as an inspiration for Rainaldi's interior of S Maria in Campitelli. Longhi's work was removed in the restoration of 1933.

Longhi's two major secular works, the stairway complexes in the Palazzo Gaetani (c. 1640; now Palazzo

2. Martino Longhi II: loggia of the *piano nobile*, Palazzo Ginnetti, Velletri, c. 1642 (destr. 1944)

projections and adding a rich assortment of sculptural accents such as the Braganza coat of arms, trumpeting angels and winged cherubim. In the late 1630s Longhi submitted a project for the completion of SS Ambrogio e Carlo al Corso, which called for a façade of great originality consisting of two boldly projecting towers and a wealth of free-standing and engaged columns. This elaborate proposal was never executed, nor was one of equal imagination (1644; Vienna, Albertina) that he made for S Giovanni Calibita on the Isola Tiberina. There Longhi proposed a façade that would have been concave in plan with paired columns flanking the single doorway. Such a plan, had it been built, would have been the first of its kind in Rome, anticipating such later façades as Carlo Fontana's S Marcello al Corso (1682–3).

The façade of the Hieronymite church of SS Vincenzo ed Anastasio (1646–50), commissioned by Cardinal Jules Mazarin, is unquestionably Longhi's masterpiece (plans, Rome, Archv Cent. Stato). Its bold elevation (see fig. 1) may rightly be called the first uncompromisingly High Baroque façade in Rome. Although its two-storey profile was part of an established Roman tradition, Longhi articulated the composition with 16 detached columns, sharply projecting wall planes and an array of free-standing and relief sculpture (not all of which was executed according to plan). A number of architectural features, such as compound or encased pediments, fully detached columns and the treatment of the corners so as to guide

Ruspoli), Rome, and the Palazzo Ginnetti (*c.* 1642; destr. 1944) in nearby Velletri are equally worthy of note. In the former he juxtaposed two long and sparsely ornamented ascending corridors with a more elegant loggia on the first floor. It was praised as one of the finest staircases in all Italy, although its Mannerist details probably contributed to his reputation for being *capricciosissimo*, first referred to by Franzini (p. 118) and followed by most early biographers. The staircase in the Palazzo Ginnetti was a free-standing, five-storey block with arched openings on three sides that afforded views of the surrounding countryside. It contrast to the dry treatment of the Gaetani staircase, this was richly embellished with stucco reliefs of the most imaginative variety, including herms, shells and cornucopias (see fig. 2).

Longhi had a competing interest in writing poetry, published as *Poesie amorose, sacre, varie* (Rome, 1639), and discourses, such as a treatise on architecture that he wrote at the age of 23.

### WRITINGS

*Epilogismo di architettura del Sig. Martino Lunghi alli nobilissimi della detta scienza studiosi* (Bracciano, 1625)
*Discorso di Martino Lunghi delle cagioni delle ruine della facciata e campanile del famoso tempio di S Pietro in Vaticano* (Rome, 1645)

### BIBLIOGRAPHY

F. Franzini: *Descrittione di Roma antica e moderna* (Rome, 1653)
G. B. Passeri: *Vite* (1679); ed. J. Hess (1934), pp. 225–33
L. Pascoli: *Vite* (1730–36), ii, pp. 515–21
J. Varriano: 'Martino Longhi the Younger and the Façade of San Giovanni Calabita in Rome', *A. Bull.*, lii (1970), pp. 71–4
——: 'The Architecture of Martino Longhi the Younger', *J. Soc. Archit. Hist.*, xxx (1971), pp. 101–18
A. Pugliese and S. Rigano: 'Martino Lunghi il Giovane', *Architettura barocca a Roma* (Rome, 1972), pp. 7–186

JOHN VARRIANO

**Longhi (iii).** Italian family of artists. They were active in Venice. (1) Pietro Longhi was the son of Alessandro Falca, who has been variously noted as a painter and goldsmith. It is not known when or why Pietro adopted the name of Longhi, under which he always worked. He was best known for his small genre paintings that were outside the mainstream of contemporary Venetian art. His son (2) Alessandro Longhi was also individualistic in approach and was most admired for the realistic qualities of his unofficial portraits, many of which depict humble subjects.

**(1) Pietro Longhi** [Pietro Falca] (*b* Venice, 1700–02; *d* Venice, 8 May 1785). Painter and draughtsman. His father, Alessandro Falca, encouraged his natural talent for drawing, and he studied under Antonio Balestra for 'several years', according to his son, (2) Alessandro Longhi. Balestra probably took Pietro to Bologna and recommended him to Giuseppe Maria Crespi. No documents exist on Longhi until 1732, the year he married, and some doubt has been expressed about his study with Crespi. There is no trace of Crespi's influence in Longhi's altarpiece for the parish church of S Pellegrino in Bologna, *St Pellegrino Condemned to Death*, installed in 1732; Crespi's style is an intimate one, however, and would have been inappropriate for such a large altarpiece. One of Longhi's first independent works, the St Pellegrino altarpiece recalls his Venetian origins and training in its broken brushwork and colour glazes. In another early work, the *Adoration of the Magi* (Venice, Scuola Grande S Giovanni Evangelista),

1. Pietro Longhi: *The Rhinoceros*, oil on panel, 489×603 mm, *c.* 1744 (Venice, Ca' Rezzonico)

documented in 1733 as at S Maria Materdomini, Venice, the subject-matter lends itself to a more domestic treatment, and Crespi's influence is evident. Both these works contain passages anticipating Longhi's subsequent development as a genre painter; in each picture a boy or young man, perhaps a self-portrait, gazes out at the spectator, unconcerned with events in the painting. The *Adoration* and the *St Pellegrino* relate to Longhi's earliest-known genre subjects, the five scenes of individual shepherd children (Bassano del Grappa, Mus. Civ., and Rovigo, Pin. Semin.).

The frescoes showing the *Fall of the Giants* (1734; Venice, Pal. Sagredo) are ambitious works with much foreshortening and many convoluted poses, which may suggest the desire of a thrifty patron to own a painting in the style of Giambattista Tiepolo. Longhi was undoubtedly aware of his limitations (or indeed gifts) as an artist, and although his career is undocumented from 1734 to 1737 (when he is first listed in the Fraglia, the Venetian painters' guild), during this period he moved away from grand historical compositions and in the second half of the 1730s began painting the small-scale genre works for which he is renowned. The dearth of dated works throughout his career makes chronological reconstruction of his oeuvre difficult, but it is generally agreed that his earliest works of this nature were scenes of peasant life, such as *The Polenta* (Venice, Ca' Rezzonico). A number of drinking, dancing and tavern scenes exist as well, such as *The Drunkard* (Biella, priv. col.; see Pignatti, 1969, pl. 35), the *Merry Couple* (Venice, Ca' Rezzonico) and *Peasants Dancing* (Ferrara, Paulucci Col.; see Pignatti, 1969, pl. 20). In

1741 Longhi signed and dated *The Concert* (Venice, Accad.), an interior view of Venetian noble life. As his first surviving signed and dated work after the Ca' Sagredo frescoes, it is a key work for Longhi studies. Sources suggested for Longhi's genre pictures include Crespi and also William Hogarth and Antoine Watteau. Longhi's scenes of tavern life, however, recall works by such northern artists as Adriaen Brouwer, David Teniers the younger and Adriaen van Ostade. Similarly such fashionable interior scenes as *The Concert* or *The Introduction* (Paris, Louvre), where most or all of the figures are related to events within the picture, appear to derive, at least in part, from 17th-century Dutch genre pictures, which were far from rare in 18th-century Venice.

From the 1740s Longhi continued to paint Venetian interior scenes; they are small, rarely taller than 650 mm, almost never show more than one wall and rarely include windows. They are painted in colours that are clear and clean, and they show a deep appreciation of the texture of fabrics, which are occasionally enlivened with flickering splashes of colour. That doll-like figures are a conscious mannerism is indicated not only by the evidence of his earlier history paintings but also by his numerous surviving drawings (over 150 in Venice, Correr). These excellent examples of draughtsmanship effortlessly capture the gesture and features of his subjects, some of which were observed from life. He drew in black chalk or pencil heightened with white chalk on light brown or blue-grey paper. His abilities were such that he was instructor to the life class at the Accademia dei Pittori until 1780 and the founder-director of the academy of drawing and engraving at the Palazzo Pisani. Occasionally, poses derived from the Antique can be seen in his pictures; in the *Adoration of the Magi*, for example, the camel holder is adapted from the *Horse Tamers* on the Quirinal Hill, Rome. Longhi's pictures are documentary (e.g. *The Rhinoceros*, *c*. 1744; Venice, Ca' Rezzonico; see fig. 1) and anecdotal of Venetian noble life (e.g. *Fortune Teller*; London, N.G.) and often both together. In the 1750s, however, he painted two series of pictures—the *Seven Sacraments* and *Shooting in the Valley* (Venice, Gal. Querini-Stampalia)—both of which depict primarily the lives of the ordinary people of Venice, and appropriately they recall stylistically the tenebrous work of Crespi. The seven paintings of the *Sacraments* are devotional works inspired by the series painted by Crespi (1712; Dresden, Gemäldegal. Alte Meister). The *Shooting in the Valley* series and his finest landscape, the *Shooting in the Lagoon* (Venice, Gal. Querini-Stampalia; see fig. 2), are realistic depictions of the work that servants put into a hunt. There is none of the sense of light usually associated with Venetian outdoor scenes, and the rough style of some of the figures anticipates Goya.

2. Pietro Longhi: *Shooting in the Lagoon*, oil on canvas, 560×720 mm, 1750s (Venice, Galleria Querini-Stampalia)

In his mature work Longhi produced both peasant scenes and interiors depicting noble life. He did not hesitate to copy compositions from all periods of his career, and consequently autograph (and non-autograph) versions of his pictures abound. Longhi was immensely popular in his day; he was lionized as an outstanding imitator of nature and was even compared favourably to Tiepolo (Gozzi). In a society that constantly looked to its past greatness and whose contemporary art was almost entirely allegorical, his scenes of 18th-century life were a novelty. In the late 20th century his work was appreciated for his charming doll-like interiors. His pictures contain many things, including portraits now unrecognized, which were undoubtedly part of their attraction. They may also hold specific meanings, now obscure, which made them a visual complement to the works of his friend and admirer the playwright Carlo Goldoni (1707–93).

BIBLIOGRAPHY

G. Gozzi: *Gazzetta veneta*, lv (13 Aug 1760)
A. Longhi: *Compendio delle vite de' pittori veneziani istorici . . .* (Venice, 1762)
F. Valcanover: 'Postilla su Pietro Longhi "pittore di storia"', *A. Ven.*, v (1951), pp. 169–70
V. Moschini: *Pietro Longhi* (Milan, 1956)
R. Pallucchini: *La pittura veneziana del settecento* (Venice and Rome, 1960)
T. Pignatti: *Pietro Longhi* (Venice, 1968; Eng. trans. London, 1969)
——: *Pietro Longhi: Opera completa* (Milan, 1974)
T. Pignatti, ed.: *Pietro Longhi: Dal disegno alla pittura* (Venice, 1975)
P. L. Sohm: 'Pietro Longhi and Carlo Goldoni: Relations between Painting and Theatre', *Z. Kstgesch.*, xlv (1982), pp. 256–73
*Giuseppe Maria Crespi and the Emergence of Genre Painting in Italy* (exh. cat., ed. J. T. Spike; Fort Worth, TX, Kimbell A. Mus., 1986)
*The Glory of Venice: Art in the Eighteenth Century* (exh. cat., ed. J. Martineau and A. Robison; London, RA; Washington, DC, N.G.A.; 1995)

**(2) Alessandro Longhi** (*b* Venice, 1733; *d* Venice, Nov 1813). Painter, engraver and writer, son of (1) Pietro Longhi. He must have received his first artistic training from his father, although the only evidence of this is the similarity of their styles. He was apprenticed to Giuseppe Nogari, one of the better Venetian portrait painters of the first half of the eighteenth century, and his earliest works are bust-length, mostly life-size portraits in Nogari's style. He first exhibited in 1757 and by 1758 must have been considered a reasonably established artist, for by the end of that year he had painted two life-size group portraits of the Pisani family. One of these—the *Family of the Procurator Luigi Pisani* (Venice, Bentivoglio d'Aragona priv. col.)—survives. It includes a number of allegorical figures and, despite a certain facility in the handling of the sitters' clothes, is reminiscent of a work by Pietro Longhi, only enlarged to life size.

In 1759 Alessandro was elected a member of the Accademia dei Pittori, for which he later painted imaginary portraits of the great artists of Renaissance Venice. His reputation was secured in 1760 when he exhibited a portrait of an innkeeper that was praised for its 'nuova maniera'. Considering the exalted portraiture typical of Venice over the preceding century the subject was novel—the innkeeper is depicted with hand raised, ready to carve a roast—and Longhi was praised for his rendering of 'reality'.

The scarcity of documented works by Alessandro has made attribution and chronology of his oeuvre difficult to establish. His style appears to have varied little; his formal state portraits woodenly depict gentlemen in full wigs and brocade costumes, with appropriately grand background trappings: imagery that accurately reflected the ossified ritualism of the dying Venetian republic. It is his portraits of less noble patrons that display his gifts. The *Portrait of a Nun* (1771; Milan, priv. col., see Pallucchini, pl. 560) is sombre and straightforward; the portrait of *Captain Pietro Buldinich* (1781; Venice, I. Brass priv. col.) is a sensitively rendered likeness that suggests that Longhi may have been familiar with English portrait mezzotints. An undated *Portrait of a Wine Butler* (Venice, P. Mentasti priv. col.) is a good example of Alessandro's skill. Its subject is shown coming through a doorway on to a balustraded porch; carrying a rough-hewn basket of wine flasks in his right hand, he gestures back inside with his left hand, while his severely rendered face confronts the viewer. There appears to be little flattery in the likeness but considerable sympathy for the man's well-worn countenance. The difference between this and Longhi's official portraits is almost shocking and enables the viewer to appreciate Longhi's reputation for realism. Yet, although such works are lively in relation to portraits painted by his immediate predecessors, they seem distinctly *retardataire* when compared to contemporary French or English portraits.

Alessandro made engravings of his own and his father's works. In 1762 he published his *Compendio delle vite de' pittori veneziani istorici . . .*, a group of biographies of contemporary Venetian artists, each illustrated with an engraved portrait by himself.

WRITINGS
*Compendio delle vite de' pittori veneziani istorici . . .* (Venice, 1762)

BIBLIOGRAPHY
V. Moschini: 'Per lo studio di A. Longhi', *L'Arte*, 34 (1932), pp. 110–47
M. Levey: *Painting in Eighteenth-century Venice* (London, 1959, rev. Ithaca, 2/1980)
R. Pallucchini: *La pittura veneziana del settecento* (Venice and Rome, 1960)
*Painting in Italy in the Eighteenth Century* (exh. cat., ed. J. Maxon and J. J. Richel; Chicago, IL, A. Inst.; Minneapolis, MN, Inst. A.; Toledo, OH, Mus. A.; 1970–71)
G. Briganti, ed.: *La pittura in Italia: Il settecento*, 2 vols (Milan, 1989, rev. 1990), ii, pp. 769–70
*The Glory of Venice: Art in the Eighteenth Century* (exh. cat., ed. J. Martineau and A. Robison; London, RA; Washington, DC, N.G.A.; 1995)

JOHN WILSON

**Longhi, Giuseppe** (*b* Monza, 13 Oct 1766; *d* Milan, 12 Jan 1831). Italian printmaker and writer. He trained with Vincenzo Vangelisti (1728–98), and went to Rome to copy Old Masters before dedicating himself completely to engraving, a field in which he did much to promote the Neo-classical movement in Milan. In 1794 he engraved Guido Reni's *Genius of Music* and in 1795 Daniele Crespi's *St Jerome*. He established his reputation in 1797 with his engraving of Napoleon Bonaparte I (from the original by Antoine-Jean Gros). In 1798 he succeeded Vangelisti as professor of engraving at the Accademia di Brera in Milan. In 1801 he was part of the Consulta Cisalpina in Lyon; he then visited Paris, where he met many artists, including Jacques-Louis David and Nicolas-Henri Tardieu.

In 1810 Longhi began engraving his most famous work, a large print from Raphael's *Marriage of the Virgin* which he finished in 1820. He also wrote on art and engraving, producing two *Discorsi accademici intorno alla pittura* (1808 and 1814) and *Vita di Michelangelo* (1816). In the last years of his life, while continuing to engrave, he began work on his treatise, the *Trattato sull'arte d'incidere*. The first volume, *Concernente la teorica dell'arte*, which was to have been followed by a second dedicated to the practical aspects of engraving, was a fundamental text for his numerous pupils.

### WRITINGS

*Trattato sull'arte d'incidere in rame all'acquaforte col bulino e colla punta: Concernente la teorica dell'arte* (Milan, 1830)

### BIBLIOGRAPHY

Thieme–Becker

G. Beretta: *Della vita, delle opere ed opinioni del Cav. G. Longhi* (Milan, 1837)

L. Servolini: 'Giuseppe Longhi', *Dizionario illustrato degli incisori italiani moderni e contemporanei* (Milan, 1955), pp. 444–6

STEFANIA MASSARI

**Longhi, Roberto** (*b* Alba, Cuneo, 28 Dec 1890; *d* Florence, 3 June 1970). Italian art historian and critic. He studied in Turin, first in the *liceo* and then at the university, where he wrote his thesis on Caravaggio under Pietro Toesca. From 1912 to 1915 he attended Adolfo Venturi's School of Advanced Studies in Rome, which gave him the opportunity to travel all over Italy and to study 15th-century painting at first hand, discovering links between Piero della Francesca and the development of Venetian painting. He also studied paintings associated with Caravaggio, by his forerunners in Lombardy and by his followers in Rome and Naples. These, especially 17th-century art, remained the fields in which Longhi specialized, paying particular attention to contemporary critical sources. He began a translation of Bernard Berenson's *Italian Painters of the Renaissance* (1894–1907), but this remained unpublished because of differences of opinion between him and the older, more established American scholar. Between 1912 and 1914 he contributed to the journal *La voce*, where he participated in the debate over the recognition of Impressionist painting in Italy, and supported Umberto Boccioni and the Futurists. Longhi's involvement with contemporary art and with that of the immediately preceding period in France (together with his vigorous opposition to Pittura Metafisica) had a decisive influence on his approach to earlier traditions. This is confirmed by the unusual photographic illustrations he chose for his books, and by contemporary artists' enthusiasm for his interpretations of the Old Masters.

While on leave from military service Longhi worked for the journal *L'arte* (1917–20), for which he reviewed many current books. Aware of the aesthetic principles formulated by Benedetto Croce, he took a formalist critical approach and strove to find verbal equivalents for his perceptions of works of art. His success was due to his uncommon literary gifts, and his subtle and passionate prose later attracted the attention of distinguished literary critics and philologists such as Gianfranco Contini and Giuseppe De Robertis. Between 1920 and 1922, together with the antiquarian and collector Alessandro Contini-Bonacossi, Longhi visited the galleries of Spain, France, Germany, Austria and Hungary. He settled in Rome, where he married Lucia Lopresti, a scholar and noted writer under the pseudonym of Anna Banti. He taught at the university and published some of the results of his researches in Italian and foreign galleries in *Vita artistica*

and *Pinacotheca* (which he edited, with Emilio Cecchi, from 1927 to 1929).

Longhi became the most important Italian art historian and critic of his time. He engaged in a polemic with Lionello Venturi regarding the importance of connoisseurship as the basis of art history, his attitudes informing his *Officina ferrarese* (1934). In 1934 he became professor of art history at the University of Bologna. Some of his pupils there, such as Attilio Bertolucci, Giorgio Bassani and Pier Paolo Pasolini, later became celebrated writers. In the course of his teaching he broadened his research on the painting of Emilia and the Po Valley, which he saw as an alternative to Florentine painting in the 14th century. The work of the contemporary painter Giorgio Morandi convinced him that 'pure painting' still existed. In 1935 Longhi organized the *Mostra del settecento bolognese*.

After acting as editor of *Critica d'arte* together with Ranuccio Bianchi Bandinelli (1900–75) and Carlo Ludovico Ragghianti (1910–87), and as part of the jury for the award of the Bergamo Prize from 1939, during temporary work for the Ministero dell'Educazione Negronde, Longhi started the journal *Proporzioni*, in which he proposed a new interpretation of the Tuscan Renaissance and the advent of Giotto's style of painting. From 1949 he taught at the University of Florence. There he founded the journal *Paragone* (which included contributions from his pupils), with alternating issues on art and literature, so creating a specialized, international periodical committed to scrutinizing contemporary cultural policy. He collaborated with the cinema critic Umberto Barbaro (1902–59) in making documentary films on art and promoted a spectacular series of exhibitions in Milan: *Mostra di Caravaggio e dei Caravaggeschi* (1951), *Pittori della realtà in Lombardia* (1953) and *Arte lombarda dai Visconti agli Sforza* (1958). The volumes of Longhi's *Opere complete* are being published (Florence, 1961–) in accordance with a scheme specified by Longhi himself.

### UNPUBLISHED SOURCES

Florence, Fond. Longhi [many unpublished MSS and lett.; also Longhi's library and collection of paintings]

Pavia, U. Stud., Cent. Ric. Trad., MS. Aut. Mod. & Contemp. [MSS and lett. received in Longhi's youth]

### WRITINGS

*Piero della Francesca* (Rome, 1927, rev. 1963), iii of *Opere complete* (Florence, 1963)

*Officina ferrarese* (Rome, 1934, rev. 1956), v of *Opere complete* (Florence, 1963)

*Caravaggio* (Milan, 1952, rev. Rome, 1968/R 1982) [with intro. by G. Previtali and bibliog. of writings on Longhi]

*Scritti giovanili* (1961), i of *Opere complete* (Florence, 1961–)

*Opere complete* (Florence, 1961–)

G. F. Contini, ed.: *Da Cimabue a Morandi* (Milan, 1973) [anthol. of Longhi's writings]

T. Graziani Longhi, ed.: *Scritti e lettere di Alberto Graziani*, 2 vols (Bologna, 1993) [incl. letters by Longhi]

F. Frangi and C. Montagnani, eds: *Anthology of Longhi's Writings* (Milan, in preparation)

### BIBLIOGRAPHY

*La fiera letteraria*, x/4 (1955) [issue devoted to Longhi]

A. Boschetto, ed.: *Bibliografia di Roberto Longhi* (Florence, 1973)

G. Previtali, ed.: *L'arte di scrivere sull'arte: Roberto Longhi nella cultura del nostro tempo. Atti del convegno: Firenze, 1980*

G. Agosti: 'Roberto Longhi al cinema (appunti su alcuni film, a Parigi, nel 1932)', *Paragone*, xl/15 (1989), pp. 1–18

C. Montagnani: *Glossario longhiano* (Pisa, 1989)

*Piero della Francesca e il novecento* (exh. cat., Sansepolcro, Mus. Civ., 1991)

G. Agosti: 'Questioni di "logica degli occhi": Cinque lettere di Lionello Venturi a Roberto Longhi', *Autografo*, ix/26 (1992)

C. Garboli and C. Montagnani, eds: *Bernard Berenson and Roberto Longhi: Lettere, 1912–1957* (Milan, 1993)

GIACOMO AGOSTI

**Longhi [Lunghi], Silla** [Giacomo, Scilla; Silla, Giacomo; Silla da Viggiù] (*b* Viggiù, nr Varese, 1569; *d* ?Rome, *c*. 1622). Italian sculptor. He executed reliefs (*c*. 1557) for pinnacles on the façade of S Petronio, Bologna, according to Baglione. In 1568–72 he completed eight reliefs from scenes from the *Life of St Sylvester* for the abbey of Nonántola (Modena). By 1578 he was established in Rome, where he executed a *Triton* for Giacomo della Porta's *Fontana del Moro* in Piazza Navona *c*. 1581. In Naples that year he completed the tomb of *Caterina Orsini* (Naples, S Caterina a Formiello). His drily carved relief of the *Coronation of Pope Pius V* (Rome, S Maria Maggiore, Cappella Sistina) was completed by 1586. In 1588–90 he worked on reliefs of the *Story of Aaron* and on a single figure of *Aaron* for the Cappella del SS Sacramento and an *Angel* for the transept of the S Giovanni in Laterano, Rome. His later works in Rome include the meticulously carved kneeling figure of *Pope Paul V* (1608), the statically posed statue of *Pope Clement VIII* (both S Maria Maggiore, Cappella Paolina) and the reclining figure of *Cardinal Alessandrino* for his tomb by Giacomo della Porta (*c*. 1611; S Maria sopra Minerva), in which the rippling draperies and characterization of the head give a more lively feeling than Longhi's earlier works.

BIBLIOGRAPHY

G. Baglione: *Vite* (1642); ed. V. Mariani (1935), pp. 120–21

A. Venturi: *Storia* (1901–40), x, pp. 601–6

J. Pope-Hennessy: *Italian High Renaissance and Baroque Sculpture* (Oxford, 1963, rev. 2/1985), pp. 423, 426

M. C. Donati: 'Gli scultori della Cappella Paolina in Santa Maria Maggiore', *Commentari*, xviii (1967), pp. 231–60

ANTONIA BOSTRÖM

**Longhurst, Margaret (Helen)** (*b* 5 Aug 1882; *d* Aldbourne, Wilts, 26 Jan 1958). English museum curator and art historian. She started voluntary work in the Department of Architecture and Sculpture at the Victoria and Albert Museum after World War I. Although she had no formal education, by the time she joined the staff officially in 1926 she was already known as an authority on medieval sculpture, in particular ivory carvings, and a stream of important publications followed her appointment. She pioneered the study of English medieval ivory carvings and published numerous new discoveries, such as the walrus ivory *Virgin and Child* from Dorchester (*c*. 1150; London, V&A), producing her classic survey of English ivories in 1926. Her other major interest was in Italian medieval and Renaissance sculpture; together with Eric Maclagan she published a catalogue of the Italian sculpture in the Victoria and Albert Museum; her corpus on Italian monuments of the 12th to 16th centuries was left unfinished. She was also the first woman keeper of a department in any British national museum (1938–42).

UNPUBLISHED SOURCES

*Notes on Italian Monuments of the 12th to 16th Centuries* [photocopied typescript, copies in London, V&A, and U. London, Warburg Inst., [?1963]]

WRITINGS

*English Ivories* (London, 1926)

*Catalogue of Carvings in Ivory, Victoria and Albert Museum* (London, 1927, 2/1929)

with E. Maclagan: *Catalogue of Italian Sculpture, Victoria and Albert Museum* (London, 1932)

Numerous contributions to *Burl. Mag.*

BIBLIOGRAPHY

Obituary, *The Times* (28 Jan 1958), p. 10

PAUL WILLIAMSON

**Longmen** [Lung-men]. Site of Buddhist cave temples located 12 km south of Luoyang, Henan Province, China. From the end of the 6th century AD to the mid-8th century many caves were excavated into the low limestone hills that run along the northern and southern banks of the Yi River. The sculptures and reliefs they contain, also carved from the living rock, range in size from the small to the colossal. Work was begun under the patronage of the Northern Wei dynasty (AD 386–534), the capital of which was moved in AD 493–4 from Datong, Shanxi Province, to Luoyang. Construction continued until 755, the year of the rebellion of An Lushan against the Tang dynasty (AD 618–907). The caves thus provide evidence both of the development of Buddhist sculpture and of the imperial patronage of the Northern Wei and Tang dynasties between the late 5th century AD and the mid-8th century. The scale and ambition of the project is evoked in the *Wei shu* ('History of the Wei', compiled in the Northern Qi period (AD 550–77)), which states that from AD 500 to 523, 800,000 workers and artisans were engaged in construction of the cave temples at Longmen. Calligraphic

1. Longmen, central Binyang cave, Shakyamuni Buddha with the disciples Kashyapa and Ananda, limestone, 6th century AD

2. Longmen, colossal statues flanking the north wall of Fengxian Temple, 7th century AD

inscriptions provide names for the caves and further evidence for their dates.

The earliest important cave at Longmen is the Guyang cave with its many inscriptions, some bearing dates; the earliest date, which indicates the beginning of construction at the site, can be interpreted as either AD 488 or 498.

The first cave commissioned by the court is the central Binyang cave, begun by Emperor Xuanwudi in AD 505 (the north and south sections were added later). Grand and unified in design, the theme is taken from the Lotus Sutra, which formed the basis of contemporary popular Buddhism. Shakyamuni, the historical Buddha (see fig. 1), accompanied by his disciples Kashyapa and Ananda and flanked by two *bodhisattvas*, occupies the back wall; a standing triad of a Buddha and two *bodhisattvas* occupies each of the two side walls. In addition to the main Buddhist figures, ten deities sculpted in the indigenous Chinese style are carved at the bottom of the front wall on the two sides of the entrance to this cave. Originally there were two reliefs above these deities: one shows the emperor and high court officials (New York, Met.), and the other shows the empress and court ladies (Kansas City, MO, Nelson–Atkins Mus. A.).

All the surfaces of the central Binyang cave are carved in meticulous detail and were once painted in colours; only traces of the original paint remain. The ceiling is decorated with a large lotus medallion. Four medallions are carved at the corners of the floor, and a walk lined

with petals leads from the entrance to the sculpture of Shakyamuni. On a low platform below Shakyamuni's dais is an area carved with water patterns in which human figures, ducks and lotuses are depicted among the ripples. The sculptures, as well as the decoration, are highly detailed and executed in carved lines. This linearity is accentuated wherever possible: for example, the eyebrows and eyelids of the Buddhist figures are depicted with fine ridges, and their robes and scarves are covered with fine lines indicating folds. Combined with the elaborate curvilinear carvings on the *mandalas*, ceilings and floor, this creates a compelling impression of the Buddhist paradise. Other Northern Wei caves are smaller in scale and less linear in their style of carving, and the evidence for their patronage is not as conclusive as that of the central Binyang cave.

The major construction of the Northern Qi period is the Yaofang cave. There the sculptures represent a transitional stage between the styles of the Northern Wei and those of the Tang; they are stocky and lack the refinement of both the Northern Wei and Tang works. Sculptures of the Sui (AD 581–618) and early Tang periods are represented by three large caves: the north and south Binyang caves and the Qianxi cave. The proportions of the figures are closer to those of the human body than those of the earlier sculptures.

The greatest sculptural undertaking of the Tang is at the Fengxian Temple, which was commissioned by Emperor Gaozong (*reg* AD 649–83) and completed in AD 675.

It was carved into the middle part of the west hill, and the colossal sculptures (see fig. 2), now standing in the open air, are visible from a considerable distance. Characterized by the realism of the Tang period, the main figure is of Vairochana Buddha (h. including the pedestal 13.37 m) flanked by Kashyapa, Ananda, *bodhisattvas*, the Guardians of the Four Quarters and Vajrapani. In the caves on the east hill the sculptures are poised and austere, reflecting the taste of the court during the rule of the Empress Wu (*reg* AD 690–705), who commissioned them.

*See also* CHINA, §III, 1.

BIBLIOGRAPHY

S. Mizuno: *Ryūmon sekkutsu no kenkyū/The Lung-men Buddhist Cave Temples* (Tokyo, 1941) [Eng. abstract]
*Rikuchō no bijutsu* [Arts of the Six Dynasties] (exh. cat., Osaka, Mun. Mus. A., 1976)
*Longmen shiku* [The stone cave temples at Longmen] (Beijing, 1980)
Gong Dazhong: *Longmen shiku yishu* [The art of the stone cave temples at Longmen] (Shanghai, 1981)
*Ryūmon sekkutsu* [The Longmen grottoes], 2 vols (Tokyo, 1987–8)

MOLLY SIUPING HO

**Longo, Robert** (*b* New York, 7 Jan 1953). American painter, sculptor, performance artist and video artist. He received his BFA in 1975 from the State University College in Buffalo, NY, with a professed ambition to reach the largest possible audience. In his early work, notably a series of large-scale drawings in charcoal and graphite entitled *Men in the Cities* (e.g. *Untitled*, 1.52×1.98 m, 1981; Atlanta, GA, High Mus. A.), he treated contorted, life-size human figures in isolation or in group situations in which the struggle for power created a menacing atmosphere. He also produced monumental works combining flat images derived from photographs with elements in sculptural relief, such as *Sword of the Pig* (2.48×5.88×0.51 m, 1983; London, Tate). During the late 1980s he was increasingly involved with films such as *Arena Brains* (30 minutes, 1988), which depicts life in the SoHo district of Manhattan.

BIBLIOGRAPHY

C. Ratcliff: *Robert Longo* (New York, 1985)
*Robert Longo: Men in the Cities, 1979–1982* (New York, 1986), intro. R. Prince [incl. interview]
H. Fox: *Robert Longo* (New York, 1989)
C. Lewis: 'Mondo Longo', *A. America*, lxxvii/3 (1989), pp. 35–9
*Robert Longo* (exh. cat., ed. H. Fox; Los Angeles, CA, Co. Mus. A.; Chicago, IL, Mus. Contemp. A.; Hartford, CT, Wadsworth Atheneum; 1989–90)
K. Tsuzuki: *Robert Longo* (Kyoto, 1992)
W. Saunders: 'Robert Longo', *A. America*, lxxxi/1 (1993), pp. 84–6

DANIEL E. MADER

**Longshan** [Lung-Shan]. Chinese Neolithic culture (*c.* 2500–*c.* 2000 BC), named after the type site at Longshan, Chengziyai, Zhangqiu County, in Shandong Province. The site was excavated in 1930–31 by Johan Gunnar Andersson (1874–1960). Remains of the Longshan culture have been identified in two distinct areas: in the provinces of Shandong and Jiangsu and, further west, in the provinces of Hebei, Henan, Shanxi and Shaanxi. The classic Longshan culture originated in central Shandong Province and was a development of the DAWENKOU culture, whereas the western Longshan had its sources in the Yangshao culture (*see also* CHINA, §VII, 3(i)(c)).

The best known pottery of the Longshan culture is a hard, black, egg-shell thin pottery, although grey pottery was also common, especially in the west, and a few pieces with a brown, red or white body have been found. Sophisticated kilns with firing chambers on top of the furnaces have been found at Longshan sites. Most of the pottery was wheelmade, but this technique was less prominent in the western areas. The black pottery has burnished surfaces often decorated with incised lines and hollows. The grey type is usually plain, but incised decoration, impressed cord and basket patterns and appliqué, mainly rings and twisted bands, are common. A few black pieces have incised cloud and thunder patterns (*leiwen*) or *taotie* animal-masks; animal and human masks were used to ornament the legs of some tripods. Small clay fragments of human and bird figurines have also been found.

Typical vessel shapes include tripods with solid or hollow legs (*see* CHINA, fig. 181), jars, steamers, cups with handles, lidded vessels or boxes and pitchers with hollow legs and bodies in the shape of an animal with two short front legs and one large leg at the back. The forms made on the wheel are characterized by their angular shapes, a feature that would normally indicate a close connection with metalworking. No metal vessels have been found at Longshan sites, however, although many of the forms occur in the bronze vessels of the Shang period (*c.* 1600–*c.* 1050 BC; *see* CHINA, §VI, 3(ii)(a)). Stemmed cups and bowls are the most characteristic shapes of Longshan pottery. Sometimes the stems are ornamented with a belt of grooves, hollowed-out circles, ovals and triangles or protruding parts. Some beakers have a rather flat, large lip resembling a brim on a hat; occasionally they have a lid in the shape of a bowl with a rim foot.

Ordinary implements were made of stone, bone and shell, and two copper-alloy awls have been found. Some ritual tools were made of jade, and jade axes were carved with cloud patterns and *taotie* animal-masks (*see* CHINA, §VIII, 1). There is evidence that scapulimancy was performed— numerous burnt and consequently cracked oracle bones (scapulae of deer and other mammals) have been found—although by the 1990s no oracle bone with inscribed characters had yet been discovered. In 1992 an inscribed Longshan pottery shard with 11 unintelligible characters was found. The characters seem to be different from later oracle bone inscriptions.

The towns of the Longshan culture were surrounded by walls up to *c.* 6 m in height, with a width of *c.* 12 m at the bottom and *c.* 9 m at the top. In one town two gatehouses have been found. Most of the houses were built on the ground or on a low platform of tamped earth. The walls of the houses were made of wattle and daub or sun-dried clay slabs or bricks. The houses were either round, square or rectangular and had one or more rooms with tamped and lime-plastered floors. The roofs were supported by wooden posts and beams and the walls. Pottery pipes were used for drainage. From burials of infants in urns or pit graves and skulls of adults that have been found close to the houses, it has been inferred that ritual offerings were made in connection with house-building. The cemeteries lie outside the towns, and the varying sizes of graves and the lavishness of grave goods indicate a highly stratified society.

BIBLIOGRAPHY

K. C. Chang: *The Archaeology of Ancient China* (New Haven, 1963, rev. New Haven and London, 3/1986), pp. 242–53, 256–80

A. E. Dien, J. K. Riegel and N. T. Price, eds: *Prehistoric to Western Zhou* (1985), ii of *Chinese Archaeological Abstracts* (Los Angeles, 1978–85), pp. 191–7

B. Watson: *Pre-Tang Ceramics of China* (London and Boston, 1991), pp. 14–17, 50–57, pls 26–33

Cai Fengshu and Cai Fengshi: *Shandong Longshan wenhua yanjiu wenji* [Collected research works on the Shandong Longshan culture] (Ji'nan, 1992)

BENT L. PEDERSEN

**Longstaff, Sir John (Campbell)** (*b* Clunes, Victoria, 10 March 1861; *d* Melbourne, 1 Oct 1941). Australian painter. From 1882 he studied at the Art School of the National Gallery of Victoria, Melbourne, where he was awarded the first travelling scholarship in 1887 for a sentimental narrative painting, *Breaking the News* (Perth, A.G. W. Australia). He left for Paris in 1887, studying at Fernand Cormon's studio and the Académie Colarossi. While in France, Longstaff visited his compatriot John Peter Russell at Belle Ile in 1889 and was influenced briefly by the latter's 'impressionist' style. Certain works by Longstaff from this period, such as *Lady in Grey* (1890; Melbourne, N.G. Victoria), reveal the influence of Whistler and the Aesthetic movement, as well as the portraiture of Velázquez, which he had studied in Spain for three months. While the bulk of his oeuvre was portraiture, his large allegorical work *The Sirens* (Melbourne, N.G. Victoria) was acclaimed at the Salon of 1892 in Paris and at the Royal Academy, London, in 1894.

Returning to Australia in 1895, Longstaff established himself successfully as a portrait painter. In 1901 he was commissioned by the National Gallery of Victoria to paint a celebrated moment in Australian history: *Arrival of Burke, Wills and King at the Deserted Camp at Coopers Creek, Sunday Evening 21 April 1861* (1902–7; Melbourne, N.G. Victoria). This work was executed in London, where Longstaff had gone in September 1901, and where he also enjoyed success as a society and royal portraitist. Longstaff served as official war artist with the Australian Imperial Force (1918–19) in France and in 1920 returned permanently to Australia.

BIBLIOGRAPHY

*AUDB*

N. Murdoch: *Portrait in Youth of Sir John Longstaff, 1861–1941* (Sydney, 1948)

*Sir John Longstaff (1861–1941)* (exh. cat. by P. Timms, Shepparton, Victoria, A.G., 1975)

BRIDGET WHITELAW

**Longthorpe Tower.** Medieval house near Peterborough, Cambs, containing the most important surviving medieval domestic paintings in England. They decorate the Great Chamber, an upper room of a tower, which was added to an earlier manor house. This section of the building seems to have been erected in the early 14th century, possibly by Robert de Thorpe, steward of Peterborough Abbey from 1330 and tenant of Longthorpe Tower. The paintings are generally dated to *c.* 1330 on stylistic grounds. The decoration covers all the walls, the window splays and the vault (*see* GOTHIC, fig. 62). In the vault are the four *Evangelist Symbols* and *David with his Musicians*. On the walls and the window splays are the *Labours of the Months*, various birds and animals, the *Apostles* holding scrolls with the

articles of the Creed accompanied by personifications of the Church, a scene involving a hermit, the *Seven Ages of Man*, the *Nativity*, the *Three Living and the Three Dead*, a *Wheel of the Five Senses* and seated figures of *Edward III* and *Edmund Woodstock, Earl of Kent*. There are several other subjects, the meaning of which is uncertain owing to the loss of the accompanying inscriptions. The reason for the inclusion of Edmund Woodstock (1301–30), who was executed in 1330, is not clear: he was the most important tenant of nearby Peterborough Abbey, but there may have been some political meaning to his portrayal with Edward III. The programme is encyclopaedic in character, combining religious and moral teachings with secular themes and including some unusual representations: the *Wheel of the Five Senses*, of which there is a related late 13th-century version in Tre Fontane Abbey, Rome, shows a wheel held steady by a king, possibly personifying common sense, with various creatures personifying the senses around its perimeter.

BIBLIOGRAPHY

E. C. Rouse and A. Baker: 'The Wall Paintings at Longthorpe', *Archaeologia*, xcvi (1955), pp. 1–57

R. M. Ogilvie: 'The Longthorpe Murals', *J. Warb. & Court. Inst.*, xxii (1959), pp. 361–2

W. B. Yapp: 'The Birds and Other Animals of Longthorpe Tower', *Antiqua. J.*, lviii (1978), pp. 355–8

G. Casagrande and C. Kleinhenz: 'Literary and Philosophical Perspectives on the Wheel of the Five Senses in Longthorpe Tower', *Traditio*, xli (1985), pp. 311–27

NIGEL J. MORGAN

**Longueil, Joseph de** (*b* Givet, Ardennes, 16 Nov 1730; *d* Paris, 17 July 1792). French engraver. After taking drawing lessons in Liège, he went to Paris, where he acquired a sound technique in the studios of Jacques-Philippe Lebas and Jacques Aliamet but principally in that of Jean-Georges Wille. Following a journey to Italy, Germany and the Netherlands he returned to Paris, where he established himself mainly as an engraver of book illustrations. His earliest datable works are 21 plates after François Eisen for the edition of Jean de La Fontaine's *Contes* known as that of the 'Fermiers généraux' (1762). The same year, for his former teacher Wille, he engraved two pictures by Pierre-Joseph Mettay (1728–59), *Shipwreck near Naples* (Panhard, no. 1) and *View of the Environs of Naples* (P 2), for which he was paid the considerable sum of 650 livres each. He seldom made individual prints, although he did engrave several scenes after Eisen, and *The Fishermen* (*c.* 1770; P 9) after Joseph Vernet for Charles-Nicolas Cochin II; and, most important of all, the *View of the Unveiling of the Pont de Neuilly* (1772; P 3) after Eustache Saint-Far (1746–1822). These plates were generally commissioned, by a variety of publishers, and often Longueil was only asked to engrave the outlines, with others such as Emmanuel de Ghendt and Augustin de Saint-Aubin doing the etching. He did, however, engrave on his own behalf, in 1776, two allegories dedicated to Louis XVI and Marie-Antoinette, *Louis XVI Supported by Minerva and Venus* and *Marie-Antoinette Receiving France's Homage*, for which he asked Cochin to do the drawings, Pierre-Philippe Choffard to do the frames, and Saint-Aubin to make the etchings. These allegories earned him a patent as Graveur du Roi and the title of Graveur du Prince de Condé.

However, it is Longueil's book illustrations, mostly after Eisen, that constitute the essence of his work. He achieved great delicacy in a type of engraving that had previously been handled much more freely; he excelled in rendering the most precise nuances by the variety of ways in which he treated texture. Since public taste was for very careful and finished illustrations, Longueil soon came to be sought out by draughtsmen and booksellers. Among his greatest successes may be numbered various illustrations for works by Claude-Joseph Dorat, such as his *Recueil de contes et de poèmes* (1770); for Voltaire's *La Henriade*, after drawings by Eisen (1770); and for Jean-François Marmontel's *Contes moraux*, after Gravelot (1765). His oeuvre amounts to over 500 works.

BIBLIOGRAPHY

F. Panhard: *Joseph de Longueil, graveur du roi, 1730–1792: Sa Vie, son oeuvre* (Paris, 1880) [P]

CHRISTIAN MICHEL

**Longueil, René de**, Marquis de Maisons (*d* 1 Sept 1677). French administrator and patron. He served the French crown in various ministerial posts. He was one of a group of rich ennobled bourgeois in royal service who were the principal patrons of François Mansart in the middle years of the 17th century. Longueil's principal act as patron was the commissioning from Mansart of the Château de Maisons (now Château de Maisons-Laffitte) near Paris, one of the earliest and finest domestic buildings in what was to become the Louis XIV style. The top-lit, square-caged staircase, decorated by Gérard van Opstal, is one of its most remarkable features. Jacques Sarazin executed the sculptured groups in the vestibule, which also contained bas-reliefs by Gilles Guérin representing the *Four Quarters of the World*. The vestibule was decorated with two iron grilles (now Paris, Louvre, Galerie d'Apollon, Pavillon de l'Horloge). Guérin was also responsible for two chimney-pieces; that of the Salon Royal has Longueil's coat of arms and eagle. The court stayed at Maisons on two occasions, in 1651 and 1671. (For further information about the château *see* MANSART, (1) and fig. 1.) Guérin also sculpted for Longueil models for an altarpiece for a church of which his son, Guillaume de Longueil, was priest, in Conches, Seine-et-Marne.

BIBLIOGRAPHY

G. Brice: *Description nouvelle de ce qu'il y a de plus remarquable dans la ville de Paris* (Paris, 1684, rev. 8/1752, *R* 1971)
E. Bonnaffé: *Dictionnaire des amateurs français au XVIIe siècle* (Paris, 1884, rev. 1966)
L. Hautecoeur: *Architecture classique* (Paris, 1943–57)

PATRICK LE CHANU

**Longuelune, Zacharias** (*b* ?Paris, 1669; *d* Dresden, 30 Nov 1748). French architect and teacher, active in Germany and Poland. He probably trained in Paris with either Antoine Le Pautre or Pierre Le Pautre (i). In 1699 he may have accompanied Jean de Bodt to Berlin, where his presence was recorded between 1704 and 1713. He worked under de Bodt's direction on the completion of the Arsenal (1706) in Berlin. In 1710 Frederick I, King of Prussia, granted Longuelune a bursary to enable him to travel to Italy, but when Frederick William I came to the throne in

1713, he was dismissed. In 1717 he secured a post at the court of Saxony in Dresden, working for Augustus II, King of Saxony and Poland (also known as Augustus the Strong). After Longuelune's appointment in 1722 as Oberlandbaumeister, he was involved in all the King's building projects, but, owing to the collaborative method used to produce designs in the building office, it is difficult to attribute many works specifically to him.

When the Holländisches Palais in Dresden was transformed into the Japanisches Palais (begun 1722), Longuelune designed the central projection on the court façade and the view overlooking the Elbe in a restrained style, using pilaster strips. Between 1721 and 1724 he collaborated closely with the King as interior designer, converting the monarch's Schatzkammer, known as the Grünes Gewölbe, into a public museum. His plans for extending the castle (1724–30) were never implemented, while his designs for the blockhouses on the bridgehead in Dresdner Neustadt were only partially realized. The original scheme envisaged two guard posts on either side of the road, to close the vista down the Hauptstrasse. Each building was to be crowned by a stepped pyramid, one topped by a statue of *Augustus the Strong*, the other by one of *Minerva*. Longuelune's influence on designs for Schloss Grosssedlitz (destr.) and its park (1719–32), and for Schloss Pillnitz, near Dresden, was of an indirect nature, but he was in charge of building work when alterations were carried out to Schloss Moritzburg (from 1720/21), to Matthäus Daniel Pöppelmann's overall design. He is traditionally credited with designing the Neptune Fountain in the garden of Palais Marcolini in Friedrichstadt, Dresden, which was executed by Lorenzo Mattielli in 1741–4; with its grottoes and rockery it constitutes the finest fountain ensemble in Dresden.

Longuelune exercised a powerful and lasting influence on Saxon and Polish architecture through his work as a teacher at the school for cadets of the engineering corps. He also invented an ingenious system of articulation based principally on the use of pilaster strips, pilasters and columns, which originated from late 17th-century French classical architecture. With the works and ideas of Longuelune (and Jean de Bodt), architecture of southern German origin lost ground in Dresden; through his famous pupil Johann Christoph Knöffel, Longuelune became the 'father of Classicism in Saxony' (Löffler), as may be seen, for example, in the simple pilastered articulation of Knöffel's Wackerbarth (1723–8) and Kurländer (1728–9) palaces, both in Dresden and built soon after the exuberant Zwinger, commissioned in 1711. After the death of Augustus II in 1733, Longuelune withdrew into the background, although he continued to promote his ideas in his role as a teacher.

BIBLIOGRAPHY

*Macmillan Enc. Architects*; Thieme–Becker
H. G. Franz: *Zacharias Longuelune und die Baukunst des 18. Jahrhunderts in Dresden* (Berlin, 1953)
W. Hentschel: *Die sächsische Baukunst des 18. Jahrhunderts in Polen* (Berlin, 1967)
F. Löffler: *Das alte Dresden* (Leipzig, 1981), p. 470

BRUNO B. HEIM

**Longwood Gardens.** Botanical gardens in Kennett Square, *c.* 50 km south-west of Philadelphia, PA, USA. An

Englishman, George Pierce, bought the estate in 1700 and in 1720 built a brick house (now a wing of the present house). From 1800 his descendants, the twin brothers Joshua Pierce (1766–1851) and Samuel Pierce (1766–1836), planted the estate with exotic trees, and the collection grew rapidly, including laurels, copper beeches, yews, European and American horse-chestnuts, Norway spruce, several varieties of magnolia, Japanese ginkgos, empress trees and hollies, with evergreens predominating. In 1906 the property, known as Pierce's Park, was bought by Pierre Samuel du Pont (1870–1954) primarily to save the arboretum. Du Pont built the present house and developed the estate, preserving and enhancing the original garden, planting in harmony with the existing scheme. He built the extensive conservatories and in 1937 created the Longwood Foundation, which searches the world for ornamental plants to introduce to the USA. Longwood covers 400 ha, including woodlands and open spaces, with the formal and informal aspects of the garden carefully harmonized. Among its features are a Fountain Garden, an Italian water garden laid out to the plan of the Villa Gamberaia at Settignano (18th century), a series of garden courts and terraced flowerbeds. The design of the open-air theatre was inspired by the 'green theatre' at the Villa Gori near Siena (1620s), and much of the sculptural ornament was brought from Italy.

BIBLIOGRAPHY

J. T. Faris: *Old Gardens in and about Philadelphia* (Indianapolis, 1932), pp. 215–26

**Lonhy, Antoine de.** *See* MASTERS, ANONYMOUS, AND MONOGRAMMISTS, §I: MASTER OF THE TRINITY OF TURIN.

**Lönn, Wivi** (*b* Tampere, 20 May 1872; *d* Helsinki, 27 Dec 1966). Finnish architect. She qualified as an architect in 1896, and in 1898 she travelled on a scholarship in central Europe, England and Scotland studying stone and brick construction, as well as school architecture. Lönn was based in Tampere between 1898 and 1911. Her first projects were houses and schools in various parts of Finland—for which she adapted the innovations she had seen in Britain. The Tampere Central Fire Station (1908), her best building, is still in use: its picturesque, loose massing reflects a ground-plan that enhances the building's efficiency. It also suits the castle-like character lent by such details as the turrets, characteristic of NATIONAL ROMAN-TICISM in Finland—of which this station is a good example. She was in Jyväskylä from 1911 to 1918 and was invited to design buildings for Johannes Parviainen Factories Ltd in Säynätsalo. She in fact designed them all. Estonia Theatre in Tallinn (1913) is the most notable result of her collaboration with Armas Lindgren. In her work of this period she moved away from National Romanticism towards a more classical style.

Lönn moved to Helsinki in 1918. The most outstanding buildings of her later years are the two YWCA headquarters. The first, completed in 1928, also contained the home Lönn shared with Hanna Parviainen, the businesswoman who had financed the enterprise. The second, a 'women's house' in Savonlinna, was completed in 1933. In both projects Lönn was assisted by a young woman architect, Aili-Salli Ahde-Kjäldman (1892–1979), with whom she

also worked on the design of a monumental warehouse for the Verkatehdas cloth factory at Tampere (1923). The prevailing classicism became increasingly austere in these buildings. Lönn's last work was a modest observatory, Tähtelä (Fin.: 'star building') in Sodankylä, in the far north of Finland, completed in 1950.

Architecta, an association for Finnish women architects, was founded in 1942 in honour of Lönn's work. When Lönn was made a professor in 1959, Alvar Aalto characterized her work as 'a beautiful illustration of the idea rightly prevalent abroad, that the creative work of women has from very early times been one of the most important influences in Finnish culture' (*Uusi Suomi* [New Finland], 15 March 1959).

BIBLIOGRAPHY

P. Kivinen: *Tampereen jugend: Arkkitehtuuri-taideteollisuus* [Tampere *jugend*: architecture-applied arts] (Helsinki, 1982)
*Profiles: Pioneering Women Architects from Finland* (exh. cat., Helsinki, Mus. Fin. Archit., 1983)

PAULA KIVINEN

**Lonsdale**, 1st Earl of. *See* LOWTHER, (2).

**Lonsing, François-Louis** (*b* Brussels, 27 May 1739; *d* Léognan, Gironde, 11 April 1799). Flemish painter and engraver, active in France. He trained at the Antwerp Academie and under the painter Martin Geeraedts (1707–91); this Flemish training had a decisive influence on his style throughout his career. Early on he found a generous patron in Charles de Lorraine (1712–80), Governor of the Habsburg Netherlands, who paid for him to make a visit to Rome, where he remained for 17 years apparently without going through any significant artistic development. His only known works of that time are some reproductive engravings of mediocre quality, which the artist completed for the Scottish painter and dealer Gavin Hamilton. Lonsing left Rome in 1778 and spent a few years in Lyon, finally moving in 1783 to Bordeaux, where, until the Revolution (1789–95), he built up an important practice as a portrait painter. Among his portraits of the 1780s are those of *Maréchal de Mouchy* (Bordeaux, Mus. A. Déc.) and *Lt-Gen. de Larose* (Brussels, Mus. A. Anc.), both formal works that show Baroque influence. Like many artists, Lonsing lost his former patrons as a result of the Revolution. He moved to Paris, where he lived in poverty, although he produced an aquatint engraving of *Jean-Baptiste Lacombe* in 1794. Not until 1798 did he receive another major commission, from a prosperous merchant of Bordeaux: the painted double portrait of *J. B. Mareilhac and his Wife*, in which the young couple are depicted with their arms around each other in the grounds of Mareilhac's château, La Louvière, at Léognan near Bordeaux. This portrait, like the drawings and other portraits Lonsing completed during the Revolution, displays a Romantic sensibility. He was working on the decoration of the salon at La Louvière when he died.

BIBLIOGRAPHY

Thieme–Becker

M. Meaudre de Lapouyade: *Un Maître flamand à Bordeaux: Lonsing* (Paris, 1911)
H. Duriot: 'Le Château de Louvière à Léognan', *Bull. Mém. Soc. Archéol. Bordeaux*, lxv (1963–9), pp. 291–302
O. Michel: 'L'Apprentissage romain de François Joseph Lonsing', *Mél. Ecole Fr. Rome: Moyen Age, Temps Mod.*, lxxxiv (1972), pp. 493–509

**Loo, Andreas de** (*d* London, 1590). Flemish merchant and collector, possibly of Italian birth. He is important in English diplomatic history for using his position as a well-connected merchant in London and the Netherlands to attempt mediation between England and Spain in the years before the Spanish Armada (1588). He was later to claim that this fruitless enterprise cost him his fortune. De Loo also has a place in the history of collecting: van Mander described him as 'an enthusiastic lover of painting . . . who lived in London and bought all the works of Holbein on which he could lay hands'. Scholars have not always agreed on which specific versions of Holbein portraits de Loo owned, but it appears that he had the original of *Thomas More and his Family* (destr. 1752), painted in tempera on linen; the earlier of the two versions of *Archbishop William Warham*; and the portrait of Henry VIII's astronomer, *Nicholas Kratzer* (both Paris, Louvre). He also owned a version of *Thomas Cromwell* (probably that now in J. Chichester Constable priv. col., Burton Constable, Humberside). All these works later passed into the celebrated collection of Thomas Howard, 2nd Earl of Arundel. Walpole claimed that de Loo also owned one of Holbein's portraits of Erasmus, which Charles I was later to own, though he exchanged it subsequently for a picture by Leonardo da Vinci.

BIBLIOGRAPHY

K. van Mander: *Schilder-boeck* ([1603]–1604), fol. 223*a*

H. Walpole: *Anecdotes of Painting in England* (1762–71); ed. R. N. Wornum (1849), i, pp. 79, 91

C. Read: *Lord Burghley and Queen Elizabeth* (Oxford, 1960)

J. Rowlands: *Holbein* (Oxford, 1985)

MAURICE HOWARD

**Loo, Georges Hulin de.** *See* HULIN DE LOO, GEORGES.

**Loo, van** [Vanloo]. French family of artists of Flemish origin. They were the descendants of the genre painter Jan van Loo (*b* Sluis, nr Bruges, 1585). His son (1) Jacob van Loo was a history and genre painter working in Amsterdam in the Flemish tradition before moving to Paris, where he distinguished himself as a portrait painter. His two sons were both painters in southern France: Jean van Loo (*fl* 1682–94) worked in Toulon, and Louis-Abraham van Loo (*c.* 1656–1712) in Nice, Toulon and Aix-en-Provence. Of the latter's three sons, (2) Jean-Baptiste van Loo was a successful history painter in Italy and France before achieving even greater success as a portrait painter in England. He had earlier furthered the career of his brother (3) Carle Vanloo, the family's most famous member, whose illustrious career was notable for its eclectic diversity of subject and style; he was acclaimed for his history and genre paintings and also for his portraits and decorative work, and his style encompassed influences ranging from Mannerism to Rococo. The third son of Louis-Abraham, Joseph van Loo (*fl c.* 1732), became an engraver. Three of his nephews, the sons of Jean-Baptiste, became painters. The eldest, (4) Louis-Michel van Loo, worked in Rome and Paris but is chiefly distinguished for the powerful influence that he exerted on the development of Spanish painting while working as portrait painter to the Spanish court. The promising career of François van Loo (1708–32) was cut short by his early death. The youngest of the three, (5) Amédée van Loo, became court painter to

Frederick the Great of Prussia, producing history paintings and portraits. The family's last recorded artist was (6) César van Loo, the son of Carle; he worked in Paris and Turin, making a speciality of winter landscapes.

**(1) Jacob van Loo** (*b* Sluis, nr Bruges, 1614; *d* Paris, 27 Nov 1670). Painter. He first trained with his father, Jan van Loo, and seems to have been influenced in his youth by Thomas de Keyser and Jacob Backer. From 1642 he lived and worked in Amsterdam, where he married a sister of the painter Maerten Lengele (*d* 1668). The works of his first ten years in Amsterdam are Flemish in feeling, as is demonstrated by a comparison between his *Coucher à l'italienne* (1650; Lyon, Mus. B.-A.) and Jacob Jordaens's the *Wife of King Candaules* (Stockholm, Nmus.). The provocatively posed figure of a naked woman seen from behind, portrayed by Jordaens with Baroque exuberance, receives a somewhat calmer treatment from van Loo in terms of line and composition; nevertheless, the motif of the naked woman turning towards the viewer and the structure of the painting are clearly inspired by Jordaens. The same ten years produced more complex figure compositions based on mythological themes, in which Flemish monumentality and animation were again translated into quieter compositions of a more classical nature. Examples of this development include van Loo's portrayals of *Diana with her Nymphs* (Berlin, Bodemus., and Brunswick, Herzog Anton Ulrich-Mus.). Similar stylistic features can be recognized in the *Allegory of Wealth* (Chantilly, Mus. Condé).

In the 1650s van Loo ranked with Rembrandt, Bartholomeus van der Helst, Willem Kalf and Ferdinand Bol as one of the most important painters in Amsterdam. The conversation pieces that he produced during this period are considered the earliest examples of that genre and provided the inspiration for similar later works by Vermeer. In these amorous scenes, showing informal gatherings of musicians, soldiers and young women, van Loo stressed the relationships between the characters and gave his pictures a narrative dimension. The *Interior with Figures* (1649; ex-Mssrs Duits Ltd, London, 1955; see Burl. Mag., pl. xvi) derives from the juxtaposition of two couples: in the right-hand foreground a soldier is trying to embrace a playfully coy woman, while in the background a man is playing music with a young woman, who is looking out of the picture at the viewer.

Van Loo must have been well regarded as a portrait painter, for in 1658 he was commissioned to paint two group portraits of the *Regentesses* and the *Regents of the Haarlem Almshouse* (Haarlem, Frans Halsmus.). These portraits likewise demonstrate his ability to employ subtle gesture and eye contact to fuse his characters into a balanced but animated overall composition; animation and intensification of expression are the distinguishing characteristics of his work. In *Portrait of a Boy* (1658; Gray, Mus. Martin), depicting a boy with his dog, he combines stately van Dyckian motifs, such as draperies, architectural backdrop and landscape view, with an expression of spontaneity and intimacy. The harmonious palette is based on a delicate balance of yellow, red and grey-white, and points in its precise modulations to van Loo's closeness to Vermeer.

In 1660 a charge of manslaughter forced Jacob van Loo to flee to Paris. In 1663 he was admitted (*reçu*) by the Académie Royale de Peinture et de Sculpture as a portrait painter. His *morceau de réception* was the three-quarter-length portrait of the painter *Michel Corneille the Elder* (*c.* 1661–4; Paris, Louvre), whom he portrayed without attributes: the sitter's eloquent gestures suffice to characterize him as a person of intellect.

BIBLIOGRAPHY
Thieme–Becker
A. von Schneider: 'Jacob van Loo', *Z. Bild. Kst*, lix (1925–6), pp. 66–78
R. Jullian: 'Le "Coucher à l'italienne" de Jacob van Loo', *Proporzioni*, 3 (1950), pp. 199–203
'Notable Works of Art Now on the Market', *Burl. Mag.*, xcvii (1955), pl. xvi
J. Cailleux: 'Jacob van Loo, Greuze et Porporati: A propos d'un dessin du Musée des Beaux Arts de Lyon', *Bull. Mus. & Mnmts Lyon*, ii (1960), pp. 289–97
H. Steszewska: 'Nieznany obraz Jacoba van Loo w zbiorach Muzeum Narodowego w Poznaniu' [An anonymous portrait of Jacob van Loo in the collection of the National Museum, Poznań], *Stud. Muz.*, ix (1972), pp. 88–94
W. L. van Watering: 'On Jacob van Loo's *Portrait of a Young Woman*', *Bull. Minneapolis Inst. A.*, lxiii (1976–7), pp. 33–41
*La Collection A. P. de Mirimonde (Legs aux musées de Gray et de Tours)* (exh. cat., ed. E. Foucart-Walter; Paris, Louvre, 1987), pp. 46–8

CATHRIN KLINGSÖHR-LEROY

**(2) Jean-Baptiste van Loo** (*b* Aix-en-Provence, 11 Jan 1684; *d* Aix-en-Provence, 19 Sept 1745). Painter, grandson of (1) Jacob van Loo. He showed early artistic promise; first trained by his father Louis-Abraham van Loo, he acquired a reputation by painting religious pictures for churches at Aix-en-Provence and Toulon, including the *Agony of St Joseph* for the Ste Marie-Madeleine at Aix (*in situ*). In 1712 he visited Nice, Monaco and Genoa and during the following year worked for Victor Amadeus II, Duke of Savoy, and other noblemen. The patronage he received enabled him in 1714 to go to Rome, where he studied under Benedetto Lutti and painted works for churches, including a *Flagellation* (Rome, S Maria della Scala). There he also helped to restore 16th-century paintings by Giulio Romano and Primaticcio.

Around 1719 van Loo moved to Paris, where he continued to produce work for churches, for example *Christ's Entry into Jerusalem* (St Martin-des-Champs). He also painted history pictures, including the *Triumph of Galatea* (*c.* 1719; St Petersburg, Hermitage), which was purchased much later by Catherine the Great, through the agency of Denis Diderot. He was approved (*agréé*) by the Académie Royale in 1722 and received (*reçu*) as a full member on 23 February 1731. His *morceau de réception* was a painting of *Diana and Endymion* (1731; Paris, Louvre), which exemplifies his fleshy historical style and skilled brushwork. Van Loo's success gained him a European reputation, and he was called upon to paint numerous portraits at foreign courts.

In 1737 van Loo moved to London. There he abandoned history painting for an elegant form of portraiture, which was sufficiently free from flamboyancy to satisfy the English taste for unaffected realism. Because he had come to England without prior invitation, he initially demonstrated his ability by painting an uncommissioned portrait of the actor *Colley Cibber and his Daughter* (1737; untraced, mezzotint by Edward Fisher, 1757–8), in which the latter is tweaking Cibber's pen from behind. His

obvious ability as a portrait painter at a time when English art was at a momentary low ebb meant that his business had increased to five sittings a day by April 1738 at his studio in Henrietta Street, Covent Garden. His success was assured when he secured the patronage of the prime minister Sir Robert Walpole, who expressed a personal wish that the artist might gain a salaried post as official court painter. Van Loo's portrait of *Sir Robert Walpole* (1740; replica, London, N.P.G.) reveals the flattering courtly style he had adopted, which also appealed to those other leading Whigs who sought to project a cultivated image of themselves. He also gained the patronage of Frederick, Prince of Wales, painting *Augusta, Princess of Wales, with Members of her Family and Household* (*c.* 1739; London, St James's Pal., Royal Col.), and also *Frederick, Prince of Wales* and *Augusta, Princess of Wales* (both 1742; London, Buckingham Pal., Royal Col.). His popularity increased so rapidly that prospective sitters were forced to apply six weeks in advance, while native artists continued to worry about the dearth of available commissions and patronage that his success had caused them.

Health problems induced van Loo to return to Aix-en-Provence in October 1742. He spent the last three years of his life working both there and in Paris, and training his brother (3) Carle Vanloo and his sons (4) Louis-Michel van Loo and (5) Amédée van Loo.

BIBLIOGRAPHY
M. F. Dandré-Bardon: *Vie de Carle Vanloo* (Paris, 1765)
'The Note-books of George Vertue', *Walpole Soc.*, xxii (1934), pp. 82–4
E. Waterhouse: 'English Painting and France in the 18th Century', *J. Warb. & Court. Inst.*, xv (1952), pp. 122–35
W. G. Kalnein and M. Levey: *Art and Architecture of the Eighteenth Century in France*, Pelican Hist. A. (Harmondsworth, 1972), pp. 116, 120

SHEARER WEST

**(3) Carle** [Charles-André] **Vanloo** (*b* Nice, 15 Feb 1705; *d* Paris, 15 July 1765). Painter, brother of (2) Jean-Baptiste van Loo. After his father's death in 1712, he travelled to Turin to join his elder brother, (2) Jean-Baptiste van Loo, who took charge of his education. When they moved to Rome in 1714, Vanloo began formal studies with the painter Benedetto Lutti and the sculptor Pierre Legros *le jeune*. In 1719 the brothers moved to Paris, where the younger artist gained practical experience by assisting his brother on such commissions as the restoration of the Galerie François I at the château of Fontainebleau. He also studied at the Académie Royale, where he won first prize for drawing in 1723. The following year he was awarded the Prix de Rome, but the money that was to finance his studies in Italy was withheld, and he was forced to raise the necessary funds himself by painting society portraits and stage decorations for the opera in Paris. His few extant paintings from this period demonstrate, by their combination of Mannerist figural proportions with a fashionable Rococo palette, Vanloo's ability to assimilate various stylistic influences (e.g. the *Presentation in the Temple*, 1728; Lyon Cathedral). In early 1728 he was at last able to set out for Rome, in the company of his nephews (4) Louis-Michel Vanloo and François van Loo, and of his friend and future rival François Boucher.

In Rome, Vanloo quickly gained favour. By December 1728 one of his drawings had taken first prize at the Accademia di S Luca, and he had attracted the attention of Cardinal Melchior de Polignac, the French Ambassador to Rome, who intervened to obtain for him his long-delayed pension. While in Rome, Vanloo developed the two distinctive styles that he employed throughout his career. His small *Marriage of the Virgin* (1730; Nice, Mus. B.-A.), probably executed out of gratitude to de Polignac, exhibited a sweet, refined classicism reminiscent of Raphael and Carlo Maratti; he was also capable, as in his *Aeneas and Anchises* (1729; Paris, Louvre), of an altogether more dynamic, fluid style that invoked his contemporary Placido Costanzi. His most important Roman work was the illusionary ceiling fresco of the *Apotheosis of St Isidore* (1729; Rome, S Isidoro), which both established his reputation as a painter in the Grand Manner and set the stage for future large-scale decorations.

In 1732 Vanloo decided to return to France via Turin; by a tragic mishap his nephew François was jolted from the carriage and trampled to death by the horses. This may have been why Vanloo stayed on in Turin, where he produced some of his most elegant works in the service of Charles-Emanuel III, Duke of Savoy and King of Sardinia. Characteristic of this period is his ceiling fresco for the Palazzo Mauriziano, Stupinigi, of *Diana and her Nymphs Resting* (1733; *in situ*), a graceful and witty display of Olympians. He also decorated a salon in the Palazzo Reale with 11 paintings (1733; *in situ*) illustrating scenes from Torquato Tasso's *Gerusalemme liberata*. These works were strikingly situated between mirrors and subsequently became so famous through engravings that Turin became an obligatory stop on the Grand Tour.

In 1733 Vanloo married Christina Antonia Somis, a celebrated opera singer. A year later the couple left for France, probably to escape the escalating warfare in Piedmont. His return to Paris marked the beginning of a brilliant career. In 1735 he was admitted (*reçu*) by the Académie Royale with a painting of *Apollo Flaying Marsyas* (1735; Paris, Ecole N. Sup. B.-A.) that demonstrated his Italianate mastery of anatomy and Classical antiquity. Official commissions immediately followed. He contributed, along with Boucher and Charles Parrocel, two Rubensian paintings of a *Bear Hunt* (1736) and an *Ostrich Hunt* (1738; both Amiens, Mus. Picardie) to a decorative series of exotic hunts for the Petits Appartements of Louis XV at the château of Versailles. He also produced a succulent, Watteau-like *Rest on the Hunt* (1737; Paris, Louvre) as a pendant to a work by Parrocel for the Petits Appartements at the château of Fontainebleau. His other royal commissions included a cartoon of *Theseus Overcoming the Minotaur* (1746; Nice, Mus. B.-A.) for the Gobelins, and the *Allegory of Painting* (1752–3; San Francisco, CA, Pal. Legion of Honor) for Mme de Pompadour's château of Bellevue. With the versatility of his period, Vanloo also produced a number of portrait paintings that included sitters from the royal family (e.g. *Queen Marie Leczinska*, 1747; Versailles, Château; and *Louis XV*, 1748; Versailles, Mus. Hist.). His most dramatic portrait was that of *Mlle Clairon as Medea* (exh. 1759 Salon; Potsdam, Park Sanssouci).

Besides his work for the court, Vanloo produced paintings for Parisian high society. To appeal to its taste, he often employed a sensuous Rococo style that rivalled that of Boucher. His five history paintings for the decoration of the Hôtel de Soubise, Paris (e.g. *Castor and Pollux*, 1737; Paris, Archvs N.), demonstrate this ability to tailor styles to patrons' demands. His most popular paintings, however, were *turqueries*, a type of genre scene that depicted contemporary figures in Turkish or other exotic dress. The collectors Jean de Jullienne and Louis Fagon commissioned respectively the *Pasha Having his Mistress Painted* (*c.* 1737; Richmond, VA Mus. F.A.) and the *Sultan Giving a Concert to his Mistress* (*c.* 1737; London, Wallace). Mme Geoffrin, whose salon Vanloo frequented, also ordered two exotic scenes as pendants: the *Spanish Conversation Piece* (1754) and the *Spanish Lecture* (*c.* 1758; both St Petersburg, Hermitage); in these Vanloo portrayed his wife in Spanish costume.

Vanloo also made a significant contribution to religious painting. His early Parisian works continued the stylistic diversity of his Roman period, as in the refined *Virgin and Child* (1738; Rouen, Mus. B.-A.) and the more dynamic and agitated *Martyrdom of St Stephen* (1740; Valenciennes, Mus. B.-A.). By the 1740s, however, a new emphasis on grandeur and monumentality had begun to appear, as in his Rubensian altarpieces of *St Denis* and *St George* for the charterhouse of Champmol. By the 1750s he had developed a style of religious painting that fully incorporated the Italian Grand Manner, while moving beyond it in its uniquely French idiom of clarity, nobility and compositional reserve. This style is best exemplified by the six scenes from the *Life of St Augustine* that he painted between 1746 and 1755 for the choir of Notre-Dame-des-Victoires, Paris. Still *in situ*, these enormous paintings transform their stylistic precedents in Raphael, Eustache Le Sueur and Bon Boullogne into an unparalleled, 18th-century orchestration of monumental form, grey-blond colour harmonies and dramatic pictorial light. The cycle's *St Augustine Preaching before Bishop Valerius* (see fig.) is one of the artist's most admired works. Other notable paintings include his *Vow of Louis XIII at the Battle of La Rochelle* (1746; Paris, Notre-Dame des Victoires); the series of paintings of the *Life of the Virgin* (*c.* 1748) for St Sulpice, Paris; and *St Clotilda Praying at the Tomb of St Martin* (1752; Brest, Mus. Mun.).

While Vanloo's stylistic eclecticism and the wide range of his subjects make him difficult to categorize in 18th-century art, it was precisely these qualities that his contemporaries admired. To them, he seemed to possess a total mastery of artistic traditions, and as a consequence he was immensely successful. Baron von Grimm called him the greatest painter in Europe, and Voltaire compared him to Raphael. He never lacked commissions, and his works were generally acclaimed at the Salons. He also enjoyed many prestigious appointments, such as professor at the Académie Royale (1737); Director of the Ecole Royale des Elèves Protégés (1749); Premier Peintre du Roi (1762); and Director of the Académie Royale (1763). He was ennobled in 1751. He was highly regarded by his students, who included Jean-Honoré Fragonard, Gabriel-François Doyen, Bernard Lépicié and Louis Lagrenée. His considerable reputation was short-lived, however; even before his death he began to witness an increasing vogue for Neo-classicism among the precursors of Jacques-Louis David. Two decades later, at the height of the Davidian

Carle Vanloo: *St Augustine Preaching before Bishop Valerius*, oil on canvas, 4.0×8.4 m, 1755 (Paris, Notre-Dame-des-Victoires)

revolution in painting, Vanloo's eclecticism was blindly condemned in the purging of the Rococo style, giving rise to the derisive slogan 'Vanloo, Pompadour, Rococo'. His reputation has only begun to be re-evaluated in the late 20th century.

BIBLIOGRAPHY

M.-F. Dandré-Bardon: *Vie de Carle Vanloo* (Paris, 1765; R/2 Geneva, 1973)

C. Blanc: *Histoire des peintres de toutes écoles: Ecole française*, ii (Paris, 1865), pp. 1–12

L. Réau: 'Carle Vanloo, 1705–1765', *Archvs A. Fr.*, xix (1938), pp. 7–96

*The Age of Louis XV: French Painting, 1710–1774* (exh. cat. by Pierre Rosenberg, Toledo, OH, Mus. A.; Chicago, IL, A. Inst.; Ottawa, N.G.; 1975–6), pp. 76–8

*Carle Vanloo: Premier peintre du roi* (exh. cat. by M.-C. Sahut, Nice, Mus. Chéret, 1977) [numerous pls]

P. Conisbee: *Painting in Eighteenth-century France* (Ithaca, 1981), pp. 54–9

F. H. Hazlehurst: 'The Wild Beasts Pursued: The *Petite Galerie* of Louis XV at Versailles', *A. Bull.*, lxvi (1984), pp. 224–36

D. Wakefield: *French Eighteenth-century Painting* (New York, 1984), pp. 101ff

*Diderot et l'art de Boucher à David* (exh. cat., ed. M.-C. Sahut and N. Volle; Paris, Hôtel de la Monnaie, 1984), pp. 368–82

*The Loves of the Gods: Mythological Painting from Watteau to David* (exh. cat., ed. C. Bailey; Fort Worth, TX, Kimbell A. Mus., 1992), pp. 429–35

M. Levey: Painting and Sculpture in France, 1700–1789, Pelican Hist. A. (New Haven, 1993), pp. 173–8

LAURIE G. WINTERS

**(4) Louis-Michel van Loo** (*b* Toulon, 2 March 1707; *d* Paris, 20 March 1771). Painter, son of (2) Jean-Baptiste van Loo. He trained with his father in Turin and Rome, later attending the courses of the Académie Royale in Paris. He received the institution's first prize for painting in 1726, and in 1728, accompanied by his brother, François, and his uncle, Carle, returned to Rome where he was associated with François Boucher. On his way back to France, he stayed for a time in Turin, painting portraits (untraced) of the royal family of Sardinia, the Duke and Duchess of Savoy. In Paris he was admitted (*reçu*) to membership of the Académie Royale and in 1735 was appointed assistant teacher at the Académie, becoming renowned as a specialist in portrait painting. Most of his portraits from this period are half-length, combining ideas from Hyacinthe Rigaud's later work with other more natural and innovative ones. On the death of Jean Ranc, Philip V of Spain asked Rigaud to suggest a substitute, and van Loo was proposed. He arrived in Madrid in 1737 and remained there as Pintor de la Corte until 1752, responding with modern aesthetic ideas to the demands of the Spanish monarchs for pomp and splendour. He carried out court commissions but devoted part of his time to teaching, his pupils often becoming studio assistants. He also took an active part in meetings held over a number of years to establish the Real Academia de Bellas Artes de S Fernando, for which he produced the canvas, the *Education of Cupid by Venus and Mercury* (1748; Madrid, Real Acad. S Fernando, Mus.), in which the three figures appear in a garden set in an architectural background. In 1752 he was appointed director of painting, a post he barely enjoyed, since he returned to Paris that year.

At the Madrid court van Loo produced a large number of portraits of the royal family, of which, over the years, replicas and studio copies were made; the latter were the work of both Spanish and French copyists, among them Benoît Verdot, who was appointed honorary Pintor de la Corte in 1739. Many of these paintings were destined to be sent to the various European courts, in line with the requirements of dynastic marriages. They also had an official function in connection with the various institutions and administrative departments of the Spanish empire, as well as important Spanish families, and served as gifts for friends and relations.

Van Loo's historical standing has been that of official portrait painter to the Spanish royal house throughout an important part of the middle of the 18th century. His most famous work is the *Family of Philip V* (1743; Madrid, Prado; see fig.), an enormous group canvas (4.06×5.11 m) showing the members of the royal family in a variety of poses in a spacious hall with red velvet hangings, in front of a musicians' tribune, underlining the family's taste for music. Van Loo is also renowned for a number of

preparatory sketches, such as that for the *Family of Philip V* (1739; Madrid, Real Acad. S Fernando, Mus.); for the great court portraits of other members of the royal family, which include those of *Louise Elizabeth of Bourbon, Duchess of Parma* (1745) and *Philip of Bourbon, Duke of Parma* (both Madrid, Prado); and for his portraits of various private individuals.

Van Loo also produced paintings with mythological content and compositions with popular themes, in the style of David Teniers II, as tapestry cartoons for the Real Fábrica de S Bárbara. Extant tapestries, probably made *c.* 1740–45 from van Loo's cartoons, depict themes such as *Couples Dancing before a Blind Musician* and *The Alchemist*. When Philip V died in 1746, his successor, Ferdinand VI, not only confirmed van Loo's appointment but also nominated him Primer Pintor, thus allowing him to continue in the service of the court and to paint the monarch and his wife, Barbara of Braganza.

In France between 1760 and 1770 van Loo painted *Louis XV* and every member of the French royal family in such portraits as that of the *Dauphin Louis* (later Louis XVI; Versailles, Château). He also succeeded his uncle Carle Vanloo as Director of the Ecole Royale des Elèves Protégés. From 1753 to 1769 he regularly showed his pictures in the Salon, achieving great success; they included

Louis-Michel van Loo: *Family of Philip V*, oil on canvas, 4.06×5.11 m, 1743 (Madrid, Museo del Prado)

a portrait of *Denis Diderot* (exh. 1767 Salon; Paris, Louvre; for illustration *see* DIDEROT, DENIS).

Through the Salon van Loo became acquainted with the bourgeois, social and scientific worlds of the last years of the reign of Louis XV. Many half-length, full-length and group portraits from this period are extant, both official and private, always skilfully and correctly executed. The collaboration of a large studio is evident in many of these portraits and would have been necessary to enable van Loo to complete his many commissions. His work influenced Goya, particularly in some portaits, and the still-life painter Luis Meléndez, as well as other artists, both Spanish and French.

BIBLIOGRAPHY
A. B. di Vesme: 'I Van Loo in Piemonte', *Archv Stor. A.*, vi (1893), pp. 333–68
Y. Bottineau: *L'Art de cour dans l'Espagne de Philippe V* (Bordeaux, 1960)
J. J. Luna: 'Louis-Michel van Loo en España', *Goya*, 144 (1978), pp. 330–37
——: 'Nuevas apreciaciones sobre las obras de Louis-Michel van Loo en el Museo del Prado', *Bol. Mus. Prado*, iii (1982), pp. 181–90
JUAN J. LUNA

**(5) (Charles-)Amédée(-Philippe) van Loo** (*b* Rivoli, nr Turin, ?25 Aug 1719; *d* Paris, 15 Nov 1795). Painter, son of (2) Jean-Baptiste van Loo. He studied with his father and at the Académie Royale, Paris; in 1738 he won the Prix de Rome. He spent three and a half years in Italy, and another two and a half with his father in Aix-en-Provence, before returning to Paris in 1745. He was received (*reçu*) as a full member of the Académie in 1747 and in the same year married his cousin Marie-Marguerite Lebrun, daughter of the painter Michel Lebrun (*d* 1753).

Van Loo's official success was confirmed in 1748, when he was appointed painter to the francophile Frederick the Great of Prussia, a post his uncle Carle Vanloo had declined. He spent the years 1748–59 and 1763–9 in Berlin, where his work for the King consisted principally of decorative schemes for the royal palaces, including the ceiling of the Court Theatre (*Apollo and the Muses*, completed 1748) and the ceiling of the Marble Room (the *Glorification of the Great Elector*, completed 1751); he also executed paintings for Schloss Sanssouci, Potsdam, including the *School of Athens* (1748) and the *Sacrifice of Iphigenia* (1749). In addition, he made a great many portraits, culminating in the full-length state portrait of the *King of Prussia* (exh. Salon 1769; London, Buckingham Pal., Royal Col.). Van Loo exhibited regularly at the Paris Salon between 1761 and 1785; the critics generally preferred his portraits and mythologies to his many conscientious but pedestrian religious works. He also made several designs for tapestries, such as the *Costume turc* (1773–5), commissioned by Mme Du Barry and woven at the Gobelins. He was appointed Professor at the Académie in 1770, but his later years showed a marked decline in his powers.

BIBLIOGRAPHY
M. Fenaille: *Etat général des tapisseries de la manufacture des Gobelins 1600–1900*, iv (Paris, 1907), pp. 329–36
C. Oulmont: 'Amédée van Loo: Peintre du roi de Prusse', *Gaz. B.-A.*, n. s. 3, viii (1912), pp. 139–50, 223–34
*Friedrich II und die Kunst: Ausstellung zum 200. Todestag* (exh. cat., ed. H.-J. Giersberg and C. Meckel; Potsdam, Sanssouci, 1986), i, p. 27; ii, pp. 176–9

**(6) (Jules-)César(-Denis) van Loo** (*b* Paris, 20 May 1743; *d* Paris, 1 July 1821). French painter, son of (3) Carle Vanloo. He studied with his father and, from 1757, at the Académie Royale, Paris. In 1767 he was approved (*agréé*) by the Académie, and in the same year was awarded a special bursary to study at the Académie de France in Rome, although his repeated attempts between 1764 and 1776 to win the Prix de Rome were all unsuccessful. In 1784 he was received (*reçu*) as a full member of the Académie Royale, on submission of *Landscape with a Storm* (untraced; formerly Paris, Louvre) and *Landscape by Moonlight* (Paris, Louvre), both in the manner of Joseph Vernet. He first exhibited at the Salon in 1785, showing his two *morceaux de réception* and another landscape, the *Temple of the Sibyl at Tivoli* (untraced); from then until 1817 he missed only the Salon of 1795. He is recorded in Rome in 1785 and probably returned to Paris in 1789, when he was appointed *adjoint au recteur* at the Académie.

In 1791 van Loo emigrated to Turin and, like his father before him, worked for the Piedmontese court. The first of his winter landscapes, a genre for which he became especially celebrated, was exhibited at the Salon of 1799, and was influenced not only by the Netherlandish masters of the 17th century, but also, more immediately, by Italian artists such as Francesco Foschi (*d c.* 1805) and the Piedmontese Giovanni Michele Granieri (*fl* 1736–78). The best of van Loo's snow scenes, such as the *Ruins of a Gothic Church* (1799; exh. Salon 1801; Fontainebleau, Château), show a careful finish combined with a strong sense of atmosphere, and place him among the most interesting and individual artists of the period. In addition to landscapes, he made at least one portrait, that of Louis XVI's secretary, the *Comte de Mirbel* (1780; Caen, Mus. B.-A.), and was the author of an open letter, *César van Loo aux amateurs des beaux-arts* (Paris, 1817).

BIBLIOGRAPHY
*French Painting, 1774–1830: The Age of Revolution* (exh. cat., ed. F. J. Cummings, P. Rosenberg and R. Rosenblum; Paris, Grand Pal.; Detroit, MI, Inst. A.; New York, Met.; 1974–5), pp. 647–9
J.-F. Heim, C. Beraud and P. Heim: *Les Salons de peinture de la révolution française, 1789–1799* (Paris, 1989), p. 370

**Looking-glass.** *See* MIRROR.

**Loomis, Roger Sherman** (*b* Yokohama, Japan, 31 Oct 1887; *d* Waterford, CT, 11 Oct 1966). American writer. He taught English at Columbia University, New York, from 1919 to 1958, and became professor there in 1947. He devoted a lifetime's research to tracing the origins of the legends of King Arthur, and to proving that they had their roots in Celtic mythology and were passed to the Continent by Breton and other story-tellers. Loomis also pursued an interest in art and art history; many of his early publications dealt with aspects of medieval Arthurian iconography, and it was this art-historical research that led him to postulate the Celtic origins of the legends. He continued, where relevant, to use his knowledge of medieval art to support his arguments. His *Arthurian Legends in Medieval Art* (1938), written in collaboration with his wife, was a comprehensive survey of Arthurian iconography up to 1500, the result of nearly 30 years' research. His continuing interest in art history is evident in *A Mirror of*

*Chaucer's World* (1965), in which he assembled paintings, manuscript illuminations and sculpture relating to the poet and his times.

WRITINGS

*Illustrations of Medieval Romance on Tiles from Chertsey Abbey*, University of Illinois Studies in Language and Literature, ii/2 (Chicago, 1916)
'The Date, Source and Subject of the Arthurian Sculpture at Modena', *Medieval Studies in Memory of Gertrude Schoepperle Loomis* (New York, 1927), pp. 209–29
with L. H. Loomis: *Arthurian Legends in Medieval Art* (New York, 1938)
*A Mirror of Chaucer's World* (Princeton, 1965)
*Studies in Medieval Literature: A Memorial Collection of Essays* (New York, 1970) [with complete bibliog.]

□

**Loon, Theodoor van** (*b* ?Brussels, 1581–2; *d* Leuven, 1667). Flemish painter. His style was developed in Rome, where he worked from 1602 to 1608, taught by, among others, the little-known Jacob de Haze (1575–1634). Van Loon was again in Rome in 1617 and 1628; during this last visit he executed a *St Anne* (untraced) for S Maria dell'Anima, the parish church of the German nation (which included the Netherlanders). Apart from these interludes, he was active mainly in Brussels and after *c.* 1639 also in Leuven. In Brussels he benefited from the patronage of the Archdukes Albert and Isabella, through whom in 1613 he was commissioned to make a cycle of paintings on the *Life of the Virgin* for the church of the Discalced Carmelites, which had been built on the Archduke's initiative. In 1620 van Loon produced three paintings, two of them representing *St Hubert*, for the archducal hunting lodge at Tervuren (now Brussels, Musées Royaux B.-A.). Between 1623 and 1628, and again in 1632, he painted seven monumental scenes from the *Life of the Virgin* for the pilgrims' church founded by the Archdukes at Scherpenheuvel (*in situ*). These commissions involved close collaboration with the court architect, Wenceslas Cobergher. Van Loon spent his later life in the university town of Leuven, where he had long-standing contacts stemming from his friendship with the humanist scholar Erycius Puteanus (*d* 1625), whose portrait he painted.

From early in his career van Loon's work had a strongly Italianate character, his choice of motifs and style being much indebted to the work of the artists who between *c.* 1590 and 1620 determined the direction of so-called proto- and early Baroque. Works such as the *Adoration of the Shepherds* (1613; Brussels, Mus. A. Anc.; see fig. 1) and the *Martyrdom of St Lambert* (1617; Sint-Lambrechts-Woluwe, St Lambertuskerk) are very much in the style of Caravaggio, particularly in the way the foregrounds are foreshortened and partly cut off by the edge of the painting, and in the light effects and expressive realism. The animated pathos of Federico Barocci also seems to have impressed van Loon, judging from the St Lambertuskerk altarpiece. His most obvious affinity, however, seems to have been with the work of the more classicizing representatives of early Baroque painting: Annibale Carracci and Domenichino. Van Loon sometimes borrowed motifs directly from their works and in general adopted their academically classical manner, especially after 1620. The well-modelled, smooth and idealized figures, posing symmetrically and serenely within a monumental composition, are the most obvious characteristics of this style, of which

1. Theodoor van Loon: *Adoration of the Shepherds*, oil on canvas, 2.07×1.54 m, 1613 (Brussels, Musée d'Art Ancien)

his impressive *Birth of the Virgin* (*c.* 1623–8; Scherpenheuvel, Onze-Lieve-Vrouwekerk; see fig. 2) is one of the most striking examples. He employed the idiom throughout his career, apparently feeling no need to adapt stylistically, as did many of his contemporaries, to the more dynamic High Baroque, as practised by Rubens and van Dyck *c.* 1625–30.

Van Loon was one of the most important painters of his time in Brussels, which was then, with Antwerp, of major artistic importance in the southern Netherlands. His stately altarpieces, Italianate and classical, fulfilled the demands of the Counter-Reformation as far as form and decorum are concerned, but his style lacked the radiant characteristics of Rubens's paintings, which were present in such remarkable profusion in Brussels churches. Competition from those and from the works of his very Rubensian contemporary and fellow citizen Gaspar de Crayer meant that van Loon remained somewhat eclipsed.

BIBLIOGRAPHY

T. Cornil: 'Theodore van Loon et la peinture italienne', *Bull. Inst. Hist. Belge Rome*, xvii (1936), pp. 187–211
J. S. Held: 'Notes on Flemish Seventeenth-century Painting: Jacob van Oost and Theodoor van Loon', *A. Q.* [Detroit], xviii (1955), pp. 147–57
A. Boschetto: 'Di Theodoor van Loon e dei suoi dipinti a Montaigu', *Paragone*, xxi (1970), pp. 42–59
D. Coeckelberghs: '*Le Martyre de Saint Lambert* (1617): Tableau caravaggesque de Theodore van Loon', *Bull. Inst. Royal Patrm. A.*, xvii (1978–9), pp. 138–52

HANS VLIEGHE

**Loos, Adolf** (*b* Brünn [now Brno], Moravia, 10 Dec 1870; *d* Kalksburg, Austria, 23 Aug 1933). Austrian architect,

2. Theodoor van Loon: *Birth of the Virgin*, oil on canvas, 2.57×1.80 m, *c.* 1623–8 (Scherpenheuvel, Onze-Lieve-Vrouwekerk)

theorist and writer. He was an often satirical critic of the Vienna Secession, an early advocate of the Functionalist aesthetic, a radical polemicist and one of the most important and influential pioneers of the Modern Movement, achieving in his buildings of *c.* 1910 the style generally adopted elsewhere only a decade later.

1. Training and early work, before 1910. 2. Mature and late work, 1910 and after.

1. TRAINING AND EARLY WORK, BEFORE 1910. His father had studied painting but worked as a sculptor and mason in Brünn, then an important industrial centre of the Austro-Hungarian empire, and early contact with his father's workshop probably influenced Loos's choice of career as well as his understanding of and respect for natural materials. In 1887 he obtained a bricklayer's certificate, in 1887–8 he studied at the Gewerbeschule in Reichenberg and he eventually completed a building engineering course at the Gewerbeschule in Brünn. He then decided to train as an architect and in 1889 attended the Technische Hochschule, Dresden. His course was interrupted by army service and a period at the Akademie der Bildenden Künste, Vienna; he returned to Dresden (1892–3) to complete his studies. In 1893 Loos left Europe for a three-year study trip to the USA, supporting himself with menial work while he visited Chicago and the World's Columbian Exposition (1893); New York and its early

skyscrapers; Philadelphia; and St Louis, where Louis Sullivan's Wainwright Building had recently been completed. In addition to the contrast apparent between the classical buildings of the Exposition and the innovative work of the Chicago school, Loos no doubt also noted Sullivan's writings, including 'Ornament in Architecture' (1892), which advocated the temporary abandonment of ornament until the architect was better able to manipulate unadorned forms, and which must have influenced his own later essay 'Ornament und Verbrechen' (see below).

In 1897, a year after Loos returned to Vienna, the Vienna Secession was founded (*see* SECESSION, §3), and he lost no time in establishing himself as a formidable critic of its *fin-de-siècle* culture, seen in the burgeoning *Sezessionstil* and the *Gesamtkunstwerk* ideal of such architects as Josef Hoffmann and Joseph Maria Olbrich. In October 1897 Loos's radical polemic began to appear in *Die Zeit* and turned into a spate of articles in the following year, mainly in the *Neue Freie Presse*. These covered a wide range of subjects, including, in addition to architecture, furnishings, dress and music, on which Loos adopted a puritanical approach. His professional design work of this period consisted mainly of interiors (mostly destr.), in which furniture was built in where possible. The best-known examples include the elegant shop interior (1898; destr.) for Goldman & Salatsch, men's clothiers, in the Graben, and the Café Museum (1899; partly destr.) opposite Olbrich's newly completed Secession Building; Loos's design for the Café Museum attained such an extreme of unornamented simplicity, with plain segmental ceiling and undecorated walls, that it became known as 'Café Nihilismus', much to Loos's satisfaction. His use of commercially available furniture, such as Thonet bentwood chairs, reflected his view that the architect's design should not inhibit the occupants' choice of everday products for comfort and convenience.

At the same time Loos developed an affinity for the underplayed styles emerging from the English Arts and Crafts movement, admiring the simplification of form and unadorned surfaces of the English domestic revival of the 1890s. His idealized vision set up the English gentleman, with his simple and functional clothes and accoutrements, as a model worthy of emulation by the *nouveaux riches* of the German-speaking world, whose pretentious historicist stucco mansions around Vienna's Ringstrasse (then still under development) he satirized in his 'Die Potemkinsche Stadt' (*Ver Sacrum*, vii, 1898). The English clothes he admired were advertised in the new and short-lived periodical he published in 1903, *Das Andere*, the sub-title of which stated that it was for the 'introduction of western civilization into Austria', while the interior (1903; partially destr.) he designed for his own house in the Bösendorferstrasse, which is well known from published photographs, had an exposed-brickwork, metal-canopied and timber-beamed inglenook fireplace that was redolent of the English tradition. The first house designed by Loos was the Villa Karma (1904–6), Clarens, Montreux, where an existing dwelling was completely enclosed in a new one, consisting of a four-storey stuccoed house of classical simplicity, with a flat roof and recessed attic storey (completed by HUGO EHRLICH). In 1908 he designed the

1. Adolf Loos: Goldman & Salatsch Building (Looshaus), Vienna, 1910

famous interior of the American Bar (Kärntner Bar), Durchgang Kärntner, Vienna, which, with its coloured glass, marble floor and panelled ceiling, continued the '... confluence of ... ideas ... some drawn from Neo-classicism, some from the influence of Ruskin and Morris, which constitutes the essence of Loos's philosophy' (Summerson; see 1985 exh. cat., p. 7).

2. MATURE AND LATE WORK, 1910 AND AFTER. Loos's career culminated in the decade before World War I, when he built his one major urban building and a series of influential private houses. The Goldman & Salatsch Building (1910; now widely known as the Looshaus; see fig. 1), Vienna, is a plain, six-storey block of residential accommodation above a large shop. It faces the Hofburg in the Michaelerplatz. Loos admired Karl Friedrich Schinkel as the last architect he considered able to use the architectural orders without rhetoric, and in the Goldman & Salatsch Building his own classicism found expression in the marble columns of the entrance canopy and the entablature raised above the mezzanine. The interior of this building, with its marble veneers and mahogany joinery, also reveals clearly Loos's preference for the use of rich materials in place of applied ornamentation, evident as well in the character of two small shops of this period: Knize & Company (1910–13) in the Graben and the Buchhandlung Manz (1912), Kohlmarkt.

It is, however, the series of private houses, beginning with the Steiner House (1910; partially altered), Weitgasse, that places Loos among the pioneers of the Modern Movement. With the Horner House (1912; partially altered), Northargasse, and the Scheu House (1912–13; restored 1971), Larochegasse, the series represents a turning point in 20th-century architecture. The Steiner

House, for example, is one of the first private houses to be built in reinforced concrete, and its flat-roofed, three-storey garden front, with an abstract cubic form, smooth white surfaces and horizontal windows, prefigures the International Style by nearly a decade. More importantly perhaps, it was in these houses, especially the Scheu House, that Loos began to develop his concept of the Raumplan, the free disposition of volumes within a simple building form to give more complex interior spaces than are possible with continuous horizontal floor divisions. Loos was thus among the first to attempt the reconciliation of internal spatial complexity with prismatic external forms, which was one of the major difficulties facing architects of the early Modern Movement and was only fully resolved with Le Corbusier's development of the completely free plan, postulated as one of his 'five points of a new architecture' (1925).

Of some 30 articles written by Loos during 1904–14, the most influential were undoubtedly 'Ornament und Verbrechen' and 'Architektur'. The former, which equates human cultural development with the progressive shedding of ornament, is widely dated to 1908 and used to exemplify Loos's early influence in determining the character of Modernist architecture. Recent scholarship (see Rukschio), however, suggests that a talk with this title was given to the Akademischer Verband für Literatur und Musik, Vienna, on 21 January 1910, repeated twice in 1913, but published first in French (Les Cahiers d'aujourd'hui, June 1913, and L'Esprit nouveau, 15 Nov 1920), and published in German in 1929 (Frankfurter Zeitung, 24 Oct). In this case any widespread influence, such as that sponsored by the founder-editors of L'Esprit nouveau, the poet Paul Dermée and the Purist painters Amédée Ozenfant and Charles-Edouard Jeanneret (Le Corbusier), seems most likely to date from about 1912.

An extract only of the paper 'Architektur' (read to a meeting of architects in Berlin in October 1910) appeared in Der Sturm on 15 December 1910, and again it was first published as a whole in French (Les Cahiers d'aujourd'hui, Dec 1912). It is clearly related to the essay on ornament, begins in praise of architecture without architects, recommends a modified Arts and Crafts philosophy of craft design and ends with a panegyric on Neo-classicism and an invocation of the spirit of Schinkel to inspire 'our forthcoming generation of architects'. Loos's advocacy of simplicity stemmed from his view that since the modern bourgeois urban dweller was alienated from both the rural vernacular and the aristocratic building traditions, for most modern urban buildings it was necessary 'to do no more than design a building with technical correctness, guided by the right human approaches, and leave the right and truly contemporary form to emerge spontaneously'. There was a clear difference between his rejection of the superfluous, seen in his plain façades, and the position of the architects of the Bauhaus who adopted simplicity as a conscious aesthetic.

During World War I Loos built a sugar refinery and a house for its director (1916–18; partially destr.) at Hrysovany (Rohrbach), near his birthplace, and he was subsequently given Czechoslovak citizenship (1918). In 1920 he was appointed chief architect to the housing department of the city of Vienna, which was suffering from a chronic shortage of housing. He produced a number of housing projects in which he tried to break away from the conventional courtyard plan, including the innovative Heubergsiedlung (1921; partially destr.) at the junction of Röntgengasse and Plachygasse, which incorporated stepped terraces and greenhouses. Frustrated by post-war austerity and inflation, however, he became disillusioned and resigned. He decided to move to Paris at the invitation of the Dadaist poet Tristan Tzara, but he first completed the Rufer House (1922), Schliessmanngasse, Vienna, the first of the cubiform houses in which he further developed the *Raumplan* concept: it is one of the well-known images of the early Modern Movement, with its classical cornice and plain frieze above plain wall surfaces and an asymmetrical arrangement of windows that reflected the free planning of the spaces within.

Loos's essays of 1897–1900 were published in German over a French imprint as *Ins Leere gesprochen* in 1921; together with the French-language publication of the more controversial articles (see above), they prepared the way for his move to Paris and a welcome from the Dadaist circle. He was in Nice when he prepared his entry for the *Chicago Tribune* Tower competition (1922; unexecuted), a skyscraper in the form of a giant Doric column with 22 floors of offices, which was one of the most widely published project drawings of the 20th century. Other designs of this period, all unexecuted, included that for a house on the Venice Lido (1923) for the actor Alexander Moissi, in which he took the *Raumplan* concept a stage further; a Grand Hotel Babylon (1923) on the Promenade des Anglais, Nice; and hotels in the Champs Elysées (1923) and Bois de Boulogne (1924), an opera house for his friend Arnold Schoenberg (1926) and a house for the dancer Josephine Baker (1928), all in Paris. A house was built, however, for Tristan Tzara (1925–6; see fig. 2) on the Avenue Junot, Montmartre, the only substantial commission he executed in Paris and regarded as a canonical example of what has been called Classical Modernism. Loos also became the correspondent in Paris for the review *Die Wohnungskultur*, a German version of *Bytová Kultura* established by Karel Teige and the Czech avantgarde with whom Loos had renewed contacts.

In 1928 Loos returned to Vienna, and in a series of houses built in Vienna and Prague towards the end of his career he fully developed the *Raumplan* concept. The Moller House (1928), Starkfriedgasse, Vienna, and the Müller House (1928–30), Střešovice, Prague, were both houses with plain exteriors, while the Khuner House (1930), near Payerbach, Lower Austria, was more contextual, with pitched roofs, but all incorporated important contributions to the development of the free plan: the Müller House in particular is one of the earliest examples of a split-level *Raumplan* domestic interior, creating dynamic, interlocking spaces across levels. A collection of some 30 of Loos's essays dating from 1903, including 'Ornament und Verbrechen' and 'Architektur', was published under the title *Trotzdem* (1931), and it is perhaps fitting, if ironic—in view of his erstwhile bourgeois clientele—that Loos's last works were unglamorous workers' houses, including the simple terraces of the Arbeitssiedlung (1932; partially destr.), Babi bei Nachod, Czechoslovakia,

2. Adolf Loos: Tzara House, Paris, 1925–6

and the simple, semi-detached houses of the Werkbundsiedlung exhibition (1932) at Woinovichgasse, Vienna.

### WRITINGS
*Ins Leere gesprochen* (Paris and Geneva, 1921/*R* 1981; rev. 2, Innsbruck, 1932); Eng. trans. by J. O. Newman and J. H. Smith as *Spoken into the Void: Collected Essays, 1897–1900* (Cambridge, MA, 1982)
*Trotzdem* (Innsbruck, 1931/*R* 1982)
F. Gluck, ed.: *Sämtliche Schriften*, i (Vienna, 1962)
*Die Potemkinsche Stadt: Verschollene Schriften aus den Jahren 1897–1933* (Vienna, 1983)

### BIBLIOGRAPHY
B. Markalous: *Adolf Loos* (Prague, 1929)
*Adolf Loos: Festschrift zum 60. Geburtstag am 10.12.1930* (Vienna, 1930)
F. Gluck: *Adolf Loos* (Paris, 1931)
H. Kulka: *Adolf Loos: Das Werk des Architekten* (Vienna, 1931, 2/1979)
C. Loos: *Adolf Loos Privat* (Vienna, 1936, 2/1985)
L. Loos: *Das Buch ohne Titel: Erlebte Geschichten* (Vienna, 1947); rev. as *Mein Leben mit Adolf Loos* (Vienna, 1986)
L. Munz: *Adolf Loos* (Milan, 1956)
L. Munz and G. Künstler: *Der Architekt Adolf Loos* (Vienna, 1964); Eng. trans. by H. Meek as *Adolf Loos: Pioneer of Modern Architecture* (London, 1966)
F. Altmann-Loos: *Adolf Loos: Der Mensch* (Vienna, 1968)
H. Czech and W. Mistelbauer: *Das Looshaus* (Vienna, 1976)
K. Frampton: *Modern Architecture: A Critical History* (London, 1980, rev. 1985), pp. 90–95
B. Gravagnuolo: *Adolf Loos: Theory and Work* (New York, 1982)
B. Rukschio and R. Schachel: *Adolf Loos: Leben und Werk* (Vienna, 1982)
*Adolf Loos, 1870–1933* (exh. cat., ed. B. Volkmann and R.-F. Raddatz; Berlin, Akad. Kst., 1983–4)
B. Rukschio: 'Ornament und Mythos', *Ornament und Askese*, ed. A. Pfahigan (Vienna, 1985), p. 57f
*The Architecture of Adolf Loos* (exh. cat., ed. Y. Safran and W. Wang; Oxford, MOMA, 1985)

L. Munz: *Adolf Loos: Mit Verzeichnis der Werke und Schriften* (Vienna, 1989)

YEHUDA SAFRAN

**Loos, Daniel Friedrich** (*b* Altenburg, 15 June 1735; *d* Berlin, 1 Oct 1819). German medallist and die-cutter. He trained as an engraver in Altenburg under Johann Friedrich Stieler (1729–90). In 1756 he entered the service of the Prussian Mint in Magdeburg, the importance of which increased when the Berlin Mint was forced to close because of the Seven Years War. In 1768 Loos moved to the reopened Berlin Mint, and in 1787 he was given the title of Prussian Court Medallist, which ensured his advance in society and brought him membership of the Berlin academy. As well as producing coin dies and interesting himself in questions of minting technique, Loos produced, in collaboration with his son Gottfried Bernhard Loos, more than 300 medals of personages and historical events. An example of his work is the medal to commemorate the *Marriage of Frederick, Duke of York, and Princess Friederica of Prussia* (1791; Munich, Staatl. Münzsamml.). He also made 'Gelegenheitsmedaillen' (occasional medals), which, sometimes produced in great numbers, were given as gifts on birthdays, weddings or religious family festivals (e.g. *Taufgeschenk*, *c.* 1800; Hamburg, Mus. Hamburg. Gesch.). The sale of these medals, excellently suited to the taste of his period, brought Loos considerable extra income. A private mint founded in Berlin by his son enjoyed a good reputation throughout the 19th century because of the quality of the medals produced.

BIBLIOGRAPHY
*ADB*; Forrer; Thieme–Becker
K. Sommer: *Die Medaillen des königlich preussischen Hof-Medailleurs Daniel Friedrich Loos und seines Ateliers* (Osnabrück, 1981)

HERMANN MAUÉ

**Looy, Jacobus van** (*b* Haarlem, 13 Sept 1855; *d* Haarlem, 24 Feb 1930). Dutch painter, draughtsman and writer. He was an orphan and received his first artistic training in Haarlem from D. J. H. Joosten (1818–82), the flower and still-life painter. In 1837 he became an active member of the Haarlem drawing society Kunst Zij ons Doel ('Let art be our aim'). With the help of the curator of the Teylers Museum, Haarlem, he prepared himself for a course at the Rijksakademie voor Beeldende Kunsten in Amsterdam. Between 1877 and 1884 he was taught there by various artists including August Allebé. In 1880 he set up the Kunstenaars-vereniging St Lucas (St Luke Society of Artists), together with Willem Witsen and Antoon Derkinderen. He moved in literary circles and in 1885 made his début as a writer in the avant-garde magazine *De Nieuwe Gids* ('The new guide').

Van Looy had won the Dutch Prix de Rome in 1884; between 1885 and 1887 he visited Italy, Spain and the Spanish section of Morocco. Although he began his career as a fairly academic painter, partly as a result of this tour, he became not only a fluent draughtsman and a good colourist but also a poet and writer. As a painter he joined a group of artists later known as the Amsterdam school, which consisted exclusively of former pupils of Allebé, among them Witsen, Jan Pieter Veth and Georg Hendrik Breitner. His paintings include portraits such as *Jacobus Batavier* (1890; The Hague, Gemeentemus.) and *Frederik*

van Eeden (1884) and scenes such as *The Café* (1890). About 1900 he discovered pastel as a particularly lively material for drawing, for example, the series *Harvesters* (Haarlem, Frans Halsmus.).

The only retrospective exhibition held during van Looy's lifetime took place at the Arti et Amicitiae gallery in Amsterdam in 1901. After reading the reviews of this exhibition, he decided never to show his work again. It is partly for this reason that he is known primarily as a poet, novelist and translator of plays. His writing allied him with the Tachtigers ('Eighties movement'), and he developed an impressionistic use of language. The Jacobus van Looy Trust in Haarlem administers part of his artistic estate; the collection is housed in the Frans Halsmuseum, Haarlem.

WRITINGS
M. J. Brusse, ed.: *Jacobus van Looy over zijn werk* [Jacobus van Looy on his own work] (Rotterdam, 1930)
F. P. Huygens, ed.: *Wie dronk toen water!* [Who drank water then!] (Amsterdam, 1975) [Van Looy's corr. with August Allebé, 1885–7]

BIBLIOGRAPHY
G. H. Marius: *Jac. van Looy* (Amsterdam, 1912)
A. M. Hammacher: *Amsterdamsche Impressionisten en hun kring* [Amsterdam Impressionists and their circle] (Amsterdam, 1941), pp. 52–7, 69–72
P. Winkels and C. Will: *Jacobus van Looy: Schilder van huis uit, schrijver door toevallige omstandigheden* [Jacobus van Looy: originally painter, writer by accident] (The Hague, 1982)
*Jacobus van Looy* (exh. cat. by M. van der Wal, Haarlem, Frans Halsmus. and Teyler, 1982)
C. Will and P. Winkels: *De dubbelbegaafdheid van Jacobus van Looy* [The double talent of Jacobus van Looy] (Haarlem, 1988)
*The Age of Van Gogh: Dutch Painting, 1880–1895* (exh. cat., ed. R. Bionda and C. Blotkamp; Glasgow, Burrell Col.; Amsterdam, Van Gogh Mus.; 1990–91)

CHR. WILL

**Lopes.** Portuguese family of painters.

**(1) Gregório Lopes** (*b* Lisbon, *c.* 1490; *d* Lisbon, 1550). He is perhaps the most cosmopolitan painter of the brief Portuguese Renaissance. Early in his career he moved away from the vestiges of Gothic in which his art originated and from the professional limitations of close collaboration with more traditional artists. During the 1530s and 1540s he developed a courtly style of painting, which is at the same time deeply spiritual and based on broader compositions that emphasize his modelling, draughtsmanship and rich colouring and show his concern with the effects of light. Lopes expressed in a very individual way the ideological spirit of the reign of John III. Lopes's artistic personality, which is close to early Antwerp Mannerism, is seen in his use of descriptive architectural backgrounds and lively graduations of colour in richly coloured textiles. In this way he distanced himself from the more traditional style of the court painter Jorge Afonso and his contemporaries and followed a more international style concerned with the definition of space, the detailed description of ornaments, arms and clothes, and the creation of individual faces and poses that stylistically have certain affinities with the work of Hans Sturm in Seville.

Lopes's career is documented from 1513, when he had opened his own workshop in Lisbon. He was court painter to Manuel I (date of appointment unknown) and in 1522 to John III, and he was made a knight of the Order of Santiago in 1524, an honour not accorded to any other

16th-century court painter. By 1514 he was married to Isabel Jorge, daughter of Jorge Afonso, to whom he had been apprenticed together with Garcia Fernandes, Pero Vaz ( *fl* 1473–1514) and Gaspar Vaz. These professional connections were strengthened in 1518–19 when Lopes collaborated in a series of paintings for the Tribunal de Relação (Court of Appeal), Lisbon, under the direction of Francisco Henriques, with Cristóvão de Figueiredo, Garcia Fernandes and André Gonçalves. This series has disappeared, though the *Inferno* panel (?*c.* 1519; Lisbon, Mus. N.A. Ant.), attributed to the Master of Lourinhã, may have belonged to it.

In 1525, together with Jorge Leal, Lopes was commissioned to paint the retable of the Saviour in the monastery of S Francisco in Lisbon. This ensemble of paintings, valued by Jorge Afonso at 66,000 reis, was moved at the end of the 16th century to the monastery of S Bento da Saúde. Four of the original five paintings, the *Visitation*, the *Adoration of the Magi*, the *Presentation in the Temple* and *Christ among the Doctors* (all 1525; Lisbon, Mus. N.A. Ant.), incorrectly attributed to the Master of S Bento ( *fl* 16th century), are the first documented works of Lopes and of Jorge Leal. In these panels the artists avoided workshop conventions and paint with clarity, firmness of line and a touching delicacy, as in the heads of the donors in the *Adoration*. Attributed to the same partnership is the retable of the church of the Paraíso, Lisbon, with eight large paintings of the *Life of the Virgin* (including the *Death of the Virgin*, dated 1527) and four predella panels with heads of Virgin Martyrs, including *St Margaret* and *St Mary Magdalene* (both Lisbon, Mus. N.A. Ant.) and *St Catherine* and *St Barbara* (both Poznań, E. Raczyński Mun. Pub. Lib.). In this expressive, though at times uneven, group of paintings the elegant costumes and details provide something of a historical document of courtly life, depicted with brilliant colouring and graceful modelling.

In 1533 Lopes worked in Lamego in collaboration with Cristóvão de Figueiredo, Garcia Fernandes and Cristóvão de Utrecht (1498–1557) on commissions for Bishop Fernando de Menezes Coutinho e Vasconcelos, and for King Henry. One of these altarpieces, of which eight are *in situ* at Ferreirim Monastery (*Annunciation, Nativity, Christ Carrying the Cross, Calvary, Deposition, Resurrection, Death of the Virgin* and *Immaculate Conception*), was a work of such close collaboration that it is difficult to establish Lopes's contributions.

From September 1536 Lopes worked at the Convent of Christ, Tomar, on the altarpieces in the Charola, for which he received 168,000 reis: *St Anthony Preaching to the Fishes* and *St Bernard* (the latter much repainted, both *in situ*); and the *Martyrdom of St Sebastian* and the *Virgin, Child and Angels in a Garden* (both Lisbon, Mus. N.A. Ant.). The *Martyrdom of St Sebastian* shows Lopes's detailed characterization of small figures and his use of related planes, as in the distant background where a dramatic *auto-da-fé* is taking place.

In 1538–9 Lopes painted the altarpiece in the church of S João Baptista, Tomar, with scenes from the *Life of St John the Baptist* and scenes relating to the Eucharist (*Beheading of John the Baptist, Salome, Abraham and Melchizedek, Fall of Manna, Last Supper* and *Mass of St*

Gregório Lopes: *Christ Appearing to the Virgin*, oil on panel, 1.30×1.09 m, *c.* 1530–40 (Setúbal, Museu de Setúbal)

*Gregory; in situ*). His paintings frequently display the work of the goldsmiths of the period, and he exploited the effects of light, as in the *Mass of St Gregory* in which great attention is given to candlesticks and censer and the glittering surface of the arch that frames the choir. Characteristic of Lopes's highly personal style in the decade of the 1530s are the fine panel of the *Madonna of Mercy* in the Misericórdia Church, Sesimbra; the four paintings in the Museu da Sé (cathedral museum) at Évora (the *Raising of the Widow's Son of Nain, St Peter, St Paul* and the *Raising of the Cross, c.* 1535); the *Presentation in the Temple* in the church of S Iria at Azóia; and *Christ Appearing to the Virgin* (see fig.) and the *Ascension* (both Setúbal, Mus. Setúbal).

During the 1540s Lopes painted the retables for the Bom Jesús Church, Valverde, from which come the panels of the *Adoration of the Shepherds, Calvary* and the *Resurrection* (*c.* 1544; Évora, Mus. Évora). His use of dramatic highlights, as well as the emotional contortion of his figures, is seen in the background of the *Passion* altarpiece from the monastery of Santos-o-Novo, Lisbon (*Annunciation, Adoration of the Shepherds, Adoration of the Magi, Agony in the Garden, Entombment* and *Resurrection, c.* 1540–45; Lisbon, Mus. N.A. Ant.). Probably of the same late period is *SS Anne and Joachim* (Lisbon, Mus. N.A. Ant.).

### BIBLIOGRAPHY
S. Viterbo: *Noticia de alguns pintores portuguezes* [Biographies of some Portuguese painters], 1st ser. (Lisbon, 1903), pp. 104–9

J. de Figueiredo: 'Gregório Lopes e a Infanta D. Maria', *Lusitânia*, x (1927), pp. 95–104

V. Correia: *Pintores portugueses dos séculos XV e XVI* (Lisbon, 1928), pp. 58–61

R. dos Santos: *Os primitivos portugueses* (Lisbon, 1940), pp. 29–33

A. de Gusmão: 'Os primitivos e a renascença', *Arte portuguesa: Pintura* (Lisbon, 1951), pp. 245–50

L. Reis-Santos: *Gregório Lopes* (Lisbon, *c*. 1954)

A. de Gusmão: *Mestres desconhecidos do Museu Nacional de Arte Antiga* [Anonymous masters from the Museu Nacional de Arte Antiga] (Lisbon, 1957)

M. Malkiel-Jirmounsky: *Pintura à sombra dos mosteiros* [Paintings in the seclusion of monasteries] (Lisbon, 1957), pp. 48–52

L. Reis-Santos:'Uma obra-prima de Gregório Lopes em França', *Colóquio*, 42 (1966), pp. 20–25

*Os mestres do Sardoal e de Abrantes* (exh. cat. by J. Paulo de Abreu e Lima, Lisbon, Mus. Gulbenkian, 1971)

M. M. Barradas Calado: *Gregório Lopes: Revisão da obra do pintor régio e sua integração na corrente maneirista* [Gregório Lopes: an analysis of the work of the royal painter and his integration into the mannerist current] (diss., U. Lisbon, 1973)

**(2) Cristóvão Lopes** (*b* Lisbon, *c*. 1516; *d* Lisbon, 1570). Son of (1) Gregório Lopes. He was probably taught by his father and was particularly distinguished as a portraitist. He followed the example of the early Antwerp Mannerism that strongly characterized his father's work.

In August 1551 Cristóvão Lopes was appointed court painter by John III, occupying his deceased father's position and earning the same annuity of 5,000 reis, and in 1552 he became examiner of painters of Lisbon. He was knighted by King John, according to Francisco Pacheco (1649). Lopes's early activity has still to be clarified, as some earlier attributions, such as the panels from the polyptych at the monastery of Madre de Deus, Xabregas, once attributed to Cristóvão Lopes, have now been attributed to the workshop of Jorge Afonso.

Lopes's portraits of *John III with St John the Baptist* and *Queen Catherine with St Catherine* (both *c*. 1555; Lisbon, Mus. N. A. Ant.) accord with the formal Mannerist state portrait in their spatial ambiguity, the robust bearing of the figures, the delicacy of the drapery and the fine modelling of the heads. Second versions by Lopes of these portraits, with some variations in the treatment of the backgrounds and details, hang in the lower choir of the monastery of Madre de Deus, Lisbon. The humanism of these works reflects the influence of Anthonis Mor, who came to Lisbon in 1552 to paint the royal family. Mor's portraits of *John III* and *Queen Catherine* (both 1552–3; Madrid, Prado) especially influenced Lopes in the modelling of faces and the minute detail of costume.

BIBLIOGRAPHY

F. Pacheco: *Arte* (1649); ed. F. Sánchez Cantón (1956), i, p. 150

R. dos Santos: 'A pintura da segunda metade do século XVI ao final do século XVII', *A. Port.* (1951)

J.-A. França: *O retrato na arte portuguesa* (Lisbon, 1981), p. 23

V. Serrão: *A pintura maneirista em Portugal* (Lisbon, 1982), pp. 45–6

VITOR SERRÃO

**Lopes, Sebastião** (*fl* Portugal, *c*. 1555; *d* between 1585 and 1596). Portuguese cartographer. His known work consists of a signed map, dated 1558, and five other cartographic works, which were attributed to him on stylistic grounds by Cortesão (1960). These are: a map of *Europe and the Mediterranean* region (*c*. 1555; London, N. Mar. Mus.); an *Atlantic Chart* (1558; London, BL); an unfinished *World Atlas* (*c*. 1565; Chicago, IL, Newberry Lib.), which contains additional folios of cosmographical information relevant to navigation, such as quadrennial charts with the sun's declination and the course of the North Star; a chart of the *Atlantic Ocean and West Indian Ocean* (Vila Viçosa, Ducal Pal.); a fragment of a map of *South America* (*c*. 1581; Madrid, Mus. Naval); and a map of the *World* (*c*. 1581; Paris, Bib. N.).

There is little evidence about Lopes's life, but his attendance is recorded in 1587 at the examination of a candidate to the title of master maker of clocks, astrolabes and marine compasses, and in a document dated 10 October 1596 the name Pedro le Lemos appears as his replacement in the post that Lopes had held in the Armazém da Guiné e da India (Guinea and India Trading Company). Lopes was a skilled cartographer and an accomplished artist who illustrated his work with meticulous drawings and used well-selected colours. There are highly expressive scenes that show a group of Arab horsemen on parade in North Africa on the 1558 chart; a caravan to the south of a range of mountains appears on the *Atlas* (*c*. 1565); and in the same work there is a scene showing a family of Native Americans with a man cutting down a brazil-wood tree. In several of these works the details, such as flags, the points of the compass and coats of arms, as well as ships, castles and 'Prester John' (the mythical Christian hero identified with the negus or king of Ethiopia), are painted with the delicacy of an accomplished miniaturist. The drawing of the *Crucifixion* on the second folio of his *Atlas* (*c*. 1565) suggests a knowledge of Italian High Renaissance art.

BIBLIOGRAPHY

A. Cortesão: *Portugaliae monumenta cartographica*, iv (Lisbon, 1960), pp. 3–24

LUIS DE ALBUQUERQUE

**López, Cándido** (*b* Buenos Aires, 29 Aug 1840; *d* 31 Dec 1902). Argentine painter. He is thought to have studied under the Italian painters Gaetano Descalzi and Baldassare Verazzi (1819–86). Joining an infantry battalion in San Nicolás de los Arroyos when the Triple Alliance of Argentina, Uruguay and Brazil declared war on Paraguay, he subsequently made the war the main theme of his art. While in the army he made many descriptive drawings and accumulated facts and details that guaranteed the fidelity of his retrospective rendering of events. His right wrist was shattered in the battle of Curupaytí in 1866, and when he returned to Buenos Aires he underwent two amputations and was thereafter restricted to the use of his left hand. From his sketches he produced a series of oil paintings that constitute an extraordinary historical record, moving in its sincerity.

López's characteristic pictures, such as *Landing of the Argentine Army in front of the Trenches of Curuzu* (1891), one of 29 paintings by him housed at the Museo Histórico Nacional in Buenos Aires, are executed in an unusual oblong format in a proportion of one to three, which allowed him to convey the expansiveness of the Argentine landscape. His figures are small, disproportionate to their surroundings and painted in minute detail; his colours are pure, flat and thinly applied; and the uniform and intense lighting gives the scenes an air of unreality accentuated by the simultaneity of the actions and a descriptive power that transforms them into poetic metaphor. In spite of the plethora of figures inhabiting his paintings, the action appears to have been frozen and the events framed in absolute immobility.

BIBLIOGRAPHY

J. L. Pagano: *El arte de los Argentinos* (Buenos Aires, 1937), pp. 67–8
*Cándido López* (exh. cat. by M. Gil Solá and M. Dujovne, Buenos Aires, Mus. N. B.A., 1971)
H. Safons: 'El manco de Curupaytí', *Primera Plana*, 452 (1971), pp. 48–9
J. E. Payró: *23 pintores de la Argentina, 1810–1900* (Buenos Aires, 1973), pp. 9, 48–9

HORACIO SAFONS

**López, Nacho** [Ignacio] (*b* Tampico, 19 Nov 1923; *d* Mexico City, 24 Oct 1986). Mexican photographer. He studied at the Instituto de Artes y Ciencias Cinematográficas, Mexico City, and with Manuel Alvarez Bravo. He developed a reputation as an outstanding photojournalist, and he used his politically combative vision to record social contradictions and conflicts in Mexico City. The photo-essays he published in *Hoy*, *Mañana*, and *Siempre!* during the 1950s were among the most critical of the period; notable among them are 'Prison of Dreams' (*Mañana*, 25 Nov 1950) and 'Once We Were Human Beings' (*Siempre!*, 19 June 1954). López was also a news cameraman and made documentary films.

WRITINGS

*Yo, el ciudadano* (Mexico City, 1984)

BIBLIOGRAPHY

J. Mraz: 'From Positivism to Populism: Towards a History of Mexican Photojournalism', *Afterimage* (Jan 1991)

PATRICIA MASSE

**López Aguado, Martín** (*b* 1796; *d* Madrid, 3 Dec 1866). Spanish architect. He was a son of Antonio López Aguado (1764–1831), the architect of the Teatro Real, Madrid, and he trained under his father in the Real Academia de Bellas Artes de San Fernando in Madrid. Between 1823 and 1827 he was in Rome, apparently on a scholarship, where he worked on projects for a prince's country house and a stock exchange building in order to be elected as an architect of merit by the Academia in Madrid. His father's requests to Ferdinand VII obtained the post, but the drawings were later withdrawn on the pretext that they had been plagiarized. Martín López Aguado was familiar not only with Italian architecture, in particular Palladio's Mannerist works, but also with works by his French contemporary Jean-Nicolas-Louis Durand and the Englishmen Colin Campbell, John James, Robert Adam and John Nash. He was also influenced, as a result of his father's teaching, by the work of the great Neo-classical architect Juan de Villanueva, but he modified this influence by achieving a more refined manipulation of the architectural elements and introducing a clearly Romantic spirit. This is particularly evident in the picturesque effects obtained by combining and offsetting his buildings with the gardens surrounding them.

López Aguado's artistic output cannot be compared to that of such contemporaries as Francisco Pascual y Colomer, Francisco Jareño y Alarcón and Aníbal Alavrez Bouquel, since he received no official commissions. He found an exceptional patron, however, in the 11th Duque de Osuna, Don Pedro de Alcántara Téllez Girón (1810–44), who employed him in 1834–44 to remodel the family property of El Capricho, near Barajas (Madrid), also known as the Palacio de Alameda, or Alameda de Osuna ('Grove of Osuna'). The most outstanding Neo-classical suburban complex in Spain, it was originally built for the 9th Duquesa de Osuna (*see* OSUNA, (3)) by the French landscape designers Mulot and Provost together with Antonio López Aguado. Martín López Aguado's contribution was to design the various Neo-classical features that decorate the English garden. Central to the entire ensemble is the Plaza de los Emperadores, or 'Exedra', which is a monument to the Duquesa. Other elements are the miniature temple, the apiary and the landscape design. López Aguado also designed the palace façade overlooking the garden, inspired by Palladian colonnades. The ensemble suffered considerable destruction in subsequent years until a programme of restoration was initiated in the 20th century. It was the most ambitious scheme that López Aguado was able to realize, though he continued to prepare projects of a comparable scale, for example for a museum of paintings and sculpture and for a theatre.

López Aguado's other commissions for the aristocracy and upper middle classes included numerous residential complexes, notably those for the Marqués de Alcañices in the Calle de Alcalá (1847) and for the Conde de Cerbellón in the Calle de Santa Isabel, both in Madrid. Both are built in a style that heralds Eclecticism.

BIBLIOGRAPHY

F. Iñiguez: 'El arquitecto Martín López Aguado y la Alameda de Osuna', *Archv Esp. A.*, xviii (1945), pp. 219–35
J. A. Gaya: *Arte del siglo XIX* (Madrid, 1966)
P. Navascués: *Arquitectura y arquitectos madrileños del siglo XIX* (Madrid, 1973)
——: 'La Alameda de Osuna: Una villa suburbana', *Estud. Pro A.*, 2 (1975), pp. 6–26
P. Navascués and others: *Del Neoclasicismo al Modernismo* (Madrid, 1979)
*Guía de arquitectura y urbanismo de Madrid* (Madrid, 1982–3)

ALBERTO VILLAR MOVELLÁN

**López Bueno, Diego** (*b* ?1568; *d* Seville, 1632). Spanish sculptor, wood-carver and architect. He was trained in the Sevillian sculptural tradition of the late 16th century, subsequently using wood as the medium for most of his work and coming to architecture via wood-carving. His most notable work includes a retable (1601) for the church of the Hospital de las Cinco Llagas, Seville, to a design of Asensio de Maeda (*fl* 1563–1601), and the retable (1619) in the chapel of S Pedro, Seville Cathedral, both of which, like the rest of his oeuvre, display the growing turgescence characteristic of early Baroque architecture in the first decades of the 17th century.

From *c*. 1612 to 1628 Diego was diocesan architect in Seville: his plan for the north portal of the church of S Lorenzo (1625) demonstrates a masterful use of the Mannerist vocabulary. As surveyor to the fabric of the Alcázar (1628–32), Seville, he was responsible for dismantling (8 March 1629) the Monte Parnaso, an artificial hill located in the Jardín del Laberinto, and its later reconstruction to the design of Jerónimo de Guzmán. López Bueno was an outstanding practitioner of the early Baroque in the first third of the 17th century in Seville.

BIBLIOGRAPHY

C. López Martínez: *Arquitectos, escultores y pintores vecinos de Sevilla* (Seville, 1928)

——: *Retablos y esculturas de traza sevillana* (Seville, 1928)
A. J. Morales Martinez: *La iglesia de San Lorenzo de Sevilla* (Seville, 1981)
A. Pleguezuelo Hernandez: *Diego López Bueno y la arquitectura del manierismo sevillano* (diss., U. Seville, 1987)
A. Marín Fidalgo: *El Alcázar de Sevilla bajo los Austrias*, 2 vols (Seville, 1990)

ANA MARÍN FIDALGO

**López-Castro, Leandro de Saralegui y.** *See* SARALEGUI Y LÓPEZ-CASTRO, LEANDRO DE.

**López Cepero, Manuel** (*b* Jerez de la Frontera, Cádiz, 7 March 1778; *d* Seville, 12 April 1858). Spanish patron and collector. He studied canon law, theology and jurisprudence at the Universidad Literaría de Sevilla from 1802 to 1807 and was ordained a priest. After being appointed to a Chair in Theology he began to collect works of art, and his house became an important centre for literary and artistic discussion. He was also interested in politics, and his constitutional and liberal ideas resulted in his election in 1813 to represent the province of Cádiz at the Cortes. With the return of King Ferdinand VII and the resultant revival of absolutism in 1814 he was confined to a monastery until 1820, when a new political upheaval brought his return to the Cortes to represent the provinces of Cádiz and Seville. He retired from public life from 1823 until 1834, when he returned to Seville to occupy various political, religious and academic offices. He was friendly with important men in the political and cultural life of his times, including Juan Augustín, Ceán Bermúdez, Alberto Lista, José-Maria Blanco White, Baron Isidore-Justin-Séverin Taylor and George Borrow. He was a great lover and student of art, a co-founder of the Museo de Bellas Artes in Seville (1835) and president of the commission that catalogued and cared for works of art throughout Seville and its province. In his house in Seville he had a collection of paintings, sculptures, books and coins that included works of the Italian, Flemish, German and Spanish schools (e.g. by Murillo, Velázquez, Zurbarán and Goya), including over a thousand pictures. At that time his collection was wider in scope than that of the newly created Museo de Bellas Artes.

BIBLIOGRAPHY
M. Teruel: *Rasgos claves de la vida de Manuel López Cepero* (Seville, 1964)
M. Ruiz Lagos de Castro: *El deán López Cepero y la ilustración romántica* (Jerez de la Frontera, 1970)
R. Merchan Cantisan: *El deán López Cepero y su colección pictórica* (Seville, 1979)

PILAR BENITO

**López de Arenas, Diego** (*b* Marchena, ?1579–80; *d* Seville, ?1638–40). Spanish architect, master carpenter and writer. He was active in Andalusia, chiefly Seville, until *c.* 1637. He trained in Seville and studied the theories of Sebastiano Serlio and Jacopo Vignola. In addition, he learnt Hispano-Islamic carpentry techniques; early in his career he earned his living mainly by repairing *mudéjar* wooden ceilings. By 1605 López de Arenas had risen to prominence and soon afterwards became a municipal architect in Seville. At least twice before 1619 he was the city assessor of buildings and had served two terms as an examination official for the building profession, testing those individuals who wished to advance through the grades of apprentice, journeyman and master builder in Seville. His superior skill and artistry in designing and constructing *mudéjar* wooden ceilings earned López de Arenas great praise from his contemporaries. In 1608 he executed the ceiling of the choir for the church of S Domingo de Portaceli, Seville. Before 1613 he completed those of the church of Mairena and the conventual churches of S Paula and María de las Dueñas, Seville. He was possibly also responsible for the ceilings of the churches of Omnium Sanctorum, Seville, and S Francisco, Granada, as well as that of the palace of the Duque de Arcos in Seville (all before 1619).

López de Arenas exerted the greatest influence on his profession through his writings. Between 1613 and 1619 he wrote the draft for a manual and treatise on the techniques of *mudéjar* ceiling carpentry. He completed the text in 1632, and the book was published a year later. This important work codifies, and therefore preserves, the rapidly disappearing art of Hispano-Islamic wooden ceiling design and construction. Largely because of this book, ceilings designed in the Hispano-Islamic manner continued to be built in Spain until the 19th century. However, it was in Latin America that the book had its greatest impact, especially in Colombia (e.g. church of the Trinity, Cartagena de Indias, 1642–88), Ecuador (e.g. cloisters, church of La Merced, Quito, 1648) and Venezuela (e.g. Trinity Chapel, Caracas Cathedral, 1698) during the 17th and 18th centuries, and in Cuba (e.g. church of S Domingo, Guanabacoa, by Lorenzo Camacho, 1728–48) during the 18th and 19th centuries.

WRITINGS
*Primera y segunda parte de las reglas de la carpintería* (MS. 1619); ed. with intro. and glossary, M. Gómez-Moreno (Madrid, 1966)
*Breve compendio de la carpintería de lo blanco, y tratado de alarifes, con la conclusión de la regla de Nicolás Tartaglia, y otras cosas tocantes a la geometría, y puntas de compás . . . : Por . . . maestro de dicho oficio, y alcalde de alarife* (Seville, 1633, rev. 2/1727; 4th edn G. Sánchez Lefler and E. de Mariategui, Madrid, 1912)

BIBLIOGRAPHY
A. Prieto Vives: 'La carpintería hispano-musulmana', *La Arquitectura*, xiv (1932), pp. 263–302
E. Nuere: *La carpintería de lo blanco* (Madrid, 1985)

FRANÇOIS-AUGUSTE DE MONTÉQUIN

**López de Arteaga, Sebastian** (*b* Seville, 1610; *d* Mexico City, 1652). Spanish painter. A pupil of Zurbarán, in 1640 he settled in Mexico, where he went as part of the retinue of the Viceroy, the Marqués de Villena. Although López de Arteaga produced only a limited amount of work in Mexico, he influenced local painters and was probably mainly responsible for introducing the tenebrist style from Seville. His paintings in Mexico include a *Crucifixion*, an *Incredulity of Thomas*, a *Betrothal of the Virgin*, another *Crucifixion* (dated 1643) and a *Stigmatization of St Francis* (dated 1650; all Mexico City, Pin. Virreinal).

BIBLIOGRAPHY
G. Kubler and M. S. Soria: *Art and Architecture in Spain and Portugal and their American Dominions, 1500–1800*, Pelican Hist. A. (Harmondsworth, 1959)
M. Toussaint: *Pintura colonial en México* (Mexico City, 1965)
J. Fernandez: *Arte mexicano de sus orígenes a nuestros días* (Mexico City, 1968)
E. Marco Dorta: *Arte en América y Filipinas*, A. Hisp., xxi (Madrid, 1973)

MARIA CONCEPCIÓN GARCÍA SÁIZ

**López de Mendoza.** *See* MENDOZA.

**López Enguidanos (y Perles), Tomás** (*b* Valencia, 1760 or 1773; *d* Madrid, 1812 or 1814). Spanish printmaker and illustrator. He studied at the Academia de S Carlos, Valencia, and the Real Academia de S Fernando, Madrid, obtaining prizes in 1781 and 1784. In 1804 he was given the title of 'grabador de Cámara honorario', and in the same year he was appointed académico de S Carlos. López Enguidanos engraved portraits of *Manuel Godoy, Prince de la Paz* and *Ferdinand VII*, and he contributed to the illustrations of many important works published in Madrid: *Las vistas de los puertos de España* (1785); *Icones et descriptiones plantarum* (1791–1801) by Antonio Cavanilles; *Los quatro libros de arquitectura* (Sp. edn of 1797) by Andrea Palladio; *Don Quixote* (edn of 1797); *Vistas de El Escorial* (1800–07). His other prints include *Roman Charity* (1809) after the painting (1670s; destr. 1845) by Murillo. His brothers José López Enguidanos (1760–1812) and Vicente López Enguidanos were painters and engravers.

Ceán Bermúdez

BIBLIOGRAPHY

Marques de Alcahali: *Diccionario biográfico de artistas valencianos* (Valencia, 1897)
F. Esteve Botey: *Historia del grabado* (Barcelona, 1935), p. 310
E. Paez: *Repertorio de grabados españoles en la Biblioteca Nacional* (Madrid, 1981–5)
A. Tomás San Martín and M. S. Silvestre Visa: *Estampas y planchas de las Real Academia de S Carlos en el Museo de Bellas Artes* (Valencia, 1982)
J. Carrete, F. Checa and V. Bozal: *El grabado en España: Siglos XV al XVIII*, Summa A., xxxi (Madrid, 1987)

BLANCA GARCÍA VEGA

**López García, Antonio** (*b* Tomelloso, La Mancha, 6 Jan 1936). Spanish painter, draughtsman and sculptor. He lived in Madrid from 1949 and studied painting there from 1950 to 1955 at the Escuela de Bellas Artes de San Fernando. He came from a prosperous farming family and continued to reflect the cycles of nature in his work even after his move to the capital. His art evolved from primitivist and Surrealist influences to a strict realism that hinted at profound truths beyond surface appearances, for example in drawings such as *Remainder from a Meal* (1971; Baltimore, MD, Mus. A.) and in oil paintings such as *Death Mask of César Vallejo* (1962; Cleveland, OH, Mus. A.). He also occasionally produced sculptures, which he sometimes worked on over a long period, including life-size human figures in painted wood (e.g. *Man and Woman*, 1968–86; see 1986 exh. cat., pp. 10–11), editioned bronzes of heads and figures, and bronze reliefs cast from plaster originals (e.g. the *Apparition of the Little Brother*, 1959–86; see 1986 exh. cat., p. 38). The classes in colour that he gave at the Escuela de Bellas Artes de San Fernando from 1964 to 1969 had a strong impact on his students. In spite of the small production and consequently rare exhibitions dictated by his scrupulous methods, he continued to be regarded as an artist of international standing within the post-war movement of Spanish realism.

BIBLIOGRAPHY

*A. López García* (exh. cat. by F. Nieva and others, Brussels, Europalia, 1985)
*Antonio López García: Paintings, Sculptures and Drawings, 1965–1986* (exh. cat., intro. F. Nieva; New York, Marlborough Gal., 1986)
*Antonio López* (exh. cat. by A. Bonet Correa and others, Madrid, Mus. N. Cent. A. Reina Sofía, 1993)

JOSÉ CORREDOR-MATHEOS

**López Loza, Luis** (*b* Mexico City, 1939). Mexican painter, printmaker and sculptor. He studied in Mexico City at the Escuela de Pintura y Escultura La Esmeralda and the Centro Superior de Artes Aplicadas before moving for several years to New York, where he studied at the Pratt Graphic Center. From the end of the 1950s he exhibited in Mexico alongside other young artists whose rebellious stance led them to be referred to as the 'generación de ruptura'.

López Loza developed his personal abstract style from the mid-1960s, after his return to Mexico, using decorative devices based on sharply defined formal structures, either in serial form within an enclosed space, as in *Metamorphosis of a Shoe* (1969; Monterrey, Nue. Léon Grupo Indust. ALFA), or distributed in syncopated rhythms. In the 1980s he began also to produce sculptures carved in wood or stone.

BIBLIOGRAPHY

T. del Conde and others: *Doce expresiones plásticas de hoy* (Mexico City, 1988)
*Ruptura* (Mexico City, 1988)

JORGE ALBERTO MANRIQUE

**López Méndez, Luis Alfredo** (*b* Caracas, 23 Nov 1901). Venezuelan painter. In 1912 he began studying at the Academia de Bellas Artes, Caracas, under Pedro Zerpa and Cirilo Almeida Crespo, among others. He became dedicated to landscape painting and received lessons from Samys Mützner and Emilio Boggio. In 1919 López Méndez travelled to Puerto Rico for political reasons; from there he went to Mexico, the USA, Cuba and finally Europe, returning to Venezuela in 1936 where he held important posts in artistic and political fields. In his work he depicted the valley of Caracas, El Avila mountain, the eastern Venezuelan beaches and exotic women (e.g. *Nude*, 1941; Caracas, Gal. A. N.). His work reflected the artistic concerns of the generation of the reformist, anti-academic movement the Círculo de Bellas Artes and of the school of Caracas. In 1943 he was awarded the national painting prize.

WRITINGS

*Círculo de Bellas Artes* (Caracas, 1969)

BIBLIOGRAPHY

J. Denis: *La obra de Luis Alfredo López Méndez* (Caracas, 1980)

YASMINY PÉREZ SILVA

**López y Portaña, Vicente** (*b* Valencia, 19 Sept 1772; *d* Madrid, 22 April 1850). Spanish painter. At the age of 13 he entered the Real Academia de Bellas Artes de S Carlos in Valencia where he was initially a pupil of Antonio de Villanueva (1714–85). In 1789 he won prizes for *Tobias Restoring his Father's Sight* (Valencia, Mus. B.A.), among other paintings, and the grant of a scholarship to the Academia San Fernando in Madrid. His period there coincided with the ascendancy of the followers of Anton Raphael Mengs, and he was particularly influenced by Gregorio Ferro and Mariano Salvador Maella. In 1790 he returned to Valencia where he subsequently became vice-director of painting at the Academia. He married and had two sons, Bernardo (1800–74) and Luis (1802–65) López y Piquer, both of whom became artists. On his wife's death in 1814, López was summoned to the court of Ferdinand VII in Madrid as Pintor de Cámara and within a short time he was jointly appointed first court painter with Francisco de Goya, to replace Mariano Salvador Maella. He remained in Madrid for the rest of his life, established as one of the major Spanish painters of the period.

López proved himself ready to attempt a variety of techniques, including fresco, oil and miniature painting, and many different genres: the portrait, allegory, biblical, mythological and historical themes. He had a notable sympathy with popular feeling in his treatment of religious subjects and a conventional attitude to portrait painting; but he proved inventive in some of his allegorical schemes in the Palacio Real in Madrid. He is most highly regarded for his large number of portraits of members of the royal family, the aristocracy and the bourgeoisie, including statesmen, academics, generals and virtually everyone of importance in Spanish history during the first half of the 19th century. Outstanding among these are the portraits of *Fray Tomás Gasco* (Madrid, Prado), *Joaquín Pareja y Obregón* (Valencia, Mus. B.A.), *Vicente Blasco* (Madrid, Mus. Galdiano), *Pedro Aznares* (Barcelona, Mus. A. Mod.), *Francisco de Goya* (Madrid, Prado; see fig.), *Amalia Augusta of Saxony* (Madrid, Pal. Real) and *Ferdinand VII* (several versions; New York, Hisp. Soc. America; Rome, Pal. Spagna).

Vicente López was one of the few painters of his day to commit himself with real fervour to religious subjects. To these he brought a fresh approach, marking a strong contrast to the conventionalism into which the genre had declined in Spain. Fine examples of his work are the *Virgin of Mercy* (Valencia, Mus. B.A.) and the *Coronation of the Virgin* (Madrid, Mus. Románico). His work as a fresco painter in several rooms of the Palacio Real, Madrid, is in the late 17th-century tradition: the *Exercise of Sovereign Power* and the *Founding of the Order of Charles III* (*in situ*). His work as a miniaturist profited from his great skill in drawing: a notable example is the portrait of *Francis I, King of the Two Sicilies* (Madrid, Pal. Real).

BIBLIOGRAPHY

*Vicente López* (exh. cat., Barcelona, 1943)
E. Aguilera: *Vicente López* (Madrid, 1946)
F. de Hornedo: 'Los retratos reales de Vicente López', *Archv Esp. A.*, xxvii (1954)
M. A. Catala Gorgues: 'Vicente López y la Real Academia de San Carlos', *Archv A. Valenc.* (1972)
J. L. Morales y Marín: *Vicente López* (Zaragoza, 1980)

JOSÉ LUIS MORALES Y MARÍN

**Lo P'ing.** *See* LUO PING.

**L'Orange, Hans P(eter)** (*b* Oslo, 2 March 1903; *d* Rome, 5 Dec 1983). Norwegian art historian and archaeologist. Founder of the Norwegian Institute in Rome, he played a major part in establishing late Antique art as an independent and worthy subject of research. His early work concentrated on portraiture, where he collected, published and analysed many little-known late Roman busts and portraits. In 1939 he produced with A. von Gerkan an unsurpassed study of the Arch of Constantine in Rome, which interpreted the monument as a crucial link between late Classical and early medieval art. His treatment of the composite nature of the construction and hierarchy of figures on the arch was particularly significant. His interest in art and political power led to studies on the symbolism of monarchy and the heavens in history, from the Ancient Near East to 11th-century Europe. He also studied the civic art of the later Roman empire, revealing the richness and variety of its themes. A collection of articles published on his 70th birthday (1973) reproduced his most influential papers on the subjects of ancient portraits, monuments and the depiction of apotheosis.

WRITINGS

with A. von Gerkan: *Der spätantike Bildschmuck des Konstantinsbogen* (Berlin, 1939)
*The Roman Empire: Art Forms and Civic Life* (Milan, 1965/*R* 1985)
*Likeness and Icon* (Odense, 1973)

JOHN CURRAN

**Lorangère, Quentin de.** *See* QUENTIN DE LORANGÈRE.

**Lorca, Federico García** (*b* Fuente Vaqueros, nr Granada, 5 June 1898; *d* Alfacar, nr Granada, ?18 Aug 1936). Spanish writer and draughtsman. From 1915 he studied law and literature at the Universidad de Granada but found greater stimulation among the literary and artistic circle centred on the Café Alameda. In 1919 he moved to the Residencia de Estudiantes in Madrid, where he met, notably, Luis Buñuel and SALVADOR DALÍ; Dalí, in particular, became Lorca's close friend, and later designed the scenery for his first play, *Mariana Pineda* (1927). In 1928 Lorca published the only two issues of the avant-garde review *gallo*, the second of which contained the first Spanish translation of the Catalan anti-artistic *Manifest groc*, written by Dalí and others. The themes that characterize Lorca's writings—rural Andalusia and its gypsies, empathy for the plight of women and the oppressed, and

Vicente López y Portaña: *Francisco de Goya*, oil on canvas, 930×750 mm, 1826 (Madrid, Museo del Prado)

an obsession with fate and death—also influenced many of his drawings (executed in pen and ink or coloured pencil). These often served as graphic expressions of literary or dramatic ideas (e.g. costume for *Leonarda*, 1932; Granada, Casa–Mus. Huerta S Vicente) or as an outlet for personal frustrations. *Self-portrait of the Poet in New York* (*c.* 1929; untraced, see Oppenheimer, fig. 47) portrays, in a style influenced by Joan Miró, Lorca's sense of alienation in the dehumanizing metrópolis, where he wrote his most surrealistic poetry in 1929–30. Lorca was at the height of his career when, early in the Spanish Civil War (1936–9), he was shot by the Nationalist forces, ostensibly for being a subversive.

WRITINGS

A. Gallego Morell, ed.: *Cartas, postales, poemas y dibujos* (Madrid, 1968)

BIBLIOGRAPHY

H. Oppenheimer: *Lorca: The Drawings* (London, 1986)
*Dibujos de Federico García Lorca* (exh. cat. by M. Zambrano and M. Hernández, Paris, Cent. Lang. Cult. Espagne, 1990) [Sp. and Fr. text]

CHARLOTTE RUNDALL

**Lörcher, Alfred** (*b* Stuttgart, 30 July 1875; *d* Stuttgart, 26 March 1962). German sculptor and draughtsman. He trained as a designer of casting moulds in the workshop of Paul Stotz's bronze foundry in Stuttgart from 1892 to 1894. This was followed by two years' training at the Kunstgewerbeschule, Karlsruhe, and from 1897 to 1898 he was a specialist craftsman, producing designs for iron stoves at the craft workshops of W. Wächter in Kaiserslautern. He then continued his studies with the sculptor Wilhelm von Rümann at the Akademie der Bildenden Künste, Munich, from 1898 to 1901. There he was particularly interested in Adolf von Hildebrand's theories on sculpture. In 1905 he travelled to Rome, Naples and Sicily. The study he made there of antique and early Classical art is reflected in his own sculptures in a simple treatment of body volumes based on early Classical models. During his period in Berlin (1908–14), when he discovered the work of Aristide Maillol among others, the subject emerged that was to dominate his art until the 1940s: the nude, usually female (e.g. *Girl Standing*, h. 1.38 m, 1921; Stuttgart, Staatsgal.). Most of his seated or crouching figures are engaged in some simple, unpretentious occupation such as reading, looking into a mirror or washing.

In 1919 Lörcher was appointed professor at the Kunstgewerbeschule, Stuttgart, a post that led to another at the Akademie der Bildenden Künste in 1936. He retired in 1945, after which he produced his most important works, abandoning the individual figure in favour of small-scale group studies (e.g. *Panic II*, bronze, 1959; Hannover, Niedersächs. Landesmus.). He continued to use his favourite material, terracotta, and based his studies on actual events that he had observed. Throughout his productive period Lörcher also worked as a draughtsman, using a swift, annotational line that became more urgent in his later years, and he also produced medals, plaques and some portraits.

BIBLIOGRAPHY

E. Petermann: *Alfred Lörcher zum 80. Geburtstag gewidmet von seinen Freunden* (Stuttgart, 1955)
M. Grüterich: *Alfred Lörcher: Skulptur, Relief, Zeichnungen* (Stuttgart, 1976)
*Alfred Lörcher* (exh. cat. by M. Droste, Stuttgart, Staatsgal., 1978)
*Alfred Lörcher* (exh. cat., E. Berlin, Staatl. Museen, 1988)

ANGELA SCHNEIDER

**Lorck** [Lorichs; Lorch], **Melchior** (*b* Flensburg, 1526/27; *d* ?Silesia, after 31 Dec 1588). Danish draughtsman, engraver, woodcut designer, painter, architect, surveyor and author. Facts about his highly productive career, which ranged from Denmark to Turkey, come primarily from an autobiographical letter of 1 January 1563 (free English trans. in Fischer, 1990) to King Frederick II of Denmark to whom he owed allegiance by birth; also from inscribed works, his letters and mostly unpublished material in archives in Vienna, Hamburg, Antwerp and Copenhagen.

1. TRAVELS IN EUROPE AND TURKEY, TO 1559. With some effort Lorck persuaded his well-connected parents to let him become an artist: he became apprenticed to a Lübeck goldsmith, whom he accompanied on business voyages in the Baltic and western Scandinavia. His earliest works are two engravings, one dated 1543, copying engravings by Heinrich Aldegrever. Prompted by the goldsmith, Lorck continued his training in South Germany and Italy. Engravings such as the *Pope as a Wild Man* (1545; Hollstein, no. 44), *St Jerome in the Desert* (1546, H 9; copy from etching by Dürer), *The Bagpiper* (1547; H 13), *The Basilisk* (1548; H 16), *The Mole* (1548; H 18) and *Martin Luther* (1548; after Reifenstein's drawing, 1545), *Albrecht Dürer* (1550; H 21) and *Haman* (1550; H 11, after Michelangelo), together with the broadsheet woodcuts of the *Dead Father and his Three Sons* (1551; H 14), the *Sibylla Tiburtina* (1551; H 50, republished as *Eer und lob* . . . , in both cases with poems by Hans Sachs) and *The Deluge* (drawing, Berlin), together with the drawing of *A Landscape* (1549; Copenhagen, Stat. Mus. Kst), testify to connections with the Little Masters, masters of the Danube School such as Augustin Hirschvogel and the broadsheet production of Nuremberg. Allegedly he was present at the Diet of Augsburg in 1548, where he obtained contacts with Henry, Elector Palatine of the Rhine, to which the drawing of *Two Horsemen* (1553; Copenhagen, Stat. Mus. Kst) inscribed 'zu Neuburg an der Donau' may testify. Drawings and prints inscribed with souvenir dedications to fellow artists like Christoph Amberger, Lorenz Stör and Franz Buch may indicate that during September 1551 Lorck left for Italy where, he wrote, he visited Venice, Bologna, Florence and Rome. A number of archaeological drawings (1551; Weimar, Erlangen; Copenhagen, Stat. Mus. Kst; London, BM) testify to his studies. His only signed painting, a *Virgin and Child with St John* (1552; Copenhagen, Stat. Mus. Kst) includes an angel vaguely reminiscent of one in Tintoretto's *St Mark Rescuing a Slave* (1548).

Although under obligation to enter Danish royal service, Lorck remained abroad and somehow caught the interest of the Emperor, Ferdinand I, who ordered him to join his embassy to Constantinople, headed by the learned A. G. Busbeq. He probably left late in 1555 and returned to Vienna some time during 1559. He produced small engraved portraits of the members of the embassy: *Antonius Verantius* (1556), *Busbeq* (1557; Sthyr, p. 43)

Melchior Lorck: *Prince Isma'il*, engraving, ?1562 (Copenhagen, Kongelige Kobberstiksamling, Statens Museum for Kunst)

and *Franciscus Zay* (1557; H 37), and later the magnificent engravings of *Süleyman the Magnificent* (bust, ?1562; Sthyr, p. 46: standing, 1574; H 35) and *Prince Isma'il* (bust, ?1562, H 28, see fig.; standing, 1573; H 29). Numerous drawings with Turkish subjects survive (Copenhagen, Stat. Mus. Kst; St Petersburg, Hermitage; Paris, Louvre, Bib. N.; London, BM; Leiden, Bib. Rijksuniv.), mostly, however, redrawn from preliminary sketches, such as the very fine unfinished *View over Roofs in Constantinople* (Copenhagen, Stat. Mus. Kst): they were intended for publication as engravings and woodcuts in books. Subjects include: antiquities, like the *Pedestal of the Thutmosis-obelisk* (?1561) and the four *Sarcophagi* (?1563; both Copenhagen, Stat. Mus. Kst); military, costume, daily life; and topography, pre-eminently in the *c.* 12 m *Prospect of Constantinople* (Leiden, Bib. Rijksuniv.), evidently finished only after Lorck's return to Vienna. Lorck may have projected antiquarian and topographical publications about Turkey, but only realized in part a volume about the Turkish military, costume and daily life, producing 127 woodcuts between 1570 and 1583, which were published posthumously with some texts by him in *Dess Weitberühmten, Kunstreichen…Melchior Lorichs… Wolgerissene und Geschnittene Figuren…* (Hamburg, 1626; 2/1646, with fragments of his texts; blocks reissued 1680s, in publications by Eberhard Werner Happel).

2. IMPERIAL AND DANISH COMMISSIONS, AFTER 1559. Returning to Vienna, Lorck worked up his Turkish material and then in 1563 was commissioned to design three triumphal arches and three fountains (designs for two fountains, Copenhagen, Stat. Mus. Kst) to mark the entry of the future Emperor Maximilian II, recently elected Roman King—the iconography being devised by the historian Wolfgang Lazius (1514–65) who was drawn by Lorck (1563; Copenhagen, Stat. Mus. Kst). A woodcut with printed text of a triumphal arch (Munich, Bayer. Staatsbib.) indicates that Lorck planned to publish his decorations. From this period may date the large painting *Esther and Ahasuerus* (Innsbruck, Schloss Ambras), with its Turkish reminiscences; stylistically it reflects the later history paintings made by Hans Schöpfer and Ludwig Refinger for Duke William IV of Bavaria. Two smaller paintings of this subject (Winnipeg, A.G.; Philadelphia, PA, Mus. A.) are probably also Lorck's.

In 1564 Ferdinand I reconfirmed the nobility of the Lorck family, and Maximilian II, now Emperor, appointed Lorck *Hartschier* (a type of court official), a position he held until 1579. Lorck however continued to travel, following the army during the 1566 campaign against the Turks. In 1567 he designed one of the Hamburg town gates (*Schartor*) and produced a 12 m long map-like *Prospect of the Mouths of the Elbe* (Hamburg, Staatsarchiv). Two drawings probably of the 1560s, a *Stone Setting* (Copenhagen, Stat. Mus. Kst) and *Lucus* (Edinburgh, N.G.) indicate an interest in ancient Germanic history, while some costume drawings (1567–73; ex-Evelyn col.) may be preparatory to a publication. During 1573–4 Lorck was in Antwerp where in 1574 he published his book *Soldan Soleyman Turckischen Khaysers…Whare und eigendrliche conrafectung und bildtnuss* of which apparently no copy survives; apart from texts, it included all four portraits of Süleyman and Isma'il. He provided five woodcuts for Christoph Plantin's folio-missal of 1575 (blocks, Antwerp, Mus. Plantin-Moretus), made friends with Abraham Ortelius (entry in the latter's *album amicorum*, Cambridge, U. Lib.), with Hubertus Goltzius (engraved portrait, 1574; H 25) and with Phillip Galle who, in 1574, dedicated to Lorck his edition of Hans Vredeman de Vries's *Fountains*. Back in Hamburg that year, Lorck produced a map of *Vierlande* (Hamburg, Staatsarchv).

On 19 February 1580 King Frederick II of Denmark appointed Lorck his court painter, an appointment of short duration: by decree of 10 November 1582, the King dismissed him. Only two works are known from this period: the *Emblem of the Order of the Elephant* (woodcut, 1580; Copenhagen, Stat. Mus. Kst) and the engraved portrait of *Frederick II* (1582; Sthyr, p. 47). Later than this, two drawings, a *Woman of Gambia* and a *Nigerian Woman* (ex-Evelyn col.), and a single Turkish woodcut, all dated 1583, are known by Lorck. A few vague entries in the Imperial archives in Vienna may indicate that Emperor Rudolf II granted him retirement in Silesia.

BIBLIOGRAPHY

Hollstein: *Ger.*

E. Oberhummer: *Konstantinopel unter Sultan Suleiman dem Grossen* (Munich, 1902)

H. Harbeck: *Melchior Lorichs* (diss.; U. Kiel, 1911)

J. Sthyr: *Dansk Grafik, 1500–1800* [Danish graphic arts, 1500–1800] (Copenhagen, 1943/*R* 1970), pp. 16–38

A. Lorck Schierning: *Die Chronik der Familie Lorck* (Neumünster, 1949)

P. Ward-Jackson: 'Some Rare Drawings by Melchior Lorichs', *Connoisseur*, cxxxv (1955), pp. 83–93

M. J. Libmann: 'The Drawings by Melchior Lorichs in the Hermitage and in the Pushhkin-Museum in Moscow', *Trudy Gosudarstvennogo Ermitazha*, vi (1962), pp. 213–23

*Melchior Lorck. Drawings from the Evelyn collection at Stonor Park, England, and from the Department of Prints and Drawings, the Royal Museum of Fine Arts* (exh. cat. by E. Fischer, Copenhagen, Stat. Mus. Kst, 1962)

J. Bolland: *Die Hamburger Elbkarte von Melchior Lorichs* (Hamburg, 1964)

E. Fischer: 'Melchior Lorck', *Fund & Forsk.*, xi (Copenhagen, 1964), pp. 33–72

W. Kayser: 'Melchior Lorichs Ehrenpforten und Weinbrunnen zum Einzug Kaiser Maximilians II. in Wien', *Philobiblon*, xix (1979), pp. 279–95

*Zeichnung in Deutschland: Deutsche Zeichner, 1540–1640*, ii (exh. cat. by H. Geissler, Stuttgart, 1979–80), pp. 173–6

E. Fischer: 'Melchior Lorck', *Biographisches Lexikon für Schleswig-Holstein und Lübeck*, vi (Neumünster, 1982), pp. 174–80 [bibliog.]

——: *Melchior Lorck in Turkey* (Copenhagen, 1990)

ERIK FISCHER

**Loredan, Leonardo**, Doge of Venice (*b* 6 Nov 1436; elected 1501; *d* Venice, 22 June 1521). Italian ruler and patron. He was born into a noble family of Venetian rulers and patrons. Apart from Leonardo, the family's most conspicuous patron in the 15th century was Andrea di Nicolo Loredan (*d* 1513), who paid for the choir of S Michele in Isola, Venice (begun 1469), by Mauro Codussi, and employed Codussi to design his palace at S Marcuola, Venice (begun *c*. 1502; now Palazzo Vendramin-Calergi; *see* CODUSSI, MAURO, fig. 2). Leonardo Loredan received a humanist education, subsequently making his fortune in Levantine trade while rising through the governing hierarchy of Venice. By 1489 he was an overseer of the building of S Maria dei Miracoli, Venice, by Pietro Lombardo, his only known involvement with the arts until his election as Doge. His long reign was dominated by the wars of the League of Cambrai (1508–17), but despite this the visual arts flourished. Although Venetian rulers were discouraged from commemorating themselves in public monuments or images, Loredan did not observe this tradition. There are relief portraits of him on the three bronze bases for standards (1505–6) by Alessandro Leopardi (for illustration *see* LEOPARDI, ALESSANDRO) in front of S Marco, Venice, and he is glorified in inscriptions on the Porta d'Ognissanti (now Porta Portella) in Padua by Guglielmo de' Grigi. His projects included the renovation of the Doge's Palace in Venice, where his arms are displayed on the exterior of the chapel of S Nicolo (1505–*c*. 1520), by Giorgio Spavento and Antonio Scarpagnino, and the upper two storeys of the façade on the Rio di Palazzo, by Antonio Rizzo and Lombardo. For the Sala degli Scarlatti he commissioned an unusual and influential votive relief, attributed to Lombardo, in which he is presented to the Virgin and Child by three saints. Fires at the Rialto necessitated the rebuilding of the Fondaco dei Tedeschi by Giorgio Spavento and Scarpagnino (1505–8) with façade frescoes (destr.) by Giorgione and Titian, and the Palazzo dei X Savi by Scarpagnino (1520–21). Portraits of Loredan by Giorgione and Titian are untraced, but among surviving likenesses are Giovanni Bellini's masterpiece (London, N.G.; *see* BELLINI, GIOVANNI, fig. 4), a votive portrait by Vincenzo Catena (Venice, Correr), Bellini's portrait of the Doge with his four sons (Berlin, Bodemus.), and six portrait medals.

BIBLIOGRAPHY

M. Brunetti: 'Due dogi sotto inchiesta: Agostino Barbarigo e Leonardo Loredan', *Archv Ven.-Trident.*, vii (1925), pp. 278–329

O. Logan: *Culture and Society in Venice, 1470–1790* (London, 1972)

B. Jestaz: 'Requiem pour Alessandro Leopardi', *Rev. A.*, lv (1982), pp. 23–34

G. Gullino: 'I Loredan di Santo Stefano: Cenni storici', *Palazzo Loredan e l'istituto veneto di scienze, lettere ed arti* (Venice, 1985), pp. 11–33

E. Merkel: 'Il mecenatismo artistico dei Loredan e il loro palazzo a Santo Stefano', *Palazzo Loredan e l'istituto veneto di scienze, lettere ed arti* (Venice, 1985), pp. 53–71

J. Meyer zur Capellen: *Gentile Bellini* (Stuttgart, 1985), pp. 187–90

PAUL H. D. KAPLAN

**Lorena, Nicolò da.** *See* CORDIER, NICOLAS.

**Lorent, Jakob August** (*b* Charleston, SC, 12 Dec 1813; *d* Meran, Austria [now Merano, Italy], 9 July 1884). German photographer. He moved with his family to Mannheim in 1818, later studying zoology, botany and chemistry at the Ruprecht-Karls-Universität in Heidelberg. After taking his doctorate in 1837 he became a naturalist, undertaking research trips in North Africa (1840), Asia Minor and Egypt (1842–5), on which he named eight new types of plants. He took up photography because of his deep admiration for the Egyptian and East Asian culture and architecture. On a longer trip to England he learnt about William Henry Fox Talbot's negative–positive process on paper. His first surviving photographs are of Venice and North Italy, signed 'A. Lorent' and dated 1853. He used the dry wax paper negative process (developed by Gustave Le Gray in 1850), whereby the paper negative is made more transparent by treating it with hot wax. According to his own description, he needed approximately 37 hours to process the negatives alone, from the first stage of production, through to the developing and drying. He used formats measuring from 380×470 mm (1853) to 570×800 mm (1857), and the time of exposure could vary depending on the type of motif and the brightness, from five minutes (marble in the sun) to three hours (interiors of a palace). About 50 albumen photographs have survived from this period. In 1858 he moved from Venice to Mannheim, and after inheriting a fortune from his foster-father devoted himself to photography without having to consider the saleability of his photographs. He made extended photographic trips to southern Spain (Granada) and Algeria (1858–9), to Egypt and Nubia (1859–60) and to Greece (1860–61). There are still 233 wax paper negatives (450×440 mm) and 133 original albumen prints from these trips. He received the highest honours at numerous European exhibitions, for example, Munich (1854), Paris (1855), Brussels (1856), London (1862), Berlin (1865) and Vienna (1881). His last foreign trips were to Palestine (1864) and Sicily (1865); the 35 photographs that have survived from the Sicilian trip were made according to the wet collodion process. In 1865 Lorent began to photograph medieval buildings, particularly complete or ruined Romanesque and Gothic monasteries in Württemberg. Around 400 photographs have survived of 23 places (wet collodion process, 190× 240 mm). He also researched the early history of the places and buildings that he photographed, publishing three volumes of text with over 1000 pages. After his move to Meran in 1873 he developed his skills further with, for example, action shots and platinotypes. Over 100 photographs of South Tirol, taken in the last decade of his life, have been preserved.

WRITINGS

*Denkmale des Mittelalters in dem Königreiche Württemberg*, 3 vols (Mannheim, 1866–9)

PHOTOGRAPHIC PUBLICATIONS

*Egypten, Alhambra, Tlemsen, Algier* (Mannheim, 1861/*R* Mainz, 1985) [contains biog. by F. Waller]

BIBLIOGRAPHY

F. Waller: 'Jakob August Lorent: A Forgotten German Travelling Photographer', *Phot. Colr*, iii (1982), pp. 21–40; v (1984), pp. 186–96

F. WALLER

**Lorente Germán, Bernardo** (*b* Seville, 1680; *d* Seville, 1759). Spanish painter. He was a pupil of Cristóbal López (*d* 1730), and he was trained in a style imitative of Murillo. He probably began to paint *c.* 1700, but his earliest work is undocumented. Ceán Bermúdez stated that Lorente Germán worked as a royal portrait painter during the residence of the court of Philip V and Isabel Farnese in Seville between 1707 and 1734. He acquired a high reputation, and he was nominated for the appointment of Painter to the King when the court returned to Madrid in 1734. Lorente Germán refused the appointment, preferring to remain in Seville. Ceán Bermúdez also stated that the artist was not better known or more widely patronized because of his reserved and melancholic character.

Lorente Germán's production was very uneven, especially in his paintings of subjects of popular devotion such as the *Divine Shepherdess*. He produced many versions of this (e.g. Madrid, Prado), most of which were conventional and carelessly executed. His earliest known work is *St Francis Xavier* (1727; Seville, priv. col., see Valdivieso, p. 303), painted with great care and deliberation. His portrait of the *Infante Don Felipe* (*c.* 1730; Barcelona, priv. col., see Valdivieso, p. 304), of high technical quality, reveals the influence of the French artist Jean Ranc, who was then working in Seville in the service of the King. Lorente Germán's present-day fame rests principally on his *trompe l'oeil* paintings, such as the *Allegory of Taste* and the *Allegory of Smell* (both Paris, Louvre). Both works adhere to Seville traditions in this genre of painting, and they may have formed part of a moralizing series representing the five senses. The former depicts a shelf, probably in an artist's studio, with rags, flasks, a scroll on which is written a *regula vitae* and several scrolls of drawings. Above the shelf is a small painting of Bacchus, and over this hangs an engraving alluding to the Flemish painter and engraver Pedro Campolargo (*fl* 1640–70), who was active in Seville. The second painting similarly depicts a shelf in the corner of an artist's studio, above which hang plaster heads and pictures, one of which shows pipe-smokers.

BIBLIOGRAPHY

Ceán Bermúdez

*Pintura española de bodegones y floreros de 1600 a Goya* (exh. cat. by A. E. Pérez Sánchez, Madrid, Prado, 1983–4), pp. 145–6, 211

E. Valdivieso: *Historia de la pintura sevillana* (Seville, 1986), p. 291

A. Perez Sanchez: *Pintura barroca en España, 1600–1750* (Madrid, 1992), p. 418

ENRIQUE VALDIVIESO

**Lorenzetti** [Laurati; Laurentii]. Italian family of painters. Two members of this Sienese family, the brothers (1) Pietro Lorenzetti and (2) Ambrogio Lorenzetti, were artists. While Ghiberti regarded Ambrogio as the greatest of Sienese 14th-century painters, he was apparently unaware of Pietro's existence. Vasari, who misread the inscription on a panel of the *Virgin and Child Enthroned with Angels* (Florence, Uffizi) as PETRUS LAURATI DE SENIS, did not recognize Pietro's connection with Ambrogio. The fraternal relationship was specified, however, in a lost inscription below frescoes on the façade of the hospital of S Maria della Scala, Siena, first recorded by Ugurieri-Azzolini: HOC OPUS FECIT PETRUS LAURENTII ET AMBROSIUS EIUS FRATER M.CCC.XXX.V. There is also evidence that the brothers borrowed tools from each other, although it is unlikely that they collaborated regularly or that they maintained a joint workshop over any lengthy period. There is no doubt that they shared artistic ideas and ambitions, not so much as a result of their family connection, but because they were both major masters and exponents of naturalism. Both painters' innovations were too radical to be assimilated by their immediate followers, but they foreshadow developments in the 15th century.

BIBLIOGRAPHY

L. Ghiberti: *I commentarii* (*c.* 1457); Ger. trans., ed. J. von Schlosser, as *Lorenzo Ghibertis Denkwürdigkeiten* (Berlin, 1912)

G. Vasari: *Vite* (1550, rev. 2/1568); ed. G. Milanesi, i (1878), pp. 471–9, 521–35

I. Ugurieri-Azzolini: *Le pompe sanesi* (Pistoia, 1649)

G. Della Valle: *Lettere sanesi*, ii (Rome, 1785), pp. 203–27

G. Milanesi: *Documenti per la storia dell'arte senese*, i (Siena, 1854), pp. 193–7

G. Sinibaldi: *I Lorenzetti* (Siena, 1933)

J. White: *The Birth and Rebirth of Pictorial Space* (London, 1957, rev. Cambridge, MA, 2/1987)

P. Torriti: *La Pinacoteca Nazionale di Siena: I dipinti dal XII al XV secolo* (Genoa, 1977)

K. Frederick: 'A Program of Altarpieces for Siena Cathedral', *Rutgers A. Rev.*, iv (1983), pp. 18–35

C. Frugoni: *Pietro e Ambrogio Lorenzetti* (Florence, 1988)

H. Maginnis: 'The Lost Façade Frescoes from Siena's Ospedale di S Maria della Scala', *Z. Kstgesch.*, li (1988), pp. 180–94

**(1) Pietro Lorenzetti** (*fl c.* 1306–45). Although deeply indebted to the art of Duccio and his circle and inclined to be retrospective, he was an artist of considerable originality: his naturalistic figures, influenced by sculpture, are imbued with intense emotions and set within innovative illusionistic space.

1. Life and work. 2. Workshop.

### 1. LIFE AND WORK.

(i) Before 1326. (ii) 1326 and after.

*(i) Before 1326.* Documents referring to Pietro and his works are comparatively scant. It is not certain whether he is identifiable with a 'Petruccio Lorenzo' who, on 25 February 1306, was paid 1 lira and 10 soldi for a picture on a 'panel' of the nine governors of Siena. Although Pietro's earliest surviving works date to the second decade of the 14th century, the course of his career suggests that he was an independent master by the first decade. A single panel of the *Virgin and Child* (on dep. Siena, Pin. N.) from Castiglione d'Orcia (Siena) is the earliest surviving work attributed to him and is technically unusual in that the image was painted on a silver ground. The composition is a modification of a type current in Duccio's circle. A dismembered polyptych from SS Leonardo e Cristoforo in Monticchiello (Pienza), composed of a half-length

*Virgin and Child* (*in situ*), a *St Margaret* (Le Mans, Mus. Tessé) and *St Benedict, St Catherine of Alexandria* and *St Agnes* (Florence, Mus. Horne), similarly dates to *c.* 1315.

It may have been between these latter works that Pietro executed a frescoed, fictive triptych of the *Virgin and Child with SS John the Baptist and Francis* in the chapel of St John the Baptist at the end of the left (south) transept in the Lower Church of S Francesco, Assisi, although the date of his activity at Assisi is controversial. The chapel was built by Cardinal Napoleone Orsini and, appropriately, Pietro's image is a reflection of the fictive altarpiece in Napoleone's other chapel, dedicated to St Nicholas, at the end of the right transept (*see* ASSISI, §II, 2). This project possibly led to Pietro receiving the commission to fresco the main body of the left transept. In the Lower Church decoration had proceeded from the St Nicholas Chapel to the right transept and then to the crossing. Around 1315 Pietro was to complete the programme of decoration with an elaborate cycle recording the events of the *Passion* and including a depiction of the *Stigmatization of St Francis* as well as a number of illusionistic elements. The *Passion* cycle begins with the *Entry into Jerusalem* and continues to the *Resurrection.*

The Assisi frescoes offered following generations a panoply of artistic ideas. The star-filled night skies of the *Last Supper* (see fig. 1) and the *Betrayal* provided a precedent for Taddeo Gaddi's exploration of nocturnal lighting in his *Annunciation to the Shepherds* in the Baroncelli

Chapel of Santa Croce, Florence, although only in the early 15th century were such devices to be fully developed. Similarly, a fictive niche below the *Crucifixion* (*see* ASSISI, fig. 5) was the antecedent of Taddeo's frescoed niches below the narratives of the Baroncelli Chapel. The fictive scdilia below the *Deposition* is perhaps the most remarkable illusionistic device of the period, and the unified field and general conceit of the transept's fictive altarpiece, below the *Crucifixion*, anticipates panel paintings of a century later.

To the years immediately following the Assisi frescoes belong a signed *Virgin and Child Enthroned with Angels*, a monumental *Crucifix*, a portable *Crucifix* (all Cortona, Mus. Dioc.), a *Crucifixion* (Cambridge, MA, Fogg) and the main tiers from a signed polyptych, commissioned on 17 April 1320 by Guido Tarlati, bishop of Arezzo, for the pieve di S Maria (main panel, *in situ*). Notices referring to testamentary bequests in aid of the project occur on 18 March, 22 July, 6 August–3 September and 8–15 September 1320. In a will of 21 September 1321, Pietro and another Sienese artist, Mino Parcis, are named as witnesses, indicating the painter's continued presence in Arezzo. Further documents relating to bequests or promised donations for the altarpiece are dated 4 January and 25 June 1322 and 20 May 1324.

These works reveal a great deal about the painter's background, his talent and the influences that shaped his early career. That Duccio and his immediate circle were

1. Pietro Lorenzetti: *Last Supper* (*c.* 1315), fresco, Lower Church, S Francesco, Assisi

the principal early influences cannot be doubted: the majority of the Assisi narratives derive from the *Passion* scenes of Duccio's *Maestà*, the front of which also provided a model for the Cortona *Madonna* (*see* DUCCIO, §I). The Cortona *Crucifix* mingles influences from Segna di Bonaventura and Ugolino di Nerio. There are, however, indications of other sources of inspiration. The compositional principles of the Assisi frescoes are not Ducciesque, but rather shaped by Pietro's experience of earlier works at Assisi. Such technical features as the use of *cangianti*, and the figure style of the late scenes, betray the gradual and growing impact of the works from Giotto's circle in the right transept. Finally, Pietro's images of the Virgin and Child, particularly that of the Arezzo Polyptych, display the influence of the work of Giovanni Pisano, specifically his half-length sculpture of the *Virgin and Child* in the Camposanto of Pisa. Yet all these sources are brought together in a highly individual way and in an idiom that frequently combines high naturalism with the exploration of emotional states.

From the decade following the commission for the Arezzo Altarpiece few works remain. Vasari, who worked in the pieve of Arezzo and was himself responsible for the removal of Pietro's polyptych from the high altar, records that the painter frescoed the apse of that church with 12 episodes from the *Life of the Virgin*. Presumably this cycle was executed during the painter's stay in the city in the early 1320s. A comparatively modest *Virgin and Child Enthroned* in the Johnson collection (Philadelphia, PA, Mus. A.) elevates the Ducciesque motif of the Christ Child blessing a donor from the realm of private devotional work to that of public image. A slightly later *St Leonard* (Riggisberg, Abegg-Stift.), patron saint of prisoners, is likewise modest in scale.

*(ii) 1326 and after*. A number of Sienese documents dated between 1324 and 1333 mention a 'Pietro' and a 'mastro Petro', but there is no reason to suppose that they refer to Pietro Lorenzetti. On 27 June 1326, however, he was paid 26 lire for 'stories' in the Siena Opera del Duomo and for the colours he had used in that work. Two important works of this period survive. A frescoed *Crucifixion* (Siena, S Francesco) was originally painted for the chapter house of S Francesco, and it seems to have been part of a collaborative project with Ambrogio. It is characterized by the clarity and broader compositional principles that are also found in the last frescoes at Assisi, the *Deposition* and *Entombment*.

The second work was an altarpiece for the Carmelites of Siena. At meetings on 24, 25 and 26 October 1329 the Consiglio Generale of Siena discussed and awarded a 50-lire grant towards the altarpiece Pietro had executed for the Carmelites, the total cost of which was said to have been 150 florins; the grant was paid directly to Pietro on 29 November 1329. The altarpiece originally stood on the high altar of the Sienese church of S Niccolò. Its central panel, the *Virgin and Child with St Nicholas and Elijah* (Siena, Pin. N.), in which Christ turns to acknowledge the figure of Elijah at his side, combines elements from the face of Duccio's *Maestà* with the motif of Christ acknowledging a figure other than the Virgin that is derived from such private devotional works from Duccio's circle as

Tabernacle no. 35 (Siena, Pin. N.). The main panel was flanked by full-length standing figures of *SS Catherine and Agnes* (Siena, Pin. N.) and *St John the Baptist and Elisha* (Pasadena, CA, Norton Simon Mus.). Although full-length standing lateral saints may have appeared earlier in Florentine painting, these figures constitute the first known instance in Siena and thus provide important precedents for the side panels of the altarpieces dedicated to the city's four patron saints in Siena Cathedral. Indeed, the composition, involving such figures to left and right of what is here a quasi-narrative scene, relates closely to the design of those altarpieces. The scenes of the predella, particularly that of the central panel, provided a precedent for the large-scale narrative and panoramic predella panels to follow. The (overtly propagandist) conception of the altarpiece, in which the Carmelites' claim to have been the one religious order with roots in the Old Testament is made visible, is one of the most original conceits of the early 14th century.

In the 1330s Pietro began work on the S Savino Altarpiece, for which in November 1335 he received a first payment of 30 florins from the Opera del Duomo of Siena (see below). By 1335 the façade frescoes for the hospital of S Maria della Scala were complete. As far as the collaboration between Pietro and Ambrogio on these can be reconstructed, it seems that Pietro was responsible for the first narrative in the cycle, the *Birth of the Virgin*, and Ambrogio for the second scene, the *Presentation of the Virgin*. Simone Martini also participated in this project, making it one of the very few instances in Siena where different artists, responsible for separate scenes, were engaged on a single fresco cycle.

Early secondary sources describe a panel dated 1337 (untraced) in the Sienese church of S Martino, and on 3 November 1337 Pietro paid the Commune of Siena for the right to bear arms; this privilege was apparently renewed on 7 November 1338. The next documentary reference occurs on 27 October 1340, when Pietro promised to paint two panels for a certain Paolo di Tingo de' Pilestri, from whom he had already received the significant sum of 40 florins. In the same year Pietro signed the *Virgin and Child Enthroned with Angels* (Florence, Uffizi), originally for the church of S Francesco, Pistoia. The work, cut at the top, is a reworking of the composition of the early Cortona *Virgin and Child*, here modified to enhance the sculptural qualities of the figures and the spatial force of the throne, reducing the gold ground to a minimum. The fragmentary red wings at the top of the panel and a variation on the composition produced by a follower indicate that the apex was originally filled with cherubim. The idea of severely limiting the ground and allowing the forms of the image to generate the very space they occupy probably stemmed from Pietro's work on his last surviving panel, the S Savino Altarpiece for Siena Cathedral.

Apart from the initial payment for this altarpiece, a document of December 1335 records payment to a 'maestro Ciecho del la grammatica' for translating the story of St Sabinus into the vernacular to be used in the work, presumably for the predella. A fragment of the predella has been identified as *St Sabinus before the Emperor* (London, N.G.). According to a cathedral inventory of

1429, the central panel (completed 1342), the signed *Birth of the Virgin* (Siena, Mus. Opera Duomo; see fig. 2), was flanked by images of St Sabinus and St Bartholomew (untraced).

To this work Pietro brought the experience of a long career: his repeated explorations of naturalistic devices and perhaps two previous treatments of the principal subject. Although the shape of the main panel derives from the centre of Simone Martini's nearby S Ansano Altarpiece (1333; Florence, Uffizi), the image is very different in character. The scene is rich in circumstantial detail: the double-vaulted bedchamber of St Anne and the passageway at the left where Joachim and a friend receive news of the Virgin's birth; beyond Joachim, an internal courtyard rises beyond our view. The most startling aspect

of the work, however, is the conception of space in which, in anticipation of images in the following century, the painted architecture is identified with the actual frame. Small areas of gold, glimpsed through windows, no longer serve as ground but are here equated with light. Across the three sections of the panel, Pietro gently shifted the viewpoint to increase legibility and to unify the design.

Pietro is mentioned in a handful of documents from the 1340s: he and his wife paid a forced loan to the Commune of Siena on 26 February 1341; a lost document of 24 September 1342 may have recorded Pietro's purchase of land on behalf of Cola and Martino, sons of the sculptor Tino di Camaino. Between 18 September 1344 and 19 February 1345 the artist sold land to them, valued at 150 lire, which is the last reference to the painter.

2. Pietro Lorenzetti: *Birth of the Virgin*, tempera on panel, 1.87×1.82 m, completed 1342 (Siena, Museo dell'Opera del Duomo)

2. WORKSHOP. Vasari claimed that BARTOLOMMEO BULGARINI was Pietro's pupil, but although Bulgarini, like other mid-century artists, drew upon Pietro's work, the direct relationship is unlikely. One clearly identifiable disciple is the Master of the Loeser Madonna (Maginnis, 1976); another, the Master of the Beata Umiltà, is named after an altarpiece now in the Uffizi, Florence. There are other works that are certainly the productions of assistants and followers, but generally we are left with the impression that the painter's circle was not large.

BIBLIOGRAPHY

P. Bacci: *Dipinti inediti e sconosciuti di Pietro Lorenzetti, Bernardo Daddi etc. in Siena e nel contado* (Siena, 1939)

F. Zeri: 'Pietro Lorenzetti: Quattro pannelli dalla pala del 1329 al Carmine', *A. Illus.*, vii (1974), no. 58, pp. 146–56

H. Maginnis: 'Assisi Revisited: Notes on Recent Observations', *Burl. Mag.*, xcvii (1975), pp. 511–17

——: 'Pietro Lorenzetti's Carmelite Madonna: A Reconstruction', *Pantheon*, xxxiii (1975), pp. 10–16

M. Frinta: 'Deletions from the Oeuvre of Pietro Lorenzetti and Related Works by the Master of Beata Umiltà, Mino Parcis da Siena and Jacopo di Mino del Pellicciaio', *Mitt. Ksthist. Inst. Florenz*, xx (1976), pp. 271–300

H. Maginnis: 'The Passion Cycle in the Lower Church of San Francesco, Assisi: The Technical Evidence', *Z. Kstgesch.*, xxxix (1976), pp. 193–208

——: 'The So-called Dijon Master', *Z. Kstgesch.*, xlii (1980), pp. 121–38

M. Seidel: 'Das Frühwerk von Pietro Lorenzetti', *Städel-Jb.*, viii (1981), pp. 79–158

H. Maginnis: 'Pietro Lorenzetti: A Chronology', *A. Bull.*, lxvi (1984), pp. 183–211

A. Guerrini: 'Intorno al polittico di Pietro Lorenzetti per la pieve di Arezzo', *Riv. A.*, xl (1988), pp. 3–29

H. Maginnis: 'A Lorenzettian Crucifix in Cortona', *Racar*, xv (1988), pp. 59–61

C. Volpe: *Pietro Lorenzetti* (Milan, 1989)

**(2) Ambrogio Lorenzetti** (*fl c.* 1317; *d* before May 1348). Brother of (1) Pietro Lorenzetti. Ghiberti styled Ambrogio a 'most perfect' and learned master. He was certainly the most inventive Sienese artist of the early 14th century. Many of his innovations in naturalism are without parallel; many of his works are characterized by iconography that is equally original. His lost 'Roman stories' from the exterior of the Palazzo Pubblico, Siena, suggest an ability to deal with highly unusual subject matter; the lost Mappamondo, an ability to create new forms (*see* §1(ii) above). His career is marked by periodic shifts and a constant search for innovation: works of the 1310s and 1320s display a pursuit of naturalism that recurred throughout his career; those from the early 1330s suggest that the artist was seeking to emulate the decorative effects of Simone Martini and his circle; in Ambrogio's late work much of this ornament disappears, or is severely restrained, while his distinctive use of inscribed banderoles implies the desire to push content beyond the traditional pictorial means of monumental painting.

1. Life and work. 2. Workshop.

1. LIFE AND WORK.

(i) Before *c.* 1337. (ii) After *c.* 1337.

*(i) Before* c. *1337.* The formulation of the inscription below the Siena hospital façade frescoes has suggested to many critics that Ambrogio was younger than Pietro; the surviving works point towards a similar conclusion. A panel of the *Virgin and Child* (Milan, Brera) is widely, although not universally, thought to be the painter's earliest extant panel. Dating to *c.* 1317, it combines forms typical of Ambrogio with marked influence from both Pietro and Simone Martini. It is, however, with the dated *Virgin and Child Enthroned* (1319; Florence, Mus. Dioc.) that Ambrogio emerges as a recognizable artistic individual. Created for the church of S Angelo in Vico l'Abate (Florence), the painting possesses great monumentality, and if the style is thoroughly Sienese the design indicates close attention to the works of Florentine contemporaries.

Some documentation survives from the 1320s. A Florentine document of 30 May 1321 records the seizure of goods belonging to a certain Ambrogio, painter of Siena, for debts owed to Mei Lapi and Justus Pauli; the connection with Ambrogio Lorenzetti is likely but speculative. On 2 January 1324 Ambrogio sold land in Siena valued at the significant sum of 200 lire. Autograph works from the period, however, are few. Two frescoes from the chapter house of S Francesco, Siena (detached and now in the church), depict the *Ordination of St Louis of Toulouse* and the *Martyrdom of Seven Franciscans at Ceuta*. The former is remarkable for its evocation of interior space, the latter for its novel use of orientalizing costume and physiognomies. On the basis of circumstantial evidence, these frescoes have been related to Ambrogio's fragmentary fresco of the *Franciscan Martyrdom at Bombay* (see below) from the adjoining cloister, and both dated to *c.* 1336 (Seidel, 1979; Frugoni). The chapter house frescoes, however, were part of a scheme to which Pietro's *Crucifixion* belonged, and the stylistic evidence places that work in the mid-1320s (*see* (1) above). Moreover, the setting for the scene of *St Louis* was adapted by Pietro for two scenes in the predella of his Carmelite Altarpiece of 1329.

Ambrogio matriculated in the Florentine painters' guild, the Medici e Speziali, in 1327, suggesting that he had a commission or commissions in that city, although no work can be associated with this specific date. Ghiberti recorded that in Florence Ambrogio decorated the chapter house of S Agostino with stories of the *Credo* in the vaults, a *Crucifixion*, a scene of *St Catherine of Alexandria Expounding her Faith* and *St Catherine Disputing with the Sages*. He also cited decorations for a chapel in S Procolo, a painted panel for the same church and an *Annunciation* for the 'Scala, where the foundlings are kept'. There survive, however, the remains of two works from the church of S Procolo. One of these, four scenes on panel of the *Life of St Nicholas of Bari* (Florence, Uffizi), probably belonged to a work resembling Simone Martini's *Blessed Agostino Novello* (Siena, Pin. N.). It contains remarkable spatial effects: a church interior, two street scenes and a seascape, undoubtedly reflecting the artist's previous experience of composing for fresco. The other work from S Procolo, three panels of the *Virgin and Child*, *St Nicholas* and *St Proculus* (Florence, Uffizi), were part of the altarpiece that once bore Ambrogio's name and a date of 1332, as recorded in early secondary sources. These panels raise the complex problem of workshop participation.

The large number of works that survive from the years after the S Procolo Altarpiece imply that Ambrogio's career acquired momentum in the 1330s, and there is no doubt that, after Simone Martini's departure for Avignon in 1336, Ambrogio replaced him as the quasi-official

1. Ambrogio Lorenzetti: *Maestà*, tempera on panel, *c.* 1335 (Massa Marittima, Museo Archeologico)

painter to the Sienese Commune and thus received more commissions, although the Commune was not his only patron. Several documents from this period appear to refer to Ambrogio: on 15 August 1334 'Ambroxio de Senis pictore' acted as witness to the authorization of a land sale signed in the cloister of the Cistercian abbey of S Galgano; a notice of 1335 records payment by the Opera del Duomo of Siena to a 'maestro Ambrogio dipegnitore' for restoring the face, hands and 'book' of 'our Lady of the cathedral'.

The *Franciscan Martyrdom at Bombay* is a fragment of Ambrogio's cloister decoration at S Francesco, which dates from the 1330s. The historian Sigismondo Tizio (*d* 1528) dated the decoration to 1331; Seidel (1979), however, proposed *c.* 1336 and argued that the wall, over 100 feet long, was divided into separate scenes; Rowley maintained it held one vast, continuous narrative. Ghiberti's description indicates extraordinary naturalistic features (e.g. 'a storm with much hail, flashes of lightning, and thundering earthquakes').

Four panels, *St Catherine*, *St Benedict*, *St Francis* and *St Mary Magdalene* (Siena, Mus. Opera Duomo), and a reframed altarpiece, dedicated to St Michael the Archangel (Asciano, Mus. A. Sacra), belong to the early 1330s and, like the S Procolo Altarpiece, show extensive workshop participation. The *St Michael*, shown full-length and in the course of slaying a dragon, is among the most complex figures of the first half of the 14th century. To *c.* 1335 belongs an extraordinary *Maestà* (Massa Marittima, Mus. Archeol.; see fig. 1). A response to the Sienese tradition of treating the subject (e.g. by Duccio and Simone Martini) and perhaps to the Baroncelli Altarpiece of Santa Croce, Florence, the work is more complex than earlier versions by other artists. The *Virgin and Child* are accompanied by 120 figures as well as personifications of Faith, Hope and Charity. The Virgin sits not on a throne but on a cushion, borne aloft by two angels whose wings replace the absent throne's back. An equally remarkable frescoed *Maestà* (Siena, S Agostino) dates just after the work in Massa. It introduces the novel motif of the Christ Child frightened by a goldfinch, symbolic of his future Passion. Here the Virgin is sustained merely by cherubim. Both aspects foreshadow developments in central Italian painting after 1348.

*(ii) After c. 1337.* Among Ambrogio's most significant works are those for the Palazzo Pubblico in Siena. The chronicler Agnolo di Tura stated that in 1337 Ambrogio painted 'Roman stories' on the exterior of the palace, although these have not survived. A lengthy series of payments for the decoration of the Sala della Pace in the Palazzo Pubblico begins on 26 February 1338. In total

some 14 notices, sometimes overlapping, running until 29 May 1339 provide what is perhaps the only complete record of payment for a major fresco project in the first half of the 14th century. The commission lasted approximately 16 months and earned the artist 357 lire, 11 soldi and 4 denarii. The frescoes, in the meeting chamber of the governing Nine and in the first room at the top of the palace's original stairway, were both an admonition to the governing oligarchy and a propagandist statement of the regime's success. Of the three decorated walls, one bears a depiction of the *Effects of Good Government on Town and Country*; another an *Allegory of Good Government*; and the third displays a combined *Allegory of Bad Government and its Effects on Town and Country*. There are significant areas of late 14th-century restoration at both ends of the *Effects of Good Government* and at the right side of the *Allegory of Good Government*.

Several interpretations of the programme of decoration have been proposed, but no consensus has emerged. While the room is an important historical document, its pictorial innovations are still more significant. In the *Effects of Good Government*, the cityscape (see fig. 2) displays a spatial organization unique for the period, although it is perhaps partially inspired by the setting of Pietro's *Road to Calvary* in the *Passion* cycle in the Lower Church in Assisi. Even more dramatic is the depiction of the surrounding countryside: the first panoramic landscape since antiquity, it is

organized in a manner that would ultimately influence painters as far afield as France and the Netherlands. Individual components are as startling as the broad conceptions. The countryside provides views of villas and farms in the area around Siena and a nascent conception of aerial perspective. In the *Allegory of Good Government* (*see* SIENA, fig. 12) the figure of Peace was inspired by antique sculpture. Among the quatrefoils of the upper borders is a figure of Winter, holding a snowball and surrounded by falling snow.

In the late 1330s Ambrogio also painted the *Madonna del Latte* (Siena, Semin.) that inspired Nino Pisano's sculpted *Madonna della Spina* (Pisa, S Maria della Spina). According to Agnolo di Tura, it was in 1340 that the painter frescoed a *Virgin and Child with the Cardinal Virtues* for the loggia of the Palazzo Pubblico, Siena. Only a portion of this survives, on the first floor of the palace, but it must have been as complex and original in its iconography as other works by the artist, for the Virgin holds a globe that Christ blesses while in his left hand he holds a banderole with an inscription from John 13:34: MANDATUM NOVUM DO VOBIS UT DILIGATIS INVICEM. Although the original location of the work and the presence of the Cardinal Virtues place it in a political context, no viewer could fail to recognize the reference in the inscription to Maundy Thursday. A debt to the hospital of S Maria della Scala, Siena, was cancelled on 12 September 1341, as Ambrogio was painting the chapel of the

2. Ambrogio Lorenzetti: *Effects of Good Government* (1338–9; detail), fresco, Sala della Pace, Palazzo Pubblico, Siena

hospital's cemetery. Another unusual payment involves the hospital: on 9 June 1344 Ambrogio received 10 soldi for having buried a poor woman.

On 3 June 1337 the Siena Opera del Duomo purchased wood for the altarpiece dedicated to S Crescenzio for the cathedral. In July 1339 Ambrogio was given an interim payment of 30 florins for his work on the altarpiece and was also paid for painting an angel, presumably sculpted, and a candlestick for the high altar of the cathedral. Another 30 florins was paid to the artist for the altarpiece in January 1340. Other notices relating to this project and dealing with the carpentry or acquisition of wood survive from July 1339 and January and May 1340. Ambrogio's signed panel, the *Presentation in the Temple* (Florence, Uffizi; see fig. 3), once the centre of the S Crescenzio Altarpiece in Siena Cathedral, was begun in 1337 but not completed until 1342. A 15th-century cathedral inventory states that the central image was flanked by figures of St Crescentius and St Michael the Archangel. Of the cathedral altarpieces dedicated to Siena's patron saints it was the largest and the most complex in content. Basing his image of the temple on the architecture of Siena Cathedral, Ambrogio created an architectural interior view of unprecedented complexity and spatial depth. By including inscriptions in his composition, he departed from the conventional treatment of the subject in order to enhance the theological significance of the event depicted. The image makes the Presentation critical in the history of salvation; in this it is unique. The central predella panel of the altarpiece was probably the *Allegory of Sin and Redemption* (Siena, Pin. N.). If this is the case, this predella was the precedent for the exceedingly large predellas of the 15th century.

Sigismundo Tizio reported that Ambrogio painted an *Annunciation* on the façade of the Sienese church of S Pietro in Castelvecchio in 1343 as well as the high altarpiece of that church. A signed *Annunciation* (Siena, Pin. N.) of 1344 was executed for the office of the Gabella in the Palazzo Pubblico, Siena. The work exhibits a spatial sophistication rivalling that of the *Presentation*: almost all the orthogonals of the tile floor run roughly to a single vanishing point. Like the careful organization of the pavement in the *Presentation*, this feature of the *Annunciation* testifies to the artist's preoccupation with the problem of rationalizing pictorial space.

To the 1340s also belong the S Petronilla Altarpiece and the 'Small' Maestà (both Siena, Pin. N.). Employing a device that appears to have become typical at this period, the artist gave the Christ Child of the S Petronilla Altarpiece a banderole inscribed with words from Luke 6:20, BEATI PAUPERES, a text suited to the Order of the Umiliati for whom the altarpiece was painted. The 'Small' Maestà, probably the centre of a triptych, is a work of great refinement, particularly noteworthy for incisions in the ground that suggest a radiance emanating from the central figures, so bright that it partially dissolves the forms of the surrounding angels.

On 31 October 1345 the Commune of Siena paid Ambrogio 85 lire for 'ornamento' executed in the Palazzo Pubblico, and on 22 November of the same year he received 3 lire for figures painted in the rooms of the Nine. It was perhaps in 1345 that he executed the lost,

3. Ambrogio Lorenzetti: *Presentation in the Temple*, tempera on panel, 1337–42 (Florence, Galleria degli Uffizi)

rotating world map for the Sala del Mappamondo in the palace, which is mentioned by Ghiberti and Tizio; no comparable image is known from the period. Two small, undated panels, *City by the Sea* and *Castle by the Sea* (both Siena, Pin. N.), are likely to belong to the second half of Ambrogio's career. Their original context is unknown, but, along with the *Effects of Good Government*, they are crucial documents in the rise of landscape painting. A summary of the painter's will is dated 9 June 1348, and surviving notices regarding the sale of his bequeathed property in May 1349 and in 1350 suggest that he and his family died in the bubonic plague (1348–9).

2. WORKSHOP. The sheer number of surviving and documented works from the 1330s and 1340s indicates the probability of assistants, and it is likely that Ambrogio had established a sizeable workshop by the late 1320s. Significant workshop participation is evident in the S Procolo Altarpiece, the Asciano *St Michael* Altarpiece and the four saints in the Museo dell'Opera del Duomo, Siena. In addition, the 1330s marked the appearance of works that evince more than workshop assistance. If Ambrogio provided ideas for the mid-1330s frescoes in the chapel of S Galgano, Montesiepi (near Siena), his hand is little if

at all evident in the execution, and even some of the compositions seem unduly dull. Such panel paintings as the half-length *Virgin and Child* from Rapolano or the Crucifix (both Siena, Pin. N.) may well be workshop productions, but there are several works in the Pinacoteca entirely by followers. From the 1340s there survive elements of two sizeable works by followers: an altarpiece in SS Pietro e Paolo, Roccalbegna (Siena), and a *Virgin and Child Enthroned* (Budapest, Mus. F.A.). The former seems to have been an unusual combination of a central *Maestà* (now a fragment) with enthroned saints in lateral panels. The latter, also a fragment of a larger composition, derives partly from the Palazzo Pubblico loggia fresco. Rowley may have exceeded the necessary distinctions among followers (and certainly erred regarding the chronological place of several of their works), but he was correct in seeing a situation of more than ordinary complexity.

BIBLIOGRAPHY

G. Rowley: *Ambrogio Lorenzetti* (Princeton, 1958)
E. Borsook: *Ambrogio Lorenzetti* (Florence, 1966)
——: *Gli affreschi di Montesiepi* (Florence, 1969)
V. Wainwright: 'The Will of Ambrogio Lorenzetti', *Burl. Mag.*, cxvii (1975), pp. 543–4
E. Skaug: 'Notes on the Chronology of Ambrogio Lorenzetti and a New Painting from his Shop', *Mitt. Ksthist. Inst. Florenz*, xx (1976), pp. 300–32
A. Luchs: 'Ambrogio Lorenzetti at Montesiepi', *Burl. Mag.*, cxix (1977), pp. 187–8
N. Muller: 'Ambrogio Lorenzetti's *Annunciation*: A Re-examination', *Mitt. Ksthist. Inst. Florenz*, xxi (1977), pp. 1–12
M. Seidel: 'Die Fresken des Ambrogio Lorenzetti in S. Agostino', *Mitt. Ksthist. Inst. Florenz*, xxii (1978), pp. 185–252
——: 'Gli affreschi di Ambrogio Lorenzetti nel chiostro di San Francesco a Siena', *Prospettiva*, xviii (1979), pp. 10–20
E. Southard: 'Ambrogio Lorenzetti's Frescoes in the Sala della Pace: A Change of Names', *Mitt. Ksthist. Inst. Florenz*, xxiv (1980), pp. 361–5
L. Cateni: 'Un polittico "too remote from Ambrogio" firmato da Ambrogio Lorenzetti', *Prospettiva*, xl (1985), pp. 62–7
H. Maginnis: 'Chiarimenti documentari: Simone Martini, i Memmi e Ambrogio Lorenzetti', *Riv. A.*, xli (1989), pp. 3–23
——: 'Ambrogio Lorenzetti's *Presentation in the Temple*', *Stud. Stor. A.*, ii (1991), pp. 33–50
R. Starn and L. Partridge: *Arts of Power: Three Halls of State in Italy, 1300–1600* (Berkeley, 1993)

H. B. J. MAGINNIS

**Lorenzetto.** *See* LOTTI, LORENZO.

**Lorenzi.** Italian family of artists.

**(1) Battista (di Domenico) Lorenzi** (*b* Settignano, *c.* 1527–8; *d* Pisa, 7 Jan 1592). Sculptor and architect. He trained in the Florentine workshop of Baccio Bandinelli from 1540. Between 1558 and 1559 he collaborated with Vincenzo de' Rossi in Rome on a statue for the monument to *Paul IV* (destr.). Battista had returned to Florence by 1563, when he undertook a cycle of the *Four Seasons* (completed *c.* 1570; untraced) for the residence in Paris of the abate Giovambattista Guadagni (*d* 1591). In 1564, the year of his election to the Florentine Accademia del Disegno, he provided a figure of *Painting* for Michelangelo's catafalque and for Michelangelo's tomb in Santa Croce, Florence, the portrait of *Michelangelo* and the figure of *Sculpture* (later transformed into *Painting*). His terracotta model for *Sculpture* (London, V&A) differs considerably from the final more complex and monumental figure (completed 1574).

In 1568 Alamanno Bandini commissioned one of Battista's most successful compositions, the group of *Alpheus and Arethusa* (New York, Met.). At the same date Battista carved a fountain figure of a *Triton with Dolphins* (Palermo, Mus. Reg.) for Cosimo I de' Medici. A figure of *Ganymede* (Florence, Boboli Gdns) has been attributed to him (Keutner). In 1573 Battista began his association with Jacopo Salviati, for whose Florentine palazzo in the Via del Corso (formerly Palazzo Salviato-Capponi, now Palazzo Nonfinito) he carved a marble figure of *Perseus*, sandstone figures of the river god *Mugnone* (*c.* 1577; *in situ*) and a *Washerwoman* (*c.* 1577–82; Florence, Giard. Gherardesca). From 1583 to 1588 Battista was sculptor and architect to the Opera del Duomo in Pisa. There he was engaged on the rebuilding of several areas of the cathedral, and he designed the bronze *Lampada di Galileo*, erected in 1586, and *St Ephysius* (erected in 1592) for the transept. In 1588–9 he contributed to the decorations for the wedding of Ferdinando de' Medici and executed the façade figures of *St Miniatos* and *St Antoninus* for Florence Cathedral.

BIBLIOGRAPHY

G. Vasari: *Vite* (1550, rev. 2/1568); ed. G. Milanesi (1878–85), vi, p. 82; vii, p. 305; viii, p. 618
R. Borghini: *Il riposo* (Florence, 1584); ed. M. Rosci (Florence, 1967)
L. Tanfani Centofani: *Notizie di artisti tratte dai documenti pisani* (Pisa, 1897), pp. 51, 77–9, 205–7, 217, 454, 473
R. Papini: *Catalogo delle cose d'arte e di antichità d'Italia*, part 1, fasc. II (Rome, 1912), pp. 59, 63, 67, 74–5, 94, 189
H. Utz Kissel: *Battista Lorenzi: Studien zur Entwicklung der Florentiner Skulptur in der zweiten Hälfte des 16. Jh.* (Munich, 1968)
H. Utz: 'Skulpturen und andere Arbeiten des Battista Lorenzi', *Met. Mus. J.*, vii (1973), pp. 37–64
*Il Ganimede di Battista Lorenzi* (exh. cat., ed. H. Keutner and others; Settignano, Misericordia, 1982)
R. P. Ciardi, C. Casini and L. Tongiorgi Tomasi: *La scultura a Pisa fra quattrocento e seicento* (Pisa, 1987), pp. 25, 100, 152, 178, 183, 218–25, 227, 230, 233, 236, 247

ANTONIA BOSTRÖM

**(2) Stoldo (di Gino) Lorenzi** (*b* Settignano, 1534; *d* Pisa, 2–6 Sept 1583). Sculptor, nephew of (1) Battista Lorenzi. He was first apprenticed as a carver in his father's workshop and then trained as a painter with Michele Tosini in Florence. By 1550, however, he was apprenticed to the sculptor Niccolò Tribolo. Stoldo's first patron was Luca Martini (*d* 1561), a poet and writer, who was the administrator of Pisa under Cosimo I de' Medici, Grand Duke of Tuscany. Martini housed Stoldo in Pisa *c.* 1555–62, during which time the sculptor also received commissions from S Maria della Spina for an Annunciation group and from Cosimo I for a marble *stemma* flanked by personifications of *Religion* and *Justice* for the palazzo of the Cavalieri di S Stefano. His most notable work for Martini is a marble relief of *Cosimo I Receiving Tribute from the Towns of Tuscany* (*c.* 1555; Holkham Hall, Norfolk). Once thought to be by Michelangelo, the relief was commissioned as a pendant to Pierino da Vinci's *Pisa restaurata* (Rome, Pin. Vaticana; for illustration *see* PIERINO DA VINCI), which Stoldo completed after Pierino's death. In 1565, he worked on the decorations for the wedding of Francesco I de' Medici and Joanna of Austria, which gained him a series of important commissions in Florence, including the statue of *Abraham* (1565) for the chapel of S Luca in SS Annunziata, the bronze *Neptune* (1565–8; Florence, Boboli Gdns) for Cosimo I, and the bronze *Amphitrite* (or *Galatea*, 1573; Florence, Pal. Vecchio) for the *studiolo* of Francesco, commissioned by the Accademia del Disegno, of which Stoldo was now a member. In the autumn of 1573 he went to Milan to work on sculpture for S Maria presso S Celso, including statues of the *Annunciation* and reliefs of the *Flight into Egypt* and the *Adoration of the Magi* on the façade. Apparently due to differences with Annibale Fontana, with whom he shared the commission, Stoldo returned to Tuscany in 1582. At the time of his death he was working for Pisa Cathedral.

BIBLIOGRAPHY
J. Pope-Hennessy: *Italian High Renaissance and Baroque Sculpture* (Oxford, 1963, rev. New York, 2/1985), pp. 87, 100, 360, 377, 380, 400
H. Utz: 'Pierino da Vinci e Stoldo Lorenzi', *Paragone*, xviii/211 (1967), pp. 47–69
W. O. Hassall and N. B. Penny: 'Political Sculpture at Holkham', *Connoisseur*, cxcv/785 (1977), pp. 207–11

CORINNE MANDEL

**Lorenzino da Bologna.** *See* SABATINI, LORENZO.

**Lorenzo**, Duke of Urbino. *See* MEDICI, DE', (11).

**Lorenzo, Antonio di Niccolò di.** *See* ANTONIO DI NICCOLÒ DI LORENZO.

**Lorenzo (di Cecco di Pascolo), Fiorenzo di.** *See* FIORENZO DI LORENZO.

**Lorenzo da Bologna** (*fl* 1465–1508). Italian architect. A document dated 1467 states that he lived in Candiana, near Padua, and possibly worked at the monastery of S Michele. Another document of the same year states that he had married 2 years earlier in or around Padua (Rigoni, p. 165). Lorenzo worked in Vicenza from 1476 on the extension of the choir and sacristy at the basilica of Monte Berico (completed 1480 and 1481 respectively; destr. 1824). In 1480 he joined the Vicenza corporation of masons and stonecutters as an engineer and began work on the Casa Valmarana, (now Casa Bertolini); its façade is characterized by a rhythmic composition that updates the Venetian Late Gothic tradition through the use of the architectural vocabulary of the early Renaissance. From 1481 Lorenzo worked on the new choir, presbytery and crypt of the 13th-century church of S Corona, Vicenza, where, possibly at the patron's wishes, Renaissance stylistic elements define a space that remains Gothic. This effect can also be observed in the contemporary apse of the cathedral (completed 1558–65, with the drum and dome by Andrea Palladio), and in the chapel of the Most Holy, which was annexed to the same building in 1483. Other notable buildings in Vicenza that can be attributed to Lorenzo include the 15th-century part of the Palazzo Thiene (*c.* 1489), its façade (rest. 1872) characterized by a plinth in smooth ashlar and by faceted quoins framing a richly painted architecture at first-floor level. The harmonious balance of the proportions in the church of S Rocco (1485; *see* SCREEN, fig. 3), which has a single space covered by a vault and interrupted halfway by a *cantoria* (singing gallery) on round arches supported by polygonal columns, represents his best achievement.

From 1489 Lorenzo was active in Padua, where he built the upper gallery of the double cloister in the monastery of S Giovanni di Verdara (1490) and began work on the great cloister (1496; with the intarsia artist Pietro degli Abati from Modena). His work on the transept, presbytery and apse of Montagnana Cathedral, which contains recurrent motifs from his religious architecture, such as semidomes and small hanging arches in terracotta decorated with shells, probably dates from the late 1490s. Lorenzo da Bologna was an eclectic architect, employing motifs derived from the architectural work of Filippo Brunelleschi and Leon Battista Alberti that he saw in Mantua. He may thus be considered the first disseminator of Tuscan Renaissance architecture in the Venetian hinterland.

BIBLIOGRAPHY
G. Lorenzoni: *Lorenzo da Bologna* (Venice, 1963)
R. Cevese: 'L'architettura vicentina del primo rinascimento', *Boll. Cent. Int. Stud. Archit. Andrea Palladio*, vi/2 (1964), pp. 199–213
E. Rigoni: *L'arte rinascimentale in Padova: Studi e documenti* (Padua, 1970), pp. 141–85
M. Morresi: 'Contra' Porti a Vicenza: Una famiglia, un sistema urbano e un palazzo di Lorenzo da Bologna', *An. Archit. Cent.*, ii (1990), pp. 97–120
——: 'Palazzo Porto-Breganze a Vicenza: Una precisazione per Lorenzo da Bologna', *An. Archit. Cent.*, iii (1991), pp. 32–9

ADRIANO GHISETTI GIAVARINA

**Lorenzo di Bicci** (*b* Florence, *c.* 1350; *d* Florence, ?second decade of the 15th century or ?1427). Italian painter. He was the first important artist in a family of artists that ran a workshop that passed from father to son for more than a century. His father was probably also a painter but all that is known of him is the name Bicci, the patronymic of Lorenzo (and probably a nickname for Jacopo). By 1370 Lorenzo had enrolled in the Florentine painters' guild. His first documented work, datable to shortly after April 1380, is a panel depicting *St Martin Enthroned* (Florence, Depositi Gal.) painted for the Arte dei Vinattieri (the wine-merchants' guild), to be mounted in the Florentine church of Orsanmichele on a pilaster assigned to that guild on 30 April 1380. The predella (Florence, Accad.) depicts the episode of *St Martin Dividing his Cloak with the Beggar*. In 1385, together with the painters Agnolo Gaddi, Corso di Jacopo and Jacopo di Luca and two goldsmiths, Piero del Migliore and Niccolò de Luca, Lorenzo was called on to value the statues of *Faith* and *Hope* by Giacomo di Piero, created for the spandrels of the Loggia della Signoria in Florence (*in situ*). He was also commissioned to apply the blue enamelled ground and to gild the statues, for which work he was paid in several instalments, on 8 and 28 June, 12 October and 22 November 1386.

The other major project in progress in Florence in that period was the decoration of the cathedral, on which Lorenzo was employed in 1387. His colleagues included two other noted painters of the time, who shared his formal inclinations: Spinello Aretino and Agnolo Gaddi. With them he produced drawings for the statues of four *Apostles*, to be executed in marble for the façade of the church. When the series of statues was completed in 1394 by Piero di Giovanni Tedesco (*fl* 1386–1402), Lorenzo was commissioned, with Agnolo Gaddi, Jacopo di Cione and Lapo di Corso, to paint and gild them.

In 1394 Lorenzo also returned to the Loggia della Signoria, where he painted and gilded the statue of *Charity* by Jacopo di Piero Guidi ( *fl* 1379–1405). For this he was paid on 6 August and 6 October of that year. On 3 June 1395 he was paid for a valuation of a statue of *St Victor* by Piero di Giovanni Tedesco for the façade of Florence Cathedral. In 1398, for the altar of the *Madonna delle Grazie* in the cathedral nave, Lorenzo executed three *compassi*—polylobed panels—for the wooden canopy of the chapel. These contained half-length images of *St John the Evangelist*, *St Matthew* and *St Mark*. Pesello painted the *Agnus Dei* (untraced) at the centre of the vault of the canopy, while Lorenzo painted the curtain to be placed before the image of the Virgin. Documents record payments on 22 May and 13 June 1398, totalling 6 florins for each of the Evangelists and another payment on 30 October 1398 of 2 lire and 10 soldi for the curtain. The canopy has since been dismantled and the panels with the Evangelists are now in the Sagrestia dei Canonici (the Old Sacristy) in the cathedral. In 1399 Lorenzo was commissioned by the Compagni della Croce di S Stefano, Empoli, to produce a triptych, of which only the central panel, a *Crucifixion* (Empoli, Mus. S Andrea; see fig.), survives. Records of payments for this work exist dated 16 September 1399 and amount to 52 florins and 3 lire. After this date there is no information on Lorenzo until 1410, when he was paid 14 florins for a figure of *St Nicholas* for the lunette of the portal of the Ospedale di S Matteo, Florence (*in situ*), now the site of the Accademia di Belle Arti. There is no certain information on Lorenzo after the first decade of the 15th century.

Despite the scarcity of biographical data and the small number of surviving documented works securely attributable to him, Lorenzo di Bicci ranks as one of the most important painters in Florence during the second half of the 14th century. The origins of his style can be traced to the group of late 14th-century painters influenced by Andrea Orcagna, which includes Jacopo di Cione and Niccolò di Pietro Gerini. His works share their very simple compositional structure and their clear and lively use of colour, and also exhibit similar round, rather inexpressively rendered faces. Lorenzo's particular characteristic, however, was the luminosity of his colours and an accuracy of execution that was aided by a considerable drawing ability at the preparatory stage of the paintings. Scholars have noted that many of his commissions came from the country clergy and from the lower-middle class Florentine guilds (for example the *St Martin* for the wine-merchants). Patronage from such sectors continued in the workshop under his successors: his son BICCI DI LORENZO and his grandson NERI DI BICCI. His only documented collaborator outside the family was Cenni di Francesco di ser Cenni, with whom he executed frescoes in S Barnaba, Florence (fragments *in situ*).

The catalogue of Lorenzo di Bicci's works has been considerably amplified (see Boskovits) but still very few of his most significant works have been identified. Apart from the above-mentioned works his oeuvre now includes the *Madonna of Humility with Saints* (*c.* 1375–80; Loro Ciuffenna, S Maria Assunta); the *Virgin Enthroned with Two Saints and Angels* (*c.* 1375–80; Rome, Pal. Venezia); a triptych reconstructed by Boskovits (*c.* 1390–95: central panel, London, Drey priv. col.; side panels, Pisa, Mus. N. S Matteo) and the *Virgin of the Holy Girdle* (1395–1400;

Lorenzo di Bicci: *Crucifixion*, tempera on panel, 1.28×0.68 m, 1399 (Empoli, Museo della Collegiata di Sant'Andrea)

Arcetri, S Leonardo) previously attributed to Neri di Bicci. The large frescoed tabernacle from Via Aretina in a suburb of Florence, depicting the *Virgin and Child Enthroned with Saints*, the so-called *Madonnone*, now reduced to the *sinopia* (1st decade of the 15th century; Florence, Sopr. B.A. & Storici Col.; copy *in situ*) and a panel depicting *Two Saints* (?1380; Fiesole, Mus. Bandini) are almost unanimously attributed to Lorenzo (exh. cat. 1993). Frosinini, however, assigned these works to his son Bicci di Lorenzo on the evidence of stylistic features that tend towards the Late Gothic, discernible in the drawing and the ornamental details. This raises an interesting issue with regard to the family workshop, not only in terms of its management but also in relation to the persistence and evolution of various formal characteristics in the paintings through three generations.

The succession passed to Bicci di Lorenzo without particularly noticeable changes in style, except for a slight accentuation of the Gothic tendency around the middle of the first decade of the 15th century, a little before it became commonly accepted. This accords well with the theory (Frosinini) that Lorenzo's death occurred within the second decade of the century, a hypothesis supported by the lack of credibility now given to a document dated 21 June 1427 (Poggi, 1909) mentioning a payment to Lorenzo for a fresco (untraced) for Florence Cathedral.

BIBLIOGRAPHY

Bolaffi; Colnaghi; Thieme–Becker

G. Poggi: 'Masolino e la Compagnia della Croce in Empoli', *Riv. A.*, iii (1905), pp. 46–53 (47–8)

——: *Il Duomo di Firenze* (Berlin, 1909), p. lvii, documents 1009–10, 1015

M. Salmi: 'Due tavole di Lorenzo di Bicci', *Riv. A.*, xii (1930), pp. 81–4

R. Salvini: 'Un affresco e una tavola di Lorenzo di Bicci', *Riv. A.*, xiv (1932), pp. 475–83

H. D. Gronau: 'Lorenzo di Bicci: Ein Rekonstruktionversuch', *Mitt. Ksthist. Inst. Florenz*, iv/2–3 (1933), pp. 103–18

G. Vigni: *Pittura del due e trecento nel Museo di Pisa* (Palermo, 1950), p. 62

W. Cohn: 'Un quadro di Lorenzo di Bicci e la decorazione primitiva della chiesa di Orsanmichele a Firenze', *Boll. A.*, xlvi (1956), pp. 171–7

L. Marcucci: *Gallerie nazionali di Firenze: I dipinti toscani del secolo XIV* (Rome, 1965), pp. 127–8

M. Boskovits: *Pittura fiorentina alla vigilia del rinascimento, 1370–1400* (Florence, 1975), pp. 107–9

C. Frosinini: 'Il passaggio di gestione in una bottega pittorica fiorentina del primo rinascimento: Lorenzo di Bicci e Bicci di Lorenzo', *Ant. Viva*, xxv/1 (1986), pp. 5–15

*Il Museo Bandini di Firenze* (exh. cat., Fiesole, Mus. Bandini, 1993), p. 113

BRUNO SANTI

**Lorenzo di Credi** [Lorenzo d'Andrea d'Oderigo] (*b* Florence, *c.* 1457; *d* Florence, 1536). Italian painter and draughtsman. He was a fellow pupil of Leonardo da Vinci and Perugino in the workshop of Andrea del Verrocchio. In 1482–3 he took over the workshop, and by 1500 he occupied an important position in Florentine art life. He is known primarily for his devotional paintings, although he was also much in demand as a portrait painter and was a sensitive draughtsman.

1. 1457–*c.* 1480. 2. *c.* 1480–1500. 3. 1501–36.

1. 1457–*c.* 1480. He was the son of the goldsmith Andrea di Oderigo Barducci who died leaving his family in difficult economic circumstances. The name Credi (Tancredi) had belonged to a forebear and was also given to an elder brother of Lorenzo's. By 1480, according to the *catasto* (land registry declaration) made by Lorenzo's mother, Lisa, he was already working in Andrea del Verrocchio's workshop for the very low wages of 12 florins a year. However, it is not known precisely how Verrocchio's workshop was organized, and it is possible that in addition to official wages his pupils were also given partial payment for the work they executed to Verrocchio's designs or on which they collaborated.

Besides Leonardo and Perugino, it is probable that other artists were associated with the workshop, including Botticelli, Domenico Ghirlandaio and Francesco di Simone Ferrucci. Despite their youth, these artists were entrusted with important works and often carried them out in collaboration with each other or their master. It is therefore difficult to make any firm attributions for paintings executed in Verrocchio's workshop during the 1470s and 1480s.

Lorenzo was probably singled out early as the best-suited for painting devotional works destined for an affluent but not over-sophisticated clientele. It is likely that by the age of 20, *c.* 1476, he was producing small, technically proficient panels of the Virgin and Child and of saints at prayer. These works are not particularly innovative in terms of composition, but their settings and landscapes are well constructed and painted in meticulous detail, and the figures are carefully arranged in the picture space. The clear, thin impastos of colour are painstakingly laid on and the paint surfaces appear polished and shining. Many of these works are derived from early paintings of Botticelli and Leonardo, but other features suggest an awareness of contemporary South Netherlandish painting, a common characteristic in Verrocchio's workshop. Examples of these devotional works are the Virgin and Child paintings in Dresden (Gemäldegal. Alte Meister), Strasbourg (Mus. B.-A.), Mainz (Altertumsmus. & Gemäldegal.) and Turin (Gal. Sabauda). A *St Sebastian* (Modena, Gal. & Mus. Estense) also belongs to this group.

In 1475, or soon afterwards, Verrocchio was commissioned to provide an altarpiece in memory of Donato de' Medici, Bishop of Pistoia (*d* 1466), for his tomb in the oratory of the Vergine di Piazza, near Pistoia Cathedral. The predella of this *sacra conversazione* is now dismantled: the central panel, a small *Annunciation* (Paris, Louvre) is attributed to Leonardo (sometimes to Leonardo in collaboration with Lorenzo di Credi), while a second panel showing a scene from the *Life of St Donatus of Arezzo* (Worcester, MA, A. Mus.) is entirely by Lorenzo; the third panel is untraced, though some scholars have suggested that a small *Birth of the Virgin* (Liverpool, Walker A.G.), an early work by Pietro Perugino, is the missing panel.

1. Lorenzo di Credi: *Virgin and Child Enthroned with SS John the Baptist and Donatus of Arezzo*, tempera and oil on panel, 1.87×1.90 m, *c.* 1475–80 (Pistoia Cathedral, Cappella del Sacramento)

The main panel of the altarpiece showing the *Virgin and Child Enthroned with SS John the Baptist and Donatus of Arezzo* (Pistoia Cathedral, Cappella del Sacramento; see fig. 1) is important in the development of the *sacra conversazione*, both in the rigorous perspectival construction of the architectural elements and in the use of deeply receding landscape views which open up behind the saints. Although it is probable that the work owes its conception to Verrocchio and Leonardo, it was executed by Lorenzo di Credi. There are parallels with Fra Angelico's early *sacre conversazioni* and with the work of Lorenzo's closest colleagues, particularly Leonardo, some of whose studies he may have used as a basis for the figures of the Virgin and John the Baptist. The influence of Netherlandish painting is also apparent, especially in the landscape (the trees are highlighted by tiny dots of light), and in the northern appearance of the town on the left. The splendid carpet is recognizably Anatolian in origin, of the type usually attributed to the town of Ushak, and recalls similar carpets in the work of Jan van Eyck and Hans Memling.

2. *c.* 1480–1500. About 1480 Verrocchio was called to Venice to design the equestrian monument to the condottiere Bartolomeo Colleoni (Campo SS Giovanni e Paolo). He settled in Venice and died there in 1488. After Leonardo's departure for Milan between 1482 and 1483, Lorenzo remained in Florence to run Verrocchio's workshop, taking over the many commissions which had been left incomplete at his master's departure. Before his death, Verrocchio named Lorenzo as his heir and the executor of his will. Under Lorenzo's guidance, the workshop gradually changed direction. Verrocchio's other pupils were established as independent masters and the activity of the workshop became more restricted and specialized, supplying mainly small-scale panel paintings of the *Virgin*, the *Nativity* and the *Annunciation*, as well as portraits. Lorenzo must have been much sought after as a portrait painter since he left an extensive series of small-scale drawings of heads done in silverpoint and white lead on pink, grey, yellow and brown paper. These vary from smooth-faced children and youths such as the *Portrait of a Young Boy* (Paris, Louvre, 1782) to the *Head of an Old Man* (Paris, Louvre, 1779) in which the aging skin is etched in a dense mesh of wrinkles. Vasari valued Lorenzo's drawings highly and some, including the *Portrait of a Young Girl* (Paris, Louvre, 1738) were collected in his *Libro de' disegni*.

The attributions of some of Lorenzo's most important portraits, ascribed to him by early sources, have been disputed by modern scholars. They include the presumed portrait of *Andrea Verrocchio* (Florence, Uffizi), alternatively thought to be a portrait of Perugino, and the *Portrait of a Man* (Washington, DC, N.G.A.), which an early and seemingly reliable inscription on the back describes as a self-portrait of Lorenzo. Both paintings have also been attributed to Perugino. It is particularly difficult to accept the attribution of the Washington portrait to Perugino since the pose of the lean-faced man, his head thrust slightly back and his gaze fixed on a point outside the picture, is strongly suggestive of the artist painting his reflection in a mirror.

Besides the numerous mannered devotional paintings destined for churches and chapels, Lorenzo also painted more sophisticated and original works, such as the *Venus* (Florence, Uffizi; see fig. 2), in which a naked, athletic young woman appears against a dark background, draped in a light, transparent veil. This painting of a female nude has no equal in Tuscan painting of the time, although an interesting comparison can be made with Botticelli's *Birth of Venus* (*c.* 1485; Florence, Uffizi; *see* BOTTICELLI, SANDRO, fig. 3) and there are also close affinities with the work of contemporary Flemish and German masters such as Lucas Cranach the elder and Hugo van der Goes. By

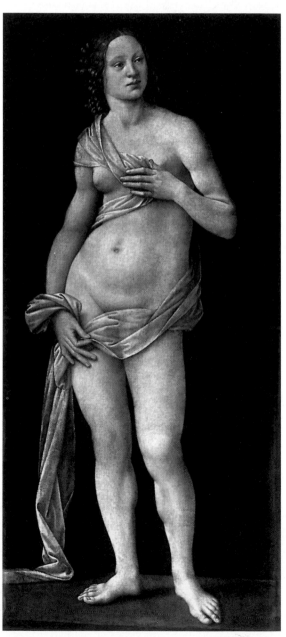

2. Lorenzo di Credi: *Venus*, oil on canvas, 1.51×0.69 m, *c.* 1490 (Florence, Galleria degli Uffizi)

the end of the 15th century the circulation of prints was fairly widespread, and paintings from north of the Alps were sought after and appreciated in Italy.

The *sacra conversazione* painted for the Cappella dei Mascalzoni in S Maria Maddalena de' Pazzi in Florence (1493; Paris, Louvre) is a more static and sentimental version of the Pistoia altarpiece, though Vasari admired it for its chromatic qualities. Vasari claimed that Lorenzo obtained particularly pure and gleaming surfaces by grinding his colours extremely fine, distilling his own oils and by keeping his colours separate by using a different brush for each one, a method that required patience and a great deal of time.

Lorenzo's fragile creativity was better expressed in the smaller works that he painted in the last years of the 15th century, such as the *Annunciation* (Florence, Uffizi), in which the two figures are shown under an exquisitely decorated loggia, and the *Virgin and Child with the Infant St John* (Rome, Gal. Borghese), a tondo based on the colour harmony of a dominant blue with white, yellow, pink and green, recalling a terracotta by Luca della Robbia, an artist whom Lorenzo admired.

In the 1490s Lorenzo appears to have been affected by Savonarola's preaching, although the extent to which he was involved in the Friar's movement is unclear. He was in contact with Fra Bartolommeo, one of Savonarola's most faithful supporters, and produced some works of a markedly devout tendency, devised in accordance with overtly didactic purposes: to this group belong an *Adoration of the Shepherds* (Florence, Uffizi) painted for the Franciscan monastery of S Chiara in Florence, a *St Mary Magdalene in Penitence* (or possibly *St Mary of Egypt*) (ex-Berlin, Kaiser-Friedrich Mus., destr.) and a *St Francis Receiving the Stigmata* (Ajaccio, Mus. Fesch). In all three paintings, the attitudes of the figures, whose faces are bent over hands clasped in prayer or raised in ecstasy towards the godhead, reveal a type of religious sentiment close to that demanded by Savonarola's most fervent supporters, the '*piagnoni*' (snivellers). The *Adoration of the Shepherds* was commissioned by Jacopo Bongianni, who had close links with Savonarola's circle. It has been suggested that the elderly man kneeling on the left of the painting is a portrait of Bongianni; certainly his sharply characterized features, which are probably copied from a portrait, distinguish him from the shepherds and the figure of St Joseph.

3. 1501–36. As a prominent member of Florentine art life, Lorenzo took part in several important arbitrations, including the installation of the lantern of Florence Cathedral, the placing of Michelangelo's statue of *David* (Florence, Accad.; *see* ITALY, fig. 54) in 1504, the appraisal of the frescoes by Ridolfo del Ghirlandaio in Palazzo Vecchio in 1514 and that of Bandinelli's *St Peter* placed in the cathedral in 1517. He also restored several famous works, including, in 1501, a *Virgin and Child Enthroned with Saints* (Fiesole, S Domenico) by Fra Angelico, which he transformed from its original triptych format into a unified space, replacing the gold background with a landscape. In Florence Cathedral he also restored Benedetto da Maiano's wooden Crucifix and the two frescoes of condottieri by Paolo Uccello and Andrea del Castagno (all *in situ*).

In common with his contemporaries, Lorenzo seems to have drawn inspiration from the experiments made by Leonardo at the end of the 15th century; Lorenzo's *Portrait of a Young Woman* (New York, Met.) suggests that he may have seen Leonardo's '*Mona Lisa*' (Paris, Louvre; *see* DRESS, fig. 22) or sketches and drawings connected with it. In another medium-sized panel, the *Virgin and Child with the Infant St John the Baptist* (Kansas City, MO, Nelson-Atkins Mus. A.) the position of the seated Virgin, whose leg is thrust forward diagonally from left to right, betrays Lorenzo's reworking of Leonardo's *Virgin and Child with SS Anne and John the Baptist* (Paris, Louvre), for which the latter had made numerous studies.

While Lorenzo was certainly aware of the innovations of Piero di Cosimo, Fra Bartolommeo and Raphael, this did not lead to any radical changes in his design of large-scale altarpieces. In the *Virgin and Child Enthroned with SS Sebastian and John the Evangelist* (before 1516; Dresden, Gemäldegal. Alte Meister), only the treatment of the drapery shows some attempt to come to terms with contemporary artistic developments, the composition is based on 15th-century prototypes. His later compositional drawings, some of them executed in pen and ink, are more crowded and dynamic than before. Only in these drawings and in his smaller paintings is there any concession to modernity. This can be seen in the panel of the *Crucifixion* (U. Göttingen, Kstsamml.), possibly a *modello*, in which the colour is laid on in a very thin layer, revealing the preliminary drawing beneath. Stylistically, the holy women, arranged rhythmically around the swooning Virgin are particularly effective.

After 1520 Lorenzo's output decreased; possibly one of his last autograph works is the *St Michael* painted for the Sagrestia dei Canonici in Florence Cathedral (*in situ*). In 1531 he put himself in the care of the Ospedale di S Maria Nuova, receiving a life annuity; in the same year he made his will, distributing his few remaining possessions among his relatives, his pupils and his serving woman. Of his numerous assistants, most of whom were mediocre painters, only Giovanni Antonio Sogliani can be easily identified. Another distinctive hand is that of the Master of the Santo Spirito Conversazione, who takes his name from the *sacra conversazione* of the *Virgin and Child with SS John the Evangelist and Jerome* in the Cappella Ridolfi in Santo Spirito, Florence.

BIBLIOGRAPHY

Thieme–Becker: 'Credi, Lorenzo di'

G. Vasari: *Vite* (1550, rev. 2/1568); ed. G. Milanesi (1878–85), vol. iv, pp. 563–76

B. Degenhart: 'Di alcuni problemi di sviluppo della pittura nella bottega del Verrocchio, di Leonardo e di Lorenzo di Credi', *Riv. A.*, xiv (1932), pp. 263–300, 403–44

——: 'Die Schüler des Lorenzo di Credi', *Münchn. Jb. Bild. Kst*, ix (1932), pp. 95–161

B. Berenson: 'Verrocchio e Leonardo: Leonardo e Lorenzo di Credi', *Boll. A.*, n.s. 3, xxvii (1933–4), pp. 193–214, 241–64

G. Dalli Regoli: *Lorenzo di Credi* (Milan, 1966)

F. W. Kent: 'Lorenzo di Credi, his Patron Jacopo Bongianni and Savonarola', *Burl. Mag.*, cxxv (1983), pp. 539–41

G. Dalli Regoli: 'La Madonna di Piazza: "... Ce n'è d'assai più bella, nessuna più perfetta"', *Scritti di storia dell'arte in onore di Federico Zeri*, i (Milan, 1984), pp. 213–32

G. DALLI REGOLI

**Lorenzo di Niccolò (di Martino)** (*fl* 1392–1412). Italian painter. The first extant record of the artist shows that he was an associate of Niccolò di Pietro Gerini in 1392, when Gerini was working on the decoration of Francesco Datini's house in Prato. Lorenzo, often wrongly described as Gerini's son, was probably trained in his workshop, and the earliest works attributable to him have much in common with the older master's style.

Lorenzo's first surviving dated work is a triptych of *St Bartholomew Enthroned, with Scenes from his Life* (1401; San Gimignano, Mus. Civ.). In the same year Lorenzo collaborated with Gerini and Spinello Aretino on an altarpiece of the *Coronation of the Virgin* (Florence, Accad.) for S Felicità, Florence. Lorenzo's contribution to this was evidently restricted to four *Saints* on the left side of the predella, but in January 1402 he himself was contracted to paint a *Coronation of the Virgin* polyptych for S Marco, Florence. This altarpiece, signed LAURENTIUS NICHOLAI ME PINSIT, was donated by the Medici family to S Domenico, Cortona, in 1440 (*in situ*). The main panel of an altarpiece of the *Virgin and Child with SS Martin and Lawrence* (Terenzano, S Martino), signed and dated 1402, is closely based on Maso di Banco's Solly *Virgin and Child* (Berlin, Gemäldegal.). The choice of this 14th-century model may be associated with a search for more monumental forms than those characteristic of the art of most of Lorenzo's contemporaries or of the preceding generation. This tendency is illustrated in a panel of *St Anthony Abbot with Angels and Donors* (*c.* 1403; Providence, RI Sch. Des., Mus. A.). Comparison with the earlier *St Bartholomew* triptych demonstrates the increasing three-dimensionality of Lorenzo's style. Other developments in Lorenzo's style are evinced by another *Coronation of the Virgin* polyptych (1410; Florence, Santa Croce). The pictorial space of the flanking panels, which contain four full-length *Saints*, is expanded compared with that in earlier works of this type by Gerini or Lorenzo himself. The horizon is higher and more clearly indicated, with broader strips of empty space left between figure and frame, and the sense of space surrounding the figures is decisively enhanced. Similarly, the central group of the *Coronation* is more obviously and coherently set back in space than in the S Felicità or S Marco versions. The figures themselves are animated, the draperies complex and flamboyant, a probable response to Late Gothic trends reflected more overtly in the work of Spinello Aretino's son Parri Spinelli, Lorenzo Monaco and Ghiberti.

Lorenzo is documented working in Florence in 1411, and the last dated work that can be attributed to him, a polyptych of the *Virgin and Child with Saints* in S Lorenzo a Collina at Mezzomonte, is dated 1412. His son Piero, also a painter, matriculated in the Arte dei Medici e Speziali in 1422, by which time Lorenzo di Niccolò is recorded as deceased. His art marks a period of transition in Florentine painting, and through his attempt to combine, in his well-crafted works, the revived spatial and volumetric concerns of early 14th-century painting with the elegance of the Late Gothic style, Lorenzo rises above the level of the largely conservative tradition in which his art was formed.

BIBLIOGRAPHY

B. Cole: 'A New Work by the Master of the Arte della Lana Coronation', *Burl. Mag.*, cx (1968), pp. 215–16

D. Wilkins: 'Maso di Banco and Cenni di Francesco: A Case of Late Trecento Revival', *Burl. Mag.*, cxi (1969), pp. 83–5

B. Cole: 'A New Work by the Young Lorenzo di Niccolò', *A. Q.* [Detroit], xxxiii (1970), pp. 114–19

R. Fremantle: *Florentine Gothic Painters* (London, 1975), pp. 391–400

E. Fahy: 'On Lorenzo di Niccolò', *Apollo*, cviii (1978), pp. 374–81

*Il polittico di Lorenzo di Niccolò della chiesa di San Domenico in Cortona dopo il restauro* (exh. cat., ed. A. Maetzke and N. Frusconi; Cortona, Pal. Casali, 1986)

JOHN RICHARDS

**Lorenzo Monaco** [Piero di Giovanni] (*b* ?1370–75; *d* ?Florence, ?1425–30). Italian painter, illuminator and draughtsman. His name means Lorenzo the Monk, and he was a member of the Camaldolese Order. His mystical and contemplative works, distinguished by their sinuous line and radiant, high-keyed colour, represent the culmination of the Late Gothic style in Florence. He is remembered principally for his paintings on panel and in illuminated manuscripts, but he also worked to a limited extent in fresco, and a few drawings have also survived. His altarpiece of the *Coronation of the Virgin* (1414; Florence, Uffizi), painted for his own monastery, is a virtuoso display of the exquisite craftsmanship and brilliant colour of late medieval art.

1. Life and work. 2. Working methods and technique. 3. Critical reception and posthumous reputation.

### 1. LIFE AND WORK.

(i) Before 1414. (ii) 1414 and after.

*(i) Before 1414.* He was born Piero di Giovanni but took the name Lorenzo when he entered the Camaldolese Order in the convent of S Maria degli Angeli in Florence. Neither the date nor the place of his birth is known. He is recorded as having taken his simple vows and received minor orders on 10 December 1391; in September 1392 he took solemn vows and was ordained subdeacon. He was ordained deacon in 1396 and, since contemporary practice appears to have been to advance to the diaconate at about the age of 21, this would suggest a birth date in the mid-1370s. His earliest identifiable works of art can be dated to the mid-1390s. The fact that he entered a Florentine convent strongly supports the idea of a Florentine origin, and early documents refer to him as of the 'popolo di S Michele Bisdomini', a parish located not far from S Maria degli Angeli. However, Siena has also been proposed as his place of birth, as his sinuous line and delicate colour are stylistically close to the art of contemporary Sienese painters. Moreover, a document of 29 January 1415 refers to him as 'don Lorenzo dipintore da siene'. Whether or not 'siene' (which would be a strange spelling) refers to the city of Siena and why he is not referred to in this way in earlier documents remain questions to plague the biographer.

It is not known where Lorenzo trained. Vasari stated that he was apprenticed to Taddeo Gaddi, but this is impossible, since Taddeo was dead by 1366. However, Lorenzo's style is akin to that of Taddeo's youngest son, Agnolo Gaddi, and he may have trained in Agnolo's shop. It has also been suggested that he was trained as a manuscript illuminator in the scriptorium of S Maria degli Angeli, which was renowned for its illuminated volumes. This latter theory is supported by similarities between his early work and the contemporary works of Don Simone Camaldolese and Don Silvestro dei Gherarducci (1339–90), major manuscript painters who worked for S Maria degli Angeli in the late 1390s.

At around the time he was made deacon (1396), Lorenzo seems to have taken up residence outside the convent and established a private workshop, although he continued to follow the religious life. The location of this shop is not known, but he is recorded as operating a shop (perhaps the same one) in the parish of S Bartolo in Corso in early 1402. January 1399 marks his earliest recorded commission, an altarpiece (untraced) executed for the second Ardinghelli Chapel in S Maria del Carmine, Florence. His earliest identifiable works are a group of miniatures representing saints and prophets in initial letters in choir-books in the Biblioteca Medicea-Laurenziana in Florence (MSS Cor. 1, 5 and 8; see fig. 1), dated 1396, 1394 and 1395 respectively. The dates inscribed in the volumes cannot be taken as the dates of the illuminations,

as they are clearly specified as the dates of the completion of the volumes, that is of the writing, and the decorations may not have been added immediately. Nevertheless, it is relatively safe to assume that these volumes were ornamented in the final years of the 14th century. They reveal a youthful hesitation in the relationship of the figures to their enframing letters and a certain dependence on the work of such older illuminators in the scriptorium as Don Simone and Don Silvestro, a hesitation and dependency not apparent in the illuminations of a choir-book dated 1409 (Florence, Bib. Medicea-Laurenziana MS. Cor. 3). However, the calligraphic use of line and the delicate colour tones that characterize Lorenzo's later works are already in evidence. The loss of the Ardinghelli altarpiece of 1399 is particularly unfortunate, as it would provide a basis for comparing Lorenzo's work in two media at approximately the same date and would possibly clear up the question of whether he was initially trained as a painter of panels or of manuscripts.

Lorenzo's large panel of the *Agony in the Garden* (Florence, Accad. B.A. & Liceo A.; see fig. 2) is a dramatic and expressive work that may date from this period. The *Virgin and Child Enthroned, with Two Angels* (Cambridge, Fitzwilliam; see fig. 3), a characteristic early work, from the first years of the 15th century, supports the Florentine origin of Lorenzo's style. The modest scale of the picture suggests a private, devotional function, perhaps as the wing of a diptych. It also places it technically within the realm of miniature painting, although the composition has a monumentality not to be found in most of Lorenzo's manuscript paintings and small-scale predella panels. The most immediate source of the composition and conception is Giotto's Ognissanti *Madonna* (Florence, Uffizi; *see* GIOTTO, fig. 6). Lorenzo has taken over the poses of the Virgin and Child and has placed them within an architectural setting similar to that used by Giotto. The pointed barrel vault of the throne's interior clearly establishes the spatial relationship between the two figures and their surroundings. The placement of the attendant angels, who envelop the finials of the arms of the throne with their sleeves and who cross the pierced openings of the structure with their torsos, further establishes a solid, tangible space. This is contrasted with the neutral gold ground with its elaborately tooled border that functions as pure ornament, almost in the way that the decorative edging of a manuscript page might function. At the same time, the colours, the Child's wrap of deep raspberry-pink fading to almost pure white in the highlights, the Virgin's steely blue mantle similarly modulated from total saturation to the palest tint, and the touches of vermilion in the cushion of the throne, the wings of the angels and the linings of their metallic blue-white mantles, all point to a dependence on the Orcagna tradition of the second half of the 14th century. At the same time, the softening of faces, both in modelling and in the mood they convey, and the humanizing of attitudes, show a familiarity with Spinello Aretino's and Agnolo Gaddi's revival of Giotto's style in the late 14th century. However, the sinuous lines of the drapery contours and the decorative features, such as the ornamentation of the throne and the delicate, golden feathering of the angels' wings, are indicative of the Late Gothic style.

1. Lorenzo Monaco: *St Romualdo*, miniature from a choir-book, *c.* 1395–1400 (Florence, Biblioteca Medicea–Laurenziana, Corale n. 8, fol. 76*r*.)

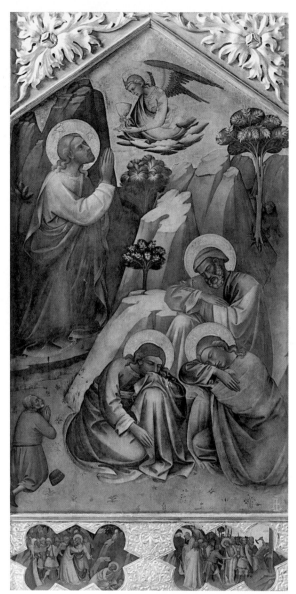

2. Lorenzo Monaco: *Agony in the Garden*, tempera on panel, 1.91×1.12 m, ?*c*. 1399 (Florence, Accademia di Belle Arti e Liceo Artistico)

Lorenzo Monaco's art is thus in the tradition of late 14th-century Florentine painting, close in time and style to that of such practitioners as Gherardo Starnina and the Master of the Bambino Vispo.

Lorenzo's only surviving documented work is the Monte Oliveto Altarpiece, with the *Virgin and Child Enthroned, Attended by SS Bartholomew, John the Baptist, Thaddeus and Benedict* (Florence, Accad. B.A. & Liceo A.), which is documented to 1407 and 1411 and bears an inscribed date of 1410. This picture draws on a similarly wide range of stylistic sources. In the same period Lorenzo painted four scenes from the *Infancy of Christ* (two, London, Courtauld Inst. Gals; one, New York, Met.; one,

Altenburg, Staatl. Lindenau-Mus.) for an untraced altarpiece, and four paintings of *Prophets* (all New York, Met.) in which the figures are more sculptural and three-dimensional and may date from *c*. 1408–10.

Among Lorenzo's paintings on panel, one of the more unusual formats, which he utilized on several occasions, is that of the *croce sagomata* (cut-out cross), in which the crucified Christ is depicted hanging on the cross as in a Crucifixion scene, but with the cross and figure free-standing. This creates something of an illusion of sculpture. The carved Crucifixes by Donatello and Brunelleschi might indicate the growing popularity of such three-dimensional images in the early 15th century, as distinguished from the painted crosses that enjoyed acclaim in the 13th and 14th centuries. Lorenzo's works of this kind include the *Crucifix* (Florence, Accad. B.A. & Liceo A.), a *Crucifix* in the museum of S Maria delle Vertighe in Monte San Savino, Tuscany, and the dramatic and expressive *Crucifix with the Mourning Virgin and St John the Evangelist* (Florence, S Giovannino dei Cavalieri), which may be the work described by Vasari as being in the church of the Romiti di Camaldoli (S Salvatore) outside Florence. In this last-named work he added cut-out figures of the Virgin and St John to create a larger tableau. Lorenzo appears to have played a major role in popularizing the *croce sagomata* form, which survived until the end of the 15th century.

3. Lorenzo Monaco: *Virgin and Child Enthroned, with Two Angels*, tempera on panel, 324×212 mm, before 1410 (Cambridge, Fitzwilliam Museum)

*(ii) 1414 and after*. The most ambitious of Lorenzo's surviving works is the great *Coronation of the Virgin* (5.12×4.50 m; Florence, Uffizi; *see* COLOUR, colour pl. II, fig. 1). This picture, painted for his own convent of S Maria degli Angeli and dated February 1413 (NS 1414), is his only signed and dated work and shows him at the height of his power. The rather lengthy inscription indicates that he was still following the religious life, though he had been living outside the convent for around 18 years. Although enclosed within a tripartite frame that recalls the triptych format popular in 14th-century altarpieces, the pictorial field is unified into a single space. In the upper centre, in front of a Gothic ciborium from which angels look on, Christ places the crown on the head of his mother, who is dressed in the white of the Camaldolese habit. Crowds of saints, ten on either side (and all male, as befits a convent of men), witness the event. From a pinnacle above the central field a Blessing Redeemer looks down, while the Annunciation is re-enacted in the two pinnacles over the side compartments. Ten prophets grace the pilasters of the frame, and a predella of six laterally elongated quatrefoils offers four stories from the *Legend of St Benedict* flanking the *Nativity* and the *Adoration of the Magi*.

The great courtly ritual represented on the principal field has its roots in Florentine tradition, going back to Giotto's Baroncelli Altarpiece (Florence, Santa Croce) of the 1330s and developed by numerous followers of Giotto in the second half of the 14th century. The graceful sway of the bodies arrayed in syncopated ranks plays against the sinuous rhythms of their drapery. The delicate colours—perhaps appearing more pastel-toned than intended, due to a 19th-century cleaning with soda—are a perfect complement to these linear rhythms, setting off the folds under a veil of almost translucent tonalities. Thus a balance is achieved between the three-dimensional elements of illusionism and the decorative qualities of pure surface pattern. The predella panels create a similar fusion of decorative line and colour with functional space and drama. The awkward frame of the quatrefoil shape is made to harmonize with the architectural and compositional elements within the paintings, so that a chevron pattern links the six subjects together horizontally, while at the same time they function individually as dramatic narratives within a functional, if abbreviated, space.

Lorenzo and his shop used the S Maria degli Angeli (Uffizi) *Coronation* as a model for another major Camaldolese commission, probably very shortly thereafter. Originally painted for the monastery of S Benedetto fuori della Porta a Pinti, outside Florence, and seen by Vasari in S Maria degli Angeli (where it was placed after the destruction of S Benedetto), this is surely the *Coronation of the Virgin* of which the major panels are now in the National Gallery, London. (For the history and reconstruction of this work, see Eisenberg, pp. 138–45.) Of generally inferior quality compared with its prototype, it demonstrates the popularity of Lorenzo's style with a segment of the artistic public, and the way in which that style was treated by his immediate following.

The *Annunciation with SS Catherine of Alexandria, Anthony Abbot, Proculus and Francis of Assisi* (*c.* 1418; Florence, Accad. B.A. & Liceo A.) develops Lorenzo's use

4. Lorenzo Monaco: *Annunciation* (Bartolini Salimbeni Altarpiece), tempera on panel, 3.00×2.74 m, after 1420 (Florence, Santa Trìnita)

of complex rhythms and lyrically graceful figures. The *Adoration of the Magi* (Florence, Uffizi), of uncertain provenance, dates from the early 1420s and is distinguished by the aristocratic elegance and exoticism of the figures. An altarpiece of the *Deposition* (Florence, Mus. S Marco) was commissioned by Palla Strozzi for the sacristy of Santa Trìnita, Florence. Begun by Lorenzo Monaco, probably *c.* 1420–22, it was finished by Fra Angelico. The painted frame by Lorenzo survives; the three pinnacle panels, with the *Resurrection*, a *Noli me tangere* and the *Holy Women at the Tomb*, remain with the altarpiece, while three small panels intended as predella scenes, the *Nativity*, the *Legend of St Onuphrius* and *St Nicholas Calming the Storm* (Florence, Accad. B.A. & Liceo A.), are now separate.

In this late period, probably after 1420, Lorenzo undertook the decoration of the Bartolini Salimbeni Chapel in Santa Trìnita, Florence, his first and only known attempt at fresco painting. The programme, probably the most complex he ever undertook, consisted of eight scenes from the *Life and Legends of the Virgin* on the walls, *Four Prophets* on the vault and *Four Saints* on the soffits of the entrance arch (all *in situ*). The scheme was completed with the addition of an altarpiece of the *Annunciation* (see fig. 4), with a predella of four scenes, the *Visitation*, the *Nativity*, the *Adoration of the Magi* and the *Flight into Egypt* (all *in situ*). The frescoed scenes were all taken from the apocryphal literature, while those that make up the altarpiece were all scriptural. On the axis of the chapel, the *Assumption of the Virgin* on the exterior wall above the entrance aligns with the *Miracle of the Snow* in the lunette of the back wall, which in turn is situated directly above the *Annunciation* in the altarpiece. It is known that two feast days were singled out for special celebration in this chapel, the Feast of the Annunciation on 25 March and an unspecified feast in August. The Miracle of the Snow was commemorated on 5 August and the Assumption of the Virgin on 15 August. Perhaps the otherwise unspecified August celebration combined and commemorated both of these events. The entire complex was undoubtedly arranged to suit the needs of particular Marian devotions associated with the chapel and its donors.

In devising the eight scenes from the Marian legend, Lorenzo depended on the numerous cycles existing in and around Florence, in particular those of the Gaddi family workshop. He once again demonstrated his reliance on Florentine traditions and, in particular, on the tradition initiated by Giotto. The altarpiece of the *Annunciation*, however, suggests that Lorenzo had encountered the new naturalism of the 1420s. Its iconography depends on a Sienese, rather than a Florentine tradition, but an attempt has been made to depict the architectural setting more convincingly, on a scale somewhat in accord with that of its occupants. The space is complex, with room opening on room, revealing a labyrinth of spaces. Nevertheless, it retains the insubstantiality of Lorenzo's earlier structures, which served more as backdrops to set the scene than as actual, inhabitable spaces. The figures, too, have become more voluminous, wrapped in fabric heavier than that of the figures in the Uffizi *Coronation*, but at the same time retaining all of their courtly elegance. As the angel Gabriel alights to deliver his greeting to Mary, he does not rest on the patterned floor so much as hover in front of it. The inverted perspective of the floor patterning might appear to encourage this perception on the main panel, but in the *Visitation* panel of the predella, Elizabeth similarly seems to float in front of the unarticulated ground rather than to rest on it; and in the *Nativity* of the predella Joseph, sitting on the ground at the lower right, appears to hover on his elegantly outspread mantle like some mystic levitating on a magic carpet. The colour scheme has altered, with greater use of more sombre, earthy colours, especially in the grounds, to set off the increasingly complex arrangements of softer, more delicate colours in the figures.

Lorenzo Monaco's death, like his birth, is not recorded. In the 14th and 15th centuries religious houses kept their own death records, separate from the secular *libri dei morti* kept by the Comune, but such records for S Maria degli Angeli have not survived. A marginal notation in another document from the convent indicates that he died on 24 May, but the year is not specified. A contract for an altarpiece dated 3 March 1421 (NS 1422) indicates that he was still living at that time. Vasari stated that he died at the age of 55, but gave no indication of the year. If his age is given correctly and the supposition of his birth date in the middle years of the 1370s is also correct, he would then have died sometime in the middle to late 1420s. This date would be consistent with the style of the works judged to be his latest, which demonstrate a growing sense of naturalism, commensurate with the developments in the art of Masaccio and Fra Angelico in the 1420s.

2. WORKING METHODS AND TECHNIQUE. Most of Lorenzo Monaco's works are in tempera on panel; he was supremely gifted as a colourist, and his sharp greens and yellows, bright pinks and blues are softly modelled and orchestrated contrapuntally; his craftsmanship in gold was exquisitely refined, and each of the haloes in the vast *Coronation of the Virgin* bears a different design. He prepared his pictures with drawings, some of which have survived; a drawing of *Six Kneeling Saints* (Florence, Uffizi) is a preparatory study for a group in either the Uffizi or the London *Coronation of the Virgin*. An unusual pair of drawings, the *Visitation* and the *Journey of the Magi* (both Berlin, Kupferstichkab.), in pen and brush with brown ink, coloured washes and tempera on parchment, fall somewhere between manuscript illuminations, presentation drawings and working drawings. A somewhat rare example of *verre églomisé* painting depicting the *Virgin of Humility with SS John the Baptist and John the Evangelist* (Turin, Mus. Civ. A. Ant.), although executed primarily by Lorenzo's shop, represents another graphic medium that Lorenzo explored.

Technical elements in the execution of the frescoes in the Bartolini Salimbeni Chapel in Santa Trinita, such as the irregularity of the *giornate*, which do not always coincide with complete figures and which occasionally cut through haloes and other elements, indicate his lack of familiarity with the medium. The blue background, painted *a secco*, has vanished. Detailed drawings must have existed for these frescoes. The *sinopie* that have been uncovered are very brief and sketchy, indicating that the compositions must have been worked out extensively on paper. The chapel was whitewashed in the early 18th century, and the paintings were unknown until 1887, when they were cleaned and restored by Augusto Burchi. A restoration in 1961–2 undid some of the damage done by Burchi's attempt to re-create the original condition of the paintings, but the paintings are in very poor condition. In places the *intonaco* has entirely fallen away, revealing the underlying *sinopie*.

Lorenzo directed a large workshop, and the inscription on the Uffizi *Coronation of the Virgin* emphasizes that it was a collaborative work. The extensive collaboration of the workshop, even in smaller works, has been discussed by Eisenberg, who has stressed that this shop produced many devotional images, such as the *Virgin and Child Enthroned* (c. 1418; Edinburgh, N.G.), for which Lorenzo supplied only the design.

3. CRITICAL RECEPTION AND POSTHUMOUS REPUTATION. Early sources, other than the scant documentation about his life and work in S Maria degli Angeli, reveal little about Lorenzo Monaco. He is not mentioned at all by Ghiberti in his autobiographical *I Commentarii* (written c. 1447–55), even though the stylistic affinity of the two artists would suggest that they represent the sculptural and painterly incarnations of the same spirit. Albertinelli (1510) said very little; *Il libro di Antonio Billi* (written c. 1516–30) and the manuscript by the Anonimo Magliabechiano (written c. 1537–42) pay him sparse attention, mentioning only a handful of works (mostly untraced). Vasari devoted a *Vita* to him but, apart from praising his virtue and listing a small number of his most important works (mostly untraced), he provides little concrete information, filling much of the chapter with an estimation of the contemplative life and of other monk painters from S Maria degli

Angeli. However, the minimal information provided by Vasari remained virtually the sole source of Lorenzo Monaco's biography and critical assessment until the latter part of the 19th century.

Modern critical assessment of Lorenzo Monaco's style began with Carlo Pini and Gaetano Milanesi in the mid-19th century. A.-F. Rio, in 1861, lumped Lorenzo together with Gentile da Fabriano and Fra Angelico as manifestations of a 'mystical school' of Florentine painters. It was J. A. Crowe and G. B. Cavalcaselle, in 1864, who set the appreciation of Lorenzo's work on a new path. Proposing him as one of the legitimate heirs of Giotto, they found in his work a depth and feeling akin to that of the earlier master, such that they recognized and identified as his paintings some that were then attributed to Giotto himself, to Taddeo Gaddi and to other 14th-century painters. Crowe and Cavalcaselle began the reconstitution of his oeuvre that culminated in the *Lists* of Bernard Berenson that first appeared in 1909. At the start of the 20th century Roger Fry recognized the quality of Lorenzo's work; but Osvald Sirén wrote the first complete monograph on the artist in 1905.

Lorenzo Monaco does not seem to have been highly regarded in the years following his death. His style was not widely imitated. Only a handful of artists followed immediately in his footsteps, though none of them ranked in the first order of 15th-century Florentine painters, and they were mostly of an archaicizing temperament. Although Lorenzo was apparently esteemed in his lifetime, especially by his brethren in S Maria degli Angeli, his work fell from favour not long after, and even his great *Coronation* altarpiece for the convent was replaced in the 16th century with a painting by Alessandro Allori, Lorenzo's work being relegated to the provincial convent of the Order at Cerretto. Many of his works hung in museums with attributions to better-known artists until the 'rediscovery' of Lorenzo in the late 19th century and in the 20th.

### BIBLIOGRAPHY

F. Albertinelli: *Memorie di molte statue et picture sono nella inclyta ciptà di Florencia . . .* (Florence, 1510/*R* Letchworth, 1909)

A. Billi: 'Il libro di Antonio Billi' (MS. *c.* 1516–30; Florence, Bib. N.); ed. C. von Fabriczy, *Archv. Stor. It.*, ser. 5, vii (1891), pp. 299–368

Anonimo Gaddiano [Magliabechiano]: 'Il codice dell'Anonimo Gaddiano nella Biblioteca Nazionale di Firenze' (MS. *c.* 1537–42; Florence, Bib. N.); ed. C. von Fabriczy, *Archv. Stor. It.*, ser. 5, xii (1893), pp. 15–94, 275–334

G. Vasari: *Vite* (1550; rev. 2/1568); ed. G. Milanesi (1878–85), ii, pp. 17–32

A.-F. Rio: *De l'art chrétien*, i (Paris, 1836, 2/1861–7)

J. A. Crowe and G. B. Cavalcaselle: *A New History of Painting in Italy* (London, 1864), i, pp. 551–8

R. E. Fry: 'Florentine Painting of the Fourteenth Century', *Mnthly Rev.*, iii (1901), pp. 112–34

——: 'Pictures in the Collection of Sir Hubert Parry at Highnam Court, near Gloucester: I', *Burl. Mag.*, ii (1903), pp. 117–31

O. Sirén: *Don Lorenzo Monaco* (Strasbourg, 1905)

R. van Marle: *Italian Schools* (1923–38), ix, pp. 115–69

M. Meiss: 'Four Panels by Lorenzo Monaco', *Burl. Mag.*, c (1958), pp. 191–8

E. Borsook: *The Mural Painters of Tuscany: From Cimabue to Andrea del Sarto* (London, 1960, rev. Oxford, 1980)

B. Berenson: *Florentine School* (1963)

G. P. de Montebello: 'Four Prophets by Lorenzo Monaco', *Bull. Met.*, xxv/4 (1966), pp. 155–68

C. Gardner von Teuffel: 'Lorenzo Monaco, Filippo Lippi und Filippo Brunelleschi: Die Erfindung der Renaissancepala', *Z. Kstgesch.*, xlv (1982), pp. 1–30

M. Eisenberg: *Lorenzo Monaco* (Princeton, 1989) [complete cat. and bibliog.]

JAMES CZARNECKI

**Lorenzo the Magnificent.** *See* MEDICI, DE', (5).

**Lorenzo Veneziano** (*fl* 1356–72; *d* ?after 1379). Italian painter. He was the leading Venetian painter of the second half of the 14th century. Major state commissions (which a generation earlier had gone to Paolo Veneziano) eluded Lorenzo—the contract for the *Paradiso* (1368; Venice, Doge's Pal.) going to the Paduan Guariento—but his influence on later Venetian painting was profound and widespread. Lorenzo seems to have worked extensively outside Venice, and he introduced to its art elements drawn from a wider experience of mainland Italian painting and Gothic art in general. The traditional view that he was trained in the studio of Paolo Veneziano is supported neither by documents nor by any certain corpus of early works. His earliest surviving signed work is the *Annunciation with Saints and Prophets* (1357; Venice, Accademia), known as the Lion Polyptych, from S Antonio Abate, Venice; its full-length saints share the elongated proportions of Paolo's figures but differ in the urbanity of expression in the faces, and the draperies already show a version of Gothic style typical of Lorenzo. In 1356 he signed a panel (untraced), formerly in Verona. A fresco of the *Madonna of Humility with Saints* (transferred to canvas; Verona, S Anastasia) and a *Crucifix* (now Verona, S Zeno Maggiore; the presence of a Dominican donor, however, suggests that it was probably also from S Anastasia) may be Lorenzo's earliest works (both *c.* 1356–7). The former has donors from the della Scala family, probably Cangrande II and his wife. Frescoes of the *Adoration of the Magi* and the *Coronation of the Virgin* (both Verona, S Fermo Maggiore) have also been attributed to Lorenzo (Cuppini, 1961). None of these works is particularly reminiscent of Paolo.

The *Annunciation* from the Lion Polyptych, the *Mystic Marriage of St Catherine* (1359; Venice, Accademia; see fig.) and a *Virgin and Child* (1361; Padua, Mus. Civ.) all show a naturalism new to Venetian art with a greater interest in the relationships between the Virgin of the *Mystic Marriage* and the typically lively child. A particular sweetness and intimacy of expression are associated with more fluent draughtsmanship and more refined and continuous modelling than was characteristic of earlier Venetian painting. The variety of Lorenzo's invention and the vitality of individual poses in the Lion Polyptych range from the gravity of St Anthony Abbot to the sympathetic and gracefully swaying stance of the Magdalene. Draperies are sometimes sharply cut and angular (e.g. Gabriel), sometimes powerfully rhythmic or more playful (e.g. St John the Evangelist and the Magdalene). Colours are bright and often juxtaposed in sharp contrasts. The complex fenestrated throne of an unsigned *Virgin and Child* closely related to this group (New York, Met.) suggests some contact with Paduan painting.

In 1366 Lorenzo painted the signed and dated polyptych of the *Death of the Virgin with Saints* for Tommaso de'

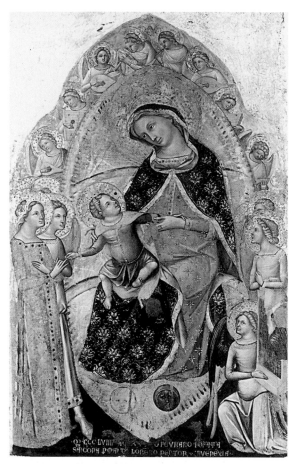

Lorenzo Veneziano: *Mystic Marriage of St Catherine*, tempera on panel, 950×580 mm, 1359 (Venice, Galleria dell'Accademia)

Proti (Vicenza Cathedral), in which the courtly, wasp-waisted figures of SS Felix and George exemplify the daintiness and elegance of Lorenzo's art. Proportions are still largely similar to Paolo's figures, but the strongly characterized kneeling apostles are set in a convincing space, suggesting contact with the more robust art of Bologna. Lorenzo signed a polyptych (untraced) for S Giacomo, Bologna, in 1368.

From the late 1360s Lorenzo's style entered a new phase. The standing saints of a polyptych of the *Delivery of the Keys to St Peter* (central panel, signed and dated Jan 1369 Venetian style, i.e. 1370, Venice, Mus. Correr; side panels and predella, Berlin, Gemäldegal.) recall earlier works, but in the densely packed central panel and the signed and dated polyptych of the *Annunciation with Saints* (1371; Venice, Accademia) figures are less elongated, more compact in design, with larger heads, modelled at times with an extraordinarily delicate *sfumato*. The figure of St James in the *Annunciation* polyptych of 1371 is typical of this later style, blending the Gothic linearity of earlier works with a new plasticity and weight. The predella of the *St Peter* polyptych demonstrates the vitality of Lorenzo's narrative gifts, with *St Peter Preaching* again reflecting Bolognese models. *Christ Walking on the Water*,

perhaps distantly echoing Giotto's Roman mosaic, is typically exuberant in design.

Architectural interests, which were present but subordinate in the central panels of the two polyptychs, come to the fore in the signed *Virgin and Child* (1372; Paris, Louvre), probably from a dismembered polyptych and his last dated work; its massive throne, rich in detail, rises through stages to a balcony, and it is topped with pinnacles.

Lorenzo was still alive in 1379 if he is the 'Lorenzo pentor di S Marina' in a document of that date. The tone of Venetian painting in the last decades of the 14th century was largely determined by his example. Catarino, Guglielmo Veneziano, Giovanni da Bologna, Stefano di Sant'Agnese and, to an extent, Jacobello di Bonomo all developed under his influence.

### BIBLIOGRAPHY

L. Venturi: *Le origini della pittura veneziana* (Venice, 1907)
E. Sandberg-Vavalà: 'A Triptych by Lorenzo Veneziano', *A. America*, xviii (1930), pp. 54–63
L. Coletti: 'Lorenzo Veneziano in neuen Licht', *Pantheon*, ix (1932), pp. 47–50
R. Longhi: *Viatico per cinque secoli di pittura veneziana* (Florence, 1946)
——: 'Calepino veneziano, ii: Il trittico di Lorenzo Veneziano per l'Ufficio della Seta', *A. Ven.*, i (1947), pp. 79–96
L. Cuppini: 'Un Lorenzo Veneziano in Siracusa', *A. Ven.*, iii (1949), pp. 159–60
S. Marconi: 'Restauro di dipinti di Lorenzo Veneziano', *Boll. A.*, xxxiv/2 (1949), pp. 156–61
F. Bologna: 'Contributi allo studio della pittura veneziana del trecento', *A. Ven.*, v (1951), pp. 15–20; vi (1952), pp. 7–18
B. Berenson: *Venetian School* (1957), pp. 98–9
L. Cuppini: 'Una croce stazionale di Lorenzo Veneziano', *Commentari*, ix (1958), pp. 235–97
M. T. Cuppini: 'Pitture del trecento in Verona', *Commentari*, xii (1961), pp. 75–83
T. Pignatti: *Origini della pittura veneziana* (Bergamo, 1961)
R. Pallucchini: *La pittura veneziana del trecento* (Venice, 1964), pp. 163–81 [full set of pls]

JOHN RICHARDS

**Lorenzo Zaragoza** [Llorenz Saragozza] (*b* Cariñena, Aragon; *fl* 1364; *d* 1401). Spanish illuminator and painter. He worked in Valencia and Barcelona and was responsible for the continuation of the so-called International Gothic style in Catalonia, Aragon and Valencia. He is recorded in Valencia from 1364 to 1366; in the latter year he was working in Barcelona, where he was paid by Queen Eleanor (*d* 1374) for two retables, one of *St Nicholas* for the Franciscan convent in Calatayud and the other of *St Catherine* for the Franciscan convent in Teruel, both of which are untraced. In 1373 King Peter IV of Aragon (*reg* 1336–87) referred to him in a letter to the Council of Albocacer as the best painter of Barcelona. Lorenzo later returned to Valencia, where he is documented from 1377 to 1401, the year of his death. His varied commissions there included an embroidered cloth for the Armourers' Guild (1390; untraced) and a series of ceiling paintings for the Casa del Peso Real (1391; untraced). Lorenzo Zaragoza remains an enigmatic figure in the history of Spanish painting, however, because of the difficulties of defining a corpus of works for him. His one authenticated surviving work is the retable of the *Virgin and Child with SS Martin and Agatha* (*c.* 1395; San Roque, Mus. Ermita), which reveals the elongations, use of gilding and refinement characteristic of the international style.

BIBLIOGRAPHY
A. José Pitarch: 'Llorenz Saragozza y los orígenes de la pintura medieval en Valencia', *D'Art* [Barcelona], v (Sept 1979), pp. 21–50

LYNETTE BOSCH

**Lorete, Francisco** [? Loret, François] (*b* France, *c.* 1490; *d* Coimbra, *c.* 1550). French sculptor, active in Portugal. He occupied an important place in the diffusion of Renaissance ornament in the central region of Portugal. Lorete settled in Coimbra *c.* 1530. He worked mainly in wood, and he is usually referred to as a cabinetmaker. His first work was a set of 12 choir-stalls for the monastery of Santa Cruz. These were later moved to a new high choir above the principal entrance of the church. His style already belonged within the Renaissance, but here he adapted it to the Late Gothic forms of the existing parts of the building. While the structure of the stalls is basically Manueline, the decoration consists of grotesque elements, coils and filigree work, a style which in contemporary documents is called 'after the Antique' or *de romano*. In 1532 he began the organ case for the same church, and the following year he was active in Tomar. He settled permanently in Coimbra around 1536, and there built his house.

BIBLIOGRAPHY
V. Correia: 'A escultura em Portugal no primeiro terço do século XVI', *A. & Arqueol.*, 1 (1930), pp. 29–48
R. dos Santos: *A escultura em Portugal*, 2 vols (Lisbon, 1950–51)

P. Dias: 'A presença de artistas franceses no Portugal de quinhentos', *Mundo A.*, 15 (1983), pp. 3–20

PEDRO DIAS

**Loreto.** Italian city in the Marches, *c.* 31 km from Ancona. It is a centre of Marian pilgrimage, the building of the Santa Casa in the sanctuary of S Maria di Loreto (*see* §II, 1, below) having served as a focus for pilgrims since the first half of the 14th century.

I. History and urban development. II. Buildings.

### I. History and urban development.

The origins of the city date from the first half of the 14th century, contemporaneous with the rise and spread of the Loretan cult of the Virgin. The cult derived from the claim that the house of the Virgin (the Santa Casa) was miraculously transported from Nazareth to Loreto. The sanctuary of S Maria (begun 1469) was built over the house and attracted numerous pilgrims. Ancillary structures for the use of the resident clergy and the pilgrims, such as houses and a hospital, developed in the immediate vicinity of the sanctuary; the townspeople, meanwhile, established themselves at the same distance towards the present north wing of the papal palace (Palazzo Apostolico; *see* §II, 2 below), along the ridge of a spur then known as Monte Prodo both owing to the conformation of the land and because the final section of the access road from Rome to the

1. Loreto, Piazza della Madonna, with (left) the Palazzo Apostolico, begun *c.* 1510 by Donato Bramante, and (right) the bell-tower (1750–54, by Luigi Vanvitelli) and façade (begun 1571, by Giovanni di Francesco Ribaldi) of the basilica of S Maria; engraving by G. Vasi, 0.87×1.32 m, Rome, 1752 (Loreto, Archivio Storico Santa Casa)

sanctuary ran along this ridge. The oldest of these houses, on the Corso Boccalini and the Via Asdrubal, are modest dwellings of one or two storeys, generally very small and often with extremely narrow doors and windows.

The urban plan was dictated by the basilica and the Palazzo Apostolico (begun in *c.* 1510 by Donato Bramante), facing each other across the Piazza della Madonna (see fig. 1), and their need for protection led to the construction of a ring of fortified walls round the whole built-up area. The fortifications, based on a plan (Florence, Uffizi) by Antonio da Sangallo (ii), were executed (1517–20) by Cristoforo Resse ( *fl* 1518; *d* 1521) from Imola. The walls were built along the crest of the hill, with two towers inserted at the most distant points and with an enlargement in the centre to accommodate the sanctuary complex. During the final two decades of the 16th century, by which time Loreto had been granted the status of a city, the process of expansion outside the walls was organized and dictated by a later ring of fortifications, known as the Sistine addition, after Pope Sixtus V. Despite the lack of continuity in the work carried out in the two previous centuries, the city at the time of Sixtus V was singularly unified and functional: the sanctuary was not only a religious centre but also the motivating element in the development of the city, representing the acropolis of the entire community.

BIBLIOGRAPHY
E. Dupré-Theseider: 'Loreto e il problema della città santuario', *Stud. Picena*, xxix (1961), pp. 96–105
K. Weil Garris: 'Cloister Court and City Square', *Gesta*, xii (1973), pp. 123–32
F. P. Fiore: 'La "città felice" di Loreto', *Ric. Stor. A.*, iv (1977), pp. 37–55
F. Grimaldi, ed.: *La città murata di Loreto* (Loreto, 1979)
——: *Felix civitas Lauretana* (Loreto, 1981)
F. Grimaldi and A. Mordenti: *Guida degli archivi lauretani*, 2 vols (Rome, 1985–6)

2. Loreto, S Maria, exterior of the east end, fortifications begun 1488

## II. Buildings.

1. S Maria di Loreto. 2. Palazzo Apostolico.

1. S MARIA DI LORETO. The sanctuary consists of the basilica of S Maria, beneath the dome of which is situated the Santa Casa (*see* §(ii) below), the Holy House of the Virgin, encased within a structure designed by Bramante in 1509. The birthplace of the Virgin in Nazareth was popularly believed to have been rescued from infidels by angels, who transported it first to Tersatto in Dalmatia on 10 March 1293, later (10 December 1294) to a forest in Recanati, and finally to its present location in December 1295. There is, however, no record of a shrine in Nazareth before the 13th century, and no record of consternation at its loss in 1293; and no account of the translation can be found before 1472. In Loreto, the original shrine seems to have consisted of a votive image of the *Virgin and Child* under a canopy. Fragments of frescoes attributed to 14th- and 15th-century Umbrian painters are visible inside the core of the Santa Casa itself, together with an early 14th-century Umbrian painted *Crucifix*. The shrine attracted pilgrims in such numbers that in 1469 Nicolò delle Aste, Bishop of Recanati, decided to build a larger church. At his death the same year Pope Paul II took over the project, and had a new plan drawn up. It was then that the legend identifying the church with the Virgin's house was propagated.

### (i) Basilica.

*(a) Architecture.* The basilica of S Maria is a domed building 93 m long, the apse, transepts and associated chapels radiating from the crossing to give an impression reminiscent of a Greek cross. The eastern arm and transepts are aisled, with apses in echelon; there are octagonal sacristies in the corners of the crossing. The nave has seven bays. Begun in Gothic style, the building was changed by subsequent alterations. The architect is unknown: the earliest evidence is a receipt left in 1470 from a master mason, Giovanni di Alberto, to the new bishop of Recanati, for payment for work in the church by him and his partners. In 1471 Marino Cedrini contracted to continue the building, but by April 1482 Giuliano da Maiano was construction engineer in charge, and he probably supervised the preparation of timber for the apse roofs and centring for the drum of the dome. The fortifications (see fig. 2) for the east end of the church are attributed to Baccio Pontelli, and building work on them began in 1488. The crenellated parapet projecting on corbels, with an internal walkway and machicolations, gives a strongly fortress-like character to the apse area. In 1499 Giuliano da Sangallo contracted to vault the dome (completed 1500); but the piers were too weak, and Pietro Amorosi ( *fl c.* 1490–1512), then Bramante, undertook consolidation work. Antonio da Sangallo (ii) later thickened the piers and added semicircular arches, thus changing the Gothic lines of the crossing into Renaissance style.

In the mid-16th century the apse chapels were modified and new chapels added along the sides of the nave, by enlarging existing niches, in response to the requirements of the Counter-Reformation. The façade of the church (see fig. 1 above) was begun in 1571 to designs by Giovanni di Francesco Ribaldi (*d*?1580), known as Boccalini, who built it up to the lower cornice. The work was completed in 1587 by Lattanzio Ventura (*fl* 1575–87). Its three bays, divided by paired Corinthian pilasters, correspond to the nave and aisles; the gable wall rises above roof level, but is in keeping with Boccalini's lower storey. The bell-tower (see fig. 1 above) was built 1750–54 in brick and Istrian stone by Luigi Vanvitelli. During the second half of the 19th century the apsidal chapels were restored to their original state by the demolition of the vaulted ceilings and the removal of the paintings from the walls (*see* §(b) below). The piers of the dome were freed of their arch supports and buttressing under the supervision of Giuseppe Sacconi.

*(b) Decoration.* The interior of the basilica is lavishly decorated. The earliest work was carried out by LUCA SIGNORELLI and Melozzo da Forlì. Signorelli painted frescoes (?1483; *in situ*) in the sacristy of St John, representing a choir of angels and beneath them the four *Evangelists* and four *Doctors of the Western Church*, the *Apostles* and the *Conversion of St Paul*. Melozzo da Forlì was responsible for the decoration (*in situ*) of the sacristy of St Mark, where in a foreshortened architectural setting he painted eight angels supporting the symbols of the Passion, together with eight prophets who foretold it. On one wall is depicted the *Entry into Jerusalem*. Signorelli returned to Loreto during the first decade of the 16th century in order to paint the medallions (*in situ*) on the vault of the church. During the 16th and 17th centuries Lorenzo Lotto, Pellegrino Tibaldi and Federico Zuccaro, among others, were responsible for the decoration of one or more of the chapels. In 1605 Cristoforo Roncalli was commissioned to decorate the sacristy of the treasury and the dome, where he exalted the Virgin in representations of her earthly life and celestial glory such as the *Coronation of the Virgin* (studies, Loreto, Santuario S Casa, Bib.).

The main entrance doors (1590–1610) to the church were cast in bronze by Antonio Lombardi and his sons; the doors depict scenes from the Old and New Testaments. Before the façade is a bronze statue (*c.* 1589) of *Sixtus V* by ANTONIO CALCAGNI, with a richly decorated pedestal incorporating reliefs of the *Four Virtues*.

From the late 19th century, artistic activity recommenced on a grand scale. The apsidal chapels were redecorated after modifications to the structure necessitated the removal of the original paintings (many now in Loreto, Pal. Apostolico). The dome was frescoed (1890–1907; cartoons, Loreto, Pal. Apostolico) by Cesare Maccari with subjects from the Loretan litanies and the events related to the definition of the dogma of the Immaculate Conception (1854).

BIBLIOGRAPHY
F. Grimaldi: *Loreto: Basilica della Santa Casa* (Bologna, 1975)
——: *La chiesa di Santa Maria di Loreto nei documenti dei secoli XII–XV* (Ancona, 1984)
G. Santarelli, ed.: *La congregazione universale della Santa Casa 1883–1983* (Loreto, 1985)
F. Grimaldi, ed.: *La basilica della Santa Casa di Loreto: Indagini archeologiche geognostiche e statiche* (Ancona, 1986)
F. Grimaldi and K. Sordi: *Scultori a Loreto: Fratelli Lombardi, Antonio Calcagni e Tiburzio Vergelli: Documenti* (Ancona, 1987)
——: *Pittori a Loreto: Committenze tra '500 e '600* (Ancona, 1988)
F. Grimaldi: *Il sacello della Santa Casa* (Loreto, 1991)
*Il progetto di Sisto V: Territorio, città, monumenti nelle Marche*, Rome, Poligrafico dello Stato cat. (Rome, 1991)
F. Grimaldi: *Historia della chiesa di Santa Maria di Loreto* (Loreto, 1993)
FLORIANO GRIMALDI

*(c) Influence.* The exceptionally large size of S Maria di Loreto, the enormous popularity of the relic it enclosed and the direct interest of the popes in the project all contributed to the fame of the church and stimulated the imitation of its spatial and structural arrangements, despite the somewhat outmoded Late Gothic style of its architecture. Already in the 1480s many architects, especially those linked with nearby Urbino, adopted the plan, often combining it with other forms. In his treatise on architecture, Francesco di Giorgio Martini discussed various forms of temple, one of which he illustrated with plans resembling Loreto. A closer similarity to S Maria is found in the plan of Pavia Cathedral; the design of 1488 was significantly influenced by Bramante, who was perhaps aware of the works at Loreto. The influence of S Maria can also be detected in some of Leonardo da Vinci's studies and drawings and in Bramante's early designs (1505–6) for St Peter's, Rome, particularly in the octagonal sacristies with entrances on the diagonals, as well as in the expansion of the central octagon, with the dome positioned above the tomb of St Peter. Distant echoes of the theme re-emerge in studies and projects by Bramante's pupils and followers, including Baldassare Peruzzi and Antonio da Sangallo (ii). A simplified form of S Maria can perhaps be seen in Girolamo Genga's S Giovanni Evangelista (begun 1543), Pesaro. Nevertheless, the Loreto plan was rarely adopted in the numerous churches which, from the 16th century onwards, were dedicated to Our Lady of Loreto, despite the fact that the appearance of S Maria was widely known from engravings and the plan was included in the Venetian edition (1567) of the *Libro d'Antonio Labacco appartenente all'architettura* and in subsequent editions. A degree of interest, even at a theoretical level, is also evident from its inclusion among the plans (Florence, Uffizi) of the churches of Tuscany and Italy drawn by Giorgio Vasari il giovane, even if its interpretation is somewhat loose or sometimes incorrect.

BIBLIOGRAPHY
L. H. Heydenreich: *Die Sakralbau-Studien Leonardo da Vinci's* (Engelsdorf-Leipzig, 1929/R Munich, 1971)
G. Giovannoni: *Antonio da Sangallo il giovane* (Rome, 1959), pp. 187–8, 252
A. Bruschi: *Bramante architetto* (Bari, 1969)
L. H. Heydenreich and W. Lotz: *Architecture in Italy, 1400–1600* (Hardmondsworth, 1974), pp. 106, 177, 235
A. Weege: 'La ricostruzione del progetto di Bramante per il Duomo di Pavia', *A. Lombarda*, lxxxvi–vii (1988), p. 140
L. Patetta: *Storia e tipologia* (Milan, 1989)
ARNALDO BRUSCHI

*(ii) Santa Casa.*

*(a) Architecture and sculpture.* In 1509 Pope Julius II commissioned Donato Bramante to construct a rectangular structure within the basilica of S Maria to enclose the Santa Casa (*see* §1 above). Bramante gave the small, humble house (*c.* 9.5×4.0 m internally) an elegant marble shell (see fig. 3). He used fluted Corinthian half columns resting on pedestals and supporting an entablature, cornice and balustrade to articulate the main storey. The structure

3. Loreto, Santa Casa, begun 1509 by Donato Bramante; sculpture by Andrea Sansovino and others

has two doorways on each of its long (north and south) sides, with an altar set against one of the short ends. Work continued after Bramante's death in 1514, the richly perforated architectural revetment being installed only in 1532–4; the balustrade was added in 1537.

The lavish sculptural decoration includes nine marble panels carved in a horizontal format in high relief depicting scenes from the *Life of the Virgin*. Bramante had chosen Giovanni Cristoforo Romano to be his sculptor, but Romano died soon after and was succeeded by Andrea Sansovino in 1513. Progress was interrupted during the papacy of Adrian VI (*reg* 1521–1523). After the Pope's death Sansovino tried, unsuccessfully, to engage Michelangelo in the project. Further delays were caused by the Sack of Rome in 1527 and Sansovino's death two years later. Sansovino's reliefs of the *Annunciation* (1518–22) and the *Adoration of the Shepherds* (1518–24) each comprise two slabs of marble; his *Marriage of the Virgin* (begun 1527) was finished by Niccolò Tribolo in 1533. The *Adoration of the Magi* by Raffaello da Montelupo dates from the period when he and Baccio Bandinelli worked on the *Birth of the Virgin*, and Tribolo and Francesco da Sangallo collaborated on the *Translation of the Holy House of Nazareth*, 1533. Also that year, Montelupo completed his *Visitation* and Sangallo added the relief of *Mary and Joseph Completing the Census*. Three years later Sangallo finished the last narrative of the *Dormition of the Virgin*.

The reliefs are framed by ten pairs of statues placed one above the other in niches flanked by half columns, with the lower niches containing seated prophets. These statues (for illustration *see* LOMBARDO) date from the 1540s; they echo the high relief of the narrative panels, as they project from the niches, but they also disrupt the harmony of the architectural planes. The Santa Casa was completed by bronze doors (installed 1568–76) with their eight scenes from the *Life of Christ*.

BIBLIOGRAPHY
J. Pope-Hennessy: *Italian High Renaissance and Baroque Sculpture* (London, 1970)

K. Weil-Garris: *The Santa Casa di Loreto; Problems in Cinquecento Sculpture*, 2 vols (New York, 1977)

EDWARD J. OLSZEWSKI

*(b) Influence.* The concept of protecting the Santa Casa beneath a dome was not new and was repeated, for example in S Maria della Consolazione, Todi, with its chapel of the Miracle, in St Peter's, Rome, with Bramante's 'tegurio' or shelter (1513; destr. 1592) over the papal altar and St Peter's tomb, and in S Maria degli Angeli, Assisi, with the chapel of the Porziuncola, as well as in many churches dedicated to Our Lady of Loreto from the 16th to the 18th centuries. While the plan of the main church is often radically different from S Maria di Loreto (*see* §1(ii) above), the small chapel within is invariably reminiscent of the Santa Casa, in a more or less literal interpretation. Meticulous attention was often paid to detail and size, and in several cases even the decoration emulated the style of Bramante, as for example in the Santuario di Macereto (begun 1538), near Visso. In the 17th and 18th centuries the Santa Casa served as a model for countless churches and chapels in such countries as Italy, Switzerland, Germany, Bohemia (*see* PRAGUE, §IV, 3), Hungary, Poland and even in Mexico and California.

BIBLIOGRAPHY
L. Patetta: *Storia e tipologia* (Milan, 1989), pp. 121–41

ARNALDO BRUSCHI

2. PALAZZO APOSTOLICO. The design of the main palazzo (see fig. 1 above) is attributed to Bramante and was probably planned when he accompanied Pope Julius II to Loreto in 1507 or 1510. According to his original conception, the palazzo was to have been erected on three sides of a piazza in front of the basilica, with an entrance portico, and a loggia running along the entire upper floor. Twin towers were to be constructed on the western side to reinforce—together with the four existing towers of the basilica—the systematically organized defences of Loreto (*see* §I above). Bramante's project therefore provided for a building that could serve as both a sanctuary and a fortress, as well as fulfilling the more regular needs of clerics and pilgrims as a hospice and a residence.

Work on the palazzo was supervised by many architects. Gian Cristoforo Romano was succeeded in 1512 by Andrea Sansovino who held control until 1517 when work was temporarily directed by Cristoforo Resse and then by Antonio da Sangallo (ii) himself. Progress was slow and at the death of Pope Clement VII in 1534 only the first eight bays on the north side were complete. By 1558 Galasso Alghisi had reached the construction of the 11th pier. The ground floor arcade supports a deep frieze decorated with triglyphs and metopes containing, in the first eight bays, the coats of arms of Pope Leo X and Pope Clement VII. In 1564 work began under Boccalini on the upper loggia. Pope Urban VIII gave instructions in 1643 for the construction of the south wing, but owing to difficulties with landowners in the area this work never got under way, and the piazza has since then remained incomplete. Vanvitelli designed (1751) the balustrade and decoration of the western section, and his designs were executed by Pietro Bernasconi (*d* 1767).

The palazzo is now the art gallery and houses many studies for works of art in the basilica along with paintings formerly hanging there, among them *Christ and the Adulteress* by Lorenzo Lotto. The ceiling of the Sala de Tinello was decorated by Gaspare Gasparini in 1584. There is an extensive collection of tapestries and pharmaceutical pottery associated with medication provided to pilgrims, including examples by Orazio Fontana.

BIBLIOGRAPHY

F. Grimaldi: *Loreto: Palazzo apostolico* (Bologna, 1977)

FLORIANO GRIMALDI

**Lorimer,** Sir **Robert S(toddart)** (*b* Edinburgh, 4 Nov 1864; *d* Edinburgh, 13 Sept 1929). Scottish architect. He trained with Robert Rowand Anderson, H. M. Wardrop (1856–87) and G. F. Bodley, before establishing a practice in Edinburgh in 1893. He soon attracted attention for his plain white cottages (1893) in Colinton, Edinburgh, which combined features of the Scottish Baronial style with English Arts and Crafts principles adopted by Lorimer after he met William Morris in 1889. These cottage designs appeared regularly in *The Builder* from 1893.

Lorimer was simultaneously developing a grander manner for his large mansions. The commission for the first of these, the rehabilitation of a 16th-century tower-house (1893–4) in Earlshall, Fife, came through family connections. There he designed much of the furniture and also an appropriately Scottish garden for the existing walled enclosure. Earlshall led to other work of this kind. Hermann Muthesius reviewed Earlshall (as well as the Colinton Cottages) at some length in *Das englische Haus* (1901), and in 1905 *Country Life* reviewed it in the first of many articles they were to run on Lorimer's work.

Lorimer kept in touch with his many Arts and Crafts friends in London, from 1893 contributing small unassuming pieces of furniture to the Arts and Crafts triennial exhibition there. In 1896 he was elected a member of the Art Workers' Guild. He had become close friends with the Scottish shipping magnate William Burrell and through him had been introduced to many other Scottish collectors, and his later designs for furniture are heavier and richer, reflecting his growing country-house practice. Nevertheless, he retained his reputation as one of Britain's leading Arts and Crafts furniture designers to the mid-1920s.

Much of Lorimer's work continued to be making alterations to existing mansions, the most impressive of which are Barton Hartshorn (1902), Bucks, Lympne Castle (1907), Kent, Dunderave Castle (1911), Argyll, and Balmanno Castle (1916), Tayside. His new mansions, each influenced by local tradition, are Brackenburgh (1901), Cumbria, in the Tudor style, and Rowallan (1902), Strathclyde, Ardkinglas (1906), Strathclyde, and Formakin (1908), Strathclyde. These are all in the Scottish Baronial style. As a Francophile, Lorimer made allusion to the 'Auld Alliance' between Scotland and France in using at the Hill of Tanit (1907), Fife, an early French classical style from the period, to use his words, 'before the pedants took over'. Wayside (1901), Fife, in sandstone is among his best medium-sized houses, and Marlyknowe (1902), East Lothian, and Woodhill (1908), Forfar, Tayside, are harled

in the Scottish tradition and whitewashed. Rhu-na-Haven (1907), Grampian, is of granite.

Garden designs were always fitted to the genius of the place. Lorimer collaborated with Gertrude Jekyll on several of them, such as Barton Hartshorn, Oxon, but none remain in their entirety. His small churches are mostly Gothic, simple and elegant in detail, preparing the way for the chapel for the Knights of the Thistle (1909–11), a small but sumptuous work, which he added to St Giles Cathedral, the High Kirk of Edinburgh. Intricately vaulted with richly carved woodwork in 16th-century manner, it was a pinnacle of Scottish achievement for which he was knighted in 1911.

Lorimer was a member of the Design and Industries Association (London) from its inception in 1915 and in 1918 was appointed a principal architect by the Imperial War Graves Commission for which his long experience in landscaping produced some particularly fine designs in Egypt, Greece and Italy, as well as Germany. His last major work was the Scottish National War Memorial (1927), Edinburgh Castle. Part old, part new and in several styles wrought by all manner of craftsmen and artists, it caught the mood of the nation and after years of political and social controversy became a great popular success. He was part of an artistically gifted family: his brother, John Henry Lorimer (1856–1936), was a painter, and his son, Hew Lorimer (*b* 1907), was a sculptor.

BIBLIOGRAPHY

L. G. Thomson: 'The Late Sir Robert Lorimer and his Work', *Royal Incorp. Architects Scotland, Q.*, xxxi (1929), pp. 63–76

F. Deas: 'The Work of Sir Robert Lorimer', *RIBA J.*, n. s. 3, xxxviii/8 (1931), pp. 239–49

C. Hussey: *The Work of Sir Robert Lorimer* (London, 1931)

P. Savage: 'The Temper of the Scots Pleasance', *Landscape*, xxiv/3 (1974), pp. 20–26

——: 'Robert Lorimer and the Garden Heritage of Scotland', *J. Gdn Hist.*, v/2 (1977), pp. 30–34

——: 'The Garden Designs of Sir Robert Lorimer', *Royal Hort. Soc. J.*, civ/8 (1979)

——: *Lorimer and the Edinburgh Craft Designers* (Edinburgh, 1980)

PETER SAVAGE

**Loring, Frances N(orma)** (*b* Wardner, ID, 14 Oct 1887; *d* Newmarket, Ont., 3 Feb 1968). Canadian sculptor of American birth. She trained briefly at the Ecole des Beaux-Arts, Geneva, and the Académie Colarossi in Paris and then attended the School of the Art Institute of Chicago (1905), the School of the Museum of Fine Arts, Boston (1906), and the Art Students' League in New York (*c*. 1910). She settled in Toronto in 1912, where she was joined soon after by her lifelong friend and colleague, the sculptor Florence Wyle (1881–1968). Significant influences included an early exposure to European art and the pioneer spirit of her father, a mining engineer who had emigrated to Canada in 1906 with a firm belief in the future of that country.

Loring was a sculptor of monuments and an architectural designer; much of her work is therefore heroic in scale and dynamic in treatment. Her early works, such as her series of munitions workers (bronze; 1918; examples in Ottawa, Can. War Mus.), commissioned for the Canadian War Records, were in a romantic-realist style. This evolved into a more stylized treatment, for example in the carved figural decorations for the Memorial Chamber of the Parliament Buildings (1928), Ottawa, and the Queen Elizabeth Monument, which commemorates the opening of the Queen Elizabeth Highway in 1939. Other work includes the Galt War Memorial (1930), the over life-size *Eskimo Mother and Child* (1938; Ottawa, N.G.; Toronto, A.G. Ont.) and a statue of *Sir Robert Borden* (1957) on Parliament Hill, Ottawa. Loring contributed to Canadian sculpture not only through the example of her own work but through her active involvement in arts organizations, particularly the Sculptors' Society of Canada, of which she was a founder-member in 1928.

BIBLIOGRAPHY
R. Sisler: *The Girls: A Biography of Frances Loring and Florence Wyle* (Toronto, 1972)
*Visions and Victories: 10 Canadian Women Artists, 1914–45* (exh. cat. by N. Luckyj, London, Ont., Reg. A.G., 1983)
*Loring and Wyle: Sculptors' Legacy* (exh. cat. by C. Boyanoski, Toronto, A.G. Ont., 1987)
CHRISTINE BOYANOSKI

**Loriyan Tangai.** Buddhist monastic site in Swat, North-West Frontier Province, Pakistan. It flourished *c.* 2nd–3rd centuries AD. The site was excavated by A. E. Caddy in 1896, but the exact location is now uncertain. ALFRED CHARLES AUGUSTE FOUCHER, who visited the site in 1896, identifies it as the ruin closest to the northern opening of the Shahkot Pass into Lower Swat, in the valley (Pasht. *tangai*) of Loriyan (or perhaps Ralyan), near Piyalana village, south-east of Allahdand. Only details of the main stupa are recorded. The 10 m square base comprised two receding diaper masonry terraces, each set on a moulded plinth and decorated with rows of evenly spaced pilasters. Nothing survived above the upper tier. A central projection on one side of the base contained steps to the top of the mound. Photographs show the stupa standing in a courtyard, with other unexcavated structures on the hillside beside it. The Loriyan Tangai schist sculptures (Calcutta, Ind. Mus.) include many Buddha and *bodhisattva* images, an intact small stupa and numerous fragments of other votive stupas and reliefs. These imply the main stupa was surrounded by the usual shrines and votive structures found at other Gandhara sites. One headless Buddha bears a Kharoshthi inscription dated in the year 318 of an unspecified era. No finds of stucco or coins are recorded.

*See also* INDIAN SUBCONTINENT, §IV, 5(i)(a).

BIBLIOGRAPHY
E. Senart: 'Deux Epigraphes du Swāt', *J. Asiat.*, n. s. 9, xiii (1899), pp. 526–37
*A List of Photographic Negatives of Indian Antiquities in the Collection of the Indian Museum, . . . [and] in the Possession of the India Office* (Calcutta, 1900) [phot. nos 1046–69 on file London, India Office Lib.]
A. Foucher: *L'Art gréco-bouddhique du Gandhâra*, i (Paris, 1905), pp. 22–5, figs 3–5
S. Konow: *Kharoshthi Inscriptions*, ii of *Corpus Inscriptionum Indicarum* (Calcutta, 1929), nos xl–xliv, pp. 106–10, pl. xxi
E. ERRINGTON

**L'Orme** [Delorme], **Philibert de** (*b* Lyon, ?3–9 June 1514; *d* Paris, 8 Jan 1570). French architect and writer. He was the most important French architect of the 16th century and, with his contemporaries Pierre Lescot and Jean Bullant, was one of the founders of the classical style in France. In his buildings he attempted to synthesize the elements of ancient Roman and Renaissance Italian archi-

tecture with French traditions of design and construction, adding innovations that stemmed from his concern with STEREOTOMY, the theory of stone-cutting. He published two treatises, of which *Le Premier Tome de l'architecture* was the most comprehensive of the 16th century in France. It remained unsurpassed until François Blondel's *Cours d'architecture* in the 18th century.

1. Life and work. 2. Writings.

1. LIFE AND WORK.

(i) Training and early works, to 1547. (ii) In the service of Henry II, 1547–59. (iii) Works for Catherine de' Medici, 1563–70.

*(i) Training and early works, to 1547.* Philibert de L'Orme presumably received his early training from his father, Jean de L'Orme I, a wealthy master mason in Lyon, working with him on his building projects, while at the same time undertaking humanistic studies. From 1533–6 he was in Rome, where he moved in humanist circles, meeting Marcello Cervini (*d* 1555), later Pope Marcellus II, and working for Paul III. It was also at this time that de L'Orme met Cardinal Jean Du Bellay (1492–1560), the French ambassador to the Holy See, and became intimate friends with François Rabelais, his secretary and physician. He also had access to the workshops of Baldassare Peruzzi and Antonio da Sangallo (ii), and he could therefore become familiar with their projects.

Shortly after de L'Orme's return to France in 1535, he built a gallery supported on pendentives on to the Hôtel Bullioud in Lyon. His next known work, and his first major construction, was the château of Saint-Maur-les-Fossés, Val-de-Marne, begun for Cardinal Du Bellay around 1541. It is possible that he spent the intervening years in Italy as a military engineer in the service of the Cardinal's brother Guillaume Du Bellay (1491–1543), French governor of Turin and Piedmont.

De L'Orme's design for Saint-Maur (published in the *Premier Tome de l'architecture*) proposed four wings around a square court. The traditional corner pavilions of French château buildings were to be omitted, and, instead of the usual high roofs, de L'Orme chose flat roofs invisible from the ground. The single storey, articulated with Corinthian columns and pilasters, was raised on a large plinth and crowned by a high attic. The latter was to have been decorated with frescoes on the courtyard side; the whole project was more like an Italian villa than a traditional château. Only the main *corps-de-logis* had been built when work stopped in 1544. In February 1545 de L'Orme was put in charge of works and fortifications in Brittany by King Francis I, a post in which he was succeeded by his brother Jean in 1549.

*(ii) In the service of Henry II, 1547–59.* De L'Orme was in the service of the Dauphin Henry by February 1547. His rise to the position of leading architect in France dates from the Dauphin's accession to the throne later that year as Henry II. On 7 April 1548 de L'Orme was appointed surveyor of the royal works, with the title 'commissaire ordonné et député par Sa Majesté'. This new office invested him with far-reaching powers, comparable to those of a Surintendant des Bâtiments du Roi in the following century. Only the building of the new Louvre in Paris, in

1. Philibert de L'Orme: *Trompe d'Anet*, 1547–55; engraving from his *Premier Tome de l'architecture* (Paris, 1567), fol. 89

the hands of Lescot, remained outside his authority. In the 11 years of Henry II's reign de L'Orme centralized the organization of royal building works, trained artisans to high degrees of skill and brought the activities of contractors under tight budgetary control. He was well rewarded by the King for his efforts, being given patents of nobility and receiving the income from a number of lucrative ecclesiastical benefices. In 1550 Cardinal Du Bellay appointed him a canon of Notre-Dame in Paris.

Among the first of the royal projects that de L'Orme undertook for Henry II was the rebuilding of the medieval château of Saint-Léger-en-Yvelines. The commission probably dates from 1547 or 1548, but work seems to have progressed slowly, and the final plan—for a large court surrounded by four wings—was only decided in 1551. Building work was carried out in 1555–7. The château was demolished in 1668, but de L'Orme's project is recorded in two drawings (Rome, Bib. Vaticana) by Jacques Androuet Du Cerceau (i). Excavations in 1977–9 revealed that of the planned four wings, only the west and south wings were ever built. The latter was the gallery, and attached to it was a square chapel with three subsidiary chapels and a cupola on pendentives, with a lantern above. This kind of arrangement, explored with increasing subtlety by de L'Orme in later projects, suggests that he must have been familiar with centralized church plans such as those of Leonardo da Vinci.

During the time that he was designing the alterations to Saint-Léger, de L'Orme was also at work on his most

famous building, the château of ANET, Eure-et-Loire. In 1547 Henry II put de L'Orme's services at the disposal of his mistress, Diane de Poitiers, who had already begun enlarging the existing buildings, in part as a memorial to her late husband, Louis de Brézé. The result of de L'Orme's intervention from 1547 to 1555 was to transform Anet into one of the most magnificent great houses in France, though only fragments now survive.

The château was laid out on an area surrounded by deep ditches. The gardens extended to the north, while the buildings, organized around three courts, were laid out to the south of the site. The main buildings surrounded the central courtyard (the Cour du Seigneur), the offices enclosed the western court (the Cour de la Fontaine), and the farm buildings enclosed the eastern court (the Basse Cour). All three courts were linked on the south by the fortress-like entrance pavilion, which survives. De L'Orme displayed considerable ingenuity in incorporating the existing buildings into his design. Among his inventions were the still extant cryptoporticus, with its twin crescent-shaped flights of steps, facing the garden in front of the north wing, the court façade of that wing (the elaborate frontispiece of which is now in the courtyard of the Ecole des Beaux-Arts, Paris) that concealed the old *corps-de-logis*, and the famous *trompe*, a turret-shaped closet supported on an undulating squinch. This last, built into a re-entrant angle of the garden front, was designed as an extension to the King's apartment and was probably the most complex stereometrical construction of its period (see fig. 1).

De L'Orme also realized some very innovative ideas in the chapel at Anet and in the entrance pavilion, both of which still stand. The chapel, a rotunda with four arms

2. Philibert de L'Orme: dome of the chapel at Anet, 1547–55

forming a Greek cross, is based on the *tepidarium* of the Baths of Diocletian in Rome and on an unexecuted design by Antonio da Sangallo (ii) for the Medici Chapel at Montecassino. The remarkable coffering of the dome (see fig. 2), made up of intersecting arcs of circles, is repeated in two dimensions on the marble pavement. In the massive and austere entrance pavilion, de L'Orme combined elements taken from a design by Sangallo for the Fortezza da Basso, near Florence, and from the portal of the Romanesque church at Saint-Gilles-du-Gard. In addition to its importance as a highly original synthesis of French, Italian and antique architectural ideas, Anet shares with Lescot's Louvre the distinction of being the first French château in which the rich decoration followed a coherent iconographic programme, its central theme of Diana and Apollo alluding to Diane de Poitiers and Henry II.

Also among de L'Orme's early royal commissions was the monument at Saint-Denis Abbey to *Francis I and Claude of France* (*see* SAINT-DENIS ABBEY, §II, 2(ii)). He probably received orders for this project late in 1547 or early in 1548, and after the death of the original contractor the work was carried out by a number of masons and sculptors, principal among them being PIERRE BONTEMPS. The finished monument was probably erected in 1558. Its design follows the traditional medieval canopy-tomb pattern, but de L'Orme recast this type in classical form, treating its four faces as triumphal arches based on the arch of Septimus Severus in Rome, while, unusually, employing an Ionic order. It is unclear if de L'Orme was

responsible for the design of the complementary monument to the *Heart of Francis I* (Saint-Denis Abbey), which was also carved by Bontemps.

De L'Orme was also employed by Henry II at the château of Vincennes, Val-de-Marne, where from 1548 he completed the vault of the medieval Sainte-Chapelle and added an internal gallery in a Late Gothic style. In 1551 a monumental staircase with an oval landing was built in front of the entrance to plans by de L'Orme. The royal château of Fontainebleau was among de L'Orme's most important responsibilities at this period. His numerous additions and alterations included the completion of Gilles Le Breton's Salle de Bal with a sumptuous coffered wooden ceiling (instead of the vault originally envisaged), executed in 1550 by Scibec de Carpi (see fig. 3). Divided into octagonal and square fields and covered with carving, it is the most magnificent French ceiling of its kind to survive from the 16th century. De L'Orme also built an exterior staircase (destr. 1634) in the Cour du Cheval Blanc. This consisted of one straight flight and two curved ones, and in *L'Architecture* he extolled it as a masterpiece of stereotomy. Among works projected, but not carried out, was a rebuilding of the wing between the Cour du Cheval Blanc and the Cour de la Fontaine, which would have featured an arrangement of colossal Doric pilasters on the Cour de la Fontaine façade.

Experiments with centralized church plans were continued by de L'Orme in the 1550s in the parks of the royal châteaux of Villers-Cotterêts, Aisne, and Saint-Germain-en-Laye, Yvelines. Both chapels are now known only through Du Cerceau's drawings (London, BM). That at Villers-Cotterêts (1552) was a rotunda with three wide secondary chapels opening off it. Its columnar portico featured shafts each made up of three drums, the joints between them concealed by carved foliate wreaths. This was de L'Orme's first realization of his 'French order'. The chapel at Saint-Germain (1555) had a hexagonal ground plan, with three curved and two rectangular spaces opening off it. It, too, featured an entrance portico. Models for the two chapels are to be found in the architectural drawings of Peruzzi and his circle, which de L'Orme must have seen during his stay in Rome.

De L'Orme was not entirely engaged on royal works. He found time to build a house (destr.) for himself in the Rue de la Cerisaie, Paris, in 1554–5. He recorded its appearance in three woodcuts in *L'Architecture*. Its noble street façade, with columnar portal, niches, plaques and delicately profiled mouldings, anticipating in some respects the 17th-century classicism of François Mansart, gives an indication of its importance in the development of the town house in France.

The year after the completion of his own house, de L'Orme was asked by Diane de Poitiers to undertake works at her newly acquired château of CHENONCEAUX, Indre-et-Loire. He began on the construction of a bridge carrying a gallery to link the existing château on the north bank of the River Cher with the south bank. When work was suspended on the death of the King in 1559, only the arches of the bridge had been completed. Works were later resumed when Chenonceaux passed to Catherine de' Medici. The magnificent plans for the further extension of the château published by Du Cerceau in *Les Plus*

3. Philibert de L'Orme: ceiling (1550, executed by Scibec de Carpi) of the Salle de Bal, château of Fontainebleau

*Excellents Bastiments* have been variously attributed to de L'Orme and to Bullant. Another project that came to a halt at the death of Henry II was the Château Neuf at Saint-Germain (for illustration *see* SAINT-GERMAIN-EN-LAYE, CHÂTEAU OF). Begun in 1557, this small pleasure palace, originally designated a *théâtre* and built to one side of the old château, was intended for court entertainments. De L'Orme's single-storey project combined traditional French château planning (a *corps-de-logis* with four corner pavilions) with elements of the Italian Renaissance villa (a square, walled courtyard with four exedrae, clearly intended for festivities). The Château Neuf was completed to different plans during the reign of Henry IV (*reg* 1589–1610).

De L'Orme's last project for Henry II, the rebuilding of the Montmartre Convent in Paris, which had been destroyed by fire in 1559, was one of his most original and extravagant. Although never completed, de L'Orme described the project in his book *Nouvelles Inventions pour bien bastir* and illustrated it with two woodcuts. The King put at the disposal of the nuns the materials of an ephemeral *salle de triomphe* in the garden of the Hôtel de Tournelles, his preferred town residence, where de L'Orme had carried out numerous temporary schemes. De L'Orme planned a vast circular building made up of two concentric walls, 48–58 m in diameter between which the nuns' cells were arranged on three floors. The inner ring wall was to have supported a gigantic wooden dome, and under the dome would have been two superimposed, circular, Ionic colonnades, giving access to the cells. As the building on its elevated site would have been visible across much of Paris, it was proposed to decorate the outer shell of the dome with the features of the earthly or celestial globe.

*(iii) Works for Catherine de' Medici, 1563–70.* Two days after Henry II's unexpected death on 10 July 1559, de L'Orme was dismissed from his royal post and replaced by Francesco Primaticcio. This was perhaps the result of intrigues by the powerful Lorraine faction at court, but de L'Orme's tight control over the royal building works and the arrogant exercise of his powers had made him many enemies. As early as 1557 Pierre Ronsard had published some satirical verses aimed at him, and the potter Bernard Palissy recorded de L'Orme's inflated opinion of himself in his *Discours admirables*. De L'Orme may have had to answer for himself before a court after his dismissal, and in his memorandum *Instruction de Monsieur d'Yvry dict de L'Orme* (reprinted in Blunt, 1958, pp. 146–51) he refuted allegations that he had unlawfully enriched himself at the King's expense. It seems that de L'Orme successfully warded off the accusations against him: in September 1561 Charles IX granted him a privilege to publish his *Nouvelles Inventions*, and in 1563 he entered the service of the Queen Mother, Catherine de' Medici.

De L'Orme had already worked for Catherine in 1557, when he had built a remarkable pavilion (destr.) at her château of Monceaux-en-Brie, Seine-et-Marne. According to the surviving contract, the ground floor, within which was an octagonal hall decorated as a grotto, was faced externally with rusticated masonry. Above this basement rose two further storeys articulated by a colossal pilaster order, probably the first appearance of this feature in France. De L'Orme's first undertaking for Catherine in the 1560s was the extension of the château of Saint-Maur, which she had acquired from Cardinal Du Bellay's heirs. To the wing that he had built two decades earlier, he attached at each end a pair of pavilions linked by a terrace supported on an arcaded cryptoporticus. He may also have been responsible for the ambitious planned extensions (shown in an illustration by Du Cerceau of *c.* 1576) to Chenonceaux, which was taken back from Diane de Poitiers by Catherine after Henry II's demise.

The biggest contract ever received by de L'Orme came in 1563–4, when Catherine de' Medici decided to build a vast palace in Paris beside the Seine and to the west of the Louvre. The place chosen had been the site of a tile works, hence the name of the new palace—the Tuileries. Between 1564 and 1572 a section of the westernmost part of the building was completed. Works then came to a halt and were not taken up again until the early years of the following century. The palace was burnt down in 1871 and subsequently demolished (a single arch of de L'Orme's loggia was rebuilt in the Tuileries Gardens). This chequered history, combined with a lack of documentation, has led to disagreement about the extent of de L'Orme's project. Plates in Du Cerceau's *Les Plus Excellents Bastiments* (drawings, London, BM) depicting a structure with three huge courtyards and twelve pavilions were dismissed by Blunt (1958) as largely the product of Du Cerceau's imagination. He suggested that de L'Orme's project was more modest, with only one court. It seems likely, however, that Du Cerceau had access to de L'Orme's own plans and models, which were seized by the Queen Mother after the architect's death.

The great central courtyard of the palace depicted by Du Cerceau (see fig. 4) has its four ranges of buildings raised on a stepped base, and the two longest sides have arcaded loggias. Beyond these loggias, to the north and south, are two smaller courts, the centres of which are occupied by oval, amphitheatre-like halls, joined to the main buildings on their longer, north–south axis. Of the twelve symmetrically placed pavilions on the outer façades of the palace, the two in the centre of the longest, east and west, fronts mark the entrances. The central pavilion in the west front, part of the range completed in de L'Orme's lifetime, housed his much praised, self-supporting, stone spiral staircase, his masterpiece of stereotomy. De L'Orme's 'French order' was much in evidence in the articulation of the façades. If Du Cerceau's engravings are taken as evidence of de L'Orme's intentions, the Tuileries Palace represents the most grandiose synthesis of French château design and Italian Renaissance architectural ideas before the construction of the château of Versailles a century later.

2. WRITINGS. De L'Orme's first treatise, *Nouvelles Inventions pour bien bastir et à petits fraiz*, appeared in 1561. His second, *Le Premier Tome de l'architecture*, incorporating the earlier work, appeared in 1567. As its title implies, de L'Orme had intended to produce a second volume, with the subtitle *Des Divines Proportions*. This was never written, however. *L'Architecture*, richly illustrated with woodcuts and written in a lively style, draws heavily on de L'Orme's own experience and buildings. It is essentially a practical

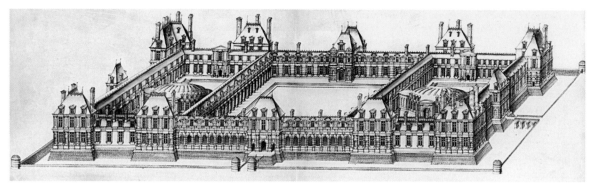

4. Philibert de L'Orme: Palais des Tuileries, Paris, begun 1564; from a drawing by Jacques Androuet Du Cerceau (i), 510×750 mm (London, British Museum)

manual for the architect and is set out in a manner that follows the processes of design and construction. Thus, Book I of the nine new sections into which it is divided (Books X and XI are the *Nouvelles Inventions*) deals with the relationship between architect and client; choice of site and orientation of the building; and selection of building materials. Book II considers the elements of geometry; the measuring and levelling of the site; and foundations. Books III and IV are of the greatest importance in the history of architectural theory and practice, containing as they do de L'Orme's discourse on stereotomy. The first of these two deals with the basis of the setting and cutting of stones for masonry, the second deals with advanced stereometrical problems—the construction of all types of arches, vaults and staircases—and includes a discussion of the famous *Trompe d'Anet*. Books V to VII deal with the orders. The Doric, Tuscan and Ionic orders are the subjects of Book V, the Corinthian of Book VI, and the Composite and 'French order' of Book VII. Although de L'Orme presented the orders according to the canons established by Vitruvius and Serlio, he also found room for deviant examples that he had himself drawn and measured in Rome. His independence can be seen in the invention of the 'French order', used by him in the chapel at Villers-Cotterêts and at the Tuileries. The great nations of history had all evolved their own column orders, so why should not a nation as great as the French have its own? The main distinguishing characteristic of de L'Orme's new column, which could be formed from any of the five Classical orders, lay in the treatment of the shaft, and was a decorative solution to what he perceived as a technical problem. Because the stones for monolithic shafts could not be quarried in France, and because he believed, erroneously, that the Greeks had made their column shafts from single stones, de L'Orme hid the construction of his own columns from joined drums by the use at the joints of carved wreaths of foliage or similar ornament. The treatment of doorways, doors and dormer windows is dealt with in Book VIII of the treatise. Book IX considers chimneys, flues and fireplaces, while Books X and XI deal with modern timber construction and its application to roofs and domes. In particular he described his novel method of supporting roofs and domes with arches assembled from many short planks, rather than using massive single beams. Not only could this reduce the expense of construction, but it could also increase the width of span, as witness the wooden dome proposed for the Montmartre Convent.

### WRITINGS

*Nouvelles Inventions pour bien bastir et à petits fraiz* (Paris, 1561, 2/1568 as suppl. to *Le Premier Tome de l'architecture*)
*Le Premier Tome de l'architecture* (Paris, 1567, 2/1568 [with *Nouvelles Inventions*]/R 1988)

### BIBLIOGRAPHY

J. Androuet Du Cerceau: *Les Plus Excellents Bastiments de France*, 2 vols (Paris, 1576–9)
C. Chevalier: *Lettres et devis de Philibert de L'Orme* (Paris, 1864)
A. Berty and H. Legrand: *Topographie historique du vieux Paris: Région du Louvre et des Tuileries II* (Paris, 1868, 2/1885)
E.-L.-G. Charvet: *Lyon artistique: Architectes* (Lyon, 1899)
H. Clouzot: *Philibert de L'Orme* (Paris, 1910)
J. Guiffrey: *Artistes parisiens des XVIe et XVIIe siècles* (Paris, 1915)
L. de la Tourasse: 'Le Château-Neuf de Saint-Germain-en-Laye', *Gaz. B.-A.*, n. s. 4, ix (1924), pp. 68–95
M. Roy: *Artistes et monuments de la Renaissance* (Paris, 1927)
J. Goldscheider: *Die Bücher des Philibert de L'Orme* (diss., U. Vienna, 1936)
L. Hautecoeur: *Histoire de l'architecture classique en France*, i/2 (Paris, 1943)
J. Prévost: *Philibert de L'Orme* (Paris, 1948)
A. Blunt: *Art and Architecture in France 1500–1700*, Pelican Hist. A. (London, 1953, 5/1982), pp. 84–94
L. Brion-Guerry: *Philibert de L'Orme* (Paris, 1955)
L. Toesca: 'The Drawings by J. A. Du Cerceau the Elder in the Vatican Library', *Burl. Mag.*, xcviii (1956), pp. 153–7
A. Blunt: *Philibert de L'Orme* (London, 1958) [extensive bibliog.]
P. Vanaise: 'La Construction de la chapelle du parc du château de Villers-Cotterêts (1552–1553)', *Bull. Soc. Hist. A. Fr.* (1967), pp. 27–38
L. Châtelet-Lange: 'Philibert de L'Orme à Montceaux-en-Brie: Le Pavillon de la Grotte', *Architectura: Z. Gesch. Archit.*, iii (1973), pp. 153–70
D. A. Chevalley: *Der grosse Tuilerienentwurf in der Überlieferung Ducerceaus* (Berne and Frankfurt am Main, 1973)
V. Hoffmann: 'Philibert Delorme und das Schloss Anet', *Architectura Z. Gesch. Archit.*, iii (1973), pp. 131–52
——: 'Artisti francesi a Roma: Philibert Delorme e Jean Bullant', *Coll. Sodalizio*, n. s., 4 (1975), pp. 55–68
J.-M. Pérouse de Montclos: 'La Vis de Saint-Gilles et l'escalier suspendu dans l'architecture française du XVIe siècle', *L'Escalier dans l'architecture de la Renaissance: Actes du colloque du Centre d'Etudes Supérieures de la Renaissance: Tours, 1979*, pp. 83–91
V. Hoffmann: 'Bemerkungen zur Verwendung der Säulenordnungen in der französischen Baukunst des 16. Jahrhunderts', *Festschrift für Wilhelm Messerer zum 60. Geburtstag* (Cologne, 1980), pp. 205–12
J.-M. Pérouse de Montclos: *L'Architecture à la française: XVIe, XVIIe, XVIIIe siècles* (Paris, 1982)
F. Boudon and J. Blécon: *Philibert Delorme et le château royal de Saint-Léger-en-Yvelines* (Paris, 1985)
W. Prinz and R. Kecks: *Das französische Schloss der Renaissance: Form und Bedeutung der Architektur, ihre geschichtlichen und gesellschaftlichen Grundlagen* (Berlin, 1985)

Yves Pauwels: 'Philibert de L'Orme et l'ordre ionique', *L'Emploi des ordres à la Renaissance: Tours, 1986*, pp. 227–36

J. Guillaume: 'De L'Orme et Michelange', *Il se rendit en Italie: Etudes offertes à André Chastel* (Rome, 1987), pp. 279–88

J.-M. Pérouse de Montclos: 'Philibert de L'Orme en Italie', *Il se rendit en Italie: Etudes offertes à André Chastel* (Rome, 1987), pp. 289–99

——: 'Les Editions des traités de Philibert de L'Orme au XVIIe siècle', *Les Traités d'architecture de la Renaissance* (Tours, 1988), pp. 355–65

V. HOFFMANN

**Loro Jonggrang** [Prambanan]. Hindu temple complex in southern Central Java. It is the largest and most important of a group of Shaivite and Buddhist temples (*candi*) on the plain of Prambanan near the village of that name, 17 km north-east of Yogyakarta. Candi Loro Jonggrang, popularly known as Candi Prambanan, is associated with an inscription with a date equivalent to AD 856, although its architecture is inconsistent with such an early date. All the temple buildings have an elevated platform, high walls divided by a horizontal moulding and a pyramidal roof that ascends without pronounced steps. The resulting slenderness is characteristic of the temple architecture of the later Singhasari period in East Java (*see* INDONESIA, §II, 1(iii)). The complex consists of more than 200 shrines of varying sizes, distributed over 2 concentric square courtyards enclosed by walls with gateways on all 4 sides. The inner courtyard is 100 m square and contains the main shrines of the compound. The outer courtyard is 200 m square and contains subsidiary temples built on four tiered platforms that descend gradually from the walls of the central square. The entire compound is enclosed by a further, lower-lying square of 365×365 m, the walls of which are not parallel to the other two enclosure walls. This square, at an angle to the others, was apparently reserved for various auxiliary buildings made of impermanent materials.

There are six principal shrines, arranged in two parallel rows of three on a north–south axis. The largest, a colossal structure 30 m square at the base rising to a height of 47 m, is dedicated to the supreme god Shiva. On either side are smaller shrines dedicated to Brahma and Vishnu (see fig.). Facing it in the middle of the parallel row is the shrine of Shiva's mount, the bull Nandi, flanked by two temple buildings of unknown purpose. Also unknown is the function of the two 'court temples' at either end of the space between the two rows of shrines. The entire complex has been successfully restored by the anastylosis (integral restoration) method. Life-size stone statues of Shiva, Brahma and Vishnu stand in their respective shrines. Only Shiva, however, is accompanied by his attendants Agastya, Ganesha and Durga, who appear in the minor cellae of his shrine.

The platforms of the three principal temples are decorated on the sides with 'Prambanan motifs': a standing lion in a niche flanked by trees of heaven guarded on either side by a pair of *kinnara*s (half-humans, half-birds),

Candi Loro Jonggrang, Prambanan, showing (from left to right) the temples of Brahma, Shiva and Vishnu, early 10th century

hares, geese or other animals. The balustrades of the processional paths to the three main shrines are decorated on the exterior with dancing figures in high relief and on the interior surface with narrative reliefs depicting episodes from the *Rāmāyaṇa* and the *Kṛṣṇāyaṇa* epics.

BIBLIOGRAPHY

V. R. van Romondt: 'De wederopbouw van de Ciwa temple te Prambanan' [The rebuilding of the Siva temple at Prambanan], *Djawa*, xx (1940), pp. 234–9
A. J. Bernet Kempers: 'Prambanan 1954', *Bijdr. Taal-, Land- & Vlkenknd*, iii (1955), pp. 7–37
——: *Ancient Indonesian Art* (Amsterdam, 1959)
——: *Herstel in eigen waarde: Monumentenzorg in Indonesie* [Restoration according to its own value: the care of monuments in Indonesia] (Zutphen, 1978), pp. 98–106, 159–73
J. Dumarçay: *The Temples of Java* (Oxford, 1986)
*The Sculpture of Indonesia* (exh. cat., Washington, DC, N.G.A., 1990)

R. SOEKMONO

**Lorrain, Claude.** *See* CLAUDE LORRAIN.

**Lorraine**, House of. Rulers and patrons. The patronage of the dukes of Lorraine was especially important between the late 16th century and the early 17th, and in the mid-18th. Although Lorraine was created as an independent hereditary duchy under the protection of the Holy Roman Empire during the early Middle Ages (*see* LOTHARINGIA), it was linked by ties of language and culture to France. Increasing French political pressure from the mid-16th century culminated in the invasion of the territory by French forces under King Louis XIII in 1633. Until then, however, by a combination of force of personality, diplomatic skill and intermarriage with the European aristocracy, the dukes had succeeded in maintaining a peaceful and relatively prosperous, if socially backward, state. From as early as the mid-15th century, the court, based in the capital, Nancy, was noted for the promotion of poetry, music, manuscript illumination and, above all, festivities (*see* NANCY, §1). The earliest surviving major building commissioned by the court is the fine Gothic church of the Cordeliers (Franciscans), erected next to the Palais Ducal by René II, Duke of Lorraine (*reg* 1473–1508; *see* ANJOU, §II(5) ) as a thank-offering after the defeat of the Burgundians at the siege of Nancy in 1477. Under René's son and successor, Anthony (*reg* 1508–44), the Palais Ducal itself was also rebuilt in Gothic style, with Renaissance ornaments. This was a structure of great splendour and was surrounded by magnificent gardens, although almost nothing of its original form remains, owing to subsequent neglect and alterations.

The court of Lorraine reached the zenith of its fame during the reigns of Charles III (*reg* 1559–1608) and Henry II (*reg* 1608–24). Constitutionally and socially the duchy remained feudal, with an absolutist system of government, a compliant States General (which kept the nobles in check), a large peasantry and only a small middle class. The religious orders, particularly the Franciscans and Jesuits, fired by the zeal of the Counter-Reformation, were a pervasive presence, and the region was devoutly Catholic. For these reasons, Lorraine escaped both the religious wars that convulsed its neighbours in the later 16th century and the early stages of the Thirty Years War (1618–48).

Culturally, the conditions in the duchy made for a court that was intellectually reactionary by European standards but was constantly active and extravagantly ostentatious; in sum, everything conspired towards the cultivation, in the arts, of the most extreme forms of Mannerism. This is not to say that Charles III neglected the modernization of Lorraine, for he founded the important university of Pont-à-Mousson in 1572 (transferred to Nancy in the early 18th century) and built the New Town of Nancy (after 1588), more than doubling the city in size. He also encouraged manufactures and commerce. It was, however, as the art-loving and energetic ruler of his court that he achieved European fame. He embellished the Palais Ducal, adding a picture gallery, a tennis-court and an orangery. Meanwhile the court festivities reached new heights of magnificence. Ballets, masquerades and jousts alternated with brilliant religious ceremonies to which the Duke, as an ardent champion of Catholicism, was strongly attached. The reception of distinguished foreign visitors provided further occasions for pageantry, as did state funerals, above all that of Charles himself in 1608 (see fig.). Following this, an octagonal funerary chapel, modelled on the Cappella dei Principi (begun 1604) attached to S Lorenzo, Florence, was added to the church of the Cordeliers to contain the tombs of the dukes. This illustrates the strong cultural links between Lorraine and Italy in this period, and most painters of any significance who were born in the duchy travelled to Italy early in their lives, some never to return, including François de Nomé, Didier Barra, Charles Mellin and François Collignon; Claude Lorrain returned briefly to Nancy in 1625–6.

Little is known of large-scale painting in Lorraine before 1600. An astonishing number of distinguished artists were born in the years around that date, however, and the region became the most interesting artistically in the French-speaking world during the early 17th century (*see* NANCY, §2). The court, however, lacked the resources to maintain permanent teams of artists and only a minority were directly employed. The principal court painters were JACQUES BELLANGE and his pupil and successor CLAUDE DÉRUET; their contribution seems smaller than it actually was, for much comprised temporary settings for the court festivities and decorative paintings (all destr.) in the Palais Ducal at Nancy. Others who worked partly for the dukes were JEAN LECLERC and the etcher and draughtsman Jacques Callot, who had previously spent ten years at the court of Florence.

The dukes were in exile during the protracted French occupation from 1633 and artistic activity virtually ceased, although Georges de La Tour worked for the French governor, Henri, Maréchal de La Ferté-Sénectère (1600–80). A measure of independence was restored to Lorraine by the Treaty of Ryswick (1697), Duke Leopold (*reg* 1697–1729) returned and building revived. This included the Baroque-classical cathedral (1703–36), Nancy, which was erected to designs by Giovanni Betto (1640–1722), revised successively by Jules Hardouin Mansart (1706) and GERMAIN BOFFRAND. After 1702 Leopold moved the court to Lunéville, where he commissioned a vast château from Boffrand (for discussion and illustration *see* LUNÉVILLE), made urban improvements and encouraged the manufacture of weapons, tapestries and ceramics. Leopold's son, Francis III (*reg* 1729–36), renounced the duchy in order

*State Funeral of Charles III, Duke of Lorraine*, engraving by Friedrich Brentel I (Nancy, Musée Historique Lorrain); from *Monumenta scenica*

to marry the Archduchess (from 1740 Empress) Maria-Theresa, whereon he became Grand Duke of Tuscany; in 1745 he was recognized as Emperor Francis I (*reg* 1745–65; *see* HABSBURG-LORRAINE).

The largest single visible memorial to ducal patronage in Nancy is also the last: the beautiful sequence of buildings and squares laid out from 1752 to 1760 to the order of STANISLAV I LESZCZYNSKI (*reg* 1736–66), who was given the vacant dukedom of Lorraine by his son-in-law, Louis XV of France, as compensation for losing the throne of Poland. The elegant architecture of this scheme (for discussion and illustration *see* HÉRÉ, EMMANUEL; *see also* NANCY, fig. 1), together with its superb Rococo ironwork (*see* NANCY, fig. 2) by Jean Lamour (1698–1771), make the town centre of Nancy one of the prettiest in France. After Stanislav's death in 1766, Lorraine was absorbed permanently into French national territory.

BIBLIOGRAPHY
R. Parisot: *Histoire de Lorraine* (Paris, 1922)
R. Taveneaux: *Histoire de Nancy* (Toulouse, 1978)
*Claude Gellée et les peintres lorrains en Italie au XVIIe siècle* (exh. cat. by J. Thuillier, Rome, Acad. France; Nancy, Mus B.-A., 1982) [intro. on Lorraine in the 17th century by R. Taveneaux]

MICHAEL KITSON

**Lorsch Abbey.** Former Benedictine abbey *c.* 15 km northwest of Mannheim, Germany.

1. ABBEY. Lorsch was one of the most important abbeys in the early Middle Ages. It was founded in 764 by Graf Cancor and settled with monks from the abbey of Gorze. The first buildings, revealed by excavation, were on the Kreuzwiese near Lorsch and consisted of a simple hall-like church with a rectangular chancel and the conventual buildings to the north grouped around a square cloister. As early as 765 Bishop Chrodegang of Metz arranged for the translation of the body of St Nazarius from Rome to Lorsch. This precious relic ensured the rapid prosperity of the monastery and in 767 resulted in the rebuilding of the abbey on the present site, about 500 m from its original location.

The new church was an aisled basilica with no transept, but with a separate sanctuary of either rectangular or apsidal plan adjoining the nave at its east end. To the west the basilica was preceded by a westwork and an almost square atrium. The westwork is the earliest known example, dating from a quarter of a century before Centula. The atrium was situated in the area of the only surviving part of the church. The church was consecrated in 774 in the presence of Charlemagne. The first monastic buildings were wooden and situated north of the church, but *c.* 800 these were replaced by a grand stone monastery to the south. These new monastic buildings included the so-called *Ecclesia triplex*, a puzzling church, aisled but very small, in the corner between the east range of the monastery and the sanctuary of the abbey church. The abbey was given special significance when King Louis the German (*reg* 817–76) decided to be buried there. Louis the younger commissioned the so-called *Ecclesia varia*, a richly decorated funerary chapel, added *c.* 870 to the choir of the church. Those buried there included Louis the German,

Louis the younger, his son Hugo, Count Werinher, Queen Kunigunde and others. After a fire in 1090, the westwork and atrium were replaced by a narthex, which survives. A new atrium extended far to the west and enclosed the surviving Torhalle (gate-house). Another gate-house was added at this time to the south-east of the monastery wall. There were minor additions in the Gothic period. In 1555 the monastery was converted to a secular college. In 1620–21 it was burnt by Spanish troops, then abandoned and dismantled except for the Torhalle and the Romanesque narthex.

2. TORHALLE. The so-called Torhalle (see fig.) is of exceptional art-historical importance. The building consists of a central transverse structure, the long sides facing east–west, with a staircase at each end. As in a gate-house, the central part is open at ground-level, through three arches; there is a wooden ceiling. The upper storey is occupied by a single large hall lit by windows placed above the ground-floor arches. The long sides of the building were intended for display and are expensively inlaid with white and red sandstone plaques. On the ground-floor the arches are flanked by engaged columns, resembling Roman triumphal arches, with excellent Carolingian composite capitals. Above the arches is a string course with palmettes, which also runs round the ends of the building, but not round the staircases. The upper walls are articulated by small fluted pilasters and pointed arches. At the top of the wall is a console cornice based on ancient models. It formerly extended to the gables and reveals the slope of the roof (c. 30°) before the gables were built to a steeper pitch probably c. 1400. The Torhalle is extraordinarily well preserved, not least because of its mortar which is almost

as hard as concrete. Of the decoration, only the slabs of inlay, the windows and a few sandstone blocks in the column bases have had to be renewed. The north staircase was rebuilt during the restoration in 1934–5 after its collapse in 1842.

The ground-floor is conceived simply as a space for passing through. The room in the upper storey was originally painted illusionistically to look like a loggia with a parapet of square plaques imitating marble, with Ionic columns above surmounted by an architrave. About 1400 this painting was replaced by depictions of angelic choirs extending up into the gables, which shows that at that time the room was used for religious purposes. Its original function is unknown; the cool architectural painting suggests a secular use, especially since there was no provision for an altar, like that created in, for example, the early Romanesque gate-house on Frauenchiemsee (Bavaria).

The Lorsch building was once completely free-standing in the middle of the open site to the west of the abbey church, almost exactly on the church's axis. As it was never the gateway to the monastery, it can therefore be called a gate-house only in a figurative sense, and scholars were quick to suggest that it should be interpreted as a triumphal arch. There is still controversy about its precise function and its date, especially since there is no documentary record of the Torhalle before 1632. Scholars agree only that it was built in the Carolingian period, and there have long been two main theories. One proposes that the Torhalle was erected in the early period of the abbey as the gate-house to the monastic precinct or as a gateway in honour of Charlemagne on his victorious return to Lorsch in 774, after his campaign against the Lombards. The other theory, based more on stylistic grounds (the antique-style capitals), is that it is a creation of the high point of the Carolingian Renaissance around 800 and may therefore be a monumental triumphal arch intended for Charlemagne's coronation as emperor. Since the Torhalle's composite capitals mentioned above are re-used, the dating 800–20 would provide only a *terminus post quem*. However, the destroyed *Ecclesia varia* can be shown to have had similar decoration, so a dating of the Torhalle to the time of the *Ecclesia varia* has been suggested (Jacobsen).

BIBLIOGRAPHY
R. Adamy: *Die fränkische Thorhalle und Klosterkirche zu Lorsch an der Bergstrasse* (Darmstadt, 1891)
W. M. Dammann, ed.: *Die Kunstdenkmäler im Grossherzogthum Hessen: Provinz Starkenburg: Kreis Bensheim* (Darmstadt, 1914)
A. Fuchs: *Die Königshalle des Klosters Lorsch* (Paderborn, 1929)
F. Behn: *Die karolingische Klosterkirche von Lorsch an der Bergstrasse. Nach den Ausgrabungen von 1927–1928 und 1932–1933* (Berlin/Leipzig, 1934)
W. Meyer-Barkhausen: 'Die "Ecclesia triplex" des Klosters Lorsch', *Z. Dt. Ver. Kstwiss.*, ii (1935), pp. 351–60
H. Walbe: 'Das Kloster Lorsch: Torhalle–Kirche–Atrium', *Dt. Kst- & Dkmlpf.* (1935), pp. 126–42
F. Behn: 'Die zweite Torhalle von Lorsch', *Das Münster*, iii (1950), pp. 336–40
W. Meyer-Barkhausen: 'Die Lorscher Torhalle und die karolingische Renaissance', *Die Starkenburg*, xii (1953), pp. 22–35; *Laurissima jubilans: Festschrift zur 1200. Jahrfeier von Lorsch 1964* (Mainz, 1964)
F. Oswald, L. Schaefer and H. R. Sennhauser: *Vorromanische Kirchenbauten: Katalog der Denkmäler bis zum Ausgang der Ottonen* (Munich, 1966–71), iii, pp. 179–83
W. Braunfels: *Die Welt der Karolinger und ihre Kunst* (Munich, 1968), pp. 112, 374

Lorsch Abbey, Torhalle, view from the west

W. Einsingbach, ed.: *Die Kunstdenkmäler des Landes Hessen: Kreis Bergstrasse* (Munich, 1969), pp. 338–60
*Die Reichsabtei Lorsch: Festschrift zum Gedenken an ihre Stiftung 764*, 2 vols (Darmstadt, 1973–7)
P. Schnitzer, ed.: *Beiträge zur Geschichte des Klosters Lorsch*, Geschichtsblätter Kreis Bergstrasse (Lorsch, 2/1980) [suppl. issue]
W. Jacobsen: 'Die Lorscher Torhalle: Zum Problem ihrer Datierung und Deutung. Mit einem Katalog der bauplastischen Fragmente als Anhang', *Jb. Zentinst. Kstgesch.*, i (1985), pp. 9–75

WERNER JACOBSEN

**Lory, (Mathias) Gabriel**, the younger (*b* Berne, *bapt* 21 June 1784; *d* Berne, 25 Aug 1846). Swiss painter, watercolourist and engraver. He was trained by his father, Gabriel Ludwig Lory (1763–1840), an engraver and watercolourist. He was a precociously talented child and soon began to earn his own living. He collaborated with his father on a number of illustrated books, including the very popular *Voyage pittoresque de Genève à Milan par le Simplon* (Neuchâtel, 1810). In Neuchâtel, Lory met the Swiss landscape painter Maximilien de Meuron. Together they travelled to Paris (1808), Milan (1809) and Rome and Naples (1811). During these trips Lory developed a freer and better organized style of painting than his father, in such paintings as *The Capucine Convent at Albano* (1811; Berne, Kstmus.). He married Louise de Meuron in 1812, and his wife subsequently took care of the production and colouring of prints, while he went in search of commissions abroad.

In 1814 Lory travelled to Guernsey and made himself known in England. The *Voyage pittoresque de Genève à Milan par le Simplon* was translated and published by Rudolph Ackermann in London in 1820, as were some plates of Swiss costumes. Returning to Neuchâtel, he became acquainted with Comte Frédéric de Pourtalès-Castellane, a banker and patron, who took him to Italy several times. Lory was an excellent watercolourist, as in for example *Departure for the Alpine Pastures* (1830; Zurich, Ksthaus), and his reputation was mainly due to his hand-coloured engravings of landscapes, genre scenes and local costumes, which were published as single plates or in works such as *Souvenirs de la Suisse* (Berne and Neuchâtel, 1829) or *Les Costumes suisses* (Neuchâtel, 1824).

In 1828 Lory again went to Paris, where he received commissions from Charles X. During the winters of 1834–5 and 1835–6 he taught drawing at the Prussian court, where he was awarded the title of visiting professor by the Akademie der Künste in Berlin.

BIBLIOGRAPHY
*Les Alpes dans la peinture suisse* (exh. cat., Chur, Bündner Kstmus., 1977)
C. De Mandach: *Deux peintres suisses: Gabriel Lory le père (1763–1840), Gabriel Lory le fils (1784–1846)* (Geneva, 1978)
*Les Petits Maîtres: Vision d'une Suisse idyllique* (exh. cat., Vevey, Mus. Jenisch, 1986)

ANNE PASTORI ZUMBACH

**Los Angeles.** North American city and seat of Los Angeles County, California. It is located on the Pacific coast in the southern part of the state, *c.* 600 km south of San Francisco and just over 200 km north of the Mexican border. It is the second largest city (population *c.* 3.4 million) in the USA. Los Angeles itself forms the hub of a vast metropolis (population *c.* 8.7 million) that comprises about 100 other urban centres, including Pasadena, Long Beach, Santa Monica and Beverly Hills; it is characterized by extensive freeway development because of lack of public transport. The city is the centre of the American film industry, around which a thriving artistic community developed; it is also a centre of high technology.

1. History and urban development. 2. Art life and organization.

1. HISTORY AND URBAN DEVELOPMENT. El Pueblo de Nuestra Señora La Reina de Los Angeles was founded on 4 September 1781 by Felipe de Neve, the Spanish governor of the Province of California, on the Los Angeles River *c.* 48 km from the Pacific Ocean. The site for the settlement was selected because of the year-round availability of water and the potential fertility of the area: it was one of the first communities in Spanish Alta California that was not founded as a mission or a military base but was intended to grow food for the province. In October 1781 Neve issued a planning ordinance for Los Angeles that was based on the 'Leyes de Indias' (1573) issued by King Philip II of Spain. As well as providing lots for agriculture and housing and land for common pasturage, Neve noted in this ordinance the settlement's existing grid plan around a central plaza; after a flood in 1815, however, its centre was moved to higher land further south. Throughout its first 40 years the community remained less important than the nearby missions of San Gabriel and San Fernando. After Mexican independence (1821), when California became a province of Mexico, Los Angeles began to assume greater economic and political importance. San Pedro and its bay to the south emerged as the port, while the town itself became increasingly cosmopolitan, attracting migrants and commercial traders from Mexico, England and elsewhere in North America. By the early 1830s Los Angeles was the largest town in Alta California, with *c.* 1200 inhabitants, and in 1835 it was raised to the status of a city by the Mexican government. Eventually Californian government was divided, with the military governor in Monterey and the civil governor in Los Angeles. By the early 1840s the area around the central plaza had a church (1818) and a number of two-storey 'Monterey style' dwellings. In 1836 a commission was appointed to 'eliminate the extreme irregularity of the streets' that had resulted from haphazard growth. The surrounding area was scattered with one- and two-storey adobe ranch-houses, with some irrigated agriculture.

The acquisition of California by the USA in 1848 did not initially disturb the slow growth of the city. In the early 1850s there was a brief economic boom based on the sale of cattle, followed by an economic decline due to a severe drought of the late 1850s. Land surveys to establish public and private ownership, first carried out in 1846, continued in the following decades, and by the early 1880s almost all the original public land had passed into private hands, the only exception being property with no apparent economic use. Some of this land eventually became public parks: Westlake, Central, Elysian and Echo parks. Problems continually occurred with sewerage, water and transportation, which were frequently the subjects of disputes between public and private interests. The problems became particularly acute in the boom years of the 1880s, when Los Angeles was being promoted as a farming

1. Los Angeles City Hall by John C. Austin, John Parkinson and Albert C. Martin, and Austin Whittlesey, 1926–8

paradise and for its healthy climate: about 50,000 migrants had arrived by the early 1890s. In 1869 the first railway was built to the port at San Pedro, where the development of wharfs and other improvements gradually took place. In 1876 Los Angeles was connected with the rest of the USA by the completion of the Southern Pacific Railroad. In the mid-1880s, as a direct response to land speculation, an electric railway was established; in 1892 this passed into the hands of Henry E. Huntington, who developed it as the Pacific Electric Railroad Co. Private interests also tended to dominate water and sewerage throughout the 1880s and 1890s: only in 1902 did the city finally acquire the Los Angeles Water Co.

By the 1890s the general pattern of Los Angeles was firmly established as a series of independent or semi-independent towns and industrial centres, separated by acres of low-density suburban districts interspersed with orchards and market gardens. The city centre of Los Angeles, which had by then moved south over Bunker and Fort hills, was only the largest of several 'downtown' areas held together by the lines of the Pacific Electric Railroad. Architecturally, by the later 1880s Los Angeles was as vigorous as any other American city. Its commercial and institutional buildings reflected the Romanesque Revival style of H. H. Richardson and the newly emerging classicism of the Beaux-Arts style, while in domestic architecture the Queen Anne Revival and COLONIAL REVIVAL held sway; in the 1890s the Los Angeles region played a major role in the introduction and adaptation of the regional Spanish Mission Revival style. Another popular form of regional architecture, which was eventually exported outside the state, was the California bungalow,

characterized by rustic interiors and exteriors, wide overhanging eaves and extensive porches (*see also* BUNGALOW).

After the World's Columbian Exposition (1893) in Chicago, Los Angeles, in common with other American cities, was strongly influenced by the City Beautiful Movement. In 1904 Los Angeles enacted one of the USA's first zoning ordinances, setting aside an area exclusively for residential use; two more far-reaching zoning ordinances followed in 1908 and 1909. These measures were upheld by the American Supreme Court in 1915, thus establishing the rights of government to regulate private property for the public good. The city's population tripled between 1900 and 1910, and in 1909 the city planner Charles Mulford Robinson was engaged to prepare general planning guidelines for its growth; in 1910 an official city planning committee was appointed, supplemented in 1913 by a private city planning association that was ultimately more influential. Los Angeles acquired an ocean port after San Pedro and Wilmington were incorporated into the city in 1909, followed by major improvements (e.g. breakwaters, dredging and docks) in these areas as well as at Long Beach during the next decade. New water supplies were provided by the construction (1907–13) of the Los Angeles Aqueduct, superseded in the late 1930s by the All American Canal. Ordinances limited buildings to no more than 150 ft (45.7 m) in height from the 1910s to the 1950s. This policy, resulting from both aesthetic and seismic considerations, encouraged the city's horizontal growth.

The question of a civic centre for the city and county of Los Angeles had surfaced as part of the City Beautiful Movement; concrete proposals were made in 1917, but little happened until the 1920s, when a number of proposals were made by Wilbur D. Cook and George O. Hall, Frank Lloyd Wright, William W. Woollett and the Allied Architectural Association. The latter's beautiful Beaux-Arts scheme was finally adopted, although the only major building carried out was the Los Angeles City Hall (1926–8; see fig. 1) by John C. Austin, John Parkinson and Albert C. Martin, and Austin Whittlesey. In the 1930s the scheme was 'modernized' by a consortium of the Southern California Chapter of the American Institute of Architects, directed by Sumner Spaulding. Its partial realization (with an entirely different Modernist architectural image) occurred only after World War II. The 1920s and 1930s were also marked by the growth of the large film studios, in particular in the Hollywood area, where the first studio was established in 1911. Despite developments in the city centre, however, planning in Los Angeles was dominated by the ideal of universal middle-class single-family housing in the suburbs, facilitated by freedom of movement provided by the motor car. This was the theme of the regional plan of 1941 for the Los Angeles Basin. Indeed from the late 1910s planning had concentrated on the road network. The concept of encouraging linear commercial strips, as eventually occurred on Wilshire Boulevard and Ventura Boulevard, for example, was formulated in the 1920s by the staff of the Regional Planning Commission, the first county-wide planning organization in the USA (established 1922). At the same time the Automobile Club of Southern California commissioned the preparation of a regional highway plan.

By the early 1920s Los Angeles and Southern California in general were committed to the ideal of creating a new Mediterranean world in California, and Hispanic and Italian architectural influences dominated the design of both buildings and landscapes. This was followed by Art Deco influence in the 1930s and buildings in the 'Streamline Moderne' style. By the mid-1920s Los Angeles had also emerged as a centre for Modernist architecture, notably through the work of IRVING GILL, RUDOLPH SCHINDLER and RICHARD NEUTRA and, in the 1930s, that of a younger generation of Modernists, Gregory Ain, Harwell Hamilton Harris and Raphael S. Soriano.

In the last years of the Great Depression, the city's first freeway, the Pasadena Freeway (1934–42), was opened, accompanied by a renaissance of 'drive-in' architecture and the first large-scale public-housing programmes. After 1945 there was a frenzy of freeway construction and suburban expansion, together with the development of regional shopping centres (closely associated with the planning firm of Victor Gruen) and additional commercial strips. By the late 1960s the region of Los Angeles encompassed an area extending from Riverside and San Bernardino in the east to Thousand Oaks and Malibu in the west, the principal public spaces comprising the luxuriously landscaped freeways and their sculptural interchanges.

After 1945 architecture in Los Angeles developed in a variety of directions. Although the California ranch-house remained the dominant form for domestic architecture, the International Style and late Modernism were employed for commercial buildings, as seen in the aluminium-clad twin Century City Towers (1968–72) by Minoru Yamasaki and in buildings erected in the commercial construction boom of the 1980s. A more idiosyncratic form of Modernism and Post-modernism was also seen, for example in the California Aerospace Museum and Theater (1982–4; for illustration see GEHRY, FRANK O.), which has a full-size jet fighter attached to the façade. Gehry also produced a temporary space for the Museum of Contemporary Art, involving rehabilitation of two old warehouse buildings owned by the city. Conservation and rehabilitation of historic buildings became increasingly popular as part of a renewed enthusiasm for California's real and imagined Hispanic heritage. The pressures of enormous growth after the mid-1950s also led to new planning and housing initiatives and efforts to solve severe pollution and traffic problems.

#### BIBLIOGRAPHY
C. Nordhoff: *California for Health, Pleasure and Residence* (New York, 1873)
J. M. Guinn: 'Los Angeles in the Adobe Age', *Hist. Soc. S. CA Q.*, iv (1897), pp. 49–55
C. M. Robinson: *The City Beautiful: Suggestions for Los Angeles* (Los Angeles, 1909)
G. Wharton James: *California, Romantic and Beautiful* (Boston, 1914)
G. Whitnall: 'Tracing the Development of Planning in Los Angeles', *Annu. Rep. LA Plan. Comm.* (1930)
G. W. Robbins and D. L. Tilton, eds: *Preface to a Master Plan* (Los Angeles, 1941)
*Los Angeles: A Guide to the City and its Environs*, Works Projects Administration (New York, 1941)
M. Scott: *Metropolitan Los Angeles: One Community* (Los Angeles, 1949)
E. McCoy: 'Wilshire Boulevard', *W. Architect & Engin.*, ccxxii/3 (1961)
P. J. Ouellet: *City Planning in Los Angeles* (Los Angeles, 1964)
R. M. Fogelson: *The Fragmented Metropolis: Los Angeles, 1850–1930* (Cambridge, MA, 1967)
R. Banham: *Los Angeles: The Architecture of Four Ecologies* (London, 1974)
D. Gebhard and H. VonBreton: *L.A. in the 30s* (Salt Lake City, 1975)
D. Streatfield: 'The Evolution of the California Landscape', *Landscape Archit.*, lxvi (1976–7), pp. 39–78, 117–27, 229–39 and 417–27
D. Brodsly: *L.A. Freeway: An Appreciative Essay* (Berkeley, CA, 1981)
P. Gleye: *The Architecture of Los Angeles* (San Diego, 1981)
D. Crouch, D. Garr and A. L. Mundigo: *Spanish City Planning in North America* (Cambridge, MA, 1982)
C. W. Moore, P. Becker and R. Campbell: *Los Angeles: The City Observed: A Guide to its Architecture and Landscape* (New York, 1984)
D. Gebhard and R. W. Winter: *Architecture in Los Angeles: A Compleat Guide* (Salt Lake City, 1985)

DAVID GEBHARD

### 2. ART LIFE AND ORGANIZATION.

(i) Art life. (ii) Museums.

*(i) Art life.* It was not until the mid-1880s that a sophisticated community of artists, most of whom were trained in Europe or on the East Coast, began to develop in Los Angeles. Between 1887 and 1892 two art schools and two art clubs were founded, and a room was set aside in the Chamber of Commerce for use as a gallery. Although some artists painted portraits and still-lifes (e.g. *Grapes* (1902; Santa Ana, CA, Bowers Mus) by Alberta McCloskey (1859–1941)), the majority painted landscapes, mostly working in conservative styles, and were influenced by German painting and the Barbizon school. By c. 1914 most artists had adopted Impressionism in one form or another. In the 1920s some landscape painters were dubbed the 'Eucalyptus school' because their favourite subject seemed to be eucalyptus trees dotting rolling plains. The most talented landscape painters were Guy Rose (1867–1925), William Wendt (1865 1946), Marian Wachtel (1876–1954), Elmer Wachtel (1864–1929), Benjamin Brown (1865–1942), Alson Clark (1876–1949), Edgar Payne (1882–1947) and Granville Redmond (1871–1935). William Wendt's *Where Nature's God hath Wrought* (1925; Los Angeles, CA, Co. Mus. A.) is a prime example.

During the Depression Los Angeles began to compete in the mainstream of American art as a result of the Federal Arts Project (see UNITED STATES OF AMERICA, §XII) and improved coast-to-coast transportation. The initiatives of the Federal Arts Project, the Public Works of Art Project and the Treasury Department encouraged artists to work in formerly neglected media, including sculpture, printmaking, drawing, murals and mosaics in public buildings. Most importantly, a small group of artists led by Millard Sheets (1907–89) developed a particularly virile style of watercolour painting. Known as the 'California watercolor style', it often utilized full sheets of watercolour paper, bold brushwork and saturated colours. Their subjects were landscapes and the activities of the average man in the local region (e.g. *Beer for Prosperity* (1933; Laguna Beach, CA, A. Mus.) by Millard Sheets). Important among these artists were Lee Blair (1911–93), Rex Brandt (*b* 1914), Phil Dike (1906–90), Emil Kosa (1903–68), Barse Miller (1904–73) and Phil Paradise (*b* 1905). Paul Sample (1896–1974) and Ben Messick (1901–81) were important regionalist painters in oil, who confronted social issues. Hollywood's film industry supported many of these artists by employing them as art directors, matte artists, animators and photographers.

2. David Hockney: *A Bigger Splash*, acrylic on canvas, 2.42×2.43 m, 1967 (London, Tate Gallery)

In the 1930s modernism began to take hold in Los Angeles. STANTON MACDONALD-WRIGHT, co-inventor of Synchronism in Paris shortly before World War I, had returned to Los Angeles in 1919 and was teaching, but it was Post-Surrealism, introduced by Lorser Feitelson (1898–1978) and Helen Lundeberg (*b* 1908) in 1933, that had the greatest influence on the West Coast. Other 1930s modernists utilizing various European styles included Peter Krasnow (1886–1979) and Knud Merrild (1894–1954). Merrild created *Flux c.* 1942, now recognized as one of the earliest forms of Abstract Expressionism. From the late 1930s several European Modernists sought refuge in Los Angeles from political developments in Europe, including the avant-garde animator Oskar Fischinger, the Romantic Surrealist Eugene Berman and the Dada artist Man Ray.

After World War II artists in Los Angeles were divided between modernists and conservatives, the latter developing a strong studio crafts movement. Rico Lebrun (1900–64), who dominated the influential Jepson Art Institute (1945–53), led many artists to the medium of drawing and to his stylistic combination of Romantic Surrealism and Abstract Expressionism. Beginning in the late 1940s four modernists, Lorser Feitelson, John McLaughlin (1898–1976), Frederick Hammersley (*b* 1919), and Karl Benjamin (*b* 1925), independently developed styles later known as Abstract Classicism, marked by flat coloured shapes with hard edges. In 1954 Peter Voulkos (*b* 1924) arrived to teach ceramics at the Otis Art Institute. In the late 1950s he moved from studio pottery to Abstract Expressionist ceramic sculpture, starting California's important fine arts ceramics movement. His most important followers were John Mason (*b* 1927) and Kenneth Price (*b* 1935). EDWARD KIENHOLZ moved to Los Angeles in

1953. He created assemblages constructed from discarded, often nostalgic objects (e.g. *Back Seat Dodge '38*, 1964; Los Angeles, CA, Lyn Kienholz col.). Other important practitioners were Wallace Berman (1926–76) and Bruce Conner (*b* 1933). Kienholz also founded the Ferus Gallery with Walter Hopps in 1957. This immediately became the focal point for avant-garde artists and remained so for ten years.

Art in Los Angeles during the 1960s was described by Peter Plagens as 'cool, semi-technological, industrially pretty' (1974, p. 120). Contemporary art benefited from the national arts explosion of the 1960s. New museums opened, existing museums expanded and a wealth of new commercial galleries were founded. For the next two decades, new styles followed each other quickly. Abstract Expressionism was represented by Richard Diebenkorn, who moved to Los Angeles in 1966, and by John Altoon (1925–69). The Pop artists Billy Al Bengston (*b* 1934), Joe Goode (*b* 1937), Edward Ruscha and transplanted Londoner DAVID HOCKNEY used locally recognized words and symbols in highly finished drawings and paintings; Hockney's work after his move to Los Angeles in 1963, for example, reflected his experience of an uninhibited lifestyle dominated by sunshine, palm trees and swimming pools (see fig. 2). Los Angeles artists also began to develop their own 'look', sometimes dubbed 'L.A. glass and plastic' or 'Finish–Fetish' because the art was made with industrial materials such as spray paints, plastic and treated glass. Leaders in the use of plastics and the interest in light were Robert Irwin, Larry Bell, Craig Kauffman (*b* 1932) and DeWain Valentine (*b* 1936), who made wall-hung and free-standing sculptures. In the 1970s this interest led to room environments where light (both natural and artificial) became the medium for creating an environment in an enclosed space, such as an empty room or museum gallery. Other practitioners were James Turrell, Douglas Wheeler (*b* 1939), Eric Orr (*b* 1939), Michael Asher (*b* 1943) and Hap Tivey (*b* 1947). Los Angeles also enjoyed a renaissance in printmaking. In 1960 JUNE WAYNE opened the internationally renowned Tamarind Lithography Workshop, which spawned Gemini G.E.L. (Graphic Editions Limited) in 1966 and Cirrus Editions, Ltd in 1970. Printmakers experimented with such techniques as double-layered torn lithographs, screenprinting on perspex and photolithography. Creative photography was practised at UCLA, where Robert Heinecken encouraged his students to print on a variety of materials and to incorporate photographs into other fine art media such as sculpture and printmaking.

From the 1970s Los Angeles artists considered themselves in the international mainstream, many of them living for part of the year on the American East Coast or in Europe. Their experimentation continued, supported by a growing group of collectors, the Museum of Contemporary Art (opened 1979) and the expanded Modern and Contemporary Art Department of the County Museum of Art. In the late 1960s and 1970s PHOTOREALISM, using banal imagery from everyday life, was developed by Robert Cottingham (*b* 1935), D. J. Hall (*b* 1951), Lawrence Dreiband (*b* 1944) and Bruce Everett (*b* 1942). Realistic figural compositions with enigmatic meanings, landscapes that made statements about society or ecology and still-lifes of new products were created by Richard Joseph (*b* 1939), Vija Celmins (*b* 1939), Paul Sarkesian (*b* 1928) and James Valerio (*b* 1938). Video art was produced by such artists as Roland Reiss (*b* 1929) and Michael McMillen (*b* 1946). The main practitioner of performance art was Chris Burden (*b* 1946). Minimalist sculptors working on a massive scale included Guy Dill (*b* 1946), Jud Fine (*b* 1944) and Michael Todd (*b* 1935).

In the 1960s and 1970s the number of women artists and artists from various ethnic minorities increased, and cultural centres specifically dedicated to their arts were established. Los Angeles, with the largest population of Mexicans outside Mexico City, has some major Chicano artists, including Frank Romero (*b* 1941), Diane Gamboa (*b* 1957) and Gronk (*b* 1954). It has also become one of the major sites for outdoor murals, ranging from those sponsored by commercial companies and government bodies to the Photorealistic murals painted by the Fine Arts Squad (five semi-anonymous muralists) to murals with a social message created by members of minorities.

From the 1980s economic recession and a decline in the frantic experimentation of the 1960s and 1970s left artists temporarily without a direction, although some exciting work was accomplished with new technologies such as computers. In the 1990s the art of many Los Angeles artists reflected a sense of psychological alienation, dispossession and disorder, dealing with such issues as AIDS, homelessness and increasing violence.

*(ii) Museums.* Los Angeles is well endowed with museums. The Museum of Contemporary Art houses a permanent collection of international range, representing art from 1940 onwards. Built of red sandstone on seven levels, with pyramidal skylights, it was designed by Arata Isozaki and opened in late 1986. Los Angeles County Museum of Art is the largest museum complex in Los Angeles, its original buildings having been supplemented in the 1980s by the Robert O. Anderson Building, built to house 20th-century art, and the Pavilion for Japanese Art, with the Sinen-Kan collection of more than 300 Japanese scroll paintings and screens. The Craft and Folk Art Museum on Wilshire Boulevard exhibits crafts from around the world, including folk art, textiles and masks from America, Japan, Mexico, and the East Indies. Santa Monica has become a major centre for the Los Angeles art community. The Santa Monica Museum of Art, designed by local architect Frank Gehry and opened in the early 1990s, presents the work of performance and video artists and exhibits works of lesser-known painters and sculptors.

The J. Paul Getty Museum building is a re-creation of a 1st-century AD Roman villa that stood on the slopes of Mt Vesuvius overlooking the Bay of Naples. The collections were established originally in Getty's home before being moved to the present building, completed in 1974. The museum houses an impressive collection of Greek and Roman antiquities, 18th-century decorative arts and Renaissance and Baroque drawings and paintings, in which all major schools of Western art from the late 13th century to the late 19th are represented. The new Getty Center complex in Brentwood, designed by Richard Meier, is due to open in 1997.

The Norton Simon Museum in Pasadena was, like the Getty, founded essentially by a single wealthy individual. Simon reorganized the failing Pasadena Museum of Modern Art in 1974 and assembled one of the world's finest collections, featuring paintings by Old Masters, Impressionists and Cubists, and sculptures from India, Thailand and Nepal. The Pacific Asia Museum is the city's most determinedly Chinese-style building outside Chinatown. It is designed in the style of a northern Chinese imperial palace, with a central courtyard. The museum is devoted entirely to the arts and crafts of Asia and the Pacific Islands.

Henry E. Huntington, a railway tycoon, laid out the foundations for the Huntington Library, Art Gallery and Botanical Gardens, in San Marino, in the early 1900s. It is one of the world's most extraordinary cultural complexes. The library contains six million items, among them first editions of Shakespeare and a Gutenberg Bible. The art gallery, devoted to 18th- and 19th-century British art, contains the *Blue Boy* by Gainsborough and *Sarah Siddons as the Tragic Muse* by Reynolds. The huge grounds contain stands of cacti and other succulents, azaleas, camellias and roses and a splendid Japanese garden.

The Natural History Museum of Los Angeles County houses not only collections of fossils and exhibits of mammals, bird, marine and insect life but also exhibits typifying various cultural groups including pre-Columbian artefacts and crafts from the South Pacific. The Spanish Renaissance main building with its inlaid marble floor is itself an attraction. Most museums in the Los Angeles area are closed on Mondays; the Pacific Asia Museum and the Santa Monica Museum of Art are closed on Mondays and Tuesdays, and the Norton Simon Monday to Wednesday.

BIBLIOGRAPHY

P. Plagens: *Sunshine Muse: Contemporary Art on the West Coast* (New York, 1974)
*California Design 1910* (exh. cat. by T. J. Andersen and others, Pasadena, CA, 1974)
N. D. W. Moure and L. W. Smith: *Dictionary of Art and Artists in Southern California before 1930* (Los Angeles, 1975)
*Painting and Sculpture in California: The Modern Era* (exh. cat., San Francisco, CA, MOMA, 1976)
*Los Angeles in the Seventies* (exh. cat. by M. Goldwater, Fort Worth, TX, Fort Worth A. Mus., 1977)
*Thames Television's The Art of Hollywood: Fifty Years of Art Direction*, (London, 1979)
*Painting and Sculpture in Los Angeles, 1900–1945* (exh. cat. by N. D. W. Moure, Los Angeles, CA, Co. Mus. A., 1980)
*Los Angeles Prints, 1883–1980* (exh. cat. by E. Feinblatt and B. Davis, Los Angeles, CA, Co. Mus. A., 1980–81)
*Art in Los Angeles: Seventeen Artists in the Sixties* (exh. cat. by M. Tuchman, Los Angeles, CA, Co. Mus. A.; San Antonio, TX, Mus. A., 1981–2)
R. L. Westphal: *Plein Air Painters of California: The Southland* (Irvine, CA, 1982)
*Drawings and Illustrations by Southern California Artists before 1950* (exh. cat. by N. D. W. Moure, Laguna Beach, CA, Mus. A., 1982)
G. T. McClelland and J. T. Last: *The California Style: California Watercolour Artists, 1925–1955* (Beverly Hills, 1985)
*Early Artists in Laguna Beach: The Impressionists* (exh. cat. by J. B. Dominik, Laguna Beach, CA, A. Mus., 1986)
*Masters of Starlight: Photographers in Hollywood* (exh. cat. by D. Fahey and L. Rich, Los Angeles, CA, Co. Mus. A., 1987)
*Regionalism: The California View. Watercolors, 1929–1945* (exh. cat. by S. M. Anderson and R. Henning jr, Santa Barbara, CA, Mus. A., 1988)
*Forty Years of California Assemblage* (exh. cat., Los Angeles, UCLA, Wight A.G., 1989)
*California Light, 1900–1930* (exh. cat. by P. Trenton and W. H. Gerdts, Laguna Beach, CA, A. Mus., 1990)

*Turning the Tide: Early Los Angeles Modernists, 1920–1956* (exh. cat. by P. J. Karlstrom and S. Ehrlich, Santa Barbara, CA, Mus. A., 1990)

R. L. Westphal and J. B. Dominik: *American Scene Painting: California, 1930s and 1940s,* (Irvine, CA, 1991)

*Helter Skelter: L.A. Art in the 1990s* (exh. cat. by P. Schimmel, Los Angeles, CA, Mus. Contemp. A., 1992)

J. Butterfield: *The Art of Light + Space,* (New York, 1993)

R. J. Dunitz: *Street Gallery: Guide to 1000 Los Angeles Murals* (Los Angeles, 1993)

*Loners, Mavericks & Dreamers: Art in Los Angeles before 1900* (exh. cat. by N. D. W. Moure, Laguna Beach, CA, A. Mus., 1993)

*Proof: Los Angeles Art and the Photograph, 1960–1980* (exh. cat. by C. Desmarais, Laguna Beach, CA, A. Mus., 1993)

O. Clarke: *New Deal Murals of Los Angeles* (Albuquerque, 1995)

NANCY DUSTIN WALL MOURE

**Lo Savio, Francesco** (*b* Rome, 28 Jan 1935; *d* Marseille, 21 Sept 1963). Italian painter, sculptor and urban planner. In 1955 he obtained his diploma at the Accademia di Belle Arti in Rome and began studying architecture, heavily influenced by Walter Gropius, the Bauhaus and De Stijl. He started work as an industrial designer in 1958. He also began to execute works devoted to the study of the dynamic qualities of light in space, which some people have seen as a forerunner of conceptual art and Minimalism. Lo Savio's first monochrome paintings, based on the study of chromatic transparency, date from 1959 (e.g. *Space-Light,* Leverkusen, Schloss Morsbroich) as do his *Filters* series, which comprised layers of opaque and semi-transparent paper squares and circles. Works of this sort were shown in the same year in a group exhibition with Franco Angeli, Tano Festa, Mario Schifano (*b* 1934) and Giuseppe Uncini at the Galleria L'Appunto in Rome, and in 1960 at the Galleria La Salita in Rome with an exhibition catalogue prefaced by the French critic Pierre Restany (*b* 1930). Lo Savio also had a one-man show at the Galleria La Selecta in Rome, entitled *Spazio-luce.* In 1960 he planned his *Metals* (executed 1961), which took the form of strips of opaque black metal, bent in different ways to modulate the incidence of light (e.g. *Uniform Opaque Black Metal,* 1960; priv. col., on loan to Düsseldorf, Kstmus.). His works became particularly popular in Germany, where he participated in the *Monochrome Malerei* exhibition in Leverkusen (1960) and made contact with the Zero group, contributing to the third issue of its magazine and to its exhibitions. In 1962 Lo Savio's book *Spazio-luce* was published, and the Galleria La Salita exhibited the last phase of his work, his *Total Articulations,* matt-white cubes with open ends containing a curved black plane. His studies of light and space extended into the realm of urban planning, where he proposed a modular system based on the structure of the human body. Lo Savio committed suicide.

### WRITINGS
*Spazio-luce* (Rome, 1962)

### BIBLIOGRAPHY
*Francesco Lo Savio* (exh. cat., ed. G. Celanti; Milan, Padiglione A. Contemp., 1979)

DANIELA DE DOMINICIS

**Losenko, Anton (Pavlovich)** (*b* Glukhov, Ukraine, 30 July 1737; *d* St Petersburg, 23 Nov 1773). Ukrainian painter, active in Russia. He trained (1753–8) under Ivan Argunov, and from 1758 he was a student at the recently founded Academy of Art in St Petersburg, where he later taught. From 1760 to 1769 he spent time in Paris, where he studied at the Académie Royale de Peinture et de Sculpture under Jean Reteux (1692–1768) and Joseph-Marie Vien. He then studied in Rome. In Moscow in 1763 he participated in preparing the coronation ceremonies on the accession of Catherine II.

In 1769 Losenko returned to St Petersburg and in 1770 became a member of the academy, and a teacher there, in recognition of his painting *Vladimir and Rogneda* (1770; St Petersburg, Rus. Mus.), one of the first pictures in Russian art to take Russian history as its subject. It shows the Polovtsian Princess Rogneda, who is forced to marry Vladimir, Prince of Novgorod. While somewhat exaggerated in its use of posture and gesture, the painting reveals an evident interest in a study of the model, an attempt to invest each character with psychological complexity, and a concern with clear exposition of the principal ideological theme, the condemnation of tyranny. Losenko also treated mythological and biblical themes, for example the subject taken from Homer's *Iliad, Hector Saying Farewell to Andromache* (1773; Moscow, Tret'yakov Gal.).

Losenko is also known as a portrait painter of some of the major figures of Russian culture, for example the actor *Fyodor Volkov* (1763; St Petersburg, Rus. Mus.; copy Moscow, Tret'yakov Gal.), the founder of the first Russian professional theatre. Losenko's drawings, mostly figure studies (e.g. St Petersburg, Rus. Mus.), are notable for precision in modelling forms and delicacy of technique. Losenko also made a contribution to the Russian theory of art as author of a textbook on human proportion (1772), intended for use at the Academy of Arts.

### WRITINGS
*Iz'yasneniye kratkoy proportsii cheloveka* [An explanation of the compact proportion of man] (St Petersburg, 1772)

### BIBLIOGRAPHY
A. L. Kaganovich: *A. Losenko i russkoye iskusstvo serediny XVIII stoletiya* [A. Losenko and Russian art of the mid-18th century] (Moscow, 1963)

G. KOMELOVA

**Los Llanos,** Conde de. *See* SALAMANCA, JOSÉ.

**Los Millares.** Site of Late Neolithic or Copper Age fortified settlement, dated *c.* 3500–*c.* 2200 BC, 1.4 km south-east of Santa Fe de Mondújar, Almería, Spain. It was excavated by the Sirets (1891–2), Martin Almagro and Antonio Arribas (1953–8), and from 1978 by Arribas and Fernando Molina. Located on a steep-sided spur at the confluence of the Andarax River and the Rambla de Huéchar, the settlement is defended by at least four successive lines of fortifications, each with exterior bastions or embedded towers. The largest of these defences is the outermost wall, measuring 310 m long×2–4 m wide. In addition to 19 square or semicircular bastions, it has a large barbican-style entrance, with a series of arrow slits and a projecting pear-shaped gateway (l. 12.5 m×w. 8–12 m) with an internal rectangular passage (l. 10 m×w. 2–3.5 m). North-east of this outer line of defence are three progressively shorter lines of fortifications.

All four lines of fortifications underwent repeated reconstruction and elaboration, although the chronological relationship between different parts of the site remains unclear. Huts from an elevated area in the innermost part of the settlement have yielded a large quantity of Beaker pottery of both the early, comb-decorated, and later, incised, types (Almería, Mus. Arqueol. Prov.; Madrid, Mus. Arqueol. N.). South-west of the outermost fortification lies a broad plateau with a large megalithic cemetery comprising 85–100 tombs. Built of stone masonry and slabs and covered by tumuli, most of the tombs have circular or ovoid burial chambers measuring 3–6 m in diameter, reached by way of rectangular passages 3–6 m long. Other types of tombs include round graves without passages, oblong or trapezoidal passage graves and a cave burial. Features of these tombs include passages blocked and divided by solid and perforated 'porthole' slabs, corbel-roofed chambers, niches, side chambers, painted gypsum walls, paved floors, and forecourts, as well as external pylons and stone alignments.

Several tombs are associated with stone enclosures containing large, undecorated stone idols known as *baetyls*. Exotic grave goods range from North African ivory and ostrich eggshell to articles of jet, amber, callaïs (green stone) and alabaster. Other luxury objects include fine flint daggers, copper weapons and ornaments, and numerous decorated objects including bone, stone and ceramic vessels, bone phalange idols and stone plaques, many of them painted or incised with an 'eye' or a 'Mother Goddess' motif. South of the cemetery are at least 14 stone-built forts on a chain of hills more than 1 km from the settlement. The largest, Fort 1, is 45 m in diameter and consists of a rectangular central tower surrounded by two concentric stone ramparts with projecting bastions, some with arrow slits; each rampart was completely encircled by a large defensive ditch.

BIBLIOGRAPHY
G. Leisner and V. Leisner: *Die Megalithgräber der Iberischen Halbinsel: Der Süden*, Römisch-Germanische Forschungen, xvii (Berlin, 1943), pp. 17–54
M. Almagro and A. Arribas: *Poblado y la necrópolis megalítica de Los Millares*, Bibliotheca Praehistorica Hispana, iii (Madrid, 1963)
A. Arribas and F. Molina: 'Bell Beakers in Los Millares', *Bell Beakers of the Western Mediterranean*, i, ed. W. H. Waldren and R. E. Kennard, Brit. Arch. Rep. Int. Ser., ccci/1 (Oxford, 1987), pp. 133–46
CLAY MATHERS

**Los Molares**, 6th Conde de. *See* RIBERA, (i), (2).

**Lossow & Viehweger.** German architectural partnership formed in 1880 by William Lossow (*b* Glauchau, Saxony, 21 July 1852; *d* Heidelberg, 24 May 1914) and Hermann Viehweger (*b* Grünhain, Erzgebirge, 14 Aug 1846; *d* Dresden, 4 Dec 1922). The firm developed by 1900 into one of the most successful practices in Saxony. Lossow studied at the Dresden Polytechnikum; Viehweger studied at the Dresden Kunstakademie (1872–3) with Christian Friedrich Arnold and Karl Robert Weissbach (1834–1912), and he worked in the latter's studio. The partnership lasted until 1906, when Lossow became director of the Dresden Kunstgewerbeschule; in 1907 he formed a partnership with his son-in-law Max Hans Kühne. Lossow & Viehweger cultivated a heavy, luxuriant Baroque Revival style, often incorporating painting and sculpture into their buildings. They broke with the contemporary predilection for the Italian High Renaissance style prevalent in Dresden. Their work included the Victoriahaus (1891–2; destr.) in

Dresden, an expensive office building modelled on the Brunswick Gewandhaus and the Rathaus (1893–4) at Plauen, near Dresden. Their most extravagant Baroque Revival buildings in the city, with profuse *Jugendstil* ornamentation, were the Zentraltheater (1898–1900; destr.) and the Herzfel department store (1901; destr.) on the Altmarkt. Their style later became less emphatic, although it remained Baroque. Characteristic of this period are the Dresden Kunstgewerbeschule and Museum (1901–6) in the Güntzstrasse, the Stadttheater (1902) in Chemnitz and Schloss Elstra (1902) near Kamenz. A further step away from the historical style, although still not a complete severance, is seen in the buildings of Lossow and Kühne after 1907. Their principal work is the monumental Hauptbahnhof (1907–16) in Leipzig.

BIBLIOGRAPHY
Thieme–Becker
Obituary [Lossow], *Dt. Bauztg* (1914), pp. 490–91
Obituary [Viehweger], *Dt. Bauztg* (1922), p. 548
V. Helas: *Architektur in Dresden, 1800–1900* (Brunswick, 1985), p. 197
VOLKER HELAS

**Lost-wax casting** [Fr. *cire perdue*]. Method of hollow casting with wax (*see* METAL, §III, 1(iv)).

☐

**Lotario dei Conti di Segni.** *See* INNOCENT III.

**Loth.** German family of painters and draughtsmen. (1) Johann Ulrich Loth brought the styles of Caravaggio and Rubens to southern Germany. By his wife Livia Krumpper (*d* 1661), a painter of miniatures, he was the father of (2) Johann Carl Loth, who made his home in Venice, where many of his religious works are still to be seen.

BIBLIOGRAPHY
Thieme–Becker
J. von Sandrart: *Teutsche Academie* (1675–9); ed. A. R. Peltzer (1925), pp. 10, 99, 198–9

**(1) Johann Ulrich Loth** (*b* Munich, *c.* 1600; *d* Munich, 1662). After an apprenticeship under Peter Candid in Munich, in 1615 he was employed by Maximilian I, Duke and future Elector of Bavaria. As he gained commissions for decorative work very early in his career, he is thought to have been involved in the decoration and furnishing of the Altes Schloss at Schleissheim, and particularly in the series of tapestries created by Candid for the Wittelsbachs, evidenced by a preliminary drawing for the tapestry *January* (before 1619; Cologne, Wallraf-Richartz-Mus.). This is the only known work preceding Loth's journey to Italy in 1619. Financed by the Duke, he travelled to Rome, where he became acquainted with the works of Caravaggio, and to Venice, where encounter with the paintings of Carlo Saraceni provided him with numerous compositional ideas. By the time he reached Mantua in 1623, he had also come into contact with engravings of the works of Rubens.

Returning to Munich, Loth married Livia Krumpper in 1624 and in 1626 left the employ of the Elector and set up on his own. His earliest dated work, the *Adoration of the Magi* (1628), opened two decades in which he devoted himself largely to religious subjects for the Church and for the Elector's painting collection at Schleissheim. Versatile and eclectic, he was much influenced by Caravaggio—as in the *Death of the Virgin* (1629; Freising Cathedral), a copy of Caravaggio's altarpiece (1605/6; Paris, Louvre). He showed his ability as a decorative painter in the ceiling pictures (*c.* 1630) in the Grosser Saal at Schloss Eurasburg, near Wolfratshausen. Depicting the *Story of Samson*, with accompanying frieze pictures of the *Seven Liberal Arts*, they are among the last great works of the period of German culture preceding the impact of the Thirty Years War and are the only Caravaggesque ceiling decoration in Germany. From the same period date Loth's high-altarpiece (1631) for the Salinenkapelle in Traunstein and the *Patron Saints* (1634) in the Maria-Himmelfahrtkirche, Bad Tölz.

Works by Loth based on models by Saraceni can be identified, including monumental versions such as the altarpiece of the *Holy Family* at Füssen. The 1640s reveal increasingly the influence of Rubens, for example in the *Assumption of the Virgin* (1641; Weilheim, Maria Himmelfahrt) and *Pentecost* (1649; Munich, Heilig Geistkirche). Late in his career Johann Ulrich also worked on miniatures, as has been established (Reinold-Kohrs), in connection with the prayer book (Munich, Bayer. Staatsbib., Cod. lat. 23640, Cim. 48) of Albert V, Duke of Bavaria.

BIBLIOGRAPHY

G. von Rambaldi: 'Geschichte des Schlosses Eurasburg und seine Besitzer', *Oberbayer. Archv Vaterländ. Gesch.*, xlviii (1893), p. 71

H. Nasse: 'Der Maler Johann Ulrich Loth', *Z. Hist. Ver. Schwaben & Neuburg*, xlvii (1927), pp. 208–16

M. Reinold-Kohrs: *Nachfolger Caravaggios in Deutschland* (diss.; Freiburg im Breisgau, 1956), pp. 4–96

*Deutsche Maler und Zeichner des 17. Jahrhunderts* (exh. cat.; W. Berlin, Schloss Charlottenburg, 1966), no. 56

B. Volk-Knüttel: *Wandteppiche für den Münchener Hof nach Entwürfen von Peter Candid* (Munich and Berlin, 1976), no. 114

E. von Knorre and G. Krämer: *Gemäldekatalog der Deutschen Barockgalerie in Augsburg* (2nd edn, Augsburg, 1984), p. 170

**(2) Johann Carl Loth** [Carlotto] (*b* Munich, 1632; *d* Venice, 1698). Son of (1) Johann Ulrich Loth. As an apprentice of his father in Munich, he came into early and crucial contact with 17th-century Roman painting, before himself going to Rome, some time after 1653. In Venice, from 1656, he worked initially in the studio of Pietro Liberi, then in that of Giovanni Battista Langetti, within whose sphere he found a new direction. He was also a close friend of the painter Antonio Zanchi of Este. Johann Carl chiefly executed altar and easel pictures dominated by the nude figure. He early attained renown and an international clientele. His painting *Jupiter and Mercury in the House of Philemon and Baucis* (Vienna, Ksthist. Mus.) was purchased before 1659 by the Holy Roman Emperor Leopold I, and many of his works were subsequently bought by monarchs and ambassadors. For example the

1. Johann Carl Loth: *Good Samaritan*, oil on canvas, 1.35×1.70 m, 1697 (Brunswick, Herzog Anton Ulrich-Museum)

*Good Samaritan* (1697; Brunswick, Herzog Anton Ulrich-Mus.; see fig. 1) was painted for Duke Anton Ulrich of Brunswick's gallery in Salzdahlum.

Hubala (1981) has commented on the 'moderation of [Loth's] naturalism … while at the same time developing athletic and stirring figure portrayal and mastering the rules of classical composition'; this manner struck a contemporary chord, and the great demand for Loth's works led to the establishment in Venice of a virtual 'picture factory'. Among his many works in Venetian churches are the *Visitation* (1664; Ospedale della Pietà), the *Death of St Joseph* (*c.*1685; Venice, S Giovanni Crisostomo), a fine example of a decorative chiaroscuro effect, and an altarpiece on the same subject in S Maria Zobenigo.

A 1688 entry in the diary of the Swedish architect Nicodemus Tessin II offers an insight into Loth's studio. Tessin found him surrounded by numerous original paintings by Tintoretto and Bassano and copies of works by Veronese and was especially struck by Loth's *Good Samaritan*, which he had painted from models, including some by Michelangelo. Although Tessin expressed a low opinion of Loth's draughtsmanship, from an early stage in Loth's career his figures received a painterly look through a tenebrist emphasis on shade, a feature also typical of his paintings (see fig. 2). An impressive illustration of this is the charcoal drawing of the *Annunciation* (Munich, Staatl. Graph. Samml.). The pen-and-ink drawing of *Soldiers in front of the Burning Tent of an Old Woman* (Augsburg, Schaezlerpal.) and two circular *Hunting Scenes* on the *verso*—disputed attributions—apparently emulate Giovanni Benedetto Castiglione's curious monotypes (Windsor Castle, Berks, Royal Lib.; Chatsworth, Derbys): Castiglione's chiaroscuro effect, combining printmaking and painting, was interpreted by Loth through the use of opaque white. If these two medallions, closely influenced by Dutch Mannerism, were intended as ceiling decorations, they would be the only known indications that Loth worked as a fresco or ceiling painter.

In 1692 Loth was appointed court painter to the Emperor. His foremost pupil was the Austrian Johann Michael Rottmayr. The inscription on a marble bust (Venice, S Luca) by Heinrich Meiring (*fl* Venice, 2nd half 17th century) commemorates Loth as an 'Apelles'.

### BIBLIOGRAPHY

G. Ewald: *Johann Carl Loth* (Amsterdam, 1965)
W. J. Müller: 'Europäische Malerei', *Kunst des 17. Jahrhunderts*, ed. E. Hubala, ix of Propyläen-Kstgesch. (Berlin, 1970), p. 197
E. Hubala: *Venedig*, ii/1 of Reclams Kunstführer Italien (Stuttgart, 1974), pp. 290, 298, 307, 341
——: *Johann Michael Rottmayr* (Vienna, Munich, 1981), p. 17
*Meisterzeichnungen des deutschen Barock* (exh. cat. by R. Biedermann; Augsburg, Zeughaus, 1987), no. 41

BERNT VON HAGEN

**Loth, Wilhelm** (*b* Darmstadt, 24 Sept 1920). German sculptor and printmaker. When he was 15 he took classes in life-drawing at the Volkshochschule in Darmstadt. He also took private lessons in painting and sculpture. Rejecting the National Socialist art of, for example, Arno Breker, he was primarily influenced by the work of Wilhelm Lehmbruck and Ernst Barlach. He entered into correspondence with Käthe Kollwitz in 1937 and visited her in

2. Johann Carl Loth: *Philosopher Contemplating Mortality* (St Petersburg, Hermitage)

Berlin a year later. She advised him not to concentrate exclusively on sculpture and so was perhaps responsible for his interest in graphic work (for examples, see 1974 exh. cat.) which, in its figurative character, relates to his sculpture. The period 1940–46 was taken up with compulsory labour and military service, as well as two years as a prisoner of war. In 1943, however, Loth had also begun to attend Toni Stadler's sculpture classes at the Städelschule in Frankfurt am Main. In 1947 he continued his studies at the newly founded Künstlerkolonie in Darmstadt, and in 1948 he began to teach as an assistant at the city's Technische Hochschule. From 1953 to 1955 he was chairman of the artists' group Neue Darmstädter Sezession. In 1958 he took up a post at the Staatliche Akademie der Bildenden Künste in Karlsruhe.

In a broad sense Loth followed the neo-classical line, before moving *c.* 1955 to informal structures, also producing figurative work. The female torso was a major theme in his work; he made repeated variations on the subject with an unusual degree of consistency. In his sculptures he first used fired clay, before moving to cast bronze or iron, which he combined in various ways with stylized metal rods. He did not restrict himself to traditional representations of the torso but moved beyond it by modelling selected individual parts such as breasts, lips and vagina, sometimes in abstract forms that almost reduce them to ciphers, sometimes with a high level of direct sexuality. The angularity of the works from the 1950s (e.g. *Head 1950*, bronze, 1953; Darmstadt, Ausstellhallen Mathildenhöhe) was replaced by a phase of softer surfaces, prompted by his encounter with the work of Bernini while on a study visit to Rome in 1959 (e.g. *Torso 3/60*, bronze, 1960; Stuttgart, Staatsgal.). Technical elements entered Loth's work in 1970, alongside luxurious, highly organic forms, giving his works an increasingly fetishistic air.

BIBLIOGRAPHY

*Wilhelm Loth: Skulpturen, Zeichnungen* (exh. cat., Recklinghausen, Städt. Ksthalle, 1970)
*Loth: Plastik und Zeichnung* (exh. cat., Darmstadt, Ksthalle, 1971)
*Wilhelm Loth: 100 Blatt Druckgraphik von 1948 bis 1973 aus der Sammlung Ernst-Heinrich Kohl-Weigand* (exh. cat., St Ingbert, 1974)
Eisenwerth [J. A. Schmoll]: *Wilhelm Loth: Bildwerke in Metall, 1947–1972* (Darmstadt, 1976)
H. Keller: *Wilhelm Loth: Handzeichnungen* (Berlin, 1976)
U. Haupenthal: *Das plastische Menschenbild bei Wilhelm Loth* (Darmstadt, 1989)

DOMINIK BARTMANN

**Lothair III**, King of Germany and Holy Roman Emperor (*b* June 1075; *reg* 1125–37; *d* Breitenwang, nr Reutte, 4 Dec 1137). German ruler and patron. He belonged to the family of the Counts of Süpplingenburg. As Duke of Saxony from 1106, he led the Saxon princes opposed to Emperor Henry V (*reg* 1106–25). Lothair was elected King of Germany in 1125, although he had no hereditary claim. He asserted his rule against the opposition of the Hohenstaufen and tried to retain imperial control over the Church. In 1133 he was crowned Emperor in the Lateran, Rome, by Pope Innocent II (*reg* 1130–43). Lothair's encouragement of missionaries, including the visit of Otto of Bamberg (*c.* 1062–1139) to Pomerania in 1127 and the work of the Premonstratensians in Brandenburg from 1134, was followed by a renewed promotion of German settlement in the east. In 1135 he founded the Benedictine abbey at Königslutter (*see* KÖNIGSLUTTER, SS PETER UND PAUL) and probably commissioned the north Italian sculptor Nicholaus to build its church. Lothair's grave at Königslutter was opened in 1620 and 1978: the objects inside included an inscribed tablet and an imperial orb of lead (Brunswick, Herzog Anton Ulrich-Mus.). Contemporary representations are recorded on his seal and coins, in wall paintings in the abbey church of St Georg at Prüfening, near Regensburg (*see* ROMANESQUE, §IV, 1), and by a carved royal head from St Bonifatius (rebuilt from 1129) at Freckenhorst.

*NDB*                    BIBLIOGRAPHY

P. J. Meier, ed.: *Die Bau- und Kunstdenkmäler des Kreises Helmstedt* (1896), i of *Die Bau- und Kunstdenkmäler des Herzogthums Braunschweig* (Wolfenbüttel, 1896–1910)
P. E. Schramm: *Die deutschen Kaiser und Könige in Bildern ihrer Zeit, 751–1190* (Leipzig, 1928); ed. F. Mütherich (Munich, 1983), pp. 124–7, 253–9
*Königslutter und Oberitalien: Kunst des 12. Jahrhunderts in Sachsen* (exh. cat., ed. M. Gosebruch and H.-H. Grote; Brunswick, Landesmus. Gesch. & Vlkstum, 1980)
H. Rotting: 'Die Grablege Lothars III. in der Stiftskirche zu Königslutter', *Kirchen, Klöster, Manufakturen: Historische Kulturgüter im Lande Braunschweig* (Brunswick, 1985), pp. 61–82
T. Gädeke: *Die Architektur des Nikolaus: Seine Bauten in Königslutter und Oberitalien* (Hildesheim, Zurich and New York, 1988)

A. HAUCAP-NASS

**Lothal** [Saragwala]. Site between the Bhogavo and Sabarmati rivers, near the head of the Gulf of Khambhavat (Cambay), in Gujarat, India. It was discovered in 1954 by Shikarpur Ranganath Rao, who excavated the site for eight seasons (1954–63). It comprises two different, but continuous, occupations: the first belongs to the Harappan Urban Phase (*c.* 2500–2000 BC); the second, much smaller occupation is part of the Harappan Post-urban Phase (*c.* 2000–1750 BC). The settlement is located further to the south-east than other Harappan sites and appears to have been a frontier town, with important commercial links with non-Harappan peoples. Identification by Rao of a large, brick-lined basin on the eastern side of the settlement as a dockyard or harbour and Lothal as a port and centre of maritime commerce linking ancient India with Mesopotamia has been disputed by a number of scholars (Leshnik; Possehl).

During the Urban Phase the settlement was about 4.2 ha in size, not counting the area of the purported dockyard. On the mound adjacent to the brick-lined enclosure is a building identified as a warehouse, a long building with bathing facilities, other structures of baked brick and a typical Harappan drainage system. To the north lay the domestic quarter with private houses, while to the west was a manufacturing area. Judging from the small part of the latter area that was excavated, it is clear that Lothal was a centre of craftsmanship. The excavations uncovered finished products and waste matter from a wide range of materials, including copper, bronze, gold, cornelian, jasper, rock crystal, other hardstones, ivory and shell. Many of these materials were associated with a bead-making shop similar to one found at CHANHU-DARO. The technology used at Lothal, as documented by drills, waste materials and broken beads, is the same as that documented at Mohenjo-daro, Mehrgarh in Balochistan and Shahr-i Sokhta in Sistan.

Typical Harappan seals and sealings were found, as well as a number of more provincial glyptic objects, in particular, the surface find of a seal of Persian Gulf type. The terracotta figurines of both humans and animals are simple, even crude, and certainly unlike those from Mohenjo-daro or Harappa. Other terracotta finds include typical Harappan weights, triangular cakes, model carts and bricks. Bun-shaped copper ingots have parallels in western Asia, but the metal implements are purely Harappan in character. Fine examples of miniature bronze animals such as a bull, hare, dog and bird-headed pin were probably cast using the lost-wax process.

A small cemetery to the north-west of the site contained a number of interments. Of the 20 graves that were opened, four seem to have been cenotaphs, as were also documented at Harappa and Kalibangan, while the remainder were extended inhumations with modest grave goods. There was one double interment. Although the skeletal remains showed the same variability as found at other Harappan sites, certain features suggest biological links with the hunting and gathering peoples of this borderland region.

BIBLIOGRAPHY

S. R. Rao: 'Excavations at Lothal', *Lalit Kala*, iii–iv (1956), pp. 82–9
——: 'Further Excavations at Lothal', *Lalit Kala*, xi (1962), pp. 14–30

——: 'A "Persian Gulf" Seal from Lothal', *Antiquity*, xxxvii (1963), pp. 96–9
L. S. Leshnik: 'The Harappan "Port" at Lothal: Another View', *Amer. Anthropologist*, lxx/5 (1968), pp. 911–22
S. R. Rao: *Lothal and the Indus Civilization* (Bombay, 1973)
G. L. Possehl: 'Lothal: A Gateway Settlement of the Harappan Civilization', *Ecological Background of South Asian Prehistory*, ed. K. A. R. Kennedy and G. L. Possehl (Ithaca, 1976), pp. 118–31
S. R. Rao: *Lothal: A Harappan Port Town, 1955–62*, 2 vols, Mem. Archaeol. Surv. Ind., lxxviii (Delhi, 1979–85)
K. A. R. Kennedy and others: 'Principal-components Analysis of Prehistoric South Asian Crania', *Amer. J. Phys. Anthropol.*, lxiv/2 (1984), pp. 105–18
B. Nath and G. V. Sreenivasa Rao: 'Animal Remains from Lothal Excavations', *Lothal: A Harappan Port Town, 1955–62*, Mem. Archaeol. Surv. Ind., lxxviii/2 (Delhi, 1985), pp. 636–50
K. Ramesh Rao and K. Rao: 'Plant Remains from Lothal', *Lothal: A Harappan Port Town, 1955–62*, Mem. Archaeol. Surv. Ind., lxxviii/2 (Delhi, 1985), pp. 667–84
S. S. Sarkar: 'Human Skeletal Remains from Lothal', *Lothal: A Harappan Port Town, 1955–62*, Mem. Archaeol. Surv. Ind., lxxviii/2 (Delhi, 1985), pp. 269–304

GREGORY L. POSSEHL

**Lotharingia.** Name given to the central lands of the extensive empire consolidated by CHARLEMAGNE and frequently used in its adjectival form to identify works of art produced in the region, particularly in the 9th century. Lotharingia lay between the East Franks and the West Franks, forming a wedge-shaped corridor that extended from the Netherlands in the north down through the Alps to Italy; its inhabitants included Frisians, Flemings, Walloons, Germans and Italians.

The region was established in AD 843 by the Treaty of Verdun, which divided Charlemagne's empire between his three grandsons and gave the central territory to the eldest, Lothair I (*reg* 817–55). His son Lothair II (*reg* 855–69) inherited the area from the North Sea to the Jura that was then named after him; Provence was given to Lothair II's brother Charles (*reg* 855–63). After Lothair's death the territory was subject to disputes between the Franks and Germans; it was partitioned by the Treaty of Meersen in 870, passed into German control from the end of the 9th century and was then known as the Duchy of LORRAINE.

The province contained the major artistic centres of Tours, Metz, Aachen and Toul, and works made there are usually referred to as Lotharingian. Classical influences survived in the frescoes of Trier Cathedral and St Germain, Auxerre, while the art of engraving on rock crystal was exemplified in the crystal (London, BM) commissioned by Lothair II to commemorate his reconciliation with his wife and acceptance of the Pope's judgement against his divorce, carved with scenes from the *Life of Susanna* in the style of the Metz school (*see* CAROLINGIAN, §§VI and VII). Other work in crystal was carried out at Tours, where there was a flourishing scriptorium (*see* TOURS, §2(i)). Artistic developments were disrupted by Viking raids in the late 9th century, ending the brief floreat of this artificially created region.

BIBLIOGRAPHY
P. Grierson: 'The Great King', *The Dark Ages*, ed. D. Talbot Rice (London, 1965), pp. 269–99
M. Backes and R. Dolling: *Art of the Dark Ages* (New York, 1969)
P. Lasko: *Ars Sacra, 800–1200*, Pelican Hist. A. (Harmondsworth, 1972)
G. Barraclough: *The Crucible of Europe* (London, 1976)

CAROLA HICKS

**Lotter, Matthias** (*b* Augsburg, *c.* 1700; *d* Cape Town, 25 Dec 1751). South African silversmith of German birth. Evidence suggests that he worked in the Netherlands for a period before moving to the Cape, in the service of the Dutch East India Company, arriving on 30 December 1733. He set up business on his own on 4 October 1735. Although only nine pieces of silverware by Lotter are known, seven of which are in the Groote Kerk, Cape Town, he is the earliest Cape silversmith with sufficient pieces extant to permit an impression of his work to be formed. All the pieces closely follow patterns popular in western Europe at the end of the 17th century and early in the 18th. Two of his six children born at the Cape, Johannes Casparus Lotter (*b* 1737) and Willem Godfried Lotter (1748–1810), became silversmiths, as did his grandson Gerhardus Lotter (1764–1824; *see* SOUTH AFRICA, §X).

BIBLIOGRAPHY
S. Welz: *Cape Silver and Silversmiths* (Cape Town, 1976)

STEPHAN WELZ

**Lotti, Cosimo** (*b* Florence, 1570–80; *d* Madrid, 24 Dec 1643). Italian architect. His career began in Florence, where he was apprenticed to Bernardino Poccetti. He collaborated with Bernardo Buontalenti on the decoration (1593) of the Boboli Gardens and created several hydraulic systems for the gardens of Pratolino and Castello. He designed trophies to adorn the Via Tornabuoni façade of the Palazzo Strozzi and worked on stage settings, mainly with the dramatist Jacopo Cicognini at the court of Grand Duke Ferdinand I of Tuscany. Lotti was sent to Spain in 1626 by Grand Duke Cosimo II to serve at the court of King Philip IV. His accomplishments enabled Philip to compete with the splendour of contemporary Italian and French courts by renovating the royal gardens, which had fallen into disrepair after the expulsion of Moorish engineers, and by producing spectacular theatre settings. Lotti designed a new theatre at the royal palace of Zarzuela (1634; destr.) and the Coliseo de Comedias (begun 1638, first performance Feb 1640; destr.) at the palace of Buen Retiro, complete with sets and stage machinery. As *fontanero* (garden engineer), he also renovated the gardens of the royal palaces of Aranjuez, El Pardo, Zarzuela and Buen Retiro in the Italian manner, with innovative hydraulic systems. Aranjuez, in particular, was based on the Boboli model, with parterres and copses interspersed with numerous fountains and water games; it was highly praised by contemporary writers.

Lotti was most celebrated, however, as a designer of stage scenery. Plays with intricate stage machinery called *comedias de tramoyas* had been performed in the early 17th century; Lotti, however, with his knowledge of Italian engineering and machinery, was able to create even more spectacular effects. His first setting (1629) was for *La selva sin amor* by Lope de Vega, in which he established two characteristic features: transformations, or sudden scene changes, and perspective and *trompe l'oeil* effects. These two features and the effective use of artificial lighting, which allowed night-time performances, became common in subsequent court theatre. Buen Retiro was the centre of court entertainment during Philip IV's reign, and Lotti made many inventions for use there. A dismountable stage system (*c.* 1633) allowed performances in the palace courtyard to be seen from the King's apartment. The stage for Pedro Calderón de la Barca's *El mayor encanto amor* (1635) appeared as an island 2 m above the lake, approached by curving staircases, with a mountain containing a cave and precipices, a thick forest with trees with human faces, and enormous fish spouting water. A carnival procession of 1637 had huge floats drawn by 48 bullocks and illuminated by 100 torches. Vicente Carducho reported in his *Diálogo de la pintura* (1633) that Lotti's work had 'provoked general astonishment with his marvellous and unheard of transformations'; his work was also celebrated in a poem by Francisco de Quevedo Villegas. There are no acknowledged drawings of sets by Lotti, but one drawing, *Apollo Enthroned on Parnassus* (1641; London, BL), may have been a sketch for a performance at the Coliseo.

BIBLIOGRAPHY

N. D. Shergold: *A History of the Spanish Stage* (Oxford, 1967)
J. Brown and J. H. Elliott: *A Palace for a King* (New Haven and London, 1980)
L. Langheri: 'Salomon de Caus de la fontana di Pratolino nell'Europa del primo seicento', *La fonte delle fonti* (Florence, 1985), pp. 35–43
B. von Barghahan: *Philip IV and the 'Golden House' of Buen Retiro*, 2 vols (New York, 1986)
J. M. Morán Turina: *Las casas del rey* (Madrid, 1986)

## Lotti, Lorenzo (di Lodovico di Guglielmo) [Lorenzetto]

(*b* Florence, 1490; *d* Rome, 1541). Italian sculptor and architect. He may have been associated with the workshop of Andrea Sansovino in Florence. The classicism of Fra Bartolommeo, Andrea del Sarto and others working in Florence during the early 16th century also seems to have influenced his artistic development. In 1514 he helped complete the cenotaph for *Cardinal Niccolò Forteguerri* (Pistoia Cathedral) begun by Andrea del Verrocchio in 1477, carving the figure of *Charity*. In Rome, according to Vasari, he worked as a sculptor and architect and restorer of antiques. He was much influenced by Raphael, whom he assisted in the decoration of the Vatican loggias (Dacos, 1977), and who was instrumental in obtaining important commissions for him in Rome. Lotti may have designed the Palazzo Vidoni–Caffarelli, though this palace is also attributed by some to Raphael.

In 1519 Lotti was designated in the will of Agostino Chigi to execute sculptures in the Chigi Chapel in S Maria del Popolo, Rome. The figures of *Elijah* and *Jonah*, as well as the relief of *Christ and the Adultress* on the chapel's altar, appear to have been based on designs by Raphael yet are rather weak in execution. The dynamic pose of *Jonah* reflects the impact of such proto-Mannerist figures as the *ignudi* painted by Michelangelo in the Sistine Chapel (Rome, Vatican), but the overall effect is awkward. Lotti carved a *Virgin and Child* (1520) for the tomb of *Raphael* in the Pantheon, Rome, the tomb of *Bernardino Cappella* in S Stefano Rotondo and also a large statue of *St Peter* (1535) for the Ponte S Angelo, Rome.

Lotti designed and decorated the garden court displaying sculpture (completed *c.* 1536) in the second, later Roman palace of Cardinal ANDREA DELLA VALLE, according to Vasari, who claims it had much influence on contemporary Roman taste.

BIBLIOGRAPHY

Thieme–Becker

G. Vasari: *Vite* (1550, rev. 2/1568); ed. G. Milanesi (1878–85), iv, pp. 248, 557, 577
J. Pope-Hennessy: *Italian High Renaissance and Baroque Sculpture*, ii (London, 1963), pp. 43–5
N. Dacos: *Le logge di Raffaelo* (Rome, 1977)
N. Nobis: *Lorenzetto als Bildhauer* (Bonn, 1979)
*Fabbriche romane del primo '500* (exh. cat., Rome, Pantheon; Bari, Castello Svevo; 1984)
C. Magnusson: 'Lorenzetto's Statue of Jonah and the Chigi Chapel in S Maria del Popolo', *Ksthist. Tidskr.*, lvi/1 (1987), pp. 19–26

STEVEN BULE

## Lotto, Lorenzo

(*b* Venice, *c.* 1480; *d* Loreto, 1556). Italian painter and draughtsman. He had a long and often prosperous career as a painter, and, although he travelled widely, his style retained a close affinity with the paintings of his native Venice. He was one of an outstanding generation of painters, including Giorgione, Titian, Palma Vecchio and Pordenone, who appeared in Venice and the Veneto during the first decade of the 16th century. In comparison with his contemporaries, Lotto was a fairly traditional painter in that he worked primarily in the long-established genres of altarpieces, devotional pictures and portraiture. Such paintings were popular in the Venetian provinces and the Marches where Lotto spent much of his career and where he often received more money for his commissions than he could obtain in Venice. His most important commissions were for altarpieces, and he is perhaps best known for a series of *sacre conversazioni* in which he skilfully varied the symmetrical groupings of figures found in earlier Venetian treatments of the subject by Giovanni Bellini and Alvise Vivarini. Precedents in Venice were also important for Lotto's early efforts in bust-length portraiture, but from 1525 he made a considerable contribution to the development of the three-quarter-length portrait. He painted many private devotional paintings but only a few of the historical, mythological or allegorical scenes that were popular in northern Italy in this period. Lotto is one of the best-documented painters of the 16th century: 40 autograph letters dating from 1524 to 1539, a personal account book covering the years 1538 to 1554 (the *Libro di spese diverse*) and many notarial acts survive, as well as 75 signed paintings and numerous securely attributed works.

1. Life. 2. Work. 3. Working methods and technique. 4. Critical reception and posthumous reputation.

### 1. LIFE.

(i) *The Veneto, the Marches and Rome, 1503–12.* In his will of 1546 Lotto claimed he was born in Venice, the son of a certain Tomaso, and was aged about 66: his birth date is derived from this statement. The first document (1503) about Lotto refers to him as the son of the 'late Thomas of Venice' and states that he was a painter in Treviso. Nothing is known about his apprenticeship, though a good knowledge of contemporary Venetian painting is apparent in his earliest works. His first paintings include two altarpieces for S Cristina al Tiverone, Treviso (1505; *in situ*) and Asolo Cathedral (1506; *in situ*), as well as several portraits and devotional paintings. While in Treviso, he enjoyed the patronage of Bishop Bernardino de' Rossi, whose portrait he painted (Naples, Capodimonte;

1. Lorenzo Lotto: *Bishop Bernardino de' Rossi*, oil on panel, 540×410 mm, 1505 (Naples, Museo e Gallerie Nazionali di Capodimonte)

see fig. 1). He left Treviso in the autumn of 1506 and travelled to Recanati to begin work on the high altarpiece of the Dominican church of S Domenico (Recanati, Pin. Civ.). The altarpiece is a large, two-tiered polyptych comprised of six panels (completed 1508). His later work for other Dominican churches and his request in 1542 to be buried in a Dominican habit suggest a close, if informal, association with the Order throughout much of his career.

Lotto was employed subsequently on the prestigious decoration of the Vatican Palace in Rome, a commission probably arranged by the papal architect Bramante, who visited Loreto, near Recanati, in 1508. On 7 March 1509 Lotto was paid for work 'in the upper rooms of the pope': exactly where and what he was painting is not known as there is no trace of his work in the Vatican. Raphael's rapid ascendancy in the Vatican project probably meant that Lotto did not continue to work there much beyond the end of 1509. He appears in the Marches again on 18 October 1511, the date of his contract for the *Entombment* (Jesi, Pin. Civ.) commissioned by the confraternity of the Buon Gesù in Jesi. He also completed two altarpieces in Recanati at this time, the *Transfiguration* (Recanati, Pin. Civ.) and the fresco of *St Vincent Ferrer* (Recanati, S Domenico).

*(ii) Bergamo, 1513–25.* In May 1513 Lotto arrived in Bergamo to paint the high altarpiece (completed 1516; Bergamo, S Bartolommeo) in the Dominican church of S Stefano. The patron of this altarpiece, one of the largest ever undertaken in northern Italy, was Conte Alessandro

Martinengo-Colleoni, the grandson of the famous condottiere Bartolomeo Colleoni. Lotto finished five other altarpieces in Bergamo between 1521 and 1523. All of them are still to be found in the city's churches, three in their original location (see fig. 2). During 1524 and 1525 he concentrated on wall paintings. The most extensive are those depicting the *Lives of SS Barbara and Brigid of Ireland* (1524; *see* DRESS, fig. 25) in the Suardi oratory of the Villa Suardi, Trescore Balneario (nr Bergamo), with the unusual portrayal of Christ with vines sprouting from his fingers in literal illustration of the words 'I am the vine, you are the branches'. Throughout his stay in Bergamo, Lotto also executed paintings for various households there. Twenty-four private paintings, mainly of religious subjects, are either documented or attributable to him during this period. He was also commissioned to design 33 Old Testament stories and their symbolic covers for the intarsia panels in the choir of S Maria Maggiore, Bergamo (1524–30; *in situ*).

*(iii) Venice, 1525–32.* Lotto arrived in Venice on 20 December 1525. He spent his first months in the Dominican monastery of SS Giovanni e Paolo, possibly in connection with the altarpiece of *St Antonino* there, which he completed in 1542. He had to leave the monastery after a few months because of a disagreement with the Dominican Fra Damiano, an intarsia artist in Bergamo and Bologna. Apart from a brief eight-day trip in early 1526, he remained in Venice until 1532. Compared to Bergamo, Venice offered the prospect of greater wealth and fame and was more convenient for shipping altarpieces to the Marches, commissions for some of which Lotto had arranged during a brief visit to the Marches in late 1523.

2. Lorenzo Lotto: *Virgin and Child Enthroned with SS Joseph, Bernardino, John the Baptist and Anthony Abbot*, oil on canvas, 3.00×2.75 m, 1521 (Bergamo, S Bernardino)

3. Lorenzo Lotto: *Andrea Odoni*, oil on canvas, 1.04×1.16 m, 1527 (London, Hampton Court, Royal Collection)

While in Venice, he painted at least five altarpieces for churches in the Marches and an altarpiece of the *Assumption* (1527) for S Maria Assunta, Celana, near Bergamo (*in situ*). The only altarpiece for a Venetian church completed during this period was that of *St Nicholas of Bari in Glory* (*c.* 1529; Venice, S Maria dei Carmini). His paintings for private households were much more in demand by Venetian patrons: eighteen such paintings can be dated between 1526 and 1532, including ten portraits. Notable among these portraits are those of three-quarter-length figures leaning against a table, as in the portrait of *Andrea Odoni* (1527; London, Hampton Court, Royal Col.; see fig. 3), which influenced Titian's portrait of *Jacopo Strada* (1568; Vienna, Ksthist. Mus.).

*(iv) Venice, the Veneto and the Marches, 1532–56.* After the relatively long periods in Bergamo and Venice, Lotto changed residence frequently during the last 24 years of his life. He had moved from Venice to Treviso by 29 August 1532. Thereafter he seems to have spent most of the next seven years in the Marches: he is documented in Jesi in 1535, in Ancona in 1538 and in Macerata in 1539, during which time he painted several altarpieces, including the *Crucifixion* (Monte San Giusto, S Maria in Telusiano) and the *Madonna of the Rosary* (Cingoli, S Nicolò). He returned to Venice in January 1540 and stayed there for two years, before moving to Treviso in October 1542. He went back to Venice in December 1545 and painted the altarpiece of the *Virgin and Child with Four Saints* (1546; Venice, S Giacomo dall'Orio). Lotto's account book shows, however, that it was becoming increasingly difficult for him to earn a living as a painter in Venice. He left Venice in 1549 to return to the Marches to paint the *Assumption* (1550) for S Francesco delle Scale, Ancona (*in situ*). He spent the final two years of his life as an oblate in the Santa Casa of Loreto, during which time he executed various decorations for the basilica of S Maria

and other works in the collection of the Palazzo Apostolico.

DAVID OLDFIELD

2. WORK.

*(i) Religious.* In the first half of the 16th century, the span of Lotto's career, painters significantly expanded the vocabulary of forms and images that had characterized religious paintings in Italy since the early 14th century. The leading innovators, Fra Bartolommeo, Raphael and Titian, were established as independent masters by the first decade of the 16th century, and Lotto was their contemporary. The paintings he executed as he travelled around northern Italy record his interest in the work of his peers and demonstrate his capacity for invention and for original syntheses of traditional forms. The largest and most costly works undertaken by Lotto were altarpieces (with the possible exception of his fresco projects). As they were in churches accessible to the public, his altarpieces helped to establish his reputation each time he moved to a new city. The extent of his travels and the distances involved were not unusual: virtually all his Venetian and Tuscan contemporaries executed long-distance commissions for altarpieces. Lotto did, however, remain for unusually long periods in places where his work was in demand, no doubt partly because he was not tied to a family workshop in Venice, like Titian and others.

The fact that many of Lotto's patrons were provincial, and not from the artistic capitals of Rome, Florence and Venice, has led writers to conclude that most were unsophisticated. This is not the case, as research since the 1970s has revealed. His private patrons were often wealthy, and they included well-educated merchants, professionals and members of the nobility; the confraternities that employed him were highly respected community institutions, and the altarpieces they commissioned were for prestigious and highly visible locations. The assumption that Lotto's career declined from the 1540s is also mistaken. In the Marches, for example, his career began auspiciously with the *Virgin and Child with Saints* (1508; Recanati, Pin. Civ.) for S Domenico in Recanati and ended with major works commissioned by noble families for prominent locations: the *Assumption* (1550) for S Francesco delle Scale, Ancona (*in situ*), and an altarpiece (1555; destr.) for Jesi Cathedral.

Lotto completed nearly 40 altarpieces, responding to the demands of a wide variety of patrons and sites and to a lively climate of artistic invention. They are as remarkable for their diversity of form and subject as they are for the acknowledged individualism of his style. The settings of his earliest *sacre conversazioni* are the luminous pavilions and vaulted halls traditional in Venetian altarpieces. His experiences in Rome in 1508–9 alongside Raphael and Bramante inspired the more grandiose architecture in the *Virgin and Child with Saints* (the 'Pala Martinengo', 1516; Bergamo, S Bartolommeo), which was supplanted from the 1520s by less defined, more dramatically lit settings that signalled the growing influence of Titian. The elegant figures of the *Virgin and Child Enthroned with Saints* (1521; Bergamo, Santo Spirito) and the dramatically foreshortened angels in another altarpiece of that subject (1521; Bergamo, S Bernardino; see fig. 2 above) are clear evidence of his study of Raphael's altarpieces. Raphael's visionary Virgins inspired Lotto's *Virgin in Glory with SS Andrew and Jerome* (1535; Rome, priv. col.; see 1983 exh. cat., fig. 51), painted for S Agostino in Fermo.

The subject-matter of Lotto's altarpieces and other religious pictures reflects the conventional attitudes and devotions of early 16th-century patrons and painters. His narrative altarpieces depicting the lives of the saints and the Holy Family and his *sacre conversazioni* are distinguished by the affecting realism of the figures' relationships to one another and to the viewer, revealed in such details as the Christ Child reaching out to St Joseph in the *Virgin and Child with Two Saints* (1526; Jesi, Pin. Civ.), and the angels throwing rose petals towards the viewer in the *Madonna of the Rosary* (1539; Cingoli, Mus. Civ.). They also indicate his willingness to experiment with novel formats, as in the *St Lucy* altarpiece (1532; Jesi, Pin. Civ.) in which a scene depicted in the main panel is repeated in the predella.

In the *Lamentation* (*c.* 1530; Monte San Giusto [Marches], S Maria della Pietà; see fig. 4), arguably Lotto's finest altarpiece, the Virgin and mourners, traditionally placed at the foot of the cross, are brought closer to the viewer. The figures are at eye-level, life-size, and painted in the brilliant colours typical of the artist's work of the 1530s. The emotive power of this altarpiece has been seen as a harbinger of Counter-Reformation piety, but it is more accurately regarded as Lotto's contribution to the development of emotionally evocative imagery of a type he may have encountered first in the late works of Sandro Botticelli.

4. Lorenzo Lotto: *Lamentation,* oil on panel, 4.5×2.5 m, *c.* 1530 (Monte San Giusto, S Maria della Pietà)

Lotto's three fresco cycles, executed in a brief period in the mid-1520s, and his devotional pictures, which occupied him throughout his career, are characterized by the same diversity of form and subject and the same novel combinations of traditional, contemporary and idiosyncratic elements. His frescoes of scenes from the *Life of St Barbara,* for example, part of the cycle (1524) for the Suardi oratory, depict the stories as a continuous narrative, a notably old-fashioned device. The settings are inspired by the tradition of perspectival illusionism in intarsia decoration (Lotto was just beginning his intarsia designs for S Maria Maggiore in Bergamo) and perhaps by early 16th-century perspectival designs for stage sets. The iconography of this particularly interesting cycle has been interpreted as a response to the threat of the Protestant Reformation. The meanings of the cycle are still debated, however, and it has yet to be considered within the context of Lotto's career as a Venetian painter working within the Venetian sphere of influence.

Lotto's devotional pictures typically follow a compositional formula derived from the Bellini workshop in Venice: a half- or three-quarter-length Virgin and Child with one or more saints arranged horizontally in front of a neutral background or a combination of architecture and landscape. He and Titian developed the expressive potential of this type of painting in such works as Titian's *Virgin with a Rabbit* (Paris, Louvre) and Lotto's *Virgin and Child with Two Saints and an Angel* (Vienna, Ksthist. Mus.), both painted *c.* 1530. Lotto's skilful depiction of the play of light and shade, the colour and texture of surfaces and the atmospheric beauty of the distant landscape demonstrate his secure position within the Venetian artistic tradition identified with his more famous contemporary. In addition, the interconnected gestures and glances that link the figures across the composition recall the works of Correggio, whose relationship to Lotto has yet to be explored.

Lotto's religious works also include his designs for a series of intarsia panels for the choir of S Maria Maggiore in Bergamo. In 1523 Lotto and another Venetian artist, Andrea Previtali, submitted designs for the choir structure and the intarsia decoration. The following year Lotto received the commission for the intarsia designs, to be executed as coloured drawings, and for intarsia covers for the 33 main panels, to be submitted as chiaroscuro drawings. The subjects for the main panels, all scenes from the Old Testament, were selected by Girolamo Terzi, a member of the Franciscan Order in Bergamo. It is clear from the correspondence, however, that Lotto was allowed to choose from a selection of subjects, that he suggested some himself and that he disagreed with some of Terzi's choices. He had more freedom with the choice of subjects for the covers, as the contract stipulated only that they should relate to the stories depicted on the panels. It has been suggested that the cover designs indicate Lotto's interest in hieroglyphics, but he referred to them as 'imprese', that is images accompanied by short phrases that together comment on the significance of the narrative.

*(ii) Portraits and mythological subjects.* Portraiture formed a significant portion of Lotto's work, and his more than 40 surviving portraits are widely admired. They are a virtual catalogue of the fertility of invention and freedom from

convention that characterized Italian painting in the first half of the 16th century. His exploration of his sitters' states of mind and of new compositional ideas demonstrates his knowledge of the refashioning of portraiture that was begun by Leonardo and continued by Raphael, Giorgione and Titian. Lotto's portraits are not, however, easily confused with those of his contemporaries, and they reflect to an unusual degree the style and approach to subject-matter of his other paintings. His subjects usually confront the viewer directly. They are idealized but particularized through specific contexts of material setting, time and circumstance.

Lotto's earliest portraits (see fig. 1 above) are bust-length and half-length figures depicted against dark grounds, and the detailed recording of their physiognomies recalls his training in the Venetian orbit of Antonello da Messina and Giovanni Bellini. During the second and third decades of the 16th century his formal repertory expanded dramatically: settings are larger and described in greater detail, figures turn and gesture in more ample spaces, and he painted portraits that include more than one figure. As has been noted, his return to Venice at the end of 1525 coincided with a change in his portraiture towards a more dramatic and sophisticated presentation, probably calculated to impress an urbane clientele, for example the portrait of *Andrea Odoni* (fig. 3 above). Although some of his late portraits are less striking, they retain the intensity of characterization that is one of his singular contributions to the history of portraiture.

Lotto's account book, the *Libro di spese diverse*, indicates that his portrait patrons belonged to the same social groups as the patrons of his religious pictures. It also provides valuable information about the identity of his sitters, although many of the portraits he described cannot be matched with surviving works. Both the account book and Lotto's numerous letters suggest that he was acutely aware of his own state of mind and reputation and very attuned to the material aspects of personal appearance, especially clothing and jewellery. It is not surprising, therefore, that his portraits show considerable sensitivity to the relationship between the sitter's inner state and its outward manifestations.

Lotto's use of puns, emblems and symbols in his portraits is only beginning to be understood. The meanings of the lizard, rose petals and gold jewellery strewn across the table in the *Portrait of a Young Man in his Study* (*c.* 1527; Venice, Accad.) or the putto supporting himself on a scale in the *Portrait of a 37-year-old Man* (*c.* 1542; Rome, Gal. Doria-Pamphili) have yet to be deciphered convincingly. In the celebrated *Triple Portrait of a Jeweller* (*c.* 1527; Vienna, Ksthist. Mus.) the sitter, who is shown in three different poses, may be participating in a commentary on his own image. Other clues to the understanding of Lotto's portrait iconography may lie in further study of his religious imagery and his few pictures of mythological and allegorical subjects, among them the *Allegory of Marriage* (*Venus and Cupid*; *c.* 1526; New York, Met.), the *Triumph of Chastity* (*c.* 1531; Rome, Pal. Rospigliosi-Pallavicini) and two early portrait covers, an *Allegory* (for the portrait of *Rossi*; see fig. 1 above) and *Plutus and the Nymph Rhodos* (both 1505; Washington, DC, N.G.A.).

LOUISA C. MATTHEW

3. WORKING METHODS AND TECHNIQUE. Information about Lotto's technique can be found in the *Libro di spese diverse*. His purchase of materials from August 1540 to June 1544 is noted in considerable detail and gives a good idea of the preliminary preparation for a painting. A typical painting would be comprised of a canvas and stretcher, a glue and gesso ground and a thin white layer of priming beneath the paint layers. Lotto also painted on wooden supports, though mainly in the first part of his career, as in the *Virgin and Child with Four Saints* of *c.* 1506 (Edinburgh, N.G.). The only documented murals by Lotto are those painted in Bergamo in 1524–5. Much of his expertise in the technique of fresco may have been gained from his work in the Vatican in 1509 rather than from his earlier training in the Veneto.

The colours that Lotto bought (listed in his *Libro*) are the common ones of the period: small quantities of *cinaprio* and *lacca di grana* for red, *verderame* for green, *giallo di Fiandra* for yellow, lapis lazuli and *azzurro grosso* for blue and large quantities of white and black. His preferred medium was linseed oil, but other oils, such as walnut, were also used. He applied his colours in smooth, meticulous brushstrokes with a distinct separation between different tones, a result of his training in the late-15th-century Venetian technique.

Lotto maintained the clear and well-defined forms of his early paintings throughout most of his career in contrast to the sketchy, hazy outlines adopted by some of his Venetian contemporaries, such as Giorgione and Titian. His traditional approach to the application of colours is not surprising when it is remembered that he was away from the Veneto (except for brief visits) from 1506 to 1525, the crucial years in the development of the new painterly style in Venice. The tone of his colours, however, underwent several changes. The works of his first years (1503–6) are distinguished by the purity of the colours and strong lighting, with the notable exception of *St Jerome* (1506; Paris, Louvre), which is a masterful imitation of the colourful and moody landscapes of Giorgione. The strong contrasts between light and dark in Lotto's early works become less harsh after his trip to Rome in 1509 when he began to add a middle tone to lighten the purity of his colours. This change can be seen when the stiff, wrinkled drapery in his early works (e.g. *Mystic Marriage of St Catherine*, *c.* 1506; Munich, Alte Pin.) is compared with the slight channels and pockets of softly curved material that are a major trait of his later style (e.g. *Virgin and Child with SS Jerome and Nicholas of Tolentino*, 1521; London, N.G.). After his arrival in Venice in 1525, Lotto increasingly adopted the mixed hues popularized by Titian (for instance, reds are tinged with blue).

Though he must have drawn extensively, drawings by Lotto are rare. Only a dozen can be securely attributed to him throughout his long career, and the earliest of these are two drawings executed during his time in Bergamo. The importance of drawing to him is shown by X-ray photographs of several of his paintings, which reveal very few changes from the original design. There is also relatively little difference between his drawings and the final painted version in the rare cases when both survive, as is the case with his squared-up drawing in black chalk of an *Apostle* (New York, Pierpont Morgan Lib., ex-Scholz priv. col.) for the *Assumption* of 1527 (Celana, S Maria Assunta). His meticulous draughtsmanship is reminiscent of late 15th-century Venetian drawings, as can be seen in his two carefully drawn poses for *St Joseph* (black chalk on grey paper, Milan, Bib. Ambrosiana) with the back view later duplicated in the S Bernardino altarpiece of 1521 (fig. 2 above). His preliminary study (pen and brown ink, *c.* 1529; New York, Pierpont Morgan Lib., ex-Scholz priv. col.) for the intarsia panel of *Samson Slaying the Philistines with a Jawbone* contains precisely drawn figures and buildings that correspond exactly with the intarsia panel even though it would have been followed by a more finished drawing with the colours noted for the intarsia worker, as in the drawing of *Judith and Holofernes* (pen and brown wash, heightened with white highlights, *c.* 1527; London, BM, ex-Pouncey priv. col.). Lotto does not appear to have adopted the method of working out poses and compositions, as was done by his Florentine and Venetian contemporaries, but some of his drawings of compositions, such as the squared-up study of a *Double Portrait* (pen and brown ink, *c.* 1523; Amsterdam, Rijksmus.) or his sketch (black chalk, *c.* 1527; Siena, Bib. Com. Intronati) of the S Floriano altarpiece, are drawn in a quick, fluid style.

The influence of Lotto's trip to Rome is noticeable in the increased complexity of the poses, gestures and arrangement of the figures in his paintings after 1509. This change coincided with an increase in his commissions with narratives after an early period dominated by *sacre conversazioni* and portraits. An example of this change can be seen in the athletic poses and skilful foreshortening of the celestial angels in his altarpieces in Bergamo. After his arrival in Venice in 1525, Lotto imitated the energetic composition of Titian's *Assumption of the Virgin* (1516–18; Venice, Frari; *see* ALTARPIECE, fig. 4) and the large, muscular figure of Pordenone's *St Christopher* (1528; Venice, S Rocco) in his own versions of those subjects (Celana, S Maria Assunta; Berlin, Gemäldegal.).

Given Lotto's peripatetic career, the contents of his workshop had to be limited and portable. He relied heavily on life studies to add variety to his work: in the *Libro di spese diverse* there are payments for the drawing of poor people, naked men and women, a child, a peasant woman's head and a beard. He also had a small collection of reliefs and statuettes, as noted in his testament of 1546. Other objects of inspiration were his own drawings and engravings by contemporary artists. These items would have been useful for the instruction of his apprentices. During his busy years in Bergamo he had at least two apprentices in his workshop, but during his last years he employed only one.

4. CRITICAL RECEPTION AND POSTHUMOUS REPUTATION. During his lifetime, Lotto's influence and reputation were greatest in the provinces of Bergamo and the Marches, where his altarpieces were among the most prominent public commissions during the first half of the 16th century. He was not as highly regarded in Venice, although his portraits achieved a certain popularity as witnessed by the large number that have survived. His portrait of *Andrea Odoni* (fig. 3 above) was mentioned by the Venetian Marcantonio Michiel, who also noted some of his public and private paintings in Bergamo. Some Venetians may have shared Ludovico Dolce's criticism of Lotto's altarpiece of *St Nicholas of Bari in Glory* for its 'bad colours'. Giorgio Vasari and Giovanni Paolo Lomazzo, however, praised the same altarpiece for its beautiful landscape. Both Vasari and Pietro Aretino, in a letter dated 1548, comment on Lotto's virtuous demeanour towards the end of his life. Carlo Ridolfi included a brief biography of Lotto with a list of paintings in his *Le meraviglie dell'arte* (1648), and in 1797 Francesco Tassi provided a good survey of Lotto's work in Bergamo.

It was only at the end of the 19th century that Lotto's paintings received any lengthy critical acclaim and attention. Berenson's monograph of 1895 was largely responsible for introducing the painter to the general public. His somewhat romantic view of Lotto as a melancholic soul constantly on the move has been gradually replaced by a more objective analysis of his works as more documents on his career have come to light. The Lotto exhibition in Venice in 1953 and the monographs of that year firmly established the artist as a major Venetian painter and emphasized his stylistic development. The discovery and publication of Lotto's letters to the Misericordia in Bergamo in 1962 by Chiodi and a new edition of Lotto's *Libro di spese diverse* by Zampetti in 1969 were major contributions to the documentation of the painter. Recent work on Lotto has focused more on his patronage, iconography and religious beliefs, as can be seen in the conference papers (1980) for the fifth centenary of his birth. The large exhibition in Ancona in 1981, *Lorenzo Lotto nelle Marche*, provided ample evidence of Lotto's importance for 16th-century painting in the Marches. His reputation within a Venetian context was enhanced by the selection of his paintings for *The Genius of Venice* exhibition in London (1983–4).

UNPUBLISHED SOURCES

Bergamo, Bib. Civ. A. Mai [letters by Lotto and other doc. relating to the intarsia panels of the choir of S Maria Maggiore, Bergamo (1525–32)]

WRITINGS

*Libro di spese diverse* (1538–54; Loreto, Archv Stor. S Casa); ed. P. Zampetti (Venice, 1969)
L. Chiodi, ed.: *Lettere inedite di Lorenzo Lotto su le tarsie di S Maria Maggiore in Bergamo* (Bergamo, 1962, 2/1968)

BIBLIOGRAPHY

EARLY SOURCES

P. Aretino: *Lettere*, 6 vols (Venice, 1538–57); ed. E. Camesasca, 3 vols (Milan, 1957–60)
G. Vasari: *Vite* (1550, rev. 2/1568); ed. G. Milanesi (1878–85), v, pp. 249–53
M. Michiel: *Der Anonimo Morelliano* (MS., before 1552); ed. T. Frimmel (Vienna, 1888), pp. 62–8, 84
L. Dolce: *L'Aretino, ovvero dialogo della pittura* (Venice, 1557)
C. Ridolfi: *Meraviglie* (1648); ed. D. von Hadeln (1914–24)
F. M. Tassi: *Vite de' pittori, scultori e architetti bergamaschi*, i (Bergamo, 1797), pp. 116–31
L. Lanzi: *Storia pittorica della Italia*, ii (Pisa, 1815), pp. 84–6
G. P. Lomazzo: *Scritti sull'arte*, ed. R. P. Ciardi (Florence, 1974), i, pp. 251, 358, 365; ii, p. 409

MONOGRAPHS, EXHIBITION CATALOGUES AND SYMPOSIA

B. Berenson: *Lorenzo Lotto* (New York, 1895, 3/1956)
A. Banti and A. Boschetto: *Lorenzo Lotto* (Florence, 1953)
L. Coletti: *Lorenzo Lotto* (Bergamo, 1953)
P. Zampetti: *Mostra di Lorenzo Lotto* (Venice, 1953)
M. Seidenberg: *Die Bildnisse des Lorenzo Lotto* (Lorrach, 1964)
P. Pouncey: *Lotto disegnatore* (Vicenza, 1965)
G. Mascherpa: *Lorenzo Lotto a Bergamo* (Milan, 1971)

G. Mariani Canova and R. Pallucchini: *L'opera completa del Lorenzo Lotto* (Milan, 1974)

F. Grimaldi, ed.: *Lorenzo Lotto a Loreto e Recanati* (Loreto, 1980)

*Bergamo per Lorenzo Lotto: Bergamo, 1980*

*Lorenzo Lotto a Treviso: Ricerche e restauri* (exh. cat., ed. G. Dillon; Treviso, Mus. Civ. Bailo, 1980)

*Lorenzo Lotto: Atti del convegno internazionale di studi per il V centenario della nascita: Asolo, 1980*

*Lorenzo Lotto nelle Marche: Il suo tempo, il suo influsso* (exh. cat., ed. P. dal Poggetto and P. Zampetti; Ancona, 1981)

SPECIALIST STUDIES
*Specific works*

G. Annibaldi: 'Dei pittori in Jesi che portano l'aggiunto da Fano', *Rass. Bibliog. A. It.*, iii (1900), pp. 205–11

G. Abbruzzeti: 'Di alcuni dipinti di Lorenzo Lotto a Jesi', *Rass. Bibliog. A. It.*, v (1902), pp. 62–71, 134–8

C. Caversazzi: 'Una dama bergamasca di quattrocent' anni fa riconosciuta in un ritratto del Lotto', *Bergomum*, vii (1913), pp. 23–5

G. Frizzoni: 'Intorno a Lorenzo Lotto e ad una sua pala smembrata', *Rass. A.*, vii (1916), pp. 45–50

A. M. Ciarafani: 'La Natività di Lorenzo Lotto nella R. Pinacoteca di Siena', *Boll. A.*, xxix (1936), pp. 319–29

J. Wilde: 'The Date of Lotto's St Jerome in the Louvre', *Burl. Mag.*, xcii (1950), p. 350

C. Gould: 'Lorenzo Lotto and the Double Portrait', *Saggi & Mem. Stor. A.*, v (1966), pp. 45–51

L. O. Larsson: 'Lorenzo Lottos Bildnis des Andrea Odoni in Hampton Court: Eine typologische und ikonographische Studie', *Ksthist. Tidskr.*, xxxvii (1968), pp. 21–33

H. A. van der Berg-Nöe: 'Lorenzo Lotto e la decorazione del coro ligneo di S Maria Maggiore in Bergamo', *Meded. Ned. Inst. Rome*, xxxvi (1974), pp. 145–60

C. Cohen: 'The Modello for a Lost Work by Lorenzo Lotto', *Master Drgs*, xiii (1975), pp. 131–5

M. von Hall: 'Messer Marsilio and his Bride', *Connoisseur*, cxci (1976), pp. 192–217

G. A. Dell'Acqua: *La Pala Martinengo di Lorenzo Lotto: Studi e ricerche in occasione del restauro* (Bergamo, 1978)

R. Goffin: 'A "Madonna" by Lorenzo Lotto', *Bull. Mus. F.A., Boston*, lxxvi (1978), pp. 34–41

F. Cortesi Bosco: *Gli affreschi dell'Oratorio Suardi* (Bergamo, 1980)

A. Chastel: 'Le Portement de croix de Lorenzo Lotto', *Rev. Louvre* (1982), pp. 266–72

*Other*

H. von Tschudi: 'Lorenzo Lotto in den Marken', *Repert. Kstwiss.*, ii (1879), pp. 280–97

G. Bampo: 'Spigolature dall'archivio notarile di Treviso: Documenti inediti intorno a Lorenzo Lotto e ad uno suo discepolo', *Archv Ven.*, xxxii (1886), pp. 169–76, 415–21

P. Gianuizzi: 'Lorenzo Lotto e le sue opere nelle Marche', *Nuova Riv. Misena*, vii (1894), pp. 35–47

A. Pinetti: 'Cronostoria artistica di S Maria Maggiore', *Bergomum*, xxii (1928), pp. 65–76, 97–111, 129–53

C. Caversazzi: 'Un discepolo bergamasco di Lorenzo Lotto', *Bergomum*, xxiv (1940), pp. 122–8

E. Zocca: 'Le decorazioni della Stanza dell'Eliodoro e l'opera di Lorenzo Lotto a Roma', *Riv. Ist. N. Archeol. & Stor. A.*, ii (1953), pp. 329–43

I. Chiappini di Sorio: 'Lorenzo Lotto nelle Marche', *A. Ven.*, xvi (1962), pp. 146–8

G. Liberali: 'Lotto, Pordenone e Tiziano a Treviso', *Mem. Ist. Ven. Sci., Lett. & A.*, xxxiii (1963), pp. 1–89

P. Zampetti and F. Cortesi Bosco: 'Lorenzo Lotto a Bergamo', *I pittori bergamaschi dal XIII al XIX secolo: Il cinquecento*, i (Bergamo, 1975), pp. 1–86

F. Cortesi Bosco: 'La letteratura religiosa devozionale e l'iconografia di alcuni dipinti di Lorenzo Lotto', *Bergomum*, lxxi (1976), pp. 3–25

L. Chiodi: 'Quattro lettere inedite di Lorenzo Lotto', *Bergomum*, lxxi (1977), pp. 17–36

D. Wronski Galis: *Lorenzo Lotto: A Study of his Career and Character, with Particular Emphasis on his Emblematic and Hieroglyphic Works* (Ann Arbor, 1980)

P. Zampetti, ed.: 'Lorenzo Lotto nel suo e nel nostro tempo', *Not. Pal. Albani*, ix/1–2 (1980) [whole issue]

P. Zampetti: 'Lorenzo Lotto', *The Genius of Venice, 1500–1600* (exh. cat., ed. C. Hope and J. Martineau; London, RA, 1983), pp. 175–82

A. Cascia, ed.: 'Omaggio a Lorenzo Lotto', *Not. Pal. Albani*, xiii/1 (1984) [whole issue]

D. Oldfield: 'Lorenzo Lotto's Arrival in Venice', *A. Ven.*, xxxviii (1984), pp. 141–5

F. Cortesi Bosco: *Il coro intarsiato di Lotto e Capoferri* (Bergamo, 1987)

L. C. Matthew: 'New Evidence for Lotto's Career in Jesi', *Burl. Mag.* (Sept 1988), pp. 693–7

DAVID OLDFIELD

**Lotus.** Term for two distinct decorative motifs based on types of water-lily; one originated in Egypt, the other in India. Lotus motifs in Egypt occur from the beginning of the Dynastic period *c.* 3000 BC in two stylized forms. The curved outline of the flower-head distinguishes the motif based on the white-flowered *Nymphaea lotus* from the more triangular outline of the motif based on the blue-flowered *Nymphaea caerulea* (see fig. (a)). Representations on the walls of tombs and temples suggest that lotus flowers were much in evidence in daily life, and the motif decorates jewellery and many domestic objects. In the tomb of Tutankhamun (reg *c.* 1332–*c.* 1323 BC), for example, the bowl of an alabaster cup represents an open white lotus, while the handles have the form of the blue lotus flower and two buds; a necklace has lotus motifs on both pendant and lock; and the pointed lotus petals form decorative borders on many objects (all Cairo, Egyp. Mus.). Lotus flowers and buds are among other plantlike capitals on stone pillars in funerary monuments and temples (see Borchardt, figs 9–11). The lotus also had some ritual significance: the flowers of water-lilies close at night and open at sunrise, a feature that came to symbolize a resurgence of life and the sun itself and became associated with the sun god Horus. The morning sun was pictured as rising from the lotus flower and settling back into the flower at night. When associated with Isis, the lotus became a fertility symbol.

Borders and overall repeat designs painted on the walls and ceilings of tombs and temples throughout the Dynastic period include lotus blossom alternating with buds or other plant elements (see fig. (b)). In the 2nd millennium BC the plant motifs of ancient Egypt became widely used in Western Asia. The lotus (and in particular the lotus border) now often in association with the PALMETTE motif, appears in Greece in 7th-century BC vase painting and architecture. A group of mouldings in the Ionic order of architecture, the EGG AND DART or leaf and dart, are ultimately derived from the lotus and bud motif, while lotus and palmette borders, made more plantlike by the addition of acanthus leaves, were sufficiently changed in appearance to be known by a new name, ANTHEMION. A fashion for the lotus and other motifs and styles of ancient Egypt in European furniture, decoration and architecture was introduced in the mid-18th century with the rise of interest in Egyptology, and its use was stimulated by Napoleon's Egyptian campaign of 1798. The discovery of Tutankhamun's tomb in 1922 initiated further Egyptian-inspired designs.

On the Indian subcontinent, the simple symbolism of the lotus motif predates its place in Buddhist iconography, but it is in Buddhist art that the lotus became an important motif. The Indian lotus motif is based on the species of water-lily typified by *Nelumbo nucifera*. With a bright pink, white or blue flower, it is a larger and more striking plant than the Egyptian water-lilies. Lotus rosettes or medallions (the flower seen from above) are prominent on the gateway structures of stupas at Sanchi and Amaravati (*c.* 2nd century BC–2nd century AD; see fig. (c)). The pointed oval petals are set in rows with stamens and the gynaeceum indicated at the centre. The lotus is one of the Buddha's auspicious signs, and images of the Buddha and *bodhisattva*s frequently sit or stand on highly stylized lotus flowers. In Buddhist architectural decoration the lotus motif became integrated with plant scrolls and other motifs of Classical origins. A scene from the life of the Buddha from Gandhara in north-west Pakistan, for example, is framed by an arch with an undulating plant scroll in the classical manner with lotus rosettes and highly stylized leaves and buds (London, BM, OA 1980.2–25.1).

The lotus rosette and lotus scroll motifs were introduced together with other features of Buddhist architecture and religious objects as Buddhism spread from India to Central Asia and China in the early centuries AD. There was no previous tradition of plant decoration in China, but when high-fired ceramics began to be produced for secular purposes in the 6th century, the imported lotus motif in more or less stylized forms dominated the designs. From the 10th century onwards the kilns at Jingdezhen began large-scale production of fine porcelain. Prominent among the motifs decorating this ware were flower scrolls of essentially Buddhist origins with highly stylized lotus-derived flower-heads with petals surrounding a gynaeceum. These are set in regular sequences within the coils of scrolls and small, unrealistic leaves (see fig. (d)). More realistic lotus plant motifs, based on observations from nature, occur on later Chinese porcelain (e.g. Vainker, figs 123, 143). In the art of Islam the lotus can be traced as flower-like features in arabesque designs, for example in the carved marble screens in the Great Mosque at Córdoba (961–76) (Ettinghausen and Grabar, fig. 117) or in carpet and other textile designs, as well as in the bizarre vegetation on Iznik plates and tiles (Rawson, pp. 145–98).

Both Chinese and Islamic forms of lotus-derived motifs greatly influenced design and taste in Europe. Large-scale imports of Chinese porcelain into Europe began in the early 17th century, alongside other oriental items such as silk and lacquer. These imports not only gave rise to chinoiserie styles but produced motifs that have become permanent features of European decoration. Such patterns as the 'pomegranate', a fantastic flower set within an ogee framework and introduced in Renaissance Italian silk-weaving under strong Islamic influence, are ultimately derived from the Indian lotus motif (e.g. Santangelo, pls 12, 21, 50, 72).

BIBLIOGRAPHY

L. Borchardt: *Die ägyptische Pflanzensäule* (Berlin, 1897)
A. Santangelo: *Tessuti d'arte italiani: Dal XII al XVIII secolo* (Milan, 1959)
I. E. S. Edwards: *Tutankhamun: His Tomb and its Treasures* (London, 1979)
E. H. Gombrich: *The Sense of Order: A Study of the Psychology of Decorative Art* (Oxford, 1979)
J. Rawson: *Chinese Ornament: The Lotus and the Dragon* (London, 1984)
*Buddhism: Art and Faith* (exh. cat., ed. W. Zwalf; London, BM, 1985)
R. Ettinghausen and O. Grabar: *The Art and Architecture of Islam, 650–1250*, Pelican Hist. A. (Harmondsworth, 1987)
S. J. Vainker: *Chinese Pottery and Porcelain* (London, 1991)

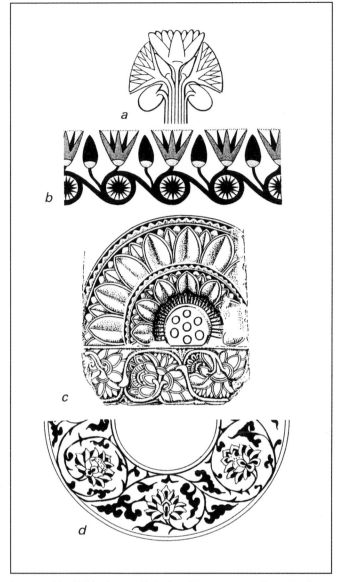

Lotus motifs: (a) blue lotus, with buds and leaves, surrounding white lotus, from a relief on a tomb at Saqqara, Egypt, *c.* 2400–2345 BC; (b) painted lotus and bud border, with flower seen from above in a connecting scroll, from the tomb of Amenhotpe-si-se, II 75, Thebes, Egypt, *c.* 1425–1379 BC; (c) detail of lotus designs on stone pillars from the Great Stupa, Amaravati, India, *c.* 2nd century BC–2nd century AD (London, British Museum); (d) detail of flower-scroll on a porcelain plate, from Jingdezhen, China, second half of 14th century (London, British Museum)

R. Knox: *Amaravati: Buddhist Sculpture from the Great Stupa* (London, 1992)
E. Wilson: *8000 Years of Ornament: An Illustrated Handbook of Motifs* (London, 1994), pp. 97–112, 143–52

EVA WILSON

**Lotz, Károly** (*b* Homburg von der Höhe, 16 Dec 1833; *d* Budapest, 13 Oct 1904). Hungarian painter and teacher. He studied under the Italian painter Jakob Marastoni (1804–60) in Pest and then under the Hungarian painter

Henrik Weber (1818–66). In 1852 he entered Carl Rahl's private school in Vienna. He painted wall and ceiling frescoes for many of the Viennese palaces, based on the cartoons of his teacher. After returning to Hungary, as an accomplished academic painter he painted numerous genre paintings, the main theme of which was the Hungarian Plain, as in *Storm on the Plain* (1861; Budapest, N.G.). He also received many commissions to decorate private houses and public buildings. His chief works were the wall paintings (1874) for the stair-well at the Hungarian National Museum in Budapest and the ceilings (1882–4) for the Budapest Opera. His other commissions in Budapest include wall paintings for the Vigado Concert Hall, for the banqueting hall of the Hungarian National Academy of Sciences (1887–8) and for the Habsburg Hall in Buda Castle (1900; destr.). Most of his works conformed to the neo-Baroque and neo-Renaissance architectural styles of the period; he painted many allegorical compositions and had a gift for narrative and a light touch (e.g. *Apotheosis of Budapest*, 1883; Budapest, Divatcsarnok Dept. Store). Lotz also painted religious works, such as the *Legend of St László* (1880; Budapest, Matthias Church), as well as mythological scenes and portraits, among the best-known of which is *Cornelia in a Black Dress* (1895; Budapest, N.G.). In 1882 he taught at the High School of Drawing (later Academy of Fine Arts) in Budapest and in 1885 in the Women Painters' School. In 1905 and 1933 retrospective exhibitions of his work were held in Budapest at the exhibition hall Műcsanok and at the Museum of Fine Arts.

BIBLIOGRAPHY

A. Feszty: 'Lotz Károly', *Művészet* (1904), pp. 358–81

A. Kriesch: 'Lotz Károlyról', *Művészet* (1905), pp. 1–6

E. Ybl: *Lotz Károly élete és művészete* [Károly Lotz's life and art] (Budapest, 1938, 2/1981)

KATALIN GELLÉR

**Lotz, Wolfgang** (*b* Heilbronn, 19 April 1912; *d* Rome, 24 Oct 1981). German architectural historian. He studied art history at the University of Munich and then at the University of Hamburg, where in 1937 he received his doctorate under the direction of Ludwig Heydenreich. His dissertation *Vignolastudien* on the Italian Renaissance architect Jacopo Vignola established the foundation for many of his subsequent academic pursuits. From 1937 to 1942 he was a Fellow and then an Assistant at the Kunsthistorisches Institut in Florence. Drafted into the German army in 1942, he was taken prisoner in 1945 and assigned to the International Commission for Monuments in Munich. When the war ended, he was appointed Deputy Director of the Zentralinstitut für Kunstgeschichte in Munich, where he remained until his departure for the USA in 1952. In America he taught first at Vassar College, NY, and then in 1959 moved to the Institute of Fine Arts at New York University. In 1962 he was appointed Director of the Bibliotheca Hertziana in Rome, the prestigious research institute for the study of Italian art. He retired from this post in 1980 in order to devote himself to his scholarly interests but died a year later and was buried in the Protestant Cemetery in Rome.

Lotz's published work is almost entirely devoted to the study of late 15th- and 16th-century Italian architecture. Complementing his lifelong occupation with the career of Vignola and later fascination with Andrea Palladio were his interests in the influential role of architectural drawings and the iconography of Renaissance building types, for example the centralized church and the urban piazza. The culmination of some five dozen articles and reviews was the Pelican History of Art volume *Architecture in Italy, 1400–1600*, in which Heydenreich covered the 15th century and Lotz the 16th. In 1981 a selection of Lotz's most important essays was published under the title *Studies in Italian Renaissance Architecture*.

WRITINGS

*Vignolastudien* (diss., U. Hamburg, 1937; Würzburg, 1938)

'Vignola-Zeichnungen', *Jb. Preuss. Kstsamml.*, lix (1938), pp. 97–115

'Michelozzos Umbau der SS Annunziata in Florenz', *Mitt. Ksthist. Inst. Florenz*, v (1940), pp. 402–22

'Die ovalen Kirchenräume des Cinquecento', *Röm. Jb. Kstgesch.*, vii (1955), pp. 7–99

'Das Raumbild in der Architekturzeichnung der italienischen Renaissance', *Mitt. Ksthist. Inst. Florenz*, vii (1956), pp. 193–226

'Architecture in the Later Sixteenth Century', *Coll. A. J.*, xvii/2 (1958), pp. 129–39

'Osservazioni intorno ai disegni Palladiani', *Boll. Cent. Int. Stud. Archit. Andrea Palladio*, iv (1962), pp. 61–8

'Mannerism in Architecture: Changing Aspects', *Studies in Western Art, 2: The Renaissance and Mannerism, Acts of the Twentieth International Congress of the History of Art: Princeton, 1963*, pp. 239–46

'The Roman Legacy in Jacopo Sansovino's Venetian Buildings', *J. Soc. Archit. Historians*, xxii (1963), pp. 3–12

'Notizen zum kirchlichen Zentralbau der Renaissance', *Studien zur toskanischen Kunst: Festschrift für Ludwig Heinrich Heydenreich* (Munich, 1964), pp. 157–65

'La Trasformazione Sansoviniana di Piazza S Marco e l'urbanistica del cinquecento', *Boll. Cent. Inst. Stud. Archit. Andrea Palladio*, viii/2 (1966), pp. 114–22

'Der Palazzo Zuccari in Rom: Ein Künstlerhaus des 16. Jahrhunderts als Sitz eines Max-Planck-Instituts', *Jb. Max-Planck-Ges. Förderung Wiss.* (1967), pp. 149–55

'Palladio e Sansovino', *Boll. Cent. Int. Stud. Archit. Andrea Palladio*, ix (1967), pp. 13–23

with J. S. Ackerman: *Essays in Memory of Karl Lehmann* (New York, 1967), pp. 1–24

'Italienische Plätze des 16. Jahrhunderts', *Jb. Max-Planck-Ges. Förderung Wiss.* (1968), pp. 41–60

'Die spanische Treppe: Architektur als Mittel der Diplomatie', *Röm. Jb. Kstgesch.*, xii (1969), pp. 39–94

'La Piazza Ducale di Vigevano: Un foro principesco del tardo quattrocento', *Studi Bramanteschi: Atti del Congresso Internazionale: Milano, Urbino, Roma, 1970*, pp. 205–21

'Gli 883 cocchi della Roma del 1594', *Studi Offerti a Giovanni Incisa della Rocchetta: Misc. Soc. Romana Stor. Patria*, xxiii (1973), pp. 247–66

'I disegni', *La vita e le opere di Jacopo Barozzi da Vignola* (Vignola, 1974), pp. 125–67

with L. H. Heydenreich: *Architecture in Italy, 1400–1600*, Pelican Hist. A. (Harmondsworth, 1974)

*Studies in Italian Renaissance Architecture* (Cambridge, MA, 1981)

BIBLIOGRAPHY

J. Ackerman: 'In Memoriam, Wolfgang Lotz (1912–1981)', *J. Soc. Archit. Historians*, xli (1982), pp. 5–6

Obituary, *Röm. Jb. Kstgesch.*, xx (1983) [dedication page]

JOHN VARRIANO

**Lötz Witwe.** Bohemian glass factory. In 1836 a glass factory was founded by Johann Eisner von Eisenstein in Klostermühle in the Bohemian forest. In 1840 production was taken over by Eisenstein's son-in-law Friedrich Hafenbrädl, who began making window and table glass. In 1851 Dr Franz Gerstner (1816–55) and his wife Susanne Lötz-Gerstner (*b* 1809), who had previously been married to Johann Lötz (1778–1848), bought the factory. From 1858 the company was named and in 1863 registered Lötz Witwe ('Lötz widow'). In 1878 the factory exhibited a range of coloured glass at the Exposition Universelle in Paris. The following year Lötz-Gerstner's grandson Max Ritter von Spaun (1856–1909) took over the company and employed Eduard Prochaska (*d* 1922) as managing director. Over the next two decades the factory was substantially enlarged, and by 1891 the company employed 200 glassworkers, 36 cutters and 30 glass painters. The company had representatives in various European cities, including E. Bakalowits & Söhne in Vienna, a company that brought the factory to the attention of many Viennese artists, L. Fränkel and Arndt & Marcus in Berlin and Fr. Krasa & Co. and Max Emanuel & Co. in London.

From the 1890s the factory specialized in the production of *Jugendstil* glass, much of which was exported to England. The influence of Louis Comfort Tiffany and Emile Gallé, whose work was shown at the 1897 glass exhibition in Reichenberg, is evident in the new forms and shapes and the use of a variety of colours iridized with gold and silver (e.g. bowl, *c.* 1900; Düsseldorf, Kstmus.; *see* GLASS, colour pl. VI, fig. 3). Particularly successful glass included 'Olympiaglas', 'Phänomenglas', 'Octopusglas', 'Papillonglas' and 'Titaniaglas'. The firm was highly acclaimed at the international exhibitions, receiving gold medals at the 1900 Exposition Universelle in Paris and the 1904 World's Fair in St Louis in the USA.

In 1908 the firm was passed on to Maximilian Robert Johann von Spaun (*b* 1883), and Adolf Beckert (1884–1929) was taken on as art director; the latter attracted the talents of such artists as Josef Hoffmann, Michael Powolny and Otto Prutscher, who all designed items for the company. Although the firm encountered financial difficulties during the early 1910s and the factory was seriously damaged by a fire in 1913, a new range of wares was created for the 1914 Deutsche Werkbundausstellung in Cologne. The company's success was briefly revived during the 1920s under Friedrich Franz von Spaun (1890–1936), but it continued to have serious financial difficulties under various owners until it was finally closed in 1947. Important collections of Lötz Witwe glass are in the Kunsthaus, Düsseldorf, and the Glasmuseum und Kochbuchmuseum, Passau.

#### BIBLIOGRAPHY

W. Neuwirth: *Loetz Witwe* (Vienna, 1986)

H. Ricke and others: *Lötz: Böhmisches Glas, 1880–1940*, 2 vols (Munich, 1989)

PETER RATH

**Loudon, John Claudius** (*b* Cambuslang, Lanark [now Strathclyde], 8 April 1783; *d* London, 14 December 1843). Scottish garden designer and writer. The son of a farmer, he was first apprenticed to a nurseryman and landscape gardener, moving to London in 1803 to set himself up as a garden designer. That year he published his 'Hints . . .[on] Laying Out the Grounds of the Public Squares in London' in the *Literary Journal* (ii/12, 31 Dec 1803, cols 739–42), advocating a judicious mixture of deciduous and evergreen plants. He also carried out work for the Duchess of Brunswick at Brunswick House, Blackheath, London, and the following year spent some time in his native Scotland, improving the estates of several aristocratic clients. The same year he exhibited three drawings at the Royal Academy and published his first book, *Observations on. . .Ornamental Plantations*. In it he emphasized his adherence to PICTURESQUE principles and those of UVEDALE PRICE in particular. From this time on, and in addition to several forays into architectural design, Loudon's career as a garden designer was inseparable from his vast publishing enterprises, by which he disseminated his advice and ideas.

In 1805 Loudon was elected a member of the Society of Arts and also published his *Short Treatise on. . .Hothouses*. The following year he became a Fellow of the Linnean Society, published his *Treatise on. . .Country Residences* and worked at Ditchley, Oxon, reshaping its lake and introducing exotic plants. He also remodelled the exterior and grounds of Barnbarrow, Wigtownshire (now Dumfries and Galloway; destr.). The following year, after a severe illness, he and his father took a lease of Wood Hall, Pinner, near London, where they set up a farm in order to demonstrate the superiority of Scottish agricultural methods. This was so successful that Loudon was invited to repeat the experiment at Great Tew, Oxon, where he established a superb *ferme ornée* at which pupils were instructed in advanced agriculture.

In 1811 the lease at Tew was sold. The following year Loudon executed his principal architectural commission at Garth, near Welshpool, Montgoms (now Powys; destr.), a house in the Gothic style, and published both his *Hints on the Formation of Gardens* and the *Observations on Laying Out Farms*. In 1813–14 he travelled abroad (the first of several trips to the Continent) and was elected to a number of learned societies in Prussia and Russia. On returning to England (to find all his financial investments had failed), Loudon became interested in glasshouse design. He invented an iron bar that made curved glass roofs for hothouses possible, and he went on to publish several books on the construction of conservatories. In 1819 he travelled through France and Italy in order to study continental garden design. The mass of information he slowly gathered together on every aspect of garden history, horticulture, aesthetics and technical development was eventually incorporated in his enormous *Encyclopaedia of Gardening* (1822), the first book to attempt such comprehensive coverage, and it established him as the foremost authority in English on the subject. He followed this in 1825 with an *Encyclopaedia of Agriculture* and the next year began his highly influential periodical, the *Gardener's Magazine*, which ran until his death. In it he wrote in support of numerous campaigns, including a successful one to encourage planting improvements in public parks.

In 1829 Loudon married Jane Webb (1807–58), who also became a popularizing horticultural writer. Some publishing failures followed, but Loudon's career as a garden designer began to re-establish itself in 1831 with his project for the Birmingham Botanic Garden, a public garden intended to be both scientific and ornamental. Two years later he and Jane Webb published their *Encyclopaedia of Cottage, Farm, and Villa Architecture*. This was immediately successful, and Loudon soon began work on his *Arboretum et Fruticetum. . .Britannicum* (1838); this proved to be a financial disaster, but, by 1836, while still preparing it, he was producing five separate monthly publications, including the *Architectural Magazine*, the first journal in Britain devoted entirely to architecture.

In 1835 Loudon laid out the Terrace Garden in Gravesend, Kent (destr.), a publicly owned open space intended specifically for recreation. In 1839 work began, following his designs, on the Derby Arboretum, and he published a catalogue of its plants the following year when it opened. The Arboretum consisted of one main walk and numerous minor 'episodal' ones, and the planting schemes were based on his Gardenesque (see GARDEN, §VIII, 5) principles, in which the presentation of flowers and shrubs was meant to feature the beauty and botanical interest of individual plants, rather than to create picturesque visual effects. The same year he edited a one-volume reprint of all Humphry Repton's writings and laid out the grounds of Castle Kennedy, near Stranraer, Wigtonshire (now Dumfries & Galloway). By 1842 Loudon was occupied with preparing *On the Laying Out . . . of Cemeteries*, a collection of articles that had first appeared in the *Gardener's Magazine*, and the single most influential work on the subject. Here Loudon was not simply concerned with utility, hygiene and function, but with Associationism as well, an aesthetic theory based on the work of Scottish rationalist philosophers such as Archibald Alison. Loudon's suggestions for appropriate types of planting for cemeteries had a widespread influence on the landscaping of burial grounds in both Britain and North America. Cemeteries as botanic gardens, as places that were instructive, morally uplifting, educational and effective, were all aspects that were discussed by him and by his followers, and during this period Loudon was responsible for designs for the cemetery at Histon Road, Cambridge (1842), the Abbey Cemetery, Bath (1843), and that at the Common, Southampton (1843). His work *On . . . Cemeteries* was the last of Loudon's books to be published in his lifetime; he died the same year and was buried in London, at Kensal Green cemetery.

## WRITINGS

*Observations on the Formation and Management of Useful and Ornamental Plantations; On the Theory and Practice of Landscape Gardening; and on Gaining and Embanking Land from Rivers or the Sea* (Edinburgh, 1804)

*A Short Treatise on Several Improvements, Recently Made in Hot-houses* (Edinburgh, 1805)

*A Treatise on Forming, Improving, and Managing Country Residences* (London, 1806)

*Designs for Laying Out Farms and Farm-buildings in the Scotch Style; Adapted to England* (London, 1811)

*Hints on the Formation of Gardens and Pleasure-grounds, with Designs in Various Styles of Rural Embellishment* (London, 1812)

*Observations on Laying Out Farms, in the Scotch Style, Adapted to England* (London, 1812)

*Remarks on the Construction of Hot-houses* (London, 1817)

*An Encyclopaedia of Gardening, Comprising the Theory and Practice of Horticulture, Floriculture, Arboriculture, and Landscape Gardening, Including . . . a General History of Gardening in All Countries* (London, 1822, rev. 3/1850)

*An Encyclopaedia of Agriculture . . . Including a General History of Agriculture* (London, 1825, rev. 8/1871)

*An Encyclopaedia of Plants* (London, 1829, rev. 3/1855)

*An Encyclopaedia of Cottage, Farm, and Villa Architecture and Furniture* (London, 1833, rev. 12/1869)

*Arboretum et fruticetum Britannicum; Or the Trees and Shrubs of Britain, Native and Foreign, Delineated and . . . Described*, 8 vols (London, 1838)

*The Suburban Gardener and Villa Companion* (London, 1938)

*The Derby Arboretum, Containing a Catalogue of the Trees and Shrubs Included in it* (London, 1840)

ed.: *The Landscape Gardening and Landscape Architecture of the Late Humphry Repton* (London, 1840)

*On the Laying Out, Planting, and Managing of Cemeteries; and on the Improvement of Churchyards* (London, 1843/R 1981)

## BIBLIOGRAPHY
Colvin

G. Taylor: *Some Nineteenth-century Gardeners* (London, 1951), pp. 17–67

G. L. Hersey: 'John Claudius Loudon and Architectural Associationism', *Archit. Rev.*, cxliv (1968), pp. 89–92

J. Gloag: *Mr Loudon's England: The Life and Work of John Claudius Loudon, and his Influence on Architecture and Furniture Design* (Newcastle upon Tyne, 1970)

L. Fricker: 'John Claudius Loudon: The Plane Truth?', *Furor hortensis: Essays on the History of the English Landscape Garden, in Memory of H. F. Clark*, ed. P. Willis (Edinburgh, 1974), pp. 76–88

M. L. Simo: *Loudon and Landscape: From Country Seat to Metropolis, 1783–1843* (New Haven, CT, and London, 1988)

J. S. Curl: *A Celebration of Death: An Introduction to Some of the Buildings, Monuments, and Settings of Funerary Architecture in the Western European Tradition* (London, 1993)

JAMES STEVENS CURL

**Lough, John Graham** (*b* Shotley, Northumb., 8 Jan 1798; *d* London, 8 April 1876). English sculptor. Apprenticed to a Northumberland stone mason, he worked as an ornamental sculptor in Newcastle upon Tyne and entered the Royal Academy Schools, London, in 1826. He became the protégé of the painter B. R. Haydon, and in 1827 he exhibited his first important work, a statue of *Milo* (bronze version, 1863; Blagdon, Northumb.), based on his studies of the Elgin marbles and the sculpture of Michelangelo. From 1834 to 1838 he worked in Rome, where his portrait style was influenced by Neo-classicism. On his return to Britain, he received commissions to execute statues of *Queen Victoria* (marble, 1845–6; untraced) and the *Prince Consort* (marble, 1845–6; London, V&A) for the Royal Exchange, London. His finest monuments are those to *Robert Southey* (marble, 1846), at St Kentigern, Crosthwaite, Cumbria, and to *George Stephenson* (bronze, 1863), near the High Level Bridge, Newcastle upon Tyne; the latter has a group of supporting figures representing engineering workers. Lough produced many ideal works on classical, historical and literary themes, including a series of marble statues of Shakespearean subjects (1843–63; e.g. Blagdon, Northumb.) for his chief patron Matthew, 4th Baronet Ridley. His powerful, imaginative and eclectic works illustrate the development of Victorian classicism towards a romantic and picturesque style.

## BIBLIOGRAPHY
Gunnis

Obituary, *A. J.* [London] (1876), pp. 202–3

T. S. R. Boase: 'John Graham Lough: A Transitional Sculptor', *J. Warb. & Court. Inst.*, xxiii (1960), pp. 277–90

B. Read: *Victorian Sculpture* (New Haven, 1982)

J. Lough and E. Merson: *John Graham Lough 1798–1876: A Northumbrian Sculptor* (Woodbridge, 1987)

MARTIN GREENWOOD

**Lough Crew.** Site of Neolithic passage grave cemetery in Co. Meath, Ireland, *c.* 40 km from the Brugh na Bóinne cemeteries of NEWGRANGE and KNOWTH (*see also* PREHISTORIC EUROPE, §IV, 2). It comprises *c.* 30 tombs, mainly spread over three hilltops, with concentrations on the central and western summits. The 110 known decorated stones are dispersed between 14 tombs; there were probably others, but many stones are missing due to damage and weathering, and in other cases the designs may have been obliterated. The largest number of surviving stones (32) is at Site T, while Site L has 21 stones; these represent the principal sites on their respective summits. Apart from one example at Site T, the kerbstones are not decorated, although the surface of the local stone used could have been weathered away. Motifs known from Megalithic art elsewhere in Ireland (*see* PREHISTORIC EUROPE, §IV, 3(i)) also occur on the decorated stones at Lough Crew. Circles, parallel lines, dot-and-circle and angular motifs and cup-marks frequently appear, but single or multiple U-shaped motifs are the most common. In comparison to the Brugh na Bóinne cemeteries, the angular element is less in evidence, although the Lough Crew artists did develop a preference for certain motifs, such as star-shaped forms, and even introduced new motifs such as the marigold design. Curvilinear motifs predominate, but the number per stone varies from one or two motifs to an overall pattern. The organization of groups of similar motifs into ordered compositions seen at Newgrange and Knowth is largely absent at Lough Crew, as is the allocation of stones with particular types of composition to special places within the tomb. On the whole, the compositions at Lough Crew are less ordered than those of the Brugh na Bóinne cemeteries and tend to resemble the motifs carved in a random manner on the backs of some of the kerbstones at Newgrange.

BIBLIOGRAPHY

E. S. Twohig: *The Megalithic Art of Western Europe* (Oxford, 1981), pp. 205–20

GEORGE EOGAN

**Louis**, Duc d'Orléans. *See* ORLÉANS, (4).

**Louis**, Duke of Orléans. *See* VALOIS, (6).

**Louis**, Duke of Savoy. *See under* SAVOY, §I, 1.

**Louis**, King of Holland. *See* BONAPARTE, (6).

**Louis**, King of Hungary and Poland. *See* ANJOU, §I(3).

**Louis I**, 1st Duke of Anjou. *See* ANJOU, §II(1).

**Louis II**, 2nd Duke of Anjou. *See* ANJOU, §II(2).

**Louis II**, King of Bohemia and Hungary. *See* JAGIELLON, (3).

**Louis II** [Louis de Mâle], Count of Flanders (*b* 25 Nov 1330; *reg* 1346–84; *d* 1384). South Netherlandish ruler and patron. He was the son of Louis I (*reg* 1322–46) and spent much of his reign reconciling the various factions in the Flemish towns' struggles for autonomy. Shortly before 1370 Louis II had his own burial chapel built next to the Onze Lieve Vrouwkerk in Kortrijk and dedicated it to St Catherine. The chapel is an early example of Gothic architecture in Brabant and may have been based on the example of the Sainte-Chapelle in Paris. Jan van Asselt (*fl* 1364–96), appointed court painter in 1365, was commissioned to decorate the chapel with frescoes, for which he received payment from 1372 until 1374. He depicted 27 Flemish counts, including *Louis de Mâle*, a few saints and the *Last Judgement* (all destr.). In 1381 van Asselt was succeeded by Melchior Broederlam, who painted leather chairs, pennons and banners for the Count. In 1374 André Beauneveu, who had earlier been in the service of Charles V, was commissioned to execute the tomb for the chapel. The tomb was never finished, however, because Louis de Mâle decided to be buried in the chapel of Notre Dame de la Treille in St Pierre, Lille. Nonetheless, Beauneveu completed an alabaster statue of *St Catherine*, which was returned to the Onze Lieve Vrouwkerk in Kortrijk by Louis's son-in-law, Philip the Bold, Duke of Burgundy (*see* BEAUNEVEU, ANDRÉ). The Missal of Louis de Mâle (*c.* 1360; Brussels, Bib. Royale Albert 1er, MS. 1217), illuminated by an unknown hand, includes a rather primitive illustration of the *Crucifixion with Donors*.

BIBLIOGRAPHY

D. Roggen: 'A. Beauneveu en het Katharinabeeld van Kortrijk' [Beauneveu and the statue of St Catherine in Kortrijk], *Gent. Bijdr. Kstgesch. & Oudhdknd.*, xv (1954), pp. 223–31

J. de Cuyper: 'De Gravenkapel van Kortrijk: Opbouw (1370–1374) en herstel na de ramp van 1382' [The chapel of the counts in Kortrijk: Works (1370–1374) and reconstruction after the disaster of 1382], *De Leiegouw*, iv (1962), pp. 5–54

L. Devliegher: 'Het Sint-Katharinabeeld van André Beauneveu' [André Beauneveu's statue of St Catherine], *De Leiegouw*, xi (1969), pp. 175–8

——: *De Onze Lieve Vrouwe Kerk te Kortrijk* (1973), vi of *Kunstpatrimonium van West-Vlaanderen* [West-Flanders art patrimony] (Utrecht, 1965–84)

M. J. T. M. STOMPÉ

**Louis IX**, King of France. *See* CAPET, (2).

**Louis XI**, King of France. *See* VALOIS, (9).

**Louis XII**, King of France. *See* VALOIS, (13).

**Louis XIII**, King of France. *See* BOURBON, §I(7).

**Louis XIV**, King of France. *See* BOURBON, §I(8).

**Louis XIV style.** Term applied to a style of architecture, interior décor and garden layout associated with the reign of Louis XIV of France (*reg* 1643–1715; *see* BOURBON, §I(8)). Once he began his personal rule in 1661, the King took a passionate interest in the building and furnishing of the royal residences, notably VERSAILLES, bringing together the most talented artists of the day to promote the power and magnificence of the monarchy. The style had its origins at VAUX-LE-VICOMTE, the opulent late Baroque château created in the 1650s for Nicolas Fouquet, Surintendant des Finances, and the collaborative effort of the architect Louis Le Vau (*see* LE VAU, (1)), the garden designer ANDRÉ LE NÔTRE and CHARLES LE BRUN, painter and designer. After Fouquet's disgrace and imprisonment in 1661, the three worked together to transform the King's hunting-lodge at Versailles into a statement of political absolutism.

The style is characterized by sumptuous materials, exquisite craftsmanship, a profusion of classical motifs and strict formality of organization. At Versailles, the layout of the gardens and the plan of the interior spaces were controlled by symmetry and axial planning. The *grands appartements* were arranged *en enfilade*, each opening on to the next with doors aligned to create lengthy vistas. Walls were covered with slabs of variegated marble divided by pilasters supporting bracketed cornices. Ceilings were painted with allegorical or mythological scenes celebrating the glory of the Sun King. Gilt stucco carved with trophies, helmets and Victories, and marble reliefs and classical busts on pedestals contributed a heavy, masculine element to the style. Pictorial tapestries were used extensively, sometimes hung above a marble dado. Plate-glass mirrors, sometimes lining the entire wall as in the Galerie des

Glaces at Versailles, lightened the whole while reflecting the rich polychromy and varied texture of the interiors (*see* FRANCE, §V, 3). In furniture the grand Italian Baroque style was allied with a more restrained French classical spirit (*see* FRANCE, §VI, 2). Cabinets, in ebony with panels of pietra dura and gilt bronze mounts, designed by Domenico Cucci and veneered with tortoiseshell and brass in the manner of ANDRÉ CHARLES BOULLE, or with floral marquetry in the Dutch fashion of PIERRE GOLE, were grand showpieces. Solid silver furniture was produced at the Gobelins manufactory for the Galerie des Glaces but was melted down in 1689 to help pay for the King's wars. The taste for exotic imports from East Asia encouraged the use of lacquered or japanned panels on many forms of furniture. Blue-and-white porcelain, avidly collected since the beginning of the 17th century, was displayed on brackets, massed on top of cabinets or used to decorate entire rooms or Porcelain Cabinets (*see* CABINET (i), §4(i)). In all media, ornament included such classical motifs as scrolls and volutes, palmettes, grotesques, satyrs' masks and caryatids as well as bands of arabesque strapwork. A lighter note appeared *c.* 1710, reflecting the influence of the ornamentalists JEAN BÉRAIN I, Claude Audran III (*see* AUDRAN, (3)) and Pierre Le Pautre III (*see* LE PAUTRE, (3)). Such new elements as lambrequins, grotesques, putti, torches, arrows and quivers linked with ribbons, garlands and interlaced initials marked the emergence of the RÉGENCE STYLE.

Despite its magnificence, or perhaps because of it, the Louis XIV style proved highly adaptable as an art of political propaganda; it was widely emulated by other European monarchs and their colonial representatives (*see* WILLIAM AND MARY STYLE). Because of the strict control and high standards of the royal manufactories (*see* GOBELINS, §1), France became pre-eminent in the arts of decoration and design during this period, and the products of French craftsmanship were widely sought after and exported. In the 20th century the term has lost the connotation of programmatic unity and is primarily used to describe the decorative arts.

BIBLIOGRAPHY
E. Dacier: *Le Style Louis XIV* (Paris, 1939)
R. A. Weigert: *Le Style Louis XIV* (Paris, 1941)
L. Hautecoeur: *L'Architecture classique en France* (Paris, 1948)
P. Pradel: *L'Art au siècle de Louis XIV* (Paris, 1949)
*Louis XIV: Faste et décors* (exh. cat., Paris, Mus. A. Déc., 1961)
P. Verlet: 'Louis XIV', *Styles, meubles, décors du Moyen Age à nos jours*, ed. P. Verlet (Paris, 1972), pp. 223–39
J. Féray: *Architecture intérieure et décoration en France, des origines à 1875* (Paris, 1988)
M. Eleb-Vidal and A. Debarre Blanchard: *Architectures de la vie privée: Maisons et mentalités XIIe–XIXe siècle* (Brussels, 1989)
                                    MONIQUE RICCARDI-CUBITT

**Louis XV**, King of France. *See* BOURBON, §I(10).

**Louis XV style.** Term used primarily in France for a style of interior decoration and decorative arts between *c.* 1700 and 1750, which roughly corresponds to the period of the

Louis XV style interior of the Salon du Prince, Hôtel Soubise (now Archives Nationales), Paris, by Germain Boffrand, late 1730s

Régence (1715–23) and the first half of the reign of Louis XV (1723–74). The term is used to describe the style that developed from the RÉGENCE STYLE and the Rococo style in France (*see* ROCOCO, §II). The style was influenced by a more informal, intimate and comfortable way of life, reflecting the increasingly important role of women in social life. The production of decorative arts was encouraged by the influential patronage of the King's mistress, the Marquise de Pompadour (*see* POISSON, (1)), and her circle at court, and by the influence on design of the marchands-merciers. The style suited the interior decoration of *petits appartements* in the HÔTEL PARTICULIER, with *boiseries* carved in the sinuous Rococo style, as for example the interiors of the Hôtel de Soubise (see fig.), or incorporating CHINOISERIE and SINGERIE motifs or the *genre pittoresque* introduced by JUSTE-AURÈLE MEISSONNIER and Nicolas Pineau (for illustration *see* PINEAU, NICOLAS), painted in light shades of colour or picked out in gilt or a contrasting colour. *Boiseries*, furniture, chimneypieces, and light fittings were often designed as an ensemble (*see* FRANCE, §VI, 3), providing a harmonious elegance to the interior. The influence of women is reflected in the new forms of furniture that appeared at this time, for example the *marquise* (sofa), the *duchesse* (chaise-longue), the *bergère* (chair), and all manner of small, delicate *bonheurs-du-jour* (work-table), many fitted with porcelain plaques from the Sèvres porcelain factory or with elaborate mechanisms. An interest in contrasting colours and luxurious materials is reflected in the use of complex pictorial or geometric marquetry by the cabinetmaker JEAN-FRANÇOIS OEBEN, the widespread use of elaborate *bronzes d'ameublement* and gilt-bronze mounts for furniture (*see* CRESSENT, CHARLES and CAFFIÉRI, (2)) and the use of lacquer and japanning (*see* VERNIS MARTIN). Porcelain, notably from the factories of Vincennes and Sèvres, and faience from Marseille and Strasbourg reflected the influence of the Rococo, as did metalwork (*see* FRANCE, §IX, 1 and 2(iii)(a)), tapestries and textiles. The Louis XV style waned in popularity from *c.* 1750, probably as a reaction against its frivolity and lightness, to be gradually replaced by the emerging Neo-classical style, which is known as the Transitional style (*see* LOUIS XVI STYLE).

BIBLIOGRAPHY
F. Kimball: *The Creation of the Rococo* (Philadelphia, 1943, rev. New York, 1980)
C. Mauricheau-Beaupré: *L'Art au XVIIIe siècle en France*, 2 vols (Paris, 1946–7)
*Louis XV et Rocaille* (exh. cat., Paris, Mus. Orangerie, 1950)
E. Dacier: *L'Art au 18e siècle en France: Régence/Louis XV* (Paris, 1951)
P. Verlet: *Les Ebénistes français du XVIIIe siècle* (Paris, 1963)
——: *French Furniture and Interior Decoration of the 18th Century* (London, 1967)

Louis XVI style boudoir of Marie-Antoinette (1786) designed by Pierre Rousseau, with paintings by Jean-Simon Berthélmy (Fontainebleau, Musée National du Château de Fontainebleau)

P. Verlet, ed.: 'Louis XV', *Styles, meubles, décors du Moyen Age à nos jours* (Paris, 1972), pp. 222–39

MONIQUE RICCARDI-CUBITT

**Louis XVI**, King of France. *See* BOURBON, §I(11).

**Louis XVI style.** Term loosely referring to a decorative style in France that first emerged in the 1750s and was fully developed before Louis XVI succeeded to the throne in 1774. In 1754 the engraver Charles-Nicolas Cochin II (*see* COCHIN (ii), (2)) appealed to craftsmen for a return to the restraint and discipline of the Antique, an appeal that reflected the larger philosophical and artistic movement of the Enlightenment. Between 1749 and 1751 Cochin undertook a tour of Italy in the company of Abel-François Poisson de Vandières (later the Marquis de Marigny and the future Directeur des Bâtiments du Roi), the architect Jacques-Germain Soufflot and the Abbé Le Blanc, which furthered the interest in the Antique. The discovery of Herculaneum (1738) and Pompeii (1748) was followed by numerous publications on antiquity, among them Cochin's own work, *Observations sur les antiquités de la ville d'Herculanum* (Paris, 1754) and *Recueil d'antiquités égyptiennes, étrusques, grecques, romaines et gauloises* (Paris, 1752–67) by the Comte de Caylus. These discoveries and subsequent publications stimulated a passion for the GOÛT GREC in France, the first, austere phase of NEO-CLASSICISM, for which such Classical motifs as the ANTHEMION, PALMETTE, BUCRANIUM, Vitruvian scroll, Greek key and GUILLOCHE were employed. Although it was the decoration and not the form of French furniture of this period that reflected the Antique, one new form that did emerge was the *athénienne*, a tripod form that could, for example, be used as a wash-stand, candelabrum or perfume burner.

This severe, pure style of decoration was superseded by the Transitional style, which moved away from the excesses of the Rococo style and heralded the Neo-classical style. *Rinceaux*, ribbon and floral motifs are used in a restrained, symmetrical manner, adding elegance and refinement to military trophies and Classical ornament (see fig.). Geometrical forms and ornament—fluting, reeding, the lozenge, wreath and rosette—were generally used to great effect in furniture, porcelain and metalwork. The Transitional style also maintained certain elements typical of the Baroque, and there was a renewed interest in pietre dure and the marquetry of André-Charles Boulle. Most specialist craftsmen adapted successfully to each different stylistic phase. By the 1770s the Transitional style had given way to the 'genre Arabesque' or 'goût étrusque' (*see* ARABESQUE STYLE and ETRUSCAN STYLE).

BIBLIOGRAPHY

S. de Ricci: *Le Style Louis XVI: Meubles et décoration* (Paris, 1913)
P. Verlet: *Le Mobilier royal français* (Paris, 1945–55)
Mauricheau-Beaupré: *L'Art au XVIIIe siècle en France* (Paris, 1947)
P. Verlet: *Les Ebénistes français du XVIIIe siècle* (Paris, 1963)
M. Gallet: *Demeures parisiennes à l'époque de Louis XVI* (Paris, 1964)
G. Janneau: *L'Epoque Louis XVI* (Paris, 1964)
P. Verlet: *Louis XVI: Styles, meubles, décors* (Paris, 1972)
S. Eriksen: *Early Neo-classicism in France* (London, 1974)

MONIQUE RICCARDI-CUBITT

**Louis XVIII**, King of France. *See* BOURBON, §I(13).

**Louis, Morris** [Bernstein, Morris Louis] (*b* Baltimore, MD, 28 Nov 1912; *d* Washington, DC, 7 Sept 1962). American painter. Born Morris Louis Bernstein, he changed his name by legal deed in 1938. He studied at Maryland Institute of Fine and Applied Arts, Baltimore (1927–32), and assisted in painting a Works Progress

Morris Louis: *Delta Beta*, acrylic on canvas, 2.62×4.40 m, 1959–60 (Boston, MA, Museum of Fine Arts)

Administration (WPA) mural for a public school in Baltimore. From 1936 to 1940 he lived in New York, where he attended the workshops of David Alfaro Siqueiros and became acquainted with the use of commercial enamel paints. A number of his WPA murals and paintings of work and workers show the influence of Max Beckmann, for example *Untitled (Two Workers)* (1939; Boston, MA, Mus. F.A.). In New York he frequently visited MOMA. He returned to Baltimore in 1940 and in 1952 moved to Washington, DC.

From the 1950s Louis devoted himself to developing a response to the avant-garde work of Jackson Pollock, Robert Motherwell, Kenneth Noland, Helen Frankenthaler and other artists of the New York School (*see* ABSTRACT EXPRESSIONISM), abandoning the late Cubist style of his previous work.

The direction of Louis's work was changed by seeing Frankenthaler's technique of 'staining' very thin pigment on to unprimed canvas in the painting *Mountains and Sea* (1953; artist's col.; for illustration *see* FRANKENTHALER, HELEN) in April 1953. A dominant feature of his work at this time was his serial paintings, which have been divided into distinct groups: *Veils* (1954), *Veils II* (1958–9), *Unfurleds* (1959–61) and *Stripes* (1961–2). In the *Veils*, for example *Untitled* (1954; Palm Beach, FL, Lannan Found.) and *Dalet Ayin* (1958; Humlebæk, Louisiana Mus.), Louis achieved this notion of interpenetration of colours by virtually staining the canvas with thinned acrylic paint so that it was difficult to see where one colour ended and another began. This technique created a wash-like transparency so that the perception of depth was problematic. The next group of paintings was the *Unfurleds*, for example *Delta Beta* (1959–60; Boston, MA, Mus. F.A.; see fig.), the majority of which were executed between June or July 1960 and some time early in 1961. In these paintings an open space of bare canvas in the centre is scored diagonally at the left and right edges with irregular stripes of colours that vanish into diminishing scales at the corner of the canvas. In the final series, the *Stripes*, for example *Third Element* (1961; New York MOMA), bunched straight vertical bands of colour, of varying thicknesses, float on a neutral ground like folds of cloth.

Louis was retrospectively named by Clement Greenberg as an exponent of POST-PAINTERLY ABSTRACTION in the exhibition of the same name held at the County Museum of Art, Los Angeles, in 1964. In the following year the painter was included as one of the WASHINGTON COLOR PAINTERS in their exhibition (1965; Washington, DC, Gal. Mod. A.).

BIBLIOGRAPHY

M. Fried: *Morris Louis* (New York, 1970)

K. Moffett: *Morris Louis in the Museum of Fine Art, Boston* (Boston, 1979)

D. Upright: *Morris Louis: The Complete Paintings* (New York, 1985) [cat. rais.]

J. Elderfield: *Morris Louis* (New York, 1986)

CHRISTOPHER BROOKEMAN

**Louis, Séraphine.** *See* SÉRAPHINE.

**Louis, Victor** [Louis-Nicolas] (*b* Paris, 10 May 1731; *d* Paris, 3 July 1800). French architect and designer. He studied at the Académie Royale d'Architecture from 1748.

He tried several times for the Prix de Rome and in 1755, although disqualified on a technicality, he was eventually awarded a bursary to study in Rome. While in Italy (1756–9) he pursued a wide range of interests, including painting and music, and he became friends with Hubert Robert and Charles-Louis Clérisseau. The end of his stay in Rome was marred, however, by the so-called 'imposture' scandal. Louis had sent the famous archaeologist, the Comte de Caylus, some imaginary drawings by Robert, claiming that they recorded recently discovered antiquities. Caylus only learnt of the deception when he was on the point of having them engraved. This episode was responsible for the lifelong hostility of the establishment towards Louis and his failure ever to be elected to the Académie Royale d'Architecture.

In 1761 Louis was entrusted with the decoration of the chapel of the Benedictine abbey of Notre-Dame de Bon Secours (destr.) in the Faubourg St Antoine, Paris. The slightly theatrical effects achieved by Louis, known from an engraving, were executed in *trompe l'oeil*. Louis's reputation as a decorator was increased by the setting he designed at the Théâtre Italien for the celebrations of the Peace of Paris (1763) between Spain and England. There followed a commission to decorate the chapel of Les Ames du Purgatoire in the church of Ste Marguerite, also in the Faubourg St Antoine. This time the desired effect was funereal, and the result much more imposing and austere than at Notre-Dame de Bon Secours, consisting of flanking colonnades of fluted Ionic columns painted on the walls and featuring an altar and sarcophagi derived from the Antique.

When Stanisław II Poniatowski was elected King of Poland in 1764, he formed a scheme to modernize the Royal Castle at Warsaw and summoned Louis, who had been recommended by his friend Marie-Thérèse Geoffrin. Louis prepared a set of designs in a transitional style between Rococo and early Neo-classicism, prompting the King to describe him as a 'génie noble, fécond et sage'. The designs remained largely unexecuted, however, due to a sudden change in the King's political fortune. Nevertheless, Louis subsequently drew on some of the same material in his designs for the Intendance (1770–76) at Besançon.

In 1773 Louis moved to Bordeaux to work on a new theatre to replace the Salle des Spectacles, destroyed by fire in 1755. Construction had begun in 1770 to designs by François Lhote (*d* 1808), but Armand, Duc de Richelieu (1696–1788), for whom Louis had already worked in Paris, secured his appointment as architect, and Louis produced new designs. The Grand Théâtre (1773–80) is his most impressive work. The façade consists of a free-standing colonnade of a giant Corinthian order, rising through two storeys to a bold unbroken cornice running around the entire building. Inside (see fig.), an extensive columnar vestibule leads to a dramatic vaulted hall of beautifully cut stone housing a monumental staircase. The combination of mysterious top-lighting and powerful, clear-cut architectural forms is the quintessence of French Neo-classicism. In addition to the circular auditorium, there was also an oval concert hall over the entrance vestibule. The building was both technically and socially innovative, bringing the format of a princely theatre to the middle

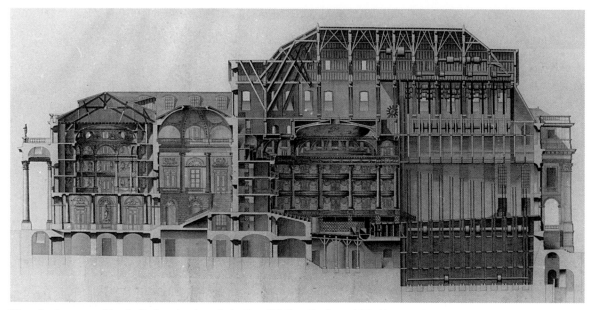

Victor Louis: measured longitudinal section through the Grand Théâtre, Bordeaux, 1773–80; engraving

classes of Bordeaux and making the process of theatre-going a spectacle in itself.

On completing the Grand Théâtre, Louis returned to Paris, where he was commissioned by the Duc de Chartres, later King Louis-Philippe, to surround the gardens of the Palais-Royal with a speculative development (1781–4); this consisted of three arcades of a sober but grand design housing a variety of shops, hairdressers, restaurants and cafés. At the end of the western arcade Louis constructed the Salle Beaujolais (1782–3; later called the Théâtre Français). Louis also designed the Théâtre du Palais-Royal (1786–90), replacing Pierre-Louis Moreau-Desproux's theatre, which had been destroyed by fire in 1781; it was renamed the Comédie Française at the end of the 18th century.

In the late 1780s Louis produced designs for a Place Louis XVI to replace the Château Trompette, Bordeaux, which it was suggested should be demolished. The sublime scale of these plans was utopian in its vision. A huge semicircular space, adjacent to the river and centred on a single monumental column, was intended to be sur-rounded by a sweeping crescent of uniform five-storey blocks articulated with a single giant order. This façade was to be continuous, though pierced at intervals by 13 triumphal arches rising the full height of the building to allow streets to radiate from the main square. Despite auspicious beginnings, the scheme foundered in 1790. The Revolution also brought to a halt Louis's most ambitious domestic project, the Château de Bouilh at Saint-André de Cubzac, near Bordeaux, designed in 1786. After this date Louis received few commissions in Paris, and in 1799 he contemplated moving to Philadelphia.

### WRITINGS
*La Salle de Spectacle de Bordeaux* (Paris, 1782)

### BIBLIOGRAPHY
C. Marionneau: *Victor Louis* (Bordeaux, 1881)
*Victor Louis, 1731–1800: Dessins et gravures* (exh. cat. by F. -G. Pariset, Bordeaux, Bib. Mun., 1980) [contains extensive bibliog.]
*Victor Louis et le théâtre, scénographie, mise en scène et architecture théâtrale aux XVIII et XIX siècles* (Paris, 1982)
C. Taillard: *Bordeaux classique* (Toulouse, 1987)

RICHARD JOHN

**Louisa Ulrica** [Lovisa Ulrika], Queen of Sweden. *See* HOLSTEIN-GOTTORP, (1).

**Louis I d'Amboise**, Bishop of Albi. *See under* AMBOISE, D'.

**Louis II d'Amboise**, Cardinal of Albi. *See under* AMBOISE, D'.

**Louis de Bourbon.** *See* BOURBON, §I(9).

**Louis de** [Lodewijk van] **Gruuthuse** [Louis of Bruges] (*b* 1422; *d* 1492). Flemish bibliophile, patron and diplomat. He was in the service of the Dukes of Burgundy, Philip the Good and Charles the Bold, and became one of the most distinguished and prominent patricians in Bruges. At the Gruuthuse Hof, Bruges (now Bruges, Gruuthuse-mus.) he assembled a rich collection of art objects and built a private library of *c.* 200 manuscripts, which could rival that of the Dukes of Burgundy themselves. Shortly after his death this was acquired by Louis XII, King of France; it remains unknown whether he was given the collection or purchased it. Most of the books entered the Bibliothèque Nationale, Paris; 119 Gruuthuse codices are still kept there. In 1831 the contents of the library were studied by Van Praet, and in 1981 Lemaire published a new contribution on the subject, assembling 140 extant manuscripts.

Apart from having new works made, Louis de Gruut-huse also bought older manuscripts. His special interests were courtly romances, edifying and moral works, Classical authors, legal and historical texts and manuscripts of music. The most famous of these older codices is the

14th-century *Liederhandschrift* (Bruges, Baron E. van Ca-loen priv. col.), which comprises a wealth of middle-Dutch lyrical poetry. Also worthy of mention is the French version of the Apocalypse (Paris, Bib. N., MS. fr. 403), written in England *c.* 1250. The contemporary codices were almost all made between 1460 and 1490, and here too the emphasis is on historical works, chivalrous romances, literary texts and edifying and devout works. They were all produced in south Netherlandish workshops, and numerous talented illuminators such as Lieven van Lathem, LOYSET LIÉDET, Philippe de Mazerolles, the MASTER OF ANTOINE OF BURGUNDY, the MASTER OF THE DRESDEN PRAYERBOOK (for the last two, *see* MASTERS, ANONYMOUS, AND MONOGRAMMISTS, §I) and the Master of 1482 illustrated them. Louis de Gruuthuse also enriched his library with first editions of contemporary publications, and he was in close contact with the printers William Caxton and Arend Keysere, and with the printer and writer Colard Mansion. A manuscript by Mansion, *La Pénitence d'Adam*, with a dedication to Louis de Gruuthuse, was discovered (sold London, Sotheby's, June 1983, lot 18); this work should be added to Lemaire's list.

Louis de Gruuthuse was also responsible for the spread of Flemish manuscript illumination in England. During the Wars of the Roses Edward IV fled from England and stayed with Louis in The Hague from 9 October to 26 December 1470, and from 13 January to 19 February 1471 he was Louis's guest in Bruges. Following the example of the codices he saw there, Edward IV subsequently had many manuscripts copied and illuminated in Flemish workshops. These formed the nucleus of the Royal Library, and 25 of them have been preserved in the British Library, London.

BIBLIOGRAPHY
J. Van Praet: *Recherches sur Louis de Bruges, Seigneur de la Gruuthuyse* (Paris, 1831)
C. Lemaire: 'De bibliotheek van Lodewijk van Gruuthuse', *Vlaamse kunst op perkament* [Flemish art on parchment] (exh. cat., Bruges, Gruuthusemus., 1981), pp. 207–29

PATRICK VALVEKENS

**Louis de Mâle.** *See* LOUIS II, Count of Flanders.

**Louis-François**, Prince de Conti. *See* CONTI, (1).

**Louis-Philippe**, Duc d'Orléans. *See* ORLÉANS, (5).

**Louis-Philippe**, King of the French. *See* ORLÉANS, (7).

**Louis-Philippe-Joseph**, Duc d'Orléans. *See* ORLÉANS, (6).

**Loukianos.** *See* LUCIAN OF SAMOSATA.

**Loukopoulos, Clearchos** (*b* Thérmon, Aitolia, Jan 1908). Greek sculptor. He studied drawing with the Greek painter Constantin Maleas (1879–1928) and sculpture with Thanassis Apartis, a pupil of Emile-Antoine Bourdelle. He was a student at the University of Athens Law School for three years and also took lessons in drama and music. He was one of the founder-members of the Armos (1949–52) and Alpha (1950) groups and of the Communication and Education in Art League. After an early period of figurative sculpture with busts and compositions in which the structural organization of masses predominated, he turned

to abstraction in about 1957. As a pioneer of non-figurative sculpture in Greece he constructed his monumental works from layers of sheet metal stuck together, as in *Cyclopean* (1966) and *Tiryns* (1965; both artist's col.), and *Acrocorinth* (bronze, 1965; Athens, N.G.), claiming that he composed them according to the laws of natural and cosmic creation. His works seek to emulate the dynamic balance of natural phenomena, formed over the centuries, but Loukopoulous's creative process condenses time in re-creating the conditions of the natural process, such as selection and rejection. Closed stereometric masses of various shapes and sizes are articulated rhythmically around an explosively condensed mass or around nuclei (e.g. *Three Forms*, bronze, 1975).

BIBLIOGRAPHY
S. Lydakis: *The Greek Sculptors*, v (Athens, 1981), pp. 130–32, 379–80
C. Christou: *Modern Greek Sculpture* (Athens, 1982), pp. 129–32, 249

MARINA LAMBRAKI-PLAKA

**Loulan** [anc. Krorayina]. Site of a town and Chinese command post (2nd–3rd centuries AD) west of the salt lake Lop Nor in south-eastern Xinjiang Uygur Autonomous Region, China. Loulan was discovered by Sven Hedin on his second expedition to Central Asia in 1900. Based on Hedin's investigations Aurel Stein started extensive excavations in 1906, uncovering a stupa and a residential district enclosed by a wall. The houses were built of clay bricks on a framework of support beams of poplar or tamarisk. In them were discovered documents (3rd–4th century AD) written on small wedge-shaped or rectangular wooden tablets (London, BM; New Delhi, N. Mus.) in Chinese and *Kharosthī* script. The wedge-shaped tablets carry orders issued by the ruler of the day, while the rectangular ones are private contracts, accounts, inventories or personal letters. All documents carried a clay seal, and the pictures on the seals were either representations of figures or Chinese ideograms. Carved, lacquered wooden components of furniture were also found (*see* CENTRAL ASIA, §II, 5(vii)).

BIBLIOGRAPHY
A. Herrmann: *Die alten Seidenstrassen zwischen China und Syrien: Beiträge zur alten Geographie Asiens* (Berlin, 1910/*R* San Francisco, 1977)
M. A. Stein: *Serindia: Detailed Report of Explorations in Central Asia and Westernmost China*, 5 vols (Oxford, 1921/*R* New Delhi, 1981)
K. Enoki: 'Yü-ni ch'êng and the Site of Loulan', *Ural-Alta. Jb.*, xxxiii (1961), pp. 52–65
——: 'The Location of the Capital of Lou-lan and the Date of the Kharosthī Inscriptions', *Mem. Res. Dept Toyo Bunko*, xxii (1963), pp. 125–71
A. F. P. Hulsewé: *China in Central Asia: The Earliest Stage, 125 B.C.–A.D. 23*, Sinica Leidensia, xiv (Leiden, 1979)

M. YALDIZ

**Loup, Jean le.** *See* JEAN LE LOUP.

**Loureiro, Artur José de Sousa** (*b* Oporto, 11 Feb 1853; *d* Gerês, 8 July 1932). Portuguese painter. He was a naturalist painter. His early training was at the Academia de Belas-Artes, Oporto, and in 1876 he went to Rome where he became a pupil of Francisco Pradilla Ortiz. In Italy he devoted himself to landscape painting. He exhibited in Paris at the Exposition Universelle (1878) and in the Sociedade Promotora de Belas-Artes in Lisbon (1880). In 1879 he was given a scholarship to go to Paris, where he stayed from 1880 to 1883. He was a pupil of Alexandre Cabanel and exhibited at the Paris Salon in 1881 and 1882.

Loureiro's landscapes of the areas around Auvers-sur-Oise and Fontainebleau show the influence of the Barbizon school, though the luminous effects and colouring of the cornfields in *Haystacks* (1883; Lisbon, Mus. N. A. Contemp.) are more Mediterranean in character than they are indebted to the example of French naturalism. In 1882 he visited London, where he exhibited a portrait of his wife, *Artist at Rest* (1883; Lisbon, Mus. N. A. Contemp.), at the Royal Academy and in 1883 at the Goupil Gallery. From 1883 until 1901 he was in Australia, where he became a teacher of drawing at the Presbyterian Ladies College, was elected to the Academy in Victoria and was influenced by the Pre-Raphaelites. In 1889 he was awarded a gold medal at the Great Britain Exhibition for his painting *Death of Burke* (untraced). He exhibited in 1900 at the Exposition Universelle, Paris.

Loureiro returned in 1904 to Oporto, where he gave painting classes. His landscapes regained their earlier characteristic use of colour and light, and he experimented more boldly in his depiction of nature but always stayed close to his Naturalistic vision, as in *Storm at Gerês* (1930; Oporto, Mus. N. Soares dos Reis).

BIBLIOGRAPHY

R. Ortigão: *Arte Portuguesa*, 3 vols (Lisbon, n.d.), pp. 7–21
R. Arthur: *Arte e artistas contemporâneos*, 3 vols (Lisbon, 1903), pp. 65–74
*Catálogo da Exposição de Pintura de Artur Loureiro* (exh. cat., Lisbon, Sociedade Nacional de Belas-Artes, 1920)
D. de Macedo: *Marquês de Oliveira; Artur Loureiro: Dois naturalistas* (Lisbon, 1953)
J. A. França: *A arte em Portugal no século XIX*, ii (Lisbon, 1966), pp. 50–52

LUCÍLIA VERDELHO DA COSTA

**Loutherbourg** [Lauterbourg; Lutherbourg], **Philippe Jacques** [Philipp Jakob; Philip James] **de** (*b* Strasbourg, 31 Oct 1740; *d* London, 11 March 1812). Alsatian painter, illustrator and stage designer, active in France and England. Loutherbourg's father, Philipp Jakob (1698–1768), was an engraver and miniature painter to the court of Darmstadt. In 1755 he took his family to Paris, where Loutherbourg became a pupil of Carle Vanloo; he also attended Jean-Georges Wille's engraving academy in the Quai des Augustins and Francesco Casanova's studio. Wille directed Loutherbourg's attention to 17th-century Dutch landscape artists, such as Philips Wouwerman and Nicolaes Berchem, and in 1763 Denis Diderot noticed the inspiration of the latter in Loutherbourg's first Salon exhibit, a landscape with figures (Liverpool, Walker A.G.). In this and other works, focus is on the foreground figures, which are framed by natural formations that occasionally fall away to reveal distant horizons. This informal style found favour with the French public; Loutherbourg's vivid, fresh colour and ability to catch specific light and weather conditions made the pastoral subjects of François Boucher and his school seem contrived and fey. Rather more romanticized were Loutherbourg's shipwreck scenes (e.g. *A Shipwreck*, exh. Salon 1767; Stockholm, Nmus.), inspired by Claude-Joseph Vernet, and pictures of banditti recalling Salvator Rosa. Loutherbourg became the most prolific painter to exhibit at the Salon between 1762 and 1771. In 1766 he

was elected to the Académie Royale de Peinture et de Sculpture and nominated as a Peintre du Roi.

Loutherbourg travelled to Marseille in the spring of 1768 and probably visited Italy, Germany and Switzerland. After a brief return to Paris, he went to London in November 1771, intending to take advantage of the wealthy English market. A letter from the director of the Opéra-Comique, Jean Monnet, introduced him to the English actor-manager David Garrick, who employed Loutherbourg as his chief scene designer at Drury Lane theatre; Richard Brinsley Sheridan, Garrick's successor from 1776, continued to use Loutherbourg's revolutionary talents. Loutherbourg was the most inventive scene designer in Europe in the 18th century, and his lighting and sound effects, his use of puppets and models, his introduction of painted act drops between scenes and the diversity of his stage pictures set a precedent for all future attempts at theatrical illusion. Loutherbourg's interest in the theatre extended to the creation in 1781 of the Eidophusikon. This miniature theatre used light effects, translucent screens and painted scenery to create an impression of motion.

Loutherbourg's scene designs also reflected his training as a landscape painter. In 1778 he visited Derbyshire for the first time to make sketches of the landscape for the Drury Lane pantomime *The Wonders of Derbyshire*. During the 1780s he travelled widely in England and Wales and exhibited large numbers of topographical views at the Royal Academy (he was elected RA in 1781). One of the most masterful of his later landscapes is the *View of Coalbrookdale by Night* (1801; London, Sci. Mus.; *see* LANDSCAPE PAINTING, colour pl. III, fig. 2). These works show a sharp break from his fanciful French landscapes in their more restrained colouring, lessened emphasis on figures, heightened atmosphere and altogether more authentic approach. The variety of his works pleased his new clients who enjoyed his Franco-Dutch landscapes and encouraged his growing interest in topography. Loutherbourg was aware of the need to be versatile, and he often adapted his art to suit the market. Among the genres he practised was a variety of elaborate caricature, the best-known example of which is *A Midsummer Afternoon with a Methodist Preacher* (1777; Ottawa, N.G.).

In 1786 Loutherbourg and his wife unwisely went to Switzerland with the self-proclaimed mystic Count Cagliostro. Loutherbourg continued to sketch during his sojourn there and planned his topographical masterpiece *Falls of the Rhine at Schaffhausen* (exh. RA 1788; London, V&A; see fig.). After six months he returned destitute to London, where he began to practise as a faith-healer. The publication of *A List of a Few Cures Performed by Mr and Mrs de Loutherbourg of Hammersmith Terrace, without Medicine* (1789) caused an outburst of public indignation, and he thereafter confined his activities to art.

The interest that Loutherbourg had developed during the 1780s in English landscape, especially the scenery of the Lake and Peak Districts, gave way in the 1790s to a more intense concentration on history painting. He was the chief contributor to Thomas Macklin's *Poets Gallery* and edition of the Bible, and he painted five large scenes from English history for Robert Bowyer's *Historic Gallery*. Contemporary fascination with the Sublime is reflected in

Philippe Jacques de Loutherbourg: *Falls of the Rhine at Schaffhausen*, oil on canvas, 1.32×1.95 m, 1788 (London, Victoria and Albert Museum)

his history paintings even more than in his landscapes. His contributions to Macklin's Bible included scenes of terrifying chaos such as *The Deluge* and the *Destruction of Pharaoh's Host* (both exh. *Poets Gallery*, 1790; London, V&A), works which made a profound impression on J. M. W. Turner and John Martin.

In Paris, Loutherbourg had exhibited five battle pieces at the Salon, including his *morceau de réception*. Later his elaborate scenery and machinery for a production of *The Camp* at Drury Lane (première 15 October 1778) led to his being chosen to commemorate in two paintings the actual event on which the play was based—George III's visit to his troops at Warley camp and the mock attack that followed (both exh. RA 1780; Brit. Royal Col.). Large scenes of contemporary history such as the *Battle of Camperdown* (1799) and the *Battle of the Nile* (1800; both London, Tate) blended documentary authenticity with epic imagination, and the bravery of the individual was emphasized to heighten the emotional impact. His battle pictures grew in size and patriotic appeal, leading to his appointment in 1807 as Historical Painter to William Frederick, Duke of Gloucester, an important promotion for a landscape artist.

Loutherbourg's activities as an illustrator included the 20 plates he contributed to John Bell's second edition of Shakespeare (1786–8). His published collections of engravings, *The Picturesque Scenery of Great Britain* (1801) and *The Picturesque and Romantic Scenery of England and Wales* (1805), contain heightened impressions of the natural beauty of Britain's landscape (*see also* AQUATINT, fig. 1).

Although Loutherbourg's importance to the history of theatre has always been recognized, his importance to the history of art has not. One of the most refreshingly original landscape artists working in France in the mid-18th century, he brought with him when he settled in London a sophisticated and ultimately influential alternative to the pervading Italianate influence in English landscape painting.

BIBLIOGRAPHY
R. G. Allen: *The Stage Spectacles of Philip James de Loutherbourg* (diss., New Haven, CT, Yale U., 1960)
R. Joppien: *Die Szenenbilder Philippe Jacques de Loutherbourgs: Eine Untersuchung zu ihrer Stellung zwischen Malerei und Theater* (diss., U. Cologne, 1972)
*Philippe Jacques de Loutherbourg, RA, 1740–1812* (exh. cat., ed. R. Joppien; London, Kenwood House, 1973)

GEOFFREY ASHTON

**Loutherburg, Johann Rudolf** (*b* Basle, 1652; *d* Basle, 1727). Swiss painter. The sparse records of his life and career show that he attended the university in Basle, and in 1679 he was painting in Berne, where he was influenced by the local landscape tradition. In 1693 he travelled to Bruges, where he was greatly impressed by Flemish and Dutch art, particularly portraiture and still-lifes. His most celebrated portrait is that of *Johann Theobald Hartmann* (1697; Solothurn, Zentbib.). His group portraits, such as *Interior with an Armenian Family* (1698; Solothurn, Kstmus.), reveal his debt to Rembrandt's portraits. While much of Loutherburg's career was devoted to portraiture, he was also a specialist in still-lifes, as in *Still-life with Books, Cards and Flowers* (1697; Basle, Kstmus.), which demonstrates his vivid use of *vanitas* iconography, then much in vogue in Swiss art. His most astonishing paintings are his *trompe-l'oeil* compositions painted late in life; the most typical example is *Quolibet* (1716; Basle, Hist. Mus.), which depicts cards, newspapers and other common objects tacked to an illusionistic board. It is equal in technique and imagination to similar paintings by the acknowledged master of the genre, Johann Caspar Füssli I. The exacting sense of naturalism that Loutherburg displayed in his still-lifes did not, however, extend to his landscape compositions, as demonstrated by his coloured engraving *Falls of the Rhine at Schaffhausen* (*c.* 1690; Basle, Kstmus.), which depicts the famous site in a distinctly primitive manner. Despite Loutherburg's originality and imagination, much of his work remains little known.

BIBLIOGRAPHY
*Schweizer Stilleben im Barock* (exh. cat., ed. P. Vignau-Wilberg; Zurich, Haus Rechberg; Sissach, Schloss Ebenrain; Solothurn, Kstmus.; Freiburg im Breisgau, Augustinmus.; 1973), pp. 50–52

WILLIAM HAUPTMAN

**Loutron.** *See under* BATH (ii), §1.

**Loutrophoros.** Ancient vessel form, often used as a funerary vase (*see* GREECE, ANCIENT, figs 71(v)k and 120). ☐

**Louvain.** *See* LEUVEN.

**Louvois**, Marquis de [Le Tellier, François-Michel] (*b* Paris, Jan 1639; *d* Paris, 16 July 1691). French statesman, administrator and collector. He served Louis XIV from 1677 as secretary of state for war and from 1683 as Surintendant des Bâtiments, Arts et Manufactures, replacing Jean-Baptiste Colbert. Louvois's first task was to put in order the finances of his office, which Colbert had been unable to control since 1679. Louvois also made changes of personnel, dismissing Charles Perrault, who had been Colbert's principal assistant. Pierre Mignard and François Girardon became Louvois's new counsellors, while Charles Le Brun, Premier Peintre du Roi, was deprived of all authority. Having brought the accounts under control, Louvois increased the sums invested in nearly all the royal buildings. Besides his major project, the completion of the Hôtel des Invalides in Paris, which had been begun in 1671, two undertakings in particular occupied his attention: the Place Vendôme in Paris, begun in 1688 and not finished in his lifetime, and the château of Versailles, where the new Grand Trianon, the Orangerie, Mansart's colonnade and various bosquets in the gardens were completed. In addition, Louvois carried on Colbert's work on the royal library and printing works.

Louvois's management of the royal collections was characterized by the same stringency as that of building projects. In 1683 he required Le Brun to draw up an inventory of the contents of the Louvre; and on the latter's death, Louvois ordered all his drawings to be seized for the king. This was thenceforth always done on the death of premiers peintres du roi. Louvois had no defined policy towards acquisitions: he usually set about them with the advice of his counsellors and civil servants. Thus in 1684 he wrote to La Teulière, whom in that year he appointed director of the Académie de France in Rome: 'As I am persuaded that ready money is a great help in getting bargains, I will forward you some as soon as you send word'. In 1685 he wrote again to La Teulière: 'Since the king wants paintings only by the great masters, as I wrote to you before, you should not even consider those by Claude Lorrain or Le Guaspre [Gaspard Dughet]'. Soon afterwards Louvois sent 'authorization for Le Sieur Blanchard to buy the *Virgin* by Van Dyck and the *Magdalen* or *Melancholy* by Feti [Domenico Fetti]' (both Paris, Louvre). And the following year he wrote: 'You are never to amuse yourself by trying to surprise me, by sending me curious items without any warning'.

The 'journal' of Gianlorenzo Bernini's visit to France records that Louvois, visiting Cardinal Mazarin's gallery, had declared that he was interested chiefly in the tapestries; he had many of them in his town house in the Rue de Richelieu, as well as paintings, for the most part copies after Poussin and Raphael, and some works by Mignard, but also some Flemish works. In all, Louvois owned about 400 paintings and many *objets d'art*; he also owned the château of Meudon, Hauts-de-Seine, bought in 1679 and refurbished by Jules Hardouin Mansart and André Le Nôtre. Also his were the château of Ancy-le-Franc, Yonne, bought in 1684, a town house at Versailles, lands at Montmirail, Mutry, Barbezieux, and in the region of Tonnerre, and a fortune of nine million livres. In 1693 his widow, Anne de Souvré, commissioned from the royal sculptors Girardon and Martin Desjardins a mausoleum (now in Tonnerre, Hôp.) for her husband.

UNPUBLISHED SOURCES
Paris, Archvs N., LXXV530 [inventory made after the death of Louvois]

BIBLIOGRAPHY
C. Rousset: *Histoire de Louvois et de son administration politique et militaire depuis la paix de Nimègue* (Paris, 1863)
L. Lalanne, ed.: *Le Journal du voyage du cavalier Bernin en France* (Paris, 1885/R Aix-en-Provence, 1981; Eng. trans., Princeton, 1985)
A. de Montaiglon and J. Guiffrey, eds: *Correspondance des directeurs de l'Académie de France à Rome*, i (Paris, 1887), pp. 143–480; ii (1888), pp. 1–474; iii (1889), pp. 121–30
A. Corvisier: *Louvois* (Paris, 1982)

PATRICK LE CHANU

**Louw.** South African family of architects. Wynand Hendrik Louw (*b* Labori et Picardi, Suider Paarl, 1883; *d* Paarl, nr Cape Town, Aug 1967) practised as an architect in the Cape Province, and his career coincided with the reassertion of the Afrikaaner after the Boer War (1899–1902). He is recognized as the first privately practising Afrikaans architect in South Africa, although he himself was not assertive politically, unlike Gerard Moerdijk. He trained under J. C. E. Seeliger in Cape Town and at the Architectural Association in London. After returning from London in 1907 he set up practice in Paarl where he received the first of his commissions for the Dutch Reformed Church, a church hall (1907) in Paarl. Thereafter Louw designed Dutch Reformed churches in many parts of Africa. His partnership (1921–6) with Moerdijk was nominal. Between them, in and out of partnership, they designed *c*. 200 Dutch Reformed churches. Both architects contributed to the evolution of a fan-shaped plan, moving away from previous Gothic-Revival style and Greek- or Latin-cross plan. Louw employed Byzantine and Romanesque elements in his churches, but the compositions were personal and bold though often awkward. The Dutch Reformed church (1912–14) at Reitz, Orange Free State, is among his better-known churches.

Louw encouraged many in their architectural careers, and in particular his brother Hendrik Jacobus Louw (*b* 1892) who worked in Louw's office from 1925, becoming a partner in 1927 (Louw & Louw). The partnership was responsible for a number of commercial buildings in Cape Town in the 1930s and 1940s, including the SANLAM building (1931–2), Wale St and the Old Mutual building (1937–8), Darling St. In 1940 Wynand Hendrik Louw was awarded the Gold Medal of Honour from the SA Akedemie vir Wetenskap en Kuns, the second architect to gain this award (Moerdijk being the first). His widespread practice and high standard of work coupled with his interest in technical developments placed his practice in the forefront of establishment architecture in South Africa in the first half of the 20th century.

BIBLIOGRAPHY
Obituary, *S. Afr. Archit. Rec.* (Oct 1967), pp. 40–41
M. A. Louw: *Wynand Louw: So het ons hom geken* (Cape Town, 1969)
D. Kesting: *Afrikaans protestante kerkbou* (diss., U. Port Elizabeth, 1978)

C. J. M. WALKER

**Louys** [Louis], **Jacob** [Jan] (*b* Antwerp, 2 Oct 1595; *d* Haarlem, after 1644). Flemish etcher, engraver and draughtsman, active in the northern Netherlands. He was probably a pupil of Pieter Claesz. Soutman in Antwerp, where he married in December 1628. In 1635 Louys was admitted to the Haarlem Guild of St Luke as an engraver. Some 18 prints by him are known, the latest of which in date are reproductive prints of royal portraits after Rubens, van Dyck and others, which he made in collaboration with Soutman (published by Soutman in 1644). Apart from these portraits, there are several etchings—occasionally lightly retouched with the burin—after genre pieces by Andries Both, Willem Kalf and Adriaen van Ostade. (This group of etchings has been attributed by some to a second, fictitious Jacob Louys.) Louys's finest work is a monumental etching with dramatic chiaroscuro effects, the *Raising of Lazarus* (Hollstein, no. 1), after Jan Lievens's painting (Brighton, A.G. & Mus.). He also produced a few drawings.

BIBLIOGRAPHY
Hollstein: *Dut. & Flem.*; *NKL*; Thieme–Becker
*Pieter Paul Rubens* (exh. cat., ed. D. Bodart; Rome, Villa Farnesina, 1977), pp. 65–7

MANFRED SELLINK

**Lovera, Juan** (*b* Caracas, 11 July 1776; *d* Caracas, 20 Jan 1841). Venezuelan painter. He studied under the Dominicans at the convent of S Jacinto in Caracas and with the painter Antonio José Landaeta, following in the traditions of the colonial period. Lovera particularly favoured portraiture, and he nearly always portrayed men with the trappings of their social class, looking ahead with the body at an angle to the right. In 1814 he followed Simón Bolívar to the east and may have stayed in Cumaná, from where he is thought to have travelled to the Antilles. In 1820 he was again in Caracas, where he painted *Divine Shepherdess* (Caracas, Gal. A. N.). In 1824 he became associated with

Colonel Francisco Avendaño, who had installed the first lithographic press in La Guaira, which was later moved to Lovera's workshop in Caracas. He began teaching in 1821, and in 1832 taught at the Academia de Dibujo in the Escuela de Primeras Letras in Caracas. His later works included *Don Marcos Borges Receiving the Academic Proposals of his Son Nicanor* (1838; Caracas, Gal. A. N.) and paintings of such historical events as *Rebellion of 19 April 1810* (1835; Caracas, Col. Concejo Mun.) and *Signing of the Act of Independence on 5 July 1811* (1838; Caracas, Col. Concejo Mun.).

BIBLIOGRAPHY
A. Boulton: *Historia de la pintura en Venezuela: Epoca nacional*, ii (Caracas, 1968/R 1973)
C. Duarte: *Juan Lovera, el pintor de los próceres* (Caracas, 1985)
MARÍA ANTONIA GONZÁLEZ-ARNAL

**Lovett Pearce, Edward.** *See* PEARCE, EDWARD LOVETT.

**Loveyko, Iosif (Ignat'yevich)** (*b* Prokhory [now in the Primorsky Kray], 19 Feb 1906). Russian architect. He studied from 1927 to 1931 in the Vkhutein (Higher Art Technical Institute), Moscow, and the Moscow Architectural Institute (MAI) under Leonid Vesnin, Aleksandr Vesnin and Konstantin Mel'nikov. The influence of Mel'nikov led to the exaggerated expressiveness of forms in Loveyko's vestibule of the Dzerzhinskaya (now Lubyanka) metro station (1935; with D. A. Fridman) in Moscow. The restrained classicism of the residential blocks (1934–8) on Kotel'nicheskaya Embankment, Moscow, and overt classicism of the administrative building (1944–7) on Ogaryova Street, Moscow, with its unwieldy Corinthian colonnade, characterized his next phase. In the same vein the Sovetskaya Hotel (1950–52), Moscow, with Viktor Lebedev and Pavel Shteller (1910–77), is more subtle. Under the influence of Moscow's tall architecture of the late 1940s, he turned to the contemporary revival of Moscow Baroque, as in the 11 to 16-storey residential complex (1952–5), Prospekt Mira 99–103 and 118–22, Moscow. From 1955 to 1960 he was Chief Architect of Moscow and, from 1961, directed the planning and construction of its northern periphery at Degunino–Beskudnikovo and Lianozovo–Bibirevo. Here, in the 1970s, he supervised the construction of vast, well-organized residential complexes, which replaced the self-contained combinations of flats and facilities (Rus. *mikrorayon*) of previous plans. He also built the Yerevan and Baykal cinemas (early 1970s; with others), Moscow, and the 26-storey Molodyozhnaya Hotel (1980), Dmitrovskoye Road, Moscow. From 1968 to 1986 he was the chief editor of the periodical *Stroitel'stvo i Arkhitektura Moskvy* ('Construction and architecture of Moscow').

BIBLIOGRAPHY
M. Astaf'yeva-Dlugach: 'Iosif Ignat'yevich Loveyko', *Arkhit. SSSR*, 7 (1977), pp. 43–9
N. P. Bilinkin and A. V. Ryabushin: *Sovremennaya sovetskaya arkhitektura* [Contemporary Soviet architecture] (Moscow, 1985), p. 94
M. Astaf'yeva-Dlugach and E. Levinskaya: *Iosif Loveyko* (Moscow, 1991)
A. V. IKONNIKOV

**Lovisa, Domenico** (*b c.* 1690; *d c.* 1750). Italian publisher. His printing press was situated 'underneath the arches at Rialto' in Venice, and he is known almost exclusively for the publication of a series of large prints, titled *Il Gran Teatro di Venezia ovvero descrizione esatta di cento delle più insigni prospettive e di altretante celebri pitture della medesima città*. The first edition is undated, but it probably came out *c.* 1717. As originally planned, the series was to include 200 prints, but this ambition was not realized, and even the second edition (1720, 2 vols) has only *c.* 120 prints. The approximately 57 plates contained in the first volume reproduce paintings that hung in Venetian public buildings, including works by Veronese, Titian, Tintoretto, Palma Giovane. They were engraved by Andrea Zucchi, Domenico Rossetti (1650–1736), Giacomo Burri, Domenico Bonavera (*b* 1640), Pietro Sante Bartoli, Agostino dalla Via and others. The second volume contains a varying number (up to 66) of views of Venice (see exh. cat., figs 279–82) engraved by Filippo Vasconi (1687–1730), Giuseppe Valeriani (*d* 1761), Carlo and Andrea Zucchi, as well as an unidentified monogrammist, S.F. This series was reprinted a number of times in the 18th century.

BIBLIOGRAPHY
G. Moschini: *Dell'incisione in Venezia* (Venice, 1924), pp. 56–70
G. Calabi: 'Note su G.B. Tiepolo incisore', *Graph. Kst.*, i (1939), pp. 7–20
R. Gallo: 'L'incisione nel '700 a Venezia e a Bassano', *Ateneo Ven.*, v–vii (1941), pp. 153–214
*Da Carlevarijs ai Tiepolo: Incisori veneti e friulani del settecento* (exh. cat., ed. D. Succi; Gorizia, Mus. Prov. Pal. Attems; Venice, Correr; 1983), pp. 230–34
DARIO SUCCI

**Low, Sir David (Alexander Cecil)** (*b* Dunedin, 7 April 1892; *d* London, 20 Sept 1963). New Zealand draughtsman. His precocious talent surfaced when he was 11 with his first political cartoon in the *Christchurch Spectator* and the Melbourne *New Idea*. Before he was 20 he moved to Australia and contributed cartoons to the famous Sydney *Bulletin*, of which he later joined the staff, sharing the important full-page cartoons with Norman Lindsay. Low's first collection of cartoons, *Caricatures by Low* (Sydney, 1915), covered all aspects of Australian life and revealed his admiration for Phil May's economy of line and indications of his own later flexibility and expressiveness. His inimitable style can be seen in his cartoons of 'Billy' Hughes, Australia's post-war Prime Minister, in *The Billy Book* (Sydney, 1918), which ran into several editions and led to his invitation to join the London *Star*. Low left Australia in 1920; his London cartoons appeared in the *Daily News* (1920), *Daily Express* (1926), and then in the Beaverbrook Press *Evening Standard* (1926–50) free, by mutual agreement, from any form of editorial control. In 1950 he joined the *Daily Herald* but left for more freedom in the *Guardian* (1953–63). Low's humour, though incisive, was essentially good-natured, without the savagery of James Gillray or the pessimism of Honoré Daumier; his narrative-commentaries accompanying the collections of cartoons were as entertaining as the drawings. His deep insight into human psychology was complemented by a keen grasp of political reality: many of his cartoons were, indeed, prophetic of later disastrous developments. He handled abstractions masterfully. British die-hard conservatism was personified in 'Colonel Blimp', forcefully pontificating in the semi-nudity of the Turkish bath. Low's post-war Britannia, unlike the majestic Britannia of John Tenniel, was a bewildered creature whose trident and shield were more likely to be broom and dustpan. Low's own philosophy and approach to his work are embodied in his book *Ye Madde Designer* (London and New York, 1935) in which he deprecated mere exaggeration in caricature. He was knighted in 1962.

BIBLIOGRAPHY

P. Coleman and L. Tanner: *Cartoons of Australian History* (Nelson, n.d.)
R. Searle: 'Master of English Caricature', *Guardian* (21 Sept 1963)
A. McCulloch: *Encyclopaedia of Australian Art* (London, 1968, rev. in 2 vols, Hawthorn, Victoria, 1984)
M. Mahood: *The Loaded Line* (Melbourne, 1973)
W. Feaver and A. Gould, eds: *Masters of Caricature* (New York, 1981)
C. Seymour-Ure and J. Schoff: *David Low* (London, 1985)

MARGUERITE MAHOOD

**Lowe, Elias Avery** [Loew, Elias] (*b* Kalvarija, Lithuania, 15 Oct 1879; *d* Bad Nauheim, Germany, 8 Aug 1969). American palaeographer of Lithuanian birth. He changed his name to Lowe during World War I. After being educated in New York and at Cornell University (graduating in 1902) he studied at Halle University for one term and then at Munich University (PhD 1907), where he was one of a group of brilliant young scholars, students of the celebrated Ludwig Traube. He was lecturer in palaeography at Oxford University from 1913 and Reader from 1927 to 1936; from 1926 he was also a research professor at the Institute of Advanced Studies at Princeton (USA). He was the recipient of many academic honours. Lowe's writings are major landmarks in the study of Western palaeography. In *The Beneventan Script* (1914) he at last laid to rest the unsatisfactory term 'Lombardic script', which had confused scholars since Jean Mabillon's time, and in his *English Uncial* (1960) he established criteria (the touchstone being the Codex Amiatinus; Florence, Bib. Medicea-Laurenziana, MS. Amiatinus 1) distinguishing English uncial script from that of the Continent. Lowe's most enduring monument is undoubtedly his *Codices latini antiquiores* (1934–66), in which more than 1800 manuscripts are palaeographically described and illustrated. The introductions to many of the volumes are basic studies of the scripts of the regions concerned. Despite the complexity of his subject-matter, Lowe's prose was unusually limpid and has been described as having 'an individual charm which lightens even the most technical of details' (Bieler p. xvii). A head of Lowe (New York, Pierpont Morgan Lib.) by Jacob Epstein is illustrated in R. Buckle: *Jacob Epstein, Sculptor* (London, 1963), pl. 562.

UNPUBLISHED SOURCES

New York, Pierpont Morgan Lib. [Lowe's col. of books, offprints, photos, notes and corr.]

WRITINGS

*The Beneventan Script* (Oxford, 1914)
*Codices latini antiquiores: A Palaeographical Guide to Latin Manuscripts prior to the Ninth Century*, 11 vols (Oxford, 1934–66, suppl 1971; vol. ii rev. 1972)
*English Uncial* (Oxford, 1960)
L. F. Bieler, ed.: *Palaeographical Papers*, 2 vols (Oxford, 1970) [articles by Lowe with bibliog. and 'Autobiographical note', pp. 594–611]

BIBLIOGRAPHY

Obituary, *The Times* (11 Aug 1969), p. 8; *Jb. Bayer. Akad. Wiss.* (1970), pp. 199–203
*Who Was Who, 1961–1970* (London, 1972), pp. 694–5
T. J. Brown: 'E. A. Lowe and *Codices latini antiquiores*', *Scritt. & Civiltà*, i (1977), pp. 177–97

ANDREW G. WATSON

**Lowe, William Drury.** *See* DRURY LOWE, WILLIAM.

**Lowell, Guy** (*b* Boston, 6 Aug 1870; *d* Madeira, Spain, 4 Feb 1927). American architect and writer. Born into a prominent New England family, he graduated from Harvard University in 1892, received a degree in architecture from Massachusetts Institute of Technology (M.I.T.) in 1894 and a diploma from the Ecole des Beaux-Arts, Paris, in 1899. On returning to the USA he opened an architectural office in Boston in 1900. Early commissions include entrances to the Boston Fenway (1902) and a lecture hall (1902) at Harvard University. These works are marked by a restrained Italianate classicism. An authority on the history of landscape architecture, Lowell lectured on this subject at M.I.T. from 1900 to 1913. He also published several books on Italian villas and gardens. This interest informs many of Lowell's works, particularly the numerous country houses and estates commissioned by wealthy patrons. The house (1903) for Bryce J. Allan, Prides Crossing, MA, is a particularly grand conception, from the arcades of its façade and classical detailing of the interior, to the layout of the gardens. Lowell made use of the traditional Georgian style in a programme of 25 buildings (1903–23) at the Phillips Academy, Andover, MA, creating a unified scheme with the existing buildings. He returned to classicism again in the Boston Museum of Fine Arts (1907–15), a complex of stolid monumentality. Extraordinarily grandiose in conception was the original plan for the New York County Courthouse (1912–27). The design for a circular building, resembling the Colosseum in Rome, but with receding tiers, was replaced by a modified, octagonal structure with a Pantheon-like temple façade. The building was dedicated shortly after Lowell's unexpected death.

WRITINGS

*American Gardens* (Boston, 1902)
*Smaller Italian Villas and Farmhouses* (New York, 1916)
*More Small Italian Villas and Farmhouses* (New York, 1920)

BIBLIOGRAPHY

*DAB*; *Macmillan Enc. Architects*
B. F. W. Russel: 'The Works of Guy Lowell', *Archit. Rev.* [Boston], xiii/2 (1906), pp. 13–40
*National Cyclopaedia of American Biography*, xxi (New York, 1931), pp. 47–8
W. M. Whitehill: *Museum of Fine Arts, Boston: A Centennial History* (Cambridge, MA, 1970)

**Löwen.** *See* LEUVEN.

**Löwenfinck, Adam Friedrich von** (*b* Kalisch, 1714; *d* Haguenau, 13 Nov 1754). German ceramics painter of Polish birth. In 1727 he began his apprenticeship at the Meissen Porcelain Factory as a flower painter. In 1734 he completed his training but was forced to flee Meissen on 3 October 1736 (allegedly as an embezzler and debtor) and began work at the faience factory in Bayreuth. In 1737, in view of his possible extradition to a Saxon commissioner, the painter Joseph Philipp Dannhofer (*fl* 1737–44) helped him escape, probably to Ansbach. It is possible that he also briefly stayed during this period at Chantilly in France. On 15 October 1741 he was appointed Hoff-Emailler-Mahler in Fulda (e.g. tureen and cover, 1745; London, V&A). On 1 March 1746, together with two merchants, he established a faience factory in Höchst and became its first director. In 1747 he attempted to bring his younger brother, Christian Wilhelm Löwenfinck, and five other painters from the Meissen factory to Höchst. Christian Wilhelm Löwenfinck (1720–53), however, remained there only until November 1748 and then escaped to Strasbourg. On 28 October 1747 Löwenfinck married the porcelain painter Maria Seraphia Susanna Magdalena Schick (1728–1805) in Fulda. Disgraced by the Elector because of his brother's escape, Löwenfinck left Höchst on 19 March 1749 for Koblenz where he probably attempted to start a faience factory in Schönbornlust. Shortly thereafter he went to the Haguenau branch of the Strasbourg Faience Factory, which belonged to the Hannong family. In 1751 he was appointed Director of the Haguenau factory. A number of irregularly marked works have been attributed to him, although the motifs, including chinoiseries, landscapes and animals (e.g. jug with hunting scene; Hamburg, Mus. Kst & Gew.), digress from the colourful flower paintings that he is known to have produced in Meissen. Löwenfinck is regarded as an outstanding porcelain- and faience painter, whose European as well as Chinese decorative schemes contributed considerably to ceramic decoration during the first half of the 18th century.

Thieme–Becker

BIBLIOGRAPHY

A. Klein: 'Ein Hauptwerk von Adam Friedrich von Löwenfinck', *Die Weltkunst*, i (1954), pp. 2–4
R. H. Wark: 'Zur Löwenfinckfrage', *Keramos*, xviii (1962), pp. 24–5
O. Walcha: 'Vorlageblätter von Adam Friedrich von Löwenfinck', *Keramos*, xxxiv (1966), pp. 130–35
S. Ducret: 'Noch einmal—Adam Friedrich von Löwenfinck', *Die Weltkunst*, xxxix (1969), pp. 9–10
P. Ducret: 'Adam Friedrich von Löwenfinck als Figuren- und Landschaftsmaler auf Fayence', *Keramos*, c (1983), pp. 117–26
R. Rückert: *Biographische Daten der Meissener Manufakturisten des 18. Jahrhunderts* (Munich, 1990), pp. 171–3

SILVIA GLASER

**Löwensprung, Paul.** *See under* MASTERS, ANONYMOUS, AND MONOGRAMMISTS, §I: CARNATION MASTERS.

**Löwenstam, Leopold** (*b* Düsseldorf, 17 Feb 1842; *d* Woodcroft, Sussex, 29 May 1898). Dutch printmaker and draughtsman. He trained at the Rijksacademie in Amsterdam from 1858 to 1864 and continued to work there until 1874. In 1871 he spent some time in Stockholm, where he established a school for the graphic arts. His prints are mostly based on compositions by other artists, such as Jozef Israëls and Lawrence Alma-Tadema, and older Dutch and Flemish masters (e.g. *Portrait of Lucas Vorstermann*, based on the etching by Anthony van Dyck). His steel engravings are remarkably delicate in tone. He worked in London from 1874 to 1883, then in Three Bridges in Sussex. His work was most appreciated in England.

Scheen

BIBLIOGRAPHY

A. J. Vervoorn: *Nederlandse prentkunst, 1840–1940* (Lochum, 1983)

CHRISTIAAN SCHUCKMAN

**Lowestoft Porcelain Factory.** English ceramics manufactory. It was founded in Lowestoft, Suffolk, in 1757 by Robert Browne (*d* 1771); the early partners included Philip Walker, Obed Aldred and James Rickman. Lowestoft produced soft-paste porcelain, which included bone-ash and is therefore chemically similar to Bow porcelain. Production included tablewares, tea caddies, inkwells and items inscribed 'A Trifle from Lowestoft'. A small selection of child and animal ornaments was also produced. Until *c.* 1765 only underglazed-blue decoration was used. Transfer-printed decoration was used later, and *c.* 1767 enamel decoration was introduced. The influence of the Worcester porcelain factory is seen in the blue-and-white wares of the 1770s and 1780s and in the use of mock Chinese landscapes, and that of the Derby porcelain factory is shown in the relief-moulded designs. Rococo and Chinese styles remained in production at Lowestoft when in other factories they had been superseded by Neo-classicism. The main painters were John Redgrave (*c.* 1721–1801), Richard Powles (1764–1808) and Robert Allen (1744–1835), who was manager at Lowestoft until the factory closed in 1802.

BIBLIOGRAPHY

W. Spelman: *Lowestoft China* (London, 1905)
G. A. Godden: *The Illustrated Guide to Lowestoft Porcelain* (Woodbridge, 1969); rev. as *Lowestoft Porcelain* (Woodbridge, 1985)

K. SOMERVELL

**Low relief.** *See* BAS RELIEF and RELIEF SCULPTURE.

**Lowry, L(aurence) S(tephen)** (*b* Stretford, nr Manchester, 1 Nov 1887; *d* Glossop, Derbys, 23 Feb 1976). English painter. On leaving school in 1904, he began work in Manchester as a clerk with a firm of chartered accountants, studying painting and drawing in the evenings at the Municipal College of Art (1905–15), where he was taught by the French painter Adolphe Valette, and at Salford School of Art (1915–25). In 1910 he became a rent collector and clerk with the Pall Mall Property Company in Manchester; he remained a full-time employee and eventually chief cashier until his retirement in 1952. Despite his unusually long period as an art student, he regarded himself as self-taught. He drew inspiration from his surroundings, particularly Pendlebury, near Manchester, where he lived from 1909 to 1948. Here were the cotton mills and factories, the coal mines and back-to-back cottages, that were to become familiar in such paintings as *The Pond* (1950) and *Industrial Landscape* (1955; both London, Tate). Lowry populated this and such neighbouring towns as Salford and Eccles with figures, at first carefully drawn, as in *Salford Street Scene* (1928; priv. col., see Levy, pl. 24). They were later realized in a more impressionistic way that suggested the routine movement of crowds of workers, as in *Coming from the Mill* (1930; Salford, Mus. & A.G.); an everyday street scene (e.g. *An Organ Grinder*, 1934; Manchester, C.A.G.); the drama of *The Arrest* (1927; Nottingham, Castle Mus.); and the festive holiday spirit in *Good Friday, Daisy Nook* (1946; priv. col., see Spalding, pl. 33).

Lowry's reputation was slow to be established. He exhibited at the Manchester Academy of Fine Art in 1918–19 and had his first exhibition, with two other artists, in an architect's office in Manchester in 1921. From 1927 to 1936 he exhibited with the New English Art Club, and in this period he had paintings exhibited in the Salon d'Automne in Paris and at the Royal Academy of Arts in

London (1932). In 1934 he was elected a member of the Royal Society of British Artists, but not until 1938, when his work was first seen by an important dealer, A. J. McNeil Reid, did Lowry have the opportunity of a one-man exhibition (1939; London, Lefevre Gal.) and more public recognition, when *Dwellings, Orsdall Lane, Salford* (1927) was purchased by the Tate Gallery in London. Subsequently he had important retrospectives at the Museum and Art Gallery, Salford (1951), the City Art Gallery, Manchester (1959), the Graves Art Gallery, Sheffield (1962), and an Arts Council of Great Britain touring retrospective in 1966–7. In 1962 he was elected an RA. Lowry remained unconcerned by his growing fame and commercial success; from 1948 until his death he lived in the same small, unmodernized house in Mottram-in-Longdendale, Cheshire.

Although Lowry is chiefly associated with street scenes and townscapes, his subject-matter was far more wide-ranging. He painted country scenes, as in *Pastoral—Lytham* (1920; priv. col., see Levy, pl. 27) and *Hillside in Wales* (1962; London, Tate), as well as views of the seaside (e.g. *Lytham Pier*, 1945; London, Crane Kalman Gal.) and of harbours, as in *River Wear at Sunderland* (1961; Sunderland, Mus. & A.G.). Though often represented as a reclusive man, his affection for relatives and close friends is shown in the *Portrait of the Artist's Mother* (1910; Salford, Mus. & A.G.), and his sympathy for those less fortunate is reflected in *An Accident* (1935) and *The Cripples* (1949; both Salford, Mus. & A.G.). Occasionally he touched on current affairs, for example in *Blitzed Site* (1942; Salford, Mus. & A.G.), depicting the damage caused by a German air raid on Manchester in World War II, although recording events of this sort was never one of his main interests. His gift for observation was put to more telling use in *Private View* (1958; London, Lefevre Gal.), which pokes fun at the art establishment as effectively as the title of *Bird Looking at Something* (1964; Monty Bloom priv. col., see Spalding, pl. 45).

BIBLIOGRAPHY

*L. S. Lowry* (exh. cat., intro. E. Mullins; London, Tate; Sunderland, Mus. & A.G.; U. Manchester, Whitworth A.G.; Bristol, Mus. & A.G.; 1966–7)

M. Levy: *The Paintings of L. S. Lowry: Oils and Watercolours* (London, 1975)

A. Andrews: *The Life of L. S. Lowry* (London, 1977)

F. Mullineux and S. Shaw: *Laurence Stephen Lowry, 1887–1976: A Catalogue of the Salford Collection* (Salford, 1977)

J. Spalding: *Lowry* (Oxford and New York, 1979)

*L. S. Lowry Centenary Exhibition* (exh. cat., ed. M. Leber and J. Sandling; Salford, Mus. & A.G., 1987)

STEPHEN STUART-SMITH

**Lowther.** English family of patrons and collectors.

**(1) Sir William Lowther**, 3rd Baronet of Marske (*b* 1727; *d* 15 April 1756). He inherited Holker Hall, Lancs (now Cumbria), in 1745 and later made the Grand Tour. His connection with Joseph Leeson, 1st Earl of Milltown, and other prominent patrons is implied by his appearance in Joshua Reynolds's caricature of Raphael's *Parody of the School of Athens* (1751; Dublin, N.G.) and a smaller caricature group (versions Holker Hall, Cumbria, and Bowood House, Wilts). While in Rome he commissioned four sea-pieces from C.-J. Vernet (one Holker Hall,

Cumbria, one destr., two apparently not supplied) and became acquainted with the landscape painter, caricaturist and dealer Thomas Patch. After his return to England, he began to buy pictures, predominantly by Dutch artists: examples by Philips Wouwerman, Salomon van Ruysdael and Isaac de Moucheron remain at Holker. His most notable purchase in the London saleroom was Rubens's *Landscape with Cattle and Duckshooters* (*c*. 1635; Berlin, Gemäldegal.) in 1756. In 1755 he inherited the very substantial estates of Sir James Lowther of Whitehaven, which may have prompted Patch to secure for him Claude Lorrain's great *'Parnassus'* (1652; Edinburgh, N.G.) from the Muti family. This did not reach England until after Lowther's premature death, when the Whitehaven estates passed to James Lowther, later Earl of Lonsdale, and Holker Hall to Lord George Cavendish.

UNPUBLISHED SOURCES

Holker Hall, Cumbria [Cavendish MSS]

BIBLIOGRAPHY

F. Russell: 'Thomas Patch, Sir William Lowther and the Holker Claude', *Apollo*, cii (1975), pp. 115–19

FRANCIS RUSSELL

**(2) William Lowther**, 1st Earl of Lonsdale (*b* 29 Dec 1757; *d* Twickenham, Middx, 19 March 1844). Distant relation of (1) Sir William Lowther. He came from a venerable Westmorland family and was made 1st Earl of Lonsdale in 1807. He was highly regarded as a patron both of the arts and literature, though there is no remaining documentary evidence to suggest the nature and scope of his collecting or patronage. William Wordsworth dedicated his poem *Excursion* (London, 1814) to him and later wrote a sonnet on the theme of the Lowther motto, *magistratus indicat virium*. Lowther was also known for pulling down Lowther Hall, Westmorland, and replacing it with a building later known as Lowther Castle. This was the first country house commission for Robert Smirke (ii) and was built between 1806 and 1811.

*DNB*                    BIBLIOGRAPHY

JULIAN SHEATHER

**Lo-yang.** *See* LUOYANG.

**Loyd, Samuel Jones**, 1st Baron Overstone (*b* London, 25 Sept 1796; *d* London, 23 Nov 1883). English banker and collector. He was the only son of Lewis Loyd, a banker, and his first wife, Sarah, daughter of the banker John Jones. He was educated at Eton College, Berks, and Trinity College, Cambridge, and was destined for the family bank, succeeding his father as head of Jones, Loyd & Co. in 1844. He was MP for Hythe from 1819 to 1826 and became perhaps the most influential financier of the mid-19th century, instrumental in the drafting of the Bank Charter Act of 1844. He acquired substantial estates at Overstone, near Northampton, and in Berkshire, and in 1850 was created a Baron. He served as a Trustee of the National Gallery from 1850 to 1871, a Commissioner for the Great Exhibition of 1851 and Chairman of the General Council of the Manchester Art Treasures Exhibition of 1857.

Loyd formed a notable picture collection reflecting the changing fashions of the 19th century, bound at the outset by conventional attitudes but responding to a growing awareness of the Renaissance, both in Italy and Germany. He began collecting *c.* 1831 with a number of minor 17th-century works. Part of Murillo's oil painting of the *Virgin and Child in Glory* (*La Vierge coupée*, Liverpool, Walker A.G.) was bought in 1838 (he acquired the rest in 1862). Loyd was one of the consortium of bankers who in 1846 acquired *en bloc* the collection of Baron Jan Gijsbert Verstolk van Soelen: his share yielded ten pictures, including a Rembrandt and several distinguished Dutch landscapes. Claude's *Enchanted Castle* (London, N.G.) followed in 1848. He was also interested in earlier schools and bought a number of Italian pictures and two panels from Lucas Cranach (i)'s *St Catherine* altarpiece (London, N.G.).

Loyd's only daughter, Harriet, married Major Robert Lindsay, VC, later 1st Lord Wantage. He was brother of Sir Coutts Lindsay and brother-in-law of Alexander William Lindsay, 25th Earl of Crawford, and Robert Staynor Holford. They added considerably to the collection with works by Pesellino, Gerard David's three scenes from the life of St Nicholas of Bari (Edinburgh, N.G.) and the same artist's three miracles of St Anthony of Padua (Toledo, OH, Mus. A.). They also acquired Turner's *Sheerness as Seen from the Nore* (1808; Japan, priv. col., see A. Wilton: *The Life and Works of J. M. W. Turner*: London, 1979, no. P76) and *Walton Bridges* (Lockinge House, Oxon; ibid., no. P60) and Corot's *Times of Day* (Lockinge House, Oxon). On Lady Wantage's death in 1920 the Lockinge collection passed to the Loyd family, while that in her London house, including the bulk of the Dutch pictures, was bequeathed to James Ludovic Lindsay, 26th Earl of Crawford.

UNPUBLISHED SOURCES

Crawford MSS
U. Reading Lib. [Overstone MSS]

BIBLIOGRAPHY
*DNB*
G. F. Waagen: *Galleries and Cabinets of Art in Great Britain* (London, 1857), pp. 130–47
[A. G. Temple]: *A Catalogue of Pictures Forming the Collection of Lady Wantage at 2 Carlton Gardens, London, Lockinge House, Berks and Overstone Park and Ardington House* (London, 1905)
[G. E. Cokayne]: *The Complete Peerage*, 14 vols (London, rev. 1910–59)
[L. Parris]: *The Loyd Collection of Paintings and Drawings at Betterton House, Lockinge, near Wantage, Berkshire* (London, 1967)
*Murillo in Focus* (exh. cat. by X. Brooke, Liverpool, Walker A.G., 1990), pp. 23–4
F. Russell: *The Loyd Collection of Paintings, Drawings and Sculptures* (London, 1991), pp. iii–vi

FRANCIS RUSSELL

**Loyet, Gerard** (*fl* 1466; *d* 1502–3). South Netherlandish goldsmith. He is cited as goldsmith and 'varlet de chambre' to Charles the Bold, Duke of Burgundy (*reg* 1433–77). Among Loyet's works for the Duke were images presented to churches, one of which survives: a gold, silver and enamel reliquary representing the kneeling Duke accompanied by St George, completed in 1466–7 and donated to St Lambert's Cathedral, Liège (*in situ*; for illustration *see* BURGUNDY, (5)), in 1471. This delicate reliquary, conceived as a votive group, provides some idea of more imposing works (all untraced), including two life-size silver statues of Charles and two portrait busts, the former for the churches in Aardenburg and Scheut (nr Brussels), the latter for churches in Geeraardsbergen and Linkebeek, listed in payments of 1477.

Loyet also worked for the Burgundian mint. In 1470 he was commissioned to engrave dies for new coinage, based on designs supplied by Jean Hennecart. On 7 November 1477, after the Duke's death, he was named mintmaster in Antwerp, although he does not appear to have assumed this position until 1495. Loyet spent his last years in Bruges, where he is cited from 1499.

*BNB*

BIBLIOGRAPHY
A. de Laborde: *Les Ducs de Bourgogne: Etude sur les lettres, les arts et l'industrie pendant le XVe siècle et plus particulièrement dans les Pays-Bas et le duché de Bourgogne*, II/i (Paris, 1849), pp. 497–8, 507–9
J. Helbig: 'Les Chasses de Saint Domitian et de Saint Mengold de l'ancienne collégiale de Huy. Le Reliquaire offert en don expiatoire à la cathédrale de Saint-Lambert de Liège: Les Auteurs et l'histoire de ces reliquaires', *Bull. Inst. Archéol. Lièg.*, xiii (1877), pp. 238–44
*Flanders in the Fifteenth Century: Art and Civilization. Masterpieces of Flemish Art: Van Eyck to Bosch* (exh. cat., Detroit, MI, Inst. A., 1960), pp. 298–300
D. Ludke: *Die Statuetten der gotischen Goldschmiede: Studien zu den 'autonomen' und vollrunden Bildwerken der Goldschmiedeplastik und den Statuettenreliquiaren in Europa zwischen 1230 und 1530* (Munich, 1983), i, pp. 93–4; ii, pp. 579–81
H. J. Van Miegroet: 'More News about Gerard David, Gerard Loyet and the Enigmatic Antheunis Huyghe', *Acad. Anlct. Kl. Wetsch.*, xlvii/1 (1986), pp. 73–107

J. STEYAERT

**Loyola.** Sanctuary complex at the birthplace of IGNATIUS LOYOLA near Azpeitia, Guipozcoa province, northern Spain. The Loyolas' manor house (1387–1405), now known as the Santa Casa, was where Ignatius resolved to become a soldier of Christ, while recovering from wounds received at the siege of Pamplona (1521). It is a relatively simple building, 16 m square, and contains the chapel of the Conversion and that of the Immaculate Conception, with its interesting decoration (1904). In 1681 Mariana of Austria, widow of Philip IV, bought the house and gave it to the Jesuits, and in the same year she commissioned Carlo Fontana to design a college and church for the site. Construction began in 1689, but the church was not consecrated until 1738, and the ensemble was not completed until 1888. The complex is in the form of a large rectangle, with the circular church at centre front. Its dome is 21 m in diameter, with its keystone at a height of 56 m. It is fronted by a convex portico and monumental steps with two bell-towers flanking the building. The model for the church was probably S Maria dei Miracoli (begun 1662) in the Piazza del Popolo, Rome, on which Fontana worked with Carlo Rainaldi.

BIBLIOGRAPHY
H. Hager: 'Carlo Fontana and the Jesuit Sanctuary at Loyola', *J. Warb. & Court. Inst.*, xxxvii (1974), pp. 280–89
I. Aspiazaim: *El santuario de Loyola* (San Sebastian, 1988)

GERMÁN RAMELLO ASENSIO

**Loyola, Ignatius.** *See* IGNATIUS LOYOLA.

**Loys, Jacob.** *See* LOIS, JACOB.

**Loza, Luis López.** *See* LÓPEZ LOZA, LUIS.

**Ltjashen** [Lchashen]. Group of Bronze Age and Iron Age archaeological sites at the village of Ltjashen on Lake Sevan, Armenia. Excavations from 1956 have uncovered a vast fortress that was in use from the 2nd millennium BC to 700 BC, and in the 9th–13th centuries AD. There are many burials in mounds, cromlechs, stone chests and other types of grave, including burial chambers similar to those at TRIALETI, with decorated ceramics and other finds in them. Most of the artefacts date to the Late Bronze Age (second half of the 2nd millennium BC). A rich collection of finds from the wooden and stone burial chambers (now Erevan, Hist. Mus. Armenia) includes ceremonial bronze weapons such as pole-axes, swords, and daggers in open-worked scabbards; a variety of cast-metal end-pieces on poles and staffs decorated with wild animals and birds; ornaments such as gold buttons and pins with encrusted gems and granulated surfaces; the statuette of a frog; and an engraved silver cup. Typical are wooden four-wheeled vehicles and two-wheeled chariots with cabs (eleven finds), decorated with geometric, spiral and zoomorphic carvings. The chariot shafts are ornamented with cast-bronze animals such as lions, deer, bulls and goats as well as images of chariots drawn by two horses, with two warriors in the cab. The pottery consists of vessels with fretted geometric designs inlaid with red and white paste. The finds from these burial mounds show that there were close links with the Ancient Near East: for example, the decorations on chariots resemble those from burials at Ur, while the weapons resemble Hittite finds.

BIBLIOGRAPHY

A. O. Mnatsakanyan: 'Drevniye povozki iz kurganov bronzovogo veka na poberezh'e ozera Sevan' [Early vehicles from the Bronze Age burial mounds on the shore of Lake Sevan], *Sov. Arkheol.*, ii (1960)

A. A. Martirosyan: *Armeniya v epokhu bronzy i rannego zheleza* [Armenia in the Bronze Age and Early Iron Age] (Yerevan, 1964)

S. A. Yesayan and A. O. Mnatsakanyan: 'Nakhodki novykh bronzovykh statuetok v Armenii' [New finds of bronze statuettes from Armenia], *Sov. Arkheol.*, ii (1970), pp. 157–68

V. YA. PETRUKHIN

**Luang Prabang.** City in northern Laos. According to the Lao dynastic chronicles, Luang Prabang was founded by two hermits at the confluence of the Mekong and Nam Khan rivers near a *mai thong* tree covered in red flowers. Initially called Muong Chawa, then Xieng Dong Xieng Thong, it may have been composed of two villages. When the court moved to Vientiane in the 1560s, it took its present name from Phra Bang, the 13th-century image of the Buddha, palladium of the kingdom, that had been brought there in 1353, when, after conquering the kingdom of Lan Xang (*see* LAOS, §I, 2), King Fa Ngum established a Khmer Buddhist monastic community to the south of the hill of Phu Si (see fig. (a)) at the centre of the city. Various Khmer remains confirm the presence of this community. One text, the Charter of Yot Kaeo (1601), lists the religious monuments: the Buddha of Vat Mano rom (1372), Vat Visun (1503), its principal stupa That Pathum (also called That Mak Mo or 'watermelon stupa') and Vat Xieng Thong (1561; b–d). In the 17th century Luang Prabang was almost completely abandoned following a cholera epidemic, and a new city, capital of one of the four kingdoms that resulted from the 1707–13 partition of Laos, was built on its ruins. Its defensive wall (e) was rebuilt and a palace (f) was constructed to the west of Phu Si. Many monasteries were established during the

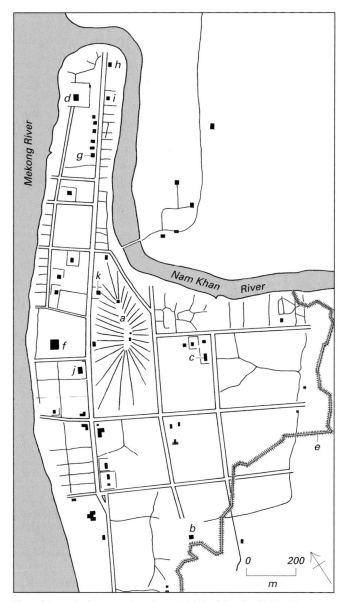

Plan of Luang Prabang, northern Laos: (a) hill of Phu Si; (b) Vat Manorom; (c) Vat Visun; (d) Vat Xieng Thong; (e) city wall; (f) palace; (g) Vat Sen; (h) Vat Pa Khan; (i) Vat Khili; (j) Vat Mai; (k) Vat Pa Ke

18th and 19th centuries. Despite the destruction inflicted on much of the city by the Ho bandit chief Deo Van Tri in 1887, all the monasteries except Vat Visun were spared, although they had to be restored in the 20th century. Some were enlarged, such as Vat Xieng Thong and Vat Sen (g). Vat Visun was reconstructed in 1898, and consequently its original walls of carved wood are known only from a drawing by L. Delaporte (1867; see Garnier, vol. 3). However, some of the 18th-century sanctuaries (Vat Pa Khan and Vat Khili (h and i), and some built in the 19th century (Vat Mai and Vat Pa Ke (j and k)) have kept their original appearance. A notable 20th-century monument, where King Sisavang Vong was cremated in 1959, is the Chapel of the Royal Funerary Chariot in Vat Xieng Thong, which has wooden panels in the walls and carved shutters showing scenes from the Hindu epic, the *Rāmāyaṇa* (*see* LAOS, §III, 2(ii) and fig. 5). The last kings amassed a collection of old pieces at the Royal Palace (1904–24), including bronze drums and objects from That Mak Mo and Vat That Luong.

BIBLIOGRAPHY

F. Garnier: *Voyage d'exploration en Indochine*, 3 vols (Paris, 1873)
M. de Barthélémy: *En Indochine* (Paris, 1901) [description of Luang Prabang in 1897]
C. Robequain: *Deux Villes du Mékong: Luang Prabang et Vieng Chane*, Cahiers de la Société de Géographie de Hanoi, xi, 1925
P. Lévy: 'Les Traces de l'introduction du bouddhisme à Luang Prabang', *Bull. Ecole Fr. Extrême. Orient*, xl (1940)
H. Parmentier: *Art du Laos*, Pubn Ecole Fr. Extrême-Orient, xxxv (1954, R 1988)
G. Sion: 'Voyage au Laos du Père Leria, 1642–1648', *Bull. Amis Royaume Lao*, iii (1970), pp. 51–8
T. B. Souk: *Louang Prabang* (Vientiane, 1974)
S. Phinith: *Contribution à l'histoire du royaume de Luang Prabang*, Pubn Ecole Fr. Extrême-Orient, cxli (1987)
M. Gîteau: 'Note sur des sculptures sur bois de Luang Prabang représentant des scènes du Rāmāyaṇa', *A. Asiatiques*, xlv (1990)
S. Bounthieng: *Luang Prabang et son art* (Paris, 1994)

MADELEINE GITEAU

**Luarasi, Skënder (Kristo)** (*b* Thessaloniki, Greece, 11 April 1908; *d* Tiranë, 20 April 1976). Albanian architect. He graduated from the Technische Hochschule, Graz, in 1936, returning to Albania in the same year and being appointed to the Ministry of Public Works in Tiranë. In his first projects he experimented with the integration of modern European architecture and the traditional architecture of Albanian cities. An example is the secondary school (1938), Gjirokastër, which combines Functionalist elements with the vernacular style of the city (*see* ALBANIA, §II). Luarasi's other works, such as the hospital (1947), Gjirokastër, the sanatorium (1957), Tiranë, and the tourist hotels at Durrës (1960) and Gjirokastër (1962), are characterized by concentration on the functional aspect, by a majestic appearance despite the modest means and by their harmonization with the historical environment. Working in the State Designing Institute (after 1965) Luarasi designed several hospitals, such as those at Sarandë (1967), Kukës (1968), Corovodë (1969), and the Hospital for Infectious Diseases (1967) and the General Hospital (1969), both in Tiranë. These buildings are examples of further experiments in improving functional aspects, economical use of resources and a tradition-based aesthetic, and they are also among those that laid the basis of a 20th-century tradition of architecture in Albania.

UNPUBLISHED SOURCES

Tiranë, U., Archv Chair Archit., [*Historia e Arkitektures Shqiptare* ('History of Albanian architecture')]

BIBLIOGRAPHY

S. Mosko: 'Për një nivel më të lartë në krijimtarinë tonë urbanistike dhe arkitektonike' [On a higher level of our urban planning and architecture], *Nëntori*, 6 (1971), pp. 5–29
——: Krijimtaria e arkitekt S. K. Laurasit [The creative work of architect S. K. Luarasi], *Ndërtuesi*, 3 (1981), pp. 22–5

GJERGJ FRASHËRI

**Luba.** Culture in Zaïre, Central Africa, that flourished from around the 17th century to the late 19th.

1. Geography and cultural history. 2. Arts of kingship. 3. Association emblems. 4. Divination arts. 5. Personal arts. 6. Artists.

1. GEOGRAPHY AND CULTURAL HISTORY. The art of the Luba is among Central Africa's exceptional visual traditions, both from an aesthetic standpoint and for the complex history and cosmology that inform it. 'Luba' is a political attribution for a number of ethnically diverse but historically related peoples located in what is now central Shaba Province (ex-Katanga) of south-eastern Zaïre, formerly the Belgian Congo. Contemporary Luba descend from an influential kingdom that flourished from approximately the 17th century to the late 19th. Yet archaeological excavations in the Luba heartland document the existence of ranked, stratified societies with advanced metalworking technologies as early as the 8th century AD. Furthermore, the continuous use of certain artefacts, such as ceremonial axes and anvils, suggests links between these early inhabitants and subsequent Luba peoples (de Maret; Childs and others).

The central Luba region extends from the Lomami River in the west to the eastern side of the Lualaba River (the name for the Zaïre River, formerly the Congo River, near its source). Natural resources, such as salt marshes and iron-rich mountains, were crucial for the economic and ideological formation of the Luba state. Close proximity to the copper belt to the south-east resulted in the manufacture and trade of copper *croisettes*, cross-shaped monies found in abundance at archaeological sites. Luba also acquired glass beads through long-distance trade, which served as currency throughout the extended Luba area. Such beads still figure importantly in the costumes and insignia of certain Luba dignitaries and ritual specialists.

The majority of Luba and Luba-related arts collected by European visitors since the late 19th century and displayed in museums around the world, including the Koninklijk Museum voor Midden-Afrika, Tervuren, the Museum für Völkerkunde, Berlin, the British Museum, London, and the Metropolitan Museum of Art, New York, belonged originally to the various branches of Luba royal culture (*see* §2 below): kingship, semi-secret associations and divination. These institutions were instrumental in the commission, production, ownership, display and use of art, which was essential to the effective performance of leadership and politico-religious authority in the precolonial and early colonial eras. Some of these institutions still thrive, and objects continue to play crucial roles in shaping contemporary Luba religious belief and political practice. The emblems referred to here as 'art' were both multi-purpose and multi-referential. They served for the display of power, as historical documents, as a means of political validation, as instruments of prophecy and problem-solving, and as receptacles of spiritual vitality. The commission and production of Luba art flourished during the period of greatest political expansion, from the early 18th century to the late 19th, when increasing numbers of rulers were installed as local manifestations of a broader concept of sovereignty. Works of art were used to forge alliances, to cement treaties and to settle debts. Every object is a historical record of the dynamic cultural, artistic and ideological exchange and borrowing that has characterized the region for several centuries.

Luba works of art are also concrete expressions of and vehicles for the ineffable dimensions of Luba ideology and religious belief that diffused over space and time. Insignia codify the secret precepts and principles of Luba government and spiritual authority, and many Luba insignia still serve as mnemonic devices, eliciting historical knowledge through their forms and iconography. Through oral narration and ritual performance, insignia serve both to conserve social values and to generate new values and interpretations of the past, as well as to effect social and political action and change.

In every domain of Luba royal art and ritual activity, female imagery and metaphor predominate. Whether in contexts of divination, kingship or secret-association emblems, the Luba female image carved from wood is meant to be a container that will attract the spirits. Luba explain that only the bodies of women are strong enough to hold such powerful spirits. Women's political and religious roles in Luba history help to explain their importance in the art (Nooter, 1991b, pp. 236–81). Certain women, especially the king's first wife and mother, were the guardians of royal interdictions. Other royal women acted as counsellors and advisers at the court or were intermarried with client chiefs to perpetuate the royal line in foreign territories. Most importantly, every deceased king was incarnated by a female spirit medium, named Mwadi, who resided in his former royal village to perpetuate the reign of the dead. Women were the guarantee of power and, though kings were men, the source of their spiritual authority resided in the deepest recesses of a woman's body. The ambiguous gendering of rulership reflects Luba notions about the complementarity and interconnection of the sexes and the important role that men and women played, and continue to play, together in the exercise of Luba political and spiritual power.

## 2. ARTS OF KINGSHIP.

*(i) Introduction.* An understanding of Luba art forms associated with the pre-colonial kingdom requires some familiarity with the kingdom itself, the origins and precepts of which are enshrined in an epic story called the 'genesis myth'. The oral account (de Heusch; Reefe, 1981) justifies and explains Luba kingship as the triumph of a progressive and enlightened political order over an earlier form of tyrannical rule. Luba express this cultural revolution in terms of archetypal characters: Nkongolo, a drunken, tyrannical ruler conceptualized as the double-headed rainbow-serpent representing the previous social order, and Mbidi Kiluwe, a hunter–prince from the east who introduces sacral kingship and practices of royal etiquette, as well as advanced technologies of metalworking and hunting. Mbidi Kiluwe's son Kalala Ilunga, conceived through Mbidi Kiluwe's union with Nkongolo's sister, ultimately overthrows his maternal uncle Nkongolo and becomes the first legitimate Luba king. All subsequent Luba kings and chiefs claim descent from Kalala Ilunga, and it is this mythical story that provides the life-line of Luba historical discourse and the explanation for the existence of most Luba art forms.

Rituals of investiture and initiation provide a mechanism through which rulers appropriate and embody the spiritual powers of the cultural bearers of Luba kingship. Through these rites, rulers incarnate the spirit personae of Nkongolo, Mbidi Kiluwe and Kalala Ilunga in a complex process that links political authority, cosmology and art. Such linkages are elucidated by Allen Roberts in his work on the Tabwa, a group closely tied to Luba history and identity. Roberts shows critical connections between rulership and the moon as source of life, renewal and divinatory wisdom. The dualism of lunar symbolism, with its monthly alternations of auspicious light and ominous darkness, provides an apt metaphor for the two-sided nature of political power and practice. (For further discussion and bibliography *see* TABWA.) Art works such as caryatid thrones and figurated spears and sceptres acquired through investiture not only validated their owners' right to rule but also activated these sources of spiritual and cosmological agency. The emblems were so potent that the mere possession of them, whether acquired by bestowal or by gift-exchange, was a sufficient premise for the exercise of power.

Luba royal arts formed part of an ensemble and were usually displayed in tandem with colourful beaded accoutrements, shell ornaments, woven mats and animal skins and furs; they were not isolated emblems as they are found today in museum and private collections. The precise composition of a treasury varies in different regions; as the missionary W. F. P. Burton explained (Burton, p. 31):

> Every chieftainship has certain objects of veneration, which may be considered as the expression of the very entity of the community. One chief will treasure a carved stool and a few headdresses of black feathers, sewn onto a strip of grass cloth. Another wears a lion's tail, some 'omanda' shells and a few ivory bracelets, while in another chieftainship the objects representing the community are a carved *kibango* staff and two carved canoe paddles.

Most Luba emblems are sculpted from wood, but many object types, including staffs, bowstands, axes, knives, spears, bells and anvils, incorporate forged iron and/or beaten or pierced copper. Luba associate blacksmithing with the origins of kingship. Through the ritual striking of an anvil against the knees, a newly invested king is created in the memory of the original culture-bearer and master blacksmith, Mbidi Kiluwe. Luba iron artefacts, widely distributed across space and time, symbolically encode a critical ideological relationship between blacksmiths and kings in Central Africa (Dewey and Childs, 1991).

Virtually all Luba insignia incorporate human imagery, often naturalistically, but also in the form of abstract geometric patterns. Yet some of the most important items in the regalia of a king are non-sculptural objects that are virtually unknown in the West because they were not considered to be collectable items by early European visitors. These include copper bracelets, beaded and conus-shell necklaces, feather headdresses, animal skins, iron bells, iron anvils and sacred baskets called *dikumbo* that contain relics of past rulers. Stools, staffs and spears, axes, bowstands, cups, drums and baskets were essential for the transfer and legitimation of power that occurred during investiture rites of a king or chief.

1. Luba caryatid stool, wood with blue-and-white beads, h. 586 mm, probably 19th century (New York, Metropolitan Museum of Art)

*(ii) Stools.* Seats are the most important symbol of Luba kingship, as they are for many African peoples. Not only is the Luba king's palace referred to as the 'seat of power' but seating is also a metaphor for the many levels and layers of hierarchy and stratification that characterize Luba royal prerogative. There are two types of Luba stools. Those that have entered Western collections are predominantly caryatid stools, supported by single or occasionally double female figures (see fig. 1). Non-figurative Luba stools also exist, however, and consist of two platforms mediated by four outwardly bowing supports embellished with deeply incised geometric patterns. It is thought that these latter may have been predecessors to the figurative stools (Kawende Fina Nkindi). Stools were such potent emblems that they were often kept secretly in a separate village from that of their owner in order to diminish the likelihood of theft. Swathed in white cloth and guarded fastidiously by an appointed official, the stool was brought out only on rare occasions. Its purpose was to serve as a receptacle for the king's spirit, rather than as a functional object. The rarity of its viewing reinforces the idea that many insignia were intended primarily not for human eyes, but for the spirit world.

*(iii) Staffs and spears.* Elegant staffs and spears were and occasionally still are the prerogative of rulers and certain dignitaries (*see* AFRICA, fig. 97). During investitures of the past, the chief's sister and wife planted these insignia in the ground at the king's left and right sides, and the chief held the two objects as he swore his oath to office. Both spears and staffs took the form of vertical elongated sceptres. The figures depicted on them represent the female founders of specific royal lines or the king himself. The double heads are those of spirit guardians, their broad sections indicate centres of political organization, and their engraved designs represent symbolic royal capitals and royal interdictions. These insignia were both prestige items and receptacles for sacral power. Sanctified by traditional priests, fortified with metal and medicine, they took on supernatural qualities and are said to have healing power. Staffs served not merely as prestige items, but primarily as genealogical and historical maps; their form and design encode secret historical knowledge about the owner's lineage history in relation to the larger Luba state.

As the property of kings and extremely powerful chiefs, spears are fewer in number than staffs, which were owned not only by chiefs but also by title-holders, land chiefs and female spirit mediums. Spears are usually double-ended with a finely sculpted female figure incorporated into the central shaft. Spears were so powerful that the mere planting of one into the ground was an act of subjugation, a sign that royalty had come to that region. Like stools, spears were shrouded in secrecy, and often the female figure carved into the shaft was covered in cloth, which was removed only for special occasions when it was out of public view.

*(iv) Axes.* Axes constitute a key component of chiefly insignia, but they are owned by other kinds of office-holders as well. Some axes consist of an engraved handle and a projecting blade of beaten copper, while others incorporate a finely sculpted human head and copper coiling around a wooden handle. Axes with sculpted heads belong to kings and high-ranking chiefs primarily, whereas title-holders, diviners and Budye members (*see* §3 below) may own axes without three-dimensional anthropomorphic elements. Engraved designs on the metal blade are a further distinguishing mark of royalty. Axes are worn over the shoulders of all royals to identify their rank, but they are also wielded in dance and other ceremonials of the court.

*(v) Bowstands.* Beautifully formed bowstands with three projecting wooden branches and iron shafts functioned as resting stands for bows and arrows, but they were primarily symbols of royal authority. Bowstands are testimony to the important relationship of hunting to kingship, for in Luba myth, the culture bearer of kingship, Mbidi Kiluwe, was a renowned hunter whose treasured emblem was his bow. Bowstands were never displayed in public; rather they were fastidiously guarded in the king's residence by a female dignitary called the Kyabuta. For public ceremonies, the Kyabuta followed the chief with a simple bow held between her breasts (Maesen). Within their protective enclosures, bowstands were regularly provided with prayers and sacrifices and were subject to elaborate ritual and taboo.

Documentation accompanying a chief's bowstand in the Koninklijk Museum voor Midden-Afrika, Tervuren, states that the sculpted female figure represents the chief's mother, who led the migration of her people from East Africa to the Luvua River, where she established an agglomeration. It is possible, then, that the figures depicted on other bowstands may also refer to particular female founders of specific royal clans. Bowstands, made from iron and wood, are unique to the regions of south-eastern Zaïre and northern Zambia. Only iron bowstands exist in Zambia, whereas both iron and wooden bowstands are known to come from Luba territories. Zambian peoples may have adopted the tradition of iron bowstands from the Luba to the exclusion of the wooden ones. Bembe, Bisa and Unga peoples all declare that bowstands originally came from Lubaland around the beginning of the 18th century when many Luba were settling the region they now inhabit.

*(vi) Cups.* Anthropomorphic cups are rare, and most seem to come from the western frontier of Luba political influence. In Luba royal investiture rites of the past, the transmission of power to a new king required the consumption of human blood from the dried cranium of his predecessor. The head was considered to be the locus of power and wisdom, and blood was the sacrificial agent that rendered a king semi-divine. Given the life-size dimensions of the few anthropomorphic cups in existence, as well as the secrecy that surrounds them, it is thought that they may have replaced actual crania after suppression of that rite during the colonial era, thus making them among the most sacred of all Luba royal emblems (Nooter, 1984, pp. 60–62).

*(vii) Drums.* Luba royal drums (*kikasa*) are used exclusively at the investiture and funeral of a ruler, or at the death of one of the ruler's children. In the collective of Kinkondja, the chief's personal court drummer is always blind; in the past, the drum was played only by a member of the slave caste. Contemporary Luba spokespersons say that in the past the inside of the drum was filled with the relics of sacrificial victims, and that the sounding chamber had a double membrane with antelope skin on one side and the finely scarified skin of a woman sacrificed for this purpose on the other. The drum was kept inside a room of the royal residence on top of an animal skin and was said to beat all by itself as a warning to members of the royal family that a death was imminent.

*(viii) Baskets.* While many items of insignia are described by the Luba as being the most important, the *dikumbo* basket lies at the root of Luba kingship. A large, woven, lidded receptacle, it contains the crania and other relics of past chiefs and kings and is guarded only by the title holder Kioni. It is forbidden for any person, royal or nonroyal, to peer inside the basket, upon pain of death. The *dikumbo* basket is used only for the investiture of a sacral king and is said to be the agent that transfers the power of kingship to the candidate from his predecessors. Like double bells and iron anvils, relic-filled baskets have widespread usage in the royal rituals of many Bantu-speaking peoples such as the KONGO and the Kuba (*see* KUBA (iii)).

3. ASSOCIATION EMBLEMS. Before and during colonialism, there existed a variety of secret and semi-secret associations, each with its own set of insignia and specialized functions of healing and litigation. One of the most important of these was the Budye association, a cross-kinship group serving as a political check and balance to kingship and as a regulatory association that guarded the precepts and principles of Luba royalty. Budye exercised considerable political control in the past, and the investiture of any king, title-holder, diviner or other office-holder included initiation into Budye. Only political and religious leaders attained the highest two grades, through which they were believed to acquire supernatural qualities.

The supreme emblem and didactic tool of the highest level of the Budye association is a memory device called *lukasa*, which consists of a rectangular wooden board embellished with clusters of beads or figures carved in relief. The latter type is characteristic of Bene Laba chiefdoms, Luba fishing groups residing along the banks of the Lualaba River. *Lukasas* from these peoples frequently incorporate two or more heads and are incised with pictorial and geometric elements. Those of the royal centre around Kabongo, by contrast, are beaded with occasional metal and shell additions and may or may not include sculptural elements.

The *lukasa*'s enigmatic signs convey to initiates the principles on which Luba politics were organized, and embody the motifs from which all other Luba royal arts were created. Its texture, pattern, colour and form convey principles of leadership, articles of law and codes of royal etiquette. The front or interior of the *lukasa* serves as a blueprint for government. Its rectangular form configures the internal order of the court. Around its perimeter, prominent beads of different colours indicate the ranks and roles of dignitaries and the hierarchy within the harem. The smaller beads prescribe the privileges and interdictions of each class and title, salutations, seating and drinking order, entrance and exit rules, dress and insignia. Divided into male and female halves, the *lukasa* also encrypts historical information about clan lists, genealogies and king lists. It also records episodes of the Luba genesis myth, a recounting of the kingdom's heroic founding. Each *lukasa* elicits some or all of this information, but the narration varies with the knowledge and oratory skill of the reader.

Another important art-producing institution that wielded considerable influence was the Bugabo association, a widespread organization dedicated to healing, hunting and fighting crime. Its principal emblem was a calabash surmounted by a sculpted female figure touching her hands to her breasts. During initiation rites, initiates placed certain sacred items inside the calabash to sanctify their oath to secrecy and their membership in the institution. These power figures (*kabwelulu*) are both divinatory and medicinal. They are catalysts to magic and agents of transformation and sorcery. Often the 'skirt' adorning the calabash is ringed by giant land snails, a symbol of the sorcerer's ability to fly in the night (A. Roberts).

An association closely linked to Budye and Bugabo and to divination practices is called Kasandji and/or Buyembe. The association was responsible for the fabrication of medicines and the preparation of healing instruments for diviners. Kasandji members collected bones, which are considered to have enormous life force and are an essential ingredient of many medicines and protective amulets against malevolent forces. The association's key emblem is a ceremonial wand with the combined head of a bird and a human. Masks in the British Museum, London, and the Linden-Museum, Stuttgart, bear the same composite features with an extended beak-like form and may also be associated with the institution. The nature of Kasandji activities, and their connection to grave sites for the retrieval of ossiferous materials, has caused them to be portrayed in the early colonial literature in a derogatory way. Yet Luba consider the association to be a positive force in the maintenance of a healthy and harmonious community.

Masking associations also existed, although they were active principally on the periphery of the Luba region. Luba call masks *bifwebe* (sing. *kifwebe*), to honour spirits of the same name. Large, round, striated masks are worn in male–female pairs for royal ceremonies and on the night of the new moon, when villagers dance to honour their ancestors (see also Neyt, pp. 200–09). There are numerous variations on the themes of *kifwebe*, the most astounding of which is an immense face-mask in the Koninklijk Museum voor Midden-Afrika, Tervuren, which is thought to be a commemorative representation of Mbidi Kiluwe, culture hero of Luba kingship and master of the forest hunt (A. Roberts). Mbidi Kiluwe is often associated with things black—a metaphorical reminder of his legendary black skin—and black cats and buffalo are common symbols of his greatness. A unique example of its kind,

2. Luba bowl figure, wood, h. 368 mm (New York, American Museum of Natural History)

this mask is a powerful evocation of the memory of Mbidi Kiluwe and the kingdom that he founded.

4. DIVINATION ARTS. Some of the finest Luba art forms are made for use in divination, the search for cause-and-effect relationships in contexts of misfortune, such as illness, pestilence and crime. One of the oldest forms of divination known to the Luba is called *kashekesheke* in the Luba heartland but is also referred to as *katatora* in the SONGYE area and generically as *lubuko*. It existed long before the introduction of sacral kingship and continues today as a personal, non-institutional form of therapeutic practice. *Kashekesheke* does not involve possession trance or clairvoyance but does require the insertion of medicinal substances into the skin of the right hand, which holds a special divining instrument.

The diminutive sculpted wooden figure used for *kashekesheke* is called by the name of the diviner's consulting spirit. Indeed, the figure's form is dictated to the diviner in a dream by the spirit itself. But, whether that ancestor is male or female, the sculpted figures are always considered to be female, even when abstracted or possessing only a head. The head often bears an intricate coiffure, and some figures display engraved designs to represent scarifications. The 'body' of the sculpture is usually a hollow rectangular form that functions as the handle, to be held by client and diviner. A smooth, worn bottom attests to considerable use and is achieved by continuous rubbing against a mat or the ground, which produces the sound 'sheke-sheke' from which its name *kashekesheke* comes. Client and diviner together hold the sculpture, which responds to their questions with coded movements. Through an extended dialogue with the figure, the diviner can unravel complex family histories and interpersonal conflicts, which may shed light on the cause of misfortune. Of this process, a Luba proverb states, 'There is not one liar alone in the *kashekesheke* divination because you are holding it and so am I.'

The institution of *bulumbu*, on the other hand, arose with sacral kingship and necessitates the invocation of the guardian spirits of Luba royalty. Royal diviners constitute an important part of dynastic rule. Once initiated into the Budye association, they incarnate the first mythical diviner, Mijibua Kalenga, who was the personal spirit medium to the first king, Kalala Ilunga. Kingship could never have been borne without the clairvoyance and the counsel of this diviner. Even today, diviners maintain a strong presence in Luba village life and continue to be consulted by chiefs in times of turmoil or social upheaval. Diviners may be male or female, although in the past most were women. As the highest rank in the order of Luba spirit mediums, these diviners are called Bwana Vidye.

Like the insignia of rulers, those of the diviner are said to have been transmitted to the original diviner by the culture hero Mbidi Kiluwe. Among the objects is the *mboko*, a sacred calabash containing a *mélange* of natural and manufactured objects, including bird claws, metal, hair, insects, fruit seeds and miniature sculpted human models. The *mboko* holds the 'promise' of clairvoyance and vision, and therefore of healing and power. As with

3. Luba figure sculpture, wood and copper, h. 445 mm (London, British Museum)

with medicinal substances that augment her powers, and she holds her own *mboko*, identical to that of the diviner, which contains kaolin and beads and visions of truth. The representation of the spirit's wife in sculptural form underscores the role of the diviner's actual wife as an intermediary in the process of invocation and consultation and reinforces the Luba notion of women as spirit containers in both life and art. Among the figure's diverse powers it is known to have curative capacities. The diviner mixes a pinch of kaolin from the figure's bowl with medicinal substances. The figure is also reputed to have oracular powers: it serves as a mouthpiece for the spirit and is capable of travelling from one place to another to gather evidence on suspected criminals.

Diviners use an array of sculpted figures that act as receptacles for medicinal substances (see fig. 3). Called *bankishi*, some serve to catch thieves, others to retrieve lost articles, still others are for curing rites. By itself, the sculpted human figure is considered to be void, until charged with substances. These compounds, called *bijimba*, contain items thought to have rare and enhanced powers, for example human bones (life force) and the hair of twins (fertility). These are embedded into the cavity of a horn, or simply wrapped in cloth and then inserted into a hole in the figure's head or stomach.

Together, these objects assist diviners in their tasks, which range from the renewal of kingship and the guardianship of natural resources to intervention in the daily lives of common people and their personal needs.

5. PERSONAL ARTS. Many Luba art works are owned by individuals for personal and practical use. These include combs, hairpins, headrests, pendants, whistles, musical instruments, dolls, pyro-engraved gourds and both figurative and non-figurative ceramics, which further attest to the extraordinary aesthetic sensibility and artistic accomplishment of the Luba.

Headrests were owned and used by Luba rulers and by other persons of high rank as pillows upon which to rest their heads at night. Headrests were not only cool and comfortable in a tropical climate but also served to protect beautiful and labour-intensive hairstyles worn by both men and women, by keeping the head raised above the surface of the bed. The sculpted caryatids are frequently depicted wearing the same coiffures worn by Luba people in the past (see fig. 4 and AFRICA, fig. 74). Headrests were highly valued by Luba people; Maesen observed that elderly people were particularly attached to them, carried them everywhere and were occasionally buried with them. Headrests were even interred in place of the deceased when the body was irretrievable, suggesting the extremely personal role of these objects. The high value accorded to headrests is further supported by the fact that, during iconoclastic upheaval with the Yeke at the end of the 19th century, the Yeke burnt all Luba headrests, while leaving other objects intact (Maesen).

Luba ivory pendants represent ancestral spirits and as such belong to a broad category of Luba sculpture called *mikisi mihasi* (Colle, p. 435). The miniature figures are portraits, or at least likenesses, and are named and honoured in memory of certain revered ancestors. Sculpted from ivory, as well as from bone and horn, these delicate

Chokwe divination baskets, Luba diviners shake the calabash and then study the configuration of objects to determine the cause and the remedy for a given problem.

Of particular importance in the diviner's kit is the sculpture of a woman holding a bowl (see fig. 2). These bowl figures have been misinterpreted as 'begging women'. In fact, the figure represents the wife of the diviner's possessing spirit. Sometimes a horn in the head is filled

4. Luba headrest, wood, h. 190 mm (Copenhagen, Nationalmuseet)

figures are suspended from bandoliers along with other objects including amulets, beads and horns. They are worn diagonally across their owner's torso or may be attached to the arm. Devotees anoint the figures with oil in homage to the ancestors, and such treatments together with regular handling and contact with the human body give the figures a smooth lustrous surface and a rich caramel colour ranging from yellowish-brown to auburn. The figures are sometimes attached to the tops of chiefs' sceptres.

The large numbers of Luba ivory figures in museums and private collections attest to their popularity and widespread ownership in the 19th century. Although each figure is slightly different in details of form and iconography, all share a minimalist conception of the human form, and hands join breasts in a gesture that signifies devotion, respect and the containment of royal secrets, according to some Luba spokespersons. The scarifications are rendered generically as incised circles, except for two sets of large raised swellings on the figure's abdomen, identifiable as *milalo*. All Luba scarifications are named and each serves a particular purpose. *Milalo* are considered to be particularly erotic and beautiful, and all women in the past were expected to have these marks of femininity and Luba social identity (Nooter, 1991b, pp. 244–7).

The Luba make and use a variety of musical instruments that are works of art in their own right. These include plucked ideophones, rattles made from seed pods and gourds, balaphones, drums of four types and whistles. Some instruments are decorated with fine geometric patterns, and some with representations of a female figure or face. The instruments accompany all rites connected with court ceremony, divination, secret-association dances and other rituals, including the worship of the new moon each month. Certain instruments, including plucked ideophones and slit drums, are used to convey messages and to invoke praise phrases through their tonal interrelationships.

6. ARTISTS. Although only a few individual Luba artists have been written about in any depth, many hands and workshops are identifiable in the corpus of Luba arts now housed in collections around the world. The best-known are the Buli Master (Olbrechts, p. 71) and the Master of the Cascade Headdress (Vogel). Also prominent is the Frobenius Master, whose repertory includes some of the most important examples of Luba art. Albert Maesen interviewed a number of artists in the 1950s and noted that master sculptors were often of Kunda origin, an aristocracy that infiltrated many regions of south-eastern Zaïre. The identification of specific, named artists from the 18th and 19th centuries is virtually impossible, however, due in part to the lack of documentation accompanying works that entered museums in the early 20th century. Furthermore, artists were often itinerant, travelling from one village to another to serve local patrons.

BIBLIOGRAPHY

V. L. Cameron: *Across Africa* (London, 1877)
P. Colle: *Les Baluba (Congo Belge)* (Brussels, 1913)
E. Verhulpen: *Baluba et Balubaïsés du Katanga* (Antwerp, 1936)
R. P. Verbeke: 'Le Bulopwe et le Kutombaka par le sang humain chez les Baluba-Shankadi', *Bull. Jur. Indig. & Droit Coutumier Congol.*, v/2 (1937), pp. 52–61
F. M. Olbrechts: *Plastiek van Kongo* (Antwerp, 1946)
E. d'Orjo de Marchovelette: 'Notes sur les funérailles des chefs Ilunga Kabale et Kabongo Kumwimba: Historique de la chefferie Kongolo', *Bull. Jur. Indig. & Droit Coutumier Congol.*, xviii/12 (1950), pp. 350–68; xix/1 (1951), pp. 1–13
W. F. P. Burton: 'Luba Religion and Magic in Custom and Belief', *An. Mus. Royal Afrique Cent.*, xxxv (1961)
L. de Heusch: *Le Roi ivre ou l'origine de l'état* (Paris, 1972; Eng. trans. by R. Willis, Bloomington, IN, 1982)
P. de Maret: 'Sanga: New Excavations, More Data, and Some Related Problems', *J. Afr. Hist.*, xviii/3 (1977), pp. 321–37
T. Q. Reefe: '*Lukasa*: A Luba Memory Device', *Afr. A.*, x/4 (1977), pp. 48–50, 88
S. M. Vogel: 'The Buli Master and Other Hands', *A. America*, lxviii/5 (1980), pp. 133–42
T. Q. Reefe: *The Rainbow and the Kings: A History of the Luba Empire to 1891* (Berkeley, 1981)
M. H. Nooter: *Luba Leadership Arts and the Politics of Prestige* (MA thesis, New York, Columbia U., 1984)
H. Womersley: *Legends and History of the Luba*, ed. T. Q. Reefe (Los Angeles, 1984)
D. P. Biebuyck: *The Arts of Central Africa: An Annotated Bibliography*, Ref. Pubns A. Hist. (Boston, MA, 1987)
S. T. Childs and others: 'Iron and Stone Age Research in Shaba Province, Zaire: An Interdisciplinary and International Effort', *Nyame Akuma*, 32 (1989), pp. 54–9
H.-J. Koloss: *Art of Central Africa: Masterpieces from the Berlin Museum für Völkerkunde* (New York, 1990) [Luba entries by M. H. Nooter]
W. Dewey and S. T. Childs: 'Forging Symbolic Meaning in Zaire and Zimbabwe', *Annual Meeting of the African Studies Association: St Louis, 1991*
M. H. Nooter: 'Secret Signs in Luba Sculptural Narrative: A Discourse on Power', *IA Stud. Afr. A.*, iii (1991), pp. 35–60
——: *Luba Art and Statecraft: Creating Power in a Central African Kingdom* (diss., New York, Columbia U., 1991)
——: 'Fragments of Forsaken Glory: Luba Royal Culture Invented and Represented (1883–1992) (Zaire)', *Kings of Africa: Art and Authority in Central Africa—Collection Museum für Völkerkunde Berlin* (exh. cat., ed. E. Beumers and H.-J. Koloss; Maastricht, Exh. & Congr. Cent., 1992), pp. 79–89
P. Petit: *Rites familiaux, rites royaux: Etude du système cérémonial des Luba du Shaba (Zaïre)*, 2 vols (diss., Brussels, U. Libre, 1992–3)
M. H. Nooter: *Secrecy: African Art that Conceals and Reveals* (New York, 1993)
F. Neyt: *Luba: To the Sources of the Zaire* (Paris, 1994)

M. H. Nooter: 'The Sculpted Narratives of Luba Staffs of Office', *Staffs of Life: Rods, Staffs, Sceptres, and Wands from the Coudron Collection of African Art*, ed. A. F. Roberts (Iowa City, 1994)

Additional information was supplied by Kawende Fina Nkindi, Albert Maesen and Allen F. Roberts.

MARY NOOTER ROBERTS

**Lubarda, Petar** (*b* Ljubotinj, nr Cetinje, 27 July 1907; *d* Belgrade, 13 Feb 1974). Montenegrin painter. He studied briefly in Belgrade and Paris, but most of his education came from time spent in Parisian galleries. Before World War II his pictures grew progressively more dramatic, their light and colouring more intense. Realism and ornament were supplanted by new forms, in which he tried to capture the essence of the landscape of Montenegro, as well as the special character of its people.

Lubarda developed the practice of spatially reducing the canvas to a two-dimensional operational surface on to which he could apply paint in an intense gestural rhythm. In the manner of American Abstract Expressionism, only the dominant features of the original motif, such as the ruggedness of the landscape, the atrocity of fighting, the animality of the depicted animal, were preserved, as in the *Buffalo* (1967; Cetinje, Crna Gora A.G.).

BIBLIOGRAPHY
L. Trifunović: *Petar Lubarda* (Belgrade, 1964)
*Petar Lubarda: Retrospektivna izložba slika* [Petar Lubarda: retrospective exhibition of pictures] (exh. cat., text M. B. Protić; Belgrade, Mus. Contemp. A., 1967)
*Petar Lubarda* (exh. cat., ed. V. Protić-Lubarda and S. Živković; Belgrade, Gal. Serb. Acad. Sci. & A., 1969)
*Lubarda* (exh. cat., text O. Perović; Ljubljana, Gal. Mod. A., 1978)

JURE MIKUŽ

**Lübeck.** German city, port and administrative district in Schleswig-Holstein, on the River Trave, *c.* 20 km from its mouth, with a population of over 200,000. Its importance as a port and trading centre was determined by its favourable location between the North Sea and the Baltic.

1. HISTORY AND URBAN DEVELOPMENT. The first small Slavic settlement ('Liubice'), with a church, a castle with ramparts and a mercantile quarter, was founded on the lower Trave by the Wendish Prince Kruto (*reg* 1066–93) but was destroyed in 1138. In 1143 a new commercial settlement was established on a better protected site (an oval enclosed by the Trave and the Wakenitz) by Count Adolf II of Schauenburg, a vassal of Henry the Lion. Henry was quick to recognize Lübeck's trade potential and, after a fire (1157), took possession of it, on the invitation of the merchants. He founded a new town in 1158–9 (episcopal see transferred there from Oldenburg, 1160) and established an unprecedented legal system. The city, which grew rapidly as a result of the arrival of Westphalian and other immigrants, was planned on a grid, with two intersecting main streets. The governor's castle was at the access point to the north, the cathedral to the south and the rest of the settlement (houses, market, town hall, main parish church) along the ridge between them. In 1226 Lübeck became an Imperial Free City; in 1227 the Danes, who had besieged the city (1201–25), were defeated, in thanksgiving for which the townspeople founded a Dominican monastery. Lübeck was head of the

Hanseatic League (first diet 1356) and in the second half of the 14th century became one of the largest towns in Germany, enjoying power, wealth and prestige. The League defeated Denmark, and the Treaty of Stralsund was concluded in 1370. The Stecknitz Canal was built in 1390–98.

Lübeck today preserves much of its appearance of the 13th and 14th centuries (see fig.) The solidly built brick town (*see* BRICK, §II, 3(i)(b)), one of the most magnificent examples of medieval town building in Germany, was the product of generous funding and high artistic aspiration. The cathedral, begun by Henry the Lion in 1173 in basilican form, was completed in the early 13th century, marking the beginning of two centuries of rivalry between the cathedral chapter and the patrician families. From *c.* 1200 the patricians constructed their main parish church, the Marienkirche (see fig.), also in basilican form. After the town fire of 1251 it was transformed into a hall church, and, from 1260, was given a new choir (*see* §2 below). This prompted the cathedral authorities (1266) to construct a hall choir and ambulatory (ded. 1341; destr. 1942; rebuilt from 1961).

The other parish churches were to varying extents based on the Marienkirche. Whereas the Petrikirche (1220–1330; destr. 1942; rebuilt from 1959) was always a hall church, the Jakobikirche (first mentioned 1227) was altered (end of 13th century) to the basilican form, then (*c.* 1300–34) converted into a larger hall church; the Ägydienkirche (first mentioned 1227) was also extended (first half of 14th century) as a hall church (choir, 1440; completed early 16th century). The Katharinenkirche (begun 1300; deconsecrated 1806) of the Franciscan monastery is a magnificent unified structure. The Dominican monastery

Lübeck, view of the old town centre from the south-west, dominated by the Marienkirche; the Rathaus is in the right middleground

(begun 1227; destr. 1276; rebuilt; ded. 1319; church destr. 1818), of which little survives, was one of the most important monastic complexes built in the North German brick idiom. Convent buildings include the former Johanniskloster (founded 1177 as a Benedictine monastery; taken over by Cistercian nuns 1245; destr. 1806) and the former St Annen-Kloster of the Augustinian nuns (1502–15; destr. 1843; now St Annen-Mus.). Of the charitable institutions built by the religious communities, the finest is the Heilig-Geist-Spital (1276–86), with its long, three-gabled façade. The Rathaus (begun 1226; Langes Haus, 1298–1308; additions, 1340–50; Kriegsstuben, 1442–4; arcade, 1570–71) is outstanding among the secular buildings and one of the finest medieval town halls in existence. Many of the houses have gabled façades with recessed entrances; some are of brick, but stone was introduced after fires in 1251 and 1276. Of the fortifications constructed from the 13th century (*see also* PASQUALINI, (4)) only the Holstentor (1467–78; *see* BRICK, fig. 9) and the 13th-century Burgtor to the north survive.

From the second half of the 14th century Lübeck was a centre for wood-carving, especially in oak, producing and exporting winged altarpieces (*see also* NOTKE, BERNT), and during the Renaissance it was the North German centre for Netherlandish art. In the 15th century it lost its supremacy as a trading centre to Bremen and Hamburg. In the 16th and 17th centuries many house fronts were plastered, and some gables were replaced by level cornices. After a decline in the 18th century, Lübeck recovered in the 19th, joining the German Confederation in 1815 and the German Empire in 1871. The demolition of the fortifications enabled the town to expand from 1864. The Elbe–Trave canal was opened in 1895. In 1937 Lübeck was transferred to Schleswig-Holstein. The city was rebuilt after large-scale destruction during World War II (1942). The Sankt-Annen-Museum and the Behnhaus contain most of the city's art collection.

BIBLIOGRAPHY

The *Hans. Geschbl.* (the yearbook of the Hansischer Geschichtsverein) invariably contains significant articles on the history and art of Lübeck.

M. Hoffmann: *Geschichte der freien Hansestadt Lübeck*, 2 vols (Lübeck, 1889–92)
H. Rahtgens and others, eds: *Die Bau- und Kunstdenkmäler der freien und Hansestadt Lübeck* (Lübeck, 1906–39)
H. A. Grabke: *Lübeck* (Berlin and Munich, 1953)
A. B. Enns: *Lübeck* (Lübeck, 1965)
H. Beseler, ed.: *Kunsttopographie Schleswig-Holstein: Die Kunstdenkmäler des Landes Schleswig-Holstein* (Neumünster, 1969)
G. Dehio: *Hamburg, Schleswig-Holstein*, ed. J. Habich, Hb. Dt. Kstdkml. (Berlin, 1971)
M. Hasse: *Lübeck* (Munich, 5/1973)

VERENA BEAUCAMP

**2. MARIENKIRCHE.** The main parish church was originally a basilica erected *c.* 1200–20 on the site of the church begun under Henry the Lion (*see* §1 above). After the fire of 1251 a new hall church was built, and a choir in basilican form was added (1260–91). The two western towers were begun in 1304 and 1310 (completed 1350–51), and the Annenkapelle (Briefkapelle) was built at the west of the south aisle from 1310. After 1315 the hall nave was abandoned and replaced (by 1330) by a basilican structure matching the chancel. Chapels were added to the aisles in 1328–85 as a result of altar donations.

The appearance of the brick building (restored after serious damage in World War II) is dominated by the two west towers and a powerful system of flying pier buttresses. Most of the brick surfaces are fairly plain, although the west towers are more richly ornamented. The church is an aisled basilica with no transept. The nine rectangular nave bays correspond to square bays in the aisles; both the nave and the aisles are rib-vaulted. The choir has a 5/8 termination and an ambulatory with radiating chapels and a standard sexpartite vault; the Lady chapel, lengthened by a rectangular bay, is separated from the ambulatory by a powerful arch. The square nave piers are articulated by astragals. There is no triforium, and the blind lower sections of the windows begin just above the apex of the arcade. The Annenkapelle has an elaborate double star vault above two slender, octagonal granite piers. Only remnants of the once very lavish furnishings have survived (*see* GOTHIC, §VIII, 5). These include the figural sculpted marble that survives from the high altar (1696–7) made by Thomas Quellinus.

In various respects (e.g. the choir and ambulatory) the Marienkirche resembles northern French and south Netherlandish cathedrals. The emulation of such models, in preference to the various abandoned hall plans, demonstrated Hanseatic patrician claims to power and prestige. The church became a prototype for parish churches in other Hanseatic towns (*see* GOTHIC, §II, 2), for Schwerin Cathedral and also for the rebuilt Cistercian abbey church in Doberan.

BIBLIOGRAPHY
M. Brix, ed.: *Lübeck: Die Altstadt als Denkmal* (Munich, 1975), i of *Die Bau- und Kunstdenkmäler der Hansestadt Lübeck* (1974–)

BETTINA GEORGI, ERNST ULLMANN

**Lubetkin, Berthold** (*b* Tbilisi, Georgia, 14 Dec 1901; *d* Bristol, 23 Oct 1990). British architect, planner and critic of Georgian birth. He was born into a prosperous Georgian family: his father was an admiral, and the family enjoyed numerous vacations throughout Europe. Lubetkin was in Moscow during the revolutionary year of 1917 and enrolled in the Vkhutemas, the school of art and architecture. He was taught by leading innovators of 20th-century art, including Kasimir Malevich, Aleksandr Rodchenko and Vladimir Tatlin. In 1922 Lubetkin went to Berlin as assistant to El Lissitsky and David Shterenberg, who were preparing the first exhibition of progressive Soviet art outside the USSR at the Van Diemen Gallery. For the next two years he studied at the Textilakademie and at the Baukunstschule, Charlottenburg, Berlin; he also worked for the architect Bruno Taut. After further study in Vienna and Warsaw, in 1924 he worked briefly for Ernst May in Frankfurt am Main. During this period he became committed to the Modernist ideals of a socially responsible architecture and the search for new forms to express this.

By 1925 Lubetkin was in Paris as architect for Konstantin Mel'nikov's Soviet Pavilion at the Exposition Internationale des Arts Décoratifs et Industriels Modernes, where he saw Le Corbusier's influential Pavillon de l'Esprit Nouveau. He stayed in Paris until the late 1920s, studying at the Ecole Spéciale d'Architecture and in the atelier of Auguste Perret at the Ecole des Beaux-Arts. Lubetkin's enthusiasm for debate led to friendships with prominent avant-garde artists, including Juan Gris, Georges Braque and Fernand Léger. Between 1926 and 1929 he worked for the USSR Trades Delegation designing demountable pavilions for regional exhibition sites, including Paris and Marseille. In 1930–32 he was in partnership with Jean Ginsberg collaborating on the block of flats (1930–31) at 25 Avenue de Versailles, Paris, that was the first successful attempt to adapt Le Corbusier's design principles to infill buildings.

In 1931 Lubetkin moved to England and the following year formed TECTON, a cooperative practice, with young graduates from the Architectural Association, London. It was immediately successful, creating the most sophisticated examples of modern British architecture of the 1930s. Their first major project, the Highpoint One block of flats in Highgate, London (1933–6), brought critical acclaim and gave Tecton an international reputation. Highpoint One offered a polished demonstration of modern construction and planning with consistent and careful attention to detailing. An eight-storey block built with a monolithic reinforced concrete structure on a double cruciform plan, it is raised on pilotis above the ground floor, planned as a series of linked free forms containing the public spaces. The floors above consist of standardized flats with services contained in the two crossings. The elevations, while clearly dependent on the contemporary work of Le Corbusier, display a strong formal tension created by the counterpoint of the structural grid and the free forms that deviate from it.

Lubetkin was convinced of the need to extend the design process out of the office and on to site as a means of advancing building technique, a legacy of his apprenticeships with May and Perret. At Tecton he was assisted by consultants who shared his ideals—most importantly Ove Arup, as in the Penguin Pool in the Zoological Gardens, Regent's Park, London (1934; for illustration *see* ARUP, OVE), and the firm of quantity surveyors Veale & Saunders. Initially, he was unable to secure commissions that matched his commitment to social change, until the mid-1930s when he was commissioned to provide a comprehensive series of social and welfare buildings, including a development plan for the socialist-led Borough of Finsbury, London. The only building of the Finsbury Plan to be completed by 1939 was the Health Centre (1935–8; see fig.), a sophisticated fusion of new formal and technical concerns. It was built with a concrete frame, faced with glazed tiles and infilled with glass. Its distinctive splayed H-plan was justified by its architects as functional, dividing permanent and public services and circulation from the flexible clinical areas, but, simultaneously, it was intended symbolically as 'a megaphone for health'. It captured public attention, but Lubetkin's modulation of the façades and rich interplay of materials was rejected by Functionalist purists in the English Modern Movement. Lubetkin's use of caryatid supports to the entrance canopy at Highpoint Two (1935–8; *see* CARYATID, fig. 2), a second block of flats in Highgate, further antagonized Modernist architects.

After World War II Tecton built several housing estates designed originally for the Finsbury Park Plan (itself abandoned), for example the Spa Green Estate (1938–46).

Berthold Lubetkin: Finsbury Health Centre, London, 1935–8

This period failed to provide Tecton with the same opportunities it had enjoyed in the 1930s, and in 1948 the practice was dissolved. Lubetkin, who was increasingly constrained by administrative inertia and the lack of proper materials (such as steel and concrete), became disillusioned with the process of reconstruction and retired to farm in Gloucestershire. He was, however, persuaded subsequently to become architect and planner for the new town of Peterlee, Co. Durham, between 1948 and 1950. To Lubetkin's disappointment, his scheme was never executed. He retired permanently from practising architecture, but in 1982 he was awarded the RIBA Gold Medal for Architecture, and he returned to architectural debate as a writer and critic, remaining an advocate of the architectural principles of the Modern Movement, which he had championed.

### WRITINGS
J. Allan and M. Reading, eds: *Writings and Speeches of Berthold Lubetkin* (in preparation)

### BIBLIOGRAPHY
G. Nelson: 'Architects of Europe Today: Tecton', *Pencil Points*, 17 (1936), pp. 527–40
R. Furneaux-Jordan: 'Lubetkin', *Archit. Rev.* [London], cxviii (1955), pp. 37–44
W. Curtis: 'Berthold Lubetkin or "Socialist" Architecture in the Diaspora', *Archit. Assoc. Q.*, viii/3 (1976), pp. 33–9
J. Thomas: 'Tecton: A Bibliography', *Archit. Assoc. Q.*, viii/3 (1976), pp. 40–50
D. Sharp, ed.: *The Rationalists: Theory and Design in the Modern Movement* (London, 1979)
J. Allan: *Lubetkin and Tecton: The Modern Architecture of Classicism* (London, 1981)
P. Coe and M. Reading: *Lubetkin and Tecton: Architecture and Social Commitment* (London and Bristol, 1981)
M. Reading: 'A Study of the Working Methods of Tecton', *RIBA Trans.*, ii (1982), pp. 57–64
D. Dean: *The Thirties: Recalling the English Architectural Scene* (London, 1983)
M. Reading: 'Tall Order', *Architects' J.*, clxxxi (1985), pp. 44–55 [on Highpoint One]
J. Allan: *Lubetkin: Architecture and the Tradition of Progress* (London, 1992)

MALCOLM READING

**Lubiąż Abbey** [Ger. Leubus]. Former Cistercian abbey near Wrocław in Silesia, south-west Poland, one of the

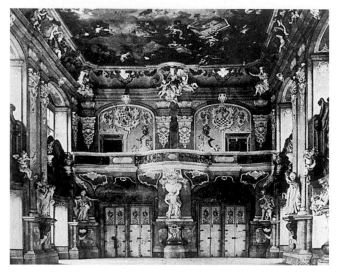

Lubiąż Abbey, Abbots' Palace, ducal hall, 1734–8

largest Baroque abbeys in central Europe (main complex: 223×118 m), situated south of Lubiąż village on the west bank of the Odra (Ger. Oder), surrounded by defence walls and moats, fields and woods. It was formerly also a centre of music. The abbey's present imposing appearance is the result of a remodelling in 1681–1739. It was founded in 1163 as the first Cistercian abbey in Silesia by Boleslav I of Silesia (*reg* 1163–1201), who brought the Order from Pforta on Saal in Thuringia. The monks settled on the site, which *c.* 1150–63 had been occupied by Benedictines. The first Romanesque church is mentioned in a document of 1208, but the only element surviving from that building is a small column (*c.* 1230–40), originally a piscina, preserved in the choir. The capital is elaborately carved with bird and plant motifs and has traces of polychromy. In the late 13th century and the early 14th that church was replaced by the existing Gothic basilica with its rectangular ambulatory; a ducal burial chapel was added in 1311–12, and notable early 14th-century monumental brasses are preserved in the choir.

In the Middle Ages the abbey prospered from its large estates, mills and fisheries, gold mines near Złotoryja, the salt and herring trade and tolls for the Odra crossing. The scriptorium, famous for faking documents, produced illuminated manuscripts, chronicles and saints' lives. Its greatest period, however, was from the mid-17th century to the mid-18th, especially under three abbots: Arnold Freiberger (*reg* 1636–72), Johann Reich (*reg* 1672–91) and Ludwig Bauch (*reg* 1696–1729). Freiberger renovated the buildings after their destruction during the Swedish wars (1655–60) and established a new library. He laid out new gardens with fountains and sculptures. In 1660 he commissioned Michael Lukus Leopold Willmann, who subsequently lived in Lubiąż for over 40 years, to execute murals and monumental paintings. Reich employed the sculptor Matthias Steinl, who took over the workshop of Matthias Knothe (*d* ?1675) and created new Baroque altars, the pulpit and choir-stalls with figures of angels playing string and wind instruments.

Between 1681 and 1739, following the examples of Lavanttal, Seckau and Lilienfeld in Austria and Czerna near Kraków in Poland, Lubiąż was transformed into a magnificent Baroque monastery-residence with interiors lavishly decorated with stuccos and frescoes. The architect, who probably came from Italy, has not been identified. The monastic buildings were all demolished except for the church, which was remodelled (1649–68) in the Baroque style. A Loreto Chapel was added *c.* 1700, and the Gothic façade was replaced *c.* 1710 by a two-tower façade forming part of the west elevation of the monastic complex. Despite the prolonged period of construction, the buildings are uniform in style and decoration. The plan had to be adjusted to the limited space and is not perfectly rectangular or symmetrical, but this impression is nevertheless given by the massive, uniform three-storey north and west elevations with pitched roofs and dormers. The Gothic church, centrally located behind the extensive west façade, forms the east–west axis of the entire complex. The monastic quadrangle was added (1619–1715) from the south, while the L-shaped Abbots' Palace (1681–99) adjoins the church from the north. Other buildings, dating mainly from the end of the 17th century or beginning of the 18th, include the church of St James and the former chancellery, hospital, bakery and brewery.

The south range includes the former refectory with ceiling frescoes (1733) by Felix Anton Scheffler (1701–60), as well as an imposing library with paintings by the Flemish artist Christian Philipp Bentum (*d* ?1750). The Abbots' Palace houses a dining-hall with frescoes by Willmann and a richly decorated ceiling, as well as a magnificent two-storey ducal hall (28.5×14.8×13.4 m; see fig.) with a musicians' gallery on the west wall. The sumptuous decoration of the hall dates from 1734–8 and relates to the dynastic ambitions of the Habsburgs. The white and gold stuccos by Albert Ignaz Provisore (*d* 1743), large-scale statues of three Holy Roman Emperors and allegorical figures by Franz Joseph Mangoldt (*fl* 1725–53) were accompanied by gold-framed paintings illustrating the life of Elizabeth Christine, wife of Emperor Charles VI, by Bentum, who also produced the illusionistic ceiling painting with the *Apotheosis of Faith* (1737). From 1740 the abbey was under Prussian occupation. It was secularized in 1810 and its extensive art collections dispersed. The abbey subsequently housed a hospital and stables and, during World War II, a munitions factory. The stalls were dismantled and remaining works of art pillaged (a *Pietà* of *c.* 1370 is now in Warsaw, N. Mus.). The abbey now serves as a store for booktraders and for the National Museum in Wrocław. The buildings were undergoing restoration in the early 1990s.

BIBLIOGRAPHY
K. Kalinowski: *Lubiąż, ślsk w zabytkach sztuki* [Monuments of art in Silesia] (Wrocław, 1970) [incl. earlier bibliog. and sources]
K. K. Jażdżewski: *Lubiąż: Losy i kultura umysłowa śląskiego opactwa cystersów (1163–1642)* [Lubiąż: a history of the Cistercian abbey and its intellectual culture (1163–1642)] (Wrocław, 1992)

ANNA BENTKOWSKA

**Lubieniecki.** Polish family of painters, draughtsmen and soldiers, active in Germany and Holland. The family left Swedish-occupied Poland and emigrated to Hamburg because of their nonconformist religion. The brothers (1)

Teodor Lubieniecki and (2) Krzysztof Lubieniecki pursued military careers before achieving recognition as painters and draughtsmen.

BIBLIOGRAPHY

*PSB*; Thieme–Becker; Wurzbach

M. Walicki: *Lubieniecy* [The Lubienieckis] (Warsaw, 1961)

**(1) Teodor (Bogdan) Lubieniecki** (*b* Szczecin, 1654; *d c.* 1718). He studied drawing from childhood while training for a military career. He did court service in Germany, Denmark and Italy, as well as pursuing military activities, until *c.* 1690, but from 1675 he was based in Amsterdam. There he received painting tuition from Gérard de Lairesse. In 1696 he began his artistic career proper in Berlin as court artist to Frederick III, Elector of Brandenburg (from 1701 Frederick I, King of Prussia). His most highly regarded drawings date from this period: now in the Albertina, Vienna, they depict masks of dying warriors, based on Andreas Schlüter's sculptures (1695–6; Berlin, Zeughaus). In 1702 Lubieniecki was appointed rector of the Kunstakademie in Berlin, but he returned to Poland via Dresden in 1706. Few of his canvases are known; among them the portrait of *Peter Schenk* (*c.* 1700; Budapest, Mus. F.A.) is outstanding. A *Family Portrait* (*c.* 1690; Warsaw, N. Mus.) was clearly painted in keeping with the late 17th-century antiquarian style of Dutch portraits.

BIBLIOGRAPHY

Thieme–Becker; Wurzbach

M. Walicki, W. Tomkiewicz and A. Ryszkiewicz: *Malarstwo polskie: Manieryzm, barok* [Polish painting: Mannerism, Baroque] (Warsaw, 1971), p. 48, footnote 387

**(2) Krzysztof [Christoffel] Lubieniecki** (*b* Szczecin, 1659; *d* Amsterdam, 1729). Brother of (1) Teodor Lubieniecki. Like Teodor, he took drawing lessons from childhood while training as a soldier, and in 1675 moved to Amsterdam. There he was taught to paint by Adriaen Backer (1635/6–84). When, at first, he was unable to support himself by painting alone, he made an income from military service. In 1693 he married into a well-known Dutch family, and he was assimilated into Amsterdam's artistic circles. Krzysztof was a talented eclectic, continuing in the waning tradition of 17th-century Dutch painting. He became a recognized portrait painter of townsfolk, scholars and the Dutch clergy. The largest collection of these portraits (about 30 survive) is now at the Rijksmuseum in Amsterdam. He also created a series of genre compositions echoing the work of Jan Steen and Adriaen van Ostade (e.g. *The Gourmets* and *The Tobacco-lovers*, both Copenhagen, Stat. Mus. Kst; and *The Game-seller*, Kraków, Wawel Castle). He also painted fantastic landscapes and biblical scenes, and his drawings have been dispersed among many European collections. Lubieniecki never disclaimed his Polish origin, always adding *Eques Polonus* after the signature on his paintings.

ANDREW STOGA

**Lubinski [Lubynski], Rudolf** (*b* Zagreb, 31 Oct 1873; *d* Zagreb, 27 March 1935). Croatian architect. After completing his studies at the Technische Hochschule, Karlsruhe, he worked in the studio of the architect Josef Durm, collaborating on projects in Offenburg, Cologne, Karlsruhe and Freiburg. After 1907 Lubinski ran his own

practice in Zagreb, where he was a leading exponent of the Vienna Secession style. His later work shows a certain amount of influence from the Modern Movement. His most important buildings in Zagreb are a residential building (1910) for priests in Palmotićeva Street; the Evangelical Centre (1909), Gundulićeva Street; the Social Insurance Building (1928), Mihanovićeva Street; and the National University Library (1911–13), Marulić Square, the finest example in Zagreb of late Secession architecture.

BIBLIOGRAPHY

I. Esih: 'Rudolf Lubinski', *Obzor* (Zagreb, 1935), p. 74

PAUL TVRTKOVIĆ

**Lübke, Wilhelm** (*b* Dortmund, 27 Jan 1826; *d* Karlsruhe, 5 April 1893). German art historian. After studying philology in Bonn, he published his first art criticism in 1850 in Friedrich Egger's *Deutsches Kunstblatt*. In 1853 he published *Geschichte der mittelalterlichen Kunst in Westphalen*, which was based on the example of Franz Kugler's *Pommersche Kunstgeschichte* (Stettin, 1832). Following the publication of *Geschichte der Architektur von den ältesten Zeiten bis auf die Gegenwart* in 1855, he became an authority on the history of architecture. The book was innovative in that it was illustrated with woodcuts. In 1857 Lübke became a lecturer in architecture at the Bauakademie in Berlin and in 1860 he became professor of art history at the Polytechnikum in Zurich. In 1863 he published *Geschichte der Plastik von den ältesten Zeiten bis zur Gegenwart*, which followed the format of his book on the history of architecture. From 1866 to 1885 he was professor of art history at the Polytechnikum and at the Kunstschule in Stuttgart. During this period, together with Karl von Lützow, he produced the new edition of the *Denkmäler der Kunst* (Stuttgart, 1863–4). He also wrote art criticism and essays and gave lectures. In 1885 he was appointed professor of art history and director of the Grossherzogliche Sammlungen in Karlsruhe. Lübke advocated a positivist approach to art history when the subject was being formulated as an academic discipline in Germany, and his writing was therefore very influential in the subsequent decades. His desire to be understood by everyone was partly responsible for some now unacceptable over-simplifications in his work. His lecture *Die Frauen in der Kunstgeschichte* (1862) aptly demonstrates the way in which the bourgeois society of his time approached the artistic work of women.

WRITINGS

*Geschichte der mittelalterlichen Kunst in Westphalen* (Leipzig, 1853)

with J. Burckhardt: *Geschichte der deutschen Renaissance*, v of *Geschichte der Baukunst*, ed. F. Kugler (Stuttgart, 1854–68)

*Geschichte der Architektur von den ältesten Zeiten bis auf die Gegenwart* (Essen and Leipzig, 1855, rev. Leipzig, 4/1875)

*Grundriss der Kunstgeschichte* (Stuttgart, 1860, rev. by E. Pernice, Esslingen, 1928; Eng. trans. of 1st edn, London, 1868); also as *Denkmäler der Kunst: Zur Übersicht des Entwicklungsganges der bildenden Kunst von den frühesten Werken bis auf die neuere Zeit* (Stuttgart, 1863–4)

*Die Frauen in der Kunstgeschichte* (Zurich and Stuttgart, 1862)

*Geschichte der Plastik von den ältesten Zeiten bis zur Gegenwart* (Leipzig, 1863, rev. 3/1880; Eng. trans. of 2nd edn, London, 1872)

ed.: K. Schnaase: *Geschichte der bildenden Künste*, 8 vols (Düsseldorf, 1876)

*Geschichte der deutschen Kunst von den frühesten Zeiten bis zur Gegenwart* (Stuttgart, 1889, rev. by A. Grebenlow, Berlin, 1927)

*Altes und Neues: Studien und Kritiken* (Breslau, 1890)

*Lebenserinnerungen* (Berlin, 1891)

BIBLIOGRAPHY
F. von Weech, ed.: *Badische Biographien*, v (Heidelberg, 1906), pp. 527–32

BARBARA LANGE

**Lublin.** Polish city (population *c.* 350,000), *c.* 160 km south-east of Warsaw on the River Bystrzyca. The earliest settlement was on Thursday (Czwartek) Hill, and dates to the 6th–7th centuries AD; the church of St Nicholas was built here in the 10th century. Also in the 10th century the royal house of Piast established a castle on the hill at the confluence of the Rivers Bystrzyca and Czechówka; it forms the centre of today's Old Town, which began to develop around the castle in the mid-13th century. In 1260 the Dominicans settled in Lublin, and in 1282 they built the church of the Archangel Michael (destr. 1846). In 1317 Vladislav IV (*reg* 1314–33; became king of Poland 1320) granted the city administrative independence according to the Magdeburg Law. In 1341 Lublin suffered heavy damage by the invading Mongol-Tatars. Rebuilding began in the following year under King Kasimir the Great; walls pierced by two entrance gates were erected around the city. The King also built a brick castle and a Gothic church for the Dominicans. In 1398 a brick town hall was completed. Several convent churches were built outside the city walls, including those of the Brigittines (1412–26), the Holy Trinity (1419) and the Bernardines (1470–87), while from the middle of the 15th century the area outside the fortifications began to be settled by Jews.

In the late 14th century and the early 15th, eight churches were built in the Gothic style and decorated with paintings in the Russian Byzantine style, reflecting the fact that the ruling monarch, Vladislav II Jagiellon (*reg* 1386–1434), had been brought up in the sphere of Russian Orthodox culture. The most important of these was the late 14th-century chapel of the Holy Trinity in the royal castle. The chapel has a square nave with a central octagonal pier supporting the cross-ribbed vaulting, and a polygonal chancel. The interior walls are covered in wall paintings by three artists (probably Ukrainian) who were led by a certain Andrew, whose name, together with the date of the work's completion (10 Aug 1418), is commemorated in a Cyrillic inscription. The application of Byzantine church decoration with its hierarchic arrangement designed for a dome and apse to a Gothic church interior presented the artists with considerable difficulties. In the vaulting above the nave are depicted *Christ Pantokrator* surrounded by the symbols of the Evangelists, angels and archangels. The paintings on the lower walls are arranged in four groups: figures from the Old Testament; the *Twelve Feasts* and the *Passion* cycle; the Fathers of the Eastern Church, hermits and martyrs; and the *Donor Standing before the Virgin*, with an equestrian image of *King Vladislav II Jagiellon* and a dedicatory inscription. Różycka-Bryzek (1983) has distinguished three styles of painting in the church: the hieratic decorative programme applied to the vaulting, generally in imitation of Byzantine models; the narrative scenes in the chancel and lower walls, based on Serbian-Atolian models and executed by Andrew, who together with the painter of the vaulting may have come from Novgorod or Tver in the Ukraine, or from neighbouring Belorussia; and the provincial, archaizing paintings by an artist of the Halicz-Volhynian school. The influence of west European painting is evident in certain scenes such as the *Communion of the Apostles*.

In 1567 King Sigismund II Augustus (*reg* 1548–72) granted the Jewish population the right to organize themselves into a commune; a Talmudic school was founded in the same year, and Lublin developed into an important centre of Jewish culture. A printing house had been founded in 1547. The main synagogue (Maharschalschul; destr. 1942–3) associated with the school was named after its first rector, Salomo Luria. It was built in the Renaissance style, with a square plan, and was the first of many such synagogues erected throughout Poland. The interior was reconstructed after a fire in 1565 and included a centrally placed square Torah shrine of the aedicular type framed by bundles of triple columns.

Lublin was already a prosperous commercial centre in 1569, when the Union of Lublin between Poland and the Grand Duchy of Lithuania was signed there. In 1571 the guild of master masons was established, and numerous local artisans became members. Their craftsmanship is attested by the fine patricians' houses with their façades richly decorated with mannerist sculpted and painted ornaments and surmounted by decorative parapets designed to hide the pitched roofs (e.g. Konopnica House, 12 Market Square; 1597). During the Counter-Reformation a few churches for the religious orders were built, including the sumptuous Jesuit church (1584–1605) by Giovanni Maria Bernardoni (*c.*1540–1605). A local variant of the late Renaissance lintel decoration of vaulting appeared in the net-coffered ceiling, called Lublin vaulting. It was first applied by the Italian builder Jacopo Balin (*fl* early 17th century) in the Bernardine church (1602–7) and soon became widespread in central Poland and Lithuania. Building activity then virtually ceased until the 18th century, when several late Baroque palaces and the churches of the Missionaries (1714–39), Capuchins (1726–8) by Carlo Bay (1678–before 1742) and Calced Carmelites (1742) by Paolo Antonio Fontana (1696–1765) were built in the suburbs. The late Baroque synagogue of Bethamidrasch (destr. 1942–3) had a square plan like the earlier Maharschalschul Synagogue, but with an interior divided into nine equal bays and covered by a vault supported on four columns. In 1795 Lublin came under Austrian rule, passing to Russian Poland in 1815, under which it flourished, and to the Polish Republic in 1918. The Jewish quarter at Podzamce was destroyed by the Nazis in 1941, together with about ten synagogues of the 16th and 17th centuries. After 1945 Lublin expanded rapidly to become a major commercial and industrial centre; it has several important museums (e.g. Mus. Lublin; N. Mus. Majdan Concent. Camp; and Skansen Mus.).

BIBLIOGRAPHY
M. Bałaban: *Die Judenstadt von Lublin* (Berlin, 1919)
M. Walicki: 'Malowidła ścienne kaplicy św. Trójcy w Lublinie' [The wall paintings in the chapel of the Holy Trinity in Lublin], *Stud. Dziejów Sztuki Polsce*, iii (1930), pp. 1–92 [with Fr. summary]
C. Osieczkowska: 'Les Peintures byzantines de Lublin', *Byzantion*, vii (1932), pp. 241–52
A. Różycka-Bryzek: *Bizantyńsko-ruskie malowidła w kaplicy zamku lubelskiego* [The Byzantine-Ruthenian wall paintings in the chapel of Lublin Castle] (Warsaw, 1983) [with Eng. summary]

JERZY KOWALCZYK

*Lubok* of a *Barber Cutting the Beard of an Old Believer*, woodcut, 353×296 mm, *c.* 1770s (St Petersburg, Russian National Library)

**Lubok.** Russian popular print, a brightly coloured woodcut or engraving produced from the mid-17th century to the late 19th. Executed in a naive yet expressive style, it may depict folktales and amusing stories while also containing elements of political propaganda or social and moral advice. *Lubki* were initially conceived as 'paper icons' and were of a religious nature. Peter the Great, however, realized their effectiveness and used them to popularize his own reforms. Those depicting the enforced cutting of beards to comply with his Europeanization programme of 1705 are particularly notable (see fig.), while others are clearly propagandist and depict the tsar as Alexander the Great or as the folk hero Il'ya Muromets. Russian peasants are often treated and are charmingly depicted in both the enchanting images and the archaic texts that usually accompany each picture. During the mid-18th century woodcuts were gradually phased out and replaced by inventive and vividly executed copper-engravings depicting the lifestyle and refined social conventions of the merchant classes.

The ruthless censorship enforced under Nicholas I in 1851 virtually destroyed the tradition of *lubki*. Early in the 20th century, however, there was a revival of interest in the *lubok* tradition. Kandinsky reproduced *lubki* in his *Blaue Reiter Almanach* (Munich, 1912) and Chagall and Natal'ya Goncharova admired their unusual subject-matter, while Mikhail Larionov possessed a large collection of them and was profoundly influenced by their distinctive stylistic qualities. They are now rare and highly prized collectors' items.

*See also* NEO-PRIMITIVISM.

BIBLIOGRAPHY

D. Rovinsky: *Russkiye narodnyye kartinki* [Russian folk pictures] (St Petersburg, 1881–93) [standard ref. work]

Y. Ovsyanikov and A. Shkarovsky-Raffe: *The Lubok: 17th–18th Century Russian Broadsides* (Moscow, 1968)

A. Sytova: *The Lubok: Russian Folk Pictures, 17th to 19th Century* (Leningrad, 1984)

ANTHONY PARTON

**Lubomirski.** Polish family of patrons and collectors. The first senator from the family was Sebastian Lubomirski (1539–1613); he made his fortune in salt-mines and acquired Wiśnicz Castle in 1593. His son (1) Stanisław Lubomirski and Stanisław's grandson (2) Stanisław Herakliusz Lubomirski were both notable magnates and patrons. (3) Henryk Lubomirski was brought up by his aunt, the patron and collector Izabella Lubomirski (1736–1816). Henryk gave his collection to the Ossoliński National Establishment (now Wrocław, Ossolineum), of which his son, Jerzy Henryk Lubomirski (*b* Vienna, 28 May 1817; *d* 25 May 1872), became curator in 1847. Jerzy developed the publishing and scientific aspects of the Establishment and initiated exhibitions of Polish art in Kraków (1858) and L'vov (now L'viv).

**(1) Stanisław Lubomirski** (*b* Wiśnicz, 1583; *d* Wiśnicz, 17 June 1649). He was educated (1593–7) in Munich by the Jesuits, then in France, the Netherlands and Italy. He began his political career in 1605. In 1613 he married Zofia Ostrogska and in the same year inherited WIŚNICZ; he employed Andrea Spezza to expand the castle there, which became his chief residence. In 1616 he founded the town of Wiśnicz Nowy ('New Wiśnicz') there. In 1621, as Commander-in-Chief at the Battle of Chocim, Lubomirski signed a favourable truce with the Turks. He vowed to found a monastery of the Discalced Carmelites in Wiśnicz and had it built (1622–35; partly destr.) by Matteo Trapolo (*fl* 1616; *d* 1637) next to his residence; it was surrounded by fortifications. Around 1629 Trapolo began remodelling Lubomirski's residence at ŁANCUT, which became the latter's second residence after 1637. Lubomirski brought the Antwerp painter Mathäus Ingermann from Rome from 1639 to 1641 to paint works for the Discalced Carmelite church in Wiśnicz. Lubomirski also employed the painter and stuccoist Stanisław Kostecki (*d* before 1651) from Kraków and Giovanni Battista Falconi and his workshop, who stuccoed the interior of the Discalced Carmelite church around 1635. Lubomirski's architectural patronage was considerable. Between 1642 and 1648 he employed such architects as Bockberger from Vienna, who built the Piarist Collegium in Lubowla, and Krzysztof Mieroszewski (*d* 1679), who built the fortifications of Przeworsk Convent. Lubomirski founded 20 churches, solely or jointly, and his projects included the decoration of the Lubomirski Chapel in Kraków, the Dominican monastery in Gródek, Kraków, the Piarist Collegium in Podliniec and the Discalced Carmelite convent and church of St Joseph in Kraków. He also built castles in Połonne, Rzemień, Lubowla, Zator, Nowy Sacz and Niepolomice. He owned a rich collection of paintings and works of art, which were mainly south Netherlandish.

UNPUBLISHED SOURCES

*Relatio fundationis conventus Visnicensis* (1624–1719, Wrocław, Ossolineum, MS. 1871)

PSB

BIBLIOGRAPHY

F. F. Buchner: *Canto concerti ecclesiastici* (Venice, 1642) [ded. to Lubomirski]

S. Czerniecki: *Dwór, wspaniałość, powaga i rządy* [The court, splendour, dignity and governments] (1697)

W. Tomkiewicz: *Z dziejów polskiego mecenatu artystycznego w XVII wieku* [From works of Polish artistic patronage of the 17th century] (Wrocław, 1952), pp. 261–304

J. Długosz: *Mecenat kulturalny i dwór Stanisława Lubomirskiego wojewody krakowskiego* [Cultural patronage and the court of Stanisław Lubomirski, Palatine of Kraków], Prace Wrocławskiego Towarzystwa Naukowego, cxlix (Wrocław, 1972)

M. Karpowicz: *Artisti ticinesi in Polonia nel '600* (Bellinzona, 1983), pp. 49–54

M. Brykowska: *Studia nad architekturą baroku: Układy przestrzenne kościołów karmelitów bosych* [Studies on Baroque architecture: spatial arrangement in Discalced Carmelite churches], Prace Naukowe Politechniki Warszawskiej, Budownictwo, lxxxvii (Warsaw, 1984)

P. S. Szlezynger: *Fundacje architektoniczne Stanisława Lubomirskiego, wojewody i generalnego starosty krakowskiego* [The architectural foundations of Stanisław Lubomirski, voivode and general starost of Kraków], Politechnika Krakowska, Arch. Ser. no. 168 (Kraków, 1994)

**(2) Stanisław Herakliusz Lubomirski** (*b* Wiśnicz, 4 March 1641; *d* Ujazdów, nr Warsaw, 16–17 Jan 1702). Magnate, philosopher, writer and patron, grandson of (1) Stanisław Lubomirski. He began his education at the court of his grandfather at Wiśnicz. He was also well educated as a military engineer, as testified by an architectural drawing (untraced, see Sawicka and Sulerzyska, p. 65) inscribed *St. Lubomirski inventit et fecit*. He contributed to the iconographic and artistic designs of his residences in Puławy (acquired through his marriage to Zofia Opalińska in 1668) and Warsaw (Czerniaków, Ujazdów Castle, Łazienki), and he wrote the inscriptions in the Bernardine church in Czerniaków, which was also his mausoleum. He brought TYLMAN VAN GAMEREN to Poland from Venice, who, with others, illustrated his *Adverbia moralia* (pubd Warsaw, 1688, 2/1691) and also designed all the buildings commissioned by Lubomirski. Francesco Antonio Giorgioli (1655–1725) and the stuccoist Carlo Giuseppe Giorgioli (1658–after 1709), responsible for the interiors of the Bernardine church in Czerniaków, worked at his artistic court between 1687 and 1689. As a neo-Stoic (*see* STOICISM) Lubormirski believed that 'every style is good when it is suitable for expressing the matter it is treating' (see Lubomirski, ed. Pollak, 1955, p. 198). Of the church in Czerniaków he wrote that 'it will not be great' but said it would be built 'in an unusual way' and 'will not yield precedence in beauty of work to any of the Polish [churches]' (letter to M. Zebrzydowski; Kraków, Library PAN, MS. 1077, fol. 137). The church was built on a Greek-cross plan with bare interior decoration and a large octagonal presbytery, joined to the convent building.

### WRITINGS

*Rozmowy Arlaksesa i Ewandra* [The conversations of Arlaxeses and Evander] (Warsaw, 1683)

*Adverbia moralia* (Warsaw, 1688, 2/1691) [in Latin]

R. Pollak, ed.: *Wybór pism* [Selected writings] (Wrocław, 1955)

### BIBLIOGRAPHY

S. Sawicka and T. Sulerzyska: *Straty w rysunkach Gabinetu Rycin Biblioteki Uniwersyteckiej* [Losses of drawings from the Cabinet of Engravings in the University Library] (Warsaw, 1960), p. 50

M. Karpowicz: 'Warszawska świątynia Amora' [Cupid's Warsaw temple], *Sekretne treści warszawskich zabytków* [The secret meaning of Warsaw's monuments] (Warsaw, 1976), pp. 30–50

J. A. Chrościcki: 'Poeta i architekt', *Poezja*, 5–6 (1977), pp. 199–202

A. Miłobędzki: *Architektura polska XVII wieku* [Polish architecture of the 17th century] (Warsaw, 1980), pp. 356–65

S. Mossakowski: 'Mecenat artystyczny Stanisława Herakliusza Lubomirskiego' [The artistic patronage of Stanisław Herakliusz Lubomirski], *Stanisław Herakliusz Lubomirski: Pisarz, polityk, mecenas* [Stanisław Herakliusz Lubomirski: writer, politician, patron], ed. W. Roszkowska (Wrocław, 1982), pp. 51–76

JULIUSZ A. CHROŚCICKI

**(3) Henryk Lubomirski** (*b* Równe, Volhynia, 15 Sept 1777; *d* Drezno, 20 Oct 1850). Great-great-nephew of (2) Stanisław Herakliusz Lubomirski. Portraits of Henryk as a young boy were executed by Antonio Canova (1786; Łańcut, Łańcut Castle), Angelica Kauffman (1786; L'viv, Pict. Gal.) and Elisabeth-Louise Vigée Le Brun (1789; Berlin, Gemäldegal.). He inherited his aunt's palace (destr.) in Vienna, along with a valuable collection of books and works of art and part of the Łańcut collections, which he moved to his own residence in Przeworsk, near Rzeszów. He often visited France, Austria, Italy, Belgium and Germany to buy works of art. In Przeworsk he created a museum with paintings, prints, weapons, medals, coins and historical objects. The most valuable part of the collection comprised over 5000 engravings and 474 drawings, including a set of drawings by Albrecht Dürer, Rembrandt van Rijn, Charles-Joseph Natoire, Annibale Carracci, François Clouet and Lorenzo di Credi. On 25 December 1823 Henryk signed a contract with Józef Maksymilian Ossoliński (1748–1826)—the founder of the Ossoliński National Establishment—agreeing to incorporate his collections into the Establishment, on the condition that his family would be its hereditary trustees and that the collections would remain separate as the museum of the Lubomirski dukes in Przeworsk. It was moved to L'viv in 1869, but since World War II most of what remains of the collection is at the Ossolineum, Wrocław. The Lubomirski trustees increased the number of drawings by about 8000: for example, 276 drawings were added from Ignacy Skarbek's collection in 1843; in 1846 Aleksander Batowski's set of drawings was acquired; and 400 drawings from Karol Kühnl's collection were added in 1868. Lubomirski left all his property to the Ossolineum. He was the author of *Zbiór widoków celniejszych ogrodów polskich* [A collection of views of the more handsome Polish gardens].

PSB

### BIBLIOGRAPHY

H. Blumówna: 'Kolekcja rycin i rysunków Henryka Lubomirskiego w zbiorach Zakładu Narodowego im. Ossolińskich' [The engravings and drawings of Henryk Lubomirski in the collection of the Ossoliński National Establishment], *Roc. Zakładu Narodowego Im. Ossolińskich*, v (1957), pp. 101–5

M. Bailey: 'Hitler, the Prince and the Dürers', *Art Newspaper*, vi/47 (April 1995), pp. 1, 6

ANDRZEJ ROTTERMUND

**Luc**, Frère. See FRANÇOIS, CLAUDE.

**Luca di Borgo.** See PACIOLI, LUCA.

**Luca di Giovanni da Siena** (*fl* 1385–90). Italian sculptor. In 1386 he was paid for a completed marble angel and was advanced funds for another, for Florence Cathedral. In the same year he began a figure of *Charity*, later finished by Jacopo di Piero Guidi (*fl* 1376–1412), for the Loggia della Signoria, Florence. In 1390 Luca was in Orvieto, where, as Master of the Works (*capomaestro*), he worked on a baptismal font begun earlier by others for the cathedral. He is last mentioned in 1390, when he was given a loan by the Orvieto Cathedral works on account of his poor health.

The identification of two *Musical Angels* (Florence, Mus. Opera Duomo) from the façade of Florence Cathedral with those mentioned in the document of 1386 is generally accepted. Becherucci has also attributed to him on the basis of style two works from the Porta del Campanile on the south flank of Florence Cathedral, the three-quarter-length figure of *Christ the Redeemer*, placed in a roundel above the door, and the large statue of the *Angel of the Annunciation* in a tabernacle above. The two *Musical Angels* suggest a mature and skilful artist who handled his assignment with vigour and originality. The faces are superbly modelled, and they reveal knowledge of the Antique not common to his Florentine and Sienese contemporaries. Carli mentioned an 18th-century source describing Luca as the teacher of Jacopo della Quercia, in whose innovative style are found resonances of this earlier master.

### BIBLIOGRAPHY

Thieme–Becker

L. Becherucci and G. Brunetti: *Il Museo dell'Opera del Duomo a Firenze*, i (Florence, 1969), pp. 247, 249

L. Becherucci: 'Un' *Annunciazione* nel Duomo di Firenze', *Scritti di storia dell'arte in onore di Ugo Procacci*, i (Milan, 1977), pp. 184–95

E. Carli: *Gli scultori senesi* (Milan, 1986), p. 27

LISBETH CASTELNUOVO-TEDESCO

**Luca di Tommè** (*fl* 1356–89). Italian painter. He worked in Siena in the second half of the 14th century and was one of the generation of artists who inherited and upheld the conventions of Duccio, Simone Martini and Pietro and Ambrogio Lorenzetti. While he was not an innovator, his extensive output helped to sustain the decorative Sienese style that was to survive well into the 15th century. Over 50 works have been attributed to him, mostly altarpieces, although it is not always possible to distinguish his hand. Documentary and inscriptional evidence shows that he was a prolific and respected artist. One of his main patrons was the Opera del Duomo, the authorities of Siena Cathedral, for which he also acted as a consultant. In style his works developed from an early, more imitative mode to a distinctive interpretation of the relationship between figures and their backgrounds, with a growing interest in line, ornament and texture.

Luca was sufficiently well established by 1356 to be recorded as a member of Siena's newly founded painters' guild. Vasari described him as a pupil of Barna, but there is little stylistic evidence for this. His paintings of the late 1350s and early 1360s were influenced by those of Pietro Lorenzetti, as is evident from the careful composition and awareness of perspective. Another influence was the delicacy and elegant linearity of Simone Martini's work, which can be recognized in Luca's *Virgin and Child Enthroned with SS Louis of Toulouse and Michael* (Los Angeles, CA, Co. Mus. A.). This work is typical of his early period: the small-scale figures show animated gestures and expressions, and they are well modelled in light tones. Luca's style was also marked by a growing ability to express emotion and to relate his figures to the areas framing them. In the *Flagellation* predella panel (Amsterdam, Rijksmus.; see fig.) Christ stands in contrapposto. The pose, which Luca used here for the first time, and the musculature of the naked torso demonstrate his understanding of anatomy. The architectural background of

Luca di Tommè: *Flagellation*, tempera on panel, 390×285 mm, *c.* 1356–61 (Amsterdam, Rijksmuseum)

columns and arches is used to structure the composition, a role that he later transferred to the frame itself.

The collaboration between Luca and Niccolò di Ser Sozzo, an older artist, is attested by their joint signatures on a polyptych with the *Virgin and Child Enthroned with SS John the Baptist, Thomas, Benedict and Stephen* (1362; Siena, Pin. N.). The inscription was not discovered until 1932, and its discovery has resulted in considerable debate regarding the artists' respective roles. The exceptional size and complexity of this work suggest that it was a prestigious commission. The central panel shows the Christ Child standing on the Virgin's lap, in the manner of Simone Martini's *Maestà* (1315; Siena, Pal. Pub.). The figures are well placed within their frames, and there is an attempt to indicate depth and perspective in the treatment of the base of the throne. It has been suggested that Luca designed the panel, which was then painted by Niccolò; it is also possible that Luca himself painted *St John the Baptist* and *St Thomas*. Whatever the nature of the partnership, whether Luca had been apprenticed to Niccolò or whether they collaborated as equals, the relationship confirmed by the signature has resulted in a reassessment of Luca's output, with some works now given to him that had formerly been attributed to Niccolò.

Another Sienese contemporary who may have influenced Luca was Bartolommeo Bulgarini. He and Luca, together with Jacopo di Mino del Pelicciaio, formed an advisory committee to Siena Cathedral to assist with the temporary removal of Duccio's *Maestà* (dispersed; main panels Siena, Mus. Opera Duomo) from the high altar during building works in 1362. The figure of *St Bartholomew* in Luca's polyptych, the *Mystic Marriage of St Catherine* (*c*. 1366; Siena, Pin. N.), is very close to Bulgarini's *St Bartholomew* (Pisa, Mus. N. S Matteo); more specifically, identical punch marks suggest tools may have been shared or borrowed.

From the mid-1360s, a more independent style emerged. Luca's output became increasingly prolific; this suggests that he ran a large workshop, where he would also have trained and influenced a younger generation of artists. He continued to work for the Opera del Duomo and also became involved in the local government of the city, evidence that he was a prosperous and respected citizen. The works of his middle period show more detailed drawing of faces and the use of contrasting colour tones to express emotion, as in the *Assumption of the Virgin* (*c*. 1365; New Haven, CT, Yale U. A.G.). His figures were becoming larger in relation to their surrounding frames, and there was an increasing sense of composition and control of space. Yet the narrative element was retained: the *Crucifixion* (1366; Pisa, Mus. N. & Civ. S Matteo) has majestic, emotionally powerful figures whose prominence within their frame brings them in direct communication with the spectator.

Although many of Luca's mature works were on an increasingly large scale, he was also capable of designing on the smaller scale required for the various predella panels that survive from complex altarpieces. He also produced a number of single panels of the *Virgin and Child Enthroned* (e.g. Cambridge, Fitzwilliam) for less prestigious commissions.

The elaborate polyptych of the *Virgin and Child with Saints and the Evangelists* (Siena, Pin. N.) is typical of Luca's work of the early 1370s and demonstrates his preoccupation with the function of the frames in relation to the figures and their background: the contrasts in scale between the central *Virgin* and the various flanking figures give an enhanced sense of depth. The grave and monumental images of the Virgin and saints of the later period, through their essentially static nature, became more decorative and, therefore, less expressive. The figures were increasingly elongated to match the growing verticality of the panels. The frames became more elaborate, and an ornamental effect began to predominate over the earlier emotional and narrative qualities. Markedly less was produced from the late 1370s, a result perhaps of Luca's civic commitments.

Luca's last recorded works, for example the *Annunciation with Saints* in the oratory of S Giovanni at Cascina, near Pisa, show the further development of these trends. The standing figures appear flat, and their drapery is stylized: they are expanded and attenuated to fill the whole area defined by the frames, which have characteristic cusped arches. The use of lettering and inscriptions adds to the effect of unreality, while gilded backgrounds increase the overwhelmingly decorative effect. These late works have been described as replacing pathos by prettiness.

Although Luca appears to have spent most of his working life in Siena, he may have accepted commissions elsewhere in Tuscany: he was recorded in 1374 as providing gold for a fresco in Orvieto Cathedral. He was still working in Siena in 1389 when he was commissioned, with Bartolo di Fredi and Andrea di Bartolo, to make an altarpiece for one of the cathedral chapels; this is the last known reference to him, but the altarpiece has not been identified.

### BIBLIOGRAPHY

P. Bacci: 'Una tavola inedita e sconosciuta di Luca di Tommè', *Rass. A. Sen. & Cost.*, i (1927), pp. 51–62
M. Meiss: *Painting in Florence and Siena after the Black Death* (Princeton, 1951)
E. Carli: *La pittura senese del trecento* (Milan, 1955)
F. Zeri: 'Sul problema di Niccolò di Ser Sozzo Tegliacci e Luca di Tommè', *Paragone*, ix/105 (1958), pp. 3–6
M. Meiss: 'Notes on Three Linked Sienese Styles', *A. Bull.*, xlv (1963), pp. 47–8
B. Berenson: *Central Italian and North Italian Schools* (London, 1968)
N. Muller: 'Observations on the Painting Technique of Luca di Tommè', *Bull. LA Co. Mus. A.*, xix (1973), pp. 12–21
P. Torriti: *La Pinacoteca Nazionale di Siena: I dipinti dal XII al XV secolo* (Genoa, 1977)
S. A. Fehm: *Luca di Tommè, a Sienese Fourteenth-century Painter* (Carbondale and Edwardsville, 1986)

CAROLA HICKS

**Lucae, Richard** (*b* Berlin, 12 April 1829; *d* Berlin, 26 Nov 1877). German architect and teacher. He took drawing lessons with Johann Gottfried Schadow at the Berlin Kunstakademie and was introduced to architecture through his uncle, August Soller, who had studied with Karl Friedrich Schinkel. After training as a surveyor (1847–9), he studied (1850–52, 1855) at the Berlin Bauakademie; in the meantime he gained practical experience (1853–5) on the building of Cologne Cathedral and Soller's Roman Catholic church at Miechowitz. At the Bauakademie he came into contact with both the classicism of Schinkel's successors, in particular Karl Bötticher, and with the eclectic historicism of Wilhelm Stier. After his architectural exams in 1859, he embarked on his first trip to Italy; further journeys, including England and France, were made in the 1860s.

Lucae's earliest works were residential buildings in Berlin, including his own house (1857–9), the Villa Soltmann (1861) and the Villa Heckmann (1868), as well as in other towns, such as Rostock, Marburg, Kassel, Erfurt and Leipzig. These buildings, since demolished, had simple cubic outlines, often enlivened with asymmetrical sections and towers in the manner of an Italian villa; the detailing, however, was late classical in style, with few Renaissance elements. Lucae's skill and style can be seen in his surviving schemes for interior decoration, as in the ballroom of the Villa Siemens (1874), Berlin. Three stylistically different façade designs for a villa in Heyden (1873–4) show that Lucae was looking for richer, more plastic styles, and this led him towards the Renaissance Revival. His Palais Borsig (1875–7; destr.), Berlin, marked this stylistic shift and represented a new trend in building for the 1870s that suited the power of the young empire, and that came between Schinkel's school and the French influence that came later.

Lucae also designed public buildings in Rostock (a school, water-tower and war memorial) and country houses and burial chapels in the Prussian province. No church designs are known of, other than an early scheme and one for the church in Kolberg. Of the competitions in which he took part (including that for the Hamburg Kunsthalle, 1863), he won those for the Magdeburg Stadttheater (1873–6) and the Frankfurt am Main Opera House (1873–88, restored 1972). His theatre buildings are particularly lavish in decoration and animated with sculpture.

Aside from his private practice, in 1869 Lucae became a member of the Technische Bau-Deputation, the highest building authority in Prussia, and in 1873 was appointed Director of the Bauakademie, where he had taught since 1859. There he designed extensions to Schinkel's building and, after the merging of the Bauakademie and the Gewerbeakademie in 1876 to form the Technische Hochschule, he was commissioned to design its new home, the most important building project in Berlin during the late 1870s. The designs, completed shortly before his death, combine the clear ordering of individual features, reflecting the discipline of Schinkel's school, and such fanciful elements as multi-domed towers. The latter were deleted from the plans by Friedrich Hitzig, who completed the building in a more conventional Renaissance Revival style.

### WRITINGS
'Über die Macht des Raumes in der Baukunst', *Z. Bauwsn*, xix (1869), pp. 294–306
'Über die ästhetische Ausbildung der Eisenkonstruktion', *Z. Bauwsn* (1870)

### BIBLIOGRAPHY
Thieme–Becker
A. Woltmann: *Die Baugeschichte Berlins* (Berlin, 1872), p. 292
H. Ende: 'Zur Erinnerung an Richard Lucae', *Dt. Bauztg*, xii (1878), pp. 51–4, 63–6
W. Lübke: 'Richard Lucae', *Z. Bild. Kst* (1878), pp. 204–9, 239–43
E. Stromeyer: *Die Wohnbauten Richard Lucaes* (Würzburg, 1941)
E. Börsch-Supan: *Berliner Baukunst nach Schinkel, 1840–1870* (Munich, 1977)
G. Peschken: 'Zur Baugeschichte der Technischen Universität Berlin', *Wissenschaft und Gesellschaft: Beiträge zur Geschichte der Technische-Universität Berlin*, ed. R. Rürup (Berlin, 1979), i, pp. 171–86
I. Schade: 'Die Bauplanung des Hauptgebäudes der Technische-Hochschule zu Berlin-Charlottenburg: Ein Vergleich der Entwürfe Richard Lucaes und Friedrich Hitzigs', *100 Jahre Technische Universität Berlin* (exh. cat., W. Berlin, Tech. U., 1979)

EVA BÖRSCH-SUPAN

**Lucas, Colin Anderson.** *See under* CONNELL, WARD AND LUCAS.

**Lucas, François** (*b* Toulouse, 1736; *d* Toulouse, 17 Sept 1813). French sculptor. The son of Pierre Lucas (1691–1752), a founder-member of the Toulouse Académie, he became the leading sculptor of the Toulouse region during the late 18th century. Lucas began to exhibit in 1759, winning the Grand Prix de Sculpture at the Toulouse Académie in 1761 with his low relief *David and Abigail* (untraced). Three years later he became a professor at the Académie; his students included Jean-Marie-Joseph Ingres (1755–1814), the father of Jean-Auguste-Dominique Ingres. By 1774 Lucas was in Carrara sketching out his great marble low relief, the *Junction of the Canal des Deux-Mers* (l. 17 m, 1775; between the Canal du Midi and the Canal de Brienne). Most of his works are in the Musée des Augustins, Toulouse, which he helped to found. They include a terracotta statuette of *Zephyr*, a seated marble

statue of *Louis XVI* (1777) in the dress of a Classical warrior, a marble low relief with the Genius of War carrying an urn, formerly part of the tomb of *Chevalier Dauvet* (Toulouse, St Jean), and portrait busts. The two elegant marble *Angels in Adoration* (1782) at the high altar of St Pierre-des-Chartreux, Toulouse, show how Lucas was inspired both by the traditions of 17th- and 18th-century French sculpture and by Italian classicism. Lucas also took part in work for the Tower of Illustrious Agenais (1806; Lacassagne, Château des Boéry), a two-storey octagonal pavilion in the Louis XVI style, for which he contributed four life-size terracotta statues: *Jules Scaliger*, *Théophile de Viau*, *Blaise de Montluc* and *Bernard Palissy*. Lucas was an avid collector of ancient medals and inscriptions; his valuable collection also went to the Musée des Augustins.

### BIBLIOGRAPHY
J. Momméja: 'Notes sur un canon en argent en 1646 et sur un amateur agenais du XVIIIe siècle: P.-F.-X. Daribeau de Lacassagne', *Réun. Soc. B.-A. Dépt.*, xxvii (1903), pp. 199–213
H. Rachou: 'Un Buste du musée des Augustins', *Bull. Soc. Archéol. Midi France*, 40 (1909–11), pp. 3–5, 173–4
[H. Rachou]: *Catalogue des collections de sculpture et d'épigraphie du musée de Toulouse* (Toulouse, 1912), pp. 369–70
B. Desazars de Montgailhard: *Les Artistes toulousains et l'art à Toulouse au XIXe siècle*, ii (Toulouse, 1925), pp. 157–60
'Classements parmi les monuments historiques', *Mnmts Hist. France*, ii (1956), pp. 238–9
P. Mesplé: 'L'Oeuvre toulousaine et régionale du sculpteur François Lucas', *Bull. Mus. Augustins* (July–Sept 1958)
——: 'L'Album de dessins de voyage d'Italie de François Lucas', *Bull. Soc. Archéol. Midi France*, xxviii (1962), pp. 75–84
R. Mesuret: *Les Expositions de l'Académie royale de Toulouse, de 1751–1791* (Toulouse, 1972), pp. 590–91 [list of works]

MICHAEL PRESTON WORLEY

**Lucas, George A(loysius)** (*b* Baltimore, MD, 29 May 1824; *d* Paris, 16 Dec 1909). American agent and collector. The son of a publisher and book illustrator, Fielding Lucas jr (*d* 1854), he worked as an engineer for the New York–New Haven Railroad, the Central Railroad of New Jersey and the Croton Aqueduct Board. In 1856 he inherited a sum sufficient to free him to pursue his interest in the arts. The following year he moved to Paris, never to return to America. In Paris, Lucas gained widespread respect in art circles through his work as agent to several American collectors and art dealers. By the mid-1880s he had expended about half a million francs at the behest of William T. Walters, a prosperous businessman also from Baltimore. Lucas was actively involved in the formation of Walters's collection of 19th-century art, noted for its outstanding works by French Realist, Academic and Barbizon school artists, with works commissioned from such artists as Honoré Daumier, Jean-Léon Gérôme and Jean-Baptiste-Camille Corot. The most representative collection in the world of the sculpture of Antoine-Louis Barye is in the Baltimore–Washington area due to Walters's and Lucas's shared enthusiasm for his work. Lucas alerted Walters to works of potential interest, for example the reduced version of the *Hemicycle* (Baltimore, MD, Walters A.G.) by Paul Delaroche. The largest sum spent by Lucas for Walters was for the *Effect of the Frost* (Baltimore, MD, Walters A.G.) by Théodore Rousseau, for which he paid the dealer Albert Goupil 112,000 francs in 1882.

For the New York art dealer Samuel P. Avery, Lucas bought even more extensively from representatives of the same artistic schools. Between the late 1860s and 1885 Lucas shipped over 2,500,000 francs' worth of art to New York on a sale or return basis. Lucas was largely responsible for assembling Avery's collection (New York, Pub. Lib.) of 19,000 graphic works, mostly 19th-century French. Lucas acquired for himself a group of about 15,000 prints, including works by Delacroix, Manet, Whistler and Mary Cassatt. He bequeathed these and over 400 19th-century French works in various media to the Maryland Institute, College of Art in Baltimore (now in Baltimore, MD, Mus. A.). Through Avery, Lucas served a number of American patrons, including John Taylor Johnston (1820–93), Cyrus J. Lawrence, William Henry Vanderbilt and Henry Field (1841–90). He also received commissions from institutions and oversaw the casting in 1888 and shipping in 1893 of Rodin's bust of *St John the Baptist* to the Metropolitan Museum of Art, New York. In the last decade of his life Lucas continued to work for select American collectors, notably Henry Walters, for whom he negotiated purchases of paintings, decorative arts, manuscripts and bookbindings. In accordance with Lucas's instructions, Walters, as his executor, arranged the transfer of his remains and his collection to Baltimore. Lucas's 51-volume diary and 45 ledgers (Baltimore, MD, Walters A.G.) provide a detailed account of his involvement in the Paris art market.

### WRITINGS
L. M. C. Randall, ed.: *The Diary of George A. Lucas: An American Art Agent in Paris, 1857–1909*, 2 vols (Princeton, 1979)

### BIBLIOGRAPHY
M. Fidell-Beaufort, H. L. Kleinfeld and J. K. Welcher, eds: *The Diaries 1871–1882 of Samuel P. Avery, Art Dealer* (New York, 1979)
W. R. Johnston: *The Nineteenth Century Paintings in the Walters Art Gallery* (Baltimore, 1982)
R. Butler: 'La Sculpture française et les Américains au XIXe siècle', *La Sculpture du XIXe siècle: Une Mémoire retrouvée* (Paris, 1986), pp. 39–50

LILIAN M. C. RANDALL

**Lucas de Montigny, Jean-Robert-Nicolas** (*b* Rouen, 9 Dec 1747; *d* Paris, 29 Jan 1810). French sculptor. He trained with Jean-Baptiste Pigalle and also from 1773 at the Académie Royale de Peinture et de Sculpture, Paris, but, despite his undoubted talents as a sculptor, he never became an academician. In 1777 he set up on his own in Paris and was soon in fashionable demand, producing portraits such as that of *Mlle d'Oligny* (terracotta, 1778; Paris, Mus. Cognacq-Jay). Portraits of actors, such as his bust of *Préville as Figaro* (patinated plaster, 1782) or the statuette of *Mme de Saint-Huberty as Dido* (plaster, 1784; both Paris, Louvre), show a responsive delicacy, but the uncompromising realism of his portraiture is seen at its best in the powerful busts of his patron Honoré Riqueti, Comte de Mirabeau, whom he sculpted in plaster in 1781 and 1790 (both in priv. cols) and in marble in 1791 (Aix-en-Provence, Mus. Arbaud). From 1781 to 1792 Lucas produced a series of plaster and terracotta statuettes of mythological subjects and historical characters, now all lost.

During the French Revolution (1789–95) Lucas de Montigny, though not an academician, was able to affirm his political sympathies by exhibiting at the Salon such works as his plaster statuette of *Voltaire* (1781; Geneva,

Mus. Voltaire) and a colossal group of the *Execution of a Vestal Virgin Found to Be with Child* (exh. Salon 1804; untraced). During the First Empire (1804–15) he received a number of official monumental commissions, of which the only works to survive are four low reliefs for the column in the Place d'Austerlitz (now Place Vendôme), Paris. His portrait busts have sometimes been confused with those of Jean-Antoine Houdon.

### BIBLIOGRAPHY
Lami
U.-R. Dessaix: 'Un Portrait de Préville en Barbier de Séville', *Interméd. Chercheurs & Curieux*, xx (1887), p. 200
H. Marcel: 'Un Oublié, le statuaire Lucas de Montigny', *Rev. A. Anc. & Mod.*, vii/36 (1900), pp. 161–8
—: 'Essai sur l'iconographie de Mirabeau', *Rev. A. Anc. & Mod.*, ix/49 (1901), pp. 269–80
—: 'L'Exposition générale d'art provençal à Marseille, sculptures', *Gaz. B.-A.*, ii/1 (1906), pp. 258–9
—: 'Sur Quelques Ouvrages peu connus de Lucas de Montigny', *Rev. A. Anc. & Mod.*, xxv/143 (1909), pp. 105–11
M. Beaulieu: 'Le Théâtre et la sculpture française au XVIIIe siècle', *Jard. A.*, xv (1956), p. 171
H. Mercier: *Jean-Robert-Nicolas Lucas de Montigny (1747–1810), sculpteur*, 2 vols (diss., Paris, Ecole Louvre, 1973)

HUGUETTE MERCIER

**Lucassen, Reinier** (*b* Amsterdam, 16 April 1939). Dutch painter and draughtsman. He studied at the Rijksnormaal-school voor Tekenleraren in Amsterdam (1957–60). From 1963 he used the works of such artists as Max Beckmann, Giorgio de Chirico, Vincent van Gogh, Piet Mondrian, James Ensor and Francis Picabia as departure points for his paintings, for example *Vincent, P.M. and Lucassen* (acrylic on canvas, 1974; Eindhoven, Stedel. Van Abbe-mus.). He combined historical connotations with the representation of interiors and people in their everyday environment. Influenced by Pop art he also depicted well-known cartoon characters. In 1966 Lucassen collaborated with Etienne Elias, Raoul de Keyser and Roger Raveel on a commission for Graaf De Kerckhove De Denterghem for paintings in the castle at Beervelde. In 1967, with Jan Dibbets and Ger van Elk he founded the Instituut vor Herscholing van Kunstenaars (Institute for the Retraining of Artists), from which manifestos and projects emerged. After 1972 Lucassen developed a partiality for the bizarre and irrational combined with elements of eroticism. Around 1977–8 another change of style occurred, in which abstract and fantastic shapes were associated with objects from reality, for example the *Spirit of Iniet* (1985; Eindhoven, Stedel. Van Abbemus.). Apart from paintings Lucassen also produced collages and assemblages.

### BIBLIOGRAPHY
R. H. Fuchs: *Dutch Painting* (London, 1978)
A. Tilroe, H. Sizoo and N. Lasseel: *Lucassen: Schilderijen, tekeningen, assemblages, 1960–1986* [Lucassen: paintings, drawings, assemblages, 1960–1986] (Amsterdam, 1986)

JOHN STEEN

**Lucas (Huyghz.) van Leyden** (*b* Leiden, *c.* 1494; *d* Leiden, 1533). North Netherlandish printmaker, draughtsman and painter, son of HUGO JACOBSZ. He was the first Dutch artist to establish an international reputation for himself as an engraver while he was still alive. His prolific output as a printmaker—*c.* 200 prints—shows the whole of his development; dated engravings survive from practically every year between 1508 and 1530. His early prints hark back to those of his slightly older German contemporary, Albrecht Dürer; later on, his work was clearly meant to compete with that of Dürer, while from 1525 onwards it was influenced mainly by examples from the Italian Renaissance, which reached Lucas through the prints by Marcantonio Raimondi and the work of Jan Gossart, the first to bring this new style to the north. Less international in outlook than his graphic work—but at least as important for the development of north Netherlandish art—is the rather small group of paintings (*c.* 15) attributable to the artist. Lucas was also an exceptionally talented draughtsman, as can be seen in the underdrawings that have been revealed in his paintings. Despite the small number of independent drawings that have been preserved (*c.* 30), they give a good impression of the quality and range of his work in this field.

1. Life and career. 2. Work. 3. Working methods and technique. 4. Critical reception and posthumous reputation.

1. LIFE AND CAREER. The main source of biographical information about Lucas van Leyden is still van Mander's extensive account of 1604, which has been supplemented to some extent by details from archival records. According to van Mander, Lucas was born in late May or early June 1494, but this has long been questioned, especially since his father, a painter, remarried late in 1494, which suggests that his mother died earlier that year or before. For van Mander's date to be correct, it must be assumed that Lucas's mother died either in childbirth or shortly thereafter. In any case, van Mander's description of Lucas as a prodigy cannot be far from the truth. Lucas's earliest dated engraving, *Mehmed and the Monk Sergius* (1508; B. 126; see fig. 1), shows him as an accomplished engraver who seems to have already been through several years of training. Since Leiden had no engraving tradition, Lucas may have first learnt the technique from a goldsmith or an engraver of arms, as van Mander supposed, or through stained-glass painting, which was then highly popular in Leiden. Technically and artistically, however, the prime example for Lucas must have been the engravings of Dürer. Those engravings by Lucas that, although undated, stylistically precede the print of *Mehmed* show how gradually he learnt to make use of the technical possibilities of engraving.

According to van Mander, Lucas was initially a pupil of his father and afterwards of the painter Cornelis Engebrechtsz. The parallels between the paintings of the father and the work of the son are primarily restricted to the figure types and the way in which landscape is structured. Engebrechtsz.'s influence is more obvious and can be seen in Lucas's prints and early paintings from 1509 onwards. It does seem likely that once Lucas had mastered the art of engraving, he took up painting, possibly as a pupil of Engebrechtsz. The latter's influence on the early paintings by Lucas is mainly a matter of technique; the choice of subjects and the general approach are highly original and closely linked with Lucas's prints.

Quite a lot is known about Lucas van Leyden's social position; from 1500 onwards his name occurs regularly in the Leiden records. As late as between 1526 and 1528 he married Lysbeth van Boshuysen, daughter of a magistrate. The marriage remained childless, although Lucas did have

1. Lucas van Leyden: *Mehmed and the Monk Sergius*, engraving, 287×216 mm, 1508 (London, British Museum)

an illegitimate daughter from a previous affair; she married in 1532, and her two sons, also painters, may have been the source of van Mander's biography of Lucas. As the husband of a magistrate's daughter and a member successively of two militia companies, Lucas must have been among the prosperous citizens of Leiden. During a visit to Antwerp he met Dürer, who recorded their encounter in his journal of his tour of the Netherlands; Dürer drew Lucas's portrait on the occasion (Lille, Mus. B.-A.), and the two artists exchanged prints.

According to van Mander, when Lucas was approximately 33 years old, he made a tour of the provinces of Zeeland, Flanders and Brabant, travelling in the company of Jan Gossart from Middelburg. He is said to have entertained his colleagues royally on this occasion. Van Mander also claimed that Lucas fell ill after this journey and remained confined to his bed thereafter, either as a result of an attempt to poison him, as van Mander suspected, or of lung disease. It seems unlikely that Lucas was suffering from any illness before 1531, for between 1526 and 1531 he produced several large, important paintings (*see* §2(ii) below). From 1528 to 1530 he was also very active as an engraver. After 1530, however, even his production of prints seems to have been curtailed. The unfinished print with *Pallas Athena* (B. 139), on which van Mander said he was working on his deathbed, must actually have been made at this time. Burial records of the Pieterskerk in Leiden have confirmed van Mander's statement that Lucas died in 1533.

## 2. WORK.

(i) Prints. (ii) Paintings. (iii) Drawings.

*(i) Prints.* Prints, mostly engravings, form the nucleus of Lucas van Leyden's oeuvre: within a period of less than 30 years he made at least 168 engravings, nearly always signed with the initial L and often dated, at least from 1508 onwards. In 1520 he experimented with the recently introduced technique of etching, producing some six works. There are also 30 separate woodcuts and almost 100 book illustrations, which are thought, on stylistic grounds, to have been designed by Lucas. The woodcuts bear neither the initial L nor a date. It remains uncertain whether they were cut by a specialized craftsman after designs by Lucas or whether he actually cut some of them himself.

Unlike Dürer's prints, the early graphic works by Lucas van Leyden do not conform to current tradition; technically as well as iconographically they are distinct. Surprisingly difficult to interpret is the *Young Boy with a Trumpet* (*c.* 1507; B. 152), which has all the characteristics of an allegorical satyr scene, except that the main figure has neither horns nor hooves. Conventional biblical themes such as the *Rest on the Flight into Egypt* (B. 38; unique impression, Vienna, Albertina) and *David and Abigail* (both *c.* 1507; B. 24) are also presented in an unusual manner. Lucas chose strange and seldomly depicted dramatic moments from the biblical stories, emphasizing their narrative character. This also applies to the earliest dated work, *Mehmed and the Monk Sergius* (see fig. 1), depicting a scene taken from one of the 14th-century travel works of Jean de Mandeville. The story relates how the prophet Mehmed met the Christian hermit Sergius on one of his journeys and subsequently became so fascinated by his sermons that, despite his servants' annoyance, he stayed out late at night to listen to the monk preach. One night, after a lot of wine, Mehmed fell asleep while listening, and his servants seized the opportunity to murder Sergius. When he woke, the servants showed him his blood-stained sword and persuaded him that he had slain the hermit while drunk. Very subtly, Lucas depicted the moment of Mehmed's deception. Psychologically, as well as spatially, the event is presented in a convincing way.

The prints of the following years show even greater variety of subjects; at the same time the choices tend to be more conventional. The *Round Passion* series (1509; B. 57–65), which reveals the influence of Engebrechtsz. in the elongated slim figures, follows current tradition. Apart from the smaller, rather intimate prints made between 1509 and 1519, there are some five engravings with a large folio format representing biblical scenes with numerous

2. Lucas van Leyden: *Lot and his Daughters*, engraving, 190×244 mm, 1530 (Amsterdam, Rijksmuseum)

figures. The *Ecce homo* (1510; B. 71) shows one of these broad compositions on a market square; the buildings form a screen, and Christ, who is exposed to the grumbling people, is pushed into the background. The emphasis falls on the spectators and their reactions rather than on the event itself. Other outstanding examples of this are the *Return of the Prodigal Son* (c. 1510; B. 78), the *Triumph of Mordecai* (1515; B. 32), *Golgotha* (1517; B. 74) and the *Dance of Mary Magdalene* (1519; B. 122). More conventional religious series include *Christ and the Twelve Apostles* (c. 1510; B. 86–99) and the *Four Evangelists* (1518; B. 100–103), as well as separate small prints of the Virgin and saints. Lucas's profane subjects are less common and more complicated to interpret. Amorous couples, soldiers and beggars are grounded in the older tradition of German printmaking. The curious *Woman Picking Fleas from a Dog* (1511; B. 154) is presumably intended as a personification of sloth. *The Milkmaid* (1510; B. 158), long regarded as a simple scene from everyday life, contains obviously erotic allusions. The *Young Man with a Skull* (c. 1519; B. 174) seems to be a *vanitas* warning: the feathered hat symbolizes his loose way of life, while the skull refers to the pointlessness of it all.

By 1520 Dürer's stylistic influence had become stronger, and Lucas began to develop a new sober and severe style. A number of his prints, including the *Small Passion* series (1521; B. 43–56), are very close to Dürer's example. Yet there was no direct borrowing, as Lucas transformed Dürer's work into his own individual style and idiom. After 1523 Dürer's influence suddenly decreased, and the sober style of the preceding years was replaced with a livelier and more expressive formal language. One of the best examples illustrating this development is Lucas's *Virgil Suspended in a Basket* (1525; B. 136), which reveals Gossart's influence in the figures and the drapery. Lucas's absorption of elements from Gossart not only injected his engravings with a new dynamism but also introduced a new concept of the human form related to the ideals of the Renaissance.

In the prints made between 1528 and 1530 an important part is played by nudes represented according to Classical ideals of beauty. With the example of other printmakers, notably Raimondi's work after Raphael, Lucas developed his own new language of form. The series of six engravings with the *Story of Adam and Eve* (1529; B. 1–6) shows the human body in various poses. In Lucas's prints from 1530 onwards, among them the *Fall of Man* (B. 10), *Mars, Venus and Cupid* (B. 137) and *Lot and his Daughters* (B. 16; see fig. 2), the nudes are more solid and the landscape is subordinated to the now monumental figures. The unambiguous way in which these prints show female sensuality indicates that these prints were intended as a warning against the power that women can exert over men. At one time this later style of Lucas met with unfavourable criticism, as he was thought to have lost his individual character through the assimilation of Renaissance influences. However, there has since been a greater recognition of Lucas's newly found ability to depict character and emotion in these works. During this late period he also produced a number of decorative prints with Renaissance motifs.

Among Lucas van Leyden's most important woodcut designs are his two series, each of six sheets, of the *Power of Women*: the first, larger series has been dated c. 1514 and the second c. 1517. They represent examples of historical moments, mostly from the Bible, at which men were ridiculed, betrayed or ruined by women, such as the *Fall of Man* (Hollstein, nos 1 and 2), *Samson and Delilah* (Hollstein, nos 5 and 6) and the *Idolatry of Solomon* (Hollstein, nos 8 and 9). Standing apart from these two series is the splendid single woodcut of *Aristotle and Phyllis* (unique impression, Paris, Bib. N.), depicting the story of the wise Aristotle, who, blinded by love, allowed the courtesan Phyllis to ride on his back.

*(ii) Paintings.* Until the late 19th century Lucas van Leyden's name was associated with hundreds of paintings of rather varied quality; by 1940 the number had been reduced to c. 35, and later some of the remaining paintings were reattributed to Lucas's contemporaries, for example the *Church Sermon* (Amsterdam, Rijksmus.), which has since been assigned to Aertgen van Leyden. Lucas's painted oeuvre is now reduced to a core of c. 15 paintings, 4 of which were described by van Mander and are still considered among his most important pictures: the *Virgin and Child with St Mary Magdalene and a Donor* (1522; Munich, Alte Pin.), the triptych with the *Last Judgement* (1526–7; Leiden, Stedel. Mus. Lakenhal; see fig. 4 below), the triptych with the *Worship of the Golden Calf* (c. 1530; Amsterdam, Rijksmus.) and the *Healing of the Blind Man of Jericho* (1531; St Petersburg, Hermitage). These paintings form the basis for further attributions, but since all four are middle or late works, it is necessary to depend largely on the prints for the stylistic analysis of the early paintings.

The paintings of the earliest period, from between c. 1508 and 1518, are all small in format; these include the *Chess-players* (c. 1508; Berlin, Gemäldegal.; see fig. 3), *Potiphar's Wife Showing Joseph's Robe to her Husband* (c. 1512; Rotterdam, Mus. Boymans–van Beuningen) and the *Card-players* (c. 1517; Wilton House, Wilts). There is a moralizing element to all of these scenes, in which women are seen playing a central role. The stress lies on the gestures, facial expression and pose of what are usually half-length figures. Within the series there is a stylistic development towards a stronger sense of three-dimensional space, a greater plasticity in the modelling of figures and more elegance in the movements and clothing. The colours are lively and quite bright in places, and the paint is applied to the panel thickly, yet in a somewhat linear (draughtsmanlike) manner.

The central piece of the middle period is Lucas's first dated painting, the panel of the *Virgin and Child with St Mary Magdalene and a Donor* (1522), which originally formed a diptych. Early in the 17th century the two halves were joined and the donor changed into the figure of St Joseph; later, the *Annunciation* (Munich, Alte Pin.), which decorated the outside of the diptych, was sawn off. Also dating from the early 1520s are several other depictions of the *Virgin and Child* (e.g. Berlin, Gemäldegal.; Oslo, N.G.) and a few portraits (e.g. London, N.G.; Brunswick, Herzog Anton Ulrich-Mus.).

Lucas's most monumental work is the triptych with the *Last Judgement* (see fig. 4), which was commissioned in

3. Lucas van Leyden: *Chess-players*, oil on panel, 270×350 mm, *c.* 1508 (Berlin, Gemäldegalerie)

1526–7 for the Pieterskerk as a memorial for the lumber merchant Claes Dircksz. van Swieten. Iconographically, the representation of the Last Judgement, which runs over all three panels, is traditional. The innovative aspect of the painting is its style: the lucid composition, structured according to various levels of perspective, the idealized nudes and the unexpectedly bright and strong colour. Impressively monumental, but darker in colour, are the outer sides of the wings, in which *St Peter* and *St Paul* are depicted, as if engaged in conversation, against a landscape with a rough sea in the distance. Of the few north Netherlandish altarpieces to have survived the iconoclastic outbreak of 1566, this is undoubtedly the most important.

On a smaller scale, but no less complicated in structure, are the other, late pictures of biblical events, usually showing a wealth of figures set against a landscape. Lucas's representation of his subjects and his strong feeling for the narrative demonstrate his thorough knowledge of the Bible, which at that time had just been made more accessible to the public in a Dutch translation. *Moses Striking Water from the Rock* (1527; Boston, MA, Mus. F.A.) is the earliest painting in this later group, and within Lucas's oeuvre it is the only known example of a painting in tempera on canvas. As is the case in the triptych with the *Worship of the Golden Calf* (*c.* 1530), the image is about the Law of Moses and how he (dis)obeyed God. The *Healing of the Blind Man of Jericho* (former date of 1531 now removed) stresses the contrast between the scribes who stubbornly adhere to the old faith and those open to Christ's message. In the 18th century the triptych was made into one panel and later transferred on to canvas; at the same time the outer wings with *Shield-bearers* (St Petersburg, Hermitage) were sawn off and displayed separately. These three late monumental paintings, of which the *Worship of the Golden Calf* is the best preserved, show a great variety of richly coloured and freely painted figures.

*(iii) Drawings.* Van Leyden's drawings are rare: there is a group of six portraits, all in an oblong format (all 1521; Leiden, Stedel., Mus. Lakenhal; Paris, Louvre; Stockholm, Nmus.; Weimar, Schlossmus.), which were probably made under the influence of Dürer. Besides black chalk, which was used only in the portraits, Lucas worked in silverpoint, pen and ink or fine brush and wash, sometimes combined with chalk. Some of the drawings were intended as preparatory studies for prints, in one case (the *Virgin and Child*; London, BM) even a painting (Oslo, N.G.), and a

few of the more elaborate drawings, for instance *Jael Killing Sisera* (*c.* 1520; Rotterdam, Mus. Boymans–van Beuningen), were presumably designs for stained-glass windows.

### 3. WORKING METHODS AND TECHNIQUE.

*(i) Prints.* Lucas seems to have mastered the language of form and the technique of engraving step by step, at first producing only small works, which still show numerous shortcomings in the technical application of the medium, anatomy and the use of space. Nevertheless, the early prints have an expressive force and directness that are lost when technical perfection is achieved in the later work. In such works as *Mehmed and the Monk Sergius*, he used extremely fine lines to produce subtly modelled forms, alternating shadows with highlights, and at the same time achieving a very convincing suggestion of depth. The prints made in the following years show greater technical variety: in some prints the manner of engraving is very fine and detailed, while in others the lines are very bold. In the best impressions of the early prints, the shadows are pitch black, whereas the best impressions of the later engravings are occasionally printed in delicate grey tones.

*(ii) Paintings.* The majority of Lucas's paintings have been examined by means of infrared reflectography, and in several cases this has revealed surprisingly elaborate underdrawings. In the early works these are executed in black paint with a fine brush and are much more elaborate than anything found beneath the works of his contemporaries. Lucas seems to have included more details than were strictly necessary for a painting, perhaps the result of his activity as a printmaker and draughtsman. In a later work such as the *Virgin and Child with St Mary Magdalene and a Donor*, the underdrawing in the interior panels, which were painted first, is still carried out with a fine brush and shows a graceful precision, but the preparation for the less delicately painted *Annunciation* on the outer wings consists of no more than a few outlines in chalk. A similar contrast can be seen in the underdrawings on the inner and outer panels of the triptych with the *Last Judgement*: on the outer wings the figures of *St Peter* and *St Paul* are painted over sketchy outlines in black chalk, while the underdrawing on the inner panels consists of an exceptionally beautiful pen-and-ink wash drawing in which the nude figures are carefully modelled. A wash underdrawing such as this has so far proved exceptional in early Dutch painting; in fact, in his later work Lucas himself used only the more schematic drawings in chalk.

*(iii) Workshop.* Although Lucas had a profound influence on his contemporaries and his work was copied a great deal, his manner of painting was never directly imitated. It seems questionable, therefore, whether Lucas ever painted with the help of assistants; certainly, within the oeuvre there is no evidence that he did. Equally, there are no records to suggest that Lucas employed apprentices in his print workshop.

4. Lucas van Leyden: *Last Judgement*, oil on panel, 3.01×4.35 m, 1526–7 (Leiden, Stedelijk Museum De Lakenhal)

4. CRITICAL RECEPTION AND POSTHUMOUS REPU-TATION. Lucas was successful and well-regarded during his lifetime; his prints sold well, not just in the Netherlands, but also in Germany, and contemporary artists recognized his genius (Dürer recorded his purchase of Lucas's complete graphic oeuvre in 1521). The copperplates passed to his heirs, who reissued his prints; they were later in the possession of Martini Petri (1500–c. 1565) in Antwerp, who reworked them. Throughout the 16th century copies of Lucas's most popular prints continued to appear, executed by such artists as Jan Muller and Hendrick Hondius the elder. Lucas's work had considerable influence, most notably on Hendrick Goltzius, Jacques de Gheyn II and Rembrandt, who owned a number of his prints, but also in Italy, where Andrea del Sarto and Pontormo knew his work. By 1550 Vasari had included a lengthy biography of Lucas in his *Vite*, praising the artist for his ability to handle perspective, and in 1604 van Mander's detailed biography of him appeared.

Although Lucas van Leyden has always been appreciated as a great artist, his graphic work has all too frequently been assessed in the context of that of Dürer, and it was not until the late 20th century that attempts were being made to formulate a more satisfactory framework in which to study his oeuvre.

BIBLIOGRAPHY

Hollstein: *Dut. & Flem.*
G. Vasari: *Vite* (1550, rev. 2/1568); ed. G. Milanesi (1878–85), v, pp. 406–11
K. van Mander: *Schilder-boeck* ([1603]–1604), fols 211–15
F. Dülberg: 'Die Persönlichkeit des Lucas van Leyden', *Oud-Holland*, xiv (1899), pp. 65–83 (66–9)
N. Beets: *Lucas de Leyde* (Brussels and Paris, 1913)
M. J. Friedländer: *Lucas van Leyden* (Leipzig, 1924); ed. F. Winkler (Berlin, 1963)
——: *Die altniederländische Malerei* (Berlin, 1924–37), x (1934), pp. 78–113, 134, 137; Eng. trans. as *Early Netherlandish Painting* (1967–76), x (1973), pp. 46–64, 81–4, 94–102; xiv, p. 112
G. J. Hoogewerff: *De noord-Nederlandsche schilderkunst*, iii (The Hague, 1939), pp. 207–320
*Middeleeuwse kunst der noordelijke Nederlanden* [Medieval art of the northern Netherlands] (exh. cat., ed. R. Luttervelt; Amsterdam, Rijksmus., 1958), pp. 106–14, 150–56
R. de Vos: *Lucas van Leyden* (Bentvelt and Maarssen, 1978)
*Lucas van Leyden: Grafiek* (exh. cat. by J. P. Filedt Kok, Amsterdam, Rijksmus., 1978)
J. P. Filedt Kok and others: *Ned. Ksthist. Jb.*, xixx (1979) [issue devoted to Lucas van Leyden]
E. S. Jacobowitz and S. L. Stepanek: 'Lucas van Leyden', *Hans Baldung Grien, Hans Springinklee, Lucas van Leyden*, xii [7–3] of *The Illustrated Bartsch*, ed. W. Strauss (New York, 1981), pp. 129–334 [B.]
*The Prints of Lucas van Leyden and his Contemporaries* (exh. cat. by E. S. Jacobowitz and S. L. Stepanek, Washington, DC, N.G.A.; Boston, MA, Mus. F.A.; 1983)
*Kunst voor de beeldenstorm* [Art before the iconoclasm], 2 vols (exh. cat., ed. J. P. Filedt Kok; Amsterdam, Rijksmus., 1986), i, pp. 15–22; ii, pp. 140–53
E. Lawton Smith: *The Paintings of Lucas van Leyden: A New Appraisal, with Catalogue Raisonné* (New York and London, 1992)

J. P. FILEDT KOK

**Lucas Velázquez** [Lucas; Lucas (y) Padilla], **Eugenio**(*b* Madrid, 17 Jan 1817; *d* Madrid, 11 Sept 1870). Spanish painter. He was long known as Lucas Padilla, but research has shown that his real surname was Lucas Velázquez. He came late to painting, in 1844 still stating his profession as that of cabinetmaker. It is possible that he studied at the Academia de San Fernando in Madrid, but he may have been largely self-taught. His early work included portraits (e.g. *Jenaro Peréz Villaamil*, 1849; Madrid, Mus. Romántico), scenes of the Spanish Inquisition and subjects from contemporary life (e.g. *Scene with Bandits*, 1855; Madrid, Mus. Romántico). By the mid-1850s he was well established: in 1853 he was appointed Pintor de Cámara Honorario to Queen Isabella II, and he was made a Knight of the Order of Carlos III as a reward for his idealized portrait of *Pedro de Valdivia*, which the Spanish government gave as a present to the cathedral of Santiago de Chile (*in situ*). Lucas Velázquez showed his work successfully at the Exposition Universelle in Paris in 1855, and in the same year he was one of three connoisseurs asked to value Francisco de Goya's *Pinturas Negras* (1820–23; Madrid, Prado), then still in the Quinta del Sordo, Goya's country house near Madrid.

Lucas Velázquez has been considered as merely an imitator of the work of Goya; yet, although Goya's influence is obvious, very few of nearly 600 paintings by Lucas Velázquez drew their inspiration from the drawings or engravings of Goya. The confusion was probably compounded by the mistaken acceptance of a dozen or so paintings by Lucas Velázquez as works by Goya—for example *The Bullfight* (*c.* 1860; Washington, DC, N.G.A.), its companion *Bullfight* (Winterthur, Samml. Oskar Reinhart) and *City on a Rock* (1860s; New York, Met.; see fig.)—which show Goya-like characteristics only in the colour and the passion and vigour of the brushwork. The true measure of Lucas Velázquez is probably as a precursor of Impressionism. Paintings dated as early as 1855 (*Packet Boats in the Cove* and *Divided Bullring*; both Madrid, priv. col., see Arnaiz, nos 219 and 147) show clear impressionistic characteristics, possibly influenced by Delacroix, whom the artist may have met in Paris in 1855. Lucas Velázquez himself in turn exercised a certain influence on Manet, whom he apparently knew, and for whom he acted perhaps as a 'translator' of Goya. Lucas Velázquez was the most important Spanish painter to work in the Goya tradition in the period following Goya's death. As such, he is one of the most interesting figures of Spanish and European Romanticism.

Two of Lucas Velázquez's sons were also painters: Julián Lucas Villamil (*b* 1865) and Eugenio Lucas Villamil (*b* Madrid, 1858; *d* Madrid, 1918). The latter is noted as a painter of pictures with an 18th-century ambience and as an imitator of his father, and difficulties of attribution created by his imitations have made the oeuvre of Lucas Velázquez difficult to assess.

BIBLIOGRAPHY

R. Balsa de la Vega: *Lucas* (Madrid, 1911)
E. Pardo Canalis: 'El mundo ignorado de Eugenio Lucas', *Goya*, 116 (1973), pp. 70–75
J. M. Arnaiz: *Eugenio Lucas: Su vida y su obra* (Madrid, 1981)

JOSÉ MANUEL ARNAIZ

**Lucca** [anc. Luca]. Italian city in Tuscany, capital of the province of Lucca. Situated about 80 km west of Florence in the Arno Valley, the walled city (population *c.* 90,000), which is known for its silk trade, retains much of its medieval urban character and rich heritage of architecture.

Eugenio Lucas Velázquez: *City on a Rock*, oil on canvas, 0.84×1.04 m, 1860s (New York, Metropolitan Museum of Art); previously attributed to Francisco de Goya

1. History and urban development. 2. Centre of silk production. 3. Cathedral.

1. HISTORY AND URBAN DEVELOPMENT. The first people to settle in the curve of the River Serchio, where Lucca now stands, were apparently Ligurian—the city's name is thought to derive from the Celtic-Ligurian root *luk* ('marshy place'). Some scholars believe the area was colonized by the Etruscans from the 7th century BC. Roman Luca was founded as a Latin colony in 180 BC and became a *municipium* in 89 BC. The grid plan of the Roman nucleus (see fig. 1), centred on the *cardo* and *decumanus* that crossed at the forum (near the present Piazza S Michele), is still discernible in the south-western part of the city. Heavy walls enclosed the city on four sides, wider on the north to include the Roman theatre (near S Agostino). The amphitheatre, also to the north, remained outside the walls; its elliptical form is preserved in the Piazza dell'Anfiteatro. Before AD 570 Lucca was conquered by the Lombards, under whom it became the seat of the most powerful of the three duchies established in Tuscany. Its importance grew when the Via Francigena (Via Romea) was routed through its territory, as this road was the main link between Rome and the transalpine lands throughout the Middle Ages. Lucca later became the capital of the marquisate of Tuscany. During the 11th-century civil wars known as the Investiture Contest it sided with the Holy Roman Emperor, subsequently gaining privileges that allowed the expansion of its silk industry and the operation of its banks throughout Europe. The city enjoyed a sustained period of prosperity in the 12th and 13th centuries and in 1162 was formally recognized as a free *comune*.

The urban fabric of medieval Lucca, most of which survives, includes many fine Romanesque churches facing piazzas, with bichrome or polychrome marble façades and rich sculptural decoration in the so-called Pisan–Luccan style. The most important churches include the cathedral (begun 1060; *see* §3 and fig. 2 below); S Michele in Foro (begun *c.* 1143), Piazza S Michele, the upper part of its tall 13th-century façade featuring four tiers of ornamented arcading; S Pietro Somaldi (begun *c.* 1200), with a striped façade and double tier of arcading in the gable; S Frediano (1112–47), which has a large mosaic on its façade; and S Maria Forisportam (early 13th century), which was built outside the walls. In secular architecture brick construction prevailed, and the commonest type of dwelling was the

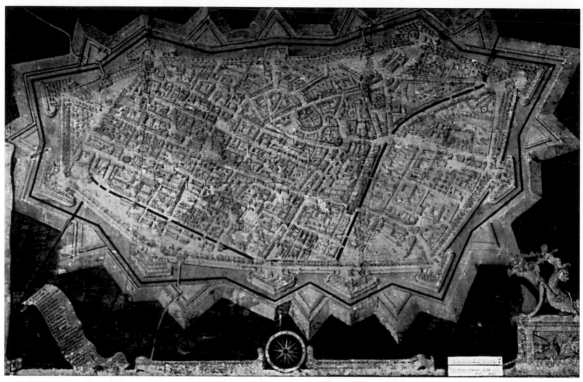

1. Lucca, perspective view showing a grid of the Roman and medieval city (left) and the new city walls (1562–1650), 1660 (Lucca, Archivio di Stato)

tower house, with a single room on each of several floors. A wider house type, with broad arches on the ground floor and a series of multi-light windows above, subsequently developed and was dominant until the late 15th century. About 1200–60 a wider circuit of walls was built, with high stone curtains punctuated by semicircular towers and four gates, two of which survive: S Gervasio and S Maria dei Borghi. The walls enclosed the north-eastern suburbs of S Gervasio, S Pietro Somaldi and S Frediano, and the western suburbs of S Donato and Pelleria. On the south side they followed the line of the old Roman walls. In the late 14th century another section of wall was added, which permitted a further expansion of the city to the east.

In the course of the 14th century Lucca was torn by internal struggles and wars with its neighbours. It was ruled by several powerful lords, notably Castruccio Castracani degli Antelminelli from 1316 to 1328. The city was later held by Pisa until 1369, when it became a republic, retaining its independence for 400 years except for a period (1400–30) of rule by Paolo Guinigi. In 1494 the Palazzo del Podestà (now Palazzo Pretorio; enlarged 1588), Piazza S Michele, was begun. During the 16th century several important urban projects were carried out. The piazzas in the religious centre around the cathedral (Piazza Antelminelli, Piazza del Duomo and Piazza S Giovanni) were regularized; and a political and business centre was established between Piazza S Michele, where the notaries' shops were concentrated, and the Palazzo Pubblico to the south, originally the 14th-century seat of the lords of Lucca. This building (later Palazzo degli Anziani; now Palazzo della Provincia) was completely rebuilt (1577–81; c. 1730) to a monumental design by Bartolomeo Ammanati.

The most important public project of this period, however, was the construction of a new circuit of city walls (see fig. 1), which still survive. Sporadic efforts had been made in the late 15th century to modernize the old walls, but the subsequent expansionist policies of Florence made it imperative to strengthen Lucca's defences. Advice and plans were sought from the most eminent fortifications experts, but no comprehensive plan was ever adopted and the construction work (1544–1650) was directed by a series of engineers, including Baldassare Lanci, FRANCESCO PACIOTTO and Muzio Oddi. The new brick walls were fortified by orillion bastions with three gates, an internal stepped rampart (now planted with trees) and a moat beyond. On the north and south sides the new walls followed the medieval line; on the west they extended out to a point, and on the east they took in a large area of gardens and vegetable plots; they never had to sustain an enemy assault, however. In the 16th and 17th centuries several palaces inspired by Florentine and Emilian architecture were built in Lucca, being harmoniously inserted into the city's medieval fabric; notable examples include the 17th-century Palazzo Mazzarosa and Palazzo Mansi. Such palaces were generally built around an inner court, with rusticated portals and quoins and grilled windows. Many fine villas were also built in the environs of the city in the 16th–19th centuries.

French troops entered Lucca unresisted in 1799, and Napoleon raised the city to a principality (1805) under his sister Elisa Bonaparte, Duchess of Lucca, and her husband Felice Baciocchi. After the Bourbon restoration, Lucca subsequently became the capital of a small duchy ruled by a local branch of the Bourbon family; it then became part of the Grand Duchy of Tuscany (1847) and finally part of the Kingdom of Italy (1860). The Baciocchi and Bourbon families sought to transform the city into a modern capital, and several public works were carried out, particularly under LORENZO NOTTOLINI, Court Architect and engineer to the Duchy of Lucca from 1818. In the first half of the 19th century two important new piazzas were constructed: the large Piazza Napoleone in front of the Palazzo Ducale and the adjoining Piazza del Giglio, opposite the Teatro del Giglio. Nottolini sensitively incorporated the ruins of the Roman amphitheatre into a new piazza, and a beautiful walk along the ramparts was created. The first attempts were also made to integrate the city into a wider territorial context; a new gate, Porta Elisa (1810), was opened facing east towards Florence, and the railway was constructed (1846) on the south side of the city. Lucca's marginal role in the war of 1847, together with an economic crisis and modest industrial development, thereafter resulted in a situation of stasis. Plans for the expansion of residential development outside the ring road, particularly near the railway, were prepared in 1887 but long delayed, as were later plans (1913, 1956). After World War II the walled city of Lucca was completely surrounded by suburbs, but its medieval fabric remained substantially intact. The city's most important art collections are held by the Museo e Pinacoteca Nazionale, housed in the Palazzo Mansi; the Museo Nazionale di Villa Guinigi, housed in the Villa Guinigi (1418) in the eastern part of the city; and the gallery in the Palazzo della Prefettura (Palazzo della Provincia). In 1980, a permanent exhibition of the costume and silks of Lucca from the 18th century to the 20th century was established in the Palazzo Controni-Pfanner.

BIBLIOGRAPHY

G. Matraia: *Lucca nel milleduecento* (Lucca, 1843); ed. I. Belli Barsali (Lucca, 1983)
J. Ross and N. Erichsen: *The Story of Lucca* (London, 1912)
A. Mancini: *Storia di Lucca* (Florence, 1950)
L. Nardi and L. Molteni: *Le case torri lucchesi* (Lucca, 1959)
P. Pierotti: *Lucca: Edilizia e urbanistica medievali* (Milan, 1965)
M. Fulvio: *Lucca: Le sue corti, le sue strade, le sue piazze* (Empoli, 1968)
G. Bedini and G. Fanelli: *Lucca: Spazio e tempo dall'ottocento a oggi* (Lucca, 1971)
P. Mencacci and M. Zecchini: *Lucca preistorica* (Lucca, 1976)
*I palazzi dei mercanti nella libera Lucca del '500: Immagine di una città-stato al tempo dei Medici* (exh. cat., ed. I. Belli Barsali; Lucca, Pal. Prefettura, 1980)
P. Mencacci and M. Zecchini: *Lucca romana* (Lucca, 1981)
R. Martinelli and G. Puccinelli: *Lucca: Le mura del cinquecento (vicende costruttive dal 1500 al 1650)* (Lucca, 1983)
R. Manselli: *La repubblica di Lucca* (Turin, 1986)
M. Paoli: *Arte e committenza privata a Lucca nel trecento e nel quattrocento* (Lucca, 1986), pp. 17–54
I. Belli Barsali: *Lucca: Guida alla città* (Lucca, 1988)

DONATA BATTILOTTI

2. CENTRE OF SILK PRODUCTION. The exact origins of the silk industry in Lucca are unknown, but documents confirm that it was firmly established by the 12th century. Lucca had by then all the prerequisites necessary to develop a silk-weaving industry, including raw materials, skilled artisans, capital and a well-developed commercial organization. Treaties with Genoa in 1153 and 1166 allowed Lucchese merchants to take goods including silks freely through Genoa and admitted her to full participation in maritime commerce so that imports of raw silk, dyestuffs and metal threads could be made from the Levant. Merchant-entrepreneurs, whose companies were recorded in the 14th century *Libro dei mercanti*, controlled both the manufacture and sale of silks and put out the work to reelers, throwsters, dyers and weavers in small workshops. Until the mid-13th century silk was sold at fairs in Europe, but the establishment of permanent agents in London, Paris and other cities allowed exotic patterned silks and velvets to be sold directly to the chief consumers, the courts, the nobility and the Church. Royal wardrobe accounts and church inventories, including the papal inventories of 1295 and 1361 and that of St Paul's Cathedral in London of 1295, list numbers of Lucchese silks, including samite, sendal, purple and camaca. The 1376 regulations dictated standards for the production of such silks and velvets, and examples in collections have the exact technical requirements prescribed. The silk industry in Lucca declined during the late 14th century, although high-quality silks continued to be sold to the courts of France and Burgundy in the 15th century.

BIBLIOGRAPHY

F. Edler de Roover: 'Lucchese Silks', *Ciba Z.*, lxxx (1950), pp. 2901–30
L. Monnas: 'Developments in Figured Velvet Weaving in Italy during the 14th Century', *Bull. Liaison Cent. Int. Etud. Textiles Anc.*, lxiii–lxiv (1986), pp. 63–100
D. King and M. King: 'Silk Weavers of Lucca in 1376', *Opera textilia variorum temporum*, ed. I. Estham and M. Nockert (Stockholm, 1988), pp. 67–77

LINDA WOOLLEY

3. CATHEDRAL. Dedicated to S Martino, Lucca Cathedral, which was built on the site of an Early Christian building, was begun in 1060 by Archbishop Anselmo da Baggio (later Pope Alexander II, *reg* 1061–73) and consecrated in 1070. The decoration on the north front, which features blind arches outlined by curved lintels decorated with delicate acanthus leaves, probably dates from this period. The main portico (see fig. 2), with three majestic semicircular arches, is derived from imperial Roman architecture and has been variously assigned to the early or mid-12th century; it is richly decorated with plant motifs and figural scenes carved on colonnettes, capitals and arches. This decoration, in its stylistic affinity with the work of both Wiligelmo and the masters of the abbey church of S Leonardo di Lama Volera (Siponto) and other Apulian monuments, represents one of the most important examples of 'pilgrim way culture' in 12th-century Italy. The bold arcaded façade above the portico was begun at the end of the 12th century by GUIDETTO, reaching the height of the first gallery by 1204 but ultimately left incomplete. Its three *loggetta* storeys are decorated with carvings and intarsia work, giving a lively polychrome effect with the use of black-and-white marble.

The decoration of the façade under the portico was begun in 1233 by a large team of Lombard masters, among whom are documented Lombardo di Guido, who supervised the work over a long period, GUIDO DA COMO and his half-brother Guidobono (*fl* 1246–58). The decorative

2. Lucca, cathedral of S Martino (begun 1060), façade, 12th and 13th centuries

scheme consists of a series of relief panels. Four panels depicting scenes from the *Life of St Martin* and symbolic representations of the months of the year are set between the three portals. The main portal displays *Christ in Glory* in the tympanum and the *Virgin with the Apostles* on the lintel; the right-hand portal features scenes from the *Life of St Regulus*. Guidetto's hand is more certainly detectable in two small panels with symbols of the *Evangelists*. The ensemble is one of the most notable examples of Lombard work in Tuscany; especially outstanding are the scenes from the *Life of St Martin*, which exhibit great coherence of form and a geometrical rigour that greatly influenced later masters from Arnolfo di Cambio onwards. Around 1258–60 Nicola Pisano (*see* PISANO (i), (1)) decorated the left-hand façade portal under the portico with reliefs of the *Nativity* and *Deposition*, thus insinuating himself into a context where the Lombard masters may still have been at work. His sculpture was executed in a radically new style that marked a sharp break with previous Luccan tradition and was the basis of further decoration carried out at the cathedral in subsequent centuries.

The interior of the cathedral was rebuilt in Gothic style in the 14th–15th centuries and has an aisled nave and transepts. It contains several works by Civitali, including an octagonal marble Tempietto (1480s) in the left aisle housing the Volto Santo, a wooden Crucifix (probably 11th century); the pulpit; and the tomb of *Pietro da Noceto* (1472; for illustration *see* CIVITALI, MATTEO). Other important works include the tomb of *Ilaria del Carretto* (1405–7/8; *see* JACOPO DELLA QUERCIA, fig. 2).

BIBLIOGRAPHY

W. Biehl: *Toskanische Plastik des frühen und hohen Mittelalters* (Leipzig, 1926)

M. Salmi: *Scultura romanica in Toscana* (Florence, 1928)

P. Guidi: 'Di alcuni maestri lombardi a Lucca nel secolo XIII', *Archv Stor. It.*, vii/12 (1929), pp. 207–31

C. Baracchini and A. Caleca: *Il Duomo di Lucca* (Lucca, 1973)

G. Kopp: *Die Skulpturen der Fassade von San Martino in Lucca* (Worms, 1981)

G. Dalli Regoli: *Dai maestri senza nome all'impresa dei Guidi* (Lucca, 1986)

ANTONIA CALECA

**Lucchese, il.** *See* FRANCHI, ANTONIO and RICCHI, PIETRO.

**Luce, Clarence Sumner** (*b* Newport, RI, 10 June 1852; *d* Staten Island, NY, 1924). American architect. He was born into an established Massachusetts family. He was in practice in Boston by the late 1870s, and by 1885 he had moved to New York. He specialized in residential buildings, although he also designed other building types, for example the Holyoke Opera House (1878–9), MA. His early work chiefly comprised Queen Anne Revival and Shingle-style houses on the East Coast, such as the Lyman Josephs House (1882–3) in Middletown, RI, but he soon graduated from timber resort and suburban houses to urban row (terraced) houses, such as the King Model Houses (1891), Striver's Row, Harlem, New York. These were sponsored by a builder, David H. King jr, who commissioned four architects to build them: Luce, Bruce Price, James Brown Lord (1859–1902) and McKim, Mead & White. Having forged a link with King, Luce went on to design for him the Renaissance Hotel (1891; destr.) on Fifth Avenue. He later built other hotels in New York, such as the Hotel Somerset (1901) on W. 47th Street, and on the East Coast, as well as apartment blocks around Fort Washington Avenue in upper Manhattan. Luce also designed exhibition buildings, including the Massachusetts pavilion for the Centennial International Exposition in Philadelphia (1876) and the New York State pavilion for the Lewis and Clark Centennial and American Pacific Exposition in Portland, OR (1905).

BIBLIOGRAPHY

G. W. Sheldon: *Artistic Country Seats* (New York, 1886)

C. W. Leng and W. T. David: *Staten Island and its People*, v (New York, 1933), p. 69

V. J. Scully: *The Shingle Style and the Stick Style* (New Haven and London, 1971)

MOSETTE GLASER BRODERICK

**Luce, Gordon (Hannington)** (*b* Gloucester, 3 May 1889; *d* London, 3 May 1979). English writer and teacher. He was born into a clerical family and studied Classics and English at Emmanuel College, Cambridge. After graduating in 1912, he was posted to Government College in Rangoon, Burma. In 1920 he was appointed Lecturer in English at the newly opened University of Rangoon, where he later became Professor of Burmese and Far Eastern History. Luce arrived in Burma at a time when the country's ancient heritage was being neglected by the British colonial authorities. A gifted linguist, he saw that the key to an understanding of Burmese history lay in a study of the country's language and literature. His particular interest in the history of PAGAN was reinforced by study leaves spent at the School of Oriental and African Studies in London (1942–6; 1950–53) and the Ecole Française d'Extrême-Orient in Paris. Although he had no formal training in archaeology, he pioneered the study of

Burma's rich architectural and epigraphic heritage and inspired a generation of scholars to continue his work.

WRITINGS

with Pe Maung Tin: *Inscriptions of Burma*, 5 port. vols (Rangoon and Oxford, 1933–56)
*Old Burma, Early Pagan*, 3 vols (Locust Valley, NY, 1969) [*Artibus Asiae* suppl. 25; contains comprehensive bibliog.]
*Phases of Pre-pagan Burma, Languages and History*, 2 vols (Oxford, 1985)

BIBLIOGRAPHY

Ba Shin and others: *Essays Offered to Gordon Luce by his Colleagues and Friends* (Ascona, 1966)
H. Tinker: 'The Place of Gordon Luce in Research and Education in Burma in the Last Decades of British Rule', *J. Asiat. Soc.*, n. s. (1986), pp. 174–90
P. Strachan: *Pagan: Art and Architecture of Old Burma* (Arran, 1989)

**Luce, Maximilien** (*b* Paris, 13 March 1858; *d* Paris, 7 Feb 1941). French painter and printmaker. He was born and brought up in the working-class surroundings of Montparnasse, and an interest in the daily routines and labours of the *petit peuple* of Paris informs much of his art. After an apprenticeship with the wood-engraver Henri Théophile Hildebrand (*b* 1824), in 1876 he entered the studio of the wood-engraver Eugène Froment where he assisted in the production of engravings for various French and foreign publications such as *L'Illustration* and *The Graphic*. He also sporadically attended classes at the Académie Suisse and in the studio of Carolus-Duran. In Froment's studio he came into contact with the artists Léo Gausson and Emile-Gustave Péduzzi (Cavallo-Péduzzi;

1851–1917) and in their company began painting landscape subjects in and around the town of Lagny-sur-Marne.

At the Salon des Artistes Indépendants in 1887 Luce's *The Toilette* (Geneva, Petit Pal.) caught the attention of Camille Pissarro, the critic Félix Fénéon and Paul Signac, who purchased the painting. *The Toilette*, which depicts a man bent over a wash-basin, is typical of Luce's handling of human subjects with a deliberate but impassive eye and is one of the first paintings in which he attempted to apply separate strokes of pure colour in accordance with the divisionist technique developed by Seurat. Henceforth he exhibited annually with the Neo-Impressionists at the Indépendants, and in 1889 and 1892 by invitation at the Salon des Vingt in Brussels.

Unlike most of the Neo-Impressionists, Luce continued to favour urban subjects throughout his career, depicting the animated bustle of streets in the Quartier Latin, construction workers on the boulevards and sweeping views of the rooftops and chimneys of Montmartre. In his portrayals of the Pont-Neuf at various times of the night and day (e.g. *Pont-Neuf*; Paris, Mus. d'Orsay) the pure colours and flat modelling suggest a familiarity with Japanese prints. Luce travelled widely during the 1890s: to London with Camille Pissarro and Saint-Tropez with Signac in 1892; to Camaret in Brittany in 1893; and repeatedly from 1895 to the Borinage, the coal-mining district of Belgium, where he painted a number of distinguished scenes, for example *Iron Foundry* (1899; Otterlo, Kröller-Müller; see fig.). He also painted stretches along the Seine west of Paris; his depiction of a bend in the

Maximilien Luce: *Iron Foundry*, oil on canvas, 1.13×1.61 m, 1899 (Otterlo, Rijksmuseum Kröller-Müller)

river, the *Seine at Herblay* (1890; Paris, Mus. d'Orsay), is a prime example of his use of stippled brushwork and high-key colour harmonies. In later years he divided his time between Paris and the riverside village of Rolleboise, painting in an Impressionist manner.

When he was 13 Luce was a witness to the Commune and its harsh suppression in the aftermath of the collapse of the Second Empire, an event that he commemorated years later in *Paris Street in May 1871* (1905; Paris, Mus. d'Orsay). The bland title of this work belies its stark portrayal of corpses beside a barricade. Luce was a staunch advocate of anarchism and occasionally contributed works of art to political fundraising events and to anarchist publications such as Jean Grave's *La Révolte* (later published as *Temps nouveaux*) and *Le Père Peinard*. In a government crackdown following the assassination of President Sadi-Carnot in 1894, Luce was arrested with other suspected agitators including Grave and Fénéon and gaoled at Mazas Prison, from which he was released six weeks later. He documented his experience of prison life in an album of ten lithographs with a text by Jules Vallès entitled *Mazas* (1894).

The most extensive collection of Luce's paintings and works on paper belongs to Jean Bouin-Luce, the artist's nephew. There is a large collection of his works at the Musée Maximilien Luce, Mantes-la-Jolie, although it includes few in his divisionist manner.

BIBLIOGRAPHY

*Exposition Maximilien Luce* (exh. cat., intro. F. Fénéon; Paris, Gal. Druet, 1904)
A Tabarant: *Maximilien Luce* (Lyon, 1928)
*Centenaire de Maximilien Luce: Peinture du travail et son milieu: Les Néo-Impressionnistes* (exh. cat., Saint-Denis, Mus. A. & Hist., 1957)
*Maximilien Luce* (exh. cat., Charleroi, Pal. B.-A., 1966)
J. Sutter: 'Maximilien Luce', *The Neo-Impressionists* (Greenwich, 1970), pp. 153–64
*Maximilien Luce* (exh. cat., Albi, Mus. Toulouse-Lautrec, 1977)
P. Cazeau: *Maximilien Luce* (Paris, 1983)
*The Aura of Neo-Impressionism: The W. J. Holliday Collection* (exh. cat. by E. W. Lee and T. E. Smith, Indianapolis, IN, Mus. A., 1983), pp. 48–54
*Maximilien Luce* (exh. cat., Paris, Mus. Marmottan, 1983)
J. Bouin-Luce and D. Bazetoux: *Maximilien Luce: Catalogue of the Paintings* (La-Celle-Saint-Cloud, 1986)
*Maximilien Luce* (exh. cat., Pontoise, Mus. Pissarro, 1987)

PETER J. FLAGG

**Lucebert** [Swaanswijk, L(ubertus) J(acobus)] (*b* Amsterdam, 15 Sept 1924). Dutch painter, draughtsman, printmaker and writer. He first trained as a painter and decorator with his father. In 1938 he spent half a year as a student at the Kunstnijverheidsschool in Amsterdam where Mart Stam was the director. During World War II he did hard labour in Germany. In 1947 he decorated the Franciscan monastery in Heemskerk and in 1948 he had his first exhibition, of drawings. He contributed some poetry to the second issue of *Reflex*, the mouthpiece of the Experimentele Groep and in 1949 he joined COBRA, although for only one year and mainly as a poet. He submitted *poèmes peintures* to the Cobra exhibition at the Stedelijk Museum in Amsterdam (1949). Between 1951 and 1956 he published six volumes of poetry.

Lucebert's painting, like that of other Cobra artists, was filled with fantastic creatures, depicted with a childlike spontaneity and naivety, for example *Orpheus and the Animals* (gouache and coloured pencil, 1952; Amsterdam,

Stedel. Mus.). In 1953 Lucebert settled in the artists' village of Bergen. In 1958 he had his first one-man exhibition at Galerie Espace, Haarlem. His work continued to be characterized by primitive qualities and a striking use of colour, for example *In Egypt* (1962; Amsterdam, Stedel. Mus.). He also produced etchings and took photographs. A large collection of his work is housed in the Groenendÿk collection, Stedelijk Museum, Amsterdam.

BIBLIOGRAPHY

*Lucebert: Gouachen und Zeichnungen, 1952–1982* (exh. cat., Mannheim, Städt. Ksthalle, 1982)
*Modern Dutch Painting* (exh. cat., Athens, N.G., 1983)
*Lucebert in the Stedelijk* (exh. cat., Amsterdam, Stedel. Mus., 1987)

JOHN STEEN

**Lucena, Víctor** (*b* Caracas, 16 June 1948). Venezuelan painter, installation artist and printmaker. He studied fine art at the Escuela de Artes Plásticas y Aplicadas 'Cristóbal Rojas' in Caracas. From 1970 Lucena lived in Milan and took part in salons and biennial exhibitions in Europe. In 1980 he held his first one-man show in Venezuela at the Museo de Arte Contemporáneo in Caracas. His work includes a series of experiments involving the spectator, whereby environments were created aimed at demonstrating the falsehood of daily visual appearances, simultaneously using both real and illusory weights, masses, colours and temperatures. He also distinguished himself with the quality of his graphic design for a series of books for the Fundación Boulton in Caracas.

BIBLIOGRAPHY

*Proposiciones de Víctor Lucena, 1969–1980* (exh. cat. by A. Boulton, Caracas, Mus. A. Contemp., 1980)

Based on information supplied by LELIA DELGADO

**Lucenti** [Lucini], **Girolamo** (*b* Rome, *c.* 1625; *d* Rome, 4 April 1698). Italian medallist, bronze-founder and sculptor. He learnt the craft of bronze-casting from his father, Ambrogio Lucenti (*d* 1656), who worked for the Fabbrica di S Pietro. He may have learnt marble carving in Bernini's workshop, as he was one of several artists who collaborated with the master on the sculptural decoration (1647–9) of the nave and aisles of St Peter's, Rome, and he also worked with Alessandro Algardi. Lucenti's best-known statue is the colossal marble figure of the *Angel Carrying the Column* (1668–9) for the Ponte Sant'Angelo, Rome. Lucenti either misunderstood the design provided by Bernini, or lacked the necessary skill as a marble carver, as the work is awkward and lacks the easy contrapposto movement of the other statues on the bridge.

Lucenti was most successful as a die-engraver and bronze-founder. He cast artillery pieces for the Castel Sant'Angelo (1658–63), and worked for the papal Mint (1668–79). He cast several works in bronze for Bernini, such as the ciborium for the chapel of the Sacrament in St Peter's, Rome (1673–4). He also worked for other artists such as Carlo Fontana, after whose designs he produced most of the bronze sculpture for the tombs of *Cardinal Girolamo Gastaldi* and *Marchese Benedetto Gastaldi*, in S Maria dei Miracoli, Rome (1679–86). Lucenti became a member of the Accademia di S Luca in 1654, and was given the title of Cavaliere by Pope Clement IX *c.* 1669.

BIBLIOGRAPHY
Thieme–Becker
R. Wittkower: *Gian Lorenzo Bernini: The Sculptor of the Roman Baroque* (London, 1955, rev. 2/1966)
Marcella Fagiolo dell'Arco and Maurizio Fagiolo dell'Arco: *Bernini: Una introduzione al gran teatro del barocco* (Rome, 1967)
M. Weil: *The History and Decoration of the Ponte S Angelo* (University Park, 1974), pp. 125–6, 144–5
J. Montagu: *Alessandro Algardi*, 2 vols (New Haven, 1985)

MARK S. WEIL

**Lucerne** [Ger. Luzern]. Swiss city and capital of the canton of Lucerne. It is situated on the River Reuss, the principal tributary of Lake Lucerne. The monastery of St Leodegar, a dependency of Murbach Abbey (Alsace), on the approximate site of present-day Lucerne, can be traced back to the mid-8th century AD. Lucerne was founded in 1178 and sold, together with the monastery, to the Habsburgs in 1291. In 1332 the town joined the Swiss Confederation and gradually detached itself from Habsburg rule. Between 1380 and 1415 it acquired subject lands of its own, the area of the present canton, and in 1417 gained independence within the Holy Roman Empire. During the Counter-Reformation Lucerne was the leading town of Catholic Switzerland; in 1798–9 it became the Helvetian capital. In the 19th century the city was one of the main centres of foreign trade in Europe.

From *c*. 1150 Lucerne developed on both sides of the Reuss bridge on the main route to the St Gotthard Pass; as traffic over the Pass increased in the 13th century, the town grew correspondingly in size. Lying between a mountainous cattle-farming area and an agricultural zone, it became the central market for an extensive region. The old wooden bridge, the Kapellbrücke, was built *c*. 1300 (destr. 1993); it had an octagonal water-tower, and it was roofed, with a series of fine paintings in the rafters that represented scenes from the town's history, some of them by Hans Heinrich Wägmann (1611; destr. 1993). In the second half of the 14th century the Musegg wall, 870 m long, with nine towers and one of the longest fortifications in Switzerland, was built round the city. Lucerne had close trading, military and religious links with Italy, and Italian influence is present in its numerous monuments dating from the late Middle Ages, the Renaissance and the Baroque periods. The Ritter'sche Palast (1556–61 and 1573–4), by Domenico de Ponte of Lugano, has a rusticated façade and a Tuscan columniated courtyard and is a rare example of Florentine early Renaissance architecture north of the Alps. The Rathaus, built 1602–4 by Anton Isenmann (*fl* 1587–1606), is one of the most important in Switzerland, combining traditional and Italian Renaissance forms. The Hofkirche SS Leodegar und Mauritius (1633–9) by Jakob Kurrer of Ingolstadt is a large and richly decorated church of the German late Renaissance. The Jesuit settlement of 1577 in Lucerne was of major importance to the city as the Order promoted schooling, the reform of religious life, Baroque culture and a theatrical tradition. The Jesuit church of St Franz Xaver (1666–9; probably to plans by a Vorarlberg architect) is the first large Baroque church built in Switzerland, a basilican structure with a polychromed façade with twin towers.

Until *c*. 1850 Lucerne grew only slowly beyond its medieval limits, despite the removal of the fortifications and the enlargement of the suburbs. It was only with the advent of the railway and tourism, which produced a basis for industrialization, new building and population growth, that the city underwent substantial changes. In order to accommodate the influx of foreign visitors, Lucerne opened up beyond the confines of the medieval quarter towards the lake, with a long waterfront (partly constructed by infilling) of fashionable hotels, for example the Schwanen (1834–5; rebuilt 1878, enlarged 1896–7) by Louis Pfyffer (1783–1845) and Placid Segesser (1803–78), and the Schweizerhof (1845–6) by Melchior Berri. Other new building projects created in response to the growth of tourism include the Gletschergarten (1876), a Romantic evocation of the glacial landscape and replicas of historic buildings; the Kursaal (1882; rebuilt 1910) by Léon Higonnet; the church of St Mark (1898–9) by Frédéric Jarrow, a 'tourist church' in an English Gothic Revival style; and numerous sports facilities (*c*. 1900). St Karli (1932–4) by Fritz Metzger (1898–1973) was the first church in central Switzerland to be built in concrete. The Lucerne Festival of international music was founded in 1938. The industrial section of the city grew up on the left bank from the end of the 19th century, and by the late 20th century Lucerne was the most important industrial centre in the canton.

BIBLIOGRAPHY
A. Reinle: *Luzern*, Kunstführer durch die Schweiz, i (Berne, 1971), pp. 309–33
H. Wickl and others, eds: *Luzern, 1178–1978: Beiträge zur Geschichte der Stadt* (Lucerne, 1978) [contains extensive bibliog.]
H. Schnyder: *Die Gründung des Klosters Luzern* (1978), v of *Historische Schriften der Universität Freiburg*, ed. G. Boesch, P. Ladner and others (Freiburg, 1976–)
*Der Geschichtsfreund*, cxxxi (1979), pp. 153–209 [issue contains bibliog. of Innerschweiz, Lucerne, Uri, Schwyz, Obwalden, Nidwalden]
F. Deuchler: *Schweiz und Liechtenstein: Kunstdenkmäler und Museen*, Reclams Kunstführer (Stuttgart, 1979), pp. 445–60
A. Dubler: *Handwerk, Gewerbe und Zunft in Stadt und Landschaft Luzern* (Lucerne, 1982)
S. Bucher: *Bauern und Patrizier in Stadt und Land Luzern im Ancien Régime* (Schüpfheim, 1986)
B. Wyss: 'Luzern', *Inventar der neueren Schweizer Architektur, 1850–1920* (Berne, 1991)

CORNELIA BAUER

**Luchese** [Lucchese]. Italian family of architects, master builders, stuccoists and masons, active mainly in Austria. Giovanni Luchese (*d* Innsbruck, Jan 1581) is known to have worked as a mason in Bohemia from 1539. After 1555 he worked at Villa Hvězda and at the Belvedere summer house (1559) in Prague. He also worked at the castle of Hradčany, probably to plans by Bonifaz Wolmut. In 1564 Luchese was summoned to the Tyrol, where from 1565 he directed the rebuilding of the Innsbruck Hofburg and of Schloss Ambras as court architect to Archduke Ferdinand II. In 1571 he built the Silver Chapel at the Innsbruck Hofkirche (*see* INNSBRUCK, §3(i)). With his son Alberto Luchese (*b* Pambio; *d* Melide, after 1600) he built the convent church at Hall, and from 1568 he directed the building of the Jesuit church at Innsbruck. Following Giovanni's death, Alberto was made master of the works at Innsbruck, where he built the ballroom (1582) in the Hofgarten and the armoury (1588) of Schloss Ambras. He was also responsible for other buildings in Günzburg, Oberkirchberg, Bressanone and Pambio.

Philiberto [Filiberto] Luchese (*b* Melide, 26 Dec 1606; *d* Vienna, 21 May 1666), the grandson of Alberto Luchese, is probably the stuccoist Philiberto, who worked on chapels (1633–6) in the collegiate church at Bielany in Poland. He entered the service of Emperor Ferdinand III before 1640, and from 1640 he worked for Count Batthyany at Schlaining, Güssing, Bernstein and Rechnitz as both stuccoist and architect and for the Counts Palffy in Pajštún, Pezinok, Bojnice, Červený Kameň and Bratislava (Slovakia) and in Marchegg (Austria). In 1642 he inspected fortifications in Hungary and Slovakia, and directed their construction at Wiener Neustadt. In 1646 he designed catafalques for Empress Maria Anna and the Spanish Infante Balthasar. Philiberto also built the chapel of St Brigitta (1650) in Vienna and in 1651, during the Danube floods, he executed various dike constructions. This work earned him the highest recognition, and he was entrusted with projects for making navigable the rivers Traun in upper Austria and Morava in Moravia. Although these were not carried out, because of lack of funds, as a result of his waterway inspections Philiberto was given the projects for the monastery church at Lambach in upper Austria and the Moravian castles at Uherský Ostroh, Holešov (with the parish church), Kvasice and the Rottal palace in Vienna.

In 1655 Philiberto designed a catafalque for the Spanish king, Philip IV, and worked on alterations to the Abensberg-Traun Palace in Vienna, and in 1657 he designed the façade of the Jesuit church Am Hof in the same city. From 1660 the Leopold range of the Vienna Hofburg was built to his plans. In 1661 he submitted plans (unexecuted) for the façade of the church of St Michael, Vienna. In Moravia he also worked for Karl Lichtenstein-Castelkorn, Bishop of Olomouc, for whom he produced the plans for the residence in Olomouc and for a garden in Kroměříž (both 1665). Before his death, Philiberto made designs for the Černín Palace in Prague, but they were not executed. Many other buildings can be attributed to him only on stylistic grounds, including the castles at Petronell and Eisenstadt, as well as the Schottenkirche, the church in Mariabrunn and the church of the Servites, all in Vienna, in which a number of collaborators must have been involved. His architecture embodies a slightly old-fashioned north Italian Mannerism and shows the influence of the style of Jacopo Vignola. His artistic strength lies in the richly structured tension of his façades, which are built up from several superimposed layers of stucco. His work in articulating the streetscape of Vienna is also notable.

BIBLIOGRAPHY
Thieme–Becker
V. Richter: 'Philiberto Luchese na Moravě' [Philiberto Luchese in Moravia], *Roč. Kruhu Pěstováni Dějin Uměni* (Prague, 1935), pp. 27–44
W. Kitlitschka: 'Das Schloss Petronell in Niederösterreich: Beiträge zur Baugeschichte und kunsthistorischen Bedeutung', *A. Lombarda*, xii (1967), pp. 105–26
K. Garas: 'Az olasz mesterek és a magyarországi barokk térhódítása' [Italian masters and the birth of the Hungarian Baroque], *Magyarországi reneszánsz és barokk* [Renaissance and Baroque in Hungary] (Budapest, 1975), pp. 211–29
P. Fidler: 'Zur Architektur des 17. Jahrhunderts im Raum Wien', *Akten des XXV. internationalen Kongresses für Kunstgeschichte: Wien, 1985*
—: 'Philiberto Luchese: Ein vergessener Pionier der österreichischen Barockarchitektur', *Röm. Hist. Mitt.*, xxx (1988), pp. 177–98
—: *Architektur des Seicento: Baumeister, Architekten und Bauten des Wiener Hofkreises* (Innsbruck, 1990), pp. 141–216

PETR FIDLER

**Lü Chi.** *See* LÜ JI.

**Luchian, Ştefan** (*b* Ştefănesti, 1 Feb 1868; *d* Bucharest, 28 June 1916). Romanian painter. He studied at the School of Fine Arts in Bucharest, graduating in 1889 and continuing his studies at the Akademie der Bildenden Künste in Munich and in Paris at the Académie Julian, where he was a student of William-Adolphe Bouguereau. He rejected the rigidity of academic painting early in his career, however. The *Last Autumn Race* (1892; Bucharest, Mus. A.), one of the few paintings known from this period, clearly illustrates the influence of Manet and Impressionism on his early work. On his return to Romania in 1892 Luchian, unwilling to restrict his work to merely copying the French artists, struggled to create an original style. In 1900 he was left partially paralysed by a spinal disease, but he continued to work, and it is during the next years that he created his most accomplished works. His self-portraits (e.g. 1907; Bucharest, Mus. A.) are clear evidence of his determination to overcome this personal tragedy; far from inspiring pity, these paintings emphasize the depth and the strength of his inner life. It is in landscapes such as *Willows at Chiajna* (c. 1907; Cluj-Napoca, Mus. A.), however, that his commitment becomes even more apparent, with joyful rhythms created by means of broad brush-strokes and contrasts of bright colours next to delicate tones. Towards the end of his life Luchian became completely immobilized. During this time flowers were his favourite subject (e.g. *Safta, the Flower Girl*; Bucharest, N. Mus. A.; *see also* ROMANIA, fig. 9), and they became a metaphorical bridge between the artist and the outside world. The colours are still bright in these last paintings, and the loss of pastel tones makes the contrast more dramatic.

BIBLIOGRAPHY
V. Cioflec: *Luchian* (Bucharest, 1924)
J. Lassaigne: *Ştefan Luchian* (Bucharest, 1947, 2/1972)
P. Comarnescu: *Luchian* (Bucharest, 1956)
M. Popescu: *Ştefan Luchian* (Bucharest, 1964)

IRINA D. COSTACHE

**Lu Chih.** *See* LU ZHI.

**Luchino di Giovanni Belbello.** *See* BELBELLO DA PAVIA.

**Luchsperger [Luchsberger], Lorenz** (*fl* Wiener Neustadt, 1486; *d* 1501). Wood-carver. He is first mentioned in 1486, married to a rich heiress and living in the elegant Deutschherrenviertel (Teutonic Knights' quarter) of the town. Mayer and Oettinger attributed to him the *Annunciation* group and *Apostle* figures in the nave of Wiener Neustadt Cathedral. A signature formerly beneath one of the *Apostles* was interpreted as his monogram. The figures originate from the circle of NICOLAUS GERHAERT: the figure types of the Nördlingen Altar (dated 1462; *see* MASTERS, ANONYMOUS, AND MONOGRAMMISTS, §I: MASTER OF NÖRDLINGEN) and in particular the pulpit of Strasbourg Cathedral (dated 1485) correspond very closely to those in Wiener Neustadt. If Luchsperger was indeed responsible for the Wiener Neustadt figures, he must have been among the sculptors who came to Austria from the Upper Rhine area in the succession of Gerhaert. Some works seem to form a link between the styles of Gerhaert and Luchsperger. A *St Sebastian* (Wiener Neustadt, Stadtpfarrkirche), which differs stylistically from the *Apostle* figures and was attributed by Wertheimer to the MASTER OF KEFERMARKT ALTAR (*see* MASTERS, ANONYMOUS, AND MONOGRAMMISTS, §I), can possibly be connected with a donation of 1495.

Luchsperger was an independent master: his masculine figure-style with strong, terse facial types is clearly distinguishable from that of Gerhaert's other followers. His monumental figures, with their forceful gestures and often fierce expressions, can be seen on a relief of the *Death of the Virgin* (Herzogenburg, Kstausstell. Stift). A fragment of a bearded saint (St Pölten, Diözmus.) can perhaps be regarded as a late work. Luchsperger's powerful, energetic style is evident finally in a figure of one of the Magi (Vienna, Belvedere), which is supposed to have come from the Hallstatt region. Other works, such as a *St John the Baptist* (Linz, Oberösterreich. Landesmus.) and a predella with *Christ and the Apostles* (Hausmannstätten, Filialkirche), can be ascribed to his workshop.

### BIBLIOGRAPHY
J. Mayer: *Geschichte von Wiener Neustadt*, i (Wiener Neustadt, 1924), pp. 415ff
G. Gugenbauer: 'Gotische Kunstdenkmäler am Heiligenstein (St. Sebald) bei Gaflenz, Oberösterreich', *Christ. Kstbl.*, lxvii (1926), pp. 33–42
O. Wertheimer: *Nikolaus Gerhaert* (Berlin, 1929), pp. 66–8
K. Oettinger: *Lorenz Luchsperger: Der Meister der Wiener Neustädter Domapostel* (Berlin, 1935)
O. Benesch: 'Lorenz Luchsperger', *Pantheon*, xviii (1936), pp. 259–64
H. Stafski: 'Der Meister der Wiener Neustädter Apostel vom Oberrhein?', *Z. Dt. Ver. Kstwiss.*, v (1938), pp. 62–76
L. Fischel: *Nikolaus Gerhaert und die Bildhauer der deutschen Spätgotik* (Munich, 1944), pp. 72–97
F. Dworschak and H. Kühnel, eds: *Die Gotik in Niederösterreich: Kunst, Kultur und Geschichte eines Landes im Spätmittelalter* (Vienna, 1963), pp. 137ff, pls 97–103
*Gotik in Österreich* (exh. cat., Krems-Stein, Minoritenkirche, 1967), pp. 214–16
E. Baum: *Katalog des Museums mittelalterlicher österreichischer Kunst* (Vienna, 1971), no. 106
G. Gerhartl: *Der Dom zu Wiener Neustadt, 1279–1979* (Vienna and Graz, 1979), pp. 27–9, pls 28–9, 44, 46–62
G. Egger and others: *Stift Herzogenburg und seine Kunstschätze* (St Pölten and Vienna, 1982), p. 125, pl. 85 [colour]
R. Recht: *Nicolas de Leyde et la sculpture à Strasbourg, 1460–1525* (Strasbourg, 1987), pp. 304ff
L. Schultes: 'Unser und des Reichs Bildhauer: Einige Aspekte des Mäzenatentums Kaiser Friedrichs III.', *Kstjb. Stadt Linz* (1992–3), pp. 169–72
——: *Die Sammlung Kastner*, i: *Mittelalter und Barock* (Linz, 1992), pp. 58ff

LOTHAR SCHULTES

**Luciani, Sebastiano.** *See* SEBASTIANO DEL PIOMBO.

**Lucian of Samosata** [Gr. Loukianos] (*b* Samosata, *c.* AD 120; *d* before 180). Author, writing in Greek, of North African birth. Towards the end of a prolific literary career, around 163 AD, he wrote the *Imagines* (Gr. *Eikones*), a panegyric couched in dialogue form, which is one of several texts surviving from the age of the Second Sophistic that include extensive descriptions of works of art (*see also* PHILOSTRATOS). Also of interest for the history of painting is Lucian's *Zeuxis*, a discussion of the idea of innovation, which includes a detailed description of a copy of the *Centaur Family*, a famous work by the

Athenian painter Zeuxis, depicting a family of centaurs in an idyllic landscape. In the Renaissance the popularity of Lucian's art writings influenced such artists as Sodoma and Botticelli; the latter incorporated many elements from Lucian's description of Aetion's *Wedding of Alexander the Great and Roxane* (327 BC; destr.) in his *Mars and Venus* (London, N.G.).

In general, the same provisos apply to the art-historical writings of Lucian as to the work of the Philostratoi: it is difficult to know whether they are describing actual works of art or fictitious ones to act as paradigms of rhetorical depiction, and thus the extent to which they can be used as sources for the actual appearance of ancient art works is limited. Lucian, however, seems to have been more genuinely interested in the plastic arts than other writers of the period, perhaps because of his supposed early apprenticeship to a sculptor. He certainly referred to statuary often, particularly in sacred contexts: see, for instance, his descriptions of the statues of Athena at Lemnos, and of Kombabos at Hierapolis in Syria, sculpted by the otherwise unattested Hermokles of Rhodes (*The Syrian Goddess* xxvi). Lucian was also unusually sensitive in his subjective responses to works of art: for instance, he says of Zeuxis' *Centaurs* that 'its other qualities are not immediately obvious to the eye of a non-specialist like myself, but nonetheless display the entire force of his skill, namely his precision of line, careful mixing of colours, felicitous application of the paint, appropriate shadowing, good perspective, proportion and balance' (*Zeuxis* v).

Lucian's aesthetic tastes were conventional and reflect those of his age. Many copies of famous statues by Pheidias, Alkamenes, Myron, Kritios and Nesiotes mentioned by Lucian were included in the decorative scheme of Hadrian's villa at Tivoli, testifying to their contemporary popularity as sculptural ideals. According to Lucian, the achievements of these Greek sculptors were so great and beautiful that 'we shall not need any artists other than them' (*Imagines* iv). In painting, he suggested that artists should first aim to imitate the great masters of the 5th and 4th centuries BC, such as Zeuxis, Apelles and Aetion, whose *Wedding of Alexander the Great and Roxane* is singled out for particular praise (*Herodotus* v–vi; *Imagines* vii). All this is in accord with Lucian's frequently asserted aesthetic doctrine that the present has to select the finest parts of antique artistic production, whether in literature or the plastic arts, before it is able to produce anything innovative or noteworthy itself (*Lexiphanes* xxii–xxiii; *Hippias* iii; *Teacher of Rhetoric* ix).

Lucian did, however, praise some buildings in the architectural style of his own time. To him, the elegant baths designed by the architect Hippias (*Hippias* v–ix) embodied the perfect blend of the best of ancient archetypes with contemporary innovation, such as coloured marble wall cladding, proper lighting, lavatories and clepsydrae. Lucian's *The Hall* (Gr. *Peri tou oikou*) is a long description of a quintessential (and certainly imaginary) public building; its ceiling, admirable for elegant plasterwork and refined symmetrical gilding, recalls the geometric coffered ceilings of such buildings as the Baths of Caracalla at Rome. Its entrance is also equipped with a picture gallery displaying mythological paintings of Perseus and Andromeda, the slaying of Aigisthos, and Medea about to murder her children, interspersed with Hellenistic genre scenes (*The Hall* xxiii–xxxii).

### WRITINGS

*Imagines* (Gr. *Eikones*) [Essays on portraiture]
*Zeuxis*

### BIBLIOGRAPHY

H. Blümner: *Archäologische Studien zu Lucian* (Breslau, 1867)
A. le Morvan: 'La Description artistique chez Lucian', *Rev. Etud. Gr.*, xlv (1932), pp. 380–90
C. Robinson: *Lucian and his Influence in Europe* (London, 1979)
K. J. Hartswick: 'The Athena Lemnia Reconsidered', *Amer. J. Archaeol.*, lxxxvii (1983), pp. 335–46
C. P. Jones: *Culture and Society in Lucian* (Cambridge, MA, 1986)

DOMINIC MONTSERRAT

**Lucini, Antonio Francesco** (*b* Florence, 1610). Italian engraver. He is best known for a series of engravings entitled *Disegni della guerra, assedio dell'armata turchesca all'Isola di Malta l'anno MDXLV* (Bologna, 1631). He also produced the plates for the monumental work by Sir Robert Dudley (1573–1649): *Dell'arcano del mare* (Florence, 1646–7), a project that took him 12 years. His style is close to that of Jacques Callot and Stefano della Bella, and his *View of Florence during a Festival* (1634) is derived from the latter.

### BIBLIOGRAPHY

Bolaffi

ANNAMARIA NEGRO SPINA

**Lucius** [Sövenbürger], **Jakob, I** (*b* ?Kronstadt, Transylvania [now Braşov, Romania], *c.* 1530; *d* Helmstedt, Oct 1597). Hungarian woodcutter, printmaker and printer of German descent, active in Germany. He was probably employed at the printing works of Gáspár Heltai (*c.* 1520–74) in Klausenburg (now Cluj) from *c.* 1545 and later probably worked in Nuremberg. From 1555 he lived in Wittenberg, at the same time as Lucas Cranach II. From 1556 he had his own printing works, and in 1564 he was appointed university book printer in Rostock. In 1579, after a dispute with the university, he moved to Helmstedt, still as a university book printer. After his death from bubonic plague, his son Jakob Lucius II (*fl* 1568–1616) carried on his printing business.

The extent of Lucius's oeuvre is difficult to ascertain, and any appreciation of his work is dominated by his major standing as a book printer. His woodcuts reflect the influence of Lucas Cranach II and attain especial quality only in his Wittenberg period, in such works as the *Adoration of the Shepherds* (Hollstein, no. 8) and *Christ Carrying the Cross* (Hollstein, no. 12). He later turned to the production and sale of metal moulds of woodcuts, making a commercial success of the technique.

### BIBLIOGRAPHY

Hollstein: *Ger.*; *NDB*; Thieme–Becker
H. Röttinger: *Beiträge zur Geschichte des sächsischen Holzschnitts* (Strasbourg, 1921), pp. 80–100
*Lucas Cranach d. Ä., Lucas Cranach d. J., Jacob Lucius d. Ä. Gemälde und Holzschnitte aus Sammlungen der DDR* (exh. cat., Bucharest, Mus. A., 1973)

MICHAEL EISSENHAUER

**Lücke** [Luick; Lukke]. German family of sculptors. The earliest known members were Carl August Lücke I (*fl* 1688) and Ernst Friedrich Lücke (*fl c.* 1700), who may have been brothers: both were ivory-carvers. One or the other of them was the father of the family's most prominent artists, (1) Johann Christian Ludwig Lücke and, putatively, (2) Carl August Lücke II. Johann Friedrich Lücke I (*fl* 1720–38), who worked as a sculptor in Freiberg and Dresden, was either their brother or their cousin. His eldest son, Johann Friedrich Lücke II (*b* Freiberg, 1727; *d* Meissen, 1797), worked as a model-maker in the porcelain manufactories of Höchst, Frankenthal and Meissen, making 'society' figures, including a fine one of the dancer *Mlle Camargo*; Christian Gottlob Lücke (*b* Freiberg, 1733; *d* Meissen, 1796), the younger son of Johann Friedrich I, worked as model-maker for the same porcelain manufactories. Karl Gottlieb Lücke (*b* 1730–40; *d* Frankenthal, 14 July 1775), who until 1757 worked with (1) Johann Christian Ludwig Lücke in Copenhagen and may have been his son, likewise made models for porcelain figures, working in Meissen and in Frankenthal: there he produced late Rococo figurines, portraying society figures in the dress of common people.

**(1) Johann Christian Ludwig (von) Lücke** (*b* Dresden, *c.* 1703; *d* Danzig [now Gdańsk, Poland], 1780). He worked as a sculptor in stone and also made small-scale sculptures in ivory, terracotta, wax and papier mâché. He probably served his apprenticeship with Balthasar Permoser in Dresden. He subsequently went on a study trip, financed by a scholarship awarded by the court in Dresden; it took him to Hamburg (1724), England (1726), the Netherlands and France. His earliest dated small sculptural work, the stone relief *Lucretia* (1728; Hannover, Kestner-Mus.), has early Rococo elements and suggests Dutch or English influence (such as that of Jan Baptist Xavery or David Le Marchand) more strongly than that of Permoser. For nine months from 1728 to 1729 Lücke worked as model-maker at the Porzellan-Manufaktur Meissen; being thought unsuited to the work, he was dismissed, but he remained in Dresden. In 1733 and 1736 he unsuccessfully applied for the post of court sculptor, in succession to Permoser. He made portraits for the royal collection, as well as *objets d'art* with mythological and religious themes, including a present to the Elector Frederick-Augustus II of an ivory group of the *Reawakening of Art* (1736) and an unusually large ivory crucifix (1737; both Dresden, Grünes Gewölbe); they exhibit the attention to minute details, such as drops of blood, which is characteristic of Lücke's work. From 1742 Lücke also worked for Charles-Leopold (1678–1747), Duke of Mecklenburg-Schwerin, making some large-scale sculptures, such as the garden statues in the park of Schloss Boitzenberg (now Schwerin); he may also have stayed in St Petersburg.

From 1747 to 1750 Lücke worked intermittently in Hamburg. Around 1750 he made an ivory portrait bust of the burgomaster of Hamburg, *David Doormann* (now Hamburg, Mus. Kst & Gew.): the sharply realistic treatment of the features gives the work a strikingly bourgeois character. Lücke next worked (1750–51) as the highly paid model-maker for the imperial porcelain manufactory in Vienna, where his signature became a mark of high quality. One of his most important works of the period after 1750 is the large ivory group, *Sleeping Shepherdess* (Munich, Bayer. Nmus.), a virtuoso work in the Rococo style, comparable in its handling, superficial charm and suggestiveness to contemporary porcelain figures.

Lücke next travelled via Hamburg to Copenhagen, where he worked for the court from 1752 to 1757. Around 1760 he moved to London, where he made from life an ivory portrait bust of *George II* (London, V&A). This is a virtuoso masterpiece without any idealization: the contrast between the splendour of the state robes and the King's plain face has an almost ironic effect. Returning to Hamburg, Lücke was again working for the Dukes of Mecklenburg-Schwerin in 1767; later he moved, first to Dresden and then to Danzig. Lücke was typical of a certain kind of many-sided peripatetic artist; his work, with its variable quality, marked the end, in Germany, of development in the art of small-scale sculpture.

**(2) Carl August Lücke II** (*b* Dresden, *c.* 1710; *d* ?Danzig [now Gdańsk, Poland], after 1777). Putative brother of (1) Johann Christian Ludwig Lücke. He specialized in making bourgeois portraits. The earliest examples of his work come from Hamburg (1738). The ivory portrait of the burgomaster of Hamburg, *Rutger Ruland* (Hamburg, Mus. Hamburg. Gesch.), is characteristic of his style in showing the subject in profile, and in its almost exaggerated attention to detail, such as hair and the pattern of cloth. Lücke's faces were always strongly characterized. From 1751 until he was dismissed in 1757, Lücke made portraits and allegorical or mythical scenes for Christian Ludwig II (1683–1756), Duke of Mecklenburg-Schwerin. Between 1757 and 1762 Lücke was in St Petersburg, returning there for two more years after a short stay in Danzig. He spent the last years of his life in Danzig, where he was reported in 1777 to be living in poverty. In his portraits Lücke sometimes used the same schema several times (including details of cloth), merely changing the sitter's head, as can be seen by comparing his *Portrait of a Young Man* (1765; Hannover, Kestner-Mus.) with his *Portrait of a Man* (Berlin, Skulpgal.).

BIBLIOGRAPHY
Thieme-Becker
C. Scherer: *Studien zur Elfenbeinplastik der Barockzeit* (Strasbourg, 1897), pp. 74–105
E. von Philippovich: *Elfenbein* (Brunswick, 1961, rev. Munich, 1982)
*Barockplastik in Norddeutschland* (exh. cat., ed. J. Rasmussen; Hamburg, Mus. Kst & Gew., 1977), pp. 568–96
C. Theuerkauff: *Die Bildwerke in Elfenbein des 16.–19. Jahrhunderts*, Berlin, Staatl. Museen Preuss. Kultbes. cat. (Berlin, 1986), pp. 193–204
A. GERHARDT

**Luckhardt.** German family of architects. Wassili (*b* Berlin, 22 July 1889; *d* Berlin, 2 Dec 1972) and his brother Hans (*b* Berlin, 16 June 1890; *d* Bad Wiessee, 1954) both studied architecture, Hans at the Technische Hochschule in Karlsruhe and Wassili at the Technische Hochschule, Charlottenburg, Berlin, and at Dresden. In 1914 Wassili took evening classes in Berlin with August Endell. After World War I both played active roles in the radical artists' groups of Berlin, including the Novembergruppe, the ARBEITSRAT FÜR KUNST and DER RING. Hans Luckhardt was the guiding spirit behind the Arbeitsrat exhibition *Neues Bauen* (May 1920), which provided a public forum for the architectural fantasists of Bruno Taut's group the Gläserne Kette. In the context of the exhibition, Hans Luckhardt sent his associates in the Gläserne Kette a Rationalist critique of the current leanings towards mysticism, primitivism and Far Eastern philosophies and suggested that the way forward and the true spirit of the age were to be found in industrial efficiency rather than the Gothic cathedral.

Expressionist traits dominated Hans Luckhardt's unexecuted project for the Deutsches Hygiene-Museum in Dresden (1921; see 1990 exh. cat., pp. 45, 186–7), however, and the crystalline fixation that the Gläserne Kette had adopted from Paul Scheerbart and Taut lingered on throughout the 1920s. Wassili used the crystal motif for a sculptural advertisement on the Avus motorway in Berlin (1921; with Rudolph Belling), and clear-cut, prismatic forms were typical of the domestic architecture of the group practice set up by the brothers in 1924, in association with Alfons Anker (1872–1958). While these forms were achieved with brick in an early group of terraced houses at Schorlemerallee 13–23 (1925; with Anker) in Dahlem, Berlin, steel-frame construction was used on four single-family houses at Schorlemerallee 7–11 and Spilstrasse 9 (1927; with Anker). A steel skeleton was also used on two houses, Heerstrasse 55 and Am Rupenhorn 24 (both 1928; with Anker), overlooking the River Havel in Charlottenburg, Berlin, which are among the most accomplished statements of the architectural purism of Neue Sachlichkeit and bear comparison with Le Corbusier's villas of the same period.

The brothers revived their Expressionist vocabulary for the 'Haus der Arbeit' competition organized by the Nazis in spring 1934 with a crystalline pavilion on the banks of the Havel. As leading proponents of the white architecture of Neue Sachlichkeit the brothers found little favour with the new regime and suffered a dearth of commissions between 1933 and 1951. This identification with the white architecture of the Weimar Republic was beneficial in the post-war years, however, when the Luckhardts were seen to represent an interrupted, democratic tradition. Their Miesian pavilion at the *Constructa* exhibition in Hannover (1951) was an expression of this continuity. The last joint scheme designed by the brothers was for a complex comprising two housing blocks and a series of shops (completed 1956) in Kreuzberg, Berlin, at Kottbusser Strasse and Skalitzer Strasse. After Hans Luckhardt's death, Wassili Luckhardt continued to practise successfully in the International Style, with designs for his own (1957) in Dahlem at Fabeckstrasse 48; an office building in Munich for the Landesversorgungsamt Bayern und Versorgungsamt München (Hessstrasse and Lothstrasse, destr. 1989); terraced housing for the *Interbau* exhibition in Berlin (Klopstockstrasse 19, 21, 23; 1955–7; with Hubert Hoffmann); the Veterinärmedizinisches Institut (1963–8; with H. J. Bandel), Koserstrasse 20, Freie Universität, Berlin; the Haus der Bürgerschaft (1962–9) in Bremen; and the Pflanzenphysiologisches Institut (1962–70), Königin-Luise-Strasse, Freie Universität, Berlin.

WRITINGS
H. Luckhardt: *Zur neuen Wohnform* (Berlin, 1930)
W. Luckhardt and W. Köhler: *Lichtarchitektur* (Berlin, 1956)

BIBLIOGRAPHY
U. Kulturmann: *Wassili und Hans Luckhardt* (Tübingen, 1958)
R. Rave and H.-J. Knöfel: *Bauen seit 1900 in Berlin* (Berlin, 1968)
H. Kliemann: *Wassili Luckhardt* (Tübingen, 1973)

I. Boyd Whyte: *The Crystal Chain Letters: Architectural Fantasies by Bruno Taut and his Circle* (Cambridge, MA, 1985)
*Brüder Luckhardt und Alfons Anker: Berliner Architekten der Moderne* (exh. cat., Berlin, Akad. Kst., 1990)

IAIN BOYD WHYTE

**Lucknow** [Lakhnau; possibly anc. Lakṣmaṇāvatī]. Capital city of Uttar Pradesh State, on the Gumti River in the flat Gangetic plain of northern India. It occupies a site topographically undistinguished except for two small hills on the river's southern bank. Fortified structures were built on these hills from an undetermined date; the earliest, according to local tradition, was established by Lakshman, brother of the epic hero Rama. Of the area's early culture nothing remains save a few unprovenanced stone sculptures (Lucknow, State Mus.). The history of Lucknow becomes clearer in the 15th century, when the area was under the Sharqi sultans of Jaunpur (*reg* 1394–1476) and locally controlled by a clan known as the Shaikhzadas. Shaikhzada 'Abd al-Rahim was appointed governor (*subadar*) of the area by the Mughal emperor Akbar (*reg* 1556–1605). 'Abd al-Rahim's tomb, known as the Nadan Mahal (*c.* 1600), is notable for its traces of fine stucco, the earliest instance of a medium that typifies the later architectural decoration of Lucknow. Another early tomb is that of Shah Mina, a celebrated Muslim mystic who settled in the city during the mid-15th century. His tomb consists of a low dome surrounded by a pillared portico (*c.* 1450).

The most important monument of Mughal rule was the fort known as Machchi Bhavan (early 17th century to 1857). The site was strategically important, being located on one of Lucknow's two hills at the point where the Gumti River was bridged. Behind the irregular bastions and walls of the fort was a series of courtyards with administrative buildings and gardens. The most striking feature was the Panch Mahalla, an airy pavilion similar to a five-storey structure known as the Panch Mahal at FATEHPUR SIKRI. A poor drawing (see Tieffenthaler) shows that the Lucknow version was of arched rather than trabeate construction, suggesting it was made of brick like most buildings in the city. The Machchi Bhavan entrance consisted of a ramped, double-doored gate flanked by octagonal bastions. The gate was illustrated in a drawing by Thomas DANIELL (see Sharar, pl. 7) prior to its destruction in 1857. The monuments within the fort also perished at that time.

British contact with Lucknow was made in the 17th century, when a factory of the East India Company, known as the Farangi Mahal ('Foreigners' House'), was established near the Chowk, or main street, which led south from the Machchi Bhavan. The town was a flourishing commercial centre, one of the first inland centres to attract British trade in cloth, sugar and indigo. There was a large bullion market and significant production of the engraved and inlaid copper vessels known as bidri ware (*see* INDIAN SUBCONTINENT, §VII, 15(v)). Some time after 1655 the Farangi Mahal was given by Emperor Aurangzeb (*reg* 1658–1707) to a Muslim scholar; it is still one of the leading Islamic colleges in India. A tangle of subsequent building inside the Farangi Mahal precinct has obscured its Mughal-period features. Also during the time of Aurangzeb a mosque was built on one of Lucknow's hills, apparently replacing a Vaishnava temple. The mosque, like many in the late Mughal period, consists of a prayer-hall flanked by minarets and crowned with three bulbous domes. As described by Joseph Tieffenthaler in 1765, Lucknow was more than 5 km square and was by then unwalled.

Lucknow flourished particularly in 1775–1856 under the nawabs of Avadh (Oudh). The fourth nawab, Asaf ud-Daula (*reg* 1775–97), transferred the capital there from Faizabad, a move that rapidly transformed the city. Originally appointed as state governors by the Mughals, the nawabs soon became hereditary rulers. During the 80 years that Lucknow was the nawabi capital, a series of complexes was built along the south bank of the Gumti to the east of the Machchi Bhavan fort. The most impressive complex is the Bara (Great) Imambara, constructed by Asaf al-Daula in 1784. By faith the nawabs were Shi'ites, and the Bara Imambara was used during the annual Muharram rite of that sect. The main building is a colossal vaulted hall richly decorated with carved stucco. The building also served as the burial place of Asaf ud-Daula and his wife. Adjacent are a mosque and a stepwell, the latter known as the Baoli Palace. Outside the complex is the Rumi Darvaza, a massive and heavily ornamented gate (*see* INDIAN SUBCONTINENT, fig. 107). In addition to the Bara Imambara, Asaf ud-Daula constructed a palace known as the Daulat Khana. This has suffered almost complete destruction, but a few structures have survived. The most important is the Asafi Kothi, probably a residence of Asaf ud-Daula. The building displays skilful adaptation of European features and avoids the fanciful qualities that dominate later architecture. Originally approached through a formal garden, the Asafi Kothi has a deep, arcaded verandah and a grand central hall two storeys high.

Adventurers such as Claude Martin (1735–1800) and Antoine Polier (1740–95) served the nawabs and influenced the development of the city's culture through their patronage of painting and architecture. Martin's first

Lucknow, Constantia (La Martinière), 1795–1800; photograph by F. Beato, *c.* 1858

residence was the Farhat Baksh, a European-style country house built on the banks of the Gumti (see INDIAN SUBCONTINENT, fig. 108). The house was partially built over the river and surrounded on the landside by a moat. During the 19th century the moat was filled, and numerous additions were made; these were subsequently demolished, and a bund was added as a protective measure. Martin's second residence, which he never lived to inhabit but in which he was interred, is the celebrated Constantia (see fig.), also known as La Martinière. Built in a unique style, Constantia is a massive square structure dominated by a five-storey tower. The heavily fortified character of the building is lightened by balustrades, classical pilasters and remarkable lions and other statuary (some replaced after the earthquake of 1803). A fluted column, added subsequently, rises from the lake in front of the house.

Constantia inaugurated a period of high eclecticism, and many of its details were copied during the first half of the 19th century. The leading architectural projects in this eclectic style were the Farhat Baksh Palace, which served as the residence of the nawabs from 1803 to 1850, and the Qaisarbagh, which was completed in 1850 and was occupied until the termination of nawabi rule in 1856. The Farhat Baksh Palace developed round Martin's first residence after Sa'adat 'Ali Khan purchased the house in June 1803. During the first half of the 19th century the term Farhat Baksh referred to the whole palace, but it is now restricted to the remaining portions of Martin's original house. After 1857 two buildings, known as the Greater and Lesser Chhatar Manzils, gave their name to the area. These structures are executed in the hybrid style typical of later Lucknow architecture. The Qaisarbagh complex, built by Wajid 'Ali Shah (reg 1847–56), was the final extravaganza of the nawabs. The complex, which embraced a number of earlier buildings, consisted of three main squares. It was damaged by military action and looting in 1858 and has steadily degenerated.

Lucknow came increasingly under British influence in the late 18th century, a development signified by the construction of the Residency c. 1800. An enclave for Europeans developed around the Residency and contained a variety of buildings. The Banqueting Hall (c. 1817) stands out as a strict exercise in 'correct' classical architecture. Many of the buildings in the complex were damaged during the prolonged siege of 1857 and now constitute a national monument.

After 1857 Lucknow served as a joint capital of the United Provinces with Allahabad. Architecture of the colonial period is abundant and includes the University of Lucknow by SAMUEL SWINTON JACOB, the Pioneer Press Building (destr. c. 1991) and two bungalows by Walter Burley GRIFFIN, a pupil of Frank Lloyd Wright. The State Museum (partially housed in a former throne building) is the premier museum of Uttar Pradesh and has an important collection of stone sculpture.

*See also* INDIAN SUBCONTINENT, §III, 7(ii)(a).

BIBLIOGRAPHY

J. Tieffenthaler: *Description historique et géographique de l'Inde* (Berlin, 1786)

W. Foster: *The English Factories in India, 1637–1654* (Oxford, 1912)

A. H. Sharar: *Lucknow: The Last Phase of an Oriental Culture* (London, 1975)

R. Llewellyn-Jones: *A Fatal Friendship: The Nawabs, the British and the City of Lucknow* (Delhi, 1985)

B. Tandon: 'The Architecture of the Nawabs of Avadh, 1722–1856', *Facets of Indian Art* (London, 1986), pp. 66–75

P. Davies: *Islamic, Rajput, European*, Penguin Guide Mnmts India (London, 1989), pp. 236–44

R. Llewellyn-Jones: *A Very Ingenious Man: Claude Martin in Early Colonial India* (Delhi, 1992)

ROSIE LLEWELLYN-JONES

**Lucy, Charles** (*b* Hereford, 1814; *d* Notting Hill, London, 19 May 1873). English painter. He studied first in London, then in Paris under Paul Delaroche at the Ecole des Beaux-Arts. In 1883 he returned as a student to the Royal Academy and then spent two years copying Old Master paintings in Paris and The Hague for a private patron. His first history painting, the *Interview between Milton and Galileo*, was hung at the Royal Academy in 1840, and thereafter he divided his time between England and France. He lived for 16 years at Barbizon but, instead of joining the landscape painters there, chose to concentrate on significant scenes from British history. In England he was a regular contributor to the fresco competitions for the New Palace of Westminster: in 1844 he was awarded a £100 premium; in 1847 his *Departure of the Pilgrim Fathers* won an award of £200. For some years he taught at a drawing school in Camden Town, London, where his pupils included Thomas Seddon, a member of the Pre-Raphaelite circle, with which he was also associated. In 1853 he was elected chairman of the committee of the new British Institution. His portrait painting was also admired, and he was commissioned to execute a series of portraits of eminent figures, past and present, which was bequeathed to the Victoria and Albert Museum in London.

BIBLIOGRAPHY

Obituary, *A. J.* [London], xii (1873), p. 208

W. M. Rossetti: *Some Reminiscences of William Michael Rossetti*, i (London, 1906), pp. 138–9

JUSTINE HOPKINS

**Ludovice, João Frederico** [Ludwig, Johann Friedrich] (*b* Hohenhart, Swabia, 1670; *d* Lisbon 1752). German goldsmith and architect, active in Portugal. The information on Ludovice is sometimes contradictory, but there is no doubt that his work contributed decisively to the creation of the courtly JOANINE style, a style named in honour of the King, John V, who was a great patron of architecture and who had colossal wealth from the Portuguese colonies at his disposal. In Ludovice he had the services of an architect of distinction, one who to a large degree determined the character of southern Portuguese architecture into the third quarter of the 18th century.

By the age of 19 Ludovice was in Augsburg where he acquired the rudiments of architecture. He served in the Imperial Army against the French. In 1697 he left for Rome, where he worked for the Jesuits and frequented the studios of other architects, including perhaps that of Carlo Fontana. In Rome he was employed on Andrea Pozzo's gilt-bronze and marble altarpiece of *St Ignatius* in the church of Il Gesù. He was commissioned by the Jesuits to make a silver sacrarium for the high altar for the church of S Antão, Lisbon (destr. 1755). He arrived in Lisbon in 1701; his early activities are unclear, but he must have failed in some way to meet his obligations to the

João Frederico Ludovice: façade of the palace and church at Mafra, 1717–35

Jesuits, who brought a lawsuit against him. It is probable that he benefited from the protection of the Germans at court, for King John II was married to Maria Anna of Austria, daughter of Emperor Leopold I.

1. WORKS AT MAFRA AND ÉVORA. Ludovice's name became associated with the principal architectural project of John V's reign, the palace, church and convent at MAFRA, built by the King in fulfilment of a pious vow that on the birth of an heir he would found a monastery there. The project, begun in 1717, was initiated by the birth in 1711 of the Infanta Maria Barbara. The extent of Ludovice's responsibility for the design of Mafra is unclear, although the great unity of the building suggests the work of a single mind. Details of the planning stages are also unclear: at first the intention was to build a small convent for 13 friars, but the project was gradually enlarged. The completed building differs greatly both in size and in quality from the traditional convents of the Arrábido (Franciscan), who were noted for their austerity and discipline. No previous architectural activity by Ludovice is known. It appears likely that the major part of the work was entrusted to him, with close supervision by the King, whose keen interest ensured that he received information from Rome on architectural developments and small-scale models of its principal buildings. The leading Portuguese architect at court, João Antunes, had died in 1712, leaving no rival of comparable stature, and the fact that Ludovice

had come from Rome with a knowledge of contemporary Italian art (and would bring, as Mafra reveals, Italian influences to Portuguese architecture) must have contributed decisively to the King's choice. Ludovice devised a rigorous system, essential for the speed with which the building was carried out (it was completed by 1735). He was assisted by the Milanese builder Carlos Baptista Garbo and, later, by his son Antonio, who took charge of some 30,000 craftsmen drawn from all over the kingdom to carry out the vast undertaking.

The building at Mafra, which occupies about 10,000 ha, is a symbol of the reign and absolute monarchy of John V, and it was paid for largely with gold from the colony of Brazil. The plan is in the form of a gridiron, formed by two rectangles. The ground floor of the principal rectangle contains the church, in the centre of the main façade, and the palace, whose rooms, surrounding courtyards, continue on the first floor. Behind this, the second rectangle houses the convent. The main long façade, facing west, measures about 220 m (see fig.). This public façade of church and palace is articulated to focus on the window of Benediction at the centre, which can be seen as emblematic of John V's unequivocal power. The architect's principal models for Mafra were selected from Rome. The front of the church suggests Carlo Maderno's St Peter's, the church towers S Agnese by Francesco Borromini, and the two flanking blocks the palace of Montecitorio by

Gianlorenzo Bernini and Carlo Fontana. Portuguese influence is seen in the end pavilions, which are reminiscent of Filippo Terzi's great 16th-century tower of the Casa da India, formerly adjacent to the Royal Palace in Lisbon (destr. 1755), and some elements of the church façade recall the church of S Vicente de Fora, Lisbon. The bulbous cupolas suggest south German architecture, and the building's general proportions are, perhaps, similar to the Dreifaltigkeitskirche, in Salzburg, by Johann Bernhard Fischer von Erlach.

The church at Mafra, consecrated in 1730, is in the form of a Latin cross crowned by a Baroque dome over the crossing. The interior is faced with local coloured marble, including the beautiful rose-coloured marble from nearby Pero-Pinheiro. Notable are the funerary Campo Santo Chapel, the chapel of Seven Altars with a Palladian loggia and the chapter house, one of the most interesting parts of Mafra, with its elliptical plan—a design rare in Portugal—and surprising effects of light filtering through windows of varied geometrical shapes. The high quality of the work set a standard, and Mafra became an important school for architects, sculptors and masons, contributing to an artistic renewal in Portugal that was brought about in part through Ludovice's central role.

At the same time Ludovice began work for the King on the renovation of the Romanesque cathedral of Évora. Between 1718 and 1746 he rebuilt the apse in order to meet the demands of the new fashion for Baroque. While part of the cost of the project was borne by the clergy of the cathedral, the work was largely paid for by the King. Ludovice opted for an Italian concept, similar to that at Mafra, and the apses of both buildings display an affinity in the use of coloured marble and their Baroque design. Court taste was thereby disseminated to southern Portugal, and Ludovice's role was fundamental both in this process of revitalization and in bringing Portuguese art into line with that in much of Europe.

2. OTHER WORKS. Ludovice's position as court architect was now firmly established, and after Mafra his name always appears in connection with the principal royal projects. In Lisbon he was responsible for improvements to the old Paço da Ribeira and the enlargement of the Royal Chapel, situated in the Terreiro do Paço, all since destroyed by the earthquake of 1755. This group of buildings had served since the 16th century as the residence of the kings of Portugal. Ludovice maintained the structure of the old building and added Italian forms of decoration using polychrome marble. Surviving descriptions of the Royal Chapel, though vague and fragmentary, emphasize the decorative richness of its altarpieces and three naves and the use of costly materials like gold, silver and precious stones. For the high altar, Ludovice followed the scheme at Mafra, with a vast painted panel flanked by columns in the Roman manner. He enriched the interior of the Royal Palace with marble decoration and laid out the gardens in terraces, exploiting Lisbon's hilly terrain alongside the River Tagus. A doorway that survived from the Royal Chapel is incorporated into the church of St Dominic, Lisbon, the interior of which Ludovice worked on, designing a new high altar (1748) in the Roman manner. Ludovice prepared plans in 1745 for a new patriarchal church in

Lisbon, which was intended to be built in Cotovia, at the edge of the Bairro Alto quarter, and which would have rivalled in scale St Peter's, Rome. This project was not carried out, probably due to the King's illness.

Ludovice's intense activity left him financially well provided. In 1727, following the practice of the nobility, who had revived the tradition, he built a small country house (the Quinta da Alfarrobeira, Benfica) on the outskirts of Lisbon. In 1747 he designed a city palace in the Rua S Pedro de Alcantara, which displays German influence and, with its vertical emphasis, is contrary to the more traditional horizontal lines prevalent in Portuguese architecture. In 1718 he became a member of the Brotherhood of St Luke, and in 1740 he was awarded the Military Order of Christ for his services to the Crown. The last important undertaking of John V's reign was a chapel dedicated to the King's patron saint, St John the Baptist, for the Jesuit church of S Roque, Lisbon. It was commissioned in 1742, in Rome, from Luigi Vanvitelli and Nicola Salvi. From correspondence between Rome and Lisbon it is clear that in Lisbon Ludovice assumed the role of 'inspector' for the work. He is shown as a staunch advocate of Baroque aesthetics in the face of Neo-classical proposals from the Italian artists. This is consistent with the work of an architect who was of fundamental importance for the development of the Baroque in Portugal. The new chapel was a compromise between different stylistic proposals and shows certain corrections imposed by Ludovice, such as the rectilinear balustrade, the royal coat of arms above the arch and the emblematic armillary sphere inlaid in the chapel floor.

On the death in 1750 of John V, the new monarch, Joseph (reg 1750–77), gave Ludovice the title of Arquitecto-Mor (Chief Architect), in recognition of his services to the court and also for his role, which had long-term importance, in training new artists at the so-called school of Mafra. The document that bestowed this exceptional honour declares that the position would cease after Ludovice's death and that it would never be bestowed again. This distinction crowned the career of the great 'Roman Frederico', as he was called. He was, by some accounts, a controversial person with a difficult temperament. The jealousy he aroused originated essentially from his rise from goldsmith to architect, a change of profession that many insisted was made possible only by the protection of the royal court. He was accused by the Swiss naturalist, Charles Frédric de Merveilleux, who was in Portugal from 1723 to 1726, of incompetence, which is said to have caused frequent demolitions during the building of Mafra. He is also recorded as a cultured man, versed in history, physics and mathematics. During his periods of absence from Mafra, João Pedro Ludovice, Ludovice's son by a first marriage in Naples, often stood in for his father, directing the building work, along with the military engineer Custódio Vieiera (d ?before 1747). The bejewelled gold monstrance of the Royal Chapel of Bemposta (Lisbon, Mus. N. A. Ant.) has been attributed to Ludovice.

BIBLIOGRAPHY
C. F. de Merveilleux: *Memórias instrutivas sobre Portugal* (Amsterdam, 1738)
C. Volkmar Machado: *Colecção de memórias* (Lisbon, 1823)

Sanches de Baena: *Apontamentos àcerca da biographia do notavel architecto Ludovice* (Lisbon, 1881)

S. Viterbo: *Dicionário dos architectos* (Lisbon, 1904)

R. Smith: 'An 18th-century Architect in Portugal', *A. Bull.*, 3 (1936)

Frazão de Vasconcelos: *A casa e a quinta de alfarrobeira dos Ludovices* (Lisbon, 1947)

——: *Novos subsídios para a biografia do Arquitecto Mor, João Frederico Ludovice* [New subsidies for the biography of chief architect, João Frederico Ludovice] (Lisbon, 1956)

H. Keilenbenz: *João Frederico Ludovice: O construtor do covento de Mafra* (Lisbon, 1959)

Ayres de Carvalho: *D. João V e a arte do seu tempo* (Lisbon, 1962)

——: 'As obras de Santo Antão e os seus artistas', *Belas A.*, 20 (1964)

J. Fernandes Pereira: *Arquitectura barroca em Portugal* (Lisbon, 1986)

JOSÉ FERNANDES PEREIRA

**Ludovisi.** Italian family of ecclesiastics, rulers, patrons and collectors. The family tradition asserts that its founder was Giovanni di Moterenzi (or Monterenzoli), who was based in a castle near Bologna. The family became noted in Bologna between 1458 and 1465, when Bertrando Ludovisi appeared in the *magistrature degli Anziani*. Girolamo Ludovisi, Bertrando's son, became a member of the Senate when it was created by Pope Julius II in 1502. Girolamo's grandson (1) Alessandro Ludovisi became Pope Gregory XV in 1621; his brother Orazio (*d* 1640) became a duke, and Orazio's son (2) Ludovico became a cardinal. The family continued from Ludovico's brother Niccolò, who inherited the principality of Piombino from his second wife, Polissena di Mendoza. Niccolò was a senator of Bologna and served in the army of Pope Innocent X against the Turks; after Innocent's death (1655), he went to Spain, where he died in 1664. His son Giambattista was also a senator of Bologna and served as Viceroy of the Indies for Philip IV, King of Spain. Giambattista died without heirs in 1699; his sister Ippolita married Gregorio Boncompagni. The Boncompagni–Ludovisi estate was dispersed in 1870; only the Casino and other garden structures remain.

BIBLIOGRAPHY

P. Litta: *Famiglie celebri italiane*, viii (Milan, 1852)

F. Haskell: *Patrons and Painters: A Study in the Relations between Italian Art and Society in the Age of the Baroque* (London, 1962; rev. New Haven and London, 1980)

**(1) Pope Gregory XV** [Alessandro Ludovisi] (*b* Bologna, 9 Jan 1554; elected 9 Feb 1621; *d* Rome, 8 July 1623). He was the son of Conte Pompeo Ludovisi and Camilla Bianchini, both of ancient Bolognese families. Between 1567 and 1571 he studied humanities, philosophy and theology at the Jesuits' Collegio Romano. He returned to Bologna to graduate in law (1575). Deciding on the priesthood, he went back to Rome; his legal expertise, coupled with diplomatic talent, became invaluable to successive popes. In 1612 Paul V appointed him Archbishop of Bologna but retained him in Rome to advise on crucial matters of international politics. He was made a cardinal in 1616 and elected pope five years later.

Gregory XV was the first pope to have had a Jesuit education. He showed his gratitude, as well as his appreciation of other Counter-Reformation orders, by canonizing Ignatius Loyola, Francis Xavier, Filippo Neri and Teresa of Avila (1622). Frail and elderly when he became pope, he nonetheless took firm control—rumours that the government was really in the hands of his nephew, (2) Ludovico Ludovisi, were greatly exaggerated.

As cardinal, Alessandro had already evinced an interest in artistic matters. On a visit to Bologna in 1620 he wrote to Ludovico in Rome, supporting Domenichino's financial claims against the Apostolic Camera. After Alessandro's election as pope, Domenichino hurried to Rome and was rewarded with the post of Papal Architect, even though he had yet to design a building. He also secured the commission to decorate the tribune of S Andrea della Valle, in place of the Parmesan Lanfranco (who was eventually allowed to paint the dome). The new pope continued existing work on his various palazzi, notably contributing two charming fountains to the gardens of the Palazzo Quirinale. He was chiefly concerned, however, with bringing to Rome artists from his native province, luring Guido Reni, albeit briefly, to paint his portrait (*c.* 1621; Corsham Court, Wilts) and more successfully the latest prodigy from the Carracci circle, Guercino. Apart from his renowned work for Cardinal Ludovico, Guercino was also awarded the coveted commission (again wrested from Lanfranco) to decorate the Benediction Loggia of St Peter's—although the Pope's death prevented its execution—and he painted an altarpiece of *St Petronilla* for the same church (1622–3; Rome, Mus. Capitolino). That altarpiece shows the first signs of the influence of Rome on Guercino's style: a turning away from lusciously tenebrist Baroque to increasingly frigid classicism. This was probably partly due to the influence of Monsignor Giovanni Battista Agucchi, private secretary to the Pope and later to Cardinal Ludovico, whose favourite painter was Domenichino and who had formulated specific theories of painting, embodied by Domenichino's most rigidly classical manner.

Although Agucchi's ideas were supported by the Cardinal and were to have lasting influence in Rome, there is no evidence that they interested Gregory XV. His taste was more fully represented by the worldly and eclectic Marchese Enzo Bentivoglio, who is said to have advised him on artistic matters. Certainly the Pope appreciated the work of Gianlorenzo Bernini, later to become anathema to the classicist camp. At this period, however, Bernini, after his triumphant series of early works for Scipione Borghese, was unrivalled as a sculptor in Rome, and even Cardinal Ludovico was eager to employ him. Bernini produced several busts of *Gregory XV*, in marble and bronze, and was knighted in reward (1621). In the same year the Pope appointed him principe of the Accademia di S Luca, an unprecedented honour for such a young artist. At the same time Gregory confirmed the statutes of the academy, thus underlining his intention that the revived institution should form an important part of the artistic life of the city, as indeed it was to do (*see* ROME, VI). An even more influential legacy of his pontificate, deriving from the sudden return to Rome of the Bolognese classicists of the Carracci tradition, was the rising tide of Baroque classicism, which eventually dominated the stylistic synthesis of the Late Baroque throughout Europe. Gregory himself was appropriately commemorated in a tomb in this style (1685; Rome, S Ignazio di Loyola). There is an oil portrait of *Gregory XV* by Ottavio Leoni in the Pantheon, Rome, and a portrait drawn in red, black and white chalk (London, BM) by the same artist (for illustration *see* LEONI, OTTAVIO).

BIBLIOGRAPHY
L. von Pastor: *History of the Popes*, xxvii, ed. E. Graf (London, 1938)
D. Mahon: *Studies in Seicento Art and Theory* (London, 1947)
D. Albrecht: *Die deutsche Politik Papst Gregors XV* (Munich, 1956)

**(2) Cardinal Ludovico Ludovisi** (*b* Bologna, 22 Oct 1595; *d* Rome, 18 Nov 1632). Nephew of (1) Gregory XV. Although his career as a collector was short, his collection of antique sculptures and contemporary paintings formed one of the most important of the 17th century. After studying law in Bologna, he went to Rome in 1619 and was made cardinal in 1621 on the election of his uncle as Pope Gregory XV, but he was able to enjoy this position for only two years. During these years he acquired the site and started the building of the Villa Ludovisi, Rome, and embarked on collecting on a large scale.

He acquired contemporary works by Bolognese artists and acknowledged masterpieces by such Venetian artists as Titian (*Worship of Venus* and *Bacchanal*; both 1518–19; Madrid, Prado), and Paolo Veronese (*Mary Magdalene*; Ottawa, N.G.). His commissions included works by Guido Reni, Domenichino (*Landscape with the Flight to Egypt*; Paris, Louvre) and Guercino (*St Jerome and the Angel*; Paris, Louvre). Guercino's *Aurora* (1621; *see* GUERCINO, fig. 2), a resolutely Baroque composition commissioned for the ceiling of the Casino of the Villa Ludovisi, is considered to be his masterpiece. Ludovico employed ALESSANDRO ALGARDI in 1625 to restore his collection of antique sculptures, and it was at the instance of Ludovico that Domenichino was awarded the commission to paint frescoes (1622–7) in S Andrea della Valle (*see* DOMENICHINO, fig. 4).

Ludovico was the patron of a new church for the Jesuit Order dedicated to S Ignatius; he had a particular affection for the Order, having been educated by them. Work began in 1626 to the design of a Jesuit priest, Orazio Grassi, but under the guidance of an architectural committee that included Carlo Maderno and Domenichino (who would have been Ludovisi's preferred choice). After Ludovico's death, the collection (recorded in an inventory of 1633) was dispersed: a large part went to the collections of Philip IV, King of Spain, through Ludovico's brother and heir Niccolò, and to Louis XIII, King of France, and Cardinal Mazarin. Approximately one-third of the collection has been identified. Ludovico is portrayed with his uncle in a double portrait by Domenichino (1621–3; Béziers, Mus. B.-A.).

BIBLIOGRAPHY
R. Wittkower: *Art and Architecture in Italy 1600–1750*, Pelican Hist. A. (Harmondsworth, 1958, rev. 1991)
K. Garas: 'The Ludovisi Collection of Pictures in 1633', *Burl. Mag.*, cix (1967), pp. 287–9, 339–47

□

**Ludwig I**, King of Bavaria. *See* WITTELSBACH, §III(3).

**Ludwig II**, King of Bavaria. *See* WITTELSBACH, §III(4).

**Ludwig IV** [Ludwig the Bavarian], Holy Roman Emperor and Duke of Bavaria. *See* WITTELSBACH, §I(1).

**Ludwig, Peter (Ernst Rudolf Georg)** (*b* Koblenz, 9 July 1925). German collector and patron. In 1945 he studied law at Bonn University and from 1946 to 1950 art history, archaeology, ancient history and philosophy at Mainz University. In 1950 he wrote his doctoral dissertation on *Das Menschenbild Picassos als Ausdruck eines generationsmässig bedingten Lebensgefühls.* The following year he married Irene Monheim. In his commercial career he began as managing director of the firm of Leonhard Monheim in 1952 and subsequently became chairman of various companies, such as Leonhard Monheim AG and Ludwig Schokolade GmbH, both in Aachen. In 1956 he became a founder-member of the Friends of the Schnütgen-Museum in Cologne; in 1957 he was made president of the Aachen Museumsverein and editor of the *Aachener Kunstblätter*; in 1972 he became a member of the purchasing commission of the Kunstsammlung Nordrhein–Westfalen in Düsseldorf. He was also a member of the council of the Museum of Modern Art, New York, in 1971.

Ludwig's interests as a collector were initially very eclectic. He acquired Greek and Italian terracottas; pre-Columbian art; medieval sculpture, enamelwork, textiles and manuscripts; faience, tiles and porcelain made after 1950; examples of Pop art, Minimal art, Op art and Nouveau Réalisme. His donations included 284 pictures and sculptures to the city of Cologne in 1976 (from 1986 in the Museum Ludwig, with the 20th-century section of the Wallraf-Richartz-Museum); 148 works of early art to the Suermondt-Ludwig-Museum, Aachen, in 1977; and 161 works to the Österreichische Ludwig-Stiftung für Kunst und Wissenschaft in Vienna, which he founded in 1981. He also donated 199 works from Antiquity to the Antikenmuseum Basel und Sammlung Ludwig, 6000 tiles to the Couven-Museum, Aachen, and 183 objects to the Rautenstrauch-Joest-Museum in Cologne, as well as founding the Ludwig-Stiftung für Kunst und Internationale Verständigung GmbH in Aachen and the Ludwig Institut für Kunst der DDR in Oberhausen.

BIBLIOGRAPHY
R. Speck: *Peter Ludwig Sammler* (Cologne, 1986)

INGRID SEVERIN

**Ludwigsburg.** German city in Baden-Württemberg and residence of the duchy of Württemberg from 1724 to 1733 and again from 1756 to 1775.

1. HISTORY AND URBAN DEVELOPMENT. The Erlachhof, a 17th-century hunting-lodge, was the site of the Schloss and later the city of Ludwigsburg; work to develop the complex began in 1704, when Eberhard-Ludwig, Duke of Württemberg, employed Philipp Jenisch (1671–1736) to design the new Schloss. The unfinished single range was taken over in 1706 and redesigned by Johann Friedrich Nette (1672–1714), who added two free-standing wings, thus creating a *cour d'honneur* of rather Italianate appearance, with banded ground floors and one-and-a-half storeys with smooth walls and flat roofs.

To the west of the Schloss, and in no axial connection, a new city was founded in 1709, which was the first in Germany without fortification. The centre is the rectangular marketplace, lined with arcaded houses and two churches. On the west side is the Protestant church (1718–26) by the Italian architect Giuseppe Donato Frisoni (1683–1735), with a twin-spired façade; directly opposite is the Roman Catholic (originally Protestant Reformed)

Ludwigsburg, aerial view from the north showing the Favorite pavilion at the bottom and the Schloss beyond, with the old *corps de logis* by Nette and the long wing of Frisoni's new *corps de logis* at the far end

sloping grounds, a terraced garden was laid out to the north, which included the Favorite, a large garden pavilion by Frisoni based on an idea by Nette (see fig.), and a parterre to the south in front of the new *corps de logis*. The interiors were richly decorated with sculpture, stucco and frescoes, and a Spiegelkabinett had been installed in 1713 in the old *corps de logis*. Other artists employed included the sculptor Diego Francesco Carlone, his brother Carlo Innocenzo Carlone and the painters Pietro Scotti ( *fl* 1703–47) and Luca Antonio Colomba. The interiors were virtually finished by 1734; Diego Francesco Carlone's sculpture and Frisoni's stuccowork are of the highest quality.

After the death of Duke Eberhard-Ludwig (1733) the official residence was moved back to Stuttgart; Ludwigsburg was used by Charles-Eugene, Duke of Württemberg, as a summer residence after 1744 and as his main residence between 1765 and 1775. Alterations were carried out after 1758 to some of the interiors by PHILIPPE DE LA GUÉPIÈRE in an elegant, French-influenced Rococo; the Duke's apartment on the second floor of the new *corps de logis* still exists. A new design for the garden was carried out after 1760, and the enlargement of the city, mainly to the south, was started.

In the final phase of interior decoration under Frederick II, Duke of Württemberg (1754–1816), who became King of Württemberg (*reg* 1806–16), all the staterooms on the first floor of the new *corps de logis*, the theatre and some other rooms were redesigned by NIKOLAUS FRIEDRICH VON THOURET, who, between 1805 and 1812, created some of the most important Neo-classical interiors, with furniture in the French Empire style. The Schloss was used throughout the 19th century and early 20th as a summer residence without undergoing any further major alterations.

BIBLIOGRAPHY

J. Nette: *Vues et parties principales de Louis-Bourg* (Augsburg, 1712)
D. Frisoni: *Vues de la residence ducale de Louisbourg* (Augsburg, 1727)
W. Fleischhauer: *Barock in Baden-Württemberg* (Stuttgart, 1958)
K. Merten: *Schloss Ludwigsburg* (Munich, 1977/R Munich and Berlin, 1984)
J. Zahlten: 'Der grosse Saal im Ordensbau des Ludwigsburger Schlosses', *Jb. Kstsamml. Baden-Württemberg*, xxii (1985), pp. 70–88
R. Weber-Stephan: 'Neue Forschungen zu Schloss Favorite in Ludwigsburg', *Jb. Kstsamml. Baden-Württemberg*, xxvii (1990), pp. 72–90
U. Esbach: *Die Ludwigsburger Schlosskapelle: Eine evangelische Hofkirche des Barock. Studien zu ihrer Gestalt und Rekonstruktion ihres theologischen Programmes*, 3 vols (Stuttgart, 1991)

JARL KREMEIER

church (1727–32). The Duke also commissioned 12 palatial houses for administrators of the Duchy's 12 districts; 8 were executed.

After Nette's death, Frisoni added two slightly set back, free-standing wings to the Schloss in the same axis, which doubled the size of the courtyard. The passages between the old and new wings led on either side to a domed pavilion, with three apses on a trefoil plan behind the wing; the court chapel inside the eastern domed pavilion was lavishly decorated, with frescoes (1720–21) by Carlo Innocenzo Carlone and Luca Antonio Colomba (1661–1737). In 1724 the Duke moved the official residence from Stuttgart to Ludwigsburg, and the Schloss was further enlarged: Frisoni added two long galleries, on the same axis but set back, leading to a new *corps de logis*, thus closing the courtyard; the galleries comprised a long range of 33 bays, three-storey to the courtyard and two-storey to the garden because of the sloping ground. After 20 years of unsystematic planning the result was a series of ranges and pavilions unified by architectural detail and colour around a huge courtyard of 160×60 m. Using the

2. CENTRE OF CERAMICS PRODUCTION. From 1724 attempts were made to produce hard-paste porcelain in Ludwigsburg at the factory of Charles-Eugene, Duke of Württemberg. Production, however, did not commence until after the arcanist Joseph Jakob Ringler (1730–1804) had taken over as technical director in January 1759. In the same year Gottlieb Friedrich Riedel (1724–84), who had previously worked at Meissen (1743–57), Höchst and Frankenthal (1757–9), was appointed director of painting (1759–79) and put in charge of the secret colour formulae. He was responsible for the painting of the wares and supervised such artists as the landscape and animal painter Johann Friedrich Steinkopf (1737–1825), the chinoiserie and landscape painter Andreas Philipp Oettner, the bird

painter Johann Jakob Höflich and the flower painters Friedrich Kirschner (1748–89) and Christian Gotthelf Grossmann ( *fl* 1775–86). Riedel was probably also responsible for the designs of such wares as those with an all-over relief scale pattern (e.g. teapot, 1768–70; Copenhagen, Kstindustmus.), table-services and luxury items.

The Duke was particularly fond of figures, and the factory is most famous for the variety and quality of its production. Allegories of the Senses, Months and Seasons were modelled as single figures, pairs or groups on rocaille bases. Among those represented are courtiers, peasants, actors, dancers, musicians, children, putti and animals as well as mythological and historical figures. The most outstanding modellers from this period were Johann Göz ( *d* 1792) and Johann Jakob Louis (1703–72), who modelled parrots, animals and genre figures, Johann Carl Vogelmann, who went to Kelsterbach in 1764, and Joseph Nees ( *fl* 1759–75); 60 different models by Nees are known, including a range of dancers. The most famous modellers working in an early Neo-classical style included the sculptor Christian Friedrich Wilhelm Beyer, who was best known for his series of musicians (e.g. cellist, 1765–6; Hamburg, Mus. Kst & Gew.), the modeller of Chinamen Joseph Weinmüller (1743–*c*. 1812) and the sculptor Valentin Sonnenschein, who created gods and goddesses, philosophers and groups depicting bloodletting, fortune-telling and shaving. The figures of Pierre François Lejeune (1721–90) and Adam Bauer (*c*. 1743–*c*. 1780) combined Baroque and Neo-classical stylistic elements, thereby achieving some very lively effects that ran counter to the fashionable trend. After 1790 the factory began steadily to decline; Philipp Jakob Scheffauer (1756–1808) and the sculptor Johann Heinrich Dannecker created some Neoclassical figures for a diminishing market, but the factory closed in 1824.

BIBLIOGRAPHY

H. Christ: *Ludwigsburger Porzellanfiguren* (Berlin, 1921)

P. Lahnstein and M. Landenberger: *Das Ludwigsburger Porzellan und seine Zeit* (Stuttgart, 1978)

WALTER SPIEGL

**Lufi, Anton (Mati)** (*b* Pljevlja, Montenegro, 6 Feb 1907; *d* Tiranë, 24 July 1980). Albanian architect, urban planner and teacher. He attended secondary school in Sarajevo (1922–6), continuing his studies (1928–31) at the Czech Technical University, Prague, and completing them at the Deutsche Technische Hochschule, Prague, where he graduated as an architect. In 1936 he began work at the Technical Bureau of the town hall of Tiranë. His first projects were villas and a few public buildings, characterized by a lyrical functionalism, for example the Vjosa Hotel (1942) and the Adriatiku Hotel (1943), both in Tiranë. More important work began with the establishment of the government run Projekti enterprise, where Lufi was head (1947–61) of the department of Architecture, Urban Planning and Housing. In 1952 he designed plans for the development of the cities of Permet, Cërrik and Pogradec, and he became one of the founders of 20th-century Albanian urban planning, introducing standard plans for housing complexes, stimulating research into exterior decoration and bringing in industrial construction methods. Lufi was also distinguished as a designer of public buildings, which reflect not only his search for a functional

compositional unity, as in the former Central Committee Building of the Albanian Labour Party (1953), Tiranë, but also his study of national style, e.g. the Migjeni Theatre (1957), Shkodër. As head (1961–7) of the Technical Branch of the Ministry of Construction and later (from 1967) as manager of Studio no. 2 in the Institute of Urban Planning and Architectural Studies and Design, Tiranë, he was mainly engaged in the study and design of eight- to nine-storey dwellings and public facilities on steep terrain, such as the Turizmi Hotel (1972), Sarandë.

UNPUBLISHED SOURCES

Tiranë, U., Archv Chair Archit., MS. (*Historia e Arkitektures Shqiptare* [History of Albanian architecture])

BIBLIOGRAPHY

S. Mosko: 'Për një nivel më të lartë në krijimtarinë tonë urbanistike dhe arkitektonike' [On a higher level of our urban planning and architecture], *Nëntori*, 6 (1971), pp. 5–29

GJERGJ FRASHËRI

**Lugano.** Swiss town in the Italian-speaking canton of Ticino, located on the north-west shore of Lake Lugano between Monte Brè and Monte San Salvatore. In AD 818 it was referred to as 'Luano' (see Anderes), and from the late 13th century it was involved in the wars between Como and Milan and the power struggle between the Ghibellines and the Guelphs. In the 15th century it belonged to the Duchy of Milan, and it was conquered in turn by the French (1499) and the Swiss (1512). Until 1798 it was under the joint jurisdiction of the 12 Confederate Regions of Switzerland, and from 1827 to 1869 it alternated with Bellinzona and Locarno as capital of the canton of Ticino, which had been established in 1803. With the opening of the Gotthard railway in 1882, Lugano developed into an international tourist centre; as a result of the prosperity this engendered, within a few decades its essentially medieval character was transformed into that of a sophisticated town with shops, offices and fine hotels. Between 1864 and 1920 the lakefront was gradually developed into an area of piers, promenades and gardens, and the Parco Civico was created on the site of a fortress that had been dismantled in 1517. After rapid but controlled development in the first half of the 20th century, the building boom of the 1960s caused the town to overspill its boundaries. As a result, the most important pieces of earlier architecture are isolated among numerous late 19th- and 20th-century structures.

S Lorenzo Cathedral, Lugano's principal church, is situated above the Old Town, and during the 13th and 14th centuries it was converted from an earlier Romanesque building. The façade (1517–*c*. 1580) is regarded as one of the finest achievements of the Italian Renaissance in Switzerland. The interior, altered in the Baroque style in the 17th and 18th centuries, contains frescoes from various periods, such as the *Glorification of St Lawrence* (1764) by the brothers Giuseppe Antonio Torricelli (1710–1808) and Giovanni Antonio Torricelli (*b* 1716) from Lugano. The monumental *Crucifixion* (1529–32) by BERNARDINO LUINI, made for the rood screen of S Maria degli Angioli, a church dedicated in 1515, is the most significant Renaissance fresco in Switzerland. The 17th-century churches of S Antonio Abate and S Carlo Borromeo have several works by GIUSEPPE ANTONIO PETRINI (e.g. *Glorification of St Anthony*, *c.* 1734, in S Antonio Abate).

Three palazzi of the first half of the 18th century, connected with the influential Riva family of Lugano, are examples of secular Baroque architecture. One of them, the Palazzo Riva, is now the Banca della Svizzera Italiana. Both the Municipio (1844–5) by GIACOMO MORAGLIA and the Villa Ciani (*c.* 1840) by Luigi Clerichetti are Classical Revival buildings; the latter houses the Museo Civico di Belle Arti's collection of the art of Ticino from the 17th to the 20th century. The head office of the Banca del Gottardo (1982–8) by MARIO BOTTA is one of his several commercial and residential buildings and an outstanding example of 20th-century architecture. Until 1992 the Villa Favorita in Castagnola, near Lugano, housed most of the important THYSSEN-BORNEMISZA collection; some pieces remain, though the majority of the collection was transferred to Madrid.

BIBLIOGRAPHY

E. Pometta, V. Chiesa and V. Maestrini: *Storia di Lugano*, 2 vols (Lugano, 1975)
B. Anderes: *Kunstführer Kanton Tessin* (Wabern, 1977); It. trans. as *Guida d'arte della Svizzera italiana* (Porza-Lugano, 1980)
A. Hauser: 'Lugano', *Inventar der neueren Schweizer Architektur, 1850–1920*, vi (Berne, 1991), pp. 205–355
M. Kahn-Rossi: *Museo Cantonale d'Arte: Lugano*, Musei Svizzeri, iv (Geneva, 1994) [Eng., Fr. and Ger. text]

CHRISTIAN BÜHRLE

**Lugano, Giroldo da.** *See* GIROLDO DA COMO.

**Lugano, Tommaso da.** *See* LOMBARDO, TOMMASO.

**Luginbühl, Bernhard** (*b* Berne, 16 Feb 1929). Swiss sculptor, film maker and writer. Initially he worked in stone and wood but later turned to iron. His exhibits at the first Swiss open-air sculpture exhibition in Biel in 1954 earned him official selection for the Venice Biennale of 1956. His work then developed through series and such recurring themes as *Aggression* and *Searchlights*. His use of animal metaphor became established in *Bulldogs* (1963–4), *Elephants* (1964–6) and *Giraffes* (1968), which reflected the sense of humour also found in *Sapperlot*, his autobiography, which he executed (as he did his numerous films) in collaboration with the photographer Leonardo Bezzola (*b* 1929). In heavy industrial machinery Luginbühl discovered the 'poetics' of the scrap heap: he endowed giant blades and fins, components of turbines, massive girders and bolts with a slow but inexorable movement. *Cyclops* (1967; Hamburg, Ksthalle), *Pegasus* (1966–8), *Atlas* and *Sisyphus* (1970–77) revitalized ancient myth by means of an imaginary symbolism based on the archaeology of mechanization. His use of static machines tended towards gigantism, as in *Tell* (exh. 1967, Montreal, Universal Exhibition) and *Osaka Punch* (exh. 1970, Osaka, Universal Exhibition), even before he began working, in 1972, on the *Milly Monster* (Paris) with Jean Tinguely and Niki de Saint-Phalle, as well as on the *Crocodrome* (1977), an installation for the Centre Beaubourg, Paris, with Tinguely, Saint-Phalle and Daniel Spoerri. In 1974 Luginbühl and Tinguely set fire to a large sculpture in wood, entitled *Wrath*, as a protest against the destruction of the environment; the last explosive happening in the *Wrath* series took place in 1983. By the 1990s his sculpture in wood,

for which he used assemblage techniques, acquired an increasing importance, side by side with his imposing works in iron, such as *Helvetia* (1991; temporary installation, Lausanne).

WRITINGS
*Sapperlot: Der Eisenplastiks Bernhard Luginbühl* (Berne, 1967)

BIBLIOGRAPHY
*Bernhard Luginbühl, Figuren, 1947–1989* (exh. cat., Berne, Reithalle and Kstmus., 1989) [incl. bibliog., filmography and list of exhs]
P.-A. Jaccard: 'La Génération du fer', *La Sculpture*, A. Helv., vii (Disentis, 1992), pp. 279–82                                           □

**Lugt, Frits** [Frederik] **(Johannes)** (*b* Amsterdam, 4 May 1884; *d* Paris, 15 July 1970). Dutch collector, connoisseur and art historian. He was the son of Frederik Johannes Lugt, an engineer, and Jeanette Petronella Verschuur, who was related to the horse painter Wouterus Verschuur. By the age of eight, Frits had compiled a catalogue of his 'rarities' (including a shell collection) entitled *Museum Lugtius*. He attended Hendrik de Keyser's drawing school in Amsterdam and, from the age of ten, regularly visited the Rijksmuseum, especially the museum's print room, where, owing to the lack of a printed catalogue of the Dutch drawings, he began to describe the sheets himself (by late 1899 he had completed 955 entries, with biographies, and had reached Jordaens). At the time of the 1898 Rembrandt exhibition, he produced an illustrated biography of the artist; the manuscript was seen by the director of the Amsterdam auction-house Frederik Muller for whom Lugt went to work after a visit to London in 1901, when he learnt about English museums and art dealers. Between 1901 and 1915 he catalogued numerous collections for sale, including those of Steengracht and Heseltine, and organized and catalogued exhibitions (e.g. van Goyen and Rembrandt), as well as writing several articles.

Lugt married Jacoba Klever (1889–1969) in 1910 and left Muller in 1915. His *Wandelingen met Rembrandt* appeared in the same year and *Le Portrait miniature* in 1917. Meanwhile he was researching into the origin and significance of collectors' marks and, while acting as an adviser and agent for collectors, began to assemble his own collection of drawings and prints. His *Redderen van den nationale kunstboedel* ('Administration of the national art collections'), which appeared in 1918, was strongly critical of current Dutch museum policy and made it virtually impossible for him to pursue an administrative career in art in his native country.

Lugt's great reference work, *Les Marques de collections*, appeared in 1921; in it he laid the foundations of the history of collecting prints and drawings, and the following year he was commissioned to catalogue the northern school drawings in the principal public institutions in Paris. From 1927 to 1968 nine volumes appeared, and, with their concise but complete descriptions and categorization of the artists and drawings, the catalogues became the basis for all later research. Lugt travelled throughout Europe for the Paris catalogue and at the same time, with the help of assistants, began an inventory of sales catalogues, which resulted in four large volumes (the last appeared posthumously in 1987). He donated his sale catalogues and collection of reproductions to the Rijksbureau voor Kunsthistorische Documentatie (R.K.D.) in The Hague, founded in 1930, to which he also lent his large art library. In 1932 he moved to The Hague, taking two large houses on the Lange Vijverberg. In 1935 his wife inherited a large fortune, which enabled them greatly to extend their own collection, although the core works were already in Lugt's possession. His phenomenal visual memory and sharp eye gave him a great advantage when, during the 1920s, he bought from the many collections that came on to the market. His purchases included a small, outstanding collection of English portrait miniatures, Flemish and Dutch paintings, antiquarian books and furniture, Chinese porcelain, Asian miniatures, Egyptian and Greek antiquities and some artists' letters. But the emphasis was on European prints and drawings, particularly 16th- and 17th-century Flemish and Dutch masters, with Rembrandt as his favourite.

At the outbreak of World War II, Lugt sent the most valuable of his drawings and prints to Switzerland by registered post. The Lugt family later moved to the USA via Switzerland and settled in Oberlin, OH. Lugt travelled, gave lectures and collected a number of publications, which he donated to the R.K.D. on his return to the Netherlands in 1945. The Lugt family decided it wanted its collection to remain intact for posterity (the antiquarian books had been stolen), and it established the Fondation Custodia in Basle in 1947. In 1953, in cooperation with the Dutch government, the Institut Néerlandais, a cultural foundation, was established by the Lugts at 121, Rue de Lille, Paris, to house the collection. The Institut Néerlandais was officially opened in 1957, and Lugt and his wife devoted themselves to the development of this cultural centre, while he continued to pursue his catalogue of the Louvre collection and the enrichment of his own collection.

WRITINGS

*Wandelingen met Rembrandt in en om Amsterdam* [Walks with Rembrandt in and around Amsterdam] (Amsterdam, 1915; Ger. trans., Berlin, 1920)
*Le Portrait miniature: Illustré par la collection de S M. la Reine des Pays-Bas* (Amsterdam, 1917)
*Les Marques de collections de dessins et d'estampes* (Amsterdam, 1921); *Supplément* (The Hague, 1956)
*Les Dessins des écoles du nord de la collection Dutuit au Musée des beaux-arts de la ville de Paris* (Paris, 1927)
*Musée du Louvre, inventaire général des dessins des écoles du nord: Ecole hollandaise*, 3 vols (Paris, 1929–33)
'Beiträge zu dem Katalog der niederländischen Handzeichnungen in Berlin', *Jb. Preuss. Ktssamml.*, lii (1931), pp. 36–80
'Italiaansche kunstwerken in Nederlandsche verzamelingen van vroeger tijden', *Oud-Holland*, liii (1936), pp. 97–135
with J. Vallery-Radot: *Bibliothèque nationale, Cabinet des estampes: Inventaire général des dessins des écoles du nord* (Paris, 1936)
*Répertoire des catalogues de ventes publiques*, 3 vols (The Hague, 1938–64)
*Musée du Louvre, inventaire général des dessins des écoles du nord: Ecole flamande*, 2 vols (Paris, 1949)
*Ecole nationale supérieure des beaux-arts, inventaire général des dessins des écoles du nord: Ecole hollandaise* (Paris, 1950)
*Musée du Louvre, inventaire général des dessins des écoles du nord: Maîtres des anciens Pays-Bas nés avant 1550* (Paris, 1968)

BIBLIOGRAPHY

*BWN*
M. F. Hennus: 'Frits Lugt: Kunstvorser, Kunstkeurder, Kunstgaarder' [Frits Lugt: art researcher, connoisseur, protector], *Mdbl. Beeld. Kst.*, xxvi (1950), pp. 77–140
J. G. van Gelder, H. Gerson and others: *Frits Lugt, zijn leven en zijn verzamelingen, 1949–1964* (The Hague, 1964)
J. G. van Gelder: 'In Memoriam Frits Lugt', *Jb. Kon. Ned. Akad. Wet.* (1971), pp. 261–7; also in *Flemish Drawings of the Seventeenth Century from the Collection of Frits Lugt* (exh. cat., London, V&A; Paris, Fond.

Custodia, Inst. Néer.; Berne, Kstmus.; Brussels, Bib. Royale Albert 1er; 1972), pp. ix–xv
M. Sérullaz: 'Hommage à Frits Lugt', *Rev. Louvre*, xxi (1971), pp. 39–44, 51–4 [with a complete bibliog.]
D. Sutton, ed.: 'Treasures from the Collection of Frits Lugt at the Institut Néerlandais, Paris', *Apollo*, civ/176 (1976), pp. 242–305; civ/177 (1976), pp. 332–404 [issue devoted to the Lugt collection]; as book (London, 1976)

MÀRIA VAN BERGE-GERBAUD

**Luhn, Joachim** (*b c.* 1640; *d* Hamburg, 4 July 1717). German painter. He is thought to have studied in the Netherlands, as a pupil of Adriaen Backer (*fl* 1635/6; *d* 1684), although the influence of the late work of Ferdinand Bols (1616–80) is also apparent in his portrait of *Georg Hertel* (1672; Brunswick, Herzog Anton Ulrich-Mus.). In 1672 he visited Brunswick and painted the portrait of *Henning Luhn* (Hamburg, Ksthalle). In 1673 he became a citizen of Hamburg, where he entered the painters' guild and married Hanna Margarete Weyer (*d* 1730), daughter of the painter Jacob Weyer (1623–70). In 1681 he collaborated with Erich Schröder (*fl* 1659–81) in executing ten paintings of *Old Testament Kings* (ex-Rathaus, Hamburg) and also painted a large *View of Hamburg* (4.76×1.8 m; ex-Rathaus and Jakobikirche, Hamburg). From 1689 to 1692 he served as court painter to the dukes of Brunswick at Schloss Salzdahlum, then returned to Hamburg to head the painters' guild. In 1714 and 1715 he painted several coats of arms for Hamburg Council's *Kammerei-Wappenbuch*.

BIBLIOGRAPHY

E. Rump: *Lexikon der bildenden Künstler Hamburgs, Altonas und der näheren Umgebund* (Hamburg, 1912, 2/1980)
H. Röver: *Die Hamburgischen Maler Otto Wagenfeldt und Joachim Luhn und ihre Schüler* (Hamburg, 1926)

KARIN KLEINEWEFERS

**Lu Hsün.** *See* LU XUN.

**Luick.** *See* LÜCKE.

**Luigi Primo.** *See* PRIMO, LUIGI.

**Luini, Bernardino** (*b* ?Luini, *c.* 1480–85; *d* ?Lugano, before 1 July 1532). Italian painter and draughtsman. He was one of the generation of Lombard painters active around 1500 who, influenced by Leonardo and Raphael, blended High Renaissance innovations with indigenous Milanese elements to create a Lombard Renaissance style. Luini's paintings were extremely popular with both collectors and critics from *c.* 1790 to the end of the 19th century. This widespread popularity, however, had unfortunate consequences: many of his frescoes were detached from their original settings, many of the panel paintings were transferred to canvas and other works were heavily restored. As a result few survive in a good state. About 700 works are attributed to Luini, but many of these attributions are over optimistic. An additional problem is the scarcity of documentation on the painter's life and work.

1. Life and work. 2. Critical reception and posthumous reputation.

1. LIFE AND WORK. According to Lomazzo (1585, p. 421), both Luini and Gaudenzio Ferrari were taught by Gian Stefano Scotto, an obscure artist who worked at Milan Cathedral from 1485 to 1520 but to whom no works

can be securely attributed. Vasari mentioned Luini among Leonardo's Milanese followers. Lomazzo (1585, 1590) further said that Luini's son Aurelio possessed a small book (untraced) containing about 50 caricatures drawn in red chalk by Leonardo and also owned Leonardo's cartoon of the *Virgin and Child with St Anne and the Infant St John* (London, N.G.), which he may have bought from the estate of Francesco Melzi. Bernardino Luini painted a copy (Milan, Ambrosiana) of Leonardo's cartoon, suggesting that there was probably some connection between the two artists. Quotations from Leonardo can be recognized in many of Luini's works: the head of the Virgin in the *Virgin and Child of the Rose Garden* (Milan, Brera) is very Leonardesque, the various versions of *Salome with the Head of the Baptist* (Boston, MA, Mus. F.A.; Paris, Louvre) show the use of Leonardo's *sfumato*, while the *Christ Blessing* (Milan, Ambrosiana) is based on a compositional device of Leonardo's. Several of Luini's works were formerly attributed to Leonardo himself.

Cesariano mentioned that Luini visited Rome but failed to give the date. Luini would seem to have been familiar with Raphael's Roman paintings and adopted his innovations in terms of design and the depiction of space. He seems to have known Peruzzi's frescoes in the Bishop's Palace at Ostia and in the Villa Farnesina in Rome and also Sodoma's frescoes in the monastery of Monteoliveto Maggiore, outside Siena, and at S Anna in Camprena, Siena (Binaghi Olivari, 1985). Critics have rightly stressed Luini's stylistic relationship with Milanese painters such as Foppa, Bergognone, Solario, Bramantino and Zenale. They have also traced the roots of his classicism to Florentine and Venetian influences, even postulating that Luini was in contact with Venetian culture on the assumption that it was he who signed himself 'Bernardinus Mediolanensis' on the *Virgin and Child with Saints* (1507; Paris, Mus. Jacquemart-André); however, this painting is manifestly not the work of Luini and stylistically would seem to be of Veronese origin.

The earliest known work by Luini is the polyptych with the *Virgin and Child*, the *Annunciation*, *God the Father* and various saints in the parish church of Maggianico, Como, painted shortly after 1510. Its vertical, multi-partite format is retardataire, but the figures show that Luini's style was already fully developed. The fresco of the *Virgin and Child Enthroned with Musician Angels* painted in 1512 in the abbey of Chiaravalle, near Milan, is also conventional in design but has an attractive landscape setting. No earlier works can be securely attributed to Luini. The altarpiece of the *Virgin and Child with SS James and Philip and Members of the Busti Family* (Milan, Brera), dated 1515 and often attributed to him, cannot be included in his oeuvre and is stylistically closer to Zenale.

The small chapel of the Sacrament in S Giorgio al Palazzo, Milan, was entirely decorated by Luini in 1516, with frescoes on the walls of scenes from the *Passion* and an altarpiece of the *Deposition* (see fig.). Against a dark ground, 16 mourners grieve over the body of Christ, laid horizontally in the foreground. Although the facial expressions owe much to Leonardo, the hieratic gestures and the suppression of extraneous detail are Luini's own contribution. In 1516–17 he executed the frescoes and panel paintings for the new church of the monastery of S Marta,

of which some fresco fragments and the altarpiece of the *Annunciation* (all Milan, Brera) survive. The *Annunciation* combines an ambitious, classicizing architectural setting with a flurry of quintessentially Lombard angels.

In the decade from 1510 to 1520 Luini was apparently fully aware of the innovations of Leonardo and Raphael and was able to apply them in part to his own work, but his style remained archaic in his use of rigid gestures, which emphasize the symbolic significance of each figure but fail to characterize the individuals or unite the composition. The curious mixture of the innovative and the archaic is also present in the work of several of Luini's Lombard contemporaries; it would seem to have been unique to the Duchy of Milan around this time.

The frescoes of scenes from the *Life of St Joseph* (Milan, Brera) from S Maria della Pace can be dated *c.* 1520–21; the fresco of the *Virgin and Child with SS Anthony Abbot and Barbara* (Milan, Brera) is dated 1521 and the fresco of *Christ Crowned with Thorns* (Milan, Ambrosiana) was painted between October 1521 and March 1522 for the oratory of S Corona, Milan. For Gerolamo Rabia, Luini frescoed two buildings, a palazzo near S Sepolcro in Milan and a country house, the Villa Pelucca, at Sesto San Giovanni, near Monza. The frescoes were later detached, and only fragments of each cycle survive. Those for the palazzo, probably executed between 1521 and 1523, illustrated the stories of *Cephalus and Procris* and of *Europa* (Washington, DC, N.G.A.; Berlin, Bodemus.). The more extensive frescoes for the Villa Pelucca (?1524) included a chapel dedicated to St Catherine, a large saloon decorated with scenes from the book of Exodus and smaller rooms with stories from Ovid (fragments in Milan, Brera). These are decorative narrative scenes in landscape settings; the colour is light and fresh, as in the *Gathering of Manna*, but in treatment and style the frescoes look back to the 15th century.

Luini worked on three separate fresco campaigns in S Maurizio, Milan. He frescoed scenes from the *Passion* and saints for Alessandro Bentivoglio and his wife, Ippolita Sforza, probably *c.* 1513–15, and for Giovanni Paolo and Violante Sforza da Caravaggio he painted the *Martyrdom of St Maurice* and saints and donors in 1522–4 (Binaghi Olivari, 1979). These frescoes were painted on both sides of the transverse chancel arch. Finally, in 1530, he frescoed the *Flagellation* and scenes from the *Life of St Catherine* in the Besozzi Chapel.

Another important fresco campaign was the scenes from the *Life of the Virgin* (1525) in the sanctuary of S Maria dei Miracoli, Saronno. The combination of severe classicizing architecture and solemn, idealized figures in the *Marriage of the Virgin* and the soaring architecture, freely painted landscape and fresh colour of the *Presentation in the Temple* make this cycle one of the high points in Lombard Renaissance art. In 1531 Luini received payment for further frescoes in the sanctuary, on the ceiling of the chapel of the Last Supper (now badly damaged) and four saints on the end walls of the nave.

The gigantic fresco of the *Crucifixion* (1529–32) in S Maria degli Angioli, Lugano, is a work of great stylistic and compositional novelty. Behind the crosses Luini introduced the complete story of the *Passion* in a series of small scenes set in a continuous landscape. The visual

Bernardino Luini: *Deposition*, panel, 2.07×1.75 m, 1516 (Milan, S Giorgio al Palazzo)

unity of this complex work is maintained by the simplicity of the forms. Situated on the transverse arch at the church's crossing, it visually overwhelms the congregation, impressing on them the significance of the Passion. In the same church he frescoed a *Virgin and Child with the Infant St John* in 1530.

Even with Luini's securely dated works it is difficult to trace any stylistic evolution. The *Virgin and Child with SS Anthony Abbot and Barbara* of 1521 is very similar to the painting of the same subject of 1512; the compositional schemes of the two polyptychs in Legnano and Mendrisio painted in 1523 are archaic compared with the *Christ Crowned with Thorns* of 1521–2, and the innovative Lugano *Crucifixion* of 1529 was followed by the outdated schemes of the late frescoes at Saronno. Luini's numerous easel paintings are almost impossible to date. These include the famous *Virgin and Child of the Rose Garden* (Milan, Brera), in which the Virgin and Child, set before a rose-garlanded trellis, are portrayed with a bland, idealized classicism. Also of uncertain date are the Leonardesque *Christ among the Doctors* (London, N.G.) and the *Christ among the Children* (sold London, Colnaghi's, 1984; see *Burl. Mag.*, xccvi, 1984, p. xl).

Luini used drawings primarily to determine compositional schemes, as in the pen study of the *Deposition* (Paris, Louvre) for the painting in S Giorgio in Palazzo. From Leonardo he borrowed certain facial types and the use of chiaroscuro, later also adopting red chalk as a medium. With this he achieved a delicate tonality, as in the *Studies of the Face and Bust of a Woman* (Milan, Ambrosiana), in which, typically, he idealized the model.

During the period of French rule in Milan at the beginning of the 16th century a group of influential people were drawn by the teachings of Amedeo Mendez da Silva (1420–82) and the order he founded in Lombardy, the Amadeiti. They shared Mendez's expectations of radical civil and religious reforms, which he had prophesied in his text *Apocalypsis nova* (Milan, Castello Sforzesco). Many members of this circle were Luini's patrons, notably Cardinal Bernardino Carvajal, who commissioned the *Virgin and Child* in the abbey of Chiaravalle, and Gerolamo Rabia. Luini's relationship to this politically powerful, culturally heterodox group makes it necessary to reassess his work.

2. CRITICAL RECEPTION AND POSTHUMOUS REPUTATION. Vasari first praised the grace of Luini's images,

and that theme was taken up by the few commentators in the 17th and 18th centuries. Caravaggio, however, responded differently in adapting more enigmatic or dramatic compositions from Luini in his *Salome* (London, N.G.) and the angel in the *Seven Acts of Mercy* (Naples, Pin. Pio Monte della Misericordia).

With the advent of Neo-classicism in Europe, the formal elegance of Luini's style and the richness of his repertory of classical forms made him one of the most studied, collected and popular painters of the 19th century. Lanzi's authoritative study (1789), which eulogizes the painter and discusses his work at length, had done much to spread his fame. In 1811 Fumagalli reproduced some of his paintings and thereafter many reproductive engravings were made of Luini's works, which helped to popularize them. Between 1811 and 1821 the Brera Accademia detached Luini's most important fresco cycles from the Milanese monasteries of S Maria della Pace and the Vetere and from the Villa Pelucca in Sesto San Giovanni and displayed them in the Pinacoteca. Public and private collectors began to compete for his paintings; Giovanni Battista Sommariva, one of the most important collectors of the early 19th century, possessed four works by Luini, of which three were fresco fragments from the Villa Pelucca. Burckhardt (1855) valued the painter highly.

In England, Ruskin made a decisive contribution to the appreciation of Luini (see Evans and Whitehouse). In 1846 he praised his paintings in Como Cathedral; in 1862 he copied the *St Catherine* (Milan, Monastero Maggiore) and visited the sanctuary at Saronno. In 1864 the Arundel Society issued colour prints of the *Presentation in the Temple* and the *Dispute* at Saronno.

Beltrami's monograph of 1911 concluded more than a century of research. Luini's reputation as a 'graceful' painter came to an end when Venturi characterized him as a 'genteel painter, but without much imagination, monotonous in his inventions, unable to create a style of his own'. Post-war studies have attempted to set the painter in his historical context and to assess his role in the creation of an indigenous Milanese style.

BIBLIOGRAPHY

C. Cesariano: *Di Lucio Vitruvio Pollione de architectura libri dece* (Como, 1521), fol. 48 *v*

G. Vasari: *Vite* (1550, rev. 2/1568); ed. G. Milanesi (1878–85), iv, p. 585; vi, pp. 519–20

G. P. Lomazzo: *Trattato dell'arte della pittura, scoltura et architettura* (Milan, 1585), pp. 171, 360, 421

——: *Idea del tempio della pittura* (Milan, 1590); ed. R. P. Ciardi as *Gian Paolo Lomazzo: Scritti sulle arti* (Florence, 1973–4), i, p. 290

G. C. Sacco: *Stato della veneranda ed insigne Confraternità del SS Sacramento* (Monza, 1652), p. 8

S. Latuada: *Descrizione di Milano* (Milan, 1737–8)

L. Lanzi: *Storia pittorica della Italia* (Bassano, 1789); ed. M. Capucci (Florence, 1968–74), ii, pp. 310–13

I. Fumagalli: *Scuola di Leonardo da Vinci in Lombardia* (Milan, 1811)

J. Burckhardt: *Der Cicerone* (Basle, 1855; It. trans., Florence, 1952), i, pp. 949–51

A. Ratti: 'Il secolo XVI nell'abbazia di Chiaravalle di Milano', *Archv Stor. Lombard.*, 3rd ser., ix (1896), p. 99

A. Venturi: *Storia: IX* (1901–40/*R* 1967), ii, pp. 744–68

L. Beltrami: *Luini, 1512–1532* (Milan, 1911)

A. Ottino Della Chiesa: *Bernardino Luini* (Novara, 1956)

J. Evans & J. H. Whitehouse, eds: *John Ruskin: The Diaries* (Oxford, 1956–9), i, p. 349; ii, pp. 561–4, 722, 905

M. L. Ferrari: 'Zenale, Cesariano e Luini: Un arco di classicismo lombardo', *Paragone*, xviii/211 (1967), pp. 18–38

*Sacro e profano nella pittura di Bernardino Luini* (exh. cat., ed. G. Mulazzani and M. T. Binaghi; Luini, 1975)

M. T. Binaghi Olivari: 'I francesi a Milano (1499–1525): Arti figurative e moda', *An. Ist. Stor. It.-Ger. Trento*, v (1979), pp. 104–6

L. Mravik: 'Stefano Scotto, maître de Gaudenzio Ferrari?', *Bull. Mus. Hong. B.-A.*, liii (1979), pp. 59–68

*Zenale e Leonardo* (exh. cat., ed. C. Pirovano; Milan, Mus. Poldi Pezzoli, 1982), pp. 101–4

M. T. Binaghi Olivari: Notes in *Andrea Solario en France* (exh. cat., ed. S. Béguin; Paris, Louvre, 1985), n. 2, p. 102

F. Moro: 'Il polittico di Maggianico e gli esordi di Bernardino Luini', *Archv Lecco* (1986), pp. 129–71

G. Bora: 'Per un catalogo dei disegni dei leonardeschi a Milano: Indicazioni e problemi di metodo', *Rac. Vinc.*, xxii (1987), pp. 139–82 (174–6)

*Disegni e dipinti leonardeschi dalle collezioni milanesi* (exh. cat., Milan, Pal. Reale, 1987)

*Pinacoteca di Brera: Scuola lombarda e piemontese, 1300–1535* (Milan, 1988)

M. T. BINAGHI OLIVARI

**Luini, Tommaso.** *See* DONINI, TOMMASO.

**Luis**, Duque de Beja. *See* AVIZ, (8).

**Lui Shou-kwan** [Lü Shou-k'un] (*b* Guangzhou [Canton], Guangdong Province, 11 Nov 1919; *d* Hong Kong, 26 Sept 1975). Chinese painter. Son of a scholar–artist, he essentially taught himself to paint by copying the works of ancient masters of various schools. In 1948 he moved to Hong Kong, and while working as a clerk for a living he joined the local art scene as a teacher, critic and creative artist, becoming one of the most influential figures in Hong Kong art. He advocated the modernization of Chinese painting by a return to inspiration from nature and the release of personal creativity. Prompted by enthusiasm for Abstract Expressionism and other modern art movements, he explored the expressive potential of pure form with Chinese brush, ink and paper and thus initiated the New Ink Painting movement. Lui sought an identity for Hong Kong art through the merging of Chinese and Western art.

Lui's work of the 1950s reveals his fascination with the visual poetry of light and atmosphere. Using the scenery in and around Hong Kong as the basis of his imagery, he gradually experimented more boldly with new compositional devices, linear configurations and tonal changes. As his style became more abstract and unrestrained, he turned to the theme of the lotus, which he painted with broad flat brushes in contrasting wet and dry ink. The resulting works, which came to be known as Lui's Chan paintings, are striking discoveries of form as well as symbols of the artist's search for spiritual sublimity.

BIBLIOGRAPHY

Lui Shou-kwan: 'Symbolism and Zen: A Contemporary Chinese Approach to Abstract Painting', *Orient. A.*, n. s., xix/3 (1973), pp. 302–5

*Lui Shou-kwan: 1919–1975* (Hong Kong, 1979)

F. K. Chan: *The Development of Lu Shoukun's Art* (diss., U. Hong Kong, 1991)

MAYCHING KAO

**Lü Ji** [Lü Chi; *zi* Tingzhen; *hao* Leyu] (*b* Yin xian (modern Ningbo), Zhejiang Province, *c.* 1420; *d c.* 1504). Chinese painter. He was a prolific master of Chinese bird-and-flower painting (*see* CHINA, §V, 3(v)). Probably because he and his works had no literary dimensions, little was recorded about his life. One Ming (1368–1644) collection claimed to have included over 100 paintings by Lü;

however, later imitations and copies from less talented artists have polluted the true corpus of his extant works.

Lü Ji was from a region of natural beauty and one with a distinguished artistic tradition. Both factors are present in Lü's work. A prominent collector in the area invited young Lü to live with him and copy his paintings by early masters. Lü's fame grew, and he was summoned to the imperial court, where he eventually reached the rank of Commander of the Embroidered-uniform Guard during the Hongzhi reign period (1488–1505). While at court the Emperor remarked that Lü used his artistry as an excuse to admonish the throne, perhaps evidence that Lü Ji felt secure in his art and confident of his favour with the Emperor. More importantly, this comment suggests one of Lü's greatest innovations, namely using flowers and birds to invest his paintings with meanings that elevated them beyond images of nature. The interpretations are generated by the rich tradition of literary imagery for flowers and birds, which was then already three thousand years old, and because in the Chinese language many different words exist for similar sounds, facilitating visual puns or rebuses.

Tradition holds that Lü Ji first studied Bian Wenjin ( *fl* early 15th century) and then blended the strengths of all the masters since antiquity. His emphasis on representation rather than technique is empathic with that of earlier Song (AD 960–1279) Academy artists, who were renowned for the verisimilitude of their work (*see* CHINA, §V, 4(i)(c)). However, features such as abrupt juxtapositions of different techniques in Lü's early works also clearly reveal the impact of Yuan (1279–1368) painting. The continuity and balanced assimilation of antecedents in Lü's work indicate an evolutionary synthesis of his style rather than a revolutionary departure along eccentric lines. Lü used tight, methodical strokes and the colourful details of nature to dazzle viewers with his startlingly realistic, tangible motifs. With their fluid compositions and exceptional clarity, his paintings presented a profoundly evocative view of a luxuriant world, for example *Flowers and Birds of the Four Seasons* (Tokyo, N. Mus.; *see* CHINA, fig. 123). Lü Ji's grand yet intricate images of nature in all its beautiful detail represent the climax of bird-and-flower painting in the Ming Academy.

For further discussion of painting of the period *see* ZHE SCHOOL.

DMB: 'Lü Chi'                    BIBLIOGRAPHY
J. Cahill: *Parting at the Shore: Chinese Painting of the Early and Middle Ming Dynasty, 1368–1580* (New York and Tokyo, 1978)
M. Loehr: *The Great Painters of China* (New York, 1980)
*Painters of the Great Ming: The Imperial Court and the Zhe School* (exh. cat., ed. R. M. Barnhart; New York, Met., Dallas, TX, Mus. A.; 1993)
Hou-mei Sung: 'Lü Ji and his Pheasant Painting', *Pal. Mus. Q.*, x/4 (July 1993), pp. 1–22

JAMES ROBINSON

**Lukasbrüder.** *See* NAZARENES.

**Luke** (*b* Antioch, 1st century AD; *d* Greece; *fd* 18 Oct). Saint, evangelist and patron of artists. One of the Four Evangelists, he was a gentile and a doctor, according to St Paul, who called him 'our beloved Luke, the physician' (Colossians 4:14). He wrote the third Gospel and the Acts of the Apostles. He earned a reputation as an accurate observer, particularly of women, in his Gospel. His identification as 'an artist with words' probably led to the assumption that he also worked as a painter. In Byzantium mention of St Luke the Evangelist painting a portrait of the Virgin arose between the 5th and 6th centuries (Mango, p. 40). The Byzantine author John of Damascus (*c.* 675–*c.* 749) identified St Luke as the painter of the Virgin's portrait in his defence of sacred images. References to Luke as a painter did not appear in Latin literature until the late 12th century. In the West the association took hold quickly, transmitted by sources such as the *Legenda aurea* by Jacobo da Voragine. Because Luke was both doctor and artist, the medieval trade system placed physicians, apothecaries and painters in the same guild under his protection, and thus St Luke became the patron of painters. Tuscan artists began to name their companies after him by the mid-14th century, and subsequently art academies were named after him, especially in the Netherlands and in Italy. He is frequently portrayed at the easel, painting the Virgin's portrait (*see* PORTRAITURE, fig. 12). His symbols include an ink pot and pen (the attributes of a writer), the winged ox or calf and the half-length portrait of the Virgin.

Tradition holds that St Luke painted a half-length portrait from life of the Virgin holding the Child in her arms on the Mountain of Jerusalem. One account relates that St Luke gave it to Theophilus, to whom he had dedicated the Gospel and the Acts. A popular legend tells that Eudokia, wife of Emperor Theodosios II (*reg* 408–50), acquired the portrait when she made a pilgrimage to the Holy Land in 438–9 (see Mango, p. 40). The Empress sent it to her sister-in-law Pulcheria (later sanctified), who had it placed in a sanctuary near the banks of the Bosphorus in Constantinople (now Istanbul). This icon came to be accepted as a portrait from life made by St Luke, and the designation Hodegetria ('she who points the way') for icons of this sort may have derived from the name of the building in which it was housed, the monastery of the Hodegon. It has been said that the original icon was destroyed by the Turks during the conquest of Constantinople in 1453; however, an alternative tradition maintains that this image and others painted by St Luke eventually found their way to the West during the Crusades. Installed in churches, these icons became objects of veneration, stimuli to the growth of the Marian cult. Examples were found in Aachen, Venice, Bologna and Rome. Another tradition relates that St Luke produced paintings of the Virgin when he was in Rome: the *Virgin and Child* in Maria in Via Lata, Rome, was supposedly excavated from the site where St Luke preached and composed the Acts of the Apostles.

These icons were valued both for their historical importance and for their ability to work miracles. They were believed to be indestructible, and efficacious in troubled times. Lengthy histories confirmed their provenance and special powers. The *Vergine del Popolo* was thought to have come from Constantinople to the Sancta Sanctorum at the Lateran, from where it was moved to S Maria del Popolo, Rome, on the order of Gregory IX (*reg* 1227–41). During the Renaissance it became the focus of artistic commissions as the church was rebuilt and decorated under Sixtus IV and again under Julius II. Many such icons attributed to St Luke were copied by 15th-century artists or overpainted in an effort to restore their original lustre. Melozzo da Forlì reproduced the *Vergine del Popolo* (*c*. 1461; untraced) for his patron Alessandro Sforza, and other painters of the Roman and Umbrian schools modelled their works after this sacred image. A fine example attributed to the circle of Antoniazzo Romano is the *Virgin and Child* (ex-Loeser priv. col., Florence, see van Marle, xv, p. 247).

The Hodegetria has come to be accepted as one of the earliest images representing the Virgin and Child: the Virgin, bust-length and facing frontally, holds the seated child to one side, usually cradled against her left arm. Her right hand directs the faithful to him, showing him as the way. The fully clothed figure of the infant Christ may bless onlookers with his right hand and hold a scroll in his left. The icon has a gold background often with Greek inscriptions identifying mother and child.

The Hodegetria was adopted as an official image of Rome in late antiquity. St Luke was believed to have painted the icon of the *Virgin and Child* in S Maria Maggiore (see fig.), for which reason there is an oratory in the church dedicated to the saint by the Company of Painters. By 1211 the painting, now thought to date from the late 12th century or early 13th, was housed in a tabernacle donated by the Senate and people of Rome and was given the popular title of *Salus populi Romani* ('The saviour/prosperity of the Roman people'). It seems to

have remained under a ciborium to the right of the apse, until it was finally transferred to the Pauline Chapel in a sacred procession in 1613. Giovanni Rucellai mentioned the painting on the occasion of his pilgrimage to Rome for the Holy Year of 1450. Copies made by Antoniazzo Romano and Melozzo da Forlì helped ensure its enduring fame.

There are numerous icons attributed to St Luke that conform to Byzantine prototypes other than the Hodegetria: the Virgin Glykophiloussa, where the Child presses his face to his mother's; the Virgin Galactotrophousa, in which the mother suckles the Child; and the Virgin Kyriotissa, where the standing Virgin holds the Child to her chest. These have all been identified as portraits from the hand of St Luke. The Virgin Haghiosoritissa, known in Italian as Avvocata, a popular image during the Middle Ages and Renaissance, was also deemed to be the invention of St Luke; it shows the solitary Virgin turned to the side with raised arms. The iconographic type recalls the theme of the Deësis (Christ flanked by the Virgin and John the Baptist) and the Virgin as intercessor. A diminutive figure of Christ may appear in an upper corner of these images of the Avvocata.

Tradition associates St Luke with the *Virgin Avvocata* of S Maria in Aracoeli, Rome, a miraculous image of great renown. The icon represents the figure of the Virgin in half-length, turning to her right while her eyes address the viewer. The history of this painting was traced back to the 6th century by medieval and Renaissance chroniclers, who occasionally confused it with the icon of S Maria Maggiore. It was exhibited on special occasions, but otherwise was kept in a closed tabernacle on the altar associated with the vision of Augustus.

A portrait of the Virgin attributed to St Luke could take on the function of a palladium when displayed in public procession. St Gregory the Great (*c.* 540–604), according to an account in *The Golden Legend*, carried St Luke's portrait of the Virgin from S Maria Maggiore around the city in an effort to stop the plague. The apotropaic potency of the icon of S Maria in Aracoeli, also supposedly by St Luke, was invoked during the plague of 1348 when it was carried through the streets of Rome. During the early Renaissance the icons were frequently paraded in papal processions. Pope Paul II invoked the powers of the *Vergine del Popolo* in his attempt to start a crusade against the Turks on at least two occasions. Again in 1476, when the plague raged through Rome, the *Virgin* from S Maria Maggiore was carried through the streets.

Despite modern restoration campaigns, precise dating of the images will remain controversial until they are analysed technically. The *Virgin* in S Maria in Aracoeli has been dated variously to the 6th–7th, 10th and 13th centuries; the *Virgin* in S Maria Maggiore probably originated in the late 12th or early 13th century, although it was undoubtedly modelled after an earlier image mentioned in 9th-century sources. Those scholars who prefer to attach the earlier dates to the panels tend to attribute them to Byzantine painters active in Rome. Although some of the later icons may have been produced in the workshops of Tuscan painters, it is more likely that 13th-century Roman artists working as mosaicists in the apse

St Luke (traditional attrib.): icon of the *Virgin and Child*, tempera on panel, 1170×790 mm (Rome, S Maria Maggiore)

of S Maria in Trastevere fashioned the miracle-working icons after Byzantine prototypes.

### BIBLIOGRAPHY

John of Damascus: *Logoi apologitikoi pros tous diabollontas tas agias eikonas* [Apologia against the slander of the holy icons] (MS.; 7th century); Eng. trans. by D. Anderson as *On the Divine Images* (Crestwood, NY, 1980)
A. B. Jameson: *Legends of the Madonna* (London, 4/1867)
R. van Marle: *Italian Schools* (1923–38)
D. Klein: *St Lukas als Maler der Maria: Ikonographie der Lukas-Madonna* (Berlin, 1933)
E. B. Garrison: *Italian Romanesque Panel Painting: An Illustrated Index* (Florence, 1949)
H. Hager: 'Rückgewonnen Marienikone des frühen Mittelalters in Rom', *Römische Qschr.*, lxi (1966), pp. 209–16
G. Schiller: *Ikonographie der christlichen Kunst*, 4 vols (Gütersloh, 1966–80)
H. Holländer: 'Lukasbilder', *Lexikon der christlichen Ikonographie*, ed. Herder, iii (Rome, 1971), pp. 122–3
C. Mango: *The Art of the Byzantine Empire, 312–1453* (Englewood Cliffs, NJ, 1972/R Toronto, Buffalo and London, 1986)
M. Warner: *Alone of All her Sex* (New York, 1976)
A. Grabar: 'Remarque sur l'iconographie byzantine de la Vierge', *Cah. Archéol.*, xxvi (1977), pp. 169–78
G. Kaftal: *Iconography of the Saints in the Painting of North-East Italy* (Florence, 1978)
G. Kraut: *Lukas malt die Madonna: Zeugnisse zum künstlerischen Selbstverständnis in der Malerei* (Worms, 1986)
G. Gharib: *Le icone mariane: Storia e culto* (Rome, 1987) [good illustrations]

EUNICE D. HOWE

**Lukke.** *See* LÜCKE.

**Lukomsky, Georgy (Kreskent'yevich)** [Rokh, Yury] (*b* Kaluga, 14 March 1884; *d* Nice, 25 March 1952). Russian architectural historian, designer and illustrator. He studied at the St Petersburg Academy of Arts (1903–15) and in Paris and Rome (1905–9), during which time he developed his concern for the protection of the artistic heritage of Russia and began to publish both his graphic art and his essays in *Apollon* and *Staryye gody*. This work, mainly dedicated to Russian and Ukrainian architecture, provided a unique record of many provincial estates, as in his book on Galicia and its heritage (1915), among others. His illustrations for these, in watercolour and crayon, comprise some of the finest examples of Russian architectural graphic art. Also an ardent enthusiast for the architectural styles seen in Russia during the late 18th century and the early 19th, he studied the buildings of St Petersburg and its environs and also supported contemporary architects working in the neo-classical style. Of particular interest to him, especially after he was appointed head of the commission for the preservation of the artistic properties of the Detskoye Selo palaces (1917–18), were the palace complexes at Tsarskoye Selo (now Pushkin). Lukomsky was also prominent in the reorganization of the Khanenko collection, the best collection of western European, Oriental and Old Russian art in Ukraine, into the Second State Museum in Kiev (1919–20; now the Kiev Museum of Western and Oriental Art), of which he was Keeper. An émigré living in Germany, France and Italy from the early 1920s, he continued to publish prolifically on Russian art and architecture and edited the art journal *Zhar-ptitsa* (Paris and Berlin, 1921–4). In Paris, he also worked as a stage designer and created the decorative schemes for various mayoral offices.

### WRITINGS

*O proshlom i sovremennom sostoyanii provintsial'noy arkhitektury Rossii* [On the past and contemporary state of the provincial architecture of Russia] (St Petersburg, 1912)
*Galitsiya v yeyo starine* [Galicia in its antiquity] (Petrograd, 1915)
*Sovremennyy Peterburg: Ocherk istorii vozniknoveniya i razvitiya klassicheskago stroitel'stva, 1900–1915* [Modern St Petersburg: an essay on the history of the origin and development of classical construction, 1900–1915] (Petrograd, 1917)
*Russische Baukunst* (Munich, 1924)
*Andrea Palladio* (Paris, 1927)
*Kiev, la ville sainte de Russie* (Paris, 1929)
*Les Sangallo* (Paris, 1934)
*Charles Cameron, 1740–1812* (London, 1943)
*History of Modern Russian Painting* (London, 1945)

### BIBLIOGRAPHY

P. Dul'sky: *Kazan' v grafike G. K. Lukomskogo* [Kazan' in the graphic art of G. K. Lukomsky] (Kazan', 1920)
*Georgy Kreskent'yevich Lukomsky* (exh. cat., intro. by E. Gollerbakh; Kazan', Mus. Tatar. ASSR, 1928)

JEREMY HOWARD, SERGEY KUZNETSOV

**Luks, George (Benjamin)** (*b* Williamsport, PA, 13 Aug 1867; *d* New York, 29 Oct 1933). American painter and draughtsman. He lived as a child in the mining town of Shenandoah, PA, but moved to Philadelphia in 1883. The facts of his early career were later confused by the wild stories fabricated by him. After a short stint in vaudeville, he spent a year at the Pennsylvania Academy of Fine Arts, Philadelphia. From 1885 he was in Europe, living most of the next decade in Düsseldorf, Munich, Paris and London, intermittently attending German and French art academies. In 1894 Luks became an artist–reporter for the *Philadelphia Press*, where he befriended Robert Henri, John Sloan, William J. Glackens and Everett Shinn. In late 1895 he went to Cuba as a war correspondent; the following year he moved to New York and joined the staff of the *New York World* as a cartoonist.

In 1897 Luks began to paint. Working with dark, slashing strokes, akin to the style of Henri, he sympathetically portrayed New York's social outcasts, as in the *Spielers* (1905; Andover, MA, Phillips Acad., Addison Gal.). This subject-matter and Luks's treatment of it led critics to characterize him later as part of the Ashcan school. Luks exhibited at the National Arts Club in 1904 and four years later, as a member of THE EIGHT (i), participated in their exhibition at the Macbeth Galleries, New York. In 1913 he exhibited at the Armory Show. Luks taught at the Art Students League from 1920 to 1924 and then established his own school. His paintings from the late years lack the strength of his early works. Luks died at the age of 66 after being beaten in a bar-room brawl.

### BIBLIOGRAPHY

E. L. Cary: *George Luks* (New York, 1932)
E. Shinn: 'Everett Shinn on George Luks: An Unpublished Memoir', *Archv Amer. A. J.*, vi/2 (1966), pp. 1–12
*George Luks* (exh. cat. by B. Danenburg, New York, Her. Gal., 1967)
*George Luks: An Exhibition of Paintings and Drawings Dating from 1889 to 1931* (exh. cat. by I. Glackens and J. Trovato, Utica, NY, Munson-Williams-Proctor Inst., 1973)
*City Life Illustrated, 1890–1940: Sloan, Glackens, Shinn, their Friends and Followers* (exh. cat., Wilmington, DE A. Mus., 1980)

For further bibliography *see* ASHCAN SCHOOL and THE EIGHT (i)

JANET MARSTINE

**Lu'lu'.** *See* BADR AL-DIN LU'LU'.

**Lulumbaba Pucará de.** *See* PUCARA DE RUMICUCHO.

**Lumague** [Lumagne]. Franco-Italian family of bankers and patrons. By the beginning of the 17th century several members of the family, originally from the Grisons, had become established as bankers in France and Italy. Little biographical information is available, although inventories reveal that three of the sons of Marc-Antoine Lumague (i) (*d* 1619) became notable patrons: Barthélémy (*b* Piuro, Grisons; *d* Lyon, 17 April 1641), Marc-Antoine (ii) (*b* 1566; *d* Milan, 1655) and Charles [Carlo] Lumague. The eldest, Barthélémy Lumague, settled in Lyon, where he made gifts to religious foundations, paying for an Italian tabernacle (untraced) for the Convent of the Visitation in 1627 and in 1634 commissioning from Guercino a *Christ Showing Heaven to St Theresa* (Aix-en-Provence, Mus. Granet) to decorate the family chapel in the church of the Discalced Carmelites. He also built an ambitious country house, the Château de l'Haye at Saint-Genis-Laval, near Lyon; part of its original decoration, including a monumental marble chimney-piece with his coat of arms dated 1631, survives. Marc-Antoine Lumague (ii) was established in Genoa before 1619, but he also spent some time in Paris. The engraver Claude Mellan dedicated to him his print after a *Jacob and Rachel at the Well* (London, priv. col.), then thought to be by Tintoretto but attributed to Veronese in 1972 (see Perez, p. 163, n. 1); according to Mariette this painting was once in Marc-Antoine's collection. Marc-Antoine Lumague (ii) was certainly the first owner of Nicolas Poussin's *Landscape with Diogenes* (1648; Paris, Louvre), and he is mentioned several times in the painter's correspondence in connection with financial matters. According to Malvasia, Charles Lumague settled in Paris and in 1641 owned works by Guercino; he presumably also owned Veronese's *Christ in Glory between SS Peter and Paul* (after 1580; Caen, Mus. B.-A.), an engraving of which, by Michel Lasne, is dedicated to him. The family is known to have bought Italian pictures through the German dealer Philipp Hainhofer.

BIBLIOGRAPHY
Mariette
C. C. Malvasia: *Felsina pittrice* (1678); ed. M. Brascaglia (1971), pp. 369, 373
J. Tricou: 'Le Guerchin des Carmes déchaussés de Lyon au musée d'Aix-en-Provence', *Nouv. Rev. Héraldique*, ii (1946), pp. 49–56
O. Aureggi: 'I Lumaga di Piuro e di Chiavenna', *Archv Stor. Lombardo* (1962), pp. 222–89
M.-F. Perez: 'Le Mécénat de la famille Lumague (branche française) au XVIIe siècle', *Actes du colloque. La France et l'Italie au temps de Mazarin: Grenoble, 1985*, pp. 153–65
MARIE-FÉLICIE PÉREZ

**Lumbini** [Rummindei]. Site of the Buddha's birth, in Bhairhwa District, Nepal. A pillar dating from the 3rd century BC identifies the site as Lumbini and carries an inscription commemorating a visit of the emperor Ashoka (*reg* 269–232 BC) to the Buddha's birthplace. It is similar in form to other pillars erected by Ashoka at Buddhist sites, for example the better preserved one at Lauriya Nandangarh. The crowning element at Lumbini, a horse, according to the 7th-century Chinese pilgrim Xuan Zang, is now missing. A large relief illustrating Maya giving birth to the Buddha is enshrined in a nearby modern temple. Though almost completely effaced, the sculpture shows sensuous lines that suggest a 5th-century AD date. Other sculptures from Lumbini include two small bronze male figures (*c.* 4th century), a head of Buddha (*c.* 2nd century) in mottled red sandstone, in a style characteristic of Mathura, and several *bodhisattva* figures (9th–10th centuries). After the 10th century it appears that Lumbini ceased to be an active centre.

The firm identification of Lumbini, the garden where the Buddha was born, has led to speculation on the location of Kapilavastu, his home city and the capital of his clan, known to be near by. Suggestions include Tilaurakot, an urban site in Nepal near Lumbini, and Piprahwa, a religious site just across the border in Basti District, Uttar Pradesh, India. Finds at Piprahwa are convincing: a 3rd century BC stupa and relics, seals inscribed with the name Kapilavastu and sculptures dating from the 1st and 2nd centuries AD. It is possible, however, that Tilaurakot was the site of the city and Piprahwa the site of a monastery on its outskirts, the modern Indo-Nepalese border making them appear more distant than they are.

BIBLIOGRAPHY
A. Führer: *Antiquities of Buddha's Birthplace in the Nepalese Terai*, ASNI, vi (Allahabad, 1897/*R* Varanasi, 1972)
P. C. Mukherji: *A Report on a Tour of Exploration of the Antiquities of Kapilavastu, Tarai of Nepal*, Archaeol. Surv. India, Imp. Ser., xxvi/1 (Calcutta, 1901/*R* Varanasi, 1969)
E. Hultzch: *Inscriptions of Aśoka*, Corp. Insc. Ind., i (Oxford, 1925), pp. 22–3
D. Mitra: *Excavation at Tilaurakot in the Nepalese Tarai* (Kathmandu, 1972)
Z. Nakamura, T. Kubo and H. Sakazume, eds: *The Rissho University Nepal Archaeological Research Report* (Tokyo, 1978)
K. Rijal: *Archaeological Remains of Kapilavastu, Lumbini and Devadala* (Kathmandu, [1979])
K. M. Srivastava: *Discovery of Kapilavastu* (New Delhi, 1986)
FREDERICK M. ASHER

**Lumiares, Manuel de Moura y Corte Real**, Conde de. *See* CASTEL RODRIGO.

**Lumikangas, Pentti** (*b* Kylmäkoski, nr Tampere, 23 Nov 1926). Finnish printmaker. He graduated as a graphic designer from the Central School of Applied Arts in Helsinki in 1949. A few years later he obtained a small press of his own and began to produce free, expressive prints, which he exhibited in Finland from 1954 and abroad from 1959. At that time his themes were minimalist, architectonic forms (e.g. *Pillar Landscape*, *Gate*, *Stone Wall* and *Shadow on the Wall*; all Stockholm, Nmus.). He used both drypoint and aquatint and produced large sketches for the finished prints.

The scale of Lumikangas's work gradually increased. The prints often represent imaginative monumental architecture set in a motionless, timeless context, at times peaceful and poetic, at times uncompromisingly stark and empty, close to the landscapes of Surrealism and Pittura Metafisica. Behind the *Open Door* lies emptiness, the *Spiral Staircase* leads nowhere, the *Road* (all Helsinki, N.G.) and the *Jetty* (artist's col.) lead into the unknown, and the *Temple* and *Tower* (both Helsinki, N.G.) are imbued with a strange, still silence. Human beings appear only as small particles of any composition. The loneliness and starkness of Lumikangas's work, which cannot easily be divided into separate stylistic periods, is relieved, however, by the vigorous quality of the prints, a result of his tonal sensitivity to air, light and shadow.

BIBLIOGRAPHY

*Pentti Lumikangas* (exh. cat. by L. Peltola, Venice, Biennale, 1972)

M. Komonen: 'Syövytettyä arkkitehtuuria' [Architecture in etchings], *Arkkitehti/Arkitekten* (1977), no. 6, pp. 10–11

J. Pallasmaa: 'Piirrettyä aikaa–kaiverrettua valoa' [Time in drawings–light in etchings], *Taide* (1977), no. 4, pp. 32–7

L. Peltola: *Pentti Lumikangas: Grafiikkaa/Graphics, 1947–1978* (Helsinki, 1980) [bilingual text]

LEENA PELTOLA

**Luminance** [luminosity; luminousness]. Term for the quantity of light that reaches the eye (or another detector) from a reflecting surface. Luminance partially accounts for the visual sensation of brightness or darkness. Luminance is a product of the intensity of illumination and the reflectance of the illuminated surface. *See* LIGHT.

**Luminism (i).** Term coined *c.* 1950 by the art historian John I. H. Baur to define a style in 19th-century American painting characterized by the realistic rendering of light and atmosphere. It was never a unified movement but rather an attempt by several painters working in the USA to understand the mysteries of nature through a precise, detailed rendering of the landscape. Luminism flourished *c.* 1850–75 but examples are found both earlier and later. Its principal practitioners were FITZ HUGH LANE, MARTIN JOHNSON HEADE, ALFRED THOMPSON BRICHER, DAVID JOHNSON and Francis Augustus Silva (1835–86). Several artists of the HUDSON RIVER SCHOOL, among them SANFORD ROBINSON GIFFORD, JOHN FREDERICK KENSETT and ALBERT BIERSTADT, painted works that could be considered examples of Luminism, as did such Canadian painters as LUCIUS R. O'BRIEN (e.g. *Sunrise on the Saguenay*, 1880; Ottawa, N.G.).

The Luminists concentrated on nuances of light and atmosphere, an approach that may have been suggested by the new, dispassionate medium of photography. The work of slightly earlier 19th-century European artists, such as the German Caspar David Friedrich and the Dane Christen Købke, may also have been influential. Even earlier precedents for Luminist paintings are the works of such 17th-century Dutch masters as Jacob van Ruisdael. *Atmospheric Landscapes of North America*, a series of watercolours by George Harvey (1800–78) executed in the mid- and late 1830s, was perhaps the first purely Luminist manifestation in American art. Lane's work recalls the earlier paintings of Thomas Birch and especially those of ROBERT SALMON, an English marine painter active in Boston in the 1830s. However, a more direct influence came from the Transcendentalists, such as Ralph Waldo Emerson (1803–82), who saw nature as the ultimate expression of God's will. In a manner akin to pantheistic communion, Luminist painters strove for this sharpened sense of the awareness of nature's mysteries through concentrated meditation on the landscape.

Luminist paintings have several common characteristics. They show no picturesque details of landscape, have a great sense of interior depth and are usually sparsely composed and peopled with few or no figures, as in Kensett's *Marine off Big Rock* (1864; Jacksonville, FL,

Cummer Gal. A.) or Lane's *Owl's Head, Penobscot Bay, Maine* (1862; Boston, MA, Mus. F.A.; for illustration *see* LANE, FITZ HUGH). Their dimensions are broad and horizontal, though not encompassing the spectacular panoramic sweep typical of the work of Thomas Cole and Frederic Edwin Church. The main subjects are often sunlight or moonlight, which shines through a cloudless sky revealing crisply outlined forms. The mood tends to be one of magical and eerie stillness, enhanced by the inclusion of calm, glossy surfaces of water. Sometimes, however, impending storms were portrayed, as in Heade's *Thunderstorm over Narragansett Bay* (1868; Fort Worth, TX, Amon Carter Mus.). In Lane's *Western Shore with Norman's Woe* (1862; Gloucester, MA, Cape Ann Hist. Assoc.) a background haziness characteristically gives way to a pellucid foreground. Brushstrokes are generally invisible, and there is evidence of careful draughtsmanship. Lane, for example, painted his works in the studio using detailed pencil drawings, which he squared for transfer. The preferred locales were New England, New Jersey and Long Island. Among other regions, Heade favoured upstate New York (e.g. *Lake George*, 1862; Boston, MA, Mus. F.A.; for illustration *see* HEADE, MARTIN JOHNSON). By the 1870s Luminist paintings began to be superseded by less detailed views rendered in the looser brushstrokes of the Impressionist technique.

BIBLIOGRAPHY

J. I. H. Baur: 'Early Studies in Light and Air by American Painters', *Brooklyn Mus. Bull.*, ix/2 (1948), pp. 1–9

——: 'Trends in American Painting, 1815–1865', *M. and M. Karolik Collection of American Paintings, 1815 to 1865* (Cambridge, MA, 1949)

——: 'American Luminism, a Neglected Aspect of the Realist Movement in Nineteenth-century American Painting', *Persp. USA*, 9 (1954), pp. 90–98

*Luminous Landscape: The American Study of Light, 1860–1875* (exh. cat. by G. Davidson, P. Hattis and T. Stebbins jr, Cambridge, MA, Fogg, 1966)

W. J. Naef and J. N. Wood: *Era of Exploration: The Rise of Landscape Photography in America* (New York, 1974)

*The Natural Paradise: Painting in America, 1800–1950* (exh. cat., ed. K. McShine; New York, MOMA, 1976)

B. Novak: *Nature and Culture: American Landscape and Painting, 1825–1875* (New York, 1980)

*American Light: The Luminist Movement, 1850–1875: Paintings, Drawings, Photographs* (exh. cat., ed. J. Wilmerding; Washington, DC, N.G.A., 1980)

E. G. Garrett: *The British Sources of American Luminism* (diss., Cleveland, OH, Case W. Reserve U., 1982)

JOHN I. H. BAUR

**Luminism (ii).** Term applied generally to Belgian Neo-Impressionism and more specifically to the work produced after 1904 by the movement's exponents, in which they combined aspects of Realism, Impressionism and Neo-Impressionism; it was also applied from 1910 in the Netherlands to describe the late phase of Dutch Impressionism that is comparable stylistically with Fauvism. The term derives from *Vie et Lumière*, the name of a group formed by EMILE CLAUS and others. After Georges Seurat's death in 1891 some Belgian Neo-Impressionists turned away from the painting movement in favour of decorative arts. When the avant-garde group Les XX was superseded in 1894 by the Libre Esthétique (1894–1914), Claus and other Belgian Impressionists sought a more national, often Flemish identity, enhanced by the nationalist tendency to pay homage to the century-old Dutch

Flemish tradition of landscape painting, and by the Romantic–Realist style taught at Belgian academies and practised by the schools of Kalmthout, Tervuren and Dendermonde.

At the Salon of the Libre Esthétique in Brussels in 1904, Octave Maus exhibited a huge collection of Impressionists' works, all French except for those by the pointillist Théophile Van Rysselberghe, who had settled in Paris. Although the show inspired a second wave of Neo-Impressionist followers, critics found Maus's Salon too French. In this climate Claus founded the group Vie et Lumière with GEORGE MORREN and ADRIEN JOSEPH HEYMANS, the leader of the Kalmthout school; it included Claus's pupils Jenny Montigny (1875–1937), Anna De Weert (1867–1950), Georges Buysse (1864–1916) and Modest Huys (1875–1932), as well as William Degouve de Nuncques, and some former members of Les XX: Georges Lemmen, James Ensor and Anna Boch (1848–1936), the last a disciple of Van Rysselberghe. In 1905, perhaps under pressure from the critics, Maus organized a second, but this time international, Impressionist exhibition, *L'Evolution externe de l'impressionnisme*, in which the members of Vie et Lumière exhibited for the first time under the group's name. The group's work was characterized by a preference for depicting the Flemish countryside (with or without figures), in particular the area where Claus lived, around the River Lys between Deinze and Ghent, bathed in sunlight. Claus's villa, Zonneschijn, at Astene became a magnet for numerous followers from Ghent, Paris and even the USA and Japan. The work also reflected academic training that most members had undertaken, and which remained visible in the importance given to accurate drawing and solidly constructed compositions. Colour or technique never overwhelmed the subject-matter. The work of the Belgian Luminists, however, has been criticized as 'Impressionist academicism'; this was perhaps why some artists moved towards a more genuine, natural art that became known as Flemish Expressionism.

Luminism in the Netherlands developed after Belgian Neo-Impressionism had been imported by Jan Toorop and Henry Van de Velde. In 1901 Toorop and Johan Thorn Prikker organized the 'First International Exhibition' in The Hague with Claus, Van Rysselberghe and others, as well as Vincent van Gogh and the French artists Paul Signac, Odilon Redon, Edouard Vuillard, Camille Pissarro and Paul Cézanne. Dutch Impressionists, including Piet Mondrian, began to move from the expressive brushwork of the 1880s towards an emphasis on firmly defined forms in balanced compositions of horizontals and verticals; Jan Sjuijters began to use colour expressively, rather than naturalistically. Under his influence, and after meeting Toorop in 1908, Mondrian broke away from Impressionism. The following year they exhibited with Leo Gestel in the St Lucas exhibition. It was at this point that their work became 'Luminist'; it showed their interest in light and the autonomy of colour and emphasized order and structure. By contrast with the work of the Belgian Luminists, their style had characteristics similar to those of French Fauvism and to German Expressionism.

BIBLIOGRAPHY

A. Santon: *Un Prince du luminisme, E. Claus* (n.p., 1946)
*Les Jeux de la lumière dans la peinture belge* (exh. cat., Brussels, Musées Royaux B.-A., 1965)
*Peintres belges, lumière française* (exh. cat., Brussels, Musées Royaux B.-A., 1969)
*Licht door kleur: Nederlandse Luministen* (exh. cat., The Hague, Gemeentemus., 1977)
M.-A. Stevens: 'Belgian Art: Les XX and the Libre Esthétique', *Post-Impressionism: Cross-currents in European Painting* (exh. cat., London, RA, 1979–80), pp. 252–9
C. Van Damme: 'De Vlaamse Impressionisten' [The Flemish Impressionists], *Openb. Kstbez.* (1982), 2, pp. 43–79
S. Polden: *A Clear View: The Belgian Luminist Tradition* (exh. cat., London, Whittford and Hughes, 1987)
S. Goyens de Heusch: 'Die belgischen Luministen und ihre Vorläufer', *Landschaft im Licht: Impressionistische Malerei in Europa und Nordamerika (1870–1910)* (exh. cat., ed. G. Crymmek; Cologne, Wallraf-Richartz Mus.; Zurich, Ksthaus; 1990), pp. 95–102
*Néo et post-impressionnistes belges dans les collections privées de Belgique* (exh. cat., Pontoise, Mus. Pissarro; Charleroi, Mus. Com. B.-A.; 1990)
S. Goyens de Heusch: 'Impressionism, Neo-Impressionism and Luminism', *Impressionism to Symbolism: The Belgian Avant-garde, 1880–1900* (exh. cat., London, RA, 1994), pp. 35–9

ROBBERT RUIGROK

**Lumley, John**, 1st Baron (*b* Chester-le-Street, Co. Durham, *c.* 1535; *d* Cheam, Surrey, 11 April 1609). English collector. He was the head of a family that had a long, proud Catholic tradition, and as such he was deeply involved in the unsuccessful Ridolfi Plot of 1571, which attempted to replace Queen Elizabeth I with the Roman Catholic Mary, Queen of Scots. Lumley married Jane (*d* 1576), daughter of HENRY FITZALAN, 12th Earl of Arundel. Lumley's career at court was sponsored by Arundel, who treated him as his son and heir, leaving him the palace of Nonsuch and its contents (*see* NONSUCH PALACE, §1), including a library, the core of which Arundel had acquired from Archbishop Thomas Cranmer (1489–1556). Lumley expanded the library further: the catalogue of 1609 lists more than 3000 volumes, making it the largest in England of this period. On Lumley's death it passed to Henry, Prince of Wales, and forms the core of the royal collection in the British Library, London.

Lumley is best known as one of the few Elizabethan nobles who travelled to Italy and brought back objects of art-historical significance. In fact it was Arundel (Lumley's father-in-law) and the Welsh antiquary Humphrey Lhuyd (1527–68; Lumley's brother-in-law and Arundel's librarian) who went to Padua in 1566–7. The confusion that has arisen over this journey to Italy is partly due to the pictorial evidence that remains of Lumley's collection of sculpture, which was unusually Italianate. The sculptures are illustrated in the first few pages of the *Red Velvet Book*, an inventory made of all Lumley's possessions in 1590. The most markedly classical sculptures illustrated are those that were made for the Privy Garden of Nonsuch (*see* NONSUCH PALACE, §2). In this formal part of the garden a series of fountains, columns and obelisks were erected, many carrying the Lumley popinjay. The Fountain of Venus is particularly Italianate and bears a close resemblance to the fountains that were made for the Medici villas outside Florence. The Grove of Diana that Lumley built at Nonsuch in homage to Elizabeth I after the Ridolfi Plot is not illustrated in the *Red Velvet Book*. Various written descriptions of it exist, however, attesting to its allegorical nature and showing that it was based on Italian and French examples.

Lumley's collection of paintings was one of the largest in Elizabethan England. The *Red Velvet Book* lists more than 300 pictures, some of which are attributed by its author John Lampton. It has been invaluable to 20th-century scholars trying to reconstruct the oeuvres of a number of artists; in particular the works of Hans Eworth and Gerlach Flicke have been established using the Lumley inventory as a basis for attribution. Among the paintings listed are the portrait of *Christina of Denmark, Duchess of Milan* (1538; London, N.G.) by Hans Holbein (ii) and his own portrait by 'the famous painter Steven', who was probably Steven van der Meulen.

Lumley was a keen amateur antiquarian and was proud (almost to the point of obsession) of the length of his ancestry. He transformed Lumley Castle, his ancestral seat at Chester-le-Street, Co. Durham, into a celebration of his family's longevity. His acts included the setting up of the *Lumley Horseman* (Leeds Castle, Kent), a life-size painted wooden sculpture of King Edward III, and the commissioning of 12 huge portraits of his ancestors, which hung in the Great Hall where the *Horseman* stood. These remain in the possession of the family at Sandbeck Park, S. Yorks.

UNPUBLISHED SOURCES
Sandbeck Park, S. Yorks [MS. of J. Lampton: *A Certyficate of . . all his Lo: Monumentes of Marbles, Pictures and Tables in Paynture with other his Lordshippes Howseholde Stuffe, and Regester of Bookes* (1590)] [*Red Velvet Book*]
Cambridge, Trinity Coll., MS. R. 722 [A. Watson: *Magnificae, et plane regiae domus, quae vulgo vocatur Nonesuch, brevis et vera descriptio*]

BIBLIOGRAPHY
L. Cust: 'The Lumley Inventories', *Walpole Soc.*, vi (1918), pp. 15–35
S. Jayne and F. R. Johnson: *The Lumley Library* (London, 1956)
J. Dent: *The Quest for Nonsuch* (Sutton, Surrey, 1988)

KATHRYN BARRON

**Luna (i)** [now Luni]. Site in Liguria, north-west Italy, of a Roman colony (*fl* 2nd century BC–4th century AD). The town was a port, known for its export of white Carrara marble, which first began to be systematically quarried in the Apuan Alps in the 1st century BC. Luna's decline in the 4th century AD was partly due to a crisis in the marble trade. The first excavations were carried out in 1837 by the Marchese Remedi (material now in Florence, Mus. Archeol.) and by C. Promis (material now in Turin, Mus. Ant.). At the end of the 19th century C. Fabbricotti carried out further excavations (material now in La Spezia, Mus. Civ. Archeol., and Carrara, Accad. B.A.). Luna has a quadrangular layout, but the side facing the sea is irregular, probably reflecting the original coastline. The Via Aemilia Scauri crossed the town and formed its *decumanus maximus*, although unusually it is not crossed by the *cardo maximus*, which linked the harbour with the town centre. Rebuilding works during the Augustan age (27 BC–AD 14) enlarged the forum, which had a portico running along its two longer sides. The improvements were possible due to the prosperity brought to the town by the export of marble, used not only to pave the main square but also for statues; these included portraits of members of the Julio-Claudian Imperial family. The works are of almost the same quality as those sculpted in Rome (for example *Augustus* wearing the *corona civica*, *Agrippina the Elder*

and *Tiberius Gemellus*; all Luni, Mus. N.). Public buildings on the fringes of the city and outside it, such as the Great Temple from the Republican era, with terracotta pediment decorations (2nd century BC; Florence, Mus. Archeol.), underwent rebuilding during the 2nd century AD. The amphitheatre, probably from the same period, has marble cladding and stairways.

BIBLIOGRAPHY
L. Banti: *Luni* (Florence, 1937)
A. Frova: *Luni, Parma, Velleia: Ricerche sulla decorazione architettonica romana* (Milan, 1968)
*Scavi di Luni*, 6 vols (Rome, 1973–7)
B. Ward-Perkins: 'L'abbandono degli edifici pubblici a Luni', *Cent. Stud. Lunensi, Quad.*, iii (1978), pp. 33–46

GIOVANNA TEDESCHI GRISANTI

**Luna (ii).** Spanish noble family of patrons. It was one of the more important houses of the Kingdom of Aragon. Its most outstanding ecclesiastical representative was Pedro de Luna, who was elected anti-pope as Benedict XIII at Avignon on the death of Clement VII (1394). He became one of the main protagonists in the Great Schism and, refusing to resign, died at Peñíscola in 1424. The most important lay member of the Luna family, however, was to make his career in Castile.

Don Álvaro de Luna (*d* Valladolid, 1453) was the illegitimate son of Álvaro de Luna, cupbearer to Henry III of Castile (*reg* 1390–1406). He was introduced into the King's service by another Pedro de Luna, Archbishop of Toledo (*d* 1414), and, once established at the Castilian court, he made his way rapidly and became the right-hand man of John II (*reg* 1406–54). He was made 1st Conde de San Esteban de Gormaz (1421), Constable of Castile (1423) and Master of Santiago (1445), and, after the death of his first wife, Elvira Portocarrero, in 1431 he married Juana Pimentel (*d* 1488), the daughter of Rodrigo Alonson, 2nd Conde de Benavente (*d* 1440). Granted Escalona Castle (Toledo) in 1435, he rebuilt it, adding a *Mudéjar* Gothic palace inside and constructing a patio and a tilt-yard outside. He was the donor of the richly decorated, Flamboyant chapel of Santiago in Toledo Cathedral, the first Late Gothic chapel in Spain (*see* TOLEDO, §IV, 1). This was to be his funerary chapel, and during his lifetime he had constructed for himself and his wife elaborate tombs, but these were severely damaged by his political enemies. Don Álvaro fell from power, and he was executed at Valladolid in 1453. His daughter María (*d* 1502), however, who had married Iñigo López de Mendoza, 2nd Duque de Infantado, had magnificent new effigies made by Pablo Ortiz (*fl* 1489) and commissioned famous portraits of her parents to adorn the retable behind the altar in the chapel. The retable, made in 1488–9 by Pedro Gumiel and others, cost 105,000 maravedis. As a result the chapel of Santiago is one of the most outstanding features of Toledo Cathedral.

BIBLIOGRAPHY
B. Bevan: *History of Spanish Architecture* (London, 1938)
C. Silio: *Don Álvaro de Luna* (Buenos Aires, 1939)
J. De Mata Carriazo, ed.: *Crónica de don Álvaro de Luna* (Madrid, 1940)
L. Torres Balbás: *Arquitectura gótica*, A. Hisp., vii (Madrid, 1952)
A. Durán Sanpere and J. Ainaud de Lasarte: *Escultura gótica*, A. Hisp., viii (Madrid, 1956)
E. Cooper: *Castillos señoriales de Castilla de los siglos XV y XVI*, 2 vols (Madrid, 1980)

N. Round: *The Greatest Man Uncrowned: A Study of the Fall of Don
Álvaro de Luna* (London, 1986)

J. R. L. HIGHFIELD

**Lunacharsky, Anatoly (Vasil'yevich)** (*b* Poltava, 24
Nov 1875; *d* Menton, France, 26 Dec 1933). Russian
statesman, critic and theorist. The son of a leading civil
servant, he studied at Zurich University. He was attracted
at an early age by Marxist ideas and became involved in
the revolutionary movement; in 1895 he joined the Russian
Social Democratic Workers' Party (RSDRP; later the
Communist Party). He was not a committed follower of
Lenin and his policies and was often at loggerheads with
the Bolshevik ideologists and with Lenin himself.

From 1917 to 1928 Lunacharsky was People's Com-
missar (Minister) for Education (*see* NARKOMPROS) and a
central figure in the cultural life of the Soviet Union. Well-
educated, tolerant and broad-minded, he did what he
could to preserve the old intelligentsia and to prevent the
destruction of cultural monuments. His views were, however, informed by the Marxist approach to history and
culture and he perpetually asserted the value of the new,
'socialist' culture, elaborating its theoretical tenets and
helping artists to orientate themselves within the new,
'proletarian' system of values. His key essay, 'Lenin and
the study of literature', is not only a tribute to semi-official
aesthetics, but also a well-argued and convincing manifesto
for Soviet culture, utilizing a class-based theory and
Marxist postulates and striving to retain links with the
classical heritage.

Lunacharsky's critical writings gave rise to accusations
of inconsistency, but he was a true art lover and a sensitive
and involved reader and critic. He wrote on the theatre,
music, painting and literature as an essayist rather than as
a scholar, but with great knowledge and professionalism.
Of particular interest was his attempt to see Soviet culture
in the context of world culture, for instance in the essay
'Culture in the West and here'. He was among the first to
notice and analyse new trends in the fine arts but, while
often criticizing them severely, he did nothing to hinder
their development. He did much to bring together the
culture of the new Russia and the Western intelligentsia
and, as a liberal of European education, was on friendly
terms with such writers as George Bernard Shaw (1856–
1950), Romain Rolland (1866–1944) and Bertolt Brecht
(1898–1955). Lunacharsky wrote several plays and a book
of memoirs which, together with his works on philosophy,
aesthetics, literature and art history, form a significant
contribution to the culture of the first post-Revolutionary
decade. In the last years of his life he worked in the
diplomatic service. He was inevitably subjected to the
mechanism of a developing totalitarian culture but he
nevertheless managed to retain a desire to protect and
encourage all that was best in the intellectual life of his
time.

WRITINGS
*Kul'tura na Zapade i u nas* [Culture in the West and here] (Moscow and
Leningrad, 1928)
'Lenin i literaturovedeniye' [Lenin and the study of literature], *Literatur-
naya entsiklopediya*, vi (1932)
*Sobraniye sochineniy: Literaturovedeniye, kritika, estetika* [Collected works:
literary studies, criticism, aesthetics], 8 vols (Moscow, 1963–7)
*Ob izobrazitel'nom iskusstve* [On fine art], 2 vols (Moscow, 1967)

*Vospominaniya i vpechatleniya* [Reminiscences and impressions] (Moscow,
1968)

BIBLIOGRAPHY
N. A. Lunacharskaya-Rozenel': *Pamyat' serdtsa: Vospominaniya* [Memory
of the heart: reminiscences] (Moscow, 1965)
A. A. Lebedev: *Esteticheskiye vzglyady A. V. Lunacharskogo*
[A. V. Lunacharsky's aesthetic views] (Moscow, 1969)

MIKHAIL GUERMAN

**Lunar, Emerio (Darío)** (*b* Cabimas, 27 Jan 1940; *d*
Cabimas, 22 Nov 1990). Venezuelan painter. He was self-
taught and is best known for his depiction of female
figures and his architectural landscapes, which showed his
appreciation of Renaissance art. Characteristic of his
painting was the portrayal of solitary figures in a posed,
wild-eyed attitude, enveloped in unreal surroundings and
in wide spaces containing solid architectural structures, as
in *Mona Lisa* (1970; Caracas, Gal. A. N.). The volume of
the figures was achieved with a flattening effect that gave
the work an archaic character. Among his most important
paintings are *Sadness* (1970; Maracaibo, priv. col.) and
*Woman in Green* (1975; Caracas, Mus. A. Contemp.).

BIBLIOGRAPHY
J. Calzadilla: *Emerio Darío Lunar* (Maracaibo, 1979)
*Emerio Darío Lunar* (exh. cat., Coro, Mus. Dioc. Monseñor Guillermo
Castillo, 1991)

MARÍA ANTONIA GONZÁLEZ-ARNAL

**Lunardi, Camillo.** *See* LEONARDI, CAMILLO.

**Lund.** Swedish city in the province of Skåne (part of
Denmark until 1658). The old centre of Lund can be
traced to the 11th century. In 1060, when the diocese of
Roskilde was divided, Lund was one of two sees established in Skåne. King Knut IV (*reg* 1081–6) founded the
first cathedral of St Laurentius, which was under construction in 1085 (*see* §1 below). The network of modern city
streets was established in the 12th century, the only major
changes occurring at the Reformation in 1536, when the
layout of streets around the demolished churches was
regulated. Nineteen medieval churches and several monasteries are known, many located through excavations. Of
special interest are the many traces of wooden churches,
whose remains date from the mid-11th century.

During the 14th century Lund was overtaken as a
commercial city by Malmö. The Mint was moved to
Malmö in the 1440s, and when the church buildings were
demolished at the Reformation, their stones were used in
the building of the Royal Castle there. The only surviving
monastic church is the 14th-century Benedictine nuns'
church of St Petri, a gabled structure related stylistically to
north German brick Gothic. The contemporary library
attached to the college of the cathedral clergy survives in
a restored condition, south of the cathedral. Some brick
houses also survive. Lund University was established in
1668 and is the second oldest in Sweden. The city centre
is still concentrated in the area around the cathedral and
the City Square, with the oldest university buildings and
the University Square across the park from the cathedral.
This was originally the site of the Archbishop's palace.

1. CATHEDRAL.

*(i) Architecture.* The first cathedral, dedicated to St Laurentius, did not long survive the elevation of Lund to an

archbishopric c. 1104, when the Archbishop became Primate of all Scandinavia and a larger church was needed. The present cathedral was probably begun soon after. During the comprehensive restoration of the cathedral from 1954 to 1963, Cinthio identified the location and plan of the cathedral founded by Knut IV. The building lay inside the present cathedral walls, in the north-east part of the nave, and it was demolished when the crypt came into use in 1131. It had a single-aisle nave, a choir with a tower of the same width and a narrower, quadrangular sanctuary or presbytery to the east. This single-nave church with eastern tower is considered by Cinthio to be 'a representative of a church type strongly marked by Anglo-Saxon features, of which no unaltered example survives in England'.

The high altar in the crypt of the present cathedral was consecrated in 1123, the north side-altar in 1126 and that to the south in 1131. The high altar and south side-altar of the upper church were consecrated in 1145 and the north side-altar in the following year. The cathedral is built in sandstone from the Höör district. It is a basilica with nave, side aisles, transept, choir and apse. A rectangular transept chapel with a sacristy flanks either side of the choir. The crypt under the transept and choir is built to the same plan. Before the late 19th-century rebuilding of the western tower area, there was a narthex with two towers. Apart from the west entrance, the nave also has a portal in the eastern part of each aisle. Two smaller doors have also been found towards the west end. In each transept arm there is a door facing east. In the north transept a door has also been found on the north side just over the entrance to the crypt. The vaulted hall-crypt, which has massive columns with block capitals, is reached from the aisles of the upper church. Eight of the columns are decorated with different types of grooved ornament. Six of these indicate the position of the altar in the presbytery.

The 12th-century cathedral was built in two stages. The architectural elements were mostly built during the first phase, while in the second, apart from some changes in the architecture, there was a concentration on the sculptural decoration. The first phase, which lasted from the first decade of the 12th century until around 1130, shows the influence of the area around the English Channel: the crypt has close connections with the crypt of St Hermès in Ronse, Belgium. Work went on simultaneously at the east and west ends of the cathedral in order to keep the older building in use as long as possible. The original intention seems to have been for a vaulted nave with a triforium. During the second stage this idea was abandoned. The nave has a double-bay system of broad piers with attached shafts alternating with plain rectangular ones. The building was finished off c. 1160 with the richly designed apse exterior (see fig. 1). This stage can be associated with Italian influence, which is also very apparent in the contemporary sculpture.

In 1234 the cathedral was badly burnt, and the main nave was rebuilt with sexpartite rib vaults resting on colonnettes. During the 19th-century restoration, when the existing quadripartite rib vaults were built, the superfluous colonnettes between the clerestory windows were allowed to remain. After the fire, the barrel vault of the

1. Lund Cathedral, exterior of apse, c. 1160

choir was replaced by a rib vault. From the start the cathedral interior was divided into two parts: the elevated transept and choir for the archbishop and clergy, and the nave, at a lower level, for the laity. The rood screen that divided the two areas was demolished in the 1830s, when the present steps were constructed.

At the beginning of the 16th century a thorough restoration of the cathedral was undertaken under the direction of ADAM VAN DÜREN. Changes in the wall construction can be clearly identified through the masons' marks. Earlier mason's marks can also be found, the earliest dating to the period after the fire of 1234. During the 19th century the cathedral underwent major changes. From 1860 to 1880 the task of the director of the works, Helgo Zettervall, was to re-create what was then thought to be as stylistically pure a Romanesque cathedral as possible; at this time the present west end was built. During the restoration from 1954 to 1963 the weathered sandstone surfaces of the walls were cleaned, and new stone was brought from the original quarry.

(ii) Sculpture. The cathedral's 12th-century sculptural decoration is among the richest in Scandinavia. The building's show-façade is the apse, with the storeys divided by blind arcades and a colonnaded gallery, where the corbels and capitals are decorated with elegant and richly varied Romanesque motifs (see fig. 1 above). Much care was devoted to the two doors in the side aisles. The north aisle door is the more ornamented and consists of a baldacchino supported on colonnettes with a series of decorated arches, added during the 1150s. The south door, which has no baldacchino, is probably earlier. There is equally rich decoration on the interior, especially in the transept area.

The 12th-century sculpture has two styles. The first, dating from the 1130s, is a Cosmati–Lombard style with distinctive ribbon-arabesques, knot patterns and rinceaux with entwined fruit or animals; the slightly later style, seen

2. Lund Cathedral, crypt column with sculpture of a figure known as the Giant Finn, 12th century

on the reset door in the north transept, is classicizing, with rich mouldings ornamented with dogtooth and egg-and-dart ornament, as well as Corinthian capitals. The figural elements and sculptures of lions and angels show Byzantine influence. New stylistic features appear towards the end of the 12th century and in conjunction with the rebuilding works after the fire in 1234.

Two sculptures that have been variously interpreted are the two crypt columns with mysterious depictions of human figures (see fig. 2). These partly damaged figures, normally called the Giant Finn and his wife and child, have been connected with a legend about the giant who built the mighty cathedral using magical powers. Reutersvärd associated the figures with the raising of the columns and an eventual miracle associated with this.

BIBLIOGRAPHY
E. Cinthio: *Lunds domkyrka under romansk tid* [Lund Cathedral during the Romanesque period] (Lund, 1957) [Ger. summary]
O. Reutersvärd: 'Simson, styrkebältet och den sakrala kraften' [Samson, the belt of strength and sacred power], *Genesis Profeta: Nordiska studier i gammaltestamentlig ikonografi* [Nordic studies in Old Testament iconography], Acta U. Stockholm.: Stud. Hist. A., xxxiii (Stockholm, 1980), pp. 59–65 [Ger. summary]

MARIAN ULLÉN

**Lund, Christian Tetzen-.** *See* TETZEN-LUND, CHRISTIAN.

**Lund, Frederik (Ludvig) Konow** (*b* Bergen, 20 Oct 1889; *d* Bergen, 30 Aug 1970). Norwegian architect. He was educated as an architect (1910–14) at the Königliche Sächsische Technische Hochschule, Dresden, and then studied in the USA (1916–17). In 1919 he started his own practice in Bergen. His intentions were already evident in the holiday house at Godøysund (1919), where, inspired by Frank Lloyd Wright (whom he had met), he gave a new interpretation to traditional, western Norwegian architectural forms. The building resembled a farmhouse that had been added to over the years: the use of different types of doors and windows contributed to this picturesque and organic effect, and the house was built on many levels. Lund became the major exponent of the 'Bergen school', which, between the wars, developed an approach to house design inspired by the free plans of Wright and of such English architects as Edwin Lutyens. Lund's many houses in Fana and Bergen of the 1920s and 1930s were distinguished by the free composition of volumes, which was adapted to the irregular sites of western Norway, and by their varied and carefully executed detailing. Other characteristics of these houses were their dry-stone walling, such traditional exterior colours as ochre and dark red, and wooden cladding chemically treated to achieve the greyness of naturally weathered wood.

Lund was never influenced by the various currents of Modernism, and he retained his personal style throughout his career. He was one of the most original talents of Norwegian 20th-century architecture. His major post-war works were the hotel at Tafjord (1946), a villa at Gausel (1948), Stavanger, and and the chapel of Marias Minde Our Lady (1957), Bergen. In the last, Lund, who also restored several churches in Bergen and western Norway after World War II, referred back to medieval ecclesiastical architecture. The brick chapel, which forms one wing of an L-shaped layout, consists of a simple barrel-vaulted nave ending in an apse, with a slender, free-standing italianate clock tower.

*NKL*                      BIBLIOGRAPHY
*En arkitekt morer seg: Festskrift til Frederik Konow Lund* [An architect enjoys himself: Festschrift for Frederik Konow Lund] (Bergen, 1959)
C. Norberg-Schulz: *Modern Norwegian Architecture* (Oslo, 1986)

CHRISTIAN NORBERG-SCHULZ

**Lundberg, Gustaf** (*b* Stockholm, 17 Aug 1695; *d* Stockholm, 18 March 1786). Swedish painter and pastellist. He was orphaned early and brought up by his grandfather, the goldsmith Fredrik Richter (1636–1714). In 1710 he was briefly apprenticed to David von Krafft (1655–1724). Against von Krafft's advice, and at his own expense, he travelled to Paris in 1717. He studied first with Hyacinthe Rigaud, Nicolas de Largillierre and Jean-François de Troy, learning to paint in a Régence style less heavy and serious than that taught by von Krafft in Sweden. He also studied drawing under Pierre-Jacques Cazes at the Ecole des Beaux-Arts. In 1720 Rosalba Carriera came to Paris from Italy, bringing with her the fashionable technique of drawing in pastel chalks. Lundberg became her pupil and within a year had mastered the medium, charming the Parisians with his portraits. Until the arrival of Carriera, he had worked only in oils (e.g. the portrait of *Gabriel Sack and his Wife Eva Bielke*, 1730; priv. col.), but he now turned exclusively to pastels. He received portrait commissions from Louis XV (*reg* 1715–74), notably for those of his young queen *Maria Leszczyńska* and of her parents *Stanislav I Leszczyński and Catherine Opalińska* (both 1725; Upplands Väsby, priv. col.), who at that time were living at Chambord. Through the agency of Carl Gustav Tessin, Lundberg was received (*reçu*) at the Académie Royale de Peinture et de Sculpture in 1741. As his *morceaux de réception* he executed two portraits of *François Boucher* and *Charles-Joseph Nattier*, shown at the Salon of 1743.

News of Lundberg's popularity quickly reached Sweden, and Swedes visiting Paris commissioned their portraits from him. Although enormously productive, he was often accused of deficiencies in drawing. In the 1740s, with the emergence of such French pastellists as Maurice-Quentin de La Tour and Jean-Baptiste Perronneau, the competition stiffened. On the advice of Axel Fleming, the Swedish ambassador in Madrid, Lundberg travelled to the Spanish capital in 1745. He evidently had no success, despite a royal portrait commission, and returned to Sweden that year. In Stockholm, Tessin introduced Lundberg at the court, and in 1750 he was appointed Court Portrait Painter. His return to Sweden was a great setback for the more traditional Swedish portrait painters such as Johan Henrik Scheffel (1690–1781) and Olof Arenius (1701–66). They worked in the older tradition of David Klöcker, David von Krafft and Engelhardt Schröder (1684–1750) and consequently saw their work passed over in favour of Lundberg's portraits, which perfectly expressed the Rococo spirit in their treatment of colour and handling of material and in their superficial but charming depictions of the sitter. In his court portraits (e.g. *Queen Ulrika Louisa*, 1777; Stockholm, Nmus.) he preserved the tradition of Rigaud. The royal family is presented in full regalia with symbols glorifying their power. These symbols can also be found in the portraits of the royal children (e.g. *Crown Prince Gustav Adolf*, 1779; Stockholm, Kun. Husgerådskam.). In 1776 he became Director of the Kungliga Akademi för die Fria Konsterna. Many of his portraits are in private collections in Sweden and have, over the years, been ruined through careless treatment. Among his many pupils, the best-known is Peter Adolf Hall.

SVKL

BIBLIOGRAPHY

O. Levertin: *Gustaf Lundberg, en studie* [Gustaf Lundberg, a study] (Stockholm, 1902)
U. G. Johnsson, ed.: *Porträtt, porträtt: Studier i statens porträttsamling på Gripsholm* [Portrait, portrait: studies of the state portrait collection at Gripsholm] (Stockholm, 1987), pp. 85–8

A.-G. WAHLBERG

**Lundbye, Johan Thomas** (*b* Kalundborg, 1 Sept 1818; *d* Bedsted, 25 April 1848). Danish painter. He studied at the Kongelige Akademi for de Skønne Kunster, Copenhagen, under Johan Ludvig Lund (1777–1867) and the animal painter Christian Holm (1804–46) between 1832 and 1842. Early on he was influenced by the ideas of the art historian N. L. Høyen, especially his concept of a truly national school of landscape painting. *Kalundborg Church* (1837; Copenhagen, Stat. Mus. Kst) depicts a historical monument familiar to all Danes, and one that had a

particular nostalgic attraction for a painter born in Kalundborg. The picture is both sharply naturalistic and emphatically painterly. In *Landscape Near Arresø* (1838; Copenhagen, Thorvaldsens Mus.) Lundbye was more occupied with the representation of light and space. There is no anecdotal element; the lake, the open sky, the low hills, the ancient cairn, the cattle and the playing children sum up a typical Danish summer landscape. His larger canvases emphasize openness; flat expanses of land terminate in low tree-fringed horizons below vast skies. They have little of Constable's temperament or the broadness of Corot but are close to the elegiac mood of Caspar David Friedrich and Johan Christian Dahl. Danish landscape painting during the mid-1830s was greatly influenced by Romanticism; Danish and German Romantic literature was an important element in the nationalist movement of those years.

Lundbye once stated that his sole wish was to paint 'dear Denmark'. His highly charged Danish patriotism led him to treat local landscapes with an idealized adaptation of the Grand style, as in *Zealand Landscape* and *Danish Coast* (both 1842; Copenhagen, Stat. Mus. Kst), two pictures that were in fact made up of various studies pieced together. In *Danish Coast* he makes the steep slopes appear monumental by diminishing the size of the trees above them and the figures on the beach below, the nearest approach to the sublime possible in a mountainless country. References to ancient Danish culture often appear in his work, as in the *Tumulus 'Hankehøj'* (1847; Copenhagen, Hirschsprungske Saml.). His own words express the essential simplicity of such works: 'It is autumn, and the cows go loose, a boy is herding them, and on the tumulus grow a couple of whitethorns which have been bowed by the frequent gusts of the north-wester' (Madsen, 1918).

Lundbye's animal paintings are more intimate than his landscapes; his main sources of inspiration were Paulus Potter and Josse II de Momper, whose works he had studied in the Netherlands on his way back from Italy in 1847. One of his best animal pieces, *Cow-shed in a Farm in Vejlby* (1844; Copenhagen, Stat. Mus. Kst), met with strong criticism because of its forthright realism. The king was said to have commented that it smelt of cow-dung. Each animal is carefully characterized; the sun creeps through the door into the warm atmosphere of the shed. At the age of 29 Lundbye was killed by an accidental shot shortly after he had volunteered for the Danish–German war of 1848–51.

BIBLIOGRAPHY

K. Madsen, ed.: *J. Th. Lundbye: Dagbogsoptegnelser* [Diaries] (Copenhagen and Kristiania, 1918), p. 57
K. Madsen: *Johan Thomas Lundbye, 1818–1848* (Copenhagen, 1895/R 1945)
*Akademiet og Guldalderen, 1750–1850* [The Academy and the Golden Age, 1750–1850], *Dansk Kunsthistorie*, iii (Copenhagen, 1972), pp. 430–42
*Johan Thomas Lundbye, 1818–1848. . .at male det kjare Danmark* [Johan Thomas Lundbye, 1818–1848. . .to paint dear Denmark] (exh. cat., ed. E. Henschen, T. Melander and S. Miss; Copenhagen, Thorvaldsens Mus., 1994)

JENS PETER MUNK

**Lundquist, Evert** (*b* Stockholm, 17 July 1904; *d* Stockholm, 4 Nov 1994). Swedish painter and engraver. He studied at Carl Willhelmson's art school in Stockholm

(1924), the Académie Julian in Paris (1924–5) and the Konsthögskola in Stockholm (1925–31), during which time he produced *Oscarskyrkan* (1928; see Wretholm, p. 43) in a dry, realistic style. In 1931–2 and again in 1933 he was in Paris, where he painted such works as *Luxembourg Garden* (1933–4; see 1974 exh. cat., p. 10) using impasto paint, simplified forms and restrained colour. He had his first one-man show in 1934 at the Konstnärhus in Stockholm. A bout of deep depression (1936–7) led him to paint such works as *The Butler* (1937; Stockholm, Mod. Mus.) in a swift, expressionist style; shortly after this he painted a number of grotesque canvases showing the influence of James Ensor, such as *Fête champêtre* (1937; see Wretholm, p. 69). After a number of tightly structured, impastoed works (e.g. *Woman in Garden (Margit)*, 1939; Stockholm, Mod. Mus.), in the early 1940s his style became more gestural, as in *Wave* (1942–3; Stockholm, Mod. Mus.). Also in the early 1940s Lundquist was loosely associated with the Swedish artists Olle Nyman (*b* 1909), Roland Kempe (*b* 1907) and Staffan Hallström (*b* 1914) in a group sometimes called the Saltsjö-Duvnäs group after the place where they often met. Lundquist travelled to France and Italy in 1947, after which he painted such thickly impastoed, near abstract works as *The Reeds* (1949; see Wretholm, p. 98). In 1952 he first experimented with drypoint engraving and later produced such dramatic prints as *Explosion* (1959; see Wretholm, p. 159). He moved in 1953 to Drottningholm, near Stockholm, where he painted interior scenes such as the *Table, Drottningholm* (1955; see Wretholm, p. 114). He also reworked Old Master paintings, as in *The Draughtsman* (1955–6; Paris, Pompidou), based on the work by Chardin. In 1956 he produced the mosaic *The Tree* for the newly built town hall at Skellefteå. In 1960 and 1962, through the introduction of the English artist Cliff Holden (*b* 1919), he was given exhibitions in London at the Beaux Arts Gallery, which also sponsored similar work by Frank Auerbach and Leon Kossoff. In 1960 he was appointed a professor at the Konsthögskola, and his work of the 1960s continued the earlier simplified, impastoed style, as in *In the Field* (1963; Stockholm, Mod. Mus.). Later paintings often depicted figures in a highly abstracted and disturbing manner, as in *Head of a Woman* (1974; Stockholm, Mod. Mus.), where the subject appears almost to dissolve in light, and the facial features are reduced to a minimum.

BIBLIOGRAPHY

*Evert Lundquist* (exh. cat. by P. von Schantz and U. Linde, Stockholm, Mod. Mus., 1974)
E. Wretholm: *Evert Lundquist* (Stockholm, 1977) [Eng./Swed. text]
*Evert Lundquist: Malerier og raderinger* [Evert Lundqvist: painter and engraver] (exh. cat. by E. Blomberg, Oslo, Kstnernes Hus, 1985)

**Lund & Slaatto.** Norwegian architectural partnership formed in 1958 by Kjell (Arve) Lund (*b* Lillehammer, 18 June 1927) and Nils Slaatto (*b* Lillehammer, 22 June 1923). Both graduated as architects from the Norwegian Polytechnic in Trondheim, Lund in 1950 and Slaatto in 1947. From its inception the partnership played a leading role in Norwegian architecture, producing a large amount of fine work. Such early works as the Vik Secondary School (1958–60), Hole, still retain an air of late Modernism, with flat roofs and ribbon windows. The Asker Town Hall (1958–63) has the same characteristics, although here more substantial, robust forms appear. These are fully evident in St Hallvard church and Franciscan monastery (1958–66), Oslo, where the basic theme is extremely simple: a circular chapel is placed at the centre of a square block. The block, although small, makes a powerful impact; the church's interior provides a restful contrast to the complexities of the area's surrounding tower blocks. St Hallvard met with general approval, but the design of the Student Union Building in Oslo, Chateau Neuf (1961–71) was attacked for its uncompromising Brutalism and technological character.

The Veritas Centre (1972–6; 1981–4) in Bærum outside Oslo is Lund & Slaatto's largest work. The architects used a prefabricated infrastructure, which provided the flexibility necessary to house a variety of functions. Its internal organization is spacious and open. It was designed to harmonize with the beautiful site on the Oslo Fjord; though large, the complex blends with its surroundings, and when seen from the fjord it conveys the impression of a village. Lund & Slaatto's ability to adapt designs to an urban environment is particularly well demonstrated by the Bank of Norway (1973–86) in Oslo and the House of Culture (begun 1979) in Stavanger, although the partnership designed a number of other important public buildings, including the European Youth Centre (1958–70), Strasbourg, and houses. Their flexible 'Ål' building system for holiday cottages (1966) is particularly interesting, since it revives basic elements of old Norwegian wooden architecture in a creative way.

NKL
BIBLIOGRAPHY
K. Lund: 'Arkitektur og identitet' [Architecture and identity], *Bygknst*, xlvii (1965), pp. 85–90
C. Norberg-Schulz: *Modern Norwegian Architecture* (Oslo, 1986)
CHRISTIAN NORBERG-SCHULZ

**Lundsten, Bengt** (*b* Turku, 1928). Finnish architect. He graduated from the Technical University in Helsinki in 1954. Lundsten worked first in Viljo Revell's office on such projects as the prizewinning entry for the Town Hall, Toronto, also acting as job architect during building. In 1962 he set up his own practice in Helsinki. In 1968 he became Professor of Building Technology at the Technical University. His work of the 1960s and 1970s shows a sensitive development of Finnish constructivist architectural expression. This is represented, in particular, by a passengers' pavilion (1965) for the Silja shipping company in Langsnäs, Åland. Mainly glass-walled, it is suspended by wires from an external steel frame. The light, right-angled prism of the building is placed perpendicularly to the pier; only its landward gable meets the rising ground. The pavilion itself, which also contains a cafeteria, guides passengers from bus to ship; a roofed area below is intended for customs' inspection of cars. Both functionally and structurally the building can be compared to a bridge. Among Lundsten's other important works are two developments of terraced houses, which apply new techniques to the tradition of Finnish wooden towns. He also developed a living environment through linking interior and exterior spaces, as visible in the street plans, which quite freely follow the grid principle. In Kortepohja,

Jyväskylä (street plan, 1965; houses, 1968–9; with Esko Kahri), two to two-and-a-half storey houses are naturally situated in undulating land so that, within the development, there are varying views despite the apparent strictness of the grid plan. Pedestrian and motor traffic are separated. The right-angled, prism-shaped, flat-roofed houses are built on a concrete frame; the cross-wall areas, which divide the flats from each other on the long side, are formed from prefabricated wooden elements complete with windows and doors. The light fences that surround the gardens also refer to the wood-town tradition. The range of external colouring is characteristic of some areas of wooden housing built in the 1920s. One of Lundsten's most important restoration projects is also from the 1960s: the Käpylä wooden suburb in Helsinki. The refurbishment of these two-storey dwellings (1970–78) was carried out with as few changes as possible to the existing buildings, and a detailed inventory of the building components that were to be replaced was drawn up. In his subsequent work Lundsten 'softened' his formal language.

MARJA-RIITTA NORRI

**Lundstrøm, Vilhelm (Henry)** (*b* Sundbyerne, 26 May 1893; *d* Copenhagen, 9 May 1950). Danish painter. He trained as an artisan painter (1908–12), and he went to the Kunstakademi in Copenhagen, where he studied (1913–15) under Peter Rostrup-Bøyesen (1882–1952) among others. He made his début at the *Kunstnernes Efterårsudstilling* ('Artists' Autumn Exhibition') in Copenhagen in 1916 and exhibited there in subsequent years. Lundstrøm was a modernist, and with Svend Johansen (1890–1970), Axel Salto and Karl Larsen (1897–1977) he formed the group De Fire (the Four), active between 1920 and 1929. They were also all associated with the avant-garde periodical *Klingen*. Lundstrøm later took his place in the artistic establishment: from 1937 as a member of the Academy council, and from 1944 as a professor at the Kunstakademi.

Lundstrøm was the first to introduce abstract art to a Danish audience. Shortly before World War I he visited Berlin, where he saw Expressionist and Cubist works, in which he maintained an interest in the following years through art books, publications and through visits to the private collection of Christian Tetzen-Lund, which included late Cubist work by Picasso and Braque. Lundstrøm began to experiment with Cubism's formal language. At the *Kunstnernes Efterårsudstilling* of 1917 he showed small collages containing pieces of newspaper, lace and silver paper. The attention these aroused erupted into a scandal at the same exhibition the following year, where Lundstrøm exhibited 'packing-case pictures' (Dan.: 'pakkasse billeder'). These abstract geometric compositions were made from pieces of packing-case wood glued and nailed together with stencilled lettering and added colour, so that they played with the tension between two and three dimensions; they were inscribed in ovals, which further underscored his affinity with Picasso and Braque. Since three of the pictures were entitled *Bud* ('Commandment'), Lundstrøm was further accused of blasphemy. They were also used by critics as examples of a mental disorder shared by young modern artists, which led them to reproduce nature in distorted form.

After his Cubist experiments Lundstrøm adopted a more emotional, expressive style in the period 1919–23 (the 'Krøllede Periode'), with heavy brushstrokes. The transition was manifested in a series of paintings, including the *Explanation of Cubism* (priv. col., see Wilmann and Brøns, p. 49) and *Goodbye to Cubism* (priv. col., see Wilmann and Brøns, pl. 50), which show his abandonment of geometric abstraction for the depiction of the luxuriant figure of a female model. She often appears in the work from this period, during which Lundstrøm was preoccupied by such painters as El Greco, Tintoretto, Rubens and Titian. Among the better-known examples is the large *Lunch on the Grass* (Humlebæk, Lousiana Mus.), for which the artist borrowed motifs from Manet's *Déjeuner sur l'herbe*, transformed into a much more vigorous, almost caricatured, image painted with coarse brushstrokes, palette knife and fingers. Lundstrøm also produced a number of paintings of everyday objects, including the *Arrangement with Pitcher, Sauce-boat and Bottle* (1920; Copenhagen, Stat. Mus. Kst), and self-portraits. From this period also came his *Hommage aux peintres artistes* (1920; Ålborg, Nordjyllands Kstmus.), a tribute to De Fire. *The Four Seasons* (Århus, Kstmus.), in the form of four buxom females, was created in cooperation with Poul Henningsen as a decoration for the *Kunstnernes Efterårsudstilling* of 1921.

After journeys to Italy and France, among other places, in the early 1920s, Lundstrøm lived with his painting comrades, at Cagnes-sur-Mer from 1923 to 1932. There he worked in the Purist style for which he is best known. He created strict geometric simplifications of various subjects, such as arrangements of a white enamel pitcher, or oranges, against a blue background. These were called 'laboratory-like' when they were exhibited in 1925 and Lundstrøm himself said that paintings should be 'uncontaminated by irrelevant things', and anonymous and impersonal. This also applied to his figure paintings, although in spite of their rigorous simplification they never entirely lost the quality of portraiture. Back in Denmark, between 1933 and 1938 Lundstrøm executed his only large decorative commission, five wall mosaics at the Frederiksberg Swimming-baths. The subject is bathing men and women, in ochre and cobalt-blue colours, and his studies of Antique sculpture, manifested in the attitudes of the figures, are applied to simplified forms. In his last decade of work he allowed more colour and detail to enter the compositions.

BIBLIOGRAPHY
'Interview med Lundstrøm', *Gads Dan. Mag.*, xxxi (1937), pp. 148–56
A. Rode: 'Interview med Lundstrøm', *Tilskueren* (Sept 1939), pp. 225–35
*Lundstrøm's Mindeudstilling* [Lundstrøm's memorial exhibition] (exh. cat., foreword A. Salto; Copenhagen, Charlottenborg, 1951)
P. Wilmann and M. Brøns: *Lundstrøm* (1977, 2/1987) [with bibliog. and Eng. résumé]

BIRGIT HESSELLUND

**Lüneburg.** German town known as a centre of tapestry production during the 16th century (*see* GERMANY, §XI, 3(ii) and (iii)).

**Lunette** [Fr.: 'little moon']. Semicircular space on a wall or ceiling, framed by an arch or vault. The term can also be applied to a window or a work of art in this format.

**Lunéville.** French town in the Meurthe-et-Moselle département. It is 30 km south-east of Nancy on the Vezouze River.

1. HISTORY AND URBAN DEVELOPMENT. The origins of the town can be traced back to the 10th century when it was a seigneurie belonging to the Folmar family, the counts of Metz. The town originated around a château and an abbey. In 1243 the seigneurie was sold to Matthew II, Duke of Lorraine (*reg* 1220–50). In 1593 the artist Georges de La Tour was born in Vic-sur-Seille, north of Lunéville, and in 1620 he settled in Lunéville, where he painted all of his works, casting off the legacy of Caravaggio in favour of a more contemplative spirituality. In 1638, during the Thirty Years War, the town was destroyed by fire, probably resulting in the loss of many of La Tour's paintings; none remains in Lunéville.

The presence of a French garrison in Nancy from 1702 prompted Leopold, Duke of Lorraine (*reg* 1697–1729), to leave his capital and establish his court at Lunéville, where he entrusted the building of a vast château (see fig.) to GERMAIN BOFFRAND. Rather than a design in the elaborate Baroque style, a less costly classically inspired design was settled on, influenced by the general layout of the château of Versailles. The main, two-storey buildings frame three sides of a courtyard and forecourt facing west to the town. Eastwards, the main ducal building gives on to a terrace that leads to formal gardens designed by Yves des Ours (*d* 1746) and Louis-Ferdinand de Nesle, known as 'Gervais' (*d* 1756). Leopold undertook plans for urban development around the Old Town, which was rebuilt after the fire in 1638 using the medieval plans. He first had new districts built in a regularly laid-out pattern, followed in 1706 by the Hôpital St Jacques. In 1728 he had a small, elliptical Italianate residence, 'La Favorite', built to the south-east of the château gardens for his youngest son Prince Charles-Alexandre; it was probably designed by Boffrand. During Leopold's reign a weapons factory and a tapestry works were founded; a pottery was also established *c.* 1728 by Jacques Chambrette (1705–58; *see* §2 below).

In 1730 Francis III (*reg* 1729–36) built the abbey church of St Rémy (now St Jacques; see HALL CHURCH, fig. 2), in the centre of the Old Town. Plans for the church were probably drawn up by Nicolas Jenneson (1686–1753), and the façade (unrealized) was designed by Jean-Nicolas Jadot de Ville-Issey. In 1737 Grand Duke STANISLAV I LESZCZYŃSKI (*reg* 1736–66), the deposed King of Poland and father-in-law of Louis XV of France, installed himself and his court at Lunéville, where he ruled until his death in 1766. He commissioned his architect EMMANUEL HÉRÉ and his Premier Peintre Jean Girardet (1709–78) to finish St Rémy in the Rococo style (1743–7). The two belfries

Lunéville, east (garden) façade of the château by Germain Boffrand (from 1708), with alterations by Emmanuel Héré (1740s)

and the organ-loft were completed in 1747. The still-life and *trompe-l'oeil* painters Jean-François Foisse, known as 'Brabant' (1708–63), and Dominique Pergaut (1729–1808) also worked for Stanislav. Nothing remains of the buildings Stanislav had Héré build in and beyond the gardens of the château: for example the salon at Chanteheux (1740) and the Théâtre d'Automates du Rocher (1742), the latter a miniature water-powered village and landscape. These were demolished from 1766, after the regions of Lorraine and Bar once again became part of France. In 1785 Charles-Augustin Piroux (1749–1805) built the synagogue, the façade of which shows the influence of Boffrand.

In the 19th century embroidery on tulle (using stitches, beads or sequins) began to be produced in Lunéville. The town also became a prominent centre of Art Nouveau design in Lorraine through the glassworks of the Muller brothers, who were followers of the potter, glassmaker and cabinetmaker Emile Gallé and who worked in Lunéville from 1895 to 1936.

BIBLIOGRAPHY

H. Beaumont: *Histoire de Lunéville* (Lunéville, 1900)
E. Delorme: *Lunéville et son arrondissement* (Lunéville, 1927)
J. Choux: *Lunéville* (Colmar-Ingersheim, 1972)
J. Rau: *Emmanuel Héré* (Berlin, 1973)
*Germain Boffrand, 1667–1754: L'Aventure d'un architecte indépendant* (exh. cat., ed. M. Gallet and J. Garms; Paris, Mairie IVe, 1986)

2. CENTRE OF CERAMICS PRODUCTION. The pottery was founded *c.* 1728 by Jacques Chambrette (1705–58), who was a Lunéville pottery vendor and produced Rococo-style faience decorated with flowers, birds, landscapes and Chinese figures. From 1749 Chambrette also introduced objects made in *terre de pipe*, a soft, white lead-glazed *faïence fine* (creamware), which was to rival porcelain. In 1757 he founded a second pottery in the neighbouring village of Saint-Clément. About 1765 Paul-Louis Cyfflé (1724–1806), sculptor to Stanislas I, also established a factory in Lunéville, which until 1780 made many biscuit figures in *terre de Lorraine*, a type of soft *terre de pipe*, whitened with lime phosphate.

In 1772 Richard Mique, architect to Marie-Antoinette, became the principal owner of the Saint-Clément pottery. The style there was Neo-classical with polychrome decoration and gilding. In 1788 the Lunéville factory was sold to Sebastian Keller (?1749–1829). From 1864 to 1876 the glassmaker and potter Emile Gallé and his father produced some of their wares in a workshop at Saint-Clément, which was then owned by the Thomas family. In 1892 the Keller and Guérin families, who owned the pottery at Lunéville, bought Saint-Clément. From 1894 Lunéville produced Art-Nouveau style hard-fired stoneware with flambé glazes. In 1922 the Fenal family acquired the two potteries. Production at Lunéville ceased in 1981, but continued at Saint-Clément.

BIBLIOGRAPHY

*Céramique lorraine: Chefs-d'oeuvre des XVIIIe et XIXe siècles* (exh. cat. by G. de Meaux, Nancy and Metz, 1990)

PIERRE CHANEL

**Lunghi.** *See* LONGHI (i).

**Lunghi, Silla.** *See* LONGHI, SILLA.

**Lung-men.** *See* LONGMEN.

**Lungren, Fernand Harvey** (*b* Hagerstown, MD, 13 Nov 1857; *d* Santa Barbara, CA, 9 Nov 1932). American painter and illustrator. Of Swedish descent, the family moved to Toledo, OH, when Lungren was four years old. He showed an early talent for drawing but was intended by his father for a professional career and in 1874 entered the University of Michigan, Ann Arbor, to study mining engineering. He left in 1876, however, determined to become an artist. After a protracted dispute with his father he was allowed briefly to attend the Pennsylvania Academy in Philadelphia, where he studied under Thomas Cowperthwaite Eakins and had Robert Frederick Blum, Alfred Laurens Brennan (1853–1921) and Joseph Pennell as fellow students. In the winter of 1877 he moved to New York, where he worked as an illustrator for *Scribner's Monthly* (renamed *Century* in 1881) during the period known as 'the golden age of American illustration'. His first illustration appeared in 1879 and he continued to contribute to the magazine until 1903. He was also an illustrator for the children's magazine *St Nicholas* from 1879 to 1904 and later for *Harper's Bazaar*, *McClure's* and *The Outlook*. For all these periodicals he produced landscapes, portraits and social scenes to illustrate articles and stories, being noted for his New York street scenes.

In 1882 Lungren travelled to Europe, visiting Antwerp and then Paris. In Paris he studied briefly at the Académie Julian and saw Impressionist works at first hand. He found the visit largely disappointing, however, and returned to New York late in 1883. Soon after his return he set up a studio in Cincinnati, OH, and in 1892 made a trip to Santa Fe, NM, where he first encountered Native American culture and the desert landscape. This was the beginning of a lifelong association with the region and its people, leading to such works as *In the Abyss: Grand Canyon* (*c.* 1895; Santa Barbara, U. CA, A. Mus.) and the huge *Snake Dance* (*c.* 1895; Santa Barbara, U. CA, A. Mus.). He showed a number of these works in 1899 at the American Art Galleries in New York, together with works by Maurice Boutet de Monvel.

After marrying Henrietta Whipple in 1898 Lungren travelled with her in the following year to London, where his desert pictures were given a mixed reception initially. He produced a number of pictures of London street life, particularly using pastels, a medium in which he had become very proficient, as shown by *Where Fog is King* (1899; Santa Barbara, U. CA, A. Mus.). He also met many artists, including Whistler, and exhibited at the Royal Academy in London and at the Walker Art Gallery in Liverpool. Late in 1900 he travelled with the medical scientist Henry Solomon Wellcome to Egypt, where he produced such works as the pastel *Pyramids at Ghizeh* (1901; Santa Barbara, U. CA, A. Mus.). In mid-1901 he returned to London, and to New York later that year.

The Lungrens moved in 1903 to California and settled in Santa Barbara in 1906. Lungren made his first trip to Death Valley in 1909, the first of many visits, and produced the painting *Death Valley, Sunrise* (1909; Toledo, OH, Mus. A.). At about this time he began work on a series of paintings designed to show the desert in all its conditions, a project that resulted in such works as *Desert Dawn*

(Santa Barbara, U. CA, A. Mus.). He remained based in Santa Barbara and on his death ensured that his paintings were left there. After a legal dispute over his planned foundation of a museum in the town, his collection of some 300 works were donated to Santa Barbara State College, now part of the University of California. Lungren's many depictions of the American desert at their best succeed in recreating its solitary atmosphere and established it as a subject worthy of attention in art.

BIBLIOGRAPHY

J. A. Berger: *Fernand Lungren: A Biography* (Santa Barbara, 1936)

**Lung-shan.** *See* LONGSHAN.

**Luny, Thomas** (*b* St Ewe, Cornwall, 20 May 1759; *d* Teignmouth, Devon, 29 Sept 1837). English painter. He was a member of the Thames group of marine painters around Deptford, following the tradition of the van de Velde (ii) family, Dutch 17th-century marine painters. Luny was a pupil of Francis Holman (*fl* 1760–90) by 1773 and first exhibited in 1777 at the Society of Artists, showing *Storm and Shipwreck* (untraced). He exhibited regularly at the Royal Academy from 1780 until 1793 and then only in 1802 and in the year of his death. His absence from the Academy exhibitions after 1793 gave rise to the erroneous assumption of his enlistment in the navy during the Napoleonic conflict, but there is no mention of Luny in Admiralty records.

Luny's prolific output of representations of naval engagements, such as the *Battle on the Nile* (1798; London, N. Mar. Mus.) and paintings of Honourable East India Company Ships, enabled him in 1807 to leave London for Teignmouth, where he had a substantial house built. This move was probably prompted by the retirement of his naval patrons to the resort after the war and by the onset of rheumatoid arthritis. After 1807 he increasingly depicted the local coastal scenery and associated maritime pursuits.

Luo Ping: *Guiqu tu* ('The fascination of ghosts'; detail), handscroll, ink on paper, 235×344 mm, before 1772 (Hong Kong, Huo Baocai private collection)

Luny compiled an inventory from 1807 until 1835, listing over 2800 paintings, giving details of size, subject, price and purchaser. His best work is generally considered to be from his middle period, from 1807 to 1817, before his physical disabilities took too firm a hold. Only known to have one pupil, a Captain Hulme, Luny had a limited influence on his contemporaries.

UNPUBLISHED SOURCES

London, Soc. Geneal. [inventory of paintings, 1807–35]

Archibald

BIBLIOGRAPHY

R. Dymond: 'Thomas Luny, Marine Painter', *Trans. Devon Assoc.*, xviii (1886), pp. 442–9

W. Gaunt: *Marine Painting: An Historical Survey* (London, 1975)

R. G. VIGG

**Luo Ping** [Lo P'ing; *zi* Dunfu; *hao* Liangfeng, Yiyun Heshang, Huazhi Siseng] (*b* Yangzhou, Jiangsu Province, 1733; *d* 1799). Chinese painter and writer. Luo was the youngest of the major YANGZHOU SCHOOL painters of the 18th century and a significant innovator in the genres of portraiture and depiction of ghosts. Born into a family of scholar–officials, in his early career Luo was much influenced by JIN NONG, his teacher in poetry and painting from about 1757. After Jin's death in 1763 Luo undertook the editing of some of his mentor's writings, together with other quasi-filial duties. Jin's historical and selfconscious exploration of a broad range of genres, including plum and bamboo painting, portraiture and Buddhist figure painting, clearly influenced Luo's choice of subject-matter. However, the relationship was not one-sided: Luo was more technically accomplished than his teacher and probably painted works to which Jin signed his own name. Luo's portrait *Jin Nong Taking a Noon Nap* (hanging scroll; 1760; Shanghai Mus.) is notably informal and irreverent in style.

Several other paintings from Luo's early career document both his entrance, by the early 1760s, into the cultured circles of south-east China and his exploration of the significance of portraiture. A second portrait, *Jin Nong*, and an image of the antiquarian and seal-carver *Ding Jing* (hanging scrolls on paper; both Hangzhou, Zhejiang Prov. Mus.) depict the scholars as *luohan* (Skt: *arhat*s) and reflect Luo's religious interests as well as his flexible conception of the self. Related to these paintings is a portrait of the *Chan Buddhist Master Tan* (hanging scroll; 1763; Suzhou Mus.), the inscription on which suggests a composite identity for the sitter, part contemporary monk and part legendary Chan eccentric. Luo's probing of the conceptual boundaries of portraiture recurs in a portrait of the eminent writer, *Yuan Mei* (1781; Princeton U., NJ, A. Mus.), where the problematic nature of the identity of the subject is noted by the sitter in his long and witty inscription.

After Jin's death, Luo travelled widely: in 1764 and 1765 he visited parts of Jiangsu, Anhui and Jiangxi provinces, and in 1771 and 1779 he went to Beijing, where he remained until the last months of his life. As earlier in Yangzhou, Luo associated with many leading scholar–officials and literary men of the capital. His greatest success, though a qualified one, was an eight-section scroll, the *Guiqu tu* ('The fascination of ghosts'; see fig.), painted before 1772. One of Luo's several variations on the theme, this painting bears a number of appreciative and critical inscriptions. Luo's ghost scenes reflect, and perhaps exploit, a broad contemporary taste for the literary genre of ghost stories. Nonetheless, the sincerity of his interest in ghosts and other occult phenomena is certain; his essay collection *Woxin lu* ('Record of my beliefs'; 1791) has chapters on reincarnation, ghosts and spirits, as well as on the significance of many of his paintings. Moreover, in comparison to the merely humorous grotesqueries of contemporary standard ghost paintings, Luo's *Guiqu tu* is distinguished both by its subtly appropriate technical devices—murkily suffused ink washes, bleeding, indistinct contours and eerily unnatural colours—and by its glimpses of anguish, confusion and terror associated with the human world.

Luo's largest body of work comprised minor technical and compositional variations on the standard Yangzhou school themes of bamboo, plum and epidendrum. He also painted explicitly Buddhist themes, sometimes on temple walls. Two landscape albums from around the 1770s best display his technical mastery, together with a thematic subtlety and ingenuity to rival anything of his century: *Landscapes* (Princeton U., NJ, A. Mus.) and *Landscapes Illustrating the Poems of Jiang Kui of the Southern Song* (1774; Washington, DC, Freer). The latter includes such inventive scenes as a rabbit fleeing the vividly realized chaos of a forest fire.

Despite his originality and early success, Luo spent his later years living quietly in Beijing temples or at the residences of patrons, and he died almost destitute, exemplifying the precarious position of the institutionally independent artist of the 18th century, subject to financial pressures and shifting tastes.

### BIBLIOGRAPHY

Luo Ping: *Woxin lu* [Record of my beliefs] (preface 1791); *R* in *Haibin zazu* (Nanling, 1908)
S. Shimada: 'Ra Hei hitsu Kyō Hakuseki Shiizu satsu' [Luo Ping's album paintings of Jiang Baishi's *Poetic Intent* pictures], *Kokka*, 748 (July 1954), pp. 194–204
J. Cahill: 'A Rejected Portrait of Lo P'ing: A Pictorial Footnote to Waley's *Yuan Mei*', *Asia Major*, n. s., vii/1–2 (1959), pp. 32–9
Luo Ping: *Luo Ping Guiqu tu juan* [Luo Ping's *Fascination of Ghosts* scroll] (Hong Kong, 1970)
Zhang Wanli and Hu Renmo, eds: *The Selected Painting and Calligraphy of the Eight Eccentrics of Yangchow*, 8 vols (Hong Kong, 1970)
Zhuang Shen: 'Luo Ping yu qi *Guiqu tu*' [Luo Ping and his *Fascination of Ghosts*], *Zhongyang Yyanjiuyuan Lishi Yuyan Yanjiusuo Jikan*, xliv/3 (1972), pp. 403–34
Chen Jinling: *Luo Liangfeng* (Shanghai, 1981)
Mayching Kao, ed.: *Painting by Yangzhou Artists of the Qing Dynasty from the Palace Museum* (Hong Kong, 1984)
J. H. Chou and C. Brown, eds: *The Elegant Brush: Chinese Painting under the Qianlong Emperor, 1735–1795* (Phoenix, 1985)
Mu Yiqin: 'Jin Nong de huihua yu Luo Ping de daibi' [Jin Nong's paintings and Luo Ping's substitutes], *Mingbao Yuekan*, xx/i (Jan 1985), p. 58

RICHARD VINOGRAD

**Luoyang** [Lo-yang]. Major Chinese city in western Henan Province, formerly capital of the Zhou (*c.* 1050–256 BC), Eastern Han (AD 25–220) and Northern Wei (AD 386–534) dynasties, and eastern capital of the Tang dynasty (AD 618–907).

Remains of Eastern Han and Northern Wei Luoyang are located some 15 km east of the modern city, between the Luo River and Mt Mang. The city became prominent after the fall of the usurper Wang Mang (*reg* AD 9–23),

when the population rose to more than 50,000 households. However, a large Western Han (206 BC–AD 9) tomb with wall paintings and numerous grave goods excavated near Mt Mang indicates that Luoyang was an important cultural centre even before becoming the Eastern Han capital. The Han city was surrounded by an outer wall of rammed earth coated with bricks, more than 14 km in circumference and of varied thickness. Inside this outer wall were three lesser enclosures, and the city was further surrounded by a deep moat connected to the Luo River. There were 12 gates in the outer wall, each with gate towers on either side. Inside the city were eight main avenues. From each gate ran a street divided into three lanes, the central one reserved for the emperor and his retinue. The main palace complex was located in the northern part of the city, occupying roughly one-tenth of the entire area. The palace wall (up to 20 m thick) enclosed several large buildings, including the main imperial hall, built on raised foundations of rammed earth. According to popular tradition, the first Buddhist temple in the city, the Baima si (White Horse Temple), was established during the Eastern Han, though none of the present structures are earlier than the Ming period (1368–1644).

In AD 493–4 Luoyang was rebuilt by Emperor Xiao-wendi (*reg* 471–99) of the Northern Wei, who transferred his capital there from Datong in northern Shanxi Province. Northern Wei Luoyang (see fig.) was essentially established on top of the Han city. According to the *Luoyang qielan ji* ('Record of the temples in Luoyang'), written in AD 547 by Yang Xuanzhi (*fl* 6th century), the city was crowded with Buddhist temples. Of these, the Yongning si, built in AD 516 and covering an area of more than

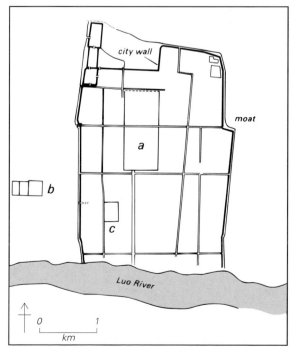

Luoyang, plan of the city during the Northern Wei period (AD 386–534): (a) palace precinct; (b) Baima si; (c) Yongning si

1 sq. km, was the most majestic. At its centre was a pagoda (h. *c.* 150 m) covered with coloured ceramic tiles. The pagoda and the temple were burnt down in a fire in AD 536, when the city was destroyed by civil war.

Under the Sui dynasty (AD 581–618) in AD 605–6 Luoyang was moved west to between the Chan and Jian rivers, so that the Luo River ran through it. Each side of the city walls measured between 6.14 and 7.31 km, with up to three gates from which major avenues ran. The walled imperial quarter was in the north-western corner, with the palace orientated on a north–south axis. The city was divided into 103 wards intersected by crossroads, and there were three major markets that covered entire wards.

Under the Tang the area of Luoyang expanded, and the population rose markedly. In AD 691 Empress Wu Zetian (*reg* 690–705) renovated palace buildings, temples and walls. Buddhist temples were dominant, existing in every quarter of the city and on the surrounding upland. There were also a number of Daoist and Zoroastrian institutions in the city. After the collapse of the Tang in AD 907, Luoyang was devastated and then abandoned. Modern industrial Luoyang bears little resemblance to the imperial and religious centre of the past.

BIBLIOGRAPHY

Yang Xuanzhi: *Luoyang qielan ji jiaoshi* [Record of the temples in Luoyang] (AD 547); ed. by Zhou Zumu (Beijing, 1963–87)

M. Loewe: *Everyday Life in Early Imperial China* (London and New York, 1968)

'Han–Wei Luoyang cheng chubu kancha' [First steps in the investigation of the city of Luoyang during the Han and Wei periods] *Kaogu* (1973), no. 4, pp. 198–208

Su Bai: 'Sui–Tang Chang'an cheng he Luoyang cheng' [The cities of Chang'an and Luoyang during the Sui and Tang], *Kaogu* (1978), no. 6, pp. 409–25

W. J. F. Jenner: *Memories of Luoyang: Yang Hsüan-chih and the Lost Capital (493–534)* (Oxford, 1981)

HENRIK H. SØRENSEN

**Luo Zhenyu** [Lo Chen-yü; *zi* Xuetang; *hao* Chensuntang] (*b* Huaian, Jiangsu Province, 3 Aug 1866; *d* Lüshun, Liaoning Province, 19 June 1940). Chinese writer, collector and calligrapher. He is particularly well known for his studies of oracle bone script (*jiagu wen*), the earliest Chinese writing, so called because it was found on animal bones and shells used for divination (*see* CHINA, §IV, 2(i)(a)). Luo's friend Wang Yirong (1845–1900) and Liu E (1857–1909) were the first to collect the bones, which they discovered and rescued from pharmacists, who ground them up for medical prescriptions. The importance of oracle bones for early Chinese history was more widely recognized in 1899 after large quantities of them were unearthed at the Yinxu site in ANYANG, Henan Province. Sun Yirang (1848–1908), Wang Guowei (1867–1927) and Luo investigated the texts on the oracle bones, and Luo dated them to the latter part of the Shang period (*c.* 1600–*c.* 1050 BC); before the discovery of these artefacts, many Western scholars believed the Shang dynasty to be a myth. Luo published many reproductions of oracle bones from his own and Lin E's collections, but he was not only interested in oracle bones: he also wrote extensively about the scripts on Han (206 BC–AD 220) wooden slips and calligraphy from the Six Dynasties (AD 222–589), Sui (AD 581–618) and Tang (AD 618–907) periods.

Luo was a respected calligrapher and the first to use oracle bones as a model in calligraphy. He also followed the early, unstandardized seal script (*zhuanshu*) inscribed on bronze vessels; models of both scripts were easily available from his own collection. This writing is remarkable for its simple strokes and ungainly, childlike composition. Luo attained a unique freshness and ease in his work in these scripts and established them as a new model for calligraphers. After a distinguished career as an adviser in agriculture and education, Luo was involved in the attempt to re-establish the dynasty of the former emperor Pu Yi (1906–67) in Manchukuo (Manchuria and Mongolia) in collaboration with the Japanese. He joined Pu Yi's circle in 1931 and accompanied it to Mongolia the year after, serving until 1938, when he retired.

BIBLIOGRAPHY

K. Shimonaka, ed.: *Shodō zenshū* [Complete collection of calligraphy], xxiv (Tokyo, 2/1961), pp. 167–77, 181, pls 102–3

H. L. Boorman, ed.: *Dictionary of Republican China* (New York, 1971), pp. 228–33

Yu Jianhua, ed.: *Zhongguo huajia da zidian* [Dictionary of Chinese artists] (Shanghai, 1981), p. 1506

*Last of the Mandarins: Chinese Calligraphy and Painting from the F. Y. Chang Collection* (exh. cat., ed. J. K. Murray; Cambridge, MA, Sackler Mus., 1987), no. 4

ELIZABETH F. BENNETT

**Lupardo di Benincasa.** *See under* BERLINGHIERI.

**Lupas, Ana** (*b* Cluj-Napoca, 1940). Romanian tapestry designer and installation artist. She studied tapestry design at the 'Ion Andreescu' Institute of Fine and Decorative Art in Cluj-Napoca, first exhibiting her work at the National Exhibition for Decorative Arts, Bucharest, in 1965. She evolved from a two-dimensional concept of tapestry towards an original attempt to work in a three-dimensional context. She was quickly recognized internationally as an innovative designer, whose suppleness of technique (passing from high warp to ikat, or the Oriental tassel technique) enabled her to move beyond the confines of conventional tapestry design to participate in installations and happenings. In her work the textile is set in opposition to hard elements, such as wood or stone, or unexpected ones, such as leather or fruit, forming only the ambient structure of an idea of a space. An organic and disquieting element appeared in her *Flying Machines* and *Nests*, small works that attempt a Dadaist effect by being absurd and aggressive. Lupas's ecological concerns, which dominate much of her work, were first expressed in optimistic works made from wheat sheaves and by installations such as the one executed with the help of peasant women in a Transylvanian village, who unfolded on a hill huge rolls of white hand-woven fabric. In the 1970s and 1980s, however, she became more pessimistic about the future of mankind, expressing her more morbid attitude in photographs, videos, drawings and texts as well as further installations. The festive installation of bleached hand-woven fabric was repeated in an urban context, with tar-spread fabric and funerary symbols (Bucharest, 1991). Among her many prizes were the Gold Medal at the Triennial of Decorative Arts, Stuttgart (1973) and the Gold and Silver Medals at the Triennial of Tapestry, Łódź (1979).

BIBLIOGRAPHY
M. Grozda, ed.: *Tapiseria contemporana româneasca* (Bucharest, 1982)
CĂLIN DAN

**Lüpertz, Markus** (*b* Liberec, Czech Republic, 25 April 1941). German painter and sculptor of Bohemian origin. He moved with his family in 1948 from Czechoslovakia to Rheydt in the Rhineland and studied from 1956 to 1961 at the Werkkunstschule in Krefeld and at the Kunstakademie in Düsseldorf. In 1963 he settled in W. Berlin, where in 1964 he was one of the founders of the gallery Grossgörschen 35, which was run as an artists' cooperative. During these years he experimented with styles as diverse as Constructivism and Expressionism. In 1966, however, he published the *Dithyrambisches Manifest* to describe the frenzied working methods that he had evolved in paintings such as *Dithyrambic with Red Stripe* (2.16×1.37 m, 1964–5; Berlin, Dr Peter Pohl priv. col., see 1984 exh. cat., p. 146) to express his Dionysian attitude to life, in marked contrast to the social criticism and realism that increasingly characterized the work produced by his colleagues at Grossgörschen 35.

In his paintings of the mid-1960s (see 1977 exh. cat., pp. 64–5) Lüpertz took as his subject-matter such ordinary images as tree trunks, tents or asparagus fields, but treated them as signs of concealed tension in order to distance them from their usual meaning. While never abandoning recognizable imagery, Lüpertz treated his motifs as if they were abstractions, an effect reinforced by the production of groups of pictures executed as almost identical replicas rather than as serial variations. In the *Motif Paintings* of 1970–75 Lüpertz made broad allusions to German ideology, for example to militarism in works such as *Black—Red—Gold Dithyrambic I, II and III* (3 canvases, each 2.60×1.97 m; Cologne, priv. col.; *see* GERMANY, fig. 26). In his later '*Stil*' *Paintings* (exh. London, Whitechapel A.G., 1981), for example *Death and the Singer* (oil and mixed media on canvas, 1.90×2.45 m, 1978; Aachen, Neue Gal.), he quoted arbitrarily from various styles, arranging the planar forms, lines or graphic patterns as if on an imaginary stage; he took this theatrical quality to its logical conclusion in producing his first stage designs, for Rainer Kunad's opera *Vincent*, performed at the Staatstheater, Kassel, in 1982. In 1981 Lüpertz produced the first of a number of painted bronze sculptures, such as *Titan* (h. 2.53 m, 1985; Zurich, Gal. Maeght-Lelong, see insert to 1987 exh. cat.), and sculptures in clay. He also painted murals on commission, for example in the Ruhleben Crematorium in Berlin (1977), finding them an appropriate outlet for his taste for monumentality. Lüpertz was teaching at the Karlsruhe Akademie from 1974 and the Düsseldorf Kunstakademie from 1986.

BIBLIOGRAPHY
*Markus Lüpertz* (exh. cat. by W. Hofmann and S. Holsten, Hamburg, Ksthalle, 1977)
*Markus Lüpertz: Gemälde und Handzeichnungen, 1964–1979* (exh. cat., ed. S. Gohr; Cologne, Josef-Haubrich-Ksthalle, 1979)
'*Stil*' *Paintings* (exh. cat. by S. Gohr, London, Whitechapel A.G., 1981)
*Markus Lüpertz: Bilder, 1970–1983* (exh. cat., ed. C. Haenlein; Hannover, Kestner-Ges., 1983)
*Origen y visión* (exh. cat., intro. C. M. Joachimides and interviews W. Grasskamp; Madrid, Pal. Velázquez; Barcelona, Cent. Cult. Caixa Pensions; 1984), pp. 53–7, 145–53
DOMINIK BARTMANN

**Lupi, Miguel Ângelo** (*b* Lisbon, 8 May 1826; *d* Lisbon, 26 Feb 1883). Portuguese painter of Italian descent. He studied in Lisbon, 1841–6, at the Academia de Belas-Artes, where he was a pupil of Joaquim Rafael (1783–1864) and of António Manuel da Fonseca. He spent the years 1851–3 in Luanda (Angola) as a Treasury official, returning to Lisbon in 1855 as a secretary in the Audit Department, but in 1860 he left for Rome with an official bursary. There he copied the paintings of Old Masters. In 1864 he was elected *académico de mérito* for his painting of the Infante *Dom João of Portugal* (Lisbon, Mus. N. A. Contemp.). He went on to Paris, where he came under the influence of the Realist School. Returning to Lisbon in 1864, he exhibited in the Salons of the Sociedade Promotora de Belas Artes from 1864 to 1868. He specialized in portraiture, and in this field he was the most realistic Portuguese painter of his time, using an innovative technique of obtaining colour resonance by means of sponging, a practice that produced very subtle nuances of tone.

From 1864 Lupi was Professor of History Painting at the Academia and continued to work in this genre with works such as *Tintoretto Painting his Dead Daughter* (Caldas da Rainha, Mus. Malhoa), which he sent to the Paris Exhibition of 1867. Within this academic genre is the *Marqués de Pombal Examining the Plans for the Rebuilding of Lisbon* (1881–3, unfinished; Lisbon, Câmara Mun.), an official commission that shows his skill as a portrait painter. His extensive gallery of portraits demonstrates his austere and objective approach, but these are also psychological interpretations, original representations of the society in which he lived. He painted portraits of kings, including *Ferdinand II of Saxe-Coburg-Gotha* (1875); aristocrats, like the *Marquesa de Belas* (1874); writers such as *A. Feliciano de Castilho* (1873), which is a moving portrait of a blind man; politicians, like the celebrated portrait of the *Duque de Ávila* (1880)—sharply observant of the sitter; and members of the middle classes, such as the *Mother of Dr Sousa Martins* (1878), acute and penetrating in her questioning gaze (all Lisbon, Mus. N. A. Contemp.). Lupi's portraits combined bourgeois realism with aristocratic dignity. He preferred indoor settings and a subtle, delicate atmosphere rather than the strong play of light and colour. The intimate quality of his work is manifest in the portraits of his wife, as in *Effects of Light* (1878; Azeitão, priv. col., see 1987 exh. cat., pl. 94, p. 145), in which she is seen against the light, and of his daughters in domestic situations.

He exhibited widely, including at the Paris Salon in 1866 and 1872 and the Expositions there in 1876 and 1878. He refused to show his work in Portugal, where he was always the target of criticism, but his influence as professor at the Academia was enormous. In 1879 he published *Projects for the Reform of the Royal Academy of Fine Arts* in Lisbon.

WRITINGS
*Indicações para a reforma da Real Academia das Belas-Artes de Lisboa* (Lisbon, 1879)
BIBLIOGRAPHY
R. Ortigão: *Arte portuguesa*, iii (Lisbon, n.d.)
Diogo de Macedo: *A exposição de Miguel Ângelo Lupi* (Lisbon, 1945)
——: *Síntese de uma obra* [Analysis of a work] (Lisbon, 1947)
——: *Miguel Lupi* (Lisbon, 1952)

J.-A. França: *A arte em Portugal no século XIX*, i (Lisbon, 1966), pp. 440–46

*Soleil et ombre: L'Art portugais du XIXème siècle* (exh. cat. by. J.-A. França, Paris, Petit Pal., 1987–8)

LUCÍLIA VERDELHO DA COSTA

**Lupiae.** *See* LECCE.

**Lupton, Thomas Goff** (*b* London, 3 Sept 1791; *d* London, 18 May 1873). English engraver. In 1805 he was apprenticed to George Clint, and he subsequently worked for S. W. Reynolds. He was one of the engravers employed on Turner's *Liber studiorum* (1807–19), and from 1858 to 1864 re-engraved 15 of the plates for a projected series that was never published. Following William Say's lead in 1820 in engraving mezzotints on steel plates rather than on copper ones, Lupton, after experiments on various metals, engraved on soft steel a portrait by Clint of the comedian *Joseph Munden* (O'Donoghue, no. 1), which was published in 1822 and which that year was awarded the Isis Gold Medal of the Society of Arts. Lupton subsequently became one of the most esteemed engravers of singly issued mezzotints to use steel plates. He produced over 100 portraits (e.g. *Wellington*, 1840; after Henry W. Briggs), as well as many prints after subject pictures by Turner and others (e.g. *Sheerness from the Nore*, 1828; after Turner). He also worked on Turner's *Rivers of England and Wales* (1823–7) and *Ports of England* (1826–8).

BIBLIOGRAPHY
O'Donoghue

Society of Arts: *Transactions of the Society Instituted at London, for the Encouragement of Arts, Manufactures and Commerce*, xl (1823), pp. 41–3

Obituary, *A. J.* [London] (1873), p. 208

A. Graves: *The Royal Academy of Arts: A Complete Dictionary of Contributors and their Works from its Foundation in 1769 to 1904*, v (London, 1906)

R. Engen: *Dictionary of Victorian Engravers, Print Publishers and their Works* (Cambridge, 1979), pp. 130–31

C. Wax: *The Mezzotint: History and Technique* (London and New York, 1990), pp. 102, 118, 120

DAVID ALEXANDER

**Lurago (i).** Italian family of architectural sculptors and stone masons. They originated from Pellio Superiore Intelvi, near Como, and worked in Genoa during the mid- to late 16th century. The brothers (1) Giovanni Lurago and (2) Rocco Lurago played an important part as artisans in translating the abstract ideas of Galeazzo Alessi, Bernardino da Cantone, Giovanni Battista Castello and other architects who worked in and around the Strada Nuova (now the Via Garibaldi) into the finely carved details that distinguish the Genoese High Renaissance school.

**(1) Giovanni Lurago** (*fl* Genoa, *c.* 1548–71). He worked for Galeazzo Alessi, carving columns for the loggia of the villa of Luca Giustiniani in Albaro. He executed the carved ornament of the Fontana Moroza (1558; destr.) in the piazza at the east end of the Strada Nuova, in light-coloured Finale stone, which often appears as his preferred material for architectural decoration. Giovanni was elected Console dell' Arte dei Maestri Antelami with Filippo Carabio in 1560. On the Strada Nuova, Giovanni and members of his workshop carved the beautiful front and side façades of the palazzo of Agostino Pallavicino in grey charcoal-coloured Promontorio stone, which interplays with the cream marble elements in Alessi's Mannerist façade. Giovanni's workshop sculpted 16 columns for the courtyard of the Palazzo Spinola (now Doria) in 1564, according to designs by Castello. Another major work is the beautiful façade of the Palazzo Grimaldi (now Tursi, the Municipio) on the Strada Nuova. Giovanni, together with Gioannetto Carlone and their workshops, executed this after designs by Domenico Ponzello and Giovanni Ponzello in Finale stone in high relief with socles, rusticated and fluted pilasters, grotesque frames, medallions and masks.

From the late 1540s until 1571 Giovanni was probably Genoa's most famous mason. He provided many palazzi, villas, churches, chapels, piazzas and streets with finished carved stone decorations, either pre-made or on commission. He worked within a highly specialized market system of construction trades and workshops. Although he did not design any of the major palazzi of his day, Giovanni certainly added to their architectural splendour.

**(2) Rocco Lurago** (*fl* Genoa, *c.* 1558–97). Brother of (1) Giovanni Lurago. He rented space in one of Giovanni's workshops in 1558. Between 1567 and 1571 he was commissioned to work on stone carvings on the façade of Santa Croce di Bosco Marengo in Piedmont, where he played a minor role under the architects Ignazio Danti and Martino Longhi the elder. By 1571 he was referred to as a master stone-carver. Rocco's major Genoese commission was his carving (1583) with Giovanni Pietro Orsolino of the Doric columns and balustrades for the seaward loggia of Giovanni Andrea I Doria's villa in Fassolo after designs by Giovanni Ponzello and Giuseppe Forlano (*d* 1593) (documents, Rome, Pal. Doria-Pamphili). Rocco enjoyed particular fame after Soprani's attribution to him of the Palazzo Grimaldi on the Strada Nuova. However, Poleggi proved that this was in fact the work of the Ponzello brothers.

BIBLIOGRAPHY
R. Soprani: *Vite* (1674); ed. C. G. Ratti (1768–9), i, pp. 419–20 [unreliable]

E. Poleggi: *Strada Nuova: Una lottizzazione del cinquecento a Genova* (Genoa, 1968–72)

E. Poleggi, ed.: *Galeazzo Alessi e l'architettura del cinquecento, Atti del convegno internazionale di studi: Genova, 1974* (Genoa, 1975)

GEORGE L. GORSE

**Lurago (ii)** [Lorago; Luragho]. Italian family of architects, active mainly in Bohemia. Members of the family, presumably distantly related to the 16th-century Lurago (i) family, who were active in Genoa, were resident in Prague from the 1630s, when (1) Carlo Lurago is documented there. Domenico Antonio Lurago (*b* Pellio Superiore Intelvi, nr Como, *bapt* 16 Jan 1638; *d* Prague) and Francesco Anselmo Lurago (*b* Pellio Superiore Intelvi; *d* Prague, *bur* 30 May 1693), who were possibly Carlo's nephews, also worked in Prague, mainly to others' plans although the latter designed the Jesuit House (from 1680) and St Wenceslas, both in the Malá Strana quarter of the city. Giovanni Antonio Lurago (*b* Pellio Superiore Intelvi, *bapt* 3 Jan 1653; *d* Prague, 9 June 1727) built St Procopius (1689–93) in Malá Strana as well as fortifications and barracks (from 1712) in Prague. His nephew (2) Anselmo Martino Lurago was perhaps the best known member of the family, and he worked in Prague until 1765. The family played an important role in the development of Baroque architecture in Bohemia and the transition to Rococo.

BIBLIOGRAPHY

F. Cavarocchi: 'I Lurago, quali stuccatori, nei secoli XVII e XVIII', *L'arte e artisti dei laghi lombardi*, ii (Como, 1964), pp. 33–48; review by V. Naňková in *Umění*, xiv (1966), pp. 167–9

O. J. Blazícek: 'Contributi lombardi al barocco boemo', *A. Lombarda*, 14 (1974), pp. 147–62

**(1) Carlo Lurago** (*b* Pellio Superiore Intelvi; *bapt* 14 Oct 1615; *d* Passau, 12 Oct 1684). He is documented in Prague from 1638 and was involved in building the fortifications there in 1648–59. He became one of the most sought-after architects in Bohemia. Much of his work was commissioned by the Jesuits, for example at Prague, Březnice, Hradec Králové, Klatovy, Chomutov and Svatá Hora. The aristocratic patrons he worked for included the Černín, Lobkovic, Losy, Piccolomini and Thun families. His form of aisleless hall church with basilican cross-section, side chapels and galleries was adopted for many Jesuit churches in 17th-century Bohemia. St Ignatius in the New Town (1665–71), Prague, has innovative sail vaults in the side chapels and an interesting façade with rounded corners to the central projecting bay. He also developed unusual forms of articulation for monastery façades that were employed in Bohemia for many years. Particularly interesting is the little Humprecht Castle (1666–8), near Sobotka, which he built for Count Černín. It has an oval plan with an oval inner hall that penetrates the building to rise above it like a cylinder. From 1668 he worked mostly on the monumental Baroque reconstruction of Passau Cathedral to his own plans.

BIBLIOGRAPHY

Thieme–Becker

J. E. Kappel: *Der Dom des Hl. Stephan zu Passau* (Regensburg, 1912)

A. Duras: *Die Architektenfamilie Lurago* (Prague, 1933)

H. G. Franz: *Bauten und Baumeister der Barockzeit in Böhmen* (Leipzig, 1962)

P. Preiss: *Italstí umelci v Praze* [Italian artists in Prague] (Prague, 1986), pp. 169–96

G. Skalecki: *Deutsche Architektur zur Zeit des dreissigjährigen Krieges* (Regensburg, 1989), pp. 161–70

VĚRA NAŇKOVÁ

**(2) Anselmo Martino Lurago** (*b* Como, 9 Jan 1701; *d* Prague, 29 Nov 1765). According to his own account he was brought to Prague by his uncle, Giovanni Antonio Lurago, and studied architecture with František Maximilián Kanka. He was granted citizenship of Prague in 1727. From the following year he studied fortification with another uncle, B. Scotti (*d* 1737) and continued to work for him, completing the chapel at Osov after Scotti's death. During 1740 he worked at Lysa nad Labem, completing the parish church and building the Augustinian church. His other churches include the castle chapel at Horin (1742) and those at Duba (1744), Jezve (1746), Velíš (1747) and Braniš (1749). In Prague he was responsible for reworking the church of the Assumption at the Strahov Monastery (*see* PRAGUE, §IV, 5); the reconstruction of the Černín Palace (1746), where he attempted to relieve the endless façade by introducing balconies and three portals, the central one of which has a terrace; and the completion of the observatory tower at the Clementinum (1748).

In 1752 Lurago was appointed Royal Architect. Nikolaus Pacassi's plans for the reconstruction of Hradčany Castle, Prague, were continued under his supervision, involving the conversion of the Rožmberk Palace and the adjoining houses into the Institute of Gentlewomen (from 1754), building the court chapel of the Holy Rood (1756–64) and laying out the *cour d'honneur* (from 1759; *see* PRAGUE, §IV, 1). Much of Lurago's other work was commissioned by the Černín, Dietrichstein, Kounic, Salm, Schlick and other aristocratic families. After the death of Kilian Ignaz Dientzenhofer in 1751 he completed the Sylva-Taroucca (1743–51) and Kinsky palaces (1755–65), and the upper part of the tower of St Nicholas, Malá Strana (1752–4), all in Prague. He succeeded Dientzenhofer as architect of the Augustinian Order, for whom he built churches at Dolní Ročov and St Thomas's, Prague. He also served as architect to the Jesuits in Prague and to the Benedictines at Prague-Břevnov, Broumov and for the deanery at Přeštice (1751–65). Lurago was the most frequently employed architect in Bohemia during the second third of the 18th century. His designs, which regularly involve a distinctive type of well-proportioned church with a prominent portal, were inspired by Johann Lukas von Hildebrandt and Dientzenhofer, and they represent the transition in Bohemia from High Baroque to Rococo.

BIBLIOGRAPHY

Thieme–Becker

P. Toman: *Nový slovník československých výtvarných umělců* [New dictionary of Czechoslovak artists], ii (Prague, 1950), pp. 50–51

I. Kořán: 'Prostorotvorné iluze Anselma Luraga' [Space-creating illusions of Anselmo Lurago], *Umění*, xxi (1973), pp. 54–65

*Dějiny českého výtvarného umění* [History of Czech fine art], ii/2 (Prague, 1989), p. 664

IVO KOŘÁN

**Lurçat.** French family of artists.

**(1) Jean Lurçat** (*b* Bruyères, Vosges, 1 July 1892; *d* Saint-Paul-de-Vence, 6 Jan 1966). Tapestry designer and painter. He was introduced to art by his parents and by Victor Prouvé, the founder of the Ecole de Nancy. In October 1912 he went to Paris, where he put into practice Prouvé's ideas at the Ecole des Beaux-Arts and later at the Académie Colarossi as a pupil of the engraver Bernard Naudin (1876–1946). In November 1912 Lurçat founded the review *Les Feuilles de mai*, which contained articles on art by Elie Faure and Antoine Bourdelle and his own essays on 'the positive sense of life and art'. In 1914 he volunteered for the infantry; after being wounded, he was evacuated to his parents' home in Sens. Watching his mother sewing inspired him to have her transpose his first tapestries, on canvas, based on his gouaches *Little Green Girls* (Berkeley, U. CA, A. Mus.) and *Evening in Granada* (Paris, priv. col.), which combine severe design with rich colour. In 1917 he held his first exhibition in Zurich, of paintings inspired by Cubism (in particular the work of Georges Braque) and by Matisse's drawings. Several were subsequently produced as tapestries by the Hennebert workshops in Toulon (1920–24). Until 1931 Lurçat intermittently attempted to produce murals, but these works always disappointed him: for example the large mural decoration for the Bernheim family's château in Villefix, near Paris (1922; destr.).

In the 1920s Lurçat travelled widely, visiting the Middle East, Sicily and North Africa. He was very active, painting effortlessly and revelling in his skill as a colourist. His wide circle of friends included Pierre Chareau, Max Jacob, Louis Marcoussis, Amédée Ozenfant and Walter Hasenclever. During this period he produced a series of large figure paintings, including *The Hangman* (1926; Angers, Mus. Lurçat), the *Turkish Woman* (1927; priv. col.) and the *Armenian Woman* (1927; Angers, Mus. Lurçat). Influenced by Surrealism and by his travels, his landscapes, which were painted in muted colours, became increasingly nightmarish and desolate, the sea, rafts and ruins being recurring themes. After 1930 his output increased, and his works became even larger. He began the series of *Masts and Sails* (example 1930; Amsterdam, Stedel. Mus.) and in 1931 produced the powerful *Bathers* (Amsterdam, Stedel. Mus.), which owed much to Picasso.

In 1933 Marie Cuttoli, who had already encouraged many avant-garde artists (including Matisse, Raoul Dufy, Fernand Léger, Georges Rouault and Braque) to weave tapestries after their paintings, asked Lurçat for his first tapestry cartoon, *Storm* (Paris, Pompidou). He received his first important tapestry commission from the Gobelins in 1936, the *Illusions of Icarus* (The Hague, Kon. Huisarchf).

Lurçat went to Angers in July 1937 to study the great series of *Apocalypse* tapestries (1373–82; Angers, Château, Col. Tap.; *see* ANGERS, fig. 4), from which he learnt much about the rigorous and economical techniques of medieval weaving. The experience encouraged him to visit Aubusson, the centre of traditional weaving in France, where he watched how the craftsmen of his day worked. His close friendship with François Tabard (1902–69), the head of the workshop, led him to develop new methods based on medieval practice, using coarse weaving with *gros point*, graded tones and numbered cartoons. The resultant speedier production, more accurate cartoon colours and reduction in wool stocks lowered the price of tapestries and gave new life to the workshops. Lurçat could not divorce his artistic and managerial roles, and he did much to reform the working practices in the Aubusson workshops. From 1937 he produced a series of outstanding tapestries at Aubusson (*see* TAPESTRY, §II, 6). With Marcel Gromaire and others, including Pierre Dubreuil (1891–1970), he was commissioned by the Ministry of Education in 1939 to create four monumental tapestries, the *Four Seasons* (Paris, Mobilier N.). He also worked in association with other painters such as Dufy and André Derain.

After World War II, during which he served in the Resistance, Lurçat settled in Tours-Saint-Laurent at Saint-Céré (Lot); his home was later given to the département by his widow and opened as a museum (Atelier-Musée Jean Lurçat). Henceforth he devoted his energies almost exclusively to tapestry. He contributed to national and international exhibitions, published several books on the history of tapestry and set up the Association des Peintres-Cartonniers and the International Biennale of Tapestry in Lausanne. Lurçat received many significant State commissions (e.g. Council of Europe, Strasbourg; Mobilier National, Paris; Rathaus, Cologne) and also commissions from private companies (KLM, Bayer, Sandoz and Nestlé). Although he gave up oil painting, he continued to paint prolifically in gouache and to draw. He illustrated in a

more intimate style the writings of Patrice de la Tour du Pin, Seghers, André de Richaud, Jean de La Fontaine, Jean-Henri Fabre and Jules Supervielle, and his own work (*Mes Domaines*, 1956–7). Through his work, travels and public appearances he gave what he flippantly described as 'the tapestry virus' to numerous artists.

In old age Lurçat undertook at his own expense a monumental tapestry series (the projected size was 500 sq. m), the *Song of the World* (Angers, Mus. Lurçat; see fig.), which was his response to the Angers *Apocalypse*. It attempted to portray the dangers and joys of the modern world. Between 1957 and 1964 he produced nine bright and lyrical tapestries with the same black background, which conveyed his message of life, death and hope. (The tenth and final tapestry was completed posthumously.) Lurçat's tapestries celebrate life and the world through his favourite themes: the sun, animals, the stars and especially man, whom he saw as the centre of the universe.

These elements are combined with a dreamlike quality reminiscent of Surrealism and enlivened through emphasizing the rhythmic quality of luxuriant natural forms (in particular leaves), picked out against flat, often black, backgrounds. The results, on the vast scale of his public commissions, make an overwhelmingly powerful impact. Lurçat's main contribution was to promote the revival of tapestry in France, its international recognition as an art form and its development as a craft.

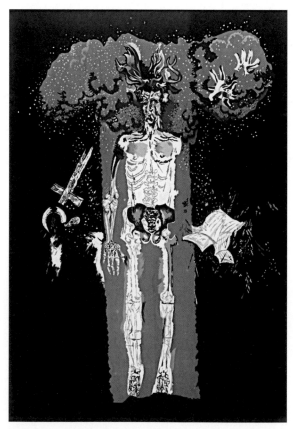

Jean Lurçat: *Man from Hiroshima*, from the tapestry series *Song of the World*, 4.37×2.92 m, 1957–64 (Angers, Musée Jean Lurçat)

WRITINGS

*Le Bestiaire de la tapisserie du moyen âge* (Geneva, 1947)
*La Tapisserie française des origines à nos jours* (Paris, 1947)
*Le Travail dans la tapisserie du moyen âge* (Geneva, 1947)

BIBLIOGRAPHY

J. Marcenac: *L'Exemple de Jean Lurçat* (Paris, 1952)
M. Braun: *Jean Lurçat: Art Documents* (Geneva, 1955–66)
C. Roy: *Jean Lurçat* (Geneva, 1956)
*Tapisseries de Jean Lurçat, 1939–1957* (Belvès, 1957)
C. Faux: *Lurçat à haute voix* (Paris, 1962)
*Lurçat, 10 ans après* (exh. cat., Paris, Mus. A. Mod. Ville Paris; Angers, Mus. B.-A.; 1976)
*Les Domaines de Jean Lurçat* (exh. cat., Angers, Mus., B.-A., 1986)

VIVIANE HUCHARD

**(2) André (Emile Lucien) Lurçat** (*b* Bruyères, Vosges, 27 Aug 1894; *d* Sceaux, Hauts-de-Seine, 11 July 1970). Architect, urban planner and writer, brother of (1) Jean Lurçat. He began his studies in Nancy, at the studio of the painter Victor Prouvé, and continued them in Paris at the Ecole des Beaux-Arts, where he was admitted in July 1914 to the studio of Edmond Paulin (1848–1915). During the 1920s Lurçat became known for the theoretical designs that he presented at the Salon d'Automne of 1923. Through his brother he won a commission for a group of artists' studios and residences in Paris, which he executed between 1924 and 1926 at the Villa Seurat; there he successfully created the image of a modern complex with sharp edges and geometric openings. He also designed other houses in Versailles and Paris, although he failed to impose his ideas in the field of public housing.

In 1926 Lurçat organized the architecture section of the *Architecture internationale* exhibition in Nancy, where Bauhaus architecture was shown in France for the first time. He was a member of CIAM from its foundation in 1928 (for photograph of congress members *see* CIAM) and sided with the German and Austrian members against Le Corbusier. As Lurçat built up and established a position during the course of his development, Josef Frank invited him to design four houses for the model estate that the Austrian Werkbund inaugurated in Vienna in 1932. Lurçat published *Architecture*, a manifesto for moderate Modernism in 1929, the year in which he built the Hôtel Nord–Sud in Calvi, Corsica. The following year he was commissioned to execute the Ecole Karl Marx complex of buildings in Villejuif, whose long horizontal windows, pilotis, accessible terrace and high-quality fittings all marked it out as a striking example of the new French architecture. In 1933 he opened a teaching studio where the German philosopher Max Raphaël lectured on aesthetics. He was invited to Moscow, and in January 1934 he was commissioned to execute a residential building for the engineers of the Moscow underground railway. He remained in the USSR until 1937, working at first for the Moscow Soviet and later heading a studio for the People's Commissariat of the Ministry of Health. Using rudimentary materials, Lurçat worked on designs for a number of projects, including the school in Mashinostroenia Street and the Children's Hospital for Contagious Diseases, whose symmetrical and hierarchically arranged elements restored a decorative quality that had disappeared from his last Parisian buildings. Far from passively accepting the pressures to produce work in the style of Socialist Realism, Lurçat strove to preserve Modernist ideas while

at the same time returning to a more monumental style, as can be seen in the project for the Academy of Sciences (1934) and in the theoretical work in which he argued for a reasoned return to the great 'laws' of architecture. None of his Soviet projects was executed, however.

On his return to France Lurçat joined the Communists in the Resistance. When France was liberated he was made a professor at the Ecole des Beaux-Arts, but he resigned under pressure from the traditionalists in charge of the individual studios. At Saint-Denis, Lurçat devoted himself to designing prefabricated 'vertical garden estates' (in fact, high-rise slabs), whose distinctive form, linking housing with collective facilities, made them stand out in the town as clearly identifiable units. The Fabien 'neighbourhood unit' was the prototype for these complexes. Lurçat was responsible for the reconstruction of Maubeuge (Nord), a city destroyed in 1940, where he paid considerable attention to the preferences of the inhabitants themselves, to the town's former appearance and to some delicate problems of land ownership; he succeeded in making use of standard prefabricated units without producing work condemned to monotony. From then on he was inundated with commissions from the municipalities of outer Paris, and he began to publish his theoretical ideas on architectural aesthetics, formulated in response to his experience in the USSR, in *Formes, composition et lois d'harmonie*. In his last works, for example the town hall (1964) at Le Blanc-Mesnil, Lurçat combined the solemnity of great symmetrical forms with the simplicity of geometrical motifs that had been a constant in his architecture since the earliest years of his career.

WRITINGS

*Architecture* (Paris, 1929)
*Formes, compositions et lois d'harmonie: Eléments d'une science de l'esthétique architecturale*, 5 vols (Paris, 1953–7)
*Oeuvres récentes I* (Paris, 1961)

BIBLIOGRAPHY

*André Lurçat architecte, projets et réalisations* (Paris, 1929)
*Archit., Movt, Cont.*, 40 (1976) [entire issue]
J.-L. Cohen: *L'Architecture d'André Lurçat (1894–1970): L'Autocritique d'un Moderne* (diss., Paris, Ecole Hautes Etud., 1985)

JEAN-LOUIS COHEN

**Luristan** [Pers. Luristăn]. Region of Iran, near the border with Iraq, which has given its name to a remarkable series of ancient bronze objects, especially those produced between *c.* 1200 and 600 BC.

1. Introduction. 2. The early periods. 3. The period of the typical Luristan bronzes. 4. Rediscovery.

1. INTRODUCTION. Luristan is situated in the central part of the Zagros mountain range, which runs north-west to south-east along Iran's frontier with Iraq. The region can be divided into two parts: to the west is the Pusht-i Kuh ('behind the mountain'), which descends towards the plains of Mesopotamia and Susiana, while to the east, at a higher altitude, lies the Pish-i Kuh ('before the mountain'). Nomadic Lurs inhabit its high, fertile valleys.

The nomads who lived in the valleys of Luristan in antiquity were shepherds, horse-breeders, hunters and warriors. It is not known what they were called, for they have left no written sources, and suggestions that they might have been Kassites or Cimmerians must be rejected.

They should perhaps be equated with the Ellipi, whose kingdom was overthrown by the Medes in 650–625 BC. The continuity of their material culture from prehistoric times until *c.* 600 BC indicates that the population remained remarkably stable. They practised transhumance (as do the Lurs of today) between the warm lower valleys where they settled in winter and the high pastures where they grazed their flocks in summer. They came into contact with the urban civilizations of the plains, with whom they traded the animals they reared and, especially, metal, which was completely absent both in Mesopotamia and in Susiana. They obtained the metal from the plateau and, as well as trading in it, fashioned it into bronzes. The lush vegetation of Luristan provided the necessary fuel for the furnaces.

The bronzes are small and easy to carry, as befits the art of a nomadic people, and consist of tools, pieces of harness, decorative plaques for quivers, votive objects, vessels and items for personal adornment and use. The bronzes show an openness to technical and aesthetic innovation and are largely inspired by the animals on which the nomads depended. A good representative collection of the various types of Luristan bronzes is in the Ashmolean Museum, Oxford.

2. THE EARLY PERIODS. At the end of the 5th millennium BC and during the whole of the 4th, related nomadic and sedentary cultures (e.g. that at TEPE GIYAN) developed in the high valleys of Luristan. The dead were buried in large cemeteries, generally singly in stone-lined graves. Burial goods consisted of plain or painted pottery, baked clay anthropomorphic and animal figurines, together with bowls, weapons, tools and seals made of stone.

1. Luristan, handle of whetstone featuring stylized ibex, bronze, h. 75 mm, late 2nd millennium BC (Brussels, M.-T. Ullens de Schooten private collection)

Both in Luristan and in Susiana, pottery was decorated with stylized representations of the long-horned mountain goat (ibex). The iconography of the prehistoric stamp seals shows links between these areas and northern Mesopotamia, with frequent depictions of ibexes and snakes and, especially, of the 'master of the animals'. The last is an ibex-headed figure (a genie, masked priest or sorcerer rather than a god) shown in association with snakes, caprids and birds. This imagery reveals the existence of a primitive mythology that gave rise to ceremonial or magic rites.

Simple copper weapons and pins with animal heads appear alongside pottery in the graves of the first three centuries of the 3rd millennium BC. From *c.* 2700 BC the bronze industry of Luristan began to develop. Huge stone tombs between 6 and 16 metres long, roofed with large stone slabs laid either flat or to form a ridge, housed multiple burials with abundant grave goods, including pottery, bronze weapons and vessels, and cylinder seals. In the last third of the 3rd millennium BC the reappearance of individual burials alongside the larger tombs may indicate the arrival of a new ethnic group. Contact continued with the rich cities of the plain, whose need for metals encouraged trade. Painted pottery is related to that of Susa, while cylinder seals and bronze weapons and tools resemble those of Susa and Mesopotamia, but by this period Luristan had developed its own distinctive metal-working tradition. The lost-wax process of casting was known, and animal decoration was often added to objects. Maces and axe-shaft holes were decorated with animals; axe blades issued from the mouth of a lion or were lion-shaped. These forms were to be revived one thousand years later. However, from *c.* 1700 BC to *c.* 1200 BC there was a break in this metallurgical tradition, probably owing to a shift in the trade routes that brought metal to Luristan.

3. THE PERIOD OF THE TYPICAL LURISTAN BRONZES. Towards the end of the 2nd millennium BC the arrival of the Iranian tribes led to a new political and economic situation; trade resumed between the plateau and the plains, and passed once more through Luristan. Locally made, inscribed bronzes bear witness to the presence in Luristan of Elamite and, especially, of Babylonian merchants and diplomats. In the earliest phase (*c.* 1200–*c.* 900 BC) small tombs were built and roofed with blocks or slabs of stone, often with a slab set on edge to form a door at one end. Buff pottery often bore incised decoration or knobs; there are bowls, goblets, cups, small two-handled vessels, jugs, vessels with open or tubular spouts, and vessels with fenestrated or tripod stands. Iron was still extremely rare, and most of the metal objects were made of bronze. Some can be securely dated by their inscriptions or by their archaeological context. This early phase is characterized by naturalism and simple decoration. Typical objects are: axes with the shaft decorated with spikes; daggers with flanged hilts; stylized ibex protomes used as handles for whetstones (see fig. 1); arrowheads; simple horse bits and harness rings; finger-rings and situlae (bucket-shaped vessels).

At the beginning of the middle phase (*c.* 900–*c.* 700 BC) the Babylonian presence seems to have vanished from the uplands of Luristan, which came under Assyrian influence and became extremely prosperous. A political organization developed that was adapted to the society and way of life of the nomads, who were henceforth grouped round permanent establishments such as sanctuaries (e.g. the temple at Surkh Dum) and the fortified residences of chiefs (e.g. the 'manor' and fort at BABA JAN). New types of tomb appeared and were often reused; some were built of square slabs set on edge, and others were simply cut into the ground. Both types were of various shapes and were occasionally roofed with stones. The pottery in the graves is difficult to distinguish from that of the early phase. Iron was often used for ornament, although bronze was still more popular; in the objects combining bronze and iron that are characteristic of this phase, the former was generally used for the functional part. Bronzework reached its apogee. A new technique consisted of adding detail in the form of coils to the wax model, the whole being destroyed when the bronze was cast by the lost-wax process. This gave the castings, for instance the heads of lions, their distinctive appearance. The typological repertory increased, and the artist found new methods of expression, naturalism being replaced by daring stylization in which the forms were narrowed or drawn out, taken to pieces and reconstituted in the most unexpected ways to form hybrid or deformed creatures. Some old themes were revived, and once again axe blades issued from the mouths of lions, and shaft holes were ornamented with a couchant lion. Horse harnesses and bits were decorated. Hollow, tube-shaped human figures, either free-standing ('idols') or flanked by pairs of rampant animals ('standards' or 'finials'), could have been mounted on bottle-shaped supports. 'Standards' also occured with linked pairs of animals only, such as confronted ibexes or lions. Tubular finials and groups of pinheads returned to the theme of the 'master of the animals'.

The late phase (*c.* 700–*c.* 600 BC) coincides with the period of Assyrian expansion. There were incursions into the Zagros valleys, and Syrian prisoners of the Assyrians were settled on the eastern borders of Mesopotamia (i.e. to the west of Luristan). These events were to have repercussions on the local bronze industry; Assyrian influence became more marked, and objects similar to those from Luristan were depicted on Assyrian reliefs. A pin, the head of which is in the shape of a couchant lion, and a simple tubular idol (Tehran, Archaeol. Mus.) were found at Baba Jan. The temple at Surkh Dum was also rebuilt. The most remarkable of the votive bronzes deposited there are cast pins with heads in the shape of an openwork 'standard' depicting the 'master of the animals' (for a similar piece see fig. 2) and pins with hammered discoidal heads decorated in repoussé and illustrating the religious beliefs and sacred liturgy of Luristan (Tehran, Archaeol. Mus.; New York, Met.; U. Chicago, IL, Orient. Inst. Mus.).

More than 450 graves in some 15 cemeteries belonging to this late phase have been properly excavated. These were single burials, either stone-roofed simple inhumations or cists. Rich grave goods included pottery, ranging from coarse handmade wares to finer wheel-made buff and burnished grey wares, as well as bull-shaped vessels. Men were buried with weapons and women with bronze ornaments, necklaces of semi-precious stones, faience and

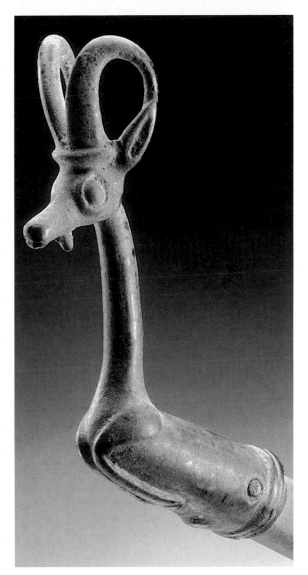

2. Luristan, pinhead decorated in the form of the 'master of the animals', bronze, h. 59 mm, 8th–7th centuries BC (Brussels, M.-T. Ullens de Schooten private collection)

shell and, occasionally, with silver earrings. Iron metallurgy had made considerable strides, and iron was used for utilitarian objects such as axes, swords, daggers, spearheads, arrowheads, tools and simple horse bits, sometimes ornamented with bronze studs and rivets. A new weapon was a forged iron sword, often more than 500 mm long, with elaborate hilt and a discoidal pommel decorated with two bearded human heads and lions; this was mass-produced according to a standard model, and hundreds of examples have survived. Other categories of object were made of bronze, such as ceremonial maces, shields and decorated plaques for quivers, votive objects, pins, bracelets, rings, belt buckles, decorated horse bits and luxury vessels that sometimes bore incised decoration. It is possible that different types of bronzes reflected an aristocracy composed of the owners of herds on the one hand ('standards' with ibex, probably on either side of a 'tree of life') and a warrior class on the other ('standards' with confronted lions). The objects are characterized by a baroque exuberance, and tubular finials of the 'master of the animals' are adorned with multiple human masks and birds' heads growing from the necks of the lions. There is a vast repertory of imaginary creatures, hybrids and winged monsters. Naturalism is still apparent, however, for instance in the horses that form the cheek pieces of some horse bits. Towards the end of the period, gadrooned cups, fibulae and spiked horse bits foreshadow Achaemenid developments. The animal art of Luristan influenced the Achaemenid Persians and, possibly, the Scythians.

4. REDISCOVERY. Towards the middle of the 19th century AD some of the Luristan bronzes reached the West, although it was not then known whence they originated, and they were wrongly attributed to Cappadocia or Armenia. From 1928 they began to flood the antiquities market, and it became known that they were from burial grounds in Luristan that the local inhabitants were robbing. Private collectors and museums bought them up enthusiastically; in order to satisfy their demands the cemeteries were systematically looted of tens of thousands of bronzes, while other burial goods were cast aside or smashed because of their lack of commercial value. Thus, although the bronzes revealed a hitherto unknown civilization in Iran, they had no archaeological context. Archaeologists sought to remedy the situation by scientific study of the bronzes and exploration of the region from which they originated. Although Luristan was difficult to reach and unsafe to travel in, Ernst Herzfeld, André Godard and Aurel Stein carried out surveys, the site of Tepe Giyan was excavated and Erich Schmidt cleared the sanctuary of Surkh Dum before World War II. Systematic exploration began in the 1960s with surveys by Jørgen Meldgaard and Henrik Thrane, and the excavation of cemeteries by Louis Vanden Berghe and of the site of Baba Jan by Clare Goff. It is unfortunate that few bronzes recovered during these controlled excavations are typical of the fully developed Luristan bronzes.

After World War II illicit digging spread beyond Luristan, and the material that reached the dealers under the name 'Luristan' was of mixed provenance; it was also often of doubtful authenticity. In establishing which are truly Luristan bronzes, the early publications of homogeneous material from a single source and the excavated pieces are of great value. Typological, iconographic and scientific studies also have their part to play. It is necessary to differentiate between the typical products of Luristan and those that are not exclusive to the culture and show analogies with the products of Mesopotamia, Elam, northern Iran and south Russia. These latter should not always be explained away as booty or imports; they are in many cases of local manufacture.

BIBLIOGRAPHY

G. Contenau and R. Ghirshman: *Fouilles de Tépé Giyan, près de Néhavand, 1931–32* (Paris, 1935)
H. Thrane: 'Tepe Guran and the Luristan Bronzes', *Archaeology*, xxiii (1970), pp. 26–35
P. R. S. Moorey: *Catalogue of the Ancient Persian Bronzes in the Ashmolean Museum* (Oxford, 1971)
P. Calmeyer: *Reliefbronzen in babylonischem Stil* (Munich, 1973)
P. Amiet: *Les Antiquités du Luristan: Collection David Weill* (Paris, 1976)
C. Goff: 'Excavations at Baba Jan: The Pottery and Metal from Levels III and II', *Iran*, xvi (1978), pp. 29–65
O. W. Muscarella: 'Surkh Dum at the Metropolitan Museum of Art: A Mini-report', *J. Field Archaeol.*, viii (1981), pp. 327–59
E. De Waele: *Bronzes du Luristan et d'Amlash: Ancienne collection Godard*, Publications d'histoire de l'art et d'archéologie de l'université catholique de Louvain, xxxiv (Leuven, 1982)
*Luristan: Een verdwenen bronskunst uit West-Iran* (exh. cat. by L. Vanden Berghe, Ghent, Cent. Kst & Cult., 1982–3)
L. Vanden Berghe and E. Haerinck: 'Prospections et fouilles au Pusht-i Kuh, Luristan', *Archv Orientforsch.*, xxxi (1984), pp. 200–09

ERIC DE WAELE

**Lu Shoukun** [Lu Shou-k'un]. *See* LUI SHOU-KWAN.

**Lusitano, Francisco Vieira.** *See* VIEIRA LUSITANO, FRANCISCO.

**Lusson, Adrien-Louis** (*b* La Flèche, Sarthe, 4 Aug 1788; *d* Rome, 9 Feb 1864). French architect. He settled in Paris, possibly in 1806, and studied architecture at the Ecole des Beaux-Arts under Abel Lahure, Charles Percier and Pierre-François-Léonard Fontaine, winning the silver medal at the Ecole d'Architecture in 1812 and at the Académie d'Architecture in 1814. After competing unsuccessfully for the Prix de Rome, he was appointed deputy inspector of public works to the city of Paris, in which capacity he built the Saint-Germain market (1813–18), publishing a description of it with Jean-Baptiste Blondel in 1816. He occupied a number of important official posts in the Paris municipal administration and was eventually appointed architect of public works to the city of Paris in 1835.

His duties allowed him to travel widely, and he visited Italy (1817–18), Sicily (1820), England (1826), Spain (1833) and Germany and Austria (1841), drawing the buildings and monuments. Some of these drawings he later worked up for exhibition at the Salon or for publication, as in the case of his *Description pittoresque de la Sicile* (Paris, 1820). He also built up a large collection of drawings by other architects and engineers, which he bequeathed to the Bibliothèque Municipale, Le Mans.

Very few of Lusson's projects were brought to a successful conclusion, and his contribution was largely that of a theorist who wished to combine the aesthetics of Classical—particularly Roman—architecture with the new forms of iron-framed construction. Among his completed works are La Rotonde, Place des Halles, Le Mans (1818–26), the customs house, Rue Chauchat, Paris (1821–6), the château of Voisin (1837–9) and the Cité Vindé, 13–17, Boulevard de la Madeleine, Paris (1843–4). In 1829–34 he designed a scheme that won the competition for 'the Embellishment of Paris: Place de la Concorde and Thirty Fountains', but changed circumstances after the 1830 Revolution prevented its realization. He also took part in the competitions of 1846 and 1861 for the reconstruction of the Paris Opéra, and he was involved in the initial design of the controversial iron-framed Gothic church of St Eugène, Paris (built 1854–5) but became embroiled in a lawsuit with its builder, the architect Louis-Auguste Boileau. His most important project was his design for the church of St François-Xavier in Paris (1861–4), which was completed in much modified form and on a reduced scale in 1877 by François Uchard (1809–91), who altered its original aiseless plan and substituted Italian Renaissance detailing for Lusson's Roman conception.

### WRITINGS

with J.-B. Blondel: *Plan, coupe, élévation et détails du nouveau marché Saint-Germain* (Paris, 1816)

*Projets de trente fontaines pour l'embellissement de la ville de Paris* (Paris, 1835)

*Projet d'un théâtre d'opéra définitif pour la ville de Paris* (Paris, 1846)

*Plans, coupes, élévations et détails de l'église rue de Montyon, à Paris. . . sous l'invocation de Saint Eugène* (Paris, 1855)

*Programme d'une église paroissiale pour la ville de Paris* (Paris, 1858–9)

### BIBLIOGRAPHY

L. Wasserman: 'Eglise Saint-François-Xavier, boulevard des Invalides', *Univl: Illus. Contemp.*, iv/81 (1863), pp. 45–8

L. Hublin: *La Place de la République au Mans* (Le Mans, 1887)

R.-A. Weigert: 'Eglise de la Rédemption, ancienne halle de déchargement de l'octroi', *Gaz. B.-A.*, n. s. 6, xxxvi (1949), pp. 279–90

S. Damiron: 'Projets pour l'embellissement en 1829 de la place Louis XVI, actuellement place de la Concorde', *Bull. Soc. Hist. A. Fr.* (1962), p. 159

ANNE CLERT

**Lutf 'Ali Khan** [Luṭf 'Alı Khān Shīrāzī] ( *fl* 1840–70). Persian painter. He is often designated *ṣūratgar* ('painter') to distinguish him from the Zand monarch of the same name (*reg* 1789–94). The artist continued the flower-and-bird tradition associated with 'ALI ASHRAF and is best known for flower paintings, such as one dated 1841 of a hand holding a rose blossom (priv. col.; see Robinson, 1979, fig. 240). Lutf 'Ali also illustrated manuscripts, and he signed most of the illustrations in a copy (1854–64; Shiraz, Vcsal priv. col.) of the *Shāhnāma* ('Book of kings'). His working methods can be seen from his album (Tehran, Riza 'Abbasi Mus., 1299–1309, 1311–1510), which contains a dozen folios of pounces, drawings and studies for penboxes, caskets, daggers and manuscript illumination. A few are in Lutf 'Ali's own style of floral sprays and flowering hazelnut branches within cartouches and medallions, including the pounce used for a painted and varnished ('lacquered') penbox (1849; Tehran, Mus. Dec. A.) decorated with a floral design incorporating European figures. Other materials in the album range in style and show the variety of compositions and designs readily available to Iranian artists in the 19th century.

### BIBLIOGRAPHY

B. W. Robinson: 'Persian Painting in the Qajar Period', *Highlights of Persian Art*, ed. R. Ettinghausen and E. Yarshater (Boulder, CO, 1979), pp. 331–62

M. A. Karimzada Tabrizi: *Ahvāl u āthār-i naqqāshān-i qadīm-i īrān* [The lives and art of old painters of Iran] (London, 1985), no. 835

L. S. Diba: 'Persian Painting in the Eighteenth Century: Tradition and Transmission', *Murqarnas*, vi (1989), pp. 147–60

B. W. Robinson: 'Persian Painting under the Zand and Qājār Dynasties', *From Nadir Shah to the Islamic Republic* (1991), vii of *The Cambridge History of Iran* (Cambridge, 1968–91), pp. 870–90

**Luther, Martin** (*b* Eisleben, Saxony, 10 Nov 1483; *d* Eisleben, 18 Feb 1564). German theologian and writer. He had begun law studies in 1505 when, following a sudden conversion, he entered an Augustinian monastery in Erfurt and was ordained in 1507. Five years later he obtained a doctorate in theology and a professorship in scripture in Wittenberg. His profound spiritual anxieties over the question of the justice of God were allayed during the course of his lectures on Psalms and Romans (1513, 1515–16), when he came to understand that sinful man becomes just before God only through belief in his mercy. From this conception he developed his doctrine of the Justification by Faith Alone. Luther's 95 theses against indulgences (1517) found wide popular support but were judged heretical. At Augsburg he refused to retract before the papal legate Cajetan (1518), and during the Leipzig disputation with Johann Eck (1519) he attacked Church doctrine. His reform tracts of 1520, the address *To the Christian Nobility of the German Nation*, *The Babylonian Captivity of the Church* and *The Freedom of Christian Man*, made the break with the Roman Catholic church inevitable. He was excommunicated by Leo X in 1520 and outlawed by Charles V's Edict of Worms of 1521. Deploring the iconoclasm instigated by Andreas Bodenstein von Karlstadt in Wittenberg, Luther returned there to promote the evangelical movement and the reform of worship. In 1525 he castigated the excesses of the Peasant War and also married a former nun. His controversy with Ulrich Zwingli over the Lord's Supper divided Protestants into the Reformed and Lutheran churches. As the control of the latter passed to the Protestant princes and free cities (Confession of Augsburg, 1530), Luther concentrated on the consolidation of his exegetical work and on evangelical education. His last years were clouded by ill-health and the growing religious and political disunity.

Luther's impact on the visual arts was considerable. In *Eight Sermons* (1522) and *Against the Heavenly Prophets in the Matter of Images and Sacraments* (1525) he defended *Merkbilder* (mnemonic images) for their didactic value and wished 'the whole Bible painted inside out for everyone to see'. His friend Lucas Cranach the elder illustrated his translation of the Bible. He fiercely opposed the veneration of images and belief in their miraculous powers (e.g. bleeding crucifixes), however, and promoted the removal from churches of pictures donated for merit. As a result of Luther's teachings, the numbers of such devotional images as the *Pietà* decreased in Germany, while other themes were emphasized or transformed. The *Last Judgement* is shown without the Virgin as intercessor, the *Ecce homo* without demonstration of the wounds of Christ, and the eucharistic *Last Supper* (instead of the historic one) signals the reformed sacrament. Luther's doctrine of Justification by Faith was addressed by themes such as *Christ and the Adulteress*, *Christ and the Woman of Samaria*, *Job with Eliu* and, especially, by a new, popular subject, the *Justification of the Sinner before the Law by the Grace of God and Faith*, associated with Cranach (1530). Cranach was also the painter and designer of numerous portraits of Luther, and he illustrated the first Reformation pamphlet, the *Passional Christi und Antichristi* (Wittenberg, 1521), juxtaposing Christ and the Pope in pairs of antithetical woodcuts. Luther was indirectly responsible for a proliferation of popular illustrated broadsheets, serving the Reformation. These polemical prints were often designed by such artists as Georg Pencz, Barthel and Sebald Beham, Peter Flötner, Erhard Schön, Leonhard Beck and Jörg Breu the elder, while many texts came from the cobbler poet Hans Sachs. Mainly tools of anticlerical propaganda, they also served to instruct the common man in Luther's theology.

WRITINGS

*D. Martin Luthers Werke: Kritische Gesamtausgabe* (Weimar, 1883–; R Graz, 1964–)

BIBLIOGRAPHY

R. H. Bainton: *Here I Stand* (Nashville, 1950)

O. Thulin: 'Luther in the Arts', *Encyclopedia of the Lutheran Church*, ii (Minneapolis, 1965), pp. 1433–42

C. C. Christensen: 'Luther's Theology and the Use of Religious Art', *Lutheran Q.*, xxii (1970), pp. 147–65

C. Harbison: 'Reformation Iconography: Problems and Attitudes', *Prt Rev.*, v (1976), pp. 78–87

M. Stirm: *Die Bilderfrage in der Reformation* (Gütersloh, 1977)

C. C. Christensen: *Art and the Reformation in Germany* (Athens, OH, 1979)

R. Bergmann: 'A "tröstlich pictura": Luther's Attitude in the Question of Images', *Ren. & Reformation*, n. s., i (1981), pp. 15–25

R. W. Scribner: *For the Sake of Simple Folk: Popular Propaganda for the German Reformation* (Cambridge, 1981)

*Martin Luther und die Reformation in Deutschland* (exh. cat., Nuremberg, Ger. Nmus., 1983)

M. Warnke: *Cranachs Luther: Entwürfe für ein Image* (Frankfurt am Main, 1984)

R. Bergmann: 'Hans Sachs Illustrated: Pamphlets and Broadsheets in the Service of the Reformation', *Racar*, xvii/1 (1990), pp. 9–16, 89–91

ROSEMARIE BERGMANN

**Lutheranism.** Christian Protestant denomination based on the teachings of MARTIN LUTHER. Luther's doubts concerning the effectiveness of the Catholic Church's teachings on personal salvation and the perceived ills of religious and social institutions were widely distributed after 1517 (*see* CHRISTIANITY, §I, 3(iii)(b)). The reforms in Church structure and liturgy that he proposed gained the support of territorial rulers and city governments, notably in many parts of Germany. Conflicts regarding the degree of reforms, often fuelled by political interests, led to the breakdown of religious authority and unity in the Holy Roman Empire. Albert of Hohenzollern (*d* 1568), Grand Master of the Teutonic Order, became a Protestant in 1525 and converted the Order's lands in Prussia and along the Baltic into a secular duchy. Frederick I, King of Denmark (*reg* 1523–33), permitted Lutheran preaching in Denmark and Norway from 1527 and made it the sole religion in 1529, banning Roman Catholic doctrines. Sweden broke with Rome in 1527, and the first Swedish service book was published in 1529; Catholic worship was banned in 1544. In order to avoid armed conflict in the Empire, the Peace of Augsburg (1555) introduced the principle of *cuius regio, eius religio*, by which the territorial ruler's religion would determine his subjects' religious affiliation. This did not ensure complete stability, however, since a change in ruler or his convictions, sometimes chosen for political rather than doctrinal reasons, might result in a sudden reversion to Catholicism, for example at Neuburg an der Donau in 1614, or a change to Calvinism, as at Heidelberg in the 1560s. By the late 16th century Lutheranism remained the largest Protestant body, with further significant minorities in Bohemia, Hungary, Poland, Austria and the Netherlands.

Lutheran teaching accepts only the sacraments of baptism and holy communion and holds that Christ is corporeally present in the eucharistic bread and wine, both of which are received by all believers. Despite objections to the Mass as a sacrifice, initially the main structure of the liturgy was retained with a reduction in ceremonial. Church government varied according to the requirements of the state or local congregation. In Scandinavia and some parts of Germany the new state churches were still governed by bishops, although consistorial government was common in most of Germany, and Calvinist influence in the Netherlands resulted in a congregational system. Scandinavian, German and Dutch traditions were introduced to North America from the 17th century, and the immigrants were absorbed into the English-speaking populace. In the 19th century, however, immigrants established their own church organizations, especially in the Mid-West, arranged by congregations and synods on national lines with little supervision from Europe. Towards the end of the 19th century some congregations returned to 17th-century Lutheran orthodoxy, and in the 20th many have come together in such bodies as the Lutheran World Federation (1947).

Luther opposed the iconoclasm that accompanied the early Reformation and accepted the presence of appropriate images that promoted evangelical worship and did not contribute to idolatry (*see* CHRISTIANITY, §III, 3(ii)(b)). The earliest visual expressions of Lutheran ideas appear in woodcuts in the vernacular Bible translations, catechisms (see fig.), service books and theological commentaries that spread the new doctrines, and also in the extensive anti-papal literature (for discussion and illustration *see* GERUNG, MATTHIAS). Otto Henry, Elector Palatine, became a Lutheran in 1542, and his chapel at Schloss

Lutheran illustration to the first petition of the Lord's Prayer; woodcut from Martin Luther: *Deutsch Catechismus* (Wittenberg, Lutherhalle Wittenberg, Reformations Geschichtliches Museum)

Neuberg, decorated in 1543 by Hans Bocksberger I, contains the earliest surviving Lutheran iconographic programme, with the *Ascension* in the centre of the vault, medallions illustrating *Baptism* and *Communion*, and Old Testament scenes on the walls. The iconography adopted in many lesser churches was often drawn from woodcuts, and later engravings (*see also* DENMARK, §III, 2; FINLAND, §III, 1; and NORWAY, §III, 2). Portraits of Luther and other reformers, such as Philipp Melancthon (1497–1560), sometimes replaced images of saints.

Civil disturbance in Germany during the first few decades of the Reformation did not encourage church building, and existing churches were adapted to the new liturgy (*see* CHURCH, §II, 4). In 1554–5, for example, galleries were inserted above the aisles of the Marktkirche (begun 1529), Halle an der Saale. Subsidiary altars were removed, but monumental altarpieces were retained as the eastern focus, sometimes with the pulpit, which was now the centre of the liturgy, placed above, for example in the chapel (1586–90) decorated by Hans Becher and WILHELM VERNUCKEN in Schloss Wilhelmsburg, Schmalkalden. The numbers of new churches increased in the late 16th century, usually still drawing on Late Gothic elements, and elaborate carved and painted furnishings were characteristic of both converted and new Lutheran structures, set in simple, almost vernacular, architecture, such as in the estate churches at Breese im Bruch (begun 1592) and Bristow (completed 1601). The parapet of the former's west and north galleries has small painted panels with scenes from the *Life of Christ* and seated figures of *St Paul* and *David* above.

Late Gothic styles were often retained into the 17th century, and the commonest ground-plans remained the hall church (e.g. 1617–28; Kristianstad, Trefaldighetskyrkan, possibly by Hans van Steenwinckel (ii)) and the barnlike, galleried chapel. The L-shaped church built by Heinrich Schickhardt II at Freudenstadt in 1601–14, intended for Lutherans expelled from southern Austria, has the altar placed at the eastern angle, opposite the organ, and galleries across both ends and the west sides of the arms; the shallow rib vault is decorated with carved medallions. One of the most complete early 17th-century interiors is at Frederiksborg Castle (1606–17; for discussion and illustration *see* HILLERØD, FREDERIKSBORG CASTLE). The interior of the Unionskirche (remodelled 1665–77), Idstein, demonstrates the lavish painted decoration permitted by some Lutheran bodies. The church of Zum Heiligen Geist (completed 1618, by Jakob Wustmann), Nidda, was a more influential design that introduced the rectangular meeting-house with a square or pentagonal apse; this plan remained in use in the 18th century (e.g. 1764–7; Lauterbach Church, by Georg Koch) and became particularly common in America.

After the Peace of Westphalia (1648) it was agreed that the Silesian Lutherans could build three large 'Peace Churches' outside the town walls, without bell-towers and using no stone or brick. The colourful interior of the half-timbered church at Jauer (now Jawor; 1654–5, by Albrecht von Säbisch) has four tiers of galleries and can hold up to 6000 worshippers. Six 'Grace Churches' were also conceded after 1707, including the stone Holy Cross Church (1709–18, by Marcin Frantz), Hirschberg (now Jelenia

Góra), where the organ is placed above the altar. Its design was based on Swedish models, notably the Katarinakyrka (1656–82), Stockholm, which had been devised by Jean De La Vallée as an ideal Protestant church (*see also* SWEDEN, §II, 2(iii)).

The flexibility of Lutheran liturgy and attitudes to iconography has permitted widely varying ground-plans and decorative schemes since the 18th century. Some new churches maintained traditional galleried forms, for example at the Dreifaltigkeitskirche (1701–17, by Johann Peter Graber), Speyer. More centralized plans included square forms, for example at Dresden in the Frauenkirche (1726–34, by George Bähr; destr. 1945; rebuilt from 1992; *see* DRESDEN, IV, 1), a Greek-cross plan with rounded corners at the Ludwigskirche (1762–75, by FRIEDRICH JOACHIM M. STENGEL; rebuilt 1965–75), Saarbrücken, and the oval St Michaelis (1751–62, by Johann Leonhard Prey and Ernst Georg Sonnin; rebuilt after World War II), Hamburg. Historicist styles were later adopted, even mixing a Romanesque Revival structure with rich gold mosaic and marble decoration of Byzantine inspiration, for example at the Erlöserkirche (1912–18), Bad Homburg.

### BIBLIOGRAPHY
P.-M. Hamberg: *Tempelbygge för protestanter* [Protestant church-building] (Uppsala, 1955)
C. C. Christensen: *Art and the Reformation in Germany*, ed. R. C. Walton (Athens, OH, 1979)
H.-R. Hitchcock: *German Renaissance Architecture* (Princeton, 1981)
C. E. Nelson: *The Rise of World Lutheranism* (Philadelphia, 1982)
*Luther und die Folgen für die Kunst* (exh. cat., ed. W. Hofmann; Hamburg, Kstalle, 1983–4)
E. T. Bachmann and M. B. Bachmann: *Lutheran Churches in the World: A Handbook* (Minneapolis, 1989)

For further bibliography *see* LUTHER, MARTIN.

□

**Lutherbourg, Philippe Jacques de.** *See* LOUTHERBOURG, PHILIPPE JACQUES DE.

**Lüthi, Urs** (*b* Kriens, 10 Sept 1947). Swiss printmaker and painter. He attended the Kunstgewerbeschule, Zurich (1963–4). He worked as a graphic artist, executing a number of coloured screenprints that were exhibited at the Stedelijk Museum in Amsterdam (1968), at the Kunstmuseum, Lucerne (1970 and 1974) and at the Museum Bochum Kunstsammlung (1974). His work was strongly connected with body art although it was purely graphic until 1980; he produced black-and-white series of two or three offset prints drawn from photographs, in which he juxtaposed a self-portrait (sometimes together with a portrait of his wife Elke) and views of buildings or of interiors. Each component image was opposed or contradicted by the conjunction of all the images. He also produced a number of screenprints on canvas, such as *Lüthi Also Cries for You* (1970; see 1991 exh. cat., pl. 16). Lüthi gradually moved towards painting and working in colour, although he maintained the same central interest in his own body as the subject; as he grew older and heavier, his images grew increasingly sexual and provocative. He executed a number of oil paintings influenced by the work of Giorgio de Chirico and Francis Picabia, and he also began to work in aquatint and drypoint, principally depicting himself and his second wife Ulrike together. In the series *Universal Order* (1989; see 1991 exh. cat., pls 197–207) his earliest narcissistic explorations are combined with his later technical experiments, using combinations of photogravure and aquatints, some of which depict his own contorted chest.

BIBLIOGRAPHY

*Transformer: Aspekte der Travestie* (exh. cat. by J.-C. Amman and R. M. Mason, Lucerne, 1974)
*Urs Lüthi: L'oeuvre multipliée* (exh. cat. by R. M. Mason, Genève, Cab. Est. Mus. A. & Hist., 1991)

VINCENT LIEBER

**Luti, Benedetto** (*b* Florence, 17 Nov 1666; *d* Rome, 17 June 1724). Italian painter, draughtsman, collector, dealer and teacher. He was one of the most significant and influential artists active in Rome in the first quarter of the 18th century. The son of a Florentine artisan, he trained in his native city under the direction of Anton Domenico Gabbiani and thoroughly absorbed the style of Pietro da Cortona and his late Baroque successors. In 1690 he left Florence for Rome, where in 1692 he made his artistic début in the annual St Bartholomew's Day exhibition with a monumental painting of *God Cursing Cain after the Murder of Abel* (Kedleston Hall, Derbys). He quickly rose to prominence and in 1694 was elected to the Accademia di S Luca. He produced a variety of works for the leading Roman families—the Torri, Colonna, Pallavicini, Barberini and Odescalchi—and enjoyed the patronage of Pope Clement XI, Cardinal Pietro Ottoboni, Cardinal Carlo Agosto Fabbroni and Padre Antonin Cloche, Master General of the Dominican Order. He was invited to participate in the most important papal commission to painters in Rome in the first quarter of the 18th century, that for the series of Old Testament prophets above the nave arcade in S Giovanni in Laterano; his contribution was *Isaiah* (1718; *in situ*). With many of the same artists who painted for Pope Clement XI—Giuseppe Bartolomeo Chiari, Francesco Trevisani, Andrea Procaccini, Sebastiano Conca, Luigi Garzi—he was also involved in the major secular commission of the time in Rome, a series of ceilings in the Palazzo de Carolis (now the Banca di Roma), contributing an *Allegory of Diana* (*c.* 1720; *in situ*). In Florence he enjoyed the support of Grand Duke Cosimo III de' Medici, and it was through his connection with the Tuscan court that his artistic reputation spread to France, England and Germany.

Like many young artists in Rome around 1700, Luti consciously adapted his native style of painting to conform to the Roman classical tradition and devoted years to the study of the paintings of Raphael, Annibale Carracci, Domenichino, Reni and Maratti, the grand exemplars of Roman *disegno*. His long years of study were rewarded in 1712, when he produced the *Investiture of St Ranieri* (Pisa Cathedral), his first major work to reveal on a grand scale the traditional Roman conventions of invention, expression, composition and anatomy. This brilliant rephrasing of Roman classicism according to the lighting, colour and handling of Florentine Baroque painting resulted in a style that was distinguished, within the context of contemporary

Benedetto Luti: *St Carlo Borromeo Administering Extreme Unction to the Plague Victims*, oil on canvas, 1.08×1.59 m, 1713 (Schleissheim, Staatsgalerie im Neuen Schloss Schleissheim)

painting in Rome, by its effects of luminosity, colour, painterly richness and naturalism. Its grand, rhetorical manner, which formed the basis of all Luti's subsequent works, was demonstrated again in one of his greatest pictures, *St Carlo Borromeo Administering Extreme Unction to the Plague Victims* (1713; Schleissheim, Neue Schloss; see fig.), painted for John William, Elector Palatine. In 1713 he also dispatched the first of his paintings commissioned by the Electoral Archbishop of Mainz, Lothar Franz von Schönborn: *Diana and Endymion* and *Venus and Adonis* (Pommersfelden, Schloss Weissenstein). Following the death of Maratti in 1713, Luti's reputation in Rome was greater than that of any other painter in the city, and during his lifetime it was seriously rivalled only by that of Trevisani and Chiari.

Luti was one of the great colourists of 18th-century Rome, and his influence on later artists, such as Pompeo Batoni, was considerable. He was not, however, a prolific painter (only some 75 autograph paintings survive), and he is probably better known today for his pastel (e.g. *Portrait of a Man*, 1718; London, V&A) and coloured chalk drawings. These studies of single heads and bustlengths of apostles, saints, angels and children are remarkably fresh and brilliant. They were deliberately imitative of the art of Correggio, which enjoyed an enormous vogue in the 18th century, and share with the paintings of the 16th-century Emilian master similar qualities of sweetness, charm, suavity and, above all, grace of colour and drawing.

One explanation for Luti's restricted artistic production is his activity in the Roman art world as connoisseur, collector and academician. Owing to the patronage of Grand Duke Cosimo III, Luti received countless opportunities to meet foreign visitors and their agents in Rome. With a reputation as the 'best connoisseur in the city' (Richardson), he was one of the principal dealers on the Roman art market. He maintained close relationships with foreign collectors in Rome, in particular with Pierre Crozat and Pierre-Jean Mariette, and he was involved in the sale and dispatch of Queen Christina of Sweden's famous collection of paintings to Philippe II, Duke of Orléans, in Paris. As a collector, Luti achieved an even greater reputation, among Romans and foreigners alike, and one contemporary estimated his collection of drawings to number around 15,000. He was active also as a teacher and academician. He held private drawing classes and maintained a large studio on a more formal basis, especially between 1710 and 1720. Among his more notable pupils were Pietro Bianchi (i), Placido Costanzi, William Kent, Jean-Baptiste van Loo, Carle Vanloo and Giovanni Paolo Panini. He exercised an important teaching and administrative role in the Accademia di S Luca: from at least 1704 he was elected annually as one of the judges for the academy's competitions; he frequently taught the life drawing classes; he played a prominent role in 1715 in the deliberations leading to the major changes in the institution's statutes intended to consolidate its authority in the Roman art world; and in 1720 he was elected Principe.

BIBLIOGRAPHY

J. Richardson: *An Account of Some of the Statues, Bas-reliefs, Drawings and Pictures in Italy & c.* (London, 1722), p. 182
N. Pio: *Vite* (1724); ed. C. Enggass and R. Enggass (1977), pp. 24–5
L. Pascoli: *Vite* (1730–36), i, pp. 228–34
G. G. Bottari and S. Ticozzi: *Raccolta di lettere sulla pittura, scultura, ed architettura*, 8 vols (Milan, 1822–5/R Olms, 1976), ii, pp. 70–84; v, pp. 304–5; vi, pp. 165–70 [artist's letters]
V. Moschini: 'Benedetto Luti', *L'Arte*, xxvi (1923), pp. 89–114
H. Voss: *Die Malerei des Barocks in Rom* (Berlin, 1924), pp. 360–66, 608–11
*Quellen zur Geschichte des Barocks in Franken unter dem Einfluss des Hauses Schönborn*, i, ed. P. H. Hantsch and A. Scherf (Augsburg, 1931); ii, ed. M. H. von Freeden (Würzburg, 1955) [artist's letters]
F. H. Dowley: 'Some Drawings by Benedetto Luti', *A. Bull.*, xliv (1962), pp. 219–36
B. Heinzl: 'The Luti Collection: Towards the Reconstruction of a Seventeenth-century Roman Collection of Master Drawings', *Connoisseur*, clxi (1966), pp. 17–22
G. Sestieri: 'Il punto su Benedetto Luti', *A. Illust.*, vi (1973), pp. 232–55
E. P. Bowron: *The Paintings of Benedetto Luti (1666–1724)* (diss., New York U., Inst. F.A., 1979) [standard ref. with cat. of autograph works]
——: 'Benedetto Luti's Pastels and Coloured Chalk Drawings', *Apollo*, cxi (1980), pp. 440–47
S. Rudolph: *La pittura del '700 a Roma* (Milan, 1983), pp. 404–10, 783
M. Coccia: 'Benedetto Luti', *La pittura in Italia: Il settecento*, ed. G. Briganti, 2 vols (Milan, 1990), ii, pp. 773–4 [with further bibliog.]

EDGAR PETERS BOWRON

**Lutma.** Dutch family of artists. They were active mainly in Amsterdam. (1) Johannes Lutma (i) worked mostly as a silversmith, and his designs were published in engravings by his two sons (2) Johannes Lutma (ii) and Jacob Lutma (*b* after 1624; *bur* 24 June 1654). Jacob's small oeuvre of prints includes portraits and reproductive engravings after other artists.

**(1) Johannes** [Jan; Janus; Joannes] **Lutma (i)** (*b* Emden [now in Germany], ?1584; *d* Amsterdam, *bur* 29 Jan 1669). Silver- and goldsmith and possible engraver. After a period spent in Paris *c.* 1615, he established himself in Amsterdam in 1621, where he married in 1623. He was a friend of Rembrandt, who etched his portrait (B. 276). Johannes (i) has wrongly been thought to have been a pupil of the goldsmith Paulus van Vianen. He is best known for the choir-screen in the Nieuwe Kerk, Amsterdam (etched by Johannes (ii), Hollstein, no. 11), and his designs for zoomorphic ornaments. This 'auricular' style was briefly influential among a small group of artists in the Netherlands (*see* AELST, WILLEM VAN), Germany and possibly Denmark. Lutma's ornamental designs (*see* FRAME, §V) were published in four series of prints, mostly by his sons Jacob and Johannes (e.g. a series of frames by Jacob Lutma, Hollstein, nos 8–19). There is also an engraving of three ovals with river gods, thought to be the work of Johannes Lutma (i) (Hollstein, no. 1).

**(2) Johannes** [Jan; Janus] **Lutma (ii)** (*b* Amsterdam, *bapt* 1 Sept 1624; *d* Amsterdam, *bur* 11 Nov 1689). Printmaker, gold- and silversmith and draughtsman, son of (1) Johannes Lutma (i). He became a master in 1643. In 1651 he was in Rome, where he made drawings (e.g. the *Farnese Hercules*, 1651; Amsterdam, Rijksmus.) and engraved several fountains (e.g. the engraving of the fountain in Piazza Navona, 1652; Hollstein, no. 9). In the etched portrait of his father (1656; Hollstein, no. 5) Johannes (ii) began to exploit tonal effects through the additional use of punch and roulette. In the later hammered or punched prints of *c.* 1681 (for illustration *see* PUNCHED PRINT) he managed to produce quite exceptional grey tones by a combination of roulette accents in the outlines and fine punching; Ackley has compared these grey tones with those found in a wash drawing.

BIBLIOGRAPHY

Hollstein: *Dut. & Flem.* [H]; Thieme–Becker
A. von Bartsch: *Le Peintre-graveur* (1803–21) [B.]
*Printmaking in the Age of Rembrandt* (exh. cat. by C. S. Ackley, Boston, MA, Mus. F.A., 1980–81), no. 195
*Dutch Figure Drawings from the 17th Century* (exh. cat. by P. Schatborn, Amsterdam, Rijksmus.; Washington, DC, N.G.A.; 1981–2), p. 66

CHRISTIAAN SCHUCKMAN

**Luttrell** [Lutterell], **Edward** (*fl c.* 1680–1724). English draughtsman, engraver and writer. He was probably related to the Luttrell family of Saunton Court, Devon; the tradition that he was born in Dublin is not substantiated. He apparently settled early in London and studied law, but abandoned it for art. He first turned to drawing for his own amusement but then, according to Bainbridge Buckeridge, received instruction in pastel portraiture (Luttrell's speciality) from Edmund Ashfield; in his manuscript on techniques, *An Epitome of Painting*, Luttrell made favourable mention of his teacher.

Luttrell's portraits in pastels, which he sometimes mixed with gouache, are closely dependent on those by Ashfield but are distinguished by coarser handling and hot, reddish-brown flesh tones. He sometimes signed them with variants of his name, or with his initials in monogram. He made numerous copies after other artists, including Rembrandt and Otto van Veen, and his work for engravers includes some portraits of earlier kings and queens for Kennet's *History of England* (1706). A pioneer of mezzotint, Luttrell adapted the technique for his pastels (e.g. *Unknown Gentleman*, 1699; Dublin, N.G.), using copperplates roughened with a rocker, as if for mezzotinting, claiming the method to be his own invention, although it was also used by William Faithorne.

Luttrell seems to have lived in Westminster, to judge from the addresses on examples of his work. George Vertue listed him in his 'Note-books' as one of the 'living painters of Note in London' and included his name among the 12 founder-members of the Great Queen Street Academy in 1711.

UNPUBLISHED SOURCES

New Haven, CT, Yale Cent. Brit. A. [MS., *An Epitome of Painting, Containing Breife Directions for Drawing, Painting, Limning and Cryoons . . . and How to Lay the Ground, and Work in Mezzo Tinto*, (1683)]

PRINTS

W. Kennet, ed.: *History of England*, 3 vols (London, 1706)

BIBLIOGRAPHY

B. Buckeridge: 'An Essay towards an English School of Painters', in R. de Piles: *The Art of Painting*, 3rd edn (London, 1750), p. 355
C. F. Bell: 'English Seventeenth Century Portrait Drawings in Oxford Collections', *Walpole Soc.*, v (1915–17), pp. 1–18
E. Croft-Murray and P. Hulton: *XVI and XVII Centuries* (1960), i of *British Museum Catalogue of British Drawings* (London, 1960–), pp. 434–5

DAVID BLAYNEY BROWN

**Luttrell Psalter.** Elaborately decorated 14th-century English Psalter (354×244 mm; London, BL, Add. MS. 42130) made, as the scribe wrote on folio 202*v*, for Sir Geoffrey Luttrell (1276–1345), Lord of Irnham, Lincs. The initials to the major liturgical divisions are historiated with scenes from the *Life of David*, forming part of the profuse decoration of borders and *bas-de-page* scenes that frame almost every page (*see* LANDSCAPE PAINTING, fig. 2). These contain a vast range of religious and secular subject-matter, seldom relevant to the psalm text. Although some of the border decoration includes episodes from the *Life of Christ* and figures of saints, more attention is devoted to contemporary genre scenes of peasant and courtly life and to grotesque hybrid creatures, often treated on an unusually large scale: no other English painting of the 14th century provides such a wealth of contemporary genre scenes, some perhaps illustrating the activities on the Luttrell manor. In a miniature (fol. 202*v*) facing Psalm 109, the owner is represented on horseback being handed his helmet, banner and shield by his wife Agnes Sutton (*d* 1340) and his daughter-in-law, Beatrice Scrope. The latter was betrothed to Geoffrey's son, Andrew Luttrell (1313–90), in 1320, when the boy was only seven. It is unlikely that she would have been formally married to him much before he came of age in 1334, although the exact date of their marriage is not known. The arms of the family members, Luttrell, Sutton and Scrope are found throughout the manuscript. Two main artists, one specializing in religious subjects and the other in the secular subject-matter, worked on the manuscript. One of these has some relation to the group of manuscripts related to the Fitzwarin Psalter (*c.* 1350–60; Paris, Bib. N., MS. lat. 765). This figure style, found in several manuscripts for the diocese of Ely, and also the costumes suggest that the Psalter was made *c.* 1330–40, although some scholars have argued for an earlier date.

BIBLIOGRAPHY

E. G. Millar: *The Luttrell Psalter* (London, 1932)
L. Freeman Sandler: *Gothic Manuscripts, 1285–1385* (1985), v of *A Survey of Manuscripts Illuminated in the British Isles*, ed. J. J. G. Alexander (London, 1975–), no. 107
L. Dennison: 'The Fitzwarin Psalter and its Allies: A Reappraisal', *England in the Fourteenth Century: Proceedings of the 1985 Harlaxton Symposium* (Woodbridge, 1986), pp. 58–61
M. Camille: 'Labouring for the Lord: The Ploughman and the Social Order in the Luttrell Psalter', *A. Hist.*, x (1987), pp. 423–54
J. Backhouse: *The Luttrell Psalter* (London, 1989)

NIGEL J. MORGAN

**Lutyens,** Sir **Edwin (Landseer)** (*b* London, 29 March 1869; *d* London, 1 Jan 1944). English architect. His biographer asserted that 'In his lifetime he was widely held to be . . . [Britain's] greatest architect since Wren if not, as many maintained, his superior' (Hussey, 1950, p. xvii). In an extensive and wide-ranging oeuvre Lutyens's successful integration of the romantic and classical traditions sustained his pre-eminence in British architecture for nearly half a century through a complex period of its development. He may be regarded as representing an alternative tradition to that which led to the acceptance of the Modern Movement in Britain.

1. Life and work. 2. Critical reception and posthumous reputation.

1. LIFE AND WORK. Lutyens's father, Charles Henry Augustus Lutyens (*b* 1829), who came from a family of Dutch origin, was a soldier turned painter and a pupil and friend of Sir Edwin Landseer, after whom his son was named. Because of poor health, Lutyens spent much of his childhood and youth at home in Thursley, a village in

Surrey, where he learnt about traditional crafts by observing builders at work, perhaps acquiring his remarkable sense of three-dimensional form and perspective by drawing the outlines of old farm buildings allegedly traced on a sheet of glass held up to the view, using a finely pared piece of soap. In 1885 Lutyens enrolled at the Kensington School of Art (now the Royal College of Art), London, to study architecture; he left in 1887, however, to become a pupil in the office of George & Peto, where he first met Herbert Baker (*see* §(iii) below). Early in 1889 Lutyens received a commission to build Crooksbury, a house near Farnham in Surrey; he immediately set up an office in London and, at the age of 20, began his long and fruitful career.

(i) Romantic vernacular, before *c.* 1905. (ii) Classicism and castles, *c.* 1905–10. (iii) Edwardian Baroque and New Delhi, *c.* 1910–18. (iv) 'Arches of Triumph': Late work, *c.* 1918–40.

*(i) Romantic vernacular, before* c. *1905.* Lutyens's design for Crooksbury, and indeed all his work in the first half of the 1890s, clearly shows the influence of Ernest George as well as that of R. Norman Shaw and Philip Webb, but none of it is particularly remarkable. He then began to work with GERTRUDE JEKYLL in a collaboration that was significant both for his architecture and for the development of his career. The redoubtable Miss Jekyll, who had come under the influence of John Ruskin, had abandoned painting for gardening because of failing eyesight, and she pursued her interest in country traditions at her home in Munstead, near Godalming. Munstead Wood (1896) is Lutyens's first masterpiece and demonstrates his ability to handle roof planes, gables and chimneys. The subtle use of traditional building materials, however, and the close relationship between house and garden, also reflect the contribution of 'Aunt Bumps', who described the building of her house in her book *Home and Garden* (London, 1900). Jekyll worked with Lutyens over the next two decades, creating for his houses gardens that combine the formal and the picturesque, with garden walls, steps and terraces placed along axes that extended from interior to exterior in a manner analogous to some early work of Frank Lloyd Wright (for further discussion and illustration *see* GARDEN, §VIII, 5 and fig. 60). Jekyll also introduced Lutyens to many of his important early clients as well as to his wife, Lady Emily Lytton, daughter of a former Viceroy of India, whom he married in 1897.

The houses Lutyens designed in the following decades, mostly for middle-class clients in the Home Counties, are among his most accomplished and inventive; Fulbrook in Elstead and Orchards in Munstead (both 1897–9; Surrey), for example, display an assured development of traditional forms with superb craftsmanship enhanced by personal mannerism and originality in the treatment of conventional elements. Further away from the influence of Gertrude Jekyll, however—as at Roseneath House (1896–7), Strathclyde, Scotland, Les Bois des Moutiers (1898), Varengeville, France, and Overstrand Hall (1899–1901), Cromer, Norfolk—there is a deliberate eccentricity reminiscent of the work of his contemporary Charles Rennie Mackintosh and other designers influenced by Art Nouveau. Lutyens's growing interest in geometry can be seen in the sophisticated stone forms of Tigbourne Court (1899–1901), Witley, Surrey, but perhaps the quintessential example of

his romantic vernacular manner is Deanery Garden (1899–1902; see fig. 1), Sonning, Berks. This red brick and tile house was designed for a supremely important client, Edward Hudson, the founder of *Country Life* (1897), which became the vehicle both for rural nostalgia and the promotion of Lutyens's architecture. At Sonning, Lutyens created a house within an existing walled garden that he related with axes to the interior of the building, which was distinguished by a double-height hall.

Contemporary with Tigbourne was the Red House (1899), Godalming, in which Lutyens began to develop his 'castle' style (*see* §(ii) below), elements of which also appeared at Overstrand. The projecting bays of the Red House rise to a continuous parapet, giving a pronounced castle-like impression on the steeply sloping site when viewed from below. Another early expression of this interest is seen at Lindisfarne Castle on Holy Island, Northumbria, which he was commissioned to restore and enlarge (1903) by Hudson a year after completing Deanery Garden. While respecting the existing silhouette of the castle, Lutyens designed interiors that revel in the simplicity of bare stone and plaster, Romanesque columns and arches on a succession of floor levels.

Lutyens's houses were classic statements of Edwardian Romanticism, but by the early years of the 20th century they also began to display a love of ambiguity in addition to the skilful handling of detail; at Grey Walls (1901), Gullane, Scotland, for example, where house and garden are related on 45° axes, there are three ambiguities of direction on the journey from the entrance gates to the drawing room; but his continuing emphasis on geometry did not overwhelm Lutyens's feeling for materials and detail. He was a master of house-planning, managing to combine comfort with unusual juxtapositions and control of movement through spaces that were always enclosed and often arranged around a central, dominant hearth with one of his inventive chimney-pieces. His staircases opened up unexpected vistas and gave an expansiveness to movement: it has been observed that his circulation spaces are often more generously planned than individual rooms.

Soon after the turn of the century, an increasing eclecticism in style began to mark Lutyens's house designs: Little Thakeham (1902), Thakeham, W. Sussex, for example, has a mellow stone Tudor-style exterior enclosing a double-height neo-classical hall with a gallery and staircase. At Marsh Court (1901–4), Stockbridge, Hants, which is built of clunch (a type of chalk), mannerist classical details are integrated into the Tudor style of the exterior. It is clear that Lutyens was responding to the growing enthusiasm for classicism (the 'grand manner') in the years around 1900, and he may have been tiring of his essays in roofs, gables, chimneys and leaded-light windows. Another notable example of this tendency is Homewood (1901), Knebworth, Herts, which was built for his mother-in-law, the Dowager Countess of Lytton; here Ionic pilasters rise to an enclosing sweep of roof, while on the entrance front, which comprises three weather-boarded gables, the segmentally arched portal has an open tympanum above a keystoned lintel. Such mannerism, leaving classicist elements hanging in space, had also appeared at Overstrand Hall, and it remained a characteristic of Lutyens's work throughout his career.

1. Edwin Lutyens: garden front of Deanery Garden, Sonning, Berkshire, 1899–1902

*(ii) Classicism and castles, c. 1905–10.* Lutyens's move towards classicism was evident in his design for Papillon Hall (1903–4; destr.), Market Harborough, Leics, where he employed forms reminiscent of the architecture of Claude-Nicolas Ledoux, for example in the powerful entrance porch. He also built some offices (1904) in Tavistock Street, London, for *Country Life* that were a subtle variation on the brick-and-stone theme of Wren's Hampton Court. The house that marked his complete acceptance of classicism, however, was Heathcote (1906; see fig. 2), Ilkley, W. Yorks, an opulent palazzo in which he adopted the Doric order used by Michele Sanmicheli and the mannerism of pilasters that 'disappear' into rustication between base and capital. This house has been seen as marking Lutyens's move from a progressive, free-style vernacular to a stiff and reactionary classicism, but it was not at all typical of his domestic practice. Nor can generalizations easily be made about Lutyens's architectural development: for example, he built the first part of Folly Farm, Sulhampstead, Berks, in 1906 in a reticent classical manner reminiscent of Wren, but when he came to extend the house in 1912 he added one of his most extravagant and romantic vernacular designs. Lutyens's later domestic work, like that of Shaw and Ernest Newton, typically adopted the simple brick manner of the late 17th century and eschewed the use of the giant order. Perhaps the Salutation (1911), Sandwich, Kent, is Lutyens's most perfect essay in the simple Georgian style.

At the same time, with the Red House at Godalming and Lindisfarne Castle behind him (*see* §(i) above), Lutyens also developed and used his 'castle' style during this period. His work at Lambay Castle (1905–12), Lambay Island, off the coast of Ireland, involved the repair and enlargement of an old house to create an intricate pattern of buildings and gardens within a huge circular rampart wall. His most extravagant work in this style was Castle Drogo, a new building on a dramatic bluff at Drewsteignton, Devon, for Julius Drewe, a successful grocer who wished to build a castle as might have belonged to a fictitious 13th-century ancestor. Building began in 1910, but only about a third of the proposed design was ever completed. However, with its subtly modelled granite walls, mullioned and transomed windows and especially its corridors and staircases planned on a heroic scale, Drogo could not be mistaken for a real castle (*see* CASTLE, fig. 13). Lutyens would have preferred to design a straightforward brick house in the manner of Wren for this client, since by this time he had his mind on grand conceptions in the classical language; but Drogo shows his willingness to build in whatever style his clients required, as well as his ability to do so without compromising the distinctive character of his work.

*(iii) Edwardian Baroque and New Delhi, c. 1910–18.* Lutyens was eager to secure a 'big job' in which he could exploit the classical language in a manner appropriate to the new mood in Britain during the Edwardian period, but he did not obtain any of the commissions for the large Edwardian Baroque public buildings being constructed in London and elsewhere at the time (*see* BAROQUE REVIVAL). His competition entry (1908) for the new County

2. Edwin Lutyens: side view of Heathcote, Ilkley, West Yorkshire, 1906

Hall in London, much influenced by Wren's Royal Hospital (now Royal Naval College) at Greenwich, was not successful, and his largest London commission—to design a formal town centre (1908–11) for Parker & Unwin's Hampstead Garden Suburb—was not in a truly urban context. At Hampstead he designed two Nonconformist churches that dominate the unfinished square; of similar configuration, they bring together the vernacular and the classical in a careful response to their location. This project was followed by the headquarters for the Theosophical Society (1911–13; now occupied by the British Medical Association), Tavistock Square, London; although his original design was never fully built, the completed central section has a grand and simple façade reminiscent of an Italian palazzo.

The big jobs eventually came to Lutyens, but initially from distant parts of the empire. In 1910 he was invited to South Africa to design the Johannesburg Art Gallery. This unfinished building has a portico derived from that at St Paul's, Covent Garden, London, by Inigo Jones, together with giant blank aedicula niches that may have been inspired by Old Newgate Prison by George Dance the younger, to which Lutyens had taken the artist William Nicholson shortly before it was demolished (1902). Lutyens also designed the Rand Regiments' Memorial (1911) in Johannesburg, the first of his many war memorials on the theme of the triumphal arch. At this time HERBERT BAKER was designing his monumental classicist Union Buildings in Pretoria, which strongly influenced the British government on the style to be adopted for the proposed

new capital of India upon its transfer from Calcutta to Delhi in 1911. The following year Lutyens was appointed as architect to the Delhi Planning Commission and, on his recommendation, Baker joined him in 1913.

Lutyens's plan for New Delhi (see fig. 3; *see also* DELHI, §I, 8, and INDIAN SUBCONTINENT, §III, 8(i)), influenced by that of Washington, DC, was based on the equilateral triangle and focused upon the Viceroy's House (1912–30; now the Rashtrapati Bhavan); this was sited at the head of the principal vista (King's Way; now Raj Path), which is also the ceremonial approach to the administrative centre of the city. Once preliminary proposals were approved in London, Lutyens lost no time in preparing sketches for the Viceroy's House, which is of immense size and highly complex in plan. In many ways his greatest achievement, it demonstrates his profound and instinctive understanding of the geometrical essence of classical architecture and his ability to transform it into something new and appropriate to India. Although Lutyens developed his own version of Roman Doric—the 'Delhi order', with bells on the capitals, which rises to the same entablature height from different levels—the character of the Viceroy's House is not given by the use of classical elements but by the dynamic monumentality of its form, with battered walls stepping back at a series of string courses that run around and through the building. Lutyens resisted demands to use an Indian style for New Delhi rather than a Western one, but he nevertheless incorporated Indian elements in his design, for example the roof-top *chatris* (domed pavilions), the deeply projecting *chajjā* (cornice)

3. Edwin Lutyens: New Delhi, aerial photograph of 1947 looking up the King's Way (now Raj Path) with the Viceroy's House (now Rashtrapati Bhavan), 1912–30, in the foreground; Herbert Baker's Secretariat buildings and Legislative Assembly (now Samsad Bhavan) are also shown

and the stupa railing motif that encircles the dome. His Mughal Garden (1918–25) to the west of the Viceroy's House, inspired by the water gardens of Iran and Kashmir, is enlivened by stone walls and pergolas in curious, abstracted forms (*see* GARDEN, §IV, 3 and fig. 12).

Baker designed the Secretariat buildings flanking the approach to the Viceroy's House and the circular Legislative Assembly (now Samsad Bhavan; see fig. 3), and although Lutyens and Baker quarrelled bitterly over the gradient of the central axis leading to the Viceroy's House, the two architects together created one of the finest and most sophisticated examples of monumental classicist urban planning of the 20th century. Several of the buildings Lutyens planned for New Delhi were not built and, apart from the Viceroy's staff quarters and a few official bungalows, Lutyens's only other executed works there were the All India War Memorial Arch and the George V Memorial, both at the approach end of King's Way; the Record Office; and palatial town houses for the Nizam of Hyderabad and the Gaekwar of Baroda. Most of the other buildings were designed by the younger architects working with Lutyens and Baker on the project, by whom they were strongly influenced, notably Arthur Shoosmith, Henry Medd, Robert Tor Russell and Walter Sykes George.

*(iv) 'Arches of Triumph': Late work, c. 1918–40.* World War I intervened in the early years of Lutyens's work at New Delhi, and although it undermined his comfortable Edwardian world, it brought him the immediate opportunity to exercise his skills in creating monumental structures in a poignant way in many war memorials, including the principal British national memorial, the Cenotaph, Whitehall, London. This was originally erected as a temporary structure in 1919 and recreated in stone the following year; it takes the form of a sarcophagus on a tall, narrow pylon, the planes of which curve and converge according to geometrical principles inspired by the entasis on the Parthenon in Athens, while the mass itself steps back alternately on each plane as it rises. This personal, abstracted classicism, described by Hussey as Lutyens's 'elemental mode', came increasingly to characterize his work. Anxious to avoid overt religious or national symbolism in his designs for the Cenotaph and other memorials, and increasingly obsessed by the subtleties of geometry, Lutyens was concerned with the emotional power of pure monumental form comprehensible within the European classical tradition.

Together with Baker, Lutyens became one of the principal architects to the Imperial War Graves Commission in 1917, and most British war cemeteries contain a Great War Stone designed by Lutyens, typically a monolithic altar modelled with characteristic entasis. He designed 126 war cemeteries in France, and his ideas on the relationship of planting to masonry walls and structures strongly influenced the general policy of the Commission, as did his desire for secular forms. Among his larger cemeteries, the most notable is perhaps that at Etaples (1923–4), where a pair of arched cenotaphs is flanked by stone flags—an enrichment of the architectural vocabulary that he had wanted to employ in Whitehall. Lutyens also designed the memorial at Thiepval to *The Missing of the Somme* (1927–32; see fig. 4), which is the finest executed statement of his abstracted and geometrical classicism and Roman triumphal arch form. The complex, stepped-back mass of the memorial is penetrated by a hierarchy of arched tunnels on 2 axes, so creating 16 piers on which are carved the names of 73,000 missing servicemen. One of his last works was the Australian National Memorial (1936–8) at Villers-Bretonneux, where the forms are severely abstracted but tempered by classical aediculae standing free in arched openings—so harking back to some of his first experiments in mannerist classicism.

In Britain, Lutyens was much less occupied with domestic commissions, and the few he did undertake, such as Gledstone Hall (1922–6), W. Yorks, and Middleton Park (1938), Oxon, developed further the classical themes of his pre-war houses. Lutyens's only venture into the design of public housing was undertaken in 1929 when he provided chequer-board façades for blocks of flats in Page Street, Westminster. An important commission was the design of the British Embassy (1927–8) in Washington, DC, which combined public and domestic accommodation in a neo-Georgian manner; the rather vertical proportions of the Embassy impart an American colonial character. The essential whimsicality of much of his work had earlier found suitable expression in the dolls' house he presented to Queen Mary in 1924 (now on display in Windsor Castle).

In addition to his work at New Delhi (the city was inaugurated in 1931) and on war memorials in Europe, Lutyens began to undertake commercial projects in Britain in the 1920s and 1930s. In London he designed classical stone façades for steel-framed office buildings, which were often planned by other firms, and in these, for example Brittanic House (1920–24), Finsbury Circus, he attempted to relieve the bulk of the structure by set-backs, varied

4. Edwin Lutyens: memorial to *The Missing of the Somme*, Thiepval, 1927–32

window treatments and imaginative classical details. An important client was the Midland Bank, for whom he designed a branch in Piccadilly (1921–5) that was an essay on the theme of Wren, and whose headquarters in Poultry (1924–39), City of London, exhibit 'disappearing' Doric pilasters and unprecedented modelling of the upper floors with precisely diminishing width and set-backs as it rises. Lutyens also designed university buildings for Magdalene College (1928–32), Cambridge, and Campion Hall (1935–42), Oxford; these were sophisticated versions of traditional styles.

After 1929, however, Lutyens was principally concerned with the design of a new Roman Catholic cathedral for Liverpool, which was intended to vie with the Anglican cathedral then rising to the Gothic designs of Giles Gilbert Scott (ii): Lutyens's classical building, of granite and red brick, was to have a dome larger than that of St Peter's, Rome, and its design was a development of the cruciform, centralized plans proposed for St Peter's, employing the hierarchy of arches that Lutyens had used for the memorial at Thiepval. The massive, battered external walls were designed to be penetrated by vast, arched openings reflecting the interior space, and the composition of spires and belfries around the great dome paid tribute to Wren's City of London skyline. Only part of the crypt had been constructed before work on the project ceased in 1940,

however (*see* CRYPT), and the complexity and intellectual rigour of this design can now only be appreciated from the wooden model first exhibited in 1934 (Liverpool, Walker A.G.). Nevertheless, the design represented Lutyens's ultimate statement in the architectural tradition that he thought justified both by its use of pure geometry and by its humanist ideals; his cathedral has been described as 'perhaps ... the latest and supreme attempt to embrace Rome, Byzantium, the Romanesque and the Renaissance in one triumphal and triumphant synthesis' (Summerson, 1990, p. 256).

Lutyens's last project was his involvement in the early years of World War II in the work of the Royal Academy Planning Committee in producing a scheme for the reconstruction of London. However, these proposals, which were dominated by traffic planning and the sterile symmetry of the Beaux-Arts tradition, were more representative of the utopian and megalomaniac spirit of the wartime years than of the subtlety and sense of national tradition that characterized his earlier work. Lutyens was knighted in 1918 and awarded the Order of Merit in 1942. He received the RIBA Gold Medal in 1921 and the American Institute of Architects Gold Medal in 1924. He was President of the Royal Academy from 1938 until his death.

2. CRITICAL RECEPTION AND POSTHUMOUS REPU-
TATION. When Lutyens died on New Year's Day, 1944,
surrounded by the drawings of his unbuilt cathedral, there
was no doubt of his greatness, and the subsequent
memorial volumes published in 1950 paid him a tribute
not granted to any other British architect since Wren. It
was principally as a classicist that he was admired by many
of his contemporaries who also adhered to the classical
tradition, but Lutyens was not an orthodox classicist either
by training or by inclination. He developed the classical
language through a geometric abstraction unparalleled
among the work of his contemporaries, yet he remained
indebted both to the English Arts and Crafts movement
and to the Gothic Revival in his treatment of mass and
attention to detail. The result was an architecture of
peculiar emotional intensity.

Lutyens's early romantic vernacular houses, which
played a significant role in the achievement of the Arts
and Crafts movement, were subject to unreserved admiration from C. F. A. Voysey and Frank Lloyd Wright.
Both, however, greatly regretted Lutyens's adoption of
classicism, which they felt reduced the possibility of a
modern, craft-based architecture being developed by the
younger generation of architects. Whether or not this is
true, Lutyens must bear much of the responsibility for the
direction taken by British architecture in the first 30 years
of the 20th century. He was always sympathetic to the
aspirations of younger architects, but he regarded the
European Modern Movement with suspicion because of
its lack of subtlety, its industrial aesthetic and its rejection
of craftsmanship and tradition. However, in refusing to
allow his own craftsmen any creative independence, instead insisting on complete aesthetic control of all sculpture and mural decoration, Lutyens himself betrayed the
ideals of the Arts and Crafts movement. Lutyens's move
from a free interpretation of the Surrey vernacular to the
grand manner of Renaissance classicism was seen by many
as leading down a reactionary cul-de-sac, but it came to be
widely recognized, even by the critics, that his reinterpretation of tradition was unique and personal. In 1951, for
example, Pevsner wrote of '. . . the paradox of the revivalist
in whose work geometry is more insistent than in any
living architect bar Corbusier'. Lutyens's son, Robert
Lutyens, and his biographer, Christopher Hussey, both
tried to identify a set of architectural principles and
geometrical theory that governed his later work, but
Lutyens himself was impatient with theory and affected to
find some of the claims made in his son's book
incomprehensible.

Lutyens was not a distinguished formal draughtsman,
but his 'worm's eye view' sketches were extremely expressive, and he was a brilliant caricaturist. He considered
himself to be verbally inarticulate, communicating his
architectural ideas best on paper, yet he also delighted in
puns and jokes; this perhaps partly explains both his social
success and the character of his work, the deliberate
dualities of his plans and his mannerist detailing reflecting
ambiguity and wit. The whimsicality that was often present
in his work was perhaps best expressed in designs for
furniture and light fittings, yet he was an artist of profound
seriousness who depended greatly on his subconscious
imagination.

Inevitably, Lutyens's reputation declined in the decades
following his death, notably in the 1960s, but later, after
the 1970s, it revived again. Despite the essentially English
character of his work, he was the subject of a pioneering
exhibition at MOMA, New York, in 1978, and in 1981 an
influential Lutyens exhibition was held in London, reflecting the pluralistic direction of contemporary architecture.
The American interest in Lutyens tended to interpret his
work in terms of Beaux-Arts classicism, but the paradoxes
and jokes in his architecture had much appeal for Post-
modern architects, who were anxious to be free of the
strict canons both of the orthodox Modern Movement
and of academic classicism.

### WRITINGS

'What I Think of Architecture', *Country Life*, lxix (1931), pp. 775–7
'Tradition Speaks', *Archit. Rev.* [London], lxxii/432 (1932), pp. 163–4
C. Percy and J. Ridley, eds: *The Letters of Sir Edwin Lutyens* (London, 1985)

### BIBLIOGRAPHY

L. Weaver: *Houses and Gardens by Edwin Lutyens* (London, 1913/R 1981)
A. C. Benson, L. Weaver and E. V. Lucas: *The Book of the Queen's Dolls' House* (London, 1924)
R. Byron: 'New Delhi', *Archit. Rev.* [London], lxix/410 (1931), pp. 1–30
A. G. Shoosmith: 'The Design of New Delhi', *Ind. State Rlwys Mag.*, iv/5 (1931), pp. 423–33
R. Lutyens: *Sir Edwin Lutyens: An Appreciation in Perspective* (London, 1942)
*London Replanned: The Royal Academy's Planning Committee's Interim Report* (London, 1942)
H. S. Goodhart-Rendel: 'Sir Edwin Lutyens: An Appreciation', *Architect & Bldg News*, clxxvii (1944), pp. 59–60
——: 'The Work of the Late Sir Edwin Lutyens, OM', *RIBA J.*, lii (1945), pp. 123–31
A. S. G. Butler: *The Lutyens Memorial: The Architecture of Sir Edwin Lutyens*, 3 vols (London and New York, 1950/R 1989)
C. Hussey: *The Lutyens Memorial: The Life of Sir Edwin Lutyens* (London and New York, 1950/R 1984); reviews of both books (the 'Memorial Volumes') by F. Lloyd Wright in *Building* [UK], xxvi (1951), pp. 260–62; and J. Summerson in *RIBA J.*, lviii/10 (1951), pp. 390–91
N. Pevsner: 'Building with Wit: The Architecture of Sir Edwin Lutyens', *Archit. Rev.* [London], cix (1951), pp. 217–25
A. Greenberg: 'Lutyens's Architecture Restudied', *Perspecta*, xii (1969), pp. 129–52
R. Venturi and D. Scott Brown: 'Learning from Lutyens', *RIBA J.*, lxxvi (1969), pp. 353–4
R. Lutyens: *Notes on Sir Edwin Lutyens: Two Sets of Notes for a Lecture to the Art Workers Guild, June 18th 1969* (London, 1970)
M. Richardson: *Edwin Lutyens: Catalogue of the Drawings Collection of the Royal Institute of British Architects* (London, 1973)
D. Mangin and J.-C. Tougeron: 'News from Nowhere: Lutyens à Va-rengeville sur Mer', *Archit., Movt, Cont.*, 43 (1977), pp. 43–54
*Silent Cities: An Exhibition of the Memorial and Cemetery Architecture of the Great War* (exh. cat. by G. Stamp, London, RIBA, 1977)
P. Inskip: *Edwin Lutyens* (London, 1979)
M. Lutyens: *Edwin Lutyens: A Memoir by his Daughter* (London, 1980)
D. O'Neill: *Edwin Lutyens: Country Houses* (London, 1980)
*Buildings for Bankers: Sir Edwin Lutyens and the Midland Bank, 1921–1939* (exh. cat. by E. Green, London, Midland Bank, 1980)
R. Gradidge: *Edwin Lutyens: Architect Laureate* (London, 1981)
R. G. Irving: *Indian Summer: Lutyens, Baker and Imperial Delhi* (London and New Haven, 1981)
G. Stamp: 'The Rise and Fall and Rise of Edwin Lutyens', *Archit. Rev.* [London], clxx/1017 (1981), pp. 311–18
*Lutyens: The Work of the English Architect Sir Edwin Lutyens (1869–1944)* (exh. cat. by C. Amery and others, London, ACGB, 1981)
J. Brown: *Gardens of a Golden Afternoon: The Story of a Partnership: Edwin Lutyens and Gertrude Jekyll* (London, 1982)
G. Stamp: 'India: End of the Classical Tradition', *Lotus Int.*, 34 (1982), pp. 67–81
G. Stamp and M. Richardson: 'Lutyens in Spain', *Quad. Arquit. & Urb.*, 155 (1982), pp. 58–81

J. A. Cortes: 'The Autonomy of Contour in the Houses by Sir Edwin Lutyens', *Comp. Arquit., A. & Archit.*, 1 (1988), pp. 103–22
P. Inskip: 'Sir Edwin Lutyens: The Gardens', *Comp. Arquit., A. & Archit.*, 1 (1988), pp. 123–50
M. Stewart-Wilson: *Queen Mary's Dolls' House* (London, 1988)
J. Summerson: 'Arches of Triumph: The Design for Liverpool Cathedral', *The Unromantic Castle* (London, 1990), pp. 245–56

GAVIN STAMP

**Lutz, Hans** (*b* Schussenried, Upper Swabia, 1473; *d* ?Bozen [now Bolzano, Italy], 1525). German architect. An official portrait of 1519 (Bolzano, Mus. Civ.) gives his place of birth and his age. He may have been a son of Master Georg Lutz, who is mentioned in 1486 in the service of the Premonstratensian abbey of Schussenried. Hans probably received his early training in Upper Swabia and may have made contact with the Augsburg lodge through working at Ulm Minster. In 1500 a Hans Lutz is listed as a taxpayer without citizen's status in the Augsburg tax records. On 3 February 1501, as foreman of Burkhard Engelberg, he was put in charge of rebuilding the tower of the parish church of St Maria Himmelfahrt (now Bolzano Cathedral), where he was to execute the spire to the design made by Engelberg in 1500. In 1505 Lutz renewed his contract, and until 1517 he is mentioned in the building accounts as the master in charge. His younger brothers Georg (*fl* 1501–7) and Peter (*fl* 1507–12) worked under him on the building of the steeple. In 1513/14 he built a pulpit in the church, the decorative forms and tracery details of which are clearly based on Engelberg's work. From 1510 Lutz owned a house and between 1509 and 1520 he was master bricklayer of the Heilig-Geist-Spital in Bozen: he had now attained social respectability. He seems also to have dealt in wine, receiving payment on several occasions in the form of considerable quantities of wine.

Lutz also worked outside Bozen: at Brunico (Ger. Bruneck) in 1508 he settled the payment of 11 masons who had made stone cannon-balls for Emperor Maximilian I, and in 1513/14 the account books of the parish church in Vipiteno (Ger. Sterzing) mention him as the master of works; the slender nave piers date from his time. In 1516 Lutz got the contract to build the nave and side aisle of the parish church of St Peter, in Auer. He was also involved in the construction of the Erasmus Chapel in Gries, near Bozen, and the churches of St Michael in St Pauls in Eppan and St Lorenzen. The parish church of Lengmoos am Ritten (Tyrol), dating from between 1502 and 1514, must also have been built under his direct influence. Indebted to the traditions of Engelberg, Lutz introduced Augsburg Late Gothic models into the south Tyrol. In so doing, he showed himself to be an outstanding technically versed stone mason rather than an independent designer.

BIBLIOGRAPHY
C. Fischnaler: 'Beiträge zur Geschichte der Pfarre Sterzing und des Pfarrkirchenbaus', *Z. Ferdinandeums Tirol & Vorarlberg*, n. s. 2, xxviii (1884), pp. 138–151
D. P. Beck: 'Burkhard Engelberg und sein Schüler Hans Lutz in Botzen', *Münster-Bl.*, iv (1888), pp. 52–64
K. T. Hoeniger: 'Hans Lutz von Schussenried und der Bozner Pfarrturm', *Schlern: Illus. Mnft. Heimat & Vlksknd.*, xx (1946), pp. 34–9
E. Egg: *Kunst in Tirol* (Innsbruck, 1973), pp. 61, 96, 116
F. Bischoff: *Burkhard Engelberg und die süd-deutsche Architektur um 1500: Anmerkungen zur sozialen Stellung und zur Arbeitsweise spätgotischer Steinmetzen und Werkmeister* (diss., U. Bamberg, 1987)
——: 'Burkhard Engelberg und Tirol', *Schwaben und Tirol. Historische Beziehungen zwischen Schwaben und Tirol von der Römerzeit bis zur Gegenwart* (Rosenheim, 1989), pp. 378–84
I. Severin: *Baumeister und Architekten. Studien zur Darstellung eines Berufsstandes in Porträt und Bildnis* (Berlin, 1992), p. 190
W. Schneider: 'Die Ziegelei des Heilig-Geist-Spitals von Bozen', *Schlern: Illus. Mhft. Heimat- & Vlksknd.*, 67 (1993), pp. 264–296

FRANZ BISCHOFF

**Lützelburger, Hans** [Franck, Hanns] (*fl c.* 1517; *d* Basle, before 23 June 1526). German woodcutter and possible medallist. His career is thought to have taken him from Augsburg, via Mainz, to Basle. In Augsburg a Hanns Franck worked *c.* 1517 in the team of woodcutters who executed series such as *Habsburg Saints* and the *Triumphal Procession* for Emperor Maximilian I—employment requiring a gifted worker. A woodcut of outstanding quality, *Fight between Peasants and Naked Men in the Forest* designed by an artist signing himself NH (Nikolaus Hogenberg, *d* 1539), appeared in 1522 with the full signature 'Hanns Leuczellburger Fvrmschneider' and an alphabet, probably intended to advertise his ability as a cutter of lettering. Thus *Model Alphabets* (1522; Mainz), published by Johann Schöffer (*fl c.* 1503–30) and signed 'HLF', may be attributed to Lützelburger. From 1523 onwards he worked almost exclusively for Hans Holbein (ii) in Basle. His reputation rests pre-eminently on his series of miniature Bible illustrations, his lettering, including a fully signed *Holbein's Alphabet with Representations of Death*, and Holbein's well-known series the *Dance of Death* (designed *c.* 1523–6; first published in entirety 1538, Lyons). Lützelburger's technical brilliance, consisting in a clarity and delicacy of line that fulfil all the designing artist's intentions, remained unsurpassed in the 16th century.

BIBLIOGRAPHY
*NDB*; Thieme–Becker

TILMAN FALK

**Luxembourg**, Grand Duchy of [Fr. Grand-Duché du Luxembourg; Ger. Luxemburg]. Country in Europe, bordered to the north and west by Belgium, to the east by Germany and to the south by France. In early 1990s the population was *c.* 390,000 in an area comprising barely 2600 sq. km. It took its name from the fortress of Lucilinburhuc (or Lützelburg), from which the capital city, also known as Luxembourg, developed. Established in AD 963 by Siegfried of Lorraine (*reg* 963–98), this fortified nucleus survived numerous political upheavals: until 1443 the area was independent, and four dukes of Luxembourg became German emperors (Henry VII, Charles IV, Wenceslas II and Sigismund; *see* LUXEMBOURG, House of); then the region fell in turn to the Burgundians, the Habsburgs, the Spanish Netherlands, France, Austria and again to France; in 1815 it was made a state in the Germanic Federation. In 1867 Luxembourg achieved neutrality and independence. The form of government is a constitutional monarchy under the Grand-Ducal family of Nassau. Luxembourg's prosperity in the late 20th century was mainly due to steel (the ARBED steelworks) and the presence of such European Union institutions as the European Commission, Parliament, Court of Justice and

Luxembourg, Vianden Castle, begun 11th century

Bank. As a borderline state of peoples, languages and cultures occupying a confined space, Luxembourg has not been in a position to develop outstanding artistic traditions of its own.

Archaeological finds, mainly located in the southern part of the country, date from the Palaeolithic age (e.g. at Herrenberg near Diekirch, Loschbur, Weiler-la-Tour), the Bronze Age (e.g. at Hünsdorf, Niederdonven, Alttrier, Goeblange) and the Celtic Iron Age (e.g. at Titelberg near Differdingen). During Roman occupation the roads laid by the Gauls were extended, and many villas, village-type settlements (e.g. at Titelberg, Dalheim, Goeblange, Mersch and Diekirch) and funerary monuments (e.g. at Greven-macherberg) were built. Frankish burial grounds with rows of graves were found at Altwies, Ellingen, Grevenmacher, Greisch and Steinsel.

The most important centres architecturally are ECHTER-NACH, the city of Luxembourg and Vianden. Echternach Abbey, founded in 698 by the Anglo-Saxon Benedictine monk Willibrord (658–739), is particularly important because it was the centre from which the country was converted to Christianity and given new artistic and economic impetus. The monastic masons' lodges were renowned; St Willibrord basilica (rebuilt after World War II) was built in 1031 over a 9th-century crypt. An example of Merovingian sculpture dating from the 8th century, an altarpiece known as the 'Rosport retable' (Luxembourg, Mus. Etat), was also located at Echternach. The church of SS Peter and Paul was built in the 11th century and is notable for its Romanesque towers. Other buildings dating partially from the Romanesque period are the churches of

St Michael in Luxembourg City and St Laurentius in Diekirch. The country's rural character resulted in a marked delay in the acceptance of the Gothic style, but once established it persisted until the mid-16th century. Surviving examples of religious Gothic buildings can be found at Vianden, where the Trinitary Church (1250) was once part of the Trinitarian Abbey, of which restored 14th-century cloisters remain, and at St Michael in Luxembourg City.

The development of feudalism resulted in the many castles that are such a characteristic feature of Luxembourg, for example the castle at Vianden with its three-stage castle chapel (see fig.) and the Rocher du Bock in Luxembourg. Little has survived of civic buildings except for the Denzelt, the 15th-century town hall in Echternach, and the Marché aux Poissons in Luxembourg. The houses of this period were very simple as the townspeople of Luxembourg were never very rich. The same is true of Gothic statuary in Luxembourg: most of it is only second-rate and was influenced by Lotharingian workshops or in the Late Gothic period by Peter von Wenderath, who worked in Trier. The unusual Helzingen altar (1544) is in the tradition of Brabant. Graf Peter Ernst von Mansfeld was appointed governor by Charles V, and during his regency (1545–1604) there was a change of direction: he was responsible for the construction of the first Renaissance building in the city of Luxembourg, the Palais Grand-ducal (originally the new town hall), begun in 1572. Notre-Dame Cathedral was built in 1613–18 as a Jesuit church by Jean Du Blocq, in Gothic style but with a Renaissance portal by the German sculptor Daniel Müller.

The Baroque period in Echternach was dominated by the Mungenast family of architects from Tyrol (new abbey building) and in Luxembourg by the French military engineer SÉBASTIEN LEPRESTRE DE VAUBAN, who built the Citadelle du Saint Esprit in 1685. In the 19th century the capital city was modernized, and many bridges were built (there are 95 altogether). While in the 20th century Luxembourg produced such architects of distinction as Rob and Léon Krier (see KRIER), there are few of their buildings in the Grand Duchy (e.g. Rob Krier's Dickes House, Bridel, 1974–5, a private commission). In the city of Luxembourg most modern buildings have been built on the Plateau de Kirchberg (e.g. the Centre Européen and other European institutions).

The scriptorium at Echternach was one of the foremost schools of copying and illumination in the Carolingian period and again in the Ottonian period (e.g. *Codex Aureus Epternacensis*, *c.* 1030; Nuremberg, Ger. Nmus., MS. 156142). There are 11th-century frescoes in St Willibrord basilica and Gothic frescoes (15th–16th century) in the church at Rindschleiden. It was only in the 19th century, however, when the landscape painters Jean-Baptiste Fresez (1800–67), Nicolas Liez (1809–92) and Michel Engels (1851–1901) were active, that a particular Luxembourg style of painting developed. The watercolourist Sosthène Weis (1872–1941) and the painters Jean-Pierre Lamboray (1882–1962) and Jean-Pierre Beckius (1899–1946) clung to Impressionism well into the 20th century. Luxembourg artists, who often studied in Germany, did not turn to Expressionism until after World War I (e.g. Nico Klopp (1894–1930) and Jean Schaack (1895–1959)). With the work of Joseph Kutter (1894–1941), an outstanding artist who painted mainly tragic portraits, still-lifes, townscapes and landscapes, Luxembourg painting began to win acclaim outside the country. After World War II such painters as Joseph Probst (*b* 1911) turned to abstract art under the influence of the Ecole de Paris; reacting against the traditional Cercle Artistique de Luxembourg (founded in 1893), they formed the Salon des Iconomaques in 1954. In the 1970s the strongest impact was made by such artists as Roger Bertemes (*b* 1927) and Ben Hayart (*b* 1927), while a boom in commercial galleries throughout the country in the late 1980s attested to the vitality of such younger painters as Patricia Lippert (*b* 1956) and Robert Brandy (*b* 1946).

The most important museum in Luxembourg City is the Musée de l'Etat, which offers a comprehensive survey of the history, archaeology, popular traditions and art of the Grand Duchy. The Musée J. P. Pescatore in the Villa Vauban, also in Luxembourg City, has a collection of 17th–19th-century Dutch, French and Belgian masters.

For ceramic and glass production in Luxembourg see VILLEROY & BOCH.

### BIBLIOGRAPHY
C. Arendt: *Das Luxemburger Land* (Luxembourg, 1903)
J.-E. Muller: 'L'Art contemporain au Luxembourg', *Encyclopédie contemporaine* (Paris, 1958), pp. 205–8
H. Kuhn and J. P. Koltz: *Burgen und Schlösser in Lothringen und Luxemburg* (Frankfurt am Main, 1964)
*L'Art au Luxembourg* (Luxembourg, 1966)
J. P. Koltz: *Les Châteaux historiques de Luxembourg* (Luxembourg, 1975)
G. Thill: *Vor- und Frühgeschichte Luxemburgs* (Luxembourg, 1977)
P. Margue: *Luxemburg im Mittelalter und Neuzeit* (Luxembourg, 1978)
U. Moll: *Luxemburg: Entdeckungsfahrten zu den Burgen, Schlössern, Kirchen und Städten des Grossherztums* (Cologne, 1983)
N. von Werveke: *Kulturgeschichte des Luxemburger Landes*, 2 vols (Esch-sur-Alzette, 1984)

INGEBORG KUHN-RÉGNIER

**Luxembourg, House of.** Dynasty of rulers and patrons. The election of (1) Henry VII, Count of Luxembourg, as King of Germany (1308) and later Holy Roman Emperor, initiated a series of advantageous dynastic marriages that greatly increased the territory under the family's control, in addition to that gained through conquest. By this means his son (2) John became King of Bohemia in 1310 and powerful links were established with France. (3) Charles IV regained the Empire and consolidated Luxembourg power, adding Lusatia and the Margravate of Brandenburg to the family lands and promulgating the Golden Bull of 1356, which made Bohemia foremost among the lay electors. He was succeeded in Bohemia by his eldest son, (4) Wenceslas, whose inability to deal with factions within the Bohemian nobility led to his deposition in 1400. Wenceslas's half-brother (5) Sigismund became King of Hungary through marriage, although he was unable to secure Poland. After a troubled reign, he was eventually elected Holy Roman Emperor. Since he had no male heir, the kingdoms of Bohemia and Hungary passed to his Habsburg son-in-law Albert V, Duke of Austria (*reg* 1404–39).

**(1) Henry VII**, Holy Roman Emperor (*b* 1274/5; *reg* 1312–13; *d* Buonconvento, ni Siena, 24 Aug 1313). He was Count of Luxembourg before being elected King of Germany in 1308. He managed to acquire Bohemia for Luxembourg and to reach agreement with the Habsburgs. In October 1310 he embarked on an Italian campaign with the aim of re-establishing imperial power and the peace that had been disrupted by fighting between the Guelphs and the Ghibellines. After being crowned King of Lombardy in Milan in January 1311 he used force to procure his coronation as Holy Roman Emperor in S Giovanni in Laterano in Rome the following year. He died in a campaign against King Robert of Naples (*reg* 1309–43) and was buried in Pisa Cathedral.

There are some important works of art associated with Henry's Italian campaign. He first visited Pisa in the spring of 1312 and it must have been then that the Pisans commissioned Giovanni Pisano to erect a group of marble statues in the south transept of the cathedral above the Porta S Ranieri (Pisa, Mus. Opera Duomo). It represented the Virgin and Child enthroned between the kneeling figures of Henry VII (destr.) and a personification of Pisa presented by angels. The tomb of Henry's wife Margaret of Luxembourg (fragments in Genoa, S Agostino, Palazzo Bianco and Palazzo Rossi; Basel, priv. col.) who had died in Genoa in December 1311 was probably also commissioned from Giovanni Pisano at this time by Henry (see PISANO (i), (2)). Around 1315 the Pisans commissioned TINO DI CAMAINO to erect a marble tomb for the Emperor in the main apse of Pisa Cathedral (Pisa, Cathedral and Camposanto). The precise reconstruction of this now fragmentary monument is uncertain. The sarcophagus, with the Twelve Apostles on its long side, was placed in a niche from which angels held back curtains. The effigy of the deceased lay on the sarcophagus; above must have been the enthroned figure of the Emperor surrounded by his counsellors.

Around 1340 Henry VII's brother Archbishop Baldwin of Trier (*reg* 1307–54) commissioned the Codex Balduini, which was produced in Trier (Koblenz, Landeshauptarchv, Inventory I C, no 1); this is a pictorial chronicle of the Emperor's Roman campaign.

BIBLIOGRAPHY
F.-J. Heyen: *Kaiser Heinrichs Romfahrt: Die Bilderchronik von Kaiser Heinrich VII. und Kurfürst Balduin von Luxemburg (1308–1313)* (Boppard am Rhein, 1965)
P. E. Schramm and H. Fillitz: *Ein Beitrag zur Herrschergeschichte von Rudolf I. bis Maximilian I., 1273–1519* (1978), ii of *Denkmale der deutschen Könige und Kaiser* (Munich, 1962–78), pp. 52–4
G. Kreytenberg: 'Das Grabmal Kaiser Heinrichs VII. in Pisa', *Mitt. Ksthist. Inst. Florenz*, xxviii (1984), pp. 33–64

ULRIKE LIEBL

**(2) John**, King of Bohemia (*b* Luxembourg, 10 Aug 1296; *reg* 1310–46; *d* Crécy, 26 Aug 1346). Son of (1) Henry VII. His mother was Margaret of Brabant. In 1310 he became King of Bohemia on his marriage to Elizabeth (1292–1330), the last Přemyslid heiress, but retained his mistrust of the Bohemian nobility. His attempts to strengthen Luxembourg power met with varying success and much of his reign was spent away from Bohemia, fighting in Germany, Italy and on the Lithuanian crusades. His marriage in 1334 to Beatrice of Bourbon (*d* 1383) brought him still closer to the French court and further influenced his artistic tastes. At Prague he built in the Rayonnant style in Hradčany Castle and in the Old Town from 1335, donated one-tenth of the Bohemian silvermines' production for the rebuilding of the cathedral in 1341 and also founded the Smíchov charterhouse (destr.). Much of the sculptural decoration from the façade of By the Bell House (U Zvonu), Prague, has been destroyed, but two of the figures may represent John and Elizabeth. He also appears, together with his son (3) Charles IV, on the tympanum (Prague, N.G., Convent of St George) from St Mary of the Snows, Prague. Surviving seals (1310–19; Prague, Cent. State Archv) are of high quality. The royal bust on a *grosso* of 1331–5 minted in his Italian lands is slightly antique in character, suggesting an interest that is further documented in Guillaume de Machaut's *Jugement du Roy de Behaigne* (before 1342). He became blind in the 1340s, yet died at the Battle of Crécy (1346), fighting for the French.

**(3) Charles IV**, Holy Roman Emperor, King of Bohemia (*b* Prague, 14 May 1316; *reg* Bohemia 1346–63, Emperor 1355–78; *d* Prague, 29 Nov 1378). Son of (2) John.

1. LIFE. From 1323 Charles was brought up at the French court, and his tutor Pierre Roger de Beaufort (later Pope Clement VI) sent him to the university at Paris, probably from 1328. Charles assisted in the administration of the Luxembourg lands in Italy (1331–3) and then Bohemia, until he fell out of favour with his father. In 1336–7 he served Venice as a condottiere and was awarded the towns of Belluno and Feltre as lifetime fiefs. He was elected King of Germany in 1346 through the influence of his great-uncle, Archbishop Baldwin of Trier, and

succeeded his father as King of Bohemia. In 1354–5 he returned to Italy, received the iron crown of Lombardy in Milan and was crowned Holy Roman Emperor in Rome.

Charles was one of the most active rulers in the Middle Ages. Much of his life was spent travelling, often incognito, throughout his lands in southern and eastern Europe. He spoke fluent Czech, German, French, Italian and Latin, and his love of learning is evident in the foundation of universities at Prague (1347–8), Arezzo, Pavia, Lucca, Orange and Geneva. He was also the author of several works in Latin, notably his autobiography (?1350–53). He was a friend of Petrarch and employed numerous outstanding scholars and artists. Although he promoted Bohemia as the centre of the Empire, during his reign German was introduced as the official written language at the court chancery.

2. PATRONAGE. Charles's interest in art was awakened by early exposure to the latest developments in France and Italy. As early as 1333 he founded the castle and town of Montecarlo, near Lucca. Another early commission was the completion of the Astronomical Almanac of the Kings of Bohemia (1334; Bernkastel-Kues, St-Nikolaus-Hosp., cod. Cus. 207), which was to form part of an extensive scientific collection. With the assistance of a circle of learned advisers, he systematically devoted himself, as his power increased, to the creation of artistic works as both an instrument of sovereignty and a reflection of his personal taste. He was especially concerned with the embellishment of Prague as the new seat of the Empire—as Uberto Decembrio (*d* 1427) noted, 'What Augustus did for Rome, Charles IV did for Prague'—and craftsmen were imported to meet the increasing patronage at court (*see* PRAGUE, §§I, 1 and II, 1).

The buildings that Charles erected on Hradčany, overlooking the River Vltava, form an impressive complex that dominates the city. Immediately after his return to Prague in 1333 he started to build a new castle (*see* PRAGUE, §IV, 1), based on the Palais de la Cité in Paris. The foundation stone of the new cathedral of St Vitus was laid near by in 1344 (*see* PRAGUE, §IV, 2(i)(c) and figs 13 and 14). The first Master of the Works, Mathias of Arras, died in 1352 and was succeeded by Peter Parler (*see* PARLER, (3)), whose influence as architect and sculptor spread across much of Europe, especially through his workshop's provision of six royal tombs (begun 1373) and the cycle of portrait busts in the lower triforium (after 1375; *see* PRAGUE, §IV, 2(ii); GOTHIC, §III, 1(iii)(c)); both projects were intended as an affirmation of Luxembourg legitimacy. Next to the royal palace Parler also built All Saints Chapel (1370–87), a slender, single-aisled sanctuary reminiscent of the Sainte-Chapelle, Paris.

In 1348 Charles extended the city by founding the New Town, which encircled the old nucleus, and protected this with a new defensive wall (l. 3.4 km). Over the next two decades 1450 houses were built in the New Town, together with five new monasteries, four churches, two hospitals and a town hall, laid out around broad streets and spacious squares. Similarly at Vyšehrad the palace was renovated (1348–50), the basilica of SS Peter and Paul was rebuilt (1369) and the fortifications strengthened. The remodelling of the city culminated in the construction across the

Vltava of the Charles Bridge (begun 1367; l. 516 m; *see* PRAGUE, fig. 2) and the Old Town bridge tower (begun 1373; see fig.), both to designs by Peter Parler.

Away from Prague, Charles commissioned the Frauenkirche (1355–8), Nuremberg, and the Wenzelsschloss (1357–60) at Lauf an der Pegnitz. The enormous complex of KARLŠTEJN CASTLE (begun 1348) was intended to protect the crown jewels and the state treasure of the Empire. Although the decoration of the imperial apartments and the great hall has not survived, its exceptionally rich wall paintings are represented in the chapels by extensive cycles that exemplify French realistic portraiture (*see* KARLŠTEJN CASTLE, fig. 2). The decoration of the chapel of the Holy Cross was begun by the Master of the Emmaus Cycle (*fl* before 1360) and completed before 1367 (for discussion and illustration *see* THEODORIC, MASTER; *see also* GOTHIC, §IV, 5(viii) and fig. 83). The complex scenes from the *Life of St Wenceslas* and the *Life of St Ludmilla* (after 1370) on the walls of the staircase leading to the chapel of the Holy Cross reveal the influence of north Italian painting and are attributed to MASTER OSWALD, who later worked in the St Wenceslas Chapel in Prague Cathedral. The latter's decoration shares with the Karlštejn chapels of the Holy Cross and St Catherine the use of gold leaf, gilded glass and hardstones to give an effect reminiscent of *opus sectile*. Traces of decoration using glass stars and polished hardstones have also been found at Tangermünde Castle (Brandenburg), which the Emperor built after 1373. His fondness for ancient techniques is further apparent in the mosaic of the *Last Judgement* (1370–71) made by Venetian artists for the cathedral's Golden Gate (*see* PRAGUE, §IV, 2(iii)).

The Emperor's interest in scholarship was demonstrated in his library, which was to form the basis of the extensive collection of his son (4) Wenceslas, although not all the manuscripts were illuminated: in the Chronicle of Přibík Pulkava of Radenin (*c.* 1374; Kraków, Czartoryski Lib., cod. 1414), for example, which he commissioned for Wenceslas, the only miniature is a depiction of the Emperor on the frontispiece. Much more expense, however, was lavished upon his passion for collecting relics and the commissioning of elaborate reliquaries (*see* CZECH REPUBLIC, §VIII, 1). These were donated to churches throughout Bohemia and the Empire, notably to Aachen Cathedral, including the Three Tower Reliquary and the bust reliquary of Charlemagne (both Aachen, Domschatzkam.). The principal collection (now Prague, St Vitus Cathedral, Treasury) included gold bust reliquaries of SS Wenceslas and Sigismund, and reliquaries for the tablecloth from the Last Supper (before 1354), made from a large crystal table ewer, and Christ's loincloth, which is decorated with engravings in black enamel of the *Crucifixion* and kneeling figures of Pope Urban V, Cardinal Pietro de Bellifortis, Charles IV and Wenceslas. The Emperor's patronage of the Prague goldsmiths is also evident in secular items from the so-called Karlštejn Treasury (now Prague, Mus. Dec. A.; *see* CZECH REPUBLIC, fig. 29). A visit to Mühlhausen in 1375 was recorded in an unusual figural group (*c.* 1380) above the south porch of St Maria (for discussion and illustration *see* MÜHLHAUSEN, §1).

Prague, Old Town bridge tower, east façade, commissioned by Charles IV, designed by Peter Parler, begun 1373

### WRITINGS
ed. E. Hillenbrand: *Vita Caroli Quarti: Die Autobiographie Karls IV.* (Stuttgart, 1979)

### BIBLIOGRAPHY
B. Jarrett: *The Emperor Charles IV* (London, 1935)
J. Šusta: *Karel IV*, 2 vols (Prague, 1946–8)
V. Kotrba: 'Baukunst und Baumeister der Spätgotik am Prager Hof', *Z. Kstgesch.*, xxxi (1968), pp. 181–215
H. Pantze, ed.: *Kaiser Karl IV., 1316–1378* (Göttingen, 1978)
F. Seibt: *Karl IV.: Ein Kaiser in Europa, 1346–1378* (Munich, 1978)
F. Seibt, ed.: *Kaiser Karl IV.: Staatsmann und Mäzen* (Munich, 1978)
K. Stejskal: *European Art in the 14th Century* (Prague and London, 1978)

*Die Parler und der Schöne Stil, 1350–1400*: Europäische Kunst unter den Luxemburgern, ii (exh. cat., ed. A. Legner; Cologne, Schnütgen-Mus., 1978)

W. Braunfels: 'Das Prag Karls IV.', *Die Kunst im Heiligen Römischen Reich Deutscher Nation*, v (Munich, 1985), pp. 92–106

F. Unterkircher: *König Wenzels Bibelbilder: Die Miniaturen aus Genesis der Wenzelsbibel* (Graz, 1983)

J. Spevácek: *Václav IV, 1361–1419: K Předpokladum Husitské Revoluce* [Václav IV, 1361–1419: towards a theory of the Hussite revolution] (Prague, 1986)

KAREL STEJSKAL

**(4) Wenceslas** [Wenzel], King of Germany [Václav IV, King of Bohemia] (*b* Nuremberg, 26 Feb 1361; *reg* Bohemia 1363–1400; *d* Prague, 16 Aug 1419). Son of (3) Charles IV. He received an excellent education. He was crowned King of Bohemia in 1363 and King of Germany in 1376. His reign, however, was marked by family dissent and a lack of determination to resolve the political, social and ecclesiastical crises that developed towards the end of the 14th century. He was deposed in 1400.

The continuity that Wenceslas encouraged on the various building projects in Bohemia initiated by his father is illustrated by their statues (*c*. 1378) placed side by side, together with the two Bohemian patron saints, on the east façade of the Old Town bridge tower, Prague (for illustration *see* (3) above). The passageway beneath the tower was originally decorated with wall paintings (destr.) showing barber-surgeons and the instruments of their trade; a contemporary report states that the same subject also decorated one of the King's houses in Prague. The royal apartments at castles built by the King were also decorated by accomplished artists attached to the court workshops. Their quality may be judged by the Březnická *Virgin and Child* (1396; Prague, N.G., Convent of St George), based upon Byzantine icons, that he commissioned for the Augustinian monastery at Roudnice (*see also* MASTERS, ANONYMOUS, AND MONOGRAMMISTS, §I: MASTER OF TŘEBOŇ).

Wenceslas was a passionate bibliophile and extended his father's library (*see* (3) above). Ten richly illuminated manuscripts made for Wenceslas have been preserved. A copy of the chivalric epic *Willehalm* (1387; Vienna, Österreich. Nbib., Cod. s.n. 2643) is the earliest of these to contain various characteristic symbols that draw upon Wenceslas's badge (a kingfisher enclosed by a veil tied in a bow) and such elements as the barber-surgeon and wild men. These symbols are further embellished in the secular scenes, in some of which the King is himself portrayed, that decorate the borders of the six-volume Wenceslas Bible (*c*. 1390–95; Vienna, Österreich. Nbib., Cods 2759–64), the German translation of which was made in Prague (for discussion and illustration *see* WENCESLAS BIBLE). This contains almost 600 completed miniatures, often incorporating drolleries with Czech captions, and its artists appear to have enjoyed a somewhat broad-minded freedom that is not apparent in their other identified works. Variants of these symbols also appear in German copies of Heinrich von Mügeln's commentary on the Psalms by Nicholas of Lyra (U. Salzburg, Bib., Cod. M. III, 20) and St Paul's *Epistles* (Vienna, Österreich. Nbib., Cod. 2789), and in three books on astronomy, including Ptolomy's *Tetrabiblos* (Vienna, Österreich. Nbib., Cod. Vindob. 2352). Perhaps the most attractive single example is the frontispiece of the Golden Bull of 1400 (Vienna, Österreich. Nbib., Cod. 338).

BIBLIOGRAPHY

H. Rieder: *Wenzel: Ein unwürdiger König* (Vienna and Hamburg, 1970)

J. Krása: *Die Handschriften König Wenzels IV.* (Prague, 1971)

**(5) Sigismund** [Zsigmond], Holy Roman Emperor, King of Hungary and King of Bohemia (*b* Nuremberg, 28 June 1368; *reg* Hungary 1387–1437, Emperor 1410–37, Bohemia 1420–37; *d* Znojmo, 9 Dec 1437). Son of (3) Charles IV. In 1385 he married Mary, Queen of Hungary (*reg* 1382–95), and was himself crowned King of Hungary after defeating the Angevin claim to the throne. Although he organized the defence of the south-east frontier against the Turks and strengthened the defences at Buda Castle (*see* BUDAPEST, §IV, 1), his army was defeated at Nicopolis in 1396. He was held prisoner by members of the Hungarian nobility in 1401 but managed to secure the loyalty of another faction. As Holy Roman Emperor he promoted the Council of Konstanz (1414–17), which ended the papal schism, and travelled to Paris and London as a mediator for an Anglo-French peace. Defeat by the Hussites made his rule in Bohemia ineffective until 1436.

Documentary sources state that Sigismund took a keen personal interest in the supervision of his artistic projects, recruited artists in Paris (1416) and south Germany (1419), and even acquired the architectural drawings for the Palais des Papes at Avignon (1416). The damaged statues excavated at Buda Castle in 1974 (*c*. 1419–33; Budapest, Hist. Mus.) were probably intended for the Frischer Palast (destr.; *see* BUDAPEST, §IV, 2 and fig. 3). In the mid-1420s, however, he moved his seat to Pozsony (now Bratislava) and extended the castle (completed after 1434). A number of items are associated with the Order of the Dragon, which he founded in 1405, including his embroidered badge (1408; Munich, Bayer, Nmus.), its small silver copy (*c*. 1429; Berlin, Tiergarten, Kstgewmus.) and his sword (1416; York, Town Hall). The sword (1425; Dresden, Hist. Mus.) that he presented to Frederick I, Elector of Saxony (*reg* 1423–8), is an easily dated example of 'Hungarian enamel', a technique characteristic of his court goldsmiths. Few manuscripts may be identified from his library, which was later seized by Emperor Frederick III, although one may be a copy of Konrad Kyeser's *Bellifortis* (Budapest, Lib. Hung. Acad. Sci.). Works on military engineering were dedicated to him, including Mariano Taccola's *Liber tertius de ingeneis ac edifitiis non usitatis* (1433; Florence, Bib. N. Cent., MS. Palat. 766) and the *Colcodei seu liber de peste* (*c*. 1431: Vienna, Östereich. Nbib., Cod. 2349) by Bartolus de Squarcialupus de Plumbino.

Easier to identify are the many representations of the Emperor that appear from the first half of the 15th century and in later copies. Among the illustrated Chronicles that cover his reign, the original copy of the *Chronicle of the Council of Konstanz* (1420) by Ulrich Richental (*d* 1437/8) has not survived, but there are nine remaining 15th-century copies (e.g. 1450–60; New York, Pub. Lib.). Sigismund's visit to Italy in 1432–3 resulted in several portraits, including a profile drawing (1433; Paris, Louvre, Cod. Vallardi, 2339) attributed to Pisanello (*see* PISANELLO, §1(ii)), an allegorical portrait (1433; Florence, Bib.

N. Cent.) by Taccola, and representations of his coronation at Rome on a *biccherna* (1434; Siena, Pal. Piccolomini, Archv Stato) and on Filarete's bronze door (1445) for St Peter's, Rome. Hans Multscher's figures (*c.* 1427–30; Ulm, Ulm. Mus.) from the east façade of the Ulm Rathaus are the most important of a series showing the Emperor with the Electors. He also appears in various allegorical contexts, for example as St Sigismund (*see* PIERO DELLA FRANCESCA, fig. 2), King David (for illustration *see* WITZ, KONRAD) and as the centurion in Jan van Eyck's *Road to Calvary* (1420s; untraced; copy in Budapest, Mus. F.A.).

### BIBLIOGRAPHY
H. Horváth: *Zsigmond király és kora* [King Sigismund and his age] (Budapest, 1937)
B. Kéry: *Kaiser Sigismund Ikonographie* (Vienna and Munich, 1972)
E. Mályusz: *Zsigmond király uralma Magyarországon, 1387–1437* [King Sigismund's reign in Hungary, 1387–1437] (Budapest, 1984)
*Művészet Zsigmond király korában, 1387–1437* [Art in the age of King Sigismund, 1387–1437], 2 vols (exh. cat., ed. E. Marosi; Budapest, Hist. Mus., 1987)

ERNŐ MAROSÍ

**Luxenstein, Frans von.** *See* LUYCKX, FRANS.

**Luxor.** *See* THEBES (i), §III.

**Lu Xun** [Lu Hsün; Chou Shu-jen; Zhou Shuren] (*b* Shaoxing, Zhejiang Province, 25 Sept 1881; *d* Shanghai, 19 Oct 1936). Chinese woodcut-printmaker, writer and critic. Already in childhood his imagination was caught by popular fiction illustrations, which were to resurface in his later writing. His sojourn in Japan (1902–9) was a turning-point, convincing him that literature and art rather than medicine made a nation healthy. From 1912 to 1926 he was employed in the Ministry of Education in Beijing, supervising and coordinating art-related affairs. For the next year he taught at Xiamen University in Fujian Province; later he chaired the Department of Literature at Sun Yat-sen (Zhongshan) University, Guangzhou (Canton). The last ten years (1927–36) of Lu's life in Shanghai were the most productive in terms of publication.

Lu was an anti-formalist. He believed that artists fulfil a Messianic role in expressing the collective soul. In *Ni bobu meishu yijianshu* ('Views on the promulgation of fine arts'; 1913), one of the first modern Chinese art manifestos, Lu Xun boldly attempted a new definition of art, distinguishing it from relics and rarities and emphasizing its conceptual base ('no art without thought'). The chief virtue he saw in Western art was the primacy of social urgency, and he ardently commended to a Chinese audience the works of such artists as Käthe Kollwitz and Carl Meffert (*b* 1903). In support of his beliefs he assimilated features of Western art, a process he called 'appropriationism' (*nalai zhuyi*). At the same time, however, he retained his enthusiasm for his artistic heritage, as embodied in monumental stone carvings of the Han period (206 BC–AD 220), in the linearity of Tang-period (AD 618–907) drawing and in the simple yet festive nature of folk art.

His editions of *Beiping jianpu* ('Collection of writing-paper designs from Beijing'; 6 volumes containing 332 examples of high-quality notepaper, chosen by Lu; *c.* 1934) and *Shizhu zhai jianpu* ('Ten Bamboo Studio decorative writing papers'; 1644; Lu's edition, Beijing, 1934) are evidence of his keenness to preserve artistic traditions. Lu Xun almost single-handedly revived the art of woodblock-printing in China (*see* CHINA, §XIII, 19(ii)) and re-energized book illustration. He published Western and Soviet woodblock-prints, such as *Yinyu ji* ('Bricks for jade'; 1934; Lu sent Chinese paper ('bricks') to the USSR in exchange for original engravings ('jade') by Soviet artists), gave public lectures and organized training courses in woodblock-printing for young people. Together with some friends, he started the first art journal in China, *Yiyuan chao hua* ('New glories in the realm of art'; five volumes, two being collections of woodcuts; 1929–30). His translation from the Japanese of *Kindai bijutsu shichoron* ('Historical trends in modern art', 3 vols, Shanghai and Beijing, 1924) was one of the first comprehensive books on Western art history to appear in China. His literary journals also served as a forum for discussion on art. With his support and guidance, an upsurge of woodblock-printing occurred in China, culminating in an exhibition in Paris (1934) and another in Moscow for which Lu himself wrote the catalogue. Dismissive of pretension and élitism, he also promoted the genre of sequential narrative drawing (*lianhuan hua*), which quickly became popular.

Lu Xun was also a tireless collector, eventually owning 5000 rubbings of ancient stone tablets and stelae and the largest contemporary collection of Soviet Russian woodblock-prints. The edition he owned (Shanghai, 1935) of the illustrations of Nikolay Gogol's *Myortvyye dushi* ('Dead Souls'; 1842) was the most comprehensive of its time.

### WRITINGS
Cai Yuanbei and others, eds. *Lu Xun quanji* [Complete works of Lu Xun] (Shanghai, 1938)

### BIBLIOGRAPHY
Chen Yanqiao and others: *Lu Xun yu muke* [Lu Xun and woodcuts] (Chishi, 1944)
Wang Guanquan: *Lu Xun meishu jinian* [Lu Xun and art: a chronicle] (Beijing, 1977)
Chen Yanqiao and others: *Xuexi Lu Xun de meishu sixiang* [Studying Lu Xun's thoughts on art] (Beijing, 1977)
Wang Guanquan: *Lu Xun yu meishu* [Lu Xun and art] (Shanghai, 1979)
L. Ou-fan Lee: *Voices from the Iron House: A Study of Lu Xun* (Bloomington and Indianapolis, 1987)

EUGENE YUEJIN WANG

**Luyckx** [Leux; Luycks; von Luxenstein], **Frans** (*b* Antwerp, *bapt* 17 April 1604; *d* Vienna, 1 May 1668). Flemish painter. He entered the Antwerp Guild of St Luke as a master in 1620 and was probably active in Rubens's workshop. In 1635 Luyckx visited Rome, and in 1638 he became court painter to Emperor Ferdinand III in Prague. He was much favoured by the Emperor, who ennobled him. In 1652 Luyckx made a short trip to the Netherlands before returning to Prague. Emperor Ferdinand died in 1657, but his successor, Leopold I, maintained Luyckx as a court painter, and from 1657 Luyckx worked in Vienna. His juvenilia, inevitably under Rubens's influence, consist mainly of historical and New Testament themes. However, he abandoned these subjects soon after his first appointment as court painter and devoted himself to portraits of the imperial family, courtiers, generals and other important figures. Often repetitive in composition, his Viennese court style betrays Italian and Spanish influences. The majority of his oeuvre is divided among the museums in Prague (N.G., Šternberk Pal.), Vienna (Ksthist. Mus.) and Stockholm (Nmus.).

BIBLIOGRAPHY
Thieme–Becker
E. Ebenstein: 'Der Hofmaler Frans Luycks', *Jb. Ksthist. Samml. Allerhöch. Ksrhaus.*, xxvi (1906–7), pp. 183–254
W. Bernt: *Die niederländischen Maler und Zeichner des 17. Jahrhunderts*, ii (Munich, 1980), pp. 37–8
*Master Drawings from the Collection of John and Alice Steiner* (exh. cat., ed. A. Moir; Santa Barbara, U. CA, A. Mus., 1986), pp. 186–7, no. 80 [entry by H. J. Van Miegroet]

HANS J. VAN MIEGROET

**Luyken.** Dutch family of artists. In the 1690s Jan Luyken (*b* Amsterdam, 16 April 1649; *d* Amsterdam, 1 April 1712) and his son Casper Luyken (*bapt* Amsterdam, 18 Dec 1672; *bur* Amsterdam, 4 Oct 1708) were the most productive and renowned illustrators in Amsterdam, at that time the publishing centre of the world. Jan was apprenticed to Martinus Zaagmolen (*b c.* 1620; *d* 1669) to train as a painter, although no paintings by him have been identified. He is best known as a designer and printmaker who produced title-pages, author portraits and illustrations for books and pamphlets. Around 3200 prints by him, mainly etchings, have survived. There are also many preparatory drawings, the early ones being the most detailed, the later often no more than shorthand scribbles, comprehensible only to Jan himself when it came to etching the copperplates. Many of his illustrations were made to accompany his own literary works; one early and fairly licentious collection of his poems, *Duytse lier* ('Dutch lyre'; 1671), however, was illustrated by another artist. His later, and very popular, anthologies were of an emblematic nature, consisting of moralizing and pietistic poetry, mottoes, biblical texts and illustrations. The prints in these books are almost invariably square (*c.* 100×100 mm) and depict some aspect of everyday human activity set in a landscape, the scene being represented with maximum precision of detail so as to drive home the emblematic meaning elaborated in the text. *Menselyk bedryf* was a particularly influential work: long after its publication in 1694 its illustrations of trades and professions were copied or used to inspire similar images.

Between 1689 and 1699 Jan was assisted by his son Casper, who afterwards travelled in Germany (*c.* 1699–1705) and worked for a period with the print publisher Cristoph Weigel (1654–1725) in Nuremberg. Together, father and son illustrated bibles and modern histories, travel-books, natural histories, pharmaceutical texts, books on religion and philosophy and literary works. They also executed the decorative work in atlases. It is not always possible to distinguish the two hands: they may even have collaborated on some plates. For their illustrations they tended to select the most emotional, active or bloodthirsty moment in a story. In their biblical illustrations, such as those for the so-called Great Bible of Mortier (1700), and in the illustrations for the work of Flavius Josephus, they produced compositions in a highly visionary manner; in other works, such as the numerous travel-books, the illustrations are sometimes stereotyped and cluttered. The size of their output over a relatively short time resulted in a tendency to repeat both themes and compositions. Critical assessment is further complicated by the enormous number of imitations produced during their lifetimes, let alone in later years and into the 19th century.

The largest collection of work by the Luykens is in the Historisch Museum, Amsterdam: *c.* 90% of Jan's prints, both loose and bound; more than 900 of his drawings; some of his illustrated manuscripts and letters; and nearly all of the 1200 plates attributed to Casper, together with over 60 of his drawings. Not all of the drawings correspond to known prints.

PRINTS
*Jezus en de ziel* [Jesus and the soul] (Amsterdam, 1678/*R* with new plates, 1714)
*Voncken der liefde Jesu* [Sparks of the love of Jesus] (Amsterdam, 1687)
*Menselyk bedryf* [Human affairs] (Amsterdam, 1694)
*De onwaardige wereld* [The unworthy world] (Amsterdam, 1710)
*De bykorf des gemoeds* [The beehive of the spirit] (Amsterdam, 1711)
*Het leerzaam huisraad* [The edifying furniture] (Amsterdam, 1711)
*'s Menschen begin, midden en einde* [Man's beginning, middle and end] (Amsterdam, 1712)

BIBLIOGRAPHY
Hollstein: *Dut. & Flem.*
P. van Eeghen and J. P. van der Kellen: *Het werk van Jan en Casper Luyken*, 2 vols (Amsterdam, 1905)
*Jan en Casper Luyken* (exh. cat., preface by I. Q. van Regteren Altena, Amsterdam, Fodor Mus., 1933)
H. Vekeman: 'Taufe in Feuer und Wasser, Jan Luyken und Jacob Böhme', *Wort und Bild in der niederländischen Kunst und Literatur des 16. und 17. Jahrhunderts*, ed. H. Vekeman and J. Müller Hofstede (Erfstadt, 1984), pp. 163–72

MICHIEL JONKER

**Luynes, Jeanne-Baptiste d'Albert de,** Comtesse de Verrue. *See* VERRUE, JEANNE-BAPTISTE D'ALBERT DE LUYNES.

**Luzarches, Robert de.** *See* ROBERT DE LUZARCHES.

**Luzern.** *See* LUCERNE.

**Lu Zhi** [Lu Chih; *zi* Shuping; *hao* Baoshan] (*b* Suzhou, Jiangsu Province, 1496; *d* Suzhou, 1576). Chinese painter and minor poet. He is associated with the WU SCHOOL of painters active in Suzhou during the Ming period (1368–1644). Lu's surviving paintings date to 1523–74; the most distinctive, executed between 1547 and 1555, represent a synthesis between the literati style of painting (*wenren hua*), as exemplified by Wen Zhengming (*see* WEN, (1)), and the professional tradition, as epitomized by QIU YING. Lu himself was a literatus: after he passed the local civil-service examination, his studies were supported by the prefectural government, though he never succeeded in the provincial examination. In 1557, at the age of 61, he was awarded the largely honorary *gongsheng* degree and allowed to retire.

Lu lived a life of genteel poverty. With the exception of two years as an instructor in a Confucian school in the early 1520s, he did not accept employment, refusing the hopeful students who sought him out. In the mid-1550s he built a retreat outside Suzhou on Mt Zhixing, where he lived in relative seclusion until the age of 80, when failing health forced him to return to the city. His biographer Wang Shizhen noted that Lu was somewhat misanthropic: he barred the door and hid at the approach of unwanted guests, though he might talk the night away over home-made chrysanthemum wine with a few select friends.

Lu moved only on the fringes of the artistic and intellectual circles surrounding Wen Zhengming and probably did not study directly with the older artist, although

Lu Zhi: *Jade Field*, handscroll, ink and colours on paper, 0.24×1.12 m, 1549 (Kansas City, MO, Nelson–Atkins Museum of Art)

Wen's paintings, ubiquitous in Suzhou, exerted a seminal influence on his development. In fact, two major lines of interest are revealed in Lu's early works: one is exemplified by the hanging scroll *Reading the* Yijing *by a Snowy Window* (1524; Taipei, N. Pal. Mus.), which explores the fine textures and traceries of bare branches in a mode characteristic of Wen Zhengming; the other is represented by the handscroll *Combined Painting and Calligraphy of Wen Zhengming and Lu Zhi* (*Wen Zhengming Lu Zhi shuhua hebi juan*, 1535; Beijing, Pal. Mus.), which features swelling volumes and packed spaces in a style associated with Wen's teacher SHEN ZHOU. The two lines of interest are combined in Lu's paintings of the 1540s. For example, a landscape hanging scroll (*c.* 1540; Chicago, IL, A. Inst.) explores the tensions between surface and depth and between linear pattern and volumetric form.

Such juxtapositions continued into Lu's artistic maturity, as for example in the masterwork *Jade Field* (see fig.). In this painting, a complex of motifs centres on a cave entrance, evoking the literary and artistic theme of the Peach Blossom Spring, land of the immortals. The cave depicted in the scroll is recognizable as a specific place, the Zhang Gong Stalactite Grotto in Yixing County, a subject that had also been painted by Shen Zhou, but it is identified with the cave-entrance to paradise by the use of the Blue-and-green (*qinglü*) colour scheme and angular brushwork associated with both antique painting styles and paradisaical imagery. The composition is close in style to the tradition of the Yuan master of literati painting WANG MENG, as transmitted by Wen Zhengming, though the angular brushwork and crystalline rock forms are based on the professional version of the Blue-and-green tradition practised by Qiu Ying.

Lu continued to depict complexes of real and mythical imagery in a similar style until the mid-1550s. He then developed a quieter vision, executing several topographical paintings, including the 16-leaf album, *Journey to Baiyue* (1554; Kyoto, Fujii Yurinkan Mus.), and a handscroll painted during a trip to Nanjing (1558; Tianjin, Mus. A.).

Several important works from the 1560s are in the styles of old masters, notably *Daoist Retreat among Streams and Mountains* (1567; Cleveland, OH, Mus. A.) in the style of Ni Zan and *Hermit Fisherman at Huaqi* (1568; Taipei, N. Pal. Mus.). From 1565 until his death, Lu was in at least occasional contact with Wang Shizhen, a leading literary figure who lived in nearby Taicang and collected works by many Wu school painters. Lu executed many paintings at Wang's request, including his latest surviving work, a copy (1574; Shanghai Mus.) of the 40-leaf album of Mt Hua by Wang Li (*b* 1332). Lu was influential mainly for his combining of literati and professional devices in his painting, which prepared the way for later artists in Suzhou and elsewhere.

BIBLIOGRAPHY
Wang Shizhen: 'Lu Shuping xiansheng zhuan' [Biography of Lu Zhi], *Yanzhou Shanren sibu gao* [Writings of Yanzhou Shanren [Wang Shizhen]] (1577/*R* Taipei, 1979), chap. 83
Lu Min, ed.: *Lu Baoshan yi gao* [Extant writings of Lu Zhi] (1665/*R* Taipei, 1970)
S. Wilkinson: 'Lu Chih's Views on Landscape', *Orient. A.*, xv/1 (1969), pp. 27–37
L. Yuhas: *The Landscape Art of Lu Chih (1496–1576)* (diss., Ann Arbor, U. MI, 1979)
——: 'Lu Chih and the Literati Tradition: Paintings in the Style of Ni Tsan', *A. Orient.*, xiii (1982), pp. 31–57
S. Nelson: 'On through to the Beyond: The Peach Blossom Spring as Paradise', *Archvs Asian A.*, xxxix (1986), pp. 23–47

LOUISE YUHAS

**Luzio, Alessandro** (*b* San Severino Marche, 25 Sept 1857; *d* Mantua, 20 Aug 1946). Italian writer, historian and archivist. His main contribution to art history lies in his copious research into the patronage and collections of the Gonzaga family. His book (1913) on the subject and on the Mantuan acquisitions of Charles I of England remains indispensable, though, like his work in general, it is essentially a miscellany of articles. He published prodigiously, citing original documents in abundance but not without errors of transcription and usually without exact archival references. He uncovered new material about numerous Renaissance humanists, literary figures and artists; thanks to his research, for instance, Tintoretto's series of paintings of Gonzaga triumphs (Munich, Alte Pin.) was identified, and in 1919 the Gonzaga set of Raphael tapestries (Mantua, Pal. Ducale) was returned to Mantua from Austria. Above all, Luzio was 'the great revealer of Isabella d'Este' (Gabriele D'Annunzio; see *Ad Alessandro Luzio*, p. 31). Inspired to carry on the work of Wilhelmo Braghirolli (*d* 1885), Luzio wrote over 20 articles about her, some in collaboration with Rodolfo Renier, between 1883 and 1915. His accusations of triviality and plagiarism against Julia Cartwright (*Fanfulla della Domenica*, 28 June 1903) reflect his frustration at this intrusion on research in progress, but he was polemical and irascible by nature.

Luzio's knowledge of the Gonzaga archives, though owing much to the archivist Stefano Davari, was enormous; numerous scholars benefited greatly from it (e.g. Paul Kristeller in his documentation of Mantegna's life) and from his magisterial descriptive guide to the correspondence files in the archives (1922). In Mantua he served as Director of the Archivio di Stato (1899–1918) and President of the Works Committee of the church of S Andrea, hoping to save its works of art from ruin; he was also a member of the committee responsible for the Palazzo Ducale, the restoration of which he had done much to instigate through newspaper articles. Luzio's interest in the Renaissance was based on its testimony of Italian cultural superiority; he was an ardent patriot, a liberal monarchist who eventually became a Fascist, and he also wrote extensively on the Risorgimento. In his earlier career as a political journalist at Macerata and Mantua, his forthright views (particularly hostile to radicals, socialists and freemasons) led to six duels and a succession of court cases. When sentenced to prison for defamation of character he fled to Vienna (1893–8) and returned to Mantua only after the death of his antagonist and receipt of a royal pardon. This exile, during which he studied in Austrian archives, made him decide to abandon journalism but also to concentrate on study of the Risorgimento. His appointment as Director of the Archivio di Stato in Turin (1918–31) gratified this sense of priority and forced him finally to renounce his ambitions to write a book about Isabella d'Este and a general history of the Gonzagas. In 1937 he helped organize the international exhibition of Gonzaga art in Mantua. His inaugural speech is a period-piece of chauvinistic bombast. Luzio bequeathed half his private archive and books to the Archivio di Stato, Mantua, and half to the Archivio di Stato, Turin.

#### WRITINGS

For full list see *Ad Alessandro Luzio* (1933).

'Lettere inedite di Fra Sabba da Castiglione', *Archv Stor. Lombardo*, xiii/3 (1886), pp. 91–112
*I precettori d'Isabella d'Este* (Ancona, 1887)
'Ancora Leonardo da Vinci e Isabella d'Este', *Archv Stor. A.*, i (1888), pp. 181–4
'Giulio Campagnola fanciullo prodigio', *Archv Stor. A.*, i (1888), pp. 184–5
'Isabella d'Este e due quadri di Giorgione', *Archv Stor. A.*, i (1888), pp. 47–8
*Pietro Aretino nei suoi primi anni a Venezia e la corte dei Gonzaga* (Turin, 1888)
with R. Renier: 'Di Pietro Lombardo architetto e scultore veneziano', *Atti Reale Accad. Sci. Torino* (1888), pp. 433–8

'Fasti gonzagheschi dipinti dal Tintoretto', *Archv Stor. A.*, iii (1890), pp. 397–400
'Tre lettere di Tiziano al cardinale Ercole Gonzaga e altre spigolature tizianesche', *Archv Stor. A.*, iii (1890), pp. 207–10
with R. Renier: 'Delle relazioni d'Isabella d'Este Gonzaga con Ludovico e Beatrice Sforza', *Archv Stor. Lombardo*, n.s. 2, vii (1890), pp. 74–119, 346–99, 619–74
with R. Renier: *Mantova e Urbino: Isabella d'Este ed Elisabetta Gonzaga nelle relazioni familiari e nelle vicende politiche* (Turin, 1893)
with R. Renier: 'Il lusso d'Isabella d'Este', *Nuo. Ant.*, lxiii (1896), pp. 441–69
'La Madonna della Vittoria del Mantegna', *Emporium*, x (1899), pp. 358–74
'I ritratti d'Isabella d'Este', *Emporium*, xi (1900), pp. 344–59, 427–42; also in *La galleria dei Gonzaga venduta all'Inghilterra nel 1627–8* (Milan, 1913), pp. 183–238
'Isabella d'Este e la corte sforzesca', *Archv Stor. Lombardo*, n.s. 3, xv (1901), pp. 145–76
'Il museo gioviano descritto da A. F. Doni', *Archv Stor. Lombardo*, n.s. 3, xvi (1901), pp. 143–9
'Le strane vicende di un quadro del Rubens (la SS Trinità)', *Archv Stor. It.*, xlvii (1911), pp. 406–13
*La galleria dei Gonzaga venduta all'Inghilterra nel 1627–8* (Milan, 1913/R Rome, 1974)
'Contributo alla storia delle suppellettili del Palazzo Ducale di Mantova', *Atti & Mem. Reale Accad. Virgil.*, vi (1914), pp. 71–2
*L'archivio Gonzaga di Mantova*, ii: *La corrispondenza familiare, amministrativa e diplomatica dei Gonzaga* (Verona, 1922)
'Discorso inaugurale', *Mostra iconografica gonzaghesca* (exh. cat., ed. N. Giannantoni and A. Rezzaghi; Mantua, Pal. Ducale, 1937), pp. xi–xxiv

#### BIBLIOGRAPHY
*Ad Alessandro Luzio: Gli Archivi di Stato italiani: Miscellanea di studi storici*, i (Florence, 1933) [with full list of Luzio's writings on art, pp. 38–40]
M. Bianchedi, ed.: *La figura e l'opera di Alessandro Luzio nel centenario della nascita* (San Severino Marche, 1957)

D. S. CHAMBERS

**Luzzo, Lorenzo** (*b* Feltre, *c.* 1485; *d* Venice, 14 Dec 1526). Italian painter. He signed his works *feltrensin* (or, on documents, 'zaroto'), which suggests that he moved between the two cities of Feltre and Venice. He trained first in the circle of Giovanni Bellini and then in that of Giorgione. Works by him documented in Feltre between 1511 and 1522 include frescoes, altarpieces and banners for confraternities. Many are untraced, and exact dating is difficult. His *Virgin and Saints* (Feltre, Pal. Bellati-Villabruna), with its disturbingly shadowy atmosphere and northern elements, is clearly a deviation from the tradition of Giorgione. *St Francis* and the *Blessed Bernardino Tomitiano* (both oil on panel; Feltre, S Maria degli Angeli), probably parts of a polyptych, are reminiscent of Bartolomeo Montagna. The *Virgin and Saints* (1511; Berlin, Bodemus.) came from S Stefano (destr.) in Feltre; there were also frescoes by Luzzo on the façade of this church and on the adjacent Loggia Pubblica. The attribution to him of the *Lamentation* (Feltre, Mus. Civ.) has provoked debate. An altarpiece of the *Virgin and Saints* (Feltre, Mus. Civ.) has drawings by Luzzo on the back. He also executed frescoes on façades of houses in Feltre, of *Curtius Flinging himself into the Gulf*, a *Nymph and Satyr*, *Christ and the Woman Taken in Adultery* and *St Christopher*; these, and especially *Christ with SS Anthony Abbot and Lucy* on the church of Ognissanti, Feltre, testify to a monumental manner based on a knowledge of the works of Raphael and, very probably, a journey to Rome. Venturi (1910) established that Luzzo cannot be identified with the Morto da Feltre in Vasari's account, which is probably a conflation of two separate artists.

BIBLIOGRAPHY
Thieme–Becker: 'Morto da Feltre'
G. Vasari: *Vite* (1550, rev. 2/1568); ed. G. Milanesi (1878–85), v, pp. 201–6
L. Venturi: 'Pietro, Lorenzo Luzzo e il Morto da Feltre', *L'Arte*, xiii (1910), pp. 362–76
M. Gaggia: 'Intorno a Lorenzo Luzzo detto Zarotto (Morto da Feltre)', *Riv. A.*, xii (1930), pp. 421–9
P. Zampetti: *Giorgione e i giorgioneschi* (Venice, 1955), pp. 264–9
S. Claut: 'Nuovi contributi sul pittore Lorenzo Luzzo', *Dolomiti* (1981), no. 1, pp. 35–8; no. 2, pp. 29–34
——: 'Il "caso" Lorenzo Luzzo', *Giornata di studio sul Pordenone: Piacenza, 1981*, pp. 44–57

SERGIO CLAUT

**L'viv** [Ger. Lemberg; Pol. Lwów; Rus. L'vov]. Major industrial city in western Ukraine. From 1939 to 1991 it was the capital of the Ukrainian Republic of the Soviet Union. The region initially belonged to the Halych–Volodymyr (Galician–Volhynian) state, and later (1349–1772 and 1918–39) it was in Poland, L'viv serving as an area capital. During the Partitions of Poland it was capital of the lands annexed by Austria. Until 1944 L'viv was the seat of Roman Catholic, Greek Catholic (Orthodox before 1700) and Armenian archbishoprics.

In the Middle Ages the town played an increasingly important part in commercial exchanges between western Europe and the Levantine colonies around the Black Sea. At the same time it became the chief artistic and cultural centre of central-eastern Europe. Its period of greatest growth was between the end of the 16th century and the beginning of the 18th; by 1800 it was a large modern city and in 1939 it had a population of *c.* 400,000, mainly Ukrainians, Germans, Jews, Greeks, Armenians and Poles. From the 16th century Poles were in a majority, giving a distinctly Polish character to L'viv's cultural life, although most emigrated after 1944. L'vivian artists were influenced by ideas from the south, east and west, and in turn influenced the artistic life of the entire Ukraine and lands populated by Poles and Romanians. Architecture, sculpture and craftsmanship produced in L'viv *c.* 1590–1670 and *c.* 1740–75 have an original and individual character.

In 1356 King Casimir the Great of Poland founded the town near an existing Ruthenian castle. The plan was based on a grid layout with a square market-place and encircling walls and has survived as the centre of present-day L'viv. The fortifications, built 1356–68, were modernized several times to the end of the 17th century but were demolished from 1787.

Throughout the Middle Ages Polish and German burghers favoured conventional Gothic art inspired by Kraków and Wrocław (Ger. Breslau, Silesia), but the Ruthenian population maintained its preference for the Byzantine artistic tradition. L'viv was the most north-western outpost of artistic influences from the Black Sea area, the most important monument being the Armenian Cathedral, built 1356–63 and inspired by the architecture of Kaffa, a Genoese colony in the Crimea. Kaffa was the home of both the founders of the cathedral, who were Armenian merchants, and the Italian architect Dorchi (Doring; *d* 1384). The cathedral design, with its cross-plan and dome, was based on old Armenian models but also shows the influence of Byzantine architecture and Islamic ornament.

From the mid-16th century, after the arrival of north Italian builders, L'viv's art began to flourish. From *c.* 1590 L'vivian masons were building the city-fortress of Zamość, and L'viv's architectural style changed from provincial Post-Renaissance to early Venetian Mannerism, the style favoured by Bernardo Morando, the architect and urban planner of Zamość. Between 1598 and 1629 Ambrosius Nutclauss 'the Benevolent' (*d* 1641) applied this style to the three-domed Byzantine-Ruthenian-style Russian Orthodox Church of the Assumption (also known as 'Walachian'), which had been begun in 1591 by Paolo Dominici (*b* Rome; *fl* 1585; *d* L'viv, 1618). The church was founded by the Ukrainian religious Stauropigia Brotherhood, aided by the Walachian Hospodars (Dukes), and was widely copied in eastern Europe. Dominici (from 1600) and Nutclauss (from *c.* 1614) later built the Minorite Church, consecrated in 1630, a basilica that is a reduced version of the mannerist Collegiate Church in Zamość. Its gables, with Netherlandish ornament, and its slender tower, derived from Silesian town halls, were added *c.* 1617–21 by Andreas Bemer (*b* Breslau [now Wrocław, Poland]; *fl* 1592; *d* L'viv, 1625).

Bemer was one of a number of German artists arriving from Silesia from *c.* 1570 who specialized in stone sculpture as well as architecture. These artists introduced a richly decorated Netherlandish mannerism which blended with oriental Armenian motifs and with a Venetian version of the Tuscan and Doric orders. This became the standard style for the L'viv burgher class and appears in the houses around the town square, as well as in altars, tombstones and funerary chapels. The Boimi Chapel (see fig.) is the most outstanding example of this style. Commissioned as the Boim family mausoleum, it was built in two stages from 1609 to 1611 and 1612 to 1615. The architecture is by Bemer, while the sculpture and decorations are attributed to several artists, including Hans Pfister and Hans Scholtz (*fl* 1615–18; *d* Landsberg, East Prussia [now Poland]).

The Boimi Chapel belongs to a series of domed mausolea, initiated by the Renaissance chapels of Kraków. Its rich decoration reflects Netherlandish and German mannerist models. The exaggerated decorative form is unstructural and does not follow any particular pattern but appears to be inspired by fantastical *horror vacui* taken from L'viv's existing Oriental influences. In the 17th century the extremely rich Baroque decoration in church interiors and their timber furnishings became increasingly heavy and provincial. A good example is the chapel of the Three Saints, annexed to the Walachian Russian Orthodox church, built from *c.* 1578–90 but redecorated after 1671 in this type of local Baroque.

L'viv was an important centre of craftsmanship, and in the second half of the 17th century artefacts were imported from all areas of the Polish-Lithuanian Commonwealth, to satisfy the Orient-inspired tastes of the nobility. L'viv craftsmen, many of Armenian origin, applied various Islamic, especially Persian and Turkish, motifs to Western forms such as textiles, carpets, ornate cloth belts worn by noblemen, metalwork, armour and items related to horse dress.

L'viv, Boimi Chapel by Andreas Bemer, 1609–11 and 1612–15

In the 18th century L'viv was under the influence of the foremost late Baroque. The Dominican Church of Corpus Christi represents the culmination in Europe of the development of the great domed church. It was designed in 1744 by Jan de Witte, Captain and later General of the Polish Army (1716–85), and built by Martin Urbanik (*fl* 1745; *d* L'viv, 1764) from 1745 to 1764; the façade was completed by Klemens Ksawery Fesinger (*d c.* 1815) between 1792 and 1798. Although this church is built on a smaller scale than its model, the Karlskirche in Vienna, it has far richer ornament and more innovative spatial solutions. The details and décor as well as the famous circle of sculpted wooden statues in the cupola drum are Rococo. These figures are light and dynamic, in sentimental or ecstatic poses, with expressively arranged drapery, and are typical of L'vivian Rococo sculpture, which is outstanding and unique in Europe, but of uncertain origin, although it shows some links with south German art. It is the work of a generation of sculptors, mostly of Polish background and interrelated through

family or workshops. They include Sebastian Fesinger (*fl* 1750; *d c.* 1769), Antoni Osiński (*d c.* 1777), Maciej Polejowski (*fl* 1761–91) and Jan Obrocki (*fl* 1764–94). Examples of their work may be found throughout central-eastern Europe. The Greek Catholic Cathedral of St George, founded by Bishop Atanaze Szeptycki (1715–46) and built from 1744 to 1764, is the most noteworthy of a series of churches built by Bernard Meretyn. They have conventional plans and rich Rococo decoration. St George is on a grand scale: its plan is based on the five-domed Russian Orthodox model but adapted to the centralized Catholic type, extended along one axis and surmounted by a massive dome.

In the hundred years or so after 1770, L'viv was artistically a provincial centre of the Habsburg empire, but with the introduction of an architectural course (1872) at the city's Polish Polytechnic Institute, architectural activity in L'viv entered a new phase; until 1939 the L'viv School of Architecture trained architects who later worked in southern Poland and Ukraine. These young architects produced work comparable to much in western and central Europe: though of high quality, it was rather cosmopolitan and was not innovative. L'viv kept up with the most modern styles in architecture such as Art Nouveau, early Modernism, the avant-garde of the 1920s and the International Style. The Department Store built *c.* 1913 to a design by Roman Feliński (*b* L'viv, 7 Feb 1886; *d* Wrocław, 22 March 1953) is interesting as an original example of early Modernism.

The lingering influence of Post-Impressionism is apparent in the art of L'viv between the two World Wars, but the influence of contemporary Western artistic ideas is also discernible. The avant-garde was rather weak there, with more Polish than Ukrainian artists. After World War II the Poles emigrated to Kraków and Wrocław, where they continued their work in a Polish cultural context. L'viv became a centre of Ukrainian art, which at first continued with Western styles but moved to Socialist Realism.

The city's numerous museums include the L'viv Art Gallery (Lvivs'ka Kartynna Halereya), with *c.* 20,000 paintings including works by Titian, Rubens, de La Tour and Goya. A major part of these works comes from former Polish museums and private collections.

BIBLIOGRAPHY

Z. Hornung: *Antoni Osiński, najwybitniejszy rzeźbiarz lwowski XVIII stulecia* [Antoni Osiński, L'viv's most outstanding 18th-century sculptor] (Warsaw, 1937)

T. Mańkowski: *Lwowska rzeźba rokokowa* [L'vivian Rococo sculpture] (Lwów, 1937)

J. Witwicki and W. Tomkiewicz: *Obwarowania miasta Lwowa* [L'viv's fortifications] (Warsaw, 1959)

M. Gębarowicz: *Studia nad dziejami kultury artystycznej późnego renesansu w Polsce* [Studies in the history of late Renaissance artistic culture in Poland] (Toruń, 1962)

——: *Szkice z historii sztuki XVII w* [Essays in the history of 17th-century art] (Toruń, 1966)

J. Witwicki and W. Tomkiewicz: 'Obwarowania śródmieścia miasta Lwowa i ich przemiany do XVIII wieku' [The fortifications of L'viv's town centre and their changes until the 18th century], *Kwart. Archit. & Urb.*, xvi (1971), pp. 91–204

T. Mańkowski: *Dawny Lwów: Jego sztuka i kultura artystyczna* [Old L'viv: its art and artistic culture] (Londyn, Poland, 1974)

ADAM MIŁOBĘDZKI

**L'vov, Nikolay (Aleksandrovich)** (*b* Nikol'skoye-Che-renchitsy estate, nr Torzhok, 1751; *d* Moscow, 2/3 Jan 1804). Russian architect, theorist, illustrator, poet, musician and inventor. An enlightened dilettante and encyclopedist from a princely family, he studied architecture on his own and travelled in western Europe (1775, 1776–7), above all in France and Italy. On his return to Russia L'vov worked at the Foreign Ministry and acquired a reputation as an architect from the early 1780s. His earliest works—the Neva Gate (1780–87) of the Peter and Paul Fortress in St Petersburg, the single-domed cathedral of St Joseph (1780–98) in Mogilyov and the similar five-domed church (1785–96) at the monastery of SS Boris and Gleb in Torzhok—are characterized by their austere simplicity, spareness of form and pronounced monumentality. They became the model for many Russian Neo-classical churches of the late 18th century and the early 19th. L'vov's works for St Petersburg include the Post Office (1782–9), unexecuted designs for the Cabinet on the Nevsky Prospect (1786–7) and for Kazan' Cathedral (1787–91), various private houses, and, on the Aleksandrovskoye estate of Aleksandr Vyazemsky, the elegant church of the Trinity (1785–7), a rotunda with a novel pyramidal bell-tower.

L'vov's enthusiasm for the artistic ideas of the 18th century found full expression in his architecture for country estates. He was particularly active in Tver' Province, where his own estate of Nikol'skoye was located. The estate houses that he designed, surrounded by landscaped parks and sited to afford splendid views from the windows, combined Neo-classical beauty with comfort. He planned mainly small buildings, which recalled, albeit in a more modest version, the Palladian composition of Pavlovsk Palace (1781–96) by Charles Cameron. On prosperous estates L'vov created magnificent entrance vistas by connecting the main house to the outbuildings with colonnades, for example at Znamenskoye-Rayok (begun 1788). Conversely, however, his proposals for clients of moderate wealth dispensed with grand entrance courts. A typical feature of his designs is the central, circular, domed hall. L'vov's interiors sometimes achieved remarkable effects with slender resources.

His park buildings are of equal artistic value. In the designs for these he developed ideas similar to those of GIACOMO QUARENGHI, whom he met frequently. These buildings include poetic pavilions and summer-houses—predominantly rotundas but sometimes oval in plan with porticos (e.g. design for a summer-house (1780s) for the Lyalichi estate)—grottoes, small bridges and modest service buildings. An integral part of his picturesque estate compositions was the church, usually a rotunda encircled by a colonnade, for example the church of St Catherine (1793) in Valday. Not all his estate churches conform to this pattern, however: some are square in plan with detached bell-towers (e.g. Arpachevo, 1783–91), while the church of St Catherine (1785–90) on the estate of Murino, near St Petersburg, is essentially an oval surmounted by a well-proportioned columnar rotunda.

Structural logic and the precise calculation of loads were invariably incorporated into L'vov's works. Of particular interest was his search for new materials and methods of fireproofing country buildings, examples of which included his experimental rammed-earth structures, notably at Pavlovsk, a small house (1797) in the village of Aropokazi, near Gatchina, and at Priorat Castle (1797–9), Gatchina, for which he opened 'Schools of Rammed-earth Building' at Nikol'skoye and near Moscow. L'vov had wide-ranging interests. He illustrated Ovid's *Metamorphoses* (1799) and the works of Derzhavin (before 1795), studied and recorded the words and music of Russian folk-songs, which he published in 1790, wrote librettos for comic operas, and wrote and translated poems, narrative verse and fables. He published a translation of the first book of Palladio's treatise (St Petersburg, 1798), inserting into the text his own ideas about the value of Palladio's legacy. While praising Palladio, L'vov rejected some tenets of his treatise as being unsuited to the conditions of the Russian climate and way of life.

BIBLIOGRAPHY

Thieme–Becker
F. L'vov: 'L'vov', *Syn otechestva*, lxxvii (1822), pp. 108–21
M. A. Il'in: 'Chertezhi arkhitektora N. A. L'vova' [Drawings of the architect N. A. L'vov], *Arkhit. Leningrada*, ii (1941), pp. 64–6
A. Lipman: 'Neizvestnyye postroyki Nikolaya L'vova' [The unknown buildings of Nikolay L'vov], *Arkhit. Leningrada*, ii (1941), pp. 67–9
M. V. Budylina: 'Nikolay Aleksandrovich L'vov: K 150-letiyu so dnya rozhdeniya' [Nikolay Aleksandrovich L'vov: for the 150th anniversary of his birth], *Sov. Arkhit.*, v (1954), pp. 75–87
G. G. Grimm: 'Proyekt parka Bezborodko v Moskve' [A design for Bezborodko's park in Moscow], *Soobshcheniya Inst. Istor. Isk. AN SSSR*, iv–v (1954), pp. 107–35
M. V. Budylina, O. I. Braytseva and A. M. Kharlamova: *Arkhitektor N. A. L'vov* [The architect N. A. L'vov] (Moscow, 1961)
N. A. Nikulina: *Nikolay L'vov* (Leningrad, 1971)
A. Glumov: *N. A. L'vov* (Moscow, 1980)

N. A. YEVSINA

**Lwena.** *See under* CHOKWE AND RELATED PEOPLES.

**Lwów.** *See* L'VIV.

**Lyalevich, Marian-Lyudovik.** *See* LALEWICZ, MARIAN.

**Lycia.** Ancient name of the south-western corner of Anatolia, now the Teke peninsula in Turkey, bounded by Telmessos (Fethiye) on the west, Antalya on the east and the Elmalı plateau on the north. The region is mountainous, and the Beydağları and Akdağ (Massikytos) massifs rise to over 3000 m. According to Strabo (*Geography* XIV.iii.2), its coast was 1720 stades long, rugged and difficult to navigate, but its harbours were excellent. The cities of Lycia are located along four river valleys. Most lie on a line from north to south along the valley of the River Xanthos (Kocaçay): Kadyanda (Üzümlü), Tlos (Düver), Pinara (Minare), XANTHOS (Kınık) and Letoon (Bozoluk). Patara (Gelemiş) is on the coast; to its east are Antiphellos (Kaş), MYRA, with its harbour Andriake, Phoinikos (Finike), Olympos (Çıralı) and Phaselis (Tekirova). Arycanda (Arif) and Limyra (Zengerler) lie in the valleys of the Arycandus and the Limyrus respectively.

1. History. 2. Art and architecture.

1. HISTORY. Because of its position, Lycia has been an important region since the earliest historical periods. The earliest evidence that the region lay on the Mediterranean trade routes are the finds from an Early Bronze Age wreck found at Ulu Burun near Antiphellos, by the late 20th

century the oldest extant wreck (late 14th century BC; Bodrum Mus.). They show that the ship was on its way from Syria-Palestine via Cyprus, southern Anatolia and the Lycian coast to either the Aegean or Egypt. Excavations in Elmalı at Karataş and Semayük, and surface surveys in the same area, seem to show that settlement started there in the Neolithic Age and continued through the Chalcolithic and Early Bronze Age. According to Herodotus (*Histories* I.clxxiii.1–3), the earliest inhabitants of Lycia were immigrants from Crete called the Termilai, but the Lycians were actually an Indo-European people who spoke a language akin to Luwian, and they appear in Hittite and Egyptian documents of the 2nd millennium BC as the Luqqu, Luqqa or Luqa. Their early burial customs and the small finds discovered at the sites on the Elmalı plateau resemble those of the Hittites. In the *Iliad* (II.876–7) the Lycians fought under Sarpedon on the Trojan side against the Achaians, while the name Xanthos occurs only as that of a river. Archaeological evidence from the Late Bronze Age to the 7th century BC is scant. The discovery in 1986–7 of Phrygian tumuli containing abundant Phrygian artefacts at Çagıltemeller (late 8th century BC to early 7th) shows that Phrygian domination extended as far as central Lycia. Subsequently, the kingdom of Lydia, one of the great powers in Anatolia in the 7th century BC, was unable to establish sovereignty over Lycia (Herodotus: I.xviii). However, from the 7th century BC Greek colonies were founded on the Lycian coast, beginning, according to Herodotus (II.178), with Phaselis in 690 BC. Greek culture began to influence Lycia at the same time.

The Persians conquered Lycia in 545 BC and incorporated it in a satrapy (administrative region). The inscription on the Inscribed Pillar at Xanthos, which is mainly in Lycian but with 12 lines in Greek, reveals that Kherei, son of the famous Persian commander Harpagos, was active in its administration. Nonetheless, Lycia had some political autonomy, while resistance to both the Greeks and Persians developed under the leadership of Perikles of Limyra, who seized Telmessos and issued coins in his own name. Despite this, Lycians fought at the battles of Salamis and Plataia (480–479 BC) on the Greek side. It is uncertain how many Lycian cities joined the Athenian dominated Delian League: after 470 BC some cities in western Lycia appeared in the tribute lists, but around 440 BC the cities of south-west Anatolia began to be omitted.

Alexander the Great put an end to Persian rule in Lycia, and during the Hellenistic period the region changed hands a number of times between his successors. The political confusion gave rise to the establishment of a Lycian League (2nd century BC) of twenty-three cities with voting rights proportionate to their importance, the six largest being Xanthos, Patara, Pinara, Olympos, Myra and Tlos. The 1st century BC was also a period of turmoil. Mithradates, King of Pontus, occupied Lycia in 88 BC, but after his defeat by the Romans, Lycia recovered its independence as a reward for having supported Rome. Immediately afterwards the Romans helped to deliver Lycia from the Cilician pirates, and Rome gradually increased its activities in the region, until it was declared a Roman province in AD 43. Under the Roman Empire the Lycians began to adopt Roman customs, and several buildings and monuments necessary for this new way of life were constructed as a result of the interest shown by Roman emperors. From the 2nd century AD the imperial cult became widespread, Roman names were adopted by Lycian families and even Greek athletics competitions were abandoned in favour of gladiatorial contests and wild beast shows.

The wealth and splendour of the region began to decline after the 3rd century AD. In the 4th century AD the Lycian cities were converted to Christianity and equipped with churches; in Late Antiquity the coastal centres were gradually abandoned or became depopulated, although new settlements and monasteries were founded in the interior. A plague in AD 542 drastically reduced the population, while Persian invasions and Arab raids took their toll in the 7th century AD. During the late 18th century and 19th, Lycia was visited by European travellers, notably Charles Fellows (1799–1860), who carried off a number of important artefacts to the British Museum, London.

2. ART AND ARCHITECTURE. Most information on the art and architecture of Lycia, especially in the early period, comes from its monumental tombs. Thousands of these are to be found scattered over almost the whole region, emphasizing their great cultural importance. A common feature of Lycian tombs—whether rock-cut or free-standing—is that they were raised above ground-level. In rock-cut tombs this was achieved by exploiting natural outcrops, while in free-standing monuments the burial chamber or sarcophagus was raised on a pedestal or tower (see fig. 1). This feature perhaps reflects a belief that the dead should be raised towards the sky. The earliest Lycian funerary monuments probably date to the 6th century BC and provide vital evidence for the forms of other early Lycian buildings, which were principally of wood and thus no longer survive. A large number of rock-cut tombs carved to resemble the façades of flat-roofed wooden houses, complete with beam ends and joints, have been found in Myra, Tlos, Pinara, Telmessos and elsewhere, although some scholars now argue that the façades are based on the banqueting halls of Lycian houses. Similarly, the decoration of Lycian stone sarcophagi is based on wooden architectural elements. In the sarcophagi, beams placed horizontally and vertically form the body, from which the beam ends protrude, while the lid too has a fake ridge-beam, purlins and posts, and panelling in the gable. Monumental tombs in the form of flat-roofed wooden houses appear as reliefs on the exterior of the sarcophagi.

The earliest extant Lycian funerary monument is the Lion Tomb in Xanthos (?c. 550 BC; see fig. 2), with reliefs (London, BM) including scenes that may be connected with the life of the hero to whom the tomb belonged. In the scene on the west side the hero's fight with a lion is portrayed; on the east side a warrior and a horseman are shown, perhaps the hero returning after his victory in this struggle. A tomb from Isinda (525 BC; Istanbul, Archaeol. Mus.) seems to be a copy of it. Echoes of the Greek Archaic style can be seen in the sculptures on these tombs, although they are purely Lycian in their architectural forms, and this is also true of other 6th- and 5th-century BC tombs. The famous Harpy Tomb at Xanthos (c. 480 BC) consists of a monolithic tower 5.43 m high hollowed out at the top and covered by a flat roof to form the burial tombs acquired the appearance of Greek temple façades, while free-standing funerary monuments became models of Greek temples. The principal Lycian rock-cut tombs that have Greek temple façades are the Amyntas Tomb at Telmessos and the Bellerophon Tomb at Tlos, named after a frieze depicting *Bellerophon and Pegasus*, both of which date from the 4th century BC and have the appearance of an Ionic temple *in antis*. The most important structure reflecting the Hellenization of Lycian tomb architecture, the Nereid Monument from Xanthos (*c.* 425–*c.* 400 BC; London, BM), is in the form of a peripteral Ionic temple with 6×4 columns on a podium. Its elevation on a podium seems to be a continuation of the ancient Lycian tomb tradition. The two relief friezes on the monument's podium and on the pediment contain scenes connected with the life of the owner of the tomb, and this is also a Lycian tradition that can be traced back to the Harpy Monument and to a number of other Lycian tombs. Persians and Greeks are depicted in battle in the lower of the two friezes on the monument's podium, a scene that reflects Greek concepts and style, but the upper frieze, which depicts the siege of a city, appears to be a reflection in Greek art of an eastern tradition that goes back to the battle-scene reliefs in the palaces of Assyria. On the pediment the owner of the tomb and his wife are depicted seated on thrones in a manner resembling Zeus and Hera, that is, in the Greek tradition. The Nereid Monument must be seen as a Lycian monument that contains elements of Persian and eastern art but in which the influence of

1. Lycia, Antiphellos, raised sarcophagus, 4th century BC

chamber. Its marble reliefs (London, BM) surround the tomb chamber on four sides. The half-bird, half-female figures in the reliefs on the northern and southern faces, previously thought to be harpies, have given the monument its name, although it has now been suggested that they are sirens. At the centre of the relief on the eastern face, a male figure is seated on a throne with two male figures standing behind him; in front of him there is a figure presenting him with an offering and another man standing with a dog. The theme of a ruler seated on a throne surrounded by his servants while he is presented with an offering is derived from Persian palace ceremonial (compare the reliefs in the palace at PERSEPOLIS). As Lycia was under Persian control when the Harpy Tomb was built, it must have belonged to a Persian ruler. However, the style of the reliefs is East Greek, thus making the Harpy Tomb a revealing synthesis of Lycian, Greek and Persian traditions. A similar synthesis is apparent in the frescoes found in the burial chambers of the Kızılbel and Karaburun tumulus tombs (*c.* 525 BC and *c.* 475 BC respectively) near ELMALI.

From the end of the 5th century BC the traditional forms of Lycian tomb monuments and the elements reflecting wooden architecture were abandoned, and Greek architectural forms began to be used. Rock-cut

2. Lycia, Xanthos, relief from the west side of the Lion Tomb, h. 670mm, ?*c.* 550 BC (London, British Museum)

the Greek Classical style predominates. Other features of this Lycian masterpiece are its Ionic capitals, which resemble those of the Erechtheion in Athens, its Ephesus-type column bases and the carving of its architrave in the form of a relief frieze in a manner reminiscent of the Temple of Athena at Assos.

Another tomb monument that is an amalgam of Lycian, Greek and Persian influences is the heroon at Limyra (4th century BC), which resembles a small amphiprostyle temple (10.4×6.8 m) raised on a terrace 3.4 m high. It is especially interesting because four caryatids have taken the place of columns on the north and south façades. Although their posture resembles that of the Erechtheion caryatids, they are more massive, and features such as their bracelets, libation vessels and rhytons reflect eastern influences.

In the Roman period too the forms of Lycian tombs underwent certain changes. For example, some sarcophagi had lids with triangular pediments and were decorated with handles or garlands. Temple tombs in the tradition of the Nereid Monument and the Limyra heroon continued, for example the tomb in the form of a Roman temple in the Corinthian order at Myra (2nd century AD). The process of Romanization also led to the construction of splendid monumental buildings in the Roman tradition. The emperor Vespasian visited Lycia in AD 69, and in his honour a Doric arch was built at Xanthos, a bath at Patara and a bath and temple at Kadyanda. A stoa was built at Limyra and dedicated to Domitian (reg AD 81–96). Hadrian visited Lycia in AD 130, and the nymphaeum at Letoon and the granaries at Patara and Audriake were built in his reign, the granaries testifying to the increased agricultural and commercial activity in the Roman period. The building of theatres in most of the cities of Lycia in Roman times is a sign of the flourishing cultural life.

Enemy raids and the spread of Christianity in Late Antiquity resulted in the shrinkage of the great urban centres of Lycia and their fortification. Thus the settlement at Xanthos withdrew into the fortified acropolis, while churches were built from spolia and rubble from earlier structures. Nonetheless, the 6th-century AD churches at Alacahisar, Karabel, Dikmen, Devekuyusu, Muskar and Alakilise in the interior of the region contain architectural sculpture and stone-carving of the highest quality.

BIBLIOGRAPHY

C. Bayburtluoğlu: *Lykia* (Ankara, n.d.)
F. J. Tritsch: 'The Harpy Tomb at Xanthus', *J. Hell. Stud.*, lxii (1942), pp. 39–50
E. Akurgal: *Die Kunst Anatoliens von Homer bis Alexander* (Berlin, 1961)
——: Ancient Civilisations and Ruins of Turkey (Istanbul, 1969, 3/1978)
M. J. Mellink: 'Archaeology in Asia Minor: Limyra', *Amer. J. Archaeol.*, lxxiv (1970), p. 169
O. Akşit: *Hellenistik ve Roma devrinde Likya* [Lycia in Hellenistic and Roman times] (Istanbul, 1971)
S. Haynes: *Land of Chimaera: An Archaeological Excursion in the South-west of Turkey* (London, 1974)
A. Shapur Shahbazi: *The Irano-Lycian Monuments* (Persepolis, 1975)
R. M. Harrison: 'Lycia in Late Antiquity', *Yayla: Report of the Northern Society for Anatolian Archaeology*, i (Newcastle, 1977), pp. 10–15
G. E. Bean: *Lycian Turkey* (London, 1978)
W. A. P. Childs: *The City Reliefs of Lycia* (Princeton, NJ, 1978)
R. M. Harrison: 'Upland Settlements in Early Medieval Lycia', *Actes du colloque sur la Lycie antique: Paris, 1980*, pp. 109–18
W. A. P. Childs: 'Lycian Relations with Persians and Greeks in the Fifth and Fourth Centuries Re-examined', *Anatol. Stud.*, xxxi (1981), pp. 55–80
V. İdil: *Likya lahitleri* [Lycian sarcophagi] (Ankara, 1985)
M. J. Mellink: 'The Remains of Second Millennium BC Habitation at Karataş-Semayük', *The Proceedings of the 7th Symposium of Excavations: Ankara, 1985*, pp. 287–91
——: 'The Painted Tomb at Karaburun (Elmalı): Problems of Conservation and Iconography', *The Proceedings of the 10th Symposium of Excavations: Ankara, 1988*, pp. 271–3

EMEL ERTEN YAĞCI

**Lycopolis.** *See* ASYUT.

**Lydia.** Region in western Asia Minor (now Turkey) that formed an independent kingdom ruled from Sardis during the 7th century BC and earlier 6th, but later fell under Persian, Greek and Roman control. It covered an area of 24,000–25,000 sq. km consisting of mountain ranges and fertile valleys (of the rivers Hermos, Kayster and Maeander, now respectively Gediz, Kücük Menderes and Menderes), which created natural corridors, and thus trade routes, between the Aegean and the central Anatolian plateau.

1. HISTORY. The history of Lydia before the 7th century BC is shrouded in legend. In the *Iliad* Lydian heroes were allies of the Trojans, while the early Lydian kings Meles and Kambles have the same semi-mythological status as Tantalos, Niobe, Omphale and Arachne, whose stories were also set in Lydia. During its period of independence (c. 680–546 BC) Lydia controlled an empire that extended over most of western Asia Minor, as far east as the River Halys (now Kızıl ırmak), and was ruled by a dynasty of native kings, of whom the most celebrated are the first and last, Gyges and Croesus. After its conquest by Persia in 546 BC, Lydia became part of the Persian empire and Sardis the seat of a Persian satrap (viceroy); Persian rule lasted until the conquest by Alexander the Great in 333 BC. During the following two centuries Lydia belonged to several Hellenistic kingdoms, notably Seleucid Syria and Pergamon, before becoming part of the Roman province of Asia (133 BC). Between the late 3rd century AD and 8th, Lydia was a Roman province in its own right. Three of its cities, Sardis, Philadelphia (now Alaşehir) and Thyateira (now Akhisar), were among the 'seven churches which are in Asia' (Revelation 1:11) on account of their prominent Christian communities. Lydia was a bishopric and Sardis the seat of its bishop from the 2nd century AD to the 14th (although bishops rarely left Constantinople after the 8th century AD).

2. ARCHITECTURE AND ARTEFACTS. The earliest major monuments of Lydia are Hittite-style reliefs of the late 2nd millennium BC (with Hittite hieroglyphic inscriptions) carved on cliffs near Nymphaeum and Magnesia ad Sipylum (now respectively Karabel and Manisa). Before the 7th century BC the culture of Lydia closely resembled that of other regions of western Anatolia and the eastern Aegean, while during Hellenistic and later times it was subsumed into the cultural spheres of Greece, Rome and Byzantium. Between the 7th century BC and the Hellenistic age, however, Lydian culture was unique, distinguished by its own Indo-European language and writing system (documented by about 110 texts on stone and pottery) and by its own religious, social and artistic traditions.

Much in Lydian art was derivative, with Greece, particularly the East Greek world (of the eastern Aegean islands and the western coast of Anatolia), providing the main inspiration. Anatolian traditions, especially those of Phrygia, were also present; but influences from further east were minimal, except for that of Persia on sumptuary arts (e.g. jewellery and plate) after the Persian conquest.

That Lydian art flourished during the 6th century BC is clear from finds at SARDIS and from aristocratic graves at other settlements and country estates throughout Lydia, about which little is otherwise known, as well as from Greek and Latin literature. To Greek contemporaries of the Lydian and Persian empires, Lydia was a land of fabulous wealth and fashion. Splendid offerings dedicated by Lydian kings at Greek sanctuaries were reported by Herodotus (I.xiv.1–3; xxv; l–lii; xcii) and other ancient writers, as well as in inscriptions at Delphi. Of eight lots of offerings in precious metal that Croesus dedicated at Delphi, three weighed a total of at least nine tons; Delphi also received offerings of gold, silver and electrum (alloy of gold and silver) from two of Croesus' predecessors, and four other sanctuaries attracted further offerings from Croesus himself. Like other exotic goods for which Lydia was celebrated—pile carpets, crimson dye, the unguents *brenthion* and *bakkaris*—these treasures have left no trace. Signets of lustrous hardstones exquisitely carved with intricate intaglio devices, and magnificent silver and silver-gilt plate from Sardis and Bagis (now Gure) in eastern Lydia, confirm the fabled wealth of the Lydians; but almost all date to the first century after the Persian conquest.

According to Herodotus (I.xciii.2–5), the most impressive monument at Sardis was the tumulus tomb of King Alyattes (*d c.* 560 BC), the father of Croesus. Its great mound, over 60 m high and 350 m in diameter, may still be seen in the cemetery of Bin Tepe, where there are more than 100 large tumuli. Many of the burial chambers in these tumuli, including that of Alyattes, were plundered in Roman times, so that no intact burial deposits have been uncovered by modern excavations. The well-preserved tumuli themselves, however, furnish abundant evidence for certain aspects of Lydian architecture. As early as the 7th century BC some of their chambers were built of precisely cut, smooth-finished limestone and marble masonry. Individual blocks were frequently carved to imitate features such as inner corners and doorframes and were designed to make maximum structural use of bedrock. Exceptionally fine is a chamber with corbel-vaulted ceiling (now known as Aktepe I) at Bagis (late 6th century BC). On the acropolis of Sardis, terraces faced with such masonry revet the slopes and landscape the natural contours (early 6th century BC). Sophisticated wall paintings also occur in tumulus chambers (late 6th century BC) at Bagis and Nakrason (now Harta or Dönertaş), but painted pots constitute the most abundant surviving Lydian works of art. In high-quality wares, such as the brilliant Ephesian ware, East Greek orientalizing styles are sometimes combined with traditional Anatolian techniques and motifs, while the abstract decorative convention of 'marbling' (see fig.) was a distinctive Lydian invention.

There is no archaeological evidence for the ancient tradition that the Etruscans were descended from Lydian

Lydia, skyphos with abstract decorative 'marbling', h. 143 mm, first half of 7th century BC (Boston, MA, Museum of Fine Arts)

migrants (Herodotus: I.xciv.2–7; *see* ETRUSCAN, §I, 1), but Greek literary sources and archaeological finds both suggest that Lydia played a leading part in the development of coinage, although the dates and identities of the earliest issues are disputed. The first coins were produced before the end of the 7th century BC and were made of electrum, while gold and silver coins were first issued in the mid-6th century BC (*see also* COINS, §I).

In Hellenistic and Roman times Lydia had many prosperous cities, notably Philadelphia, Thyateira, Magnesia ad Sipylum, Julia Gordos and Nyssa. The Ionic temple of Artemis at Sardis was one of the largest Greek temples (early 3rd century BC with Roman additions); also at Sardis, the largest extant ancient synagogue (*c.* 85×20 m) was incorporated into a major bath–gymnasium complex in late Roman times. To posterity, however, ancient Lydia has left more legend than legacy. The impact of Lydian military power and wealth on the ancient Greeks secured a permanent niche for Lydia in Classical and Western tradition. The riches of Lydia and the mercurial fortunes of Lydian kings became common paradigms in Greek and Latin literature. Croesus was commemorated in Greek vase painting and Gyges in Greek tragedy (see Page); both figures recur in western European poetry, drama and art.

Pauly–Wissowa

BIBLIOGRAPHY

G. Radet: *La Lydie et le monde grec au temps des Mermnades (687–546)* (Paris, 1893)
D. Magie: *Roman Rule in Asia Minor to the End of the Third Century after Christ* (Princeton, 1950)
D. L. Page: *A New Chapter in the History of Greek Tragedy* (Cambridge, 1951)
A. Pigler: *Profane Darstellungen*, ii of *Barockthemen: Eine Auswahl von Verzeichnissen zur Ikonographie des 17. und 18. Jahrhunderts* (Budapest, 1956, 2/1974), pp. 277–349 [on Gyges and Croesus]
G. M. A. Hanfmann: *From Croesus to Constantine: The Cities of Western Asia Minor and their Arts in Greek and Roman Times* (Ann Arbor, 1975)

——: *Sardis from Prehistoric to Roman Times: Results of the Archaeological Exploration of Sardis, 1958–1975* (Cambridge, MA, 1983)

CRAWFORD H. GREENEWALT JR

**Lydos.** *See* VASE PAINTERS, §II.

**Lye, Len** [Huai, Leonard Charles] (*b* Christchurch, 5 July 1901; *d* New York, 15 May 1980). American film maker, sculptor and painter of New Zealand birth. He began work in New Zealand, then moved to Australia, Samoa and England (where he settled in 1926). *Tusalava* (1929) was the first of his 24 films. He pioneered various methods of 'direct' film making, eliminating the camera by painting directly on to clear film (*Colour Box*, 1935), developing the 'rayogram' technique (*Colour Cry*, 1952) and scratching black film (*Free Radicals*, 1958). He experimented with colour processing in *Rainbow Dance* (1936) and *Trade Tattoo* (1937).

The batiks (e.g. *Polynesian Connection*, 1928) and oil paintings (e.g. *Jam Session*, 1936; both New Plymouth, NZ, Govett-Brewster A.G.) that Lye exhibited with the Seven and Five Society (1927–34) and in the International Surrealist Exhibition (1936) were influenced by his profound study of tribal art. In 1944 he moved to New York and continued film making until 1958, when he turned to motorized kinetic sculpture. His sculpture was exhibited at the Museum of Modern Art (1961) and in international exhibitions of kinetic art. Lye based his kinetic sculpture and experimental film making on his concept of 'a new art of motion' that heightened the sense of 'physical empathy'. In his later years he resumed film making (*Particles in Space*, 1979) and theorized about 'motion composition' and about connections between art and science. In 1980 a Len Lye Foundation was established at the Govett-Brewster Art Gallery in New Zealand, whose collection includes such major sculptures as *Fountain* (1963), *Universe* (1963) and *Flip and Two Twisters* (1967), all made of stainless steel on wood bases with motors.

WRITINGS

*Figures of Motion: Selected Writings* (Auckland, 1984)

BIBLIOGRAPHY

*Len Lye: A Personal Mythology* (exh. cat., ed. A. Bogle; Auckland, C.A.G., 1980)
*Film Lib. Q.*, xiv/3–4 (1981) [issue devoted to Len Lye]

ROGER HORROCKS

**Lykios** (*b* Eleutherai, Boiotia; *fl c.* mid-5th century BC). Greek sculptor. He was trained by his father, the famous sculptor Myron (Pliny: *Natural History* XXXIV.xix.50). He was active in Athens and Olympia. None of his works survives; they included a bronze statue of a youth holding a basin on the Athenian Acropolis (Pausanias: *Guide to Greece* I.xxiii.8), of which the inscribed marble base perhaps survives (*Inscr. Gr./2*, I, 537). He also produced two bronze equestrian statues, which were erected at the entrance to the Acropolis, and remains of an inscribed base (*Inscr. Gr./2*, I, 400) show that it was a votive gift dedicated by the cavalry to commemorate the victories of Pericles (*c.* 446 BC). Another statue in Athens, near the prytaneion, depicted *Autolykos*, a champion wrestler at the Panathenaic games of 422 BC (Pausanias: I.xviii.3 and IX.xxxii.5), while the statues of *The Argonauts* and a youth blowing on a dying fire were also attributed to Lykios by

Pliny (XXXIV.xix.79). The Ionians from Apollonia commissioned Lykios to set up a monument near the hippodameion at Olympia to commemorate a military victory of the mid-5th century BC. The long, semicircular base held 13 statues of gods and mythological figures (Pausanias: V.xxii.2–3).

BIBLIOGRAPHY

Pauly–Wissowa
J. Overbeck: *Die antiken Schriftquellen zur Geschichte der bildenden Künste bei den Griechen* (Leipzig, 1868/*R* Hildesheim, 1959), nos 861–7
V. H. Poulsen: 'Myron: Ein stilkritischer Versuch', *Acta Archaeol.*, xi (1940), pp. 1–42 (28–33)
G. Lippold: *Die griechische Plastik* (1950), III/i of *Handbuch der Archäologie*, ed. W. Otto and R. Herbig (Munich, 1939–), pp. 183–4

DIANE HARRIS

**Lykosoura.** *See under* MEGALOPOLIS.

**Lyle, John M(acIntosh)** (*b* Connor, Ireland, 13 Nov 1872; *d* Toronto, 19 Dec 1945). Canadian architect and urban planner of Irish birth. He attended the Hamilton School of Art, Ontario, and trained as an architect at the School of Arts, Yale University, New Haven, CT, before enrolling in the Ecole des Beaux-Arts, Paris (1894). His training was reinforced by 12 years' work in New York for several large firms. Upon return to Canada (1906) he was instrumental in disseminating the Beaux-Arts ideals to the architectural profession through the Atelier Lyle and lectures at the University of Toronto. Throughout his career his works reflected the Beaux-Arts style, for example the Royal Alexandra Theatre, King Street West (1906), and Union Station, Front Street (1911–27) (both Toronto), Memorial Arch, Royal Military College, Kingston, and Bank of Nova Scotia, Ottawa (both 1923).

In the 1920s, through an examination of Canada's architectural heritage, Lyle went on to develop a distinctive Canadian style of architecture. His integration of Canadian flora and fauna motifs into the design of his buildings parallels the artistic development of the painters in the Group of Seven; for example in 1929 he designed three bank branches that codified his nationalistic feelings: Dominion Bank, Yonge & Gerrard, Toronto, Bank of Nova Scotia, 8th Avenue South West, Calgary, and Bank of Nova Scotia, Head Office, Halifax. In these buildings he integrated elaborate sculptural motifs in stone, metal, plaster, fresco, glass and mosaic to express the Canadian landscape. In 1930 he built the Runnymede Library, Toronto, which combined colonial Georgian, North American Indian and early Quebec motifs. His work in urban and regional planning made him a spokesperson for the City Beautiful Movement, and he developed visionary designs for Toronto's Civic Improvement League. His designs submitted to the Dominion Coin Competition (1936) influenced the adoption of animal and leaf motifs in Canadian coinage.

BIBLIOGRAPHY

*John M. Lyle: Toward a Canadian Architecture* (exh. cat. by G. Hunt, Kingston, Ont., Queen's U., Agnes Etherington A. Cent., 1982)

GEOFFREY HUNT

**Lyman, John (Goodwin)** (*b* Biddeford, ME, 29 Sept 1886; *d* Christchurch, Barbados, 26 May 1967). Canadian painter and writer of American birth. He studied painting in Paris at the Académie Julian and at the Académie Henri

Matisse from 1907 to 1910. He lived and painted in Europe until 1931, basing himself in Paris and only occasionally returning to Canada for short visits. Lyman never had to earn a living from his art as he was from a well-to-do family. This financial security allowed him to travel extensively in France, Spain and Tunisia and to purchase several apartments and villas.

For the first 15 years after settling again in Canada in 1931, Lyman contributed significantly to the artistic growth of Quebec through his frequent exhibition reviews and articles on art in *The Montrealer* and other periodicals. In 1939 he founded the Contemporary Arts Society in Montreal, a group of progressive professional artists who advocated an international outlook as opposed to the nationalist sentiments espoused by the recently disbanded Group of Seven; he served as the Society's first President from 1939 to 1945.

Lyman worked mainly as an oil painter, exhibiting in his art an emotional reserve much in keeping with his personality. More concerned with the formal compositional structure than with anecdotal or narrative details, he held carefully orchestrated colour in place with dark enclosing outlines; often there is a sharp contrast between raking light and deep shadow, as in the portrait of *Jack Hoare* (1923; Montreal, Mus. F.A.). In his subject-matter he remained faithful to themes popularized by Matisse and other contemporary French painters, with a predominance of portraits, female nudes posed in the studio and beach and harbour scenes. Figures are often placed in sparse landscapes and turned away from the viewer, creating a psychological distance, as in *On the Beach (Saint-Jean-de-Luz)* (1929–30; Ottawa, N.G.). Those in interior settings are usually engaged in some quiet, noncommittal activity, such as reading or playing cards, for example the *Card Game* (c. 1935; Ottawa, N.G.). His portrait subjects are posed against neutral backgrounds and display a prim and static elegance, as in *Woman with a White Collar* (c. 1936; Ottawa, N.G.).

BIBLIOGRAPHY
G. Corbeil: 'John Lyman', *A. & Pensée*, iii/15 (1954), pp. 75–83
*John Lyman* (exh. cat. by P. Surrey, Quebec, Mus. Qué., 1966)
*The Contemporary Arts Society/La Société d'art contemporain* (exh. cat. by C. Varley, Edmonton, Alta, A.G., 1980)
*John Lyman, 1886–1967: I Live by my Eyes/Je vis par les yeux* (exh. cat. by L. Dompierre, Kingston, Ont., Queen's U., Agnes Etherington A. Cent., 1986)

KIRK MARLOW

**Lynar** [Linar], **Rochus Quirinus** [Guerini, Rochus], Graf zu (*b* Maradia, Tuscany, 25 Dec 1525; *d* Spandau, nr Berlin, 22 Dec 1596). Italian architect and merchant, active in Germany. He had a French training and went to work in France from 1542 to 1554. In 1561 he supervised the construction of the Citadel of Metz. As a Huguenot, Lynar was later forced to flee France, and by 1569 he had entered the service of Augustus I, Elector of Saxony, who sent him to oversee the construction of the fortifications at Dresden and Freiberg. In 1572 he superseded Hieronymus Lotter (1540–84) at the Augustusburg fortress. Personal attacks connected with anti-Protestant feeling prevented his rising to a leading position as a regional Minister of Works and Artillery Commander. In 1571 he organized the mining industry for Saxony and completed designs for ideal fortifications in 1575. His services were in demand from patrons outside Saxony: he worked in Kassel, Friedelheim and Dessau (from 1577). In 1578 he was appointed by John George, Elector of Brandenburg, to a supervisory position similar to the one he had originally held in Dresden. Between 1578 and 1583 he constructed the fortifications at Spandau and Peitz. He also worked on the Berlin Schloss. In 1580 he set up his own saltworks in Beelitz and was active in the salt trade. A few of his buildings, for example the eastern curtain and the Kronprinz and Brandenburg bastions of the Citadel at Spandau, have survived. In his day Lynar had an unrivalled reputation as a fortifications architect and artillery expert; Korn, however, questioned his abilities as an architect. In 1582 he commissioned his own epitaph, which also serves as high altar at St Nikolai, Spandau: a three-winged altarpiece with Renaissance detail, executed in stone and painted in 1591–2 by Hieronymus Rosenbaum (*fl* 1580–97).

BIBLIOGRAPHY
R. Korn: *Kriegsbaumeister Graf Rochus zu Linar* (Dresden, 1905)
T. Biller: 'Rochus Guerini Graf zu Lynar', *Baumeister, Architekten, Stadtplaner: Biographien zur baulichen Entwicklung Berlins*, ed. W. Ribbe and W. Schäche (Berlin, 1987), pp. 13–34

WERNER SCHADE

**Lynch, Kevin** (*b* Chicago, IL, 7 Jan 1918; *d* Gayhead, Martha's Vineyard, MA, 25 April 1984). American urban planner, teacher and theorist. His early training included an apprenticeship (1937–9) with Frank Lloyd Wright at Taliesin, Spring Green, WI. Lynch received a bachelor's degree in urban planning from the Massachusetts Institute of Technology (MIT), Cambridge, in 1947 and then began a long teaching career there. A major influence on his work was provided by Gyorgy Kepes (*b* 1906), his teacher and then colleague at MIT. Lynch is best known for his theoretical studies, put forth primarily in a series of books. *The Image of the City* (1960), his most influential work, has 'imageability' as its central idea, and Lynch argued for clarity, cohesiveness, legibility and identifiable structuring in urban planning in order to create this quality. *Site Planning* (1962) is more technical than theoretical and subsequently became a standard introductory textbook on urban planning. *The View from the Road* (1964) is concerned with the problems generated by the introduction of motor vehicles into the city, and it presents ways in which highways might be more thoughtfully planned. *What Time Is This Place* (1972) is the culmination of Lynch's theories, arguing that 'a desirable [urban] image is one that celebrates and enlarges the present while making connections with the past and future' (p. 1). Lynch was also engaged in private practice as a consultant with Carr Lynch Associates. He assisted in the development of plans for Boston's Government Center (late 1950s–c. 1960), in the redevelopment of Boston's city waterfront area (1960s), and in the creation of Columbia (1969), a new town in Maryland. He retired from MIT in 1978. Through his teaching and writing, Lynch had a significant influence on a generation of urban planners and architects.

WRITINGS
*The Image of the City* (Cambridge, MA, 1960); review by E. H. Chapman in *J. Aesth. & A. Crit.*, xxi/1 (1962), p. 91
*Site Planning* (Cambridge, MA, 1962, rev. 2/1971)
*The View from the Road* (Cambridge, MA, 1964)

*What Time Is This Place?* (Cambridge, MA, 1972)
*A Theory of Good City Form* (Cambridge, MA, 1981)

BIBLIOGRAPHY
L. K. Eaton: 'Imageability: A Shock to Architects', *Progr. Archit.*, xlii/9 (1961), pp. 226, 232, 236
R. Campbell: 'A Giant among City Planners', *Boston Globe* (16 May 1984)
R. Severo: 'Kevin A. Lynch, 66, Pioneer Urban Theorist', *New York Times* (3 May 1984), p. D26
T. Banerjee and M. Southworth, eds: *Kevin Lynch, 1918–1984* (Cambridge, MA, 1990)

WALTER SMITH

**Lynes, George Platt** (*b* East Orange, NJ, 15 April 1907; *d* New York, 6 Dec 1955). American photographer. After a visit to Paris in summer 1925 to meet Gertrude Stein, and to pursue his interest in art and literature, he returned there for subsequent summers. He was a self-taught photographer and was inspired to take up photographic portraiture after being given a view-camera. His early subjects included *André Gide* (1982 exh. cat., no. 4) and *Gertrude Stein.* Influenced by Man Ray, Lynes began using less conventional methods of lighting and posing, and of cropping images. In 1932 his friendship with Julien Levy, the New York art dealer specializing in Surrealist art, led to his first exhibition. Publication of his celebrity portraits in *Vogue* and *Harper's Bazaar* created enough interest in his work that in 1933 he was able to open a New York studio. Throughout the 1930s his commercial success in portraiture and as a fashion photographer continued and included a collaboration with George Balanchine's American Ballet company. From 1934 Lynes created one of the finest photographic documents of this great company, its productions and dancers.

During the 1930s Lynes began to experiment with homoerotic subjects, for example *Untitled, 1935* (Santa Fe, NM, Jack Woody Col.; see fig.), and mythological themes; sometimes he combined the two, as in *Mythological Figure* (undated; see 1982 exh. cat., no. 82). Although he considered his most controversial work his finest, it was not published during his lifetime, for fear of destroying his commercial career. In private, and to the detriment of his commercial work, Lynes continued his photographic exploration of a sexual landscape in such photographs as *Paul Cadmus, J. French* (*c.* 1940; see 1982 exh. cat., no. 36), using devices such as half-smoked cigarettes, beds and backward glances. By the late 1940s neglect had bankrupted his studio, ending a career he had long considered artistically worthless.

Friends and odd jobs were Lynes's only means of support during his last years. Later photographs took a harsher, less romantic look at sexuality: couples eye each other more suspiciously; their bodies are less beautiful. Terminally ill with lung cancer, he suffered a debilitating cycle of radium treatments and wasting illness. He began systematically to destroy large portions of his surviving archives. Most of his 8×10 negatives of fashion and commercial portraiture were discarded, as were a number of his nudes. Lynes's surviving work, rediscovered 25 years after his death, established him as one of America's pre-eminent Surrealist-influenced photographers.

BIBLIOGRAPHY
J. Woody, ed.: *George Platt Lynes: Photographs, 1931–1955* (Pasadena, 1981)
——: *George Platt Lynes: Ballet* (Pasadena, 1985)

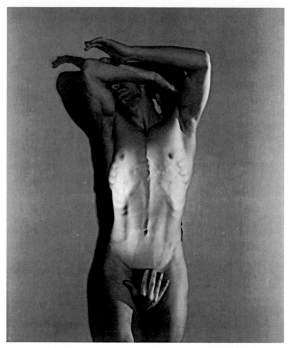

George Platt Lynes: *Untitled, 1935*, photograph (Santa Fe, NM, Jack Woody Collection)

James Crump: *George Platt Lynes: Photographs from the Kinsey Institute* (Boston, 1993)
J. Woody, ed.: *George Platt Lynes: Portraits 1927–1955* (Santa Fe, 1994)

JACK WOODY

**Lynn, Vivian** (*b* Wellington, NZ, 30 Nov 1931). New Zealand sculptor and printmaker. She was one of the most technically and stylistically diverse of the feminist artists to emerge in New Zealand in the 1970s. In such works as her screenprinted *Playground* series (1975; Wellington, Mus. NZ, Te Papa Tongarewa) she was concerned to show how women's identities have been constructed by cultural forces. In exploring how attitudes to women are rooted historically, culturally and psychologically, she drew her imagery from throughout history and from various cultures. In the 1980s much of her work used hair as a medium because of its association with femininity and sexuality. For instance, her *Guardian Gates* (1982; Wellington, Mus. NZ, Te Papa Tongarewa) is a cycle of seven metal cyclone gates dressed with hair; and in a temporary installation called *Stain* (1984) a carpet woven from hair and resembling dried trickles of blood was placed on the steps of a cathedral in Dunedin to protest against the Church's suppression of women.

BIBLIOGRAPHY
A. M. Johnston: 'Vivian Lynn', *Sculpture 2* (exh. cat., Auckland, C.A.G., 1982)
*Vivian Lynn: Anxious Images* (exh. cat. by A. M. Johnston, Auckland, C.A.G., 1984), pp. 41–6

ROBERT LEONARD

**Lynn, William Henry** (*b* St John's Point, Co. Down, 27 Sept 1829; *d* Belfast, 12 Sept 1915). Irish architect. He was apprenticed to CHARLES LANYON in Belfast in 1846, serving as clerk of works on Lanyon's Queen's College and County Court House. In 1854 he was taken into partnership by Lanyon and remained with him until 1872 when the firm was dissolved and Lynn set up practice on his own. He was a prolific designer with an eclectic taste and a scholarly interest in historic styles, at first mainly medieval but later also classical.

Early works by Lynn included the Belfast Bank (now Northern Bank) branches at Newtownards (1854) and Dungannon (1855), which are among the earliest examples of Venetian Gothic detailing in Ireland, and the similarly Ruskin-inspired Sinclair Seamen's Presbyterian Church (1856–7), Belfast, in Lombardic Romanesque style. His most conspicuous warehouse in Belfast, built for Richardson, Sons & Owden in Donegall Square (1865–9), was also Italian Gothic in style. His main interest was in ecclesiastical design, usually English Gothic in style, as at the Church of Ireland St Andrew's (1860), Dublin, but at St Patrick's (Church of Ireland; 1865–8), Jordanstown, Co. Antrim, he produced a rare essay in Celtic Romanesque style. He also produced Scottish Baronial designs for several country houses in Ulster. Lynn was very successful in competitions, both at home and abroad. The most important in his time with Lanyon were the unexecuted design (1861) for the New South Wales Parliament Building in Sydney, Australia, and Chester Town Hall (1863–9). Competition successes continued in his independent practice, as at the George A. Clark Town Hall (1875–82), Paisley, Scotland, and Barrow-in-Furness Town Hall (1877–87), both designed in his later classical manner.

Most of Lynn's important later work is to be seen in Belfast, where he built the Carlisle Memorial Methodist Church (1874–5) in English Gothic style and the Central Library (1883–8), Royal Avenue, the Harbour Office extension (1891–5) and the Bank Buildings (1895–1900), all in classical style; Campbell College (1891–4) was designed in Tudor style. From 1910 to 1915 he was architect for St Anne's Church of Ireland Cathedral (begun in 1896 by Thomas Drew), Belfast, where he designed the baptistery in 1915 (built 1922–4). Lynn's honours included the award of a gold medal for architectural drawing at the Exposition Universelle (1867), Paris, and his election as President of the Royal Institute of Architects of Ireland for 1885–9. He was an accomplished landscape watercolourist as well as a brilliant architectural draughtsman, while his competition design successes gave Irish architecture a greater prestige than it had ever had before.

BIBLIOGRAPHY

C. E. B. Brett: *Buildings of Belfast, 1700–1914* (London, 1967, rev. Belfast, 1985)

H. Dixon: 'William Henry Lynn', *Q. Bull. Irish Georg. Soc.*, xvii/1–2 (1974), pp. 25–30

*W. H. Lynn, 1829–1915: Watercolours and Building Perspectives* (exh. cat. by H. Dixon, Belfast, Ulster Mus., 1978)

P. Larmour: *Belfast: An Illustrated Architectural Guide* (Belfast, 1987)

PAUL LARMOUR

**Lyon** [Lat. Lugdunum]. French city near the confluence of the rivers Rhône and Saône, and préfecture of the Rhône département, with a population of *c.* 1,100,000.

1. History and urban development. 2. Art life and organization. 3. Centre of production. 4. Cathedral.

## 1. HISTORY AND URBAN DEVELOPMENT.

(i) Lugdunum. (ii) Modern city.

*(i) Lugdunum.* The Roman colony founded in 43 BC by Julius Caesar's lieutenant, Lucius Munatius Plancus, at the confluence succeeded two Gaulish settlements on Fourvière Hill to the west and at Condate on the low ground between the rivers. Lugdunum was the focal point of Gaul's road system, laid out by Agrippa, and the political centre of the Three Gauls (the provinces of Lugdunensis, Aquitania and Belgica), whose council met annually in the amphitheatre above Condate, beside the ceremonial Altar of Rome and Augustus; this altar had been inaugurated in AD 12 by Drusus, father of the future emperor Claudius (*reg* AD 41–54), who was born at Lugdunum. The other public buildings were all on Fourvière Hill, and included two fora, the first Augustan (27 BC–AD 14), the second Antonine (AD 138–93), and several temples, of which the east front of the podium of Cybele's temple still stands. The Gier aqueduct, of Hadrianic date (AD 117–38), is unusual outside Italy in being faced in reticulate masonry and reached the city's height by means of a siphon. Apart from Vienne, Lugdunum was the only city in Gaul with two theatres, which are its best-preserved Roman buildings. The larger open theatre was originally Augustan, rebuilt and enlarged under Hadrian to seat over 10,000 spectators. The orchestra was paved in coloured marbles, and the stage building had three curved exedrae. The smaller, covered odeon was built close to it, also Hadrianic, and equally magnificent in its marble decoration. Several luxurious houses with good mosaic pavements have been excavated on Fourvière Hill. The finest mosaic, showing chariot-racing in the circus, was found in another rich residential area in Ainay, formerly on an island between the rivers. At Condate there were workshops of bronze founders, glaziers and potters, some of the latter having come from Arezzo in Italy, introducing the manufacture of fine-quality red *terra sigillata* (*see* ROME, ANCIENT, §X, 8). Remains of several 5th-century AD churches survive (*see* §(ii)(a) below).

BIBLIOGRAPHY

P. Wuilleumier: 'Fouilles de Fourvière à Lyon', *Gallia-Suppl.*, iv (1951) [whole issue]

A. Audin: *Lyon, miroir de Rome dans les Gaules* (Paris, 1965)

T. F. C. BLAGG

*(ii) Modern city.*

*(a) AD 300–1499.* Between the 3rd and 4th centuries profound changes occurred in the urban landscape of Lyon: the upper town on Fourvière Hill was progressively abandoned in favour of the lower east bank of the Saône and the peninsula. Additionally, the arrival of Christianity resulted in the building of the first cathedral complex in the second half of the 4th century (*see* §4 (i) below), and of the necropolis of the upper town, where the tombs were gathered around the venerated graves of SS Irenaeus (*d c.* 202) and Justus (*d c.* 390) in the present Rue des Macchabées.

During the Burgundian occupation of the region around Lyon from before 469 the town became a capital, and was enriched with numerous monuments, some of which were described by Sidonius Apollinaris. The quality of the monuments, the continued use of Roman architectural techniques and the appearance of new kinds of religious building (e.g. churches with transepts, such as St Just (begun 4th century; destr. 1562) and St Laurent (6th century; destr. 8th century)) demonstrate a certain sophistication. The arrival of the Franks in 534 changed little. Although Lyon was no longer a regional capital, it remained a religious metropolis; the powerful bishops of Lyon were descended from the senatorial aristocracy, for example, St Nicetius (*reg* 553–73), the uncle of St Gregory of Tours (*c.* 538–94). Following the Arab raids of 725–31 Bishop Leidrade (*reg* 797–816) restored order and rebuilt most of the churches. At that time the layout of the city was already complicated: on the west bank of the Saône was the cathedral complex and the collegiate churches of St Paul (12th–16th century) and St Georges (rest. 802; rebuilt 1844); on the peninsula, despite the presence of Ainay Abbey (of which St Martin survives), the population shifted from the southern point to the St Nizier district where the Carolingian *burgus* (destr.) was situated.

From the second half of the 10th century the bishops of Lyon established undivided power over the city. This power was eventually contested by the counts of Forez, who were victorious in 1173. The urban landscape was profoundly changed by the rebuilding (1052–77) of the bridge over the Saône. Ecclesiastical buildings were restored, including the abbeys of Ile-Barbe, Ainay (ded. 1107) and St Pierre (begun 5th century; rebuilt 1659; now Musée des Beaux-Arts; *see* §2 below and fig. 2 below), and the churches of St Paul (12th century) and St Just, and in the 12th century work began on the new cathedral of St Jean in Romanesque style. By the 13th and 14th centuries the bishop was firmly established in the Château de Pierre Scize (11th–13th century), and work on the cathedral continued in Gothic style. Episcopal power, however, was eventually destroyed by the bourgeoisie, who, somewhat belatedly, obtained a charter of franchise. Philip IV used the situation to take control of the town (1311–12). The Franciscans and Dominicans settled on the peninsula, and with the building of the bridge over the Rhône (1180–90) a line of communication crossing the peninsula was created.

The Hundred Years War (1337–1453) thwarted development until the four public annual fairs, formally established by Louis XI in 1462, proved successful. Lyon became one of the centres of European trade, and with this new prosperity the buildings were altered and housing increased in density. The city became more Gothic than Renaissance in appearance, especially round the cathedral, in the lawyers' quarter near the Hôtel de Roanne (14th century; destr. 1835), in the money-changers' district near St Paul, and in the tradesmen's quarter around St Nizier (13th–15th century; rest. 19th century). Town houses from this period are characterized by narrow street façades with many openings and tiny courtyards linked by *traboules* (Fr.: 'narrow passages').

BIBLIOGRAPHY

N. Gonthier: 'Une Esquisse du paysage urbain au Moyen Age', *'Le Paysage urbain au Moyen-Age.' Actes du XIe Congrès des historiens médiévistes de l'enseignement supérieur: Lyon, 1981*, pp. 253–75

J. F. Reynaud: 'Lyon du IVe au VIIIe siècle: Edifices religieux, nécropoles et topographie urbaine', *Recherches récentes en archéologie gallo-romaine et paléochrétienne sur Lyon et sa région*, ed. S. Walker, Brit. Archaeol. Rep., International Series, clviii (1981), pp. 119–56

——: *Lugdunum Christianum: Lyon du IVe au VIIIe siècles: Topographie, nécropoles et édifices religieux* (in preparation)

J. F. REYNAUD

*(b) 1500 and after*. In the 16th and 17th centuries the urban structure centred on the Saône was essentially preserved. The ramparts enclosed rural zones to the north and east on the hills of La Croix-Rousse and Fourvière; the south of the peninsula was divided into lots from 1560, and hôtels particuliers were built. At the heart of the peninsula public squares were laid out, the most important of which was the Place Bellecour (1562; altered during the 17th century; see fig. 1). It contains a bronze equestrian statue of *Louis XIV* (1820–25) by François-Frédéric Lemot, replacing an earlier one by MARTIN DESJARDINS.

The principal 17th-century buildings included new convents on the periphery of the city, Etienne Martellange's Jesuit college (1607; mostly destr.; rebuilt by Simon Maupin; now the Lycée Ampère), the Hospice de la Charité (1622; destr. 1934), and the Hôtel-Dieu (1739–48; *see* SOUFFLOT, JACQUES-GERMAIN). The Hôtel de Ville (rest.), built by the consulat (city council) from 1655 to 1704, first under Simon Maupin (*d* 1668), and then Jules Hardouin Mansart, is noted for its decoration by THOMAS BLANCHET.

In the 18th century the city spread east towards the Rhône. An embankment (1738–78) was built on the site of the old ramparts, and a second bridge was constructed across the Rhône in 1774. The consulat commissioned a granary (1729) and Soufflot's Loge du Change (1747–9; now a Protestant church) and his Théâtre (1751–6; destr. 1828). Middle-class businessmen put up blocks of flats, sometimes luxurious, as in the Quartier St Clair (1760–90), built on reclaimed land to the north of the Rhône. By the time of the collapse of the *ancien régime* in 1789, the development of the east bank of the Rhône proposed by Jean Antoine Morand (1727–94) was barely started, while the project of the architect Antoine-Michel Perrache (1726–79) to push back the confluence of the rivers meant that a large area of land was made available at the south of the peninsula.

These projects were more fully developed in the 19th century. The Quartier des Brotteaux on the east bank was built up as a residential area, while the Perrache district became less salubrious, with the creation of a prison, warehouses, factories and so on. La Croix-Rousse Hill was covered with a working-class settlement of large buildings for the silk-weavers, and heavy industry arrived in the suburbs. In 1852 the suburbs of La Croix-Rousse, La Guillotière and Vaise became part of the city.

During the second half of the 19th century great vistas were carved through the peninsula in a style similar to those created by Georges-Eugène Haussmann in Paris. This disrupted the old pattern of land ownership. In the same period a number of grand public buildings were constructed. Following the new Opéra (1828–32) by ANTOINE-MARIE CHENAVARD and the Palais de Justice (begun in 1835; *see* LAW COURT) by Louis-Pierre Baltard (*see* BALTARD, (1)), the city was provided with a Palais du

1. Lyon, looking south with Place Bellecour to the left of centre and the cathedral beyond, across the river; engraving by Simon Maupin, 1635 (Lyon, Musée Gadagne)

Commerce (1855–62) by Gaspard André (1840–86), Préfecture (1879–90) by Antonin Georges Louvier (1818–92), university (1890–98) by Abraham Hirsch (*b* 1828; *d* after 1898), and two railway stations, the Gare de Perrache (1856) by François-Alexis Cendrier (1803–93) and the Gare des Brotteaux (1904–8) by V. L. Rascol and P. d'Arbaut, and its skyline was crowned with Notre-Dame de Fourvière (1872–96) by PIERRE BOSSAN.

The great 20th-century amenities were only built after 1920, although Tony Garnier, supported by the mayor Edouard Herriot (1872–1957), had started some major projects before 1914 (*see* GARNIER, TONY, §2). Urban development after World War II was characterized by the housing schemes built to the east (Bron-Parilly, Vaulx-en-Velin, Vénissieux) and west (La Duchère). The city acquired international links such as airports and motorways, sometimes at the expense of urban design, as at the Centre d'Echanges at Perrache. Since 1968 a new city, the Ile d'Abeau, about 30 km away, had continued the eastwards thrust that has characterized the growth of Lyon. A planned community, associated with a commercial centre (La Part-Dieu), was created from 1970 on the east bank and completed by a new railway station (1983) for high-speed trains. Cars, photographic and pharmaceutical products are made in Lyon, and the city is renowned for its medical research. In 1994 Santiago Calatrava completed Lyon Airport Railway Station, a dramatic structure with the main station hall having angled roofs in the form of outstretched wings.

BIBLIOGRAPHY

A. Kleinklausz: *Lyon des origines à nos jours: La Formation de la cité* (Lyon, 1925)

D. Bertin and A.-S. Clémençon: *Lyon-Guide* (Paris, 1986)

2. ART LIFE AND ORGANIZATION. From the 17th century many of Lyon's finest artists were attracted to Paris and elsewhere; for example the Audran family of engravers all worked in Paris. Although ANTOINE COYZEVOX wished to sculpt and teach in his native city, he was enticed to Paris by royal favour, taking his nephews, the sculptors Nicolas Coustou and Guillaume Coustou (i), with him. By contrast, the sculptor JOSEPH CHINARD spent most of his career in Lyon, and maintained Lyonnais contacts even when he worked elsewhere. The city acquired its own school of design in 1756, founded by a group of amateurs who wanted a pool of artists and designers in Lyon for the silk trade.

The Musée des Beaux-Arts was one of 15 provincial museums set up in 1801. Though formed around a nucleus of confiscated works brought together at the convent of St Pierre in 1791, the core of its collection comprised those placed on permanent loan from the state in 1803, 1805 and 1811. It also contained an archaeological section, the first curator of which was the antiquary François Artaud (1767–1838). From 1807 to 1842 the Salon des Fleurs (*see* FLOWER PAINTING) was organized at the museum and displayed Dutch flower paintings by such artists as Jan van Huysum and Gerard van Spaendonck next to those by Lyonnais artists in order to educate future silk designers (*see* §3(ii) below). One of the most important sections of the Ecole des Beaux-Arts, established in 1803 in the Palais des Beaux-Arts (now the Musée des Beaux-Arts; see fig 2), was the flower class. A number of successful 19th-century artists, for example Victor Orsel, the FLANDRIN brothers, Paul Chenavard, Michel Dumas (1812–85), JOSEPH GUICHARD, CLAUDIUS JACQUAND and Louis Appian (1862–96), studied at the Ecole under teachers such as PIERRE RÉVOIL and FLEURY RICHARD. The term 'Lyon school' is sometimes applied to their work (*see* TROUBADOUR STYLE). The Ecole left the Palais des Arts in 1918, but survives as the Ecole Nationale des Beaux-Arts (4).

2. Lyon, main façade (north) of the former Palais des Beaux-Arts (now the Musée des Beaux-Arts)

Local learned societies such as the Athénée and the Académie des Sciences, Belles-Lettres et Arts (refounded 1800) also flourished. Members of the latter often contributed to the *Revue du Lyonnais*, which was founded (1835) by Léon Boitel (1806–55) and directed by him until 1852, after which it was run (1853–90) by Aimé Vingtrinier (1812–1903). It contained reviews of the exhibitions that were organized from 1836 by the Société des Amis des Arts and held in the Palais des Arts. At these exhibitions the city purchased works by local artists, which were then entrusted to the Musée des Beaux-Arts. In 1864 the Musée d'Art et d'Industrie was established by the chamber of commerce in its trade centre. From 1878 the archaeological department of the Musée des Beaux-Arts flourished under the direction of Paul Dissard (1852–1926); it was expanded and its staircase decorated by Puvis de Chavannes. The committee controlling the museum was chaired from 1872 by Edouard Eynard (1857–1913), a collector who also founded the Musée Historique des Tissus in 1890 to replace the Musée d'Art et d'Industrie. In 1887 the exhibitions of the Société des Amis des Arts were discontinued, after which artists organized their own, for example the Salon des Artistes Lyonnais (1906) and the Salon d'Automne (1907).

In 1914, however, Lyon was still predominantly a centre of learning with a marked interest in archaeology, religious history and the industrial arts. From 1920 to 1940 there were a number of attempts to bring Lyon up to date, as well as a renewed interest in 16th-century printers, which led to the revival of the *Revue du Lyonnais*. The same spirit, and often the same individuals, also inspired a number of associations such as La Belle Cordière (1929) and the Cercle Sébastien Gryphe (1933). Both societies sought to revive the tradition of producing books illustrated with prints, often wood-engravings. Eugène Vial (1863–1941), among others, was behind the foundation of the Musée Historique de Lyon in 1924 in the Renaissance Hôtel de Gadagne. In 1925 the chamber of commerce founded the Musée des Arts Décoratifs, which contains an important collection of prints and drawings acquired since 1865.

Art life in Lyon in the 20th century was dominated by such figures as Dr Emile Malespine (1892–1953), who founded the review *Manomètre* (1922–8). He solicited contributions from such well-known artists as Hans Arp, Piet Mondrian and László Moholy-Nagy. Only eight Lyonnais wrote for the periodical. It was in touch with avant-garde movements, for instance, de Stijl, Der Sturm, Merz (the work of Kurt Schwitters) and the Bauhaus, and although short-lived, it was influential. In 1936, for example, Marcel Michaud (1898–1958) founded the Témoignage group, which brought together painters, sculptors, poets and musicians. A number of exhibitions were also established which represented a variety of artistic trends, primarily traditionalist: the Salon du Sud-Est (1925), the Salon des Artistes Femmes (1927) and Regain (1938). Additionally, the Folklore gallery displayed sculptures by ETIENNE-MARTIN and François Stahly, paintings by Jean Le Moal (*b* 1909) and the Lyonnais painters René Burlet (*b* 1905) and Camille Niogret (*b* 1910). After World War II the gallery continued to pursue its activities in a more eclectic spirit until 1966.

Lyon was the refuge of many artists during World War II, but this dynamism did not endure; in the 1950s such artists as André Cottavoz (*b* 1922), Jean Fusaro (*b* 1925) and Jacques Truphémus (*b* 1922), who represented a Lyon school distinguished by its restraint and distance from abstraction, achieved success. Abstract art was brought to Lyon by a new generation of galleries, including L'Oeil Ecouté (founded 1962), Galerie du Griffon, Verrière (1962) and Le Lutrin (1964). They all displayed works by the new generation of Lyonnais painters (e.g. Jean Janoir (*b* 1929), Pierre Montheillet (*b* 1923), Michel Moskovtchenko (*b* 1935) and Max Schöndorff (*b* 1934)) side by side with those of well-known French and foreign artists. Exhibitions of this period include *Art et verité* (1969), and in the late 20th century there were also salons held in the spring and autumn. The Musée de la Civilisation Gallo–Romaine, designed by Bernard Zehufuss, was opened on Fourvière Hill in 1976. Also in the 1970s attempts were made to put Lyon on the international modern art circuit. In 1976, for example, an initiative by the association of Lyon art critics led to the establishment of the Espace Lyonnais d'Art Contemporain. In 1978 the Nouveau Musée was founded by private patrons, although it later sought museum status.

In 1983 decentralization brought the Rhône–Alpes region its first regional modern art fund, which launched a number of young artists such as Stéphane Braconnier (*b* 1958), Philippe Favier (*b* 1957) and Denis Laget (*b* 1958), and built up a collection of international works; it sought to link contemporary art forms, including film, video, installations, painting and sculpture. New galleries, run by entrepreneurs, attracted a new clientele from the world of advertising and business. In the 1980s initiatives designed to interest the public in contemporary art included Artothèques (art libraries) and Centres d'Art Contemporain. The Musée Saint Pierre Art Contemporain, a section of the Musée des Beaux-Arts, began to acquire its own collection in 1983; it organized a number of remarkable exhibitions, such as Le Monochrome (1988), but lacked a permanent site. In 1986 plans were drawn up for the rebuilding of the Musée des Beaux-Arts, which had outgrown its premises in the Palais des Arts: work began in 1989 and the second stage of the project was completed in 1993.

BIBLIOGRAPHY

M. Audin and E. Vial: *Dictionnaire des artistes et artisans d'art du Lyonnais* (Lyon, 1918)

*Lyon, 1882–1982, entre création et récréation* (exh. cat., Lyon, Espace Lyon. A. Contemp., 1982)

*20 Ans d'une galerie de province: L'Oeil écouté* (exh. cat., Lyon, Espace Lyon. A. Contemp., 1982)

P. Durey: *Le Musée des Beaux-Arts de Lyon*, Musées et Monuments de France (Paris, 1988)

G. Chomer: 'Quelques traits de la vie artistique', *Le Rhône: Naissance d'un département, ouvrage collectif* (Lyon, 1990), pp. 279–81

*Edouard Aynard: Le Fondateur du Musée, 1890–1990* (exh. cat., Lyon, Mus. Hist. Tissus, 1990)

N. Chiron: 'Un Exemple de critique d'art en province: La Peinture des années 1852–80 à travers la *Revue du Lyonnais*', *Gaz. B.-A.*, n. s. 5, cxxxiii (1991), pp. 42–52

MARIE FÉLICIE PÉREZ

## 3. Centre of production.

**(i) Faience.** In the late 16th century faience was produced in Lyon by such Italian potters as Sebastiano Griffo from Genoa, and Giulio Gambino and Guillaume Tardessire from Faenza; in 1574 they received permission to make and sell 'vaisselle de terre à la façon de Venise'. Work produced by these potters is unknown, but a circular *istoriato* (pictorial) plate (London, BM; *see* FRANCE, fig. 64) inscribed *La Verba di faraô/in serpentte/1582/ GT..VF/lyon* remains the basis for work attributable to Lyon in the late 16th century and early 17th. Several apothecary albarelli and spouted wet-drug jars are also attributable to Lyon; the form of the double-gourd albarelli in particular reveals a Venetian influence. The decoration of these wares (examples in Louhans, Apothicairie l'Hôtel-Dieu and Lyon, Mus. Hospices) is similar to that found on Italian maiolica at the end of the 15th century and on Hispano-Moresque wares, with large Gothic inscriptions, ivy and oak leaves, geometric patterns and fleurs-de-lis. The palette is strong with a rich, dark blue and deep orange-yellow. *Faience blanche* was also produced in Lyon during this period. The first identifiable production of faience in Lyon in the 18th century is that of Joseph Combe, a potter from Moustiers, and his Lyonnais partner, Jacques-Marie Ravier, who in 1733 obtained a royal privilege to produce it. In 1737 the factory passed to Dame Lemasle, and in 1753 to her son-in-law, François-Joseph Patras. The factory continued to produce faience until 1770. The two known pieces by Combe (Sèvres, Mus. N. Cér.; Lyon, Mus. Hist.) are marked *lyon C.F.* and bear the arms of Camille Perrichon, Provost of the Merchants of

Lyon between 1730 and 1739. The mythological scene *en camaïeu bleu* on each plate is surrounded by a border with decoration typical of wares from Moustiers. Pierre Mongis (1712–56), a faience painter, is known by a plate (1739; Lyon, Mus. Hist.) decorated with a central medallion of a townscape and broderie borders in a style similar to that used at Rouen. Plates and dishes painted with figures and architectural motifs (e.g. in Paris, Mus. A. Déc.) are also attributable to Lyon, and again reveal the influence of Moustiers. Characteristic of Lyon ware is an ochre-yellow palette. Documentary evidence attests to a number of factories operating in Lyon from the 1750s, among them that of Pierre Rogé.

BIBLIOGRAPHY

C. Damiron: *La Faience de Lyon* (Paris, 1926)

J. Chompret: 'Les Céramiques du Musée des Hospices civils de Lyon', *Albums crocodile*, v (Sept–Oct 1937) [whole issue]

——: 'Le Musée des Hospices civils de Lyon', *Bull. Amis Sèvres*, xxxiv (1939), pp. 69–76

BET MCLEOD

**(ii) Silk.** During the Middle Ages, Lyon was situated at the centre of a network of European trade routes running from northern Europe to the Mediterranean. By 1450 Lyon was granted exclusive rights to customs tariffs on all goods passing through the town. When Louis XI attempted to found a silk industry at Lyon in 1466 his plans were greeted with hostility as the merchants were unwilling to have their lucrative trade in Italian and Near Eastern silks threatened by a domestic industry; production was therefore moved to Tours. A silk industry was finally established in Lyon in 1536 after the Consulate had witnessed the success of the industry at Tours. In 1536 Lyon was given the same privileges as Tours and in 1554 the first set of regulations were issued. At this time most silks were still imported from such centres as Lucca. Lyon was producing only plain or very simple patterned silks as French craftsmen lacked the technical knowledge and expertise to produce such sophisticated types as the Italian figured silks.

The example of Claude Dangon, a Milanese weaver in Lyon, gave the industry a boost. The technical improvements he made to the draw loom in 1604–5 enabled him to produce elaborate brocaded velvets and silks. By 1656 the lustring technique had been discovered, reputedly by Octavio May (lustring involved treating the warp before weaving by stretching and heating, sometimes coating with beer, to produce a very lightweight, glossy dress silk). These technical advances, coupled with the new regulations of 1619 which made the distinction between master weavers, master workers and merchants, encouraged the burgeoning industry and by 1660 there were in the region of 3000 looms in Lyon. The silks were becoming increasingly elaborate and it was at this time that the French industry began to overtake the Italian.

There was, however, little control over the quality of silk produced as the industry was mainly organized around small workshops. In 1665 Jean-Baptiste Colbert, Surintendant et Ordonnateur Général des Bâtiments, Arts et Manufactures, laid down regulations governing the width of the silks and their inspection. He also attempted to organize the structure of the industry, which consisted of rival groups of master weavers and master workers (*see* SILK).

In spite of these internal problems the silk industry at Lyon continued to expand throughout the 17th century. The revocation of the Edict of Nantes (1685) had little effect on it, although the economic problems caused by the wars at the end of Louis XIV's reign caused some weavers to emigrate. With the end of the War of the Spanish Succession (1713), foreign markets were once more open and the financial situation of the crown and court, the main consumers of silk, strengthened. Louis XIV had succeeded in making France the leader of European fashion, with the result that the ever-changing French silk patterns were extremely popular abroad. The demand was so high that English mercers often paid to have the latest patterns from Lyon smuggled over the Channel.

The 18th century was a very prosperous period for the Lyon silk industry. French competitors, particularly those in Tours, no longer seriously threatened its position, and by the 18th century Italy was no longer producing elaborate figured silks on a grand scale. Lyon was the main production centre for dress silk in Europe, and by 1739 there were approximately 8000 looms in the city. Part of the success of Lyon silk was due to the outstanding skills of the designers. Jean Revel (1684–1751), one of the most influential, invented a system of shading in silk called *point rentré*, which enabled a subtle gradation of colour to be achieved by interlocking the threads of adjacent colours. This meant that silks could be woven with naturalistic patterns, realistically shaded, that gave a three-dimensional impression. Revel's silks were extremely popular, and during the 1730s many silks were produced in Lyon with lifelike fruits and flowers, which showed the influence of Revel's love of naturalism. The Lyonnais were well aware of the importance of the silk designers in contributing to their success. In 1756 a school of design was founded and by 1759 there were approximately 60 designers in Lyon. The school emphasized the importance of technical training as well as artistic ability and encouraged regular visits to Paris so that the designers could keep up to date.

The most famous Lyon silk designer was PHILLIPE DE LASALLE, who was active in Lyon from the 1750s until the Revolution. His designs, which often depict such birds as partridges or pheasants among realistic flower sprays or foliage (*see* FRANCE, fig. 96), were the final extension of Revel's naturalism and have been described as 'pictures in silk'. The extent of his commissions from both Marie-Antoinette and Catherine the Great demonstrate the high regard for Lyon silk.

Throughout the 18th century the silk industry continued to expand. Occasional slumps were caused by wars, court mournings and internal quarrels among the weavers but by the 1770s there were some 12,000 looms in Lyon and by the 1780s half the silk in France was produced there. The French Revolution caused a dramatic slump in demand for luxury fabrics but production picked up during the Napoleonic period and high-quality furnishing fabrics were made for the Imperial residences. An outstanding designer of Empire silks was Jean-François Bony (1754–1825), who provided silks for the Château de Malmaison. The industry adapted to new demands for lighter silks

with smaller patterns and even exploited the new vogue for composing patterns for embroidery, which became an important part of industrial production in the 19th century. Although production was high at this time, the introduction of the Jacquard loom, perfected in 1802, meant that quality was often sacrificed. The production of sumptuous floral silks was encouraged in the 19th century by the establishment of the Salon des Fleurs at the Musée des Beaux-Arts, Lyon, which, between 1807 and 1842, displayed Netherlandish flower paintings intended to inspire silk designers (*see* FLOWER PAINTING). Production continued on a reduced scale in the late 20th century.

BIBLIOGRAPHY

B. M. Borland: *Philippe de Lasalle* (Chicago, 1936)
C. G. E. Bunt: *The Silks of Lyon* (Leigh on Sea, 1960)
P. Thornton: *Baroque and Rococo Silk* (London, 1965)
M. Carlano and L. Salmon: *French Textiles: From the Middle Ages through the Second Empire* (Hartford, 1985)
*Ancien Régime-Premier Empire, 1785–1805* (exh. cat. by A. Gruber, Riggisberg, Abegg-Stift., 1989)
P. Arizzoli-Clémentel: *Le Musée des tissus de Lyon* (Paris, 1990)
N. Rothstein: *Silk Designs of the Nineteenth Century* (London, 1990)

DIANA FOWLE

### 4. CATHEDRAL.

#### (i) Architecture.

(a) First cathedral complex. The *ecclesia* of Lyon, situated between the hill and the Saône, was described by Sidonius Apollinaris in AD 469. It was remarkable for its forest of columns in Aquitainian marble, for the goldwork on the ceiling and for its atrium and porticos. To the north of the cathedral, excavations have uncovered the remains of the churches of St Etienne and Ste Croix, destroyed during the Revolution. They are set out behind a wall 1.80 m thick. The earliest distinguishable structure comprises two rectangular chambers, heated by radiant ducts, dating from the first half and middle of the 4th century. The small, south chamber became a baptistery dedicated to St Etienne at the end of the 4th century, with the construction of an octagonal cistern. It was succeeded by a cruciform church with three eastern apses, transept, short nave and porch, probably in the Carolingian, but certainly by the Romanesque period; and this church was enlarged towards the west in the 12th and 13th centuries. The remains of Ste Croix to the north are fragmentary, consisting of a broken mosaic pavement and remnants of walls. A large, aisled church without a transept was built in the 11th and 12th centuries and rebuilt on the same foundations in the mid-15th century. To the south, remains of the apse of the *maxima ecclesia*, dedicated to St John the Baptist, lie under the crossing of the existing cathedral. There were five building campaigns from the 5th century to the 12th: under Bishop Patiens in 469, in the Merovingian period, in the time of Bishop Leidrade at the beginning of the 9th century and in the 11th and early 12th centuries with the mosaic of Bishop Gaucerand.

(b) Cathedral of St Jean. Renovated at the beginning of the 12th century, the cathedral was rebuilt from 1170 to 1180 by Bishop Guichard. Construction began at the east. The conservatism of the canons is apparent in such archaisms as a bench for the clergy round the inside of the apse; in the very traditional plan (a seven-sided polygonal apse leading out of a straight-ended choir, with squared-off side chapels); and in the style, which is still Romanesque, with blind arcading, fluted pilasters in the triforium, and triple windows in the straight bays recalling those of the cathedrals of Lausanne and Geneva.

The Gothic style first appears in the transept (with pointed arches in the triforium). Regional traditions are, however, maintained with square towers over the transept ends, as at Aosta (Italy), Champagne (Ardèche) and Saint-Chef (Dauphiné); and local conservatism is seen in the use of sexpartite vaulting in the nave, which may indicate that Lyon, like Dijon Cathedral, was one of the group of buildings, identified by Bony, that resisted the solutions used at Chartres Cathedral. The clerestory passage (on the exterior in the choir, interior in the transept and nave) shows the influence of the northern Ile-de-France. The nave was built during the 13th century, the two western half-bays dating from the end of the 14th century. The chapel of the Bourbons, built in the second half of the 15th century on the south side of the nave, is the most beautiful example of Flamboyant in the Lyonnais.

The exterior is built in fine masonry with re-used Romanesque ashlar at the east end. The west façade is more sober in design than those further north: it is bare, with a flat wall without buttresses and the whole is articulated by a single horizontal line, the balustrade over the portals. To the south-west stands the Manécanterie, a Romanesque construction with delicately carved arcades.

BIBLIOGRAPHY

R. L. Begule and M. C. Guigue: *Monographie de la cathédrale de Lyon* (Lyon, 1880)

M. Aubert: 'Lyon, Cathédrale', *Congr. Archéol. France*, xcviii (1935), pp. 54–90

J. Bony: 'The Resistance to Chartres in Early Thirteenth-century Architecture', *J. Brit. Archaeol Assoc.*, n. s. 3, xx–xxi (1957–8), pp. 35–52

J. F. Reynaud: 'Lyon du IVe au XVIIIe siècle: Edifices religieux, nécropoles et topographie urbaine', *Recherches récentes en archéologie gallo-romaine et paléochrétienne sur Lyon et sa région*, ed. S. Walker, Brit. Archaeol. Rep., International Series, cviii (1981), pp. 119–56

——: 'Le baptistère Saint-Etienne du groupe episcopal de Lyon', *Actes du Xe congrès international d'archéologie chrétienne: Thessalonike, 1984*, pp. 463–75

——: *Lugdunum Christianum: Lyon du IVe au VIIIe siècle: Topographie, nécropoles et édifices religieux* (in preparation)

*(ii) Sculpture.* Fragments of early medieval sculpture were found during excavations. They include pieces of palm-tree ornament, perhaps bordering a central cross and dating from the 6th or 7th century, from the site of St Etienne and numerous choir-screen fragments bearing interlace decoration from the *maxima ecclesia*, some of which are preserved *in situ*. Mosaic pavements were discovered during the excavation of the earlier apse under the crossing of the cathedral in 1935. An ornamental border, showing a chain motif, is still in place along the interior curve of the apse, while a fairly large fragment, depicting a tower and the start of an inscription, is preserved under a later wall to the south-west of the apse. This work has been compared to other mosaics in the Rhône Valley (e.g. Cruas, Abbey Church, 1098; Saint-Paul-Trois-Châteaux) and dated to the early 12th century.

At the east end of the cathedral, Romanesque sculptors from Vienne were probably responsible for the white marble friezes with red mastic inlay and the expressive animal heads and base spurs, dating from the last quarter of the 12th century. Parallels can be drawn between sculpture at St André-le-Bas, Vienne, which shows antique influence, and the capitals of the lower apse arcade of the cathedral at Lyon (e.g. Christ with his hands raised beneath the corners of the capital, the Adoration of the Magi and the Bathing of the Infant Christ). Four reliefs are set into the west façade of the Manécanterie, perhaps representing the Liberal Arts. Their style (supple draperies combined with monumental but relaxed poses) suggests that the figures date from the second quarter of the 12th century.

The cathedral is famous for the 325 reliefs decorating the embrasures of the west portals, which date from the episcopate (1308–22) of Pierre de Savoie. The medallions, mostly quatrefoils, are executed in low relief and arranged in seven tiers. They include episodes from the Old and New Testaments, the lives of saints (particularly the patrons SS John and Peter), bestiaries and scenes of everyday life, treated with great animation; the delicacy of composition and execution is reminiscent of manuscript illumination. The sculptures may possibly be related to the reliefs on the transept portals of Rouen Cathedral. The sculpted consoles flanking the portals bear the finest examples of Gothic sculpture in Lyon. The reliefs representing frolicking lovers from the Lai d'Aristote are remarkable for their subtle modelling and the composition of the figures in relation to the frame. The tympana of the portals were lost during the Wars of Religion (1562–98).

BIBLIOGRAPHY

R. L. Begule and M. C. Guigue: *Monographie de la cathédrale de Lyon* (Lyon, 1880)

M. Aubert: 'Lyon, cathédrale', *Congr. Archéol. France*, xcviii (1935), pp. 54–90

R. Jullian: 'Lyon et l'Italie au moyen âge: Histoire et art', *Rev. Etud. It.*, n.s., v/2–3 (1958), pp. 133–46

J. F. REYNAUD

**Lyon, Corneille de.** *See* CORNEILLE DE LYON.

**Lyon, Danny** (*b* Brooklyn, NY, 16 March 1942). American photographer and film maker. He began photographing in 1962 and became the staff photographer for the Student Nonviolent Coordinating Committee (SNCC). From images of racial strife taken during this time Lyon produced two books, which reported on contemporary American culture and political life. In 1967 he published his first important photographic essay, *The Bikeriders*, a look at the Chicago Outlaws, a renegade motorcycle club. As an independent photographer he worked in Latin America, photographing prostitutes in Colombia and experimenting with colour for the first time.

In 1967 Lyon began to work for the photographic agency Magnum. He assisted Robert Frank in 1969 on the film *Life Raft Earth*, then produced the films *Social Science 127* and *Llanito*. These projects were followed by *Conversations with the Dead* in 1971, a book that is his best-known work and that shows life in Texan prisons through Lyon's strong images and texts written by the inmates. During the 1970s Lyon continued to make films. In 1980 he published *The Paper Negative*, an autobiographical account of life in New Mexico as told through a fictional character, and in 1981 *Pictures from the New World*, a retrospective of his photographic career. Lyon's photographs are motivated by a combination of humanism and militancy and often picture downtrodden people as social heroes. He followed the tradition of personal interactive journalism also found in the work of Robert Frank and, like Larry Clark, involved himself in the lives he photographed in order to evince an uncompromising realism.

PHOTOGRAPHIC PUBLICATIONS

*The Bikeriders* (New York, 1967)
*Conversations with the Dead* (New York, 1969)
*Pictures from the New World* (Millerton, 1981)

BIBLIOGRAPHY

*Danny Lyon, Photo, Film* (exh. cat., ed. U. Eskildsen and T. Pitts; Heidelberg, 1991)

SHERYL CONKELTON

**Lyrical Abstraction.** *See* ART INFORMEL and TACHISM.

**Lys, Johann.** *See* LISS, JOHANN.

**Lysippides Painter.** *See* VASE PAINTERS, §II.

**Lysippos** (*fl c.* 370–*c.* 300 BC). Greek sculptor. He was the greatest sculptor from the school at Sikyon, then an artistic centre second only to Athens, and ancient sources classed him with Myron of Eleutherai, Pheidias and Polykleitos.

1. Career. 2. Works.

1. CAREER. Establishing accurate dates for Lysippos' career is problematic, both because no original works survive and because of disputes over the attribution of copies and the dates of signed statue bases. Pliny dated the height of his activity to 328–325 BC (XXXIV.xix.51) because of his close connection with Alexander the Great. Other literary and epigraphic sources, however, indicate that he had a long and active career that probably spanned much of the 4th century BC.

Lysippos was probably influenced by the Sikyonian painter Eupompos (*fl c.* 410–*c.* 310 BC), but there is no evidence that they were contemporaries. A statue of Troilos, set up at Olympia to commemorate equestrian victories in 372 BC, was ascribed to Lysippos by Pausanias (*Guide to Greece* VI.i.4–5) and is often cited as his earliest work. The letter forms of the dedicatory inscription may, however, be as late as 350 BC. Nonetheless, a signed base found at Delphi (see Marcadé, i, p. 66) naming Lysippos as the sculptor of a statue of the Theban general Pelopidas (*c.* 410–364 BC) indicates that he was active by the 360s BC. Although it is difficult to identify other individual mid-4th-century BC works, by the 340s BC his reputation was such that he was summoned to Pella to become Alexander's court sculptor. Towards 340 BC he also completed a family monument for the Thessalian dynast Daochos (*fl c.* 338–*c.* 334 BC) at Pharsalos. In addition to sculpting a series of portraits of Alexander, which began with him as a boy, Lysippos produced an elaborate monument commemorating the deaths of 25 of Alexander's entourage at the Battle of the River Granikos in 334 BC (see Arrian: *Anabasis* I.xvi.4), the only securely dated work of his connected with Alexander. He later worked with the sculptor LEOCHARES on a monument at Delphi depicting the lion hunt of Alexander and Krateros (Plutarch: *Alexander* xl.4). The dedicatory inscription indicates that, though the monument was vowed by Krateros before his death in 321 BC, it was erected some time later by his son. Epigraphic evidence suggests that the sculptural group was probably completed in the 3rd century BC, perhaps after Lysippos' death. It appears, however, that he was still active as a sculptor after Alexander's death, since he produced special jars for the export of Mendaian wine after Kassander (*c.* 358–*c.* 297 BC) had established his new capital of Kassandreia in 316 BC (Athenaeus: *Deipnosophists* xi.784c). It is uncertain when Lysippos' career ended, although a signed base for a statue of Seleukos I (*c.* 358–281 BC), with the epithet *basileos*, may be one of his last works (see E. Löwy: *Inschriften griechischer Bildhauer*, Leipzig, 1885, no. 487), since Seleukos adopted this royal title in 306 BC. The epithet may, however, have been added by a Roman copyist. Lysippos certainly lived to a good age and was referred to as an 'old man' (*Palatine Anthology* XVI.332). Petronius' story (*Satyricon* LXXXVIII) that he died of starvation as he brooded over a statue should be discounted.

2. WORKS. Lysippos began his career as a bronzesmith (Pliny: XXXIV.xix.61), and most, if not all, of his statues were of bronze. He was exceptionally prolific (Pliny: XXXIV.xvi.37): reputed to have set aside a gold coin for every statue that he completed, he had apparently accumulated 1500 coins by his death. As head of a large workshop, however, he had many students, some of whom worked in a style that was indistinguishable from his own (Pliny: XXXIV.xix.66–7). Unfortunately, despite the number and exceptional quality of his works, not a single original statue survives. Many Roman copies have been attributed to Lysippan originals on the basis of ancient descriptions of his works and style, though few of these attributions are sound.

Lysippos' repertory was varied and included portraits and statues of deities, athletes, heroes and animals. Among his most famous was a statue of a youth scraping himself, which so enthralled the emperor Tiberius that he had it removed to his bedroom, though the displeasure of the Roman people forced him to restore it to its original location. This statue is generally associated with a Roman marble copy, the *Apoxyomenos* (Rome, Vatican, Mus. Pio-Clementino; see fig.), which has the characteristics of Lysippos' style listed by Pliny (XXXIV.xix.65): a small head, slim body, long legs and carefully modelled hair. A marble statue of *Agias*, one of nine sculptures that originally composed the family monument of Daochos II in Delphi (*c.* 338–*c.* 334 BC; Delphi, Archaeol. Mus.; *see also* GREECE, ANCIENT, fig. 64), was probably a contemporary copy of the Lysippan original at Pharsalos, since it was accompanied by a similar epigram. Given Lysippos' preference for bronze, however, he probably did not execute the *Agias* himself, and there is even controversy as to whether it reflects his style. The *Apoxyomenos* and the *Agias* certainly differ, in that the *Agias* is squarer with softer musculature and less carefully modelled hair. The *Agias* may belong to a different phase in Lysippos' career or even be the work of a pupil.

Lysippos: *Apoxymenos*, marble copy of lost original of *c*. 330 BC, h. 2.05 m (Rome, Vatican, Museo Pio-Clementino)

Lysippos made many statues of Zeus, including a colossal bronze at Tarentum over 40 cubits (20.22 m) high. His bronze *Zeus* in the agora at Sikyon may be depicted on a Sikyonian coin of Imperial date (see Sjöqvist, 1966, fig. 18) showing the god nude, holding a thunderbolt in his right hand and a sceptre in his left. Other ancient coins may depict his bronze *Zeus* at Argos as well as his statue of the god at Megara (Pausanias: II.xx.3 and I.xliii.6). A bronze *Poseidon*, which Lysippos made for the Corinthians, was mentioned by Lucian (*Zeus Tragoedus* 9), and other statues of divinities included a *Dionysos* on Mt Helicon in Boiotia, a youthful *Eros* made for the Thespians and *Helios in a Chariot* at Rhodes. His many statues of Herakles were famous, especially the *Weary Herakles Resting after his Labours* (Libanios: *Descriptions* xv). Over 50 statues, torsos and heads copy this work, the most notable being the marble statue in Florence (Uffizi).

Detailed descriptions of Lysippos' *Herakles Epitrapezios* (Martial: *Epigrams* IX.43–4.; Statius: *Silvae* IV.vi.32–58) indicate that this bronze statuette (a table ornament) depicted the hero seated on a rock covered by lion skin holding a wine-cup in his right hand and a club in his left (copy in London, BM). The work was admired by Alexander and its base carried Lysippos' signature. Other statues of Herakles included a colossus at Tarentum, a bronze at Sikyon, a group in Alyzia in Akarnania depicting the labours and *Herakles Overcome by Love*. Lysippos' celebrated allegorical statue of *Kairos* (Opportunity) brilliantly captured the ephemeral nature of its subject: a winged youth stood on tiptoe on a sphere, his right hand holding a razor, his left a balance; long hair curled beside his face, but his head was bald behind (Kallistratos: *Descriptions* vi.897–8; see also the copy on a relief, Turin, Mus. Civ. A. Ant.; *see* ICONOGRAPHY AND ICONOLOGY, fig. 3).

Lysippos' many portraits included ones depicting Alexander's friend Hephaistion, the Theban poetess Praxilla, Aesop of Samos and two portraits of the soldier Pythes. His bronze of Socrates may be represented by a bust in Rome (Mus. N. Romano) and the 'Socrates Statue' of a seated philosopher (Copenhagen, Ny Carlsberg Glyp.). His best-known portraits were of Alexander, capturing the manliness and majesty of their subject so effectively that Alexander allegedly permitted no other sculptor to depict him (Plutarch: *Alexander* iv.1). Lysippos also made victory statues at Olympia for the famous pancratiast Polydamas of Skotoussa, the charioteer Troilos, the wrestler Cheilon, the armed runner Kallikrates and the pancratiast Xenarches.

Lysippos' style is elusive, since there are no certain copies of his works and the references in ancient literary sources are difficult to interpret. According to Cicero (*Brutus* lxxxvi.296) he studied under no one but learnt from the *Doryphoros* of Polykleitos (*see* POLYKLEITOS, §1), so that its structural qualities may have influenced his early work. Pliny (XXXIV.xix.61, 65) stated, however, that Lysippos argued for working not from other artists' works but from nature. Thus, whereas earlier sculptors had depicted men as they were, he showed them as they appeared to be. Lysippos' efforts to imitate nature led him to introduce a new canon of proportions with slimmer figures with smaller heads, making his statues appear taller. His chief characteristic was his skill in imparting vitality even to his sculptures' smallest details (Pliny: XXXIV.xix.65), and later sources commented that his works lacked only movement and breath.

BIBLIOGRAPHY
Pauly–Wissowa
Pliny: *Natural History*
J. Overbeck: *Die antiken Schriftquellen* (Leipzig, 1868/R Hildesheim, 1959), nos 1443–1512
T. Homolle: 'Lysippe et l'ex-voto de Daochos', *Bull. Corr. Hell.*, xxiii (1899), pp. 421–85
P. Gardner: 'The *Apoxyomenos* of Lysippus', *J. Hell. Stud.*, xxv (1905), pp. 234–59
F. P. Johnson: *Lysippos* (Durham, NC, 1927)
C. H. Morgan: 'The Style of Lysippos', *Hesperia*, viii (1949) [suppl.], pp. 228–34
E. Sjöqvist: 'The Early Style of Lysippus', *Opuscula Athen.*, i (1953), pp. 87–97
J. Marcadé: *Recueil des signatures de sculpteurs grecs*, 2 vols (Paris, 1953–7)

E. Sjöqvist: 'Lysippus', *Lectures in Memory of Louise Taft Semple*, ii (Cincinnati, 1966)

T. Dohrn: 'Die Marmor-Standbilder des Daochos-Weihgeschenks in Delphi', *Ant. Plast.*, viii (1968), pp. 33–53

P. Moreno: *Testimonianze per la teoria artistica di Lisippo* (Treviso, 1973)

C. Vermeule: 'The Weary Herakles of Lysippos', *Amer. J. Archaeol.*, lxxix (1975), pp. 323–32

A. F. Stewart: 'Lysippan Studies', *Amer. J. Archaeol.*, lxxxii (1978), pp. 163–71, 301–13, 473–82

NANCY SERWINT

**Lysippus the younger** (*fl* Rome, *c.* 1470–84). Italian medallist. The identity of this medallist, who named himself after the ancient Greek sculptor Lysippos of Sikyon, has not been established, although Raffaele Maffei in 1506 (*Commentariorum urbanorum* (Rome, 1506), xxi, p. 300 *v*) said he was the nephew of the Mantuan medallist Cristoforo di Geremia. Maffei referred to him by his pseudonym, and two of his medals are signed with this name, one of them, that of *Martinus Phileticus*, Professor of Greek at Rome, in Greek. Maffei also stated that in his youth Lysippus produced a medal of *Sixtus IV*, and it would appear that Lysippus spent his career at the papal court in Rome, modelling a large number of medallic portraits of papal officials.

Lysippus's style is established by the two signed medals, that of *Martinus Phileticus* (*c.* 1473; Hill, *Corpus*, no. 789) and one of *Giulio Marascha*, known only from a 17th-century engraving (H 788). Working from these two medals, approximately 28 others have been attributed to Lysippus. They are distinguished by inscriptions in fine, clear and balanced classical lettering, both Greek and Latin; the frequent use of a heavy foliate moulded border; a delicate, detached leaf or pair of leaves; and a consistency of portrait types. They usually show a young cleric with longish hair wearing a round cap and a high-necked gown. The truncation of the bust is almost always hollow, steeply curved and ends in a sharp point at the sternum. Although the busts are standardized and have a rather static quality, the portraits themselves are sensitively modelled, refined and individualized.

From his classical pseudonym and the style and iconography of his work, Lysippus the younger appears to have been a member of a humanist circle in Rome. The subject-matter of the reverses of his medals is neither imaginative nor visually exciting and includes simple inscriptions, heraldic devices, classical figures derived from Roman coins, and emblems. The reverse of the *Phileticus* medal, the Pelican in her Piety, is copied from Pisanello's medal of *Vittorino da Feltre* (H 38).

Two of the medals attributed to Lysippus, those of *Catelano Casali of Bologna* (H 790) and *Raffaello Riario, Cardinal of San Giorgio* (H 791), are dated 1478. Among the medals attributed to him, several are representative of his style: *Malitia Gesualdi* (Hill, *Corpus*, no. 795), *Francesco Massimi* (H 799), *Sixtus IV* (H 806) and a series of medals of the jurist and poet *Giovanni Alvise Toscani* (*d* 1475), of which the largest (72 mm; H 812) is one of his most impressive works. Somewhat atypical of his work, though generally included in his oeuvre, is the large medal of *Raffaele Maffei da Volterra* (H 797), which does not have the characteristic sharp truncation of the bust, but which is otherwise very much in Lysippus's style, and that of *Giovanni Battista Orsini* (H 801), which, although similar

in many respects to the Maffei medal, is even less like Lysippus's known style.

One securely attributed medal has often been proposed as Lysippus the younger's self-portrait. It depicts a young man facing left with a ring of curly hair showing beneath the edge of a round hat and wearing a high-necked, buttoned gown (H 796). The inscription, DI LA IL BEL VISO E QUI IL TVO SERVO MIRA ('On that side admire your own beautiful visage and on this that of your servant'), implies that the plain reverse was originally polished as a mirror in which his lovers could catch their own reflection.

BIBLIOGRAPHY

Forrer

J. Friedländer: *Die italienischen Schaumünzen des fünfzehnten Jahrhunderts* (Berlin, 1880/R Bologna, 1976), pp. 126–7

A. Armand: *Les Médailleurs italiens des quinzième et seizième siècles* (Paris, 1883/R Bologna, 1966), pp. 54–6

C. von Fabriczy: *Medaillen der italienischen Renaissance* (Leipzig, 1903), pp. 79–80

G. F. Hill: 'The Medallist Lysippus', *Burl. Mag.*, xiii (1908), pp. 274–86; xvi (1909), pp. 25–6

G. Habich: *Die Medaillen der italienischen Renaissance* (Stuttgart, 1924), pp. 82–3

G. F. Hill: *Corpus*, i (1930), pp. 205–11 [H]

R. Weiss: 'Une Médaille à demi connue de Lysippus le jeune', *Schweiz. Münzbl.*, x/37 (1960), pp. 7–10

G. F. Hill and G. Pollard: *Renaissance Medals from the Samuel H. Kress Collection at the National Gallery of Art* (London, 1967), p. 43

G. Pollard: *Italian Renaissance Medals in the Museo Nazionale del Bargello*, i (Florence, 1984), pp. 334–41

*The Currency of Fame: Portrait Medals of the Renaissance* (exh. cat., ed. S. K. Scher; Washington, DC, N.G.A.; New York, Frick; 1994), pp. 120–21, 387

STEPHEN K. SCHER

**Lysistratos** (*fl* later 4th century BC). Greek sculptor, brother of LYSIPPOS. Pliny dated the artist, like his brother, from Sikyon, to the 113th Olympiad (328–325 BC) and wrote that he developed a method of taking plaster casts from the human body and face, then pouring wax into this to produce a perfect portrait likeness that was ready for moulding and casting. (Early studies of Greek bronze-casting misinterpreted this to mean that he actually invented the indirect method of lost-wax casting, which is clearly untrue: the indirect method is known in large-scale sculpture two full centuries before.) Surviving bronzes from this and the Hellenistic period suggest that these wax likenesses were almost certainly selectively retouched in order to heighten key features and so bring out the character of the sitter.

Nevertheless, Pliny's observation that portraits thenceforth aimed at likeness rather than beauty is correct, for Hellenistic sculptors usually began with the individual rather than taking an ideal type and individualizing it to a greater or lesser extent, as earlier. Lysistratos also used master-moulds for overcasting variations on the same type, and he and his brother certainly made innovations in casting technique (such as smaller piece-moulds and thinner plates of wax) which enabled them to use less bronze per statue. His technique of overcasting was enthusiastically adopted by Hellenistic and Roman copyists, who used it to cast replicas, thinly disguised versions or pastiches of existing statues (*see* ROME, ANCIENT, §IV, 1(iii)(c)). Lysistratos' only attested portrait was of *Melanippe the Wise*: evidently he was more of a technician than a sculptor in his own right.

BIBLIOGRAPHY

Pliny: *Nat. Hist.* XXXIV.51 and XXXV.153

P. C. Bol: *Antike Bronzetechnik* (Munich, 1985), pp. 124–5

D. Haynes: *The Technique of Greek Bronze Statuary* (Mainz, 1992), pp. 42–7

For further bibliography *see* LYSIPPOS.

ANDREW F. STEWART

**Lythrankomi, Panagia Kanikaria.** Byzantine church on the Karpas peninsula of Cyprus *c.* 85 km north-east of Nicosia. The original basilica church was probably constructed in the late 5th century and restored after the Arab raids of the mid-7th. A second major restoration, perhaps after an earthquake *c.* 1160, is attributed to the late 12th century, when the church received a narthex, a dome and three barrel-vaulted aisles.

This building is known principally for a fragmentary mosaic (probably *c.* AD 526–30; untraced), formerly preserved in the irregularly shaped conch of the apse until it was stolen between 1974 and 1979. It originally occupied the entire conch and was composed of a central mandorla showing the Virgin seated on a lyre-back throne with the Child on her lap. The combination of these iconographical elements has been interpreted as a relatively early depiction of the Incarnation, a theme apparently originating from Constantinople (Megaw and Hawkins). The presence of the mandorla may also have signified an assertion of Chalcedonian doctrine (Sacopoulo). An archangel and a palm-tree were depicted on either side of the mandorla; 12 medallion busts of the Apostles and one of St Paul were on the fore-edge of the conch. Ten of these portraits were completely or partly preserved and identified by inscription. The mosaic combines both formalizing and classicizing stylistic elements.

Among the fresco fragments still *in situ* are those of the *Archangel Gabriel* and *St Barbara* (late 12th century), the figure of *St George* executed during the 13th-century reconstruction of the south aisle and a *Last Judgement* attributed to the 14th century. About 1500 the dome was rebuilt on new supporting arches and a programme of repainting was undertaken in the central part of the church, of which the *Pantocrator*, the *Nativity*, the *Annunciation*, the *Ascension* and individual figures survive.

BIBLIOGRAPHY

A. Stylianou and J. Stylianou: *The Painted Churches of Cyprus* (Stourbridge, 1964); rev. as *The Painted Churches of Cyprus: Treasures of Byzantine Art* (London, 1985), pp. 43–8

M. Sacopoulo: *La Théotokos à la mandorle de Lythrankomi* (Paris, 1975)

A. H. S. Megaw and E. J. W. Hawkins: *The Church of the Panagia Kanakariá at Lythrankomi: Its Mosaics and Frescoes*, Dumbarton Oaks Studies, xiv (Washington, DC, 1977)

SUSAN YOUNG

**Lytras, Nikiforos** (*b* Tinos, 1832; *d* Athens, 14 June 1904). Greek painter and teacher. He studied at the School of Fine Arts in Athens (1850–56) and then at the Akademie der Bildenden Künste in Munich (1860–1865) under Karl Theodor von Piloty. Among his fellow pupils were Hans Makart, Franz Defregger, Franz von Lenbach and Wilhelm Leibl. Returning to Athens in 1866, Lytras became professor of painting in the Art School of the Polytechnic. The subjects of Lytras's first paintings are historical and mythological, for example the *Burning of the Turkish Flag-ship by Canaris* (1866–70), *Antigone Confronted with the Dead Polynices* (1865; Athens, N. Gal.). After 1870, however, he turned to genre painting and portraits, responding to the wishes of the wealthy members of the new Athenian bourgeoisie. Characteristic examples from this period include *Return from the Fair at Penteli* (*c.* 1870; Athens, N.G.), of primarily sociological interest; *The Kalanda Carol Singing* (1870–75; Athens, Serpieri Col.); *Lamentation at Psara* (*c.* 1880; Athens, N.G.) with a strong folkloric character; and portraits such as that of *Lysander Kavtandzoglou* (1885–90; Athens, N.G.). Lytras was one of the main Greek representatives of the Munich-trained painters. Although he adhered to the tenets of academic realism, he was able to bring to his work a significant element of personal distinction.

BIBLIOGRAPHY

N. Athanassoglou: *Oi Ellines zografoi apo ton 19o aiona ston 20o* [Greek painters from the 19th century to the 20th] (Athens, 1974), i, pp. 100–37

——: *O zografos Nikiforos Lytras* [The painter Nikiforos Lytras] (diss., U. Athens, 1976)

C. Christou: *Elliniki zographiki, 1832–1922* [Greek painting, 1832–1922] (Athens, 1981), pp. 44–9

N. Misirli: *Elliniki zographiki, 18os–19os aionas* [Greek painting, 18th–19th century] (Athens, 1993), pp. 70–85, 206–7

ALKIS CHARALAMPIDIS

**Lyubitel'.** *See* ETTINGER, PAVEL.

**Lyveden.** English centre of ceramic production. Excavations have revealed potters' settlements dating to between the 13th century and early 15th at Lyveden in the Rockingham Forest, Northants. The tenements incorporated workshops with hearths, deposits of unused clay in stone-lined pits, drains, industrial waste, kilns, knives, hones and a bone stamp. Sometimes clays from within the tenement boundary were used with such tempers as crushed shell and limestone. Decoration embellished several forms and included rouletting and applied strips on kitchen wares and white slip and applied pads on jugs. Forms included cooking pots, bowls, shallow dishes, cisterns, curfews and building materials.

BIBLIOGRAPHY

J. M. Steane and G. F. Bryant: 'Excavations at the Deserted Medieval Settlement at Lyveden, Northants', *J. Northampton Mus. & A.G.*, xii (1975) [whole issue]

MICHAEL R. McCARTHY

# M

**Ma.** Chinese family of painters. The Ma family was from Hezhong (modern Yongqi) in Shanxi Province. They established an unbroken line of five generations of artists: Ma Fen (*b* 1080–90); Ma Xingzu (*b* 1105–15); Ma Gongxian and Ma Shirong (*b* 1130–40); (1) Ma Yuan (*d* after 1225); Ma Kui (*b* 1155–65); and (2) Ma Lin (*d* after 1256). This continuity appears to have resulted from a decree (1056) of the emperor Renzong (*reg* 1023–63) to the effect that court painters were forbidden to transfer into the regular system of civil service and the advancement this implied, 'so that their arts can be handed down and specialized for generations to come' (see 1980–81 exh. cat., p. xxviii).

BIBLIOGRAPHY

*Eight Dynasties of Chinese Painting: The Collections of the Nelson Gallery–Atkins Museum of Art, Kansas City, and the Cleveland Museum of Art* (exh. cat. by Wai-kam Ho and others, Kansas City, MO, Nelson–Atkins Mus. A.; Cleveland, OH, Mus. A.; Tokyo, N. Mus.; 1980–81)

**(1) Ma Yuan** [*zi* Qinshan] (*b* Qiantang, Lin'an [modern Hangzhou], Zhejiang Province, *c.* 1155; *d* after 1225). Together with XIA GUI, he is often mentioned in Chinese criticism as epitomizing the highest level of painting at the Southern Song (1127–1279) Academy centred in Lin'an (within the area of modern Hangzhou), Zhejiang Province (*see* CHINA, §V, 4(i)(c)).

There is no clear account of Ma Yuan's life. He appears to have served as *zhihou* (usher) and *daizhao* (painter in attendance) under three emperors: Guangzong (*reg* 1190–94), Ningzong (*reg* 1195–1224) and Lizong (*reg* 1225–64). He was certainly a mature and celebrated painter by 1200. In that year Ningzong's favourite concubine, surnamed Yang (1162–1232), was elevated to empress and thereafter, as a skilled calligrapher and patron of the arts, often added inscriptions and seals to Ma Yuan's paintings. For example, the small, unsigned hanging scroll *Solitary Fisherman* (Tokyo, N. Mus.) bears such a seal with the name of the empress's palace, Kunning, and a date corresponding to 1211. The handscroll *Twelve Scenes of Water* (Beijing, Pal. Mus.) bears a seal with a legend referring either to the year 1200 or 1222. This scroll also bears an inscription noting that it was presented to the *da liangfu* ('elder two authorities'), a term for the two heads of the military and civilian administration, further confirming that Ma Yuan's art reached the highest official circles. Empress Yang's calligraphy or seals occur on a further important group of Ma Yuan paintings, including the two flower studies *Apricot* and *Peach*, *Banquet by Lantern Light* and *On a Mountain Path in Spring* (all Taipei, N. Pal. Mus.), as well as on the

hanging scrolls depicting 9th- and 10th-century Chan Buddhist patriarchs *Yunmen* and *Fayan* (both Kyoto, Tenryūji) and *Dongshan* (Tokyo, N. Mus.). Ma Yuan was a friend of Zhang Zi (1153–*c.* 1212), a wealthy aristocrat, official and sometime recluse noted for his elegant gardens and the lavish entertainments held there. In a poem for Ma Yuan, inspired by the painting *View beneath Groves*, which he had commissioned, he equated Ma's passion for painting with his own passion for poetry.

Ma Yuan's paintings themselves indicate what motivated his art. His subjects are consistent with courtly taste: paintings described above depict evening entertainment in an elegant villa, a flowering branch that might have grown in the garden of such a villa and the scholarly aristocrat in nature. His relationship with Chan Buddhism is reflected not only in the portraits of Tang-period (AD 618–907) patriarchs, but also in his somewhat enigmatic treatment of ordinary subjects, such as the quiet huddle of birds in *Egrets in the Snow* (Taipei, N. Pal. Mus.) and the chilled fuel-gatherer in *Through Snowy Mountains at Dawn* (late 12th century; see fig.). Confucian tradition influenced Ma Yuan's *Two Scholars under a Plum Tree* (Boston, MA, Mus. F.A.), as well as two scrolls often attributed to him: *Composing Poetry on a Spring Outing* (Kansas City, MO, Nelson–Atkins Mus. A.; a recent hypothesis connects this painting with Zhang Zi's garden) and *Four Sages of Mt Shang* (Cincinnati, OH, A. Mus.). The world of the immortals is treated in *Riding a Dragon* (Taipei, N. Pal. Mus.) or in the representation of the Daoist figure *Lü Dongbin* (Chongqing, Mun. Mus.), and the three sages of Buddhism, Daoism and Confucianism (Shakyamuni, Laozi and Confucius) were depicted in *Three Teachings*, a painting no longer extant mentioned by the 13th-century critic Zhou Mi. There are also paintings of more complete landscapes, notably *Bare Willows and Distant Mountains* (Boston, MA, Mus. F.A.) and the attributed *Landscape in Wind and Rain* (Tokyo, Seikadō Bunko). A recently discovered album (New York, C. C. Wang priv. col.) may further expand the range of this genre.

Ma Yuan's style is particularly characteristic. Words in Chinese criticism used to define it convey notions of condensed concentration: 'exact severity' (*yanzheng*), charcoal or 'burnt ink' (*jiaomo*) and 'squeezed brush' (*jiabi*). His rocks are described as 'square and hard' (*fangying*), and a sharp jab of the brush in defining surfaces, especially of mountain and rock, is termed 'axe-stroke' (*fupi*). His line might be short, broken and abbreviated; the term 'nail-head, rat tail' (*dingtou shuwei*) is applied to

Ma Yuan: *Through Snowy Mountains at Dawn*, album leaf, ink and colours on silk, 276×400 mm, late 12th century (Taipei, National Palace Museum)

it, meaning a line that begins strongly and then tapers. Modern scholars have noted his use of a vibrant stroke known as 'tremulous brush' (*zhanbi*).

A striking feature of Ma Yuan's compositions is the emphasis on one corner. The earliest traced comment on this is from the critic Rao Ziran (*fl c.* 1340), who pointed out that most compositions considered to be by Ma Yuan were 'side-cornered' (*bianjiao*), although there were also 'complete compositions' (*quanjing*). It was the former, however, that became most persistently associated with Ma; in the 15th century the term 'one-corner Ma' appeared. In the early part of the Ming period (1368–1644) the court painter Guo Shun (1370–1444) attached political meaning to Ma Yuan's striking brevity: 'the remains of mountains and rivers mean the partial peace of Song'.

Ma Yuan's style, along with that of Xia Gui, was a corner-stone for the development of the ZHE SCHOOL in the Ming period. By the early 17th century Dong Qichang had identified Ma Yuan with a category of painting he designated the NORTHERN SCHOOL, connoting lack of individual spontaneity and scholarly refinement. In modern times this narrow view is greatly questioned, and Ma Yuan is considered one of the giants of Chinese painting.

### BIBLIOGRAPHY

*EWA*: 'Ma Yüan'; Franke: 'Ma Yüan'
Zhou Mi: *Qi dong yeyu* [Eastern Qi jottings] (1291); *R* in *Lidai xiaoshi* (Shanghai, 1940), *juan* 59
Xia Wenyan: *Tuhui baojian* [Precious mirror for examining painting] (1365/*R* Shanghai, 1936)
O. Sirén: *Chinese Painting: Leading Masters and Principles* (London and New York, 1956–8), ii, pp. 112–19; iii, pls 284–91
Deng Bai and Wu Fuzhi: *Ma Yuan yu Xia Gui* [Ma Yuan and Xia Gui] (Shanghai, 1958)
*Song Ma Yuan shuitu* [Ma Yuan's water paintings] (Beijing, 1958)
M. Loehr: 'Chinese Paintings with Sung Dated Inscriptions', *A. Orient.*, iv (1961), pp. 253, 259–60, 269, 274
Chiang Chao-shen: 'The Identity of Yang Mei-tzu and the Painting of Ma Yüan', *N. Pal. Mus. Bull.*, ii/2 (May 1967), pp. 1–4; ii/3 (July 1967), pp. 9–14
Gao Huiyang: *Ma Yuan huihua zhi yanjiu* [Research on the painting of Ma Yuan] (Taipei, 1978)
M. Sullivan: 'Ma Yuan', *The New Encyclopedia Britannica: Macropaedia* (Chicago, 1979), xi, pp. 723–5
J. Cahill: *An Index of Early Chinese Painters and Painting: T'ang, Sung and Yüan* (Berkeley and Los Angeles, 1980), pp. 152–61
M. Loehr: *The Great Painters of China* (New York, 1980), pp. 199–207

**(2) Ma Lin** (*b* probably Qiantang, Lin'an (modern Hangzhou), Zhejiang Province, *c.* 1185; *d* after 1256). Son of (1) Ma Yuan. All that is known of Ma Lin relates to Lin'an, and it is assumed he was born and lived there most of his life. His painting activity was centred at the imperial academy in the city.

Short notices of Chinese criticism rate him less highly than his father. In the Academy he reached only the position of *zhihou* (usher) under Emperor Ningzong and never the more honoured position of *daizhao* (painter in attendance). Zhuang Su, in the earliest recorded mention of Ma Lin (1298), stated that he was less talented than both his uncle, Ma Kui, and his father, but that Ma Yuan, moved by affection, often signed 'Ma Lin' to his own

Ma Lin: *Fragrant Spring: Clearing after Rain*, album leaf, ink and colour on silk, 275×416 mm, early 13th century (Taipei, National Palace Museum)

paintings to bring his son fame; Xia Wenyan essentially repeats this information in *Tuhui baojian* ('Precious mirror for examining painting', 1365).

Certainly his father must have enabled Ma Lin to be accepted at court. Extant works, spanning a 40-year period, bear inscriptions or seals indicative of imperial patronage. Empress Yang inscribed Ma Lin's spare, selective *Plum Blossoms* (Beijing, Pal. Mus.) and imprinted it with a seal bearing a date equivalent to 1216. The complex, elegant album leaf, *Fragrant Spring: Clearing after Rain* (see fig.), bears no date, but the title was inscribed by either Empress Yang or Emperor Ningzong and thus cannot post-date the Empress's death in 1232. Ma Lin's *Listening to the Wind in the Pines* (Taipei, N. Pal. Mus.) carries the inscription of Emperor Lizong and a seal imprint with a date equivalent to 1246. *Evening* (Tokyo, Nezu A. Mus.) is also inscribed by Lizong and is dated 1254. The fan-shaped album leaf *Watching the Time the Clouds Arise* (Cleveland, OH, Mus. A.) bears calligraphy by Lizong dated 1256. Ma Lin's figure paintings include a series of 13 ancient heroes commissioned by Lizong in 1241 for the Imperial Academy and inscribed by him. Five of these survive (Taipei, N. Pal. Mus.), the first, *Fu Xi*, a hanging scroll (l. *c.* 2.5 m), bearing Ma Lin's signature.

Ma Lin's painting fits closely with the style established by Ma Yuan and perhaps even that of earlier members of the Ma family. However, his subtleties of individual expression bring his work to a level of excellence whereby it stands in its own right. A 17th-century recording of a colophon reads 'Ma Lin's brush concept was lofty and

antique; why need he take advantage of his father's great reputation?' (see Wang Keyu). Chen Ji (1370–1434) comments on two Ma Lin paintings of beautiful women (destr.), stating that the artist followed the 12th-century style of Jia Shigu, who in turn followed the almost legendary master of figure painting, Li Gonglin. A brilliant recorder of sensibilities at the close of a sophisticated era, Ma Lin extended his family style to its limits. His impeccable *Waiting for Guests by Lamplight* (Taipei, N. Pal. Mus.) develops Ma Yuan's conception of moonlight in a villa's garden, and *Evening* pushes his father's one-corner brevities to the very edge of non-definition.

### BIBLIOGRAPHY
Franke: 'Ma Lin'
Zhuang Su: *Hua ji buyi* [Painting continued: a supplement] (1298); *R* in *Hua ji, hua ji buyi* by Deng Chun and Zhuang Su (Beijing, 1963), p. 14
Xia Wenyan: *Tuhui baojian* [Precious mirror for examining painting] (1365/*R* Shanghai, 1936), p. 81
Wang Keyu: *Shanhu wang hualu* [The coral net: record of paintings] (1643/*R* Shanghai, 1936), ii, *juan* 5, p. 843
W. Speiser: 'Ma Lin', *Festschrift für Baron Eduard v. d. Heydt* (Ascona, 1952), pp. 40–57
O. Sirén: *Chinese Painting: Leading Masters and Principles* (London and New York, 1956–8), ii, pp. 117–18; iii, pls 292–4
J. Cahill: *An Index of Early Chinese Painters and Painting: T'ang, Sung and Yüan* (Berkeley and Los Angeles, 1980), pp. 148–51

RICHARD EDWARDS

**Ma'abad, Tell al-.** *See* UBAID, TELL AL-.

**Maas [Maes], Dirk** (*b* Haarlem, 12 Sept 1659; *d* Haarlem, 25 Dec 1717). Dutch painter, draughtsman and engraver. He was a pupil of Nicolaes Berchem and Hendrick

Mommers (1623–1693). He entered the Haarlem Guild of St Luke in 1678, later moving to The Hague, where he entered the Guild in 1697. He accompanied William III, Prince of Orange Nassau, to England and joined him on his Irish campaign. A large drawing of the *Battle of the Boyne*, signed and dated 1 July 1690 (Windsor Castle, Royal Lib.), served as the basis for an unknown number of paintings (e.g. Petworth House, W. Sussex, NT). He also made two engravings of the battle. He was back in the Netherlands by 1693 and apparently continued working for William III, decorating his hunting lodge at Soestdijk. He painted three versions of *William III Stag Hunting*, one dated 1696 (two in Apeldoorn, Pal. Het Loo; one in Dublin, N.G.). Most of Maas's pictures contain horses. His preferred subjects include cavalry skirmishes, hunting parties, horse fairs and, occasionally, winter scenes. Their settings are sometimes Italianate, but the costumes are usually northern and often military. His style stems from his teachers and from his friend Jan van Huchtenburg (1647–1733), who was an important influence, but his colour scheme, predominantly green, is more sombre than theirs. His numerous drawings are in red or black chalk, often with watercolour. A group of 33 in the Staatliche Graphische Sammlung in Munich includes watercolour pastoral landscapes and rapid chalk sketches of cavalry battles and military manoeuvres.

BIBLIOGRAPHY

Thieme–Becker

W. Bernt: *Niederländische Maler des 17. Jahrhunderts*, 3 vols (Munich, 1948, rev. 3/1969–70)

——: *Niederländische Zeichner des 17. Jahrhunderts*, 2 vols (Munich, 1957)

W. Wegner: *Die niederländischen Handzeichnungen des 15.–18. Jahrhunderts* (1973), i of *Kataloge der Staatlichen Graphischen Sammlung München* (Berlin, 1973–), pp. 102–4, pl. 289–300

GEORGE GORDON

**Maasai** [Masai]. Eastern Nilotic, Olmaa-speaking African people numbering *c.* 350,000, living in Kenya and Tanzania. Their pastoralist culture is related to that of several Olmaa-speaking groups, including the pastoral Samburu and the non-pastoral Arusha, Parakuyu and Njemps. The Maasai try to live off just their herds of cattle, goats and sheep but most in fact rely to some extent on employment and agriculture. They live in semi-arid plains, plateaux and open grasslands, shunning hilly country and forests as unsuitable for herding livestock. According to Maasai oral history and the archaeological record, they originated in the north near Lake Turkana, where they apparently separated from the ancestors of the modern Turkana and Kalenjin. They are the southernmost Nilotic speakers and, like the other Nilotes, absorbed a number of other peoples during their migrations.

1. BEADWORK. Since nomadic and semi-nomadic pastoralists carry few possessions with them, East African peoples, such as the Maasai, have made the human body the locus of artistic expression. The epitome of beauty is the well-ornamented warrior or the young married woman. Through dress, scarification, paint and jewellery the body becomes a mobile, three-dimensional art form and a significant identity-marker. Thus the most important artistic activity of the Maasai is ornamental beadwork in the form of jewellery and embroidery, mostly using glass beads imported from the Czech Republic. Although governed by conventions of form, colour and pattern, beadwork allows artists great creative freedom while enabling them collectively to express ideals and ideas of major importance to them as individuals and groups. They also incorporate wire, chain, plastic, leather, buttons and various recycled materials, including metal zip-fasteners, safety-pins and flashlight bulbs. Beadwork contains both two- and three-dimensional elements, incorporating flat patterns with sculptural construction and form. The geometric patterns consist of stripes, bands, registers, blocks, triangles and numerous shapes named after parts of the body, such as the eye, or after such objects as windows and stools. Only women and girls may create beadwork, although men and boys may make suggestions.

Body ornaments are concentrated around the neck and head, and include headbands, upper and lower earrings, chokers, collars and long ropes and bandoliers of beads or chain (see fig.). Cuffs and bangles are placed on the upper arms and wrists, sometimes leaving only the elbows bare. Belts, thigh- and calf-bands and anklets complete the assemblage of body attachments. Personal objects such as snuffboxes, fly-whisks, milk gourds and clothing, especially skirts and capes, are also decorated with beadwork. The Maasai style, which is brighter and more flamboyant than that of many neighbouring and related groups, is well displayed in wide and rigid, discoid collars, worn singly and in sets, which flap like the dewlap of a cow when a woman dances.

Ornamental beadwork is a visible manifestation of the thought patterns that organize the Maasai universe, being intimately connected with and reflecting their philosophy

Maasai woman with characteristic beadwork adornment; from a photograph by Duncan Willetts

and social structure. In Maasai thought the harmonious interaction of opposites is an ideal based on complementarity and alternation. Thus, for example, night and day, although opposite and mutually exclusive, complete each other through the cyclical alternation of dark and light. Male and female are unified through marriage, but their activities in life are alternative and complementary. Pastoralist and non-pastoralist complement each other economically through exchange, which is a form of alternation. These dualities, however, are mitigated by the potential of pairs to recombine into triads, thus allowing the manipulation and inclusion of exceptions or anomalies.

The organization of colour and pattern in Maasai beadwork follows this principle. The basic dual opposition is black and white or dark and light. In beadwork, black/white/red (with blue often used as the equivalent of black) forms the basic colour set called *narok* (black), which stands for the black aspect of God. The resulting pairs of opposites, black and white or dark and light (red/white, black/red), are the basis of colour organization in ornament. This conceptualization is used in visual descriptions of the natural environment, such as the coat patterns of domestic livestock, particularly cattle. The appropriate mixing or balance of colours and the names of patterns derive from the size and distribution of units of dark colour on a light ground or vice versa.

The opposite colour set to *narok*, equated to white, is variously known as *tara* (multicoloured in small units), *imuatat* (meaning the tightly twined sections of a sheep-pen as well as cells of colour) and *muain sidain* ('beautiful colours', the sets of colours that look best together). It is composed of pairs of complementary colours, namely green/red and blue/orange, separated by white. Red and blue are considered strong colours while green and orange are weak. Just as blue equals black, so yellow equals green; accordingly this set may also be expressed as yellow/red/white/black/orange. It has been the predominant element in Maasai ornament since the 1940s, although *narok* always appears as its complement. In the 1970s and 1980s inspiration was taken from the colours of commercially manufactured blankets, the national flag and the clothing of tourists, leading to the use of red/black/yellow and red/green/yellow sets in limited contexts.

The form and colour of body ornaments are indices of the wearer's age, gender, role and position within the social structure. Each of the Maasai's politically autonomous sub-groups or sections (*iloshon*, sing. *olosho*) has its own style of ornament and colour preferences that parallel the preferred colours of its cattle. In each section there are regional and possibly neighbourhood variants, as well as individual aesthetic expressions relating to the kind, quantity and quality of ornaments. As a person passes from one stage of life to the next he or she must change ornaments. Babies have their special toy medley necklaces with religious and medicinal charms, along with belts and wristlets that monitor their growth. At circumcision boys and girls replace their childhood ornaments with the ornaments of warriorhood and marriage respectively. The most elaborate and fastidious dressers are male warriors and uncircumcised girls, who spend much time grooming and dressing themselves. Young mothers gradually relinquish their wedding ensembles as they have more children, while grandmothers adopt specially revered ornaments that indicate the number of grandchildren who will inherit from them. Elders tone down their ornamentation to distinguish themselves from warriors and to look respectable.

Maasai mark the passage of time with deliberately contrived changes in ornament styles and fashions. When a warrior set is formed by the circumcision of an age cohort, the boys and their girlfriends agree on new styles, patterns, colours or materials that will distinguish them from their predecessors. The Ilmirisho, for example, the senior warriors in the late 1980s, recognize each other by the prominence of the eye motif in their ornaments and the representation of a helicopter on women's necklaces. Ornaments are often named after the particular warrior set that developed them: for example, a necklace known as Enkirupi is named after the Ilkirupi age set. This process may also result in the rejection of a certain type of bead, colour or shade. Certain key features of each age set have been identified, documented and dated back to the mid-to late 19th century (Klumpp, 1987).

Before the colonial incursion at the turn of the 20th century, Maasai ornament was made of metal (mostly iron) and a variety of seeds, grasses, leather, bone, ivory, wood and sometimes shell. With the completion of the Kenya–Uganda railway in 1902, 'many beads fell into the land', according to Maasai informants. The Maasai changed from metal ornaments to beaded ones, giving women creative control over what was once the domain of male blacksmiths. In comparison to the limitations of metal as a medium, beads also provided additional potential for aesthetic expression owing to their modularity and colour. With the emphasis on colour and pattern modifications in form and structure, changes occurred. Heavy wire spirals, for example, gave way to those made of fine wire on which to string beads. Thus the use of colour enabled the Maasai to refine their aesthetic principles and cultural identity.

2. OTHER ARTS. Among the range of other Maasai art works are sculptures of people, animals and such objects as cars and radios, made by children from mud and cow dung to use in their play. Uncircumcised boys whittle ear sticks and ear stretchers as well as small charms for their necklaces; they may also make the wooden weaning devices placed in calves' noses.

Maasai do not make pottery because it entails breaking the earth, a religious taboo. Weaving and twining are done only in basketry form, as in the construction of thonged leather or skin doors that double as carriers when moving the household. Other forms of leather- or skinwork produced by Maasai women include garments and the backings for beadwork. The Maasai house is like a huge basket of spiriform plan smeared with cow dung. Metalwork, comprising spears, swords, bells, branding irons and iron jewellery, is the speciality of blacksmiths called Ilkunono, a marginal group who are somewhat isolated from the main body of Maasai.

Formerly, warriors devised and painted their own shields according to heraldic conventions, but these have been banned, except for sale to tourists. Painting is now done primarily on the body, especially the face, and this only on special or ceremonial occasions. More permanent paintings are made by warriors on rock walls at secluded meat-feasting sites, using pigment, usually ochre, mixed with fat and/or water. The designs are usually silhouettes, outlines or stroked impressions of warriors, shields, cattle brands, ornaments or wild animals. Some comprise chevrons, dots and other abstract motifs, which are also used in beadwork structures.

In the 1980s a group of entrepreneurs developed a pseudo-Maasai style of sculpture using game animal bones, ivory and rhinoceros-horn. An elaborate story was created to promote and reify this material as part of a long-standing tradition of secret ceremonial use by Maasai diviners or *laibons* (*iloibonok*). The objects, numbering in the thousands, have been distributed on international art markets and are in continuous production.

BIBLIOGRAPHY

J. Thomson: *Through Masailand: A Journey of Exploration among the Snowclad Mountains and Strange Tribes of Eastern Equatorial Africa* (London, 1885/*R* 1968)
S. L. Hinde and H. Hinde: *The Last of the Masai* (London, 1901)
M. Merker: *Die Masai: Ethnographische Monographie eines Ostafrikanischen Semitenvolkes* (Berlin, 1904, rev. 1910/*R* New York, 1968)
A. C. Hollis: *The Masai: Their Language and Folklore* (Oxford, 1905/*R* Westport, CT, 1970)
C. W. Hobley: *Ethnology of A-Kamba and other East African Tribes*, Cambridge Archaeological and Ethnological Series (Cambridge, 1910, rev. London, 1919/*R* 1971)
J. Adamson: *The Peoples of Kenya* (London and New York, 1967)
A. H. Jacobs: *The Traditional Political Organization of the Pastoral Masai* (diss., Oxford U., 1967)
——: 'A Chronology of the Pastoral Maasai', *Hadith*, i (1968), pp. 10–31
S. S. O. Sankan: *The Maasai* (Nairobi, 1971)
H. M. Cole: 'Vital Arts in Northern Kenya', *Afr. A.*, vii/2 (1974), pp. 12–23, 82
J. G. Galaty: *In the Pastoral Image: The Dialectic of Maasai Identity* (diss., U. Chicago, IL, 1977)
J. C. Winter: 'Maasai Shield Patterns: A Documentary Source for Political History', *Zur Sprachgeschichte und Ethnohistorie in Afrika: Neue Beiträge afrikanistischer Forschungen*, ed. W. J. G. Möhlig, F. Rottland and B. Heine (Berlin, 1977), pp. 324–47
S. Somjee: *On the Material Culture of the Nationalities and the Formation of a National Art*, Institute of African Studies, University of Nairobi, Discussion Paper, 89 (Nairobi, 1978)
E. C. Burt: *An Annotated Bibliography of the Visual Arts of East Africa*, Trad. A. Africa (Bloomington, IN, 1980)
C. Beckwith and T. O. Saitoti: *Maasai* (London and New York, 1980)
A. Fisher: *Africa Adorned* (London and New York, 1984/*R* 1989)
M. Carey: *Beads and Beadwork of East and South Africa*, Shire Ethnography, 3 (Princes Risborough, 1985)
M. Amin, D. Willetts and J. Eames: *The Last of the Maasai* (London and Nairobi, 1987)
D. R. Klumpp: *Maasai Art and Society: Age and Sex, Time and Space, Cash and Cattle* (diss., New York, Columbia U., 1987)
D. R. Klumpp and C. Kratz: 'Aesthetics, Expertise and Ethnicity: Okiek and Maasai Perspectives on Personal Ornament', *Being Maasai: Ethnicity and Identity in East Africa*, Eastern African Studies, ed. T. Spear and R. Waller (London, Dar es Salaam, Nairobi and Athens, OH, 1993), pp. 195–221
G. Turle: *The Art of the Maasai: 300 Newly Discovered Objects and Works of Art* (New York, 1992); review by D. K. Pido in *Afr. A.*, xxvii/2 (1994), pp. 15–19

DONNA KLUMPP PIDO

**Maaskant, Hugh Aart** (*b* Rotterdam, 17 Aug 1907; *d* Rotterdam, 27 May 1977). Dutch architect and urban planner. He studied at the Middelbaar Technische School, Rotterdam, then worked for various architects until 1934, when he joined the office of Wilhem van Tijen in Rotterdam. From 1937 to 1954 he formed a partnership with van Tijen: together they produced one of the first high-rise residential blocks in Holland, the Plaspolder

Building (1938), Rotterdam, where they experimented with flexible floor-plans and broke the minimum living requirements as defined by the CIAM. Their constructional method followed the practice of Johannes Duiker and L. C. van der Vlugt (*see* BRINKMAN), using a skeleton of reinforced concrete. During World War II Maaskant drew up plans (with van Tijen, J. A. Brinkman and J. H. van den Broek (*see* VAN DEN BROEK & BAKEMA)) for the redevelopment of the inner city of Rotterdam, which had been completely destroyed (1940). After the war he was given the chance to set a firm stamp on the city's architecture; a characteristic work is the Groothandelsgebouw (1953), Stationsplein 45, Rotterdam. The majority of Maaskant's buildings are utilitarian. In spite of the critical reception with which his work met in the course of the 1960s, he remained loyal to the principles of Functionalism. He used the earnings from his extensive architectural activity to endow the Maaskant Prize, awarded by the Stichting Rotterdam–Maaskant for advances in architectural scholarship.

WRITINGS

'Naar aanleiding van de huisjes afgebeeld in dit nummer' [Concerning the cottages pictured in this issue], *De 8 & Opbouw*, v (1937), p. 121
'Van Ravesteyn', *De 8 & Opbouw*, ix (1941), p. 66
with W. van Tijen, J. H. van den Broek and J. A. Brinkman: *Woonmogelijkheden in het Nieuwe Rotterdam* [Housing possibilities in the New Rotterdam] (n.p., 1941)

BIBLIOGRAPHY

G. Fanelli: *Architettura moderna* (1968)
H. J. F. de Roy van Zuydewijn: *Amsterdamse bouwkunst, 1815–1940* (Amsterdam, 1970), p. 202
*Rotterdams jaarboekje*, vi (Rotterdam, 1978)
M. Fluks, M. Vink and S. Umberto Barbieri, eds: *Architekt H. A. Maaskant* (Amsterdam, 1984)

DIANNE TIMMERMAN, FRANK VAN DEN HOEK

**Maastricht** [Maestricht]. Dutch city, capital of Limburg Province. It is situated on the River Meuse in the extreme south of the Netherlands and has a population of *c.* 115,000.

1. History and urban development. 2. St Servatius.

1. HISTORY AND URBAN DEVELOPMENT. The Roman settlement of Mosae Trajectum was founded under Emperor Augustus at a bridging point across the Meuse on the route from Cologne to the sea. Building remains and sculptured stones from the 1st to the 4th centuries AD have been excavated. There are late Roman fortifications, dated 333 AD, and early Christian gravestones (Maastricht, St Servatius) dating from the 5th to the 6th centuries, and a church was founded *c.* 550 outside the settlement over the grave of St Servatius (*d* 384), the first Bishop of Tongres (Tongeren, Belgium). The see was transferred to Maastricht in the 6th century and moved to Liège after 700, the period when the settlement at Maastricht began to flourish from trade. It had a mint, and by the 8th century it was an inland port, with a toll-house. The abbey of St Servatius (*see* §2 below), first mentioned in 743, played a large part in its development.

Maastricht benefited from the wealth of the Meuse region as a whole during the Middle Ages, and it was the intended capital of the Duchy of Lower Lorraine in the

10th century. The church of St Servatius and the Onze-Lieve-Vrouwekerk both had elaborate building programmes, the latter with a precipitous westwork flanked by round towers (*see* NETHERLANDS, THE, fig. 2), dating from *c.* 1000, and a two-storey eastern ambulatory of the 12th century. It was the development of Maastricht during the 13th century, however, that consolidated it as a fortified town. Much of what was possibly the first city wall, begun 1229, and one gate, the Helpoort, survive, but by the end of the century the city had expanded to 114 ha and a new wall was built. In 1284 the 'Alde Caerte' confirmed that the city government should be shared between the Prince-bishop of Liège and the Duke of Brabant, an arrangement that persisted until 1795. Its prosperity based on weaving, tanning and general trade, by the late 14th century Maastricht was as big as Utrecht, with *c.* 9000 inhabitants. Of the numerous churches and monasteries, few survived the French occupation (1794–1814) or the Industrial Revolution; but the medieval street plan has survived, although the house façades are mainly 17th- and 18th-century, either in the local Renaissance style, with transomed windows and polychrome masonry of brick, stone and marl, or in contemporary French styles. The Stadhuis (1659–64), which dominates the market square, was built by Pieter Post.

From the 16th century, and particularly after the Dutch conquest of 1632, the location of Maastricht made it one of the most important strongholds in north-western Europe, with its outworks (Hoge Fronten and Lage Fronten) and casemates, built mainly between *c.* 1770 and 1785. Culturally, however, it suffered from being a garrison town, although the Rococo theatre of 1784 in the former Jesuit church was one of the earliest in the Dutch Republic. The industrial expansion of the city began with the ceramics and glassworks of Petrus Regout (1801–78), the building of canals and an inner harbour, workers' hostels and the demolition of much of the abandoned fortifications (1867). Maastricht was the birthplace of Victor de Stuers, the founder of the movement to preserve monuments and historic buildings in the Netherlands. At the end of the 19th century suburbs were built outside the former city walls, but the greatest expansion started after World War II, when the city was tripled in size, with some exemplary new housing estates. A notable project begun in the 1990s is the development of the Céramique area across the river from the historic centre; this is designed to provide residential areas, offices, shops, hotels and other facilities, including the new Bonnefanten Museum (opened 1995), designed by Aldo Rossi. After 1987 the European Fine Art Fair was held in Maastricht.

BIBLIOGRAPHY

G. W. A. Panhuysen: *Studieën over Maastricht in de dertiende eeuw* (Maastricht, 1933)

R. Meischke: 'Het Maastrichtse burgerhuis', *Kon. Ned. Oudhdkd. Bond: Bull. KNOB*, lxxii (1973), pp. 83–103

T. A. S. M. Panhuysen: *Maastricht staat op zijn verleden* (Maastricht, 1984)

*Sint-Servatius, bisschop van Tongeren-Maastricht: Het vroegste christendom in het Maasland: Handelingen van het Colloquium te Alden Biesen: Tongeren en Maastricht, 1984*

*Een seer magnifick Stadthuys: Tien studies over de bouw en de inrichting van het stadhuis te Maastricht*, Leids Studenten Streekgezelschap 'Limburgia' (Delft, 1985)

T. A. S. M. Panhuysen and P. H. D. Leupen: 'Maastricht in het eerste millennium', *Actes du XIV colloque international: Spa, 1988*, pp. 411–55

*Kon. Ned. Oudhdkd. Bond: Bull. KNOB*, lxxxviii/3 (1989) [whole issue on Maastricht]

TITUS A. S. M. PANHUYSEN

2. ST SERVATIUS. The former collegiate church is the most significant surviving Romanesque church of the Netherlands. About 560–80 Bishop Manulf replaced a wooden church on the site of St Servatius's grave with a large new church, probably of stone. A monastery is first mentioned in 743. Under Provost Geldulf (*d* 1051) a new church was built, dedicated in 1039. Between 1063 and 1073 Provost Humbert renewed and decorated the choir, and in 1087 St Servatius was made an exempt imperial college of canons. In 1797 the chapter was abolished and the church deconsecrated, becoming a parish church in 1804. During the 1860s Baroque decorations were removed from the choir and in the 1880s the crossing crypt (destr. 1812) was rebuilt, the exterior masonry of the choir was renewed and the upper sections of the eastern towers were rebuilt. The decorative elements of the interior were given an oil-based polychromy. The western towers were burnt in 1955. Since 1960 the interior has been comprehensively restored.

*(i) Architecture.* The present church (interior length 86.7 m) is an aisled basilica of eight bays with a western choir and, on the east, a projecting transept with a central apse preceded by a single choir bay. A series of crypts extends under the choir, the crossing and the two eastern bays of the nave. The structure is mostly of sandstone.

The earliest surviving sections are the confessio (3.2×2.8 m) under the second bay west of the crossing and the small barrel-vaulted crypt (5.33×2.75 m) abutting it to the east. They probably lay underneath the sanctuary of the pre-1039 building. The present nave, probably belonging to the church dedicated in 1039, originally had a timber roof and arcades supported by unarticulated piers. The exterior was decorated with the blind arcading (still visible in a few bays) typical in the Mosan area. An eastern choir with three aisles has been postulated, extending at least to the eastern arch of the present crossing. Beyond the choir the present eastern crypt, attributed to the early 11th century, may have continued as an outer crypt. It is now a nine-bay hall crypt, but excavations in 1915 revealed that it originally extended at least two bays further and was shortened when the present apse was built.

The existing transept, originally lower than the nave, is slightly later and has been attributed to Provost Humbert's restoration (1063–73), along with the crossing crypt, a hall crypt three bays wide and four deep. The two chapels flanking the apse served originally as entrance halls into the church. Abutting the north wall of the transept and attributed to the same period is the Chapel of the Chapter, a two-storey rectangular structure (*c.* 20×7 m) with an exterior decoration of Lombard bands. In the 13th century the choir bay was vaulted, the apse exterior was rebuilt with superimposed colonnettes supporting blind arcades and crowned by an open loggia, and flanking towers were erected. It is closely comparable to Rhenish apse decorations of the 1150s, especially those of Bonn Minster, which was built by Gerhard von Are, later provost at St Servatius (1154–60).

The western choir is a massive rectangular block (w. 34 m) supporting twin towers (*see* WESTWORK, fig. 3). The most elaborate of the Mosan western choirs, it is attributed by Mekking to Provost Christian von Buch and dated between 1165 and 1200. The exterior is articulated by blind arcading and pilaster-strips and pierced by a variety of windows on the upper levels. The interior is organized around a central bay two storeys high, where an altar to the Virgin was located under the arch leading into the nave. At the second level, galleries surround the central bay on three sides. On the third level the Keizerzaal under the patronage of Charlemagne, vaulted by a dome on squinches, may have originally opened to the nave through a low arcade.

There are two entrances on the north side of the nave; the main south portal (Bergportaal) may have replaced an earlier entrance. Chapels were added along the sides of the nave and the nave and transept were vaulted *c.* 1425, when the windows were changed and the walls slightly heightened.

Maastricht, St Servatius, west choir, capital showing masons at work, *c.* 1165–80

### BIBLIOGRAPHY

Gregory of Tours: *Liber de gloria beatorum confessorum* (6th century); ed. W. Arndt and B. Krusch, Mnmt. Ger. Hist.: Scriptores Rerum Merovingicarum, i/2 (Hannover, 1885/*R* 1969), p. 340

P. H. J. Cuypers: 'De restauratie van de Sint-Servaaskerk te Maastricht,' *Bull. Kon. Ned. Oudhdknd. Bond*, v (1903–4), pp. 19ff, 124ff; vi (1905) pp. 76ff

L. Weischer: *Studien zur holländisch-limburgischen Romanik* (Strasbourg, 1934), pp. 73–99

A. Verbeek: 'Romanische Westchorhallen an Maas und Rhein', *Wallraf-Richartz-Jb.*, ix (1936), pp. 59–87

O. Lehmann-Brockhaus: *Schriftquellen zur Kunstgeschichte des 11. und 12. Jahrhunderts für Deutschland, Lothringen und Italien* (Berlin, 1938/*R* 1971), i, nos 1881–2

J. J. M. Timmers: *De Sint-Servaaskerk te Maastricht* (Utrecht, 1955)

J. Deeters: *Servatiusstift und Stadt Maastricht: Untersuchungen zu Entstehung und Verfassung*, Rheinisches Archiv, lxxiii (Bonn, 1970)

A. J. J. Mekking: *De Sint-Servaaskerk te Maastricht* (Zutphen, 1986)

*(ii) Sculpture.* The sculpture of St Servatius consists of capitals on the eastern apse and in the western choir, portals on the north and south sides of the nave, and reliefs from the altar of the Virgin. All but the Bergportaal are attributable to a single workshop, known as the Heimo workshop (from the mason represented offering a capital to the Virgin on a capital in the choir of Onze Lieve Vrouwe), which was active in the later 12th century.

The capitals are cubic, carved with dense designs of foliage, animals and human figures, in a style clearly derived from northern Italy. Those in the western choir (*c.* 1165–80) bear lively depictions of what appear to be scenes from everyday life, among them a group of masons at work, inscribed *operarii lapis* (see fig.). The two north portals were both originally decorated with reliefs, but only the tympanum of the eastern portal has survived, carved with *Christ in Majesty* in a hard marl (*see* ROMANESQUE, fig. 41). Dated variously between *c.* 1150 and *c.* 1200, it has been compared to the so-called Madonna of Dom Rupert (Liège, Mus. Curtius), included by Brenk in the Heimo workshop. Brenk further suggested that the reliefs from the altar of the Virgin were the latest products of the shop. Set up in 1881 as an altarpiece in the western choir, they originally crowned the central section of a

choir-screen (destr. early 19th century). The lower, rectangular, relief (severely damaged early 19th century; rest. with plaster 1852) represents the *Virgin and Child* in a mandorla supported by angels; the upper, semicircular, relief shows *Christ Enthroned Crowning SS Peter and Servatius*. The reliefs are variously dated between *c.* 1160 and 1200, and Brenk saw the influence of Cologne.

The Mariological sculptures of the Bergportaal (*c.* 1230), the present main south door, are derived both stylistically and iconographically from the northern French tradition stemming from the west portal of Senlis Cathedral.

### BIBLIOGRAPHY

R. Ligtenberg: *Die romanische Steinplastik in den nördlichen Niederlanden* (The Hague, 1918)

H. Beenken: *Romanische Skulptur in Deutschland* (Leipzig, 1924)

E. Kluckhohn: 'Die Bedeutung Italiens für die romanische Baukunst und Bauornamentik in Deutschland', *Marburg. Jb. Kstwiss.*, xvi (1955), pp. 1–120

J. Raspi Serra: 'Lapicidi lombardi ed emiliani nel xii secolo a Maastricht in Olanda', *Commentari*, xx (1970), pp. 27–43

J. J. M. Timmers: *De kunst van het Maasland* (Assen, 1971)

R. Haussherr: 'Die Skulptur des frühen und hohen Mittelalters an Rhein und Maas', *Rhein und Maas: Kunst und Kultur, 800–1400* (exh. cat., ed. A. Legner; Cologne, Josef-Haubrich-Ksthalle; Brussels, Musées Royaux A. & Hist.; 1973), ii, pp. 387–406

B. Brenk: 'Die Werkstätten der Maastrichter Bauplastik des 12. Jahrhunderts', *Wallraf-Richartz-Jb.*, xxxviii (1976), pp. 46–63

ELIZABETH B. SMITH

*(iii) Treasury.* The treasury of St Servatius was already mentioned in the second part of Henric van Veldeke's *Servaaslegende* (1174–83): the relics were kept in the 'tresoer', a small double chapel, built *c.* 1170 against the north wall of the choir at the corner with the transept. It served primarily as a safe for the relics and treasure belonging to the church. The *ordinarius custodum* ('sacristan's book'), probably dating from the 14th century but surviving in a copy of *c.* 1600 (Maastricht, Rijksarchf Limburg, St Servaaskapittel Archf, no. 166), concerns the function of the treasury. The heart of the treasure is the shrine of St Servatius. The reliquary itself (made of gilded copper, bronze, enamel, vernis-brun and filigree, completed

1198–1200), the 'emergency coffer' and four associated gable fragments (Brussels, Musées Royaux A. & Hist.) were made in the Rhine–Meuse region. They originally stood behind the high altar. Around 1400 the skull of Servatius was provided with a reliquary in the form of a bust, replaced in the late 16th century by the present silver-gilt copper reliquary bust (eight silver reliefs from the pedestal of the early 15th-century reliquary now in Hamburg, Mus. Kst & Gew.).

The so-called 'Servatiana', objects considered to have been the personal property of St Servatius, occupy a prominent place in the treasure of the church. The most important is the silver key of Servatius (l. 285 mm), made in the early 9th century by the workshop that produced the bronze gates of the Palatine chapel at Aachen (*see* AACHEN, §2(ii)(b)). This was presumably originally intended as a symbol of authority, as the *clavis David* ('key of David') for Charlemagne, and was ascribed to Servatius from the 11th century onwards, the saint supposedly having received it in Rome from the Apostle Peter as one of the keys to Heaven. Among the other Carolingian objects that once formed part of this treasure are the Einhard arch (untraced; known from a 17th-century drawing, Paris, Bib. N., MS. Fr. 10440, fol. 45; for illustration *see* EINHARD) and an ivory pyx (London, BM, BM 1903 5–14/1).

Many objects from the treasuries of both St Servatius and Onze Lieve Vrouwe were lost in the 18th century during the occupation of Maastricht by French revolutionary troops, but in the early 19th century both treasuries were restored to their former glory. As many as possible of the earlier relics and other treasures were reassembled. Both Roman Catholic parishes expanded their 'treasuries' considerably in the 19th and 20th centuries. Publication of the first thorough description of the collections (Bock and Willemsen) also signalled a major restoration campaign for the treasures of both churches.

BIBLIOGRAPHY

F. Bock and M. Willemsen: *Antiquités sacrées conservées dans les anciennes collégiales de S Servais et de Notre-Dame à Maestricht* (Maastricht, 1873)
G. A. van Es: *Sint Servaes legende* (Antwerp, Brussels and Leuven, 1950/*R* Culemborg, 1976)
*Rhein und Maas: Kunst und Kultur, 800–1400* (exh. cat., ed. A. Legner; Cologne, Josef-Haubrich–Ksthalle; Brussels, Musées Royaux A. & Hist.; 1972)
A. M. Koldeweij: *Der gude Sente Servas: De Servatiuslegende en de Servatiana*, Maaslandse Monografieën Groot Formaat, v (Assen and Maastricht, 1985)
R. Kroos: 'Der Schrein des heiligen Servatius in Maastricht und die vier zugehörigen Reliquiare in Brüssel', *Veröff. Zentinst. Kstgesch. München*, viii (1985)
*Schatkamers uit het Zuiden* (exh. cat., ed. A. M. Koldeweij and P. M. L. van Vlijmen; Utrecht, Catharijneconvent, 1985)
T. J. van Rensch and others: *Hemelse trektochten*, Vierkant Maastricht, xvi (Maastricht, 1990) [incl. A. M. Koldeweij: 'De Schatkamer van de Sint-Servaaskerk', pp. 13–50, 160–61; M. L. de Kreek: 'De Schatkamer van de O. L. Vrouwekerk', pp. 123–35, 159–60]
M. L. de Kreek: *De kerkschat van het Onze-Lieve-Vrouwekapittel te Maastricht*, Clavis Kunsthistorische Monografieën, xiv (Utrecht and Amsterdam, 1994)

A. M. KOLDEWEIJ

**Maatkare.** *See* HATSHEPSUT.

**Mabasa** [Mabaso], **Noria** (*b* Thsigalo, Ramukhumba district, northern Transvaal, 10 May 1938). South African sculptor. She had no formal art training but used her rural

woman's skill of modelling clay when she first made sculptures in the early 1970s. These were inspired by dreams, which continue to prompt her work. Her earliest figures resembled representational carvings for Venda initiation ceremonies, but as her small images had no ritual function they soon proved saleable. From figures in traditional dress, she extended her range to include others in her village community, such as preachers, politicians and policemen. Shaped in clay in simple but carefully observed detail, they were fired and then painted. Her market was dramatically augmented when her work was included in two exhibitions in Johannesburg; *Tributaries*, at the Africana Museum in Progress in 1985, followed by a solo exhibition at the Goodman Gallery the next year.

Commercial success widened Mabasa's horizons, both through material possessions like television and through visits to the city, which engendered new subject-matter and also increased contacts with other artists, such as the carver Nelson Mukhuba (1925–87), who had adapted traditional skills to the art market with equal success. Although carving was the preserve of men, Mabasa too began to work in wood. Her complex monumental carvings of intertwined human and animal forms, such as *Carnage II* (0.79x1.97x2.18 m, 1988; Johannesburg A. G.), seem to fuse images of real-life disasters with dream visions. Such work rapidly achieved acclaim and was included in the Cape Town Triennial in 1988. The later casting of a few of Mabasa's clay figures in bronze confirmed her reputation in art circles.

BIBLIOGRAPHY

E. Dell: 'Transitional Sculpture', *Ten Years of Collecting* (exh. cat., ed. D. Hammond-Tooke and A. Nettleton; Johannesburg, U. Witwatersrand, 1989), pp. 45–53
S. Williamson: *Resistance Art in South Africa* (Cape Town, 1989), pp. 50–51
E. Rankin: *Images of Metal: Post-war Sculptures and Assemblages in South Africa* (Johannesburg, 1994), pp. 144–8

ELIZABETH RANKIN

**Mabe, Manabu** (*b* Kumamoto, Japan, 1924). Brazilian painter of Japanese birth. At the age of ten he was taken by his family to Brazil, where he first worked in the coffee plantations in the interior of São Paulo State. After moving to the state capital he painted his first pictures *c*. 1945. Initially, he painted still-lifes and landscapes influenced by Braque and Picasso, such as *Still-life* (1952; Rio de Janeiro, Mus. N. B.A.), but he developed a calligraphic abstraction of compact brushstrokes, abrupt lines and dramatic bursts of paint generally against monochrome backgrounds. Even at his most abstract he continued to use referential titles alluding to the real world and to human emotions, as in *Agony* (1963; Washington, DC, Mus. Mod. A. Latin America).

BIBLIOGRAPHY

F. Aquino: *Museu Manchete* (Rio de Janeiro, 1982), pp. 22–9
J. Maurício: 'Abstração' [Abstraction], *Seis décadas de arte moderna na Coleção Roberto Marinho* [Six decades of modern art in the Roberto Marinho Collection] (Rio de Janeiro, 1985), pp. 350–61
M. Mabe and others: *Vida e obra* [Life and work] (São Paulo, 1986)

ROBERTO PONTUAL

**Mabillon, Jean** (*b* Saint-Pierremont, Ardennes, 23 Nov 1632; *d* Paris, 27 Dec 1707). French historian and antiquary. A member of the Benedictine Order from 1654, he was called to St Germain-des-Prés Abbey in Paris in 1664 as an assistant to the aged scholar Luc d'Achery and remained a member of that house until his death. Although a monk of great piety, Mabillon was not remote from the world: his Order was in touch with the learning of Paris, and he travelled widely and maintained a vast correspondence with contemporary scholars. Added to his distinguished mind and character he possessed a fine sense of judgement and the ability to digest and order an immense range of material, and he was able to express himself in Latin of unusual clarity. Although he made errors of judgement (for example in his dating of the statues of kings and queens at St Germain-des-Prés, where he may have been influenced by a desire to give as impressively early a date as possible to the founding of the Abbey), and many of his conclusions have been discredited (Vanuxem), his writings remain of value due to the method they expound. *De re diplomatica* is generally regarded as his masterpiece. Written in reply to the Jesuit Daniel Papebroch who attempted in his *Editoris acta sanctorum* (1675) to formulate rules for establishing the genuineness of medieval charters and other documents, Mabillon's treatise laid the foundations for deciphering charters and PALAEOGRAPHY, stating that only after the examination of the material used, the script, grammar, wording, seal and signature, could any decision be made about date, origin and authenticity.

WRITINGS

*Acta sanctorum ordinis Sancta Benedicti*, 9 vols (Paris, 1668–1701)
*De re diplomatica*, 2 vols (Paris, 1681–1704)
*De liturgica gallicana* (Paris, 1685)
*Sancti Bernardi opera* (Paris, 1690)
*Traité des études monastiques* (Paris, 1691)
*Annales ordinis Sancti Benedicti*, 4 vols (Paris, 1703–39)

BIBLIOGRAPHY

M. D. Knowles: 'Jean Mabillon', *J. Eccles. Hist.*, x (1950), pp. 153–73
H. Leclercq: *Mabillon*, 2 vols (Paris, 1953–7) [with 1856 letters calendared]
J. Vanuxem: 'The Theories of Mabillon and Montfaucon on French Sculpture of the Twelfth Century', *J. Warb. & Court. Inst.*, xx (1957), pp. 45–58

ANDREW G. WATSON

**Mabuse.** *See* GOSSART, JAN.

**Mabuseus.** *See* RÉGNIER, NICOLAS.

**MAC.** *See* MOVIMENTO ARTE CONCRETA.

**Macagnino, Angelo del.** *See* ANGELO DEL MACAGNINO.

**Macalister, Molly (Morell)** (*b* Invercargill, 18 May 1920; *d* Auckland, 12 Oct 1979). New Zealand sculptor. She studied at the Canterbury School of Art (1938–40), where the guidance of Francis Shurrock (1887–1977) encouraged her to take up sculpture. Her principal subjects were human figures, heads and animals in attitudes of stillness and repose. Among her early works in wood are *Head* (1948; Auckland, Haydn priv. col., see 1982 exh. cat., no. 8), which depicts a Maori woman, and *Mask* (1948–50; Auckland, Haydn priv. col., see 1982 exh. cat., no. 16), which is influenced by Pacific carving. In 1952 Macalister's work was the New Zealand entry in a competition organized by the Institute of Contemporary Arts in London for a statue of the *Unknown Political Prisoner* (unexecuted). Her maquette, in concrete, was exhibited at

the Tate Gallery, London, in 1953. The scale of her work increased after 1957, when she began working in cast and moulded concrete. Her principal European influences were Henry Moore and Marino Marini, but a Pacific and Maori awareness is always evident. An exhibition of new work in concrete, with two other sculptors, Alison Duff (*b* 1914) and Ann Severs (*b* 1931), at the Auckland City Art Gallery in 1959 was acclaimed as a landmark in New Zealand sculpture. She received a number of large public commissions, including a monumental bronze *Maori Figure* (1964–6; Auckland, Queen Street; for illustration *see* NEW ZEALAND, fig. 8).

BIBLIOGRAPHY

P. Tomory: 'New Zealand Sculpture', *A. & Australia*, iii/2 (1965), pp. 108–13
C. McCahon: 'Molly Macalister, 1920–1979', *A. NZ*, 14 (1979), pp. 26–7
*Molly Macalister: A Memorial Exhibition* (exh. cat. by A. M. Johnston, Auckland, C.A.G., 1982)

ALEXA M. JOHNSTON

**Macao** [Macau; Aomen]. Portuguese-administered territory on a peninsula attached to Guangdong Province in southern China. Present-day Macao includes the islands of Taipa and Coloane. The territory is 40 km west of Hong Kong and 145 km south of Guangzhou (Canton) along the Pearl River delta.

1. HISTORY AND URBAN DEVELOPMENT. Macao was founded by the Portuguese *c*. 1557 and was the earliest European city to be built in China. Before the arrival of the Portuguese, the area had been settled by Chinese fishermen from Fujian Province. The temple to A-Ma or Tin-Hau (Tian Hoa), the goddess of the sea, was built, probably on the site of a pre-existing shrine, during the Ming period (1368–1644). The earliest Chinese building is the Kunyam (Guanyin; Goddess of Mercy) Temple, which is believed to date to the Yuan period (1279–1368).

An important colonial port from the 16th to the 17th century, Macao was also the headquarters of the Roman Catholic missions to China and Japan. Among the most valued commodities traded from Macao were Chinese export porcelains and ceramics, including Shekwan (*see* SHIWAN) glazed wares and figures (*see also* CERAMICS, §II), paintings, Chinese and Indo-Portuguese silverware and Japanese *Nanban* art objects (*see* JAPAN, §X, 2(vi) (b) ). Macao owed its wealth to trade with Japan and Manila: every year Portugal's black carracks left for Japanese ports loaded with Chinese silks, which were traded for silver. The trade rose in value from one million taels in the 16th century to over three million in the 1630s.

Christened Porto do Nome de Deus, Macao was governed by the Captain-Major of the Japan trade, who was appointed by the viceroys of the Portuguese colony of Goa in India. The Portuguese erected military and religious buildings, which either have survived or are known from drawings. A diocese was established in the colony in 1576. The church and the missionary orders with headquarters in the city—the Franciscans, Augustinians, Dominicans and the Jesuits—played a significant role in the development of the colony's art and architecture. The Jesuits were the most active patrons during the late 16th century and early 17th. Some of the city's main religious, educational, social and military structures were built under their auspices, including the São Paulo Fort, the seminary and church of S José (early 17th century) and the church of S Paulo (church of Madre de Deus; 1602–40; destr. 1835; see fig. ). Only the 24-m granite façade of S Paulo still stands, but according to contemporary descriptions the vault was made of rare Japanese wood carved by Chinese craftsmen in the Portuguese style known as *talha* (gilded carved wood; *see* PORTUGAL, §V). Macao's earlier Western architecture adopted Cantonese building methods. Brick, coated with painted stucco, gave buildings a Latin appearance, with often unorthodox decorations and structural members moulded in stucco.

After the tragic death of Sebastian, King of Portugal (*reg* 1557–78), during the union of the Spanish and Portuguese crowns between 1580 and 1641, Macao became embroiled in the conflict between Catholic Spain and the Protestant Low Countries. The Macanese narrowly repulsed a Dutch invasion in 1622. This period also coincided with Macao's most important cultural flowering. Profits from the Japan trade increased manyfold, and an illicit trade with the Spanish Philippines flourished. In 1586 the colony acquired the status of a city (Cidade do Nome de Deus) with its own municipal chamber (*senado*). Its first governor was appointed in 1623. The Spanish established several religious foundations, including the monasteries of S Agostinho (1586; rest. 18th century) and S Domingos (1588) and the convent of S Clara (1633), and built the church of S Francisco (destr.; later rebuilt in

Rococo style by the Portugese). The columns of the 18th-century façade of S Domingos are of brick overlaid with stucco decoration.

In 1641 Macao could once again look to a Portuguese monarch—John IV—in Lisbon; however, the city had already begun to decline in importance. Rather than English and Dutch attacks, this was brought about by the exclusion edicts of 1639 issued by shogun Tokugawa Iemitsu (1604–51), which barred all foreign traders from Japan except the Chinese and Dutch, who were allowed limited access to Nagasaki.

In 1770 a Chinese edict forbidding Europeans to reside in Guangzhou outside the trading season obliged foreign merchants to rent and later buy houses in Macao. The wealthiest of these, the traders of the British East India Company, rented the Casa Garden, where an English garden was laid out. The East India Company was so influential that it almost took over the colony, and the main items of trade began to include opium as well as porcelain, tea and silk. During the 19th century English Neo-classical mansions dominated the Praia Grande (the outer harbour promenade), and during the second half of the century Macao produced its own style of Neo-classical architecture.

In the 20th century mediocre high-rise and restoration projects were the norm, apart from the St Lazarus urbanization project, several public and domestic buildings dating to the first three decades of the century, the restoration of a few old buildings, such as the Bela Vista Hotel, and several notable exceptions in the late part of the century.

2. ART LIFE AND ORGANIZATION. Most art in Macao from before the end of the 18th century can be classified as colonial Portuguese *arte sacra* produced under the patronage of the Church, though Macao's forts attest to the existence of lay patronage. By the 19th century patronage had moved from the church to the wealthy merchant class. China trade art (*see* CHINA, §I, 4(ii)) reached an unprecedented artistic level with the arrival of the English painter GEORGE CHINNERY (see fig.) in 1825 and of the French painter Auguste Borget (1809–77) in 1838. After Chinnery's death production became more commercialized, even among his more gifted pupils, who included Lamqua (*see* GUAN, (2)) and the Macanese Marciano Baptista (1826–96), who later established himself in Hong Kong.

In the 20th century urban decay and the destruction of Macao's architectural heritage were reflected in the watercolours of George Smirnoff (1903–47) and Lui Shoukwan. Gao Jianfu and Lui Shoukwan, respectively the founders of Lingnan and Hong Kong painting, and Smirnoff were only visitors to the colony. The Macanese painter Luís Demée (*b* 1929), Smirnoff's pupil, emigrated to Portugal. An influx of Portuguese and Chinese painters working in vigorous abstract styles raised standards from 1980.

BIBLIOGRAPHY
J. de Jesus Maria: *Asia sinica de Japónica*, 2 vols (Macao, 1740–45); intro. C. R. Boxer (Macao, 1988)
J. E. McCall: 'Early Jesuit Art in the Far East: China and Macao', *Artibus Asiae*, xi (1948), pp. 45–69
J. M. Braga: *The Western Pioneers and their Discovery of Macao* (Macao, 1949)

Macao, S Paulo, 1602–40, destroyed (except for façade) 1835; detail (182×103 mm) of drawing by George Chinnery, pen and ink, 182×146 mm, 1834 (London, Victoria and Albert Museum)

J. B. Bury: 'A Jesuit Façade in China', *Archit. Rev.* [London], cxxiv (1958), pp. 412–13

C. R. Boxer: *The Great Ship from Amacon* (Lisbon, 1959)

M. da Silva Mendes: *Colectânea de artigos de Manuel da Silva Mendes* (Macao, 1963)

S. K. Wong: *Macao Architecture: An Integration of Chinese and Portuguese Influences* (Macao, 1970)

H. Chan: *A Catalogue of Chinese Paintings in the Luis Camões Museum, Macau* (Macao, 1977)

R. Hutcheon: *Souvenirs of Auguste Borget* (Hong Kong, 1979)

C. R. Boxer: *Seventeenth Century Macao* (Hong Kong, 1984)

C. Clunas: *Chinese Export Watercolours* (London, 1984)

J. Graça: *The Fortifications of Macao* (Macao, 1984)

C. Guillén-Nuñez: *Macau, Images of Asia* (Hong Kong, 1984)

M. Teixeira: *Macau no século XVIII* (Macao, 1984)

G. W. Bonsall: *George Chinnery: His Pupils and Influence* (Hong Kong, 1985)

C. Guillén-Nuñez: 'Buildings from Macao's Past', *A. Asia*, xvi/1 (Jan–Feb 1986), pp. 66–71

R. Ptak, ed.: *Portuguese Asia: Aspects in History and Economic History, 16th and 17th Centuries* (Stuttgart, 1987)

H. Cameron: *Barbarians and Mandarins* (Hong Kong, 1989)

A. Coates: *Macao and the British, 1637–1842: Prelude to Hong Kong* (Hong Kong, 1989)

R. L. Edmonds: *Macau*, World Bibliography Series (Oxford, 1989)

R. D. Cremer, ed.: *Macau: City of Commerce and Culture* (Hong Kong, 1991)

P. Conner: *George Chinnery, 1774–1852: Artist of India and the China Coast* (Woodbridge, 1993)

J. A. Prescott, ed.: *Macaensis monumentum* (Macao, 1993)

CÉSAR GUILLÉN-NUÑEZ

**McArdell, James** (*b* Dublin, ?1728; *d* London, 1 June 1765). Irish engraver. In 1746 he moved to London with his master, the engraver John Brooks (*fl* 1730–56), in order to further his artistic career. By 1750 he had branched out on his own, determined to make a living as a mezzotint engraver. His success soon attracted a group of his Dublin friends to London, and with the arrival of Richard Houston, Charles Spooner (1720–67) and Richard Purcell (*d* 1766) a group of Irish engravers began to become established. In the course of his career McArdell engraved about 200 mezzotints after other artists, nearly all of which are portraits. Early acclaim for his work was for such prints as *Lord John and Lord Bernard Stuart*, after Anthony van Dyck, and *Elizabeth Hamilton, Comtesse de Grammont*, after Peter Lely. He also produced prints after Rembrandt, Peter Paul Rubens, William Hogarth and others.

In 1754 McArdell began an association with Joshua Reynolds: that year Reynolds, who realized the potential advantages of having his portraits popularized through prints, paid McArdell to engrave a mezzotint after his painting of *Lady Charlotte Fitzwilliam* (Wentworth Woodhouse, S. Yorks). This print was probably the first McArdell made after a work by Reynolds, and he went on to produce 38 of them during the next decade, among them *Miss Frances Anne Greville and her Brother, as Psyche and Cupid* (1762; painting now Cambridge, Fitzwilliam). McArdell's Irish background and contacts helped him to gain commissions from Dublin printsellers and Irish patrons; included among the latter were Sir Charles Burton (*d* 1775), Dublin's Lord Mayor in 1752–3, and James Fitzgerald (1722–73), 20th Earl of Kildare (Duke of Leinster from 1766). McArdell was the undisputed leader of the Irish engravers in London.

BIBLIOGRAPHY

J. Chaloner Smith: *British Mezzotinto Portraits* (London, 1884), ii, pp. 834–907

G. Goodwin: *James McArdell*, British Mezzotinters (London, 1903)

W. Strickland: *A Dictionary of Irish Artists*, 2 vols (Dublin, 1913)

D. Alexander: 'The Dublin Group: Irish Mezzotint Engravers in London, 1750–1775', *Bull. Irish Georg. Soc.*, xvi (1973), pp. 73–90

FINTAN CULLEN

**McArthur, John**, jr (*b* Bladnock, Scotland, 13 May 1823; *d* Philadelphia, PA, 8 Jan 1890). American architect. He came to Philadelphia *c.* 1833, where he was apprenticed as a carpenter with an uncle but studied architecture at the Carpenters' Company and attended lectures by Thomas Ustick Walter at the Franklin Institute. By the 1840s McArthur had become an architect and in the 1850s won numerous mercantile commissions for buildings that he usually designed in one of the 19th-century classical styles. Particularly noteworthy were the Italianate hotels La Pierre and Continental (1853 and 1858 respectively; destr.) and the Public Ledger offices (1866; destr.), a handsome Second Empire building crowned by a massive mansard roof, all in Philadelphia.

McArthur is best known as the architect of City Hall (formerly the Public Buildings) in Philadelphia, for which he twice won competitions, first in 1860 and again in 1869. The scheme as built was the third design (1871) and consisted of four L-shaped structures at each corner of Center Square, representing the city, county, judiciary and regulatory branches of government. The corners are joined into a single unit by great archways that frame vistas of avenues and unified by a monumental Second Empire overlay of columns and statues beneath a crowning mansard roof. On the north façade there is an immense tower capped by a statue of Pennsylvania's founder, William Penn (1644–1718), which acts as a landmark for the centre of the city. It is the second tallest masonry structure in the world, exceeded only by Robert Mills's Washington Monument, Washington, DC, a hierarchy that Philadelphians thought appropriate. When City Hall was finally completed (1901), its architect was long dead and its style was out of fashion. After World War II it was saved from demolition only by its bulk; hemmed in later by austere post-war office slabs, McArthur's masterpiece afforded much needed visual relief in the redeveloped city centre, but it was finally overshadowed in 1986 by a taller commercial skyscraper.

BIBLIOGRAPHY

*DAB*; *Macmillan Enc. Architects*

L. Wodehouse: 'John McArthur jr, 1823–1890', *J. Soc. Archit. Hist.*, xxviii (1969), pp. 271–83

S. Tatman and R. Moss: *Biographical Dictionary of Philadelphia Architects, 1700–1930* (Boston, 1985), pp. 510–12

J. Cohen: 'John McArthur jr, AIA, 1823–1890', *Drawing towards Building: Philadelphia Architectural Graphics, 1732–1986* (exh. cat. by J. O'Gordon and others, Philadelphia, PA Acad. F.A., 1986), pp. 111–14

GEORGE E. THOMAS

**McBean, Angus** (*b* Newbridge, Gwent, 8 June 1904; *d* 9 June 1990). British photographer. A self-taught photographer, he worked as a bank clerk in Monmouth from 1923 to 1926 and then moved to London, where he worked for Liberty's until 1933. Following this he spent a year making decorative masks and theatre props as well as taking photographs. He greatly improved his technical competence working as a photographic assistant to Hugh

Cecil in 1934–5. He then set up a studio in London, where he produced photographs of leading actors and actresses. He soon became the official photographer for the Old Vic, Sadlers Wells, Stratford-on-Avon and Glyndebourne theatres and also for the theatrical productions of H. M. Tennent. The resulting works, such as *Vivien Leigh as Cleopatra and Laurence Olivier as Mark Antony* (1951; see Woodhouse 1982, pl. 80), were widely distributed for over 30 years and provide invaluable records of that distinguished period in British theatre. Having started with his studio in Victoria in London, he moved to Covent Garden in 1945, to Islington in 1960 and in 1966 moved out of London into Suffolk. By 1970 he had largely given up professional photography, and by this time the prevailing emphasis on theatrical realism had made his composed, artificial style unfashionable.

While producing theatre photographs, McBean also made light-heartedly Surrealist studio portraits of actors and actresses, which appeared first in *The Sketch* and later in *The Tatler* as well. Using theatrical props and elaborate sets he created works such as *Dorothy Dickson* (1938; see Woodhouse 1982, pl. 26) in which, characteristically, most of the sitter's body was concealed beneath the props. From 1945 McBean began making sophisticated photographic Christmas cards, employing the Surrealist style of his studio portraits; these images became widely influential despite their originally private distribution. In the 1950s he began to produce photographs for the covers of record albums, including several for the Beatles' records, such as the cover for their 1970 album *Let it Be*.

BIBLIOGRAPHY
A. Woodhouse: *Angus McBean* (London and New York, 1982)
——: *Masters of Photography: Angus McBean* (London, 1985)

**Macbeth, Robert Walker** (*b* Glasgow, 30 Sept 1848; *d* London, 1 Nov 1910). Scottish painter, illustrator and printmaker. The son of the Scottish portrait painter Norman Macbeth (1821–88), he studied at the Royal Scottish Academy Painting Schools, Edinburgh. He first exhibited in London, at the Dudley Gallery, in 1869; he moved in 1870 to London, where he attended the Royal Academy Schools (1871–2). During the 1870s he worked as an illustrator for the *Graphic* magazine. Among his many semi-journalistic illustrations, his scenes of life in Paris during the Franco–Prussian War were vividly realistic.

Macbeth revered and emulated the 'Idyllist' group of illustrators and painters, which had formed in the 1860s around the artist Fred Walker. Macbeth adapted from the works of Walker, George John Pinwell, George Heming Mason and John William North his own approach to rustic figurative subjects, and, like them, he combined a poignant romanticism with accuracy of naturalistic detail. In the mid-1870s Macbeth repeatedly visited Lincolnshire, and a series of large paintings of Fenland life resulted, including *A Lincolnshire Gang* (exh. RA 1876; untraced) and the *Potato Harvest* (exh. RA 1877; sold London, Sotheby's, 15 March 1983, lot 66). Both of these include heroically scaled figures set among dour farm buildings or bleak landscapes and evoke the physical hardship of working on the land. Later Macbeth adopted a gentler mood: his gouache *Greeting the Postman* (1880; London,

V&A) is typical of the intimate genre subject that Macbeth inherited from Walker. In the mid-1880s Macbeth moved to Somerset to live near North; as a result Macbeth's work both in oil and in watercolour gained a new brilliancy of colour and a more vibrant technique. In 1897 Macbeth moved back to London, where he continued to paint pastoral and rustic subjects.

Macbeth was also a distinguished printmaker. From *c.* 1878 onwards he made original etchings of the subjects he was painting; these frequently appeared in the *Portfolio* or other art magazines, occasionally before the equivalent painting was completed. Macbeth was also widely admired for his reproductive prints, which included the *Harvest Moon* after Mason, of 1883; the *Pied Piper* after Pinwell, of 1884; and *The Plough* after Walker, of 1887. Other contemporary painters whose works he copied were Millais and Burne-Jones, and he also etched subjects after Titian and Velázquez.

BIBLIOGRAPHY
[P. G. Hamerton]: 'The Ferry: Etched by Robert W. Macbeth', *Portfolio* [London] (1881), p. 21
W. Armstrong: 'Scottish Painters X', *Portfolio* [London] (1887), pp. 227–34
[P. G. Hamerton]: 'Art Chronicle', *Portfolio* [London] (1887), p. 64
A. L. Baldry: 'R. W. Macbeth, A.R.A.', *A. J.* [London] (1900), pp. 289–92
                                    CHRISTOPHER NEWALL

**MacBryde, Robert** (*b* Maybole, Ayrshire [now Strathclyde], 5 Dec 1913; *d* Dublin, 6 May 1966). Scottish painter. He was closely associated with Robert Colquhoun, whom he met as a student at Glasgow School of Art in 1932 and with whom he travelled to France and Italy from 1937 to 1939. Exempt from military service in World War II, he followed Colquhoun to London where they entered the Neo-Romantic circle, sharing the same friends and influences (*see* NEO-ROMANTICISM). Although his work is sometimes considered derivative of Colquhoun's, some of his still-lifes, for example *Table in a Red Room* (1950; AC Eng), show him to have been a competent painter. Notorious figures of Fitzrovia, London's wartime bohemia, he and Colquhoun feature in many literary memoirs, regarded as casualties of a 'lost generation'. His loyal support of Colquhoun was essential to the latter's success. He was constantly in debt, his work declined in the late 1950s and he produced little after his friend's death.

BIBLIOGRAPHY
*A Paradise Lost: The Neo-Romantic Imagination in Britain, 1935–55* (exh. cat., ed. D. Mellor; London, Barbican A.G., 1987)
M. Yorke: *The Spirit of the Place: Nine Neo-Romantic Artists and their Times* (London, 1988)
                                    VIRGINIA BUTTON

**McCahon, Colin (John)** (*b* Timaru, 1 Aug 1919; *d* Auckland, 27 May 1987). New Zealand painter. He was the outstanding figure in New Zealand visual art of the 20th century. His continuing themes were the landscape of New Zealand and the paradoxes of faith and doubt in a secular world. During the 1940s he depicted a number of biblical events set in the New Zealand landscape. Words appeared as titles written on to the works, as in the *Promised Land* (1948; Auckland, C.A.G.), or in speech balloons issuing from the mouths of the figures, as in *King* *of the Jews* (1947; Wellington, Mus. NZ, Te Papa Tongarewa). The scornful responses to these works, which he painted in a consciously naive style hoping for ease of communication, created a long-lasting bitterness.

After travelling to America in 1958 McCahon began producing long series of paintings designed for the viewer to walk past. The first of these was *Northland Panels* (1958; Wellington, Mus. NZ, Te Papa Tongarewa). These 'journey' works often included numbers referring to the Stations of the Cross (e.g. *Te Tangi o te Pipiwhararua* ('The song of the shining cuckoo', 1974; Dunedin, NZ, U. Otago, Hocken Lib.). His works became increasingly abstract and his landscapes more schematic though he did not subscribe to a modernist rejection of content. Narrative was contained in his chosen texts, which were usually quotations from the Bible or from Maori and English poetry. After 1965 he worked principally in black and white, writing in white on a black ground, the words enlightening the dark landscape. In 1970 he painted *Victory Over Death 2* (Canberra, N.G.) in which the words 'I AM' dominate the 7 m long canvas, and other texts are the words of Christ and the crowd around the foot of the cross.

For illustration *see* NEW ZEALAND, fig. 6.

BIBLIOGRAPHY
*Colin McCahon: A Survey Exhibition* (exh. cat. by C. McCahon, Auckland, C.A.G., 1972)
G. H. Brown: *Colin McCahon: Artist* (Wellington, 1984, rev. 1993)
*I Will Need Words* (exh. cat. by W. Curnow, Wellington, NZ, N.A.G., 1984)
*Colin McCahon: Gates and Journeys* (exh. cat. by A. Johnston and others, Auckland, C.A.G., 1988)
*Colin McCahon: The Last Painting* (Auckland, 1993)

ALEXA M. JOHNSTON

**Maccari, Cesare** (*b* Siena, 1840; *d* Rome, 1919). Italian painter. He studied decoration at the Istituto d'Arte in Siena and also observed the sculptor Tito Sarrocchi (1824–1900) at work in his studio. Maccari became a friend of Luigi Mussini and Alessandro Franchi, and he decided to devote himself to painting. On winning a scholarship, he studied in Rome. He achieved success with *Fabiola* (Siena, Col. Chigi–Saracini) and afterwards he worked on the decoration of the church of the Sudario.

From 1872 to 1882 he worked for Goupil and other dealers, and he came to know the Spanish painter Mariano Fortuny y Marsal. From 1882 to 1888 he painted frescoes of scenes from Roman history in the Sala Gialla in the Senate at Rome. In the Palazzo Pubblico at Siena (1886–7) he painted the *Presentation to Victor Emmanuel II of the Plebiscite of Rome by Duke Caetani* and the *Transport of the Mortal Remains of Victor Emmanuel II to the Pantheon* (*in situ*).

Maccari was in contact with the painter Nino Costa (1827–1903), and he took part in exhibitions organized by watercolourists in Rome. It is possible that he also exhibited with the group In Arte Libertas in London in 1890. He received several church commissions, working in churches in Genova and Imperia between 1886 and 1889, and in Loreto, on the dome of the basilica, between 1888–9 and 1907. In his later work he adopted a style combining neo-Renaissance, Venetian and realistic elements.

BIBLIOGRAPHY
O. Roux: *Artisti*, ii of *Infanzia e giovinezza di illustri italiani contemporanei: Memorie autobiografiche* (Florence, 1909), pp. 43–51
G. Marziali: 'Cesare Maccari', *Siena tra Purismo e Liberty* (exh. cat., ed. M. Batazzi; Siena, Pal. Pub., 1988), pp. 153–9

BERNARDINA SANI

**McCarter Nairne.** Canadian architectural partnership formed in 1921 in Vancouver by John Young McCarter (*b* Victoria, British Columbia, 12 Aug 1886; *d* Vancouver, 21 May 1981) and George Colvill Nairne (*b* Inverness, Scotland, 14 Nov 1884; *d* Vancouver, 18 April 1953). McCarter trained in Victoria and then with Thomas Hooper (1859–1931) in Vancouver (1907–12). Nairne practised in Cardiff, Wales, Seattle and Nanaimo, British Columbia, before joining Hooper (1911–13). With the completion in 1925 of the modern Gothic David Spencer Store (now part of the Sears Tower complex) they became the most celebrated exponents in Vancouver of contemporary architectural trends, remaining so until the 1950s. The Medical–Dental Building (1928–9; destr. 1989) was their first essay in Art Deco, which they perfected with the Marine Building (1928–30), 335 Burrard Street, Vancouver, an Art-Deco masterpiece upon which their reputation chiefly rests; it is ornamented with terracotta panels and was then the tallest building in Vancouver. McCarter Nairne's sophisticated eclecticism is particularly evident in the Federal Office Building (1935–8), and elements remain in the formalism of their later interpretations of the International Style in Vancouver, typified by the dignified functionalism of the General Post Office (1953–8; with the Federal Department of Public Works). The franker Modernism of the Stock Exchange (1953) and Wosk's Warehouse Store (1956) was replaced in the firm's later phase by an inventive New Brutalism, at its most adept in the Shaughnessy Place housing development (1976), all in Vancouver. The firm, renamed McCarter, Nairne and Partners in 1953, remained in practice until 1983.

BIBLIOGRAPHY
H. Kalman and J. Roaf: *Exploring Vancouver 2* (Vancouver, 1978)
A. Rogatnick: 'Everything Was Up-to-date in the 1930s', *Vancouver: Art and Artists, 1931–1983*, ed. L. Rombout (Vancouver, 1983), pp. 42–6

R. WINDSOR LISCOMBE

**McCarthy, J(ames) J(oseph)** (*b* Dublin, 6 Jan 1817; *d* Dublin, 6 Feb 1882). Irish architect. He was educated at the Christian Brothers' School, Dublin, and entered the Figure and Ornament Schools of the Royal Dublin Society in 1834. In 1837 he moved to the Architecture School and in the same year began to exhibit designs at the Royal Hibernian Academy. He was articled to the architect William Farrell (*d* 1852). He probably spent the years 1843–6 in England, where he came under the influence of A. W. N. Pugin and the Ecclesiological movement. By 1846 he was back in Ireland and embarked on his first major commission, St Kevin's, Glendalough, Co. Wicklow, which he described as 'the first uncompromisingly true church of the old type erected in the archdiocese of Dublin'. It followed Ecclesiological recommendations for a small rural church, with a nave and carefully differentiated chancel, a bell cote, south porch and a sacristy, and was built of local granite with limestone dressings. He planned a richly decorated interior, with rood screen, sedilia and founder's tomb, stained glass, encaustic tiles and stencilled walls, but little of this was achieved. St Kevin's launched McCarthy on a successful career. His religion was no disadvantage, as the Catholic church began a vigorous building campaign. McCarthy was a skilled self-publicist, writing about the new architecture in Duffy's *Irish Catholic Magazine*. As a founder and joint honorary secretary of the Irish Ecclesiological Society, he was in a position to influence the Catholic hierarchy and obtain many commissions. The society published his pamphlet *Suggestions on the Arrangement and Characteristics of Parish Churches* in 1851. In 1852 Pugin offered McCarthy the supervision of his Irish work, but the proposed partnership came to nothing owing to Pugin's death in the same year.

Throughout the 1850s McCarthy consolidated his position as Ireland's leading Catholic architect, a position vividly illustrated in the number of cathedrals he designed or completed. In 1853 he was given the supervision of Pugin's Killarney Cathedral, and he also completed work at Enniscorthy in 1857. He took over the design of St Patrick's, Armagh, in 1854 and turned Thomas Duff's spiky Perpendicular into soaring Decorated Gothic. He completed St Eugene's, Derry, in the mid-1850s. His first independent cathedral commission was St Macartan's, Monaghan, begun in 1861, an ambitious essay in full-blown and vigorous High Victorian Decorated. His Cathedral of the Assumption, Thurles, Co. Tipperary (1865–72), on the other hand, is Italian Romanesque, with an arcaded front and circular baptistery as at Pisa. McCarthy handled these commissions with confidence, even panache, but he was at his best in small parish churches, clearly and coherently planned, with strong sculptural forms built of local materials. Generally in Early English style, as at Portlaw, Co. Waterford (1858–9), or Decorated Gothic, as at Kilskyre, Co. Meath, they are occasionally Romanesque, the rather bleak Ballitore, Co. Kildare (1860–63), for example. McCarthy was very much influenced by the development of the Gothic Revival in England and kept abreast of the literature on the subject. On the whole he drew on English or French models for his designs, though occasionally, where there were suitable local examples, as at Kilmallock, Co. Limerick (1878), he turned to Irish medieval architecture. His practice was almost wholly ecclesiastical, though he made Gothic additions to Castleforbes, Co. Longford, in 1859, and designed Cahirmoyle House, Co. Limerick, in full-blooded Ruskinian polychromy in 1870. Not, it appears, a popular man, he was professionally successful. He was a member of the Royal Irish Academy, the Royal Institute of the Architects of Ireland and the Royal Hibernian Academy. In 1867 he became Professor of Architecture at the Catholic University in Dublin.

WRITINGS

'Ecclesiastical Architecture', *Ir. Catholic Mag.*, iv (1847), p. 110

BIBLIOGRAPHY

J. Sheehy: *J. J. McCarthy and the Gothic Revival in Ireland* (Belfast, 1977)

JEANNE SHEEHY

**MacCarthy-Reagh, Count Justin** (*b* Springhouse, Scotland, 18 Aug 1744; *d* Toulouse, 1811). French book collector of Scottish birth. Having promised his father that he would leave Britain and never return while Catholicism was not the dominant religion, MacCarthy-Reagh settled in Toulouse. In 1776 he was granted naturalization as a Frenchman. He collected books from his youth and amassed one of the finest libraries in Europe, concentrating particularly on the acquisition of rare early printed books and illuminated manuscripts. He acquired a fine series of books printed at Mainz in the early days of printing, rare books printed in the late 15th century and the 16th, books printed on parchment, and very early books printed from woodblocks, regarded as the first experiments in printing. Among his collection he had a number of finely illuminated early printed books; one of these is a Latin Bible (sold Paris, de Bure, at Hôtel de Bullion, 27 Jan–6 May 1817, lot 66) published in Venice by Nicolas Jenson in 1476, with an ornamental frontispiece, a full-page miniature and over 60 pages of decorated borders. His collection of illuminated manuscripts included two Books of Hours executed by Nicolas Jarry in 1645 and 1652 (sold Paris, de Bure, at Hôtel de Bullion, 27 Jan–6 May 1817, lots 436 and 427).

BIBLIOGRAPHY

Hoefer

J. R. de Bure and M. J. de Bure: *Catalogue des livres rares et précieux de la bibliothèque du feu M. le Comte de Mac-Carthy Reagh*, 2 vols (Paris, 1815) [record of col., later advertised at time of sale]

**Macchiaioli.** Group of Italian artists based in Tuscany during the second half of the 19th century. The formation of the group between 1853 and 1860 coincided with the Paris Exposition Universelle and popular acceptance of the Barbizon school and of Camille Corot, who influenced them indirectly. In 1854 Serafino De Tivoli (1826–92) was one of a group of *plein-air* painters who called themselves the Scuola di Staggia. At about the same time Telemaco Signorini, Vincenzo Cabianca (1827–1902) and Odoardo Borrani (1834–1905) formed their own group, which was joined by Giovanni Fattori and Vito D'Ancona (1825–84) in 1855, Raffaello Sernesi (1838–66) and Silvestro Lega in 1859, and by Cristiano Banti (1824–1904) and Giuseppe Abbati (1836–68) in 1860. United by common artistic and political sentiments of opposition to the formal teaching of the Florentine Accademia di Belle Arti and support for Italian unification, these ten artists formed the first nucleus of the *Macchiaioli* group.

Isolated in their early years by the repressive political situation preceding Italian unification, the group kept up with wider European artistic trends through banned foreign periodicals and contact with artists who had been abroad. Domenico Morelli, Saverio Altamura (1826–97) and De Tivoli brought news from the Paris art world in 1855. Signorini and others met Edgar Degas in Florence in 1856. Giovanni Costa came to Florence in 1859 and for ten years was their friend and adviser. Marcellin Desboutin, French writer, poet, painter and antiquarian, was influential between 1857 and 1874. By 1861, when they were able to travel abroad, numerous artists, especially Signorini, began to make regular trips to Paris, London and Edinburgh.

While in Florence, the *Macchiaioli* frequented the Caffè Michelangiolo, which was favoured by artistic and political rebels until 1860. It was there that Signorini met DIEGO MARTELLI, whose moral and material support became vital to the group. His farm at Castiglioncello in the Tuscan Maremma was a gathering-place for the *Macchiaioli*, especially between 1861 and 1867, and many works were produced there (e.g. Odoardo Borrani, *Sea coast at Castiglioncello*, c. 1864–5; Florence, Pitti).

At first the *Macchiaioli* called themselves *Effettisti*, probably deriving the term from the French *effet*, used to describe the results of light and shade distribution in paintings and photographs. Their painting technique eschewed half-tones; they claimed that 'effect' was achieved through the use of broad patches of colour, *macchie*, which moved abruptly from dark to light. *Macchia* translates as spot, blot or daub. In 1862 a Florentine critic dubbed them *Macchiaioli*, or spot-makers, ridiculing them as daubers who left their paintings unfinished; the name was then adopted by the group. Because the theories of the *Macchiaioli* were not written down until the 1870s and 1880s, its contemporary historians, Martelli, Signorini and Adriano Cecioni, may have shaped their descriptions of the early movement to conform with later experiences; thus Martelli saw Fattori's works as 'impressions' after becoming acquainted with Impressionism. According to Martelli, the *macchia* was 'the theory of chiaroscuro and the relationship of one colour with another, whether they were found next to one another on the canvas on the same perspective plane or ... juxtaposed on the canvas but in different perspective planes'. Cecioni wrote: '*Il vero* [nature, as we see it] results from *macchie* of *colour* and of *chiaroscuro*, each one of which has its own value, which is measured by means of *relationship*. In every *macchia* this relationship has a double value: as light or dark, and as colour.' Cecioni also spoke of the use of a black mirror, or 'Claude glass', to help establish colour values and relationships. Such theories and research were inspired by two 19th-century concerns, the search to understand colour through science and the revival of interest in the Italian artistic past.

The word *macchia* had been part of the artistic vocabulary of the Italian Renaissance; it was used by Vasari in 1550 to describe the stage in a painting when the colours are blocked out in a flat, simplified scheme before the execution of the finished painting. Some scholars have accepted this traditional practice as the source of the *macchia* adopted by the *Macchiaioli* in their small, sketch-like paintings. Vasari also used the term in describing the loose finish in Titian's late manner. In 1660 Marco Boschini wrote a lengthy poetic description of the Venetian *macchia*, in which gesture, impasto, blurring of outline, colour reflections and the optical interplay of warm and cool colours were preferred to the smooth surfaces and hard outlines of Florentine painting. There are many points of similarity between Renaissance and 19th-century uses of the *macchia*, and in many ways the works of the *Macchiaioli* are part of a specifically Italian tradition of painting.

Nationalist sentiments were an important element of their ethos as a group; in their adoption of the local landscape as their main subject and in their identification with the ideals of Garibaldi and Mazzini, they were thoroughly bound up with the contemporary world. Their depiction of ordinary folk engaged in everyday activities in traditional Renaissance pictorial space was typically Realist (Silvestro Lega, *The Pergola*, 1868; Milan, Brera). They were not Impressionists, and did not wish to be, in spite of Martelli's attempts to link them with contemporary French painting. While Impressionists and *Macchiaioli* both aimed for spontaneity and immediacy of effect, the Impressionists pursued effects of light and colour at the expense of form and depth, while *macchia* painting used light and colour to create form and pictorial space. Furthermore, the Impressionists used the 'scientific' colours of Isaac Newton, while the *Macchiaioli* palette, though bright, remained more traditionally Romantic.

Modern technology was not shunned, however; the use of photographs, documented by Signorini in 1874, can be detected in the group's more topographical views and in some figurative works that resemble photomontages, such as Signorini's *Leith* (1881; Florence, Pitti). The experiments of Fattori and Signorini with the colours and spatial organization of Japanese prints were noted at the time and have been documented (Gray Troyer, 1978). Some of the *macchia* paintings from as early as 1860 show a remarkable geometric reduction and abstract simplicity for their dating (Giuseppi Abbati, *Cloister*, c. 1861–2; Florence, Pitti).

Most *Macchiaioli* works have remained in Italian collections, and most of the literature on the group is in Italian. Scholars outside Italy have recently given the *Macchiaioli* a broader historical viewpoint and audience. A second generation of Italian *macchia* painters carried the technique into the 20th century.

#### BIBLIOGRAPHY
T. Signorini: 'Cose d'arte', *Il Risorgimento* (June 1874); repr. in E. Somaré: *Signorini* (Milan, 1926), pp. 256–9
A. Cecioni: 'Vincenzo Cabianca', *Scritti e ricordi*, ed. G. Uzielli (Florence, 1905)
D. Martelli: 'Giuseppi Abbati', *Scritti e ricordi di Diego Martelli*, ed. A. Boschetto (Florence, 1952)
N. Broude: *The Macchiaioli: Academicism and Modernism in Nineteenth Century Italian Painting* (diss., New York, Columbia U., 1967)
——: 'The Macchiaioli: Effect and Expression in Nineteenth-century Florentine Painting', *A. Bull.*, lii (1970), pp. 11–21
——: 'The Macchiaioli as "Proto-Impressionists": Realism, Popular Science and the Re-shaping of *Macchia*: Romanticism, 1862–1886', *A. Bull.*, lii (1970), pp. 404–14
——: 'An Early Friend of Degas in Florence: A Newly Identified Portrait Drawing of Degas by Giovanni Fattori', *Burl. Mag.*, cxv (1973), pp. 726–35
*I Macchiaioli* (exh. cat. by D. Durbé and S. Pinto, Florence, Forte Belvedere, 1976)
N. Gray Troyer: *The Macchiaioli: Effects of Modern Color Theory, Photography and Japanese Prints on a Group of Italian Painters, 1855–1900* (diss., Evanston, IL, Northwestern U., 1978)
*I Macchiaioli: Peintres en Toscane après 1850* (exh. cat. by D. Durbé, Paris, Grand Pal., 1978)
D. Durbé and G. Matteucci: *30 Macchiaioli inediti* (Rome, 1980)
N. Gray Troyer: 'Telemaco Signorini and Macchiaioli *Giapponismo*', *A. Bull.*, lxvi (1984), pp. 136–45
N. Broude: *The Macchiaioli: Italian Painters of the Nineteenth Century* (New Haven and London, 1987)
A. Boime: *The Art of the Macchia and the Risorgimento: Representing Culture and Nationalism in Nineteenth-century Italy* (Chicago, IL, 1993)

NANCY GRAY TROYER

**Macchietti, Girolamo (di Francesco di Mariotto)** [Girolamo del Crocifissaio] (*b* c. 1535; *d* Florence, 3 Jan 1592). Italian painter. He trained in Florence with Michele Tosini, whose studio he left c. 1556 to work for six years under Vasari on the redecoration of the Palazzo Vecchio, Florence; there he was apparently employed as a designer of tapestries. This was followed by two years of study in Rome. By 1563 he had returned to Florence, where he became a member of the newly founded Accademia del Disegno. Under the academy's auspices he collaborated in 1564 with his friend MIRABELLO CAVALORI on a grisaille painting of *Lorenzo de' Medici Receiving Michelangelo* (untraced) for the catafalque of Michelangelo's funeral in S Lorenzo, Florence. For the academy's next major project, the decorations for Duke Francesco I de' Medici's wedding in 1565 to Joanna of Austria (1547–78), Macchietti contributed a monochrome painting of the *Establishment of the Monastery of Monte Oliveto Maggiore* (untraced) towards a festive 'Arch of Religion'.

Macchietti may have visited Rome again before executing the *Adoration of the Magi* (1568; Florence, S Lorenzo, Cappella della Stufa). This altarpiece chiefly reflects Vasari's elaborate Mannerist style, but numerous details derive from paintings by Parmigianino and the school of Raphael; and the composition was based on a version of the theme by Taddeo Zuccaro (Cambridge, Fitzwilliam). In Macchietti's *Holy Family with St Anne* (*c*. 1568; Budapest, Mus. F.A.) and the *Madonna della cintola* (*c*. 1569; Florence, S Agata), his Mannerism yielded to a more restrained style. This may be due to contemporary works he viewed in Rome, or to pictures conceived in the spirit of the Counter-Reformation in Florence, such as Santi di Tito's *Adoration of the Shepherds with St Francis* (*c*. 1566; Florence, S Giuseppe) and Cavalori's *Pentecost* (*c*. 1567–8; Florence, Badia Fiorentina).

The two paintings Macchietti contributed to the *studiolo* of Francesco I in the Palazzo Vecchio, the *Baths of Pozzuoli* and *Medea and Jason* (*c*. 1570–72), were indebted to Cavalori's *studiolo* pictures in their naturalism of light and space and in the graceful figure-types derived from Pontormo and Andrea del Sarto. The beautiful lighting of these pictures is also found in Macchietti's *Allegory of Wealth* (Venice, Ca' d'Oro). For his *Martyrdom of St Lawrence* (1573; Florence, S Maria Novella, Cappella Giuochi) Macchietti turned to Venetian models, particularly Titian's rendition of the subject in S Maria Assunta (Venice, Chiesa dei Gesuiti). Macchietti's later altarpieces, such as the *St Lawrence in Glory* (Empoli, Mus. S Andrea), were less adventurous and more schematic. His last years were spent mainly in Naples and Benevento (1578–84) and in Spain (1587–9).

BIBLIOGRAPHY

L. Marcucci: 'Girolamo Macchietti disegnatore', *Mitt. Ksthist. Inst. Florenz*, vii (1955), pp. 121–32
P. Pouncey: 'Contributo a Girolamo Macchietti', *Boll. A.*, xlvii (1962), pp. 237–40
V. Pace: 'Contributi al catalogo di alcuni pittori dello studiolo di Francesco I', *Paragone*, xxiv (1973), pp. 69–84
J. Spalding: 'Two Florentine Altarpieces by Girolamo Macchietti', *Pantheon*, xlii (Oct–Dec 1984), pp. 367–9
L. Feinberg: *The Works of Mirabello Cavalori* (diss., Cambridge, MA, Harvard U., 1986)

LARRY J. FEINBERG

**Macció, Rómulo** (*b* Buenos Aires, 29 April 1931). Argentine painter. He was self-taught and showed Surrealist-influenced pictures at his first one-man exhibition in 1956. After a brief period of lyrical abstraction, he returned to figurative references within an essentially Abstract Expressionist style under the influence of Willem de Kooning. After 1961, when he, Ernesto Deira, Luis Felipe Noé and Jorge de la Vega held an exhibtion, *Otra figuración*, at the Galería Peuser, Buenos Aires, he adopted a more monumental style concerned with gesture and expression in works such as *Living a Little Every Day* (1963; Buenos Aires, Mus. N. B.A.), often using innovative supports and submerging the human figure in a virtually abstract setting; in these works he favoured violent colours and graphic devices borrowed from the mass media, reflecting his own experience in the advertising business. From 1977 Macció no longer treated figures in a fragmented form, picturing them instead like distorted shapes in an early stage of development. From 1982 he turned his attention to archetypes painted in a wild Neo-Expressionist style, using humour and fantasy to create a disconcerting world.

He received various important awards, including the Primer Premio Internacional of the Instituto de Artes Visuales Torcuato Di Tella in Buenos Aires (1963) and the Guggenheim International Prize in New York (1964). He also showed in the Argentine pavilion at the Venice Biennale in 1968.

BIBLIOGRAPHY

A. Pellegrini: *Panorama de la pintura argentina contemporánea* (Buenos Aires, 1967)
*Rómulo Macció* (exh. cat., preface J. Lassaigne; Milan, Gal. Incisione, 1974)

NELLY PERAZZO

**McClymonds, Ruth.** *See* MAITLAND, RUTH.

**MacColl, Dugald Sutherland** (*b* Glasgow, 10 March 1859; *d* London, 21 Dec 1948). Scottish writer, critic and painter. Born and educated in Scotland, he spent most of his working life in London, writing art criticism for the *Spectator*, *Saturday Review* and *Week-end Review*, and exhibiting with the New English Art Club, which he joined in 1896. He painted mostly in watercolour, combining fluid washes with an interest in topography, as in *A Mill at Tewkesbury* (1910; London, V&A). He was also editor of the *Architectural Review* (1901–5), Keeper of the Tate Gallery (1906–11) and Keeper of the Wallace Collection (1911–24). He was the first to propose the idea, in his three reports published in September 1900 in the *Saturday Review*, for the National Art-Collection Fund, which he helped found. He was also an outspoken critic of the use to which the Chantry Bequest had been put. His book *Nineteenth Century Art* (1902), based on the paintings exhibited at the International Exhibition at Glasgow in 1901, helped direct attention away from the Royal Academy and towards the Glasgow school and the New English Art Club. Its chapter 'The Spectral Palette' revealed an intelligent understanding of Impressionist theory and practice and helped establish MacColl as an interpreter of this movement. The book also promoted an artist on whom MacColl later wrote the monograph *Life, Work and Setting of Philip Wilson Steer* (1945). Like his mentor R. A. M. Stevenson (1847–1900), MacColl emphasized technique and painting method over representational content, but he could not accept Post-Impressionism and all his life remained hostile to Cézanne's work. He first voiced his objections in his article 'A Year of Post-Impressionism' (*19th C. & After*, lxxi (1912), pp. 285–302) and remained Roger Fry's most serious critic.

WRITINGS
*Nineteenth Century Art* (Glasgow, 1902)
*Confessions of a Keeper and Other Papers* (London, 1931)
*Life, Work and Setting of Philip Wilson Steer* (London, 1945)

BIBLIOGRAPHY
*DNB*
J. V. Falkenheim: *Roger Fry and the Beginnings of Formalist Art Criticism* (Ann Arbor, MI, 1980) [chap. 3 discusses the debate between Fry and MacColl]
M. Lago: *Christiana Herringham and the Edwardian Art Scene* (in preparation)

FRANCES SPALDING

**McCollum, Allan** (*b* Los Angeles, CA, 4 Aug 1944). American sculptor. He did not have a formal art education. McCollum has stated that formative influence in his work included the Fluxus movement of the 1960s and the work of conceptual artists, such as Sol LeWitt and Daniel Buren. In 1975 he moved to New York. Departing from the notion of a work of art as a rare object of unique value, he introduced a procedure of studio manufacture of precast models made in unlimited editions. The series of *Perfect Vehicles* (exh. New York, Cash–Newhouse Gal., 1986) resembled large vessels, sealed and painted in Moorglo on concrete. *Over 10,000 Individual Works* (exh. New York, John Weber Gal., 1987) comprised precise rows of miniature units moulded from found objects, painted in enamel on solid-cast Hydrocal (fibreglass and concrete). McCollum scrupulously avoided aspects of ironical parody typical of Pop art. His works were not presented as decorative accessories or social commentary but as physical signs of the mechanical drives of existence—of repetitious behaviour and patterns of market-based relationships.

BIBLIOGRAPHY
C. Owens: 'Allan McCollum: Repetition and Difference', *A. America*, lxxi/8 (1983), pp. 130–32
*Allan McCollum: Perfect Vehicles* (exh. cat. by J. Jacobs, Sarasota, FL, Ringling Mus. A., 1988–9)
*Allan McCollum* (exh. cat. by A. Rorimer and L. Cooke, Eindhoven, Stedel. Van Abbemus., 1989)

☐

**McComb, John**, jr (*b* New York, 17 Oct 1763; *d* New York, 25 May 1853). American architect. The leading architect in New York during the Federal period, he was trained by his father, John McComb sr (1732–1811), a mason and builder–architect. The younger McComb began his career in the 1790s in a style combining Colonial Palladian tendencies with a Neo-classicism inspired by Robert Adam, and he retained the latter character in his work to the end. In his unexecuted designs, this quality is especially seen in unusual room shapes, but in his completed buildings it is most revealed in proportions and in decorative detail. His architectural work comprised town and country houses for the leading citizens of New York, a number of churches and a variety of semi-public buildings in that city, two college buildings in New Jersey and a series of lighthouses stretching from Virginia to the eastern end of Long Island.

McComb's best-known work is New York City Hall, the execution of which, based on the competition-winning design submitted jointly by him and Joseph François Mangin, he supervised from 1803 to 1812. That design, in a French Neo-classical vein, was primarily the work of Mangin, but McComb refined the design and created the

interior decoration, introducing significant elements from his English-influenced background. His other major works include Alexander Hamilton's country house, The Grange (1801–02; then outside the city but now in New York); and St John's Chapel (1803–07; destr.) and Washington Hall (1809–14; destr.), both in New York. He largely retired from active practice *c.* 1826.

BIBLIOGRAPHY
D. Stillman: *Artistry and Skill in the Architecture of John McComb jr* (diss., Newark, U. DE, 1956)
——: 'New York City Hall: Competition and Execution', *J. Soc. Archit. Historians*, xxiii (1964), pp. 129–42
A. A. Gilchrist: 'Notes for a Catalogue of the John McComb (1763–1853) Collection of Architectural Drawings at the New-York Historical Society', *J. Soc. Archit. Historians*, xxviii (1969), pp. 201–10
——: 'John McComb, sr and jr, in New York, 1784–1799', *J. Soc. Archit. Historians*, xxxi (1972), pp. 10–21

DAMIE STILLMAN

**McConnel, Smith & Johnson.** *See under* JOHNSON, RICHARD NORMAN.

**McCubbin, Frederick** (*b* Melbourne, 25 Feb 1855; *d* Melbourne, 20 Dec 1917). Australian painter and teacher. A baker's son, he trained from 1869 at the local Artisans' School of Design in Carlton and by 1872 was at the School of Design, National Gallery of Victoria, Melbourne. It was not until the Munich-trained George Folingsby (1828–91) was appointed master of the Gallery Art School in 1882 that McCubbin received a thorough academic training in figure painting. Folingsby evoked McCubbin's interest in large-scale history pieces with a pronounced national flavour. From the colonial artist and Swiss émigré Abram-Louis Buvelot, McCubbin absorbed a more intimate, Barbizon-style vision of the Australian landscape. Julian Ashton directed his attention to subjects from contemporary life and introduced him to *plein-air* painting. In the mid-1880s McCubbin's growing adherence to *plein-air* Realism was strengthened by the influence of Portuguese-born Arthur Loureiro (1853–1912) and, more dramatically, by the impact of Tom Roberts, recently returned from Europe in 1885. With Roberts and Arthur Streeton he founded the painting camp at Box Hill, in the suburbs of Melbourne, that became known as the HEIDELBERG SCHOOL. The Realists' concern with the integrity and significance of the subject shaped McCubbin's fundamental attitudes to art. Unlike Roberts and Charles Conder (a fellow Heidelberg painter), McCubbin was only marginally influenced by the Aesthetic Movement, and he exhibited a token five works at the famous *9 by 5 Impression Exhibition* in Melbourne in 1889.

McCubbin's major achievement was probably his series of large subject pictures that paid tribute to the heroism of the pioneers in settling the land and establishing the Australian nation. Such pioneer subjects as the *North Wind* (1891), *The Pioneer* (1904; both Melbourne, N.G. Victoria) and the *Bush Burial* (1890; Geelong, A.G.; see fig.) relate to earlier traditions in Australian colonial art, but McCubbin laid new emphasis on the hardships endured by women and children alongside the men. He successfully combined the style and iconography of European Realism with local, popular imagery found in illustration and photography. The strain of melancholy and residue of 19th-century sentiment in McCubbin's

Frederick McCubbin: *Bush Burial*, oil on canvas, 1.23×2.25 m, 1890 (Geelong, Art Gallery)

pictures distinguish their mood and conception from comparable pastoral subjects painted by Roberts.

In the early 1890s McCubbin gradually adopted a more painterly style and technique in tune with contemporary foreign developments. In the later 1890s he became increasingly preoccupied with capturing the lyrical beauty of the bush landscape for its own sake; the influence of Jules Bastien-Lepage, so evident in his earlier pioneer subjects, slowly gave way to the more evocative, intimate effects of such artists as Camille Corot (e.g. *Winter Evening*, 1897; Melbourne, N.G. Victoria). The final phase of McCubbin's development began around 1904 with a deepening appreciation of the late works of J. M. W. Turner. His enthusiasm for Turner was confirmed in 1907 during his only visit to Europe, though he was also impressed by George Clausen's recent works and the art of the Impressionists. On his return to Australia he concentrated on painting light-filled Impressionistic landscapes, strongly poetic in mood; these pictures have brilliant, broken colour, palette-knife effects and a richly textured surface (e.g. *Autumn Morning, South Yarra*, 1916; Melbourne, N.G. Victoria). McCubbin evidently valued these works as highly as his earlier, better-known figure compositions. In his later years he also received an increasing number of portrait commissions.

McCubbin believed that artists should primarily derive their inspiration from direct experience of their environment. From 1886 he was drawing-master at the School of Design at the National Gallery of Victoria. His teaching was rarely systematic, but he was remembered fondly by his many students. His son, Louis McCubbin (1890–1952), was director of the Art Gallery of South Australia, Adelaide, from 1936 to 1950.

### WRITINGS
*The Art of Frederick McCubbin, and Some Memoirs on Australian Art by the Artist*, intro. by J. S. MacDonald (Melbourne, 1916)

A. Galbally, ed.: 'Notes by Frederick McCubbin', *La Trobe Lib. J.*, vi/24 (1979), pp. 69–78

### BIBLIOGRAPHY
*AUDB*
U. Hoff: 'The Phases of McCubbin's Art', *Meanjin*, x (1951), pp. 301–6
D. Thomas: 'Frederick McCubbin', *A. & Australia*, vii/1 (1969), pp. 66–73
A. Galbally: *Frederick McCubbin* (Melbourne, 1981)
L. Astbury: *City Bushmen: The Heidelberg School and the Rural Mythology* (Melbourne, 1985)

LEIGH ASTBURY

**McCullin, Don(ald)** (*b* London 9 Oct 1935). English photographer. He won a Trade Arts Scholarship to study painting at the Hammersmith School of Arts and Crafts in 1948, but he had to abandon his studies to work when his father died in 1950. One of his jobs was as a messenger and colour-mixer for W. M. Larkins, a firm of London film animators. In 1954 he joined the RAF as a photographic printer for aerial reconnaissance, stationed in Oxfordshire, Suez, Kenya and Cyprus. At the end of his service he returned to Larkins's where he worked as a photographic printer for three years while pursuing his own work privately.

McCullin's photographs of 'The Guv'nors', a London gang of which he had been a member, were first published in *The Observer* in 1959. In 1964 he won the World Press Photographers' Award and the Warsaw Gold Medal for war photographs taken in Cyprus. His images, characterized by a refusal to shy away from the misery and extremes of suffering, often attain an almost hallucinatory intensity, as in *Starving Albino Boy, Biafra* (1970; see Haworth-Booth, p. 32), where the figure is bent over clutching a ration tin, his huge pale head offset by his emaciated body.

McCullin's first book of photographs, *The Destruction Business* (London, 1971), depicted unflinchingly the real horrors of war in Vietnam, Biafra, the Lebanon and elsewhere, in stark images such as *Two Dead Khmer Rouge*

*Soldiers, Praveng* (1970; see *Hearts of Darkness*, p. 52). His book of photographs, *Homecomings* (London, 1979), documented the grim social deprivation in Britain, with single or grouped figures of derelicts or struggling families in stark and impoverished surroundings, such as *Mother and Child in their Kitchen, Bradford* (1978; see Haworth-Booth, p. 19).

PHOTOGRAPHIC PUBLICATIONS
*The Destruction Business* (London, 1971); *R* as *Is Anyone Taking Any Notice?* (Cambridge, MA, 1973)
*The Palestinians* (London, 1979/*R* 1981)
*Beirut: A City of Crisis* (London, 1983)

BIBLIOGRAPHY
J. Le Carré: 'Homecoming', *Amer. J. Phot.* (1979)
J. Le Carré, ed.: *Hearts of Darkness* (London, 1980)
M. Haworth-Booth: *Donald McCullin* (London, 1983)

KENNETH G. HAY

**McCulloch, George** (*b* Glasgow, 22 April 1848; *d* London, 12 Dec 1907). Scottish mining speculator and collector. His uncle appointed him manager of a large sheep station near Broken Hill, NSW, shortly before the rich mining potential of that region was discovered in 1883. McCulloch became privy to this information and immediately organized the Broken Hill Mining Co. syndicate, investing in Australian gold and silver mines.

In 1893 McCulloch returned to London a rich man. He spent £200,000 on his collection of modern art, constructing a mansion in Queen's Gate, which he filled with large-scale canvases by Frederic Leighton (*Garden of the Hesperides*, *c.* 1892; Port Sunlight, Lady Lever A.G.), Edward Burne-Jones, G. F. Watts, Jean-Léon Gérôme and Jules Bastien-Lepage. The most remarkable feature of McCulloch's opulent house was its picture gallery, which incorporated the latest advances in lighting, temperature control and fireproofing. A separate sculpture hall included a marble version of Rodin's *The Kiss* (untraced), which was sold with the rest of his collection at Christie's on 23 and 29–30 May 1913 by his widow, who married the Scottish painter James Coutts Michie (1861–1919) following McCulloch's death.

McCulloch's taste was criticized by the *Burlington Magazine* at the time of the posthumous exhibition of his collection at the Royal Academy in 1909. It charged that the collector's choices were too limited because he bought exclusively at official exhibitions in England and France rather than at more adventurous smaller galleries.

*AUDB*
BIBLIOGRAPHY
C. Phillips: 'The Collection of George McCulloch, Esq.', *A. J.* [London] (1896), pp. 1–5, 37–40, 65–8, 355–6
A. L. Baldry: 'The Collection of George McCulloch, Esq.', *A. J.* [London] (1897), pp. 1–4, 68–72, 217–19, 325–8, 372–6
*The McCulloch Collection of Modern Art* (exh. cat., London, RA, 1909); review in *Burl. Mag.*, xiv (1909), pp. 263–4, 329–31
D. S. Macleod: 'Art Collecting and Victorian Middle-class Taste', *A. Hist.*, x (1987), pp. 328–50 (344–5)

DIANNE SACHKO MACLEOD

**McCulloch, Horatio** (*b* Glasgow, Nov 1805; *d* Edinburgh, 24 June 1867). Scottish painter. He was trained in the studio of the Glasgow landscape painter John Knox (1778–1845) and at first earned his living as a decorative painter. By the early 1830s McCulloch's exhibits with the Glasgow Dilettanti Society and with the Royal Scottish Academy had begun to attract buyers, notably the newly instituted Association for the Promotion of the Fine Arts in Scotland. Commissions from book and print publishers allowed him to concentrate on easel painting. On his election as full Academician of the Scottish Academy in 1838, McCulloch settled in Edinburgh and soon became a prominent figure in the artistic life of the capital and a prolific contributor to the Royal Scottish Academy exhibitions. At the same time contact with Glasgow was maintained: McCulloch's favourite sketching grounds were in the west, he exhibited regularly in the city and his most loyal patrons were wealthy Glasgow industrialists such as David Hutcheson (1799–1881), the steamship owner. He seldom exhibited outside Scotland and only once at the Royal Academy, London (1843), but he kept in touch with London artist–friends, John Phillip, David Roberts and John Wilson (1774–1855), through correspondence and visits. His own art collection was evidence of his admiration for 17th-century Dutch painters, for J. M. W. Turner and Richard Wilson and for contemporaries such as Clarkson Stanfield; his extensive library was indicative of literary, antiquarian and musical interests.

During his lifetime Horatio McCulloch became the best-known and most successful landscape painter in Scotland. He was admired chiefly for his large and highly finished oil paintings of loch and mountain scenery such as *Glencoe* (1864; Glasgow, A.G. & Mus.) and *Loch Katrine* (1866; Perth, Tayside, Mus. & A.G.). His constant aim was to paint 'the silence of the Highland wilderness where the wild deer roam' with the kind of poetic truthfulness he admired in Wordsworth. The accomplished watercolours and broadly painted oil sketches that he produced throughout his career attracted little notice at the time and have remained comparatively unknown.

BIBLIOGRAPHY
A. Fraser: *Scottish Landscape: The Works of Horatio McCulloch RSA* (Edinburgh, 1872)
D. Irwin and F. Irwin: *Scottish Painters at Home and Abroad* (London, 1975), pp. 353–7
S. Smith: *Horatio McCulloch, 1805–1867* (exh. cat., Glasgow, A.G. & Mus., 1988)

SHEENAH SMITH

**McCutcheon, Osborn.** *See under* BATES SMART & MCCUTCHEON.

**Macdonald.** British family of decorative artists and painters. Margaret Macdonald (*b* Tipton, nr Wolverhampton, 5 Nov 1864; *d* London, 10 Jan 1933) and her sister Frances (Eliza) Macdonald (*b* Kidsgrove, nr Stoke-on-Trent, 24 Aug 1873; *d* Glasgow, 12 Dec 1921) were two of the most original artists working in Glasgow in the 1890s. Together with Charles Rennie Mackintosh and HERBERT MACNAIR they became known as The Four (*see* MACKINTOSH, CHARLES RENNIE, §2). The group created a distinctive decorative style that was disseminated internationally through exhibitions, in particular the fifth exhibition of the Arts and Crafts Society in London (1896), the eighth exhibition of the Vienna Secession (1900) and the Esposizione Internazionale d'Arte Decorativa in Turin (1902), as well as through periodicals, notably *The Studio, Dekorative Kunst, Deutsche Kunst und Dekoration* and *Ver Sacrum*. In this way, though they had few direct imitators, they provided substantial impetus for the development and recognition in Britain and on the Continent of a distinctive GLASGOW STYLE.

The sisters attended Glasgow School of Art (1890–94), then under the enlightened directorship of Francis H. Newbery (1853–1946), before opening a city centre studio. During the 1890s they worked so closely together, in a variety of media and occasionally in collaboration with MacNair, that much of their work from this period cannot be differentiated. Their output included illustrations for a manuscript *Christmas Story* (1896; U. Glasgow, Hunterian A.G.) and an unpublished edition of William Morris's *Defence of Guenevere and Other Poems* (1896–7; untraced, contemporary photographs, U. Glasgow, Hunterian A.G.), a series of four watercolours *The Seasons* (1897–8; Glasgow, A.G. & Mus.), a few textile designs and some remarkable graphics and metalwork. At times whimsical and weak in design and execution, their productions are often of considerable originality and are characterized by the use of decorative linear patterns and gaunt, stylized human and plant forms. Their style suggests an awareness of Jan Toorop, Aubrey Beardsley and 19th-century Japanese prints, probably through illustrations in periodicals such as *The Studio*. The enigmatic symbolism of such watercolours as *Ill Omen* (1893; U. Glasgow, Hunterian A.G.) and the treatment of abstract themes, as in the decorative screen depicting the legend of the *Birth and Death of the Winds* (*c.* 1898; untraced, see 1983 exh. cat., no. 5), earned the Macdonalds, together with Mackintosh and MacNair, the sobriquet the 'Spook School'.

Following the marriage of Frances Macdonald and MacNair in 1899, the sisters' collaboration ended and their careers diverged. Frances joined MacNair in Liverpool,

where she taught embroidery at the School of Architecture and Applied Art, University College, until 1909. During these years she concentrated on painting watercolours, also designing and executing jewellery and embroidery. She embroidered four figurative panels with motifs based on Maurice Maeterlinck's *Seven Princesses* (untraced; contemporary photographs, U. Glasgow, Hunterian A.G.) intended for Mackintosh's music room (1902) at the Viennese home of Fritz Wärndorfer (1868–1939), a notable patron of Secession art. At the Turin exhibition of 1902 she contributed embroidery, jewellery and beaten metalwork for the writing-room designed by MacNair (see *The Studio*, 1902). After the couple's return to Glasgow in 1909, Frances taught design in metalwork, enamel and embroidery at the School of Art until 1911. An exhibition of 34 watercolours by the MacNairs was held in 1911 at the John Baillie Gallery, London; examples of her watercolours include *The Choice* and *Tis a Long Path which Wanders to Desire* (both *c.* 1909–15; U. Glasgow, Hunterian A.G.). As much of her work was destroyed by MacNair after her death it is difficult to assess her career. Nearly half of her documented output is untraced; a beaten lead mirror known as the 'Dreamboat' (1921; priv. col.) is the only known work that she began after 1911.

Margaret Macdonald married Mackintosh in 1900, and her subsequent career is well documented, largely through the Mackintosh estate of drawings, watercolours and archival material (U. Glasgow, Hunterian A.G.), which contains more than half of her total output. Following the student and studio work of the 1890s, her career can be divided into the years of collaboration with Mackintosh and a period of declining activity from 1910. The wide-ranging activity of the 1890s helped to define her style and preferred media. From 1900 she continued with watercolours, also producing some graphics and textile designs and a few pieces of beaten metalwork. She concentrated, however, on gesso and embroidery because their potential for including a variety of materials and colours suited the development of her decorative style better than metalwork did. She showed considerable technical skill and draughtsmanship in working an awkward plaster medium into such highly finished, complex gesso compositions as the *Heart of the Rose* (1901; Glasgow, School A., A. Col.; see fig.) and *O Ye that Walk in Willowwood* (1903; LRT Pension Fund Trustee Co. Ltd, on loan to Glasgow, A.G. & Mus.). Her themes are primarily romantic, as may be seen in her watercolours the *Flowery Path* (1901; untraced, see *Dek. Kst*, v (1902), p. 218) and *The Sleeper* (*c.* 1903; untraced, see *Dt. Kst & Dek.*, vi (1905), p. 361). While most of her subject-matter is drawn from her imagination, she occasionally used literary sources such as Dante Gabriel Rossetti's poetry and in particular Maeterlinck's writings. Her compositions frequently comprise stylized female figures set against a decorative linear background incorporating rose motifs in muted tones of pink, green and violet.

Margaret's work with Mackintosh in the early 1900s consisted principally of panels in metal, gesso and embroidery designed to contribute to the thematic and symbolic content of his furniture and interiors. Her work was included in 11 of his projects, notably the music room for the Art Lover's House (a competition devised by

Margaret Macdonald: *Heart of the Rose*, gesso, 969×940 mm, 1901 (Glasgow, School of Art, Art Collection)

*Zeitschrift für Innendekoration*, 1900–01), the Rose Boudoir, Turin (1902), and the Room de Luxe for the Willow Tea Room, Glasgow (1903; see Billcliffe, 1979, pp. 97–103, 119–22, 130–31), to which she contributed characteristic decorative motifs and colour schemes of silver, white, pink and grey. After 1910 her output lessened due in part to poor health but also because of Mackintosh's declining career. Only 20 works are known, predominantly water-colours of obscure symbolism, for example *Mysterious Garden* (1911) and *Pool of Silence* (1913; both priv. col., see Billcliffe, 1978, pp. 104–5). Collaboration appears to have been essential to Margaret's creativity. More than two-thirds of her output was produced in association with her sister or her husband. Of Mackintosh's few commissions after 1910, only his additional decorative scheme for the Willow Tea Room, the *Dug-out* (1916), included work by his wife, a two-panel oil painting, the *Little Hills* (1914; Glasgow, Hunterian A.G.). Deprived of the impetus of Mackintosh's creativity and unable to diversify or develop her limited formal vocabulary, Margaret reverted to a by then outmoded symbolism. Her last documented work (*Legend of the Blackthorns*, watercolour, exh. Royal Scottish Society of Painters in Water-colours; priv. col.) dates from 1922.

BIBLIOGRAPHY

G. White: 'Some Glasgow Designers and their Work', *The Studio*, xi (1897), pp. 86–100, 223–36; xii (1897), pp. 47–51

'The International Exhibition of Modern Decorative Art in Turin: The Scottish Section', *The Studio*, xxvi (1902), pp. 91–104

E. Bird: 'Ghouls and Gas Pipes: Public Reaction to the Early Work of The Four', *Scot. A. Rev.*, xiv (1975), pp. 13–16

R. Billcliffe: *Mackintosh Watercolours* (London, 1978)

——: *Charles Rennie Mackintosh: The Complete Furniture, Furniture Drawings and Interior Designs* (Guildford, 1979, rev. London, 3/1986)

*Margaret Macdonald Mackintosh* (exh. cat. by P. Reekie, Glasgow, Hunterian A G , 1983) [with bibliog.]

J. Burkhauser, ed.: *Glasgow Girls* (Edinburgh, 1990)

PAMELA REEKIE ROBERTSON

**MacDonald, J(ames) E(dward) H(ervey)** (*b* Durham, 12 May 1873; *d* Toronto, 22 Nov 1932). Canadian painter and designer. He emigrated to Canada with his parents in 1887, initially to Hamilton, Ontario, and then settling early in 1889 in Toronto. He joined the leading Toronto design firm of Grip Ltd as an artist in 1894, after serving an apprenticeship with a lithography company; he possibly also worked as a stone-engraver. He attended evening and Saturday classes (1891–8) at the new Central Ontario School of Art and Design in Toronto, as well as the informal classes of the Toronto Art Students' League, which undertook summer sketching trips in the country. While this activity developed his technique and established his habit of developing major canvases during the winter from sketches done in the summer, it was from reading that his thoughts on art derived. Apart from his youthful attraction to Ruskin, he was drawn to the writings of Walt Whitman and Henry David Thoreau, who both dealt with the relationship between man and nature.

In 1903 MacDonald went to England to work at the Carlton Studio, a London firm of designers and illustrators. He had been recommended as the outstanding designer of the emerging generation in Canada, a reputation he enjoyed all his life; however, little documentation survives on this aspect of his career. Only after his return to Canada in the spring of 1907 did the tentative artistic aspirations expressed in earlier years take a positive form, and from 1908 he participated regularly in regional and national exhibitions. Colleagues praised the 'native spirit' of his sketches and the absence of 'European formula'. After 1911 his sketching trips took him to the Laurentian highlands, Georgian Bay and Algonquin Park, and his paintings increasingly dealt with the rugged nature and monumentality of the landscape. Vigorous, rough paint surface and sombre colour helped to express those qualities. A visit in 1913 with Lawren S. Harris to Buffalo to see the exhibition *Contemporary Scandinavian Art* confirmed his aspirations for an art that was Canadian in spirit and expression as well as content; his determination to realize this is shown in the *Tangled Garden* (1916; Ottawa, N.G.) and *The Elements* (1916; Toronto, A.G. Ont.).

MacDonald associated with artists whose training and experience of Canada were varied but who shared his belief in a Canadian art. In 1920 the group presented their first exhibition as the GROUP OF SEVEN, and for the next ten years they exhibited together annually. His friendship with Tom Thomson, who shared his intuitive sensitivity to the forces of nature, helped him to clarify his objectives. In the autumn of 1918, 1919 and 1920 MacDonald joined Harris in Algoma, north of Lake Superior. *Falls, Montreal River* (1920; Toronto, A.G. Ont.), *Solemn Land* (1921) and *Algoma in Autumn* (1922; both Ottawa, N.G.) derive from those trips. In composition the paintings are tightly disciplined, with colour, line and brushwork rhythmically developing the forms found within the elements of nature. While less dramatic than earlier works they are more powerful in their statement of physical and spiritual forces.

In 1921 MacDonald joined the staff of the Ontario College of Art, Toronto, and could no longer travel in the autumn. In 1922 he went to Nova Scotia and in August 1924 he made the first of six trips to the Rocky Mountains. These landscapes demanded new forms of expression, and he experimented with a poster-like format of broad flat planes and simplified colour (e.g. the *Front of Winter*, 1928; Montreal, Mus. F.A.). MacDonald later modified this technique and compositional structure; *Goat Range, Rocky Mountains* (1932; Kleinburg, Ont., McMichael Can. A. Col.) is notable for its grainy texture, subdued colour and tight three-dimensional composition.

BIBLIOGRAPHY

*J. E. H. MacDonald, R.C.A., 1873–1932* (exh. cat. by N. E. Robertson, Toronto, A.G.; Ottawa, N.G.; 1965)

*The Group of Seven* (exh. cat. by D. Reid, Ottawa, N.G., 1970)

For further bibliography *see* GROUP OF SEVEN.

NANCY E. DILLOW

**Macdonald, Jock** [J(ames) W(illiamson) G(alloway)] (*b* Thurso, Highland, 31 May 1897; *d* Toronto, Ont., 3 Dec 1960). Canadian painter and teacher of Scottish birth. He graduated from the Edinburgh College of Art in 1922. He was employed as a designer and educator in England and was appointed head of design at the Vancouver School of Decorative and Applied Art in 1926. His early landscapes were strongly influenced by the style of the Group of Seven. Although he painted landscapes and continued to draw inspiration from nature throughout his life, he is best known as a pioneer in the development of abstract painting in Canada.

In 1934 Macdonald began work on the semi-abstract and abstract paintings he called 'modalities'. In 1943 (under the influence of British psychiatrist and surrealist artist Grace Pailthorpe, then resident in Vancouver) he began to experiment with 'automatic' painting. During the next ten years he confirmed his reputation as a leading exponent of abstraction and of watercolour painting in Canada. He was a key member of the Toronto-based PAINTERS ELEVEN. The bold, often majestic, later abstract paintings such as *Heroic Mould* (1959; Toronto, A.G. Ont.) represent the culmination of his artistic achievement. One of the most important teachers in modern Canadian art history, Macdonald was mentor to several generations of younger artists. With Fred Varley he co-founded the innovative British Columbia College of Art, Vancouver (1933–5). He taught at the Provincial Institute of Technology, Calgary, Alberta (1946–7), where he was instrumental in founding the Calgary Group. From 1947 until his death he taught at the Ontario College of Art, Toronto.

BIBLIOGRAPHY

R. A. Pollock and D. Reid: *Jock Macdonald—a Retrospective* (Ottawa, 1969)

J. Zemans: *Jock Macdonald: The Inner Landscape* (Toronto, 1981)

JOYCE ZEMANS

**Macdonald, Lawrence** (*b* Gask, Tayside, 15 Feb 1799; *d* Rome, 4 March 1878). Scottish sculptor. He worked as an ornamental sculptor before entering the Trustees' Academy, Edinburgh, in 1822. In Rome in 1823 he was one of the founders of the British Academy of Art. He returned to Edinburgh in 1826 and became a member of the Royal Scottish Academy in 1829. Four years later he settled in Rome, and from 1844 he worked in Bertel Thorvaldsen's former studio. He became the city's most fashionable portrait sculptor and, according to the *Art Journal* (1854), his studio was filled with 'the peerage done into marble, a plaster galaxy of rank and fashion'. His sitters included the essayist *Henry Taylor* (marble, 1843; London, N.P.G.), *Prince Adolphus Frederick, 1st Duke of Cambridge* (marble, 1846; Windsor Castle, Berks, Royal Col.), *Lady Herbert of Lea* (marble, 1848; Wilton House, Wilts) and the *2nd Earl of Yarborough* (marble, 1854; Brockenhurst Park, Hants).

Macdonald obtained the patronage of Prince Albert, for whose sculpture gallery at Osborne House he executed ideal works such as *Hyacinthus* (marble, 1852; Windsor Castle, Berks, Royal Col.). His finest statue is a monumental reclining figure of the *Countess of Winchelsea* (marble, 1850; London, V&A), based on Roman prototypes. His work is characteristic of later Neo-classical sculpture in which the severe style gives way to a measured elegance. He could idealize the features of any sitter while retaining, in the Roman manner, the costumes and accessories of current fashion.

BIBLIOGRAPHY

*DNB*; Gunnis

*A. J.* [London] (1854), pp. 351–2

Obituary, *A. J.* [London] (1878), p. 135

P. R. Drummond: *Perthshire in Bygone Days* (London, 1879), pp. 109–26

R. L. Woodward: *19th-century Scottish Sculpture* (diss., U. Edinburgh, 1977)

B. Read: *Victorian Sculpture* (New Haven, 1982)

*Virtue and Vision: Sculpture in Scotland, 1540–1990* (exh. cat., ed. F. Pearson; Edinburgh, N.G., 1991), pp. 65–72

MARTIN GREENWOOD

**Macdonald-Wright, Stanton** (*b* Charlottesville, VA, 8 July 1890; *d* Pacific Palisades, CA, 22 Aug 1973). American painter. He was brought up in Santa Monica, CA, and first studied art from 1904 to 1905 at the Art Students League, New York, under Warren T. Hedges (1883–1910). In 1907 he went to Paris and enrolled at the Sorbonne (1908–12), also studying briefly at the Ecole des Beaux-Arts, Académie Colarossi and Académie Julian. He exhibited for the first time at the Salon d'Automne in 1910.

In 1911 Macdonald-Wright met Morgan Russell and they studied under Ernest Percyval Tudor-Hart (1873–1954), a Canadian painter, whose colour theory was analogous to that of musical harmonies. Macdonald-Wright and Russell collaborated on developing their own theory of colour abstraction, which they called SYNCHROMISM; its emphasis lay in colour rhythms. Synchromist paintings, such as *Abstraction on Spectrum (Organization No. 5)* (1914; Des Moines, IA, A. Cent.), often had a superficial resemblance to the Orphist works of Robert Delaunay and Sonia Delaunay; both Synchromism and Orphism, however, had their roots in Cubism. Unlike the Orphist concern for coloured light, Synchromism used colour to convey the three-dimensionality of objects. The different parts of Macdonald-Wright's paintings were not meant to be perceived simultaneously, but through the development of colour rhythms.

Macdonald-Wright first exhibited his Synchromist works with Russell at the Neue Kunstsalon, Munich, in 1913, and then at Bernheim-Jeune, Paris; they exhibited in New York at the Carroll Galleries in 1914. The compositions of his earlier *Synchromies* were based on the human figure and often used the contrapposto pose of Michelangelo's sculpture as a major design element. He experimented with pure abstraction only briefly *c.* 1914, preferring to find inspiration in landscapes, still-lifes and, in works such as *Synchromy in Blue* (1916; New York, Weyhe Gal.), in the human figure. From 1916 to 1919 he worked in New York, contributing to the landmark *Forum Exhibition of Modern American Painters* (1916), and he had his first one-man exhibition in New York at Stieglitz's gallery, 291, in 1917.

In 1919 Macdonald-Wright returned to California and was based in Los Angeles for the rest of his life. From 1922 he directed the Art Students League of Los Angeles. At that time his art was less Cubist and more representational, although he retained a preference for heroic figures, prismatic hues and crystalline planes. From 1935 to 1937 he directed the Southern California region of the Works Progress Administration's Federal Art Project (WPA-/FAP) and later served as technical adviser for the Western region of the FAP. In the latter position he was influential in encouraging the revival of mosaic murals in Southern California, particularly the invention of new, inexpensive mural techniques such as petrachrome; this new mosaic process used tinted concrete as opposed to pieces of glass embedded in concrete, as in the ancient *opus sectile* method. He also received several mural commissions, including one for 38 panels on the theme 'Invention and Imagination' for the Santa Monica Public Library (1934–5; on dep. Washington, DC, N. Mus. Amer. A.).

Macdonald-Wright became increasingly involved with Zen and oriental art, in which he found a source for creating a more serene and transcendent vision. By the 1930s his themes were inspired by oriental legends and philosophies. He first visited Japan in 1937, and from 1956 he began spending five months each year at a Zen monastery in Kyoto. In the 1940s he painted Synthetic Cubist works, but following Russell's death he returned to Synchromist paintings. During the 1950s there was renewed interest in his art. From 1942 he taught oriental philosophy as well as art history at the University of California in Los Angeles. His last significant work was the *Haigo* folio, a series of 20 woodblock prints illustrating haiku poems (1965–6; unpublished).

UNPUBLISHED SOURCES
Washington, DC, Smithsonian Inst., Archvs Amer. A. [papers]

BIBLIOGRAPHY
*The Art of Stanton Macdonald-Wright* (exh. cat., intro. D. W. Scott; Washington, DC, N. Col. F. A., 1967) [includes excerpts and treatise on colour by Macdonald-Wright]
D. W. Scott, H. Clausen and J. A. Walker: 'Macdonald-Wright', *Amer. A. Rev.*, i/2 (1974), pp. 48–68
*Synchromism and American Colour Abstraction, 1910–1925* (exh. cat. by G. Levin, New York, Whitney, 1978)

ILENE SUSAN FORT

**MacDowell, Patrick** (*b* Belfast, 12 Aug 1799; *d* London, 9 Dec 1870). Irish sculptor. He was apprenticed to a coachbuilder in London in 1813 and lodged with the sculptor Pierre Chenu from whom he learnt to model. He first exhibited at the Royal Academy in 1822 and in 1830 entered the Royal Academy Schools on the recommendation of John Constable. His first important work was the memorial to *William Tennant* (*d* 1832) in the Rosemary Street Presbyterian Church, Belfast. His chief patron, T. W. Beaumont, MP for Northumberland, commissioned busts and ideal subjects in marble such as *Early Sorrow* (1847; Belfast, Ulster Mus.). Beaumont paid for MacDowell to study in Italy following his election as ARA in 1841.

In 1846 he became an RA and submitted a *Nymph* (London, RA) as his diploma piece, continuing to exhibit at the Royal Academy until his death. His finest work is the memorial to *Frederick Richard Chichester, Earl of Belfast* (*d* 1853) at Belfast Castle, which combines observation and sentiment within a Neo-classical format. However, MacDowell is best known for the allegorical group, *Europe*, on the Albert Memorial, London, completed after his death.

BIBLIOGRAPHY
Gunnis; Strickland
H. Potterton: 'Patrick McDowell, 1799–1870', *Hibernia* (10 Sept 1971)

JOHN TURPIN

**Macedo, Manuel de** (*b* Verride, 1 May 1839; *d* Lisbon, 20 Oct 1915). Portuguese engraver. He studied in Lisbon in 1857–8 with Tomás José da Anunciação and in Oporto in 1858. Macedo used his many talents to observe and depict the customs of his day in a humorous manner. During a stay in Coimbra in 1860 he published two albums of engravings, *Narcotique* and *Banhos de Mar*. He was invited by the engraver João Pedroso (1823–90) to illustrate *A gravura em madeira em Portugal* (Lisbon, 1872). He collaborated with Alfredo Roque-Gameiro on an edition of *The Lusiads* (Lisbon, 1900), and between 1872 and 1874 he contributed a series of engravings of characters of Lisbon, along the lines of the work of Paul Gavarni and Honoré Daumier, to the Lisbon journal *Artes e letras*. The periodical *Diário ilustrado* (Lisbon) published his everyday scenes (*cenas de costumes*) from 1872 to 1880. The picturesque and expressive scenes that Macedo contributed to *Almanaque ilustrado horas românticas* and to *Album humorístico* (both Lisbon) are reminiscent of the work of Cham (Amedée-Charles-Henri, Comte de Noe). These same qualities are apparent in Macedo's work for *Lanterna mágica* (Lisbon, 1875): a constant tendency towards realism in the portrayal of characters, who are also depicted in strong and contrasting chiaroscuro. Popular types were also the subject of *Album de costumes portugueses* (Lisbon, 1888) and of Macedo's work between 1878 and 1914 for *O Ocidente*, a review that he founded with the aim of perfecting the art of wood-engraving.

Macedo was curator of the Museu Nacional de Belas-Artes, Lisbon, from 1884, a teacher at the Instituto Industrial de Lisboa from 1886, and around 1895 he contributed articles to the series *A arte portuguese* under the pseudonyms of Spectator and Pin-Sel.

WRITINGS
*Restauração de quadros e gravuras* (Lisbon, 1885)
*Manual de pintura* (Lisbon, 1898)

PRINTS
J. C. Machado: *Lisboa na rua* (Lisbon, 1874)
A. Ennes: *História de Portugal*, 6 vols (Lisbon, 1876)
L. Bastos: *Crimes de Diogo Alves* (Lisbon, 1877)
R. Camara: *Viagens em Marrocos* (Oporto, 1879)
A. D. da Cruz e Silva: *O Hyssope* (Lisbon, 1879)
L. Bastos: *A comédia burguesa: Sapatos de defunto* (Lisbon, 1882)
G. Junqueiro and G. Azevedo: *Viagem à roda da Parvónia* (Lisbon, 1893)

BIBLIOGRAPHY
C. Alberto: 'A arte do pintor Manuel de Macedo apreciada por um contemporâneo', *Diário Lisboa*, xci (1924), p. 3
A. Meira: 'Autodidacta notável', *O Panorama*, xii (1947), pp. 277–81
E. Soares: *Evolucão da gravura de madeira em Portugal* (Lisbon, 1951), pp. 48–9
J. A. França: *A arte em Portugal no século XIX*, i (Lisbon, 1966), p. 447
E. Soares: *História da gravura artística em Portugal: Os artistas e as suas obras* (Lisbon, 1971)

MARIA DE AIRES SILVEIRA

**Macedonia (i).** Region in northern Greece between the Aegean Sea and Balkan massif. Its location, climate and natural resources fostered the development of a distinctive culture but also attracted invaders and settlers. Alone of the provinces of Greece, it provides fertile, well-watered plains, cut by the great rivers Haliakmon, Axios and Strymon, and mountains rich in mineral resources, such as the gold of Mt Pangaion. The Mediterranean climate of Chalkidike encourages widespread olive production while, inland, cereals are widely cultivated and there is good grazing for cattle and sheep. From the Classical period (*c.* 480–323 BC), if not earlier, the surplus cereal production of the lowlands and the abundant shipbuilding timber of the hills were the envy of those in the south of Greece. Good harbours provide easy access to the trade routes of the eastern Mediterranean while the river valleys and mountain passes leading west, north and north-east allow good routes of communication.

Around 6000 BC a new way of life was established in Greece, based on cereal agriculture and stock raising. Villages in Macedonia such as NEA NIKOMEDIA are some of the earliest Neolithic settlements known in Europe. The pottery vessels, stone tools and clay figurines found here have parallels at early farming villages in the(former Yugoslavia) Republic of Macedonia and Serbia as well as Albania—a clear indication that the new techniques were passed on to south-east Europe from Macedonia. Bronze tools first appeared around 2500 BC, but their use in Macedonia was not accompanied by the widespread economic success and social change apparent in southern Greece and the Cyclades.

A thousand years later a more sophisticated society had developed in central Macedonia. Here the landscape is dotted with small steep-sided settlement mounds which were fortified centres, each serving as the focal point for a community scattered in the surrounding landscape. At Assiros, for example, the well-planned buildings within the walls included granaries holding vast stores of wheat and barley. One room alone is estimated to have contained over 10 tons of cereals, enough to feed ten families for a year. The total of stored crops was far more than that needed for the number of people who could have lived on the summit of the mound (perhaps between 50 and 100 adults) and must have provided a reserve for the whole community. At Assiros and many other sites influence from southern Greece is shown by imported Mycenaean pottery and its local imitations, while locally made incised ware shows regular contact with the peoples living in the lower Danube valley.

At the end of the Bronze Age (c. 1000 BC) social and economic change occurred throughout Greece following the destruction of the Mycenaean palatial centres. In Macedonia these processes were gradual. The small mounds with tightly packed buildings were abandoned for more spacious sites, perhaps to bring the whole community within a single defensible perimeter. Although new styles of decoration were used on pottery, there is little to support theories of invasion by northern peoples, sometimes equated with the Dorians of Classical tradition.

Numerous Iron Age tombs provide further evidence of Macedonian civilization. Cemeteries near the coast at Dion and Torone have yielded many examples of southern Greek style Protogeometric pottery (in museums at Dion and Polygyros) which represent the first tentative colonial movement from the south. Local forms predominated inland at Vergina and on the island of Thasos. Prosperity, especially from the 8th century BC onwards, is shown by bronze ornaments such as armbands, figure-of-eight brooches and cast pendants in the form of globes, vases, birds and other shapes. Such objects are commonly found in burials in Macedonia and the western Balkans but in southern Greece are only found at sanctuary sites.

By the early 7th century BC Greek colonies such as Pydna, Mende, Torone and Thasos allowed a much closer relationship to develop between Macedonia and southern Greece. These contacts are illustrated by abundant imports of pottery and other goods, even including decorated clay coffins from Clazomenai (Thessaloniki, Archaeol. Mus.)

in Asia Minor. The colony on THASOS, which also controlled the neighbouring part of the mainland, exploited sources of gold on the island and on Mt Pangaion to become one of the wealthiest Greek cities in the northern Aegean. Cemeteries at Sindos, Ayia Paraskeve and Amphipolis all illustrate the wealth of Macedonia at this period. At Sindos, in particular, the gold panned from the River Gallikos enabled the inhabitants to acquire elaborate gold jewellery, probably of southern manufacture, bronze helmets, high-quality Athenian pottery vases and fine glass bottles (artefacts in Thessaloniki, Archaeol. Mus.). They often furnished their dead with gold face masks and model tables, chairs and carts.

This wealth even attracted the interest of Darius, King of Persia (reg 521–486 BC). During his campaigns against the Scythians (c. 513 BC), Darius' commander, Megabazus, gained control of the area between the Strymon and the Axios and, according to Herodotus (Histories V.xvii), received the submission of the Macedonian king, Amyntas, since his son, Bubares, was married to Amyntas' daughter. About this time silver coins were minted in large numbers in central Macedonia, particularly at Liti, and found their way eastward across the Persian Empire, some as far as Afghanistan. Inland Macedonia still had a tribal organization in contrast to the colonial city states on the coast, and the king of the Macedonians was only one of many local rulers between the Pindos mountains in the west and the River Nestos in the east. The dispute about the 'Greekness' of the Macedonians was already in existence since Amyntas' son Alexander I (reg c. 495–450 BC) had to prove his Argive descent when entering for the Olympic games. Their original language was probably a dialect of Greek.

The dynastic marriage between Amyntas' daughter and the Persian noble was a critical factor in the increasing domination of northern Greece by the Macedonian kings, whose traditional capital was at VERGINA. The Thracians, who formerly had inhabited the whole area east of the Axios valley, were pushed steadily eastwards. Alexander I, however, was not slow to oppose the Persians when the time was right and to annex the areas that Xerxes abandoned when his army retreated from Greece in 478 BC. From this point on, the power of the king of Macedon was an important factor in the delicate balance between the Greek cities of the south, particularly Athens and Sparta, who sought to expand their influence amongst the colonies on the Macedonian coast.

Following the defeat of Athens at the end of the Peloponnesian War (404 BC), Olynthos in Chalkidike and Amphipolis at the mouth of the River Strymon took a leading role in opposing the ambitions of the Macedonian kings. Macedonia was no longer on the fringe of the Greek world but home to every aspect of Greek culture. At OLYNTHOS excavation has revealed the grid plan of a thriving town with spacious mosaic-floored houses, together with a host of objects that illustrate everyday life in Greece at the beginning of the 4th century BC.

With the accession of Philip II (reg 359–336 BC), a vigorous and talented general, as king of Macedonia, the balance of power changed. One by one the Greek city states were brought under Philip's control. The new Macedonian capital of Pella (see PELLA (ii)) became a focus of political and artistic activity. Here, for a time, the philosopher Aristotle acted as tutor to Philip's son, the young Alexander the Great. Excavations have uncovered the large agora (200×180 m) and the palace on the acropolis hill as well as splendid town houses with internal porticos and superb mosaic floors.

By 336 BC Philip's generals were poised to challenge the Persians in Asia itself, but before the campaign could begin, Philip was murdered near the theatre at Vergina during the ceremonies to celebrate the marriage of his daughter. Even though he had been murdered, he received a lavish burial at Vergina. The barrel-vaulted tomb had a painted façade and contained gold burial chests, armour and weapons, as well as a profusion of bronze and silver vessels.

ALEXANDER THE GREAT first had to secure his throne, then his control of Greece, before he too was free to turn eastwards and to complete his father's plans—and to outstrip them beyond the bounds of imagination. The conquests of Asia Minor, Babylonia, Egypt and the lands of the Indus Valley followed one after the other. In 13 years he gained a vast empire and then died without securing any succession. For the next 150 years Alexander's successors fought each other to gain a larger share of this empire. The noble families built elaborate tombs which were covered with tumuli and filled with rich offerings (see fig.). By the beginning of the 2nd century BC the Romans began to encroach on the eastern Mediterranean. When they defeated Perseus, the last King of Macedon (reg 179–168 BC), at Pydna in 168 BC, they carried off much of the wealth of the nobles, and Macedonia became rather a backwater in the Roman Empire.

The strategic importance of Macedonia reappeared as the Roman Empire became more oriented towards its eastern provinces. The Via Egnatia, starting at Dyrrachion on the Adriatic coast, crossed the mountains to reach the Aegean at Thessaloniki, and thence followed the coast eastwards. In eastern Macedonia the armies of Mark Antony and Octavian (later Augustus), controlling Italy and the West, met in the plain of Philippi with those of Julius Caesar's murderers, Brutus and Cassius, who had the support of the eastern legions. For the moment, the outcome assured the supremacy of the West, but the contest was regularly replayed between rival contenders for imperial power. Three and a half centuries later the Emperor Galerius (reg AD 305–11) saw in the thriving city of THESSALONIKI a base for his rule over the Empire. Here he erected the great arch commemorating his victories over the Persians and built his palace and mausoleum: he persecuted Christians savagely, including the patron of Thessaloniki, St Demetrius. After his death Constantine (reg AD 306–37) gained sole power, Christians ceased to be persecuted, and the capital moved east to Constantinople.

BIBLIOGRAPHY

N. G. L. Hammond, G. T. Griffith and F. W. Walbank: *A History of Macedonia*, 3 vols (Oxford, 1972–87)

M. B. Sakellariou, ed.: *Macedonia: 4000 Years of Greek History and Civilization* (Athens, 1983)

*Sindos: Katalogos tis ekthesis* [Sindos: catalogue of the exhibition] (exh. cat. by I. B. Vokotopoulou and others, Thessaloniki, Archaeol. Mus., 1985)

G. Jones and others: 'Crop Storage at Assiros', *Sci. Amer.* (March 1986), pp. 96–103

*Ancient Macedonia* (exh. cat., Melbourne, Mus. Victoria, 1988) [excellent plates]

R. Ginouvès: *Macedonia from Philip II to the Roman Conquest* (Athens, 1993)

K. A. WARDLE

Macedonia, set of jewellery, thought to be from Thessaloniki, *c.* 330–*c.* 300 BC (New York, Metropolitan Museum of Art)

**Macedonia (ii).** Republic of the former Yugoslavia in the Balkan peninsula, south-eastern Europe. It is bordered by Serbia, Bulgaria, Albania and Greece (see fig. 1). It is a region of high mountains and broad plains covering 25,713 sq. km with a population of *c.* 2 million, 67% of whom are Slav Macedonians and 20% are ethnic Albanians, with small minorities of Turks, Serbs and other nationalities. Orthodox Christians predominate, but there is a sizeable minority of Muslims. The capital is SKOPJE.

The territory of the present republic formed part of the ancient kingdom of Macedonia (see MACEDONIA (i)), which was conquered by the Romans in the 2nd century BC. Christianity was adopted there in the 4th century AD. In the 7th century AD the area, part of the Byzantine empire, was occupied by Slavonic tribes, who adopted Christianity in the second half of the 8th century AD. In 864 Macedonia and Epir were conquered by the Bulgarian prince Boris (see BULGARIA). From 976 to 1018 it was the centre of the great Slavic Kingdom ruled by Samuil, with capitals in Prespa and Ohrid, but it was reincorporated into the Byzantine empire in 1018. It was appropriated by the Kingdom of SERBIA in the 13th century, and in the late 14th century it was annexed by the Ottoman empire; it subsequently remained under Ottoman rule until 1912, when it was taken over by Serbia. Macedonia was part of the Kingdom of Yugoslavia before World War II and later

1. Map of Macedonia; those areas with separate entries in this dictionary are distinguished by CROSS-REFERENCE TYPE

became a constituent republic of the Federal Socialist Republic of Yugoslavia (1945–92).

I. Architecture. II. Painting, graphic arts and sculpture. III. Decorative arts. IV. Museums.

### I. Architecture.

Examples of Early Christian architecture in Macedonia include the remains of the tetraconch basilica with narthex, atrium and baptistery at Ohrid (5th century) and those of the 4th- and 5th-century basilicas at STOBI with their fine wall paintings and floor mosaics. In the 8th century, prior to the Bulgarian conquest, and subsequently in the 9th century the Slavonic settlers were constructing churches under Byzantine influence, as in St Panteleimon, Ohrid (9th century; destr.), built to a triconch plan. The three-aisled basilica at PRESPA was constructed in 983 and may have been restored in 1078. The three-aisled transept basilica of St Sophia at Ohrid (1036–57) acquired an exonarthex in 1313–17 (see OHRID, fig. 1). Notable churches continued to be built under Byzantine spiritual and cultural influence, usually to a cruciform plan, on a small scale, with simple materials but with a complex structure. They include: the Virgin Eleousa at Strumica (11th century); St George at STARO NAGORIČANO (11th century; rebuilt 14th century); St Panteleimon at Nerezi (1164; rest. 1960s; see NEREZI, ST PANTELEIMON); St Clement (originally dedicated to the Virgin Peribleptos) and St John Kaneo, both at Ohrid (13th century); and the

14th-century church in the monastery of St Andrew, near Skopje.

Under Ottoman rule architecture in Macedonia was predominantly Islamic, with the most intensive building activity occurring in the 15th and 16th centuries. Notable examples of Ottoman architecture in Macedonia include: the Sultan Murat Mosque (1436) in SKOPJE; the Hadji Kaddi Mosque (1561) in BITOLJ; the Daut-Pasha Hammam (baths; 1480–97) and the Suli Han caravanserai (15th century), both in Skopje; the 17th-century Bezistan (covered market) in Bitolj; and the 18th-century dervish school (now the municipal museum) in Tetovo.

Christian religious building was curtailed until the 19th century, but under a special licence from the Ottoman authorities monastic life continued; existing monasteries could be restored and new ones built. Depending on religious requirements and financial resources, a monastery might consist simply of a church and a building for the monks or might be more complex, perhaps comprising a church, cells for monks, guest quarters, domestic offices, a school for fresco and icon painters, seminary, library, hospital etc. These were always surrounded by stone or wooden walls. Prominent monasteries were those at Treskavac (13th century), Zrze (14th century) and Slepče (14th–17th centuries), all near Prilep; the Markov Monastery (14th century) near Skopje; the monastery of St John Osogovski (11th–12th centuries) at Kriva Palanka; that of St John Bigorski (14th century) at Debar and that of St Naum (founded c. 900; rebuilt 14th century; see fig. 2) on Lake Ohrid. Many monasteries were partially

2. Monastic church of St Naum, Lake Ohrid, Macedonia, founded *c.* 900, rebuilt 14th century and later

rebuilt in the 20th century. Examples of vernacular architecture include Christian and Muslim houses that express their different cultural traditions, with Christian houses facing towards the public world of the street and Muslim houses opening on to internal courtyards. Typical houses can be found in Ohrid, Kruševo, Veles (now Titov Veles) and Kratovo.

In the 19th century ANDREJA DAMJANOV drew on Romanesque traditions in designing churches in Macedonia and Serbia, notably the large three-aisled basilicas of St Panteleimon (1840) in Veles and St Joachim Osogovski (1845), near Kriva Palanka. Numerous buildings for the Ottoman administration, consular corps and prominent families were constructed in the 19th century in Bitolj, Skopje, Ohrid and Resen in academicist Neo-classical and Neo-Romantic styles. In the early 20th century academicism predominated in urban planning, as in the plans (1914) for Skopje by Dimitrije Leko (1863–1914) and those (1929) by Josif Mihajlović (1887–1941), and the plans for development along the shore of Lake Ohrid. Building regulations were made more rigorous, and public tenders were invited, resulting in the Governor's Palace (1931; by J. Dubai) and the National Bank (1932) by Bogdan Nestorović (1901–75) in Skopje. Mihajlović's urban project was followed by the construction of residential quarters on the right bank of the River Vardar in Skopje. Ivan Artemuskin constructed many buildings in a Functionalist style while Sotir Tomovski (1899–1985) applied a similar approach in the Girls' Lyceum (1935–8) in Skopje and the Radio Skopje Building (1938). Miko Čakelja (1909–76) followed the same trend in his Ibni

Pajko building (1937). DRAGO IBLER constructed the District Labour Insurance Building (1932) in Skopje, which introduced Le Corbusier's principles to Yugoslavia, and Milan Zlokovic (1898–1965) designed Skopje's Chamber of Commerce (1935).

After World War II programmes of Socialist urbanization were carried out in Skopje, Prilep, Ohrid, Veles and Štip by Ludjek Kubeš (*b* 1914), V. Antolić, Ljube Pota (*b* 1918), Risto Galić (1926–85), Dusko Pecovski (*b* 1924) and Vlado Čosevski (*b* 1921), while the first modern buildings for industry, education, health and social welfare institutions were built by Dusko Petkov (*b* 1922), Slavko Brezoski (*b* 1922), Aleksandar Serafimovski (*b* 1923), Dragan Tomovski (*b* 1911) and Risto Šećerinski (*b* 1925). In the same period B. Čipan and K. Tomovski initiated work on the conservation of the architectural heritage. In 1949 a department of architecture was opened at the Technical Faculty in Skopje, the first university-level school of architecture in Macedonia. It is now the Faculty of Architecture. After an international competition for the reconstruction of the centre of Skopje after an earthquake in 1963, there was an influx of fresh ideas, including a plan by Kenzō Tange (1965; unexecuted; for further discussion *see* SKOPJE). In the 1970s and 1980s efforts were made to find new methods of linking form and function within the architectural tradition of Macedonia, as in the architectural production of George Konstantinovski (*b* 1930), Kliment Zarov (*b* 1931), Aleksandar Nikoljski (*b* 1937) and others. Interesting examples are the Retirement Home in Ohrid (1972) and the Skopje Market Centre (1973), both by Živko Popovski (*b* 1934), and the Skopje Main Post Office (1980) by Janko Konstantinov (*b* 1926).

BIBLIOGRAPHY

G. Ostrogorski: *Istorija Vizantije* [A history of Byzantium] (Belgrade, 1957)

S. Tomovski: *Makedonska narodna arhitektura* [Macedonian folk architecture] (Skopje, 1960)

*Istorija na makedonskiot narod* [A history of the Macedonian people], 2 vols (Skopje, 1966)

A. Deroko: *Folklorna arhitektura vo Jugoslavija* [Folk architecture in Yugoslavia] (Belgrade, 1974)

*Makedonska arhitektura* [Macedonian architecture] (Skopje, 1974)

G. Bošković: *Arhitektura srednjeg veka* [Medieval architecture] (Belgrade, 1976)

P. Miljković: *Veljuša* (Skopje, 1981)

Ž. Popovski: 'O mladoj makedonskoj arhitekturi' [On modern Macedonian architecture], *Arhitektura* (1981), pp. 176–7

N. V. Belousov: *Sovremena jugoslovenska arhitektura* [Contemporary Yugoslav architecture] (Moscow, 1986)

I. Štraus: *Arhitektura Jugoslavije* (Sarajevo, 1991)

ŽIVKO POPOVSKI

## II. Painting, graphic arts and sculpture.

Among the earliest examples of wall painting, mosaics and sculpture in Macedonia are those excavated in the Early Christian basilicas (4th and 5th centuries AD) at STOBI. The earliest series of wall paintings in the cathedral of St Sophia at Ohrid are probably contemporary with its construction (1037–56; *see* OHRID, §3), with subsequent paintings executed in the late 11th century. The wall paintings (*c.* 1294–5; rest.) in the church of St Clement, also at Ohrid, by Michael and Eutychios (*see* ASTRAPAS), are among the most vivid representations of early Palaeologan art and include Old Testament, Eucharist and Feast scenes as well as portraits of saints and Apostles (*see* OHRID, fig. 2).

In the early 14th century a new narrative style of wall painting appeared, with smaller, more realistic figures, muted colours and a greater variety of subject-matter, as in the fragments of wall paintings (mid-14th century) in the church of the Matejić Monastery near Kumanovo. Later artists painted in a somewhat superficial narrative style. Artistic activity around Ohrid and PRESPA in the second half of the 15th century was considerable, with wall paintings showing a fusion of Palaeologan iconography and elements derived from 15th-century Italian art, as in St Nicholas Bolnički (1480/81) at Ohrid (*see* POST-BYZANTINE ART, §III, 2(iii)). In the 16th century wall painting around Ohrid and Štip became repetitive, while in the Skopje region it benefited from the influence of Greek artists, as in the church of St Andrew's Monastery (rest. 1559/60) near Skopje.

During the 16th century the main centres of icon painting were the Debar and Ohrid regions, although few icons have survived. The art of these areas was extremely conservative: 17th-century icons were based on 15th-century prototypes and were painted in a harsh linear style. The decoration of iconostases, however, was often magnificent, with ornate wood-carvings. Medieval traditions survived into the 19th century (see fig. 3), when they began to combine with other influences; for example the prolific icon painter DIČO ZOGRAF KRSTEV blended Post-Byzantine symbolism with Baroque ornament. Elements from folk art as well as realism made an impact, too; these trends are reflected in the work of Dimitrija Andonov Papradiški (1859–1953), Ǵorǵi Zografski (1871–1946) and Mihailo Šojlev (1887–1971), who taught such painters as

3. Carved wooden iconostasis, St Saviour, Skopje, first half of the 19th century

LAZAR LIČENOSKI and NIKOLA MARTINOSKI, both of whom went on to study abroad. Martinoski helped establish the Art School in Skopje in 1945; in 1948 it was transformed into the School of Applied Arts. Another important figure in the early 20th century was Milton Manaki (1880–1964) from Bitolj, who helped introduce photography into Macedonia. Among those influenced by his work were Mihailo Šojlev, Gogo Popov (1908–79) and Blagoja Drnkov (*b* 1914).

Among painters active in the early 20th century, the impact of Expressionism and Fauvism was reflected in the work of such artists as Borislav Traikovski (*b* 1917) and PETAR MAZEV. The latter was also influenced by Surrealist, Constructivist and post-Cubist trends, as was Spase Kunovski (1929–78). A consistent simplification of forms based on the Byzantine tradition is found in the work of Dimitar Kondov (1927–93) and Bogoljub Ivkovič (*b* 1924). In the 1960s RODOLJUB ANASTASOV produced non-figurative paintings, focusing on the structural qualities of a painting's surface. In the second half of the 1970s such painters as Aleksandar Risteski (*b* 1937) and Risto Kalčeski (1935–89) developed an abstract style alongside an enhanced interest in tradition and a new approach to the physical and social ambience of Macedonia. Also from the mid-1970s some painters, including Gligor Čemerski (*b* 1940) and Ilinka Gligorova (*b* 1940), adopted modern forms of figurative expression (Pop art, Neo-Expressionism, science fiction). At the end of the 1970s there was a synthesis of geometric abstraction and Systems art. A desire to 'wage war against' kitsch in the urban and natural environment underpinned the work of Simon Šemov (b 1941) and Nicola Fidanovski (b 1946), among others. GLIGOR STEFANOV created his installations from crumbling natural materials.

Modern graphic art in Macedonia had emerged before World War II, predominantly in the form of wood-engraving and linocuts by Vasilie Popovič-Cico (1914–63), Borko Lazevski (1917–93) and Nikola Martinoski, but the establishment of the department of graphic art at the School of Applied Arts in Skopje in 1948 speeded up its development. Wood-engravings, linocuts and lithographs ranged from poetic realism and Expressionism to geometric composition and stylized decoration, as in the work of Mira Spirovska (b 1939) and Spase Kunovski. After 1970, however, the academies in Belgrade, Zagreb and Ljubljana and the School of Applied Arts in Skopje reared the first generation of artists to devote themselves exclusively to this form of art, among them Dragan Bikov (b 1933) and Tomislav Krmov (b 1938). In sculpture heterogeneous trends existed side by side with academic approaches and both non-figurative and figurative work being represented. Realistic forms with elements of Impressionism, Expressionism and Cubism are found in the work of Dimo Todorovski (1907–83), Borka Avramova (b 1924) and Tome Serafimovski (b 1935), while a stylized anthropomorphism is evident in the work of Vangel Naumovski (b 1924), PETAR HADJI BOŠKOV and Ilija Lafazanovski (b 1939). Elements of primitive, archaic and folk art are reflected in the sculptures of Krsto Slavkovski (b 1928), Aneta Svetieva (b 1944) and Nikola Šentevski (b 1945), among others. The influence of Nouveau Réalisme is evident in the work of Aleksandar Ivanovski-Karadare (b 1943), while Surrealist elements are found in the sculptures of Olga Milik (b 1948). Organic and abstract forms with elements of Minimalism as well as Constructivism appear in the sculptures of, for example, JORDAN GRABULOSKI-GRABUL and Dragan Popovski-Dada (b 1933).

After 1973 a new type of art emerged, with artists using photography, film and video to record experimental work. The aim was to introduce new approaches to the meaning and function of objects, and to the use of colour and materials as three-dimensional interventions in space. The initiators of Environmental art, Simon Šemov and Nicola Fidanovski, sometimes collaborated with students of the Faculty of Visual Arts in Skopje. Similar projects were undertaken by the Aesthetic Laboratory in Skopje as well as by a group of young architects from Kavadarci. The architect Sime Uzunov (b 1949), for example, used 'cheap' materials to build evocative plastic 'flashes' in galleries. Alongside intimate sculpture, monumental sculpture went through a phase of intensive development when numerous monumental sculptures, reliefs and busts were erected. These works ranged from realism through stylized figuration, geometrical vertical sculptures and relief compositions with Cubist stylized images to abstract forms. Photography also remained an important medium in its own right, with such figures as Robert Jaki (b 1951), Rumen Čamilov (b 1946) and Marin Dimes (b 1948) coming to prominence in the late 20th century.

BIBLIOGRAPHY

Makedonski pejzaž [Macedonian landscape] (exh. cat. by E. Macan, Skopje, A.G., 1961)
Aspekti na crtežot vo Makedonija [Aspects of drawing in Macedonia] (exh. cat. by B. Petkovksi, Skopje, 1967)
M. Protić: Jugoslovensko slikarstvo, 1900–1950 [Yugoslav painting, 1900–1950] (Belgrade, 1973)
V. J. Djurić: Vizantijske freske u Jugoslaviji [Byzantine frescoes in Yugoslavia] (Belgrade, 1974; Ger. trans., Belgrade 1976)
A. Nikolovski: 'Razvojni tendencii na sovremenata makedonska umetnost vo povoeniot period' [Trends in contemporary Macedonian art in the post-war period], Kult. Naslestvo, vi (1975), pp. 7–18
B. Petkovski: Otkrivanja [Discoveries] (Skopje, 1977)
S. Abadžieva Dimitrova: Spase Kunovski (Skopje, 1977)
B. Petkovski: 'Sovremeno makedonsko slikarstvo' [Contemporary Macedonian painting], Makedonska Rev. (1981), pp. 5–79
Oto Bihalji-Merin: 'Vangel Naumovski', Kultura (1983)
S. Janevski, I. Mikulčić and others: Kulturno bogatstvo na Makedonija [Cultural treasures of Macedonia] (Skopje, 1984)
Novi pojavi vo makedonskata likovna umetnost vo poslednata decenija [New trends in Macedonian visual arts in the last decade] (exh. cat. by V. Veličkovski, Skopje, 1984)
Jugoslavenska likovna enciklopedija [Yugoslav fine arts encyclopedia], 2 vols (Zagreb, 1987)

ŽARKO TOZI

### III. Decorative arts.

The decorative arts in Macedonia have been subject to the influences of Byzantine, Romanesque, Gothic and, during the Turkish occupation of the Balkans, Islamic art. The embroidery and textiles are particularly striking, especially those used in traditional costumes, which vary greatly in style according to region. The embroidery was done in wool and occasionally worked with gold and silver thread, although the most popular colours were shades of red, dark pink, black, dark blue and occasional touches of yellow and green. Until the beginning of the 20th century, vegetable dyes were used. These were subsequently replaced by aniline dyes, which produced a greater variety but generally a more crude selection of colours. Embroidery was used on the collars, sleeves and fronts of dresses and shirts and on the woollen jackets and waistcoats. The hems of women's dresses were often embroidered several inches up and further embellished with braid, beads and sequins. Textiles were woven from hemp, flax, wool and (more recently) cotton and, for special items, silk. Like embroidery, weaving was an important art form produced by women, who also knitted socks, some of which were very ornate and intended as part of their dowry. Carpets, bedspreads, aprons, belts and towels were also made in the home. The making of kilims developed from the 16th century. These richly coloured carpets were woven on vertical looms and were initially used to decorate mosques but were later adopted by the Christian population. The most common colours were red, black, blue, green and brown on a cream or red ground, with geometric patterns, identical on both sides. Cloth for dresses, shirts, towels etc was woven on horizontal looms and belts on special tablet looms. The designs on textiles and on the pottery and metalware were geometric, usually comprising various forms of S shape—swastikas, spirals and rhombs—or flowers, birds, animals and dancers.

Byzantine and Mediterranean influences were found in both men's and women's jewellery. Perhaps most interesting were the women's huge belt buckles (pafti), made of metal, engraved with floral or plant motifs and sometimes embellished with mother-of-pearl and/or gold wire. Heavy metal bracelets, coin necklaces and headdresses were also worn—in particular by brides who were weighed down by the gold and silver coins adorning their bridal costumes. Earlier jewellery was mainly of gilt bronze, cast and beaten into shapes, while later items were of silver or silver alloy made with filigree decoration and frequently embellished with cornelian, mother-of-pearl, coral and coloured glass. Heavy coin chains and decorated daggers were made for the men. Macedonian pottery preserved Greco-Roman and Byzantine forms, with thick walls and covered in a light brown or green glaze decorated with geometric patterns. Ornate flower carvings were often found on chests in which linen and dowry items were kept. The production of decorative art objects declined in the mid-20th century, however, as imported and mass-produced goods became easier to obtain.

BIBLIOGRAPHY
*Folk Art in Macedonia* (Skopje, 1971)
N. Pantelic: *Traditional Arts and Crafts in Yugoslavia* (Belgrade, 1984)

DIANE WALLER

## IV. Museums.

The Art Gallery in Skopje (founded 1949) contains medieval art, Macedonian art and paintings, sculptures, prints and drawings by artists from other republics of the former Yugoslavia. The Moša Pijade Art Gallery in Bitolj (1957) also contains work by artists of the former Yugoslavia. In Skopje the Archaeological Museum of Macedonia (1949), which has Classical and medieval collections, and the Ethnographical Museum (1949), which contains textiles, metalwork and woodwork, are the two foremost institutions of their kind in Macedonia. There are provincial museums at Titov Veles (1951; for archaeology); Štip (1950; archaeology, numismatics, ethnography and paintings); Strumica (1952; ethnography); and Prilep (1948), which has a rich archaeological collection. The Archaeological Museum in Bitolj (1937) contains archaeological findings from Herakleia Linkestis. The National Museum in Ohrid (1951) contains archaeological and ethnographical collections as well as 9th–14th-century icons. Many museums contain paintings of partisan exploits during World War II that are of limited artistic interest. The Museum of Djordji Pulevski (Galičnik, 1952) contains memorabilia of the Macedonian writer and educationalist.

BIBLIOGRAPHY
*Enciklopedija likovnih umjetnosti* [Encyclopedia of fine arts], ii (Zagreb, 1962), p. 347; iii (Zagreb, 1964), p. 517
*Muzeji Jugoslavije* [The museums of Yugoslavia] (Belgrade, 1962)

PAUL TVRTKOVIĆ

**Macedonian dynasty.** Line of Byzantine emperors and art patrons (867–1056). The dynasty was founded by (1) Basil I, whose family had settled in the military and administrative zone of Macedonia; it became extinct on the death of the empress Theodora (*reg* 1042 and 1055–6) in 1056. The earlier Macedonian emperors from Basil I to (3) Constantine VII Porphyrogenitus took an active part in the artistic renewal that followed the end of iconoclasm, and this has given rise to the concept of a 9th- to 11th-century 'Macedonian Renaissance'; but contemporary sources offer little evidence in support, and the military

emperors of the late 10th century and the early 11th, Nikephoras Phokas (*reg* 963–9), John Tzimiskes (*reg* 969–76) and Basil II (*reg* 976–1025), were not active patrons of art. Moreover, the characteristics usually associated with an artistic renaissance such as creativity, progress or close study of the art of antiquity are scarcely to be found in the Macedonian period (see Walter). Such claims as have been made for a revival of Classical art (see Weitzmann) have largely been based on a small number of manuscripts and *objets d'art* said to have been commissioned in imperial circles: some imperial commissions, however, such as the votive crown of (2) Leo VI and the two enamelled chalices probably commissioned by Romanos II (*reg* 959–63; all now Venice, Tesoro S Marco; *see* VENICE, §IV, 1(iv)), suggest that the argument may not be viable even for court circles and that the few works that do exist point more to a love of luxury than to a deep-seated concern for Classical values.

*See also* EARLY CHRISTIAN & BYZANTINE ART, §I, 3.

BIBLIOGRAPHY
K. Weitzmann: 'The Character and Intellectual Origins of the Macedonian Renaissance', *Studies in Classical and Byzantine Manuscript Illumination*, ed. H. L. Kessler (Chicago, 1971), pp. 176–223
C. Walter: 'Expressionism and Hellenism: A Note on Style and Tendencies in Byzantine Figurative Art from Spätantike to the Macedonian "Renaissance"', *Rev. Etud. Byz.*, xlii (1984), pp. 265–87

BARBARA ZEITLER

(1) Emperor **Basil I** (*b* nr Adrianople, *c.* 820–40; *reg* 867–886; *d* Constantinople, 29 Aug 886). Born into an obscure provincial family of Armenian descent, Basil became a court official, attracting the favour of Emperor Michael III (*reg* 842–67), who made him co-emperor. He became sole ruler through Michael's murder, in which he was himself involved, and thereafter devoted a large proportion of his energies to legitimizing his position. The main source for his life is the *Vita Basilii* (ed. I. Bekker in *Theophanes Continuatus*, Bonn, 1838), a eulogistic biography written by his grandson Constantine VII Porphyrogenitus which attempts to blacken the memory of the preceding Armorian dynasty and to present Basil's accession as the beginning of an imperial revival: it is now recognized, however, that both Michael III and his father THEOPHILOS had many political and cultural achievements to their credit.

Basil's most significant contribution to the arts was his ambitious building programme described in the *Vita* and chronicle sources. He restored 25 churches throughout Constantinople, including those of the Holy Apostles and Hagia Sophia. He also built several new churches and secular buildings in the area of the Great Palace, which he extended to the south-east. The most notable of these were the Nea Ekklesia (Gr.: 'New Church'; 877–80; destr.) and the Kainourgion (Gr.: 'New Hall'). The former, built with conscript labour and recycled material, was the largest ecclesiastical construction in Constantinople since the 6th century, and its five-domed structure was widely copied; the latter was decorated inside with mosaics depicting Basil in a style reminiscent of the triumphal art of Justinian I.

All that survives of Basil's building work are his repairs to the fabric of Hagia Sophia (*see* ISTANBUL, §III, 1(ii)), which include some figural mosaics. The only surviving work of art attributable to his patronage is the illustrated manuscript of the *Homilies of St Gregory of Nazianzus* (879–80; Paris, Bib. N., MS. gr. 510), which contains portraits of Basil and his family on its opening folios.

BIBLIOGRAPHY

G. Moravcsik: 'Sagen und Legenden über Kaiser Basileios I.', *Dumbarton Oaks Pap.*, xv (1961), pp. 61–126

E. Kislinger: 'Der junge Basileios I. und die Bulgaren', *Jb. Österreich. Byz.*, xxx (1981), pp. 137–50

——: 'Eudokia Ingerina, Basileios I. und Michael III.', *Jb. Österreich. Byz.*, xxxiii (1983), pp. 119–36

L. Brubaker: 'Politics, Patronage and Art in Ninth-century Byzantium: The *Homilies* of Gregory of Nazianzus in Paris (B.N. gr. 510)', *Dumbarton Oaks Pap.*, xxxix (1985), pp. 1–13

P. Magdalino: 'Observations on the Nea Ekklesia of Basil I', *Jb. Österreich. Byz.*, xxxvii (1987), pp. 51–64

——: 'Basil I, Leo VI, and the Feast of the Prophet Elijah', *Jb. Österreich. Byz.*, xxxviii (1988), pp. 193–6

PAUL MAGDALINO

**(2) Emperor Leo VI** [Leo the Wise; Leo the Philosopher] (*b* ?Constantinople [now Istanbul], 19 Sept AD 866; *reg* 886–912; *d* Constantinople, 11 May 912). Son of (1) Basil I. He was a devout ruler with marked ecclesiastical and theological interests, which he expressed in numerous liturgical poems, sermons and addresses for church festivals. He also wrote several secular verses. He completed the revision of the law of Justinian I begun by his father, so producing the greatest collection of laws of the medieval Byzantine empire, the *Basilika*. His first three wives Theophano (*d* 896 or 897), Zoe (*d* 899) and Eudokia (*d* 901) all died prematurely without leaving any heirs. In 906, he married his mistress Zoe Karbonopsina ('coal-eyes'; *reg* 914–19) a few days after she had given birth to a son, the future Constantine VII (*see* (3) below).

Leo is known to have built several churches and monasteries in Constantinople and, according to an early 10th-century EKPHRASIS by Leo Choirosphaktes, a sumptuously decorated bathhouse in the Great Palace. It has been suggested that this bathhouse was one of the most ambitious classicizing works produced by the Macedonian dynasty (Magdalino, 1988). Among extant images of Leo are several miniatures depicting episodes in his life in an illustrated version of the *Chronicle of John Skylitzes* (12th century; Madrid, Bib. N., MS. Vit. 26–2). They include scenes of *Leo Enthroned Receiving Homage* after the death of Basil I (fol. 106*r*); *Leo Being Presented with a Petition for Peace from Emperor Simeon of Bulgaria* (*reg* 893–927; fol. 109*r*); *Leo receiving News of an Arab Attack* (fol. 111*r*); the *Baptism of Leo's Son* (fol. 112*r*); and *Leo on his Deathbed* (fol. 116*r*). In an illustrated 9th-century collection of Gregory of Nazianzus' homilies (Paris, Bib. N., MS. gr. 510, fol. Br.), young Leo is shown with his mother Eudokia Ingerina and brother Alexander. Leo is usually identified with the emperor depicted on one of the eight surviving enamelled medallions, out of an original 14, that decorate a Byzantine votive crown (late 9th century or early 10th; Venice, Tesoro S Marco). He is shown wearing the imperial *loros* (tabard) and a diadem. Another likely portrait of Leo is the mosaic (late 9th century or early 10th) of an anonymous emperor kneeling in front of *Christ Enthroned* in the lunette over the central door of Hagia Sophia (*see* ISTANBUL, §III, 1(ii)(b) and CHRISTI-ANITY, fig. 1). Medallions of the *Virgin* and an *Archangel*

(?Michael) complete the scene. Oikonomides has suggested that this image represents the occasion when Leo knelt in penitence before Patriarch Nicholas Mystikos at the same door, humbled as a result of their quarrel over Leo's marriage to his fourth wife Zoe. The mosaic was allegedly set up by Nicholas Mystikos after the council of 920, which posthumously pardoned Leo's tetragamy. It may, however, have been donated by Leo, who is known to have set up metrical inscriptions (destr.) in the church.

BIBLIOGRAPHY

H. Omont: *Miniatures des plus anciens manuscrits grecs de la Bibliothèque nationale du VIe au XIVe siècle* (Paris, 1929)

A. Vogt and I. Haussherr: *Oraison funèbre de Basile Ier par son fils Léon le Sage* (Rome, 1932)

C. Mango: 'The Legend of Leo the Wise', *Zborn. Radova Vizant. Inst.*, vi (1960), pp. 59–93

N. Oikonomides: 'Leo VI and the Narthex Mosaic of Saint Sophia', *Dumbarton Oaks Pap.*, xxx (1976), pp. 151–72

I. Spatharakis: *The Portrait in Byzantine Illuminated Manuscripts* (Leiden, 1976)

A. Grabar and M. Manoussacas: *L'Illustration du Manuscrit de Skylitzès de la Bibliothèque nationale de Madrid* (Venice, 1979)

R. Cormack: 'Interpreting the Mosaics of S Sophia at Istanbul', *A. Hist.*, iv (1981), pp. 138–41

P. Magdalino: 'The Bath of Leo the Wise', *Maistor: Classical, Byzantine and Renaissance Studies for Robert Browning*, ed. A. Moffatt, Byzantina Australiensia, v (Canberra, 1984), pp. 225–40

——: 'The Bath of Leo the Wise and the "Macedonian Renaissance" Revisited: Topography, Iconography, Ceremonial, Ideology', *Dumbarton Oaks Pap.*, xlii (1988), pp. 97–118

SUSAN PINTO MADIGAN

**(3) Emperor Constantine VII (Porphyrogenitos)** (*b* Constantinople [now Istanbul], *bapt* Jan 905; *reg* 912–59; *d* Constantinople, 15 Nov 959). Son of (2) Leo VI. The name Porphyrogenitos (Gk: 'born in the purple') refers to Constantine's birth in the Purple Chamber of the Great Palace in Constantinople, used to legitimize his rule. His name is associated with a number of encyclopedic and other works, such as the *De Thematibus* (932–44), *De Administrando imperii* (948–52) and the *Book of Ceremonies* (*c*. 959), in which the principles of Byzantine diplomacy and traditional court ceremonies were brought together. The anonymous *Theophanes continuatus* (*c*. 949–50), a chronicle written during his reign, as well as other sources suggest that although Constantine had a wide-ranging interest in the arts, his patronage of architectural projects was modest in contrast with that of other rulers of the Macedonian dynasty. However he was more interested in the decorative and particularly the luxury arts. During his reign, restoration work was undertaken in the Great Palace in Constantinople. Several rooms, including the Chryso-triklinos (throne room), were lavishly decorated with mosaics. A pair of silver doors was also made for the Chrysotriklinos. The description of the ornately gilded ceiling in the Hall of the Nineteen Couches (*Theophanes continuatus* vi 15) suggests that this interior was similar to those of contemporary Islamic courts. Many of Constantine's other commissions were destined for churches, among these being the precious liturgical vessels and fabrics for the church of Hagia Sophia in Constantinople.

Despite Constantine's documented activity as a prolific patron, the attribution of extant works of art to his patronage is problematic. A number of mid-10th-century manuscripts and luxury objects may have been commissioned by him. These include the JOSHUA ROLL (Rome,

Vatican, Bib. Apostolica, MS. Pal. gr.), the PARIS PSALTER (Paris, Bib. N., MS. grec 139), an ivory panel showing *Christ Crowning Constantine* (Moscow, Pushkin Mus. F. A.) and a glass bowl featuring pastiches of classical motifs (Venice, S Marco). Most of these works are characterized by a classicizing style and by the use of formal and iconographical elements derived from the art of the Classical and Early Christian periods. They originated in the court at Constantinople and are considered to exemplify the so-called 'Macedonian Renaissance', yet these works attest to Constantine's love of luxury rather than his interest in Classical values. An artefact undoubtedly associated with his patronage is in the Limburg Staurothek, elaborately decorated with enamel work and precious jewels.

BIBLIOGRAPHY

K. Weitzmann: 'The Character and Intellectual Origin of the Macedonian Renaissance', *Studies in Classical and Byzantine Manuscript Illumination*, ed. H. L. Kessler (Chicago, 1971), pp. 176–223

A. Toynbee: *Constantine Porphyrogenitus and his World* (Oxford, 1973)

H. Buchtal: 'The Exaltation of David', *J. Warb. & Court. Inst.*, xxxvii (1974), pp. 330–33

A. Cutler: 'The Mythological Bowl in the Treasury of S Marco', *Studies in Honor of George C. Miles*, ed. D. K. Kouymjian (Beirut, 1974), pp. 235–54

N. P. Ševčenko: 'The Limburg Staurothek and its Relics', *Thumiama ste mnème tes Laskarinas mpoura, Tomos I* (Athens, 1994), pp. 289–94

**(4)** Emperor **Constantine IX (Monomachos)** (*reg* 1042–55). As a member of the Byzantine civil aristocracy and an eminent senator, he was crowned Emperor in 1042 on becoming the third husband of Empress Zoe, great-great niece of (3) Constantine VII. His patronage of secular and ecclesiastical architecture, mosaics, manuscripts and small luxury objects was lavish. In Constantinople (now Istanbul) he founded the vast monastery of St George of the Mangana (destr.), of which the katholikon (1042–7; destr.) was described by the 11th-century historian Michael Psellos (*Chronographia* vi. 185–6) and the Spanish ambassador Clavijo in 1403 (p. 77) as being richly decorated with marble revetment and mosaics. Some sculptural pieces from this building survive, including a marble relief panel of the *Virgin at Prayer* (Istanbul, Archaeol. Mus.).

Constantine was also responsible for additions to the Great Palace, as well as providing gifts of precious vessels and a large financial donation to the church of Hagia Sophia in Constantinople to ensure the daily celebration of the liturgy. This is commemorated by a mosaic in the south gallery of the church depicting *Constantine and Zoe*, both nimbed and standing on either side of a seated Christ. The scene is a reworking of an earlier donor representation showing Zoe and her first husband Romanos III Argyros (*reg* 1028–34).

Outside Constantinople, Constantine built the monastery of Nea Moni on Chios (1045; *see* CHIOS, §2) and also rebuilt the rotunda in the complex of the church of the Holy Sepulchre in Jerusalem (1048; *see* JERUSALEM, §II, 2(i)), which had been destroyed by the Fatimid caliph al-Hakim in 1009. Constantine probably commissioned the cloisonné enamel crown that was sent as a diplomatic gift to a member of the Hungarian royal family and includes portraits of *Constantine, Zoe* and her sister *Theodora* among its six surviving panels (Budapest, N. Mus.; *see* EARLY

CHRISTIAN AND BYZANTINE ART, §VII, 6). The same three figures are depicted on the title page of a copy of the *Homilies of St John Chrysostomos* (Mt Sinai, Monastery of St Catherine, Codex Sinaiticus, gr. 364). An important purpose of this representation was to legitimize Constantine's rule as emperor.

BIBLIOGRAPHY

R. G. de Clavijo: *Embassy to Tamerlane, 1403–1406*, ed. G. le Strange (London, 1928)

E. R. A. Sewter: *The Chronographia of Michael Psellos* (New Haven, 1953, Bungay, 2/1966)

R. Cormack: *Writing in Gold* (London, 1985)

R. Ousterhout: 'Rebuilding the Temple: Constantine Monomachos and the Holy Sepulchre', *J. Soc. Archit. Historians* (1989), pp. 66–78

H. Maguire: 'The Mosaics of Nea Moni: An Imperial Reading', *Dumbarton Oaks Pap.*, 46 (1992), pp. 205–14

N. Oikonomedes: 'La Couronne dite de Constantin Monomaque', *Trav. & Mém.*, xii (1994), pp. 241–62

BARBARA ZEITLER

**Macehead.** *See* MATTOIR.

**Macellum** [Gr. makellon: 'enclosure'; Lat.: 'food market']. Type of enclosed market built in ancient Rome. Fish, meat and other perishable foods were sold there. Although the term is derived from the Greek word *makellon*, it was first used to signify this type of market by the Romans. As a building type the macellum is probably a Roman adaptation of the Greek commercial agora, although it has also been suggested that its origins are Punic. Such buildings as the 4th-century BC North Agora at Miletos, which was a rectangular space completely surrounded by porticos and shops, separated from the rest of the agora, are likely forerunners. In ancient Greece, as in Rome, such markets were designed to segregate unsightly food stalls from an increasingly monumental civic centre. In Rome the first macellum was built in the 3rd century BC, on a site in the Forum Romanum later covered by the eastern portion of the Basilica Aemilia and part of the Temple of Antoninus and Faustina. After the construction of the Basilica Aemilia (179 BC), a new macellum was built by M. Fulvius Nobilior slightly to the north, on the site later occupied by the Templum Pacis. In the later 2nd century BC macella were built at Pompeii, Morgantina and Alatri, and in the 1st century BC at other towns such as Alba Fucens and Ostia. The third macellum in Rome, the Macellum Liviae, built by Augustus (*reg* 27 BC–AD 14) on the Esquiline Hill, comprised an elongated rectangular area (80×25 m) surrounded probably on all four sides by porticos and shops. In AD 59 Nero inaugurated the largest of all macella, the Macellum Magnum, on the Caelian Hill; it measured about 93×70 m according to a fragment of the Severan marble plan of Rome. Coins show it to have been surrounded by a two-storey portico in the middle of which was a large tholos covered by a cupola. During the 2nd century AD many new macella were built in the interior of Italy, while older ones were rebuilt. The earliest macellum in North Africa was that at Leptis Magna (9–8 BC; see fig.), but the prosperity of the 2nd and 3rd centuries AD resulted in the building of many new markets in that region, such as those at Hippo Regius, Thuburbo Maius and Djemila.

Macella vary considerably in layout. The simplest are square in plan with shops and porticos on all four sides and a tholos in the middle. This type, which most closely

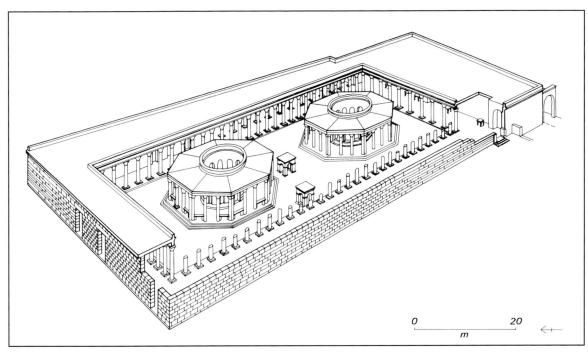

Macellum, Leptis Magna, 9–8 BC; surrounding porticos, AD 31–7; reconstruction

resembles the Greek commercial agora, is particularly common in Anatolia, for example at Perge (2nd century AD), although the macellum at Djemila in Algeria is also of this type. A related type has shops on only three sides, the fourth side forming the main entrance to the complex. Examples from the 2nd century AD occur at Viroconium, Thuburbo Maius and Hippo Regius. A third type of macellum is axially planned with an entrance on one side and opposite it a set of rooms of particular significance. The macellum at Pompeii follows this layout: on the side opposite the entrance are three rectangular rooms, all richly marbled, the central one built like a temple and containing an imperial statue. In some cases the central room was apsidal, as at Dougga (AD 54, with later alterations), Paestum and Bulla Regia (both late 2nd century AD or early 3rd) and PUTEOLI (late 1st century AD). The macellum at Puteoli was an exceptionally large building (75×58 m) and may have been influenced by the Macellum Magnum of Nero. A variant of this type, frequently found in North Africa, comprised a rectangular enclosure with a hemicycle of shops at the end opposite the main entrance. This layout is found at Gigthis (mid-2nd century AD) and in the two markets at Thamugadi (both early 3rd century AD), although the central market there has two hemicycles of shops instead of one. The macellum at Leptis Magna is unusual in consisting of a rectangular peristyle enclosure surrounding two large tholoi. Finally, several towns in central Italy, such as Herdonia and Aeclanum, have a distinctive type of macellum with the shops arranged around a circular courtyard (both 2nd century AD). The macellum of Alba Fucens was rebuilt on a similar plan in the 2nd century AD; a variant of this plan, with a hexagonal courtyard, can be seen at Saepinum (2nd century AD or later).

BIBLIOGRAPHY

J. S. Rainbird, J. Sampson and F. B. Sear: 'A Possible Description of the Macellum Magnum of Nero', *Pap. Brit. Sch. Rome*, xxxix (1971), pp. 40–46

N. Nabers: 'The Architectural Variations of the Macellum', *Opuscula Romana*, ix (1973), pp. 173–6

C. De Ruyt: 'L'Importance de Pouzzoles pour l'étude du macellum romain', *Puteoli: Studi di storia antica*, i (Naples, 1977), pp. 128–39

N. Nabers: 'The Roman Macellum: The Archaeological Evidence and the Written Evidence', *J. Field Archaeol.*, iv (1977), p. 262

C. De Ruyt: *Macellum: Marché alimentaire des Romains* (Leuven, 1983) [with cat. of sites and useful bibliogs]

F. B. SEAR

**McEntee, Jervis** (*b* Rondout, NY, 14 July 1828; *d* Rondout, 27 Jan 1891). American painter. His only period of professional painting instruction was with Frederic Edwin Church in New York during the winter of 1850–51, after which his family steered him into business. By 1859, however, he had decided to devote himself to painting as a career; he took a studio in the Tenth Street Studio Building in New York and travelled regularly between there and Rondout on the Hudson River. McEntee's speciality was the sober autumnal and winter landscape (e.g. *Autumn, Landscape*, 1868; priv. col., see 1987 exh. cat., p. 278); he crafted his imagery from recollections of solitary walks taken in the Rondout area to palliate the effects of his own melancholic temperament. Simple landscape forms, narrow ranges of tone and subdued atmospheric effects distinguish McEntee's work from the dramatic topography and light preferred by many artists associated with the Hudson River school and link his sensibility with those American painters inspired by the Barbizon school. Following his sole trip abroad, to Europe, in 1868–9, he occasionally produced Italian subjects, such as the *Ruins of Caesar's Palace* (*c*. 1869; Philadelphia, PA, Acad. F.A.), and experimented with figural imagery in the 1870s and 1880s. McEntee exhibited landscapes at the National Academy of Design, New York, almost every year between 1850 and 1890. Beginning in 1872 he kept a diary, chronicling two decades of the social life and views of the conservative faction within the National Academy of Design.

UNPUBLISHED SOURCES

Washington, DC, Smithsonian Inst., Archv Amer. A., microfilm, roll no. D180 [McEntee's diaries, 1872–90]

BIBLIOGRAPHY

G. W. Sheldon: *American Painters: With Eighty-three Examples of their Work Engraved on Wood* (New York, 1879), pp. 51–6
'The Jervis McEntee Diary', *J. Archv Amer. A.*, viii (July–Oct 1968), pp. 1–29
*American Paradise: The World of the Hudson River School* (exh. cat. by J. K. Howat, New York, Met., 1987)

DAVID STEINBERG

**MacEntyre, Eduardo** (*b* Buenos Aires, 20 Feb 1929). Argentine painter. After studying technical drawing, he decided in the late 1940s to become an artist. After producing detailed drawings influenced by Dürer and still-lifes reminiscent of Chardin and Zurbarán, in the early 1950s he turned his attention to the work of Seurat and Cézanne and then to Cubism. He came to prominence, however, as one of the principal practitioners of a form of geometric abstraction called ARTE GENERATIVO in the late 1950s, basing his work on the articulation of an extremely simple basic element: a curved line. Believing the circumference of a circle to be the purest means of expressing movement, he favoured regular and symmetrical patterns of development in paintings such as *Red, Orange and Black* (1965; New York, MOMA) and explored the rhythmic possibilities of curved lines in impeccably executed paintings that suggest the perfection of geometry, such as *Variable Polyptych II* (1973–5; Washington, DC, Kennedy Cent. Perf. A.).

BIBLIOGRAPHY

O. Haedo: *MacEntyre* (Buenos Aires, 1980)
R. Squirru: *Eduardo MacEntyre* (Buenos Aires, 1981)

NELLY PERAZZO

**McEvoy, Ambrose** (*b* Crudwell, Wilts, 12 Aug 1878; *d* London, 4 Jan 1927). English painter. On the advice of James McNeill Whistler, he attended the Slade School of Fine Art, London, from 1893 to 1896. His important early pictures were atmospheric studies of figures in interiors, for example *Interior* (1903; London, Pyms Gal., see 1986 exh. cat., p. 85). He exhibited with the New English Art Club from 1900 and is recorded as a member in 1902. In 1906 he bought 107 Grosvenor Road, overlooking the River Thames in Chelsea, where he lived and worked the rest of his life, often painting his portraits there. McEvoy slowly added to the number of his patrons and extended the range of his work to include portraits, cityscapes and landscapes, much in the manner of Walter Sickert, for example *Bessborough Street, Pimlico* (1900; London, Tate). Portraits became his main interest, not least because of the way he strove to appeal to the imagination in order to suggest more than the mere appearance of his sitters. Not all these were female, but he certainly established a reputation with portraits of fashionable women, such as *The Hon. Mrs Cecil Baring* (*c*. 1917; London, Tate). Between 1911 and 1913 he had some success at the New English Art Club with his portraits of Gerald Brockhurst's future wife, Dorette (*The Ear-ring*; 1911; London, Tate), and by 1916 his work was much in demand. He developed a bravura technique that enhanced his sitters' charms as much as it paid tribute to their social status.

BIBLIOGRAPHY

J. Rothenstein: *Modern English Painters, Sickert to Smith* (London, 1952)
*Ambrose McEvoy* (exh. cat. by C. C. Thomson, Belfast, Ulster Mus., 1968)
*The New English Art Club Centenary Exhibition* (exh. cat. by A. Robins, London, Christie's, 1986)

THEO COWDELL

**McEwen, Jean (Albert)** (*b* Montreal, 14 Dec 1923). Canadian painter. From 1944 to 1949 he studied for a degree in pharmacy in the University of Montreal, during which time he wrote poetry and taught himself painting. On graduation he began work as a pharmacist and met Paul-Emile Borduas, who soon became an influence on his work. In 1951 he had his first one-man show at the Galerie Agnès Lefort in Montreal. Soon afterwards he was persuaded by Borduas to travel to meet Jean-Paul Riopelle in Paris, where he also saw for the first time the work of Jackson Pollock and Sam Francis. During a trip to Brittany he produced such works as the ink and watercolour *Untitled* (1952; Montreal, Mus. F.A.), showing the influence of his companion Riopelle. In 1955, with the series of *White Works* such as *The Millstones* (1955; Quebec, Mus. Qué.), he departed from the characteristic Automatiste attempt to create spatial depth in painting. These works were largely white, while allowing some of the underlying colours to seep through. This technique of layering of colour remained important in his later work.

From 1957 McEwen's painting developed in a succession of series experimenting with the properties and visual depth of colour. The first of the series were the 'Margin' and 'Cell' works of the late 1950s, such as *Black Cell* (1959; Montreal, Mus. F.A.), which consisted of large blocks of overlaid colours. The margins in the former series allowed him to reveal the underlying colours. In the late 1960s, with works such as *I Hate Movement which Displaces Lines* (1965; Toronto, A.G. Ont.), he used rigidly geometrical monochrome blocks of colour in his paintings. He then returned to the more diffuse brushwork of strong, multi-layered colours, as in *Elegy Riddled with Blue No. 3* (1986; Montreal, priv. col., see 1987 exh. cat., p. 118).

BIBLIOGRAPHY

*McEwen, 1953–73* (exh. cat. by F. Saint-Martin, Montreal, Mus. A. Contemp., 1973)
*Jean McEwen: Colour in Depth* (exh. cat. by C. Naubert-Riser, Montreal, Mus. F.A., 1987)    □

**McGrath, Raymond** (*b* Sydney, 7 March 1903; *d* Dublin, 23 Dec 1977). British architect and decorative artist of Australian birth. He studied at Sydney University (BArch, 1926). Moving to England in 1926, he gained a research fellowship at Clare College, Cambridge, under the patronage of Mansfield Forbes (1890–1936), a fellow of Clare

College, for whom he remodelled Finella (1929), Queens Road, Cambridge, a showcase for the dramatic use of modern materials and a centre for the nascent modern movement in England. He began practice in 1930 as coordinating designer for the interiors of Broadcasting House (1930–33, with Wells Coates and Serge Chermayeff; destr.; see Hanson, p. 62), Portland Place, London. His interior work continued with the Embassy Club (1932, destr.; see *Architects' J.*, lxxvi, 1932, pp. 490–94) and Fischers Restaurant (1933, destr.; see Hanson, p. 62), New Bond Street, both London, offices and aircraft interiors for Imperial Airways, and exhibition designs. He designed much decorative work for execution on glass, of which the doors at the RIBA (1934), Portland Place, London, are among the few survivors. He also designed furniture, glassware and fabrics. His major built work was the house at St Ann's Hill (1936), Chertsey, Surrey, a circular house in reinforced concrete, beautifully detailed with built-in furniture, set in a mature landscape redesigned by Christopher Tunnard (1910–79), who occupied the house. Keene House (1938), Carrygate, Galby, Leics, was built of salvaged Tudor bricks and elm boarding with a free plan.

McGrath's elaborate plans for a factory for Aspro at Slough, Berks, were curtailed by World War II and he took a post in the Office of Works in Dublin in 1940, after a short period as a War Artist drawing aircraft production. He became Principal Architect (1948–68) and designed the Cenotaph (1950), Leinster Lawn, the Kennedy Memorial Concert Hall (1965, unexecuted; see *Builder*, ccviii/6356, 1965, p. 561) and new galleries for the Royal Hibernian Academy (1970), all Dublin. The Irish period of McGrath's career was less successful in the face of his brilliant and widely-publicized career as a Modernist in the 1930s.

WRITINGS

*Twentieth Century Houses* (London, 1934)
with A. C. Frost: *Glass in Architecture and Decoration* (London, 1937, rev. 1961)

BIBLIOGRAPHY

B. Hanson: 'Rhapsody in Black Glass', *Archit. Rev.* [London], clxii (1977), pp. 58–64 [interview]
R. Butler: *Raymond McGrath Prints* (Armadale, 1979)
A. Powers: '"Simple Intime"—the Work of Raymond McGrath', *30s Soc. J.*, iii (1983), pp. 2–11

ALAN POWERS

**Macgregor, W(illiam) Y(ork)** (*b* Finnart, Dunbartonshire [now Strathclyde], 14 Oct 1855; *d* Bridge of Allan, Stirlingshire [now Central], 28 Sept 1923). Scottish painter. He trained as a pupil of James Docharty (1829–78) and then at the Slade School of Fine Art in London under Alphonse Legros. This informal training, his slight superiority in age and his financial independence made him a natural leader of the younger painters of the GLASGOW BOYS. His studio at 134 Bath Street, Glasgow, became a meeting place for James Guthrie, John Lavery, E. A. Walton, George Henry, Joseph Crawhall and others of the group. Here they shared models and materials and discussed the new ideas of the young French painter Jules Bastien-Lepage, whose naturalist painting attracted them.

After his return to Scotland from London, Macgregor practised a form of *plein-air* painting, spending each summer on the east coast with the painter James Paterson

(1854–1932) and returning to Glasgow for the winter. In the winter of 1882–3, however, he began work on a large painting directly inspired by Bastien-Lepage, showing a girl selling vegetables from a stall. The life-size figure was removed by the artist in 1884, probably after seeing the figure paintings produced by Guthrie at Cockburnspath in 1883–4. This altered picture, the *Vegetable Stall* (Edinburgh, N.G.), remains one of the most important realist paintings produced in Scotland in the 1880s. Macgregor's other naturalist paintings, notably *Cottage Garden, Crail* (1883; priv. col., see Billcliffe, pl. 67) and *Crail* (1883; Stirling, Smith A.G. & Mus.), reflect Guthrie's use of direct sunlight but demonstrate Macgregor's weakness as a figure painter.

As Guthrie was gradually adopted as leader of the Glasgow school, Macgregor began to withdraw from the city. He suffered from severe asthma and moved to Bridge of Allan to convalesce. After spending two winters in the south of England, he lived in South Africa from 1888 to 1890. With his health improved, he returned to Bridge of Allan but remained on the fringes of the Glasgow school during the 1890s. He was elected to the Royal Scottish Academy in 1898. From the 1890s until his death, his landscapes remained bold in handling and colour but were never popular with collectors.

BIBLIOGRAPHY

E. A. Taylor: Obituary, *The Studio*, lxxxix (1925), pp. 89–92
D. Irwin and F. Irwin: *Scottish Painters at Home and Abroad, 1700–1900* (London, 1975), pp. 373–4 [excellent bibliog.]
R. Billcliffe: *The Glasgow Boys: The Glasgow School of Painting, 1875–1895* (London, 1985) [most comprehensive account and selection of pls]

ROGER BILLCLIFFE

**McGuinness, Norah** (*b* Londonderry, 7 Nov 1901; *d* Dublin, 22 Nov 1980). Irish painter and illustrator. She attended life classes at Derry Technical School and from 1921 studied at the Metropolitan School of Art, Dublin, under Patrick Tuohy (1894–1930), Oswald Reeves (1870–1967) and Harry Clarke. Through Clarke she obtained a commission to illustrate Sterne's *A Sentimental Journey* (London, 1926). She settled in 1925 in Wicklow and was involved in the literary and theatrical life of Dublin, designing for the Abbey and Peacock theatres and illustrating W. B. Yeats's *Stories of Red Hanrahan* (London, 1927). On Mainie Jellett's advice she went to Paris in 1929 to study with André Lhôte and came under the influence of the Ecole de Paris. During the 1930s she lived in London and visited the USA, returning in 1939 to Dublin, where she painted landscapes in watercolour and gouache. The loose, Fauve-influenced style of the evocative *Mount Street Bridge* (1951; Dublin, Mrs R. Jameson priv. col.) gave way to a post-Cubist style influenced by Evie Hone but distinctly her own, as in *Kitchen Table* (1960; Dublin, Trinity Coll.). Later in the decade, in such paintings as *Water Weeds* (1968; Dublin, A.C. Ireland) and *Pattern on the Featherbed Mountain* (1975; Belfast, Ulster Mus.), she returned to a looser style characterized by broad, circular sweeps of harmonious colour and pools of light. She exhibited at the Royal Hibernian Academy from 1940 and in 1943 was a founder-member of the Irish Exhibition of Living Art, becoming President on the death of Mainie Jellett.

BIBLIOGRAPHY
*Norah McGuinness* (exh. cat., intro. A. Crookshank; Dublin, Trinity Coll., 1968) [retro.]
*Irish Art, 1943–1973* (exh. cat. by C. Barrett, Cork, Crawford Mun. A.G., 1980)
*Irish Women Artists from the Eighteenth Century to the Present Day* (exh. cat., Dublin, N.G., 1987)

HILARY PYLE

**Mach, David** (*b* Methil, Fife, 18 March 1956). Scottish sculptor. In his earliest works at the Duncan of Jordanstone College of Art, Dundee (1974–9), he made use of discarded objects found in local scrap-yards, which he combined in sculpture that explored the resonance of their industrial use. He moved on to make monumental assemblages from such materials as vast stocks of magazines and directories, that were turned into, for example, life-size cars, tanks and submarines (e.g. *Silent Running*, 1982; Rotterdam, Gal. 't Venster) reflecting aspects of an aggressive and consumer-driven culture. Mach aimed to demythologize the practice of art and did not hesitate to incorporate mass-produced elements, ranging from childrens' toys to kitsch accessories, in often satirical constructions. *If You Go Down to the Woods* (1987; see 1987 exh. cat.), for example, consists of dozens and dozens of mass-produced dolls and teddy bears supporting huge wooden logs. He also rejected the traditional function of sculpture as an avenue for the contemplation of abstract ideas, preferring in his temporal installations, such as the statues of 101 Dalmatians exhibited in the grounds of the Tate Gallery, London, to make a point of contact with the urgent concerns of the modern world.

BIBLIOGRAPHY
*David Mach: Towards a Landscape* (exh. cat. by M. Livingstone, Oxford, MOMA, 1985)
*David Mach: Si avui t'endinses en els boscos* (exh. cat., Barcelona, Fund. Miró, 1987)
*David Mach: 101 Dalmatians* (exh. cat., London, Tate, 1988)
M. Livingstone, ed.: *David Mach* (Kyoto, 1990) [Eng./Jap. text]

**Machado, Alvaro** (*b* Lisbon, June 1874; *d* Lisbon, 1944). Portuguese architect. After completing his studies in architecture (1897) at the Academia de Belas Artes in Lisbon, where he was a pupil of José Luís Monteiro, Machado began his career working as an assistant to Rosendo Carvalheira on Parede Sanatorium (1901), Lisbon. This experience exposed Machado to contemporary styles, particularly the ornamental use of Art Nouveau as expressed in the fine *azulejos* (glazed tiles) that decorated the sanatorium. His own designs, however, adopted a Romanesque Revival style, for example the mausoleum of the Visconde de Valmôr (1900), Cemitério do Alto S João, Lisbon, which was his first work in this style and showed his preference for compact masses and heavy mouldings. He used similar features in the Colégio Academico (1904), 13 Avenida da Republica, which is one of the most important Romanesque Revival buildings in Lisbon, designed as a heavy circular structure on a corner site, set between two lateral blocks at right angles to each other. The suggestion of Romanesque weight is not, therefore, confined to a superficial application of motifs but is produced by the fundamental organization of the building's masses. In the Sociedade Nacional de Belas Artes building (1906), 36 Rua Barata Salgueiro, Lisbon, Machado used the same medievalist aesthetic but less effectively, failing to achieve an organic link between the interior, which opens into wide saloons, and the constricted exterior masses. He also used other styles; for example, his unexecuted design for a viaduct (1909) in Avenida Ressano Garcia was influenced by the academic grandiloquence of contemporary French design, whereas a group of houses (1909–11) at Alto Estoril shows a very contemporary approach combining decorative Art Nouveau *azulejo* panels with a plan that was almost functionalist in layout, forming an early example of Art Deco in Portugal. In several other designs for private houses Machado showed the same tendency to simplify forms, freeing architecture from eclectic ornament, and this is the most significant aspect of his professional achievement.

BIBLIOGRAPHY
J.-A. França: *A arte em Portugal no século XIX*, ii (Lisbon, 1966)

RAQUEL HENRIQUES DA SILVA

**Machado da Silva Castro e Vasconcelos, Félix** [Montebelo, Marquês de] (*b* Torre da Fonte, 1595; *d* Madrid, 1662). Spanish painter and writer, also active in Portugal. He received a classical education at Santiago de Compostela and participated at court in the activities of music, dance and painting. In Madrid he was a personal friend of Diego Velázquez. Machado wrote sonnets and picaresque novels and was also a friend of the Camões scholar Manuel de Faria e Sousa. He was interested in the history of the nobility and concerned with the defence of the Liberal Arts.

Machado made his living entirely from painting, especially portraiture. The *Portrait of the Artist's Children António, Francisco and Diogo* (*c.* 1635–40; Portugal, Countess of Figueira, priv. col., see Santos, pl. 20) is charming. A self-portrait (1635–40; Portugal, Dona Maria José Machado de Castro Branco, priv. col., see exh. cat., pl. 36) shows the artist painting his son, Francisco, with Dona Bernarda. The vibrant tonalities and the misty backgrounds are reminiscent of Velázquez's work. Machado's work should be seen in the context of Spanish portrait painting rather than as part of the less formal and plainer conception of portraiture then current in Portugal.

WRITINGS
*A terceira parte de Guzmán de Alfarache* (Lisbon, Pal. Ajuda, MSS), pubd *Rev. Hisp.*, lxix (1927), p. 155

BIBLIOGRAPHY
*Personagens portuguesas do século XVII* (exh. cat., Lisbon, Acad. B. A., 1942)
R. dos Santos: 'O significado da pintura portuguesa no século XVII', *Conferências de arte*, ii (Lisbon, 1943), pp. 37–56
J. Palma-Ferreira: *Novelistas e contistas portugueses dos séculos XVII e XVIII* (Lisbon, 1981), pp. 213–16

VITOR SERRÃO

**Machado de Castro, Joaquim** (*b* Coimbra, 1731; *d* Lisbon, 1822). Portuguese sculptor. He was the most celebrated Portuguese sculptor of the 18th century, and his reputation is based mainly on his bronze equestrian statue of *King Joseph* (Lisbon, Praça do Comércio; see fig.). He was appointed the official sculptor of Portugal in the reign of Queen Mary I. The Museu Nacional de

Machado de Castro in Coimbra, inaugurated 1913, is named after him.

Machado de Castro was the son of a sculptor of religious images and was apprenticed aged 15 in Lisbon to José de Almeida. In 1756 he settled in Mafra where he collaborated with Alessandro Giusti, who directed the sculptural work being carried out in the convent-palace. He became Giusti's principal assistant, engaged until 1770 on the marble altar reliefs there, though without producing work that can be distinguished as his. In 1771, after being chosen in a competition to make an equestrian statue of King Joseph, he set up a workshop in Lisbon to produce both official and royal works, and as a training school, or Aula Régia, and where he employed several sculptors from Giusti's studio.

The equestrian statue of *King Joseph* was designed to occupy the centre of the new Praça do Comércio, Lisbon, the broad new waterfront square that was the crowning feature of the rebuilding of Lisbon by Sebastião José Carvalho e Mello, 1st Marquês of POMBAL, after the earthquake of 1755. The statue, the first equestrian statue to be made in Portugal, was intended to add the finishing touch to this great scheme of urban reconstruction. Machado de Castro's model for the statue was accepted in 1771, and the bronze was successfully cast in one operation by General Bartolomeu da Costa (*fl* 1771–3). The statue was dedicated in a great ceremony on 6 June 1775, presided over by the Marquês de Pombal, whose portrait by Machado de Castro appears in a circular medallion below the royal coat of arms on the front of the base of the monument. The pedestal was designed by Reinaldo Manuel dos Santos. The statue was inspired by the design, prepared in 1759–60, by the architect of the square, Eugénio dos Santos, and is based on projects by Charles Perrault and Charles Le Brun for works dedicated to Louis XIV. In a European context Machado could also have been influenced at second hand by works such as *Louis XIV* by François Girardon, *Louis XV* by Edmé Bouchardon and the *Peter the Great* by Etienne-Maurice Falconet in St Petersburg, of which he wrote at length in *Descrição analítica* (1810), an account of the entire project. Here he elaborated on his aesthetic ideas and listed his varied sources, from Charles-Alphonse Dufresnoy and Jacques-François Blondel to Charles-Nicolas Cochin (ii) and Johann Winckelmann, although he probably only read the last after completing the statue.

The concept of the monument and the depiction of the King is symbolic, and with great skill Machado de Castro gives a lightness and grace to a formal academic scheme. This is seen in the way that he subordinates the King's head to the helmet, whose floating plumes launch a ripple of movement that runs through the horse, the curving serpents under its hooves and down to the elegant Rococo ornament on the base. The two allegorical groups that flank the pedestal were also made by Machado de Castro after the plan of Eugénio dos Santos, in turn inspired by Le Brun. They represent *Triumph Leading a Rearing Horse* and *Fame Conducting an Elephant*, an allusion to the Portuguese conquests in the East. On the back of the pedestal Machado sculpted in bas-relief a complex allegorical picture with seven figures according to Cesare Ripa's rules, and showing Royal Generosity rising from

Joaquim Machado de Castro: *King Joseph*, bronze, 1771–3 (Lisbon, Praça do Comércio)

the throne to bring relief to the ruined City, aided by the Government of the Republic, who leads the figure of Love of Virtue. The kneeling Commerce places her riches at the feet of royalty, while behind stand Human Providence and Architecture, the latter displaying plans for the rebuilding of the city.

Machado de Castro produced a vast amount of work that he listed in a partial inventory made in 1817; besides the equestrian statue, this included the full-length statue of his patroness *Mary I* (1783; Lisbon, Bib. N.). He made (*c.* 1785) the monumental tombs for *Dona Mariana Vitória de Bourbon* (1718–81), widow of King Joseph, in São Francisco de Paula, Lisbon, and, on the same model, for Mary I's confessor *Frei Inacio de São Caetano, Archbishop of Thessaloniki* (*c.* 1790) in the new Basílica da Estrela, or Sacred Heart, Lisbon. Between 1777 and 1783 he designed a series of colossal marble statues for the façade of the same Basilica of the Sacred Heart, allegorical figures representing *Faith*, *Adoration*, *Liberty* and *Gratitude* as well as figures of *St Teresa of Jesus*, *St Mary Madalene de Pazzi*, *St Elias* and *St John of the Cross*, and the large bas-relief representing the *Sacred Heart of Jesus*, all of which were carved by assistants. He carved a series of statues for the vestibule of the Palácio de Ajuda, Lisbon, where he was appointed director of works in 1802 and where he made three works himself, including the first of the scheme that was installed in 1817, depicting *Gratitude* (*in situ*); the others were by his collaborators, including his pupil Faustino José Rodrigues.

Another aspect of Machado's work is seen in the elaborate Christmas cribs that he made in painted terracotta. These popular genre scenes have no parallel in contemporary Portuguese painting. Though deeply Catholic in expression, their religious content is often diluted by their popular and sentimental nature. They were highly prized and collected by convents and the nobility. The *presépio* of Lisbon Cathedral, signed and dated 1766, and that of the Marqués de Belas (*c.* 1765; Lisbon, Mus. N. A. Ant.), are among the most graceful of these figure groups.

WRITINGS
*Descrição analítica da estátua equestre erigida em Lisboa, à gloria do Senhor rei fidelisimo d. José I* (Lisbon, 1810); ed. by J.-A. França (Lisbon, 1975)

BIBLIOGRAPHY
M. Mendes: *Machado de Castro* (Lisbon, 1947)
D. de Macedo: *Machado de Castro* (Lisbon, 1958)

JOSÉ-AUGUSTO FRANÇA

**Machang** [Ma-ch'ang]. Neolithic site east of Ledu in eastern Qinghai Province, China. Excavated in 1921–3 by the Swedish archaeologist Johan Gunnar Andersson (1874–1960), it is the type site of the Machang phase (*c.* 2000–*c.* 1800 BC) of the Gangsu Yangshao culture. The best-preserved remains of Machang houses are found in Majiawan in Yongjing, Gansu Province; they have round or square semi-subterranean floors, wattle-and-daub walls and probably thatched roofs. The tombs are mostly single, although multiple tombs have also been discovered; wooden coffins were often used. The pottery vessels that served as grave goods varied in number from a few to several dozen and sometimes contained grains of millet. The pottery was made of either red clay or sand-tempered red and grey clay, the most usual forms being jars, juglike vessels and bowls. The red clay vessels are either plain or painted in red, black and maroon slip. The painted designs extend two-thirds of the way down the vessel, and the black lines characteristic of Gansu Yangshao pottery are often enhanced with red lines. Common motifs include four large circles, anthropomorphic patterns, ringlets, spirals and woven and checked patterns. Much of the pottery bears painted symbols, of which 139 different signs have been identified. Small clay masks have also been found. Some large jars have been found with tops in the shape of human heads: on one there is a human figure with both female and male sexual organs and breasts (Beijing, Pal. Mus.). These human figures were probably associated with shamanistic rituals.

BIBLIOGRAPHY
K. C. Chang: *The Archaeology of Ancient China* (New Haven, 1963, rev. New Haven and London, 4/1986), pp. 138–50
A. E.Dien, J. K. Riegel and N. T. Price, eds: *Prehistoric to Western Zhou* (1985), ii of *Chinese Archaeological Abstracts* (Los Angeles, 1978–85), pp. 266–87

BENT L. PEDERSEN

**Machati, Gratiadio.** See AGUCCHI, GIOVANNI BATTISTA.

**Machaut, Guillaume de.** See GUILLAUME DE MACHAUT.

**Machek, Antonín** (*b* Podlažice, nr Chrast, 31 Oct 1775; *d* Prague, 18 Nov 1844). Bohemian painter. He was considered the leading portraitist in Bohemia during the last 40 years of his life, and most of his work is now in the Prague National Gallery. He studied under several teachers in Prague, and in 1799 in Vienna. He began work, mainly as a portraitist, in Upper Austria, primarily at Linz. In 1814 he moved back to Prague, where his subjects for portraiture were mostly from the patriotic intelligentsia, both in the city and outside it. His most notable works include portraits of representatives of the Czech national revival such as the philologists *Václav Hanka* (1826) and *Josef Jungmann* (1833; both Prague, N.G., Convent of St Agnes) and the family of the nation's leading historian, *Tereza Palacká and her Children* (*c.* 1837; Maleč Castle, nr Chotěboř). His portraits reveal the stylistic developments of the time, from the Neo-classical tradition to the Biedermeier era. In addition to portraiture he produced stage designs and history paintings. He instigated the publication of a collection of lithographs, *History of Bohemia in Pictures* (Prague, 1820–34), and in 1828 founded a workshop that pioneered the process of lithography in Prague.

BIBLIOGRAPHY
L. Novák: *Antonín Machek* (Prague, 1962) [Ger. summary]
*Die tschechische Malerei des XIX. Jahrhunderts* (exh. cat., ed. J. Kotalík; Vienna, Belvedere, 1984), pp. 1–41 [entry by M. Nováková]

ROMAN PRAHL

**Machiavelli, Zanobi (di Jacopo di Piero)** (*b* 1418–19; *d* Pisa, 7 March 1479). Italian painter. His birth date is calculated from his 1457 *catasto* (land registry declaration) in which he gave his age as 39. In neither this declaration nor that for 1469 does he mention his occupation. He was formerly confused with a painter named Zanobi who in 1453 entered into a three-year partnership with Piero di Lorenzo di Pratese di Bartolo Zuccheri (1413–87) and Pesellino, but that painter's name was Zanobi di Migliore. However, Zanobi Machiavelli's documented works do show the influence of Pesellino.

Vasari stated that Zanobi was a pupil of Benozzo Gozzoli. This is undocumented, but Zanobi may have assisted Gozzoli in Umbria during the early 1450s. He appears to have worked mainly outside Florence and the only mention of his workshop in the city is in Benedetto Dei's *Pittori nella città di Firenze* (1470). Zanobi is not mentioned in the records of the Arte de' Medici e degli Speziali, the Florentine painters' guild. In Zanobi's earliest surviving work, a *St James* (1463; Berlin, Gemäldegal.), the influence of Gozzoli is evident, while the strong light effects and rich drapery design recall Pesellino.

On 12 March 1465 Zanobi received 66 lire for three lunette overdoor paintings of the *Pietà*, *St Augustine* and *St Monica* (all untraced) for the recently completed Badia at Fiesole. A signed *Coronation of the Virgin* (Dijon, Mus. B.-A.) was commissioned in 1473 for Santa Croce in Fossabanda, just outside Pisa. It was probably executed in large part by assistants and is almost a caricature of Zanobi's style. More representative of his talents is a *Virgin and Child with Four Saints* (Pisa, Mus. N. S Matteo; see fig.), also for Santa Croce in Fossabanda. In this work and a slightly earlier *Virgin and Child with Saints* (Dublin, N.G.) the placement of figures, play of light and setting recall the *Virgin and Child with Four Saints* (Paris, Louvre, inv. no. 1661) begun by Pesellino and probably finished in Lippi's workshop. The figure of St Jerome in the Dublin picture depends on a figure in Lippi's *Coronation of the Virgin* (Rome, Pin. Vaticana). Roughly contemporary with the Dublin and Pisa paintings is a *Virgin and Child with Two Angels* (Rome, Gal. Pallavicini). The inscribed haloes and the dry, almost metallic forms also recall Gozzoli, but the vivacious faces (with almond-shaped eyes, light skin and high foreheads) and the flowing drapery are typical of Zanobi. Machiavelli is mentioned in Pisa in 1475, and on 28 September 1476 he was paid by the administrators of Pisa Cathedral for blue pigment for a painting. Further payments were made in October and November 1476 and also on 12 February 1477.

Padoa Rizzo has made a convincing case for Zanobi's activity as a painter of illuminated manuscripts. Her attributions tally well with the style of Zanobi's *St Jerome* predella panels (untraced, see Padoa Rizzo, 1984, figs 6 and 7) and share that 'sentimental tone of composed yet gentle devotion' that is a trademark of his art.

BIBLIOGRAPHY
G. Vasari: *Vite* (1550, rev. 2/1568); ed. G. Milanesi, vol. iii, pp. 53–4
G. Poggi: 'Zanobi di Iacopo Machiavelli pittore', *Riv. A.*, ix (1916–17), pp. 67–9
P. Bacci: 'Zanobi Machiavelli a Pisa', *Riv. A.*, x (1917–18), pp. 125–7
B. Berenson: 'Zanobi Macchiavelli', *Burl. Mag.*, xcii (1950), pp. 345–9 [with several superseded attributions]
A. Padoa Rizzo: 'Zanobi Machiavelli miniatore?' *Scritti di storia dell'arte in onore di Roberto Salvini* (Florence, 1984), pp. 319–24

ELIOT W. ROWLANDS

**Ma-chia-yao.** *See* MAJIAYAO.

**Machicolation.** Stone gallery supported on corbels embedded in the external wall of a fortified building, incorporating holes in the floor through which projectiles can be dropped (see fig.). It first appeared as a feature of stone fortresses in the late 12th century. In common with most developments in medieval fortification, it was created by French and Norman castle builders, inspired by Muslim fortresses encountered during the Crusades.

The earliest machicolations were simple openings between stone corbels supporting a timber war head at the top of a tower, covering the footings of the wall below. By constructing a series of small arches between the corbels—redolent of Islamic design—a stone parapet could be carried in front of the wall line, bringing the footings safely into full view at battlement height.

Machicolations on the fortified churches of the Auvergne, as in the great hall of the 12th-century cathedral of Notre-Dame at Le Puy-en-Vélay and the 13th-century church of St-Léger at Royat, were architecturally advanced but also isolated examples. The donjon of Château-Gaillard (1197–8; ruined) at Les Andelys, Normandy, the innovative castle built by Richard I of England (*reg* 1189–99), pioneered arched machicolation on both walls and towers. This required modifications to the upper walls, including the construction of a broad walkway, with 2 m high walls supported on overlapping corbels. The system was further developed in the castle (donjon destr. 1918) at Coucy-le-Château, with five towers added *c.* 1220. There, timber hoarding was replaced by a stone parapet on corbels connected by arches running beneath the battlements. Some 50 years later at Chillon Castle (1263–8), Switzerland, a continuous frieze of machicolation, covered with a roof, was added above the walls and towers.

Until the 14th century it was more common for machicolation to be confined to gateways, which were most vulnerable to assault. The Porte Narbonnaise (late

Zanobi Machiavelli: *Virgin and Child with Four Saints*, tempera on panel, 1.54×1.77 m, *c.* 1465 (Pisa, Museo Nazionale di S Matteo)

13th century) at Carcassonne had three machicolations at different heights and a square machicolation between the two towers. This defensive style was characteristic of Edward I's Welsh castles, especially Harlech and Conwy, by James of St George. The fortified hall house of Haughton Castle (mid-13th century), Northumbria, employed buttress machicolations on five arches down either side of the gate, a style more typical of Provençal architecture. At the Palais des Papes (1330s; 1340s) at Avignon, immense buttresses extending from the crenellation to the footings were connected by pointed arches. Uninterrupted openings in the walkway were wide enough for large projectiles. The Breton style of machicolation featured more delicate corbels shaped like inverted pyramids to offer the maximum field of vision from the battlements. These were seen on the Pont Valentré towers (1355) at Cahors and the later, triangular fortress (1466) at Nantes.

By the second half of the 14th century, fragile timber hoardings had been replaced with elaborate stone machicolations incorporating wide walkways on a broad parapet. The upper storey of the great tower of Nunney (*c.* 1373), Somerset, was encircled with a massive fighting gallery. The work was inspired by the *château-fort* at Pierrefonds (*c.* 1400; rebuilt 19th century), Oise, the uninterrupted oversailing machicolations of which were perhaps the most impressive of all. At Tarascon (early 15th century), Provence, defensive efficiency was improved by making the encircling bank of machicolations the same height across the towers and walls, allowing easier movement of troops. Civic architecture also incorporated stone machicolations, more for show than for defence, as in the Palazzo Vecchio (early 14th century), Florence (*see* FLORENCE, fig. 22). The palace of the dukes of Aquitaine (1380s; now part of the Palais de Justice) at Poitiers was entirely encircled by an elaborate parapet, and the Grand Master's Palace at Malbork Castle (1383–99) featured a prominently oversailing coronet of machicolation. This Rhenish style

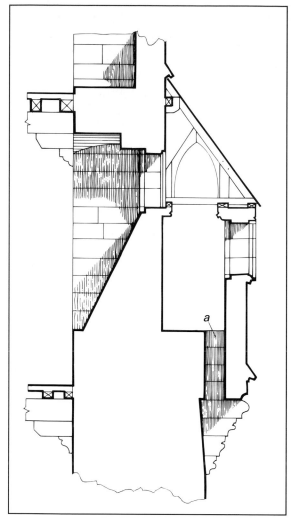

Machicolation, cross-section showing the floor opening (a) for dropping projectiles

was adopted in England at Caister (1430s), near Yarmouth, Norfolk, a brick tower inspired by the 15th-century cylindrical towers of Kempen, lower Rhineland, with their machicolation frieze, and on the great tower (1432–46) at Tattershall Castle, Lincs, crowned with enormous two-storey parapets (for illustration *see* TATTERSHALL). Hanging turrets connected by a continuous frieze of machicolations also characterized the commanding rectangular keeps that John II (*reg* 1406–54) and Henry IV (*reg* 1454–74) of Castile added to the great castles of their kingdom, as at the Alcázar (destr. 1862; rebuilt) in Segovia, the Castilo de la Mota (Medina) and Peñafiel (Valladolid), and substantial new works at Coca (Castile).

The introduction of long-range fire-artillery in the 15th century made machicolations redundant (*see* MILITARY ARCHITECTURE AND FORTIFICATION, §III, 2), although they survived in such projects as the Italian Rocca Pia (1460), Tivoli; Rocca Maggiore (rebuilt 16th century), Assisi; and the Medici fortress at Volterra (after 1472). In the 19th century such restorers as Eugène-Emmanuel Viollet-le-Duc at Pierrefonds (from 1858) and Jeffry Wyatville at Windsor Castle (Round Tower, from 1824; *see* WINDSOR CASTLE, fig. 3) made machicolation a cardinal feature of their re-created medieval military architecture.

*See also* CASTLE, §I.

BIBLIOGRAPHY
E.-E. Viollet-le-Duc: *Dictionnaire raisonné de l'architecture française du XIe au XVIe siècle*, 10 vols (Paris, 1854–67)
V. Lamperiz y Romea: *Historia de la arquitectura cristiana en la edad media* (Barcelona, 1904–9)
S. Toy: *A History of Fortification* (London, 1955)
J. F. Fino: *Forteresses de la France médiévale: Construction, attaque, défense* (Paris, 1967)
W. Anderson: *Castles of Europe from Charlemagne to the Renaissance* (London, 1970)  □

**Machine aesthetic.** Term applied to the concept of the machine as a source of beauty, a concept particularly important in the development of art and design in Europe and North America in the 20th century. It can be argued, however, that the origins of the machine aesthetic lie in the 19th century, although few 19th-century architects, designers or writers were willing to think of machines as in themselves potential sources of beauty. Such writers as John Ruskin stressed instead the close affinity between organic forms, especially in decorative ornament, and aesthetic pleasure; a wide range of 'modern' machines from locomotives to kitchen implements continued therefore to be heavily ornamented. Moreover, the introduction of MASS PRODUCTION techniques, with industrial design replacing craftsmanship, was largely seen as incompatible with individual artistry and therefore aesthetic worth. In the 20th century, however, historians and polemicists of the Modern Movement, including Nikolaus Pevsner, Lewis Mumford, Sigfried Giedion and Herwin Schaefer claimed to find the origins of a new aesthetic in some of the great achievements of the 19th century in engineering and the applied arts, such as Joseph Paxton's Crystal Palace (1851), London, the chairs of Michael Thonet (*see* INDUSTRIAL DESIGN, fig. 3) and machine shop lathes.

Numerous distinct artistic movements—all of them, however, sharing a commitment to modernism—contributed to the development of the machine aesthetic in the 20th century. In the years before World War I the Italian Futurists developed an aesthetic that celebrated the machine as the embodiment of energy and power, and this was translated visually into a kaleidoscope of different colours and complicated geometry (*see* FUTURISM). In Great Britain, from *c*. 1914 Wyndham Lewis and other artists associated with VORTICISM also sought to celebrate the arrival of the 'machine age', while working in a harsher, less romantic style than the Futurists. In France after World War I the French painter Amédée Ozenfant and the Swiss architect Le Corbusier developed a Purist aesthetic (*see* PURISM), characterized by an appreciation of the ideal purity of form of the machine. In the 1920s and 1930s this view came to be the predominant, canonical form of the machine aesthetic, and the essence of machine beauty was seen by many artists, designers and polemicists as a stark, unornamented, geometric simplicity and regularity of shape, and smooth, frequently shiny surfaces. Le

Corbusier's dictum that 'the house is a machine for living in', for example, sought to establish an architectural aesthetic analogous to the beauty of some engineering works. This view was inextricably related to FUNCTION-ALISM and was promoted by Walter Gropius at the BAUHAUS in Germany, by the DE STIJL group and by the Museum of Modern Art in New York as well as by Le Corbusier and the group associated with the journal *L'Esprit* in Paris.

Other versions of the machine aesthetic continued to evolve, however. In the 1920s, for example, the ART DECO style, characterized by a stylized and geometric approach to natural forms rather than an emphasis on functionalism, was widely popular, especially in France. PRECISIONISM celebrated modern technology in a specifically American context but continued to have affinities with Purism. In the 1930s a new approach emerged in which speed and efficiency were seen as the essential characteristics of the machine, and this was often expressed by an aerodynamic, streamlined or tear-drop shape. Such shapes, however, were applied not only where they had a real function, as with aeroplanes or automobiles, but also with stationary objects, including buildings. This approach became very popular with American industrial designers such as Norman Bel Geddes, Raymond Loewy and Walter Dorwin Teague, who favoured a streamlined approach in the design of everything from locomotives to cameras and pencil-sharpeners. A biomorphic approach also emerged in the 1930s and gained great force in the 1940s and 1950s, for example in the works of Charles Eames and Frederick Kiesler. These designers insisted that machines could conform to human bodily contours, rather than humans having to conform to the contours of the machine, and this led to the common adoption of amoeba shapes. In the 1960s the Japanese Metabolists (*see* METABOLISM) developed a mechanistic approach, based on the concept of interchangeable, renewable parts, and the English ARCHIGRAM group apotheosized the machine as raw technology. This led ultimately to the HIGH TECH approach to architecture and interior decoration and to such buildings as the Centre George Pompidou in Paris by Renzo Piano and Richard Rogers (1971–7; *see* PARIS, fig. 15). The personal and ever-changing nature of any definition of beauty, evident in these diverse approaches, and the continuing development of the forms of machinery through advances in technology will doubtless continue to necessitate a constant reassessment of machine aesthetics.

### BIBLIOGRAPHY

Le Corbusier: *Vers une architecture* (Paris, 1923); Eng. trans. as *Towards a New Architecture* (London, 1927)
N. Bel Geddes: *Horizons* (New York, 1932)
L. Mumford: *Technics and Civilization* (New York, 1934)
*Machine Art* (exh. cat., New York, MOMA, 1934)
S. Cheney and M. Cheney: *Art and the Machine* (New York, 1936)
N. Pevsner: *Pioneers of Modern Design (from William Morris to Walter Gropius)* (London, 1937)
W. Teague: *Design this Day; the Technique of Order in the Machine Age* (New York, 1940)
S. Giedion: *Space, Time and Architecture* (Cambridge, MA, 1941)
R. Banham: *Theory and Design in the First Machine Age* (New York, 1967)
*The Machine Age in America, 1918–1941* (exh. cat. by R. Wilson, D. Pilgrim and D. Tashjian; New York, Brooklyn Mus.; and elsewhere; 1968–9)
H. Schaefer: *Nineteenth Century Modern: The Functional Tradition in Victorian Design* (New York, 1970)
J. L. Meikle: *Twentieth Century Limited: Industrial Design in America, 1925–1939* (Philadelphia, 1979)
B. Constensou, ed.: *Léger et l'esprit moderne* (Paris, 1982)

RICHARD GUY WILSON

**Machinery, construction.** *See* CONSTRUCTION MACHINERY.

**Macho, Victorio** (*b* Palencia, 23 Dec 1887; *d* Toledo, 13 July 1966). Spanish sculptor. The son of a poor carpenter, he became aware of his vocation at an early age when he came into contact with the sculpture of the Mannerist and Baroque artists of Castile. At the age of 17 he entered the Escuela de Bellas Artes in Madrid but immediately demonstrated his rejection of academic teaching by joining bohemian circles. He became the friend of the most interesting realist sculptor of the day, Julio Antonio, who encouraged him to undertake journeys through the most remote and forgotten villages of Castile in an attempt to find his own roots. On these journeys, between 1910 and 1915, Macho made a series of drawings of local people, shepherds and labourers (*El hombre de Madera*, 1910–12; Toledo, Casa–Mus. Victorio Macho), and these inspired him to create his first sculptures of popular figures, for example *Marinero Vasco* (Toledo, Casa–Mus. Victorio Macho). He held his first exhibition in 1921 at the Museo de Arte Moderno in Madrid. It had considerable success and established him as one of the leading Spanish sculptors. When the Civil War broke out, Macho went into exile, first in Paris (1937) and later in Lima, Peru. He returned to Spain in 1952 and settled in Toledo, where he continued to work and where he organized a museum, the Casa–Museo Victorio Macho, which houses most of his work. Macho's sculpture was of considerable importance in the development of the young avant-garde of the 1930s. Basing his work on ancient Egyptian models, and influenced by Emile-Antoine Bourdelle as well as by the formal freedom that Cubism had created, Macho produced sculptures dominated by closed volumes, great smooth planes and an architectural sense of composition, for example the monument to *Dr Llorente* (*c.* 1918; Madrid, San Justo Cemetery) and portrait of *Miguel de Unamuno* (granite and bronze, h. 1.2 m, 1929–30, U. Salamanca, Pal. Anaya). His innovative concept of the public monument can be clearly seen in one of his most interesting works, the monument to the novelist *Benito Pérez Galdós* (1918) in the Parque del Retiro in Madrid. It depicts the writer seated in an armchair, wearing a dressing-gown and with his legs covered by a blanket.

### BIBLIOGRAPHY

F. Mon: *Victorio Macho* (Madrid, 1979)
J. Alix Trueba: *Escultura española: 1900–1936* (Madrid, 1985), pp. 76–80
J. C. Brasas Egido: *Victorio Macho: Vida, arte y obra* (Palencia, 1987)

JOSEFINA ALIX TRUEBA

# Illustration Acknowledgements

We are grateful to those listed below for permission to reproduce copyright illustrative material and to those contributors who supplied photographs or helped us to obtain them. The word 'Photo:' precedes the names of large commercial or archival sources who have provided us with photographs, as well as the names of individual photographers (where known). It has generally not been used before the names of owners of works of art, such as museums and civic bodies. Every effort has been made to contact copyright holders and to credit them appropriately; we apologize to anyone who may have been omitted from the acknowledgements or cited incorrectly. Any error brought to our attention will be corrected in subsequent editions. Where illustrations have been taken from books, publication details are provided in the acknowledgements below.

Line drawings, maps, plans, chronological tables and family trees commissioned by the *Dictionary of Art* are not included in the list below. All of the maps in the dictionary were produced by Oxford Illustrators Ltd, who were also responsible for some of the line drawings. Most of the line drawings and plans, however, were drawn by the following artists: Diane Fortenberry, Lorraine Hodghton, Chris Miners, Amanda Patton, Mike Pringle, Jo Richards, Miranda Schofield, John Tiernan, John Wilson and Philip Winton. The chronological tables and family trees were prepared initially by Kate Boatfield and finalized by John Johnson.

**Leather** *1* British Library, London (no. 66.g.9); *2–4* Board of Trustees of the Victoria and Albert Museum, London; *5* Photo: National Trust Photo Library, London

**Lebanon** Nicolas Ibrahim Sursock Museum, Beirut

**Le Brocquy, Louis** National Gallery of Ireland, Dublin

**Le Brun, Charles** *1* Trustees of Dulwich Picture Gallery, London; *2–4* Photo: © RMN, Paris

**Lecce** Photo: Scala, Florence

**Leck, Bart van der** Haags Gemeentemuseum, The Hague/© DACS, 1996

**Leclerc: (1) Sébastien Leclerc (i)** *1–2* Bibliothèque Nationale de France, Paris

**Le Corbusier** *1* University of Warwick (History of Art Photograph Collection); *2* Architectural Association, London/Photo: F. Yerbury; *3, 7–8* Fondation Le Corbusier, Paris/© DACS, 1996; *4, 6* Photo: Tim Benton, Cambridge; *5* Photo: Robert Harding Picture Library, London

**Ledoux, Claude-Nicolas** *1* Photo: British Architectural Library, RIBA, London; *2* Photo: S. Colomb

**Lefèvre, Robert** Board of Trustees of the Victoria and Albert Museum, London

**Lega, Silvestro** Photo: Soprintendenza ai Beni Artistici e Storici, Milan

**Lega and related peoples** *1–2* Koninklijk Museum voor Midden-Afrika, Tervuren

**Léger, Fernand** *1* Rijksmuseum Kröller-Müller, Otterlo/© ADAGP/SPADEM, Paris, and DACS, London, 1996; *2* Philadelphia Museum of Art, Philadelphia, PA/© ADAGP/SPADEM, Paris, and DACS, London, 1996; *3–4* Musée National d'Art Moderne, Paris/© ADAGP/SPADEM, Paris, and DACS, London, 1996

**Le Gray, Gustave** Metropolitan Museum of Art, New York (Gift of A. Hyatt Mayor, 1976; no. 1976.645.1)

**Legros: (2) Pierre Legros (ii)** Photo: Archivi Alinari, Florence

**Le Havre** Musée des Beaux-Arts, Le Havre/Photorama SA/© RMN, Paris

**Lehmbruck, Wilhelm** Wilhelm-Lehmbruck-Museum, Duisburg/Photo: Foto Schubert

**Leibl, Wilhelm** Hamburger Kunsthalle, Hamburg

**Leiden** *1* Rijksdienst voor de Monumentenzorg, Zeist; *2* Stedelijk Museum De Lakenhal, Leiden

**Leighton, Frederic** Private collection

**Leilan, Tell** Photo: Harvey Weiss

**Leinberger, Hans** *1* Photo: Bildarchiv Foto Marburg; *2* Staatliche Museen zu Berlin, Preussischer Kulturbesitz

**Leipzig** *1* Photo: Bildarchiv Foto Marburg; *2* Universitätsbibliothek, Leipzig

**Lely, Peter** *1* Trustees of Dulwich Picture Gallery, London; *2* National Trust Photo Library, London/Photo: J. Whitaker; *3* Scottish National Portrait Gallery, Edinburgh; *4* Lamport Trust, Lamport Hall, Northants

**Le Mans** *1* Photo: Conway Library, Courtauld Institute of Art, London; *2* Photo: James Austin, Cambridge

**Lemberger, Georg** Germanisches Nationalmuseum, Nuremberg

**Le Mercier, Jacques** *1–2* Photo: Conway Library, Courtauld Institute of Art, London

**Lemke, Johann Philipp** Statens Konstmuseer, Stockholm

**Le Moiturier, Antoine** Musée du Petit Palais, Avignon

**Lemoyne: (3) Jean-Baptiste Lemoyne (ii)** Photo: Arch. Phot. Paris/© DACS, 1996

**Lemoyne, François** Photo: © RMN, Paris

**Le Nain** *1, 3* Photo: Erich Lessing/AKG Ltd, London; *2* Trustees of the National Gallery, London; *4* Board of Trustees of the Victoria and Albert Museum, London

**Lenbach, Franz von** Städtische Galerie im Lenbachhaus, Munich

**Le Nôtre, André** *1* Bibliothèque Nationale de France, Paris; *2* Photo: Thomas d'Hoste, Paris

**Lens, A. C.** Photo: © ACL Brussels

**Leo, Ludwig** Photo: Reinhard Friedrich

**Leo Bible** Biblioteca Apostolica Vaticana, Rome

**León** *1, 3–4* Ampliaciones y Reproducciones MAS, Barcelona; *2* Photo: Anthony Kersting, London; *5* Photo: Zodiaque, St-Léger-Vauban; *6* Photo: John Williams

**Leonardo, Jusepe** Museo del Prado, Madrid

**Leonardo da Vinci** *1* Gabinetto Fotografico, Soprintendenza ai Beni Artistici e Storici, Florence; *2* Trustees of the National Gallery, London; *3* National Museum, Kraków; *4, 6–7* Royal Collection, Windsor Castle/© Her Majesty Queen Elizabeth II; *5* Photo: © RMN, Paris; *8* Trustees of the British Museum, London; *9* Museum of Fine Arts, Budapest

**Leone Leoni** *1* Museo del Prado, Madrid; *2* Photo: Archivi Alinari, Florence

**Leoni: (1) Ottavio Leoni** Trustees of the British Museum, London

**Leonidov, Ivan** British Architectural Library, RIBA, London/Photo: Academy Editions, London (from A. Gozak and A. Leonidov: *Ivan Leonidov: Complete Known Works*, ed. Catherine Cooke)

**Leopardi, Alessandro** Photo: Conway Library, Courtauld Institute of Art, London

**Le Pautre: (2) Antoine Le Pautre** *1* Photo: Robert W. Berger; *2* Photo: J.C. Vaysse

**Lepenski Vir** Photo: Dragoslav Srejović

**Lepère, Auguste** Photo: Bridgeman Art Library, London

**Lépicié: (2) Nicolas-Bernard Lépicié** Photo: Giraudon, Paris

**Le Prince, Jean-Baptiste** Photo: © RMN, Paris

**Leptis Magna** *1–2* Photo: Fototeca Unione, American Academy, Rome; *3* Photo: Archivi Alinari, Florence

**Le Puy** Photo: Bildarchiv Foto Marburg

**Leslie, C. R.** Yale Center for British Art, New Haven, CT

**Lesotho** Photo: Pierre Desormeaux

**Lespugue** Photothèque du Musée de l'Homme, Paris